The **Rough Guide** to

# Europe

this edition written and researched by
**Slawomir Adamczak, Thomas Brown, Jon Bousfield,
Tim Burford, Lucia Cockcroft, Sarah Gear, Lucia Graves,
Michael Harcourt, Rob Humphreys, Daniel Jacobs,
Phil Lee, Norm Longley, Lucy Mallows, Claire Morsman,
Lone Mouritsen, Roger Norum, Catherine Phillips,
James Proctor, Emma Rees, Paul Sentobe, Matthew Teller,
Geoff Wallis and Clifton Wilkinson**

ROUGH
GUIDES

NEW YORK • LONDON • DELHI

www.roughguides.com

# Contents

◄◄ Jungfrau train, Switzerland ◄ Gellért Baths, Budapest

| 0 | | 500 km |
| 0 | | 250 miles |

Metres
4000
2000
1000
400
200
0
below
sea level

Arctic Circle

REYKJAVÍK ● ICELAND

Faroes

Shetland

ATLANTIC
OCEAN

NORTH
SEA

DENMARK

Belfast ● ● Edinburgh

IRELAND
● DUBLIN
York ●

UNITED
KINGDOM

Cardiff ● ● Hamburg

NETHER-
LANDS

LONDON ● AMSTERDAM

BRUSSELS
BELGIUM GERMAN

Cologne

LUX. ● Frankfurt
PARIS ● LUXEMBOURG

Munich ●

FRANCE BERN ● Zürich
SWITZERLAND

Santiago de
Compostela ● Bordeaux ● Lyon

Milan ● Venice ●

Bilbao ●
Porto ●

SAN
MARINO

PORTUGAL ANDORRA Marseille ● MONACO Florence ●

MADRID ● I T A

LISBON ●
S P A I N Barcelona ● Corsica
(Fr.)

ROME ●

Valencia ● Ibiza

Seville ● Mallorca Sardinia

Tangier ● M E D I T E R R A

RABAT ● ALGIERS ●

Casablanca ● Fes ● TUNIS ●

Essaouira ● M O R O C C O TUNISIA

Marrakesh ● A L G E R I A

4

## Introduction to

# Europe

**Europe is one of the world's most exciting and diverse destinations: distances are short, travel is easy, and just a couple of hours will take you from one country to another, with quite radical differences of language, culture, landscape and food. Soaked in a long and rich history, Europe is nonetheless modern, dynamic and constantly reinventing itself. Travellers arriving with classic images in mind are rarely disappointed: the Eiffel Tower, the Colosseum, Big Ben and the Kremlin are all here to be**

**ticked off the list. But equally appealing are party cities like Berlin, Madrid, Prague and Tallinn, while exploring Europe's backwaters, where life seems not to have changed in centuries, can be as rewarding as visiting its major urban centres.**

Europe crams a lot of countries into a small area but open borders, an extensive transport network, and continent-wide rover tickets like Eurail, InterRail and Eurobus, make it easy to tour, and almost everywhere you'll find accommodation to meet your needs, whatever budget you are on. Exactly where Europe starts and ends is a little hazy. Conventionally, the **geographical boundaries** are the Ural Mountains in the east, the Atlantic Coast in the north and west, and the Mediterranean in the south. This guide, however, includes some countries outside this area that not everyone would

**Europe is one of the world's most exciting and diverse destinations**

call Europe (notably Turkey, Morocco, and perhaps even the British Isles), while excluding a few that are too far off the beaten track to be on most people's "Grand Tour" (into this category fall Bosnia, Albania, Macedonia, Belarus, Ukraine and Moldova). Within this book, though, you'll find an exceptional variety of **landscapes**, from the pretty, alpine scenery of Switzerland to the canal-veined flatness of the Netherlands, from the heather-coated highlands of Scotland and the rolling green countryside of England to the sandy beaches of the French riviera and the desert of southern Morocco. **Culturally** too, there's an amazing diversity, from laid-back, sun-soaked Catholic countries, where the siesta rules and dinner is rarely eaten without a bottle of good wine, to the generally colder and more austere lands of the Protestant north, where the drink is mainly beer and the partying has a harder edge. There are Slavic Christian Orthodox countries like Russia and Serbia; and Muslim countries such as Morocco and Turkey, the two, very different ends of the southern Mediterranean's Islamic crescent. Even

## Top 5 Architectural highlights

**Chartres Cathedral, France** See p.375

**Guggenheim Museum, Bilbao, Spain** see p.937

**Aya Sofya, İstanbul, Turkey** See p.1038

**The Kremlin, Moscow, Russia** See p.849

**The Alhambra, Granada, Spain** See p.969 ▼

## The European Union

The European Economic Community (EEC), formed by the Treaty of Rome in 1957, had six members: France, Germany, Italy, Belgium, the Netherlands and Luxembourg. By the time the Maastricht Treaty came into force in 1993, changing the organization's name to the **European Union** (EU), the original six had been joined by Denmark, Ireland and the UK (1973), Greece (1981), and Portugal and Spain (1986). Austria, Finland and Sweden signed up in 1995, and the latest batch of entrants were Cyprus, the Czech Republic, Estonia, Hungary, Latvia, Lithuania, Malta, Poland, Slovakia and Slovenia, who all joined in May 2004, bringing the number of member states to 25. Norway voted in a 1972 referendum to stay out.

Whether this vast union, headed by a Council of Ministers and a directly elected European Parliament, should move towards becoming a fully fledged United States of Europe, or confine itself to being just a trading bloc, is a matter of some controversy. The original six members have tended to favour further political union, leading to a federal Europe, the UK and Denmark being the countries most consistently opposed to this. In 2005. however, two previously strong advocates of the European project, France and the Netherlands, rejected the EU constitution in national referenda, possibly heralding a swing towards a looser rather than a closer union.

within countries you may think of as English-, German-, French- or Spanish-speaking, you'll find enclaves of cultures you never knew existed – the Celtic-speakers of western Wales and Ireland, the Romansh language, akin to ancient Latin, that is spoken in the valleys of southeastern Switzerland, and the Basques of northern Spain and southwestern France, whose tongue is unrelated to any other language known. Then there are **cities** like London, Europe's greatest melting-pot, where cultures from around the world mingle, followed by Paris and Berlin with a similar cosmopolitan mix. **Politically**, much of Europe has signed up to – and much of the rest wants to join – the European Union (see box, left), which, for all its teething problems, has given the "Continent" a new sense of direction and purpose, and a feeling that Europe

▲ Trevi Fountain, Rome

will continue to play a leading part in world affairs for some time to come. For the visitor, continuing integration facilitates ever-easier movement around the continent and, whether you want to drink Guinness in Ireland, eat pizza in Naples, go skiing in St Moritz, or sunbathe in St Tropez, there's a near infinite range of opportunities to make your trip unforgettable.

# When to go

Europe's **climate** is as variable as everything else about the continent. In **northwestern Europe** (Benelux, Denmark, southwestern Norway, most of France and parts of Germany, as well as the British Isles) the climate is basically a cool temperate one, with the chance of rain all year round and no great extremes of either

> there's a near infinite range of opportunities to make your trip unforgettable

## Top 5 Events

**Fiestas de San Fermín, Pamplona, Spain** See p.941

**Il Palio, Siena, Italy** See p.624

**Oktoberfest, Munich, Germany** See p.480

**Edinburgh Festival, Britain** See p.212

**World Cup 2006, Germany** See p.431 ▼

**FIFA WORLD CUP**

## Top 5 Treats

**A night in a parador, Spain** See p.915
**Soak in the baths, Budapest, Hungary** See p.541
**Tak a gondola ride, Venice, Italy** See p.606
**Champagne tasting, France** See p.377
**Ballooning in Turkey** See p.1063 ▼

cold or hot weather. There is no bad time to travel in most of this part of Europe, although the winter months (Nov–March) can be damp and miser-able, especially in the upland regions, and obviously the summer period (May–Sept) sees the most reliable and driest weather.

In **eastern Europe** (eastern Germany, Poland, central Russia, the Baltic states, southern Sweden, the Czech and Slovak republics, Austria, Switzerland, Hungary and Romania) the climatic conditions are more extreme, with freezing winters and sometimes sweltering summers. Here the transitional spring and autumn seasons are the most pleasant time to travel; deep midwinter, in contrast, can be very unpleasant, although it doesn't have the dampness associated with the northwestern European climate.

**Southern Europe**, principally the countries that border the Mediterra-

## Top 5 Drinks

**Beer, Belgium** See p.122
**Wine, France** See p.358
**Vodka, Russia** See p.846
**Mint tea, Morocco** See p.697
**Guinness, Ireland** See p.562 ▼

nean and associated seas – southern France, Italy, Spain, Portugal, Greece and western Turkey, as well as Morocco – has the most hospitable climate in Europe, with a general pattern of warm, dry summers and mild winters. Travel is possible at any time of year here, although the peak summer months can be very hot and busy, and the deep winter ones can see some rain.

There are, too, marked regional variations within these three broad groupings. As they're such large countries, Spain and France can, for example, see an inland **continental** type of weather as extreme as any in central Europe, and **mountain areas**, such as those in Italy, Austria and Switzerland, have a climate mainly influenced by altitude, which means short summers and long winters that always see snow. There are also, of course, the northern

11

## Top 5 Dishes

**Fish and chips, Britain** See p.147

**Pizza, Naples, Italy** See p.645

**Tapas, Madrid, Spain** See p.923

**Smörgåsbord, Sweden** See p.985

**Moules Frites (mussels and chips), Belgium** See p.121 ▼

regions of Russia and Scandinavia, which have an **Arctic climate** – again, bitterly cold, though with some surprisingly warm weather during the short summer when much of the region is warmed by the Gulf Stream. Winter sees the sun barely rise at all in these areas, while high summer means almost constant daylight.

There are obviously **other considerations** in deciding when to go. If you're planning to visit popular tourist areas, especially beach resorts in the Mediterranean, avoid July and August, when the weather can be too hot and the resorts at their most congested. Bear in mind, also, that in a number of countries in Europe everyone takes their vacation at the same time (this is especially true in France, Spain and Italy, where everyone goes away in August). At these times you can expect the crush to be especially bad in the resorts, while in the cities the only other people around will be fellow tourists. In northern Scandinavia the climatic extremes are such that you'll find opening times severely restricted, and even road and rail lines closed, outside the May to September period, making travel often impossible. Across the continent's mountainous areas, things stay open for the winter sports season (Dec–April), though outside the main resorts you'll again find many things closed. On the other hand, mid-April to mid-June can be a quiet period in many mountain resorts, when you may have much of the place to yourself.

## Top 5 Nightlife Spots

**London, Britain** See p.149

**Madrid, Spain** See p.924

**Berlin, Germany** See p.439

**Tallinn, Estonia** See p.324

**Ibiza, Spain** See p.958 ▶

## Average daily maximum temperatures in °C/°F

| | Jan | Feb | Mar | Apr | May | Jun | Jul | Aug | Sep | Oct | Nov | Dec |
|---|---|---|---|---|---|---|---|---|---|---|---|---|
| Amsterdam | 4/40 | 5/42 | 9/49 | 13/56 | 18/64 | 21/70 | 22/72 | 22/71 | 19/67 | 14/57 | 9/48 | 6/42 |
| Ankara | 4/40 | 6/42 | 11/51 | 17/63 | 23/73 | 26/78 | 30/86 | 31/87 | 26/78 | 21/69 | 14/57 | 6/43 |
| Athens | 13/55 | 14/57 | 16/60 | 20/68 | 25/77 | 30/86 | 33/92 | 33/92 | 29/84 | 24/75 | 19/66 | 15/58 |
| Berlin | 2/35 | 3/37 | 8/46 | 13/56 | 19/66 | 22/72 | 24/75 | 23/74 | 20/68 | 13/56 | 7/45 | 3/38 |
| Brussels | 4/40 | 7/42 | 10/51 | 14/58 | 18/65 | 22/72 | 23/73 | 22/72 | 21/69 | 15/60 | 9/48 | 6/42 |
| Bratislava | -1/30 | 0/30 | 5/41 | 10/50 | 13/58 | 12/54 | 20/68 | 19/67 | 16/61 | 10/50 | 4/40 | 0/32 |
| Bucharest | 1/34 | 4/40 | 10/50 | 18/64 | 23/74 | 27/81 | 30/86 | 30/85 | 25/78 | 18/65 | 10/49 | 4/40 |
| Budapest | 1/34 | 4/40 | 10/50 | 17/62 | 22/71 | 26/78 | 28/82 | 27/81 | 23/74 | 16/61 | 8/47 | 4/40 |
| Copenhagen | 2/36 | 2/36 | 5/41 | 10/51 | 16/61 | 19/67 | 22/71 | 21/70 | 18/64 | 12/54 | 7/45 | 4/40 |
| Dublin | 8/46 | 8/47 | 10/50 | 13/55 | 15/60 | 18/65 | 20/67 | 19/67 | 17/63 | 14/57 | 10/51 | 8/47 |
| Helsinki | -3/26 | -4/25 | 0/32 | 6/44 | 14/56 | 19/66 | 22/71 | 20/68 | 15/59 | 8/47 | 3/37 | -1/31 |
| İstanbul | 8/46 | 9/47 | 11/51 | 16/60 | 21/69 | 25/77 | 28/82 | 28/82 | 24/76 | 20/68 | 15/59 | 11/51 |
| Lisbon | 14/57 | 15/59 | 17/63 | 20/67 | 21/71 | 25/77 | 27/81 | 28/82 | 26/79 | 22/72 | 17/63 | 15/58 |
| London | 6/43 | 7/44 | 10/50 | 13/56 | 17/62 | 20/69 | 22/71 | 22/71 | 19/65 | 14/58 | 10/50 | 7/45 |
| Luxembourg | 3/37 | 4/40 | 10/49 | 14/57 | 18/65 | 21/70 | 23/73 | 22/71 | 19/66 | 13/56 | 7/44 | 4/40 |
| Madrid | 9/47 | 11/52 | 15/59 | 18/65 | 21/70 | 27/80 | 31/87 | 30/85 | 25/77 | 19/65 | 13/55 | 9/48 |
| Moscow | -9/15 | -6/22 | 0/32 | 10/50 | 19/66 | 21/70 | 23/73 | 22/72 | 16/61 | 9/48 | 2/35 | -5/24 |
| Oslo | -2/28 | -1/30 | 4/40 | 10/50 | 16/61 | 20/68 | 22/72 | 21/70 | 16/60 | 9/48 | 3/38 | 0/32 |
| Paris | 6/43 | 7/44 | 12/54 | 16/60 | 20/68 | 23/73 | 25/76 | 24/75 | 21/70 | 16/60 | 10/50 | 7/44 |
| Prague | 0/31 | 1/34 | 7/44 | 12/54 | 18/64 | 21/70 | 23/73 | 22/72 | 18/65 | 12/53 | 5/42 | 1/34 |
| Rabat | 17/63 | 18/65 | 20/68 | 22/71 | 23/73 | 26/78 | 28/82 | 30/83 | 27/81 | 25/77 | 21/70 | 18/65 |
| Rīga | -4/25 | -3/27 | 2/35 | 10/50 | 16/61 | 21/69 | 22/71 | 21/70 | 17/63 | 11/52 | 4/40 | -2/29 |
| Rome | 11/52 | 13/55 | 15/59 | 19/66 | 23/74 | 28/82 | 30/87 | 30/86 | 26/79 | 22/71 | 16/61 | 13/55 |
| Sofia | 2/35 | 4/40 | 10/50 | 16/60 | 21/69 | 24/76 | 27/81 | 26/79 | 22/70 | 17/63 | 9/48 | 4/40 |
| Stockholm | -1/30 | -1/30 | 3/37 | 8/47 | 14/58 | 19/67 | 22/71 | 20/68 | 15/60 | 9/49 | 5/40 | 2/35 |
| Tallinn | -4/25 | -4/25 | 0/32 | 7/45 | 14/57 | 19/66 | 20/68 | 19/66 | 15/59 | 10/50 | 3/38 | -1/30 |
| Vienna | 1/34 | 3/38 | 8/47 | 15/58 | 19/67 | 23/73 | 25/76 | 24/75 | 20/68 | 14/56 | 7/45 | 3/37 |
| Vilnius | -5/25 | -3/26 | 1/34 | 12/54 | 18/65 | 21/71 | 23/74 | 22/71 | 17/62 | 11/52 | 4/40 | -3/26 |
| Warsaw | 0/32 | 0/32 | 6/42 | 12/53 | 20/67 | 23/73 | 24/75 | 23/73 | 19/66 | 13/55 | 6/42 | 2/35 |
| Zürich | 2/36 | 5/41 | 10/51 | 15/59 | 19/67 | 23/73 | 25/76 | 24/75 | 20/69 | 14/57 | 7/45 | 3/39 |

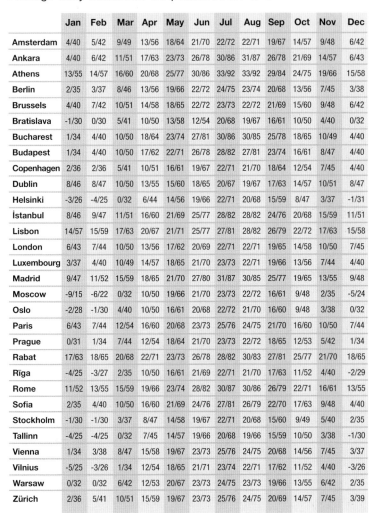

# Europe

# Itineraries

You can't expect to fit everything Europe has to offer into
one trip and we don't suggest you try. On the following
pages are a selection of itineraries that guide you through
different regions of the continent, taking you from Moorish
palaces in Spain to Santa's village in the Arctic Circle.
We've also included our own Grand Tour for those who
want to see some of the highlights of Europe but with
limited time. Each itinerary could be done in two to three
weeks, spending a couple of nights in each place, but bear
in mind that with so much to see and do it's easy to get
waylaid in a favourite place; getting off our suggested route
and taking that day-trip recommended by someone you met
on the train can easily turn into an extended exploration of
some wonderful area.

◄ Prague, Czech Republic

# Britain and Ireland

**1 London** One of the world's greatest cities, London requires lots of energy and even more money but for culture, nightlife and history there are few places to match it. **See p.149**

**2 Cambridge** The famous university town offers the chance to punt along the river, admire the university architecture or down a few in a student pub. **See p.184**

**3 York** From a Viking museum and medieval streets to a Gothic minster and national rail collection, if you want to soak up some British history, York is the place to do it. **See p.193**

**4 Edinburgh** With its stunning cityscape, lively bars and – if you time it right – international festival, the Scottish capital has something for everyone. **See p.206**

**5 The Highlands** For getting away from it all, Britain's most remote region and highest mountains are the perfect destination for some R and R. **See p.219**

▲ Big Ben, London

**6 The Lake District** With its millions of visitors don't expect to wander lonely as a cloud, but this area of lakes and mountains is still a captivating spot. **See p.190**

**7 Caernarfon Castle** Of all North Wales's splendid castles, this is the most impressive. **See p.205**

**8 Dublin** Convivial pubs, the best Guinness, Georgian architecture and a fascinating literary heritage make Ireland's capital a great introduction to the country. **See p.558**

**9 Galway** If you're looking for the legendary Irish craic, head for this West Coast town with its festivals, live music and friendly atmosphere. **See p.572**

**10 The Giant's Causeway** Long one of Ireland's top attractions, this geological wonder still amazes – 37,000 polygonal basalt columns can't be wrong. **See p.580**

# France and the low countries

**1 Amsterdam** Whether you're looking for culture, cannabis, clubs or cuisine, the Netherlands' largest city has it all. See p.726

**2 Bruges** It may be busy and touristy but this gem of Flemish architecture is still worth a visit for its atmospheric canals and beautiful buildings. See p.135

**3 Paris** Laze over a coffee in a Left Bank café, arrange a romantic rendezvous with your new Gallic friend or tick off the many museums in Europe's most enticing capital. See p.359

**4 The Loire Valley** Bucolic valley that's filled with some of the most impressive chateaux you'll see in the country. See p.385

**5 Bordeaux** Elegant bustling city and world-famous wine-growing region combine to make this a great destination. See p.390

**6 The Pyrenees** Clear your head after all that wine with the fresh air and fine walks of this mountain range bordering Spain. See p.393

**7 Avignon** A former papal residence with a suitably impressive legacy of buildings and monuments, Avignon also draws the crowds with its July drama festival. See p.411

**8 The Côte d'Azur** Nice, Cannes, St Tropez, Monaco – the names alone ooze glamour so get your glad rags on and show the world your fabulous side. See p.414

▲ Eiffel Tower, Paris

**9 Lyon** If the Côte d'Azur hasn't broken the bank, then there's no better city in which to indulge your passion for French cuisine than here in the country's gastronomic capital. See p.409

# Central Europe

**1 Berlin** Warfare, destruction, division and reunification have shaped this fascinating city, while the modern architecture and frantic nightlife give it an über contemporary feel. **See p.433**

▲ Bundestag, Berlin

**2 Dresden** Utterly destroyed in World War II, this Baroque city was carefully rebuilt and is once again Germany's most attractive. **See p.445**

**3 Prague** Whether it's beautiful architecture, great eating and drinking, or buzzing nightlife you're after, Prague has it all. **See p.275**

**4 Vienna** Former imperial headquarters, Austria's capital is chock full of palaces, museums and grand boulevards – with a coffee and cake in a grand café never too far away. **See p.94**

**5 Salzburg** From music by its most famous son, Mozart, to tours celebrating its most famous screen appearance, *The Sound of Music*, this handsome city has a few of everyone's favourite things. **See p.108**

**6 The Matterhorn** Whatever the time of year, you can enjoy winter sports here, on one of Europe's most famous mountains. **See p.1024**

**7 Zürich** Archetypal clean and efficient Swiss city worth a detour thanks to its delightful old town, wonderful lake setting and great café culture. **See p.1006**

**8 Munich** Oktoberfest (actually in late September) or not, the Bavarian capital has a lively nightlife scene and enough parks, museums and churches to occupy you till it's time for the next beer. **See p.476**

**9 The Rhine Gorge** Taking a cruise on this stretch of Germany's best-known river allows you to see the region's beautiful countryside and clifftop castles. **See p.461**

NORTH SEA

0     200 km
0     100 miles

GERMANY

Berlin ➊

The Rhine Gorge ➒     Dresden ➋

Prague ➌

CZECH REPUBLIC

Munich ➑     Vienna ➍

Zürich ➐     Salzburg ➎

SWITZERLAND     AUSTRIA

The Matterhorn ➅

# Iberia and Morocco

**1 Barcelona** Innovative architecture, city beaches, late-night bars and atmospheric old town – the Catalan capital has more than enough to have you staying longer than you planned. See p.948

**2 Madrid** Some of Europe's best museums to fill your days, some of Europe's best bars and clubs to fill your nights. If you're eating before 9pm, dancing before midnight and asleep before dawn, you haven't experienced a truly Madrileño evening. See p.917

**3 Lisbon** Portugal's immediately likeable capital has a great setting, delicious food and a huge amount of historic interest. See p.800

**4 The Algarve** Southern Portugal's beaches, especially on Ilha de Tavira, are second to none – and the nightlife isn't bad either. See p.819

**5 Seville** Learn to flamenco, knock back some fine wine or get lost in the Jewish Quarter – for many, Seville encapsulates Spain. See p.971

**6 Granada** For a taster of what's to come in Morocco, take a detour to Granada and its beautiful Alhambra Palace, an extraordinary reminder of Moorish architectural skill. See p.965

**7 Fes** Once across the Straits of Gibraltar, dive head first into Morocco with a stay in this medieval city of labyrinthine alleys, souks and mosques. See p.705

**8 Marrakesh** Stunning, atmospheric city with the Atlas Mountains as a backdrop and the live circus that is the Djemaa el Fna square at its heart. See p.713

**9 Essaouira** Lovely seaside and surfing resort that was once a hippie favourite and still retains a laid-back, arty feel. See p.717

▲ Koutoubia, Marrakesh

19

# Italy, Greece and Turkey

**1 Venice** Packed with visitors throughout the year, this unique, stunning city still has plenty of quieter corners where you can enjoy the beauty all by yourself. See p.605

**2 Florence** Birthplace of the Renaissance and a beautiful city in its own right, Florence's artistic treasures will inspire even the most uncultured visitor. See p.615

**3 Rome** More history than you can shake a toga at combined with a modern vibe make the Italian capital unmissable. See p.630

**4 Naples** The home of pizza – and best place to eat it – Naples is also a frenetic, crumblingly attractive city, while for actual ruins nearby Pompeii gives you an insight into how the ancient Romans used to live. See p.641

**5 Athens** Crowded, noisy and polluted the Greek capital may be, but its influence on Western culture and the buildings that provide tangible evidence of its former greatness are worth a few days of anyone's time. See p.490

**6 The Greek Islands** You say Cyclades, I say Dodecanese. Whatever your persuasion, island-hopping Greek style allows you to sunbathe, dine and party on a different island each day. See p.510

**7 Ephesus** Turkey's best-preserved archeological site is a treasure trove of ruined temples, public toilets, mosaics and baths. See p.1052

**8 Cappadocia** A long trip east through Anatolia but Cappadocia's rock-hewn buildings and volcanic landscape have an irresistible allure – and if you can afford a balloon trip over the area, you'll have one of the highlights of your trip. See p.1063

**9 İstanbul** Gaze in awe at the Blue Mosque, shop your way through the covered bazaar and reward your sightseeing endeavours with a genuine Turkish bath. See p.1035

◄ Santorini, Greek Islands

# Eastern Europe

**1 Warsaw** Don't be put off by the mishmash of architecture, the Polish capital has a reconstructed old town, beautiful parks and a energetic bar, club and restaurant scene. See p.777

**2 Kraków** You won't be the only one enjoying this historic city's sights but it's still a must-visit place. See p.786

**3 Budapest** Visit the museums and admire the views from hilly Buda, then cross the not-so-blue Danube for the restaurants and nightspots of Pest. See p.537

**4 Transylvania** You probably won't see any vampires but the mountain-hiking and quaint villages in this corner of Romania easily reward a visit. See p.835

▲ Parliament, Budapest

**5 Rila** South of Sofia lies Bulgaria's biggest and most revered monastery, known for its wonderful architecture and fine mountain setting. See p.235

**6 Belgrade** Not the most obvious of destinations, but the Serbian capital is fast attracting a hip crowd thanks to its cool nightlife. See p.869

**7 Dubrovnik** Dramatic views and a well-preserved medieval centre make this Adriatic port a highly recommended stop on any trip. See p.265

**8 Ljubljana** Small but perfectly formed, Slovenia's capital is a thoroughly enjoyable, easily manageable city in which to unwind. See p.900

# Scandinavia

**1 Copenhagen**
Relatively inexpensive by
Scandinavian standards, and
highly user-friendly, the Danish
capital is a lively, welcoming
introduction to the region. See
p.299

**2 Oslo** Uncrowded city,
close to equally uncrowded
woodland and beaches, make
Oslo a hugely enjoyable capital in which to stay. See p.753

**3 The fjords** No trip
to Norway would be complete
without a visit to the country's
western coastline and its
magnificent fjords. See p.758

**4 Lofoten Islands**
Try your hand at fishing, gawp
at the awe-inspiring mountain
scenery, or simply relax in the
friendly villages. See p.767

**5 Jokkmokk** Enjoy the
extremely long summer nights, local Sámi culture and traditional handicrafts in this
Arctic Circle town. See p.1000

**6 Stockholm** The handsome island setting of Sweden's capital complements the
wealth of museums and nightlife on offer. See p.986

**7 Helsinki** Distinctly Russian in atmosphere, Helsinki has a grand feel to it,
tempered by the locals' enthusiasm in summer for outdoor eating, drinking and
concerts. See p.341

**8 Rovaniemi** Back to the Arctic Circle, but this time for traditions of a very different
kind – namely a visit to Santa Claus Village and the chance to prove you've been good.
See p.350

▲ Midnight sun, Sweden

# Russia and the Baltic States

▲ St Basil's Cathedral, Moscow

**1 Moscow** From Red Square and the Kremlin to the Stalinist skyscrapers of the 1950s, the Russian capital is chaotic, beautiful in parts and always fascinating. **See p.847**

**2 St Petersburg** In a wonderful location, with jaw-dropping architecture and priceless art collections, Russia's second city is at its best during the midsummer White Nights festival. **See p.855**

**3 Tallinn** From obscure Soviet backwater to booming party town, it's been a long time since Estonia's capital has had it so good. **See p.324**

**4 Rīga** The Baltic States' one true metropolis, Latvia's capital is full of architectural treasures and is the gateway to some wonderful coastal scenery. **See p.669**

**5 Vilnius** Most beautiful of the Baltic capitals, cosmopolitan and atmospheric Vilnius's largely undiscovered status means you can get a break from the crowds. **See p.682**

**6 Couronian Spit** This narrow strip of land consisting of mountainous sand dunes is the place to get your hiking boots on and strike out on the numerous walking trails. **See p.691**

# The Grand Tour

For more information on all these see the relevant separate itinerary.

# Basics

# Basics

# Getting there

Airfares always depend on the season with the highest being roughly mid-June to early September and over the Christmas period. Note also that flying on weekends sometimes adds $25–80/£15–45 to the round-trip fare; price ranges quoted below assume midweek travel.

Barring special offers, the cheapest of the **airlines' published fares** usually require advance purchase of two to three weeks, and impose certain restrictions, such as heavy penalties if you change your schedule. These tickets sometimes go under names like "Apex" or "SuperApex". Many airlines offer youth or student fares to **under-26s**; a passport or driving licence is sufficient proof of age, though these tickets are subject to availability and can have eccentric booking conditions. Most cheap return fares will only give a percentage refund, if any, should you need to cancel or alter your journey, so check the restrictions carefully before buying.

You can often cut costs by going through a **specialist flight agent** – either a consolidator, who buys up blocks of tickets from the airlines and sells them at a reduced price, or a **discount agent**, who in addition to dealing with discounted flights may also offer special student and youth fares and a range of other travel-related services such as travel insurance, rail passes and tours. Some agents specialize in **charter flights**, which may be cheaper than anything available on a scheduled flight, but departure dates on these are fixed and withdrawal penalties are high. Be careful when choosing who to buy from, especially when dealing with small firms that are not well-established, and never deal with a company that demands cash up front or refuses to accept credit cards.

If Europe is only one stop on a longer journey, and especially if you are based in Australia or New Zealand, you might want to consider buying a **Round-the-World (RTW) ticket**. Some travel agents can sell you an "off-the-shelf" RTW ticket that will have you touching down in about half a dozen cities (London, Paris, Amsterdam, Rome, Athens and Moscow are on many such itineraries); others will assemble one for you, which can be tailored to your needs but is likely to be more expensive. Figure on US$1500–2000/Aus$2500 for a RTW ticket including one or two European stopovers. It may be worth your while if booking a RTW ticket to choose an agent with offices around the world, or at least with a 24-hour helpline in case you need to alter your itinerary en route.

## Booking flights online

Many airlines and discount travel websites offer you the opportunity to book your tickets online, cutting out the costs of agents and middlemen. Good deals can often be found through discount or auction sites, as well as through the airlines' own websites.

### Useful websites

Ⓦ **www.cheapflights.com** (in US), Ⓦ **www.cheapflights.ca** (in Canada), Ⓦ **www.cheapflights.co.uk** (in UK and Ireland), Ⓦ **www.cheapflights.com.au** (in Australia and New Zealand). Flight deals, travel agents, plus links to other travel sites.

Ⓦ **www.cheaptickets.com** Discount flight specialists (US only). Also on ☎1-888/922-8849.

Ⓦ **www.ebookers.com** Efficient, easy to use flight finder, with competitive fares.

Ⓦ **www.etn.nl/discount** A hub of consolidator and discount agent links, maintained by the nonprofit European Travel Network.

Ⓦ **www.expedia.com** (in US), Ⓦ **www.expedia.ca** (in Canada), Ⓦ **www.expedia.co.uk** (in UK). Discount airfares, all-airline search engine and daily deals.

Ⓦ **www.flyaow.com** "Airlines of the Web" – online air travel info and reservations.

Ⓦ **www.geocities.com/thavery2000** An extensive list of airline websites and US toll-free numbers.

Ⓦ **www.hotwire.com** Bookings from the US only.

Last-minute savings of up to forty percent on regular published fares. Travellers must be at least 18 and there are no refunds, transfers or changes allowed.

ⓦ **www.site59.com** (in US), ⓦ **www.lastminute .com** (in UK), ⓦ **www.lastminute.com.au** (in Australia), ⓦ **www.lastminute.co.nz** (in New Zealand). Good last-minute holiday package and flight-only deals.

ⓦ **www.opodo.co.uk** Popular and reliable source of low UK airfares. Owned by, and run in conjunction with, nine major European airlines.

ⓦ **www.orbitz.com** Comprehensive web travel source, with the usual flight, car hire and hotel deals but also great follow-up customer service.

ⓦ **www.priceline.com** (in US), ⓦ **www.priceline .co.uk** (in UK). Name-your-own-price website that has deals at around forty percent off standard fares.

ⓦ **www.skyauction.com** Bookings from the US only. Auctions tickets and travel packages to destinations worldwide.

ⓦ **travel.kelkoo.co.uk** Useful UK-only price-comparison site, checking several sources of low-cost flights (and other goods and services) according to specific criteria.

ⓦ **www.travelocity.com** (in US), ⓦ **www .travelocity.ca** (in Canada), ⓦ **www.travelocity .co.uk** (in UK), ⓦ **www.zuji.com.au** (in Australia), ⓦ **www.zuji.co.nz** (in New Zealand). Destination guides, hot fares and great deals for car rental, accommodation and lodging.

ⓦ **www.travelshop.com.au** Australian website offering discounted flights, packages, insurance, and online bookings. Also on ☏ 1300/767 908.

ⓦ **travel.yahoo.com** Incorporates some Rough Guides material in its coverage of destination countries and cities across the world, with information on places to eat, sleep, etc.

ⓦ **www.travelzoo.com** Great resource for news on the latest airline sales, cruise discounts and hotel deals. Links take you directly to the carrier's site.

# From North America

The airspace between **North America** and Europe is one of the most heavily travelled in the world and is consequently served by dozens of airlines that offer a huge range of seats at a huge range of prices. Cost depends on when and from where you're travelling, and, of course, where you want to go. The lowest fares and greatest choice of flights can be had by leaving from a US airline's "hub" – New York, Atlanta, Dallas, Chicago, Los Angeles, San Francisco, Seattle, Vancouver, Toronto and Montreal are the main ones – and into one of Europe's

"gateway" cities – London, Paris, and Amsterdam are the most popular, with Milan, Rome and Frankfurt running a close second in some cases.

## By plane from eastern and central US

There are lots of options from most of the **eastern hub cities**, though the best deals are generally out of New York and Chicago to London. Fixed-date advance-purchase tickets for midweek travel to London cost around $365 in low season (roughly speaking, winter), $685 in high season (summer, Christmas and Easter) from New York, $455/845 from Chicago. A more flexible ticket will set you back around $1560 out of New York, $1670 out of Chicago. Fixed-date advance-purchase alternatives include New York to Paris for $420/830 to Paris, $380/820 to Frankfurt, $420/820 to Madrid, or $585/1025 to Athens; flying from Chicago, discounted tickets can be had at $500/920 to Paris, $450/910 to Frankfurt, $575/920 to Madrid, or $622/1075 to Athens. Some agents and airlines may offer you an "open jaw" ticket, flying you into one city and out from another, not necessarily even in the same country, and there may also be promotional offers from time to time, especially in the off-peak seasons; Virgin Atlantic, for example, sometimes has very cheap New York–London fares in late winter with no advance purchase necessary.

## By plane from the US west coast

From the **west coast** the major airlines fly at least three times a week (sometimes daily) from Los Angeles, San Francisco and Seattle to the main European cities, with flexible economy-class tickets from LA to London at around $2270. If you don't mind buying your tickets a couple of weeks in advance and having fixed dates, you can get to London for $520/865 (low/high season), to Paris for $635/955, to Frankfurt for $545/980, to Madrid for $630/1045, or to Athens for $700/1240.

## By plane from Canada

Most of the big airlines fly to the major European hubs from **Montreal** and **Toronto** at least once daily (three times a week for the smaller airlines). From Toronto, London is your cheapest option, with the lowest direct round-trip fare around Can$650/870. For a flexible economy-class ticket on the same route, you're looking at around Can$3300. Fares from Montreal to Paris start at Can$900/1080. Vancouver has daily flights to several European cities, with round-trip fares to London from around Can$780/1115, depending on the season.

### Airlines in North America

**Aer Lingus (Irish)** ☎1-800/IRISH-AIR, ⊛www.aerlingus.com.

**Aeroflot (Russian)** US ☎1-888/340-6400, Canada ☎416/642-1653, ⊛www.aeroflot.com.

**Air Canada** ☎1-888/247-2262, ⊛www.aircanada.com.

**Air Europa (Spanish)** ☎1-800/238-7672, ⊛www.aireuropa.com.

**Air France** US ☎1-800/237-2747, Canada ☎1-800/667-2747, ⊛www.airfrance.com.

**Alitalia** US ☎1-800/223-5730, Canada ☎1-800/361-8336, ⊛www.alitalia.com.

**American Airlines** ☎1-800/433-7300, ⊛www.aa.com.

**Austrian Airlines** ☎1-800/843-0002, ⊛www.aua.com.

**bmi (British)** ☎1-800/788-0555, ⊛www.flybmi.com.

**British Airways** ☎1-800/AIRWAYS, ⊛www.ba.com.

**Continental Airlines** ☎1-800/231-0856, ⊛www.continental.com.

**Croatia Airlines** US ☎1-888/462-7628, ⊛www.croatiaairlines.hr.

**CSA Czech Airlines** US ☎1-800/223-2365, Canada 416/363-3174, ⊛www.czechairlines.com.

**Delta** ☎1-800/241-4141, ⊛www.delta.com.

**Estonian Air** US ☎1-800/397-1354, Canada ☎905/677-4295, ⊛www.estonian-air.ee.

**Finnair** ☎1-800/950-5000, ⊛www.finnair.com.

**Iberia (Spanish)** ☎1-800/772-4642, ⊛www.iberia.com.

**JAT (Serbian/Montenegrin)** US ☎212/689-1677, Canada ☎416/920 4222, ⊛www.jat.com.

**KLM/Northwest** ☎1-800/447-4747, ⊛www.klm.com, ⊛www.nwa.com.

**Lithuanian Airlines** US ☎1-800/454-8482, ⊛www.lal.lt.

**LOT (Polish)** US ☎1-800/223-0593, Canada ☎1-800/668-5928, ⊛www.lot.com.

**Lufthansa (German)** US ☎1-800/645-3880, Canada ☎1-800/563-5954, ⊛www.lufthansa.com.

**Malev (Hungarian)** ☎1-800/223-6884 or 212/566-9944, ⊛www.malev.hu.

**Martinair (Dutch)** ☎1-800/627-8462, ⊛www.martinair.com.

**Olympic (Greek)** US ☎1-800/223-1226, Canada ☎416/964-2720, ⊛www.olympic-airways.com.

**Royal Air Maroc** ☎1-800/344-6726, ⊛www.royalairmaroc.com.

**SAS (Scandinavian)** ☎1-800/221-2350, ⊛www.scandinavian.net.

**Swiss** ☎1-877/FLY-SWISS, ⊛www.swiss.com.

**TAP Air Portugal** ☎1-800/221-7370, ⊛www.tap-airportugal.pt.

**Tarom (Romanian)** ☎212/560-0840, ⊛www.tarom.ro.

**Turkish Airlines** ☎1-800/874-8875 or 212/339-9650, ⊛www.thy.com.

**United Airlines** ☎1-800/538-2929, ⊛www.united.com.

**US Airways** ☎1-800/622-1015, ⊛www.usair.com.

**Virgin Atlantic (British)** ☎1-800/862-8621, ⊛www.virgin-atlantic.com.

### Discount agents in North America

**Air Brokers International** ☎1-800/883-3273, ⊛www.airbrokers.com. Consolidator and specialist in RTW tickets.

**Airtreks** ☎1-877/AIRTREKS, ⊛www.airtreks.com. RTW specialists whose website has an interactive database that lets you build and price your own itinerary.

**Educational Travel Center** ☎1-800/747-5551 or 608/256-5551, ⊛www.edtrav.com. Student/youth discount agent.

**Flightcentre** US ☎1-866/WORLD-51, ⊛www.flightcentre.us, Canada ☎1-877/GR8-TRIP, ⊛www.flightcentre.ca. Rock-bottom fares to Europe.

**STA Travel** US ☎1-800/329-9537, Canada 1-888/427-5639, ⊛www.statravel.com. Worldwide specialists in independent travel; also student IDs, travel insurance, car rental, rail passes, and more.

**Student Flights** ☎1-800/255-8000 or 480/951-1177, ⊛www.isecard.com/studentflights. Student/youth fares, plus student IDs and European rail and bus passes.

**TFI Tours** ☎1-800/745-8000 or 212/736-1140, ⊛www.lowestairprice.com. Well-established consolidator with a wide variety of fares.

**Travel Avenue** ☎1-800/333-3335, ⊛www.travelavenue.com. Full-service travel agent that offers discounts in the form of rebates.

**Travel Cuts** Canada ☎1-800/592-CUTS, US ☎1-866/246-9762, ⊛www.travelcuts.com. Popular, long-established Canadian student-travel organization.

**Travelers Advantage** ☎1-877/259-2691, ⊛www.travelersadvantage.com. Discount travel club; annual membership fee required (currently $1 for 2 months' trial).

**Travelosophy US** ☎ 1-800/332-2687, ⊛ www .itravelosophy.com. Good range of discounted and student fares.

**Worldtek Travel** ☎ 1-800/243-1723, ⊛ www .worldtek.com. Discount travel agency.

## From Britain

Heading **from Britain** to destinations in north-western Europe, train, long-distance bus and crossing the Channel by ferry tend to be best value for money, but the further you go the less expensive air travel becomes, and it's normally cheaper to fly than take the train to most parts of southern Europe, although special deals on rail passes can bring prices down considerably.

### By plane

The best way to find the cheapest **flight** is to shop around: air travel in Europe is still highly regulated, which means that the prices quoted by the airlines can sometimes be undercut considerably by going to an agent. During the summer you can reach most of the countries of southern Europe – Portugal, Spain, Italy, Greece – on **charter flights**, block-booked by package holiday firms who usually have a few seats left over which they sell off cheaply through selected **agents**, sometimes known as "bucket shops". Though these tickets are inevitably restricted, with fixed return dates, a maximum validity of a month, and no chance of cancelling or changing after purchase, they can be very cheap – so much so in some cases that it's actually worth just using the outward portion if the return date doesn't suit. **"No frills" air-lines** such as easyJet, bmibaby and Ryanair, best booked online for the cheapest fares, offer low-cost tickets to airports around Europe (though not always the most conven-ient ones), and they often have some seri-ously cheap special offers in winter. They also have by far the least expensive flights if you only want to go one-way, as they charge for each leg of the journey separately, but some of them do have a reputation for leaving pas-sengers in the lurch if anything goes wrong or if flights have to be cancelled. It's also worth checking with flight agents who specialize

in low-cost, discounted flights (charter and scheduled), some of them – like STA Travel or Trailfinders – concentrating on deals for young people and students, though they can be a good source of bargains for eve-ryone. In addition, there are agents special-izing in offers to a specific country or group of countries on both charters and regular scheduled departures. Excellent deals can also be found on Teletext and the Internet (see p.27).

**London** is predictably Britain's main hub for air travel, offering the highest frequency of flights and widest choice of destinations from all five airports (Heathrow, Gatwick, Stansted, Luton and City), but **Manchester** has flights to most of Europe, and there are also regular services to the Continent from Birmingham, Bristol, Cardiff, Glasgow, Edinburgh, Leeds/Bradford and Newcastle. Failing that, you can get a BA or BMI flight from most UK airports (but not from Birmingham) to London, and take an onward flight from there, or fly to Paris with Air France, or Amsterdam with KLM, and change there.

To give a rough idea of **prices** booked through agents on midweek return sched-uled flights in high season reckon on paying £75–120 to Paris, Brussels or Amsterdam; £85–150 to Scandinavia; £70–150 to the major cities of Spain or Italy; £170–250 to Athens; £135–250 to Istanbul; or £80–250 to the major cities of eastern Europe. Many agents also do "open jaw" tickets, flying you into one city and out from another, not nec-essarily even in the same country.

### Airlines

**Adria (Slovenian)** ☎ 020/7734 4630 or 7437 0143, ⊛ www.adria-airways.com.
**Aer Arann** ☎ 0800/587 2324, ⊛ www.aerarann .com.
**Aer Lingus** ☎ 0845/084 4444, ⊛ www.aerlingus .com.
**Aeroflot (Russian)** ☎ 020/7355 2233, ⊛ www .aeroflot.co.uk.
**Air Baltic (Latvian)** ☎ 0870/774 5458, ⊛ www .airbaltic.com.
**Air Berlin** ☎ 0870/738 8880, ⊛ www.airberlin .com.
**Air France** ☎ 0870/142 4343, ⊛ www.airfrance .co.uk.
**Alitalia** ☎ 0870/544 8259, ⊛ www.alitalia.co.uk.

Austrian Airlines ☎0870/124 2625, ⊛www
.aua.com.
BMI ☎0870/607 0555, ⊛www.flybmi.com.
bmibaby ☎0870/264 2229, ⊛www.bmibaby
.com.
Britannia ☎0800/000 747, ⊛www
.britanniadirect.com.
British Airways ☎0870/850 9850, ⊛www
.ba.com.
Croatia Airlines ☎020/8563 0022, ⊛www
.croatiaairlines.hr.
CSA (Czech Airlines) ☎0870/444 3747,
⊛www.csa.cz.
easyJet ☎0871/750 0100, ⊛www.easyjet.com.
Estonian Air ☎020/7333 0196, ⊛www
.estonian-air.ee.
Finnair ☎0870/241 4411, ⊛www.finnair.com.
flyBE ☎0871/700 0535, ⊛www.flybe.com.
Iberia (Spanish) ☎0870/609 0500, ⊛www
.iberia.com.
JAT (Serbian) ☎020/7629 2007, ⊛www
.jatlondon.com.
Jet2 ☎0870/737 8282, ⊛www.jet2.com.
Jetmagic ☎0870/178 0135, ⊛www.jetmagic
.com.
KLM (Dutch) ☎0870/507 4074, ⊛www.klm.com.
LOT (Polish) ☎0845/601 0949, ⊛www.lot.com.
Lufthansa (German) ☎0845/773 7747, ⊛www
.lufthansa.co.uk.
Luxair ☎01293/596 633, ⊛www.luxair.lu.
Maersk Air ☎020/7333 0066, ⊛www
.maersk-air.com.
Malev (Hungarian) ☎0870/909 0577, ⊛www
.malev.hu.
Monarch ☎0870/040 5040, ⊛www.flymonarch
.com.
Olympic (Greek) ☎0870/606 0460, ⊛www
.olympic-airways.com.
Royal Air Maroc ☎020/7439 4361, ⊛www
.royalairmaroc.com.
Ryanair ☎0871/246 0000, ⊛www.ryanair.com.
SAS (Scandinavian) ☎0870/60727727, ⊛www
.scandinavian.net.
Sky Europe ☎020/7365 0365, ⊛www
.skyeurope.com.
SN (Brussels Airlines) ☎0870/735 2345,
⊛www.flysn.com.
Swiss ☎0845/601 0956, ⊛www.swiss.com.
TAP (Air Portugal) ☎0870/607 2024, ⊛www
.tap-airportugal.co.uk.
Tarom (Romanian) ☎020/7224 3693, ⊛www
.tarom.ro.
Turkish Airlines ☎020/7766 9300, ⊛www
.thy.com.
Virgin Express ☎020/7744 0004, ⊛www
.virgin-express.com.

VLM Airlines (Belgian) ☎020/7476 6677,
⊛www.vlm-airlines.com.

### Discount agents

Bridge the World ☎0870/443 2399, ⊛www
.bridgetheworld.com. Good-value flight deals aimed
at the backpacker market.
ebookers ☎0870/010 7000, ⊛www.ebookers
.com. Low scheduled fares.
Flights4Less ☎0871/222 3432, ⊛www
.flights4less.co.uk. Good discount airfares. Part of
Lastminute.com.
Flynow ☎0870/444 0045, ⊛www.flynow.com.
Large range of discounted tickets.
North South Travel ☎01245/608 291, ⊛www
.northsouthtravel.co.uk. Friendly, competitive travel
agency, offering discounted fares worldwide. Profits
are used to support projects in the developing world,
especially the promotion of sustainable tourism.
STA Travel ☎0870/160 0599, ⊛www.statravel
.co.uk. Worldwide specialists in low-cost flights
and tours for students and under-26s, though other
customers are welcome.
Top Deck ☎020/7244 8000, ⊛www
.topdecktravel.co.uk. Long-established agent dealing
in discount flights.
Trailfinders ☎0845/058 5858, ⊛www.trailfinders
.com. One of the best-informed and most efficient
agents for independent travellers.
TravelCare ☎0870/112 0085, ⊛www.travelcare
.co.uk. Discount charter flights.

### By train

Direct **trains** through the Channel Tunnel
from London to Paris (15 daily, 2hr 40min)
and Brussels (9 daily, 2hr 20min) are operated by **Eurostar**. Tickets for under-26s start
at £40 one-way, £59 return. For over-26s,
the cheapest return ticket, at £59, costs
less than a single fare, which is £149 – in
theory, the cheaper ticket involves a "compulsory return". Through-ticket combinations
with onward connections from Brussels and
Paris can be booked through Trainseurope,
International Rail and Rail Europe.

Other rail journeys from Britain involve some
kind of **sea crossing**, by ferry or, sometimes,
catamaran. Current rail–sea–rail return fares
from London (which include the crossing)
are £75 to Paris, £82 to Brussels and £85
to Amsterdam. They can be bought from
International Rail, and from some major rail
stations (in London, at Charing Cross if routed
via France or Belgium, or at Liverpool Street

or from ⊛ www.amsterdamexpress.co.uk if routed via the Hook of Holland). For some destinations, there are cheaper SuperApex fares (£50 to Amsterdam, for example) requiring advance booking and subject to greater restrictions. Five-day return tickets to Paris and Brussels are also available, at £64 and £72 respectively. Otherwise, international tickets are valid for two months and allow for stopovers on the way, providing you stick to the prescribed route (there may be a choice, with different fares applicable). One-way fares are generally around two-thirds the price of a return fare. If you're **under 26** you're entitled to all sorts of special deals, not least cut-price youth fares; examples of under-26 return ticket prices are £68 to Paris, £63 to Brussels and £68 to Amsterdam.

Trainseurope, International Rail, Ffestiniog Travel, European Rail and Rail Europe can sell **through tickets** to most Western European destinations, and some through tickets can be booked on line with Rail Europe. For destinations further afield, and especially to places like Russia, Romania, Bulgaria, Greece and Turkey, Trainseurope and Ffestiniog Travel are more likely to sell through tickets than the bigger firms, and it's worth shopping around, as some agencies can sell you tickets that others can't, and some may offer cheaper prices than others, or more convenient routes. The Europe page of The Man in Seat 61 website has more detailed advice about buying through tickets, plus detailed information on rail travel from Britain to any European country.

For **rail passes** and other types of discounted rail travel, see "Getting around", p.45.

### Rail contacts

**European Rail** ☎020/7387 0444, ⊛www .europeanrail.com.
**Eurostar** ☎0870/518 6186, ⊛www.eurostar.com.
**Eurotunnel** ☎0870/535 3535, ⊛www.eurotunnel .com.
**Ffestiniog Travel** ☎01766/512400, ⊛www .festtravel.co.uk,
**International Rail** ☎0870/751 5000, ⊛www .international-rail.com.
**The Man in Seat 61** ⊛www.seat61.com.
**Rail Europe** ☎0870/837 1371, ⊛www.raileurope .co.uk.
**Trainseurope** ☎0871/700 7722, ⊛www .trainseurope.co.uk.

## By bus

A long-distance **bus**, although much less comfortable than the train, is at least a little cheaper. The main operator based in Britain is **Eurolines**, which has a network of routes spanning the continent – north as far as Scandinavia, east to Poland and the Baltic states, and south to Spain, Portugal and Morocco. **Prices** can be up to a third less than the equivalent train fare, and there are marginally cheaper fares on most services for those under 26, which undercut youth rail rates for the same journey. Current Eurolines fares from London's Victoria Coach Station to Paris or Amsterdam are £36 for a one-way ticket booked four days in advance (£39 without a youth reduction) or a return booked fifteen days in advance (with special offer £16 one-way fares on some services). Brussels is £35 one-way, £36 return (£36 one-way or return without a youth reduction), Berlin £65/85 (£69/89), Madrid £79/129 (£89/139), Budapest £69/95 (£79/109) and Moscow £119/139 (£169/199). There's usually a discount of £4–10 if you buy your ticket at least four days in advance, and bigger discounts for return journeys booked two weeks or a month in advance. Slightly higher fares apply at Easter, in July and August, and from mid-December to the beginning of January, when reductions for two-week and one-month advance purchases do not apply. Connecting services from elsewhere in Great Britain add around £15–20 each way to the price of the ticket. The German-based firm **Gullivers** offers an alternative service to Paris, Brussels, Amsterdam, Berlin, Hamburg and Hannover via the Channel Tunnel, and Anglia International serves all of those plus Prague, Bratislava, Copenhagen and various Polish destinations, with connecting services from Glasgow and Edinburgh.

Eurolines also has **Minipass** return tickets from London to two or more European cities, valid for ninety days: London–Brussels–Paris–London or London–Amsterdam–Brussels–London costs £55, London–Amsterdam–Paris–London is £67, London–Cologne–Paris–London £73. Alternatively, you might consider Eurolines's fifteen-, thirty- and forty-day passes, or one of the various passes offered by **Busabout** for their services around the continent (see "Getting around", p.56).

### Bus contacts

**Busabout** ☎020/7950 1661, ⓦwww.busabout .com.
**Eurolines** ☎0870/514 3219, ⓦwww.eurolines .co.uk. Tickets can also be purchased from any Eurolines or National Express agent.
**Gullivers** ☎00800/4855 4837, ⓦwww.gullivers .de.

## By ferry

There are numerous **ferry services** between Britain and Ireland, and between the British Isles and the European mainland. Ferries from the southeast of Ireland and the south coast of England connect with northern France and Spain; those from Kent in southeast England reach northern France and Belgium; those from Scotland and the east coast and northeast of England cross the North Sea to Belgium, the Netherlands, Germany and Scandinavia.

### Ferry operators

**Brittany Ferries** ☎0870/366 5333, ⓦwww .brittanyferries.co.uk. Portsmouth to Caen, Cherbourg and St Malo; Poole to Cherbourg; Plymouth to Roscoff and Santander.
**Condor Ferries** ☎0845/641 0240, ⓦwww .condorferries.co.uk. Poole to Cherbourg; Portsmouth, Poole, and Weymouth to St Malo via Jersey and Guernsey.
**DFDS Seaways** ☎0870/533 3111, ⓦwww .dfdsseaways.co.uk. Harwich to Cuxhaven (Germany), Esbjerg (Denmark); Newcastle to Amsterdam, and seasonally to Gothenburg (Sweden) and Kristiansand (Norway).
**Fjord Line** ☎ 0870/143 9669, ⓦwww.fjordline .co.uk. Newcastle to Stavanger, Haugesund and Bergen.
**Hoverspeed** ☎0870/240 8070, ⓦwww .hoverspeed.co.uk. Dover to Calais; Newhaven to Dieppe.
**Norfolk Line** ☎0870/870 1020, ⓦwww .norfolkline.com. Dover to Dunkerque.
**P&O Ferries** ☎0870/600 0600 or 01304/864 003, ⓦwww.poferries.com. Hull to Zeebrugge and Rotterdam; Dover to Calais; Portsmouth to Bilbao and Le Havre.
**SeaFrance** ☎0870/571 1711, ⓦwww.seafrance .com. Dover to Calais.

**Smyril Line** ☎01595/690 845, ⓦwww.smyril-line .fo. Lerwick (Shetland) to Bergen, with connecting P&O Scottish service from Aberdeen.
**Superfast Ferries** ☎0870/234 0870, ⓦwww .superfast.com. Rosyth (near Edinburgh) to Zeebrugge (Belgium).
**Stena Line** ☎0870/400 6798, ⓦwww.stenaline .co.uk. Harwich to Hook of Holland.
**Transmanche Ferries** ☎0800/917 1201, ⓦwww .transmancheferries.com. Newhaven to Dieppe.

## From Ireland

There are direct flights **from Dublin** to most major cities in mainland Europe, and connections from those or from London to practically any airport you want to fly to. There are also one or two direct flights to the Continent **from Shannon** and **from Cork**. Bus or train/ferry combination tickets provide a slower though slightly less expensive alternative.

## By plane

The no-frills airlines, such as Ryanair, are usually the cheapest, especially in winter, and especially if you only want a one-way journey. You may save a little money travelling by land, sea or even air to London and buying your flight there, but the difference isn't much, and if you're going to London by surface routes, you may as well carry on that way into Europe. **From Belfast**, there are direct flights with easyJet to Amsterdam, Paris, Nice, Malaga and Alicante. For other destinations, you'll have to change at one of those, or at London (served by easyJet, BMI, BA and flyBE) or Manchester (served by BA and bmibaby).

### Airlines

**Aer Arann** ☎0818/210 210 or 01/814 1058, ⓦwww.aerarann.com.
**Aer Lingus** ☎0818/365 000, ⓦwww.aerlingus.ie.
**Air France** ☎01/605 0383, ⓦwww.airfrance.ie.
**Alitalia** ☎01/677 5171, ⓦwww.alitalia.ie.
**Austrian Airlines** ☎1800/509 142, ⓦwww.aua .com.
**BMI** ☎01/407 3036, Northern Ireland ☎0870/607 0555, ⓦwww.flybmi.com.
**bmibaby** ☎1890/340 122, Northern Ireland ☎0870/264 2229, ⓦwww.bmibaby.com.
**British Airways** ☎1800/626 747, Northern Ireland ☎0870/850 9850 ⓦwww.ba.com.
**CityJet** ☎01/870 0100, ⓦwww.cityjet.com.

**CSA (Czech Airlines)** ☎01/814 4626, ⊛www
.csa.cz.
**easyJet** Northern Ireland ☎0871/750 0100,
⊛www.easyjet.com.
**Finnair** ☎01/844 6565, ⊛www.finnair.com.
**flyBE** ☎1890/925 532, Northern Ireland
☎0871/700 0535, ⊛www.flybe.com.
**Iberia (Spanish)** ☎01/407 3017, ⊛www.iberia
.com.
**Jetmagic** ☎0818/200 135, ⊛www.jetmagic.com.
**LOT (Polish)** ☎1890/200 514, ⊛www.lot.com.
**Lufthansa (German)** ☎01/844 5544, ⊛www
.lufthansa.ie.
**Malev (Hungarian)** ☎01/844 4303, ⊛www
.malev.hu.
**Olympic (Greek)** ☎01/608 0090, ⊛www
.olympic-airways.com.
**Ryanair** ☎0818/303 030, ⊛www.ryanair.com.
**SAS (Scandinavian)** ☎01/844 5440, ⊛www
.scandinavian.net.
**Skynet** ☎061/234 455, ⊛www.skynet.aero.
**Swiss** ☎1890/200 515, ⊛www.swiss.com.
**TAP (Air Portugal)** ☎01/679 8844, ⊛www
.tap-airportugal.pt.

### Discount agents

**Aran Travel First Choice** ☎091/562 595,
⊛www.firstchoicetravel.ie. Good-value flights.
**ebookers** ☎01/241 5689, ⊛www.ebookers.ie.
Low fares on an extensive selection of scheduled
flights.
**Go Holidays** ☎01/874 4126, ⊛www.goholidays
.ie. City breaks and package tours.
**Joe Walsh Tours** ☎01/872 2555, ⊛www
.joewalshtours.ie. General budget fares agent.
**Lee Travel** ☎021/427 7111, ⊛www.leetravel.ie.
Flights and holidays.
**McCarthy's Travel** ☎021/427 0127, ⊛www
.mccarthystravel.ie. General flight agent.
**Neenan Travel** ☎01/607 9900, ⊛www
.neenantrav.ie. Specialists in European city breaks.
**Rosetta Travel** Northern Ireland ☎028/9064 4996,
⊛www.rosettatravel.com. Specialist in deals from
Belfast.
**Trailfinders** ☎01/677 7888, ⊛www.trailfinders.ie.
Excellent agent for independent travel.
**USIT** ☎01/602 1904, Northern Ireland ☎028/9032
7111, ⊛www.usitnow.ie. Ireland's main student and
youth travel specialists.
**World Travel Centre** ☎01/416 7007, ⊛www
.worldtravel.ie. Excellent fares to Europe.

### By bus and train

From Ireland, direct **rail** tickets to Europe
via Britain generally include both boat con-

nections, and are available from Iarnród
Éireann's Continental Rail Desk in the
Republic, or Northern Ireland Railways in
the North, with discounted under-26 tickets available from these and from USIT.
Eurolines **bus services** connect in London
for onward travel to the Continent.

### Bus and train contacts

**Eurolines** ☎01/836 6111, ⊛www.eurolines.ie.
**Iarnród Éireann** ☎01/703 1885, ⊛www.irishrail
.ie.
**Northern Ireland Railways** ☎028/9066 6630,
⊛www.translink.co.uk.

### Ferry operators

**Brittany Ferries** ☎021/427 7801, ⊛www
.brittanyferries.ie. Cork to Roscoff (March–early
Nov).
**Irish Ferries** Republic ☎0818/300 400, UK
☎0870/517 1717, ⊛www.irishferries.com. Dublin
to Holyhead; Rosslare to Pembroke, Cherbourg
(March–Dec) and Roscoff (March–Dec).
**Norse Merchant Ferries** Republic ☎01/819
2999, UK ☎0870/600 4321, ⊛www
.norsemerchant.com. Belfast and Dublin to
Birkenhead.
**P&O Irish Sea** Republic ☎1800/409 049, UK
☎0870/242 4777, ⊛www.poirishsea.com. Larne
to Cairnryan and Troon (March–Sept); Dublin to
Liverpool.
**SeaCat** Republic ☎1800/805 055, UK
☎0870/552 3523, ⊛www.seacat.co.uk. Dublin
to Liverpool.
**Stena Line** Republic ☎01/204 7777, ⊛www
.stenaline.ie, UK ☎028/9074 7747, ⊛www
.stenaline.co.uk. Rosslare to Fishguard; Dun
Laoghaire and Dublin to Holyhead; Belfast to
Stranraer; Larne to Fleetwood.
**Swansea–Cork Ferries** Republic ☎021/427
1166, UK ☎01792/456116, ⊛www
.swansea-cork.ie. Cork to Swansea (March–early
Jan).

## From Australia and New Zealand

There are **flights** from Melbourne, Sydney,
Adelaide, Brisbane and Perth to most
European capitals, and there's not a great
deal of difference in the fares to the busi-
est destinations: a scheduled return from
Sydney to London, Paris, Rome, Madrid,
Athens or Frankfurt should be available
through travel agents for around A$1900

in low season (Australia's summer, Europe's winter). A one-way ticket costs slightly more than half that, while a return flight from Auckland to Europe is approximately NZ$2000 in low season. Asian airlines often work out cheapest, and may throw in a stopover, while there are often bargain deals to be had from Melbourne to Athens on Olympic Airways. Some agents may also offer "open jaw" tickets, flying you into one city and out from another, not necessarily even in the same country. For RTW deals and other **low-price tickets**, the most reliable operator is STA Travel, who also supply packages with companies such as Contiki and Busabout, can issue rail passes, and advise on visa regulations – for a fee they'll even do all the paperwork for you.

## Airlines

**Aeroflot (Russian)** Australia ☎02/9262 2233, ⊛www.aeroflot.com.au.

**Air France** Australia ☎1300/361 400, NZ ☎09/308 3352, ⊛www.airfrance.com.

**Air New Zealand** Australia ☎13 24 76, ⊛www.airnz.com.au, NZ ☎0800/737 000, ⊛www.airnz.co.nz.

**Austrian Airlines** Australia ☎1800/642 438 or 02/9251 6155, NZ ☎09/308 5206, ⊛www.aua.com.

**British Airways** Australia ☎1300/767 177, NZ ☎0800/274 847 or 09/356 8690, ⊛www.britishairways.com.

**Cathay Pacific** Australia ☎13 17 47, NZ ☎0508/800 454 or 09/379 0861, ⊛www.cathaypacific.com.

**Croatia Airlines** Australia ☎03/9699 9388, NZ ☎09/838 7722, ⊛www.croatiaairlines.hr.

**CSA (Czech Airlines)** Australia ☎02/9247 7706, ⊛www.csa.cz.

**Emirates** Australia ☎1300/303 777 or 02/9290 9700, NZ ☎09/377 6004, ⊛www.emirates.com.

**Finnair** Australia ☎02/9244 2299, NZ ☎09/308 3365, ⊛www.finnair.com.

**Garuda Indonesia** Australia ☎1300/365 330 or 02/9334 9944, NZ ☎09/366 1862, ⊛www.garuda-indonesia.com.

**Gulf Air** Australia ☎02/9244 2199, NZ ☎09/308 3366, ⊛www.gulfairco.com.

**JAL (Japan Airlines)** Australia ☎02/9272 1111, NZ ☎09/379 9906, ⊛www.jal.com.

**KLM (Dutch)** Australia ☎1300/303 747, NZ ☎09/309 1782, ⊛www.klm.com.

**LOT (Polish)** Australia ☎02/9244 2466, NZ ☎09/308 3369, ⊛www.lot.com.

**Lufthansa (German)** Australia ☎1300/655 727, NZ ☎0800/945 220, ⊛www.lufthansa.com.

**Malaysia Airlines** Australia ☎13 26 27, NZ ☎0800/777 747, ⊛www.malaysia-airlines.com.

**Malev (Hungarian)** Australia ☎02/9244 2111, NZ ☎09/379 4455, ⊛www.malev.hu.

**Qantas** Australia ☎13 13 13, NZ ☎0800/808 767 or 09/357 8900, ⊛www.qantas.com.

**SAS (Scandinavian)** Australia ☎1300/727 707, ⊛www.scandinavian.net.

**Singapore Airlines** Australia ☎13 10 11, NZ ☎0800/808 909, ⊛www.singaporeair.com.

**Swiss** Australia ☎1800/883 199, New Zealand ☎09/977 2238, ⊛www.swiss.com.

**TAP Air Portugal** Australia ☎02/9244 2344, NZ ☎09/308 3319, ⊛www.tap-airportugal.pt.

**Tarom (Romanian)** Australia ☎02/9262 1144, ⊛www.tarom.ro.

**Thai Airways** Australia ☎1300/651 960, NZ ☎09/377 3886, ⊛www.thaiair.com.

**Turkish** Australia ☎02/9299 8400, ⊛www.thy.com.

**Virgin Atlantic** Australia ☎02/9244 2747, ⊛www.virgin-atlantic.com.

## Discount agents

**Flight Centre** Australia ☎13 31 33, ⊛www.flightcentre.com.au, NZ ☎0800/243 544, ⊛www.flightcentre.co.nz. Rock-bottom fares to Europe and worldwide.

**Holiday Shoppe** NZ ☎0800/808 480, ⊛www.holidayshoppe.co.nz. Great deals on flights, hotels and holidays.

**OTC** Australia ☎1300/855 118, ⊛www.onlinetravel.com.au. Deals on flights, hotels and holidays.

**STA Travel** Australia ☎1300/733 035, ⊛www.statravel.com.au; NZ ☎0508/782 872, ⊛www.statravel.com.au. Worldwide specialists in low-cost flights, overlands and holiday deals. Good discounts for students and under-26s.

**Trailfinders** Australia ☎1300/780 212, ⊛www.trailfinders.com.au. One of the best-informed and most efficient agents for independent travellers.

**travel.com.au** and **travel.co.nz** Australia ☎1300/130 482, ⊛www.travel.com.au, NZ ☎0800/468 332, ⊛www.travel.co.nz. Comprehensive online travel company, with discounted fares.

# Red tape and visas

Within the EU, border-crossing has become an informal procedure, with holders of most passports just having to wave their documents at border officials.

Citizens of the UK (but not other British passport holders), Ireland, Australia, New Zealand, Canada and the US do not need a visa to enter most European countries (current exceptions are listed in the next paragraph), and can usually stay for one to three months, depending on nationality; for some countries, passports must be valid at least six months beyond the end of stay. Always check **visa requirements** before travelling, as they can and do change; this especially applies to Canadian, Australian and New Zealand citizens intending to visit Eastern European countries; EU countries never require visas from British or Irish citizens.

Everyone needs a **visa** to visit Russia. **American**, **British** and **Irish** citizens need a visa for Turkey (available at the border). **Canadians** need visas for Poland and Turkey (the second available at the border). **Australians** need visas to visit Poland, Romania and Turkey (the last available at the border). **New Zealanders** need visas for Poland and Romania. You will need a **transit visa** if passing through Ukraine or Belarus (when travelling, for example, from Poland, Slovakia, Hungary or Romania to Moscow).

Fifteen countries (Austria, Belgium, Denmark, Finland, France, Germany, Greece, Iceland, Italy, Luxembourg, the Netherlands, Norway, Portugal, Spain and Sweden), known as the Schengen Group, now have joint visas which are valid for travel in all of them; in theory, there are also no immigration controls between these countries, but, in practice, there are often more ID spot-checks within their borders.

## Customs

**Customs and duty-free restrictions** vary throughout Europe, but are standard for travellers arriving in the EU at one litre of spirits, plus two litres of table wine, plus 200 cigarettes (or 250g tobacco, or fifty cigars).

There is no duty-free allowance for travel within the EU; in principle you can carry as much in the way of duty-paid goods as you want, so long as it is for personal use. However, for the time being limits still apply to cigarettes or tobacco imported to the rest of the EU from the Czech Republic, Estonia, Hungary, Latvia, Lithuania, Poland, Slovakia and Slovenia. Note that Andorra, Gibraltar, the Channel Islands, the Canary Islands, Ceuta, Melilla and northern Cyprus are outside the EU for customs purposes. Remember that **carrying contraband** such as controlled drugs, banned pornography or firearms is illegal, not to mention foolhardy in the extreme. If you are carrying prescribed drugs of any kind, it might be a good idea to have a copy of the prescription to show to suspicious customs officers. Note also that for health reasons, many countries, including all EU members, restrict the importation of meat, fish, vegetables and honey, even for personal consumption.

## European embassies

**Andorran** UK ☎020/8874 4806, US ☎212/750 8064.

**Austrian** US ☎202/895-6700, Canada ☎613/789-1444, UK ☎020/7235 3731, Ireland ☎01/269 4577, Australia ☎02/6295 1533, NZ ☎04/499 6393.

**Belgian** Australia ☎02/6273 2501, Canada ☎613/236-7267, Ireland ☎01/205 7100, NZ ☎09/915 9146, UK ☎020/7470 3700, US ☎202/333-6900.

**British** Australia ☎02/6270 6666, Canada ☎613/237-1530, Ireland ☎01/205 3700, NZ ☎04/924 2888, US ☎202/588-7800.

**Bulgarian** Australia ☎02/6286 9600, Canada ☎613/789-3215, Ireland ☎01/660 3293, UK ☎020/7584 9400, US ☎202/387-0174.

**Croatian** Australia ☎02/6286 6988, Canada ☎613/562-7820, NZ ☎09/836 5581, UK ☎020/7387 2022, US ☎202/588-5899.

**Czech** Australia ☎02/6290 1386, Canada

☎613/562-3875, Ireland ☎01/668 1135, NZ ☎09/522 8736, UK ☎020/7243 1115, US ☎202/274-9100.

**Danish** Australia ☎02/6273 2196, Canada ☎613/562-1811, Ireland ☎01/475 6404, NZ ☎04/471 0520, UK ☎020/7333 0200, US ☎202/234-4300.

**Estonian** Australia ☎02/9810 7468, Canada ☎613/789-4222, Ireland ☎01/219 6730, UK ☎020/7589 3428, US ☎202/588-0101.

**Finnish** Australia ☎02/6273 3800, Canada ☎613/288 2233, Ireland ☎01/478 1344, NZ ☎04/499 4599, UK ☎020/7838 6200, US ☎202/298-5800.

**French** Australia ☎02/6216 0100, Canada ☎613/789-1795, Ireland ☎01/277 5000, NZ ☎04/384 2555, UK ☎020/7073 1000, US ☎202/944-6166.

**German** Australia ☎02/6270 1911, Canada ☎613/232-1101, Ireland ☎01/269 3011, NZ ☎04/473 6063, UK ☎020/7824 1300, US ☎202/298-8140.

**Greek** Australia ☎02/6273 3011, Canada ☎613/238-6271, Ireland ☎01/676 7254, NZ ☎04/473 7775, UK ☎020/7229 3850, US ☎202/939-1300.

**Hungarian** Australia ☎02/6282 3226, Canada ☎613/230-2717, Ireland ☎01/661 2902, NZ ☎04/973 7507, UK ☎020/7235 5218, US ☎202/362-6730.

**Irish** Australia ☎02/6273 3022, Canada ☎613/233-6281, UK ☎020/7235 2171, US ☎202/462-3939.

**Italian** Australia ☎02/6273 3333, Canada ☎613/232-2401, Ireland ☎01/660 1744, NZ ☎04/473 5339, UK ☎020/7312 2200, US ☎202/612-4400.

**Latvian** Australia ☎03/9499 6920, Canada ☎613/238-6014, UK ☎020/7312 0040, US ☎202/726-8213.

**Lithuanian** Australia ☎02/9498 2571, Canada ☎613/567-5458, NZ ☎09/571 1822, UK ☎020/7486 6401, US ☎202/234-5860.

**Luxembourg** Australia ☎02/9253 4708, UK ☎020/7235 6961, US ☎202/265-4171.

**Moroccan** Australia ☎02/9922 4999, Canada ☎613/236-7391, Ireland ☎01/660 9449, NZ ☎09/520 4129, UK ☎020/7581 5001, US ☎202/462-7979.

**Netherlands** Australia ☎02/6220 9400, Canada ☎613/237-5030, Ireland ☎01/269 3444, NZ ☎04/471 6390, UK ☎020/7590 3200, US ☎202/244-5300.

**Norwegian** Australia ☎02/6273 3444, Canada ☎613/238-6571, Ireland ☎01/662 1800, NZ ☎04/471 2503, UK ☎020/7591 5500, US ☎202/333-6000.

**Polish** Australia ☎02/6273 1208, Canada ☎613/789-0468, Ireland ☎01/283 0855, NZ ☎04/475 9453, UK ☎0870/774 2700, US ☎202/234-3800.

**Portuguese** Australia ☎02/6290 1733, Canada ☎613/729-0883, Ireland ☎01/289 4416, NZ ☎09/259 4014, UK ☎020/7235 5331, US ☎202/328-8610.

**Romanian** Australia ☎02/6286 2343, Canada ☎613/789-3709, Ireland ☎01/269 2852, UK ☎020/7937 9666, US ☎202/232-4846.

**Russian** Australia ☎02/6295 9033, Canada ☎613/236-7220, Ireland ☎01/492 2048, NZ ☎04/476 6113, UK ☎020/7229 3628, US ☎202/298-5700.

**Serbian** Australia ☎02/6290 2630, Canada ☎613/233 6289, UK ☎020/7235 9049, US ☎202/332 0333.

**Slovakian** Australia ☎02/6290 1516, Canada ☎613/749-4442, Ireland ☎01/660 0012, NZ ☎09/366 5111, UK ☎020/7313 6470, US ☎202/237-1054.

**Slovenian** Australia ☎02/6243 4830, Canada ☎613/565-5781, UK ☎020/7222 5400, US ☎202/667 5363.

**Spanish** Australia ☎02/6273 3555, Canada ☎613/747-2252, Ireland ☎01/269 1640, NZ ☎03/366 0244, UK ☎020/7589 8989, US ☎202/452-0100.

**Swedish** Australia ☎02/6270 2700, Canada ☎613/241-8553, Ireland ☎01/671 5822, NZ ☎04/499 9895, UK ☎020/7917 6400, US ☎202/467-2600.

**Swiss** Australia ☎02/6273 3977, Canada ☎613/235-1837, Ireland ☎01/218 6382, NZ ☎04/472 1593, UK ☎020/7616 6000, US ☎202/745-7900.

**Turkish** Australia ☎02/6295 0227, Canada ☎613/789-4044, Ireland ☎01/668 5240, NZ ☎04/472 1292, UK ☎020/7393 0202, US ☎202/612-6700.

# Information, websites and maps

Before you leave, it's worth contacting the tourist offices of the countries you're intending to visit for free leaflets, maps and brochures, some of which can be quite useful for planning your trip and when travelling.

This is especially true in parts of central and eastern Europe, where up-to-date maps can be harder to find within the country. Bulgaria, Estonia and Latvia do not have official tourist offices, and neither does Russia except in the US; their embassies will have some information, but it will be about rules and regulations rather than transport and sightseeing. Go easy, though: much of the information can be picked up just as easily on your travels. Some tourist offices in the UK charge premium rates for phone enquiries (numbers beginning ☎09), making it cheaper to call their US office instead.

Once you're in Europe, on-the-spot information is easy enough to pick up. Most countries have a network of **tourist offices** that answer queries, dole out a range of (sometimes free) maps and brochures, and can often book accommodation, or at least advise you on it. They're better organized in northern Europe – Scandinavia, the Netherlands, France, Switzerland – with branches in all but the smallest village, and mounds of information; in Greece, Turkey and eastern Europe you'll find fewer tourist offices and they'll be less helpful on the whole, sometimes offering no more than a couple of dog-eared brochures and a photocopied map. We've given further details, including a broad idea of opening hours, in the introduction for each country.

## Tourist information websites and offices

If there is no office in your home country, apply to the embassy instead.

**Andorra** ⊛ www.turisme.ad. UK ☎020/8874 4806.
**Austria** ⊛ www.austria.info. Australia ☎02/9299 3621; Canada ☎416/967-3381; Ireland ☎189/093 0118; UK ☎0845/101 1818; US ☎212/944-6880.
**Belgium** ⊛ www.visitbelgium.com. Canada ☎514/457-2888; UK ☎0800/954 5245; US ☎212/758-8130;.

**Britain** ⊛ www.visitbritain.com. Australia ☎02/9021 4400 or 1300/858 589; Canada ☎1-888/VISIT-UK; Ireland ☎01/670 8000; New Zealand ☎0800/700 741; US ☎1-800/462-2748.
**Bulgaria** ⊛ www.bulgariatravel.org.
**Croatia** ⊛ www.croatia.hr. UK ☎020/8563 7979; US ☎1-800/829 4416.
**Czech Republic** ⊛ www.visitczech.cz. Canada ☎416/363-9928; Ireland ☎01/283 6068; UK ☎020/7631 0427; US ☎212/288-0830.
**Denmark** ⊛ www.visitdenmark.com. UK ☎020/7259 5959; US ☎212/885-9700.
**Estonia** ⊛ www.visitestonia.com.
**Finland** ⊛ www.finland-tourism.com. Canada & US ☎1-800/FIN-INFO; Ireland ☎01/407 3362; UK ☎020/7365 2512.
**France** ⊛ www.franceguide.com. Australia ☎02/9231 5244; Canada ☎514/288-2026; Ireland ☎1560/235 235 (premium rate); UK ☎0906/824 4123 (premium rate); US ☎410/286-8310.
**Germany** ⊛ www.germany-tourism.de. Australia ☎02/8296 0488; Canada & US ☎1-800/651-7010; Ireland ☎1800/484 480; UK ☎020/7317 0908.
**Greece** ⊛ www.gnto.gr. Australia ☎02/9241 1663; Canada ☎416/968-2220; UK ☎020/7495 9300; US ☎212/421-5777.
**Hungary** ⊛ www.hungarytourism.hu. UK & Ireland ☎00800/3600 0000; US ☎212/355-0240.
**Ireland** ⊛ www.ireland.travel.ie. Australia ☎02/9299 6177; Canada & US ☎1-800/223-6470; New Zealand ☎09/977 2255; UK ☎0800/039 7000.
**Italy** ⊛ www.enit.it. Australia ☎02/9262 1666; Canada ☎416/925-4882; UK ☎020/7399 3562; US ☎212/245-4822.
**Latvia** ⊛ www.latviatourism.lv.
**Lithuania** ⊛ www.tourism.lt. US ☎718/423-6161.
**Luxembourg** ⊛ www.ont.lu. UK ☎020/7434 2800; US ☎212/935-8888.
**Morocco** ⊛ www.tourisme-marocain.com. Australia ☎02/9299 6177; Canada ☎514/842-8111; UK ☎020/7437 0073; US ☎212/557-2520.
**Netherlands** ⊛ www.holland.com. The Netherlands has no walk-in offices, nor numbers for telephone inquiries.

**Norway** ⊛ www.visitnorway.com. UK ☎ 0906/302 2003 (premium rate); US ☎ 212/885-9700.

**Poland** ⊛ www.polandtour.org. UK ☎ 0870/067 5010; US ☎ 201/420-9910.

**Portugal** ⊛ www.portugal-insite.pt. Canada ☎ 416/921-7376; Ireland ☎ 1800/943 131; UK ☎ 0845/355 1212; US ☎ 646/723 0200.

**Romania** ⊛ www.romaniatourism.com. UK ☎ 020/7224 3692; US ☎ 212/545-8484.

**Russia** ⊛ www.russia-travel.com. US ☎ 1-877/221-7120 or 212/575 3431.

**Serbia** ⊛ www.serbia-tourism.org. UK ☎ 020/7629 2007.

**Slovenia** ⊛ www.slovenia-tourism.si. US ☎ 954/491 0112; UK ☎ 01373/814 233.

**Spain** ⊛ www.tourspain.es. US ☎ 212/265-8822; Canada ☎ 416/961-3131; UK ☎ 020/7486 8077.

**Sweden** ⊛ www.visit-sweden.com. Worldwide toll-free ☎ +800/3080 3080; Ireland ☎ 01/247 5440; UK ☎ 020/7108 6168; US ☎ 212/885-9700.

**Switzerland** ⊛ www.myswitzerland.com. Canada ☎ 011-800/1002 0030; UK ☎ 00800/1002 0030; US ☎ 1-877/SWITZERLAND.

**Turkey** ⊛ www.turizm.gov.tr. UK ☎ 020/7629 7771; US ☎ 212/687-2194.

## Maps

Whether you're doing a grand tour or confining yourself to one or two countries, you will need a decent **map**. Though you can often buy maps on the spot, you may want to get them in advance to plan your trip – if you know what you want, the best advice is to contact a firm such as Stanfords in London (arguably the world's best map shop) or Rand McNally in the US (⊛ www .randmcnally.com); both sell maps online or by mail order.

We've recommended the best maps of individual countries throughout the book. In general, the best series are Bartholomew /RV, Kümmerley & Frey, Hallwag, and the aforementioned Rand McNally. With plans of over fifty European cities, the Falk series of detailed, indexed maps are excellent, and easy to use. Geo-Center's 1:1,250,000 double-sided Europe map is one of the best covering the entire continent – clear, with a large scale, showing roads, railways and relief. Other good road maps covering the whole of Europe include Kümmerley & Frey (1:2,750,000), Michelin (1:3,000,000), Hallwag (1:3,600,000), Freytag & Berndt (1:3,500,000), and Philip's (1:3,500,000),

all of which show the road networks pretty well, though they omit most of Turkey and Morocco. Of those, only the first three show railways, and all of them omit large parts of Turkey and Morocco. Penguin's map, on a smaller scale (1:5,500,000), is less detailed but shows the main road and rail routes pretty clearly. For extensive motoring, it's better to get a large-page road atlas such as Michelin's Tourist and Motoring Atlas. If you intend to travel mainly by rail, it might be worth getting the Thomas Cook Rail Map of Europe.

### Map outlets

### Australia and New Zealand

**The Map Shop** 6 Peel St, Adelaide, SA 5000 ☎ 08/8231 2033, ⊛ www.mapshop.net.au.

**Mapland** 372 Little Bourke St, Melbourne, Vic 3000 ☎ 03/9670 4383, ⊛ www.mapland.com.au.

**Map World (Australia)** 280 Pitt St, Sydney, NSW 2000 ☎ 02/9261 3601, ⊛ www.mapworld.net .au. Also 65 Northbourne Ave, Canberra, ACT 2601 ☎ 02/6230 4097 and 1981 Logan Road, Brisbane, Qld 4122 ☎ 07/3349 6633.

**Map World (NZ)** 173 Gloucester St, Christchurch ☎ 0800/627 967, ⊛ www.mapworld.co.nz.

### UK and Ireland

**Stanfords** 12–14 Long Acre, London WC2E 9LP ☎ 020/7836 1321, ⊛ www.stanfords.co.uk. Also at 39 Spring Gardens, Manchester M2 2BG ☎ 0161/831 0250 and 29 Corn St, Bristol BS1 1HT ☎ 0117/929 9966.

**Blackwell's Map Centre** 50 Broad St, Oxford OX1 3BQ ☎ 01865/793 550, ⊛ maps.blackwell.co.uk. Branches in Bristol, Cambridge, Cardiff, Leeds, Liverpool, Newcastle, Reading and Sheffield.

**The Map Shop** 30a Belvoir St, Leicester LE1 6QH ☎ 0116/247 1400, ⊛ www.mapshopleicester.co.uk.

**National Map Centre** 22–24 Caxton St, London SW1H 0QU ☎ 020/7222 2466, ⊛ www.mapstore .co.uk.

**National Map Centre Ireland** 34 Aungier St, Dublin 2 ☎ 01/476 0471, ⊛ www.mapcentre.ie.

**The Travel Bookshop** 13–15 Blenheim Crescent, London W11 2EE ☎ 020/7229 5260, ⊛ www .thetravelbookshop.co.uk.

**Traveller** 55 Grey St, Newcastle upon Tyne NE1 6EF ☎ 0191/261 5622, ⊛ www.newtraveller.com.

### US and Canada

**110 North Latitude** US ☎ 336/369-4171, ⊛ www.110nlatitude.com.

**Book Passage** 51 Tamal Vista Blvd, Corte Madera, CA 94925 ☎1-800/999-7909, ⓦwww .bookpassage.com.
**Distant Lands** 56 S Raymond Ave, Pasadena, CA 91105 ☎1-800/310-3220, ⓦwww.distantlands.com.
**Globe Corner Bookstore** 28 Church St, Cambridge, MA 02138 ☎1-800/358-6013, ⓦwww .globecorner.com.
**Longitude Books** 115 W 30th St #1206, New York, NY 10001 ☎1-800/342-2164, ⓦwww .longitudebooks.com.

**Map Town** 400 5 Ave SW #100, Calgary, AB T2P 0L6 ☎1-877/921-6277 or 403/266-2241, ⓦwww .maptown.com.
**The Travel Bug Bookstore** 3065 W Broadway, Vancouver, BC V6K 2G9 ☎604/737-1122, ⓦwww .travelbugbooks.ca.
**World of Maps** 1235 Wellington St, Ottawa, ON K1Y 3A3 ☎1-800/214-8524, ⓦwww.worldofmaps .com.

# Insurance and health

Wherever you're travelling from, it's a very good idea to have some kind of travel insurance. Before paying for a new policy, however, it's worth checking whether you're already covered: some all-risks home insurance policies may cover your possessions when overseas, and many private medical schemes include cover when abroad.

In Canada, provincial health plans usually provide partial cover for medical mishaps overseas, while holders of official student/teacher/youth cards in Canada and the US are entitled to meagre accident coverage and hospital in-patient benefits. Students will often find that their student health coverage extends during the vacations and for one term beyond the date of last enrolment.

After exhausting these possibilities, you might want to contact a specialist **travel insurance company**, or consider Rough Guides' own travel insurance deal (see box). A typical travel insurance policy usually provides cover for the loss of baggage, tickets and – up to a certain limit – cash or cheques, as well as cancellation or curtailment of your journey. Most of them exclude so-called **dangerous sports** unless an extra premium is paid: in Europe this can mean anything from scuba-diving to mountaineering, skiing and even bungee-jumping. Many policies can be chopped and changed to exclude coverage you don't need; for example, sickness and accident benefits can often be excluded or included at will. If you do take

**medical coverage**, ascertain whether benefits will be paid as treatment proceeds or only after you return home, and whether there is a 24-hour medical emergency number. When securing baggage cover, make sure that the per-article limit will cover your most valuable possession. If you need to make a claim, you should keep receipts for medicines and medical treatment, and in the event you have anything stolen, you must obtain an official statement from the police.

## Health

There aren't many particular health problems you'll encounter travelling in Europe. You don't need to have any **inoculations** for any of the countries covered in this book, although for Morocco and Turkey typhoid jabs are advised, and in southeastern Turkey malaria pills are a good idea for much of the year – check ⓦ www.cdc.gov/travel /regionalmalaria for full details. When travelling, remember to be up-to-date with your polio and tetanus boosters.

**EU citizens** resident in the UK or Ireland are covered by reciprocal health agreements

## Rough Guides travel insurance

Rough Guides has teamed up with Columbus Direct to offer you **travel insurance** that can be tailored to suit your needs.

Readers can choose from many different travel insurance products, including a low-cost **backpacker** option for long stays; a **short break** option for city getaways; a typical **holiday package** option; and many others. There are also annual **multi-trip** policies for those who travel regularly, with variable levels of cover available. Different sports and activities (trekking, skiing, etc) can be covered if required on most policies.

Rough Guides travel insurance is available to the residents of 36 different countries with different language options to choose from via our website – ⍉www.roughguides insurance.com – where you can also purchase the insurance.

Alternatively, UK residents can call ☎0800/083 9507; US citizens should call ☎1-800 749-4922; Australians should call ☎1300 669 999. All other nationalities should call +44 870 890 2843.

for free or reduced-cost emergency treatment in many of the countries in this book (main exceptions are Morocco and Turkey). To claim this, you will often need only your passport, but you may also be asked for your NHS card or proof of residence. In EU countries plus Norway, Switzerland and Liechtenstein you'll also need a European Health Insurance card (replacing the old E111 form), which you can apply for in Britain at post offices, or on line at ⍉www .dh.gov.uk, in Ireland from your local Health Board or on line at ⍉www.ehic.ie. Allow a couple of weeks for your application to be processed.

Without a Health Insurance card, you won't be turned away from hospitals but you will almost certainly have to pay for any treatment or medicines. Also, in practice, some countries' doctors and hospitals charge anyway and it's up to you to claim reimbursement when you return home. Make sure you are insured for potential medical expenses, and keep copies of receipts and prescriptions.

**Tap water** in most countries is drinkable, and only needs to be avoided in southern Morocco and parts of Turkey. **Unfamiliar food** may well give you a small dose of the runs, but this is usually nothing to worry about, and is normally over in a couple of days; you shouldn't go plugging yourself up with anti-diarrhoea pills in the meantime. **AIDS** is of course as much of a problem in Europe as in the rest of the world, and it hardly needs saying that unprotected casual sex is extremely dangerous; members of both sexes should carry condoms – readily available and reliable across the Continent (though less so in Morocco and Turkey) – and, if it comes down to it, insist on using them.

For minor health problems it's easiest to go to the local **pharmacy** which you'll find pretty much everywhere. In more serious cases contact your nearest consulate, which will have a list of English-speaking doctors, as will the local tourist office. In the accounts of larger cities we've listed the most convenient hospital casualty units/emergency rooms.

# Costs, money and banks

It's hard to generalize about what you're likely to spend travelling around Europe. Some countries – Norway, Switzerland, the UK – are among the most expensive in the world, while in others (Turkey, for example) you can live like a lord on next to nothing. In general, countries in the north and west of Europe are more expensive than those in the south and east.

**Accommodation** will be your largest single expense, and can really determine where you decide to travel. For example, it's hard to find a double hotel room anywhere in Scandinavia – perhaps the most expensive part of the continent – for much under £45/$80 a night, whereas in most parts of southern Europe, and even in France, you might be paying under half that on average. Everywhere, though, even in Scandinavia, there is some form of bottom-line accommodation available, and there's nearly always a hostel on hand. In general, reckon on a minimum accommodation budget of around £10/US$18 a night per person in most parts of Europe.

**Food and drink** costs also vary wildly, although again in most parts of Europe you can assume that a cheap restaurant meal will cost £5–10/US$9–18 a head, with prices nearer the top end of the scale in Scandinavia, at the bottom end in eastern and southern Europe, and below that in Turkey and Morocco. **Transport** costs are something you can pin down more exactly if you have a rail pass. Nowhere, though, are transport costs a major burden, except perhaps in Britain where public transport is less heavily subsidized than elsewhere. Local city transport, too, is usually good, clean and efficient, and is normally fairly inexpensive, even in the pricier countries of northern Europe.

The bottom line for an **average daily budget** touring the continent – camping, self-catering, hitching, etc – might be around £15/$27 a day per person. Adding on a rail pass, staying in hostels and eating out occasionally would bring this up to perhaps £25/$45 a day, while staying in private rooms or hotels and eating out once a day would mean a personal daily budget of at least £30/$55.

## The euro

The **euro** (€) – made up of 100 cents – is the currency of twelve EU countries: Austria, Belgium, Finland, France, Germany, Greece, Ireland, Italy, Luxembourg, the Netherlands, Portugal and Spain. Andorra and Kosovo also use it. The ten new Union members (Cyprus, the Czech Republic, Estonia, Hungary, Latvia, Lithuania, Malta, Poland, Slovakia and Slovenia) have all committed themselves to joining the euro, but have not yet done so – they aim to join around 2007. The remaining three EU countries (the UK, Denmark and Sweden) are expected to join the euro zone eventually, though their politicians may have a hard time convincing voters that it is a good idea. The British government rashly promised a referendum before joining; Denmark had one and voted against.

Euro **coins** come as 1c, 2c, 5c, 10c, 20c, 50c, €1 and €2. One side of the coin states the denomination, and is the same everywhere, while the other side has a design unique to the issuing country. Euro **notes** come as €5, €10, €20, €50, €100, €200 and €500. All euro notes and coins are legal tender throughout the euro zone, regardless of their country of issue.

At the time of writing, £1 was worth €1.40, US$1 got you €0.75, Can$1 was €0.60, Aus$1 equalled €0.55, and NZ$1 was €0.52.

When you are travelling also makes a difference. Accommodation rates tend to go up across the board in July and August, when everyone is on vacation – although paradoxically there are good deals in Scandinavia during these months. Also bear in mind that in capital cities and major resorts in the peak season everything will be more expensive, especially if you're there when something special is going on, for example the Munich Beer Festival, the running of the bulls in Pamplona, or the Palio in Siena. These are, in any case, times when you'd be lucky to find a room at all without having booked.

As for ways of **cutting costs**, there are plenty. It makes sense, obviously, to spend less on transport by investing in some kind of rail pass. Always try to plan in advance. Although it's good to be flexible, buying one-off rail tickets can add a huge amount to your travel budget. The most obvious way to save on accommodation is to use hostels; you can also save by planning to make some of your longer trips at night, if you're able to sleep easily on trains or buses. It's best not to be too spartan when it comes to food costs, but doing a certain amount of self-catering, especially at lunchtime when it's just as easy (and probably nicer) to have a picnic lunch rather than eat in a restaurant or café, will save money.

## Youth and student discounts

If you're a student, an **International Student Identity Card** (ISIC for short) is well worth investing in. It can get you reduced (usually half-price, sometimes free) entry to museums and other sights – costs which can eat their way into your budget alarmingly if you're doing a lot of sightseeing – as well as qualifying you for other discounts in certain cities. It can also save you money on some transport costs, notably ferries, and especially if you are over 26. For Americans there's also a health benefit, providing up to $3000 in emergency medical coverage and $100 a day for sixty days in hospital, plus a 24-hour hotline to call in the event of a medical, legal or financial emergency. The card costs $22 in the US, Can$16 in Canada, £7 in the UK, €13 in Ireland, Aus$18 in Australia, and NZ$20 in New Zealand. If you're not a student but under 26, get an **International Youth Travel Card**, which costs the same and can in some countries give much the same sort of reductions. Teachers qualify for the **International Teacher Identity Card**, offering similar discounts. All these cards are available from youth travel specialists such as STA and Travel Cuts; full information is at ⊛ www.isiccard.com. Basically, it's worth flashing whichever card you've got at every opportunity – you never know what you might get.

## Carrying money

The easiest way to carry your money is in the form of plastic, though travellers' cheques and cash still have their advantages.

### Credit and debit cards

Hotels, shops and restaurants across Europe accept major **credit and debit cards**, although cheaper places may not. More importantly, you can use them 24/7 to get cash out of ATMs throughout Europe, including Morocco and Turkey, as long as they are affiliated to an international network (such as Visa, MasterCard or Cirrus). If you're not sure whether your card will work in the countries you intend to visit, check with the issuer before you leave home. Cash withdrawals and credit card transactions will often be subject to a fee, usually a percentage of the total with a minimum fee per transaction; in the case of cards issued by American banks, this can often be quite high, so it's worth finding out before you leave how much it will be. Both credit and debit cards may also impose a limit on the amount you can draw at one time, or in one day – again, check with your card issuer. In the case of credit cards, of course, if you're away for more than a month, you'll need to have someone back home taking care of the bills.

### Cash and travellers' cheques

As well as carrying a **cash back-up**, you may also want to consider **travellers' cheques**, in either US dollars, euros or UK pounds. These are available for a small commission from any bank, or direct from offices of the issuing companies; the most commonly accepted brands are Thomas Cook/MasterCard,

## Prices and exchange rates

We've quoted **prices** in local currency wherever possible, except in those countries where the weakness of the currency and the inflation rate combine to make this a meaningless exercise. In these cases we've resorted to either US dollars, British pounds or euros, depending on which hard currency is most commonly used within that country.

The current **exchange rates** are given in the "Basics" section at the beginning of each country chapter, but bear in mind that in the case of less stable currencies, the approximate rates quoted may fluctuate considerably. You can find the latest market rates (bank rates will not be as good) at ⓦ www.oanda.com – click on "Cheat Sheet" to get a printable table comparing two currencies.

For **accommodation** prices, we've used a standard coding system throughout this book: see p.57 for details.

American Express and Visa. Travellers' cheques have the major advantage over cash of being refundable if lost or stolen, but the downside is that they're expensive: you'll usually have to pay a commission fee again when you cash each cheque. It pays to get a selection of denominations, and you should keep the purchase agreement and a record of cheque serial numbers safe and separate from the cheques themselves. If cheques are lost or stolen, the issuing company will expect you to report the loss forthwith to their local office; most companies claim to replace lost or stolen cheques within 24 hours. Keep a record of the cheques as you cash them, as you can get the value of all uncashed cheques refunded immediately if you lose them.

In some countries **banks** are the only places where you can legally change money, and they often offer the best exchange rates and lowest commission. Local banking hours are given throughout this book. Outside normal hours you can normally resort to **bureaux de change**, often located at train stations and airports, though their rates and/ or commissions may well be less favourable. You'll also come across automatic money-changing machines, which can be handy out of hours, but don't give good exchange rates. You'd do best to avoid changing money or cheques in hotels, where the exchange rates are generally very poor.

A kind of compromise between plastic and travellers' cheques is **Visa travel money**, a disposable debit card that you top up with funds before you leave home and that can be used in ATMs worldwide. For more details,

see the "Debit cards" section at ⓦ www .international.visa.com.

## Wiring money

Having **money wired** from home is not cheap, and should be considered as a last resort. Funds can be sent to most countries via MoneyGram and Western Union. Both companies' fees depend on the amount being transferred, but as an example, wiring US$1000/£600 will cost around US$65/£40. The funds should be available for collection (usually in local currency) from the company's local agent within minutes of being sent; you can do this in person at the company's nearest office (in the UK all post offices are agents for MoneyGram), or over the phone using your credit card with Western Union. It's also possible, and slightly cheaper, to have money wired from a bank in your home country to one in Europe, but this is much slower (two working days is the norm, but a couple of weeks is not unheard of) and less reliable; if you go down this route, the person wiring the funds will need to know the routing number of the destination bank.

If you can't get money wired from home, and you can't find work, your could try throwing yourself on the mercy of your nearest consulate; they won't be sympathetic or even helpful, but they may cash a cheque drawn on a home bank and supported by a cheque card. They might, if there's absolutely no other possibility, repatriate you, though if they do, your passport will be confiscated as soon as you set foot in your home country and you will have to pay back all costs incurred (at top-whack rates). Consulates never lend money.

### Money-wiring companies

**MoneyGram** ⍵ www.moneygram.com. Australia ℡ 0011-800/666 3947, Canada ℡ 1-800/933-3278, Ireland and New Zealand ℡ 00-800/666 3947, UK ℡ 00-800/8971 8971, US ℡ 1-800/666 3947.
**Western Union** ⍵ www.westernunion.com. Australia ℡ 1800/173 833, Canada & US ℡ 1-800/325 6000, Ireland ℡ 66/947 5603, NZ ℡ 0800/005 253, UK ℡ 0800/833 833.

# Getting around

It's easy enough to travel in Europe, and a number of special deals and passes can make it fairly economical too. Air links are extensive, and thanks to the growing number of "no-frills" economy airlines, are often cheaper than taking the train, but you'll appreciate the diversity of Europe best at ground level, by way of its enormous and generally efficient web of rail, road and ferry connections.

## By train

Though to some extent it depends on where you intend to spend most of your time, the **train** is the best way to make a tour of Europe. The rail network in most countries is comprehensive and the continent boasts some of the most scenic rail journeys you could make anywhere in the world. Costs are relatively low, too, even in the richer parts of northwest Europe, where – apart from Britain, whose rail system suffered massively following privatization – trains are heavily subsidized, and prices are brought down further by passes and discount cards, both Europe-wide (**InterRail** for those based in Europe or the British Isles, **Eurail** for anyone based elsewhere) and on an individual country basis. We've covered the various passes here, as well as the most important international routes and most useful addresses; supplementary details, including frequencies and journey times of domestic services, are given throughout the guide in each country's "Travel details" section.

During the summer, especially if you're travelling at night or a long distance, it's best to make **reservations** wherever you can; on some trains (most French TGV services, for example) it's compulsory. At night, couchettes in six-berth compartments cost around £13 per person; sleeper cars cost around £20–50, depending on the train, and may be two-, three- or four-bed.

If you intend to do a lot of rail travel, the **Thomas Cook European Timetable** is an essential investment, detailing the main lines throughout Europe, as well as ferry connections, and is updated monthly. Thomas Cook also publishes a rail map of Europe, which may be a good supplement to our own train map on pp.48–49.

Finally, whenever you board an international train in Europe, check the route of the car you are in, since trains frequently split, with different carriages going to different destinations.

### Europe-wide rail passes

#### InterRail

For young Europeans, probably the most popular of all the ways of travelling around the continent is the **InterRail pass**, a ticket giving – in principle – free travel on rail lines the length and breadth of Europe (but you pay half fares in the country where you bought the card). InterRail passes are available from main stations and international rail agents in all countries covered by the scheme. For contacts in Britain and Ireland, see p.32 & p.34. A **zoning system** applies for the European countries valid under the pass, as follows:

**Zone A** Britain, Ireland
**Zone B** Sweden, Norway, Finland
**Zone C** Denmark, Germany, Switzerland, Austria
**Zone D** Poland, Czech Republic, Slovakia, Hungary, Croatia
**Zone E** France, Belgium, the Netherlands, Luxembourg
**Zone F** Spain, Portugal, Morocco
**Zone G** Italy, Slovenia, Greece, Turkey
**Zone H** Bulgaria, Romania, Serbia and Montenegro, Republic of Macedonia

The zones you want to travel in determine the price, which starts at £159 for those under 26 (£199 for over-26s) for a one-zone card valid for sixteen days, £165/£235 for two zones over 22 days, or £290/£409 for all the zones over a month. To qualify, you need to have been resident in one of the participating countries for six months or more; you also need a valid passport. For further details, price updates and online purchasing, see ⓦwww.raileurope.co.uk/inter-rail.

In fact, unlimited free travel is a bit of a myth. Increasingly with InterRail passes, you need to pay **supplements** on most European express trains – all of them on some routes, and certainly all the most convenient ones. Even where there is in theory no supplement, there's often a compulsory reservation fee, which may cost you double if you only find out about it once you're on the train.

### Eurail

**Non-European residents** aren't eligible for InterRail passes, though many agents don't check residential qualifications. For them, a **Eurail pass**, which should be bought outside Europe (but can be obtained from Rail Europe in London by non-residents who were unable to get it at home), gives unlimited travel in seventeen countries – Austria, Belgium, Denmark, Finland, France, Germany, Greece, Hungary, Ireland, Italy, Luxembourg, the Netherlands, Norway, Portugal, Spain, Sweden and Switzerland – fewer than InterRail (see above), but valid for more express trains, thus saving money on supplements. The **Eurailpass Youth** (for under-26s) costs US$382 for fifteen days, US$495 for 21 days, US$615 for one month,

US$870 for two months, and US$1075 for three months; if you're 26 or over you'll have to buy a first-class pass, also available for fifteen days (US$588), 21 days (US$762), one month (US$946), two months (US$1338) and three months (US$1654). If there are between two and five of you travelling together, the **Eurailpass Saver** (first class only) knocks about fifteen percent off the cost of the standard Eurail offerings.

You stand a better chance of getting your money's worth out of a **Eurailpass Flexi**, which is good for a certain number of travel days in a two-month period. This, too, comes in under-26 and first-class versions: ten days costs US$451 for under-26s (US$694 for first-class travel); and fifteen days costs US$594/914. There's also a **Eurailpass Saver Flexi** for two to five people travelling together.

If you only want to travel in a small number of adjoining countries, the **Eurail Selectpass** allows travel in 3–5 countries linked to each other by rail or boat on 5, 6, 8, 10 or 15 days in two months; overnight journeys starting after 7pm count as part of the next day; Belgium, the Netherlands and Luxembourg ("Benelux") count as a single country, as do Croatia and Slovenia, and Serbia–Montenegro and Bulgaria. Prices for under-26s and over-26s range from US$241/370 for five days in three countries to US$537/826 for fifteen days in five countries (fifteen-day tickets are not available for less than five countries). There's also a **Eurail Selectpass Saver** version for people travelling together. All Eurail passes are available from the agents listed on p.32, p.34 & p.56. For full details, price updates and online purchasing, see ⓦwww.eurail.com.

### National rail passes

Some European countries provide a **national rail pass**, which can be good value if you're doing a lot of travelling within one country, or a 3- to 8-day **EuroDomino** (also called a **Freedom Pass**), which you buy before you leave home. Main second-class options are listed below; there are, in addition, first-class versions of most EuroDominos, Railpasses and Flexipasses, plus first-class passes for Bulgaria, Portugal, Romania, Spain and Portugal combined, Austria, Slovenia and

Croatia combined, and the Balkans. In general, those passes quoted in pounds or dollars need to be bought before you leave home from the country's rail company or national tourist office, or from a general sales agent such as RailEurope (some prices may vary between agents, and some agents may offer passes that others do not). There is no pass as such for Estonia, Latvia or Lithuania.

**Austria** The VORTEILSCard rail pass gives a 45 percent discount throughout Austria for a year for €19.90 (€99.90 for over-26s). A EuroDomino pass costs from £63 (over-26s £84) for three days up to £100/140 for eight days. An Austrian Railpass gives three days' free travel in a fifteen-day period for $112, plus up to five additional days at $16 each. A Switzerland'n'Austria Youthpass gives four days' travel in two months in Austria and Switzerland for $209, with up to six additional days at $27 each (over-26s have to take a 1st-class pass for $309 with additional days at $36). Also see "Eastern Europe".

**Belgium** A EuroDomino pass costs from £30 (£41 for over-26s) for three days up to £60/78 for eight days. The Go Pass allows under-26s ten single journeys of any length in a year for €43 (the over-26 version, Rail Pass, costs €65). Also see "Benelux".

**Benelux (Belgium, Netherlands & Luxembourg)** A Benelux Tourrail card gives five days' travel in a month on all three countries' networks for $109 ($163 for over-26s, $244 for two people travelling together). The Germany'n'Benelux Pass gives unlimited rail travel throughout the Benelux countries and Germany on any five days in two months for $199 ($246 for over-26s), six days for $217 ($272), eight days for $258 ($324), or ten days for $299 ($374), with a "Saver" version giving discounts for 2–5 people travelling together.

**Britain** The BritRail Consecutive Pass, available from agents outside Britain, gives unlimited rail travel throughout England, Wales and Scotland for four days at $157 ($209 for over-26s), eight days at $225 ($299), fifteen days at $337 ($449), 22 days at $432 ($575), or a month at $510 ($679). It also gives a discount on some Eurostar (Channel Tunnel) fares. Alternatively, the BritRail Flexipass gives unlimited travel on any four days in two months for $199 ($265 for over-26s), eight days for $289 ($385) or fifteen days for $439 ($585). Other options include: the BritRail England Consecutive Pass, giving unlimited rail travel in just England for four days at $127 ($169 for over-26s), eight days at $180 ($239), fifteen days at $274 ($365), 22 days at $345 ($459), or a month at $405 ($539); the BritRail England Flexipass, giving unlimited

travel in England on any four days in two months for $157 ($299 for over-26s), eight days for $232 ($309), or fifteen days for $352 ($469); the BritRail Scottish Freedom Pass, giving four days' travel in Scotland in an eight-day period at $214, eight days in fifteen at $279; the BritRail London Plus Pass giving unlimited travel in southeastern England on any two days in eight for $52 ($69 for over-26s), four days in eight for $97 ($129), or seven days in fifteen for $127 ($169). "Party" versions of these passes give discounts for three or more people travelling together. With a BritRail Pass Plus Ireland, you get five days' travel in a month throughout Britain and Ireland (plus a round trip on Stena Line Irish Sea ferries) for $419, or ten days for $669. The Young Person's Railcard – on sale in Britain for £20 – gives a 33-percent reduction on standard fares for full-time students and under-26s for a year. A EuroDomino pass costs from €115 (€155 for over-26s) for three days up to €225 (€305) for eight days.

**Bulgaria** A EuroDomino pass costs from £24 (£30 for over-26s) for three days up to £46 (£60) for eight days.

**Croatia** A EuroDomino pass costs from £33 (£43 for over-26s) for three days up to £59 (£77) for eight days. A Hungary/Slovenia/Croatia Youth Pass gives unlimited rail travel throughout the three countries on any five days in two months for $140 (over-26s have to take a first-class pass for $200), six days for $159 ($220), eight days for $189 ($260), or ten days for $209 ($300).

**Czech Republic** A EuroDomino pass costs from £29 (£38 for over-26s) for three days up to £62 (£78) for eight days. A Czech Flexipass gives three days' free travel in a fifteen-day period for $52, plus up to five additional days at $7 each. Also see "Eastern Europe".

**Denmark** A EuroDomino pass costs from £43 (£58 for over-26s) for three days up to £88 (£117) for eight days. A Germany'n'Denmark Pass gives unlimited rail travel throughout Denmark and Germany on any five days in two months for $188 ($230 for over-26s), six days for $204 ($254), eight days for $236 ($302), or ten days for $268 ($350), with a "Saver" version giving discounts for two or more people travelling together. For ScanRail passes see "Scandinavia".

**Eastern Europe** A European East Pass gives five days' travel in a month in Austria, the Czech Republic, Hungary, Poland and Slovakia for $162, plus up to five additional days at $21 each.

**Finland** Finnrail passes are valid for unlimited rail travel on three, five or ten days in a month and cost $168, $222 and $300 respectively; add-on round-trips to Tallinn (Estonia) or St Petersburg (Russia) are available. A EuroDomino pass costs from £68 (£91 for over-26s) for three days up to £123 (£165) for eight days. For ScanRail passes see "Scandinavia".

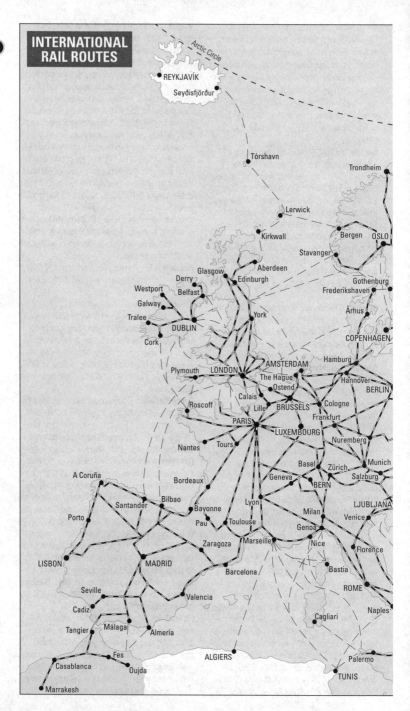

INTERNATIONAL
RAIL ROUTES

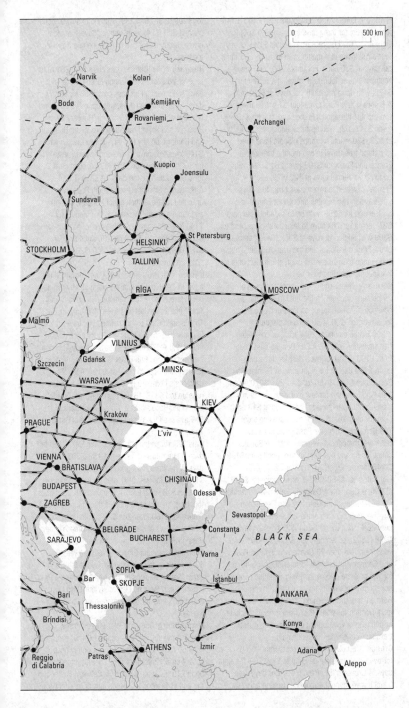

**France** A EuroDomino pass costs from £103 (£140 for over-26s) for three days up to £199 (£266) for eight days. The France Railpass costs $199 for any four days' travel in a month, with up to six additional rail days at $30 each. For under-26s, the France Youthpass gives four days' travel in a month for $172, with up to six additional days at $22 each. A France'n'Italy Pass gives four days' free travel in two months throughout France and Italy for $199 (over-26s $269), with up to six additional days at $23 ($30) each. A France'n'Spain Pass gives four days' free travel in two months throughout France and Spain for $199 (over-26s $269), with up to six additional days at $22 ($29) each. A France'n'Switzerland Youthpass gives four days' free travel in two months throughout France and Switzerland for $209, with up to six additional days at $27 each (over-26s have to take a 1st-class pass for $309 with additional days at $36). "Saver" versions of the France Railpass and the over-26 France'n'Italy and France'n'Spain passes exist, giving discounts for 2–5 people travelling together.

**Germany** The German Rail BahnCard gives a 25 percent discount on the full fare (but not on advance-purchase fares) on long-distance trains for a year for €50, a 50 percent discount for €200 (students under 26 €100), or completely free travel for €3250. A EuroDomino pass costs from £103 (£140 for over-26s) for three days up to £159 (£215) for eight days. A German Rail Pass costs $142 ($180 for over-26s, $270 for two travelling together) for any four days' travel in a month, with up to six additional days at $13 each ($24 for over-26s, $36 for two travelling together). The Germany'n'Benelux Pass gives unlimited rail travel throughout Germany and the Benelux countries on any five days in two months for $199 ($246 for over-26s), six days for $217 ($272), eight days for $258 ($324), or ten days for $299 ($374). A Germany'n'Denmark Pass gives unlimited rail travel throughout Germany and Denmark on any five days in two months for $188 ($230 for over-26s), six days for $204 ($254), eight days for $236 ($302), or ten days for $268 ($350). "Saver" versions of the over-26 Germany'n'Benelux Pass and Germany'n'Denmark Pass exist, giving discounts for two or more people travelling together. Länder tickets give free travel on local trains in any one German state from 9am on any weekday until 3am next morning for €29 (€27 from a ticket machine or online at ⓦ www.bahn.de/pv/view/int_guest/ travelservice/laender_tickets.shtml).

**Greece** A EuroDomino pass costs from £35 (£45 for over-26s) for three days up to £72 (£89) for eight days. A Greece'n'Italy Pass gives four days' free travel in two months throughout Greece and Italy

for $200 (over-26s $239), with up to six additional days at $20 ($24) each, with a "Saver" version giving discounts for two or more people travelling together.

**Hungary** A EuroDomino pass costs from £31 (£39 for over-26s) for three days up to £64/87 for eight days. A Hungarian Flexipass costs $52 for any five days' travel in fifteen days, with up to five additional rail days at $6 each. A Romania'n'Hungary Youth Pass gives unlimited rail travel throughout Hungary and Romania on any five days in two months for $140 (over-26s have to take a first-class pass for $200), six days for $154 ($220), eight days for $182 ($260), or ten days for $210 ($300). A Hungary'n'Slovenia/Croatia Youth Pass gives unlimited rail travel throughout Hungary, Slovenia and Croatia on any five days in two months for $140 (over-26s have to take a first-class pass for $200), six days for $159 ($220), eight days for $189 ($260), or ten days for $209 ($300). Also see "Eastern Europe".

**Ireland** Irish Rail's Rover ticket buys unlimited rail travel in the Republic and the North on any five days out of fifteen for €157, with an Irish Explorer Rail Ticket (the same deal in the Republic only) at €127. The Emerald Card covers rail and bus travel in the Republic and the North, at €218 for eight days in fifteen and €375 for fifteen days in thirty. The Irish Explorer Rail and Bus Ticket is valid for eight days in fifteen in the Republic only at €194. A EuroDomino pass costs from £49 (£58 for over-26s) for three days up to £98 (£113) for eight days and is valid only in the Republic. See "Britain" for details of the BritRail Pass Plus Ireland (not available in Britain or Ireland).

**Italy** A EuroDomino pass costs from £97 (£129 for over-26s) for three days up to £152 (£203) for eight days. A Trenitalia Pass gives four days in a month for $174 ($206 for over-26s), plus up to six additional days for $18 ($22) each. A France'n'Italy Pass gives four days' travel in two months throughout Italy and France for $199 (over-26s $269), with up to six additional days at $23 ($30) each. A Greece'n'Italy Pass gives four days' travel in two months throughout Italy and Greece for $200 (over-26s $239), with up to six additional days at $20 ($24) each. "Saver" versions of the over-26 Trenitalia Pass, France'n'Italy Pass and Greece'n'Italy Pass exist, giving discounts for two or more people travelling together.

**Luxembourg** One-day Oeko-Billjee passes covering rail and bus services are €4.60 each, €18.50 for a book of five. A EuroDomino pass costs from £12 (£16 for over-26s) for three days up to £15 (£23) for eight days. Between Easter and the end of October, a Luxembourg Card – that also gives free entry to various tourist attractions – costs €9 for one day, €16 for any two days in two weeks, and €22 for any three days in two weeks. See also "Benelux".

**Morocco** A EuroDomino pass costs from £25 (£26 for over-26s) for three days up to £55 (£60) for eight days.

**Netherlands** A Dagkaart (Day Card) gives a day's unlimited travel for €39.80 (an OV Dagkaart, covering buses, trams and metro too, is €44.80; a 5-Dagkaart, valid for five days, costs €189). A Zomertoer (Summer Tour) ticket giving free travel on any three days in ten during July and August costs €49 for one person, €69 for two travelling together, or €59.50 (€84) for a pass covering bus services too. A HollandRail Pass gives three days' free travel in a month at $72 ($95 for over-26s), or five days for $115 ($153). A EuroDomino pass costs from £32 (£43 for over-26s) for three days up to £84 (£109) for eight days. Also see "Benelux".

**Norway** A Norway Railpass Youth gives three days' free travel in a month for $151 (over-26s have to take a first-class pass for $209), plus up to 5 additional days for $25 ($35) each. A EuroDomino pass costs from £95 (£126 for over-26s) for three days up to £180 (£238) for eight days. For ScanRail passes see "Scandinavia".

**Poland** Polrail passes cost £58 (£82 for over-26s) for eight days travel, £68 (£96) for fifteen, (£76/£109) for 21 days, and £96 (£136) for a month. A EuroDomino pass costs from £38 (£43 for over-26s) for three days up to £78 (£92) for eight days. Also see "Eastern Europe".

**Portugal** A Bilhete Turistico pass, which costs €114 for a week's rail travel, €194 for two weeks, and €285 for three, is really only worthwhile for first-class travel, which it allows. A EuroDomino pass costs from £38 (£54 for over-26s) for three days up to £78 (£92) for eight days.

**Romania** A EuroDomino pass costs from £33 (£43 for over-26s) for three days up to £78 (£103) for eight days. A Romania'n'Hungary Youth Pass gives unlimited rail travel throughout Romania and Hungary on any five days in two months for $140 (over-26s have to take a first-class pass for $200), six days for $154 ($220), eight days for $182 ($260), or ten days for $210 ($300).

**Russia** A EuroDomino pass costs from €45 (€60 for over-26s) for three days up to €85 (€110) for eight days.

**Scandinavia** The ScanRail pass is valid on the rail networks of Denmark, Norway, Sweden and Finland, and costs $203 ($291 for over-26s) for five days' travel in two months, $273 ($390) for ten days in two months, and $316 ($453) for 21 days unlimited.

**Serbia and Montenegro** A EuroDomino pass costs from £26 (£39 for over-26s) for three days up to £41 (£65) for eight days.

**Slovakia** A EuroDomino pass costs from £23 (£31 for over-26s) for three days up to £46 (£60) for eight days. Also see "Eastern Europe".

**Slovenia** A EuroDomino pass costs from £31 (£41 for over-26s) for three days up to £53 (£71) for eight days. A Hungary'n'Slovenia/Croatia Youth Pass gives unlimited rail travel throughout Slovenia, Croatia and Hungary on any five days in two months for $140 (over-26s have to take a first-class pass for $200), six days for $159 ($220), eight days for $189 ($260), or ten days for $209 ($300).

**Spain** A EuroDomino pass costs from £71 (£84 for over-26s) for three days up to £163 (£195) for eight days. The Spain Flexipass gives three days' free travel in a two-month period for $175, plus $30 each for up to seven additional days. A France'n'Spain Pass gives four days' free travel in two months throughout Spain and France for $199 (over-26s $269), with up to six additional days at $22 ($29) each.

**Sweden** EuroDomino passes for Sweden cost from £94 (£128 for over-26s) for three days up to £153 (£209) for eight days. ScanRail passes are also valid (see "Scandinavia").

**Switzerland** A Swiss Pass, valid for unlimited travel on rail, bus and ferry routes, costs $135 for four days ($180 for over-26s, $153 each for two or more people travelling together), $192 ($255/217) for eight days, $233 ($310/264) for fifteen days, $270 ($360/306) for 22 days, and $300 ($400/340) for a month. Alternatives are the Swiss Flexi Pass (giving three to eight days in a month at $172–322, or $146–274 each for two or more people travelling together), the Half-Fare Card (50 percent discount on rail travel for a month for SFr99), and the Swiss Card (one free return journey from the border or airport to any town plus 50 percent discount on other tickets for a month at $130). A France'n'Switzerland Youthpass gives four days' free travel in two months throughout Switzerland and France for $209, with up to six additional days at $27 each (over-26s have to take a 1st-class pass for $309 with additional days at $36). A Switzerland'n'Austria Youthpass gives four days' travel in two months in Switzerland and Austria for $209, with up to six additional days at $27 each (over-26s have to take a 1st-class pass for $309 with additional days at $36). A EuroDomino pass costs from £61 (£82 for over-26s) for three days up to £95 (£126) for eight days.

**Turkey** A EuroDomino pass costs from £23 (£29 for over-26s) for three days up to £52 (£70) for eight days.

# International train routes

| FROM ⟍ TO | Amsterdam | Belgrade | Berlin | Bratislava | Brussels |
|---|---|---|---|---|---|
| Amsterdam | – | Munich | 3 (6hr) | Berlin | 20 (2hr40) |
| Belgrade | Munich | – | Munich | Budapest | Zurich |
| Berlin | 3 (6hr) | Munich | – | 2 (9hr55) | 1 (8hr35) |
| Bratislava | Berlin | Budapest | 2 (9hr55) | – | Vienna & Cologne |
| Brussels | 20 (2hr40) | Zurich | 1 (8hr25) | Cologne & Vienna | – |
| Bucharest | Vienna & Frankfurt | 1 (13hr20) | Prague | 1 (16hr) | Vienna & Cologne |
| Budapest | Munich | 2 (6hr50) | 2 (12hr) | 7 (2hr20)1 | Zurich |
| Copenhagen | Duisberg | Munich | Hamburg | Hamburg | Hamburg |
| Ljubljana | Munich | 4 (8hr30) | Munich | Vienna | Zurich |
| Luxembourg | Brussels | Zurich | Cologne | Cologne & Vienna | 23 (2hr40) |
| Milan | Basel | Venice (Mestre) & Ljubljana | Munich | Vienna | Basel |
| Moscow | Cologne[b] | 1 (49hr50)[u] | 3–6 weekly (27hr45)[b] | 1 (32hr10)[b] | 1 (37hr25)[b] |
| Munich | 1 (11hr) | 2 (12hr50) | 8 (6hr50) | Vienna | Cologne |
| Paris | 5 (4hr10) | Zurich | 1 (11hr20) | Vienna | 26 (1hr25) |
| Prague | Frankfurt | Vienna | 7 (4hr40) | 6 (4hr20) | Cologne |
| Rome | Munich | Trieste & Ljubljana | Munich | Vienna | Zurich |
| Vienna | Frankfurt | 2 (10hr20) | 2 (9hr25) | 23 (1hr)[1] | Cologne |
| Warsaw | Berlin | Vienna | 4–5 (6hr05) | 2 (7hr10) | 2 (7hr10) |
| Zagreb | Munich | 5 (6hr10) | Munich | Vienna | Vienna |
| Zurich | 1 (12hr20) | 1 (19hr20) | 1 (12hr10) | Vienna | Vienna |

This chart shows the number of **direct daily trains** between Europe's main rail hubs and the fastest scheduled time. Where there is no direct service, a suggested **interchange point** is given instead, but note that you may have to pick up your connecting service from a different terminal, and that you may have to wait several hours for your connection: you could take it as an opportunity to wander round town, with your bags at the left luggage deposit in the meantime, or to freshen up – many major stations have washing facilities. Depending on the time of day, or day of the week, you may be able to get to your destination more quickly or conveniently with one or two extra changes of train. Train connections from cities on the periphery of Europe (such as London, Athens, Stockholm and Madrid) are not shown here, but can be found in the Travel Details sections at the end of their respective chapters. Note too that most trains to Russia pass through Belarus or Ukraine, and that you may therefore need a transit visa to use them (see p.36).

| Bucharest | Budapest | Copenhagen | Ljubljana | Luxembourg |
|---|---|---|---|---|
| Frankfurt & Vienna | Munich | Duisberg | Munich | Brussels |
| 1 (13hr25) | 2 (6hr45) | Munich | 4 (9hr20) | Zurich |
| Prague | 2 (12hr15) | Hamburg | Munich | Cologne |
| 1 (17hr20) | 7 (2hr20)[1] | Hamburg | Vienna | Vienna & Cologne |
| Cologne & Vienna | Zurich | Hamburg | Zurich | 23 (2hr40) |
| – | 5 (14hr20) | Prague & Hamburg | Budapest | Budapest & Zurich |
| 5 (13hr15) | – | Munich | 3 (7hr40) | Zurich |
| Munich & Budapest | Munich | – | Munich | Cologne |
| Budapest | 3 (7hr40) | Munich | – | Zurich |
| Zurich & Budapest | Zurich | Cologne | Zurich | – |
| Vienna | Venice (Mestre) | Munich | Venice (Mestre) | Basel |
| 1 (44hr30)[u] | 1 (38hr45)[u] | Cologne[b] | Budapest[u] | Cologne[b] |
| Budapest | 2 (7hr35) | 1 (15hr) | 3 (6hr15) | Strasbourg |
| Vienna | Munich | Hamburg | Munich | 5 (3hr35) |
| 1 (23hr20) | 4 (7hr05) | Hamburg | Munich | Cologne |
| Vienna | Trieste | Munich | Trieste | Zurich |
| 1 (16hr30) | 7 (2hr35)[1] | Munich | 1 (6hr15) | Cologne |
| Krakow | 2 (10hr10) | Cologne | Vienna | Cologne |
| Budapest | 2 (5hr05) | Munich | 8 (2hr15) | Zurich |
| Budapest | 1 (12hr50) | Cologne | 1 (10hr50) | 1 (5hr25) |

1 There is also a hydrofoil service in summer.
2 Through cars are available three to five days a week; on other days, change cars between Kiev and Budapest.
3 On days when there is no direct service between Vienna and Moscow, change (also) at Warsaw.
b via Belarus – transit visa needed.
u via Ukraine – transit visa needed.

## International train routes (Contd.)

| TO<br>FROM | Milan | Moscow | Munich | Paris | Prague |
|---|---|---|---|---|---|
| Amsterdam | Basel | Cologne[b] | 1 (11hr10) | 5 (4hr10) | Frankfurt |
| Belgrade | Ljubljana & Venice (Mestre) | 1 (47hr40) | 2 (16hr10) | Zurich | Vienna |
| Berlin | Munich | 3–6 weekly (28hr50)[b] | 8 (6hr60) | 1 (11hr40) | 7 (4hr45) |
| Bratislava | Vienna | 1 (31hr05)[b] | Vienna | Vienna | 6 (4hr20) |
| Brussels | Brig | 1 (36hr50)[b] | Cologne | 26 (1hr25) | Cologne |
| Bucharest | Vienna | 1 (45hr40)[u] | Budapest | Vienna | 1 (24hr30) |
| Budapest | Venice (Mestre) | 1 (37hr50)[u] | 2 (7hr35) | Munich | 4 (7hr) |
| Copenhagen | Munich | Cologne[b] | 1 (14hr10) | Hamburg | Hamburg |
| Ljubljana | Venice (Mestre) | Budapest[u] | 3 (6hr20) | Munich | Munich |
| Luxembourg | Brig | Cologne[b] | Strasbourg | 5 (3hr45) | Cologne |
| Milan | – | Vienna[3b] | 2 (7hr20) | 4 (6hr50) | Munich |
| Moscow | Vienna[3b] | – | Hanover[b] | Brussels[b] | 1 (32hr05)[b] |
| Munich | 2 (7hr15) | Hanover[b] | – | 4 (8hr35) | 3 (6hr) |
| Paris | 4 (6hr45) | Brussels[b] | 4 (8hr35) | – | Cologne |
| Prague | Munich | 1 (30hr25)[b] | 3 (6hr) | Cologne | – |
| Rome | 24 (4hr30) | Vienna[3b] | 2 (10hr35) | 1 (15hr) | Vienna |
| Vienna | 1 (13hr25) | 4–7 weekly (30hr45)[3b] | 5 (4hr30) | 1 (13hr55) | 7 (4hr15) |
| Warsaw | Vienna | 2–3 (19hr45)[b] | Berlin | Brussels | 3 (8hr50) |
| Zagreb | Ljubljana & Venice (Mestre) | 1 (49hr)[2u] | 3 (8hr40) | Munich | Vienna |
| Zurich | 8 (3hr40) | Cologne[b] | 4 (4hr20) | 3 (5hr55) | 1 (12hr15) |

This chart shows the number of **direct daily trains** between Europe's main rail hubs and the fastest scheduled time. Where there is no direct service, a suggested **interchange point** is given instead, but note that you may have to pick up your connecting service from a different terminal, and that you may have to wait several hours for your connection: you could take it as an opportunity to wander round town, with your bags at the left luggage deposit in the meantime, or to freshen up – many major stations have washing facilities. Depending on the time of day, or day of the week, you may be able to get to your destination more quickly or conveniently with one or two extra changes of train. Train connections from cities on the periphery of Europe (such as London, Athens, Stockholm and Madrid) are not shown here, but can be found in the Travel Details sections at the end of their respective chapters. Note too that most trains to Russia pass through Belarus or Ukraine, and that you may therefore need a transit visa to use them (see p.36).

| Rome | Vienna | Warsaw | Zagreb | Zurich |
|---|---|---|---|---|
| Munich | Frankfurt | Berlin | Munich | 1 (12hr20) |
| Ljubljana & Trieste | 2 (10hr10) | Vienna | 5 (6hr45) | 1 (21hr20) |
| Munich | 2 (9hr35) | 4–5 (6hr) | Munich | 1 (11hr45) |
| Vienna | 23 (1hr)[1] | 2 (7hr25) | Vienna | Vienna |
| Zurich | Cologne | 1 (14hr40) | Zurich | 1 (8hr10) |
| Vienna | 1 (17hr) | Krakow | Budapest | Budapest |
| Trieste | 7 (2hr30)[1] | 2 (10hr20) | 2 (5hr05) | 1 (12hr30) |
| Munich | Munich | Cologne | Munich | Cologne |
| Trieste | 1 (6hr20) | Budapest | 8 (2hr15) | 1 (11hr45) |
| Zurich | Cologne | Cologne | Zurich | 1 (5hr20) |
| 24 (4hr30) | 1 (11hr40) | Vienna | Venice (Mestre) & Ljubljana | 8 (3hr40) |
| Vienna[3b] | 4–7 weekly (32hr25)[3b] | 2–3 (19hr40)[b] | 1 (51hr55)[2u] | Cologne[b] |
| 2 (10hr15) | 5 (4hr25) | Berlin | 3 (8hr35) | 4 (4hr15) |
| 1 (15hr) | 1 (13hr55) | Brussels | Munich | 3 (5hr50) |
| Vienna | 7 (4hr25) | 3 (9hr20) | Vienna | 1 (12hr05) |
| – | 1 (12hr55) | Vienna | Trieste & Ljubljana | 1 (12hr15) |
| 1 (13hr30) | – | 3 (7hr30) | 2 (6hr30) | 3 (8hr50) |
| Vienna | 3 (7hr30) | – | Vienna | Vienna |
| Ljubljana & Trieste | 2 (6hr30) | Vienna | – | 1 (14hr10) |
| 1 (10hr40) | 3 (8hr55) | Vienna | 1 (13hr10) | – |

1 There is also a hydrofoil service in summer.
2 Through cars are available three to five days a week; on other days, change cars between Kiev and Budapest.
3 On days when there is no direct service between Vienna and Moscow, change (also) at Warsaw.
b via Belarus – transit visa needed.
u via Ukraine – transit visa needed.

## Rail contacts

See p.32 for Britain and p.34 for Ireland.

### North America

**BritRail Travel** ☎1-866/BRITRAIL, ⊛www.britrail
.com. British passes.

**CIE Tours International** ☎1-800/CIE-TOUR or
973/292-3438, ⊛www.cietours.com. Irish passes.

**Europrail International** Canada ☎1-888/667-
9734, ⊛www.europrail.net. European and many
individual country passes.

**Orbis Polish Travel Bureau** ☎1-800/TO-POLAND,
⊛www.orbistravel.com. Passes for Poland.

**Rail Europe** US ☎1-877/257-2887, Canada
☎1-800/361-RAIL, ⊛www.raileurope.com. Official
Eurail agent, with the widest range of regional and
one-country passes.

**ScanTours** ☎1-800/223-7226 or 310/636-4656,
⊛www.scantours.com. Eurail, Scandinavian and
other European country passes.

### Australia and New Zealand

**CIT World Travel** Australia ☎02/9267 1255 or
03/9650 5510, ⊛www.cittravel.com.au. Eurail and
Italian rail passes.

**Rail Plus** Australia ☎03/9642 8644, ⊛www
.railplus.com.au; NZ ☎09/377 5415, ⊛www
.railplus.co.nz. Eurail and BritRail passes.

**Trailfinders** Australia ☎1300/780 2122, ⊛www
.trailfinder.com.au. All Europe passes.

## By bus

On the whole, you'll find yourself using **buses**
only for the odd local trip, since long-distance
journeys between major European cities are
generally slow, uncomfortable and not particularly cheap, especially if you have a rail
pass. With a limited itinerary, however, a
**bus pass** or **circular bus ticket** can undercut a rail pass, especially for over-26s. The
**Eurolines pass** is valid for unlimited travel
between 35 cities in Europe and the British
Isles (though, with certain exceptions, it is not
supposed to be used for journeys that do not
cross international frontiers). It costs £129
(£149 for over-26s) for fifteen days in low
season and £165 (£195) in high season; for
one month it's £169 (£209) and £235 (£290)
and for two months it's £211 (£265) and £259
(£333). Alternatively, **Busabout** run services
for their own pass holders every two to four
days in summer, covering London and the

major cities of eleven European countries,
with add-on connections to more. Two-week
Busabout passes are £229 for under-26s
and student card-holders, £259 for others,
rising to £359 (£399) for four weeks, £449
(£499) for six weeks, £539 (£599) for eight,
£649 (£739) for twelve, and £769 (£859) for
the whole season (April–Oct). Busabout also
has Flexipasses for travel on any eight days
at £259 (£299), twelve days £359 (£399),
sixteen days at £449 (£499), or twenty days
at £539 (£599), with additional days at £35.
There are sometimes discounts on passes
bought early in the year. Major youth/stu-
dent travel agents in Britain, North America,
Australia and New Zealand sell Busabout
passes; for more information, and prices,
see ⊛www.busabout.com.

## By ferry

Travelling by **ferry** is often the most practical way to get from one part of Europe to
another, the obvious routes being from the
mainland to the Mediterranean islands, as
well as moving between the countries bordering the Baltic and Adriatic seas. There are
countless routes serving a huge range of destinations, too numerous to outline here; where
possible we've given the details of ferries to
other countries within each chapter. For further details of schedules and operators, see
the *Thomas Cook European Timetable*.

## By plane

Short-haul **air travel** is no longer the
extravagance it once was. With increasing deregulation inside the EU, most large
European countries now have at least one
"no frills" airline offering low-cost flights
across Europe, usually selling tickets online,
and invariably undercutting train and bus
fares on longer international routes. Airlines
like easyJet (⊛www.easyjet.com), bmibaby
(⊛www.bmibaby.com) and flyBE (⊛www
.flybe.com) in Britain; Ryanair (⊛www
.ryanair.com) in Ireland; Hapag-Loyd (⊛www
.hlx.com), German Wings (⊛www.german
wings.com) and Air Berlin (⊛www.airberlin
.com) in Germany; and Sky Europe (⊛www
.skyeurope.com) in Hungary and Slovakia,
are best located via the Internet. Of course,
travelling by air, you miss the scenery and

the "feel" for a country that ground-level transport can give you, and there's also the inconvenience of getting between airports and the cities they serve, often quite a haul in itself, but if you're pressed for time, and especially if you want to get from one end of Europe to another, taking the plane is definitely an option.

# Accommodation

Although accommodation is one of the more crucial costs to consider when planning your trip, it needn't be a stumbling block to a budget-conscious tour of Europe. Indeed, even in Europe's pricier destinations the hostel system means there is always an affordable place to stay. If you're prepared to camp you can get by on very little while staying at some excellently equipped sites.

The one thing you should bear in mind is that in the more popular cities and resorts – Florence, Venice, Amsterdam, Prague, Barcelona, the Algarve, and so on – things can get chock-a-block during the peak summer months, and even if you've got plenty of money to throw around you should book in advance.

## Hostels

The cheapest places to stay around Europe are the innumerable **hostels** that cover the continent. Some of these are private places, but by far the majority are official hostels, members of **Hostelling International** (HI), which incorporates the national youth hostel associations of every country in the world. Youth hostelling isn't the hearty, up-at-the-crack-of-dawn and early-to-bed business it once was; indeed, hostels have been keen to shed this image of late and now appeal to a wider public. In many countries they simply

represent the best-value overnight accommodation available. Most are clean, well-run places, always offering dormitory accommodation, some – especially in Scandinavia and other parts of northern Europe – offering a range of private single and double rooms, or rooms with four to six beds. Many hostels also either have self-catering facilities or provide low-cost meals, and the larger ones have a range of other facilities – a swimming pool and a games room for example. There is no age limit (except in Bavaria, in southern Germany), but where there is limited space, priority is given to those under 26.

Strictly speaking, to use an HI hostel you have to have **membership**, although if there's room you can stay at most hostels by simply paying a bit extra – and you can often join the HI on the spot. If you do intend to do a lot of hostelling, however, it's certainly worth joining, which you can do through your home country's hostelling association.

## Accommodation price codes

Throughout this guide, accommodation is coded on a scale of ❶ to ❾, the code indicating the **lowest price per night for a double room** in each establishment in high season. The prices indicated by the codes are as follows:

❶ up to €15
❷ €15–30
❸ €31–45

❹ €46–60
❺ €61–75
❻ €76–90

❼ €91–100
❽ €101–120
❾ €121 and over

We've given the name and address of the relevant national hostelling organization in each chapter if you want further information. HI hostels can usually be booked through their country's hostelling association website, almost always over-the-counter at other hostels in the same country, and often through the international HI website, ⊛www.hihostels .com. The *HI Guide to Europe*, available from bookstores and national hostelling associations, is a good investment at £7.95/$13.95, detailing every official hostel in Europe (but not Morocco, which is covered by the *HI Guide to Africa, the Americas, Asia and the Pacific*).

### Youth hostel associations

**Australia** ☎02/9261 1111, ⊛www.yha.com.au. Annual membership A$52, renewal A$37.

**Canada** ☎1-800/663 5777 or 613/237 7884, ⊛www.hihostels.ca. Sells membership valid from 16 to 28 months, depending on when you buy it, for Can$35, life membership costs Can$175 (both plus tax).

**England & Wales** ☎0870/770 8868, ⊛www.yha .org.uk. Annual membership £15.50, under-26s £10, life membership £200.

**Ireland** ☎01/830 4555, ⊛www.irelandyha.org. Annual membership €20, life membership €100.

**New Zealand** ☎0800/278 299 or 03/379 9970, ⊛www.yha.co.nz. Annual membership NZ$40, renewal NZ$30; life membership NZ$300.

**Northern Ireland** ☎028/9032 4733, ⊛www.hini .org.uk. Annual membership £13, life membership £75.

**Scotland** ☎01786/891 400, ⊛www.syha.org.uk. Annual membership £6, life membership £60.

**USA** ☎301/495-1240, ⊛www.hiusa.org. Annual membership $28, life membership $250.

## Hotels and pensions

If you've got a bit more money to spend – or have decided to have a bit of a splurge – you may want to upgrade from hostel accommodation to something a little more comfortable and private. With **hotels** you can really spend as much or as little as you like. Most hotels in Europe are graded on some kind of star system. One- and two-star category hotels are plain and simple on the whole, usually family-run, with a number of rooms without private facilities; sometimes breakfast won't be included. In three-star hotels all the rooms will have private facilities, prices will normally include breakfast and there may well be a phone or TV in the room; while four- and five-star places will certainly have all these, plus sauna, swimming pool, and other such facilities. In the really top-level places breakfast, oddly enough, isn't always included. When it is, in the Netherlands, Britain or Germany, it's fairly sumptuous; in France it won't amount to much anyway and it's no hardship to grab a croissant and coffee in the nearest café.

Obviously prices vary greatly, but you're rarely going to be paying less than £15/$27 for a double room even in southern Europe, while in the Netherlands the average price is around £30/$55, and in Scandinavia and the British Isles somewhat higher than that. In some countries a **pension** or B&B (variously known as a guesthouse, *pensão*, *Gasthaus* or numerous other names) is a cheaper alternative, offering smaller, simpler accommodation, usually with just a few rooms. In some countries these advertise with a sign in the window; in others they can be booked through the tourist office, which may demand a small fee. There are various other kinds of accommodation – apartments, farmhouses, cottages, *paradores* in Spain, *gîtes* in France, and more – but most are geared to longer-term stays and we have detailed them only where relevant.

## Camping

The cheapest form of accommodation is, of course, a **campsite**, either pitching your own tent or parking your caravan or camper van. Most sites make a charge per person, plus a charge per plot and/or another per vehicle. Bear in mind, especially in countries like France where camping is very popular, that facilities can be excellent (though the better the facilities, the pricier the site). If you're on foot you should add in the cost and inconvenience of getting to the site, since most are on the outskirts of towns, sometimes further. Some sites have **cabins**, which you can stay in for a little extra, although these are usually fairly basic affairs, only really worth considering in regions like Scandinavia where budget options are thin on the ground. In Britain, the AA issues *Camping and Caravanning Europe* (£10.99), which provides a **list of campsites** in eleven West European countries. Alternatively, **tourist offices** can recommend well-equipped and conveniently located sites.

If you're planning to do a lot of camping, an **international camping carnet** is a good investment. The carnet gives discounts at member sites, serves as useful identification, and is obligatory on some sites in Portugal and some Scandinavian countries. Many campsites will take it instead of making you surrender your passport during your stay, and it covers you for third-party insurance when camping. However, the carnet is not recognized in Sweden, where you may have to join their own carnet scheme. In **the US and Canada**, the carnet is available from home motoring organizations, or from Family Campers and RVers (FCRV; ☎ 1-800/245-9755, ⓦ www.fcrv.org). FCRV annual membership costs $25 per family, and the carnet an additional $20. In **the UK and Ireland**, the carnet costs £4.50/€6.35, and

is available to members of the AA in Ireland or the RAC in the UK, or for members only from either of the following: the Camping and Caravanning Club (☎ 024/7669 4995, ⓦ www.campingandcaravanningclub.co.uk; annual membership £30 plus £5 joining fee), or the CTC (☎ 0870/873 0061, ⓦ www.ctc.org.uk, membership £32). For Camping and Caravanning Club members, the club's foreign touring arm, Carefree Travel Service (☎ 024/7642 2024), provides the camping carnet free if you take out insurance with them; they also book ferry crossings and inspect camping sites in Europe.

As for **camping rough**, it's a fine idea if you can get away with it – though perhaps an entire trip of rough camping is in reality too gruelling to be truly enjoyable. In some countries it's easy – in parts of Scandinavia it's a legal right, and in Greece and other southern European countries you can usually find a bit of beach to pitch down on – but in others it's almost a non-starter and can get you into trouble with the law.

# Communications

Communications throughout northern and western Europe are generally excellent: public phones are readily available and normally work, the postal system is reasonably efficient and easy to use, and the Internet and emailing websites can accessed just about everywhere. In southern Europe, services are sometimes less impressive, notably in Italy and Spain, where the post is not overly reliable; while in eastern Europe the infrastructure is poor and services consequently unpredictable.

## Mail

For buying stamps and, sometimes, making phone calls, we've listed the **central post offices** in major cities and given an idea of opening hours. Bear in mind, though, that throughout much of Europe you can avoid the queues in post offices by buying stamps from newsagents, tobacconists and street kiosks. If you know in advance where you're going to be and when, it is possible

to receive mail through the **poste restante** (general delivery) system, whereby letters addressed to you, marked "poste restante" and sent to the main post office in any town or city will be kept under your name – for at least two weeks and usually for a month – for collection at the relevant counter. When collecting mail, make sure you take your passport for identification, and bear in mind that there's a possibility of letters being misfiled by someone unfamiliar with your language;

try looking under your first name as well as your surname.

## Phones

It is nearly always possible, especially in western Europe, to make **international calls** from a public call box; this can often be more trouble than it's worth from a coin phone due to the constant need to feed in change, although most countries now have phone cards, making the whole process much easier. Otherwise, you can go to a **post office**, or a special **phone bureau**, where you can make a call from a private booth and pay afterwards. Most countries have these in one form or another, and the local tourist office will point you in the right direction. Avoid using the phone in your **hotel room** – unless you have money to burn.

To **call any country** in this book from Britain, Ireland or New Zealand, dial ☎00, then the country code (see box), then the city/area code (if there is one) without the initial zero – except for Russia, Latvia and Lithuania, where an initial 8 is omitted, Italy, where the initial zero must be dialled, and Spain, where the initial 9 must be dialled – then the local number. From the US and most of Canada, the international access code is ☎011, from Australia it's ☎0011; otherwise the procedure is the same.

To **call home** from almost all European countries, including Morocco and Turkey, dial ☎00, then the country code, then the city/area code (without the initial zero if there is one), then the local number. The exception is Russia, where you dial ☎8, wait for a continuous dialling tone and then dial ☎10, followed by the country code, area code and number.

For **collect calls**, "Home Country Direct" services are available in most of the places covered in this book. In the UK and some other countries, international calling cards available from newsagents enable you to call North America, Australia and New Zealand very cheaply. Most North American, British, Irish and Australasian phone companies either allow you to call home from abroad on a credit card, or billed to your home number (contact your company's customer services before you leave to find out their toll-free access codes from the countries you'll be visiting), or else will issue an international calling card which can be used worldwide, and for which you will be billed on your return. If you want a calling card and do not already have one, leave yourself a few weeks to arrange it before leaving.

**Cellphones** from North America are unlikely to work in Europe – for details of which phones will work outside the US and Canada, contact your provider. **Mobiles** from the British Isles, Australia and New Zealand can be used in most parts of Europe, and a lot of countries – certainly in Western Europe – have nearly universal coverage, but you may have to inform your provider before leaving home to get international access switched on, and you will be charged for receiving calls and even voicemail. Also note that it will not always be possible to charge up or replace

## Country codes

| | | |
|---|---|---|
| Andorra ☎376 | Greece ☎30 | Portugal ☎351 |
| Australia ☎61 | Hungary ☎36 | Romania ☎40 |
| Austria ☎43 | Ireland ☎353 | Russia ☎7 |
| Belgium ☎32 | Italy ☎39 | Serbia & Montenegro |
| Bulgaria ☎359 | Latvia ☎371 | ☎381 |
| Canada ☎1 | Liechtenstein ☎423 | Slovakia ☎421 |
| Croatia ☎385 | Lithuania ☎370 | Slovenia ☎386 |
| Czech Republic ☎420 | Luxembourg ☎352 | Spain ☎34 |
| Denmark ☎45 | Monaco ☎377 | Sweden ☎46 |
| Estonia ☎372 | Morocco ☎212 | Switzerland ☎41 |
| Finland ☎358 | Netherlands ☎31 | Turkey ☎90 |
| France ☎33 | New Zealand ☎64 | UK ☎44 |
| Germany ☎49 | Norway ☎47 | USA ☎1 |
| Gibraltar ☎350 | Poland ☎48 | |

your pre-paid cards, so again check beforehand and, if necessary, top up your credit before you leave. A standard two-pin socket is used on the Continent so you may also need an adaptor for charging up your phone.

The most useful resource for information on phone codes and electrical systems around the world is the encyclopedic website ⓦ www.kropla.com.

## Internet and email

Europe still lags behind the US in terms of **Internet access**, and surfing the web can be more expensive due to the high rates charged for local phone calls. Nonetheless, things are improving all the time: more and more Internet cafés are opening up, and it's becoming increasingly easy to access the web and send and receive **email**. That being the case, a good way to keep in touch is to open up an account with one of the free Internet email sites that can be accessed from anywhere, for example Yahoo Mail (ⓦ mail.yahoo.com) and Hotmail (ⓦ www .hotmail.com), so that you can receive emails while on the road.

# The media

British newspapers and magazines are widely available in Europe, sometimes on the day of publication, more often the day after. They do, however, cost around three times as much as they do at home.

Exceptions to this rule are the *Guardian* and *Financial Times*, which print European editions that are cheaper and available on the day of issue. You can also find the *International Herald Tribune* and *USA Today* just about everywhere. If you're lucky you may come across the odd *New York Times* or *Washington Post*, while *Time*, *Newsweek* and *The Economist* are all widely available.

It's cheaper to get your news by tuning a **radio** into the BBC World Service (considered to have the most reliable news of all the media), Voice of America, Radio Canada, or one of the many local news broadcasts in English. The easiest way to pick up BBC World Service is on medium wave, at 648kHz (western Europe) or 1323kHz (southeastern Europe); short wave frequencies include 6195, 9410, 12,095, 15,565 and 17,640kHz. In addition, FM stations in cities from Gibraltar to Helsinki slot the BBC news and/or some programming into their schedules; ⓦ www.bbc.co.uk has details. In northern France, the Netherlands and Belgium you can pick up BBC domestic services on medium and long wave. Voice of America (ⓦ www.voa.gov) can be found on 9825, 15,195 or 15,495kHz short wave, among other frequencies. Radio Canada (ⓦ www.rcinet.ca) broadcasts on short wave on 5850, 11,765 and 15,325kHz between 8pm and 9pm GMT.

With the advent of cable and satellite channels, **television** has become more of a pan-European medium than radio. CNN, Eurosport and MTV Europe are all popular and normally available in pricier hotels. In many parts of Europe there is, in any case, a reasonably wide choice of terrestrial channels, since a border is never far away and you can often pick up at least one other country's TV stations. For instance, in Belgium and the southern Netherlands, you can pick up all the satellite and cable channels, plus Dutch and Belgian TV, French TV, British BBC1 and BBC2, all the German stations, and even the state Italian channel.

# Festivals and annual events

There's always some event or other happening in Europe, and the bigger shindigs can be reason enough for visiting a place – some are even worth planning your entire trip around. Be warned, though, that if you're intending to visit a place during its annual festival you need to plan well in advance, since accommodation can be booked up months beforehand, especially for the larger, more internationally known events.

## Religious and traditional festivals

Many of the **festivals** and annual **events** you'll come across in Europe were – and in many cases still are – religious affairs, commemorating a local miracle or saint's day. Others are decidedly more secular – from film and music festivals to street carnivals – but just as much fun. The following are some of the biggest celebrations, further information on which can be found at local tourist offices.

### January

**Spain and Eastern Europe** Twelfth Night (Jan 6). Rather than Christmas Day, this is the time for present-giving in Spain, while in Orthodox Eastern Europe, the sixth of January *is* Christmas Day.

### February

**Berlin (Germany)** The Berlin Film Festival is more geared towards the general public than the more famous one in Cannes.

### March

**Venice (Italy)** Carnival/Mardi Gras (March 7 2006). Celebrated most famously in Venice, there are smaller events across Europe, notably in Viareggio (Italy), Luzern and Basel (Switzerland), Cologne (Germany), Maastricht (Netherlands) and tiny Binche (Belgium).

**Dublin (Ireland)** St Patrick's Day (March 17). Celebrated wherever there's an Irish community, in Dublin it's a five-day festival with music, parades and a lot of drinking.

### April

**Across Europe** Easter (April 16 2006). Celebrated with most verve and ceremony in Catholic and Orthodox Europe, where Easter Sunday or Monday is usually marked with some sort of procession; note that the Orthodox Church's Easter can fall a week or two either side of the Western festival (April 23 2006).

**Seville (Spain)** Feria. A week of flamenco music and dancing, parades and bullfights, in a frenzied and enthusiastic atmosphere.

**Netherlands** Annual displays and processions of flowers in the Dutch bulbfield towns.

**Florence (Italy)** Maggio Musicale (late April until early July). Festival of opera and classical music.

### May

**Bruges (Belgium)** Heilig Bloed procession (May 25 2006). Held on Ascension Day (forty days after Easter), when a much-venerated relic of Christ's blood is carried shoulder-high through the town.

**Landgraaf (Netherlands)** PinkPop Festival. Holland's biggest pop music festival.

**Cannes (France)** Cannes Film Festival. The world's most famous cinema festival is really more of an industry affair than anything else.

### June

**Brussels (Belgium)** Ommegang processions through the city centre (30 June–2 July) to commemorate a medieval miracle.

**Roskilde (Denmark)** The Roskilde Festival. An eclectic range of music (rock, dance, folk) and performance arts, with profits going to worthy causes.

### July

**Berlin (Germany)** The Love Parade. The world's biggest street rave, with pounding techno music and massive grins all round.

**Pamplona (Spain)** San Fermín festival. Anarchic fun, centred on the running of the bulls through the streets of the city, plus music, dancing and of course a lot of drinking.

**Siena (Italy)** The Palio. Italy's most spectacular annual event, a bareback horse race between representatives of the different quarters of the city around the main square.

**Bruges and Ghent (Belgium)** Flanders Festival. An umbrella title for all sorts of dramatic and musical events held mainly in medieval buildings during July and August.

**Montreux (Switzerland)** Montreux Jazz Festival. These days only loosely committed to jazz, this festival takes in everything from folk to breakbeats.

**The Hague (Netherlands)** North Sea Jazz Festival. For real cool cats, this one sticks more closely to its orthodox roots than Montreux.

**Salzburg (Austria)** Salzburg Music Festival. Arguably the foremost, if also the most conservative, classical music festival in Europe.

**London (England)** The Proms (July–Sept). World-famous concert series that maintains high standards of classical music at egalitarian prices.

**Cambridge (England)** Cambridge Folk Festival. Still relatively small, this is still Britain's foremost folk music gathering.

**Spoleto (Italy)** Festival dei Due Mondi. Italy's leading international arts festival, held over two weeks each summer.

**Avignon (France)** Avignon Festival. Slanted towards drama but hosts plenty of other events too and is a great time to be in town.

**Dubrovnik (Croatia)** Dubrovnik Summer Festival (July and August). A host of musical events and theatre performances against the backdrop of the town's beautiful Renaissance centre.

## August

**Siena (Italy)** Second Palio, similar to the one in July.

**London (England)** Notting Hill Carnival. Predominantly Black British and Caribbean celebration that's become the world's second biggest street carnival after Rio.

**Edinburgh (Scotland)** Edinburgh Arts Festival. Mass of top-notch and fringe events in every performing medium, from rock to cabaret to modern experimental music, dance and drama.

**Locarno (Switzerland)** Locarno Film Festival. Movies from around the world compete on the banks of Lake Maggiore (see p.1026).

## September

**Venice (Italy)** Venice Film Festival. First held in 1932, this is the world's oldest film festival.

**Venice (Italy)** Regata Storica. A trial of skill for the city's gondoliers.

**Naples (Italy)** Festa di San Gennaro. Join the devout to see the dried blood of the city's patron saint liquefy to prevent disaster befalling the place (it rarely fails).

**Munich (Germany)** Oktoberfest. A huge beer festival and fair (held in the last two weeks of September, despite the name), attracting vast numbers of people to consume gluttonous quantities of beer and food.

## October

**Morocco, Turkey and Muslim areas of Bulgaria and Greece** Ramadan (around 23 Sept 2006). Commemorating the revelation of the Koran to the Prophet Muhammad, this month of fasting from sunrise until sunset ends with a huge celebration called Eid el-Fitr, on or around 23 Oct 2006.

## November

**Venice (Italy)** Annual procession across the Grand Canal to the church of the Santa Maria della Salute (see p.609).

## December

**Christmas** Festive markets sprout up across the continent in the run-up to Christmas.

**New Year's Eve** Celebrated with fireworks, parties and some serious carousing pretty much everywhere in Europe.

# Crime and personal safety

Travelling around Europe should be relatively trouble-free, but, as in any part of the world, there is always the chance of petty theft. However, conditions do vary greatly from, say, Scandinavia, where you're unlikely to encounter much trouble of any kind, to the inner-city areas of metropolises such as London, Paris or Barcelona, where the crime-rate is higher, and poorer regions such as Morocco, Turkey and southern Italy, where street crime is low but tourists are an obvious target.

In order to minimize the risks, you should take some basic **precautions**. First and perhaps most important, you should try not to look too much like a tourist. Appearing lost, even if you are, is to be avoided, and it's not a good idea – especially in southern Europe – to walk around showing off the latest handheld camcorder or flashing an obviously expensive camera: the professional bag-snatchers who tour train stations can have your valuables off you in seconds.

Be discreet about using a mobile phone, and be sure to put it back into a secure pocket as soon as you've finished. If you're waiting for a train, keep your eyes (and hands if necessary) on your bags at all times; if you want to sleep, put everything valuable under your head as a pillow. You should be cautious when choosing a train compartment and avoid any situation that makes you feel uncomfortable. Padlocking your bags to the luggage rack if you're on an overnight train means that they're more likely to still be there in the morning.

If you're staying in a hostel, take your valuables out with you unless there's a very secure store for them on the premises; having photocopies of your passport and ID is a good idea. Storing a copy of your address book with friends or family can be worthwhile too. If you're driving, don't leave anything valuable in your parked car.

If the worst happens and you do have something stolen, inform the **police** immediately (we've included details of the main city police stations in the text); the priority is to get a statement from them detailing exactly what has been lost, which you'll need for your insurance claim back home. Generally you'll find the police sympathetic enough,

sometimes able to speak English, but often unwilling to do much more than make out a report for you.

As for **offences** you might commit, it's hardly necessary to state that **drugs** such as amphetamines, cocaine, heroin, LSD and ecstasy are illegal all over Europe, and although use of cannabis is widespread in most countries, and legally tolerated in some (famously in the Netherlands, for example), you are never allowed to possess more than a tiny amount for personal use, and unlicensed sale remains illegal. Penalties for possession of hard drugs and psychedelics can be severe; in certain countries, such as Turkey, even possession of cannabis can result in a hefty prison sentence, and your consulate is unlikely to be sympathetic.

Other, more minor, misdemeanours include **sleeping rough**, which is more tolerated in some parts of Europe than others and should be undertaken everywhere with a certain amount of circumspection, and topless **sunbathing**, which is now fairly common throughout southern Europe but still often frowned upon, especially in parts of Greece, Turkey and Italy. As always, be sensitive, and err on the side of caution.

It's also worth remembering that, in theory, it's illegal to be on the streets without an official ID card or passport throughout most of mainland Europe (except the Netherlands and Scandinavia) so it's worth carrying copies with you. Finally, although this is much less of an issue than it once was, avoid photography around sensitive military sites or installations: you may be arrested as a spy.

## Sexual harassment

One of the major irritants for women travelling through Europe is **sexual harassment**, which in Italy, Greece, Turkey, Spain and Morocco especially can be almost constant for women travelling alone or with another woman, and can put certain areas completely out of bounds. Southern European coastal areas, especially, can be a real problem, where women tourists are often regarded as being on the lookout for sex. By far the most common kind of harassment you'll come across simply consists of street whistles and cat-calls; occasionally it's more sinister and very occasionally it can be dangerous. Indifference is often the best policy, avoiding eye contact with men and at the same time appearing as confident and purposeful as possible. If this doesn't make you feel any more comfortable, shouting a few choice phrases in the local language is a good idea; don't, however, shout in English, which often seems to encourage them. You may also come across gropers on crowded buses and trains, in which case you should complain as loudly as possible in any language – the ensuing scene should be enough to deter your assailant. The best way of avoiding more dangerous situations is to simply be as suspicious as possible: don't ever get yourself into a situation where you're alone with a man you don't know.

# Gay and lesbian travellers

Gay men and lesbians will find most of Europe a tolerant part of the world in which to travel, the west rather more so than the east. Gay sex is no longer a criminal offence in any country covered by this book except Morocco, but some still have measures that discriminate against gay men (a higher age of consent for example). Lesbianism would seem not to officially exist, so it is not generally subject to such laws.

In general, the Netherlands and Scandinavia (except Finland) are the most tolerant parts of the continent, with anti-discrimination legislation and official recognition of lesbian and gay partnerships. Homophobic laws against things like "public scandal" and "luring into perversion" have gradually been abolished across Europe, though gay sex remains illegal in Morocco. For further information, check the International Lesbian and Gay Association's European region website at ⓦwww.ilga-europe.org.

Most cities of any size have a few bars or cafés frequented by **gay men**, and it's not hard to make contact with other gay people. In the major northern capitals, certainly, the gay scene is usually fairly sophisticated, with any number of bars, bookshops, clubs and gay organizations and switchboards, though things are usually firmly slanted towards gay men. The gay capital of Europe is Amsterdam, but there's plenty of interest in London, Paris and Copenhagen, and, to a lesser extent, Madrid, Barcelona, Ibiza and the Greek island of Mykonos. In southern Europe, things are less developed: the main cities may have the odd gay bar, but it may not advertise itself as such, and outside the capitals there's unlikely to be anywhere obvious to meet at all. **Lesbians** can likewise usually find somewhere to meet with other gay women in northern Europe, albeit on a much smaller scale than gay men, while elsewhere, in southern and eastern Europe, word-of-mouth is about the only course open. We've detailed the best of the gay scenes of the major cities in the guide; for further information, contact the organizations listed below.

## Contacts for gay and lesbian travellers

**Spartacus Gay Guide** Bruno Gmünder Verlag, Kleiststrasse 23–26, 10787 Berlin ☎ +49-30/615 0030, ☻ www.brunogmuender.de. US: Bookazine Co, 75 Hook Rd, Bayonne, NJ 07002 ☎ 1-800/548 3855; UK: Turnaround, Unit 3, Olympia Trading Estate, Coburg Rd, London N22 6TZ ☎ 020/8829 3000; Australia: Bulldog Books, PO Box 6406, Alexandria, NSW 2015 ☎ 02/9699 3507. International gay guide with information on meeting and cruising spots for gay men, but nothing much for lesbians.

### North America

**Damron Company** ☎ 1-800/462-6654 or 415/255-0404, ☻ www.damron.com. Publishes a men's and a women's guide, and an accommodation guide and gay road atlas, all mainly on North America but covering major European cities too.
**Gay Travel** ☎ 1-800/GAY-TRAVEL, ☻ www.gaytravel.com. Gay online travel agent, offering accommodation, cruises, tours and more.
**International Gay & Lesbian Travel Association** ☎ 1-800/448-8550 or 954/776-2626, ☻ www.iglta.org. Trade group that can provide a list of gay- and lesbian-owned or -friendly travel agents, accommodation and other travel businesses.

### UK

**Gay Travel** ☻ www.gaytravel.co.uk. Online gay and lesbian travel agent, offering good deals on all types of holiday. Also lists gay- and lesbian-friendly hotels in several European cities and resorts.
**Madison Travel** ☎ 01273/202532, ☻ www.madisontravel.co.uk. Established travel agents specializing in packages to gay- and lesbian-friendly mainstream destinations, and also to gay/lesbian destinations.
**Dream Waves Holidays** ☎ 0870/042 2475, ☻ www.gayholidaysdirect.com. Specializes in exclusively gay holidays, including skiing trips and summer sun packages.
**Respect Holidays** ☎ 0870/770 0169, ☻ www.respect-holidays.co.uk. Offers exclusively gay packages to all popular European resorts.
Also check out adverts in the weekly papers *Boyz* and *Pink Paper*, handed out free in gay venues.

### Australia

**Gay and Lesbian Tourism Australia** ☻ www.galta.com.au. Directory and links for gay and lesbian travel worldwide.
**Parkside Travel** Australia ☎ 08/8274 1222, ℮ parkside@herveyworld.com.au. Gay travel agent associated with local branch of Hervey World Travel; all aspects of gay and lesbian travel worldwide.
**Tearaway Travel** Australia ☎ 1800/664 440 or 03/9847 4732, ☻ www.tearaway.com. Gay-specific business dealing with international and domestic travel.

# Travellers with disabilities

**Prosperous northern Europe is easier for disabled travellers than the south and east, but the gradual enforcement of EU accessibility regulations is making life easier within the European Union at least.**

**Wheelchair access** to public buildings nonetheless remains far from common in many countries, as is wheelchair accessibility to public transport – indeed, the only big-city underground systems that are accessible are those in Berlin, Amsterdam, Stockholm and Helsinki, with the rest lagging far behind. Most buses are still inaccessible to wheelchair users, but airport facilities are improving, as are those on cross-Channel ferries. As for rail services, these vary greatly: France, for example, has very good facilities for disabled passengers, as have Belgium, Denmark, Switzerland and Austria, but many other countries make little if any provision.

Your particular disability may govern whether you decide to see Europe on a **package tour** or **independently**. There are any number of **specialist tour-operators**, mostly catering for physically disabled travellers, and the number of non-specialist operators who cater for disabled clients is increasing.

Pressure on space means that it is impossible for us to detail wheelchair-access arrangements for everywhere we list; neither can we detail the best and worst of the operators. For more **information on disabled travel abroad** you should get in touch with the organizations listed below. As well as their publications, look out for *Access London* and *Access Paris,* with information specific to those cities, published by Access Project in the UK.

## Contacts for travellers with disabilities

### North America

**Access-Able** ⓦwww.access-able.com. Online resource for travellers with disabilities.
**Directions Unlimited** ⓣ1-800/533-5343 or 914/241-1700. Tour operator specializing in bookings for people with disabilities.
**Mobility International USA** ⓣ541/343-1284, ⓦwww.miusa.org. Information and referral services, access guides, tours and exchange programmes.
**Society for Accessible Travel & Hospitality (SATH)** ⓣ212/447-7284, ⓦwww.sath.org. Non-profit educational organization that has actively represented travellers with disabilities since 1976.

Annual membership $45; $30 for students and seniors.
**Wheels Up!** ⓣ1-888/389-4335, ⓦwww.wheelsup.com. Offers discounted airfare, tour and cruise prices for disabled travellers, and also publishes a free monthly newsletter.

### UK and Ireland

**Access Travel** UK ⓣ01942/888844, ⓦwww.access-travel.co.uk. Small tour operator that can arrange flights, transfers and accommodation in France, Spain, Portugal and parts of Greece.
**Holiday Care** UK ⓣ0845/124 9971 or 020/8760 0072, ⓦwww.holidaycare.org.uk. Provides free lists of accessible accommodation abroad. Information on financial help for holidays available.
**Irish Wheelchair Association** Ireland ⓣ01/818 6400, ⓦwww.iwa.ie. Useful information provided about travelling abroad with a wheelchair.
**Tripscope** UK ⓣ0845/758 5641, ⓦwww.tripscope.org.uk. Registered charity providing a telephone information service offering free transport and travel advice for people with mobility problems.

### Australia and New Zealand

**ACROD (Australian Council for Rehabilitation of the Disabled)** Australia ⓣ02/6282 4333 (also TTY), ⓦwww.acrod.org.au. Provides lists of travel agencies and tour operators for people with disabilities.
**Disabled Persons Assembly** New Zealand ⓣ04/801 9100 (also TTY), ⓦwww.dpa.org.nz. Resource centre with lists of travel agencies and tour operators for people with disabilities.

# Work and study

The opportunities for working or studying your way around Europe are almost unlimited, especially for EU citizens, who can legally work in any EU state. You can fix something up before you leave home and build your trip around it, or look out for casual labour on your travels as a way of topping up your vacation cash.

The best way of discovering a country properly is to **work** there, learning the language if you can and discovering something about the culture. **Study** opportunities are also a good way of absorbing yourself in the local culture, but they invariably need to be fixed up in advance; check the newspapers for ads or contact one of the main organizations direct (see pp.68–69).

There are any number of jobs you can pick up on the road to supplement your spending money. It's normally not hard to find **bar** or **restaurant work**, especially in large resort areas during the summer, and your chances will be greater if you speak the local language – although being able to speak English may be your greatest asset in more touristy areas. In EU countries, British and Irish citizens do not need **work permits** (though other bureaucratic hurdles may be thrown in your path instead). Don't be afraid to march straight in and ask, or check the noticeboards in local bars, hostels or colleges, or the local newspapers, particularly the English-language ones. Cleaning jobs, nannying and **au pair** work are also common, if not spectacularly well paid, often just providing room and board plus pocket money. Some of them can be fixed up on the spot, while others need to be organized before you leave home. If staying in a place for a while, you can place ads offering your services. The other big casual earner is **farm work**, particularly grape-picking, an option from August to October when the vines are being harvested. The best country for this is France, but there's sometimes work in Germany too, and you're unlikely to be asked for documentation. Also in France, along the Côte d'Azur, and in other yacht-havens in Greece and parts of southern Spain, there is sometimes **crewing work** available, though you'll obviously need some sailing experience. Or try tour operators, who are often on the lookout for **travel couriers**, though this is better arranged from home. If you're really serious, get in touch with the companies that run bus tours for young people around Europe, who are often keen to take on new blood.

Rather better paid, and equally widespread, if only during the September to June period, is **teaching English** as a foreign language (TEFL), though it's becoming harder to find English-teaching jobs without a TEFL qualification. You'll normally be paid a liveable local salary, sometimes with somewhere to live thrown in, and you can often supplement your income with more lucrative private lessons. The TEFL teaching season is reversed in Britain and to a lesser extent Ireland, with plenty of work available during the summer

in London and on the English south coast (but again, some kind of TEFL qualification is pretty well indispensable).

Another pre-planning strategy for working abroad, whether teaching English or otherwise, is to get hold of one of the books on summer jobs abroad and how to work your way around the world published in the UK by Vacation Work; call ☎01865/241 978 or visit ⊛www.vacationwork.co.uk for their catalogue. Travel magazines like *Wanderlust* (every two months; £3.80) have a Job Shop section which often advertises job opportunities with tour companies. ⊛www.studyabroad.com is a useful website with listings and links to study and work programmes worldwide.

**Studying abroad** invariably means learning a language, doing an intensive course that lasts between two weeks and three months and staying with a local family. There are plenty of places you can do this, and you should reckon on paying around £200/$380 a week including room and board. If you know a language well, you could also apply to do a short course in another subject at a local university; scan the classified sections of the newspapers back home, and keep an eye out when you're on the spot. The EU runs a programme called **Erasmus** in which university students from Britain and Ireland can obtain mobility grants to study in one of 26 European countries (including other EU countries, plus Bulgaria, Iceland, Liechtenstein, Norway, Romania and Turkey) for three months to a full academic year if their university participates in the programme. Check with your university's international relations office, or see ⊛europa.eu.int/comm/education/programmes/mundus/index_en.html.

## Work and study contacts

**AFS Intercultural Programs** ⊛www.afs.org. Australia ☎1300/131736, Canada ☎1-800/361-7248 or 514/288-3282, NZ ☎0800/600 300 or 04/494 6020, UK ☎0113/242 6136, US ☎1-800/AFS-INFO, international enquiries ☎+1-212/807-8686. Global UN-recognized organization running summer programmes to foster international understanding.

**American Institute for Foreign Study** ⊛www.aifs.com. UK ☎020/7581 7300, US ☎1-800/727-2437. Language study and cultural immersion for the summer or school year, as well as au pair programmes.

**ASSE International** ⊛ www.asse.com. Australia ☎ 03/9775 4711, Canada ☎ 1-800/361-3214, UK ☎ 01952/460733, US ☎ 1-800/333-3802. International student exchanges and summer language programmes across most of Europe.

**Association for International Practical Training** ⊛ www.aipt.org. US ☎ 410/997-2200. Summer internships in various European countries for students who have completed at least two years of college in science, agriculture, engineering or architecture.

**British Council** ⊛ www.britishcouncil.org. UK ☎ 0161/957 7775. The Council's Recruitment Group (☎ 020/7389 4931) recruits TEFL teachers with degrees and TEFL qualifications for posts worldwide (check the website for a list of current vacancies), and its Education and Training Group (☎ 020/7389 4169) runs teacher exchange programmes and enables those who already work as educators to find out about teacher development programmes abroad.

**Council on International Educational Exchange (CIEE)** ⊛ www.ciee.org/study. US ☎ 1-800/40-STUDY. An international organization worth contacting for advice on studying, working and volunteering in Europe. They run summer-semester and one-year study programmes, and volunteer projects.

**International House** ⊛ www.ihlondon.com. UK ☎ 020/7518 6999. Head office for reputable English-teaching organization that offers TEFL training leading to the award of a Certificate in English Language Teaching to Adults (CELTA), and recruits for teaching positions in Britain and abroad.

**World Learning** ⊛ www.worldlearning.org. US ☎ 1-800/257-7751. The Experiment in International Living (⊛ www.usexperiment.org) has summer programmes for high-school students, while the School for International Training (⊛ www.sit.edu/studyabroad) offers accredited college semesters abroad, with language and cultural studies, homestay and other academic work, in Croatia, the Czech Republic, France, Germany, Ireland, Morocco, the Netherlands, Russia, Spain and Switzerland.

# Directory

**Bargaining** The only places where you need really do any bargaining when shopping are in Turkey – in the bazaars and carpet shops – and in the souks of Morocco. Everywhere else, even in the less developed parts of southern Italy and Greece, people would think it odd if you tried to haggle.

**Contraceptives** Condoms are available everywhere, and are normally reliable international brands such as Durex, at least

## Metric conversions

*All figures are approximate.*
**1 inch** = 2.5cm; **1 foot** = 30cm; **1 yard** = 0.91m; **1 mile** = 1.61km; **5 miles** = 8km.
**1 centimetre** = 0.39 inches; **1 metre** = 1.09 yards or 39 inches;
**1 kilometre** = 0.62 miles.
**1oz** = 28g; **1lb** = 450g/0.45kg; **1 kilo** = 2.2lb.
**1 litre** = 2.11 US pints; **1 US pint** = 0.47 litres*; **1 US quart** = 0.95 litres.
**1 litre** = 1.76 UK pints; **1 UK pint** = 0.57 litres; **1 UK gallon** = 4.54 litres.

*1 US pint = 0.83 UK pint; 1 UK pint = 1.2 US pints.

**Temperatures**

| °C | -5 | 0 | 5 | 10 | 15 | 20 | 25 | 30 | 35 |
|----|----|----|----|----|----|----|----|----|----|
| °F | 23 | 32 | 41 | 50 | 59 | 68 | 77 | 86 | 95 |

in northwestern Europe; the condoms in eastern European countries, Morocco and Turkey are of uncertain quality, however, so it's best to stock up in advance. The pill is available everywhere, too, though often only on prescription; again, bring a sufficient supply with you. In case of emergency, the morning-after pill is available from pharmacies without a prescription in Belgium, Denmark, Finland, France, Morocco, Norway, Portugal, Sweden, Switzerland and the UK.

Electric current The supply in Europe is 220v (240v in the British Isles), which means that anything on North American voltage (110v) normally needs a transformer. However, one or two countries (notably Spain and Morocco) still have a few places on 110v or 120v, so check before plugging in. Continental, Moroccan and Turkish sockets take two round pins, British and Irish ones take three square pins. A travel plug which adapts to all these systems is useful to carry. See ⓦwww.kropla.com for more.

Left luggage (Baggage deposit) Almost every train station of any size has facilities for "left luggage", either lockers or a desk that's open long hours every day. We've given details in the accounts of the major capitals.

Smoking While cigarette smoking (for cannabis see p.64) is fast going out of fashion in northwestern Europe, it remains pretty uninhibited in Eastern Europe and the Mediterranean, where it's considered quite normal for example to smoke in a restaurant without asking permission. The country leading a possible move to change all that is Ireland, where since April 2004 smoking has been illegal in all enclosed workplace environments including pubs, restaurants and even a company car. The EU is keeping an eye on the Irish smoking ban, and if successful it will almost certainly be imposed Europe-wide.

Tampons In western and southern Europe you can buy tampons in all chemists and supermarkets, although in parts of eastern Europe they can still be hard to come by. If

you're travelling in the east for any length of time, it's best to bring your own supply.

Time The places covered in this book are in four time zones. Britain, Ireland, Portugal and Morocco are in principle on GMT (Greenwich Mean Time aka UTC, or Universal Time), which is five hours ahead of Eastern Standard Time, eight hours ahead of Pacific Standard Time, eight hours behind Western Australia, ten hours behind eastern Australia, and twelve hours behind New Zealand. Most of the Continent is on GMT+1, with Finland, Estonia, Latvia, Lithuania, Romania, Bulgaria, Greece and Turkey on GMT+2, and Moscow and St Petersburg on GMT+3. All of these (except Morocco) have daylight saving time from March to October; thankfully, they usually manage to all change over at the same time nowadays, but this change, along with daylight saving in North America, Australia

and New Zealand, can affect the time difference by an hour either way.

Tipping Although it varies from one country to the next, tipping is not really the serious business it is in North America. In many countries it's customary to leave at least something in most restaurants and cafés, if only rounding the bill up to the next major denomination. Even in swankier establishments, a ten percent tip is sufficient, and you shouldn't feel obliged to tip at all if the service was bad, especially if service has been included in the bill. In smarter hotels you should tip hall porters, and cab drivers expect a tip in Britain and Ireland, but not necessarily on the Continent. The opposite is true of bartenders (but if you want to tip a bartender in Britain or Ireland, tell them to "get one for yourself" when paying – which they'll generally take in the form of the cash equivalent).

# Guide

# Guide

# Andorra

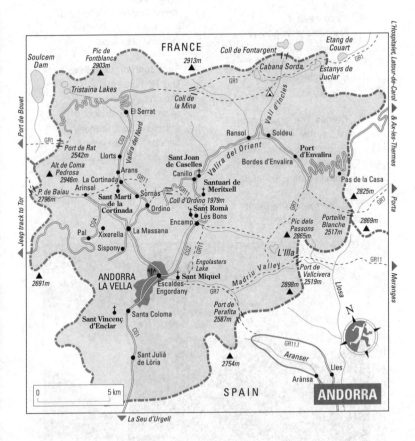

# Andorra highlights

✳ **Shopping** It's easy to max out your credit card on electronics, alcohol, cosmetics and clothing, with prices much cheaper than in France and Spain. See p.82

✳ **Casa de la Vall** Andorra's new parliament meets several times a year in this sixteenth-century edifice. See p.82

✳ **Caldea** The largest natural thermal springs in Europe, with whirlpools, saunas, waterfalls and Roman baths. See p.83

✳ **Casa Areny-Plandolit** Eighteenth-century granite and limestone mansion that was the former residence of one of Andorra's most influential barons. See p.85

✳ **The GR7** Hike along an old smugglers route, traversing the country from the French border to Spain. See p.86

✳ **Sant Joan de Caselles** This Romanesque church holds the remains of an unusual stuccoed Christ in Glory, formerly buried under the stone altar for four hundred years. See p.87

△ Sant Joan de Caselles

# Introduction and basics

Often falling off the itineraries of most European travellers, **Andorra** is a tiny country nestled in the Pyrenees. One of the oldest nations in Europe, it was one of the buffer territories set up by Charlemagne in the eighth century to keep the Islamic Moors at bay. It remained an anachronistic feudal state until 1993, when Andorrans voted for an independent, democratic principality – although technically the country's "princes" are the president of France and the Spanish Bishop of Urgell.

Andorra's forty-odd hamlets are scattered across the valleys, with several dozen Romanesque churches and chapels, and trails that wend their way to mountains and alpine lakes beyond. The capital, **Andorra La Vella**, offers a few sights and most of the shopping, while next-door **Escaldes** lays claim to the biggest thermal spa in Europe. Further north, the remote town of **Pal** remains virtually untouched by modernity while **Arinsal** makes a great stop for an *après* drink. **Ordino**'s hills have access to excellent alpine paths, while sleepy towns like **Llorts** and **El Serrat** offer breathtaking views. East of here, a road weaves through jaw-dropping mountainscapes to **Canillo**, which boasts a captivating Romanesque chapel, and further north, **Soldeu**, a sleepy place just a stone's throw from France.

## Information & maps

The Ministeri de Presidència i Turisme operates **tourist offices** in the capital and most large towns. Be sure to ask for their **brochures** *Cultural Itineraries* and *Mountain Activities*, which detail dozens of good hiking, biking and rock-climbing routes. For general walking around the country, the best map is Rando Édition's Andorra-Cadi 21. The more detailed (1:50,000) Muntanys d'Andorra charts are best for greater exploration and are available at tourist offices.

## Money and banks

Andorra uses the **euro** (€). You'll find **exchange facilities** at most post offices and banks (Mon–Fri 9am–1pm & 3–5pm, Sat 9am–noon), there are **ATMs** throughout the country and credit cards can be used just about everywhere.

## Communications

**Phonecards** (€3 or €6) are sold in shops and tourist offices. Phoning outside the country can be very expensive. The local operator is ☏ 111; international operator is ☏ 119. **Post offices** around the country are either Spanish or French – the latter's is more efficient. You'll need to buy special Andorran stamps to post anything. **Internet** access is available in all the main towns.

## Getting there and around

**Getting to Andorra** isn't the easiest of tasks. Several companies operate **buses** from Spain and France: Alsina Graells

## Andorra on the net

ⓦ **www.andorra.ad** Tourist Board site.
ⓦ **www.andorramania.com** Lots of information, largely geared towards skiers.
ⓦ **www.alltravelandorra.com** Information on getting to Andorra and accommodation.
ⓦ **www.andorraportal.com** Directory of restaurants and shopping establishments.
ⓦ **www.skiandorra.ad** Site covering Andorra's ski resorts, the largest in the Pyrenees.

(☎ 826 567, 🖰 www.alsinagraells.com) arrives daily from Barcelona (€20) and Lleida in Spain (€14); Novatel (☎803 789, 🖰www .andorrabybus.com) runs airport transfers from Barcelona and Toulouse (€25–28); and Eurolines (☎805 151, 🖰www.eurolines .es) has daily services from Madrid and Barcelona (€20) and several buses weekly from other Spanish cities. Hispano Andorra (☎821 372) has a few daily buses to all the main towns from La Seu d'Urgell (€2.40) in Spain and l'Hospitalet (€7.70) in France, where you can hop on SNCF trains.

Once in the country, the best way to tour Andorra is **on foot** – the gorgeous scenery and well-marked paths make for wonderful hiking. With limited time or energy, however, a car is your best option. Fuel is a lot cheaper than in the rest of Europe, and you can **rent a car** in the capital for around €60 per day. **Taxis** are fairly cost-effective and, if you're in a group, are a viable option – a trip from Andorra la Vella to Arinsal, nearly halfway across the country, costs €13.

# Accommodation

Good **budget accommodation** is hard to come by, and most of the cheaper options, located in the capital of Andorra la Vella, have zero charm. Prices run sky-high in high season – July to August (when reservations are a must) and December to March – expect to pay at least €40 for a double room. There's only one **hostel**, and it's stuck up in the hills west of La Massana but **camping** (€5 or less) provides a great alternative given the handsome landscape and well-maintained trails. Another popular option in the summer is staying for free in one of Andorra's 26 state-run **refugis**, simple mountain cabins. Information is available at tourist offices around the country. Camping in the wild is illegal except around these cabins.

# Food and drink

Andorran **food** is generally characterised by rich meat and cheese dishes, though there are influences from French and Spanish cuisines. Breakfasts consist of an espresso and a croissant or *tartine du pain*. Lunch at many restaurants is an inexpensive *plat du jour*, while dinner is usually a full-on Catalan affair of char-grilled fish, fowl or steak alongside fresh aubergine, tomatoes or garlic.

Typical Andorran **dishes** include *trinchat* (cabbage, potatoes and bacon), *estofat d'isard* (goat stew), *truite de ríu* (river trout), *coques* (clam-filled cakes), *xai* (roast lamb), *escudella* (chicken, sausage and meat-ball stew) and *crema catalana* (dessert custard with a caramel crust). Buying **alcohol** in supermarkets will be absurdly cheap, but drink prices can run high in some bars and restaurants. Spanish *vino* is generally the local drink of choice, house wines are a safe and inexpensive choice, though for the more discerning, the medium-bodied Buzet or exotic and fruity Penedès are both good bets.

# Opening hours, holidays and festivals

Most shops open from 9am–8pm, with a near-obligatory siesta between 1 and 4pm and reduced hours on Sundays. Shops and banks are closed on the following **public holidays**: Jan 1, Jan 6, March 14, Holy Thurs–Easter Mon, May 1, Ascension, Pentecost and Whit Mon, June 24, Aug 15, Sept 8, Nov 1, Nov 4, Dec 8, Dec 24–26, Dec 31. **Churches** open daily in July and August from 10am to 7pm. The summer months also see local **festivals** in many of Andorra's townships. The main ones are in Canillo (third Sun & Mon in July); Sant Julià de Lòria (last Sun, Mon & Tues in July); Escaldes-Engordany July 25–27; Andorra La Vella (first Sat, Sun & Mon in Aug); La Massana and Encamp (Aug 15–17); and Ordino (Sept 16–17).

# Shopping

Andorra offers **duty-free shopping** on most goods. In some smaller shops, you can ask for *el descuento,* an extra ten percent discount for foreigners, though this is at the discretion of the establishment. The official duty-free allowances for alcohol and tobacco are currently 5 litres of wine, 1.5

## Catalan (Català)

| | Catalan | Pronunciation |
|---|---|---|
| Yes | *Sí* | See |
| No | *Noh* | Noh |
| Please | *Si us plau* | See-uus-plow |
| Thank you | *Graciés* | Gra-see-ess |
| Hello/Good day | *Hola* | Oh-lah |
| Goodbye | *Adéu* | A-day-uu |
| Excuse me | *Perdoni* | Perdoni |
| Where? | *On?* | On? |
| Good | *Bon/Bona* | Bo |
| Bad | *Mal* | Mal |
| Near | *Aprop* | Aprop |
| Far | *Lluny* | Yoon |
| Cheap | *Barat* | Barat |
| Expensive | *Car* | Car |
| Open | *Obert* | Obert |
| Closed | *Tancat* | Ton-cot |
| Today | *Avui* | A-body |
| Yesterday | *Ahir* | Uh-ear |
| Tomorrow | *Demà* | De-mah |
| How much? | *Quant val?* | Kwant val? |
| What time is it? | *Quina hora és?* | Kwina ora es? |
| I don't understand | *No ho entenc* | No hoe entayn |
| Do you speak English? | *Parles anglès?* | Parles ang-lays? |
| One | *Un/Una* | Oon/Oona |
| Two | *Dos/Dues* | Dohs/Doo-es |
| Three | *Tres* | Trrhes |
| Four | *Quatre* | Kwa-trer |
| Five | *Cinc* | Seenk |
| Six | *Sis* | Sees |
| Seven | *Set* | Set |
| Eight | *Vuit* | Vweet |
| Nine | *Nou* | No |
| Ten | *Deu* | Deoo |

litres of spirits and 300 cigarettes. You'll probably slip past the French border with an extra bottle or two, but the Spanish guards are known to be much more strict.

# Emergencies

The biggest danger in Andorra is the risk of spending too much money in the ubiquitous duty-free shops. Otherwise be careful on the mountain roads which have some very sharp curves. Each commune has its own *Centro de Salud*, where you can find on-duty doctors for non-urgent health issues. For **emergencies**, call an ambulance or get to the hospital in Escaldes. At least one **pharmacy** in most big towns will be open 24-hours, the address for which one should be posted in the windows of all of them.

### Emergency numbers

Police ☎110; Ambulance and Fire ☎118; Medical ☎116; Mountain Rescue ☎112.

# Central and southern Andorra

**Andorra la Vella** is the country's largest town and a natural place to get your bearings, while the rest of southern Andorra consists of small villages packed into sheer valleys.

## Andorra la Vella

Lying at the confluence of three mountain rivers, the national capital of **ANDORRA LA VELLA** is a bit of a misnomer. "Old Andorra" is for the most part a collection of soulless tourist restaurants, ageing storefronts and neon-lit windows proclaiming final markdowns. Where once the streets bustled with shepherds and their livestock – most of the capital was farmland until a few decades ago – today it exists more or less as a base for shoppers and wealthier skiers. Since most buses arrive here, you'll probably end up passing through once or twice during your stay, and while it's not the best introduction to Andorra, the city holds a few sights to while away an afternoon – and enough bargain hunting to while away a few lifetimes.

### Arrival, information and accommodation

**International buses** arrive at the Central d'autobusos, located just southeast of the small Parc Central, five minutes south of the city centre. Domestic transport buses (7am–9pm; €1.20–4.60) leave from just west of pl Benlloch, though service is notoriously slow and unpredictable; check with the tourist office for schedules but don't expect the buses to follow them.

There's a **tourist office** for the commune at pl de la Rotonda (Jul–Aug Mon–Sat 9am–9pm, Sun 9am–7pm; Sept–June 9.30am–1.30pm & 3.30–7.30pm; ☏827 117), and a national one at pl del Poble (Mon–Sat 9/10am–1/1.30pm &

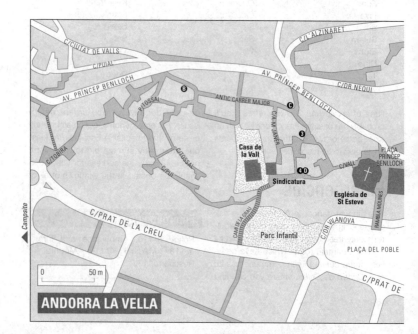

3–7pm, Sun 10am–1pm; Sept–June closed Sun; ☏820 214). They should be able to help with finding a place to stay if you need one but are otherwise not overly useful or friendly.

Being the most commercialized and least traditional of all the townships, Andorra La Vella is also the best place to find cheap **accommodation**. The not-quite-in-the-wild **camping** facilities are good out at *Valira*, av de Salou (☏722 384, ⊛www .campvalira.com; bungalows ❹), with a pool and a restaurant.

## Hotels

**Carlton Plaza** av Meritxell 23–25 ☏872 999, ⊛www.plazaandorra.com. Luxury option, with sauna, Jacuzzi and sleek decor, that has April–Aug bargains making the spacious, comfy rooms a steal. ❻

**Hostal del Sol** pl Guillemó 3 ☏823 701 ☏822 363. The cheapest singles in the country (€13.75) are at this older hotel on a central *plaça*. Though weathered, small and with shared baths, the rooms are clean enough and presided over by a very friendly mater familias. Ask for one of the brighter, balconied rooms. ❷

**Hotel Flora** Antic Carrer Major 25 ☏821 508, ⊛www.andornet.ad/flora. Spick and span place with large rooms decorated in faded floral patterns and a nice pool out back. ❺

**Pensió La Rosa** Antic Carrer Major 18 ☏ & ☏821 810. Just inside the gates of the old quarter, the 24 simply-styled rooms in this friendly pension are a bit larger than in the *del Sol* and in a quieter setting. ❷

**Racó d'en Joan** c/de la Vall 20 ☏820 689, ☏821 280. Well located in the old town next to the parliament, with friendly staff and tidy rooms. The attached restaurant serves inexpensive meals. ❸

## The City

The capital is bisected by the Avinguda del Príncep Benlloch, which further east becomes Avinguda de Meritxell and then, on towards neighboring Escaldes-Engordany, Avinguda de Carlemany. Towards the western end of town, **Barri Antic** is the capital's old quarter and with its cobbled streets and quiet *plaças* is a great escape from the shopping mall that is the rest of the city. In the centre is

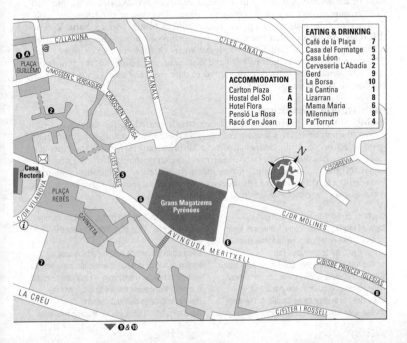

**EATING & DRINKING**

| | |
|---|---|
| Café de la Plaça | 7 |
| Casa del Formatge | 5 |
| Casa Léon | 3 |
| Cerveseria L'Abadia | 2 |
| Gerd | 9 |
| La Borsa | 10 |
| La Cantina | 1 |
| Lizarran | 8 |
| Mama Maria | 6 |
| Milennium | 8 |
| Pa'Torrut | 4 |

**ACCOMMODATION**

| | |
|---|---|
| Carlton Plaza | E |
| Hostal del Sol | A |
| Hotel Flora | B |
| Pensió La Rosa | C |
| Racó d'en Joan | D |

one of the oldest parliaments in Europe – and certainly the smallest – the **Casa de la Vall** (Mon–Sat 9.30am–1pm & 3–7pm, Sun 10am–2pm; free guided tours; bookings required on ☎829 129). Built in 1580 and complete with towers, battlements and steel-barred windows, it provides an appropriately historical base for the courts and the Sindic, Andorra's representative house. Among the rocks below, the government is busily constructing a modern parliament building, due to open in 2007. East of the Casa de la Vall, plaça Príncep Benlloch is presided over by the town's main church, **Sant Esteve**. Originally an eleventh-century construction, it's now best mostly modernised throughout, though it does retain two lovely seventeenth- and eighteenth-century altarpieces. South of here, **Plaça del Poble** makes a great hangout in the evenings and houses the **Centre de Congresos**, one of the country's only theatre and music venues, though performance season runs in winter only. To the northeast, avinguda Meritxell and the streets around have the highest concentration of shops including Andorra's largest **department store**, the Grans Magatzems Pyrénées, at no.11 (Mon–Fri 9.30am–8pm, Sat 9.30am–9pm, Sun 9.30am–7pm; Aug weeknights until 9pm), which also houses several cafeteria-style restaurants on the top floor. Just round the corner on c/Les Canals – follow your nose – is the **Casa del Formatge** with some 2000 types of cheeses, many of which you can sample. At the other end of the pungency spectrum, a fifteen-minute stroll along avinguda Meritxell brings you to the **Museu del Perfum**, av Carlemany 115 (Tues–Fri 10am–1pm & 4–8pm, Sat 10am–2pm & 3.30–8pm, Sun 10am–1.30pm; €5). The small museum displays hundreds of bottles dating from 700BC to the present and has an ingenious contraption that allows visitors to mix the essences of several dozen plants, herbs and spices, and waft the resulting bouquet.

Two kilometres south of the capital, **Santa Coloma** is the most famous church in Andorra, often seen plastered across postcards and tourist bureau walls. It was built in several stages over a few hundred years beginning in the ninth century, and the entire interior was once literally plastered in beautiful iconography, though most of the murals now reside in museums in Berlin and Massachusetts. Now all that remains of note is a small geometric Agnus Dei, just at the triumphal arch. A thirty-minute walk west up the rocky hillside brings you to **Sant Vicenç d'Enclar**, Andorra's oldest church, and the remains of a pre-medieval fortification where the Counts of Urgell – the original rulers of Andorra – once played fort. The church itself was rebuilt in 1979 and is in quite good nick, but the remains of the embrasured walls behind it, rumoured to date from the sixth century, have all but succumbed to the passage of time.

## Eating and drinking

**Eating-out** places in Andorra la Vella are largely geared up for the eat-and-run tourist, though there are a few exceptions, and the Barri Antic offers a surprisingly good selection of Andorran restaurants in all price ranges. Most restaurants and cafés in the shopping district are modernish and serve standard continental-style dishes. **Nightlife** in the capital leaves much to be desired, especially in summer – avinguda Dr Mitjavila has a half-dozen or so very local joints, or try your luck at the discos on the otherwise deserted avinguda de Tarragona.

### Cafés and Restaurants

**Café de la Plaça** pl del Poble. A fine spot for an outdoor coffee or tea, with views to the sprawling valleys that front Spain. Open late.

**La Cantina** plça Guillemó. Good-sized pizzas for €7 or lots of other dishes to choose from, eaten either inside or outside on the *plaça*.

**Casa del Formatge** c/Les Canals 4. The huge cheese shop also contains two small restaurants,

where you can linger on plates of gooey fondue or hard bricks of the stuff from all over the world.

**Casa Léon** placeta de la Consòrcia. A cosy, Franco-Andorran restaurant in the old town with a well-priced *carte*. The bargain €11.30 *menu rustic* is a regal four-course meal with soup, entrée, meat or vegetable dish and dessert.

**Gerd** c/Prat de la Creu 15–25. Modern café-style

restaurant with a terrace looking right onto the Riu Gran Valira.

**Lizarran** av Meritxell 86. Set just off the shopping thoroughfare, this pleasant traditional restaurant-bar sports a terrace and serves a large selection of tapas and sandwiches for €1.10 a pop.

**Mama Maria** av Meritxell 25. Massive tapas restaurant serving Catalan-style plates from €2.30, or try one of their large pizzas for €9.50. Open until 11pm daily.

**Pa'Torrut** c/de la Vall 18. A family-run place on a quiet *plaça* serving a wide range of local dishes

– meats are the speciality here – as well as some cheaper continental standards.

### Bars

**La Borsa** av Tarragona 36. Just around the corner from the bus station, a happening club in-season, but social rigor mortis otherwise.

**Cerveseria L'Abadia** Cap del Carrer 2. Up the stairs from the pl Guillemó, this popular local pub has Leffe and Hoegaarden on draught and is open daily until 3am.

**Millennium** av Dr Mitjavila 13. A loud disco-bar with a dartboard, table football and €2 beers.

## Listings

**Bookstore** Librería Jaume Caballé, av Fiter Rossell 31.

**Car Rental** Hertz ☎880 000; Avis ☎871 855; Europcar ☎874 290.

**Embassies** UK av Sant Antoni 32, La Massana, ☎839 840. The closest US, Canadian, Australian and New Zealand representatives are in Barcelona (see p.957).

**Hospital** Hospital Nostra Senyora de Meritxell, just next to the Caldea spa ☎871 000.

**Internet** Future@point, c/de la Sardana 6; E-Café c/l'Alziranet 5 (pl. Guillemó).

**Laundry** Grans Magatzems Pyrénées, av Meritxell 11, has per-item cleaning but no self-service.

**Pharmacy** Les Tres Creus, c/Canals 5 usually has someone who speaks English.

**Post offices** Spanish Post at C. Joan Maragall 10, French La Poste at rue Pere d'Urg 1 (Mon–Fri 8.30am–2.30pm, Sat 9.30am–1pm).

# Escaldes-Engordany

The two towns of **ESCALDES-ENGORDANY**, 1km east of Casa de la Vall, feel more or less an extension of Andorra La Vella, and are easily accessible on foot following av Meritxell. Really the only thing to draw you here is the **Caldea Spa** (daily 9am–11pm; €32 for three hours; ☎800 999, ❂www.caldea.com). This glass and steel complex is the largest health centre on the continent, pumping in water from the nearby thermal springs to offer everything from Turkish baths to bubble beds to exfoliating hydromassages. The thermal water is rich in sodium, silica and sulphur and is reputed to have considerable antalgic effects for skin and respiratory ailments. Even if the spa is not your cup of tea, the eleventh-floor bar offers some nice views. Elsewhere in town, the **Viladomat Museum** (Mon–Sat 10am–1pm & 4–8pm; €1.80) houses an impressive collection of works by twentieth-century Spanish sculptor Josep Viladomat. There's also a contemporary, Romanesque-style church in town, but much more interesting is **Sant Miquel d'Engolasters**, a few kilometres east of the centre. A twelfth-century construction, the simple, rickety church is in good condition, with a sloped roof, small nave and unadorned bell-tower, though the frescoes that once decorated the walls are currently in Barcelona and in their place hang reproductions. A fifteen-minute drive from here further into the eastern hills, **Lake Engolasters** makes for a great afternoon picnic spot, while every Saturday back in town at plaça Santa Anna and plaça de l'Església de Sant Pere Màrtir there's a great traditional **food market**.

## Sant Julià de Lòria and around

Leaving town and heading south, after 6km you arrive at the small village of **SANT JULIÀ DE LÒRIA**, a sleepy place that holds a few sights to detain you. The rebuilt parish church of **Sant Julià i Sant Germà de Lòria** stands in the centre, though the only thing originally medieval here is its three-storey bell tower, with mullioned windows and eleventh-century Lombardy arches. Just steps away is the **Museu del Tabac**, Carrer Doctor Palau 17 (Tues–Sat 10am–8pm, Sun 10am–2.30pm; €5). Since its days as a sanctuary for smugglers, tobacco has always played a role in Andorran life, and the museum presents an interesting panorama of the region's tobacco history. At the nearby plaça Laurèdia, a local market takes place every Wednesday from 9.30am to 1.30pm, with merchants sellling every-thing from honey to T-shirts. Up the hill east from Sant Julià in the small village of **NAGOL**, the church of **Sant Serni** dates from 1055, and is worth a look for the paintings around the arch, which comprise skilful depictions of an archangel dressed in Byzantine garb and Saint Michael scuffling with a serpent.

The tourist office is on plaça Francesc Cairat (summer Mon–Fri 9am–9pm, Sat & Sun 10am–2pm & 4–8pm, winter daily 10am–2pm & 4–8pm; ☎744 045). If you need to stay **overnight** here, the *Pensió Cal Jaume*, c/la Canal 2 (☎841 124; ❸), is your cheapest option. Otherwise for a bit of mountain solitude, head for the hills where the *Hotel Coma-Bella*, carretera de la Rabassa (☎841 220, ⓦwww .hotelcomabella.com; ❹), perches high above town and has a heated pool and well-kept gardens. You can also cross-country ski and rent bikes and other equip-ment at the nearby Rabassa **sports centre**. *Huguet*, c/de Fontaneda (☎843 718, Ⓔrenepujol@hotmail.com), runs a decent **campsite**.

# Northern and western Andorra

Perching above the narrow western valleys, the 2942m Coma Pedrosa is Andor-ra's largest mountain, and the snowy peaks here are drained by the Riu Valira del Nord. The main towns of **La Massana** and **Ordino** have a few sights to hold your interest, but the real joy is in the hiking. The roads that meander out to the Spanish border give access to tranquil, unspoilt towns like **Pal** and **El Serrat**, not to mention some of the most pristine countryside you'll find in the Pyrenees.

## La Massana and around

Ascending northwest out of Engordany, the CG3 follows the Valira del Nord river through a verdant valley, arriving at **LA MASSANA** five or so kilometres on. The town itself, presided over by a modern church clock tower, has little to hold you, though the trails in this area make for some excellent hiking – check with the tourist office for specifics. You're best off pressing on and up to the **Casa Rull** (Tues–Sat 9.30am–1.30pm & 3–6.30pm, Sun 10am–2pm; last entrance 45 minutes before closing; €2.40), 3km west in Sispony, an ethnographic museum built around a *borda*, a typical pre-twentieth-century Andorran household. The house itself was built in 1623, and had many different owners whose household items – baby cradles, kitchenware and bedspreads – are on display. Halfway between La Massana and Ordino (see opposite) you can book a scenic **helicopter tour** of the northern mountains and valleys through Heliand (☎837 929); a ten-minute ride costs €60, minimum four passengers.

At La Massana's **tourist office** on avinguda de San Antoni (Mon–Sat 9am–1pm 3–7pm, Sun 9am–1pm & 3–6pm, winter closed Sun afternoons; ☎835 693) be sure to ask for the informative booklet *A Walk through La Massana*. For **accommoda-tion**, there are 100 bunks at the *Borda Jovell* **hostel** (☎836 520, ⓦwww.andornet.ad /bordajovell; €14), up the steep hill in Sispony at av Jovell 18. Alternatively, far off in the northwestern hills though accessible on foot from Erts is the *Rifugi de Compadrosa* (☎327 955; open June–Oct), the only **cabin** setup that serves meals. For **camping**, try *Xixerella*, up in Erts on the carretera de Pal (☎836 613, ⓦwww.campingxixerella .com). *La Borda Xica*, just next to the church, is a traditional **restaurant** serving delicious Andorran lunch and dinner specialities for under €15 (reservation recommended, call ☎837 190). *Vesuvio*, five minutes from the tourist office on avinguda Sant Antoní, serves tasty pizzas for €7.50. *Le Cocktail*, on the same road, is a lively nightspot.

At the western end of the La Massana commune lies **PAL**, one of the best-preserved villages in Andorra, hugging the slopes which veer up to the popular ski resort of Pal-Arinsal. Strict zoning laws here have banned the development that has had such a negative effect on places like Pas de la Casa. The town's medium-sized **Sant Climent** church has a large porch that looks onto the cemetery as well as some older houses, now much dilapidated. Head back down to La Massana to take the road up to **ARINSAL**, 2km northwest, best known for its lively nightlife, though if you have a car – or strong legs – continue up the windy road to the Pal-Arinsal ski area for some great views over to the mountains that are staggered to the east. In town, up from the *telecabina*, the *Hostal Poblado* (☎835 122, closed Oct–Nov; ❸) is a cheap, central **hotel** with an **Internet** café. Opposite the *telecabina*, *Surf* is an ever-popular Argentine **restaurant**, serving mean steaks downstairs and meaner shots at the bar above. *Quo Vadis*, fifty paces away, serves nightcaps to a slightly more mature crowd.

## Ordino and north

Northeast of La Massana, the woods and river return, flanked to the west by green pastures. Though it holds only one or two sites of real interest, the quiet town of **ORDINO** makes a great base for getting out to explore Andorra's northern peaks and valleys. If coming by car, continue on after the town entrance to the small roundabout, alongside which you can park in the free lot and walk back down to enter the *peatonal*, Ordino's pedestrian walkway. On the *peatonal* the **Areny-Plandolit House** (Tues–Sat 9.30am–1.30pm & 3–6.30pm, Sun 10am–2pm; €2.40) is a luxurious mansion dating from 1633 and was the residence of the eponymous Don Guillem d'Areny-Plandolit, a wealthy and powerful nineteenth-century baron who served as president of Andorra. A mandatory guided tour explains everything you could want to know in halting English. Just next door is the **Postal Museum** (same hours and price), walking you through the history of postal Andorra with a comprehensive exhibition of national stamps. Back down the hill, the **Miniature Museum**, right at the entrance to town on c/Ordino, houses a large collection of micro-miniatures, most of which need to be viewed through a microscope. Be sure to have a squint at the palm tree, pyramid and caravan of camels which all sit in the eye of a needle as well as the silver platter with wine bottle and glasses atop a grain of salt (Tues–Sat 9.30am–1.30pm & 3.30–7pm, Sun 9.30am–1.30pm; €4).

Most of the villages that border the Valira del Nord river north of Ordino remain relatively untouched. Leaving Ordino past the tourist office on the CG3, a number of traditional houses give way to **LA CORTINADA**, whose **Església de Sant Martí** is worth a look. Transformed and extended from its original twelfth-century incarnation, it retains some lovely wooden and Baroque altarpieces, but the real draw is the decorative frescoes by the apse: a fantastical, long-limbed, three-tongued animal bearing an uncanny resemblance to Scooby-Doo, and the Nativity and Adoration paintings at the altar, all in remarkable condition. The next village that merits a stop is **LLORTS**, a nicely preserved place set amidst fields of tobacco. Rather quiet, it has a simple church and several trails leading up to the iron mines and paddocks further on. Ahead, the mountains are dominated by the 2903m Pic de Font Blanca, which forms part of the border with France. The Ordino tourist office runs tours of the ore mines here, but claustrophobes would do better to push on north along the CG3, past a waterfall a few kilometres on, to **EL SERRAT**, and the near-empty rough country around it – about the only virgin terrain Andorra has left. From here, a few seldom-beaten paths run up out of the valley, east to the lush Sorteny National Park and west to the Tristaina Lakes which border Spain.

## Ambling about Andorra

Though cars are helpful for moving between towns, hands down the best way to see Andorra is **on foot**, and you don't have to be an experienced hiker to do so. Three primary **long-distance trails** run across much of the country, and offer varying levels of trekking. They comprise the GR7, which crosses all the way from the French border to Spain via the capital; the GR11, a jagged, mountainous route across the heart of the country; and the GRP1, a perimeter trail that hugs much of the national frontier. Off these main routes, smaller *camins* connect them to the towns below and the rugged hills above. You can easily do a few day or overnight hikes, making full use of any of Andorra's several dozen *refugis*, all but two of which are free, and most have room for at least ten people, so even in the busy summer months you're likely to get one. A number of ski centres also rent out mountain bikes (around €15–20 per day) and sell lift passes during the summer: you can either bike straight up the steep slopes or ascend in a relaxing funicular, then ride leisurely down. Whatever you decide, your first stop should be one of the local tourist offices to grab a copy of *Andorra Mountain Activities*, an excellent handbook that maps out dozens of alpine paths for hiking and biking all over the country. The *Rough Guide to the Pyrenees* is also packed with helpful, detailed information on outdoor activities in the region.

The **tourist office** in Ordino, on Nou Vidal (July & Aug Mon–Sat 8am–7pm, Sun 8am–5pm; Sept–June Mon–Sat 9am–1pm & 3–7pm, Sun 9am–1pm; ☎737 080), rents out mountain bikes in the summer. The best pick of the **accommodation** is the *Santa Barbara*, located on the *peatonal* (☎837 100, ☏837 092; ❹), where many of the nicely done-up and spacious rooms have views onto the main *plaça*. Another good choice is the plusher *Hotel Coma* (☎736 100, ☼www.hotelcoma .com; ❾) with a pool and tennis courts out back, or, if money is tight, head for the friendly, cabinesque *Hotel Ordino* (☎863 700, ☏836 704; ❸), at c/General. Spectacular riverside **camping** can be found at *Borda Ansalonga*, 2km north in Ansalonga (☎850 374, ☼www.campingansalonga.com; open mid-May to Sept & Nov–April). For good **food**, go to *Topic*, located just at the entrance to the *peatonal*, a popular and spacious restaurant-bar serving traditional *plats* and a great selection of beers. Further down is the less-fancy *Armengol*, with pasta dishes for €6.50.

# Eastern Andorra

The road running east of Andorra La Vella, all the way to the French border, passes through thirty kilometres of mountain, dell, woodland, scree, river and lake topography, dominated to the east by the expansive Grand Valira ski resort. The town of **Encamp** offers a few points of interest, while Canillo is a great base for exploring the countryside. **Prats** and **Soldeu**, meanwhile, are smaller, less developed and much more serene.

## Encamp

Northeast of Engordany, the mountains ascend above the sloping road, while across the Valira d'Orient River, the hills hold a few settlements. Of these, Villa is the largest and retains some well-maintained traditional architecture. Continuing up the CG2, you arrive at **ENCAMP**, with a few museums and Andorra's largest church, the modern **Sant Eulàlia**, with its leaning belltower. The compact museum alongside presents a small exhibition of ecclesiastical art. **Cal Cristo** on carrer dels Cavallers (Sept–June Tues–Fri 3–6.30pm; July–Aug Tues–Sat 10am–1.30pm

& 3.30–8pm; €2.50), is a humble mountain home that's been turned into a museum, offering a cursory ethnography of local farming life before industrialization. There's little particularly Andorran about the **National Automobile Museum**, av Coríncep Episcopal 64 (Tues–Sat 9.30am–1.30pm & 3–6.30pm, Sun 10am–2pm; €2.40), but the collection does include some mint pieces like an 1885 steam-powered Pinette and a number of motorbikes and antique bicycles.

Just north of Encamp, about halfway to Canillo, a steep road veers up east to **MERITXELL**, where you are assaulted by the spiritual core of Andorra. Built in the image of a Greek cross, the **sanctuary** at Meritxell (daily except Tues 9.15am–1pm & 3–6pm; free) is today the most important church in the country. Our Lady of Meritxell, Andorra's patron saint, was worshipped faithfully here until 1972, when a revelrous summer feast got out of hand and the ensuing fire levelled the original seventeenth-century Romanesque structure. All that remains is the apse and western wall, now a museum dedicated to the memory of the church that once was, with huge photos of the altarpieces plastered across the walls. The massively uninspiring building that stands today as the replacement is a bizarre mix of Andorran Romanesque, Florentine classical and Islamic art influences. Inside, the wide-eyed statue of the Virgin on the eastern wall is a reproduction of the one lost in the blaze. Outside and up the stairs to the right runs a path with oratories, crosses and a pair of benches good for taking in the views.

Encamp's **tourist office** is at c/Major (☎731 000). On the road into town arriving from the south you hit a couple of plainish **hotels**, the friendlier of which is the *Montecarlo* (☎731 116, ⊛www.hotelmontecarlo.ad; ❹), av Coríncep Episcopal 104, which also runs a respectable restaurant. The *Comptes des Foix* (☎831 319; ❸), av Coríncep Francès 68, is clean enough, while *Caliu d'en Josep* (☎831 210, ⊜res. caliu.josep@andorra.ad; ❸), further up the same road at av Coríncep Francès 4, has a few rooms and serves cheap cafeteria-style **food** downstairs.

# Canillo

Continuing north, the road ascends and curves to allow for some good views down to Encamp and the central valleys, while to the west, Pic de Casamanya glistens with snow for most of the year. Four kilometres past the well-preserved hamlet of Les Bons is **CANILLO**, less commercial than other parish capitals and with many of the original granite and slate buildings in the old part still in quite good condition. For active types, the countryside around here offers some great opportunities for hiking, biking and canyoning – the tourist office can provide details (see below). Dominating the town is the Palau de Gel, a massive aluminium-sided sporting centre, though a half-hearted attempt has been made to make it look somewhat "Andorran". Atop the old quarter is the **Sant Serni** church, whose small graveyard makes for a pleasant stroll, and provides some nice views onto the town below. About a kilometre north past the town, the church of **Sant Joan de Caselles** is worth a longer visit. The interior holds a magnificent, glimmering altar retable and a twelfth-century stucco Christ in Glory, surrounded by frescoes of the cross and a scene of Roman soldiers at the crucifixion. Outside, a few tombstones are carved right out of the rock in the medieval cemetery.

From the town centre, follow the pebbly road towards the tiny village of **PRATS**, passing the stubby **Cross of the Seven Arms**. Erected in 1477, the Gothic stone bears depictions of Christ and the Virgin on two of the weather-beaten limbs; amputation of the seventh is said to be the work of the devil. A bit further on, the tiny local church of **Sant Miquel** has a Romanesque arched entrance and a belfry grown over with bulrushes. Continue on foot and you can follow a well-marked path to arrive at the Meritxell church, a few hundred metres south.

Canillo's **tourist office** (Mon–Sat 9am–1pm & 3–7pm; ☎751 090), in the centre on the main avinguda Sant Joan de Caselles, hands out *Valls de Canillo*, a brochure offering details on local walks in the hills. On summer Thursdays the small *plaça* just across from the tourist office holds an artisan market. There's little budget **accommodation** in Canillo itself, though the plain and simple *Canigó* on avinguda Sant Joan de Caselles (☎851 024, ✉hotelcanigo@hotmail.com; ❹), has smallish rooms and a restaurant below. You're better off at the more charming *Trèvol de Quatre Fulles* (☎851 352, ✉hoteltrevol@mhz.ad; ❺), which has rustic-style rooms and friendly staff, located in Prats just after the church on camí de Meritxell. Very central **camping** is at *Casal*, a few hundred metres up from the tourist office on carretera General (☎851 451, ⊛www.campingcasal.com). Just before the campsite, *Molí del Peano* is a very good traditional Franco-Andorran **restaurant**, with well-priced salads and *plats combinats* and a terrace right at the river. In town, get great burgers and fries at *Burger Roc* on avinguda Sant Joan de Caselles, while nearby *Tinc 7* serves strong **sangría** to Francophone locals and visitors.

## En route to France: Soldeu and Pas de la Casa

Past Canillo, the landscape is one of rolling hills, the odd petrol station and many more examples of the country's stone architecture. Considered the best skiing in the Pyrenees, the slopes of the Grand Valira ski resort loom east, blanketed by plenty of snowfall in the winter and verdant green after May. Just past, a river slices into the mountains in front of the Incles Valley, opening up at **SOLDEU**, a quiet place that has the vague air of a Seventies' ski village. There's little going on, but check with the tourist office in Canillo for tips on hiking routes from here. A few hundred metres back down the main road into town, the *Roc de Sant Miquel* (☎851 079, ⊛www.hotel-roc.com; ❸) is a cosy British-run **hotel** with a restaurant and live music in the evenings. The *Bruxelles* (☎851 010, ☏852 099; ❸), in the centre of town on c/General, has some nice rooms and also serves good, cheap meals. Just up from the town church, *Slim Jim's* has good, inexpensive deli-style sandwiches, as well as **Internet** access until late, while *Fat Albert's*, above, is a great live **music** venue.

The most enjoyable way to reach **PAS DE LA CASA** is the road over the Bord d'Envalira, the Pyrenees' highest pass, proffering dazzling views into the conifers and onto the mountain face ahead, but a tunnel (€5.20) now affords quicker access. "Pas" borders both on France and on the downright offensive: its chintzy dwellings evoke a high-rise dystopia. It's earned the moniker "Ibiza on ice" thanks to a rocking, spring-break style nightlife, with no fewer than twenty up-all-night bars frequented by British tourists or their young in the winter months. Outside ski season, however, Pas calms down somewhat. A small **tourist office** is right at the entrance to town (☎855 292), though there's little to see here. Cheap, central **accommodation** is at *La Forca*, c/Sant Jordi 8 (☎855 077, ✉hotellaforca@hotmail.com; ❺). For **food**, go for the Portuguese dishes at *La Borrufa*, 24 pl Co-Princeps, or, for a more upscale meal, try the big portions of Catalan *plats* at *Chez Paolo*, across from the IT shopping centre at c/Major 21. Pas de la Casa's **nightlife** centres around plaça Sant Josep, and the most popular joints include *KYU*, *West End* and *Underground*, the latter famous for its killer shots and rowdy Dutch DJs. **Internet** is at CyberPas Cafè, just above the *plaça*.

# Travel details

| Buses |
| --- |

**Andorra La Vella to:** Barcelona (9–12 daily; 3hr 30min–4hr 30min); l'Hospitalet (2 daily; 1hr 15min); La Seu d'Urgell (hourly Mon–Sat, 5 daily Sun; 30–45min); Madrid (daily; 9hr); Málaga (2 weekly; 18hr 15min); Toulouse (2–6 daily Mon, Wed, Fri & Sun; 2hr 30min); Valencia (3 weekly; 8hr 30min).

# Austria

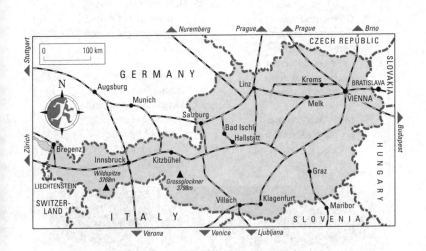

# Austria highlights

* **Staatsoper, Vienna** Drink in a performance at Vienna's ornate opera house: standing-room from just €2. See p.99

* **Schönbrunn Palace, Vienna** The epitome of opulence. See p.102

* **Coffee and cake, Vienna** An unmissable part of any trip: get your *Kaffee und Kuchen*, sit back and watch the world go by. See p.103

* **Melk** Over-the-top Baroque decor at this Benedictine monastery. See p.105

* **The Sound of Music tour, Salzburg** Cheesy but fun, whether you're into Julie Andrews or not. See p.110

* **Hallstatt** Picture-postcard village in the lovely Salzkammergut region. See p.112

* **Adventure sports, Innsbruck** Hiking, mountain-biking, canyoning and more, in the stunning setting of the Austrian Alps. See p.113

△ Schönbrunn Palace, Vienna

# Introduction and basics

Long the heart of the Habsburg Empire, with a pivotal role in the political and cultural destiny of Europe, **Austria** underwent decades of change and uncertainty in the twentieth century. The interwar state, shorn of its empire and racked by economic problems and political strife, fell prey to the promises of Nazi Germany. Postwar economic stability encouraged an emphasis on social policy as the guiding principle of national life, and the growth of a low-key patriotism. With the end of the Cold War, the country returned to the heart of Europe, finally joining the EU in 1995. From time to time, however, Austria's reactionary past and the persistence of xenophobic attitudes have come back to haunt it, most notably in recent years with the rise of Jörg Haider and the far-right Freedom Party (FPÖ).

Politics aside, Austria is primarily known for two contrasting attractions – the fading imperial glories of the capital, and the stunning beauty of its Alpine hinterland. **Vienna** is the gateway to much of central Europe and a good place to soak up the culture of *Mitteleuropa* before heading towards the Magyar and Slav lands over which the city once held sway. Less renowned provincial capitals such as **Graz** and **Linz** provide a similar level of culture and vitality. The most dramatic of Austria's Alpine scenery is west of here, in and around the **Tyrol**, whose capital, Innsbruck, provides the best base for exploration. **Salzburg**, between **Innsbruck** and Vienna, represents urban Austria at its most picturesque, an intoxicating Baroque city within easy striking distance of the mountains and lakes of the Salzkammergut.

## Information & maps

**Tourist offices** (usually *Information, Tourismusverband, Verkehrsamt, Fremdenverkehrsverein*) are plentiful, often hand out free maps and almost always book accommodation. A good general **map** is the 1:500,000 Freytag & Berndt. The 1:200,000 Generalkarte series of regional maps is useful for lengthier touring, as are the 1:50,000 Freytag & Berndt Wanderkarten and rival Kompass Wanderkarten.

## Money and banks

Austria's currency is the **euro** (€). Banking hours tend to be Mon–Fri 8am–12.30pm & 1.30 or 2–3 or 4pm; in Vienna they're mostly Mon–Fri 8am–3pm, Thurs until 5.30pm. Post offices charge slightly less commission on exchange than banks, and in larger cities are open longer hours.

## Communications

Most **post offices** are open Mon–Fri 8am–noon & 2–6pm; in larger cities they do without the lunch break and also open Sat 8–10am; a few are open 24hr. Stamps

### Austria on the net

ⓦ **www.austria.info** Austrian Tourist Board website.
ⓦ **www.wien.info** Vienna's Tourist Board website.
ⓦ **www.oebb.at** Train site, including excellent English-language journey planner.
ⓦ **www.austrosearch.at** Search engine, news and chat for all things Austrian.
ⓦ **www.tiscover.com** Detailed information on all regions of the country.
ⓦ **www.wienerzeitung.at** Website of the official Vienna city authorities' newspaper, with an English version packed with news and tourist information.

can also be bought at tobacconists (*Tabak-Trafik*). The smallest coin accepted in **public phones** is €0.20; two should suffice for a local call. Insert €0.50 and upwards if calling long distance, or buy a phone card (*Telefonkarte*), available from tobacconists. You can make international calls from all public phones, but it's easier to do so from larger post offices, which have booths. The operator and directory enquiries number is ☎118 11. **Internet access** is widespread in the big cities, less so in rural areas; expect to pay around €5/hr.

# Getting around

Austria's public transport system is fast, efficient and comprehensive. Austrian Federal Railways, or **ÖBB** (✆ www.oebb .at), runs a punctual, clean and comfortable network, which includes most towns of any size. **Trains** marked EC or EN (*EuroCity* and *EuroNight* international expresses), ICE or IC (Austrian InterCity expresses) are the fastest. Those designated D (*Schnellzug*) or E (*Eilzug*) are next, stopping at most intermediate points, while the *Regionalzug* (R) is the slowest service, stopping at all stations. InterRail and Eurail are valid.

The **Bahnbus** and **Postbus** system serves remoter villages and Alpine valleys; fares are around €10 per 100km. As a general rule, Bahnbus services, operated by ÖBB, depart from outside train stations; the *Postbus* tends to stop outside the post office. Daily and weekly regional travelcards (*Netzkarte*), covering both trains and buses, are available in many regions.

Austria is bike-friendly, with **cycle lanes** in all major towns. Many train stations rent bikes for around €15 per day (€10 with a valid rail ticket). You can return them to any station for an extra fee of €10/€5.

## Language

A high proportion of Austrians speak English, though any attempt at learning a few phrases of **German** (see p.430) will be heartily appreciated – the standard greeting throughout Austria is *Grüss Gott*.

# Accommodation

Outside popular tourist spots such as Vienna and Salzburg, **accommodation** need not be too expensive. Most tourist offices book accommodation with little fuss, sometimes for a fee (€2–3) and/or a deposit.

A high standard of cleanliness and comfort can usually be taken for granted in Austrian **hotels**. Outside Vienna, expect to pay a minimum of €50 for a double with bathroom. Good-value **B&B** is usually available in the many small family-run hotels known as *Gasthöfe* and *Gasthaüser*, with prices starting at €40 for a double. In the larger towns and cities a **pension** or *Frühstuckspension* will offer similar prices. Most tourist offices also have a stock of **private rooms** or *Privatzimmer*, although in well-travelled rural areas, roadside signs offering *Zimmer Frei* are fairly ubiquitous anyway. Prices for a double room are usually €30–45.

There are around 100 **HI hostels** (*Jugendherberge* or *Jugendgästehaus*), run by either the ÖJHV (☎01/533 5353, ✆www .oejhv.or.at) or the ÖJHW (☎01/533 1833, ✆www.oejhw.or.at). Rates are €12–18, normally including a nominal breakfast. Sheet sleeping bags are obligatory, although the cost of renting one is often included in the charge. Many hostels also serve lunch and dinner for an additional €3.50–5.50. There are also a number of excellent **independent hostels**.

Austria's high standards are reflected in the country's **campsites**, most of which have laundry facilities, shops and snack bars. Most are open May–Sept, although in the winter-sports resorts many open year-round. In general, you can expect to pay €5–6 per person, €3–9 per pitch.

# Food and drink

**Eating** out in Austria is often cheaper than self-catering, but both will take a large chunk out of your daily expenses. By contrast, **drinking** is remarkably affordable.

For ready-made snacks, try a bakery (*Bäckerei*) or confectioner's (*Konditorei*). **Fast food** centres on the *Würstelstand*, which sells hot dogs, *Bratwurst* (grilled sausage), *Käsekrainer* (spicy sausage with cheese), *Bosna* (spicy, thin Balkan sausage) and *Currywurst*, usually chopped up and served with a *Semmel* or bread roll, along with a dollop of *Senf* (mustard) and *Dose* (can) of beer. Food served up in town-centre Kaffeehäuser or cafés and bars can be great value, with light meals and snacks starting at about €5; most restaurant and café menus have filling stand-bys such as spicy *Serbische Bohnensuppe* (Serbian bean soup) and *Gulaschsuppe* (goulash soup) for less than €4. Main dishes (*Hauptspeisen*) are dominated by schnitzel (tenderized veal) often accompanied by potatoes and a vegetable or salad: Wienerschnitzel is fried in breadcrumbs, *Pariser* in batter, *Natur* served on its own or with a creamy sauce. In general you can expect to pay €5–10 for a standard main course, though set lunchtime two-course menus (*Mittagsmenü*) are always better value. Desserts (*Mehlspeisen*) include strudel, *Palatschinken* (pancake, with various nut or jam fillings) and the tasty *Moor im Hemd*, a hot chocolate pudding with chocolate sauce and whipped cream.

## Drink

For urban Austrians, daytime drinking traditionally centres on the **Kaffeehaus**, relaxed places serving alcoholic and soft drinks, snacks and cakes, alongside a wide range of different coffees: a *Schwarzer* is small and black, a *Brauner* comes with a little milk, while a *Melange* is half-coffee and half-milk; a *Kurzer* is a small espresso; an *Einspänner* a glass of black coffee topped with *Schlag*, the ubiquitous whipped cream that is offered with most pastries and cakes. A cup of coffee in one of these places is pricey at around €2.50–3 and numerous stand-up coffee bars are a much cheaper alternative at €1.50 a cup. Most cafés, particularly those dubbed *Café-Konditorei*, or *Kaffee-Konditorei*, offer a tempting array of freshly baked Austrian **cakes and pastries**. *Apfelstrudel* is apple and raisins wrapped in pastry and topped with icing sugar. *Mohnstrudel* has a poppyseed and raisin filling. *Topfenstrudel* has a sweet curd cheese filling while *Linzertorte* is a jam tart with almond pastry and

*Sachertorte* a famously rich chocolate cake.

Night-time drinking centres on **bars** and cafés, although more traditional *Bierstuben* and *Weinstuben* are still thick on the ground. Austrian **beers** are good quality. Most places serve the local brew on tap, either by the *Krügerl* (half-litre, €3), *Seidel* (third-litre, €1.80) or *Pfiff* (fifth-litre, €0.80–1.30). The local **wine**, drunk by the *Viertel* (25cl mug) or the *Achterl* (12.5cl glass), is widely consumed. The *Weinkeller* is the place to go for this or, in the vine-producing areas, a *Heuriger* or *Buschenshenk* – a traditional tavern, customarily serving cold food as well.

# Opening hours

Traditionally, opening hours for **shops** are Mon–Fri 9am–noon & 2–6pm, with late opening on Thurs till 7 or 8pm & Sat 8am–noon. It's increasingly common for shops to open all day Sat and in big cities most also stay open at lunchtimes. Many **cafés and restaurants** also have a weekly *Ruhetag* (closing day). Shops and **banks** close, and most museums have reduced hours, on **public holidays**: Jan 1, Jan 6, Easter Mon, May 1, Ascension Day, Whit Mon, Corpus Christi, Aug 15, Oct 26, Nov 1, Dec 8, Dec 25 & 26.

# Emergencies

Austria is law-abiding and reasonably safe. **Police** (*Polizei*) are armed, and are not renowned for their friendliness. As for **health**, city hospital casualty departments will treat you and ask questions later. For prescriptions, **pharmacies** (*Apotheke*) tend to follow normal shopping hours. A rota system covers night-time and weekend opening; each pharmacy has details posted in the window.

# Vienna (Wien)

Most people visit **VIENNA** (Wien in German) with a vivid image in their minds: a romantic place full of Habsburg nostalgia and musical resonances. Visually it's unlikely to disappoint: an eclectic feast of architectural styles, from High Baroque, through the monumental imperial projects of the late nineteenth century, to Modernist experiments and enlightened municipal planning. However, the capital often seems aloof from the rest of the country; Alpine Austrians look on it as an alien eastern metropolis with an impenetrable dialect, staffed by an army of fund-draining bureaucrats.

It was only with the rise of the Babenberg dynasty in the tenth century that Vienna became an important centre. In 1278 the city fell to **Rudolf of Habsburg**, but had to compete for centuries with Prague, Linz and Graz as the imperial residence on account of its vulnerability to attack from the Turks, who first laid siege to it in 1529. It was only with the removal of the Turkish threat in 1683 that the court based itself here permanently. The great aristocratic families, grown fat on the profits of the Turkish wars, flooded in to build palaces and summer residences in a frenzy of construction that gave Vienna its Baroque character. **Imperial** Vienna was never a wholly German city; as the capital of a cosmopolitan empire, it attracted great minds from all over central Europe. By the end of the Habsburg era it had become a breeding-ground for the ideological movements of the age: nationalism, socialism, Zionism and anti-Semitism all flourished here. This turbulence was reflected in the cultural sphere, and the ghosts of Freud, Klimt, Schiele, Mahler and Schönberg are nowadays bigger tourist draws than old stand-bys such as the Lipizzaner horses and the Vienna Boys' Choir. There is more to Vienna than fin-de-siècle decadence, however; a strong, home-grown, youthful culture, together with influences from former Eastern Bloc neighbours, has once more placed the city at the heart of European cultural life.

## Arrival, information and city transport

**Trains** from the west and from Hungary terminate at the **Westbahnhof**, five metro stops from the city centre; services from eastern Europe, Italy and the Balkans arrive at the **Südbahnhof**, south of the city centre (U-Bahn Südtiroler Platz and a five-minute walk or tram #D); services from Lower Austria and the odd train from Prague arrive at **Franz-Josefs-Bahnhof**, north of the centre (tram #D). Long-distance **buses** arrive at Vienna's **main bus terminal**, the City Air Terminal beside Wien-Mitte, on the eastern edge of the city centre (U-Bahn Landstrasse); while DDSG **boats** (⚑www.ddsg-blue-danube.at) from further up the Danube, or from Bratislava or Budapest, dock at the Schiffahrtszentrum by the Reichsbrücke, some way northeast of the city centre – the nearest station (U-Bahn Vorgartenstrasse) is five minutes' walk away, one block west of Mexicoplatz. The **airport**, Flughafen Wien-Schwechat (⚑english.viennaairport.com), lies around 20km southeast, connected to Wien-Mitte station by City Airport Train (CAT; every 30min; 15min; €9 single) and S-Bahn line S7 (every 30min; 30min; €3 single). Buses (every 20–30min; €6 single) run to U-Bahn Schwedenplatz (20min) in the centre and to the Südbahnhof (25min) and Westbahnhof (40min).

All points of arrival have tourist kiosks which can help with accommodation. The central **tourist office** (daily 9am–7pm; ℡24555, 🖰www.wien.info), behind the opera house on Albertinaplatz, can also arrange accommodation and hands out maps. Its excellent website, in English, has links to many of the key attractions. There's also a good **information centre for young people**, *Wienxtra-Youthinfo*, at Babenbergerstr. 1 (Mon–Sat noon–7pm; ℡17 79, 🖰www.wienxtra.at), near the Kunsthistorisches Museum.

So many attractions are in or around the Innere Stadt that you can do and see a great deal on foot. Elsewhere, you can take advantage of the fantastic **public transport** system, which runs 5am–midnight (outside these times night buses called *NightLine* run from Schwedenplatz). The network consists of **trams** (*Strassenbahn* or *Bim*), **buses**, the **U-Bahn** (metro) and the **S-Bahn** (fast commuter trains). Buy your ticket from the ticket booths or machines at U-Bahn stations and from tobacconists, and punch it on-board buses and trams or before entering the U- or S-Bahn. Fares are calculated on a zonal basis: tickets for the central zone (covering all of Vienna) cost €1.50 and allow unlimited changes on any mode of transport. Much better value is a **travel pass** (*Netzkarte*; €5/12 for 24/72hr) and the much-touted *Wien-Karte* or **Vienna Card** (€16.90); the latter includes a 72-hour travel pass and also gives minor discounts at attractions. The penalty for fare-dodging is €60, plus the fare. **Taxis** run from the ranks around town; to book, call ℡31300 or 40100 or 60160.

## Accommodation

There's no shortage of expensive **accommodation**, but extreme pressure on the cheaper end of the market means booking ahead is essential in summer and advisable during the rest of the year. The city has some excellent **hostels**, which are friendly, clean and efficient but also very popular; it's worth calling ahead. These aside, it's hard to find anything really affordable and central: the cheapest double rooms within easy reach of the centre will set you back at least €60. The likeliest hunting grounds are in the western districts between the Ring and the outer orbital road, the Gürtel (districts 5–9); places here are often on the upper floors of characterful nineteenth-century apartment buildings. The tourist offices have a limited number of **private rooms** (℡24555; from €50 for a double; min 3 nights), but these go quickly and are often in distant suburbs. You could also try the Mitwohnzentrale, 8, Laudongasse 7 (Mon–Fri 10am–2pm & 3–6pm; ℡402 6061, 🖰www.mwz.at), which tends to have cheaper properties and also offers weekly rates. Breakfast is included unless otherwise stated.

### Hostels

**Hostel Ruthensteiner** 15, Robert Hamerlinggasse 24 ℡893 4202, 🖰www.hostelruthensteiner.com. Excellent hostel within easy walking distance of the Westbahnhof. There's a nice courtyard to hang out in, a choice of dorm beds, doubles or triples (discounts for HI members), Internet and laundry facilities, plus the use of musical instruments, a (small) kitchen and barbecue. Breakfast not included. U-Bahn Westbahnhof. Dorms €11.50–15, rooms ❹

**Jugendgästehaus Wien-Brigittenau** 20, Friedrich-Engels-Platz 24 ℡332 8294, 🖰www.oejhv .or.at. Huge, modern HI hostel in a dour suburb. Three to six-bed dorms and loads of en-suite bunk-bed doubles. Tram #N from U-Bahn Schwedenplatz or Dresdnerstr. Dorms €16–19, rooms ❸

**Hostel Hütteldorf** 13, Schlossberggasse 8 ℡877 1501, 🖰www.hostel.at. A 300-bed hostel, with dorms plus some double and triple rooms. Out in the sticks, but convenient if you want to explore the wilds of the Lainzer Tiergarten and Schönbrunn. S- and U-Bahn Hütteldorf. Dorms €15, rooms ❸

**Jugendherberge Wien-Myrthengasse** 7, Myrthengasse 7 & Neustiftgasse 85 ℡523 6316, 🖰www.oejhv.or.at. A short walk up Neustiftgasse from U-Bahn Volkstheater is this most central of the HI hostels, with 260 beds (some doubles) divided between two nearby addresses. Book well

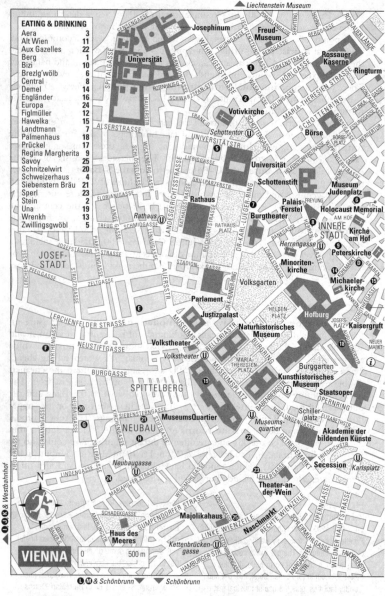

**EATING & DRINKING**

| | |
|---|---|
| Aera | 3 |
| Alt Wien | 11 |
| Aux Gazelles | 22 |
| Berg | 1 |
| Bizi | 10 |
| Brezlg'wölb | 6 |
| Central | 8 |
| Demel | 14 |
| Engländer | 16 |
| Europa | 24 |
| Figlmüller | 12 |
| Hawelka | 15 |
| Landtmann | 7 |
| Palmenhaus | 18 |
| Prückel | 17 |
| Regina Margherita | 9 |
| Savoy | 25 |
| Schnitzelwirt | 20 |
| Schweizerhaus | 4 |
| Siebenstern Bräu | 21 |
| Sperl | 23 |
| Stein | 2 |
| Una | 19 |
| Wrenkh | 13 |
| Zwillingsgwöbl | 5 |

**VIENNA**

0     500 m

in advance and go to the Myrthengasse reception on arrival. Dorms €16–19, rooms ❸

**Kolpingfamilie Jugend-gastehaus Wien-Miedling** 12, Bendlgasse 10–12 ☏ 813 5487, ⊛ www.kolpinghaus-wien12.at. Large, institutional hostel with singles and doubles as well as dorm beds. Easily reached from the city centre. U-Bahn Niederhofstr. Dorms €18.50, rooms ❹

**Westend City Hostel** 6, Fügergasse 3 ☏ 597 67 29, ⊛ www.westendhostel.at. A few minutes' walk from the Westbahnhof, this refurbished 211-bed former hotel has dorms and ensuite-doubles, friendly staff, a patio, left-luggage and laundry services. Dorms €17.20, rooms ❹

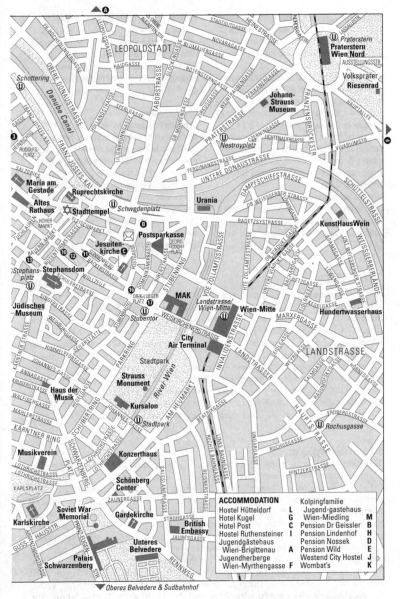

**ACCOMMODATION**

| | |
|---|---|
| Hostel Hütteldorf | **L** |
| Hotel Kugel | **G** |
| Hotel Post | **C** |
| Hostel Ruthensteiner | **I** |
| Jugendgästehaus | |
| Wien-Brigittenau | **A** |
| Jugendherberge | |
| Wien-Myrthengasse | **F** |
| Kolpingfamilie | |
| Jugend-gastehaus | |
| Wien-Miedling | **M** |
| Pension Dr Geissler | **B** |
| Pension Lindenhof | **H** |
| Pension Nossek | **D** |
| Pension Wild | **E** |
| Westend City Hostel | **J** |
| Wombat's | **K** |

▼ *Oberes Belvedere & Sudbahnhof*

**Wombat's** 15, Grangasse 6 ☎897 2336, ⓦwww
.wombats.at. Excellent hostel option a short walk
from the Westbahnhof, with dorm beds, bunk-bed
doubles and a party atmosphere (you get a free
welcome drink at the bar). Internet access, laundry
facilities and nightly movies. Breakfast €3.50.
Dorm beds €18, doubles ④

## Hotels and pensions
**Pension Nossek** 1, Graben 17 ☎533 7041,
ⓦwww.pension-nossek.at. Large family-run
pension right in the historic centre with
en-suite doubles and a few bargain singles. It's
popular so book in advance. U-Bahn Stephansplatz. ⑦

Hotel Kugel 7, Siebensterngasse 43 ☏523 3355, ⓦwww.hotelkugel.at. Plain but clean rooms with continental breakfast included. Close to Spittelberg's numerous restaurants and bars. U-Bahn Neubaugasse. ➏

Hotel Post 1, Fleischmarkt 24 ☏515 83, ⓦwww .hotel-post-wien.at. A civilized, very large central hotel with big old rooms (some with shared facilities) and modern furnishings. U-Bahn Schwedenplatz. ➎

Pension Dr Geissler 1, Postgasse 14 ☏533 28 03, ⓦwww.hotelpension.at. Anonymous modern pension on the eighth floor; all rooms have cable/ satellite TV, and those with shared facilities are among the cheapest in the Innere Stadt. U-Bahn Schwedenplatz. ➍

Pension Lindenhof 7, Lindengasse 4 ☏523 0498, ⓔpensionlindenhof@yahoo.com. Appealing rooms with creaky parquet flooring in a lugubrious building off Mariahilferstr. U-Bahn Neubaugasse. ➌

Pension Wild 8, Lange Gasse 10 ☏406 5174, ⓦwww.pension-wild.com. Friendly, laid-back pension, a short walk from the Ring in a student district behind the university, and especially popular with backpackers and gay travellers. Booking essential. U-Bahn Rathaus/Volkstheater. ➍

### Campsites

Camping Rodaun 23 An der Au 2 ☏888 4154. Nice location by a stream on the southwestern outskirts of Vienna, near the Wienerwald (Vienna Woods). Tram #60 from U-Bahn Hietzing to its terminus, then 5-min walk. April–Oct.

Wien West 14 Hüttelbergstr. 80 ☏914 2314, ⓦwww.wiencamping.at. In the plush far-western suburbs of Vienna, close to the Wienerwald, with two- and four-bed bungalows to rent (€27–37). Bus #151 from U-Bahn Hütteldorf or a 15 min walk from tram #49 terminus.

## The City

Central Vienna may well bowl you over with its grandiosity, but for all that, it's surprisingly compact: the historical centre or **Innere Stadt**, bound to the northeast by the Danube canal and surrounded on all other sides by the majestic ribbon of the **Ringstrasse**, is just 1km wide at its broadest point. Most of the important sights are concentrated in the central district and along the Ring. One of the best ways to grasp its grand sweep is to board tram #1 or #2 from outside the Staatsoper (opera house); these circle the boulevard, letting you get a taste for which areas you'd like to explore at a more leisurely pace. Important outlying sights include the imperial palace at **Schönbrunn** and the funfair and parklands of the **Prater**. Judicious use of public transport enables you to travel from one side of the city to the other in less than thirty minutes, so you should be able see a great deal in a couple of days.

### Stephansplatz

The obvious place to begin a tour of the city is **Stephansplatz**, the lively pedestrianized central square dominated by the hoary Gothic bulk of the **Stephansdom** (Mon–Sat 9am–noon & 1–5pm, Sun 12.30–5pm; free). The first thing that strikes you as you enter the gloomy, high-vaulted interior is that, despite the tourists, Stephansdom is still very much a place of worship. The highlight in the nave is the early-sixteenth-century carved stone pulpit with portraits of the four fathers of the Christian church, and a self-portrait by the sculptor who peers from a window below the pulpit stairs. The area beyond the transepts is roped off, so to get a good look at the Wiener Neustädter Altar, a masterpiece of late Gothic art, and, to its right, the tomb of the Holy Roman Emperor Friedrich III, you must sign up for a guided tour (English tours April–Oct daily 3.45pm; €4). Other features include the **catacombs** (Mon–Sat 10–11.30am & 1.30–4.30pm, Sun 1.30–4.30pm; €4), where, among other macabre remains, the entrails of illustrious Habsburgs are housed in bronze caskets; and the north or **Eagle Tower**, which can be ascended by lift (daily 8.30/9am–5/6/6.30pm; €4) for a look at the *Pummerin* (Great Bell). The more energetic might choose to climb up to the spire, 137m high and nicknamed Steffl or "Little Stephen" (daily 9am–5.30pm; €3), reached via a blind scramble up internal stairways; it has better views than the Eagle Tower.

## East and north of Stephansplatz

The warren of alleyways north and east of the cathedral preserve something of the medieval character of the city, although the architecture reflects centuries of continuous rebuilding. The medieval house at Raubensteingasse 8 where **Mozart** died while at work on his *Requiem* has long since disappeared, but is commemorated by a small memorial on the ground floor of the Steffl department store that now occupies the site. The only one of the composer's residences to survive is the so-called **Figarohaus**, immediately east of the cathedral at Domgasse 5 (Tues–Sun 9am–6pm; €4, free Fri am), though there's little to see inside. Further east, the seventeenth-century **Jesuitenkirche** on Dr.-Ignaz-Seipel-Platz is by far the most awesome High Baroque church in Vienna. Inside, the most striking features are the red and green barley-sugar spiral columns, the exquisitely carved pews and the clever trompe l'oeil dome. Nearby, on the far side of Stubenring, is Vienna's most enjoyable museum, known as the **MAK** (Tues 10am–midnight, Wed–Sun 10am–6pm; €7.90, free on Sat; ⑩www.mak.at). The highlights of its superlative, eclectic collection, dating from the Romanesque period to the twentieth century, are Klimt's *Stoclet Frieze* and the unrivalled collection of Wiener Werkstätte products.

North of Stephansdom, **Judenplatz**, one of the prettiest little squares in Vienna, is dominated by the bleak concrete **Holocaust Memorial**, designed by British sculptor Rachel Whiteread. Judenplatz stands on the site of the medieval Jewish ghetto and you can view the foundations of an old synagogue at the excellent **Museum Judenplatz** at no. 8 (Mon–Wed & Fri–Sun 10am–6pm, Thurs 10am–8pm; €3, joint ticket with Jüdisches Museum €7), which has an interactive multimedia exhibition on Jewish life in the ghetto.

## Kärntnerstrasse, Graben and Kohlmarkt

From Stephansplatz, Kärntnerstrasse leads off southwest, a continuous pedestrianized ribbon lined with street entertainers and elegant shops that ends at the city's illustrious **Staatsoper** (⑩www.wiener-staatsoper.at), opened in 1869 as the first phase of the development of the Ringstrasse. You can tour the venue (times vary – for details check at the arcades under the opera house; €4.50) but a more unusual tribute to the city's musical genius can be found down Annagasse at the **Haus der Musik**, Seilerstätte 30 (daily 10am–10pm; €10), a hugely enjoyable, state-of-the-art exhibition on the nature of sound. At the southwest exit of Neuer Markt square is the **Kaisergruft** (daily 9.30am–4pm; €4), where Habsburg family members were interred from 1633. Maria Theresa reputedly came here on the eighteenth of every month to commune with the remains of her late husband Franz Stephan, and was eventually placed beside him in a riotously ornamented sarcophagus of stunning proportions – a stark contrast to the humble, unadorned coffin of her enlightened successor, Josef II.

The prime shopping street **Graben** leads northwest off Stephansplatz; just off Graben, at Dorotheergasse 11, is the intriguing **Jüdisches Museum** (daily except Sat, 10am–6pm, Thurs until 9pm; €5, joint ticket with the Museum Judenplatz €7; ⑩www.jmw.at). The emphasis of the museum's excellent exhibitions on the first floor is on contemporary Jewish life, while on the second floor, visitors are confronted with a series of freestanding glass panels imprinted with holograms, ghostly images of the city's once vast Jewish population. At the far end of **Kohlmarkt** is Michaelerplatz, overlooked by the statue-laden nineteenth-century Michaelertor, entrance to the Habsburgs' city residence, the Hofburg.

## The Hofburg and around

The **Hofburg** (⑩www.hofburg-wien.at) is a complex of immense, highly ornate buildings that house many of Vienna's key sights. Apart from being the seat of the Austrian president, it now contains a range of museums with imperial connections, which begin with the rather dull parade of **Kaiserappartements** (daily 9am–5/5.30pm; €7.50) on the north side of the main courtyard, whose only draw is the **Sisi Museum**, retelling the story of the tragic Empress Elisabeth. To the southeast is the brightly painted entrance to the Schweizerhof, a smaller courtyard where you'll find the much more impressive **Schatzkammer** (daily except Tues 10am–6pm; €8), which holds some of the finest medieval craftsmanship and jewellery in Europe, including the imperial regalia and relics of the Holy Roman Empire as well as the Habsburgs' own crown jewels. Steps beside the Schatzkammer lead up to the **Hofburgkapelle** (Jan–June & mid-Sept to Dec Mon–Thurs 11am–3pm, Fri 11am–1pm; €1.50), primarily known as the venue for Mass with the **Vienna Boys' Choir** (mid-Sept to June Sun 9.15am; ⓦwww.wsk.at), for which you can obtain free, standing-room-only tickets from 8.30am. Another monument to the Habsburgs' hoarding instincts is the ornate Baroque **Prunksaal** (daily 10am–2/4pm, Thurs till 7pm; €5), overlooking Josefsplatz and worth a glimpse for its frescoes, globes and gold-bound volumes. On the other side of Josefsplatz, a door leads to the imperial stables, home to the performing white horses of the **Spanish Riding School** (performances March–June & Sept, Oct & Dec; standing from €26, seats from €40; training sessions same months Tues–Sat 10am–1pm; €11.50; ⓦwww.srs.at). Tickets for performances are hard to come by, but training session tickets are sold at the **Lipizzaner Museum** (daily 9am–6pm; €5) entrance in advance. You can also buy tickets on the day at the Josefsplatz entrance box office – the queue is at its worst early on, but by 11am it's usually easy enough to get in. South of Josefsplatz, down Augustinerstrasse, lies the **Albertina** (daily 10am–6pm, Wed till 9pm; €7.50; ⓦwww.albertina.at), home to one of the largest collections of graphic arts in the world, with works by Raphael, Rembrandt, Dürer, Leonardo, Michelangelo, Bosch and many more.

Southwest of the Hofburg are still more museums, with some interesting features. Across the Ring in Maria-Theresien-Platz is the **Kunsthistorisches Museum** (Tues–Sun 10am–6pm, Thurs till 9pm; €10), with Egyptian, Greek and Roman artefacts as well as Gothic-infused canvases of Danubian painters such as Altdorfer and the two Cranachs. However, it's the unparalleled collection of Pieter Bruegel the Elder that attracts most visitors: pictures such as *The Meeting of Lent and Carnival* and the famous winter scenery of the *Return of the Hunters*. Nearby is **MQ**, Vienna's **MuseumsQuartier** (ⓦwww.mqw.at), housed in the former imperial stables, and home to a whole host of new museums and galleries, the best of which is the **Leopold Museum** (daily 10am–7pm, Fri till 9pm; €9), boasting works by Klimt and a large collection by Egon Schiele.

## Rathausplatz, Freud and the Liechtenstein Museum

By now you will have crossed the **Ringstrasse**, built to fill the gap created when the last of the city's fortifications were demolished in 1857 and subsequently lined with monumental civic buildings – "Ringstrasse Historicism" became a byword for the bombastic taste of the late Habsburg bourgeoisie. The broad sweep of the Ring wasn't just a symbol of imperial and municipal prestige: it was designed to ease the mobility of cannons in the event of any rebellious incursions from the proletarian districts beyond. **Rathausplatz**, northwest of the Hofburg, is the Ringstrasse's showpiece square, framed by four monumental public buildings: the Rathaus (City Hall), the Burgtheater, Parlament and the Universität – all completed in the 1880s. The most imposing is the cathedral-like **Rathaus**, parts of which are accessible only as part of a guided tour (Mon, Wed & Fri 1pm; free). Directly opposite stands the **Burgtheater**, flanked by two grandiose staircases decorated with frescoes by, among others, Gustav Klimt (guided tours only: daily 3pm, Sun also 11am; €4.50). The **Parlament** is an imposing affair fronted by a monumental statue of Pallas Athene (guided tours only: July to mid-Sept Mon–Fri hourly 9am–3pm, except noon; mid-Sept to June Mon & Wed 10 & 11am, Tues & Thurs 2 & 3pm, Fri 11am, 1, 2 & 3pm; free).

Not far north is the former home of Sigmund Freud, who moved to the second floor of Berggasse 19, six blocks north of the Ring, in 1891 and stayed here until June 4, 1938, when he and his family fled to London. His apartment, now the **Sigmund-Freud-Museum** (daily 9am–5/6pm; €5; ✆www.freud-museum.at; tram #D to Schlickgasse), is a place of pilgrimage, even though Freud took almost all his possessions with him into exile. His hat, coat and walking stick are still here, and there's home-movie footage from the 1930s, but the only room with any original decor is the waiting room. A little further north lies the **Liechtenstein Museum** (daily except Tues 9am–8pm; €10), a grandiose Baroque palace used by the Liechtenstein royal family to display their vast private art collection which includes several works by Canova, Van Dyck, Frans Hals and a whole stash of Rubens paintings.

## Karlsplatz

South of the Hofburg in **Karlsplatz**, traffic interchanges and seedy subways dominate, but you can still see examples of Vienna's Art Nouveau, or Jugendstil (literally "Youth Style") movement. On the west side of the square is the **Secession** building (Tues–Sun 10am–6pm, Thurs till 8pm; €6; ✆www.secession.at), completed in 1898 as the headquarters of the movement in the city. Led by Gustav Klimt, this younger generation rebelled against academic historicism in favour of something more modern. Look out for the so-called "gilded cabbage" that crowns it. One of Klimt's most characteristic works, the *Beethoven Frieze*, created for an exhibition of 1902, remains on permanent display in the basement. Rising majestically above everything around it, at the other end of Karlsplatz, the **Karlskirche** (Mon–Sat 9am–12.30pm & 1–6pm, Sun 1–6pm; €4), designed by Fischer von Erlach, is one of the city's finest Baroque churches.

## South of the Ring

Immediately south of the Ring, beyond the bombastic Soviet War Memorial on Schwarzenbergplatz, near Karlsplatz, is the **Belvedere** (tram #D from the opera house), one of Vienna's finest palace complexes. Two magnificent Baroque mansions, designed for Prince Eugene of Savoy, face each other across a sloping formal garden, commanding a superb view. Today, the loftier of the two palaces, the **Oberes Belvedere** (Tues–Sun 10am–6pm; €7.50; ✆www.belvedere.at), has the best concentration of paintings by Klimt in the city, plus some choice works by Schiele and Kokoschka. The same ticket lets you into the **Unteres Belvedere**, which preserves more of its original, lavish decor.

Beyond the Belvedere and the Südbahnhof, on the other side of the Schweizer Garten is the former **Arsenal**, a huge barracks complex that also houses the **Heeresgeschichtliches Museum** (daily except Fri 9am–5pm; €5.10), built in 1856 to glorify the imperial army. Among the exhibits is the Gräf & Stift open-top car in which Archduke Ferdinand and his wife Sophie Chotek were assassinated in Sarajevo in June 1914; his bloodstained uniform lies nearby.

Ten minutes' walk from here (or tram #71 from Schwarzenbergplatz) is the **St Marxer Friedhof**, on Leberstrasse (daily 7am–dusk), Vienna's principal cemetery from 1784 to 1874. Planted with a rather lovely selection of trees, the cemetery today gives little indication of the bleak and forbidding place it must have been when, on a rainy night in December 1791, **Wolfgang Amadeus Mozart** was given a pauper's burial in an unmarked mass grave with no one present but the grave-diggers. A memorial marking the area in which the composer was interred – a broken column accompanied by a cherub – was first raised in 1859. The original, however, now stands in Vienna's greatest necropolis, the **Zentralfriedhof** (daily 7/8am–5/7pm; tram #6 or #71) on Simmeringer Hauptstrasse, in which graves of eminent Viennese are grouped by profession. The musicians, principally Beethoven, Schubert, Brahms and the Strauss family, lie a short way beyond Gate 2, to the left of the central avenue.

## East of the Ring

One of Vienna's most popular tourist attractions, the kitsch **Hundertwasser-haus** (no public access), lies in the unassuming residential area of Landstrasse, east of the Ring; take tram #N from Schwedenplatz U-Bahn to Hetzgasse. Following his philosophy that "the straight line is godless", the Austrian artist Friedensreich Hundertwasser (1928–2000) transformed some dour council housing on the corner of Löwengasse and Kegelgasse into a brightly coloured, higgledy-piggledy ensemble that caught the popular imagination. Understandably, the residents were none too happy when hordes of pilgrims began ringing on their doorbells, asking to be shown round; Hundertwasser obliged with a shopping arcade opposite, called **Kalke Village**, the most disconcerting aspect of which is his penchant for uneven floors. There's another of Hundertwasser's Gaudí-esque conversions, **KunstHausWien** (daily 10am–7pm; Mon €4.50; Tues–Sun €9; @www.kunsthauswien.com), three blocks north up Untere Weissgerberstrasse; it features a permanent gallery devoted to Hundertwasser's own life and works.

On the other side of the Danube canal, which runs east of the centre, is **Leopoldstadt**, home to a thriving Jewish community until the Nazi Holocaust. The district's main attraction is the **Prater** (U-Bahn Praterstern), a large expanse of parkland that stretches for miles between the Danube canal and the river itself – formerly the royal hunting grounds. The public were allowed access to the Prater by Josef II, who often walked here himself, quixotically ordering passing members of the public not to salute him. The funfair at the northern end near the U-Bahn stop is renowned for the **Riesenrad** (daily: March–Oct 9/10am–10pm/midnight; Nov–Feb 10am–6pm; €7.50), the giant Ferris wheel featured in Carol Reed's film *The Third Man*. You can take U1 east from Praterstern to the **Donauinsel**, an island in the middle of the Danube crisscrossed with cycle paths and the city's most popular summer bathing and barbecue area.

## Schönbrunn

The biggest attraction in the west of the city is the imperial summer palace of **Schönbrunn** (@www.schoenbrunn.at; U4 to Hietzing), a palace designed by Fischer von Erlach on the model of residences like Versailles and eventually completed during the reign of Maria Theresa. To visit the palace rooms or **Prunkräume** (daily 8.30am–4.30/5pm; July & Aug till 6pm) there's a choice of two tours: the "Imperial Tour" (€8.90), which takes in 22 state rooms, and the "Grand Tour" (€11.50), which includes all 40 rooms. However, the shorter tour misses out the best rooms – such as the Millions Room, a rosewood-panelled chamber covered from floor to ceiling with wildly irregular Rococo cartouches, each holding a Persian miniature watercolour. There are coaches and carriages to see in the **Wagenburg** (April–Oct daily 9am–6pm; Nov–March Tues–Sun 10am–4pm; €4.50) in the right wing, but it's better to concentrate on strolling through the **Schlosspark** (daily 6am–dusk; free), with its frolicking fountain statuary, its **Maze and Labyrinth** (daily: April–Oct 9am–5/6pm; Nov 10am–3.30pm; €2.60) and Gloriette – a hilltop colonnaded monument, now a café (daily 9am–dusk), from which you can enjoy splendid views back towards the city. The park also holds Vienna's excellent **Tiergarten** or Zoo (daily 9am–5/6.30pm; €12); **Palmenhaus** (daily 9.30am–4.30/5.30pm; €3.50), a glasshouse full of tropical ferns; and **Wüstenhaus** (9am–5/6pm; €3), a greenhouse filled with cacti, desert mammals, geckos and lizards. Also worth a visit is the **Technisches Museum** (Mon–Fri 9am–6pm, Sat & Sun 10am–6pm; €8; @www.technischesmuseum.at), on the opposite side of Auer-Welsbach-Park from the main gates of Schönbrunn. An innovative, hands-on museum, it has a great vintage transport section and the city's only IMAX cinema (€10).

# Eating and drinking

Vienna has a wide range of **cuisines**, from Balkan to South American, and is, of course, also the home of the Kaffeehaus. In summer a visit to a wine tavern (*Heuriger*), to sample their produce along with traditional fare, is extremely popular; you'll find *Heurigen* in Vienna's outlying districts such as Grinzing (tram #38) or Stammersdorf (tram #31). For **snacks**, head for a *Wurstelstand* or one of the lunchtime stand-up snack bars selling bite-size open-topped sandwiches (*Brötchen*) in the city centre. The Naschmarkt – the city's main fruit and veg market off Karlsplatz – is a great place to assemble a picnic or grab a takeaway. Other budget options are the student dining-halls, or *Mensas*, which serve subsidized three-course lunches (Mon–Fri); ask for details from the tourist office.

## Cafés

**Aera** 1, Gonzagagasse 11. Relaxing café upstairs serving tasty food, with live bands in the dimly lit cellar downstairs. Open till 2am. U-Bahn Schwedenplatz.

**Alt Wien** 1, Bäckerstr. 9. Dark, smoky Kaffeehaus with good food, if you can find a table. Open till 2am. U-Bahn Stephansplatz.

**Berg** 9, Berggasse 8. Trendy modern café, with good food and relaxed, mostly gay, clientele. Open till 1am. U-Bahn Schottentor.

**Central** 1, Herrengasse 14. Traditional meeting place of Vienna's intelligentsia, and Trotsky's favourite Kaffeehaus – this is probably the most ornate of Vienna's cafés. Closed Sun eve. U-Bahn Herrengasse.

**Demel** 1, Kohlmarkt 14. Vienna's most prestigious and priciest café for patisseries and cakes. U-Bahn Herrengasse.

**Engländer** 1, Postgasse 2; U-Bahn Stubentor. Great Kaffeehaus with a long pedigree that went under for a few years but has come back with a vengeance. Open till 1am.

**Europa** 7, Zollergasse 8. Lively, spacious café that attracts a trendy crowd, with a tasty mixture of Viennese and Italian food. Open till 5am. U-Bahn Neubaugasse.

**Hawelka** 1, Dorotheergasse 6. Famed for its smoky, Bohemian atmosphere, this is a popular drinking venue. Open till 2am. Closed Tues. U-Bahn Stephansplatz.

**Landtmann** 1, Dr-Karl-Lueger-Ring 4. One of the poshest of the Kaffeehäuser, it was a favourite with Freud; other famous visitors included Marlene Dietrich. Today's clientele is a mixture of politicians, actors, regulars and tourists. U-Bahn Herrengasse/Schottentor.

**Palmenhaus** 1, Burggarten. Stylish modern café set amidst the palms of the greenhouse in the Burggarten behind the Hofburg. Open till 2am. U-Bahn Karlsplatz.

**Prückel** 1, Stubenring 24. Great retro 1950s decor; opposite the MAK. U-Bahn Stubentor. Daily till 10pm.

**Savoy** 6, Linke Wienzeile 36. Wonderfully scruffy but ornate decor, packed with boho bargain-hunters during the Saturday fleamarket. Closed Sun. U-Bahn Kettenbrückengasse.

**Sperl** 6, Gumpendorferstr. 11. The fin-de-siècle interior is one of the finest of the city's coffeehouse scene. July & Aug closed Sun. U-Bahn Karlsplatz/Babenbergerstr.

**Stein** 9, Währingerstr. 6. Big, trendy, designer café, with funky music, online facilities and decent food. Open till 1am. U-Bahn Schottentor.

**Una** 7, Museumsplatz 1; U-Bahn Museumsquartier. Best of the Museums Quartier cafés, Una boasts a wonderful vaulted floral ceramic ceiling, an imaginative menu and a friendly vibe. Open till midnight; closed Sun eve.

## Restaurants

**Aux Gazelles** 6, Rahlgasse 5. The full over-the-top North African monty, this vast enterprise includes a café, brasserie, oyster bar, salon de thé and even a small hammam. Closed Mon. U-Bahn Museumsquartier.

**Bizi** 1, Rotenturmstrasse 4. Great, cheap, central, self-service stomach-filler serving salads, pizzas and other hot meals. U-Bahn Stephansplatz.

**Brezlg'wölb** 1, Ledererhof 9, off Drahtgasse. Cosy, candle-lit, cavern-like place serving Austrian favourites. Open till 1am. U-Bahn Schwedenplatz.

**Figlmüller** 1, Wollzeile 5. In a little side alley, this very popular place is famous for its Wienerschnitzel. U-Bahn Stephansplatz. Closed Aug.

**Regina Margherita** 1, Wallnerstrasse 4. Smart, bustling Neapolitan pizza and pasta joint in the inner court of the Palais Esterházy. Closed Sun. U-Bahn Herrengasse.

**Schnitzelwirt** 7, Neubaugasse 52. Another great place to eat Wienerschnitzel – and cheaper than Figlmüller. Closed Sun. Tram #49.

**Schweizerhaus** 2, Str. des 1 Mai 116. Czech-owned restaurant in the Prater, known for its

draught beer and grilled pigs' trotters (Steltzen). Closed Nov–Feb. U-Bahn Praterstern.
**Siebenstern Bräu** 7, Siebensterngasse 19. Popular modern Bierkeller that brews its own beer and serves solid Viennese food. U-Bahn Volkstheater/Neubaugasse.

**Wrenkh** 1, Bauernmarkt 10. Fashionable vegetarian restaurant just north of Stephansplatz. Open till 1am. U-Bahn Stephansplatz.
**Zwillingswöbl** 1, Universitätsstrasse 5. Popular, smoky student place, just down from the university. Open till 1am; closed Sun. U-Bahn Schottentor.

## Nightlife

Vienna's late-night **bars** are concentrated in four main areas: the Bermuda Triangle around Seitenstettengasse and the Ruprechtskirche, near Schwedenplatz; the Naschmarkt, where late-night licences abound; under the railway arches of the inner ring road or Gürtel; and Spittelberg, between Burggasse and Siebensterngasse. At **clubs**, you may have to pay admission, though it's rarely more than €7.50; for the latest information, visit ⊛www.viennahype.at. The local **listings magazine** *Falter* (⊛www.falter.at) has comprehensive details of the week's cultural programme and is pretty easy to decipher. The tourist office also publishes the free monthly *Programm*. You can catch high-class international **opera** and **ballet** at the Staatsoper, 1, Opernring 2 (⊛www.wiener-staatsoper.at). Seats often sell out weeks in advance, but hundreds of standing tickets (*Stehplätze*) go on sale each night 80 minutes before a performance from just €2/3.50. Ask at the ticket office under the arcades at the opera house for details. Opera and operetta are also staged at the Volksoper, 9, Währingerstr. 78 (⊛www.volksoper.at). The principal **classical music** venues are the Musikverein, 1, Karlsplatz 6 (⊛www.musikverein-wien.at), home of the Vienna Philharmonic, and the Konzerthaus, 3, Lothringerstr. 20 (⊛www.konzerthaus.at). Bookings for all these can be made at Bundestheaterkassen, 1, Hanuschgasse 3 (⊛www.bundestheater.at) – though, again, you can get cheap standing-room tickets by queuing up an hour before a performance.

### Musikcafés, live venues and clubs

**American Bar** 1, Kärntner Durchgang. Small, dark late-night bar off Kärntnerstrasse, with a rich interior designed by Adolf Loos. Open till 4am. U-Bahn Stephansplatz.
**B72** 8, Stadtbahnbögen 72, Hernalser Gürtel ⊛www.b72.at. Dark, designer club underneath the U-Bahn arches, that features a mixture of DJs and live indie bands. Open till 4am. U-Bahn Alserstr.
**Blue Box** 7, Richtergasse 8 ⊛www.bluebox.at. Musikcafé with resident DJs and a good snack menu. Open till 2am or later. U-Bahn Neubaugasse.
**Chelsea** 8, Gürtelbögen 29–31, Lerchenfelder Gürtel. Favourite rock venue with up-and-coming Brit guitar bands. Situated underneath the railway arches. U-Bahn Thaliastr.
**Flex** 1, Donaukanal ⊛www.flex.at. Vienna's most serious dance-music club by the canal, attracting the city's best DJs and a very young enthusiastic crowd. Open till 4am. U-Bahn Schottenring.
**Passage** 1, Babenberger Passage, Burgring/Babenbergerstrasse ⊛www.sunshine.at. The city's newest DJ club is a funky futurist conversion of a pedestrian underpass. Open till 4am. U-Bahn Museumsquartier/Volkstheater.

**Porgy & Bess** 1, Riemergasse 11 ⊛www.porgy.at. A converted porn cinema, now the home for Vienna's top jazz venue, attracting acts from all over the world. U-Bahn Stubentor.
**rhiz** 8, Gürtelbögen 37–38, Lerchenfelder Gürtel ⊛www.rhiz.org. Bar/café/club, with several DJs spinning everything from dance to trance. Open till 4am. U-Bahn Josefstädterstr.
**Rosa-Lila-Villa** 6, Linke Wienzeile 102 ⊛www.villa.at. Gay and lesbian centre housing a café/restaurant with a nice leafy courtyard. A good place to pick up information about events. Open till 2am. U-Bahn Pilgramgasse.
**U4** 12, Schönbrunnerstr. 222 ⊛www.clubnet.at. Popular with the alternative crowd, a dark, cavernous disco, playing mostly break beats and house, plus frequent gigs. Gay and lesbian night on Thurs. Open till 5am. U-Bahn Meidling-Hauptstr.
**Volksgarten** 1, Burgring 1 ⊛www.volksgarten.at. Situated in the park of the same name, Vienna's longest-running club is still a favourite with the dance crowd. Open till 5am. U-Bahn Volkstheater.
**w.u.k.** 9, Währingerstr. 59 ⊛www.wuk.at. Old school turned arts venue with a great café and a wide programme of events, including live music and DJ nights. Open till 2am. Tram #40, #41 or #42.

## Listings

**Bike rental** City Bike, self-service bike rental from Stephansplatz and other locations around the city (ⓦ www.citybikewien.at). Pedal Power, 2, Ausstellungstr. 3 (ⓣ729 7234, ⓦ www.pedalpower .at; €27/day).

**Embassies** Australia, 4, Mattiellistr. 2–4 ⓣ50674, ⓦ www.australian-embassy.at; Canada, 1, Laurenzerbergg. 2 ⓣ531 383 000, ⓦ www.kanada.at; Ireland, 1, Rotenturmstr. 16–18 ⓣ715 4246; UK, 3, Jaurèsgasse 12 ⓣ716 135 151, ⓦ www .britishembassy.at; US, 9, Boltzmanngasse 16 ⓣ31339, ⓦ www.usembassy.at.

**Exchange** Outside banking hours try the offices at the Westbahnhof (daily 7am–10pm) or the Südbahnhof (Mon–Fri 7am–7pm; July & Aug also Sat & Sun 6.15am–9pm), or the 24hr automatic exchange machines around Stephansplatz.

**Hospital** Allgemeines Krankenhaus, 9, Währinger Gürtel 18–20; U-Bahn Michelbeuern-AKH.

**Internet** Free Internet access at Amadeus bookshops, Mariahilferstrasse 99 and elsewhere (ⓦ www.amadeusbuch.co.at), plus Big Net, at Hoher Markt 8–9, Kärntnerstrasse 61 and Mariahilferstrasse 27 (ⓦ www.bignet.at).

**Laundry** Bendiz Laundrette, 7, Siebensterng. 52 (Mon, Tues & Thurs 8am–6pm, Wed 8am–4pm, Fri 8am–1pm).

**Pharmacy** Alte Feldapotheke, opposite the Stephansdom and at the Westbahnhof.

**Post offices** 1, Fleischmarkt 19; Westbahnhof; Südbahnhof (all 24hr).

# The Danube Valley

Heading west from Vienna, there are two alternative routes for onward travel: to Salzburg, around three hours away, and then on to Munich or Innsbruck; or a more leisurely route following the Danube through the **Wachau**, a winding stretch of water where vine-bearing, ruin-encrusted hills roll down to the river from the north. This is an Austria decidedly different from either cosmopolitan Vienna or the Alpine southwest. At **Melk** you'll find a superb Benedictine monastery overlooking the river, while the industrialized, but culturally vibrant, northern city of **Linz** has enough of interest to make a further stopoff worthwhile. Melk is reached on the main line from Vienna's Westbahnhof. The most stylish way to travel is **by boat**. DDSG (ⓦ www.ddsg-blue-danube.at) operates boats at weekends between Vienna, Linz and Passau during the summer, with year-round services on the most scenic stretch between the historic town of Krems and Melk. The journey takes about three hours upstream, two downstream, and costs around €15.50 each way. Making your way along the river by shorter hops will work out more expensive. Eurailers travel free; InterRailers go half-price.

## Melk

For real High Baroque excess, head for the Benedictine monastery at **MELK** – a pilgrimage centre associated with the Irish missionary St Coloman – designed by local architect Jakob Prandtauer in the first half of the eighteenth century. The monumental coffee-cake monastery, perched on a bluff over the river, dominates the town. Highlights of the interior (Easter–Oct daily 9am–5/6pm; rest of year guided tours only: 11am & 2pm; €7, €8.60 with guided tour; ⓦ www.stiftmelk.at) are the exquisite library, with a cherub-infested ceiling by Troger, and the monastery church, with similarly impressive work by Rottmayr. Melk's river station is about ten minutes' walk north of town; the train station is at the head of Bahnhofstrasse, which leads directly into the old quarter. The **tourist office**, Babenbergstr. 1 (April–Oct Mon–Sat 9am–7pm, Sun 10am–2pm; Nov–March Mon–Fri 9am–noon & 1–4pm; ⓣ02752/52307), has a substantial stock of private rooms, though most are out of the centre. The HI **hostel** is ten minutes' walk from the tourist office, at Abt Karl-Str. 42 (ⓣ02752/52681, ⓦ www.oejhv.or.at; March to mid-Dec; €15). A similar distance in the opposite direction is the town's **campsite**, *Melker Camping* (ⓣ02752/53291, ⓔ faehrhaus-jensch@melker.net; March–Nov), by the river station.

# Linz

Away from its industrial suburbs, **LINZ** is a pleasant Baroque city straddling the Danube, even though its greatest claim to fame is as the childhood home of Adolf Hitler, something about which the local tourist board is understandably coy. The heart of the city is the rectangular expanse of the main square, **Hauptplatz**, with its pastel-coloured facades and central Trinity Column, crowned by a gilded sunburst. In the nearby **Pfarrkirche**, a gargantuan marble slab contains Emperor Friedrich III's heart (the rest of him is in Vienna's Stephansdom); he made Linz the imperial capital for four years from 1489. A modern addition to the city's cultural scene nestles beside the Danube: the shimmering, hangar-like steel and glass **Lentos** (daily except Tues 10am–6pm, Thurs till 10pm; €6.50; ®www.lentos.at) shows contemporary and modern art, including Klimt, Kokoschka, and Schiele. Beside the Nibelungen bridge links Linz to its northern suburb of Urfahr. To the right is the **Ars Electronica Center**, Hauptstr. 2 (Wed–Sun 9/10am–5/6pm, Fri till 9pm; €6; ®www.aec.at), a fun museum dedicated to new technology; most of the instructions are in German, but the helpful staff speak English. You can play around with various pieces of state-of-the-art computer equipment, but the highlight is a visit to the "CAVE", a virtual reality room with 3D projections on the walls and floor – get there early to book for it. Also from Urfahr you can take a ride on the **Pöstlingbergbahn**, a narrow-gauge railway which climbs to the eighteenth-century pilgrimage church of Pöstlingberg. Trains leave from a twee station at the terminus of tram #3 (daily 6am–7pm; every 20min; €3.20).

## Practicalities

Linz's **train station** is 2km south of the centre, at the end of the city's main artery, Landstrasse; tram #3 runs to Hauptplatz. There's a **tourist office** in the Altes Rathaus, Hauptplatz 1 (Mon–Fri 8am–6/7pm, Sat & Sun 10am–6/7pm; ☎0732/7070 1777, ®www.linz.at). Affordable **accommodation** is rare: the *Wilder Mann*, ten minutes' walk from the station at Goethestr. 14 (☎0732/65 60 78, ®members.aon.at/wilder-mann; ❹), has en-suite showers but shared hallway WCs; the similarly equipped but more pleasant *Goldenes Dachl*, Hafnerstr. 27 (☎0732/77 58 97, ®goldenesdachl@gmx.at; ❸), is one block south of the cathedral. Linz has three **youth hostels**, the most central of which is the small and friendly *Jugendherberge*, Kapuzinerstrasse 14 (☎0732/78 27 20; March–Sept), five minutes' walk from Hauptplatz, with 4- and 6-bed dorms (€12). The best **campsite** is on the Pleschinger See, 3km northeast of the centre on the Danube at Seeweg 11 (☎0732/24 78 70, ®kolmer@ione.at; mid-March to Oct; bus #33 or #33a from Rudolfstrasse in Urfahr). There are plenty of central **bars** and **restaurants** around Hauptplatz. *Mangolds* at no. 6 (closed Sun) is a self-service vegetarian café with cheap but tasty food, while the former monastery *Klosterhof*, Landstr. 30, serves solid Austrian fare and boasts a large beer garden. The traditional coffee house *Traxlmayr*, Promenade 16, is a good place to treat yourself to a slice of *Linzer Torte*, the local chocolate cake. *Alte Welt*, Hauptplatz 4 (closed Sun), is a trendy **wine bar**, and there are *Weinkellers* along the riverfront in Urfahr. The characterful *Extrablatt*, Waltherstr. 15, is a studenty café-bar decked out with nostalgic posters. A welter of **nightclubs** line the Hofberg, between the Landhaus and the Danube, while *Posthof*, 2km east at Posthofgasse 43 (®www.posthof.at; bus #46), organizes regular gigs and **club nights**.

# Southeast Austria

Austria's **southeastern** corner, with the subalpine terrain of the province of Styria and the sun-baked plains of the Burgenland, is bypassed by most visitors. The area's wealth of diffuse attractions demands leisurely exploration, although the obvious focus of concentrated interest is the provincial capital of **Graz**.

# Graz

Austria's second-largest city, **GRAZ**, owes its importance to the defence of central Europe against the Turks. From the fifteenth century, it was constantly under arms, rendering it more secure than Vienna and leading to a modest seventeenth-century flowering of the arts (the Baroque style appeared first in Graz). The city's former reputation as a conservative place full of pensioners has been superseded, thanks to a clutch of modern, glass and steel architectural adventures and a large student population, creating a varied nightlife; Graz's recent UNESCO World Heritage status has also given the city a flush of confidence.

Graz is compact and easy to explore, most sights being within striking distance of the broad **Hauptplatz** square. The easiest way to get your bearings is to take a trip up the **Schlossberg**, a wooded hill overlooking the town: either walk up a balustraded stone staircase which zigzags from Schlossbergplatz to the summit or take the hi-tech lift (April–Oct daily 9am–2am, Sun till midnight; Nov–March daily 10am–11pm; €1.60) or funicular (daily: April–Sept 9am–11pm; Oct–March 10am–10pm; €1.60), which lies a little further along Sackstrasse. The Schloss, or fortress, was destroyed by Napoleon in 1809; only a few prominent features survive – most noticeably the huge sixteenth-century **Uhrturm** (clock tower), and more distant **Glockenturm** (bell tower), whose bell "Liesl" is said to be cast from 101 Turkish cannonballs.

From Hauptplatz, it's a few steps to the River Mur and two examples of Graz's architectural renaissance: **Kunsthaus Graz** (Tues–Sun 10am–6pm, Thurs till 8pm; €6; ☻www.kunsthausgraz.at), resembling a giant submarine, exhibits programmes of contemporary design, web art and photography, while the **Murinsel** is an ultra-modern floating bridge-cum-meeting place linking the two banks, inspired by an opened mussel shell. From the southern end of Hauptplatz, Herrengasse leads towards the sixteenth-century Landhaus, and the adjacent **Zeughaus** (April–Oct Tues–Sun 10am–6pm, Thurs till 8pm; Nov–March Tues–Sun 10am–3pm; €4.50), which bristles with weapons used to keep the Turks at bay. West of Herrengasse is the **Landesmuseum Joanneum** (☻www.museum-joanneum.at), a vast collection housed in different locations: one, the **Alte Galerie** at Neutorgasse 45 (Tues–Sun 10am–5pm, Thurs till 8pm; €4.50), houses Gothic devotional paintings, including a fifteenth-century altarpiece depicting the martyrdom of Thomas à Becket and a macabre *Triumph of Death* by Bruegel. On the other side of Herrengasse, Stempfergasse leads into a neighbourhood of narrow alleyways that dog-leg their way up the hill towards the **Mausoleum of Ferdinand II** (daily 10/10.30am–noon & 1/1.30–3/4pm; €4). It's a fine example of the early Baroque style, begun in 1614 when its intended incumbent was a healthy 36-year-old. The **Burg** is nearby, a former imperial residence; peer through the archway at the end of the first courtyard to view the unique double spiral of a fifteenth-century Gothic staircase. A short way north of Hauptplatz, down Sackstrasse, the **Neue Galerie** (Tues–Sun 10am–6pm, Thurs till 8pm; €6; ☻www.neuegalerie.at), displays nineteenth- and twentieth-century painting featuring Klimt, Schiele and Duchamp.

## Practicalities

Graz's **train station** is on the western edge of town, a fifteen-minute walk or short tram ride (#1, #3, #6 or #7) from Hauptplatz. There's a **tourist office** at the station (Mon–Fri 9am–6pm, Sat 9am–3pm; ☏0316/80750, ☻www .graztourismus.at) and a bigger one at Herrengasse 16 (Mon–Fri 9am–6pm, Sat 9am–3pm, Sun 10am–3pm). **Accommodation** can be found at the comfortable *Strasser*, Eggenburger Gürtel 11 (☏0316/71 39 77, ☻www.clicking.at/hotel; ❸), and *Pension Rückert*, Rückertgasse 4 (☏0316/32 30 31; ❺), 2km east of the centre; take tram #1 to Teggethofplatz. The HI **hostel** is four blocks south of the station at Idlhofgasse 74 (℡0316/70 83 50, ⊛www.jgh.at; €17) and offers dorms and en-suite doubles; it's justifiably popular so book ahead. **Camping** *Central* is south of town at Martinhofstr. 3 (℡0316/378 5102, ⊛www .tiscover.com/campingcentral; April–Oct; bus #32 from Jakominiplatz). There's **Internet** access at Sit 'n' Surf, Hans-Sachs-Gasse 10 (Mon–Sat 8am–midnight), and a coin-op **laundry** on Jakoministrasse, corner of Grazbackgasse (Mon–Fri 8am–5pm, Sat 8am–noon; tram #4 or #5).

Graz is foremost among Austria's provincial cities in preserving the culture of the **Kaffeehaus**. *Hofcafé Edegger Tax*, Hofgasse 8, is a sedate refuge; modern *Operncafé*, Opernring 22, attracts a youthful crowd and is equally popular in the evening; *Café Promenade*, Erzherzog-Johann-Allee 1, is an attractive pavilion in the Stadtpark. *Gambrinuskeller*, Farbergasse 6–8 (closed Sun), has a wide choice of **food**, including kebabs, stuffed peppers and other Balkan dishes; *Glöckl Bräu*, Glockenspielplatz 2–3, has more standard Austrian fare. In the university district *Zu den 3 goldenen Kugeln*, corner of Goethestrasse and Heinrichstrasse, doles out schnitzel-and-chips; it is easily accessible by bus #31 from Jakominiplatz to the Geidorfplatz stop. Other good eating options around the district include *Café Harrach*, Harrachgasse 24, and *Bier Baron*, Heinrichstr. 56, a student favourite, serving inexpensive food. Many of the best places to **drink** are in the alleys around Hauptplatz: *MI*, Färberplatz, is a swish designer bar, while *Flann O'Brien's*, Paradiesgasse, is the best of the Irish pubs. *Park House*, a pavilion in the Stadtpark, is a late bar with resident DJs. Other **clubs** include the *Kulturhauskeller*, a studeny dive at Elisabethstr. 31, and *Arcadium*, Griesgasse 25 (⊛www.arcadium.at), which pulls in guest DJs. Graz is also something of a **festival** city: events (June–Sept) range from story-telling, puppetry, classical, jazz and opera to street theatre.

# Salzburg and the Salzkammergut

**Salzburg**, hugging the border with Germany, is a magnet for those seeking the best of the country's Baroque heritage and a taste of subalpine scenery, and is consequently heavily touristed. The most accessible and popular of these mountain areas is the **Salzkammergut**, a peaceful region of glacier-carved lakes and craggy peaks a couple of hours east by bus or train.

## Salzburg

For many visitors, **SALZBURG** represents the quintessential Austria, offering ornate architecture, mountain air, and a musical heritage provided by the city's most famous son, Wolfgang Amadeus **Mozart**, whose bright-eyed visage peers from every box of the city's ubiquitous chocolate delicacy, the *Mozartkugeln*. The city, once home to the renowned singing Von Trapp family (immortalized in the movie **The Sound of Music**), wastes no time in cashing in on the connection via a variety of tours and shows.

### The City

Salzburg's compact centre straddles the River Salzach. The city and surrounding area used to be ruled by a series of prince-archbishops and the resulting collection of episcopal buildings on the **west bank** forms a tight-knit network of alleys and squares, overlooked by the medieval Hohensalzburg castle. From here it's a short hop over the river to a narrow ribbon of essential sights on the **east bank**.

From the Staatsbrücke, the main bridge, tourists are funneled along Judengasse and up into **Mozartplatz**, home to a statue of the composer and overlooked by the

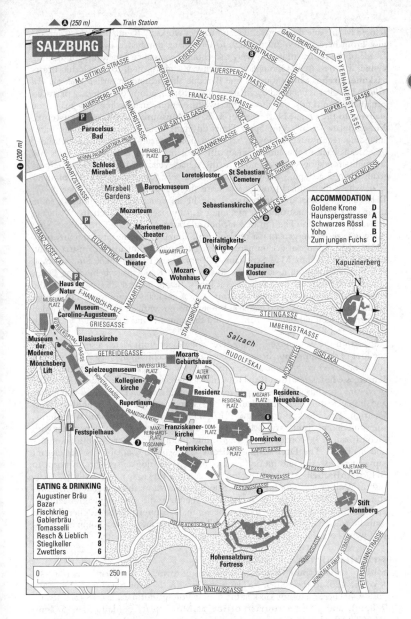

**SALZBURG**

▲ Ⓐ (250 m)    ▲ *Train Station*

**ACCOMMODATION**

| | |
|---|---|
| Goldene Krone | **D** |
| Haunspergstrasse | **A** |
| Schwarzes Rössl | **E** |
| Yoho | **B** |
| Zum jungen Fuchs | **C** |

**EATING & DRINKING**

| | |
|---|---|
| Augustiner Bräu | **1** |
| Bazar | **3** |
| Fischkrieg | **4** |
| Gablerbräu | **2** |
| Tomaselli | **5** |
| Resch & Lieblich | **7** |
| Stieglkeller | **8** |
| Zwettlers | **6** |

0 ——————— 250 m

**Glockenspiel**, a seventeenth-century musical clock whose chimes attract crowds at 7am, 11am and 6pm. The complex of Baroque buildings on the right exudes the ecclesiastical and temporal power wielded by Salzburg's archbishops, whose erstwhile living quarters – the **Residenz** – dominate the west side of Residenzplatz. You can make a self-guided audio-tour of the lavish state rooms (daily 10am–5pm; combined ticket with Residenzgalerie €7.30), and then visit the **Residenzgalerie**

**AUSTRIA** | Salzburg and the Salzkammergut

109

(closed Mon), one floor above, which includes works by Rembrandt and Caravaggio. From here arches lead through to Domplatz, dominated by the pale marble facade of the **Dom**, an impressively cavernous Renaissance structure with dazzling ceiling frescoes. Across Domplatz, an archway leads through to the Gothic **Franziskanerkirche**, which houses a fine Baroque altar around an earlier *Madonna and Child*. The altar is enclosed by an arc of nine chapels, adorned in a frenzy of stucco ornamentation. Look out also for the twelfth-century marble lion that guards the stairway to the pulpit. Northwest of here, the **Museum Carolino-Augusteum**, Museumplatz 1 (daily 9am–5pm, Thurs till 8pm; €3.50), contains Roman finds, including reconstructed mosaics retrieved from beneath Mozartplatz. Getreidegasse leads back to the centre, lined with opulent boutiques, painted facades and wrought-iron shop signs. At no. 9 is the canary yellow **Mozarts Geburtshaus** (daily 9am–5.30/7pm, ⓦwww.mozarteum.at; €6; joint ticket with Wohnhaus €9), where the musical prodigy was born (in 1756) and lived till the age of 17. Between the waves of tour parties it can be an evocative place, housing some fascinating period instruments, including a baby-sized violin used by Wolfgang Amadeus as a child. The fortified **Hohensalzburg** (daily 9am–5/6/7pm; €3.60; ⓦwww.salzburg-burgen.at) is a key landmark, looking over the city from the rocky Mönchsberg. You can get up here by using the oldest funicular in Austria (daily: Oct–April 9am–5pm; May–Sept 9am–9/10pm; every 10min; €8.50 return, €5.60 one way, includes admission to the fortress) from Kapitelplatz behind the Dom, although the walk up isn't as hard as it looks. Begun around 1070 to provide the city's archbishops with a refuge, the fortress was gradually transformed into a more salubrious courtly seat. You can visit the state rooms with an audioguide (included in entrance fee), although a roam around the ramparts and passageways is enough to gain a feel for the place.

Streets on the eastern bank of the river radiate out from Platzl, a small square at the foot of the **Kapuzinerberg**, named after a Capuchin monastery at the summit. It can be scaled in ten minutes for excellent views of Salzburg's domes and spires. Linzergasse heads east from Platzl towards the **Sebastianskirche** and its fascinating graveyard, resting-place of the Renaissance humanist and alchemist Paracelsus and home to the tiled mausoleum of the seventeenth-century archbishop Wolf Dietrich. Two blocks northwest of Platzl, on Makartplatz, is **Mozarts Wohnhaus**, the family home from 1773 to 1787 (daily 9am–5.30/7pm; €5.50; joint ticket with Geburtshaus €9), containing an engrossing multimedia history of the composer and his times. The **Dreifaltigkeitskirche** stands nearby, notable for the elegant curve of its exterior and murky frescoes inside. Dreifaltigkeitsgasse leads north to **Schloss Mirabell**, Mirabellplatz, on the site of a previous palace built by Archbishop Wolf Dietrich for his mistress Salome, with whom the energetic prelate was rumoured to have sired a dozen children. Rebuilt in the early eighteenth century, and reconstructed after a fire in the nineteenth, it features a Baroque, cherub-lined staircase and ornate gardens – the rose-filled high ground of the adjoining Kurgarten, which offers a much-photographed view back across the city.

## Practicalities

Salzburg's **main train station** is 1km north of town, with regular buses (#1, #3, #5, #6, #25) to the central F.-Hanusch-Platz. A 24-hour travel pass (*Netzkarte*) costs €4. There's a tourist kiosk at the train station (platform 2a; daily 8.15/8.45am–7/8pm), and a larger **tourist office** at Mozartplatz 5 (daily 9am–6/7pm; ☎0662/889 87-330, ⓦwww.salzburginfo.at). Both offices have accommodation details and book rooms for a fee of €3; they also sell the **Salzburg Card** (€22/29 for 24/48hr), which grants unlimited use of public transport and free admission to all of the sights. Panorama Tours on Mirabellplatz (☎0662/874 029, ⓦwww .panoramatours.com) runs what they dub "**The Original Sound of Music Tour**" (daily 9.30am & 2pm; 4 hours; €33) on which you're bussed to the key locations of the film, played the soundtrack and sent away with a free packet of edelweiss seeds. Salzburg can also serve as a base for a day trip into the **mountains**: Crocodile Sports, Gaisbergstr. 34a (℡0662/642 907, ◍www.crocodile-sports.com), runs rafting, canyoning, cave tours and canoeing from around €40 upwards.

Out of the **places to stay**, *Yoho*, Paracelsusstr. 9 (℡0662/87 96 49, ◍www.yoho .at; €15), is a great hostel; convenient for the train station and very sociable, it's large, modern and clean. The HI-affiliated *Haunspergstrasse* hostel is three blocks west of the train station at Haunspergstr. 27 (℡0662/87 50 30, ◍www.lbsh -haunspergstrasse.at; €15; July & Aug only). **Hotel** rooms fill quickly in summer and can be pricey. Spartan but clean *Zum jungen Fuchs*, Linzergasse 54 (℡0662/875 496; ❸), is a bargain, in a good location. Nearby is the wonderful, creaky old *Schwarzes Rössl*, Priesterhausgasse 6 (℡0662/87 44 26; ◍www.academia-hotels .co.at; July–Sept; ❹). *Goldene Krone*, also on the left bank at Linzergasse 48 (℡0662/87 23 00, ◒office@hotel-goldenekrone.com; ❻), is an old-fashioned place with some en suites. *Camping Nord-Sam*, Samstr. 22a, is the most convenient **campsite** (℡0662/64 04 94, ◍www.camping-nord-sam.com; April–Oct; bus #23).

Plenty of outlets offer sandwiches and **snacks**; riverside *Fischkrieg*, F.-Hanusch-Platz 4, serves up everything from fishburgers to grilled squid. Of Salzburg's elegant **cafés**, one of the most renowned is *Tomasselli*, Alter Markt 9; *Bazar*, Schwarzstr. 3, has a nice river-view terrace. The *Resch & Lieblich* **restaurant**, next to the Festspielhaus at Toscaninihof 1, offers good-value Austrian cuisine in dining rooms carved out of the Hohensalzburg cliffs. *Gablerbräu*, Linzergasse 9, serves similar traditional fare (from around €7 for a main meal) and has several vegetarian options, as does *Stieglkeller*, Festungsgasse 10 – also a good place for drinking beer on warm evenings. There are many raucous night-time **drinking** venues along Rudolfskai. *Zwettlers*, Kaigasse 3, is a relaxing pub with good food and blues music. *Augustiner Bräu*, Augustinerstr. 4–6, is an open-air courtyard fifteen minutes northwest of the centre serving huge mugs of its own brewed beer.

The city hosts dozens of **concerts** – many of them Mozart-related – all year round; check with Salzburg Ticket Service (◍www.salzburgticket.com), inside the tourist office on Mozartplatz. The **Salzburg Festival** (end-July to end-Aug; ◍www.salzburgfestival.at) is one of Europe's premier festivals of classical music, opera and theatre. The box office for tickets is on Hofstallgasse (℡0662/8045 500).

## Listings

**Consulates** UK, Alter Markt 4 ℡0662/84 81 33; US, Alter Markt 1 ℡0662/84 87 76.
**Exchange** Outside banking hours try at the main station (Mon–Fri 8.30am–8pm, Sat 8.30am–4pm).
**Hospital** Sankt Johann's Spital/Laneskranken-haus, Müllner Hauptstr. 48 ℡0662/4482.

**Internet access** Bignet, Judengasse 5–7; Piter-fun, opposite the train station.
**Laundry** Bubble Point, Karl-Wurmb-Str. 3 (daily 7am–11pm).
**Left luggage** 24hr lockers at the main station.
**Pharmacy** Elisabeth Apotheke, Elisabethstr. 1.
**Post office** Postamt 1010, Residenzplatz 9.

## The Salzkammergut

The peaks of the **Salzkammergut** may not be as lofty as those further south, but the lakes that fill the glacier-carved troughs separating them make for some spectacular scenery. Most of the settlements here are modest, quiet until the annual summer influx of visitors. The hub is the nineteenth-century spa town of **Bad Ischl**, 60km east of Salzburg, near two of the most scenic lakes – the **Wolfganger-see** and **Hallstättersee**. You can reach Bad Ischl by train, either branching off the main Salzburg–Vienna route at Attnang-Puchheim, or leaving the Salzburg–Graz line at Stainach-Irdning to the south. Once in Bad Ischl you're just a half-hour train ride from dramatic **Hallstatt** or a half-hour bus ride from idyllic **St Wolfgang**.

## St Wolfgang

Hourly buses between Salzburg and Bad Ischl run east along the southern shores of the Wolfgangersee, though they bypass the lake's main attraction, the village of **ST WOLFGANG**, on the opposite shore: get off at Strobl, at the lake's eastern end, and pick up a connecting bus from there. St Wolfgang can be crowded in summer, but is worth visiting, if only to see the **Pfarrkirche**, just above the lake shore; its high altar, an extravagantly pinnacled structure 12m high, was completed between 1471 and 1481, and features brightly gilded scenes of the *Coronation of the Virgin* in the centrepiece flanked by scenes from the life of St Wolfgang. Little trains climb the local **Schafberg** peak (May–Oct; €22 return; InterRail/Eurail discounts) from a station on the western edge of town. The **tourist office** (May–Oct Mon–Fri 9am–6/7pm, Sat 9am–noon & 2–6pm; Nov–April Mon–Fri 9am–5pm, Sat 9am–noon; ☏06138/8003, ⊛www.wolfgangsee.at) is at the eastern entrance to the road tunnel, and can help arrange accommodation.

## Bad Ischl

It was the soothing properties of the waters and tranquil ambience that still permeates the town of **BAD ISCHL** today that prompted the penultimate Habsburg emperor, Franz Josef, to summer in the **Kaiservilla** (April Wed, Sat & Sun 9.30am–4.45pm; May to mid-Oct daily 9–5pm; €9.50, park only €3.50) across the River Ischl from the centre. Beyond the villa (which is crammed with victims of the emperor's hunting expeditions) stretches a park containing the **Marmorschlössel** (April–Oct daily 9.30am–5pm; €1.50), an exquisite neo-Gothic garden retreat built for the Empress Elizabeth; it now houses a small museum of photography. Both the **bus** and **train stations** are on the eastern fringe of the centre, a few steps from the **tourist office**, Bahnhofstr. 6 (Mon–Fri 9am–5/6pm, Sat 9am–noon; July & Aug Sat till 3pm and also Sun 9am–1pm; ☏06132/27757, ⊛www.badischl.at). There's a modern, functional HI **hostel** near the swimming pool at Am Rechensteg 5 (☏06132/26577, ⊛www.oejhv.or.at; €18.50), and the clean and comfy ivy-clad *Eglmoos*, at Eglmoosgasse 14 (☏06132/23154; July–Sept; ❸). Another choice is the friendly *Steininger*, Leitenbergerstr. 2 (☏06132/25260, ⊛www.gh-steininger.at; ❹).

## Hallstatt

The jewel of the Salzkammergut is the UNESCO World Heritage Site of **HALLSTATT**, which clings to the base of precipitous cliffs on the shores of the Hallstättersee, 20km south of Bad Ischl. With towering peaks and a pristine lake, this is a stunning setting in which to hike, swim or rent a boat. Arriving **by train** is a highly evocative experience; the station is on the opposite side of the lake, and the ferry which meets all incoming trains gives truly dramatic views. (Note that after 6.30pm, trains don't stop here and instead continue to Obertraun, 5km away on the lakeshore.) Buses stop in the suburb of Lahn, a ten-minute lakeside walk away.

Hallstatt gave its name to a distinct period of Iron Age culture after Celtic remains were discovered in the salt mines above the town. Many of the finds date back to the ninth century BC, and can now be seen in the **Museum Hallstatt** (April–Oct daily 9/10am–4/6pm; Nov–March Tues–Sun 11am–3pm; €7; ⊛www.museum-hallstatt.at). The **Pfarrkirche** has a south portal adorned with sixteenth-century Calvary scenes and, inside, a Gothic winged altar on the right with heavily gilded statuettes of the Madonna and Child flanked by St Catherine (the patron of woodcutters, on the left) and St Barbara (the patron of miners). In the graveyard outside is a small stone structure known as the **Beinhaus** (daily 10am–4.30/6pm; €1), traditionally the repository for the skulls of villagers. The skulls, some of them quite recent, are inscribed with the names of the deceased and dates of their death, and are often decorated. Steep paths behind the graveyard lead up to a highland valley, the Salzachtal (1hr 30min of hard hiking), where the **salt mines** that provided the area's prosperity can be viewed (guided tour only: May–Oct daily 9.30am–3/4.30pm; €14.50). You can also take the **funicular** (May–Oct daily 9am–3/4.30pm; €7.90 return) from the nearby suburb of Lahn. A combined ticket for tour and funicular is €19.90.

Hallstatt's **tourist office** is in the centre of town (May–Oct Mon–Fri 9am–noon & 2–5pm; July & Aug no lunch break and also Sat 10am–6pm; Nov–March Mon–Fri 9am–1pm; ☎06134/8208, ⊛www.hallstatt.net). The friendly *Gasthaus zur Mühle*, set back from the landing stage at Kirchenweg 36 (☎06134/8318; ❸), has doubles and dorms (€12.50). Friendly family-run *Seethaler*, Dr F. Mortonweg 22 (☎06134/8421, ⊛pension.seethaler@kronline.at; ❸), is a great place to stay – each room has a lake-view balcony. The **campsite** *Klausner-Höll* is in Lahn by the petrol station on Lahnstrasse (☎06134/8322; mid-April to mid-Oct), a short walk from the landing stage. **Canoes** can be rented from the boatshed beside the landing stage (€7/hr). The tourist office can advise on a route for the four-hour **hike** up to the *Wiesberghaus* mountain hut (☎06134/20620; Jan–Oct; €15), and also sell you a hiking guide in English (€5). There are plenty of **places to eat**: *Bräugasthof*, Seestr. 120, does excellent Austrian food, with a lakeside terrace and competitively priced fresh fish. For **drinking**, the bar in the *Gasthaus zur Mühle* offers a warm welcome, while the one at Marktplatz 59 is popular with locals.

# Western Austria

West towards the mountain province of the **Tyrol**, the grandiose scenery of Austria's Alpine heartland begins to develop. Most trains from Vienna and Salzburg travel through a corner of Bavaria in Germany before joining the Inn valley and climbing back into Austria to the Tyrolean capital, **Innsbruck**. A less direct but more scenic route (more likely if you're coming from Graz) cuts by the majestic **Hoher Tauern** – site of Austria's highest peak, the Grossglockner – before joining the Inn valley at Wörgl. The exclusive resort-town of **Kitzbühel** provides a potential stopoff, although Innsbruck offers the most convenient mix of urban sights and Alpine splendour. Further west, **Bregenz**, on the shores of Lake Constance, makes for a tranquil stop before pressing on into Germany or Switzerland.

## Innsbruck

High in the Alps, with ski resorts within easy reach, **INNSBRUCK** is a compact city hemmed in by towering mountains. It has a rich history: Maximilian I based the imperial court here in the 1490s, placing this provincial Alpine town at the heart of European politics and culture for a century and a half. Most attractions are confined to the central Altstadt, bounded by the river and the Graben, following the course of the moat which used to surround the medieval town. Leading up to this, Innsbruck's main artery is **Maria-Theresien-Strasse**, famed for the view north towards the great rock wall of the Nordkette, the mountain range that dominates the city. At its southern end the triumphal arch, **Triumphpforte**, was built for the marriage of Maria Theresa's son Leopold in 1756. Halfway along, the **Annasäule**, a column supporting a statue of the Virgin, was erected to commemorate the retreat of the Bavarians, who had been menacing the Tyrol, on St Anne's Day (July 26), 1703. Herzog-Friedrich-Strasse leads on into the centre, opening out into a plaza lined with arcaded medieval buildings. At the plaza's southern end is the **Goldenes Dachl**, or "Golden Roof" (though the tiles are actually copper), built in the 1490s to cover an oriel window from which the court of Emperor Maximilian could observe the square below. Inside is the **Maximilianeum** (May–Sept daily 10am–6pm; Oct–April Tues–Sun 10am–5pm; €3.60;

Ⓦwww.tiroler-landesmuseum.at), a flashy museum that includes an entertaining video-style documentary about the emperor. An alley to the right leads down to Domplatz and the **Domkirche St Jakob**, home to a valuable *Madonna and Child* by German master Lucas Cranach the Elder, although it's buried in the fussy Baroque detail of the altar. The adjacent **Hofburg**, entered around the corner, has late-medieval roots but was remodelled in the eighteenth century, its Rococo state apartments crammed with opulent furniture (daily 9am–7pm; €5.45). At the head of Rennweg, entered through the Tiroler Volkskunstmuseum (see below), is the **Hofkirche**, which contains the Cenotaph of Emperor Maximilian (Mon–Sat 9am–5/5.30pm; €3, free on Sun). This extraordinary project was originally envisaged as a series of 40 larger-than-life statues, 100 statuettes and 32 busts of Roman emperors, representing both the real and the spiritual ancestors of Maximilian, but in the end only 32 of the statuettes and 20 of the busts were completed. Upstairs is the Silberkapelle or silver chapel, named after the silver Madonna that adorns the far wall. The same complex houses the **Tiroler Volkskunstmuseum** (hours as for Hofkirche; €5; combined ticket with Hofkirche €6.50) which features recreations of traditional wood-panelled Tyrolean peasant interiors. The **Tiroler Landesmuseum Ferdinandeum**, a short walk south at Museumstr. 15 (June–Sept daily 10am–6pm, Thurs till 9pm; Oct–May Tues–Sun 10am–6pm; €8), contains one of the best collections of Gothic paintings in Austria; most originate from the churches of the South Tyrol (now the Italian region of AltoAdige). Also worth a visit is **Schloss Ambras** (daily 10am–5/7pm; closed Nov; €8), 2km southeast on tram #6; this was the home of Archduke Ferdinand of Tyrol and still houses his wide-ranging collection of artworks and objects from around the globe.

The quickest route to higher altitudes is the **Hungerburgbahn** (daily 8am–5/6pm; €4.30 return), which runs from the end of Rennweg (end of tram #1) up to the Hungerburg plateau, a good base for hikes. A two-stage sequence of cable cars continues from here to just below the summit of the Nordkette range, where you can enjoy stupendous views of the high Alps.

### Practicalities

Innsbruck's **train station** has a tourist kiosk (daily 9am–7pm), while the main **tourist office** is at Burggraben 3 (daily 9am–6pm; ☎0512/59850, Ⓦwww .innsbruck.info). Both sell the "Innsbruck Card" (€21/26/31 for 24/48/72hr), which allows free travel in the centre and admission to all the sights. A 24-hour transport pass costs €3.40. An Innsbruck Club Card (given free on hotel check-in) gives free guided hikes, reduced cable-car fares and free lake bathing.

The HI *Jugendherberge Innsbruck* is 4km east of the centre, at Reichenauerstr. 147 (☎0512/346179, Ⓦwww.youth-hostel-innsbruck.at; €14.50) – take bus #O. Another option is *Torsten-Arneus-Schwedenhaus*, Rennweg 17b (☎0512/585814; €10; July and Aug only), with en-suite bathrooms, laundry facilities and Internet access; it's ten minutes' walk from the town centre or take bus #4, #D or #E. The very basic *Jugendherberge St Nikolaus*, Innstr. 95 (☎0512/286515, Ⓦwww.hostelnikolaus .at; €17), has a restaurant/bar and no night-time curfew; it's also ten minutes from town, or bus #K from the train station trundles past. *Paula*, Weiherburggasse 15 (☎0512/292262, Ⓦwww.pensionpaula.at; ❹), is a friendly **pension** on a hillside north of the river – ask for a room with balcony and mountain views. More central options are the pleasant *Innrain*, Innrain 38 (☎0512/588981, Ⓦwww.gasthof-innrain .com; ❹), and *Innbrücke*, Innstr 1 (☎0512/281 934, ✉innbruecke@nextra.at; ❹), just over the bridge from the old town. The only **campsite** is *Camping Kranebitten*, 5km west of town at Kranebittner Allee 214 (☎0512/28 41 80, Ⓦwww.campinginnsbruck .com; bus #LK from Boznerplatz, a block west of the station, to Klammstrasse).

The streets around the Goldenes Dachl are packed with old coaching inns transformed into **restaurants**; one of the more atmospheric is the *Ottoburg* (closed Sun), Herzog-Friedrich-Str. 1, with solid Austrian fare and veggie options. The slightly cheaper *Stiftskeller* is at Stiftgasse 1, offering a good choice of fresh fish; and the cheaper-still *La Cucina*, Museumstr. 26, has a wide range of pizza and pasta dishes. *Café Central*, Gilmstr. 5, is a venerable old coffeehouse serving up excellent pastries and cakes as well as decent breakfasts. There are plenty of convivial **drinking venues**: *Elferhaus*, at Herzog-Friedrich-Strasse 11, is a popular beer bar that also does good food. *Weli*, under the railway arches just east of the centre at Ing-Etzelstr. 26, is an informal café/bar with snacks. *Innkeller*, Innstr. 1, is another late-night haunt.

The Innsbruck Alpine School runs a programme of guided **hikes** (June–Sept; free with a Club Innsbruck Card), including sunrise and lantern-lit ones; the tourist office has details. **Bikes** can be rented from Sport Neuner (☎0512/561501; from €20/day). As befits such a stunning setting, there's a range of **adventure sports** on offer. Snow stays on the nearby Stubai Glacier all year, making summer skiing possible: the tourist office organizes day trips, from €49 including equipment, bus transfer and lift passes. Trips to see the glacier cost €26. Adrenaline junkies can shoot down the 1000-metre **bobsleigh run** in just over a minute (Aug–Oct Thurs & Fri 4pm & 6pm; ☎05275/5386, ☻www.sommerbobrunning.at; €25). There's **white-water rafting** (☎05234/68100; from €40) and **paragliding** through Flugschule Parafly (☎05226/3344, ☻www.parafly.at; from €95).

## Listings

Consulates UK, Kaiserjägerstr. 1 ☎0512/588320.
Hospital Universitätklinik, Anichstr. 35
☎0512/504.
Internet access Tele system, ground floor of the Rathaus Galerien, 38 Maria-Theresien-Strasse (free).

Laundry Bubble Point, Andreas-Hoferstr. 37 &
Brixnerstr. 1 (Mon–Fri 8am–10pm, Sat & Sun
8am–8pm).
Left luggage At the station 24hr lockers.
Post office Maximilianstr. 2 (24hr).

# Bregenz

On the eastern tip of the Bodensee (Lake Constance), **BREGENZ** is an obvious staging post on journeys into neighbouring Germany, Liechtenstein or Switzerland. The Vorarlbergers who live here speak a dialect close to Swiss German, and have always considered themselves separate from the rest of Austria. At first sight Bregenz is curiously disjointed, the tranquil lakeside parks cut off from town by the main road and rail links along the lakeshore. Most points of interest are in the old town, up the hill from the lake, around **St Martinsturm**, an early seventeenth-century tower crowned by a bulbous wooden dome. Up the street from here is the seventeenth-century **town hall**, an immense half-timbered construction with a steeply inclined roof. Down in the modern town near the lake on Kornmarkt, the **Kunsthaus Bregenz** (Tues–Sun 10am–6pm, Thurs till 9pm; €6; ☻www.kunsthaus-bregenz.at), known as the KUB, is a cool green cube that hosts high-profile modern art exhibitions. The **Vorarlberger Landesmuseum**, Kornmarkt 1 (Tues–Sun 9am–noon & 2–5pm; €2; ☻www.vlm.at), has some outstanding paintings by Angelika Kauffmann, a local painter who achieved success in eighteenth-century London. Beyond here, leafy parks line the lake to the **Festspielhaus**, a modern concert hall built to accommodate the Bregenz Festival (mid-July to mid-Aug; ☻www.bregenzerfestspiele.com), which draws thousands of opera lovers every year. A cable car rises from a station at the eastern end of town to the **Pfänder** (daily 9am–7pm; €9.80), a wooded hill with excellent views; you can also follow the worthwhile Pfänderweg on foot to the top (1hr 30min).

## Practicalities

The **tourist office** is at Bahnhofstr. 14 (July–Sept Mon–Sat 9am–7pm; Oct–June Mon–Fri 9am–noon & 1–5pm, Sat 9am–noon; ☎05574/49590, ☻www.bregenz.at). *Gästehaus Tannenbach*, Im Gehren 1 (☎05574/44174; May–Sept; ❸), is a friendly place with a lovely garden east of the centre; *Pension Sonne*, Kaiserstr. 8 (℡05574/42572, ⊛www.bbn.at/sonne; ❹), is a good place in the centre that hikes its rates steeply during the festival. The HI **hostel** west of the train station at Mehrerauerstr. 5 (℡05574/42867, ⊛www.jfgh.at; €18.20) offers dorms as well as swanky doubles, while *Seecamping*, Bodengasse 7, is a large **campsite** by the lake, 2km west (℡05574/71895/6, ⊛www.seecamping.at). *Gunz*, Anton-Schneider-Str. 38, serves low-priced traditional Austrian **food**; *Goldener Hirschen*, Kirchstr. 8, is a more atmospheric, pub-like venue with slightly more expensive eats. Amongst the good central **bars** are *1 Akt* (closed Sun), Kornmarktstr. 24, and the stylish but cosy *Flexibel*, Rathausstrasse 27.

# Travel details

## Trains

**Bad Ischl** to: Hallstatt (10–14 daily; 30min).
**Graz** to: Innsbruck (8 daily; 6hr); Linz (7 daily; 3hr 30min); Salzburg (8 daily; 4hr).
**Innsbruck** to: Bregenz (8 daily; 2hr 40min).
**Salzburg** to: Innsbruck (8 daily; 2hr); Linz (hourly; 1hr 20min).
**Vienna** to: Bregenz (8 daily; 8hr); Graz (hourly; 2hr 40min); Innsbruck (every 2hr; 5hr 20min); Krems (hourly; 1hr 15min); Linz (1–2 hourly; 2hr); Melk (every 1–2hr; 1hr); Salzburg (1–2 hourly; 3hr–3hr 20min).

## Buses

**Bad Ischl** to: Hallstatt (5–7 daily; 40min); Salzburg (hourly; 1hr 40min); St Wolfgang (2 hourly; 45min).
**Krems** to: Melk (3–4 daily; 1hr).
**Linz** to: St Florian (Mon–Fri 15 daily, Sat 8 daily, Sun 2 daily; 35min).
**Salzburg** to: St Wolfgang (9 daily; 1hr 40min); Hallstatt (9 daily; 2hr 30min).

# Belgium and Luxembourg

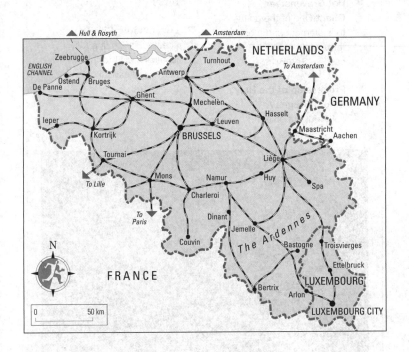

# Belgium & Luxembourg highlights

✳ **Grand-Place, Brussels** At the heart of the Belgian capital, this wonderfully well-preserved square is framed by a magnificent set of old guildhouses. See p.125

✳ **Het Gravensteen, Ghent** One of the country's sternest and most formidable medieval castles. See p.133

✳ **Procession of the Holy Blood, Bruges** A colourful but solemn religious procession held each Ascension Day. See p.135

✳ **Canoeing** Great opportunities, mostly along the River Lesse, in the wooded, hilly landscape of the Ardennes. See p.138

✳ **Luxembourg City** The spectacular setting fully justifies a visit to this pint-sized capital city. See p.148

△ Canoeing in the Ardennes

# Introduction and basics

A federal country, with three official languages and an intense regional rivalry, Belgium has a cultural diversity that belies its rather dull reputation. Its population of around ten million is divided between Flemish-speakers in the north (about sixty percent) and French-speaking Walloons to the south (forty percent), with a few pockets of German-speakers in the east. Prosperity has shifted back and forth between the two leading communities over the centuries, and relations have long been acrimonious.

Roughly in the middle of **Belgium** lies the capital, **Brussels**, a culturally varied city that is also at the heart of the European Union. North of here stretch the flat landscapes of Flemish Belgium, whose main city, **Antwerp**, is a bustling old port with doses of high art, redolent of its sixteenth-century golden age. Further west, also in the Flemish zone, are the historic cities of Bruges and Ghent, each with a stunning concentration of medieval art and architecture. Belgium's most scenic region, the **Ardennes**, is, however, in Wallonia, its deep, wooded valleys, high elevations and dark caverns sprawling away to the south with the attractive town of **Namur** the obvious gateway.

The Ardennes reach across the border into the northern part of the **Grand Duchy of Luxembourg**, a verdant landscape of rushing rivers and high hills topped with crumbling castles. The best base for rural expeditions is **Luxembourg City**, a pleasant town with a splendid rugged setting. The city has a population of around 80,000, which makes it one of Europe's smallest capitals.

## Information & maps

In both Belgium and Luxembourg, there are **tourist offices** in all but the smallest of villages. They usually provide free local maps, and in the larger towns offer a free accommodation-booking service too. The best general road **map** is the easy-to-use Baedeker & AA Belgium and Luxembourg (1:250,000) map.

## Money and banks

Belgium and Luxembourg both use the **euro** (€). **Banks** are the best places to change money and are generally open Mon–Fri 9am–4/4.30pm in both countries, though some have a one-hour lunch break between noon and 2pm. **ATMs** are commonplace.

## Communications

**Post offices** are usually open Mon–Fri 9am–noon & 2–5pm. Some urban post offices also open on Saturday mornings. Many public phones take only phonecards, which are available from newsagents and post offices. There are no area codes in either country. **Mobile** phone coverage is good. **Internet** access is widespread, with at least one or two cybercafés in all the larger cities; libraries are often a good bet where all else fails.

### Language in Belgium and Luxembourg

There are three official languages in **Belgium** (Flemish, which is effectively Dutch, French and German), but you will be able to get by in English easily in the Flemish north and just about in the French south too. Natives of **Luxembourg** speak Letzebuergesch, a dialect of German, but most people also speak French and German and many speak English too. See p.356 and p.430 for some basic French and German language tips.

# Getting around

Travelling around Belgium is rarely a problem. Distances are short, and an efficient, reasonably priced train network links all the major and many minor towns and villages. Luxembourg, on the other hand, can be a tad more problematic: the train network is not extensive and bus timetables can demand careful study for longer journeys.

**Belgium's railway system** (ⓦ www.b-rail.be) – SNCB in French, NMBS in Flemish – is comprehensive and efficient, and fares are comparatively low. InterRail and Eurail passes are valid throughout the network, as are a number of other regional passes – see p.47 for further details. SNCB/NMBS also publishes information on offers and services in their comprehensive timetable book, which has an English-language section and is available at major train stations. **Buses** are only really used for travelling short distances, or in parts of the Ardennes where rail lines fizzle out.

**Luxembourg's railways** (ⓦ www.cfl.lu) comprise one main north–south route down the middle of the country, with a handful of branch lines fanning out from the capital, but most of the country can only be reached by bus. **Fares** are comparable with those in Belgium, and there are a number of passes available, giving unlimited train and bus travel.

The modest distances and flat terrain make **cycling** in Belgium an attractive proposition. That said, only in the countryside is there a decent network of signposted cycle routes. You can take your own bike on a train for a small fee or rent one from any of around thirty train stations during the summer at about €9.50 per day; note also that some train excursion tickets include the cost of bike rental. Full details, with a list of stations offering bike rental, are on the SNCB/NMBS website and in the *Train & Vélo* leaflet (available at stations). In Luxembourg you can rent bikes for around €10 a day, and take your own bike on trains (not buses) for a minimal fee per journey. The Luxembourg Tourist Office has leaflets showing cycle routes and also sells cycling guides.

# Accommodation

Hotel **accommodation** is one of the major expenses on a trip to Belgium or Luxembourg – indeed, if you're after a degree of comfort, it's going to be the costliest item by far. There are, however, **budget alternatives**, principally the no-frills end of the hotel market, private rooms – effectively Bed and Breakfasts – arranged via the local tourist office and hostels.

In both countries **prices** begin at around €60 for a double room in the cheapest one-star hotel and climb to €90–150 for a comfortable double in a mid-range establishment. **Breakfast** is normally included. During the summer you'd be well advised to book ahead – **reservations** can be made for free through most tourist offices on the day itself; the deposit they require is subtracted from your final hotel bill. Private rooms can be booked through local tourist offices too. Expect to pay €40–60 a night for a double, but note that they're often inconveniently situated on the outskirts of cities and towns. An exception is in Bruges, where private rooms can be booked direct and many are in the centre.

## Hostels and student rooms

**Belgium** has around 30 HI **hostels**, run by two separate organizations. In Flanders (northern Belgium), this is Vlaamse

Jeugdherbergcentrale (☎ 032 32 72 18, ⓦ www.vjh.be), in Wallonia (southern Belgium) it's Les Auberges de Jeunesse de Wallonie (☎ 022 19 56 76, ⓦ www.laj .be). Most charge a flat rate per person of between €16–20 for a bed in a dormitory, €40–45 for a double – non-members a little more – and breakfast is included. Many also offer meals for €5–15. During the summer you should book ahead wherever possible. Some of the larger cities – Bruges, Antwerp and Brussels, for example – also have privately run hostels. These normally charge about €20 for a dorm bed and are often just as comfortable as their HI counterparts. You'll also find some universities offering **student rooms** for rent during the summer vacation, Ghent being a good example. Rooms are basic – reckon on about €15–25 per person per night.

There are nine HI hostels in **Luxembourg**, all of which are members of the Centrale des Auberges de Jeunesse Luxembourgeoises (☎ 26 27 66 40, ⓦ www.youthhostels .lu). Dorm-bed rates for HI members are €14.30–16.30, with non-members paying an extra €3–5. Breakfast is always included; lunch or dinner is €6–8.

## Camping

**Camping** is a popular pastime in both Belgium and Luxembourg, though many sites can only be reached by car or bike. In **Belgium**, there are literally hundreds of sites, anything from a field with a few tent pitches through to extensive complexes with all mod cons. Campsites are regulated by three governmental agencies – one for Flanders, one for Brussels and one for Wallonia – and each produces its own camping booklet. All three do, however, apply the same one- to five-star Benelux grading system. The vast majority are one- and two-star establishments, for which two adults with a car and a tent can **expect to pay** €10–20 per night. Surprisingly, most four-star sites don't cost much more – add about €5 – though the occasional five-star campsite can reach €50. All of **Luxembourg**'s campsites are detailed in the Duchy's free tourist office booklet. They are classified into three broad bands: the majority are in Category 1, the

best-equipped and most expensive classification. Prices vary considerably, but are usually €3–5 per person, plus €3–5 for a pitch. In both countries, it's a good idea to **reserve** ahead during peak season; individual campsite phone numbers are listed in the free **camping booklets**, and in Luxembourg the national tourist board (☎ 42 82 82 10, ⓦ www.ont.lu) will make a reservation on your behalf.

# Food and drink

**Belgian cuisine** is held in high international regard and is often compared in style and quality with that of France; the country also offers a competent range of ethnic food. **Luxembourg**'s food is less varied and more Germanic, but you can still eat out extremely well. As for drink, **beer** is one of the real delights of Belgium, and Luxembourg produces some very drinkable white **wines**.

## Food

**Southern Belgian** (or Wallonian) cuisine is similar to traditional French, retaining its neighbour's fondness for rich sauces and ingredients. In **Flanders** to the north the food is more akin to that of the Netherlands, with mussels and French fries the most common dish. Throughout the country, pork, beef, game, fish and seafood are staple items, often cooked with butter, cream and herbs, or sometimes in beer; hearty soups are also common. The Ardennes is renowned for its smoked ham and pâté.

In both countries, many **bars** offer inexpensive meals, at least at lunchtimes, and in addition a host of cafés serve basic dishes – omelettes, steak or **mussels with chips** for instance. **Cafés/bars** (the distinction is blurred) are often also the most fashionable places to be, especially in the cities. Most serve a dish of the day for €10–15. Restaurants are almost always more expensive – a main course will rarely cost under €15 – but the food is generally excellent.

Belgium is also renowned for its **chocolate**. The big chocolatiers, Godiva and Leonidas, have shops in all the main towns and cities, and their pralines and truffles almost make a trip to the country worthwhile in itself.

### Drink

Drinking **beer in Belgium** is a real treat. The most common brands are Stella Artois, Jupiler and Maes, but this merely scratches the surface. In total, there are about 700 speciality beers from dark stouts to fruit beers, wheat beers and brown ales – something to suit any palate and enough to overwhelm the hardiest of livers. The most famous are the strong ales brewed by the country's five Trappist monasteries, of which the most widely available is **Chimay**. **Luxembourg** doesn't really compete, but its three most popular brews – Diekirch, Mousel and Bofferding – are pleasant enough lagers. French **wines** are the most commonly available, although Luxembourg's wines, produced along the north bank of the Moselle, are very drinkable. You'll find Dutch-style **jenever** (a local gin) in most bars in the north of Belgium, and in Luxembourg home-produced, super-strong **eau-de-vie**, distilled from various fruits.

# Opening hours and holidays

In both countries, the weekend fades painlessly into the week with some shops staying closed on Monday morning, even in major cities. Nonetheless, normal **shopping hours** are Mon–Sat 9/10am–6/7pm with many urban supermarkets staying open until 8/9pm on Fridays and many smaller places shutting early on Saturday. In the big cities, a smattering of convenience stores (*magasins de nuit/avondwinkels*) stay open

either all night or until around 1/2am daily, and some souvenir shops open late and on Sundays too. At the other extreme, some shops close for a half-day (Wed or Thurs am), though this tradition has died out in all but the smaller towns and villages. Shops, banks and many museums are closed on the following **public holidays**: New Year's Day, Easter Sunday, Easter Monday, Labour Day (May 1), Ascension Day (forty days after Easter), Whit Sunday, Whit Monday, Luxembourg National Day (Luxembourg only; June 23), Belgian National Day (Belgium only; July 21), Assumption (mid-August), All Saints' Day (November 1), Armistice Day (Belgium only; November 11), Christmas Day.

# Emergencies

You shouldn't have much cause to come into contact with the **police** in either country. If you're unlucky enough to have something **stolen**, report it immediately to the nearest police station and get a report number, or better still a copy of the statement itself, for your insurance claim when you get home. With regard to **medical emergencies**, if you're reliant on free treatment within the EU health scheme, try to remember to make this clear to the ambulance staff and any medics you subsequently encounter. Outside working hours, all **pharmacies** should display a list of open alternatives. Weekend rotas are also listed in local newspapers.

# Brussels (Bruxelles, Brussel)

Wherever else you go in Belgium, it's hard to avoid **BRUSSELS**, a capital boasting architecture and museums to rank with the best in Europe, a well-preserved medieval centre and an energetic nightlife. It's also very much an international city, with European civil servants and business folk, plus immigrants from Africa, Turkey and the Mediterranean, making up a quarter of the population.

The city takes its name from Broekzele, or "village of the marsh", which grew up in the sixth century on the trade route between Cologne and the towns of Bruges and Ghent. In the nineteenth century it became the capital of the newly independent Belgium, and was kitted out with all the attributes of a modern European capital. Since World War II, the city's appointment as headquarters of both NATO and the EU has brought major developments, including a metro.

## Arrival and information

Brussels has three main **train stations** – Bruxelles-Nord, Bruxelles-Centrale and Bruxelles-Midi, each a few minutes apart; almost all domestic trains stop at all three. The majority of **international trains**, including expresses from London, Amsterdam, Paris and Cologne, stop only at Bruxelles-Midi (Brussel-Zuid). Bruxelles-Centrale is a five-minute walk from Grand-Place; Bruxelles-Nord lies in the business area just north of the main ring road; and Bruxelles-Midi is south of the city centre. To transfer from one of the three main stations to another, simply jump on the next available mainline train. **Eurolines** buses arrive at the Gare du Nord complex. The **airport** is in Zaventem, 13km northeast of the centre, served by regular trains to the city's three main stations (30min; €2.60).

There are three **tourist offices** in the city centre. The main one is the **BIT** (Bruxelles International Tourisme), in the Hôtel de Ville on the Grand-Place (May–Sept daily 9am–6pm; Oct–Dec & Easter to end-April Mon–Sat 9am–6pm, Sun 10am–2pm; Jan till Easter Mon–Sat 9am–6pm; ☎02 513 89 40, ⊛www .brusselsinternational.be). The second and much smaller **BIT office** (May–Sept Mon–Thurs, Sat & Sun 8am–8pm, Fri 8am–9pm; Oct–April Mon–Thurs 8am–5pm, Fri 8am–8pm, Sat 9am–6pm & Sun 9am–2pm) is on the main concourse of the Bruxelles–Midi train station. The third, the **Belgian tourist information centre**, is footsteps from the Grand-Place at rue du Marché aux Herbes 63 (phone for hours ☎02 504 03 90, ☎02 513 04 75), and provides information on the whole of Belgium.

## City transport

The easiest way to get around central Brussels is to **walk**, but to reach some of the more outlying attractions you'll need to use **public transport**. The system, called STIB (⊛www.stib.be), runs on a mixture of bus, tram, prémétro (underground tram) and métro lines. A single flat-fare **ticket** costs €1.50, a five-journey ticket costs €6.50, and ten costs €10 – all available from tram and bus drivers, metro kiosks and ticket machines. A day-pass (*carte de jour/dagpas*) allows unlimited travel for 24hr and is €3.80; note that most drivers will not issue this, but métro and prémétro stations will. Services run from 6am until midnight; route maps are available free from the tourist office and from STIB kiosks. **Taxis** can be picked up from ranks around the city – notably on Bourse and place De Brouckère; to book, phone Taxis Verts (☎02 349 49 49) or Taxis Orange (☎02 349 43 43).

## Accommodation

Brussels has no shortage of **places to stay**, but given the number of visitors, finding a room can be hard, particularly in summer, and it's best to **book ahead**. Belgium's central reservation agency, Resotel (℡02 779 39 39, ⓦwww.belgium-hospitality.com), operates an efficient hotel reservation service, seeking out the best deals and discounts. Alternatively, if you arrive in the city with nowhere to stay, both BIT offices (see p.123) operate a **same–night hotel booking service**. The service is provided free – you just pay a percentage of the room rate as a deposit and this is then subtracted from your final hotel bill.

### Hostels

**Bruegel** rue du Saint-Esprit 2 ℡02 511 04 36, ⓦwww.vjh.be. Official IYHF hostel, housed in a pleasantly designed modern building, with 135 beds. A basic breakfast – as well as the hire of sheets – is included in the overnight fee, and dinner costs €8.50. Check-in 10am–1pm & 2–4pm; curfew at 1am. Metro Gare Centrale. Dorms €26, rooms ❸

**Le Centre Vincent Van Gogh** rue Traversière 8 ℡02 217 01 58, ⓦwww.chab.be. A rambling, spacious, 210-bed hostel with a good reputation and friendly staff, though it can all seem a bit chaotic. Breakfast is included and there are sinks in all rooms, but sheets cost an extra €3.80. Launderette and kitchen facilities available and no curfew. Métro Botanique. Dorms €27, rooms ❸

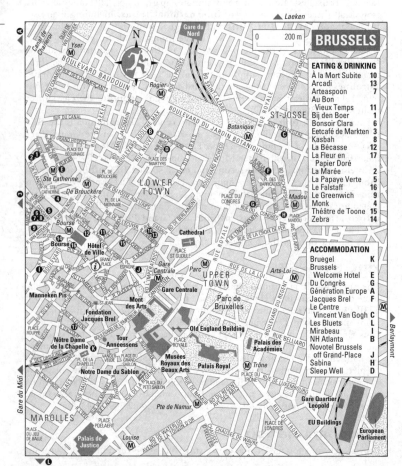

▲ Laeken

**BRUSSELS**

0      200 m

**EATING & DRINKING**

| | |
|---|---|
| À la Mort Subite | 10 |
| Arcadi | 13 |
| Arteaspoon | 7 |
| Au Bon Vieux Temps | 11 |
| Bij den Boer | 1 |
| Bonsoir Clara | 6 |
| Eetcafé de Markten | 3 |
| Kasbah | 8 |
| La Bécasse | 12 |
| La Fleur en Papier Doré | 17 |
| La Marée | 2 |
| La Papaye Verte | 5 |
| Le Falstaff | 16 |
| Le Greenwich | 9 |
| Monk | 4 |
| Théâtre de Toone | 15 |
| Zebra | 14 |

**ACCOMMODATION**

| | |
|---|---|
| Bruegel | K |
| Brussels Welcome Hotel | E |
| Du Congrès | G |
| Génération Europe | A |
| Jacques Brel | F |
| Le Centre Vincent Van Gogh | C |
| Les Bluets | L |
| Mirabeau | I |
| NH Atlanta | B |
| Novotel Brussels off Grand-Place | J |
| Sabina | H |
| Sleep Well | D |

▶ Berlaymont

**Génération Europe** rue de l'Eléphant 4 ☎02 410 38 58 ℉02 410 39 05 🌐www.laj.be. New IYHF hostel located in a modern barracks-like building in Molenbeek, an inner-city industrial district, a 15-minute walk west from the Grand-Place. Prices include breakfast and sheets. Check-in is from 7.45am–11.30pm and there's no curfew. Métro Comte de Flandre. Dorms €26, rooms ❸

**Jacques Brel** rue de la Sablonnière 30 ☎02 218 01 87, 🌐www.laj.be. This official IYHF hostel is modern and comfortable, and has a hotel-like atmosphere. Breakfast is included in the price, there's no curfew (you get a key), and cheap meals can be bought on the premises. Check-in 7.30am–1am. Métro Madou. Dorms €26, rooms ❸

**Sleep Well** rue du Damier 23 ☎02 218 50 50, 🌐www.sleepwell.be. Bright and breezy hostel close to the city centre. Hotel-style facilities include a bar-cum-restaurant, which serves traditional Belgian beers and well-priced local dishes. No curfew. Métro Rogier. Dorms €27, rooms ❹ including breakfast.

### Hotels

**Les Bluets** rue Berckmans 124, Saint Gilles ☎02 534 39 83, ✉bluets@swing.be. Charming, family-run hotel with just ten en-suite rooms in a large, handsome old stone terrace house. Immaculate decor in rich fin-de-siècle style. No lift. One block south of the "petit ring" and metro station Hôtel des Monnaies. ❺

**Brussels Welcome Hotel** quai au Bois à Brûler 23, ☎02 219 95 46, 🌐www.hotelwelcome.com. Friendly, family-run three-star in the heart of the Ste Catherine district. Each of the seventeen themed rooms is decorated in the style of a particular country or region, and there's an attractive wood-panelled breakfast room too. Métro Ste Catherine. ❼

**Du Congrès** rue du Congrès 38–44 ☎02 217 18 90, 🌐www.hotelducongres.be. Pleasant three-star occupying a set of attractive old town houses in an especially good-looking corner of the Lower Town. Each of the seventy-odd en-suite rooms is spacious and airy and decorated in plain, modern style. Métro Madou. ❼

**Mirabeau** place Fontainas 18 ☎02 511 19 72, 🌐www.hotelmirabeau.be. Friendly, medium-sized hotel with thirty, small en-suite rooms, plainly decorated. Windows are not sound proofed, so interior rooms are quieter than those on the square. Large, modern breakfast room at the front with a small bar. Prémétro Annees-sens. ❻

**NH Atlanta** boulevard Adolphe Max 7 ☎02 217 01 20, 🌐www.nh-hotels.com. The NH chain has moved in on Brussels with gusto and it now operates four hotels in and around the city centre. This is the pick of the bunch, decorated in the chain's trademark style of sleek modern furnishings and fittings matched by pastel–painted walls. Special deals and discounts bring the prices down and it's in a good central location too. Métro De Brouckère. ❾

**Novotel Brussels off Grand-Place** rue du Marché aux Herbes 120 ☎02 514 33 33, 🌐www.novotel.com. Chain hotel occupying a modern block close to Gare Centrale. The 136 rooms are decorated in brisk modern style and discounts regularly bring the price down to around €120. Métro Gare Centrale. ❾

**Sabina** rue du Nord 78 ☎02 218 26 37 ℉02 219 32 39 🌐www.hotelsabina.be. Basic pension in an attractive late nineteenth-century town house with twenty-four workaday, en-suite rooms. Triples and quads available. Discounts and cheaper weekend rates. A five- to ten-minute walk from Métro Madou. ❻

# The City

Central Brussels is enclosed within a rough pentagon of boulevards – the **petit ring** – which follows the course of the medieval city walls. The centre is also divided between the Upper and Lower Towns, the former being the traditional home of the city's upper classes who kept a beady eye on the workers down below.

## The Lower Town

The obvious place to begin any tour of the **Lower Town** is the **Grand–Place**, the commercial hub of the city since the Middle Ages. With its stupendous spired tower, the **Hôtel de Ville** (tours in English: April–Sept Tues & Wed 3.15pm, Sun 10.45am & 12.15pm; Oct–March Tues & Wed only 3.15pm; €3) dominates the square, and inside you can view various official rooms. But the real glory of the Grand-Place lies in its **guildhouses**, mostly built in the early eighteenth century, their slender facades swirling with exuberant carving and sculpture. On the west side of the square, at no. 1, stands the **Roy d'Espagne**, once the headquarters of the guild of bakers and named after its bust of Charles II, the last of the Spanish Habsburgs. Moorish and Native American prisoners flank Charles, symbolizing his mastery of a vast empire. At no. 4 is the **Maison du Sac**, the headquarters of the carpenters and coopers; the upper storeys, appropriately designed by a cabinet-maker, feature pilasters and caryatids that resemble the ornate legs of Baroque furniture. Next door, the **Maison de la Louve** was once the home of the influential archers' guild and its elegant pilastered facade is studded with pious representations of concepts like Peace and Discord. Adjoining it, at no. 6, the **Maison du Cornet** was the headquarters of the boatsmen's guild, a fanciful creation of 1697 whose top storey resembles the stern of a ship. The adjacent **Maison du Renard** started out as the home of the haberdashers' guild; on the ground floor animated cherubs in bas-relief play at haberdashery, while a scrawny, gilded fox – after which the house is named – squats above the door.

Most of the northern side of the square is taken up by the sturdy neo-Gothic **Maison du Roi**, a reconstruction of a sixteenth-century Habsburg building that now holds the **Musée de la Ville de Bruxelles** (Tues–Sun 10am–5pm; €3). Here you'll find an eclectic mix of locally manufactured tapestries, ceramics, pewter, carved altar pieces and porcelain.

## South to the Marolles quarter

Rue de l'Etuve leads south from the Grand-Place down to the **Manneken Pis**, a diminutive statue of a little boy pissing that's supposed to embody the "irreverent spirit" of the city and is today one of Brussels' biggest tourist draws. Jerome Duquesnoy cast the original statue in the 1600s, but – much to the horror of the locals – it was stolen several times and the current one is a copy. From here it's another short hop to place de la Vieille-Halle aux Blés and the **Fondation Internationale Jacques Brel** (Tues–Sun 10.30am–5pm; €5; ⓦ www .jacquesbrel.be), a small but inventive museum celebrating the life and times of the Belgian singer Jacques Brel (1933–1978).

From place de la Vieille-Halle aux Blés, it's a short walk south to boulevard de l'Empereur, a busy carriageway that scars this part of the centre. Across the boulevard, you'll spy the crumbling brickwork of **La Tour Anneessens**, a chunky remnant of the medieval city wall, while to the south gleams the immaculately restored **Notre Dame de la Chapelle** (June–Sept Mon–Sat 9am–5pm & Sun 8am–4.30pm; Oct–May daily 12.30–4.30pm; free), a sprawling Gothic structure founded in 1134 that is the city's oldest church. Running south from the church, rue Haute and parallel rue Blaes form the spine of the **Quartier Marolles**, traditionally a working–class neighbourhood. Where today, gentrification has well–nigh overwhelmed rue Blaes in an eddy of antique shops. **Place du Jeu de Balle**, the heart of Marolles, has retained its earthy character and is the site of the city's best **flea market** (daily from 7am, but at its busiest on Sundays).

## The Upper Town

The steep slope that marks the start of the **Upper Town** rises just a couple of minutes' walk to the east of the Grand-Place. Here, at the east end of rue d'Arenberg, you'll find Brussels **cathedral** (daily 8/8.30am–6pm; free), a splendid Brabantine-Gothic building begun in 1220 and sporting a striking twin-towered, whitestone facade. Inside, the triple-aisled nave is an airy affair supported by plain, heavy-duty columns and holding a massive oak pulpit featuring Adam and Eve. Look out also for the gorgeous sixteenth-century **stained-glass windows** in the transepts and above the main doors.

Five minutes' walk south of the cathedral, the so-called **Mont des Arts** also occupies the slopes of the Upper Town, its collection of severe geometric buildings given over to a variety of government- and arts-related activities. In the middle, a wide stairway climbs up towards **place Royale** and **rue Royale**, the dead-straight backbone of the Upper Town. Ahead to the left of the top of the stairway is the **Old**

England Building, one of the finest examples of Art Nouveau in the city. Once a department store, it now holds the **Musée des Instruments de Musique**, rue Montagne de la Cour 2 (Tues–Fri 9.30am–5pm, Sat & Sun 10am–5pm; €5), which contains an impressive collection of antique musical instruments and an infra–red system that triggers an appropriate burst of music in visitors' headphones when they walk past the main exhibits. A couple of minutes' walk away, off place Royale, the **Palais Royal** (late July to early Sept Tues–Sun 10.30am–4.30pm; free) is something of an anti-climax, being no more than a sombre conversion of some eighteenth-century town houses that together serve as the official residence of the Belgian royals.

Back on place Royale, at the start of rue de la Régence, the **Musées Royaux des Beaux Arts** (Tues–Sun 10am–5pm; €5 for both museums) comprise two museums: the Musée d'Art Moderne and the Musée d'Art Ancien, which together make up Belgium's most satisfying all-round collection of fine art. The permanent collection is vast, but a system of colour-coded zones makes it easy to negotiate. In the **Musée d'Art Ancien**, the **blue zone** takes in paintings of the fifteenth and sixteenth centuries. The **brown zone** concentrates on the seventeenth and eighteenth centuries, notably glorious canvases by Rubens. Moving on into the **Musée d'Art Moderne**, the **yellow zone** begins with Social Realism, continues with a collection of Neoclassical paintings, and finishes with the Symbolists and a separate section devoted to the disconcerting canvases of James Ensor. The **green zone** boasts modern art and sculpture, with fine examples of Fauvism, Cubism, Futurism, Expressionism, and, above all, Surrealism.

From the Beaux Arts it's a short stroll south along rue de la Régence to the **place du Petit Sablon**, decorated with 48 statues representing the medieval guilds, and a fountain surmounted by the Counts Egmont and Hoorn, beheaded on the Grand-Place for their opposition to Spanish tyranny in the 1500s. On the opposite side of rue de la Régence stands the fifteenth-century church of **Notre Dame du Sablon** (Mon–Fri 9am–6pm, Sat & Sun 10am–6pm; free), built after a statue of Mary with powers of healing was brought by boat from Antwerp, an event still celebrated each July by the Ommegang procession. Behind the church, the sloping wedge of **place du Grand Sablon** is the centre of one of the city's wealthiest districts and scene of a lively weekend antiques market.

### Outside the petit ring: the EU and Victor Horta

Brussels by no means ends with the petit ring. To the east of the ring road, the **Quartier Leopold** has been colonized by the huge concrete and glass high-rises of the **EU**, notably the winged **Berlaymont** building beside Métro Schuman. One of the newer additions to the sprawling EU is the lavish **European Union Parliament building** (free guided tours: usually Mon–Thurs 10am & 3pm, Fri 10am; ☎02 284 34 57 ⓦwww.europarl.eu.int), an imposing structure topped off by a spectacular curved glass roof. It's a couple of minutes' walk from place du Luxembourg, behind the Quartier Léopold train station.

## Eating and drinking

Brussels has an international reputation for the quality of its cuisine, and even at the dowdiest snack bar you'll find that the food is well prepared and generously seasoned. Furthermore, many of the city's **restaurants** are of an excellent standard, with traditional Bruxellois dishes featuring amalgamations of Walloon and Flemish ingredients and cooking styles. In addition, the city is among Europe's best for sampling a wide range of different cuisines – from the Turkish restaurants of St Josse to Spanish, Vietnamese and Japanese places. Eating out is rarely cheap, but **prices** are usually justified by the quality. You can also keep costs down by sticking to the city's **cafés** and **bars**, some of which provide food to rival that of many a restaurant.

If you're after a **drink**, the enormous variety of bars and cafés is one of the city's real joys.

## Cafés and restaurants

**Arcadi** rue d'Arenberg 18. Hard–to–beat café, decorated in brisk modern style, that is a perfect spot for lunch, tea or an early evening meal. The menu offers lots of choices, but the salads, quiches and fruit tarts are particularly delicious – and only cost a few euros. Daily 7/8am–11pm. Métro De Brouckère or Gare Centrale.

**Arteaspoon** rue des Chartreux 32. An art gallery and café rolled into one. Minimalist decor and a lovely little mezzanine, plus a variety of delicious quiches, omelettes and salads for €6–7. The art on display is mostly local. Mon–Fri 10.30am–4pm, Sat noon–5pm. Prémétro Bourse.

**Bij den Boer** quai aux Briques 60 ☎02 512 61 22. Good old neighbourhood café–restaurant serving up a wide range of tasty seafood with main courses averaging around €20–30 – less for the daily specials. Mon-Sat noon–3pm & 6–11pm. Métro Ste Catherine.

**Bonsoir Clara** rue Antoine Dansaert 22 ☎02 502 09 90. Moody, atmospheric lighting, geometrically mirrored walls and smooth jazz-meets-house background music make this one of the city's chicest restaurants. The menu is full of Mediterranean, French and Belgian classics rendered in full *nouvelle* style. Main courses average €20. Reservations recommended. Mon-Fri noon–2.30pm & daily 7–11.30pm. Prémétro Bourse.

**Eetcafé de Markten** place du Vieux Marché aux Grains. Vibrant café buzzing with chatter and activity and offering no–nonsense, good quality food at very reasonable prices. Mon–Sat 11am–11pm, Sun 11am–6pm. Métro Ste Catherine.

**Kasbah** rue Antoine Dansaert 20 ☎02 502 40 26. Popular with a youthful, groovy crowd, this Moroccan eatery is famous for its (enormous portions of) couscous and other North African specialities for €12–18. Reservations necessary at the weekend. Daily noon–3pm & 6.30pm–midnight. Prémétro Bourse.

**La Marée** rue de Flandre 99 ☎02 511 00 40. There's another La Marée on rue au Beurre, so don't get confused – this one (the better of the two) is a pocket-sized bistro specializing in fish and mussels. The decor is pretty basic, but the food is creatively made and mains go for around a reasonable €12. Wed–Sat noon–2pm & 6.30–10pm. Closed Mon & Tues. Métro Ste Catherine.

**La Papaye Verte** rue Antoine Dansaert 53. Tasty and inexpensive Thai and Vietnamese food served up in smart, authentically Southeast Asian surroundings. Main courses go from as little as €5, and there's a good range of vegetarian options too. Mon–Sat noon–2.30pm & 6.30–11.30pm,

Sun 6.30–11.30pm; closed for one month in the summer. Prémétro Bourse.

**Le Falstaff** rue Henri Maus 17–23. Long-established café-cum-restaurant much lauded for its charming Art Nouveau decoration. Attracts a mixed bag of tourists, Eurocrats and bourgeois Bruxellois. The food is fairly predictable, but the cakes and tarts are mouthwatering. Daily 10am–1am. Prémétro Bourse.

## Bars

**À la Mort Subite** rue Montagne aux Herbes Potagères 7. Infamous 1920s bar that loaned its name to a popular bottled beer. It occupies a long, narrow room with nicotine-stained walls, long tables and lots of mirrors, and on a good night is inhabited by a dissolute-arty clientele. Mon–Fri 10am–1am, Sat 11am–1am, Sun 1pm–1am. Métro Gare Centrale.

**Au Bon Vieux Temps** rue du Marché-aux-Herbes 12. Tucked away down an alley, this is a small, intimate and wonderfully cosy old bar. It's occupied by a convivial, older (and often very loaded) crew. Daily 1pm–12.30am, Fri & Sat 1pm-2am. Prémétro Bourse.

**La Bécasse** rue de Tabora 11. Down an inconsequential–looking alley, this old-fashioned bar has a sort of community-hall atmosphere and is one of the few places in Belgium to sell authentic Lambic beer, an ancient brew that relies on wild yeast for its fermentation. Avoid the food; no smoking. Mon–Thurs 2pm–midnight, Fri–Sun 2pm–2am. Prémétro Bourse.

**La Fleur en Papier Doré** rue des Alexiens 53. Locals' bar cluttered with antique bygones, its walls covered with oodles of doodles and once (one of) the chosen drinking holes of René Magritte – it's rather like sitting in a great aunt's living room. Sun–Thurs 11am–2am, Fri & Sat 11am–4am. Métro Gare Centrale.

**Le Greenwich** rue des Chartreux 7. Smoky bar patronised by chess and backgammon enthusiasts and selling beer at rock-bottom prices. Daily 11am–1am. Prémétro Bourse.

**Monk** rue Ste Catherine 42. Large and popular bar named after the jazz musician Thelonious Monk – and appropriately a grand piano has pride of place. Unusually for Brussels, the service is at the bar. Mon–Sat 11am–1am, Sun and hols 4pm–1am. Métro Ste Catherine.

**Théâtre de Toone** Impasse Schuddeveld 6. Ancient bar belonging to the Toone puppet theatre that comprises two small rooms, plus a rather unappetising outside terrace. There's a reasonably priced beer list, a modest selection of snacks, and a soundtrack of classical and jazz. There are two

alley–entrances, one on Petite rue des Bouchers, the other on rue du Marché aux Herbes, opposite rue des Harengs. Métro Gare Centrale. Daily noon–11pm.
**Zebra** place St Géry 33–35. This small but trendy bar on the corner of place St Géry attracts a young, fashionable crowd who come for the upbeat atmosphere and groovy music. Sun–Thurs noon–1am, Fri & Sat noon–3am. Prémétro Bourse.

## Listings

**Embassies** Australia, rue Guimard 6 (T02 286 05 00); Canada, avenue de Tervuren 2 (T02 741 06 11); Great Britain, rue d'Arlon 85 (T02 287 62 11); Ireland, rue Wiertz 89–93 (T02 235 66 76); New Zealand, 7th Floor, square de Meeus 1 (T02 512 10 40); South Africa, rue de la Loi 26 (T02 285 44 00); USA, boulevard du Régent 27 (T02 508 21 11).

**Left luggage** At all three main train stations.
**Pharmacies** Agora, rue du Marché aux Herbes 109; Multipharma, rue du Marché aux Poulets 37.
**Post office** First floor, Centre Monnaie, pl de la Monnaie.

# Northern Belgium

The region to the north of Brussels is almost entirely **Flemish-speaking** and possesses a distinctive and vibrant cultural identity, its pancake-flat landscapes punctuated by a string of fine historic cities. These begin with **Antwerp**, a large old port dotted with many reminders of its sixteenth-century golden age. To the west, in Flanders, lie two more fascinating cities – **Ghent** and **Bruges** – which became prosperous during the Middle Ages on the back of the cloth trade. All three cities have great bars and restaurants too.

Belgium's main international **ferry port** is **Zeebrugge**, with ferries from Hull and Rosyth in Britain. Ferries dock out on a mole 2km from the train station, so check with the ferry company to make sure they provide onward bus connections.

## Antwerp

**ANTWERP**, Belgium's second city, fans out from the east bank of the Scheldt about 50km north of Brussels. Many people prefer it to the capital and indeed it does have a denser concentration of things to see, not least some fine churches and distinguished museums – reminders of its auspicious past as centre of a wide trading empire. In recent years, the city has also become the effective capital of Flemish Belgium, acting as a lively cultural centre with a spirited nightlife.

### Arrival, information and transport
Antwerp has two mainline **train stations**, Berchem and Centraal. The latter is the one you want for the city centre. **Centraal Station** is located about 2km east of the main square, the Grote Markt. **Trams** #2 and #15 (direction Linkeroever) run from the Diamant underground tram station beside Centraal Station to the centre; get off at Groenplaats. A flat–rate single fare **ticket** on any part of the city's transport system costs €1; a 24-hour pass (*dagpas*) €3.80. Antwerp's **tourist office** is at Grote Markt 13 (Mon–Sat 9am–5.45pm, Sun 9am–4.45pm; T03 232 01 03 Wwww .visitantwerpen.be).

### Accommodation
Finding **accommodation** is rarely difficult, although there are surprisingly few places in the centre. Many mid-priced and budget establishments are around

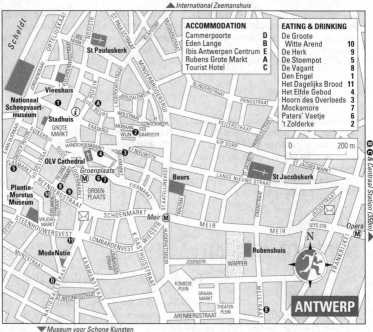

▲ *International Zeemanshuis*

| ACCOMMODATION | |
| --- | --- |
| Cammerpoorte | D |
| Eden Lange | B |
| Ibis Antwerpen Centrum | E |
| Rubens Grote Markt | A |
| Tourist Hotel | C |

| EATING & DRINKING | |
| --- | --- |
| De Groote Witte Arend | 10 |
| De Herk | 9 |
| De Stoempot | 5 |
| De Vagant | 8 |
| Den Engel | 1 |
| Het Dagelijks Brood | 11 |
| Het Elfde Gebod | 4 |
| Hoorn des Overloeds | 3 |
| Mockamore | 7 |
| Paters' Vaetje | 6 |
| 't Zolderke | 2 |

▼ *Museum voor Schone Kunsten*

Centraal Station, where you should exercise caution at night. The tourist office has a comprehensive list of places and will make bookings for you.

## Hostels

**Jeugdherberg Op Sinjoorke** Eric Sasselaan 2 ☎03 238 02 73, ℗03 248 19 32, ⊛www.vjh.be. HI hostel close to the ring road, 5km south of the centre. The 25 rooms have two, four, six, eight or twelve beds, and there's a canteen, self-catering facilities and a laundry room. Tram #2 from Centraal Station to the Bouwcentrum. Dorm beds €14, rooms ❸

**Scoutel** Stoomstraat 3 ☎03 226 46 06, ℗03 232 63 92, ⊛www.scoutel.be. Neat and trim hostel-cum-hotel offering frugal but perfectly adequate singles, doubles, triples and quadruples with breakfast. It's situated about five minutes' walk from Centraal Station: head south down Pelikaanstraat, turn left along Lange Kievitstraat, go through the tunnel and it's the first road on the right. There's no curfew (guests have their own keys), but be sure to check in before 6pm when reception closes. Reservations are advised in the summer. Dorms €25, rooms ❸

## Hotels

**Cammerpoorte** Nationalestraat 38 ☎03 231 97 36, ℗03 226 29 68. Modern, two-star hotel with 39 frugal, en-suite rooms in a building that looks a bit like a car park. The hotel has a mildly forlorn air, but is reasonably priced and has a handy location. ❻

**Eden Lange** Herentalsestraat 25 ☎03 233 06 08, ⊛www.diamond-hotels.com. Chain hotel in the diamond district, whose modern rooms are perfectly adequate but quite plain – and stand by for attack in the mosquito season. Breakfasts are very good. ❻

**Ibis Antwerpen Centrum** Meistraat 39 ☎03 231 88 30, ⊛www.ibishotel.com. Competitively priced chain hotel with routine modern rooms hidden away behind a particularly ghastly concrete exterior but compensated by a decent location, close to the Rubenshuis. ❽

**Rubens Grote Markt** Oude Beurs 29 ☎03 226 95 82, ⊛www.hotelrubensantwerp.be. Arguably the most agreeable hotel in town, the Rubens occupies attractive old premises in a handy downtown location. It's a small hotel (36 rooms) with a relaxing air, and the modern rooms are both comfortable and attractively furnished. ❾

**Tourist Hotel** Pelikaanstraat 20 ☎ 03 232 58
70, ⓕ 03 231 67 07, ⊛ www.demahotels.com.
Straightforward, modern rooms near Centraal

Station – OK for a night or two, though Pelikaanstraat can be noisy. ❹

## The City Centre

At the centre of Antwerp is the spacious **Grote Markt**, where the conspicuous
**Brabo fountain** comprises a haphazard pile of rocks surmounted by a bronze of
Silvius Brabo, the city's first hero, depicted flinging the hand of the giant Antig-
onus – who terrorized passing ships – into the Scheldt. The north side of Grote
Markt is lined with daintily restored sixteenth-century guildhouses and the west
is hogged by the **Stadhuis** (tours Mon–Thurs at 2pm; €1), a handsome structure
completed in 1566 and one of the most important buildings of the Northern
Renaissance.

Southeast of Grote Markt, the **Onze Lieve Vrouwe Cathedral** (Mon–Fri
10am–5pm, Sat 10am–3pm, Sun 1–4pm; €2) is one of the finest Gothic
churches in Europe, dating from the middle of the fifteenth century. Inside,
the seven-aisled nave is breathtaking, if only because of its sense of space, an
impression that's reinforced by the bright, light stonework revealed by a recent
refurbishment. Four early paintings by **Rubens** are displayed here, the most
beautiful of which is the *Descent from the Cross*.

It takes about five minutes to walk southwest from the cathedral to the **Plantin-
Moretus Museum**, on Vrijdagmarkt (Tues–Sun 10am–5pm; €4), which occupies
the grand old mansion of Rubens' father-in-law, the printer Christopher Plantin.
One of Antwerp's most interesting museums, it provides a marvellous insight into
how Plantin and his family conducted their printing business.

From here it's a brief stroll to the **Nationaal Scheepvaartmuseum** (Tues–Sun
10am–5pm; €4), a maritime museum which occupies the Steen, the remaining
gatehouse of what was once an impressive medieval fortress. Inside, the cramped
rooms feature exhibits on inland navigation, shipbuilding and waterfront life,
while the open-air section has a long line of tugs and barges under a rickety corrugated roof. It's a short walk east to the impressively gabled **Vleeshuis** (closed
for refurbishment), built for the guild of butchers in 1503 and distinguished by
its bacon–like brickwork. Just north of here, along Vleeshouwersstraat, **St Pau-
luskerk** (early March to mid–Oct daily 2–5pm; free) is a dignified late-Gothic
church built for the Dominicans in the early sixteenth century. Inside, the airy and
elegant nave is decorated by a series of paintings depicting the Fifteen Mysteries of
the Rosary, including Rubens' exquisite *Scourging at the Pillar* of 1617.

### East of the Grote Markt

Ten minutes' walk east of the Grote Markt is the **Rubenshuis**, Wapper 9 (Tues–
Sun 10am–5pm; €5), the former home and studio of Rubens, now restored as a
very popular museum. Rubens died in 1640 and was buried in **St Jacobskerk**, just
to the north at Lange Nieuwstraat 73 (April–Oct daily except Tues 2–5pm; €2).
The artist and his immediate family are buried in the chapel behind the high altar,
where, in one of his last works, *Our Lady Surrounded by Saints*, he painted himself
as St George, his two wives as Martha and Mary, and his father as St Jerome.

### South of the Grote Markt

South from the Groenplaats along Nationalestraat, is the **ModeNatie** (⊛ www
.modenatie.com), an ambitious complex spread over several floors that showcases
the work of local fashion designers. Part of the building contains **MoMu** (Mode
Museum; Tues–Sun 10am–6pm; €6), which has some great contemporary fashion
displays.

About fifteen minutes' walk south of ModeNatie is the **Museum voor Schone
Kunsten** (Tues–Sat 10am–5pm, Sun 10am–6pm; €5), which has one of the

country's better fine art collections. Its early Flemish section features paintings by Jan van Eyck and Quentin Matsys, while Rubens has two large rooms to himself, in which one very large canvas stands out: the *Adoration of the Magi*, a beautifully human work apparently completed in a fortnight.

## Eating and drinking

Antwerp is an enjoyable and inexpensive place to **eat**, full of informal café-restaurants that excel at combining traditional Flemish, Mediterranean and French cuisines. Several of the best are clustered on Suikerrui and Grote Pieter Potstraat near the Grote Markt, and there's another concentration in the vicinity of Hendrik Conscienceplein. For **fast food**, try the kebab and falafel places on Oude Koornmarkt. Antwerp is also an excellent place to **drink**, the narrow lanes of its centre dotted with small and atmospheric bars.

### Cafés and restaurants

**De Stoempot** Vlasmarkt 12 ☏03 231 36 86. Stoemp is a traditional Flemish dish consisting of puréed meat and vegetables – and this cosy little restaurant is the best place to eat it. Closed Wed.

**Het Dagelijks Brood** Steenhouwersvest 48. Enjoyable and distinctive café where the variety of breads is the main event, served with delicious, wholesome soups and light meals at one long wooden table. No smoking. Daily 7am–7pm.

**Hoorn des Overloeds** Melkmarkt 1 ☏03 232 83 99. Excellent, very unpretentious fish restaurant, good for lunch and dinner; look out for the daily specials. Daily noon–10pm.

**Mockamore** Groenplaats 30. Appealing little café with modern furnishings and a rickety old staircase that somehow manages to climb three floors. Great coffees; good cakes and snacks. Mon–Sat 8.30am–6.30pm, Sun 11am–6pm.

**'t Zolderke** Hoofdkerkstraat 7 ☏03 233 84 27. In an attractively converted old mansion footsteps from Hendrik Conscienceplein, this appealing restaurant offers a mix of tasty Belgian and Mediterranean dishes. Main courses average €15–20. Mon–Fri 6–11pm, Sat & Sun noon–midnight.

### Bars

**De Groote Witte Arend** Reyndersstraat 18. Attractive café-bar set around a courtyard in an old mansion; classical music sets the tone. A good range of beers – including authentic gueuze and kriek – plus pancakes, waffles and ice cream.

**De Herk** Reyndersstraat 33. Tiny bar in ancient premises set around a courtyard, offering a good range of beers and ales – including an excellent Lindemans gueuze – to a twentysomething, modish clientele.

**De Vagant** Reyndersstraat 21. Specialist gin bar serving an extravagant range of Belgian and Dutch jenevers in comfortable, laid-back surroundings.

**Den Engel** Grote Markt 3. Handily located, traditional bar with an easy-going atmosphere in a guildhouse on the main square. It attracts a mixture of businesspeople and locals from the residential enclave round the Vleeshuis.

**Het Elfde Gebod** Torfbrug 10. On one of the tiny squares fronting the north side of the cathedral, this long-established bar has become something of a tourist trap, but it's still worth visiting for the kitsch, nineteenth-century religious statues which cram the interior; don't bother with the food.

**Paters' Vaetje** Blauwmoezelstraat 1. Popular bar – the "Priests' Casket" – in the shadow of the cathedral and offering the widest range of beers and ales in this little area – over 100 at the last count. Old-fashioned main bar downstairs, gallery bar upstairs.

# Ghent (Gent)

The largest town in western Europe during the thirteenth and fourteenth centuries, **GHENT** was once at the heart of the medieval Flemish cloth trade with thousands of city folk producing cloth for the rest of Europe. The trade, however, began to decline in the early sixteenth century and Ghent decayed, until better times finally returned in the nineteenth century when the city was industrialized. It's now the third largest city in Belgium, appealing place with bags of character, great restaurants and a clutch of first-rate historic sights.

The best place to start exploring is at the mainly Gothic **St Baaf's Cathedral**, squeezed into the corner of St Baafsplein (Mon–Sat 8.30am–5/6pm,

Sun 1–5pm; free). Inside, a small chapel (April–Oct Mon–Sat 9.30am–4.45pm, Sun 1–4.30pm; Nov–March Mon–Sat 10.30am–3.45pm, Sun 1–3.30pm; €3) holds Ghent's greatest treasure, the altarpiece of the **Adoration of the Mystic Lamb**, a wonderful early fifteenth-century painting by Jan van Eyck. In addition, the cathedral **crypt** is temporarily being used to display selected medieval paintings from the city's Museum voor Schone Kunsten (Fine Art Museum; due to reopen in 2006), including two exquisite works by Hieronymus Bosch.

On the west side of St Baafsplein lurks the medieval **Lakenhalle** (Cloth Hall), a gloomy hunk of a building one of whose entrances leads to the adjoining **Belfort** (Belfry; mid-March to mid-Nov daily 10am–12.30pm & 2–5.30pm; €3), a much-amended edifice dating from the fourteenth century. A glass-sided lift climbs up to the roof for excellent views over the city centre. From the belfry, it's a few strides north to the **Stadhuis**

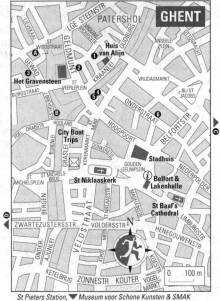

St Pieters Station, ▼ Museum voor Schone Kunsten & SMAK

| ACCOMMODATION | | EATING & DRINKING | |
|---|---|---|---|
| Boatel | C | Avalon | 2 |
| Brooderie | B | Bij den wijzen en den zot | 1 |
| Jeugdherberg | | Brooderie | B |
| De Draecke | | De Tap en de Tepel | 3 |
| HI Hostel | A | Het Waterhuis an de Bierkant | 5 |
| Monasterium | | Pink Flamingos | 6 |
| Poortackere | D | 't Dreupelkot | 4 |

(City Hall; guided tours bookable at the tourist office, May–Oct Mon–Thurs; €3), which possesses a long stone facade that was erected in two distinct phases: the earlier, fancier carving reflects the city in its pomp, but the money ran out and the building had to be completed in a much plainer style later on.

Located a short walk west of the Stadhuis, the **Graslei** forms the eastern side of the old city harbour and is home to a splendid series of medieval **guildhouses**. From here, it's another short hop to the sinister-looking **Het Gravensteen** (daily: April–Sept 9am–6pm; Oct–March 9am–5pm; €6), the Castle of the Counts of Flanders, where a self-guided tour leads through a labyrinth of cold, stark rooms and chambers. Nearby, just to the east, are the narrow cobbled lanes and alleys of the **Patershol**, a pocket-sized district that was formerly home to the city's weavers, but is now Ghent's main restaurant quarter. Here you'll find **Het Huis van Alijn**, Kraanlei 65 (Tues–Sun 11am–5pm; €2.50), a folk museum sited in a series of restored almshouses and boasting a delightful chain of period rooms depicting local life and work in the eighteenth and nineteenth centuries.

Strolling south from the centre along Ghent's main shopping street, **Veldstraat**, it takes about twenty minutes to reach the old casino, parts of which have been turned into **SMAK** (Tues–Sun 10am–6pm; €5; ⊛www.smak.be), a museum of contemporary art that is well-known for its adventurous programme of temporary exhibitions. Opposite, the **Museum voor Schone Kunsten** (Fine Art Museum), at Nicolaas de Liemaeckereplein 3, is closed for refurbishment until 2006.

## Boat trips

Throughout the year, boat trips explore Ghent's inner waterways, departing from the Graslei (April–Oct daily 10am–6pm; Nov–March Sat & Sun 11am–4pm). Trips last forty minutes, cost €5, and leave roughly once every fifteen minutes, though the wait can be longer as boats often only depart when reasonably full.

## Practicalities

Of Ghent's two **train stations**, the one you want is **St Pieters**, about 2km to the south of the city centre. From the covered stops beside St Pieters, **trams** run up to the Korenmarkt, plumb in the centre of town, every few minutes. All trams have destination signs and numbers at the front, but if in doubt check with the driver. The flat-rate fare per journey is €1. The **tourist office** (daily: April–Oct 9.30am–6.30pm; Nov–March 9.30am–4.30pm; ☎09 266 52 32, ⊛www.visitgent .be) is in the centre, in the crypt of the Lakenhalle, on the Botermarkt.

Ghent has several especially enticing **places to stay** and the tourist office publishes a free and comprehensive brochure detailing local accommodation. They also operate a free **hotel booking service**, which is especially useful in July and August, when vacant rooms are thin on the ground. As for **eating out**, Ghent's numerous cafés and restaurants offer the very best of Flemish and French cuisine. The fancier restaurants are concentrated in and around the Patershol, while less expensive spots, including a rash of fast-food joints, cluster the Korenmarkt. Ghent has lots of great **bars** too.

### Accommodation

**Boatel** Voorhoutkaai 44 ☎09 267 10 30 ⊛www .theboatel.com. The two-star Boatel is, as its name implies, a converted boat, an imaginatively refurbished canal barge to be precise. The seven bedrooms are decked out in crisp, modern style and breakfasts, taken on the deck, are first-rate. The boat is moored in one of the city's outer canals, a ten- to fifteen-minute walk east from the centre. ❽

**Brooderie** Jan Breydelstraat 8 ☎09 225 06 23. Three neat and trim little rooms above an appealing little café, handily located in the city centre. The included breakfast is excellent. ❻

**Jeugdherberg De Draecke HI Hostel** St Widosstraat 11 ☎09 233 70 50, ⊛www.vjh.be. Excellent, well-equipped HI hostel in the city centre. There are over a hundred beds, and facilities include lockers, bike rental and a bar. Breakfast is included, and lunch and dinner offered. Advance reservations advised. Dorms €16.30, rooms ❸

**Monasterium Poortackere** Oude Houtlei 56 ☎09 269 22 10 ⊛www.monasterium.be. This unusual one-star hotel-cum-guesthouse occupies a rambling former monastery dating from the nineteenth century. Guests choose between spick and spartan, en-suite rooms in the hotel section (€125); or the more authentic monastic-cell experience in the guest house, either en suite or with

shared facilities (both €100). Breakfast is taken in the old chapter house. ❼

### Cafés and restaurants

**Avalon** Geldmunt 32. This café and tearoom offers a wide range of well-prepared vegetarian food, all served in a tranquil environment. The daily lunchtime specials, at about €8, are particularly popular. Café: Mon–Sat noon–2pm; tearoom: Mon–Fri 2–6pm.

**Bij den wijzen en den zot** Hertogstraat 42 ☎09 223 42 30. One of the best restaurants in the Patershol, serving up delicious Flemish cuisine with more than a dash of French flair – house specialities include eel, cooked in several different ways. Mains around €20. Tues–Sat noon–2pm & 7–10pm.

**Brooderie** Jan Breydelstraat 8. Pleasant and informal café with a health-food slant, offering wholesome breakfasts, lunches, sandwiches and salads (from around €9), plus cakes and coffee. Also offers bed and breakfast (see above). Tues–Sun 8am–6pm.

### Bars

**Pink Flamingos** Onderstraat 55. Weird and wacky little place stuffed with everything kitsch, from plastic statues to awful religious icons. Attracts a groovy crowd, and is a great place for an aperitif or cocktails. Mon–Wed noon–midnight,

Thurs & Fri noon–3am, Sat 2pm–3am, Sun 2pm–midnight.

**De Tap en de Tepel** Gewad 7. This charming candlelit bar ("The Tap and Nipple") has an open fire and a clutter of antique furnishings. Wine is the main deal, served with a good selection of cheeses. Wed–Sat 6pm until late; closed most of Aug.

**Het Waterhuis aan de Bierkant** Groentenmarkt 9. More than a hundred types of beer are available

in this engaging, canal-side bar, which is popular with tourists and locals alike. Be sure to try a delicious local brew called Stropken (literally "noose"). Daily from 11am until late.

**'t Dreupelkot** Groentenmarkt 12. Cosy bar, down a little alley off the Groentenmarkt, specializing in jenever, of which it stocks more than 215 brands, all kept at icy temperatures. Daily: July & Aug 6pm till late; Sept–June 4pm till late.

# Bruges (Brugge)

**BRUGES'** reputation as one of the most perfectly preserved medieval cities in Europe has made it the most popular tourist destination in Belgium. Inevitably, the crowds tend to overwhelm the city's charms, but you would be mad to come to Belgium and miss the place – its intimate, winding streets, woven around a pattern of narrow canals and lined with ancient buildings, live up to even the most inflated hype.

Bruges boomed throughout the Middle Ages, sharing effective control of the Flemish **cloth trade** with its two great rivals, Ghent and Ieper (Ypres), its weavers turning English wool into items of clothing that were exported all over the world. By the end of the fifteenth century, however, Bruges was in decline, partly because of a recession in the cloth trade and partly because the Zwin river – the city's vital link to the North Sea – was silting up. By the 1530s its sea trade had collapsed completely, and Bruges simply withered away. Frozen in time, the city escaped damage in both world wars to emerge the perfect tourist attraction.

## The City

The older sections of Bruges fan out from two central squares, Markt and Burg. **Markt**, edged on three sides by nineteenth-century gabled buildings, is the larger of the two, an impressive open space flanked on its south side by the mighty **Belfort** (Belfry; Tues–Sun 9.30am–5pm; €5), built in the thirteenth century when the town was at its richest and most extravagant. The belfry is attached to the rectangular **Hallen**, a much-restored edifice dating from the thirteenth century, its style and structure modelled on the cloth hall at Ieper. Entry to the Belfry is via the Hallen and inside a tapering staircase leads up to the roof from where there are wonderful views over the city centre.

From the Markt, Breidelstraat leads through to the **Burg**, whose southern half is fringed by the city's finest group of buildings. One of the best is the **Heilig Bloed Basiliek** (Basilica of the Holy Blood; daily: April–Sept 9.30–11.50am & 2–5.50pm; Oct–March Mon, Tues & Thurs–Sun 10–11.50am & 2–3.50pm, Wed 10–11.50am; free), named after a phial of the blood of Christ brought back here from Jerusalem by the Crusaders, and one of the holiest relics in medieval Christendom. The basilica divides into a shadowy Lower Chapel, built to house another relic, that of St Basil, and an Upper Chapel where the phial is stored in a grandiose silver tabernacle. The Holy Blood is still venerated on Ascension Day, when it

## Boat trips and museum visits

Half-hour **boat trips** around the central canals leave every few minutes from a number of jetties south of the Burg; March–Nov daily 10am–6pm; €5.70. For the rest of the year there's a sporadic service on the weekend only. A €15 **combined ticket** for any five of Bruges' central museums is available at all of them, as well as from the tourist office.

is carried through the town in a colourful but solemn procession.

To the left of the basilica, the **Stadhuis** has a beautiful, turreted sandstone facade dating from 1376. Inside, the magnificent **Gothic Hall** (Tues–Sun 9.30am–5pm; €2.50) boasts fancy vault-keys depicting New Testament scenes and romantic paintings commissioned in 1895 to illustrate the history of the town. The price of admission covers entry to the former alderman's mansion, the nearby **Renaissancezaal 't Brugse Vrije** (Tues–Sun 9.30am–12.30pm & 1.30–5pm), also on the square. It has just one exhibit: an enormous sixteenth-century marble and oak chimney piece carved in honour of the ruling Habsburgs, who are flattered by their enormous cod-pieces.

From the arch beside the Stadhuis, Blinde Ezelstraat ("Blind Donkey Street") leads south across the canal to the huddle of picturesque houses crimping the **Huidenvetter-splein**, the old tanners' quarter that now holds some of the busiest drinking and eating places in town. Nearby, the Dijver follows the canal to the **Groeninge Museum**, Dijver 12 (Tues–Sun 9.30am–5pm; €8), which houses a superb sample of Flemish paintings from the fourteenth to twentieth centuries. The best section is the early Flemish work, including several canvases by Jan van Eyck, who lived and worked in Bruges from 1430 until his death eleven years later. There's also work by Hieronymus Bosch, Rogier van der Weyden and Gerard David. Further along the Dijver, at no. 17, the **Gruuthuse Museum** (Tues-Sun 9.30am–5pm; €6) is sited in a rambling fifteenth-century mansion and holds a varied collection of fine and applied art, including intricately carved altar pieces, locally–made tapestries and many different types of antique furniture. Beyond, the **Onze Lieve Vrouwekerk** (Mon-Fri 9.30am–12.30pm & 1.30-5pm, Sat 9.30am–12.30pm & 1.30-4pm, Sun 1.30-5pm; free) is a rambling shambles of a building, but among

**BRUGES**

| ACCOMMODATION | | EATING & DRINKING | |
|---|---|---|---|
| Bauhaus | | B-in | 9 |
| Budget Hotel | D | Den Dyver | 7 |
| De Goezeput | F | Het Brugs Beertje | 3 |
| Europ | C | Het Dreupelhuisje | 6 |
| Jacobs | A | L'Estaminet | 5 |
| Passage Hostel | E | Laurent | 2 |
| Snuffel | | Lokkedize | 8 |
| Backpacker Hostel | B | 't Eekhoetje | 4 |
| | | Wijnbar Est | 1 |

its assorted treasures is a delicate marble *Madonna and Child* by Michelangelo and, in the **chancel** (€2.50) the exquisite Renaissance **mausoleums** of Charles the Bold and his daughter Mary of Burgundy. In the 1970s, archeologists dug beneath the mausoleums. The hole was never filled in and today mirrors give sight of Mary's coffin along with the brick **burial vaults** of several unknown medieval dignitaries. In total, seventeen of these vaults were unearthed and three have been placed in the **Lanchals Chapel**, just across the ambulatory. Plastered with lime mortar, the inside walls of all the vaults sport brightly coloured **grave frescoes**, a specific art that flourished hereabouts from the late thirteenth to the middle of the fifteenth century.

Opposite the church, the large medieval ward of **St Jans Hospitaal** (Tues–Sun 9.30am–5pm; €8) has been turned into a lavish museum celebrating the city's history in general and St John's hospital in particular. In addition, the old hospital chapel displays a small but exquisite collection of paintings by **Hans Memling**. Born near Frankfurt in 1433, Memling spent most of his working life in Bruges, producing serene but warmly coloured and stunningly beautiful paintings. From St Jans, it's a quick stroll down to the **Begijnhof** (daily 9am–6pm or sunset if earlier; free), a circle of whitewashed houses around a tidy green. Nearby, the picturesque **Minnewater** is billed in much publicity hype as the "Lake of Love". The tag certainly gets the canoodlers going, but in fact the lake – more a large pond – started life as a city harbour, its distinctive stone lock house recalling its original function

## Practicalities

Bruges' **train station** adjoins the bus station about 2km southwest of the centre. Local buses leave from outside the train station for the main square, the Markt; flat-rate tickets cost €1. Inside the train station is a **tourist office** (April–Sept Tues–Sat 10am–1pm & 2–6pm; Oct–March Tues–Sat 9.30am–12.30pm & 1–5pm; ☎050 44 86 86), which concentrates on same-day hotel reservations. The **main tourist office** is in the city concert hall, the Concertgebouw, a ten-minute walk west of the Markt at 't Zand 34 (daily 10am–6pm, Thurs till 8pm; ☎050 44 86 86, ⊛www.brugge.be). They also offer a same-day hotel-booking service. Note, however, that you would be well advised to book **accommodation** ahead of time as vacant rooms can get very thin on the ground throughout the summer.

Most of the city's **restaurants** and **cafés** are geared up for tourists, churning out some pretty mediocre stuff. Exceptions, including the places we recommend below, are well worth seeking out. There's also a very good range of **bars**, the pick of which sell a wide range of Belgian beers.

### Hostels

**Passage Hostel** Dweersstraat 26 ☎050 34 02 32, ⊛www.passagebruges.com. The most agreeable hostel in Bruges, accommodating fifty people in ten comparatively comfortable dormitories (all with shared bathrooms). Meals are available at the bar, and guests get a free beer with food. Dorms from €14, €3 extra for breakfast. Run by the same people, the *Passage Hotel* next door offers simple but well-maintained en-suite doubles for just €60, doubles with shared facilities from €40. Advance reservations advised.

**Snuffel Backpacker Hostel** Ezelstraat 47–49 ☎050 33 31 33, ⊛www.snuffle.be. Well-run hostel to the west of the centre with four- to twelve-bed dorms and a cosy, laid-back bar which stays open till late. Rooms and bathrooms have recently been decorated in lively contemporary style by local artists and art students. Bikes are available for rent, and there are regular BBQs in summer. Reservations recommended April–Sept. Dorm beds from €13.

### Hotels

**Bauhaus Budget Hotel** Langestraat 133 ☎050 34 10 93, ⊛www.bauhaus.be. Twenty rooms with shared facilities, plus one en suite. Don't expect too much in the way of creature comforts, but the atmosphere is usually agreeable and the clientele friendly. ➍

**De Goezeput** Goezeputstraat 29 ☎050 34 26 94, ☎050 34 20 13. Set in a charming location on a quiet street near the cathedral, this outstanding two-star hotel occupies an immaculately refurbished eighteenth-century convent complete with wooden beams and oodles of antiques. ⑤

**Europ** Augustijnenrei 18 ☎050 33 79 75, ⓦwww .hoteleurop.com. Two-star in a dignified late nineteenth-century town house overlooking a canal. It's a pleasant place to stay, even if the public areas are somewhat frumpy and the modern bedrooms are a little spartan. ⑥

**Jacobs** Baliestraat 1 ☎050 33 98 31, ⓦwww .hoteljacobs.be. Creatively modernized old brick building, a ten-minute walk to the northeast of the Markt. The 23 rooms are decorated in brisk modern style, though some are a tad small. ⑥

### Cafés and restaurants

**Den Dyver** Dijver 5 ☎050 33 60 69. Top-flight restaurant specializing in traditional Flemish dishes cooked in beer – the quail and rabbit are magnificent, though the seafood runs them close. The decor is plush and antique, and the only real negative is the muzak. Reservations advised. Mains around €25. Daily noon–2pm & 6.30–9pm, closed Wed & Thurs lunch.

**Laurent** Steenstraat 79c. Cheap and cheerful café-restaurant metres from the cathedral. No points for decor or atmosphere, but the snacks are filling and fresh and the pancakes first-rate. Daily 9am–5.30pm.

**Lokkedize** Korte Vuldersstraat 33 ☎050 33 44 50. Attracting a youthful crowd, this café-bar – all subdued lighting, fresh flowers and jazz music – serves up a good line in Mediterranean food, with main courses averaging around €9 and bar snacks from €4. Wed & Thurs 7pm–midnight, Fri & Sat 6pm–1am, Sun 6pm–midnight.

**'t Eekhoetje** Eekhoutstraat 3 ☎050 34 89 79.

Bright and airy tearoom, with a small courtyard, whose efficient and friendly staff serve a good selection of tasty snacks and light meals such as omelettes, pasta and toasties. Daily except Wed 7.30am–7.30pm.

### Bars

**B-in** Mariastraat 38 ⓦwww.b-in.be. The coolest place in town, this recently opened bar-club is kitted out with eye-grabbing coloured fluorescent tubes. Guest DJs play funky, uplifting house, and there are reasonably priced drinks and cocktails. Gets going about 11pm. Free entry. Daily except Tues 10am–3am, Fri & Sat until 5am.

**Het Brugs Beertje** Kemelstraat 5. This small and friendly speciality beer bar claims a stock of three hundred beers, which aficionados reckon is one of the best selections in Belgium, and there are tasty snacks too, such as cheeses and salad. Popular with backpackers. Daily except Wed 4pm–1am.

**Het Dreupelhuisje** Kemelstraat 9. Tiny, laid-back and eminently agreeable bar specializing in jenever and advocaat, of which it has an outstanding range. Daily except Tues 6pm–2am.

**L'Estaminet** Park 5. Groovy neighbourhood café-bar with a relaxed feel and a diverse and cosmopolitan clientele. Rickety furniture both inside and on the large outside terrace adds to the flavour of the place, as does the world music backtrack, and there's a first-rate beer menu. Daily except Thursday 11.30am–1am or later.

**Wijnbar Est** Noordzandstraat 34 ☎050 33 38 39. The best wine bar in town, with a friendly and relaxed atmosphere, an extensive cellar and over twenty-five different wines available by the glass every day. There's live jazz, blues and folk music every Sunday from 8pm. Mon, Thurs & Sun 5pm till late, Fri & Sat 3pm–1am.

# Southern Belgium

South of Brussels lies **Wallonia**, French-speaking Belgium, where a belt of heavy industry interrupts the rolling farmland that itself precedes the high wooded hills of the **Ardennes**. The latter spreads over three provinces – Namur in the west, Luxembourg in the south and Liège in the east – and is a great place for hiking and canoeing. The best gateway town for the Ardennes is the lively provincial centre of **Namur**, an hour from Brussels by train.

## Namur

**NAMUR** is a pleasant and appealing, medium–sized town, whose antique centre is dotted with elegant, eighteenth-century mansions. It also possesses a number of first-rate restaurants and a lively bar scene, lent vigour by its university students.

Namur occupies an important strategic location, straddling the confluence of the rivers Sambre and Meuse, the main result being the massive, rambling **Citadel** (late March to Oct daily 11am–6pm; €6), which rolls along the top of the steep bluff overlooking the south bank of the Sambre. Its nooks and crannies can take a couple of days to explore, though you can speed things up by using the tourist mini-train, which costs a couple of euros and runs every half-hour.

Cutting through the old town centre is **rue de l'Ange** and its continuation **rue de Fer**, which together comprise the main shopping street. A few metres east of here, the **Trésor du Prieuré d'Oignies**, rue Julie Billiart 17 (Treasury of the Oignies Priory; Tues–Sat 10am–noon & 2–5pm, Sun 2–5pm; €1.50), is Namur's best – and smallest – museum. Located in a nunnery, it holds a spellbinding collection of reliquaries and devotional pieces created by local craftsman Hugo d'Oignies in the first half of the thirteenth century; the nuns give the guided tour in English.

## Practicalities

Namur's **train** and **bus stations** are on the northern edge of the city centre on place de la Station. The **tourist office** is just a few steps away on square Léopold, at the north end of rue de Fer (daily 9.30am–6pm; ☏081 24 64 49, ⊛www.ville .namur.be). They give advice on cycling, walking and canoeing in the Ardennes and will also arrange accommodation. There's also a seasonal **tourist information chalet** (April–Oct daily 9.30am–6pm), ten minutes' walk away, over the Sambre bridge on the other side of the centre. Namur has several competitively priced **hotels** and a **hostel** and there's also an excellent selection of **restaurants** and **bars**, many of them clustered in the quaint, pedestrianized squares just west of rue de l'Ange, on and around place Marché-aux-Légumes and neighbouring place Chanoine Descamps.

### Accommodation

**Auberge de Jeunesse** ave Félicien Rops 8 ☏081 22 36 88, ⊛www.laj.be. This 100-bed hostel occupies a big old house on the southern edge of town on the banks of the Meuse past the casino. There's no lock-out and the hostel has a kitchen, laundry and self-service restaurant. It's 3km from the train station; buses #3 or #4 run here from the centre. Dorms €14.30, rooms ③

**Beauregard** ave Baron de Moreau 1 ☏081 23 00 28, ⊛www.diamond-hotels.com. Part of Namur's casino complex, this hotel has attractive, large and modern rooms, some with a river-view and balcony. It's a ten-minute walk south of the centre, on the banks of the Meuse below the citadel. An excellent breakfast is included in the price. ④

**Ibis Namur Centre** rue du Premier Lanciers 10 ☏081 25 75 40, ⊛www.ibishotel.com. Straightforward, mid-range chain hotel in a handy downtown location and with comfortable, modern rooms. ⑤

**Les Tanneurs** rue des Tanneries 13 ☏081 24 00 24, ⊛www.tanneurs.com. Extremely comfortable four-star hotel in a lavishly and imaginatively renovated old brick mansion, located down a quiet alley close to the town centre. Highly recommended. ③

### Restaurants

**La Bonne Fourchette** rue Notre Dame 112 ☏081 23 15 36. Pocket-sized, informal and family-run restaurant down below the citadel on the way to the casino. A little off the beaten track, so the prices are reasonable and the food is delicious. Closed Wed.

**Le Moulin à Poivre** rue Bas de la Place 19 ☏081 23 11 20. Cosy little restaurant offering tasty French food from premises just off place d'Armes. Main courses from €15. Mon–Sat noon–2.30pm & Tues–Sat 6.30–10.30pm.

**Le Temps des Cerises** rue des Brasseurs 22 ☏081 22 53 26. Intimate little restaurant offering a quality menu of dishes prepared in the French manner. Main courses average €20. Wed–Fri noon–2.30pm & Wed–Sat 7–10pm.

### Bars

**Le Chapitre** rue du Séminaire 4. Unassuming, sedate little bar behind the cathedral, with an extensive beer list.

**Henry's Bar** pl St Aubain 3. Right by the cathedral, this is a big loud brasserie in the best tradition.

**Le Monde à L'Envers** rue Lelièvre 28. Lively, fashionable bar just up from the cathedral, that's a favourite spot for university students.

**Piano Bar** pl Marché-aux-Légumes. One of Namur's most popular bars. Live jazz Fri & Sat from 10pm.

# Luxembourg

Some 100km southeast of Namur, across the border from the Belgian province of Luxembourg, the **Grand Duchy of Luxembourg** is one of Europe's smallest sovereign states, a tiny principality with a population of around 450,000. Many travellers write the duchy off as a dull and expensive financial centre, but this is a mistake. **Luxembourg City**, the country's agreeable and dramatically sited capital, is well worth one or two nights' stay, and from here it's a short hop – by road, rail or bus – to the forested **hills** of the Ardennes that fill out the northern part of the country. Every native speaks the indigenous language, Letzebuergesch – a dialect of German that sounds a bit like Dutch – but most also speak French and German and many speak English too.

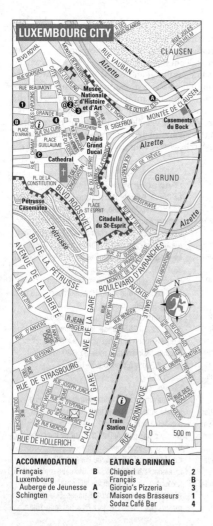

## Luxembourg City

**LUXEMBOURG CITY** is one of the most spectacularly sited capitals in Europe. The valleys of the rivers Alzette and Pétrusse, which meet here, cut a green swath through the city, their deep canyons once key to the city's defences, but now providing a beautiful setting. A tiny place, Luxembourg City divides into three distinct sections. The **old town**, on the northern side of the Pétrusse valley, is not noticeably ancient, but is very appealing and its tight grid of streets holds most of the city's sights. On the opposite side of the Pétrusse is the **modern city** – less attractive and of interest only for its train station and cheap hotels. The **valleys** themselves, far below and most easily accessible by lift from place St-Esprit, are a curious mixture of houses, allotments and parkland, banking steeply up to the massive bastions that secure the old town.

The **old town** focuses on two squares, the more important of which is **place d'Armes**, fringed with cafés and restaurants. To the north lie the city's principal shops, mainly along **Grande Rue**, while on the southern side a small alley cuts through to the larger **place Guillaume**, the venue of Luxembourg's main general market (Wed & Fri am). Nearby, on Marché aux Poissons, a group of patrician mansions holds the city's largest and choicest museum, the **Musée National d'Histoire et d'Art** (Tues–Sun 10am–5pm; €5), where there's an enjoyable sample of fifteenth- and sixteenth–century Dutch and Flemish paintings. East of the museum lie the **Casements du Bock** (daily March–Oct 10am–5pm; €1.75), underground fortifications built by the Spaniards in the eighteenth century. The city occupies an ideal defensive position and its defences were reinforced on many occasions – hence the massive bastions and subterranean artillery galleries that survive today. These particular casements are the most diverting to visit – though several others are also open throughout the summer – and afterwards you can follow the dramatic **chemin de la Corniche**, which tracks along the side of the cliff with great views of the slate-roofed houses of **Grund** down below. It leads to the gigantic **Citadelle du St-Esprit**, whose top has been levelled off and partly turned into a leafy park.

## Arrival and information

The **train station**, fifteen minutes' walk south of the old town, is the hub of all the city's **bus** lines and close to many of the cheapest (but plainest) hotels. There is a branch of the **national tourist office** inside the train station (June to mid–Sept Mon–Sat 9am–6.30pm, Sun 9am–12.30pm & 2–6pm; mid–Sept to May daily 9am–12.30pm & 1.45–6pm; ☎42 82 82 20; ⊛www.ont.lu). It sells the **Luxembourg Card**, which entitles you to unlimited use of public transport throughout the Grand Duchy and admission to selected museums and attractions from Easter to October (1/2/3 days for €9/16/22). The **city tourist office** is on place d'Armes (Mon–Sat 9am–6/7pm, Sun 10am–6pm; ☎22 28 09, ⊛www.lcto.lu). **Walking** is the best way of getting around.

## Accommodation, eating and drinking

Most **hotels** are clustered near the train station, which is the least interesting part of town. You're much better off staying in the old town and won't necessarily pay more to do so, though you're limited to just a handful of places. The old town is crowded with inexpensive **cafés** and **restaurants**. French cuisine is popular here, but traditional Luxembourg dishes are found on many menus too, mostly meaty affairs such as neck of pork with broad beans (*judd mat gaardebounen*) or black sausage (*blutwurst*). Keep an eye out also for *gromperenkichelchen* (potato cakes usually served with apple sauce) – and, in winter, stalls and cafés selling *glühwein* (mulled wine). As for **drinking**, there's a lively bar scene in the old town and Grund.

### Hostel
**Luxembourg Auberge de Jeunesse** rue du Fort Olisy 2 ☎22 68 89, ⊛www.youthhostels.lu. This barracks-like HI hostel is 3km northeast of the station on the edge of the old town in the Alzette Valley. It has a laundry and cooking facilities and breakfast is included. Dorm beds €16.30.

### Hotels
**Francais** place d'Armes 14 ☎47 45 34, ⊛www.hotelfrancais.lu. This attractive place has smart and spotless rooms furnished in crisp modern style. Great location, too, on the old town's main square, though light sleepers might do well to avoid the rooms at the front. ❽
**Schintgen** rue Notre Dame 6 ☎22 28 40, ✉schintgen@pt.lu. Bang in the middle of the old

town, this simple, unassuming hotel is short on accessories, but is reasonably priced. ❻

### Cafés and restaurants
**Francais** place d'Armes14. The pavement café of the *Hotel Francais* (see above) offers tasty salads and a wide-ranging menu including several Luxembourg favourites. Excellent–value daily specials.
**Giorgio's Pizzeria** rue du Nord 11. A sociable and eminently fashionable place tucked away off côte d'Eich in the old town. Mon–Sat 11.45am–2.30pm & 6.30–11pm.
**Maison des Brasseurs** Grande Rue 48 ☎47 13 71. On a modern shopping street just to the north of place d'Armes, this long-established and smartly decorated restaurant sells delicious

Luxembourg dishes. Sauerkraut is the house speciality. Mon–Sat 11am–10pm.

## Bars

**Chiggeri** rue du Nord 15. Groovy bar–cum–café

in the old town that has a great atmosphere, funky decor and a mixed straight and gay clientele.
**Sodaz Café Bar** rue de la Boucherie 16. Small and crowded bar serving cocktails accompanied by soul and rock music.

## Listings

**Bike rental** rue Bisserwee 8, Grund ☏ 496 23 83. Easter to Oct daily 10am–noon & 1–8pm; advance booking advised.
**Internet** Chiggeri, rue du Nord 15 ☏ 22 82 36, ⊛ www.chiggeri.lu.
**Laundry** Quick-Wash, rue de Strasbourg 31 ☏ 48 78 33.

**Left luggage** At the train station.
**Pharmacies** Goedert, pl d'Armes 5; Mortier, ave de la Gare 11.
**Post office** rue Aldringen 25 (Mon–Fri 7am–7pm, Sat 7am–5pm).

# Travel details

For information on ferry crossings, see Basics, p.56.

### Trains

**Antwerp** to: Bruges (hourly; 1hr 20min); Brussels (every 30min; 40min); Ghent (every 30min; 50min); Ostend (hourly; 1hr 40min).
**Bruges** to: Antwerp (hourly; 1hr 20min); Brussels (every 30min; 1hr); Ostend (every 20min; 15min); Zeebrugge (hourly; 15min).
**Brussels** to: Antwerp (every 30min; 40min); Bruges (every 30min; 1hr); Ghent (every 30min; 40min); Luxembourg City (every 2hr; 2hr 30min);

Namur (hourly; 50min); Ostend (hourly; 1hr 20min).
**Ghent** to: Antwerp (every 30min; 50min); Bruges (every 20min; 25min); Brussels (every 30min; 40min); Ostend (every 30min; 50min).
**Luxembourg City** to: Brussels (hourly; 2hr 30min); Namur (hourly; 1hr 40min).
**Namur** to: Brussels (hourly; 50min); Luxembourg City (hourly; 1hr 40min).
**Ostend** to: Antwerp (hourly; 1hr 40min); Bruges (every 20min; 15min); Brussels (hourly; 1hr 20min); Ghent (every 30min; 50min).

# Britain

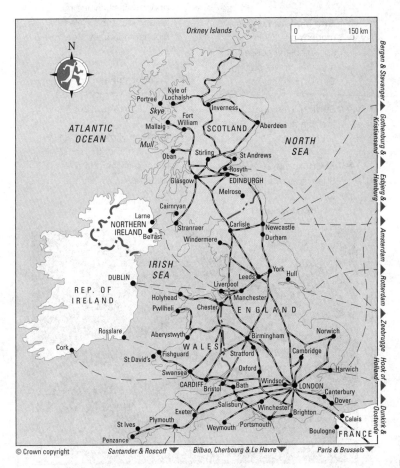

Orkney Islands

N

0        150 km

ATLANTIC
OCEAN

Portree  Kyle of
Lochalsh
Skye  Inverness
Mallaig  Fort
William  SCOTLAND  Aberdeen
Mull  NORTH
Oban  Stirling  St Andrews  SEA
Rosyth
Glasgow  EDINBURGH
Melrose
Cairnryan
Larne
NORTHERN
IRELAND  Stranraer  Carlisle  Newcastle
Belfast  Windermere  Durham

IRISH
SEA

DUBLIN

REP. OF
IRELAND  Leeds  York  Hull
Holyhead  Liverpool
Pwllheli  Chester  Manchester
E N G L A N D
Aberystwyth  Norwich
Rosslare  W A L E S  Birmingham
Cork  Stratford  Cambridge
St David's  Fishguard  Oxford  Harwich
Swansea  Windsor
CARDIFF  Bath  LONDON
Bristol  Canterbury
Salisbury  Winchester  Dover
Exeter  Brighton
St Ives  Plymouth  Weymouth  Portsmouth  Calais
Penzance  Boulogne
FRANCE

Bergen & Stavanger ▶
Gothenburg & Kristiansand ▶
Esbjerg & Hamburg ▶
Amsterdam ▶ Rotterdam ▶ Zeebrugge ▶
Hook of Holland ▶
Dunkirk & Oostende ▶

© Crown copyright    Santander & Roscoff ▼    Bilbao, Cherbourg & Le Havre ▼    Paris & Brussels ▼

# Britain highlights

✳ **A pint down the pub**
In a late-night bar or an
ancient coaching inn, a
pint is an essential part
of any visit to Britain.
See p.147

✳ **Tate Modern** London's
modern-art gallery,
spectacularly housed in
a former power station.
See p.159

✳ **Surfing, Newquay** Test
the Atlantic rollers. See
p.179

✳ **Stratford-upon-Avon**
Shakespeare's home
town and host to the
world-renowned Royal

Shakespeare Company.
See p.182

✳ **Snowdonia** Craggy
Welsh range that offers
hiking and climbing
opportunities, including
an ascent of the Wales's
highest mountain. See
p.204

✳ **Edinburgh Festival**
The world's biggest arts
festival. See p.212

✳ **Scottish Highlands**
Dramatic, moody land-
scapes in one of the last
wildernesses in Europe.
p.219

△ London pub

# Introduction and basics

The single most important thing to remember when travelling around Britain* is that you're visiting not one country, but three: England, Wales and Scotland. That means contending with three capital cities (London, Cardiff and Edinburgh) and three sets of national identity – not to mention the myriad of accent shifts as you move between them.

England remains the dominant and most urbanized member of the British partnership, but crossing the border into predominantly rural **Wales** brings you into an unmistakably Celtic land, while in **Scotland** the presence of a profoundly non-English worldview is striking.

London is a ceaselessly entertaining city, and is the one place that features on everyone's itinerary. **Brighton** and **Canterbury** offer contrasting diversions – the former an appealing seaside resort, the latter one of Britain's finest medieval cities. The southwest of England has the rugged moorlands of **Devon** and the rocky coastline of **Cornwall**, and the historic spa city of **Bath**. The chief attractions of central England are the university cities of **Oxford** and **Cambridge**, and Shakespeare's hometown, **Stratford-upon-Avon**. Further north, the former industrial cities of **Manchester**, **Liverpool** and **Newcastle** are lively, rejuvenated places, and **York** has splendid historical treasures, but the landscape is again the real magnet, especially the uplands of the **Lake District**. For true wilderness, head to the **Welsh mountains** or **Scottish Highlands**. The finest of Scotland's lochs, glens and peaks, and the magnificent scenery of the west coast islands, can be reached easily from the contrasting cities of **Glasgow** and **Edinburgh** – the latter perhaps Britain's most attractive urban landscape.

## Information & maps

Tourist information centres (TICs) exist in virtually every British town, offering a basic range of maps and information. **National Parks** (ⓦ www.anpa.gov.uk) also have their own information centres, which are better for guidance on outdoor pursuits. The most comprehensive series of maps is produced by the **Ordnance Survey** (ⓦwww .ordnancesurvey.co.uk).

## Money and banks

The **pound** (£) sterling, divided into 100 pence, remains the national currency. There are coins of 1p, 2p, 5p, 10p, 20p, 50p, £1 and £2; and notes of £5, £10, £20 and £50; notes issued by Scottish banks are legal tender but often not accepted south of the border. At the time of writing, £1 was worth €1.45 and $1.75. Normal **banking hours** are Mon–Fri 9.30am–4.30pm, but some branches open on Saturday. **ATMs** accept a wide range of debit and credit cards. Shops, hotels, restaurants and most other places readily accept **credit cards** for payment.

## Communications

**Post offices** open Mon–Fri 9am–5.30pm, and some open on Sat 9am–12.30/1pm.

---

### Britain on the net

ⓦ **www.visitbritain.com** Tourist board site with links to regional sites.

ⓦ **www.pti.org.uk** Information on public transport.

ⓦ **www.backpackers.co.uk** The low-down on independent hostels.

ⓦ **www.knowhere.co.uk** Irreverent local knowledge.

ⓦ**www.multimap.com** Town plans and area maps.

"Britain" is a geographical term, referring to the largest of the British Isles. "United Kingdom" is a political term, referring to a state comprising England, Scotland, Wales and Northern Ireland. Northern Ireland is covered with the rest of the island of Ireland in Chapter 15.

Most **public phones** are operated by BT, and take all coins from 10p upwards (minimum charge 20p), as well as £5, £10 or £20 phonecards, available from post offices and newsagents. An increasing number accept credit cards too. Newsagents can sell you good-value cards from other phone companies for making international calls. Domestic calls are cheapest from 6pm to 8am and at weekends. For the operator, call ☎ 100 (domestic) or ☎ 155 (international); of several directory enquiry lines, BT's is ☎ 118500. Internet cafés are common, and you'll also find access at some hostels and some public phones. Prices vary, but £1 should be enough for you to reply to your email.

# Getting around

Most places are still accessible by train and/or coach (as long-distance buses are known), though costs are among the highest in Europe. **Traveline** (daily 7am–9pm; ☎ 0870/608 2608, ✆ www.traveline.org .uk) is a national service that can advise on trains, coaches, ferries and, most usefully, local buses.

## Trains

The British **train** network has suffered chronic under-investment for decades, and **fares** are some of the highest in Europe. Cheap deals do exist, but the bafflingly complicated pricing system makes them hard to find. Generally speaking, avoid rush hours (especially Fri eve), and book your ticket as far in advance as you can to get the best deals. Always ask the person selling you your ticket to specify the cheapest options open to you. If you're travelling on routes between major cities at busy times, especially during public holidays or around

Christmas, you should book a seat. Reservations are usually free if made at the same time as ticket purchase. **National Rail** (☎ 0845/748 4950, ✆ www.nationalrail .co.uk) has details of all train services; or you can buy online at ✆ www.thetrainline. com. Britain is in **InterRail** Zone A; **Eurail** passes aren't valid; for details of other passes, see p.47.

## Coaches and buses

The **bus** services run by National Express (☎ 0870/580 8080, ✆ www.nationalexpress .com) duplicate many intercity rail routes, very often at half the price or less. If you're a student, under 26 or over 50 you can buy a National Express Coachcard (£10), which gives up to thirty percent off standard fares. Their BritXplorer Pass offers unlimited travel for visitors at £79 for seven days, £139 for two weeks and £219 for a month. Both the Coachcard and Pass are valid on National Express through-routes to Scotland, but not on services within Scotland itself. These are provided by the sister company **Scottish Citylink** (☎ 0870/550 5050, ✆ www .citylink.co.uk), which has its own Explorer Pass for three consecutive days (£39), five days in ten (£62) or eight days in sixteen (£85); Euro under-26 youth cardholders can save up to 20 percent on standard fares.

Easy Bus (✆ www.easybus.co.uk) offers services for as low as £1, while **Megabus** (✆ www.megabus.com/) has a range of popular city-to-city journeys, again starting at £1. **Local bus services** are run by a bewildering array of companies, but there are very few rural areas which aren't served by at least the occasional minibus.

## Minibus and bus tours

Many travellers prefer the flexibility of touring Britain on "jump-on-jump-off" **minibus** or **special tours**. Road Trip (☎ 0845/200 6791, ✆ www.roadtrip.co.uk) offers fully inclusive budget bus tours with flexible itineraries.

Similar companies operate out of Edinburgh focusing on **Scotland** including Haggis (☎ 0131/557 9393, ✆ www.haggis .com), Macbackpackers (☎ 0131/558 9900, ✆ www.macbackpackers.com), and Wild in Scotland (☎ 0131/478 6500, ✆ www.wild-in -scotland.com).

# Accommodation

**Accommodation** in Britain is expensive. Top-range hotels are often superb and budget travellers are well catered for with numerous hostels, but the standard of many B&Bs, guesthouses and simple hotels is often disappointing. It's a good idea to reserve in advance, especially for accommodation in towns and cities. Many tourist offices will book rooms for you, expect to pay a small fee for this, as well as putting down a ten-percent deposit on your first night's stay.

In tourist cities it's hard to find a double in a **hotel** for less than £50 a night but budget accommodation in the form of **guesthouses** and **B&Bs** – often a comfortable room in a family home, plus a substantial breakfast – starts at around £20 a head, more in London).

Britain has an extensive network of **HI hostels** (Ⓦ www.yha.org.uk). In Scotland (Ⓦ www.syha.org.uk), a bed for the night can cost as little as £5, except in the cities, where you might pay more than twice that. In England and Wales charges start at around £10. **Privately run hostels** are generally of a comparable standard and can be several pounds cheaper. There are more than 750 official **campsites** in Britain, charging from around £5 per tent per night. In the countryside farmers will often let you camp in a field if you ask, sometimes charging a couple of pounds. Camping rough is illegal in designated parkland and nature reserves.

# Food and drink

Though the British still tend to regard eating as a functional necessity rather than a pleasure, things are getting better. "Modern British" cuisine – in effect anything inventive – has been at the core of this change, though wherever you go you'll find places serving Indian, Italian and Chinese food. This said, the pub is still the centre of British social life.

## Food

In many B&Bs you'll be offered an **"English breakfast"** – basically sausage, bacon and fried eggs – although most places will give

you the option of cereal, toast and fruit as well. Every major town will have upmarket restaurants, but the quintessential British meal is **fish and chips**. However, the once ubiquitous fish-and-chip shop ("chippy") is now outnumbered on Britain's high streets by kebab and burger joints. Less threatened is the so-called "greasy spoon", generally a down-at-heel diner where the average menu will include variations on sausages, fried eggs, bacon and chips.

Many **pubs** also serve food including steak-and-kidney pie, shepherd's pie (minced lamb topped with potato), chops or steaks, accompanied by potatoes and veg. **Gastro-pubs** can offer menus to rival any restaurant. There's also an increasing number of **vegetarian** restaurants, especially in the larger towns, but most places – including pubs – will make some attempt to cater for vegetarians.

## Drink

**Drinking** traditionally takes place in the **pub**, where a standard range of draught beers – sold by the pint or half-pint – generates most of the business, although imported bottled beers are also popular. Beers fall into two distinct groups: cold, blond, fizzy **lager** and the very different darker ale, or **bitter**. In England, pubs are generally open Mon–Sat 11am–11pm, Sun noon–10.30pm (though some close daily 3–5.30pm); hours are often longer in Scotland, while Sunday closing is common in Wales.

In Scotland, the national drink is of course **whisky**. The best are the single malts, produced by small distilleries using local spring water.

# Opening hours and holidays

General **shop hours** are Mon–Sat 9am–5.30/6pm, although an increasing number of places in big towns are also open Sun (usually 10am–4pm) and till 7/8pm at least once a week. In England and Wales, **public holidays** ("bank holidays") are: Jan 1, Good Fri, Easter Mon, first Mon and last Mon in May, last Mon in Aug, Christmas Day and

Boxing Day (Dec 25 & 26). In Scotland, Jan 1, Jan 2 & Dec 25 are the only fixed public holidays, otherwise towns are left to pick their own.

# Museums and monuments

Many of Britain's national **museums** are free, but stately homes and monuments are often administered by the state-run **English Heritage** (given as EH in opening times through this chapter; ⓦwww.english -heritage.org.uk) and **Historic Scotland** (HS; ⓦwww.historic-scotland.gov.uk); while in Wales **CADW** (ⓦ www.cadw.wales.gov .uk) owns several dramatic ruins. The annual fee for EH is £36 (£20 if you're under 19 or a student), for HS £34 (£26 if you're a full-time student) or you can get an Explorer pass for access to 74 sites in a week (from £17). CADW's Explorer Pass is £9.50 for 3 days or £15.50 for 7 days. The privately run **National Trust** (NT; ⓦwww.nationaltrust.org .uk) and **National Trust for Scotland** (NTS; ⓦwww.nts.org.uk) also run a large number of gardens and stately homes nationwide; annual membership of NT/NTS costs £38/£35 (£17.50/£12 for under-26s), and each pass is recognized by the other. The **Great British Heritage Pass**, which covers

sites administered by all the organizations above and many others too, is available from the British Visitor Centre, Lower Regent St, London, and selected tourist information centres (£28/39/52/70 for 4/7/15/30 days; ⓦwww.visitbritain.com for details), as well as worldwide agents.

# Emergencies

**Police** remain approachable and helpful. Tourists aren't a particular target for criminals except in the crowds of the big cities, where you should be on your guard against **pickpockets**. Britain's bigger conurbations all contain inner-city areas where you may feel uneasy after dark, but these are usually away from tourist sights. **Pharmacists** dispense only a limited range of drugs without a doctor's prescription. Most are open standard shop hours, though in large towns some may stay open as late as 10pm. Local newspapers carry lists of late-opening pharmacies. For complaints that require immediate attention, go to the **accident and emergency** (A&E) department of the local hospital.

# London

With a population of just under eight million, **LONDON** is Europe's biggest city, spreading over an area of more than 600 square miles from its core on the River Thames. This is where the country's news and money are made, and if Londoners' sense of superiority causes some resentment in the regions, it's undeniable that the city has a unique aura of excitement and success. However, all this comes at a price; with high accommodation and transport costs, this is one of the most expensive cities in the world.

London's world-class museums and **galleries** – from the British Museum to Tate Modern – have been reinvented in recent years and the vast majority are free of charge. You could spend days just shopping in the city's famous department stores and the offbeat weekend **markets**. The music, **clubs** and gay scene too are second to none, while **pubs** and restaurants offer an array of world cuisine suited to any pocket. For a little respite, the city's "green lungs" are some of the best in the country. Central **parks** including Hyde Park and St James's Park are worth a stroll, as are the wilds of Hampstead Heath, Greenwich and Kew.

Founded by the **Romans** as the town of Londinium on the north bank of the Thames soon after invading Britain in 43 AD, the city didn't really begin until the eleventh century, when the last successful invader of Britain, **William of Normandy**, became in 1066 the first king of England to be crowned in Westminster Abbey. Subsequent monarchs left their imprint, but many of the city's finest structures were destroyed in a few days in 1666, when the **Great Fire of London** razed over thirteen thousand houses and nearly ninety churches. **Christopher Wren** was commissioned to replace much of the lost architecture, and rose to the challenge by designing such masterpieces as St Paul's Cathedral. Unfortunately, only a portion of the post-Fire splendours have survived, due partly to the bombing raids of the Blitz in World War II and partly to some equally disfiguring postwar development. However, recent years have seen a spate of new development and London's skyline has been enhanced by projects like the London Eye and the "Gherkin".

## Arrival and orientation

Flying into London, you'll arrive at one of the capital's five **international airports**: Heathrow, Gatwick or Stansted (@www.baa.com), Luton (@www.london-luton .co.uk) or City (@www.londoncityairport.com). From **Heathrow**, fifteen miles west, the Piccadilly Line underground runs to central London in about an hour (£3.80), or there are Heathrow Express trains to Paddington Station (every 15min; 15min; £14). National Express also runs coach services to Victoria Coach Station (every 30min; 45min; £10), while Airbus A2 stops at several central destinations before terminating at Euston (every 30min; 1hr 30min; £6 single). After midnight, night bus #N9 runs to Trafalgar Square (every 30min; 55min; £1.20). There's also a range of airport-to-hotel shuttle-buses run by Hotel Link (℡01293/532244, @www.hotelink.co.uk). **Gatwick**, thirty miles south, is connected by several train companies: the Gatwick Express speeds to Victoria Station (every 15min; 30min; £12), although South Central trains on the same route are cheaper (every 15min; 40min; £8), and Thameslink trains run to Blackfriars and King's Cross (every 15min; 45min; around £10). **Stansted**, 34 miles northeast, is served by Stansted Express trains to Liverpool Street Station (every 15/30min; 45min; £14.50 single); hop off at Tottenham Hale to join the Victoria line. National Express services A6 and A7 run to Victoria Coach Station (every 20/30min; 1hr 30min; £10), as does the Terravision Express Shuttle (@www.lowcostcoach.com; every 30min; £8.50). From **Luton**, 37 miles north, free buses shuttle to Luton Airport Parkway station, from where there are Thameslink trains to King's Cross and Blackfriars stations and Midland Mainline trains to St Pancras Station (every 15min; 30min; £11). Green

Line bus #757 runs from the airport terminal into central London (every 30min; 1hr 15min; £9). From **London City**, ten miles east, there's a green shuttle bus (£3) to Canning Town underground station, or a blue shuttle bus to Liverpool Street Station (£6.50). Eurostar trains from Paris or Brussels through the Channel Tunnel terminate at Waterloo. **Trains** from the English Channel ports arrive at Victoria, Liverpool Street or Charing Cross stations, while those from elsewhere in Britain come into one of London's numerous mainline termini (most important are Paddington or Waterloo from the west, Euston or King's Cross from the north, and Liverpool Street from the east), all of which have tube stations. **Buses** from around Britain and continental Europe arrive at Victoria Coach Station, 500m walk south of Victoria train station.

## Information

London's flagship **tourist information** centre is the **Britain and London Visitor Centre**, near Piccadilly Circus at 1 Regent St (Mon 9.30am–6.30pm, Tues–Fri 9am–6.30pm, Sat 9am–5pm, Sun 10am–4pm; ⊛www.visitbritain.com), which has multi-lingual staff and Internet facilities, and also acts as a ticket and travel agency. There are other branches at Waterloo International (daily 8.30am–10.30pm), Liverpool Street tube station (daily 8am–6/7pm), and in Victoria Station (Mon–Sat 8/9am–7/9pm, Sun 8am–6.15pm). None of these offices accepts phone queries but Visit London's well-designed website (⊛www.visitlondon.com) is crammed with useful material. The **City Information Centre** (Easter–Sept daily 9.30am–5pm, Oct–March Mon–Fri 9.30am–5pm, Sat 9.30am–12.30pm; ☎020/7332 1456, ⊛www.cityoflondon.gov.uk), St Paul's Churchyard, is another well-run option, opposite St Paul's Cathedral.

## City transport

The **Transport for London (TfL) information** office at Piccadilly Circus tube station (daily 8.45am–6pm; ⊛www.tfl.gov.uk) will provide free transport maps, with other desks at Heathrow Terminals 1, 2 and 3, and Euston, King's Cross, Liverpool Street and Victoria stations. There's also a 24-hour phone line for information on all bus, tube and river-boat services (☎020/7222 1234). The quickest way to get around London is by **Underground** (daily 5.30/7.30am–midnight). Tickets must be bought in advance from the machines or booths in station entrance halls and need to be kept until the end of your journey so that you can leave the station; if you cannot produce a valid ticket on demand, you'll be charged an on-the-spot Penalty Fare of £20. A one-way journey in central Zone 1 costs £2, or you can buy a Carnet of ten tickets for £17. Better value is a **Travelcard**, valid for buses, suburban trains and the tube. Day Travelcards come in two varieties: Off-Peak – which are valid after 9.30am on weekdays and all day during the weekend – and Peak. A Day Travelcard (Off-Peak) costs £4.70 for the central zones 1 and 2, rising to £6 for zones 1–6 (including Heathrow); the Day Travelcard (Peak) starts at £6 for zones 1 and 2.

    **Buses** are a good way to see the city especially from the top of London's famous double deckers. The majority of bus stops outside the centre are request stops so if you don't hold your arm out the bus will drive past. In most of central London – and anywhere indicated with a yellow panel on the bus stop – you need to "pay before you board". If you don't have a Travelcard you will either need to buy a set of six **Bus Saver** tickets (£6) or a **One-Day Bus Pass** (£3) from a newsagents or buy a single ticket (£1.20) from the machine at the bus stop. Show the ticket to the driver on entering. After midnight, **night buses** prefixed with the letter "N" take over; fares remain the same and Travelcards are valid until 4.30am.

    **River-boat** trips on the Thames are a great way to see the city. Westminster Pier, beside Westminster Bridge, Embankment Pier and Waterloo Pier, near the

London Eye, are the main central embarkation points and there are regular sailings to Tower Bridge, Greenwich, Kew and Hampton Court. Timings and services alter frequently so pick up the Thames River Services Booklet from a TfL travel information office, phone ☎020/7222 1234 or visit ✺www.thamesclippers.com. Tickets are pricey but Travelcards get you a third off your fare.

If you're in a group of three or more, London's metered **black cabs** (taxis) can be a viable way of riding across the centre; there's a minimum £2.20 fare and a trip from Euston to Victoria should cost around £12. However, after 8pm fares go sky high and you're best off using the tube. A yellow light in the roof above the windscreen tells you if the cab is available – just wave to hail it. To book in advance, call ☎020/7272 0272. **Minicabs** look just like regular cars and are considerably cheaper than black cabs, but they only take four people and are less regulated. There are hundreds of them so it's best to get the number of a local outfit from the pub or club you're at and best to avoid the unlicensed ones that tout for business after dark. To have a women driver, call Ladycabs on ☎020/7254 3501; for a gay/lesbian driver call Freedom Cars ☎020/7734 1313. Most minicabs are not metered, so check the fare before you get going.

**Cycling**, although not for the faint-hearted, is popular in London. A good central option for **bike hire** is London Bicycle Tour Co (£3/hr, £16/day; ☎020/7928 6838, ✺www.londonbicycle.com) in Gabriel's Wharf on the South Bank, otherwise you can source hire shops through the London cycling campaign website (✺www .lcc.org.uk). You can pick out cycle-friendly routes using the free London cycle guides available from transport information offices.

## Accommodation

London is extremely expensive, and budget **accommodation** in the centre tends to be poor quality. However, the sheer size of the city means you'll have little trouble finding a room. The Visit London **hotel booking** service (☎0845/644 3010, ✺www.visitlondon.com) will get you the best available prices with no additional charge. To book a **hostel bed**, contact the individual hostels, or for HI hostels, the YHA (☎020/7373 3400, ✺www.yha.org.uk). A good **website** for booking independent hostels is ✺www.hostellondon.com. **Student rooms** are also available over Easter and from July to September; contact Imperial College (☎020/7594 9507, ✺www.imperial.ac.uk), the LSE (☎020/7955 7370, ✺www .lse.ac.uk) or University of London (☎020/7862 8880, ✺www.housing.lon .ac.uk).

### Hostels

**City of London** 36 Carter Lane ✺www.yha.org .uk ☎020/7236 4965. 200-bed hostel right by St Paul's Cathedral with crowded dorms or private rooms. The area is very quiet at night but it's close to the centre. St Paul's or Blackfriars tube. £24.60.

**Earl's Court** 38 Bolton Gardens ☎020/7373 7083. Dorms only, but comfortable, with good-value meals. Earl's Court tube. £19.50.

**Hampstead Heath** 4 Wellgarth Rd ☎020/8458 9054. One of the biggest and best-appointed hostels, near the wilds of Hampstead Heath. Golders Green tube. £21.

**Holland House** Holland Walk ☎020/7937 0748. Fairly convenient for the centre, with a nice location overlooking parkland. Dorms only. Holland Park or High St Kensington tube. £21.60.

**Oxford Street** 14 Noel St ☎020/7734 1618. In the heart of the West End, but with only 75 beds,

it fills up fast. Discounts for weekly stays. Oxford Circus or Tottenham Court Rd tube. £22.60.

**Rotherhithe** Island Yard, Salter Rd ☎020/7232 2114. Rather far out to the east, but a viable option in peak season, with 320 beds. Canada Water tube or bus #381 from Waterloo. £23.60.

**St Pancras** 79 Euston Rd ☎020/7388 9998. In a good location opposite St Pancras station and within walking distance of both the West End and Camden Town, with small dorms and twins. King's Cross tube. £24.60.

### Other hostels

**Generator** Compton Place ☎020/7388 7666, ✺www.the-generator.co.uk. Huge 837-bed hostel with neon-lit post-industrial decor and a youthful clientele. No sharing with strangers, so prices get cheaper the bigger your group is. Russell Sq or Euston tube. £15.

**Leinster Inn** 7–12 Leinster Sq ☎020/7229 9641, ⓦwww.astorhostels.com. The biggest and liveliest of the Astor hostels, close to Notting Hill. Under 30s only. Queensway or Notting Hill Gate tube. £14.50

**Museum Inn** 27 Montague St ☎020/7580 5360, ⓦwww.astorhostels.com. The quietest of the Astor hostels, near the British Museum, with the usual young crowd. Russell Sq tube. £15.

**Piccadilly Hotel** 12 Sherwood Street ☎020/7434 9009, ⓦwww.piccadillyhotel.net. A lively and friendly hostel situated in the heart of the West End. Price includes Internet access and breakfast Piccadilly Circus tube. £12.

**St Christopher's Village** 121 Borough High St ☎020/7407 1856, ⓦwww.st-christophers.co.uk. Upbeat and cheerful hostel in a series of buildings near London Bridge, with a café and late bar onsite. London Bridge tube. £13.

### Hotels and B&Bs

**Abbey House** 11 Vicarage Gate ☎020/7727 2594, ⓦwww.abbeyhousekensington.com. Victorian B&B, offering large, bright rooms with shared facilities. High St Kensington tube. ⓺

**Cavendish** 75 Gower St ☎020/7636 9079, ⓦwww.hotelcavendish.com. Clean, tastefully decorated guesthouse, one of the best in Bloomsbury. Goodge St tube. ⓺

**Garden Court** 30–31 Kensington Gardens Sq ☎020/7229 2553, ⓦwww.gardencourthotel .co.uk. Presentable, family-run hotel in a leafy area of town, close to bustling Portobello Market. Bayswater tube. ⓻

**Melbourne House** 79 Belgrave Rd ☎020/7828 3516, ⓦwww.melbournehousehotel.co.uk. Clean and friendly B&B where all the doubles are en suite. Victoria tube. ⓼

**Morgan House** 107 & 120 Ebury St ☎020/7730 2384, ⓦwww.morganhouse.co.uk. Above-average B&B near Victoria station with some en-suite rooms. Victoria tube. ⓻

**Oxford House** 92–94 Cambridge St ☎020/7834 6467. Friendly B&B with pristine rooms and shared facilities; booking essential. Victoria tube. ⓹

**Philbeach** 30–31 Philbeach Gardens ☎020/7373 1244, ⓦwww.philbeachhotel.freeserve.co.uk. London's busiest gay hotel with a popular restaurant attached. Earl's Court tube. ⓻

**Ridgemount** 65–67 Gower St ☎020/7636 1141, ⓦwww.ridgemounthotel.co.uk. Old-fashioned family-run Bloomsbury hotel with a garden and a laundry service. Goodge St tube. ⓺

**Rushmore Hotel** 11 Trebovir Rd ☎020/7370 3839, ⓦwww.rushmore.activehotel.com. This cute Victorian townhouse with a conservatory is a bit of a gem in the often dreary Earl's Court area. Earl's Court tube. ⓼

### Campsites

**Abbey Wood** Federation Rd ☎020/8311 7708. Enormous, well-equipped Caravan Club site, east of Greenwich. Open all year. Train from Charing Cross to Abbey Wood.

**Crystal Palace** Crystal Palace Parade ☎020/8778 7155. All-year Caravan Club site, maximum two weeks' stay in summer, three in winter. Train from Victoria or London Bridge to Crystal Palace.

# The City

The majority of sights are north of the **River Thames**, but there's no single focus of interest. Most people head, at one time or another, to the area around Whitehall, with **Trafalgar Square** at one end and Parliament Square at the other. All are just a ten-minute stroll east of **Buckingham Palace**. The busiest, most popular area for visitors and Londoners alike is the **West End**, centred on Leicester Square and Piccadilly Circus, and home to the majority of the city's theatres and cinemas. The financial district lies a mile or so to the east, and is known, confusingly, as the **City of London**, at once the most ancient and most modern part of London. Over on the other side of the river, the **South Bank** has become a prime destination thanks to the London Eye, Tate Modern and Shakespeare's Globe. Further afield, **Greenwich** makes for a great day out, as do the Royal Botanic Gardens at **Kew**, and the outlying royal palaces of **Hampton Court** and Windsor Castle.

### Trafalgar Square and the National Gallery

Trafalgar Square's focal point is **Nelson's Column**, featuring the one-eyed admiral who died whilst defeating the French at the 1805 Battle of Trafalgar. Four lions guard the column's base, while two adjacent fountains are a magnet for overheating sightseers during the summer.

Extending across the north side of the square is the bulk of the **National Gallery** (daily 10am–6pm, Wed till 9pm; free; @www.nationalgallery.org.uk), one of the world's great art collections. A quick tally of the National's Italian masterpieces includes works by Raphael, Botticelli, Michelangelo, Leonardo da Vinci, Caravaggio and Titian. From Spain there are dazzling pieces by Velázquez (including the *Rokeby Venus*), El Greco and Goya. From the Low Countries there's Memlinck, van Eyck (the *Arnolfini Marriage*), Rubens, and some of Rembrandt's most searching portraits. The collection also includes several famous Impressionist and Post-Impressionist works by the likes of Seurat, Cézanne, Van Gogh and Monet. If you want to take the art chronologically, you should start in the Sainsbury Wing, a post-modern annexe on the west side. Tickets for the major exhibitions cost around £10 and should be booked in advance. Round the side of the National Gallery, in St Martin's Place, is the **National Portrait Gallery** (daily 10am–6pm, Thurs & Fri till 9pm; free; @www.npg.org.uk), which houses portraits of the great and good from Hans Holbein's larger-than-life drawing of Henry VIII to photographs of the latest pop stars.

## The Mall and Buckingham Palace

The tree-lined sweep of **The Mall** runs from Trafalgar Square through the imposing Admiralty Arch, and on to **Buckingham Palace** (Aug & Sept daily 9.30am–4.15pm; £13.50; @www.royal.gov.uk). The palace has served as the monarch's permanent residence only since the accession of Queen Victoria in 1837. The building's exterior, last remodelled in 1913, is as bland as could be, but inside it's suitably lavish. There's more high-class art on display in the **Queen's Gallery** (daily 10am–4.30pm; £7.50), on the south side of the palace. The **Royal Mews** on Buckingham Palace Road (March–Oct daily except Fri 10am–4.15pm; £6) is home to the State vehicles, most spectacular of which is Her Majesty's State Coach. A combined ticket for all of the above is available (£23.50). When Buckingham Palace is closed, most folk simply mill about outside the gates, with the largest crowds assembling for the **Changing of the Guard** (April–Aug daily 11.30am; Sept–March alternate days; no ceremony if it rains). However, you're better off heading for the **Horse Guards** building on Whitehall (see below), where a more elaborate equestrian ceremony takes place (Mon–Sat 11am, Sun 10am). Wherever you watch the Changing of the Guard, you can relax afterwards in nearby **St James's Park**, immaculately laid out south of The Mall, its lake providing an inner-city reserve for wildfowl.

## Whitehall

Heading south from Trafalgar Square is the broad sweep of **Whitehall**, lined with government buildings. The original Whitehall was a palace built for King Henry VIII and subsequently extended, but virtually the only bit to survive a fire in 1698 is the supremely elegant **Banqueting House** (Mon–Sat 10am–5pm; £4; @www .hrp.org.uk), begun by Inigo Jones in Palladian style in 1619 and decorated with vast ceiling paintings by Rubens, glorifying the Stuart dynasty. They were commissioned by James's son, Charles I – who on January 30, 1649, stepped onto the executioner's scaffold from one of the building's front windows. Further down this west side of Whitehall is **10 Downing St**, residence of the Prime Minister since 1732. During World War II, the Cabinet was forced to vacate Downing Street in favour of a bunker in nearby King Charles Street. The **Churchill Museum and Cabinet War Rooms** (daily 9.30am–6pm; £10; ☎020/7930 6961, @www.iwm .org.uk) – left more or less as they were in 1945 – provide a glimpse of the claustrophobic suites from which Winston Churchill directed wartime operations and a fascinating insight to the life of the man himself.

## The Houses of Parliament and Westminster Abbey

Clearly visible at the south end of Whitehall is one of London's best-known buildings, the Palace of Westminster, better known as the **Houses of Parliament**. The

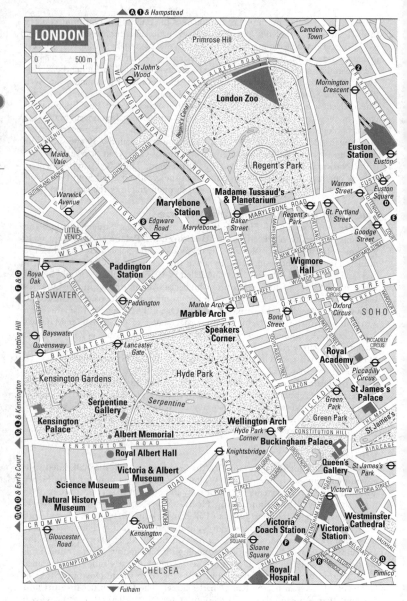

city's finest Gothic Revival building and symbol of a nation once confident of its place at the centre of the world, it's distinguished above all by the ornate, gilded clock tower popularly known as **Big Ben**, after the thirteen-ton bell that it houses. The original royal palace, built by Edward the Confessor in the eleventh century, burnt down in 1834. The only part to survive is the magnificent Westminster Hall, which can be glimpsed en route to the **public galleries** from which you can

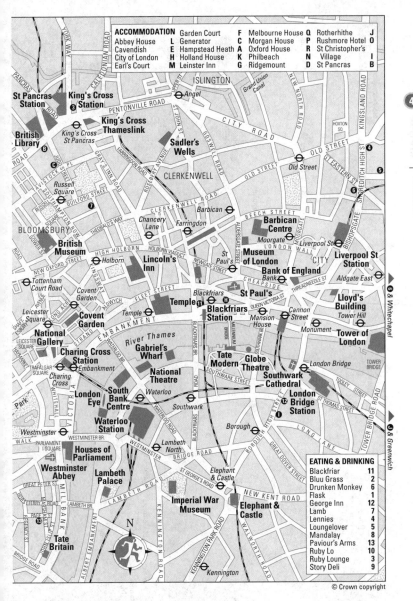

**ACCOMMODATION**

| | | | | | |
|---|---|---|---|---|---|
| Abbey House | L | Garden Court | F | Melbourne House | Q | Rotherhithe | J |
| Cavendish | E | Generator | C | Morgan House | P | Rushmore Hotel | O |
| City of London | H | Hampstead Heath | A | Oxford House | R | St Christopher's | |
| Earl's Court | M | Holland House | K | Philbeach | N | Village | I |
| | | Leinster Inn | G | Ridgemount | D | St Pancras | B |

**EATING & DRINKING**

| | |
|---|---|
| Blackfriar | 11 |
| Bluu Grass | 2 |
| Drunken Monkey | 6 |
| Flask | 1 |
| George Inn | 12 |
| Lamb | 7 |
| Lennies | 4 |
| Loungelover | 5 |
| Mandalay | 8 |
| Paviour's Arms | 13 |
| Ruby Lo | 10 |
| Ruby Lounge | 3 |
| Story Deli | 9 |

© Crown copyright

watch parliament's proceedings – Friday is the easiest day to get tickets (free), when sittings commence at 9.30am: turn up early to avoid queues.

The Houses of Parliament dwarf their much older neighbour, **Westminster Abbey** (Mon–Fri 9.30am–3.45pm, Wed until 7pm, Sat 9.30am–1.45pm; £8; ⒲www.westminster-abbey.org), yet this single building embodies much of the history of England: it has been the venue for all but two coronations since the time

156

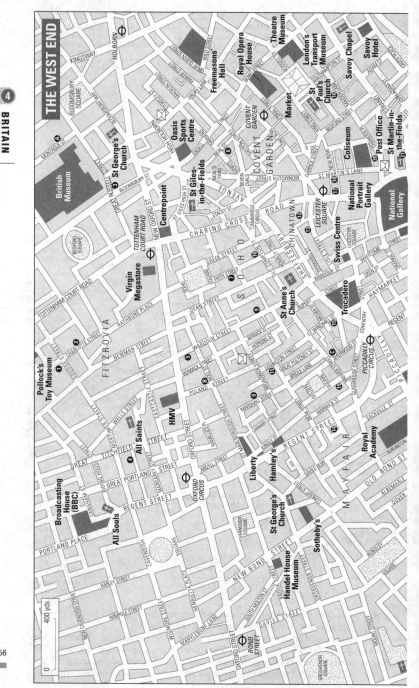

THE WEST END

British Museum

Pollock's Toy Museum

St George's Church ❸

Centrepoint

Oasis Sports Centre

St Giles-in-the-Fields

Freemasons' Hall

Royal Opera House

Theatre Museum

London's Transport Museum

Market

St Paul's Church

Savoy Chapel

Savoy Hotel

Coliseum

Post Office

St Martin-in-the-Fields ㉑

National Portrait Gallery

National Gallery

Swiss Centre

Trocadero

St Anne's Church

Virgin Megastore

HMV

All Saints

Broadcasting House (BBC)

All Souls

Liberty

Hamley's

St George's Church

Handel House Museum

Sotheby's

Royal Academy

FITZROVIA

SOHO

CHINATOWN

MAYFAIR

COVENT GARDEN

BLOOMSBURY SQUARE

BEDFORD SQUARE

SOHO SQUARE

LEICESTER SQUARE

CAVENDISH SQUARE

HANOVER SQUARE

BERKELEY SQUARE

GROSVENOR SQUARE

PICCADILLY CIRCUS

OXFORD CIRCUS

BOND STREET

TOTTENHAM COURT ROAD

CHARING CROSS ROAD

SHAFTESBURY AVENUE

OXFORD STREET

REGENT STREET

PICCADILLY

NEW BOND STREET

OLD BOND ST

PORTLAND PLACE

KINGSWAY

HOLBORN

400 yds

0

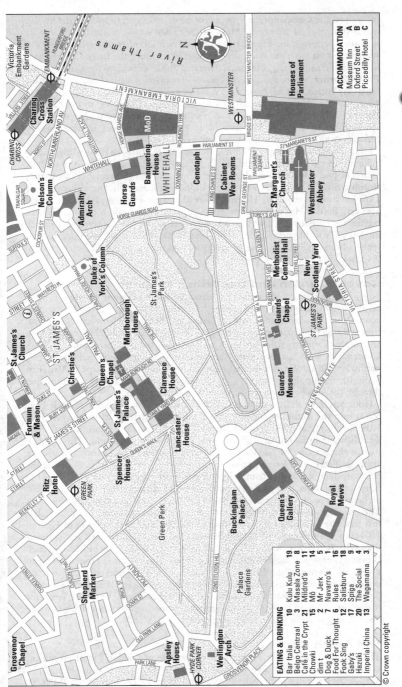

BRITAIN

4

**ACCOMMODATION**
Museum Inn                A
Oxford Street             B
Piccadilly Hotel          C

**EATING & DRINKING**

| | |
|---|---|
| Bar Italia | 10 |
| Belgo Centraal | 3 |
| Café in the Crypt | 21 |
| Chowki | 15 |
| dim t | 7 |
| Dog & Duck | 6 |
| Food For Thought | 12 |
| Fook Sing | 17 |
| Gaby's | 20 |
| Hazuki | 13 |
| Imperial China | 8 |
| Kulu Kulu | 19 |
| Masala Zone | 11 |
| Mildred's | 14 |
| Mô | 5 |
| Mr Jerk | 1 |
| Navarro's | 16 |
| Rules | 18 |
| Salisbury | 9 |
| Spiga | 4 |
| The Social | 3 |
| Wagamama | 13 |

of William the Conqueror, and the site of more or less every royal burial for five hundred years until George II. Many of the nation's most celebrated citizens are honoured here, too, and the interior is crowded with monuments, reliefs and statuary. Entry is via the north door, and the highlights include the **Lady Chapel**, with its wonderful fan vaulting, the much venerated Shrine of Edward the Confessor and **Poets' Corner**, where the likes of Chaucer, Tennyson, Charles Dickens and many others are buried, and still more, like Shakespeare, and T.S. Eliot are honoured. On your way out, don't miss the Great Cloister, which gives access to the **Chapter House** (daily 10.30am–4pm; free) with its thirteenth-century paving stones and the Norman **Undercroft Museum** (daily 10.30am–4pm; free), in which several generations of royal death-masks are displayed.

From Parliament Square, Millbank runs south to **Tate Britain** (daily 10am–5.50pm; free; ⊛www.tate.org.uk; Pimlico tube). Displaying British art from 1500 onwards, plus a whole wing devoted to Turner, it also showcases contemporary British artists. The galleries are re-hung more or less annually, but always include a fair selection of works by Hogarth, Constable, Gainsborough, Reynolds, Blake, Spencer, Bacon, Hockney and others. The gallery also runs contemporary art's prestigious Turner prize. Every autumn, the finalists' work is displayed for a month or two prior to the prize-giving. The **Tate Boat** (☏020/7887 8888) carries passengers from Millbank to Tate Modern on Bankside (see opposite; every 40min; £4 single or £2.65 with a Travelcard).

### Covent Garden and the British Museum

Northeast of Trafalgar Square lies the attractive area of **Covent Garden**, centred on the Piazza, London's oldest planned square, laid out in the 1630s, and now centred on the nineteenth-century market hall that housed the city's principal fruit and vegetable market until the 1970s. The structure now shelters a gaggle of tasteful shops and arty stalls. On the western side, by Inigo Jones's classical St Paul's Church, is a semi-institutionalized venue for buskers and more ambitious street performers. In the Piazza's southeast corner is the **London Transport Museum** (daily 10am–6pm, Fri from 11am; £5.95; ⊛www.ltmuseum.co.uk), a fun scamper through the history – and possible future – of public transport.

From here it's a short walk northwards up past the shops along fashionable Neal Street into the district of Bloomsbury, home to the **British Museum** on Great Russell Street (Sat–Wed 10am–5.30pm, Thurs & Fri till 8.30pm; free; ⊛www .british-museum.ac.uk), one of the great museums of the world. The building itself is the grandest of London's Greek Revival edifices, and is now even more amazing, thanks to Norman Foster's glass-and-steel covered Great Court, at the heart of which stands the **Round Reading Room**, where Karl Marx penned *Das Kapital*. With over four million exhibits, the BM is far too big to be seen comprehensively in one go – head for the two or three displays that interest you most. The museum's Roman and Greek antiquities are second to none, but the exhibits that steal the headlines are the **Parthenon Sculptures** – taken by Lord Elgin in 1801 and still the cause of discord between the British and Greek governments – and the **Rosetta stone**, which led to modern understanding of hieroglyphics. British archeological highlights include Saxon pieces from Sutton Hoo, the Roman silverwork known as the Mildenhall Treasure, the 2000-year-old Lindow Man, preserved in a Cheshire bog after his sacrificial death, and the twelfth-century Lewis Chessmen, carved from walrus ivory. One collection everyone heads for is the vast Egyptian mummy display upstairs, while high-profile exhibitions take place throughout the year – ticket prices vary.

### The South Bank

**The South Bank** of the Thames is home to one of London's most prominent landmarks, the **London Eye** (daily: Feb–April & Oct–Dec 9.30am–8pm, May, June & Sept 9.30am–9pm, July & Aug until 10pm; £12.50; ☏0800/500 0600,

@www.ba-londoneye.com), a 443ft-tall observation wheel that revolves above the Thames. From the Eye, a riverside footpath heads east past the strikingly ugly concrete edifices of the **South Bank Centre** (@www.sbc.org.uk) and **National Theatre** (@www.nationaltheatre.org.uk), taking in the craft shops and restaurants in Gabriel's Wharf and the OXO tower, for a mile or so before reaching Bankside, the old entertainment district of Tudor and Stuart London. Contemporary Bankside is dominated by the austere former power station, which has been transformed into **Tate Modern** (daily 10am–6pm, Fri & Sat till 10pm; free; @www.tate .org.uk). The collection is arranged thematically, and re-hangs take place every six months or so, but you're pretty much guaranteed to see works by Monet, Bonnard, Matisse, Picasso, Dalí, Mondrian, Warhol, Beuys and Rothko. For information on the Tate boat service see opposite. Major exhibitions run for about three months and tend to be very popular, so it's worth booking ahead.

Directly outside Tate Modern is Norman Foster's **Millennium Bridge**, London's famous bouncing bridge, which wobbled so worryingly when it first opened in 2000 that it was closed for repairs for almost two years. The crossing, with spectacular views, will take you effortlessly over to St Paul's Cathedral (see below).

Dwarfed by Tate Modern is the equally impressive **Shakespeare's Globe Theatre** (@www.shakespeares-globe.org), a reconstruction of the polygonal playhouse where most of the Bard's later works were first performed. The Globe's pricey but stylish exhibition (daily: May–Sept 9am–5pm; Oct–April 10am–5pm; £9) is well worth a visit, and includes a guided tour of the theatre, except in the afternoons during the summer – when you're better off watching a show.

One other national institution on the South Bank worth seeking out is the **Imperial War Museum**, on Lambeth Road, half a mile south of Waterloo Station (daily 10am–6pm; free; @www.iwm.org.uk; Lambeth North tube). By far the best museum of its type in the country, its covers British military campaigns from World War I to the present. The museum also contains the nation's only permanent **Holocaust Exhibition**, which avoids depicting the victims of the Holocaust as nameless masses by focusing on individual cases with interspersed archive footage and eyewitness accounts.

### The City of London

Once the fortified heart of the capital, the **City of London**, also known as the Square Mile, is now its financial district. Few people actually live here, making it a desolate place after nightfall and at weekends. The 1666 Fire of London destroyed most of the old City, and postwar redevelopment demolished much of the rest, but the area's finest structure, **St Paul's Cathedral** (Mon–Sat 8.30am–4pm; £8; @www.stpauls.co.uk; St Paul's tube), which was designed by Christopher Wren, remains. The most distinctive feature of this Baroque edifice is the dome, second in size only to St Peter's in Rome, and still a dominating presence on the London skyline. The interior of the church, recently cleaned and restored to its former glory, is filled with dull imperialist funerary monuments, for the most part, but a staircase in the south transept leads up to a series of galleries in the dome. The internal **Whispering Gallery** is the first, so called because of its acoustic properties – words whispered to the wall on one side are clearly audible on the other. The broad exterior Stone Gallery and the uppermost Golden Gallery both offer good panoramas over London. The **crypt** is the resting place of Wren himself, along with Turner, Reynolds and other artists, but the most imposing sarcophagi are the twin black monstrosities occupied by the Duke of Wellington and Lord Nelson.

The eastern extent of the City is marked by the **Tower of London** (March–Oct Tues–Sat 9am–6pm, Sun & Mon 10am–6pm; Nov–Feb Tues–Sat 9am–5pm, Sun & Mon 10am–5pm; £14.50; @www.hrp.org.uk), on the river a mile southeast of St Paul's. Despite all the hype, it remains one of London's most remarkable buildings, site of some of the goriest events in the nation's history, and somewhere all visitors should explore. For a start, the Tower is the most perfectly preserved (albeit heavily restored) medieval fortress in the country, begun by William the Conqueror, and pretty much completed by the end of the thirteenth century. Before you set off exploring, take one of the free tours given by the "Beefeaters", ex-servicemen in Tudor costume. The central White Tower holds part of the **Royal Armouries** collection (the rest resides in Leeds), and, on the second floor, the Norman Chapel of St John, London's oldest church. Close by is Tower Green, where the likes of Lady Jane Grey, Anne Boleyn and Catherine Howard were beheaded. The Waterloo Barracks house the **Crown Jewels**, among which are the three largest cut diamonds in the world. On the south side of the complex, the **Bloody Tower** is where the murder of the "Princes in the Tower", Edward V and his brother, is thought to have taken place. Below lies **Traitor's Gate**, through which prisoners arrived after having been ferried down the Thames from the courts of justice at Westminster. River views from here are dominated by the twin towers of **Tower Bridge**, completed in 1894 and now one of London's most famous landmarks. The raising of the bascules to allow tall ships through remains an impressive sight. Sadly, though, you can only visit the walkways linking the summits of the towers by joining a guided tour dubbed the "Tower Bridge Experience" (daily 9.30am–6pm; £5.50; ⊛www.towerbridge.org.uk).

## Hyde Park

The best way to approach **Hyde Park**, London's largest central green space, is from the southeastern corner known as Hyde Park Corner. Here, in the middle of the traffic interchange, stands the **Wellington Arch** (Wed–Sun 10am–4/5pm; £3; EH), placed here to commemorate Wellington's victories in the Napoleonic Wars. The arch now houses a small exhibition on London's outdoor memorials. Overlooking the arch is **Apsley House**, where Wellington himself used to live (Tues–Sun; April–Oct 10am–5pm; Nov–March 10am–4pm; £4.95; EH) and which now houses the Wellington Museum, holding works by Velázquez, Goya and Rubens. In the middle of Hyde Park is the **Serpentine Lake**, with a popular lido towards its centre; the nearby **Serpentine Gallery** (daily 10am–6pm; free; ⊛www.serpentinegallery.org) hosts excellent contemporary art exhibitions. Nearby stands the **Albert Memorial**, an over-decorated Gothic canopy covering a gilded statue of Queen Victoria's much-mourned consort, who died in 1861. To the west the park merges into **Kensington Gardens**, leading to Kensington Palace (daily 10am–5/6pm; £11; ⊛www.hrp.org.uk), a modestly proportioned Jacobean brick mansion that was Princess Diana's London residence following her separation from Prince Charles. The highlights of the sparsely furnished state apartments are the trompe-l'oeil ceiling paintings by William Kent, and the oil paintings in the King's Gallery.

## South Kensington museums

London's richest concentration of free museums lies to the south of Hyde Park. In terms of sheer variety and scale, the **Victoria and Albert Museum** (daily 10am–5.45pm; Wed & last Fri of month until 10pm; free; ⊛www.vam.ac.uk), on Cromwell Road, is the greatest museum of applied arts in the world. The most celebrated of the V&A's numerous exhibits are the Raphael Cartoons, seven vast biblical paintings that served as templates for a set of tapestries destined for the Sistine Chapel. Other highlights include the largest collection of Indian art outside India, the British Galleries, plaster casts of European art's greatest sculptures, fascinating displays of fashion through the ages, more Constable paintings than the Tate and a decent collection of Rodin sculptures.

Established as a technological counterpart to the V&A, the **Science Museum** on Exhibition Road (daily 10am–6pm; free; ⊛www.sciencemuseum.org.uk) is undeniably impressive. First off, visit the Making of the Modern World, a display of inventions such as Puffing Billy, the world's oldest surviving steam train, and a Ford Model T, the world's first mass-produced car. From here, the darkened, ultra-purple

Wellcome Wing beckons you in, its ground floor dominated by the floating, sloping underbelly of the museum's IMAX cinema. The four floors of the Wellcome Wing are filled with hi-tech hands-on gadgetry. Back on Cromwell Road, the nearby **Natural History Museum** (Mon–Sat 10am–5.50pm, Sun 11am–5.50pm; free; @www.nhm.ac.uk) is London's most handsome museum. Most folk come here with the kids to see the Dinosaur gallery, and wince at the creepy-crawlies. Even more stunning, however, are the Earth Galleries, a visually exciting romp through the earth's evolution. The most popular sections are the slightly tasteless Kobe earthquake simulator, and the spectacular display of gems and crystals in the Earth's Treasury.

## North London: Regent's Park to Hampstead

A short stroll southwest of Regent's Park, on busy Marylebone Road, is one of London's most enduring tourist traps, **Madame Tussaud's** (daily 9/9.30am–5.30/6.00pm; weekdays £20.99, weekends £19.99); @www.madame-tussauds .co.uk), which has been pulling in the crowds since the good lady arrived in 1802 with the sculpted heads of guillotined aristocrats. The entrance fee might be extortionate, the likenesses risible, but you can still rely on finding some of London's biggest queues here. Tickets include entrance to the Auditorium, a standard romp through the basics of astronomy accompanied by hi-tech visuals and cosmic astrobabble.

As with almost all of London's royal parks, Londoners have Henry VIII to thank for Regent's Park, which he confiscated from the Church for yet more hunting grounds. Flanked by some of the city's most elegant residential buildings, the park is best known for **London Zoo** (daily 10am–4/5.30pm; £14; @www.londonzoo .co.uk), one of the world's oldest and most varied collections of animals, which hides in the northeastern corner. Five minutes' walk from the north side of the park lies bustling **Camden Town**, host to a vast weekend market that sprawls around the canal, spilling over several locations either side of the main street.

Further north still is the affluent suburb of **Hampstead**, which gives access to Hampstead Heath, one of the few genuinely wild areas left within reach of central London. One major attraction east of Hampstead is **Highgate Cemetery**, ranged on both sides of Swains Lane (Highgate or Archway tube). Highgate's most famous corpse is Karl Marx, who lies in the East Cemetery (daily 10/11am–3.30/4.30pm; £2; @www.highgate-cemetery.org); more atmospheric is the overgrown West Cemetery (guided tours only: March–Nov Mon–Fri noon, 2pm & 4pm, Sat & Sun hourly 11am–4pm; Dec–Feb Sat & Sun hourly 11am–3pm; £3), with its spooky Egyptian Avenue and terraced catacombs.

## Greenwich

Some seven miles southeast of central London, **Greenwich** (pronounced "grenitch") is one of London's most beguiling spots. At its heart is the architectural set piece of the former Royal Naval College overlooking the Thames, while nearby are two prime tourist sights, the Royal Observatory and the National Maritime Museum. Transport links are good: boats run regularly from Westminster Pier, trains run from Charing Cross, and the Docklands Light Railway scoots east from the Bank or Tower Gateway in the City via the redeveloped Docklands, south to the **Cutty Sark** ship, which stands in a dry dock next to Greenwich pier (daily 10am–5pm; £4.50; @www.cuttysark.org.uk). This majestic vessel was one of the last of the clippers, sail-powered cargo ships built for speed and used on long-distance routes to bring wool, tea and other produce to London from the far-flung corners of the Empire. Hugging the riverfront to the east is Wren's beautifully symmetrical Baroque ensemble of the **Old Royal Naval College** (daily 10am–5pm; free; @www.greenwichfoundation.org.uk). Across the road the **National Maritime Museum** (daily 10am–5pm; free; @www.nmm.ac.uk) exhibits model ships, charts and globes, and has been wonderfully rejuvenated with some inventive new galleries under an enormous glazed roof. Inigo Jones's adjacent **Queen's House**, Britain's first Neoclassical building, also forms part of the museum. From here Greenwich Park stretches up the hill, crowned by the Wren-inspired **Royal Observatory** (daily 10am–5pm; free), home of Greenwich Mean Time and Zero Longitude. As well as housing numerous telescopes and navigational equipment, the museum also has a fascinating exhibition on the search for longitude.

## Out west: Kew to Windsor

Boats ply westwards from Westminster Pier upstream to **Kew** where you'll find the **Royal Botanic Gardens** (daily 9.30am–dusk; £10; Kew Gardens tube; ⊚www .kew.org), established in 1759, and now home to over fifty thousand species grown in the plantations and glasshouses of a beautiful 300-acre site. Further upstream, thirteen miles southwest of the centre and also served by riverboat, is the finest of England's royal mansions, **Hampton Court Palace** (April–Oct daily 10am–6pm; Nov–March closes 4.30pm; £12; ⊚www.hrp.org.uk). Built in 1516 by the upwardly mobile Cardinal Wolsey, it was enlarged and improved by Henry VIII, and later rebuilt by William III who hired Wren to remodel the buildings. The palace is laid out into six thematic walking tours, with costumed guided tours available at no extra charge. If your energy is lacking, the most rewarding sections are Henry VIII's State Apartments, which feature the glorious double hammer-beamed Great Hall, the King's Apartments, and the Tudor Kitchens. There's plenty more to see in the grounds: the Great Vine, the Lower Orangery, which houses Mantegna's *The Triumphs of Caesar*, and, of course, the famous **Maze**, laid out in 1714, lies just north of the palace.

**WINDSOR**, 21 miles west of central London and connected by train from Waterloo, is dominated by **Windsor Castle** (daily March–Oct 9.45am–5.15pm, Nov–Feb until 4.15pm; £12.50; ⊚www.royal.gov.uk). The castle began its days as a wooden fortress built by William the Conqueror, with numerous later monarchs having had a hand in its evolution. It's an undeniably awesome sight, but the small selection of rooms open to the public are relatively unexciting; the only exception is the Perpendicular Gothic glory of St George's Chapel, resting place of numerous royals.

# Eating and drinking

London is a great place in which to **eat out** with the chance to sample more or less any kind of cuisine. The only drawback is that it can be very pricey, but for those on a budget, there are still plenty of options: London has some of the best Cantonese restaurants in Europe, top Indian and Bangladeshi food, numerous French, Greek, Italian, Japanese, Spanish and Thai restaurants. The city's great period of **pub** building took place in the Victorian era, to which many taverns still pay homage; but they are increasingly difficult to find, as chain pubs are as ubiquitous in London as elsewhere in the country. As for modern **bars**, there are countless numbers of them watering an eternally young, hip clientele that's seemingly oblivious to the sky-high prices. For a break from the West End head out east to the hip Shoreditch and Old Street areas, where you'll find cool bars, restaurants and underground clubs.

### Snacks and quick meals

**Bar Italia** 22 Frith St. Open 24hr except Sun 7–4am. Tiny, buzzing café serving coffee and snacks that's a bit of a legend. Leicester Sq tube.

**Bluu Grass** 6 Plender St. Great little Vietnamese café off Camden High St, serving huge portions of noodles, curries and plenty more. Mornington Crescent tube.

**Café in the Crypt** St Martin-in-the-Fields, Trafalgar Sq. The buffet food is nothing special, but the handy location makes this an ideal refuelling spot. Charing Cross tube.

**Centrale** 7 Archer Street. Tiny, friendly Italian café that serves up huge plates of steaming, garlicky pasta. Also does omelettes, chicken and chops for around £5. Leicester Sq tube.

Food For Thought 31 Neal St. Very small vegetarian restaurant – the inexpensive food is delicious, but don't expect to linger. Covent Garden tube.

Fook Sing 25 Newport Court. No frills and not many tables at this Chinatown café, but the cooking which hails from China's Fujian province excites, as do the bargain prices. Leicester Sq tube.

Gaby's 30 Charing Cross Rd. Busy café serving a wide range of home-cooked veggie and Middle Eastern specialities. Hard to beat for value, choice and location. Leicester Sq tube.

Lennies 4 Calvert Drive. A cosy café/restaurant serving excellent Malay and Thai food. Old Street tube.

Mr Jerk 189 Wardour St. Excellent place to escape the hordes of Oxford Street shoppers, this lively, no-frills place dishes up generous portions of Caribbean staples. Oxford Circus tube.

Mô 25 Heddon St. The ultimate Arabic pastiche, and a successful one at that. This pricey tearoom, just off Regent St, serves delicious snacks from mid-morning and is a great place to pose. Piccadilly Circus tube.

Story Deli 3 Dray Walk. A bit of a departure in this area known for its curry houses but the pizzas here are among the best in town, veggie options are plentiful and all ingredients are organic. Liverpool St tube.

## Restaurants

Belgo Centraal 50 Earlham St. Hugely popular Belgian restaurant, famed for its mussels, served by waiters dressed as monks. Lunchtime deals offer best value. Covent Garden tube.

Chowki 2–3 Denman St. Stylish Indian restaurant dishing up authentic village recipes. The menu changes with the season and, given the location, prices are very reasonable. Piccadilly Circus tube.

dim t 32 Charlotte St. Great *dim sum* and filling plates of noodles and rice dishes in this cool, friendly and inexpensive restaurant. Goodge St tube.

Hazuki 43 Chandos Place. A great find, right in the heart of things, this is a classy-looking Japanese restaurant with an enticing and affordable menu. Charing Cross tube.

Imperial China White Bear Yard, 25 Lisle St. Large restaurant with excellent *dim sum*, and service that is Chinatown brusque. Leicester Sq tube.

Kulu Kulu 76 Brewer St. Fine sushi at this authentic Japanese diner. No-frills but excellent value. Piccadilly Circus tube.

Mandalay 444 Edgware Rd. Small, non-smoking restaurant that serves pure, freshly cooked, unexpurgated Burmese cuisine. Closed Sun. Edgware Rd tube.

Masala Zone 9 Marshall St. Refreshingly modern curry house where the food is imaginative and tasty and won't damage the wallet. Oxford Circus or Piccadilly Circus tube.

Mildred's 45 Lexington St. Generous portions of tasty vegetarian fare served in a lively setting. Prices are good value and the food ranges from burgers to stir-fries. Oxford Circus or Piccadilly Circus tube.

Navarro's 67 Charlotte St ☏020/7637 7713. Authentic, fairly priced Spanish tapas in an area that's not short on decent places to eat. Booking advised. Closed Sun. Goodge St tube.

Rules 35 Maiden Lane. London's oldest restaurant, dating from 1798, serves traditional British food at moderate prices, although your fellow diners are unlikely to be locals. Charing Cross tube.

Spiga 84–86 Wardour St. A pleasant Italian venue with a wood-fired oven churning out great pizzas. Leicester Square tube.

Wagamama 4 Streatham St. Minimalist canteen-style place where the diners share long benches and slurp huge bowls of noodle soup and stir-fry plates. Expect to queue but not to linger. Tottenham Court Rd tube. Branches all across town.

## Pubs and bars

Blackfriar 174 Queen Victoria St. One of the capital's most lovely and most unusual pubs, with marble walls, stained-glass windows and carved or illustrated monks in every nook and cranny. Blackfriars tube.

Dog & Duck 18 Bateman St. Tiny pub that's retained its old character and a loyal clientele. Leicester Sq tube.

Drunken Monkey 222 Shoreditch High Street. A warm, but lively ambience waits in this haven for cocktail and *dim sum* lovers. Old Street or Liverpool Street tube.

Flask 14 Flask Walk. Convivial local, close to the station and serving good food and real ale. Hampstead tube.

George Inn 77 Borough High St. Magnificent seventeenth-century coaching inn, now owned by the National Trust. Borough or London Bridge tube.

Lamb 94 Lamb's Conduit St. You can feel the history in this smoky, no-nonsense drinking den, in which the poet Dryden lost his life in a bar-room brawl. Holborn tube.

Loungelover 1 Whitby St. The current pick of Shoreditch's trendy watering holes – you'll need to dress well if you don't want to feel intimidated. Liverpool St tube.

Paviour's Arms Page St. Untouched Art Deco pub, close to Tate Britain, with cheap Thai food. Pimlico tube.

Salisbury 90 St Martin's Lane. One of the most beautifully preserved Victorian pubs in the centre. Leicester Sq tube.

The Social 5 Little Portland St. Bacchanalian, industrial club/bar, with great DJs playing everything from rock to rap for a truly hedonistic crowd. Oxford Circus tube. Closed Sun.

Ruby Lounge 33 Caledonian Road. Great pre-club bar with deep red walls and boudoir-like lighting. DJs spin some decent groove and funk tunes. Kings Cross tube.

Ruby Lo 23 Orchard Street. A gem hidden among the plethora of over-priced, suit-inhabited venues that populate the West End. Great for top-name DJs. Bond St tube.

# Nightlife

On any night of the week London offers a bewildering range of things to do after dark, ranging from top-flight opera and theatre to clubs. The **listings magazine** *Time Out* (every Tues; £3) is essential if you want to get the most out of this city and gives details of times, prices and access, plus previews and reviews. If you're looking for **dance music**, then London has it all, with everything from hip-hop to house, techno to trance, samba to soca. The **gay and lesbian** scenes in London are also livelier than almost anywhere else in Europe, with a vast range of venues from quiet pubs to frenetic clubs. London's West End **theatre** scene is dominated by big musicals, but there's plenty of other stuff on offer, too. Cut-price stand-by tickets can sometimes be had on the day, otherwise head for the large booth in Leicester Square selling half-price tickets (Mon–Sat 10am–7pm, Sun noon–3pm) for that day's performances at all West End theatres (they specialize in the top end of the price range). An even better bargain are the standing tickets for around £4 for the **Proms** (July–Sept), the annual classical music festival held at the Royal Albert Hall, or the free classical concerts that take place during weekday lunch-times in the City's churches.

## Live music venues

**Barfly** 49 Chalk Farm Road. Where a large array of punk, rock and indie bands make their debut. Camden Town or Chalk Farm tube.

**100 Club** 100 Oxford St. Unpretentious and inexpensive venue in a very central location, showcasing a variety of acts. Tottenham Court Rd tube.

**Borderline** Orange Yard, Manette St. Intimate venue best known for Indie and ska. Good place to catch new bands. Also has club nights. Tottenham Court Rd tube.

**Forum** 9–17 Highgate Rd. Perhaps the capital's best medium-sized venue – large enough to attract established bands, but also a prime spot for newer talent. Kentish Town tube.

**Jazz Café** 5 Parkway. Futuristic, white-walled venue with an adventurous booking policy including Latin, rap, funk, hip-hop and musical fusions. Camden Town tube.

**Ronnie Scott's** 47 Frith St. The most famous jazz club in London, small, smoky and rather precious, but featuring top-line names. Leicester Sq tube.

**Underworld** 174 Camden High St. This labyrinthine venue is good for new bands and has sporadic club nights. Camden Town tube.

**Water Rats** 328 Gray's Inn Road. Still well-known for showcasing indie-gigs, and its gritty interior has recently had a facelift. Kings Cross tube.

## Clubs and discos

**Bar Rumba** 36 Shaftesbury Ave. Small West End venue with a programme of Latin, jazz-based and funk dance. Piccadilly Circus tube.

**Cargo** 83 Rivington Street. Live music and bar/club with globally influenced music, trendy crowds and futuristic decor. Old Street tube.

**The End** 16a West Central St. A club designed by clubbers for clubbers – large and spacious with chrome minimalist decor. Tottenham Court Rd tube.

**Fabric** 77a Charterhouse St. If you're seriously into dance music, head for Fabric at the weekends and get there early. Farringdon tube.

**The Fridge** 1 Town Hall Parade. A haven for hardcore fans of trance in this South London institution. Brixton tube.

**Ministry of Sound** 103 Gaunt St. Corporate clubbing that still draws top talent. Elephant & Castle tube.

**Herbal** 12–14 Kingsland Road. Another of Shoreditch's cosy clubs, boasting top-name DJs and a massive sound system. Old Street or Liverpool St tube.

**Plastic People** 147 Curtain Road. An intimate venue playing a mix of house, hip-hop, funk and jazz. Old Street or Liverpool St tube

**The Scala** 278 Pentonville Rd. An eclectic club holding unusual and multi-faceted nights that take in film, live bands and music from hip-hop to deep house. King's Cross tube.

## Gay and lesbian nightlife

**Brief Encounter** 41–43 St Martin's Lane. A popular pre-Heaven or post-opera hangout; the front bar is light, the back bar dark, and both are busy. Leicester Square tube.

**Candy Bar** 4 Carlisle St. Britain's first seven-day all-girl bar offers a retro-style cocktail bar-cum-pool room upstairs; a noisy, beery ground level cruising area. Tottenham Court Rd tube.

**The Escape** 10a Brewer Street. Shiny pink balloons and glitter-ball kitsch in this tiny but trendy venue. Tottenham Court Rd tube.

**First Out** 52 St Giles High St. The West End's original gay café/bar, and still permanently packed, serving good veggie food at reasonable prices. Fridays women-only nights get busy. Tottenham Court Rd tube.

**Freedom** 60 Wardour St, Soho. Hip, busy café/bar attracting a gay and straight crowd. Leicester Sq tube.

**G.A.Y.** The Astoria, 157 Charing Cross Rd. Huge, unpretentious and fun-loving dance nights for a young crowd on Fri & Sat. Tottenham Court Rd tube.

**Heaven** under the Arches Villiers St. Britain's most popular gay club, this legendary, 2000-capacity club continues to reign supreme. Charing Cross or Embankment tube.

**Vespa Lounge** Under Centrepoint House, St. Giles High St. This heaving girl-only bar sets up shop at weekends. Tottenham Court Rd tube.

## Theatre, cinema and the arts

**Barbican Centre** Silk St ⊛ www.barbican.org. uk. Home of the London Symphony Orchestra and venue for a wide range of concerts and exhibitions from classical to world music. Barbican or Moorgate tube.

**Donmar Warehouse** Earlham St ⊛ www.donmar -warehouse.com. Formerly the spiritual home of Sam Mendes, and the best bet for a central off-West End show. Covent Garden tube.

**English National Opera Coliseum** St Martin's Lane ⊛ www.eno.org. More radical and democratic than the ROH, with opera (in English) and ballet. Leicester Sq tube.

**ICA** Nash House, The Mall ⊛ www.ica.org.uk. Theatre, dance, films and art at London's enduringly cutting-edge HQ. Charing Cross tube.

**National Film Theatre** South Bank. London's only really serious arts cinema, with six different films shown each day. Waterloo tube.

**National Theatre** South Bank Centre, South Bank ⊛ www.nationaltheatre.org.uk. The NT has three separate theatres, and consistently good productions – some sell out months in advance, but discounted day seats are available. Waterloo tube.

**Open Air Theatre** Regent's Park, Inner Circle ⊛ www.openairtheatre.org. If the weather's good, there's nothing quite like a dose of al fresco Shakespeare, or a musical, play or concert. Regent's Park tube.

**Prince Charles** 2–7 Leicester Place ⊛ www .princecharlescinema.com. The bargain basement of London's cinemas, with a programme of newish movies and cult favourites. Leicester Sq tube.

**Royal Opera House** Bow St ⊛ www.royalopera house.org. Grand home of London's opera and ballet seasons. Discounted day seats available. Covent Garden tube.

**Sadler's Wells** Rosebery Avenue ⊛ www .sadlerswells.com. London's biggest dance venue puts on a mix of the best contemporary dance, kids' shows and ballet. Angel tube.

**Shakespeare's Globe** New Globe Walk ⊛ www .shakespeares-globe.org.uk. Replica open-air Elizabethan theatre that puts on shows from mid-May to mid-Sept, with standing tickets for £5. London Bridge, Blackfriars or Southwark tube.

**Wigmore Hall** 36 Wigmore St ⊛ www.wigmore -hall.org.uk. Intimate and elegant classical recital venue that's many Londoners' favourite. Oxford Circus tube.

# Listings

**Embassies** Australia, Australia House, Strand ☏ 020/7379 4334 (Holborn tube); Canada, 38 Grosvenor Street ☏ 020/7258 6600 (Bond St tube); Ireland, 17 Grosvenor Place ☏ 020/7235 2171 (Hyde Park Corner tube); New Zealand, 80 Haymarket ☏ 020/7930 8422 (Piccadilly Circus tube); United States, 24 Grosvenor Square ☏ 020/7499 9000 (Bond St tube).

**Exchange** Shopping areas such as Oxford St and Covent Garden are littered with private exchange offices, but their rates are usually worse than the banks. You'll find branches of major banks all around the centre.

**Hospitals** St Mary's Hospital, Praed St ☏ 020/7886 6666 (Paddington tube); University College Hospital Grafton Way ☏ 020/7387 9300 (Euston Square tube).

**Internet access** easyEverything: 9 Tottenham Court Rd (Tottenham Court Rd tube), 358 Oxford St (Bond St tube), 7 Strand (Charing Cross tube) and across the city.

**Left luggage** At all airport terminals and major train stations.
**Lost property** On a bus or tube, call ☎020/7486 2496; on a train ☎0845/748 4950; in a black taxi ☎020/7918 2000.

**Pharmacy** Bliss, 5 Marble Arch, W1 (daily 9am–midnight). Marble Arch tube.
**Police** 10 Vine St, W1 ☎020/7437 1212.
**Post office** 24–28 William IV St (Leicester Sq or Charing Cross tube). Mon–Fri 8.30am–6.30pm, Sat 9am–5.30pm.

# Southeast England

Nestling in self-satisfied prosperity, **southeast England** is the richest part of the country, due to its agricultural wealth and proximity to the capital. Swift, frequent rail and coach services make it ideal for day-trips from London. Medieval ecclesiastical power-bases such as **Canterbury** and **Winchester** offer an introduction to the nation's history; while on the coast is the upbeat, hedonistic resort of **Brighton**, London's playground by the sea.

**DOVER** is the main port of entry along this stretch of coast, and the country's busiest. It's not a particularly inspiring town, and its famous White Cliffs are best enjoyed from a boat several miles out. **Ferries** sail to Calais from the Eastern Docks, which is also the starting point for SpeedFerries' catamaran service to Boulogne. Hoverspeed's catamaran service operates from the Western Docks, south of the centre. The main **train station**, for services to Canterbury and London (last one around 10pm), is Dover Priory, ten minutes' walk west of the centre and served by shuttle buses (£1) from the Eastern Docks. **Coaches** to London (last one around 8.20pm) pick up from both docks and the town-centre bus station on Pencester Road. The **tourist office** is on Biggin Street (daily 9/10am–4/5.30pm; Oct–March closed Sun; ☎01304/205108, ⊛www.whitecliffscountry.org.uk.

## Canterbury

**CANTERBURY**, one of England's oldest centres of Christianity, was home to the country's most famous martyr, Archbishop Thomas à Becket, who fell victim to Church–State rivalry in 1170. It became one of northern Europe's great pilgrimage sites, as Chaucer's *Canterbury Tales* attest, until Henry VIII had the martyr's shrine demolished in 1538. The cathedral remains the focal point of a compact centre, which is enclosed on three sides by medieval walls. Today, as well as hosting a sizeable student population, it's thronged with visitors, but remains relatively unspoilt.

Built in stages from 1070 onwards, the vast **Cathedral** (Mon–Sat 9am–5/6.30pm, Sun 12.30–2.30pm & 4.30–5.30pm; £4.50; ⊛www.canterbury-cathedral.org) derives its distinctive presence from the perpendicular thrust of the late Gothic towers, dominated by the central, sixteenth-century Bell Harry tower. Notable features of the high vaulted interior are the tombs of Henry IV and his wife, and a gilded effigy of the Black Prince, both in the Trinity Chapel behind the main altar. The site of Becket's murder is marked by a modern shrine in the northwest transept, with a crude sculpture of the supposed weapons suspended above. Steps descend from here to the Romanesque arches of the **crypt**, one of the few remaining visible relics of the Norman cathedral. East of the cathedral, across the ring road, are the evocative ruins of **St Augustine's Abbey** (April–Sept 10am–6pm, Oct–March Wed–Sun 10am–4pm; £3.70; EH), on the site of a church founded by St Augustine, who began the conversion of the English in 597. Most of the town's other sights are located on or near High Street. The **Eastbridge Hospital** (Mon–Sat 10am–4.45pm; £1; ⊛www.eastbridgehospital.org.uk), opposite the library, was founded in the twelfth century to provide poor pilgrims with shelter, and a thirteenth-century wall painting of Christ is still faintly visible in the upstairs refectory. The **West Gate**, at the far end of St Peter's Street (a continuation of High Street), is the city's last remaining medieval gate, housing a small museum (Mon–Sat 11am–12.30pm & 1.30–3.30pm; £1.15; ⓦwww.canterbury-museums.co.uk) featuring weaponry used by the medieval city guard. The best exposition of local history is provided by the interactive **Museum of Canterbury**, on Stour St (Mon–Sat 10.30am–5pm & June–Sept Sun 1.30–5pm; £3.20; ⓦwww.canterbury-museums.co.uk).

## Practicalities

Canterbury has two **train stations**, Canterbury East for most services from London Victoria and Dover Priory, and Canterbury West for services from London Charing Cross – the stations are ten minutes south and northwest of the centre respectively. The **bus station** is on St George's Lane, just below the High Street. The **tourist office** is opposite the entrance to the cathedral at 13 Sun St (daily 9.30/10am–4/5pm; Jan–Easter closed Sun; ☎01227/378100, ⓦwww.canterbury .co.uk); it will book a room for you for a small fee, a service which is often necessary in the summer months.

### Hostels

**KiPPS hostel** 40 Nunnery Fields ☎01227/786121, ⓦwww.kipps-hostel.com. A short walk south of the centre, this friendly place has Internet access and a garden with space for a couple of tents. Dorms £12, rooms ❸

**YHA** 54 New Dover Rd ☎0870/770 5744, ⓦwww.yha.org.uk. Victorian villa a mile southeast of the centre. There's a self-catering kitchen and Internet access. Closed Jan. Dorms £16.40, rooms ❸

### Guest houses

**Ann's House** 63 London Rd ☎01227/768767. Traditional Victorian villa, a short walk from West Station, offering comfortable rooms, most en suite. ❺

**St Stephen's Guest House** 100 St Stephen's Rd ☎01227/767644, ⓦwww.st-stephens.fsnet.co.uk. Ten minutes' walk north along the river Stour, this place has excellent-value en suites. ❻

**Wincheap Guest House** 94 Wincheap ☎01227/762309, ⓦwww.wincheapguesthouse.co.uk. Good-value Victorian B&B near East station. ❹

### Eating and drinking

**Bell & Crown** 10 Palace St. A friendly medieval pub with excellent home-cooked food.

**Café des Amis du Mexique** 95 St Dunstan's St. This popular place has been around for years and still has a loyal following for its authentic Mexican fare.

**Casey's** 5 Butchery Lane. Irish pub serving Irish stew and soda bread, with occasional live folk music.

**Chaopraya River** 2 Dover St. Delicious Thai food at affordable prices.

**The Goods Shed** Canterbury West Station ☎01227/459153. Making imaginative use of local produce, this place is gaining a strong reputation, so booking may be advisable.

**Simple Simon's** 3 Church Lane. Old hostelry popular with students, with live music almost nightly.

**Tapas** 13 Palace St. Tasty tapas from around £5 a dish, and occasional live music.

# Brighton

**BRIGHTON** has been a prime target for day-tripping Londoners since the Prince Regent (later George IV) started holidaying here in the 1770s with his mistress, launching a trend for the "dirty weekend". One of Britain's most entertaining seaside resorts, the city has emerged from seediness to embrace a new, fashionable hedonism, in the process becoming one of the country's premier gay centres. This factor – along with a large student presence – has endowed Brighton with a buzzing nightlife scene, and there's a colourful music and arts festival (ⓦwww .brightonfestival.org.uk), which runs for three weeks in May.

From the train station on Queen's Road it's a ten-minute stroll straight down to the seafront, a four-mile-long pebble beach bordered by a balustered promenade. The wonderfully tacky **Palace Pier** is an obligatory call, basically a half-mile amusement arcade lined with booths selling fish and chips, candyfloss and assorted tat. Near here the antiquated locomotives of **Volk's Railway** (Easter to mid-Sept daily 11am–5/6pm; £2.50 return), the first electric train in the country, run east-

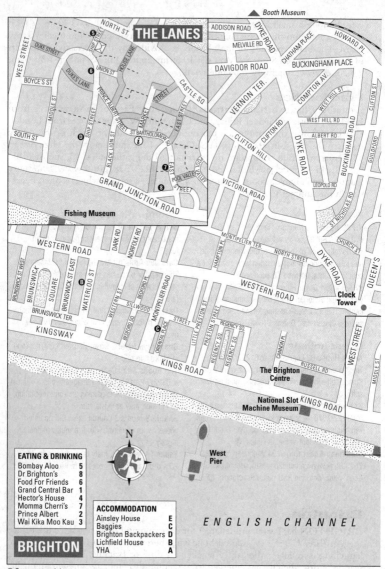

ward towards the Marina and the nudist beach. On the western seafront you can see – but not enter – the brooding **West Pier**, damaged in World War II, severed from the mainland following a hurricane in 1987, and gutted by fire in 2003. Inland, overlooking the traffic-heavy Old Steine, is the distinctive **Royal Pavilion** (daily: Oct–March 10am–5.15pm, April–Sept 9.30am–5.45pm; £6.10; @www.royal.org .uk), a wedding-cake confection of pagodas, minarets and domes built in 1817 as a pleasure palace for the Prince Regent. Just across the lawns from the pavilion is Brighton's **Museum and Art Gallery** (Tues 10am–7pm, Wed–Sat 10am–5pm,

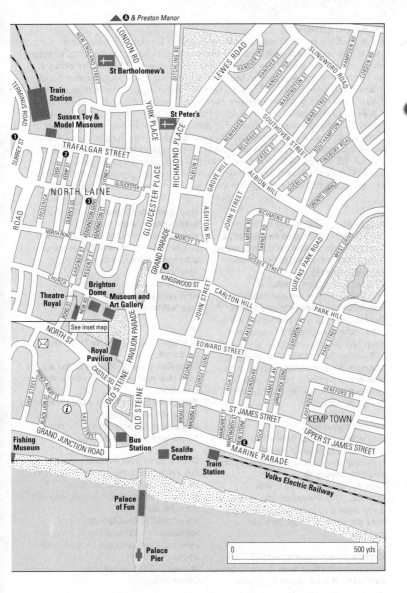

Sun 2–5pm; free; ⓦwww.brighton.virtualmuseum.info), with displays of Art Nouveau and Art Deco furniture and a pair of the corpulent Prince Regent's enormous trousers. Lying to the south and north of the Pavilion and museum are two areas of shops and cafés that are among Brighton's main draws: a block back from the seafront, the narrow alleys of **The Lanes** preserve the layout of the fishing port that Brighton once was, while to the north – on the other side of Church Street – the arty, bohemian quarter of **North Laine** has myriad secondhand clothes-, record- and junk-shops interspersed with stylish boutiques and co-op coffee houses.

## Practicalities

Brighton has a fast and frequent train service from London (Victoria, King's Cross, Blackfriars and London Bridge) and from Gatwick and Luton airports. Coaches arrive at the Pool Valley **bus station**, very near the front. The **tourist office** is at 10 Bartholomew Square in The Lanes (daily Mon–Sat 10am–5pm, summer Sundays 10am–4pm; ☎0906/711 2255, ⍟www.visitbrighton.com). Note that many of the B&Bs in town require a minimum two nights' stay at weekends and in August. **Cafés** and **restaurants** abound, with a particularly good selection in North Laine. Many also offer student discounts. For drinking, the **pubs** around The Lanes are the place to head for. Brighton has a frenetic nightlife scene, livelier than just about anywhere outside London. We've listed a few of the most highly rated places below, but for full listings, pick up a copy of the free magazines *This is Brighton* or *Insight*, available from the tourist office. Brighton also has a lively **gay scene**; for full details check out the free listings magazine *3Sixty* or ⍟www.gay.brighton.co.uk.

### Hostels

**Baggies Backpackers** 33 Oriental Place ☎01273/733740. Just beyond the West Pier this homely hostel has spacious rooms, a huge video library, guitars to strum, and occasional parties. Dorms £12, rooms ❸

**Brighton Backpackers** 75 Middle St ☎01273/777717, ⍟www.brightonbackpackers .com. Just off the seafront with good facilities. Dorm beds cost £13 in the main building, or £15 in the quieter annexe around the corner, where rooms have great sea views. ❸

**YHA** Patcham Place ☎0870/770 5724, ⍟www .yha.org.uk. Sixteenth-century manor house four miles north of Brighton on the A23 London Rd; take bus #5 or #5a. Nov–Feb closed Sun–Wed. Dorms £16, rooms ❸

### Guest houses

**Ainsley House Hotel** 13 Madeira Place ☎01273/605310, ⍟www.ainsleyhotel.com. Friendly, upmarket place in an attractive Regency terrace. No smoking. ❻

**Lichfield House** 30 Waterloo St, Hove ☎01273/777740, ⍟www.lichfieldhouse.freeserve .co.uk. Stylish place just off the seafront, about half a mile west of the centre. No smoking in rooms. ❺

### Cafés and restaurants

**Bombay Aloo** 39 Ship St. Indian place in The Lanes; check out the £5 eat-all-you-can veggie buffet.

**Food for Friends** 17 Prince Albert St. A classy budget wholefood veggie eatery.

**Momma Cherri's** 11 Little East St. Jambalaya, pig's feet and southern fried catfish are just some of the soul food delicacies on offer at this fun American diner.

**Wai Kika Moo Kau** 11 Kensington Gardens. Funky global veggie café-restaurant in North Laine, with low prices.

### Pubs

**Dr Brighton's** 16 Kings Rd. Popular gay haunt on the seafront.

**Grand Central Bar** 29–30 Surrey St. Cool and comfy place opposite the station, with live music at weekends.

**Hector's House** Grand Parade. A favourite student hangout with pre-club music.

**Prince Albert** 48 Trafalgar St. Near the station, this pub has live rock and real ales.

### Clubs and live music venues

**Audio** 10 Marine Parade. This is Brighton's trendiest club, specializing in funk and house.

**Concorde** 2 Madeira Drive. Live music venue with club nights at weekends.

**Honey Club** 214 Kings Rd Arches. By the seafront near the bottom of Ship St, this attracts a youngish crowd, dancing to garage, house and hip-hop.

**Revenge** 32 Old Steine. Predominantly gay venue. Cabaret on Mon night.

# Winchester

**WINCHESTER**'s rural tranquillity betrays little of its former role as the political and ecclesiastical power base of southern England. A town of Roman foundation fifty miles southwest of London, Winchester rose to prominence in the ninth century as King Alfred the Great's capital, and remained influential well into the Middle Ages. The shrine of St Swithun, Alfred's tutor and Bishop of Winchester, made the town an important destination for pilgrims.

Alfred's statue stands at the eastern end of the Broadway, the town's main thoroughfare, which becomes High Street as it progresses west towards the train station. To the south of here is the **Cathedral** (daily 8.30am–6pm; £4 donation; @www .winchester-cathedral.org.uk); much of its exterior is twelfth-century, although there's some Norman stonework visible in the south transept. Above the high altar are mortuary chests holding the remains of the pre-Conquest kings of England. The Angel chapel contains sixteenth-century wall paintings of the miracles of the Virgin Mary, although a modern protective replica now covers the originals. Jane Austen is buried on the north side of the nave; the inscription on the floor slab remembers her merely as the daughter of a local clergyman, ignoring her renown as a novelist. Immediately outside are traces of the original Saxon cathedral, built by Cenwalh, king of Wessex, in the mid-seventh century. The true grandeur of this structure is shown by a model in the **City Museum** (April–Oct Mon–Sat 10am–5pm; Nov–March Tues–Sat 10am–4pm, Sun noon–4pm; free) on the western side of the cathedral close; other exhibits include mosaics and pottery from Roman Winchester. Further west along High Street is the thirteenth-century **Great Hall** (daily 10am–5pm; free), a banqueting chamber used by successive kings of England and renowned for what is alleged to be King Arthur's Round Table – though the piece is probably fourteenth-century (and so several centuries too young). It seems to have been repainted with portraits and the names of King Arthur's knights for the visit of Emperor Charles V, who was entertained here by Henry VIII in 1522. South of the cathedral is the fourteenth-century Pilgrims Hall, from where a signposted route leads through a medieval quarter to **Winchester College**, the oldest of Britain's public schools. It's then a half-hour stroll across the Water Meadow to the almshouse of **St Cross** (Mon–Sat 9.30/10.30am–3.30/5pm; £2.50), founded in 1136. Continuing a medieval tradition, needy wayfarers may still apply for the "dole" here – a tiny portion of bread and beer.

### Practicalities

Winchester's **train station** is about a mile northwest of the cathedral on Stockbridge Road. The **bus terminal** is on Broadway, just opposite the Guildhall, in which the **tourist office** is situated (Mon–Sat 9.30/10am–5/5.30pm, Sun 11am–4pm; Oct–March closed Sun; @01962/840500, @www.visitwinchester.co.uk). Winchester's affluence is reflected in both the style and prices of its **B&Bs**, most of which cluster in the streets between St Cross and Christchurch roads, south of town. *The Farrells*, 5 Ranelagh Rd (@01962/869555; ④), is a good central option, or try *Sullivans*, 29 Stockbridge Rd, beside the train station (@01962/862027, @sullivans_bandb@amserve.net; ④). There's also a lovely **hostel** in the City Mill, 1 Water Lane, just east of Alfred's statue (@0870/770 6092, @www.yha.org.uk; closed Nov–Feb; dorms £10.60, rooms ④). For food, *Forte Brasserie and Tea Rooms*, 78 Parchment St, offers snacks, full meals and a buzzy atmosphere, while the cool, modern *Alcatraz Rosso*, Jewry St, provides pizzas and pastas. For more expensive fare in a traditional pub with cosy nooks and crannies, head for the *Wykeham Arms* at 75 Kingsgate Street, just outside the cathedral precinct to the south.

# England's West Country

England's **West Country** has never been a precise geographical term, but as a broad generalization, the cosmopolitan feel of the southeast begins to fade into a slower, rural pace of life from **Salisbury** onwards, becoming more pronounced the further west you travel. In Neolithic times a rich and powerful culture evolved here, as shown by monuments such as **Stonehenge** and **Avebury**, and the isolated moorland sites of inland **Cornwall**. Urban attractions of western England include **Bristol** and the well-preserved Regency spa town of **Bath**; those in search of rural peace and quiet should head for the compelling bleakness of **Dartmoor**. The southwestern extremities of Britain include some of the most beautiful stretches of coastline, its rugged, rocky shores battered by the Atlantic, although the excellent sandy beaches make **Cornwall** one of the country's busiest corners over the summer. All of the region's major centres can be reached fairly easily by train or coach from London. Local bus services cover most areas, although in the rural depths of Dartmoor they can be very sparse indeed. Check the tourist office website ⓦwww.westcountrynow.com.

## Salisbury and around

**SALISBURY**'s central feature is the elegant spire of its **Cathedral** (daily 7.15am–6.15pm; £3.80 donation; ⓦwww.salisburycathedral.org.uk), the tallest in the country, rising over 400ft. With the exception of the spire, the cathedral was almost entirely completed in the thirteenth century, and is one of the few great English churches that is not a hotch-potch of different styles. Prominent among the features of the interior are the fourteenth-century clock just inside the north porch, one of the oldest working timepieces in the country, and an exceptional Tudor memorial to the Earl of Hertford, Lady Jane Grey's brother-in-law, in the Lady Chapel at the eastern end of the church. An octagonal **chapter house**, approached via the extensive **cloisters** (Mon–Sat 9.30/10am–5.15/6.45pm, Sun noon–5.30pm; free), holds a collection of precious manuscripts, among which is one of the four extant copies of the Magna Carta. Most of Salisbury's remaining sights are grouped in a sequence of historic houses around The Close, the old walled inner town around the cathedral. The **Salisbury and South Wiltshire Museum**, opposite the main portal of the cathedral on West Walk (Mon–Sat 10am–5pm; July & Aug also Sun 2–5pm; ⓦwww.salisburymuseum.org.uk), is a good place to bone up on the Neolithic history of the region before heading out to Stonehenge and Avebury. **Mompesson House** on The Close's North Walk (April–Oct Sat–Wed 11am–5pm; £4) is a fine eighteenth-century house complete with Georgian furniture and fittings. For the postcard view of the cathedral immortalized by John Constable, wander across the meadows and over the River Avon to **HARNHAM**, about a twenty-minute walk, where you can have lunch or a drink at the *Old Mill* pub. A ten-minute hop on any Andover- or Amesbury-bound bus takes you to the ruins of **OLD SARUM** (daily 9/11am–3/6pm; £2.80), abandoned in the fourteenth century when the bishopric moved to Salisbury. Traces of the medieval town are visible in the outlines of its Norman cathedral and castle mound, but the ditch-encircled site is far older, populated in Iron Age, Roman and Saxon times.

### Practicalities

It's a short walk southeast from Salisbury's **train station** (services from London Waterloo) across the River Avon into town. **Buses** from nearby Winchester and elsewhere terminate behind Endless St, a block south of which is the **tourist office**, just off Market Square (daily 9.30/10.30am–4.30/6pm; closed Sun in winter; ☎01722/334956, ⓦwww.visitsalisbury.com).

### Hostel

**YHA** Milford Hill House, Milford Hill ☎0870/770 6018, ⓦwww.yha.org.uk. Excellent, secluded hostel five minutes' walk east of the city centre. Dorms £16, rooms ❹

### Guest houses

**Glen Lyn** 6 Bellamy Lane ☎0845/129 8149,

ⓦwww.glenlynbandbatsalisbury.co.uk. Victorian B&B in quiet location ten minutes' walk from the centre. No smoking. ❺

**Old Rectory** 75 Bellevue Rd ☎01722/502702, ⓦwww.theoldrectory-bb.co.uk. Elegant, good-value B&B with en-suite or private bathrooms. No smoking in rooms. ❺

**Wyndham Park Lodge** 51 Wyndham Rd

⊕01722/416517, ⓦwww.wyndhamparklodge.
co.uk. Solid Victorian house with period trappings
and all rooms en suite. No smoking. ❻

### Eating and drinking
**Haunch of Venison** 1 Minster St. Tiny, atmospheric old pub serving good food.

**Michael Snell's Tea Rooms** St Thomas's Square.
Patisserie and café, serving snacks and delicious
buns.
**The Mill** 7 The Maltings. Popular pub offering bar
meals and outdoor seating.
**Moloko** 5 Bridge St. Cool café and vodka bar,
open till late.

## Stonehenge
The uplands northwest of Salisbury were a thriving centre of Neolithic civilization,
the greatest legacy of which is **STONEHENGE** (daily 9/9.30am–4/7pm; £5.50;
EH). It's served by buses from Salisbury. You can also take a tour – ask at the bus
station for details – or get an Explorer (£6) or Wiltshire Day Rover (£6.50) pass,
which are valid all day and include travel to Avebury and Bath. The monument's
age is being constantly revised as research progresses, but it's known that it was
built in several distinct stages and adapted to the needs of successive cultures. The
first Stonehenge probably consisted of a circular ditch dug in around 3000 BC.
The first stones were raised within the earthworks about five hundred years later,
comprising approximately forty great blocks of dolerite (bluestone), sourced from
Preseli in Wales. During the next six hundred years, the incomplete bluestone circle
was transformed by the construction of a circle of twenty-five trilithons and an
inner horseshoe formation of five trilithons, made up of local Wiltshire sarsen stones
up to 21ft in height and topped by horizontal slabs. The smaller bluestones were
re-arranged in various patterns within the outer circle during this period. The way
in which the sun's rays penetrate the central enclosure at dawn on midsummer's day
has led to speculation about Stonehenge's role as either an astronomical observatory
or a place of sun worship, but knowledge of the cultures responsible for building it
is too scanty to reach any firm conclusions. The stones themselves are fenced off to
prevent the erosion caused by thousands of visitors, but it makes the visit a slightly
disappointing experience. The only way to enter the circle itself is take a **guided
tour** (apply on ⊕01980/626267 or at ⓦwww.englishheritage.org.uk; £10).

## Avebury
Salisbury also serves as a base for visiting the equally important – and much more
atmospheric – Neolithic site at **AVEBURY**. Bus #5 runs here daily from Salisbury. The Avebury monoliths were probably erected soon after 2500 BC, and the
main circle – with a diameter of some 1300ft – easily beats Stonehenge in terms of
scale, even if it's not as impressive for its architectural sophistication. The atmosphere here is far more relaxed, however, and you can contemplate the grassy site
armed with a pint or two from the *Red Lion* village pub, set right beside the main
stone circle. Avebury's **Alexander Keiller Museum** (daily 10am–4/6pm; £4.20)
has displays on the monoliths as well as other ancient sites in the vicinity, while the
**Barn Gallery** (same times, same ticket) favours a more interactive approach. Both
places are worth visiting before or after exploring the cluster of archeological sites
to the south of Avebury, best approached along the (signposted) **West Kennet
Avenue**, two lines of standing stones thought to have been a processional way.
Originally this ran two miles south to the so-called **Sanctuary**, possibly a gathering place of religious significance from around 3000 BC, of which little remains
today. More compelling is the enormous conical mound of **Silbury Hill** just west
of here, Europe's largest Neolithic construction, dating from around 2600 BC.
Signposted up a track on the other side of the A4, **West Kennet Long Barrow** is
an impressive stone passage grave in use for over fifteen hundred years from about
3700 BC. From the Sanctuary at Overton Hill, hikers can loop northeast on a
section of the **Ridgeway**, a 4000-year-old prehistoric highway which may once
have run the breadth of Britain; it can still be walked or cycled as far as Tring, in

the Chilterns. Get details from Avebury's **tourist office** on Green Street (daily 9.30/10am–4.30/5.30pm; ☎01672/539425, ✆www.visitkennet.co.uk).

# Bath

**BATH** is an ancient Roman spa revived in the eighteenth century as a retreat for the wealthy upper classes. Extensive reconstruction put into effect by Neoclassicist architects John Wood and his son, John Wood the Younger, gives the town its appearance, with terraces of weathered sandstone fringed by spindly black railings. The hot spring that gave the city its name was dedicated to Sulis, the Celtic goddess of the waters, and provided the centrepiece of an extensive **Roman Baths** complex, now restored and holding a fascinating museum (daily 9/9.30am–5.30/6pm; July–Aug till 10pm; ✆www.romanbaths.co.uk; £9.50). The pools, pipes and underfloor heating are remarkable demonstrations of the ingenuity of Roman engineering. The **Pump Room** (free), built above the Roman site in the eighteenth century, is now a restaurant and tea room where you can sample the waters while listening to genteel tunes from the resident chamber ensemble. Next to the Roman Baths, **Bath Abbey** (Mon–Sat 9am–4.30/6pm, Sun 1–2.30pm, also 4.30–5.30pm in summer; £2.50 donation; ✆www.bathabbey.org) is renowned for the lofty fifteenth-century vault of its choir and the dense carpet of gravestones and memorials that cover the floor. The Abbey's **Heritage Vaults** (Mon–Sat 10am–4pm; £2) house Saxon and Norman sculpture and a reconstruction of the original building.

The best of Bath's eighteenth-century architecture is on the high ground to the north of the town centre, where the well-proportioned urban planning of the Woods is showcased by the elegant **Circus** and the adjacent **Royal Crescent**. The house at **1 Royal Crescent** is now a museum (Tues–Sun 10.30am–4/5pm; closed Dec to mid-Feb; £4), showing how the Crescent's houses would have looked in the Regency period. The social calendar of Bath's elite centred on John Wood the Younger's **Assembly Rooms** (daily 11am–5/6pm; free), just east of the Circus; it includes the interesting **Museum of Costume** in the basement (daily March–Oct 11am–5pm, Nov–Feb 11am–4pm; ✆www.museumofcostume.co.uk; £6.25; joint ticket with Roman Baths £12.50). The triple arches of Pulteney Bridge, behind the abbey, lead northeast from the town centre across the River Avon and up Great Pulteney Street to the **Holburne Museum** (Tues–Sat 10am–5pm, Sun 11am–5pm; closed mid-Dec to mid-Feb; ✆www.bath.ac.uk/holburne; £3.50), which contains silver, porcelain and furniture from the Regency period, as well as some fine art, including works by Gainsborough, once a Bath resident.

## Practicalities

The **train** and **bus stations** are both on Manvers Street, five minutes south of the centre. The **tourist office** is just off the Abbey churchyard (Mon–Sat 9.30am–5/6pm, Sun 10am–4pm; ☎0906/711 2000, ✆www.visitbath.co.uk). The main tourist thoroughfares and neighbouring backstreets provide plenty of **tearooms** – we've listed some of the best, along with the best **restaurants** and **pubs**, below. Bath also hosts the eclectic **International Music Festival** (✆www.bath musicfest.org.uk) in May and June. Accommodation at this time can be hard to find – indeed, you should book early if staying in Bath at any time. For **Internet** access and coffee try the Green Park Brasserie at Old Green Park Station, off James St (☎01225/338565; £3/hr).

### Hostels

**Backpackers' Hostel** 13 Pierrepoint St ☎01225/446787, ✆www.hostels.co.uk. Relaxed and centrally located hostel, just five minutes' walk north of the train and bus stations. Dorms £12, rooms ❹

**YHA Bathwick Hill** ☎0870/770 5688, ✆www.yha .org.uk. A hillside villa a mile east of town; bus #18 or #418. Dorms £12.50, rooms ❹

### Guest houses

**Belmont** 7 Belmont, Lansdowne Rd ☎01225/423082, ✆www.belmontbath.co.uk.

Fairly large rooms in a house designed by John Wood near the Assembly Rooms and Circus. ❹
**Henry** 6 Henry St ☎01225/424052, ⊛www.thehenry.com. Near the Abbey, this friendly, recently refurbished place books up quickly. Shared facilities. ❻

### Cafés and restaurants

**Café Retro** 18 York St. Popular café and bistro with an inventive international menu and a relaxed atmosphere. Great breakfasts too.

**Demuths** 2 North Parade Passage off Abbey Green. A genuinely classy vegetarian restaurant offering an imaginative range of mouthwatering dishes, though prices are on the steep side.

**Walrus and Carpenter** 28 Barton St. Friendly place behind the theatre, serving steaks and burgers as well as veggie dishes.

### Pubs

**The Bell** 103 Walcot St. Everything you could want from a neighbourhood pub with a great range of beers, a mixed and lively crowd, garden and live music Mon and Wed eve, plus Sun lunch.

**The Porter** 15 George St. Something of a Bath institution, with decent vegetarian food at lunchtime, live music during the week and DJ sets at weekends.

**The Salamander** 3 John St. This small, characterful pub can get uncomfortably crowded with knowledgeable drinkers lapping up the locally brewed ales. The upstairs restaurant does exceptionally fine food, though it doesn't come cheap.

# Bristol

Situated on a succession of lumpy hills twelve miles west of Bath and just inland from the mouth of the Avon, the city of **BRISTOL** grew rich on transatlantic trade – slaving, in particular – in the early part of the nineteenth century. It has moved on since then, while remaining a wealthy, commercial centre, now home to computer and aviation industries, a major university and a thriving cultural scene.

The city centre – in so much as there is one – is an elongated traffic interchange, **The Centre**. Its southern end gives onto the **Floating Harbour**, an area of waterways that formed the hub of the old port and now are the location of numerous bars and restaurants as well as two of Bristol's best contemporary arts venues, housed in converted warehouses on either side of the water: the **Arnolfini** (⊛www.arnolfini.org.uk), which at the time of writing was undergoing a major redevelopment (due to reopen late 2005) and the **Watershed Arts Centre** (⊛www.watershed.co.uk), which has a pleasant, reasonably priced café serving food until late. Behind the Watershed lies the at-Bristol complex (⊛www.at-bristol.org.uk), where two interactive centres – **Explore** (daily 10am–6pm; £8), a hands-on technology park, and **Wildwalk** (same times; £6.50), a hi-tech wildlife museum – are overshadowed by a giant **IMAX cinema** (screenings 11.15am–4.30/7.15pm; £6.50); a ticket for all three costs £17. From the Arnolfini, on Prince's Wharf, a swing bridge leads to the quayside **Bristol Industrial Museum** (Sat–Wed 10am–5pm; free; ⊛www.bristol-city.gov.uk/museums), with cars and ship models. Just east of here rises the **Church of St Mary Redcliffe** (daily May–Oct 9am–5pm, Nov–March until 4pm), a glorious Gothic confection begun in the thirteenth century. A brief walk further east along busy Redcliffe Way brings you to the **British Empire and Commonwealth Museum**, attached to the main train station (daily 10am–5pm; £6.50; ⊛www.empiremuseum.co.uk), which reviews Britain's colonial empire and the trading network that succeeded it. To the west of the Industrial Museum, ten minutes' walk or a brief ride on the harbour ferry brings you to the **Maritime Heritage Centre** (daily 10am–4.30/5.30pm; £6.25), celebrating Bristol's shipbuilding past and providing access to Brunel's **SS Great Britain**, the first propeller-driven iron ship, launched from this dock in 1843, and to a replica of the *Matthew*, which carried John Cabot to North America in 1497.

The rest of your time is best spent wandering around the suburb of **CLIFTON**, whose airy terraces are reminiscent of the Georgian splendours of nearby Bath. It's a somewhat genteel quarter, but full of enticing pubs and with a spectacular focus in the **Clifton Suspension Bridge** (⊛www.clifton-suspension-bridge.org.uk), the creation of the indefatigable engineer and railway builder Isambard

Kingdom Brunel, spanning the limestone abyss of the Avon Gorge. An interpretive Visitor Centre is due to open here in early 2006. On a height above the bridge, the diminutive **Observatory** (daily 11am/noon–4/5pm; closed when cloudy; £1.50) holds a Victorian camera obscura which encompasses views of the gorge and bridge, and provides access to a steep tunnel ending at Giant's Cave, a ledge on the side of the gorge (same hours; £1.50).

## Practicalities

Bristol's main Temple Meads **train station** is a five-minute bus ride southeast of the centre, or a fifteen-minute walk. The **bus station** is close to the Broadmead shopping centre on Marlborough Street. There's a **tourist office** in the at-Bristol complex on Harbourside (daily 10/11am–4/6pm; ☎0906/711 2191, ✆www.visit bristol.co.uk). For food and drink, the stretch between Clifton and the city centre offers a vast choice of ethnic eats and late bars. For **nightlife** listings galore check out the magazine *Venue* (✆www.venue.co.uk; £3.99) available at any newsagent. Arnolfini and Watershed both have arts **cinemas**, and there's a renowned **theatre** company at the Old Vic on King St. In recent decades Bristol's vibrant music scene has produced a host of influential names (Tricky, Massive Attack, Portishead); top **clubs** are listed below.

### Hostels

**Bristol Backpackers** 17 St Stephen's St ☎0117/925 7900, ✆www.bristolbackpackers .co.uk. Friendly place in the heart of the pub district, with late bar and Internet access. Dorms £14, rooms ❹

**YHA** 14 Narrow Quay ☎0870/770 5726, ✆www .yha.org.uk. Splendidly situated hostel in an old wharfside building next to the Arnolfini. Dorms £18, rooms ❹ (prices include breakfast).

### Guest houses

**Downs View** 38 Upper Belgravia Rd ☎0117/973 7046, ✆www.downsviewguesthouse.co.uk. Overlooking Clifton Downs, with good views from the rooms, some of which are en suite. ❻

**St Michael's Guest House** 145 St Michael's Hill ☎0117/907 7820. Simple rooms, with shared facilities, above a popular café. ❹

### Eating and drinking

**Planet Pizza** 83 Whiteladies Rd. Good-value pizzeria with a mellow feel and some outside tables.

**Tantric Jazz Café** 39 St Nicholas St. Mediterranean-style cuisine, live jazz and blues and a bohemian atmosphere.

**Watershed** 1 Canons Rd. Pop in at any time of day and choose from one of the dozens of enticing specials. Portions are generous, prices are low and there are plenty of veggie options. It's a licensed bar too.

### Nightlife

**Academy** Frogmore St. Live bands and big-name DJs at this central and capacious club.

**Blue Mountain** Stokes Croft. Non-mainstream club spinning funk, hip-hop and drum'n'bass.

**Thekla** The Grove. Great riverboat venue staging eclectic events until 2am or later.

# Wells and Glastonbury

A small market town possessed of an extraordinary cathedral, **WELLS** is served by regular buses from Bristol and Bath, all arriving at Princes Road bus station, five minutes from the centre. Follow Market Street eastwards from here to the inn-lined Market Place, and the **tourist office** in the Town Hall (April–Oct daily 9.30am–5.30pm, Nov–March daily 10am–4pm; ☎01749/672552). From here a gateway leads through to The Close, bringing you face to face with an intoxicating array of Gothic statuary, mostly from the 1230s and 1240s. Inside the majestic **Cathedral** (daily 7am–6/7pm; £5 donation; ✆www.wellscathedral.org .uk), the great interlacing "scissor-arches" at the crossing were devised to support the unstable tower; in the north transept a fourteenth-century clock strikes the quarter-hours. North of the cathedral are **Vicar's Close**, a row of fourteenth-century terraced houses, and the town **museum** (Easter–Oct daily 10am–5.30pm, Aug till 8pm; Nov–Easter Mon & Wed–Sun 11am–4pm; £2.50). The nearest

**hostel** (☎0870/770 5760, ⊛www.yha.org.uk; call for opening Sept–April; dorms £11, rooms ❹) is six miles northwest in the village of **CHEDDAR**, reached on bus #126 or #826, walking distance from the dramatic **Cheddar Gorge**, formed by the collapse of a cave system.

Once- or twice-hourly buses head southwest from Wells to **GLASTONBURY**, a small rural town whose associations with the Holy Grail and King Arthur have made it a magnet for those with a taste for the mystical – the **Tor**, a natural mound overlooking the town, is identified with the Isle of Avalon. Joseph of Arimathea, a relation of the Virgin Mary, is also said to have owned land nearby, and to have brought Mary and Jesus here. Around the Market Cross, Glastonbury's High Street is overrun by New Age cafés and shops. The impressive ruins of the **Abbey** are approached from nearby Magdalene St (daily 9/10am–4.30/6pm; £4; ⊛www .glastonburyabbey.com); this was the oldest Christian establishment in continuous use in England until Henry VIII ordered its near-destruction. The choir is alleged to hold the tomb of King Arthur and Guinevere. A mile to the east is the Tor, at the base of which stands the natural spring known as **Chalice Well** (Nov–Feb daily 10am–4pm, Mar–Oct daily 10am–5.30pm; £2.85; ⊛www.chalicewell.org.uk). The ferrous waters that flow from the hillside here were popularly thought to have gained their colour from the blood of Christ, supposedly flowing from the Holy Grail, buried here by Joseph of Arimathea. On top of the Tor stands the remains of a fourteenth-century church; the views from here are spectacular and it's a popular place from which to see the sunrise on the summer solstice.

By nightfall Glastonbury reverts to sleepy rural stillness – except over the summer solstice and during the **Glastonbury Festival**, which is held on a nearby farm over the last weekend in June and draws 80,000 people to its binge of music, cabaret and all-round hedonism. Tickets (£125) are available via the website ⊛www.glastonbury festivals.co.uk or by calling ☎0870/830 2004. The **tourist office** is housed in the Tribunal on the High Street (daily 10am–4/5.30pm; ☎01458/832954, ⊛www.glaston buryric.co.uk). There's a friendly crowd at the Glastonbury Backpackers **hostel** on Market Place (☎01458/833353, ⊛www.glastonburybackpackers.com; dorms £12, rooms ❸), while the Isle of Avalon **campsite** is a short walk up Northload Street from the centre (☎01458/833618). For **food and drink**, the *Backpackers* has cheap, filling meals and a lively bar with events; you'll also find coffees, meals and music at the *Blue Note Café* on the High Street.

## Dartmoor

**Dartmoor** (⊛www.dartmoor-npa.gov.uk) is one of England's most beautiful wilderness areas, an expanse of wild uplands some 75 miles southwest of Bristol. It's home to an indigenous breed of wild pony and dotted with **tors**, characteristic wind-eroded pillars of granite. One focus for visitors in the middle of the park is **POSTBRIDGE**, reached by local bus from Exeter and Plymouth on the #82 Transmoor service (daily in summer, weekends only in winter). Famous for its medieval bridge over the East Dart river, this is a good starting point for walks in the woodlands surrounding **Bellever Tor** to the south. Postbridge's **tourist office**, on the main road through the village (daily Easter–Oct daily 10am–5pm, Nov–Dec weekends 10am–4pm, closed Jan–Easter; ☎01822/880272, ⊛www.dartmoor-npa .gov.uk), can supply information on the national park. The nearest **hostel** is at Bellever, one mile south (☎0870/770 5692, ⊛www.yha.org.uk; closed Nov–Feb; dorms £12.50).

The wildest parts of the moor, around its highest points of High Willhays and Yes Tor, are south of the market town of **OKEHAMPTON** – served by regular buses from Plymouth and Exeter. Despite the stark beauty of the terrain, this part of the moor is used by the Ministry of Defence as a firing range: details of times when it's safe to walk the moor are available from the **tourist office** on Fore Street (Mon–Sat 10am–5pm; ☎01837/53020, ⊛www.okehampton.co.uk). Surrounded by woods one mile southwest of town is the now crumbling Norman keep of Oke-hampton Castle (April–Sept daily 10am–5/6pm; £2.80). There's a YHA **hostel** in a converted goods shed at the station (℡0870/770 5978, ⊛www.yha.org.uk; closed Dec & Jan; dorms £14, rooms ➍).

# The Eden Project

In the heart of Cornwall, England's most southwesterly county, the **Eden Project** (April–Oct daily 9.30am–6pm, Nov–March daily 10am–4pm; £10; ⊛www.edenproject.com) lies four miles northeast of St Austell (bus #T9 from St Austell train station or #T10 from Newquay). Occupying a 160-foot-deep disused clay pit, the centre showcases the diversity of the planet's plant-life in a stunningly landscaped site. The centrepiece is two vast geodesic "biomes", or conservatories, one holding plants more usually found in warm, temperate zones, and the larger of the two recreating a tropical environment, with teak and mahogany trees, and even a waterfall and river gushing through. Equally impressive are the external grounds, where the various plantations are interspersed with brilliant swathes of flowers. There are timed story-telling sessions, a lawn-carpeted arena where Celtic and other music is played, and good food on hand. Allow at least half a day for a full exploration, but arrive early to avoid congestion.

# Penzance and around

The busy port of **PENZANCE** forms the natural gateway to the westernmost extremity of Cornwall – and, indeed, England – the Penwith Peninsula, and all the major sights of the region can be reached on day-trips from here. From the **train station**, at the northern end of town, Market Jew Street threads its way through the town centre, culminating in the Neoclassical facade of Market House, fronted by a statue of local-born chemist and inventor Humphry Davy. West of here, a series of parks and gardens punctuate the quiet residential streets overlooking the promenade. The **Penlee House Gallery and Museum**, off Morrab Road (Mon–Sat 10/10.30am–4.30/5pm; £2, free on Sat; ⊛www.penleehouse.org.uk), features works by members of the Newlyn school, late nineteenth-century painters of local land- and seascapes. The view east across the bay is dominated by **St Michael's Mount**, site of a fortified medieval monastery perched on an offshore pinnacle of rock. At low tide, the Mount is joined by a cobbled causeway to the mainland village of Marazion (regular buses from Penzance); at high tide, a boat can ferry you over (£1). You can amble around part of the Mount's shoreline, but most of the rock lies within the grounds of the **castle**, now a stately home belonging to Lord St Levan (April–Oct Mon–Fri 10.30am–5.30pm, plus most weekends; Nov–March in good weather only; £5.50).

The other obvious excursion is to **LAND'S END**, the extremity of the Penwith Peninsula, accessible on frequent buses from Penzance. Despite the hold it exerts over the popular imagination, the site may fail to live up to expectations – especially now that a theme park has been built here – and it's worthwhile using the coastal path to explore some of the less frequented spots of the peninsula. A mile and a half south of Land's End you'll find rugged beauty at **Mill Bay**, while there are acres of beaches the same distance north at **Whitesand Bay**, and more spectacular headlands around **Cape Cornwall**, four miles north of Land's End.

## Practicalities

Penzance **train** and **bus stations** are at the northeastern end of town, a step away from Market Jew Street. The **tourist office** (Mon–Sat 9am–5pm, Sun 10am–1pm; ℡01736/362207, ⊛www.go-cornwall.com) is by the bus station. **B&Bs** congregate at the western end of town around Morrab Rd. The YHA **hostel**, Castle Horneck, Alverton (℡0870/770 5992, ⊛www.yha.org.uk; closed Jan; dorms £14, rooms

④), is a about a mile from the centre off the Land's End road and has camping facilities, or there's *Penzance Backpackers*, Alexandra Road (☎01736/363836, ☻www.pzbackpack.com; dorms £13, rooms ❸). Near Whitesand Bay and Land's End, the excellent *Whitesands Lodge* (☎01736/871776, ☻www.whitesandslodge.co.uk) offers dorms (£12.50), private rooms (❺) and camping. *Bar Co-Co's*, 12 Chapel Street, has **snacks** and cakes as well as coffee and beer; *Archie Brown's*, on Bread Street, is a veggie café/restaurant. Town-centre **pubs** include two touristy but good-value places on Chapel Street, the seventeenth-century *Admiral Benbow* and the even older *Turk's Head*, both with maritime fittings and good food. Look out for live music and other performances at the *Acorn Arts Centre* on Parade Street.

## St Ives and the north Cornwall coast

Across the peninsula from Penzance, the fishing village of **ST IVES** is the quintessential Cornish resort, featuring a maze of narrow streets lined with whitewashed cottages, sandy beaches and lush subtropical flora. The village's erstwhile tranquillity attracted several major artists throughout the twentieth century – Ben Nicholson, Barbara Hepworth and Naum Gabo among them. You can see examples of the work of these and others at **Tate St Ives**, overlooking Porthmeor Beach (daily 10am–4.30/5.30pm; Nov–Feb closed Mon; £5.50; ☻www.tate.org.uk/stives). A combined ticket (£8.50) admits you to the **Barbara Hepworth Museum** on Barnoon Hill (same hours), which preserves the studio of the modernist sculptor. Of the town's three beaches, the north-facing Porthmeor occasionally has good surf, and boards can be rented at the beach.

The **train station** is at Porthminster Beach, just north of the **bus station** on Station Hill. The **tourist office** in the Guildhall, Street an Pol (mid-May to Aug Mon–Sat 9/9.30am–5/6pm, Sun 10am–1/4pm; Sept to mid-May Mon–Fri 9/9.30am–5pm, Sat 9/10am–2pm; ☎01736/796297, ☻www.go-cornwall.com), is a couple of minutes from both stations. Nearby is the *St Ives Backpackers* **hostel**, in a restored Wesleyan chapel on The Stennack (☎01736/799444, ☻www.backpackers.co.uk/st-ives; dorms £11–16, rooms ❸).

### Newquay, Padstow and Tintagel

Buffeted by Atlantic currents, Cornwall's north coast has a harsh grandeur, and is the area of the West Country most favoured by the **surfing** set. King of the surf resorts is **NEWQUAY**, whose somewhat tacky centre is surrounded by seven miles of golden sands, including Fistral Beach, the venue for surfing championships. There's a **tourist office** at Marcus Hill (mid-May to mid-Sept Mon–Sat 9.30am–5.30pm, Sun 9.30am–1pm; mid-Sept to mid-May Mon–Fri 9.30am–4.30pm, Sat 9.30am–12.30pm; ☎01637/854020, ☻www.newquay.co.uk), and numerous campsites and hostels, including *Newquay International Backpackers*, 69 Tower Rd (☎01637/879366, ☻www.backpackers.co.uk/newquay; dorms £9–15, rooms ④), and *Matt's Surf Lodge*, 110 Mount Wise (☎01637/874651, ☻www.matts-surf-lodge.co.uk; dorms £8–12.50, rooms ④).

However, unless you're dedicated to sand and surf, or drawn by the clubbing scene – Newquay's hectic nightlife is legendary – you could plump for less packed resorts nearby. Ten miles north, **PADSTOW** makes a more appealing base for some first-class beaches, such as Constantine Bay, four miles west, and Polzeath, on the eastern side of the Camel estuary. Primarily a fishing port, Padstow is renowned for its fish restaurants, not least those belonging to celebrity chef Rick Stein; dodge the expensive *Seafood Restaurant* and *St Petroc's Bistro* in favour of the more casual *Rick Stein's Café*, 10 Middle St, which serves lunchtime snacks and moderately priced evening meals, his *Seafood Deli* on South Quay for take-aways, and *Stein's Fish & Chips*, also on South Quay. Across the Camel estuary, twelve miles northwest, the village of **TINTAGEL** trades on its associations with King Arthur. Even if you're bored by all the hocus-pocus surrounding the legend,

Tintagel Castle (daily April–Sept 10am–6pm, Oct 10am–5pm, Nov–March 10am–4pm; £3.90), supposedly Arthur's birthplace, merits a visit, its black and tattered Norman ruins straddling an outcrop above the sea. It's an evocative spot, with splendidly craggy coastline to either side, and the coast path running along the cliff-top. Padstow **tourist office** is on the harbourside (Easter–Sept Mon–Sat 9.30am–5pm, also Sun 11am–4pm in July & Aug; Oct–Easter Mon–Fri 9am–4pm; ☏01841/533449, ⊛www.padstowlive.com) and Tintagel's is in the car park off Fore Street (daily 10/10.30am–4/5pm; ☏01841/533449, ⊛www.northcornwall -live.com). Two YHA **hostels** in the region enjoy superb locations: just off the beach at Constantine Bay, near Padstow (☏0870/770 6076, ⊛www.yha.org.uk; call for winter opening; dorms £14, rooms ❹), and about a mile south of Tintagel at Dunderhole Point (☏01840/770 6068, ⊛www.yha.org.uk; closed Nov–March; dorms £11, rooms ❹).

# Central England

Central England was the powerhouse of the Industrial Revolution and is still pre-dominantly a region of gritty manufacturing towns. Birmingham, at the hub of this industrial sprawl, boasts one of the best concert halls and orchestras in the country, but is still unlikely to feature on a whistlestop national tour. The university town of **Oxford**, and **Stratford-upon-Avon**, the birthplace of William Shakespeare, are the main draws here – and, in the east of the region, the other major university town of **Cambridge**.

## Oxford

Think of **OXFORD** and inevitably you think of its university, revered as one of the world's great academic institutions, inhabiting honeystone buildings set around ivy-clad quadrangles. Much of this is accurate enough, but although the university dominates central Oxford, the wider city has an entirely different character, its economy built on the car plants of the suburb of Cowley. The **university** has long operated a collegiate system in which many students and tutors live, work and take their meals together in the same complex of buildings – usually a couple of quadrangles ("quads") with a chapel, library and dining hall. Taken together, the colleges form a dense maze of historic buildings in the heart of the city. Note that access may be restricted during examinations – especially in May and June – conferences and functions.

The main point of reference is **Carfax**, a central crossroads overlooked by the chunky **Carfax Tower** (daily 10am–4.30pm; £1.50), one of many opportunities to enjoy a panorama of Oxford's "dreaming spires". From here, head south down St Aldates to the biggest of Oxford's colleges, **Christ Church** (Mon–Sat 9.30am–5.30pm, Sun noon–5.30pm; £4). The main entrance – though visitors are usually ushered in further south – is overlooked by the imposing Tom Tower, built in 1681 by Wren, and opens onto the vast expanse of Tom Quad, mostly dating from the college's foundation in the sixteenth century. An indication of the prestige and wealth of the college is that the city's late Norman **cathedral** also serves as the college chapel. A short stroll west along Pembroke Street is **Modern Art Oxford** (Tues–Sat 10am–5pm, Sun noon–5pm; free; ⊛www.modernart oxford.org.uk), which features excellent temporary exhibitions of contemporary art. South of Christ Church, **Christ Church Meadow** offers gentle walks – either east along Broad Walk to the River Cherwell or south along New Walk to the Thames (referred to hereabouts as the Isis). From the Broad Walk, paths lead to **Merton** (Mon–Fri 2–4pm, Sat & Sun 10am–4pm; free), perhaps the prettiest of

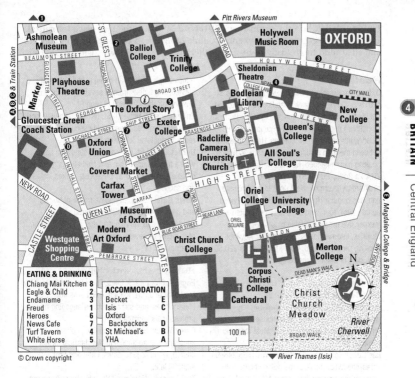

**Map labels:**

Ashmolean Museum
Balliol College
Trinity College
Holywell Music Room
Playhouse Theatre
Sheldonian Theatre
Bodleian Library
New College
The Oxford Story
Gloucester Green Coach Station
Exeter College
Queen's College
Oxford Union
Radcliffe Camera
University Church
All Soul's College
Covered Market
Carfax Tower
Museum of Oxford
Oriel College
University College
Modern Art Oxford
Christ Church College
Merton College
Westgate Shopping Centre
Corpus Christi College
Christ Church Cathedral
Christ Church Meadow
River Cherwell
New College
City Wall

▲❶❷❸❹ & Train Station
Market
◀ ▲ Gloucester Green Coach Station
▲ ❺ Magdalen College & Bridge

N
0   100 m

DEAD MAN'S WALK
BROAD WALK

EATING & DRINKING
Chiang Mai Kitchen 8
Eagle & Child 2
Endamame 3
Freud 1
Heroes 6
News Cafe 7
Turf Tavern 4
White Horse 5

ACCOMMODATION
Becket E
Isis C
Oxford
  Backpackers D
St Michael's B
YHA A

© Crown copyright                    ▼ River Thames (Isis)

the city's colleges, and Rose Lane, which emerges at the eastern end of the High St opposite **Magdalen College** (pronounced "maudlin"; Mon–Fri noon–6pm, Sat & Sun 2–6pm; £3). From here, it's a brief stroll to the bridge over the River Cherwell, where you can rent **punts** in summer.

Many of the university's most important and imposing buildings lie just north of the High Street. The most dramatic is the Italianate **Radcliffe Camera**. Built in the 1730s by James Gibbs, it is now used as a reading room for the **Bodleian Library**, whose main building is immediately to the north in the Old Schools Quadrangle. Most of the library is closed to the general public, but you can see several parts of it on an hour-long guided tour (Mon–Fri 2–4pm daily; £4). The adjacent **Sheldonian Theatre** (Mon–Sat 10am–12.30pm & 2–3.30/4.30pm; £1.50), a copy of the Theatre of Marcellus in Rome, was designed by Christopher Wren and is now a venue for concerts and university functions. A couple of hundred yards north along Parks Road lies the **Pitt Rivers Museum** (Mon–Sat noon–4.30pm, Sun 2–4.30pm; free), a fascinating anthropological hoard, while five minutes west of the Sheldonian is the mammoth **Ashmolean Museum** (Tues–Sat 10am–5pm, Sun noon–5pm; June–Aug Thurs till 7pm; free; ℗www .ashmol.ox.ac.uk). Highlights include the Egyptian rooms with their well-preserved mummies and sarcophagi; the Islamic and Chinese art sections, which both hold superb ceramics; and the rich collections of French and Italian paintings.

### Practicalities

From Oxford's **train station**, it's a five- to ten-minute walk to the centre. Long-distance buses terminate at the central Gloucester Green **bus station**. The **tourist office** is at 15 Broad St (Mon–Sat 9.30am–5pm, Easter–Oct also Sun 10am–3.30pm; ℗01865/726871, ℗www.visitoxford.org). Bike Zone at 6 Lincoln

House, Market St, off Cornmarket (☎01865/728877), is the best place for **rental**. For listings of gigs and other events, consult *Daily Info*, a poster put up in colleges and all around town (daily term-time, otherwise weekly; ☜www.dailyinfo.co.uk).

### Hostels

**Oxford Backpackers Hostel** 9a Hythe Bridge St ☎01865/721761, ☜www.hostels.co.uk. Independent hostel, with ten bunkrooms holding a maximum of eighteen people each. Fully-equipped kitchen, laundry, bar and Internet facilities. Handy location, between the train station and the centre. Advance booking recommended. No curfew. Dorm beds £13. **YHA** 2a Botley Rd ☎0870/770 5970, ✉oxford@yha.org.uk. Next door to the train station, this popular HI hostel has 184 beds divided up into two-, four- and six-bedded en-suite rooms. Inexpensive meals available plus self-catering facilities, Internet access and laundry. Advance booking recommended. No curfew. Dorms £20.50 (including breakfast), rooms ⑤

### Guest houses and B&Bs

**Becket Guest House** 5 Becket St ☎01865/724675. Modest but well-run bay-windowed, non-smoking guest house in a plain terrace close to the train station. Most rooms are en suite. ⑤
**Isis Guest House** 45–53 Iffley Rd ☎01865/248894, ✉isis@herald.ox.ac.uk. Large college house with some en-suite rooms, just across Magdalen Bridge. Good value, but spartan. July–Sept only. ⑥
**St Michael's Guest House** 26 St Michael's St ☎01865/242101. Often full, this friendly, well-kept B&B in a cosy three-storey terrace house, has unsurprising furnishings and fittings, but a very central location. ⑥

### Cafés and restaurants

**Chiang Mai Kitchen** Kemp Hall Passage, 130A High St ☎01865/202233. Superb Thai food

– including a vegetarian menu – and excellent service, in a timber-framed seventeenth-century building off the west end of High St.
**Endamame** 15 Holywell St. Terrific Japanese food and modest prices have quickly secured this tiny restaurant a loyal following.
**Heroes** 8 Ship St. Oxford's best sandwich bar, with a huge range of hot and cold fillings to eat in or take away, as well as breakfasts, cakes, salads and soups.
**News Café** 1 Ship St. A wide range of salads and daily-special hot dishes offered at this good-value and very central day-and-night café, plus plenty of newspapers and satellite news channels on TV.

### Pubs, bars and clubs

**Eagle & Child** 49 St Giles. This pub was once the haunt of J.R.R. Tolkien, C.S. Lewis and other literary types, and still attracts an engaging mix of professionals and academics.
**Freud** Walton St. Classy café-bar – pizzas a speciality – in an imposing Neoclassical former church, with live jazz, blues, Latin and funk every night till late.
**Turf Tavern** Off Holywell St. This atmospheric pub, tucked down a winding alleyway (which also connects with New College Lane), offers good food, fine ales and outdoor seating.
**White Horse** 52 Broad St. A tiny, old pub with a coveted "crow's nest" snug, pictures of old university sports teams on the walls and real ales.
**Zodiac** 190 Cowley Rd ☎01865/420042, ☜www.thezodiac.co.uk. Oxford's most respected live music and dance venue, with bands and club nights throughout the week.

# Stratford-upon-Avon

**STRATFORD-UPON-AVON** makes the most of its association with William Shakespeare, who was born here on April 23, 1564. There are five restored properties recalling the Bard, three in the town itself and two on the outskirts. If you've time to visit them all, it's worth considering a **combined ticket** on sale at all five sites (£10/three town properties, £13/all five); otherwise save your money and go and watch the excellent Royal Shakespeare Company instead (see box, p.183). Top of everyone's Bardic itinerary is **Shakespeare's Birthplace Museum** (Jan–March & Nov–Dec Mon–Sat 10am–4pm, Sun 10.30am–4pm; April–May & Sept–Oct Mon–Sat 10am–5pm, Sun 10.30am–5pm; Jun–Aug Mon–Sat 9am–5pm, Sun 9.30am–5pm; £6.70), on Henley Street, comprising an ugly modern visitor centre attached to the heavily restored half-timbered building where the great man was born. A short walk away is the engaging **Nash's House**, Chapel

## The Royal Shakespeare Company

The Royal Shakespeare Company, or **RSC** (☎01789/403444, ⊛www.rsc.org.uk), works on a repertory system, which means you could see four or five different **plays** in a visit of a few days. Tickets start at around £5 for standing room and a restricted view, rising to £40 for the best seats in the house, though note that the most popular shows get booked up months in advance. There are two adjoining theatres – the Swan and the Royal Shakespeare – and one **box office** (Mon–Sat 9.30am–6pm; ☎0870/609 1110).

Street (Jan–March & Nov–Dec daily 11am–4pm; Apr–May & Sept–Oct daily 11am–5pm; June–Aug Mon–Sat 9.30am–5pm, Sun 10am–5pm; £3.50), once the property of Thomas Nash, first husband of Shakespeare's granddaughter, Elizabeth Hall. The house is kitted out with period furnishings and has a display on the history of Stratford illustrated by various archeological bits and pieces. Chapel Street continues south as Church Street. At the end, turn left along Old Town Street for the impressive medieval **Hall's Croft** (opening hours as Nash's House; £3.50), former home of Shakespeare's elder daughter, Susanna, and her doctor husband, John Hall. Immaculately maintained, with its creaking wooden floors, beamed ceilings and fine kitchen range, it holds a fascinating display on Elizabethan medicine. Beyond, Old Town Street steers right to reach the handsome **Holy Trinity Church** (Mon–Sat 8.30/9am–4/5/6pm, Sun noon–5pm; free), whose mellow, honey-coloured stonework is enhanced by its riverside setting. Shakespeare lies buried here in the chancel (£1). About a mile west of the town centre in Shottery is **Anne Hathaway's Cottage** (daily 9/9.30/10/10.30am–4/5pm; £5.20), whose wooden beams and thatching were home to Anne before she married Shakespeare. **Mary Arden's House**, three miles northwest of the centre in Wilmcote (daily 9.30/10/10.30am–4/5pm; £5.70), was the home of Shakespeare's mother and is now a well-furnished example of an Elizabethan farmhouse.

### Practicalities

Stratford's **train station** is on the northwestern edge of town, ten minutes' walk from the centre; it's served by hourly shuttles from Birmingham and frequent trains from London Paddington and Marylebone. Long-distance **buses** pull into the Riverside Station on the east side of the town centre, off Bridgeway. The **tourist office** (Mon–Sat 9.30am–5pm, Sun 10.30am–4.30pm; ☎0870/160 7930, ⊛www.shakespeare-country.co.uk) is a couple of minutes' walk from the bus station by the bridge at the junction of Bridgeway and Bridgefoot; it operates an efficient accommodation booking hotline. **Bike rental** is available at Clarke's Cycles, 3 Guild St (☎01789/205057).

#### Hostel

**YHA Hemmingford House**, Alveston ☎0870/770 6052, ⊛www.yha.org.uk. HI hostel occupying a rambling Georgian mansion on the edge of the pretty village of Alveston, two miles east of the town centre on the B4086. Dormitories, doubles and family rooms, some en suite, plus laundry, Internet access, cafeteria and self-catering. Regular buses from Stratford's Riverside bus station. Dorms £18, rooms **❹**

#### Guest houses

**Chadwyns Guest House** 6 Broad Walk

☎01789/269077, ⊛www.chadwyns.co.uk. Just off Evesham Place, this well-maintained guest house occupies pleasant Victorian premises and offers en-suite rooms. Great breakfasts with vegetarian options. **❼**
**Parkfield Guest House** 3 Broad Walk ☎01789/293313, ⊛www.parkfieldbandb.co.uk. Very pleasant, non-smoking B&B in a rambling Victorian house down a residential street off Evesham Place. Most of the rooms are en suite. Less than 10mins walk from the centre. **❻**
**Woodstock Guest House** 30 Grove Rd ☎01789/299881, ✉woodstockhouse@compuserve.com.

A smart, non-smoking B&B ten minutes' walk from the centre, by the start of the path to Anne Hathaway's Cottage. It has five extremely comfortable bedrooms, most of them en suite. No credit cards. ⑥

### Campsite

**Stratford Racecourse** Luddington Rd ☏01789/201063. Well-equipped camping and caravan site one mile southwest of the town centre. Regular buses into town (not Sun). Closed Oct–March.

### Cafés, restaurants and pubs

**Callands** 13–14 Meer St. An enticing little restaurant with an eclectic menu offering traditional English fare alongside more exotic dishes. The set-price lunch and dinner menus are a bargain.
**Dirty Duck** (aka *The Black Swan*) 53 Waterside.

The archetypal actors' pub, stuffed to the gunwales every night with a vocal entourage of RSC employees and hangers-on. Essential viewing, plus good food.
**Garrick Inn** 25 High St. Arguably the town's most photogenic and best-preserved old ale house: exposed beams, real ales and decent food.
**Lamb's restaurant** 12 Sheep St ☏01789/292554. Smart restaurant in a sixteenth-century building serving a wide range of stylish dishes, including plenty for veggies; lunch and pre-theatre set menus. Booking advisable.
**Russons** 8 Church St ☏01789/268822. Excellent, good-value cuisine, featuring interesting meat and vegetarian dishes on the main menu and an extensive blackboard of seafood reflecting the catch of the day; cheaper lunch and pre-theatre menus. Closed Sun & Mon.

# Cambridge

Tradition has it that the University of **CAMBRIDGE** was founded by refugees from Oxford, who fled that town after one of their number was lynched by hostile townsfolk in the 1220s; there's been rivalry between the two institutions ever since. What distinguishes Cambridge is "**the Backs**", the green swath of land straddling the River Cam, which overlooks the backs of the old colleges, and provides the town's most enduring image of grand academic architecture. Note that, as in Oxford, access to the colleges may be restricted during examinations – especially in May and June – conferences and functions.

A logical place to begin a tour is **King's College**, whose much celebrated **chapel** (term time Mon–Fri 9.30am–3.30pm, Sat 9.30am–3.15pm, Sun 1.15–2.15pm; rest of year Mon–Sat 9.30am–4.30pm, Sun 10am–5pm; £4.50) is an extraordinarily beautiful building, home to an almost equally vaunted choir (term-time evensong Tues–Sat 5.30pm). King's flanks King's Parade, originally the medieval High Street, at the northern end of which is the **Senate House**, the scene of graduation ceremonies on the last Saturday in June, when champagne corks fly. Adjacent Trinity Street holds the main entrance to **Gonville and Caius College**, known simply as Caius (pronounced "keys"), whose two adjoining courts boast three fancy gates representing different stages on the path to academic enlightenment. On the south side, the "Gate of Honour" leads into Senate House Passage, which itself heads west to **Clare College** (daily 10am–5pm; £2). One of seven colleges founded by women, Clare's plain period-piece courtyard leads to one of the most picturesque of all the bridges over the Cam, **Clare Bridge**. Beyond lies the Fellows' Garden, one of the loveliest college gardens open to the public (times as college). Just north of Caius, **Trinity College** (daily 10am–4.30pm; £2) is the largest of the Cambridge colleges. A statue of Henry VIII, who founded it in 1546, sits in majesty over Trinity's Great Gate, his sceptre replaced with a chair leg by a student wit. Beyond lies the vast asymmetrical expanse of Great Court, which displays a fine range of Tudor buildings, the oldest of which is the fifteenth-century clock tower – the annual race against its midnight chimes is now common currency thanks to the film *Chariots of Fire*. To get through to Nevile's Court – where Newton first calculated the speed of sound – you must pass through "the screens", a passage separating the Hall from the kitchens, a common feature of Oxbridge colleges. The west end of Nevile's Court is enclosed by the beautiful Wren Library (term time Mon–Fri noon–2pm, Sat 10.30am–12.30pm; rest of year Mon–Fri

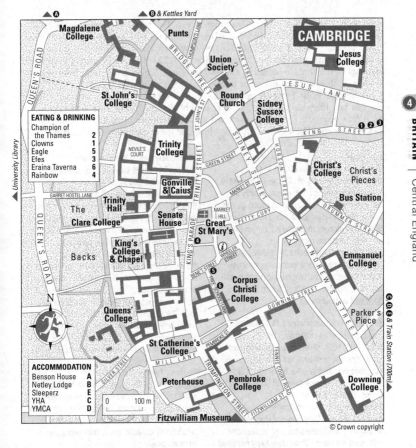

© Crown copyright

**Map labels and legend (within image):**

▲ Ⓐ  ▲ Ⓑ & Kettles Yard

CAMBRIDGE

Magdalene College
Punts
Jesus College
Union Society
St John's College
Round Church
Sidney Sussex College
JESUS LANE
KING STREET
Trinity College
Christ's College
Christ's Pieces
Gonville & Caius
Bus Station
Trinity Hall
Senate House
Great St Mary's
The Clare College
King's College & Chapel
Backs
Emmanuel College
Corpus Christi College
Queens' College
Parker's Piece
St Catherine's College
Peterhouse
Pembroke College
Downing College
Fitzwilliam Museum

QUEEN'S ROAD
University Library
NEVILE'S COURT
GARRET HOSTEL LANE
GREEN STREET
MARKET ST
MARKET HILL
PETTY CURY
WHEELER STREET
BENE'T STREET
FREE SCHOOL LANE
DOWNING STREET
SILVER STREET
MILL LANE
PEMBROKE ST
TRUMPINGTON STREET
TENNIS COURT RD
ST ANDREW'S STREET
DRUMMER STREET
HOBSON STREET
SIDNEY STREET
TRINITY STREET
KING'S PARADE
ST JOHN'S ST
BRIDGE STREET
THOMPSON'S LANE
PARK STREET

Ⓒ Ⓓ Ⓔ & Train Station (700m)

N

0   100 m

**EATING & DRINKING**
| | |
|---|---|
| Champion of the Thames | 2 |
| Clowns | 1 |
| Eagle | 5 |
| Efes | 3 |
| Eraina Taverna | 6 |
| Rainbow | 4 |

**ACCOMMODATION**
| | |
|---|---|
| Benson House | A |
| Netley Lodge | B |
| Sleeperz | E |
| YHA | C |
| YMCA | D |

---

only; free). Back outside Trinity, it's a short hop to the River Cam, where you can go **punting** – the quintessential Cambridge activity. Amongst several places, **punt rental** (£12/hr) is available at the bridge on Garret Hostel Lane.

Doubling back along King's Parade, it takes about five minutes to reach **Queens' College** (daily 10am–4.30pm; £1.50), accessed through the gate on Queen's Lane, just off Silver Street. Here, the Old Court and the Cloister Court are twin fairy-tale Tudor courtyards, with the first the perfect illustration of the original collegiate ideal with kitchens, library, chapel, hall and rooms all set around a tiny green. Equally eye-catching is the wooden **Mathematical Bridge** over the Cam, a copy of the mid-eighteenth-century original which, it was claimed, would stay in place even if the nuts and bolts were removed. From Queens', it's a short stroll to the **Fitzwilliam Museum** (Tues–Sat 10am–5pm, Sun noon–5pm; free; ⓦwww .fitzmuseum.cam.ac.uk). Of all the museums in Cambridge, this is the best, with the Lower Galleries containing a wealth of classical antiquities, while the Upper Galleries display European painting, sculpture and furniture, including masterpieces by Rubens, Hogarth, Renoir and Picasso.

## Practicalities

Cambridge **train station** is a mile or so southeast of the city centre, off Hills Road. It's a twenty-minute walk into the centre, or take shuttle bus #3. The **bus** station is centrally located on Drummer Street. The **tourist office** is on Wheeler Street, off King's Parade (Mon–Sat 10am–5/5.30pm, plus Easter–Oct Sun 11am–4pm; premium line ☎09065/862526, ⓦwww.visitcambridge.org), and operates a useful **accommodation booking service** (☎01223/457581). Currently, the best **listings** is the free, bi–monthly *Cambridge Agenda*. There are several **bike rental** outlets, including Station Cycles outside the train station (☎01223/307125). The **Cambridge Folk Festival** (ⓦwww.cambridgefolkfestival.co.uk), held over four days in late July, has become one of the highlights of the summer festival season. In recent years the festival has widened its boundaries to include acts as diverse as Nick Cave and The Divine Comedy, alongside more traditional folk sounds.

### Hostels

**YHA** 97 Tenison Rd ☎0870/770 5742, ⓔcambridge@yha.org.uk. This well-equipped HI hostel has dorms and twin rooms, laundry and self-catering facilities, a small courtyard garden, and serves breakfast and evening meals. It's close to the train station, off Station Rd. Dorms £16 including breakfast, rooms ❸

**YMCA** Gonville Place ☎01223/356998, ⓦwww .theymca.org.uk. Central location on the south side of Parker's Piece. Singles and doubles, with breakfast included. Very busy during summer; book well in advance. ❹

### Guest houses and B&Bs

**Benson House** 24 Huntingdon Rd ☎01223/311594, ⓔbensonhouse@btconnect .com. Pleasant, well-kept, non-smoking accom-modation in a demure brick house, north of Magdalene Bridge near New Hall College. Five rooms, three en suite. ❼

**Netley Lodge** 112 Chesterton Rd ☎01223/363845. Cosy, non-smoking B&B in a Victorian town house a long but manageable walk from the centre. Three attractively furnished bedrooms, one en suite. No credit cards. ❻

**Sleeperz Hotel** Station Rd ☎01223/304050, ⓦwww.sleeperz.com. This popular hotel is in an imaginatively converted granary warehouse, right outside the train station. Most of the rooms are bunk-style affairs done out in the manner of a ship's cabin, and there are a few doubles too. All are en suite, with shower and TV. ❻

### Restaurants and cafés

**Clowns** 54 King St. Licensed, day-and-night Italian café with a roof garden, serving cakes, sandwiches, all-day breakfasts, pasta and daily specials.

**Efes** 80 King St ☎01223/350491. Intimate Turkish restaurant, with chargrilled meats prepared under your nose and a decent *meze* selection.

**Eraina Taverna** 2 Free School Lane ☎01223/368786. Packed Greek taverna near the tourist office that satisfies the hungry hordes with huge platefuls of stews and grills, as well as pizzas and curries.

**Rainbow Vegetarian Bistro** 9a King's Parade ☎01223/321551. Vegetarian restaurant opposite King's College with main courses – ranging from salads to *enchiladas* – all under £8. Organic wines, beers and ciders served with meals. Closed Sun.

### Pubs, bars and clubs

**Eagle** Bene't St. An ancient inn with good food, and a cobbled courtyard where Crick and Watson sought inspiration in the 1950s, at the time of their discovery of DNA. It's been tarted up since and gets horribly crowded, but is still worth a pint of anyone's time.

**Champion of the Thames** 68 King St. Gratify-ingly old–fashioned central pub with decent beer and a student/academic clientele.

**Junction** Clifton Rd ☎01223/511511, ⓦwww .junction.co.uk. Live bands, club nights, comedy, drama, dance, performance and digital art at this popular and eclectic venue.

# Northern England

The main draw of **northern England** is the **Lake District**, a scenic region just thirty miles across, taking in stone-built villages, sixteen major lakes and the steeply pitched faces of England's highest mountains. However, to restrict yourself purely to the outdoors would be to do a disservice to cities such as **Manchester** and **Liverpool** in the northwest, and **Newcastle** in the northeast, whose centres are alive with the ostentatious civic architecture of nineteenth-century capitalism and twenty-first-century renewal. An entirely different angle on northern history is provided by the great ecclesiastical centres of **Durham** and **York**, where famous cathedrals provide a focus for extensive medieval remains.

# Manchester

Few cities in the world have embraced social change so heartily as **MANCHES-TER**. From engine of the Industrial Revolution to cutting–edge metropolis, the city has no real rival in England outside of London. After a massive IRA bomb destroyed a chunk of the centre in 1996, rebuilding has transformed the city, and with a huge student population, a lively **Gay Village**, and a strong history of churning out talent for the twin glories of British culture – music and football – Manchester hosts one of the country's most vibrant social and cultural scenes. From the main Piccadilly train station, it's a few minutes' walk northwest to **Piccadilly Gardens** (hub of the local tram and bus network). North of the gardens is what's been dubbed the **Northern Quarter**, an edgy, old wholesale district full of boutiques, music stores, bars and cafés. West of the gardens, **St Ann's Square** has been transformed into a pedestrianized shopping area, and is home to the **Royal Exchange** building, which houses the famous Royal Exchange Theatre. New Cathedral Street runs through the landscaped expanse of Exchange Square to the demure fifteenth-century **Cathedral**, and beyond to **Urbis** in Cathedral Gardens (daily 10am–6pm; free; ⊛www.urbis.org.uk), a spectacular glass building with interactive displays exploring life in different world cities. South down Deansgate and right into Liverpool Road is a celebration of the triumphs of industrialization at the superb **Museum of Science and Industry** (daily 10am–5pm; free; ⊛www .msim.org.uk), where exhibits include working steam engines, textile machinery, a hands-on science centre and a glimpse of the Manchester sewer system. Fifteen minutes' walk northeast, on Albert Square, stands the city's finest Victorian Gothic building, its **Town Hall**, whilst a block to the east is the **Manchester Art Gallery** on Mosley St (Tues–Sun 10am–5pm; free; ⊛www.manchestergalleries.org), which includes a fine collection of pre-Raphaelite paintings.

Metrolink trams run from Mosley Street to **Salford Quays**, scene of a massive urban renewal scheme in the old dock area. Centrepiece is the spectacular waterfront **Lowry Centre** (Tues–Sat 9.30am–8pm, Sun & Mon until 6pm; free; ⊛www.thelowry.com), where, as well as theatres and galleries, room is always made for the work of the artist L.S. Lowry, best known for his "matchstick men" scenes. To get here, take the tram to Broadway, or walk down the docks from the Salford Quays stop. A footbridge runs across the docks to the **Imperial War Museum North** (daily 10am–6pm March–Oct, 10am–5pm Nov–Feb; free; ⊛www.iwm.org.uk/north), a striking aluminium-clad building designed by Daniel Libeskind, where imaginative exhibits explore the effects of war since 1900. It's as resonant in its way as the other great building that looms in the near distance, Old Trafford, home of **Manchester United Football Club**, whose museum is sited in the North Stand (daily 9.30am–5pm; museum & tour £9, museum only £5.50; Metrolink to Old Trafford; advance booking essential for tours, ☎0870/442 1994, ⊛www.manutd.com).

## Practicalities

Most **trains** arrive at Piccadilly station, on the city's east side. Long–distance **buses** stop at Chorlton Street, just west of Piccadilly station. The **airport** is ten miles south, with a fast and frequent train service to Piccadilly. The **Manchester Visitor Centre** is in the town hall extension on Lloyd Street, facing St Peter's Square (Mon–Sat 10am–5.30pm, Sun 10.30am–4.30pm; ☎0161/234 3157, ⊛www .manchester.gov.uk/visitorcentre), with branches at the airport too. For budget **eating**, head a couple of blocks east of the visitor centre to Chinatown. Alternatively, the scores of restaurants along Wilmslow Road in Rusholme (buses #40–49), otherwise known as "Curry Mile", feature some of Britain's best (and least expensive) Asian cooking. The grooviest places to **drink** are in the Castlefield area around Liverpool Road; under the railway arches along Deansgate Locks (Whitworth Street West); in the Northern Quarter around Oldham Street; and the Gay Village around Canal Street.

For details of **nightlife**, consult the weekly magazine *City Life* or Friday's *Manchester Evening News*. Top clubs of the moment include *Music Box*, 65 Oxford St (℡0161/236 9971, 🖰www.themusicbox.info), and *Sankey's Soap*, Beehive Mill, Jersey St, Ancoats (℡0161/661 9668, 🖰www.tribalgathering.co.uk). The *Cornerhouse*, 70 Oxford St (℡0161/200 1500, 🖰www.cornerhouse.org), is the best bet for art-house film releases, special screenings and **cinema**–related talks and events.

### Hostels

**The Hatters** 50 Newton St ℡0161/236 9500, 🖰www.hattersgroup.com. A recently converted listed building in the Northern Quarter is home to this bright and modern hostel. A good range of facilities is available and staff will provide tourist information and book tours. Dorms from £14, rooms ❹

**YHA** Potato Wharf, Castlefield ℡0870/770 5950, 🖰www.yhamanchester.org.uk. Opposite the Science and Industry Museum, this well-designed HI hostel (all dorm rooms have private bathroom) comes with all mod cons. Dorm beds £20.50, including breakfast, rooms ❺

### Hotels

**Jury's Inn** 56 Great Bridgewater St ℡0161/953 8888, 🖰www.jurys.com. Very handy location for this large, three-star hotel. Rates, which are room only, are discounted on the weekend. ❾

**The Ox** 71 Liverpool Rd ℡0161/839 7740, 🖰www.theox.co.uk. Nine rooms above a classy bar-restaurant opposite the Science and Industry Museum. ❼

**Premier Lodge** 7 Lower Mosley St ℡0870/700 1476, 🖰www.premierlodge.com. Good-value, city-centre, motel-style rooms from this standard modern chain. Several other Manchester locations too. ❻

### Cafés and restaurants

**Dimitri's** 1 Campfield Arcade, Deansgate. Pick and mix from the Greek/Spanish/Italian menu, or grab an arcade table and sip a drink.

**Earth** 16–20 Turner St. Gourmet veggie food – curries, pies, salads and juices – in a stylish

Northern Quarter café in the Manchester Buddhist Centre. Closes 5pm Sat & Sun.

**Eighth Day** 107–111 Oxford Rd. Manchester's premier vegetarian and vegan joint with a shop, takeaway and juice bar upstairs, café/restaurant below.

**Shere Khan** 52 Wilmslow Rd, Rusholme ℡0161/256 2624. Popular Indian brasserie, serving marvellous kebabs, and great karahi and biryani dishes.

**Wong Chu** 63 Faulkner St. The best of the budget Chinatown eateries, this no-frills joint serves up enormous portions of Cantonese staples.

### Bars and pubs

**Britons Protection** 50 Great Bridgewater St. Elegantly decorated traditional pub, with good home-made food, comedy nights and other events, and a beer garden.

**Dry Bar** 28–30 Oldham St. The first of the designer café-bars on the scene, and catalyst for much of what goes on in the Northern Quarter.

**Dukes '92** Castle St, Castlefield. Former stable-block for canal horses, now a large, sociable pub with terrace seating, a woodfire pizza oven and a great-value range of pâtés and cheeses.

**Mr Thomas' Chop House** 52 Cross St. Victorian pub with a Dickensian feel to its nooks and crannies, serving Lancashire hotpot and other good-value traditional dishes.

**Temple of Convenience** Great Bridgewater St. A tiny, converted public toilet – yes that's right – stocking a wide selection of Belgian beers.

# Liverpool

Once Britain's main transatlantic port and the empire's second city, **LIVERPOOL** spent too many of the twentieth-century postwar years struggling against adversity. Things are looking up at last, as regeneration projects brighten the centre and the old docks on the River Mersey, while the successful bid to be European Capital of Culture for 2008 promises to transform the way outsiders see the city. Acerbic wit and loyalty to one of the city's two great football teams are the linchpins of Liverpudlian or "Scouse" culture, along with an underlying pride in the local musical heritage – fair enough from the city that produced The Beatles.

Just north of the main Lime Street station, on William Brown Street, is the renowned **Walker Art Gallery** (Mon–Sat 10am–5pm, Sun noon–5pm; free; ⊛www.thewalker.org.uk), including a representative jaunt through British art history, with Hogarth, Gainsborough, Stubbs and Hockney all well represented. From here it's a fifteen-minute walk west to the **Pier Head** and Liverpool's waterfront, where it's worth taking a "Ferry 'cross the Mersey" (*à la* Gerry and the Pacemakers) to Birkenhead for the views back towards the city; ferries serve commuters during morning and evening rush hours (£2.10 return), but in between operate hourly cruises with commentary (⊛www.merseyferries.co.uk; £4.65). A short stroll south is the **Albert Dock**, showpiece of the renovated docks area, whose main focus is **Tate Liverpool** (Tues–Sun 10am–6pm; free; ⊛www.tate.org.uk/liverpool), northern home of the national collection of modern art. Occupying the other side of the dock is the **Maritime Museum** (daily 10am–5pm; free; ⊛www.merseysidemaritimemuseum.org.uk), housing – amongst other highlights – a shocking exhibition detailing Liverpool's key role in the slave trade. The Albert Dock is also home to **The Beatles Story** (daily 10am–6pm; £8.99; ⊛www.beatlesstory.com), a multimedia attempt to capture the essence of the Fab Four's rise. Continuing the theme, the city centre area around **Mathew Street** has been designated the **Cavern Quarter**, its pubs and shops providing an excuse to wallow in nostalgia, especially at the rebuilt version of the *Cavern Club* (hosting live bands Thurs–Sun), where The Beatles played in the 1960s. You can take a two-hour "Magical Mystery Tour" of other sites associated with the band, such as Penny Lane and Strawberry Fields, on a bus that departs from The Beatles Story and ends up at the *Cavern Club* (daily tours; book at The Beatles Story or tourist offices; £11.95; ⊛www.cavern-liverpool.co.uk). Real fans also won't want to miss touring **20 Forthlin Rd**, home of the McCartney family from 1955 to 1964, and **Mendips**, the house where John Lennon lived between 1945 and 1963. Both are preserved by the National Trust and only accessible on a pre-booked minibus tour (Easter–Oct Wed–Sun; ☎0870/900 0256; £12), departing twice daily from Albert Dock. Back in town, in the revived Ropewalks area, **FACT** at 88 Wood St shelters two galleries showing film, video and new media projects (Tues & Wed 11am–6pm, Thurs–Sat 11am–8pm, Sun noon–5pm; free; ⊛www.fact.co.uk), as well as an arthouse cinema, café and bar. To the east, at either end of Hope Street, stand the city's two eye-catching twentieth-century cathedrals: the Roman Catholic **Metropolitan Cathedral** (daily 8am–5/6pm; suggested £3 donation), ten minutes' walk up Mount Pleasant, is a vast inverted funnel of a building, while the pale red neo-Gothic Anglican **Liverpool Cathedral** (daily 8am–6pm; suggested £3 donation) is the largest in the country, designed by Sir Giles Gilbert Scott in 1903, but not completed until 1978.

## Practicalities

**Trains** arrive at Lime Street Station, on the eastern edge of the city centre; **coaches** stop on Norton Street, northeast of the station. **Ferry** arrivals – including from Dublin and Belfast – dock just north of Pier Head. **Tourist information** (☎0906/680 6886, ⊛www.visitliverpool.com) is available from two downtown offices: one in **Queen Square** (Mon–Sat 9am–5.30pm, Sun 10.30am–4.30pm), the other at **Albert Dock** (daily 10am–5.30pm); both can book accommodation (☎0845/601 1125). Budget **accommodation** includes, from mid-June to early September, self-catering student halls at John Moores University (☎0151/231 3511, ⊛www.livjm.ac.uk) and the University of Liverpool (☎0151/794 6402, ⊛www.liv.ac.uk).

Inexpensive **food** can be found around Mount Pleasant and Hardman and Bold streets, while Berry and Nelson streets to the south form the heart of **Chinatown**. As for **pubs and bars**, Fleet, Slater and Wood streets and Concert Square (off Bold Street) are where all the action is. The *Liverpool Academy*, 160 Mount Pleasant (☎0151/794 6868, ⊛www.liverpoolacademy.co.uk), is the best **live music venue** (and has good club nights), while the *Royal Court Theatre*, Roe St (☎0151/709

4321, ⓦwww.royalcourttheatre.net), gets the major touring bands and stand-up comedians. At the Bluecoat Arts Centre on School Lane (ⓣ0151/709 5297, ⓦwww .bluecoat.com; closed until 2006), regular **arts and drama** events combine with a good veggie café, while the Everyman Theatre and Playhouse on Hope Street (ⓣ0151/709 4776, ⓦwww.everymanplayhouse.com) presents drama, dance, poetry and music – not to mention cheap food and a great bar. The evening paper, the *Liverpool Echo*, has what's-on **listings**, while annual **festivals** like the Summer Pops (July) and International Beatles Festival (August) are when the city lets its hair down.

## Accommodation

**Aachen** 89–91 Mount Pleasant ⓣ0151/709 3477, ⓦwww.aachenhotel.co.uk. The most popular and central budget hotel, with value-for-money rooms and big "eat-as-much-as-you-like" breakfasts. ❻

**International Inn** 4 South Hunter St, off Hardman St ⓣ0151/709 8135, ⓦwww.internationalinn .co.uk. Converted Victorian warehouse with en-suite dorms for 2–10 people, really helpful staff, plus kitchen, laundry and no curfew. Adjacent café has Internet access. Dorms £15, rooms ❹

**YHA** Wapping ⓣ0870/770 5924, ⓦwww.yha.org .uk. One of the best HI hostels, just south of Albert Dock. Smart three-, four- or six-bed rooms, all with private bathroom, plus licensed café, laundry and 24hr reception. Dorms £20.50 including breakfast, rooms ❺

## Eating and drinking

**The Baltic Fleet** 33a Wapping. Restored maritime pub with real ales and a great period feel.

**The Casa** 29 Hope St. A good, cheap community meeting place for drinks (until 2am at weekends) and daytime bistro food.

**The Magnet** 45 Hardman St. Blood-red decor and a bit of Barry White – it's groovy, plus there's a funky club downstairs and a diner that stays open until 2am.

**May Sum** 180-181 Elliot St. There are some fifty-plus dishes to choose from at this hugely popular eat-all-you-can Chinese buffet. It's not the place for a relaxing meal, but the food's not bad and can't be faulted for value.

**Number Seven Café** 7 Falkner St. Terrific sandwiches, salads, soups and cakes to eat inside or out at the streetside tables, or to take away.

**The Philharmonic** 36 Hope St. Huge, ornate pub boasting mosaic floors, gilded wrought-iron gates and marble decor in the gents.

**Tabac** 126 Bold St. Contemporary café-bar, serving a wide-ranging menu.

**Tea Factory** 79 Wood St. Very cool, very chic "bar and kitchen" in the Ropewalks neighbourhood.

**Yuet Ben** 1 Upper Duke St. The very reasonably priced Peking cuisine here is authentic and, refreshingly, vegetarians are not given the cold shoulder – try the set vegetarian banquet for £12.50.

# The Lake District

The site of England's highest peaks and its biggest concentration of lakes, the glacier-carved **Lake District National Park** is the nation's most popular walking area. The weather here in Cumbria changes quickly, but the sudden shifts of light on the bracken and moorland grasses, and on the slate of the local buildings, are part of the area's appeal. The most direct access is via the mainline **train** route from London Euston towards Glasgow, disembarking at Lancaster, from where bus #555 runs to Kendal, Windermere, Ambleside, Grasmere, Keswick and Carlisle – the open-top #599 bus is a summer alternative between Windermere and Grasmere. Alternatively, you could get off the train at **Oxenholme**, connecting with a branch line service to Kendal and Windermere; or take a direct train from Manchester to Windermere. A National Express **coach** service runs daily from London Victoria and Manchester to the Lake District, while local **Stagecoach buses** go everywhere in the region – an **Explorer Ticket** (£8.50/day, £18/four days, £25/seven days), valid on their entire network and available on the bus, is just one of many local passes, including bus-and-boat tickets. The region boasts 26 youth hostels and dozens of campsites, covering all the destinations described below. For more **information** visit ⓦwww.lake-district.gov.uk; the official site of the Cumbria Tourist Board is ⓦwww.golakes.co.uk.

## Windermere, Bowness, Ambleside and around

**Windermere** is the largest of the lakes, with its main town of **WINDERMERE** (where the train from Oxenholme/Kendal stops) set a mile or so back from the water. Other than the short climb up to the viewpoint of **Orrest Head** (30min), it offers little to do, though it is the region's main service centre. The **tourist office** is just outside the train station (daily 9am–6/7.30pm; ☎ 015394/46499), steps from the cosy *Lake District Backpackers' Lodge* (☎01539/446374, ✆www.lakedistrictbackpackers.co.uk; £12 including breakfast). A top B&B choice is *Brendan Chase*, 1–3 College Rd (☎01539/445638; ❹). **Bikes** can be rented from Country Lanes at the train station (☎01539/444544, ✆www.countrylanes.co.uk). The

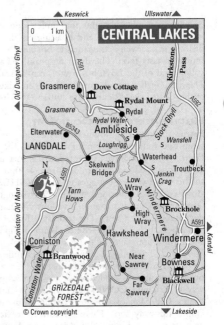

nearest HI **hostel** is at Troutbeck, two miles northwest of Windermere town (☎01539/443543; £12.50); a shuttle-bus (£2) meets trains at the station. For the lake itself, catch the bus from outside Windermere station to the prettier lakeshore town of **BOWNESS**, where you can rent a rowboat or take a steam launch cruise from the **Steamboat Museum** (Easter–Oct daily 10am–5pm; museum £4.75, cruises £5.50; ✆www.steamboat.co.uk). A mile and a half south of Bowness on foot, there's the rare chance to visit a house designed by one of the major exponents of the Arts and Crafts Movement, Mackay Hugh Baillie Scott's **Blackwell** (mid-Feb to Dec daily 10am–4/5pm; £5; ✆www.blackwell .org.uk). Accommodation in Bowness tends to be more expensive, but don't miss a drink or a bar meal in *The Hole in't Wall* **pub**, behind the church, the town's oldest hostelry. Lake **ferries** (☎01539/531188, ✆www.windermere-lakecruises .co.uk) run to Lakeside at the southern tip (£7.20 return) or to Waterhead (for Ambleside) at the northern end (£6.95 return). A 24-hour Freedom-of-the-Lake ticket costs £12.50. There are also boats (£5.50 return) to the excellent **Lake District National Park Visitor Centre** at Brockhole (April–Oct daily 10am–5pm; free; ☎01539/446601; bus #555 or #599).

From Waterhead, it's a mile north to **AMBLESIDE** – or take bus #555 or #599 from Windermere and Bowness – whose **Ambleside Museum** (daily 10am–5pm; £2.50) has the lowdown on lakeland writers and artists. The **tourist office** is in the Central Buildings by the Market Cross (daily 9am–5.30pm; ☎01539/432582). One of the Lake District's best-sited HI **hostels** fronts the lake at Waterhead (☎0870/770 5672; £18.50), or there's the independent *Ambleside Backpackers* on Old Lake Road (☎01539/432340, ✆www.englishlakesbackpackers.co.uk; £14 including breakfast). **B&Bs** line central Ambleside streets, with the cheapest rates at *Linda's B&B*, Shirland, Compston Road (☎01539/432999; ❹), or splash out on *Compston House*, Compston Rd (☎01539/432305, ✆www.compstonhouse. co.uk; ❻), an American-themed B&B with great breakfasts. *Zeffirelli's*, a cinema on Compston Road, specializes in inexpensive vegetarian food, either in the daytime café or upstairs in the dinner-only pizza **restaurant**. The #516 bus (April–Oct only) from Ambleside runs four miles west to the hamlet of **ELTERWATER**, centred on a tiny green and boasting another HI hostel, *Elterwater* (☎0870/770 5816; £11), as well as the fantastic *Britannia Inn* (☎015394/37210), an old lakeland pub with tasty food. The dramatic peaks of **Langdale**, three miles further up the valley (end of the #516 bus route), can be scaled from the equally venerable *Old Dungeon Ghyll*, a pricey hotel with terrific hikers' bar. Canny campers stay nearby at the *Great Langdale* **campsite** (☎01539/437668).

## Hawkshead and Coniston

Ferries shuttle from Bowness piers across the lake to Sawrey, from where it's a steep two-mile walk (or minibus ride) to the hamlet of **NEAR SAWREY** and Beatrix Potter's beloved seventeenth-century house and garden, **Hill Top** (April–Oct Mon–Wed, Sat & Sun 10.30am–4.30pm; £5; NT). It's another two miles to the whitewashed cottages of **HAWKSHEAD** (bus #505 from Windermere, Bowness and Ambleside), which is refreshingly peaceful after the hurly-burly of Windermere and has some marvellous village pubs (the *King's Arms*, which serves decent food, is the best). The **tourist office** at the main car park (daily: April–Oct 9.30am–5.30/6pm; Nov–March 10am–3.30pm; ☎01539/436525) handles B&Bs and farmhouse stays, or there's the family-oriented HI **hostel**, *Esthwaite Lodge* (☎0870/770 5856; £12.50 per person), a mile south of the village.

From Hawkshead, walking through **Grizedale Forest**, with its startling outdoor sculptures, and descending towards graceful Coniston Water is a good way of reaching **CONISTON** village, a cluster of houses nestling beneath the craggy Old Man of Coniston (which you can climb in two hours). Bus #505 comes this way too. There's a **tourist office** on Ruskin Avenue (April–Oct daily 9.30am–5.30pm; Nov–March Fri–Sun 10am–3.30pm; ☎01539/441533), as well as an HI **hostel** just north of the village at *Holly How* (☎0870/770 5770; £12.50), and another more isolated one, great for hikers, above Coniston, on the slopes of Old Man, at *Coppermines House* (☎0870/770 5772; £11). Closest **campsite** is at *Coniston Hall* (☎01539/441223; reservations essential), a mile south of town by the lake. The *Beech Tree Guesthouse*, a friendly vegetarian place on Yewdale Road, just past the museum (☎01539/441717; ❺), is pick of the B&Bs; best **pub** is the *Sun Hotel*, an old inn serving good meals and real ale 200m uphill from the bridge in the centre. The most popular walk from Coniston is to **Tarn Hows**, two miles northeast, a serene lake with several vantage points across the hills. On **Coniston Water**, the wooden *Coniston Launch* (☎01539/436216, ☯www.conistonlaunch.co.uk) operates a year-round ferry service on two routes, north and south (£4.60 & £6.80 return). This, along with the *Steam Yacht Gondola* (April–Oct; £5.80 return, ☎01539/463864, ☯www .nationaltrust.org.uk/gondola), is the best means of reaching the elegant lakeside villa, **Brantwood** (mid-March to mid-Nov daily 11am–5.30pm; mid-Nov to mid-March Wed–Sun 11am–4.30pm; £5.50, gardens only £3.75; ☯www.brantwood .org.uk), once home of artist and critic John Ruskin. The house is full of Ruskin's own drawings and sketches, as well as items relating to the pre-Raphaelite painters he inspired; there are also beautiful gardens and a good café.

## Rydal and Grasmere

From Windermere and Ambleside, the #555 bus connects to **RYDAL**, three miles northwest of Ambleside, where Wordsworth made his home from 1813 until his death in 1850; his house, **Rydal Mount** (daily 9.30/10am–4/5pm; Nov–Feb closed Tues; £4.50, gardens only £2; ☯www.rydalmount.co.uk), is famous largely for the gardens laid out by Wordsworth himself. Paths on either side of Rydal Water cover the two miles to **GRASMERE**, site of Wordsworth's better-known abode, **Dove Cottage** (daily 9.30am–5.30pm; closed Jan; £6; ☯www.wordsworth.org.uk). The ticket gets you a guided tour of the cottage, while the adjoining museum has portraits and manuscripts relating to Wordsworth, his friend Samuel Taylor Coleridge and Thomas De Quincey, author of *Confessions of an English Opium-Eater*. Wordsworth and his sister Dorothy lie in simple graves in the churchyard of St Oswald's, in the village. Grasmere's **tourist office** is on Redbank Road, by the main car park (April–Oct daily 9.30am–5.30pm; Nov–March Fri–Sun 10am–3.30pm; ☏01539/435245). The *Jumble Room Café* on Langdale Road (closed Mon & Tues) is a funky **café-restaurant** with an organic touch, or there are tearoom favourites at the *Dove Cottage Tea Rooms and Restaurant* (at night, prices shoot up for fashionable dinners; ☏01539/435268). The HI **hostel** choices are *Butharlyp Howe* (£14), 150 yards north of the green on Easedale Road, and simpler *Thorney How* (£11), under a mile further along the unlit road (both ☏0870/770 5836). There's also the excellent *Grasmere Independent Hostel* at Broadrayne Farm (☏01539/435055; £14.50), just north of town on the A591, near the *Travellers' Rest* **pub** (which serves bar meals).

## Keswick and Derwent Water

Principal hiking and tourist centre for the northern lakes, **KESWICK** (pronounced "kez-ick") lies on the shores of **Derwent Water**. The **Keswick Launch** (mid-March to Nov daily; Dec to mid-March Sat & Sun; £5.70 round trip; ☏01768/772263, ✇www.keswick-launch.co.uk) runs right around the lake and you can get off at Hawes End for the climb up **Cat Bells** (1481ft), best of the lakeside vantage points. The trek up **Skiddaw** (3000ft; 5hr), north of town, is more demanding, but the easiest of the many true mountain hikes around and about. Otherwise, stroll a mile and a half eastwards to **Castlerigg Stone Circle**, a Neolithic monument commanding a spectacular view, or take the #77/77A/79 bus ride down into **Borrowdale**, south of town, perhaps the most beautiful valley in England. **Buses** use the terminal behind Lakes Foodstore, off Main Street. Keswick's **tourist office** is in the Moot Hall, Market Square (daily 9.30am–4.30/5.30pm; ☏01768/772645), and there's **bike rental** from Keswick Mountain Bikes on Southey Hill (☏01768/775202, ✇www.keswickmountain .co.uk). The local HI **hostel** is on Station Road by the river (☏0870/770 5894; £12.50); there's another on the eastern shores of Derwentwater, two miles south, in Barrow House (☏0870/770 5792; £12.50); buses #77/77A/79 come this way. **B&Bs** cluster all around town, especially on Southey, Blencathra and Eskin streets – *Bridgedale Guesthouse*, near the bus station at 101 Main St (☏01768/773914; ❺), has bargain room-only deals (mention Rough Guides for a small discount), while *Bluestones*, 7 Southey St (☏01768/774237, ✇www.bluestonesguesthouse.co.uk; ❺), is a welcoming guest house that offers big buffet breakfasts. Keswick's most agreeable **café** is the *Lakeland Pedlar*, Henderson's Yard, off Main Street, and there are fine **pub** meals and good beer at the *Lake Road Inn* and the *Four In Hand*, both on Lake Rd. **Theatre by the Lake** (☏01768/774411, ✇www.theatrebythelake .com) hosts drama, dance and music.

# York

It's the spectacular Gothic Minster, cobbled alleyways and ancient walls that draw tourists to **YORK**, but the city's character-forming experiences go back a lot further than that. It was the principal northern headquarters of the Romans, while the city's position as the north's spiritual capital dates from 627, when Edwin of Northumbria adopted Christianity. Northumbrian power crumbled in the face of a Danish invasion that swept through York in 866, and by 876 the Vikings were firmly entrenched in "Jorvik", beginning a century of Scandinavian rule.

Best introduction to York is a stroll around the **city walls** (daily till dusk), a three-mile circuit – two miles of it on the walls themselves – that takes in the various medieval "bars", or gates, and grants fine views of the Minster. A free two-hour **guided walk** (daily at 10.15am, plus additional tours April–Oct at 2.15pm, & June–Aug 6.45pm), led by the York Association of Voluntary Guides, departs from outside the art gallery in Exhibition Square; just turn up. Ever since Edwin built a

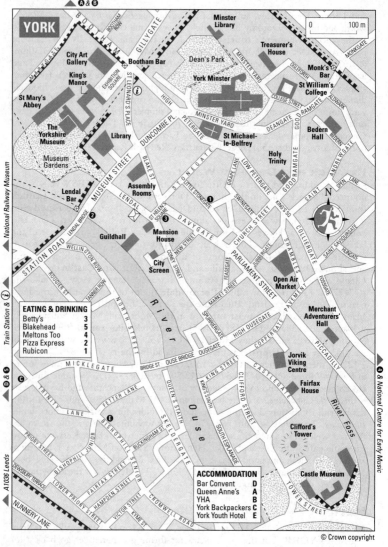

EATING & DRINKING

| | |
|---|---|
| Betty's | 3 |
| Blakehead | 5 |
| Meltons Too | 4 |
| Pizza Express | 2 |
| Rubicon | 1 |

ACCOMMODATION

| | |
|---|---|
| Bar Convent | D |
| Queen Anne's | A |
| YHA | B |
| York Backpackers | C |
| York Youth Hotel | E |

© Crown copyright

wooden chapel on the site, **York Minster** (daily 7am–6.30pm; £5/7; @www.york minster.org) has been the centre of religious authority for the north of England. Most of what's visible now was built in stages between the 1220s and the 1470s, and today it ranks as the country's largest Gothic building. Inside, the scenes of the East Window, completed in 1405, and the abstract thirteenth-century Five Sisters window represent the finest collection of stained glass in Britain. Various parts of the Minster have separate admission charges, though the full £7 ticket covers all the attractions – don't miss climbing the central tower, which gives views over the medieval pattern of narrow streets to the south, known as the **Shambles**. Southwest of the Minster, just outside the city walls, Museum Gardens lead to the ruins of the

Benedictine abbey of St Mary and the **Yorkshire Museum** (daily 10am–5pm; £4; ⊛www.yorkshiremuseum.org.uk), which contains much of the abbey's medieval sculpture, and a selection of Roman, Saxon and Viking finds. The shopping streets spread south and east from here, focusing eventually on Coppergate, former site of the city's Viking settlement. The blockbuster experience that is **Jorvik** (daily April–Oct 10am–5pm, Nov–March 10am–4pm; £7.45; ⊛www.vikingjorvik.com) provides a taste of the period through a re-creation of Viking streets, complete with appropriate smells and recorded sounds, to the accompaniment of an informative commentary. Further south, the superb **Castle Museum** (daily 9.30am–5pm; £6.50; ⊛www.yorkcastlemuseum.org.uk) indulges in full-scale re-creations of life in bygone times, with evocative street scenes of the Victorian and Edwardian periods. Another museum worth a call is the excellent **National Railway Museum**, ten minutes' walk from the station on Leeman Rd (daily 10am–6pm; free; ⊛www .nrm.org.uk), which includes the nation's finest collection of steam locomotives.

## Practicalities

York's **train station** lies just outside the city walls, with services from Manchester, as well as fast trains from London and Edinburgh; long-distance **coaches** drop off and pick up here, as well as on Rougier Street, two hundred yards north of the train station, just before Lendal Bridge. There's a **tourist office** at the train station (Mon–Sat 9am–5/6pm, Sun 9.30/10am–4/4.30pm), though the main office is over Lendal Bridge, in the De Grey Rooms on Exhibition Square (Mon–Sat 9am–5/6pm, Sun 10am–4/5pm; ☎01904/621756, ⊛www.visityork.org).

There's some good **hostel** accommodation, and tons of **B&Bs** (many concentrated off Bootham, west of Exhibition Square), while the **University of York** offers good-value rooms and self-catering flats during Easter and summer holidays (☎01904/432222, ⊛www.york.ac.uk). Cultural entertainment is wide and varied, with the **National Centre for Early Music** in St Margaret's Church, Walmgate (☎01904/658338, ⊛www.ncem.co.uk), hosting a prestigious early music festival in July, plus world, jazz and folk **gigs**. Indie and guitar-pop bands play most nights of the week at *Fibbers*, Stonebow House, Stonebow (☎01904/651250, ⊛www.fibbers.co.uk), while there's an art-house **cinema**, City Screen, 13 Coney St (☎01904/541155, ⊛www.picturehouses.co.uk), with riverside café-bar and live music and DJ nights.

### Hostels

**York Backpackers Hostel** Micklegate House, 88–90 Micklegate ☎01904/627720, ⊛www .yorkbackpackers.co.uk. Dorm space, doubles and family rooms in a rather grand building, former home of the High Sheriff of Yorkshire. There's a café, kitchen, laundry and bar, plus Internet access. Dorms £13–14, rooms ❹, including breakfast.
**York YHA** Water End, Clifton ☎0870/770 6102. HI hostel twenty minutes' walk along Bootham from the tourist office. Four-bedded dorms and some private rooms (book in advance), a licensed café, laundry, self-catering facilities, Internet access, bike rental and large garden. Dorms £18, rooms ❺
**York Youth Hotel** 11–13 Bishophill Senior, off Micklegate ☎01904/625904, ⊛www.yorkyouth hotel.com. Dorms, singles and twin/double rooms in characterful city-centre hostel, with a kitchen, laundry and bar; bike rental and meals available. Dorms £14, rooms ❺

### Guest houses

**The Bar Convent** 17 Blossom St ☎01904/643238, ⊛www.bar-convent.org.uk. Lovely Georgian building, just south of the train station next to Micklegate Bar, offering good-value rooms (continental breakfast included) with self-catering kitchens and a café. ❼
**Queen Anne's Guest House** 24/26 Queen Anne's Road ☎01904/629389, ⊛www .queen-annes-guesthouse.co.uk. Welcoming B&B a short walk northwest of Bootham Bar. Clean, comfortable rooms, most with en-suite facilities. ❻

### Cafés and restaurants

**Betty's** 6–8 St Helen's Sq. If there are tea shops in heaven they'll be like *Betty's*, a York institution which also serves main courses, to the accompaniment of a pianist, until 9pm.
**Blake Head Vegetarian Café** 104 Micklegate.

Bookstore/café with patio for freshly baked cakes, breakfasts, quiches, salads and soups.

**Melton's Too** 25 Walmgate. Exposed brickwork, scattered cushions and the daily papers set the tone for this relaxed café-bar and bistro.

**Pizza Express** River House, 17 Museum St. Grand old riverside club rooms with sought-after balcony, the venue for this chain's usual menu of good-quality pizzas.

**The Rubicon** 5–7 Little Stonegate ☏01904/676076. Contemporary style and vegetarian world flavours, from moussaka and lasagna to Thai red curry and cinnamon couscous.

### Pubs

**Black Swan** Peasholme Green. York's oldest (sixteenth-century) pub with some superb stone flagging and wood panelling, and regular singer-songwriter and folk nights.

**Judge's Lodging Cellar Bar** 9 Lendal. Lively drinking hole in the eighteenth-century cellars of a smart hotel, with a large outdoor terrace and regular DJ nights.

**Three-Legged Mare** 15 High Petergate. York Brewery's cosy outlet for its own quality beer and definitely a pub for grown-ups – no jukebox, no video games and no kids.

## Durham

Seen from the train, **DURHAM** presents a magnificent sight, with cathedral and castle perched atop a bluff enclosed by a loop of the River Wear (pronounced "weer"), and linked to the suburbs by a series of sturdy bridges. Nowadays a quiet provincial town with a strong student presence, Durham was once one of northern England's power bases: the Bishops of Durham were virtual royal agents in the north for much of the medieval era, responsible for defending a crucial border province frequently menaced by the Scots. The town initially owed its reputation to the possession of the remains of St Cuthbert, which were evacuated to Durham in the ninth century because of Viking raids. Since then, his shrine has dominated the eastern end of the spectacular **Cathedral** (Mon–Sat 9.30am–6.15/8pm, Sun 12.30–5pm; £3 donation requested; ⓦwww .durhamcathedral.co.uk). The cathedral itself is the finest example of Norman architecture in England, and also contains the tomb of the Venerable Bede, the country's first historian. The **Treasures of St Cuthbert** exhibition is in the undercroft (Mon–Sat 10am–4.30pm, Sun 2–4.30pm; £2), while the **tower** gives breathtaking views (Mon–Sat 9.30/10am–3/4pm; £2). On the opposite side of Palace Green is the **castle** (Easter & July–Sept daily 10am–12.30pm & 2–4pm; rest of the year Mon, Wed, Sat & Sun 2–4pm; tours £5; ⓦwww.durhamcastle .com), a much-refurbished Norman edifice that's now a university hall of residence. A half-hour stroll follows a pathway on the wooded river bank below the cathedral and castle, all the way around the peninsula, passing a succession of elegant bridges.

Durham **train station** is ten minutes' walk from the centre, via either of two river bridges. The **bus station** is just south on North Road. The **tourist office** is at Millennium Place (Mon–Sat 9.30am–5.30pm, Sun 11am–4pm; ☏0191/384 3720, ⓦwww.durhamtourism.co.uk), where there's also a theatre, library, café and bar. There's no hostel, but Durham University has **rooms** available – including within the castle – at Easter and from July to September (☏0800/289970, ⓦwww.dur.ac.uk/conference_tourism), while good-value **B&Bs** include *Green Grove*, 99 Gilesgate (☏0191/384 4361; ❹), east of the city centre. For well-priced **food**, *Vennel's Café*, Saddler's Yard, serves everything from cakes to pasta in a lovely little hidden courtyard off Saddler St – the upstairs bar here kicks into action after 7pm. The *Almshouse* on Palace Green, near the cathedral, conjures up tasty dishes for around £6 (till 8pm in summer), while the *Court Inn* on Court Lane is the best dining **pub** in town, a favourite with students and locals. Or there's the *Swan & Three Cygnets* by Elvet Bridge, which has cheap beer and a riverside terrace. The **Gala Theatre** at Millennium Place hosts drama, music, comedy and the arts (☏0191/332 4041, ⓦwww .galadurham.co.uk).

# Newcastle upon Tyne

Once a tough, industrial city with a proud shipbuilding heritage, **NEWCASTLE** has retained its undeniable raw vigour, most conspicuously in its famously high-spirited nightlife. These days, it's streets ahead of its rivals in the northeast, and has a slew of fine galleries and arts venues, as well as a handsome Neoclassical downtown area fanning out from the lofty Grecian column of **Grey's Monument**, the city's central landmark. Arriving by train, your first view is of the **River Tyne** and its redeveloped quaysides, along with the Norman keep of the castle itself. A famous series of bridges spans the Tyne, linking Newcastle to the Gateshead side of the river – the single steel arch of the **Tyne Bridge**, built in 1929, contrasts with the hi-tech "winking" **Millennium Bridge**. The northeast's main art collection is housed in the **Laing Gallery** on New Bridge Street (Mon–Sat 10am–5pm, Sun 2–5pm; free; ⓦwww.twmuseums.org.uk), but it has been overshadowed by the opening of **BALTIC**, the Centre for Contemporary Art (daily 10am–6pm, Thurs until 8pm; free; ⓦwww.balticmill.com), on the Gateshead side of the Tyne next to the Millennium Bridge. Second only in scale to London's Tate Modern, this converted former flour mill accommodates exhibition galleries, artists' studios, a café-bar and two restaurants. The Baltic has been joined by the similarly ambitious **The Sage Gateshead** (ⓦwww.thesagegateshead.org), a billowing steel, aluminium and glass structure by Norman Foster that's home to the Northern Sinfonia, one of Europe's most acclaimed chamber orchestras. A full programme of concerts, classical and contemporary, and activities runs throughout the year – a free monthly guide to events at The Sage can be obtained here or at the tourist office. Easy out-of-town trips on the Metro can take you to **Bede's World** (Mon–Sat 10am–4.30/5.30pm, Sun noon–4.30/5.30pm; £4.50; ⓦwww.bedesworld.co.uk; Bede station), five miles east in Jarrow, which imaginatively evokes the life and times of the great early

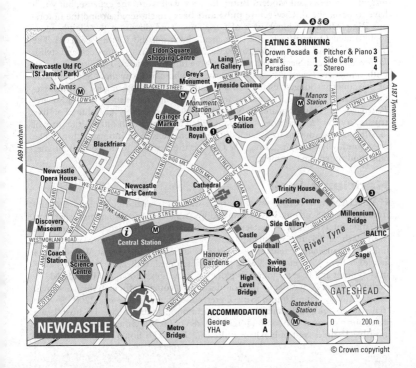

© Crown copyright

Christian scholar, alongside the remains of Bede's monastery; and to the excavations at **Segedunum** (daily April–Aug 9.30am–5.30pm, Sept & Oct 10am–5pm, Nov–March 10am–3pm; £3.50; ⊛www.twmuseums.org.uk/segedunum), the "strong fort" four miles east of Newcastle that was the last outpost of Hadrian's great border defence.

## Practicalities

Newcastle's **Central Station** is five minutes' walk south of Grey's Monument; the **coach station**, on St James's Boulevard, a few minutes' walk west of the station. The **ferry port** (for crossings from Amsterdam and Scandinavia) is in North Shields, seven miles east, with connecting buses running to the centre, and the **airport** is six miles north, served by the local **Metro** system (Day Saver for unlimited rides, £2–3 after 9am depending on the day). There are **tourist offices** in Central Station (Mon–Fri 9.30am–5pm, Sat 9am–5pm; ☎0191/277 8000, ⊛www.visitnewcastlegateshead.com) and at 132 Grainger St (Mon–Sat 9.30am–5.30pm, Thurs till 7.30pm, plus June–Sept Sun 10am–4pm; same number). The HI **hostel** is at 107 Jesmond Rd (☎0870/770 5972; £16). Jesmond – a mile north of the centre and on the Metro – is the main location for budget hotels and **B&Bs**, with the *George*, 88 Osborne Rd (☎0191/281 4442; ⑤), about the cheapest. The University of Northumbria (☎0191/227 3215) and Newcastle University (☎0191/222 6296) offer good-value, summertime B&B (mostly single rooms) in their halls of residence.

Local institutions for cheap **meals** are the *Side Café Bistro*, near the Quayside at 1–3 The Side; *Pani's*, an Italian café-restaurant at 61 High Bridge St, off Grey St (closed Sun); *Paradiso* nearby at 1 Market Lane, a mellow café-bar with great food (closed Sun); and *Uno's*, 18 Sandhill, with happy hour pizzas and pasta for under £3 (weekdays before 7pm, Sat before 5pm). For a blow-out, the top table in town (quite literally) is the Baltic's *Rooftop Restaurant* (☎0191/440 4949), whose magnificent views and Modern British food are well worth the expense, but you'll have to book ahead. City-centre **pubs and bars** are clustered around the notorious **Bigg Market**, a block west of Grey Street, and down on the slightly more sophisticated **Quayside**. In the latter area, check out the *Crown Posada*, 31 The Side, a traditional drinking den, or by the Millennium Bridge, the sleek and stylish *Pitcher & Piano* and *Stereo*, both of which have fine river views. The city's foremost **club** venues are *Foundation*, 57 Melbourne St, whose Saturday night Shindig is one of the country's longest established and most revered house nights; and the six-floor (including a skatepark and an art gallery) *World Headquarters*, Carliol Square. *Powerhouse* in Times Square, is Newcastle's only exclusively gay club. For **live music**, try the *Head of Steam* opposite Central Station, which offers a fine mix of local bands and touring national and international acts in an intimate setting. The free monthly **listings** magazine, *The Crack*, is the best way to find out about gigs, clubs and other entertainment.

## Hadrian's Wall

**HADRIAN'S WALL** (⊛www.hadrians-wall.org), separating Roman England from barbarian Scotland, was punctuated by "mile castles", strongpoints spaced at one-mile intervals, and by sixteen more substantially garrisoned forts. **Hadrian's Wall Path**, an 84-mile waymarked trail (5–7 days), now runs from coast to coast, linking the substantial remains – the start is at Segedunum fort at Wallsend (see above), where you get your "walk passport" stamped. Otherwise, the best jumping-off point and base for longer exploration is the abbey town of **HEXHAM**, 45 minutes west of Newcastle by train or bus. It has a **tourist office**, in the main town car park (daily 9am–5/6pm; Nov–Easter closed Sun; ☎01434/652200, ⊛www.tynedale.gov.uk), and plenty of accommodation including a basic HI **hostel** two miles north of town in Acomb (☎01434/602864; £8.50). Other accommodation is available 15 miles west of Hexham at the *Once Brewed* HI hostel (☎0870/770 5980;

£12.50) and the nearby *Twice Brewed Inn* (℡01434/344534, ⓦwww.twicebrewedinn
.co.uk; ④; closed Jan), a friendly **pub** with simple rooms, food until
8.30pm, local beers and Internet access. Both of these options lie near some of
the finest preserved sections of wall, including **Housesteads** (daily 10am–4/6pm;
£3.10), the most complete Roman fort in Britain, set in spectacular countryside,
and the partly recreated fort and lively museum at **Vindolanda** (daily: April–Sept
10am–6pm; Oct/Nov & Feb/March 10am–5pm; Dec/Jan Wed–Sun 10am–4pm;
£4.50; ⓦwww.vindolanda.com). The **Hadrian's Wall #AD122 bus** (Easter–Oct:
up to 4 daily in summer, restricted services at other times; 1-day ticket £6, 3-days
£10) runs between Hexham and Carlisle via all the main sites; at least once a day
it links through to Newcastle and Wallsend. The year-round #685 bus runs from
Carlisle to Housesteads via Haltwhistle (on the Newcastle–Carlisle train line).

# Wales

The relationship between England and **Wales** (Cymru in Welsh) has never been
entirely easy. Impatient with constant demarcation disputes, the eighth-century
Mercian king Offa constructed a dyke to separate the two countries; today, the
177-mile **Offa's Dyke Path** follows its route from near Chepstow in the south to
Prestatyn in the north, still marking the border to this day. During Edward I's reign
in the late thirteenth century, the last of the Welsh native princes, Llywelyn ap
Gruffudd, was killed, and Wales passed uneasily under English rule. Trouble flared
again with the rebellion of Owain Glyndŵr in the fifteenth century, but the Welsh
prince Henry Tudor's defeat of Richard III at the Battle of Bosworth crowned him
King Henry VII of England and paved the way for the 1536 Act of Union, which
joined the English and Welsh in restless but perpetual partnership. The arrival of
the 1999 National Assembly for Wales, the first all-Wales tier of government for
nearly six hundred years, may well indicate that power is shifting back, though so
far it's a slow trickle. Indigenous Welsh culture survives largely through language
and song. The **Eisteddfod festivals** of Welsh music, poetry and dance still take
place throughout the country in summer – the annual Royal National Eisteddfod
(ⓦwww.eisteddfod.org.uk), a very Welsh affair that breaks out in a different location
during the first week of August, and the Llangollen International Musical Eisteddfod (ⓦwww.internationaleisteddfod.co.uk), held on the first full week in July, being
the best-known examples. The Welsh language is undergoing a revival and you'll
see it on bilingual road signs all over the country, although you're most likely to
hear it spoken in the north, west and mid-Wales. Some Welsh place-names have
never been anglicized, but where alternative names do exist, we've given them in
the text.

Much of the country, particularly the **Brecon Beacons** in the south and Snowdonia in the north, is relentlessly mountainous and offers wonderful walking and
climbing terrain. **Pembrokeshire** to the west boasts a spectacular rugged coastline,
dotted with offshore island nature reserves. The biggest towns, including the capital
**Cardiff** in the south, **Aberystwyth** in the west, and **Caernarfon** in the north,
all cling to the coastal lowlands, but even then the mountains are no more than a
bus-ride away. **Holyhead**, on the island of **Anglesey**, is the main British port for
ferry sailings to the Irish capital, Dublin.

## Cardiff

Though once shackled to the fortunes of the coal-mining industry, Wales's largest
city, **CARDIFF** (Caerdydd), 150 miles west of London, has made its mark as the
vibrant Welsh capital, and since 1999 has been the home of the Welsh Assembly.

The city's narrow Victorian arcades are interspersed with new shopping centres and wide pedestrian precincts. The geographical and historical heart of the city is **Cardiff Castle** (tours daily 9.30am–5pm; £6.25 full tour, £3.70 short tour, grounds only £3). Standing on a Roman site developed by the Normans, the castle was embellished by William Burges in the 1860s, and each room is now a wonderful example of Victorian "medieval" decoration; best of all are the Chaucer Room, the Banqueting Hall, the Arab Room and the Fairy-tale Nursery. Five minutes' walk northeast, the **National Museum and Gallery** in Cathays Park (Tues–Sun 10am–5pm; free; ⓦwww.nmgw.ac.uk) houses a fine collection of Impressionist paintings, and natural history and archeological exhibits. A half-hour walk south of the centre is the **Cardiff Bay** area, also reached by bus #8 from Central Station, or a train from Queen Street. Once known as Tiger Bay, the long-derelict area (birthplace of singer Shirley Bassey) has seen massive redevelopment since the opening of the Welsh Assembly. The area is now dominated by the imposing **Wales Millennium Centre** (ⓣ0870/040 2000, ⓦwww.wmc.org .uk), which houses a huge theatre for the performing arts. Nearby is the **Visitor Centre** (daily 9.30/10.30am–5pm, ⓣ029/2046 3833), known popularly as "The Tube" for its unique, award-winning design. Pleasant waterfront walks, glittering architecture and an old Norwegian seamen's chapel converted into a cosy café add to the new air of refinement. The **Museum of Welsh Life** is at St Fagans, four miles west of the centre on bus #320. This 100-acre open-air museum is packed with reconstructed rural and industrial heritage buildings (daily 10am–5pm; free; ⓦwww.nmgw.ac.uk). Fans of William Burges' elaborate interiors shouldn't miss the fairy-tale **Castell Coch** at Tongwynlais, five miles north of town on bus #26 (April–Oct daily 9.30am–5/6pm; Nov–March Mon–Sat 9.30am–4pm, Sun 11am–4pm; £3; closed for six weeks every Jan & Feb). Perched dramatically on a steep, forested hillside, Burges' lavish Victorian showpiece was commissioned by the third Lord Bute as a country retreat, complete with turrets.

### Practicalities

Long-distance coaches, and buses from the airport, arrive at the **bus terminal**, right beside Cardiff Central **train station**, south of the city centre off Penarth Road (local trains use Queen Street station instead, east of the centre). The **Visitor Centre** is at The Old Library (Mon–Sat 9.30am–6pm, Sun 10am–4pm; ⓣ029/2022 7281, ⓦwww.visitcardiff.info). Cardiff's **HI hostel** is a couple of miles north of the centre at 2 Wedal Rd (ⓣ0870/770 5750, ⓦwww.yha.org.uk; £16), or you could try the excellent *Cardiff International Backpacker*, just west of the centre across the River Taff at 98 Neville St (ⓣ029/2034 5577, ⓦwww.cardiffbackpacker .com; dorms £16.95, rooms ❹). **B&Bs** include *Acorn Lodge*, 182 Cathedral Rd, Pontcanna (ⓣ029/2022 1373; ❺), fifteen minutes' walk west of the centre; the best budget hotel is the trendy **Big Sleep Hotel**, Bute Terrace (ⓣ029/2063 6363, ⓦwww.thebigsleephotel.com; ❻), opposite the Cardiff International Arena. To **eat** laver bread and other Welsh delicacies, head for *Celtic Cauldron* in the shopping arcade opposite the castle. *Cibo*, 83 Pontcanna St, is a small Italian trattoria serving sandwiches and more substantial fare, while the café in the Norwegian church by Cardiff Bay is great for salads and snacks. For a drink, *The Owain Glyndwr* on John's Street is one of the few central pubs to retain a degree of character. For a more cutting-edge venue, try *BSB* on Windsor Place, one of the new breed of style bars. *Barfly* at Kingsway is the best place to go for live music.

## South Wales

The most urbanized part of the country nevertheless contains a wealth of historic and rural attractions, all within striking distance of Cardiff or of Newport, first stop for buses and trains arriving from Bristol and London, and unexceptional but for the fact that Kurt Cobain proposed to Courtney Love in the town's *TJ's* pub.

## Chepstow and Tintern Abbey

South Wales' most spectacular historic monument is accessible from the old market town of **CHEPSTOW** (Cas-Gwent), itself ringed on three sides by thirteenth-century walls and on the fourth by the River Wye. Within the town, the Wye bridge gives stunning views of cliff-faces soaring above the river and of the first stone **castle** in Britain, built by the Normans in 1067, a year after William the Conqueror's victory at Hastings (April–Oct daily 9.30am–5/6pm; Nov–March Mon–Sat 9.30am–4pm, Sun 11am–4pm; £3). Nothing within the town can match the six-mile stroll north along the Wye to the romantic ruins of **Tintern Abbey**, built in 1131, rebuilt 150 years later and now in a state of majestic disrepair (same hours as castle; £2.50). The nave walls rise to such a height that, from a distance, you might think the magnificent Gothic church still stood intact beneath the overhang of the wooded cliff. If you don't fancy walking, catch bus #69 (every 2hr), which runs from Chepstow to Tintern and on to Monmouth, eight miles north. You can fill up for the return journey in the fourteenth-century *Moon and Sixpence* pub – almost a mile north of the Abbey by the river – which does excellent food. For information on Chepstow and the popular **Offa's Dyke Path** contact the **tourist office** on Bridge St (daily 10am–4/6pm; ☎01291/623772, ✉chepstow.tic@monmouthshire .gov.uk). The *Coach and Horses Inn* on Welsh Street offers B&B (☎01291/622626; ⑤). The cheapest options are some way out of town: the superb St Briavels Castle HI **hostel** (☎0870/770 6040, ✉stbriavels@yha.org.uk; dorms £11.25) is set in a moated Norman castle seven miles northeast of Chepstow, reached by bus #69; and the St Pierre Caravan & **Camping**, at Portskewett (☎01291/425114), is four miles west, reached on the Caldicot and Newport bus.

# The Brecon Beacons

The **Brecon Beacons National Park** (✆www.brecon-beacons.com) occupies a vast area of rocky uplands that are perfect walking territory. The Beacons themselves, a pair of hills 2900ft high accessed from Brecon town, share the limelight with the **Black Mountains** north of Crickhowell. Bus #21 (every 2hr, not Sun) runs from Newport to Brecon, passing through Abergavenny and Crickhowell, but trains from Newport veer off into England after Abergavenny.

The market town of **ABERGAVENNY** (Y Fenni) sits in a fold between seven green hills at the eastern edge of the park, about fifteen miles north of Newport. Before setting out for the mountains, pick up maps from the combined **tourist office** and **national park information office** (daily 9.30/10am–4.30/6pm; ☎01873/857588, ✉abergavenny.tic@monmouthshire.gov.uk) at Swan Meadow beside the bus station – and check what sort of weather you can expect, as conditions change rapidly. The most accessible walking areas are the **Sugar Loaf** (1955ft), four miles northwest, and **Holy Mountain** (Skirrid Fawr; 1595ft), three miles north. The *Black Sheep* **hostel** opposite the train station has dorm beds (☎01873/859125, ✆www.blacksheepbackpackers.com; £11). Plenty of **B&B**s line Monmouth Rd on the five-minute walk between the train station and the town centre; *Maes Glas* on Raglan Terrace is best (☎01873/854494, ✉maesglasBB@amserve.com; ⑤). For good-value **eating** try the *Greyhound Vaults* on Market Street or the upmarket *Trading Post*, 14 Neville Street. **CRICKHOWELL** (Crughywel), a friendly village with a fine seventeenth-century bridge five miles west of Abergavenny, is more picturesque. A great six-mile hike into the Black Mountains from here takes you through remote countryside to tiny **Partrishow Church**; inside, you'll find a rare carved fifteenth-century rood screen complete with dragon, and an ancient mural of the grim reaper. Beaufort Street in Crickhowell holds both the **tourist office** (April–Oct daily 9.30am–5pm; ☎01873/812105, ✆www.crickhowell.org.uk) and *Greenhill Villas* **B&B** (☎01873/811177, ✉ionamorgan@greenhillvillas1.fsnet.co.uk; ④). To the north of the Black Mountains, on the border with England, is the small town of **Hay-on-Wye**, famous as the secondhand book capital of the world. As well as being piled high with bargain books, the charming town hosts an important literature festival in June every year and has more than its fair share of great pubs and places to eat.

The largest of the central Brecon Beacons rise just south of **BRECON** (Aberhonddu), a lively little town eight miles west of Crickhowell that springs to life in mid-August for the huge international Brecon Jazz Festival (@www.breconjazz .co.uk). For details of the numerous trekking routes and an extensive programme of guided walks, call in at the park's **information office**, which shares premises with the **tourist office** in the Cattle Market car park beside Safeway (daily 9/10am–5/6pm; ☎01874/622485). **B&Bs** abound; both *Pickwick House*, St John's Rd (☎01874/624322, @www.pickwick-house.brecon.co.uk; ❻), and *Beacons*, in a rambling town house at 16 Bridge St (☎01874/623339, @www.beacons.brecon .co.uk; ❺), also cook excellent evening meals. Take the #39 bus a few miles north of Brecon just off the A470 to *The Griffin Inn* (☎01874/620111, @www.eatdrinksleep .ltd.uk; ❾), in Felin Fach. It's the area's best pub and also offers rooms and excellent, if pricey, food. The Ty'n-y-Caeau HI **hostel** is two miles east of Brecon at Groesfford (☎0870/770 5718, @www.yha.org.uk; £12.50), a mile off the Abergavenny bus route, while the *Held Bunkhouse* hostel is in Cantref (☎01874/624646, @www .heldbunkhouse.co.uk; £10.50), a mile southwest of town.

### Pembroke and the southwest

**PEMBROKE** (Penfro), birthplace of Henry VII, is a sleepy town, easily accessible by train from Cardiff. Centrepiece is the magnificent water-girt castle (daily April–Sept 9.30am–6pm, March & Oct 10am–5pm, Nov–Feb 10am–4pm; £3; @www.pembrokecastle.co.uk), whose circular keep, dating from 1200, offers fine views of the countryside. The castle overshadows the high street where shops are shoehorned into an assortment of Tudor and Georgian buildings. The Visitor Centre on Commons Road includes the **tourist office** (Easter–Oct daily 10am–5.30pm; ☎01646/622388). *Beech House* is the best-value **B&B** in town, 78 Main St (☎01646/683740; ❹). The nearest **HI hostel** is six miles east at Manorbier (☎0870/770 5954; £12.50), accessible by train. Regular **ferries** to Rosslare in Ireland (4hr) leave from Pembroke Dock, two miles north of the town.

The **Pembrokeshire Coast National Park** sweeps all the way around the edge of the southwestern peninsula of Wales, and the coastal path includes some of the country's most stunning and remote scenery, offering sheer cliff-faces, panoramic sea views and excellent seabird-watching. From Pembroke, bus #349/359 runs north to Haverfordwest where you can catch bus #411 sixteen miles west to **ST DAVID'S** (Tyddewi), one of the most enchanting spots in Britain, with a beautiful **cathedral** (@www.stdavidscathedral.org.uk), delicately tinted purple, green and yellow by a combination of lichen and geology, hidden in a dip below the High Street. Constructed between 1180 and 1522, but heavily restored in the nineteenth century, it hosts a prestigious classical music festival in late May or early June. Across a thin trickle of river thousands of jackdaws congregate around the extensive remains of the magnificent fourteenth-century **Bishop's Palace** (Easter–Oct daily 9.30am–5/6pm; Nov–Easter Mon–Sat 9.30am–4pm, Sun noon–4pm; £2.50), which adds to the beauty of the setting. Bus #411 runs two miles northwest to the St David's **HI hostel** at Llaethdy (☎0870/770 6042; £10), and seven miles southeast to the Penycwm HI hostel, near the attractive little village of Solva (☎0870/770 5988; £14). *Pen Albro*, 18 Goat St (☎01437/721865; ❹), is a central **B&B**. The **tourist office** is at the top of the High Street (Easter–Oct daily 9.30am–5.30pm; Nov–Easter Mon–Sat 10am–4pm; ☎01437/720392, @www.stdavids.co.uk).

About 17 miles further north on bus #411 – at the end of the main train line from Cardiff and London – is **FISHGUARD** (Abergwaun), an attractive fishing port that's another embarkation point for Rosslare, with ferries and catamarans departing daily from alongside the train station. *Hamilton Backpackers Lodge*, a **hostel** near the tourist office at 21 Hamilton St (☎01348/874797, @www.fishguard -backpackers.com; £12), is a good option.

# Mid-Wales

**Mid-Wales**, an area of wild mountain roads, hidden valleys and genteel ex-spa towns, is the least visited part of the country, perhaps because access is a little trickier than elsewhere. Nevertheless, it's worth making the effort, because it's here that you'll discover the traditional rural Wales, in quiet towns where the pub conversation takes place in Welsh rather than English. But this is also Wales at its most "alternative": look out for healthfood shops and trendy bookshops, their owners often escapees from England's industrial Midlands sprawl.

Trains run from Shrewsbury across the border, accessible on the main line north from Cardiff. Three miles inside Wales is **WELSHPOOL** (Y Trallwng), a market town full of the distinctive black-and-white half-timbered houses typical of the Marches, the Welsh–English borders. It's worth a stop simply to visit the thirteenth-century **Powis Castle**, a gorgeous red limestone building that's been continuously inhabited for five hundred years (April–Oct Thurs–Sun 1–4/5pm; £8.80). The castle houses a fine collection of furniture, tapestries and pictures, as well as the Clive of India collection of Indian treasures. The famous eighteenth-century landscape gardener Capability Brown designed the lovely terraced **gardens** (same days 11am–6pm; free with castle ticket, or £6.20). The **tourist office** is on Church Street (daily 9.30am–5.30pm; ☎01938/552043). One of the many **B&Bs** is *Montgomery House* on Salop Rd (☎01938/552693; ⑤).

Trains terminate at **ABERYSTWYTH**, a lively, thoroughly Welsh seaside resort of neat Victorian terraces and a thriving student culture. The train station is ten minutes south of the seafront, reached by walking up Terrace Rd past the **tourist office** (July & Aug daily 10am–6pm, Sept–June Mon–Sat 10am–5pm; ☎01970/612125, ✉aberystwythTIC@ceredigion.gov.uk). Upstairs, the **Ceredigion Museum** (free) contains coracles once used by local fishermen as well as a reconstructed cottage interior. The flavour of the town is best appreciated on the seafront, where one of Edward I's castles bestrides a windy headland to the south. There's also a Victorian **camera obscura** further north, which can be reached via the clanking **cliff railway** (March–Nov daily 10am–5/6pm; £2.50 return). For a more extended rail trip, you could take the very popular **Vale of Rheidol** narrow-gauge steam train to **Devil's Bridge**, a canyon where three bridges span a dramatic waterfall (April–Oct; 3hr return trip, 1hr to Devil's Bridge; £12). The town seafront is lined with genteel **guest houses**; try *Yr Hafod*, 1 South Marine Terrace (☎01970/617579; ⑤). Out of term-time, contact the University of Wales about beds in **student halls** (☎01970/621960; £12). *The Treehouse*, on Eastgate, is a great daytime vegetarian café. Check out the university's Arts Centre on Penglais Hill for films, plays, exhibitions and other events.

North of Aberystwyth the train passes through a succession of seaside resorts before reaching **HARLECH**, where one of the best of Edward I's great castles, later Owen Glyndŵr's residence, towers above everything else on a rocky crag overlooking the sea (April–Oct daily 9.30am–5/6pm; Nov–March Mon–Sat 9.30am–4pm, Sun 11am–4pm; £3); the ramparts offer panoramic views over the mountains of Snowdonia on one side and Tremadog Bay on the other. The town itself huddles apologetically behind the castle; if you want **to stay**, try the *Arundel B&B*, High Street (☎01766/780637; ④), or the *Plas Newydd* HI **hostel**, three miles south by bus #38 or train in Llanbedr (☎0870/770 5926, ⊛www .yha.org.uk; £11). Midway between Aberystwyth and Harlech is down-at-heel **Barmouth**, from where you can catch bus #94 inland to **DOLGELLAU**, a base for exploring **Cadair Idris** (2930ft). The mountain looms over the southern side of town, its summit accessible via a tough six-mile, five-hour trek along the Pony Path starting three miles south of Dolgellau at Ty Nant – just one of the many walks in the area. Dolgellau **tourist office** is on central Eldon Square, right by the bus stop (Easter–Oct daily 10am–5/6pm; Nov–Easter closed Tues–Thurs; ☎01341/422888, ✉ticdolgellau@hotmail.com). *Tan-y-Fron* (☎01341/422638,

@www.tanyfron.co.uk; ❺), half a mile east along Arran Road, is a handily located **B&B,** or you could make for *Kings* HI **hostel** at Penmaenpool, four miles west, off the #28 bus route (☎0870/770 5900; £11).

# North Wales

**Snowdonia National Park** is the glory of **North Wales**, with some of the most dramatic mountain scenery Britain has to offer – jagged peaks, towering waterfalls and glacial lakes decorating every roadside. Walkers congregate here in large numbers, and the villages around the area's highest peak, Snowdon (3560ft), see steady tourist traffic even in the bleakest months of the year. Whatever season you're here, make sure you're equipped with suitable shoes, warm clothing, and food and drink to see you through any unexpected hitches. There are two main access routes. From Porthmadog, a few miles north of Harlech, **buses** skirt the base of Snowdon west to Caernarfon and Llanberis, and east to Blaenau Ffestiniog; while mainline **trains** from Crewe and Chester hug the north coast through Conwy and Bangor to Holyhead, with a branch line heading south to Betws-y-Coed and Blaenau Ffestiniog.

## Blaenau Ffestiniog and Betws-y-Coed

The narrow-gauge **Ffestiniog Railway** (call for times; ☎01766/516024, @www .festrail.co.uk) loops inland from Porthmadog for 14 miles up to the slate-quarrying town of **BLAENAU FFESTINIOG**. On a grey day, Blaenau Ffestiniog can look particularly desolate, but it's worth a call for the **Llechwedd Slate Caverns** a mile north, reached by bus. One train tour takes visitors into the side of the mountain, while the Deep Mine tour visits an underground lake and spectacular caverns on Britain's steepest train incline (daily 10am–5/6pm; one tour £7.50, both £11.50; @www.llechwedd-slate-caverns.co.uk). Should the brooding scenery cast its spell over you, **B&B** can be had at *Afallon*, Manod Rd (☎01766/830468; ❹).

Most people push on to **BETWS-Y-COED**, ten miles northeast by ordinary train. A popular base for Snowdonia National Park – though no serious walks start here – the town has one of the prettiest settings in Wales but is overrun with visitors in summer, many coming here just to see the **Swallow Falls** in the wooded Llugwy Valley, two miles west of town. Mountain biking in the nearby Gwydyr Forest Park may be more tempting. *Swallow Falls* HI (☎01690/710796, @www .yha.org.uk; £12.50) is a recent addition to the numerous places to stay in the area, two miles west of Betws-y-Coed on the A5. There's another HI hostel at Capel Curig (☎0870/770 5746; £14.40) a further four miles west. Half a mile from Betws-y-Coed on the A470 is the *Rose Hill* **B&B** (☎01690/710455, @www.rosehill -snowdonia.co.uk; ❺). In town *The Royal Oak Hotel* and *Three Gables*, both on Holyhead Road, do meals and the *Royal Oak* is the liveliest place to drink. Beside the station sits the **tourist office** (daily 9.30/10am–5/6pm; ☎01690/710426, @ticbetws@hotmail.com). From Betws-y-Coed there are trains and buses to Llandudno Junction, on the main Chester–Holyhead line.

## Conwy and Caernarfon

A couple of miles west of Llandudno Junction is **CONWY**, where Edward I's magnificent **castle** (April–Oct daily 9.30am–5/6pm; Nov–March Mon–Sat 9.30am–4pm, Sun 11am–4pm; £4) and the town walls are a UNESCO World Heritage Site. The entrance contains the **tourist office** (same hours; ☎01492/592248). The ramparts offer fine views of Thomas Telford's recently restored 1826 suspension bridge (April–Oct daily; £1.40) over the River Conwy. For **B&B** try the popular *Gwynedd Guesthouse*, 10 Upper Gate St (☎01492/596537, @abs.conwy@virgin .net; ❺). Otherwise, there's Conwy **HI hostel**, Lark Hill, just west of the centre (☎0870/770 5774, @www.yha.org.uk; £14). West of Conwy, trains pass through **Bangor** on the way to Holyhead. To get to **CAERNARFON** – the springboard for trips into Snowdonia from the north – you'll need bus #88 from the bus station off Bangor High St. **Caernarfon Castle** (daily: April–Oct 9.30am–5/6pm; Nov–March 9.30/11am–4pm; £4.75), built in 1283, is arguably the most splendid castle in Britain. Little of the interior has survived, however, and the three-acre space is largely grassed over; it's here that the Princes of Wales are invested. Buses stop on Penllyn, just across Castle Square from the **tourist office**, Castle Street (daily 10am–4.30/6pm; Nov–Easter closed Wed; ☎01286/672232, ✉caernarfon .tic@gwynedd.gov.uk). In town, the cheapest place to stay is *Totters*, an excellent backpacker hostel at 2 High St (☎01286/672963; £12); *Isfryn Guesthouse*, 11 Church St (☎01286/675628; ❺), is another good bet.

## Llanberis and Snowdon

Regular buses run the seven miles east from Caernarfon to **LLANBERIS**, a lakeside village in the shadow of **Snowdon**, at 3560ft the highest mountain in England and Wales. With the biggest concentration of guest houses, hostels and restaurants close to the mountains, Llanberis offers the perfect base for even the most tentative Snowdonian exploration. The longest but easiest ascent of the mountain is the Llanberis Path, a signposted five-mile hike (3hr) that is manageable by anyone reasonably fit. Alternatively, you can cop out and take the generally steam-hauled **Snowdon Mountain Railway** (daily mid-March to October; £20; ☎www.snow donrailway.co.uk), which operates from Llanberis to the summit café, pub and post office, weather permitting (note that in adverse conditions trains may terminate at Clogwyn, three-quarters of the way up the mountain). Return tickets permit half an hour's viewing from the summit. The slate quarries that seared Llanberis's surroundings now lie idle, with the **Welsh Slate Museum** (Easter–Oct daily 10am–5pm; Nov–Easter daily except Sat 10am–4pm; free; ☎www.nmgw .ac.uk) remaining as a memorial to the workers' tough lives. Nearby, the Dinorwig Pumped Storage Hydro Station is carved out of the mountain and can be visited on underground tours (£6.50) starting at the **Electric Mountain Museum** (daily 9.30/10.30am–4.30/5.30pm; Feb–Easter Thurs–Sun only; closed Jan; free), which has a good café and interesting displays on ancient wooden boats recovered locally.

Buses stop near the **tourist office**, 41 High St (Easter–Oct daily 10am–6pm; Nov–Easter Wed & Fri–Sun 11am–4pm; ☎01286/870765, ✉llanberis .tic@gwynedd.gov.uk). Walkers have a good choice of **accommodation**. The Sherpa Bus services (£3 all-day) collectively encircle Snowdon providing access to several HI **hostels** (☎www.yha.org.uk), each at the base of a footpath up the mountain: *Llanberis*, Llwyn Celyn (☎0870/770 5932; £12.50); *Snowdon Ranger*, Rhyd Ddu (☎0870/770 6038; £10.60); *Bryn Gwynant*, Nantgwynant (☎0870/770 5732; £11); and *Pen-y-Pass*, Nantgwynant (☎0870/770 5990; £12.50). Llanberis's High Street is lined with small **hotels**: try *The Heights* at no. 74 (☎01286/871179, ☎www.heightshotel.co.uk; dorms £14, rooms ❺), which also has eight-bed dorms (£17.50), or *Dolafon*, another pleasant B&B (☎01286/870993, ☎www.dolafon.com; ❻). The enduringly popular *Pete's Eats*, 40 High St, satisfies walkers' appetites.

## Anglesey – and boats to Dublin

The Menai Bridge was built by Thomas Telford in 1826 to connect North Wales with the island of **Anglesey** (Ynys Môn) across the Menai Straits, and it's one of the two chief sights on the little island, even though it's been superseded by a newer rival alongside. The other draw is the last of Edward I's masterpieces, **Beaumaris Castle** (April–Oct daily 9.30am–5/6pm; Nov–March Mon–Sat 9.30am–4pm, Sun 11am–4pm; £3), reached by bus #53, #57 or #58 from Bangor. The giant castle was built in 1295 to guard the straits and has a fairy-tale moat enclosing its twelve sturdy towers. Nonetheless, most tourist traffic in this direction speeds past to **HOLYHEAD** (Caergybi), the busiest Welsh **ferry-port**, with several daily ferry and catamaran sailings leaving for Dublin. **B&Bs** galore are within a few minutes' walk of the combined bus, train and ferry terminal, including *Orotavia*, 66 Walthew Ave (☎01407/760259; ❹), and others on nearby Newry Street. The **tourist office** (daily 8.30am–6pm; ☎01407/762622, ✉holyhead@nwtic.com) is inside the ferry terminal.

# Scotland

**Scotland** is a model example of how a small nation can retain its identity within the confines of a larger one. Down the centuries the Scots, unlike the Welsh, successfully repulsed the expansionist designs of England, and when the "old enemies" first formed a union in 1603, it was because King James VI of Scotland inherited the English throne, rather than the other way around. Although the two countries' parliaments merged one hundred years later, Scotland retained many of its own institutions, notably distinctive legal and educational systems. However, the most significant reawakening of Scottish political nationalism since then has been in the last few years, with a separate parliament looking after most of Scotland's day-to-day affairs being re-established in Edinburgh in 1999.

Most of the population clusters in the narrow "central belt" between the two principal cities: stately **Edinburgh**, the national capital, with its magnificent architecture and imperious natural setting, and earthy **Glasgow**, a powerhouse of the Industrial Revolution but now as well known for its cultural core as its rough edges. Although the third city, Aberdeen, perched on the North Sea coast, has grown wealthy on the proceeds of offshore oil, Scotland is overwhelmingly rural outside the Central Belt. Only pockets of the land are particularly fertile, yet in the **Highlands and Islands**, which comprise over two-thirds of the total area, the harsh, mountainous landscape is spectacularly beautiful, its rugged landscapes enhanced by the volatile climate, producing an extraordinary variety of moods and colours. It's a terrific place for those keen on outdoor activities such as hiking and mountain biking, though even the highest mountain, **Ben Nevis**, is an uncomplicated ascent for the average walker and much of the scenery – such as the famous **Loch Lomond** and **Loch Ness** – is easily accessible.

## Edinburgh

**EDINBURGH**, the showcase capital of Scotland, is a historic, cosmopolitan and cultured city. Its stone-built houses, historic buildings and fairy-tale castle, perched on a rocky crag right in the heart of the city, make it visually stunning and it is little surprise that this city is the most popular draw for tourists in Scotland. The 430,000 population swells massively in high season, peaking in mid-August during the **Edinburgh Festival**, by far the biggest arts event in Europe. Yet despite this annual invasion, the city is still emphatically Scottish in character and atmosphere, mixing rich history with fast-moving current affairs that have seen the re-establishment of a Scottish parliament and the consequent reaffirmation of Edinburgh as a dynamic European capital.

The centre has two distinct parts. The castle rock is the core of the medieval city, where nobles and servants lived side by side for centuries within tight defensive walls. Edinburgh earned the nickname "Auld Reekie" for the smog and smell generated by the cramped inhabitants of this **Old Town**, where the streets flowed with sewage tipped out of tenement windows and disease was rife. The **New Town** was begun in the late 1700s on farmland lying to the north of the Castle. Edinburgh's wealthier residents speculated profitably on tracts of this land and engaged the services of eminent architects in their development. The result is an outstanding example of Georgian town planning, still largely intact.

## Arrival, information and accommodation

Edinburgh airport is seven miles west of the centre; there are bus connections around the clock to the city. **Trains** pull into Waverley Station, bang in the centre; the New Town and Princes Street lie to the north, the Old Town and the castle to the south. The **bus** terminal is on St Andrew Square, just north of Princes Street. The best way to get around the city centre is on foot. There's also a good local bus service; day passes (£2.30; off-peak £1.80) are available on board. An **Edinburgh Pass** secures free airport transfer, unlimited bus travel and access to 27 of the city's attractions (one-day pass £26, two-day £34, three-day £40). The pass can be obtained from the main **tourist office** at 3 Princes St, above the station on the top level of Princes Mall (July & Aug Mon–Sat 9am–8pm, Sun 10am–8pm; Sept–June Mon–Sat 9am–5/7pm, Sun 10am–5/7pm; ☏0845/225 5121, ⊛www.edinburgh .org). The tourist office has full listings of accommodation, and will book rooms for a £3 fee. Central hotels and hostels book up quickly in peak season, but B&B is easier to come by, with prices starting from £15 per person. In addition, you can get student rooms over the summer, though they're not cheap; try Napier University (☏0131/455 3738; ⑨) or Pollock Hall, Edinburgh University (☏0131/667 1971; ⑨). Campsites are on the fringes of the city. If you want to stay during the Festival (early Aug to early Sept), you'll need to book months in advance.

### Hostels

**Argyle** 14 Argyle Place, Marchmont ☏0131/667 9991, ⊛www.argyle-backpackers.co.uk. Quieter hostel, with small dorms and a dozen double/twin rooms. Pleasant location in studenty Marchmont. Dorms £12, rooms ④

**Brodies** 12 High St, Old Town ☏0131/556 6770, ⊛www.brodieshostels.co.uk. Tucked down a typical Old Town close, it's cosier than many others, but with limited communal areas. £16.50.

**Bruntsfield** 7 Bruntsfield Crescent, Bruntsfield ☏0870/004 1114. Large HI hostel a mile south of Princes Street. £16.

**Castle Rock** 15 Johnston Terrace, Old Town ☏0131/225 9666, ⊛www.scotlands-top-hostels .com. Busy 200-bed hostel tucked below the castle ramparts. £14.

**Edinburgh Backpackers** 65 Cockburn St, Old Town ☏0131/220 1717, ⊛www.hoppo.com. Big hostel with a great central location in a side street off the Royal Mile. Dorms £17.50, rooms ⑥

**Eglinton Hostel** 18 Eglinton Crescent, Haymarket ☏0870/004 1116. The more central of the two HI hostels, in a characterful town house west of the centre. £16.

**High Street Hostel** 8 Blackfriars St, Old Town ☏0131/557 3984, ⊛www.scotlands-top-hostels .com. Large, lively well-known hostel in a sixteenth-century building just off the Royal Mile. £14.

**Royal Mile Backpackers** 105 High St, Old Town ☏0131/557 6120, ⊛www.scotlands-top-hostels .com. Small hostel popular with longer-term residents; shares facilities with the nearby *High Street Hostel*. £14.

**St Christopher's Inn** 9–13 Market St, Old Town ☏0131/226 1446, ⊛www.st-christophers.co.uk. Edinburgh's first mega-hostel; 110 beds (all bunks) with smaller rooms as well as dorms. Dorms £18, rooms ⑥

### Hotels and B&Bs

**Ardenlee Guest House** 9 Eyre Place ☏0131/556 2838, ⊛www.wayfarerguesthouse.co.uk. Welcoming, non-smoking guest house near the Royal Botanic Garden, with spacious rooms. ⑦

**Bar Java** 48–50 Constitution St, Leith ☏0131/553 2020, ⊛www.hotelbarjava.com. Simple but brightly designed rooms above one of Leith's funkiest bars. Food and drink available till late in the bar itself. ⑥

**Cluaran House** 47 Leamington Terrace, Viewforth ☏0131/221 0047, ⊛www.cluaran-house -edinburgh.co.uk. Pleasant B&B in a nicely deco-rated, non-smoking house near Bruntsfield serving wholefood breakfasts. ⑨

**The Greenhouse** 14 Hartington Gardens, Viewforth ☏0131/622 7634, ⊛www.greenhouse -edinburgh.com. A fully vegetarian/vegan guest house, where a relaxed atmosphere prevails. ⑧

**International Guest House** 37 Mayfield Gardens, Mayfield ☏0131/667 2511, ⊛www .accommodationedinburgh.com. One of the best Southside guest houses, with comfortable well-equipped rooms. ⑧

**Six Mary's Place** Raeburn Place ☏0131/332 8965, ⊛www.sixmarysplace.co.uk. Collectively run "alternative" guest house; has a no-smoking policy and offers excellent home-cooked vegetar-ian meals. ⑧

**Stuart House** 12 East Claremont St ☎0131/557 9030, ⓦwww.stuartguesthouse.co.uk. Cosy, bright Georgian house in the Broughton area. No smoking. ⑨

**Teviotdale House Hotel** 53 Grange Loan, Grange ☎0131/667 4376, ⓦwww.teviotdalehouse.com. Peaceful non-smoking hotel, offering luxurious standards at reasonable prices. Particularly good (and huge) home-cooked Scottish breakfasts. ⑨

### Campsites

**Edinburgh Caravan Club** Marine Drive, Silverknowes ☎0131/312 6874. Pleasantly located close to the shore in the northwestern suburbs, 30min from the centre on bus #28.

**38 Mortonhall Gate** Frogston Rd ☎0131/664 1533. A good site, five miles south of the centre, near the Braid Hills; take bus #11 (marked Captain's Rd) or #31 from the centre of town. Closed Jan–March.

## The Old Town

The cobbled **Royal Mile** – composed of Castlehill, Lawnmarket, High Street and Canongate – is the central thoroughfare of the **Old Town**, running down a prominent ridge to the Palace of Holyroodhouse (see opposite) from the **Castle** (daily 9.30am–5/6pm; £9.80). The castle is thought to have evolved from an Iron Age fort, the sheer volcanic rock on which it stands providing formidable defence on three sides. Within its precincts are St Margaret's Chapel, probably the oldest building in the city, containing the ancient crown jewels of Scotland and the even older Stone of Destiny, coronation stone of the kings of Scotland. There's a large military museum here, too, and the castle esplanade provides a dramatic setting for the world-famous Military Tattoo, an unashamed display of martial pomp staged during the Festival. Year round, at 1pm (not Sun) a cannon shot is fired from the battlements.

Descending Castlehill from the Esplanade you'll pass the **Scotch Whisky Heritage Centre** (daily 10am–5.30pm, longer hours in summer; £8.50; ⓦwww .whisky-heritage.co.uk), which offers an informative and entertaining introduction to Scotland's national beverage. A little further down in an imposing black Gothic church building is **The Hub** (daily 9.30am–late; free), permanent home of the Edinburgh International Festival, where you'll find a pleasant café/bistro, a bookshop and various quirky art installations. Still further down, leading off the far side of Lawnmarket, Lady Stair's Close is home to the **Writers' Museum** (Mon–Sat 10am–5pm; during Festival also Sun noon–5pm; free), dedicated to Sir Walter Scott, Robert Burns and Robert Louis Stevenson.

At the southern end of Lawnmarket, George IV Bridge leads south from the Royal Mile to Chambers Street; here the **Museum of Scotland** (Mon–Sat 10am–5pm, Tues till 8pm, Sun noon–5pm; free; ⓦwww.nms.ac.uk), housed in an imaginatively designed modern sandstone building, is home to many of the nation's principal historical treasures, ranging from Celtic pieces to twentieth-century icons. Immediately next door is the **Royal Museum** (same times), a soaring Victorian pile housing a rich collection of colonial acquisitions. The area south of here is dominated by **Edinburgh University**, Scotland's largest with over 15,000 students.

Back on the Royal Mile, High Street starts at Parliament Square, dominated by the **High Kirk of St Giles** (daily 9am–5/7pm; donation £2), whose beautiful crown-shaped spire is an Edinburgh landmark. Inside, the Thistle Chapel (entry £1) is an amazing display of mock-Gothic woodcarving. Outside, near the west door, the heart-shaped cobble pattern set in the cobbles is the Heart of Midlothian – traditionally, passers-by spit on it for luck. On the south side of Parliament Square are the Neoclassical law courts, incorporating the seventeenth-century **Parliament House**, under whose spectacular hammerbeam roof the Scottish parliament met until the 1707 Union. This stretch of the Royal Mile is the starting point for entertaining **ghost tours** which prowl around the spookiest of the medieval nooks and crannies, including some underground streets. Look out for information boards on the street or contact Mercat Tours (☎0131/557 6464) or Witchery Tours (☎0131/225 6745).

The final section of the Royal Mile, Canongate, starts just beyond medieval **John Knox's House** (Mon–Sat 10am–6pm; £3; note that these opening hours are temporary while the site is incorporated into what will be the Scottish Storytelling

Centre. For further details, check the website ⓦwww.scottishstorytellingcentre
.co.uk). Reputedly the home of the city's famously fierce Calvinist cleric, its
bare interiors give a good idea of the labyrinthine layout of Old Town houses.
The final section of Canongate is dominated by the new **Scottish Parliament**
a costly and controversial but undoubtedly striking piece of contemporary architecture. In complete contrast is the **Palace of Holyroodhouse** (daily April–Oct
9.30am–6pm, Nov–March 9.30am–4.30pm; £8.50), the Royal Family's official
Scottish residence, which principally dates from the seventeenth century. The
public are admitted to the sumptuous state rooms and historic apartments unless the
royals are in residence. The **Queen's Gallery** (same opening hours; £5) displays
works of art from the royal collection. The palace looks out over Holyrood Park,
650 acres of wilderness in the heart of the city, where fine walks lead along the
**Salisbury Crags** and up **Arthur's Seat** beyond; a fairly stiff climb is rewarded by
magnificent views over the city and out to the Firth of Forth.

## The New Town

The clear divide between the Old and **New Town** is the wide grassy valley of
Princes Street Gardens, along the north side of which runs **Princes St**, the main
shopping area, with chain stores crammed in cheek-by-jowl. Splitting the gardens
halfway along is the **National Gallery of Scotland** (daily 10am–5pm, Thurs till
7pm; free), an Athenian-style sandstone building. One of the best small collections
of pre-twentieth-century art in Europe, it includes works by major European artists including Botticelli, Raphael, Titian, Rembrandt, Vermeer, Degas, Gauguin
and Van Gogh. The Scottish collection is relatively limited, though it's worth
looking out for the charming *Reverend Robert Walker Skating* by Henry Raeburn – a
postcard favourite. The National is linked, via a splendid neo-classical underground
chamber, to the **Royal Scottish Academy** (same opening hours; free). Originally
designed by William Playfair in 1826, the building has been sensitively refurbished
and is now a major exhibition space, with a lecture theatre and restaurant.

East of the National Gallery the peculiar Gothic spire of the **Scott Monument** (daily March–May 10am–6pm, June–Sept 9am–8pm/6pm, Oct 9am–6pm,
Nov–Feb 10am–4pm; £2.50), a tribute to Sir Walter Scott, stands out. You can
climb the tightly winding internal spiral staircase for heady views of the city below
and hills beyond. Nearby George Street, which runs parallel to Princes Street, is fast
becoming the domain of designer-label shops, while suave Charlotte Square, at its
western end, remains the most elegant square in the New Town. North of George
Street is the broad avenue of Queen Street, at whose eastern end stands the **Scottish
National Portrait Gallery** (daily 10am–5pm, Thurs till 7pm; free). The remarkable red sandstone building is modelled on the Doge's Palace in Venice; inside the
collection of portraits offers an engaging procession through Scottish history with
famous Scots such as Bonnie Prince Charlie and Mary, Queen of Scots on display
alongside contemporary heroes such as Sean Connery and Alex Ferguson.

East of here, best approached along Waterloo Place (an extension of Princes
Street), **Calton Hill** rises up above the New Town and is worth heading up both
for the views you'll get across the city, and for an odd collection of Neoclassical
buildings including the **National Monument**, perched on the very top of the
hill. It was begun in 1822 to imitate the Parthenon in Athens, but funds quickly
ran out and only twelve of its massive columns were built, earning it the nickname
"Edinburgh's Disgrace".

In the northwest corner of the New Town lies **Stockbridge**, a smart residential
suburb with bohemian pretensions – especially noticeable around the huddle of old
mill buildings known as Dean Village. From here Belford Road leads up to the
**Scottish National Gallery of Modern Art** and the **Dean Gallery** extension
opposite (both daily 10am–5pm, Thurs till 7pm; free); the two offer an accessible introduction to all the notable movements of twentieth-century art and the
sculpted garden area by Charles Jencks has become a popular work of art in itself.

Inverleith Park

Royal Botanic Garden
INVERLEITH TERRACE
WATER OF LEITH WALKWAY
INVERLEITH PL
WARRISTON PL
BROUGHTON RD
ROONEY STREET

GLENOGLE ROAD

Mansfield Place Church

BELLEVUE CRESCENT
EAST CLAREMONT STREET

HENDERSON ROW
EYRE PLACE
H

STOCKBRIDGE
RAEBURN PLACE
i
GLANVILLE PLACE
HAMILTON PLACE
DEANHAUGH STREET
KERR STREET

Theatre Workshop
ST STEPHEN STREET

CUMBERLAND STREET

SCOTLAND STREET
DRUMMOND PLACE
LONDON ST

DUBLIN ST

BARONY STREET

ST BERNARDS CRES
LESLIE PLACE
DEAN TERRACE
ANN STREET

GREAT KING STREET

NORTHUMBERLAND ST

ALBANY STREET

COMELY BANK AVENUE
DEAN PARK CRESCENT
CIRCUS PLACE
ROYAL CIRCUS
HOWE STREET
DUNDAS STREET
ABERCROMBY PLACE

NEW
TOWN

QUEENSFERRY ROAD

MORAY PLACE
JAMAICA STREET
HERIOT ROW
Gardens
Queen Street

Scottish National Portrait Gallery
YORK PLACE
ELDER ST

Queen
QUEEN STREET
FREDERICK STREET
THISTLE STREET
ST ANDREW SQUARE
Bus Station

WEST REGISTER ST

DEAN VILLAGE

Water of Leith
WATER OF LEITH WALKWAY
DEAN BRIDGE
ANSLIE PLACE

Georgian House
CHARLOTTE

6
St Andrew & St George

7
Princes Mall

i

BELFORD ROAD
RANDOLPH CLIFF
DOUGLAS CRES
RANDOLPH CRES
QUEENSFERRY STREET
CHARLOTTE SQUARE

West Register House
HILL STREET
YOUNG STREET
CASTLE STREET
GEORGE STREET
8
Assembly Rooms
ROSE STREET
HANOVER STREET

Scott Monument

Royal Scottish Academy
THE MOUND

East Princes Street Gardens

National Gallery of Scotland

WEST END
ROTHESAY PL
MELVILLE STREET
WALKER ST
STAFFORD ST
COATES CRES
NTS Headquarters
WEST MAITLAND ST

PRINCES STREET
WEST END
St John
St Cuthbert

West Princes Street Gardens

Assembly Hall (NTS)

Gladstone's Land (NTS)

MARKET ST
WAVERLEY BRIDGE

WAVERLEY ST
NORTH BRIDGE

St Mary's Episcopal Cathedral
PALMERSTON PLACE
WILLIAM STREET
SHANDWICK PL

LOTHIAN ROAD
KING'S STABLES RD

The Castle

OLD TOWN
CASTLEHILL
LAWNMARKET
The Hub
JOHNSTON TERRACE
Central Library
VICTORIA ST
GEORGE IV BRIDGE
COWGATE

St Giles
HIGH ST

9
National Library

HAYMARKET
MORRISON STREET
Edinburgh Conference Centre
Film House
CAMBRIDGE STREET
Traverse Theatre
Usher Hall
Royal Lyceum Theatre
GRINDLAY STREET
SPITTAL ST
GRASSMARKET
WEST PORT
Magdalen Chapel
Statue of Greyfriars Bobby
Greyfriars Kirk
10
11
12
Museum of Scotland
13

Haymarket Train Station
14
Odeon Cinema
BREAD STREET
Museum of Fire
George Heriot's School
LAURISTON PLACE

WESTERN APPROACH ROAD
FOUNTAIN BRIDGE
TOLLCROSS

Cameo Cinema
HOME STREET
LOCHRIN PLACE
BROUGHAM PLACE

The Meadows

0        300 yds

GILMORE PLACE
LEVEN STREET
15
King's Theatre
GLENGYLE TERR
L

M
Bruntsfield Links

© Crown copyright

A702 Bruntsfield, Morningside, Biggar & Carlisle

## Eating, drinking and nightlife

Edinburgh is well served with **restaurants**, while its **cafés** are among the most enjoyable spots in the city, sometimes doubling as exhibition and performance spaces during the Festival. The city's many **pubs** and **bars** are among the most congenial in the country; live music is a frequent bonus and you'll easily find places open after midnight. The city has a lively **nightlife**, and venues change

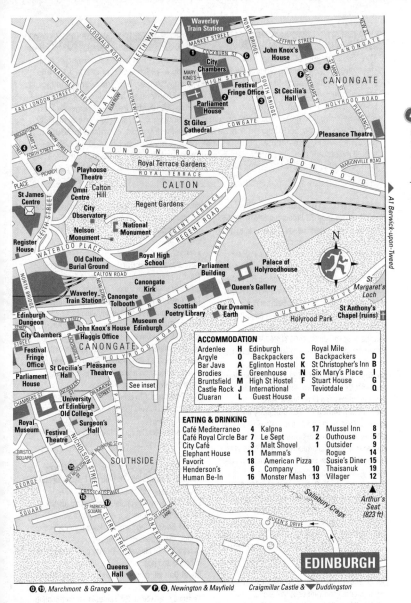

**ACCOMMODATION**

| | | | | | |
|---|---|---|---|---|---|
| Ardenlee | H | Edinburgh | | Royal Mile | |
| Argyle | O | Backpackers | C | Backpackers | D |
| Bar Java | A | Eglinton Hostel | K | St Christopher's Inn | B |
| Brodies | E | Greenhouse | N | Six Mary's Place | I |
| Bruntsfield | M | High St Hostel | F | Stuart House | G |
| Castle Rock | J | International | | Teviotdale | Q |
| Cluaran | L | Guest House | P | | |

**EATING & DRINKING**

| | | | | | |
|---|---|---|---|---|---|
| Café Mediterraneo | 4 | Kalpna | 17 | Mussel Inn | 8 |
| Café Royal Circle Bar | 7 | Le Sept | 2 | Outhouse | 5 |
| City Café | 3 | Malt Shovel | 1 | Outsider | 9 |
| Elephant House | 11 | Mamma's | | Rogue | 14 |
| Favorit | 18 | American Pizza | | Susie's Diner | 15 |
| Henderson's | 6 | Company | 10 | Thaisanuk | 19 |
| Human Be-In | 16 | Monster Mash | 13 | Villager | 12 |

**EDINBURGH**

name and location with such speed that the only way to keep up with what's going on is to get hold of *The List,* a comprehensive **listings** magazine published fortnightly. The best **theatre** is the Traverse, 10 Cambridge St, and there's an excellent art-house **cinema**, The Filmhouse, nearby at 88 Lothian Road. **Gay nightlife** is centred on the top of Leith Walk, notably at *C.C. Bloom's* and *Planet Out*, next to the Playhouse on Greenside Place.

## The Edinburgh Festival

The city's essential cultural event is the **Edinburgh Festival** (ⓦ www.edinburgh
-festivals.com), by far the world's largest arts jamboree, which was founded in 1947 and
now attracts thousands of artists from August to early September. The event is, in fact,
several different festivals taking place at around the same time: the Edinburgh International Festival traditionally presents highbrow fare; but it's the frenetic **Fringe** (ⓦ www
.edfringe.com) that gives the city its unique buzz during August, with all sorts of unlikely
venues turned into performance spaces for a bewildering array of artists. In addition,
there's a Film Festival focusing on the latest movies, a Jazz Festival, and a Book Festival. **Tickets** are available at the venues and from the International Festival Office, The
Hub, Castlehill (ⓣ 0131/473 2000), or the Fringe Office, 180 High St (ⓣ 0131/226 0026).

### Cafés and restaurants

**Café Mediterraneo** 73 Broughton St ⓣ 0131/557
6900. Deli with a small dining space serving good-
quality Italian food at great prices.

**Elephant House** 21 George IV Bridge. Popular café
near the university with a cavernous back room.

**Favorit** Teviot Pl and 30–32 Leven St, Bruntsfield.
Modern café/diner open till the wee small hours.

**Henderson's** 94 Hanover St. Self-service
restaurant with a lively atmosphere, good-value
vegetarian food and occasional live music.

**Kalpna** 2 St Patrick Sq ⓣ 0131/667 9890.
Prize-winning vegetarian Indian; great prices for
superb food.

**Le Sept** 5 Hunter Sq ⓣ 0131/225 5428. An old
favourite, this French brasserie serves filling
savoury crepes and good fish dishes.

**Mamma's American Pizza Company** 30 Grassmarket. Good pizzas and a lively atmosphere that
often spills out onto the Grassmarket cobbles.

**Monster Mash** 4a Forrest Rd ⓣ 0131/225 7069.
Hugely popular newcomer, serving quality rendi-
tions of British standards at small cost.

**Mussel Inn** 61–65 Rose St ⓣ 0131/225 5979.
Owned by two Scottish shellfish farmers, you can
feast here on a kilo of mussels and a basket of
chips for under £10.

**The Outsider** 15–16 George IV Bridge ⓣ 0131/226
3131. Stylish, vibrant restaurant in the Old Town
serving modern, filling and affordable food.

**Rogue** 67 Morrison St ⓣ 0131/228 2700 Stunning
design and immaculately prepared modern Scottish fare combined with sensible prices.

**Susie's Diner** 51 West Nicolson St. Popular
student veggie/vegan café.

**Thaisanuk** 21 Argyle Place ⓣ 0131/228 8855. A

haven for cheap, authentic Thai food in the student
quarter of Marchmont. It's always packed, so
expect to wait for a table.

### Pubs and bars

**Café Royal Circle Bar** 19 West Register Street.
Make a point of visiting this Grade A listed pub,
arguably Edinburgh's most beautiful watering-hole.

**City Café** 19 Blair St. A bar, club and internet café
rolled into one. The food is good too.

**Human Be-In** 2–8 West Crosscauseway. Airy,
laid-back bar whose outdoor seating and stylish
clientele make it an ideal spot for people-watching.

**Malt Shovel** 11 Cockburn St. Good beer, plenty
of local colour and a wide choice of single malt
whiskies; live jazz some evenings.

**The Outhouse** 12a Broughton St Lane. A heated
outdoor area makes this the venue for year-round
alfresco drinking.

**Villager** 49–50 George IV Bridge. Busy new bar-
cum-diner in the Old Town.

### Live music venues and clubs

**Cabaret Voltaire** 36–38 Blair St. Eclectic beats
and the occasional live band.

**Ego** 14 Picardy Pl. Popular club playing anything
from house to swing to a mixed crowd.

**Liquid Room** 9c Victoria St. Holds house and indie
nights; also a popular live venue.

**Massa** 36–39 Market St. Dressy club that grooves
to house and pop.

**Royal Oak** Infirmary St. Venue for Scottish folk
music.

**Venue** 17–21 Calton Rd. Features up-and-coming
indie bands as well as a range of club nights.

**Whistlebinkies** 4–6 South Bridge. Late-night rock
and folk venue.

## Listings

**Banks and exchange** Several big branches on
and around Andrew, Hanover and George squares.
**Bike rental** Biketrax, 11 Lochrin Place

ⓣ 0131/228 6333, ⓦ www.biketrax.co.uk; Edinburgh Cycle Hire, 29 Blackfriars St ⓣ 0131/556
5560, ⓦ www.cyclescotland.co.uk.

Consulates Australia, 69 George St ☎0131/624 3333; Canada, 30 Lothian Rd ☎0131/220 4333; USA, 3 Regent Terrace ☎0131/556 8315. Hospital Royal Infirmary, Old Dalkeith Rd ☎0131/536 1000. Laundry Sundial, 7 East London St; Tarvit Launderette, 7 Tarvit St.

Left luggage At Waverley Station and in lockers by St Andrew Square bus station. Pharmacy Boots, 48 Shandwick Place. Police St Leonards Street ☎0131/662 5000. Post office St James' Shopping Centre, near the east end of Princes St.

# Glasgow

**GLASGOW** is the largest city in Scotland, home to 750,000 people. It once thrived on the tobacco trade with the American colonies, on cotton production and, most famously, on the shipbuilding on the River Clyde, with the civic architecture of Victorian Glasgow as grand as any in Britain, and the West End suburbs regarded as among the best designed in the country. Since this heyday, however, it has not enjoyed the best of reputations. The Gorbals area became notorious as one of the worst slums in Europe, and the city's association with violence and heavy drinking stuck to it like a curse. However, like many British cities, rejuvenated Glasgow has undergone another change of image, symbolized by its selection as the European City of Culture in 1990 and City of Architecture and Design in 1999, titles which recognize that it has broken the industrial shackles of the past and evolved into a city of stature and confidence.

## The City

Glasgow's centre lies on the north bank of the Clyde, around the grandiose **George Square**, a little way east of Central Station. Just south of the square, down Queen Street, is the **Gallery of Modern Art** (Mon–Thurs & Sat 10am–5pm, Fri & Sun 11am–5pm; free). Formerly a "temple of commerce" built by one of the eighteenth-century tobacco lords, it now houses an exciting collection of contemporary Scots art, notably works by Peter Howson and John Bellany. A short way west on Mitchell Lane, just off Buchanan Street, **The Lighthouse** (Mon–Sat 10.30am–5pm, Tues from 11am, Sun noon–5pm; £3; @www .thelighthouse.co.uk) was the first commission of Glasgow's famous architect Charles Rennie Mackintosh, whose distinctively streamlined Art Nouveau designs appear in shops all over the city; inside is an exhibition devoted to the man. Northeast of George Square is the **cathedral** on Castle Street (Mon–Sat 9.30am–4/6pm, Sun 1–4/5pm). Built in 1136, destroyed in 1192 and rebuilt soon after, it's the only Scottish mainland cathedral to have escaped the hands of the country's sixteenth-century religious reformers, whose hatred of anything that smacked of idolatry wrecked many of Scotland's ancient churches. Just as interesting as the cathedral is the adjacent **Necropolis**, a hilltop cemetery for the magnates who made Glasgow rich; there are great views across the city from here.

North and west of George Square, on Glasgow's most famous thoroughfare, Sauchiehall St (pronounced "socky-hall"), the **McLellan Galleries** (Mon–Thurs & Sat 10am–5pm, Fri & Sun 11am–5pm; free) are a temporary home for some of the best pieces from the Glasgow Art Gallery and Museum, which is currently undergoing renovation (due to reopen March 2006). The collection has notable pieces by Rembrandt, Degas, Millet, Van Gogh and Monet, as well as an impressive body of Scottish painting. Just off Sauchiehall Street is the **Glasgow School of Art**, 167 Renfrew St, a remarkable building designed by Mackintosh that is a fusion of Scottish manor house solidity and modernist refinement. The interior, making maximum use of natural light, was also furnished and fitted entirely by the architect, and can be seen on a guided tour (daily between 10.30am and 2.30pm; Oct–March closed Sun; £5; ☎0141/353 4526, @www.gsa.ac.uk). A short distance north is the **Tenement House**, 145 Buccleuch St (March–Oct daily 1–5pm; £5; @www.nts.org.uk), an intriguing if sanitized vision of twentieth-century Glaswegian working-class life.

About four miles south of the centre, in **Pollok Country Park** (bus #45, #48 or #57 from Union St, or train to Pollokshaws West), is the astonishing **Burrell Collection**, housed in a custom-built gallery (Mon–Thurs & Sat 10am–5pm, Fri & Sun 11am–5pm; free). Sir William Burrell began collecting at the age of 15 and kept going until his death at 96, buying an average of two pieces a week. Works by Memling, Cézanne, Degas, Bellini and Géricault feature among the paintings, while in adjoining galleries there are pieces from ancient Rome and Greece, medieval European arts and crafts, and a massive selection of Chinese artefacts, with outstanding ceramics, jades and bronzes.

## Practicalities

**Glasgow International airport** (☎0141/887 1111) is eight miles west of the city, with regular buses shuttling to Buchanan Street Bus Station; **Glasgow Prestwick airport** (☎01292/511000), thirty miles south, is connected to the city centre by train. Glasgow has two main **train stations**: Central serves all points south and west, Queen Street serves Edinburgh and the north. It's an easy city to explore on foot – the grid pattern of the centre makes navigation relatively simple. The **Underground** is cheap and easy, operating on a circular chain of fifteen stations with a flat fare of £1 (day-pass £1.70). The **Strathclyde Travel Centre**, above St Enoch underground station (Mon–Sat 8.30am–5.30pm), has information on all public transport, as well as discount passes. The helpful **tourist office** is on the south side of George Square, near the top of Queen Street (Mon–Sat 9am–6/8pm, Sun 10am–6pm; Oct–April closed Sun; ☎0141/204 4400, ⊛www.seeglasgow.com); there's a smaller office at the airport (Mon–Sat 7.30am–5pm; April–Sept Sun 7.30am–5pm, Oct–March Sun 8am–3.30pm; ☎0141/848 4440). During summer, the universities of Glasgow (☎0141/330 5385) and Strathclyde (☎0141/553 4148) let out **rooms** (❻).

There are plenty of inexpensive eating options in the city centre and a huge number of pubs in which to down a pint. As for nightlife, the fortnightly magazine *The List* is the best source of club information, but pick of the crop are *The Arches*, on Midland Street, and Glasgow School of Art, which hosts several top club nights. You can often find innovative, challenging theatre at the Citizens' or Tramway theatres, both on the south side of the river, pop gigs at the Barrowland (244 Gallowgate) and the Carling Academy (121 Eglinton St), while the Centre for Contemporary Arts or CCA, 346 Sauchiehall St, has a reputation for a programme of controversial performances and exhibitions. The wonderful Glasgow Film Theatre, Rose Street (☎0141/332 8128, ⊛www.gft.org.uk), shows art films and old favourites.

### Hostels and B&Bs

**Adelaide's** 209 Bath St ☎0141/248 4970, ⊛www.adelaides.co.uk. City-centre guest house in a converted church providing simple but comfortable accommodation. Breakfast not included. ❺

**Alamo** 46 Gray St ☎0141/339 2395, ⊛www.alamoguesthouse.com. Quiet and attractive option near the university that offers good value for money. ❺

**Euro Hostel** 318 Clyde St ☎0141/222 2828, ⊛www.euro-hostels.co.uk. Huge 360-bed hostel on the banks of the River Clyde. A convenient if somewhat soulless option Dorms £14. ❹

**Glasgow SYHA** 8 Park Terrace ☎0870/155 3255, ⊛www.syha.org.uk. Refurbished hostel in a listed building beside Kelvingrove Park. Good facilities. £16.

### Campsite

**Craigendmuir Park** Campsie View ☎0141/779 4159. Four miles northeast of the centre; take a train to Stepps, from where it's a fifteen-minute walk.

### Cafés and restaurants

**Café Hula** 321 Hope St. A haven for unfussy, but very good, cooking in the city centre. Servings are generous, prices low.

**Corinthian** 191 Ingram Rd. Pillars, chandeliers and beautifully ornate decoration greet the diner here. Worth paying a little extra for the sheer opulence.

**Grassroots Café** 97 St George's Rd. Innovative organic food in bright and airy surroundings.

**Kember and Jones** 134 Byres St. Deservedly popular café near the university, serving

Spanish-influenced salads and huge sandwiches. Very good coffee too.

**Stravaigin Café Bar** 28 Gibson St. Imaginative bistro fare, more affordable than the basement restaurant of the same name.

**University Café** 87 Byres Rd. An original Art Deco-style café, something of an institution. The menu is of the unreconstructed kind – think steak pie and Knickerbocker Glory.

**The Wee Curry Shop** 7 Buccleuch St and 29 Ashton Lane. Tiny establishments offering excellent-value Indian meals.

**Willow Tea Rooms** 217 Sauchiehall St. Designed by Rennie Mackintosh, a required stop for Art Nouveau fans, although the unimaginative menu is disappointing.

### Pubs and live music venues

**Bar 10** 10 Mitchell St. A good example of a traditional Glasgow style bar. The modish design epitomizes the city's rejuvenation as a centre of style and culture.

**Bargo** Albion St. A trendy pre-club DJ bar in fashionable Merchant city. Works by local artists adorn the walls.

**Mercury** 142 Bath Lane. Lively addition to the gay scene with wild weekend nights and chilled mid-week drinking.

**The Horseshoe Bar** 17 Drury St. Rarely a quiet moment at this city-centre pub which features the longest bar in the UK.

**King Tut's Wah Wah Hut** 272a Vincent St. Famous as the place where Oasis were discovered, and still hosts excellent gigs.

**Scotia** 112 Stockwell St. Atmospheric Glasgow favourite, one of the best places to catch live folk and blues musicians.

### Listings

**Bike rental** Dales, 150 Dobbies Loan ℡0141/332 2705; West End Cycles, 16 Chancellor St ℡0141/357 1344.

**Hospital** Royal Infirmary, 84 Castle St ℡0141/211 4000.

**Laundry** Bank Street Laundry, 39–41 Bank St; Majestic Launderette, 1110 Argyle St.

**Pharmacy** Boots, Buchanan Galleries.

**Police** Pitt St ℡0141/532 2000.

**Post office** 47 St Vincent St.

# Melrose

If you've only time to visit one town in the Scottish Borders, the upland region lying between England and Scotland, then **MELROSE**, 37 miles south of Edinburgh, is the obvious choice. Tucked in between the River Tweed and the gorse-backed Eildon Hills, this is the most beguiling of towns, its narrow streets trimmed by a harmonious ensemble of styles, from pretty little cottages and tweedy shops to high-standing Georgian and Victorian facades. Its chief draw is its ruined **abbey** (April–Sept daily 9.30am–6.30pm; Oct–March daily 9.30am–4.30pm; £4), best seen on a bright morning, with the sun streaming through the tracery of the exquisite east and south windows and illuminating the richly sculpted capitals and cornices of the nave. The Scots Baronial house of **Abbotsford** (daily March–Oct 9.30am–5pm, Sun March–May 2pm–5pm; £4.50; ⊛www.scottsabbotsford.co.uk), three miles west of Melrose, was designed to satisfy the Romantic inclinations of **Sir Walter Scott**, who lived here from 1812 until his death twenty years later. Despite all the exterior pomp, the interior is surprisingly small and poky, with just six rooms open for viewing, starting with the wood-panelled study where Scott banged out the Waverley novels at a furious rate to try and pay off his debts. Even more aesthetically pleasing is Scott's burial place, **Dryburgh Abbey** (hours as for Melrose Abbey; £3.30), five miles southeast of Melrose. The romantic setting is second to none, though the abbey ruins are much less substantial than those at Melrose. Virtually nothing survives of the nave, but the transepts have fared better and now serve as a burial ground for Scott and Field Marshal Haig, the World War I commander responsible for the needless slaughter of millions.

**Buses** to Melrose stop in Market Square, from where it's a short walk north to the abbey ruins and the **tourist office**, opposite (Mon–Sat 9.30/10am–5/6.30pm; ℡0870/608 0404). The **HI hostel** is in an old Victorian villa overlooking the abbey (℡0870/155 3255, ⊛www.syha.org.uk; £13.50). There's a plentiful supply of **B&Bs**, most notable of which is *Braidwood*, on Buccleuch St (℡01896/822488, ⊛www.braidwoodmelrose.co.uk; ⑥). The old coaching inns in the village offer quality **food**: *Burt's* does good bar meals, as does *The Ship*.

# Stirling

Occupying a key strategic position between the Highlands and Lowlands at the easiest crossing of the River Forth, **STIRLING** has played a major role throughout Scottish history. With its castle and steep, cobbled streets, it can appear like a smaller version of Edinburgh. Imperiously set on a rocky crag, the atmospheric and explorable **castle** (daily 9.30am–5/6pm; £8) combined the functions of a fortress with those of a royal palace. Highlights within the complex are the **Royal Palace**, dating from the late Renaissance, and the earlier **Great Hall**, where recent restoration, including a complete rebuilding of the vast hammerbeam roof, has revealed the original form and scale. The oldest part of Stirling is grouped around the streets leading up to the castle. Look out for the Gothic **Church of the Holy Rude** (daily 10am–5pm), with its fine timber roof, where the infant James VI – later James I of the United Kingdom – was crowned King of Scotland in 1567. From here, Broad Street slopes down to the lower town, passing the **Tolbooth**, the city's newly restored arts and cultural centre. Stirling is famous as the scene of Sir William Wallace's battlefield victory over the English in 1297, a crucial episode in the Wars of Independence. The Scottish hero was commemorated in Victorian times by the **Wallace Monument** (daily 9.30am–6.30pm, shorter hours in winter; £6), about a mile north near the university. Though the refurbished building seems ugly close up, compensation comes in the stupendous views – finer even than those from the castle.

The train and bus stations are both five minutes' walk from the **tourist office**, 41 Dumbarton Rd, in the lower part of town (July & Aug daily 9am–7pm; Sept–June Mon–Sat 9/10am–5/6pm; ☎08707/200 620, ☻www.visitscottishheartlands.com). The *HI hostel*, St John Street, is a little characterless but occupies a great setting at the top of town in a converted church (☎0870/004 1140, ☻www.syha.org .uk; £15), while *Willy Wallace Independent Hostel*, 77 Murray Place, is a lively, welcoming backpacker hostel (☎01786/446773, ☻www.willywallacehostel.com; £12). Of the many guest houses, *No.10*, 10 Gladstone Place, is especially friendly (☎01786/472681, ☻www.cameron-10.co.uk; ⑤). The picturesque *Witches' Craig* campsite is three miles east of town on bus #62, off the St Andrews road (☎01786/474947, ☻www.witchescraig.co.uk; closed Nov–March). Try *Sarah Jane's*, a bustling little café on Pitt Terrace, for hearty Scottish breakfasts, while *Barnton Bar and Bistro*, Barnton Street, is a good choice for a relaxed meal.

# St Andrews

Well-groomed **ST ANDREWS**, on the coast 56 miles northeast of Edinburgh, has the air of a place of importance. Retaining memories of its days as medieval Scotland's metropolis, it is the country's oldest university town, the Scottish answer to Oxford or Cambridge, with a snob-appeal to match. St Andrews has an exalted place in Scottish sporting history too. Entering the town from the Edinburgh road, you pass no fewer than four golf links, the last of which is the **Old Course**, the most famous and – in the opinion of Jack Nicklaus – the best in the world. At the southern end of the Old Course, down towards the waterfront, is the award-winning **British Golf Museum** (April–Oct Mon–Sat 9.30am–5.30pm, Sun 10am–5pm; Nov–March daily 10am–4pm; £5; ☻www.britishgolfmuseum.co.uk); if you want to step onto the famous fairways, head to the **Himalayas** putting green, located right by the first hole and only £1 per round. Sweeping north from the Old Course is a great crescent of sandy beach; immediately south of the Old Course begins North Street, one of St Andrews' two main arteries. Much of it is taken up by university buildings, with the tower of **St Salvator's College** rising proudly above all else. Together with the adjoining chapel, this dates from 1450 and is the earliest surviving part of the university. Further east, you can reach the ruined **castle** on North Castle Street (April–Sept daily 9.30am–6.30pm; Oct–March daily 9.30am–4.30pm; £4, or combined ticket with cathedral £5). A short distance further along the coast is the equally ruined Gothic **cathedral** (same hours; £3), the mother church of medieval Scotland and the largest and grandest ever built in the country. Even though little more than the cemetery survives, the intact east wall and the exposed foundations give an idea of the vast scale of what has been lost. With the cathedral entrance ticket you can get a token to ascend the austere Romanesque **St Rule's Tower** – part of the priory that the cathedral replaced – for superb views over the sea and town.

### Practicalities

You can reach St Andrews by **bus** on a day-trip from Edinburgh or Stirling. There are no direct trains, though frequent buses connect with the train station five miles away in Leuchars (where the parish church incorporates the most beautiful and intact piece of Norman architecture in Scotland). St Andrews' **tourist office**, 70 Market St (Mon–Sat 9.30am–7pm, Sun 10.30am–5pm; shorter hours and closed Sun in winter; ℡01334/472021, ✆www.standrews.com/fife), will book rooms for a ten percent deposit – worth paying in the summer and during big golf tournaments, when **accommodation** is in short supply. The only **hostel** in the area is *St Andrews Tourist Hostel* on St Mary's Place (℡01334/479911; £16). *Doune House*, 5 Murray Place (℡01334/475195, ✆www.dounehouse.com; ❽), and *Craigmore*, 3 Murray Park (℡01334/472142, ✆www.standrewscraigmore.com; ❽), are two options of the many on those streets. For eating, student favourites are *The Inn on North Street*, 127 North St, and the Mexican *La Posada* on St Mary's Place; for a more stylish contemporary bistro try *The Doll's House* at 3 Church Sq (℡01334/477422). Most pubs are concentrated on Market and South streets; best of the bunch are *Central*, 1 Market St, *Ma Belle's*, 40 The Scores, both popular student joints, while *Broons Bistro and Bar* beside the New Picture House cinema on North Street is a trendier spot with live music sessions.

## Loch Lomond and the Trossachs

**Loch Lomond** – the largest stretch of fresh water in Britain – is the epitome of Scottish scenic splendour, thanks in large part to the ballad that fondly recalls its "bonnie, bonnie banks". The easiest way to get to the loch is to take one of the frequent trains from Glasgow Queen Street Station to **BALLOCH** at its southwestern tip, from where you can take a cruise around the 33 islands nearby. The **western shore** is very developed, with the upgraded A82 zipping along its banks. The only place to find any peace and quiet now is on the **eastern shore**, large sections of which are only accessible via the footpath which forms part of the West Highland Way. The easiest access to the graceful peak of **Ben Lomond** (3192ft) is from Rowardennan, from where it's a straightforward three-hour hike to the summit; in summer you can reach Rowardennan by ferry from Inverbeg on the western shore.

Loch Lomond is at the heart of the **Trossachs National Park**, Scotland's first national park, opened in 2002. A huge development called Lomond Shores incorporating shops, information points and cafés has been built at Balloch; the Gateway Centre here is the best place for information (daily 9/10.30am–4.30/7pm; ℡0845/345 4978, ✆www.lochlomond-trossachs.org) and a taste of the park if you're not able to explore further. A couple of miles northwest of Balloch is Scotland's most beautiful **HI hostel**, complete with resident ghost (℡0870/004 1136; March–Oct; (£15.50); and there's another alluringly sited HI hostel at Rowardennan (℡0870/004 1148; March–Oct; £13.50). The tourist office has details of the wide choice of **campsites** and **B&Bs** in all the villages.

## The isles of Mull and Iona

The **ISLE OF MULL** is the most accessible of all the Hebridean islands off the west coast of Scotland: just forty minutes by ferry from **Oban**, which is linked by train to Glasgow. The chief appeal of the island is its remarkably undulating coastline – three hundred miles of it in total. Despite its proximity to the mainland, the slower pace of life is clearly apparent: most roads are single lane, with only a handful of buses linking the main settlements. **CRAIGNURE**, the ferry terminal for boats from Oban (4–6 daily; 45min; £3.95 single), is little more than a smattering of cottages. It does, however, have the island's main **tourist office** (daily 8.30/10.30am–5/7pm; ☎0870/720 0610), a decent pub, bike rental and a campsite. On its way into Craignure, the ferry passes the dramatic **Duart Castle** (April Sun–Thurs 11am–4pm; May to mid-Oct daily 10.30am–5.30pm; £4.50; ⊕www .duartcastle.com), two miles' walk along the bay. The stronghold of the MacLean clan from the thirteenth century, it was restored earlier last century – you can peek in the dungeons and ascend to the rooftops. Mull's "capital", **TOBERMORY**, 22 miles northwest of Craignure, is easily the most attractive fishing port on the west coast of Scotland, its clusters of brightly coloured houses and boats sheltering in a bay backed by a steep bluff. For a list of the local **B&Bs** head for the **tourist office** (April–Oct daily 9/10am–5/6pm; ☎0870/720 0625), in the Mac ferry ticket office at the northern end of the harbour. The **HI hostel** (☎0870/004 1151; £13; closed Nov–Feb) is on Main Street, near *Harbour House*, an inexpensive guest house (☎01688/302209; ❺; closed Nov–Feb). Also on Main Street is the *Mishnish Hotel* pub, popular for live folk music at the weekends.

At the opposite end of Mull, 35 miles west of Craignure, is the **ISLE OF IONA**. Just three miles long and not much more than a mile wide, Iona has been a place of pilgrimage for several centuries: it was to this flat Hebridean island that St Columba fled from Ireland in 563 and established a monastery that was responsible for the conversion of more or less all of pagan Scotland. No buildings remain from Columba's time: the present **Abbey** (daily 9.30am–4/6pm; £3.30), which dominates all views of the island, dates from a re-establishment of monasticism here by the Benedictines in around 1200; it was extensively rebuilt in the fifteenth and sixteenth centuries, and restored wholesale last century. Iona's oldest building, **St Oran's Chapel**, lies south of the abbey, and boasts an eleventh-century door. It stands at the centre of the sacred burial ground, Reilig Odhrain, which is said to contain the graves of sixty kings of Norway, Ireland, France and Scotland, including the two immortalized by Shakespeare – Duncan and Macbeth. In front stand three delicately carved crosses from the eighth and ninth centuries, among the masterpieces of European sculpture of the Dark Ages. Iona is a very popular day-trip in summer, reached in a few minutes by regular ferry from **Fionnphort** at the western tip of Mull. To appreciate its special atmosphere, it's best to stay the night. Camping is not permitted, but the excellent *Iona Hostel* (☎01681/700781, ⊕www.ionahostel.co.uk; £15), a mile or so from the ferry, past the abbey, has comfortable beds and superb views. For B&B, try *Sithean House* (☎01681/700331; ❺; April–Oct), a mile from the ferry on the west side of the island; the better of the two **hotels** – if you can afford it – is the *Argyll* (☎01681/700334, ⊕www .argyllhoteliona.co.uk; ❾).

A basaltic mass rising direct from the sea, the **Isle of Staffa** is the northern end of the Giant's Causeway (see p.580), and is the most romantic and dramatic of Scotland's many uninhabited islands. On one side, its perpendicular rockface has been cut into caverns of cathedral-like dimensions, notably **Fingal's Cave**, whose haunting noises inspired Mendelssohn's *Hebrides Overture*. To get to Staffa, jump aboard the *Iolaire* (☎01681/700358; £17.50), which sails out of Fionnphort and Iona.

## The Isle of Skye

Jutting out from the mainland, the bare and bony promontories of the **ISLE OF SKYE** fringe a deeply indented coastline. The most popular destination on the island is the **Cuillin ridge**, whose jagged peaks dominate the island during clear weather; equally dramatic in their own way are the rock formations of the

Trotternish peninsula in the north. The easiest way to reach Skye is either to catch a **ferry** from the train terminus of Mallaig, or by **bus** (via the Skye Bridge) from the train terminus of Kyle of Lochalsh. Either way, you'll end up in the southeast corner of the island, where there's a concentration of hostels. From Mallaig, you disembark in **ARMADALE**, where there's an *HI hostel* (☎0870/004 1103; £12; closed Oct to mid-March) along the shore from the harbour. From Kyle of Lochalsh, you arrive in **KYLEAKIN**, which has an *HI hostel* a few minutes' walk from the dock (☎0870/004 1134; £12.50) with the laid-back *Skye Backpackers* nearby (☎01599/534510; £13). Further up the road at **KILMORE** the *Flora MacDonald Hostel* is open all year (☎01471/844272; £10). These places are preferable to those on offer in **BROADFORD**, a charmless village, which does, however, have a small **tourist office** (April–June & Oct Mon–Sat 9.30am–5.30pm; July & Aug 9am–7pm, also Sun 10am–5pm; ☎01471/822361).

The best approach to the Cuillin is via **ELGOL**, fourteen miles southwest of Broadford at the end of the most dramatic road in Skye and served by postbus #106. From here there are boat trips on the *Bella Jane* (☎0800/731 3089, ⊛www .bellajane.co.uk; one way £15, return trip £20) to Loch Coruisk, after which you can walk the eight miles up gentle Glen Sligachan to the welcoming *Sligachan Hotel* (☎01478/650204, ⊛www.sligachan.co.uk; ❾) and adjacent campsite (closed Nov–March). Serious hikers head for **GLENBRITTLE**, ten miles southwest of Sligachan and west of the Cuillin, where there's an *HI hostel* (☎0870/004 1121; £13; closed Oct–Feb) and a campsite not far away by the sandy beach (☎01478/640404; closed Nov–March). The only real town on Skye is the "capital", **PORTREE**, an attractive fishing port in the north of the island. Here you'll find the island's main tourist office just off Bridge Street (Mon–Sat 9am–5.30/7pm; April–Oct also Sun 10am–4pm; ☎01478/612137). The town has several hostels, smartest of which is the *Portree Independent Hostel* (☎01478/613737; £13), housed in the Old Post Office on the Green. Of the dozens of B&Bs, *Balloch* in Viewfield Road (☎01478/612093, ⊛www.balloch-skye.co.uk; ❻) is a comfortable and friendly option. Food in Portree can be pricey, but the fish and chips down by the harbour are excellent. If you can dip further into your pocket, the welcoming *Isles Inn* serves hearty portions of traditional Scottish fare, including haggis.

From Portree, head north up the east coast of the **Trotternish** peninsula. Some nine miles from Portree, at the edge of the Storr ridge, is a distinctive 165-foot obelisk known as the **Old Man of Storr**, while a further ten miles north, rising above Staffin Bay, are the **Quiraing** – a spectacular forest of mighty pinnacles and savage rock formations, including the Needle, the Prison and the Table. The straggling village of **UIG**, on the west coast, has ferries to the islands of the Outer Hebrides, including Harris and North Uist, as well as an HI hostel (☎0870/004 1155; £13; closed Oct–March), high up above the harbour, a mile or so from the ferry terminal.

## Inverness and the Highlands

Capital of the Highlands, **INVERNESS** is 160 miles north of Edinburgh, the train line between the two traversing the gentle countryside of Perthshire before skirting the stark Cairngorm mountains. Approaching from Skye in the west, there's the magnificent eighty-mile train journey from Kyle of Lochalsh. Inverness **airport** (☎01667/464000) is seven miles northeast. The town has a fine setting astride the River Ness at the head of the Beauly Firth, but despite having been a place of importance for a millennium – it was probably the capital of the Pictish kingdom and the site of Macbeth's castle – there's nothing remarkable to see, nor any particularly strong sense of character. The chief attractions of historical interest lie some six miles east of town, reached by regular buses. **Culloden Moor** was the scene in 1746 of the last pitched battle on British soil, when the troops of "Butcher" Cumberland crushed Bonnie Prince Charlie's Jacobite army in just forty minutes. This ended forever Stuart ambitions of regaining the monarchy, and marked the beginning of the break-up of the clan system which had ruled Highland society for centuries. A **visitor centre** (daily 9/10am–4/7pm; closed Jan; £5) has displays describing the action.

As well as the only big choice of shops, restaurants and nightlife in the Highlands, you'll find B&Bs by the score in Inverness. These tend to fill up in summer, and the **tourist office** on Castle Wynd (March–Sept Mon–Fri 9am–7pm, Sat 9am–6pm, Sun 9.30am–5pm; Oct–Feb Mon–Fri 9am–5pm, Sat 10am–4pm; ☏01463/234353, ✆www.visithighlands.com) charges £3 to find a room. The modern **HI hostel** is on Victoria Drive, off Milburn Road (☏0870/004 1127; £15); there are plenty of independent hostels, including the non-smoking *Bazpackers*, at the top of Castle Street (☏01463/717663; £11). Also try the *Eastgate Backpackers*, 38 Eastgate (☏01463/718756, ✆www.eastgatebackpackers.com; £11), which has a wide range of facilities including Internet access and bike rental. There are **campsites** at Culloden (closed Nov–Feb), on the road to Loch Ness, and within Inverness at Bught Park, west of the river. The area is best explored by bike: contact *Barney's*, 35 Castle St (☏01463/232249).

## Loch Ness

**Loch Ness** forms part of the natural fault line known as the Great Glen, which slices across the Highlands between Inverness and Fort William. In the early 1800s, Thomas Telford linked the glen's lochs by means of the **Caledonian Canal**, enabling ships to pass between the North Sea and the Atlantic without having to navigate Scotland's treacherous northern coast. Today, pleasure-craft galore ply the route, with cruises from Inverness (summer only; book at tourist office) providing the most straightforward way of seeing the terrain. Most visitors are eager to catch a glimpse of the elusive **Loch Ness Monster**: tales of "Nessie" date back at least as far as the seventh century, when the monster came out second best in an altercation with St Columba. However, the possibility that a mysterious prehistoric creature might be living in the loch only attracted worldwide attention in the 1930s, when sightings were reported during the construction of the road along its western shore. Numerous appearances have been reported since, but even the most hi-tech surveys of the loch have failed to come up with conclusive evidence. To find out the whole story, take a bus to **DRUMNADROCHIT**, fourteen miles southwest of Inverness, where the most informative displays are at the **Loch Ness 2000 Exhibition** (daily: July & Aug 9am–8pm; shorter hours at other times; £5.95; ✆www.loch-ness-scotland.com). Most photographs allegedly showing the monster have been taken around the ruined **Castle Urquhart** (daily April–Sept 9.30am–6.30pm, Oct–March until 4.30pm; £6, includes entry to the visitor centre), one of Scotland's most beautifully sited fortresses, a couple of miles further south.

## Into the Highlands

With its beguiling mix of bare hills, green glens and silvery lochs and rivers, the spectacular scenery of the **Highlands** (which covers most of Scotland north of the Central Belt and west of Aberdeen) is a major draw. The distances involved, however, as well as poor public transport, mean that you really need a few days to explore any one part of it properly. Coachloads of sightseers take in what they can from carefully positioned viewpoints on the main roads, but **outdoor activities** are a major reason to visit: most tourist information centres and backpacker hostels carry information on good local hiking routes, bike rental and adventure sports. While you can get a taste of the Highlands as far south as Loch Lomond and the Trossachs National Park, barely an hour from Edinburgh or Glasgow, any trip to Inverness, Mull or Skye will take you through some magnificent upland country. Obvious stopping-points for further exploration include **AVIEMORE**, at the foot of the looming Cairngorm range, which offers challenging hiking, ancient pine forests, and skiing and other winter sports in season. On the west coast, the town of **FORT WILLIAM** is a great base for draws such as **Ben Nevis** (the UK's highest peak), the **West Highland Way** long-distance footpath and **Glen Coe**, where soaring scenery and poignant history combine like nowhere else in the country.

**Getting around** the Highlands without a car does require patience, although good-value travel passes are available on First ScotRail's **train** network (ⓦwww .firstscotrail.com), which has some superbly scenic stretches including the famous **West Highland Line** from Glasgow to Oban, Fort William and Mallaig. Alternatively, a couple of rival companies offer lively **minibus tours** designed specifically for backpackers: Haggis (ⓣ0131/557 9393, ⓦwww.haggisadventures.com) and Macbackpackers (ⓣ0131/558 9900, ⓦwww.macbackpackers.com) depart from Edinburgh on trips lasting between one and seven days; you can also buy a jump-on/jump-off ticket allowing you to cover their circuits (which generally take in Inverness, Skye, Oban and Stirling) at your own pace.

# Aberdeen

On the east coast 120 miles north of Edinburgh, **ABERDEEN** is the third city of Scotland. Solid and hard-wearing like the distinctive silver-grey granite used for so many of its buildings, it has been nicknamed the "Silver City", although its wealth is built on black gold – North Sea oil. Until a hundred years ago, Aberdeen was two separate towns a couple of miles apart, based around the mouths of the rivers Dee and Don. While Old Aberdeen slumbered in academic and ecclesiastical tranquillity, the newer town became a major port and commercial centre, and was subject to grandiose planning schemes. The most ambitious of these, in the early nineteenth century, included the layout of spacious **Union Street**, a block north of the bus and train stations, which runs for more than a mile east–west across the centre. Despite the grand buildings, Union Street today is fairly tawdry, with uninspiring shops and the continual drone of traffic. Best of the sights is down Shiprow, near the eastern end, where Provost Ross's House, a sixteenth-century mansion, now abuts the award-winning **Maritime Museum** (Mon–Sat 10am–5pm, Sun noon–3pm; free). The collection here describes Aberdeen's relationship with the sea through imaginative displays, films and models, including a thirty-foot oil rig. A further short walk downhill is the bustling **harbour** area, seen at its best in the early morning, before the daily fish market winds down at 8am. Across Union Street from Shiprow is Broad Street, dominated by **Marischal College**, the younger half of Aberdeen University. Its facade, a century-old historicist extravaganza, is probably the most spectacular piece of granite architecture in existence. Less than a mile east of Union Street is the best **beach** to be found in any British city, a great two-mile sweep of clean sand, very popular in summer.

The **bus** and **train** stations are on Guild Street, 200m south of Union Street. The **tourist office**, 23 Union St (June–Sept Mon–Sat 9am–7pm, Sun 10am–4pm; Oct–May Mon–Sat 9.30am–5.30pm; ⓣ01224/288800), can help with finding B&B. The **HI hostel** is at 8 Queen's Rd (ⓣ0870/004 1100; £14.75); take buses #14, #15, #23 or #27. One of Aberdeen's perennially popular spots for **eating** is the *Ashvale*, 46 Great Western Rd, long rated as one of Britain's best fish-and-chip shops. Cheap meals can also be found at *Café 52*, on The Green near Union Street, and at the café at the Lemon Tree arts centre, 5 West North St. For **drinking**, the *Prince of Wales* on St Nicholas Lane is Aberdeen's most colourful real ale pub, while *Cameron's Inn*, 6 Little Beaumont St, is a popular hangout.

# Travel details

## Trains

**Bristol** to: Bath (every 20min; 20min); Birmingham (every 30min; 1hr 30min); Cardiff (hourly; 50min); Salisbury (hourly; 1hr 10min); York (hourly; 4hr 10min).

**Edinburgh** to: Aberdeen (hourly; 2hr 50min); Durham (hourly; 2hr); Glasgow (every 15min; 50min); Inverness (6 daily; 3hr 50min); Newcastle (hourly; 1hr 30min); Leuchars for St Andrews (hourly; 1hr 20min); Stirling (every 30min; 50min); York (hourly; 2hr 30min).

**Glasgow** to: Aberdeen (hourly; 2hr 35min); Inverness (3 daily; 3hr 25min); Mallaig for Skye (Mon–Sat 3 daily; Sun 1 daily; 5hr 15min); Oban for Mull (3 daily; 3hr); Preston for Liverpool & Manchester (13 daily; 1hr 30min); Newcastle (every 2hr; 2hr 30min); Stirling (hourly; 30min).

**Inverness** to: Aberdeen (10 daily; 2hr 15min); Kyle of Lochalsh for Skye (Mon–Sat 3 daily; Sun 1 daily; 2hr 40min); Stirling (some change at Perth; 9 daily; 2hr 30min).

**Liverpool** to: Cardiff (some change at Crewe; 13 daily; 4hr); Manchester (hourly; 50min); York (hourly; 2hr 20min).

**London** to: Aberdeen (6 daily; 7hr 30min); Aberystwyth (change at Birmingham; 14 daily; 5hr); Bath (1–2 hourly; 1hr 30min); Brighton (every 15min; 1hr–1hr 20min); Bristol (every 30min; 1hr 45min); Cambridge (every 15min; 45min); Canterbury (1–2 hourly; 1hr 20min–1hr 40min); Cardiff (hourly; 2hr–2hr 20min); Dover (every 30min; 1hr 45min); Durham (hourly; 2hr 45min); Glasgow (hourly; 5hr 30min); Liverpool (hourly; 2hr 50min); Manchester (20 daily; 2hr 30min); Newcastle (every 30min; 3hr); Newport (every 30min; 1hr 45min); Oxford (every 20–30min; 1hr); Penzance (9 daily; 5hr 15min–7hr); Salisbury (hourly; 1hr 30min); Stratford-upon-Avon (5 daily; 2hr 15min); Winchester (every 15–30min; 1hr–1hr 10min); York (every 30min; 2hr 15min).

**Manchester** to: Newcastle (10 daily; 3hr); Windermere (5 daily; 1hr 45min); York (every 30min; 1hr 40min).

## Buses

**Bristol** to: Bath (every 15–30min; 50min); Birmingham (5–8 daily; 2hr–2hr 30min); Cardiff (3–5 daily; 1hr 10min); 1hr 45min–2hr); Oxford (1 daily; 2hr 40min); Salisbury (1 daily; 2hr); Wells (hourly; 50min).

**Edinburgh** to: Aberdeen (hourly; 3hr 20min); Durham (1 daily; 4hr 30min); Glasgow (every 20min; 1hr 10min); Inverness (hourly; 4hr); Kyle of Lochalsh for Skye (2 daily; 7hr); Manchester (3 daily; 5hr 30min); Melrose (hourly; 1hr); Newcastle (3 daily; 3hr); St Andrews (every 30min; 2hr–3hr); Stirling (every 30min; 1hr 15min).

**Glasgow** to: Aberdeen (hourly; 3hr 20min); Inverness (every 2hr; 4hr); Liverpool (2 daily; 4hr 40min–5hr 15min); Manchester (3 daily; 5hr 30min); Newcastle (every 2hr; 2hr 30min); Oban for Mull (3 daily; 3hr); St Andrews (12 daily; 2hr 20min); Stirling (every 30min; 30min).

**Inverness** to: Aberdeen (10 daily; 2hr 15min); Stirling (2 daily; 3hr 20min).

**Liverpool** to: Cardiff (4 daily; 5hr 40min–6hr 40min); Manchester (hourly; 1hr); Newcastle (3 daily; 4hr 30min–7hr 30min); Oxford (4 daily; 5hr 30min); York (2 daily; 3hr 40min–5hr).

**London** to: Aberdeen (2 daily; 12hr); Aberystwyth (1 daily; 6hr 45min); Bangor (for Holyhead; 1 daily; 8hr 30min); Bath (11 daily; 2hr 30min–3hr 40min); Brighton (hourly; 1hr 15min); Bristol (hourly; 2hr 30min); Cambridge (hourly; 2hr); Canterbury (hourly; 2hr); Cardiff (6 daily; 3hr 10min); Dover (hourly; 2hr 25min); Durham (5 daily; 5hr 30min); Edinburgh (4 daily; 8hr 30min–9hr 10min); Glasgow (5 daily; 7hr 45min–8hr 50min); Inverness (2 daily; 12hr 20min–13hr 10min); Liverpool (5 daily; 4hr 45min); Manchester (7 daily; 4hr 35min); Newcastle (5 daily; 6hr 30min); Newport (6 daily; 2hr 45min); Oxford (every 15min; 1hr 40min); Penzance (6 daily; 7hr 30min–9hr 30min); Salisbury (3 daily; 2hr 45min–3hr 15min); Stirling (2 daily; 9hr); Stratford (3 daily; 2hr 45min–3hr 15min); Winchester 10 daily; 1hr 30min–2hr 10min); York (3 daily; 4hr 30min).

**Manchester** to: Durham (3 daily; 4hr 30min); Glasgow (2 daily; 4hr 30min–5hr); Newcastle (6 daily; 4hr 50min); York (3 daily; 3hr 20min).

# Bulgaria

# Bulgaria highlights

✳ **Aleksandâr Nevsky Cathedral, Sofia** One of the most awe-inspiring buildings in the Balkans. See p.233

✳ **Rila Monastery** Bulgaria's largest and most beautiful monastery, in the mountains south of Sofia. See p.235

✳ **Old Quarter, Plovdiv** A wealth of brightly painted National Revival houses, art galleries and Roman remains. See p.237

✳ **Koprivshtitsa** This picturesque village boasts Bulgaria's finest ensemble of National Revival architecture. See p.239

✳ **Archeology Museum, Varna** A treasure trove of Neolithic and Roman antiquities. See p.242

✳ **Nesebâr** The Black Sea Coast's prettiest resort, with several fine medieval churches. See p.243

△ Aleksandâr Nevsky Cathedral, Sofia

# Introduction and basics

If Westerners have an image of **Bulgaria**, it tends to be coloured by the murky intrigues of Balkan politics, with tales of poisoned umbrellas and plots to kill the pope. The nation has come a long way, though, since it threw off the 500-year yoke of the Ottoman Empire in the 1870s, and is now struggling to cope with the aftermath of Communist misrule. The Socialists retained power through the early 1990s, and moves towards free-market reforms were slow. The election of a right-of-centre government in 1997 brought some measure of economic stability, and in 2001, the former king, Simeon II, was democratically elected as prime minister. His party has pledged to fight institutional corruption, speed up the privatization process and, now safely in NATO, to prepare the country for membership of the EU (slated for 2007). In the meantime, however, low wages and high unemployment remain ever-present features of life.

Independent travel in Bulgaria is slowly becoming more common; costs are low, and for the committed there is much to take in. The main attractions are the mountainous scenery and the web of towns and villages with a crafts tradition, where you'll find the wonderfully romantic architecture of the National Revival era. Foremost among these are **Koprivshtitsa** in the Sredna Gora range, **Bansko** in the Pirin mountains and **Plovdiv**, the second largest city. The monasteries are stunning, too – the finest, Rila, should be on every itinerary. For city life, the bustling, if rather faded capital, **Sofia**, and the cosmopolitan coastal resort of **Varna** are the places to aim for.

## Information & maps

There are few publicly funded **tourist offices** in Bulgaria, and those that do exist are fairly basic. Most main towns have agencies, working on commission, who will book accommodation and transport for you, but are of little use for other information. The best **maps** of Bulgaria and of Sofia are produced by Datamap and are widely available.

## Money and banks

The Bulgarian currency is the **lev** (Lv), which is divided into 100 stotinki (st) and pegged to the euro. There are notes of 1Lv, 2Lv, 5Lv, 10Lv, 20Lv and 50Lv, and coins of 1st, 2st, 5st, 10st, 20st and 50st, and 1Lv. Since it was revalued in 1999, the lev has been stable, although hotels, travel agencies and the like frequently quote prices in euros. Nonetheless, you can always pay in the local currency, and many places prefer it. At the time of writing, €1 was equal to around 2Lv, $1 to 1.60Lv, and £1 to 3Lv. Museums and galleries charge in leva, and foreigners are currently required to pay more for entry than Bulgarians, although this is due to change soon. Producing a student ID card will often get you a discount. Be sure to keep a ready supply of coins for small purchases, as shops are often unable to change larger denomination notes.

**Banks** are open Mon–Fri 9am–4pm, and there are ATMs in most towns. Private exchange bureaux, offering variable rates, are widespread – but beware of hidden commission charges. Also watch out for

---

### Bulgaria on the net

ⓦ **www.bulgaria.com** Comprehensive travel information.
ⓦ **www.discover-bulgaria.com** Travel information and hotel booking.
ⓦ **www.sofiaecho.com** News site.
ⓦ **www.travel-bulgaria.com** Information on history and culture, as well as travel.

black market moneychangers who approach unwary foreigners with offers of better rates; if they sound too good to be true, they are. Many smaller banks and offices won't take travellers' cheques, and while Visa and MasterCard are gaining greater acceptance, credit cards are generally acceptable only at the more expensive shops and hotels.

# Communications

**Post offices** (*poshta*) are usually open Mon–Sat 8.30am–5.30pm, longer in big towns. The main office will have a poste restante facility, but postal officers tend to return mail to sender if it's not claimed immediately.

Card-operated **public phones** are on the whole reliable and can be used to make international calls. **Phonecards** (*fonkarta*) are available from post offices and many street kiosks and shops. The operator number for domestic calls is ☏121, for international calls ☏0123.

You'll find **Internet cafés** in most towns and cities, where you'll rarely pay more than 1.50Lv per hour.

## Body language

Bulgarians shake their heads when they mean "yes" and nod when they mean "no". Sometimes they reverse these gestures if they know they're speaking to foreigners, thereby complicating the issue further. Emphatic use of the words *da* (yes) and *ne* (no) should avoid misunderstandings.

# Getting around

**Public transport** in Bulgaria is inexpensive but notoriously slow and not always clean or comfortable. Travelling by **bus** (*avtobus*) is usually the quickest way of getting between major towns and cities, and an ever-growing number of privately run – and generally faster and more comfortable – services ply these routes. Generally, you can buy **tickets** at the bus station (*avtogara*) at least an hour in advance when travelling between towns, but on some routes they're only sold when the bus arrives. On rural routes, tickets are often sold by the driver.

**Bulgarian State Railways** (BDZh; ☻www .bdz.bg) can get you to most towns; trains are punctual and fares low. Express services (*ekspresen*) are restricted to main routes, but on all except the humblest branch lines you'll find so-called Rapid (*bârz vlak*) trains. Where possible, use these rather than the snail-like *pâtnicheski* services. Long-distance/overnight trains have reasonably priced couchettes (*kushet*) and/or sleepers (*spalen vagon*). For these, on all expresses and many rapids, you need seat **reservations** (*zapazeni mesta*) as well as **tickets** (*bileti*). To ensure a seat in a non-smoking carriage (*myasto nepooshachi*), you will have to specify this when booking. In large towns, it's usually easier to obtain tickets and reservations from **railway booking offices** (*byuro za bileti*) rather than at the station, and wise to book a day in advance at weekends and in summer. Tickets can only be bought on the day of travel at the station. Advance bookings are required for **international tickets** and are bought through the Rila Agency (☻www.bdz-rila.com); branches can be found in all major cities. Most stations have **left-luggage offices** (*garderob*). InterRail, EuroDomino, Balkan Flexipass and Bulgarian Flexipass are valid, although it can easily work out cheaper to buy your rail tickets as you go.

# Accommodation and red tape

All foreigners are supposed to register their passports at their **accommodation** within five days of arrival, and continue to register themselves every time they move on. Hotels automatically issue you with a stamped **Foreigner Registration Form** that lists every night of your stay, although hostels may be less inclined to do so. Officially you can be asked to show these forms on leaving the country, although in practice this hardly ever happens. However, it's best to be aware that if you don't have proof of address for every night of your stay, the police can fine you up to €250. If you're not given a registration form, you're within your rights to request one. Traditionally, foreigners are charged twice the rate paid by Bulgarians for accommodation – though this is still cheap by Western standards – but since 2005, changes in the law mean that there should be one price for all. However, at the time of writing it was not clear whether this would be enforced. In the meantime, the prices quoted throughout this chapter are all foreigner prices.

Most one- and two-star **hotels** (for the most part uninspiring high-rise blocks) rent double rooms from around €35, a little more in Sofia and Plovdiv. Cosier family-run hotels are common on the coast and in village resorts such as Koprivshtitsa and Bansko. **Private rooms** (*chastni kvartiri*) are available in most large towns, and are usually administered by accommodation agencies, although in the smaller resorts you can usually find a room by asking around; expect to pay around €15–20 for a double, more in Sofia and Plovdiv. Single travellers usually get a small reduction on the price of a double. The quality varies enormously, and

## Bulgarian

Hotel and travel agency staff in Sofia and the larger towns generally speak some **English**, but knowledge of foreign languages elsewhere in the country is patchy; younger people are more likely to know a few words of English, but German and French are the preferred second languages in the coastal resorts. Most street signs, menus and so on are written in the **Cyrillic** alphabet, but an increasing number have English transliterations.

|  | Bulgarian | Pronunciation |
|---|---|---|
| Yes | *Da* | Da |
| No | *Ne* | Ne |
| Please | *Molya* | **Mol**ya |
| Thank you | *Blagodarya* | Blago**dar**ya |
| Hello/Good day | *Dobâr den* | **Do**bur den |
| Goodbye | *Dovizhdane* | Do**vizh**danye |
| Excuse me | *Izvinyavaïte* | Izvin**yav**itye |
| Where? | *Kude* | Kud**e** |
| Good | *Dobro* | **Dobro** |
| Bad | *Plosho* | **Losh**o |
| Near | *Blizo* | **Bliz**o |
| Far | *Daleche* | Dal**eyche** |
| Cheap | *Eftino* | **Eft**ino |
| Expensive | *Skupo* | S**kup**o |
| Open | *Otvoreno* | Ot**vor**eno |
| Closed | *Zatvoreno* | Zat**vor**eno |
| Today | *Dnes* | Dnes |
| Yesterday | *Vechera* | Ve**cher**a |
| Tomorrow | *Utre* | **Utre** |
| How much is...? | *Kolko stroova?* | **Ko**lko str**oo**va? |
| What time is it? | *Kolko e chasut?* | **Ko**lko ai cha**su** |
| I don't understand | *Ne razbiram* | Ne raz**bir**am |
| Do you speak English? | *Govorite li Angliski?* | Go**vor**ite li Angliski? |
| One | *Edin/edna* | Ed**in**/ed**na** |
| Two | *Dve* | Dve |
| Three | *Tri* | Tree |
| Four | *Chetiri* | **Chet**iri |
| Five | *Pet* | Pyet |
| Six | *Shest* | Shest |
| Seven | *Sedem* | **Sed**em |
| Eight | *Osem* | **Os**em |
| Nine | *Devet* | **Dev**yet |
| Ten | *Deset* | **Des**yet |

it's rarely possible to inspect the place first, but as a rule, private rooms in big cities will be in large residential blocks, while those in village resorts can often be in atmospheric, traditional houses.

The number of good quality private **hostels** (*turisticheska spalnya*) is growing, and they now exist in most places of interest. Some towns have a **campsite** (*kamping*; usually summer only) on the outskirts, although these are few and far between, and can be unkempt affairs with poor connections to the town centre. Many also feature two-person chalets (€10–15 per night). **Camping rough** is illegal and punishable with a fine.

# Food and drink

Fresh fruit and vegetables have long formed the basis of **Bulgarian cuisine**, a tradition rarely reflected in restaurants, where menus have become pretty standardized and uninspiring. Grilled meats are the focus of most restaurant meals, although you'll sometimes find more traditional roasted or stewed dishes.

Sit-down meals are eaten in either a **restorant** (restaurant) or a **mehana** (tavern). There's little difference between the two, save for the fact that a *mehana* is likely to offer folksy decor and a wider range of traditional Bulgarian dishes. Wherever you go, you're unlikely to spend more than 15Lv for a main course, salad and drink. The most characteristic **traditional Bulgarian dishes** are those baked and served in earthenware pots. The best-known dish is *gyuvech* (which literally means "earthenware dish"), a rich stew comprising peppers, aubergines and beans, to which is added either meat or meat stock. *Kavarma*, a spicy meat stew (either pork or chicken), is prepared in a similar fashion. Fish dishes (*riba*) are most common on the coast. **Vegetarian meals** (*yastia bez meso*) are hard to obtain, although *gyuveche* (a variety of *gyuvech* featuring baked vegetables) and *kachkaval pane* (cheese fried in breadcrumbs) are worth trying, as is *tarator*, a traditional cold summer soup, made with cucumber and yoghurt.

Foremost among **snacks** are *kebapcheta* (grilled sausages), or variations such as *shishche* (shish kebab) or *kiofteta* (meatballs). Another favourite is the *banitsa*, a flaky-pastry envelope with a filling – usually cheese – sold by street vendors in the morning and evening, to people going to and from work. Elsewhere, *sandvichi* (sandwiches) and *pitsi* (pizzas) dominate the fast-food repertoire. Pork (*svinsko*), veal (*teleshko*), chicken (*pile*) and offal, in various forms, all make appearances on restaurant menus, usually accompanied by potatoes (*kartofi*) and a couple of vegetables, as well as bread. Bulgarians consider their **yoghurt** (*kiselo mlyako*) the world's finest, and hardly miss a day without consuming a glass.

The quality of Bulgarian **wines** is constantly improving, and the industry now exports worldwide. Among the best reds are the heavy, mellow Melnik, and rich, dark Mavrud. Dimyat is a good, dry white wine. If you prefer the sweeter variety, try Karlovski Misket (Muscatel) or Tramminer. Cheap native **spirits** are highly potent, and should be drunk diluted with water in the case of *mastika* (like ouzo in Greece) or downed in one, Balkan-style, in the case of *rakiya* – brandy made from either plums (*slivova*) or grapes (*grozdova*). Bulgarian **beer** is as good as any, and brands such as Kamenitza and Zagorka are preferable to pricey imported alternatives.

**Coffee** (*kafe*) usually comes *espresso* style. **Tea** (*chai*) is nearly always herbal – ask for *cheren chai* (literally "black tea") if you want the real stuff, normally served with lemon.

# Opening hours and holidays

Big-city **shops and supermarkets** are generally open Mon–Fri 8.30am–6pm or later; on Sat they close at 2pm. In rural areas and small towns, an unofficial siesta may prevail between noon and 3pm. Many shops, offices, banks and museums are closed on the following **public holidays**: Jan 1, March 3, Easter Sun, Easter Mon, May 1, May 24, Sept 6, Sept 22, Dec 25 & Dec 31. Additional public holidays may occasionally be called by the government.

# Emergencies

Petty theft is a danger on the coast, and the Bulgarian **police** can be slow in filling out insurance reports unless you're insistent. Foreign tourists are no longer a novelty in much of the country, but **women** travelling alone can expect to encounter stares, comments and sometimes worse from macho types, and clubs on the coast are pretty much seen as cattle-markets. A firm rebuff should be enough to cope with most situations. Note that everyone is required to carry some form of **ID** at all times.

## Emergency numbers

Police ☏166; Ambulance ☏150; Fire ☏160.

If you need a **doctor** (*lekar*) or dentist (*zâbolekar*), go to the nearest *poliklinika* (health centre), whose staff might speak English or German. Emergency treatment is free of charge although you must pay for **medicines** – larger towns will have at least one 24-hour pharmacy.

**BULGARIA** | Basics

5

# Sofia

One of Europe's least known and least glamorous capital cities, **SOFIA** can appear an uninspiring place to first-time visitors, with its drab suburbs and crumbling old buildings. However, much has been done in recent years to revitalize the heart of the city, and once you've settled in and begun to explore, you'll find it a surprisingly laid-back place, especially on fine spring days, when its lush public gardens and pavement cafés buzz with life. Urban pursuits can be combined with the outdoor possibilities offered by verdant **Mount Vitosha**, just 12km to the south.

Sofia was founded by a Thracian tribe some 3000 years ago, and various **Roman ruins** attest to its zenith as the regional imperial capital of Serdica in the fourth century. The Bulgars didn't arrive on the scene until the ninth century, and with the notable exception of the thirteenth-century Boyana Church, their cultural monuments largely disappeared during the Turkish occupation (1396–1878), of which the sole visible legacy is a couple of stately **mosques**. The finest architecture postdates Bulgaria's liberation from the Turks: handsome public buildings and parks, and the magnificent **Aleksandâr Nevsky Cathedral.**

## Arrival and information

Trains arrive at **Central Station** (Tsentralna Gara), a concrete hangar harbouring a number of exchange bureaux and snack bars, but little else to welcome the visitor. Five minutes' ride along bul Knyaginya Mariya Luiza (tram #1 or #7) is pl Sveta Nedelya, within walking distance of several hotels and the main accommodation

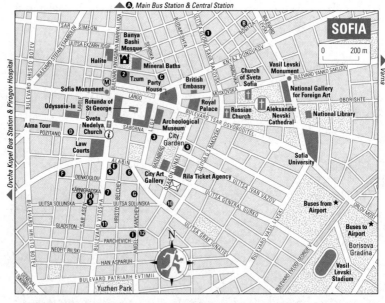

| ACCOMMODATION | | | | EATING & DRINKING | | | | Perfect | 2 |
|---|---|---|---|---|---|---|---|---|---|
| Art Hostel | I | Hostel Sofia | D | Art Club | | Club Lavazza | 7 | Pizza Troll | 7, 10 |
| Baldzhieva | H | Internet Hostel | E | Museum Café | 3 | Divaka | 12 | Pri Yafata | 9 |
| Enny Pop | A | Kervan Hostel | B | Baalbek | 4 | Dream House | E | Trops-kâshta | 6 |
| Hostel Mostel | F | Lyulin | C | Chen | 1 | J.J. Murphy's | 8 | Ugo | 11 |
|  |  | Red Star Hostel | G |  |  |  |  |  |  |

agencies. Most buses arrive in the new **bus station**, just next to the train station, although some Bansko services and Blagoevgrad buses (for connections to Rila Monastery) use the Ovcha Kupel terminal, 5km southwest of the centre along bul Tsar Boris III (tram #5 from behind the Law Courts). The best way to get into town from **Sofia airport** is to catch minibus #30, which runs until around 10pm (every 15–30min), and operates like a shared taxi; it will take you to the city centre for 1Lv. Bus #84 (every 10–20min, until around 11.30pm), takes a more tortuous route and drops you, rather inconveniently, outside Borisova Gradina, at the southeastern edge of the city centre. Waiting taxis might well try to charge you an exorbitant €20 or more, so it's wise to book one at the booth in the arrivals hall (7-10Lv).

Sofia does have an official **tourist office**, the National Information and Advertising Centre on Sveta Nedelya (Mon–Fri 9am–5.30pm; ☎02/987-9778, ⓦwww.bulgariatravel.org), but a better bet is the friendly travel agent Odysseia-In, at bul Stamboliiski 20 (entrance on ul Lavele; Mon–Fri 9am–7.30pm, daily in summer; ☎02/980-5102, ⓦwww.odysseia-in.com) who charge a €5 consultation fee, although not for accommodation booking. The free quarterly *Sofia Inside & Out* and the monthly *Sofia City Guide*, available from some hotel reception desks, contain general information and **listings**, while the English-language weekly *Sofia Echo*, sold at newsstands around Tzum, is a good source for local news and events.

## City transport

The **public transport** network – consisting of buses (*avtobus*), trolleybuses (*troleibus*), a one-line metro system, and trams (*tramvai*) – runs between 5am and midnight and is cheap and efficient. There's a **flat fare** of 50st on all urban routes; tickets (*bileti*) are sold from street kiosks, and, occasionally, on board, and must be punched as you enter the vehicle (inspections are frequent and there are spot fines of 5Lv for fare-dodgers). Note that if you're travelling with luggage, you should buy and punch two tickets. Kiosks at the main tram stops sell one-day tickets (*karta za edin den*; 2Lv) and five-day tickets (*karta za pet dena*; 9Lv). Metro tickets must be bought from the station; a "combination ticket" (*kombiniran bilet*) costs 80st and is valid for one metro and one bus or tram journey. The most reliable **taxis** are the yellow OK taxis, who set the standard fares, and should charge about 39st per kilometre until nightfall, and 45st afterwards, as well as an additional 12st per minute, and 40st initial fare; make sure the driver has his meter running. Additionally, there's a fleet of private **minibuses** (*marshrutka*), acting like shared taxis and covering around forty different routes across the city for a flat fare of 1Lv. Destinations and routes are displayed on the front of the vehicles – in the Cyrillic alphabet – and passengers flag them down like normal taxis, calling out when they want them to stop.

## Accommodation

Accommodation tends to be slightly dearer than in other towns, but there are a number of small, reasonably priced **hotels** and the growing number of good **hostels** means that prices are kept competitive. All fill up quickly, though, especially in summer, and advance bookings are advisable. **Private rooms** (❸) can be booked by agencies such as Odysseia-In (see above) and Alma Tour, at bul Stamboliiski 27 (Mon–Fri 9am–6.30pm, Sat 10.30am–4pm; ☎02/987-7233, ⓦwww.almatour.net).

### Hostels

**Art Hostel** Angel Kânchev 21a ☎02/987-0545, ⓦwww.art-hostel.com. Sofia's trendiest hostel, hosting art exhibitions, live music and drama performances. Guests have access to a kitchen, tea room, and free Internet. Breakfast included. €10 or €5 for floor space only.

**Hostel Mostel** Denkoglu 2 ☎0889/223-296, ⓦwww.hostelmostel.com. Modern, welcoming hostel with free 24-hour Internet access and all-you-can-eat breakfast. Two seven-bed dorms, and three doubles. Dorms €10, €5 for floor space; rooms ❸

**Hostel Sofia** Pozitano 16 ☎02/989-8582, ⓦwww.hostelsofia.com. Clean and well-run two-dorm, fourteen-bed hostel, just behind the Law Courts, with shared kitchen, bathroom and cable TV. Breakfast and drinks included. €9.

**Internet Hostel** Alabin 50a ℡02/989-9419, ✉interhostel@yahoo.co.uk. Friendly hostel, with doubles, triples and quads. Located inside a shopping arcade on the second floor, above the Dream House restaurant. Internet access and kitchen. Breakfast included. €10 per person, €5 for floor space only.

**Kervan Hostel** Rositza 3 ℡02/983-9428, ⊛www .kervanhostel.com. Three-dorm bohemian-style hostel in a quiet area of central Sofia, minutes from Nevsky Cathedral. Bike rental is available, and there's also a kitchen. Breakfast included. €10.

**Red Star Hostel** Angel Kânchev 6 ℡02/986-3341, ✉redstarhostel@yahoo.com. Modern hostel with clean and cosy doubles, triples and dorms.

Breakfast included, along with free Internet access. Dorms €10, rooms ❸

### Hotels

**Baldzhieva** Tsar Asen 23 ℡02/981-1257, ✉baldjievahotel@yahoo.com. Small hotel in a smart town house one block west of bul Vitosha. Rooms are clean and cosy, all with phone, fridge, TV and bathroom. ❺

**Enny** Pop Bogomil 46 ℡02/983-1649. Good-value small hotel – one of the cheapest in central Sofia – just off bul Knyaginya Mariya Luiza, and not far from the train station. Rooms come with cable TV but shared bathrooms. ❷

**Lyulin** Serdika 8 ℡02/940-2147. Well-located, if somewhat characterless hotel, offering small en-suite rooms in an anonymous apartment block right behind Tzum. ❺

## The City

At the heart of Sofia is **Ploshtad Sveta Nedelya**, a pedestrianized square dominated by the **Sveta Nedelya Church**, built after the liberation as the successor to a number of churches that have stood here since medieval times. Running south of the square is **bulevard Vitosha**, Sofia's main shopping street, which leads to **Yuzhen Park**. An underpass gives access from pl Sveta Nedelya to a sunken shop-lined plaza, with the tiny **Church of Sveta Petka Samardzhiiska** (Mon–Sat 9am–7pm, Sun 9am–2pm; 5Lv) at its centre. Dating back to the fourteenth century, the church contains fragmentary and much-restored frescoes.

Heading north, you'll come to the **Largo**, an elongated plaza flanked on three sides by severe monumental buildings, the most arresting of which is the towering monolith of the former **Party House**, originally the home of the Communist hierarchy, and now serving as government offices. The plaza extends westwards to the Serdika metro station, watched over by the city's symbol, the **Sofia Monument**, representing the eponymous Goddess of Wisdom. On the northern side of the Largo is the Council of Ministers (Bulgaria's cabinet) and Sofia's upmarket shopping mall, **Tzum**.

Just beyond, on bulevard Knyaginya Mariya Luiza, you'll find the **Banya Bashi Mosque**, built in 1576 by Hadzhi Mimar Sonah, who also designed the great mosque at Edirne in Turkey. Behind stand Sofia's **mineral baths**, housed in a yellow and red-striped fin-de-siècle building, currently being restored. Locals gather daily to bottle the hot, sulphurous water that gushes into long stone troughs outside. Opposite the mosque is the **Halite**, an elegant building dating from the early 1900s, housing the city's central food hall, with three floors of shops and restaurants.

On the southern flank of the Largo, the *Sheraton Hotel*'s sombre wings run round a courtyard containing Sofia's oldest church, the fourth-century **Rotunda of St George**. It houses frescoes from the eighth century onwards, although most eyes are drawn to the fourteenth-century Christ Pantokrator, surrounded by a frieze of 22 prophets, in the dome. Next to the church is the **Presidency**, guarded by soldiers in colourful nineteenth-century garb (Changing of the Guard hourly). Immediately to the east, a fifteenth-century mosque now holds the **Archeological Museum** (Tues–Sun 10am–5pm; 5Lv), whose prize exhibit is a magnificent gold cauldron and cups of the Thracian Vâlchitrân treasure. Also on show is a collection of Thracian armour, medieval church wall paintings and numerous Roman tombstones.

A little further to the east is **Ploshtad Aleksandâr Battenberg**, named after the German aristocrat chosen to be the newly independent country's first monarch in 1878. The square, surfaced with attractive yellow bricks, was once the scene of Communist rallies and, until its demolition in 1999, was dominated by the mausoleum of Georgi Dimitrov, first leader of the People's Republic of Bulgaria. On the northern side of the square is the dilapidated former **Royal Palace**, today home to the National Art Gallery and Ethnographic Museum, though these are of little note; instead, try the **City Art Gallery** (Tues–Sat 10am–6pm, Sun 11am–5pm; free) in the City Garden, immediately to the south, which stages monthly exhibitions of contemporary Bulgarian art.

Follow the yellow-brick bulevard Tsar Osvoboditel east, and you'll see the **Russian Church**, a stunning golden-domed building, with an emerald spire and an exuberant mosaic-tiled exterior, concealing a dark, candle-scented interior. Just beyond is a particularly busy road junction; turn left, up ul Rakovski, where a glint of gold betrays the proximity of the **Aleksandâr Nevsky Cathedral**, one of the finest pieces of architecture in the Balkans. Financed by public subscription and built between 1882 and 1924 to honour the 200,000 Russian casualties of the 1877–78 War of Liberation, it's a magnificent structure, bulging with domes and semi-domes and glittering with gold leaf. Within the gloomy interior, a beardless Christ sits enthroned above the altar, and numerous scenes from his life, painted in a humanistic style, adorn the walls. The crypt, entered from outside (Tues–Sun 10.30am–6.30pm; 4Lv), contains a superb collection of icons from all over the country. Pride of place goes to a fifteenth-century double-sided icon from Sozopol, carrying an image of the Virgin and Child on one side and the Crucifixion on the other.

On the northeastern edge of the cathedral square, an imposing white building houses the **National Gallery for Foreign Art** (Mon & Wed–Sun 11am–6.30pm; 10Lv), which devotes a lot of space to Indian wood-carvings and second-division French and Russian artists, though there are a few minor works by the likes of Rodin, Chagall and Kandinsky. Heading west across the square, you'll pass two recumbent lions flanking the Tomb of the Unknown Soldier, set beside the wall of the plain, brown-brick **Church of Sveta Sofia**. Originally erected during the sixth century, it has been much restored since. The best route from here is to cut down past the **Parliament** building onto pl Narodno Sâbranie, watched over by an equestrian statue of the Russian Tsar Alexander II, known as the "Liberator" (*Osvoboditel*). From here, it's a brief stroll along bul Tsar Osvoboditel, past Sofia University, to **Borisova Gradina**, named after Bulgaria's interwar monarch, Boris III. The park – the largest in Sofia – has a rich variety of flowers and trees, outdoor bars, two football stadiums and two huge Communist monuments, still impressive despite the graffiti and rubbish scattered around them.

## Mount Vitosha

A wooded granite mass 20km long and 16km wide, **Mount Vitosha**, 12km south of the city, is where Sofians come for picnics and skiing – and the ascent of its highest peak, the 2290-metre **Cherni Vrâh**, has become a traditional test of stamina. Getting here on public transport is straightforward, although there are fewer buses on weekdays than at weekends. One approach is to take tram #5 from behind the Law Courts to Ovcha Kupel bus station, then change to bus #61, which climbs through the forests towards **Zlatni Mostove**, a beauty spot on the western shoulder of Mount Vitosha beside the so-called **Stone River**. Beneath the large boulders running down the mountainside is a rivulet, which once attracted gold-panners. Trails lead up beside the rivulet towards the mountain's upper reaches: Cherni Vrâh is about two to three hours' walk from here.

Another route is on tram #9 from the train station or #14 from Graf Ignatiev to the Hladilnika terminus on bul Cherni Vrâh, and then bus #66 to the resort centre of **Aleko**. Aleko can also be reached by taking bus #64 or #93 from Hladilnika to the suburb of **Dragalevtsi**, where there's a chairlift (*lifta*; daily in winter; rest of year weekends only); or taking bus #122 from Hladilnika to **Simeonovo**, starting point for the Aleko-bound gondola (daily). **Aleko** is a thriving winter sports centre, with pistes to suit all and a couple of ski schools that also rent out gear; outside the ski season, there are plenty of walking trails to explore (Cherni Vrâh is an easy forty-minute walk from here). The resort is well-served with snack bars and restaurants throughout the year.

## Eating, drinking and nightlife

**Eating and drinking** in Sofia can be remarkably cheap and quite varied. Numerous fast-food outlets serve up the usual range of burgers, sandwiches and kebabs, while pizza parlours and restaurants offering grilled meats, salads and chips are also common. In addition, there are plenty of pricier restaurants offering a range of international cuisine, but don't expect total authenticity. The cheapest places to grab a beer or a coffee are the many cafés and kiosks around bul Vitosha or in the city's public gardens, while for evening entertainment, there's an ever-growing number of **clubs**, most playing a mix of pop and the ubiquitous local "folk pop"(*chalga*). Jazz and Latino music are also popular.

### Restaurants

**Baalbek** Dyakon Ignati 4. Highly regarded Lebanese establishment, with sit-down restaurant upstairs and fast-food counter offering kebabs, shawarma and falafel on the ground floor.

**Chen** Rakovski 86. Popular Chinese with authentic food, opposite the opera house.

**Divaka** Gladston 54. Bright and busy restaurant, just west of Graf Ignatiev, behind the Art Hostel, serving excellent, meat-heavy Bulgarian dishes. Open 24 hours.

**Dream House** Alabin 50a. Only real vegetarian restaurant in Sofia, with good choice of meals, snacks and herbal teas. On the first floor above the shopping mall.

**Perfect** In the sunken plaza beneath Tzum. Spacious, modern place, offering reasonably priced Bulgarian and international dishes, including grills, salads and pizzas.

**Pizza Troll** Vitosha 27. One of the better pizza and pasta restaurants in the centre, with vaguely Art Nouveau decor. There's another branch on Graf Ignatiev.

**Pri Yafata** Solunska 28. Brash but fun take on a traditional Mehana, complete with live music, costumed staff, and a great Bulgarian menu.

**Trops-kâshta** Graf Ignatiev 12. Good-value buffet-style chain restaurant, with several branches around town, offering tasty – if invariably luke-warm – Bulgarian standards.

**Ugo** Vitosha 45. Popular pizza and pasta joint, with a good range of dishes, and an upwardly mobile clientele. Open 24-hours.

### Cafés, bars and clubs

**Art Club Museum Café** Cnr of Sâborna & Lege. Chic café with a pleasant patio set amid Thracian tombstones next to the Archeological Museum. Serves a variety of drinks, light meals and desserts.

**Bibliotekata** Vasil Levski 88. Glitzy nightclub beneath the National Library building, drawing in a moneyed young crowd.

**Blaze** Slavyanska 36. Lively bar and club near the university, with a good sound system and trendy clientele.

**Caramba** Tsar Osvoboditel 4. Sofia's premier Latino club, featuring different Latin rhythms nightly.

**Club Lavazza** Vitosha 13. Smart place for coffee and cakes, which also offers light meals and an excellent-value English breakfast.

**J.J. Murphy's** Kârnigradska 6. Sofia's top Irish bar, offering filling pub grub, big-screen sports and live music at the weekends.

**Life House** Vitosha 12. An exclusive club on the main drag, with some of the best house music in town.

**My Mojito** Ivan Vazov 12. One of Sofia's trendiest clubs with regular DJ slots and a laid-back crowd.

**Pri Kmeta** Parizhka 3. Roomy basement beer hall, serving good food, with nightly disco music and the occasional live band.

**Spartacus** Located in the underpass by the university, the city's only real gay club is a welcoming, laid-back place to spend an evening.

**Swingin' Hall** Dragan Tsankov 8. Cheap, cheerful and crowded bar, with live music (usually pop/rock or jazz) on two stages.

## Listings

**Embassies & consulates** Australia, Trakia 37
℡ 02/946-1334; Canada, Moskovska 9 ℡ 02/969-
9717; UK, Moskovska 9 ℡ 02/933-9222; US,
Kozyak 16 ℡ 02/937-5100.
**Gay Sofia** Bulgarian Gay Organization, bul Vasil
Levski 3 (℡ 02/987-6872, ☜ www.bgogemini
.org).

**Internet access** Cyber Zone, Angel Kânchev 22a;
Gattaca, Sveta Sofia 10; both open 24 hours.
**Hospital** Pirogov hospital, bul General Totleben 21
℡ 02/51531.
**Pharmacy** No. 7, pl Sveta Nedelya 5.
**Post office** Ul General Gurko 6 (daily 7am–
8.30pm).

# Southern Bulgaria

Trains heading from Bulgaria to Greece follow the Struma Valley south from Sofia, skirting some of the country's most grandiose mountains on the way. Formerly noted for their bandits and hermits, the Rila and Pirin Mountains contain Bulgaria's highest peaks, swathed in forests and dotted with alpine lakes. If time is short, the place to head for is the most revered of Bulgarian monasteries, **Rila**, lying some 30km east of the main southbound route. **Bansko**, on the eastern side of the Pirin range, is a small detour from the main north–south route, and boasts a wealth of traditional architecture, as well as being a burgeoning **ski** resort and a good base for **hiking**. Another much-travelled route heads southeast from Sofia towards Istanbul, through the Plain of Thrace, a fertile region that was the heartland of the ancient Thracians, whose origins date back to the third millennium BC. The main road and rail lines now linking Istanbul and Sofia essentially follow the course of the Roman Serdica–Constantinople road, past towns ruled by the Ottomans for so long that foreigners used to call this "European Turkey". Of these, the most important is **Plovdiv**, Bulgaria's second city, whose old quarter is a wonderful mixture of National Revival mansions and classical remains. Some 30km south of Plovdiv is **Bachkovo Monastery**, containing Bulgaria's most vivid frescoes.

## Rila Monastery

As the most celebrated of Bulgaria's religious sites, famed for its fine architecture and mountainous setting – and declared a world heritage monument by UNESCO – the **Rila Monastery** receives a steady stream of visitors, many of them day-trippers from Sofia. Joining one of these one-day tours from the capital is the simplest way of getting here, but can work out expensive (most tours cost around €70). Far cheaper is to travel by public transport, though realistically you'll have to stay the night. There are three daily buses from Sofia's Ovcha Kupel terminal to **RILA village**, from where four buses a day make the 27km run up to the monastery. Otherwise, you'll need to catch the bus or train to Dupnitsa or Blagoevgrad in the Struma Valley, and then change to a local bus for Rila village.

The road from Rila village to the monastery runs above the foaming River Rilska, fed by springs from the surrounding pine-clad mountains. Even today there's a palpable sense of isolation, and it's easy to see why **Ivan Rilski** chose this valley to escape the savagery of feudal life and the laxity of the established monasteries at the end of the ninth century. The current foundation, 4km from Ivan's original hermitage, was plundered during the eighteenth century and repairs had hardly begun when the whole structure burned down in 1833. Its resurrection was presented as a religious and patriotic duty: public donations poured in throughout the nineteenth century, and the east wing was built as recently as 1961 to display the treasury.

Ringed by mighty walls, the monastery has the outward appearance of a fortress, but this impression is negated by the beauty of the interior, which even the crowds can't mar. Graceful arches above the flagstoned courtyard support tiers of monastic cells, and stairways ascend to wooden balconies. Bold red stripes and black-and-white check patterns enliven the facade, contrasting with the sombre mountains behind and creating a harmony between the cloisters and the **church**. Richly coloured frescoes shelter beneath the church porch and cover much of its interior. The iconostasis is particularly splendid, almost 10m wide and covered by a mass of intricate carvings and gold leaf. Beside the church is **Hrelyo's Tower**, the sole remaining building from the fourteenth century. Cauldrons, which were once used to prepare food for pilgrims, occupy the soot-encrusted kitchen on the ground floor of the north wing, while on the floors above you can inspect the spartan refectory and panelled guest rooms. Beneath the east wing is the **treasury** (daily 8.30am–4.30pm; 5Lv), where, amongst other things, you can view a wooden cross carved with more than 1500 miniature human figures by the monk Raphael during the 1790s.

It's possible to **stay** in the monastery, although most of the rooms come without showers or hot water (gates close at dusk; €15 per person). The handful of **restaurants** outside the east gate are decent, but sometimes overcharge stray foreigners. For cheap **snacks**, delicious bread and doughnuts, you should head for the bakery opposite the east gate. The primitive *Bor* **campsite** (follow the signs) occupies an attractive riverside spot.

## Bansko

Lying some 40km east of the main Struma Valley route, **BANSKO** is the primary centre for walking and skiing on the eastern slopes of the Pirin mountains. It's a traditional agricultural centre and a rapidly growing tourist resort, boasting a wealth of stone-built nineteenth-century farmhouses and numerous small hotels. Though connected to Sofia and other towns by bus, Bansko can also be reached by a **narrow-gauge railway**, which leaves the main Sofia–Plovdiv line at **Septemvri** and forges its way across the highlands. It's one of the most scenic trips in the Balkans, but also one of the slowest, taking five hours to cover just over 100km.

Bansko centres on the modern pedestrianized pl Nikola Vaptsarov, where the **Nikola Vaptsarov Museum** (Mon–Fri 8am–6pm, Sat & Sun 8am–noon & 2–6pm; 2Lv) contains a display relating to the local-born poet and socialist martyr. Immediately north of here, pl Vâzrazhdane is watched over by the solid stone tower of the **Church of Sveta Troitsa**, whose interior contains exquisite nineteenth-century frescoes and icons. On the opposite side of the square, the **Rilski Convent** contains an icon museum (summer only; Mon–Fri 9am–noon & 2–5pm; 2Lv) devoted to the achievements of Bansko's nineteenth-century icon painters. From the main square, ul Pirin leads north towards the new **cable car,** along with its buzzy collection of ski-hire shops, bars and restaurants. The cable car (daily 8.30am–5pm, 16Lv) allows easy access to **hiking trails** in the summer, and the popular winter **ski slopes**. Ski passes start at 50Lv per day to 280Lv for 6 days, with ski and snowboard hire at around 30Lv per day. In the summer months, the other option for reaching the summit is to head west – on foot or by taxi – via a steep fourteen-kilometre uphill climb to the Vihren hut, where cheap dorm accommodation is available. This is the main trail-head for hikes towards the 2914-metre summit of **Mount Vihren** (Bulgaria's second-highest peak), or gentler rambles around the meadows and lakes nearby.

There are five buses a day to Bansko from Sofia, although if you're approaching the area from Rila, it's far easier to head for **Blagoevgrad** and change buses there. Bansko Travel (℡029/585347; ⊛www.banskotravel.com) provides a wide range of information on both skiing and hiking in the region, and can also arrange walking guides, ski lessons and good-value private accommodation.

At Bansko, the **bus and train stations** are on the northern fringes of town, ten minutes' walk from pl Vaptsarov, where you'll find the main **tourist office** (irregular hours; ☏07443/4611). Best of the family-run **hotels** are in the old town centre; the friendly *Dvata Smârcha* near Sveta Troitsa at Velyan Ognev 2 (☏07443/2632; ❷), and the welcoming *Dzhangal*, at Gotse Delchev 24 (☏07443/2661, ☻hotel _djangal@abv.bg; ❷), which features a sauna and can arrange transfers from Sofia. The nearby *Durchova Kushta* also has a sauna and can arrange car rental (☏07443/8223, ☯www.durchova-kashta.com; ❹). For **eating** and entertainment, there are over forty *mehanas* offering traditional specialities and folk music at weekends: *Sirleshtova Kâshta, Momini Dvori* and *Dyado Pene*, all around the main two squares, are among the most atmospheric.

# Plovdiv and around

Bulgaria's second largest city, **PLOVDIV**, has more obvious charms than Sofia, which locals tend to look down on. The old town embodies Plovdiv's long history – Thracian fortifications subsumed by Macedonian masonry, overlaid with Roman and Byzantine walls, and by great timber-framed mansions erected during the Bulgarian renaissance, symbolically looking down upon the derelict Ottoman mosques and artisans' dwellings of the lower town. But Plovdiv isn't just another museum town: the city's arts festivals and trade fairs are the biggest in the country, and its restaurants and bars are equal to those of the capital.

### The City

Plovdiv centres on the large **Ploshtad Tsentralen**, dominated by the monolithic *Hotel Trimontium Princess*. Heading north from here, the pedestrianized ul Knyaz Aleksandâr I Battenberg, lined with shops, cafés and bars, leads onto the attractive **Ploshtad Dzhumaya**, where stallholders gather to sell a range of touristy knick-knacks, including paintings, jewellery and icons. The ruins of a **Roman Stadium**, visible in a pit beneath the square, are just a fragment of the arena where up to 30,000 spectators watched gladiatorial spectacles. Among the variously styled buildings here, the **Dzhumaya Mosque**, with its diamond-patterned minaret and lead-sheathed domes, steals the show; it's believed that the mosque, sadly now looking a little dilapidated, dates back to the reign of Sultan Murad II (1359–85).

With its cobbled streets and colourful mansions covering one of Plovdiv's three hills, the **Old Quarter** is a painter's dream and a cartographer's nightmare. As good a route as any is to start from pl Dzhumaya and head east up ul Sâborna. Blackened fortress walls dating from Byzantine times can be seen around Sâborna and other streets, sometimes incorporated into the dozens of timber-framed National Revival houses that are Plovdiv's speciality. Outside and within, the walls are frequently decorated with niches, floral motifs or false columns, painted in the style known as *alafranga*. Turn right, up the steps beside the Church of Sveta Bogoroditsa, and continue, along twisting cobbled lanes, to the **Roman Theatre** (daily 9am–5pm; 3Lv), the best preserved in the country, and still an impressive **venue for regular concerts and plays** (advertised around the town and in the local press). Back on Sâborna, the **State Gallery of Fine Arts** (Mon–Fri 9am–12.30pm & 1–5.30pm, Sat 10am–5.30pm; 2Lv, free Thurs) holds an extensive collection of nineteenth- and twentieth-century Bulgarian paintings, including some fine portraits by Stanislav Dospevski. Further along, the **Church of SS Constantine and Elena** contains a fine gilt iconostasis, partly decorated by the prolific nineteenth-century artist Zahari Zograf, whose work also appears in the adjacent **Museum of Icons** (Mon–Fri 9am–12.30pm & 1–5.30pm, Sat 10am–12.30pm; 2Lv, free Thurs). A little further uphill is the richly decorated **Kuyumdzhioglu House**, now home to the **Ethnographic Museum** (Tues–Thurs, Sat & Sun 9am–noon & 2–5pm, Fri 9am–noon; 4Lv). Folk costumes and crafts are on display on the ground floor, while upstairs, the elegantly furnished rooms reflect the former owner's taste for Viennese and French Baroque. Heading west from the Hisar Gate, a road leads downhill to ul Artin Gidikov, where, at no. 4, the **Hindlian House** (daily

## Travelling on from Plovdiv

There's a nightly **train** to Istanbul, which leaves Plovdiv at 9.30pm; Turkish visas can be bought at the Kapikule frontier (UK citizens £10; US citizens US$20; Canadian citizens US$45; Australian and New Zealand citizens US$20) – have the exact sum ready in cash, as they don't always have change and won't let you in without the visa. Other nationals should contact the Turkish consulate at ul Filip Makedonski 10 in Plovdiv (☎032/632309) for current visa prices. Several agencies at the Yug bus station sell tickets for **international buses**; Hebros Bus (daily 7.30am–7pm; ☎032/626916), a Eurolines agent, can book seats on buses to Greece, Turkey and Western Europe.

9.30am–5pm; 3Lv), the former home of an Armenian merchant, harbours some of Plovdiv's most evocative nineteenth-century interiors.

### Practicalities

Plovdiv's **train station** is on the southern fringe of the centre, on bul Hristo Botev, and the two **bus stations** are nearby: Rodopi, serving the mountain resorts to the south, is just on the other side of the tracks; while Yug, serving Sofia and the rest of the country, is one block east. **Private rooms** (❷) can be booked through *Esperansa*, Ivan Vazov 14 (☎032/260653). The welcoming *Raisky Kat* **hostel** (☎032/268849, ✉acommodacion_svetla@yahoo.com; €10 per person) offers doubles and triples in the old town at ul Slaveikov 6, whilst across the road at Slaveikov 5, *Sportna Sreshta* (☎032/635115; €10) offers dorm accommodation in a fabulous seventeenth-century town house, and runs eco-tours in the area. The hostel is too cold for a comfortable stay in winter though. In the town centre, the modern *PBI Hostel* at Naiden Gerov 13 has twenty dorm beds, a bar and Internet access (☎032/638467, ✇www.pbihostel.com; €10). **Hotel** prices are relatively high, but you can get decent-value rooms at the friendly *Trakia*, near the train station at ul Ivan Vazov 84 (☎032/624101; ❷), with its own restaurant. The *Gorski Kat* **campsite** (☎032/551360) is located some 4km west, reached by bus #222 from outside the train station.

The best **restaurants** are in the old town, many occupying elegant old houses and serving good, traditional Bulgarian food; try *Apoloniya*, ul Vasil Kânchev 1, the excellent *Philipopol*, ul Konstantin Stoilov 56b, or the cheaper *Hushove*, at the top of the lane opposite the *Raisky Kat* hostel. In the new town, ul Knyaz Aleksandâr I is awash with cheaper fast-food outlets, though better quality can be found away from the main drag; the *Red Dragon*, on the corner of bul Ruski and ul Filip Makedonski, is a good Chinese restaurant, serving generous portions, while *Malâk Bunardzhik*, ul Volga 1, in the park at the foot of the Hill of the Liberators, is a smart but surprisingly cheap restaurant serving excellent Bulgarian cuisine. **Drinking** takes place in the pavement cafés of ul Knyaz Aleksandâr I. *Dreams*, at Knyaz Aleksandâr I 42, is a popular spot for coffee, cocktails and cakes, while *Dzhumayata*, built into the side of the Dzhumaya mosque, serves authentic Turkish coffee and sweets, such as baklava. The Kapana area just north of the Dzhumaya mosque is the best place to head for late-night drinks and dancing, while *Morris*, north of the river at bul Maritsa 122, is a trendy nightclub with regular live music. For **Internet** access try Elite at ul Patriarch Evtimi 24, or Fantasy, ul Knyaz Aleksandâr I 31.

### Bachkovo Monastery

The most attractive destination south of Plovdiv is **Bachkovo Monastery**, around 30km away and an easy day-trip from the city (hourly buses from Rodopi station to Smolyan). Founded in 1038 by two Georgians in the service of the Byzantine Empire, this is Bulgaria's second-largest monastery and, like Rila, has been declared a UNESCO World Heritage Site.

A great iron-studded door admits visitors to the cobbled courtyard, surrounded by wooden galleries and adorned with colourful frescoes. Along one wall is a pictorial narrative of the monastery's history, showing Bachkovo roughly as it appears today, and watched over by the Madonna and Child. Beneath the vaulted porch of Bachkovo's principal church, **Sveta Bogoroditsa**, are frescoes depicting the horrors in store for sinners; the entrance itself is more optimistic, overseen as it is by the Holy Trinity. Floral motifs in a naive style decorate the beams of the interior, where you can view a fourteenth-century Georgian icon of the Virgin, though legend claims it to be the original handiwork of St Luke. The church of **St Nicholas**, originally founded during the nineteenth century, features a fine *Last Judgement* covering the porch exterior, which includes a portrait of the artist, Zahari Zograf. Finally, just outside the main gate is the recently restored **Ossuary**, which dates from the eleventh century and contains a number of early medieval frescoes, but sadly, it's rarely open to visitors. It's possible to **stay** in recently refurbished rooms in the monastery (☎03327/277; €5 per person), and there are three **restaurants** just outside; *Vodopada*, with its mini-waterfall, is the best.

# Northern Bulgaria

Routes from Sofia to the Black Sea coast take you through the mountainous terrain of central and northern Bulgaria – a gruelling eight- or nine-hour ride that's worth interrupting to savour something of the country's heartland. For over a thousand years, Stara Planina – known to foreigners as the **Balkan range** – has been the cradle of the Bulgarian nation. It was here that the Khans established the First Kingdom, and here, too, after a period of Byzantine control, that the Boyars proclaimed the Second Kingdom and created a magnificent capital at **Veliko Târnovo**. Closer by, the **Sredna Gora** (Central Mountains) was inhabited as early as the fifth millennium BC, but for Bulgarians this forested region is best known as the Land of the April Rising, the nineteenth-century rebellion for which the picturesque town of **Koprivshtitsa** will always be remembered.

Although they lie a little way off the main rail lines from Sofia, neither Veliko Târnovo nor Koprivshtitsa is difficult to reach. The former lies just south of Gorna Oryahovitsa, a major rail junction midway between Varna and Sofia, from where you can pick up a local train or bus; the latter is served by a stop on the Sofia–Burgas line, whose four daily trains in each direction are met by local buses to ferry you the 12km to the village itself.

## Koprivshtitsa

Seen from a distance, **KOPRIVSHTITSA** looks almost too lovely to be real, its half-timbered houses lying in a valley amid wooded hills. It would be an oasis of rural calm if not for the tourists drawn by the superb architecture and Bulgarians paying homage to a landmark in their nation's history. From the Bridge of the First Shot to the Place of the Scimitar Charge, there's hardly a part of Koprivshtitsa that isn't named for an episode or participant in the **April Rising of 1876**. As neighbouring towns were burned by the Bashibazouks – the irregular troops recruited by the Turks to put the rebels in their place – refugees flooded into Koprivshtitsa, spreading panic. The rebels eventually took to the hills while local traders bribed the Bashibazouks to spare the village – and so Koprivshtitsa survived unscathed, to be admired by subsequent generations as a symbol of heroism.

Buses arrive at a small station 200m south of the main square, where you'll find the **tourist office** (daily 9am–5pm; ☎07184/2191) and a **museum centre** (Wed–Sun 9.30am–5.30pm; ☎07184/2191) selling tickets for Koprivshtitsa's six house museums. The entry fee for each museum is 3Lv, but you can buy a combined ticket covering entry to all six for 5Lv; if the centre is closed, you can buy the combined ticket at any of the museums, and it's also possible to hire an English-speaking guide for a two-hour tour (15Lv). All of the museums are open 9.30am–5.30pm, with half of them closing on Mondays, and the other half on Tuesdays.

A street running off to the west of the main square leads to the **Oslekov House** (closed Mon), where pillars of cedar wood support a facade decorated with scenes of Italian cities. Its Summer Guest Room is particularly impressive, with a vast wooden ceiling carved with geometric motifs. Further along, the street joins ul Debelyanov, which straddles a hill between two bridges and boasts some more lovely buildings. Near the Surlya Bridge is the birthplace of the poet **Dimcho Debelyanov** (closed Mon), who is buried in the grounds of the hilltop **Church of the Holy Virgin**, just to the south. Built in 1817 and partly sunk into the ground to comply with Ottoman restrictions, the church contains icons by nineteenth-century artist Zahari Zograf. A gate at the rear of the churchyard leads to the birthplace of **Todor Kableshkov** (closed Mon), leader of the local rebels. Kableshkov's house now displays weapons used in the Rising and features a wonderful circular vestibule. Continuing south, cross the **Bridge of the First Shot**, which spans the Byala Reka stream, and head up ul Nikola Belodezhdov, and you'll come to the **Lyutov House** (closed Tues), once home to a wealthy yoghurt merchant and today housing some of Koprivshtitsa's most sumptuous interiors. The house is especially notable for its colourful murals depicting palaces, temples and world cities. On the opposite side of the River Topolnitsa at the southern end of the village, steps lead up to the birthplace of another major figure in the Rising, **Georgi Benkovski** (closed Tues). A tailor by profession, he made the insurgents' uniforms and famous silk banner embroidered with the Bulgarian Lion and "Liberty or Death!" as well as commanding a rebel band on Mount Eledzhik, which fought its way north until it was wiped out near Teteven. Returning towards the main square along the eastern bank of the river, you'll find the birthplace of **Lyuben Karavelov** (closed Tues), who published émigré newspapers from exile in Bucharest, advocating armed struggle against the Ottomans. His printing press and other oddments are on display.

The tourist office (see p.239) books **private rooms** in charming village houses (❶). The nearby *Trayanova Kâshta* (℡07184/3057; ❷), just up the street from the Oslekov House, has delightful rooms in the National Revival style, while *Zdravets*, near the Lyutov House at ul Nikola Belovezhdov 3 (℡07184/2286; ❷), has neat modern rooms in an attractive wooden house with a large garden. For **eating and drinking**, the best places to sample traditional food are the *Dyado Liben Inn*, in a fine nineteenth-century mansion opposite the main square, and *Lomeva Kâshta*, a folk-style restaurant just north of the square.

## Veliko Târnovo

With its dramatic medieval fortifications and huddles of antique houses teetering over the lovely River Yantra, **VELIKO TÂRNOVO** holds a uniquely important place in the minds of Bulgarians. When the National Assembly met here to draft Bulgaria's first constitution in 1879, it did so in the former capital of the Second Kingdom (1185–1396), whose civilization was snuffed out by the Turks. It was here, too, that the Communists chose to proclaim the People's Republic in 1944.

Modern Târnovo centres on **Ploshtad Mayka Bâlgariya**: from here bul Nezavisimost (which becomes ul Stefan Stambolov after a few hundred metres) heads northeast into a network of narrow streets that curve above the River Yantra and mark out the old town, with its photogenic houses. Alleyways climb from Stefan Stambolov to the peaceful old **Varosh Quarter**, where you'll find a couple of nineteenth-century churches. Continuing along Stefan Stambolov, you'll notice steps leading downhill to ul General Gurko; don't miss the **Sarafina House** at no. 88 (Mon–Fri 9am–noon & 1–6pm; 4Lv), whose elegant restored interior is notable for its splendid octagonal vestibule and a panelled rosette ceiling. Rejoining Stefan Stambolov and continuing downhill, you'll find the blue-and-white building where the first Bulgarian parliament assembled in 1879. It's now home to the **Museum of the Bulgarian Renaissance and Constituent Assembly** (Mon & Wed–Sun 8am–noon & 1–6pm; 4Lv), where you can see a reconstruction of the original assembly hall, and a collection of icons. From here, Ivan Vazov leads directly to the medieval fortress, **Tsarevets** (daily 8am–7pm; 4Lv). The boyars Petâr and Asen led a successful rebellion against Byzantium from this citadel in 1185, and Tsarevets remained the centre of Bulgarian power until 1393, when, after a three-month siege, it fell to the Turks. The partially restored fortress is entered via the **Asenova Gate** halfway along the western ramparts. To the right, paths lead round to **Baldwin's Tower**, where Baldwin of Flanders, the so-called Latin Emperor of Byzantium, was incarcerated by Tsar Kaloyan. Above lie the ruins of the royal palace and a reconstruction of the thirteenth-century Church of the Blessed Saviour.

All **trains** between Sofia and Varna stop at Gorna Oryahovitsa, from where local trains and frequent buses cover the remaining 13km to Veliko Târnovo, although it is much easier to travel here by bus directly from Sofia or Varna. From Târnovo train station, 2km south of the city centre, buses #4 and #13 run to pl Mayka Bâlgariya, where you'll find a **tourist office** (Mon–Fri 8am—6pm, summer also Sat 8am–6pm; ☎062/600768) and 24-hour **Internet** access nearby at Matrix at Nezavisimost 32. The *Comfort* **hotel**, in the Varosh quarter at ul Paneyot Tipografov 5 (☎062/628728; ❸), is a spotless, family-run place, with splendid views of the Tsarevets. Just up the road from here at Rezervoarska 91 is the friendly *Hikers Hostel* (☎088/9691661, ⓦwww.hikers-hostel.org; €10 per person) which offers yet more striking views, along with excellent dorm accommodation, free Internet access and kitchen. The best **restaurants** are the traditional *mehanas* off Stefan Stambolov – try *Mecha Dupka*, which serves authentic Bulgarian fare in a cellar below ul Rakovski, often with music and dancing. The popular *Shastlivetsa* restaurant, at Stambolov 79, also serves local dishes, as well as a large range of pizzas and pastas. A good cheap option – with a great view – is the *Rich* restaurant, down some steps off Stefan Stambolov at ul Yantra 1. For **drinking**, there are numerous cafés and bars around town; *Yasna*, on pl Slaveykov, is a good spot for coffee or cocktails.

# The Black Sea coast

Bulgaria's **Black Sea** resorts have been popular holiday haunts for more than a century, though it wasn't until the 1960s that the coastline was developed for mass tourism, with Communist party officials from across the former Eastern Bloc descending on the beaches each year for a spot of socialist fun in the sun. Since then, the **resorts** have mushroomed, growing increasingly sophisticated as the prototype mega-complexes have been followed by holiday villages. With fine weather practically guaranteed, the selling of the coast has been a success in economic terms, but with the exception of ancient **Sozopol** and touristy **Nesebâr**, there's little to please the eye. Of the coast's two cities – **Varna** and **Burgas** – the former is by far preferable as a base for getting to the less-developed spots.

## Varna

**VARNA**'s origins date back almost five millennia, but it wasn't until seafaring Greeks founded a colony here in 585 BC that the town became a port. The modern city is used by both commercial freighters and the navy, as well as being a popular tourist resort in its own right. It's a cosmopolitan place, and nice to stroll through: Baroque, nineteenth-century and contemporary architecture are pleasantly blended with shady promenades and a handsome seaside park.

Social life revolves around **Ploshtad Nezavisimost**, where the opera house and theatre provide a backdrop for restaurants and cafés. The square is the starting point of Varna's evening promenade, which flows eastward from here along bul Knyaz Boris I and towards bul Slivnitsa and the seaside gardens. Beyond the opera house, Varna's main lateral boulevard cuts through pl Mitropolit Simeon to the domed **Cathedral of the Assumption**. Constructed in 1886, it contains a splendid iconostasis and bishop's throne, with armrests carved in the form of magnificent winged panthers. The **Archeology Museum** on the corner of Mariya Luiza and Slivnitsa (Tues–Sun 10am–5pm; winter closed Sun; 4Lv) houses one of Bulgaria's finest collections of antiquities. Most impressive are the skeletons and gold jewellery, some dating back almost 6000 years, recovered from a Neolithic necropolis on the outskirts of town. There's also an array of Greek and Roman artefacts, including an extensive display of funerary sculpture, and a gallery of icons.

South of the centre, on ul Han Krum, are the extensive remains of the third-century **Roman baths**, which played a central role in the social life of the city. It's still possible to discern the various bathing areas and the once huge exercise hall. Ten minutes west of here on ul Panagyurishte is the **Ethnographic Museum** (Tues–Sun 10am–5pm; 2Lv), where you can see displays illustrating traditional local crafts, folk costumes and reconstructions of nineteenth-century interiors. At the southern edge of the Sea Gardens, the **Navy Museum** (Mon–Fri 10am–5pm; 2Lv) houses a musty collection of naval relics, with some rusting armaments, including a couple of helicopters, in the gardens. Meanwhile, the boat responsible for the Bulgarian Navy's only victory – the *Drazki* – is embedded in the pavement outside; it sank the Turkish cruiser *Hamidie* off Cape Kaliakra in 1912.

### Practicalities

Each of the main points of arrival has good bus connections with the centre: the **bus terminal** (bus #1, #22 or #41) is a ten-minute journey northwest on bul Vladislav Varnenchik; Varna **airport** is about a 50-minute ride (#409) in the same direction; and the **train station** is ten minutes' walk south along ul Tsar Simeon.

**Private rooms** in central Varna (❶) can be obtained from Astra Tour in the railway station (daily; summer 7am–10pm; winter 9am-6pm ☎052/605861, ✉astratur@yahoo.com). Alternatively, you could try Victorina, across the road at Tsar Simeon 36v (daily 9am–5pm; winter closed Sat & Sun; ☎052/603541, ✉victorina_m@top.bg), which also sells a good city map. The central *Flag Hostel*, Opalchenska 25 (☎052/648877, ✉flagvarna@yahoo.com; €10 per person) is brand-new and friendly, with 18 beds and kitchen access. **Hotels** in Varna are generally expensive, but the best of the cheaper options are the *Three Dolphins*, near the train station at ul Gabrovo 27 (☎052/600911, ✉three_dolphins@abv.bg; ❸), which has a pleasant café downstairs, whilst centrally located *Astra* at Opolchenska 9 has excellent en-suite rooms (☎052/630524; ❸).

Varna has no shortage of **eating and drinking** venues. For authentic Bulgarian dishes, try *Arkitekt*, a traditionally furnished wooden town house with a pleasant courtyard garden at ul Musala 10, while for a more American theme, the *Happy Bar and Grill* on Ploshtad Nezavisimost is a good bet. There are plenty of other bars to choose from along bul Knyaz Boris I, while in summer, the **beach**, reached by steps from the Sea Gardens, is lined with open-air bars, fish restaurants and a seemingly unending strip of nightclubs. Outside high season, though, it's pretty dismal. For **Internet** access, try Doom, ul 27 July 13, or Cyber X, Knyaz Boris I 53, both open 24 hours.

# Burgas and around

The south coast's prime urban centre and transport hub, **BURGAS**, can be reached by train from Sofia and Plovdiv, or by bus from Varna, and provides easy access to the picture-postcard town of Nesebâr to the north and Sozopol to the south. Burgas's train and bus stations are both located at the southern edge of town, near the port. Bypassed by most tourists, the pedestrianized city centre, lined with smart boutiques, bars and cafés, is pleasant enough, though Burgas's best features are the well-manicured **Sea Gardens**, overlooking the beach and its rusting pier at the eastern end of town. If you want to stay, contact Dimant, ul Tsar Simeon 15 (street sign reads Republikanska; Mon–Sat: summer 8.30am–8.30pm; winter 8.30am–6.30pm; ☎056/840779, ✆dimant91@abv.bg), which can book **private rooms** (**①**). The city's few **hotels** are pricey; *Hotel Elite*, ul. Morska 35 (☎056/845780; **❸**) is the only reasonable hotel in the town centre.

## Nesebâr

Founded by Greek colonists from Megara, **NESEBÂR** – 35km northeast of Burgas and served by buses every twenty minutes – grew into a thriving port during the Byzantine era, and ownership alternated between Bulgaria and Byzantium until the Ottomans captured it in 1453. The town remained an important centre of Greek culture and the seat of a bishop under Turkish rule, which left Nesebâr's **Byzantine churches** reasonably intact. Nowadays the town depends on them for its tourist appeal, demonstrated by the often overwhelming stream of summer visitors crossing the man-made isthmus that connects the old town with the mainland. Outside the hectic summer season, the place seems eerily deserted, with little open other than a few sleepy cafés.

Buses arrive at either the harbour at the western end of town, or further up Han Krum before turning around to head for the nearby Sunny Beach resort. The **Archeological Museum** (summer daily 8am–8pm; winter Mon–Fri 9am–5pm; 2.50Lv) stands just inside the city gates and has an array of Greek tombstones and medieval icons on display, as well as an intriguing small Hellenistic statue showing a triple image of Hecate, goddess of witches. Immediately beyond the museum is **Christ Pantokrator**, the first of Nesebâr's churches, currently in use as an art shop. Dating from the fourteenth century, its ceramic inlays and red-brick motifs are characteristic of late Byzantine architecture, and it features an unusual frieze of swastikas – an ancient symbol of the sun and continual change. Downhill on ul Mitropolitska is the eleventh-century church of **St John the Baptist** (now an art gallery), only one of whose frescoes – a seventeenth-century depiction of St Marina – still survives. Overhung by half-timbered houses, ul Aheloi branches off from ul Mitropolitska towards the **Church of Sveti Spas** (summer only: Mon–Fri 10am–1.30pm & 2–5.30pm, Sat & Sun 10am–1.30pm; 2Lv), outwardly unremarkable but filled with seventeenth-century frescoes. Down an alley from here are the now ruined **Church of the Archangels Michael and Gabriel** and the **Church of Sveta Paraskeva**, patterned with green ceramic inlays. A few steps to the east lies the ruined **Old Metropolitan Church**, dominating a plaza filled with pavement cafés and street traders. The church itself dates back to the sixth century, and it was here that bishops officiated during the city's heyday. South of the town's main street, down ul Ribarska, lies the **New Metropolitan Church** (Sveti Stefan; daily 9am–1pm & 2–6pm; 2Lv), whose interior fresco of the Forty Martyrs, on the west wall, gives pride of place to the patron who financed the church's enlargement during the fifteenth century. Downhill from here is the ruined **Church of St John Aliturgetos**, standing in splendid isolation beside the shore and representing the zenith of Byzantine architecture in Bulgaria. Its exterior employs limestone, red bricks, crosses, mussel shells and ceramic plaques for decoration.

**Accommodation** can be hard to come by during the busy summer season, and advance bookings are advisable. **Private rooms** (**❷**), many in fine old houses, can be booked through Messemvria, Messembria 10 (☎0554/45880, ⓔmessemvria@tourism.bg), near St John Baptist church. *Hotel Tony*, at ul Kraybrezhna 20 (☎0554/42403; ❷), and the nearby, summer-only *Hotel Rai*, at ul Sadala 7 (☎0554/46094; ❷), are small and comfortable family-run pensions on the northern side of the peninsula. There are plenty of places to **eat**, although most restaurants are aimed at the passing tourist crowd, serving predictably mediocre food. Two of the better options are the *Kapetanska Sreshta*, overlooking the harbour, and the sea-facing *Neptun*, towards the far end of town. Snacks are available from summertime kiosks along the waterfront.

## Sozopol

**SOZOPOL**, the oldest settlement in Bulgaria, was founded in the seventh century BC by Greek colonists from Miletus, who called the town Apollonia and prospered by trading textiles and wine for honey and corn. The town's charm owes much to its **architecture**, the old wooden houses jostling for space, their upper storeys almost meeting across the town's narrow cobbled streets. Today it's a busy fishing port and holiday resort, especially popular with East European tourists. The **Archeological Museum** (summer 8am–5pm; winter 8am–noon; 2Lv) behind the library holds a worthwhile collection of ancient ceramics, as well as a number of artefacts uncovered in the local area. Further into the town, follow the signs to the **Southern Fortress Wall and Tower Complex** (summer only, 10am–7pm; 4Lv) which gives access to a beautifully restored defence tower dating from the 4th century BC. Half-hourly **buses** from Burgas arrive at the southern edge of the old town. **Accommodation** can be even harder to find during summer than in Nesebâr, and most places shut down for the rest of the year. The Amon-Ra bureau at ul Republikanska 1, in the new part of town (irregular hours; ☎05502/2208), can arrange rooms (❷). Right next door to the bureau, at Republikanska 3, is a private guesthouse with balconies and en-suite bathrooms (☎05502/3021; ❷). Along the same street, *Alfa-Beta*, at no. 9 (☎05502/3021; ❷), is a small pension with a pleasant breakfast garden. The *Poseidon*, ul Apoloniya 7, and the *Vyatarna Melnitsa*, ul Morski Skali 27, are a couple of good, if touristy **restaurants**.

# Travel details

| Trains | Buses |
|---|---|
| **Gorna Oryahovitsa** to: Veliko Târnovo (10 daily; 20min). **Plovdiv** to: Burgas (4–6 daily; 4–5hr); Sofia (13 daily; 2hr–3hr 30min); Varna (3 daily; 5hr). **Septemvri** to: Bansko (2 daily; 5hr). **Sofia** to: Blagoevgrad (6 daily; 2hr 30min–3hr 30min); Burgas (5 daily; 6–8hr); Gorna Oryahovitsa (10 daily; 4hr 30min); Koprivshtitsa (4 daily; 1hr 50min); Plovdiv (13 daily; 2hr–3hr 30min); Septemvri (16 daily; 1hr 30min–2hr 15min); Varna (6 daily; 8–9hr). | **Blagoevgrad** to: Bansko (hourly; 1hr 20min); Rila village (hourly; 40min); Sofia (5 daily; 1hr 30min). **Burgas** to: Nesebâr (every 20min; 50min); Sozopol (every 30min; 40min); Varna (hourly; 3hr). **Gorna Oryahovitsa** to: Veliko Târnovo (every 15min; 30min). **Plovdiv** to: Bachkovo (hourly; 40min); Sofia (hourly; 2hr). **Rila village** to: Rila Monastery (4 daily; 30min). **Sofia** to: Bansko (10 daily; 3hr); Burgas (8 daily; 7hr); Koprivshtitsa (1–2 daily; 2hr); Plovdiv (hourly; 2hr); Rila village (2 daily; 2hr); Varna (hourly; 6hr); Veliko Târnovo (every 30min; 3hr). |

# Croatia

# Croatia highlights

✴ **Amphitheatre, Pula** This magnificent arena is the sixth largest in the world. See p.256

✴ **Diocletian's Palace, Split** This extraordinary 1700-year-old palace houses shops, restaurants and bars, as well as some fascinating remains. See p.259

✴ **Windsurfing, Bol** The Adriatic's most attractive beaches also provide the best windsurfing opportunities. See p.261

✴ **Vis Island** One of the coast's lushest and most peaceful islands. See p.263

✴ **City Walls, Dubrovnik** Sensational views of the Old Town and the Adriatic from the 25-metre high city walls. See p.266

✴ **Dubrovnik Summer Festival** Classical concerts and theatre at Croatia's most prestigious festival. See p.265

△ Dubrovnik

# Introduction and basics

An independent kingdom in the tenth century, **Croatia** (Hrvatska) was subsequently absorbed by the Austro-Hungarian Empire before becoming part of the new state of Yugoslavia in 1918. Under Communist rule (from 1945), it declared its independence in 1991. War raged until 1995, when a return to stability saw tourists flooding back to a country that boasts one of Europe's finest stretches of coastline, and an array of impressive architecture, dating back to Roman times.

The capital, **Zagreb**, is a lively central European metropolis, combining elegant nineteenth-century architecture with plenty of cultural diversions and a vibrant café scene. The peninsula of **Istria** contains many of the country's most developed resorts, with old Venetian towns like **Rovinj** rubbing shoulders with the raffish port of **Pula**. Further south lies **Dalmatia**, a dramatic, mountain-fringed stretch of coastline studded with islands. Dalmatia's main towns are **Zadar**, an Italianate peninsula town, and **Split**, an ancient Roman settlement and modern port which provides a jumping-off point to a series of enchanting **islands**. South of Split lies the medieval walled city of **Dubrovnik**, site of an important festival in the summer and a magical place to be, whatever the season.

## Information & maps

Most towns of any size have a **tourist office** (*turističke informacije*) which will happily give out brochures and local maps; English is widely spoken in these places. Few offices book private rooms, but they will at least direct you to an agency that does. Freytag & Berndt produce a good 1:600,000 **map** of Croatia, Slovenia and Bosnia-Herzegovina, as well as 1:100,000 regional maps of Istria and the Dalmatian coast.

## Money and banks

The local currency is the **kuna** (kn), which is divided into 100 lipa. There are coins of 1, 2, 5, 10, 20 and 50 lipa, and 1kn, 2kn and 5kn; and notes of 5kn, 10kn, 20kn, 50kn, 100kn, 200kn, 500kn and 1000kn. Accommodation and ferry prices are often quoted in euros, but you still pay in kuna. **Banks** (*banka*) are open Mon–Fri 9am–5pm (sometimes with longer hours in the summer), Sat 7.30am–1pm. Money can also be changed in post offices, travel agencies and **exchange bureaux** (*mjenjačnica*). Credit cards are accepted in a large number of hotels and restaurants, and you can use them to get cash from ATMs. At the time of writing, €1 was equal to around 7kn, $1 to 6kn, and £1 to 11kn.

## Communications

**Post offices** (*pošta* or HPT) open Mon–Fri 7/8am–8pm, Sat 8am–1pm. In big towns and resorts, some are open daily and until 10pm. Stamps (*marke*) can also be bought at newsstands.

Public **phones** use magnetic cards (*telekarta*), which come in denominations of 15kn, 25kn, 50kn and 100kn; you can

---

### Croatia on the net

ⓦ **www.adriatica.net** General info about the Adriatic resorts, and an online booking service with a wide range of apartments, villas and hotels.

ⓦ **www.croatia.hr** Croatia's tourist board site.

ⓦ **www.istra.com** Covers the Istrian peninsula.

ⓦ **www.dalmacija.net** Comprehensive coverage of the Dalmatian islands.

ⓦ **www.dubrovnik-online.com** Excellent city site, including message board.

buy these from post offices or newspaper kiosks. When making long-distance and international calls, you can also go to the post office, where you're assigned a cabin and given the bill afterwards.

**Internet access** is readily available in the capital and most towns and cities; expect to pay around 25kn per hour.

# Getting around

**Croatian Railways** (*Hrvatske željeznice*; ⓦ www.hznet.hr) runs a smooth and efficient service. Trains (*vlak*, plural *vlakovi*) are divided into *putnički* (slow ones which stop at every halt) and IC (intercity trains which are faster and more expensive). Tilting trains have recently been introduced on the Zagreb–Split line, halving the journey time. Timetables (*vozni red*) are usually displayed on boards in stations – *odlazak* means departure, *dolazak* arrival.

The **bus** network is run by a confusing array of small local companies, but services are well integrated and bus stations tend to be well-organized affairs. If you're at a big city bus station, tickets (*karta*) must be obtained from ticket windows before boarding the bus. Elsewhere, they can be bought from the driver. You'll be charged around 6kn for items of baggage to be stored in the hold.

Jadrolinija (ⓦ www.jadrolinija.hr) operates **ferry** services down the coast on the Rijeka–Split–Korčula–Dubrovnik route at least once a day in both directions between June and August, and two or three times weekly for the rest of the year. Rijeka to Dubrovnik is a 22-hour journey, involving one night on the boat. In addition, ferries, and faster catamarans, link Split with the islands of Brač, Hvar, Vis and Korčula. Ferries are also a good way of moving on from Croatia, with connections to Italy (Split and Zadar to Ancona, Pula and Rovinj to Trieste, Dubrovnik to Bari, Rovinj to Venice). Fares are reasonable for short trips: Split to Hvar costs around €4. For longer journeys, prices vary greatly according to the level of comfort you require. Book in advance for longer journeys wherever possible; addresses and phone numbers are provided in the text where relevant.

# Accommodation

**Private rooms** (*privatne sobe*) have long been the mainstay of Croatian tourism. Bookings are made through the local tourist office or private travel agencies (usually open daily 8am–8/9pm in summer. Prices are around €20/150kn per person for a simple double sharing a toilet and bathroom, €25/200kn for a double with en-suite facilities; stays of less than three nights are often subject to a surcharge of thirty percent or over. Places fill up quickly in July and August, when it's a good idea to arrive early or book ahead. Single travellers will sometimes find it difficult to get a room at all at this time, unless they're prepared to pay the price of a double; at other times, you could expect to get a thirty percent discount on the room rate. It's very likely you'll be offered rooms by elderly ladies waiting outside train, bus and ferry stations, particularly in southern Dalmatia. Don't be afraid to take a room offered in this manner, but be sure to establish the location of the room and agree a price before setting off. If taking a room this way expect to pay around twenty percent less than you would with an agency. However you find a room, you can usually examine it before committing to paying for it.

Croatian **hotels** are generally modern multi-storey affairs providing modern comforts but little atmosphere. One-star hotels have rooms with shared toilet and bathroom; two-stars have rooms with en-suite facilities; three-stars have slightly larger en-suite rooms and, most probably, a TV; while four- and five-stars are in the international luxury bracket. One-star establishments are in short supply, however, and in most places you'll be dependent on two-star hotels, where you should expect to pay €50–70/400–550kn for a double room. In addition to hotels, there's a growing number of family-run **pensions**, offering 2- or 3-star comforts at a slightly cheaper price – €40–60/300–450kn a double being the average.

HI **hostels** are thin on the ground, although those that exist – mostly in the big cities – are generally clean and well run. You can get details, and make reservations, from Hrvatski Ferijalni i Hostelski Savez, Dežmanova 9, Zagreb (☏ 01/48-47-474, ⓦ www.hfhs.hr).

|  | Croatian | Pronunciation |
|---|---|---|
| Yes | *Da* | Dah |
| No | *Ne* | Neh |
| Please | *Molim* | Mo-leem |
| Thank you | *Hvala* | Hvahlah |
| Hello/Good day | *Bog/Dobar dan* | Dobahr dan |
| Goodbye | *Bog/Dovidjenja* | Doh veedehnyah |
| Excuse me | *Izvinite* | Izvineet |
| Where? | *Gdje* | Gdyeh |
| Good | *Dobro* | Dobroh |
| Bad | *Loše* | Losheh |
| Near | *Blizu* | Bleezoo |
| Far | *Daleko* | Dalekoh |
| Cheap | *Jeftino* | Yeftinoh |
| Expensive | *Skupo* | Skoopoh |
| Open | *Otvoreno* | Otvoreenoh |
| Closed | *Zatvoreno* | Zatvoreenoh |
| Today | *Danas* | Danass |
| Yesterday | *Juče* | Yoocheh |
| Tomorrow | *Sutra* | Sootrah |
| How much is....? | *Koliko stoji...?* | Koleekoh sto-yee? |
| What time is it? | *Koliko je sati?* | Koleekoh yeh satee? |
| I don't understand | *Ne razumijem* | Neh rahzoomeeyehm |
| Do you speak English? | *Govorite li engleski?* | Govoreeteh lee ehngleskee? |
| One | *Jedan* | Yehdan |
| Two | *Dva* | Dvah |
| Three | *Tri* | Tree |
| Four | *Četiri* | Cheteeree |
| Five | *Pet* | Pet |
| Six | *Šest* | Shest |
| Seven | *Sedam* | Sedam |
| Eight | *Osam* | Osam |
| Nine | *Devet* | Devet |
| Ten | *Deset* | Deset |

In addition, student rooms are often let out cheap to travellers during the summer vacation (usually mid-July to Aug). For both, expect to pay €40–50/300–400kn for a double room. **Campsites** (most open May–Sept) abound on the Adriatic coast, and tend to be large-scale, well-appointed affairs with plentiful facilities, restaurants and shops. Two people travelling with a tent can expect to pay roughly €15–20/50–100kn each.

# Food and drink

There's a varied and distinctive range of **cuisine** on offer, largely because Croatia straddles two culinary cultures: the fish- and seafood-dominated cuisine of the Mediterranean and the hearty meat-oriented fare of central Europe.

Basic **self-catering** and picnic ingredients such as cheese (*sir*), vegetables (*povrće*) and fruit (*voće*) can be bought at supermarkets (*samoposluga*) or open-air markets (*tržnica*). Bread (*kruh*) is bought from either a supermarket or a *pekarna* (bakery). For breakfasts and fast food, look out for street stalls or snack-food outlets selling *burek*, a flaky pastry filled with cheese; or grilled meats such as *ćevapčići* (rissoles of minced beef, pork or lamb), and *pljeskavica* (a hamburger-like mixture of the same meats).

For a more relaxed, sit-down meal, a **restaurant** menu (*jelovnik*) will usually include speciality starters such as *pršut* (home-cured ham) and *paški sir* (piquant hard cheese), as well as a range of soups (*juha*). Typical main courses include *punjene paprike* (peppers stuffed with rice and meat), *gulaš* (goulash) or some kind of *odrezak* (fillet of meat, often pan-fried), usually either *svinjski* (pork) or *teleški* (veal). *Mješano meso* is a mixed grill. Lamb, often roasted, is *janjetina*. Traditional dishes from the area around Zagreb include *purica z mlincima* (turkey with pasta noodles) and *strukli* (ravioli-like blobs of pasta dough with a cheese filling). One typically Dalmatian dish is *pašticada* (beef and bacon cooked in vinegar and wine). On the coast, you'll be regaled with every kind of seafood. *Riba* (fish) can come either *na žaru* (grilled) or *u pečnici* (baked). *Brodet* is a hot peppery fish stew. Otherwise, the main menu items to look out for on the coast are *lignje* (squid), *škampi* (unpeeled prawns eaten with the fingers), *rakovica* (crab), *oštrige* (oysters), *kalamari* (squid), *školjke* (mussels) and *jastog* (lobster); *crni rizoto* is risotto with squid. No town is without at least one pizzeria, serving good stone-baked pizzas, making them the cheapest, tastiest places to eat and also the easiest, if not the most imaginative, sources of a **vegetarian** meal. Typical **desserts** include *palačinke* (pancakes), *voćna salata* (fruit salad) and *sladoled* (ice cream).

### Drink

Daytime **drinking** takes place in a *kavana* (café) or a *slastičarnica* (patisserie). Coffee (*kava*) is usually served black unless specified otherwise – ask for *mlijeko* (milk) or *šlag* (cream). Tea (*čaj*) is widely available, but is drunk without milk. Night-time drinking takes place in a growing number of small *kafići* or café/bars. Croatian **beer** (*pivo*) is of the light lager variety; Karlovačko and Ožujsko are two good local brands to look out for. The local **wine** (*vino*) is consistently

good and reasonably cheap. In Dalmatia there are some pleasant whites, crisp dry wines such as Kastelet, Grk and Posip, as well as reds such as the dark heady Dingač and Babić. In Istria, Semion is a bone-dry white, and Teran a light fresh red. Local spirits include *loza*, a clear grape-based spirit; *travarica*, herbal brandy; *vinjak*, locally produced cognac, and *Maraskino*, a cherry liqueur from Dalmatia.

# Opening hours and holidays

Most **shops** open Mon–Fri 8am–8pm, Sat 8am–1pm, although many supermarkets, outdoor markets and the like are open daily 7am–7pm. **Museum and gallery** times vary from place to place, although most are closed Mon. All shops and banks are closed on the following **public holidays**: Jan 1, Jan 6, Easter Mon, May 1, Corpus Christi, June 22, June 24, Aug 5, Aug 15, Oct 8, Nov 1, & Dec 25 & 26.

# Emergencies

The crime rate is low by European standards. **Police** (*policija*) are generally helpful when dealing with holiday-makers, although they can be slow when filling out reports. They also often make routine checks on identity cards and other documents; always carry your passport. **Hospital** treatment is free to EU citizens. **Pharmacies** (*ljekarna*) tend to follow normal shopping hours, and a rota system covers night-time and weekend opening; details are posted in the window of each pharmacy.

### Emergency numbers

Police ☏92; Fire ☏93; Ambulance ☏94; Sea rescue and diving alert ☏9155.

# Zagreb

Capital of an independent state since 1991, **ZAGREB** has served as the cultural and political focus of Croatia since the Middle Ages. The city grew out of two medieval communities, Kaptol, to the east, and Gradec, to the west, each sited on a hill and divided by a river long since dried up but nowadays marked by a street known as Tkalčićeva. Zagreb grew rapidly in the nineteenth century, and the majority of its buildings are relatively well-preserved, grand, peach-coloured monuments to the self-esteem of the Austro-Hungarian Empire. Nowadays, with a population topping one million, Zagreb is the trendy, boisterous capital of a newly self-confident nation. A handful of good museums and a vibrant nightlife ensure that a few days here will be well spent.

## Arrival, information and city transport

Zagreb's central **train station** is on Tomislavov Trg, on the southern edge of the city centre, a ten-minute walk from Trg bana Jelačića, the main square. The main **bus station** is a fifteen-minute walk east of the train station, at the junction of Branimirova and Držićeva – trams #2, #3 and #6 run between the two stations, with #6 continuing to the main square. Zagreb **airport** is 10km southeast of the city; Croatia Airlines buses run to the main bus station (7am–8pm, every 30min; 25kn). There are two **tourist offices** in central Zagreb; the main one is at Trg bana Jelačića 11 (Mon–Fri 8.30am–8pm, Sat 9am–5pm, Sun 10am–2pm; ☎01/48-14-051, ☒www.zagreb-touristinfo.hr), the other is at Trg N. Zrinskog 14 (Mon, Weds & Fri 9am–5pm; Tues & Thurs 9am–6pm, Sat & Sun 9am–6pm; ☎01/49-21-645). Both sell the **Zagreb Card** (72hr, 90kn), which gives unlimited city transport and good discounts in museums and restaurants. The superb and free *Zagreb In Your Pocket* (☒www.inyourpocket.com), available from the tourist offices, hotels and shops, is by far the best source of information on the city.

Zagreb has an efficient and comprehensive **tram** network and, to a lesser extent, **bus** network, though much of the city centre can easily be seen on foot. Flat-fare tram and bus **tickets** (*karte*) are sold from cigarette and newspaper kiosks (6.50kn) or from the driver (8kn). Day tickets (*dnevne karte*) cost 18kn. Validate your ticket by punching it in the machines on board the trams. The train station and Trg bana Jelačića are the two main hubs of the city transport system.

## Accommodation

Zagreb has very little in the way of budget accommodation. **Private rooms** (❸) can be arranged through the Evistas agency at Šenoe 28, midway between the train and bus stations (Mon–Fri 9am–8pm, Sat 9.30am–5pm; ☎01/48-39-546, ✉evistas@zg.htnet.hr). In addition to the hostels listed below, some **student rooms** are available (mid-July to late Sept only; ❹). The two main locations are at Cvijetno naselje, Odranska 8 (☎01/61-91-245; tram #14 or #17 from Trg bana Jelačića), and Stjepan Radić, Jarunska 2 (☎01/36-34-255; tram #17 from Trg bana Jelačića). The nearest **campsite** (☎01/65-30-444, ☒www.motel-plitvice.hr) is 10km southwest of town at the *Plitvice Motel* beside the main Zagreb–Ljubljana motorway; there's no public transport to it.

### Hostels

**Bagaj** Trg bana Jelačića 1 ☎01/48-35-865 ☒www.bagaj.hr. Great little hostel located in the Aplo Language Centre right on the main square. Open July and Aug. 110kn per person.

**Omladinski Hostel** Petrinjska 77 ☎01/48-41-

261. Large, run-down hostel near the train station. A little better than sleeping in the station itself. 80kn per person.

**Ravnice Hostel 1.** Ravnice 38b ☎01/233-23-25, ☒www.ravnice-youth-hostel.hr. Fabulous, welcoming hostel east of the centre. Tram #4,

**ZAGREB**

Museum of Zagreb ❶
Popov Toranj
GORNJI GRAD

Meštrović Atelier ■

St Mark's
Croatian Parliament
Ribnjak
Historical Museum
RADICEV TRG
Kamenita Vrata
Gallery of Naïve Art
GRADEC ❷
Cathedral ❸
JEZUITSKI TRG
Archbishop's Palace
Kula Lotrščak ❹
Funicular
Dolac Market
KAPTOL
VLASKA

ILICA
TRG BANA JELACICA ℹ
JURISICEVA
MARTICEVA

PRERADOVICEV TRG
BOGOVICEVA
TESLINA
TRG JOZE VLANOVICA

VARSAVSKA
MASARYKOVA
Archeological Museum

Museum of Art and Crafts
DONJI GRAD
TRG NIKOLE ZRINSKOG
➕ Hospital
TRG ZRTAVA
FAŠIZMA
ZVONIMIROVA

TRG MARSALA TITA
National Theatre
ℹ
BOSKOVICEVA

ROOSEVELTOV TRG
MAZURANICEV TRG
HEBRANGOVA

Ethnographic Museum
ŽERJAVICEVA
STROSSMAYEROV TRG
HATZOVA
KNEZA BORNE

Mimara Museum
MARULICEV TRG
Art Pavilion
TOMI-SLAVOV TRG
SENOE
PALMOTICEVA

SAVSKA CESTA
VODNIKOVA
PRERADOVICEVA
MIHANOVICEVA
Train Station
BRANIMIROVA
Bus Station

Botanic Gardens

0   250 m

N

**EATING & DRINKING**

| | | | |
|---|---|---|---|
| Boban | 11 | Nokturno | 2 |
| Bulldog | 13 | Pivnica | |
| Cantinetta | 12 | Medvedgrad | 17 |
| Club Havana | 15 | Pod Grickim | |
| Dobar Zvuk | 16 | Topom | 5 |
| Hemingway | 6 | Purger | 14 |
| K.&K | 10 | Rubelj | 9 |
| Kerempuh | 3 | Tolkien's | 4 |
| Makronova | 8 | Vincek | 7 |
| Melin Monroe | 1 | | |

**ACCOMMODATION**

| | |
|---|---|
| Bagaj | C |
| Dora | G |
| Ilica | D |
| Jadran | B |
| Omladinski Hostel | E |
| Ravnice Hostel | A |
| Slisko | F |

#11, #12 or #7 to the Ravnice stop, by the Kraš chocolate factory, then five minutes' walk south along 1. Ravnice. 112kn per person.

### Hotels

**Dora** Trnjanska 11f ☎01/63-11-900, @www .zug.hr. This simple but cheery place, ten minutes' walk south of the train station (via the subterranean Importanne shopping mall), has clean, wood-furnished rooms. Breakfast included. ❻

**Ilica** Ilica 102 ☎01/37-77-522, @www.hotel-ilica .hr. Modern, smart and friendly hotel with en-suite rooms and apartments 1.5km west of the main square. Popular, so book in advance. ❺

**Jadran** Vlaška 50 ☎01/45-53-777, @www .hup-zagreb.hr. Cheapest of the central hotels, with en-suite rooms. Just east of the city centre and fifteen minutes' walk from the train station at the top end of Draskovićeva. ❼

**Slisko** Supilova 13 ☎01/61-84-777, @www .slisko.hr. Clean, comfortable and welcoming hotel, 300m east of the main bus station. ❺

## The City

Zagreb falls neatly into three parts. **Donji Grad** or "Lower Town", which extends north from the train station to Trg bana Jelačića, the main square, is the bustling centre of the modern city. Uphill from here, to the northeast and the northwest, are the older quarters of **Kaptol** (the "Cathedral Chapter") and **Gradec** (the "Upper Town"), both peaceful districts of ancient mansions, quiet squares and leafy parks.

### Donji Grad

**Tomislavov Trg**, opposite the train station, is the first in a series of three shaded, green squares that form the backbone of the lower town. Its main attraction is the **Art Pavilion** (Mon–Sat 11am–7pm, Sun 10am–2pm; 20kn, Mondays free; ⓦwww.umjetnicki-paviljon.hr), built in 1898 and now hosting art exhibitions in its gilded stucco and mock-marble interior. There's little to divert you in the second of the squares, but beyond, in the last of the three – **Trg Nikole Zrinskog** – lies the **Archeological Museum** (Tues–Fri 10am–5pm, Sat & Sun 10am–1pm; 20kn; ⓦwww.amz.hr); the museum has pieces from prehistoric times to the Middle Ages, including pottery fragments from the fourth-century-BC Vučedol culture, ancient Roman and Greek artefacts and Egyptian antiquities.

Walk up from here and you're on **Trg bana Jelačića**, flanked by cafés, hotels and department stores, and hectic with the whizz of trams and hurrying pedestrians. The statue in the centre is of the nineteenth-century governor of Croatia, Josip Jelačić. Running west from the square, below Gradec hill, is **Ilica**, the city's main shopping street. A little way along it and off to the right, you can take a **funicular** (daily 6.30am–9pm, every 10min; 3kn) up to Strossmayerovo Šetalište; alternatively, head south via **Preradovićev Trg**, a small lively square where there's a flower market, to **Trg maršala Tita**. This is a grandiose open space, centred on the late nineteenth-century **National Theatre**, a solid ochre-coloured pile behind a water sculpture by Ivan Meštrović, the strangely erotic *Well of Life*. Across the square, the **Museum of Arts and Crafts** (Tues–Sat 10am–7pm, Sun 10am–2pm; 20kn; ⓦwww.muo.hr) boasts an impressive display of furniture, ceramics, clothes and textiles from the Renaissance to the present day. On the southern side of the square, on Mažuranićev Trg, the **Ethnographic Museum** (Tues–Thurs 10am–6pm, Fri–Sun 10am–1pm; 15kn, Thurs free) has a collection of costumes from every corner of the country, as well as an engaging heap of artefacts brought back from the South Pacific, Asia and Africa.

A couple of minutes west, on Rooseveltov Trg, lies Zagreb's most prestigious art collection, the **Mimara Museum** (Tues–Weds & Fri–Sun 10am–5pm, Thurs 10am–7pm; 20kn), housing the art and archeological collection of Ante Topić Mimara, a native of Zagreb who spent much of his life in Austria. Ground-floor exhibits include ancient glass from Egypt, Greece, Syria and the Roman Empire, and Chinese art from the Shang through to the Song dynasty. Upstairs, there's a fine collection of European paintings, including works by Rembrandt, Rubens and Renoir.

## Kaptol and Gradec

Behind Trg bana Jelačića, the filigree spires of Zagreb's **cathedral** mark the edge of the district (and street) known as **Kaptol**, ringed by the ivy-cloaked turrets of the eighteenth-century **Archbishop's Palace** – a "southern Kremlin" fancied the archeologist Arthur Evans before its destruction by an earthquake in 1880. After the disaster, the cathedral was rebuilt in neo-Gothic style, a high, bare structure inside, with very little left from the years before the earthquake. Behind the altar lies a shrine to Archbishop Stepinac, head of the Croat church in the 1940s, imprisoned by the Communists after World War II, and beatified by the Pope in 1998.

Immediately west of Kaptol, **Gradec** is the most ancient and atmospheric part of Zagreb, a leafy, tranquil backwater of tiny streets, small squares and Baroque palaces, whose mottled brown roofs peek out from the hill to the west. From Trg bana Jelačića, make your way to the **Dolac market**, which occupies several tiers immediately beyond the square; this is the city's main food-market, a feast of fruit, vegetables, meat and fish held every morning. From the far side of Dolac market, **Tkalčićeva** spears north, following the course of the river which once formed the boundary between Kaptol and Gradec. Entry to Gradec proper from here is by way of **Krvavi Most**, which connects the street with Radićeva. On the far side of Radićeva, the **Kamenita Vrata** is a gloomy tunnel with a small shrine that formed part of Gradec's original fortifications. Close by, the fourteenth-century **Kula Lotrščak** (May–Oct Tues–Sun 11am–8pm; 10kn) marks the top station of the funicular (see above). There are fantastic views from here over the rest of the city and the plains beyond. North of the tower, the **Gallery of Naive Art**, Ćirilometodska 3 (Tues–Fri 10am–6pm, Sat & Sun 10am–1pm; 10kn; ⊛www .hmnu.org), is an impressive collection of work by peasant artists. At the northern end of Ćirilometodska, **Markov Trg** marks the centre of Gradec – fringed by government offices, the square's focus is the squat **Church of St Mark**, a much renovated place whose tiled roof displays the coats-of-arms of the constituent parts of Croatia.

Just north of Markov Trg, at Mletačka 8, is the **Meštrović Atelier** (Tues–Fri 10am–6pm, Sat & Sun 10am–2pm; 20kn), an exhibition dedicated to Croatia's most famous twentieth-century artist – in the sculptor's former home and studio. On display are sketches, photographs, memorabilia from exhibitions worldwide, and small-scale studies of his more familiar public creations. Left off Markov Trg, the **Historical Museum of Croatia**, at Matoševa 9 (Mon–Fri 10am–5pm, Sat & Sun 10am–1pm; 10kn; ⊛www.hismus.hr), is the venue for prestigious temporary exhibitions. The **Museum of Zagreb**, at Opatička 20 (Tues–Fri 10am–6pm, Sat & Sun 10am–1pm; 20kn), close to the thirteenth-century **Popov Toranj** (Priests' Tower), is perhaps the more appealing, telling the tale of Zagreb's development from medieval times to the early twentieth century with the help of paintings and lumber from the city's wealthier households, and the original seventeenth-century statues that once adorned the portals of the city's cathedral.

## Eating and drinking

Whilst not outstanding, Zagreb's **restaurant** scene is becoming more varied, and there's no shortage of budget places to eat. There's a wide range of Croatian cuisine, including several superb seafood restaurants, and any number of pizzerias. Expect to pay 50–70kn for a decent meal in any of the places listed below. For **snack food**, head to the area around Dolac market. **Picnic supplies** can be purchased from Dolac, or from the supermarkets in the subterranean Importanne shopping centre in front of the train station. Zagreb has a wealth of **cafés and bars** offering outdoor seating in the pedestrian area around Gajeva and Bogovićeva – particularly along trendy Tkalčićeva, just north of Trg bana Jelačića.

### Restaurants

**Boban** Gajeva 9. Popular and central pasta place in the vaulted basement of the stylish café of the same name.

**Cantinetta** Teslina 14. Good-quality Croatian and Italian food just south of the main square. Chic, but not too expensive. Closed Sun.

**Club Havana** Perkovčeva 2 This brilliant Cuban restaurant, located under the Press Club on a side street behind the Ethnographic Museum, has high-class food, sophisticated decor and attentive waiting staff, making It the most engaging place in town to eat. Closed Sun.

**Kerempuh** Dolac bb. Hidden away behind the main fruit-and-veg market, this is one of the best places in town to fill up on traditional Croatian pork-based favourites. Cheap lunchtime specials.

**Makronova** Ilica 72. Friendly, stylish and compact vegetarian restaurant serving imaginative and tasty fare. Shares its first-floor location with Zagreb's premier health food shop.

**Nokturno** Skalinska 4. One of the better budget eateries in the area, with good pizza and pasta and serviceable salads. In a buzzy little side street just off Tkalčićeva.

**Pivnica Medvedgrad** Savska 56. Located 1.5km southwest of the centre, this huge beer hall serves up large, cheap portions of grilled meats; the beer, brewed on the premises, is excellent, too.

**Pod Grickim Topom** Zakmardijeve stube. Good Croatian food in a cosy restaurant on the steps leading down from Strossmayerovo Šetalište to Trg bana Jelačića.

**Purger** Petrinjska 33. Great local restaurant that's not particularly stylish, but serves excellent-value Croatian dishes.

**Rubelj** Frankopanska 2 & Dolac market. Cheapest central place for simple but tasty grilled-meat standards.

### Cafés and bars

**Bulldog** Bogovićeva 6. A typically elegant Zagreb bar and pavement café, this is one of the most popular meeting places in the town centre.

**Dobar Zvuk** Gajeva 18. Popular café-bar with cheap drinks and a moderately bohemian clientele.

**Hemingway** Dežmanova. Funky cocktail bar, popular with Zagreb's smart set.

**K.&.K** Jurišićeva 3. Intimate split-level café, whose every spare inch of wall space is covered in old pictures of Zagreb.

**Melin Monroe** Košarska 19. This energetic pub is a terrific alternative to the posier establishments nearby on Tkalčićeva.

**Tolkien's** Katarinin Trg. Funky, *Lord of the Rings* inspired place on a quiet square, next to the Kula Lotršćak in Gradec.

**Vincek** Ilica 18. The very best place in town to stop for ice cream, cakes and hot chocolate.

# Nightlife

Zagreb offers a rich and varied diet of high culture, with the **National Theatre**, Trg maršala Tita 15 (ticket office Mon–Fri 10am–1pm & 5–7.30pm, Sat 10am–1pm & 90min before each performance, Sun 30min before each performance; ☎01/48-28-532, ⓦwww.hnk.hr), providing the focus for serious, Croatian-language drama, as well as opera and ballet. The city's main orchestral music venue is the **Lisinski Concert Hall** south of the train station at Trg Stjepana Radića 4 (ticket office Mon–Fri 9am–8pm, Sat 9am–2pm; ☎01/61-21-166, ⓦwww.lisinski .hr). Intimate chamber-music concerts take place at the **Croatian Musical Institute**, Gundulićeva 6 (☎01/48-30-922). The free monthly pamphlet *Events and Performances*, available from the Zagreb tourist office, contains **listings** in English of all forthcoming events. Nightlife centres on a clutch of established, and reasonably varied, **discos** and **clubs**, many presenting the best opportunities for catching live rock and jazz – check the posters plastered liberally around the city centre or pick up flyers from record shops for an idea of what's on.

## Discos and clubs

**Aquarius** Aleja Mira bb. At the eastern end of Lake Jarun, 4km southwest of the centre, this place specializes in techno and drum 'n' bass. Occasional live bands too. Thurs–Sun.

**BP Club** Teslina 7. Established jazz club and relaxed late-night drinking haunt.

**Global** Hatzova 14. Laid-back gay club with a good mix of people. Women's nights on Wednesdays, and men only Mon and Tues.

**Mocvara** Tvornica Jedinstvo building, Trnjanski nasip. Unpretentious cultural centre in an old factory on the banks of the River Sava. Live gigs (usually alternative rock), film shows and club

nights – something happening every night. Take any bus heading for Novi Zagreb and alight just before the bridge – the club is on your right.

**Saloon** Tuškanac 1a. Legendary meeting place in a leafy corner of town, 500m west of the centre. Music is an enjoyable mish-mash of commercial disco. Tues–Sat.

**Sax** Palmotićeva 22. Large, comfortable basement club, two blocks east of Trg N. Zrinskog, with live music (with a jazz bias) most nights.

**Tvornica** Šubićeva 1. Former ballroom just north of the bus station, now hosting live rock, club nights and theatre.

# Listings

**Embassies** Australia, Nova Ves 11 ☎01/48-91-200; Canada, Prilaz Gjure Deželića 4 ☎01/48-81-200; UK, Ivana Lučića 4 ☎01/60-09-100; US, Thomasa Jeffersona 2 ☎01/66-12-200.

**Exchange** In the main post office.

**Hospital** Draskovićeva 19 ☎01/46-10-011.

**Internet access** Aquarius, Kralja Držislavova 4; Art Net Club, Preradovićeva 25; Charlie's, Gajeva 4a; Sublink, Teslina 12.

**Laundry** Predom, Draškovićeva 31 (Mon–Fri 7am–7pm, Sat 8am–noon).

**Left luggage** At the train and bus stations (both 24hr).

**Pharmacy** Ilica 43 (24hr).

**Police** Petrinjska 30.

**Post offices** Branimirova 4 (24hr); Jurišićeva 13 (Mon–Fri 7am–9pm, Sat 7am–7pm, Sun 8am–2pm).

# Istria

A large peninsula jutting into the northern Adriatic, **Istria** offers Croatian tourism at its most developed. Many of the towns here were resorts in the nineteenth century, and in recent years their proximity to northern Europe has ensured an annual influx of sun-seekers from Germany, Austria and the Netherlands. Yet the growth of modern hotel complexes, sprawling campsites and (mainly concrete) beaches has done little to detract from the essential charm of the region. This stretch of the coast was under Venetian rule for 400 years and there's still a fair-sized Italian community, with Italian very much the second language. Istria's largest centre is the port city of **Pula**, which, with its Roman amphitheatre and other relics of Roman occupation, is a rewarding place to spend a couple of days. On the western side of the peninsula, the resort town of **Rovinj**, with its cobbled piazzas and shuttered houses, is almost overwhelmingly pretty.

## Pula

Once the chief port of the Austro-Hungarian Empire, **PULA** is an engaging combination of working port, naval base and brash riviera town. The Romans put the city squarely on the map when they arrived in 177 BC, transforming it into an important commercial centre. The most obvious relic of their rule is the first-century-BC **Amphitheatre** (daily: June–Sept 24hrs; Oct–May 8.30am–4.30pm; 16kn) just north of the centre, a great grey elliptical skein of connecting arches, silhouetted against the skyline. It's the sixth largest in the world, and once had space for over 23,000 spectators. The outer shell is fairly complete, as is one of the towers, up which a slightly hair-raising climb gives a good sense of the enormity of the structure and a view of Pula's industrious harbour. The cavernous rooms underneath, which would have been used for keeping wild animals and Christians before they met their death, are now given over to piles of crusty amphorae and reconstructed olive presses.

South of the amphitheatre, central Pula circles a pyramidal hill, scaled by secluded streets and topped with a star-shaped Venetian fortress. On the eastern side of the hill, Istarska – which later becomes Giardini – leads down to the first-century-BC **Triumphal Arch of the Sergians**, through which ul Sergijevaca, a lively pedestrianized thoroughfare, leads in turn to a square known as **Forum** – site of the ancient Roman forum and now the centre of Pula's old quarter. On the far side of here, the slim form of the **Temple of Augustus** was built between 2 BC and 14 AD to celebrate the cult of the emperor; its imposing Corinthian columns, still intact, make it one of the best examples of a Roman temple outside Italy.

Heading north from Forum along Kandlerova leads to Pula's **cathedral** (June–Aug daily 10am–1pm & 5–8pm; 5kn), a broad, simple and very spacious structure that is another mixture of periods and styles: a fifteenth-century renovation of a Romanesque basilica built on the foundations of a Roman temple. From

---

### Moving on from Istria: Rijeka

Travelling on from Istria towards Zagreb or Dalmatia, most routes lead through the port city of **RIJEKA**, hardly worth a stopoff in its own right but an important transport hub for onward travel: regular **buses** run from here to Zagreb, Zadar, Split and Dubrovnik, and it's the starting point for the Jadrolinija coastal **ferry**, which calls in at Zadar, Split and Dubrovnik on its way south. Rijeka's train and bus stations are about 400m apart; the former at the western end of Trpimirova, the latter at the eastern end of the same street on Trg Žabica. The Jadrolinija ferry office (daily 7am–6/9pm; ☎051/211-444) is along the waterfront from the bus station at Riva 16.

the cathedral, you can follow streets up to the top of the hill, the site of the original Roman Capitol and now the home of a mossy seventeenth-century **fortress**, built by the Venetians and housing a pretty inessential local museum. You're better off following tracks to the far side of the fortress where there are the remains of a small **Roman Theatre** (free) and the **Archeological Museum** (May–Sept Mon–Sat 9am–8pm, Sun 10am–3pm; Oct–April Mon–Fri 9am–2pm; 12kn), which has pillars and toga-clad statues mingling haphazardly with ceramics, jewellery and trinkets from all over Istria, some dating back to prehistoric times.

## Practicalities

Pula's **train station** is a ten-minute walk north of the centre, at the far end of Kolodvorska; the **bus station** is a similar distance northeast of the centre, along Istarska Divizije. The **tourist office** is in the Forum (June–Sept daily 9am–10pm; Oct–May Mon–Fri 8am–7pm, Sun 10am–4pm; ☎052/219-197, ⓦwww.pulainfo .hr) and can provide information for all of Istria. **Private rooms** (❷) can be booked through Arenatours, Splitska Ulica 1 (☎052/529-400, ⓦwww.arenaturist .hr), or Atlas, Ulica Starih Statuta 1 (☎052/393-040). There's an HI **hostel** at Valsaline bay, 4km south of the centre (☎052/391-133; 90kn); take bus #2 from Giardini to Vila Idola and then bear right towards the bay. Cheapest of the hotels is the *Omir*, slightly uphill from Giardini at Sergia Dobrića 6 (☎052/210-614; ❺). The plush *Scaletta*, just north of the amphitheatre at Flavijevska 26 (☎052/541-599, ⓦwww.hotel-scaletta.com; ❻), is one of the best family-run **hotels** in Croatia. The nearest **campsite** is *Stoja*, on a rocky wooded peninsula 3km southeast of town (☎052/387-144); take bus #1 from Giardini.

The vast **market** on Narodni Trg will yield all the provisions you'll need. Most **eating out** options are around the amphitheatre. For a treat, the *Scaletta* restaurant, opposite the hotel (see above) is the best Italian in town. *Jupiter*, below the fortress at Castropola 38, is easily the best of the pizzerias, and *Pompei*, just off Sergijevaca at Clarissova 1, does good pasta dishes and salads. Best of the **drinking** haunts are *Ulix*, an elegant bar next to the triumphal arch; *Zen*, Cesta Prekomorski Brigada, a lively late-night drinking spot on the ring road, about 10 minutes' walk west from the bus station, and *Uljanik*, Dobrilina 2, a counter-cultural club of many years' standing that has DJ nights at weekends and live music in summer. Otherwise, during the summer, the liveliest party venues are in Verudela, 3km south of town.

# Rovinj

**ROVINJ** lies 40km north of Pula, its harbour a likeable mix of fishing boats and swanky yachts, its quaysides a blend of sunshaded café-tables and the thick orange of fishermen's nets. From the main square, **Trg maršala Tita**, the Baroque **Vrata svetog Križa** leads up to Grisia Ulica, lined with galleries selling local art. It climbs steeply through the heart of the old town to **St Euphemia's Church** (June–Sept daily 10am–5pm), dominating Rovinj from the top of its peninsula. This eighteenth-century church, Baroque in style, has the sixth-century sarcophagus of the saint inside; you can climb its 58-metre-high tower (same times; 10kn). Back on maršala Tita, the **Town Museum** (May–Sept Mon–Sat 9am–1pm & 5–9pm; Oct–April Tues–Sat 10.30am–1.30pm; 10kn) has the usual collection of archeological bits and pieces, antique furniture and Croatian art. North of here is **Trg Valdibora**, home to a small fruit and vegetable market. Paths on the south side of Rovinj's busy harbour lead south towards **Zlatni rt**, a densely forested cape, crisscrossed by tracks and fringed by rocky **beaches**. Other spots for bathing can be found on the two islands just offshore from Rovinj – **Sveta Katarina**, the nearer of the two, and **Crveni otok**, just outside Rovinj's bay; both are linked by boats from the harbour (every 30min).

Rovinj's **bus station** is five minutes' walk southeast of its centre, just off Trg na lokvi, at the junction of Carrera and Carducci. The **tourist office** is located just back from the waterfront at Obula Pina Budicin 12 (June–Sept daily 8am–10pm; Oct–May Mon–Fri 8am–3pm, Sat 8am–1pm, Sun 9am–1pm; ☎052/811-566, ✺www.tzgrovinj.hr). **Private rooms** (❷) can be organised from Natale, opposite the bus station at Carducci 4 (☎052/813-365). The only reasonably priced **hotel** in town is the *Rovinj*, Svetoga Križa 59 ☎052/811-288, ✉hotel-rovinj@pu.hinet.hr; ❻), while the nearest **campsite** is the *Porton Biondi* (☎052/813-557, ✺www.cel .hr/porton-biondi), which occupies a pine-shaded site right by the sea 1km north of town. The harbourfront area is teeming with places to **eat and drink**, the best summer spot being *Valentino*, Svetoga Križa, an outdoor bar perched on the rocks over the Adriatic. Away from here, *da Sergio*, at Grisia 11, is the best place for pizza; while *Konoba Veli Jože*, at Svetog Križa 1, has top-notch seafood.

# Dalmatia

Stretching from Zadar in the north to the Montenegrin border in the south, **Dalmatia** possesses one of Europe's most dramatic shorelines, the sheer wall of Croatia's mountain ranges sweeping down to the sea from stark, grey heights, scattering islands in their path. For centuries, the region was ruled by Venice, spawning towns, churches and an architecture that wouldn't look out of place on the other side of the water. All along, well-preserved medieval towns sit on tiny islands or just above the sea on slim peninsulas, beneath a grizzled karst landscape that drops precipitously into some of the clearest – and cleanest – water in the Mediterranean. In northern Dalmatia, the busy port city of **Zadar** provides a vivacious introduction to the region. Otherwise, the main attractions are in the south: the provincial capital **Split** is served by trains from Zagreb and provides onward bus connections with the walled city of **Dubrovnik**. Ferry and catamaran connections to the best of the islands – **Brač**, **Hvar**, **Vis** and **Korčula** – are also from Split.

## Zadar

A bustling town of around 100,000 people, **ZADAR** boasts a compact historic centre crowded onto a tapered peninsula jutting northwest into the Adriatic. It displays a pleasant muddle of architectural styles, with Romanesque churches competing for space with café-bars. Near the northwestern end of the peninsula, Zadar's main square or **Forum** is dominated by the ninth-century **St Donat's Church** (summer only: daily 9am–10pm; 5kn), a hulking cylinder of stone built – according to tradition – by St Donat himself, an Irishman who was bishop here for a time. The cavernous, bare interior makes the perfect venue for summer chamber concerts. Opposite, the **Archeological Museum** (Mon–Sat 9am–1pm & 5–7pm; 10kn) has an absorbing collection of Neolithic, Roman and medieval Croatian artefacts. The adjacent **Permanent Exhibition of Church Art** (Mon–Sat 10am–1pm & 6–8pm, Sun 10am–1pm; 20kn) is a storehouse of Zadar's finest church treasures. On the northwestern side of the Forum, the twelfth- and thirteenth-century **Cathedral of St Anastasia** has an arcaded west front reminiscent of Tuscan churches. Around the door frame stretches a frieze of twisting acanthus leaves, from which various beasts emerge – look for the rodent and bird fighting over a bunch of grapes. Southeast of the Forum is **Narodni Trg**, an attractive Renaissance square overlooked by the clock tower of the sixteenth-century **Guard House**. A little further southeast, on Trg Petra Zoranića, the Baroque **St Simeon's Church** houses the exuberantly decorated reliquary of St Simeon, ordered by Queen Elizabeth of Hungary in 1377 and fashioned from 250kg of silver by local artisans.

## Practicalities

**Ferries** arrive on Liburnska obala, from where the town centre is a five-minute walk uphill. Zadar's **train** and **bus stations** are about 1km east of the town centre, a fifteen-minute walk or a quick hop on municipal bus #5 – tickets cost 8kn from the driver or 10kn (valid for two journeys) from kiosks. The **tourist office** is on Narodni Trg (May–Sept daily 8am–midnight; Oct–April Mon–Fri 8am–8.30pm, Sat & Sun 8am–2.30pm; ☏023/316-166, ⊛www.zadar.hr). **Private rooms** (❸) in the old town are available from Aquarius, Nova Vrata bb (☏023/212-919, ⊛www .jureskoaquarius.com), and Miatours, Vrata sv. Krševana (☏023/254-300, ⊛www .miatours.hr), both located under arches in the town wall, near the ferry quays. *Venera*, Šime Ljubića 4a (☏023/214-098; ❸), is an old-town **pension** offering minuscule but neat en suites. About 4km northwest at the beach resort of Borik (bus #5 from the bus and train stations) is a big, friendly **hostel** on the waterfront at Obala kneza Trpimira 76 (☏023/331-145, ✉zadar@hfhs.hr; 90kn), and the well-equipped *Borik* **campsite** (☏023/332-074). In Zadar, old-town **eating** opportunities include *Foša*, Ante Kuzmanića, a fish restaurant set in a small harbour just outside the town walls, with outdoor dining; and *Dva Ribara*, Borelli 7, with tasty pizzas. Atmospheric café-bars are tucked into the alleys off Narodni Trg – head down Klaiča and its continuation Varoška to find them. In the summer months **drinking** takes place at *Garden*, Bedemi zadarskih pobuna, on top of the city walls, whilst **dancing** happens year-round at *Gotham City*, Marka Oreškovića.

# Split

The largest city in the region, and its major transit hub, **SPLIT** is a hectic place, but one of the most enticing spots on the Dalmatian coast. At its heart lies a crumbling old town built within the precincts of **Diocletian's Palace**, one of the most outstanding classical remains in Europe. Built as a retirement home by Dalmatian-born Roman Emperor Diocletian in 305 AD, it has been modified over the centuries, but has remained the core of Split. The best place to start a tour of the palace area is on the seaward side, through the **Bronze Gate**, a functional gateway giving access to the sea that once came right up to the palace itself. Inside, you find yourself in a vaulted hall, from which imposing steps lead through the now domeless vestibule to the **Peristyle**. Once the central courtyard of the palace complex, these days the Peristyle serves as the main town square, crowded with cafés and surrounded by remnants of the stately arches that once framed the square. At the southern end, steps lead up to the **vestibule**, a round, formerly domed building that is the only part of the imperial apartments to be left anything like intact. You can get some idea of the grandeur of the old apartments by visiting the **subterranean halls** (daily: July & Aug 8am–8pm; Sept–June 8am–noon & 4–7pm; 10kn) beneath the houses which now stand on the site; the entrance is to the left of the Bronze Gate.

On the east side of the Peristyle stands one of two black granite Egyptian sphinxes, dating from around 15 BC, that flanked the entrance to Diocletian's mausoleum; the octagonal building, surrounded by an arcade of Corinthian columns, has since been converted into Split's **cathedral** (Mon–Sat 8am–8pm). On the right of the entrance is the **campanile** (same hours; 5kn), a Romanesque structure much restored in the late nineteenth century – from the top, the views across the city are splendid. As for the cathedral itself, the walnut and oak main **doorway** is one of its most impressive features – carved in 1214 with an inspired comic strip showing scenes from the life of Christ. Inside is a hotchpotch of styles, the dome ringed by two series of decorative Corinthian columns and a frieze that contains portraits of Diocletian and his wife. The **pulpit** is a beautifully proportioned example of Romanesque art, sitting on capitals tangled with snakes, strange beasts and foliage. But the church's finest feature is on the Altar of St Anastasius – a cruelly realistic *Flagellation of Christ*, completed by local artist Juraj Dalmatinac in 1448.

North of the cathedral and reached by following Dioklecijanova is the grandest and best preserved of the palace gates, the **Golden Gate**. Just outside there's a piece by Mestrović, a gigantic statue of the fourth-century Bishop **Grgur Ninski**. Fifteen minutes' walk northwest of here, the **Archeological Museum** at Zrinsko Frankopanska 25 (June–Sept Tues–Sat 9am–1pm & 4–7pm, Sun 10am–noon; Oct–May Tues–Sat 9am–2pm, Sun 10am–noon; 20kn) contains comprehensive displays of Illyrian, Greek, medieval and Roman artefacts. Outside, the arcaded courtyard is crammed with a wonderful array of Greek, Roman and early Christian gravestones, sarcophagi and decorative sculpture.

If you want some peace and quiet, head for the woods of the **Marjan peninsula** west of the old town. It's accessible from Obala hrvatskog narodnog preporoda via Sperun and then Senjska, which cuts up through the slopes of the **Varoš** district. Most of Marjan's visitors stick to the road around the edge of the promontory with its scattering of tiny rocky **beaches**; the Bene beach, on the far northern side, is especially popular. From the road, tracks lead up into the heart of the Marjan Park, which is thickly wooded with pines. The main historical highlight of the area lies some fifteen minutes west of the centre (bus #12 from the seafront). The **Meštrović Gallery**, Ivana Meštrovića 46 (daily 10am–dusk/7pm; 20kn, includes entrance to Kaštelet), is another Croatian shrine, housed in the ostentatious Neoclassical building that was built – and lived in – by Croatia's most famous twentieth-century artist, the sculptor Ivan Meštrović (1883–1962). This fabulous collection consists largely of boldly fashioned bodies curled into elegant poses. Mestrović's former workshop, **Kaštelet** (same times and ticket), is 300m up the same road, and contains a chapel decorated with one of his most important set-piece works: a series of wood-carved reliefs showing scenes from the Stations of the Cross.

## Practicalities

Split's main **bus** and **train stations** are next to each other on Obala Kneza Domagoja, five minutes' walk round the harbour from the centre; the **ferry terminal** for both domestic and international ferries – and the Jadrolinija booking office – is a few hundred metres south of here. Split **airport** is 16km west of town; Croatia Airlines buses connect with scheduled flights and run to the waterfront Riva (30kn); alternatively the #37 Split–Trogir bus runs from the main road outside the airport to the suburban bus station (15kn). The **tourist office** is in the Peristyle of the Palace (June–Sept daily 8am–8pm; Oct–May Mon–Fri 8am–8pm, Sat & Sun 8am–1pm; ☏021/345-606, ⓦwww.visitsplit.com). **Private rooms** (❸) can be booked through Turist Biro, on the waterfront at Obala narodnog preporoda 12 (☏021/347-100, ⓔturist-biro-split@st.t-com.hr). Cheapest of the central **hotels** is the newly refurbished *Slavija* at Buvinova 3 in the old town (☏021/323-840, ⓦwww.hotelslavija.com; ❻). The only **hostel** is at Velebitska 27 (☏021/538-025; 100kn), a fifteen-minute walk out of town along Slobode (or bus #9 from the harbour).

The daily **market** at the eastern edge of the old town is the place to shop for fruit, veg and local cheeses. Most **restaurants** are just outside the old town: *Ponoćno sunce*, Teutina 15, has a good range of meat and fish dishes as well as excellent salads. Further afield, *Konoba kod Joe* at Sredmanuška 4, 10 min northeast of the old town, is an atmospheric place specializing in seafood; while *Konoba Varoš*, at ban Mladenova 7, is another traditional Dalmatian restaurant. Nearby, *Šperun*, Šperun 3, offers tasty seafood in an atmospheric tavern. The bustling waterfront is lined with decent **cafes**, whilst the old town's many small squares yield clusters of options: on Mihovilova Širina, *Shook* is fairly upbeat, whilst just around the corner you'll find *Puls*, at Buvinina 1, and opposite at Dosud 10, the *Ghetto Club*; both are welcome alternatives to the posier establishments round about. For quieter, more reflective options, head for the cafes such as *Teak*, *Porta* and *Dante* on the tiny square just off Majstora Jurja. *Planet Jazz* is a popular bohemian hangout on Grgura Ninskog, whilst the beach at Bačvice, a few minutes' walk south past the railway station, is a popular party place in summer. For **Internet access** head to *Backpacker's Caffe* near the bus station, which also sells secondhand books in English.

# The island of Brač

**BRAČ** is famous for its milk-white marble, which has been used in places as diverse as Berlin's Reichstag, the high altar of Liverpool's Metropolitan Cathedral, the White House in Washington – and, of course, Diocletian's Palace. In addition to the marble, a great many islanders were once dependent on the grape harvest, though the phylloxera (vine lice) epidemics of the late nineteenth century and early twentieth century forced many of them to emigrate. Even today, as you cross Brač's interior, the signs of this depopulation are all around in the tumbledown walls and overgrown fields. The easiest way to reach Brač is by **ferry** from Split to **Supetar**, an engagingly laid-back fishing port on the north side of the island, from where it's a straightforward hour's bus journey to **Bol**, a major windsurfing centre on the island's south coast and site of one of the Adriatic's most beautiful beaches.

## Supetar

Though the largest town on the island, **SUPETAR** is a rather sleepy village onto which package tourism has been painlessly grafted. There's little of specific interest, save for several attractive shingle **beaches** which stretch west from the harbour, and the **Petrinović Mausoleum**, a neo-Byzantine construction on a wooded promontory 1km west of town, built by sculptor Toma Rosandić to honour a local businessman. Supetar's **tourist office** beside the ferry dock at Porat 1 (July & Aug daily 8am–10pm; June & Sept daily 8am–4pm; Oct–May Mon–Fri 8am–4pm; ☎021/630-551, ◎www.supetar.hr) has information on the whole island. **Private rooms** (❷) are available from Atlas (☎021/631-105) on the harbourfront. The *Palute,* 1.5km west of the harbour at Put pašike 16 (☎021/631-541; ❸), is a friendly **pension**, but soon fills up. The *Supetar* **campsite** is 1.5km east of the ferry dock. Best of the places to eat on the harbourfront is *Palute* at Porat 4, which serves good grilled fish. *Vinotoka*, just inland from the harbour at Dobova 6, has a wide range of traditional Croatian food and an extensive choice of local wines. The clear waters around Supetar are perfect for **scuba diving**; the Dive Center Kaktus in the *Kaktus Hotel* complex (☎021/630-421; closed Nov–March) rents out gear and arranges scuba and snorkelling courses (from 220kn), as well as renting out mountain bikes (120kn/day).

## Bol

Stranded on the far side of the Vidova Gora mountains, there's no denying the beauty of **BOL**'s setting, or the charm of its old stone houses. However, the main attraction of the village is its beach, **Zlatni rat**, which lies to the west of the centre along the wooded shoreline. The pebbly cape juts into the sea like an extended finger, changing shape from season to season as the wind plays across it. Unsurprisingly, it does get very crowded during summer. While you're here, look in at the late-fifteenth-century **Dominican Monastery** (daily 10am–noon & 5–9pm; 10kn), dramatically perched on a bluff just east of central Bol. **Buses** from Supetar stop just west of Bol's harbour, at the far end of which stands the **tourist office** (June–Aug daily 8am–10pm; Sept–May Mon–Fri 8.30am–2pm; ☎021/635-638, ◎www.bol.hr) by the *Big Blue Cafe*. **Private rooms** (❷) can be booked through Boltours, 100m west of the bus stop at Vladimira Nazora 18 (☎021/635-693, ◎www.boltours.com), or Adria, just beyond it at Vladimira Nazora 28 (☎021/635-966). There are a couple of **campsites**, the *Ranč* (☎021/635-635) and the *Meteor* (☎021/635-630), on Hrvatskih Domobrana uphill from the centre. For **eating**, there are numerous places along the waterfront, although *Gust*, above the harbour at F. Radića 14, has the widest range of traditional food. Big Blue (☎021/635-614, ◎www.big-blue-sport.hr), on the path leading to Zlatni rat, is the best of several **windsurfing** centres; as well as board rental (€15/hr) and a range of courses for beginners, they also rent out sea kayaks (€3.75/hr) and **mountain bikes** (€1.90/day). Free cycling maps are available from the tourist office.

## The island of Hvar

One of the most hyped of all the Croatian islands, **HVAR** is undeniably beautiful – a slim, green slice of land punctured by jagged inlets and cloaked with hills of spongy lavender. Tourist development hasn't been too crass, and the island's main centre, **Hvar Town**, retains much of its old Venetian charm. At least one daily hydrofoil from Split arrives at Hvar Town itself; numerous ferries head for Stari Grad, 4km east, from where buses run into Hvar Town.

The best view of **HVAR TOWN** is from the sea, the tiny town hugging the bay, grainy-white and brown with green splashes of palms and pines bursting from every nook and cranny. At the centre, the main square is flanked to the south by the arcaded bulk of the **Venetian arsenal**, the upper storey of which was added in 1612 to house a **theatre** (daily: June–Aug 9am–1pm & 5–11pm; Sept–May 11am–noon; 10kn), the oldest in Croatia. The theatre has since been converted into a cinema, but its painted Baroque interior has survived pretty much intact. At the eastern end of the square is Hvar's **cathedral** (usually open mornings), a sixteenth-century construction with an eighteenth-century facade that's a characteristic mixture of Gothic and Renaissance styles. Inside is routine enough, but the **Bishop's Treasury** (daily: June–Aug 9am–noon & 5–7pm; Sept–May 10am–noon; 10kn) is worth the entry fee for its small but fine selection of chalices and reliquaries. The rest of the old town stretches back from the piazza in an elegant confusion of twisting lanes and alleys. Up above, the **fortress** (April–Sept daily 8am–dusk; 10kn) is a good example of sixteenth-century military architecture, and is also home to a popular summer nightclub. The views over Hvar and the islands beyond are well worth the trek to the top. From the fort you can pick out the fifteenth-century **Franciscan Monastery** (Mon–Fri 10am–noon & 5–7pm; 15kn), to the left of the harbour; next door, the monastic church is pleasingly simple, with beautifully carved choir stalls.

The **beaches** nearest to town are rocky and crowded, and it's best to make your way towards the **Pakleni otoci**, just to the west. Easily reached by water taxi from the harbour (about 20kn each way), the Pakleni are a chain of eleven wooded islands, three of which cater for tourists with simple bars and restaurants: Jerolim, a naturist island, is the nearest; next is Marinkovac; then Sv Klement, the largest of the islands. Bear in mind that camping is forbidden throughout Pakleni, and that naturism is popular.

### Practicalities

Hvar Town's **tourist office** (July & Aug daily 8am–2pm & 3–10pm; June & Sept Mon–Sat 8am–1.30pm & 4–9pm, Sun 10am–noon & 6–8pm; Oct–May Mon–Sat 8am–1pm; ☎021/741-059, ✆www.tzhvar.hr) is on the waterfront below the theatre. For **private rooms** (❸), head for Atlas, also on the harbour (☎021/741-911, ✉atlas-hvar@st.htnet.hr), or Pelegrin, by the ferry dock (☎021/742-743, ✉pelegrin@inet.hr). Of the **hotels**, *Dalmacija*, on the eastern side of the harbour (☎021/741-120, ✆www.suncanihvar.hr; ❹) is as reasonable as you'll get here. The small *Jagoda & Ante Bracanović House* at Poviše Škole 21 (☎021/741-416; ✉virgilye@yahoo.com; 110kn per person; free pickup from bus station) is an excellent budget choice with apartments, balconies and shared kitchen. The *Milna* **campsite** (☎021/745-027) is 3km southeast of town on Milna Bay – most Hvar Town–Stari Grad buses drop off nearby. There are dozens of **restaurants** in Hvar Town, none of which is too expensive. *Junior*, at Pučkog ustanka 4, does a mean shrimp pasta and other reasonably priced seafood dishes in a narrow street that runs parallel to the ferry dock; while *Hanibal*, on the main square, has a slightly pricier, but wider ranging, menu. *Macondo*, signposted in a backstreet uphill from the harbour, is the best place for meat and fish. For **drinking**, there are several cafés and bars around the harbour: *Loco* and *Gromit* are good, while *Carpe Diem* is said to be the best cocktail bar in Croatia.

## The island of Vis

Compact, humpy, and at first glance a little forbidding, **VIS** is situated further offshore than any other of Croatia's inhabited Adriatic islands. Closed to foreigners for military reasons until 1989, the island has never been overrun by tourists, and even now depends much more heavily on independent tourism than its package-oriented neighbours. Croatia's bohemian youth seem to have fallen in love with the place over the last decade, drawn by its wild mountainous scenery, two good-looking towns, **Vis Town** and **Komiža**, and a brace of fine wines, including the white Vugava and the red Viški plavac. Ferries and, in summer, catamarans from Split arrive at Vis Town, from where buses depart for Komiža on the western side of the island.

### Vis Town

**VIS TOWN** is attractively sited, a sedate arc of grey-brown houses on a deeply indented bay, above which looms a steep escarpment covered with the remains of abandoned agricultural terraces. The most attractive parts of town are east of the ferry landing in the suburb of **Kut**, a largely sixteenth-century tangle of narrow cobbled streets overlooked by the summer houses built by nobles from Hvar. A kilometre further on lies a small British war cemetery, and just behind it, a wonderful pebbly **beach**. Heading west around the bay soon brings you to a small peninsula, from which the campanile of the Franciscan **monastery of St Hieronymous** rises gracefully alongside a huddle of cypresses. The **tourist office** (May–Sept daily 8am–2pm & 5–8pm; Oct–April Mon–Fri 8am–2pm; ☏021/717-017, ⊛www.tz-vis.hr) is just to the right of the ferry dock. **Private rooms** (➋) can be booked through Ionios, Obala Sv Jurja 37 (☏021/711-532, ⓔionios @st.hinet.hr). Best of the **hotels** are the stately early twentieth-century *Tamaris*, on the waterfront at Obala Sv Jurja 20 (☏021/711-350, ⓔtamaris@st.t-com.hr; ➏), and the smaller, pension-like *Paula*, at Petra Hektorovića 2 (☏021/711-362; ➍), in Kut. *Pizzeria Katerina* near the ferry dock is good for a quick bite; while *Pojoda* and *Vatrica*, both in Kut, are worth splashing out on for sumptuous **seafood**.

### Komiža

**KOMIŽA**, 10km from Vis Town, is the island's main fishing port – a compact town with a palm-fringed seafront on one side and a ring of mountains on the other. Dominating the southern end of the harbour is the **Kaštel**, a stubby sixteenth-century fortress which now holds a **Fishing Museum** (June–Sept Mon–Sat 10am–noon & 7–10pm, Sun 7–10pm; 10kn). Komiža's nicest **beaches** are a further ten minutes south of the museum, where you'll find a sequence of pebbly coves. Each morning small boats leave Komiža harbour for the nearby island of Biševo in order to visit the so-called **Blue Cave**. A grotto filled with eerie shimmering light, it's well worth seeing – expect to pay around 120kn for the trip. Buses from Vis Town terminate about 100m behind the harbour, from where it's a short walk southwards to the **tourist office** (July & Aug Mon–Sat 8am–noon & 6–10pm; Sept–June Mon–Fri 8am–1pm; ☏021/713-455), on the Riva just beyond the Kaštel. The town's **hotel**, the *Biševo* (☏021/713-095; ➎), is at the northern end of the bay, and there are **private rooms** (➋) available through Darlić & Darlić, on the harbourfront (☏021/713-760, ⊛www.darlic-travel.hr), and Srebrnatours at Ribarska 4 (☏021/713 668, ⊛www.srebrnatours.hr). There are a couple of pizzerias on the harbour, and one very good seafood **restaurant**,

*Bako*, just off Ribarska. For **drinking**, head for the tiny main square, Škor, which is ringed by lively café-bars.

## The island of Korčula

Like so many islands along this coast, **KORČULA** was first settled by the Greeks, who gave it the name Korkyra Melaina or "Black Corfu" for its dark and densely wooded appearance. Even now, it's one of the greenest of the Adriatic islands, and one of the most popular. The island's main settlement is **Korčula Town**, and the rest of the island, although beautifully wild, lacks any real centres. The main coastal **ferry** docks at Korčula Town harbour. In addition, local ferries travel daily between Split and Vela Luka at the western end of Korčula island, from where there's a connecting bus service to Korčula Town. There's also a **bus service** from Dubrovnik, which crosses the narrow stretch of water dividing the island from the mainland by ferry from Orebić.

**KORČULA TOWN** sits on a beetle-shaped hump of land, a medieval walled city ribbed with a series of narrow streets that branch off the spine of the main street like the veins of a leaf. The Venetians first arrived here in the eleventh century, and stayed, on and off, for nearly eight centuries. Their influence is particularly evident in Korčula's old town, which huddles around the **Cathedral of St Mark**, squeezed into a space between the buildings that roughly passes for a main square. The cathedral facade is decorated with a gorgeous fluted rose window and a bizarre cornice frilled with strange gargoyles. The interior, reached through a door framed by statues of Adam and Eve, is one of the loveliest in the region – a curious mixture of styles, ranging from the Gothic forms of the nave to the Renaissance northern aisle, tacked on in the sixteenth century. The best of the church's treasures have been removed to the **Bishop's Treasury** (July & August: daily 10am–noon & 5–7pm; at other times enquire at the tourist office; 10kn), a couple of doors down. This small collection of fine and sacral art is one of the best in the country, with an exquisite set of paintings, including a striking *Portrait of a Man* by Carpaccio and a Leonardo da Vinci sketch of a soldier wearing a costume bearing a striking resemblance to that of the Moreška dancers (see below). Opposite the treasury, a former Venetian palace holds the **Town Museum** (July & August daily 9am–1pm & 5–7pm; rest of year Mon–Sat 9am–1pm; 10kn), whose more modest display contains a plaster cast of a fourth-century-BC Greek tablet from Lumbarda – the earliest evidence of civilization on Korčula. Close by the main square, down a turning to the right, is another remnant from Venetian times, the so-called **House of Marco Polo** (July & Aug daily 9am–1pm & 5–7pm; Sept–June Mon–Sat 9am–1pm; 10kn). Korčula claims to be the birthplace of Marco Polo, although it seems unlikely that he had any connection with this seventeenth-century house, which these days is little more than an empty shell with some terrible twentieth-century prints.

Your best bet for **beaches** is to head off by water taxi from the old harbour to one of the **Skoji islands** just offshore. The largest and nearest of these is **Badija**, where there are some secluded rocky beaches, a couple of snack bars and a naturist section. There's also a sandy **beach** just beyond the village of **Lumbarda**, 8km south of Korčula (reached by hourly bus in the summer).

### Practicalities

Korčula's **bus station** is 400m southeast of the old town. Work your way round to the northwestern side of the peninsula to find the **tourist office** (June–Sept daily 8am–9pm; Oct–May Mon–Sat 8am–noon; ☎021/715-701, ⊛www.korcula .net). **Private rooms** (❸) are handled by Marko Polo (☎020/715-400, ⊜marko -polo-tours@du.tel.hr), whose office is between the bus station and the entrance to the old town. Hotels are generally expensive; the *Park* is a package-tour-oriented place in a bay southeast of the centre (☎020/726-004; ❺). The nearest

**campsite** is *Autocamp Kalac* (☏020/711-182), about 3km southeast of town and reached by hourly buses for Lumbarda. Not surprisingly, most **restaurants** in the old town tend to be pricey. One exception is the excellent *Adio Mare*, near Marco Polo's House and justifiably popular; arrive early to get a table. Another good choice is *Gradski Podrum*, just inside the main gate of the old town. A cheaper and more functional alternative is *Planjak* at Plokata 21. Wherever you eat, do try some of the excellent **local wines**: the delicious dry white Grk from Lumbarda, Posip from Smokvica, or the headache-inducing red Dingač from Postup on Peljesac. Performances of Korčula's famous **folk dance**, the Moreška, take place outside the main gate to the old town in summer every Thursday evening (tickets from Marko Polo; 50kn). This frantic, sword-based dance is the story of a conflict between the Christians (in red) and the Moors (in black): the heroine, Bula, is kidnapped by the evil foreign king and his army, and her betrothed tries to win her back in a ritualized sword fight which takes place within a shifting circle of dancers.

# Dubrovnik

**DUBROVNIK** is a beautifully preserved medieval fortified city. First settled by Roman refugees in the early seventh century and given the name Ragusa, the town soon exploited its favourable position on the Adriatic with a maritime and commercial genius. By the mid-fourteenth century, having shaken off the yoke of first the Byzantines and then the Venetians, it had become a successful and self-contained city state, its merchants trading far and wide. Dubrovnik fended off the attentions of the Ottoman Empire and continued to prosper until 1667, when an earthquake devastated the city. Though the city-state survived, it fell into decline and, in 1808, was formally dissolved by Napoleon. An eight-month siege by Yugoslav forces in the early 1990s caused much destruction, but the city swiftly recovered. The prestigious **Summer Festival** (July 10 to Aug 25; ☏020/326-100, ⓦwww.dubrovnik-festival.hr) is a good, if crowded, time to be around, with classical concerts and theatre performances in most of the city's courtyards, squares and bastions. Book tickets well in advance.

## Arrival, information and accommodation

The **ferry** and **bus terminals** are located in the port suburb of Gruž, 3km west of town. The main western entrance to the old town, the Pile Gate, is a thirty-minute slog along ul Ante Starčevića; you'd be better off catching a bus – #1a and #3 from the ferry terminal; #1a, #3 or #6 from behind the bus station. Tickets for local buses are bought from the driver (10kn; exact change only) or from newspaper kiosks (8kn). The main **tourist office** is in the old town on the Stradun (June–Aug daily 8am–midnight; Sept–May daily 8am–8pm; ☏020/321-561, ⓦwww.tzdubrovnik.hr), although there are branches just up from Pile Gate at Ante Starčevića 7 (June–Aug daily 8am–8pm, Sept–May Mon–Fri 9am–4pm & Sat 9am–1pm), and opposite the ferry terminal in Gruž (same hours). **Private rooms** (❸) can be booked through Gulliver, opposite the ferry terminal at Obala Stjepana Radića 32 (☏020/313-300), and Dubrovnikturist, 100m east of the bus station at put Republike 7 (☏020/356-969, ⓦwww.dubrovnikturist.hr). There's a basic, well-run HI **hostel** at bana Jelačića 15/17 (☏020/423-241, ⓔdubrovnik@hfhs .hr; dorms 105kn) – head up Ante Starčevića from the bus station and turn uphill to the right after five minutes. *Vila Micika*, Mata Vodopica 10, Lapad (bus #6 to Lapad post office; ☏020/437-332, ⓦwww.vilamicika.hr; ❹), is a family-run **pension** offering hostel-style arrangements (a bed in a clean and comfortable 1-, 2- or 3-person room) as well as bright en-suite doubles. Nearby, the *Begović Boarding House*, Primorska 17 (☏020/435-191, ⓔbega@beg-board.com; 120kn) has friendly, clean, hostel-style accommodation. Affordable **hotels** are in short supply: *Petka*, opposite the ferry terminal at Obala Stjepan Radića 38 (☏020/418-008, ⓦwww.hotelpetka.com☆ ❽), and *Lero*, 1.5km west of Pile Gate at Iva Vojnovića

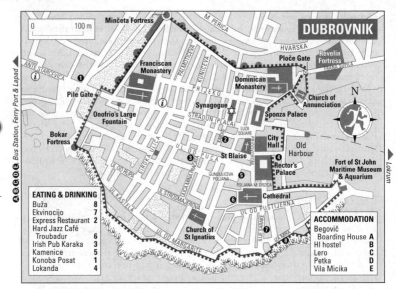

**DUBROVNIK**

**EATING & DRINKING**

| | |
|---|---|
| Buža | 8 |
| Ekvinocijo | 7 |
| Express Restaurant | 2 |
| Hard Jazz Café Troubadur | 6 |
| Irish Pub Karaka | 3 |
| Kamenice | 5 |
| Konoba Posat | 1 |
| Lokanda | 4 |

**ACCOMMODATION**

| | |
|---|---|
| Begovič Boarding House | A |
| HI hostel | B |
| Lero | C |
| Petka | D |
| Vila Micika | E |

14 (☎ 020/341-333, ⍟ www.hotel-lero.hr; ⑧) are the best options. The free, monthly *Dubrovnik Riviera Guide*, available from hotels and the tourist office, lists bus and ferry timetables as well as forthcoming events.

### The City

The **Pile Gate**, main entrance to the old town, is a fifteenth-century construction complete with a statue of St Blaise, the city's protector, set in a niche above the arch. The best way to get your bearings is by making a tour of the fabulous **city walls** (daily: May–Sept 9am–7pm; Oct–April 10am–3pm; 30kn), 25m high and with all five towers intact. Of the various towers and bastions that punctuate the walls, the 1455 **Minčeta fortress**, which marks the northeastern side, is by far the most imposing.

Within the walls, Dubrovnik is a sea of roofs faded into a pastel patchwork, punctured now and then by a sculpted dome or tower. At ground level, just inside the Pile Gate, **Onofrio's Large Fountain**, built in 1444, is a domed affair at which visitors to this hygiene-conscious city had to wash themselves before they were allowed any further. Across the street is the fourteenth-century **Franciscan Monastery** complex (free access); its treasury (daily 9am–5pm; 10kn) holds some fine Gothic reliquaries and manuscripts tracing the development of musical scoring, together with relics from the apothecary's shop, dating from 1317 and claiming to be the oldest in Europe. From outside the monastery church, **Stradun** (also known as Placa), the city's main street, runs dead straight across the old town, its limestone surface polished to a slippery shine by the tramping of thousands of feet. Its far end broadens into the pigeon-choked **Luža Square**, the centre of the medieval town and even today hub of much of its activity. On the left, the **Sponza Palace** was once the customs house and mint, with a facade that's an elegant weld of florid Venetian Gothic and more sedate Renaissance forms; its majestic courtyard is given over to contemporary art exhibitions. Across the square, the Baroque-style **Church of St Blaise**, built in 1714 to replace an earlier church, serves as a grace-ful counterpoint to the palace. Outside the church stands the carved figure of an armoured knight, known as **Orlando's Column** and once the focal point of the city-state. On the eastern side of the square a Gothic arch leads through to an alley which winds past the **Dominican monastery**. Here, an arcaded courtyard filled with palms and orange trees leads to a small **museum** (daily 9am–5pm; 10kn), with outstanding examples of local sixteenth-century religious art. Back on Luža, a street leads round the back of St Blaise towards the fifteenth-century **Rector's Palace**, the seat of the Ragusan government, in which the incumbent Rector sat out his month's term of office. Today it's given over to the **City Museum** (May–Sept daily 9am–6pm; Oct–April Tues–Sun 9am–2pm; 20kn), though for the most part it's a rather paltry collection, with mediocre sixteenth-century paintings and dull furniture.

Immediately south of the Rector's Palace, Dubrovnik's seventeenth-century **cathedral** is a rather plain building, although there's an impressive Titian polyptych of *The Assumption* inside. The **Treasury** (Mon–Sat 8am–5pm, Sun 11am–5pm; 7kn) boasts a twelfth-century reliquary containing the skull of St Blaise; an exquisite piece in the shape of a Byzantine crown, the reliquary is stuck with portraits of saints and frosted with delicate gold and enamel filigree work. From the cathedral, it's a short walk through to the small harbour, dominated by the monolithic hulk of the **Fort of St John**, which now houses a downstairs **aquarium** (May–Sept daily 9am–6pm; Oct–April Mon–Sat 9am–1pm; 20kn); upstairs is the **maritime museum** (May–Sept daily 9am–7pm; Oct–April Tues–Sun 9am–2pm; 15kn), which traces the history of Ragusan sea power through a display of naval artefacts and model boats. Walking back east from here, you skirt one of the city's oldest quarters, **Pustijerna**, much of which predates the seventeenth-century earthquake. On the far side, the **Church of St Ignatius**, Dubrovnik's largest, is a Jesuit confection, modelled, like most Jesuit places of worship, on the enormous church of Gesù in Rome. The steps that lead down from here also had a Roman model – the Spanish Steps – and they sweep down to **Gundulićeva Poljana**, the square behind the cathedral which is the site of the city's morning fruit and vegetable market.

The noisy and crowded main city **beach** is a short walk east of the old town; a better bet is to head for the less crowded, and somewhat cleaner, beach on the Lapad peninsula, 5km to the west, or to catch one of the **boats** from the old city jetty (April–Oct 8am–5pm, every 30min, journey time 10min; 25kn return) to the wooded island of **Lokrum**. Crisscrossed by shady paths overhung by pines, Lokrum is home to an eleventh-century Benedictine monastery-turned-palace and has some extensive rocky beaches running along the eastern end of the island – with a naturist section (FKK) at the far eastern tip.

## Eating and drinking

For self-catering, there are morning fruit-and-vegetable **markets** (not Sun) on Gundulićeva Poljana. For **snacks**, try the sandwich bars lining the alleys running uphill from Stradun. *Express Restaurant*, Kaboge 1, is a decent self-service canteen with vegetarian options. There's no shortage of **restaurants** in the old town, though many on Prijeko, the street running parallel to Stradun to the north, make too much of a hard sell, which is generally offputting: head instead for *Lokanda* right on the old harbour, serving a small but fantastic seafood menu; *Kamenice*, at Gundulićeva Poljana 8, a simple place serving up cheap portions of *girice* (tiny deep-fried fish) and *kamenice* (oysters); or *Ekvinocijo*, a family-run seafood eatery at Ilije Sarake 10; alternatively, there's *Konoba Posat*, uz Posat 1, a large garden terrace just outside the Pile Gate which is good for grilled meats.

The pavement cafés at the eastern end of Stradun are popular spots for daytime and evening drinking, but for something with a bit more character, head for the smaller **café-bars** in the backstreets: *Hard Jazz Café Troubadur*, on Bunićeva Poljana, has live jazz most nights; *Buža*, Iza Mira, is an atmospheric outdoor bar perched on rocks through a hole in the city walls; and *Irish Pub Karaka*, Izmełu polača 5, will satisfy those seeking a more beery evening. Outside the centre, ulica bana Jelačića, just above the bus station, is lined with bars buzzing until late on summer evenings. For **clubbing**, *Latino Club Fuego*, outside the Pile Gate, and *Ragusea*, in the Revelin Fortress, are mainstream places. Live music and themed disco nights take place at Lazaretti, a cultural centre just beyond Pile Gate on Frana Supila.

## Listings

**Consulates** UK, Petilovrijenci 2 ☎311-466.
**Exchange** Nova Banka, Stradun (Mon–Fri 7.30am–8pm, Sat 7.30am–1pm).
**Hospital** Roka Mišetića bb ☎020/431-777.
**Internet access** Dubrovnik Internet Centar, Brsalje 1 (daily 9am–9pm); Netcafe, Prijeko 21 (daily 9am-11pm).

**Left luggage** At the bus station (daily 6am–9.30pm).
**Pharmacy** Kod Zvonika, Stradun (Mon-Fri 7am-8pm, Sat 7.30am-3pm).
**Post office** A. Starčevića 2 (Mon–Fri 7am–9pm, Sat 7am–7pm, Sun 9am–2pm).

# Travel details

## Trains

**Zagreb** to: Pula (4 daily; 6hr 40min); Rijeka (2 daily; 5hr); Split (July & Aug 2 daily; Sept–June 1 daily; 4hr 40min).

## Buses

**Dubrovnik** to: Korčula (1 daily; 3hr 30min); Rijeka (6 daily; 11hr 30min); Split (18 daily; 4hr 30min); Zadar (9 daily; 8hr 30min); Zagreb (8 daily; 11hr).
**Hvar Town** to: Stari grad (7 daily; 35min).
**Pula** to: Dubrovnik (1 daily; 14hr); Rijeka (every 30min); Rovinj (20 daily; 1hr); Split (3 daily; 10hr); Zagreb (17 daily; 6hr).
**Rijeka** to: Dubrovnik (4 daily; 13hr); Pula (hourly; 2hr 30min); Split (4 daily; 8hr); Zagreb (hourly; 4hr).
**Rovinj** to: Pula (hourly; 1hr); Rijeka (8 daily; 5hr).
**Split** to: Dubrovnik (hourly; 4hr 30min); Pula (3 daily; 10hr); Rijeka (13 daily; 8hr); Zadar (5 daily; 4hr); Zagreb (every 30min; 7–9hr).
**Supetar** to: Bol (8 daily; 1hr).
**Vis Town** to: Komiža (5 daily; 25min).
**Zadar** to: Dubrovnik (9 daily; 8hr 30min); Pula (3 daily; 6hr); Rijeka (13 daily; 4hr 30min); Split (every 30min; 3hr 30min); Zagreb (every 30min; 5hr).

**Zagreb** to: Dubrovnik (6 daily; 11hr); Pula (12 daily; 6hr); Rijeka (hourly; 4hr); Rovinj (5 daily; 9hr); Split (hourly; 8hr).

## Ferries

*Services from Dubrovnik and Rijeka run daily in summer and twice-weekly at other times.*
**Bram** to: Split (7 daily; 1hr).
**Dubrovnik** to: Korčula (3–4hr); Hvar Stari Grad (7hr); Rijeka (22hr); Split (9hr).
**Hvar Town** to: Korčula (2 weekly; 45min); Split (1 daily; 2hr); Vis (1 weekly; 1hr 15min).
**Hvar Stari Grad** to: Split (3–5 daily; 2hr).
**Korčula** to: Hvar (2 weekly; 45min); Split (1–2 daily; 3hr).
**Rijeka** to: Split (12hr); Hvar Stari Grad (14hr); Korčula (18hr); Dubrovnik (20hr); Zadar (6hr).
**Split** to: Dubrovnik (1 daily; 9hr); Hvar Town (1 daily; 2hr); Hvar Stari Grad (3–5 daily; 2hr); Korčula (1–2 daily; 3hr); Rijeka (1 daily; 12hr); Supetar (7 daily; 1hr); Vis (1–2 daily; 2hr 30min); Zadar (summer 1 daily; winter 2 weekly; 5hr 15min).
**Vis** to: Hvar (1 weekly; 1hr 15min); Split (1–2 daily; 2hr 30min).

# Czech Republic

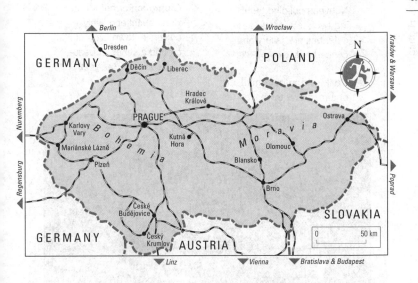

# Czech Republic highlights

✳ **Prague Castle** Home to the cathedral, royal palace and numerous art galleries, with great views across the city. See p.279

✳ **Obecní dům, Prague** The city's finest Art Nouveau building, housing two restaurants, a café, bar, art gallery and concert hall. See p.282

✳ **Český Krumlov** A gem of a medieval town, tucked into a bend of the River Vltava. See p.285

✳ **Brewery, Plzeň** Take a tour of the Pilsner Urquell brewery, home of the world's first lager. See p.286

✳ **Olomouc** Former Moravian capital and lively university town laid out around a series of beautiful squares. See p.291

△ Prague Castle

# Introduction and basics

Czechoslovakia's "Velvet Revolution" of 1989 was the most unequivocally positive of Eastern Europe's anti-Communist upheavals, as the Czechs and Slovaks shrugged off 41 years of Communist rule without a shot being fired. Just four years on, however, the country split into two separate states: the Czech Republic and Slovakia. The Czechs – always the most urbane, agnostic and liberal of the Slav nations – have fared well, joining the European Union in 2004, although they have had to contend with rising crime and an increasing cost of living. For coverage of Slovakia, see Chapter 27.

Almost untouched by the wars of the twentieth century, the Czech capital **Prague** is justifiably one of the most popular destinations in Europe. An incredibly beautiful city with a wealth of architecture, it's also a lively meeting place for young people from all over Europe. The rolling countryside of **Bohemia** is swathed in forests and studded with well-preserved medieval towns and castles, especially in the south around **České Budějovice**. In the west, you'll find the spa towns of **Karlovy Vary** and **Mariánské Lázně**. The country's eastern province, **Moravia**, is every bit as beautiful, only less touristed. **Olomouc** is the most attractive town here, but **Brno**, the regional capital, has its own pleasures and lies within easy reach of Moravia's spectacular **karst region**.

## Information & maps

Most cities and towns have their own **tourist offices** (*informační centrum*), where you should find at least one English-speaker. A comprehensive range of **maps** is usually available, often very cheaply, either from the tourist office or from bookshops, petrol stations and some hotels. Ask for a *plán města* (town plan) or *mapa okolí* (regional map).

For hiking, Klub českých turistů produces a 1:50,000 *turistická mapa* series detailing the country's complex network of marked footpaths.

## Money and banks

The local currency is the Czech **crown**, or *koruna česká* (Kč), which is divided into one hundred hellers or *haléřě* (h). Crowns come in coins of 1Kč, 2Kč, 5Kč, 10Kč and 20Kč; notes are in denominations of 20Kč, 50Kč, 100Kč, 200Kč, 500Kč, 1000Kč and 2000Kč (less frequently 5000Kč). **Banks** are by far the best places to change money and normally open Mon–Fri 8am–5pm. Given the abundance of **ATMs**, credit and debit cards are a cheaper and more convenient way of carrying funds than **travellers' cheques**, though it's a good idea to keep some hard currency in cash for emergencies. At time of writing, €1 was equal to 30Kč, $1 to 23Kč, and £1 to 44Kč.

## Communications

Most **post offices** (*pošta*) are open Mon–Fri 8am–5pm, Sat 8am–noon. Look for the right

---

## The Czech Republic on the net

ⓦ**www.czech.cz** Basic information on the whole country.

ⓦ**www.pis.cz** Prague's tourist office site.

ⓦ**www.praguepost.com** Online version of the capital's own English-language paper.

ⓦ**www.radio.cz/english** Updated news and cultural features.

ⓦ**www.ticketpro.cz**, ⓦ**www.ticketstream.cz**, ⓦ**www.ticketsbti.cz** Three good sites for finding out what's on in Prague and booking tickets online.

sign to avoid queuing: *známky* (stamps), *dopisy* (letters) or *balky* (parcels). You can also buy stamps from newsagents, tobacconists and kiosks. The majority of public **phones** only take phonecards (*telefonní karty*), available from post offices, kiosks and some shops. You can make local and international calls from all card phones, all of which have instructions in English. You'll find **Internet cafés** in almost every Czech town; charges are usually 60–100Kč/hr.

# Getting around

The Czech Republic has one of the most comprehensive **rail** networks in Europe. Czech Railways (*České dráhy* or ČD; ⓦwww.cd.cz) runs two main types of **trains**: *rychlík* (R) or *spěšný* (Sp) trains are the faster ones which stop only at major towns, while *osobní* trains stop at just about every station, averaging as little as 30kph. Fast trains are further divided into SuperCity (SC), which are first class only, EuroCity (EC) or InterCity (IC), for which you need to pay a supplement, and Expres (Ex), for which you don't. **Tickets** (*jízdenky*) for domestic journeys can be bought at the station (*nádraží*) before or on the day of departure. ČD runs reasonably priced **sleepers** to and from a number of cities in neighbouring countries, for which you must book as far in advance as possible. **InterRail** and **EuroDomino** passes are valid in the Czech Republic; **Eurail** passes are not.

Regional **buses** – mostly run by the state bus company, *Česká státní automobilová doprava* (ČSAD) – travel to most destinations, with private companies such as ČEBUS providing an alternative on popular intercity routes. Bus stations are usually next to the train station, and though some have ticket offices you can usually buy your ticket from the driver. For long-distance journeys it's a good idea to book your ticket at least a day in advance. A useful **website** for train and bus times is ⓦwww.vlak.cz.

# Accommodation

**Accommodation** can be the most expensive aspect of travelling in the Czech Republic. There is no organized hostel system, as such, though some places are now affiliated with Hostelling International (HI). Private rooms are available all over the country and are usually good value. To book accommodation **online**, try ⓦwww.avetravel.cz or ⓦwww.marys.cz.

**Hotels** are fairly expensive, especially in Prague. Most old state hotels have been refurbished by their new owners, and many new hotels and pensions have opened, particularly in the more heavily touristed areas. In the newer places, continental or buffet-style breakfast is normally included. Ignore the star system as it's no guarantee of quality, service or atmosphere.

**Private rooms** are available in Prague, Brno and many of the towns on the tourist trail, and are a good bet – keep your eyes peeled for signs saying *Zimmer Frei* or book through the local tourist office. Prices start at around 300Kč per person per night, more in Prague.

The capital has a number of **hostels**, many of which are very centrally located. The student travel organization CKM at Mánesova 77 in Prague (☎222 721 595, ⓦwww.ckm.cz) can arrange cheap **student accommodation** in the big university towns during July and August and usually charge from 250Kč per person for dorm beds. The KMC (Young Travellers Club), at Karolíny Světlé 31 in Prague (☎222 220 347, ⓦwww.kmc.cz), is an umbrella organization for youth hostels throughout the Republic which can also help organize accommodation for you.

**Campsites**, known as *autokemp*, are plentiful all over the Republic; the facilities are often basic and the ones known as *tábořiště* are even more rudimentary. Most have simple **chalets** (*chaty* or *bungalovy*) for anything upwards of 500Kč for two people. The Shocart map *Kempy a chatové osady ČR* lists Czech campsites and is sold in many bookshops.

# Food and drink

The good news is that you can eat and drink very cheaply in the Czech Republic. The bad news is that forty years of culinary isolation and centralization under the Communists allowed few innovations in **Czech cuisine**.

## Czech

| | Czech | Pronunciation |
|---|---|---|
| Yes | *Ano* | **Uh**-no |
| No | *Ne* | Neh |
| Please | *Prosím* | **Pro**-seem |
| Thank you | *Děkuji vam* | **Dye**-koo-yi vam |
| Good day/Hello | *Dobry den/Ahoj* | **Dob**-rie den/**A**-hoy |
| Goodbye | *Na shledanou* | Nu **shle**-dan-uh |
| Excuse me | *Promiňte* | **Prom**-in-teh |
| Where? | *Kde* | Gde |
| Good | *Dobrý* | **Dob**-rie |
| Bad | *Špatný* | **Shput**-nie |
| Near | *Blízko* | **Blee**-sko |
| Far | *Daleko* | **Duh**-lek-o |
| Cheap | *Levný* | **Lev**-nie |
| Expensive | *Drahý* | **Dru**-hie |
| Open | *Otevřeno* | **Ot**-evrsh-en-o |
| Closed | *Zavřeno* | **Zavrsh**-en-o |
| Today | *Dnes* | Dnes |
| Yesterday | *Včera* | **Ftch**-er-a |
| Tomorrow | *Zítra* | **Zeet**-ra |
| How much is...? | *Kolík stojí...?* | **Kol**-ik **sto**-yee |
| What time is it? | *Kolík je hodin?* | **Kol**-ik ye **hod**-in |
| I don't understand | *Nerozumím* | **Ne**-ro-zoom-eem |
| Do you speak English? | *Mluvíte Anglicky?* | **Myuv**-ee-te **ang**-lits-ky |
| One | *Jeden* | **Yed**-en |
| Two | *Dva* | Dva |
| Three | *Tři* | Trshi |
| Four | *Čtyři* | **Chtirsh**-i |
| Five | *Pět* | Pyet |
| Six | *Šest* | Shest |
| Seven | *Sedm* | **Sed**-um |
| Eight | *Osum* | **Oss**-um |
| Nine | *Devět* | **Dev**-yet |
| Ten | *Deset* | **Dess**-et |

Still, washed down with divine Czech beer, anything tastes good.

The whole concept of **breakfast** (*snidaně*) is alien to the Czechs. Popular street **snacks** include *bramborák*, a potato pancake with flecks of bacon, *párek*, a frankfurter dipped in mustard or ketchup and shoved in a white roll, and *smažený sýr* – a slab of melted cheese fried in breadcrumbs and served in a roll (*v housce*) with tartar sauce. The better Czech cafés have proper espresso machines

serving decent **coffee** (*káva*); elsewhere, the Czechs drink Turkish-style or *turecká*, with grains at the bottom of the cup. The **cake shop** (*cukrárna*) is an important part of the country's social life, particularly on Sundays when it's often the only place that's open.

**Restaurants** (*restaurace*) always display their menus and prices outside. They serve hot meals from about 11am until 9pm. Most **pubs** (*pivnice*) also serve basic hot dishes, as do **wine bars** (*vinárna*) – often the most stylish places around. Lunchtime menus start with soup (*polévka*), one of the country's culinary strong points. **Main courses** are overwhelmingly based on pork (*vepřový*) or beef (*hovězí*), but one treat is carp (*kapr*), traditional at Christmas and cheaply and widely offered just about everywhere, along with trout (*pstruh*). Goose (*husa*), duck (*kachna*) and wild boar (*kanci maso*) dishes are also generally delicious. Main courses are served with different varieties of **dumpling** (*knedlíky*) or **vegetables**, most commonly potatoes (*brambory*) and cabbage (*zelí*). With the exception of *palačinky* (pancakes), filled with chocolate or fruit and cream, fruit dumplings (*ovocné knedlíky*) and ice cream, **desserts** can be pretty uninspiring.

### Drink

Even the simplest *bufet* (self-service cafeteria) in the Czech Republic almost invariably has beer (*pivo*) on draught. **Pubs**, most of which close around 11pm, are still a predominantly male affair, with heavy drinking the norm; **wine bars** are more upmarket, and **cocktail bars** have opened up in larger towns.

The Czech Republic tops the world league table of **beer** consumption – hardly surprising since its beer ranks among the best in the world. The most natural starting point for any beer tour is the Bohemian city of **Plzeň** (Pilsen), whose local lager is the original Pils. The other big brewing town is **České Budějovice** (Budweis), home to Budvar, a mild beer by Bohemian standards but still leagues ahead of the American Budweiser. There's also a modest selection of medium-quality **wines**; the largest wine-producing region is southern Moravia. The home-production of firewater is a national pastime, resulting in some almost terminally strong concoctions, most famously a plum brandy called **slivovice**. The best-known Czech **spirit** is Becherovka, a medicinal herbal tipple from Karlovy Vary, known as a *beton* when ordered with ice and tonic.

# Opening hours and holidays

**Shops** are open Mon–Fri 9am–5pm, with some, especially in Prague, and most supermarkets staying open till 6pm or later. Smaller shops close for lunch between noon and 2pm, while others stay open late on Thursdays. In larger towns, some shops stay open all day at weekends, and the **corner shop** (*večerka*) stays open daily till 11pm. **Public holidays** include Jan 1, Easter Mon, May 1, May 8, July 5 & 6, Sept 28, Oct 28, Nov 17, Dec 24–26.

# Emergencies

**Pickpockets** are as rife in the centre of Prague as in any European capital, particularly in the Old Town Square, on the #22 tram, in the metro and in the main railway stations. Theft from cars is also a problem. You should theoretically carry your **passport** with you at all times though, you're unlikely to get stopped.

Minor ailments can be easily dealt with at a **pharmacy** (*lékárna*), but language is likely to be a problem outside the capital. If it's a repeat prescription you want, take any empty bottles or remaining pills along with you. If the pharmacist can't help, they'll be able to direct you to a **hospital** (*nemocnice*).

| **Emergency numbers** |
| :--- |
| Police ☏158; fire ☏150; ambulance ☏155. |

# Prague (Praha)

Architecturally, **PRAGUE** (Praha) is a revelation: few other cities anywhere in Europe look so good, and no other European capital can present six hundred years of architecture so untouched by war; even the severe floods of 2002 have left little trace. Alongside its heritage, Prague has a lively atmosphere, and is a great place to enjoy a variety of nightlife – from traditional pubs to funky bars – or just relax and soak up the view in one of the city parks and gardens.

The city has its **origins** in the ninth century under Prince Bořivoj, its first Christian ruler and founder of the Přemyslid dynasty. His grandson, Prince Václav, became the **Good King Wenceslas** of the Christmas carol and the country's patron saint. The city prospered from its position on the central European trade routes, but it was after the dynasty died out in 1306 that Prague enjoyed its golden age. In just thirty years Holy Roman Emperor Charles IV transformed it into one of the most important cities in fourteenth-century Europe, founding the university and an entire new town, Nové Město. Following the execution of the reformist preacher Jan Hus in 1415, the country became engulfed in **religious wars**, and trouble broke out again between the Protestant nobles and the Catholic Habsburg rulers in 1618. The full force of the Counter-Reformation was brought to bear on the city's people, though the spurt of Baroque rebuilding that went with it gave Prague some of its most striking buildings.

After two centuries as little more than a provincial town in the Habsburg Empire, Prague was dragged out of the doldrums by the **Industrial Revolution** and the **národní obrození**, the Czech national revival that led to the foundation of the **First Republic** in 1918. After World War II, which it survived substantially unscathed, Prague disappeared completely behind the Iron Curtain. The city briefly re-emerged onto the world stage during the Prague Spring in 1968, but the decisive break came in November 1989, when a peaceful student demonstration, brutally broken up by the police, triggered off the **Velvet Revolution**, which eventually toppled the Communist government. The popular unity of that period is now history, but there is still a great sense of new-found potential in the capital. Ongoing restoration of buildings and a substantial influx of foreign businesses, workers and visitors have once again made Prague a smart and cosmopolitan European capital.

## Arrival, information and city transport

Prague's **airport**, Ruzyně, is 10km northwest of the city. The cheapest way of getting into town is to take local bus #119 (4am–midnight; every 7–15min; 20min) to Dejvická metro station, the start of line A, which will take you directly to the centre of town. Alternatively, there's the ČEDAZ **express minibus** (5.30am–9.30pm; every 30min; 20min to Dejvická, 40min–1hr to city centre), which stops first at Dejvická metro station, and ends up at náměstí Republiky (90Kč). This service will also take you straight to your accommodation for around 480Kč per drop-off – a bargain if there's a few of you (960Kč for 5–8 people). "Fixed-price" taxis are best avoided, at around 700Kč to the centre. Arriving by **train** from the west, you're most likely to end up at **Praha hlavní nádraží**, the main station. It's only a short walk to Wenceslas Square from here (though inadvisable at night), and the station has its own metro stop. International expresses passing through Prague usually stop only at **Praha Holešovice** station, north of the city centre (metro Nádraží Holešovice). Some trains from Moravia and Slovakia wind up at the central **Praha Masarykovo** station (metro Náměstí Republiky), and trains from the south at **Praha Smíchov** station (metro Smíchovské nádraží). The main **bus station** is Praha-Florenc on the eastern edge of Staré Město (metro Florenc). The best place to go for information

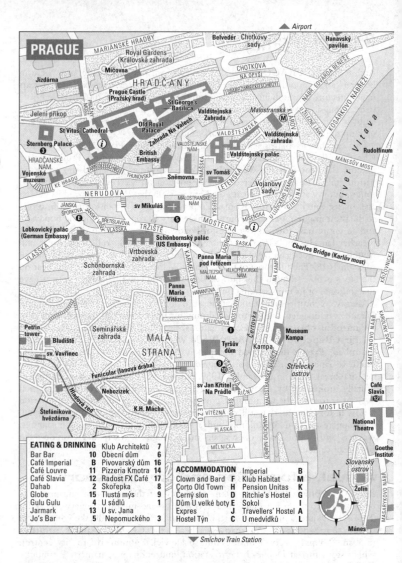

PRAGUE

Airport

MARIÁNSKÉ HRADBY — Royal Gardens (Královská zahrada) — Belvedér — Chotkovy sady — Hanavský pavilón — CHOTKOVA — NA OPYŠI — Jízdárna — Míčovna — HRADČANY — Jeleni příkop — Prague Castle (Pražský hrad) — St George's Basilica — Valdštejnská Zahrada — Malostranská Ⓜ — KLÁROV — Sternberg Palace — St Vitus' Cathedral — Old Royal Palace — Zahrada Na Valech — VALDŠTEJNSKÁ — Valdštejnská zahrada — Rudolfinum — HRADČANSKÉ NÁM. ❸ — VALDŠTEJNSKÉ NÁM. — British Embassy — Valdštejnský palác — MÁNESŮV MOST — Vojenské muzeum — KE HRADU — THUNOVSKÁ — Sněmovna — sv Tomáš — River Vltava — NERUDOVA — JÁNSKÁ — SPORKOVA Ⓔ — BŘETISLAVOVA — sv Mikuláš — MALOSTRANSKÉ NÁM. — Vojanovy sady — Lobkovický palác (German Embassy) — VLAŠSKÁ — TRŽIŠTĚ ❺ — MOSTECKÁ — MÍŠEŇSKÁ ⓘ — Charles Bridge (Karlův most) — Schönbornský palác (US Embassy) — SASKÁ — Vrtbovská zahrada — Panna Maria pod řetězem — MALTÉZSKÉ NÁM. — VELKOPŘEVORSKÉ NÁM. — NA KAMPĚ — Schönbornská zahrada — HARANTOVA — Panna Maria Vítězná — HELLICHOVA — Petřín tower — Seminářská zahrada — MALÁ STRANA — Tyršův dům — Kampa — Museum Kampa — Střelecký ostrov — Bludiště — sv. Vavřinec — Funicular (lanová dráha) — Nebozízek — sv Jan Křtitel Na Prádle — ŘÍČNÍ — Café Slavia ⑫ — Štefánikova hvězdárna — Hladová zeď — K.H. Mácha — ÚJEZD — VÍTĚZNÁ — MOST LEGIÍ — National Theatre — PLASKÁ — Goethe Institut — MĚLNICKÁ — Slovanský ostrov — Žofín — N — Mánes — Smíchov Train Station

CZECH REPUBLIC | Prague (Praha)

| EATING & DRINKING | |
|---|---|
| Bar Bar | 10 |
| Café Imperial | B |
| Café Louvre | 11 |
| Café Slavia | 12 |
| Dahab | 2 |
| Globe | 15 |
| Gulu Gulu | 4 |
| Jarmark | 13 |
| Jo's Bar | 5 |
| Klub Architektů | 7 |
| Obecní dům | 6 |
| Pivovarský dům | 16 |
| Pizzeria Kmotra | 14 |
| Radost FX Café | 17 |
| Skořepka | 8 |
| Tlustá mýš | 9 |
| U sádlů | 1 |
| U sv. Jana Nepomuckého | 3 |

| ACCOMMODATION | | | |
|---|---|---|---|
| Clown and Bard | F | Imperial | B |
| Corto Old Town | H | Klub Habitat | M |
| Černý slon | D | Pension Unitas | K |
| Dům U velké boty | E | Ritchie's Hostel | G |
| Expres | J | Sokol | I |
| Hostel Týn | C | Travellers' Hostel | A |
| | | U medvídků | L |

is the **Prague Information Service**, or PIS (Pražská informační služba), which has several branches around town; the main office is at Na příkopě 20 (Mon–Fri 9am–6/7pm, Sat 9am–3/5pm; April–Oct also Sun 9am–5pm; Ⓦwww.pis.cz). The staff speak English, but their helpfulness varies; they can usually answer most enquiries, and organize accommodation, sell maps, guides and theatre tickets. As for events, it's worth getting hold of the English-language monthly *Prague Events* or *Heart of Europe*, both with good listings sections.

### City transport

Prague's city centre is reasonably small and best explored on foot, but to cross the city quickly, or reach some of the more widely dispersed attractions, you'll need

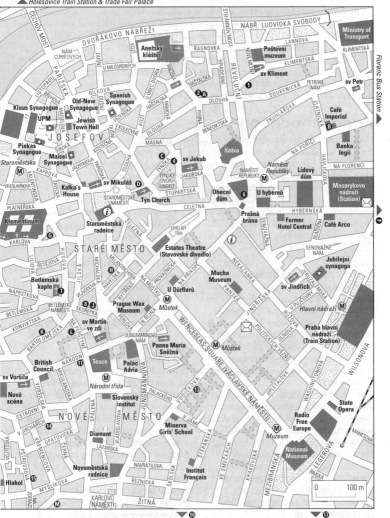

to use the public transport system. There are two main **tickets**: the 12Kč *přestupní jízdenka* is valid for an hour (1hr 30min off-peak), and allows you to change metro lines, trams and buses as often as you like; the 8Kč *nepřestupní jízdenka* allows you to travel for up to fifteen minutes on a single tram or bus, or up to four stops on the metro. Buy tickets from a tobacconist, kiosk or one of the ticket machines inside metro stations and at some tram stops and then validate them on board or at the metro entrance. To take a large backpack on public transport you'll need an extra half-fare ticket. If you're going to be using the system a lot, it's worth getting hold of a **travel pass** (*Časová jízdenka*; 70Kč/24hr, 200Kč/72hr, 250Kč/week); remember to validate it when you first use it. Plain-clothes inspectors check tickets – it's a fine of 400Kč on the spot if it's not valid.

The fast, Soviet-built **metro** (daily 5am–midnight) is the most useful form of city transport. The trams (every 10–15min) navigate Prague's hills and cobbles with remarkable dexterity. Tram #22, whose run includes Vinohrady and Hradčany, is a good way to sightsee, though beware of pickpockets. Night trams #51–59 (midnight–4.30am; every 30min) all pass by Lazarská in Nové Město. The horror stories about Prague **taxi** drivers ripping off tourists are too numerous to mention, so your best bet is to call the English-speaking AAA (☎140 14; 34Kč plus 25Kč per 1km), rather than go to the mafia-controlled taxi ranks.

## Accommodation

Prague's **hotels** are exorbitant for what you get, and booking ahead is essential. As a result, most tourists on a budget now stay in private rooms or **hostels**, both of which are easy to organize on arrival. The main international train stations and the airport have numerous **accommodation agencies** dealing with hotels, pensions and sometimes **private rooms**: the largest is AVE (☎251 091 111,ⓦwww.avetravel.cz), with over 1500 beds in hotels and pensions on its books. Prague's university, the Karolinum, rents out over a thousand **student rooms** in summer; contact the booking office at Voršilská 1, Nové Město (Mon–Fri only; ☎224 930 010; beds available July to mid-Sept; from around 250Kč).

### Hostels

**Clown and Bard** Bořivojova 102, Žižkov ☎222 716 453, ⓦwww.clownandbard.com. Laid-back atmosphere and loads of events, plus laundry service and Internet access. Tram #5, #9 or #26 to Lipanská from metro Hlavní nádraží. Dorms 250Kč, rooms ❷

**Hostel Týn** Týnská 21, Staré Město ☎224 828 519, ⓦwww.hostel-tyn.web2001.cz. Central hostel, offering four- and five-bed dorms and simple doubles. Metro Náměstí Republiky. Dorms 450Kč, rooms ❸

**Klub Habitat** Na Zderaze 10, Nové Město ☎224 918 252, ⓦwww.klubhabitat.cz. A fairly basic but friendly place, a short walk from Karlovo náměstí. Book ahead. Metro Karlovo náměstí. 450Kč.

**Ritchie's Hostel** Karlova 9, Staré Město ☎222 221 229, ⓦwww.ritchieshostel.cz. A hostel-cum-hotel wonderfully located between the Staroměstské náměstí and the Charles Bridge. Dorms and rooms with or without en-suite bathrooms. Internet access. Metro Staroměstská. Dorms 300Kč, rooms ❹–❺

**Sokol** Nosticova 2, Malá Strana ☎257 007 397, ⓦwww.sokol-cos.cz/hostel.html. Student hostel in a great location near the river and castle. Tram #12, #20 or #22 from metro Malostranská. 350Kč.

**Travellers' Hostel** Dlouhá 33, Staré Město ☎224 826 662, ⓦwww.travellers.cz. Centrally located hostel, with dorms and one- to six-bed rooms. There's also a bar, laundry and Internet access. Metro Náměstí Republiky. Dorms 380Kč, rooms ❹

### Hotels and pensions

**Corto Old Town** Havelská 15, Staré Město ☎224 215 313, ⓦwww.corto.cz. Perfect location right over the market on Havelská, though the rooms are pretty spartan. Metro Můstek. ❽

**Černý slon** Týnská 1, Staré Město ☎222 321 521, ⓦwww.hotelcernyslon.cz. A four-star hotel with beautifully refurbished rooms and a wine cellar, in a medieval house near the Staroměstské náměstí. Metro Náměstí Republiky. ❽

**Dům U velké boty** Vlašská 30, Malá Strana ☎257 533 234, ⓦwww.dumuvelkeboty .cz. If you can afford to splash out, try this delightful, tastefully decorated pension, run by a very welcoming couple. Metro Malostranská. ❽

**Expres** Skořepka 5, Staré Město ☎224 211 801, ⓦwww.pragueexpreshotel.cz. Friendly staff and a reasonable price, so long as you don't mind the peepshow across the street. The cheapest rooms come without en-suite facilities. Metro Národní třída. ❹

**Imperial** Na Poříčí 15, Nové Město ☎222 316 012, ⓦwww.hotelimperial.cz. Atmospheric and spotless rooms with shared facilities in an Art Nouveau hotel on the edge of the old town, with a great café below. Metro Náměstí Republiky. ❺

**Pension Unitas** Bartolomějská 9, Staré Město ☎224 221 802, ⓦwww.unitas.cz. Hotel-cum-hostel in a former nunnery; rooms range from the clean and bright to claustrophobic converted secret-police prison cells (where the former Czech president Václav Havel was once detained). Breakfast included. Metro Národní třída. ❹

**U medvídků** Na Perštýně 7 ☎224 211 916, ⓦwww.umedvidku.cz. Friendly, central place with plainly furnished rooms above a famous Prague pub. Metro Národní třída. ❽

# The City

The River Vltava divides the capital into two unequal halves: the steeply inclined left bank, where you'll find the castle district of Hradčany and Malá Strana, and the gentler, sprawling right bank, which includes Staré Město, Josefov and Nové Město. **Hradčany**, on the hill, contains the most obvious sights – the castle, the cathedral and the old royal palace. Below Hradčany, **Malá Strana** (Little Quarter), with its narrow eighteenth-century streets, is the city's ministerial and diplomatic quarter, though its Baroque gardens are there for all to enjoy. Over the river, on the right bank, **Staré Město** (Old Town) is a web of alleys and passageways centred on the city's most beautiful square, Staroměstské náměstí. Enclosed within the boundaries of Staré Město is **Josefov**, the old Jewish quarter, now down to a handful of synagogues and a cemetery. **Nové Město** (New Town), the focus of the modern city, covers the largest area, laid out in long wide boulevards – most famously Wenceslas Square – stretching south and east of the old town.

## Hradčany

**Hradčany** is wholly dominated by the city's omnipresent landmark, **Prague Castle** (daily 5/6am–11pm/midnight; most sights 9am–4/5pm; ⊛www.hrad.cz). Viewed from the Charles Bridge, the castle stands aloof from the rest of the city, protected by a rather austere palatial facade that's breached only by the gothic mass of **St Vitus Cathedral**.

Work on the cathedral started under Charles IV, who employed the precocious 23-year-old German mason Peter Parler; by the time Charles died in 1399, however, only the choir and the south transept were finished, and the whole structure wasn't finally completed until 1929. The cathedral is the country's largest church, and, once inside, it's difficult not to be impressed by its sheer height. The grand **chapel of sv Václav**, by the south door, is easily the main attraction. Built by Parler, its rich decoration resembles the inside of a jewel casket: the gilded walls are inlaid with over 1300 semiprecious stones, set around ethereal fourteenth-century biblical frescoes, while above, the tragedy of Wenceslas unfolds in later paintings. A door in the south wall leads to the coronation chamber, which houses the Bohemian crown jewels, including the gold crown of St Wenceslas. At the centre of the choir, within a fine Renaissance grill, cherubs lark about on the sixteenth-century marble **Imperial Mausoleum**, commissioned by Rudolf II for his grandfather, Ferdinand I, and father, Maximilian II.

If you want to see the choir, crypt or tower you'll need to buy a ticket (350Kč; valid for two days), which also gives you entry into a handful of other sights in the castle, including the **Old Royal Palace** (Starý královský palác), just across the courtyard from the south door of the cathedral, and home to the princes and kings of Bohemia from the eleventh to the seventeenth centuries. It's a sandwich of royal apartments built by successive generations – these days you enter at the third floor, built at the end of the fifteenth century. The massive Vladislav Hall (Vladislavský sál) is where the early Bohemian kings were elected, and where every president since Masaryk has been sworn into office. The palace's basement holds "The story of Prague Castle" exhibition (daily 9am–5pm), including a 40-minute film (in English every 90min; first at 9.45am).

---

## Museum and building entry

If you want to see the interior of a building in Prague, often the only way is to go on a **guided tour** that will last at least 45 minutes; the last tour usually leaves an hour before the advertised closing time. Ask for an anglický text, an often unintentionally hilarious English résumé. **Entrance tickets** to most sights of interest throughout the Czech Republic rarely cost more than 50–100Kč, so prices are only quoted in this chapter where the admission fee is prohibitively high.

Don't be fooled by the uninspiring red facade of the **Basilica of St George** (Bazilika sv Jiří), on the square to the east of St Vitus – this is Prague's most beautiful Romanesque monument, its inside meticulously restored to recreate the honey-coloured basilica which replaced the original tenth-century church in 1173. Next door, the **Convent of St George** (Jiřský klášter), founded in 973, now houses the National Gallery's **Rudolfine and Baroque art collection** (Tues–Sun 10am–6pm; 50Kč; ®www.ngprague.cz), mostly of specialist interest only, though including a brief taste of the overtly sensual and erotic Mannerist paintings from the reign of Rudolf II (1576–1612). Round the corner from the convent is the **Golden Lane** (Zlatá ulička), a blind and crowded alley of miniature sixteenth-century cottages in dolly-mixture colours. A plaque at no. 22 commemorates Franz Kafka's brief sojourn here during World War I.

North of the castle walls, across the **Powder Bridge** (Prašný most), is the entrance to the **Royal Gardens** (Královská zahrada; April–Oct daily 10am–6pm), founded in the early sixteenth century and still the best-kept gardens in the country, with fountains and immaculately cropped lawns. At the end of the gardens is Prague's most celebrated Renaissance legacy, the **Belvedér**, a delicately arcaded summer house.

**Hradčanské náměstí** fans out from the castle's main gates, surrounded by the oversized palaces of the old nobility. A passage down the side of the Archbishop's Palace leads to the early eighteenth-century **Šternberg Palace** (Tues–Sun 10am–6pm; 60Kč; ®www.ngprague.cz), housing the National Gallery's relatively modest **Old European art collection** (ie non-Czech), which primarily consists of works from the fifteenth to eighteenth centuries, the most significant of which is the *Festival of the Rosary* by Dürer.

## Malá Strana

**Malá Strana** conforms to the image of Prague as the quintessential Baroque city. Its focus is the sloping, cobbled **Malostranské náměstí**, a busy square split in two by the former Jesuit seminary and church of **sv Mikuláš** (daily 9am–4/5pm; tower: April–Oct daily 10am–6pm; Nov–March Sat & Sun 10am–5pm; free), possibly the most magnificent Baroque building in the city. Nothing of the plain west facade prepares you for the overwhelming High Baroque interior – the fresco in the nave alone covers over 1500 square metres, and portrays some of the more fanciful feats of St Nicholas.

Follow Tomášská north from the square and you'll enter Valdštejnská, flanked on one side by the gargantuan Valdštejn Palace, and on the other by the **Valdštejnská zahrada** (April–Oct daily 10am–6pm). These terraced gardens, which connect higher up with the Zahrada na valech (The Gardens on the Ramparts), are one of the chief joys of Malá Strana. This is where the royal vineyards used to be and the gardens command superb views over Prague.

South of the main square, a continuation of Karmelitská brings you to the funicular railway up **Petřín** hill (daily 9am–11.20/11.30pm; every 10–15min), a better green space than most in Prague, and a good place for a picnic and views from the **Petřín tower** (April, Sept & Oct daily 10am–6/7pm; May–Aug daily 10am–10pm; Nov–March Sat & Sun 10am–5pm).

## Staré Město

**Staré Město**, founded in the early thirteenth century, is where most of the capital's shops, restaurants and pubs are located. It is linked to Malá Strana by the city's most familiar monument, the **Charles Bridge** (Karlův most), begun in 1357. The statues that line it – brilliant pieces of Jesuit propaganda added during the Counter-Reformation – have made it renowned throughout Europe and choked with tourists throughout the year. Cross to Staré Město and head down the narrow, crowded **Karlova**, which winds past the massive **Klementinum** (March–Oct Mon–Fri 2–6/7pm, Sat & Sun 10/11am– 6/7pm; Nov–Feb Sat &

Sun 11am–6pm), the former Jesuit College, completed just before the order was turfed out of the country in 1773. The Klementinum is now home to the collections of the national library and you can take a tour of the spectacular Baroque Library and the astronomical tower.

At the end of the street lies **Staroměstské náměstí**, the most spectacular square in Prague and the city's main marketplace from the eleventh century. At its centre is the dramatic Art Nouveau **Jan Hus Monument**, featuring the great fifteenth-century religious reformer. The best-known sight on the square, however, is the **Astronomical Clock** (chimes hourly 9am–9pm), which features a mechanical performance by Christ and the Apostles. The clock is an integral part of **Staroměstská radnice**, the town hall, inside which you can view a few chambers (Mon 11am–5/6pm, Tues–Sun 9am–5/6pm), climb the tower and get a close-up view of the mechanical figures. Staré Město's most impressive Gothic structure is the mighty **Týn Church**, whose towers rise above the two arcaded houses which otherwise obscure its facade. Behind, at the end of Týnská, lies the **Týnský dvur**, a stunning fortified courtyard where customs used to be collected; it houses the Renaissance Granovský Palace plus some upmarket shops and cafés.

## Josefov

Within Staré Město lies **Josefov**, the Jewish quarter of the city until the end of the nineteenth century, when this ghetto area was demolished in order to create a beautiful bourgeois district on Parisian lines. The writer **Franz Kafka** spent most of his life in and around Josefov, and the destruction of the Jewish quarter, which continued throughout his childhood, had a profound effect on his psyche; a small exhibition (Tues–Fri 10am–6pm, Sat 10am–5pm) on the site of his birthplace, at náměstí Franze Kafky 5, tells the story of his life.

The synagogues and sights of Josefov are covered by one ticket, available from any of the quarter's box offices (daily except Sat & Jewish holidays 9am–4.30/6pm; 300Kč, plus another 200Kč for the Old-New Synagogue; ✪www.jewishmuseum .cz). The best place to begin is the **Pinkas Synagogue** on Široká, which contains a chilling memorial to the 77,297 Czechoslovak Jews who were killed during the Holocaust – the names of all the victims cover the walls, while children's drawings from the Theresienstadt (Terezín) camp are displayed in the women's gallery. From here, you enter the **Old Jewish Cemetery** (Starý Židovský hřbitov), established in the fifteenth century and in use until 1787, by which time there were some 100,000 graves here piled on top of one another. The jumble of Gothic, Renaissance and Baroque tombstones are a poignant reminder of the ghetto, its inhabitants subjected to overcrowding even in death. By the exit to the cemetery on U Starého hřbitová is the Baroque **Klaus Synagogue**, which, along with the neo-Gothic **Maisel Synagogue** on Maiselova, displays some beautiful religious objects and portrays the history of the Jews in the Czech lands until the eighteenth century.

Halfway down **Pařížská** is the steep brick gable of the **Old-New Synagogue**, completed in the fourteenth century and still the religious centre of Prague's Jewish community. Originally it was known simply as the New Synagogue, but after several fires gutted the ghetto it became the oldest synagogue building in the quarter – hence its name. Opposite the synagogue is the **Židovská radnice**, the old Jewish town hall founded in the sixteenth century and later turned into a creamy-pink Baroque house crowned by a wooden clocktower. In addition to the four main clocks, there's one on the north gable, which (like Hebrew script) goes "backwards". A couple of blocks east of Pařížská, at Věženská 1, is the highly ornate neo-Byzantine **Spanish Synagogue**, which contains an exhibition on the history of the city's Jewish community from 1781.

## Nové Město

**Nové Město**, now a sprawling quarter of late nineteenth-century bourgeois dwellings, was actually founded in 1348 by Charles IV. The borderline between Staré and Nové Město is made up by the continuous boulevards of **Národní** and **Na příkopě**, a boomerang curve that follows the course of the old moat. The former was the unlikely setting for the November 17 demonstration that sparked off the Velvet Revolution.

At the river end of Národní is the gold-crested **National Theatre**, completed in 1881, a proud symbol of the Czech nation. Refused money by the Austrian state, Czechs of all classes dug deep into their pockets to raise funds for the venture themselves. Halfway along Na příkopě, you can visit the **Mucha Museum**, at Panská 7 (daily 10am–4/6pm; 120Kč; ✆www.mucha.cz), dedicated to the most famous Czech practitioner of Art Nouveau, Alfons Mucha.

At the far end of Na příkopě, on náměstí Republiky, stands the **Obecní dům**, where you can see more of Mucha's work. Begun in 1903, it was decorated inside and out with the help of almost every artist connected with the Czech Art Nouveau, or Secession, movement. The easiest way of soaking up the dramatic interior, covered with mosaics and pendulous chandeliers, is to have a reasonably pricey but delicious meal in the French restaurant to the right of the entrance or a coffee in the equally dazzling café to the left. Alternatively, you can go on a guided tour of the interior (also in English); tickets are available from the information centre inside (daily 10am–6pm; 150Kč; ✆www.obecnidum.cz).

Cross Na příkopě at its central point and you're into the pivot of modern Prague and the political focus of the events of 1989 – the wide, gently sloping **Wenceslas Square** (Václavské náměstí). The square's history of protest goes back to the Prague Spring of 1968: towards the top end, there's a small memorial to the victims of Communism, the most famous of whom, the 21-year-old student Jan Palach, set himself alight on this very spot in 1969 in protest against the Soviet occupation. A six-lane freeway effectively cuts off the square from the **National Museum** (daily 9/10am–5/6pm; 100Kč), one of the great symbols of the nineteenth-century Czech national revival, with its monumental glass cupola, sculptural decoration and frescoes from Czech history. However, unless you're a geologist or a zoologist you're likely to remain unmoved by the exhibits.

### Trade Fair Palace: The Museum of Modern Art

One excellent reason to hop on a tram is to visit the city's modern art museum, housed in a stylish 1920s functionalist building, known as the **Trade Fair Palace** (Veletržní palác; Tues–Sun 10am–6pm; 100Kč for each floor visited or 250Kč for all four; ✆www.ngprague.cz;), on Dukelských hrdinů 47 (tram #5 from nám. Republiky). The museum's *raison d'être* is its unrivalled collection of nineteenth- and twentieth-century Czech art, but it also houses the National Gallery's modest collection of nineteenth- and twentieth-century European art, including works by Klimt, Schiele, Picasso and the French Impressionists, as well as temporary exhibitions of contemporary Czech and foreign art.

## Eating

While traditional Czech food still predominates in the city's pubs, Prague now has a wide range of **restaurants** offering anything from French to Japanese cuisine. Steer clear of places in the main tourist areas, such as either side of the Charles Bridge, which tend to be overpriced and of indifferent quality.

**Bar Bar** Všehrdova 17, Malá Strana. Arty crêperie with generous, cheap salads and sweet and savoury pancakes.

**Jarmark** Vodičkova 30, Nové Město. Popular, inexpensive self-service steak and salad buffet in the Lucerna pasáž, where the chef prepares your food in front of you; a few veggie dishes on offer, too.

**Klub Architektů** Betlémské nám. 5, Staré Město ✆224 401 214. Attractive, lively cellar restaurant serving tasty Czech and vegetarian cuisine. Booking recommended.

**Pizzeria Kmotra** V Jirchářích 12, Nové Město. Hugely popular basement pizza place in the backstreets behind Národní.

**Radost FX Café** Bělehradská 120, Vinohrady. Outstanding veggie food attracts ultra-fashionable crowd; open till very late, brunch at weekends.

**Skořepka** Skořepka 1, Staré Město. Czech and international dishes served in this pleasant, folk-style restaurant with vaulted ceiling, hidden in the backstreets of Staré Město.

**Tlustá mýs** Všehrdova 19, Malá Strana. Cosy cellar bar, restaurant and gallery, offering reasonably priced hearty Czech food washed down with Pilsner Urquell.

**U sádlů** Klimentská 2, Staré Město. Deliberately over-the-top themed medieval banqueting hall serving inexpensive hearty fare and lashings of frothing ale.

**U sv. Jana Nepomuckého** Hradčanské nám. 12, Hradčany. Stylish, old-fashioned restaurant in the former archbishop's stables. In summer, there are tables on the quiet, cobblestoned patio.

# Drinking

The choice of Prague **cafés** is pretty varied – from Art Nouveau relics, which also do food, and swish espresso bars (both of which are called *kavárna* and are licensed), to simple sugar and caffeine joints (*cukrárna*). For no-nonsense boozing you need to head for a **pub** (*pivnice*), which invariably serves excellent beer by the half-litre, but many of which close around 11pm. For late-night drinking, head for one of the clubs or all-night bars.

**Café Imperial** Na poříčí 15, Staré Město. An endearingly shabby yet still grand Habsburg-era Kaffeehaus, which has retained its original, tiled decor.

**Café Louvre** Národní 20, Nové Město. Resurrected Habsburg-era Kaffeehaus with high ceiling, mirrors, daily papers and a billiard hall.

**Café Slavia** Národní 1, Nové Město. Famous café opposite the National Theatre, with great riverside views, decent meals and Manet's *Absinthe Drinker* on the wall.

**Dahab** Dlouhá 33, Staré Město. The mother of all Prague teahouses, a vast Bedouin tent of a place offering tasty Middle Eastern snacks and hookahs to a background of funky world music.

**Globe** Pštrossova 6, Nové Město. Large, buzzing café, at the back of the English-language bookstore of the same name. A serious expat hangout, but enjoyable nevertheless.

**Gulu Gulu** Týnská 12, Staré Město. Several pretty spartan rooms opposite the *Hostel Týn*, with world music in the evenings and cheap pizzas.

**Jo's Bar** Malostranské náměstí 7, Malá Strana. A narrow bar in Malá Strana that is the original expat/backpacker hangout. Tex-Mex food served all day, bottled beer only and a heaving crowd guaranteed most evenings. Downstairs is *Jo's Garáž* disco.

**Obecní dům** Nám. Republiky 5, Nové Město. Glorious Art Nouveau decor, impeccable service and a good cake trolley.

**Pivovarskýdům** Lipova 15, Nové Město. In-house brewery offering everything from wheat- to banana-beer, along with excellent Czech pub grub and good service.

# Nightlife

Predictably enough for a nation which began life with a playwright for a president, **theatre** in Prague is thriving; unless you know the language your scope is limited, but there's also a tradition of innovative mime and puppetry in the city. Tickets are cheap and available from various agencies around town, including Ticketpro, as well as from tourist offices and the venues themselves.

As far as **live music** is concerned, the classical scene still has the edge in Prague, though there are also good **jazz clubs** and **nightclubs**. Classical concerts take place throughout the year in concert halls and churches, the biggest event being the Prague Spring international music festival (@www.festival.cz), which traditionally begins on May 12, the day of Smetana's death, with a performance of *Má vlast*, and finishes on June 2 with a rendition of Beethoven's Ninth. Watch out for concerts in the churches and palaces, as well as in the main venues (listed below), and in the summer for the many open-air concerts and plays held at Hradčany.

## Classical music and theatre

**Estates Theatre** (Stavovské divadlo) Ovocný trh 1, Staré Město ⓦwww.narodni-divadlo.cz. Theatre, ballet and opera in the venue that premièred Mozart's *Don Giovanni*.

**Národní Divadlo** Národní 2, Nové Město ⓦwww.narodni-divadlo.cz. Grand nineteenth-century theatre with a highly ornate interior showing theatre, ballet and opera.

**Rudolfinum** Alsovo nábřeží 12, Staré Město ⓦwww.rudolfinum.cz. Stunning Neo-Renaissance concert hall and home to the Czech Philharmonic.

**Smetana Hall** Obecní dům, náměstí Republiky 5, Nové Město. Fantastically ornate and recently renovated Art Nouveau concert hall, which is home to the excellent Prague Symphony Orchestra.

**Prague State Opera** Wilsonova 4, Nové Město ⓦwww.opera.cz. The former German opera house and the city's second-choice venue for opera and ballet.

## Clubs and live venues

**AghaRTA Jazz Centrum** Železná 16, Staré Město ⓦwww.agharta.cz. Prague's best jazz club, with a good mix of top-name foreigners and locals.

**Karlovy lázně** Novotného lávka 1, Staré Město ⓦwww.karlovylazne.cz. Mega, high-tech club by the Charles Bridge; techno on the top floor, progressively more retro as you descend to the Internet café on the ground floor.

**Lucerna Music Bar** Vodičkova 36, Nové Město ⓦwww.musicbar.cz. Central, small dance space, with live music.

**Palác Akropolis** Kubelíkova 27, Vinohrady ⓦwww.palacakropolis.cz. Decent live arts/world music venue in the backstreets of Žížkov, renowned for Romany and other ethnic music festivals. Tram #5, #9 or #26.

**Radost FX** Bělehradská 120, Vinohrady ⓦwww.radostfx.cz. Still the slickest (and latest-opening – till 5am) all-round dance club venue in Prague, with a great veggie café-restaurant attached.

**Roxy** Dlouhá 33, Staré Město ⓦwww.roxy.cz. Once a cinema, now a major venue with gallery, theatre and club nights.

# Listings

**Embassies and consulates** Australia (honorary), Klimentská 10, Nové Město ☎296 578 350; Canada, Muchova 6, Hradčany ☎272 101 800; New Zealand, Dykova 19, Vinohrady ☎222 514 672; Ireland, Tržiště 13, Malá Strana ☎257 530 061; UK, Thunovská 14, Malá Strana ☎257 402 111; US, Tržiště 15, Malá Strana ☎257 530 663.

**Gay & lesbian Prague** The city doesn't have a large gay and lesbian scene, but there are a few bars and clubs worth checking out: *Friends*, Náprstkova 1, Staré Město, is a friendly, laid-back gay/lesbian cellar bar in the old town, while *Gejzee…r*, Vinohradská 40 (open Thurs–Sat), is the largest and most popular gay club, with dance floor, DJs and darkroom.

**Internet access** Globe (see p.283) has several fast terminals; Bohemia Bagel at Újezd 16, Malá Strana & Masná 2, Staré Město, also serve great bagels, while Káva Káva Káva, Národní 37, Nové Město, is renowned for its coffee.

**Laundry** Laundryland, Londýnska 71, Nové Město (daily 8am–10pm) has a basement bar. Several other locations around town.

**Left luggage** There are lockers or left-luggage offices at all of the train stations.

**Pharmacies** Palackého 5, Nové Město ☎224 946 982 (Mon–Fri 7am–7pm, Sat & Sun 8am–noon); Štefánikova 6, Malá Strana ☎257 320 918 (24hr); plenty of others round town.

**Post office** Jindřišská 14, Nové Město (daily 2am–midnight).

# Bohemia

Prague is the natural centre and capital of **Bohemia**; the rest divides easily into four geographical districts. South Bohemia, bordered by the Šumava Mountains, is the least spoilt; its largest town by far is the brewing centre of **České Budějovice**, and its chief attraction, aside from the thickly forested hills, is a series of well-preserved medieval towns, whose undisputed gem is **Český Krumlov**. Neighbouring West Bohemia has a similar mix of rolling woods and hills, despite the industrial nature of its capital **Plzeň**, home of Pilsen beer and the Škoda empire. Beyond here, as you approach the German border, Bohemia's famous spa region unfolds, with magnificent resorts such as **Mariánské Lázně** and **Karlovy Vary** enjoying sparkling reputations. North Bohemia has real problems: devastated by industrialization, many parts are virtually uninhabitable. East Bohemia has suffered indirectly from the polluting industries of its neighbour, but remains relatively blight-free. There's some great walking and climbing country here, but the only essential stop on a quick tour is the silver-mining centre of **Kutná Hora**.

# České Budějovice

Since its foundation in 1265, **ČESKÉ BUDĚJOVICE** has been a self-assured town, convinced of its own importance. In medieval times the town made its money from silver mining and taxing salt as it passed through from Linz to Prague. In the seventeenth century war and fire pretty much destroyed the place but it was rebuilt by the Habsburgs in lavish style. If you're travelling on to Český Krumlov you'll almost certainly have to change trains here – České Budějovice is a great place to stretch your legs and try the tasty local Budvar **beer**.

The compact old town is only a five-minute walk from the **train** and **bus** stations, both to the east of the city centre: head along the pedestrianized Lannova třída. The medieval grid plan leads inevitably to the magnificent central **náměstí Přemysla Otakara II**, one of Europe's largest market squares. Its buildings are elegant enough, but it's the arcades and the octagonal **Samson's Fountain** – once the only tap in town – that make the greatest impression. The 72-metre status symbol, the **Black Tower** (Černá věž), one of the few survivors of the 1641 fire, leans gently to one side of the square; its roof gallery (10am–6pm: April–Oct Tues–Sun; July & Aug Mon–Sat) provides superb views. The **Budvar brewery** is 2.5km up the road to Prague, on Karolíny Světlé (bus #2), and has a modern *pivnice* inside the nasty titanium-blue headquarters. You'll need to book ahead for tours (☎387 705 341, ⓦwww.budweiser.cz).

There's a friendly **tourist office** at no. 2 on the main square (May–Sept Mon–Fri 8.30am–6pm, Sat 8.30am–5pm, Sun 10am–noon & 12.30–4pm; Oct–April Mon–Fri 9am–4pm, Sat 9am–noon & 1–3pm; ☎386 801 413, ⓦwww.c-budejovice.cz). České Budějovice is popular and **hotels** tend to be expensive. Not cheap but excellent value is the canalside *Hotel Klika*, Hroznova 25 (☎387 318 171, ⓦwww.hotelklika.cz; ⑤). Slightly cheaper and also good is the hotel *U solné brány*, Radniční 11 (☎386 354 121, ⓦwww.hotelusolnebrany.cz; ⑤). From July to September rooms are available in **student halls** at Studentská 15 (☎387 774 201; ❷). There's also a decent **campsite**, *Dlouhá louka*, at Stromovka 8 (☎387 210 601; bus #16 from Lidická třída). The Budvar-run *Malý pivovar* serves great pub **food** and **beer**, as does the cheap *Hospůdka U žáby* (closed Sun), near the *Hotel Klika*.

# Český Krumlov

**ČESKÝ KRUMLOV** is a tiny, near-perfect medieval town with a fantastically over-the-top Renaissance castle and beautiful houses on its narrow cobbled streets. Despite the crowds of trippers in high summer it's still a relaxing place to spend a couple of days and by rented bike or canoe, or on foot, you can easily venture out into the surrounding countryside.

The town lies twenty minutes' walk from the **train station** down a steep cobbled path, while the bus station is just outside the old town. The twisting River Vltava divides the town into two: the circular Staré Město on the right bank and the Latrán quarter on the hillier left. For centuries, the focal point has been the **castle** in Latrán (Tues–Sun: April–May & Sept–Oct 9am–5pm; June–Aug 9am–6pm). There's a choice of two tours: Tour 1 (160Kč) concentrates on the stunning Renaissance parts of the castle and Tour 2 (140Kč) will take you into the slightly less remarkable eighteenth- and nineteenth-century quarters. From the castle, a covered walkway puts you high above the town in the unexpectedly expansive terraced **gardens**. Back down in Latrán a wooden bridge crosses the Vltava leading into the Staré Město. Head straight up the soft incline of Radniční to the main square, náměstí Svornosti, where a long, white Renaissance arcade connects two-and-a-half Gothic houses to create the **town hall**. On the other side, the high lancet windows of the church of **sv Vitus** rise above the red rooftops. Continuing east off the square, down Horní, the beautiful sixteenth-century Jesuit college now provides space for the town's grandest hotel, the *Hotel Růže*. Opposite, the local **museum** (March–April & Oct–Dec Tues–Fri 9am–4pm, Sat & Sun 1–4pm; May, June & Sept daily 10am–5pm; July & Aug daily 10am–6pm) includes a reconstructed seventeenth-century shop interior among its exhibits. West of the square, on Široká, the excellent **Egon Schiele Art Centrum** (daily 10am–6pm; 180Kč; ⑩www.schieleartcentrum.cz) has a series of galleries and exhibition halls housed in a fifteenth-century former brewery, devoted in part to the Austrian painter Egon Schiele, who lived here briefly in 1911.

The helpful **tourist office** (daily: April, May & Oct 9am–6pm; June & Sept 9am–7pm; July–Aug 9am–8pm; Nov–March 9am–5pm; ☎380 704 622, ⑩www .ckrumlov.cz) is situated on the main square. For **accommodation**, the friendly pub/hotel *Na louži*, Kájovská 66 (☎380 711 280, ⑩www.nalouzi.cz; ③), is a good bet. There are lots of **hostels** in Český Krumlov, including the central HI *Travellers Hostel* at Soukenická 43 (☎380 711 345, ⑩www.travellers.cz; 270Kč) and the more attractive *Merlin*, down by the river at Kájovská 59 (☎606 256 145; 250Kč), both of which offer Internet access. There are several **campsites** south of town along the road to Rožmberk but you'll need your own transport to get there. As far as **eating** goes, there's a wide choice: *Papa's Living Restaurant*, Latrán 13, offers funky Mexican, Italian and veggie dishes, while the *U písaře Jana*, Horní 151, has a vast menu, including fish. **Drinking** is best done at the *Eggenberg*, "the brewery tap", on the eastern edge of the Latrán quarter, or at the aforementioned *Na louži*.

## Plzeň

**PLZEŇ** (Pilsen) is Bohemia's second city, with a population of around 175,000. Despite its industrial character, there are compensations – eclectic architecture and an unending supply of (probably) the best beer in the world. Plzeň's **train stations** are works of art in themselves: your likeliest point of arrival is Hlavní nádraží, just a little east of the city centre. The **bus terminal** is on the west side of town. From both stations, the city centre is only a short walk away. The main square, **náměstí Republiky**, presents a full range of architectural styles, starting with the exalted heights of the Gothic cathedral of **sv Bartoloměj**, its green spire (daily 10am–6pm) reaching up almost 103m. Over the way rises the sgraffitoed Renaissance **Old Town Hall**, self-importantly one storey higher than the rest of the square. Here and there other old structures survive, but the vast majority of Plzeň's buildings hail from the city's heyday during the industrial expansion around the beginning of the twentieth century.

The reason most people come to Plzeň, however, is to sample its famous 12° (extra-strong) Plzeňský Prazdroj, better known as **Pilsner Urquell** abroad. Beer has been brewed in the town since it was founded in 1295, but it wasn't until 1842 that the famous Bürgerliches Brauhaus was built, after a near-riot by the townsfolk over the declining quality of their brew. For a guided tour of the **brewery** (☎377 062 888, ⑩www.beerworld.cz; 120Kč), you can either book in advance or simply show up at 12.30pm or 2pm for tours in English. You could, of course, just settle for a half-litre or two at the vast *Na Spílce* pub (daily 11am–10pm), just inside the brewery's triumphal arch.

The **tourist office** (April–Sept daily 9am–6pm; Oct–March Mon–Fri 10am–5pm, Sat–Sun 10am–3.30pm; ☎378 035 330, ⑩www.plzen-city.cz), at nám.

Republiky 41, can arrange **private rooms**. Finding a vacancy in one of Plzeň's **hotels** presents few problems, though they don't come cheap. The best-value rooms in town are the three at *Pension V Solní*, Solní 8 (☎377 236 652, ⓦwww .volny.cz/pensolni; ❸), just off the main square; alternatively, try the *U Salzmannů* pub at Pražská 8 (☎377 235 855, ⓦwww.usalzmannu.cz; ❹). There are a handful of **hostels** in town, including the grubby *Zahradní*, at Zahradní 21 (☎377 443 262; dorms 150Kč, rooms ❶; tram #1 goes down Slovanská, the parallel street). Bus #20 from the main square will drop you at the *Bílá hora* **campsite** (☎377 562 225; April–Sept) on 28 Října in the northern suburb of the same name. For cheap meals you might as well combine your **eating** with your **drinking**. Apart from *Na Spílce*, you can get cheap, hearty grub at the wood-panelled *U Salzmannů* (see above), while Gambrinus, Plzeň's other main beer, is best at *Žumbera* at Bezručova 14.

# Mariánské Lázně

Once one of the most fashionable European spas, **MARIÁNSKÉ LÁZNĚ** is not quite so exclusive today. The riotous fin-de-siècle architecture is gradually being restored, and the spa now serves busloads of elderly Germans getting the full works. Buses and trains stop 3km from the spa, from where trolleybus #5 runs up Hlavní třída to the centre. Sumptuous, regal buildings, most dating from the second half of the nineteenth century, rise up from the pine-clad hills – an appropriate backdrop for the classical music festivals hosted here annually. The focal point of the spa is the **Kolonáda**. This beautiful wrought-iron colonnade gently curves like a whale-ribbed railway station, the atmosphere relentlessly genteel and sober, although the view has been marred by a functionless concrete splat left by Communist planners. The spa's first and foremost **spring**, Křížový pramen, has its own adjoining Neoclassical colonnade (daily 6am–6pm). Mariánské Lázně's altitude lends an almost subalpine freshness to the air, and walking is as important to "the cure" as the various specialized treatments; maps showing marked walks in the area are available in hotels and shops.

The **tourist office**, at Hlavní 47 (daily 10am–noon & 1–6pm; ☎354 622 474, ⓦwww.marienbad.cz), has Internet access and can arrange cheap **accommodation**. While the cure hotels are extremely pricey, there are a few cheaper places to stay. The *Zlatý zámek*, Klíčová 167 (☎354 623 924; ❸), offers exceptional value for its central locale. The *Oradour*, Hlavní třída 43 (☎354 624 304, ⓦwww.penziono radour.wz.cz; ❷), also has a great location and offers large rooms without en-suite facilities, while the fin-de-siècle *Polonia*, Hlavní třída 50 (☎354 622 451; ❸), has rooms overlooking the spa gardens – the *Café Polonia* here is probably Mariánské Lázně's most opulent **café**, offering stucco decoration as rich as its cakes. A little way down the street, near the *Hotel Excelsior*, is *Churchill's* **pub** and **restaurant**, serving local food and salads, washed down with Guinness.

# Karlovy Vary

**KARLOVY VARY**, undisputed king of the Bohemian spas, is one of the most cosmopolitan Czech towns. Its international clientele – largely Russians – annually doubles the local population, which is further supplemented by thousands of able-bodied tourists in summer, mostly German. Trains from Prague arrive at **Horní Nádraží** to the north of town while trains from Mariánské Lázně come in at **Dolní nádraží** close to the main **bus station** and the town centre. Buses run to the spa area from all stations. If you're bussing it from Prague get off one stop early at Tržnice, even closer to the spa area.

The best way to take in Karlovy Vary is to wander up the river stopping to sip the medicinal water at the springs along the way. You can buy kitsch teapot-like drinking cups at souvenir kiosks. The water's hot and surprisingly salty – the delicious sweet wafers you'll see people munching are designed to take away the taste. Start at the

Thermal, a fairly brutal Communist-era construction that has an open-air, spring-water **swimming pool** (Mon–Sat 8am–9.30pm, Sun 9am–9.30pm) with fantastic views over the town. As the valley narrows, the river disappears under a wide terrace in front of the graceful **Mlýnská kolonáda**, each of whose four springs is more scalding than the last. Most powerful of the town's twelve springs is the **Vřídlo**, which belches out over 2500 gallons every hour. The smooth marble floor of the modern **Vřídelní kolonáda** (the old fountain was melted down for armaments by the Nazis) allows patients to shuffle up and down contentedly, while inside the glass rotunda the geyser shoots hot water forty feet upwards. Clouds of steam obscure a view of Dientzenhofer's Baroque masterpiece, the church of **sv Maria Magdaléna**, pitched nearby on a precipitous site. South of the Vřídlo is Karlovy Vary's most famous shopping street, the Stará louka. At no. 30, *Grand Hotel Pupp*, founded in 1701 as the greatest hotel in the world, maintains a certain snooty grandeur.

The town's **tourist office** is next to the Mlýnská kolonáda at Lázeňská 1 (Mon–Fri 8am–5pm, Sat & Sun 10am–4pm; ☎353 224 097, ✆www.karlovyvary .cz). It's best to start looking for **accommodation** early in the day – Karlovy Vary is a very fashionable spa town so nothing comes dirt cheap. W Privat, an office on náměstí Republiky (Mon–Fri 8.30am–5pm, Sat 9am–1pm; ☎353 227 768, ✉wprivat@volny.cz), can organize **private rooms** (❷). Moderately priced **hotels** include the very central *Hotel Kučera*, Stará louka 2 (☎353 235 053, ✆www .pensionkucera.cz; ❸). A bit cheaper but about fifteen minutes' walk from the spa is the *Hotel Kavalerie*, T.G. Masaryka 43 (☎353 229 613, ✉kavalerie@volny.cz; ❸). For **eating**, head for the *Zámecký vrch*, an intimate restaurant up at no. 14 on the street of the same name, or *U Švejka*, Stará louka 10, a slightly themed but cheery place up a little alley off the main street. The *Elefant* on Stará louka is Karlovy Vary's swishest café.

## Kutná Hora

**KUTNÁ HORA**, 60km east of Prague, is a sleepy country town but was once one of the most important centres in Bohemia. The medieval lanes are dominated by the massive towers of sv Jakub and sv Barbora, while the ground beneath the town is riddled with old silver workings. From 1308 Bohemia's royal mint at Kutná Hora converted the silver into coins called *Groschen* which were used all over Central Europe. The most straightforward way to get here is to take a bus from Florenc in Prague – it's an easy day-trip.

From the pretty but unassuming main square Palackého naměstí, head down 28 října to the **Italian Court** where Florentine craftsmen minted the coins. Guided tours in English take around thirty minutes (daily: April–Sept 9am–6pm; March & Oct 10am–5pm; Nov–Feb 10am–4pm). The **park** next door runs down to the river and is a good picnic spot. Carry on past **sv Jakub** – the tower leans slightly due to subsidence in the mines below – to the **Mining Museum** (April–Oct Tues–Sun 9/10am–5/6pm; 130Kč) in a tiny medieval fort. You can see a collection of silver and go right down into the mines. Continuing up the hill you come to a road lined with Baroque sculptures of saints similar to those on the Charles Bridge in Prague. These lead to the imposing **Cathedral of sv Barbora** (Tues–Sun: April & Oct 9am–noon & 1–4.30pm; May–Sept 9am–6pm; Nov–March 10am–noon & 1–4pm). Not to be outdone by St Vitus Cathedral in Prague, the miners of Kutná Hora financed the construction of a great cathedral of their own, dedicated to Barbara, the patron saint of miners and gunners. The foundations were probably laid by Peter Parler in the 1380s, but the church remained unfinished until the late nineteenth century. From the outside it's an incredible sight, bristling with pinnacles, finials and flying buttresses supporting a roof of three tent-like towers and unequal needle-sharp spires. Inside, light streams through the plain glass, illuminating a vaulted nave whose ribs form branches and petals stamped with coats of arms belonging to Václav II and the miners' guilds.

While you're in Kutná Hora, don't miss the weird subterranean *kostnice* or **ossuary** (daily: April–Sept 8am–6pm; Oct–March 9am–noon & 1–4/5pm), overflowing with 40,000 complete sets of bones, moulded into sculptures and decorations by František Rint in the nineteenth century. To get there, take bus #1 or #4 to the giant tobacco factory 3km northeast of the centre; you'll find the ossuary behind a Baroque church.

The **tourist office** at Palackeho náměstí 377 (April–Sept daily 9am–6pm; Oct–March Mon–Fri 9am–5pm, Sat & Sun 10am–4pm; ☏327 512 378, ⦿www.kh.cz) can book **private rooms** and has **Internet access**. *Penzion Centrum*, at Jakubská 57 (☏327 514 218; ❸), has rooms on a pleasant courtyard right by sv Jakub, while *Hotel Anna*, Vladislavova 372 (☏327 516 315, ⦿sweb.cz/hotel.anna; ❸), is a bit more upmarket, with its own restaurant and pub under a Renaissance vaulting. The nearest **campsite** is the unlikely sounding *Santa Barbara* on Česká (☏327 512 051; April–Oct), northwest of the town centre with hot showers and a restaurant.

# Moravia

Wedged between Bohemia and Slovakia, **Moravia** is the smallest of the three provinces that once made up Czechoslovakia, but perhaps the prettiest, friendliest and most bucolic. Although the North Moravian corridor is heavily industrialized – and towns and cities here suffer more from unemployment than any other region – in the Czech Republic – much of Moravia is rural and folk roots, traditions and religion are strongly felt. The Moravian capital, **Brno**, a once-grand nineteenth-century city, is within easy striking distance of Moravia's spectacular **karst region**. In the northern half of the province, the Baroque riches of the Moravian prince-bishopric have left their mark on the old capital, **Olomouc**, now a thriving university town and one of the region's main attractions.

## Brno

**BRNO** is the Czech Republic's second-largest city after Prague and though it hasn't got the capital's gobsmacking beauty it does have a couple of really excellent museums and galleries and a fair bit of nightlife, enlivened by the large student population. After the milling tourist crowds of Prague, Brno can feel like a refreshing dose of real life. In the nineteenth century it was a major textile centre and known as "rakousky Manchestr" (Austrian Manchester). Between the wars the city enjoyed a cultural boom, heralded by the 1928 Exhibition of Contemporary Culture, which provided an impetus for much of the city's pioneering functionalist architecture. After the war, Brno's German-speakers (one quarter of the population) were sent packing on foot to Vienna. Capital fled with the capitalists and centralized state funds were diverted to Prague and Bratislava.

### The City

Running from the train and bus stations at the southern edge of the city centre is Masarykova, lined either side with five-storey mansions, some embellished with fantastic decorations. Follow the flow of shoppers north and you'll end up at **náměstí Svobody**. To the left, halfway up Masarykova, is **Zelný trh**, a vegetable market on a sloping cobbled square, with a huge fountain at its centre. At the top of the square, the plain mass of the Dietrichstein Palace contains the **Moravian Museum** (Tues–Sat 9am–5pm), a worthy collection of ancient and medieval artefacts. Much more interesting, if only for its macabre value, is the **Capuchin Crypt** (March–Sept Mon–Sat 9am–noon & 2–4.30pm, Sun 11–11.45am & 2–4.30pm; Oct–Feb closed Mon), to the far south of the square, a gruesome collection of dead monks and top nobs mummified in the crypt of the Capuchin church. Clearly visible from Zelný trh is the **Old Town Hall**. Anton Pilgram's Gothic doorway is its best feature: the thistly pinnacle above the statue of Justice symbolically twisted – Pilgram's revenge on the town aldermen who short-changed him for his work. Inside, the courtyards and passageways are jam-packed with tour groups, most of them here to see the so-called Brno dragon (actually a stuffed crocodile) and the Brno Wheel, made in 1636 by a cartwright from nearby Lednice. The **tower** (April–Sept daily 9am–5pm) is worth climbing for the panorama across the red-tiled rooftops.

Southwest of the square, the Petrov hill – on which the **Cathedral of SS Peter and Paul** stands – is one of the best places to escape from the streets below. The cathedral's needle-sharp Gothic spires dominate the skyline for miles around, but close up the crude nineteenth-century rebuilding has made it a lukewarm affair. On the western edge of the city centre, the **UPM** at Husova 14 (Wed–Sun 10am–6/7pm) contains one of the country's best collections of applied art, displaying everything from medieval textiles to swirling Art Nouveau vases; it also has excellent temporary shows. At the **Pražák Palace** (Wed–Sun 10am–6/7pm), a little further down the road, there's a very good cross-section of twentieth-century Czech art on display. Skulking in the woods above the gallery is the barely visible **Špilberk Castle**, one of the worst prisons in the Habsburg Empire, and later a Gestapo jail; the **dungeons** (daily: 9am–5/6pm; ⍟www.spilberk.cz) are open to the public, while the **city museum** (May–Sept Tues–Sun 9am–6pm; April & Oct Tues–Sun 9am–5pm; Nov–March Wed–Sun 10am–5pm) occupies the upper floors.

## Practicalities

Brno's main **train** and **bus stations** sit closely together, on the edge of the city centre; the train station has lockers and a 24-hour left-luggage office. It's an easy walk to all the sights but if you do want to take a **tram** it's 8Kč for a 10-minute ticket (plenty of time to get anywhere in the city centre) and 13Kč for a 40-minute ticket. You'll need to pay a half-fare for your bag, too, if it's bulky. Buy your ticket from one of the yellow machines or kiosks near the stop and validate it on board. The main **tourist office** is in the Old Town Hall at Radnická 8 (April–Sept Mon–Fri 8.30am–6pm, Sat & Sun 9am–5.30pm; Oct–March Mon–Fri 9am–6pm, Sat 9am–5.30pm, Sun 9am–3pm; ☎542 211 089, ⍟www.ticbrno.cz). Brno hosts many trade fairs, so it's wise to book **accommodation** ahead. One of the cheapest **hotels** is the *Amphone*, třída. Kpt. Jaroše 29 (☎545 428 310; ➍), a short walk from the old town. *Pegas*, Jakubská 4 (☎542 210 104, ⍟www.hotelpegas.cz; ➍), just off Česká, is more central and above a microbrewery (see below). Best of Brno's **campsites** is the *Radka* (☎546 215 821; June–Aug; tram #1, #3 or #11), 10km northwest of the city on the shores of the Brno dam, at Brneňska prehrada-kninia. There's plenty of choice for **eating** and **drinking**: *Arca di Adria*, in a sixteenth-century building at Náměstí Svobody 17, is a popular Italian-run café serving great ice cream and pizzas, while Czech and international dishes are served in *U rudého vola* at Kobližná 2, just off the opposite end of the square, which is an elegant restaurant with a peaceful arcaded patio under a glassy roof. Good beer and food can be had at the microbrewery *Pegas*, or at the *Elektra* at Běhounská 7. Another decent pub is *Špalíček*, at the top of Zelný trh, which has tables outside in summer and lashings of the local Starobrno beer. **Internet cafés** include *Internet Centrum Coffee* at Masarykova 22–24 and *@ Internet Café* at Lidická 17.

## The Moravian karst region

Lying 25km northeast of Brno, the **Moravian karst** is a region of rolling fields, forests and limestone hills. Over thousands of years the limestone has eroded creating deep and dramatic caves: you can take guided tours of some at **Skalní Mlýn** – catch an early morning train from Brno to Blansko and then hop on a connecting bus. If you don't make the bus it's a beautiful 8km hike through the beech woods: follow the green and white waymarkers from outside the train station. Tickets for the caves are sold at the Skalní Mlýn ticket office. Following the stream for another kilometre (or taking the Eko-train), you'll come to **Punkevní** (July & Aug Mon 10am–3.50pm, Tues–Sun 8.20am–5pm; April–June & Sept Mon 10am–3.50pm, Tues–Sun 8.20am–3.50pm; Oct Tues–Fri 8.40am–2pm, Sat & Sun 8.20am–3.40pm; Nov–March Tues–Sun 8.40am–2pm; Ⓦwww.cavemk .cz), the most dramatic cave, with an underground boat ride. Back at the ticket office there's a **hotel**, **café** and **bike rental**.

# Olomouc

Once capital of Moravia and seat of the bishopric, **OLOMOUC** (pronounced "olla-moats") has a lot going for it: a well-preserved old town, spacious cobbled squares and a plethora of Baroque fountains, not to mention a healthy quota of university students and a few interesting festivals. The **Staré Město** is a strange contorted shape, squeezed in the middle by an arm of the Morava. In the western half of the old town, all roads lead to the city's two central squares, which are hinged to one another at right angles. At the centre of the upper square, the irregular **Horní náměstí**, stands the amalgamation of buildings that collectively make up the **town hall**. From its creamy rendering the occasional late Gothic or Renaissance gesture emerges – notably the handsome lanterned tower soaring to its conclusion of baubles and pinnacles. On the north side is an astronomical clock – a modern reconstruction of the original, which was destroyed in World War II. The remake chimes all right, but the hourly mechanical show is disappointing. Big enough to be a chapel, the **Holy Trinity Column** to the west of the town hall is the country's largest plague column; many such monuments were erected as thanksgiving for deliverance from the forces of Protestantism, but few are left standing. Set into the west facade of the square is the **Moravian Theatre**, where Mahler arrived as the newly appointed Kapellmeister in 1883; the local press took an instant dislike to him, and he lasted just three months. **Fountains** grace each of Olomouc's six ancient market squares. Horní náměstí boasts three: Hercules, looking unusually athletic for his years, Julius Caesar bucking on a steed that coughs water from its mouth and a modern fountain on a marine theme featuring giant tortoises and a naked lady prancing with a dolphin.

Two of the city's best-looking backstreets, Školní and Michalská, lead southeast from Horní náměstí up to the **church of sv Michál**, plain on the outside but inside clad in a masterly excess of Baroque. Firmly wedged between the two sections of the old town is the Jesuit church of **Panna Maria Sněžná**, deemed particularly necessary in a city where Protestantism had spread like wildfire in the sixteenth century. Jutting out into the road, it signals the gateway to the less hectic part of town. The great mass of the former Jesuit College, now the **Palacký University**, dominates the first square, náměstí Republiky, opposite which is the dull town museum and, next door, the vastly superior **Museum of Art** (Tues–Sun 10am–6pm); the top floor houses a fascinating selection of twentieth-century works by local-born artists and features a viewing tower. Three blocks east of náměstí Republiky, the **cathedral of sv Václav** comes into view. Though it started life as a Romanesque basilica, the current structure is mostly nineteenth-century neo-Gothic. However, the walls and pillars of the nave are prettily painted in Romanesque style. The **crypt** (Tues & Thurs–Sat 9am–5pm, Wed 9am–4pm, Sun 11am–5pm) has a wonderful display of gory reliquaries and priestly sartorial wealth.

## Practicalities

The **train station** is 1.5km east of the Staré Město, so on arrival take any tram heading west up Masarykova and get off after three or four stops; the **bus station** is even further out, and connected to the centre by tram #4. The **tourist office** in the town hall (daily 9am–7pm; ☎585 513 385, ⊛www.olomouc-tourism.cz) will book **private rooms** for you. The best-value **hotel** is *Na hradbách*, Hrnčířská 14 (☎585 233 243; ✉aquaveri@iol.cz; ❷), a spotless, three-room pension hidden away in one of the city's prettiest backstreets. The cheapest **hostel**-style option is the *Ubytovna Zora*, U stadionu 2 (☎585 234 709; ❶), a ten-minute walk north from the centre. Note that rooms can be hard to come by in May when the spring **Music Festival** follows the **Flora Festival**.

For **restaurants**, *U červeného volka* on Dolní náměstí is a cheap place with a wide range of veggie dishes, while *Caesar* in the cobbled vaults under the town hall is the most popular pizza joint in town. A good range of cakes can be found in *Maruška* on 28 Října or the *Café Mahler*, at Horní náměstí 11. In the evening, head for the *U-Klub*, at the Studentcentrum at the far end of Křížovského, which has occasional DJs and bands.

# Travel details

## Trains

**Brno** to: Olomouc (up to 7 daily; 1hr 25min).
**České Budějovice** to: Brno (4–5 daily; 4hr 20min); Český Krumlov (8 daily; 1hr); Plzeň (12–13 daily; 2hr–3hr 25min).
**Mariánské Lázně** to: Karlovy Vary (6–7 daily; 1hr 40min–2hr 20min); Plzeň (hourly; 1hr 10min–1hr 35min).
**Prague** to: Brno (every 1–2hr; 2hr 40min–3hr 40min); České Budějovice (up to 14 daily; 2hr 15min–3hr); Karlovy Vary (3 daily; 4hr 5min–5hr 10min); Mariánské Lázně (10 daily; 2hr 55min); Olomouc (1–2 hourly; 3hr 10min–3hr 30min); Plzeň (hourly; 1hr 40min).

## Buses

**Brno** to: Olomouc (hourly; 1hr 20min–1hr 50min).
**České Budějovice** to: Brno (3–6 daily; 3hr 30min–4hr 30min); Český Krumlov (every 15–30min; 25–50min).
**Mariánské Lázně** to: Plzeň (up to 7 daily; 1hr25min).
**Prague** to: Brno (every 30min–1hr; 2hr 20min–3hr 30min); České Budějovice (up to 8 daily; 2hr 30min–3hr 25min); Český Krumlov (2–6 daily; 2hr 40min–3hr 25min); Karlovy Vary (hourly; 2hr 10min–2hr 20min); Kutná Hora (hourly on week-days; 1hr 15min); Mariánské Lázně (2–5 daily; 2hr 45min–3hr 15min); Olomouc (up to 8 daily; 3hr 50min–5hr).

# Denmark

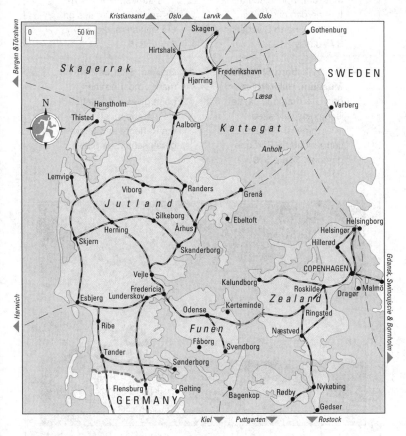

# Denmark highlights

* **Ny Carlsberg Glyptotek**
Copenhagen's finest gallery houses an extensive collection of Etruscan art outside Italy. See p.303

* **Louisiana, Humlebæk** A magnificent modern art museum, whose sculpture garden overlooks the Øresund to Sweden. See p.308

* **Frederiksborg Slot and Museum, Hillerød** Frederik II's dramatic castle is impressively sited over three islands and surrounded by Baroque gardens. See p.310

* **Viking Ship Museum, Roskilde** Check out the delicately renovated Viking ships retrieved from the Roskilde fjord. See p.310

* **Den Gamle By, Århus** This atmospheric open-air museum recreates an old Danish market town. See p.315

* **Grenen, Skagen** Denmark's most northerly point gives a dramatic view of the meeting of the Kattegat and Skaggerak seas. See p.317

△ Skagen

# Introduction and basics

Between Scandinavia proper and mainland Europe, Denmark is a difficult country to pin down. In many ways it shares the characteristics of both regions: it's an EU member, and has prices and drinking laws that are broadly in line with those in the rest of Europe. But Denmark's social policies and its style of government are distinctly Scandinavian: social benefits and the standard of living are high, and its politics are very much that of consensus.

Denmark is the easiest Scandinavian country in which to travel, but its landscape is the least dramatic: very green and flat, largely farmland interrupted by pretty villages. Apart from a scattering of small islands, three main landmasses make up the country – the islands of **Zealand** and Funen and the peninsula of Jutland, which extends northwards from Germany. Most visitors make for Zealand (Sjælland), and, more specifically, **Copenhagen**, an exciting focal point with a beautiful old centre, a good array of museums and a boisterous nightlife. **Funen** (Fyn) has only one real urban draw, **Odense**; otherwise, it's renowned for cute villages and sandy beaches. **Jutland** (Jylland) has, as well as some varied scenery, ranging from soft green hills to desolate heathlands, **Århus** and **Aalborg**, two of the liveliest Danish cities.

## Information & maps

Most places have a **tourist office** that can help with accommodation. They're open daily, with long hours, in the most popular spots, but have reduced hours from October to March. All airports and many train stations also offer a hotel booking service. A good general **map** is by *Hallwag*, but the HI Association map is excellent and available free at @www.danhostel.dk.

## Money and banks

Currency is the **krone** (plural *kroner*), made up of 100 øre. It comes in notes of 50kr, 100kr, 200kr, 500kr and 1000kr, and coins of 25øre, 50øre, 1kr, 2kr, 5kr, 10kr and 20kr. **Banking hours** are Mon–Fri 9.30/10am–4pm, Thurs till 5.30/6pm. Banks are plentiful and the easiest place to **exchange cash** and travellers' cheques although they charge 30kr per transaction. Forex bureaux charge only 20kr to exchange cash and 10kr per travellers' cheque but are much rarer. Most airports and ferry terminals have late-opening exchange facilities, and ATMs are widespread. At the time of writing, €1 was equal to 7.5kr, $1 to 6kr and £1 to 11kr.

## Communications

**Post offices** are open Mon–Fri 9.30/10am–5/6pm and Sat 9.30/10am– noon/2pm, with reduced hours in smaller communities. You can also buy stamps from most newsagents. Coin-operated **phones** are white and require a minimum of 3kr for a local call (they swallow one of the coins if the number is engaged), and 5kr for international calls; **phonecards** for the blue phones (which are a little cheaper) come as 30kr, 50kr and 100kr. The operator number is ☏118 (domestic), ☏113 (international) – both 8kr/

---

### Denmark on the net

@**www.visitdenmark.com** Official Danish tourist board site with links to all regional sites.
@**www.useit.dk** For budget travellers; focuses mainly on Copenhagen.
@**www.aok.dk** Listings for most of Zealand.
@**www.woco.dk** Official Wonderful Copenhagen tourist site.
@**www.rejseplanen.dk** Public transport journey planner.

min. **Internet access** is free at most libraries and some tourist offices, otherwise most towns have cybercafés.

# Getting around

Denmark has swift and easy-to-use **public transport**. Danish State Railways (Danske Statsbaner or DSB; Ⓦwww.dsb.dk) runs an exhaustive and reliable **rail** network co-run on some stretches by private networks and supplemented by a few privately owned rail lines. Train types range from the large inter-city expresses (*Lyntog*) to smaller local trains (*regionaltog*). **InterRail**, **Eurail** and **Scanrail** passes (see p.47) are valid on all DSB trains, with reduced rates on most privately owned lines. Ticket prices are worked out according to a countrywide zonal system and travel by local transport within the zone of departure and arrival is included in the price. Everywhere not served by train can be easily reached by buses, which often supplement the train **timetable** – some operated privately, some by DSB itself – and on these, railcards are valid. DSB timetables or *Køreplan* (free) detail train, bus and ferry services, including the S-train and Metro systems in Copenhagen. The only buses not included are the few private companies competing with the state-controlled monopoly. These are slower but generally cheaper; details can be found at railway and bus stations.

**Ferries** or bridges link all the Danish islands. Where applicable, train and bus fares include the cost of crossings (although with ferries you can also pay at the terminal and walk on). Routes and prices are covered on the very useful HI map.

**Cycling** is the best way to appreciate Denmark's flat landscape, which is crisscrossed by cycle routes (maps and information at Ⓦ www.dcf.dk). Most country roads have sparse traffic and all large towns have cycle tracks. Bikes can be rented at hostels, tourist offices and some train stations, as well as from bike rental shops (50–75kr/day, 250–350kr/week; 200–500kr deposit). All trains and most long-distance buses accept bikes, but you'll have to pay according to the zonal system used to calculate passenger tickets – 50kr to take your bike from Copenhagen to Århus by train with 20kr on top if you want to reserve a space in advance; 80kr by bus.

# Accommodation

**Accommodation** is a major expense. Hotels, however, are by no means off-limits if you're prepared to seek out the better offers. Expect to pay around 400–600kr for a shared facilties/en-suite double **hotel** room and note that this nearly always includes an all-you-can-eat breakfast. It's a good idea to book in advance, especially in peak season. You can do this either through tourist-office websites or by checking the individual hotel websites where major discounts can be had. Tourist offices can also supply details of **private rooms**, which cost 300–400kr a double. **Farmstays** (*Bondegårdsferie*) are becoming increasingly popular; see Ⓦwww .bondegaardsferie.dk.

**Hostels** are the cheapest option. Every town has one and they offer a high degree of comfort. Most have a choice of private rooms, often with en-suite toilets and showers, as well as dorm accommodation; nearly all have cooking facilities. Rates are around 120kr per person for a dorm bed; non-HI members pay an extra 35kr a night (160kr for a one-year HI membership). Danhostel Danmarks Vandrerhjem (☎ 33.31.36.12, Ⓦwww.danhostel.dk) produces a free hostel guide. For a similar price, **sleep-ins** (smaller hostels geared towards backpackers and often run by volunteer staff) can be found chiefly in major towns though are often only open in summer (May–Aug). You need your own sleeping bag, sometimes only one night's stay is permitted and there can be an age restriction. Local tourist offices have details.

If you plan to **camp**, you'll need an International Camping Card, or a Camping Card Scandinavia (80kr), which is available at official campsites. A Transit Pass (20kr) can be used for a single overnight stay. All sites are open at least from June to August, many from April to September, while a few stay open all year. There's a rigid **grading system**: one-star sites have toilets and at least one shower; two-stars also have basic cooking facilities and a food shop within

2km; three-stars include a laundry and a TV-room, four-stars also have a shop, while five-stars include a cafeteria. Prices are around 55–65kr per person. Many campsites also have **cabins** to rent, usually with cooking facilities, for 2000kr–4000kr per week for a six-berth place, although they are often fully booked in summer. Tourist offices have a free leaflet listing all sites. **Camping rough** without permission is illegal, and an on-the-spot fine may be imposed. However, the Danish Forest and Nature Agency has initiated a two-year trial which allows free low-impact camping in some two-hundred designated woodland areas. The rules are strict: only one night at each site, only two tents per site, no open fire or camping stoves allowed and the site has to be left as you found it. Check ֍www2.skovognatur .dk for a list of sites and more info.

# Food and drink

Traditional Danish **cooked meals** centre on meat and fish, served with potatoes and another, usually boiled, vegetable. **Breakfast** (*morgenmad*) can be the tastiest Danish meal, and almost all hotels and hostels offer a sumptuous spread: a table laden with cereals, freshly made bread, cheese, ham, fruit juice, milk, coffee and

| Danish | | |
| --- | --- | --- |
| | **Danish** | **Pronunciation** |
| Yes | *Ja* | Ya |
| No | *Nej* | Nye |
| Please | *Vær så venlig* | Verso venly |
| Thank you | *Tak* | Tagg |
| Hello/Good day | *Goddag* | Go-dah |
| Goodbye | *Farvel* | Fah-vell |
| Excuse me | *Undskyld* | Unsgul |
| Where? | *Hvor* | Voa |
| Good | *God* | Gouth |
| Bad | *Dårlig* | Dohli |
| Near | *Nær* | Neh-a |
| Far | *Fjern* | Fee-ann |
| Cheap | *Billig* | Billie |
| Expensive | *Dyr* | Duy-a |
| Open | *Åben* | Oh-ben |
| Closed | *Lukket* | Lohggeth |
| Today | *Idag* | Ee-dah |
| Yesterday | *Igår* | Ee-goh... |
| Tomorrow | *Imorgen* | Ee-mon |
| How much is....? | *Hvad koster....?* | Vath kosta....? |
| What time is it? | *Hvad er klokken?* | Vath ea cloggen? |
| Where is....? | *Hvor er.....?* | Voa ea...? |
| I don't understand | *Jeg forstår ikke* | Yai fusto igge |
| Do you speak English? | *Taler de engelsk?* | Tayla dee engellsgg? |
| One | *En* | Ehn |
| Two | *To* | toh |
| Three | *Tre* | Tray |
| Four | *Fire* | Fee-a |
| Five | *Fem* | Fem |
| Six | *Sex* | Segs |
| Seven | *Syv* | Syu |
| Eight | *Otte* | Oddeh |
| Nine | *Ni* | Nee |
| Ten | *Ti* | Tee |

tea, for around 40–50kr if not included in the price of the room. **Brunch**, served in most cafes from 11am until mid-afternoon, is a popular and filling option for late starters and costs 60–120kr. Traditional **lunch** (frokost) is smørrebrød – open sandwiches heaped with meat, fish or cheese, and assorted trimmings – sold for 10–35kr a piece and very filling.

For daytime **snacks**, there are hot dog stands (pølsevogn) in all main streets and at train stations, serving hot dogs (pølser), toasted ham and cheese sandwiches (parisertoast) and chips (pommes frites). Bakeries and cafés sell Danish pastries (wienerbrød), tastier and much less sweet than the imitations sold elsewhere, and you can usually get a generous sandwich or filling portion of salad (usually served with fresh bread) for around 60kr. An excellent-value set lunch can usually be found at restaurants and bodegas (bars that sell no-frills food). Tilbud is the "special", dagens ret the "dish of the day", and you can expect to pay around 50kr for these, 80–120kr for a three-course set lunch. Open **buffets**, where you help yourself to as much as you like, will set you back 80–100kr. Kebabs and Chinese food are easy to find in most larger towns; a filling snack will cost around 25–30kr. You can also get a self-service meat, fish or omelette lunch in a supermarket cafeteria for 50–90kr. Restaurants that are promising for lunch turn into expense-account affairs at night, although some still will have good-value buffets for **dinner** (aftensmad). Many hostels serve filling evening meals for 50–75kr. If you plan to save money by **self-catering**, head for Netto or Fakta supermarkets, where the food and drink are good value. Alternatively Brugsen and Irma supermarkets are more expensive but sell top-of-the-range stuff.

The most sociable places to **drink** are pubs (aka værtshus, bar or bodega) and cafés, where the emphasis is on lager. The cheapest is bottled – the so-called gold **beer** (Guldøl or Elefantøl; 20–30kr/bottle) is

the strongest. Draught lager (Fadøl) is more expensive and a touch weaker, but tastes fresher. The most common brands are Carlsberg and Tuborg although small independent breweries are beginning to make their mark. Most international **wines** (from 25kr) and **spirits** (15–35kr) are widely available. There are many varieties of **schnapps**; a tasty relative is the hot and strong Gammel Dansk Bitter – drunk occasionally at breakfast time.

# Opening hours and holidays

Standard **shop hours** are Mon–Fri 9.30/10am–5.30/7pm, Sat 9/9.30am–2/5pm. All shops and banks are closed, and public transport and many museums run to Sunday schedules on **public holidays**: Jan 1; Maundy Thurs to Easter Mon; Prayer Day (4th Fri after Easter); Ascension (40th day after Easter); Whit Sun & Mon; Constitution Day (June 5); Dec 24 (pm only); Dec 25 & 26. On **International Workers' Day**, May 1, many offices and shops close at noon.

# Emergencies

You're unlikely to have much contact with **police**, as street crime and hassle are minimal; however, they're helpful and most speak English. For **prescriptions**, doctors' consultations and dental work – but not hospital visits – you have to pay on the spot; to get a full refund, take your receipt, European Health Insurance Card (formerly the E111) and passport to the local health office.

# Copenhagen (København)

**COPENHAGEN** is Scandinavia's most affordable capital, and one of Europe's most user-friendly cities: welcoming and compact, with a centre largely given over to pedestrians. It is the seat of all national institutions – politics, finance and the arts – and dominates any visit to Denmark; its first-rate galleries, museums and summertime street entertainers fill your days, while by night its live music and an intimate bar and club scene are rivalled only by those on offer in Århus. There was no more than a tiny fishing settlement here until the twelfth century, when **Bishop Absalon** built a castle on Christiansborg's present site. Prosperity and trade flourished with the introduction of the Sound Toll on vessels in the Øresund, and after the demise of the Hanseatic ports, the city became the Baltic's principal harbour, earning the name **København** ("merchant's port"), and in 1443 it was made the Danish capital. A century later, Christian IV created Rosenborg Slot, Rundetårn and the districts of Nyboder and Christianshavn, and in 1669 Frederik III graced the city with its first royal palace, Amalienborg.

## Arrival, information and city transport

Kastrup **airport** is 8km southeast of the centre, and connected to it by trains (6 hourly 5am–midnight; hourly overnight; takes 13min; 25.50kr), which pull into Københavns Hovedbanegård (**Central Station**), near Vesterbrogade. **Long-distance buses** from elsewhere in Denmark stop either at various points round Central Station or a short bus or S-train ride from the centre. **Ferries** from Oslo and Poland dock an S-train ride away north of the centre at Nordhavn. The **tourist office**, across from the Central Station at Vesterbrogade 4a (May–Aug Mon–Sat 9am–6/8pm; July & Aug also Sun 10am–6pm; Sept–April Mon–Sat 9am–2pm; ☎70.22.24.42, ⊛www.woco.dk), can help with accommodation for a 75kr fee. Far better for youth and budget-oriented information, however, is **Use-It**, centrally located in the Huset complex at Rådhusstræde 13 (mid-June to mid-Sept daily 9am–7pm; mid-Sept to mid-June Mon–Wed 11am–4pm, Thurs 11am–6pm, Fri 11am–2pm; ☎33.73.06.20, ⊛www.useit.dk). Its friendly staff provide poste restante and free Internet access, luggage storage and a useful free magazine, *Playtime*, as well as a list of current hostel availability and a free private room booking service. If you're sightseeing on a tight schedule, consider the **Copenhagen Card** (199/429kr for 24/72hr), which is valid for the entire public transport network (including much of eastern Zealand) and gives entry to most museums and attractions in the area. It's available at tourist offices, hotels, travel agents and the train station.

An integrated network of **buses**, electric **S-trains** (*S-tog*) and an expanding **metro** covers the city (5am–1am); night buses (*natbus*) take over after 1am, and there's a less frequent metro service on Thursday, Friday and Saturday nights. Night fares are double daytime fares. You can get a free route map from stations. Ticket options include a Copenhagen Card (see above); the **24-timer billet** (100kr), which covers the same area for 24 hours, but doesn't include admission to museums; and the **Klippekort** (110/150kr for two/three zones), which consists of ten stamps, each giving unlimited travel for one hour within the designated zones (make sure you stamp your ticket when boarding the bus or in machines on station platforms). For a single journey, get a **Billet** (17kr), valid for an hour's unlimited travel in two zones. *Billets* can be bought on board buses or at train stations; *Klippekort* and *24-timer billet* at stations, HT Kortsalgs kiosks and newsagents. Travelling without a ticket can get you an instant 500kr fine. In summertime, under the **City Bike scheme** (⊛www.bycyklen.dk), you can borrow bikes from racks across the city for a deposit of 20kr, which is returned when the bike is locked back into any other city rack after use. You'll be fined up to 1000kr if you use the bikes outside the city limits (the old rampart lakes mark the border) and you'll need to get yourself some lights if you want to cycle at night, as you'll be fined if you're caught without.

## Accommodation

**Accommodation** can be difficult to come by, especially if you arrive late, or during July and August, when it's a good idea to book in advance. Most of the cheaper **hotels** are around Istedgade, a slightly seedy area on the far side of the train station. Check with the tourist office early in the day and they may find you a double room for as little as 450kr; **private rooms** (③) are usually an S-train ride away from the centre, best-value places found through Use-It (see p.299). There's a great, though less central, selection of **hostels**; space is only likely to be a problem in the peak summer months, when you'll have to book in advance or turn up as early as possible to be sure of a place (Use-It keeps a daily list of availability). Breakfast is not included in the prices given, unless otherwise stated.

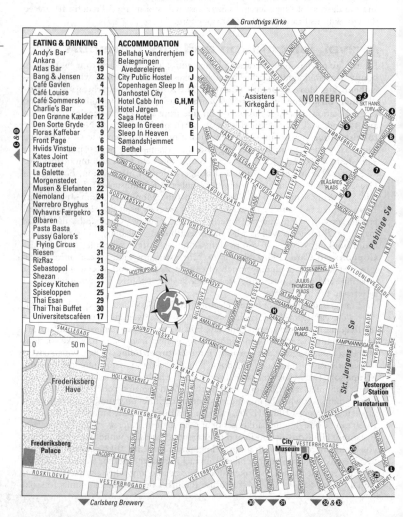

▲ Grundtvigs Kirke

**EATING & DRINKING**

| | |
|---|---|
| Andy's Bar | 11 |
| Ankara | 26 |
| Atlas Bar | 19 |
| Bang & Jensen | 32 |
| Café Gavlen | 4 |
| Café Louise | 7 |
| Café Sommersko | 14 |
| Charlie's Bar | 15 |
| Den Grønne Kælder | 12 |
| Den Sorte Gryde | 33 |
| Floras Kaffebar | 9 |
| Front Page | 6 |
| Hviids Vinstue | 16 |
| Kates Joint | 8 |
| Klaptræet | 10 |
| La Galette | 20 |
| Morgenstedet | 23 |
| Musen & Elefanten | 22 |
| Nemoland | 24 |
| Nørrebro Bryghus | 1 |
| Nyhavns Færgekro | 13 |
| Ølbaren | 5 |
| Pasta Basta | 18 |
| Pussy Galore's Flying Circus | 2 |
| Riesen | 31 |
| RizRaz | 21 |
| Sebastopol | 3 |
| Shezan | 28 |
| Spicey Kitchen | 27 |
| Spiseloppen | 25 |
| Thai Esan | 29 |
| Thai Thai Buffet | 30 |
| Universitetscaféen | 17 |

**ACCOMMODATION**

| | |
|---|---|
| Bellahøj Vandrerhjem | C |
| Belægningen Avedørelejren | D |
| City Public Hostel | J |
| Copenhagen Sleep In | A |
| Danhostel City | K |
| Hotel Cabb Inn | G,H,M |
| Hotel Jørgen | F |
| Saga Hotel | L |
| Sleep In Green | B |
| Sleep In Heaven | E |
| Sømandshjemmet Bethel | I |

NØRREBRO

Assistens Kirkegård

0 — 50 m

Frederiksberg Have

Frederiksberg Palace

▼ Carlsberg Brewery

Vesterport Station

Planetarium

City Museum

## Hostels and sleep-ins

**Bellahøj Vandrerhjem** Herbergsvejen 8, Brønshøj ☎38.28.97.15, ⊛www.youth-hostel.dk. Cosy HI hostel with large dorms, located in a peaceful lakeside setting just fifteen minutes from the city centre on buses #2a, #11 and #13, nightbus #82N. Closed mid-Dec to early Jan. Check in 2–5pm. 100kr.

**Belægningen Avedørelejren** Vester Kvartergade 22, Hvidovre ☎36.77.90.84, ⊛www.belaegningen. dk. Clean and tidy hostel with four-bed rooms in the former army barracks of Avedøre, which also house the Zentropa film production company made famous by Lars Von Trier. There's an excellent restaurant here too, but it's a good distance from town. Bus #133 from Avedøre S-train station. Check-in 2–7.30pm, Sat & Sun until 5.30pm. 110kr including bedding.

**City Public Hostel** Absalonsgade 8, Vesterbro ☎33.31.20.70, ⊛www.city-public-hostel.dk. Noisy sixty-bed dorm on the lower floor, less crowded conditions on other levels. Just ten minutes' walk from the train station. Buses #6a and #26 stop close by. May to mid-Aug. 130kr, 150kr including breakfast.

**Copenhagen Sleep In** Blegdamsvej 132, Østerbro ☎35.26.50.59, ⊛www.sleep-in.dk. North of the

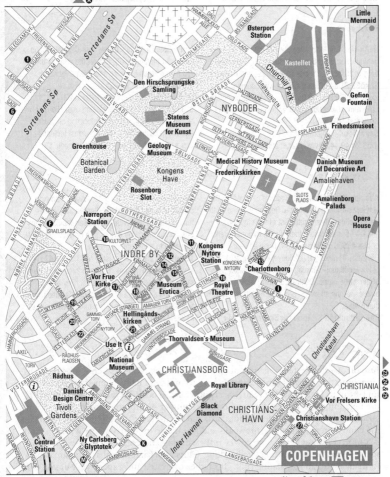

**COPENHAGEN**

*Airport & Amager* ▼

centre, next to Fælledparken and within walking distance of lively Sankt Hans Torv. Basic but adequate four- and six-bed dorms. Bus #1a, #3a, #14 or #15, nightbus #80N, #85N or #95N. July & Aug only. 110kr.

**Danhostel Copenhagen City** H C Andersens Boulevard 50 ☎33.11.85.85, ⊛www.danhostel .dk. A brand spanking new, seven-hundred bed, five-star HI hostel housed in a multi-storey building overlooking the harbour and the green copper spires of the city. Priding itself on being the largest city hostel in Europe, rooms come in four-to eight-bed versions. A short walk from the Central Station or bus #5a. 120kr.

**Hotel Jørgensens** Rømersgade 11 ☎33.13.81.86, ⊛www.hoteljoergensen.dk. A stone's throw from Nørreport station on Israels Plads. Mostly dorms of six, nine and fourteen beds, with a few decent-sized doubles (**❼**, **❻** with shared facilities). Dorms 135kr including breakfast.

**Sleep in Green** Ravnsborggade 18, Nørrebro ☎35.37.77.77, ⊛www.sleep-in-green.dk. In the centre of hip Nørrebro, with bright rooms of eight, twenty and thirty-eight beds, and a fabulous organic breakfast for 40kr. Ten minutes from the centre by bus #5a or #16, nightbus #81N and #84N. 100kr.

**Sleep in Heaven** Struensegade 7, Nørrebro ☎35.35.46.48, ⊛www.sleepinheaven.com. Two vast halls, the largest with 76 beds divided into four- and eight-bed compartments. Pleasant atmosphere, with youthful staff and occasional free gigs. Age limit 35. Ten minutes from the centre by bus #12 or #69, nightbus #92N. 130kr.

## Hotels

**Hotel Cab Inn** Mitchellsgade 14 ☎33.46.16.16, behind Central Station; Vodroffsvej 55, Frederiksberg ☎35.36.11.11, bus #2a or #29; and Danasvej 32 ☎33.21.04.00; bus #29; ⊛www.cabinn .com. Inspired by the Oslo ferry, these three hotels have almost identical good-value en-suite cabins. Breakfast 50kr. **❻**

**Saga Hotel** Colbjørnsensgade 18–20 ☎33.24.49.44, ⊛www.sagahotel.dk. Cheap,

family hotel, a stone's throw from Central Station (head out the back exit), and on the edge of the red light district. En-suite and shared facilities. Breakfast included. **❺–❻**

**Sømandshjemmet Bethel** Nyhavn 22 ☎33.13.03.70, ⊛www.hotel-bethel.dk. Former seaman's home in a fantastic location on Nyhavn and worth paying the extra. Breakfast included. Bus #19 or Kongens Nytorv metro station. **❽**

## Campsites

**Absalon** Korsdalsvej 132, Rødovre ☎36.41.06.00, ⊛www.camping-absalon.dk. Reasonable site, with basic facilties, 9km southwest of the city. S-train line B to Brøndbyøster, then fifteen minutes' walk or bus #550S, nightbus #93N. Open all year.

**Bellahøj Camping** Hvidkildevej 66 ☎38.10.11.50, ⊛www.bellahoj-camping.dk. Near the hostel of the same name. Central but grim, with long queues for the showers. Bus #2a, nightbus #82N. June–Aug.

**Charlottenlund Strandpark** Strandvejen 144,

Charlottenlund ☎39.62.36.88, ⊛www.camping copenhagen.dk. Beautifully situated at Charlottenlund Beach and with good, clean facilities. Very busy in summer. Bus #1a or #14 or nightbus #85N. Mid-May to mid-Sept.

**Tangloppen** Ishøj Havn, Ishøj ☎43.54.07.67, ⊛www.fdmcamping.dk. Fourteen kilometres from the centre, but a fantastic location near both a beach and a plethora of watersports facilities. S-train A or E to Ishøj then a ten-minute walk or bus #128. May to mid-Sept.

# The City

Just off hectic Vesterbrogade outside the station is Copenhagen's most famous attraction, the **Tivoli Gardens** (mid-April to mid-Sept daily 11am–11pm/1am and mid-Nov to Dec daily 10/11am–9/11pm; 68kr), whose opening each April marks the beginning of summer. Throughout the summer season, the gardens feature fairground rides, flower gardens, fountains, and a variety of nightly entertainment in the central arena, including fireworks and live music on Fridays. The winter season is a more low-key affair with fewer rides working and emphasis on the Christmas spirit – spectacular lighting, stalls selling Christmas paraphernalia, Christmas performances and an ice-skating rink. It's rather overrated and expensive, but you can still have an enjoyable evening wandering among the revellers of all ages. On the south side of Tietgensgade, the **Ny Carlsberg Glyptotek** (Tues–Sun 10am–4pm; 20kr, Wed & Sun free; @www.glyptoteket.dk) is Copenhagen's finest gallery, with an array of Greek, Roman and Egyptian art and artefacts, as well as one of the biggest and best collections of Etruscan artefacts outside Italy. There are also excellent examples of modern European art, including some Degas casts, Monet's *The Lemon Grove* and works by Gauguin, Toulouse-Lautrec and Van Gogh.

Directly behind the train station begins **Vesterbro**, the former red-light district. The area once housed a large immigrant community, but has recently undergone major gentrification and is now popular with students and young families. In the dark streets between Vesterbrogade and Istedgade, a few porno shops remain as evidence of the area's past. At Vesterbrogade 59 (bus #6a and #26 or 15min on foot), the **City Museum** (Mon & Wed–Sun 10am–4pm, Wed until 9pm; 20kr, free on Fri) contains reconstructed ramshackle house fronts and tradesmen's signs from early Copenhagen, a large room recording the form Christian IV gave the city, and a collection of memorabilia concerning the nineteenth-century Danish philosopher Søren Kierkegaard. Further along Vesterbrogade, down Pile Allé and along Gamle Carlsberg Vej (buses #6a and #26), the exhibition at **Carlsberg Brewery Visitors Center** (Tues–Sun 10am–4pm; free), with a new brewhouse producing smaller batches of speciality beer, and a free tasting session, is well worth a visit.

## Indre By

**Indre By**, an intricate maze of streets, squares and alleys, forms the city's inner core. The main way in is from the buzzing open space of Rådhuspladsen on the north side of the Tivoli Gardens, where you'll find the **Rådhus** (Mon–Fri 10am–4pm; tours: Mon–Fri 3pm, Sat 10am & 11am; 30kr), which has an elegant fin-de-siècle hall and a **bell tower** (separate tours: Mon–Sat noon, June–Sept Mon–Fri 10am & 2pm; 20kr) that gives wonderful views over the city. Jens Olsen's World Clock (10kr), in a room close to the entrance, took 27 years to perfect; it contains a 570,000-year calendar, plotting solar and lunar eclipses and various planetary orbits, as well as telling the local time – all with astounding accuracy.

Beyond Rådhuspladsen, **Strøget**, a busy pedestrianized street, leads into the heart of the city. The liveliest part is around Gammeltorv and Nytorv, squares on either side of Strøget, where there's a small morning fruit and vegetable market, jewellery and bric-à-brac stalls, and outdoor cafés. A few minutes further on is the **Helligånds Kirke** (daily noon–4pm) founded in the fourteenth century and largely rebuilt from 1728 onwards, it is one of the oldest churches in the city. Strøget ends at **Kongens Nytorv**, the city's largest square, with an equestrian statue of its creator, Christian V, in the centre and a couple of grandly ageing structures around two of its shallow angles, most notably the Danish Royal Theatre and Charlottenborg – finished in 1683, at the same time as the square itself, for a son of Frederik III. Since 1754 Charlottenborg has been the home of the **Royal Academy of Art** (daily 10am–5pm, Wed till 7pm; 30kr; @www .charlottenborg-art.dk), which hosts decidedly eclectic art exhibitions in its spacious rooms.

There's more to see among the tangle of buildings and streets **northwest of Strøget**, not least the old university area, sometimes called the Latin Quarter, where Copenhagen's cathedral, the **Vor Frue Kirke** (Mon–Thurs & Sat 8.30am–5pm, Fri 8.30am–10.30am, Sun noon/3–4.30pm), dates from 1829 and boasts a figure of Christ behind its altar and solemn statues of the Apostles, crafted by Bertel Thorvaldsen (see p.305) and his pupils. Northeast, the **Rundetårn** round tower (Mon–Sat 10am–5/8pm, Sun noon–5/8pm; 20kr), whose summit is reached by a spiral ramp, was built by Christian IV as an observatory. Close by, the **Musikhistorisk Museum**, just off Kultorvet at Åbenrå 30 (daily except Thurs 1–3.50pm, Oct–April also closed Tues and Fri; 40kr), holds an impressive collection of musical instruments and sound-making devices, spanning the globe and the last thousand years. Over Nørre Voldgade, the **Arbejdermuseet** (Workers Museum) at Rømersgade 22 (daily 10am–4pm; Nov–June closed Mon; 50kr) is an engrossing guide to working-class life in Copenhagen from 1930 to 1959. Formerly seedy and crime-ridden, **Nørrebro**, northwest of the train station, is now a lively, young area that houses an increasing number of trendy fashion shops and stays up through the night.

## North of Indre By

There's a profound change of mood once you cross Gothersgade: the congenial alleys of the old city give way to long, broad streets and proud, aristocratic structures. Running from Kongens Nytorv, a slender canal divides the two sides of **Nyhavn**, picturesquely lined by colourful eighteenth-century houses – now bars and cafés, and very busy in summer. Just north, the cobbled **Amalienborg Plads** centres on a statue of Frederik V flanked by four identical Rococo palaces. Two serve as royal residences, and there's a changing of the guard at noon, if the monarch is at home. Between the square and the harbour are the modern gardens of **Amaliehaven** looking over at the grand new opera house on the bank of Holmen; in the opposite direction is the great marble dome of **Frederikskirke**, also known as "Marmorkirken" or marble church (Mon–Thurs 10am–5pm, Wed till 6pm, Fri–Sun noon–5pm; admission to the dome mid-June to Aug daily 1 & 3pm, Sept to mid-June only Sat & Sun; 20kr), which was modelled on St Peter's in Rome. Begun in 1749, it remained unfinished until a century and a half later because of the enormous costs involved. Further along Bredgade, a German armoured car commandeered by Danes to bring news of the Nazi surrender marks the entrance to the **Frihedsmuseet** (Museum of the Danish Resistance Movement; Tues–Sun 10am–3/5pm; 40kr, free on Wed). The road behind the museum crosses into the grounds of the **Kastellet** (daily 6am–sunset; free), a fortress built by Christian IV and expanded by his successors through the seventeenth century. On a nearby corner, overlooking the harbour, the diminutive **Little Mermaid** has been a magnet for tourists since its unveiling in 1913. A bronze statue of a Hans Christian Andersen character, it was sculpted by Edvard Erichsen and paid for by the founder of the Carlsberg brewery. A short walk to the south, the spectacular **Gefion Fountain** shows the goddess Gefion with her four sons, whom she's turned into oxen having been promised, in return, as much land as she can plough in a single night.

West of here lies **Nyboder**, a curious area of narrow streets lined with rows of compact yellow dwellings, originally built by Christian IV to encourage his sailors to live in the city. Across Sølvgade from Nyboder is the main entrance to **Rosenborg Slot** (May–Oct daily 10/11am–3/5pm; Nov–April Tues–Sun 11am–2pm; 60kr). This Dutch-Renaissance-style palace served as the main residence of Christian IV and, until the end of the nineteenth century, of the monarchs who succeeded him. The main building includes the rooms and furnishings used by the regal occupants, although the highlight is the downstairs treasury, which displays the crown jewels and rich accessories worn by Christian IV. Adjacent to Rosenborg Slot is **Kongens Have**, the city's oldest public park and a popular place for picnics, while on the west side is the **Botanical Garden** (Botanisk Have; daily 8.30am–4/6pm; winter closed Mon; free). The neighbouring **Statens Museum for Kunst** (Tues–Sun 10am–5pm, Wed till 8pm; 50kr, free on Wed; ❀www.smk .dk) holds a mammoth collection of art, from minor Picassos to major works by Matisse and Braque, Cranach, El Greco, Titian, Rubens, Poussin and Claude Lorrain – although it's the grotesque pieces by Emil Nolde that steal the show. Across the park, **Den Hirschsprungske Samling** on Stockholmsgade (Mon & Wed–Sun 11am–4pm; 35kr, free on Wed; ❀www.hirschsprung.dk) contains a collection of twentieth-century Danish art, including work by the Skagen artists (see p.317), renowned for their interesting use of light.

## Christiansborg

**Christiansborg** sits on the island of Slotsholmen, with several short bridges tenuously connecting it to Indre By. It was here, in the twelfth century, that Bishop Absalon built the castle that instigated the city. The drab royal palace completed in 1916 that now occupies the site is primarily given over to government offices and the state parliament, or **Folketinget** (guided tours in English 2pm; free). Close to the bus stop on Christiansborg Slotsplads is the doorway to the **Ruins beneath Christiansborg** (daily 10am–4pm; Oct–April closed Mon; 30kr), where a staircase leads down to the remains of Absalon's original building; it's surprisingly absorbing, the mood enhanced by the semi-darkness and lack of external noise. In the palace's north wing, the **Royal Reception Rooms** (guided tours in English: May–Sept daily 11am, 1pm & 3pm; Oct–April Tues–Sun 3pm; 60kr) are used by the royal family to entertain important visitors. On the north side of Slotsholmen, the **Thorvaldsens Museum** (Tues–Sun 10am–5pm; 20kr, Wed free) is the home of an enormous collection of work and memorabilia (and the body) of Denmark's most famous sculptor, who lived from 1770 to 1844. There's another major collection a short walk away over the Slotsholmen moat, in the **National Museum** (same hours; 50kr, free on Wed; ⊛www.natmus.dk), which has excellent displays on Denmark's prehistory and Viking days – jewellery, sacrificial gifts, and even bodies, all remarkably well preserved by Danish peat bogs.

### Christianshavn and Christiania

From Christiansborg, a bridge crosses to **Christianshavn**, built by Christian IV as an autonomous new town in the early sixteenth century as housing for shipbuilding workers. Its features were more common to Dutch ports of the time, even down to small canals, and in parts it's more redolent of Amsterdam than Copenhagen. Reaching skywards on the far side of Torvegade is one of the city's most recognizable features, the copper and golden spire of **Vor Frelsers Kirke** (daily 11am/noon–3.30pm; tower April–Aug only; free, tower 20kr); its external staircase was added to the otherwise plain church in the mid-eighteenth century. A few streets from Vor Frelsers Kirke, **Christiania** is a former barracks area that was colonized by hippies after declaring itself a "free city" in 1971. It has since evolved into a self-governing entity with quirky buildings housing alternative small businesses such as the Christiana Bike and the Women's Smithy, as well as shops, cafés, restaurants, music venues, and – most famously – an open hash market on Pusherstreet. Bob Marley and John Lennon blare out from the bars and the area is awash with psychedelic painting. There are guided tours of the area (July & Aug daily 3pm, rest of the year Sat & Sun only; 30kr; ☎32.95.65.07, ⊛www.christiania.org), starting at the main gate by Princessegade, but it's just as fun to wander around on your own: no photos allowed.

## Eating and drinking

There's a wide choice of **eating** options in the city centre; check out the areas around Kultorvet and along Studiestræde. Further afield, the Sankt Hans Torv area of Nørrebro across Peblinge Søen draws in the crowds, and Vesterbrogade turns up a number of good value lower-key places. If you're **self-catering**, numerous bakeries sell freshly made *rundstykker* (crispy rolls) and flaky Danish pastry – still oven-warm – in the early hours of the morning. Rhein van Hauen on Mikkelbryggersgade 8 near Rådhuspladsen are acknowledged pastry masters, and Emerys with bakeries at Vesterbrogade 34, Nørrebrogade 8, and Østerbrogade 51 do outstanding all-organic bread and rolls. For take-away *smørrebrød* try the outlets at Domhusets Smørrebrød, Kattesundet 18, Centrum Smørrebrød, Vesterbrogade 6C, and Klemmen at the Central Station. There's a Netto supermarket at Nørre Voldgade 94, Nørrebrogade 43, Landemærket 11 and Store Kongensgade 47. Fakta is on Nørrebrogade 14–16 and on Borgergade 27.

# Brunches and light meals

**Bang & Jensen** Istedgade 130. Popular café at the quieter end of Istedgade, serving a breakfast buffet until 11am, filling brunch until 4pm, and sandwiches and light meals all day. Turns into a busy bar at night, especially when there's music on at Vega nearby (see p.308).

**Café Gavlen** Ryesgade 1. Small, good-value café near the pricier places on Sankt Hans Torv. Basic egg-and-bacon brunch for 40kr, three pieces of smørrebrød for 40kr, and a daily special for 55kr.

**Café Sommersko** Kronprinsensgade 6. A golden oldie French-style café whose popularity hasn't diminished one bit since it opened in the mid-70s. Particularly recommended is the filling Sunday brunch (veggie options available). Late opening bar during the weekends.

**Den Sorte Gryde** Istedgade 108. Legendary huge burgers, as well as good traditional Danish fare, mostly take-away.

**Floras Kaffebar** Blågårdsgade 27. A temple to coffee with outdoor seating in summer, this place also does a good chilli con carne (69kr) and homemade burgers.

**Front Page** Sortedams Dosseringen 21. With its lakeside setting, this is a perfect spot for a quiet coffee or a cool beer and tapas sundowner.

**Klaptræet** Kultorvet 11. Popular refuelling spot for shoppers, serving coffee, sandwiches, quiches and snacks.

**La Galette** Larsbjørnstræde 9. Authentic Breton pancakes made with organic buckwheat and an array of fillings – from smoked salmon to chocolate and chestnut mousse.

**Morgenstedet** Langgade, Christiania. Tasty and mostly organic vegan and vegetarian salads and light meals at very affordable prices. No smoking or alcohol. Closed Mon.

**Pussy Galore's Flying Circus** Sankt Hans Torv 30. Trendy brunch spot with outdoor seating on the square, that's also popular in the evening, when beer and wine take priority.

# Restaurants

**Ankara** Vesterbrogade 35. Popular Turkish restaurant with all-you-can-eat buffets for 49/69kr (lunch/eve) as well as good-value à la carte deals. Also branches at Vesterbrogade 96 and Krystalgade 8–10.

**Atlas Bar** Larsbjørnstræde 18. Eco-restaurant/café serving tasty Asian and South American dishes. The portions are enormous, with main courses at lunchtime from 95kr and in the evening from 120kr. Closed Sun.

**Den Grønne Kælder** Pilestræde 48. A simple, tiled-floor cellar joint serving affordable gourmet-style vegetarian meals. Lunch starts at 65kr for a main course, and the scrumptious evening à la carte menu won't break the bank. Closed Sun.

**Kates Joint** Blågårdsgade 12. Small funky place serving quality dishes from around the globe. A few regulars include Jamaican Jerk Chicken and Chicken Tikka for 65kr, and there's always at least one vegetarian option.

**Nyhavns Færgekro** Nyhavn 5. Slightly pricey, but the lunchtime fish-laden buffet (89kr) cannot be surpassed. Outdoor seating in summer.

**Pasta Basta** Valkendorfgade 22. Late-closing place with a wide range of pasta dishes – from simple pesto to lobster salad – and a good-value buffet at 79kr. Mon–Thurs & Sun open till 3am, Fri & Sat till 5am.

**RizRaz** Kompagnistræde 20. Excellent-value Mediterranean food.

**Shezan** Viktoriagarde 22. Copenhagen's first Pakistani restaurant is still going strong, with authentic, spicy main courses from 52kr, plenty of vegetarian options, and a great view of Istedgade's shady dealings.

**Spicey Kitchen** Torvegade 56. Popular small restaurant serving lightly spiced Indian and Pakistani fare (with eight veggie options) for under 50kr a main course. Also take-away.

**Spiseloppen** Christiania. It's won culinary accolades, and hiked up its prices, but the *Spiseloppen* is still great and the portions generous. Meals from 135kr. Evening only, closed Mon.

**Thai Esan** Lille Istedgade 7. Bargain Thai food in a very popular restaurant. If it's full, try *Thai Esan 2* around the corner at Halmtorvet 44.

**Thai Thai Buffet** Valdemarsgade 46. Open Thurs–Sat for dinner only, this take-away joint does a fabulous all-you-can-eat buffet for 129kr.

# Bars

**Andy's Bar** Gothersgade 33B. Packed late-night bar with a very jovial vibe – you'll end up leaving the place with lots of new friends. Daily 11pm to 6am.

Café Louise Nørrebrogade 5. Legendary last stop after a big night out. Ring the door bell to get in. Daily 1–7am, weekends till 9am.

Charlie's Bar Pilestræde 33. Award-winning Real Ale pub that gets very busy, so arrive early if you want a seat.

Hviids Vinstue Kongens Nytorv 19. Old-fashioned bar with crowded rooms patrolled by uniformed waiters. Outdoor seating in summer.

Musen og Elefanten Vestergade 21. Small bar on two floors, serving Carlsberg's draught Elefant Beer from a carved trunk.

Nemoland Christiania. Despite a government crackdown on Christiania, *Nemo* is still one of the city's most popular open-air bars. In winter, the punters move indoors to the pool tables and backgammon boards.

Nørrebro Bryghus Ryesgade 3. Immensely popular brewery pub with a range of home brews that sell out quicker than they can be bottled. Also has a pricey restaurant.

Riesen Oehlenschlægersgade 36. Small crowded neighbourhood bar featuring Indie rock and affordable draught beer.

Sebastopol Sankt Hans Torv 2. Trendy café on the Sankt Hans Torv square that catches the last rays of sun and gathers large crowds in summer. Good brunches too.

Universitetscaféen Fiolstræde 2. A prime location, long hours (until 5am), outdoor seating in summer and live blues or rock every Thurs.

Ølbaren Elmegade 2. Literally "beer bar", with an incredible range from around the world, and a bartender that knows them all and can advise accordingly. Always packed. No smoking Mon & Sat.

# Nightlife

Copenhagen is a pretty good place for **live music**. Major international names visit regularly, and there are always plenty of minor gigs in cafés and bars, which are often free during the week. For **listings** of what's on, pick up the free *Gaffa*, from cafés and music shops. Clubs are busy from midnight to 5am, with fairly easy-going dress codes; drinks and admission (from 50kr) are fairly cheap.

## Live music and clubs

Club Mambo Vester Voldgade 85. Popular Latin dance venue. Free Salsa and Merengue lessons 10–11pm. Open Thurs, Fri & Sat.

Copenhagen JazzHouse Niels Hemmingsensgade 10 ⊛ www.jazzhouse.dk. The city's top jazz venue, hosting live jazz gigs – jazz in its broadest sense from world music to fusion – followed by a funky late night disco.

Drop Inn Kompagnistræde 34. Laid-back, unpretentious place near Huset with live blues or rock most nights. Cheap beer and late opening hours.

JazzHuset Vohnporten Rådhusstræde 13. In the same building as Use-It (see p.299), with regular live bands. Monday is big band night, Tuesday features superjam, and Friday and Saturday are jazz. Happy hour 8–9pm.

Loppen Christiania ⊛ www.loppen.dk. Christiania's

### Gay and lesbian Copenhagen

The Danish capital has a small but lively **gay scene**. For **information**, contact the National Organization for Gay Men and Women, Teglgårdstræde 13 (☎33.13.19.48, ⊛ www.lbl.dk), or get hold of the free Copenhagen Gay Map, the free supplement to *Out and About* magazine or the monthly Danish *Pan* magazine. **Places to go** include the *Cosy Bar*, Studiestræde 24, a late-night place popular with gay men of all ages; *Oscars*, Rådhuspladsen 77, the city's only gay café-lounge and typically the first port of call on a night out; and *Heaven*, Kompagnistræde 10, which draws a predominantly young trendy crowd. *Pan Club*, Knabrostræde 3, part of the largest gay centre in Scandinavia, has a good disco, and *Masken*, Studiestræde 33, has a great bar and disco (women only Thursday 9pm–2am). Further up the road at no. 12, the wildly popular *Jailhouse* has a basement bar designed as a jail with drinking "cells". For lesbians, *Les Ziraf*, Sankt, Pederstræde 34, is a restaurant/bar with regular live gigs, and a 5–8pm happy hour, and *Kvindehuset*, Gothersgade 37, has a café and the *XXBar* disco every third Friday of the month, as well as other regular events.

main rock and jazz venue. DJs follow live music events on Fri & Sat. Closes 5am.

**Mojo** Løngangstræde 21. Atmospheric low-key blues venue where live music fills the place every night. Happy hour 8–10pm.

**Park Café** Østerbrogade 79. Plush high-ceilinged café/bar in grand surroundings. Thurs–Sat, it's home to a nightclub upstairs, with a cocktail bar downstairs sometimes featuring live pop/rock music. Friday over-20s, Saturday over-22.

**Pumpehuset** Studiestræde 52 ⊛ www.pumpehu set.dk. Copenhagen's former pumping station is now a hip venue for mainstream rock, pop and funk from around the world.

**Rust** Guldbergsgade 8 ⊛ www.rust.dk. Large complex hosting live indie-rock, pop and hiphop bands

on its main stage, and three dancefloors playing everything from breakbeat to latin jazz.

**Stengade 30** Stengade 18 ⊛ www.stengade30. dk. Popular hardcore metal, punk and indie venue. Closed Mon.

**Stereo Bar** Linnésgade 16A. Once-trendy bar that's mellowed with age, with a dance-floor in the basement playing mostly latin, house and drum'n'bass. Free entry. Closes 3am. Closed Sun–Tues.

**Vega** Enghavevej 40 ⊛ www.vega.dk. The city's premier music venue that caters for most tastes. Two concert halls, Lille Vega and Store Vega, with international acts, a nightclub (Fri & Sat, free admission until 1am, over-20s only) and Ideal Bar (Wed–Sat).

## Listings

**Bike rental** Københavns Cykelbørs, Gothersgade 157; Københavns Cykler, Reventlowsgade 11; Østerport Cykler, Oslo Plads 9.

**Embassies** Australia, Dampfærgevej 26 ☎ 70.26.36.76; Canada, Kristen Bernikowsgade 1 ☎ 33.48.32.00; Ireland, Østbanegade 21 ☎ 35.42.32.33; Netherlands, Toldbodgade 33 ☎ 33.70.72.02; New Zealand, use UK; UK, Kastelsvej 40 ☎ 35.44.52.00; US, Dag Hammerskjölds Allé 24 ☎ 35.55.31.44.

**Exchange** Den Danske Bank at the Airport (daily 6am–8.30pm); Forex and X-Change at the Central

Station (daily 7/8am–9pm). Kontanten ATMs everywhere.

**Hospital** Rigshospitalet, Blegdamsvej 9 ☎ 35.45.35.45.

**Left luggage** Free for a day at Use-It, Rådhus-stræde 13. Otherwise, lockers at Central Station, from 25kr for 24hr.

**Pharmacies** Steno Apotek, Vesterbrogade 6C; Sønderbro Apotek, Amagerbrogade 158. Both 24hr.

**Police** ☎ 33.25.14.48.

**Post office** Købmagergade 33, and at Central Station.

## Short trips from Copenhagen

If the weather's good, you can top up your tan at the Amager **beaches** (buses #2a, #12, or #250S along Øresundsvej). On the other side of the airport from the beaches lies **DRAGØR**, an atmospheric, cobbled fishing village which has good local history collections in the harbourside **Dragør Museum** (May–Sept Tues–Sun noon–4pm; 20kr), and the **Amager Museum** (same hours, plus Oct–April Wed & Sat noon–4pm), just off the Copenhagen road at the western edge of the village. From the city, take bus #30, #31, #32 or #350S. If you're in the mood for an amusement park but don't fancy the neatness of Tivoli, venture out to **BAKKEN** (mid-March to early Sept daily noon/2pm–10pm/midnight; free; 119/239kr day pass, cheaper mid-week and during low season; ⊛ www.bakken.dk), close to the Klampenborg stop at the end of lines C and F+ on the S-train. Besides swings and rollercoasters it offers pleasant woods of oak and beech, which were once royal hunting grounds.

Two more excellent attractions are on Zealand's northeastern coast. Fifteen minutes' walk from Rungsted Kyst train station, the peaceful **Karen Blixen Museum** (May–Sept Tues–Sun 10am–5pm; Oct–April Wed–Sun 11am/1pm–4pm; 40kr) presents a moving testament of this remarkable woman's life, best known as the author of *Out of Africa*. In **HUMLEBÆK**, 10km further north and a short walk from its train station, is **Louisiana**, an outstanding modern art gallery, at Gammel Strandvej 13 (daily 10am–5pm, Wed till 10pm; 76kr; ⊛ www.louisiana.dk); its setting alone is worth the journey, harmoniously combining art, architecture and the natural landscape.

# The rest of Zealand

As home to the capital, **Zealand** is Denmark's most important and most visited region, and, with a swift metropolitan transport network covering almost half of the island, you can always make it back to the capital in time for an evening drink. North of Copenhagen, **Helsingør**, the departure point for ferries to Sweden, is the site of the Kronborg Slot, with nearby **Hillerød** being home to its rival, the Frederiksborg Slot. West of Copenhagen, and on the main train route to Funen, is **Roskilde**, its extravagant cathedral the resting place for Danish monarchs, and with a gorgeous location on the Roskilde fjord, from where five Viking boats were salvaged and are now restored and displayed in a specially built museum.

## Helsingør

First impressions of **HELSINGØR** are none too enticing, but away from the bustle of its train and ferry terminals it's a quiet and likeable town. Its position on the four-kilometre strip of water linking the North Sea and the Baltic brought the town prosperity when, in 1429, the Sound Toll was imposed on passing vessels. Today, it's once again an important waterway, with ferries to Swedish Helsingborg accounting for most of Helsingør's through-traffic and innumerable cheap booze shops. The town's great tourist draw is **Kronborg Slot** (May–Sept daily 10.30am–5pm; Oct–April Tues–Sun 11am–3/4pm; 50kr, 75kr joint ticket with the Maritime Museum; Copenhagen Card not valid), principally because of its literary associations as Elsinore Castle, whose ramparts Shakespeare's Hamlet supposedly strode. The playwright never actually visited Helsingør, and the tenth-century character Amleth on whom his hero was based long predates the castle, but nevertheless there's a thriving Hamlet souvenir business. The present castle dates from the sixteenth century when it stood out like a raised fist into the sound warning passing ships not to consider dodging the toll. Though various parts have been destroyed and rebuilt since, it remains a grand affair, enhanced immeasurably by its setting; the interior, particularly the royal chapel, is spectacularly ornate. The castle also houses the surprisingly captivating national **Maritime Museum** (40kr, 75kr joint ticket with the castle), which, apart from a motley collection of model ships and nautical knick-knacks, contains relics from Denmark's conquests in Greenland, India, the West Indies and West Africa, as well as, from 1852, the world's oldest surviving ship's biscuit.

The **tourist office**, opposite the train station at Havnepladsen 3 (Mon–Fri 10am–4/5/6pm, Sat 10am–1/3pm; ☎49.21.13.33, ⊛www.helsingorturist.dk), leads into Helsingør's well-preserved medieval quarter. **Stengade** is the main pedestrianized street, linked by a number of narrow alleyways to Axeltorv, the town's small market square and a nice place to enjoy a beer. Near the corner of Stengade and Skt. Annagade is Helsingør's cathedral, **Skt. Olai's Kirke** (Mon–Fri 10am–2pm), with its renovated spire. Just beyond is Skt. Mariæ Kirke, whose **Karmeliterklostret**, built circa 1400, is now the best-preserved medieval monastic complex in Scandinavia (Mon–Fri 10am–2/3pm; 20kr). Its former hospital contains the **Town**

---

### Across to Sweden

Three **ferry** lines make the twenty-minute crossing from Helsingør to Helsingborg in Sweden every 20/30min. All ferries leave from the main terminal by the train station; Scandlines (34kr return) and Sundbusserne (daytime and foot passengers only; 34kr) arrive at central Helsingborg while HH Ferries (30kr) dock a good walk from the centre. Eurail and Scanrail passes are valid on Scandlines and Interrail and the Copenhagen Card gives a fifty percent discount.

**Museum** (daily noon–4pm; 10kr), which prided itself on brain operations – the unnerving tools of which are still here, together with diagrams of the procedures used. For **food**, *Rådmands Davids Hus*, Strandgade 70, is a prime lunchtime spot for its daily specials; *Møllers Conditori*, Stengade 39, Denmark's oldest bakery, has sizeable sandwiches and Danish pastries to follow; or try the varied delights in the courtyard at Stengade 26, including *Biocafeen*, with live music in the evenings.

## Hillerød

Last stop on lines A and E of the S-train, or thirty minutes by train from Helsingør, **HILLERØD**'s highlight is the lovely **Frederiksborg Slot** (daily 10/11am–3/5pm; 60kr), lying decorously across three small islands in an artificial lake and lined by a beautifully manicured Baroque garden. The tiny Frederiksborg ferry does a half-hour trip on the castle lake in summer (20kr). Buses #701 and #702 run from the train station to the castle, but it's only a twenty-minute signposted walk. The castle was rebuilt at the turn of the seventeenth century in Dutch Renaissance style and the unusual design – prolific use of towers and spires, pointed Gothic arches and flowery window ornamentation – still dominates. In 1878, a museum of national history was established here and provides a magnificent setting for the country's finest collection of historical and portrait paintings as well as furniture. There's an illustrated guide to the castle and museum (60kr), but most rooms have detailed descriptions in English pasted on the walls. Two rooms deserve special mention: the exquisite chapel, where monarchs were anointed between 1671 and 1840, and the Great Hall above, bare but for the staggering wall- and ceiling-decorations: tapestries, wall-reliefs, portraits and a glistening black marble fireplace. The *Spisestedet Leonora*, in one of the castle's gatehouses, serves fantastic *smørrebrød* (from 42kr a piece), should you get peckish.

## Roskilde

**ROSKILDE** was the base of the Danish church in the twelfth century and as a consequence became the nation's capital. Its importance waned after the Reformation, but its ancient centre is one of Denmark's most appealing – well worth a look on your way west. Its showpiece is the fabulous **Roskilde Domkirke** (April–Sept Mon–Fri 9am–4.45pm, Sat 9am–noon, Sun 12.30–4.45pm; Oct–March Tues–Sat 10am–3.45pm, Sun 12.30–3.45pm; 25kr), founded in 1170 and largely completed by the fourteenth century, although bits have been added since. Four royal chapels house a magnificent collection of regal remains: twenty-one kings and eighteen queens. The most richly endowed chapel is that of Christian IV, a previously austere resting place jazzed up in the early nineteenth century with bronze statues, frescoes and vast paintings of scenes from his reign. Upstairs in the Great Hall, a small **Cathedral Museum** (April–Sept Mon–Fri 11am, 1pm & 3pm, Sat 10am, Sun 1pm & 2pm; Oct–March Tues–Fri noon & 1pm, Sat noon, Sun 1pm & 2pm; access only with Cathedral staff) provides an engrossing introduction to the Cathedral's colourful history. A roofed passageway, the Arch of Absalon (not open to the public), runs from the Cathedral into the **Roskilde Palace** next door, housing the **Palace Collections** (mid-May to mid-Sept daily 11am–4pm; mid-Sept to mid-May Sat noon–4pm; 25kr), with its paintings, furniture and other artefacts belonging to the wealthiest Roskilde families of the eighteenth and nineteenth centuries. In the same building, the **Museum of Contemporary Art** (Tues–Fri 11am–5pm, Sat & Sun noon–4pm when there are exhibitions on; 30kr, Wed free) hosts temporary exhibitions and includes a charming sculpture garden. The town's history is recorded in the **Roskilde Museum** at Skt. Ols Gade 18 (daily 11am–4pm; 25kr), with strong sections on medieval pottery and toys, although more absorbing is the modern **Viking Ship Museum** (daily 10am–5pm; 75kr; ⊛www.vikingeskibsmuseet.dk), at Vindeboder 12, on the banks of the fjord. Inside, five excellent specimens of

Viking shipbuilding are displayed: a deep-sea trader, a merchant ship, a warship, a ferry and a longship, each one retrieved from the fjord where they had been sunk to block invading forces. Outside, on Museum Island, you can watch boat-building and sail-making using only tools and materials available during the Viking era; when the weather allows you can also experience the ship's seaworthiness on the fjord – you'll be handed an oar when you board and be expected to pull your weight as a crew member (50min; 50kr on top of the museum ticket).

The **tourist office** (Mon–Fri 9am–4/5/6pm, Sat 10am–1/2pm; ☎46.31.65.65, ⑩www.visitroskilde.dk) is at Gullandsstræde 15, a short walk from the main square. For **lunch**, head to *Café Satchmo*, down a passageway between the *Hotel Prindsen* and Bryggergården on Algade. Contact the tourist office well in advance if you wish to stay during the **Roskilde Festival** (⑩www.roskilde-festival.dk), one of the largest open-air rock events in Europe, attracting almost 100,000 people annually. Note that tickets go on sale in December and tend to sell out quickly. The festival takes place late June/early July and there's a special free camping ground beside the festival site, to which shuttle buses run from the train station every few minutes.

# Funen

Known as the Garden of Denmark, partly for the lawn-like neatness of its fields, partly for the fruit and vegetables grown in them, **Funen** is the smaller of the two main Danish islands. The pastoral outlook of the place and the coastline draw many visitors, but its attractions are low-profile cultural sights, such as the collections of the "Funen painters" and the birthplaces of writer Hans Christian Andersen and composer Carl Nielsen. **Odense**, Denmark's third city, is the island's main urban settlement, with the surrounding coastline dotted with laid-back former fishing towns, and the nearby picturesque Hindsholm peninsula.

## Odense

**ODENSE** loves to remind you it's the birthplace of Denmark's best-loved writer, Hans Christian Andersen. Named after Odin, chief of the pagan gods, Odense is one of the oldest settlements in the country. The inner core of the city is pedestrianized with a range of good museums to visit; the nightlife is surprisingly lively, with a focus on live music and jazz.

The city's major attraction is the **Hans Christian Andersen Hus** at Bangs Boder 29 (June–Aug daily 9am–6pm; Sept–May Tues–Sun 10am–4pm; ⑩www .odmus.dk; 50kr), where the writer was born in 1805. The museum includes a library of Andersen's works, audio collections of his best-known works and the intriguing paraphernalia of his life, including school reports, manuscripts, paper cuttings and drawings from his travels. For some local history, the **Bymuseet Møntergården**, a few streets away at Overgade 48–50 (Tues–Sun 10am–4pm; free; ⑩www.odmus.dk), has an engrossing collection of artefacts dating from the city's earliest settlements to the Nazi occupation. There's more about Andersen at Munkemøllestræde 3–5, between Skt. Knud Kirkestræde and Horsetorvet, in the tiny **Hans Christian Andersen's Barndomshjem** (Childhood Home; daily 10/11am–3/4pm; 10kr), where Andersen lived from 1807 to 1819. Nearby, the crypt of **Skt. Knud's Kirke** (Mon–Sat 9/10am–4/5pm, Sun noon–5pm; free), holds the remains of King Knud II and his brother Benedikt, both murdered in 1086 at the altar of nearby Skt. Albani Kirke. The cathedral is the only example of pure Gothic church architecture in the country; its enormous and finely detailed sixteenth-century altarpiece, coated in twenty-three carat gold leaf, is one of the greatest works of the Lübeck master, Claus Berg.

At Jernbanegade 13, the **Fyns Kunstmuseum** (Funen Art Gallery; Tues–Sun 10am–4pm; ⊛www.odmus.dk; 30kr), just a few minutes' walk from Skt. Knud's, gives a good introduction to the Danish art world during the late nineteenth century; the collection contains some stirring works by Vilhelm Hammershøi, P.S. Krøyer, Michael and Anne Ancher, and H.A. Brendekilde's emotive *Udslidt*. A short walk east, at Claus Bergs Gade 11, in a wing of Odense's Concert Hall, is the **Carl Nielsen Museet** (Thurs & Fri 4–8pm, Sun noon–4pm; 25kr; ⊛www.odmus.dk). Born in a village just outside Odense, Nielsen is best remembered in Denmark for his popular songs, though it was his operas, choral pieces and symphonies that established him as a major international composer.

West of the centre is the **Brandts Klædefabrik**, on Brandts Passage just off Vestergade, a large former textile factory now given over to an art school, a cinema, a music library, several cafés and restaurants, and three museums (July & Aug daily 10am–5pm; Sept–June closed Mon; 50kr combined ticket; ⊛www.brandts.dk). In the large hall that once housed the huge machinery is the **Brandts Kunsthallen** (30kr), which displays works by the cream of new talent in art and design, and the **Museet for Fotokunst** (25kr), featuring changing exhibitions of photography. On the third floor the **Danmarks Mediemuseum** (25kr), displaying bulky machines and devices, chronicles the development of printing, book binding and illustrating from the Middle Ages to the present. Further down Brandts Passage, upstairs at no. 29, the tiny **Tidens Samling** (daily 10am–5pm; ⊛www.tidenssamling.dk; 30kr) gives an intimate insight into the changing fashions of sitting-rooms and clothing since the beginning of the twentieth century.

South of the centre at Sejerskovvej 20 is **Den Fynske Landsby** (Funen Village; April–May and Sept–Oct Tues–Sun 10am–5pm, 40kr; June–Aug daily 10am–7pm, 55kr; Nov–March Sun only 11am–3pm, free; ⊛www.odmus.dk), a reconstructed nineteenth-century village made up of buildings from all over Funen. In summer, some of the old trades are revived in the former workshops and crafthouses, and free shows are staged at the open-air theatre. Bus #42 runs to the village from the city centre.

## Practicalities

Odense **train station** is a ten-minute walk from the city centre, and is also the terminus for all long-distance **buses**. The **tourist office** (mid-June to Aug Mon–Fri 9.30am–6pm, Sat & Sun 10am–3pm; Sept to mid-June Mon–Fri 9.30am–4.30pm, Sat 10am–1pm; ⊕66.12.75.20, ⊛www.visitodense.com) is on the Vestergade side of the Rådhus – follow the signs – and sells the useful **Adventure Pass** (120/160kr for 24/48hr), which gives free entry to most museums and unlimited travel on all local buses.

There are a number of inexpensive **hotels** near the centre, with the best value being *Det Lille Hotel*, Dronningensgade 5 (⊕66.12.28.21, ⊛www.lillehotel.dk; ❹), and *Ydes*, Hans Tausens Gade 11 (⊕66.12.11.31, ⊛www.ydes.dk; ❺), both of which include breakfast. There are two **hostels**: one alongside the train station at Østre Stationsvej 31 (⊕66.11.04.25, ⊛www.cityhostel.dk; 120kr); and a quieter one at Kragsbjergvej 121 (⊕66.13.04.25, ⊛www.odense-danhostel.dk; 105kr; closed Dec–March) – take bus #61 or #62 south to Tornbjerg and get off along Munkebjergvej at the junction with Vissenbjergvej. The closest **campsite** (⊕66.11.47.02) is due south at Odensevej 102, near Den Fynske Landsby, and also has cabins to rent – take buses #21, #22 or #23 from the Rådhus or train station to Højby. There's free **Internet** access in the library at the train station.

There are plenty of **restaurants** and **snack bars** in the city centre. *Den Gyldne Ovn* bakery on Fisketorvet is a reliable spot for freshly made pastries and sandwiches, while the best pizzeria is *Italiano*, at Vesterbro 9. *Tortilla Flat*, Frederiksgade 38, is a popular Mexican restaurant, or you could try the inexpensive café (35kr for the daily special) in the Badstuen cultural centre, Østre Stationsvej 26. Vegetarians should make for *Kærnehuset*, Nedergade 6, where at 6pm (Tues–Fri) you can eat as much as you like for a bargain 40kr. For **drinks**, *Carlsen's Kvarter*, on the corner of Hunderupvej and Læssøgade, is an inexpensive pub serving fruity Belgian beers and English ales and occasionally hosting Danish folk music, while the fashionable *Café Biografen* in Brandts Passage is also worth a visit. As for **nightlife**, *Jazzhus Dexter*, Vindegade 65 (ⓦwww.dexter.dk), is the place to head for jazz, while the Badstuen cultural centre (ⓦwww.badstuen.dk) has popular folk nights and *Rytmeposten*, across the road at Østre Stationsvej 35 (ⓦwww.rytmeposten.dk), hosts raucous live bands.

# Jutland

Long ago, the Jutes, the people of **Jutland**, were a separate tribe from the more warlike Danes who occupied the eastern islands. In pagan times, the peninsula had its own rulers and it was here that the ninth-century monarch Harald Bluetooth began the process that turned the two tribes into a unified Christian nation. By the Viking era, however, the battling Danes had spread west, absorbing the Jutes, and real power gradually shifted towards Zealand, where it has largely stayed ever since. Unhurried lifestyles and rural calm are thus the overriding impression of Jutland for most visitors; indeed, its distance from Copenhagen makes it the most distinct and interesting area in the country. In the south, Schleswig is a territory long battled over by Denmark and Germany, though beyond the immaculately restored **Ribe** town, it holds little of abiding interest. **Århus**, halfway up the eastern coast, is Jutland's main urban centre and Denmark's second city. Further inland, the countryside is the country's most dramatic – stark heather-clad moors, dense forests and swooping gorges. North of vibrant **Aalborg**, sited on the bank of the Limfjord, the landscape reaches a crescendo of storm-lashed savagery around **Skagen**, on the very tip of the peninsula.

## Ribe

Exquisitely-preserved **RIBE** was once a major stopover point for pilgrims on their way to Rome, as well as a significant port, until the Reformation and the silting-up of the harbour in the Middle Ages. Since then, not much appears to have changed, making it a delight to wander around. From the train station, Dagmarsgade leads to Torvet and the towering **Domkirke** (daily 10am/noon–4/5.30pm; 12kr), begun around 1150. Only the Cat's Head Door on the south side remains from the original construction; much more modern are the interior's colourful mosaics, stained-glass windows and paintings, completed by COBRA member Carl-Henning Pedersen in 1984. You can normally climb the red-brick tower and peer out over the town and beyond to the Wadden Sea. Behind the cathedral, the **Weis' Stue** is a tiny inn built around 1600, from which the nightwatchman of Ribe makes his rounds – a throwback to the days when Danish towns were patrolled by singing guards looking for unattended candles and warning residents of storms, though these days he stops at points of interest to explain the town's history to tourists (May to mid-Sept 10pm; June–Aug also 8pm; free).

### Practicalities

The **tourist office** (Mon–Fri 9/9.30am–4.30/6pm, Sat 10am–1/5pm; ☏75.42.15.00, ⓦwww.visitribe.dk) is behind the cathedral, opposite the Weis' Stue, with a full list of **private rooms** to rent (❹). It also sells a map (15kr) with directions for a wonderfully quiet and relaxing bicycle ride to the nearby Wadden Sea and island of Mandø; you can rent a bike for 60kr per day from the **hostel** at Skt. Pedersgade 16 (☏75.42.06.20, ⓦwww.danhostel.dk/ribe; 120kr; closed Dec & Jan).

To get there from the station follow Skt. Nicolai Gade onto Saltgade, then turn left in Skt. Pedersgade. If the hostel's full, try the *Weis' Stue* on Torvet (☎75.42.07.00, ⓦwww.weis-stue.dk; ⑥), opposite the atmospheric but expensive *Hotel Dagmar* (☎75.42.00.33, ⓦwww.hoteldagmar.dk; ⑨), the oldest hotel in Denmark. The nearest **campsite** is *Ribe Camping*, which is 1.5km from Ribe along Farupvej, and also has cabins (☎75.41.07.77; bus #715 on weekdays; closed mid-Oct to Easter). For **food**, try *Restaurant Backhaus*, Grydergade 12, with good value steaks and burgers. Traditional Danish dishes can be found at *Restaurant Sælhunden*, Skibroen 13, in a wood-beamed, listed building overlooking the harbour, while nearby *Kolvig Café and Restaurant* offers filling, reasonably-priced salads and sandwiches in a relaxed riverside setting. There's excellent coffee in *Valdemar Sejr* next to the art gallery on Skt. Nicolaj Gade, which is also a good spot for **drinks** and **music** in the evening. *Stenbohus*, at Stenbogade 1, has live blues, folk or rock bands at least once a week.

# Århus

Tempted by the shelter of the Århus Å river, Vikings first settled here in Aros ("river mouth" in old Nordic) over a thousand years ago. **ÅRHUS** (or Aarhus) is now Denmark's second-largest city, an instantly likeable assortment of intimate cobbled streets, sleek modern architecture, brightly painted houses and laid-back students. It's small enough to get to grips with in a few hours, but lively enough to make you linger for days – its excellent music scene, interesting art, pavement cafés and energetic nightlife all earn it the unofficial title of Denmark's culture capital.

### Arrival, information and accommodation

**Trains**, **buses** and **ferries** all stop on the southern edge of the city centre. Frequent buses from the **airport** run to the train station (45min; 80kr). The **tourist office** is a short walk from the stations, in Park Allé (Mon–Fri 9/9.30am–4/6pm, Sat 10am–1/5pm; mid-June to mid-Sept also Sun 9.30am–1pm; ☎89.40.67.00, ⓦwww .visitaarhus.com), on the first floor of the city's Rådhus, and can arrange private rooms (③) for a 25kr booking fee. Pick up a city map plus film, music and theatre listings for free. Buses form the city's **public transport system**, which is divided into four zones: one and two cover the centre; three and four reach into the country. A basic ticket costs 17kr from machines in the back of the bus and is valid for any number of journeys for two hours from the time stamped on it. And while it's easy to get around on foot – you'll need buses only to get to Moesgård Museum, the beaches and woods on the outskirts – it might be worth considering the **Århus Pass** (97/121kr for 24/48hr), which, along with unlimited bus travel, covers entrance to most museums and sightseeing tours (book these at the tourist office first).

There's an idyllic **hostel**, *Pavillonen*, 3km from the centre at Marienlundsvej 10 (☎86.16.72.98, ⓦwww.hostel-aarhus.dk; 108kr; buses #1, #6, #8, #9, #16,

#56 and #58), in the middle of Risskov Wood and close to Den Permanente beach, to which locals flock in summer. Much more central is the *Århus City Sleep-In*, Havnegade 20 (☎86.19.20.55, ⓦwww .citysleep-in.dk; 110kr), with picnic tables and a barbecue in its courtyard, Internet access and TV/pool rooms. The only reasonably priced **hotel** is *Hotel Cab Inn Århus*, Kannikegade 14 (☎86.75.70.00, ⓦwww .cab-inn.dk; ⓒ). Next in price is the luxurious *Hotel Guldsmeden* at Guldsmedgade 40 (☎86.13.45.56, ⓦwww.hotel guldsmeden.dk; ⓒ, cheaper rooms with shared facilities). To the northwest near the University there's a good B&B, *Get In*, Jens Baggesens-vej 43 (☎86.10.86.14, ⓦwww .get-in.dk; ⓒ; bus #4 or #7). Of a number of **campsites**, the two most accessible are *Blommehaven* (☎86.27.02.07, ⓦ www.blommehaven.dk;

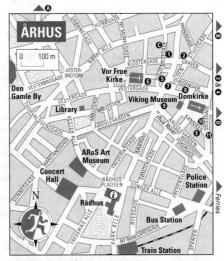

| ACCOMMODATION | | EATING & DRINKING | | | |
|---|---|---|---|---|---|
| Pavillonen hostel | B | Athena | 7 | Restaurant Pinden | 10 |
| Århus Sleep In | D | Café Jorden | 5 | Restaurant Gyngen | 4 |
| Cab Inn | E | Café Smagløs | 6 | Under Engle | 3 |
| Hotel Guldsmeden | C | Cross Café | 9 | Under Masken | 8 |
| Get In | A | Emmerys | 1 | | |
| | | Englen | 2 | | |
| | | Pind's Café | 11 | | |

closed mid-Oct to mid-March; bus #6 or #19), overlooking the bay 3km south of the city centre, and *Århus Nord*, 8km north (☎86.23.11.33, ⓦwww.dk-camp .dk/aarhusnord; bus #117 or #118 from the bus station); both have cabins.

## The City

**Søndergade** is the main street, a pedestrianized strip that leads down into Bispe-torvet and the old centre, the streets of which form a web around the **Domkirke** (Mon–Sat 9.30/10am–3/4pm), a massive Gothic church, most of which dates from the fifteenth century. The area to the north, known as the Latin Quarter, is crammed with browsable shops, galleries and enticing cafés. Across the road from the cathedral, the basement in Nordea bank houses the **Viking Museum** (Mon–Fri 10am–4pm, Thurs till 5.30pm; free), with a skeleton and a reconstructed sunk pit house. West along Vestergade, the thirteenth-century **Vor Frue Kirke** (Mon–Fri 10am–2/4pm, Sat 10am–noon) has some interesting medieval frescoes, depicting local workers rather than biblical scenes, and an atmospheric eleventh-century crypt church below. The **Rådhus**, home to the tourist office and one of the modern city's major sites, is a controversial 1940s building clad in Norwegian marble. Above the entrance hangs Hagedorn Olsen's huge mural, *A Human Society*, symbolically depicting the city emerging from World War II. You can wander in and investigate this for yourself, but to see Albert Naur's subversive murals in the civic room and to enjoy a view over the city and bay from the bell tower, you'll need to take a guided tour (mid-June to Aug Mon–Fri 11am; 10kr). It's a short walk from here to one of the city's best-known attractions, **Den Gamle By**, on Viborgvej (daily: mid-June to Aug 9am–6pm; Sept to mid-June 10/11am–3/5pm; 80kr; ⓦwww.dengamleby.dk), an open-air museum of traditional Danish life, with seventy-odd half-timbered town houses from around the country. Many of the craftsmen's buildings are used for their original purpose, the overall aim of the place being to give an impression of an old Danish market town, something it does very effectively. For more contemporary architecture, check out the new art museum, **ARoS** (Tues–Sun 10am–5pm, Wed till 10pm; 60kr; ⊛www.aros.dk), behind the Rådhus, next to the Concert Hall. Designed by the same architects as the Black Diamond extension to the Royal Library in Copenhagen, it contains seven floors of works from the late eighteenth century to modern day.

### The outskirts
On Sundays Århus resembles a ghost town, most locals spending the day in the parks or beaches on the city's outskirts. The closest **beaches** are north of the city at Riis Skov, easily reached by bus #6 or #16. Otherwise, Marselisborg Skov, south of the centre, is the city's largest park, and home to the **Marselisborg Slot**, summer residence of the Danish royals: its landscaped grounds can be visited when the monarch isn't staying. Further east, paths run down to quiet pebbly beaches, and, near the junction of Ørneredevej and Thorsmøllevej, to the Dyrehave or Deer Park. A few kilometres further south, the **Moesgård Prehistoric Museum** (daily 10am–4/5pm; Oct–March closed Mon; 45kr; ⊛www.moesmus.dk), reached direct on bus #6, details Danish civilizations from the Stone Age onwards. Its most notable exhibit is the "Grauballe Man", a body dating from 80 BC discovered in a peat bog west of town and amazingly well preserved. Also remarkable is the Illerup Ådal collection of weapons and military paraphernalia, dating from around 200 BC. From the museum, a scenic "prehistoric trail" runs 3km to the sea, past a scattering of reassembled dwellings, monuments and burial places.

### Eating, drinking and nightlife
Many of the old-town **cafés** and **restaurants** offer lunchtime specials for around 65kr; try theatrical *Pind's Café* at Skolegade 11, for excellent *smørrebrød*, not to be confused with *Restaurant Pinden* at no 29 which does traditional Danish fare. *Café Jorden* is a popular brunch hangout, with pavement seating overlooking Rosengade. *Athena*, on the first floor on Storetorv, is also good value, as are the highly rated **veg-etarian** meals at *Restaurant Gyngen*, Mejlgade 53, and *Under Engle*, Mejlgade 28. The classy architecture of Åboulevarden, overlooking the Århus Å river, towers above a string of trendy eating and drinking venues; try *Cross Café* for generous brunch plat-ters. The sun-drenched steps outside are a popular picnic spot. For superb organic Danish bread and pastries, head to *Emmerys*, Guldsmedgade 24–26, housed in the city's oldest patisserie; the coffee is freshly ground and the cakes to die for. For **self-catering**, there's a late-opening supermarket (8am–midnight) at the train station. Århus and Aalborg, further north, are the only places in Denmark with a **nightlife** to match that of Copenhagen. The city has particularly good **bars**, many situated in the streets close to the cathedral, including *Under Masken* at Bispegade 3, *Smagløs* at Klostertorv 7, and *Englen* on Studsgade (which also does good food). The cream of Danish and international rock acts can be found at *Voxhall*, Vester Allé 15, and *Train*, Toldbogade 6; *Fatter Eskil*, Skolegade 25, and *Kulturgyngen*, Fronthuset, Mejlgade 53, have more run-of-the-mill rock/jazz/blues bands. The country's leading **jazz** venue is the smoky, atmospheric *Bent J*, at Nørre Allé 66.

## Aalborg
The main city of north Jutland, **AALBORG** hugs the southern bank of the Limfjord and boasts a nightlife to rival Copenhagen's. The most obvious place to spend a night or two before venturing into the wilder countryside beyond, Aalborg is the main transport terminus for the region, and boasts a well-preserved centre dating from its seventeenth-century trading heyday. The era is perhaps best exemplified by the **Jens Bangs Stenhus** opposite the tourist office, a grandiose five-storey affair in the Dutch Renaissance style, today housing a pharmacy. The commercial roots of the city are further evidenced by the collection of

religious paintings sponsored by the town's merchants that hang inside the **Budolfi Domkirke** (Mon–Fri 9am–3/4pm, Sat 9am–noon/2pm), behind. The cathedral is a small but elegant Gothic building, built on the site of an eleventh-century wooden church, from which a few tombs remain, embedded in the walls close to the altar. In July and August it also hosts small **concerts**. Outside, across the square, the **Aalborg Historical Museum** at Algade 48 (Tues–Sun 10am–5pm, 20kr; ⊛www.aahm.dk) depicts the region's history and has an impressive silverware collection.

On the other side of Østerågade, the sixteenth-century **Aalborghus Slot** is worth a visit for its **dungeon** (May–Oct Mon–Fri 8am–3pm; free) and underground passages (till 9pm). Fifteen minutes' walk southwest out of the centre on Kong Christians Allé, the **North Jutland Art Museum** (Tues–Sun 10am–5pm, 40kr, Dec free; ⊛www.nordjyllandskunstmuseum.dk; bus #15) designed by Alvar Aalto is one of the country's best modern art collections, featuring works by Max Ernst, Andy Warhol, Le Corbusier and Claes Oldenburg, alongside many Danish contributions.

### Practicalities

The **tourist office** is centrally located at Østerågade 8 (Mon–Fri 9am–4.30/5.30pm, Sat 10am–1/4pm; ☎98.12.60.22, ⊛www.visitaalborg.com). The best of the inexpensive **hotels** are the *Prinsen Hotel* across from the train station at Prinsensgade 14 (☎98.13.37.33, ⊛www.prinsen-hotel.dk; ❻), and *Hotel Krogen*, Skibstedvej 4 (☎96.30.39.50, ⊛www.krogen.dk; ❻–❽), with a few basic rooms with shared facilities. There's a large, well-equipped **hostel** (☎98.11.60.44, ⊛www.danhostelnord.dk/aalborg; 120kr), 3km west of the town on the Limfjord bank beside the marina – take bus #13 to the Egholm ferry junction and continue on foot for five minutes following the signs. In the same direction is a **campsite**: *Strandparken* (☎89.12.76.29, ⊛www.strandparken.dk; closed mid-Sept to March) with cabins. For a little more adventure, catch the half-hourly **ferry** (☎98.11.78.23; 6.30am–11.15pm; 14kr) from near the campsite to Egholm, an island in Limfjord with free camping under open-sided shelters.

For **food and nightlife**, head for the lively Jomfru Ane Gade, a small street off Bispensgade that's crammed with eateries and pubs; try the medieval-looking *Fyrtøjet* at no.7. Aalborg Kongres & Kultur Center at Europa Plads 4 (☎99.35.55.55, ⊛www.akkc.dk) is the city's grand **theatre** and **concert venue**. For smaller gigs head for *Skråen*, Standvejen 19 (☎98.12.21.89, ⊛www.skraaen.dk).

# Skagen

About 100km north of Aalborg, **SKAGEN** perches at the very top of Jutland amid a breathtaking landscape of heather-topped sand dunes. It can be reached by private train (50 percent discount with Eurail, ScanRail and InterRail) roughly once an hour. Sunlight seems to gain extra brightness as it bounces off the two seas which collide off Skagen's coast, something which attracted the **Skagen artists** in the late nineteenth century. They arrived in the small fishing community between 1873 and 1874 and often met in the bar of *Brøndum's Hotel*, off Brøndumsvej, the grounds of which now house the **Skagen Museum** (May–Sept daily 10am–5pm; Nov–March Wed–Sun 10am–3pm; 60kr; ⊛www.skagensmuseum.dk). Many of the canvases depict local scenes, using the town's strong natural light to capture subtleties of colour. Nearby, at Markvej 2–4, is the home of one of the group's leading lights and his wife, herself a skilful painter: the **Michael and Anna Anchers' Hus** (April–Oct daily 10/11am–3/6pm; Nov–March Sat 11am–3pm; 50kr). The exhibition evokes the atmosphere of the time through an assortment of used tubes of paint, piles of canvases, paintings, sketches, books and ornaments.

The forces of nature can be appreciated at **Grenen**, 4km north of Skagen (hourly bus #79 in summer), along Sct. Laurentii Vej, Fyrvej and the beach, where two seas – the Kattegat and Skaggerak – meet, often with a powerful clashing of waves.

You can get to the tip by a tractor-drawn bus (mid-April to mid-Oct; 15kr return) – although it's an enjoyable walk through some beautiful scenery.

## Practicalities

The **train station** on Sct. Laurentii Vej also incorporates the **tourist office** (June–Aug Mon–Sat 9am–5/6pm, Sun 10am–2/4pm; Sept–May Mon–Fri 9/10am–4pm, Sat 10am–1pm; ☎98.44.13.77, ⊛www.skagen-tourist.dk). If you can afford it, *Brøndum's Hotel*, Anchervej 3 (☎98.44.15.55, ⊛www.broendums-hotel .dk; ❸), is by far the most atmospheric spot to stay – book well ahead in summer. Slightly cheaper are *Clausens Hotel*, Sct. Laurentii Vej 35 (☎98.45.01.66, ⊛www .clausenshotel.dk; ❻), and *Skagen Sømandshjem*, Østre Strandvej 2, close to the harbour (☎98.44.25.88, ⊛www.skagenhjem.dk; ❼). There's an excellent **hostel** at Rolighedsvej 2 (☎98.44.22.00, ⊛www.danhostelnord.dk/skagen; 120kr). Of a number of **campsites**, the most accessible are *Grenen* (☎98.44.25.46, ⊛www .grenencamping.dk; closed mid-Sept to early May), to the north along Fyrvej, with cabins, and *Poul Eeg's* (☎98.44.14.70, ⊛www.pouleegcamping.dk; closed Sept to mid-May), on Batterivej, left off Oddenvej just before the town centre.

# Travel details

## Trains

**Århus** to: Aalborg (34 daily; 1hr 15min–1hr 30min); Copenhagen (38 daily; 3hr–3hr 15min); Odense (40 daily; 1hr 30min–1hr 45min).
**Copenhagen** to: Aalborg (28 daily; 4hr 10min–4hr 50min); Frederikshavn (hourly until 8pm; 6hr); Helsingør (every 20min; 50min); Odense (56 daily; 1hr 30min); Roskilde (8 hourly; 25min).

**Frederikshavn** to: Aalborg (24 daily; 1hr 10min); Skagen (20 daily; 35min).
**Helsingør** to: Hillerød (hourly; 30min).
**Ribe** to: Esbjerg (22 daily; 40min).
**Roskilde** to: Odense (56 daily; 1hr 10min).

## Buses

**Copenhagen** to: Aalborg (3–5 daily; 4hr 30min); Århus (6–7 daily; 3hr–4hr).

# Estonia

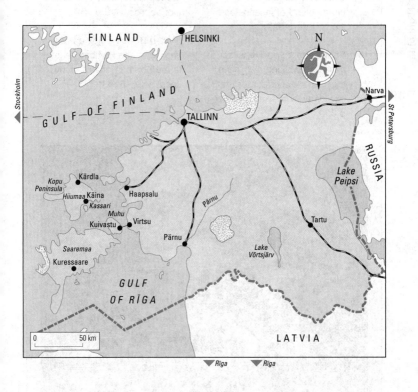

# Estonia highlights

* **Tallinn's Old Town** Within medieval turreted walls, this ancient corner of the city is beautifully preserved. See p.326

* **Alexander Nevsky Cathedral, Tallinn** This Russian Orthodox cathedral is a heady blend of incense and icons. See p.327

* **Saaremaa** If you like wilderness and walking or cycling, this island is perfect for that get-away-from-it-all trip. See p.330

* **Kuressaare Castle, Saaremaa Island** The best-preserved medieval castle in the region. See p.331

* **Café Wilde, Tartu** A relaxed tea house in the heart of Estonia. Huge pots of tea, newspapers, cake and Internet access. See p.332

* **Pärnu Beach** Enjoy a bracing dip in the Baltic or take a mud bath in one of many local spas. See p.333

△ Alexander Nevsky Cathedral, Tallinn

# Introduction and basics

It's a tribute to the resilience of the people of **Estonia** that, since independence in 1991, they've transformed their country from a dour outpost of the Soviet Union into a confident and technologically advanced EU member. The Estonians have had the misfortune to be surrounded by powerful, warlike neighbours. Conquered by the Danes in the thirteenth century, then German crusading knights, then Swedes and Russians, the country snatched independence at the end of World War I. This brief freedom was extinguished by the Soviets in 1940 and the country disappeared from view again only to emerge from the Soviet shadow in 1991.

Estonia's capital, **Tallinn**, is an atmospheric city with a magnificent medieval centre and lively nightlife. Two other major cities, **Tartu**, a historic university town, and **Pärnu**, a popular seaside resort, are worth a day or so each. To get a feel for the unspoilt countryside head for the island of **Saaremaa**: the island capital **Kuressaare** is home to one of the finest castles in the Baltics.

## Information & maps

**Tourist offices** can be useful for booking B&Bs and hotel rooms, as well as good-quality free **maps**; most bookstores also have good map sections. **Addresses** often include *mantee* (mnt.), meaning road; *puistee* (pst.), avenue; and *tänav* (tn.), street its *väljak* square.

## Money and banks

Currency is the **Eesti kroon** (Estonian Crown), pegged to the euro at €1 to 15.65EEK, and divided into 100 sents. Notes come as 2, 5, 10, 25, 50, 100 and 500 EEK and coins as 0.10, 0.20, 0.50, 1 and 5 EEK. **Bank** (*pank*) opening hours are Mon–Fri 9am–4pm, many staying open in larger towns till 6pm and

most also open Sat 9am–2/4pm. **ATMs** are widely available. **Credit cards** can be used in most hotels, restaurants and stores, but outside urban areas cash is preferred.

## Communications

**Post offices** (*postkontor*) open Mon–Fri 9am–6pm & Sat 9am–3pm. You can buy stamps here and at some shops, hotels and kiosks. Most public **phones** take phonecards (of 30, 50 and 100EEK; available at kiosks and post offices) for local and long-distance calls. You'll find **Internet** cafés in most towns; expect to pay 25–60EEK/hr.

## Getting around

Places covered in this chapter are all reached easily by **bus**, and schedules are posted on-line with an English version (@ www .bussireisid.ee). **Tickets** can be bought either from the bus station ticket office or direct from the driver. Buy tickets in advance if you're travelling in the height of summer or at weekends and opt for an express (*ekspress*) bus if possible. Buses are also the best method for travelling to the other Baltic countries, with services linking Tallinn, Vilnius and Riga.

---

### Estonia on the net

@ **www.visitestonia.com** Tourist board site.

@ **www.weekend.ee** Entertainment listings.

@ **www.balticsworldwide.com** News, listings and links from the bi-monthly Baltic *City Paper*.

@ **www.baltictimes.com** English-language weekly newspaper.

The **rail** network has been cut back drastically, but the routes still in operation are as fast as buses and slightly cheaper. The only international service is an overnight train to Moscow; book seats for this in advance. Ticket windows at stations are marked *linnalähedanel* for suburban lines, *piletite müük* for national services and *rahvusvaheline* for international. Both train and bus **information** is available from station timetable boards – departure is *väljub*, arrival is *saabub*.

## Accommodation

Though cheaper than in Western Europe, **accommodation** in Estonia will still take a large chunk out of most budgets. Booking a **private room** is often the cheapest option (usually 250–400EEK per person). This can be arranged through tourist offices or private agencies. You should be able to find plain but clean **hotel** or **pension** rooms for 300–500EEK per person including breakfast, though the cheapest of these are not usually centrally located. Outside of Tallinn **hostels** are often just student dorms converted for the summer; the Estonian Youth Hostel Association (☎372/6461 455, ⊛www .baltichostels.net) has details. Beds cost 100–200EEK per person. An ex-Soviet phenomenon is the **cabin campsite** (*kämping*), offering accommodation in three- to four-bed cabins (shared facilities) for 180–260EEK per

## Estonian

| | Estonian | Pronunciation |
|---|---|---|
| **Yes** | *Jah* | Yah |
| **No** | *Ei* | Ey |
| **Please** | *Palun* | Palun |
| **Thank you** | *Aitäh/tänan* | Ayteh, tanan |
| **Hello/Good day** | *Tere* | Tere |
| **Goodbye** | *Head aega* | Heyad ayga |
| **Excuse me** | *Vabandage* | Vabandage |
| **Where?** | *Kus* | Kus |
| **Good** | *Hea* | Heya |
| **Bad** | *Halb* | Holb |
| **Near** | *Lähedal* | Lahedal |
| **Far** | *Kaugel* | Cowgal |
| **Cheap** | *Odav* | Odav |
| **Expensive** | *Kallis* | Kallis |
| **Open** | *Avatud* | Avatud |
| **Closed** | *Suletud* | Suletud |
| **Today** | *Täna* | Tana |
| **Yesterday** | *Eile* | Eyle |
| **Tomorrow** | *Homme* | Homme |
| **How much is....?** | *Kui palju maksab...?* | Kuy palyo maksab...? |
| **What time is it?** | *Mis kell praegu on?* | Mis kell prego on? |
| **I don't understand** | *Ma ei saa aru* | May saaru |
| **Do you speak English?** | *Kas te räägite inglise keelt?* | Kas te raagite inglise kelt? |
| **One** | *Uks* | Uks |
| **Two** | *Kaks* | Koks |
| **Three** | *Kolm* | Kolm |
| **Four** | *Neli* | Neli |
| **Five** | *Viis* | Vees |
| **Six** | *Kuus* | Koos |
| **Seven** | *Seitse* | Seytse |
| **Eight** | *Kaheksa* | Koheksa |
| **Nine** | *Üheksa* | Ooheksa |
| **Ten** | *Kümme* | Koome |

person; many of them will also let you pitch a tent.

# Food and drink

Not many people come to Estonia for the **food**. Soup (*supp*), dark bread (*leib*), and sour cream (*hapukoor*) and herring (*heeringas*) all figure prominently, a culinary legacy of the country's largely peasant past. A typical **national dish** is *verevorst* and *mulgikapsad* (blood sausage and sauerkraut), and various kinds of smoked fish, particularly eel (*angerjas*), perch (*ahven*) and pike (*haug*), are also popular, as are Russian dishes such as *pelmeenid* (ravioli with meat or cabbage and mushrooms). You'd have to be invited into a local home to enjoy Estonian food at its best, as the average **restaurant** (*restoran*) serves up hearty meat dishes such as pork chop in batter (*karbonaad*) or roast chicken (*kanapraad*). There are, however, a few good places to try Estonian food in Tallinn, and both the capital and Tartu boast an impressive choice of ethnic restaurants. Outside these two cities, **vegetarians** will find little to choose from.

When eating out, it's cheaper to head for bars and cafés, many of which serve snacks like pancakes (*pannkoogid*) and salads (*salatid*). In a café you should be able to have a modest meal for 60–90EEK, while in a typical restaurant two courses and a drink would come to around 160EEK. If you really want to keep costs down then try one of the various **fast-food options**. Some places going under the name of café (*kohvik*) are canteen-style restaurants with dishes-of-the-day (*päevapraad*) for as little as 30EEK. **Self-catering** poses no major problems: supermarket staples such as bread, cheese, smoked meat and tinned fish can be supplemented by fruit and vegetables from markets.

## Drink

Estonians are enthusiastic drinkers, with **beer** (*õlu*) being the most popular tipple.

The principal local brands are Saku and A. Le Coq, both of which are rather tame light lager-style brews, although both companies also produce stronger, dark beers – the most potent are found on the islands (Saaremaa õlu is the best known). In bars a lot of people favour **vodka** (*viin*) with mixers which, thanks to generous measures, is a more cost-effective route to oblivion. Local alcoholic specialities include **hõõgvein** (mulled wine) and *Vana Tallinn*, a pungent dark liqueur which some suicidal souls mix with vodka. Pubs and bars – most of which imitate Irish or American models – are beginning to take over, especially in Tallinn; if you're not boozing, head for a *kohvik* (café), where alcohol is still served but getting drunk is not a priority. **Coffee** (*kohv*) is usually of the filter variety, and **tea** (*tee*) is served without milk.

# Opening hours and holidays

Most **shops** open Mon–Fri 9/10am–6/7pm & Sat 10am–2/3pm, but many larger ones stay open later and are also open Sun. **Public holidays**, when most shops and all banks are closed, are: Jan 1, Feb 24, Good Fri, Easter Mon, May 1, Whitsun, June 23 & 24, Aug 20, Dec 25 & 26.

# Emergencies

Theft and **street crime** are at relatively low levels, and if you keep your wits about you you should come to no harm. The **police** (*politsei*) are mostly very young and some speak English. Emergency **health care** is free, and, at least in Tallinn, emergency operators speak English.

> ### Emergency numbers
>
> Police ☎110; fire & ambulance ☎112.

# Tallinn

The port city of **TALLINN**, Estonia's compact capital, has been shaped by nearly a millennium of outside influence. Its name, derived from the Estonian for "Danish Fort" (*taani linnus*), recalls that the city was founded by the Danes at the beginning of the thirteenth century, and since then political control has nearly always been in the hands of foreigners. Tallinn was one of the leading cities of the Hanseatic League, the German-dominated association of Baltic trading cities, and for centuries it was known to the outside world by its German name, Reval. Even when Estonia was ruled by Sweden and Russia, the city's public life was controlled by the German nobility and its commerce run by German merchants. Today reminders of foreign rule abound in the streets, where each of the city's one-time rulers has left their mark. Once the staple crumbling backdrop for Soviet fairy-tale films, Tallin has been busy reinventing itself as a weekend getaway for Europeans, especially young Scandinavians in search of fun and cheap booze, and these days its buzzing cafés, pubs and clubs can offer a variety of hedonistic pursuits on a night out.

## Arrival, information and city transport

Tallinn's **train station** is at Toompuiestee 35, just northwest of the Old Town, while the city's **bus terminal** is at Lastekodu 46, 2km southeast of the centre – trams #2 and #4 run from nearby Tartu mnt. to Viru väljak at the eastern entrance to the Old Town. Arriving by **sea**, the passenger port is just northeast of the centre at Sadama 25. The **airport** is 3km southeast of the city centre and linked to Viru väljak by bus #2. The **tourist office**, in the Old Town at Kullasseppa 4 (April–Oct Mon–Fri 9am–6pm, Sat & Sun 10am–5pm; Nov–March Mon–Fri 9am–5pm, Sat 10am–3pm; ☎0/645 7777, ⊛www.tourism.tallinn.ee), sells various maps and city guides. You can also buy a Tallinn Card here (90/250/300/350EEK for 6/24/48/72hr) which gives free entry to all museums and churches, unlimited use of public transport and other discounts. The widely available free paper *Tallinn This Week* (⊛www.ttw.ee), the excellent *City Paper* (⊛www.balticsworldwide .com; 33EEK) and the informative *Tallinn In Your Pocket* (⊛www.inyourpocket .com; 35EEK) city guide have what's-on listings.

Though most sights can be covered on foot, Tallinn has an extensive tram, bus and trolleybus network. Tickets (*talongid*) common to all three systems are available from kiosks near stops for 10EEK or from the driver for 15EEK. Validate your ticket using the on-board punches. Taxis are reasonably cheap (around 10EEK/km, slightly more after 10pm) though as a foreigner you may occasionally find your meter running faster than it should. Most companies have a minimum charge of 35EEK, but a taxi from one point in the city centre to another rarely exceeds 50EEK.

## Accommodation

Though the range of hostel and budget accommodation in central Tallinn is improving, demand still outstrips supply in summer, and if arriving without a reservation you may find yourself forced to stay in a distant suburb. Beyond what's listed below, you can book central and excellent-value **private rooms** with Bed & Breakfast Rasastra, a few steps north of Viru väljak at Mere 4 (daily 9.30am–6pm; ☎0/661 6291, ⊛www.bedbreakfast.ee), an agency offering rooms (❷–❸) in family homes throughout the Baltics, and private apartments (❹–❺) for longer stays. Many of the places listed below have 10 percent discounts for ISIC card holders.

### Hostels

**Alur** Rannamäe 3 ☎0/631 1531, ⊛www .alurhostel.com. Friendly and well-run place in an old wooden house next to the train station. One of the most pleasant hostels in Tallinn, and a good breakfast is included. Dorms 270EEK, rooms ❸

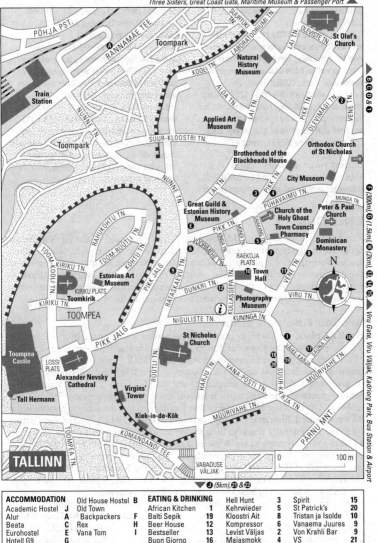

**TALLINN**

9 | **ESTONIA** | Tallinn

| ACCOMMODATION | | EATING & DRINKING | | Hell Hunt | 3 | Spirit | 15 |
|---|---|---|---|---|---|---|---|
| Academic Hostel | J | African Kitchen | 1 | Kehrwieder | 5 | St Patrick's | 20 |
| Alur | A | Balti Sepik | 19 | Kloostri Ait | 8 | Tristan ja Isolde | 10 |
| Beata | C | Beer House | 12 | Kompressor | 6 | Vanaema Juures | 9 |
| Eurohostel | E | Bestseller | 13 | Levist Väljas | 2 | Von Krahli Bar | 9 |
| Hotell G9 | G | Buon Giorno | 16 | Maiasmokk | 4 | VS | 21 |
| Old House | | Café Anglais | 7 | Miny Many | 14 | Woodstock | 22 |
| Guest House | D | Elevant | 11 | Nimeta Baar | 18 | X-Baar | 17 |
| Old House Hostel | B | | | | | | |
| Old Town | | | | | | | |
| Backpackers | F | | | | | | |
| Rex | H | | | | | | |
| Vana Tom | I | | | | | | |

**Beata** Uus 35 ☎0/641 1171. Modest and slightly careworn hostel on the edge of the Old Town. Quiet, and likely to have a free bed when other places are full. Dorms 240EEK, rooms ❸

**Eurohostel** Nunne 2 ☎0/644 7788, ⓦwww .eurohostel.ee. Anonymous but competently managed Old Town hostel set in an attractive location at the base of Toompea Hill. 225EEK.

**Old House Hostel** Uus 26 ☎0/641 1281, ⓦwww .oldhouse.ee. Rambling Old-Town house with a small dorm and a handful of cosy doubles with shared bath. Dorms 260EEK, rooms ❸

**Old Town Backpackers** Uus 14 ☎0/517 1337, ⓦwww.balticbackpackers.com. Clean one-room place where the price includes breakfast and free use of sauna. May expand to a larger building across the street in the near future. 225EEK.

**Rex** Tartu mnt. 62 ☎0/633 2181, ⊛www.hot .ee/allarp3. Functional hostel around the corner from the bus station, with basic but adequate dorms as well as a few doubles and singles with shared bath. Dorms 200EEK, rooms ❸

**Vana Tom** Väike-Karja 1 ☎0/631 3252, ⊛www .hostel.ee. Large Old-Town hostel with dorms and doubles. Popular with backpackers for its location and keen staff, but could be a bit cleaner. Breakfast included. Dorms 235EEK, rooms ❸

### Guest houses and B&Bs

**Academic Hostel** Akadeemia 11 ☎0/620 2275, ⊛www.academichostel.com. Renovated student dorm 5km southwest of the centre, with well-furnished doubles. Trolleybus #3 or bus #E11 from Vabaduse väljak to Keemia. ❸

**Hotell G9** Gonsiori 9 ☎0/626 7100, ⊛www .hotelg9.ee. Sparsely-furnished but comfy en suites on the third floor of an apartment building, nicely poised between the Old Town and the bus station. Breakfast costs 50EEK extra. ❹

**Old House Guest House** Uus 22 ☎0/641 1464, ⊛www.oldhouse.ee. Second branch of the *Old House* has five small but handsome rooms with shared facilities (❸) and a comfortable seven-bed dorm (290EEK). The first-class breakfast here makes the higher prices worth paying. Also has a number of apartments (❹–❽).

# The City

The heart of Tallinn is the **Old Town**, still largely enclosed by the city's medieval walls. At its centre is the **Raekoja plats**, the historic marketplace, above which looms **Toompea**, the hilltop stronghold of the German knights who controlled the city during the Middle Ages. Outside the city centre, **Kadriorg Park**, a peaceful wooded area to the east with a cluster of historic buildings and a view of the sea, and the **Open-Air Museum**, to the west, are both worth a visit.

## Around Raekoja plats

**Raekoja plats,** the cobbled, gently sloping market square at the heart of the Old Town, is as old as the city itself. On its southern side stands an imposing reminder of the Hanseatic past: the fifteenth-century **Town Hall** (Tallinna Raekoda), which boasts an elegant arcade of Gothic arches at ground level, and a delicate steeple at its northern end. Near the summit of the steeple, Vana Toomas, a sixteenth-century weather vane depicting a medieval town guard, has become Tallinn's city emblem. Of the other old buildings that line the square, the most venerable is the **Town Council Pharmacy** in the northeastern corner, with a white facade dating from the seventeenth century, though the building is known to have existed in 1422 and may be much older. If the tiny museum inside (Mon–Fri 9am–7pm, Sat 9am–5pm; free) leaves you underwhelmed, head for the former Town Jail behind the town hall at Raekoja 4/6, which now houses the **Museum of Photography** (March–Oct Thurs–Tues 10.30am–6pm; Nov–Feb Thurs–Mon 10.30am–5pm; 10EEK), an entertaining little collection with English captions.

Close to Raekoja plats are a couple of churches that neatly underline the social divisions of medieval Tallinn. The fourteenth-century **Church of the Holy Ghost** (May–Sept Mon–Sat 10am–5pm; Oct–April Mon–Sat 10am–4pm; 10EEK), tucked away on Pühavaimu and reached via a small passage called Saiakang tänav next to the Town Council Pharmacy, is the city's most appealing church, a small Gothic building with stuccoed limestone walls, stepped gables and a tall, verdigris-coated spire. Originally the Town Hall chapel, it later became the place where the native Estonian population worshipped, and in 1535 priests here compiled an Estonian-language Lutheran catechism, an important affirmation of identity at a time when most Estonians had been reduced to serf status. The ornate clock set in the wall above the entrance dates from 1680 and is the oldest in Tallinn. Contrasting sharply is the late Gothic **St Nicholas Church**, sitting on raised open ground just southwest of Raekoja plats. Rebuilt after being more or less destroyed in a 1944 Soviet air raid, these days the church serves as a museum and concert hall (Wed–Sun 10am–4.30pm; 35EEK) displaying a stunning collection of medieval altarpieces. It also hosts free organ music recitals (Sat & Sun 4pm) as well as evening concerts (around 100EEK).

## Toompea

**Toompea** is the hill where the Danes built their fortress after conquering what is now Tallinn in 1219. According to legend, it is also the grave of Kalev, the mythical ancestor of the Estonians. The most atmospheric approach is through the sturdy gate tower – built by the Teutonic Knights to contain the Old Town's inhabitants in times of unrest – at the foot of Pikk jalg. This is the cobbled continuation of Pikk, the Old Town's main street, and climbs up to Lossi plats, dominated by the incongruous-looking **Alexander Nevsky Cathedral** (daily 8am–7pm). This gaudy, onion-domed concoction, complete with souvenir shop, was built at the end of the nineteenth century for the city's Orthodox population; it is an enduring reminder of the two centuries Tallinn spent under tsarist rule.

At the head of Lossi plats is **Toompea Castle**, on the site of the original Danish fortification. Today's castle is the descendant of a stone fortress built by the Knights of the Sword, the Germanic crusaders who kicked out the Danes in 1227 and controlled the city until 1238 (when the Danes returned). The castle has been altered by every conqueror who raised their flag above it since then; these days it wears a shocking-pink Baroque facade, the result of an eighteenth-century rebuild for Catherine the Great. The northern and western walls are the most original part of the castle, and include three defensive towers, the most impressive of which is the fifty-metre **Tall Hermann** at the southwestern corner, dating from 1371. Toompea Castle is now home to the Riigikogu, Estonia's parliament, and is therefore out of bounds to the public, but nearby a couple of the towers that formed part of the Old Town fortifications are accessible. A narrow archway in the medieval walls just south of the Alexander Nevsky Cathedral leads to the ironically named **Virgins' Tower**, which was once a prison for prostitutes and is now home to a café/bar. A little south of here on Komandandi tee is the imposing **Kiek-in-de-Kök tower** dating from 1475; it is now a **museum** (Tues–Sun 10.30am–5/6pm; 25EEK) containing a jumble of displays on the city's history and fortifications.

From Lossi plats, Toom Kooli leads north to the **Toomkirik** (Tues–Sun 9am–6pm), the city's outwardly understated Lutheran cathedral, boasting an interior spectacularly covered with elaborately carved heraldic emblems. A stone's throw from the Toomkirik, in a peppermint green neo-Renaissance palace, is the **Estonian Art Museum**, Kiriku plats 1 (Wed–Sun 11am–6pm; 20EEK), housed here temporarily, pending the construction of a new building in Kadriorg Park, and with space to display only a handful of its vast holdings. At any given time you're likely to find nineteenth-century studies of Tallinn and Estonian rural life as well as twentieth-century works influenced by artistic trends like Expressionism and Cubism.

## Elsewhere in the Old Town

The remainder of the Old Town contains the commercial streets of medieval Tallinn, lined by merchants' residences and warehouses. Pikk tänav, running northeast from Pikk jalg gate and linking Toompea with the port area, has some of the city's most important secular buildings from the Hanseatic period, kicking off with the **Great Guild** at Pikk 17. Completed in 1430 this was the city's main guild, meeting place of the German merchants who controlled the city's wealth. Its gloomy Gothic facade now fronts the **Estonian History Museum** (11am–6pm; closed Wed; 10EEK) where a bland array of weaponry, domestic objects and jewellery traces the history of Estonia up to the eighteenth century. If the appearance of their headquarters is anything to go by, the guild who occupied the **Brotherhood of the Blackheads House**, Pikk 26, were a more exuberant bunch than the merchants of the Great Guild. The Renaissance facade of this building, inset with an elaborate stone portal and richly decorated door, cuts a dash amid the stolidity of Pikk. The Brotherhood moved here in 1531 and remained until the guild was abolished by the Soviets in 1940. A short detour eastwards to the parallel street of Vene brings you to the outstanding **City Museum** at no. 17 (Wed–Mon: March–Oct 10.30am–6pm, Nov–Feb 10.30am–5pm; 35EEK), which recounts the history of Tallinn, from the thirteenth century through the Soviet period and beyond, in imaginative multimedia style.

Continuing north along Pikk brings you to **St Olaf's Church**, first mentioned in 1267 and named in honour of King Olaf II of Norway, who was canonized for battling against pagans in Scandinavia. Extensive renovation left this enormous Gothic structure with an unexceptional nineteenth-century interior, and the church is chiefly famous for its 124-metre spire, which you can climb (daily 10am–5pm; 25EEK). According to local legend the citizens of Tallinn wanted the church to have the highest spire in the world to attract passing ships and trade. Whether Tallinn's prosperity during the Middle Ages had anything to do with the church spire is not known, but between 1625 and 1820 the church burned down eight times as a result of lightning striking the tower. Various Old Town merchants' houses bear witness to the city's medieval wealth, but the best examples are the **Three Sisters**, a gabled group at Pikk 71. Supremely functional with loading hatches and winch-arms set into their facades, these would have served as combined dwelling places, warehouses and offices; today they are home to a luxury hotel. At its far end Pikk is straddled by the **Great Coast Gate**, a sixteenth-century city gate flanked by two towers. The larger of these, the aptly named Fat Margaret Tower, has walls four metres thick and now houses the **Estonian Maritime Museum** (Wed–Sun 10am–6pm; 25EEK; some English captions), a surprisingly diverting collection of model boats, swimming costumes and nautical ephemera.

West of Lai street is one of the longest extant sections of Tallinn's medieval **city wall**; to reach it, head down Suur-Kloostri. The 4km of walls that surrounded the Old Town were mostly constructed during the fourteenth century, and enhanced over succeeding centuries. Today, 2km are still standing, along with twenty-six of the original forty-six towers.

## Out of the centre

**Kadriorg Park**, a heavily wooded area 2km east of the Old Town, was laid out according to the instructions of Russian tsar Peter the Great, who first visited Tallinn in 1711, the year after the Russian conquest. The main entrance to the park is at the junction of Weizenbergi tänav and J. Poska (tram #1 or #3 from Viru väljak). Weizenbergi cuts through the park, running straight past **Kadriorg Palace**, a Baroque residence designed by the Italian architect Niccolò Michetti, which Peter had built for his wife Catherine. These days the palace houses the **Museum of Foreign Art** (May–Sept Tues–Sun 10am–5pm; Oct–April Wed–Sun 10am–5pm; 45EEK), with a fine collection of Dutch and Russian paintings. While waiting for the palace to be completed, Peter lived in a humble cottage in the park grounds, at the junction of Weizenbergi and Mäekalda.

The path down Mäekalda from Peter's cottage leads, after around fifteen minutes, to Narva mnt. On the other side of this busy road is the **Lauluväljak**, a vast amphitheatre that's the venue for Estonia's Song Festivals. These gatherings, featuring massed choirs thousands strong, have been an important form of national expression since the first all-Estonia Song Festival was held in Tartu in 1869, and are held every two years. The present structure, which can accommodate 15,000 singers (with room for a further 30,000 or so on the platform in front of the stage), went up in 1960. The grounds were filled to capacity for the 1988 festival – a significant public expression of longing for independence from Soviet rule, which gave rise to the epithet "Singing Revolution". A tree-lined avenue heads downhill from the amphitheatre to Pirita tee, which runs along the seashore.

At the other end of Tallinn, on the western outskirts, is the **Open-Air Museum** (daily: May–Aug 10am–8pm; Sept & Oct 10am–6pm; Nov–April 10am–4pm;

25EEK; bus #21 from the train station), a collection of eighteenth- and nineteenth-century village buildings gathered here from around the country. You can also view a wooden church and several windmills, though for many the biggest attraction is the *Kolu Kõrts* café which serves up traditional bean soup and beer.

## Eating, drinking and nightlife

The variety and quality of **restaurants** in Tallinn keeps getting better, and though meat and potatoes figure prominently on many menus, the choice of international cuisines you'll find around the Old Town would be impressive anywhere. These are the best places for vegetarians, though conventional restaurants usually offer one or two meat-free options. Most of the **cafés** and **bars** listed below also offer snacks and full meals, and are usually a cheaper option; many feature live music or dancing. Most of Tallinn's highly popular **clubs** cater for a mainstream crowd. More underground, cutting-edge dance music events change location frequently and are advertised by flyposters, or try asking around in the city's hipper bars; expect to pay 50–150EEK admission.

### Cafés and snacks

**Balti Sepik** Suur-Karja 3. Cheap, central bakery/café that's good for a quick breakfast.

**Bestseller** Viru väljak 4/6. Popular café on the top floor of the Viru Centre mall, inside the Rahva Raamat bookstore. Great juices, wraps and salads.

**Kehrwieder** Saiakang 1. Sagging sofas ideal for curling up with a top-quality coffee in this dimly lit cellar café, with big windows looking out on Raekoja plats.

**Kompressor** Rataskaevu 3. Roomy café-bar popular with a youngish crowd, and famous for its Estonian pancakes – wonderfully stodgy and filling.

**Maiasmokk** Pikk 16. Tallinn's most venerable café – founded in 1864 – with a beautiful wood-panelled interior. Queue up for your coffee and pastry, then, like the regulars, take your used dishes back when you're done.

**Miny Many** Maakri 26, behind the *Radisson Hotel*. Cheap, old-fashioned lunch spot in the new town, with filling meat-and-potatoes dishes at around 35EEK. Mon–Fri till 7pm, Sat till 5pm.

**Spirit** Mere pst. 6e. Ultra-chic café/sushi bar in a restored nineteenth-century warehouse just east of the Old Town.

**Tristan ja Isolde** Raekoja plats 1. Dark, atmospheric café in the Town Hall with a full range of drinks and tasty salads and cakes.

### Restaurants

**African Kitchen** Uus 34. Intriguing selection of peanut, coconut and rice dishes, some spicy and many vegetarian, prepared by a Nigerian chef and served in a jungle-themed lounge.

**Beer House** Dunkri 5. Busy, roomy beer cellar which brews its own ales and serves up hearty pork-and-potato meals.

**Buon Giorno** Müürivahe 17. Genial atmosphere and affordable pizza and pasta; popular with Tallinn's resident Italians.

**Café Anglais** Raekoja plats 14. Upstairs in one of the houses on the square, with live piano music, excellent coffee and hot chocolate, and a sumptuous range of salads, sandwiches and sweets.

**Elevant** Vene 5. Chic Indian restaurant with affordable range of dishes, including plenty of vegetarian choices.

**Kloostri Ait** Vene 14. With its enormous open fire and relaxed crowd, the spacious dining room here is ideal for a quiet meal. Good, reasonably-priced international dishes, and frequent live jazz, classical or folk music.

**Vanaema Juures** Rataskaevu 10/12. The most amenable and affordable of the Estonian restaurants in the Old Town, "Grandma's Place" serves quality traditional food in an unpretentious setting. Closes 6pm Sundays.

### Bars

**Hell Hunt** Pikk 39. What claims to be Estonia's oldest pub (with just a 15-year history) is spacious, friendly and serves its own excellent dark Hunt beer.

**Levist Väljas** Olevimägi 12. Grungy cellar bar offering cheap drinks and strictly non-top 40 music. There's no sign – look for a low door at the intersection of Olevimägi and Vene.

**St. Patrick's** Suur-Karja 8. The pick of Tallinn's Irish pubs, set in a beautifully restored medieval house and popular with expats, tourists and locals alike. Your fourth beer comes free.

**Nimeta Baar** Suur-Karja 4/6. Along with its sister venture the *Nimega Baar* at Suur-Karja 13, this lively bar draws in an expat crowd. DJs and live music at weekends, international football matches screened live.

**Von Krahli Bar** Rataskaevu 10/12. Hip hangout that's always packed with a bohemian crowd. Frequent live music and dancing, and good, cheap food.

**VS** Pärnu mnt. 28. The industrial decor, late-night DJs, hip clientele and great Indian food all make this one of the top spots in Tallinn.

**Woodstock** Tatari 6. Hippy-retro bar with psychedelic murals, cheap meals, and occasional live bands.

**X-Baar** Sauna 1. Relaxed gay bar with bright pink decor. The adjacent *Angel* (Wed–Sat only), Tallinn's premier gay club, is notoriously difficult to get into.

### Live music and clubs

**Café Amigo** In the *Viru Hotel*, Viru väljak 4. Heaving but likeable place playing mainstream dance music for locals and tourists into the early hours. Frequent appearances by Estonian bands.

**Club Privé** Harju 6. Style-conscious temple to cutting-edge dance culture, attracting big-name DJs and live bands. Dress up in club gear or risk being left out in the cold.

**Guitar Safari** Müürivahe 22. Popular, unpretentious venue for live cover-bands and dancing.

**Hollywood Club** Vana-Posti 8. Popular Old-Town dance club specializing in commercial techno. Wed–Fri only.

**Moskva** Vabaduse väljak 10. Polished and deservedly popular club/café/restaurant that buzzes with a see-and-be-seen crowd. DJs at weekends.

**Terrarium** Sadama 6. Visiting international DJs and beautiful young things in this minimalist club by the port. Closed Sun–Tues.

## Listings

**Embassies** Canada, Toom-Kooli 13 ☏0/627 3311; Ireland, 2nd floor, Vene 2 ☏0/681 1888; UK, Wismari 6 ☏0/667 4700; US, Kentmanni 20 ☏0/668 8100.

**Exchange** Outside banking hours, try the Monex exchange offices in the ferry dock, or the Kaubamaja or Stockmann department stores (all daily 9am–8pm).

**Hospital** Ravi 18 ☏0/620 7015.

**Internet access** Kohvik@Grill, Aia 3 (daily 9am–9pm; 25EEK/hr); Neo, Väike-Karja 12 (24hr; 35EEK/hr).

**Laundry** Sauberland, Maakri 23; Seebimull, Liivalaia 7.

**Left luggage** At the bus station (Mon–Sat 6.30am–10.20pm, Sun 7.45am–8.20pm).

**Pharmacies** Aia Apteek, Aia 10; Tallinna Linnaapteek, Pärnu mnt. 10.

**Police** Pärnu mnt. 11 ☏0/6123 523.

**Post office** Narva mnt. 1, opposite the *Viru Hotel*.

# The rest of Estonia

The island of **Saaremaa**, off the west coast of Estonia, is easily reached from Tallinn yet under-exploited as a holiday destination, its forests and coastline ripe for exploration. On the mainland some 190km southeast of Tallinn, **Tartu**, the former Hansa city of Dorpat, is regarded by many Estonians as the spiritual capital of Estonia, thanks to its role in the nineteenth-century National Awakening. These days it's a laid-back university town with a population of 100,000 and a small but lively Old Town. **Pärnu**, Estonia's fifth-largest city, lies west of Tartu. There are a handful of sights in its Old Town, but the city's chief claim to fame is as the country's main resort, its sandy beach drawing thousands of visitors every summer – especially in July, for its jazz festival.

## The island of Saaremaa

Cloaked with pine trees and juniper bushes, and littered with glacial boulders, the island of **SAAREMAA** is a tranquil place. It was the last part of Estonia to come under foreign control (when the Knights of the Sword captured it in 1227) and the locals have always maintained a strong-minded indifference to the influence of foreign occupiers, leading many to claim that the island is one of the most authentically Estonian parts of the country. Buses from Tallinn, Tartu and Pärnu come here via a ferry running from the mainland village of Virtsu to Muhu island, which is linked to Saaremaa by a causeway.

Approaching **KURESSAARE**, Saaremaa's main town, don't be put off by its grey, low-rise suburbs – the centre remains much as it was before World War II and is home to one of the finest castles in the Baltic region. From the bus station on Pihtla turn left onto Tallinna in order to reach **Kesk väljak**, the main square. Here you'll find Kuressaare's second oldest building (after the castle), the yellow-painted **Town Hall**, dating from 1670, its door guarded by stone lions; facing it is the **Weigh House**, another yellow building with a stepped gable. From the square, Lossi runs south past a monument to the dead of the 1918–20 War of Independence, past the eighteenth-century **Nikolai kirik**, a white Orthodox church with green onion domes, and on to the magnificent **Kuressaare Castle**, a vast fortress built from locally quarried dolomite. Surrounded by a deep moat, the castle was founded during the 1260s as a stronghold for the bishop of Ösel-Wiek, who controlled western Estonia from his base at Haapsalu on the mainland. The formidable structure you see today dates largely from the fourteenth century and is protected by huge, seventeenth-century ramparts. The labyrinthine keep houses the **Saaremaa Regional Museum** (May–Sept daily 11am–7pm; Oct–April Wed–Sun 11am–7pm; 30EEK), an interesting if somewhat confusingly laid-out collection covering the history and culture of the island from prehistoric times. The various sections are summarized in English. It's also possible to view the spartan living quarters of the bishops on the ground floor and climb the watchtowers, one of which houses art exhibitions. **Tall Hermann**, the eastern (and thinner) corner tower, is linked to the rest of the keep only by a wooden drawbridge.

The **tourist office** is in the town hall (June–Aug daily 9am–7pm; Sept–May Mon–Fri 9am–5pm; ☎45/33120, ⊛www.saaremaa.ee), and will book **private rooms** across the island for around 200EEK per person. The most affordable **hotel** in town is the *Guesthouse Mardi*, Vallimaa 5a (☎45/24633, ⊛www.saaremaa .ee/mardi; ❸), which has spartan but clean doubles and triples with bathrooms shared between two rooms. On the outskirts of town at Piibelehe 4, *Piibelehe Holiday Home* (☎45/36206, ⊛www.piibelehe.ee; ❷) has several guest rooms with shared facilities; it also offers camping (50EEK for 4 people). Alternatively, try the *Kraavi Holiday Cottage*, 500m southeast of the castle at Kraavi 1 (☎45/55242, ⊛www.kraavi.ee; ❷), where there are modest doubles and bicycles to rent. *Ovelia Majutus* nearby at Suve 8 (☎45/55732; ❷) is another good family-run B&B. For **food**, the *Classic* café, Lossi 9, has an excellent selection of pasta, salads, omelettes and pancakes, or pour your own coffee and select from a tempting array of pastries at the *Vannalinna Kohvipood* café at Kauba 10. The sweet, strong local beer, Saaremaa, can be hard to find in bars, but more conventional brews are served at the family-friendly *Veski*, Pärnu 19, a pub in an old windmill, which also dishes up standard meat dishes. *Vana Konn*, a more youth-oriented drinking spot at Kauba 6, has Czech and German beers on tap, a pool table and pub grub, Estonian-style. **Internet** access is at the public library, Raekoja 1 (Mon–Fri 9am–6pm, Sat 10am–4pm).

### Around the island

Public transport on the island is limited, though regular services to **Leisi** on its northern tip make both Kaali and Angla within day-trip distance. A more attractive option, thanks to Saaremaa's largely flat terrain, is to explore the island by bicycle; Bivarix Rattapood, next to the Kuressaare bus station at Tallinna 26, rents sturdy bikes (Mon–Sat 10am–6pm; 80EEK/4hrs or 150EEK/day). **KAARMA**, just over 10km north of Kuressaare, is the location of the thirteenth-century Kaarma kirik, a large, red-roofed church containing a christening stone from the same period. In woods at the edge of the village of **KAALI**, 10km northeast of Kaarma and 2.5km southeast of the Leisi road, is a round, murky green pool about 100m in diameter, created by the impact of a meteorite during the eighth century BC. A curiously mysterious, if not very spectacular place, it is one of the world's few easily accessible meteorite craters and the locals are very proud of it. Around 15km north of Kaali and right on the Leisi road is **ANGLA**, with five much-photographed wooden windmills by the roadside. A right turn just past the windmills leads to the thirteenth-century Karja kirik, a plain white village church with an unusual crucifixion carving above its side door. Inside the church are more stone carvings and medieval ceiling frescoes depicting odd and arcane symbols.

## Tartu

The main sights of **TARTU**, less than three hours from Tallinn by bus, lie between Cathedral Hill, right in the centre, and the River Emajõgi. The train station is about 500m southwest of the centre at Vaksali 6, and the bus station is just east of the centre at Turu 2. The city's focal point is its cobbled **Town Hall Square**, lined by prim Neoclassical buildings, the most eye-catching of which is the **Town Hall**, a pink-and-white toytown edifice topped by a bell-tower at the head of the square. The Neoclassical theme continues in the cool white facade of the main **Tartu University** building at Ülikooli 18, a couple of hundred metres north of the square. About 100m beyond the university is the red-brick Gothic **St John's Church**, founded in 1330, bombed out in 1944, and completely restored over the last fifteen years. The building is most famous for the pint-sized terracotta sculptures set in niches around the main entrance. Depicting Biblical figures, local citizens and fantastic creatures, roughly half of the original two thousand sculptures have survived. From behind the Town Hall, Lossi climbs **Cathedral Hill**, now a pleasant park with a few historic buildings dotted among its trees. On the way up, the street passes beneath the brightly painted wooden **Inglisild**, or Angel's Bridge, dating from the nineteenth century. At the top of the hill you'll find the remains of the red-brick **Cathedral**, built by the Knights of the Sword in the thirteenth century. Tacked onto the end of the cathedral is a newer building housing the rather dull **University History Museum** (Wed–Sun 11am–5pm; 20EEK). A few minutes' walk southeast of Cathedral Hill is the **Estonian National Museum**, J. Kuperjanovi 9 (Wed–Sun 11am–6pm; 20EEK). Devoted to peasant life and the development of agriculture, it includes some imaginatively recreated farmhouse interiors and a detailed display of folk costume from all over the country; there's good English labelling, too.

### Practicalities

Tartu's **tourist office** is at Raekoja plats 14 (Mon–Fri 9am–5pm, Sat 10am–3pm; May–Sept also Sun 10am–3pm; ☎7/442 111, ⦿www.tartu.ee). Central Tartu suffers from a shortage of affordable hotels, but there are a few small, friendly guest houses in the suburbs (❷). Most central of these is *Herne*, 1km north of the main square at Herne 59 (☎7/441 959, ⦿www.hot.ee/supilinn; ❷). The tourist office will also advise on which of the university **hostels** have vacancies; the clean and modern *Pepleri Hostel* at Pepleri 14 (☎7/427 608, ⦿www.kyla.ee) is only ten minutes from the centre and has en-suite doubles (❷) throughout the year but no dorms. For **food** try *Vanalinna Söögituba*, a pleasant and cheap Estonian restaurant with English menu, opposite St. John's Church at Rüütli 23. Better for vegetarians is *Tsink Plekk Pang*, Küütri 6, which serves Chinese and Indian food in an arty café ambience, while *Gruusia Saatkond*, around the corner at Rüütli 8, has excellent Georgian dishes. For a **drink**, the superb *Café Wilde*, Vallikraavi 4, offers tea, coffee, alcohol and light meals amidst sepia photographs and nineteenth-century cotton looms. Alternatively, head to *Zavood*, a bohemian dive just north of the centre at Lai 30. *Atlantis*, on the opposite bank of the river from the centre at Narva mnt. 2, is a large and lively mainstream disco; although *Club Tallinn*, Narva mnt. 27, attracts more renowned DJs. **Club** nights also take place at *Varjend 2000*, a graffiti-covered bunker 500m south of the centre on Pargi. There's **Internet** access at *Zum Zum*, Küüni 2 (daily 9am–11pm; 35EEK/hr).

# Pärnu

The main town on Estonia's southwestern coast, **PÄRNU** comes into its own in summer, when the faded beach resort fills with visitors intent on making the most of the brief good weather. The sandy beaches are popular with young families, but the festivals cater to an alternative, cultural crowd and the mud baths of the many sanatorium spas are a must. The few historic sights are mostly clustered in its **Old Town**. The bus station is on Pikk at the northeastern edge of the Old Town (information & ticket office at Ringi 3, round the corner), and the **train station** is about 5km east of the centre on Riia mnt. 116. **Rüütli**, lined with two-storey wooden houses, is the Old Town's main thoroughfare, cutting east–west through the centre. Near the junction with Aia is the **Pärnu Museum**, Rüütli 53 (Wed–Sun 10am–6pm, 30EEK), devoted to local history and archeology. The oldest building in town is the **Red Tower**, a fifteenth-century remnant of the medieval city walls on Hommiku, running north from Rüütli a few blocks west of the museum. Despite its name the tower is white – only the roof and window frames are red – and it now houses an antiques shop. At the end of Uus, on the western edge of the Old Town, the **Catherine Church** is a green-domed Orthodox church dating from 1760 and named after the Russian empress Catherine the Great. The interior is abundantly furnished with icons but open on Sundays. Follow Nikolai south from the centre and you'll come to the **Chaplin Centre** (daily 9am–9pm; 25EEK), which occupies the former Communist party HQ at Esplanaadi 10. Taken over by local artists in the post-independence years, it holds regular shows, film festivals and a collection of contemporary Estonian paintings and other works donated by international artists, including Yoko Ono. South of here Nikolai joins Supeluse, which runs down to the city's **resort area**, passing beneath the trees of the Rannapark, a shady park separating the town from the beach. At the southern end of Supeluse are the grand, colonnaded Neoclassical **Pärnu Mud-Baths**, built in 1926, with Pärnu's sandy, white beach just beyond, packed at weekends and on public holidays.

## Practicalities

The **tourist office** is at Rüütli 16 (June–Aug Mon–Sat 9am–6pm, Sun 10am–3pm; Sept–May Mon–Fri 9am–5pm; ☎44/73000, ⊛www.parnu.ee). **Private rooms** (❶) are available from Majutusbüroo, a block east of the bus station at Hommiku 5 (☎44/31070, ✉majutus@tanni.ee). The best hotels and guesthouses lie between the town centre and the beach, though these are expensive in season: try the *Terve Hostel* at Ringi 50, offering clean doubles with shared facilities (☎50/77332, ⊛www.terve.ee; ❹). The **hostel** *Lõuna*, centrally located at Lõuna 2 (☎44/30943, ⊛www.hot.ee/hostellouna), with comfortable and spacious dorms (200EEK) and modest doubles (❷–❸), has English-speaking staff and can provide breakfast. *Konse Holiday Village*, 2km east at Suur-Jõe 44a (☎53/435092, ⊛www .konse.ee; ❸), has rooms as well as tent pitches. For **food**, try *Kohvik Georg*, Rüütli 43, an inexpensive self-service restaurant open until 7.30pm; *Steffani*, Nikolai 24, which has a big choice of pizza and pasta dishes; or *Mõnus Margarita*, Akadeemia 5, a lively Tex-Mex joint with reasonable prices. The best of the **drinking** venues also do good food – try *Viies Villem*, a pub-style venue at Kuninga 11 with a meat and pancakes menu. *Sunset Club*, Ranna pst. 3, on the Baltic shore, hosts beach-side music events. For **Internet** access, head to the Chaplin Centre (see above; 30EEK/hr).

# Travel details

## Trains

Tallinn to: Pärnu (2 daily; 3hr); Tartu (3 daily; 3hr 20min).

## Buses

Kuressaare to: Leisi (4–5 daily; 1hr 10min); Tallinn (6 daily; 4hr 30min).
Pärnu to: Kuressaare (4 daily; 3hr); Tallinn (every 30min; 2hr); Tartu (20 daily; 2hr 30min).

Tallinn to: Kuressaare (6 daily; 4hr 30min); Pärnu (every 30min; 2hr); Tartu (every 30min; 2hr 30min).
Tartu to: Kuressaare (6 daily; 6hr); Pärnu (20 daily; 2hr 30min); Tallinn (every 30min; 2hr 30min).

## Ferries

Tallinn to: Helsinki, Finland (15–25 daily; 1hr 40min-4hr).
Virtsu to: Kuivastu for Saaremaa (12–20 daily; 30min).

# Finland

# Finland highlights

* **Senate Square, Helsinki**
The capital's main square,
dominated by the awe-
inspiring Lutheran cathedral,
Tuomiokirkko. See p.343

* **Aura river, Turku** Sip a cool
beer on board a boat-café,
moored in the heart of the
former capital. See p.347

* **Lenin museum, Tam-
pere** Fascinating col-
lection delving into the
long, mutually respectful
relationship between
Lenin and Finland. See
p.348

* **Olavinlinna castle, Savonlinna** The best preserved
medieval castle in Finland.
See p.349

* **Crossing the Arctic Circle,
Rovaniemi** The trip everybody wants to make – to
visit Father Christmas. See
p.351

* **Pielpajärvi wilderness
church, Inari** Trek across the
tundra of Lapland to reach
this former Saami outpost.
See p.351

△ Reindeer, Lapland

# Introduction and basics

Scandinavia's most culturally isolated and least understood country, **Finland** has been independent only since 1917, having been ruled for hundreds of years by first the Swedes and then Tsarist Russia. Much of its history involves a struggle for recognition and survival, and so modern-day Finns have a well-developed sense of their own culture, manifest in the popular Golden Age paintings of Gallen-Kallela and others, the music of Sibelius, the National Romantic style of architecture, and the ingrained values of rural life.

The country is mostly flat and punctuated by huge forests and lakes, but has wide regional variations. The south contains the least dramatic scenery, but the capital, **Helsinki**, more than compensates, with its brilliant architecture and superb collections of national history and art. Stretching from the Russian border in the east to the industrial city of **Tampere**, the vast waters of the **Lake Region** provide a natural means of transport for the timber industry – indeed, water here is a more common sight than land with towns lying on narrow ridges between lakes. North of here, Finland ranges from the flat western coast of **Ostrobothnia** to the thickly forested heartland of **Kainuu** and gradually rising fells of **Lapland**, Finland's most alluring terrain and home to the Saami, semi-nomadic reindeer herders.

## Information & maps

Most towns have a **tourist office**, which sometimes books accommodation. In summer they generally open daily 9am–7pm in more popular centres; in winter, hours are much reduced and some don't open at all. The best general **map** is by *Freytag & Berndt*; there's also an excellent publication *Finland facts and map*, available from tourist offices.

## Money and banks

Finland's currency is the **euro** (€). Banks are open Mon–Fri 9.30am–4.15pm. Some **banks** have exchange desks at transport terminals, and **ATMs** are widely available. You can also change money at hotels, but the rates are generally poor. **Credit cards** are widely accepted right across the country.

## Communications

Communications are dependable and quick. **Post offices** are generally open 9am–6pm, with later hours in Helsinki. Public **phones** are ubiquitous; you'll need a phone card (*puhelinkortti*; €6–20), available at post offices and tourist offices; some phones also accept credit cards. International calls are cheapest between 10pm and 8am. Operator numbers are ☏118 (domestic) and ☏92020 (international); directory enquiries is ☏020208. Free **Internet access** is readily available, even in the most out-of-the-way places – most likely at the local library (though you may need to book a few hours in advance) or the tourist office.

## Getting around

For the most part trains and buses integrate well, and you'll only need to plan with care

---

### Finland on the net

ⓦ**www.visitfinland.com** The Finnish tourist board site.
ⓦ**www.finland.org** General facts about Finland.
ⓦ**www.sauna.fi** The Finnish Sauna Society.
ⓦ**www.srmnet.org** Finnish Youth Hostel Association.

when travelling through the remoter areas of the far north and east. **Trains** are operated by Finnish State Railways (VR; ⊛ www.vr.fi). Comfortable Express and InterCity trains, plus tilting Pendolino trains, serve the principal cities several times a day. Elsewhere, especially on east–west hauls through sparsely populated regions, trains are often tiny or replaced by buses on which rail passes are still valid. **InterRail** and **ScanRail** passes (see p.47) are valid on all trains. The best timetable is the *Rail Pocket Guide* published by VR and available from all train stations and tourist offices. **Buses** – privately run, but with a common ticket system – cover the whole country, but are most useful in the north. Tickets can be purchased at bus stations and most travel agents; only ordinary one-way tickets can be bought on board. The timetable (*Pikavuoroaikataulut*), available at all main bus stations, lists all bus routes.

Domestic **flights** can be comparatively cheap as well as time-saving, especially if you're planning to visit Lapland and the far north. Finnair (⊛ www.finnair.com) and Blue1 (⊛ www.blue1.com) are the main operators, though, generally, cheaper tickets are only available if booked well in advance. One-way tickets with Blue1 can be especially good value.

# Accommodation

**Hotels** are expensive. Special offers in summer mean that you'll be able to sleep well on a budget in high season, but may have difficulty finding anything affordable out of season – the reverse of the norm. You can **book** through Hotel Booking Centre (☏ 09/2288 1400), inside the train station in Helsinki. The free *Finland: Budget Accommodation* booklet, available from any tourist office, contains a comprehensive list of hostels and campsites.

Most hotels come with TV, phone and private bathrooms, and all-you-can-eat buffet breakfasts. Taking advantage of discount schemes and summer reductions, such as the **Finncheque**, can cut prices to either €36 or €45 per person for a double room depending on standard. Finncheques must be arranged through the Finnish Tourist

Board or a specialist travel agent before arriving in Finland; each cheque entitles the holder to one night's accommodation with breakfast in participating chains, for use daily between June and Sept and Fri–Sun all year; there's a surcharge (€25–35) for single room occupancy. More information can be obtained from Suomen Hotellivaraukset on ☏ 09/686 0330. In many towns you'll also find **tourist hotels** (*matkustajakoti*), offering fewer frills for €35–50 per person, although they are often full during summer. **Summer hotels** (*kesähotelli*; June–Aug only) are another option, offering decent accommodation in student blocks for €25–45 per person, normally with breakfast thrown in.

Each city has at least one **HI hostel** (*retkeilymajat*; ⊛ www.srmnet .org), usually the cheapest option and always spotlessly clean. It's advisable to book ahead, especially between June and August, and note that many close altogether from mid-August till June. Hostels range from the basic dormitory type to those with two-bedded rooms and a bathroom between three. Bed linen, if not included, costs an extra €3.50–5 – Finnish health regulations prohibit the use of sleeping bags in hostels. HI cards reduce overnight charges by €2.50.

Official **campsites** (*leirintäalue*) are plentiful. Most open from May or June until August or September, although some stay open longer and a few all year round. Many three-star sites also have cottages, often with TV, sauna and kitchen. Two people sharing a tent pay €5–15, depending on site facilities; cabins cost €100–500 per week (book cabins as far ahead as possible for July & Aug). You'll need either an International Camping Card or a National Camping Card; the latter (€3.40), available at all sites, is valid for a year.

# Food and drink

**Restaurants** can be pricey so take advantage of special lunchtime deals and self-catering. Though tempered by many regulations, **alcohol** is more widely available and considerably less expensive than in the rest of Scandinavia.

Though it may at first seem a stodgy, unsophisticated cuisine, **Finnish food** is an interesting mix of Western and Eastern influences, with Scandinavian-style fish specialities and exotic meats such as reindeer and elk alongside dishes that bear a Russian stamp – pastries, and casseroles strong on cabbage and pork. **Breakfasts** (*aamiainen*) are sumptuous buffets of herring, eggs, cereals, cheese, salami and bread. You can lunch on the economical **snacks** sold in market halls (*kauppahalli*) or adjoining cafés. Most train stations and some bus stations and supermarkets also have cafeterias offering a selection of snacks and light meals, and the *Grilli* street stands turn out burgers and hot dogs for €2.50–3.50. Otherwise, campus **mensas** are the cheapest places to get a hot dish (€2–4). Theoretically, you have to be a student, but you're unlikely to be asked for ID. In regular restaurants or *ravintola*, **lunch** (*lounas*) deals are good value, with many places offering a lunchtime buffet table (*voileipäpöytä* or *seisovapöytä*) stacked with a choice of traditional goodies for a set price of €8.50–13. Pizzerias are another good bet, serving lunch specials for €6–9. For **evening meals**, a cheap pizzeria or *ravintola* will serve up standard plates of meat and two veg. In Helsinki and the big towns there's usually a good range of options, including Chinese and Thai. Prices run from €6 for a cheap pizza to €50 for a substantial meal plus drinks in a smart restaurant.

## Finnish

Stress on all Finnish words always falls on the first syllable.

|  | Finnish | Pronunciation |
|---|---|---|
| **Yes** | *Kyllä* | Koo-leh |
| **No** | *Ei* | Ay |
| **Please** | *Olkaa hyvä* | Olcar hoo-veh |
| **Thank you** | *Kiitos* | Keetos |
| **Hello/Good day** | *Hyvää päivää* | Hoo-veh pai-veh |
| **Goodbye** | *Näkemiin* | Nek-er-meen |
| **Excuse me** | *Anteeksi* | Anteksi |
| **Where?** | *Missä?* | Miss-eh |
| **Good** | *Hyvä* | Hoo-veh |
| **Bad** | *Paha* | Paha |
| **Near** | *Lähellä* | Le-hell-eh |
| **Far** | *Kaukana* | Kau-kanna |
| **Cheap** | *Halpa* | Halpa |
| **Expensive** | *Kallis* | Kallis |
| **Open** | *Avoin* | Avoyn |
| **Closed** | *Suljettu* | Sul-yet-oo |
| **Today** | *Tänään* | Ten-ern |
| **Yesterday** | *Eilen* | Aylen |
| **Tomorrow** | *Huomenna* | Hoo-oh-menna |
| **How much is....?** | *Mitä maksaa?* | Mee-teh maksaa |
| **What time is it?** | *Paljonko kello on?* | Palyonko kello on |
| **I don't understand** | *En ymmärrä* | Enn oomerreh |
| **Do you speak English?** | *Puhutteko englantia?* | Poohut-tuko englantia |
| **One** | *Yksi* | Uxi |
| **Two** | *Kaksi* | Caksi |
| **Three** | *Kolme* | Col-meh |
| **Four** | *Neljä* | Nel-yeh |
| **Five** | *Viisi* | Veesi |
| **Six** | *Kuusi* | Coosi |
| **Seven** | *Seitsemän* | Sayt-se-men |
| **Eight** | *Kahdeksan* | Car-deksan |
| **Nine** | *Yhdeksän* | Oo-deksan |
| **Ten** | *Kymmenen* | Kummenen |

Whilst the attitude to **drinking** can seem austere, Finland has a huge problem with alcoholism: bars in smaller towns can be quite depressing. In Helsinki and bigger cities, however, the drinking culture is more sophisticated and appealing. Most restaurants are fully licensed, and many are frequented more for drinking than eating. **Bars** are usually open till midnight or 1am and service stops half an hour before closing. You have to be 18 to buy beer and wine, 20 to buy spirits. Expect to queue to get into popular bars, as there's no standing allowed, so you'll only be let in if there's a seat free. Remember to tip the doorman (*portsari*; €1), if there is one, on leaving; if there isn't, then there'll almost certainly be an obligatory cloakroom fee (also €1). The main – and cheapest – outlets for take-out alcohol are the ubiquitous government-run **ALKO** shops (Mon–Thurs 10am–5pm, Fri 10am–6pm; Oct–April also Sat 9am–2pm).

**Beer** (*olut*) falls into three categories: "light beer" (I-Olut), like a soft drink; "medium strength beer" (*keskiolut*, III-Olut), perceptibly alcoholic, sold in supermarkets and cafés; and "strong beer" (A-Olut or IV-Olut), on a par with the stronger European beers, and only available at licensed restaurants, clubs and ALKO shops. Strong beers, such as Lapin Kulta and Koff, cost about €2.25 per 500ml can. Imported beers go for €2.50–2.80 per can. Finlandia **vodka** is €16 for a 700ml bottle; Koskenkorva, a rougher vodka, is €15.

# Opening hours and holidays

**Shops** open Mon–Fri 9am–6pm, Sat 9am–4pm. Along with banks, they close on **public holidays**, when most public transport and museums run to a Sunday schedule: Jan 1, Jan 6 (Epiphany), Good Fri & Easter Mon, May 1, June 21, Nov 1, Dec 6, Dec 24, 25 & 26.

# Emergencies

You won't have much cause to come into contact with the Finnish **police**, though if you do they are likely to speak English. As for **health problems**, if you're insured, you'll save time by seeing a doctor at a private health centre (*lääkäriasema*) rather than waiting at a national health centre (*terveyskeskus*). Medicines must be paid for at a **pharmacy** (*apteekki*), generally open daily 9am–6pm; outside these times, a phone number for emergency help is displayed on every pharmacy's front door.

# Helsinki

The southern coast of Finland is the most populated, industrialized and richest part of the country, with the densest concentration, not surprisingly, around the capital, **HELSINKI**. A city of 560,000 people, Helsinki is quite different from the other Scandinavian capitals, closer both in mood and looks to the major cities of eastern Europe. For a century an outpost of the Russian Empire, its very shape and form is derived from its powerful neighbour. Yet during the twentieth century it became a showcase for independent Finland, much of its impressive architecture drawing inspiration from the dawning of Finnish nationalism and the rise of the republic. Today, the streets have a youthful buzz, the short summer bringing crowds along the boulevards and to outdoor cafés and restaurants, while at night the pace picks up, with a great selection of pubs and clubs and free rock concerts in the numerous parks.

## Arrival, information and city transport

All points of arrival are close to the city centre: the **ferry** terminals are less than 1km from the centre; the **train station** is in the heart of the city; the **long-distance bus station** is a short way up Simonkatu; and the **airport**, Vantaa, is 20km to the north, connected by Finnair buses to the central train station (every 20min; €4.90).

The **City Tourist Office** at Pohjoisesplanadi 19 (Mon–Fri 9am–6/8pm, Sat & Sun 9/10am–4/6pm; ☎09/169 3757, ⌨www.hel.fi/tourism) stocks the useful, free listings magazines *Helsinki This Week*, *City* and *Helsinki Happens*. If you're staying a while, consider purchasing a **Helsinki Card** (€25/35 for 24/48hr), giving unlimited travel on public transport and free entry to more than forty museums. For information on the rest of the country, use the **Finnish Tourist Board** across the road at Eteläesplanadi 4 (Mon–Fri 9am–5pm; May–Sept also Sat & Sun 11am–3pm; ☎09/4176 9300, ⌨www.visitfinland.com). Most sights are within easy walking distance of each other. However, quick hops across the centre are easily done on the efficient **public transport** system (trams, buses and a small metro). One-way tickets can be bought on board (€2) or from the bus station, tourist office or kiosks around the centre, while a **tourist ticket** (€5.40/10.80/16.20 for one/three/five days) permits unlimited use of the whole network for the period covered. **Tram #3T** follows a useful figure-of-eight route around the centre.

## Accommodation

There's plenty of **accommodation**, the bulk of it mid-range **hotels**. However, there are a number of cheaper, if less luxurious, **tourist hotels**, providing basic accommodation in private rooms without bathrooms, and a few **hostels**, though space can be tight in summer. You can book hotel rooms and hostel beds at the **Hotel Booking Centre** at the train station for a fee of €5 in person or for free by email or phone (June–Aug Mon–Fri 9am–7pm, Sat 9am–6pm, Sun 10am–6pm; Sept–May Mon–Fri 9am–6pm, Sat 9am–5pm; ☎09/2288 1400, ⌨hotel@helsinkiexpert.fi).

### Hostels and tourist hotels

**Academica** Hietaniemenkatu 14 ☎09/1311 4334. On the fringes of the city centre with dorms and double rooms. HI and student card discounts. Breakfast included in price. June to Aug only. Dorms €18, rooms ❺

**Erottajanpuisto** Uudenmaankatu 9 ☎09/642 169. A good central location close to Mannerheimintie with singles to quadruples. Breakfast is €5. Dorms €20, rooms ❸–❻

**Eurohostel** Linnankatu 9 ☎09/622 0470. The biggest hostel in Finland, close to the ferry terminals and with a free sauna. Breakfast is €6.10. Dorms €20.40, rooms ❸

**Omapohja** Itäinen teatterikuja 3 ☎09/666 211. No dorms here, just rooms, some of which are en-suite. Breakfast costs €6 extra. ❺

**Stadion Hostel** Olympic Stadium ☎09/477 8480. Some 2km out of the centre and often crowded, but cheap and open all year. Trams #3T, #7A, #7B and #10 to stadium, then follow the signs. Breakfast is €5.30. Dorms €15, rooms ❸

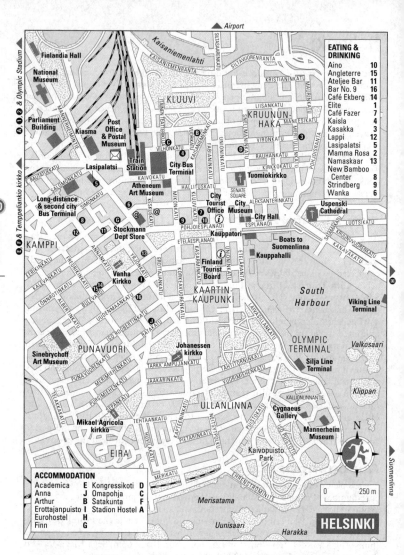

EATING & DRINKING

| | |
|---|---|
| Aino | 10 |
| Angleterre | 15 |
| Ateljee Bar | 11 |
| Bar No. 9 | 16 |
| Café Ekberg | 14 |
| Elite | 1 |
| Café Fazer | 7 |
| Kaisla | 4 |
| Kasakka | 3 |
| Lappi | 12 |
| Lasipalatsi | 5 |
| Mamma Rosa | 2 |
| Namaskaar | 13 |
| New Bamboo Center | 8 |
| Strindberg | 9 |
| Wanka | 6 |

ACCOMMODATION

| | | | |
|---|---|---|---|
| Academica | E | Kongressikoti | D |
| Anna | J | Omapohja | C |
| Arthur | B | Satakunta | F |
| Erottajanpuisto | I | Stadion Hostel | A |
| Eurohostel | H | | |
| Finn | G | | |

**Summer Hotel Satakunta** Lapinrinne 1 ☎09/6958 5231. Centrally located place that doubles as an HI hostel. June–Aug only. Dorms €19, rooms ❹; breakfast included.

### Hotels

**Anna** Annankatu 1 ☎09/616 621. Small and central, with a cosy atmosphere though the rooms are a little cramped. ❽

**Arthur** Vuorikatu 19 ☎09/173 441. Good-quality choice, with some en-suite rooms. ❼

**Finn** Kalevankatu 3b ☎09/684 4360. A peaceful, modern option, virtually in the city centre, and a good place to meet other travellers. ❺

**Kongressikoti** Snellmaninkatu 15a ☎09/135 6839. Clean and cosy place close to Senate Square. Discounts for longer stays. ❹

### Campsite

**Rastila** Karavaanikatu 4 ☎09/321 6551. Located 13km east of the city centre, at the end of the metro line and served by night buses #90N and #93N till 1.30am. Also has cabins (❸).

# The City

Following a devastating fire in 1808, and the city's appointment as Finland's capital in 1812, Helsinki was totally rebuilt in a style befitting its new status: a grid of wide streets and Neoclassical brick buildings modelled on the then Russian capital, St Petersburg. From **Senate Square** to **Esplanadi** the grandeur has endured. The square itself is dominated by the exquisite form of the recently renovated **Tuomiokirkko** (cathedral; Mon–Sat 9am–6pm, Sun noon–6pm; free), designed by Engel and completed after his death in 1852. After the elegance of the exterior, the spartan Lutheran interior comes as a disappointment; better is the gloomily atmospheric **crypt** (same times as cathedral; entrance on Kirkkokatu), now often used for exhibitions. Walking east, the square at the end of Aleksanterinkatu is overlooked by the onion domes of the Russian Orthodox **Uspenski Cathedral** (Mon–Sat 9.30am–4pm, Sun noon–3pm, Oct–April closed Mon; tram #3). Inside, a rich display of icons glitters while incense mingles with the sound of Slavonic choirs. Beyond is Katajanokka, a wedge of land extending between the harbours, where a dockland development programme is converting the old warehouses into pricey new restaurants and apartments. Just a block south of Senate Square, the new **City Museum** at Sofiankatu 4 (Mon–Fri 9am–5pm, Sat & Sun 11am–5pm; €3) offers a hi-tech record of Helsinki life in an impressive permanent exhibition called "Time".

## From Mannerheimintie to Kaivopuisto park

Across a mishmash of tramlines from the harbour is Esplanadi, a wide tree-lined boulevard that is Helsinki at its most charming. Southwest of here, on Annankatu, is the **Vanha kirkko**, Engel's humble wooden structure, the first Lutheran church to be built in Helsinki after it became the capital. A few blocks from the end of Kasarmikatu is the large and rocky **Kaivopuisto** park, where nobility from St Petersburg came to sample the waters at its 1830s spa house. However, it's north of Bulevardi that most of the city's attractions can be found. On the corner of Aleksanterinkatu and Mannerheimintie is the Constructivist brick exterior of the **Stockmann Department Store**. Europe's largest, it sells everything from bubble gum to Persian rugs. Further along Mannerheimintie, steps head down to the **Tunneli** shopping complex, which leads to one of the city's most enjoyable structures, **Helsinki train station**, a solid yet graceful building dating from 1914. Beside the station is the imposing granite **National Theatre**, home of Finnish drama since 1872. Directly opposite the bus station is the **Atheneum Art Museum**, Kaivokatu 2 (Tues–Fri 9am–6/8pm, Sat & Sun 11am–5pm; €5.50). Its stirring selection of late-nineteenth-century works – including Akseli Gallén-Kallela and Albert Edelfelt's scenes from the Finnish epic, the *Kalevala*, and Juho Rissanen's moody studies of peasant life – recalls a time when the spirit of nationalism was surging through the country.

**Mannerheimintie** spears north from the city centre, past the striking **Kiasma**, Helsinki's museum of contemporary art (Tues 9am–5pm, Wed–Sun 10am–8.30pm; €5.50). Its gleaming steel-clad exterior and hi-tech interior make it well worth a visit, and its collection includes installations in which sound, moving images and smell add a sensory dimension to the experience. Opposite is the **Lasipalatsi**, a multimedia complex situated in a recently renovated 1930s classic Functionalist building, inside which are trendy shops and cafés. Further along on the left, the **Parliament Building** (guided tours Sat 11am & noon, Sun noon & 1pm; July & Aug also Mon–Fri 2pm; free), with its pompous columns and choking air of solemnity, was completed in 1931. There's more information on the parliament from the attached visitor centre, Arkadiankatu 3 (Mon–Fri 10am–4pm, Tues–Thurs till 6pm; free). North of here is the **National Museum** (Tues–Sun 11am–6/8pm; €5.50), its design drawing on the country's medieval churches and granite castles. The exhibits, from prehistory to the present, are exhaustive; it's best to concentrate on a few specific sections, such as the marvellously restored seventeenth-century manor house interior and the ethnographic displays from the nation's varied regions.

Diagonally opposite the National Museum, **Finlandia Hall** (guided tours by appointment; ☎09/402 4246; €6) was designed in the 1970s by the country's premier architect, Alvar Aalto. Inside, Aalto's characteristic asymmetry and wave pattern (his surname means "wave") are everywhere, from the walls and ceilings through to the lamps and vases. A little further up Mannerheimintie, the **Olympic Stadium** is clearly visible; originally intended for the 1940 Olympics, it hosted the second postwar games in 1952. Its **tower** (Mon–Fri 9am–8pm, Sat & Sun 9am–6pm; €2) gives an unsurpassed view over the city and a chunk of the southern coast. Back towards the city centre, the **Hietaniemi Cemetery** houses the graves of some of the big names of Finnish history – Mannerheim, Engel and Alvar Aalto, whose tombstone, with its chopped Neoclassical column, stands beside the main entrance. East of here, at Lutherinkatu 3, is the late-1960s **Underground Church** (Temppeliaukio kirkko; Mon–Fri 10am–8pm, Sat till 6pm, Sun noon–1.45pm & 3.15–5.45pm; closed Tues 1–2pm and during services; tram #3B). Blasted from a single lump of granite beneath a domed copper roof, it's a thrill to be inside.

### Suomenlinna

Built by the Swedes in 1748 to protect Helsinki from seaborne attack, the fortress of **Suomenlinna** stands on five interconnected islands and is the biggest sea fortress in the world. It's reachable by ferry (every 30min; €2 single or €3.60 return) from the harbour: you can either visit independently, or take one of the hour-long summer **guided walking tours**, beginning close to the ferry stage and conducted in English (June–Aug daily 10.30am, 1pm & 3pm; €5). Suomenlinna has a few museums, none particularly riveting. The best of the lot is **Suomenlinna Museum** (daily 10/11am–4/6pm; Oct–April closed Mon; €5) which contains a permanent exhibition on the island, but it's the views from the island back across the water towards the capital that are truly superb.

## Eating, drinking and nightlife

Many places offer good-value **lunchtime** deals, and there are plenty of affordable ethnic **restaurants** and fastfood *grillis* for the evenings. At the end of Eteläesplanadi the old market hall, Kauppahalli (Mon–Fri 8am–7pm, Sat 8am–4pm), is good for snacks and reindeer kebabs. Helsinki has several **student mensas**, two of which are centrally located at Aleksanterinkatu 5 and Yliopistonkatu 3; both are open during term time, and one or the other will be open through summer. **Drinking** can be enjoyed in the city's many pub-like restaurants; on Fridays and Saturdays it's best to arrive as early as possible to get a seat. Most places also serve food, although the grub is seldom at its best in the evening. There are ALKO shops at Fabianinkatu 9–11 and Kaivokatu 10.

Helsinki has a vibrant night scene, with several venues putting on a steady diet of **live music** and free gigs almost every summer Sunday in Kaivopuisto park. There's also a wide range of **clubs and discos**, which charge a small admission fee (around €5). For details of **what's on**, read the entertainments page of *Helsingin Sanomat*, or the free fortnightly paper, *City*, found in record shops, bookshops, department stores and tourist offices. **Tickets** can be booked at Tiketti, Yrjönkatu 29c (Mon–Fri 9am–5pm; ☎0600/11 616, premium-rate call).

### Restaurants and cafés

**Aino** Pohjoisesplanadi 21. Justifiably popular place in the centre of town, serving up delicious and hearty Finnish food. Closed Sun.

**Café Ekberg** Bulevardi 9. Nineteenth-century fixtures and a fin-de-siècle atmosphere, with starched waitresses bringing expensive sandwiches and pastries to marble tables.

Café Fazer Kluuvikatu 3. Owned by Finland's biggest chocolate company, with celebrated pastries.

Kasakka Meritullinkatu 13. Great atmosphere and food in this old-style Russian restaurant.

Lappi Annankatu 22. Authentic Lapland food in a restaurant done out in tacky log-cabin style. Lunchtime specials are good value, but prices escalate in the evenings.

Lasipalatsi Mannerheimintie 22–24. Decent modern Finnish food served in a classic Functionalist-style building with great views of the street life below.

Mamma Rosa Runeberginkatu 55. A classic pizzeria also serving fish steaks and pasta.

Namaskaar Bulevardi 6 & Mannerheimintie 100. Popular evening buffet and plenty of vegetarian options.

New Bamboo Center Annankatu 29. Cheap, cheerful and fast – one of the more authentic Indian restaurants currently hitting Helsinki.

Strindberg Pohjoisesplanadi 33. The upstairs restaurant serves contemporary Scandinavian cuisine, while the street level café is one of the places in town to see and be seen.

## Bars

Angleterre Fredrikinkatu 47. Well-known for its massive selection of traditional British beers on draught and in bottles.

Ateljee Bar roof of *Hotel Torni*, Yrjönkatu 26. The best views of Helsinki in a stylish atmosphere.

Bar Nº9 Uudenmaankatu 9. A popular hangout for professionals at lunchtime and bohos in the evening,

it has a beer list and menu as cosmopolitan as its staff. Food is reasonably cheap and filling and there is always a vegetarian option.

Elite Eteläinen Hesperiankatu 22. Once the haunt of the city's artists, many of whom settled their bill with the paintings that line the walls. Especially good in summer, when you can drink on the terrace.

Kaisla Vilhonkatu 4. One of the city's most popular drinking establishments known for its extensive selection of different types of beer. Always popular.

Wanha Mannerheimintie 3. Self-service and comparatively cheap café/bar. Arrive early for a seat on the balcony overlooking the streets below. The cellar is given over to a smoky beer hall, whilst other parts of the building serve as an indie/rock concert venue.

## Nightlife

Botta Museokatu 10. Vibrant dance music of various hues most nights.

Heartbreakers Mannerheimintie 5. This incredibly central club is *the* place to dance the night away and is accordingly stuffed full of beautiful people.

Kaarle X11 Kasarmikatu 40. The latest nightclub in town sprawling over two levels. One of the dance-floors bounces to the sounds of Finnish pop music.

Saunabar Eerikinkatu 27. With a sauna attached and a legendary Sunday night DJ spot, this is one of the most unusual places in town.

Storyville Museokatu 8. Popular venue for nightly live jazz. Good food, too.

## Gay Helsinki

Finland decriminalized homosexuality in 1971 and introduced partnership laws in 2001. In recent years the gay scene in Helsinki has flourished and there's an impressive number of exclusively gay and gay-friendly establishments. For the latest details, pick up a copy of the monthly *Z* **magazine** – in Finnish only but with a useful listings section – widely available in larger newsagents, or drop into the state-supported gay organization SETA, Hietalahdenkatu 2b 16 (T09/681 2580, Wwww.seta.fi).

Con Hombres Eerikinkatu 14. The most popular bar in Helsinki and one of the oldest in the country. If it's quiet elsewhere, the chances are there'll be people here. Very cruisy at weekends.

dtm (Don't Tell Mamma) Annankatu 32 Wwww .dtm.fi. The capital's legendary night club and *the* place to go, with occasional drag shows and house music most nights.

Hercules Lönnrotinkatu 4b. Not quite as trendy as *dtm*, this club plays varied music, including some of Finland's best offerings.

Lost & Found Annankatu 6. Two bars on two floors, with a small dance-floor downstairs. Very popular at weekends with a mixed crowd.

Mann's Street Mannerheimintie 12 (upstairs). If you're looking for karaoke, Finnish music and older gay men, you'll find generous helpings here.

Room Erottajankatu 5. Next to *Lost and Found* and one of Helsinki's better neighbourhood bars; attracts the young and beautiful.

## Listings

**Embassies** Canada, Pohjoisesplanadi 25b
⊕09/228 530; Ireland, Erottajankatu 7A ⊕09/646
006; UK, Itäinen Puistotie 17 ⊕09/2286 5100;
US, Itäinen Puistotie 14a ⊕09/616 250. Australia,
contact Stockholm embassy (see p.991).
**Exchange** Other than the banks, try Travelex at
the airport (5.30am–11.30pm) or Forex at the train
station (daily 8am–9pm).
**Hospital** Marian Hospital, Lapinlahdenkatu 16
⊕09/4711.
**Internet** Akateeminen Kirjakauppa (Micronia
department), Keskuskatu 2; Netcup,

Aleksanterinkatu 52; *mbar* in the Lasipalatsi,
Mannerheimintie 22–24.
**Laundry** Rööperin pesulapalvelut, Punavuorenkatu
3 and Easywash, Topeliuksenkatu 21.
**Left luggage** At the train station.
**Pharmacy** Yliopiston Apteekki, Mannerheimintie
96 (24hr).
**Police** Pieni Roobertinkatu 1–3 ⊕1891.
**Post office** Mannerheiminaukio 1.
**Sauna** Kotiharjun sauna (Tues–Fri 2–8pm, Sat
1–7pm; ⊕09/753 1535), Harjutorinkatu, near the
Sörnäinen metro station.

## Around Helsinki: Porvoo

About 50km east of Helsinki, **PORVOO** is one of the oldest towns on the south
coast and one of Finland's most charming. Its narrow cobbled streets, lined by
small wooden buildings, give a sense of the Finnish life which predated the capital's
bold squares and Neoclassical geometry. Close to the station, the **Johan Ludwig
Runeberg House**, Aleksanterinkatu 3 (Mon–Sat 10am–4pm, Sun 11am–5pm;
Sept–April closed Mon & Tues; €5), is where the famed Finnish poet lived from
1852 while a teacher at the town school; despite writing in Swedish, one of his
poems provided the lyrics for the Finnish national anthem. The old town is built
around the hill on the other side of Mannerheimkatu, crowned by the fifteenth-
century **Tuomiokirkko** (May–Sept Mon–Fri 10am–6pm, Sat 10am–2pm, Sun
2–5pm; Oct–April Tues–Sat 10am–2pm, Sun 2–4pm), where Alexander I proclaimed Finland a Russian Grand Duchy and convened the first Finnish Diet. This,
and other aspects of the town's past, can be explored in the **Porvoo Museum**
(daily 10am/noon–4pm; Sept–April closed Mon & Tues; €5) at the foot of the
hill in the main square; the collection of furnishings, musical instruments and oddities mostly date from the days of Russian rule.

**Buses** run daily from Helsinki to Porvoo (€8.70 one-way; 1hr), arriving opposite the **tourist office**, which is at Rihkamakatu 4 (Mon–Fri 9.30am–4.30/6pm,
Sat & Sun 10am–2/4pm; Sept to early June closed Sun; ⊕019/520 2316, ⊛www
.porvoo.fi). There's a **hostel** at Linnankoskenkatu 1–3 (⊕019/523 0012, ⊛www
.porvoohostel.cjb.net; €18), and a **campsite** (⊕019/581 967; June–Aug), 1.5km
from the town centre. The cheapest place **to eat** is *Rosso* at Piispankatu 21.

# Southwest Finland

The area west of Helsinki is probably the blandest section of the country – endless
forests interrupted only by modest-sized patches of water and virtually identical
villages and small towns. The far **southwestern** corner is more interesting, with
islands and inlets around a jagged shoreline and some of the country's distinctive
Finnish-Swedish coastal communities. The former capital **Turku** is historically and
visually one of Finland's most enticing cities.

## Turku

**TURKU** was once the national capital, but lost its status in 1812 and most of
its buildings in a ferocious fire in 1827. These days it's a small and sociable city,

bristling with history and culture and with a sparkling nightlife, thanks to the students from its two universities.

To get to grips with Turku and its pivotal place in Finnish history, cut through the centre to the river. This tree-framed space was, before the great fire of 1827, the bustling heart of the community, and is overlooked by Turku's **Tuomiokirkko** (daily 9am–7/8pm except during services), erected in the thirteenth century and still the centre of the Finnish Church. Despite repeated fires, a number of features survive, notably the ornate seventeenth-century tomb of Torsten Stålhandske, commander of the Finnish cavalry during the Thirty Years War. On top of a small hill near the cathedral, you'll see the wooden dome of the **Engel Observatory**, which currently houses the **Turku Art Museum** (Tues–Fri 11am–7pm, Sat & Sun 11am–5pm; €6). The museum contains one of the better collections of Finnish art, with works by all the great names of the country's golden age plus a commendable stock of modern pieces. Retrace your steps to the riverbank to find Turku's newest and most splendid museum, the combined **Aboa Vetus and Ars Nova** (daily 11am–7pm; mid-Sept to March closed Mon; €8). Digging the foundations of the modern art gallery revealed a warren of medieval lanes, now on view beneath the glass floor of the building. The gallery comprises 350 striking works plus temporary exhibits, and there's a great café too.

Just north of the cathedral is the sleek, low form of the **Sibelius Museum** (Tues–Sun 11am–4pm, Wed also 6–8pm; €3), which – although Sibelius had no direct connection with Turku – displays family photo albums and manuscripts, the great man's hat, walking stick and even his final half-smoked cigar. A short walk away, on the southern bank of the river at Itäinen Rantakatu 38, the **Wäinö Aaltonen Museum** (Tues–Sun 11am–7pm; €4) is devoted to the best-known modern Finnish sculptor, who grew up close to Turku and studied at the local art school – his imaginative and sensitive work turns up in every major Finnish town. Crossing back over Aurajoki and down Linnankatu and then heading towards the mouth of the river will bring you to **Turku Castle** (daily 10am–3/6pm; mid-Sept to mid-April closed Mon; €6.50). The featureless exterior conceals a maze of cobbled courtyards, corridors and staircases, with a bewildering array of finds and displays. The castle probably went up around 1280; its gradual expansion accounts for the patchwork architecture.

## Practicalities

The river Aura splits the city, its tree-lined banks forming a natural promenade as well as a useful landmark. On the northern side of the river is Turku's central grid, where you'll find the **tourist office** at Aurakatu 4 (Mon–Fri 8.30am–6pm; also Sat & Sun: April–Sept 9am–4pm, rest of year 10am–3pm; ☎02/262 7444, ⊛www .turkutouring.fi). Both the **train** and **bus station** are within easy walking distance of the river, just north of the centre; for the Stockholm ferry, stay on the train for the terminal, 2km west, or catch bus #1 on Linnankatu.

There are some good deals to be had at Turku's mid-range **hotels**, especially if you make an early reservation and pick a weekend. Try *Hotel Julia*, Eerikinkatu 4 (☎02/336 000; ❻), or for a real slice of luxury and character try *Park Hotel*, Rauhankatu 1 (☎02/273 2555, ⊛www.parkhotelturku.fi; ❽). Alvar Aalto fans should stay at *Omena Hotelli* (☎020/424 4034; ❻), Humalistonkatu 7, housed in a building designed by Finland's most famous architect; ask for room no. 422 or 534. The excellent **hostel**, *Hostel Turku*, is by the river at Linnankatu 39 (☎02/262 7680, ⊛hostel@turku.fi; €14); take bus #1 or #30. The nearest **campsite** (☎02/262 5100; June–Aug; bus #8) is on the island of Ruissalo, which has two sandy beaches and overlooks Turku harbour.

For excellent **food** at sensible prices, it's worth trekking out to *Alabama Datacity* restaurant in the Data Centre, close to Turku hospital (take the train one stop to Kupittaa; 5min), run by the catering college; the food and service are excellent. In the centre, *Baan Thai*, Kauppiaskatu 17, has great Thai food at respectable prices;

or there's *Pizzeria Dennis*, Linnankatu 17, for affordably priced pizza. Near the tourist office **Market Square** (*Kauppatori*) sells fresh produce, and in summer is full of open-air cafés; nearby, the effervescent market hall or **Kauppahalli** (Mon–Fri 8am–5pm, Sat 8am–2pm) offers a slightly more upmarket choice of delis and other eateries. Top-notch food can be had at *Herman*, Läntinen Rantakatu 37, in a bright, airy storehouse dating from 1849, with excellent lunches (€7.10). Floating bar-restaurants change each summer, but look out for *Papa Joe*, *Svarte Rudolph* and *Donna*. Otherwise, the most popular **drinking** venue is *Uusi Apteekki*, Kaskenkatu 1, which, true to its name, is an old pharmacy complete with ancient fittings.

# ⑩ Finland's Lake Region

About a third of Finland is covered by the **Lake Region**, a huge area of bays, inlets and islands interspersed with dense forests. Despite holding much of Finland's industry, it's a tranquil, verdant area, and even **Tampere**, the major industrial city, enjoys a peaceful lakeside setting. The eastern part of the region is the most atmospheric, slender ridges furred with conifers linking the few sizeable landmasses. The regional centre, **Savonlinna**, stretches delectably across several islands and boasts a superb medieval castle.

## Tampere

**TAMPERE**, a leafy place of parks and lakes, is Scandinavia's largest inland city. Its rapid growth began just over a century ago, when the Scot James Finlayson opened a textile factory, drawing labour from rural areas where traditional crafts were in decline. Metalwork and shoe factories soon followed, their owners paternally promoting a vigorous local arts scene for the workforce. Free outdoor concerts, lavish theatrical productions and one of the best modern art collections in Finland maintain such traditions to this day. Almost everything of consequence is within the central section, a thin strip of land bordered on two sides by lakes Näsijärvi and Pyhäjärvi. The main streets run off either side of Hämeenkatu, which leads directly from the train station across Hämeensilta bridge. Left off Hämeenkatu, up slender Hämeenpuisto, the **Lenin Museum** at no. 28 (Mon–Fri 9am–6pm, Sat & Sun 11am–4pm; €4) remembers the time when Lenin lived in Finland and attended the Tampere conferences, held in what is now the museum. Nearby, at Puutarhakatu 34, the **Art Museum of Tampere** (Tues–Sun 10am–6pm; €5) holds temporary art exhibitions, but if you're looking for Finnish art you might be better off visiting the **Hiekka Art Gallery**, a few minutes' walk away at Pirkankatu 6 (Tues–Thurs 3–6pm, Sun noon–3pm; €5), which has sketches by Gallen-Kallela and Helene Schjerfbeck. Better still is the tremendous **Sara Hildén Art Museum** (daily 11am–6pm, closed Mon Oct–April; €4), built on the shores of Näsijärvi, a quirky collection of Finnish and foreign modern works; take bus #16 from the centre.

Tampere's **tourist office** is by the river, 500m from the **train station** at Verkatehtaankatu 2 (Mon–Fri 9am–4/5/8pm; June–Sept also Sat & Sun 10am–5pm; ☎03/3146 6800, ⊛www.tampere.fi), and a similar distance along Hatanpään from the **bus station**. Central, moderately priced **hotels** include the *Victoria*, Itsenäisyydenkatu 1 (☎03/242 5111; ❼), and *Sokos Hotel Villa*, Sumeliuksenkatu 14 (☎020/1234 633; ❻). There are various **hostels**, the best being the *Uimahallin maja*, an HI hostel centrally located at Pirkankatu 10–12 (☎03/222 9460; €27); and the *NNKY* opposite the cathedral at Tuomiokirkonkatu 12a (☎03/254 4020; June–Aug; €22). The nearest **campsite** is *Härmälä*, 5km south (☎03/265 1355; mid-May to late Aug; bus #1), which also has cabins (❸).

The cheapest places to eat are the **student mensas** at the university at the end of Yliopistonkatu; the usual pizza joints such as *Paprilla* on the second floor of the *Hostel Uimahallin Maja*, Pirkankatu 10–12; and, for relaxed posing, *Café Strindberg*, opposite the train station. For a local speciality, try *mustamakkara*, a type of black sausage, at the Laukontori open-air **market** by the rapids. For **drinking**, the busiest and trendiest place is *Cafe Europa* at Aleksanterinkatu 29, which, despite its name, is more bar than café. Also worth a look is *Plevna*, a German-style beer hall in Finlayson's converted factory at Itäinenkatu 8, which is especially busy at weekends; for live music, head for *Tullikammari*, a **nightclub** in an old customs house on Itsenäisyydenkatu behind the train station.

# Savonlinna and around

**SAVONLINNA** is one of the most relaxed towns in Finland, a woodworking centre that also makes a decent living from tourism and its renowned **opera festival** (☎015/476 750, ⊛www.operafestival.fi) in July. It's packed throughout summer, so book well ahead if you're visiting at this time. Out of peak season, its streets and beaches are uncluttered, and the town's easy-going mood makes it a pleasant place to linger. The best locations for soaking up the atmosphere are the **harbour** and **market square** at the end of Olavinkatu, where you can cast an eye over the grand *Seurahuone Hotel*, with its Art Nouveau fripperies. Follow the harbour around Linnankatu, or better still around the sandy edge of Pihlajavesi, which brings you to atmospheric and surprisingly well-preserved **Olavinlinna Castle** (guided tours daily 10am–3/5pm; €5), perched on a small island. Founded in 1475, the castle witnessed a series of bloody conflicts until the Russians claimed possession of it in 1743 and relegated it to the status of town jail. Nearby is the **Savonlinna Regional Museum** in Riihisaari (July to August daily 11am–5pm; rest of the year closed Mon; €4), which occupies an old granary and displays an intriguing account of the evolution of local life, with rock paintings and ancient amber carved with human figures.

There are two **train stations**: be sure to get off at Savonlinna-Kauppatori, just across the main bridge from the **tourist office**, Puistokatu 1 (June & Aug daily 9am–5pm, 8am–10pm during July; Sept–May Mon–Fri 9am–5pm; ☎015/517 510, ⊛www.savonlinnatravel.com). The **bus station** is off the main island, but within easy walking distance of the town centre. **Bikes** can be rented at several places on Olavinkatu, including at Koponen, no. 19–21 (☎015/533 977); for **canoes** and **rowing boats** try Saimaan Vuokravenko at Kivrunkatu 15 (☎015/273 101). For information and tickets for the **festival** visit the opera office, Olavinkatu 27. The most central **accommodation** is at the *Perehotelli Hospitz*, Linnankatu 20 (☎015/515 661; ❻). Another good choice (June–Aug only), *Malakias*, Pihlajavedenkatu 6 (☎015/533 283; ❻), is 2km west of the centre along Tulliportinkatu and then Savontie. The best-value place in town is the summer hotel (June–Aug) *Vuorilinna*, on Kasinosaari (☎015/739 5494; ❺), five minutes over the bridge from the marketplace. The nearest **campsite** is 7km from the centre at Vuohimäki (☎015/537 353; June–Aug; bus #4). Good, cheap **food** is available at the pizza joints along Olavinkatu and Tulliportinkatu. *Majakka*, Satamakatu 11, offers good Finnish nosh at lunchtime.

## Around Savonlinna

Savonlinna boasts beautiful scenery all around, and the place to sample it is **Punkaharju Ridge**, a narrow strip of land between the Puruvesi and Pihlajavesi lakes, 28km from town. Locals say it has the healthiest air in the world, super-oxygenated by abundant conifers. This is the Lake Region at its most breathtakingly beautiful. The ridge is traversable by road and rail, both running into the town of Punkaharju and passing the incredible **Retretti Arts Centre** (June–Aug daily 10am–5pm/6pm; €15), set in caves and with a large sculpture park. Trains and buses make the short journey between Savonlinna and Retretti.

# Northern Finland

The northern regions take up a vast portion of Finland: one third of the country lies north of the Arctic Circle. It's sparsely populated, with small communities often separated by long distances. The coast of **Ostrobothnia** is affluent due to the adjacent flat and fertile farmland; busy and expanding **Oulu** is the region's major city as well as a centre of high-tech expertise, though it maintains a pleasing small-town atmosphere. Further north, **Lapland** is a remote and wild territory whose wide open spaces are home to several thousand Saami, who have lived in harmony with this harsh environment for millennia. Here, the long winters are eerily dark, while summer days are long and bright with the midnight sun. There is an extensive bus service and regular flights from Helsinki. Make sure you try Lappish cuisine, too – fresh cloudberries, smoked reindeer and wild salmon are highlights. **Rovaniemi** is the rather bland gateway to the Arctic North; from here a road leads north towards **Inari** and on to Norway.

## Oulu

**OULU**, with its renowned university, is a leading light in Finland's burgeoning computing and microchip industries. During the nineteenth century it was the centre of the world's tar industry and the city's affluence and vibrant cultural scene date from that time. In the centre of town on Kirkkokatu, the **City Hall** retains some of the grandeur of the late nineteenth century when it was a luxury hotel, and you can peek in at the wall paintings and enclosed gardens. Further along Kirkkokatu, the copper-domed and stuccoed **Tuomiokirkko** (daily: June–Aug 11am–8/9pm; Sept–May Mon–Fri noon–1pm) seems anachronistic amid the bulky blocks of modern Oulu. Across the small canal just to the north, the **North Ostrobothnia Museum** (daily 10/11am–6/7pm; closed Mon; €3) has a large regional collection with a good Saami section.

The connected **train and bus stations** are linked to the city centre by several parallel streets feeding down to the *kauppatori* and *kauppahalli* (**markets**) by the water beyond. The **tourist office** is at Torikatu 10 (Mon–Fri 9am–4pm; mid-June to Aug until 6pm also Sat & Sun 10am–3pm; ☎08/5584 1330, ⓦwww.oulutourism.fi). For **Internet** connections, head for the library at Kaarenväylä 3. Low-cost **accommodation** in the centre is available at the *Hotel Turisti* (☎08/563 6100; ⑤), opposite the train station at Rautatienkatu 9, which provides good-value accommodation during summer. Alternatively *Hotel Oppimestari* (☎08/8848 527; ④) at Nahkatehtaankatu 3 offers more no-nonsense hostel-style rooms. There's a **campsite** (☎08/5586 1350) with cabins on Hietasaari Island, 4km from town; take bus #17 from Isokatu in the town centre. Oulu boasts some charming **cafés** including *Sokeri Jussi* in an old salt warehouse on Pikisaari just over the bridge from Kauppatori square, while *Katri Antell* on Rotuaari (Mon–Fri 8am–6pm, Sat 9am–3pm) is justly famed for its luscious cakes. Cheapest **meals** are at the pizzerias – *Fantasia,* Isokatu 30, serves the best (buffet €8) and also has a selection of Finnish dishes; *Oskarin Kellari*, opposite the train station, serves a stuff-your-face lunch buffet for about €7.50. For **nightlife** the busiest pubs are *Jumpru*, Kappurienkatu 6, and *Graali* at Saaristonkatu 5, both generally stuffed with the city's young and trendy.

## Rovaniemi

Easily reached by train, **ROVANIEMI** is touted as the capital of Lapland, though its administrative buildings and busy shopping streets are a far cry from the surrounding rural hinterland. The elegant wooden houses of old Rovaniemi were razed by departing Nazis at the close of World War II, and the town was completely rebuilt during the late 1940s. Aside from eating reindeer in the local restaurants, the best way to prepare yourself for what lies further north is to visit the 172m-long glass tunnel of **Arktikum**, Pohjoisranta 4 (daily 9/10am–5/7pm; Sept to mid–May closed Mon; €11; ⓦwww.arktikum.fi). Subterranean galleries along one side house the **Provincial Museum of Lapland** with genuine Saami crafts and costumes alongside the imitations sold in souvenir shops to emphasize the romanticization of their culture. Across the corridor is the **Arctic Centre**, which gives a thorough treatment of all things circumpolar. For a couple of weeks either side of midsummer, the **midnight sun** is visible from Rovaniemi, the best vantage points being either the striking bridge over the Ounaskoski or atop the forested and mosquito-infested hill, Ounasvaara, across the bridge. The remaining sight is on the south side of town near the bus and train stations, where pristine Aalto-designed civic buildings line Hallituskatu. The city **library** (Mon–Thurs 11am–8pm, Fri 11am–5pm, Sat 11am–4pm) has a Lapland Department with a staggering hoard of books in many languages covering every Saami-related subject. Most other things of interest are outside town, not least the **Arctic Circle**, 8km north and connected by the hourly bus #8 from the railway station (€5.20 return). On the circle is the **Santa Claus Village** (daily 9/10am–5/7pm; free), a large log cabin where you can meet Father Christmas all year round and leave your name for a Christmas card from Santa himself.

The **tourist office** is at Rovakatu 21 (Mon–Fri 8am–5pm; June–Aug also Sat & Sun 10am–4pm; ☎016/346 270, ⓦwww.rovaniemi.fi). Rovaniemi's new **youth hostel** (June–Aug €23, Sept–May €34) is at Koskikatu 41, a 10-minute walk from the centre at the junction of Koskikatu and Tukkipojantie. Check-in and reservations though are made at *Quality Hotel Santa Claus*, Korkalonkatu 29 (☎016/321 321). Otherwise you can fall back on the **guest houses**, the best of which are within five minutes' walk of the train station: *Matka Borealis* is nearest at Asemieskatu 1 (☎016/342 0130; ⑤), whilst *Matka Outa*, Ukkoherrantie 16 (☎016/312 474; ④), is towards the town centre. The only other budget accommodation is the **campsite** (☎016/345 304; June–Aug) on the far bank of Ounaskoski, facing town, a thirty-minute walk from the station. For filling **food** at very reasonable prices try the buffet (€7.99) at *Rax*, Koskikatu 11, or *Martina*, also Koskikatu 11, for good value pizzas and pasta dishes. The liveliest bars are *Zoomit*, Korkalonkatu 29, and *Hemingways*, once again, Koskikatu 11.

# Inari

A half-day bus ride north of Rovaniemi, **INARI** lies along the fringes of Inarijärvi, one of Finland's largest lakes, and makes an attractive base from which to further explore this part of Lapland. The **bus** stops outside the **tourist office** (Mon–Fri 9/10am–4/7pm; June–Sept also Sat & Sun 10am–3pm; ☎016/661 666, ⓦwww .inarilapland.org), on the main street, Inarintie, before continuing to Karasjok in Norway and – from June to late August only – the North Cape. Staff here have information on guided snow-scooter trips in winter and fishing trips around the lake in summer. Close by is the excellent "Siida", the **Saami Museum** (daily 9/10am–5/8pm; Oct–May closed Mon; €8). An outstanding outdoor section gives you an idea of how the Saami survived in Arctic conditions in their tepees, or *kota*, while the indoor section has a well-laid-out exhibition on all aspects of life in the Arctic. Towards the northern end of the village, summer boat tours (€12) depart from under the bridge to the ancient Saami holy site on the island of **Ukonkivi**; a plaque marks an ancient site of worship rumoured to have been a place of sacrifice. If walking's your thing then check out the pretty **Pielpajärvi Wilderness Church**, a two-hour well-signposted 7km hike from the village. There was a church on this site as far back as 1646, though the present one dates from 1754.

**Accommodation** should not be too problematic, though Inari does get very busy during the summer. The *Inarin Kultahovi* (☎016/671 221; ✆inarin .kultahovi@co.inet.fi; ⓞ) at Saarikoskentie 2 is a basic hotel with a decent **restaurant**. The *Uruniemi* **campsite** (☎016/671 331, ✆pentti.kangasniemi@uruniemi .inet.fi; Oct–April advanced booking obligatory) is about 3km south of the village in a lovely location right by the lake.

# Travel details

## Trains

**Helsinki** to: Oulu (8 daily; 7hr); Rovaniemi (5 daily; 9hr 45min); Tampere (hourly; 2hr); Turku (12 daily; 2hr).
**Oulu** to: Rovaniemi (5 daily; 3hr).
**Rovaniemi** to: Helsinki (5 daily; 9hr 45min); Oulu (5 daily; 3hr).
**Savonlinna** to: Parikkala for Helsinki (2 daily; 50min).
**Tampere** to: Helsinki (hourly; 2hr); Oulu (7 daily; 5hr); Savonlinna (2 daily; 5hr); Turku (8 daily; 2hr).
**Turku** to: Tampere (8 daily; 2hr).

## Buses

**Helsinki** to: Porvoo (15 daily; 1hr).

**Inari** to: North Cape (June to late Aug 1 daily; 5hr 30min); Rovaniemi (4 daily; 5hr 30min).
**Rovaniemi** to: Inari (4 daily; 5hr 30min); North Cape (June to late Aug 1 daily; 10hr 30min).

## Flights

**Helsinki** to: Ivalo for Inari (2–3 daily; 1hr 40min); Oulu (10–15 daily; 1hr); Rovaniemi (5–7 daily; 1hr 20min).

## Ferries

**Helsinki** to: Rostock, Germany (June to early Sept 3 weekly; 24hr); Stockholm, Sweden (2 daily; 17hr); Tallinn, Estonia (15–25 daily; 1hr 40min–4hr).
**Turku** to: Stockholm (4 daily; 10–11hr).

# France

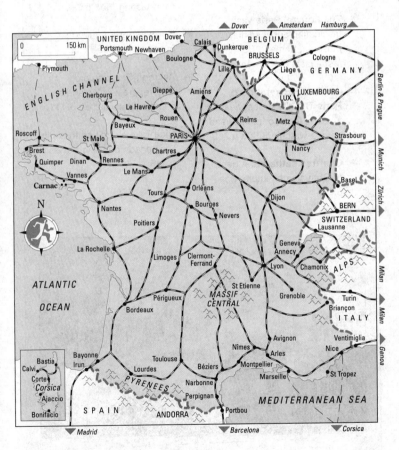

# France highlights

✳ **Food and wine** Pamper your tastebuds – from humble coffee-and-croissant breakfasts to the highest of *haute cuisine*, via 265 kinds of cheese. See p.357

✳ **The Louvre, Paris** Vast, fascinating and inspiring museum, home to Da Vinci's *Mona Lisa*. See p.364

✳ **Jardin du Luxembourg, Paris** The city's most beautiful park, ideal for picnics and people-watching. See p.369

✳ **Chartres cathedral** A gem of Gothic architecture. See p.375

✳ **Reims** The heart of the Champagne region. See p.377

✳ **The Loire Valley** Studded with châteaux, a fine area for wine-tasting. See p.385

✳ **Carcassonne** A fairy-tale medieval city. See p.397

✳ **Avignon** Stunning architecture, great cafés and a summer festival. See p.411

✳ **Nice** Take a stroll on the chic Promenade des Anglais. See p.418

△ Chenonceaux, Loire Valley

# Introduction and basics

**France** is a core country on any European tour and it would be hard to exhaust its diversity in a lifetime of visits. Each area looks different, feels different, has its own style of architecture and cuisine and often its own *patois* or dialect too.

If you arrive from the north, you may pass through the Channel ports or **Normandy**, with its considerable allure, to **Paris**, one of Europe's most elegant and compelling capitals. To the west lie the rocky coasts of **Brittany** and, just south, the grand **Loire** valley, though most people push on further south to the limestone hills of **Provence**, the canyons of the **Pyrenees** mountains on the Spanish border, or the glamorous Riviera coastline of the **Côte d'Azur**. There are good reasons, however, for taking things more slowly, not least the Germanic towns of **Alsace** in the east, the gorgeous hills and valleys of the **Lot** and the **Dordogne**, and, more adventurously, the high and rugged heartland of the **Massif Central**.

## Information & maps

Most towns and villages have a Syndicat d'Initiative (SI) or Office de Tourisme, giving out local **information** and free maps. Some can book accommodation anywhere in France, and most can find you a local room for the night. In larger cities and resorts offices will be open all day, every day, during high season, though in winter the hours are generally reduced. The best **map** is the red Michelin no. 721/989 (1:1,000,000); the Michelin yellow series (scale 1:200,000) is better for regional detail. If you're planning to walk or cycle, check out the IGN green (1:100,000 and 1:50,000) and blue (1:25,000) maps.

## Money and banks

Currency is the **euro** (€). Standard **banking hours** are Mon–Fri 9am–noon & 2–4.30pm; some also open on Saturday. The Banque Nationale de Paris often gives the best rates and the lowest commissions. **Exchange** counters – at the train stations in all big cities and usually a few in the town centre as well – have longer opening hours, though these normally offer a much worse deal. You can also change money at post offices and some tourist offices, and draw cash direct from ever-present **ATMs**. Credit cards are generally accepted by shops and most restaurants and hotels.

## Communications

**Post offices** (*la Poste*) are generally open Mon–Fri 8.30am–6.30pm, Sat 8.30am–noon. **Stamps** (*timbres*) are also sold in *tabacs* (tobacconist shops). International **phone calls** can be made from any box (*cabine*), using phonecards (*télécartes*), available from post offices, *tabacs* and train station ticket counters. For calls within France – local or long-distance – you must dial all ten digits. Directory enquiries is ☎12. To call Monaco, prefix the eight-digit number with ☎00377. Cybercafés offering **Internet access** are everywhere, charging around €4/hr.

---

## France on the net

- ⓦ **www.tourisme.fr** French Tourist Board.
- ⓦ **www.franceguide.com** Excellent resource, with links to many tourist offices.
- ⓦ **www.discoverfrance.net** Useful tourist information, with links to other sites.
- ⓦ **www.viafrance.com** Information on festivals, expos, events and concerts.
- ⓦ **www.parissi.com** Up-to-date tips for Paris by night (in French).

# Getting around

France has the most extensive **rail** network in Western Europe, run by SNCF (ⓦ www .sncf.com). The only areas not well served are the mountains, where rail routes are replaced by SNCF buses. Private bus services tend to be uncoordinated.

Fares are reasonable. InterRail, Eurail and EuroDomino passes are valid, though high-speed TGVs (*Trains à Grande Vitesse*) require compulsory reservations (€5), plus a supplement at peak times. All tickets (not passes) must be stamped in the orange machines in the foyer of the train station (*gare SNCF*) on penalty of a steep fine. Rail journeys may be broken any time, anywhere, for up to 24hr. All but the smallest stations have an information desk and most have *consignes automatiques* – coin-operated left-luggage lockers.

*Autocar* on a timetable column means it's an **SNCF bus service**, on which rail tickets and passes are valid. Apart from these, the only time you'll need to take a bus is in cities. Buses rarely serve regions outside the SNCF network.

**Cyclists** are much admired. Traffic keeps at a respectful distance (except in the big cities) and restaurants and hotels go out of their way to find a safe place for your bike. Bikes go free on some SNCF trains, though

| French | | |
|---|---|---|
| | **French** | **Pronunciation** |
| **Yes** | *Oui* | Whee |
| **No** | *Non* | No(n) |
| **Please** | *S'il vous plaît* | Seel voo play |
| **Thank you** | *Merci* | Mersee |
| **Hello/Good day** | *Bonjour* | Bo(n)joor |
| **Goodbye** | *Au revoir/à bientôt* | Orvoir/abyantoe |
| **Excuse me** | *Pardon* | pardo(n) |
| **Where?** | *Où?* | Oo |
| **Good** | *Bon* | Bo(n) |
| **Bad** | *Mauvais* | Movay |
| **Near** | *Près* | Pray |
| **Far** | *Loin* | Lowa(n) |
| **Cheap** | *Bon marché* | Bo(n) marchay |
| **Expensive** | *Cher* | Share |
| **Open** | *Ouvert* | Oovair |
| **Closed** | *Fermé* | Fermay |
| **Today** | *Aujourd'hui* | Ojoordwee |
| **Yesterday** | *Hier* | Eeyeah |
| **Tomorrow** | *Demain* | Duhma(n) |
| **How much?** | *Combien?* | combyen |
| **What time is it?** | *Quelle heure est-il?* | Kel ur et eel |
| **I don't understand** | *Je ne comprends pas* | Je nuh compron pah |
| **Do you speak English?** | *Parlez-vous anglais?* | Parlay voo onglay |
| **One** | *Un* | Uh(n) |
| **Two** | *Deux* | Duh |
| **Three** | *Trois* | Twoi |
| **Four** | *Quatre* | Kattre |
| **Five** | *Cinq* | Sank |
| **Six** | *Six* | Seess |
| **Seven** | *Sept* | Set |
| **Eight** | *Huit* | Wheat |
| **Nine** | *Neuf* | Nurf |
| **Ten** | *Dix* | Deess |

the standard charge is €10. Some SNCF stations and tourist offices also rent bikes for around €10–15 per day.

# Accommodation

Outside high season it's generally possible to turn up in any town and find **accommodation**. However, booking in advance is essential from mid-July to end-Aug.

All **hotels** are officially graded, and prices are relatively uniform. Nearly all post their tariffs inside the entrance. Ungraded and single-star hotels cost €20–30 per double room, two-stars €30–55; breakfast is usually extra. Increasingly common, especially in rural areas, are **chambres d'hôtes** – B&B in a house or on a farm. These vary in standard and usually cost the equivalent of a two-star hotel. Full lists of accommodation for each province are available from any tourist office. It's worth getting hold of these, together with a handbook for the **Logis de France** – recommended, independent hotels (⊛ www .logis-de-france.fr).

There's a wide range of official **hostels** (*auberges de jeunesse*), and most are of a high standard. However, at €8–17 for a dorm bed (more in Paris), they are sometimes no less expensive than the cheapest hotel room. There are two national associations: Federation of Youth Hostels (⊛ www .fuaj.org) and French Hostels League (⊛ www.auberges-de-jeunesse.com) as well as several other unofficial ones. HI membership covers all official hostels, though only hostels of the FUAJ are detailed in the HI handbook. A few large towns provide more luxurious hostel accommodation in **Foyers des Jeunes Travailleurs/-euses**, residential hostels for young workers and students, charging around €15 for a room. Most have a good, inexpensive canteen. In rural areas, **gîtes d'étape** provide bunkbeds and simple kitchen facilities: they are listed, along with mountain refuges, on ⊛ www .gites-refuge.com.

**Campsites** are ubiquitous. The cheapest – starting at €5 per person per night – is usually the *Camping Municipal*, generally clean, well-equipped and in a prime location. Ask tourist offices for lists of sites or consult ⊛ www.campingfrance.com. **Rough camping** (*camping sauvage*) is also a possibility but be sure to ask permission from the landowner first.

# Food and drink

**Food** in France is art. Eating out isn't particularly cheap, but as long as you avoid tourist hotspots, you should be able to get decent *plats du jour* with wine for less than €15.

Generally the best place to eat **breakfast** is in a bar or café. Most serve *tartines* (*baguette* – French bread – with butter) and croissants. **Coffee** is invariably black and strong. *Un café* or *un express* is black; *un crème* is with milk; *un grand café* is a large cup; *un café au lait/un grand crème* is a large cup with plenty of hot milk. **Tea** (*thé*) is less popular, though most cafés and restaurants serve it. Hot chocolate (*chocolat chaud*) is also widely available.

Cafés are often the best option for a light **lunch**, serving omelettes, sandwiches (generally half-baguettes filled with cheese or meat), and *croques-monsieur* and *-madame* (variations on a toasted ham or cheese sandwich). On street stalls you'll also find *frites* (chips/french fries), *crêpes*, *galettes* (wholewheat pancakes) and *gaufres* (waffles). For **picnics**, nothing can beat the salads and ready-made main courses from a *charcuterie* (delicatessen), also available at supermarkets.

You can also eat lunch at a **brasserie** – like a restaurant, but open all day and geared to quicker meals. **Restaurants** tend to stick to the traditional meal times of noon–2pm & 7–9/9.30pm. City-centre brasseries often serve until 11pm or midnight. Prices at both are posted outside. Look out at lunchtime and in the evening for the **plat du jour** (daily special), which for as little as €10–15 will often be the most interesting and best-value item on the menu. *Service compris* means **service** is included. Wine or a drink may be included in a *menu fixe*, but when ordering your own wine ask for *un quart*, *un demi-litre* or *une carafe* (a litre) – it'll be house wine unless you specify otherwise.

## Drink

Where you can eat you can usually drink,

and vice versa. **Drinking** is done most often at a café and at a leisurely pace, whether taken as an *apéritif* before eating, a *digestif* after eating, or as a meal's accompaniment. **Wine** (*vin*) is drunk at just about every meal or social occasion. *Vin de table* or *vin ordinaire* (table wine) is cheap and generally drinkable but serious wines command serious prices. In a café, a glass of wine is simply *un rouge* (red) or *un blanc* (white). If you select an AOC (Appellation d'Origine Contrôlée) wine you may have the choice of a round glass (*un ballon*) or a smaller glass (*un verre*). A popular aperitif is *kir*, white wine with crème de cassis (blackcurrant liqueur).

Most of the **beers** you'll find are the familiar Belgian and German names, plus home-grown brands. Beer on tap (*à la pression*) is France's cheapest alcoholic drink, alongside wine – just ask for *une pression*. Stronger alcohol is drunk by some folk from 5am as a pre-work fortifier, right through the day: **cognac** or **armagnac** brandies, dozens of *eaux-de-vie* (spirits distilled from fruit) and liqueurs. Measures are generous, but don't come cheap. **Pastis** is a refreshing and inexpensive aniseed-flavoured liquor, drunk diluted with water and ice (*glaçons*).

# Opening hours and holidays

Basic **working hours** are 9am–noon/1pm & 2/3–6.30/7.30pm. Sun and/or Mon are the standard **closing days**, though you'll always find at least one *boulangerie* (bakery)

open. **Museums** open at around 9/10am and close 5/6pm, with reduced hours outside the mid-May to mid-Sept season, sometimes even outside July and Aug; they also tend to shut on Mon or Tues. All shops, museums and offices are closed on the following **national holidays**: Jan 1, Easter Sun & Mon, Ascension Day, Pentecost, May 1, May 8, July 14, Aug 15, Nov 1, Nov 11, Dec 25.

# Emergencies

There are two main types of **police**, the Police Nationale and the Gendarmerie Nationale. You can report a theft, or other incident, to either. You can be stopped at any time and asked to produce ID, so always carry your passport. Every **hospital** visit, doctor's consultation and prescribed medicine is charged. To find a **doctor**, stop at any *pharmacie* and ask for an address. Consultation fees for a visit should be €20–25 and in any case you'll be given a *Feuille de Soins* (Statement of Treatment) for your insurance claims. Prescriptions should be taken to a *pharmacie*, which is also equipped – and obliged – to give first aid (for a fee), and all towns and cities have a 24-hour pharmacy on-call. For minor illnesses **pharmacists** will dispense free advice and a wide range of medication.

# Paris

PARIS is the paragon of style and arguably the most captivating city in Europe. It's an artistic, intellectual and sartorial pacesetter, and yet at the same time a deeply traditional and village-like metropolis. Neighbourhood shops stand alongside famous fashion boutiques, and old-fashioned cafés next to trendy nightspots.

Even the city's history is glamorous, a long tale of extravagant monarchs and world-shaking revolutions. From a shaky start, the kings of France gradually extended their control from Paris over their feudal rivals, centralizing administrative, legal, financial and political power as they did so. The supremely autocratic Louis XIV made the city into a glorious symbol of the pre-eminence of the state, a tradition his successors have been happy to follow. Napoleon I added to the Louvre and built the Arc de Triomphe, the Madeleine and the Arc du Carrousel, while Napoleon III had Baron Haussmann redraw the city centre. The habit of breaking architectural moulds has continued with the Pompidou Centre's luridly coloured tubing, the landmark steel-and-glass Louvre Pyramid and the enormous hollow cube of the Grande Arche de la Défense.

The most tangible pleasures of Paris are to be found in its **street life** and along the lively banks of the River Seine. Few cities can compete with the cafés, bars and restaurants – trendy and traditional, local and cosmopolitan, humble and pretentious – that line every street and boulevard. And the city's compact size makes it possible to experience the individual feel of the different *quartiers*. You can move easily, even on foot, from the calm, almost small-town atmosphere of **Montmartre** and the **Latin Quarter** to the busy commercial centres of the **Bourse** and **Opéra** or the relaxed chic of the **Marais**. An imposing backdrop is provided by the monumental architecture of the **Arc de Triomphe**, the **Louvre** and the **Eiffel Tower**, and by the endless parade of bridges over the river. As for entertainment, Paris is a world **cinema** capital and has a **club** scene renowned across Europe, incorporating the continent's most vibrant African music scene.

Paris is divided into twenty postal districts, known as **arrondissements**, which are used by everyone to locate addresses. The first, or *premier* (abbreviated as 1$^{er}$), is centred on the Louvre, with the rest (abbreviated as 2$^e$, 3$^e$, 4$^e$) spiralling outwards in a clockwise direction. The inner hub of the city, where most of the major sights and museums are located, is covered by the first six *arrondissements*.

## Arrival and information

Paris has two main **airports**: Roissy-Charles de Gaulle and Orly. A much smaller one, Beauvais, is used primarily by the discount airlines Ryanair and Wizzair. **Charles de Gaulle** (CDG) is 23km northeast and connected to the Gare du Nord train station by Roissyrail, on the RER train line B (every 15min, 5am–midnight; 30min; €7.85). You can pick it up direct from terminals CDG2 and 3, but from CDG1 you have to take the free shuttle bus to the station. There's also the Roissybus, which departs from both CDG1 and CDG2 and terminates at M° Opéra (every 15min, 5.45am–11pm; 45min; €8), or two Air France bus lines, which depart from all terminals to M° Charles-de-Gaulle-Étoile (every 15min, 5.45am–11pm; €12), or to Gare de Lyon and Gare Montparnasse (every 30min, 7am–9pm; €12). **Orly** (ORY), 14km south of Paris, has two bus–rail links: Orly-Rail, a shuttle bus then RER line C to the Gare d'Austerlitz and other Left Bank stops (every 15–30min, 5.50am–10.50pm; 35min; €5.25); and Orlyval, a fast train shuttle link to RER line B station Antony then connection to M° Denfert-Rochereau, St-Michel and Châtelet (every 4–8min, 6am–11pm; 35min; €8.85). Air France buses go to the Gare des Invalides via Montparnasse (every 15min, 6am–11.40pm; 35min; €8), Orlybus goes to M° Denfert-Rochereau (every 15min, 6am–11.30pm; 30min; €5.50) and Jetbus (every 15min; 6.15am–10.15pm,

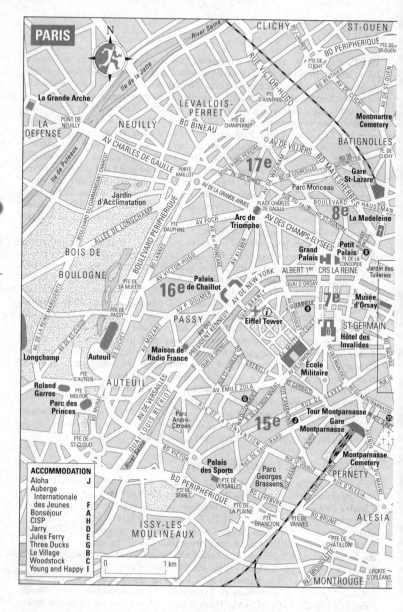

**PARIS**

Accommodation

| ACCOMMODATION | |
|---|---|
| Aloha | **J** |
| Auberge | |
| Internationale | |
| des Jeunes | **F** |
| Bonséjour | **A** |
| CISP | **H** |
| Jarry | **D** |
| Jules Ferry | **E** |
| Three Ducks | **G** |
| Le Village | **B** |
| Woodstock | **C** |
| Young and Happy | **I** |

15min; €5.15) goes to Mº Villejuif-Louis Aragon at the end of line 7. If you call 48 hours in advance, you can book Blue Vans' door-to-door **minibus** service from either airport (€14.50 per head if there are two or more people, €22 for a single person; 6am–7.30pm; ☎01.30.11.13.00, ⊛www.bluvan.fr).

Paris has six mainline **train** stations, all served by the métro. You can buy national and international tickets at any of them. Eurostar trains from London, as

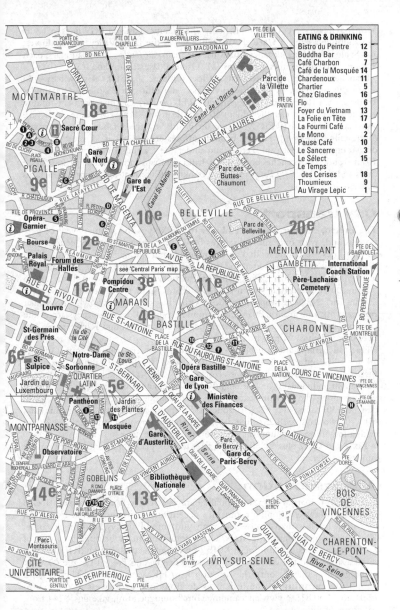

well as trains from northern France, Belgium, the Netherlands, northern Germany and Scandinavia, arrive at the **Gare du Nord**; Eurostar has its own booking offices at one side of the station. The **Gare de l'Est** serves eastern France, Luxembourg, southern Germany, northern Switzerland, Austria and eastern Europe; **Gare St-Lazare** serves the Normandy coast; **Gare de Lyon** serves the south, the Alps, western Switzerland, Italy, Greece and TGV lines to southeast France; **Gare**

**Montparnasse** serves Chartres, Brittany, the Atlantic coast and TGV lines to Tours and southwest France; **Gare d'Austerlitz** serves the Loire Valley, the southwest and Spain. Most long-distance **buses** use the main *gare routière* (International Coach Station) at Bagnolet in eastern Paris (Mº Gallieni, last stop on line #3).

Branches of the Paris **tourist office** (℡08.92.68.30.00, ⊛www.paris-info .com) can be found all over the city. The main office, at 25 rue des Pyramides 1ᵉʳ (Mon–Sat 10am–7pm; Mº Pyramides/RER Auber), can help with last-minute accommodation, as can the offices at Gare de Lyon (RER/Mº Gare de Lyon), and Gare du Nord (RER/Mº Gare du Nord), by the Grandes Lignes arrivals (both daily 8am–6pm). Further **branch offices** are located at 11 rue Scribe, 9ᵉ, on Montmartre's place du Tertre, and under the Carrousel du Louvre (all daily 10am–7pm). The branches book hotels, hand out maps and sell travel passes, phone cards and the *Paris City Passport* (€5), a booklet of discounts on various attractions and activities.

## City transport

The **métro,** or métropolitain (abbreviated as Mº) is the simplest way of getting around, with only short distances between stations in the city centre. The various lines are colour-coded and numbered, and the name of the train's final destination is always signposted to let you know its direction. The métro operates from 5.30am to 12.30am, after which **night buses** *(Noctambus)* run from 1am to 5.30am on eighteen routes from place du Châtelet near the Hôtel de Ville (every 30min–1hr). Nightbus stops are marked with a black and yellow owl. The regular **bus** network runs from 6.30am until around 8.30pm. Longer journeys across the city, or out to the suburbs, are best made on the underground **RER** express rail network, which overlaps with the métro.

Free route **maps** are available at métro stations, bus terminals and tourist offices; ask for a "Grand Plan de Paris". Flat-fare **tickets** (€1.40) are valid on buses, the métro and, within the city limits (zones 1–2), the RER rail lines; tickets can be bought individually or, for slightly less, in **carnets** of ten (€10.50). If you plan on using the network extensively, then consider buying a one-day *Mobilis* pass (€5.30/zones 1–2, €12.10/zones 1–5) or the *Paris Visites* (€8.35/one day, €13.70/two days, €18.25/three days, €26.65/five days), valid for zones 1–3 and with a few minor discounts on admission to monuments.

**Taxis** start at €2 plus €0.60 per km; fares to most places in the city centre usually run well under €10.

## Accommodation

Compared to many European capitals, Paris is a relatively inexpensive place to spend the night – a double room in a decent and centrally located **hotel** can be found for less than €40 – although you should always book in advance. There are also numerous **hostels**, either independent or belonging to one of four organizations: the unofficial MIJE (⊛www.mije.com) and UCRIF (⊛www .ucrif.asso.fr), and the official FUAJ (⊛www.fuaj.fr) and French League (⊛www .auberges-de-jeunesse.com), the latter open to HI members only. There's good Seine-side **camping** in the lush Bois de Boulogne park, west of the centre (℡01.45.24.30.81; ⊛www.abccamping.com/boulogne.htm); take bus #244 from Mº Porte Maillot.

### Hostels

**Aloha** 1 rue Borromᵉ, 15ᵉ ℡01.42.73.03.03, ⊛www.aloha.fr. Popular, young and noisy independent hostel with its own bar serving cheap beer. Popular with Americans. Mº Volontaires. Dorms €22, doubles ❹

**Auberge Internationale des Jeunes** 10 rue Trousseau, 11ᵉ ℡01.47.00.62.00, ⊛www.aijparis.com. Laid-back but noisy independent in a great location, 5min from the Bastille. Mº Ledru-Rollin. €15–17.
**BVJ Paris Quartier Latin** 44 rue des Bernardins, 5ᵉ ℡01.43.29.34.80, ⊛www.bvjhotel.com.

Central, efficient and slightly institutional UCRIF hostel. M° Maubert-Mutualité. Dorms €26, doubles **④**

**CISP** 6 av Maurice Ravel, 12ᵉ ☏01.44.75.60.00, ⦿www.cisp.asso.fr. Large dorm-style rooms in a good location for barhopping. Also runs a second hostel at 17 bd Kellermann, 13ᵉ ☏01.44.16.37.38 (M° Porte d'Italie). M° Porte Vincennes. Dorms €18, doubles **④**

**Jules Ferry** 8 bd Jules-Ferry, 11ᵉ ☏01.43.57.55.60, ⦿www.fuaj.org. The smaller and more central of the two FUAJ hostels, in a lively area alongside the Canal St-Martin. Get there early – it fills up fast. M° République. €20.

**Le Fauconnier** 11 rue du Fauconnier, 4ᵉ ☏01.42.74.23.45. MIJE hostel in a superbly renovated seventeenth-century mansion with a courtyard. Breakfast included. M° St-Paul. Dorms €27, doubles **⑤**

**Le Fourcy** 6 rue de Fourcy, 4ᵉ ☏01.42.74.23.45, ⦿www.mije.com. MIJE hostel in a beautiful mansion with small, four- to eight-bed dorms. Breakfast included and restaurant on site. M° St-Paul. Dorms €27, doubles **⑤**

**Le Village** 20 rue d'Orsel, 18ᵉ ☏01.42.64.22.02, ⦿www.villagehostel.fr. Attractive new independent hostel with good facilities and a terrace with a Sacré-Coeur view. The generally older clientele don't seem to mind the 2am curfew. M° Anvers. Dorms €23, doubles **④**

**Maubuisson** 12 rue des Barres, 4ᵉ ☏01.42.74.23.45, ⦿www.mije.com. Central MIJE hostel in a magnificent medieval building on a quiet street. Breakfast included. M° Pont-Marie. Dorms €27, doubles **⑤**

**Three Ducks** 6 place Étienne-Pernet, 15ᵉ ☏01.48.42.04.05, ⦿www.3ducks.fr. Lively, independent hostel with bar, beer and use of kitchen. Book ahead May–Oct. M° Félix Faure. Dorms €23, doubles **④**

**Woodstock** 48 rue Rodier, 9ᵉ ☏01.48.78.87.76, ⦿www.woodstock.fr. Fiercely independent place in the heart of Montmartre, with friendly staff, cheap bar and courtyard, though less of a party atmosphere than others. 2am curfew. M° Anvers. Dorms €21, doubles **④**

**Young and Happy** 80 rue Mouffetard, 5ᵉ ☏01.45.35.09.53, ⦿www.youngandhappy.fr. Rowdy, student place right on the Latin Quarter

party strip, though beware the strict 2am curfew. M° Monge/Censier-Daubenton. Dorms €22, doubles **④**

## Hotels

**Bonséjour** 11 rue Burq, 18ᵉ ☏01.42.54.22.53, ⓟ01.42.54.25.92. Friendly place with clean, excellent-value rooms on a quiet street in the centre of Montmartre. M° Abbesses. **③**

**Du Commerce** 14 rue de la Montagne-Ste-Geneviève, 5ᵉ ☏01.43.54.89.69, ⦿www.commerce-paris-hotel.com. Professionally run budget hotel in the heart of the Quartier Latin, with bright, if garishly decorated rooms. M° Maubert-Mutualité. **④**

**Grand Hôtel du Loiret** 8 rue des Mauvais-Garçons, 4ᵉ ☏01.48.87.77.00, ⓟ01.48.04.96.56. A simple but good-value hotel at the heart of the Marais. M° Hotel-de-Ville. **④**

**Henri IV** 25 place Dauphine, 1ᵉʳ ☏01.43.54.44.53. Well-known cheapie in the beautiful place Dauphine on the Île de la Cité. Breakfast included. Booking essential. M° Pont-Neuf. **③**

**Jarry** 6 rue Jarry, 10ᵉ ☏01.47.70.70.38, ⓟ01.42.46.34.45. Simple, clean hotel in a lively immigrant quarter. Much fresher than the cheap dives on the same street. M° Gare-de-l'Est/Château-d'Eau. **③**

**Marignan** 13 rue du Sommerard, 5ᵉ ☏01.43.54.63.81, ⦿www.hotel-marignan.com. Excellent if relatively pricey backpacker-oriented hotel, with free laundry and self-catering facilities, and lots of triples and singles. Book well ahead. M° Maubert-Mutualité. **⑤**

**Médicis** 214 rue St-Jacques, 5ᵉ ☏01.43.54.14.66, ⓔhotelmedicis@aol.com. Rumoured to have hosted Jim Morrison for a week in 1970, this basic, tatty old hotel has a great location and low prices, making it quite popular, and the elderly owners are full of charm. RER Luxembourg. **③**

**Rivoli** 44 rue de Rivoli, 4ᵉ ☏01.42.72.08.41. Older rooms with shared bathrooms and some street noise, but the location, right at the Hôtel de Ville, can't be beat. M° Hôtel de Ville. **②**

**Tiquetonne** 6 rue Tiquetonne, 2ᵉ ☏01.42.36.94.58, ⓟ01.42.36.02.94. Good-value, old-fashioned place on a small, attractive street. Closed Aug. M° Étienne-Marcel. **④**

# The City

Paris is split into two halves by the Seine. On the north of the river, the **Right Bank** *(rive droite)* is home to the *grands boulevards* and most monumental buildings, many dating from Haussmann's nineteenth-century redevelopment, and is where you'll probably spend most time, during the day at least. The top museums are here – the Louvre and the Pompidou Centre, to name just two – as well as the city's widest range of shops around rue de Rivoli and Les Halles; and there are also fashionable quarters like the Marais for strolling. The **Left Bank** *(rive gauche)* has a noticeably different feel, its very name conjuring up images of Bohemians and intellectuals, and something of this atmosphere survives in the city's best range of bars and restaurants, and its most wanderable streets: the areas around St-Germain and St-Michel are full of nooks and crannies to explore. Parts of Paris, of course, don't sit easily in either category. **Montmartre**, rising up to the north of the centre, has managed to retain a village-like atmosphere despite the daily influx of tourists, while the dilapidated quarters of **eastern Paris**, undisturbed by tourism, offer a rich, ethnically diverse slice of Parisian streetlife.

## The Arc de Triomphe, Champs-Élysées and around

There's no better place to drink in the city's grandeur than from the top of the imposing **Arc de Triomphe** (daily 10am–10.30/11pm; €8; Mº Charles-de-Gaulle-Étoile), built by Napoleon in homage to the armies of France and himself. To its west rears the Grande Arche de la Défense (see p.370), connected to the mighty Louvre in the east by a monumental, nine-kilometre axis, known as the **Voie Triomphale**, or Triumphal Way. Part of this axis, the celebrated **avenue des Champs-Élysées**, sweeps gracefully down from the Arc de Triomphe to the vast **place de la Concorde**, whose centrepiece, a gold-tipped obelisk from the temple of Luxor, was given to the city by the viceroy of Egypt in 1829. Beyond lies the formal **Jardin des Tuileries** (daily 8/9am–7/8pm; Mº Concorde), with its grand vistas and symmetrical flowerbeds. Towards the river, the **Orangerie** displays Monet's largest water-lily paintings, as well as works by Cézanne, Matisse, Utrillo and Modigliani.

A short walk south of the Arc de Triomphe is the **Musée d'Art Moderne de la Ville de Paris** in the Palais de Tokyo, 11 av du Président-Wilson (Tues–Sun 10am–5.30pm; free; Mº Iéna; currently closed for renovation – check with the tourist office for the latest details), a veritable goldmine of major early twentieth-century artists, particularly those working in France, but the centrepieces are the leaping figures of Matisse's *La Danse* and Dufy's 250-panel mural illustrating the story of electricity. Located in the deliberately semi-derelict western wing of the palace is the **Site de Création Contemporaine** (Tues–Sun noon–midnight; cost varies according to exhibitions), given over to cutting-edge contemporary art exhibitions. A short walk down the river, at **Trocadéro**, the terrace of the Palais de Chaillot gives splendid vistas across the river to the Eiffel Tower.

## The Louvre

On the east side of the Jardin des Tuileries is the home of the *Mona Lisa*, the mighty **Louvre** (daily except Tues 9am–6pm; Wed & Fri open until 9.45pm; €8.50; after 6pm €6; Mº Palais Royal-Musée du Louvre/Louvre-Rivoli; ⓦwww .louvre.fr). The building was first opened to the public in 1793, during the Revo-lution, and within a decade Napoleon had made it the largest art collection on earth with the takings from his empire.

I.M. Pei's stunning glass pyramid is the main entrance, with an alternative entrance at the Portes des Lions. At both, picking up a free "Plan/Information"

## Museum entry

Many museums offer **discounted entry** to the under-26s with reduced fees for all on Sundays – and are often free on the first Sunday of every month. Most are closed on Mondays or Tuesdays. Unless you plan to camp out in Paris's museums, the *Carte Musées et Monuments* pass (€18/36/54 for one/three/five days), available at partici-pating museums, probably isn't worth it.

# CENTRAL PARIS

0    250 m

## EATING & DRINKING

| | |
|---|---|
| Berthillon | 10 |
| Bistro de la Sorbonne | 13 |
| Café Véry | 1 |
| Chez Georges | 8 |
| The Frog and Princess | 7 |
| Goldenberg | 5 |
| Grand Appétit | 9 |
| L'As du Falafel | 4 |
| La Petite Légume | 15 |
| Le Loir dans la Théière | 6 |
| Le Potager du Marais | 2 |
| Le Rubis | 14 |
| Lô Sushi | 3 |
| Perraudin | 16 |
| Polidor | 11 |
| Rhubarb | 12 |
| Taverne Henri IV | B |

## ACCOMMODATION

| | |
|---|---|
| BVJ Paris | K |
| Quartier Latin | J |
| Du Commerce | F |
| Le Fauconnier | G |
| Le Fourcy | C |
| Grand Hôtel du Loiret | B |
| Henri IV | H |
| Marignan | E |
| Maubuisson | I |
| Médicis | D |
| Rivoli | A |
| Tiquetonne | |

brochure will make navigating the vast premises a bit easier, and each of the gallery rooms has an information sheet that details specific works of the collections. **Oriental Antiquities** covers the Sumerian, Babylonian, Assyrian and Phoenician civilizations – including Hammurabi's two-metre-high law code – plus Islamic and Persian art. **Egyptian Antiquities** comprises a wealth of jewellery, domestic objects, sarcophagi and statues like the pink granite *Mastaba Sphinx*. **Greek and Roman Antiquities**, divided between the Denon and Sully wings, is mostly nude statuary, notably the famous *Venus de Milo*. The **Objets d'Art** collection is a chronology of the finest tapestries, ceramics, jewellery and furniture commissioned by France's wealthiest patrons, from medieval times to the nineteenth century. **Sculpture** covers the entire development of the art in France from Romanesque to Rodin, all in the Richelieu wing, plus Italian and northern European sculpture in Denon, including Michelangelo's *Slaves*, designed for the tomb of Pope Julius II.

The largest and busiest section is **Painting**. French from the year dot to mid-nineteenth century – notably works by Poussin – is covered in the Richelieu wing, which also houses the Dutch, German and Flemish collections – look out for Rembrandt's masterful *Supper at Emmaus* and two exquisite Vermeers. Over in the Denon wing, the Italians attract the biggest crowds, Leonardo's *Mona Lisa* most of all. Other Leonardos hang more peacefully in the nearby Grande Galerie, along with an amazing parade of works by Giotto, Botticelli, Titian, Tintoretto and Mantegna, including, most strikingly, Paolo Veronese's huge *Marriage at Cana*. Two rooms behind house epic canvases by the great nineteenth-century artists David, Ingres and Delacroix, as well as Géricault's harrowing *Raft of the Medusa*.

### The Opéra, Les Halles and the Pompidou Centre

A short walk north of the Louvre is the preposterously ornate **Opéra-Garnier**, on place de l'Opéra. Built in 1875 as the venue for opera, since the completion of the Opéra-Bastille in 1989 it has been used chiefly for ballet. You can see the splendid interior (daily 10am–4.30pm; €7; M° Opéra), including the auditorium, where the domed ceiling is the work of Chagall. Southeast of here is the area around the former **Les Halles** (a covered market), which was redeveloped in the 1970s amid widespread opposition, and is scheduled for more redevelopment in the coming years. A young, international crowd shops and hangs out in the pedestrianized streets, but the shopping precinct at the area's core, the **Forum des Halles**, is a tacky affair, and it can be unsafe, too, especially at night. During the day the main flow of feet is from here a little way east to the **Pompidou Centre** (M° Rambuteau). This seminal 1977 design by Renzo Piano and Richard Rogers was the first public structure to manifest the hi-tech notion of displaying its services on the outside, the tubing colour-coded according to function, leaving maximum space for the interior. Inside is the hugely popular **Musée National d'Art Moderne** (11am–9pm, closed Tues; €5.50), a superb collection that ranges from Fauvism and Cubism through Pop Art to the present day, and at the very top buzzes a swank minimalist bar with great city-wide panoramas.

### The Marais, the Bastille and Île St-Louis

Just east of the Pompidou Centre lies the **Marais**, one of the most seductive areas of central Paris. Formerly a fashionable aristocratic district that then became one of the city's poorer quarters, the area has recently undergone regentrification, its beautiful Renaissance mansions turned into museums, offices and chic apartments flanked by designer clothes shops, trendy cafés and gay nightspots. A little way down the main drag, **rue des Francs-Bourgeois**, one of the grandest Marais mansions houses the excellent **Musée Carnavalet** (entrance around the corner at 23 rue de Sévigné; Tues–Sun 10am–6pm; free; M° St-Paul), which presents the history of Paris from the reign of François I to the early twentieth century, with paintings, reconstructions of sumptuous interiors and mementoes of the

1789 Revolution. Slightly further north, at 71 rue du Temple, the **Musée d'Art et d'Histoire du Judaïsme** (Sun–Fri 10/11am–6pm; €6.80, €4.50 for under 26s; Mº Rambuteau) has a fascinating display of Jewish artefacts and historical documents as well as paintings by Chagall and Soutine. A short walk east, another mansion, the proud seventeenth-century Hôtel Juigné Salé at 5 rue de Thorigny, is home to the **Musée Picasso** (daily except Tues 9.30am–5.30/6pm; €6.70; Mº St-Paul). It's an overwhelming collection, much of which was the artist's personal property, and comprises the largest number of his works anywhere.

At the far end of rue des Francs-Bourgeois, off to the right, **place des Vosges** is a masterpiece of aristocratic urban planning, a vast square of stone and brick symmetry built for Henri IV and Louis XIII. At no. 6, the **Maison Victor Hugo** (Tues–Sun 10am–6pm; free; Mº Bastille) is the former home of the writer of *Les Misérables*.

A short walk southeast, heading for the landmark column with the gilded "Spirit of Liberty", is **place de la Bastille**, the site of the Bastille that was famously stormed in 1789. The column was erected to commemorate not the surrender of the prison, which was subsequently demolished, but the July Revolution of 1830 – although it is the 1789 Bastille Day that France celebrates every July 14. The Bicentennial in 1989 was marked by the inauguration of the **Opéra-Bastille**, on the far side of the square, a bloated building that caused great controversy when it went up – a "hippopotamus in a bathtub", one critic called it.

Just south of here, across Henri IV bridge, the **Île St-Louis** is one of the centre's swankier quarters, with no monuments or museums, just high houses on single-lane streets. It's a peaceful and atmospheric route through to the Île de la Cité, strolling down either the centre, along the shop-filled rue St-Louis-en-l'Île – a real weekend promenade with pedestrians taking over the street, many queuing for an ice cream at the famous *Berthillon* – or along the tree-lined *quais* down by the Seine.

## Île de la Cité

**Île de la Cité** is where Paris began. It's the original site of the Roman garrison and later of the palace of the Merovingian kings and the counts of Paris, who in 987 became kings of France. Nowadays the main lure is the astounding Gothic **Cathédrale de Notre-Dame** (daily 7.45am–6.45pm, closed Sat 12.30–2pm; Mº Cité), begun in 1163 under the auspices of Bishop de Sully and completed around 1345. In the nineteenth century, Viollet-le-Duc carried out extensive renovation work, remaking most of the statuary and adding the steeple and baleful-looking gargoyles, which you can see close up if you brave the 387-step ascent of the **towers** (daily 9/10am–5/9pm; €5.50). The sculpture of the west front portals is amazingly detailed, dating mainly from the twelfth and thirteenth centuries, while inside, the immediately striking feature is the dramatic contrast between the darkness of the nave and the light falling on the first great clustered pillars of the choir. In front of the cathedral, the **crypte archéologique** (Tues–Sun 10am–6pm; €3.30) holds the remains of the original cathedral, as well as of streets and houses of the Cité back as far as the Roman era.

At the western end of the island, the dull mass of the **Palais de Justice** swallowed up the palace that was home to the French kings until the bloody revolt of 1358 frightened them into the greater security of the Louvre. The only part of the older complex that remains in its entirety is Louis IX's **Sainte-Chapelle** at 4 bd du Palais (daily 9.30/10am–5/6.30pm; €6.10, €9 joint ticket with the Conciergerie; Mº Cité). This was built to house a collection of holy relics and is one of the finest achievements of French Gothic style, lent a fragility by its height and huge expanses of glorious stained glass, most of which is original. You should also visit the **Conciergerie**, Paris's oldest prison, whose entrance is around the corner facing the river on quai de l'Horloge (same times and prices). This was where Marie-Antoinette and, in their turn, the leading figures of the Revolution were incarcerated before execution. Its chief interest is the enormous late-Gothic Salle des Gens d'Armes (canteen and recreation room of the royal household staff), as well as Marie-Antoinette's cell and various macabre mementoes of the guillotine's victims. Outside the Conciergerie is Paris's first public clock, the **Tour de l'Horloge**, built in 1370.

## The Eiffel Tower, Les Invalides and the Musée d'Orsay

Though no conventional beauty, the **Eiffel Tower** is nonetheless an amazing structure, at 300m the tallest building in the world when it was completed by Gustave Eiffel in 1889. Reactions to it were violent, but it stole the show for the two million who climbed it at the 1889 Exposition, for which it had been constructed. Lifts take you straight to the top (daily 9/9.30am–11pm/midnight; €10.70; M° Bir Hakeim/RER Champ de Mars); if you're fit enough, you can save money by walking up as far as the second level (704 stairs; €3.50), from where you can join the lift for the final leg (€3). The queues can be dispiriting on clear summer days, so think about going at night, when the views can be even more impressive.

To the east, the **Esplanade des Invalides** strikes south from the river to the wide facade of the **Hôtel des Invalides**, built as a home for invalided soldiers on the orders of Louis XIV and topped by a distinctive gilded dome which is a real Paris landmark. It now houses the giant **Musée de l'Armée** (daily 10am–5/6pm; €7), with a vast collection of armour, uniforms, weapons and Napoleonic relics, and a more rewarding wing devoted to World War II. The same ticket allows entry to Napoleon's grandiose tomb, accessed from the south side. Immediately east, on the corner of rue de Varenne, the **Musée Rodin** (Tues–Sun 9.30am–4.45/5.45pm; €5; M° Varenne), houses many of the sculptor's best-known works, including a version of *The Kiss*, in a beautiful eighteenth-century mansion.

A little way northeast along the river, on the quai d'Orsay, the **Musée d'Orsay** (Tues–Sun 9/10am–6pm, Thurs till 9.45pm; €5.50/7.50; free 1st Sun of month and to under-18s; RER Musée d'Orsay/M° Solférino; ®www.musee-orsay.fr), converted from a disused train station in the 1980s, houses an outstanding collection of painting and sculpture from the pre-modern period (1848–1914). On the ground floor are works by the likes of Ingres, Delacroix, Degas, Daumier, Corot and Millet; in the top floor attics are the Impressionists and post-Impressionists, ranging from Manet, Renoir, Pissarro and Monet through to Cézanne, Van Gogh, Gauguin and Toulouse-Lautrec. The middle floor is dominated by sculpture, with some amazing works by Rodin.

## The Latin Quarter, St-Germain and Montparnasse

The neighbourhood around the broad boulevards St-Michel and St-Germain has been known as the **Quartier Latin** since medieval times, because it was the home of the Latin-speaking universities. It is still a student-dominated area, its pivotal point being **place St-Michel**, whose cafés and shops are jammed with people – mainly young and, in summer, largely foreign. The warren of streets around rue de la Huchette, gathering-place of beatniks and bums in the 1950s, is now a tacky tourist trap. Close to the St-Michel/St-Germain junction, the walls of the third-century Roman baths are visible in the garden of the Hôtel de Cluny on place Paul-Painlevé. This sixteenth-century mansion, built by the abbots of the powerful Cluny monastery as their Paris *pied-à-terre*, now houses the **Musée National du Moyen Age – Thermes de Cluny** (daily except Tues 9.15am–5.45pm; €5.50; M° Cluny-La Sorbonne), a treasure-house of medieval art that includes some wonderful tapestries. The real masterpieces are the six fifteenth-century panels depicting *The Lady with the Unicorn*, which symbolize the five senses and the Christian virtue in resisting them.

Immediately south of here, the Montagne Ste-Geneviève slopes up to the domed **Panthéon**, Louis XIV's thankyou to Geneviève, patron saint of Paris, for curing him of illness, which was transformed during the Revolution into a mausoleum for the great: its incumbents include Voltaire, Rousseau, Zola and Hugo (daily 10am–6.15/6.30pm; €7; M° Cardinal Lemoine/RER Luxembourg). Just next door stand the prestigious Sorbonne and Collège de France universities, age-old bulwarks of the European intellectual tradition. Down rue Soufflot, across boulevard St-Michel, you might prefer to while away a few hours in the elegant surrounds of the **Jardin du Luxembourg** (daily dawn to dusk; M° Luxembourg), laid out by Marie de Médici, Henri IV's widow, to remind her of the Palazzo Pitti and Giardino di Bóboli of her native Florence. They are the chief recreation grounds of the Left Bank, with tennis courts, a *boules* pitch, toy yachts to rent on the pond and wooded and grassy areas much used by students for sunbathing and socializing.

Beyond the Luxembourg gardens, the northern half of the 6$^e$ *arrondissement* is one of the most attractive parts of the city, full of bookshops, art galleries, antique shops, cafés and restaurants. It is also, perhaps, its most culturally historic: Picasso painted *Guernica* in rue des Grands-Augustins; in rue Visconti, Delacroix painted and Balzac's printing business went bust; and in parallel rue des Beaux-Arts, Oscar Wilde died and the crazy poet Gérard de Nerval went walking with a lobster on a blue ribbon. **Place St-Germain-des-Prés**, the hub of the *quartier*, is the site of the *Flore* and *Deux Magots* cafés, renowned for the number of politico-literary backsides that have shined their seats. Head east to the Seine and you will come upon the **Institut du Monde Arabe** (Tues–Sun 10am–6pm; €4; M° Jussieu), an awesome structure swathed in aluminum and glass with museum exhibits on the ancient and modern Middle East.

On the southern side of the Luxembourg gardens, **Montparnasse** also trades on its association with the colourful characters of the interwar years, many of whom were habitués of the cafés *Select*, *Coupole*, *Dôme* and *Rotonde* on boulevard du Montparnasse. Close by, the colossal 59-storey skyscraper **Tour Montparnasse**, avenue du Maine, has become one of the city's most hated landmarks since its construction in 1973; ugly it may be, but it's less expensive and far quicker to climb than the Eiffel tower, and you can look across to the more beautiful structure (daily 9.30am–10.30/11/11.30pm; €8.50; M° Montparnasse-Bienvenue). A short walk down boulevard Edgar-Quinet, the **Montparnasse cemetery** (daily 8/9am–5.30/6pm; free; M° Raspail) has plenty of illustrious names, from Baudelaire to Sartre and André Citroën to Serge Gainsbourg.

## Montmartre and eastern Paris

**Montmartre** lies in the middle of the 18$^e$ *arrondissement*. It's topped by the **Butte Montmartre**, whose central **place du Tertre** is a touristic honeypot – photogenic but totally bogus, jammed with day-trippers, overpriced restaurants and "artists" painting garish Eiffel Towers. Crowning the hill is the nineteenth-century, neo-Byzantine **Sacré-Cœur** (daily 6am–10.30pm; free; M° Anvers/Abbesses), a classic of the Paris skyline; you can climb to the top of the pimply dome (daily 10am–5.45pm; €5) for a wonderful view. To get to the top of the Butte, take the funicular from place Suzanne-Valadon (ordinary métro tickets and passes are valid) or, for a quieter, prettier approach, climb the steep stairs via place des Abbesses. The streets around this square are lined with cool boutique clothes shops, trendy bars and good restaurants. Off the curving rue Lepic, the **Moulin de la Galette**, immortalized by Renoir, is the only visible survivor of Montmartre's forty-odd windmills. Down the hill on boulevard de Clichy, the notorious Moulin Rouge was never a windmill, and these days it's a package-tour-oriented version of its former self. The stretch of road around it, known as **Pigalle**, has always been a sleazy neighbourhood of peepshows and transvestite prostitution. At the western end of Pigalle, a little way up rue Caulaincourt, the **Montmartre cemetery** (daily 8/9am–5.30/6pm; M° Place de Clichy) holds the graves of Zola, Berlioz and Degas, among others.

East of Montmartre, the **Bassin de la Villette** and the **canals** at the northeastern gate of the city were for generations the centre of a densely populated working-class district but have recently become the subject of yet another big Paris redevelopment. The area's major extravagance is the **Cité des Sciences et de l'Industrie** (Tues–Sun 10am–6/7pm; €7.50; M° Porte de la Villette) in the **Parc de la Villette**, built into the concrete hulk of the abandoned abattoirs on the north side of the canal de l'Ourcq. Three times the size of the Pompidou Centre, this is the most astounding monument to be added to the capital in the last two decades, and is worth visiting for the interior alone – all glass and stainless steel, cantilevered platforms and suspended walkways. Its permanent exhibition, Explora, on the top two floors, is the science museum to end all science museums, covering everything from microbes to outer space.

South of La Villette, Paris's **eastern** districts – **Belleville** and **Ménilmontant** – are among the poorest of the city and not on most visitors' itineraries. However, the **Père-Lachaise cemetery**, on boulevard de Ménilmontant, draws a fair number of tourists (daily 8/9am–5.30/6pm; M° Père-Lachaise), most of them heading for Jim Morrison's small, guarded grave and Oscar Wilde's more extravagant tomb. There are countless famous others buried here – Chopin, Edith Piaf, Modigliani, Abélard and Héloïse, Sarah Bernhardt, Ingres, Delacroix and Balzac, to name only a few.

### The Beaux Quartiers, Bois de Boulogne and La Défense

South and west of the Arc de Triomphe extend the so-called **Beaux Quartiers**, the 16ᵉ and 17ᵉ *arrondissements*, in turns aristocratic and rich, bourgeois and staid. They hold little of interest save the wonderful **Musée Marmottan**, 2 rue Louis-Boilly (Tues–Sun 10am–6pm; €7; M° La Muette), housing the world's largest collection of Monet paintings. Among them is the canvas called *Impression, Soleil Levant*, an 1872 rendering of a misty sunrise over Le Havre, whose title unwittingly gave the Impressionist movement its name. Beyond the museum, the **Bois de Boulogne**, running down the west side of the 16ᵉ, is the city's largest open space, its prime attraction the **Parc de Bagatelle** with its beautiful rose garden.

In stark contrast, further west lies Paris's avant-garde business district, **La Défense**, a dizzying complex of steel, glass and marble skyscrapers. Dominating all is Mitterand's breathtaking **Grande Arche** (M° Grande-Arche-de-la-Défense), a 112-metre-high hollow cube clad in white marble. Suspended within its hollow are open lift shafts and a "cloud canopy". You can ride up to the roof (daily 10am–7pm; €7), but the views from the front steps are just as impressive.

# Eating

**Eating out** in Paris need not be an extravagant affair. Numerous fixed-price menus provide simple but tasty French fare from around €12, or for a similar price you could choose from a wide range of ethnic restaurants – North and West African, Chinese, Japanese, Vietnamese, Greek and lots more. Being vegetarian in Paris is not always easy, but veggie and vegan places are becoming more popular; Indian, Jewish and Italian cuisine is also a good bet for non-meat dishes. Anyone in possession of an ISIC card is eligible to apply for tickets for the **university restaurants** run by CROUS – see ⓦwww.crous-paris.fr for a list of addresses, and buy your ticket from the restaurants themselves.

### Snacks, sandwiches, cakes and ice cream

**Berthillon** 31 rue St-Louis-en-l'Île, 4ᵉ. Expect long queues for the best ice creams and sorbets in the city. Closed Mon & Tues. M° Pont Marie.

**Café de la Mosquée** 39 rue Geoffroy-St-Hilaire, 5ᵉ. Mint tea and Middle Eastern cakes in this oasis of calm, next to an excellent Turkish bath. Open daily till midnight. M° Jussieu.

**Café Véry** (aka *Dame Tartine*) Jardin des

Tuileries, 1<sup>er</sup>. The best of a number of café-restaurants in the gardens, serving toasted sandwiches and more substantial snacks, and popular among artsy types. Daily noon–7pm. M° Concorde.

**Le Loir dans la Théière** 3 rue des Rosiers, 4<sup>e</sup>. Peaceful, sometimes quirky retreat with leather armchairs and a laid-back atmosphere. Midday *tartes* and omelettes, fruit teas and cakes served all day, and a great Sunday brunch. M° St-Paul.

**Le Sancerre** 35 rue des Abbesses, 18<sup>e</sup>. Hangout for the young and trendy in the Abbesses area of Montmartre. Daily 7am–2am. M° Abbesses.

**Taverne Henri IV** 13 pl du Pont-Neuf, Île de la Cité, 1<sup>er</sup>. Old-style wine bar serving generous plates of meats and cheeses. Closed Sun & Aug. M° Pont-Neuf.

### Restaurants and brasseries

**Au Virage Lepic** 61 rue Lepic, 18<sup>e</sup>. Simple, good-quality meaty fare served in a noisy, friendly, old-fashioned bistro. M° Abbesses.

**Bistro de la Sorbonne** 4 rue Toullier, 5<sup>e</sup>. Large portions of traditional French and North African dishes at good prices in a buzzing and occasionally clamorous ambience. M° Place Monge.

**Bistro du Peintre** 116 av Ledru-Rollin, 11<sup>e</sup>. A charming Art Nouveau bistro serving copious salads and hearty Auvergnat cuisine – beef dishes with pungent cheeses and potato sides. M° Ledru-Rollin.

**Chardenoux** 1 rue Jules-Vallès, 11<sup>e</sup>. An authentic oldie that still serves solid meaty fare at moderate prices. Closed Sun & Aug. M° Faidherbe-Chaligny.

**Chartier** 7 rue du Faubourg-Montmartre, 9<sup>e</sup>. Good inexpensive food and cheap wine in an original and splendid early-twentieth-century soup kitchen. Expect to queue. M° Le Peletier.

**Chez Gladines** 30 rue des Cinq-Diamants, 13<sup>e</sup>. Tiny, welcoming corner bistro serving hearty Basque dishes. Close to the cool bars of the Butte-aux-Cailles. M° Corvisart.

**Flo** 7 cours des Petites-Écuries, 10<sup>e</sup>. Handsome pre-war-styled Alsatian brasserie, where you eat elbow-to-elbow at long tables. Excellent food and thoroughly enjoyable atmosphere. M° Château d'Eau.

**Foyer du Vietnam** 80 rue Monge, 5<sup>e</sup>. Very popular student place where you can eat well for under €10, including wine. M° Monge.

**Goldenberg** 7 rue des Rosiers, 4<sup>e</sup>. Paris's best-known Jewish restaurant. Its borscht, blinis, strudels and other central European dishes are a real treat. Go for the beef goulash. M° St-Paul.

**Grand Appétit** 9 rue de la Cerisaie, 4<sup>e</sup>. Vegetarian and macrobiotic meals for around €15 served by dedicated eco-veggies at the back of this unassuming shop. M° Bastille.

**L'As du Falafel** 34 rue des Rosiers, 4<sup>e</sup>. Well-known as the city's best falafel; try their pitta special – cabbage, eggplant, hummus and tabasco sauce. Sun–Thurs till midnight M° St-Paul.

**Le Mono** 40 rue Véron, 18<sup>e</sup>. Togolese restaurant serving delicous grilled fish and meats in a lively, Afro-styled atmosphere. Closed Wed. M° Abbesses.

**La Petite Légume** 36 rue des Boulangers, 5<sup>e</sup>. Tiny, homely vegetarian café with an organic approach. Health-food grocery store next door. Closed Sun. M° Jussieu.

**Le Potager du Marais** 22 rue Rambuteau, 3<sup>e</sup>. Light, modern and all-organic vegetarian and fish dishes, served at a long communal table. Closed Sun. M° Rambuteau.

**Le Temps des Cerises** 18–20 rue de la Butte-aux-Cailles, 13<sup>e</sup>. A well-established and excellent-value workers' co-op restaurant with convivial packed-in seating offering hearty French dishes and a decent wine list. M° Corvisart.

**Lô Sushi** 1 rue de Pont-Neuf, 8<sup>e</sup>. The sushi (€2–7) is good, but the real excitement comes from computer terminals at your seat that allow you to chat online with anyone else in the restaurant. Daily until midnight. M° Pont-Neuf.

**Perraudin** 157 rue St-Jacques, 5<sup>e</sup>. Well-known traditional Latin Quarter bistro with moderate-value menus. M° Cluny-La Sorbonne.

**Polidor** 41 rue Monsieur-le-Prince, 6<sup>e</sup>. A classic bistro since 1845, today it's packed with noisy regulars tucking into well-made French standards till late. M° Odéon.

**Thoumieux** 79 rue St-Dominique, 7<sup>e</sup>. Cavernous and deeply old-fashioned brasserie in a smart district near the Eiffel Tower. Meals from around €20. M° Invalides.

# Drinking

Most squares and boulevards have **cafés** spreading out onto the pavements and, although these are usually the priciest places to drink, it can be worth shelling out for a coffee if only to take in the streetlife. The Left Bank has some of the city's best-known and longest-established cafés and **bars**, especially around the university quarter and near St-Germain-des-Prés. The Bastille is livelier than ever, while the Marais has small, crowded café-bars and some upbeat gay establishments. The *quais* of the Canal St-Martin also offer a few trendy, bohemian bars. For old-fashioned **wine bars**, often serving food, Montmartre is a good bet, while bars and **pubs** inspired by Belgian or British watering holes can be found throughout the city. Places listed below are open all day until around 2am unless otherwise stated, and many offer an early evening "happy hour", with inexpensive drinks until around 8pm.

**Buddha Bar** 8 rue Boissy d'Anglas 8ᵉ. Once the centre of posh Paris nightlife, the beautiful people still drop in sometimes for a drink, and the awesome Oriental decor is worth a gander. Daily 4pm–2am. Mᵒ Concorde.

**Café Charbon** 109 rue Oberkampf, 11ᵉ. Hugely successful revival of a fin-de-siècle café, packed in the evenings with a young pre-club clientele but relaxed during the day. DJs hit the turntables at weekends. Mᵒ St-Maur/Parmentier.

**Chez Georges** 11 rue des Canettes, 6ᵉ. Old-fashioned, tobacco-stained wine bar upstairs, lively cellar-bar below, both very popular with local students. Tues–Sat noon–2am; closed Aug. Mᵒ Mabillon.

**La Folie en Tête** 33 rue de la Butte-aux-Cailles, 13ᵉ. Alternative-spirited, laid-back bar on a lively street, serving cheap drinks and daytime snacks. Mon–Sat 5pm–2am. Mᵒ Place-d'Italie.

**The Frog and Princess** 9 rue Princesse, 6ᵉ. It's spring break every night at this English chain pub,

with happy hours until 8pm. Open till 2am. Mᵒ St-Germain-des-Prés/Mabillon.

**La Fourmi Café** 74 rue des Martyrs, 18ᵉ. High-ceilinged café-bar full of trendy young Parisians. Daily 8/10am–2/4am. Mᵒ Pigalle.

**Pause Café** 41 rue de Charonne, 11ᵉ. A fashionable café-bar, with pavement tables, relaxed music and a lively buzz day and night. Tues–Sat 8am–2am, Sun till 9pm. Mᵒ Ledru-Rollin.

**Rhubarb** 18 rue Laplace, 5ᵉ. Loud, Irish-run student pub with €2 shots all day Mon–Thurs and happy hour until 10pm. Till 2am. Mᵒ Maubert-Mutualité.

**Le Rubis** 10 rue du Marché-St-Honoré, 1ᵉʳ. One of the oldest wine bars in Paris, with excellent snacks and *plats du jour*. Mon–Fri 7.30am–10pm, Sat 9am–3pm; closed mid-Aug. Mᵒ Tuileries.

**Le Sélect** 99 bd du Montparnasse, 6ᵉ. The least spoilt of the swanky Montparnasse cafés, still thriving since its 1920s heyday when Picasso and Fitzgerald came to drown their sorrows. Open till 3/4am. Mᵒ Vavin.

## Nightlife

Paris's reputation for **live music** is impeccable: its world music is second to none, live jazz continues to be excellent, and there's an almost limitless choice of classical music and opera. **Clubs** come and go as rapidly as in any other large city, but there are one or two long-established places that won't let you down; most clubs open around 11pm and get going from around 1am; some stay open until dawn and beyond. For **what's on listings**, the best weekly guides are either *Pariscope* (€0.40), with a small section in English, or *L'Officiel des Spectacles* (€0.35). The best places to **buy tickets** are FNAC, Forum des Halles, 1–5 rue Pierre-Lescot, level 3 (Mᵒ Les Halles), and the Virgin Megastore, 56–60 av des Champs-Élysées (Mᵒ Franklin Roosevelt).

There are over 350 **films** showing in Paris in any one week. Tickets cost around €8, €5 for students. Almost all of the huge selection of foreign films will be shown at some cinemas in their original language – *v.o.* in the listings (as opposed to *v.f.*, which means it's dubbed into French). Committed film freaks should head to the small *cinémathèques*, which show a choice of over fifty movies a week; tickets are only €4.75. The Forum des Images in the Forum des Halles, 2 Grande Galerie, Porte Eustache (Mᵒ Les Halles), is an excellent-value venue for the bizarre or obscure on celluloid, with themed repertoires and a *vidéothèque* where you can call up a huge range of films for private viewing on video.

### Live music venues

**Au Limonaire** 8 Cité Bergère, 9ᵉ ☎01.45.23.33.33, @limonaire.free.fr. Tiny backstreet venue, featuring Parisian *chanson* and poetry acts. Inexpensive dinner beforehand

gets you a seat for the 10pm show; otherwise take your chances getting in. Mᵒ Grands Boulevards.

**Caveau de la Huchette** 5 rue de la Huchette, 5ᵉ. Very popular basement jazz club featuring excellent bebop and big-band groups, often with dancing. €10 cover. M° St-Michel.

**House of Live** 124 rue de la Boétie, 8ᵉ ☎01.42.25.13.28, ⓦwww.houseoflive.com. Large bar-restaurant featuring live, up-and-coming, French rock/pop/soul acts, with after-show club-bing. Free entry. M° Franklin D. Roosevelt.

**Le Bataclan** 50 bd Voltaire, 11ᵉ ⓦwww.bataclan .fr. Classic ex-theatre with one of the best line-ups of any venue, covering anything from inter-national and local dance and rock musicians to opera, comedy and techno nights. M° Oberkampf.

**Le Divan du Monde** 75 rue des Martyrs, 18ᵉ ⓦwww.divandumonde.com. Café with one of the city's most exciting programmes, ranging from techno to Congolese rumba, with dancing till dawn on weekend nights. M° Pigalle.

**La Guinguette Pirate** Quai François Mauriac, 13ᵉ ⓦwww.guinguettepirate.com. Beautiful Chinese barge, moored alongside the quay in front of the Bibliothèque Nationale, hosting world music nights Tues–Sun. M° Quai de la Gare.

### Clubs

**Batofar** Quai de la Gare, 13ᵉ. A good bet for a not-too-expensive club night out, with a cool setting in an old lighthouse boat outside the Bibliothèque Nationale. M° Quai de la Gare.

**Les Bains** 7 rue du Bourg-l'Abbé, 3ᵉ. As posey as they come, set in an old Turkish bathhouse with a plunge pool. A youngish crowd bangs its head to house, hip hop and garage. Daily midnight–dawn. M° Étienne-Marcel.

**Man Ray** 32 rue Marboeuf, 8ᵉ. The hippest of the hip; if you can convince the bouncers to let you into this ultra-exclusive lounge, splurge on one of their €11 cocktails. M° Blanche.

**Nouveau Casino** 109 rue Oberkampf, 11ᵉ ⓦwww.nouveaucasino.net. Eclectic, innovative mix of musical styles spun at this large, trendy club. M° Parmentier.

**Point Ephémère** 200 Quai de Valmy, 10ᵉ ⓦwww .pointephemere.org. A new cultural space with modern art, DJs, live music and dance shows. Open until 2am. M° Pigalle.

**Rex Club** 5 bd Poissonnière, 2ᵉ. The clubbers' club: spacious and serious about its music, which is strictly electronic, and offering big-name DJs. M° Grands-Boulevards.

**Triptyque** 142 rue Montmartre, 2ᵉ ⓦwww .letriptyque.com. Acid jazz, trip hop and electronica spun every day of the week for €10. M° Bourse/ Grands Boulevards.

### Classical music, opera and ballet

**Cité de la Musique** 221 av Jean-Jaurès, 19ᵉ ☎01.44.84.84.84, ⓦwww.cite-musique.fr. Concert hall seating 800–1200, with an eclectic programme that covers Baroque, contemporary works, jazz, *chansons* and world music. M° Porte-de-Pantin.

**Opéra-Bastille** 120 rue de Lyon, 12ᵉ ☎08.36.69.78.68, ⓦwww.opera-de-paris.fr. Paris's ultra-modern opera house. Tickets cost €10–160, with the cheapest seats only available to personal callers; unfilled seats are sold at a discount to students five minutes before curtain. M° Bastille.

**Opéra-Garnier** place de l'Opéra, 9ᵉ ☎08.92.89.90.90. The original opera house now stages smaller operas and ballet productions. Tickets and website as above. M° Opéra.

**Théâtre des Champs-Élysées** 15 av Montaigne, 8ᵉ ☎01.49.52.50.50, ⓦwww.theatre champselysees.fr. Home to the Orchestre National de France, but also hosts international superstar conductors, ballet troupes and operas. M° Alma-Marceau.

**Théâtre Musical de Paris (Châtelet)** 1 place du Châtelet, 1ᵉʳ ☎01.40.28.28.40, ⓦwww .chatelet-theatre.com. As well as operas, the programme includes visiting ballets, concerts and solo recitals. M° Châtelet.

## Gay and lesbian Paris

Paris has a well-established **gay scene** concentrated mainly in the Halles, Marais and Bastille areas, and there are numerous gay organizations. For information, check out *Têtu* (ⓦwww.tetu.com), France's main gay monthly magazine, which is full of contact details, addresses and reviews, or visit the main information centre, Centre Gai et Lesbien de Paris, 3 rue Keller, 11ᵉ (☎01.43.57.21.47, ⓦwww .cglparis.org; M° Ledru-Rollin/Bastille).

**Banana Café** 13 rue de la Ferronnerie, 1ᵉʳ. Seriously hedonistic club-bar, packing in the punters with up-tempo clubby tunes. Happy hour 6.30–9.30pm. M° Châtelet.

**Bar Central** 33 rue Vieille-du-Temple, 4ᵉ. An old, dimly-lit standby in the Marais, attracting a quieter,

more laid-back clientele. Paris's sole gay-only hotel is just above. Mon–Fri 4pm–2am, Sat & Sun 2pm–2am. M° St-Paul.

**Le Mixer** 23 rue Ste-Croix-de-la-Bretonnerie, 4ᵉ ☎01.48.87.55.44. Popular gay, lesbian and straight-friendly bar with futuristic decor, a good atmosphere and a tiny dance-floor. Mº Hôtel-de-Ville.

**Le Pulp** 25 bd Poissonnière, 2ᵉ ⓦ www.pulpeclub .com. Done up In the style of a nineteenth-century music hall, this popular lesbian bar is well-known for its untamed parties. Cover around €10; open till dawn. Mº Grands-Boulevards.

**Le Tango** 13 rue au Maire, 3ᵉ. Gay and lesbian dance-hall with a traditional *bal* until midnight, then house and mainstream dance later on. Mº Arts-et-Métiers.

**Redlight** 34 rue du Départ, 15ᵉ ⓣ01.42.79.94.53, ⓦ www.enfer.fr. Popular club with huge weekend house nights that kick off in the early hours. Mº Montparnasse-Bienvenüe.

## Listings

**Bike rental** From €14 a day. Paris-Vélo, 2 rue du Fer-à-Moulin, 5ᵉ ⓣ01.43.37.59.22 (Mº Censier-Daubenton); Paris à Vélo C'est Sympa, 22 rue Alphonse Baudin, 11ᵉ ⓣ01.48.87.60.01, ⓦ www.parisvelosympa.com (Mº Richard Lenoir); Bike N'Roller, 38 rue Fabert, 7ᵉ ⓣ01.45.50.38.27, ⓦ www.bikenroller.fr (Mº Invalides), which also rents out rollerblades; RATP, 1 passage Mondétour, opposite 120 rue Rambuteau, 1ᵉʳ ⓣ08.10.44.15.34, ⓦ www.rouelibre.fr (Mº Les Halles).

**Bookstore** Shakespeare & Co, 37 rue de la Bûcherie, 5ᵉ.

**Embassies** Australia, 4 rue Jean-Rey, 15ᵉ ⓣ01.40.59.33.00 (Mº Bir Hakeim); Canada, 35 av Montaigne, 8ᵉ ⓣ01.44.43.29.00 (Mº Franklin Roosevelt); Ireland, 4 rue Rude, 16ᵉ ⓣ01.44.17.67.00

(Mº Charles-de-Gaulle-Étoile); New Zealand, 7 rue Léonard-de-Vinci, 16ᵉ ⓣ01.45.01.43.43 (Mº Victor Hugo); UK, 35 rue du Faubourg-St-Honoré, 8ᵉ ⓣ01.44.51.31.00 (Mº Concorde); US, 2 rue St Florentin, 1ᵉʳ ⓣ01.43.12.22.22 (Mº Concorde).

**Hospital** 24hr medical help from SOS-Médecins ⓣ01.43.37.77.77; ⓣ15 for emergencies.

**Left luggage** Lockers (€3.50–9.50) at all train stations and *consignes* for bigger items.

**Pharmacies** English spoken at Swann, 6 rue Castiglione, 1ᵉʳ (Mº Tuileries); Dérhy, 84 av des Champs-Élysées, 8ᵉ (Mº Georges V), is open 24hr.

**Police** ⓣ17 in emergencies; for thefts, report to the *commissariat de police* of the arrondissement in which the theft took place.

**Post office** 52 rue du Louvre, 1ᵉʳ (Mº Les Halles).

## Day-trips from Paris

Around 32km east of the city is **Disneyland Paris** (daily 9/10am–8/11pm; €40; RER line A to Marne-la-Vallée; ⓦ www.disneylandparis.com), a 5000-acre slice of the hyperreal. It's predictably commercial, but with enough thrill and technology-based rides to make it Europe's leading theme park. Aside from this, the most popular day-trip is to **Versailles**, but the most rewarding is the cathedral at **Chartres**, while **Giverny** is a haven for acolytes of Monet.

### Versailles

The **Palace of Versailles** (Tues–Sun 9am–5.30/6.30pm; €7.50, €5.30 after 3.30pm; ⓦ www.chateauversailles.fr) is one of the three most visited monuments in France, and a twenty-year, €400 million restoration project is seeing that it stays that way. Sixteen kilometres west of Paris, it's the apotheosis of French regal indulgence, its decor an unrestrained homage to two of the greatest of all self-propagandists, Louis XIV (the "Sun King") and Napoleon. It's more impressive for its size than anything else, which, by any standards, is incredible. The most amazing room is perhaps the **Hall of Mirrors**, although the mirrors are not the originals; this is, more importantly, the room in which the Treaty of Versailles was signed, so bringing World War I to an end. You can also visit the state apartments of the king and queen, and the **royal chapel**, a grand structure that ranks among France's finest Baroque creations. Outside, the **park** is something of a relief, and you could wander for hours through its vast extent. It's inevitably a very ordered affair, but the scenery becomes less formal the further you go from the palace, especially around the **Grand** and **Petit Trianons** (Tues–Sun noon–5/6pm; €5 for both). Beyond is **Le Hameau**, an area of thatched cottages, a mill and a dairy set around a lake where Marie Antoinette played at being a shepherdess. The easiest way to get to Versailles is the half-hourly RER line C5 from Gare d'Austerlitz to Versailles-Rive Gauche (40min; €5 return).

## Chartres

About 35km southwest of Versailles, an hour by frequent train (€10) from Paris-Montparnasse, **CHARTRES** is a pretty but undistinguished town. However, its **Cathédrale Notre-Dame** (daily 8am–7.15/8pm) is one of the finest examples of Gothic architecture in Europe. The heart-lifting space is unique in being almost unaltered since its consecration in 1225, lit by 130 stunning and mostly original stained-glass windows. The stonework is just as wonderful, with a Renaissance choir screen and a host of sculpted figures above each door. There's also a treasury and crypt, and you can climb the north **tower** (€4). Though the cathedral is the main reason for visiting, Chartres town is not entirely without appeal, with a small old quarter and a picturesque district of bridges and old houses down by the River Eure. The **Musée des Beaux-Arts** in the former episcopal palace just north of the cathedral (Mon & Wed–Sat 10am–noon & 2–5/6pm, Sun 2–5/6pm; €2.50) has some beautiful tapestries, a room full of Vlaminck paintings, and Zurbarán's *Sainte Lucie*, as well as good temporary exhibitions. The **tourist office** is in front of the cathedral, at place de la Cathédrale (Mon–Sat 9/10am–6/7pm, Sun 9.30/10am–1pm & 2.30–4.30/5.30pm; ☎02.37.18.26.26, ✆www.ville-chartres .fr), and can help with accommodation. For a snack, the simple *Café Serpente* is usefully located opposite the south side of the cathedral, or for something more hearty, head for *Le Pichet* at 19 rue du Cheval Blanc.

## Giverny

Less than an hour west of Paris, **GIVERNY** is famous for **Monet's house and gardens**, complete with water-lily pond (April–Oct Tues–Sun 9.30am–6pm; €5.50, €4 gardens only; ✆www.fondation-monet.com). Monet lived here from 1883 until his death in 1926 and the gardens that he laid out were considered by many – including Monet himself – to be his "greatest masterpiece"; the best months to visit are May and June, when the rhododendrons flower around the lily pond and the wisteria hangs over the Japanese bridge, but it's overwhelmingly beautiful at any time of year. There aren't any original paintings on show, however; the house is filled with Monet's collection of Japanese prints. To get here, take a train to nearby **VERNON** from Paris-St-Lazare (4–5 daily; 45 min), then either rent a bike or take the *Gisor* bus from the station (not Mon). Giverny's only **hotel** is the small, elegant *Auberge La Musardière*, 123 rue Claude Monet (☎02.32.21.03.18; ❹), with attached restaurant.

# Northern France

**Northern France** includes some of the most industrial and densely populated parts of the country. However, there are curiosities within easy reach of the Channel ports – of which **Boulogne** is the prettiest. Further south, the *maisons* and vineyards of **Champagne** are the main draw, for which the best base is **Reims,** with its fine cathedral.

The main port of entry is **CALAIS**, France's busiest passenger port with the shortest and most frequent connections to Dover, England. There's a **free bus** service during the day from the ferry dock alongside Calais-Maritime train station to place d'Armes and on to the central Calais-Ville **train station** in Calais-Sud. The **tourist office** is at 12 bd Clemenceau (Easter–Aug Mon–Sat 9am–7pm, Sun

10am–1pm; Sept–Easter Mon–Sat 10am–1pm & 2–6.30pm; ☎03.21.96.62.40, ⓦwww.ot-calais.fr). There's a beachside **hostel** at avenue Maréchal de Lattre de Tassigny (☎03.21.34.70.20, ⓦwww.auberge-jeunesse-calais.com; €16.20).

## Boulogne

**BOULOGNE** is the one northern Channel port that might tempt you to stay. Its **Ville Basse** (Low Town), centring on place Dalton, is home to some of the best butchers and *pâtisseries* in the north, as well as an impressive array of fish restaurants. Rising above, the **Ville Haute** (Upper Town) is one of the gems of the northeast coast, flanked by grassy ramparts that give impressive views over the town and port. Inside the walls, the **Basilique Notre-Dame** is something of an oddity, raised by the town's vicar in the nineteenth century without any architectural knowledge or advice. Its crypt (Tues–Sun 2–5pm; €2) has frescoed remains of the previous Romanesque building and relics of a Roman temple to Diana, while the main part of the church has a curious statue of the Virgin and Child on a boat-chariot, drawn here on its own wheels from Lourdes. The **tourist office** (July & Aug daily 9am–7pm; Sept–March Mon–Sat 9am–12.30pm & 2–6pm; April–June also Sun 10am–1pm; ☎03.21.10.88.10, ⓦwww.tourisme -boulognesurmer.com) is at 24 Quai Gambetta, beside the fish market and ferry terminal, and can advise on availability of rooms, which in summer fill early. Your best bet is the friendly **hostel** in front of the train station, 56 place Rouget de Lisle (☎03.21.99.15.30; €15.80). Most of the budget **hotels** are around the port area: try *Alexandra*, 93 rue Thiers (☎03.21.30.52.22, ⓦwww.hotel-alexandra.fr; ④), or *Hôtel des Arts*, 102 bvd Gambetta (☎03.21.31.53.31, ℗03.21.33.69.05; ③). For **eating**, there are dozens of possibilities around place Dalton and the cathedral, but you need to be selective. The brasserie *Chez Jules*, 8 place Dalton, is always a good bet and serves food all day.

Opposite the cathedral on rue de Lille, *Estaminet du Château* offers inexpensive menus in a pleasant setting. At 31 Grande Rue, the fishermen's cooperative *Aux Pêcheurs d'Étaples* offers excellent seafood, while *La Houblonnière*, 8 rue Monsigny, has a vast international selection of brews to wash down its *plats du jour*.

## Lille

The very symbol of French industry and working-class politics, **LILLE** has traditionally suffered from some of the country's worst poverty, crime and racial conflict. In recent years, however, it has shaken off its negative image, aided by being designated European City of Culture in 2004. A stop for Eurostar trains between London and Paris, it's well worth at least a night for its lovely old quarter, some serious gourmet eating and its lively nightlife. Marking the southern boundary of

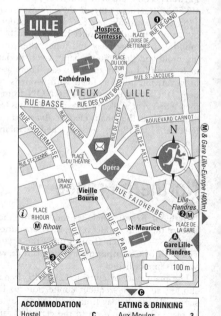

| ACCOMMODATION | | EATING & DRINKING | |
|---|---|---|---|
| Hostel | C | Aux Moules | 3 |
| Hôtel de France | B | Les Brasseurs | 2 |
| Hôtel Faidherbe | A | T'Rijsel | 1 |

the old quarter, the **Grand Place**, also known as place du Général de Gaulle (he was born here in 1890), is a busy square dominated by the old exchange building, the lavishly ornate **Vieille Bourse**, or old stock exchange. A few minutes' walk north is the **Hospice Comtesse**, 32 rue de la Monnaie, a former hospital now containing a selection of Dutch, Flemish and French paintings on loan from the Palais des Beaux-Arts in its old ward, the **Salle des Malades** (Mon 2–6pm, Wed–Sun 10am–12.30pm & 2–6pm; €2.30). South of the old quarter lies the modern place Rihour, beyond which the stylish rue de Béthune leads into café-lined place Béthune, and on to boulevard de la Liberté and the city's **Musée des Beaux-Arts**, a well-stocked fine arts museum, on place de la République (Mon 2–6pm, Wed–Sun 10am–6pm, Fri till 7pm; €4.60).

## Practicalities

The **train station** is only a few minutes' walk from the old town. The **tourist office** is in the old Palais Rihour on place Rihour (Mon–Sat 9.30am–6.30pm, Sun 10am–noon & 2–5pm; ☎03.21.21.94.21, ⊛www.lilletourism.com). *Hôtel Faidherbe*, at 42 place de la Gare (☎03.20.06.27.93; ❸), is clean, welcoming and just opposite the station; alternatively *Hôtel de France,* at 10 rue de Béthune (☎03.20.57.14.78, ℻03.20.57.06.01; ❸), is very central, as is the excellent **hostel,** near the Hôtel de Ville at 12 rue Malpart (☎03.20.57.08.94; €13.80). The main area for **restaurants** is around place Rihour and place Béthune. For mussels – the local speciality – head for *Aux Moules,* 34 rue de Béthune, or any of the brasseries around the station. Excellent **beer** flows freely at *T'Rijsel,* 25 rue du Gand, and *Les Brasseurs,* 18–22 place de la Gare by the station, or venture to rue Solferino for a pick of trendy student bars.

# Reims

Devastated by World War I artillery, **REIMS** is not the most inspiring of cities, although there are two good reasons for visiting: the champagne, and one of France's finest Gothic cathedrals, formerly scene of the coronations of French monarchs. The battered west front of the **Cathédrale** (daily 8am–7pm) is a delight, with an array of restored and expressive statuary. Inside, the stained glass includes stunning designs by Marc Chagall in the east chapel and glorifications of the champagne-making process in the south transept. Beside the cathedral, the **Palais du Tau** (May–Aug Tues–Sun 9.30am–6.30pm; Sept–April Tues–Sun 9.30am–12.30pm & 2–5.30pm; €6.10), the former bishop's palace, is worth a visit to see some of the dislodged west-front figures: there are grinning angels, friendly-looking gargoyles and a superb Eve. The building also preserves the paraphernalia of Charles X's coronation in 1824. Most of the early kings were buried in Reims's oldest building, sited 1km east of the cathedral – the eleventh-century **Basilique St-Rémi** (daily 8am–7pm). Part of a former Benedictine abbey, it's an immensely spacious building that preserves its Romanesque transept walls and ambulatory chapels.

If you're in town for the **champagne**, head to place des Droits-de-l'Homme and place St-Niçaise, around which most of the Reims *maisons* congregate; the majority charge a small fee for their tours and many require prior appointment. Of those that don't, Mumm and Piper-Heidsieck are perhaps the best: Mumm, 34 rue du Champ-de-Mars (March–Oct daily 9.30–11am & 2–4.30pm; Nov–Feb Sat & Sun 2–5pm; €6), is informative but informal, whilst Piper-Heidsieck, 51 bd Henry Vasnier (daily 9.30–11.45am & 2.30–6pm; closed Jan & Feb; €7.50), is slightly more tacky, focusing on its longstanding links with Hollywood. Of those you have to book, **Veuve Clicquot**, 1 place des Droits-de-l'Homme (April–Oct Mon–Sat; Nov–March Mon–Fri; 7 visits a day by appointment only; €7; ☎03.26.89.53.90), is the least pompous.

## Practicalities

Reims **train station** is on the northwest edge of the town centre, on Square Colbert. A five-minute walk leads to the **tourist office**, 2 rue Guillaume de Machault (daily Easter to mid-Oct 9/10am–6/7pm, mid-Oct to Easter Mon–Sat 10/11am–4/5pm; ☎03.26.77.45.00, ⊛www.reims-tourisme.fr). Of the central **hotels**, the *Thillois*, 17 rue de Thillois (☎03.26.40.65.65; ❷), and the *Alsace*, 6 rue Général Sarrail (☎03.26.47.44.08, ☎03.26.47.44.52; ❸), are the most affordable, and there's a *Centre International de Séjour* with **dorms** and doubles south of the centre at Parc Léo Lagrange (☎03.26.40.52.60, ⊛www.cis-reims.com; dorms €12.30–16.80, doubles ❸), fifteen minutes' walk from the station. For **food**, place Drouet d'Erlon is lined with cafés and restaurants: try *A Casa Mia* at no. 84 or the more upmarket *l'Apostrophe* at no. 59. There's **Internet** access at Clique et Croque, 27 rue de Vesle.

# Normandy

To the French, the essence of **Normandy** is its produce. This is the land of butter and cream, cheeses and seafood, cider and calvados, and yet parts of Normandy are among the most economically depressed of the whole country. The Normans themselves have a reputation for being insular and conservative, with a muttered hatred of Parisians who own weekend homes in the region. Along the coast, there are occasional surprises, notably the picturesque harbour at **Honfleur** and the astounding architectural feat of **Mont St-Michel**. Inland, it's hard to pin down specific highlights; the pleasures lie in the feel of particular landscapes – lush meadows and orchards, half-timbered houses, and the food and drink for which the region is famous. Of urban centres, **Rouen**, the Norman capital, is by far the most compelling, while more subdued **Bayeux** houses its eponymous tapestry and is close to the famous Normandy beaches.

The main ports of entry along this stretch of coast are Le Havre, Cherbourg and Dieppe, of which **DIEPPE** is the most enjoyable, with a good market, a castle and some decent restaurants. Its **tourist office** is beside the ferry terminal on Pont Ango (Mon–Sat 9am–noon/1pm & 2–6/8pm; summer also Sun 10am–1pm & 3–6pm; ☎02.32.14.40.60, ⊛www.dieppetourisme.com); the **train station** is about 800m southwest.

## Honfleur

**HONFLEUR** is the best-preserved of the Normandy ports and a near-perfect seaside town. The ancient port still functions and although only pleasure craft now make use of the moorings in the harbour basin, fishing boats tie up alongside the pier close by, and there are usually freshly caught fish for sale either directly from the boats or from stands on the pier. It's all highly picturesque, and not so different from the town that had such appeal for artists in the late nineteenth century.

It's this artistic past – and a present-day concentration of galleries and artisanal shops – which dominates Honfleur. The town owes most to Eugène Boudin, forerunner of Impressionism, who was born and worked here, trained the eighteen-year-old Monet, and was joined for various periods by Pissarro, Renoir and Cézanne. There's a good selection of his work in the **Musée Eugène Boudin**, west of the port on place Erik-Satie (mid-March to Sept daily except Tues 10am–noon & 2.30–6pm; Oct–Dec & mid-Feb to mid-March Mon & Wed–Fri 2.30–5pm, Sat & Sun 10am–noon & 2.30–5pm; closed Jan to mid-Feb; €4.40), along with an impressive set of works by Dufy and Monet. The composer, musician, artist and author Erik Satie was also born in Honfleur, and the rooms of his childhood home have been converted into an exhibition of his life and works. **Les Maisons Satie**, 67 bd Charles V (daily except Tues 10/11am–6pm; closed Jan to late Feb; €5.10), is no conventional museum, however. Visitors are conducted through a series of innovative "stage sets" by the man himself – or rather his words and music – by way of an infra-red controlled headset. Expect flying giant pears and indoor rain showers, rather than dusty artefacts. Back at the docks, you can take an hour-long **boat tour** of the coast for €6.50.

### Practicalities

Honfleur is on the direct **bus** route between Mont St-Michel and Le Havre (8 buses Mon–Sat); the town's nearest **train station** is at Deauville, connected by bus #20 to the town's central gare routière (takes 20min). The **tourist office** is on quai Lepaulmier (daily July & Aug 10am–5/7pm; Sept–June 10am–12.30pm & 2–5/6pm; ☎02.31.89.23.30, ⓦwww.ot-honfleur.fr). None of Honfleur's **hotels** is very affordable – the *Cascades*, 17 place Thiers (☎02.31.89.05.83; ➌), is the best bet, or there's a **campsite**, *Du Phare*, at the west end of boulevard Charles V on place Jean de Vienne (☎02.31.89.10.26; closed Oct–March). The most reasonable **restaurants** and **bars** are on rue Haute, on the way up to the Boudin museum: try *Au P'tit Mareyeur* at no. 4. At the harbour itself, it's hard to beat *Le Vieux Honfleur*, 13 quai St Étienne, while *Goutillon*, 5 cours des Fosses, has great coffee. For **Internet**, head to Cyber Pub, 55 rue de la République.

# Bayeux

**BAYEUX**'s magnificent cathedral and world-famous tapestry depicting the 1066 invasion of England by William the Conqueror make it one of the high points of Normandy. The town also makes a good jumping-off point for trips to the D-Day beaches, but it receives an influx of summer tourists that can make its charms pall somewhat. The famous **Bayeux Tapestry** is housed in the **Centre Guillaume le Conquérant**, clearly signposted on rue de Nesmond (daily 9/9.30am– 6/6.30/7pm; Nov to mid-March closed 12.30–2pm; €7.40). A 70m strip of linen gorgeously embroidered over nine centuries ago with coloured wools, it records scenes from the Norman Conquest, as well as incidental details of domestic and daily life, which run along the bottom as a counterpoint. The tapestry was commissioned for the consecration of the nearby **Cathédrale Notre-Dame** in 1077 where, despite some eighteenth-century vandalism, the Romanesque plan of the church is still intact. The crypt, entirely unaltered, is a beauty, its columns graced with frescoes of angels playing trumpets and bagpipes. Also well worth a visit is the **Memorial Museum to the Battle of Normandy** on boulevard Fabian Ware (daily 9.30/10am–6/6.30pm; Oct–April closed 12.30–2pm; €5.50). The numerous original documents, life-sized models, equipment and videos dramatically capture the most decisive chapter in the 1944 Allied invasion of Europe. For tours of the Normandy beaches, try ringing D-Day Tours (☎02.31.51.70.52; €35).

### Practicalities

Bayeux's **train station** is on the southern side of town, on boulevard Sadi Carnot. The **tourist office**, at Pont St Jean (Mon–Sat 9am–7pm, Sun 9am–12.30pm & 2–6.30pm; Oct–June closed Mon–Sat 12.30–2pm & all day Sun; ☎02.31.51.28.28, ⓦwww.bayeux-tourism.com), might be able to help you find reasonable **accommodation**. Most affordable of the **hotels** are the *Maupassant*, 19 rue St-Martin (☎02.31.92.28.53, ⓔmaupassant14@hotmail.com; ➌), and *La Gare*, 26 pl de la Gare (☎02.31.92.10.70; ➍). The *Family Home* at 39 rue du Général de Dais (☎02.31.92.15.22; €18), north of the cathedral, functions as a friendly and decent **hostel**, and serves good food too. The nearest **campsite** is on boulevard d'Eindhoven, a fifteen-minute walk from the centre (☎02.31.92.08.43; closed Oct–April). Most of the **restaurants** are on the pedestrianized rue St-Jean – *La*

*Fringale* at no. 43 is quite popular, while just off the end of the cobbles, *Djerba*, 57 rue St. Martin, dishes up good Tunisian food.

## Mont St-Michel

On the far western edge of Normandy, the island of **Mont St-Michel** is the site of a marvellous **Gothic abbey** (tours daily 9/9.30am–6/7pm; €7). The abbey church, long known as the Merveille, is visible from all around the bay, and it becomes more awe-inspiring the closer you get; it's especially striking at night, when bathed in white and amber light from below. The granite structure was sculpted to match the contours of the hill, and though space was always limited, the building has grown through the centuries in ever more ingenious uses of geometry. However, the current dour state of the stone walls is a far cry from the way the monastery would have looked in medieval times, brightly painted and festooned with tapestries. **To stay** on the island, head up the one twisting street to the *Du Guesclin* (☎02.33.60.14.10, ⊕02.33.60.45.81; ❺), with excellent rooms and a run-of-the-mill **restaurant**. There's a **campsite** (☎02.33.60.22.10; closed mid-Nov to Jan) near the causeway to the island, or a **hostel** at boulevard du Général Patton, 6km south in Pontorson (☎02.33.60.18.65; €7.30). The nearest **train station** is also here and you can either rent a bike or take a bus to the Mont.

## Rouen

**ROUEN** was flattened during World War II, following which a flood of money was spent on restoring it to an attractive, if in parts fake, medieval centre complete with half-timbered houses, cobbled streets and impressive churches. A prominent point in the centre, between place du Vieux-Marché – where Joan of Arc was burned at the stake in 1431 – and the cathedral, is the Gros-Horloge, a colourful one-handed clock that spans the street named after it. Just off here is the **Cathédrale de Notre-Dame** (Mon 2–6pm, Tues–Sun 8am–6pm; free), a Gothic masterpiece built in the twelfth and thirteenth centuries. The west facade, intricately sculpted like the rest of the exterior, was Monet's subject for his series of celebrated studies of changing light. The church of **St-Ouen**, in a park a short walk northeast, is larger than the cathedral and has far less decoration, so that the Gothic proportions have a more instant impact. Close by, the church of St-Maclou is more flamboyant, although perhaps the real interest is in its adjacent **Aître St-Maclou**, once a cemetery for plague victims, which still has its original macabre decorations. Also worth a visit is the **Musée Flaubert et d'Histoire de la Médecine** in the Hôpital Hôtel-Dieu on the corner of rue de Lecat and rue du Contrat-Social (Tues 10am–6pm, Wed–Sat 10am–noon & 2–6pm; €2.20), dedicated to Rouen's most famous novelist, Gustave Flaubert, whose father was chief surgeon at the medical school here.

### Practicalities

The main **train station**, Rouen Rive-Droite, is a ten-minute walk or one métro stop from the centre. The **bus station** is just off the southern end of the main rue Jeanne d'Arc. The **tourist office** is opposite the cathedral at 25 pl de la Cathédrale (Mon–Sat 9am–12.30pm & 1.30–6/7pm, Sun 9.15/10am–12.30/1pm & 2–6pm; Oct–April closed Sun afternoon; ☎02.32.08.32.40, ⓦwww.rouentourisme .com). Inexpensive **hotels** include: the bare-bones *Sphinx*, 130 rue Beauvoisine (☎02.35.71.35.86; ❸) and *Le Palais*, 12 rue du Tambour (☎02.35.71.41.40; ❸). The town's **campsite** is 5km northwest on rue Jules-Ferry in Déville-lès-Rouen (☎02.35.74.07.59; bus #2 from Théâtre des Arts). Rouen has a reputation for good **food**, and its most famous dish, duckling (*caneton*), can be enjoyed quite affordably at *Pascaline*, 5 rue de la Poterne. For excellent basic meals, the south side of place du Vieux-Marché and the north side of St-Maclou church are both lined with good-quality restaurants. There's **Internet** access at Cyber Net, 59 pl du Vieux-Marché.

# Brittany

For generations the people of **Brittany** risked their lives fishing and trading on the violent seas or struggling with the arid soil of the interior, and their resilience is tinged with Celtic culture: mystical, musical, sometimes morbid, sometimes vital and inspired. Unified with France in 1532, the Bretons have seen their language steadily eradicated, and the interior severely depopulated. Today, the people still tend to think of France as a separate country, even if few of them actively support Breton nationalism. The recent economic resurgence, helped partly by summer tourism, has largely been due to local initiatives. At the same time, a Celtic artistic identity has been revived at festivals of traditional Breton music, poetry and dance, and today 700,000 people speak Breton as a first or second language. For most visitors to Brittany, the **coast** is the dominant feature. After the Côte d'Azur, this is the most popular summer resort area in France, and the attractions are obvious – white sand beaches, towering cliffs and offshore islands. Whether you approach across the Channel by ferry, or along the coast from Normandy, the River Rance, guarded by **St-Malo** on its estuary and **Dinan** 20km upstream, makes a spectacular introduction to the region. Brittany's southern coast takes in France's most famous prehistoric site, the alignments of **Carnac**, and although the beaches are not as spectacular as Finistère's, the water is warmer. Of the cities, **Vannes** has one of the liveliest medieval town centres.

Brittany's main port apart from St-Malo is **ROSCOFF**, close to the northwestern tip. Follow the signs from the **ferry terminal** to the town centre; the **train station** is 100m south of the town on rue Ropartz Morvan. The **tourist office** is at 46 rue Gambetta (Mon–Sat 9am–noon/12.30pm & 1.30/2–6/7pm, also July & Aug Sun 10am–12.30pm; ☎02.98.61.12.13, ⊛www.roscoff-tourisme.com), where there are a few **Internet** terminals.

## St-Malo

**ST-MALO**, walled and built with the same grey granite as Mont St-Michel, presents its best face to the River Rance and the sea. Once within the old ramparts it can seem a little grim and squat, and overrun by summer tourists, but away from the thoroughfares of the tiny **citadel**, with its high seventeenth-century houses, random exploration is fun. The **town museum**, in the castle to the right as you enter the main city gate, Porte St-Vincent (daily 10am–noon/12.30pm & 2–6pm; winter closed Mon; €5), devotes several exhausting floors to St-Malo's sources of wealth and fame – colonialism, slave-trading and privateering among them. **Buses** drop you at Porte St-Vincent, while **trains** stop on the other side of the docks, a ten-minute walk away. The **tourist office** is on the Esplanade St-Vincent, right in front of the gate (Mon–Sat 9/10am–12.30pm & 1.30/2.30–6/7.30pm; July & Aug open through lunch; winter closed Sun; ☎02.99.56.64.48, ⊛www.saint-malo-tourisme.com). It's always hard to find **accommodation** in the old city, despite the extraordinary number of hotels, but rooms at Le Nautilus, 9 rue de la Corne de Cerf (☎02.99.40.42.27, ℮nautilus-st-malo@wanadoo.fr; ❹), and Le Louvre, 2 rue des Marins (☎02.99.40.86.62; ❹), are worth trying. Otherwise, there's an array of places near the train station. In the suburb of Paramé, 2km northeast of the station, is an often-crowded **hostel** at 37 av R.P. Umbricht (☎02.99.40.29.80, ⊛www.centrevarangot.com; €12.40; bus #2 or #5). There's a municipal **campsite**, Cité d'Aleth, on allée Gaston Buy (☎02.99.81.60.91), near some shops and the beach.

Most of the citadel's **restaurants** are pricey tourist traps, though *Coquille d'Oeuf*, 20 rue de la Cerf Corne de has cheap traditional meals. Otherwise, there's a slew of Breton *crêperies* and *mouleries,* such as *La Brigantine*, 13 rue de Dinan, and *Le Brick*, 5 rue Jacques-Cartier. **Internet** access is at Cop Imprime, 39 bd des Talards.

# Dinan

A short distance from St-Malo along the River Rance lies **DINAN**, one of the most enjoyable towns in Brittany. Its **citadel** has been preserved almost intact within a three-kilometre circuit of walls, inside which lies a warren of beautiful late-medieval houses. It's almost too good to be true and time is easily spent rambling from *crêperie* to café, admiring the houses on the way. Unfortunately, there's only one small stretch of the **ramparts** that you can walk along – from the gardens behind St-Sauveur to just short of the Tour Sillon – but you get a good general overview from the **Tour de l'Horloge** (April & May daily 2–6.30pm; June–Sept daily 10am–6.30pm; €2.70). Another good view can be had from the **Château Duchesse Anne** (June–Sept daily 10am–6.30pm; Oct–May closed noon–1.30pm & Tues; closed Jan; €4). An inevitable target of any Dinan wanderings is the church of **St-Sauveur**, a real mix of styles, with a Romanesque porch and eighteenth-century steeple.

## Practicalities

Dinan's **train station** is a ten-minute walk away from the central place du Guesclin. The **tourist office** (daily 9am–6/7pm; closed lunch Sun & Oct to mid-June; ☎02.96.87.69.76, ⊛www.dinan-tourisme.com) is at the southwest corner of the *place*, at 9 rue du Château. The cheapest **hotels** are near the station, but it's nicer within the walls: try *La Duchesse Anne* at 10 pl du Guesclin (☎02.96.39.09.43, ☎02.96.85.09.76; ➍). Dinan's **hostel** (☎02.96.39.10.83; €13.30; closed Jan) is attractively set in the Moulin de Méen near the port at Taden, about 3km away, while the closest **campsite** is at 103 rue Châteaubriand (☎02.96.39.11.96; closed late Sept to late May), which runs parallel to the western ramparts. Of the wide choice of **eating places**, two good bets are *Crêperie Ahna*, 7 rue de la Poissonnerie and *La P'tite Pizz'*, 9 rue de l'Horloge.

# Quimper and around

**QUIMPER**, capital of the ancient diocese and kingdom of Cornouaille, is the oldest Breton city, founded according to legend by St Corentin, who came here across the channel to the place they named Little Britain some time between the fourth and seventh centuries. It's a laid-back town, with old granite buildings, two rivers and the rising woods of Mont Frugy overlooking the centre. Quimper focuses on the enormous Gothic Cathédrale St-Corentin, while the **Musée des Beaux-Arts**, alongside at 40 pl St-Corentin (July & Aug daily 10am–7pm; Sept–June closed noon–2pm & Tues; Nov–March also closed Sun 10am–noon; €4), has an amazing collection of drawings by Cocteau, Max Jacob and Gustave Doré (shown in rotation) and nineteenth- and twentieth-century paintings of the famed Pont-Aven school. To see pottery made on an industrial scale, and an exhibition of the changing styles since the first Quimper *ateliers* of the late seventeenth century, head for rue Jean-Baptiste Bosquet, where you'll find the **Faïenceries de Quimper** (hourly guided visits only; €3.50; ☎02.98.90.09.36) and the **Musée de la Faïence** (mid-April to mid-Oct Mon–Sat 10am–6pm; €4).

## Practicalities

The adjacent **train** and **bus stations** are a short walk east along the river from the town centre. The **tourist office** is on the south bank at 7 rue de la Déesse, place de la Résistance (July & Aug Mon–Sat 9am–7pm, Sun 10am–12.45pm &

3–5.45pm; June & Sept closed Sun afternoon; Oct–May closed all Sun & Mon–Sat 12.30–1.30pm; ℡02.98.53.04.05, ⓦwww.quimper-tourisme.com). Budget **hotels** include the *Hôtel le Derby*, near the station at 13 av de la Gare (℡02.98.52.06.91, ℉02.98.53.39.04; ❸), and *TGV*, nearby at 4 rue de Concarneau (℡02.98.90.54.00, ⓦwww.hoteltgv.com; ❹). The **hostel** (℡02.98.64.97.97, ℮quimper@fuaj.org; €9.10) and **campsite** (℡02.98.55.61.09; reserved for caravans in winter) are downstream on avenue des Oiseaux in the Bois du Séminaire – take bus #1 from place de la Résistance. For **food**, go for the *crêpes* at *La Krampouzerie*, 9 rue du Sallé, on the lively little place au Beurre, north of the cathedral. Note that rooms book up fast for the last full week of July, when the town hosts the **Festival de Cornouaille**, a jamboree of Breton music, costume and dance.

**Boats** down the Odet to the coast leave from the end of quai de l'Odet, opposite the Faïenceries, making a winding journey to the upmarket resort of **BÉNODET**, where there's a long sheltered beach; for times and prices call ℡02.98.52.98.41. Hotels here are comparatively expensive, but there are several large campsites. There are more **beaches** along the coast between Penmarch and Loctudy and beyond, about an hour by bus from Quimper. Another possibility is a trip to the **Pointe du Raz**, the Land's End of France, a series of plummeting fissures, filling and draining with deafening force, above which you can amble along precarious paths.

# Carnac and Quiberon

About 30km southeast along the coast from the functional port of Lorient, **CARNAC** is home to one of the most important prehistoric sites in Europe, a congregation of some two thousand or so semi-megalithic **menhirs** stretching for more than 4km to the north of the village, long predating the Pyramids or Stonehenge. The stones may have been part of an observatory for the motions of the moon, but no one really knows. The main alignments, fenced from the public, are viewed from a raised platform at one end of the plain. There's plenty of information on them at the **Musée de la Préhistoire**, 10 pl de la Chapelle, near rue du Tumulus in Carnac-Ville (daily 10am–12.30pm & 1.30–6/7pm, closed Wed am; €5). Carnac itself, made up of Carnac-Ville and the newer seaside resort of Carnac-Plage, is extremely popular, though deserted out of season. **Buses** arrive at the main **tourist office** at 74 av des Druides in Carnac-Plage (July & Aug Mon–Sat 9am–7pm, Sun 3–7pm; Sept–June closed lunch & Sun; ℡02.97.52.13.52, ⓦwww.ot-carnac.fr). Among the town's **hotels**, the *Ratelier*, 4 chemin du Douet (℡02.97.52.05.04, ⓦwww.le-ratelier.com; ❺; closed Oct–March), with its eight well-styled rooms is a good deal, as is the central *chambres d'hôte Chez Nous*, 5 pl de la Chapelle (℡ & ℉02.97.52.07.28, ℮chez.nous56@wanadoo.fr; ❹; closed Nov–March). The best of the many **beaches** is the smallest, the Men Dû, just off the road towards La Trinité. For **camping** by the sea, head for *Men Dû* (℡02.97.52.04.23, ⓦwww.camping-du-mendu.com; closed Oct–Easter), though the best site is opposite the stones, *La Grande Métairie* (℡02.97.52.24.01; closed mid-Sept to March).

South of Carnac, the town of **QUIBERON** is a lively port and provides a jumping-off point for boats out to the nearby islands or simply a base for the peninsula. The ocean-facing shore, known as the **Côte Sauvage**, is a wild and unswimmable stretch, but the sheltered eastern side has safe and calm sandy beaches, and offers plenty of **campsites**. In Quiberon, **Port Maria**, the fishing harbour, is the most active part of town and has the best concentration of **hotels**, though they're often full in high season – try *Le Neptune* at 4 quai de Houat (℡02.97.50.09.62; ❺), or *Au Bon Accueil*, 6 quai de Houat (℡02.97.50.07.92; ❸), which also has a very good fish restaurant. The spartan **hostel**, *Les Filets Bleus*, 45 rue du Roch-Priol (℡02.97.50.15.54, ℮quiberon@fuaj.org; €7.70; closed Oct–March), is set back from the sea about 1km southeast of the train station. Fish **restaurants** line the seafront: *Le Port Maria* is one good option, while the **cafés** by the long bathing beach are also enjoyable. The **train station**, with services in July and August only, is a couple of minutes north of the centre on place de la Gare, and buses, which run year-round, arrive here as well. The **tourist office** is at 14 rue de Verdun (July & Aug Mon–Sat 9am–7.30pm, Sun 9.30am–12.30pm & 2.30–7pm; Sept–June Mon–Sat 10am–noon & 2–6pm; ℡02.97.50.45.12, ✆www.quiberon.com).

## Vannes and the Golfe de Morbihan

**VANNES**, whose old centre is a chaotic web of streets crammed around the cathedral and enclosed by ramparts and gardens, is one of the most historic towns in Brittany. It was here that the Breton assembly ratified the Act of Union with France in 1532, in the building known as **La Cohue**, opposite the cathedral, which now houses the **Musée de Vannes** (June–Sept daily 10am–6pm; Oct–May Mon & Wed–Sat 10am–noon & 2–6pm, Sun 2–6pm; €4). Vannes' harbour is a channelled inlet of the ragged-edged **Golfe de Morbihan**, which lets in the tides through a narrow gap. By popular tradition, the **islands** scattered around this enclosure used to number the days of the year, though for centuries the waters have been rising and there are now fewer than one for each week. Of these, forty-one are privately owned, while two – the Île aux Moines and Île d'Arz – have small communities and regular ferry services, and end up being crowded in summer. You can take a **boat tour** around the rest, a compelling trip through a baffling muddle of channels, megalithic ruins, stone circles and solitary menhirs; contact Navix (℡02.97.46.60.00) or Compagnie des Îles (℡02.97.46.18.19) for details.

### Practicalities

It's twenty minutes' walk south from the **train station** to the centre at place de la République. The **tourist office** is at 1 rue Thiers (daily July & Aug 9am–7pm; Sept–June Mon–Sat 9am–12.30pm & 2–6pm; ℡02.97.47.24.34, ✆www.pays-de -vannes.com/tourisme). Vannes has the best choice of **hotels** anywhere around the Golfe de Morbihan: two good ones are *Le Bretagne*, 36 rue du Mené, in the old town (℡02.97.47.20.21, ✆www.bretagne-hotel.com; ❸), and *Le Marina* over-looking the port at 4 pl Gambetta (℡02.97.47.22.81; ❸). For **food**, the *Crêperie La Cave St-Gwenaël*, 23 rue St-Gwenaël, is good value, set in a lovely old house facing the cathedral.

## Nantes

Though **NANTES**, the former capital, is these days not officially a part of Brittany, it remains for its inhabitants integral to the province. Crucial to its self-image is the **Château des Ducs**, subjected to a certain amount of damage over the centuries, but still preserving the form in which it was built by two of the last rulers of independent Brittany, François II and his daughter Duchess Anne, who was born here in 1477. You can walk into the courtyard and up onto the low ramparts for free, and visit temporary exhibitions in the Harnachement building, but the rest of the castle is under renovation until late 2006. In 1800 the castle's arsenal exploded, shattering the stained glass of the **Cathédrale de St-Pierre et St-Paul**, 200m away, just one of many disasters that have befallen the church. Its soaring heights are home to the tomb of François II and his wife, Margaret. Back past the château, the **Île Feydeau**, once an island, was the birthplace of **Jules Verne**; the museum dedicated to him is at 3 rue de l'Hermitage (Mon & Wed–Sat 10am–noon & 2–6pm, Sun 2–6pm; €1.50). The **train station** is a short way east of the castle. For **accommodation**, try the central *Hôtel Rénova*, 11 rue Beauregard (℡02.40.47.57.03, ✆www.hotel-renova.com; ❸), *Hôtel de l'Océan,* 11 rue du Maréchal-de-Lattre-de-Tassigny (℡02.40.69.73.51, ✆www.hotel-nantes.com; ❸), or *Fourcroy*, 11 rue Fourcroy (☎02.40.44.68.00; ❸). The city's **hostel**, at 2 pl de la Manu (☎02.40.29.29.20; €12.55), is a ten-minute walk east of the train station along the tram tracks, or take tram #1 to Beaujoire. The **tourist office** is on place du Commerce, in a large FNAC book and music store (Mon–Sat 10am–6pm; ☎02.40.20.60.00, ⊛www.nantes-tourisme.com) in an appealing, largely pedestrian area that is a good source of **restaurants**. There's **Internet** access at Cyber City, 14 rue de Strasbourg.

# The Loire Valley

The sheer density of châteaux can be daunting when choosing where to go in the **Loire**, but if you pick selectively – the best are those at **Chenonceaux** and **Loches** – this can be one of the most enjoyable of all French regions. The Loire itself is known as the last wild river in France, as well as the longest; no one swims in it, nor are any goods carried along it. The stretch above Saumur is the loveliest on the lower reaches, the land to the south planted with vines and sunflowers. Other than the châteaux, the region has few sights; of the towns, **Tours** is good for low-key bustle, while **Saumur** and **Chinon** are perfect for provincial indolence.

## Tours and around

The regional capital **TOURS** makes a good base for châteaux-hunting. The city has two main areas, sited either side of the central rue Nationale. To the east loom the extravagant towers and stained-glass windows of the **Cathédrale St-Gatien**, with some handsome old streets behind. Adjacent, the **Musée des Beaux-Arts**, on place François Sicard (9am–12.45pm & 2–6pm, closed Tues; free), has some beauties in its rambling collection, notably Mantegna's *Christ in the Garden of Olives* and *Resurrection*. Tours' **old town** meanwhile crowds around medieval place Plumereau, on the west side of the city. It's crammed with cafés, bars and restaurants, and in the winding streets around the square, the medieval half-timbered houses and bulging stairway towers are the city's showpieces.

### Practicalities

The **tourist office** is in front of the **train station** at 78–82 rue Bernard-Palissy (8.30/9am–6/7pm, Sun 10am–12.30/1pm & 2.30–5pm; mid-Oct to mid-April closed lunch and Sun afternoon; ☎02.47.70.37.37, ⊛www.ligeris.com). There are plenty of reasonably priced **hotels** in the cathedral quarter: the *Regina*, 2 rue Pimbert (☎02.47.05.25.36, ☎02.47.66.08.72; ❷), and *Art Hôtel*, 40 rue de la Préfecture (☎02.47.05.67.53; ❷), are decent places, as is *Hôtel du Cygne*, 6 rue du Cygne (☎02.47.66.66.41, ⊛perso.wanadoo.fr/hotelcygne.tours; ❹). There's no campsite in town, but there's an HI **hostel** behind place Plumereau, at 5 rue Bretonneau (☎02.47.37.81.58; €17). The commercial area around rue du Grand-Marché, on the periphery of old Tours, and rue Colbert, which runs down to the cathedral, are the most promising streets for **restaurants**: try *Le Petit Patrimoine*, at 58 rue Colbert, for good regional cuisine. Nightlife gallivants around Place Plumereau.

### Villandry, Chenonceaux and Loches

The most popular attraction close to Tours is the **château** of **VILLANDRY**, about 13km west, where there are some extraordinary Renaissance **gardens** – the largest in France – set out on several terraces with marvellous views over the river (daily 9am–5/6.30pm; gardens till 5.30/7.30pm; €8, €5.50 gardens only). The handsome château holds Spanish paintings and a Moorish ceiling from Toledo. There's no public transport, but if you rent a bike at Tours it's a wonderful ride along the banks of the Cher. Perhaps the finest Loire **château**, however, is that straddling the river at **CHENONCEAUX** (daily 9am–4.30/7pm; €8), about 15km from Villandry and accessible by train from Tours. The building went up in the 1520s and was the home of first Diane de Poitiers and then Catherine de Médicis, respectively the lover and wife of Henry II. There are numerous gorgeous rooms of tapestries, paintings and furniture, but the views onto the placid Cher river are the highlight – you can rent boats in summer. The **château** at **LOCHES**, an hour by train southeast of Tours, is visually the most impressive of the Loire fortresses, with ramparts and a huddle of houses below still partly enclosed by the outer wall of the medieval town (daily 9/9.30am–5/7pm; €7). You can climb to the top of the ruined keep, poke around in the dungeons and torture chamber and visit the royal lodgings, where Charles VII had his residence.

### Chinon

The ruined **château** at **CHINON** (daily 9/9.30am–5/7pm; €6), where Henry II of England died cursing his rebellious sons Richard and John, was later one of the few places in which Charles VII could stay while Henry V of England held Paris and the title to the French throne. Charles' situation changed with the arrival here in 1429 of Joan of Arc, who persuaded him to give her an army in the ruined Grande Salle. To the west, the **Tour Coudray** preserves thirteenth-century graffiti carved by imprisoned and doomed Templar knights. Wedged between the castle and the river Vienne, the town of Chinon is ancient and attractive, with the tiny *Hôtel de la Treille*, 4 pl Jeanne d'Arc (℡02.47.93.07.71; ❷), being an excellent place to **stay**. Alternatively, try charming *Menestrel* (℡02.47.93.07.20, ⓦwww .lemenestrel.com; ❷), with both an inexpensive brasserie and **Internet** café. Across the river at Île-Auger, the **campsite** (℡02.47.93.08.35) rents out kayaks in summer on the River Vienne. The **tourist office** is on place Hofheim (daily 10am–7pm; Oct–April closed lunch & Sun; ℡02.47.93.17.85, ⓦwww.chinon .com). *La Treille* is a wonderfully old-fashioned **restaurant**, while *La Maison Rouge*, 38 rue Voltaire, features decent regional specialities.

### Saumur and around

**SAUMUR** is a peaceful, pretty riverside town, and a good place to base yourself, with Tours and Chinon within easy reach, and the local sparkling wines available everywhere. Its **château** (10am–12.30/1pm & 2–5.30/6pm; closed Tues; €2) is dramatically perched above town, though there's little to see thanks to a current restoration project, scheduled to finish in 2007. The immense **Abbaye de Fontevraud** (daily 9/10am–5.30/6.30pm; €6.10), 13km on bus #16 (4–6 daily; 35min), was founded in 1099 as both a nunnery and a monastery with an abbess in charge. Its chief significance is as the burial ground of the Plantagenet kings and queens, notably Henry II, Eleanor of Aquitaine and Richard the Lionheart. Saumur's **train station** is on the north bank of the river; from here cross over the bridge to the island, then over another bridge to the main part of the town on the south bank. The **tourist office** is at the foot of the second bridge, on place de la Bilange (Mon–Sat 9.15am–7pm, Sun 10/10.30am–noon/12.30pm & 2.30–5.30pm; mid-Oct to mid-May closed lunch and Sun afternoon; ℡02.41.40.20.60, ⓦwww.ot-saumur.fr). The best **hotel** is *Le Cristal*, 10 place de la République (℡02.41.51.09.54, ⓔcrystal@saumur.net; ❹), with river views from most rooms and **Internet** access; alternatively there's the charming *Le Volney*, 1 rue Volney (℡02.41.51.25.41, ⓦwww.levolney.com; ❸), on the south side of town. On the Île d'Offard, connected by bridges to both banks of the town, there's a good **hostel** at the eastern end of rue de Verdun (℡02.41.40.30.00; €22), and a **campsite** next door. The best area for **eating** is around place St-Pierre: *Auberge St-Pierre*, at no. 6, has a fairly inexpensive menu, or try *Les Forges de St-Pierre*, at no.1.

## Orléans

Due south of Paris, **ORLÉANS** continually harks back to the glory it enjoyed when Joan of Arc delivered the city from the English in 1429. Stained-glass windows in the nave of the enormous, Gothic **Cathédrale Sainte-Croix** (daily 9.15am–noon & 2.15–5pm; free) tell the story of her life, with caricatures of the loutish Anglo-Saxons and snooty French nobles, while a fine sculpture of the "Maid of Orléans" stands nearby, outside the sixteenth-century Hôtel de Ville. Immediately opposite, the **Musée des Beaux-Arts** (Tues–Sat 9.30am–12.15pm & 1.30–5.45pm, Sun 2–6.30pm; €3) has an excellent collection of French painting.

The **train station** and **tourist office** (daily 9.30am–6.30pm except Sept–March closed lunch & Sun; ☎02.38.24.05.05, ⊛www.ville-orleans .fr) are both on the busy place d'Arc, north of the town centre, connected by rue de la République to the central place du Martroi. Just back from the station there's an inexpensive **hotel**, *Hôtel de Paris*, 29 rue Faubourg-Bannier (☎02.38.53.39.58; **②**), or, more central, there's the *Charles Sanglier*, 8 rue Charles Sanglier (☎02.38.53.38.50; **③**), and *Le Brin de Zinc*, 62 rue Ste-Catherine (☎02.38.53.88.77), which has a lively restaurant with outdoor seating. The **hostel** is at boulevard de la Motte-Sanguin, twenty minutes' walk to the east of town, and accessible on bus #4 from the train station (☎02.38.54.83.31; €8.80; private room **②**). Bus #26 goes to the **campsite** at St-Jean-de-la-Ruelle, 3km out on the Blois road on rue de la Roche (☎02.38.88.39.39, open July–Aug). Rue de Bourgogne, parallel to the river, has an excellent choice of bars and **restaurants** of which *La Petite Marmite*, at no. 178, serving traditional French food, is one of the best.

# Poitou-Charente and the Atlantic coast

Vast horizons punctuated by fields of sunflowers, fertile farmland and groves of poplars typify **Poitou-Charente**, whose timeless, siesta-silent air gives the first exciting promise of the south. The coast – distinctly Atlantic, with dunes, pine forests and misty mud flats – has copious charm, though lacks the glitz and glamour of the Côte d'Azur. The principal port, **La Rochelle**, is one of the prettiest and most distinctive towns in France, while the nearby islands of **Ré** and, further south, **Oléron**, out of season at least, are lovely, with kilometres of sandy beaches and ancient oyster beds. **Poitiers** is a good starting point for the region, a pleasant town with an attractive old centre. South of here, the valley of the Charente river, slow and green, epitomizes blue-overalled, peasant France, accessible on boat trips from **Cognac**, famous for its brandy.

## Poitiers

**POITIERS** is a charming country town whose eclectic noble architecture derives from its enduring and often influential history as seat of the dukes of Aquitaine. The tree-lined **place Leclerc**, and **place de Gaulle**, a few streets north, are the two poles of communal life, flanked by cafés and market stalls. A tantalising web of streets lies between, with rue Gambetta cutting past the **Palais de Justice** (daily 8.45am–noon & 1.45–5.30pm; free), whose nineteenth-century facade hides the twelfth-century great Gothic hall of the dukes of Aquitaine. This magnificent room is where Jean, Duc de Berry, held his sumptuous court in the late fourteenth century, seated on the intricately carved dais at the far end of the room. In one corner, stairs give access to the old castle keep and lead out onto the roof with a memorable view over the town. Across from the Palais is one of the most idiosyncratic churches in France, **Notre-Dame-la-Grande** (Mon–Sat 8.30am–7pm, Sun 2–7pm; free), whose elaborate, almost fussy west façade holds a number of enthralling sculpted figures, from a detailed bathing Jesus to a perched demoiselle, hair blowing in the wind. There's another unusual church a little way east, literally in the middle of rue Jean-Jaurès as you head towards the River Clain. Reputedly the oldest Christian building in France, the fourth-century **Baptistère St-Jean** (daily April–Sept 10.30am–12.30pm & 3–6pm; Oct–March 2.30–4.30pm; Sept–June closed Tues; €1) was until the seventeenth century the only place in town to conduct a proper baptism; the font was the octagonal pool sunk into the floor. A sprinkling of ancient and faded frescoes can be seen on its walls, including one of the Emperor Constantine on horseback.

## Practicalities

At the foot of the hill that forms the kernel of the town is Poitiers **train station,** a ten-minute walk up the stairs flanking the city walls from the centre. Cheap **hotels** nearby include the *Bistrot de la Gare* at 131 bd du Grand-Cerf (℡05.49.58.56.30; ❷), and the *Petite Villette*, 14 bd de l'Abbé de Frémont (℡05.49.41.41.33, ℡05.49.50.09.77; closed mid-July to mid-Aug; ❸). In the town centre there's the attractive *Plat d'Étain*, 7–9 rue du Plat d'Étain (℡05.49.41.04.80, ℗www .hotelduplatdetain.com; ❷). The **hostel** is at 1 allée Roger Tagault (℡05.49.30.09.70; €8.85; bus #3 or #7) and there's a municipal **campsite** on rue du Porteau, 2km north of town (℡05.49.41.44.88, ℡05.49.46.41.91; closed Sept–June; bus #7). The **tourist office** is at 45 pl Charles de Gaulle (Mon–Sat 9.30/10am–6/7/11pm; April–Oct also Sun 10am–6pm; ℡05.49.41.21.24, ℗www.ot-poitiers.fr). *Le St-Hubert*, 13 rue Cloche Perse, serves regional **food** at reasonable prices, while *La Serrurerie*, on 28 rue des Grandes Écoles, is a buzzing bistrot-bar very popular with students.

## La Rochelle

**LA ROCHELLE** is the most attractive seaside town in France, with a beautiful seventeenth- and eighteenth-century centre and waterfront and a lively, bustling air. Granted a charter by Eleanor of Aquitaine in 1199, it rapidly became a port of major importance, trading in salt and wine. The heavy Gothic gateway of the **Porte de la Grosse Horloge** straddles the entrance to the old town, dominating the pleasure-boat-filled inner harbour, guarded by two sturdy towers (10am–12.30/1pm & 2–5.30/7pm; €4.60). Behind the Grosse Horloge, the main shopping street of **rue du Palais** is lined by eighteenth-century houses and arcaded shop fronts. To the west, especially in **rue de l'Escale**, are the discreet residences of the eighteenth-century ship owners and chandlers, while to the east, rue du Temple leads to the Franco-Italian-style **Hôtel de Ville**, begun in the reign of Henri IV, whose initials, intertwined with those of Marie de Medici, are carved on the ground-floor gallery (guided tours: June–Sept daily 3pm; July & Aug daily 3 & 4pm; Oct–May Sat & Sun 3pm; free). Further riches lie inside the **Musée du Nouveau Monde**, 10 rue Fleuriau (Mon & Wed–Sat 10am–12.30pm & 2–6pm, Sun 2.30–6pm; €3.50), which occupies the former residence of the Fleuriau family, who, like many of their fellow *Rochelais*, made fortunes from slavery, sugar, spices and coffee. For **beaches**, you're best off crossing over to the **Île de Ré**, a long narrow island immediately west of La Rochelle (buses from place de Verdun or pricey boat trips from the Vieux Port), which is surrounded by sandy strands. Out of season it has a slow, misty charm, centred around the cultivation of oysters and mussels; in summer it's packed to the gills. **Île d'Oléron**, just south of La Rochelle, is flatter and more wooded, but also has a number of excellent beaches as well as a lovely bird sanctuary, the Marais aux Oiseaux.

## Practicalities

From the **train station**, it's ten minutes down avenue du Général de Gaulle to the town centre. The **tourist office** is by the harbour on place de la Petite Sirène, Quartier du Gabut (daily July & Aug 9am–8pm; Sept–June Mon–Sat 9/10am–6/7pm, Sun 10/10.30am–1/5.30pm; ☎05.46.41.14.68, ⊛www.larochelle-tourisme .fr). You should book accommodation in advance in summer, though the tourist office can help you find something if you arrive *sans réservations*. There's a **hostel** in avenue des Minimes to the west (☎05.46.44.43.11; €12.70; bus #10 from place de Verdun or the train station) and two **campsites** – the *Soleil* by the hostel (☎05.46.44.42.53; closed mid-Sept to mid-May) and the *Port Neuf*, on the northwestern side of town on boulevard A. Rondeau (☎05.46.43.81.20; bus #6 from Grosse Horloge). Of the handful of budget **hotels**, the best central bets are the *Bordeaux*, 45 rue St-Nicolas (☎05.46.41.31.22, ⊛www.hotel-bordeaux-fr.com; ❸), which is atmospheric but a bit noisy, and the newly-renovated *Henri-IV*, 31 rue des Gentilshommes (☎05.46.41.25.79, ℮HENRI-IV@wanadoo.fr; ❹). For **food**, try the area around rue du Port and rue Saint-Sauveur just off the waterfront, or *Café de la Poste*, on place de l'Hôtel de Ville, for good menus. Alternatively, rue St-Nicolas is a good bet with *À Côté de Chez Fred*, at no. 34, serving unforgettable fish (menu lunchtimes only), and **Internet** access just opposite, at Squat, no. 63.

## Cognac

The prosperous little town of **COGNAC** is best known for its brandy distilleries, whose heady scent pervades the air. The **tourist office**, close to the central place François I, 16 rue du 14-juillet (daily: July & Aug 9am–7pm; Sept–June 9.30/10am–5/5.30pm; ☎05.45.82.10.71, ⊛www.tourism-cognac.com), has information on visiting the various cognac *chais*, most of which are at the end of Grande-Rue, which winds through the old quarter of town. Hennessy, at 1 rue de la Richonne (March–Dec daily 10am–5/6pm; Jan & Feb Mon–Fri by appointment only; ☎05.45.35.72.68, €5.30), offers one of the best tours: the seventh-generation family firm of Irish origin keeps 180,000 barrels in stock, with various blends of brandy made under the guidance of the *maître du chai*'s expert eye, nose and palate. Aside from cognac, the town has a charming old centre dotted with ancient palaces and half-timbered buildings. The centre is five minutes' walk from the **train station**: take rue Mousnier, then rue Bayard, which leads up rue du 14-Juillet to place François I. For **accommodation**, try the friendly *Le Cheval Blanc*, 6–8 pl Bayard (☎05.45.82.09.55, ⊛www.lechevalblanc.fr; ❹), with good-value rooms, or the *Hotel d'Orléans*, at 25 rue d'Angoulême (☎05.45.82.01.26, ℮VRBonnin@aol .com; ❸), with its spectacular staircase, a garden and a decent restaurant. Upstream from the bridge, the oak woods of the Parc François I stretch along the riverbank to the lovely town **campsite** (☎05.42.32.13.32; closed mid-Oct to April). Food can be pricey – try the **brasseries** on place François I, or the Charentais plates – *cagouilles* (snails cooked in white wine) or *daube de boeuf* (hearty beef stew) – at *La Bonne Goule*, 42 allées de la Corderie.

# Aquitaine, the Dordogne and the Lot

Lush, steamy and green, the southwest of France can feel like a lower-latitude England, and is particularly popular with the British. Although undoubtedly beautiful, the most famous spots in the **Dordogne** heartlands can become oppressively crowded in summer. The main entry point to the region is **Bordeaux**, the largest city in Aquitaine, and an obvious stop for those interested in wine. East of Bordeaux, the **Périgord Blanc** is named after the white of its rocky outcrops

– undulating, fertile, wooded country, rising in the north and east to the edge of the Massif Central. The regional capital is **Périgueux**, whose central position and good transport make it a good base, especially for the cave paintings at **Les Eyzies** and around. The **Périgord Noir** is the stretch of territory from Bergerac to Brive, the area most people think of when you say Dordogne, with its picture-book villages and rich cuisine. To the south lies the drier, poorer and more sparsely populated region through which the **River Lot** flows, ideal for hiking, cycling and camping.

# Bordeaux

Famous the world over for the wines of the surrounding countryside, **BOR-DEAUX** is a large, bustling city, with an enviable nightlife and a grand eighteenth-century centre. Wine *aficionados* won't want to miss a wine tour or the biennial **Fête de Vin**, a four-day celebration of local viticulture and gastronomy held in June. Although the surrounding landscape is nothing special, within a day-trip from Bordeaux you can enjoy the vast pine-covered expanses of Les Landes and wild Atlantic **beaches**. The centre of the city is **place Gambetta**, conceived in the time of Louis XV. In one corner, the eighteenth-century arch of the Porte Dijeaux spans the street. East, cours de l'Intendance, full of chic shops, leads to the impeccably classical 1780 **Grand Théâtre** on place de la Comédie. Cours du 30-Juillet leads into **Esplanade des Quinconces**, said to be Europe's largest municipal square, with a memorial to the Girondins, the influential local deputies to the Revolutionary Assembly of 1789, purged by Robespierre as counter-revolutionaries. Rue Ste-Catherine leads down from place de la Comédie towards the city's best museum, the **Musée d'Aquitaine** at 20 cours Pasteur (Tues–Sun 11am–6pm; €4), illustrating the history of the region from prehistoric times through to the 1800s. To the east stand the cathedral of **St-André** (Mon–Fri 7.30–11.30am & 2–6/6.30pm; free), with its exquisite stained-glass windows and slender twin spires, and the classical **Hôtel de Ville**. Around the corner at 20 cours d'Albret, the **Musée des Beaux-Arts** (daily except Tues 11am–6pm; €4) displays works by Rubens, Matisse and Renoir, as well as Lacour's 1804 evocative Bordeaux dockside scene, *Quai des Chartrons*.

Along with Burgundy and Champagne, the **wines** of Bordeaux form the Holy Trinity of French viticulture. The reds in particular – known as claret to the English – have graced the tables of the discerning for centuries, produced from districts such as Médoc, Haut-Médoc, Bourg, Blaye, Pomerol and St-Émilion. South of the city is the domain of the great whites, notably the super-dry Graves and the sweet dessert wines of Sauternes. The **Maison du Vin de Bordeaux**, at 3 cours du 30-Juillet (Mon–Fri 8.30am–5.30/6pm, late-May to mid-Oct also Sat 9am–4.30pm; ☎05.56.00.22.66), has information on châteaux visits and wine-tasting, as does the Bordeaux tourist office, which also organizes half-day English-language **wine tours** (May–Oct daily at 1.30pm; Nov–April Wed & Sat only; €26) and two-hour *dégustations* (Aug Thurs & Sat 4.30pm; rest of year Thurs only; €20, including meal).

## Practicalities

Bordeaux **airport**, 12km west, is connected by regular shuttle **bus** (daily 7am–10.45pm; 30–45min; €6) to place Gambetta and the **train station**, the gare St-Jean (from here take the tram or bus #7 or #8 to the centre, €1.30). There's a small **tourist office** at the station, but the main office is near the Grand Théâtre at 12 cours du 30-Juillet (Mon–Sat 9am–6/7.30pm, Sun 9.30am–6.30pm; ☎05.56.00.66.00, ⓦwww.bordeaux-tourisme.com).

For **accommodation**, try the *Résidence la Terrasse*, 20 rue St-Vincent de Paul (☎05.56.33.46.46, ⓦwww.hotellaterrasse.fr; ❹); the several buildings operated by the *Bristol*, on place Gambetta (☎05.56.81.85.01, ⓦwww.hotel-bordeaux.com; ❸);

or *Acanthe,* 12–14 rue St-Rémi (☎05.56.81.66.58, ⓦwww.acanthe-hotel-bordeaux .com; ❹). The **hostel** is near the station, at 22 cours Barbey (☎05.56.33.00.70; €18). There are several inexpensive **restaurants** around the station area, and along the left bank of the river nearby. More centrally, try the *Café des Arts,* on rue Ste-Catherine, or the charming, if touristy *Bistrot Edouard,* on Place du Parlement. Both *Chez Dupont,* 45 rue de Notre-Dame, and *Croc-Loup,* 45 rue du Loup, serve typical French dishes, or try the Brazilian specialities at *Carioca,* 30 rue du Dr. Nancel-Pénard. The city's lively **bars** include the Irish pub *Connemara,* 18 cours d'Albret, and the Cuban *Calle Ocho* at 24 rue des Pilliers-de-Tutelle. **Internet access** is at Artobas, 7 rue Maucoudinat.

## Périgueux

The bustling market town of **PÉRIGUEUX**, with its beautiful Renaissance and medieval centre, makes a fine base for visiting the Dordogne's prehistoric caves. The centre of town focuses on **place Bugeaud**, a ten-minute walk from the train station. Ahead, down rue Taillefer, the **Cathédrale St-Front** – its square, pineapple-capped belfry surging above the roofs of the surrounding medieval houses – is one of the most distinctive Romanesque churches in France, and the inspiration behind Paris' Sacré Coeur. Outside, place de la Clautre opens on to Périgueux's renovated old quarter, with a number of fine Renaissance palaces, particularly along rue Limogeanne and on place St-Louis. The **Musée du Périgord**, on rue St-Front, at 22 cours Tourny (Mon & Wed–Fri 10am–5.30pm, Sat & Sun 1–6pm; €4), boasts some beautiful Gallo-Roman mosaics found locally. The **tourist office** is at 26 pl Francheville (daily 9/10am–1pm & 2–6pm; ☎05.53.53.10.63, ⓦwww.perigueux.fr), next to the Tour Mataguerre, the last remnant of the town's medieval defences. Inexpensive **hotels** include the riverside *Hôtel des Barris*, 2 rue Pierre Magne (☎05.53.53.04.05, ℉05.53.05.19.08; ❸), with a great view of the cathedral, though the *Ibis* opposite (☎05.53.53.64.58, ℉05.53.07.51.79; ❹) is more reliable. Alternatively, try the *Comfort Hôtel Régina,* facing the station at 14 rue Denis-Papin (☎05.53.08.40.44, ℮comfort.perigueux@wanadoo.fr; ❸). The **campsite** *Barnabé Plage* (☎05.53.53.41.45, ⓦwww.barnabé-perigord.com) is at 80 rue Bains, near the Stade Jules Dubois. There's no shortage of **restaurants** and **bars**, most tucked away in the pedestrian zones: *L'Amandier,* 12 rue Eguill-erie, has good menus featuring local specialities; *Le Chameau Gourmand,* 2 rue des Farges, serves excellent couscous; and *Le Gouter du Charlotte,* place St-Louis, is a charming *crêperie.*

## The Vézère valley caves

Half-an-hour or so by train southeast from Périgueux is a luxuriant cliff-cut region riddled with **caves** and subterranean streams. Cro-Magnon skeletons were first unearthed here in 1868, and an incredible wealth of archeological evidence of the life of late Stone Age people has since been found. The paintings that adorn the caves – perhaps to aid fertility or hunting rituals – are remarkable not only for their age, but also for their exquisite colouring and the skill with which they are drawn.

 **LES EYZIES** is the centre of the region, a rambling, somewhat unattractive village dominated by tourism. **Trains** run daily to Les Eyzies; the Périgueux tourist office has a factsheet detailing how to get there and back in a day. Worth a glance before or after visiting the caves is the **Musée National de la Préhistoire** (July & Aug 9.30am–6.30pm; Sept–June daily except Tues 9am–12.30pm & 2.30–5.30pm; €4.50), which exhibits prehistoric artefacts, including copies of one of the most beautiful pieces of Stone Age art – two clay bison from the Tuc d'Audoubert cave in the Pyrenees. Just outside Les Eyzies, off the road to Sarlat, the tunnel-like **Grotte de Font de Gaume** (daily except Sat: mid-May to mid-Sept 9.30am–5.30pm;

mid-Sept to mid-May 9.30am–12.30pm & 2–5.30pm; €6.10) contains dozens of polychrome paintings, most miraculous of which is a frieze of five bison, the colour remarkably preserved by a protective layer of calcite. To be sure of a place, reserve in advance on ☎05.53.06.86.00, though the ticket office does have a number of last-minute tickets every morning at opening time. Les Eyzies' **tourist office** at 19 rue de la Préhistoire (Mon–Sat 9am–7pm, Sun 9/10am–noon & 2–5/6pm; Oct–May closed lunch; ☎05.53.06.97.05, ⊛www.leseyzies.com) has information on private rooms in the area and rents out bikes for €14 per day.

**Abri du Cap Blanc** (daily: April–June, Sept & Oct 10am–noon & 2–6pm; July & Aug 10am–7pm; ☎05.53.59.21.74; €5.90) is a steep but manageable 7km bike ride from Les Eyzies. Not a cave but a rock shelter, its 15,000-year-old sculpted frieze of horses and bison is polished and set off against a pockmarked background in extraordinary high relief. Of the surviving prehistoric sculptures in France, this is the best. The road continues past the **Grotte des Combarelles** (June–Sept daily 9.30am–5.30pm; Oct–May daily 9am–12.30pm & 2–5.30pm; Jan–April closed Mon & Tues; €6.10), whose engravings of humans, reindeer and mammoths dating from the Magdalanian period (about 20,000 years ago) are also worth a visit.

Up the valley of the Vézère river to the northeast, **MONTIGNAC** is more attractive than Les Eyzies though its prime interest is the cave paintings at nearby **Lascaux** – or, rather, for a tantalizing replica, Lascaux II (April–Sept daily 9.30am–7pm; July & Aug daily 9am–8pm; Oct–March daily 10am–12.30pm & 2–5.30pm; mid-Nov to March closed Mon; forty-minute guided tour €8); the original has been closed since 1963 due to deterioration caused by the breath and body heat of visitors. Executed 17,000 years ago, the paintings are said to be the finest prehistoric works in existence. There are five or six identifiable styles, and subjects include the bison, mammoth and horse, plus the biggest-known prehistoric drawing in existence of a bull with astonishingly expressive head and face. The **tourist office** is at place Bertran-de-Born (Mon–Sat 10am–1pm & 3–6pm; ☎05.53.51.82.60, ⊛www.bienvenue-montignac.com). Montignac is short on moderately priced **accommodation**, with the best option being the *Hôtel de la Grotte*, 63 rue du 4 Septembre (☎05.53.51.80.48, ⊛www.hotel delagrotte.fr; ❷), with a nice restaurant. There's also a **campsite**, *Le Moulin du Bleufond*, on the riverbank (☎05.53.51.83.95, ⊛www.bleufond.com; closed mid-Oct to March).

# Bergerac

On the banks of the Dordogne south of Périgueux, **BERGERAC** is the main market town for the surrounding maize, vine and tobacco farms. Devastated in the sixteenth-century Wars of Religion, when most of its Protestant population fled overseas, it's essentially a modern town with a small, rather charming old quarter. In rue de l'Ancien-Pont, the seventeenth-century Maison Peyrarède houses a fascinating **tobacco museum** (Tues–Sat 10am–noon & 2/2.30–6/6.30pm, Sun 2.30–6.30pm; €3), detailing the history of the weed, with collections of pipes and tools of the trade. The **train station** is on avenue du 108ᵉ Régiment d'Infanterie, a short walk north of the town centre. The **tourist office** is at 97 rue Neuve-d'Argenson (July & Aug daily 9.30am–7/7.30pm; Sept–June Mon–Sat 9.30am–1pm & 2–7pm; ☎05.53.57.03.11, ⊛www.bergerac-tourisme.com). For **accommodation**, try the American-run *Le Colombier de Cyrano et Roxanne*, 17 pl de la Myrpe (☎05.53.57.96.70, ✉bluemoon2@club-internet.fr; ❹), a tiny b&b in a renovated sixteenth-century house, or for a bit more luxury, the *Hôtel de Bordeaux*, 38 pl Gambetta (☎05.53.57.12.83, ⊛www.hotel-bordeaux-bergerac .com; ❺), a three-star option with a swimming pool and relaxing garden. There's also a **campsite**, *La Pelouse* (☎ & ☎05.53.57.06.67), ten minutes' walk north of the centre, by the river.

# The Pyrenees

Basque-speaking and damp in the west, snowy and Occitan-speaking in the middle, dry and Catalan in the east, **the Pyrenees** are physically beautiful, culturally varied and decidedly less developed than the Alps. The entire range is marvellous walking country, especially the central **Parc National des Pyrénées**, with its 3000-metre-high peaks, streams, forests, flowers and wildlife. If you're a serious hiker, you can walk all the way across from Atlantic to Mediterranean between June and September, following the GR10 or the harder *Haute Randonnée Pyrénéenne* (HRP) between well-spaced alpine refuges. Bear in mind that these are big mountains, and to do any of the trail sections you'll need hiking boots and, despite the southerly latitude, warm and windproof clothing. Down at sea level, the **Basque coast** is lovely but very popular, suffering to a large extent from seaside sprawl and a surfeit of caravan sites. **St-Jean-de-Luz** is much the prettiest resort, while **Bayonne** is the most attractive town, with an excellent Basque museum and art gallery; **Biarritz** has the best surf and the liveliest nightlife. The foothill towns are generally dull, though the château at **Pau** makes a nice afternoon stop, while **Lourdes** is a monster of kitsch that has to be seen to be believed.

## Biarritz

**BIARRITZ** is a nineteenth-century resort once patronized by French Emperor Napoleon III – who built a seaside palace for Empress Eugénie here – and an impressive list of European aristocracy and royalty. Today, its air of faded gentility is still discernible out of season, while in summer the crashing waves attract surfers from across the world, with a prestigious competition held every July. The town's beaches – particularly the central **Grande Plage** – are the main attraction, though its few museums provide enough diversion for a rainy day. The **Musée de la Mer**, on the Esplanade du Rocher de la Vierge (daily: July & Aug 9.30am–midnight; Sept–June 9.30am–12.30pm & 2–6pm; Nov–March closed Mon; €7.20), has an interesting collection from the Bay of Biscay in its aquarium, plus a rooftop seal pool. Sweet-toothed visitors will relish the intricate chocolate sculptures at the **Musée du Chocolat**, 14 av Beau Rivage (daily 10am–noon & 2.30–6pm; €6), while **Asiatica**, at 1 rue Guy Petit (Mon–Fri 10.30am–7pm, Sat & Sun 2–8pm; €7), houses one of Europe's most important collections of oriental art, dating from prehistoric to modern times.

### Practicalities

Biarritz's **train station** lies 3km southeast of the centre in La Negresse district, at the end of avenue Kennedy. Buses #2 and #9 run from there to square d'Ixelles, where you'll find the **tourist office** (July & Aug daily 8am–8pm; Sept–June Mon-Sat 9-6pm, Sun 10am-5pm; ☏05.59.22.37.10, ⓦwww.biarritz.fr).

There's a limited amount of reasonably priced **accommodation** in town, which must be booked weeks in advance during summer. Try *Le Baron de Biarritz*, just south of the centre above an affordable Vietnamese restaurant at 13 av Maréchal Joffre (☏05.59.22.08.22; ❷), or the *Rocher de la Vierge*, 13 rue du Port-Vieux (☏05.59.24.11.74; ❸), towards the quieter end of this central street leading down to a sheltered beach. There's a **hostel** at 8 rue Chiquito de Cambo (☏05.59.41.76.00; €17), 2km southwest of town at the Mouriscot lake, and **camping** a few kilometres away in Anglet on rte de l'Aviation (☏05.59.23.00.23, ⓦwww.campingdeparme.com). For **food** – specifically grills and seafood for under €25 – head to *Le Surfing*, behind Plage de la Côte-des-Basques, festooned with antique boards. With Spain just a stone's throw away, tapas bars are much in evidence; longest-running and most affordable is *Bar Jean* at 5 rue des Halles, beside the market. Start the day at *Salon de Thé L'Orangerie*, 1 rue Gambetta, where juice, cereal and yoghurt breakfasts go for under €8.

## Bayonne

Capital of the French Basque country and home of the bayonet, **BAYONNE** lies 6km inland at the junction of the Nive and Adour rivers. Having escaped the worst effects of mass tourism, it remains a cheerful and pretty town, with the shutters on the older half-timbered houses painted in the distinctive Basque tones of green and rust-red. The two main medieval quarters line the banks of the Nive, whose quays are home to many bars and restaurants. Close to the confluence of the two rivers, **Place de la Liberté** is the main square, with a stop for bus #1 (for Biarritz and the beaches) alongside the Hôtel de Ville. In "Petit Bayonne", on the Nive's right bank, stands the **Musée Basque** on Quai des Corsaires (Tues–Sun: April–Oct 10am–6.30pm; Nov–March 10am–12.30pm & 2–6pm; €5.50), giving a comprehensive overview of modern Basque culture. The city's second museum, the **Musée Bonnat** on nearby rue Jacques Laffitte (daily except Tues: May–Oct 10am–6.30pm; Nov–April 10am–12.30 & 2–6pm; €5.50, €9 with the Musée Basque), is an unexpected treasury of art, with works by, among others, Goya, El Greco, Rubens and Degas. Across the Nive in "Grand Bayonne", the **Cathédrale Ste-Marie** looks best from a distance, its twin spires rising with airy grace above the houses; the **cloister** (Sun–Fri 9.30am–12.30pm & 2–5pm; free) rewards a visit with a good view of the stained glass and buttresses.

### Practicalities

Bayonne's **train station** is in the St-Esprit quarter on the opposite bank of the Adour from the centre, ten minutes' walk over the Pont St-Esprit. The **tourist office** is five minutes west of the Hôtel de Ville, on place des Basques (Mon–Sat 7/9am–6/7pm; July & Aug also Sun 10am–1pm; ☎05.59.46.01.46, ⌨www.bayonne-tourisme.com). CyberNetCafé, place de la République, has **Internet** terminals.

Budget **accommodation** is available at the basic *Hôtel des Basques* at 4 rue des Lisses (☎05.59.59.08.02; ➋). A more comfortable choice is the *Monbar* at 24 rue Pannecau, Petit Bayonne (☎05.59.59.26.80; ➌). The closest **campsite** is well-equipped *La Chêneraie* (☎05.59.55.01.31; closed Oct–Easter), in the St-Frédéric quarter on the north bank of the Adour. Most **cafés** and **restaurants** line the Nive quays; you can eat stylishly for under €20 at *Bar du Marché* at 39 rue des Basques (lunch only), and *Le Bistrot Ste-Cluque* at 9 rue Hugues in St-Esprit. Make sure you try the famed local ham, flavoured with salt from nearby mines. For **live music** and a pint of Guinness, head for *Katie Daly's* on place de la Liberté.

## St-Jean-de-Luz

**ST-JEAN-DE-LUZ** is by far the most attractive resort on the Basque coast. Although crowded and with an undistinguished seafront, it boasts a long curve of beautiful fine sand while still thriving as a fishing port; the old houses around the harbour, both in St-Jean and across the water in Ciboure (essentially the same town) are very picturesque. At its heart is **place Louis XIV**, with cafés, a bandstand and plane trees. The seventeenth-century **Maison Louis XIV** (June–Sept Mon–Sat 10.30am–12.30pm & 2.30–5.30/6.30pm; €4.50), on the harbour side of the square, was where Louis XIV stayed at the time of his marriage to Maria Theresa in 1660, and the suitably stately nails-and-beams building houses a fine array of period furnishings. A short distance up rue Gambetta, on the town side of the square, is the large thirteenth-century church of **St-Jean-Baptiste** (daily 9am–noon & 3–6.30pm), where Louis and Maria Theresa were married. The **train station** is on place de Verdun, close to the **tourist office** on place du Maréchal-Foch (Mon–Sat 9am–7/8pm, Sun 10/10.30am-1pm & 3–7pm; Sept–June closed lunch

& Sun afternoon; ☎05.59.26.03.16, ⊛www.saint-jean-de-luz.com). The cheapest **hotels** are near the train station: try *Le Verdun*, 13 av de Verdun (☎05.59.26.02.55, ⊛www.hotel-leverdun.com; ❸), with a good restaurant, or *Hôtel de Paris*, at 1 bd du Commandant Passicot (☎05.59.85.20.20, ⊛www.hoteldeparis-stjeandeluz .fr; ❸). There are plenty of **campsites** in the vicinity, all grouped together a few kilometres northwest of the town, including the *Chibau Berria* (☎05.59.26.11.94), off the N10 towards Guéthary.

## Lourdes, Pau and the mountains

In 1858 Bernadette Soubirous, 14-year-old daughter of a poor local miller in **LOURDES**, 30km southeast of Pau, had eighteen visions of the Virgin Mary in a spot called the Grotte de Massabielle. Miraculous cures at the grotto soon followed and Lourdes grew exponentially, now catering for six million Catholic pilgrims a year, with whole streets devoted to the sale of religious kitsch. At the **grotto** itself – a moisture-blackened overhang by the riverside with a statue of the Virgin inside – long queues of the faithful process through clockwise. Above looms the first, neo-Gothic church built here, in 1871, while nearby a massive subterranean **basilica** has a capacity of 20,000. Lourdes **train station** is on the northeastern edge of town. At avenue Francis Lagardère a **funicular** makes the 1000m ascent through the pines up to the Pic de Jer, where the Pyrenees begin. For the **tourist office** on place Peyramale turn right outside the station, then left down Chaussée Maransin (Mon–Sat 9am–noon & 2–6/7pm; Easter–Oct also Sun 11am–6pm; ☎05.62.42.77.40, ⊛www.lourdes-france.com). There's an abundance of inexpensive **hotels** on avenue de la Gare, and more en route to the grotto and around the castle. **Hostel** accommodation is at *Pension Familiale*, 44 rue de l'Égalité (☎05.62.94.26.75; €20.20 including meals). Closest of several **campsites** is *La Poste*, 26 rue de Langelle (☎05.62.94.40.35; closed mid-Oct to Easter), between the train station and post office.

Lying 30km northwest of Lourdes, and accessible by regular train and bus, the town of **PAU** sits quietly on a steep scarp over a still river. At the western end of boulevard des Pyrénées stands a pretty **château** (daily 9.30am–11.45/12.15pm & 1.30/2–5/5.45pm; 1hr guided visits €4.50), while the same boulevard offers unrivalled views of the surrounding mountainscape. Pau is also a great source of information for the Parc National des Pyrénées Occidentales; stop in for hiking advice at the **Club Alpin Français**, 5 rue René Fournets (Mon–Fri 5–7pm).

From Lourdes train station, several SNCF buses run daily to Gavarnie and Barèges, two resorts near the heart of the **Parc National des Pyrénées Occidentales**. From either, a few hours on the GR10 or HRP bring you to staffed alpine refuges (rough camping is not generally allowed in the park). **GAVARNIE** is smaller and pricier, but has an incomparable namesake cirque towering above, forming the border with Spain. You can **stay** hostel-style at *Le Gypaète* (☎05.62.92.40.61; ❷), or **camp** at the primitive but superbly set *La Bergerie* (☎05.62.92.48.41), towards the cirque. **BARÈGES** is more of a real village, with a good streamside **campsite** – *La Ribère* (☎05.62.92.69.01) – and two high-quality **gîtes** next to each other: *L'Oasis* (☎05.62.92.69.47, ⊛www.gite-oasis.com; ❸) and *L'Hospitalet* (☎05.62.92.68.08; ❷). During mid-July, the Tour de France often passes through; in winter, Barèges offers some of the best downhill skiing in the Pyrenees.

# Languedoc and Roussillon

**Languedoc** is more an idea than a geographical entity. The modern region covers a mere fraction of the lands that stretched south from Bordeaux and Lyon into

Spain and northwest Italy, where once *Occitan* or the *langue d'Oc* was spoken. Although things are changing, the sense of being Occitanian remains strong, a territorial identity that dates back to the Middle Ages, when the castles and fortified villages were the final refuges of the Cathars, a heretical religious sect. The old Roman town of **Nîmes** is one gateway, while **Montpellier** also makes a good base. The nearby coast, however, is not generally noteworthy, with most of the beaches windswept and cut off from their hinterland by marshy lakes. The picturesque medieval town of **Carcassonne** is enjoyable, as is **Toulouse**, the elegant cultural capital. South of Languedoc, **Roussillon**, or French Catalonia, maintains much of its Catalan identity, though there is little support nowadays for political independence or reunification with Spanish Catalunya, to which it belonged until the seventeenth century. Its hills and valleys provide some fine walking, and although the coast again is something of a disappointment, the region's main town, **Perpignan**, is a likeable place.

# Nîmes

**NÎMES** is intrinsically linked to two things: Rome – whose influence is manifest in some of the most extensive Roman remains in Europe – and denim, a word corrupted from *de Nîmes*. Denim was first manufactured as *serge* in the city's textile mills and exported to the USA to clothe workers; a certain Mr Levi-Strauss made it world famous. The old centre of Nîmes spreads northwards from place des Arènes, site of the magnificent first-century **Les Arènes** (daily 9/10am–5/6.30pm; €4.80), one of the best-preserved Roman arenas in the world, still capable of holding 20,000 spectators. Four centuries after it was built, and with the Roman Empire crumbling away, the arena was turned into a fortress by invading Visigoths. Eventually, it became a slum, home to some two thousand people until the early 1800s. Now fully restored, with a retractable roof, it hosts opera, an international summer jazz festival and the high-spirited *Feria* in May, with bullfights galore. Another Roman survivor can be found northeast along boulevard Victor Hugo: the **Maison Carrée** (daily 9/10am–5/7pm; free), a compact temple built in 5 AD and celebrated for its harmony of proportion. Other worthwhile sights include the **Musée Archéologique** and the **Muséum d'Histoire Naturelle** (Tues–Sun 10/11am–6pm; both museums free), housed in a seventeenth-century chapel on boulevard Amiral-Courbet, which hold a sizeable collection of Roman artefacts. Further out, across bd de la Libération, the **Musée des Beaux-Arts** on rue Cité Foulc (Tues–Sun 10am–6pm; €4.80) prides itself on a huge Gallo-Roman mosaic showing the *Marriage of Admetus*, while the **Musée d'Art Contemporain** (Tues–Sun 11am–6pm; €4.80), holds an impressive collection of post-1960 art. If you're here for more than a day, it might be worth investing in a **monument and museum pass** (€10.20), which gives access to the town's attractions for three days.

## Practicalities

Nîmes **train station** is at the end of avenue Feuchères. The main **tourist office** is at 6 rue Auguste, by the Maison Carrée (Mon–Sat 8.30/9am–7/9pm, Sun 10am–5/6pm; ☎04.66.58.38.00, ✆www.ot-nimes.fr).

To **stay** in the heart of things, try the modern *Hôtel Central*, at 2 place du Château (☎04.66.67.22.85, ✆www.hotel-central.org; ❸), or nearby *Cat*, 22 bd Amiral-Courbet (☎04.66.67.22.85; ❸). There's a **hostel** 2km northwest of town on Chemin de la Cigale (☎04.66.68.03.20; €9.65), which also has tent space (bus #2). The main **campsite** is the *Domaine de la Bastide* on route de Générac (☎04.66.38.09.21), 3km south of the centre. For good regional food at reasonable prices, try *L'Ancien Théatre*, 4 rue Racine, or along rue de l'Étoile. **Cafés** and **restaurants** abound on Place du Marché and boulevard Amiral-Courbet, while boulevard Victor Hugo has plenty of lively watering holes. Netgames offers **Internet** access just behind the temple, at place de la Maison Carrée.

# Montpellier

**MONTPELLIER** is a vibrant city, renowned for its ancient university, once attended by such luminaries as Petrarch and Rabelais. Ruled over by the Kings of Mallorca for almost a hundred and fifty years during the Middle Ages, today it's the regional capital of Languedoc-Roussillon and a cosmopolitan youthful place. At the town's hub is **place de la Comédie**, a grand oval square paved with cream-coloured marble and surrounded by cafés. The **Opéra**, an ornate nineteenth-century theatre, presides over one end, while the other end leads onto the pleasant Champs du Mars park. Nearby, the much-vaunted **Musée Fabre** is closed until 2006. Behind the Opéra lie the tangled, hilly lanes of Montpellier's **old quarter**, full of seventeenth- and eighteenth-century mansions and small museums. One of the more interesting, at 7 rue Jacques-Coeur, is the **Musée Languedocien** (Mon–Sat 2/3–5/6pm; €5), which houses an eclectic display of ceramics, furniture and tapestries. At the end of rue Foch, on the western edge of town, are the formal gardens of the Promenade du Peyrou. The **Jardin des Plantes** (Tues–Sun noon–6/8pm; free), just north of here, with its alleys of exotic trees, is France's oldest botanical garden, founded in 1593.

## Practicalities

The **train station** is next to the **bus station** on the southern edge of town, a short walk down rue de Maguelone. The main **tourist office** is at 13 rue de la République (Mon–Sat 9/10am–6.30/7.30pm, Sun 9/9.30am–1pm & 2/2.30–4/6pm; ☎04.67.60.60.60, ✆www.ot-montpellier.fr); there's also a desk in the train station during July and August.

There are numerous **hotels** between the stations and place de la Comédie: the basic *Floride*, 1 rue François-Perrier (☎04.67.65.73.30, ✆www.hotelfloride.fr; ❹), and *Des Étuves*, 24 rue des Étuves (☎04.67.60.78.19, ✆www.hoteldesetuves.fr; ❸), are both good bets. The **hostel** is on rue des Écoles-Laïques (☎04.67.60.32.22; €12.50), and there's a municipal **campsite** (☎04.67.15.11.61) just south of town on the D21 (bus #28). Of the large number of **restaurants**, *La Diligence*, 2 pl Pétrarque, is excellent if expensive, while the lively *Caves Jean-Jaurès*, 3 rue Callot, serves quite good local cuisine in a seventeenth-century hotel. Vegetarians should head for *Tripti Kulai*, 20 rue Jacques-Coeur. **Nightlife** centres around place de la Comédie, place du Marché-aux-Fleurs and place Jean-Jaurès; *Fizz*, 4 rue Cauzit, is a very popular dance club. For **Internet** access, make for Cybercafé, 5 rue des clos René.

# Carcassonne

**CARCASSONNE**, on the main Toulouse–Montpellier train link, is one of the most dramatic (if also most commercialized) towns in Languedoc. It owes its division into two separate "towns", the Cité and Ville Basse, to the Cathar wars of the Middle Ages. Following Simon de Montfort's capture of the town in 1209, its people tried to restore their traditional ruling family, the Trencavels, in 1240. In reprisal King Louis IX expelled them, only permitting their return on condition they built on the low ground by the River Aude. The main attraction is the **Cité**, a double-walled and turreted **fortress-town** crowning the hill above the Aude like a scene from a medieval fairy-tale. Viollet-le-Duc rescued it from ruin in 1844, and his rather romantic restoration has been furiously debated ever since. Inevitably, it's become a real tourist trap, with its narrow lanes lined with innumerable souvenir shops and regularly crammed with hordes of day-trippers. There's no charge for admission to the main part of the city, or the grassy *lices* (moat) between the walls. However, to see the inner fortress of the **Château Comtal**, with its small **museum** of medieval sculpture, and to walk along the walls, you may have to join one of the hourly guided tours from the ticket office (daily 9.30am–5/6.30pm; €6.10). In addition to wandering the narrow streets, don't miss the beautiful church of **St-Nazaire** at the end of rue St-Louis (daily 9–11.45am & 1.45–5/7pm; free), a serene combination of Romanesque nave with carved capitals, and Gothic transepts and choir. Especially attractive are the two colourful Rose windows, dating from the thirteenth and fourteenth centuries.

### Practicalities

The **tourist office** is at 28 rue de Verdun, next to place de Lattre de Tassigny (Mon–Sat 9am–6pm; Sept–June closed lunch; ☎04.68.10.24.30, ⊛www .carcassonne-tourisme.com), with an annexe in the Tours Narbonnaises in the Cité (daily 9am–5/7pm) and also at the station in summer.

Accommodation in the Cité is pricey, apart from the 120-bed **hostel** on rue du Vicomte Trencavel (☎04.68.25.23.16; €15.80; closed mid-Dec to mid-Jan), and you're better off at a **hotel** in the Ville Basse, such as the *Cathare*, 53 rue Jean Bringer (☎04.68.25.65.92; ❸). The nearest **campsite**, *Camping de la Cité*, is off route de St-Hilaire (☎04.68.25.11.77) just west of the Cité (bus #8). There's an abundance of reasonably priced **restaurants** in the Cité, with several touristy, but very good, brasseries located around place Marcou – try *Auberge de Dame Carcas*, 3 pl du Château, which serves good regional dishes, especially *cassoulet*, the famed French peasant stew with goose confit, pork sausages and butter beans. For a night out, head to the bars around place Verdun.

## Toulouse and around

**TOULOUSE** is one of the most vibrant provincial cities in France, a result of a policy to make it the centre of hi-tech industry. Always an aviation centre – St-Exupéry and Mermoz flew out from here on their pioneering flights over Africa in the 1920s – Toulouse is now home to Aérospatiale, the driving force behind Airbus and the Ariane space rocket. Added zest comes from its large student population, second only to that of Paris. The centre of Toulouse is a rough hexagon clamped around a bend in the wide, brown river Garonne. The **Musée des Augustins**, 21 rue de Metz (Mon & Thurs–Sun 10am–6pm, Wed 10am–9pm; €2.40), incorporates the two cloisters of an Augustinian priory and houses collections of outstanding Romanesque and Gothic sculpture, much of it saved from the now-vanished churches of Toulouse's golden age in the late sixteenth century. Outside the museum, the main shopping street, **rue Alsace-Lorraine**, runs north. West of here are the cobbled streets of the **old city**, lined with the ornate *hôtels* of the merchants who grew rich on the woad trade, the city's economic base until the sixteenth century. The predominant building material is the flat Toulousain brick, whose cheerful rosy colour gives the city its nickname of *ville rose*. Best known of these palaces is the **Hôtel d' Assézat**, towards the river end of rue de Metz, which houses the marvellous private art collection of the **Fondation Bemberg** (Tues–Sun 10am–12.30pm & 1.30–6pm, Thurs till 9pm; €4.60), and includes excellent works by Bonnard. Modern art is on display at **Les Abattoirs**, a vaulted nineteenth-century building on the west bank of the Garonne at 76 allées Charles de Fitte (Tues–Sun 11am/noon–7/8pm; €6.10). One highlight is an enormous theatre backdrop painted by Picasso, *La Dépouille du Minotaure en Costume d'Arlequin* (*The Minotaur Dressed as a Harlequin*).

The **place du Capitole** is the site of Toulouse's town hall and prime meeting-place, with numerous cafés and a weekday market. Rue du Taur leads northwards to place St-Sernin and the largest Romanesque church in France, the **Basilique de St-Sernin**. Begun in 1080 to accommodate passing hordes of pilgrims, it is one of the loveliest examples of its kind. Inside, the ambulatory (daily 10am–5.45pm; €1.10) is well worth a visit for its succession of richly housed relics and exceptional eleventh-century marble bas-reliefs. Opposite the church, the **Musée St-Raymond** (daily 10am–6/7pm; €2.40) houses exhibits charting the history of the

Roman town of *Tolosa*, as Toulouse was then known. West of place du Capitole, on rue Lakanal, the church of **Les Jacobins** is another unmissable ecclesiastical building, a huge fortress-like rectangle of unadorned brick, with an interior divided by a central row of slender pillars from whose capitals spring a colourful splay of vaulting ribs. Beneath the altar lie the bones of the philosopher St Thomas Aquinas, while the north side reveals a tranquil cloister (daily 10am–7pm; €2.40).

Toulouse also serves as a good base for a visit to **ALBI**, an hour's train ride away and the birthplace of bohemian poster artist Toulouse-Lautrec. Here you can visit his museum (daily 9/10am–noon & 2–5/6pm; Oct–March closed Tues; €4.50) or, next door, gawk at the mammoth **Cathédrale Ste-Cécile** (daily 9am–6.30pm, Oct–May closed noon–2pm; guided tours in summer only; €1).

## Practicalities

Trains and buses arrive at the **gare Matabiau**, fifteen minutes' walk from the centre down allées Jean-Jaurès, or a five-minute métro ride. The **tourist office** is just behind place du Capitole, in a restored medieval tower on place Charles de Gaulle (Mon–Sat 9am–6/7pm, Sun 10/10.30am–7pm; Oct–May closed Sat–Sun 12.30–2pm; ☎05.61.11.02.22, ⊛www.ot-toulouse.fr).

Best of the city's central **hotels** are the *Castellane*, 17 rue Castellane (☎05.61.62.58.04, ⊛www.castellanehotel.com; ⑤), *Des Ambassadeurs*, 68 rue Bayard (☎05.61.62.65.84, ℮hotel.ambassadeurs@gofornet.com; ③), and *Ours Blanc*, next to the covered market at 25 pl de Victor-Hugo (☎05.61.23.14.55, ⊛www .hotel-ours-blanc.fr; ⑤). The **hostel** is at 2 av Yves Brunaud (☎05.34.30.42.80; €13.72). The closest **campsite** is on the chemin du Pont de Rupé, just north of the city (☎05.61.70.07.35; bus #59 from place Jeanne-d'Arc).

There are plenty of very good **restaurants** in town. *Au Chat Deng*, 37 rue Peyrolières, offers a good-value menu in trendy surroundings, while for more classical regional cuisine try *La Bascule*, near the Palais de Justice at 14 av Maurice-Hauriou. Excellent steaks and delicious homecooking are served at *La Côte de Boeuf*, 12 rue des Gestes, while pasta-lovers can fill up at *Mille et Une Pâtes*, 1 rue Mirepoix. The food **market** on place Victor Hugo also houses several good, small lunchtime restaurants, or if you're just looking for a snack, try *Jour de Fête*, 43 rue du Taur. *Le Chat d'Oc*, at 7 rue de Metz, has a wide range of **beers**, and for cocktails, tapas and dancing try *Maximo Café*, 3 rue Gabriel Péri or *Bodega-Bodega*, 1 rue Gabriel Péri. The streets around the train station are chock full of **Internet** cafés.

# Perpignan

This far south, climate and geography alone would ensure a palpable Spanish influence, but **PERPIGNAN** is actually Spanish in origin and home to refugees from the Spanish Civil War and their descendants. This southern atmosphere is intensified by its sizeable North African community, including Arabs and white French settlers repatriated after Algerian independence in 1962. It's a cheerful city, with Roussillon's red and yellow striped flag atop many a building, and makes an ideal stop-off en route to Spain or Andorra. Its heyday was the thirteenth and fourteenth centuries, when the kings of Mallorca held their court here, and it wasn't until 1659 that it finally became part of the French state. The centre of Perpignan is marked by the palm trees and smart cafés of **place Arago**. From here rue Alsace-Lorraine and rue de la Loge lead past the massive iron gates of the classical Hôtel de Ville to the tiny **place de la Loge**, the focus of the renovated old core, dominated by the **Loge de Mer**, a late fourteenth-century Gothic building designed to hold the city's stock exchange and a maritime court. Just north up rue Louis-Blanc is one of the city's few remaining fortifications, the crenellated fourteenth-century gate of **Le Castillet**, now home to the **Casa Païral**, a fascinating museum of Roussillon's Catalan folk culture (daily except Tues 10/11am–5.30/6/30pm; €4). In the gloomy nave of the fourteenth-century **Cathédrale St-Jean**, down rue

St-Jean and across place Gambetta, are some elaborate Catalan altarpieces, while a side-chapel houses a Rhenish altarpiece dating from around 1400. Through place des Esplanades, crowning the hill that dominates the southern part of the old town, is the **Palais des Rois de Majorque** (daily 10am–6pm; €4), a two-storey palace with a great, arcaded courtyard dating from the late thirteenth century.

### Practicalities

To reach the centre from the **train station**, follow avenue Général-de-Gaulle to place de la Catalogne, then continue along boulevard Clemenceau as far as Le Castillet. The **tourist office** is a short stroll from here, in the Palais des Congrès at the end of boulevard Wilson (Mon–Sat 9am–6/7pm, Sun 9/10–noon/4pm; ☏04.68.66.30.30, ☒www.perpignantourisme.com). The **bus station** is by Pont Arago, on avenue Général-Leclerc.

Lodging is plentiful and cheap around the train station, or try the central and spacious *Hotel de la Loge*, 1 rue Fabriques-Nabot (☏04.68.34.41.02; ☒www .hoteldelaloge.fr; ❹). The **hostel** (☏04.68.34.63.32; €9.10) is about 1km from the train station in Parc de la Pépinière by the river, and there's a **campsite**, *Le Catalan*, on route de Bompas (☏04.68.63.16.92), north of town. Inexpensive **food** abounds around the station, or for traditional Catalan fare, try the *Bodega du Castillet*, 13 rue Fabriques-Couberts, just around the corner from draft Guinness at *O'Shannon*, place de la Loge.

# The Massif Central

Thickly forested, and sliced by numerous rivers and lakes, the **Massif Central**, occupying a huge part of the middle of France, is geologically the oldest part of the country, and culturally one of the most firmly rooted in the past. Industry and tourism have made few inroads here, and the taciturn population has an enduring sense of regional identity. The heart of the region is the **Auvergne**, a wild, inaccessible, almost lunar, landscape dotted with extinct volcanic peaks known as *puys*, much of it now incorporated into the **Parc Naturel Régional des Volcans d'Auvergne**. To the southeast are the gentler wooded hills of the **Cévennes** that form part of the **Parc National des Cévennes**. Only a handful of towns have gained a foothold in this rugged terrain. **Le Puy**, spiked with jagged pinnacles of lava and with a majestic cathedral, is the most compelling, but there is appeal, too, in the provincial capital, **Clermont-Ferrand**.

## Clermont-Ferrand

**CLERMONT-FERRAND** is an incongruous capital for rustic Auvergne. A lively, youthful city with a major university and a manufacturing base, it's best known as home to Michelin. However, it also has a pretty, well-preserved historic centre and makes a good base for exploring the Massif and the nearby **Puy de Dôme** and the Natural Volcano Park (☒www.vulcania.com). Clermont and neighbouring Montferrand, to the east, were united in 1630 to form a single city, but you're likely to spend most of your time in the former. Clermont's most immediate feature is its *ville-noire* aspect – so-called for the local black volcanic rock used in many of its buildings. On the edge of old Clermont, the huge and soulless **place de Jaude** is the city hub and main shopping area. In the centre stands a rousing statue of the mythologised Gallic chieftain Vercingétorix, who in 52 BC led his people to their only – and indecisive – victory over Julius Caesar. North from place de Jaude, **place St-Pierre** is the site of Clermont's food **market** (Mon–Sat 7am–7.30pm), at its liveliest on Saturdays. The central **Musée**

d'archéologie Bargoin, at 45 rue Ballainvilliers (Tues–Sat 10am–noon & 1–5pm, Sun 2–7pm; closed Nov–Dec; free), has some especially good Gallo-Roman collections. The streets run up to the dark and soaring **Cathédrale Notre-Dame**, whose strong volcanic stone made it possible to build vaults and pillars of unheard-of slenderness and height. Surprisingly light inside, the cathedral boasts wonderful stained-glass windows; off the nave, the **Tour de la Bayette** (daily 9–11.15am & 2–5pm; €1.50) gives extensive views across the city. A short step northeast, on place Delille, stands the beautiful **Basilique Notre-Dame du Port**, a gem of Auvergnat Romanesque.

### Practicalities

Clermont-Ferrand **train station** is on avenue de l'URSS, east of the centre and connected by frequent buses with place de Jaude. The **tourist office** is on place de la Victoire (Mon–Fri 9am–6/7pm, Sat & Sun 9.30/10am–12.30/1pm & 2–6/7pm; ☏04.73.98.65.00, ✉www.clermont-fd.com), with copious literature and advice on **hiking** and **mountain-biking** in the Massif. Of the cluster of **hotels** outside the station, the *Grand Hôtel du Midi*, 39 av de l'URSS (☏04.73.92.44.98, ☏04.73.92.29.41; ❸), is the best value, while a ten minute walk away is the *Deux Avenues*, 4 av de la République (☏04.73.92.37.52, ✉hotel.2avenues@wanadoo.fr; ❷). More central is the *Foch*, 22 rue Maréchal-Foch (☏04.73.93.48.40, ✉regina.foch@wanadoo.fr; ❸), with a terrace. The nearest **campsite**, *L'Oclède*, is at Royat to the west (☏04.73.35.97.05, ✉oclede@camping-indigo.com; closed Nov–March; bus #41). For **food**, *Crêperie 1513* on 3 rue des Chaussetiers has a fine setting in a sixteenth-century mansion, while nearby *Le Café Pascal* and *Le Bar d'O*, both on place de la Victoire opposite the cathedral, offer excellent-value *plats du jour*. **Internet** access is at Cyberfrag, 3 rue de la Boucherie.

## Le Puy-en-Velay

**LE PUY** sprawls across a broad basin in the mountains in a muddle of red roofs barbed with poles of volcanic rock; both landscape and architecture are totally theatrical. Since medieval times it has been a starting point for pilgrims bound for Santiago de Compostela in Spain, and amid the cobbled streets of the old town are some of the most richly endowed churches in the land. Lush farming country surrounds the town, still producing its famous green lentils and a powerful local liqueur made from verbena – the Saturday morning market is the place to purchase them. The **old town**, reached by climbing the series of steep streets and steps that terrace the town's *puy* foundation, is dominated by the **Cathedral** – almost Byzantine in style, striped with alternate layers of light and dark stone and capped with a line of small cupolas. The Black Virgin inside is a copy of a revered original burned during the Revolution, and is still paraded through the town every August 15. Other, lesser treasures are on display in the sacristy, beyond which is the entrance to the beautiful twelfth-century **cloister** (daily: July & Aug 9am–6.30pm; Sept–June 9am–noon & 2–5/6.30pm; €4.60). A giant crimson statue of the **Virgin and Child** perches on the highest *puy*, fashioned from the metal of Russian guns captured in the Crimean War; you can climb to the top for some stunning views (€3). The nearby church of **St-Michel** (daily: May–Sept 9am–6.30pm; Oct–April 9.30am–noon & 2–5.30pm; €2.75), atop a steeper *puy*, the Rocher d'Aiguilhe, is an eleventh-century construction that seems to grow out of the rock itself. It's a tough ascent, but one you should definitely make: St-Michel is a quirky little building decorated with mosaics, arabesques and trefoil arches, its bizarre shape dictated by the lay of the land. Back down below, Le Puy's old lanes form a wonderful maze, while the new part of town, beyond the squat Tour Pannessac around place du Breuil and place Michelet, is home to the spacious public gardens and the **Musée Crozatier** (daily except Tues 10am–noon & 2–6pm; Oct–April closes at 4pm and on Sun afternoons; €3), with exhibits illustrating the local lace industry. The Monument/Museum Card (€7.50) gives entry to the town's major sights, and can be bought either from attractions themselves or the tourist office.

## Practicalities

**Buses and trains** arrive at place du Maréchal-Leclerc, a fifteen-minute walk from place du Breuil and the **tourist office** (Sept–June Mon–Sat 8.30am–noon & 1.30–6pm, Sun 10am–noon; July & Aug daily 8.30am–7.30pm; ☎04.71.09.38.41, ⓦwww.ot-lepuyenvelay.fr), and within easy striking distance of good value **hotels**, such as the dirt cheap *Régional*, 36 bd Maréchal Fayolle (☎04.71.09.37.74; ❷). There's a **hostel** at the *Centre Pierre Cardinal*, 9 rue Jules Vallès (☎04.71.05.52.40; closed weekends Oct–March; €7), and a municipal **campsite**, *Bouthézard*, a half-hour's walk from the station along chemin de Roderie (☎04.71.09.55.09; bus #6). For inexpensive regional **food**, try *L'Âme des Poètes,* on rue Séguret, by the cathedral, or the creative *crêperie*, *La Main à la Pâte*, 59 rue Chaussade.

# Burgundy

Peaceful, rural **Burgundy** is one of the most prosperous regions of modern France and was for a long time independent from the French state. In the fifteenth century its dukes ruled an empire that embraced much of northeastern France, Belgium and the Netherlands, with revenues equalled only by Venice. Everywhere there is evidence of this former wealth and power, both secular and religious. **Dijon**, the capital, is a slick and affluent town with many remnants of old Burgundy. South, there are the famous **vineyards**, a major moneymaker since Louis XIV's doctor prescribed the local tipple for the royal dyspepsia. **Beaune** is a good centre for sampling the best of the wine, and be sure to try local specialities such as *escargots à la bourguignonne*, *bœuf bourguignon* and *coq au vin*.

## Dijon

**DIJON** grew out of its strategic position on the merchant route from Britain up the Seine and across the Alps to the Adriatic. But it was as capital of the dukes of Burgundy from 1000 until the late 1400s that it knew its finest hour. The dukes used their tremendous wealth and power to make Dijon one of Europe's greatest centres of art, learning and science. Though it lost some of this status with incorporation into the French kingdom in 1477, it has remained one of the pre-eminent provincial cities, especially since the industrial boom of the mid-nineteenth century. You sense Dijon's former glory more in the lavish houses of its burghers than in the former seat of the dukes, the **Palais des Ducs**, an undistinguished building from the outside and one that has suffered substantial alterations, especially in the sixteenth and seventeenth centuries when it became the Parliament of Burgundy. The only outward reminders of the dukes' building are the fifteenth-century **Tour Philippe le Bon** (tours every 45 min: April–Nov daily 9am–noon & 1.45–5.30pm; Dec–March Sat & Sun 9am–3.30pm, Wed 1.30–3.30pm; €2.30), from whose terrace you can see Mont Blanc on a clear day, and the fourteenth-century **Tour de Bar**. The latter now houses Dijon's wonderful **Musée des Beaux-Arts** (daily except Tues 9.30/10am–5/6pm; €3.40), with a collection of paintings ranging from Titian and Rubens to Monet and Manet. The museum ticket also allows you to visit the vast kitchen and magnificent **Salle des Gardes**, richly appointed with panelling, tapestries and a minstrels' gallery, as well as the tombs of the dukes of Burgundy, Philippe le Hardi and Jean sans Peur, and Jean's wife, Marguerite de Bavière. The palace looks onto **place de la Libération**, a gracious semicircular space designed in the late seventeenth century and bordered by houses of honey-coloured stone. Behind it is the tiny, enclosed **place des Ducs** and a maze of lanes flanked by beautiful old houses, best of which are those on **rue des Forges**. Parallel to rue des Forges, **rue de la Chouette** passes the north side of the impressive thirteenth-century Gothic church of **Notre-Dame**, whose north wall holds a small sculpted owl (*chouette*), which people touch for luck and which gives the street its name. At the end of the street is the attractive **place François-Rude**, a favourite summer hangout, crowded with café tables. Just to the south, the **Musée Archéologique**, 5 rue Docteur-Maret (daily except Tues 9am–6pm; Oct to mid-May also closed 12.30–1.30pm; free), has interesting Gallo-Roman funerary bas-reliefs depicting the perennial Gallic preoccupation with food and wine.

### Practicalities

Dijon **train station** is at the end of avenue Maréchal-Foch, beside the **bus station** and five minutes from place Darcy, site of the main **tourist office** (daily: May to mid-Oct 9am–7pm; mid-Oct to April 10am–6pm; ☎03.80.44.11.44, ⊛www.dijon-tourism.com). Another tourist office is at 34 rue des Forges (Mon–Sat 9am–noon & 2–6pm).

The official **hostel** is 4km from the centre at 1 bd Champollion (☎03.80.72.95.20; €15) – take bus #5 from place Grangier. As for **hotels**, try the old-fashioned *Le Jacquemart*, at 32 rue Verrerie (☎03.80.60.09.60, ⊛www.hotel-lejacquemart.fr; ❸), the well-kept *Chambellan*, 92 rue Vannerie (☎03.80.67.12.67, ✉hotelchambellan@aol.com; ❷) or the *Hostellerie Le Sauvage*, at 64 rue Monge (☎03.80.41.31.21; ❸), a former coaching inn with a good restaurant. The nearest **campsite** is *Camping du Lac*, off boulevard Chanoine Kir (☎03.80.43.54.72; closed Nov–March; bus #12). Excellent **restaurants** abound in this centre of *haute cuisine*, though locating affordable places is hard, especially on a Sunday evening when almost all close. Good bets are the bustling rue Berbisey and place Émile Zola, where the lively *Verdi* serves pizzas and grills. For great Burgundian cuisine at very reasonable prices, try the *Clos des Capucines*, 3 rue Jeannin at the end of rue Jean-Jacques-Rousseau. Alternatively, there's the more refined *Le Chabrot*, at 36 rue Monge. For **drinks**, there's the studenty *Au Vieux Léon*, 52 rue Jeannin or *Shanti*, 69 rue Berbisey, a popular sheesha tea house, open late. Multirezo, in the bus station, offers **Internet** access.

## Beaune and the Burgundy vineyards

Burgundy's best wines come from a narrow strip of hillside – the **Côte d'Or**, which runs southwest from Dijon to Santenay. Its principal town, rather overrun by wine tourists, is **BEAUNE**, whose chief attraction is the fifteenth-century hospital, the **Hôtel-Dieu** on the corner of place de la Halle (daily 9am–6.30pm; €5.40). The vast stone-flagged hall has an impressive painted timber roof and until quite recently continued to serve its original purpose. It is here that the Hospices de Beaune's wines are auctioned every third Sunday in November during the *Trois Glorieuses* festival, the prices paid setting the pattern for the season. The private residence of the dukes of Burgundy on rue d'Enfer contains the **Musée du Vin** (daily 9.30am–5/6pm; Dec–March closed Tues; €5.40), with giant winepresses and interesting associated paraphernalia. From Beaune **train station**, the town centre is 500m up avenue du 8 Septembre, across the boulevard and left onto rue des Tonneliers. **Buses** leave from rue Maufoux, beyond the walls. The **tourist office**, opposite the Hôtel-Dieu (Mon–Sat 9/10am–5/7pm, Sun 10am–1pm & 2–5/6pm; ☎03.80.26.21.30, ⊛www.ot-beaune.fr), has information on wine tours. **Accommodation** is pricier than in nearby Dijon – best bets are the central *Hôtel Foch*, 24 bd Maréchal Foch (☎03.80.24.05.65, ☎03.80.24.75.59; ❸), the *Arcantis Hôtel au Grand St Jean*, 18 rue du Faubourg Madeleine (☎03.80.24.12.22, ⊛www.hotel-au-grand-st-jean.com; ❹) and the **campsite**, *Les Cent Vignes* (☎03.80.22.03.91), 1km out on rue Auguste Dubois off rue du Faubourg-St-

Nicolas. **Food** can be disappointing but try *Piqu' Boeuf Grill*, 2 rue Faubourg Madeleine, or the tiny *Bistrot Bouguignon*, 8 rue Monge. *Grand Café du Lyon*, on place Carnot, serves snacks accompanied by good wine by the glass.

The Côte d'Or is divided into two wine regions – **Côte de Nuits** and **Côte de Beaune**. With few exceptions, the reds of the Côte de Nuits are superior, while the whites of the Côte de Beaune are some of the most prestigious and pricey whites in France. The villages, strung along the N74 through Beaune and beyond, are sleepy and exceedingly prosperous, full of houses inhabited by well-heeled *vignerons*, and *caves* at which to sample wines before you buy.

# Alsace and Lorraine

France's eastern borderlands were a battleground for centuries. Disputed since the Middle Ages, in the twentieth century they became the scene of some of the worst fighting in the two world wars. The democratically minded burghers of **Alsace**, the more beautiful of the two provinces, created a plethora of well-heeled semi-autonomous towns for themselves centuries before their seventeenth-century incorporation into the French state. These are neat, well-ordered places full of Germanic fripperies adorning the houses – but the Alsatian people remain fiercely and proudly French, despite the German dialect spoken by many. The *mélange* of cultures is at its most vivid in the string of little wine towns that punctuate the *Route du Vin* along the eastern margin of the wet and woody **Vosges** mountains, and in the great cathedral city of **Strasbourg**. By comparison, the province of **Lorraine**, though it has suffered much the same vicissitudes, is rather wan, the elegant eighteenth-century provincial capital of **Nancy** being the main exception.

## Nancy

**NANCY**, capital of Lorraine, has a relatively untouched eighteenth-century core that was the work of the last of the independent dukes of Lorraine, Stanislas Leczynski, dethroned King of Poland and father-in-law of Louis XV. During the twenty-odd years of his office in the mid-eighteenth century he ordered some of the most successful urban redevelopment of the period in all France. The centre of this is **place Stanislas**, a supremely elegant, partially enclosed square at the far end of rue Stanislas, whose south side is taken up by the **Hôtel de Ville**, its roof line topped by florid urns and lozenge-shaped lanterns dangling from the beaks of gilded cockerels. On the west side of the square, the excellent **Musée des Beaux-Arts** (daily except Tues 10am–6pm; €4.60) boasts work by Caravaggio, Dufy, Modigliani and Matisse. A little to the north, at 64 Grande-Rue, is the **Musée Lorrain** (daily except Tues 10am–12.30pm & 2–6pm; €3.10), under renovation but fully open and devoted to Lorraine's history and with a room of etchings by the seventeenth-century artist, Jacques Callot, whose concern with social issues presaged much nineteenth- and twentieth-century art. It's then a twenty-minute walk to the **Musée de l'École de Nancy**, 36–38 rue du Sergent Blandan (Wed–Sun 10.30am–6pm; €4.60), which holds a collection of Art Nouveau furniture and furnishings, arranged as if in a private house.

### Practicalities

Nancy **train station** is at the end of rue Stanislas, a five-minute walk from place Stanislas, where you'll find the **tourist office** (Mon–Sat 9am–6/7pm, Sun 10am–1/5pm; ☏03.83.35.22.41, ⊛www.ot-nancy.fr). The best of the budget **hotels** is the *Poincaré*, 81 rue Raymond Poincaré, west of the train station (☏03.83.40.25.99, ⊛www.hotel-poincare.fr.st; ❸), or there's a **hostel** out at the *Centre d'Accueil*,

Château de Rémicourt, Villers-lès-Nancy (☎03.83.27.73.67; €13.50; bus #126 to St-Fiacre). *Camping de Brabois* (☎03.83.27.18.28, @campeoles.brabois@wanadoo .fr; closed mid-Oct to March) is the nearest **campsite**. For reasonably priced **food**, head to Grande-Rue or rue des Ponts – *Chez Bagot*, at 45 Grande-Rue, has good fish dishes. The ornate café *L'Excelsior*, across place Thiers from the train station, is a beautiful place for a coffee and a hearty meal. For **Internet** access, head to e-café, 11 rue des Quatre Églises.

# Strasbourg

The prosperous and attractive capital of Alsace, **STRASBOURG** is big enough to have a metropolitan air, but with a cheerful cosiness that prevents it from being overwhelming. It has one of the loveliest cathedrals in France, an ancient but active university and is the current seat of the Council of Europe and the European Court of Human Rights, and part-time base of the European Parliament. Even if you're not planning to spend much time in eastern France, Strasbourg is a genuine highlight and well worth a detour.

Strasbourg focuses on two main squares, the busy **place Kléber**, and, to the south, **place Gutenberg**, named after the pioneer of printing type, who lived here in the early fifteenth century. Christened "pure beauty" by Goethe, the nearby **Cathédrale de Notre-Dame** (daily 7–11.30am & 12.40–7pm; free) soars from a square of crooked-roofed medieval houses, with a spire of such delicate, flaky lightness it seems the work of confectioners rather than masons. In the south transept the slender triple-tiered thirteenth-century column, the Pilier des Anges, is decorated with some of the most graceful and expressive statuary of its age. Climb to the top platform for stunning views to the Black Forest, and don't miss the tremendously complicated **astrological clock** (open only noon–12.20pm; €1), built by Schwilgué of Strasbourg in 1842. Visitors arrive in droves to witness its crowning performance – striking the hour of noon with unerring accuracy at

12.30pm. South of the cathedral the **Musée de l'Oeuvre Notre-Dame**, 3 pl du Château (Tues–Sun 10am–6pm; €4), houses the original sculptures from the cathedral exterior, damaged in the Revolution and replaced today by convincing copies. There's also the eleventh-century *Wissembourg Christ*, perhaps the oldest representation of a human figure in stained glass, retrieved from the previous cathedral. Just north of the old centre, across the river, **place de la République** is surrounded by vast German neo-Gothic edifices erected during the Prussian occupation (1870–1918), a few hundred metres beyond which are the imposing pieces of contemporary architecture that are home to the European Court of Human Rights and the European Parliament. The western edge of the city centre is much more picturesque. Around quai Turckheim, four square towers guard the so-called **Ponts Couverts** over a series of canals. This beautiful area, known as the Petite France, has winding streets bordered by sixteenth- and seventeenth-century houses with carved woodwork and decked with flowers; the neighbourhood was called "Little France" by the Alsatians as it was once a quarantine for patients of a devastating sixteenth-century venereal disease, attributed to the French. The **Musée d'Art Moderne et Contemporain**, 1 pl Jean-Hans Arp (Tues, Wed, Fri & Sat 11am–7pm, Thurs noon–10pm, Sun 10am–6pm; €5), stands on the west bank of the river and houses an impressive collection featuring Monet, Klimt, Ernst and Klee. **Kronenbourg**, 68 route d'Oberhausbergen (℡03.88.27.41.59; daily except Sat Oct–April and Sun), runs daily **brewery** tours.

### Practicalities

From the **train station** take rue du Maire Kuss, cross the river into rue du 22 Novembre and continue to place Kléber, from where rue des Grandes-Arcades heads south to place Gutenberg and the **tourist office** at 17 place de la Cathédrale (daily 9am–6/7pm, shorter hours in winter; ℡03.88.52.28.28, ✆www.ot -strasbourg.fr). The tourist office also has annexes in the underground shopping centre in front of the train station and at the Pont de l'Europe, at the German border. **Internet** access is at Midi Minuit, 5 pl du Corbeau.

Hotels are expensive and often fully booked weekdays, but the city does have several good **hostel** choices: the clean and tour group-happy *CIARUS*, 7 rue de Finkmatt, (℡03.88.15.27.88, ✆www.ciarus.com; bus #10; dorms €17.40, rooms ❸) or, on rue des Cavaliers by the Pont de l'Europe, the more sedate *Des Deux Rives* (℡03.88.45.54.20; bus #21; €18). **Hotels** include the upmarket *Hôtel des Arts*, 10 pl du Marché-aux-Cochons-de-Lait (℡03.88.37.98.37, ✆www.hotel-arts .fr; ❹) and the elegant *Hôtel du Rhin*, 7–8 pl de la Gare (℡03.88.32.35.00, ✆www .hotel-du-rhin.com; ❸). The nearest campsite, *La Montagne Verte*, is at 2 rue Robert Forrer (℡03.88.30.25.46); take bus #2/13 to *Auberge de Jeunesse*. Eating can be quite pricey, but for inexpensive options, try rue des Tonneliers, just south of place Gutenberg. The *FEC Student Canteen* at place St-Étienne also serves good meals at rock-bottom prices. Alternatively, try the down-market *Bistrôt de la Gare*, 18 rue du Vieux-Marché-aux-Grains, for good pasta and salads, or the more traditional *La Victoire*, 24 quai des Pêcheurs. At night, the city comes to life in its **wine bars** and **beer halls**. *L'Académie de la Bière*, 17 rue Adolphe-Seyboth, is the city's most serious beer palace, frequented by locals and tourists alike, while *La Salamandre*, 3 rue Paul-Janet, is great for live music and dancing.

# The French Alps

Rousseau wrote in his *Confessions*, "I need torrents, rocks, pine trees, dark forests, mountains, rugged paths to go up and down, precipices at my elbow to give me a good fright." And these are, in essence, the principal joys of the **French Alps**.

Along the mountains' western edge, **Grenoble** and **Annecy** are the gateways to the highest parts, although you really need to spend several days here to create time for anything more strenuous than viewing the peaks from your hotel window. There are six **national or regional parks** – Vanoise, Écrins, Bauges, Chartreuse, Queyras (the least busy) and Vercors (the gentlest) – each of which is ideal walking country, as is the professionals' **Route des Grandes Alpes**, which crosses all the major massifs from Lake Geneva to Menton. But if you're pushed for time, go to **Chamonix**, principal base for accessing Mont Blanc and revered by extreme sports enthusiasts, or simply do day-walks from any of the main centres. All **routes** are clearly marked and equipped with refuge huts and *gîtes d'étape* (⊛www .gites-refuges.com). The Maison de la Montagne in both Grenoble and Chamonix provides detailed information on GR paths, and local tourist offices often produce maps of walks in their areas. Bear in mind that anywhere above 2000m will only be free of snow from early July until mid-September.

## Grenoble

The economic and intellectual capital of the French Alps, **GRENOBLE** is a thriving city, beautifully situated on the Drac and Isère rivers. The old centre, south of the Isère, focuses on place Grenette and place Notre Dame, both popular with local students lounging in the many outdoor cafés. For a good introduction to the region, visit the **Musée Dauphinois**, 30 rue Maurice-Gignoux (daily except Tues 10am–6/7pm; free), which occupies the former convent of Ste-Marie-d'en-Haut on rue Maurice-Gignoux. The French Resistance was particularly active in the Vercors Massif near Grenoble during World War II, and is commemorated – along with victims of the Holocaust – in the **Musée de la Résistance et de la Déportation**, 14 rue Hébert (daily except Tues 9/10am–6/7pm; free). Highlight of Grenoble, however, especially in good weather, is the trip by *téléphérique* from the riverside quai Stéphane Jay up to **Fort de la Bastille** on the steep slopes above the north bank of the Isère (daily 9.15/11am–6.30pm/12.15am; €5.70 one-way). It's a hair-raising ride to an otherwise uninteresting fort, but the view over the surrounding mountains and valleys, and down onto the town, is stunning.

### Practicalities

The **train** and **bus stations** are on the western edge of the centre, at the end of avenue Félix Viallet. The **tourist office,** at 14 rue de la République, near place Grenette (Mon–Sat 9am–noon & 2–6pm, Sun 10am–1pm; April–Sept also Sun 2–5pm; ☏04.76.42.41.41, ⊛www.grenoble-isere.info), also houses the **Maison de la Montagne** desk, where you can pick up detailed information on hiking and climbing.

Several **hotels** cluster near the station – the *Alizé,* 1 pl de la Gare (☏04.76.43.12.91, ⊛www.hotelalize.com; ❸), is probably the best bet. More centrally, try the quiet and old-fashioned *Du Moucherotte*, on 1 rue Auguste Gâché, near place Grenette, (☏04.76.54.61.40, ☏04.76.44.62.52; ❸). There's a **hostel**, 4km to the south of town in Échirolles (☏04.76.09.33.52; €15.60; bus #16), and a **campsite**, *Les Trois Pucelles*, 4km to the west, in Seyssins (☏04.76.96.45.73, ⊛www.camping -trois-pucelles.com; open all year). For reasonably priced local food there's a wide selection of **cafés and brasseries** between place St-André and place Notre-Dame; try the popular *Le Valgodemar,* at 2 rue St-Hugues, or lively *Caffé Forte*, 4 pl Lavalette. For **Internet** access go to Neptune, 2 rue de la Paix.

## Annecy

Attracting holiday-makers and serious hikers alike, the touristy yet undeniably pretty town of **ANNECY** sits in a glorious lake setting, with a warren of picturesque seventeenth-century lanes intersected by the Canal du Thiou. Though the town's attractions are more scenic than historic, it's worth wandering down to the south bank of the canal for the **Musée-Château** (June–Sept daily 10.30am–6pm; Oct–May daily except Tues 10am–noon & 2–5pm; €4.70), which houses some interesting archeological finds and offers splendid views to the lake below. The **Palais de l'Île** (June–Sept daily 10.30am–6pm; Oct–May daily except Tues 10am–noon & 2–5pm; €3.10) is a small twelfth-century fort-turned-museum and was used as a prison in World War II. Annecy's **train** and **bus** station complex is five minutes' walk northwest of the centre, while the **tourist office** is by the lake at 1 rue Jean-Jaurès (July & Aug Mon–Sat 9am–6/6.30pm, Sun 9/10am–noon/1pm & 1.45–6.30pm; Sept–June closed lunch; also Nov–March closed Sun; ☎04.50.45.00.33, ⓦwww.lac-annecy.com). The local **hostel** is at 4 route du Semnoz (☎04.50.45.33.19; €15), and **hotels** fill up fast, so it's advisable to book. For rooms in the centre, try the *Hôtel Alexandra*, 19 rue Vaugelas (☎04.50.52.84.33, ☎04.50.45.49.06; ❸), just across from the tourist office, or *Hotel Central*, 6 bis rue Royale (☎04.50.45.05.37, ⓦwww.hotelcentralannecy.com; ❸), overlooking the canal. The **campsite** is off boulevard de la Corniche, just south of town (☎04.50.45.48.30; closed mid-Oct to March). A variety of **restaurants** can be found in the old centre, many fairly average – *l'Étage*, 13 rue du Pâquier, is one of the best.

## Chamonix and Mont Blanc

At 4810m, **Mont Blanc** is both Europe's highest mountain and the Alps' biggest draw. At Le Fayet the **tramway du Mont-Blanc** (1hr 15min; €22) begins its haul to the **Nid d'Aigle**, a vantage point on the northwest slope. Thirty kilometres further on, at **CHAMONIX**, an expensive **téléphérique** (€35 return) soars to the **Aiguille du Midi** (3842m), a terrifying granite pinnacle on which the cablecar station and a restaurant are precariously balanced. Here, the view of Mont Blanc, and the altitude, will literally leave you breathless. At your feet is the snowy plateau of the **Col du Midi**, with the glaciers of the Vallée Blanche and Géant advancing at their millennial pace. To the right, a steep snowfield leads to the "easy" ridge route to the summit with its cap of ice. Try to book the *téléphérique* ahead to avoid the queues (☎08.92.68.00.67) and go before 9am: the summit usually clouds over towards midday and the crowds become intolerable. Bring warm clothes, too, as it can be chilly at the top.

### Practicalities

Chamonix' **tourist office** and **Maison de la Montagne,** near the church at place du Triangle-de-l'Amitié (daily 8.30am–12.30pm & 2–7pm; ☎04.50.53.00.24, ⓦwww.chamonix.com), can provide details of all local sporting activities. From the train station, in the centre of town, the spectacular mountain train line **Mont-Blanc Express** starts its slow, precipitous journey to the Swiss town of Martigny (at least 5 daily; 1hr 40min; €37 return; ⓦwww.momc.ch), where you can connect to Milan. SAT **buses** leave from the train station for Geneva via Le Fayet (5 daily; 2hr; €33) and Courmayeur in Italy (3 daily; 20min; €9.50).

Finding **accommodation** can be a problem and you should book ahead. Rue Vallot has a couple of options worth trying: *Hotel Touring* at no. 95 (☎04.50.53.59.18, ⓦwww.hoteltouring-chamonix.com; ❹), and *La Boule de Neige* at no. 362 (☎04.50.53.04.48, ☎04.50.55.91.09; ❹) or best of all, the popular *Vagabond*, 365 av Ravanel-le-Rouge (☎04.50.53.15.43, ⓦwww.gitevagabond.com; €12.50), a comfortable **hostel** with adjacent restaurant, bar and **Internet**. **Campsites** are numerous: *Les Molliases* (☎04.50.53.16.81; closed mid-Sept to May) is off the main road west of Chamonix heading for the Mont Blanc tunnel, whilst *Les Rosières* is on route des Praz (☎04.50.53.10.42). Alternatively, try the inexpensive **mountain cabins** run by the Alpine Club of Chamonix (☎04.50.53.16.03, ⓦwww.clubalpin-chamonix.com) **Restaurants** and **bars** include *La Calèche*, 18 rue Paccard, serving Savoyard specialities, and Ozzie favourite *Wild Wallabies*, rue de la Tour, for late-night drinking.

# Rhône Valley and Provence

Of all the regions of France, **Provence** is the most irresistible, with attractions that range from the high mountains of the southern Alps to the wild plains of the Camargue. Yet, apart from the coast, large areas remain remarkably unscathed by development. Its complete integration into France dates only from the nineteenth century and, although the Provençal language is rarely heard, the accent is distinctive even to a foreign ear. The main problem is choosing where to go. The **Rhône valley**, north–south route of ancient armies, medieval traders and modern rail and road, is nowadays fairly industrialized, and other than the big city delights of **Lyon** – not strictly in Provence but the main gateway for the region – there's not much to detain you before the old papal stronghold of **Avignon**, which also hosts a wonderful summer festival. Deeper into Provence, on the edge of the flamingo-filled lagoons of the **Camargue**, the ancient settlement of **Arles** boasts an impressive Roman legacy.

## Lyon

**LYON**, France's third-largest city, became a UNESCO World Heritage site in 1998, one of only six urban sites in the world thus honoured. Its charms are manifold, not least its gastronomy: there are more restaurants per square metre here than anywhere else on earth. It also has a beautifully preserved old Renaissance quarter and an elegant town centre of grand boulevards and public squares. With a population of more than two million, including over 100,000 university students, there's a vibrant nightlife and cultural scene, boasting one of the few national operas outside Paris and a major summer-long **festival**, *Les Nuits de Fourvière*, celebrating theatre, cinema (the Lumière brothers were Lyonnais), music and dance.

### Arrival, information and accommodation

Lyon-St-Exupéry **airport** is 45 minutes from the centre by bus (daily 6am–11.20pm, every 20min; €8.50). The main TGV train station, **Gare de la Part Dieu**, is on boulevard Marius-Vivier-Merle, in the heart of the commercial district on the east bank of the Rhône, and connected to the centre by a regular métro service. Other **trains** arrive at the **Gare de Perrache**, on what was once the tip of the peninsula, near the **tourist office** on place Bellecour (daily 9/10am–6/7pm; ☎04.72.77.69.69, ⊛www.lyon-france.com), where you can pick up local transport maps and book guided tours. Tickets for **city transport** cost a flat €1.50, or buy the tourist office's **liberté ticket** for a day's unlimited travel on trams, buses and métro (€4.20). The **City Card**, also available at the tourist office, covers entry to all museums, monuments, tours and transport (€18/28/38, for 1, 2 or 3 days respectively). *Le Petit Bulletin* is a useful, free weekly listings newspaper, available from shops and restaurants.

For **accommodation** close to the centre, try the comfortable *Élysée*, 92 rue Edouard-Herriot (☎04.78.42.03.15, ⊛www.elysee-hotel.com; ❺). Nearer the Gare de Perrache is the clean and homely *Vaubecour*, 28 rue Vaubecour (☎04.78.37.44.91, ☎04.78.42.90.17; ❷). The modern *Athéna Part-Dieu*, 45 bd Marius-Vivier-Merle (☎04.72.68.88.44, ⊛www.athena-hotel.fr; ❸), next to the TGV station, is a very handy option that fills up fast. Vieux Lyon has a **hostel** at 41–45 montée du Chemin Neuf (☎04.78.15.05.50; €13.80), with great city views.

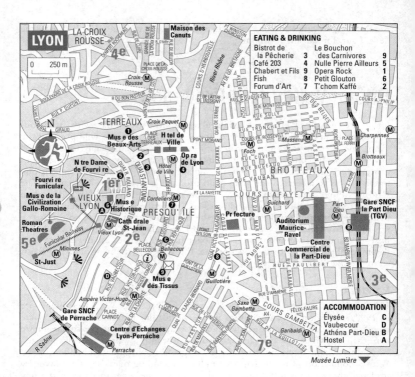

**LYON**
LA-CROIX ROUSSE

0   250 m

Maison des Canuts

Musée Lumière ▼

The closest **campsite** is the *Porte de Lyon* at Dardilly (℡04.78.35.64.55, ⊕www
.camping-lyon.com), a ten-minute ride by bus #89 from the bus station in Gare
de Vaise, north of the city.

### The City

Directly in front of Gare de Perrache is the green square of **place Carnot** which
leads to the pedestrian rue Victor-Hugo, in turn opening out onto the vast **place
Bellecour**, where even the statue of Louis XIV on horseback looks small. On
rue de la Charité, which runs parallel to rue Victor-Hugo on the Rhône side, is
is the **Musée des Tissus** (Tues–Sun 10am–5.30pm; €4.60; Mº Victor Hugo),
a surprisingly interesting collection of fabrics, clothes and tapestries dating from
ancient Egypt to the present. From here, push straight on up the busy rue de la
République, past place Bellecour. Turning left leads to quai St-Antoine, lined
in the mornings with a colourful food market; a Sunday book market lies just
upriver. Heading north, to **Place des Terreaux**, the centrepiece is an imposing
nineteenth-century fountain sculpted by Bartholdi, more famously responsible
for New York's Statue of Liberty. The square also features the splendidly ornate
**Hôtel de Ville**, as well as the **Musée des Beaux-Arts** (daily except Tues
10/10.30am–6pm; €6; Mº Hôtel de Ville). This absorbing collection includes
ancient Egyptian, Greek and Roman artefacts as well as works by Rubens, Renoir
and Picasso.

   North of Place des Terreaux, the old silk weavers' district of **La Croix Rousse**
is still a working-class area, but today only twenty or so people work on the
computerized looms that are kept in business by the restoration and maintenance
of France's palaces and châteaux. You can watch traditional looms in action at **La**

**Maison des Canuts** at 10 rue d'Ivry, one block north of place de la Croix Rousse (Tues–Sat 10am–6.30pm; free; M° Croix Rousse). From here, cut through to the river and cross to **Vieux Lyon**. The tangled streets on the left bank of the Saône form an attractive muddle of cobbled lanes and Renaissance facades, riddled with the famous *traboulés*, or covered alleyways, running between streets. Originally used to transport silk safely through town, they later served as escape routes and hideouts for the resistance during World War II. The **Musée Historique de Lyon** and **Musée de la Marionnette,** place du Petit Collège, are under renovation, so check with the tourist office. **Théâtre Guignol**, 2 rue Louis-Carrand (Wed & Sat 3pm & 4.30pm; Sun 3pm; €8), puts on popular puppet theatre shows.

Rue St-Jean ends at the **Cathédrale St-Jean**, and though damaged during World War II, its thirteenth-century stained glass (above the altar and in the rose windows of the transepts) is in perfect condition, as is the magnificent fourteenth-century mechanical clock (it strikes at noon, 2pm, 3pm and 4pm). Just beyond the cathedral, at M° Vieux Lyon on avenue Adolphe-Max, is a **funicular station**, from which you can ascend to the two **Roman theatres** on rue de l'Antiquaille (daily 9am–7pm; free), and the excellent **Musée de la Civilisation Gallo-Romaine** at 17 rue Cléberg (Tues–Sun 10am–6pm; €3.80), containing mosaics and artefacts from Roman Lyon.. From here, it's a short walk to the late nineteenth-century **Basilique de Notre-Dame** (daily 8am–7pm), a gaudy showcase of multicoloured marble and mosaic. The belvedere (€4) behind the church affords an impressive view of Lyon and its curving rivers. Reminders of the war are never far away in France and this is particularly true of Lyon where the **Centre d'Histoire de la Résistance et de la Déportation**, at 14 av Berthelot (Wed–Sun 9am–5.30pm; €3.80), tells of the immense courage and ingenuity of the French resistance, and also serves as a poignant memorial to the city's deported Jews. To the southeast of town, the new **Musée Lumière**, 25 rue du Premier-Film, houses the Lumière brothers' cinematograph, which in 1895 projected the world's first film (Tues–Sun 11am–6.30pm; €6; Métro D to Monplaisir-Lumière).

### Eating, drinking and nightlife

Lyon is the self-proclaimed gastronomic capital of France, and with good reason. It has hundreds of **restaurants** offering delicious, if somewhat heavy, Lyonnais fare. Vegetarians will be disappointed, however, as specialities focus on meat and offal, most famously in its *quenelles* (soufflé-like dumplings) and *andouillettes* (hefty tripe sausages). Lyon is crammed with touristy restaurants claiming to be *bouchons*, typical Lyon wine bars serving food. For the real thing, try *Chabert et Fils*, 11 rue des Marroniers, for excellent local fare; or, opposite at no. 8, *Le Bouchon des Carnivores*, which offers a beef-heavy menu and walls covered with paintings, photos and models of bulls. Other options include the bargain bistro *Le Petit Glouton*, 56 rue St-Jean; *Nulle Pierre Ailleurs*, 2 Quai R Rolland, for its generous portions; and *Café 203*, by the Opera House at 9 rue du Garet, which is popular with Lyon's trendy set and offers excellent-value menus all day. For **Internet** access, there's Raconte-moi La Terre, 38 rue Thomassin, with a bookshop specializing in travel literature (closed Sun). For **nightlife**, both *Opera Rock*, 7 rue Terme, and *Bistrot de la Pêcherie*, 1 rue de la Platière, have live DJs and late-night dancing, while *Fish*, 21 quai Victor-Auganeur, is a buzzing house club favoured by under-thirtysome-things. Lyon also boasts a few **gay bars**: head for the 1930s *Forum d'Art*, 15 rue des Quatre-Chapeaux, or *T'chom Kaffé*, 26 rue Hippolyte-Flandrin.

## Avignon

**AVIGNON**, great city of the popes and for centuries one of the major artistic centres of France, is today one of the country's biggest tourist attractions and always crowded in summer. It's an immaculately preserved medieval town, and it's worth putting up with the inevitable queues and camcorder-wielding hordes to enjoy its unique stock of monuments, churches and museums. During the drama festival in July, it's the only place to be, though as around 200,000 spectators come here for the show, doing any normal sightseeing becomes virtually impossible.

Central Avignon is enclosed by intimidating medieval **walls**, built by one of the nine popes who based themselves here in the fourteenth century, away from the anarchic feuding and rival popes of Rome. Centre of town is **place de l'Horloge**, lined with cafés and market stalls on summer evenings, just beyond which is the enormous **Palais des Papes** (daily 9/9.30am–5.45/7/8pm; €9.50, joint ticket with Pont d'Avignon €11.50). The denuded interior gives little indication of the richness of the papal court, although the building is impressive for sheer size alone. The nearby **Musée du Petit Palais** (daily except Tues 9.30/10am–1pm & 2–5.30/6pm; €6) houses a collection of religious art from the thirteenth to sixteenth centuries, while more modern works are on show at the **Musée Calvet**, 65 rue Joseph-Vernet (daily except Tues 10am–1pm & 2–6pm; €6) and in the **Collection Lambert**, 5 rue Violette (Tues–Sun 11am–6/7pm; €5.50). Jutting out halfway across the river is the famous **Pont St-Bénézet** (same hours as Palais des Papes; €4). The struggle to keep the bridge in good repair against the ravages of the Rhône was finally abandoned in 1660, three-and-a-half centuries after it was built, and today just four of the original 22 arches survive.

### Practicalities

Avignon's **train station** is by the porte de la République on boulevard St-Roch, on the southern edge of the centre. There's a separate **TGV station** in the Quartier de Courtine, to the west, reached by regular shuttle bus from the stop just inside the main gate. The **tourist office** is a short walk from the main station at 41 cours Jean-Jaurès (daily 9/10am–5/6pm, winter closed Sun afternoons; ☎04.32.74.32.74, ⊕www.ot-avignon.fr); ask for the free **Avignon Pass**, offering great discounts on entrance fees to all monuments and museums. During Avignon's July **festival** (☎04.90.27.66.50, ⊕www.festival-avignon.com, ⊕www.avignon-off .org), theatre dominates, but opera, classical music and film also feature, with the streets given over to the fringe.

Even outside festival time, finding **accommodation** can be a problem. One of the cheaper options is the *Monclar*, 13 av Monclar (☎04.90.86.20.14, ⊕www .hotel-monclar.com; ❸), an attractive eighteenth-century house just round the corner from the train station. Other reasonable choices include *Alizea*, 38 cours Jean Jaurès, (☎04.90.82.03.21, ⊕www.hotelalizea.com; ❸), and the *Innova*, 100 rue Joseph-Vernet (☎04.90.82.54.10, ✉hotel.innova@wanadoo.fr; ❸). There's a **hostel**, the *Auberge Bagatelle* (☎04.90.86.30.39; dorms €11, rooms ❷), across the river on Île de la Barthelasse, which also has a **campsite**; take bus #10 or #11 to the bridge, from where you can cross to the island. **Eating** on a budget is easy. The touristy brasseries on place de l'Horloge all do well-priced meals and have outdoor seating – *Les Domaines* is a good choice. Alternatively, the lively and local *Maison Nani*, 29 rue Théodore Aubanel does good *plats du jour*, while *Tapalocas*, 10 rue Galante, buzzes with tasty tapas and sangría. At night, both *RedZone*, 25 rue Carnot, and *Bokao's*, rue Rempart-St-Lazare, are cool places for drinking and dancing. Place de l'Horloge also has plenty of places to sip an early evening **drink**, and there's **Internet** access at Webzone, place Pie XII.

## Arles

Around 25km south of Avignon, **ARLES** was one of Gaul's most important settlements, providing grain for most of the western Roman empire, as well as being a crucial port and shipbuilding centre – indeed, in the fourth century it became the capital of Gaul, Britain and Spain. Today, Arles is a picturesque town with a laid-back Mediterranean atmosphere and well-preserved vestiges of its illustrious past – not least a marvellous Roman amphitheatre. Arles' most famous inhabitant, Vincent van Gogh, spent a turbulent year here – an ear was lost – with his friend Paul Gauguin, but managed to produce some of his most famous works, including *Starry Night* and *Night Café*. No original Van Gogh paintings remain in the town, but the **Fondation Van Gogh** in the Palais de Luppé, 24 Rond Point des Arènes (April–Oct daily 10.30am–8pm; Nov–March Tues–Sun 11am–5pm; €7), exhibits works based on his masterpieces by well-known contemporary artists, such as Hockney and Bacon. **Boulevard des Lices** is Arles' main street, along with rue Jean-Jaurès and its continuation, rue Hôtel-de-Ville. The central **place de la République** runs between rue Jean Jaurès and rue Hôtel-de-Ville and is home to the **Cathédrale St-Trophime**, whose doorway is one of the most famous bits of twelfth-century Provençal carving, depicting a *Last Judgement* trumpeted by angels playing with the enthusiasm of jazz musicians. The cloister (daily 9/10am–4.30/6pm; €3.50), with its mix of Romanesque and Gothic architecture, is also worth a look. Immediately east of the cathedral is the **Théâtre-Antique** (daily: May–Sept 9am–noon, 2–6pm; Oct–April 9/10–11.30am & 2–4.30/5.30pm; €3), though a better insight into Roman Arles can be found at the **Musée de l'Arles Antique** (daily 9/10am–5/7pm; €5.50), west of the town centre on the spit of land between the Rhône and the Canal du Rhône. Its fabulous mosaics, sarcophagi and sculpture illuminate Arles' early history, while alongside lies the town's most impressive Roman structure, the **Cirque Romain**, built in the first century AD and originally seating 20,000. Housed in a splendid medieval building once used by the Knights of the Order of Malta, the **Musée Réattu** (March–Oct daily 10am–noon & 2–5pm; Nov–Feb daily 1–5pm; €4) hosts a fine collection of modern art, including sketches and sculptures by Picasso. Opposite are the remains of the fourth-century **Roman baths** (daily: May–Sept 9am–noon, 2–6pm; Oct–April 9/10–11.30am & 2–4.30/5.30pm; €3).

## Practicalities

The **train station** is a few blocks north of the Cirque Romain, close to the Porte de la Cavalerie. The **tourist office** is opposite rue Jean Jaurès on boulevard des Lices (April–Sept daily 9am–5.45/6.45pm; Oct–March Mon–Sat 9am–4.45/5.45pm, Sun 10am–2.15pm; ☏04.90.18.41.20, ⊛ www.tourisme.ville-arles.fr), and provides a hotel booking service.

For central **accommodation**, try the *Mirador*, at 3 rue Voltaire (☏04.90.96.28.05, ⊛ www.hotel-mirador.com; ❸), or *De l'Amphithéâtre*, at 5 rue Diderot (☏04.90.96.10.30, ⊛ www.hotelamphitheatre.fr; ❺), a wonderfully renovated seventeenth-century mansion with small, neat rooms. There's a **hostel** at 20 av Maréchal-Foch (☏04.90.96.18.25; €11.50; closed Jan), a five-minute walk from the tourist office. Of the five **campsites** within easy reach of the city, the most pleasant is *La Bienheureuse* (☏04.90.98.48.06), 7km out on RN453 at Raphèle-lés-Arles, with a restaurant and regular bus connections; closer to town is *Camping City*, 67 route de la Crau (☏04.90.93.08.86, ⊛ www.camping-city.com). To sample traditional Provençal **cuisine**, try *La Gueule du Loup*, 39 rue des Arènes, or *Lou Peyrou*, 18 bd Georges Clemenceau. **Internet** is available at Hexaworld, on rue du 4 Septembre, by the train station.

## The Camargue

The flat, marshy delta immediately south of Arles – the **Camargue** – is a beautiful area, used as a breeding-ground for the bulls which participate in local *corridas*, and the white horses ridden by their herdsmen. The true wildlife of the area is made up of flamingos, marsh- and seabirds, and a rich flora of reeds, wild flowers and juniper trees. The only town is **SAINTES-MARIES-DE-LA-MER**, best known for the annual **Gypsy Festival** held each May, and which is linked by a regular bus service to Arles. It's a pleasant, if touristy, place, with some fine sandy beaches; if you're interested in bird-watching or touring the lagoons, your first port of call should be the **tourist office** on 5 av Van Gogh (daily: July & Aug 9am–8pm; Sept–June 9am–5/7pm; ☎04.90.97.82.55, ⊛www.saintesmaries .com), which has information on a number of organized cycle, horse and boat tours of the Camargue. There are also several places to **rent bicycles, horses or 4x4s**, if you prefer to explore alone. For **hotels**, try the basic *Delta*, 1 place Mireille (☎04.90.97.81.12; ❸), the central *Camille* (☎04.90.97.80.26, ⊛www .hotel-camille.camargue.fr; ❹) or the quiet *Mirage* (☎04.90.97.80.43, ⊛www .lemirage.camargue.fr; ❹).

# Marseille and the Côte d'Azur

The **Côte d'Azur**, synonymous with glamour, wealth and luxury, is one of the prettiest and most built-up stretches of coast in the world. While its reputation as a pricey playground for the super-rich still holds, holidaying here need not necessarily be more expensive than elsewhere in France, providing you avoid the more obvious tourist traps. The coast's eastern reaches are its most spectacular, the mountains breaking their fall just a few metres before levelling off to the shore. **St-Tropez** is an expensive high spot, though **Nice** trumps in real substance, while at the opposite end of the coast, the vast, cosmopolitan sprawl of **Marseille** is quite different, with its big-city buzz and down-to-earth charm. July and August are the busiest months of the year, when accommodation can be hard to come by; and May can be equally hectic, with both **Monaco**'s Grand Prix and **Cannes**' Film Festival pulling in the crowds.

## Marseille

France's most populous city after Paris, **MARSEILLE** has been a major centre of international maritime trade ever since it was founded by Greek colonists 2500 years ago. Like the capital, the city has suffered plagues, religious bigotry, republican and royalist terror and had its own Commune and Bastille-storming. It was the presence of so many revolutionaries from this city marching to Paris in 1792 that gave the name *Marseillaise* to the national anthem. A working city with little of the glamour of its ritzy Riviera neighbours, it is nevertheless a vibrant, exciting place, with a cosmopolitan population including many Italians and North Africans. It's also a world-class diving and sailing centre, and, surprisingly, France's second fashion capital.

The old harbour, or **Vieux Port**, is a good place to indulge in the sedentary pleasures of observing the city's streetlife over a pastis. Two **fortresses** guard the entrance to the harbour, a little way south of which is the **Abbaye St-Victor** (daily 8.30am–6.30pm), the city's oldest church. It looks and feels like a fortress – the walls of the choir are almost 3m thick – and you can visit the crypt and catacombs (daily 9am–7pm; €2). On the northern side of the harbour is the former old town of Marseille, known as **Le Panier**, a densely populated area that was dynamited by the Nazis, who deported around 20,000 people from here. Largely rebuilt, it's still a working-class quarter, although fashionable with the young and bohemian. After the war, archeologists reaped the benefits of the destruction by finding remains of the Roman docks equipped with vast storage jars for foodstuffs, now housed in the small **Musée des Docks Romains** on place Vivaux (Tues–Sun 10/11am–5/6pm; €2). The quarter's main attraction, though, is **La Vieille Charité**, a Baroque seventeenth-century church and hospice complex, on rue de la Charité, now home to several museums, including the **Musée d'Archéologie**

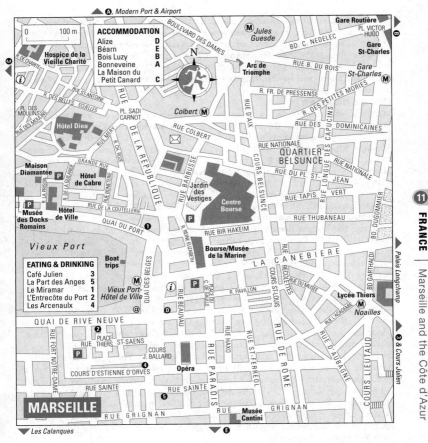

**ACCOMMODATION**

| | |
|---|---|
| Alize | **D** |
| Béarn | **E** |
| Bois Luzy | **B** |
| Bonneveine | **A** |
| La Maison du Petit Canard | **C** |

**EATING & DRINKING**

| | |
|---|---|
| Café Julien | **3** |
| La Part des Anges | **5** |
| Le Miramar | **1** |
| L'Entrecôte du Port | **2** |
| Les Arcenaulx | **4** |

**MARSEILLE**

▼ *Les Calanques*

**Méditerranéenne** (Tues–Sun 10/11am–5/6pm; €2), housing a superb collection of Egyptian mummified animals.

Leading east from the Vieux Port is **La Canebière**, Marseille's main street. Just off the lower end, on busy cours Belsunce, the **Centre Bourse** is a giant mall, also home to an excellent museum of finds from Roman Marseille, the **Musée d'Histoire de Marseille** (Tues–Sun 10/11am–5/6pm; €2), which includes the well-preserved remains of a third-century Roman merchant vessel. At the far eastern end of La Canebière, the **Palais Longchamp** (bus #81) was the grandiose conclusion of an aqueduct bringing water from the outlying hills to the city. Water is still pumped into the middle of the central colonnade of the building, which houses the **Musée des Beaux-Arts** (Tues–Sun 10/11am–5/6pm; €2). South of La Canebière are Marseille's main shopping streets, rue Paradis, rue St-Ferréol and rue de Rome, and the **Musée Cantini**, 19 rue Grignan (Tues–Sun 10/11am–5/6pm; €2), a fine collection of twentieth-century art with works by Dufy, Léger and Picasso.

A twenty-minute boat ride offshore is the **Château d'If** (daily 9.30am–5.30/6.30pm; Oct–March closed Mon), the notorious island fortress that figured in Dumas' great adventure story, *The Count of Monte Cristo*. In reality, no one ever escaped, and most prisoners, incarcerated for political or religious reasons, ended their days here. Hourly boats leave for the island from the Quai des Belges (€10 return, plus €4.70 admission to the château). Twenty minutes southeast of Marseille (bus #21), **Les Calanques**, beautiful rocky inlets carved from white limestone, provide fine bathing, diving and walking. To reach the Plage du Prado, Marseille's main sand **beach**, take bus #83 or #19 to the Promenade Pompidou.

### Practicalities

Marseille's main train station, **gare St-Charles**, is on the northern edge of the 1$^{er}$ *arrondissement*, round the corner from the **bus station** on place Victor-Hugo. The best way of getting around is to walk, although if you need to cover longer distances fast, the **public transport** system – bus, tram and métro – is efficient enough: tickets cost €1.40 from métro stations and on buses. The **tourist office**, at 4 La Canebière, down by the harbour (Mon–Sat 9am–7/7.30pm, Sun 10am–5/6pm; ☏04.91.13.89.00, ☻www.marseille-tourisme.com), offers a free accommodation booking service, as well as selling the **City Pass** for free entry to all museums and the boat ride and visit to the Château d'If (€16/23, for one/two days). **Internet** access is at Infocafé, 1 Quai de Rive Neuve.

Among the budget **hotels**, *La Maison du Petit Canard*, 2 impasse Ste-Françoise (☏04.91.91.40.31, ☻maison.petit.canard.free.fr; ❹), is a small, friendly place in the middle of the Panier district; *Alizé*, 35 quai des Belges (☏04.91.33.66.97, ☻www .alize-hotel.com; ❺), is right opposite the port; while the *Béarn*, 63 rue Sylvabelle (☏04.91.37.75.83, ☏04.91.81.54.98; ❸), offers all the mod cons a few blocks east of the harbour. There are two **hostels**, the *Bois Luzy*, allée des Primevères (☏04.91.49.06.18; €8.90; bus #6 or #8; 10.30pm curfew), housed in an old château; and the *Bonneveine*, on avenue Joseph Vidal (☏04.91.17.63.30; €15.70; bus #44), three miles from the city near Les Calanques.

Marseille's culinary speciality is *bouillabaisse*, a delicious fish stew served in most **restaurants** around the Vieux Port; the finest place to try it is *Le Miramar*, 12 quai du Port, a local institution that books up fast. You can eat cheap, if unexceptional, meals on the fashionable cours d'Estienne-d'Orves: *Les Arcenaulx* at no. 25 has a wonderful tearoom, surrounded by shelves of books. Better food can be found behind on rue Sainte – *La Part des Anges* at no.33 is great fun – or around trendy cours Julien. Beside the port, the popular *L'Entrecôte du Port*, 6 Quai de Rive Neuve, serves steak and mussels. The cours d'Estienne-d'Orves and cours Julien are the places to head for **nightlife** – *Café Julien*, 39 cours Julien, is a popular **bar** with live music at weekends.

## St-Tropez and around

The heart of **ST-TROPEZ** oozes village charm, set around an ancient Greek port and made up of a web of cobbled alleys and butter-coloured houses. Rustic it is not, however: following Roger Vadim's 1956 filming of Brigitte Bardot in *Et Dieu Créa La Femme* (*And God Created Woman*), the hamlet was transformed into a social mecca for the richer-than-thou and their acolytes. The road into St-Tropez splits in two as it enters the village, with the bus station between them. A short distance beyond on place Georges Grammont is the **Musée de l'Annonciade** (daily except Tues 10am–noon & 2/3–6/7pm; €4.60) – a reason in itself for coming here, with works by Matisse, Signac and Derain. Beyond the museum, the **Vieux Port** is the centre of the town, a regular promenade for orange-tanned yacht owners and an internationalista crowd of wealthy style-slaves. Up from here, at the end of quai Jean-Jaurès, rue de la Mairie passes the **Hôtel de Ville**, not far from the rocky **Baie de la Glaye**, and the fishing port with a tiny **beach**. Beyond the fishing port, roads lead up to the sixteenth-century **Citadelle**, with an interesting museum and marvellous views from the ramparts, or along to Les Graniers and further **beaches** on Baie des Canoubiers – accessible by a coastal path and frequent bus service.

St-Tropez has no train service: the nearest station is St-Raphaël. **Buses** from here run every few hours and arrive on avenue Général de Gaulle, a short walk from quai Jean Jaurès, home of the **tourist office** (daily: July & Aug 9.30am–8pm; Sept–June 9.30am–12.30pm & 2–6/7pm; ☏04.94.97.45.21, ⊛www.saint-tropez .st). **Hotels** are pricey and often booked up – and few stay open in winter: try *Baron Lodge*, 23 rue de l'aïoli (☏04.94.97.06.57, ⊛www.hotel-le-baron.com; ➎), open year round; cheaper are *La Belle Isnarde*, route de la Plage de Tahiti (☏04.94.97.13.64, ☏04.94.97.57.74; closed mid-Oct to mid-April; ➎) and *Lou Riou*, chemin de la Moutte, (☏04.94.97.03.19, ⊛www.louriou.com; ➍). There's a better choice of accommodation in **ST-RAPHAËL**, north of St-Tropez; try *Hotel Bellevue*, 22 bd Félix-Martin (☏04.94.19.90.10, ⊛www.hotelbellevue.150m.com; ➍). There's also *La Bonne Auberge*, 54 rue de la Garonne (☏04.94.95.69.72; ➌), or the *Centre International*, 5km east of town at the beach, 100m from Boulouris train station (☏04.94.95.20.58; €20); both closed mid-Nov to mid-March). **Camping** poses similar problems: the two closest sites to St-Tropez are a few kilometres southeast on the plage du Pampelonne and cost a fortune. Better is *Les Tournels*, inland on route de Camarat near Ramatuelle (☏04.94.55.90.90, ⊛www .tournels.com). There are plenty of **restaurants** in St-Tropez, on rue Clemenceau, and place des Lices – try *Café des Arts* at no.1 – but don't expect any bargains. In St-Raphaël, the portside *Le Sirocco* and, further down, *La Moule Joyeuse,* both have good seafood menus.

# Cannes

Fishing village turned millionaires' playground, **CANNES** is best known for the International Film Festival, held in May, during which time the place is overrun by the denizens of Movieland, their hangers-on, and a small army of paparazzi. The seafront promenade, **La Croisette**, and the **Vieux Port** form the focus of Cannes's eye-candy life, while the old town, **Le Suquet**, on the steep hill overlooking the bay from the west, with its quaint winding streets and eleventh century castle, is a pleasant place to wander. Meanwhile, the attractive **Îles des Lérins**, composed of touristy Ste Marguerite and the quieter St Honorat, home to a Cistercian monastery, are just a ten-minute ferry ride from the Vieux Port (€10).

### Practicalities

The **train station** is on rue Jean Jaurès, a short walk north of the centre along rue des Serbes. There's a **tourist office** at the station, with the main office in the Palais des Festivals on the waterfront (both Mon–Sat 9am–7pm; ☏04.93.39.24.53, ⊛www.cannes.fr).

Finding accommodation can be a problem during high season, and all but impossible during the Film Festival, when prices are bumped up considerably. There are several budget **hotels** along rue du 24 Août near the train station: try the *Bourgogne*, at no. 11 (☏04.93.38.36.73, ⊛www.hotel-de-bourgogne.com; ➌), or, closer to the seafront, is the cosy *Albe*, 31 rue Bivouac Napoléon (☏04.97.06.21.21, ⊛www .albe-hotel.com; ➍). The **hostel**, *Le Chalit*, 27 av Galliéni (☏04.93.99.22.11, ⊛www.le-chalit.com; €20), is just minutes from the *gare SNCF*. The nearest **campsite** is *Parc Bellevue*, 67 av Maurice Chevalier (☏04.93.47.28.97, ⊛www .parcbellevue.com; bus #2 or #9). Le Suquet is full of **restaurants**, which get cheaper as you reach the top. *Au Bec Fin*, 14 rue du 24 Août, has superb traditional cooking and good *plats du jour; Le Sevrina*, 3 rue Félix-Faure, serves pizza, pasta and fondue; and *Le Bouchon d'Objectif*, 10 rue de Constantine, is an excellent, reasonably priced bistro. Cannes abounds with **nightclubs**, though prices, as you might expect, are high: *Brumel*, 3 bd de la République, is ever trendy, while *Le Zanzibar*, 85 rue Félix-Faure, is one of the oldest gay bars in France. **Internet** access is available at Dream Cybercafé, 6 rue du Commt. Vidal.

# Nice

**NICE**, capital of the French Riviera and France's fifth-largest city, grew into a major tourist resort in the nineteenth century, when large numbers of foreign visitors – many of them British – were drawn here by the mild Mediterranean climate. The most obvious legacy of these early holiday-makers is the famous **promenade des Anglais** stretching along the pebble beach, laid out by nineteenth-century English residents to facilitate their afternoon stroll by the sea, while Russian aristocrats erected an **Orthodox Cathedral** at the end of avenue Nicolas II, not far from the train station. These days, Nice is a busy, bustling city with an incredible amount of traffic, but it's still a lovely place, with a beautiful location and attractive historical centre. The city also makes the best base for visiting the Riviera coast, which stretches for 30km, east to the Italian border and west to Cannes. **Carnival** (Feb/early March) packs out the town, with parades and music culminating at Mardi Gras, a city-wide party that takes up every street. The old town, **Vieux Nice**, nestles around the hill of Nice's former château, a rambling collection of narrow alleys lined with tall, rust-and-ochre houses, and centring on place Rossetti and the Baroque **Cathédrale Ste-Réparate**. Nearby is the entrance to the **Parc du Château** (there's an elevator and stairway by the Tour Bellanda, at the eastern end of quai des États-Unis), decked out in a mock-Grecian style harking back to the original Greek settlement of Nikea. The point of climbing the stairs, apart from enjoying the perfumed greenery, is the view stretching west over the bay. Nearby, on promenade des Arts, is the **Musée d'Art Moderne et d'Art Contemporain** (Tues–Sun 10am–6pm; €4), with a collection of Pop Art and neo-Realist work, including pieces by Andy Warhol and Roy Lichtenstein. The **Musée des Beaux-Arts** (Tues–Sun 10am–6pm; €4), meanwhile, is on the other side of town at 33 av des Baumettes, with a superb collection of works dating from the fifteenth to the twentieth century.

Up above the city centre, **Cimiez**, a posh suburb reached by bus #15 from just in front of the train station, was the social centre of the town's elite some seventeen centuries ago, when the city was capital of the Roman province of Alpes-Maritimae. Excavations of the Roman baths are housed, along with accompanying archeological finds, in the **Musée d'Archéologie**, 160 av des Arènes (daily except Tues 10am–6pm; €4). Overlooking the baths is the wonderful **Musée Matisse** (daily except Tues 10am–6pm; €4): Nice was the artist's home for much of his life, and the collection covers every period. Nearby, the beautiful, uplifting **Musée Chagall**, 16 av du Doct. Ménard (daily except Tues 10am–5/6pm; €5.50),

*▲ Musée Matisse & Musée Chagall*

**NICE**

**ACCOMMODATION**

| | |
|---|---|
| Les Camélias | C |
| Carlyna | D |
| Chez Patrick | A |
| Cronstadt | E |
| Les Orangers | B |

N

0   250 m

**EATING & DRINKING**

| | |
|---|---|
| Fenocchio | 4 |
| Chez René Socca | 3 |
| Passez à Table | 1 |
| Pasta Basta | 6 |
| Le Saint Geran | 2 |
| Thor | 7 |
| Wayne's | 5 |

exhibits dazzlingly colourful Biblical paintings, stained glass and book illustrations. Both museums have lovely gardens.

## Practicalities

Nice **airport** is 6km southwest, connected to its train station by bus #99 or #23 (daily 8am–9pm, every 30min; €4) and centre by bus #98 (daily 6am–9.30pm, every 10–15min; €4). The main **train station**, Nice-Ville, is ten minutes' walk northwest from the centre, at the top of avenue Jean-Médecin. The main **tourist office** is at 5 promenade des Anglais (Mon–Sat 8/9am–6/8pm; June–Sept also Sun 9am–6pm; ☎08.92.70.74.07, ⓦ www.nicetourism.com), with branches at the airport and on avenue Thiers next to the *gare*. For **city transport**, single bus tickets (€1.30) can be bought on board, while *carnets* of ten (€10) are available from kiosks and *tabacs*, who also sell the one- and seven-day **bus pass** (€4/€15). For **Internet** access, there's Cyberpoint at 10 avenue Félix-Faure.

## Accommodation

There are lots of cheap, though not terribly attractive, **hotels** around the train station. There's a better choice in the centre of town, where you'll also find two **hostels**. The area around Nice is filled with **campsites**; check the tourist office and take your pick.

**Carlyna** 2 rue Sacha Guitry ☎04.93.80.77.21, ⓦ www.int1.com/carlyna. Spic-and-span "modern" hotel just paces from the Promenade des Anglais. Service is adequate, and the 24 rooms have TV, phone and a/c. ❹

**Chez Patrick** 32 rue Pertinax ☎04.93.80.30.72, ⓦ www.backpackerschezpatrick.com. Excellent student-happy hostel in the old town, with dorm beds for €21. No curfew or lockout.

**Cronstadt** 3 rue Cronstadt ☎04.93.82.00.30, ⓦ www.hotelcronstadt.com. A block from the sea, this exquisite courtyard hotel run by a friendly Swedish couple has ten charming rooms and delicious breakfasts. ❺

**Les Orangers** 10bis av Durante ☎04.93.87.51.41, ⓕ04.93.82.57.82. Ignore the chipping paint, as it's one of the better economy finds around the station. ❸

**Les Camélias** 3 rue Spitalieri ☎04.93.62.15.54. Popular, bright and cheery central hostel with showers and sinks in the dorm rooms and shared toilets. €18.50.

## Eating and drinking

The old town is full of **restaurants** and likes to stay up late. Marché aux Fleurs (not to be missed in the mornings for its colourful market) is lined with restaurants, their tables spilling outdoors, but they tend to be quite pricey. For nightlife, Cours Saleya and the parallel rue de la Préfecture are the places to be.

**Fenocchio** place Rossetti. The best ice cream in town, with novel flavours including lavender, jasmine and tomato.

**Chez René Socca** 2 rue Miralhéti. The place to try Niçois specialities, including great *socca*, a pancake made from chickpea flour. Closed Mon.

**Passez à Table** 30 rue Pertinax. Classic French restaurant with a number of inexpensive vegetarian meals and organic produce. Great large pasta dishes for under €10, or try the tasty *potage de légumes* (vegetable soup), under €5.

**Pasta Basta** 18 rue de la Préfecture. Dependable Italian *plats du jour* for under €13.

**Le Saint Geran** 12 rue Paganini. Delicious food from the island of Mauritius, with seafood menus from €11.50. Closed Sun eve & Mon.

**Thor** 32 cours Saleya. The fifty different beers and cheap menus on offer here attract the locals in droves.

**Wayne's** 15 rue de la Préfecture. Live music bar very popular with imbibing backpackers.

# Monaco

The tiny independent principality of **MONACO** rears up over the rocky Riviera coast like a Mediterranean Hong Kong. The ruling family, the Grimaldis, have held power here for more than seven centuries. Prince Rainier III, who famously put Monaco on the map when he married American actress Grace Kelly, firmly held on to the throne for 56 years. After Rainier's death in April, 2005, his son Albert took over rule, though if he fails to marry and produce a legitimate heir, Monacan rule may pass to either of his two sisters, Princesses Caroline and Stéphanie. The three-kilometre-long state consists of the old town of Monaco-Ville; Fontvieille; La Condamine by the harbour; Larvotto – with its artificial beaches of imported sand – and, in the middle, **MONTE CARLO**. There are relatively few conventional sights; best is the superb aquarium at the **Musée Océanographique** on avenue St-Martin (daily 9.30/10am–6/7.30pm; €11), which displays a living coral reef, transplanted from the Red Sea into a 40,000-litre tank. There's also, of course, the famous **Casino** (daily noon–dawn; €15; over-18s only), though you may be refused entry if you don't look like a serious gambler.

### Practicalities

The **train station** is on avenue Prince-Pierre in La Condamine, a short walk from the **bus station** on place d'Armes. Bus #4 (direction Larvotto) takes you from the train station to the Casino-Tourism stop, near the **tourist office** at 2a bd des Moulins (Mon–Sat 9am–7pm, Sun 10am–noon; ☏92.16.61.16, ⊛www .monaco-tourisme.com). The efficient and free lift and escalator system spares steep north-south journeys. **Accommodation** is in short supply, especially when the Grand Prix is in town (end of May/beginning of June); La Condamine is your best bet with the cheapest option being the *Hôtel de France,* 6 rue de la Turbie (☏93.30.24.64, ⊛www.monte-carlo.mc/france; ⑥). **Dorms** are available from April–Oct at *RIJ Villa Thalassa,* on the coast at Cap d'Ail, 3km from Monte Carlo towards Nice (☏04.93.78.18.58; €15). La Condamine and the old town are the places to look for **restaurants**; try the well-priced *Le Pinocchio* for some of the best pasta dishes in town, 30 rue Félix-Gastaldi.

# Corsica

Despite nearly two-and-a-half centuries of French rule, the island of **CORSICA** has more in common culturally with Italy than with its governing country, with which it has been locked in a grim – and often bloody – struggle for autonomy since 1974. A history of repeated invasion has strengthened the cultural identity of an island whose reputation for violence and xenophobia has overshadowed the more hospitable nature of its inhabitants. An amazing diversity of landscapes is to be found in Corsica, one third of which is protected as a National Park: its magnificent rocky coastline is interspersed with outstanding beaches, while the mountains soar to 2706m at Monte Cinto – one of a string of Pyrenean-scale peaks lining the island's granite spine. The extensive forests and sparkling rivers provide the locals with a rich supply of game and fresh fish: regional specialities include wild boar, chestnut-flour dishes, a soft ewe's cheese called *brocciu* and some of France's most prized *charcuterie* (cured meats).

Two French *départements* divide Corsica, each with its own capital: Napoleon's birthplace, **Ajaccio**, is on the southwest coast, while **Bastia** faces Italy in the north. The old capital of **Corte** dominates the interior, backed by a formidable wall of mountains. Of the coastal resorts, **Calvi** draws tourists with its massive citadelle and long sandy beach; while **Bonifacio**, huddled on the southernmost point facing Sardinia, is superbly located, with a tightly packed grid of Genoan houses perched atop limestone cliffs overseeing the clearest water in the Mediterranean. Still more dramatic landscapes lie around the **Golfe de Porto** in the far northwest, where the famous red cliffs of the Calanches de Piana rise over 400m.

Corsica's narrow-gauge **train** crosses the mountains to connect the island's main towns. Interail and other cards are valid for all services, or you could buy a Carte Zoom, which gives one week's unlimited train travel for €47. The cards are available from any station and also cover use of left-luggage rooms (*consignes*). Otherwise you're reliant on **buses**, which run regularly between the larger towns but rarely reach the interior villages; services are scaled back drastically between November and May.

## Ajaccio

Set in a magnificent bay, **AJACCIO** combines all the ingredients of a Riviera-style town with its palm trees, spacious squares, glamorous marina and street cafés. **Napoleon** was born here in 1769, but did little for the place except to make it the island's capital for the brief period of his empire. It is, however, a pleasant place to spend time, particularly around the harbour and narrow streets inland from the fifteenth-century Genoese *citadelle*. Halfway down rue Cardinal-Fesch, the **Musée Fesch** (Mon 1.30–5.15/6pm, Tues–Sun 9.15am–12.15pm & 2.15–5.15/6.30pm; €5.35) is home to the country's most important collection of Renaissance paintings outside Paris, including works by Botticelli, Titian and Poussin. As for **beaches**, avoid the Plage St-François, below the citadel, in favour of the cleaner Plage Trottel, ten minutes further southwest from the centre along the promenade.

### Practicalities

The **airport**, Campo dell'Oro, is 8km southeast and connected to the town by shuttle bus, *navette* (€4.50); taxis cost around €25. The **ferry port** and **bus station** occupy the same building in the town centre, while the **train station** is a ten-minute walk north along the seafront. The **tourist office** (summer Mon–Sat 9am–8.30pm, Sun 9am–1pm; winter Mon–Fri 8am–6pm, Sat 8am–noon & 2–5pm; ☏04.95.51.53.03, ⓦwww.tourisme.fr/ajaccio) is on the Place du Marché, directly behind the Hôtel de Ville on Place Foch. Budget **accommodation** is thin on the ground and books up fast: try *Le Dauphin*, just north of the ferry port/bus station at 11 bd Sampiero (☏04.95.21.12.94, ⓦwww.ledauphinhotel .com; ❺); or the *Marengo*, twenty minutes' walk from the centre at 2 rue Marengo

### Ferries

For full details, go to ⓦwww.corsicaferries.com, ⓦwww.happylines.it, ⓦwww .mobylines.it, ⓦwww.saremar.it or ⓦwww.sncm.fr. Routes marked * are covered by superfast NGV hydrofoils in summertime only. The cheapest crossings are from Nice (€21–50) and the mainland Italian ports (€23–36).

**From France**
**Marseille** to: Ajaccio (3–7 weekly; 4hr 30min–11hr); Bastia (1–3 weekly; 10hr).
**Nice** to: Ajaccio* (1–6 weekly; 3–12hr); Bastia* (3–24 weekly; 5hr); Calvi* (1–5 weekly; 3hr 45min).
**Toulon** to: Ajaccio (2–6 weekly; 5hr); Bastia (6 weekly; 8hr 30min).

**From Italy**
**Genoa** to: Bastia (June–Sept 1 daily; 9hr).
**La Spezia** to: Bastia (May–Sept 5–7 weekly; 5hr).
**Livorno** to: Bastia* (April–Oct 1–6 daily; 2–10hr).
**Piombino** to: Bastia (July to mid-Sept; 1 daily).
**Santa-Teresa-di-Gallura** (Sardinia) to: Bonifacio (2–4 daily).
**Savona** to: Bastia (June–Sept; 2–3 weekly).

(☎04.95.21.43.66, ✆www.hotel-marengo.com; ④). The most convenient **campsite** is *Le Barbicaja*, 5km west (☎04.95.52.01.17; closed Oct to mid-April); take bus #5 from place de Gaulle. For location, the **restaurants** along the quai de la Citadelle are hard to beat, though the seafood served up tends to be mediocre – stick to pizza and a *pichet* (small jug) of house red. Out on the route des Sanguinaires (near the *Barbicaja* campsite; bus #5), the *Ariadne* (☎04.95.52.09.63) has a much funkier atmosphere, with World cuisine, live salsa or reggae most nights and a terrace on the beach. Hanging out in bars dressed up to the nines is a favourite pastime in Ajaccio, and cafés, cocktail joints and *glaciers* line most of the pavements and squares. At weekends, *Safari* and its neighbours next to the casino (behind the plage St-François) is where *le beau monde* strut their stuff. Game.net, on the corner of cours Napoléon and place de Gaulle offers **Internet** access.

## Le Golfe de Porto

Corsica's most startling landscapes surround the **Golfe de Porto**, in the west of the island. A deep blue bay enfolded by outlandish red cliffs – among them the famous **Calanches de Piana** rock formations – the gulf is framed by snow-topped mountains and a vast Laricio pine forest. The entire area holds endless possibilities for outdoor enthusiasts, with a superb network of waymarked trails (free maps available from the Ajaccio tourist office) and canyoning routes, perfect kayaking bays and some of the finest diving sites in the Mediterranean. Less adventurous visitors can explore the coast on one of the excursion boats from the village of **PORTO**, the gulf's main tourist hub, where there's a **tourist office** (☎04.95.26.10.55, ✆www.porto-tourisme.com) and a huge range of **accommodation**. Best value among the cheap hotels is *Le Golfe*, 1km from the sea opposite the Genoese watchtower (☎04.95.26.13.33; ③). Of the four campsites, the *Camping Sol e Vista*, behind the supermarkets just off the main road, is the most pleasant. For an inexpensive **restaurant** meal, try one of the lookalike pizzerias lining the roadside above the marina.

## Calvi

Seen from the water, the great *citadelle* of **CALVI** resembles a floating island, sharply defined by a hazy backdrop of snowcapped mountains. Home to the Paratroop Regiment of the Foreign Legion, this is the island's third port and draws thousands of tourists for its 6km of sandy beach. The **Haute Ville**, a labyrinth of cobbled lanes and stairways, rises from **place Christophe Colomb**, the square linking the two parts of town. The name of the *place* derives from the local belief that the discoverer of the New World was born here, in a now ruined house on the edge of the *citadelle*. Although this is hotly disputed by historians, you'll come across his image in many of the shops, restaurants and hotels scattered around the **Basse Ville**, which backs onto the marina. To reach the **beach**, keep walking past the boats.

### Practicalities

Calvi's Ste-Catherine **airport** is 8km southeast, with only **taxis** (€16–18) to get you into town. **Trains** stop behind the marina, near the stop for **buses** to and from Bastia, and also close to the **tourist office** (daily 9am–5/7pm; winter closed noon–2pm & all Sun; ☎04.95.65.16.67, ✪www.tourisme.fr/calvi). The **ferry port** is on the opposite side of the marina, below the *citadelle*. If the cheap and central BVJ hostel (☎04.95.65.14.15) at the marina is still under renovation (due to reopen in 2006), the most convenient budget **accommodation** is the *Hôtel du Centre* (☎04.95.65.02.01; ❸), hidden away in the Basse Ville at 14 rue Alsace-Lorraine. Otherwise, the *Relais International de la Jeunesse* (☎04.95.65.14.16; €23.50) is in a great spot 5km out of town; from the station, turn left on avenue de la République, right on rte de Pietramaggiore and keep walking. The long pine forest behind the sands shelters a string of large **campsites**, of which *la Pinède* (☎04.95.65.17.80, ✪www.camping-calvi.com; summer only), 2km out of town, is one of the smartest; you can reach it on the hourly trains from Calvi. **Restaurants** cram the streets of the Basse Ville; of the options along quai Landry, the *Pizzeria Cappuccino* has cheap *calzones* and pasta. Further into the old quarter, *U San Carlu*, place St-Charles, serves excellent seafood at reasonable prices, while the lively but touristy *La Santa Maria*, 14 rue Clemenceau, turns out some unusual Corsican specialities such as *stifatu*, a tasty blend of stuffed meats. The famous piano bar and restaurant *Chez Tao* is worth a visit for its impressive views of the bay.

## Bastia

**BASTIA** is a charismatic harbour town, its crumbling buildings set against a backdrop of bare hills. Now a thriving commercial port, it was the island capital under the Genoese and has remained a working town with few concessions to tourism. It has much to recommend it: the dilapidated Vieux Port, a sprinkling of Baroque churches, the imposing citadel, or bastion, from which the town gets its name, and the vast place St-Nicolas, lined with trees and cafés open to the sea.

The most appealing area is the **Vieux Port**, the site of the original fishing village around which the town grew. Dominating the harbour are the twin towers of **Église St-Jean-Baptiste** (daily 9am–6pm), the largest church in Bastia, which shoulders the place du Marché, where a lively **market** takes place each morning. A flight of steps leads from the southern edge of the harbour up through a small park to the *citadelle*, or **Terra Nova**. Worth hunting out amid the grid of colour-washed old tenements is the **Oratoire Sainte-Croix** (daily 9am–6pm), a splendidly gaudy Baroque chapel renowned for its miracle-working black crucifix.

### Practicalities

Bastia's **airport**, Poretta, is 16km south of town off RN197. Shuttle **buses** (35min; €8) meet all flights and whisk you to the centre opposite the **train station**, located above place St-Nicolas; other buses stop opposite the **tourist office** on the north side of place St-Nicolas (9am–6/8pm; Oct–May closed Sun; ☎04.95.54.20.40, ✪www.bastia-tourisme.com) – only worth dropping into for bus timetables. **Accommodation** can be hard to find, especially in high season. Pick of the bunch is the *Central*, 3 rue Miot (☎04.95.31.71.12, ✪www.centralhotel.fr; ❹), just off the south side of place St-Nicolas; alternatively, there's the *Posta-Vecchia*, near the Vieux Port on the quai-des-Martyrs (☎04.95.32.32.38, ✪www.hotel-postavecchia.com; ❹). Top **campsite** is *Camping*

*Casanova* (☎04.95.33.91.42; closed Nov–Feb), 5km north at Miomo; buses run until 7.30pm from the top of place St-Nicolas opposite the tourist office (Mon–Sat every 30min, Sun hourly). The Vieux Port and nearby market place are crammed with **restaurants**. In the evening, head for the outdoor **cafés** on the harbour-side or the quirky *La Braise*, two minutes' walk from the marina on boulevard Hyacinthe-de-Montrea. *Le Pub Assunta*, at 5 place Fontaine-Neuve (just off the south end of the town's main street, boulevard Paoli), is a dependably lively **bar**, hosting live music on Thursdays. **Internet** access is at *Café Albert*, 11 bd Général de Gaulle by the place St-Nicholas.

# Corte

Set against a spectacular backdrop of craggy mountains, **CORTE**, the island's only interior town, is regarded as the spiritual capital of Corsica, as this is where Pasquale Paoli had his seat of government during the brief period of independence in the eighteenth century. Paoli founded a university here which reopened in the early 1980s, and its student population add a much-needed bit of life. For outdoor enthusiasts, this is also an ideal base for trekking into the island's watershed, with two superb gorges stretching west into the heart of the mountains.

The main street, **cours Paoli**, runs the length of town, culminating in place Paoli, a pleasant market square lined with cafés. A cobbled ramp leads from here up to the Ville Haute, where you can still see the bullet marks made by Genoese soldiers during the War of Independence in tiny **place Gaffori**. Continuing north you'll soon come to the gates of the **Citadelle**, whose well-preserved ramparts enclose the **Museu di a Corsica** (Tues–Sun 10am–6/8pm; June–Sept also Mon; Nov & Dec closed Sun; €5.30), hosting a collection of old farming implements that's far less compelling than the building itself. Best views of the *citadelle*, the town and its valley are from the **Belvédère**, a platform opposite the tower which you don't have to pay to reach.

### Practicalities

Corte's **train station** is 1km east of town at the foot of the hill near the university. **Buses** stop at the south end of cours Paoli. The **tourist office**, within the *citadelle* (Mon–Fri 9am–1pm & 2–6/8pm; ☎04.95.46.26.70, ⓦwww.corte-tourisme.com), also houses the Parc Naturel Régional Corse, the best information source on the island for walkers.

Places to stay are plentiful and relatively inexpensive: head for the *Hôtel HR*, near the train station on allée du 9 Septembre (☎04.95.45.11.11, ⓦwww.hotel-hr.com; ❷), a charmless, but cheap, converted police station. For more comfort, try the characterful *De la Poste*, 2 place Padoue (☎04.95.46.01.37, ℻04.95.46.01.37; ❹), or the smart, friendly and efficient *Du Nord et de L'Europe*, halfway along cours Paoli (☎04.95.46.00.68, ⓦwww.hoteldunord-corte.com; ❻). Of the seven **campsites**, much the nicest is the *Ferme Equestre l'Albadu* (☎04.95.46.24.55), fifteen minutes' walk away – follow the main road south down the hill from place Paoli and take the second right after crossing the second river bridge – with superb views. The area around place Gaffori has several **restaurants** – *Paglia Orba* on avenue Xavier Luciani is your best bet – with plenty of inexpensive vegetarian options; for a more inspiring location try *U Museu*, huddled beneath the *citadelle* walls and serving a superb goat's cheese salad and tasty wild boar stew.

# Bonifacio

The port of **BONIFACIO** is superbly isolated on a narrow peninsula of dazzling white limestone at Corsica's southernmost point, only minutes by boat from Sardinia (see p.657). For hundreds of years the town held the most powerful fortress in the Mediterranean and was a virtually independent republic, and a sense of detachment from the rest of Corsica persists, with many Bonifaciens still speaking their own dialect. It has become a chic holiday spot and sailing centre, and can be unbearably overcrowded in midsummer.

The **Haute Ville** is connected to the marina by a steep flight of steps at the west end of the quay, at the head of which are revealed glorious views across the straits to Sardinia. Within the massive fortifications of the *citadelle* is packed an alluring maze of cobbled streets. Heading west you emerge from the houses at the **Cimetière Marin**, a walled cemetery at the far end of the promontory filled with elaborate mausoleums. Down in the marina, a **boat excursion** (around €14) round the base of the cliffs gives a fantastic view of the town and the **sea-caves**, grottoes where the rock glitters with rainbow colours and the turquoise sea is deeply translucent. Some outstanding beaches lie near Bonifacio, most notably the shell-shaped **plage de la Rondinara**, 10km north; further north still, off the main Porto-Vecchio road, the **plages de Santa Giulia** and **Palombaggia** wouldn't look outclassed in the Maldives.

### Practicalities

**Ferries** from Santa-Teresa-di-Gallura on Sardinia dock at the far end of the quay; **buses** from Ajaccio stop in the car park by the marina. The **tourist office** is in the Haute Ville, at the bottom of rue Fredi-Scamaroni (May–Sept daily 9am–8pm; Oct–April Mon–Fri 9am–noon & 2–6pm; ☎04.95.73.11.88, ⊛www.bonifacio .fr). The most affordable **hotel** is *Étrangers*, 1km out of town from the marina on avenue Sylver Bohn (☎04.95.73.01.09, ☎04.95.73.16.79; ❹). En route to it you pass the nearest campsite, *L'Araguina* (☎04.95.73.02.96). For **food**, *Cantina Doria*, up in the Haute Ville on rue Doria (☎04.95.73.40.59), offers inexpensive Bonifacien specialities such as stuffed aubergine. *Lollapalooza*, on the marina near the ferry dock, is a trendy, lively **bar** that stays open late. For **Internet** access, try Boni Boom on quai Comparetti.

# Travel details

### Trains

**Ajaccio** to: Bastia (4 daily; 3hr 15min); Calvi (2 daily; 4hr 30min); Corte (2–4 daily; 2hr).

**Bastia** to: Ajaccio (4 daily; 3hr 15min); Calvi (2 daily; 3hr); Corte (2–4 daily; 1hr 30min).

**Bordeaux** to: Bayonne-Biarritz (8 daily; 1hr 45min–3hr 30min); Bergerac (8 daily; 1hr 25min); Marseille (6 daily; 5hr 45min–7hr 15min); Nice (3 daily; 8hr 30min–10hr 10min); Périgueux (10 daily; 1hr–1hr 40min); Toulouse (frequent; 2hr–2hr 45min).

**Calvi** to: Ajaccio (2 daily; 4hr 30min); Bastia (2 daily; 3hr); Corte (2 daily; 2hr 30min).

**Clermont-Ferrand** to: Marseille (6 daily, 1 direct, the rest changing at Lyon; 4hr 40min–8hr 30min); Nîmes (3 daily; 4hr 50min–8hr); Toulouse (4 daily; 6hr–8hr 20min).

**Corte** to: Ajaccio (2–4 daily; 2hr); Bastia (2–4 daily; 1hr 30min); Calvi (2 daily; 2hr 30min).

**Dijon** to: Beaune (frequent; 20min); Lyon (frequent; 1hr 30min–2hr 15min).

**Le Puy** to: Lyon (3 daily, 1 direct, 2 changing at St Etienne; 2hr 25min).

**Lyon** to: Avignon (frequent; 1hr 5min–2hr 45min); Grenoble (frequent; 1hr 45min–3hr 45min); Marseille (frequent; 1hr 45min–3hr 45min).

**Nancy** to: Strasbourg (8–13 daily; 1hr 30min).

**Nice** to: Marseille (every 40min; 2hr 45min); St-Raphaël (every 20min; 1hr 15min).

**Nîmes** to: Arles (frequent; 20min); Avignon (frequent; 30min); Clermont-Ferrand (frequent; 4hr 50min–5hr 30min); Marseille (14 daily; 50min–1hr 20min); Montpellier (frequent; 30min); Perpignan (frequent; 2hr 10min–2hr 40min).

**Paris** to: Avignon (13 daily; 2hr 40min–3hr 30min); Bayonne (7–10 daily; 4hr 45min); Bordeaux (hourly; 3hr); Boulogne (4–6 daily; 2hr 10min); Brest (8 daily; 4hr 20min–5hr 20min); Caen (hourly; 2hr–2hr 30min); Calais (9 daily;

1hr 40min–3hr 15min); Carcassonne (hourly; 5hr 10min–8hr); Cherbourg (9 daily; 3hr–3hr 30min); Clermont-Ferrand (5–7 daily; 3hr 30min); Dieppe (hourly; 2–3hr); Dijon (hourly; 1hr 40min); Grenoble (frequent; 3–4hr); Le Havre (10–14 daily; 2hr); Lille (hourly; 1hr); Lyon (hourly; 2hr); Marseille (hourly; 3hr 10min); Metz (10 daily; 2hr 50min); Montpellier (10 daily; 3hr 25min); Nancy (12 daily; 3hr); Nantes (frequent; 2hr); Nice (frequent; 5hr 30min–6hr); Nîmes (10 daily; 3hr); Pau (9–10 daily; 5hr 15min–7hr 20min); Poitiers (frequent; 1hr 40min); Reims (frequent; 1hr 40min); Rennes (hourly; 2hr 15min); Rouen (hourly; 1hr 15min); Strasbourg (12–13 daily; 4hr); Toulouse (10 daily; 5hr–6hr 30min); Tours (hourly; 1hr–2hr 30min).

**Périgueux** to: Les Eyzies (2–6 daily; 30min).
**Poitiers** to: Bordeaux (15 daily; 1hr 45min); La Rochelle (10–17daily; 1hr 35min–2hr 10min).
**Rennes** to: Nantes (12 daily; 2hr); Quimper (4–10 daily; 2hr 30min); St-Malo (frequent; 1hr 15min).

**Toulouse** to: Albi (9–19 daily; 1hr); Bayonne-Biarritz (4 daily; 3hr–3hr 45min); Bordeaux (frequent; 2hr 20min); Clermont-Ferrand (6 daily, most changing at Lyon; 6hr–7hr 50min); Lourdes (9–10 daily; 2hr); Lyon (10 daily changing at Montpellier; two direct trains daily; 4hr–4hr 40min); Marseille (9 daily; 4hr); Pau (8–10 daily; 2hr 40min–3hr 10min).
**Tours** to: Chenonceaux (5–7 daily; 30min); Chinon (5–10 daily; 45min); Orléans (frequent; 1hr–1hr 30min); Saumur (frequent; 45min).

## Buses

**Ajaccio** to: Bastia (2 daily; 3hr); Bonifacio (2 daily; 4hr); Corte (2 daily; 2hr).
**Corte** to: Ajaccio (2 daily; 2hr); Bastia (2 daily; 1hr 15min).

## Ferries

For Channel crossings, see p.33; for Corsica crossings, see p.421.

# Germany

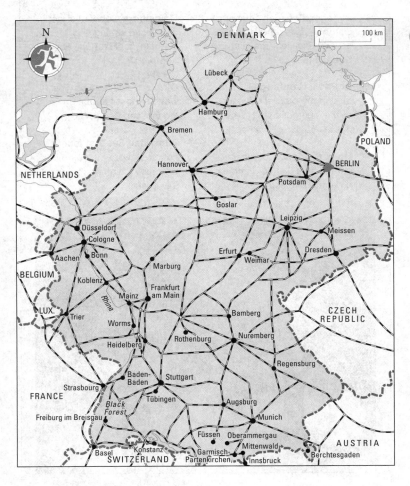

# Germany highlights

* **Berlin** Dramatic history and gritty modernity combine in this most untamed of European capitals. See p.433

* **Zwinger, Dresden** Stunning Baroque palace housing several excellent museums. See p.446

* **St Pauli, Hamburg** Go clubbing in the buzziest district of this energetic port. See p.450

* **Dom, Cologne** Cologne's cathedral is Gothic grandeur on a massive scale. See p.456

* **Rhine Gorge** Sit back for a half-day cruise through some spectacular scenery. See p.461

* **Heidelberg** Cobbled streets, a majestic setting and Germany's oldest university. See p.467

* **Oktoberfest, Munich** The world's most famous drinking festival. See p.480

* **Zugspitze** See into four countries from the summit of Germany's highest mountain. See p.481

△ Oktoberfest, Munich

# Introduction and basics

The stereotype of **Germany** as a great monolith has always been a long way from the truth. Regional characteristics are a strong feature of German life, and there are many hangovers from the days when the country was a patchwork of independent states. To travel from the ancient ports of the north, across the open fields of the German plain, down through the Ruhr conurbation, and on to the forests, mountains and cosmopolitan cities of the south is to experience a variety as great as any European country can offer.

Several cities have the air of national capitals. **Cologne**, with a spectacular cathedral, is rich in monuments. **Munich** is another star attraction, with great museums and thriving nightlife. **Berlin** has an engaging, and sometimes electrifying, atmosphere, while **Nuremberg** retains more than a trace of its bygone glory. **Hamburg**, burned to the ground in 1943, is now a pleasant city with nightlife comparable to Berlin's, while **Frankfurt**'s skyscrapers testify to its role as the economic dynamo of postwar reconstruction. In the east, as well as Berlin, there's the Baroque splendour of **Dresden**. However, in many respects the smaller towns of Germany offer a richer experience. There's nowhere as well loved as the university city of **Heidelberg**, while **Trier**, **Regensburg** and **Rothenburg** in the west and **Potsdam** and **Meissen** in the east are all attractive places that reward exploration.

Among the scenic highlights are the **Bavarian Alps** on Munich's doorstep, the **Bodensee** (Lake Constance) marking the Swiss border, the **Black Forest** and the **Rhine Valley**, whose majestic sweep has spawned a rich fund of legends and folklore.

## Information & maps

You'll find a **tourist office** (*Fremdenverkehrsamt*) in virtually every town. Staff are invariably friendly and efficient, providing large amounts of literature and maps. The major cities share the same phone number for information: simply dial the local code followed by ☎19 433. The best general **map** is Kümmerly and Frey's 1:500,000. Specialist cycling or hiking maps can be bought in the relevant regions. **Altstadt**, widely used in this chapter and on streetsigns, means "Old Town".

## Money and banks

German currency is the **euro** (€). **Exchange facilities** are in most banks, post offices and commercial exchange shops called *Wechselstuben*. The Deutsches Reisebank has branches in the train stations of most main cities (generally open daily, often till 10/11pm). Basic **banking hours** are Mon–Fri 9am–noon & 1.30–3.30pm, Thurs till 6pm. **Credit cards** are used relatively infrequently, except for withdrawing cash from **ATMs**, which are widespread.

## Communications

**Post offices** are open Mon–Fri 8am–6pm & Sat 8am–noon. **Poste restante** is available at main post offices: head for the counter marked *Postlagernde Sendungen*. You can **phone** abroad from all payphones except

---

**Germany on the net**

ⓦ **www.germany-tourism.de** Official tourist board site.
ⓦ **www.stadtplan.de** City maps.
ⓦ **www.webmuseen.de** Information on the country's museums.
ⓦ **www.galerie.de** Digest of the country's galleries and artists.
ⓦ **www.party.de** Nightlife and events listings.

those marked "National"; phonecards (€5) are widely available. The operator is on ☏03. Internet access is easy to find in larger towns and cities, and many department stores (notably the Karstadt chain) also offer the facility. Expect to pay €3–4/hr.

# Getting around

While it may not be cheap, getting around Germany is quick and easy. **Trains** are operated by Deutsche Bahn (DB; ⓦ www .db.de). Fares cost €0.14/km second class, exclusive of supplements, and a return costs the same as two one-way tickets. The most luxurious service is the InterCityExpress (ICE); otherwise the fastest trains are Inter-City (IC) and EuroCity (EC). InterRegio (IR) trains run on less heavily used routes. Major cities often have an **S-Bahn** commuter rail network. InterRail and Eurail are both valid (including on S-Bahn trains). Some also have a **U-Bahn**, or metro system. Supplements

| German | | |
| --- | --- | --- |
| | **German** | **Pronunciation** |
| **Yes** | Ja | Yaa |
| **No** | Nein | Nine |
| **Please** | Bitte | Bitter |
| **Thank you** | Danke | Danker |
| **Hello/Good day** | Güten Tag | Gooten Targ |
| **Goodbye** | Auf Wiedersehen | Owf veederzain |
| **Excuse me** | Entschuldigen Sie, bitte | Entshooldigen zee bitter |
| **Where?** | Wo? | Vo |
| **Good** | Gut | Goot |
| **Bad** | Schlecht | Shlect |
| **Near** | Nah | Naa |
| **Far** | Weit | Vite |
| **Cheap** | Billig | Billig |
| **Expensive** | Teuer | Toyer |
| **Open** | Offen | Offen |
| **Closed** | Geschlossen | Geshlossen |
| **Today** | Heute | Hoyter |
| **Yesterday** | Gestern | Gestern |
| **Tomorrow** | Morgen | Morgan |
| **How much is....?** | Wieviel kostet...? | Vee feel costet...? |
| **What time is it?** | Wieviel Uhr ist es? | Vee feel ur ist es? |
| **I don't understand** | Ich verstehe nicht | Ik vershtayer nikt |
| **Do you speak English?** | Sprechen Sie Englisch? | Sprecken zee eng-lish? |
| **One** | Eins | Einz |
| **Two** | Zwei | Zwi |
| **Three** | Drei | Dry |
| **Four** | Vier | Fear |
| **Five** | Fünf | Foonf |
| **Six** | Sechs | Sex |
| **Seven** | Sieben | Seeben |
| **Eight** | Acht | Acct |
| **Nine** | Neun | Noyn |
| **Ten** | Zehn | Zain |

apply on sleepers, and for InterRailers on fast trains as well. All stations have free pocket timetables for local routes.

Many **buses** are run by regional cooperatives in association with DB, although there are also a few privately operated routes. You're most likely to need buses in remote rural areas, or along designated "scenic routes" where scheduled services are more luxurious than on standard routes and buses pause at major points of interest.

**Cyclists** are well catered for: many smaller roads have cycle paths, and bike-only lanes are a common sight in cities. Between April and October, the best place to rent a bike is from a railway station participating in the *Fahrrad am Bahnhof* scheme (around €6/day). You can return it to any other participating station; rail-pass-holders pay half-price.

## Accommodation

Nearly all tourist offices will book **accommodation** for a fee, and it's advisable to book ahead, especially in 2006 when the **football World Cup** (see box) will see rooms in host cities snapped up well in advance.

You're never far away from a large, functional HI hostel (*Jugendherberge*) – run by DJH (☎52 31/74 010, ⊛www.djh.de) – but at any time of the year (especially summer weekends) they're liable to be block-booked by school groups, so reserve as far in advance as possible. Hostels divide into categories according to location and facilities. A bed in the most basic costs around €13; the most luxurious – which go under the title *Jugendgästehaus* (youth guesthouse) – charge upwards of €20. Except in youth guesthouses, HI members over 27 pay around €2 extra per night; non-members, if admitted at all, also pay an extra €2 per night. Note that in the southern province of Bavaria people over 27 cannot use hostels at all, unless they're accompanying children. In larger cities, **independent hostels** tend to have less stringent rules and more personalized accommodation and service. Expect to pay from €12.

**Hotels** are all graded, clean, comfortable and functional. In country areas, rock-bottom prices start at about €30 for a double room; in cities, add roughly €10. Hotels in eastern Germany are overwhelmingly geared to the business market, but the situation is much better for the budget traveller in holiday areas. **Pensions** are plentiful, either rooms above a bar or restaurant or in a private house. An increasingly popular budget option is **B&B** (look for signs saying *Fremdenzimmer* or *Zimmer frei*). Cheapest rates start around €25 for a double. Particularly plentiful along the main touring routes are country inns or guesthouses (*Gasthöfe* or *Gasthäuser*). The best budget option in the East is a room in a **private house**, though prices vary widely and may cost as much as €25 per person in the cities.

Even the most basic **campsites** have toilets, washing facilities and a shop, while the grandest have swimming pools and supermarkets. Prices usually comprise a fee per person and per tent (each €2.50–5), plus extra for vehicles. Many sites are full from June to September, so check-in early in the afternoon. Aside from those in popular skiing areas, most close for winter.

## Food and drink

German **food** is both good value and high quality, but it helps if you share the national penchant for solid, meat-heavy fare and fresh salads. The majority of hotels and guesthouses include **breakfast** in the price of the

---

### World Cup 2006

The **World Cup** is being hosted by twelve German cities in 2006: Berlin, Cologne, Dortmund, Frankfurt, Gelsenkirchen, Hamburg, Hannover, Kaiserlautern, Leipzig, Munich, Nuremberg and Stuttgart. The official **website** is ⊛www.fifaworldcup.com which lists all the match **dates** of the competition which runs from June 9 to July 9. Tickets are already on sale and start at €35, going all the way up to €600 for the final in Berlin. If you want to see a match, or will be in a host city at the time of the competition, make sure to book accommodation as far in advance as your plans allow.

room – typically, a small platter of cold meats and cheeses, with a selection of breads, marmalades, jams and honey, and sometimes muesli and yoghurt. Elegant cafés are a popular institution, serving *Kaffee und Kuchen*, a choice of coffee and cream cakes or pastries. At **butcher's shops** you can generally choose from a variety of freshly roasted meats to make up a hot sandwich, though the easiest option for a snack is to head for the ubiquitous **Imbiss** stands and shops, which serve sausages, meatballs, hamburgers and fries, plus sometimes soup, schnitzels, chops, spit-roasted chicken and salads.

In **restaurants**, hot meals are usually served throughout the day; lunch tends to be treated as the main meal, with good-value menus on offer. Most of the *Gaststätte*, *Gasthaus*, *Gasthof*, *Brauhaus* or *Wirtschaft* establishments belong to a brewery and function as a *gemütlich* (cosy) meeting-point, drinking haven and cheap restaurant. Their cuisine resembles hearty home-cooking, and portions are usually generous. Main courses are overwhelmingly based on pork, served with a variety of sauces. Sausages feature regularly, with distinct regional varieties. **Vegetarians** will find Germany fairly difficult – menus are almost exclusively for carnivores – though student towns and the larger cities are slowly becoming more veggie-friendly. Germany's multicultural society is mirrored in its wide variety of ethnic eateries: Italian restaurants are the most reliable, but there are also plenty offering Balkan, Greek, Turkish and Chinese cooking.

### Drink

For **beer** drinkers, Germany is paradise; around forty percent of the world's breweries are found here, with over six hundred in Bavaria alone. Munich's beer gardens and beer halls are the most famous drinking dens in the country, offering a wide variety of premier products, from dark lagers through tart *Weizens* to powerful *Bocks*. Cologne holds the world record for the number of city breweries, all of which produce the beer called *Kölsch*, but wherever you go you can be fairly sure of getting a locally brewed beer. Most people's knowledge of German **wine** starts and ends with Liebfraumilch, a medium-sweet wine. Sadly, its success has obscured

the high quality of other German wines, especially those made from the Riesling grape. **Apfelwein** is a variant of cider beloved in and around Frankfurt. The most popular **spirits** are the fiery *Korn* and after-dinner *Schnapps*, which are usually fruit-based.

# Opening hours and holidays

**Shops** open at 8.30am and close around 6.30pm weekdays, 2pm Saturdays, and all Sunday (except for bakers, who may open for a couple of hours between 11am and 3pm, petrol stations and train stations). Smaller shops also close noon–2pm. Exceptions are pharmacies and shops in and around train stations, which stay open late and at weekends. **Museums** and **historic monuments** are, with few exceptions (mainly in Bavaria), closed on Monday. Most museums offer half-price entry for students with valid ID and a few even have a free day once a week. **Public holidays** are: Jan 1, Jan 6 (regional), Good Fri, Easter Mon, May 1, Ascension Day, Whit Mon, Corpus Christi (regional), Aug 15 (regional), Oct 3, Nov 1 (regional), Dec 25 & 26.

# Emergencies

The **police** (*Polizei*) usually treat foreigners with courtesy. Reporting thefts at local police stations is straightforward, but inevitably there'll be a great deal of bureaucracy to wade through. The level of theft in eastern Germany has increased dramatically, but provided you take the normal precautions, there's no real risk. Doctors generally speak English. **Pharmacies** (*Apotheken*) can deal with many minor complaints and staff will often speak English. All display a rota of local pharmacies open 24hr. In western Germany you'll find international *Apotheken* in most large towns who'll be able to fill a prescription in English.

> **Emergency numbers**
>
> Police ☎110; Fire & Ambulance ☎112

# Berlin

Energetic and irreverent, **BERLIN** is a welcoming, exciting city where the speed of change in the past few years has been astounding. With a long history of decadence and cultural dynamism, the revived national capital has become a magnet for artists and musicians, who were quick to see the opportunities that the cheap properties of the former East provided. Culturally, it has some of the most important archeological collections in Europe. Its nightlife is an exuberant, cutting-edge mix that could keep you occupied for weeks. And in 2006, the city's Olympiastadion will stage the finals of the football World Cup, affirming Berlin's role as a world city.

The city reeks of modern European history, having played a dominant role in Imperial Germany, during the Weimar Republic after 1914, and in the Nazis' Third Reich. After 1945, the city was partitioned by the victorious Allies, and as a result was the frontline of the Cold War. In 1961, its division into two hostile sectors was given a very visible expression by the construction of the notorious Berlin Wall. After the Wall fell in 1989, Berlin's status as national capital was confirmed. These days, parliament sits in the renovated Reichstag (Bundestag), and some of the city's excellent museum collections have been put back together again, housed in buildings at the forefront of architectural design. The central district of **Mitte** – extending either side of the main Unter den Linden boulevard, in what was formerly the Communist East – **Kreuzberg** and bohemian **Prenzlauer Berg** are where things are liveliest.

## Arrival, information and city transport

From Berlin's **Tegel airport** (TXL; ⓦwww.berlin-airport.de), frequent #X9 express or local #109 buses (€2) run to Bahnhof Zoologischer Garten (shortened to **Bahnhof Zoo**), the most important train station in Berlin until June 2006 when the Hauptbahnhof will assume this role, relegating Bahnhof Zoo to a local train and S-Bahn station. From Berlin's **Schönefeld airport** (SXF), S-Bahn trains run to Ostbahnhof, Friedrichstrasse (just off Unter den Linden) and Bahnhof Zoo (€2; every 30min; 20–30min). Some trains from Poland and the East terminate at **Bahnhof Lichtenberg**, easily accessible on the S-Bahn. Most international buses stop at the **bus station** near the Funkturm, linked to the centre by bus #149 or U-Bahn from Kaiserdamm.

Berlin's **tourist office** is in the Europa Center at Budapester Str. 45 (daily 10am–7pm; ☎030/25 00 25, ⓦwww.berlin-tourism.de), with additional offices in Prenzlauer Berg, at Schönhauser Allee 36 (Mon–Wed & Sun noon–6pm, Thurs–Sat noon–8pm; ☎030/44 35 21 70, ⓦwww.tic-prenzlauerberg.de), and the Fernsehturm on Alexanderplatz and at Brandenburger Tor (both daily 10am–6pm). Berlin has two **listings magazines**, Zitty (€2.50; ⓦwww.zitty.de) and Tip (€2.70; ⓦwww.tip-berlin.de), and an invaluable guide in English, New Berlin (free; ⓦwww.newberlinmagazine.com) and New Berlin Weekly, the supplement (ⓦwww.NewBerlin-Weekly.com), found in most hostels.

The **U-Bahn** metro system is efficient and extensive; trains run daily 4am–12.30am (Fri & Sat all night). The **S-Bahn**, whose stops are further apart, travels to the outer suburbs (such as Wannsee) and out of the city boundaries (eg Potsdam). The city **bus network** – and the **tram system** in eastern Berlin – covers most of the gaps left by the U-Bahn: night buses run at intervals of around twenty minutes, although the routes often differ from daytime ones; free maps are available at most stations. **Tickets** can be bought from machines at U-Bahn station entrances, on trams, or from bus drivers; good for any mode of transport, they cost €2, allow you to travel in two of the three tariff zones, and are valid for a single trip once validated (entwerten) in the yellow machines on platforms. The transport police are rigorous, issuing on-the-spot fines of €40 for those without a valid ticket or pass. Longer trips, from central Berlin to Potsdam for example, cost €2.60. A **Kurzstreckentarif** (short-trip ticket; €1.20) allows you to travel up to three train or six bus stops. A **day ticket** is €5.60 for two tariff zones, €6 for all three. The three-day **Welcome Card** (€22) provides free travel in all zones and up to 50 percent off at many of the major tourist sights.

## Accommodation

**Accommodation** in high season can be hard to find – especially if there's a festival or major event taking place – and it's best to call at least a couple of weeks in advance. The tourist office in the Europa Center offers a free **hotel-booking service**; most of the accommodation listed can be booked on their website.

### Hostels

**Bax Pax** Skalitzer Str. 104 ☏030/69 51 83 22, ⍟www.baxpax.de. Laid-back with clean, bright-as-a-button rooms, this backpacker outfit offers cooking facilities and a rare chance to sleep in a VW Beetle. Görlitzer Bahnhof U-Bahn. Dorms €15, rooms ❹

**The Circus** Rosa-Luxemburg-Str. 39–41 & Weinbergsweg 1a ☏030/28 39 14 33, ⍟www.circus-berlin.de. Two welcoming, clean, fun and deservedly popular bases near the action in the east, with helpful staff and breakfast service. Rosa-Luxemburg-Platz U-Bahn & Rosenthaler Platz U-Bahn. Dorms €15, rooms ❹

**City Stay Hotel** Rosenstr. 16 ☏030/23 62 40 31, ⍟www.citystay.de. Brand-new bright and airy hostel in the bustling heart of Mitte which, thanks to its off-street location, is a peaceful and safe base for travellers. Hackescher Markt S-Bahn. Dorms €15, rooms ❹

**Heart of Gold Hostel** Johannisstr. 11 ☏030/29 00 33 00, ⍟www.heartofgold-hostel.de. Fantastic location in the heart of downtown Mitte, this *Hitchhiker's Guide*/starship-themed place has a relaxing bar, spotless rooms and friendly pilots. Oranienburger Tor U-Bahn. Dorms €14, rooms ❹

**Lette'm Sleep** Lettestr 7 ☏030/44 73 36 23, ⍟www.backpackers.de. Chilled-out and comfortable hostel with free Internet, newly renovated kitchen and ideal Prenzlauer Berg location. Eberswalder Str. U-Bahn. Walk down Danziger Str., take first left and then second right onto Lettestr. Dorms €15, rooms ❹

**Meininger** Meininger Str. 10 & Hallesches Ufer 30 ☏030/66 63 61 00, ⍟www.meininger-hostels.de. Justifiably claiming to offer hotel-quality rooms and beds at hostel prices, both these places are modern, friendly, centrally located and include breakfast. Rathaus Schöneberg U-Bahn & Möckernbrücke U-Bahn. Dorms €14, rooms ❹

**Odyssee Globetrotter Hostel** Grünberger Str. 23 ☏030/29 00 00 81, ⍟www.globetrotterhostel.de. Young, well-organized hostel with individually designed rooms, ideally situated for the Friedrichshain nightlife scene. Frankfurter Tor U-Bahn. Dorms €13, rooms ❸

### Hotels

**Acksel Haus** Belforter Str. 21 ☏030/44 33 76 33, ⍟www.ackselhaus.de. Small, stylish hotel in the midst of the lively Prenzlauer Berg scene. Senefelderplatz U-Bahn. ❺

**Bogota** Schlüterstr. 45 ☏030/88 15 001, ⍟www.hotelbogota.de. Traditional-style place, with a dozen four-bed rooms, in a stuffy but comfortable 1911 (ask about the history) building. Savignyplatz U-Bahn. ❺

**Bregenz** Bregenzer Str. 5 ☏030/88 14 307, ⍟www.hotelbregenz-berlin.de. Very quiet and cosy family-run set-up only a 5min walk from the Ku'damm. Adenauer-Platz U-Bahn. ❹

**Charlot** Giesebrechtstr. 17 ☏030/32 79 660, ⍟www.hotel-charlot.de. Neatly restored but impersonal mid-range hotel near Adenauerplatz. Good value for money. Adenauerplatz U-Bahn. ❺

---

### Museum entry

Berlin's **state museums and galleries** (Gemäldegalerie, Kunstgewerbemuseum, Neue Nationalgalerie, Alte Nationalgalerie, Altes Museum, Pergamonmuseum, Ägyptisches Museum, Berggruen Collection: Picasso and His Era and the Dahlem Museums; ⍟www.smb.spk-berlin.de) are all **free** to visit on **Thursdays**, 4hr before closing. A **day ticket** for all Berlin's state-owned museums costs €10.

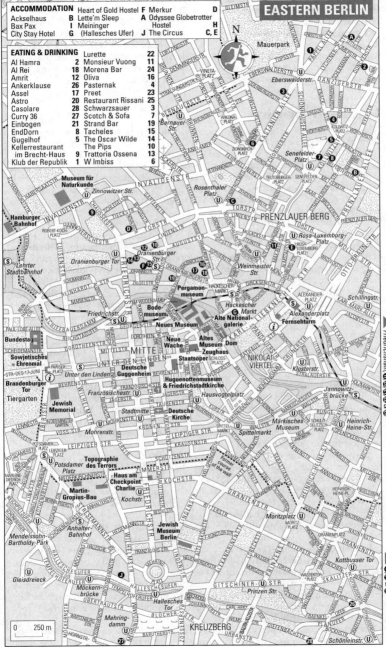

**Hotel Berolina** Stuttgarter Platz 17 ☎ 030/32 70 90 72, ⊛ www.hotel-berolina.de. Friendly, functional place where all rooms have TV and desk. Breakfast not included. Right next to Charlottenburg S-Bahn. ❸

**Korfu 11** Rankestr. 35 ☎ 030/21 24 790, ⊛ www .hp-korfu.de. Unexciting but clean and simple rooms in a central location. Breakfast not included

but free Internet access. Kurfürstendamm U-Bahn. ❹

**Merkur** Torstr. 156 ☎ 030/28 28 297, ⊛ www .hotel-merkur-berlin.de. Comfortable rooms, including one with five beds, within easy walking distance of city-centre attractions and late nightlife. Most rooms have showers. Rosenthaler Platz U-Bahn. ❺

# Eastern Berlin

The most atmospheric approach to eastern Berlin starts at the **Brandenburg Gate**, built as a city gate-cum-triumphal arch in 1791 and now – since it stands at the fulcrum between the city's eastern and western halves – the much-photographed symbol of German reunification. North of here stands the Bundestag (see opposite), while to the south lies the newly built, bold and contentious **Jewish Memorial**, whose 2700 concrete slabs are arranged in a grid for the public to walk through.

East of the gate stretches **Unter den Linden**, a stately broad boulevard that is rapidly reassuming its prewar role as one of Berlin's most important thoroughfares. The **Deutsche Guggenheim Berlin** at nos. 13–15 (daily 11am–8pm, Thurs till 10pm; €4; ⊛ www.deutsche-guggenheim-berlin.de), hosts three to four major exhibitions of modern and contemporary art per year, while nearby **Bebelplatz** was the site of the infamous Nazi bookburning of May 10, 1933; an unusual, but poignant, memorial – an underground room housing empty bookshelves visible through a glass panel set in the centre of the square – marks the event. More than anyone, it was Karl Friedrich Schinkel who shaped nineteenth-century Berlin and one of his most famous creations can be found opposite the Staatsoper further along Unter den Linden: the **Neue Wache**, a former royal guardhouse resembling a Roman temple and now a memorial to victims of war and tyranny. Next door is Berlin's finest Baroque building, the old Prussian **Zeughaus** (Arsenal), containing the **Deutsches Historisches Museum**, scheduled to reopen in early 2006 (⊛ www.dhm.de).

Following Charlottenstrasse south from Unter den Linden leads to the **Gendarmenmarkt**, much of whose appeal is derived from the **Friedrichstadtkirche** on the northern side of the square. Built as a church for Berlin's influential Huguenot community at the beginning of the eighteenth century, it also now houses the **Hugenottenmuseum** (daily 11am/noon–2/6pm; €3), documenting their way of life. Friedrichshain, a high-class shopping district with an eclectic mix of modernist architecture, lies a block west of here.

At the eastern end of Unter den Linden lies the **Schlossplatz**, former site of the imperial palace, now overlooked by the abandoned parliament building of the former East Germany and, to the north, the uninspiring Dom cathedral. The *platz* stands at the midpoint of a city-centre island whose northwestern part, **Museumsinsel**, is the location of some of Berlin's best museums. An extensive reconstruction programme has closed the **Bodemuseum** until October 2006, and the **Neues Museum**, shut until 2009. But there's plenty left, starting with the **Alte Nationalgalerie** (Tues–Sun 10am–6pm, Thurs till 10pm; €8), which houses a collection of nineteenth-century European art. In the **Altes Museum** (Tues, Wed & Fri–Sun 10am–6pm Thurs 10am–10pm; €8) are Greek and Roman antiquities, though it's the **Pergamonmuseum** (Tues–Sun 10am–6pm, Thurs till 10pm; €8) that houses the real treasure-trove of the ancient world unearthed by German archeologists in the nineteenth century. Two must-sees here are the spectacular Pergamon Altar, which dates from 160 BC, and the huge Processional Way from sixth-century-BC Babylon.

To reach **Alexanderplatz**, the commercial hub of eastern Berlin, head along Karl-Liebknecht-Strasse (the continuation of Unter den Linden), past the Neptunbrunnen fountain and the thirteenth-century Marienkirche. Like every other building in the vicinity, the church is overshadowed by the gigantic **Fernsehturm** (TV tower), known locally as "the Alex" (daily 9/10am–midnight/1am; €7.50; ⓦwww.berlinerfernsehturm.de), whose observation platform and revolving café offer unbeatable views from 203m. Southwest of here lies the **Nikolaiviertel**, a modern development that attempts to re-create the winding streets and small houses of this part of prewar Berlin, which was razed overnight on June 16, 1944.

## Western Berlin

**Bahnhof Zoo** (Zoo Station) is at the centre of the city's western side – a short walk south and you're at the eastern end of the Kurfürstendamm, or **Ku'damm**, a 3.5-kilometre strip of ritzy shops, cinemas, bars and cafés. A landmark here is the **Kaiser-Wilhelm-Gedächtniskirche** church, destroyed by British bombing in 1943 and left as a reminder of the horrors of war. There's little to do on the Ku'damm other than stroll, window-shop and spend money; the main cultural attraction nearby is the **Käthe-Kollwitz-Museum** at Fasanenstr. 24 (Mon & Wed–Sun 11am–6pm; €5; ⓦwww.kaethe-kollwitz.de), devoted to the drawings and prints of the left-wing pacifist artist Käthe Kollwitz.

The zoo itself, beside Zoo Station, forms the beginning of the **Tiergarten**, a restful expanse of woodland and a good place to wander along the banks of the Landwehrkanal. Strasse des 17 Juni heads all the way through the Tiergarten to the Brandenburg Gate, from where a short stroll north leads to the **Bundestag** (formerly the Reichstag), the nineteenth-century home of the German parliament. Remodelled by Norman Foster for the resumption of its historic role in 1999, its glass cupola has become a landmark, and the popular trip to the top (daily 8am–midnight; free) affords a stunning view. Immediately behind here, it's now only just possible to make out the course of the **Berlin Wall**, which divided the city for 28 years until November 9, 1989. The heart of prewar Berlin used to be to the south of the Brandenburg Gate, its core formed by **Potsdamer Platz**. A huge commercial project here, involving various eateries, theatres and a shopping mall built within the impressive Sony Center, attempts to re-create the area's former liveliness. Just to the east, near the corner of Wilhelmstrasse and An der Kolonnade, lies the site of **Hitler's bunker**, where the Führer spent his last days, issuing meaningless orders as the Battle of Berlin raged above.

West of Potsdamer Platz lies the Kulturforum, a series of museums centred on the unmissable **Gemäldegalerie**, Matthäikirchplatz 8 (Tues–Sun 10am–6pm, Thurs till 10pm; €6). Inside is a world-class collection of old masters, covering all the main European schools from the Middle Ages to the late eighteenth century. One highlight of the German section is Cranach's tongue-in-cheek *The Fountain of Youth*. The interconnected building to the north houses the **Kunstgewerbemuseum** (Tues–Sun 10/11am–6pm; €6), a sparkling collection of European arts and crafts. At Potsdamer Str. 50, a couple of minutes' walk to the south, the **Neue Nationalgalerie** (Tues–Sun 10/11am–6pm, Thurs till 10pm; €6) has a good collection of twentieth-century German paintings, best of which are the Berlin portraits and cityscapes by George Grosz and Otto Dix.

Southeast of here, the **Martin-Gropius-Bau**, at Niederkirchnerstr. 7 (Mon & Wed–Sun 10am–8pm; admission varies; ⓦwww.gropiusbau.de), is now a venue for prestigious art exhibitions. Next door, the open-air exhibition **Topography of Terror** (daily 10am–6/8pm; free; ⓦwww.topographie.de) occupies the former site of Gestapo and SS headquarters, and documents their history. From here it's a ten-minute walk on Wilhelmstrasse and Kochstrasse to the site of the notorious Checkpoint Charlie, the most infamous crossing-point between East and West Berlin in the old days; evidence of the trauma the Wall caused is still on hand in the

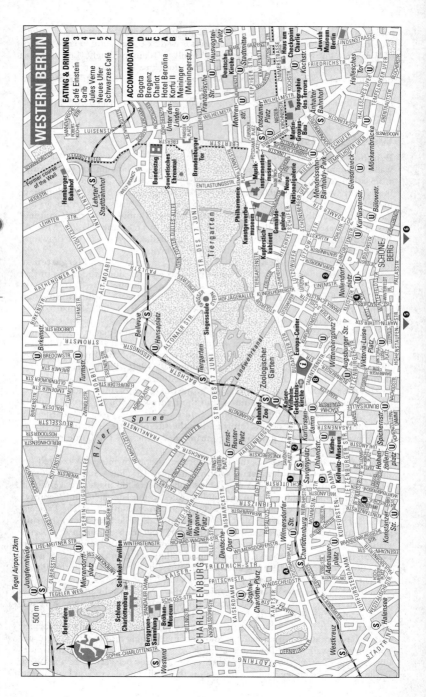

## WESTERN BERLIN

### EATING & DRINKING

| | |
|---|---|
| Café Einstein | 3 |
| Carib | 4 |
| Jules Verne | 1 |
| Neues Ufer | 5 |
| Schwarzes Café | 2 |

### ACCOMMODATION

| | |
|---|---|
| Bogota | D |
| Bregenz | E |
| Charlot | C |
| Hotel Berolina | A |
| Korfu II | B |
| Meininger (Meiningerstr.) | F |

Tegel Airport (2km)

Jungfernheide

Former course of the Wall

Schloss Charlottenburg

Belvedere

Berggruen-Sammlung

Brohan-Museum

Schinkel-Pavillon

Spree River

CHARLOTTENBURG

SCHÖNE-BERG

Tiergarten

Zoologischer Garten

Bahnhof Zoo

Kaiser-Gedächtnis-kirche

Europa-Center

Käthe-Kollwitz-Museum

Siegessäule

Philharmonie

Kunstgewerbe-museum

Kupferstich-kabinett

Gemälde-galerie

Neue Nationalgalerie

Musik-instrumenten-museum

Bundestag

Sowjetisches Ehrenmal

Brandenburger Tor

Martin-Gropius-Bau

Topographie des Terrors

Deutsche Kirche

Checkpoint Charlie

Jewish Museum Berlin

Unter den Linden

500 m

popular **Haus am Checkpoint Charlie** at Friedrichstr. 43–45 (daily 9am–10pm; €9.50; ⓦwww.mauer-museum.com), which tells the history of the Wall and the desperate stories of those who tried to cross it.

The checkpoint area marks the northern limit of **Kreuzberg**, famed for its large immigrant community and its self-styled "alternative" inhabitants and nightlife. Daniel Libeskind's striking zinc-skinned **Jewish Museum Berlin**, at Lindenstr. 10 (daily 10am–8/10pm; €5; ⓦwww.jmberlin.de), documents the culture, notable achievements, and tragic history of Berlin's Jewish community using a plethora of multimedia exhibits, art installations, religious artefacts and historic manuscripts.

## Out of the centre

Northwest of the Tiergarten is the sumptuously restored **Schloss Charlottenburg** (Tues–Sun 9/10am–4.30/5.30pm; €8; ⓦwww.spsg.de), commissioned by the future Queen Sophie Charlotte in 1695, it was added to throughout the eighteenth and early nineteenth centuries. Admission includes a tour of the main state apartments, self-guided visits to the private chambers (where the Prussian crown jewels can be seen), the Knobelsdorff-Flügel with its wonderful array of paintings by Watteau and other eighteenth-century French artists, and the Belvedere and Mausoleum in the park.

For a break from the bustle of the city centre, head out to the **Grunewald** forest and its beaches on the Havel lakes. Take S-Bahn #1 or #7 to Nikolassee station, from where it's a ten-minute walk to **Strandbad Wannsee** (April–Sept daily 7am–8pm; €4), a one-kilometre strip of pale sand that's the largest inland beach in Europe.

A very different excursion is to **Sachsenhausen concentration camp**, 35km north of the city (daily: April–Sept 8.30am–6pm; Oct–March 8.30am–4.30pm; free; ⓦwww.gedenkstaette-sachsenhausen.de), a sobering place where roughly 100,000 victims died at the hands of the Nazis. Take S-Bahn1 to Oranienburg, and then bus #804 (hourly) or a twenty-minute walk.

## Eating, drinking and nightlife

The range and quality of **restaurants** in Berlin is unmatched in any other German city, and there's a wealth of **bars**, from Bavarian-style beer halls to sleek cocktail lounges. The cheapest way of warding off hunger is to use the *Imbiss* snack stands, or one of the *Mensas*, officially for German students but usually open to anyone who looks the part. Eating out in a restaurant won't break the bank, though, with prices for a main course usually between €6 and €16.

**Nightlife** in the city outstrips many other European capitals. In **Eastern Berlin** there's a fast-developing scene: Oranienburger Strasse and Rosenthaler Strasse in the Mitte neighbourhood host dozens of new bars and clubs that attract a young professional crowd as well as tourists, while the streets, such as Kastanienallee, further north around Prenzlauer Berg and to the east around Boxhagener Strasse in Friedrichshain, and a little further south, Kreuzberg, are more alternative. **Western Berlin** has three focal points for drinking: Savignyplatz is for conspicuous good-timers; the area around Nollendorfplatz (northwestern Schöneberg) and Winterfeldtplatz is the territory of sped-out all-nighters and the pushing-on-forty crew; and central Schöneberg bars are on the whole more mixed and more relaxed. Unless you're into drunken businessmen, avoid the Ku'damm and the rip-off joints around the Europa Center. Berlin's diverse **gay scene** is spread across the city, but with a focus of sorts in Schöneberg, around Nollendorfplatz. The informative magazine, *Siegessäule*, has current listings and can be picked up in many cafés, libraries and shops.

Don't bother turning up before midnight for the all-night clubs in Kreuzberg and Schöneberg. To find out what's on, buy one of the listings magazines (see p.433).

## Snacks

**Al Rei** Grosse Hamburger Str. 20/21, Mitte. Informal place where you can linger over tea and Arab dishes such as couscous and falafel.

**Curry 36** Mehringdamm 36, Kreuzberg. One of the best places to try Berlin Currywurst – a traditional fast-food combination of grilled sausage, hot tomato sauce and curry powder. Open until 4am every day.

**Oliva** Oranienburger Str. 84, Mitte. Great pizza and fresh pasta dishes plus lunchtime deals. Convenient location for grabbing a snack after sightseeing.

**W Imbiss** Kastanienallee 49, Mitte. Unique pizza creations on naan bread in cheap, stomach-filling proportions.

## Restaurants

**Amrit** Oranienburger Str. 45, Mitte. Medium-priced Indian food, a huge outdoor candlelit seating area, and cheap lunchtime deals. Oranienburger Tor U-Bahn.

**Assel** Oranienburger Str. 21, Mitte. A vine-covered restaurant/bar with streetside tables, a bohemian air, and a fast trade in quality breakfasts. Oranienburger Tor U-Bahn.

**Carib** Motzstr. 30, Schöneberg. Caribbean cuisine, friendly service and lethal rum cocktails. Nollendorfplatz U-Bahn.

**Casolare** Grimmstr. 30, Kreuzberg. A wonderful, always packed Italian restaurant offering great pizzas and with a unique line in punk poster interior decor. Schönleinstr. U-Bahn.

**Einbogen** Simon Dach Str. 1, Friedrichshain. Stylish bar/restaurant serving decent German cuisine, with outdoor seating and all-you-can-eat deals on Sundays. Boxhagener Str. U-Bahn.

**EndDorn** Belforter Str. 27, Prenzlauer Berg. Brick-walled eatery/ bar where every dish (pasta, chilli con carne, baguettes, breakfast etc) is less than €5. Senefelderplatz U-Bahn.

**Gugelhof** Kollwitzstr. 59, Prenzlauer Berg. Stylish and popular Alsatian restaurant in the trendy Kollwitzplatz neighbourhood; the set meals are the best value. Senefelderplatz U-Bahn.

**Jules Verne** Schlüterstr. 61, Charlottenburg. Near Zoo Station, meals here are international, unusual, delicious and affordable. Savignyplatz U-Bahn.

**Kellerrestaurant im Brecht-Haus** Chausseestr. 125, Mitte ☎030/28 23 843. Formal restaurant in the basement of Brecht's old house, decorated with Brecht memorabilia and boasting Viennese specialities supposedly dreamt up by Brecht's wife, Helene Weigel. Booking advised. Zinnowitzer Str. U-Bahn.

**Monsieur Vuong** Alte Schönhauser Str. 45, Mitte. Small and popular Vietnamese place with a high-quality, low-price menu that changes daily. Rosa-Luxemburg-Platz U-Bahn.

**Pasternak** Knaackstr. 24. Intimate Russian restaurant in the thick of the bustling scene in Prenzlauer Berg; also open for breakfast. Senerfelderplatz U-Bahn.

**Preet** Boxhagener Str. 17, Friedrichshain. Popular, pukka and cheap Punjabi restaurant in the thick of the bars and clubs. Boxhagener Str. U-Bahn.

**Restaurant Rissani** Spreewaldplatz 4, Kreuzberg. Next to the park off Wiener Strasse, this place has a relaxed atmosphere and platefuls of mouthwatering Moroccan food at low prices. Görlitzer Bhf U-Bahn.

**Trattoria Ossena** Oranienburger Str. 39, Mitte. High-quality yet inexpensive Italian food in an aroma-filled trattoria setting. Oranienburger Tor U-Bahn.

## Bars and cafés

**Al Hamra** Raumerstr. 16, Prenzlauer Berg. Relaxed, extremely popular Arabian-style café/bar. Good food and cheap drinks every day – Sunday's "Orientale Brunch" until 5pm is especially tasty.

**Ankerklause** Kottbusser Damm 104, Kreuzburg. Cosy, relaxed bar with a terrace overlooking the riverbank; draws an unpretentious crowd.

**Astro** Simon-Dach-Str. 40, Friedrichshain. Always packed pre-club kitsch bar with different DJs nightly.

**Café Einstein** Kurfürstenstr. 58, Charlottenburg. Housed in a seemingly ancient mansion, this exudes the formal ambience of the prewar Berlin Kaffeehaus, with international newspapers, breakfast served daily till 2pm and delicious *Kuchen*.

**Klub der Republik** Pappelallee 81, Prenzlauer Berg. Cheap drinks in this fabulous chilled-out lounge/bar with comfy sofas. Fire-escape steps up to the entrance.

**Lurette** Boxhagener Str. 105, Friedrichshain. Retro bar/club, complete with Sixties wall projections, dishing up cheap cocktails to an upbeat lounge crowd.

**Morena Bar** Wiener Str. 60, Kreuzberg. Studenty, blue-tiled bar that opens early for good breakfasts.

**Neues Ufer** Hauptstr. 157, Schöneberg. Cramped, cool yet casual and kitschy gay café. Near Kleistpark U-Bahn.

**The Oscar Wilde** Friedrichstr. 112, Mitte. A large pub near Oranienburger Tor U-Bahn, for those who prefer their pints black and with a creamy white head. Live music and TV sports coverage most weekends.

**The Pips** Auguststr. 84, Mitte. Packed, welcoming and friendly bar with vibrant designer furnishings and different cocktail offers every day.

**Schwarzes Café** Kantstr. 148, Charlottenburg. Kantstrasse's best hangout for the young and chic, with a bohemian atmosphere, good music and Kölsch on tap. Great 24-hour breakfasts too.

**Schwarzsauer** Kastanienalle 13/14, Prenzlauer Berg. Large, ragged alternative bar/café that is popular with students.

**Scotch & Sofa** Kollwitzstr. 18, Prenzlauer Berg. Trendy, relaxed pre-club bar with free Internet and a loyal crowd.

**Strand Bar** Monbijoustr. 3, Mitte. Seasonal (April–Oct) but popular beach-themed bar with sand and deckchairs overlooking the River Spree.

**Tacheles** Oranienburger Str. 54–56, Mitte. Squatters' alternative arts centre that's something of an institution. It includes a cinema, three bars and beer garden.

## Discos, clubs and live music venues

**Grüner Salon & Roter Salon** Rosa-Luxemburg-Platz, Mitte. Two clubs in one building. 1920s ballroom ambience with live music, DJs and various musical styles depending on day of week.

**Junction Bar** Gneisenaustr. 18, Kreuzberg. A fixture on the local jazz circuit, with nightly live music and DJs at the weekends.

**Kaffee Burger** Torstr. 60, Mitte. Small, meandering bar decorated in deep flushed red, with an attached live music venue and infamously funky Russian disco.

**Matrix** Warschauer Platz 18, Friedrichshain. Famous disco that aims to satisfy all tastes across three dance floors. House, soul, rock and more.

**Pfefferberg** Schönhauser Allee 176, Prenzlauer Berg. Bars, dance floors, techno basement club and wonderful beer garden in summer with live music.

**Privat Club** Pücklerstr. 34, Kreuzberg. Highly

intimate basement club with an eclectic and unpredictable lightshow, drawing in a dance-orientated crowd of all ages.

**Sage Club** Köpenicker Str. 78, Mitte. Very popular club with 3 dance floors and a swimming pool. Occasional strict door policy but worth persevering.

**SO 36** Oranienstr. 190, Kreuzberg. Dark, punky cult club with a large gay and lesbian following. Live music and techno – spontaneous outbreaks of belly dancing are not unknown.

**WMF** Karl-Marx-Alle 34, Mitte. Housed in an old East German building, this place has two dance floors and a chill-out room. Pricey, but people still line up round the block at weekends.

## Classical music

**Deutsche Oper** Bismarckstr. 35 ☏030/34 10 249, ⊛www.deutscheoperberlin.de. Opera and ballet in a large, modern venue, plus good classical concerts too.

**Komische Oper** Behrenstr. 55–57 ☏030/47 99 74 00, ⊛www.komische-oper-berlin.de. Some very good opera productions are staged here and the house orchestra performs classical and contemporary music.

**Konzerthaus Berlin** Schauspielhaus am Gendarmenmarkt, Gendarmenmarkt 2 ☏030/2 03 09 21 01, ⊛www.konzerthaus.de. Home to the Berlin Sinfonie Orchester and host to visiting orchestras.

**Philharmonie** Herbert-von-Karajan-Str. 1 ☏030/25 48 80, ⊛www.berliner-philharmoniker .de. Custom-built home of the world's most celebrated orchestra, the Berlin Philharmonic.

**Staatsoper** Unter den Linden 7 ☏030/20 35 45 55, ⊛www.staatsoper-berlin.org. Excellent operatic productions in one of central Berlin's most beautiful buildings.

# Listings

**Bike rental and tours** Fahrradstation, Friedrichstrasse station ☏030/20 45 45 00; Pedal Power, Grossbeerenstr. 53 ☏030/78 99 19 39. From €10/day, €35/week; deposit, insurance payment and passport required. Fat Tire bike tours are a handy way to see the city with a friendly guide showing you all the Berlin unmissables on a six-mile, five-hour tour with beer-garden pit stop (☏030/24 04 79 91, ⊛www.fattirebiketoursberlin.com; €20).

**Embassies and consulates** Australia, Wallstr. 76–79 ☏030/88 00 880; Canada, Friedrichstr. 95 ☏030/20 31 20; Ireland, Friedrichstr. 200 ☏030/22 07 20; New Zealand, Friedrichstr. 60 ☏030/20 62 10; UK, Wilhelmstr. 70–71 ☏030/20 45 70; US, Neustädtische Kirchstr. 4–5 ☏030/83 050.

**Exchange** Reisebank, at the main entrance to

Zoo Station (daily 7.30am–10pm), Friedrichstrasse station (daily 7am–8pm) and Ostbahnhof (daily 7am–10pm).

**Hospitals** Charité University Clinic, Schumannstr. 20/21 ☏030/4 50 50; Prenzlauer Berg Hospital, Fröbelstr. 15 ☏030/4 24 20; Spandau Hospital, Neue Bergstr. 6 ☏030/3 38 70.

**Internet** easyEverything, Kurfürstendamm 224, and Alexanderplatz, Rathaus Passage; Surf and Sushi, Oranienburgerstr. 17.

**Laundry** Rosenthaler Str. 71; Hermannstr. 74–75.

**Left luggage** At major stations.

**Pharmacies** Europa-Apotheke, Europa Center, Tauentzienstr. 9.

**Post office** Joachimsthaler Str. 7 (daily 8am–midnight).

# Eastern Germany

By the time the Communist GDR (German Democratic Republic, or East Germany) was fully incorporated into the Federal Republic (West Germany), one year after the peaceful revolution (or Wende) of 1989, most vestiges of the old political system had been swept away. Yet there remains a long way to go before the two parts of the country achieve parity, and the cities of eastern Germany are still in the process of social and economic change. Berlin stands apart from the rest of the East, but its sense of excitement finds an echo in the two other main cities – **Leipzig**, which provided the vanguard of the revolution, and **Dresden**, the beautiful Saxon capital so ruthlessly destroyed in 1945. Equally enticing are some of the smaller places, notably **Weimar**, the fountainhead of much of European art and culture. The small town of **Meissen** and the old Prussian royal seat of **Potsdam** retain more of the appearance and atmosphere of prewar Germany than anywhere in the West.

## Potsdam

**POTSDAM** is an excellent day-trip from Berlin, linked to the capital by S-Bahn line #7 or most westbound mainline trains which stop at the main station (though some go to Park Sanssouci station). Potsdam's historic centre, whose skyline is dominated by the huge dome of the Nikolaikirche, is 2km east of **Park Sanssouci** (bus #695; daily 9am–dusk; free; joint ticket covering entry to all sights below €15; ⑩www.spsg.de), the fabled retreat of the Prussian kings. To avoid the crowds, visit on a weekday. Frederick the Great worked closely with his court architect on designing **Schloss Sanssouci** (tours Tues–Sun 9am–4/5pm; €8), which was to be a pleasure palace where the king could escape Berlin and his wife Elizabeth Christine. Begun in 1744, it's a surprisingly modest one-storey Baroque affair, topped by a copper dome and ornamental statues looking out over vine terraces. The most eye-catching chambers are the opulent Marble Hall and the Concert Room, where the flute-playing king had eminent musicians play his own works on concert evenings. West of the palace, overlooking the ornamental Holländischer Garten, is the **Bildergalerie** (mid-May to mid-Oct Tues–Sun 10am–5pm; €2), a restrained Baroque creation that contains paintings by Rubens, Van Dyck and Caravaggio. On the opposite side of the Schloss, steps lead down to the **Neue Kammern** (mid-May to mid-Oct Tues–Sun 10am–5pm; €3), the architectural twin of the Bildergalerie, originally used as an orangery and later as a guest house. Immediately to the west of the Neue Kammern is the prim Sizilianischer Garten, crammed with coniferous trees and subtropical plants, complementing the Nordische Garten just to the north. From the west of the Sizilianischer Garten, Maulbeerallee cuts through the park and ascends to the **Orangerie** (mid-May to mid-Oct Tues–Sun 10am–5pm; €3), clearly showing the king's love of Italian architecture. To the west through the trees rises the **Neues Palais** (Mon–Thurs, Sat & Sun 9am–4/5pm; €5), another massive Rococo extravaganza from Frederick's time. The interior is predictably opulent, though a couple of highlights stand out: the vast and startling Grottensaal on the ground floor decorated entirely with shells and semiprecious stones to form images of lizards and dragons, and the equally huge Marmorsaal, with its beautiful floor of patterned marble slabs. The southern wing (which these days houses a small café) contains Frederick's apartments and the theatre where the king enjoyed Italian opera and French plays.

## Leipzig

**LEIPZIG** has always been among the most dynamic of German cities. With its influential and respected university, and a tradition of trade fairs dating back to the Middle Ages, there was never the degree of isolation from outside influences experienced by so many cities behind the Iron Curtain. Leipzigers have embraced the challenges of reunification and its imposing monuments, narrow cobbled back-streets and wide-ranging nightlife make for an inviting visit. Most points of interest lie within the old centre. Following Nikolaistrasse due south from the train station brings you to the **Nikolaikirche**, a rallying point during the Wende. Although a sombre medieval structure outside, inside the church is a real eye-grabber thanks to rich decoration, works of art and columns designed to resemble palms. A couple of blocks west is the Markt, whose eastern side is entirely occupied by the **Altes Rathaus** (Tues–Sun 10am–6pm; €2.50, free on 1st Sun of month), built in the grandest German Renaissance style with elaborate gables, an asymmetrical tower and the longest inscription to be found on any building in the world. On the north side of the square is the handsome **Alte Waage**, or weigh house. To the rear of the Altes Rathaus, approached by a graceful double flight of steps, is the **Alte Handelsbörse**, a Baroque gem that was formerly the trade exchange headquarters. Five minutes' walk away, further along Katharinenstrasse, is the **Museum der Bildenden Künste** (Tues & Thurs–Sun 10am–6pm, Wed noon–8pm; €5), a distinguished collection of old masters, including Cranach and Rubens. Following Barfussgässchen off the west-ern side of the Markt brings you to Kleine Fleischergasse and the cheerful Baroque **Zum Coffe Baum**. One of the German pioneers of the coffee craze that followed the Turkish invasion of central Europe in the late seventeenth century, it gained further fame courtesy of the composer Robert Schumann, who came here regularly. Klostergasse leads southwards to the **Thomaskirche**, where Johann Sebastian Bach served for the last 27 years of his life. Predominantly Gothic, the church has been altered down the centuries. The most remarkable feature is its musical tradition: the Thomanerchor choir, which Bach once directed, can usually be heard on Fridays (6pm), Saturdays (3pm) and during the Sunday service (9.30am). Directly across from the church is the **Bach-Museum** (daily 10am–5pm; €3; ⓦwww.bach-leipzig .de), with an extensive show of mementos of the great composer. Close by, at Dittrichring 24, is another historically important museum, the Round Corner or **Runde Ecke** (daily 10am–6pm; free), a fascinating trawl through the methods and machinery of the Stasi, East Germany's secret police.

## Practicalities

Leipzig's enormous **train station** is at the northeastern end of the Ring, which encircles the old part of the city. The **tourist office**, directly opposite at Richard-Wagner-Str. 1 (Mon–Fri 10am–6pm, Sat 10am–4pm, Sun 10am–2pm; ☎0341/71 04 260, ⓦwww.leipzig.de), can book private rooms (❸) and sells the Leipzig Card (€7.40/15.50 for one/three days), which covers public transport and museum admission. Two well-run backpacker **hostels** are the *Hostel Sleepy Lion*, just west of the centre at Käthe-Kollwitz-Str. 3 (☎0341/99 39 480, ⓦwww.hostel-leipzig .de; dorms €14, rooms ❸); and, three minutes west of the station, the popular *Central Globetrotter*, Kurt-Schumacher-Str. 41 (☎0341/14 98 960; dorms €13, rooms ❸). The HI hostel is at Volksgartenstr. 24 (☎0341/24 57 000; €20; tram #1 to Löbauer Str.), and the **campsite**, *Auensee*, at Gustav-Esche-Str. 5 (☎03 41/46 51 600; tram #10).

Three main areas hold the **eating** and **nightlife** options: the medieval Barfussgässchen, Gottschedstrasse just to the west, and the student area of Karl-Liebknecht-Strasse in Südvorstadt. At the start of Barfussgässchen, *Zum Coffe Baum* serves excellent *Kaffee und Kuchen*, though it's often swamped with tour groups during the day. *Zur Pleissenburg*, Schulstr. 2, is a homely bar/restaurant with good-value hearty German food and outdoor tables. Nearby, at the south-eastern end of the Markt, in the Mädler-Passage, is *Auerbachs Keller*, a historic and quite formal restaurant that was the setting for a scene in Goethe's *Faust*. *Apels Garten*, Kolonnadenstr. 2, is a traditional restaurant that uses recipes from a 300-year-old cookbook. South of the centre, students hang out in the cool *NATO* bar, Karl-Liebknecht-Str. 46, while nearby *Ilses Ericka*, on Bernhard-Göring

Str. 152, is a grungy bar and music venue. Also south of the centre, back in the Altstadt, housed beneath the medieval city fortifications of the Moritzbastei is *MB*, a tightly packed collection of bars and clubs including the biggest student club in Europe.

# Weimar

Despite its modest size, **WEIMAR** has played an unmatched role in the development of German culture: Goethe, Schiller and Nietzsche all made it their home, as did the Cranachs and Bach, and the architects and designers of the Bauhaus school. The town was also chosen as the seat of government of the democratic republic established after World War I, a regime whose failure ended with the Nazi accession. Birthplace of the Hitler Youth movement, Weimar is also where Buchenwald, one of the most notorious concentration camps, was built, and its preservation here is a shocking reminder of the Nazi era. Weimar's cobbled streets and laid-back, quietly highbrow atmosphere are worth a day's detour.

Weimar's former seat of power was the **Schloss** (Tues–Sun 10am–4.30/6pm; €4; ⊛www.swkk.de), set by the River Ilm at the eastern edge of the town centre, a Neoclassical complex of a size more appropriate for ruling a mighty empire. On the ground floor is a collection of old masters, including pieces by both Cranachs, and Dürer's portraits of the Nuremberg patrician couple, Hans and Elspeth Tucher. South of nearby Herderplatz is the spacious **Markt**, lined by an unusually disparate jumble of buildings, of which the most eye-catching is the green and white gabled Stadthaus on the eastern side, opposite the neo-Gothic Rathaus. Schillerstrasse snakes away from the southwest corner of the Markt to the **Schillerhaus** (Mon & Wed–Sun 9am–4/6pm; €3.50), the home of the poet and dramatist for the last three years of his life. Beyond lies Theaterplatz, in the centre of which is a large monument to Goethe and Schiller. The **Nationaltheater** on the west side of the square was founded and directed by Goethe, though the present building, for all its stern Neoclassical appearance, is a modern pastiche. On Frauenplan, south of the Markt is **Goethewohnhaus und Nationalmuseum** (Tues–Sun 9am–4/6pm; €5), where Goethe lived for some fifty years until his death in 1832. From here, Marienstrasse continues to the **Liszthaus** (April–Oct Tues–Sun 10am–6pm; €2), home of the Hungarian composer and pianist for the last seventeen years of his life, when he was director of Weimar's orchestra and opera. A few minutes' walk west down Geschwister-Scholl-Strasse is the **Hochschule für Architektur und Bauwesen**, where Walter Gropius established the original Bauhaus in 1919. The **Park an der Ilm** stretches from the Schloss to the southern edge of town on both sides of the river; aim for the southern suburb of Oberweimar, where stands the full-blown summer palace of **Schloss Belvedere** (Tues–Sun 10am–4/6pm; €3.50; ⊛www.swkk.de), whose light and airy Rococo forms a refreshing contrast to the Neoclassical solemnity of so much of the town. The **Konzentrationslager Buchenwald** (Tues–Sun 10am–4/6pm; free; ⊛www.buchenwald.de) is situated north of Weimar on the Ettersberg heights, and can be reached by bus (hourly from just south of the train station). Over 240,000 prisoners were incarcerated in this concentration camp, with 65,000 dying here.

## Practicalities

Weimar's **train station**, on the Leipzig line, is a twenty-minute walk north of the main sights. One of the **tourist offices** (daily 10am–8pm) is there; another, larger one is in the Stadthaus at Markt 10 (Mon–Fri 9.30/10am–6pm, Sat & Sun 9.30/10am–3pm; ☎036 43/74 50, ⊛www.weimar.de). The cheapest and most central **hostel** is the environmentally minded and cosy *Hababusch* at Geleitstr. 4 (☎036 43/85 07 37, ⊛www.hababusch.de; dorms €10, rooms ❷). There are neat and tidy HI **hostels** at Humboldt Str. 17 (☎036 43/85 07 92; €21.70) and

Carl-August-Allee 13 (☎036 43/85 04 90; €21.70). Reasonably priced **pensions** include the recently refurbished *Savina*, Meyerstr. 60 (☎036 43/8 66 90, ✆www .pension-savina.de; ❹). Weimar's range of **eating and drinking** spots comes as a surprise, given its relatively small size. Centrally located *Zum Zwiebel*, Teichgasse 6, is a deservedly popular, cosy and lively restaurant serving local specialities at cheap prices. The *Residenz-Café* on Grüner Markt, though rather plush, has good coffee and cakes; nearby *A.C.C.*, Burgplatz 1, is a more relaxed bar and restaurant with quiet candlelit tables lining a cobbled sidestreet.

# Dresden

Generally regarded as Germany's most beautiful and culturally significant city, **DRESDEN** survived World War II largely unscathed until the night of February 13, 1945. Then, in a matter of hours, it was reduced to ruins in saturation bombing – according to official figures at least 35,000 civilians died (though the total was probably considerably higher), as the city was packed with people fleeing the advancing Red Army. With this background, it's all the more remarkable that Dresden is the one city in the former East Germany that has slotted easily into the economic framework of the reunited Germany, and the post-Communist authorities are now brilliantly restoring the historic buildings.

## Arrival, information and accommodation

Dresden has two main train stations – the **Hauptbahnhof**, south of the Altstadt, and **Neustadt Bahnhof**, at the northwestern corner of the Neustadt, convenient for the backpacker hostels and nightlife. One of the **tourist offices** is in a pavilion at Prager Str. 10 (Mon–Fri 10am–6pm, Sat 10am–4pm; ☎0351/49 19 20, ✆www .dresden-tourist.de), a short walk from the Hauptbahnhof; the other is in the heart of the Altstadt, in the Schinkelwache on Theaterplatz (Mon–Fri 10am–6pm, Sat & Sun 10am–4pm). Both sell the **Dresden Card** (€19/two days) or the **Dresden Regio-Card** (€29/three days), which cover public transport, museum admission and sundry discounts. Otherwise, there's a day **transport ticket** (€4.50) and a separate **day ticket** for the museums (€10).

The tourist offices can book private rooms and pensions (❸). There are three backpacker **hostels** in Neustadt, well placed for nightlife in the Hechtviertel artists' ghetto: the wonderfully cosy *Lollis Homestay*, Görlitzer Str. 34 (☎0351/81 08 458, ✆www.lollishome.de; dorms €13, rooms ❸); the relaxed *Mondpalast*, Louisenstr. 77 (☎0351/56 34 050, ✆www.mondpalast.de; €13.50); and *Die Boofe*, Hechtstr. 10 (☎0351/8 01 33 61, ✆www.boofe.de; dorms €15, rooms ❸), ten minutes north of Neustadt Bahnhof, which has its own sauna. For a slightly soulless but hotel-quality hostel, go to the bright and quiet *Hostel Louise 20*, Louisenstr. 20 (☎0351/8 89 48 94, ✆www.louise20.de; dorms €15, rooms ❸). The *Mockritz* **campsite** is at Boderitzer Str. 30 (☎0351/47 15 250, ✆www.camping-dresden .de; bus #76 from Hauptbahnhof).

## The City

If you arrive at the Hauptbahnhof, you see the worst of modern Dresden first: the **Prager Strasse**, a vast Stalinist pedestrian precinct with a few fountains and statues thrown in for relief, though undergoing something of a facelift at the moment. At the far end, beyond the inner ring road, is the **Altmarkt**, much extended after its wartime destruction; the only building of note that remains is the **Kreuzkirche**, a church that mixes a Baroque body with a Neoclassical tower. On Saturdays at 6pm, and at the 9.30am Sunday service, it usually features the Kreuzchor, one of the world's leading church choirs. North of here, the **Albertinum** (Wed–Mon 10am–6pm; €6; ✆www.skd-dresden.de) houses one of the greatest of Romantic paintings, Friedrich's *Cross in the Mountains*. West of the Albertinum is the **Neumarkt**, dominated by the round, domed

**Frauenkirche**. Only a fragment of wall was left standing after the war, and after fierce controversy, the decision was taken in 1991 to rebuild the church completely, with much of the funding coming from the UK and US. The colossal **Residenzschloss** (Wed–Mon 10am–6pm; €6; @www.skd-dresden.de) was also wrecked in the war, and the rebuilding programme now under way is a massive task, though the projected completion date of 2006 – the city's 800th anniversary – looks achievable. The recently moved **Grünes Gewölbe** or Green Vault, a dazzling array of treasury items, can now be admired here. Sooner or later, the miraculously preserved **Mirror Rooms** (currently closed) will re-house the entire Grünes Gewölbe collection. At the end of nearby Augustusstrasse is the Baroque **Hofkirche**, or Kathedrale. The existence of this Catholic church in a staunchly Protestant province is explained by the fact that the Saxon rulers converted in order to gain the Polish throne.

Baroque Dresden's great glory was the palace known as the **Zwinger** (@www .skd-dresden.de; individually priced or €10 for all), which faces the Residenzschloss and now contains several museums. Beautifully displayed in the southeastern pavilion, entered from Sophienstrasse, is the **Porzellansammlung** (Tues–Sun 10am–6pm; €5); products from the famous Meissen factory are extensively featured. The southwestern pavilion is known as the **Mathematisch-Physikalischer Salon** (Tues–Sun 10am–6pm; €5), and offers a fascinating array of globes, clocks and scientific instruments. In the nineteenth-century extension is the **Gemäldegalerie Alte Meister** (Tues–Sun 10am–6pm; €6), whose collection of old masters ranks among the dozen best in the world, and includes some of the most familiar Italian Renaissance paintings: Raphael's *Sistine Madonna*, Titian's *Christ and the Pharisees* and Veronese's *Marriage at Cana*. The German section includes Dürer's *Dresden Altarpiece*, Holbein's *Le Sieur de Morette*, Cranach's *Duke Henry the Pious*, and there's a Low Countries section in which Rubens and Rembrandt are extensively featured. On the north side of the Zwinger stands the **Rüstkammer** (Tues–Sun 10am–6pm; €3), a wonderful collection of weaponry that includes a magnificent Renaissance suit of armour for man and horse, depicting scenes from the Trojan War.

Across the River Elbe, the **Neustadt** was a planned Baroque town and its layout is still obvious, even if few of the original buildings survive. Today it's the focus of the city's gentrification with a burgeoning art scene, and you can wander through the bohemian **Kunsthofpassage** with its courtyards, houses and arty shops. In the park overlooking the Elbe is the most esoteric creation of Dresden Baroque, the **Japanisches Palais** (Tues–Sun 10am–6pm; €4), which now contains archeological and ethnographic museums focusing largely on the South Seas. You don't have to pay to see the courtyard, a fantasy inspired by the eighteenth-century infatuation with the Orient.

## Eating, drinking and nightlife

There's a wide choice of **restaurants**, and with over 130 **bars and clubs** clustered around a handful of cobbled, narrow streets, the Neustadt provides something for everyone. For up-to-date nightlife **listings**, pick up a copy of *Sax*, *Dresdner* or *Fritz* from kiosks or backpacker hostels.

### Cafés and restaurants

**Am Thor** Hauptstr. 35, Neustadt. A worthy survivor from Communist days, serving traditional fare.

**Bauernstuben im Kügelgenhaus** Hauptstr. 13, Neustadt. Atmospheric restaurant-cum-beer cellar in a fine Baroque building.

**Dürüm Kebap Haus** Rothenburger Str. 41. A rock-bottom favourite, serving as a cheap takeaway, quick restaurant and general meeting place.

**El Perro Borracho** Kunsthof alleyway, off Alaunstrasse, Neustadt. A highly regarded, lively Spanish eatery.

**Kartoffelkeller** Nieritzstr. 11. All you could ever dream of doing with a potato, at good rates.

**Oosteinde** Preissnitzstr. 18. Delicious, good-value food served inside under narrow arches or outside in a peaceful beer garden.

**Pfund's** Bautzner Str. 79, Neustadt. Touristy

café/restaurant attached to a dairy shop, with immaculately restored Jugendstil decor.

**Schlemmerland** Pragerstr. You'll find plenty of cheap and cheerful fast-food outlets under one roof here.

**Szeged** Wilsdruffer Str. 4, Altstadt. It's worth dining here in order to sample the rich Hungarian and German cuisine and the local wines, and enjoy the occasional bouts of live traditional music.

### Neustadt bars

**Blue Note** Görlitzer Str. 2b. Dark, cavernous, smoke-filled blues bar that gets packed to the gills every night for its live music.

**Bottoms Up** Martin-Luther-Str. 31. Down a quiet backstreet away from the main action, this large easy-going bar and beer garden is an unpretentious favourite.

**El Cubanito** Sebnitzer Str. 8b. A cramped but cosy Cuban tapas and cocktail bar.

**Groove Station** Katherinenstr. 11–13. Situated at the back of a courtyard, this rough-and-ready rock bar and live venue has been a Neustadt cornerstone for years.

**Hebeda's** Rothenburger Str. 30. A large, crumbling and basic pub that epitomizes the Neustadt alternative scene.

**Raskolnikov** Böhmische Str. 34. A large, rambling, bohemian Russian bar/café and restaurant. Great food and atmospheric beer garden.

**Scheune** Alaunstr. 36–40. Neustadt arts centre with a welcoming bar, large beer garden, live music, theatre, and gay and lesbian nights.

**Trotzdem** Alaunstr. 81. Chilled, funky bar with intimate corners and a good choice of beer.

# Meissen

The cobbled square and photogenic rooftop vistas are reason alone to make the effort to visit the porcelain-producing town of **MEISSEN** which, unlike its neighbour Dresden, survived World War II almost unscathed. Walking towards the centre from the train station, you see the commandingly sited castle almost immediately. The present building, the **Albrechtsburg** (daily 10am–5/6pm; closed Jan; €3.50; ⓦwww.albrechtsburg-meissen.de), is a late fifteenth-century combination of military fortress and residential palace. Cocooned within the castle precinct is the **Dom** (daily 9/10am–4/6pm; €2.50); inside, look out for the superb brass tombplates of the Saxon dukes and the rood screen with its colourful altarpiece. Between the castle hill and the Elbe lies the atmospheric **Altstadt**, a network of twisting and meandering streets whose centrepiece is the **Markt**, dominated by the Renaissance Rathaus. On its own small square to the side is the Flamboyant Gothic **Frauenkirche**, whose carillon, fashioned from local porcelain, can be heard six times daily. On the terrace just above is the celebrated **Gasthaus Vinzenz Richter**, a half-timbered tavern that preserves an eighteenth-century winepress. The wines served here are said to be the best in eastern Germany. The **Staatliche Porzellan-Manufaktur Meissen** (tours daily 9am–5/6pm; €3; ⓦwww.meissen.de), about 1.5km south of the Markt, is most easily reached by going down Fleischer Gasse, then continuing straight down Neugasse; it's also close to the S-Bahn terminus, Meissen-Triebischtal, and there's a city bus from the station (hourly 10am–5pm). This is the latest factory to manufacture Dresden china, whose invention came about when Augustus the Strong imprisoned the alchemist Johann Friedrich Böttger, ordering him to produce some gold. Instead, he invented the first true European porcelain, according to a formula that remains secret. In addition to seeing the works, you can also view the **museum** (same hours; €4.50), which displays many of the factories' finest achievements, most notably some gloriously over-the-top Rococo fripperies made by the most talented artist ever employed here, Johann Joachim Kaendler. Meissen's **tourist office** at Markt 3 (Mon–Fri 10am–6pm, Sat & Sun 10am–4pm; Jan closed weekends; ⓣ035 21/41 940, ⓦwww.touristinfo-meissen.de) books private rooms (❸). There's also a trio of reasonably priced central **pensions**: *Burkhardt*, Neugasse 29 (ⓣ035 21/45 81 98; ❹), *Schweizerhaus*, Rauhentalstr. 1 (ⓣ035 21/45 71 62; ❸), and *Meissner Arkaden*, Burgstrasse 24 (ⓣ035 21/45 86 84; ❷). The one unmissable **restaurant** is the *Gasthaus Vincenz Richter*, which specializes in local and national dishes. Other possibilities include *Domkeller*, Domplatz 9, and the traditional *Bauernhaus'l*, Oberspaarer Str. 20.

# Northern Germany

**Hamburg**, Germany's second city, is infamous for the sleaze and hectic nightlife of the Reeperbahn strip – yet it also has a more sophisticated cultural scene. In this unprepossessing region, another maritime city, **Lübeck**, has the strongest pull, with a similar appeal to the mercantile towns of the Low Countries. To the north, Schleswig-Holstein's mix of dyke-protected marsh, peat bog and farmland holds few rewarding sights on the way to mainland Denmark. To the south lies the region's capital, **Hannover**; worth a short visit for its museums and gardens. The province's smaller towns present a fascinating contrast – the former silver-mining town of **Goslar**, in particular, is unusually beautiful.

## Hamburg

Stylish media centre and second-largest port in Europe, **HAMBURG** is undeniably cool – more laid-back than Berlin or Frankfurt, more sophisticated than Munich or Cologne, and with nightlife to rival the lot. Its skyline is dominated by the pale green of its copper spires and domes, but a few houses and the churches are all that's left from older times. The Great Fire of 1842 was a main cause of this loss, plus wartime bombing. Much of the subsequent rebuilding might not be especially beautiful, but the result is an intriguing mix of old and new, coupled with an appealing sense of open space – two thirds of Hamburg is occupied by parks, lakes or tree-lined canals, adding some much-needed leafiness to this major industrial centre.

### Arrival, information and accommodation

An Airport Express connects the **airport** to the main train station, the **Hauptbahnhof**, at the eastern end of the city centre (every 15min; 20min; €4.60). The helpful **tourist office** in the Hauptbahnhof (daily 7am–11pm; ☏040/30 05 13 00, ⊛www.hamburg-tourismus.de) has a room-finding service (€4). Pick up the **Hamburg Card** (€7.30/15 for 1/3 days) here, which gives free or reduced admission to some of the city's museums as well as free use of public transport. Under-30s can pick up a similar, cheaper card, called the **Hamburg Power-Pass** (€6.70 for 1 day/€3 per day for additional days). A one-day travel card (S- and U-Bahn) costs €5.50.

Close to Sternschanze station (north of St Pauli; U-Bahn #3, S-Bahn #21 or #31) are two **hostels**: *Backpacker Hostel Instant Sleep*, Max-Brauer-Allee 277 (☏040/43 18 23 10, ⊛www.instantsleep.de; dorms €15, rooms ❸), and the more comfortable *Schanzenstern*, Bartelsstr. 12 (☏040/439 84 41, ⊛www.schanzenstern .de; dorms €18, rooms ❺). *Schanzenstern* now has an additional hostel in Altona at Kleine Rainstr. 24–26 (☏040/39 91 91 91, ⊛www.schanzenstern.de; dorms €18, rooms ❹). The cheapest, and most popular, **hotels** are near the train station. *Annenhof*, Lange Reihe 23 (☏040/24 34 26, ⊛www.hotel-annenhof.de; ❸; reception closes at 9.30pm), is good value; or there's the small but stylish *Sarah Petersen* at no. 50 (☏040/24 98 26; ❹). **B&B** is available through *bed&breakfast*, Müggenkampstr. 35 (☏040/491 56 66; book in advance Mon–Fri; ❸).

### The City

A good place to begin your exploration is the oldest area, the **harbour**, dominated by the clock tower and green dome of the St Pauli Landungsbrücken. The main tourist draw is a one-hour **boat tour** of the harbour (many companies operate these; prices start at €8.50), but they are best avoided unless you have a fascination for industrial containers. More interesting is the late nineteenth-century **Speicherstadt** lying a little to the east, filled with tall, ornate warehouses and the smell of spices and coffee wafting on the breeze. As the Speicherstadt is within the

# HAMBURG

**EATING & DRINKING**

| | | | | |
|---|---|---|---|---|
| Alt Hamburger | | Erika's Eck | 4 |
| Aalspeicher | 8 | Frank & Frei | 1 |
| Bok | 5 | Petisco | 3 |
| Café Koppel | 7 | Noodles | 6 |
| Einstein | 2 | Sagres | 9 |

**ACCOMMODATION**

| | |
|---|---|
| Annenhof | E |
| Backpacker Hostel | A |
| Instant Sleep | C |
| bed&breakfast | D |
| Sarah Petersen | B |
| Schanzenstern | B |
| Schanzenstern Altona | F |

ST GEORG

Deutsches
Schauspielhaus

Hauptbahnhof
Hauptbahnhof-Süd
ZOB

Hauptbahnhof

Museum für Kunst
und Gewerbe

Deichtorhallen

KLOSTERWALL

Aussenalster

Kunsthalle

Galerie der
Gegenwart

St Jakobi

St Petri

Chilehaus

Massberg

Binnenalster

BALLINDAMM

Jungfernstieg

St Katharinen

Rathaus
& Börse

St Nicolai

SPEICHERSTADT

Hamburgische
Staatsoper

Binnenhafen

Bahnhof Dammtor

Damntor

Stephansplatz

ESPLANADE

COLONNADEN

Alsterfleet

Musikhalle

Messehallen

Kramerants-
wohnungen

Johannes-
Brahms-
Museum

St Michaelis

Museum für
Hamburgische
Geschichte

Fernsehturm

Sternschanze

ST PAULI

St Pauli
Landungsbrücken

Rickmer
Rickmers

HAMBURG

River Elbe

▼ Cap San Diego

SCHULTERBLATT

BUDAPESTER STR

REEPERBAHN

0   250 m

449

Freihafen (customs-free zone) you can walk around unrestricted and crisscross the bridges (Hamburg has more than Venice or Amsterdam). Just to the north from the Landungsbrücken is the nightlife centre of **St Pauli**, whose main artery is the notorious **Reeperbahn** – ugly and unassuming by day, blazing with neon at night. Running off here is Grosse Freiheit, the street that famously hosted The Beatles' first gigs. The main road along the waterfront on St Pauli's edge is the Hafenstrasse, which runs west to the trendy suburb of **Altona**. Its reputation for racial tolerance is one of the reasons it grew, and it still has a large Portuguese population – and good, cheap Portuguese restaurants. On the waterfront here, one of the city's main weekly events takes place: the **Fischmarkt**. Come early on Sunday and you'll find yourself in an amazing trading frenzy; everything is in full swing by 5am and by 10am it's over.

The commercial and shopping district centres on **Binnenalster** lake and the neo-Renaissance **Rathaus** (guided tours in English: Mon–Thurs 10.15am–3.15pm, Fri–Sun 10.15am–1.15pm; €1.50), a magnificently pompous demonstration of the city's power and wealth in the nineteenth century. From the Rathausmarkt, continue up **Poststrasse** to the heart of Hamburg's exclusive shopping area. Away to the east, north of the Hauptbahnhof is the **Kunsthalle**, the unmissable art collection (Tues–Sun 10am–6pm, Thurs till 9pm; €8.50; ⑳www.hamburger-kunsthalle.de). There are three altarpieces by Master Bertram, the first German painter identifiable by name, and a Dutch and Flemish section where two Rembrandts take centre stage, but it's the nineteenth-century German section that is the museum's main strength. Next door is the **Galerie der Gegenwart** (same hours and ticket), showing contemporary art. Nearby is the **Museum für Kunst und Gewerbe** (same hours; €8.20; ⑳www.mkg-hamburg.de) which hosts exciting exhibitions from graphic design to the latest in furniture.

## Eating, drinking and nightlife

Some of the best **places to eat** are northwest of the city centre, in the Univiertel or the Schanzenviertel, around Schulterblatt and Schanzenstrasse (two minutes' walk south of Sternschanze station). For **snacks**, the stalls in front of the Rathaus are varied and delicious, while most café-bars have food as well as drinks. Hamburg's **nightlife** is outstanding, including a good bar scene and a wide range of excellent clubs. For up-to-the-minute listings, look out for a number of free mags in bars such as *Nachtlichter* (for clubs) or *Kultur News* for more artistic pursuits. St Pauli is the city's main venue for clubbing and live music, with big-name DJs and bands playing at weekends. Admission is generally about €10. The student bar scene is in Schanzenviertel, while Altona attracts young professionals. The best way to find out what's on in the lively **gay scene** is through *Hinnerk* magazine, available from the tourist office. They also have a free, short gay city guide, *Hamburg's Pride*, in German and English.

### Cafés and restaurants

**Alt Hamburger Aalspeicher** Deichstr. 43. One of the best-known addresses in the city centre for traditional German cuisine and fish dishes. Pricey but worth it.

**Bok** Schulterblatt 3. An outlet of the excellent local Thai eatery and convenient if you're staying in the Sternschanze area. Continue north of Budapester Stra. onto Stresemannstr., turn right and continue down Max-Brauer-Allee – Schulterblatt is first on the left.

**Café Koppel** Koppel 66. Best known for its delicious wholemeal chocolate cake, this place also serves a good range of vegetarian dishes and has a summer garden.

**Einstein** Bahrenfelder Chaussee 45. The place to seek out if an inexpensive fill-up is a priority, with pizzas figuring heavily – on the road that leads into Stresmannstr. Feldstrasse or Sternschanze U-Bahn.

**Erika's Eck** Sternstr. 98. Best breakfast in the city and a firm student favourite.

**Frank & Frei** Schanzenstr. 93. Enormous salads, pasta and pizza.

**Noodles** Schanzenstr.2–4. Daily noodle-based specials sit alongside more typical German crowd pleasers.

Petisco Schulterblatt 78. A popular Portuguese restaurant, serving authentic, inexpensive fare.
Sagres Vorsetzen 42. Good and inexpensive Portuguese restaurant in the vicinity of the harbour. Generous portions.

### Clubs and music venues

Betty Ford Klinik Grosse Freiheit 6. The finest in house and techno. Fri & Sat.
Cotton Club Alter Steinweg 10. Traditional jazz club, with live music Mon–Sat 8.30pm.
Fabrik Barnerstr. 36. Major live music and party venue in Altona, with an emphasis on world music, jazz and dance.
Grosse Freiheit Grosse Freiheit 36. A tourist attraction in itself, Hamburg's leading live venue books major acts most weekends. Emphasis on goth and rock.
Grünspan Grosse Freiheit 58. Uncompromisingly heavy rock. Wed–Sat.
Gum Hamburger Berg 12–13. The name stands for Global Underground Music; probably the best place for serious techno, trance and house.
Kaiserkeller *Grosse Freiheit* club basement. Massive subterranean club playing mostly alternative music; famous for hosting The Beatles in the early 1960s.
Lounge Gerhardstr. 16. House, Latin and jazz mix happily in this intimate venue.

### Gay Hamburg

Café Gnosa Lange Reihe 93. Well-known bar/restaurant with marvellous cakes. Packed at weekends.
Frauenkneipe Stresemannstr. 60. The city's leading address for women only. Occasionally organizes lesbian club nights elsewhere. Feldstrasse or Sternschanze U-Bahn.
Juice Club Stresemannstr. 30. Hosts lesbian club nights, with mostly house and disco music; accompanied gay men welcome.
Purgatory Friedrichstr. 8. Relaxed gay and lesbian bar with eccentric decor.

## Listings

Bike rental At left luggage in the train station's travel centre.
Consulates UK, Harvestehuder Weg 8a ☎040/44 80 320; Ireland, Feldbrunnenstr. 43 ☎040/44 18 62 13; US, Alsterufer 28 ☎040/411 71 10.
Hospital Krankenhaus Bethesda, Glindersweg 80 ☎040/46 680.

Internet access Baff Internetcafe, Schulterblatt 116; Int. Telecom, Kirchenallee 9; also at Hauptbahnhof-Süd station.
Left luggage At the train station.
Pharmacy Bergstr. 14.
Post office At the Kirchenallee exit of the train station.

# Lübeck

Just an hour from Hamburg, **LÜBECK** makes a great day-trip. Set on an egg-shaped island surrounded by the water defences of the Trave and the city moat, the pretty Altstadt is a five-minute walk from the train station, past the twin-towered **Holstentor** (Tues–Sun 10am–4/5pm; €4), the city's emblem. On the waterfront to the right of the Holstentor is a row of lovely gabled buildings – the **Salzspeicher**. Straight ahead, over the bridge and up Holstenstrasse, the first church on the right is the Gothic **Petrikirche**; an elevator goes to the top of its spire (daily 9am–7pm; closed Oct–Feb; €2.50) for city-wide views. Back across Holstenstrasse is the Markt and the elaborate **Rathaus**. Opposite is **Konditorei-café Niederegger**, renowned for its vast marzipan display; its old-style first-floor café is surprisingly affordable and crammed with marzipan products, whilst the top floor is a free museum dedicated to the sugary substance. Behind the north wing of the town hall is the **Marienkirche**, Germany's oldest brick-built Gothic church. The interior makes a light and lofty backdrop for the church's treasures: a magnificent 1518 carved altar, a life-sized figure of John the Evangelist dating from 1505, a beautiful Gothic gilded tabernacle and an ornate astronomical clock. **Katharinenkirche**, on the corner of Königstrasse and Glockengiesserstrasse, boasts three sculptures on its west facade by Ernst Barlach; he was commissioned to make a series of nine in the early 1930s, but had completed only these when his work was banned by the Nazis. To the north at Königstr. 9–11 are the **Behnhaus** and the **Drägerhaus**, two patricians' houses now converted into a museum (Tues–Sun 10am–5pm; €4). The former has a good collection of modern paintings, including works by Kirchner and Munch, whilst the latter is crammed with nineteenth-century furniture and porcelain. Across from the nearby **Jakobikirche**, on Breite Strasse, is a Renaissance house that used to belong to the sailors' guild, the **Haus der Schiffergesellschaft**. A tavern since 1535, it's decked out with all sorts of seagoing paraphernalia.

At the opposite end of the Altstadt is the **Kunsthalle Museum St Annen** displaying art from the fifteenth to the nineteenth century within the St Annen wing and contemporary art in the recently attached Kunsthalle, which includes a Warhol.

Lübeck **train station** is just west of the Altstadt. The main **tourist office** is at Breite Str. 62 (Mon–Fri 9.30am–6pm, Sat 10am–3pm; June–Sept also Sun 10am–2pm; ☎0180/58 82 233, ⓦwww.luebeck-tourismus.de). The best **hostel** is in the Werkhof complex at Kanalstr. 70 (☎0451/70 68 92, ⓦwww.people.freenet .de/rucksackhotel; €24), while the two HI hostels are in the centre of the old town, one at Grosse Petersgrube 11 (☎0451/71 920, ⓦwww.cvjm-luebeck.de; €12.50), the other, more luxurious one, at Mengstr. 33 (☎0451/702 03 99; €17.50). A good-value **hotel** is the very convenient *Stadt Lübeck*, Am Bahnhof 21 (☎0451/83 8 83, ⓦwww .stadt-luebeck-hotel.de; ❹). Lübeck has a good choice of **cafés** and **restaurants**. Traditional cuisine can be found at the *Ratskeller*, Markt 13; *Schmidt's*, Dr-Julius-Leber-Str. 60–62, has an eclectic menu; and informal *Tipasa*, Schlumacherstr. 12–14, has cheap pizzas and pastas and eccentric decor. *Café Affenbrot*, part of the Werkhof (Kanalstr. 70), has tasty veggie food and cakes. Mühlenstrasse is the best street for **bars**.

# Hannover

**HANNOVER** has a closer relationship with Britain than any other German city, a consequence of the 1701 Act of Settlement, which resulted in Georg Ludwig of Hannover becoming the British George I in 1714. Anticipating the accession, the court director of music, Georg Friedrich Händel, had established himself in London by the time his employer arrived, and went on to write his finest works there. Hannover's showpiece – refreshingly – is not a great cathedral, palace or town hall, but a series of **gardens**. Add this to a number of first-class museums and it's worth spending a day here.

Starting at Hannover's most popular rendezvous, the **Kröpcke** café, the most imposing building in view is the vast Neoclassical **Opernhaus**. A short distance southwest, a few streets of rebuilt half-timbered buildings convey some impression of the medieval town; the elaborate brickwork of the high-gabled fifteenth-century **Altes Rathaus** is clearly visible, despite the interior now housing more modern shops. Alongside is the fourteenth-century **Marktkirche**, with some miraculously preserved stained glass. Southwards, across the Friedrichswall, is the massive **Neues Rathaus**, a Baroque-cum-neo-Gothic extravaganza whose dome gives the best views of the city (April–Oct daily 10am–6pm; free). Next door, the **Kestner-Museum** (Tues–Sun 11am–6pm, Wed till 8pm; €4; ⓦwww.kestner.org) is a compact and eclectic decorative arts museum. Round the back of the Rathaus on Willy-Brandt-Allee is the **Niedersächsisches Landesmuseum** (Tues–Sun 10am–5pm, Thurs till 7pm; €4; ⓦwww.nlmh.de), housing an excellent collection of paintings from the Middle Ages to the early twentieth century. A bit further down the road lies the **Sprengel-Museum** (Tues–Sun 10am–6/8pm; €7; ⓦwww.sprengel -museum.de), with much of the display space given over to changing exhibitions of contemporary photography, graphics and experimental art-forms, but there's also a first-rate permanent display of twentieth-century painting and sculpture.

The royal gardens of **Herrenhausen**, featuring Europe's biggest fountain, can be reached by U-Bahn #4 or #5 from the Kröpcke. Proceeding north from town along Nienburgerstrasse, head past the Welfengarten on the right. To the left, the dead-straight Herrenhäuser Allee cuts through the **Georgengarten**, an English-style landscaped garden with an artificial lake, created as a foil to the magnificent formal **Grosser Garten** (daily 9am–4.30/6/7/8pm; €4, free mid-Oct to early

April), the city's pride and joy. If possible, time your visit to coincide with the playing of the fountains (April–Sept daily 11am–noon & 2/3–5pm), when the illuminations are switched on (May–Aug after sunset; €3), or during one of the concerts and fireworks displays (check with tourist office for programme; €16). Just inside the entrance gate is the striking **Hedge Theatre**, a permanent amphitheatre whose hedges double as scenery and changing rooms. Across Herrenhäuser Strasse north of the Grosser Garten is the **Berggarten** (daily 9am–7/8pm; €2, or free with Grosser Garten ticket), set up to shelter rare and exotic plants.

## Practicalities

The **train station** is in the centre of town; behind is the **bus station**. The **tourist office** is beside the train station in the post office, Ernst-August-Platz 2 (Mon–Fri 9am–6pm, Sat 9am–2pm; April–Oct also Sun 9am–2pm; ☏0511/12 34 51 11, ⊛www.hannover-tourism.de). Pick up a Hannover Card here (€8/12 for 1/3 days), covering public transport and entrance to the main museums and sights. There's an HI **hostel** at Ferdinand-Wilhelm-Fricke-Weg 1 (☏0511/13 17 674; €20); take U-Bahn #3 or #7 to Fischerhof, from where it's a five-minute walk to the left over the bridge, then right. For €6.50 the tourist office will book you into a **hotel** (the service is free if arranged in advance). Hannover charges fancy business prices; the lowest rates in the centre are at the spotless *Flora*, offering an excellent breakfast, Heinrichstr. 36 (☏0511/38 39 10; ❹), and *Gildehof*, Joachimstr. 6 (☏0511/36 36 80; ❺); or you could also try *Reverey*, Aegidiendamm 8 (☏0511/88 37 11; ❹). For **snacks** head for the Markthalle, where German, Italian, Spanish and Turkish stalls sell great-value meals. Alternatively, try the shops around Goetheplatz, or pop into the Mövenpick complex, Joachimstr. 1–3, which has self-service (vegetarian) and sit-down restaurants. *Café Kröpcke*, Georgestr. 35, has an abundant selection of cakes, while *Fire*, Knochenhauerstr. 30, is a trendy **bar** serving food. Popular **clubs** include *Zaza*, Hamburger Allee 4a, which offers house, funk and soul, and *H.De.M.* on Windmühlenstr. 1, more geared towards techno and trance. **Internet** access is at Surf Inn, Seilwinderstr. 8 and at Tele Klick Schillerstr. 23.

# Goslar

**GOSLAR** is an absurdly picturesque mining town located at the northern edge of the gentle wooded Harz mountains. Silver was discovered in the nearby Rammelsberg in the tenth century, and Goslar soon became the "treasure chest of the Holy Roman Empire". The presence of a POW hospital during World War II spared the town's attractive architecture from bombing and the UNESCO World Heritage status, awarded in 1992, has increased the tourist crowds. The central **Marktplatz** hosts a morning market (Tues & Fri), but is best seen empty to fully appreciate its visual variety, with an elegantly Gothic **Rathaus** (daily 11.30am–3pm; €2) and roofs of bright red tiles and contrasting grey slate. The **Huldigungssaal** in the Rathaus contains a dazzling array of medieval wall and ceiling paintings, with the most valuable items hidden in altar niches and closets behind the panelling. Just behind the Rathaus is the **Marktkirche**, facing the sixteenth-century **Brusttuch**, with its top storey crammed with satirical carvings. Goslar's half-timbered beauty begins in earnest in the streets behind the church – the Frankenberg Quarter – the oldest houses lying in the Bergstrasse and Schreiberstrasse areas. Down Peterstrasse, past a variety of attractive buildings, lies the remarkable **Kaiserpfalz**, built in the early eleventh century; much of the interior (daily 10am–4/5pm; €4.50) is occupied by the vast Reichssaal, decorated with romantic depictions of the emperors. Below, a car park fills the former site of the **Dom**, pulled down in 1822 due to lack of funds for restoration: only the entrance hall with its facade of thirteenth-century statues survived. A ten-minute walk northwest of Marktplatz brings you to the **Mönchehaus Museum** (Tues–Sat 10am–5pm, Sun 10am–1pm; €3; ⊛www .moenchehaus.de). A black-and-white half-timbered building over 450 years old, it's the curious home to Goslar's modern art collection which includes a Joseph Beuys room. East of here, the **Jakobikirche** contains a moving *Pietà* by the great but elusive sixteenth-century sculptor, Hans Witten, while to the north, the early thirteenth-century **Neuwerkkirche** (Mon–Fri 10am–noon & 2.30–4.30pm, Sat & Sun 2.30–4.30pm; free) is dominated by its two striking polygonal towers.

Goslar's **tourist office** is at Marktplatz 7 (Mon–Fri 9.15am–5/6pm, Sat 9.30am–2/4pm, Sun 9.30am–2pm; Nov–April closed Sun; ☏053 21/78 060, ⓦwww.goslarinfo.de). A few minutes' walk from the **train station** at the northern end of town is the excellent *Gästehaus Möller*, Schieferweg 6 (☏05321/23 098; ❹). The quaint HI **hostel**, Rammelsberger Str. 25 (☏053 21/22 240; €15.90), is twenty minutes' walk southwest from the centre. The eighteenth-century *Zur Börse*, Bergstr. 53 (☏05321/34 510, ⓦwww.hotel-boerse-goslar.de; ❹), is one of the prettiest **hotels**. Marktplatz is a good place to pick up **snacks** of sausages and fish rolls on market mornings (Tues & Fri). For **restaurants**, try *Köpi am Markt*, Worthstr. 10, which does salads and steaks; *Worthmühle*, Worthstr. 4, good for provincial cooking; or, almost opposite the Rathaus at Marktkirchhof 3, *Butterhanne*, serving coffee and cakes as well as full meals.

# Central Germany

**Central Germany** is the most populous region of the country and home to the zone of heaviest industrialization – the Ruhrgebiet. Within this conurbation, **Cologne** stands out, managing to preserve many of the splendours of its long centuries as a free state. Neighbouring **Bonn** is another historic city, renowned for being the birthplace of Beethoven. The other city of historical interest is **Aachen**, the original capital of the Holy Roman Empire. To the south the Rhineland-Palatinate is the land of the national epic, of the alluring Lorelei, of robber barons and of the traders who used the river routes to make the country rich. Nowadays pleasure cruisers run through the **Rhine Gorge**, past a wonderful landscape of rocks, vines, white-painted towns and ruined castles. Industry exists only in isolated pockets, and **Mainz**, the state capital, only just ranks among the forty largest cities in Germany. Its monuments, though, merit more than a passing glance, while **Trier** preserves the finest buildings of classical antiquity this side of the Alps. In the province of Hesse, dynamic **Frankfurt** dominates, with its banking and communications industries providing the region's real economic base.

## Cologne (Köln)

**COLOGNE** (Köln) has a population of just over a million, and its huge Gothic Dom is the country's most visited monument. Try and coincide your visit with the annual **carnival** in early spring – Cologne boasts the largest street parties in Germany and the entire city does little but celebrate for a full three days. In a similar vein, the city ranks high as a **beer** centre, with several breweries producing the distinctive **Kölsch**. Another good time to visit is during the **Christmas market**, which attracts visitors from all over Europe.

Founded by the Romans in 33 BC, Cologne acquired the relics of the Three Magi from Milan in the twelfth century, increasing its standing as one of the greatest centres of pilgrimage in northern Europe. Situated on the intersection of the Rhine and several major trade routes, medieval Cologne became immensely rich – and the largest city in Germany. Later decline was partially reversed in the eighteenth century with the exploitation of an Italian recipe for distilling flower blossoms into almost pure alcohol. Originally created as an aphrodisiac, it was marketed here as a toilet water, achieving worldwide fame as **eau de Cologne**.

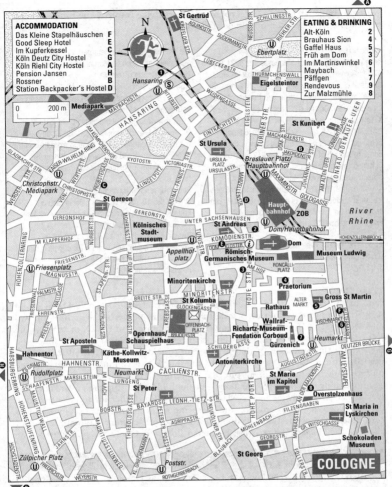

### Arrival, information and accommodation

The main train station, the **Hauptbahnhof**, is immediately below the Dom; directly behind is the **bus station** – take exit Breslauer Platz. Coming from the **airport**, bus #170 runs from both terminals (every 12min; 20min; €5) to the Hauptbahnhof, or take the train line S13 (terminal 2; every 20min; 20min; €2). The **tourist office**, Unter Fettenhennen 19, in front of the Dom (Mon–Sat 9am–9/10pm, Sun 10am–6pm; ☎0221/22 13 04 00, ⍟www.koeln.de), publishes a monthly guide to what's on, *Köln-Im* (€1). Far better are *Kölner Illustrierte* (€1) and *Stadt Revue* (€2), both available at newsagents. The **public transport** network is a mixture of buses and trams, the latter becoming the U-Bahn around the centre. Fares can be complicated, and it makes sense to buy a pass if you plan to make use of the system (€5.70 for 1 day) or the **Welcome Card** (€9/19 for 1/3 days), which also covers entrance to some sights. **Accommodation** is mainly geared to trade fairs. For a hotel room, the best advice is to pay the tourist office's €3 search fee; they often offer special discounts.

### Hostels

**Köln Deutz City Hostel** Siegesstr. 5 ☏0221/81 47 11, ⌨www.jugendherberge.de/jh/koeln-deutz. HI hostel close to Deutz station, directly across the Rhine from the Altstadt. Large and functional with little character. Dorms €23, rooms ❹

**Köln Riehl City Hostel** An der Schanz 14 ☏0221/76 70 81, ⌨www.koeln-riehl.jugendher berge.de. Large HI hostel tucked away in the quiet northern suburb of Riehl; U-Bahn #17 or #19 to Boltensternstrasse. Dorms €22.20, rooms ❹

**Station Backpacker's Hostel** Marzellenstr. 44–48 ☏0221/91 25 301, ⌨www.hostel-cologne .de. Best choice in town is this large, privately run hostel with an excellent central location, kitchen and free-internet. Dorms €16, rooms ❸

### Hotels and pensions

**Das Kleine Stapelhäuschen** Fischmarkt 1–3 ☏0221/25 77 862, ⌨www.koeln-altstadt .de/stapelhaeuschen. Characterful hotel/restaurant very near the Gross St Martin. Rooms overlooking the river are the nicest. ❺

**Good Sleep Hotel** Komödienstr. 19–21 ☏0221/25 72 257, ⌨www.goodsleep.de. Clean and friendly with good central location. ❹

**Im Kupferkessel** Probsteigasse 6 ☏0221/27 07 96 0, ⌨www.im-kupferkessel.de. Good-value rooms in a location just far enough from the centre to be peaceful. Head up Dompropst-Ketzer-Str. from the Dom; Probsteigasse is a road on the right. ❺

**Pension Jansen** Richard-Wagner-Str. 18 ☏0221/25 18 75, ⌨www.pensionjansen.de. Friendly, simple six-room pension; all rooms have TV. Rudolfplatz U-Bahn. ❹

**Rossner** Jakordenstr. 19 ☏0221/12 27 03. Homely and clean, and looking exactly as it must have in the 1950s, this is the pick of the cluster of hotels behind the station. ❸

## The City

One of the largest Gothic buildings ever constructed, Cologne's **Dom** (daily 6am–7.30pm; free) is built on a scale that reflects its power – the archbishop was one of the seven Electors of the Holy Roman Empire, and the Dom remains the seat of the Primate of Germany. The chancel was completed in 1322, but then the extravagant ambition of the plans began to take its toll. In 1560 the project was abandoned, to be resumed only in the nineteenth century, so what you see today is an act of homage from one age to another. From the west door your eye is immediately drawn down the length of the building to the high altar, with the spectacular golden shrine to the Magi, made in 1181. Other masterpieces include the ninth-century Gero crucifix, the most important monumental sculpture of its period, and the greatest achievement of the fifteenth-century Cologne school of painters, the *Adoration of the Magi* by Stefan Lochner. Climb the 509 steps to the

---

### Cologne's carnival

Though Cologne's **carnival** actually begins as early as November 11, the real business starts with Weiberfastnacht on the Thursday prior to the seventh Sunday before Easter. A ceremony at 10am in the Alter Markt leads to the official inauguration of the festival, with the mayor handing over the keys of the city to Prinz Carnival, who assumes command for the duration. At 3pm there's the first of the great processions and in the evening the series of costume balls begins – with singing and dancing in the streets and taverns as an alternative. On the Saturday morning there's the Funk-enbiwak, featuring the Rote und Blaue Funken: men who, dressed up in eighteenth-century military outfits, disobey every order. On Sunday the Schul- und Veedleszög, largely featuring children, forms a prelude to the more spectacular Rosenmontagzug (Rose Monday Parade). After this, the festival runs down, but there are numerous smaller parades in the suburbs on Shrove Tuesday, while the restaurants offer special fish menus on Ash Wednesday. The grandstand seats along the route are expensive for the Rose Monday Parade but good value on the Sunday. However, it's free, and certainly more fun, simply to mingle with the crowds.

top of the south tower for a breathtaking panorama over the city and the Rhine (daily 9am–5pm; €2). The **Domschatzkammer** (daily 10am–6pm; €4, joint ticket with tower €5) in the cellars, entered from the north side of the building, contains a stunning array of treasury items, the original sculptures from the medieval south portal and items excavated from Merovingian royal graves.

In a modern building next to the Dom, the outstanding **Museum Ludwig** (Tues–Sun 10am–6pm; €7.50; ⊛www.museenkoeln.de) is huge, and one of Germany's premier collections of modern art, particularly strong on the German Expressionists. Attached is the Agfa-Foto-Historama, which shows old photographic equipment and a selection of prints from the vast holdings of the local company. The neighbouring **Römisch-Germanisches Museum** (Tues–Sun 10am–5pm, Wed till 8pm; €6; ⊛www.museenkoeln.de) has a collection of Roman glass reckoned to be the world's finest, but of more general appeal is the dazzling array of jewellery on the first floor, mostly dating from the Dark Ages. Its star exhibit is the Dionysus Mosaic, the finest work of its kind in northern Europe, created for a patrician villa in about 200 AD.

For nearly 600 years, **Gross St Martin**'s tower, surrounded by four turrets, was the dominant feature of the Cologne skyline. From the cobbled **Alter Markt** just beyond, you can see the irregular octagonal tower of the **Rathaus**, a real fricassee of styles, the highlight being the graceful Renaissance loggia. Just in front of the entrance to the Rathaus, a steel and glass pyramid stands over the **Mikwe** (Mon–Thurs 7.30am–4pm, Fri 7.30am–2pm, Sat and Sun 11am–3pm; free). This is the only remnant of the Jewish ghetto, which was razed soon after the expulsion order of 1424. Proceeding south, you come to the strikingly angular **Wallraf-Richartz-Museum** (Tues–Sun 10/11am–6/8pm; €5.80; ⊛www .museenkoeln.de), whose holdings centre on the fifteenth-century Cologne school as well as a fine Impressionist collection. The gems of the display are the two large triptychs by the Master of St Bartholomew, from the school's final flowering at the beginning of the sixteenth century. Then go down Rheingasse to see the step-gabled **Overstolzenhaus**, the finest mansion in the city. Further south, on the banks of the Rhine, is the **Schokoladenmuseum** (Tues–Fri 10am–6pm, Sat & Sun 11am–7pm; €6; ⊛www.schokoladenmuseum.de), a thoroughly enjoyable museum focusing on the history and production of chocolate. Highlight is the "factory", with machines producing milk chocolate tablets, truffles and moulded animal shapes – don't miss the chocolate fountain where white-clad attendants hand out freshly created samples. The museum also has an excellent **café**.

## Eating, drinking and nightlife

Cologne crams over three thousand pubs, bars and cafés into a relatively small area. Their ubiquitous feature is the city's unique beer, **Kölsch**. Light and aromatically bitter, it's served in a small, thin glass (*Stange*), which holds only a fifth of a litre – hence its rather effete image among other German beer-drinkers. Best places to try it are the **Brauhäuser**, brewery-owned beer halls, which, although staffed by horribly matey waiters called *Köbes*, are definitely worth sampling, not least because they serve some of the cheapest and tastiest food in the city. **Nightlife** is concentrated in several distinct quarters. Gross St Martin in the Altstadt catches the tourists and businessmen, with the student area focusing on Zülpicher Strasse (in the southwest of the city), lined with cheap restaurants and lively bars, while the area south of Heumarkt has a handful of popular **gay and lesbian** bars.

### Beer halls and restaurants

**Alt-Köln** Trankgasse 7–9. Notable for both the intricate clock mechanism on the outside and the no-nonsense slabs of salmon steak served inside.

**Brauhaus Sion** Unter Taschenmacher 5. Fre-
quented mainly by locals, despite its proximity to the Dom; the menu concentrates on variations of *Wurst* and knuckles of pork leg.

**Früh am Dom** Am Hof 12–14. Located opposite the Dom, this heavily touristed *Brauhaus* serves excellent food.

Gaffel Haus Alter Markt 20–22. One of the most genuine old-style restaurants serving huge portions of schnitzel; much cosier than most beer halls.

Im Martinswinkel Fischmarkt 9. The cheapest and least touristy of the riverfront restaurants, serving salads and sausages, coffee and cake.

Maybach Maybachstr. 111. One of the best beer gardens in town, with a pleasant leafy courtyard lit by fairy lights at night. Hansaring U-Bahn.

Päffgen Friesenstr. 64–68. Less touristy than the places near the Dom with a younger clientele, and Kölsch brewed on the premises.

Rendevous Zülpicher Str. 11a. One of a handful of good-value Italian restaurants in this area. Big portions and a young, friendly crowd.

Zur Malzmühle Heumarkt 6. Traditional home-brew tavern that produces its own malty Malzmühlenkölsch. Few tourists and always popular.

### Bars and clubs

Apollo Hohenzollernring 79–83. On a road in the west of the city dotted with clubs, this one is spread over two floors and hosts mainly R&B, techno and disco nights.

Biermuseum Buttermarkt 39. Small bar tucked away near the river serving eighteen types of beer on tap and over fifty types of bottled beer.

Blue Note Brüsseler Str. 96. Trendy drum'n'bass and hip-hop club, catering to a young, studenty crowd – a few minutes west of Hohenzollernring.

Filmdose Zülpicher Str. 39. Fun pub that's packed with students enjoying a post-lecture Kölsch; it has a tiny cabaret stage and also shows films in English. All-day breakfasts.

Gebaude 9 Deutz-Mühlheimer-Str. 127–129. Intimate bar, club and theatre hall where events and exhibitions take place, as well as drum' n'bass/live gigs.

Opera Alteburger Str. 1. Brightly coloured, youth-oriented place, in the south of the city, with daily specialities on the menu.

Quo Vadis Vor St Martin 8–10. Cosy gay bar between Neumarkt and Heumarkt serving light meals. Hosts popular Eighties themed nights.

Roxy Aachener Str. 2. Midnight until 7am, this is the place to hit at the end of the night. Two bars, one packed dance floor and an eclectic music mix.

Schmelztiegel Luxemburger Str. 34. Located in a former pharmacy, the relaxed "melting pot" now offers eleven varieties of Kölsch to combat most ailments. Tram #16, #18 or #19 to Barbarossaplatz.

Underground Vogelsanger Str. 200. Great for live gigs, especially rock and punk, the *Underground* has a big indie and alternative following. Free entry mid-week, and beer garden.

### Listings

Bike rental Rent-a-Bike and tours, Markmanns-gasse in the Altstadt ☏0221/72 36 27.
Hospital Alexianer Krankenhaus, Kölner Str. 64 ☏02203/91 700.
Internet Via Phone, Marzellenstr. 3–5.

Laundry Pantaleonsmühlengasse 42, in the south of the city near Barbarossaplatz.
Left luggage At the train station.
Pharmacy At the station & Neumarkt 2.
Post office At the station & Breite Str. 6.

# Bonn

**BONN**, Cologne's neighbour, served as West Germany's capital from 1949 until the unification of 1990, when Berlin was restored to its former status. Although Bonn's administrative role has diminished, it still remains an important cultural centre, and despite its provincial reputation it's a surprisingly interesting place to visit, not least for its superb museums – and for being the birthplace of Beethoven. The small **Altstadt** is now a pedestrianized shopping area centred on two spacious squares. The square to the east is named after the huge Romanesque **Münster**, whose central octagonal tower with its soaring spire is the city's most prominent landmark. The pink, chocolate-box Rococo **Rathaus** adds a touch of colour to the other square, the **Markt**, which still hosts a market every day except Sunday. A couple of minutes' walk north of here, at Bonngasse 20, is the **Beethoven-Haus** (Mon–Sat 10am–5/6pm, Sun 11am–5/6pm; €4; ⊕www.beethoven-haus-bonn .de), one of the few old buildings in the centre to have escaped wartime devastation. Beethoven served his musical apprenticeship at the Electoral court, but left the city for good at the age of 22, though this hasn't deterred Bonn from building up the best collection of memorabilia of its favourite son. To the east is the

Baroque **Schloss**, an enormously long construction that was formerly the seat of the Archbishop-Electors of Cologne and is now used by the university. Bonn's **government quarter**, a mile south of the centre, was saddled with a temporary status. As a result, nothing was custom-built, but rather government offices utilized existing buildings, such as the **Villa Hammerschmidt** and the **Palais Schaumburg** – they now serve as the second residences of the President and Chancellor respectively. The **Museumsmeile**, planned as a cultural accompaniment to the government quarter, is home to the **Kunstmuseum** (Tues–Sun 11am–6pm, Wed till 9pm; €3.50), with a fine Expressionism collection. Next door is the **Kunst- und Ausstellungshalle** (Tues–Sun 10am–7/9pm; €7; ⓦwww.bundeskunsthalle. de), a monumental postmodern arts centre for important temporary exhibitions.

Bonn **train station** lies in the middle of the city; just to the east is the **bus station**, whose local services, along with the trams (which become the U-Bahn in the city centre), form part of a system integrated with Cologne's. As the attractions are well spaced out, it's a good idea to buy a public transport pass (€5.70 for 1 day) or the **Welcome Card** (€9/14 for 1/2 days), which covers public transport plus some museum admission. You can get them from the **tourist office**, Windeckstr. 1 (Mon–Sat 9am–4/6.30pm, Sun 10am–2pm; ⓣ0228/77 50 00, ⓦwww.bonn.de). An HI **hostel** is at Haager Weg 42 (ⓣ0228/28 99 70, ⓦwww.bonn.jugendherberge. de; €21.50) in the suburb of Venusberg; take bus #621. Central **hotels** include the basic *Daufenbach*, Brüdergasse 6 (ⓣ0228/96 94 600; ❸), or the more homely *Deutsches Haus*, Kasernenstr. 19 (ⓣ0228/63 37 77, ⓦwww.deutscheshaus-bonn.de; ❺). For **places to eat** try *Cassius Garten*, Maximilianstr. 28d, which offers mouthwatering veggie choices, or *Em Höttche*, Markt 4, a traditional *Gaststätte* next to the Rathaus. Many of the best **bars** are in the Altstadt. *Brauhaus Bönnsch*, Sterntorbrücke 4, produces a distinctive blond ale and does good-value meals, while *Zebulon*, Stockenstr. 19, is a big favourite with arts students, particularly for breakfast.

## Aachen

**AACHEN** – bordering both Belgium and the Netherlands – was the hub in the eighth century of the great empire of Charlemagne, a choice made partly for strategic reasons but also because of the presence of hot springs. Exercising in these waters was one of the emperor's favourite pastimes and today a thriving industry is based around the health-enriching properties of these waters – see the tourist office for details. Aachen has a laid-back atmosphere that reflects its large student population, making it a good day-trip from Cologne, or stop-off point between countries.

Although the surviving architectural legacy of Charlemagne is small, Aachen retains its crowning jewel, the former **Palace chapel**. Now the heart of the **Dom** (daily 7am–7pm), the original octagon had to be enlarged by adding the Gothic chancel to accommodate the number of pilgrims that poured in. At the end of the chancel, the gilded shrine of Charlemagne, finished in 1215 after fifty years' work, contains the remains of the emperor, while in the gallery is the imperial throne, which you can only see on a tour (daily; €2.50). Next to the Dom, the **Schatzkammer** (Mon 10am–1pm, Tues, Wed & Fri–Sun 10am–6pm, Thurs 10am–9pm; €4) is a dazzling treasury and UNESCO World Heritage site. Highlights among its collections are the tenth-century Lothar Cross and a Roman sarcophagus once used as Charlemagne's coffin. The emperor's palace once extended across the Katschhof to the site of the fourteenth-century **Rathaus**, which incorporates two of the palace's towers and has a facade lined with the figures of fifty Holy Roman Emperors, 31 of whom were crowned in Aachen. The glory of the interior (daily 10am–1pm & 2–5pm; €2) is the much-restored Kaisersaal, repository of the crown jewels – in reproduction. The Rathaus fronts the expansive **Markt**, which boasts the finest medieval houses left in the city.

The centre is ten minutes from the **train station** – down Bahnhofstrasse then left into Theaterstrasse. The **tourist office** occupies the Atrium Elisenbrunnen on

Friedrich-Wilhelm-Platz (Mon–Fri 9am–6pm, Sat 9am–2pm; April–Dec also Sun 10am–2pm; ☏0241/18 02 960, ⊛www.aachen.de). The HI **hostel** is southwest of the centre, at Maria-Theresia-Allee 260 (☏0241/71 10 10, ⊛www.aachen .jugendherberge.de; dorms €21.50, rooms ❹); take bus #2 as far as Ronheide. The cheaper **hotels** are near the train station; try *Dura*, Lagerhausstr. 5 (☏0241/40 31 35; ❹), or *Marx*, Hubertusstr. 33–35 (☏0241/37 541, ⊛www.hotel-marx.de; ❺). A spiced gingerbread called Printen is the main local speciality, and the place to eat it is the old coffeehouse *Leo van den Daele*, Büchel 18. The most celebrated **bar/restaurant** is *Postwagen*, Markt 40, with a cheerful Baroque exterior and wonderful cramped rooms inside. The student quarter centres on Pontstrasse, which is lined with bars and cheap eateries. The bistro-style *Egmont* at no. 1 is a popular haunt, as is relaxed *Café Kittel*, at no. 37. *Labyrinth* at no. 156 is a large pub serving Greek-style food.

## Mainz and beyond

At the confluence of the Rhine and Main rivers, **MAINZ** is an agreeable mixture of old and new, with an attractive restored centre and a jovial populace – it's second only to Cologne in the carnival stakes. Ecclesiastical power aside, prestige came through Johannes Gutenberg, who revolutionized the art of printing here. Rearing high above the centre of Mainz is the **Dom** (April–Sept Mon–Fri 9am–6.30pm, Sat 9am–4pm, Sun 12.45–3pm & 4–6.30pm; Oct–March Mon–Fri 9am–5pm, Sat 9am–4pm, Sun 12.45–3pm & 4–5pm; free), crowded in by eighteenth-century houses. Choirs at both ends of the building indicate its status as an imperial cathedral, with one area for the emperor and one for the clergy. Visit the spacious **Markt**, with its riotously colourful fountain, when it's packed with market stalls (Tues, Fri & Sat mornings). Dominating the adjoining Liebfrauenplatz is the **Gutenberg Museum** (Tues–Sat 9am–5pm, Sun 11am–3pm; €3.50; ⊛www.gutenberg.de) – a fitting tribute to one of the greatest inventors of all time, whose pioneering development of movable type led to the mass-scale production of books. In 1978, the museum acquired the last Gutenberg Bible still in private hands – made in the 1450s, it's one of only forty-odd surviving examples. Across Schöfferstrasse from the Dom, Ludwigstrasse runs to Schillerplatz and Schillerstrasse, both lined with Renaissance and Baroque palaces. Up the hill by Gaustrasse is the Gothic **St Stephan** (Mon–Sat 10am–noon & 2–5pm; free), whose priest persuaded Marc Chagall to make a series of atmospheric stained-glass windows. Symbolizing the reconciliation between France and Germany, Christian and Jew, the nine windows were finished in 1984, a few months before the artist's death.

The **train station** is northwest of the city centre, while the **tourist office** (Mon–Fri 9am–6pm, Sat 10am–3pm; ☏061 31/28 62 10, ⊛www.info-mainz .de) is in the Brückenturm am Rathaus at the corner of Rheinstrasse. Near the station are some of the least expensive **hotels**; try the *Terminus*, Alicenstr. 4 (☏061 31/22 98 76, ⊛www.hotel-terminus-mainz.de; ❺), which has en-suite rooms. *Stadt Coblenz*, Rheinstr. 49 (☏061 31/22 76 02; ❹), is more conveniently located near the Dom, though the rooms suffer from street noise. The HI **hostel** at Otto-Brunfels-Schneise 4 (☏061 31/85 332; €17.50; buses #62 & #63) is in the wooded heights of Am Fort Weisenau. Mainz boasts more **vineyards** than any other German city; some *Weinstuben* (wine bars) are open in the evenings only, such as the oldest, *Alt Deutsche Weinstube*, Liebfrauenplatz 7, which offers cheap daily dishes. Even better **food** is available at *Weinhaus Schreiner*, Rheinstr. 38 (closed Sat night & Sun); *Am Fischtor*, Fischtorstr. 1, although rather dark, is also worth a try. Mainz also has an excellent home-brew **pub**, *Eisgrub-Bräu*, Weissliliengasse 1a, which serves inexpensive buffet lunches. *Havana*, below the *Stadt Coblenz* hotel at Rheinstr. 49, is a Cuban/Mexican bar and restaurant which gets packed out at weekends.

# The Rhine Gorge to Koblenz

North of Mainz, the Rhine bends westwards and continues undramatically until **BINGEN**, where it widens and swings north into the spectacular 80km **Rhine Gorge**. This waterway has become one of Europe's major tourist magnets, but the pleasure steamers are still outnumbered by commercial barges – a reminder of the river's crucial role in the German economy. Spring and autumn are the best times to visit, since in summer inexpensive accommodation is scarce and heavily booked. Rail and road lines lie on each side of the river and, although there are no bridges between Bingen and Koblenz, there are fairly frequent ferries, enabling you to hop from one bank to the other. However, it's undeniably most fun to travel by boat. Some **river cruises** (mainly April–Oct) depart from Mainz, where there's a K-D Line office (T061 31/23 28 00, Wwww.k-d.com), although more regular through-services start from Bingen. The full one-way boat fare from Bingen to Koblenz is €23.20 (takes 3hr 40min) – though Eurail is valid and other rail passes attract a discount; two cyclists travel for the price of one on Tuesdays.

At **BACHARACH**, 10km downstream from Bingen, the chunky castle of Burg Stahleck houses an HI **hostel** (T06743/12 66; €21.40) – it's a steep climb up the hill to get there, but the views are worth it – and there's a **campsite** at Strandbadweg. From **KAUB**, a few kilometres on, you get a great view of the appealing **Pfalz**, a white-walled toll fortress standing on an island that has become a famous Rhineland symbol (Tues–Sun 9am–1pm & 2–5/6pm; €3.60 including ferry). The most famous point along the Rhine is the **Lorelei**, a much-photographed rocky projection a little downstream from Kaub, where, legend has it, a blonde woman would lure passing mariners to their doom with her siren song. The rock can also be spotted from trains heading between Mainz and Koblenz, since the track runs right along the banks of the Rhine as it passes through the gorge.

Quiet **KOBLENZ** stands where the Rhine and Mosel meet. The centre is at its most appealing in the area around the confluence at **Deutsches Eck**, which is also home to the giant **Monument of German Unity**, built as homage to Kaiser Wilhelm I for uniting a divided nation. More commanding sights are across the Rhine in the district of **Ehrenbreitstein**, overshadowed by the **Festung**. One of the largest fortresses in the world, it's now home to the **Landesmuseum Koblenz** (mid-March to Nov Tues–Sun 10.30am–5pm; €2.50) and one of the best **hostels** in Germany (T0261/97 28 70, Wwww.jugendherberge.de; €21.40). The Festung and hostel can be reached by chairlift (€5.80 return; check with the tourist office for operating times) or a 1.5-kilometre walk. Koblenz's main **tourist office** (Mon–Fri 9am–6/8pm, Sat & Sun 10am–4/6/8pm; T0261/30 38 80, Wwww.koblenz.de) is opposite the **train** and **bus stations**, a little southwest of the centre. **Hotel** rooms are reasonably priced: try *Sessellift*, Obertal 22, near the Festung – take bus #9 or #10 (T0261/7 52 56; ❸); or the more central *Jan van Werth*, Van-Werth-Str. 9 (T0261/3 65 00; ❸). The **campsite** (T0261/82 719; April to mid-Oct) is opposite Deutsches Eck; a ferry crosses the Mosel here in summer, while another crosses the Rhine further south.

# Trier

Birthplace of Karl Marx and the oldest city in Germany, **TRIER** was once the capital of the western Roman Empire. Nowadays, it has the less exalted role of regional centre for the upper Mosel valley, its relaxed air a world away from the status it formerly held. Despite a turbulent history, an amazing amount of the city's past has been preserved, in particular the most impressive group of Roman monuments north of the Alps.

The centre corresponds roughly to the Roman city and can easily be covered on foot. From the train station, it's a few minutes' walk down Theodor-Heuss-Allee to the **Porta Nigra**, northern gateway to Roman Trier. Nearby, housed in a former monastery, is the **Städtisches Museum Simeonstift** – closed until early 2007 – which contains medieval sculptures and a good ancient Egyptian and Roman section. From here, Simeonstrasse runs down to the **Hauptmarkt**, a busy pedestrian shopping area, with stalls selling fruit and flowers. At the southern end of the Hauptmarkt a Baroque portal leads to the Gothic **St Gangolf**, built by the burghers of Trier in an attempt to aggravate the archbishops, whose political power they resented. Up Sternstrasse from the Hauptmarkt is the magnificent Romanesque **Dom** (6.30am–5.30/6pm; free) on the site of an original built in the fourth century for Emperor Constantine. The present building dates from 1030, and the facade has not changed significantly since then. Inside, the **Schatzkammer** (Mon–Sat 10/11am–4/5pm; Sun 2–4/5pm; €1.50) has many examples of the work of local goldsmiths, notably a tenth-century portable altar. From here, Liebfrauenstrasse goes past the ritzy **Palais Kesselstadt** to the **Konstantinbasilika**. Built as Constantine's throne hall, its dimensions are awe-inspiring: 30m high and 75m long, it is completely self-supporting. It became a church for the local Protestant community in the nineteenth century. Next door, the **Rokoko-Palais der Kurfürsten** was built in 1756 for an archbishop who felt that the adjoining old Schloss wasn't good enough for him. Its pink facade overlooks the Palastgarten, setting for the **Rheinisches Landesmuseum** (daily 9.30/10am–5pm; Nov–April closed Mon; €5.50). Easily the best of Trier's museums, its collection brings to life the sophistication and complexity of Roman civilization; prize exhibit is the Neumagener Weinschiff, a Roman sculpture of a wine ship. A few minutes further south, the **Kaiserthermen** (daily 9am–4/5/6pm) was once one of the largest bath complexes in the Roman world. The extensive underground heating system has survived, and you can walk around the service channels and passages. From here, the route to the **Amphitheatre** (daily 9/10am–4/5/6pm), oldest of Trier's surviving Roman buildings, is well signposted.

Trier's **tourist office**, An der Porta Nigra (Mon–Sat 9/10am–5/7pm, Sun 10am–1/5pm; ☎0651/97 80 80, ⊛www.trier.de), sells the **Trier-Card** (€9/3 days), which covers entrance to the museums and other discounts. There's homely *Hille's* **hostel** at Gartenfeldstr. 7 (☎0651/710 27 85, ⊛www.hilles-hostel-trier.de; dorms €15, rooms ❸), providing a clean and sociable base for travellers. *Warsberger Hof*, Dietrichstr. 42 (☎0651/97 52 50, ⊛www.warsberger-hof.de; ❸), is the best-value **hotel**, with dorms from €19 as well as rooms, and it's ideally situated in the Altstadt. Another to try is *Hotel Handelshof* on Lorenz-Kellner-Str. 1 (☎0651/73 933; ❹). There's a **campsite**, *Trier City*, Luxemburger Str. 81 (☎0651/82 00 911; closed Dec & Jan), on the western bank of the Mosel. It's easy to get good and inexpensive **food** thanks to the student population: the best bet is *Astarix*, Karl-Marx-Str. 11, a relaxed student bar; or *Zum Domstein*, Hauptmarkt 5, whose eclectic menu includes dishes from the only remaining Roman cookbook. Among the many possibilities for tasting the local wines is the late-opening, prestigious **bar**, *Weinstube Palais Kesselstatt*, at Liebfrauenstr. 10. The bright and breezy *InFlagranti*, Viehmarkt 14, is a student favourite serving food, while *Forum*, Hindenburgstr. 4, is an invariably packed café/bar/club.

# Frankfurt

Straddling the River Main just before it meets the Rhine, **FRANKFURT AM MAIN** (usually abbreviated to just Frankfurt) is a city with two faces. The cut-throat financial capital of Germany, with its fulcrum in the Westend district, it's also a civilized place that spends more per year on the arts than any other city in Europe. It has one of the best ranges of museums in the country, and some excellent (if expensive) nightlife. Over half of the city, including almost all the centre, was destroyed during the war and the rebuilders opted for innovation rather than restoration, resulting in an architecturally mixed skyline – half intimidating sky-scrapers, half sweetly Germanic red-brick buildings.

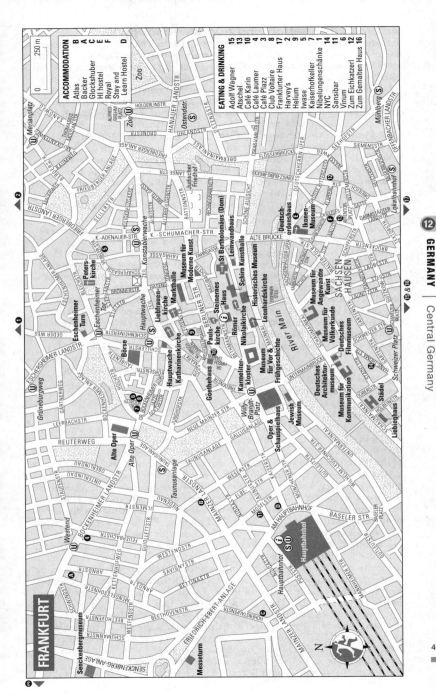

# FRANKFURT

## ACCOMMODATION
| | |
|---|---|
| Atlas | B |
| Backer | A |
| Glockshuber | C |
| HI hostel | E |
| Royal | F |
| Stay and Learn Hostel | D |

## EATING & DRINKING
| | |
|---|---|
| Adolf Wagner | 15 |
| Atschel | 13 |
| Café Karin | 10 |
| Café Laumer | 4 |
| Café Plazz | 3 |
| Club Voltaire | 8 |
| Frankfurter Haus | 17 |
| Harvey's | 2 |
| Heilom | 9 |
| Iwase | 5 |
| Kaiserhofkeller | 7 |
| Nibelungenschänke | 11 |
| NYC | 14 |
| Sansibar | 6 |
| Vinum | 12 |
| Zum Eichkatzerl | 12 |
| Zum Gemalten Haus | 16 |

## Arrival, information and accommodation

Frankfurt **airport** has regular rail links to most German cities, with a frequent service (every 15min; 11min; €2) to the main **train station**. The airport is also linked to the train station by two S-Bahn lines, run by the regional transport company (RMV). Local transport ticket prices vary according to the time of travel, making it better to invest in the one-day ticket (€4.80) or the **Frankfurt Card** (€7.80/11.50 for 1/2 days), which can be bought from tourist offices and allows travel throughout the city, plus reduced entry charges to most museums. From the Hauptbahnhof it's a fifteen-minute walk to the centre, or take U-Bahn line #4 or #5, or tram #11. There are two main **tourist offices**: in the train station (Mon–Fri 8am–9pm, Sat & Sun 9am–6pm; ☎069/21 23 88 00, ✆www.frankfurt-tourismus.de), and at Römerberg 27 (9.30am–4/5.30pm). Free listings magazines, *Fritz* and *Strandgut*, are available at both, although *Prinz* (€3), from newsagents, is more comprehensive.

**Accommodation** is pricey, thanks to the expense-account clientele. Most reasonably priced options are in the sleazy environs of the train station, close to the Kaiserstrasse red-light district. For a €3 fee the tourist office will book a room.

### Hostel

**HI hostel** Deutschherrnufer 12, Sachsenhausen ☎069/61 00 150, ✆www.jugendherberge -frankfurt.de. Around 470 places in dorms of up to twelve beds each. Internet, café and 2am curfew. Bus #46 from the train station – in the evenings take tram #16 to Lokalbahnhof. Dorms €18, rooms ❹
**Stay and Learn Hostel** Kaiserstr. 74 ☎069 25 39 52, ✆www.room-frankfurt.de. The best budget option in town; fabulously central with clean dorms, Internet and common room/kitchen. €20

### Hotels

**Atlas** Zimmerweg 1 ☎069/72 39 46, ✆www .hotel-atlas-frankfurt.de. Friendly place with bright, airy rooms close to the station but away from the sleazy side of things. ❺
**Backer** Mendelssohnstr. 92 ☎069/74 79 92. Clean and close to the university, although use of the showers costs €2 a time. U-Bahn line #6 or #7 to Westend. ❸
**Glockshuber** Mainzer Landstr. 120 ☎069/74 26 28, ✉glockshuber@t-online.de. Pleasant budget hotel just north of the train station, away from the sleazier streets. ❹
**Royal** Wallstr. 17 ☎069/62 30 26. Good-value hotel in the heart of Sachsenhausen, close to some of the well-known apple-wine taverns. ❺

## The City

The city centre is defined by the old city walls, now transformed into a semicircular stretch of public gardens. **Römerberg** is the historical and geographical centre. Charlemagne built his fort on this low hill to protect the original *frankonovurd* (Ford of the Franks), but the whole quarter was flattened by bombing in 1944. The most significant survivor was the thirteenth-century St Bartholomäus or **Dom**, and even that emerged with only its main walls intact. To the right of the choir is the restored Wahlkapelle, where the seven Electors used to make their final choice of Holy Roman Emperor. To the north, in Domstrasse, is the **Museum für Moderne Kunst** (Tues–Sun 10am–5pm, Wed till 8pm; €6; ✆www.mmk-frankfurt .de), a three-storey affair featuring major modern artists and innovative temporary exhibitions. At the opposite end of the Römerberg is the **Römer**, formerly the Rathaus. The **Imperial Hall** (Kaisersaal; daily 10am–1pm & 2–5pm; €2), with its distinctive facade of triple-stepped gables, has recently been restored and fronts the Römerplatz market square, home to a twinkling **Christmas Market** in December. The **Saalhof**, an amalgamation of imperial buildings now housing the **Historisches Museum**, (Tues, Thurs, Fri & Sun 10am–5pm, Wed 4–8pm, Sat 1–5pm; €4; ✆www.historisches-museum.frankfurt.de), is nearby on Mainkai, overlooking the river. Its twelfth-century chapel is all that remains of the palace complex, which grew up in the Middle Ages. The museum contains a good local history collection, with an eye-opening section on the devastation caused by the bombing. A short distance to the west, on Untermainkai, is the **Jewish Museum** (Jüdisches Museum; Tues–Sun 10am–5pm, Wed till 8pm; €2.60; ✆www.juedischesmuseum.de), providing an interesting look at the city's Jewish community, which lost 10,000 people to the Nazis.

A little to the northwest of the **Hauptwache** (originally a guard house, now a café close to the main shopping area), near the Börse, Frankfurt's stock exchange, are two of the most expensive shopping streets in the city: **Goethestrasse** is all expensive jewellers and designer clothes shops, while **Grosse Bockenheimer Strasse** is home to upmarket delicatessens and smarter restaurants. This area is characterized by gleaming skyscrapers; the **Mainturm** (daily 10am–7/9pm; €4.50) admits the public to its outside viewing platform on the 56th floor, for some unparalleled vistas.

For a laid-back evening out, head for **Sachsenhausen**, the city-within-a-city on the south bank of the Main. The network of streets around Affentorplatz is home to the famous apple-wine (*Ebbelwei*) houses, while on Schaumainkai – also known as **Museumsufer** – the Saturday **flea market** is worth a browse. Museumsufer is also lined with excellent museums, pick of the bunch being the **Städel**, located at no. 63 (Tues–Sun 10am–5pm, Wed & Thurs till 9pm; €6; ⍾www.staedelmuseum .de), one of the most comprehensive art galleries in Europe. All the big names in German art are represented, including Dürer, both Holbeins, Cranach and Altdorfer. The **Deutsches Filmmuseum**, at no. 41 (Tues–Sun 10am–5pm, Wed till 8pm, Sat 2–8pm; €2.50; ⍾www.deutsches-filmmuseum.de), has its own cinema and is a popular spot for foreign films and art house-screenings. The **Deutsches Architekturmuseum**, no. 43 (Tues & Thurs–Sun 10am–5pm, Wed till 8pm; €4; ⍾www.archaeologisches-museum.frankfurt.de), is also worth a visit, installed in an avant-garde conversion of a nineteenth-century villa; the highpoint is the "house within a house" which dominates the museum like an oversized dolls' house.

## Eating, drinking and nightlife

Frankfurt has a wealth of gastronomic possibilities. One of its best-known locales is Kleine Bockenheimer Strasse, aka Jazzgasse, the centre of Frankfurt's jazz scene; while the trendiest bars and clubs can be found around the Salzhaus in the centre, in the Westend district, or the Ostend, around Hanauer Landstrasse.

### Apple-wine taverns

**Adolf Wagner** Schweizer Str. 71, Sachsenhausen. One of the best of the taverns, with a lively clientele of all ages and a cosy garden terrace.

**Atschel** Wallstr. 7. This place offers a more extensive menu than many of its counterparts, and has bargain set lunches. Closed Mon.

**Zum Eichkatzerl** Dreieichstr. 29, Sachsenhausen. An excellent, traditional tavern with a large courtyard and low-priced food. Closed Mon.

**Zum Gemalten Haus** Schweizer Str. 67, Sachsenhausen. A bit kitsch with its oil-painted facade and stained-glass windows, but quite intimate and lively, with long rows of tables outside. Closed Mon & Tues.

### Bars and cafés

**Café Karin** Grosser Hirschgraben 28. Frankfurt institution that's friendly, unpretentious and well worth a visit. Breakfast all day and bistro/bar in the evenings.

**Café Laumer** Bockenheimer Landstr. 67. One of Frankfurt's oldest cafés, halfway up the Westend's main thoroughfare. The all-day breakfasts are a true indulgence.

**Club Voltaire** Kleine Hochstr. 5. Tasty, good food with a Spanish bias, and an eclectic clientele. Frequent events include musical improvisation evenings and political debates. From 6pm.

**Harvey's** Bornheimer Landstr. 64. Slick, high-ceilinged colonnaded bar in an appealing end-of-terrace building, in the northeast of the city, which in the evening hosts a mainly gay and lesbian crowd.

**Helium** Bleidenstr. 7. High-quality world cuisine served to a well-heeled crowd in this fashionable bar. Also popular for after-work drinks.

**Kaiserhofkeller** Kaiserhofstr.18. Buzzing underground beerhall that's popular with all ages for its good-value food.

**NYC** Hans-Thoma-Str. 1. Funky café/bar with tasty pancakes, a young crowd and outside tables.

**Sansibar** Taunustor 2. Arabic-styled rooftop bar offering great views and cocktails.

### Restaurants

**Café Plazz** Kirchplatz 8. Stupendous selection of drinks and generous portions of food, including delicious home-made cakes. Inviting atmosphere. U-Bahn Kirchplatz.

**Frankfurter Haus** Darmstädter Landstr. 741. Old-style restaurant serving typical Frankfurt dishes such as *Grüne Sosse* (a green sauce made with at least five types of fresh herbs, served with egg and potatoes) and *Handkäs mit Musik* (a strong cheese smothered with chopped onions, vinegar and oil). In the southern part of the Sachsenhausen.

**Iwase** Vilbeler Str. 31. Reasonably priced Japanese place, with seating at the counter or the few tables. Closed Sun.

**Nibelungenschänke** Nibelungenallee 55. Typical Greek food at very reasonable prices. Attracts a young crowd and is usually open till 2am. Nibelungenallee/Deutsche Bibliothek U-Bahn.

**Vinum** Kleine Hochstr. 9. Rustic wine cellar with local range of wines to try. Slightly pricey food but in the heart of Frankfurt.

### Clubs and live music

**190east** Hanauer Landstr. 190. Top club in Frankfurt's latest hip area. Packed out at weekends, with excellent house, techno and funk nights.

**Batschkapp** Maybachstr. 24. Grimy, sweaty venue for top-rank indie bands – avoid the school-age club nights though. S-Bahn #6 to Eschersheim.

**Brotfabrik** Bachmannstr. 2–4. One of the city's fading stars, featuring live and dance music, plus occasional salsa nights. Fischstein/Grosse Nelkenstrasse U-Bahn.

**Cooky's** Am Salzhaus 4. Hip-hop, house and soul club, north of Berliner Strasse, hosting popular DJ nights plus occasional live acts.

**Jazzkeller** Kleine Bockenheimer Str. 18a. This atmospheric cellar is Frankfurt's premier jazz venue. Often closed Sun.

**U60311** Rossmarkt Unterführung. Long-standing favourite and one of the best techno clubs in town. Be prepared to queue. Hauptwache U-Bahn.

**Unity** Hanauer Landstr. 2. Intimate, crowded and fun club, playing house music daily until 5am. Zoo U-Bahn.

### Listings

**Bike rental** Per Pedale, Leipziger Str. 4 ☎069/70 76 91 10.

**Consulates** UK, Bockenheimer Landstr. 42 ☎069 /17 00 020; US, Siesmayerstr. 21 ☎069/75 350.

**Hospital** Bürgerhospital, Nibelungenallee 37–41 ☎069/15 000.

**Laundry** Wash World, Moselstr. 17 (east of the Hauptbahnhof).

**Left luggage** At the train station.

**Pharmacy** At the train station.

**Post office** Goetheplatz 2–4.

# Southern Germany

The southwestern province of **Baden-Württemberg** is the most prosperous part of the country. The motor car was invented here in the late nineteenth century, and the region has stayed at the forefront of world technology ever since, with **Stuttgart** still the home of Daimler-Chrysler and Porsche. Germany's most famous university city, **Heidelberg**, is here, and the spa resort of **Baden-Baden** remains wonderfully evocative of its nineteenth-century heyday as the playground of Europe's aristocracy. The scenery is wonderful too: its western and southern boundaries are defined by the Rhine and its bulge into Germany's largest lake, the **Bodensee** (Lake Constance). Within the curve of the river lies the **Black Forest**, source of another of the continent's principal waterways, the Danube.

**Bavaria** (Bayern), which occupies the whole southeastern chunk of the country out to the Austrian and Czech frontiers, is the home of all the German clichés: beer-swilling men in *Lederhosen*, sausage-dogs, sauerkraut and *Wurst*. But that's only a small part of the picture, and almost entirely restricted to the Alpine region south of the magnificent state capital, **Munich**. In the western parts, around pristine **Augsburg**, the food is less pork and sausage and more pasta and sauce, and the landscape gentle farming country ideal for camping and cycling holidays. To the north lies **Nuremberg**, centre of a region of vineyards and nature parks. Eastern Bavaria – apart from its capital **Regensburg** – is relatively poor; life in its highland forests revolves around logging and workshop industries such as glass production. One practical note: travellers over the age of 27 are barred from using Bavarian hostels, although you'll almost always be able to find a reasonable alternative.

# Heidelberg

Home to Germany's oldest university, **HEIDELBERG** is majestically set on the banks of the swift-flowing Neckar, 70km south of Frankfurt. For two centuries, it has seduced travellers like no other German city. Centrepiece is the Schloss, a compendium of magnificent buildings, somehow increased in stature by their ruined condition. The rest of the city has some good museums, but the main appeal is its picturesque cobbled streets, crammed with old-style eateries and student pubs. In spring and early summer, the streets hum with activity and late-night parties – by July and August, most students have left, only to be replaced by swarms of tourists.

The dominating **Schloss** can be reached from the Kornmarkt by funicular (€5 return), which continues to the Königstuhl viewpoint; you can also walk up in ten minutes via the Burgweg. At the southeastern corner is the most romantic of the ruins, the Gesprengter Turm; a collapsed section lies intact in the moat, leaving a clear view into the interior. The **Schlosshof** (daily 8am–6pm; €3) holds a group of Renaissance palaces that now contain the diverting Pharmacy Museum and the Grosses Fass, an eighteenth-century wine-barrel capable of holding 220,000 litres. The finest building is the swaggering **Friedrichsbau** (tours only; in English hourly April–Oct 10.15am–4.15pm; Nov–March 11.15am–12.15pm & 2.15–4.15pm; €3.50), which supports a pantheon of the House of Wittelsbach. The original statues can be seen inside, along with a number of restored rooms that have been decked out in period style.

The **Altstadt**'s finest surviving buildings are grouped around the sandstone **Heiliggeistkirche** on Marktplatz. Note the tiny shopping booths between its buttresses, a feature ever since the church was built. The striking Baroque **Alte Brücke** is reached from the Marktplatz down Steingasse; dating from the 1780s, it was painstakingly rebuilt after being blown up during World War II. The **Palais Rischer** on Untere Strasse was the most famous venue for the university's *Mensur*, or fencing match; wounds were frequent and prized as badges of courage – for optimum prestige, salt was rubbed into them, leaving scars that remained for life. Universitätsplatz, the heart of the old town, is flanked by the eighteenth-century **Alte Universität** (April–Oct Mon–Sat 10am–4pm; Nov–March Tues–Fri 10am–4pm; €2.50) and the **Neue Universität**, erected with US funds in 1931. The oddest of Heidelberg's traditions was that its students used not to be subject to civil jurisdiction: offenders were dealt with by the university authorities, and could serve their punishment at leisure. The **Students' Prison** (same hours and ticket as Alte Universität) was used from 1712 to 1914; its spartan cells are covered with graffiti.

## Practicalities

Heidelberg's **train** and **bus stations** are in an anonymous quarter west of the centre; trams #1 and #4 run to Bismarckplatz at the end of the Altstadt. The main **tourist office** is on the square outside (April–Oct Mon–Sat 9am–7pm, Sun 10am–6pm, Nov–March Mon–Sat 9am–6pm; ☎06221/19 433, ✆www.cvb-heidelberg .de), while another well-run office at the other end of town, Touristen-Shop, Am Neckarmönzplatz (April–Oct daily 9am–5pm; ☎06221 60 26 23), – has Internet access. The **hostel** is on the north bank of the Neckar, about 4km from the centre, at Tiergartenstr. 5 (☎06221/65 11 90; €21; bus #33 from Hauptbahnhof or Bismarkplatz, direction Schwimmbad). **Hotels** are often booked solid; the chart outside the tourist office lists any vacancies. A good option is *Jeske*, a few steps off Marktplatz at Mittelbadgasse 2 (☎06221/23 733, ✆www.pension -jeske-heidelberg.de; ❸). *Elite* is a friendly place ten minutes from the centre at Bunsenstr. 15 (☎06221/25 734, ✆www.hotel-elite-heidelberg.de; ❺) €75). The **student taverns** are a must, known for their basic dishes at reasonable prices. At the eastern end of Hauptstrasse are the two most famous: *Zum Sepp'l* at no. 213 and *Roter Ochsen* at no. 217. Slightly less touristy is the oldest tavern, *Schnookeloch*, at Haspelgasse 8. *Essighaus*, Plöck 97, is a traditional **restaurant** serving large set menus at low prices, while *Weisser Schwan Biermuseum*, Hauptstr. 143, offers 24 types of beer with its meals. Characterful *Destille* is the best of the buzzing **drinking spots** along Untere Strasse. To try the famous Heidelberger Studentenkuss, a dark chocolate filled with praline and nougat, visit nineteenth-century *Knösel* at Haspelgasse 20. *Café Gekco*, Bergheimer 8, has a respectable range of salads and serves breakfast. It also has two **Internet** terminals; Webdome, Sofienstr. 25, has many more.

# The Black Forest region

Home of the cuckoo clock and source of the celebrated Danube river, the **Black Forest**, stretching 170km north to south, and up to 60km east to west, is Germany's largest and most beautiful forest. Its name reflects the mountainous landscape darkened by endless pine trees and, as late as the 1920s, much of this area was an eerie wilderness, a refuge for boars and bandits. Nowadays, many of its villages are geared toward the tourist trade, brimming with shops selling tacky souvenirs; the old forest trails have become gravel paths smoothed down for easier walking. The modernization, however, has also brought several of the most spectacular railway lines in Europe here, although trains tend to stick to the valleys and bus services are much reduced outside the tourist season. Most of the Black Forest is associated with the Margravate of Baden, whose old capital, **Baden–Baden**, is at the northern fringe of the forest, in a fertile orchard and vine-growing area. **Freiburg im Breisgau**, one of the most enticing cities in the country, is surrounded by the forest.

## Baden-Baden

The therapeutic value of the town's hot springs, first discovered by the Romans, is still the main draw in **BADEN-BADEN** – hardly the recipe for a party atmosphere. Nevertheless, it's a pretty town for an afternoon's stroll. South of the original **Kurhaus** (casino) runs Baden-Baden's most famous thoroughfare, the Lichtentaler Allee, landscaped with exotic trees and shrubs. It's flanked by the **Kunsthalle**, an exhibition venue for international modern and contemporary art that also contains the famously opulent Casino, the oldest in Europe, whose gilded frescoes and chandeliers are well worth a peek. (Daily tours 9am–12pm; €4.80 or visit in the evening for a flutter, €3). Smart clothes and passports are obligatory. North of the Kurhaus is the **Trinkhalle**, whose arcades shelter frescoes illustrating local legends. Halfway up the Florintinerberg is the **Marktplatz** and the **Stiftskirche**, a Gothic hall church containing one of the masterpieces of European sculpture, an enormous sandstone *Crucifixion* by Nicolaus Gerhaert von Leyden. Above the Römerbad, just east on Römerplatz, is the **Friedrichsbad** (Mon–Sat 9am–10pm, Sun noon–8pm); begun in 1869, it's as grand as a Renaissance palace. Speciality of the house is a three-hour "Roman-Irish Bath" that will set you back €21 (€29 for soap-brush massage). The **train station** is 4km northwest in the suburb of Oos; buses #201, #205 or #216 all go to the centre. The main **tourist office** is in the Trinkhalle on Kaiserallee (Mon–Sat 10am–5pm, Sun 2–5pm; ☎072 21/27 52 00, ⊛www.baden-baden.de), and has details of a few private rooms (❷). An uninspiring HI **hostel** is between the train station and the centre at Hardbergstr. 34 (☎072 21/52 223, ⊛www.jugendherberge-baden-baden. de; €20.90; bus #201). It's signposted from the Grosse-Dollen-Strasse bus stop. *Löwenbräu*, Gernsbacher Str. 9, is a good **place to eat**, and has a beer garden in summer. *Leo's*, Luisenstr. 10, is a trendy café-bar, opposite the tourist office, while for reasonably priced German food, there's *Rathausglöckel*, Steinstr. 7.

## Freiburg im Breisgau

**FREIBURG IM BREISGAU** – midway between Strasbourg (France) and Basel (Switzerland) – basks in a laid-back atmosphere that seems completely un-German. A university town since 1457, its youthful presence is maintained all year round with the help of a varied programme of festivals. It's a thoroughly enjoyable place to visit, and makes the perfect base for exploring the surrounding Black Forest. Highlight is the dark red sandstone **Münster**, towering above the main square (which hosts a daily market). Begun in about 1200, the church has a masterly Gothic nave, resplendent with flying buttresses, gargoyles and statues – the magnificent sculptures of the west porch are the most important German works of their time. From the tower (April–Oct Mon–Sat 9.30am–5pm, Sun 1–5pm; closed Mon Nov–March; €1.50) there's a fine panorama of the city and the surrounding forest-blanketed hills. A local peculiarity is the system of rivulets known as the **Bächle**, which run in deep gulleys all over the city. Formerly used for watering animals and as a fire-fighting provision, they have their purpose even today, helping to keep the city cool. Following the main channel of the Bächle, you come to the **Schwaben Tor**, one of two surviving towers of the medieval fortifications. On Oberlinden, just in front, is *Zum Roten Bären*, generally considered Germany's oldest inn. Further south, on Marienstrasse, the **Museum für Moderne Kunst** (Tues–Sun 10am–5pm; €2) has a good cross-section of twentieth-century German art. From here, follow Fischerau, the old fishermen's street, and you come to the other thirteenth-century tower, the **Martinstor**, in the middle of Freiburg's central axis, Kaiser-Josef-Strasse.

The **train station**, with the **bus station** on its southern side, is about ten minutes' walk west from the city centre. Following Eisenbahnstrasse, you come to the **tourist office** at Rotteckring 14 (Mon–Fri 9.30am–6/8pm, Sat 9.30am–2.30/5pm, Sun 10am–noon; ☎0761/38 81 880, ⊛www.freiburg.de). For €3, they'll find you a room; after closing time, an electronic board (with phone) lists vacancies. The cheapest central **hotel** is *Schemmer*, Eschholzstr. 63 (☎0761/20 74 90, ⓔangelavr @t-online.de; ➍). The inviting *Black Forest Hostel* at Kartäuserstr. 33 (☎0761/881 78 70, ⊛www.blackforest-hostel.de; dorms €15, rooms ➌), built in an old factory, is the best place to stay and has a well-equipped kitchen. The HI **hostel** is at Karthäuserstr. 151 (☎0761/67 656; €19.50; tram #1 to Römerhof), at the eastern end of the city. Nearby is one of Freiburg's three **campsites**, the *Hirzberg* (☎0761/35 054) at no. 99. A pricey but excellent **restaurant** is *Oberkirchs Weinstube*, Münsterplatz 22, serving Baden specialities; *Kleiner Meyerhof*, Rathausgasse 27, offers hearty South German cooking. A student favourite for cheap, filling meals is the seafood chain *Nordsee* – there are outlets on Kaiser-Joseph-Strasse and in the train station. One of the hippest spots for a bite to eat is *Uni-Café*, Niemensstr. 7, serving a wide selection of coffees and snacks. Also worth trying is the *Art Café* just opposite, offering the pizza-like *Flammenkuchen*. Both cafés are situated at the hub of Freiburg's **nightlife** scene, which revolves around the junction of Universitätstrasse and Niemenstrasse. The city ranks as one of the country's best places to hear **jazz**, thanks to the *Jazzhaus* at Schnewlinstr. 1, which has gigs nightly. *Shake n Surf*, Bismarckallee 5, is a cheap **Internet café** near the station (daily 10am–10pm).

## Stuttgart

In the centre of Baden-Württemberg, 85km southeast of Heidelberg, **STUTTGART** is home to the German success stories of Bosch, Porsche and Daimler-Chrysler. Founded around 950 as a stud farm (Stutengarten), it became a town only in the fourteenth century. Though certainly not the comeliest of cities, it has a range of superb museums, and a sophisticated cultural scene and nightlife. From the train station, Königstrasse passes the dull modern Dom and enters Schlossplatz, on the south of which is the **Altes Schloss**, home to the **Württembergisches Landesmuseum** (Tues 10am–1pm, Wed–Sun 10am–5pm; €3; ⊛www.landes museum-stuttgart.de). Highlight of this richly varied museum is the *Kunstkammer* of the House of Württemberg; the first floor has small bronze sculptures of mainly Italian origin, while the second is laid out in the manner of a Renaissance curio cabinet. North of Schlossplatz is the **Staatsgalerie** (Tues–Sun 10am–6pm, Thurs till 9pm;

first Sat in month till midnight; €4.50; ⓦ www.staatsgalerie.de), whose most startling work is the violently expressive *Herrenberg Altar* by Jörg Ratgeb. On the other side of Schlossplatz, the Altes Schloss overlooks **Schillerplatz**, Stuttgart's sole example of an old-world square. Two of Stuttgart's most famous names put corporate propaganda to work with outstanding results. The **Mercedes–Benz–Museum** (Tues–Sun 9am–5pm; free; ⓦ www.daimler-benz.com) is an absolute must. Take S-Bahn #1 to Gottlieb-Daimler-Stadion, then follow the signs to the museum bus stop at the factory's doorstep. Because of the company's concerns about industrial espionage, you then have to wait for a sealed bus for the one-minute ride to the museum. The earliest vehicle on display is the Daimler Reitwagen of 1885, the first-ever motorbike, which was capable of 12kph. Daimler's first Mercedes dates from 1902. There are various vehicles on display, but it's the luxury cars and the machines specially designed for world-record attempts that steal the show. The **Porsche–Museum**, Porschestrasse 42 (Mon–Fri 9am–4pm; weekends till 5pm; free), is beside Neuwirtshaus station on S-Bahn line #6. The vehicles on show illustrate all the company's cars, from the 356 Roadster of 1948 to current models.

## Practicalities

Stuttgart's **train and bus stations** are in the centre of town. S-Bahn #2 and #3 link to the **airport** (every 10/20min; 30min) – a day ticket for the extensive integrated **public transport** network costs €5. The **tourist office**, opposite the train station at Königstr. 1a (Mon–Fri 9am–8pm, Sat 9am–6pm, Sun 11am/1pm–6pm; ⓣ 0711/22 28 0, ⓦ www.stuttgart-tourist.de), offers the **StuttCard Plus** (€17/three days), which covers public transport, admission to most museums and numerous freebies; the basic StuttCard (€11.50/three days) gives the same benefits without public transport. The HI **hostel**, Haussmannstr. 27 (ⓣ 0711/24 15 83; €17.90), is a short ride on bus #42 to Eugensplatz from the train station; independent hostels include *Jugendgästehaus*, Richard-Wagner-Str. 2–4a (ⓣ 0711/24 11 32, ⓦ www.hostel-stuttgart.de; dorms €18.50; rooms ❸), and the friendly and convenient *Alex 30*, Alexanderstr. 30 (ⓣ 0711/83 88 950, ⓦ www.alex30-hostel.de; dorms €18, rooms ❹). The cheapest **hotel** deals are at the central *Museum-Stube*, Hospitalstr. 9 (ⓣ 0711/29 68 10; ❹).

Stuttgart is surrounded by vineyards, and the numerous **Weinstuben** are excellent places to try good-quality, traditional noodle-based dishes and local wines at low cost. *Zur Kiste*, Kanalstr. 2, is the best known of these, but the widest choice of wines is at *Weinhaus Stetter*, Rosenstr. 32. For good beer and food, head for **microbrewery** *Calwer-Eck-Bräu*, Calwerstr. 31. *Lift* and *Prinz Stuttgart*, available from newsagents, have complete **nightlife** listings, while helpful Tips'n'trips, Lautenschlagerstr. 22 (Mon–Fri noon–7pm, Sat 10am–2pm; ⓣ 0711/22 22 730, ⓦ www.jugendinformation -stuttgart.de), maintains a list of the city's 25 clubs. Current hotspots are *M1*, below the ultra-modern Bosch-Areal complex at Breitscheider 12 (closed Mon & Tues), and the laid-back *Bett im Filmhaus*, Friedrichstr. 23, popular, and open every night. There are **bars** scattered all over town; a good one to try is *Palast der Republik*, a tiny funk-shack on the square where Bolzstrasse meets Lautenschlagerstrasse. **Internet** access is at Level One, Schlossplatz 22.

## Tübingen

**TÜBINGEN** is sited above the willow-lined banks of the Neckar, 55km upstream (southwest) from Stuttgart. It's a youthful, lively place – over half the population of 70,000 is connected with its university and the old town is a visual treat, a mixture of brightly painted half-timbered and gabled houses grouped into twisting and plunging alleys. **Holzmarkt** forms the heart of the town and is dominated by the **Stiftskirche** (daily 9am–4/5pm; free), a gaunt, late-Gothic church with a fine interior. The chancel (daily: 11.30am–5pm Easter–Oct; Nov–Easter Fri–Sun only; €1 including access to the tower) contains an outstanding series of stained-glass windows which cast reflections on the thirteen tombs of the House of Württemberg. Overlooking the banks of the Neckar on Bursagasse is the **Hölderlinturm** (Tues–Fri 10am–noon & 3–5pm, Sat & Sun 2–5pm; €1.50). Originally part of the medieval fortifications, it contains memorabilia of the poet Friedrich Hölderlin, hopelessly but harmlessly insane, who lived here in the care of a carpenter's family for 36 years; Hölderlin is now regarded as one of the greatest of all German poets. The **Markt**, heart of old Tübingen (markets Mon, Wed & Fri), is a short walk uphill from here. It preserves many of its Renaissance mansions, along with a fountain dedicated to Neptune. Burgsteige, one of the oldest and handsomest streets in town, climbs steeply from one corner to **Schloss Hohentübingen**, housing the **Schausammlungen der Universität** (Wed–Sun 10am–4/5pm; €3), one of the largest university museums in the world, with archeology, history and ethnology displays. The northwestern part of town, immediately below the Schloss, has some spectacular half-timbered buildings, such as the old municipal **Kornhaus** and **Fruchtschranne** on Bachgasse.

The adjacent **train** and **bus stations** are five minutes' walk from the old town. At the edge of Eberhardsbrücke is the **tourist office** (Mon–Fri 9am–7pm, Sat 9am–5pm; May–Oct also Sun 2–5pm; ☎070 71/91 360, ⊛www.tuebingen-info .de), with details of outlying private rooms (④–⑥). **Hotels** are expensive; the pleasant *Am Schloss*, Burgsteige 18 (☎070 71/92 940; ⑦), and *Hospiz*, a few doors down (☎070 71/92 40, ⊛www.hotel-hospiz.de; ⑦), both offer a couple of simple, bathless singles (⑤) in addition to their pricier doubles. The HI **hostel** is on the banks of the Neckar, a short walk from the station at Gartenstr. 22/2 (☎070 71/23 002, ⊛www .jugendherberge-tuebingen.de; €22). To reach the **campsite**, Rappenberghalde 61 (☎070 71/43 145; open March–Sept), turn left on leaving the train station and cross at Alleenbrücke. Tübingen has a number of good **restaurants**, including upmarket *Forelle*, a *Weinstube* at Kronenstr. 8. *Krumme Brüke*, Kornhausstr. 17, does giant schnitzels, while the bar/café *Schloss Café* at Burgsteige 7 serves good-value and tasty food in relaxed alcoves and has a lively club downstairs. *Jazz Keller*, Haaggasse 15, is one of many popular student **bars** and has live music or DJs nightly.

## Konstanz and the Bodensee

In the far south, hard up against the Swiss border, **KONSTANZ** lies at the tip of a tongue of land sticking out into the **Bodensee** (Lake Constance). The town itself is split by the water; the **Altstadt** is an enclave on the southern shore. It's a cosy little town, with a convivial atmosphere in summer, when street cafés invite long pauses and the water is a bustle of sails. The most prominent church is the **Münster**, set on the highest point of the Altstadt. The regional highlight is the nearby **Insel Mainau** (daily: April–Oct 7am–8pm; Nov–March 9am–6pm; bus #4 from the train station; €11; ⊛www.mainau.de), an island occupied by a royal park featuring magnificent floral displays, formal gardens, greenhouses, forests and a handful of well-placed restaurants. Konstanz **tourist office** is beside the **train station** at Bahnhofplatz 13 (Mon–Fri 9.30am–12.30pm & 2–6.30pm; April–Oct also Sat 9am–4pm & Sun 10am–1pm; ☎075 31/13 30 30, ⊛www.konstanz.de); they can book accommodation in private rooms (②). The **hostel** is *Jugendwohnheim Don Bosco* at Salesianerweg 5 (☎075 31/622 52, ⊛www.donbosco-kn.de; €21.60; bus #1 or #4 to Tannenhof). **Pension** *Graf* is at Wiesenstrasse 2 (☎075 31/12 86 890, ©pension.graf@t-online.de; ③). You can get information on **cruises** and **ferries** from the Bodensee-Schiffsbetriebe at Hafenstr. 6 (☎075 31/36 40 389, ⊛www .bsb-online.com). Ferries depart regularly around the lake, as well as on a scenic trip to the impressive Rhine falls in Switzerland (€20), covered in Chapter 31.

## Augsburg

**AUGSBURG**, where Martin Luther's Protestant reforms found their earliest support, lies 60km west of Munich. Heart of the city is the cobbled **Rathausplatz**, which turns into a massive open-air café during the summer and into a glittering market at Christmas. Inside the **Rathaus**, the gold-leaf pillars and marble floor of the Goldener Saal (daily 10am–6pm; €2) recall the period when the Fugger banking dynasty made Augsburg one of Europe's financial centres. To the south, **Maximilianstrasse** is lined with merchants' palaces and punctuated by fountains. At the other end of the town's axis stands the **Dom**; its Romanesque bronze doors are on view in the **Diocesan Museum St Afra** (Tues–Sat 10am–5pm, Sun 2–5pm; €2.50) in the cloisters. For a charge of one "Our Father", one "Hail Mary" and one Creed daily, plus €0.90 per annum, good Catholic paupers can retire to the sixteenth-century **Fuggerei** at the age of 55. With an entrance in Jacoberstrasse, it's a town within a town, and compared with modern housing estates is a real idyll, the cloister-like atmosphere disturbed only by the odd ringing doorbell. No. 13 (March–Dec daily 9am–6pm; €1) is one of only two houses from the original foundation; today it's full of furnishings from the sixteenth to the eighteenth centuries. The **tourist offices** (☎0821/50 20 70, ⊛www.augsburg -tourismus.de) are at Bahnhofstr. 7 (Mon–Fri 9am–6pm), a couple of minutes from the **train station**, and on Rathausplatz (April–Oct Mon–Fri 9am–6pm, Sat & Sun 10am–1pm; Nov–March Mon–Fri 9am–5pm, Sat 10am–2pm). The cheapest central **pension** is *Jakoberhof*, Jakoberstr. 41 (☎0821/51 00 30, ⊛www.jakoberhof .de; ❸), a friendly place close to the Fuggerei. The central HI **hostel** is at Beim Pfaffenkeller 3 (☎0821/33 909; €19.45). The cheapest places for **snacks** are in the Stadtmarkt meat halls off Annastrasse. For **drinking**, take your pick of the **café/ bars** along Maximilianstrasse, or head to *Mojo* cocktail bar at Jakoberstr. 7.

# Rothenburg ob der Tauber

The **Romantic Road** winds its way along the length of western Bavaria, running through the most visited – and most beautiful – medieval town in Germany: **ROTHENBURG OB DER TAUBER**. Located 50km west of Nuremberg, it's connected by a branch railway with Steinach on the Augsburg–Würzburg line. This fairy-tale town is besieged with tour groups during the day, so make a point of spending a night so as to appreciate it in relative peace. The views of the surrounding countryside from the fourteenth-century town walls are magnificent, but Rothenburg's true charms lie amongst its medieval half-timbered houses and cobbled streets. The sloping **Marktplatz** is dominated by the arcaded front of the Renaissance Rathaus; the sixty-metre tower of the older **Gotisches Rathaus** behind (daily: April–Oct 9.30am–12.30pm & 1–5pm; Dec noon–3pm; Nov & Jan–March weekends only noon–3pm; €1) provides the best views. The other main attractions on the Marktplatz are the figures on each side of the three clocks of the **Ratsherrntrinkstube**, which seven times daily re-enact an episode that allegedly occurred during the Thirty Years War. The fearsome Johann Tilly agreed that Rothenburg should be spared if one of the councillors could drain in one draught a tankard holding over three litres of wine. A former burgomaster duly sank the contents of the so-called *Meistertrunk*, then needed three days to sleep off the effects. On the opposite side of the Marktplatz is the Gothic **St Jakob-Kirche** (daily: April–Oct 9am–5.30pm; Nov & Jan–March 10am–noon & 2–4pm; Dec 10am–5pm; €1.50), with its massive towers and exquisitely carved altars. Of the local museums, the most interesting is the **Kriminalmuseum** at Burggasse 3 (daily: April–Oct 9.30am–6pm; Nov, Jan & Feb 2–4pm; Dec & March 10am–4pm; €3.50), containing collections of medieval torture instruments and related objects such as the beer barrels that drunks were forced to walk around in.

Rothenburg's **tourist office** is in the Ratstrinkstube on Marktplatz (Mon–Fri 9am–noon & 1–5/6pm, Sat 10am–1/3pm; ☎09861/40 4800, ⊛www.rothenburg .de). The HI **hostel**, Mühlacker 1 (☎09861/94 160; €18.50), is housed in two beautifully restored houses off the bottom of Spitalgasse. Rothenburg is full of cheap **pensions** and **inns**; worth trying are the charming *Pöschel*, Wenggasse 22

(☎09861/34 30, ✉pension.poeschel@t-online.de; ❸), wonderfully creaky *Raidel*, in a medieval house on the same street at no. 3 (☎09861/31 15, ⓦwww.romanticroad .com/raidel; ❸), and friendly *Zur Goldenen Rose*, Spitalgasse 28 (☎09861/46 38, ⓦwww.zur-goldenen-rose.de; ❸; closed Jan & Feb). The latter has pleasant rooms and serves great home-cooked food in one of the town's many fine **restaurants**. Be sure to try the ubiquitous *Schneeball* (snowball), a rich pastry dusted with sugar, in one of the **cafés** dotted around town. **Internet** access is at Inter@Play, Milchmarkt 3.

# Nuremberg (Nürnberg)

Founded in the eleventh century, **NUREMBERG** (Nürnberg) – halfway between Frankfurt and Munich – quickly grew into an economic and political centre. In the twentieth century it become a focal point for the Nazis' infamous rallies and, after the war, it served as the site of the war-crimes trials. Yet the infamy caused by the city's recent past seems a world away from the friendly, bustling town that greets visitors today. Nuremberg has a relaxed air that makes whiling away a day or two amongst its half-timbered houses, fine museums and beer halls an altogether enjoyable experience.

On January 2, 1945, a storm of bombs reduced ninety percent of Nuremberg's centre to ash and rubble, but you'd never guess it from the meticulous postwar rebuilding. The reconstructed medieval core is surrounded by its ancient city walls and is neatly spliced by the River Pegnitz. To walk from one end to the other takes about twenty minutes, but much of the centre, especially the area around the castle – known as the **Burgviertel** – is on a steep hill. One of the highest points of the city is occupied by the **Kaiserburg** (daily: April–Sept 9am–6pm; Oct–March 10am–4pm; €6), whose **Sinwellturm** can be ascended for great views. The area around the **Tiergärtner Tor** next to the Kaiserburg is one of the most attractive parts of the old centre, a meeting point for summertime street vendors, artists and musicians. Virtually next door, the **Albrecht-Dürer-Haus** (June–Aug Tues–Sun 10am–5pm, Thurs till 8pm; €5) is where the painter, engraver, scientist, writer, traveller and politician lived from 1509 to 1528, and is one of the very few original houses still standing. Heading south, the church of **St Sebaldus** is the city's oldest,

| ACCOMMODATION | | EATING & DRINKING | |
| --- | --- | --- | --- |
| Goldener Adler | B | Barfüsser | 7 |
| HI Hostel | A | Bratwürst - Häusle | 2 |
| Lett'm Sleep | C | Bratwürst - Herzle | 5 |
| Vater Jahn | D | Meisengeige | 1 |
| | | Mohr | 4 |
| | | Souptopia | 6 |
| | | Treibhaus | 3 |

a thriteenth-century construction, dripping with sculpture on the outside and containing the impressive bronze shrine of St Sebald within. Continuing south, the **Hauptmarkt**, commercial heart of the city and the main venue for weekly markets, has, on its east side, the **Frauenkirche**, on whose facade a clockwork mechanism, known as the *Männleinlaufen*, tinkles away at noon. South of the Hauptmarkt the Museumsbrücke crosses the river, providing a good view of the Fleischbrücke to the right and the Heilig-Geist-Spital – one of the largest hospitals built in the Middle Ages – on the left. Passing the oldest house in the city, the thirteenth-century **Nassauer Haus**, you shortly come to the church of **St Lorenz**, a graceful, late fifteenth-century tabernacle, some 20m high. The man who carved it, Adam Kraft, depicted himself as a pensive figure crouching at the base. The **Germanisches Nationalmuseum** (Tues–Sun 10am–6pm, Wed till 9pm; €5, free after 6pm on Wed; ✆www.gnm.de) – perhaps the most important collection of the country's arts and crafts – occupies a fourteenth-century monastery on Kornmarkt. On the ground floor the displays follow a roughly chronological layout, beginning with Bronze Age items and moving on to medieval sculptures and carvings. German painting at its Renaissance peak dominates the first floor, while subsequent rooms focus on the Renaissance. Look out for the first globe of the earth, made by Martin Behaim in 1491 – just before Columbus "discovered" America.

In many minds, Nuremberg conjures up images of **Nazi** rallies and war-crimes trials. Indeed, the "**Nuremberg Laws**" of 1935, which deprived Jews of their citizenship and forbade relations between Jews and Gentiles, were the device by which the Nazis justified their extermination of six million Jews, 10,000 of whom came from Nuremberg. However, as the city council is eager to point out, the Nazis' choice of Nuremberg had less to do with local support of Nazi ideology, and more to do with what medieval Nuremberg represented in German history: Adolf Hitler considered it to be the "most German of all German cities". The rallies were held on the **Zeppelin and March fields** in the suburb of Luitpoldhain (tram #9 from the centre). Nearby, in the gargantuan but never-completed Congress Hall, the **Dokuzentrum's Fascination and Terror** is a multimedia exhibition documenting the history of the rally grounds and the ruthless misuse of power under National Socialism (Mon–Fri 9am–6pm, Sat & Sun 10am–6pm; €5; tram #6 or #9 to Dokuzentrum).

### Practicalities

The main **tourist office** (Mon–Sat 9am–7pm; ✆0911/23 36 132, ✆www.nuernberg .de) is at the entrance to the Altstadt in the Künstlerhaus opposite the **train station**. There's a smaller office at Hauptmarkt 18, within the Altstadt (Mon–Sat 9am–6pm; May–Oct also Sun 10am–4pm; ✆0911/23 36 135). The **Nürnberg Card** (€18/two days) covers public transport plus entrance to museums. There's 24-hour **Internet** access at Flat-S, on the top floor of the train station. The friendly and popular *Lett'm Sleep* hostel at Frauentormauer 42 (✆0911/99 28 128, ✆seeyou@backpackers.de; €15) offers free Internet access. The HI **hostel** has a wonderful location within the Kaiserburg, overlooking the Altstadt (✆0911/23 09 360; €20.45). The cheapest central **pensions** include *Vater Jahn*, Jahnstr. 13 (✆0911/44 45 07; ❸), just south of the Opernhaus on the other side of railway tracks, and, in the Altstadt, *Goldener Adler*, Hallplatz 21 (✆0911/22 13 60; ❸), which serves good home cooking downstairs.

Nuremberg is the liveliest Bavarian city after Munich, with a wealth of *Studentenkneipen* and café-bars catering for students. The cheapest meals in town are to be found in the university *Mensa*, in the northeastern corner of the Altstadt. There are plenty of *Imbiss*-type **snack-joints** in the pedestrian zone around St Lorenz. Good places to eat include *Bratwurst-Häusle*, Rathausplatz 1, the most celebrated and touristy of the city's sausage **restaurants**, and the more down-to-earth *Bratwurst Herzle*, Brunnengasse 11. *Barfüsser*, Hallplatz 2, occupying the cavernous cellars, brews its own beer and serves good food. If you're sick of sausage, head for *Souptopia*, Lorenzerstr. 27, where five types of soup are on offer daily, including at least one vegan option. Fashionable **café-bars** include *Treibhaus*, south of Maxbrücke on Karl-Grillenberger-Str. 28, *Mohr*, Färberstr. 3, and tiny *Meisengeige*, Am Laufer Schlagturm 3. The last is one of several cafés on the street and has a small cinema showing an offbeat selection of films; follow Theresienstrasse east to get here. The trendiest **club** is *Mach 1*, Kaiserstr. 1–9, with four different bars (closed Mon & Tues); lounge-like *Stereo Deluxe*, Klaragasse 8, is more chilled-out (Thurs–Sat only). To find out what else is going on, get the monthly *Dopplepunkt* magazine from the tourist office, or *Plärrer* magazine from any kiosk.

# Regensburg

The undisturbed medieval ensemble of central **REGENSBURG**, stunningly located on the banks of the Danube midway between Nuremberg and Munich, can easily be visited as a day-trip. Getting lost in the web of cobbled medieval lanes and nursing a drink in one of the wide, sunny squares are the main draws here. A good place to start is the twelfth-century **Steinerne Brücke**, the only safe crossing along the entire length of the Danube at the time it was built. To the left, the **Historische Wurstküche** (daily 8am–7pm) originally functioned as the bridge-workers' kitchen. This local institution, run by the same family for generations, serves little else but delicious Regensburg sausages. The Gothic **Dom** (Mon–Sat 10/11am–4/5pm, Sun 2–4/5pm; €2.50), begun around 1250, replaced a Romanesque church of which only the Eselsturm ("donkey tower") remains above ground. Highlights include the fourteenth-century stained-glass windows. The cathedral's Domspatzen boys' choir is famous throughout Germany; catch them performing during Sunday services at 10am. A short way south is Neupfarrplatz, below which lies **Document Neupfarrplatz**, a grid of **archeological excavations** including a Roman camp and the medieval Jewish quarter (entrance with tour only; Thurs, Fri & Sat 2.30pm; €5). Today's Neupfarrkirche occupies the site of the old synagogue, wrecked during the 1519 expulsion. **Schloss Thurn and Taxis** (tours April–Oct Mon–Fri 11am, 2pm, 3pm & 4pm, Sat & Sun also 10am; Nov–March Sat & Sun 10am, 11am, 2pm & 3pm; €10.50), the largest aristocratic residence in Europe, is in the converted monastic buildings of the abbey of St Emmeram in the city's southern quarter. The former cloisters are fine Gothic, while the nineteenth-century state rooms contain some interesting Brussels tapestries recording the Thurn und Taxis family's illustrious history.

Maximilianstrasse leads straight from the **train station** to the centre. The **tourist office** is in the Altes Rathaus (Mon–Fri 9.15am–6pm, Sat 9.15am–4pm, Sun 9.30am–4pm; ☎0941/50 74 410, ⓦwww.regensburg.de). A brand-new and very welcoming backpackers *Brook Lane Hostel*, Obere Bach Gasse 21 (☎0941/690 0966, ⓦwww.hostel-regensburg.de; dorms €15, rooms ❸), is in a handy location, has a kitchen and is above a food shop. The HI **hostel**, Wöhrdstr. 60 (☎0941/57 402, ⓦwww.regensburg.jugendherberge.de; €17.85), is a good ten minutes' walk from the centre. A good **hotel** choice, especially for solo travellers, is *Spitalgarten*, St Katharinen-Platz 1 (☎0941/8 47 74, ⓦwww.spitalgarten.de; ❹). Located on the other side of the Steinerne Brücke, on one of the Danube islands, it also has the best **beer garden** in town. *Goldene Ente*, Badstr. 32, is another beer garden popular with students. Neupfarrplatz has a number of stalls selling cheap **sausages** and fresh fruit. Cozy and friendly *Oma Plüsch*, Rote-Stern-Gasse 6, has reasonably priced food and beer; nearby *Hemingways*, on the corner of Augustinergasse and Obere Bachgasse, is a classy **bar** popular with foreigners. *Netzblick*, Am Römling 9, is a café/bar with **Internet** access.

# Munich (München)

Founded in 1158, **MUNICH** (München) has been the capital of Bavaria since 1503, and as far as the locals are concerned it may as well be the centre of the universe. The city is impossibly energetic, bursting with a good-humoured self-importance that is difficult to dislike. After Berlin, Munich is Germany's most popular city – with its compact and attractive old centre, it is certainly much easier to digest. It also has a great setting, with the mountains and Alpine lakes just an hour's drive away. The best time of year to come here is from June to early October, when the beer gardens, street cafés and bars are in full swing – not least for the world-famous **Oktoberfest** beer festival.

## Arrival, information and accommodation

Munich's **airport**, Franz Josef Strauss Flughafen, is connected to the **Hauptbahnhof** by S-Bahn #1 or #8. There are **tourist offices** (℡089/23 39 65 00, ⓦwww .muenchen-tourist.de) at Bahnhofplatz 2 (Mon–Sat 9am–6.30/8pm, Sun 10am–6pm) and in the Rathaus on Marienplatz (Mon–Fri 10am–8pm, Sat 10am–4pm), either of which can book rooms. Day tickets, valid for all **public transport** in the central city area, are a good investment at €4.50. The **Munich Welcome Card** (€6.50/16 for 1/3 days) covers all public transport and gives big discounts on attractions. Also available are **strip cards** (€9.50 for 10); stamp two strips for every zone crossed – the zones are shown on maps at stations and tram and bus stops. For journeys of up to two S- or U-Bahn stops, or up to four bus or tram stops, only one strip needs to be cancelled. Individual and day tickets and strip cards can be bought from automatic machines in all U-Bahn stations, at some bus and tram stops, and inside trams.

Cheap **accommodation** can be hard to find, especially in summer. If you're going to be in town during the Oktoberfest, it's essential to book well in advance; be warned that prices tend to rise during this period.

## Hostels

**4you München** Hirtenstr. 18 ℡089/55 21 660, ⓦwww.the4you.de. Scruffy but lively outfit very close to the main station, with some singles and doubles as well as standard dorms. Dorms €18.50, rooms ➍

**Easy Palace** Mozartstr. 4 ℡089/55 87 97 0, ⓦwww.easypalace.com. Welcoming hostel with en-suite toilets/showers, 15min walk from the train station or U-Bahn to Goetheplatz. No age limit. Dorms €16.90, rooms ➍

**Euro Youth Hotel** Senefelderstr. 5, ℡089/59 90 88 11, ⓦwww.euro-youth-hotel.de. Good atmosphere and location with late-closing bar and helpful staff. Dorms €15, rooms ➍

**Jugendherberge München** Wendl-Dietrich-Str. 20 ℡089/13 11 56. The largest, most central and most basic HI hostel. U-Bahn to Rotkreuzplatz. €19.55.

**Meininger** Landsberger Str. 20 ℡0800 634 64 64 (freephone), ⓦwww.meininger-hostels.de. Brand-new, clean accomodation with pricey doubles and kitchen facilities. Price includes breakfast and sheets. Dorms €19, rooms ➎

**Wombats** Senefelderstr. 1 ℡089/59 98 91 80, ⓦwww.wombats-hostels.com. Modern, lively, central backpackers with a great bar, winter garden and friendly staff. Dorms €22, rooms ➍

## Hotels and pensions

**Am Kaiserplatz** Kaiserplatz 12 ℡089/34 91 90. Very friendly place in a good location with big rooms, each done in a different style – from red satin to Bavarian rustic. Six-bed rooms can be arranged. U-Bahn to Münchener Freiheit. ➍

**Am Siegestor** Akademiestr. 5 ℡089/39 95 50, ⓦwww.hotel-siegestor.de. Friendly place and good location in the lively area of Schwabing, north of the centre. Some rooms more modern than others. ➍

**Eder** Zweigstr. 8 ℡089/55 46 60, ⓦwww.hotel-eder.de. Cosy hotel in a quiet road near the train station, offering nicely appointed rooms. ➍

**Frank** Schellingstr. 24 ℡089/28 14 51, ⓦwww.pension-frank.de. A good choice in the student quarter for both price and atmosphere, with homely rooms in a creaky old building. ➍

**Jedermann** Bayerstr. 95 ℡089/54 32 40, ⓦwww .hotel-jedermann.de. Classy, family-run hotel just 5min walk from the train station. The buffet breakfast is especially good and free Internet is available. ➎

**Steinberg** Ohmstr. 9 ℡089/33 10 11, ⓦwww .pension-steinberg.de. Friendly and in a good location near Giselastr. U-Bahn station. ➎

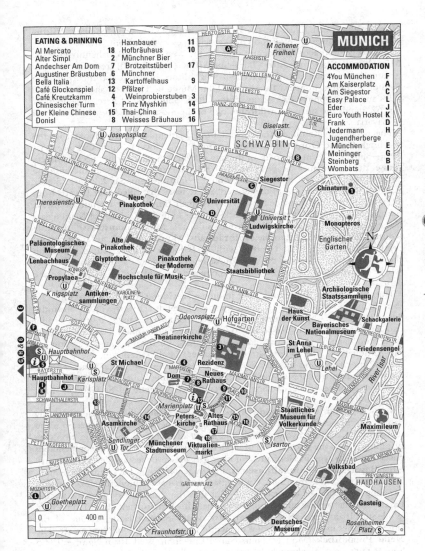

**EATING & DRINKING**

| | |
|---|---|
| Al Mercato | 18 |
| Alter Simpl | 2 |
| Andechser Am Dom | 7 |
| Augustiner Bräustuben | 6 |
| Bella Italia | 13 |
| Café Glockenspiel | 12 |
| Café Kreutzkamm | 4 |
| Chinesischer Turm | 1 |
| Der Kleine Chinese | 15 |
| Donisl | 8 |
| Haxnbauer | 11 |
| Hofbräuhaus | 10 |
| Münchner Bier | |
| Brotzeitstüberl | 17 |
| Münchner | |
| Kartoffelhaus | 9 |
| Pfälzer | |
| Weinprobierstuben | 3 |
| Prinz Myshkin | 14 |
| Thai-China | 5 |
| Weisses Bräuhaus | 16 |

**MUNICH**

**ACCOMMODATION**

| | |
|---|---|
| 4You München | F |
| Am Kaiserplatz | A |
| Am Siegestor | C |
| Easy Palace | L |
| Eder | J |
| Euro Youth Hostel | K |
| Frank | D |
| Jedermann | H |
| Jugendherberge | |
| München | E |
| Meininger | G |
| Steinberg | B |
| Wombats | I |

**12**

**GERMANY** | Southern Germany

## The City

The central **Marienplatz** is the bustling heart of Munich and is always thronged with crowds being entertained by street musicians and artists. At 11am and noon, the square fills with tourists as the tuneless carillon in the **Rathaus** tower jingles into action. The Rathaus itself is a late nineteenth-century neo-Gothic monstrosity whose only redeeming features are the café in its cool and breezy courtyard and the view from the **tower** (May–Oct daily 9/10am–7pm; Nov–April Mon–Thurs 9am–4pm, Fri 9am–1pm; €2). To the right is the plain Gothic tower of the Altes Rathaus, which now houses a vast toy collection in the **Spielzeugmuseum** (daily

10am–5.30pm; €3). Close by, the **Peterskirche** looks out across the busy **Viktu-alienmarkt**, a huge open-air food market selling everything from *Weisswurst* (white herb sausage) and beer to fruit and veg. To the west of the Viktualienmarkt is the **Münchener Stadtmuseum** (Tues–Sun 10am–6pm; €2.50, free Sun; @www .stadtmuseum-online.de); this excellent local history museum also incorporates a Fashion Museum, Puppet Museum and Film Museum. The latter shows art-house films and has a popular café on its ground floor. Southwest of here, at Sendlinger Str. 62, stands the small **Asamkirche**, one of the most splendid Rococo churches in Bavaria.

The pedestrian Kaufingerstrasse, west from Marienplatz, is overlooked by the red-brick Gothic **Dom**, whose twin onion-domed **towers** (April–Oct Mon–Sat 10am–5pm; €3) form the focus of the city's skyline. A little further up Kaufinger-strasse, the Renaissance facade of **St Michael** stands unassumingly in line with the street's other buildings. In the crypt (Mon–Fri 9.30am–4pm, Sat 9.30am–2.30pm; €2) you'll find the coffins of the Wittelsbach dynasty that ruled over Bavaria from 1180 until 1918 and provided two Holy Roman Emperors – a candle is always burning at the foot of that of mad castle-builder Ludwig II. North of Marienplatz is the posh end of the city centre. From fashionable **Maximilianstrasse**, the little Kosttor alley leads straight to the **Hofbräuhaus**, Munich's largest and most famous drinking hall (see p.481). Nearby, with its Baroque facade standing proud on the Odeonsplatz, is one of the city's most regal churches, the **Theatinerkirche**, whose golden-yellow towers and green copper dome add a splash of colour to the roofscape.

The palace of the Wittelsbachs, the immense **Residenz** (daily: April to mid-Oct 9am–6pm; mid-Oct to March 10am–4pm; €6), stands across the square from the Theatinerkirche. One of Europe's finest Renaissance buildings, it was so badly damaged in the last war that it had to be almost totally rebuilt. To see the whole thing you have to go on two consecutive visits: on the morning tour you see the Antiquarium, the oldest part of the palace; in the afternoon, the two very contrasting chapels and the Baroque Golden Hall. A separate ticket is necessary to see the fabulous treasures of the **Schatzkammer** (same hours; €6, €9 combined ticket); star piece is the dazzling stone-encrusted statuette of St George, made around 1590.

Munich's most overwhelming museum – the **Deutsches Museum** (daily 9am–5pm; €7.50; @www.deutsches-museum.de) – occupies the mid-stream island of Isarinsel. Covering every conceivable aspect of technical endeavour, from the first flint tools to the research labs of modern industry, this is the most compendious collection of its type in Germany. Another gargantuan collection lies further north – the **Bayerisches Nationalmuseum**, Prinzregentenstr. 3 (Tues–Sun 10am–5pm, Thurs till 8pm; €3, free Sun; @www.bayerisches-nationalmuseum.de), houses a rambling collection of decorative arts. But it is the Pinakothek museums around Barerstrasse that are the city's main draw. The **Alte Pinakothek** (Tues 10am–8pm, Wed–Sun 10am–5pm; €5, €1 Sun; @www.alte-pinakothek.de) is one of the largest galleries in Europe, housing the world's finest assembly of German art. The **Neue Pinakothek** (Mon & Thurs–Sun 10am–5pm, Wed 10am–8pm; €9, €5 Sun; @www.neue-pinakothek.de) holds a fine collection of nineteenth-century art. The **Pinakothek der Moderne** (Tues, Wed, Sat & Sun 10am–5pm, Thurs & Fri 10am–8pm; €9; @www.pinakothek-der-moderne.de) is worth visiting for its stun-ning architecture alone. The stark glass and concrete structure presents an impressive collection, from Dalí and Picasso to German greats such as Beckmann and Polke, and features exhibitions about design, architecture and graphics.

### Around Munich: Nymphenburg and Dachau

**Schloss Nymphenburg** (daily: April to mid-Oct 9am–6pm; mid-Oct to March 10am–4pm; €5, €10 combined ticket with pavilions and Marstall), the summer residence of the Wittelsbachs, is reached by tram #17 from the train station. Its kernel is a small Italianate palace begun in 1664 for the Electress Adelaide, who dedicated it to the goddess Flora and her nymphs – hence the name. The **Marstall**, or stables, contain notable collections of historic coaches and porcelain, but more enticing than the palace itself are the wonderful park and its four distinct pavilions. Three were designed by Joseph Effner: the **Magdalenenklause**, built to resemble a ruined hermitage; the **Pagodenburg**, used for the most exclusive parties thrown by the court; and the **Badenburg**, which, like the Pagodenburg, reflects an interest in the art of China. For all their charm, Effner's pavilions are overshadowed by the stunning **Amalienburg**, the hunting lodge built behind the south wing of the Schloss by his successor as court architect, François Cuvilliés. This supreme expression of the Rococo style marries a cunning design – which makes the little building seem like a full-scale palace – with the most extravagant decoration imaginable.

On the northern edge of Munich, the picturesque town of **Dachau** was the site of Germany's first **concentration camp** (Tues–Sun 9am–5pm; free; ⑩www .kz-gedenkstaette-dachau.de), and the motto that greeted arrivals at the gates has taken its chilling place in the history of Third Reich brutality: *Arbeit Macht Frei*, "Work Brings Freedom". Original buildings still standing include this gateway, the administration block, the deeply unsettling bunker cell-block, two crematoria and the gas chambers, which were never used. A replica hut gives an idea of the conditions under which prisoners were forced to live, and there's a permanent exhibition of photographs. Turn up at 11.30am or 3.30pm and you can also view the short, disturbing documentary *KZ-Dachau* in English. There are also weekend **tours** in English at 1.30pm. Get there by taking bus #724 or #726 from Dachau S-Bahn station.

## Eating and drinking

*Mensas* are the cheapest places to **eat**; though you're supposed to have a valid student card, no one seems to check. The most central one is at Leopoldstr. 15 (closed Sat & Sun), and there are two more in the main building at Schellingstrasse and at the Technical University, Arcisstr. 17. *Gaststätten* offer filling soups, salads and sandwich-type dishes. An excellent place to stock up on fresh bread, sausages and fruit is the bustling Viktualienmarkt, which offers an array of outdoor eateries in summer. **Drinking** is central to social life in Munich and, apart from the *Gaststätten* and beer gardens, the city has a lively café-bar culture that carries on well into the early hours. For a good alternative to glitzy Schwabing, head for Haidhausen, across the river to the southeast of the centre; it has a good mix of bars, cafés and restaurants.

### Cafés, café-bars and wine bars

**Alter Simpl** Türkenstr. 57. Famous literary café-bar that spawned the satirical magazine *Simplicissimus*, now a favoured student haunt.

**Café Glockenspiel** Marienplatz 28 (5th floor). Classy café-bar with a fusion menu and surprisingly few tourists; it has a rooftop terrace and a direct view across to its namesake. The entrance is in the passageway behind the shops.

**Café Kreutzkamm** Maffeistr. 4. Airy and elegant; one of the best (and most expensive) *Kaffee und Kuchen* establishments, just off Theatinerstrasse.

**Pfälzer Weinprobierstuben** Residenzstr. 1. Despite the chandeliers, this has an unpretentious buzz, serving excellent wines from western Germany.

### Restaurants

**Al Mercato** Prälat-Zistl-Str. 12. No-frills Italian serving cheap pizzas and pasta dishes, just south of the Viktualienmarkt. Closed Sun.

**Andechser am Dom** Behind the Dom, off Weinstr. Traditional place serving beer from the Andechs monastic brewery and solid Bavarian fare to a cheerful crowd.

**Bella Italia** Herzog-Wilhelm-Str. 8. One of a small chain of inexpensive Italian restaurants, south of Karlsplatz.

**Der Kleine Chinese** Im Tal 28. Cheap, filling Chinese dishes served all day in this tiny eatery near Marienplatz.

**Donisl** Weinstr. 1. A fine old Munich *Gaststätte* with an ornate eighteenth-century gallery and good prices.

**Haxnbauer** Corner of Sparkassenstr. and

Ledererstr. Specializes in Germany's famous roasted pork knuckles; the lamb version is no less tasty.

**Münchner Kartoffelhaus** Hochbrücken Str. 3. Cosy restaurant celebrating the humble potato. Good-value selection of carbohydrate-rich dishes. Head down Ledererstrasse from *Haxnbauer*, then right.

**Prinz Myshkin** Hackenstr. 2. Best vegetarian place in the centre, with international dishes served beneath a high, vaulted ceiling.

**Thai-China** Bahnhofplatz 1 (entrance on Schützenstr.). Unbeatable value for Indian food too; also does take-out.

### Beer gardens and beer halls

**Augustiner Bräustuben** Landsbergerstr. 19. Off the tourist track, this was once the house of Augustinian monks and now serves marvellous food in a great atmosphere.

**Chinesischer Turm** Englischer Garten 3. One of several beer gardens in the lovely Englischer Garten. Frequent live Bavarian brass band appearances.

**Hofbräuhaus** Platzl 9. Famous and touristy *Bierkeller*, but beer and food prices are reasonable.

**Münchner Bier Brotzeitstüberl** Viktualienmarkt. Popular beer garden in the centre of the market, with wooden trestles set under oak trees. Closes at 7pm.

**Weisses Bräuhaus** Im Tal 7. Famous for its wheat beer and the favourite Munich *Weisswurst*, a white veal (brain) sausage, best enjoyed with sweet mustard.

## Nightlife and entertainment

Munich has a vibrant nightlife scene, ranging from classical concerts and jazz bars to full-on dance clubs. The best sources of **information** are *In München*, a free magazine handed out in bars and restaurants, the monthly *Monatsprogram* from the tourist office, or the English-language *Munich Found*. Munich has three first-rate symphony **orchestras** – the Münchener Philharmoniker, the Bayrisches Rundfunk Sinfonie Orchester and the Staatsorchester – as well as eleven major and numerous fringe **theatres**. Advance tickets for plays and concerts can be bought at the box offices or commercial ticket shops such as the one located in the Marienplatz U-Bahn station. Munich's **club** scene centres around the popular *Kultfabrik* and its neighbour *Optimolwerke*, although there are plenty of other good dance venues scattered around town.

The huge **Oktoberfest**, held on the Theresienwiese fairground for sixteen days following the penultimate Saturday in September, is an orgy of beer drinking, spiced up by fairground rides that are so hairy they're banned in the US. The fairgrounds are divided along four main avenues, creating a boisterous city within a city, heaving from morning till night. The event began when a fair held to celebrate a Bavarian royal wedding in October 1810 proved so popular that it's been repeated ever since. For more information, check out ⊛www.oktoberfest.de. **Fasching**, Munich's carnival, is an excuse for fancy-dress balls and general shenanigans from mid-January until the beginning of Lent. More sedate is **Auer Dult**, a traditional market that takes place on the Mariahilfplatz during the last weeks of April or May, July and October each year; there are stalls selling food, crafts and antiques, and there's also a fairground.

### Clubs and live music venues

**Atomic Café** Neuturm Str. 5. Retro-style bar and club near Hofbräuhaus catering to a fashionable crowd.

**Kultfabrik** Grafinger Str. 6, S- or U-Bahn to Ostbahnhof. Along with adjacent *Optimolwerke* at Friedenstr. 10, this mini-city of clubs and bars housed in a network of old factory buildings attracts upwards of 30,000 ravers on any given weekend. A mix of musical genres and locales makes this Munich's premier nightspot.

**Muffathalle** Zellstr. 4, Haidhausen. Converted waterworks featuring live music and regular dance nights.

**Nachtwerk** Landsberger Str. 185. Draws a young crowd for its chart dance nights on Fri and Sat, and stages occasional up-and-coming live acts. Take tram #18 or #19 east from the centre.

**Olympiapark** Free rock concerts by the lake in summer; they usually get going around 2pm at weekends.

**Soul City** Maximilianplatz 6. Gay/mixed disco in the heart of the city – inhibitions best left at home.

**Unterfahrt** Einsteinstr. 42, Haidhausen. Showcase for avant-garde jazz, with many big names gracing the stage.

**Vorraum** Tal 15. Tiny chilled-out lounge across from the *Münchner Kartoffelhaus* that stays open late and has DJs nightly; closed Sun.

## Listings

**Bike rental** Radius, at the train station near platform 32.
**Consulates** UK, Bürkleinstr. 10 ℡089/21 10 90; Canada, Tal 29 ℡089/2 19 95 70; Ireland, Denningerstr. 15 ℡089/20 80 59 90; US, Königinstr. 5 ℡089/28 880.
**Gay Munich** Despite Bavaria's deep conservatism, Munich has an active and visible gay scene, centred primarily around Gärtnerplatz. *OurMunich* is a gay listings mag, and the *Columbia Fun Map* is a gay guide to the city. *Inge's Karotte*, Baaderstr. 13, is a café predominantly for lesbians; *Mylord*,

Ickstattstr. 2a, is a popular lesbian club. *Fortuna*, Maximiliansplatz 5, is a popular club with both gays and lesbians.
**Hospital** Technische Universität München, Ismaninger Str. 22 ℡089/4 14 00; Bereitschaftsdienst der Münchener Ärtze, Elisenstr. 3 (℡01805 19 12 12), is a late-night clinic near the train station.
**Internet** easyInternetcafé, Bahnhofplatz 1. Open 24hr.
**Laundry** City-Waschcenter, Paul-Heyse Str. 21.
**Pharmacy** Bahnhof-Apotheke, Bahnhofplatz 2.
**Post office** Bahnhofplatz 1.

# The Bavarian Alps

It's among the picture-book scenery of the **Alps** that you'll find the Bavarian folklore and customs that are the subjects of so many tourist brochures. The region also encompasses some of the most famous places in the province, such as the Olympic ski resort of **Garmisch-Partenkirchen**, and the fantasy castle of **Neuschwanstein**, just one of the lunatic palaces built for King Ludwig II of Bavaria. The western reaches are generally cheaper and less touristy, partly because they're not so easily accessible to Munich's weekend crowds. Much of the eastern region to **Berchtesgaden** is heavily geared to the tourist trade, but outside July and August, it's considerably quieter.

## Füssen and around

Lying between the Forggensee reservoir and the Ammer mountains, around 100km by rail from Munich, **FÜSSEN** and the adjacent town of **SCHWANGAU** are the bases for visiting Bavaria's two most popular castles. **Schloss Hohenschwangau** (daily: April–Sept 9am–6pm; Oct–March 10am–4pm; €9), originally built in the twelfth century but heavily restored in the nineteenth, was where Ludwig II spent his youth. A mark of his individualism is left in the bedroom, where he had the ceiling painted with stars that were spot-lit in the evenings. **Schloss Neuschwanstein** (same hours; €9, €17 combination ticket for both castles), the ultimate storybook turreted castle, was built by Ludwig a little higher up the mountain. The architectural hotchpotch includes a Byzantine throne hall and an artificial grotto. Left incomplete at Ludwig's death, it's a monument to a very sad and lonely man. The nearest HI **hostel** is in Füssen, at Mariahilferstr. 5 (℡08362/77 54; €19.40), otherwise the **tourist office** at Kaiser-Maximilian-Platz 1 in Füssen (Mon–Fri 9am–5pm, Sat 10am–12pm; ℡083 62/93 850, ⊛www.fuessen.de) can book accommodation. Füssen is also the end of the much-publicized **Romantic Road** from Würzburg via Augsburg, served by special tour buses in season.

## Garmisch-Partenkirchen and around

**GARMISCH-PARTENKIRCHEN** is the most famous town in the German Alps, partly because it's at the foot of the highest mountain – the **Zugspitze** (2966m) – and partly because it hosted the 1936 Winter Olympics. It has excellent facilities for skiing, skating and other winter sports, as well as abundant accommodation (❷–❾); the **tourist office** at Richard-Strauss-Platz 2 (Mon–Sat 8am–6pm, Sun 10am–noon; ℡088 21/18 07 00, ⊛www.garmisch-partenkirchen.de) has a full list. The ascent of Zugspitze by **rack-railway** or **cable car** (both €44 return, €35 in winter) is the most memorable local excursion. **MITTENWALD**, which remains a community rather than a resort, is 15km from Garmisch-Partenkirchen, cuddled up against the Austrian border. The Karwendel mountain towering above is a popular climb, and the view from the top is exhilarating; a **cable car** goes there (€20 return). The **tourist office**, at Dammkarstr. 3 (Tues–Fri 8.30am–5pm, Mon from 8am; June–Sept also Sat 9am–noon & Sun 10am–noon; ☏088 23/33 981, ⊛www.mittenwald.de), provides free maps of the area. There are plenty of good **guesthouses**, such as *Franziska*, Innsbrucker Str. 24 (☏088 23/92 030, ⊛www.franziska-tourismus.de; ❹), and *Sonnenheim*, Dammkarstr. 5 (☏088 23/82 47, ⊛www.sonnenheim-tourismus.de; ❸). The nearest **campsite** is 3km north, on the road to Garmisch.

### Berchtesgaden

Almost entirely surrounded by mountains at Bavaria's southeastern extremity – but easily reached by rail from Munich – the area around **BERCHTESGADEN** has a magical atmosphere, especially in the mornings, when mists rise from the lakes and swirl around lush valleys and rocky mountainsides. A star attraction is the stunning **Königssee**, Germany's highest lake, which bends around the foot of the towering Watzmann, 5km south of town – regular buses run out here – and has year-round **cruises** (every 30min; €15 return). You can also take a cable car up the **Jenner**, immediately above the lake (€18.80 return), used mostly by skiers in the winter months. Berchtesgaden is still indelibly associated with **Adolf Hitler**, who rented a house in the nearby village of Obersalzberg, which he later enlarged into the **Berghof**, a stately retreat where he could meet foreign dignitaries. It was blown up by the Allies, and the ruins are now overgrown. High above the village, Hitler's Kehlsteinhaus, or **"Eagle's Nest"**, survives as a restaurant, and can be reached by special bus from Obersalzberg once the snow has melted (April to mid-Oct; €14 return). Berchtesgaden has some great **mountain walks** to take you away from the crowds in summer – maps of suggested walking routes can be bought at the **tourist office** (mid-May to mid-Oct Mon–Fri 8.30am–6pm, Sat 9am–5pm, Sun 9am–3pm; mid-Oct to mid-May Mon–Fri 8.30am–5pm & Sat 9am–noon only; ☏086 52/96 70, ⊛www.berchtesgaden.de) opposite the train station. **Guesthouse** options include the friendly *Haus am Hang*, Göllsteinbichl 3 (☏086 52/43 59, ⊛www.hausamhang.de; ❸), and *Haus Achental*, Ramsauer Str. 4 (☏086 52/45 49, ⊛www.berchtesgaden.de/achental; ❹), where all rooms have bathrooms. The tourist office can direct you to any of the five **campsites** in the valley.

# Travel details

## Trains

**Berlin** to: Dresden (hourly; 2hr); Frankfurt (hourly; 4hr); Hamburg (hourly; 2hr 30min); Hannover (hourly; 1hr 30min); Leipzig (hourly; 2hr); Munich (frequent; 6hr 30 min); Weimar (every 2hr; 3hr).

**Cologne** to: Aachen (every 30min; 1hr); Frankfurt (2 hourly; 1hr 25min); Heidelberg (2 hourly; 2hr); Mainz (every 20min; 1hr 45min); Stuttgart (frequent; 2hr 15min).

**Dresden** to: Meissen (every 30min; 50min).

**Frankfurt** to: Baden-Baden (hourly; 1hr 30min); Berlin (every 30min; 4hr); Cologne (every 30min; 1hr 30min); Hamburg (frequent; 3hr 45min); Hannover (frequent; 2hr 20min); Heidelberg (every 30min; 1hr); Munich (hourly; 4hr); Nuremberg (every 30min; 2hr 30min).

**Hamburg** to: Hannover (every 30min; 1hr 25min); Lübeck (every 30min; 40min).

**Hannover** to: Goslar (2–3 hourly; 1hr 20min–2hr); Heidelberg (hourly; 4hr).

**Koblenz** to: Trier (hourly; 1hr 30min).

**Leipzig** to: Dresden (hourly; 1hr 40min); Meissen (hourly; 2hr); Weimar (frequent; 50min–1hr 40min).

**Mainz** to: Koblenz (frequent; 50min).

**Munich** to: Augsburg (every 20min; 30min); Nuremberg (hourly; 1hr 30min–2hr 30min); Regensburg (1–2 hourly; 1hr 30min).

**Nuremberg** to: Munich (hourly; 1hr 40min); Regensburg (hourly; 1hr).

**Stuttgart** to: Freiburg (hourly; 2hr); Heidelberg (every 30min; 1hr); Konstanz (frequent; 2hr 10min–3hr 30min).

# Greece

# Greece highlights

* **The Acropolis, Athens** One of the archetypal images of Western culture. See p.494

* **Mystra** A fortified Byzantine town with frescoed monasteries, tumbling down the slopes of Mt Taïyettos. See p.499

* **Olympia** Atmospheric ancient site where the Olympic Games were born. See p.502

* **Delphi** Centre of the world according to the ancient Greeks, and site of the famous oracle. See p.503

* **Metéora** Awe-inspiring Byzantine monasteries perched atop extraordinary rock formations. See p.505

* **Santoríni (Thíra)** Volcanic island with spectacular sunsets from the caldera cliff. See p.515

* **Knossos, Crete** This 3700-year-old palace is the largest and most impressive Minoan site. See p.526

* **Samarian Gorge, Crete** The longest gorge in Europe, and one of the most beautiful. See p.529

△ The Acropolis, Athens

# Introduction and basics

With 166 inhabited islands and a landscape that ranges from Mediterranean to Balkan, **Greece** has enough appeal to fill months of travel. Its historic sites span four millennia of civilization, ranging from the renowned – Olympia, Delphi and the Parthenon in Athens – to the obscure, where a visit can still seem like a personal discovery. The beaches are distributed along a long, convoluted coastline, and garland cosmopolitan resorts as well as remote islands where boats may call only once or twice a week. The landscapes of Greece encompass the stony deserts of the Máni, the lush Peloponnesian coastal hills, the resin-scented ridges of Skiáthos and Sámos and the wind-blasted rocks of the central Aegean. The simple pleasures of the natural environment, and of the country's climate and food, are what make Greece special.

The country is the sum of an extraordinary diversity of influences. Romans, Arabs, Frankish Crusaders, Venetians, Slavs, Albanians, Turks, Italians, as well as the thousand-year Byzantine Empire, have all been and gone since the time of Alexander the Great. Each has left its mark: the **Byzantines** through countless churches and monasteries, particularly at the ghost town of Mystra; the **Venetians** in impregnable fortifications such as Monemvasiá in the Peloponnese; the **Franks** with crag-top castles, again in the Peloponnese but also in the Dodecanese and east Aegean. Most obvious, perhaps, is the heritage of four hundred years of **Ottoman Turkish** rule which exercised an inestimable influence on music, cuisine, language and way of life.

Even before the fall of Byzantium in the fifteenth century, the Greek country people – peasants, fishermen, shepherds – had created one of the most vigorous and truly **popular cultures** in Europe, which endured until quite recently in songs and dances, costumes, embroidery, furniture and the whitewashed houses of popular image. Since the 1970s much of this has disappeared under the impact of Western consumer values, relegated mostly to museums, but Greek architectural and musical heritage in particular has undergone a recent renaissance.

## Information & maps

The **National Tourist Organization (EOT)** publishes an array of free regional pamphlets and maps, though many are years out of date. There are EOT offices in most larger towns and resorts; in other places, try equally good **municipal tourist offices**. The **tourist police** often have lists of rooms to let, but are mostly there to assist if you have a serious complaint about a hotel or restaurant. The most reliable **maps** are published in Athens. Road Editions (ⓦ www.road.gr) has the best range for mainland regions and islands; maps by Emvelia Editions (ⓦ www.emvelia.gr) include useful town plans; and Anavasi (ⓦ www.anavasi.gr) produce the best mountaineering maps, plus excellent coverage of the Sporades and Cyclades.

---

### Greece on the net

ⓦ**www.culture.gr** Ministry of Culture site; lots of info on ruins and museums.
ⓦ**www.athensnews.gr** Useful and literate English-language weekly.
ⓦ**www.gnto.gr** Greek National Tourist Organisation site.
ⓦ**www.poseidon.ncmr.gr** Sophisticated oceanographer's site that's the best window on current Greek weather.
ⓦ**www.gtp.gr** Information on all ferry and hydrofoil schedules except some minor local lines.

# Money and banks

Greece's currency is the **euro** (€). **Banks** are normally open Mon–Thurs 8am–2.30pm, Fri 8am–2pm. They charge a flat fee (€2–3) to change money, the National Bank usually being the cheapest; travel agencies and designated money-exchange booths give a poorer rate, but often levy a sliding two-per-cent commission, which makes them better than banks for changing small amounts. Plenty of **ATMs** accept foreign cards; in isolated areas without ATMs, a small quantity of US dollar/sterling notes – not travellers' cheques – will prove useful. **Credit cards** are generally accepted in more upmarket hotels, restaurants and shops.

# Communications

Most **post offices** operate Mon–Fri 7.30am–2pm, and into the evening and even weekends in the largest cities and major resorts. **Stamps** can also be bought at designated postal agencies inside newsstands or stationers. **Poste restante** is reasonably efficient. **Public phones** are mainly card-operated, though many cafés and kiosks have counter-top coin-op models. Buy phone cards from newsagents and kiosks. It's possible to make collect (reverse-charge) or charge-card calls from these phones, but you need credit on a Greek phone-card to begin. There are no area codes per se; you merely dial all ten digits of every phone number. The operator is on ☎132 (domestic) or ☎139 (international). All big towns have several places with **Internet** access, and there's usually at least one place on the more visited islands. Prices are €4.50–6/hr.

# Getting around

The **rail** network is limited, and trains are slower than the equivalent buses – except on the showcase IC (intercity) lines, which cost more. However, most trains are cheaper than buses, and some of the routes are highlights in their own right. If you're starting a journey at the initial station of a run

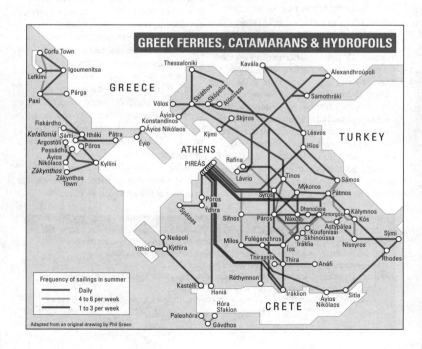

**GREEK FERRIES, CATAMARANS & HYDROFOILS**

Corfu Town, Igoumenítsa, Lefkími, Párga, Paxí, Fiskárdho, Kefalloniá, Sámi, Argostóli, Pessádha, Áyios Nikólaos, Zákynthos, Zákynthos Town, Kyllíni, Itháki, Póros, Pátra, Éyio, Vólos, Áyios Konstandínos, Áyios Nikólaos, Thessaloníki, Skiáthos, Skópelos, Alónissos, Skýros, Kými, Kavála, Alexandroúpoli, Samothráki, Lésvos, Híos, TURKEY, GREECE, ATHENS, PIREÁS, Rafína, Lávrio, Tínos, Sámos, Pátmos, Mýkonos, Sýros, Dhonoússa, Amorgós, Kálymnos, Kós, Póros, Ýdhra, Spétses, Sífnos, Páros, Náxos, Koufoníssi, Astypálea, Skhinoússa, Iráklia, Sými, Níssyros, Rhodes, Neápoli, Kýthira, Mílos, Folégandhros, Íos, Thirassía, Thíra, Anáfi, Yíthio, Réthymno, Kastélli, Haniá, Iráklion, Áyios Nikólaos, Sitía, Paleohóra, Hóra Sfakíon, Gávdhos, CRETE

Frequency of sailings in summer
Daily
4 to 6 per week
1 to 3 per week

Adapted from an original drawing by Phil Green

you can reserve a seat; at most intermediate points, it's first-come, first-served. **Eurail** and **InterRail** are valid, though passholders must reserve like everyone else, and there's a small supplement on the intercity services.

**Buses** form the bulk of public land transport, and service on the major routes is efficient, with companies organized nationally into a syndicate called **KTEL** (ⓦ www .ktel.org). Larger towns can have several widely spaced termini for departures in different directions, so ensure you aim for the right station. Ticketing is computerized for major intercity lines, which can get booked up. On rural routes, tickets are dispensed on the spot, with some standing allowed. On many islands, a bus runs between the port and main town to coincide with ferry arrivals and departures.

Schedules for **sea transport** are notoriously erratic. The most reliable, up-to-date information is available from the local port police (*limenarhío*) at Pireás and on all sizeable islands. Regular ferry tickets are best bought on the day of departure, unless you need to reserve a cabin – although from March 23 to 25, the weeks before and after Orthodox Easter and during August it's best to book several days in advance. The cheapest ticket is "deck class". Hydrofoils and high-speed catamarans are roughly twice as fast and twice as expensive as ordinary ferries. In season, *kaḯkia* (caiques) sail to more obscure islets.

Once on the islands, almost everybody rents a **scooter** or a **bike**. Scooters cost from €12 a day, mountain bikes a bit less. To rent a motorbike (anything over 50cc) you usually need to show an appropriate licence. You should make sure your travel insurance covers spills and damage to the bike, as bike-agency insurance is usually deficient.

## Accommodation

Most of the year you can turn up pretty much anywhere and find a **room**. Only around Easter (Orthodox, see p.489) and during July and August are you likely to experience problems; at these times, it's worth booking well in advance. If that's not possible, head off the standard tourist routes, or arrive at each new place early in the day.

**Hotels** are categorized from "Luxury" down to "E-class" – slowly being replaced by a five-to-no-star system – but these ratings have more to do with amenities and number of rooms than pricing. In resorts and throughout the islands, you have the additional option of **privately let rooms** (*dhomátia*). These are divided into three classes (A–C), and are usually cheaper than hotels. As often as not, rooms find you: owners descend on ferry and bus arrivals to fill any space they have. Increasingly, rooms are being eclipsed by **self-catering facilities**, which can be equally good value; if signs or touts are not apparent, ask for studios at travel agencies. There's a handful of **hostels** outside Athens; with few exceptions, they're run-down and not HI-affiliated, and charge around €8–12 a night.

Official **campsites** range from basic island compounds to highly organized complexes, mostly closed in winter (Nov–April). Casual places rarely cost more than €4 a night per person; however, at fancier sites it's possible for two people and a tent to pay almost as much as for a basic room. Rough camping is forbidden and the regulations do get enforced occasionally.

## Food and drink

**Eating out** in Greece is popular and reasonably priced: €14–20 per person for a meal with beer or cheap wine. Greeks generally don't eat breakfast. **Snacks**, however, can be one of the distinctive pleasures of Greek eating. *Tyrópites* and *spanakópites* (cheese and spinach pies respectively) are on sale everywhere, as are *souvlákia* (small kebabs) and *yíros* (doner kebab), served in *píta* bread with garnish. In choosing a **taverna**, the best strategy is to go where the locals go. Typical dishes to try include *moussakás* (aubergine and meat pie), *yígandes* (white haricot beans in red sauce), *tzatzíki* (yoghurt, garlic and cucumber dip), *melitzanosaláta* (aubergine dip), *khtapódhi* (octopus), and *kalamarákia* (fried baby squid). Note that people eat late: 2.30–4pm for lunch & 9–11.30pm for dinner.

The traditional coffee shop or **kafenío** is the central pivot of life in rural villages; like tavernas, these range from the sophisticated to the old-fashioned. Their main business is Greek coffee, but they also serve spirits such as aniseed-flavoured *oúzo* and brandy, as well as beer and soft drinks. Islanders take pre-dinner *oúzo* an hour or two before sunset: you'll be served a glass of water alongside, to be tipped into your *oúzo* until it turns milky white. **Bars**, often housed in buildings of historic interest, are now ubiquitous in the largest towns and resorts. Drinks, at €5.50–9, are invariably more expensive than at a *kafenío*. Tavernas offer a better choice of **wines**: Boutari, Tsantali and Calliga are good, low-priced labels. Otherwise, ask for the local bulk wines – *hýma* or *varelísio* – at around €4–6 per litre.

# Opening hours and holidays

**Shops** generally open at 8.30–9am, then take a long break at 2–2.30pm before reopening in the late afternoon (5.30/6pm–8.30/9pm) on Tuesday, Thursday and Friday only. However, tourist areas have shops and offices often staying open right through the day. Opening hours for **museums** and **ancient sites** change with exasperating

## Greek

| | Greek | Pronunciation |
|---|---|---|
| **Yes** | *Néh* | Ne |
| **No** | *Óhi* | Oxhi |
| **Please** | *Parakaló* | Parakalo |
| **Thank you** | *Efharistó* | Efharisto |
| **Hello/Good day** | *Yás sas/Hérete* | Yas sas/Xherete |
| **Goodbye** | *Adío* | Adio |
| **Excuse me** | *Signómi* | Siynomi |
| **Where?** | *Pou?* | Poo? |
| **Good** | *Kaló* | Kalo |
| **Bad** | *Kakó* | Kako |
| **Near** | *Kondá* | Konda |
| **Far** | *Makriá* | Makria |
| **Cheap** | *Fthinó* | Fthino |
| **Expensive** | *Akrivó* | Akrivo |
| **Open** | *Aniktó* | Anikto |
| **Closed** | *Klistó* | Klisto |
| **Today** | *Símera* | Simera |
| **Yesterday** | *Khthés* | Khthes |
| **Tomorrow** | *Ávrio* | Avrio |
| **How much is....?** | *Póso káni...?* | Poso kani...? |
| **What time is it?** | *Ti óra íneh...?* | Ti ora ine...? |
| **I don't understand** | *Dhen katalavéno* | en katalaveno |
| **Do you speak English?** | *Xérete angliká?* | Xherete anglika? |
| **One** | *Éna/mía* | Ena/mia |
| **Two** | *Dhýo* | Thio |
| **Three** | *Trís/tría* | Tris/tria |
| **Four** | *Tésseres/* | Tesseris/ téssera tessera |
| **Five** | *Pénde* | Pende |
| **Six** | *Éxi* | Exhi |
| **Seven** | *Eftá* | Efta |
| **Eight** | *Októ* | Okto |
| **Nine** | *Enéa* | Enea |
| **Ten** | *Dhéka* | Theka |

frequency. Smaller sites generally close for a long siesta (even when they're not supposed to), as do monasteries. Many state-owned museums and sites are free for students from EU countries (a valid card is required, but not necessarily an ISIC). Non-EU students, and all over-65s, generally pay half-price. Most museums and archeological sites are free on the following days; every Sunday Nov to end of March; 1st Sunday of April, May, June & Oct; 2nd Sunday of July–Sept; all national holidays. There's a vast range of **public holidays** and **festivals**. The most important, when almost everything will be closed, are: Jan 1 & 6, 1st Mon of Lent, March 25, May 1, Orthodox Easter Sun & Mon (April 23 in 2006, April 8 in 2007), Pentecost/Whit Mon, Aug 15, Oct 28, Dec 24–27.

# Emergencies

The most common causes of a run-in with the **police** are drunken loutishness,

breaking into archeological sites after-hours, and camping outside an authorized site. Topless bathing is now legal on virtually all Greek beaches but, especially in smaller places, be aware of local sensitivities before stripping off (and full nudity is tolerated only at designated or isolated beaches). For minor medical complaints go to the local **pharmacy**, usually open Mon–Fri 8am–2pm. Details of pharmacies open out-of-hours are posted in all pharmacy windows. For serious medical attention you'll find English-speaking doctors in all bigger towns and resorts; consult the tourist police for names. Emergency treatment is free in state hospitals, though you'll only get the most basic level of nursing care.

13

GREECE | Basics

489

# Athens

**ATHENS** has been inhabited continuously for over seven thousand years. Its acropolis, protected by a ring of mountains and commanding views of all seagoing approaches, was a natural choice for prehistoric settlement. Its development as a city-state and artistic centre reached its zenith in the fifth century BC with a flourish of art, architecture, literature and philosophy that has pervaded Western culture ever since. Following World War II, the city's population has risen from 700,000 to four million – over a third of the country's population. – and the speed of this process is reflected in Athens' chaotic mix of retro and contemporary: cutting-edge clothes shops and designer bars stand by the remnants of the Ottoman bazaar, while brutalist 1960s apartment blocks dwarf crumbling Neoclassical mansions. The ancient sites are the most obvious of Athens' attractions, but the attractive cafés, landscaped stair-streets, and markets, the startling views from the hills of Lykavitós and Filopáppou, and, around the foot of the Acropolis, the scattered monuments of the Byzantine, medieval and nineteenth-century town all have their appeal. Outside the city, the **Temple of Poseidon** at Sounion is the most popular trip, justified by its dramatic clifftop position.

The port of **PIREÁS**, effectively an extension of Athens, is the main terminus for international and inter-island **ferries**. Get there from Athens by metro: Pireás is the last stop heading southwest from Monastiráki. The other ports on the east coast of the Attic peninsula, **RAFÍNA** and **LÁVRIO**, are alternative departure points for many of the Cycladic and northeast Aegean islands. Frequent buses connect them with central Athens.

## Arrival, information and city transport

A light-rail line (€5–8 depending on number of people in party) whisks you from Eleftherios Venizelos **airport** to Dhoukíssis Plakendías station, easterly terminus of the metro network. The X95 express **bus** (24hrs; every 20–40min) from outside Arrivals goes direct to Sýndagma square, the X94 heads for Ethnikí Ámyna metro station, whilst the X96 express bus (same times, price and location) heads to Pireás port; these cost €2.90 single. For a separate €3, you can buy a day ticket valid on all Athens public transport for 24hr. International **trains** arrive at the Stathmós Laríssis in the northwest of the city centre, with its own metro station. The nearly adjacent Stathmós Peloponníssou handles traffic to and from the Peloponnese. Buses from northern Greece and the Peloponnese arrive at Kifissoú 100, ten minutes from the centre by bus #051. Buses from central Greece arrive closer to the centre at Liossíon 260, north of the train stations (bus #024 to Sýndagma). Most international buses drop off at the train station or Kifissoú 100; a few will drop you right in the city centre. Arriving by boat at Pireás, the simplest access to the centre is by metro, with the station being a few steps from the quay on Platía Odhissoú. The city's main EOT **tourist office** is at Leofóros Amálias 26 (Mon–Fri 9am–7pm; ☎210 33 10 392).

All **public transport** operates daily from around 5am to midnight. Athens' bus and trolley network is extensive but very crowded at peak times. A **tram** line built for the Olympiad runs from Sýndagma to the seaside resorts of Glyfadha and Faliro. Line #1 of the **metro** runs from Pireás to Kifissiá, with central stops at Thissío, Monastiráki and Omónia; Line #2 runs from Áyios Andónios to Áyios Dhimítrios via Sýndagma and a station at the foot of the Acropolis; Line #3 heads east from Monastiráki to Dhoukíssis Plakendías (with special metro cars continuing direct to the airport). Tickets (€0.70) are available at all stations from automatic coin-op dispensers or staffed windows. Tickets for **buses** must be bought in advance from kiosks and validated once on board. **Taxis** can be surprisingly difficult to hail, but are very inexpensive: fares around the city centre should rarely come to more than

€4. Taxi drivers will often pick up a whole string of passengers along the way, each passenger paying the full fare for their journey – so if you're picked up by an already occupied taxi, memorize the meter reading; you'll pay from then on, including a €1.50 minimum charge.

## Accommodation

**Accommodation** can be packed to the gills in July and August but for much of the rest of the year there is good availability.

### Hostels

**Athens Backpackers** Makri 12 ☎210 92 24 044, ⓦwww.backpackers.gr. Excellent hostel with clean spacious dorms, Internet access, laundry, BBQ and rooftop bar with Acropolis views. €18–23

**Hostel #5** Dhamáreos 75, Pangráti ☎210 75 19 530, ⓦwww.athens-yhostel.com. In a congenial (if remote) neighbourhood – trolleys #2 or #11 stop nearby – with cooking and laundry facilities, and no curfew. €14.

**International Youth Hostel** Víktoros Ougó 16, near Metaxouryío metro ☎210 52 32 540. Central Athens' cheapest option, an official HI hostel with a cheerful atmosphere, well-kept facilities and helpful staff, though the location isn't wonderful. €8–11.

**Student and Travellers' Inn** Kydhathinéon 16 ☎210 32 44 808, ⓦwww.studenttravellersinn .com. Popular, clean and well-run hotel-cum-hostel in a prime location. Singles, doubles, triples and dorms, most with shared bathrooms, as well as luggage storage and Internet access. Dorms €15–23, doubles ❹

### Hotels

**John's Place** Patróöu 5, Pláka ☎210 32 29 719. Dark rooms with baths in the hall, but neat and well-kept. In a peaceful backstreet off Mitropóleos, with a cheap restaurant on the ground floor. ❸

**Marble House** Cul-de-sac off Anastasíou Zínni 35, Koukáki ☎210 92 28 294, ⓦwww.marblehouse .gr. Peaceful, welcoming pension south of the Acropolis. Most rooms en suite and with balcony; all rooms have fans and fridge. Reservations essential. ❸

**Orion** Emm. Benáki 105, corner Anexartisías, Exárhia ☎210 33 02 387, ⒺOrion-dryades@mail .com. Quiet, well-run budget hotel across from the Lófos Stréfi park – a steep final walk to get there, yet close to many attractions. Rooftop kitchen and common area with an amazing view. ❹

**Phaedra** Adhriánou & Herefóndos 16, Pláka ☎210 32 38 461. All the cheerful, air-con rooms, just over half en suite. Excellent location on pedestrian street overlooking a Byzantine church and the Acropolis. ❹

### Campsites

**Nea Kifissia** Potamoú 60, Néa Kifissiá ☎210 62 05 646. In a leafy suburb, this year-round place has its own swimming pool. Metro to Kifissiá then bus #528 behind the station.

**Várkiza Camping** Km27 on the Athens–Sounion road ☎210 89 73 614. Large year-round site by the beach, 20km south of the centre. Bus #A3 from Amalías Avenue to Glyfáda, then #115 to Várkiza.

## The City

**Pláka** is the best place to begin exploring the city. One of the few parts of Athens with charm and architectural merit, its narrow streets and stepped lanes are flanked by nineteenth-century Neoclassical houses. An attractive approach follows **Odhós Kydhathinéon**, a pedestrian walkway starting on Odhós Filellínon, south of Sýndagma. It continues through café-crowded Platía Filomoússou Eterías to **Odhós Adhrianoú**, which runs nearly the whole east–west length of Pláka from Hadrian's Arch to the Thissíon. From the Roman Forum uphill, Adhrianoú is tattily commercial, but just past the end of Kydhathinéon, there's a quiet and attractive sitting space around the fourth-century-BC **Monument of Lysikratos**, erected to celebrate the success of a prize-winning dramatic chorus. Continuing straight ahead from the Kyd-hathinéon–Adhriánou intersection up **Odhós Théspidhos** you reach the edge of the Acropolis precinct. Up to the right, the whitewashed Cycladic houses of

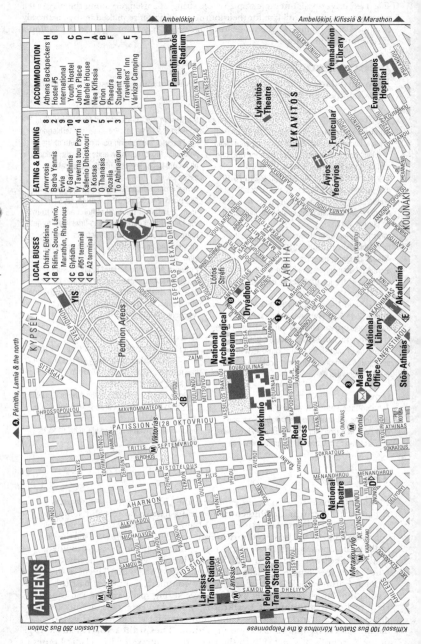

**13**

**GREECE** | Athens

**ATHENS**

**ACCOMMODATION**
| | |
|---|---|
| Athens Backpackers | H |
| Hostel #5 | G |
| International Youth Hostel | C |
| John's Place | D |
| Marble House | I |
| Nea Kifissia | A |
| Orion | B |
| Phaedra | F |
| Student and Travellers' Inn | E |
| Várkiza Camping | J |

**EATING & DRINKING**
| | |
|---|---|
| Amvrosia | 8 |
| Barba Yannis | 2 |
| Evvia | 9 |
| Iy Gardhinia | 10 |
| Iy Taverna tou Psyrri | 4 |
| Kafenio Dhioskouri | 6 |
| O Kostas | 7 |
| O Thanasis | 5 |
| Rozalia | 1 |
| To Athinaïkon | 3 |

**LOCAL BUSES**
- ◁ A   Dháfni, Eléfsina
- ◁ B   Ráfina, Soúnio, Lávrio, Marathón, Rhámnous
- ◁ C   Glyfádha
- ◁ D   #051 terminal
- ◁ E   A2 terminal

Panathinaïkos Stadium

LYKAVITÓS

Lykavitós Theatre

Funicular

Áyios Yeóryios

Vennádhion Library

Evangelismos Hospital

KOLONÁKI

Akadhimía

National Academy

National Library

Stoá Athinás

EXÁRHIA

Lófos Stréfi

Dryádhon

Pedhíon Áreos

KYPSÉLI

VIS

National Archeological Museum

Polytekhnío

Red Cross

Viktorías

Omonia

Main Post Office

Metaxouryío

National Theatre

Lárissis Train Station

Peloponníssou Train Station

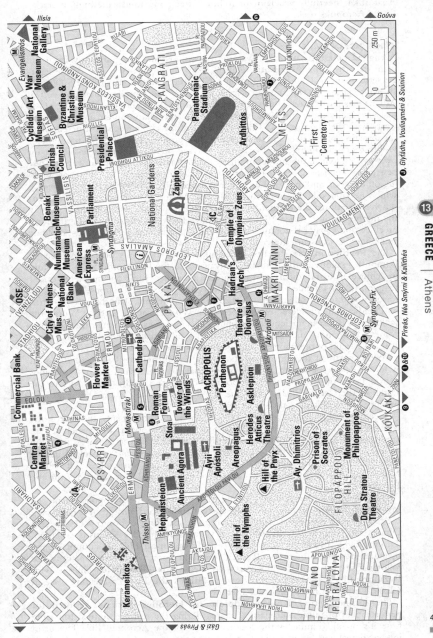

GREECE | Athens

13

Anafiótika cheerfully proclaim an architect-free zone amidst the highest crags of the Acropolis rock.

## The Acropolis

A rugged limestone outcrop, watered by springs and rising abruptly from the plain of Attica, the **Acropolis** (daily 8.30am–2.30/5pm) was one of the earliest settlements in Greece, supporting a Neolithic community around 5000 BC. By Mycenaean times it sported a fortified palace and temples where the cult of Athena was introduced. During the ninth century BC, it became the heart of the first Greek city-state, and in the wake of Athenian military supremacy and a peace treaty with the Persians in 449 BC, Pericles had the complex reconstructed under the direction of architect and sculptor Pheidias, producing most of the monuments visible today, including the Parthenon. Having survived more or less intact for over two millennia, the Acropolis finally fell victim to the vagaries of war. In 1687 besieging Venetians ignited a Turkish gunpowder magazine in the Parthenon, blasting off the roof, and in 1801 Lord Elgin removed the frieze (the "Elgin Marbles"), which he later sold to the British Museum. Meanwhile, generations of visitors slowly wore down the Parthenon's surfaces; more recently, smog has been turning the marble to dust. Since 1981, visitors have been barred from the Parthenon's precinct, and a major restoration programme is proceeding sporadically; scaffolding and cranes may obscure the view.

The **Parthenon** was the first great building in Pericles's plan. Designed by Iktinos, it exploits all the refinements available to the Doric order of architecture to achieve an extraordinary and unequalled harmony. Built on the site of earlier temples, it was intended as a new sanctuary for Athena and a house for her cult image, a colossal wooden statue decked in ivory and gold plate that was designed by Pheidias and considered one of the Seven Wonders of the Ancient World; the sculpture was lost in ancient times, but its characteristics are known through later copies. "Parthenon" means "virgins' chamber" and initially referred only to a room at the west end of the temple occupied by the priestesses of Athena.

To the north of the Parthenon stands the **Erechtheion**, the last of the great works of Pericles. Here, in symbolic reconciliation, Athena and the city's previous patron Poseidon-Erechtheus were both worshipped. On the south side, in the Porch of the Caryatids, the Ionic line is transformed into six maidens (caryatids) holding the entablature on their heads.

Placed discreetly on a level below that of the main monuments, the **Acropolis Museum** (Mon 10am–2.30pm, Tues–Sun 8.30am–2.30pm; price included in admission to Acropolis) contains nearly all the portable objects removed from the Acropolis since 1834. Prize exhibits include the *Moschophoros*, a painted marble statue of a young man carrying a sacrificial calf; the graceful sculpture of Athena Nike adjusting one sandal, known as *Iy Sandalízoussa*; and four caryatids from the Erechtheion.

Rock-hewn stairs immediately below the entrance to the Acropolis ascend the low hill of the **Areopagus**, site of the ancient court of criminal justice. Following the road or path over the flank of the Acropolis, you come out onto pedestrianized Dhionysíou Areopayítou, just above the Odeion of Herodes Atticus (see below). Turning right, a network of paths leads up **Filopáppou Hill**, its summit capped by a grandiose monument to a Roman consul. Just north of the main path, which follows a line of truncated ancient walls, sits **Áyios Dhimítrios** church, with Byzantine frescoes. North of this rises the **Hill of the Pnyx**, a meeting place in Classical times for the democratic assembly.

The second-century Roman **Odeion of Herodes Atticus**, restored for performances of music and classical drama during the summer festival (the only time it's open), dominates the southern slope of the Acropolis hill. The main interest hereabouts lies in earlier Greek sites to the east, pre-eminent among them the **Theatre of Dionysos**. Masterpieces of Aeschylus, Sophocles, Euripides and Aristophanes were first performed here, at one of the most evocative locations in the city. The ruins are impressive; the theatre, rebuilt in the fourth century BC, could hold some seventeen thousand spectators.

### The Agora and Roman Forum

Northwest of the Acropolis, the **Agora** was the nexus of ancient Athenian city life, where acts of administration, commerce and public assembly competed for space. The site is a confused jumble of ruins, dating from various stages between the sixth century BC and the fifth century AD. For some idea of what you are surveying, head for the **museum** in the rebuilt Stoa of Attalos. At the far corner of the agora precinct sits the nearly intact but distinctly clunky Doric **Temple of Hephaistos**, otherwise known as the Thissíon from the exploits of Theseus depicted on its friezes.

The **Roman Forum**, or Roman agora, was built as an extension of the Hellenistic agora by Julius Caesar and Augustus. The best-preserved and most intriguing of the ruins, though, is the graceful, octagonal structure known as the **Tower of the Winds**. It was designed in the first century BC by a Syrian astronomer, and served as a compass, sundial, weather vane and water-clock powered by a stream from one of the Acropolis springs. Each face of the tower is adorned with a relief of a figure floating through the air, personifying the eight winds.

### Sýndagma Square, National Gardens and Lykavitós

All roads lead to Platía Syndágmatos – **Sýndagma Square** – with its pivotal metro station. Geared to tourism, with a main post office, banks, luxury hotels and travel agents grouped around, it has little to recommend it. Behind the parliament buildings on the square, the **National Gardens** provide the most refreshing spot in the city, a shady oasis of trees, shrubs and creepers. South of the gardens stands **Hadrian's Arch**, erected by the Roman emperor to mark the edge of the Classical city and the beginning of his own. Directly behind are sixteen surviving columns of the 104 that originally comprised the **Temple of Olympian Zeus** – the largest in Greece, dedicated by Hadrian in 131 AD.

At the northeastern corner of the National Gardens is the fascinating and much-overlooked **Benáki Museum**, Koumbári 1 (Mon & Wed–Sat 9am–5pm, Thurs 9am–midnight, Sun 9am–3pm; €6, free on Thurs), with a well-organized collection that features Mycenaean jewellery, Greek costumes, memorabilia of the Greek War of Independence and historical documents, engravings and paintings.

Taking the second left off Vassilísis Sofías after the Benáki Museum will bring you to the **Museum of Cycladic and Ancient Greek Art**, Neofýtou Dhouká 4 (Mon & Wed–Fri 10am–4pm, Sat 10am–3pm; €5), impressive for both its subject and the quality of its displays.

North, past the posh shopping district of Kolonáki, a path through woods begins its ascent to the summit of **Lykavitós**. On top, a chapel of Áyios Yeóryios provides the main focus. A pair of nearby cafés both have views spectacular enough to excuse their high prices.

To the northwest, beyond Omónia, the fabulous **National Archeological Museum**, Patissíon 44, contains gold finds from the grave circle at Mycenae, including the so-called Mask of Agamemnon, along with an impressive classical art collection and findings from the island of Thíra, dating from around 1450 BC, contemporary with the Minoan civilization on Crete.

## Eating, drinking and entertainment

Pláka's stepped lanes provide a pleasant evening's setting for a meal, despite the touts and tourist hype, but for good-value, good-quality fare, outlying neighbourhoods such as Psyrrí, Koukáki and Exárhia are better. Quintessentially Greek **ouzerí** and **mezedhopolía** serve filling *mezédhes* (the Greek version of tapas) along with drinks, adding up to a substantial meal. Athens probably has Europe's most expensive coffee at €3 for an espresso even at ordinary places: developing a taste for Greek coffee (*ellinikós*) will prove slightly cheaper. Bars, cinemas, exhibitions and nightlife venues change frequently, so it's useful to have a copy of the English-language weekly *Athens News* (Fri; ⊛www.athensnews.gr), which has **listings** for clubs, galleries, concerts and films. The summer **Athens Festival** (late May to late Sept) encompasses classical Greek theatre, established and contemporary dance, classical music, big-name jazz, traditional Greek music and a smattering of rock shows. Most performances take place at the Herodes Atticus theatre, which is memorable in itself on a warm summer's evening. There are also special bus excursions to the great ancient theatre at Epidaurus. The main **festival box office** (☏210 92 82 900, ⊛www.greekfestival.gr) is at Hatzikhrístou 23.

### Restaurants

**Amvrosia** Dhrákou 3-5, right by Syngroú-Fix metro, Veíkoú. The best grill on this pedestrian street; always packed. Good takeaway *ghýros* (Greek kebabs), or enjoy a whole roast chicken at outdoor tables.

**Barba Yannis** Emmanouíl Benáki 94, Exárhia. Vast menu of inexpensive oven-cooked food, served indoors and out. Food is best at lunch, but it's open till 2am Mon–Sat, 6pm Sun.

**Iy Gardhinia** Anastasíou Zínni 29, Koukáki. Basic but inexpensive oven-casserole food in a cool, cavernous premises run by a friendly couple. Open 11am–9pm, closes earlier in midsummer.

**Iy Taverna tou Psyrri** Eskhýlou 12, Psyrrí. Straightforward taverna that excels in grilled/fried seafood, vegetable starters and wine from basement barrels. Arrive early (supper only) or wait for a table.

**O Kostas** Ekális 7, Platía Varnáva, Pangráti. Among the oldest, cheapest tavernas in town, there's a brief, lovingly cooked menu of bean dishes, meatballs and fried fish, accompanied by palatable bulk wine, served at indoor/outdoor tables. Closed Sun.

**O Thanasis** Mitropóleos 69, Monastiráki. Reckoned the best *souvláki* and Middle Eastern kebab in this district. Always packed with locals at lunchtime; worth the wait. Take out or eat in.

**Rozalia** Valtetsíou 58, Exárhia. The best all-round *mezédhes*-and-grills taverna with a garden open in summer.

### Ouzerí and mezedhopolía

**To Athinaïkon** Themistokléous 2, cnr Panepistimíou. Long-established *ouzerí* with marble tables and old posters, popular with local workers at lunch; strong on fresh seafood. Closed Sun.

**Kafenio Dhioskouri** Dhioskoúron, Pláka. Popular, shady bar/café with an unbeatable view of the ancient agora, where cold drinks and coffees take precedence over slightly pricey snacks.

**Evvia** Yeoryíou Olymbíou 8, Koukáki. Fresh dips and seafood titbits, plus good bulk wine or *oúzo*; sidewalk seating on this pedestrian street. Daily except Aug.

## Listings

**Bookshops** Compendium, Níkis 28 off Sýndagma, has books on Greece, travel guides (including Rough Guides), magazines and a secondhand section. Eleftheroudhakis, Panepistimíou 17 plus other branches, has the largest foreign-language stock in town, plus maps. Iy Folia tou Vivlíou, arcade at Panepistimíou 25, has a good travel guide/map section.

**Embassies and consulates** Australia, Cnr Kifissias & Alexandras, Ambelokipi ☏210 870

4000; Canada, Ioánni Yennadhíou 4 ☎210 727
3400; Ireland, Vassiléos Konstandínou 7 ☎210
723 2771; New Zealand, Kifissías 268 ☎210 687
4700; UK, Ploutárhou 1, Kolonáki ☎210 727 2600;
US, Vassilísis Sofías 91 ☎210 721 2951.
**Hospitals** Evangelismós, with its own metro
stop, is the most central, but KAT, way out in
Maroússi, is the designated Greater Athens
emergency ward.
**Internet** easyeverything, main branch over
*Everest* at Pl. Syndágmatos; Museum Internet

Café, Patissíon 46; Sofokleous.com Internet Café,
Stadhíou 5.
**Laundry** Angélou Yerónda 10, off Platía Filomoússou Eterías, Pláka.
**Pharmacies** These are numerous, but unlike other
shops open only Mon–Fri 8am–2pm. Outside these
hours, check any pharmacy window for the nearest duty pharmacy.
**Post offices** Main branch Eólou 100, just off
Omónia; more convenient one on Mitropóleos,
corner Sýndagma.

## The Temple of Poseidon at Sounion

The 70km of shoreline south of Athens has good but highly developed beaches.
At weekends the sands fill fast, as do innumerable bars, restaurants and clubs. But
for most visitors, this coast's attraction is at the end of the road. **Cape Sounion**
is among the most imposing spots in Greece, and on it stands the fifth-century
BC Temple of Poseidon (daily 10am–sunset; €4), built in the time of Pericles as
part of a sanctuary to the sea god. In summer you've faint hope of solitude unless
you arrive before the tours do, but the temple is as evocative a ruin as Greece can
offer. Doric in style, it preserves sixteen of its thirty-four columns, and the view
is stunning. Below the promontory lie several coves, the most sheltered of which
is a five-minute walk east from the car park and site entrance. The main Sounion
**beach** is more crowded, but has a group of tavernas at the far end, which – considering the location – are reasonably priced. There's a single **campsite** about 5km
short of the cape, the *Bacchus* (☎229 20 39 572). Buses to Sounion leave every
thirty minutes from the KTEL terminal on Mavromatéon at the southwest corner
of the Pédhion Áreos park in central Athens. They alternate between coastal and
inland services, the latter slightly longer and more expensive (the coastal route
takes around 2hr).

# The Peloponnese

The appeal of the **Peloponnese** is hard to overstate. This southern peninsula seems
to have the best of almost everything Greek. Its **beaches** are among the finest
and least developed in the country. Its ancient sites include the Homeric palace of
Agamemnon at **Mycenae**, the Greek theatre at **Epidaurus** and the sanctuary of
**Olympia**, host to the Olympic Games for a millennium. Medieval remains run
from the fabulous castle at **Acrocorinth** and the strange tower-houses and frescoed churches of the **Máni**, to the extraordinary Byzantine towns of **Mystra** and
**Monemvasiá**. The Peloponnese also boasts Greece's most spectacular train route, an
hour-long journey on the **rack-and-pinion rail line** from Dhiakoftó to Kalávryta,
that follows the Vouraikós River through a narrow and vertiginous gorge.

The usual approach from Athens is on the frequent buses and trains that run via
modern **Kórinthos**. From Italy and the Adriatic, **PÁTRA** is the **main port** of
the Peloponnese. Its tourist police (☎2610 451 833) is at the Italian ferry terminal
entrance, with the helpful City Info Center, providing information on all of Greece
(☎2610 461 740, ⊛www.infocenterpatras.gr), main bus station (☎2610 273 936)
and train station midway along the waterfront. Pátra's youth **hostel** (☎2610 427
278; €10) past the ferry port along the waterfront, is cheap, but 1.5km north of
the centre, at Iróon Polytekhníou 62.

# Ancient Corinth

Whoever possessed **CORINTH** – the ancient city that displaced Athens as capital of the Greek province in Roman times – controlled both the trade between northern Greece and the Peloponnese, and the short-cut between the Ionian and Aegean seas. It's unsurprising, therefore, that the city's history is a catalogue of invasions and power struggles, until it was razed by the Romans in 146 BC. The site lay in ruins for a century before being rebuilt, on a majestic scale, by Julius Caesar in 44 BC. Nowadays, the remains of the city occupy a rambling site below the acropolis hill of Acrocorinth, itself littered with medieval ruins. To explore both you need a full day, or better still, to stay close by. The modern village of **ARHÉA KÓRINTHOS** spreads around the main archeological zone, where you'll find good **accommodation** at *Hotel Shadow* (☎27410 31 481; ❹); there's also a scattering of **rooms** to rent in the backstreets. Frequent bus and train services run from Athens and Pátra to modern Kórinthos, from where you can catch a local bus from the main square to Arhéa Kórinthos and the adjacent site.

The main excavated site (daily 8am–5/7pm; €6) is dominated by the remains of the Roman city. You enter from the south side, which leads straight into the **Roman agora**. The real focus, however, is a survival from the classical Greek era: the fifth-century BC **Temple of Apollo**, whose seven austere Doric columns stand slightly above the level of the forum. Towering 575m above the lower town, **Acrocorinth** (summer daily 8am–7pm; winter Tues–Sun 8.30am–3pm; free) is an amazing mass of rock still largely encircled by 2km of wall. During the Middle Ages this ancient acropolis of Corinth became one of Greece's most powerful fortresses. It's a 4km climb up (about 1hr), but well worth it. Amid the sixty-acre site, you wander through a jumble of semi-ruined chapels, mosques, houses and battlements, erected in turn by Greeks, Romans, Byzantines, Franks, Venetians and Ottomans.

# Mykínes (Mycenae)

Southwest of Corinth, the ancient site of **MYCENAE** is tucked into a fold of the hills just 2km northeast of the modern village of **MYKÍNES**. Agamemnon's citadel, "well-built Mycenae, rich in gold", as Homer wrote, was uncovered in 1874 by the German archeologist Heinrich Schliemann, who was convinced of a factual basis to Homer's epics. Brilliantly crafted gold and sophisticated architecture bore out the accuracy of Homer's epithets. The buildings unearthed by Schliemann show signs of having been occupied from around 1950 BC until 1100 BC, when the town, though still prosperous, was abandoned. No coherent explanation has been found for this event, but war between rival kingdoms was probably a major factor.

You enter the **Citadel of Mycenae** (daily 8.30am–3/5pm; €8) through the mighty **Lion Gate**. Inside the walls to the right is **Grave Circle A**, the cemetery which Schliemann believed contained the bodies of Agamemnon and his followers, murdered on their triumphant return from Troy. In fact the burials date from about three centuries before the Trojan war, but they were certainly royal, and the finds (now in Athens' National Archeological Museum; see p.495) are among the richest yet unearthed. Schliemann took the extensive **South House**, beyond the grave circle, to be the Palace of Agamemnon. But a much grander building, which must have been the **Royal Palace**, was later discovered on the summit of the acropolis. Rebuilt in the thirteenth century BC, probably at the same time as the Lion Gate, it is, like all Mycenaean palaces, centred on a **Great Court**. The small rooms to the north are believed to have been royal apartments and in one of them the remains of a red stuccoed bath have led to its fanciful identification as the place of Agamemnon's murder. Only the ruling elite were permitted to live within the citadel itself; outside the walls lay the main part of the town and extensive remains of **merchants' houses** have been uncovered near to the road. A few minutes' walk down the road is the astonishing **Treasury of Atreus**, a royal burial vault entered through a majestic fifteen-metre corridor. Set above the chamber doorway is a lintel formed by two immense slabs of stone, one of which – a staggering 9m long – is estimated to weigh 118 tonnes.

There's a **train station** at Fíkhti, 2km west of Mykínes; most long-distance KTEL buses will also drop you off here, whilst four daily buses from Náfplio (see below) stop at the site entrance. There are also numerous bus tours here from Athens, making this a popular day-trip destination. **To stay**, try the *Rooms Dassis*, on Mykínes main street (☎27510 76 123; ❸), with its own Internet café, or *Hotel Belle Hélène* (☎27510 76 225; ❸), up the hill towards the site; alternatively there are a couple of campsites, *Mycenae* (☎27510 76 121) and *Atreus* (☎27510 76 221). The village has many **restaurants**, though all are aimed at the lunchtime bus-tour trade.

## Náfplio and Epidaurus

**NÁFPLIO**, a lively, beautifully sited town with a faded elegance, inherited from when it was briefly modern Greece's first capital, makes an attractive base for exploring the area or for resting up by the sea. The main fort, the **Palamídhi** (daily 8am–3/5pm; €4), is most directly approached by 899 stone-hewn steps up from Polyzoïdhou Street. Within its walls are three self-contained castles, all built by the Venetians in the 1710s. To the west, the **Acronafplía** fortress occupies the ancient acropolis, whose walls were adapted by successive medieval occupants. The third fort, the photogenic **Boúrtzi**, occupies the islet offshore from the harbour and allowed the Venetians to close the shallow shipping channel with a chain. In the town itself, Platía Syndágmatos, the main square, is a great place to relax over a coffee. **Buses** arrive on Syngroú, just south of the interlocking squares Platía Trión Navárhon and Platía Kapodhístria, while the **train station** is on the waterfront around 600m north. The unreliable EOT **tourist office** is at 25-Martíou 2 (daily 9am–1pm & 4–8pm; ☎27520 24 444). **Hotels** are generally overpriced, the most reasonable being *Hotel Economou* (☎27520 23 955; ❷), fifteen minutes' walk from the centre at Argonaftón 22, between the roads to Árgos and Toló. Private **rooms**, most of which cluster on the north slope of the Acronafplía, can also be a good deal. For **eating**, try *Kakanarakis*, Vassilísis Ólgas 18, or *Omorfi Tavernaki* at no. 16.

From the sixth century BC to Roman times, **EPIDAURUS**, 30km east of Náfplio, was a major spa and religious centre; its **Sanctuary of Asclepius** was the most famous of all shrines dedicated to the god of healing. The magnificently preserved 14,000-seat theatre (daily 8am–5/7pm; €6), built in the fourth century BC, merged so well into the landscape that it was rediscovered only in the nineteenth century. Constructed with mathematical precision, it has near-perfect acoustics: from the highest of the 54 tiers of seats you can hear coins dropped in the orchestra. Close by is a small **museum** (Mon noon–5/7pm, Tues–Sun 8am–5/7pm; same ticket as theatre) containing various statuary and frieze fragments. The sanctuary itself encompasses hospitals, dwellings for the priest-physicians, and hotels and amusements for the fashionable visitors. Most people take in Epidaurus as a day-trip from Náfplio, but a memorable experience is to catch an evening classical theatre **performance** (June–Aug Fri & Sat; ⊛www.greekfestival.gr). You can sometimes camp near the car park, or **stay** in **LYGOURIÓ**, 5km north, at *Hotel Alkyon*, Asklipíou 195 (☎27530 22 002; ❸). There are four campsites on the beach at Paléa Epídhavros; *Verdelis* (☎27530 41 425) is the best bet. The nearest **restaurant** to the theatre is *Oasis* on the Lygourió road, though *Leonides* in the village proper is better.

## Mystra

A glorious, airy place, hugging a steep flank of Taïyetos, **MYSTRA** is an astonishingly complete Byzantine city that once sheltered a population of some twenty thousand. The castle on its summit was built in 1249 by Guillaume II de Villehar-douin, fourth Frankish Prince of the Morea (as the Peloponnese was then known), and together with the fortresses of Monemvasiá and the Máni it guarded his territory. In 1262 the Byzantines drove out the Franks and established the Despotate of Mystra. This isolated triangle of land in the southeastern Peloponnese enjoyed considerable autonomy from Constantinople, flowering as a brilliant cultural centre in the fourteenth and early fifteenth centuries and only falling to the Ottomans in 1460, seven years after the Byzantine capital was conquered.

The site of the **Byzantine city** (daily 8/8.30am–3/7pm; €5) has two entrances on the road up from Néos Mystrás: it makes sense to take the bus from Spárti (see below) to the top entrance, then explore a leisurely downhill route. Following this course, the first identifiable building that you come to is the fourteenth-century church of **Ayía Sofía**. The chapel's finest feature is its floor, made from polychrome marble. The **Kástro**, reached by a path that climbs directly from the upper gate, maintains the Frankish design of its thirteenth-century construction, though modi-fied by successive occupants. Heading down from Ayía Sofía, there is a choice of routes. The right fork winds past the ruins of a Byzantine mansion, while the left fork is more interesting, passing the massively fortified **Náfplio Gate** and the vast, multi-storeyed complex of the **Despots' Palace**, which is currently being restored. At the **Monemvasiá Gate**, linking the upper and lower towns, turn right for the **Pandánassa convent**. The church, whose name means "Queen of the World", is perhaps the finest that survives in the town, a perfectly proportioned blend of Byzantine and Gothic. Further down on this side of the lower town make sure you see the diminutive **Perívleptos monastery**, whose single-domed church, partly carved out of the rock, contains Mystra's most complete cycle of frescoes, almost all of which date from the fourteenth century. The **Mitrópolis**, or cathedral, immedi-ately beyond the gateway, ranks as the oldest of Mystra's churches, built from 1270 onward. A marble slab set in its floor is carved with the symbol of the Paleologos dynasty, the double-headed eagle of Byzantium, commemorating the spot where Constantine XI Paleologos, the last emperor, was crowned in 1449.

The modern village, **NÉOS MYSTRÁS**, is a small roadside community whose half-dozen tavernas are crowded with tour buses by day and revert to a low-key life at night. **Accommodation** is limited to the *Hotel Byzantion* (March–Oct only; ☏27310 83 309, ✉byzanhtl@otenet.gr; ❹) and *Khristina Vahaviolou* (☏27310 20 047; ❸). Nearby **SPÁRTI** (ancient Sparta, though there's little left to see) is a good alternative base, with the friendly *Hotel Cecil*, Paleológou 125, near the top of Paleológou (☏27310 24 980; ❸), or *Apollon*, Thermopýlon 84 (☏27310 22 491; ❹). One **campsite**, 2.5km from Spárti, is *Paleologio Mystras* (☏27310 22 724); closer to Mystra itself is *Castle View* (☏27310 93 303). There are a number of reasonable **restaurants** in Spárti, including *Akrolithi*, Odhós ton 118, no. 75, and *Diethnes*, Paleológou 105, and an **Internet café**, *Lasa*, off the main square at Likoúrgou 130. Spárti's **bus station** is at the far eastern end of Lykoúrgou, a 10min walk from the centre.

## Monemvasiá

Set impregnably on a great eruption of rock connected to the mainland by a causeway, the Byzantine seaport of **MONEMVASIÁ** is a place of grand, haunted atmosphere. At the start of the thirteenth century it was the Byzantines' sole possession in the Morea, eventually being taken by the Franks in 1249 after three years of siege. Regained by the Byzantines as part of the ransom for the captured Guillaume de Villehardouin, it served as the chief commercial port of the Despot-ate of the Morea. At its peak in the Byzantine era, Monemvasiá had a population of almost sixty thousand. **Buses** connect with Spárti and Athens four times daily, and with Yíthio twice daily in season only, arriving in the village of **YÉFIRA** on the mainland, where most **accommodation** is located. There are several reasonable hotels near the causeway – try the spotless *Akrogiali* next to the bus stop (℡27320 61 360; ❸) – plus numerous cheaper pensions and rooms, but it's worth splashing out to stay on the rock itself – the long-established *Malvasia* (℡27320 61 323, ✉malvasia@otenet.gr; ❹) is a good choice. The nearest **campsite**, *Kapsis Paradise* (℡27320 61 123), is 3.5km south of Yéfira near a decent beach. The best **taverna** in the old town is *Matoula* on the main street.

The **Lower Town** once sheltered forty churches and over 800 homes though today a single main street harbours most of the restored houses, plus cafés, tavernas and a scattering of shops. The foremost monument is the **Mitrópolis**, the cathedral built by Emperor Andronikos II Komnenos in 1293, and the largest medieval church in southern Greece. Across the square, the tenth-century domed church of **Áyios Pétros** was transformed by the Ottomans into a mosque and is now a small **museum** of local finds (unpredictable opening hours). Towards the sea is a third church, the **Khrysafítissa**, with its bell hanging from an old acacia tree in the courtyard. The climb to the **Upper Town** is highly worthwhile, not least for the solitude. Its fortifications, like those of the lower town, are substantially intact; within, the site is a ruin, though infinitely larger than you could imagine from below.

## Yíthio and the Máni peninsula

**YÍTHIO**, Sparta's ancient port, is the gateway to the dramatic Máni peninsula and one of the south's most attractive seaside towns. Its somewhat low-key harbour, with occasional ferries, has a graceful nineteenth-century waterside, while out to sea, tethered by a long narrow causeway, is the islet of **Marathoníssi** (ancient Kranae), where Paris and Helen of Troy spent their first night after her abduction from Sparta. **Buses** from Spárti (as Sparta is now known) drop you close to the centre of town, and finding **accommodation** should be a matter of a stroll along the waterfront Vassiléos Pávlou, where there is, amongst others, the *Matina* pension, at no. 19 (℡27330 22 518; ❷). There are several summer **campsites** (*Meltemi* and *Gythion Bay* are good choices) along the huge Mavrovoúni beach, which begins 3km south of town off the Areópoli road. For **eating**, try the *Iy Nautilia* or *Korali ouzerís* at the head of the port.

The southernmost peninsula of Greece, the **Máni peninsula**, stretches from Yíthio in the east and Kalamáta in the west down to Cape Ténaro, mythical entrance to the underworld. It's a wild and arid landscape with an idiosyncratic culture and history: nowhere in Greece seems so close to its medieval past. The quickest way into it is to take a bus from Yíthio to **AREÓPOLI**, gateway to the so-called Inner Máni. There are **rooms** at a number of tower-houses, including *Pyrgos Tsimova* (℡27330 51 301; ❹), or there's the *Hotel Kouris* on the main square (℡27330 51 340; ❹). There are buses from here north to Stoúpa, Kardhamýli and Kalamáta, though a change in Ítylo is usually involved.

More attractions lie to the north of Areópoli, along the eighty-kilometre road to Kalamáta, which has views as dramatic and beautiful as any in Greece. There are numerous cobbled paths for hiking and a series of **small beaches**, beginning at **ÁYIOS NIKÓLAOS**, which has fish tavernas and rooms such as the *Skafidakia* (℡27210 77 698; ❸), and extending more or less through to Kardhamýli. **STOÚPA**, which has possibly the best sands, is now geared very much to British tourism, with several small hotels – friendliest of which is *Leftron* (℡27210 77 322; ❹) – two **campsites**, supermarkets and tavernas. **KARDHAMÝLI**, 8km north, remains a beautiful place despite its commercialization and busy road, with a long pebble beach and a restored tower-house quarter. *Lela's* (℡27210 73 541, or ℡6977 71 6017 in winter; ❹) has some good rooms. If you get as far as **Kalamáta** – the largest city in the area – then ancient **Pýlos**, the impressive medieval fortresses of **Methóni** and **Koróni** and the superb beaches at **Yiálova** are all close enough to be taken in as day-trips.

## Olympia

The historic resonance of **OLYMPIA**, which for over a millennium hosted the Panhellenic Games, is rivalled only by Delphi or Mycenae. Its site, too, ranks with this company, for although the ruins are confusing, the setting is as perfect as could be imagined: a luxuriant valley of wild olive and plane trees beside the twin rivers of Alfiós and Kladhéos, overlooked by the pine-covered hill of Krónos. The contests at Olympia probably began around the eleventh century BC, slowly developing over the next two centuries from a local festival to a major quadrennial celebration attended by states from throughout the Greek world. From the very beginning, the main Olympic events were athletic, but the great gathering of people expanded the games' importance: nobles and ambassadors negotiated treaties here, while merchants chased contacts and sculptors and poets sought commissions. The games eventually fell victim to the Christian Emperor Theodosius's crackdown on pagan festivities in 391–2 AD, and his successor ordered the destruction of the temples, a process completed by invasion, earthquakes and, finally, by the river Alfiós changing its course to cover the sanctuary site. There it remained, covered by seven metres of silt and sand, until the 1870s.

The entrance to the **ancient site** (daily 8/8.30am–3/7pm; €6, joint ticket with museum €9) leads along the west side of the sacred precinct wall past a group of public and official buildings, including a structure adapted as a Byzantine church. This was originally the studio of Pheidias, the fifth-century BC sculptor responsible for the great gold and ivory cult statue in the focus of the precinct, the great Doric **Temple of Zeus**. Built between 470 and 456 BC, it was as large as the Parthenon and its decoration rivalled the finest in Athens. The Pheidias statue was displayed in the *cella*, and here, too, the Olympian flame was kept alight from the time of the games until the following spring – a tradition continued at an altar for the modern games. The smaller **Temple of Hera**, behind, was the first built here; prior to its completion in the seventh century BC, the sanctuary had only open-air altars, dedicated to Zeus and a variety of other cult gods. Rebuilt in the Doric style in the sixth century BC, it's the most complete structure on the site. However, it's the 200-metre track of the **Stadium** itself that makes sense of Olympia: the start and finish lines are still there, as are the judges' thrones in the middle and seating banked to each side. The tiers accommodated up to thirty thousand spectators, with a smaller number on the southern slope overlooking the **Hippodrome** where chariot races were held. Finally, in the **archeological museum** (Mon 11am/noon–5/7pm, Tues–Sun 8/8.30am–5/7pm; €6), the centrepiece is the statuary from the Temple of Zeus, displayed in the vast main hall. Most famous of the individual sculptures is the **Hermes of Praxiteles**, dating from the fourth century BC; one of the best-preserved of all Classical sculptures, it retains traces of its original paint.

Most people arrive at Olympia via Pýrgos, which has frequent buses and trains to the site, plus numerous connections to Pátra and a couple daily to Kalamáta. The modern town of **OLYMBÍA** has developed to serve the excavations and tourist trade. Among **hotels**, the least expensive is *Hermes*, by the Shell garage (☎26240 22 577; ❸), or try the **hostel** at Praxitéles Kondhýli 18 (☎26240 22 580; €12). The closest **campsite**, *Diana* (☎26240 22 314), 1km from the site, has a pool and good facilities. For **eating**, most of the tavernas offer standard tourist meals at inflated prices; an exception is *O Kladhios*, a beautiful and authentic grill near the river.

# Central and northern Greece

Central Greece has an indeterminate character, consisting mostly of vast agricultural plains dotted with rather drab market towns, and ringed by low hills. The highlights lie at the fringes: **Delphi** and **Ósios Loukás** above all, and further northeast the forested slopes of **Mount Pílio** with magnificent villages and alluring beaches, or northwest at the otherworldly rock-monasteries of **Metéora**. Access to these monasteries is through **Kalambáka**, beyond which the **Katára pass** over the Píndhos Mountains brings you into **Epirus**, the poorest – but one of the most distinctive – mainland regions. En route lies **Métsovo**, perhaps the easiest location for a taste of mountain life, though blatantly commercialized. Nearby **Ioánnina**, once the stronghold of the notorious Ali Pasha, retains some character, and serves as the main transport hub for trips into the relatively unspoilt villages of **Zagóri**, around the **Víkos gorge**. The northern provinces of Macedonia and Thrace have only been part of the Greek state since 1913 and 1923 respectively. As such, they stand slightly apart from the rest of the nation – an impression reinforced for visitors by scenery and climate that are essentially Balkan. The only areas to draw more than a sprinkling of summer visitors are **Mount Olympus** and **Halkidhikí**, the latter a beach-playground for the Macedonian capital of **Thessaloníki** and also sheltering the "Monks' Republic" of **Mount Áthos**.

**IGOUMENÍTSA** is Greece's third **passenger port** after Pireás and Pátra, with almost hourly ferries to Corfu; several daily to and from Italy make it a likely arrival point. The tourist office is next to the customs house on the old quay (daily 8am–2pm; ☏26650 22 227), whilst the bus station, with connections to Athens, Thessaloniki and Pátra sits two blocks back from here in the town centre. There are frequent bus and train services from **Thessaloníki** on to Bulgaria, Romania or Turkey, though you should get any necessary visas in Athens.

# Delphi

Access to the extraordinary site of **DELPHI**, 150km northwest of Athens, is simple: six buses arrive from the capital daily, passing through **Livádhia**, the nearest rail terminus, on their way. With its position on a high terrace overlooking a great gorge, in turn dwarfed by the ominous crags of Parnassós, it's easy to see why the ancients believed Delphi to be the centre of the earth. But what confirmed this status was the discovery of a chasm that exuded strange vapours and reduced all comers to frenzied, incoherent and obviously prophetic mutterings. For over a thousand years a steady stream of pilgrims toiled their way up the dangerous mountain paths to seek divine direction, until the oracle eventually expired with the demise of paganism in the fourth century AD.

You enter the **Sacred Precinct of Apollo** (daily: 7.30am–2.45/6.45pm; €6, or €9 with museum) by way of a small agora, enclosed by ruins of Roman porticoes and shops for the sale of votive offerings. The paved **Sacred Way** begins after a few stairs, zigzagging uphill between the foundations of memorials and treasuries to the **Temple of Apollo**. Only the foundations stood when it was uncovered in the 1890s; archeologists, however, re-erected six Doric columns, giving a vertical line to the ruins and providing some idea of its former dominance over the sanctuary. In the inner sanctum of the temple was a dark cell where the priestess would officiate; no sign of cave or chasm has been found, but it was probably closed by earthquakes. The theatre and stadium used for the main events of the Pythian games are on terraces above the temple. The **theatre**, built in the fourth century BC, was closely connected with Dionysos, god of the arts and wine, who reigned in Delphi over the winter months when Apollo was absent and the oracle silent. A steep path leads up through pine groves to the stadium, which was banked with stone seats in Roman times. The **museum** (same hours as site) contains a collection of Archaic sculpture matched only by finds on the Acropolis in Athens; the most famous exhibit is *The Charioteer*, one of the few surviving bronzes of the fifth century BC. Following the road east of the sanctuary towards Aráhova, you reach a sharp bend. To the left, marked by niches for votive offerings and the remains of an Archaic fountain house, the celebrated **Castalian spring** still flows from a cleft in the cliffs. Visitors to Delphi were obliged to purify themselves in its waters, usually by washing their hair, though murderers had to take the full plunge. Across and below the road from the spring is the **Marmaria** or Sanctuary of Athena Pronoia (same hours as main site; free), the "Guardian of the Temple". The precinct's most conspicuous building is the **Tholos**, a fourth-century BC rotunda whose purpose remains a mystery. Outside the precinct on the northwest side, above the Marmaria, a **gymnasium** also dates from the fourth century BC though it was later enlarged by the Romans.

The modern village of **DHELFÍ** has a quick turnaround of visitors, so **accommodation** should present few problems. There are over twenty hotels and pensions, plus a few rooms to let, though low seasons are brief: in winter, skiers throng the place. Opt for the en-suite *Sibylla* at Pávlou ke Fredheríkis 9 (☎22650 82 335, ✉sibydel@otenet.gr; ❷), or the *Athina* at no. 55 of the same street (☎22650 82 430, ☎22650 82 239; ❸). The nearest official **campsite** is *Apollon* (☎22650 82 750; open June–Sept), 1500m west towards Ámfissa. **Restaurant** options aren't great; try *Taverna Vakhos* on Apóllonos Street, or *Iy Skala*, on the stair-street up from the road on which the *Sibylla* is. The helpful **tourist office** in the town hall on Pávlou ke Fredheríkis (Mon–Fri 7.20am–2.30pm; ☎22650 82 900), has up-to-date transport schedules.

## Ósios Loukás

The beautifully positioned monastery of **Ósios Loukás** (daily: May to mid-Sept 8am–2pm & 4–7pm; mid-Sept to April 8am–5pm; €3), some 32km east of Delphi in a remote valley beneath Mt Elikónas, is a pain to reach by public transport but worth the effort – even if you have to hire a taxi from **DHÍSTOMO**, the nearest village. Its eleventh-century church contains superb mosaics, particularly in the narthex (portico), of events from the life of Christ, including the *Washing of the Disciples' Feet*, the *Resurrection* and, high up in the dome, the *Baptism*.

## The Pílio (Pelion) peninsula

With its lush orchards and dense broadleaf forests, the **Pílio peninsula** seems decidedly un-Mediterranean. Water tumbles in rivulets beside every road, and summers are rather cooler than in the rest of central Greece. Pílio villages are idiosyncratic too, scattered affairs with sumptuous mansions and barn-like churches lining their cobbled streets. Add to the scenery and architecture a score of excellent beaches, a tiny ski centre, plus easy access from Athens and Thessaloníki, and it's no wonder that this is a well-loved corner of Greece. Avoid July, August, Easter and Christmas unless you're happy to camp out.

The most visited part of Pílio lies just north and east of the industrial city of **Vólos**. The town's bus station, catering for the peninsula's villages, is at Grigoríou Lambráki, a short walk south of the train station. If time is limited, the best single targets are Makrinítsa and Vyzítsa. **MAKRINÍTSA** has become very commercialized, and whilst you can stay there affordably at *Hotel Theophilos* (☎24280 99 435; ❷), eating is much better at *Kritsa* in the neighbouring village of Portariá. Remoter **VYZÍTSA** has equally good bus connections, with budget accommodation in the *Xenon Thetis* (☎24230 86 211; ❸), west of the square, and the decent *Taverna O Yiorgaras* on the road east. Generally, you must go to extremes (literally) to save money in Pílio; at the end of the bus lines to the southern peninsula, in the coastal hamlets of **KATIYIÓRYIS** and **PLATANIÁ**, are (respectively) *Flisvos Rooms* (☎24230 71 071; ❷), with an excellent ground-floor fish restaurant, and *Hotel Platania* (☎24230 71 266; ❸), with more good food at its restaurant *To Steki*.

The largest village on the Pílio is **ZAGORÁ**, destination of fairly regular buses northeast across the peninsula's summit ridge. It's more appealing than first impressions suggest, and unlike its seashore neighbours has a life independent of tourism. You're also more likely to find a room here in season, for example at *Yian-*

*nis Halkias* (☎24260 22 159; ❷), than down at **HOREFTÓ** beach, 8km below, where you might try *Hotel Erato* (☎24260 22 445; ❸). In Horeftó, you can eat at year-round *Ta Dhelfínia*, whilst in Zagorá choice is ample, starting with *Venizelos* (under *Yiannis Halkias*). Just before Zagorá, a junction funnels traffic southeast to **TSANGARÁDHA**, also the terminus of two daily buses from Vólos. Nearly as extensive as Zagorá, it's divided into four distinct quarters along several kilometres of road. Reasonable accommodation is scarce – try *Villa ton Rodhon* (☎24260 49 340; ❹) in Ayía Paraskeví – as are decent restaurants – *Apostolís*, beneath the police station, is the best bet. There's more choice, however, at **MOÚRESSI**, 3km northwest, where several year-round tavernas dish out local specialities at fairly moderate prices. **KISSÓS**, still further towards Zagorá, is another possibility for lodging and dining, with its modern *Rooms Sofia Gloumi* (☎24260 31 267; ❸) and cosy *Makis Taverna*.

Most visitors, however, stay at several nearby beaches, the best on this shore of the peninsula. **ÁYIOS IOÁNNIS**, 6km below Kissós, is an overblown resort with plenty of accommodation – you can try *Hotel Evripidis* (☎24260 31 338; ❸), and eat affordable fish at *Posidhonas*. If it's too busy for your tastes, head south along the sand, past the crowded campsite, to Papá Neró beach or further still to postcard-perfect **DAMOÚHARI**, with its tiny ruined castle and fishing anchorage. The area's most scenic beach is reached by following a winding 7km road from the south end of Tsangarádha to Mylopótamos, packed-out in high season. For more solitude, you can undertake the ninety-minute walk from Damoúhari to **Fakístra beach**, even lovelier, but without facilities.

## Kalambáka and Metéora

Few places are more exciting to arrive at than **KALAMBÁKA**. The shabby town itself you hardly notice, for your eye is immediately drawn to the weird grey cylinders of rock overhead. These are the outlying monoliths of the extraordinary valley of **Metéora**. To the right you can make out the monastery of Ayíou Stefánou, firmly planted on a massive pedestal; beyond stretches a chaos of spikes, cones and stubbier, rounded cliffs – river sediment twisted into bizarre shapes as it flowed into the sea that covered the Plain of Thessaly some twenty-five million years ago. The earliest religious communities in the valley emerged during the late tenth century, when hermits made their homes in the caves that score many of the rocks. In 1336 they were joined by two monks from Mount Áthos, one of whom established the first monastery here. Today, put firmly on the map by films such as the James Bond *For Your Eyes Only*, the four most visited monasteries are essentially museums. Only two others, Ayías Triádhos and Ayíou Stefánou, continue to function with a primarily religious purpose. Each monastery levies an **admission charge** of €2 and operates a strict **dress code**: skirts for women (supplied at the monasteries), long trousers for men and covered arms for both sexes.

From Kastráki the road loops between huge outcrops of rock before reaching a path to the left, which winds up a low rock to the fourteenth-century **Ayíou Nikoláou Anápavsa** (9am–3.30pm, closed Fri). A small, 1980s-restored monastery, this has superb sixteenth-century frescoes in its main chapel. Some 250m past the car park and stairs to Ayíou Nikoláou, a clear path leads up a ravine between assorted monoliths; soon, at a fork, you've the option of bearing left for Megálou Meteórou or right to Varlaám, the two also linked by a higher access road. **Varlaám** (9am–4pm, closed Thurs) ranks as one of the oldest and most beautiful monasteries in the valley. It also preserves its old ascent tower; until 1923 the only way of reaching the monasteries was by being hauled up in a net drawn by rope and windlass, or by equally perilous retractable ladders. Today, however, you reach Varlaám safely, if breathlessly, via steps cut into the side of the rock. From the fork below Varlaám the path also takes you northwest to **Megálou Meteórou** (9am–5pm, closed Tues). This is the grandest of the monasteries and also the highest, built 400m above the valley floor. Next you follow trails, or the main access road east, ignoring the turning back down for Kastráki, until you reach the signed access path for the tiny, compact convent of **Roussánou** (daily 9am–6pm), approached in the final moment across a dizzying bridge from an adjacent rock. This has perhaps the most extraordinary site of all the monasteries, its walls built right on the edge of a sheer pinnacle. It's less than a half-hour from Roussánou to the vividly frescoed **Ayías Triádhos** (9am–5pm, closed Thurs), approached up 130 steps carved through a tunnel in the rock. Although Ayías Triádhos teeters above a deep ravine and its little garden ends in a precipitous drop, there is a 3km, well-marked cobbled trail at the bottom of the monastery's steps back to Kalambáka, which saves a tedious retracing of steps. **Ayíou Stefánou** (9am–2pm & 3.30–6pm, closed Mon), the last of the monasteries, lies a further fifteen minutes' walk east of Ayías Triádhos; bombed in World War II, it's the one to omit if you've run out of time.

Visiting the monasteries demands a full day, which means staying two nights in Kalambáka or at the village of Kastráki, right in the shadow of the rocks. **KALAMBÁKA** is characterless but pleasant enough, with plentiful **accommodation**. Good budget choices in the quieter, upper portion of town towards Kastráki include *Hotel Meteora*, Ploutárhou 13 (T24320 22 367, Wwww.meteorahotels.com; ➌), and *Koka Roka Rooms*, Kanári 21, at the end of the trail from Ayías Triádhos (see above), with a cheap taverna on the ground floor (T24320 24 554, Ekokaroka@yahoo .com; ➋). To **eat,** the best restaurants line Trikalon leading from the main square; there's also an Internet café, *Surf City*, at no. 73. **KASTRÁKI** is twenty minutes' walk out of Kalambáka; there are hourly buses in season. Along the way you pass the busy *Vrahos*, the first of two **campsites**, offering rock-climbing lessons and bike hire (T24320 22 293); the other, *The Cave* (T24320 24 802), is smaller but quieter, grassier and incomparably set beneath the pinnacles. Kastráki also has hundreds of **rooms** to rent, mostly better value than in Kalambáka (though avoid the main road); good examples include those offered by *The Cave* (see above; ➍), *Ziogas Rooms* (T24320 24 037; ➌) and *Hotel Tsikelli* (T24320 22 438; ➌). **Eat** at *Paradhissos*, on the through road, for grills and dips, or *Bakalarkaia* below the square and church, for cheap fried hake and house wine.

## Métsovo and Ioánnina

West of Kalambáka, the **Katára pass** cuts across the Píndhos mountains to link Thessaly and Epirus. The route is one of the most spectacular in the country, covered by just two buses daily between **Tríkala** and **Ioánnina**. **MÉTSOVO** spreads just west of the Katára pass, a high mountain town built on two sides of a ravine and encircled by a mighty range of peaks. From below the main road, eighteenth- and nineteenth-century stone houses, with their wooden balconies and modern tile roofs, spill down the hillside to the main *platía*, where a few old men, magnificent in full traditional dress, still loiter after Sunday Mass. The town **museum** occupies the Arhondikó Tosítsa (tours only 9.30am–1.30pm & 4–6pm, closed Thurs; €3), an eighteenth-century mansion restored to former glory, with a fine collection of crafts and costumes. Métsovo boasts quite a range of **accommodation** and apart from around July 26, date of the main local **festival**, and during skiing season, you'll have little difficulty getting a room. Try the *Filoxenia* (T26560 41 021; ➋), below the *platía* with ravine views from some rooms, or the *Flokas* on the lane leading south from the square (T & F26560 41 309; ➌). For **eating**, the *To Koutouki tou Nikola* beneath the post office has some vegetarian dishes.

Descending from Métsovo, you approach **IOÁNNINA** through more spectacular folds of the Píndhos Mountains. The fortifications of the old town, former capital of the Albanian Muslim chieftain Ali Pasha, are punctuated by towers and minarets. From this base Ali, "the Lion of Ioánnina", prised from the Ottoman Empire a fiefdom encompassing much of western Greece, an act of rebellion that foreshadowed wider defiance in the Greeks' own War of Independence in the 1820s. Disappointingly, most of the city is modern and undistinguished; however, the fortifications of Ali's citadel, the **Kástro**, survive more or less intact. Apart from this, the most enjoyable quarter is the old **bazaar** area, outside the citadel's main gate.

On the far side of the lake from Ioánnina, the island of **Nissí** is served by water-buses (every 30min) from the quay northwest of the Froúrio. Its village, founded during the sixteenth century, is flanked by several beautiful, diminutive monasteries, with the best thirteenth-century frescoes in **Filanthropinón**. You can stay on the island at the basic **rooms** kept by the Dellas family (☎26510 84 494; ❷). In Ioánnina itself, budget lodging is in the area between the bazaar and the central plazas; try *Esperia*, Kaplání 3 (☎26510 24 111; ❸). The pleasant lakeshore *Limnopoula* **campsite** (☎26510 25 265) is 2km out of town on the Pérama/airport road. For **food**, head just outside the Kástro's main gate to *To Metsovo*, on Ethnikís Andístasis, for grills, or *Fysa Roufa*, at Avéroff 55, for oven dishes. The main **bus** station is at Zozimádhon 4, serving most points north and west; a smaller terminal at Bizaníou 19 connects villages south and east. The **tourist office** at Dhodhónis 39 (Mon–Fri 7.30am–2.30pm, also open evenings and Sat am in summer), south of the centre, can provide information on the whole Epirus region, and there's an **Internet café** nearby, just off the main square

## Zagóri and the Víkos Gorge

Few parts of Greece are more surprising, or beguiling, than **Zagóri**, the rugged, infertile region to the north of Ioánnina. It's the last place you'd expect to find some of Greece's most imposing architecture, yet the *Zagorohória*, as the region's 46 villages are called, are full of grand stone mansions, enclosed by semi-fortified walls and with deep-eaved gateways opening on to immaculately cobbled streets. In the northwest corner of the region, the awesome trench of the **Víkos Gorge** – its walls nearly 1000m high in places – separates the villages of western and central Zagóri. A hike through or around Víkos is the highlight of any visit to the area, the usual starting point being the handsome village of **MONODHÉND-HRI**. There are twice-daily buses from Ioánnina (Mon, Wed & Fri only); the only real budget option here is *Katerina's Pension* (☎26530 71 300; ❷). The most used **path into the gorge**, marked as the long-distance O3, starts beside Áyios Athanásios church; the route is fairly straightforward, and it takes under five hours to reach the point where the gorge begins to open out. From here the best option is to follow the O3 path to **MEGÁLO PÁPINGO**, two hours further on. A hillside village of fifty or so houses along a tributary of the Voïdhomátis river, it offers abundant if pricey **accommodation**; most reasonable are the *dhomátia* kept by Lakis Kotsoridhis (☎26530 41 087; ❷) and *Xenonas Kalliopi* (☎26530 41 081; ❸). Around half the size of its neighbour, **MIKRÓ PÁPINGO**, just uphill, has one main inn, *Xenon O Dhias* (☎26530 41 257; ❹). Bus services to Ioánnina are erratic (in theory four weekly in summer). The alternative is to trail-walk west two and a half hours from Pápingo to the village of **Káto Klidhoniá**, where there are regular buses along the Kónitsa–Ioánnina highway.

## Mount Olympus

Highest, most magical and most dramatic of all Greek mountains, **Mount Olympus** – the mythical seat of the gods – rears straight up nearly 3000m from the shores of the Thermaïkos gulf. Dense forests cover its lower slopes and its wild flowers are gorgeous. If you're well-equipped, no special expertise is necessary to reach the top between mid-June and October, though it's a long hard pull, and its weather is notoriously fickle. The usual approach is via **LITÓHORO** on the eastern slopes. Hourly buses ply the route from Thessaloniki. If travelling by train, head to Katerini from where hourly buses make the 25min journey. Best-value **accommodation** is the hotel *Enipeas*, with balconied rooms and breakfast right on the main square (☎23520 84 328; ④). Best **eats** are at *To Pazari*, uphill on 25 Martou, or *Psistaria Zeus*, at the start of the road up the mountain. You'd do well to buy a proper **map** of the range in Athens or Thessaloníki (#31 Road Editions 1:50,000 is adequate). Four to five hours' walking along the well-marked, scenic E4 long-distance path up the Mavrólongos canyon brings you to **Priónia**, from where there's a sharper three-hour trail-climb to the *Spílios Agapitos* **refuge** (☎23520 81 800; €10 per person; closed mid-Oct to mid-May). It's best to stay overnight here, as you need to make an early start for the three-hour ascent to **Mýtikas**, the highest peak (2917m), as the summit frequently clouds over towards midday. The path continues behind the refuge, reaching a signposted fork above the tree line in about an hour; straight on, then right, takes you to Mýtikas via the ridge known as Kakí Skála, while the abrupt right reaches the *Yiosos Apostolidhis* **hut** in one hour (no phone; €10 per person; closed mid-Sept to mid-June). From the hut there's an enjoyable loop down to the **Gortsiá** trailhead and from there back down into the Mavrólongos canyon, via the medieval monastery of Ayíou Dhionysíou.

# Thessaloníki

Second city of Greece, **THESSALONÍKI** feels more Balkan-European and modern than Athens. During the Byzantine era, it was the second city after Constantinople, reaching a cultural "Golden Age" until the Ottoman conquest in 1430. As recently as the 1920s, the city's population was as mixed as any in the Balkans: besides the Ottoman Turks, who had been in occupation for close on five centuries, there were Slavs, Albanians and the largest European **Jewish** community of the period – eighty thousand at its peak. Today, however, there is little to detain you aside from the excellent archeological museum, and a couple of frescoed Byzantine churches full of mosaics. You can also arrange a permit for Mt Áthos here, or make onward connections to the Halkidhikí beaches, and to Bulgaria or Turkey. The renovated **Archeological Museum** (daily 8.30am–3/5pm; €4) is a few paces from the White Tower, the last surviving bastion of the city's medieval walls. The museum contains finds from the tombs of Philip II of Macedon and others at the ancient Macedonian capital of Aegae (Vergina). They include startling amounts of gold and silver – masks, crowns, necklaces, earrings, bracelets – all of extraordinary craftsmanship, although the exhibits are now depleted following the transfer of the star items back to a purpose-built subterranean gallery at Vergína itself (see opposite). Among the city's many **churches**, the best three are Áyios Yeóryios, originally a Roman rotunda, decorated with superb mosaics emerging from long restoration; Áyios Dhimítrios, with more seventh-century mosaics of the patron saint in various guises; and still-later Ayía Sofía, with mosaics of the *Ascension* and the *Virgin Enthroned*.

### Practicalities

The **train station** on the west side of town is a short walk from the central grid of streets and the waterfront. Except for Halkidhikí services, **buses** use a KTEL terminal 3km southwest of the centre; city buses #1 & #32 go there. From the **airport**, 16km out at Mikrá, bus #78 runs hourly to the train station and KTEL terminal (6am–11pm). There's a **tourist office** (Mon–Fri 8am–2pm) in the greying port building.

Outside the fair-and-festival season (Sept–Nov), **hotel** vacancies are easy to find, though not, as a rule, attractive or good value. Shun the poor-value "budget" hotels clustered along the noisy beginning of busy Egnatía in favour of *Orestias Kastoria* at Agnóstou Stratiótou 14 (☎2310 276 517, ⊛www.okhotel.gr; ④); *Nea Mitropolis*, just north of Egnatía at Syngroú 22 (☎2310 525 540, ⊛www .neametropolis.gr; ❸); or *Bill*, Syngroú 29, corner Amvrossíou (☎2310 537 666; ❸). To **eat**, *Platia Athonos* on Dhragoúmi, an alley off Platía Áthonos, is one of the more dependable of several *ouzerís* in this area, or try *Koumbarakia*, behind a Byzantine chapel at Egnatía 140. **Bars** and **clubs** concentrate in the rehabilitated warehouse area southeast of Platía Eleftherías known as Ladhádhika; *Zythos*, Platía Katoúni 5, is one of the best bar-restaurants, with dozens of well-kept foreign beers. The main indoor **music** venue is the multidisciplinary complex *Mylos*, out in an old flour mill at Andhréou Yeoryíou 56, where you'll find more bars, a summer cinema and exhibition galleries.

## Listings

**Consulates** Australia, Archeologikou Mousiou 28, ☎2310 827 494; Canada, Tsimiskí 17 ☎2310 256 350; UK, Aristotelous 21 ☎2310 278 006; US Tsimiskí 43 ☎2310 242 905. If you need a visa for onward Balkan travel, best get it in Athens.
**Hospital** Yenikó Kendrikó, Ethnikís Amýnis 41 ☎2310 211 211.
**Internet** Atlantic City, Venizelou; Internet Café, Kitrous Episkopou 2.

**Laundry** Bianca, Antoniádhou 3; Freskadha, Filíppou 105.
**Mount Áthos permits** Take your passport to the Grafío Proskynitón Ayíou Órous (Mount Áthos Pilgrims' Office), Egnatia 109 (Mon–Fri 9am–2pm, Sat 10am–noon; ☎2310 252 578); they will issue an entry permit for a specified day.
**Post office** Aristotélous 26; open all day Mon–Fri, Sat & Sun am.

## Vergína (Ancient Aegae)

In 1977, archeologists discovered the burial sanctuary of the ancient Macedonian dynasty which culminated in Alexander the Great at the hitherto insignificant village of **VERGÍNA**. The four **Royal Tombs** (daily 8am–3/6pm; €8) constitute the focus of an unmissable underground museum, featuring delicate gold and silver funerary artefacts, the facades of the tombs, and the bones of the deceased in ornate ossuaries. It's easy to make this a day-trip from Thessaloníki: hourly buses ply to Véria, from where eleven onward buses per day cover the final 20min to modern Vergína village.

## Halkidhikí and Mount Áthos

The squid-shaped peninsula of **Halkidhikí** begins at a perforated edge of lakes east of Thessaloníki and extends into three prongs of land – Kassándhra, Sithonía and Áthos – trailing like tentacles into the Aegean Sea. **Kassándhra** and **Sithonía** are Thessaloníki's beach-playground, hosting some of the largest holiday resorts in Greece. Both are linked to Thessaloníki by bus, but neither peninsula is easy to travel around on public transport – you really have to pick a spot and stay there, perhaps renting a scooter for local excursions. Áfytos is by far the most attractive place on Kassándhra, while Sithonía is marginally less packaged, with low-key resorts at Kalamítsi, Pórto Koufó and Toróni. **Mount Áthos** (⊚www.inathos .gr), the easternmost peninsula, is in all ways separate: a "Holy Mountain" whose monastic population, semi-autonomous from the Greek state, excludes all women – even as visitors. Men who are over-18, and can demonstrate a religious or scholarly interest in Áthos, can make a reservation at the pilgrims' office in Thessaloníki (detailed above) for up to four days' stay in a different monastery each night. A visit is highly recommended, though you can't hope to see more than a fraction of the twenty main monasteries in the time allotted. Choose between the "museum monasteries" of Meyístis Lávras, Vatopedhíou, Ivíron or Dhionysíou with their wealth of treasures and art, or the more modestly endowed cloisters – Osíou Grigoríou, Pandokrátoros and Ivíron – where the brothers will make more time for you.

Both Ierissós and Ouranópoli, villages at the top of the peninsula and the usual gateways to Áthos, are served by several daily buses from Thessaloníki. **IERISSÓS** has many **rooms** to let and the friendly if slightly noisy *Hotel Marcos* (☎23770 22 518; ➍); in summer boats sail four times a week at 8.30am, weather permitting, to the monasteries of Áthos's northeast shore. It's often best to continue to the busy resort of **OURANÓPOLI**, the last settlement before you reach the monastic domains. **Accommodation** is plentiful, with numerous rooms and a few budget hotels, such as *Diana* (℗23770 71 250; ❷). From Ouranópoli the most reliable ferries depart for the southwest shore of monastic Áthos, daily at 9.45am. Allow time to queue at the Grafío Proskynitón (Pilgrims' Bureau) to exchange your reservation from the Thessaloníki office for a **pass** (€30, €15 for students) allowing you to stay overnight at any of the major monasteries. From the usual entry port of **DHÁFNI** on the southwest coast, there are more possibilities of moving about by boat and bus, but walking between the religious communities on a dwindling trail network is an integral part of the Athonite experience, so you should be reasonably fit and self-sufficient in dry snack food, as the two meals offered each day tend to be spartan. Most monks pay scant attention to foreigners, so you get more of an idea of the magnificent scenery and architecture than of the religious life, though it's hard to avoid tangling with the disorienting daily schedule, dictated by the hours of sun and darkness. Also, many monasteries have become so visited that you must book a bed by phone in advance; the Pilgrims' Bureau provides a list of contact numbers.

# The southern Aegean islands

The **Argo–Saronic** islands are the nearest archipelago to Athens and one of the busiest, with **Ídhra** being the most popular. More than any other group, these islands, are at their best outside peak season. To the east, the **Cyclades** is the most satisfying Greek archipelago for island-hopping, with its vibrant capital on **Sýros**. The majority of the islands are arid and rocky, with brilliant-white, cubist architecture, making them enormously popular with tourists. **Íos**, the original hippie island, is still a backpackers' paradise, while **Mýkonos** – with its teeming old town, nude beaches and highly sophisticated clubs and bars (many of them gay) – is by far the most visited of the group. Arriving by ferry at the partially submerged volcanic caldera of **Santoríni**, meanwhile, is one of the world's great travel adventures. **Páros**, **Náxos** and **Sífnos** are nearly as popular, while the one major ancient site worth making time for is **Delos**, the commercial and religious centre of the classical Greek world. Almost all of the Cyclades are served by boats from Pireás, but there are also ferries from Rafína.

Further east still, the **Dodecanese** islands lie so close to the Turkish coast that some are almost within hailing distance of the shore. They were only included in the modern Greek state in 1948 after centuries of occupation by Crusaders, Ottomans and Italians. Medieval **Rhodes** is the most famous, but almost every one has its classical remains, its Crusaders' castle, its traditional villages and grandiose, Italian-built Art Deco public buildings. The main islands are connected almost daily with each other, and none is hard to reach. Rhodes is the principal transport hub, with ferry services to Turkey and Cyprus, as well as connections with Crete, the northeastern Aegean islands, the Cyclades and the mainland (Kavála, Alexandhroúpoli and Pireás).

## Ídhra

The port and town of **ÍDHRA**, with its tiers of stone mansions and tiled white houses climbing up from a perfect horseshoe harbour, forms a beautiful spectacle. Unfortunately, from Easter to September it's often packed to the gills, and the seafront becomes one uninterrupted outdoor café (there are no private cars on Ídhra). Dozens of mansions were built here, mostly during the eighteenth century, on the accumulated wealth of a merchant fleet which traded as far afield as America. There's no lack of expensive cafés and **restaurants** on the waterfront, but better value eating lies inland, for example at *To Steki* and the much-loved *Yeitoniko* (alias *Manolis & Christina's*). **Hotels** and pensions are overpriced; reasonable-value places include *Alkionides* (☎22980 54 055, ⊛www.alkionideshydra.com; ❹) and, near the back of town, *Theodoros* (☎22980 52 810; ❹). As far as beaches are concerned, from the west side of the harbour a coastal path leads to a pebbly but popular stretch, just before **KAMÍNI**, where there are a pair of reasonable pensions – try *Antonia* (☎22980 52 481; ❸) – and a good year-round taverna, *Christina*. Thirty minutes' walk beyond Kamíni (or a taxi-boat from the port) brings you to islet-sheltered **VLYHÓS**, a small hamlet with pricier rooms, two tavernas, and a pebble beach. For more sheltered bathing, head for Limnióniza on the south coast (75-min walk), or Bísti and Áyios Nikólaos on the west tip (boat-bus late May to early Oct 4 daily).

## Sýros

Home to the capital of the Cyclades, **Sýros** is the most populous island in the archipelago. The main town and port of **ERMOÚPOLI** is a lively spot, bustling with a commercial life that extends far beyond tourism. Crowned by two imposing churches, the Catholic Capuchin **Monastery of St Jean** in the medieval quarter of Ano Sýros and the Orthodox **Anástasis**, the city is one of the most religiously and culturally diverse places in the whole of Greece. **Accommodation** is plentiful and most conveniently booked at the Rooms and Apartments Association of Sýros (☎22810 82 252) on the waterfront. Good choices include *Kastro Rooms*, Kalomenopoúlo 12 (☎22810 88 064; ❹), *Dream*, on the seafront near the bus station (☎22810 84 356, ℻22810 86 452; ❹), and *Hotel Nisaki*, on Papadhám behind the port authority (☎22810 88 200, ℻22810 82 000; ❺). The most authentic and reasonably priced **places to eat** on the harbour are *Yiannena Estiatorio* on Platía Kanári, and the popular *Psaropoula Ouzerí*. Around Platía Miaoúli, there are some good traditional tavernas – *Manousos*, on the square itself, is the best choice. For a **drink**, head to the seafront with its collection of lively bars.

## Sífnos

Although **Sífnos** – notable for its classic Cycladic architecture and pottery – often gets crowded, its modest size makes exploring the picturesque island a pleasure, whether by the excellent in-season bus service or on foot over a network of old stone pathways. **KAMÁRES**, the port, is tucked at the base of high bare cliffs in the west. **Accommodation** can be expensive – the best budget option is *Hotel Stavros* (☎22840 33 383; ℻22840 31 709; ❹), towards the beach from the quay. A steep twenty-minute bus ride takes you up to **APOLLONÍA**, a rambling collage of flagstones, belfries and flowered courtyards. The island bank, post office and tourist police are all here, while the Aegean Thesaurus agency (☎22840 31 151, ⊛www.thesaurus.gr) should be able to help with rooms. As an alternative base, head for **KÁSTRO**, a forty-minute walk or regular bus ride below Apollonía on the east coast; built on a rocky outcrop with an almost sheer drop to the sea on three sides, this medieval capital of the island retains much of its character. There are plenty of rooms in the village – the modernized year-round *Aris Rafeletos Apartments* (☎ & ℻22840 31 161; ❹) is a good bet. At the southern end of the island, 12km from Apollonía by frequent bus, lies the busy beach resort of **PLATÝS YIALÓS**, with an uninspiring campsite and numerous rooms to let, as well as tavernas, bakeries and supermarkets. Alternatively, ask the driver to drop you off at the bus stop for Chrissopigí (from where it's a ten-minute walk down a path), where the beach is less crowded and where there's an excellent taverna and a postcard-perfect monastery. The island's finest walk is through the hills to **VATHÝ**, around three hours from Apollonía's Katavatí "suburb". A fishing and ex-pottery village on a stunning funnel-shaped bay, Vathý is the most attractive base on the island. Its cheapest **rooms** are at the taverna *Manolis* (℡22840 71 111; ③); there's also another taverna, *Tò Tsikali,* behind the tiny monastery.

## Mýkonos

**Mýkonos** has become the most popular and expensive of the Cyclades, visited by nearly a million tourists a year. If you don't mind the crowds, the upmarket capital is one of the most beautiful and vibrant of all island towns. Dazzlingly white, it's the archetypal island-postcard image, with sugar-cube buildings stacked around a cluster of seafront fishermen's dwellings.

The airport is about 3km out of **MÝKONOS TOWN** (also known as **HÓRA**), a short taxi ride away. Cruise ships dock at the northern port, while island **ferries** arrive at the more central northern jetty, where they are met by a horde of **hotel** and **room** touts; you'd do better to proceed to the helpful Mýkonos Accommodation *Center* in town (℡22890 23 160, ⓦwww .mykonos-accommodation. com), or try the comfortable *Stelios Pension* (℡22890 24 641, ℱ22890 26 779; ③), on steps leading up from near the jetty. More central options include the *Terra Maria* at Kaloyéra 18 (℡22890 24 212, ℱ22890 27 112; ⑤) and the *Philippi* at Kaloyéra 25 (℡22890 22 294, ℱ22890 24 680; ⑤). Otherwise there's a very lively **campsite** at Paradise (℡22890 22 129, ⓦwww .paradisemykonos.com). Back in town, the harbour curves around past the dull, central beach, behind which is the **bus station** for Áyios Stéfanos. Continue along the seafront to the southern jetty for the **tourist and port police** and *kaïkia* to Delos. A second bus terminus, for beaches to the south of town, is right at the other end of Hóra, beyond the windmills.

There's no shortage of **dining** options in the town's labyrinthine centre, with *Kostas,* near Mitropóleos and *Yiavroutas Estiatorio,* a bit further along

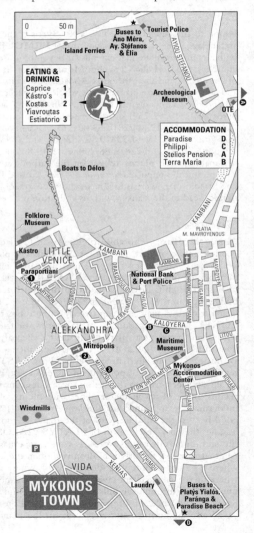

Mitropóleos, among the more traditional and affordable options. For **nightlife**, *Kástro's* and *Caprice*, on the waterfront in Little Venice, are good for an early-evening cocktail, followed by the *Skandinavian Bar-Disco* and the *Irish Bar* for the backpacker set. The more sophisticated clubs tend to centre on and around Andhroníkou Matoyiánni, known as "Fifth Avenue" for the nightly fashion parade along its cobblestone catwalk, with *Space* on Lákka Square being the largest dance club in town.

The closest decent **beach** is **Áyios Stéfanos**, 4km north and connected by a very regular bus service, though **Platýs Yialós**, 4km south, is marginally less crowded. A *kaïki* service from Mýkonos town connects almost all the beaches east of Platýs Yialós: gorgeous, pale-sand **Paránga** beach, popular with campers; **Paradise**, well sheltered by its headland and predominantly nudist; and **Super Paradise**, which has a friendly atmosphere and two bars. Probably the island's best beach is **Eliá** on the southeast coast: a broad sandy stretch with a verdant backdrop, split in two by a rocky area. Less busy, but harder to get to, is **Pánormos Bay** on the island's wind-swept northern coast, with its relatively sheltered Pánormos and Áyios Sostis beaches.

# Delos

The skeletal remains of ancient **DELOS** (Tues–Sun 8.30am–3pm; €5) give some idea of the past grandeur of this sacred isle a few sea-miles west of Mýkonos. Accessible only as a day-trip by *kaïki* (€6) from the southern jetty in Mýkonos Town, this tiny island can be thoroughly explored in a few hours. Delos' ancient claim to fame is as the place where Leto gave birth to the divine twins Artemis and Apollo; one of the first things you see on arrival is the **Sanctuary of Apollo**, while three Temples of Apollo stand in a row along the Sacred Way. To the east towards the museum you pass the **Sanctuary of Dionysos** with its marble phalluses on tall pillars. To the north is the **Sacred Lake** where Leto gave birth: guarding it is a group of lions, masterfully executed in the seventh century BC. Set out in the other direction from the agora and you enter the residential area, known as the **Theatre Quarter**. There are some nice mosaics to be seen: one in the **House of the Trident** – better ones in the **House of the Masks** – including a vigorous portrayal of Dionysos riding on a panther's back. A steep path from here leads up **Mount Kýnthos** for spectacular views back down over the ruins and out to the surrounding Cyclades.

# Páros and Andíparos

With its old villages, monasteries, fishing harbour and labyrinthine capital, **Páros** has everything one expects from a Greek island, including boat connections to virtually the entire Aegean. All ferries dock at **PARIKÍA**, the main town, with its ranks of white houses punctuated by the occasional Venetian-style building and church domes. Just outside the centre, the town also has one of the most interesting churches in the Aegean – the sixth-century **Ekatondapyliani**, or "Church of One Hundred Gates". The town culminates in a seaward Venetian **kástro**, whose surviving east wall incorporates a fifth-century-BC round tower.

You'll be met off the ferry by locals offering **rooms**: alternatively, try the peaceful *Hotel Captain Manolis* (☎22840 21 244, @www.paroswelcome.com; ❸), or the smart *Hotel Argonauta* (☎22840 21 440, @www.argonauta.gr; ❺), both close to the National Bank. There's a crowded **campsite**, the *Koula* (☎22840 22 081), at the northern end of the town beach, or the better *Krios Camping* (☎22840 21 705, @www.krios-camping.gr), across the bay to the north. For food, the *Hotel Argonauta* has a reliable **restaurant**, while *Trata*, behind the ancient cemetery, is good for fish. The most popular cocktail **bars** extend along the seafront, tucked into a series of open squares.

The second village of Páros, **NÁOUSSA** (reached by regular buses from the stop 100m or so to the left of the ferry dock), retains much of its original character as a fishing village with winding, narrow alleys and simple Cycladic houses. Though very busy in summer, it makes a good base for exploring nearby beaches. For inexpensive **accommodation**, try *Stella,* several blocks inland from the old harbour (☎22840 52 198; ❸), or one of the **campsites** out of town towards the beaches of Kolymbíthres (☎22840 51 565) or Sánta María (☎22840 51 013), both better than the mosquito-plagued one in Parikía.

There are boats from Parikía to the island of **ANDÍPAROS** (hourly in high season; 40min), making it a convenient day-trip. There's plenty of **accommodation**, including a campsite. The best beaches are at Psaralíki, Glýfa, Ághios Yeóryios and Kalógeros; *kaïkia* make daily trips around the island, stopping at them all, as well as the impressive **cave** (daily 10.45am–3.45pm; €3).

## Náxos and the minor Cyclades

**Náxos** is the largest and most fertile of the Cyclades with high mountains, intriguing central valleys, a spectacular north coast, sandy beaches in the southwest and Venetian towers and fortified mansions scattered throughout. A long causeway protecting the harbour connects **NÁXOS TOWN** with the islet of Palátia, where the huge stone portal of an unfinished sixth-century-BC **Temple of Apollo** still stands. Most of the town's life goes on down by the port or in the streets just behind it; stepped lanes behind lead up past crumbling balconies and through low arches to the fortified medieval **kástro**, near the **Archeological Museum** (Tues–Sun 8.30am–3pm; €3), with its important early sculpture collection and a Hellenistic mosaic on the roof terrace. For **accommodation**, avoid the touts greeting the ferry and head for the Náxos Tourism Office near the jetty (☎22850 25 201; daily 9am–11pm), which can book rooms around the island. Alternatively, the best budget options near the *kástro* are the rooms of *Despina Panteleou* (☎22850 22 356; ❸) and the *Hotel Panorama* (☎22850 24 404, ✉panoramanaxos@in.gr; ❹). Along the quayside, **cafés** and **restaurants** are abundant: favourites include *Ouzerí Gatis* (aka *To Limanaki*) and its neighbour *Popi's*, which has its own wine and cheese shop.

The island's best **beaches** are regularly served by buses in season. Within walking distance is **Áyios Yeóryios**, a long sandy bay south of the hotel quarter, with several tavernas. An hour's walk further south, however, you'll find the more inviting **Áyios Prokópios** and **Ayía Ánna** beaches, with plenty of rooms to let and a few modest tavernas. Beyond the headland stretches **Pláka** beach, a 5km-long vegetation-fringed expanse of white sand, which comfortably holds the summer crowds of nudists and campers from its two friendly campsites, *Maragas* (☎ & ☎22850 24 552), which also has double rooms (❷), and the newer *Plaka* (☎22850 42 700).

Náxos also serves as a convenient entry point to the **MINOR CYCLADES**, a chain of small islands that have become fashionable destinations for those seeking seclusion in recent years. In August, local boat *Express Skopelitis* leaves Náxos Town almost daily, calling at **Áno Koufoníssia**, **Skhinoússa**, **Irakliá** and **Donoússa**, where you'll find basic accommodation and good beaches. The end point of this journey is the island of **AMORGÓS**, with dramatic mountain scenery and crystal-blue seas. It's best to stay at the port of **Eyiáli**, where there's a welcoming campsite (☎22850 73 050) and plenty of rooms to let. Be sure to visit the pretty village of **Hóra**, and the spectacular monastery of Hozoviótissa, dramatically situated on a cliff high above the sea.

## Íos

Although no other island attracts more under-25s, **Íos**, party capital of the Aegean, has miraculously maintained much of its traditional Cycladic charm. Arriving in

YIALÓS, you'll find plenty of accommodation – there's a refurbished **campsite** (☎22860 91 329) near the harbour, while nearby Yialós beach is fringed by hotels and lodgings – though most of the budget **rooms** are in **HÓRA**, a twenty-minute walk (or a short bus ride) up the mountain behind the port. Every evening the streets throb to music with the larger **clubs** (mostly free, though drinks tend to be expensive) clustered near the bus stop. For up-to-date listings see ⓦwww.iospartyisland .com. The most popular stop on the island's bus routes is **MYLOPÓTAS**, site of a magnificent beach and mini-resort. It gets very crowded, so for a bit more space, head away from the terminus where there are dunes behind the beach. There are two **campsites**, *The Purple Pig* (☎22860 91 302, ⓦwww.purplepigstars.com) and *Far Out* (☎22860 91 468, ⓦwww.faroutclub.com), which also has bungalows. For rooms, try *Dracos Pension* (☎22860 91 281; ❹) to the right of the bus stop. From Yialós, boats depart daily at around 10am to **MANGANÁRI** on the south coast, the beach to go to for a serious tan. There's a better atmosphere, though, at **ÁYIOS THEODHÓTIS**, up on the northeast coast, served by daily buses from Yialós.

## Santoríni (Thíra)

As the ferry manoeuvres into the great bay of **Santoríni** (a partially submerged volcanic caldera poking above the ocean's surface in five places), gaunt, sheer cliffs loom hundreds of feet above. Nothing grows to soften the view, and the only colours are the reddish-brown, black and grey pumice strata layering the cliff face of **THÍRA**, Santoríni's largest island. Despite a past every bit as turbulent as the geological conditions that formed it, the island is now best known for its spectacular views, dark-sand beaches and light, dry white wines.

Most boats arrive at the somewhat grim port of **Órmos Athiniós** from where buses meeting the ferries make their way to the island's capital **FIRÁ;** half-rebuilt after a devastating earthquake in 1956 and lurching dementedly at the cliff's edge. Besieged by day-trippers from cruise-ships, it's somewhat tacky and commercialized, though watching the sunset from a cliff-hugging terrace of any of the overpriced restaurants you'll understand why. There's no shortage of **rooms** in the area, though most are expensive. The town boasts a couple of **museums** (Tues–Sun 8.30am–2.30pm; €3 for both): the Archeological Museum, near the cable car to the north of town, and the Museum of Prehistoric Thíra, between the cathedral and the bus station. **Bus** services are plentiful enough between the town and beaches.

Near the northwest tip of the island is one of the most dramatic towns of the Cyclades, **ÍA**, a curious mix of pristine white reconstruction and tumbledown ruins clinging to the cliff face. With a post office, travel agencies and an excellent **youth hostel** (☎22860 71 465; dorms €10), it makes a good base from which to explore the island. Santoríni's **beaches** are bizarre: long black stretches of volcanic sand which get blisteringly hot in the afternoon sun. There's little to choose between **KAMÁRI** and **PERÍSSA**, the two main resorts: both have long beaches and a mass of restaurants, rooms and apartments. Períssa gets more backpackers, has the better campsite and a well-run hostel, *Anna* (☎22860 82 182, ☎22860 81 943; €10–12).

At the southwest tip of the island, evidence of a Minoan colony was found at **Akrotíri** (summer Tues–Sat 8.30am–2.30pm; €5; bus from Firá or Períssa), a town buried under banks of volcanic ash. Tunnels through the ash uncovered structures two and three storeys high, and you can now walk down an authentic Minoan street. Nearby is the spectacular, red sand **Kókkini Ámmos** beach, and *Caldera View Camping* (☎22860 82 010). Daily **boat trips** run from either Firá or Ía (€10–30) to the charred volcanic islets of **PALEÁ KAMÉNI** and **NÉA KAMÉNI**, and on to the relatively unspoiled islet of **THIRASSÍA**, which was once part of Thíra until shorn off by an eruption in the third century BC.

# Rhodes

It's no surprise that **Rhodes** is among the most visited of Greek islands. Not only is its east coast lined with sandy beaches, but the core of the capital is a beautiful and remarkably preserved medieval city. **RHODES TOWN** divides into two unequal parts: the compact old walled city, and the new town sprawling around it in three directions. First thing to meet the eye, and dominating the northeast sector of the city's fortifications, is the **Palace of the Grand Masters** (summer Mon 12.30–6.40pm, Tues–Fri 8am–6.40pm; winter Mon 12.30–3pm, Tues–Sun 8.30am–3pm; €6, or €10 combo ticket with other museums). Two excellent **museums** occupy the ground floor: one devoted to medieval Rhodes, the other to ancient Rhodes. The heavily-restored **Street of the Knights** (Odhós Ippotón) leads due east from the front of the palace. The "Inns" lining it housed the Knights

Map legend:

**ACCOMMODATION**
- Apollo Tourist House — D
- Hotel Spot — A
- Pension Niki's — C
- Youth Hostel — B

**EATING & DRINKING**
- L'Auberge Bistrot — 5
- Lefteras — 2
- Megaro — 4
- Mikes — 3
- Niohori — 2
- Sakis — 6

RHODES TOWN

of St John for two centuries, and at the bottom of the slope the Knights' Hospital now houses the **Archeological Museum** (Tues–Sun 8am–6.40pm; €3, or €10 combo ticket), where the star exhibits are two statues of Aphrodite. Across the way is the **Byzantine Museum** (same hours; €1.50 or €10 combo ticket), housed in the Knights' chapel and highlighting the island's icons and frescoes. Heading south, it's hard to miss the most conspicuous Ottoman monument in Rhodes, the candy-striped **Süleymaniye Mosque** (Fri noon–2pm; free).

Affordable **accommodation** abounds in the old town. Quiet, good-value places include the newly refurbished *Apollo Tourist House*, Omírou 28C (☎22410 32 003, ⑭www.apollo-touristhouse.com; ❸); the friendly, helpful *Pension Niki's*, Sofokléous 39 (☎22410 25 115, ⑭www.nikishotel.gr; ❸), and the modernized, en-suite *Hotel Spot*, Perikleous 21 (☎22410 34 737, ⑯spothot@otenet.gr; ❸). There's a good **hostel** at Eryíou 12, just off Ayíou Fanouríou (☎22410 30 491; €8). **Eating** cheaply can be more of a problem; try the little alleys and backstreets south of Sokrátous. Here you'll find home-style cooking at *Lefteras*, Evdhóxou 49, or some of the cheapest fish in town at *Mikes*, in an alley off Sokrátous. Better value can be had just outside the walls at *Sakis*, on the corner of Kanadhá and Apostólou Papadhiamándi, near Zéfyros Beach, or *Niohori*, Ioánni Kazoúli 29, by the Franciscan monastery, whilst for a treat, try *L'Auberge Bistrot* at Praxitélous 21. The **post office**, most banks, the EOT **tourist office** (Mon–Fri 7.30am–2.30pm; ☎22410 23 255) and the municipal tourist office (June–Sept Mon–Sat 8am–9.30pm, Sun 9am–3pm) are arrayed around the Italian-built New Market. **Buses** for the rest of the island leave from two terminals within sight of the market. Most central **Internet** cafés are *Rock Style* at Dhimokratías 7, just southwest of the old town, and *Cosmonet*, at Platía Evreon Martyon 45.

Heading down the east coast from Rhodes Town, the giant promontory of **Tsambíka**, 26km south, is the first place to seriously consider stopping – there's an excellent eponymous beach just south of the headland. The best overnight base on this stretch of coast is probably **HARÁKI**, a tiny port with rooms and tavernas overlooked by a ruinous castle. **LÍNDHOS**, Rhodes' number-two tourist attraction, erupts 12km south of Haráki. Its charm is undermined by commercialism and crowds, and there are relatively few self-catering units that aren't block-booked through package companies – find vacancies through Pallas Travel (T22440 31 494, Wwww.pallastravel.gr). On the hill above the town, the Doric **Temple of Athena** and Hellenistic stoa (porch-like building used for meetings and commerce) stand inside the inevitable knights' castle (summer Mon noon–6.40pm, Tues–Sun 8am–6.40pm; winter Tues–Sun 8.30am–3pm; €6). Líndhos' beaches are crowded and overrated, but you'll find better ones heading south past Lárdhos, the start of 15km of intermittent coarse-sand beach up to and beyond the growing resort of **Yennádhi**. Inland near here, the late Byzantine frescoes in the village church of **Asklipió** are among the best on Rhodes.

## Kós

**Kós** is the largest and most popular island in the Dodecanese after Rhodes, and there are superficial similarities between the two. Like its rival, the harbour here is also guarded by a castle of the Knights of St John, the streets are lined with ambitious Italian public buildings, and minarets and palm trees punctuate extensive Greek and Roman remains. Except for Kós Town and Mastihári, there aren't many non-package travellers: in high season you'll be lucky to find any sort of bed at all, except perhaps at the far west end of the island. Mostly modern **KÓS TOWN**, levelled by a 1933 earthquake, fans out from the harbour. The helpful municipal **tourist office** (Mon–Fri: May–Oct 8.30am–2.30pm & 5.30–8.30pm; Nov–April 8.30am–2.30pm; T22420 24 460), 500m south of the ferry dock on the shore road, offers maps and ferry schedules. **Buses** arrive inland 500m west of the tourist office. Among budget **accommodation**, try the clean, friendly *Pension Alexis*, Irodhótou 9, two blocks back from the harbourfront (T22420 25 594; ❷; closed Nov–Feb), or *Hotel Afendoulis*, 600m southeast, near the tourist office at Evripýlou 1 (T22420 25 321, Eafendoulishotel@kos.forthnet.gr; ❸; closed Nov–March). Avoid the harbourfront **restaurants** in favour of *Ambavris*, 1.5km inland in the eponymous hamlet, or *Koakon* at Artemisías 56. Apart from the **castle** (Tues–Sun 8.30am–3pm; €3), the town's main attraction is its wealth of Hellenistic and Roman remains, including mosaics and statues displayed in the Italian-built **Archeological Museum** (Tues–Sun 8am–2.30pm; €3). Next to the castle, scaffolding props up the branches of the so-called Hippocrates plane tree, which does have a fair claim to be one of the oldest trees in Europe. Hippocrates is also honoured by the **Asklepion** (summer Tues–Sun 8am–6.30pm; winter closes earlier; €3), a temple to Asklepios and renowned centre of Hippocratic teaching, 45 minutes on foot (or a short bus ride) from town. The road to the Asklepion passes through the village of **PLATÁNI**, where the island's ethnic Turkish minority run the *Arap* and *Sherif* tavernas (summer only), serving excellent, affordable food.

For **beaches** you'll need to use buses or rent scooters or pedal-bikes. Around 12km west of Kós town, **Tingáki** is easily accessible but busy. **Mastihári**, 30km from Kós town, has a decent beach and non-package-tour rooms. Continuing west, buses run as far as **Kéfalos**, which covers a bluff looking back along the length of Kós. Well before Kéfalos are **Áyios Stéfanos**, where the exquisite remains of a mosaic-floored fifth-century basilica overlook tiny Kastrí islet, and **Kamári**, the package resort just below Kéfalos. Beaches begin at Kamári and extend east past

Áyios Stéfanos for 7km, almost without interruption; "Paradise" has the most facilities, but "Magic" (officially Polémi) and Langádhes are calmer and more scenic.

## Pátmos

St John the Divine reputedly wrote the Book of Revelation in a cave on **Pátmos**, and the monastery which commemorates him, founded here in 1088, dominates the island both physically and politically. While the monks no longer run Pátmos as they did for more than six centuries, their influence has stopped most of the island going the way of Rhodes or Kós. **SKÁLA**, the port and main town, is the chief exception, crowded with day-trippers from Kós and Rhodes or cruise-ship shoppers. **Accommodation** touts meet all ferries and hydrofoils, and their offerings can be a long walk inland – not necessarily a bad thing, as the waterfront is noisy. Less expensive hotels to book in advance include *Australis* in Netiá district (☏22470 31 576; ❹), who will refer you to relatives' pensions if they're full. Among **restaurants**, try the reliable seafood *Ouzerí To Hiliomodhi*. The next bay north of the main harbour shelters **Méloï Beach**, with a well-run campsite and an excellent taverna, *Stefanos*. For swimming, the second beach north, **Agriolivádhi**, is usually less crowded.

The **Monastery of St John** (daily 8am–1.30pm; Tues, Thurs & Sun also 4–6pm; monastery free, treasury €5) shelters behind massive defences in the hilltop capital of **HÓRA**. Buses go up, but the thirty-minute walk along a beautiful old cobbled path puts you in a more appropriate frame of mind. Just over halfway is the **Monastery of the Apocalypse**, built around the cave where St John heard the voice of God issuing from a cleft in the rock. This is merely a foretaste, however, of the main monastery, whose fortifications guard a dazzling array of religious treasures dating back to medieval times. Hóra itself is a beautiful little town whose antiquated alleys conceal over forty churches and monasteries, plus dozens of shipowners' mansions dating from the island's heyday in the seventeenth and eighteenth centuries. **Rooms** are limited, so advance reservations are required, and stays of three nights or more are preferred – *Yeoryia Triandafyllou* (☏22470 31 963; ❸) is a good bet. From Hóra a good road runs above the package resort of Gríkou – where *Ktima Petra* is one of the best tavernas on the island – to the isthmus of **Stavrós**, from where a thirty-minute trail leads to the excellent beach, with one seasonal taverna, at **Psilí Ámmos** (summer *kaïki* from Skála). There are more good beaches in the north of the island, particularly **Livádhi Yeránou**, shaded by tamarisk groves and with a decent taverna, and **Lámbi** with volcanic pebbles and another quality taverna, *Leonidas*.

# The northern Aegean islands

The seven scattered islands of the **northeastern Aegean** form a rather arbitrary archipelago. Local tour operators do a thriving business shuttling passengers for absurdly high tariffs between the easternmost islands and the Turkish coast. **Sámos** is the most visited, and was – until a week-long forest fire devastated a fifth of the island in 2000 – perhaps the most verdant and beautiful. **Híos** is culturally fascinating, while **Lésvos** is more of an acquired taste, though once smitten you may find it hard to leave. The **Sporades**, in the northwestern Aegean, are an easier group to island-hop and well connected with Athens by bus and ferry via Áyios Konstandínos or Kými (for Skýros only), and with Vólos.

## Sámos

**Sámos** was the wealthiest island in the Aegean during the seventh century BC, but fell on hard times thereafter; today its economy is heavily dependent on package tourism. All ferries to and from Pireás and the Cyclades call at both Karlóvassi in the west and Vathý in the east; additionally there are services to the Dodecanese out of Pythagório in the south. **VATHÝ**, the capital, lines the steep-sided shore of its namesake bay and is of minimal interest except for its hill quarter of tottering, tile-roofed houses, Áno Vathý, and an excellent **archeological museum** (Tues–Sun 8.30am–3pm; €3), containing a wealth of peculiar votive offerings and a huge, five-metre statue of an idealized youth. **Accommodation** includes the welcoming *Pension Avli*, housed in a former convent at Áreos 2 (☏22730 22 939; ❷), and the partly en-suite *Pension Trova*, Manóli Kalomíri 26 (☏22730 27 759; ❷). For **food**, *T'Ostrako*, on the waterfront by the police station, serves affordable seafood, while just north of the ferry dock *Artemis* is more versatile. West of Vathý, the busy resort of **Kokkári** is enchantingly set between twin headlands at the base of still partly forested mountains. Nearby beaches are pebbly and exposed, prompting its role as a major windsurfers' resort. Some 13km west is untouristed **ÁYIOS KONSTAND-ÍNOS**, with several modest pensions and hotels, plus three excellent **tavernas**, the most reliably open being *To Kyma*. Less than an hour's walk west from functional Karlóvassi, **Potámi** is a popular beach ringed by forest and weird rock formations; for more solitude you can continue another hour or so on foot to the two bays of **Mikró Seïtáni** (pebbles) and **Megálo Seïtáni** (sand). But for an amenitied beach resort in the west of the island, shift south to **ÓRMOS MARATHAKÁMBOU**, adjacent to 2km of sand and pebbles at Votsalákia package resort. In Órmos itself, *Lekatis*, at the east end of the front, serves inexpensive seafood.

# Híos

Increasing numbers of foreigners are discovering **Híos** beyond its port city and single resort strip – fascinating villages, an important Byzantine monument and a healthy complement of beaches. **HÍOS TOWN** is always full of life, with a shambling old bazaar district, some excellent authentic tavernas, and a regular evening promenade along the waterfront. There's relatively cheap **accommodation** along and just behind the waterfront; the helpful **tourist office**, Kanári 18 (daily 7am–2.30/10pm; winter closed Sat & Sun; ☏22710 44 389), has comprehensive lists. The best-value include *Híos Rooms*, Kokáli 1 (☏22710 20 198, ⓦwww .chiosrooms.gr; ❷). For **eating out** head for *Inomayirio Iakovos*, Ayíou Yeoryíou Frouríou 20, inside the *kástro*, or *O Hotzas*, inland at Yeoryíou Kondhýli 3. Green long-distance **buses** run from the terminal south of the central park to most of the villages, though services to the north are sparse. The closest decent beach is **KARFÁS** (7km; frequent blue urban bus), a long if narrow sweep of sand, unfortunately overwhelmed by package tours; the best independent **accommodation** here is *Marko's Place* (☏22710 31 990, ⓦwww.marcos-place.gr; ❷; closed Dec–March), in a disused monastery. The monastery of **Néa Moní** (daily 8am–1pm & 4–8pm; free), founded by Byzantine emperor Constantine IX in 1042, is the most beautiful and important medieval building on the Greek islands. There are special KTEL bus excursions from the long-distance bus station (see above) in summer (Mon, Wed & Fr at 10am), or pricier agency excursions including Anávatos (see below). Once a community of six hundred monks, the monastery was pillaged during Ottoman atrocities in 1822 and most of its inmates killed. The deserted medieval village of **Anávatos**, about 9km to the northwest of Néa Moní, is set on a dramatic 300-metre-high rock formation. The hillsides of **southern Híos** are home to the mastic bush, whose resin – for centuries the base of paints and cosmetics – was the source of local wealth before petrochemicals came along. **PYRGÍ**, 24km from the port, is one of the liveliest and most colourful of the "mastic villages", its houses elaborately embossed with geometric patterns cut into the plaster and then outlined with paint. Pyrgí has a handful of rooms and some good beaches nearby, the closest being **Emborió**, 5km from Pyrgí and served by occasional buses in summer; eating is, however, better at the equally impressive

**MESTÁ**, 11km west, with the decent *Mesaionas* taverna on its square, and more accommodation.

## Lésvos

Lésvos, birthplace of Sappho, the ancient world's foremost woman poet, may not at first seem particularly beautiful, but the craggy volcanic landscape of pine and olive groves grows on you. Despite the inroads of tourism, this is still essentially a working island, with few large hotels outside the capital, Mytilíni, and the resorts of Skála Kallonís and Mólyvos. Few people stay in **MYTILÍNI**, but do pause long enough to **eat** at *Paradhosiako Kalderimi* at Thássou 2, and peek at the **archeological museum**, with its superb Roman mosaics (Tues–Sun 8.30am–3pm; €3). **MÓLYVOS**, on the northwestern coast, is easily the most attractive spot on Lésvos. Tiers of sturdy, red-tiled houses mount the slopes between the picturesque harbour and the Genoese castle. There are plenty of rooms to let – the **tourist office** by the bus stop (summer daily 8am–3pm & 6.30–8.30pm; ☎22530 71 347) can book them – and a campsite east of town. The main lower road, past the tourist office, heads towards the picturesque harbour, where *The Captain's Table* is the best-value taverna. Lésvos' best beach is at **SKÁLA ERESSOÚ** in the far southwest, with rooms far outnumbering hotels. Tavernas with wooden terraces line the beach – try *Eressos Palace* or *Blue Sardine*. **PLOMÁRI** in the southeast, long the *oúzo* capital of Greece, is another good base, though beaches lie some distance either side; **stay** at *Pension Lida*, in a restored mansion (☎22520 32507; ②).

## The Sporades

The three northern **Sporades** – package-tourist haven Skiáthos, Alónissos and **Skópelos**, the pick of the trio – have good beaches, transparent waters and thick pine forests. **Skýros**, the fourth Sporade, is isolated from the others and less scenic, but with perhaps the most character; for a relatively uncommercialized island within a day's travel of Athens it's unbeatable.

### Skópelos

More rugged yet better cultivated than neighbouring Skiáthos, **Skópelos** is also very much more attractive. **SKÓPELOS TOWN** slopes down one corner of a huge, almost circular bay. There are dozens of rooms to let – take up one of the offers when you land or call the Roomowners Association (☎24240 24 576) for vacancies. The most reliable **tavernas** are *Molos*, on the front, and *Alexander*, inland and uphill. Within the town, spread below the oddly whitewashed ruins of a Venetian *kástro*, are an enormous number of churches – 123 reputedly, though some are small enough to be mistaken for houses. **Buses** run along the island's one asphalt road to Loutráki about seven times daily, stopping at the turn-offs to all the main beaches and villages. **Stáfylos** beach, 4km out of town, is the closest, but it's small, rocky and increasingly crowded; the overflow, much of it nudist, flees to **Valanió**, just east. Much more promising, if you're after relative isolation, is sandy **Limnonári**, a fifteen-minute road-walk or short *kaïki* ride from **AGNÓNDAS** (tavernas and rooms). The large resort of **Pánormos** has become overdeveloped, but slightly further on, **Miliá** offers a tremendous 1500m sweep of tiny pebbles beneath a bank of pines.

### Skýros

**Skýros** remained until the 1980s a very traditional and idiosyncratic island. The older men still wear the vaguely Cretan costume of cap, vest, baggy trousers, leggings and clogs, while the women favour yellow scarves and long embroidered skirts. Skýros also has a particularly lively *Apokriátika* or pre-Lenten **carnival**, featuring the "Goat Dance", performed by masked revellers in the village streets. A **bus** connects Linariá – a functional little port with a few tourist facilities – to **SKÝROS TOWN**, spread below a high rock rising precipitously from the coast. Traces of Classical walls can still be made out among the ruins of the Venetian *kástro*; within the walls is the crumbling, tenth-century monastery of **Áyios Yeóryios**. There are several hotels and plenty of **rooms** to let in private houses; you'll be met with offers as you descend from the bus, or Skyros Travel (T22220 91 123, Wwww.skyrostravel.com) on the main street can help with accommodation. Skyrian **tavernas** are of reasonably high quality; choose from among *O Pappous k'Ego*, *Khristina's* and *Maryetis*. The campsite is down the hill at the fishing village of **MAGAZIÁ**, with rooms and tavernas fronting the island's best beach.

# The Ionian islands

The six **Ionian islands** are, both geographically and culturally, a mixture of Greece and Italy. Floating on the haze of the Adriatic, their green silhouettes come as a surprise to those more used to the stark outlines of the Aegean. The islands were the Homeric realm of Odysseus and here alone of all modern Greek territory the Ottomans never held sway. After the fall of Byzantium, possession passed to the Venetians, and the islands became a keystone in that city-state's maritime empire from 1386 until its collapse in 1797. Tourism has hit **Corfu** in a big way but none of the other islands has endured anything like the same scale of development, although the process seems well advanced on parts of **Zákynthos**. For a less sullied experience, head for **Kefalloniá** or **Itháki**.

## Corfu (Kérkyra)

**Corfu**'s natural appeal remains an intense experience, if sometimes a beleaguered one, for it has more package hotels and holiday villas than any other Greek island. The commercialism is apparent the moment you step ashore at the ferry dock, or cover the 2km from the airport (local buses #2 and #3 leave from 500m north of the terminal gates). **KÉRKYRA TOWN**, the capital, has a lot more going for it than first exposure to the summer crowds might indicate. The cafés on the Esplanade and in the arcaded Listón have a civilized air, and the Palace of SS Michael and George at the north end of the Spianádha is worth visiting for its **Asiatic museum** (Tues–Sun 8.30am–3pm; €2) and **Municipal Art Gallery** (daily 9am–9pm; €1.50). The **Byzantine Museum** (Tues–Sun 9am–3pm; €3) and the cathedral are both interesting, as is the **Archeological Museum**, Vraíla 3 (Tues–Sun 8.30am–3pm; €3), where the small but intriguing collection features a 2500-year-old Medusa pediment. The island's patron saint, Spyrídhon, is entombed in a silver-covered coffin in his own church on Vouthrótou, and four times a year, to the accompaniment of much celebration and feasting, the relics are paraded through the streets. Some 5km south of town lies the picturesque convent of **Vlahérna**, which is joined to the plush mainland suburb of Kanóni by a short causeway; the tiny islet of **Pondikoníssi** in the bay can also be visited by a frequent *kaíki* service (€1.50 return). The best source of independent **accommodation** in Corfu Town and around the island is the Roomowners Association at D. Theotóki 2 near the archeological museum (Mon–Fri 9am–1.30pm; Tues, Thurs & Fri also 6–8pm; T26610 26 133, Eoitkcrf@otenet.gr). Otherwise, try the least expensive old-town **hotel**, *Europa*, Yitsiáli 10, near the new port (T26610 39 304; **③**). The nearest **campsite** is *Dionysos Camping Village* (T26610 91 417) at Dhassiá, 8km north. For **eating out**, try *Aleko's Beach*, at the jetty below the Palace of SS Michael and George, or the friendly *To Paradosiakon* at Solomoú 20.

**Buses** for the rest of the island leave from the long-distance KTEL terminal near the new fortress.

The coast north of the port has been remorselessly developed as far as Pyrgí; the best spot is **PEROULÁDHES**, a genuine, somewhat run-down village with a spectacular beach of brick-red sand below wind-eroded cliffs. On the west coast, **PALEOKASTRÍTSA** has gone the way of all package locations, though its coves are on a beautiful stretch of coast. Expensive villas and hotels are present in abundance, plus a few campsites, though these are some distance from the town. If you just want a room, search uphill in the villages of Lákones and Makrádhes, 5km away. The tiny village of **VÁTOS**, just inland from west-coast Érmones, is the one place within easy reach of Kérkyra Town that has an easy, relaxed feel to it and reasonable rooms and tavernas. The nearest campsite to picturesque Myrtiótissa Beach is *Vatos Camping*, near the village of Vátos. Nearby **PÉLEKAS** is rather busy, but it's a good alternative base, with simple tavernas and rooms – try *Pension Paradise* (T26610 94 530; **③**) – and the excellent *Zanzibar* pub. Further south, **ÁYIOS GÓRDHIS** beach is more remote but that hasn't spared it from the crowds who come to admire the cliff-girt setting or patronize the *Pink Palace* (T26610 53 103; €17–26 per person half board), a youth-oriented holiday village/resort that sprawls from the sand up the hill behind. Also here, the HI *Corfu Travelers Inn* (T26610 53 935, Wwww.corfutravelersinn.com; dorms & half board €15) offers beachside accommodation. Beyond Messongí stretches the flat, sandy southern tip of Corfu. **Áyios Yeóryios**, on the southwest coast, consists of a developed area just before its beautiful beach, which extends north alongside the peaceful Korissíon lagoon. **Kávos**, near the cape itself, rates with its many clubs and discos as the nightlife capital of the island; for daytime solitude and swimming, you can walk to beaches beyond the nearby hamlets of Sparterá and Dhragotiná.

## Kefalloniá

**Kefalloniá** is the largest, and at first glance least glamorous, of the Ionian islands; the 1953 earthquake that rocked the archipelago was especially devastating here, with almost every town and village levelled. Couple that with the islanders' legendary eccentricity, and with poor infrastructure, it's no wonder tourism didn't take off until the late 1980s. Already popular with Italians, the island has, more recently, been attracting large numbers of British tourists, in no small part thanks to Louis de Bernières' novel, *Captain Corelli's Mandolin*, which was set here. There's plenty of interest: beaches to compare with the best on Corfu or Zákynthos, good local wine, and the partly forested mass of Mount Énos (1628m). The island's size, skeletal bus service and shortage of summer accommodation make renting a motorbike or car a must for extensive exploration. **Ferries** mostly dock at **SÁMI** on the east coast, where the main *Corelli* set was built; few people linger here, though there is an excellent campsite, *Karavomilos Beach* (T26740 22 480). **AYÍA EFIMÍA**, 10km north, makes a far more attractive base, with the small but smart *Moustakis* hotel (T26740 61 030, Wwww.moustakishotel.com; **④**) and highly rated *Dendrinos* taverna. Between the two towns, 3km from Sámi, the **Melissáni cave** (daily 8am–sunset; €6) a partly submerged Capri-type "blue grotto", is well worth a stop. Southeast from Sámi are the resorts of **PÓROS**, with ferries to Kyllíni on the Peloponnese. You may have to continue around the cape, past excellent beaches, to find accommodation in the coastal village of Lourdháta. Just inland, detour to the Venetian castle of **Áyios Yeóryios** (Tues–Sun 8.30am–3/7pm; free). **ARGOSTÓLI**, with occasional ferries to Kyllíni and Zákynthos, is the bustling, concrete island capital. The waterfront **tourist office** (Mon–Fri 7.30am–2.30pm; in summer also Mon–Fri 6–10pm & Sat–Sun 9am–2pm & 6–10pm; T26710 22 248) keeps comprehensive lists of **accommodation**; you're best off with private rooms as hotels are expensive. The town's **Archeological Museum** (Tues–Sun 8.30am–3pm; €3) is second only to Corfu's in the archipelago. Heading north, you come to the beach of **Mýrtos**, considered the best on the island, although lacking in facilities; the closest places to **stay** are nearby Dhiváráta and almost bus-less **Ássos**, a beautiful fishing port perched on a narrow isthmus linking it to a castellated headland. At the end of the line, **Fiskárdho**, with its eighteenth-century houses, is the most expensive place on the island; the main reason to come would be for the daily **ferry** to Lefkádha island, and crossings to Itháki.

## Itháki

Despite its proximity to Kefalloniá, there's still very little tourist development to spoil **Itháki**, Odysseus's capital. There are no sandy beaches, but the island is good walking country, with a handful of small fishing villages and various coves to swim from. Most **ferries** from Pátra and Kefalloniá land at the main port and the village-sized capital of **VATHÝ**, at the back of a deep bay within a bay: some ferries from Kefalloniá, however, arrive at the busless Piaetós Wharf, 6km out of town on the west coast, where you'll be met by taxis. **Rooms** in Vathý are fairly easy to come by; they tend, however, to be inconspicuous, and are best sought by nosing around the backstreets south of the ferry dock. There's ample choice for **food**, with seven or eight tavernas, the seafront *To Kohyli* being the best of a remarkably similar bunch. In season the usual small boats shuttle tourists from the harbour to a series of tiny coves along the peninsula northeast of Vathý. The pebble-and-sand **beaches** between Cape Skhinós and Sarakíniko Bay are excellent. Two daily **buses** run north along the main road out of Vathý to **STAVRÓS**, a fair-sized village with a couple of tavernas and some rooms. There's a Homeric site nearby that may be the location for Odysseus's castle. **FRÍKES**, a thirty-minute walk downhill beyond Stavrós, is smaller but has a handful of tavernas, rooms and a pebbly strip of beach. This is where the seasonal **ferries** dock, to and from Lefkádha and Fiskárdho on northern Kefalloniá; the port is linked to Vathý by the same bus as Stavrós.

## Zákynthos

**Zákynthos** was hit hardest by the 1953 earthquake, and the island's grand old capital was completely destroyed. Although some of its beautiful Venetian churches have been restored, it's a town of limited appeal and the attraction for travellers lies more in the thick vineyards, orchards and olive groves of the interior, and some excellent beaches. Under two hours from Kyllíni on the mainland, Zákynthos now gets close to half a million visitors a year. Most tourists, though, are conveniently housed in one place, Laganás, on the south coast; if you avoid July and August, and steer clear of Laganás and the developing villages of Argási and Tsiliví, there's still a peaceful Zákynthos to be found.

The most tangible hints of the former glory of **ZÁKYNTHOS TOWN** are in **Platía Solomoú**, the grand and spacious main square. At its waterside corner stands the beautiful fifteenth-century sandstone church of **Áyios Nikólaos**, whose paintings and icons are displayed in the imposing **Byzantine Museum** (Tues–Sun 8am–2.30pm; €3), by the town hall. The large church of **Áyios Dhionýsios** was one of the few buildings left standing after the earthquake, and newly painted murals cover the interior. If you've a couple of hours to fill, walk up the cobbled path to the town's massive Venetian fortress (daily 8am–2/7.30pm; €1.50) for great views across the town and sea. The **tourist police** on waterfront Lombárdhou have information about **accommodation** and **bus** services. The Roomowners Association (☎26950 49 498) also has vacancies all over the island. Good-value hotels include *Egli* at the corner of Loútzi and Lombárdhou (☎26950 28 317; ❸). There are plenty of **eating places**, especially on the seafront on the north side of town; *Taverna Arekia* is excellent and has authentic live music, but it's a twenty-minute walk. To get to the **beaches**, buses depart from the station on Filitá (one block back from the seafront), but since the island is fairly flat, apart from the north and west, it's an ideal place to rent a **bike** – available from Moto-Saki, opposite the phone office. In the summer a number of boats depart from the quay for day-trips around the island.

# Crete

With its flourishing agricultural economy, **CRETE** is one of the few islands that could probably support itself without tourists. Nevertheless, mass tourism is all too evident. Much of the north coast, in particular, is overdeveloped and, though there are coastal areas that have not been spoiled, they are getting harder and harder to find. By contrast, the high mountains of the interior – capped with snow right through to June – are barely touched. Crete is distinguished as the home of the **Minoan** civilization, Europe's earliest, which made the island the centre of a maritime trading empire as early as 2000 BC and produced artworks unsurpassed in the ancient world. The island's strategic position means that it has seen a succession of influences since: control passed from Greeks to Romans to Saracens, through the Byzantine Empire to Venice, and finally to Turkey for more than two centuries before reunion with modern Greece. Almost wherever you go, you'll find some reminder of the island's history. The capital, **Iráklion**, is not the prettiest town on the island, although visits to its superb archeological museum and the Minoan palace at nearby **Knossos** are all but compulsory. There are other great Minoan sites at **Malia** on the north coast and at **Phaestos** in the south. Near the latter are the remains of the Roman capital at **Gortys**. For many people, unexpected highlights also turn out to be Crete's **Venetian forts** and its **Byzantine churches**. Historical heritage apart, the main attractions are that inland this is still a place where traditional rural life continues, and that the island is big enough to ensure that, with a little effort, you can still get away from it all. To do so, head for the far west, the far east or the harder-to-reach places along the south coast. If you want it, there's also a surprisingly sophisticated club scene

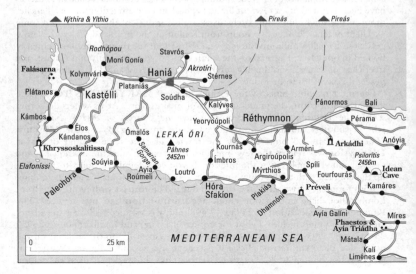

in the north-coast cities, and plenty of manic, beer-soaked tourist fun in the resorts in between.

Transport connections are excellent. There are daily **ferries** from Pireás to Iráklion, Réthymnon, Haniá and Áyios Nikólaos, as well as regular connections to Kastélli and Sitía (all on the north coast), a constant stream of **buses** plying between these places, and onward bus connections from these main centres to much of the rest of the island. Thanks to the tourists, there are also plenty of day-trips available in season, and small **boats** linking villages on the south coast. Rather than head for Iráklion, you're better off basing yourself initially in the beautiful city of **Haniá** (for the west, the mountains and the famous **Samarian Gorge**), in **Réthymnon** (only marginally less attractive, and handy for Iráklion, the major Minoan sites and the south), or **Sitía** to explore the far east.

## Iráklion and around

The best way to approach **IRÁKLION** is by sea; that way you see the city as it should be seen, with Mount Ioúktas rising behind and the Psilorítis range to the west. As you get closer, it's the fifteenth-century city walls which first stand out, still dominating and fully encircling the oldest part of town, and finally you sail in past the great Venetian fort defending the harbour entrance. Unfortunately, big ships no longer dock in this old port but at great modern concrete wharves alongside – which neatly sums up Iráklion itself: many of the old parts have been restored, but they're of marginal relevance to the dust and noise which characterize much of the modern city today. The only real sight of interest is the **Archeological Museum**, just off the north side of the main square, Platía Eleftherías (April–Sept Mon noon–7pm, Tues–Sun 8am–7pm; €6). It hosts a collection that includes almost every important prehistoric and Minoan find on Crete (go early or late in the day to avoid tour groups).

Directly opposite the museum is the tiny EOT **tourist office** (Mon–Fri 9am–2.30pm; ☎2810 228 225, ⓦwww.heraklion-city.gr). You're probably better off treating Iráklion and Knossos as a day-trip – **rooms** are hard to come by in high summer – but if you want to stay try the non-HI **hostel** at Víronos 5 (☎2810 286 281, ⓔheraklioyouthhostel@yahoo.gr; €10) or *Rent Rooms Hellas*, Hándhakos 24

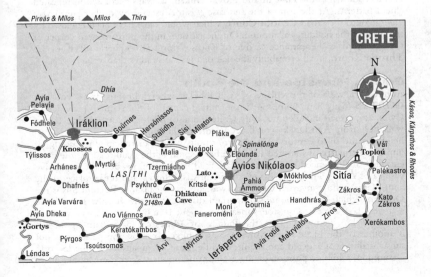

(☎2810 288 851; dorms €10, doubles ❷). The nearest **campsite**, *Creta Camping* at Káto Goúves (☎28970 41 400), lies 16km east; Hersónissos-bound buses will drop you there. One thing Iráklion does have going for it is a great **café** life: the pedestrianized alleys off Dedhálou, especially Koraï, are crammed with tables and packed evenings and weekends. **To eat**, you're better off at the fast food places around Fountain Square (Platía Venizélou). One of the few reasonably priced central tavernas is *Ouzerí Mezes Ligeros* at Títou 22, near the back of the church of Áyios Títos while, just west of here, along a small alley (Odhós Marinélli), a line of economical *ouzerí* serve up great *mezédhes* – *Fos Fanari* and *Katsina* are recommended. **Internet** access is available at Gallery Games, Koraï 14, or Konsova, Dhikeosínis 25, near the market. **Buses** for all points along the north-coast highway use the Bus Station by the ferry dock; services on inland routes to the south and west (for Phaestos for example) leave from a terminal outside the city walls at Haniá Gate. For Knossos, city bus #2 sets out every 10mins from the Bus Station by the dock, stopping at Fountain Square on its way through town.

### Knossos

The largest of the Minoan palaces, **KNOSSOS** (daily: April–Sept 8am–7pm, Oct–Mar 8.30am–5pm; €6) reached its cultural peak over 3500 years ago, though a town of some importance survived here well into the Roman era. It lies on a low hill some 5km southeast of Iráklion amid country rich in lesser remains spanning twenty-five centuries. As soon as you enter the palace of King Minos through the West Court, the ancient ceremonial entrance, it is clear how the legends of the Labyrinth of the Minotaur grew up around it. Even with a detailed plan, and despite extensive and controversial reconstruction by the original excavator, Sir Arthur Evans, it's almost impossible to find your way around the site systematically, although newly constructed timber walkways, built to protect the monument from further damage, guide you towards the most important bits. Evidence of a luxurious lifestyle is plainest in the **Queen's Suite**, off the grand **Hall of the Colonnades** at the bottom of the stunningly impressive **Grand Staircase** (which visitors are no longer allowed to use but which can be viewed from above). On the floor above the Queen's domain, you can glimpse a set of rooms in a sterner vein, generally regarded as the **King's quarters**. The staircase opens into a grandiose reception chamber known as the **Hall of the Royal Guard**, its walls decorated in repeated shield patterns. At the top of the staircase (visitors ascend by timber steps) you emerge onto the broad **Central Court**, which would once have been enclosed by the walls of the buildings all around. On the far side, in the northwestern corner of the courtyard, is the entrance to one of Knossos' most atmospheric survivals, the **Throne Room**, in all probability the seat of a priestess rather than a ruler.

### Gortys, Phaestos and the south

About 1km west of the village of Áyii Dhéka, where the bus drops you off, **GORTYS** (daily 8am–6pm; €4) is the ruined capital of the Roman province of Cyrenaica, which included not only Crete but also much of North Africa. If you walk here from Áyii Dhéka you'll get an idea of the huge scale of the place at its height in the third century AD. An enormous variety of remains, including an impressive **theatre**, is scattered across the fields south of the main road. At the main entrance to the fenced site, north of the road, is the ruinous but still impressive basilica of **Áyios Títos**, the island's first Christian church and burial place of the saint (Titus) who converted Crete and was also its first bishop. Beyond this is the **Odeion**, which houses the most important discovery on the site, the **Law Code** – ancient laws inscribed on stones measuring about 10m by 3m.

Some 17km west of Gortys, the **Palace of Phaestos** (daily 8am–6pm; €4) is another of the island's key Minoan sites. Unlike Knossos, the palace was not substantially reconstructed and requires a little more imagination, but the location is stunning, a hillside position giving a commanding view over the Messará plain.

Merely following your nose will enable you to find the **Theatral Area** with an imposing staircase, royal apartments, storerooms with huge ceramic *pithoi* for storing oil, wine and grain, and a magnificent **Central Court**, the focus of all Minoan palaces. If this fires your imagination, a 45-minute walk will take you to **Ayía Triádha** (daily 10am–4pm; €3), a tiny but beautiful and much less crowded site, thought to have been a summer palace or noble's villa.

From here you could continue towards the south coast. The easiest destination – some buses from Phaestos continue there – is **Mátala**, formerly a 1960s hippie hangout, and now a pretty commercialized resort. In **Ayía Galíni**, likewise, the beach is overwhelmed by the number of visitors. A better bet, if you're hoping to escape, would be **Léndas** and the beaches to the west of there.

## Eastern Crete

The coast east of Iráklion was the first to be developed, and is still the domain of the package tourist. There are some good beaches, but all of them fully occupied. The heart of the development lies around **HERSÓNISSOS** and **MÁLIA**, which these days form virtually a single resort. If it's the party-holiday spirit you're after, this is the place to come. Hersónissos is perhaps slightly classier, but Mália was a bigger place to start with, which means there's a real town on the south side of the main road, with more chance of reasonably priced food and accommodation. Wherever you go, you'll have no problem finding bars, clubs and English (or Irish or even Dutch) pubs. If you're looking for somewhere **to stay** try the unofficial *Youth Hostel* at the junction of the old and new roads just east of Hersónissos (☎28970 23 674; dorms €10), or *Pension Menios*, on Konstandínou Yiamboudháki (☎28970 31 361; ❸), for basic rooms in Mália old town not far from where the bus drops you. Some of the better beaches stretch east from Mália, where the atmospheric ruins of the **Palace of Mália** (daily 8.30am–3pm; €4), much less visited than Knossos or Phaestos, boast a virtually intact ground plan.

After Mália the road cuts inland, past the turning to the spectacular **Lasíthi Plateau**, before re-emerging on the coast at **ÁYIOS NIKÓLAOS**. The town's beautiful setting, around a supposedly bottomless salt lake now connected to the sea to form an inner harbour, was spotted long ago, and lake and port are surrounded by pricey restaurants and bars. In season, it's also jammed with tourists, many of them staying in hotels on the beaches north and east of town. There's little chance of finding a cheap **room** in season, though at quiet times there are bargains to be had; check at the helpful **tourist office** (summer daily 8am–9/10pm; ☎28410 22 357), by the bridge dividing the lake and harbour.

Sleepy **SITÍA**, the port and main town of the relatively unexploited eastern edge of Crete, may be about to wake up. A new international airport (originally slated for 2005) will eventually bring overseas tourists direct, bypassing the sinuous and spectacular coast road that has discouraged most in the past. For the moment, though, Sitía still offers a plethora of waterside restaurants, a long sandy beach and a lazy lifestyle little affected by the thousands of visitors in peak season. The **tourist office** is on the seafront (☎28430 28 300), and there are several **rooms** in places around Kondhiláki, a few streets back from the harbour – try the welcoming *Hotel Arhontiko*, Kondhiláki 16 (☎28430 28 172; ❸). For **food**, there are inexpensive options in the streets behind the waterfront, such as *Mixos*, Kornárou 117. At the eastern end of the island, **VÁÏ BEACH** is the most famous on Crete thanks to its ancient grove of palm trees. In season, though, its undoubted charms, now fenced off, are diluted by crowds of day-trippers. Other beaches at nearby **Ítanos** or **Pálekastro** – Crete's main windsurfing centre – are less exotic but emptier. Or head further south – at **Káto Zákros** the pebbly beach is right by another important Minoan palace, while beyond that you're really off the beaten track (and also beyond the reach of the bus network).

# Western Crete

West of Iráklion, the major centres of Réthymnon and Haniá are both surrounded by extensive tourist development these days, but they're historical, lively and attractive towns in their own right, and the gateways to less-travelled areas in the south and far west. The old town of **Réthymnon** is a labyrinthine tangle of Venetian and Turkish houses set around an enclosed sixteenth-century harbour and wide sandy beach. Medieval minarets lend an exotic air to the skyline, while dominating everything from the west is the superbly preserved outline of the **Venetian fortress** (Sat–Thurs 8am–7pm; €2.90). From the **bus station**, head around the inland side of the fortress to reach the beach and the centre; the **tourist office** (Mon–Fri 8am–2.30pm, Sat 10am–4pm; ☎28310 29 148, ⊛www .rethymnon.com) is right on the beach. There are plenty of **rooms**; try *Olga's Pension*, Soulíou 57 (☎28310 54 896, ℗28310 29 851; ❸) or the unofficial **youth hostel**, Tombázi 45 (☎28310 22 848, ⊛www.yhrethymno.com; €8). *Camping Elizabeth* (☎28310 28 694) is in the hotel strip about 4km east along the beach, served by frequent buses from the main bus station. Much of the pleasure here is just in wandering the streets of the old town; there's an unbroken line of **tavernas**, cafés and cocktail bars right around the waterside and into the area around the old port. Better-value places are around the seventeenth-century Venetian **Rimóndi Fountain**, an easily located landmark: *Stella's Kitchen* at Soulíou 55, a couple of minutes east, is good for breakfasts and great-value daily specials, a couple of which are always vegetarian. *Messologiou*, slightly north of the fountain at the corner of Salamínos, has good value *yíros* and pizzas. Just round the corner from here, on Salamínos, a line of clubs make up the heart of Réthymnon's **nightlife**.

Réthymnon lies at one of the narrower parts of Crete, so it's relatively quick to cut across from here to the south coast. The obvious place to head is **PLAKIÁS**, a growing resort which has managed to retain a small-town atmosphere. There are numerous **rooms**, very busy in August, as well as a relaxed and friendly youth **hostel** (☎28320 32 118, ⊛www.yhplakias.com; €7.50) at the back of the town, and *Camping Appolonia* (☎28320 31 507) on the road in from Réthymnon. Locals can point you in the direction of quieter beaches all around, with boat trips to many of them.

## Haniá

**HANIÁ** is the spiritual capital of Crete; for many, it is also the island's most attractive city – especially in spring, when the snowcapped peaks of the Lefká Óri (White Mountains) seem to hover above the roofs. Although it is for the most part modern, the small harbour is surrounded by a jumble of Venetian streets that survived the wartime bombardments. The **bus station** is on Odhós Kydhonías, within easy walking distance of the centre: turn right, then left down the side of Platía 1866, and you'll emerge at a major road junction opposite the top of Halídhon, the main street of the old quarter. The very helpful municipal **tourist office** (summer only Mon–Fri 9am–2pm; ☎28210 36 155) is in the *Dhimarhío* (town hall) at Kydhonías 29, four blocks east of the bus station. They will provide a free town map plus help with accommodation when things get tight in high summer. **Ferries** dock about 10km away at the port of Soúdha: there are frequent city buses which will drop you by the market on the fringes of the old town. The **port area** is the oldest and the most interesting part of town. The little hill that rises behind the landmark domes of the quayside Mosque of the Janissaries is called **Kastélli**, site of the earliest Minoan habitation and core of the Venetian and Turkish towns. Beneath the hill, on the inner harbour, the arches of sixteenth-century Venetian arsenals survive alongside remains of the outer walls. Behind the harbour lie the less picturesque but more lively sections of the old city. Around the cathedral on Halídhon are some of the more animated shopping areas, particularly leather-dominated **Odhós Skrídhlof**. In the direction of the **Splántzia** quarter are ancient alleys with tumbledown Venetian stonework and overhanging wooden balconies that appear little touched by modern tourism. Haniá's **beaches** all lie to the west: the packed city beach is a ten-minute walk beyond the Maritime Museum, but for good sand you're better off taking the local bus from the east side of Platía 1866 along the coast road to Kalamáki. In between you'll find emptier stretches if you're prepared to walk some of the way.

There are plenty of **rooms** on offer, but in season you may face a long search. The friendly *Pension Fidias*, Kalinikoú Sarpáki 8, behind the cathedral (☎28210 52 494; dorms €9, doubles ❷) is run along hostel lines and has the cheapest beds in town. Walk across the old town from here to *Pension Nora*, Theotokopoúlou 60 (☎28210 72 265; ❸), near the Maritime Museum and Byzantine Collection, and you'll pass dozens of other options, some in wonderfully chic restored mansions (with prices to match). There's a **campsite**, *Camping Hania* (☎28210 31138), on the coast 4km west, served by city bus from Platía 1866. Both the inner and outer harbours are circled by **cafés**, **tavernas** and **bars**, although you pay for the location. You can stock up on food at the bustling and colourful **market**, three blocks east from the northern end of Platía 1866. The bars and clubs around the harbour are obvious enough, but you won't find many locals there. Young Haniotes tend to start their evening in the bars and cafés along Aktí Miaoúli, east of the harbour, and then move on to *Daz* beneath the Schiavo bastion in the ancient walls, or *Premier*, on Tsoudéron, at the back of the market. Alternatively, after midnight, the beachside clubs to the west of the town are popular. Haniá is also a good place to catch local Cretan **lýra** music; keep an eye out for posters or ask the locals what's on. **Internet** access is at *Café Vranas*, Isodhíon 12, next to *Vranas Studios*.

## Gorges and beaches

The **Samarian Gorge** – Europe's longest – is an easy day-trip from Haniá (May–Oct only; four buses daily to Omalos when the gorge is open). If you do it, though, be warned that you will not be alone: dozens of coachloads set off before dawn from all over Crete for the dramatic climb into the White Mountains and the long (at least 4hr) walk down. At the bottom of the gorge is the village of **AYÍA ROÚMELI** from where boats will take you east to **Hóra Sfakíon** and your bus home, or west towards the pleasant resorts of **Soúyia** and **Paleohóra**. The mountains offer endless other **hiking** challenges to help you escape the crowds. Soúyia and Paleohóra are both good starting points, as is **Loutró**, a tiny place halfway to Hóra Sfakíon, accessible only by boat. These places also have decent beaches, and from Paleohóra you can reach more at the far west of the island where only **Elafoníssi**, an isolated beach with an almost tropical lagoon feel, ever sees crowds.

# Travel details

## Trains

**Athens** to: Corinth (12 daily; 1hr 30min–2hr); Kalamáta (3 daily; 6hr 30min–7hr); Mycenae (4 daily; 2hr 30min); Náfplio (2 daily; 3hr); Olympia (2 daily; 5hr 30min); Pátra (8 daily; 3hr 45min–4hr).
**Dhiakoftó** to: Kalávryta (4 daily; 1hr 10min).
**Pátra** to: Corinth (8 daily; 2hr–2hr 30min); Kalamáta (1 daily; 5hr); Pýrgos (8 daily; 1hr 40min).
**Thessaloníki** to: Litóhoro (6 daily; 1hr 40min); Vólos (2 daily; 3hr).

**Vólos** to: Athens (2 daily; 5hr); Kalambáka (2 daily; 2hr 45min); Lárissa (13 daily; 1hr).

## Buses

**Athens** to: Corfu (4 daily; 11hr); Corinth (hourly; 1hr 30min); Delphi (6 daily; 3hr); Ioánnina (8 daily; 7hr 30min); Kalamáta (13 daily; 4hr 30min); Kefalloniá (3 daily; 7hr); Kými, for Skýros ferries (3 daily; 3hr 30min); Mycenae-Fíkhti (hourly; 2hr); Náfplio (hourly; 2hr 50min); Olympia (4 daily; 5hr 30min); Pátra (every 30min; 3hr); Rafína (every 30min; 1hr 30min); Sounion (every 30min; 2hr);

Spárti (10 daily; 3hr 30min); Thessaloníki (10 daily; 7hr 30min); Vólos (10 daily; 5hr 20min); Zákynthos (5 daily; 6hr).

**Corinth** to: Ancient Corinth (hourly; 20min); Árgos (hourly; 1hr); Kalamáta (7 daily; 3–4hr); Mycenae-Fíkhti (hourly; 30min); Náfplio (hourly; 1hr 20min); Spárti (8 daily; 3–4hr).

**Ioánnina** to: Igoumenítsa (7–9 daily; 2hr); Métsovo (4 daily; 1hr 30min); Tríkala (2–3 daily daily; 4hr).

**Kalamáta** to: Areópoli (4 daily; 1hr 30min–2hr 30min); Kóroni (8 daily; 1hr 30min); Methóni via Pýlos (5 daily; 1hr 30min); Pátra (2 daily; 4hr); Pýlos (8 daily; 1hr).

**Lárissa** to: Kalambáka (hourly; 2hr).

**Náfplio** to: Epidaurus (4 daily; 45min); Mycenae (4 daily; 50min).

**Pýrgos** to: Kalamáta (2 daily; 2hr); Olympia (hourly; 45min); Pátra (6–11 daily; 2hr).

**Sparti** to: Monemvasía (4 daily; 3hr); Mystra (5 daily; 15min); Yíthio (3 daily; 1hr).

**Thessaloníki** to: Delphi (2 daily; 6hr); Ierissós (5–7 daily; 3hr 30min); Ioánnina (5 daily; 7hr); Kalambáka (7 daily; 4hr 30min); Litóchoro (hourly; 1hr 30min); Ouranoúpoli (5–7 daily; 3hr 45min); Vólos (4 daily; 4hr).

**Vólos** to: Áyios Ioánnis (2–3 daily; 2hr 30min); Kalambáka (2 daily; 3hr); Lárissa (hourly; 1hr 15min); Makrinítsa (10 daily; 50min); Miliés (5–6 daily; 1hr); Tsangarádha (2–3 daily; 2hr); Vyzítsa (5–6 daily; 1hr 10min); Zagorá (4 daily; 2hr).

## Ferries, catamarans and hydrofoils

The following information is based on high-season travel from late June to early September and is intended as an approximate guide: for specific, up-to-date information on ferries, check ⓦ www .gtp.gr.

**Áyios Konstandínos** to: Skópelos (2–3 daily; 2hr 15min).

**Crete**: Iráklion to Pireás (4 daily; 6–12hr); Iráklion to Mýkonos (1 daily; 9hr); Iráklion to Páros &

Cyclades (daily catamaran or twice daily ferry; 2hr 45min or 6hr); Kastélli to Yíthio (2 weekly; 8hr); Áyios Nikólaos and Sitía to Rhodes (3 weekly; 11hr).

**Kefalloniá** to: Zákynthos (summer 2 daily; 1hr 30min); Itháki (2–4 daily; 30–45min).

**Kós** to: Pátmos (2–4 daily; 2hr 30min–5hr); Rhodes (2–4 daily; 2–4hr).

**Kyllíni** to: Kefalloniá (2–4 daily; 1hr 30min–2hr 30min); Zákynthos (6 daily, 2 in winter; 1hr 15min).

**Kými** to: Skýros (1–2 daily; 2hr 30min).

**Lésvos** to: Híos (6–10 weekly; 1hr 30min–3hr 30min); Thessaloníki (2 weekly; 14hr).

**Pátra** to: Corfu (3–5 daily; 7–10hr); Igoumenítsa (2–3 daily; 5–8hr); Itháki (2 daily; 3–4hr); Kefalloniá (2 daily; 2hr 30min).

**Pireás** to: Crete (2–4 daily; 12hr); Híos (6–9 weekly; 6hr–10hr 30min); Íos (2–4 daily; 5–10hr); Kós (13 weekly; 7–12hr); Lésvos (6–10 weekly; 8–14hr); Mýkonos (2–4 daily; 2hr 30min–5hr); Náxos (2–4 daily; 4–8hr); Páros (2–4 daily; 3hr 30min–7hr); Pátmos (2 daily; 11hr); Rhodes (19 weekly; 18–23hr); Sámos (daily; 7hr 30min–14hr); Sífnos (2 daily; 3–5hr); Sýros (2–3 daily; 2hr–4hr); Thíra (Santorini) (2–4 daily; 6–12hr).

**Rafína** to: Mýkonos, Náxos, Páros, Sýros (all 1–2 daily; 3–5hr).

**Rhodes** to: Crete (Sitía/Áyios Nikólaos; 3 weekly; 11hr); Kós (2 daily; 4hr); Pátmos (2 daily; 8hr).

**Sámos** to: Híos (2–3 weekly; 3hr); Kós (4–11 weekly; 3hr 45min–4hr 15min); Pátmos (2–11 weekly; 1hr 30min–3hr); Rhodes (1–2 weekly; 6hr 30min–9hr).

**Thessaloníki** to: Cyclades, including Mýkonos, Náxos, Páros, Skiáthos, Tínos, Sýros, and Thíra (1–3 weekly; 10–15hr); Híos (1–2 weekly; 18hr 30min); Iráklion (1–3 weekly; 21hr); Lésvos (1–2 weekly; 15hr).

**Vólos** to: Skópelos (3–4 daily; 2hr–3hr 30min); Lésvos (1 weekly; 12hr).

# Hungary

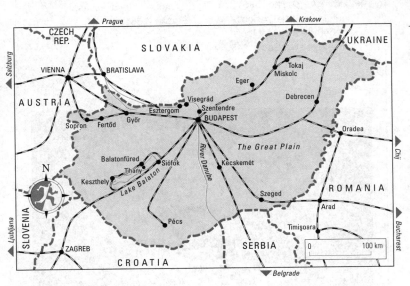

# Hungary highlights

**✱ Communist Statue Park, Budapest** Graveyard for statues of old dictators, an ironic open-air museum. **See p.541**

**✱ Széchenyi Baths, Budapest** Beat the locals at chess or simply relax in the steamy, healing waters. **See p.542**

**✱ Hévíz** A genuine Hungarian health experience at Europe's largest thermal-lake spa. **See p.548**

**✱ Pécs** Terrace cafés, brightly coloured buildings and laid-back attitude; a young, fun destination. **See p.550**

**✱ Szépasszony Valley, near Eger**. No trip to Eger should omit the "Valley of the Beautiful Woman", a horseshoe of cellars offering a terrific range of local wines. **See p.551**

△ Széchenyi Baths, Budapest

# Introduction and basics

Visitors who refer to **Hungary** as a Balkan country risk getting a lecture on how this small, landlocked nation of ten million people differs from "all those Slavs": locals are strongly conscious of themselves as Magyar – a race that transplanted itself from Central Asia into the heart of Europe over a thousand years ago.

The magnificent capital **Budapest** (split into historic Buda and vibrant Pest), with its coffee houses, Turkish baths and fad for Habsburg bric-á-brac, has a strong whiff of Mitteleuropa – that ambient culture that welcomed Beethoven in Budapest and Hungarian-born Liszt in Vienna, and continues with a new wave of writers, film directors, artists and other media figures. But there's also an eager modern feel to the place, with international fashions snapped up and adapted to local tastes. Outside the capital, there's much to explore: a short way north of Budapest, on a beautiful stretch of the River Danube, is **Szentendre**, while to the west lies **Lake Balaton**, the "nation's playground", encircled with a string of brash resorts such as **Siófok** and **Keszthely**. Other highlights include the delightful city of **Sopron**, on the border with Austria, and Turkish-flavoured Pécs, in the south. The forested Northern Uplands in the far northeast towards Ukraine envelop the beautiful Baroque town of **Eger**, also famed for its wine.

## Information & maps

You'll find branches of **Tourinform**, the Hungarian National Tourist Office, in the capital and in just about every other town across the country; branches are open Mon–Fri 9am–5/8pm; summer also open Sat & Sun. They don't book accommodation, but do have information on where rooms and beds are available, including the booklets *Hungarian Hotel Guide* and *Camping*. There are also **local tourist offices** in larger towns (such as Balatontourist around Lake Balaton), where you can **book rooms**; opening hours are Mon–Fri 9am–4/6pm; summer also Sat 8am–1pm. It's cheapest to buy your **maps** in Hungary: the best is Cartographia's full-country fold-out sheet (1:450,000).

## Money and banks

Currency is the **forint** (Ft), which comes in notes of 200Ft, 500Ft, 1000Ft, 2000Ft, 5000Ft, 10,000Ft and 20,000Ft, and in coins of 1Ft, 2Ft, 5Ft, 10Ft, 20Ft, 50Ft and 100Ft (the 50Ft coin is easily confused with the 10Ft coin). The best rates of exchange are offered by regional tourist offices and the banks. At the time of writing, €1 was worth around 250Ft, US$1 got you 190Ft, and £1 equalled 360Ft. Standard **banking hours** are Mon–Thurs 8am–4pm, Fri 8am–3pm. **ATMs** are widespread throughout the country, and you can use a **credit card** to pay in many hotels, restaurants and shops.

## Communications

Larger **post offices** (*posta*) are usually open Mon–Fri 8am–6pm, Sat 8am–1pm. Smaller branches close at 3pm and don't always open on Sat. Address poste restante

---

### Hungary on the net

ⓦ**www.hungarytourism.hu** National tourist office.
ⓦ**www.travelport.hu** Excellent general site.
ⓦ**www.wherebudapest.com** Extensive listings, updated monthly.
ⓦ**www.elvira.hu** Train timetables and information.
ⓦ**www.pecs.hu** A young, fun site with loads of info.

mail "Poste restante, Posta", followed by the name of the town. You can make local calls from **public phones**, where 20Ft is the minimum charge (40Ft if you're calling a mobile phone), or, better, from cardphones, which come in 50 and 120 units and can be bought from post offices and newsstands. To make national calls, dial ☎06, wait for the buzzing tone, then dial the area code and number. You can make international calls from most public phones: dial ☎00, wait for the buzzing tone, then dial the country code as usual. **Internet access** is widely available (usually 500–800Ft/hr) in most towns.

# Getting around

**Public transport** in Hungary is, generally speaking, cheap, clean and fairly reliable. The only problem is getting information – staff rarely speak anything but Hungarian.

The centralization of the MÁV **rail network** means that many cross-country journeys are easier if you travel via Budapest. Intercity trains are the fastest way of getting to the major towns, though seat reservations, made at any MÁV office, are compulsory and cost an extra 350–480Ft; *személyvonat* trains, which stop at every hamlet en route, do not incur the reservation fee. You can buy tickets (*jegy*) for domestic services at the station (*pályaudvar* or *vasútállomás*) on the day of departure, but it's best to buy tickets for international trains (*nemzetközi gyorsvonat*) at least 36hr in advance. You're permitted to break your journey once. When buying your ticket, specify whether you want a one-way ticket (*egy útra*), or a return (*retur* or *oda-vissza*). For a journey of 100km, travelling second-class on an express train, expect to pay around 1300Ft. **InterRail** and **Eurail** passes are valid.

Volán runs the bulk of Hungary's **buses**, which are often the quickest way to travel between the smaller towns. Arrive early to confirm the departure bay and get a seat. For **long-distance services** from Budapest and the major towns, you can buy tickets with a seat booking up to 30min before departure; after that, you get them from the driver (and risk standing). In rural areas, tickets are only available on board and there

may be only one or two buses a day. For a journey of 100km, expect to pay around 1200Ft.

# Accommodation

**Accommodation** costs have risen dramatically in recent years. More upmarket places tend to quote prices in euros (they'll usually accept US dollars or pounds sterling too); private rooms and hostels charge in forints. The cheapest places tend to fill up during high season, so it's wise to book ahead.

Outside Budapest and Lake Balaton (where prices are thirty percent higher), a three-star **hotel** (*szálló* or *szálloda*) will charge from around 12,000Ft for a double room with bath and TV; solo travellers often have to pay this too, since singles are rare. A similar rating system is used for **inns** (*fogadó*) and **pensions** (*panzió*), which tend to be more charismatic than hotels, and also charge a little less.

**Hostels** go under various names: in provincial towns they're *turistaszálló*, in the highland areas *turistaház*. Local tourist offices can provide details and make bookings; check ⊛ www.backpackers.hu. They can also guide you to student dormitories, which are usually even cheaper: rooms are rented out in July and August, and are often available at weekends year-round.

**Private rooms** (*fizető vendégszoba*) – B&B-style in a private home – are an inexpensive way of staying near town centres. Such accommodation can be arranged through Ibusz, the nationwide agency, or local tourist offices. Alternatively, look for signs saying *szoba kiadó* or *Zimmer Frei*. Doubles range from 4000Ft in provincial towns to around 6000Ft in Budapest and around Balaton. Rooms in a town's Belváros (inner sector) are likely to be much better than those in outlying zones.

**Bungalows** (*faház*) proliferate around resorts and on the larger campsites. The first-class bungalows – with kitchens, hot water and a sitting room or terrace – are excellent, and will cost a few thousand forints, while the most primitive at least have clean bedding and don't leak. Campsites (usually signposted *Kemping*) likewise range

| | Hungarian | Pronunciation |
|---|---|---|
| Yes | *Igen* | I-gen |
| No | *Nem* | Nem |
| Please | *Kérem* | Kay-rem |
| Thank you | *Köszönöm* | Kur-sur-nurm |
| Hello/Good day | *Jó napot* | Yo nopot |
| Goodbye | *Viszontlátásra* | Vee-sont-lar-tarsh-rar |
| Excuse me | *Bocsánat* | Botch-ah-not |
| Where? | *Hol?* | Hall? |
| Good | *Jó* | Yo |
| Bad | *Rossz* | Ross |
| Near | *Közel* | Kur-zel |
| Far | *Távol* | Tah-vol |
| Cheap | *Olcsó* | Ol-cho |
| Expensive | *Drága* | Drah-ga |
| Open | *Nyitva* | Nyeet-va |
| Closed | *Zárva* | Zah-rva |
| Today | *Ma* | Ma |
| Yesterday | *Tegnap* | Teg-nop |
| Tomorrow | *Holnap* | Hall-nop |
| How much is....? | *Mennyibe kerül...?* | Men-yi-beh keh-rool...? |
| What time is it? | *Hány óra van?* | Hine-ora von |
| I don't understand | *Nem értem* | Nem ear-tem |
| Do you speak English? | *Beszél Angolul?* | Beh-sail ong-olool? |
| One | *Egy* | Edge |
| Two | *Kettö* | Ket-tur |
| Three | *Három* | Hah-rom |
| Four | *Négy* | Naidge |
| Five | *Öt* | Urt |
| Six | *Hat* | Hot |
| Seven | *Hét* | Hait |
| Eight | *Nyolc* | Nyolts |
| Nine | *Kilenc* | Kee-lents |
| Ten | *Tíz* | Teez |

**14**

**HUNGARY** | Basics

from de luxe to third class. In high season, expect to pay anything up to 3500Ft, more around Lake Balaton.

# Food and drink

For foreigners, the archetypal **Hungarian dish** is goulash (*gulyásleves*) – historically a soup made of potatoes and meat, which was later flavoured with paprika. Hungarians like a calorific **breakfast** (*reggeli*) that includes cheese, eggs or salami, plus bread and jam. **Coffee houses** (*kávéház*) are coming back into fashion and you'll find many serving breakfast and a coffee with milk (*tejeskávé*) or whipped cream (*tejszínhabbal*). Most Hungarians take their coffee short and strong (*eszpresszó*). A whole range of places sell **snacks**, including bakeries and delicatessens (*csemege*), and numerous patisseries (*cukrászda*) pander to the Magyar fondness for sweet things. Pancakes (*palacsinta*) with fillings are very popular, as are strudels (*rétes*). On the streets you can buy, in summer, corn-on-the-cob (*kukorica*) and in winter, roasted chestnuts (*gesztenye*); while stalls selling fried fish (*sült hal*) are common in towns near rivers or lakes.

In theory an *étterem* is a proper restaurant, while a *vendéglő* approximates to the

Western notion of a bistro; however, these distinctions are thin. The old word for a roadside inn, *csárda*, is often used by folksy, touristy restaurants. The main meal of the day is **lunch**, when some places offer set menus (*napi menü*), a basic meal at moderate prices. There are plenty of places where you can eat well and sink a few beers for under 2000Ft (and aways check your bill carefully as foreigners are a common target for being ripped off). **Starters** (*előételek*) range from soup (*leves*) to the popular *Hortobágyi palacsinta* (pancakes stuffed with mince and doused in a creamy paprika sauce), though nobody will mind if you just have a **main course** (*főételek*). Hungarians like most things fried in breadcrumbs, such as *rántott csirkecomb* (chicken drumstick), but they also have a taste for *marhapörkölt* (beef stew). In traditional places, the only choice for **vegetarians** will be breaded and fried cheese, mushrooms or cauliflower (*rántott sajt/gomba/karfiol*).

Hungary's mild climate and diversity of soils is perfect for **wine** (*bor*), which is perennially cheap, whether you buy it by the bottle (*üveg*) or the glass (*pohár*). Wine bars (*borozó*) are ubiquitous, while true grape devotees make pilgrimages to the wine cellars (*borpince*) around Pécs and Eger. The best-known types of **brandy** (*pálinka*) are distilled from apricots (*barack*) and plums (*szilva*), the latter often available in private homes in a mouth-scorching, home-distilled version. **Beer** (*sör*) of the lager type (*világos*) predominates, although you can also find **brown ale** (*barna*): these come in draught form (*csapolt sör*) or in bottles (*üveges sör*). Local brands to look out for are Pécsi Szalon sör and Soproni Ászok.

# Opening hours and holidays

**Shops** are generally open Mon–Fri 10am–6pm, Sat 10am–1pm. Most things close down for the following public holidays: Jan 1, March 15, Easter Mon, May 1, Whit Mon, Aug 20, Oct 23, Nov 1, Dec 25 & 26.

# Emergencies

Tourists are treated with respect by the police (*rendörség*) – unless they're suspected of black-marketeering, drug smuggling or driving under the influence of alcohol. Most have a smattering of German, but rarely any other foreign language. Be sure to always carry your passport or a photocopy.

All towns and some villages have a pharmacy (*gyógyszertár* or *patika*), with staff – often German-speaking – authorized to issue a wide range of drugs. Opening hours are generally Mon–Fri 9am–6pm, Sat 9am–noon or 1pm; signs in the window give the location of all-night pharmacies (*ügyeletes gyógyszertár*). Tourist offices can direct you to local medical centres or doctors' surgeries (*orvosi rendelő*); these will probably be in private (*magán*) practice, so be sure to carry health insurance. EU citizens have reciprocal arrangements for emergency treatment, but only at state hospitals.

> **Emergency numbers**
>
> Police ☏107; Ambulance ☏104; Fire ☏105.

# Budapest and around

The importance of **BUDAPEST** to Hungary is difficult to overestimate. Around two million people – one-fifth of the population – live in the city, and everything converges here: wealth, political power, cultural life and transport. Surveying the city from Castle Hill, it's obvious why Budapest was dubbed the "Pearl of the Danube" – its grand buildings and sweeping bridges look magnificent, especially when floodlit.

**Castle Hill** (Várhegy) is the most prominent feature of the **Buda** district, a plateau one mile long laden with old mansions and a huge palace, commanding the **Watertown**. Buda and its twin across the river, **Pest**, have a plethora of other fine sights, including museums and galleries, restaurants, bars and a wide variety of entertainments, accessible by efficient, inexpensive public transport. Ease yourself into Budapest life by wallowing away an afternoon in one of the city's **thermal baths** (gyógyfürdő). A basic ticket covers three hours in the pools, sauna and steam-rooms (gőzfürdő), while supplementary tickets are available for such delights as the mud baths (iszapfürdő) and massages (masszázs).

Each of Budapest's 23 districts (kerületek) is designated on maps, street signs and at the beginning of addresses by a Roman numeral; "V" is Belváros (inner city), on the Pest side; "I" is the Castle district in Buda.

## Arrival, information and city transport

There are three main **train stations**, all of which are directly connected by **metro** with the central **Deák tér** metro station in the Belváros, in the city-centre district of Pest: Keleti station handles most international trains, including those from Vienna (Westbahnhof), Belgrade, Bucharest, Zagreb and Bratislava, as well as domestic arrivals from Sopron and Eger; Nyugati station handles trains from Prague and Bratislava, some from Bucharest, and domestic ones from the Danube Bend; and Déli station has one train a day from Vienna (Südbahnhof), the occasional train from Zagreb, and domestic services from Pécs and Lake Balaton. From Ferihegy **airport**, an Airport Minibus will take you to wherever you're staying (2100Ft; book it in the terminal building). By public transport, take the Reptér-busz (airport bus) to the final stop Kőbánya-Kispest and from there the metro ten stops to the centre, Deák tér. The airport taxi-drivers are notorious sharks and best avoided. The central **bus station** is at Népliget (blue metro 3), serving international destinations and routes to Transdanubia. Also in Pest, Stadion bus station (red metro) serves areas east of the Danube; and Árpád híd bus station (blue metro) serves the Danube Bend. **Hydrofoils** from Vienna dock alongside the Danube embankment on the Pest side.

The best source of information is **Tourinform** (daily 8am–8pm; ☎1/438-8080, ⓦwww.tourinform.hu), just around the corner from Deák tér metro at Sütő utca 2, behind the big yellow Lutheran church; other branches are on Liszt Ferenc tér (daily 9am–7pm) and in the Castle District on Szentháromság tér (daily 9am–9pm). Other useful offices include the **Vista Tourist Center**, Paulay Ede utca 7 (Mon–Fri 9am–8pm, Sat & Sun 10am–6pm; ☎1/267-8603, ⓦwww.vista.hu) and **Budapest Tourist**, in the subway in front of Nyugati train station (Mon–Fri 9am–4pm; ☎1/342-6521). **Mitch's Tours** (☎1/221-8864, ⓦwww.mitchstours .com) offers a door-to-door minibus service Budapest–Vienna catering to back-packers (tickets €29 one way). The Discover Hungary agency (☎1/266-8777, ⓦwww.discoverhungary.com), Sütő utca 2, offers a varied programme of citywide excursions, bike rides and pub crawls.

A great source of what's-on **listings** is *Budapest In Your Pocket*, available from hotel foyers and bookshops. A **Budapest Card** (4700/5900Ft for two/three days), available at the airport and town centre tourist offices, hotels and major metro

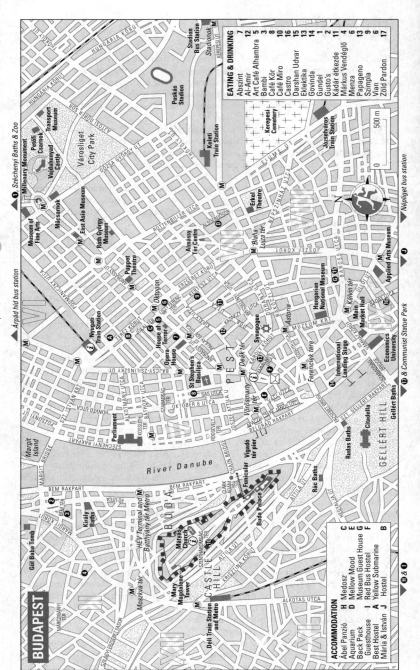

**BUDAPEST**

**ACCOMMODATION**
| | |
|---|---|
| Ábel Panzió | H |
| Aquarium | D |
| Back Pack | G |
| Guesthouse | I |
| Best Hostel | A |
| Mária & István | B |
| Medosz | H |
| Mellow Mood | D |
| Museum Guest House | G |
| Red Bus Hostel | I |
| Yellow Submarine | A |
| Hostel | J |

**EATING & DRINKING**
| | |
|---|---|
| Abszint | 7 |
| Al-Amir | 12 |
| Art Café Alhambra | 5 |
| Bambi | 3 |
| Café Kör | 8 |
| Café Miró | 10 |
| Castro | 16 |
| Darshan Udvar | 15 |
| Eklektika | 13 |
| Govinda | 14 |
| Gundel | 1 |
| Gusto's | 2 |
| Kádár étkezde | 11 |
| Márkus Vendéglő | 4 |
| Menza | 6 |
| Papageno | 13 |
| Szimpla | 9 |
| Vian | 6 |
| Zöld Pardon | 17 |

stations, gives unlimited travel on public transport, free museum admission, reductions on the airport minibus and other discounts. Tourist offices supply free **maps**, but far better is the wirebound 1:25,000 Budapest Atlas (1700Ft), from newsstands, bookshops and Tourinform offices.

The **metro** (daily 4.30am–11.15pm) has three lines intersecting at Deák tér. There's little risk of going astray once you've learned to recognize the signs: *bejárat* (entrance), *kijárat* (exit), *vonal* (line) and *felé* (towards). A basic 160Ft ticket (190Ft if bought on the bus) is valid for a journey along one line, and is also valid for a single journey on buses, trolleybuses, trams and the **HÉV suburban train** as far as the city limits. On the metro you can also buy 120Ft tickets for journeys of up to three stops, and combination tickets for transferring to another metro line. Buy tickets from metro stations or (quicker) from street stands or newsagents, and punch them in the machines at the station entrance (or on board buses, trolleybuses and trams): inspectors often wait at the bottom of the escalators to check tickets and hand out fines. **Buses** (*busz*) with red numbers make limited stops, while those with the red suffix "E" go nonstop between termini; all run every ten minutes or so during the day – as do **trams** (*villamos*) and **trolleybuses** (*trolibusz*) – and every thirty to sixty minutes between 11pm and dawn along routes with a night service (denoted with the black suffix "E"). Either get a **pass** (1350/2700Ft for one/three days), or buy a book of tickets (ten 1375Ft, twenty 2650Ft) – don't tear them out, as they are only valid if kept in the book. **Taxis** are inexpensive, but are also a common rip-off. Go for Főtaxi (Ⓣ1/222-2222) or the English-speaking Citytaxi (Ⓣ1/211-1111): both charge a basic fee of around 300Ft plus up to 240Ft per kilometre.



## Accommodation

**Hotels** are generally expensive, and many of the better places expect payment in euros. For bookings, contact the Vista Visitor Center, VI, Paulay Ede utca 7 (Ⓣ1/429-9950, Ⓦwww.vista.hu). There are plentiful **hostels** in Budapest, bookable through the Hungarian Youth Hostel Association near Keleti Station (Ⓣ1/413-2065, Ⓦwww.youthhostels.hu). **Private rooms** downtown cost from 4500Ft a night, rising to 10,000Ft or more in high season. **Apartments**, rented out per night from 8500Ft (12,500Ft high season), are good value for groups. Preferable locales are districts V, VI and VII in Pest, and the parts of Buda nearest Castle Hill. Both rooms and apartments can be booked through IBUSZ, Ferenciek tere 10 (Mon–Fri 8.15am–5pm; Ⓣ1/485-2716, Ⓦwww.ibusz.hu), and the To-Ma Travel Agency at V, Október 6 utca 22 (Ⓣ1353-0819, Ⓦwww.tomatour.hu). Best Hotel Service, V, Sütő utca 2 (8am–8pm; Ⓣ1/318-4848, Ⓦwww.besthotelservice.hu), in a courtyard behind the main Tourinform office, books hostels, rooms and apartments.

### Hostels

**Aquarium** VII, Alsóerdősor utca 12 Ⓣ1/321-8444, Ⓦwww.budapesthostel.com. Bright and clean, with kitchen facilities, laundry, free Internet and travel guides. Young, friendly staff. Ten minutes' walk from Keleti railway station. Dorms 2600Ft, one double ❸

**Back Pack Guesthouse** XI, Takács Menyhért utca 33 Ⓣ1/385-8946, Ⓦwww.backpackbudapest.hu. Charming, clean place, with a shaded garden, and only 20min from the centre. Lots of city information, plus rock climbing and cave trips. Tram #49 or bus #7 to Tétényi út stop in Buda. Dorms 2000–2800Ft, one double ❷

**Best Hostel** VI, Podmaniczky utca 27, 1st floor Ⓣ1/332-4934, Ⓦwww.besthostel.hu. Situated in a group of converted apartments this central choice is five minutes' walk from Nyugati train station. Dorms 3000–4200Ft, rooms ❸

**Mellow Mood** V, Bécsi utca 2 Ⓣ1/411-1310, Ⓦwww.mellowmoodhostel.com. Friendly, well-run and very centrally located hotel with 270 beds in doubles and rooms of four, six and eight beds, all overlooking the street. Book in Keleti Station and you get a lift in the Mellow Mood van. Dorm beds from 3200Ft, doubles ❷

**Museum Guest House** VIII, Mikszáth Kálmán tér 4, 1st floor Ⓣ1/318-9508, Ⓦwww.budapesthostel.com. Behind the National Museum and handy for central bars and cafés, there are three clean

dorms here, each with seven or eight mattresses on the floor. Free Internet. Dorms 2600Ft.
**Red Bus Hostel** V, Semmelweis utca 14 ☎1/266-0136, ⓦwww.redbusbudapest.hu. Clean, quiet hostel with basic facilities but a great, central location. Red Bus Books next door will swap all your dog-eared paperbacks. Dorms 2900Ft, rooms ❷
**Yellow Submarine Hostel** VI, Teréz körút 56 ☎1/331-9896, ⓦwww.yellowsubmarinehostel.com. Compact, warm and friendly, with cheap dorms and a bustling common-room kitchen. Ten minutes from Nyugati. Dorms 2800Ft (with breakfast), rooms ❸

### Hotels and pensions
**Ábel Panzió** XI, Ábel Jenő utca 9 ☎1/381-0553, ⓦwww.hotels.hu/abelpanzio. Fantastic 1913 villa with beautiful Art Nouveau fittings in a quiet street thirty minutes' walk from the Belváros. Just ten rooms, so essential to book in advance. Discount for cash payments. ❺

**Mária & István** IX, Ferenc körút 39 ☎1/216-0768, ⓔmariaistvan@axelero.hu. Friendly couple who rent out rooms in their flat, each with own fridge, shower and WC. ❷
**Medosz** VI, Jókai tér 9 ☎1/374-3000, ⓔHotelMedosz@budapest-hotel.hu. Comfortable lodging in a well-located but ugly building near the Oktogon. ❺

### Campsites
**Csillebérc Camping** XII, Konkoly Thege M. út 21 ☎1/395-6537, ⓦwww.datanet.hu/csill. Large, well-equipped site also offering a range of bungalows. A short walk from the last stop of bus #21 from Moszkva tér. Open all year.
**Római Camping** III, Szentendrei út 189 ☎1/368-6260, ⓔromai@matavnet.hu. Another huge site beside the road to Szentendre in Rómaifürdő (25min by HEV). Rates include use of the nearby swimming pool. Open all year.

## The City

The **River Danube** (Duna) determines basic orientation, with **Pest** sprawled across the eastern plain and **Buda** reclining on the hilly west bank. Castle Hill is the historic focal point of Buda, home of the Royal Palace and for many years the government. Across the water, Pest has always been the commercial focus, with its hub around the old city centre or Belváros. Construction of the first permanent bridge between the two in 1849 led to rapid expansion, then unification in 1873.

### Buda

Seen from the embankments, **Buda** looks irresistibly romantic with its palatial buildings, archaic spires and outsize statues rising from rugged hills. Its centre, **Castle Hill**, is easily reached via the **Chain Bridge**, opened in 1849 and the first permanent bridge between Buda and Pest. From the busy square on its western side, Clark Ádám tér, you can ride up Castle Hill on the nineteenth-century funicular or **Sikló** (daily 7.30am–10pm; 600Ft up, 500Ft down). Alternatively, take the red metro to Moszkva tér and the Várbusz from there.

By midday, **Szentháromság tér**, the square at the heart of the district, is crammed with tourists, buskers, handicraft vendors and other entrepreneurs, a multilingual spectacle played out against the backdrop of the wildly asymmetrical **Mátyás Church** (Mon–Sat 9am–5pm, Sun 1–5pm; 600Ft). The church is a riotous nineteenth-century recreation grafted onto those portions of the thirteenth-century structure that survived one hundred and fifty years of Ottoman rule – when the church was turned into a mosque – and the siege of 1686, which brought the Ottoman occupation to an end. An equestrian statue of **King Stephen** stands just outside the church, commemorating the ruler who forced Catholicism onto his subjects, thus aligning Hungary with the culture of Western Europe. Behind the church, the **Fishermen's Bastion** or Halászbástya (daily mid-March to Oct 8.30am–11pm; 100–200Ft) is a white rampart with cloisters and seven turrets, framing the view of Parliament across the river. Medieval architectural features have survived along **Országház utca**, at the northern end of which the quasi-Gothic **Mary Magdalene Tower** still dominates Kapisztrán tér, albeit gutted and transformed into an art gallery. To the south of Szentháromság tér the street widens as it approaches the **Buda Palace**. The fortifications and dwellings built by

Béla III after the thirteenth-century Mongol invasion were replaced by ever more luxurious palaces; the most recent reconstruction dates from after the devastation wrought in World War II. The **National Gallery** (Tues–Sun 10am–4/6pm; free, 800Ft for visiting shows), occupying the central wings B, C and D, contains Hungarian art since the Middle Ages. Gothic stone-carvings, altars and painted panels fill the ground floor, while nineteenth-century painting dominates upstairs. On the far side of the Lion Courtyard, the **Budapest History Museum** in Wing E (daily 10am–4/6pm; 800Ft) gives the history of the territory that makes up the city, from prehistoric finds on display on the top floor down to the marbled and flagstoned halls of the Renaissance palace deep underground.

**Watertown** (Víziváros), a wedge-shaped tangle of narrow streets between Castle Hill and the river to the north of the Chain Bridge, was once the poor quarter housing fishermen, craftsmen and their families. Today it's a reclusive neighbourhood of old mansions meeting at odd angles on the hillside, reached by alleys which mostly consist of steps rising from the main street, Fő utca. North along Fő utca stand the **Király baths** (men only Tues, Thurs & Sat 9am–8pm; women only Mon, Wed & Fri 7am–6pm; 1100Ft), distinguishable by four copper cupolas.

South of Watertown rises **Gellért Hill** (Gellérthegy), crowned by the **Liberation Monument**, one of the few Soviet monuments to survive the fall of the Iron Curtain, and the **Citadella**, a low fortress built by the Habsburgs to cow the population after the 1848–49 revolution. Nowadays the fort contains nothing more sinister than a few exhibits, a tourist hostel, a new terrace bar and an overpriced restaurant. Descending the southern slopes of the hill through the playgrounds of Jubileumi Park, you'll come to the **Gellért baths**, at the side of *Hotel Gellért*. The best publicized of the city's baths, they were built in 1913, and the grandeur of the entrance hall is continued in the main pool (Mon–Fri 6am–7pm, Sat & Sun 6am–5/7pm; 2400Ft pool and locker, 2900Ft pool and cabin). You can get cheaper tickets just for the stunning thermal baths (which close earlier at weekends; separate baths for men and women), but it's worth paying to enjoy the beauty of the whole complex. Further north, by the Erzsébet Bridge, are the men-only **Rudas baths** (Mon–Fri 6am–7pm, Sat & Sun 6am–1pm; 1100Ft for steam bath), Budapest's most atmospheric Turkish baths, whose interior has hardly changed since it was constructed in 1556.

Budapest's ironically nostalgic **Communist Statue Park** (Szoborpark; daily 10am–sunset; 600Ft; ◉www.szoborpark.hu) also lies on this side of the river and is well worth a detour to see the monumental statues of Marx, Engels and Lenin. It's stuck out in district XXII; take the direct bus from Deák tér (daily: July & Aug 10am, 11am, 3pm, 4pm; March–June, Sept & Oct 11am & 3pm; Nov–Feb 11am; 1950/2450Ft return, includes entry fee).

## Pest

**Pest**, busier than Buda, is the place where things are decided, made and sold. Much of the architecture and general layout dates from the late nineteenth century, when boulevards, public buildings and apartment houses were built on a scale appropriate to the Habsburg Empire's second city and the capital of Hungary, which celebrated its 1000th anniversary in 1896. The **Belváros** revels in its cosmopolitanism, with shops selling the latest fashions, posters proclaiming the arrival of international rock groups, and streets noisy with the sound of foreign cars and languages.

The main square, **Vörösmarty tér** is dominated by crowded café terraces; the most venerable institution here is the **Gerbeaud** patisserie, the favourite of Budapest's high society since the late nineteenth century, and now packed with tourists. The city's most chic shopping street, **Váci utca**, runs south from the square. Passing the Pesti Theatre, where twelve-year-old Liszt made his concert debut, the crowds flow down to **Ferenciek tere**, overlooking which is a slab of gilt-and-gingerbread architecture, the **Párizsi udvar**, home to an ice-cream parlour and IBUSZ office, but chiefly known for its "Parisian arcade", adorned with arabesques and stained glass. Váci utca continues south to the **Main Market Hall**, with its fancy ironwork, porcelain tiles and stalls festooned with strings of paprika and garlic. Ten minutes' stroll north of the market is the **National Museum** (Tues–Sun 10am–6pm; free), sensitively renovated and showing a comprehensive display of Hungarian history from the Magyar tribes' arrival in 896 through to the collapse of communism in 1989.

Peering over the rooftops to the north of Vörösmarty tér is the dome of **St Stephen's Basilica**, from the top of which there's a good view over the city (dome: April–Oct daily 10am–4/6pm; 500Ft). On his name day, August 20, St Stephen's mummified hand and other holy relics are paraded round the building; the rest of the year, the hand is on show in a side chapel. Just north of the basilica, dominating the banks of the Danube, is the large dome of the **Parliament**, a stupendous nineteenth-century creation that houses the old **Coronation Regalia**. Reputedly the very crown, orb and sceptre used by King Stephen, the regalia are now thought to be a combination of two crowns used by Stephen's successors; nevertheless they are still seen as a symbol of Hungarian statehood. There are daily **tours** of the building – in English – if parliamentary business allows (10am, noon, 2pm & 6pm; free for EU citizens, 2070Ft for others; tickets from Gate X, half-way along the east front).

To the east of the basilica, **Andrássy út** runs dead straight for 2.5km, a parade of grand buildings laden with gold leaf, dryads and colonnades, including the magnificent Opera House at no. 22. Its shops and sidewalk cafés retain some of the style that made the avenue so fashionable in the 1890s. A little further along, at no. 60, is the **House of Terror** (Tues–Fri 10am–6pm, Sat & Sun 10am–7.30pm; 1200Ft). Once the headquarters of the dreaded secret police, the building now houses a collection of sobering exhibits pertaining to Stalin, the Nazis and the Holocaust, as well as the Soviet "liberation" and the 1956 uprising. The boulevard culminates at **Hősök tere**, built to mark the 1000th anniversary of the Magyar conquest. Its centrepiece is the **Millenary Monument**, portraying the great Magyar leader Prince Árpád and his chieftains grouped around a 36-metre-high column topped by the Archangel Gabriel, and half-encircled by a colonnade displaying statues of Hungary's most illustrious leaders, from King Stephen to Kossuth. Also on the square, the **Museum of Fine Arts** (Tues–Sun 10am–6pm; free) contains Egyptian funerary relics, Greek and Roman ceramics, and paintings and drawings by European masters from the thirteenth to twentieth centuries, including Dürer, El Greco, Velázquez and Bronzino. Behind the museum lies **Budapest Zoo** (daily 9am–4/7pm; 1300Ft), worth a visit for the architecture alone – the Palm House, the Elephant House and the Aviary in particular. Opposite the zoo, the yellow neo-Baroque walls of the **Széchenyi baths** (daily 6am–7pm; 1900Ft) contain one of Europe's largest spa complexes. Watch locals play chess on floating boards while wallowing in the steam. Note that the Széchenyi and Gellért baths both offer money back on the ticket, depending on how long you stay; if you stay just an hour, you can get 300Ft back, decreasing each hour to three hours maximum time for a rebate.

Back towards the centre of the Belváros, on the corner of Wesselényi and Dohány utca, stands the dramatic main **Synagogue** (Mon–Thurs 10am–3pm, Fri 10am–2pm, Sun 10am–2pm; 1000Ft including entrance to Jewish Museum) whose Byzantine-Moorish architecture was restored; the interior is now complete and utterly magnificent with shimmering golden geometric shapes and a 5000-tube organ, played in the past by Liszt and Saint Saëns. In the **National Jewish Museum** next door (same times), exhibits dating back to the Middle Ages are contrasted by a harrowing Holocaust exhibition, which casts a chill over the third section, portraying Jewish cultural life today. In the streets behind the synagogue lies Pest's main **Jewish quarter**. In recent years the small Jewish community that survived the Holocaust has become much more visible in the city, although even here, where the community is strongest, it keeps a low profile. Along Dob utca there is the *Fröhlich* kosher coffee shop at no. 22, a wigmaker at no. 31, and at no. 35, by the entrance to the orthodox community buildings, a kosher butcher.

## Eating and drinking

Magyar cooking has been overtaken in Budapest's **restaurants** by scores of places devoted to international cuisine. Prices by Western European standards are very reasonable, and your budget should stretch to at least one binge in a top–flight place. The following categories – *cukrászdas* (patisseries) for sweet pastries and coffee, restaurants (for eating), and bars and beer halls (for drinking) – are to an extent arbitrary, since almost all restaurants serve alcohol and all bars serve some food, while *eszpresszós* (cafés) feature both, plus coffee and pastries.

### Patisseries

**Ági Rétes** II, Retek utca 9. Best *rétes* (strudel) in town, all baked on the premises. Located near Moszkva tér.

**Angelika** I, Batthyány tér 7. This former convent has been modernized with techno soundtrack and a lively terrace, though elderly locals are still hanging in there.

**Central** V, Károlyi Mihály utca 9. Large old coffee house, three minutes' walk south from Ferenciek tere, restored to its former glory, with a broad menu ranging from cheap to very expensive.

**Eckermann** VI, Andrássy út 24. Big coffees in this popular café next to the Goethe Institute. Closed Sun.

**Fröhlich** VII, Dob utca 22. A kosher patisserie five minutes' walk from the Dohány utca synagogue, presided over by the Fröhlich family. Specialities include *flódni* (an apple, walnut and poppy-seed cake). Closed Sat & Jewish holidays.

**Gerbeaud** V, Vörösmarty tér 7. A popular, very grand place in central Pest. A coffee and a *torte* will set you back around 1000Ft; the same rich pastries are cheaper in *Kis Gerbeaud* around the corner.

**Müvész** VI, Andrássy út 29. Grand old coffee house that's less touristy and cheaper than *Gerbeaud*.

**Múzeum Cukrászda** VIII, Múzeum körút 10. Friendly hangout by the National Museum, where fresh pastries arrive at dawn.

**Ruszwurm** I, Szentháromság utca 7. Excellent cakes, served production-line fashion to those taking a break from sightseeing on Castle Hill.

### Fast food, self-service and snack bars

**Buddha** VI, Teréz körút 46. Friendly Thai noodle bar with baguettes and coffee too.

**Duran Sandwich Bar** V, Október 6 utca 15. A sandwich and coffee bar – still, oddly enough, a rare combination in Budapest. Closed Sun.

**Falafel Faloda** VI, Paulay Ede utca 53. Best of the city's falafel joints. Closed Sat & Sun.

**Karma Café** VI, Liszt Ferenc tér 11. Beautifully decorated café with excellent tapas, situated on Pest's trendiest square.

**Marie Kristensen Sandwich Bar** IX, Ráday utca 7. A decent sandwich bar behind Kálvin tér. Closed Sun.

**Szahara** VIII, József körút 82. Clean, bright joint offering a good range of Middle Eastern food. No smoking.

### Restaurants

**Abszint** VI, Andrássy út 34. Reasonably priced Provençal cuisine in a fun setting. Budding visionary poets can taste a version of absinthe, dripped through a sugar cube.

**Al-Amir** VII, Király utca 17. Syrian restaurant serving excellent salads and hummus, making it a haven for vegetarians in a city of carnivores. No alcohol.

**Art Café Alhambra** VI, Jókai tér 3. Gorgeous interior, heavenly tapas, exhibitions and Moroccan teas to aid chilling out in style.

**Café Kör** V, Sas utca 17 ☎1/311-0053. Popular place near the basilica with excellent food and fine wines. Menu supplemented by specials written up on the wall. Booking essential. Closed Sun.

**Govinda** V, Vigyázó Ferenc utca 4. An oasis of spiritual calm in a little side street, just north of Roosevelt tér, serving a good range of Indian vegetarian dishes and salads.

**Gundel** XIV, Állatkerti út 2 ☎1/468-4040. Priding itself as the flagship of Hungarian cuisine this place has correspondingly high prices. On Sunday, though, you can eat your fill for 4700Ft at their bargain brunch. Booking essential. Closed Sun eve. Right next to the zoo's main entrance on the northern edge of the City Park.

**Kádár étkezde** VII, Klauzál tér 9. Jewish home-cooking in the old quarter, where friendly staff serve lunches of boiled beef in fruit sauces. Closed Sun.

**Márkus Vendéglő** II, Lövőház utca 17. Welcoming, inexpensive Hungarian restaurant near Moszkva tér.

**Menza** VI, Liszt Ferenc tér. Stylish, retro-looking place offering excellent and moderately priced Hungarian dishes.

**Papageno** V, Semmelweis utca 19. Small, friendly establishment, with top chefs specializing in French and Italian cuisine. Closed Sun.

### Bars, wine bars and beer halls

**Bambi** I, Bem tér. Wonderful old bar from the socialist era serving breakfast, snack lunches, cakes and alcohol.

**Café Miro** I, Úri utca 30. A trendy bar in the Castle district, which often has live music.

**Castro** IX, Ráday utca 35. A lively place on Ráday utca, a street popular with students and lined with cafés and bars. Internet access too.

**Darshan Udvar** VIII, Krúdy Gyula utca 7. The largest bar in a growing complex of bars, cafés and shops. Set at the back of the courtyard, with oriental/hippie decorations, good food, world music and leisurely service.

**Eklektika** V, Semmelweis utca 21. Arty, gay-friendly bar with 1960s furniture, art exhibitions, a pasta/salad menu and women-only evenings on the second Saturday of the month.

**Gusto's** II, Frankel Leó út 12. Tiny bar near Buda side of Margit Bridge, serving the best tiramisu in town. Closed Sun.

**Szimpla** VII, Kertész utca 48. The *Szimpla* folk keep the spirit of grunge alive and also organize outdoor bar venues during the summer months.

**Vian** VI, Liszt Ferenc tér 11. One of the best, and least posey, bars on the square, with pleasant staff and a cool atmosphere.

**Zöld Pardon** XI, by the Buda end of Petőfi Bridge. Giant outdoor bar, with live music, sprawling across the grass near the university quarter. May–Oct. Tram #4 or #6 to Petőfi Bridge.

## Entertainment, nightlife and festivals

The four main venues for **alternative concerts**, **folk music** and **modern dance** events are the Petőfi Csarnok in the Városliget (@www.petoficsarnok.hu); the Almássy tér Cultural Centre at VII, Almássy tér 6; the Trafó, a revamped transformer station in Pest, at IX, Liliom utca 41 (@www.trafo.hu); and the Fonó in Buda at XI, Sztregova utca 3 (@www.fono.hu). **Tickets** for most events can be had through Ticket Express for classical and pop, VI, Andrássy út 18 (☎1/312-0000, @www.tex.hu); or Publika for rock and jazz, VII, Károly körút 9 (☎1/322-2010). New **clubs** are opening all the time, and the rave and floating party scene (held on river boats) is growing constantly: check flyers and posters around town, or look in the "Könnyű" section of *Pesti Est*, the free listings magazine in cinema foyers. There's also a variety of cheap **student clubs**, and keep an eye out for the steamy parties organized in the thermal spas by the Cinetrip crew. Entry costs anything from 1000–4000Ft.

Star events in the cultural year are the **Budapest Spring Festival** (two weeks in March or April) and the **Autumn Music Weeks** (late Sept to late Oct), both of which attract top international acts. There are also scores of classical and popular concerts during the summer, chief amongst which is the superb **Sziget Festival**, attracting some of the biggest rock and pop acts going. On **St Stephen's Day** (Aug 20) the area around the Royal Palace becomes one big folk and crafts fair, and in the evening people line the embankments to watch the fireworks.

### Clubs

**Angyal** VII, Szövetség utca 33. Budapest's premier gay club, in a side street leading off Almássy tér. It looks like an airport lounge but has an interesting crowd. Sat is men only. Closed Mon–Wed.

**Buddha Beach** IX, Közraktár utca 9–11 ☎1/476-0433. Outside bar attracting a wealthy young crowd, that's one of the few places you can dance outside until the early hours. Good bar food so it's worth booking a table if you're eating. March–Oct.

**Capella** V, Belgrád rakpart 23. Drag queens, jungle music and lots of kitsch: just the place for a night on the town.

**Cha Cha Cha** IX, Kálvin tér subway. Despite its strange location, this place attracts a big crowd spilling out into the concourse, and has DJs at weekends. Closed Sun.

**Süss Fel Nap** V, Honvéd utca 40. Heaving, lively place attracting a young crowd.

**Trocadero Café** V, Szent István körút 15. Excellent Latin music and dancing just up from Nyugáti Station. Closed Sun & Mon.

**West Balkan** IX, Kisfaludy utca 16. Superb, and very upbeat, club with both indoor and outdoor dance areas. May–Sept.

## Listings

**Embassies and consulates** Australia, XII, Királyhágó tér 8–9 ☎1/457-9777; Canada, XII, Budakeszi út 32 ☎1/392-3360; Ireland, V, Szabadság tér 7, 7th floor, Bank Center ☎1/302-9600; New Zealand, VI, Teréz körút 38, ☎1/428-2208; UK, V, Harmincad utca 6 ☎1/266-2888; US, V, Szabadság tér 12 ☎1/475-4400.

**Exchange** Gönc Szövetkezeti Takarékpénztár at V, Rákóczi út 5; Magyar Külkereskedelmi Bank at Türr István utca at the top of Váci utca, Pest; Tribus tourist office V, Apáczai Csere János utca 1.

**Hospitals** V, Hold utca 19, behind the US embassy ☎1/311-6816; II, Ganz utca 13–15 ☎1/202-1370.

**Internet** CEU Net, V, Október 6 utca 14 (daily 11am–10pm); Electric Café, VII, Dohány utca 37 (daily 9am–midnight); Millenarium Park C Building (free for one hour); Matávpont, V, Petőfi utca 17–19 and all large shopping malls (daily 9am–8pm).

**Pharmacies** Alkotás utca 1B, opposite Déli station, and Teréz körút 41, near Oktogon, are both open 24hr.

**Police** Tourists can report a crime at V, Kecskeméti út (☎1/317-0711) or V, Szalay utca (☎1/373-1000) police stations.

**Post office** V, Petőfi utca 13.

# Around Budapest: Szentendre

To escape Budapest's humid summers, many people flock north of the city to the **Danube Bend**, one of the grandest stretches of the river. The historic town of **SZENTENDRE** on the west bank is the most popular day-trip from the capital (40min by HÉV train from Batthyány tér; 1hr 30min by boat from Vigadó tér pier), a friendly maze of houses painted in autumn colours, secret gardens, and alleys leading to hilltop churches – the perfect spot for an artists' colony, which is what it became in the 1920s, when artists moved out from the city to make the most of the superb natural light. Szentendre's original character was largely shaped by Serbs seeking refuge from the Ottomans. Their townhouses – now converted into galleries, shops and cafés – form a set piece around **Fő tér**, now a stage for musicians and mime-artists. On the north side of the square is **Blagovestenska Church** (Tues–Sun 10am–5pm; winter open for worship only; 200Ft), whose iconostasis, painted by Mikhail Zivkovic (1776–1824), suggests the richness of the Serbs' artistry and faith. Just around the corner at Vastagh György utca 1 stands the wonderful **Margit Kovács Museum** (daily 10am–5/6pm; closed Mon in winter; 600Ft), displaying the lifetime work of Hungary's best-known ceramicist, born in 1902. Above Fő tér there's a fine view over Szentendre's steeply banked rooftops and gardens from the hilltop **Templom tér**, where frequent craft fairs help finance the restoration of the Catholic parish church there. Opposite the church, paintings whose fierce brush strokes and sketching were a challenge to the canons of classicism during the 1890s hang in the **Béla Czóbel Museum** (April–Oct Tues–Sun 10am–6pm; 400Ft), beyond which the spire of the **Serbian Orthodox Cathedral** pokes above a walled garden; tourists are generally not admitted, but you can see the cathedral iconostasis and treasury in the adjacent **museum** (April–Oct Wed–Sun 10am–5pm; 400Ft). Hourly buses run from the HÉV terminal out along Szabadságforrás út to Szentendre's fascinating **Village Museum** (Tues–Sun 9am–5pm; 700Ft; ⊛www.skanzen.hu), which has reconstructed villages from six regions of Hungary with three more planned. During the summer, on alternate weekends, there are demonstrations of traditional craft techniques, including pottery, baking and basket-making.

**Information**, both on the town and the Danube Bend, is available from Tourinform at Dumtsa Jenő utca 22 (June–Aug Mon–Fri 9am–7pm, Sat & Sun 9am–6pm; Sept–May Mon–Sat 9.30am–4.30pm, Sun 10am–2pm; ☎26/317-965, ✉szentendre@tourinform.hu). For **accommodation**, the cheapest option is a **private room**, advertised widely throughout town, while two good-value pensions are the *Horváth Panzió*, to the north of the centre at Daru piac 2 (☎26/313-950, ⊛www.option.hu/horvath; ❷); and the *Ilona Panzió*, Rákóczi utca 11 (☎ & ☎26/313-599; ❷), in a pleasant location in the heart of the old quarter. While many people end up camping rough on Szentendre Island, the official **campsite** is on Pap Island (☎26/310-697, ⊛www.pap-sziget.hu; May–Sept), 1.5km north of town – take any bus heading towards Visegrád or Esztergom and get off by the *Danubius Hotel*. The best of the **restaurants** is the superb Mexican, *Palapa*, at Dumtsa Jenő utca 22. Most others are concentrated in and around Fő tér, including *Aranysárkány*, Alkotmány utca 1/a, and *Rab Ráby*, Kucsera Ferenc utca 1, both of which offer traditional, and very filling, Magyar cuisine. The most enjoyable **cafés** are the Balkan-themed *Café Adria* towards the bottom of town at Kossuth utca 4 and *Avakum*, near the *Aranysárkány* restaurant at Alkotmány 4. **Internet access** is available at Game Planet, Petőfi utca 1 (daily 10am–10pm).

# Western Hungary

The major tourist attraction to the west of the capital is **Lake Balaton**, over-romantically labelled the "Hungarian sea", but very much the nation's playground, with vacation resorts lining both shores. The more built-up southern shore features the livelier resorts, chief amongst which is **Siófok** – the lake's number one party place – while, on the western tip, lies the appealing university town of **Keszthely** and Europe's largest thermal lake at **Hévíz**. By way of contrast development on the northern bank has been limited to some extent by reedbanks and cooler, deeper water, giving tourism a different slant – the historic **Tihany** peninsula, with its quaint village, is the main draw here. Most of these places are connected by regular ferry services during the summer months.

More than other regions in Hungary, the western region of **Transdanubia** is a patchwork land, an ethnic and social hybrid. Its valleys and hills, forests and mud flats have been a melting pot since Roman times: settled by Magyars, Serbs, Slovaks and Germans; torn asunder and occupied by Ottomans and Habsburgs; transformed from a state of near-feudalism into brutal collectives; and now operating under modern capitalism. All the main towns display evidence of this evolution, especially **Sopron**, with its gorgeous, and well-preserved, medieval centre, and **Pécs**, which boasts an Ottoman mosque and minaret.

## Siófok

The largest, busiest and most vibrant resort on Balaton, **SIÓFOK** is *the* place to come for bathing, boozing and dancing. The two main waterfront resort areas are Aranypart (Gold Shore) to the east of the Sió Canal, and Ezüstpart (Silver Shore) to the west. Though the central stretch of shoreline consists of paying **beaches** (daily mid-May to mid-Sept 7am–7pm; 700Ft), there are free *strand* (beaches) 1km further along at both resort areas. You can rent **windsurfing** boards and small **sailing** boats at most beaches.

From the **bus** and **train stations,** next to each other on Fő utca, it's a five-minute walk to the Tourinform office in the water tower (Víztorony) on Szabadság tér (mid-June to mid-Sept Mon–Fri 8am–8pm, Sat & Sun 9am–6pm; mid-Sept to mid-June Mon–Fri 9am–4pm; ☎84/315-355, ⊛www.siofok.com). They also book **private rooms**, as can Ibusz, inside the atrium at Fő utca 176 (June–Aug Mon–Fri 8am–6pm, Sat 9am–6pm, Sun 9am–1pm; Sept–May Mon–Fri 8am–4pm; ☎84/510-720, ✉i081@ibusz.hu). The largest **campsites** in town are *Aranypart Camping*, 5km east of the centre (bus #2) at Szent László utca 183–185 (☎84/352-801; chalets ④; mid-April to mid-Sept), and *Ezüstpart Camping*, 4km west of the centre (bus #1 from the Baross Bridge) at Liszt Ferenc sétány 5 (☎84/350-374; chalets ❸; May–Sept). There are also two **hostels** west of the centre: the *Youth Holiday Home*, Erkel Ferenc utca 46 (☎84/310-131; 2500Ft; June–Aug), and the *Touring Hotel* (☎84/350-185; 2500Ft; May–Sept), Cseresznye utca 1/0.

Two great **restaurants** are *Amigo*, Fő utca 99, which has a varied menu including a fantastic range of pizzas, and *Café Roxy*, Szabadság tér 1, offering a good selection of salads, stews and grills. Petőfi sétány, the shore front strip, is crammed with **bars** and **clubs**, though serious clubbers head for the *Palace Dance Club*, to the west of town at Deák Ferenc utca 2, or *Flört*, a high-energy techno club just off Fő utca on the east bank of the canal. There are also regular **pop and rock concerts** on one of the *strand* by the hotels in the centre of town.

## Keszthely and Hévíz

Gracefully absorbing thousands of visitors, **KESZTHELY** runs Siófok a close second as Balaton's best hangout, with some good eating and drinking options, several beaches, and a university to give it some life of its own. Keszthely's waterfront has two bays (one for swimming, the other for ferries) formed by man-made piers, a slew of parkland backed by plush hotels and miniature golf courses, and dozens of fast-food joints. In the evenings, action shifts from the water to the centre, where the bars and restaurants work at full steam. Walking up from the train station along Mártírok útja, you'll pass the **Balaton Museum** at the junction with Kossuth Lajos utca (Tues–Sun 9am–5pm; 300Ft), with exhibits on the region's history and wildlife. From Fő tér onwards, with its much-remodelled Gothic church, Kossuth utca is given over to cafés, vendors, buskers and strollers and leads up towards the **Festetics Palace**, founded in 1745 by Count György Festetics (Tues–Sun 10am–5/6pm; 1200Ft), which attracted the leading lights of Magyar literature from the nineteenth century onwards. The building's highlights are its gilt, mirrored ballroom and the Helikon Library, a masterpiece of joinery and carving built in 1801. The palace stages regular summer concerts – check with Tourinform. To the rear of the palace grounds, in the former stables, is the splendid **Coach Museum** (Tues–Sun 10am–5/6pm; 500Ft), displaying a fine assortment of eighteenth- and nineteenth-century carriages.

The **dock** is roughly ten minutes' walk south of the centre along Erzsébet királyné útja, and the **train** and **bus** stations five minutes' walk southwest of the cluster of lakeside hotels along Kazinczy utca. Some **buses**, however, drop off on Fő tér, halfway along Kossuth utca, the main drag. The **Tourinform** office is at Kossuth utca 28 (June to mid-Sept Mon–Fri 9am–8pm, Sat & Sun 9am–6pm; mid-Sept to May Mon–Fri 9am–5pm, Sat 9am–1pm; ☎83/314-144, ⊛www.keszthely .hu). For budget **accommodation**, private rooms are your best bet, advertised widely throughout town or bookable through Keszthely Tourist, Kossuth utca 25 (June–Aug daily 9am–8/9pm, Sept–May Mon–Sat 8am–5pm; ☎83/312-031, ⊛www.keszthelytourist.hu). For information on rooms in college **dorms** (July & Aug daily; rest of year weekends only), check with Tourinform. There are two **campsites** just south of the train station; *Sport Camping* (☎83/313-777; mid-May to Sept) and *Zalatour Camping* (☎83/312-782; mid-April to mid-Oct); and the larger, more expensive *Castrum Camping* (☎83/312-120; April–Oct), 1500m along the shore in the opposite direction.

Good **restaurants** include the *Béke Vendéglő*, Kossuth utca 50, which offers homestyle Hungarian food; the rustically-styled *Di Marcello Pizzeria* at Városház utca 4; and *Oázis*, down Szalasztó utca from the palace at Rákóczi tér 3 (Mon–Fri

11am–4pm), which has an excellent salad and vegetarian self-service bar. Local student hangouts are the trio of **bars** opposite the post office on Kossuth Lajos utca, whilst the smart *Café Pelso*, next to the Gothic parish church on Fő tér, is ideal for a coffee stop. There's **Internet access** at *Stones Cyber-Café*, Kisfaludy utca 17.

Half-hourly buses from Keszthely train station run to **HÉVÍZ**, a spa based around Europe's largest thermal lake, **Hévízi Gyógy-tó**. The wooden terraces surrounding the **Tófürdő** ("lake bath"; daily 8.30/9am–5/6pm; entry tickets: 3hr 900Ft, all day 1600Ft) have a vaguely fin-de-siècle appearance, but the ambience is contemporary, with people sipping beer while bobbing on the murky, egg-scented lake in rented inner-tubes. Having had a soak, there's no real reason to hang around, but if you do want to **stay**, then Hévíz Tourist, Rákóczi utca 2 (Mon–Fri 8.30am–5.30pm, Sat 9am–1pm; ☎83/341-348, ✉heviztour@axelero.hu), can book **private rooms**; alternatively, two great-value hotels are the colourful *Pannon*, Széchenyi utca 23 (☎83/340-482, ⊛www.hotels.hu/pannon_heviz; ❹), and the *Napfény* across the road at no. 21 (☎83/340-642, ⊛www.napfenyhotelheviz.hu; ❺). The best central **restaurant** is the *Rózsakert* opposite the baths, and there's a late-night **bar** and **casino** in the *Hotel Thermál*.

## Tihany

The historic centre of **TIHANY**, self-proclaimed "Pearl of the Balaton", sits above the harbour where the **ferries** from the southern shore dock; follow the winding steps up between a screen of trees, until you get to the mass of tourist boutiques and stalls crowding the streets. Tihany's **Benedictine Abbey**, 2km north of the docks, on top of the hill, was established in 1055. A few paces north from the abbey is the **Open-Air Folk Museum** (May–Sept Tues–Sun 10am–6pm; 330Ft), a collection of old cottages giving a feel of life in the village in the early twentieth century. Around Petőfi and Csokonai streets, houses are built of grey basalt tufa, with windows and doors outlined in white, and porticoed terraces. Even without a map it's easy to stumble upon the **Inner Lake** (Belső-tó), whose sunlit surface is visible from the abbey. From its southern bank, a path runs through vineyards, orchards and lavender fields past the Aranyház geyser cones and down to Tihanyi-rév, the ferry dock. Your alternative method of arrival is by **bus** from the neighbouring resort of Balatonfüred. There's a **Tourinform** office up by the abbey at Kossuth utca 20 (☎87/438-016, ⊛www.tihany.hu), though Tihany Tourist, Kossuth utca 11 (April–Oct daily 9am–4/8pm; ☎87/448-481, ⊛www.tihanytourist.hu), are more helpful and can also help out with **private rooms** in the village. Hotel prices are well above the average here, though the restful *Kántás Panzió*, just behind the post office at Csokonai utca 49 (☎87/448-072, ⊛www.hotels.hu/kantas; ❹), offers reasonable value. The best of the brazenly tourist-oriented **restaurants** lining Kossuth utca are the *Fogas Csárda* at no. 9, with good fish, and the *Két Fazék* at no. 23, with traditional food, very friendly staff and a vociferous mynah bird. There's good pizza and beer at the *Stég Pub and Pizzeria*, Kossuth utca 18.

## Sopron and around

**SOPRON** – the nearest big Hungarian town to Vienna and consequently a popular destination – has 240 listed buildings, which allow it to claim to be "the most historic town in Hungary". The horseshoe-shaped Belváros (inner town) is north of Széchenyi tér and the main train station. At the southern end, **Orsolya tér** features Renaissance edifices dripping with loggias and carved protrusions, and a Gothic church. Heading north towards the main square, **Új utca** (New Street – one of the town's oldest thoroughfares) is a gentle curve of arched dwellings painted in red, yellow and pink, with chunky cobblestones and pavements. At no. 22 stands one of the **synagogues** (May–Oct Tues–Sun 10am–6pm; 400Ft) that flourished when the street was known as Zsidó utca (Jewish Street); Sopron's Jewish community survived the expulsion of 1526 only to be all-but-annihilated during World War II. The main source of interest is up ahead on Fő tér, a parade of Gothic and Baroque architecture partly overshadowed by the **Goat Church** – so called, so legend has it, because its construction was financed by a goatherd whose flock unearthed a cache of loot. The Renaissance **Storno House**, also on the square, exhibits an enjoyable collection of Roman, Celtic and Avar relics, plus mementoes of Liszt (Tues–Sun: April–Sept 10am–6pm; Oct–March 10am–2pm; 600Ft). North of here rises Sopron's symbol, the **Firewatch Tower** (April–Oct Tues–Sun 10am–6pm; 500Ft), founded upon the stones of a fortress originally laid out by the Romans. From the top there's a stunning view of the town's narrow streets and weathered rooftops. The "Gate of Loyalty" at the base of the tower commemorates the townfolk's decision, when offered the choice of Austrian citizenship in 1921, to remain Magyar subjects. Walk through it and you'll emerge onto Előkapu, a short street where the houses are laid out in a saw-toothed pattern.

The **train station** is on Mátyás Király utca, 500m south of Széchenyi tér and the old town; Sopron is linked to Vienna by a fast intercity service, though it's not on the main Budapest–Vienna route. The **bus station** is to the northwest of the old town, five minutes' walk along Lackner Kristóf utca from Ógabona tér. **Information** is available from Tourinform, inside the Liszt Cultural Centre at Liszt utca 1 (mid-June to mid-Sept Mon–Fri 9am–7pm, Sat & Sun 9am–6pm; mid-Sept to mid-June Mon–Fri 9am–5pm, Sat 9am–3pm; ☏99/517-560, ⊛www.tourinform .sopron.hu), and there's **Internet access** at Új utca 3 (Mon–Wed 1–7pm, Thurs & Fri 11am–7pm). The *Brennbergi* youth hostel is sited 4km west of town at Brennbergi utca 82 (☏99/313-166; 2200Ft), and reached by buses #3 and #10 from the bus station, while **private rooms** and student accommodation can be arranged through Ciklámen Tourist, Ógabona tér 8 (Mon–Fri 8am–4.30pm, Sat 8am–noon; ☏99/312-040). For other **accommodation**, try *Bástya Panzió*, Patak utca 40 (☏99/325-325, ⊛ www.bastya-panzio.hu; ❸), or *Jégverem Panzió*, Jégverem utca 1 (☏99/510-113, ⊛www.jegverem.hu; ❸), both good-value pensions just across the Ikva stream to the northeast of town. The *Lövér* **campsite** is 4km south of town – take bus #12 from Deák tér.

The best of the town's **restaurants** include *Várkerület Söröző*, Várkerület 83, serving Hungarian dishes; *Rókalyukhoz*, opposite, with an extensive and eclectic international menu; and the *Fórum Pizzeria* at Szent György utca 3, which also does a good line in pastas and salads. Two fabulous **cafés** are the *Liszt Szalon Café* (and chocolate shop), opposite the *Fórum Pizzeria* at Szent György utca 12 (daily 10am–10pm), and the cosy *Teaház* at Széchenyi tér 16 (daily 10am–10pm), which offers a complete range of teas alongside some delicious strudels and roulades. The sociable *Hungariá Kaveház* in the Liszt Cultural Centre has the best summer terrace (daily 9am–10pm). There's good local **wine** to be had at the atmospheric *Cézár* cellar, Hátsókapu utca 2, or *Gyógygödör Borozó*, Fő tér 4 (both daily until 10pm).

## Esterházy Palace

Some 27km east of Sopron (hourly buses), in the village of Fertőd, lies a monument to one of the country's most famous dynasties: the **Esterházy Palace**. Originally minor nobility, the Esterházy family began its rise thanks to Miklós Esterházy I (1583–1645), who married two rich widows, sided with the Habsburgs, and got himself elevated to count. The palace itself was begun by his grandson, Miklós the Ostentatious, who inherited 600,000 acres and a dukedom in 1762. Fronted by a vast horseshoe courtyard where Hussars once pranced to the music of Haydn – Esterházy's resident maestro for many years – the palace was intended to rival Versailles. **Guided tours** (every 40min; April–Oct Tues–Sun 10am–6pm; Nov–March Fri–Sun 10am–4pm; 1000Ft) cover 23 of the 126 rooms in the palace, including several blue-and-white chinoiserie salons, the Banqueting Hall with its superb ceiling fresco, and one room displaying **Haydn memorabilia**. There's a Tourinform office opposite the palace gates (April–Oct Mon–Sat 9am–5pm; Nov–March Tues–Sat 10am–4pm; ☎99/370-544, ⓔfertod@tourinform.hu), and should you wish to **stay**, try the *Újvári Panzió*, about 500m from the palace at Kossuth utca 57a (☎99/537-097, ⓦwww.extra.hu/ujvaripanzio; ❸), or the *Kata Vendégház*, 1km down Vasút utca at Mikes Kelemen utca 2 (☎99/370-857, ⓦwww.hotels .hu/kata_fertod; ❸).

# Pécs

The town of **PÉCS** is one of Transdanubia's largest and most attractive towns; indeed, it lays claim to being the finest town in the country, with its tiled rooftops climbing the vine-laden slopes of the Mecsek range. Besides some good museums, the fifth-oldest university in Europe (founded in 1367) and a great market, Pécs contains Hungary's best examples of **Islamic architecture**, a legacy of the long Ottoman occupation. Heading up Bajcsy-Zsilinszky út from the bus terminal, or by bus #30 from the train station towards the centre, you'll pass Kossuth tér and Pécs's **synagogue** (May–Oct Mon–Fri & Sun 10am–5pm; 300Ft). The beautiful nineteenth-century interior is a haunting place, with Romantic frescoes swirling around a space emptied by the murder of almost 3500 Jews – ten times the number that live in Pécs today. During the Ottoman occupation (1543–1686), a similar fate befell the Christian population, whose principal church was converted into the **Mosque of Gázi Kászim Pasha** (mid-April to mid-Oct Mon–Sat 10am–noon/4pm, Sun 11.30am–2/4pm; donations) to the north on Széchenyi tér. In a twist of history, the mosque has changed sides again and operates as the City Centre Catholic Parish Church. Behind the mosque is an **Archeological Museum** (Tues–Sun 10am–4pm; 300Ft) displaying items testifying to a Roman presence between the first and fifth centuries. From here you can follow either Káptalan or Janus Pannonius utca towards the **cathedral** (Mon–Sat 9am–5pm, Sun 1–5pm; 700Ft, which includes a glass of wine at the Bishop's Wine Cellar just around the corner from the main entrance). Though its architects have incorporated a crypt and side-chapels from eleventh- to fourteenth-century churches, the cathedral is predominantly nineteenth-century neo-Romanesque.

**Pécs Fair**, held on the morning of the first Sunday of each month – and the Friday and Saturday immediately before – sees some hard bargaining and hard drinking, and there are smaller markets on the same site every Sunday. Bus #50 carries local shoppers from outside the Konzum store in Rákóczi utca to the brand new Pécs Plaza mall opposite the fair; get a ticket from a newsstand or the train station before boarding. Pécs is also an excellent starting-point for heading to the nearby **wine region** of Villány to the south – ask at Tourinform for further information.

The **train station** is a twenty-minute walk south of the centre on Indoház tér, and the **bus station** a short walk northeast of the train station on Zsolyom utca. **Tourinform** is at Széchenyi tér 9 (June–Sept Mon–Fri 9am–6pm, Sat & Sun 9am–3pm; Oct–May Mon–Fri 8am–4pm; ☎72/213-315, ⓔbaranya-m@tourinform .hu), while the adjoining office offers **Internet access** (same hours).

For inexpensive, central accommodation, you can book a **private room** or **student hostel bed** through Mecsek Tours, Széchenyi tér 1 (☎72/513-370, ⓔutir@mecsektours.hu), or Ibusz, Király utca 11 (Mon–Fri 9am–5pm; ☎72/212-157, ⓔi077@ibusz.hu). The best-value option **hotels** in the centre are the *Főnix Hotel* just north of Széchenyi tér at Hunyádi út 2 (☎72/311-680, ⓦwww.fonixhotel .hu; ❸), and the *Víg Apát Hotel*, 200m west of the train station at Mártírok utca 14 (☎72/313-340, ⓦwww.hotels.hu/vig_apat_pecs; ❸). There's also the *Laterum Hotel/Youth Hostel*, 3km west of the centre (bus #2 or #4) at Hajnóczi utca 37 (☎72/252-113; 2500Ft), and two **campsites**, *Família Privát Camping*, 3km east at Gyöngyösi utca 6 (☎72/327-034; open all year; bus #31), and *Mandulás Camping*,

Ángyán János utca 2 (☎72/515-655; mid-April to mid-Oct; bus #34), 2km north of the centre near the woods.

When it comes to **eating**, *Az Elefántos*, Jokai tér 6, has simple but tasty and filling pizza and pasta dishes, or there's the magnificently decorated *Dóm Étterem*, Király utca 3, offering some excellent house specialities; and the *Cellárium*, a cavernous cellar restaurant next to the *Főnix Hotel* serving up high quality Hungarian cuisine. Two of the most popular places for **drinking** are the hip *Coffeein Café* at Széchenyi tér 9 (daily 8am–midnight, Fri & Sat till 2am), and the full-on *Replay Café and Bar* at Király utca 4 (daily 10am–2am) – both also offer a decent food menu. For a daytime coffee head to the lovely *Kávéház*, adjacent to *Az Elefántos*, and for cakes the *Virág Cukrászda* opposite Mecsek Tours.

# Eastern Hungary

The hilly and forested northern region of **eastern Hungary** will not feature prominently in any hurried tour of the country, but nobody should overlook the gorgeous wine-producing town of **Eger**, and the nearby "Valley of the Beautiful Woman", famed for its wine cellars.

## Eger

Its colourful architecture suffused by sunshine, **EGER** seems a fitting place of origin for Egri Bikavér, the famous red wine marketed abroad as "Bull's Blood", which brings hordes of visitors to the town. Despite occasional problems with accommodation, it's a fine place to hang out and wander around, not to mention all the opportunities for drinking. The Neoclassical **cathedral**, designed by József Hild and constructed between 1831 and 1836, is five minutes' walk southwest from Dobó István tér, the main square. The florid **Lyceum** directly opposite the cathedral is worth visiting for its library (Tues–Sun 9.30am–3.30pm; 450Ft), whose beautiful floor and fittings are made of polished oak. While in the building, check out the **observatory**, at the top of the tower in the east wing (same hours; 450Ft), where a nineteenth-century camera obscura projects a view of the entire town. Close by, facing Széchenyi utca, stands the **Archbishop's Palace** (10am–4/5pm; 250Ft), a U-shaped Baroque pile with fancy wrought-iron gates; in its right wing you'll find the treasury and a history of the bishopric of Eger. Heading back towards the centre along Bajcsy-Zsilinsky utca you'll come out on the pleasant **Dobó István tér**. Cross the bridge and head to the left to find Eger's most photographed structure, a slender fourteen-sided **minaret** (April–Oct 9am–6pm; 140Ft), looking rather lonely without its mosque, which was demolished during a nineteenth-century building boom. Alternatively, head uphill from the square to the gates of the **castle** (daily 8/9am–5/8pm; 800Ft). From the bastion overlooking the main gate, a path leads up to the ticket office and the fifteenth-century **Bishop's Palace**. Here, tapestries, ceramics, Turkish handicrafts and weaponry fill the museum upstairs, while downstairs are temporary exhibits and a Hall of Heroes, where a life-size marble István Dobó lies amid a bodyguard of heroes of the 1552 siege in which two thousand soldiers and Eger's women repulsed a Turkish force six times their number.

Just west of town, in the Szépasszony Valley, local **vineyards** produce four types of wine – Muskotály (Muscatel), Bikavér (Bull's Blood), Leányka (medium-dry white with a hint of herbs) and Medoc Noir (rich, dark and sweet red) – and it's possible to sample all of them in the cellars here. Finding the best cellar is a matter of luck and taste, but you could try Auntie Anci's Olaszrizling at no. 28 or the Medoc Noir in Sándor Arvai's at no. 31. Cellars tend to close by 8pm. Take a

**taxi** (around 800Ft; ☎36/411-222) or tackle the twenty-minute walk back uphill to town.

**Trains** from Budapest-Keleti arrive at the station on Állomás tér; to reach the centre, walk up the road to Deák Ferenc út, catch bus #10 or #12, and get off when you see the cupola of the cathedral. The **Tourinform** office is at Bajcsy-Zsilinszky utca 9 (mid-June to Aug Mon–Fri 9am–6pm, Sat & Sun 9am–1pm; Sept to mid-June Mon–Fri 9am–5pm, Sat 9am–1pm; ☎36/517-715, ✉www.tourinform.hu/eger). For **student hostels** and **private rooms** contact Ibusz, Széchenyi utca 9 (☎36/311-451, ✉i047@ibusz.hu), or Express, Széchenyi utca 28 (☎36/427-757). Alternatively, along from the castle, there's the *Tourist Motel*, Mekcsey utca 2 (☎36/429-014; ❷); the *Hotel Minaret*, Harangöntő utca 5 (☎36/410-020, ✉hotelminaret@axelero.hu; ❹); or the classier *Senator Ház Hotel*, Dobó István tér 11 (☎36/320-466, ✉www.hotels.hu/senatorhaz; ❻). There are two **campsites**: *Autós Caraván Camping* to the north, Rákóczi út 79 (☎36/410-558; mid-April to mid-Oct; bus #10/#11), and *Tulipán* in the Szépasszony Valley (☎36/410-580; open all year). Two **restaurants** serving reasonably priced, large portions of traditional Hungarian food are *Efendi*, Kossuth utca 19, and *Fehérszarvas Vadásztanya*, Klapka utca 8, while the marvellous *Palacsintavár*, Dobó utca 9, has a terrific range of sweet and savoury pancakes. A good drinking spot is the *Egri Est Café*, Széchenyi utca 16, which occasionally has live music.

# Travel details

## Trains

Budapest to: Balatonfüred (every 1–2hr; 2hr 15min); Pécs (11 daily; 2hr 40min–3hr); Siófok (8 daily; 1hr 45min); Sopron (7 daily; 3hr); Szentendre (every 10–20min; 40min); Eger (8 daily; 1hr 50min–2hr 30min).

## Buses

Balatonfüred to: Tihany (hourly; 15min).
Budapest to: Balatonfüred (5 daily; 2hr 15min–3hr); Eger (hourly; 2hr–3hr 20min); Hévíz (5 daily; 3hr–3hr 20min); Keszthely (7 daily 3hr 15min–4hr 15min); Pécs (5 daily; 4hr); Siófok (7 daily; 1hr 35min–2hr 10min); Sopron

(5 daily; 3hr 45min); Szentendre (every 30min, 30–45min).
Keszthely to: Hévíz (every 15min; 10–20min).

## Ferries

*Usually operating April–Oct/Nov, weather permitting*
Budapest to: Szentendre (1–3 daily; 1hr 40min).
Siófok to: Tihany (4–7 daily; 1hr 20min).
Tihany to: Siófok (4–7 daily; 1hr 20min).

## Hydrofoils

*Usually operating April–Oct/Nov, weather permitting*
Budapest to: Vienna (1–2 daily; 6hr 20min).

# Ireland

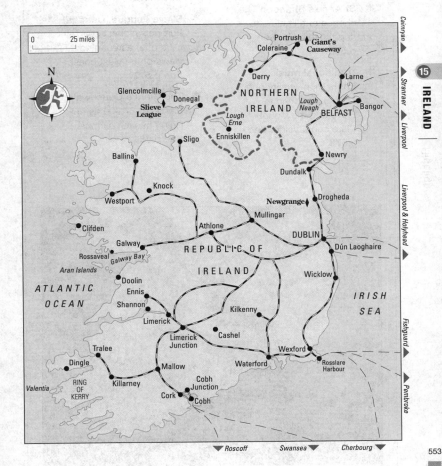

# Ireland highlights

* **The Guinness Storehouse, Dublin** High-tech temple to Ireland's national brew. See p.562

* **St Anne's Shandon** The chance of a lifetime to ring those bells. See p.568

* **Traditional music, Ennis** High-quality pub sessions abound in Ennis and the County Clare countryside. See p.572

* **The Aran Islands** Spectacular setting for some of Ireland's finest archeological remains. See p.573

* **Slieve League, Donegal** Europe's highest sea cliffs offer astounding views of the west coast. See p.577

* **The Giant's Causeway** Marvel at 37,000 astonishing basalt columns. See p.580

△ Guinness Storehouse, Dublin

# Introduction and basics

In both **Northern Ireland** and the **Republic** (respectively a part of the UK and an independent country, separated by partition in 1921), Ireland's lures are its landscape and people — the rain-hazed loughs and wild coastlines, the talent for conversation and wealth of traditional music. While economic growth has transformed Ireland's cities, the rural landscape remains relatively unchanged.

Ireland's **west** draws most visitors; its coastline and islands – especially Aran – combine vertiginous cliffs, boulder-strewn wastes and violent mountains. The interior is less spectacular, but the southern pastures and low wooded hills are the classic landscapes. Northern Ireland's principal draws are the bizarre basalt formation of the **Giant's Causeway** and the alluring, island-studded **Lough Erne**.

**Dublin** is an extraordinary mix of youthfulness and tradition, of rejuvenated Georgian squares and vibrant pubs. **Belfast**, victim of a perennial bad press, has a lively nightlife, while the cities of **Cork** and **Galway**, in particular, sparkle with new-found energy.

No introduction can cope with the complexities of Ireland's **politics**, which permeate most aspects of daily life, especially in the North. However, regardless of partisan politics, Irish hospitality is as warm as the brochures say, on both sides of the border.

## Information & maps

**Bord Fáilte** provides tourist information in the Republic, and the **Northern Ireland Tourist Board** in the North. The best **maps** are the Michelin 1:400,000 (#405) and the AA 1:350,000. The Ordnance Survey's four 1:250,000 regional Holiday Maps are useful; its 1:50,000 Discovery series is the best option for walkers.

## Money and banks

Currency in the Republic is the **euro** (€), in Northern Ireland the **pound sterling** (£). Standard **bank hours** are Mon–Fri 10am–4pm (Republic) and Mon–Fri 9.30am– 4.30pm (Northern Ireland). There are **ATMs** throughout Ireland – though not in all villages – and most accept a variety of cards.

## Communications

Main **post offices** are open Mon–Fri 9am–5.30pm, Sat 9am–1pm. Stamps and phonecards are often available in newsagents. **Public phones** are everywhere, and usually take **phonecards** (available at post offices and many newsagents); coin-operated phones are rare in rural areas. **International calls** are cheaper at weekends or after 6pm (Mon–Fri). For the **operator** in the Republic call ☎10 (domestic) or ☎114 (international); in Northern Ireland ☎100 or ☎155. To call the Republic from Northern Ireland dial ☎00353 followed by the area code (without the initial 0) and the local number (note cross-border calls are charged at the international rate). To call the North from the Republic use the code ☎048, followed by the eight-digit local number. **Internet access** is widely available.

---

### Ireland on the net

ⓦ**www.ireland.travel.ie** Bord Fáilte.
ⓦ**www.discovernorthernireland.com** Northern Ireland Tourist Board.
ⓦ**www.ireland.com** Irish Times site with up-to-date info on Dublin.
ⓦ**www.browseireland.com** Useful site with a massive number of Irish links.
ⓦ**www.ntni.org.uk** Details of the National Trust's properties in Northern Ireland.

# Getting around

In the Republic, Iarnród Éireann (@ www
.irishrail.ie) operates **trains** to most major
towns and cities. Few routes run north–
south across the country, so, although you
can get to the west coast easily by train,
you can't use the railways to explore. The
Dublin–Belfast line is the only **cross-border
service**. NI Railways (@ www.translink
.co.uk) operates just a few routes in Northern
Ireland. With the **InterRail** pass, visitors travel
free in the Republic while Irish citizens travel
half-price; with InterRail in Northern Ireland,
all visitors (including Irish citizens) travel free,
and UK citizens get a 75-percent discount.

The express **buses** of the Republic's Bus
Éireann (@ www.buseireann.ie) cover most of
the island, including several cross-border services. Fares are generally cheaper than trains,
especially midweek. Remote villages may only
have a couple of buses a week, so knowing
their times is essential – major bus stations
stock free timetables. Private buses operate
on major routes throughout the Republic and
are often cheaper than Bus Éireann. In the
North, Ulsterbus (@ www.translink.co.uk) runs
regular and reliable services.

**Cycling** is an enjoyable way to see Ireland.
In the Republic, bikes can be rented in most
towns and Raleigh is the main operator
(€20/day, €80/week; from €100 deposit,
depending on the dealer; ☎ 01/465 9659,
@ www.raleigh.ie); local dealers (including
some hostels) are cheaper. It costs an extra
€10 to carry a bike on a bus, and €3–10
on a train, though not all buses or trains
carry bikes; check in advance. In the North,
bike rental (around £15/day) is more limited;
tourist offices have lists of local operators.
Taking a bike on a bus costs half the adult
single fare (up to a maximum of £5) and, on
a train, a quarter of the adult single fare (with
no upper limit).

# Accommodation

**Hostels** run by **An Óige** (the Irish Youth
Hostel Association; @ www.irelandyha.org)
and **HINI** (Hostelling International Northern
Ireland; @ www.hini.org.uk) are affiliated to
Hostelling International. Overnight prices
start at €11–17 in the Republic and £8–12
in the North. **Independent hostels** are
very often cosy and informal; they don't
have curfews, though some cram people
in to the point of discomfort. They usually
belong to either Independent Holiday Hostels (☎ 01/836 4700, @ www.hostels-ireland
.com) or the Independent Hostels Owners
network (☎ 074/973 0130, @ www.hostel
lingireland.com). There's a few disreputa-
ble hostels around, so it's a good idea to
enquire locally before booking in at a non-
approved place. In the Republic, expect
to pay €12–15 for a dorm bed (more in
Galway, Cork and Dublin), €15–30 (rising to
€44 in some Dublin hostels) per person for
private rooms where available; in the North,
it's £7–11/£12–16.

**B&Bs** vary enormously, but most are
welcoming, warm and clean. Expect to pay
from around €28/£20 per person; en-suite
facilities are usually a little more and most
**hotels** are generally pricier. For an extra €4
(Republic) or £2 (Northern Ireland), you can
book through tourist offices or by phoning
the international toll-free line ☎ +800/668
668 66. Booking ahead is always advisable
during high season and major festivals.

**Camping** usually costs around €10 a
night in the Republic, £7 in the North. In
out-of-the-way places nobody minds where
you pitch. Farmers in popular tourist areas
may ask for a small fee to use their land,
but other than this you can expect to camp
for free in areas where there's no official
site. Some hostels also let you camp on
their land for around €8/£5 per person.

## The Irish language

Though **Irish** is the first language of the Republic, you'll rarely hear it spoken outside
the areas officially designated as *Gaeltacht* ("Irish-speaking"), namely West Cork,
West Kerry, Connemara, some of Mayo and Donegal, and a tiny part of Meath. However, two important words you may encounter sometimes appear on the doors of pub
toilets – *Fir* (for men) and *Mná* (for women).

# Food and drink

Irish **food** is meat-orientated. B&Bs usually provide a "traditional" **Irish breakfast** of sausages, bacon and eggs, although many now offer vegetarian alternatives. **Pub lunch** staples are usually meat or fish and two veg, sometimes with a few veggie options, while specifically vegetarian places are sparse outside major cities and popular tourist areas. All towns have fast-food outlets, but old-fashioned fish-and-chips is a better bet, especially on the coast. For the occasional treat, there are some very good seafood restaurants, particularly along the southwest and west coasts. Most towns have daytime cafés serving a selection of hot dishes, salads, soups, sandwiches and cakes.

Especially in rural areas, the **pub** is the social heart of the community and the focus for the proverbial **craic** (pronounced "crack"), a particular blend of Irish fun involving good company, witty conversation and laughter, frequently against a backdrop of music. The classic Irish drink is **Guinness**, best in Dublin, home of the brewery, while the Cork stouts Beamish and Murphy's have their devotees. For English-style keg **bitter**, try Smithwicks, while **lager** brands include Carlsberg, Harp and Budweiser. Irish **whiskeys** may seem expensive, but the measures are large: try Paddy, Jameson's, Powers or Bushmills. In the Republic of Ireland, **smoking** is now banned in all indoor public places, including pubs, cafés and restaurants.

# Opening hours and holidays

**Opening hours** are roughly Mon–Sat 9am–6pm, with some late evenings (usually Thurs or Fri), half-days and Sunday opening. In rural areas, hours are often more flexible, with later closing times. The main **museums and attractions** will normally be open regular shop hours, though, outside the cities, many only open during the summer. Possession of a **student card** often gives reduced entrance charges and, if you're visiting sites run by the Heritage Service in the Republic (Ⓦ www.heritageireland.ie), it's worth buying a **Heritage Card** (€20, students €7.50) which provides a year's unlimited admission. **Public holidays** in 2006 in the Republic are: Jan 1, St Patrick's Day (March 17), Easter Mon, May 1, June 5, Aug 7, Oct 30, Dec 25 & 26. In the North: Jan 1, St Patrick's Day (March 17), Good Fri, Easter Mon, May 1 & 29, July 12, Aug 28, Dec 25 & 26.

# Emergencies

The Republic's police are known as the **Gardaí** (pronounced "gar-dee"), while the **PSNI** (Police Service of Northern Ireland) operates in the North. **Hospitals** and medical facilities are high quality; you'll rarely be far from a hospital, and both Northern Ireland and the Republic are within the European Health Insurance Card scheme (formerly E111). Most **pharmacies** open standard shop hours, though in large towns some may stay open as late as 10pm; they dispense only a limited range of drugs without a doctor's prescription.

> ## Emergency numbers
>
> In the Republic ☎ 112 or ☎ 999; in Northern Ireland ☎ 999.

# Dublin

Set on the River Liffey's banks, **DUBLIN** is splendidly monumental, but also a youthful city with a lively nightlife. Ireland's vibrant economy has brought extensive urban regeneration, but there's still much deprivation here. It's this collision of the old and the new, the slick and the shabby, which makes Dublin the exciting, aggravating, energetic place it is.

Dublin began as the Viking trading post Dubh Linn (Dark Pool), which soon amalgamated with the Celtic settlement of **Baile Átha Cliath** (Town of the Hurdle Ford) – still the Irish name for the city. Most early buildings were wooden, so only the two cathedrals, part of the castle and several churches are pre-seventeenth century. The city's fabric is essentially **Georgian**, when the Anglo-Irish gentry began to invest their income in new townhouses. After the 1801 Act of Union Dublin entered a long economic decline, but remained the focus of much of the agitation that eventually led to independence. The 1829 Emancipation Act secured a limited role for Catholics in the administration of the city, and Dublin was later the birthplace of the Gaelic League which helped catalyse an Irish national consciousness by nurturing the native language and culture. The long struggle for freedom reached a head during the **Easter Rising** of 1916, a rebellion commemorated by a host of monuments in Dublin, and culminated in the bitterly fought, but successful War of Independence of 1919–1921.

## Arrival, information and city transport

**Trains** terminate at either **Connolly Station** on the Northside, or **Heuston Station** on the Southside. All Bus Éireann **coaches** arrive at Busáras, the main bus station off Beresford Place, just behind The Custom House; private buses use a variety of central locations. From the **airport**, six miles north, Airlink buses #747 and #748 run to Busáras (every 10–20 min; €5 single, €9 return; 30min), and the AerDart service #A1 (every 15 min; €5.50 single) connects with the DART railway at Howth Junction, or there are regular Citybus services #16A, #41, #41B & #41C (every 10–20 min; €1.75). **Ferries** dock at either **Dún Laoghaire**, nine miles southeast, connected to the centre by the **DART** railway (every 20 min; €1.90; 20min), or at the closer **Dublin Port** where an unnumbered Citybus service (€2.50; 15min) meets arriving ferries; through-coaches from Britain usually drop you at Busáras.

The main **tourist office** is on Suffolk Street, off College Green (Mon–Sat 9am–5.30/7pm; July & Aug also Sun 10.30am–3pm; ⓦwww.visitdublin.com), with branches at 14 Upper O'Connell St, the Dún Laoghaire ferry terminal and the airport. USITNow on Aston Quay, by O'Connell Bridge (Mon–Fri 9.30am–6.30pm, Thurs till 8pm, Sat 9.30am–5pm; ⓣ01/602 1600, ⓦwww.usitnow.ie), also books B&Bs during the summer and includes a travel agency offering student discounts. For what's-on **listings**, see the free *Event Guide*, *In Dublin* and *Totally Dublin* or, for music events, *Hot Press* (€3.50).

Dublin has an extensive **bus** network and all buses are **exact fare only**. Fares are €0.90–1.85, a one-day bus pass is €5, with a pack of five one-day passes costing only €16, or there are bus and rail passes (including DART) for one day/three days (€7.70/€15). Free bus timetables are available from Dublin Bus, 59 Upper O'Connell St. The **LUAS tram** service operates along two routes: from Connolly Station to Tallaght via Abbey Street to Heuston Station, and from St Stephen's Green to Sandyford. Tickets cost €1.30–€2 single, €2.50–€3.80 return. A one-day pass is €4.50 and a combined bus/LUAS one-day pass €6. The **DART railway** links Howth and Malahide to the north of the city with Bray to the south via Pearse, Tara St and Connolly stations in the city centre (maximum fare €3.50). **Nitelink** buses cost €4–6, depending on your destination.

# Accommodation

Although Dublin has stacks of **accommodation**, anywhere central will probably be full at weekends, around St Patrick's Day (March 17), at Easter and in high summer so it's always wise to **book ahead**. **Hotels** are generally expensive, and sometimes no more comfortable than good **B&Bs**, but off-season and mid-week reductions can be considerable. Most of the better B&Bs are in the suburbs, but this isn't a problem, given the good public transport. All hotels and B&Bs listed have en-suite facilities. All **hostels** listed provide free breakfast, unless stated.

## Hostels

**Abbey Court** 29 Bachelors Walk ☎01/878 0700, ⓦwww.abbey-court.com. Well-equipped and with all rooms en-suite. Dorms €23, rooms ⓺

**Avalon House** 55 Aungier St ☎01/475 0001, ⓦwww.avalon-house.ie. Friendly, if sometimes noisy, hostel with cramped dorms but plenty of twin or four-bedded rooms, and a good café. Dorms €20, rooms ⓹

**Brewery Hostel** 22–23 Thomas St ☎01/473 8600, ⓔbreweryh@indigo.ie. Housed in a fine converted library, this small hostel often has space when others are full. Breakfast not provided. Dorms €21, rooms ⓹

**Dublin International Youth Hostel** 61 Mountjoy St ☎01/830 1766. An Óige's Dublin flagship, occupying a former convent, this massive, well-equipped hostel houses 293 beds, including a few private rooms, in a rather dreary Northside location. Dorms €18, rooms ⓸

**Globetrotters Tourist Hotel** 46 Gardiner St Lower ☎01/873 5893, ⓦwww.globetrottersdublin .com. Upmarket hostel where security-locked dorms and individual bed lights make for a peaceful night's sleep. Also some spacious private rooms. Dorms €25, rooms ⓻

**Goin' My Way** 15 Talbot St ☎01/878 8484, ⓔgoinmyway@esatclear.ie. Small, family-run, value-for-money place near O'Connell St. Its midnight curfew makes this one of Dublin's quieter hostels. Dorms €15, rooms ⓷

**Isaacs Hostel** 2–5 Frenchman's Lane ☎01/855 6215, ⓦwww.isaacs.ie. Housed in an eighteenth-century wine warehouse with its own restaurant on site, offering eight- and ten-bed dorms and a few cosy twins, none en-suite. Dorms €18, rooms ⓺

**Jacobs Inn** 21–28 Talbot Place ☎01/855 5660, ⓦwww.isaacs.ie. Sister hostel to *Isaacs* offering comfortable accommodation, a restaurant and Internet access. Dorms €22, rooms ⓺

**Kinlay House Christchurch** 2–12 Lord Edward St ☎01/679 6644, ⓦwww.kinlayhouse.ie. Bright and cheerful hostel offering doubles, quadruples and six-bed dorms with en-suite. Café, laundry facilities and kitchen too. Dorms €20, rooms ⓺

**Litton Lane Hostel** 2–4 Litton Lane ☎01/872 8389, ⓦwww.irish-hostel.com. This converted warehouse off Bachelor's Walk on the Northside has excellent showers and good security. Dorms €25, rooms ⓺

## Guesthouses, B&Bs and hotels

**Clifden Guesthouse** 32 Gardiner Place ☎01/874 6364, ⓦwww.clifdenhouse.com. Friendly guesthouse in a slightly run-down Northside street half-a-mile north of the city centre. ⓼

**Egan's Guesthouse** 7/9 Iona Park, Glasnevin ☎01/830 3611, ⓦwww.eganshouse.com. Comfortable Northside option with well-appointed rooms, just a mile from the city centre. ⓻

**Harding Hotel** Copper Alley, Fishamble St ☎01/679 6500, ⓦwww.hardinghotel.ie. Extremely popular, well-furnished budget hotel in a prime Christchurch location. Breakfast extra. ⓻

**Jurys Inn Christchurch** Christchurch Place ☎01/454 0000, ⓦwww.bookajurysinn.com. Bang opposite Christ Church Cathedral, this large modern hotel has rooms capable of accommodating up to three adults, making it an economic option for sharers. ⓼

**Marian Guesthouse** 21 Upper Gardiner St ☎01/874 4129, ⓦwww.marianguesthouse.ie. Friendly, good-value, family-run guest house about a mile north of the city centre. ⓹

# The City

Dublin's fashionable **Southside** can lay claim to the city's trendy bars, restaurants and shops – especially in the cobbled alleys of buzzing **Temple Bar** leading down to the **River Liffey** – and most of its historic monuments, centred on **Trinity College**, **Grafton Street** and **St Stephen's Green**. But the **Northside**, with its long-standing working-class neighbourhoods and inner-city communities,

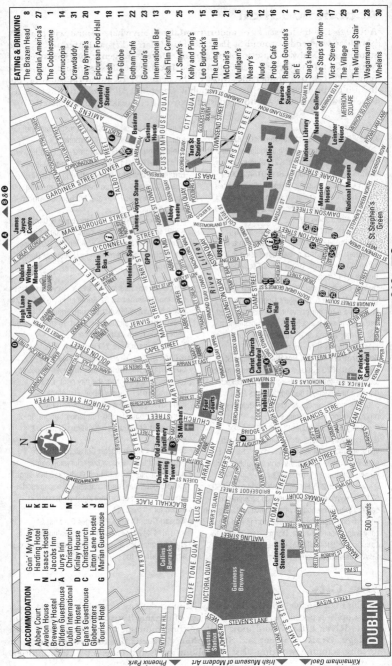

**DUBLIN**

**ACCOMMODATION**

| | |
|---|---|
| Abbey Court | E |
| Avalon House | K |
| Brewery Hostel | H |
| Clifden Guesthouse | F |
| Dublin International Youth Hostel | A |
| Egan's Guesthouse | D |
| Globetrotters | C |
| | |

| | |
|---|---|
| Goin' My Way | I |
| Harding Hotel | N |
| Isaacs Hostel | L |
| Jacobs Inn | A |
| Jurys Inn Christchurch | M |
| Kinlay House Christchurch | D |
| Litton Lane Hostel | K |
| Marian Guesthouse | J |
| Tourist Hotel | B |

**EATING & DRINKING**

| | |
|---|---|
| The Brazen Head | 8 |
| Captain America's | 27 |
| The Cobblestone | 1 |
| Cornucopia | 14 |
| Crawdaddy | 31 |
| Davy Byrne's | 20 |
| Epicurean Food Hall | 4 |
| Fresh | 18 |
| The Globe | 11 |
| Gotham Café | 22 |
| Govinda's | 23 |
| International Bar | 13 |
| Irish Film Centre | 9 |
| J.J. Smyth's | 25 |
| Kelly and Ping's | 3 |
| Leo Burdock's | 15 |
| The Long Hall | 19 |
| McDaid's | 21 |
| Mulligan's | 6 |
| Neary's | 26 |
| Nude | 12 |
| Probe Café | 16 |
| Radha Govinda's | 2 |
| Sin É | 7 |
| Stag's Head | 10 |
| The Steps of Rome | 24 |
| Vicar Street | 17 |
| The Village | 29 |
| The Winding Stair | 5 |
| Wagamama | 28 |
| Whelans | 30 |

vaunts itself as the real heart of the city. Across the bridges from Temple Bar are the shopping districts around **O'Connell Street**, where you'll find a taste of the old Dublin. You'll also find here a fair amount of graceful – if slightly shabby – residential streets and squares, with plenty of interest in the museums and cultural centres around **Parnell Square**.

## The Southside

The Vikings sited their assembly and burial ground near what is now **College Green**, where **Trinity College** is the most famous landmark. Founded in 1592, it played a major role in the development of a Protestant Anglo-Irish tradition: right up to 1966, Catholics had to obtain a special dispensation to study here, though nowadays they make up roughly seventy percent of the students. The stern grey- and mellow red-brick buildings are ranged around cobbled quadrangles in a grander version of the quads at Oxford and Cambridge. **The Old Library** (Mon–Sat 9.30am–5pm, Sun 9.30am/noon–4.30pm; €7.50; ⊛www.tcd.ie/library) owns numerous Irish manuscripts. Pride of place goes to the ninth-century **Book of Kells**, which totals 680 pages but was rebound in the 1950s into four volumes, of which two are on show at any one time, one open at a completely illuminated page, the other at a text page, itself adorned with patterns and fantastic animals intertwined with the capitals. The **Book of Durrow** is equally interesting, being the first of the great Irish illuminated manuscripts, dating from between 650 and 680, and has, unusually, a whole page given over to abstract ornament. In the Arts block, the **Dublin Experience** (late May to early Oct daily 10am–5pm; €4.20) provides an audiovisual account of the city's history.

Just south of here, the streets around pedestrianized **Grafton Street** frame Dublin's quality shopping area – chic, sophisticated and expensive. At its southern extremity lies **St Stephen's Green**, whose pleasant gardens and pools are the focus of Georgian city planning. Running parallel to Grafton Street, Kildare Street harbours the imposing Leinster House, built in 1745 as the Duke of Leinster's townhouse, and now the seat of the Irish parliament, the **Dáil** (pronounced "doyle"). Alongside is the **National Museum** (Tues–Sat 10am–5pm, Sun 2–5pm; free; ⊛www.museum.ie), the repository of the treasures of ancient Ireland. Much of its prehistoric gold was found in peat bogs, as were a sacrificed human and the Lurgan Longboat. The Treasury and the Viking exhibition display such master-pieces as the Ardagh Chalice and Tara Brooch – perhaps the greatest piece of Irish metalwork – and St Patrick's Bell.

Around the block, the other side of Leinster House overlooks **Merrion Square**, the finest Georgian plaza in Dublin. No. 1 was once the home of Oscar Wilde, and a flamboyant statue on the green opposite shows the writer draped insouciantly over a rock; on Sundays the square's railings are used by artists selling their works. Here, the **National Gallery** (Mon–Sat 9.30am–5.30pm, Thurs until 8.30pm, Sun noon–5.30pm; free; ⊛www.nationalgallery.ie) owns a fair spread of European old masters and French Impressionists, but the real draw is the trove of Irish paintings, best of which is the permanent exhibition devoted to Ireland's best-known painter, Jack B. Yeats, tracing his development from Dublin illustrator to expressionist interpreter of Connemara sea- and landscapes.

## From Temple bar to Kilmainham

Dame Street, leading west from College Green, marks the southern edge of the **Temple Bar** quarter, whose fashionable restaurants, pubs, boutiques and arts centres make this one of the liveliest parts of town.

Uphill, tucked away behind City Hall, **Dublin Castle** (Mon–Fri 10am–4.45pm, Sat & Sun 2–4.45pm; €4.50; ⊛www.dublincastle.ie) was founded by the Nor-mans, and symbolized British power over Ireland for seven hundred years. Though parts date back to 1207, it was largely rebuilt in the eighteenth century. Tours of the State Apartments reveal much about the tastes and foibles of the viceroys and while you can see the lovely Chapel Royal, the real highlights are the excavations of Norman and Viking fortifications in the Undercroft. The Clock Tower building now houses the **Chester Beatty Library** (Mon–Fri 10am–5pm, Sat 11am–5pm, Sun 1–5pm; Oct–April closed Mon; free; ⊛www.cbl.ie), a sumptuous and massive collection of books, objects and paintings amassed by Sir Arthur Chester Beatty on his travels around Europe and Asia. Over the brow of Dublin Hill, **Christ Church Cathedral** (daily 9.45/10am–5pm; €5; ⊛www.cccdub.ie) is a resonant monument built between 1172 and 1240 and heavily restored in the 1870s. The north wall of the nave has leaned eighteen inches outwards since the roof collapsed in 1562. The crypt museum now houses a small selection of the Cathedral's treasures. The former Synod Hall, connected to Christ Church by an overhead bridge, contains **Dublinia** (daily 10/11am–4/5pm; €6; ⊛www.dublinia.ie), an array of presentations, models and tableaux depicting Dublin's medieval past and Viking and Norman artefacts excavated at nearby Wood Quay. Five minutes' walk south from Christ Church is Dublin's other great Norman edifice, **St Patrick's Cathedral** (daily 9am–5/6pm; Nov–Feb Sun closes 3pm; €4.50; ⊛www.stpatrickscathedral .ie), founded in 1191, and replete with relics of Jonathan Swift, its dean from 1713 to 1747. Near the entrance are memorials to both him and Esther Johnson, the "Stella" with whom he had a passionate though apparently platonic relationship, while the north pulpit contains Swift's writing table, chair, portrait and death mask. Handel's *Messiah* received its first performance here in 1742.

A mile west of Christ Church, the **Guinness Brewery** covers 64 acres on either side of James's Street. Founded in 1759, Guinness has the distinction of being the world's largest single beer-exporting company, dispatching some 300 million pints a year. Set in the centre of the brewery, the **Guinness Storehouse** (daily 9.30am–5/9pm; €14.50; ⊛www.guinness-storehouse.com) presents a comprehensive account of the history of the famous stout, visits ending with reputedly the best pint of Guinness in Dublin, in the panoramic *Gravity* bar with superb views over the city.

Regular buses (#26, #51, #79 and #90) run along The Quays to Heuston Station from where it's a five-minute walk to the **Royal Hospital Kilmainham**, Ireland's first Neoclassical building, dating from 1680, which now houses the **Irish Museum of Modern Art** (Tues–Sat 10am–5.30pm, Sun noon–5.30pm; free; ⊛www.modernart.ie), with excellent temporary exhibitions. Exiting via the west wing and following the avenue to the gateway, you'll emerge near **Kilmainham Gaol** (daily 9.30/10am–4/5pm; €5; ⊛www.heritageireland.ie), where the British incarcerated patriots such as Charles Stewart Parnell, Pádraig Pearse and James Connolly (the last two were executed here). A superb museum on both political history and crime sets the tone for guided tours of the gaol.

## The Northside

Crossing O'Connell Bridge, the view of the Georgian **Custom House** downstream is marred by a railway viaduct, and many of the handsome buildings on **O'Connell Street**, the main avenue on the Northside, have been spoiled by tacky facades. Halfway up O'Connell Street looms the **General Post Office** (Mon–Sat 8am–8pm; free), the insurgents' headquarters in the 1916 Easter Rising; only the frontage survived the fighting, and its pillars are still scarred by bullets. Across the road on the corner of Essex Street North is a **statue of James Joyce**. At the same junction, where the city's most famous landmark once stood, Nelson's Pillar (it was blown up by the IRA on the fiftieth anniversary of the Easter Rising in 1966), stands a huge, illuminated stainless-steel spike – the **Monument of Light** – representing the city's hopes for the new millennium.

At the northern end of O'Connell Street lies Parnell Square, one of the first of Dublin's Georgian squares. Its plain red-brick houses are broken by the grey stone **Hugh Lane Municipal Art Gallery** (due to reopen March 2006; ☎01/ 222 5550, ⊛www.hughlane.ie), once the Earl of Charlemont's townhouse and the focus of fashionable Dublin. The gallery exhibits work by Irish and international masters, and features a reconstruction of Francis Bacon's working studio. Almost next door, the **Dublin Writers Museum** (Mon–Sat 10am–5/6pm, Sun 11am–5pm; €6.50; ⊛www.visitdublin.com) whisks you through Irish literary history from early Christian writings up to Samuel Beckett. Two blocks east of Parnell Square, at 35 North Great George's St, the **James Joyce Centre** (Mon–Sat 9.30am–5pm, Sun 12.30–5pm; €5; ⊛www.jamesjoyce.ie) runs intriguing walking tours of the novelist's haunts (€11; ☎01/878 8547).

Ten minutes west of O'Connell Street, on Church Street, stands **St Michan's Church** (March–Oct Mon–Fri 10am–12.30pm & 2–4.30pm, Sat 10am–12.45pm; Nov–Feb Mon–Fri 12.30–3.30pm, Sat 10am–12.45pm; €3.50), the oldest on the Northside, founded in 1095. The crypt is famous for its "mummified" bodies, preserved by the constant temperature and dry air pervaded by methane gas. One, thought to have been a Crusader, dates back seven hundred years. At the bottom of Church Street, on the Liffey bank, stands **The Four Courts**. Like The Custom House down river, it's a grand eighteenth-century edifice by James Gandon that was restored after serious damage during the Civil War, which followed the 1921 treaty of independence.

One block west on Bow Street is the **Old Jameson Distillery** (daily 9.30am– 6pm; €8.75; ⊛www.irishwhiskeytours.ie); tours cover the history and method of distilling what the Irish called *uisce beatha* (anglicized to whiskey and meaning "water of life") – which differs from Scotch whisky by being thrice-distilled and lacking a peaty undertone – and end with a tasting session involving different types of whiskey, Scotch and bourbon. Outside, a lift conveys you to the top of the old distillery **chimney** (Mon–Sat 10am–5.30pm, Sun 11am–5.30pm; €5), where an observation platform provides panoramic views of the city.

Further west on Benburb Street is the **Collins Barracks** (Tues–Sat 10am–5pm, Sun 2–5pm; free; ⊛www.museum.ie), housing the National Museum's decorative arts collection and occasional special exhibitions. Finally, there's **Phoenix Park**, one of the world's largest urban parks (bus #10 from O'Connell Street or #25 from Wellington Quay); originally priory land, it's now home to the Presidential Lodge and attractions such as **Dublin Zoo** (Mon–Sat 9.30am–4/6pm, Sun 10.30am–4/6pm; €13; ⊛www.dublinzoo.ie). The **visitor centre** (daily 10am–5/6pm; €2.75; ⊛www.heritageireland.ie) covers the park's history and wildlife and tickets include a tour of the adjacent **Ashtown Castle**, a seventeenth-century tower house.

## Eating, drinking and entertainment

A wide range of **food** is on offer in Dublin. Many **cafés** and **restaurants** serve lunch at much lower prices than they'll charge in the evening (when it's wise to reserve a table), while Dublin's eight hundred **pubs** offer anything from soup and sandwiches to a full carvery. The **music** scene – much of which is pub-based – is volatile, so it's always best to check the listings magazines (see p.558). The best clubs can be found around Temple Bar and on Harcourt Street, off St Stephen's Green. Dublin's **theatres** are among the finest in Europe.

### Restaurants and cafés

**Captain America's** 44 Grafton St. Reasonably priced burgers, steaks and seafood served amidst a host of rock'n'roll memorabilia.

**Cornucopia** 21 Wicklow St. One of the city's few vegetarian cafés and highly popular too. Closed Sun.

**Epicurean Food Hall** Liffey Street Lower. Offers a host of dining opportunities including Asian street food, fish and chips or traditional lunches and dinners.

**Fresh** 2nd floor, Powerscourt Townhouse Centre, off Grafton St. Delicious vegetarian food, at tables overlooking the atrium. Closed Sun.

**Gotham Café** 8 South Anne St. Lively place offering an extensive and reasonably priced global menu.

**Govinda's** 4 Aungier St. Huge helpings of dhal and rice and tasty vegetarian curries plus daily veggie specials, served by very friendly teams. The sister restaurant is *Radha Govinda's*, 84 Abbey Street Middle.

**Irish Film Centre** 6 Eustace St, Temple Bar. Delicious, inventive food in elegantly minimal surroundings. Watch a film or just soak up the atmosphere.

**Kelly and Ping's** Smithfield Village. Splendid Thai-style restaurant next to the Old Jameson Distillery offering an excellent, filling early-bird menu.

**Leo Burdock's** 2 Werburgh St. Dublin's best fish-and-chips – takeaway only. Closed Sun.

**Nude** 21 Suffolk St. Canteen-style café serving hot and cold wraps, panini, soups and salads.

**Probe Café** Market Arcade, South Great George's St. Excellent, reasonably priced café offering everything from Irish stew to fajitas. Reductions for students. Closed Sun.

**The Steps of Rome** 1 Chatham Court. Limited seating area, though has great slabs of highly original pizza available to take away. Good vegetarian options. If it's full, try its larger branch at St Andrew's Lane.

**Wagamama** South King St. Japanese-style noodle dishes served in a near-clinical atmosphere, but great soups, dumplings and juices.

**The Winding Stair** 40 Lower Ormond Quay. Quaint bookshop downstairs, wholefood café and coffee shop upstairs with great-value hearty lunches.

## Pubs

**Davy Byrne's** 21 Duke St. An object of pilgrimage for *Ulysses* fans, since Leopold Bloom stopped here for a snack. Despite the pastel-toned refit, it's still a good pub.

**The Globe** South Great George's St. Trendy hangout with loud music. Backs onto *RiRá*, an intimate but very lively club.

**The Long Hall** South Great George's St. Victorian pub encrusted with mirrors and antique clocks.

**McDaid's** 3 Harry St. Excellent Guinness in Brendan Behan's former local.

**Mulligan's** 8 Poolbeg St. Down-to-earth, but always packed in the evenings; many claim that it serves the best Guinness in Dublin.

**Neary's** 1 Chatham St. Plenty of bevelled glass and shiny wood, plus Liberty-print curtains to show some style appropriate for its theatrical clientele.

**Sin É** Ormond Quay Upper. Cool and popular Northside bar with a great range of beers and splendid soundtracks.

**Stag's Head** Dame Court, Dame St, almost opposite the Central Bank. Wonderfully intimate pub, full of mahogany, stained glass and mirrors. It does good lunches, too.

## Music pubs and venues

**The Brazen Head** 20 Lower Bridge St. The oldest pub in Dublin, with traditional music nightly from 9.30pm.

**The Cobblestone** 77 North King St, Smithfield. Popular old-fashioned bar with nightly traditional music sessions.

**Crawdaddy** 35 Harcourt St. New intimate venue with an eclectic programme of live music.

**International Bar** 23 Wicklow St. Large saloon with rock bands and a comedy club upstairs or in the cellar.

**J.J. Smyth's** 12 Aungier St. One of the few places to catch local jazz and blues talent.

**Vicar Street** 58–59 Thomas St, ⊛www.vicar-street.com. One of the city's finest music venues, offering a varied programme of major music and comedy acts, plus assorted club nights.

**The Village** 26 Wexford St. Excellent venue with an eclectic schedule and a late club (Thurs–Sat).

**Whelans** 25 Wexford St. Very lively place with nightly gigs and frequent bar extensions.

## Clubs

**Gaiety Theatre** South King St. The theatre transforms itself into one of Dublin's major clubs on Friday and Saturday nights, with DJs on three levels and the city's latest-serving bar.

**The Hub** 23–24 Eustace St. Plenty of indie-inspired rock bands in the evening, plus punk to funk club nights into the small hours.

**Red Box/POD** 35 Harcourt St. Two hugely popular clubs, housed in an old railway station, offering a variety of different regular nights and events.

**RiRá** Dame Court. Everything from funky house to eclectic electrics – one of the city's longest-standing venues.

**Spirit** Middle Abbey Street. The club's Revelation on Fridays, with three local DJs plus international guests, is one of Dublin's hottest nights out.

## Theatres

**Abbey Theatre** Lower Abbey St ☎01/878 7222, ⊛www.abbeytheatre.ie. Founded in 1904 by W.B. Yeats and Lady Gregory, the Abbey's golden era featured Yeats, J.M. Synge and later Sean O'Casey as house playwrights. The building also contains the Peacock Theatre, which stages experimental shows.

**Gate Theatre** Cavendish Row, Parnell Square ☎01/874 4045, ⊛www.gatetheatre.ie. Another of Dublin's literary institutions, staging classic and modern Irish theatre.

**Project** 39 Essex St East, Temple Bar ☎01/679 6622. This long-standing arts venue continues to mount experimental and politically sensitive theatre.

## Listings

**Bike rental** Cycle Ways, 185 Parnell St ☏01/873 4748.

**Embassies** Australia, Fitzwilliam House, Wilton Terrace ☏01/664 5300; Canada, 64–65 St Stephen's Green ☏01/417 5000; UK, 31–33 Merrion Rd ☏01/205 3700; US, 42 Elgin Rd, Ballsbridge ☏01/668 8777.

**Exchange** Thomas Cook, 118 Grafton St; General Post Office; most city centre banks.

**Hospitals** Southside: St James's, James St ☏01/410 3000; Northside: Mater Misericordiae, Eccles St ☏01/885 8888.

**Internet cafés** Central Cybercafé, 6 Grafton St; Global Internet Café, 8 Lower O'Connell St; Oz Cyber Café, 39 Abbey St Upper; Planet Cyber Café, 13 St Andrew's St.

**Laundry** All American Launderette, Wicklow Court, South Great George's St.

**Left luggage** Busáras, Heuston and Connolly stations.

**Pharmacies** Dame Street Pharmacy, 16 Dame St; O'Connell's, 55 O'Connell St.

**Police** Harcourt Terrace ☏01/666 6666.

**Post offices** O'Connell St; St Andrew's St.

## North of Dublin: Newgrange and Drogheda

The main N1 Belfast road and the railway pass through **Drogheda**, from where it's a short bus hop to the great **NEWGRANGE** tumulus (daily 9/9.30am–5/7pm; €5.50; ⓦwww.heritageireland.ie), entered by the **Brú na Bóinne** visitor centre. Raised around five thousand years ago and completely restored, the mound of earth and loose stone covers the chambers of a remarkable **passage grave**, surrounded by a unique outer ring of standing stones, of which only twelve uprights now remain. The most intriguing feature is the **roof-box**, several feet in from the tunnel mouth and containing a slit through which, at the **winter solstice**, the rays of the rising sun fill the chamber with a sudden blaze of orange light. The entry passage, about three feet wide, leads into the **central chamber**, where the stones are carved with intricate decoration.

**DROGHEDA** itself is a lively town whose layout reflects its medieval origins and is best viewed from the summit of **Millmount** hill, south of the River Boyne. The **Millmount Museum** (Mon–Sat 10am–6pm, Sun 2.30–5.30pm; €4.50; ⓦwww.millmount.net) is one of Ireland's finest town museums and contains a wealth of exhibits and artefacts recounting the area's history. The **tourist office** (Mon–Sat 10am–1pm & 2–5pm; March–Oct also Sun 11.45am–5pm; ☏041/983 7070, ⓦwww.drogheda-tourism.com) is in the **bus station** on Donore Road – the **train station** is ten minutes' walk to the east, off Dublin Road. A good central **place to stay** is the *Green Door* hostel, 47 John St (☏041/983 4422, ⓦwww .hostel-lodge.com; dorms ⑤). The centre offers plenty of **eating** options, especially along West Street where *Weavers* cooks good-value meals and *Lucky Ned Peppers* serves Mexican specials. The most atmospheric **pub** is *Carbery's* on North Strand, while *Peter Matthews* on Laurence Street has music most nights.

# From Wexford to Cork

The southeast is Ireland's sunniest and driest corner, and the region's medieval and Anglo-Norman history is richly concentrated in **Kilkenny**, a bustling, quaint inland town, while to the west, at the heart of County Tipperary is the **Rock of Cashel**, a spectacular natural formation topped with Christian buildings from virtually every period. In the southwest, **Cork** is both relaxed and spirited, the perfect place to ease you into the exhilarations of the west coast.

**Ferries** from Wales (Fishguard and Pembroke) and France (Cherbourg and Roscoff) arrive at **ROSSLARE HARBOUR**, on the southeastern corner of

Ireland. Daily trains leave here for Wexford, Waterford and Dublin, and there are also daily bus services to Dublin and the west. The ferry terminal's **tourist desk** is open for incoming sailings (May–Sept, except early mornings; ☎053/33622); otherwise, try the Kilrane tourist office, just over a mile from the dock along the N25 (May–Sept daily 11am–8pm; Oct–April Tues–Sun 2–8pm; ☎053/33232). The nearest **hostel** is thirteen miles away in **WEXFORD** – *Kirwan House Hostel*, 3 Mary St (☎053/21208, ✉kirwanhouse@eircom.net; dorms €16, rooms ❸).

# Kilkenny

**KILKENNY** is Ireland's finest medieval city, its castle set above the broad sweep of the River Nore and its narrow streets laced with carefully maintained buildings. In 1641, the city became virtual capital of Ireland, with the founding of a parliament known as the Confederation of Kilkenny. The power of this short-lived attempt to unite resistance to English persecution of Catholics had greatly diminished by the time Cromwell's wreckers arrived in 1650. Kilkenny never recovered its prosperity, but enough remains to indicate its former importance.

The **bus and train stations** are just north of the centre off John Street. Following this road over the river and climbing Rose Inn Street leads to the **tourist office** (Mon–Sat 9am–5/7pm, July & Aug also Sun 11am–1pm & 2–5pm; ☎056/775 1500, ⊛www.southeastireland.com), based in the sixteenth-century **Shee Alms House**. Left at the top of Rose Inn Street is the broad **Parade**, which leads up to the castle. To the right, the High Street passes the eighteenth-century **Tholsel**, once the city's financial centre and now the town hall. Beyond is **Parliament Street**, the main thoroughfare, where the **Rothe House** (Mon–Sat 10.30am/1–5pm, Sun 3–5pm; Nov–Feb closed Sun; €3) provides a unique example of an Irish Tudor merchant's home, comprising three separate houses linked by cobbled courtyards. This end of town's highlight is the thirteenth-century **St Canice's Cathedral** (Mon–Sat 9/10am–1pm & 2–4/6pm, Sun 2–4/6pm; €3), which has a fine array of sixteenth-century monuments, many in black Kilkenny limestone. The **round tower** next to the church (same hours; €2; combined ticket with cathedral €4) is the only remnant of a monastic settlement reputedly founded by St Canice in the sixth century; there are superb views from the top. It's the imposing **Castle**, though, which defines Kilkenny (tours daily: April–Sept 9.30/10.30am–5/7pm; Oct–March 10.30am–12.45pm; €5; ⊛www.heritageireland.ie). Seat of the Butler family, the castle was founded in the twelfth century and radically altered by the nineteenth century. Its library, drawing room, bedrooms and Long Gallery of family portraits are open for viewing, as is the **Butler Gallery**, housing exhibitions of modern art.

## Practicalities

Kilkenny is well served by **B&Bs**, although advance booking is advisable in summer, especially during festival weeks in June and August. Near the centre is *Celtic House*, 18 Michael St (☎056/776 2249, ⊛www.celtic-house-bandb.com; ❻), and the equally pleasant *Banville's*, 49 Walkin St (☎056/777 0182, ✉mbanville@eircom.net; ❺). The *Kilkenny Tourist* **hostel**, 35 Parliament St (☎056/776 3541, ✉kilkennyhostel@eircom.net; dorms €16, rooms ❸), is an excellent budget option and there's **camping** at *Tree Grove* (☎056/777 0302), a mile south of the city on the R700. Among popular **eating-places**, *Café Sol* (closed Sun) on William Street is great for lazy breakfasts and wholesome lunches, while *M.L. Dore*, 65 High St, serves inexpensive sandwiches and full meals. *Kyteler's Inn*, St Kieran Street, provides food in medieval surroundings, and *Billy Byrne's* on John Street has fine bar lunches. For **traditional music** try *John Cleere's* or *The Pumphouse*, both on Parliament Street, or *Anna Conda* on Watergate. *Tynan's* on the Bridge is worth visiting for its cosy Victorian interior. The weekly *Kilkenny People* has information about what's on. The town is renowned for The Cat

Laughs comedy **festival** in June (@www.thecatlaughs.com) and its Arts Festival in August (@www.kilkennyarts.ie).

# The Rock of Cashel

Approached from north or west, the **ROCK OF CASHEL** (daily 9am–4.30/7.30pm; €5; @www.heritageireland.ie) appears as a mirage of crenellations rising bolt upright from the vast encircling plain. The rock, less than a quarter of a mile wide, is one of Ireland's most extraordinary architectural sites and is also where St Patrick reputedly used a shamrock to explain the doctrine of the Trinity.

Walking from **Cashel** town, ten minutes to the east, the first sight you'll encounter on the Rock is the fifteenth-century **Hall of the Vicars**, whose vaulted undercroft contains the original **St Patrick's Cross**. The cross's huge plinth was reputedly the coronation stone of the High Kings of Munster. **Cormac's Chapel**, built in the 1130s, is the earliest and most beautiful of Ireland's Romanesque churches; both north and south doors feature intricate carving, while inside, the alleged sarcophagus of King Cormac has an exquisite design of interlacing serpents and ribbon decoration. The graceful limestone **Cathedral**, begun in the thirteenth century, is Anglo-Norman in conception, with its Gothic arches and lancet windows; a door in the south transept gives access to the tower, and in the north transept some panels from sixteenth-century altar-tombs survive. The tapering **round tower** is the earliest building on the Rock, dating from the early twelfth century. Cashel's **tourist office** (Mon–Sat 9.15am–6pm; July & Aug also Sun 11am–5pm; Sept–March closed Sat; ☎062/61333) is on Main Street alongside the **Cashel of the Kings Heritage Centre** (9.30am–5.30/8pm; Sept–March closed Sat & Sun; free), where a small exhibition covers the history of the town. Cashel has two excellent and central **hostels**: *O'Brien's Holiday Lodge*, off the Dundrum Road (☎062/61003, @www.cashellodgeandcampsite.com; dorms €18, rooms ❹; also has camping), and *Cashel Holiday Hostel*, 6 John St (☎062/62330, @www.cashelhostel.com; dorms €15, rooms ❹). For **B&B**, try *Abbey House*, 1 Dominic St (☎062/61104, @www.southeastireland.com/michelle; ❺), or *Rockside House*, Rock Villas (☎062/63813, @joyrocksidehouse@eircom.net; ❻), both near the Rock.

# Cork

Everywhere in **CORK** there's evidence of its history as a great mercantile centre, with grey stone quaysides, old warehouses, and elegant, quirky bridges spanning the River Lee to each side of the city's island core – but the lively atmosphere and large student population, combined with a vibrant social and cultural scene, are equally powerful draws. **St Finbarre** founded an abbey here in the seventh century, but the Vikings wrecked it in 820 before building a new settlement on one of the islands in the marshes, and eventually integrating with the native Celts. Massive stone walls built by invading Normans in the twelfth century were destroyed by William III's forces during the **Siege of Cork** in 1690, after which waterborne trade brought increasing prosperity, as witnessed by the city's fine eighteenth-century bow-fronted houses and ostentatious nineteenth-century churches.

The graceful arc of **St Patrick's Street** – which with **Grand Parade** forms the commercial heart of the centre – is crammed with major chain stores and, just off here on Princes Street, the sumptuous **English Market** offers the chance to sample local delicacies like drisheen (a peppered sausage made from a sheep's stomach lining and blood). On the far side of St Patrick's Street, chic Paul Street is a gateway to the bijou environs of French Church Street and Carey's Lane. The downstream end of the island, where many of the quays are still in use, gives the clearest sense of the old port city. In the west the island is predominantly residential, though Fitzgerald Park is home to the **Cork Public Museum** (Mon–Sat 11am–1pm & 2.15–5/6pm, Sun 3–5pm; free), which focuses on Republican history.

North of the River Lee is **Shandon**, a reminder of Cork's eighteenth-century status as the most important port in Europe for dairy products. The most striking survivor is the **Cork Butter Exchange**, stout nineteenth-century Neoclassical buildings recently given over to craft workshops. The old butter market itself, now housing a theatre, sits in a cobbled square. To the rear is the pleasant Georgian church of **St Anne Shandon** (Mon–Sat 9am–6pm; €5), easily recognizable from all over the city by its weather vane – an eleven-foot salmon. The church tower gives excellent views and an opportunity to ring the famous bells: a good stock of sheet tunes is provided. Around two miles west of here in Sunday's Well is the nineteenth-century **Cork City Gaol** (daily 9.30/10am–4/5pm; €5), with an excellent taped tour focusing on social history. From here, you can walk back to the town centre via the Shaky Bridge and Fitzgerald Park.

### Practicalities

The **bus station** is on Parnell Place alongside Merchant's Quay, while the train station is about one mile east of the city centre on Lower Glanmire Road. **Ferries** from Swansea and Roscoff arrive at Ringaskiddy, some ten miles out, from where there's a bus into the centre. The **tourist office** is on Grand Parade (Mon–Sat 9/9.15am–4.30/6pm; July & Aug also Sun 10am–5pm; ☎021/425 5100, ⊛www.corkkerry.ie). For **B&B**, try *Number Forty Eight*, 48 Lower Glanmire Rd (☎0121/450 5790, ⊜jerryspillane48@hotmail.com; ❻), *Redclyffe Guest House*, near the University on Western Road (☎021/427 3220, ⊛www.redclyffe.com; ❻), or the many others along these two roads. **Hostels** include: *Sheila's*, 4 Belgrave Place, Wellington Road (☎021/450 5562, ⊛www.sheilashostel.ie; dorms €16.50, rooms ❹); *Kinlay House*, Bon & Joan's Walk, Shandon (☎021/450 8966, ⊛www.kinlayhouse.ie; dorms €16, rooms ❹); *Kelly's Hostel*, 25 Summerhill South (☎021/431 5612, ⊛www.kellyshostel.com; dorms €18, rooms ❹); and An Óige's *Cork International*, 1–2 Redclyffe, Western Road (☎021/454 3289; €19), fifteen-minutes' walk from the centre or bus #8 to the University. Internet Exchange on Wood Street provides **Internet** access. For **food**, *The Quay Co-op*, 24 Sullivan's Quay, and *Café Paradiso*, 16 Lancaster Quay, are excellent vegetarian restaurants using local produce. *Zanzibaar*, 34 Patrick St, serves tasty pasta and seafood, while *Oz Cork,* on Grand Parade, offers everything from pasta to panini at reasonable prices. There's plenty of **traditional music** around: try *Corner Bar* and *Sin É*, both on Coburg Street; *An Spailpín Fánach*, South Main Street; *The Gables*, Douglas Street; and *The Lobby Bar*, Union Quay (which has rock bands too). Cork's premier **club** is *The Savoy* on Patrick Street, with DJs and live music. *The Bodega* on Cornmarket Street is a popular late café-bar with regular DJs; and there's an international **jazz festival** in late October (⊛www.corkjazzfestival.com). For **theatre**, the Triskel Arts Centre in Tobin Street (☎021/427 2022, ⊛www.triskelartscentre.com) is a lively spot with a cinema, exhibitions, readings and concerts. The Kino Cinema on Washington Street screens independent films and co-hosts the excellent **film festival** in mid-October (⊛www.corkfilmfest.org). For **listings** of what's on get the free *Whazon?* (⊛www.whazon.com) or the *Evening Echo*.

# The west coast

If you've come to Ireland for mountainous scenery, sea and remoteness, you'll find them all in County Kerry. By far the most visited areas are the town of **Killarney** and a scenic route around the perimeter of the Iveragh Peninsula known as the **Ring of Kerry**. County Clare's **Ennis** and the more tourist-ridden **Doolin** are marvellous spots for **traditional music**. **Galway** is an exceptionally enjoyable, free-spirited sort of place, and a gathering point for young travellers. To its west lies **Connemara**, a magnificently wild coastal terrain, with the nearby, elementally beautiful **Aran Islands**, in the mouth of Galway Bay. Up the coast the landscape softens around the historic town of **Westport**, while further north, **Sligo** has many associations with the poet Yeats and a lively, bustling feel. In the far northwest **County Donegal**'s scenery is especially rich with a spectacular two-hundred-mile folded coastline whose highlight is **Slieve League**'s awesome sea cliffs, the highest in Europe. There are plenty of international flights directly into the region (to Shannon and Knock airports).

## Killarney and around

**KILLARNEY** has been heavily commercialized and has little of architectural interest, but its location amid some of the best lakes, mountains and woodland in Ireland definitely compensates. **Cycling** is a great way of seeing the terrain, and makes good sense because local transport is sparse. Around the town, three spectacular lakes – Lough Leane, Muckross Lake and the Upper Lake – form an appetizer for MacGillycuddy's Reeks, the highest mountains in Ireland. The entrance gates to the **Knockreer Estate**, part of the **Killarney National Park**, are just over the road from Killarney's cathedral. A short walk through the grounds takes you to the banks of **Lough Leane**, where tall wooded hills plunge into the water, with the peaks rising behind to the highest, **Carrantuohill** (3414ft). The main path through the estate leads to the restored fifteenth-century tower of **Ross Castle** (April–Sept daily 9/10am–5/6.30pm; Oct Tues–Sun 10am–5pm; €5; gardens free), the last place in the area to succumb to Cromwell's forces in 1652.

A mile or so south of Killarney is the **Muckross Estate**; aim first for **Muckross Abbey**, for the ruin itself and its calm, contemplative location. Founded by the Franciscans in the mid-fifteenth century, it was suppressed by Henry VIII; the friars returned, but were finally driven out by Cromwell. Back at the main road, signposts point to **Muckross House** (daily 9am–5.30/7pm; €5.50 or €8.25 joint ticket with farm; ⊛www.heritageireland.ie), a solid nineteenth-century neo-Elizabethan mansion with wonderful gardens and also a traditional working farm. The estate gives access to well-trodden paths along the shores of the Muckross Lake where you can see one of Killarney's celebrated beauty spots, the **Meeting of the Waters**. Actually a parting, it has a profusion of indigenous and flowering subtropical plants on the left of the Old Weir Bridge. Close by is the massive shoulder of Torc Mountain, shrugging off **Torc Waterfall**. The Upper Lake is beautiful, too, with the main road running along one side up to Ladies' View, from where the view is truly amazing.

West of Killarney lies the **Gap of Dunloe**, a natural defile formed by glacial overflow that cuts the mountains in two. **Kate Kearney's Cottage**, a pub located six miles from Killarney at the foot of the track leading up to the Gap, is the last place before **Lord Brandon's Cottage**, a summer tearoom (June–Aug), seven miles away on the other side of the valley. The track winds its way up the desolate valley between high rock cliffs and waterfalls, past a chain of icy loughs and tarns, to the top, where you find yourself in what feels like one of the remotest places in the world: the **Black Valley**. Named after its entire population perished during the famine (1845–49), it's now inhabited by a mere handful of families, and was the very last valley in Ireland to get electricity. There's a wonderfully isolated *An Óige* **hostel** here too (March–Nov; ☏064/34712, dorms €13). From here, the quickest way to Killarney is to carry on down to Lord Brandon's Cottage and take the boat back across the Upper Lake.

### Practicalities

**B&Bs** abound in Killarney, though in high season it's worth booking ahead through the **tourist office**, on Beech Road off New Street (Mon–Sat 9.15am–5.15pm;

June–Sept also Sun 10am–1pm & 2–6pm; ☎064/31633, ☺www.corkkerry.ie). The *An Óige* **hostel** (☎064/31240; dorms €20.50) is three miles west of town along the Killorglin road at Aghadoe, but there are several alternatives in Killarney itself: *Killarney Railway Hostel* opposite the station (☎064/35299, ☺www.hoztel.com; dorms €14, rooms ❹); *The Súgan Hostel* minutes away on Lewis Road (☎064/33104, ☺www.killarneysuganhostel.com; dorms €15, rooms ❷); bustling *Neptune's Town Hostel* in the middle of town on New Street (☎064/35255, ☺www.neptuneshostel. com; dorms €17.50, rooms ❸); and *Park Hostel* up the hill off Cork Road, opposite the petrol station (June–Aug; ☎064/32119; dorms €14). **Camping** is available at *Killarney Flesk* (April–Sept; ☎064/31704), a mile south on the N71 Kenmare road. **Eating and drinking** places are thick on the ground: one of the best is *Bricín*, on High Street, along with *The Caragh* on New Street; or try *Cronin's* on College Street, all serving hearty food. Internet Leaders, 12 Beech Rd, and Web-Talk, 53 High St, provide **Internet** access. O'Sullivan's, 18 New St rents **bikes**. Evening **entertainment** is everywhere as you walk the streets; pick up *The Kerryman* for **listings**.

# The Ring of Kerry

Most tourists view the spectacular scenery of the 110-mile **Ring of Kerry**, west of Killarney, without ever leaving their tour coach or car, so anyone straying from the road or waiting until the afternoon when the buses stop running will experience the slow twilights of the Atlantic seaboard in perfect seclusion. **Cycling** the Ring takes three days, and a bike provides access to the largely deserted mountain roads. Buses from Killarney circle the Ring in summer (May–Sept two daily); for the rest of the year they travel only as far as Caherciveen.

## Valentia Island to Waterville

Heading anticlockwise on the main N70 around the Ring of Kerry, at **Kells Bay** the road veers inland towards **CAHERCIVEEN**, the main shopping centre for the western part of the peninsula. It has an independent **hostel**, *Sive*, 15 East End (☎066/947 2717, ✉sivehostel@oceanfree.net; dorms €15, rooms ❸). Beyond here, lanes lead out to **VALENTIA ISLAND**, Europe's most westerly harbour, its position on the Gulf Stream providing a mild, balmy climate. A **ferry** (April–Sept; single €1.50, return €2) crosses from Reenard Point (two-and-a-half miles from Caherciveen) to **Knightstown** whose main street has a few shops, a post office and a couple of bars. The much-touted **Grotto** – Valentia's highest point – is a gaping slate cavern with a crude statue of the Virgin perched two hundred feet up amid dripping icy water. More exciting is the spectacular cliff scenery to the northwest. For **B&B** there's *Spring Acre* (March–Nov; ☎066/947 6141, ✉rforan@indigo.ie; ❺) opposite the ferry, while *The Ring Lyne* (☎066/947 6103, ✉seanosullivan@hotmail.com; dorms €15) provides **hostel** accommodation in Chapeltown, four miles west.

The stretch of coast south of Valentia is wild and almost deserted, apart from a scattering of farms and fishing villages. Sweet-smelling, tussocky grass dotted with wild flowers is raked by Atlantic winds, ending in abrupt cliffs or sandy beaches. In **BALLINSKELLIGS** the *Skellig* (☎066/947 9942; dorms €15, rooms ❻) provides **hostel** accommodation. The village is a focus of the Kerry Gaeltacht (Irish-speaking area), busy in summer with schoolchildren and students learning Irish. Formerly a popular resort, **WATERVILLE**, across the bay from Ballinskelligs, is the best base on the Ring for exploring the coast and the mountainous country inland. For **B&B** try *The Old Cable House* in the former transatlantic Cable Station (☎066/947 4233, ☺www.oldcablehouse.com; ❺), or *Klondyke House*, New Line Road (☎066/947 4119, ☺homepage.eircom.net/~klondykehouse; ❹). Alternatively, there's the *Bru na Domoda* **hostel** at Maistir Gaoithe, seven miles up the Inny Valley (May–Oct; ☎066/947 4782, ✉maistirgaoithe@eircom.net; dorms €19, rooms ❹).

# The Dingle Peninsula

The **Dingle Peninsula** is a place of intense, shifting beauty. Spectacular mountains, long sandy beaches and the splinter-slatted mass of rocks that defines the extraordinary coast at **Slea Head** all conspire to ensure that, remote though it is, the peninsula is firmly on the tourist trail. Here is one of the greatest concentrations of Celtic ruins in Ireland, and the now uninhabited Blasket Islands once generated a wealth of Irish literature. The best base for exploring the peninsula is **DINGLE**, little more than a few streets by the side of **Dingle Bay**. Formerly Kerry's leading port in medieval times, then later a centre for smuggling, the town's main attractions nowadays are aquatic: the star of the show is undoubtedly **Fungi** the dolphin who's been visiting the town's natural harbour for some twenty years (a number of boats offer trips out to see him from around €15). Alternatively, there's **Oceanworld** on the waterfront (daily 10am–6pm; €8.50; ⓦwww.dingle-oceanworld.ie), whose numerous aquaria include a touch pool and shark tank as well as a turtle exhibition.

There's no shortage of **accommodation**, and the **tourist office** on The Quay (Mon–Fri 9/10am–5/7pm; July & Aug also Sat 9am–7pm, Sun 10am–6pm; ☎066/915 1188) will book places. Although many of Dingle's **B&B**s are fairly expensive, the *Mainstay Guesthouse*, Dykegate Street (☎066/915 1598, ⓦwww.mainstaydingle.com; ➐) offers excellent rooms, while *Boland's* on Upper Main Street (☎066/915 1426, ⓦwww.bolandsdingle.com; ➏) is another reliable choice. For **hostels**, try the *Grapevine*, Dykegate Street (☎066/915 1434, ⓦwww.grapevinedingle.com; dorms €13, rooms ➋), or *Ballintaggart House*, one mile east of Dingle town (Easter–Oct; ☎066/915 1454, ✉info@dingleaccommodation.com; dorms €18, rooms ➎) which also has a campsite. Dingle's top **restaurants** serve excellent seafood, landed just a few hundred yards away. Try *Doyle's* or the *Half Door* on John Street for good, if pricey, meals. *The Oven Doors*, Holyground, serves everything from tea and scones to inexpensive pizzas. **Internet** access is at *Dingle Internet Café* on Main Street. The best **pubs** for traditional music are *An Droichead Beag* on Main Street (nightly) and *O'Flaherty's* on Bridge Street (Fri & Sat).

## West of Dingle town

Public transport in the west of the peninsula amounts to a **bus** from Dingle to Dunquin, making **cycling** the best way to explore; bikes are available at Foxy John's on Main Street. The Irish-speaking area west of Dingle is rich with relics of the ancient Gaelic and early Christian cultures and the main concentration of monuments lies between Ventry and Slea Head. First off there's the spectacular **Dún Beag** (daily 9am–6/8pm; €2), about four miles west of Ventry. A promontory fort, its defences include four earthen rings, with an underground escape route by the main entrance. West of here, the hillside above the road is studded with stone **beehive huts**, cave dwellings, forts, churches, standing stones and crosses – over five hundred in all. The beehive huts were being built and used for storage until the late nineteenth century, but among ancient buildings like the **Fahan group** you're looking over a landscape that's remained essentially unchanged for centuries.

At **Slea Head** the view encompasses the desolate, splintered masses of the **Blasket Islands**, uninhabited since 1953, though there are some summer residents. In the summer, boats bound for **Great Blasket** depart daily from the pier just south of Dunquin (June–Aug every 30min, Easter–May & Sept to mid-Oct hourly; ☎066/915 6422; €20 return). Great Blasket's delights are simple ones: tramping the footpaths that crisscross the island, sitting on the beaches watching the seals and dolphins, or savouring the amazing sunsets. The only **accommodation** is provided by the *Great Blasket Hostel* (April–Sept; ☎086/852 2321, ⓦwww.greatblasketisland.com; dorms €25, rooms ➍), though you can camp for free and there's a café serving good, cheap vegetarian meals. At **DUNQUIN**, there's an *An Óige* **hostel** (Feb–Nov; ☎066/915 6121; dorms €15).

A couple of miles north around the headland from Dunquin stands **BALLY-FERRITER** where little northward lanes lead to the five-hundred-foot cliffs at Sybil Head or to Smerwick Harbour and **Dún an Óir** (Golden Fort). The single most impressive early Christian monument on the peninsula is the dry-stone **Gallarus oratory** (April–Oct daily 9am–5/9pm; €2.50), three miles further east, built some time between the ninth and twelfth centuries and still watertight. It's the best-preserved example of around twenty such oratories in Ireland, and represents a transition between the round beehive huts and the later rectangular churches, an example of which is to be found a mile to the north at **KILMALKEDAR**, with a nave dating from the mid-twelfth century and a corbelled stone roof.

## County Clare

Clare is one of the best spots in Ireland to catch a traditional music session, and a good place to start is its county town, **ENNIS**. In daytime hours there's little of interest in the narrow bustling streets, though the **Clare Museum** on Arthur's Row (June–Sept Mon–Sat 9.30am–5pm, Sun 2–5pm; Oct–May Tues–Sat 9.30am–1pm & 2–5pm; €3.50) offers a detailed account of local history from Bronze Age times onwards. Ennis' traditional music centre, **Glór** on Friar's Walk (ⓦwww .glor.ie), hosts regular evening concerts, but it's the **pub sessions** that remain the local music scene's lifeblood. Safe bets for high-standard sessions include: *Cruise's*, Abbey Street (nightly); *Ciarán's*, Francis Street (Wed–Sun); and *Kelly's*, Carmody Street (Sat & Sun) – Custy's Music Store on Francis Street is an excellent source of information. Additionally, the town hosts a couple of **festivals**: Fleadh Nua (ⓦ www.fleadhnua.com) in the last week of May, and the Ennis Trad Festival (ⓦ www.ennistradfestival.com) in mid-November.

The **bus** and **train** stations sit alongside one another, a ten-minute walk southeast of the town centre down Station Road. The **tourist office** (ⓣ065/682 8366, ⓦwww.shannonregiontourism.ie) is in the same building as the Clare Museum, with the same opening hours. **Hostel** accommodation is provided by the *Abbey Tourist Hostel*, Harmony Row (ⓣ065/682 2620, ⓦwww.abbeytouristhostel.com; dorms €14, rooms ❸). **B&Bs** near the centre include the very comfortable *Banner Lodge*, Market Street (ⓣ065/682 4224, ⓦwww.bannerlodge.com; ❺), and the welcoming *Cloneen*, Clonroad (April–Oct; ⓣ065/682 9681; ❺). For **meals** try *Punjab*, 59 Parnell St, a superb-value Indian restaurant, or *Numero Uno*, 3 Barrack St, a cheery pizza place. **Bikes** can be rented from Tierney's Cycles, 17 Abbey St.

Some twenty-five miles northwest of Ennis is the seaside village of **DOOLIN**, famed for a steady, year-round supply of **traditional music** in its three pubs, though these can often be crowded with tourists. There's plenty of accommodation including four **hostels**, all charging around €14 for a dorm bed: *Paddy's Doolin Hostel* (ⓣ065/707 4421, ⓦwww.doolinhostel.com; ❸); *Rainbow Hostel* (ⓣ065/707 4415, ⓦwww .rainbowhostel.com; ❷); *Flanagan's Village Hostel* (ⓣ065/707 4564; ❸); and *Aille River Hostel* (ⓣ065/707 4260, ⓦwww.esatclear.ie/ailleriver; ❸). All Doolin's pubs serve excellent **food**; the *Lazy Lobster* and *Doolin Café* are two of the best restaurants. A **ferry** (April–Sept) runs from the pier to the **Aran Islands**. **The Cliffs of Moher**, four miles south of Doolin, are the area's most famous tourist spot, their great bands of shale and sandstone rising 660 feet above the waves.

## Galway and around

The city of **GALWAY** continues to justify its reputation as the party capital of Ireland. University College guarantees a high number of young people in term-time, but the energy is most evident during Galway's **festivals**, especially the **Arts Festival** in the last two weeks of July (ⓦwww.galwayartsfestival.ie). For locals the most important event is the **Galway Races** (ⓦwww.galwayraces.com), held in the last week of July, when booking accommodation in advance is essential.

Galway began as a crossing point on the River Corrib, and developed as a strong Anglo-Norman colony. Granted city status in 1484, it developed a flourishing trade with the Continent, especially Spain. When Cromwell's forces arrived in 1652, however, the city was besieged for ninety days and went into a decline from which it has only recently recovered. The prosperity of maritime Galway was expressed in the distinctive townhouses of the merchant class, remnants of which are littered around the city, even though recent development has destroyed some of its character. The **Browne doorway** in Eyre Square is one such monument, a bay window and doorway with the coats of arms of the Browne and Lynch families, dated 1627. Just about the finest medieval townhouse in Ireland is fifteenth-century **Lynch's Castle** in Shop Street – along with Quay Street, the social hub of Galway. Now housing the Allied Irish Bank, it has a stone facade decorated with carved panels, gargoyles and a lion devouring another animal. Down by the River Corrib stands the **Spanish Arch**; more evocative in name than in reality, it's a sixteenth-century structure that was used to protect galleons unloading wine and rum. Across the river lies the **Claddagh** district, the old fishing village that once stood outside the city walls and gave the world the Claddagh ring as a symbol of love and fidelity. Past the Claddagh the river widens out into **Galway Bay**; for a pleasant sea walk follow the road until it reaches **Salthill**, the city's seaside resort. There are several beaches along the prom, though for the best head two miles from Salthill to **Silverstrand** on the Barna road.

## Practicalities

The **bus** and **train** stations are off Eyre Square, on the northeast edge of the city centre. The **tourist office** (May–Sept daily 9am–5.45/7.45pm; Oct–April Mon–Fri 9am–5.45pm, Sat 9am–12.45pm; ☏091/537700, ✆www.irelandwest.ie) is a short stroll down Forster Street and can book **B&B** accommodation. The best **hostels** include *Kinlay House Galway*, Merchant's Road (☏091/565244, ✆www .kinlayhouse.ie; dorms €16, rooms ❹); *Sleepzone*, Bóthar na mBan, Wood Quay (☏091/566999, ✆www.sleepzone.ie; dorms €18, rooms ❹); and *Barnacles Quay Street House*, 10 Quay St (☏091/568644, ✆www.barnacles.ie; dorms €22, rooms ❹). There's **camping** at *Ballyloughnane Caravan Park*, Ballyloughlane, Renmore (April–Sept; ☏091/752029), three miles east of the centre. Netaccess, Olde Malte Arcade, High Street and E-2008, Forster Street provide **Internet** facilities.

Good-value pub **food** is served around midday at *The Quays*, Quay Street; *Busker Browne's*, Kirwans Lane; and *McSwiggan's* in Eyre Street. For a more adventurous menu with a Latin influence, head for *BarCuba* on Eyre Square. In Quay Street, *McDonagh's Seafood Bar* is a must for seafood at any time of day, while *Get Stuffed*, 4b St Anthony's Place, Wood Quay, is a reliable vegetarian option. *Fat Freddy's*, Quay Street, is a busy pizza place, while excellent noodle dishes can be enjoyed at *Da Tang Noodle House*, Middle Street. The Quay Street area leading down to the river is known as the "**left bank**" due to the proliferation of popular pubs, restaurants and cafés. *The Quays* bar is one of the city's best loved, along with the nearby *Front Door* on Cross Street. Among the best places to hear **traditional music** are *Taaffe's* on Shop Street, the old-fashioned *Tigh Neachtain* on Cross Street and *The Crane* bar across the river on Sea Road (all nightly). For varied live music gigs, *Róisín Dubh* in Dominick Street attracts leading Irish and international names, while *Sally Long's*, Upper Abbeygate Street, is a decidedly hard-rock venue. Galway also has its fair share of **clubs**: *Cuba*, Eyre Square, is a huge draw while other popular venues include *GPO* on Eglinton Street, and *Boo Radley's* on Forster Street. For **listings**, see the weekly *Galway Advertiser* or *Galway City Tribune*.

## The Aran Islands

The **ARAN ISLANDS** – Inishmore, Inishmaan and Inisheer, lying thirty miles out across the mouth of Galway Bay – make spectacular settings for a wealth of early remains and some of the finest archeological sites in Europe. The isolation of the Irish-speaking islands prolonged the continuation of a unique, ancient culture into the early twentieth century. There are daily **ferries** to Inishmore year-round (less frequently to the other islands), departing from Galway city, Rossaveal (twenty miles west by bus) and Doolin in County Clare – the cost of a return trip starts at around €25, depending on the season, with some student reductions and good-value accommodation packages. Book tickets in Galway city through Aran Island Ferries, 4 Forster St (☎091/568903, ⊛www.aranislandferries.com); Inismór Ferries, 29 Forster St (☎091/566535, ⊛www.queenofaran2.com); or O'Brien Shipping (☎065/707 4455 or ☎091/567283, ⊛www.doolinferries.com) – all three companies have desks in Galway tourist office. You can also **fly** with Aer Árann Islands (☎091/593034, ⊛www.aerarannislands.ie) for around €45 return; book at Galway tourist office.

Although **INISHMORE** is very tourist-orientated, its wealth of dramatic ancient sites overrides such considerations. It's a long strip of an island, a great tilted plateau of limestone with a scattering of villages along the sheltered northerly coast, and land that slants up to the southern edge, where tremendous cliffs rip along the entire shoreline. As far as the eye can see is a tremendous patterning of stone, some of it the bare pavements of grey rock split in bold diagonal grooves, latticed by dry-stone walls. The ferry docks at **Kilronan**, where you'll find the *Kilronan Hostel* (☎099/61255, ⊛www.kilronanhostel.com; dorms €14), though the island's tranquillity is best enjoyed at the relaxing *Mainistir House Hostel* (☎099/61318, ⊛www.mainistirhousearan.com; dorms €15, rooms ❹), twenty minutes' walk west from the pier. **B&Bs** can be booked through the Kilronan **tourist office** (daily 10am–4/6.30pm; ☎099/61263), or when you buy your ferry ticket. Seafood is the island's great speciality, with most of the popular **restaurants** located in Kilronan: *Dún Aonghasa* has a varied and somewhat pricey menu; more budget-conscious meals are available at *The Pier House*, while *Joe Watty's* bar serves good soups and stews. For **bike rental**, there's *Mullin's* and *BNN* near the pier. Alternatively, take the seasonal **minibus** (€10) up through the island's villages and walk back down from any point.

Most of Inishmore's sights are to the northwest of Kilronan. The first hamlet in this direction is Mainistir, from where it's a short signposted walk to the twelfth-century church of **Teampall Chiaráin**, the most interesting of the ecclesiastical sites on Inishmore. Three miles or so down the main road is Kilmurvey, a fifteen-minute walk from the most spectacular of Aran's prehistoric sites, **Dún Aonghasa**. Accessed via the **visitor centre** (daily 10am–4/6pm; €2; ⊛www.heritageireland.ie), this massive ring fort, lodged on the edge of three-hundred-foot sea cliffs, has an inner citadel of precise blocks of grey stone, their symmetry echoing the almost geometric regularity of the land's limestone pavementing. Nearby **Dún Eoghanachta** is a huge drum of a stone fort, set in a lonely field with the Connemara mountains as a backdrop. It's accessible by tiny lanes from Dún Aonghasa with a detailed map; otherwise retrace your steps to Kilmurvey and follow the road west for just over a mile. At the **seven churches**, just east of Eoghannacht, there are ancient slabs commemorating seven Romans who died here, testifying to the far-reaching influence of Aran's monasteries. The site is, in fact, that of two churches and several domestic buildings, dating from the eighth to the thirteenth centuries, and includes St Brendan's grave, adorned by an early cross with interlaced patterns.

From Inishmore, it's an easy hop by boat to the other two islands; all the ferry companies run daily services. In comparison with Inishmore, **INISHMAAN** is lush, its stone walls forming a maze that chequers off tiny fields of grass and clover. The island's main sight is **Dún Chonchubhair**: built some time between the first and seventh centuries, its massive oval wall is almost intact and commands great views. Inishmaan's indifference to tourism means that amenities for visitors are minimal; if you arrive on spec ask at the pub for information (☎099/73003) – it's a warm and friendly place that also serves snacks in summer. For **B&B** try *Ard Álainn* (April–Sept; ☎099/73027; ⑤) or *An Dún* (☎099/73047, ⓦinismeainaccommodation.com; ⑤), both near Dún Chonchubhair.

**INISHEER**, less than two miles across, is the smallest of the Aran Islands, and tourism plays a key role here. A great plug of rock dominates the island, its rough, pale-grey stone dripping with greenery, topped by the fifteenth-century **O'Brien's Castle**, standing inside an ancient ring fort. Set around it are low fields, a small community of pubs and houses, and windswept sand dunes. The **Inisheer Island Cooperative** hut by the pier (June–Sept daily 10am–7pm; ☎099/75008) will give you a map and a list of **B&Bs**; *Radharc an Chláir*, by the castle (☎ & ☎099/75019; ⑤), is a good bet. There's also a **hostel**, *Brú Radharc na Mara* (mid-March to Oct; ☎099/75024, ⓔmaire.searraigh@oceanfree.net; dorms €13, rooms ③), and a **campsite** near the pier. Meals are available at the *Óstán Inis Oírr* hotel. For **music**, head for *Tigh Ned's* bar.

# Westport

Set on the shores of Clew Bay, **WESTPORT** is one of the west's liveliest spots. Planned by the eighteenth-century architect James Wyatt, its formal layout comes as quite a surprise in the midst of its rural surrounds. The craggy **Croagh Patrick** makes an imposing background to the town, standing at 2510 feet above the bay – the climb is a strenuous one, but rewarded by spectacular views. St Patrick reputedly prayed on the mountain for forty days for the conversion of the Irish to Christianity, and on the last Sunday of July, known as "Reek Day" which coincides with the Celtic festival of Lughnasa, many tackle the pilgrimage to the summit barefoot. Another attraction is **Westport House** (March–Sept; call ☎098/27766 for opening times; €15; ⓦwww.westporthouse.ie), a mile or so out of town towards the bay. The beautifully designed house dates from 1730 and is privately owned: the present family are direct descendants of legendary pirate Grace O'Malley of Clew Bay. Inside the house is a *Holy Family* by Rubens and an upstairs room with intricate Chinese wallpaper dating from 1780 – outside there's a giant water flume, train rides, boating and a bird and animal park.

**Buses** drop off on Mill Street in the centre; the **train** station is on Altamount Street, ten minutes north of the centre. Westport's best **hostel** is the *Old Mill* on James Street (☎098/27045, ⓦireland.iol.ie/~oldmill/; dorms €16, rooms ③). There are plenty of **B&Bs** – check for availability at the **tourist office** on James Street (Mon–Sat 9am–1pm & 2–5.45pm; June–Aug also Sun; ☎098/25711, ⓦwww.irelandwest.travel.ie). On Bridge Street *McCormack's* is a popular daytime **eating** choice, while the Mediterranean-style *Sol Rios* is a good lunch option. The *Quay Cottage*, by the entrance to Westport House, serves enormous salmon salads and plenty of vegetarian food; the nearby complex of refurbished waterside buildings brims with people, pubs and more expensive restaurants. The best **music** pubs are on Bridge Street – *The West* is hugely popular and *Matt Molloy's*, owned by the eponymous Chieftains' flute player, occasionally features visiting celebrities. **Internet** access is available at *Dunnings Cyberpub*, The Octagon, James Street.

# Sligo and around

**SLIGO** is, after Derry, the biggest town in the northwest of Ireland. The legacy of **W.B. Yeats** – perhaps Ireland's best-loved poet – is still strongly felt here: the **Yeats Memorial Building** on Hyde Bridge (Mon–Fri 10am–5.30pm; €4; ⓦwww.yeats-sligo.com) features a photographic exhibition and film on his life, while the poet's Nobel Prize for Literature and other memorabilia are on show in the **Sligo County Museum** on Stephen Street (May–Sept Tues–Sat 10am–noon & 2–5pm; Oct–April 2–5pm only; free). **The Model Arts Centre** on The Mall (Tues–Sat 10am–5.30pm; also April–Oct Sun noon–5.30pm; free;

@www.modelart.ie) houses works by the poet's brother **Jack B. Yeats** and also displays a broad representation of modern Irish art. Across the River Garavogue on Abbey Street stands the thirteenth-century **Dominican Friary** whose visitor centre (mid-March to Oct daily 10am–6pm; Nov & Dec Fri–Sun 9.30am–4.30pm; €2; @www.heritageireland.ie) provides an informative introduction to many of its existing features, including the last remaining sculptured high altar in the country.

**Buses** and **trains** arrive at the stations on Lord Edward Street and Union Street respectively, five minutes west of the centre. The **tourist office** is on Temple Street (June–Aug daily 9/10am–6/7pm; Sept–May Mon–Fri 9am–5pm; ☎071/916 1201, @www.sligotourism.ie). For **B&B** try *Lissadell*, Mailcoach Road (☎071/916 1937; ❺), ten minutes south of the centre, or *Tree Tops*, Cleveragh Road (☎071/916 0160, @www.sligobandb.com; ❻), a mile southeast along Pearse Rd. **Hostels** include the well-equipped *Eden Hill*, Pearse Road (☎071/914 3204, @homepage.eircom.net/~edenhill; dorms €14, rooms ❸), by the junction with Mailcoach Rd, and the central, popular *White House* on Markievicz Road (☎071/914 5160; dorms €14), by the river north of Hyde Bridge. There are **campsites** (Easter–Sept) five miles from town at Rosses Point to the north (bus #473) and Strandhill to the west (bus #472): both have fine beaches and Strandhill, while unsafe for swimming, attracts plenty of surfers. Several **pubs** in Sligo serve decent bar **lunches**: *Hargadon's* on O'Connell Street has fine old traditional snugs; the *Garavogue* on Stephen Street offers excellent international food and bar snacks all day. For top pizza head for *Bistro Bianconni* on O'Connell Street; *The Loft* on Lord Edward Street, near the bus station, has an extensive menu of world cuisine. Sligo's best **traditional music pubs** are *Sheela na Gig* (nightly) on Bridge Street, owned by local stars **Dervish**, and *Earley's* (Thurs) just opposite. Popular **clubs** include *Envy*, on Teeling Street and *Toff's*, on Kennedy Parade. Check the weekly *Sligo Champion* for **listings**. For **bike rental**, try Flanagan's, Market Yard. **Internet** access is provided by *Cygo Internet Café*, 19 O'Connell St.

## Donegal Town

**DONEGAL town** is a busy place focused around its old marketplace, The Diamond, and a fine base for exploring the stunning coastal countryside and inland hills and loughs. Just about the only sight in the town itself is the well-preserved shell of **O'Donnell's Castle** on Tirchonaill Street by The Diamond (mid-March to Oct daily 10am–6pm; Nov & Dec Fri–Sun 9.30am–4.30pm; €3.50; @www .heritageireland.ie), a fine example of Jacobean architecture. On the left bank of the River Eske stand the few ruined remains of **Donegal Friary**, while on the opposite bank a woodland path known as Bank Walk offers wonderful views of **Donegal Bay** and towards the **Blue Stack Mountains**.

There are dozens of **B&Bs** here, but to avoid a lot of walking it's simplest to call at the **tourist office** on The Quay (Easter–Sept Mon–Sat 9am–5/8pm; July & Aug also Sun 9am–8pm; ☎074/972 1148, @www.irelandnorthwest.ie). The only **hostel** is just past the roundabout on the Killybegs road, *Donegal Town Independent Hostel* (☎074/972 2805, @www.donegalhostel.com; dorms €13, rooms ❸). **Eating-places** are plentiful, including excellent burgers and pizzas at the *Harbour*, opposite the tourist office, and substantial cheap meals at the *Atlantic Café*, Main Street. Many **pubs** serve lunches and are good evening watering holes. The *Olde Castle Bar*, next to the castle, is fine for a quiet daytime drink; *McGroarty's* on The Diamond has a good bar menu; and *The Scotsman* on Bridge Street has regular traditional music sessions.

## Slieve League and Glencolmcille

To the west of Donegal town lies one of the most stupendous landscapes in Ireland – the stark and beautiful **Teelin Bay** and the majestic Slieve League cliffs. An ideal **base** for exploring the region is the busy, but always welcoming, *Derrylahan Independent Hostel* (☎074/973 8079, ✉derrylahan@eircom.net; dorms €12, rooms ➌), a two-mile walk from Kilcar along the coastal road to Carrick.

There are two routes up to the ridge of **Slieve League**: a back way following the signpost to Baile Mór just before Teelin, and the road route from Teelin to Bunglass, a thousand sheer feet above the sea. The former path has you looking up continually at the ridge known as One Man's Pass, on which walkers seem the size of pins, while the frontal approach swings you up to one of the most thrilling cliff scenes in the world, the **Amharc Mór**. On a good day you can see a third of Ireland from the summit.

One Man's Pass across the summit, only a few feet wide in places and dangerous in windy weather, leads via Malinbeg – where there's the excellent *Malinbeg Hostel* (☎074/973 0006, ⊛www.malinbeghostel.com; dorms €12, rooms ➋) – and Malinmore to **GLENCOLMCILLE**, the Glen of St Columbcille, the name by which Columba was known after his conversion. A place of pilgrimage since the seventh century, following Columba's stay in the valley, every June 9 at midnight the locals commence a three-hour barefoot itinerary of the cross-inscribed slabs that stud the valley basin, finishing up with Mass at 3am in the small church. If you want to attempt Turas Cholmcille ("Columba's Journey") yourself, get a map of the route from the **Folk Village Museum** (Easter–Sept Mon–Sat 10am–6pm, Sun noon–6pm; €3; ⊛www.glenfolkvillage.com), a cluster of replica, period-furnished thatched cottages, including a National School and a Shebeen house. A path up to the left from here leads to the wonderfully positioned *Dooey Hostel* (☎074/973 0130, ⊛www.dooeyhostel.com; dorms €11.50, rooms ➋), while **B&Bs** include *Corner House* (April–Sept; ☎074/973 0021; ➎), four hundred yards down the Ardara road from *Biddy's Bar* in the village centre. The best **food** in Glencolmcille is at *An Cistín*, part of the Foras Cultúir Uladh complex.

# Northern Ireland

Both the pace of political change and the uncertainty of its future continue to characterize Northern Ireland. In 1998, after thirty years of "The Troubles", its people overwhelmingly voted in support of a political settlement and, it was hoped, an end to political and sectarian violence. For a time the political process gradually inched forwards, hampered by deep mistrust and suspicion on both sides, with issues such as the decommissioning of IRA weaponry paramount, and inter-community tensions still rife in parts of Belfast. At the time of writing, the process was in a state of impasse, with the Northern Ireland Assembly suspended amidst fears of a political collapse. Despite the instability, the North remains a pretty safe place for tourists. **Belfast** and **Derry** – two lively and attractive cities – have no obvious security presence beyond the occasional hovering army helicopter. The northern coastline – especially the weird geometry of the **Giant's Causeway** – is as spectacular as anything in Ireland, while to the southwest is the great **Lough Erne**, a huge lake complex, and **Enniskillen**, a town resonant with history.

## Belfast

A quarter of Northern Ireland's population lives in the capital, **BELFAST**. While the legacy of "**The Troubles**" is clearly visible in the landscape of areas like West Belfast – the peace walls, derelict buildings and political murals – security measures have been considerably eased, though there are certain flashpoints such as the Short Strand and the Ardoyne which are inadvisable to visit.

Belfast began life as a cluster of forts guarding a ford across the River Farset, which nowadays runs beneath High Street. However, its history doesn't really begin until 1604, when Sir Arthur Chichester was "planted" in the area by James I. By the eighteenth century the cloth trade and shipbuilding had expanded tremendously, and the population increased ten-fold in a century. It was then noted for its liberalism, but in the nineteenth century the sectarian divide became wider and increasingly violent. Although **Partition** in 1921 and the creation of Northern Ireland with Belfast as its capital inevitably boosted the city's status, the Troubles exacerbated the industrial decline that hit much of the British Isles during the 1980s. A massive programme of regeneration commenced in the 1990s at the first signs of peace, and this economic rejuvenation coupled with optimism generated by the early years of the peace process brought a new zest to the city. However, on weekday nights the city centre can resemble a ghost town, even though there's no doubt that Belfast's arts scene continues to thrive.

## Arrival, transport and information

Flights arrive at **Belfast International Airport** (☎028/9448 4848, ⓦwww.belfastairport.com), nineteen miles west of town (buses every 30min to Europa bus station; £6 single, £9 return), or **Belfast City Airport**, three miles northeast (☎028/9093 9093, ⓦwww.belfastcityairport.com; bus #600 every 40min to city centre; £2.50). **Ferries** from Stranraer dock at Corry Road (taxi £6); and those from Liverpool further north on West Bank Road (taxi £7); while ferries from Cairnryan dock twenty miles north at Larne (bus or train into centre). Most **trains** call at the central Great Victoria Street Station, though those from Dublin and Larne terminate at Central Station on East Bridge Street. **Buses** from Derry, the Republic, the airports and ferry terminals arrive at Europa bus station beside Great Victoria Street train station; buses from the north coast use Laganside Buscentre in Queen's Square. A regular Centrelink bus connects all bus and train stations. Covering most places the excellent **Metro** bus service costs £0.70–£1.50. Passes allowing travel anywhere on the network cost £3 for all day Monday to Saturday (£2 after 10am) or just £1 on Sundays. The Metro kiosk in Donegall Square West provides free bus maps. **Ulsterbus** serves the outlying areas; and there are Saturday **late-night buses** from Donegall Square West (1–2am; £3.50). Information on all buses and trains is available at ☎028/9066 6630 or ⓦwww.translink.co.uk.

The **Belfast Welcome Centre**, 47 Donegall Place (Mon 9.30am–5.30pm, Tues–Sat 9am–5.30/7pm; also June–Sept Sun noon–5pm; ☎028/9024 6609, ⓦwww.gotobelfast.com), provides information and an accommodation booking service as well as left-luggage facilities and an **Internet** café. **Bord Fáilte**, for information about the Republic, is at 53 Castle St (Mon–Fri 9am–5pm; March–Sept also Sat 9am–12.30pm; ☎028/9032 7888).

## Accommodation

Most of Belfast's accommodation is south of the city centre in the University area.

### Hostels

**The Ark** 18 University St ☎028/9032 9626, ⓦwww.arkhostel.com. Friendly, comfortable hostel close to the university. Dorms £9.50, rooms ❸

**Arnie's Backpackers** 63 Fitzwilliam St ☎028/9024 2867, ⓦwww.arniesbackpackers.co.uk. Cheerful and relaxed independent hostel, also near the university. Dorms £9.50, rooms ❸

**Belfast International Youth Hostel** 22–32 Donegall Rd ☎028/9031 5435. Large, well-equipped but characterless modern HINI hostel, just west of Shaftesbury Square. Dorms £9, rooms ❸

### B&Bs

**Avenue House** 23 Eglantine Ave ☎028/9066 5904, ⓔavenueguesthouse@ntlworld.com. Comfortable two-star guesthouse off Malone Road, south of the University, with well-equipped en-suite rooms. ❺

**Kate's B&B** 127 University St ☎028/9028 2091, ⓔkatesbb127@hotmail.com. Popular B&B, off University Road, offering an "all you can eat" breakfast. ❺

**Malone Guest House** 79 Malone Rd ☎028/9066 9565, ⓔmaloneguesthouse@maloneroad.fsnet.co.uk. Victorian house with thirteen comfortable

en-suite bedrooms, south of the University. **⑥**
**Marine House** 30 Eglantine Ave ☎028/9066
2828, ©marine30@utvinternet.com. A large
Victorian three-star guesthouse in a quiet setting
off Malone Road, offering attractive, spacious
rooms. **⑤**

**Pearl Court House** 11 Malone Rd ☎028/9066
6145, ©pearlcourtgh@hotmail.com. Spacious
bedrooms, including some triples, in this large
house just south of the University. Excellent
breakfasts too. **⑤**

## The City

**Belfast City Hall**, presiding over central Donegall Square, is an austere building (tours June–Sept Mon–Fri 11am, 2pm & 3pm, Sat 2.30pm; Oct–May Mon–Fri 11am & 2.30pm, Sat 2.30pm; free; ⓦwww.belfastcitygov.uk), its civic purpose almost subservient to its role in propagating the ethics of Presbyterian power. At the northwest corner of the square stands **The Linen Hall Library** (Mon–Fri 9.30am–5.30pm, Sat 9.30am–4pm; ⓦwww.linenhall.com), entered on Fountain Street, where the Political Collection houses over eighty thousand publications covering Northern Ireland's political life since 1966. Nearby is the branch of the **Northern Bank** which was the subject of the UK's biggest bank robbery (£26m), allegedly undertaken by the IRA, in 2004. The streets heading north off Donegall Square North lead to the main shopping area. Towards the river, either side of Ann Street, you're in the narrow alleyways known as **The Entries**, with some great old saloon bars. At the end of High Street the clock tower is a good position from which to view the world's second- and third-largest cranes, Goliath and Samson, across the river in the Harland & Wolff shipyard where the **Titanic** was built. North of the clock tower is a series of grand edifices that grew out of the same civic vanity as invested in the City Hall. The restored **Customs House**, a Corinthian-style building, is the first you'll see, but the most monolithic is the Church of Ireland **St Anne's Cathedral** at the junction of Donegall and Talbot streets, a neo-Romanesque basilica started in 1899 (Mon–Sat 10am–4pm, Sun noon–3pm; free; ⓦwww.belfastcathedral .org). Across the river from the Customs House is the face of new Belfast, the ambitious **Odyssey** complex (ⓦwww.theodyssey.co.uk) housing a sports arena doubling as a concert venue, ten-pin bowling alley, Sheridan IMAX cinema (ⓦwww.belfastimax.com) and twelve-screen multiplex, **W5 science discovery centre** (Mon–Sat 10am–6pm, Sun noon–6pm; £6; ⓦwww.w5online.co.uk) and numerous restaurants. Further along the waterside is the impressive Waterfront Hall concert venue (ⓦwww.waterfront.co.uk).

The area of **South Belfast** known as "The Golden Mile" stretches from the **Grand Opera House** on Great Victoria Street down to the university, and has plenty of eating-places, pubs and bars at each end. Its attractions include the **Crown Liquor Saloon**, one of the greatest of the old Victorian gin palaces. Further south on University Road, **Queen's University** is the architectural centrepiece, flanked by the most satisfying Georgian terrace in Belfast, University Square. Just south of the university are the verdant **Botanic Gardens** whose Palm House (Mon–Fri 10am–4/5pm, Sat & Sun 2–4/5pm; free) was the first of its kind in the world. Also in the Botanic Gardens is the **Ulster Museum** (Mon–Fri 10am–5pm, Sat 1–5pm, Sun 2–5pm; free; ⓦwww.ulstermuseum.org.uk), with its collection of Irish art, history and natural sciences exhibits, and treasures salvaged from the Spanish Armada ships that foundered off the Giant's Causeway in 1588.

## Eating, drinking and entertainment

Many of the best places to **eat** and the liveliest **pubs** can be found around Great Victoria Street and in the university area, and Belfast's best entertainment is pub music. There's also a vibrant **club** scene and plenty of DJ bars; check out *The Big List* (ⓦwww.thebiglist.co.uk; free), available in pubs and record shops, the web-based *wheretonight.com* (ⓦwww.wheretotonight.com) and the *Belfast Evening Telegraph*.

### Restaurants and cafés

**Archana** 53 Dublin Rd ☎028/9032 3713. Fine curries and balti dishes upstairs and superb-value vegetarian dishes in its ground-floor *Little India* offshoot.

**Ba Soba** 38 Hill St ☎028/9058 6868. Belfast's first and most popular noodle bar, packed even at lunchtime. Closed Mon.

**Bewley's** Donegall Arcade. Excellent coffee house serving good-value breakfasts, lunches and snacks.

**Café Vincents** 78 Botanic Ave. Fine breakfasts, value-for-money high teas and plenty of pizzas.

**Delaney's** 19 Lombard St. Good value, wholesome food from a daytime restaurant handily placed in the main shopping area. Thurs until 9pm.

**Gingeroot** 73–75 Great Victoria St ☎028/9031 3124. Indian café-bar offering very reasonably priced lunches and evening specials.

**Maggie May's** 45 Botanic Ave. Huge, economically priced portions in this cosy café with lots of veggie choices.

**Red Panda** 60 Great Victoria St & Odyssey Pavilion. Very pleasant establishments specializing in dim sum and other authentic Chinese dishes.

### Pubs and live music

**Crown Liquor Saloon** 46 Great Victoria St. The city's most famous pub, decked out like a spa bath, with a good range of Ulster food, such as champ and colcannon (both potato dishes) and Strangford oysters in season.

**The Empire** 42 Botanic Ave. Music hall and cellar bar in a converted church, with nightly live music or comedy.

**The John Hewitt** Donegall St. Owned by Belfast Unemployed Resource Centre, this popular bar has some of Belfast's best traditional music sessions (Tues 9.30pm, Weds 9pm, Sat 6pm).

**Kelly's Cellars** 30 Bank St. One of the city's oldest and finest traditional bars.

**Madden's** Smithfield. Unpretentious and atmospheric pub, with regular traditional music sessions (Fri & Sat).

**The Morning Star** 17 Pottinger's Entry. Old-fashioned bar serving great food in the restaurant upstairs, with a very reasonable lunchtime buffet downstairs.

**The Rotterdam** 54 Pilot St. Names big and small play in this docklands venue, plus traditional music on Thurs (9.30pm).

**Wetherspoon's** 35–37 Bedford St. Belfast's cheapest pint of stout and a range of good-value meals on offer all day.

### Clubs and DJ bars

**Apartment** 2 Donegall Square. Swish, recently renovated bar where bright young Belfast goes to be seen; DJs most nights.

**The Fly** 5–6 Lower Crescent. About as hip as Belfast gets – three floors of music and occasional mayhem.

**The Kremlin** 90 Donegall St. Ireland's biggest gay venue with a host of events throughout the week.

**La Lea** 43 Franklin St. Hugely popular club, especially for its Saturday night funked-up house session.

**The Limelight** 17 Ormeau Ave. A serious dance club with various club nights.

**The Menagerie** 130 University St. Leftfield venue offering a broad range of musical entertainment.

**Milk Bar Club** 10–14 Tomb St. Ever-popular and ever-packed club playing dance music for all tastes every night of the week.

**Northern Whig** 2–10 Bridge St. Massive bar in the premises of the old newspaper, featuring pre-club DJs most nights.

## Listings

**Bike Rental** Lifecycles, Unit 35, Smithfield Market.

**Exchange** Thomas Cook, 11 Donegall Place (☎028/9055 0030); and the Belfast Welcome Centre (see p.578).

**Hospitals** Belfast City Hospital, Lisburn Rd (☎028/9032 9241); Royal Victoria, Grosvenor Rd (☎028/9024 0503).

**Internet** Belfast Welcome Centre, 47 Donegall Place; Friends Café, 109–113 Royal Avenue; ITXP, 175–177 Ormeau Rd; Revelations, 27 Shaftesbury Square.

**Left luggage** Belfast Welcome Centre, 47 Donegall Place.

**Police** North Queen St ☎028/9065 0222.

**Post office** Castle Place.

## The Giant's Causeway and around

Since 1693, when the Royal Society publicized it as one of the great wonders of the natural world, the **Giant's Causeway**, 65 miles north of Belfast on the coast, has been a major tourist attraction. Consisting of an estimated thirty-seven thousand polygonal basalt columns, it's the result of a massive subterranean explosion some sixty million years ago which spewed out a huge mass of molten basalt onto the surface and, as it cooled, solidified into massive polygonal crystals. **Trains** from Belfast go to **COLERAINE**, where there's a regular connection to **PORTRUSH**; from either, you can catch the "**open-topper**" bus (June–Aug 5 daily; £2.70 single, £4 return) to the Causeway, or from Portrush there's bus #172, both running via Bushmills. A restored **narrow-gauge railway** runs between Bushmills and the Causeway (mid-May to Sept 3–5 daily plus some days in other months; 20min; single £2.50, return £4.50). The Antrim Coaster coach (Goldline Express #252) runs from Larne direct to the Causeway (2 daily; Oct–June not Sun; 2hr 30min), taking in the gorgeous scenery of the Antrim Glens and stunning seascapes en route.

The Causeway's **visitor centre** (daily 10am–5/7pm; ✆028/2073 1855; free; car parking £5) has information and a small exhibition. Taking the path down the cliffs from the visitor centre (or the shuttle bus; every 15min; £1.20 return) brings you to the most spectacular of the blocks where many people linger, but if you push on, you'll be rewarded with relative solitude and views of some of the more impressive formations high in the cliffs. One of these, **Chimney Point**, has an appearance so bizarre that the ships of the Spanish Armada opened fire on it, believing that they were attacking Dunluce Castle, a few miles further west. An alternative two-mile circuit follows the spectacular cliff-top path from the visitor centre, with views across to Scotland, to a flight of 162 steps leading down the cliff to a set of forty-ft basalt columns known as the **Organ Pipes**, from where paths lead round to the shuttle-bus stop alongside the Causeway proper.

**BUSHMILLS** makes a reasonable base, as there's an HINI **hostel**, *Mill Rest*, at 49 Main St (✆028/2073 1222; dorms £11) and several **B&B** options. While here you could tour the **Old Bushmills Distillery** (April–Oct Mon–Sat 9.30am–5.30pm, Sun noon–5.30pm; Nov–March call ✆028/2073 1521 for tour times; £5; ⊛www.bushmills.com) and sample whiskeys from the world's oldest licit distillery, founded in 1608.

# Derry

**DERRY** lies at the foot of Lough Foyle, less than three miles from the border with the Republic. The city presents a beguiling picture, its two hillsides terraced with pastel-shaded houses punctuated by stone spires, and, being seventy per cent Catholic, has a very different atmosphere from Belfast. However, from Partition in 1921 until the late 1980s Derry's Catholic majority was denied its civil rights by gerrymandering, which ensured that the Protestant minority maintained control of all important local institutions. The situation came to a head after the Protestant Apprentice Boys' March in August 1969, when the police attempted to storm the Catholic estates of the Bogside. In the ensuing tension, British troops were widely deployed for the first time in Northern Ireland. On January 31, 1972, the crisis deepened when British paratroopers opened fire on civilians, killing thirteen unarmed demonstrators in what became known as **Bloody Sunday**. Derry is now greatly changed: tensions eased considerably here long before Belfast, thanks in part to a determinedly even-handed local council, although defiant murals remain and marching is still a contentious issue. The city centre has undergone much regeneration too, and Derry has a justifiable reputation for innovation in the arts.

## The City

You can walk the entire mile-long circuit of Derry's seventeenth-century **city walls** – some of the best-preserved defences left standing in Europe. Reinforced by bulwarks, bastions and a parapeted earth rampart, the walls encircle the original medieval street pattern with four gateways – Shipquay, Butcher, Bishop and Ferryquay – surviving from the first construction, in slightly revised form.

The best starting point is the **Guildhall Square**, once the old quay, where most of the city's cannons are lined up, between Shipquay and Magazine gates, their noses peering out above the ramparts. A reconstruction of the medieval **O'Doherty Tower** houses splendid displays on the city's turbulent political history and a new exhibition on the Spanish Armada (check with the tourist office for opening times). Turning left at **Shipquay Gate**, the promenade doglegs at Water Bastion where the River Foyle once lapped the walls at high tide. Continue on to Newgate Bastion and **Ferryquay Gate**, where you can look out across the river to the Waterside area, once primarily Protestant, now almost half Catholic – further evidence of the lessening of the city's political tensions. Between Ferryquay and Bishop's Gate the major sight is the Protestant **St Columb's Cathedral** (Mon–Sat 9am–1pm & 2–4/5pm; £1.50; ⊛www.stcolumbscathedral.org), just within the southern section of the walls; it overlooks **The Fountain**, the Protestant enclave immediately outside the same stretch of walls, and offers one of the best views of the city. Built in 1633, it was Ireland's first post-Reformation cathedral. In 1688/89 Derry played a key part in the Williamite victory over the Catholic King James II by holding out against a fifteen-week siege that cost the lives of one-quarter of the city's population. The cathedral was used as a battery during the siege, and in the entrance porch you'll find the cannonball shot into the grounds by the besieging army with proposals for the city's surrender.

Back on the walls, pass the white sandstone **courthouse** next to Bishop's Gate and you'll see, downhill to the left, the only remaining tower of the old Derry jail. At the **Double Bastion** sits the Roaring Meg cannon, used during the siege, while down in the valley below are the streets of the Bogside. These were once the undisputed preserve of the IRA, and **Free Derry Corner** marks the site of the original barricades erected against the British army at the height of the Troubles. Nearby are the Bloody Sunday and Hunger Strikers' memorials. Further along the city wall is the **Royal Bastion**, former site of the Rev. George Walker statue which was blown up in 1973. It is in Walker's and their predecessors' memory that the Protestant Apprentice Boys march around the walls every August 12.

## Practicalities

**Trains** from Belfast arrive on the east bank of the Foyle with a free connecting bus to the **bus station** on Foyle Street beside Guildhall Square. City of Derry **airport** (☎028/7181 0784, ⊛www.cityofderryairport.com) is seven miles northeast, connected to the centre by bus. The **tourist office** is at 44 Foyle St (July–Sept daily 9/10am–5/7pm; Oct–June Mon–Fri 9am–5pm, mid–March to June also Sat 10am–5pm; ☎028/7126 7284, ⊛www.derryvisitor.com) and has a **bureau de change**.

**Hostel** accommodation includes the *Derry City Independent Hostel* at 44 Great James St, north of the city walls, half-a-mile down Strand Road (☎028/7137 7989, ⊛www.derry-hostel.co.uk; dorms £10, rooms ❸), with a smaller sister, *Derry Backpackers Hostel* (same contact details and prices), at 4 Asylum Rd. For **B&B** try the excellent-value *The Saddler's House*, 36 Great James St (☎028/7126 9691, ⊛www.thesaddlershouse.com; ❺), or *Clarence House*, 15 Northland Rd (☎028/7126 5342, ⊜clarencehouse@zoom.co.uk; ❺).

**Eating** out options include *The Leprechaun*, 23 Strand Rd, for delicious home-baking and hot meals; the *Aroma Bistro*, Union Hall Place, for reasonably priced snacks and lunches; the stylish *Mange 2* on Clarendon St, offering a variety of meat and fish dishes; and *Badger's Bar*, 16 Orchard St, offering good-value pub lunches. **Internet** access is available at *Webcrawler Cyber Café*, 52 Strand Rd. **Pubs** host most entertainment, and Waterloo Street just outside the northern walls is the best bet for traditional and other live music venues, including *Bound for Boston* and *Peadar O'Donnell's*, or try *Sandino's* on Water Street. Students congregate at *Café Roc*, where Rock and Strand roads meet; upstairs *Earth Niteclub* is hugely popular. *Downey's*, on Shipquay Street, claims to be "Ireland's largest R&B club" and has music most nights while other clubs to try include DJ bars such as *The Strand Bar* and *The Carraig*, all on Strand Road. Check the bi-weekly *Derry Journal* for **listings**.

## Enniskillen and Lough Erne

**ENNISKILLEN** sits on a lake island, a narrow ribbon of water passing each side of the town between Lower and Upper **Lough Erne**. The water loops its way around the core of the town, its glassy surface lending Enniskillen a sense of calm and reflecting the mini-turrets of **Enniskillen Castle**. Rebuilt by William Cole, to whom the British gave Enniskillen in 1609, the castle houses the **Fermanagh County Museum** and the **Regimental Museum of the Royal Inniskilling Fusiliers** in the keep (July & Aug Tues–Fri 10am–5pm, Sat–Mon 2–5pm; May, June & Sept closed Sun; Oct–April closed Sat & Sun; £2.50; ⓦwww.enniskillencastle.co.uk), a proud, polished display of paraphernalia of the town's historic regiments. A mile along the Belfast road stands **Castle Coole** (noon–6pm: mid-March to May & Sept Sat & Sun; June Wed–Mon; July & Aug daily; £4.20). A perfect Palladian building of Portland stone, with an interior of fine plasterwork and superb furnishings, it sits in a beautiful landscaped garden (daily 10am–4/8pm; free).

Opposite the **bus station** on Wellington Road is the **tourist office** (Mon–Fri 9am–5.30/7pm; Easter–Sept also Sat & Sun 10/11am–5/6pm; ☎028/6632 3110, ⓦwww.fermanagh-online.com), which can help finding B&Bs, most of which are some distance from the town centre. The modern HINI **hostel**, *The Bridges*, is on Belmore Street by the war memorial (☎028/6634 0110; dorms £10, rooms ❸). For **eating** out, try *Oscar's* in Belmore Street, or *Franco's* in Queen Elizabeth Road. Several **bars** along High Street and its continuation, Townhall Street, provide pub food, particularly *The Linen Hall* and *Pat's*. You'll find occasional traditional music at *Blakes of the Hollow* on Townhall Street, while *The Fort Lodge Hotel* and *Railway Hotel*, both on Forthill Street, have live music and DJs at weekends.

### Lough Erne

The earliest people to settle in this region lived on and around the two lakes of **Lough Erne** which features many crannogs (artificial islands). The maze of waterways protected the settlers from invaders and created an enduring cultural isolation. Stone carvings suggest that Christianity was accepted far more slowly here than elsewhere: several pagan idols have been found on Christian sites, and the early Christian remains on the islands reveal the influence of pagan culture.

The easiest place to visit is **Devenish Island**, two miles northwest of Enniskillen. St Molaise founded a monastic settlement here in the sixth century and it remained an important religious centre up until the early seventeenth century. It's a delightful setting and the considerable ruins span the entire medieval period. There are regular ferries (April–Sept Tues–Sat 10am–6pm, Sun 2–6pm; £2.25) from Trory Point, three miles north of Enniskillen on the A32 road. Four miles further north along the Kesh road lies **Castle Archdale** forest park from whose marina ferries (April–June Sat & Sun 11am–1pm; July & Aug daily 11am–6pm; £3) depart to **White Island**. The island's ruined abbey is known for its early Christian carvings that look eerily pagan: the most disconcerting is the lewd female figure known as a Sheila-na-Gig, with bulging cheeks, a big grin, open legs and arms pointing to her genitals.

# Travel details

### Trains

Details are for weekday services; extra services may run on Mondays and Fridays, fewer on Sundays.

**Belfast** to: Coleraine (9–10 daily; 1hr 30min); Derry (7–8 daily; 2hr 15min); Dublin (8 daily; 2hr 5min); Larne Harbour (12–16 daily; 55min).
**Coleraine** to: Portrush, for Giant's Causeway (21 daily; 15min).

**Cork** to: Dublin (9 daily; 2hr 35min–3hr 35min); Killarney (6 daily; 1hr 30min–1hr 45min).
**Derry** to: Belfast (7–8 daily; 2hr 15min); Coleraine (8 daily; 40min).
**Drogheda** to: Dublin (32 daily; 30min–1hr).
**Dublin (Connolly)** to: Belfast (8 daily; 2hr 5min); Drogheda (33 daily; 30min–1hr); Rosslare (3 daily; 3hr 5min–3hr 25min).
**Dublin (Heuston)** to: Cork (9 daily; 2hr 35min–3hr 20min); Ennis (5 daily; 2hr 55min–3hr 40min); Galway (6–7 daily; 2hr 20min–2hr 50min); Kilkenny (5 daily; 1hr 35min–1hr 50min); Killarney (7 daily; 3hr 30min–3hr 50min); Sligo (3 daily; 3hr 10min–3hr 30min); Westport (3 daily; 3hr 20min–3hr 40min).
**Ennis** to: Dublin (7 daily; 3hr 5min–4hr 45min).
**Galway** to: Dublin (6–7 daily; 2hr 25min–2hr 50min).
**Kilkenny** to: Dublin (5 daily; 1hr 40min–1hr 55min).
**Killarney** to: Cork (5 daily; 1hr 20min–1hr 40min); Dublin (5 daily; 3hr–4hr.
**Rosslare Harbour** to: Dublin (3 daily; 3hr–3hr 10min).
**Sligo** to: Dublin (3 daily; 3hr–3hr 10min).
**Westport** to: Dublin (3 daily; 3hr 30min–3hr 40min).

## Buses

Details below cover Bus Éireann or Ulsterbus services on summer weekdays; extra services may run on Fridays, fewer in winter and on Sundays.
**Belfast** to: Derry (15 daily; 1hr 40min); Dublin (7 daily; 2hr 55min); Enniskillen (8–10 daily; 2hr 35min).
**Cashel** to: Cork (6 daily; 1hr 35min); Dublin (6 daily; 2hr 50min).
**Cork** to: Cashel (6 daily; 1hr 35min); Dublin (6 daily; 4hr 25min); Galway (12 daily; 3hr 15min); Kilkenny (5 daily; 2hr 45min–3hr 35min); Killarney (12 daily; 2hr).

**Derry** to: Donegal (4–5 daily; 1hr 30min); Dublin (5 daily; 4hr 30min); Enniskillen (7 daily; 1hr 30min); Sligo (5 daily; 2hr 30min).
**Donegal town** to: Derry (4–5 daily; 1hr 30min); Dublin (6 daily; 3hr 45min–4hr 10min); Glencolmcille (3 daily; 1hr 25min); Sligo (6 daily; 1hr).
**Dublin** to: Belfast (7 daily; 2hr 55min); Cashel (6 daily; 2hr 50min); Cork (6 daily; 4hr 25min); Derry (5 daily; 4hr 30min); Donegal town (6 daily; 3hr 45min–4hr 10min); Doolin (2 daily; 6hr 15min); Drogheda (35 daily; 1hr 15min); Ennis (12 daily; 4hr 20min–6hr 50min); Enniskillen (6 daily; 2hr 20min–3hr); Galway (15 daily; 3hr 30min); Kilkenny (6 daily; 2hr 10min–2hr 30min); Killarney (5 daily; 6hr 10min); Newgrange (3 daily; 1hr 40min–1hr 55min); Portrush (1/2 daily; 5hr 40min); Rosslare Harbour (13 daily; 3hr 20min); Sligo (6 daily; 4hr); Westport (3 daily; 5hr–5hr 40min).
**Ennis** to: Doolin (3 daily; 1hr 25min); Dublin (15 daily; 4hr 10min–6hr 50min).
**Enniskillen** to: Belfast (8–10 daily; 2hr 35min); Derry (7 daily; 1hr 30min); Dublin (6 daily; 2hr 20min–3hr).
**Galway** to: Cork (12 daily; 3hr 15min); Doolin (2 daily; 1hr 30min); Dublin (15 daily; 3hr 30min); Killarney (6 daily; 4hr 35min); Westport (6 daily; 1hr 50min).
**Kilkenny** to: Cork (4 daily; 2hr 50min–3hr 35min); Dublin (7 daily; 2hr 15min–2hr 45min).
**Killarney** to: Cork (12 daily; 2hr); Dingle (2–5 daily; 1hr 45min–2hr 30min); Dublin (6 daily; 5hr 15min–6hr 20min); Waterville via Caherciveen (1–3 daily; 1hr 45min).
**Rosslare Harbour** to: Dublin (13 daily; 3hr 20min); Wexford (13 daily; 35min).
**Sligo** to: Derry (5 daily; 2hr 30min); Dublin (6 daily; 4hr); Enniskillen (4 daily; 1hr 25min); Galway (5 daily; 2hr 30min).
**Westport** to: Dublin (5 daily; 5hr); Galway (3 daily; 1hr 50min).

# Italy

# Italy highlights

* **Grand Canal, Venice**
Catch a waterbus at night
for the most romantic
views. See p.605

* **The Palio, Siena** The
event of the year, a
frenetic horse race in this
wonderfully preserved
medieval town centre. See
p.624

* **Spanish Steps, Rome**
Hang out here in the
evening and be serenaded
by guitar-strumming
locals. See p.635

* **Villaggio Globale** Rome's
most interesting music is
played at this alternative
venue. See p.640

* **Pompeii** The excava-
tions of this Roman town,
buried by volcanic ash
in 79 AD, are hauntingly
evocative. See p.647

* **Pizza, Naples** Sample
pizza in its home town,
made with fresh tomatoes,
basil and topped with buffalo mozzarella. See p.645

* **Sassi, Matera** Sleep in a
cave in one of Italy's most
fascinating southern cities.
See p.650

* **Valle dei Templi, Agrigento** Wander around this
stunning string of Greek
temples to rival any in
Greece. See p.656

△ The Palio, Siena

# Introduction and basics

Of all the countries in Europe, **Italy** is perhaps the hardest to classify. It is a modern, industrialized nation; it is the harbinger of style, its designers leading the way with each season's fashions. But it is also a Mediterranean country, with all that that implies. Agricultural land covers much of the country, a lot of it, especially in the south, still owned under almost feudal conditions. In towns and villages all over the country, life stops during the middle of the day for a long lunch. It remains strongly family-oriented, with an emphasis on the traditions and rituals of the Catholic Church, and it is not unusual to find people living with their parents until their early thirties.

If there is a single national characteristic, it's to embrace life to the full, manifest in the hundreds of local **festivals** taking place on any given day, and the importance placed on good food. There is also, of course, the country's enormous cultural legacy: Tuscany alone has more classified historical monuments than any country in the world and every region retains its own relics of an artistic tradition generally acknowledged to be the world's richest.

Italy wasn't unified until 1861, a fact that's borne out by the regional nature of the place today. The north is one of the most advanced industrial societies in the world; the south is by contrast one of the most economically depressed areas in Europe. In the northwest, the regions of Piemonte and Lombardy – and the two main centres of **Turin** and **Milan** – epitomize the wealthy north. Liguria, the small coastal province to the south, has long been known as the "Italian Riviera". It's a beautiful stretch of coast, whose provincial capital, **Genoa**, is a bustling port with a long seafaring tradition. The interest of the northeastern regions is of course **Venice** itself – a unique city, and every bit as beautiful as its reputation would suggest, though you won't be alone in appreciating it. If the crowds are too much, aim for the arc of historic towns nearby – **Verona**, **Padua** and **Vicenza**. To the south,

Emilia-Romagna has been at the heart of Italy's postwar industrial boom. Its coast is popular, especially brash **Rimini**, and there are also the ancient centres of **Ravenna**, **Parma** and **Bologna**, the latter one of Italy's liveliest but least appreciated cities.

The centre of the country, specifically **Tuscany**, with its classic rolling countryside and the art-packed towns of **Florence**, **Pisa** and **Siena**, represents the most commonly perceived image of Italy. Neighbouring **Umbria** is similar but quieter, though visitors flock into towns such as **Perugia** and **Assisi** – and unspoilt **Urbino** nearby. Lazio, to the south, is a poor and desolate region whose focal point is **Rome**, the national capital. South of here in Campania, **Naples**, a petulant, unforgettable city, is the spiritual heart of the Italian south, and is close to the fine ancient sites of **Pompeii** and **Herculaneum**, not to mention the spectacular stretch of coast around **Amalfi**. Puglia, the "heel" of Italy, has underrated pleasures – the souk-like quality of its capital, **Bari**, and more notably **Lecce**, a Baroque gem of a city. **Sicily** is a law unto itself, with attractions ranging from Hellenic remains to the drama of Mount Etna, and the fascinating city of Palermo. **Sardinia**, too, feels far removed from the mainland, especially in its relatively undiscovered interior.

## Italy on the net

ⓦ **www.enit.it** Official Tourist Board site.
ⓦ **www.virgilio.it** Search engine with good travel and tourism links.
ⓦ **www.paginegialle.it** Italian Yellow Pages.
ⓦ **www.trenitalia.com** Italian rail timetables.

# Information & maps

Most towns, major train stations and airports have a **tourist office** (*ufficio turistico*) and/or a **Pro Loco** information service. Most tourist offices will give out **maps** for free, but if you want an indexed town plan, get Studio FMB's or Falk's. The clearest and best-value large-scale road maps are by Michelin: a 1:1,000,000 map, or 1:400,000 maps of the north and south, Sicily and Sardinia.

# Money and banks

Italy's currency is the **euro** (€). **Banking hours** are Mon–Fri 8.30am–1.30pm & 3.30–7.30pm. ATMs are widespread. To change cash or travellers' cheques, **exchange bureaux** tend to give a better rate than the banks. Otherwise, larger hotels will change money and travellers' cheques. Under 25s and students are often allowed free entry or reduced rates upon production of a valid student card or proof of age.

# Communications

**Post office** opening hours are Mon–Fri 8am–6.30pm, with branches in towns and cities also open on Sat. Stamps can also be bought at *tabacchi* – ask for *posta prioritaria* if you want letters to arrive home before you do. Public **phones** are card-operated; get a phone card (*scheda telefonica*) from *tabacchi* and newsstands for €5/10. For landline calls – local and long-distance – dial all digits, including the area code. **Directory enquiries** are pricey – call ☏176 (international) or ☏412 then 3 (domestic). Most towns have at least one place with **Internet** access. Hourly rates vary from €3/hour to €10/hour in big cities.

# Getting around

Apart from a few private lines in the north and Sardinia, **trains** are operated by Italian State Railways (*Ferrovie dello Stato* or FS; Ⓦwww.trenitalia.it). For most journeys you'll have a choice between Eurostar/Intercity – for which you have to pay a supplement of thirty percent (and reserve for Eurostar) – and ordinary trains, *Diretto*, *Interregionale* and *Regionale*, which can be extremely slow. InterRail, Eurail and the Italian Trenitalia **passes** are valid on the whole FS network, though you'll pay supplements for the fast trains, and most long-distance trains. Almost everywhere has some kind of **bus** service, but schedules can be sketchy. Buy tickets at *tabacchi* or the bus terminal rather than on board.

# Accommodation

Most tourist offices have details of **hotel** rates. Book ahead in the major cities and resorts, especially in summer. Hotels in Italy come with a confusing variety of names (*locanda*, *pensione*, *albergo*) but all are star-rated. Rates vary greatly but on average you can expect to pay €60 for a double without private bathroom (*senza bagno*) in a one-star hotel, and a minimum of €80 for a double in a three-star. In very busy places you might have to stay a minimum of three nights.

**B&Bs** and **agriturismi**·(farm-stays) can make a good-value alternative. They are often in spectacular locations and provide excellent Italian home cooking, though you may need a car to get to them: ask for a list from the tourist office.

There are also more than a hundred **hostels** in Italy, charging €14–26 per person for a dorm bed, though for two people travelling together, this isn't much cheaper than a budget hotel room. You can get a full list of HI hostels from the Associazione Italiana Alberghi per la Gioventù (Ⓦwww.ostellionline.org). Alternatively, ask the tourist board about local **case per ferie**, usually religious houses with rooms or beds to let. They can be better value than hostels but often have curfews.

There are plenty of **campsites** and in most cases you pay for location rather than facilities, which can vary enormously. Daily prices are around €5–9 per person, plus the same for a tent and around €5 for a vehicle. Check out Ⓦwww.camping.it.

## Italian

Italian is the country's official language, but many people also speak a localized dialect - some of which, such as Sard, now have language status.

|  | Italian | Pronunciation |
|---|---|---|
| Yes | Sì | See |
| No | No | Noh |
| Please | Per favore | Pear fah-vure-ay |
| Thank you | Grazie | Grraat-see-ay |
| Hello/Good day | Ciao/buon giorno/salve | Chow/bon jaw-noh/salvay |
| Goodbye | Ciao/arrivederci | Chow/arriva-derchee |
| Excuse me | Mi scusi/prego | Mee scoo-see/ pray-go |
| Where? | Dove? | Doh-vay? |
| Good | Buono | Bwo-noh |
| Bad | Cattivo | Cat-ee-voh |
| Near | Vicino | Vih-chee-noh |
| Far | Lontano | Lont-ah-noh |
| Cheap | Buon mercato | Bwon mare-cart-oh |
| Expensive | Caro | Car-oh |
| Open | Aperto | Apairt-oh |
| Closed | Chiuso | Queue-soh |
| Today | Oggi | Ojj-ee |
| Yesterday | Ieri | Ee-air-ee |
| Tomorrow | Domani | Doh-mahn-ee |
| How much is....? | Quanto è...? | Cwan-to ay? |
| What time is it? | Che ore sono? | Keh orr-ay son-noh |
| I don't understand | Non ho capito | Non oh kapee-toe |
| Do you speak English? | Parla Inglese? | Parr-la inglay-zay? |
| One | Uno | Oo-noh |
| Two | Due | Doo-ay |
| Three | Tre | Tray |
| Four | Quattro | Cwattr-oh |
| Five | Cinque | Chin-cway |
| Six | Sei | Say |
| Seven | Sette | Set-tay |
| Eight | Otto | Ot-toe |
| Nine | Nove | Noh-vay |
| Ten | Dieci | Dee-ay-chee |

# Food and drink

There are few places in the world where you can eat and drink as well as in Italy. If you eat only pizza and *panini* (rolls), you'll be missing out on the distinct regional cuisines; don't be afraid to ask what the *piatti tipici* (local dishes) are. Most Italians start their day in a bar, with a cappuccino and a *cornetto* (croissant), a **breakfast** that should cost around €2 if you stand up. At **lunchtime**, bars sell *tramezzini*, sandwiches on white bread, and *panini*. Another stopgap is *arancini,* fried meat- or cheese-filled rice balls. Markets are also a good source of cheap food. Many places have no seating and bars charge up to three times more if you sit down. Italian **ice cream** (*gelato*) is justifiably famous: a cone (*un cono*) is an indispensable accessory to the evening *passeggiata*. For the best choice go to a *gelateria*.

For sit-down food, the cheapest is **pizza** – if you're lucky, cooked in the traditional way in wood-fired ovens. Although a **trattoria** or **ristorante** often does a fixed-price *menu turistico*, it's not always very good. Traditionally, a trattoria is cheaper than a restaurant, offering *cucina casalinga* (home-style cooking). But in either, pasta dishes go for around €6–9, and although pasta is considered a starter there's usually not a problem just having this; the main fish or meat courses will normally be €9–15. Order vegetables (*contorni*) separately; salads (*insalate*) are either green (*verde*) or mixed (*mista*). Afterwards there's fruit (*frutta*) and desserts (*dolci*). As well as the **cover charge** (*coperto*), service (*servizio*) will often be added, generally about ten percent (if it isn't, you should tip the same amount). Note that **smoking** is now outlawed in most public places, including restaurants and trains, and you can be fined for lighting up.

### Drink

**Bars** are less social centres than functional places for a quick coffee or beer. You pay first at the cash desk (*la cassa*), present your receipt (*scontrino*) and give your order. In the south it's customary to leave a small tip on the counter. **Coffee** comes small and black (*espresso*, or just *caffé*), with a dash of milk (*macchiato*) or cream (*con panna*); or white and frothy (*cappuccino*); try a *granita* – cold coffee with crushed ice, usually topped with cream. **Tea** (*te*) comes with lemon (*con limone*) unless you ask for milk (*con latte*); there are usually several types, and it's also served cold (*te freddo*). A *spremuta* is a fresh fruit **juice**; there's also crushed-ice fruit *granites*, while the Italian version of cola, *chinotto*, is a refreshing alternative. In winter, try a hot punch – *punch alla livornese*, an alcoholic coffee drink found in Tuscany, is one of the best. **Wine** is invariably drunk with meals, and is very cheap. Go for the local stuff: ask for *un mezzo* (a half-litre) or *un quarto* (a quarter). Bottles are pricier but still good value; expect to pay around €12 a bottle in a restaurant. **Beer** (*birra*) usually comes in bottles of one-third or two-thirds of a litre. Cheapest and most common are the Italian brands Peroni and Dreher, or you could choose draught beer (*alla spina*). A generous shot of spirits costs from about €3. There's also fiery **grappa**, made from grape pips and stalks. Of the **liqueurs**, Amaro is a bitter after-dinner drink, Amaretto sweeter with a strong taste of marzipan, and Sambuca a sticky-sweet aniseed concoction.

There are now **pubs** all over Italy but drinking is often pricey: €6 for a beer, and €7–10 for a cocktail. Drinking in **nightclubs** can be ruinous – the entrance fee of €10–15 usually includes one drink.

# Opening hours and holidays

Most **shops and businesses** open Mon–Sat 8/9am–1pm & 4–7/8pm, though in the north, offices work a 9am–5pm day. Just about everything except bars and restaurants closes on Sunday. Most **churches** keep shop hours: note that many will not let you in with bare shoulders or wearing short trousers or skirts. **Museums** traditionally open Tues–Sat 9am–2pm, Sun 9am–1pm, and are closed on Mon; but some have extended hours. Most **archeological sites** open daily from 9am until about an hour before sunset. Everything closes for **national holidays**: Jan 1, Jan 6, Easter Mon, April 25, May 1, Aug 15, Nov 1, Dec 8, Dec 25 & 26.

# Emergencies

Most of the **crime** you're likely to come across is small-time. You can minimize the risk of this by being discreet, not flashing anything of value (including phones), keeping a firm hand on your camera and bag, and never leaving anything valuable in your car. The **police** come in many forms: the *Polizia Urbana/Vigili Urbani* deal with traffic offences; but you should report thefts to the *Polizia Statale*. It is worth noting that Italy is currently cracking down on soft **drugs** offences and treating them as severely as hard drugs.

**Pharmacies** (*farmacie*) can give advice and dispense prescriptions; there's one open all night in towns and cities (find the address of the nearest on any pharmacy door). For serious ailments, go to the *Pronto Soccorso* (casualty) section of the nearest **hospital** (*ospedale*).

### Emergency numbers

Police ☎112; Ambulance ☎133; Fire ☎115.

# Northwest Italy

While the northwest of Italy is many people's first experience of the country, it represents its least "Italian" aspect, at least in the regions of **Piemonte** and **Val d'Aosta**, where French is still spoken by some as a first language. **Turin**, on the main rail and road route from France to Milan, is the obvious initial stop, the first capital of Italy after the Unification in 1860 and a grand city with many reminders of its past. To the east, **Lombardy** was long viewed by northerners as the heart of Italy – emperors from Charlemagne to Napoleon came here to be crowned – and northern European business magnates continue to take its upbeat capital, **Milan**, more seriously than Rome. The region's landscape has paid the price for economic success: industry chokes the peripheries of towns and spreads its tentacles into the northern lakes and mountain valleys. Nonetheless, Lombardy has its attractions, notably **Mantua**, which flourished during the Middle Ages and Renaissance. The region of **Liguria** to the south has perhaps the country's most spectacular stretch of coastline. Chief town of the province is the sprawling port of **Genoa**, while southeast, towards Tuscany, the mix of mountains and fishing villages "discovered" by the Romantics in the late eighteenth century prepared the way for the first package tourists in the early twentieth century. Now the whole area explodes every July and August, with people coming to resorts like **Portofino** strictly for pose value – although stretches like the **Cinque Terre** are still well worth discovering.

## Turin (Torino)

After a recent clean up, **TURIN** (Torino) – a virtual Fiat company town - has emerged resplendent with gracious avenues, opulent palaces and splendid galleries. It is a lively, bustling place with cafés and nightlife to rival any European city, as well as Italy's most vibrant contemporary art scene, while the 2006 Winter Olympics have provided the impetus for some major redevelopment. The grid plan of the Baroque centre makes finding your way around easy. **Via Roma** is the central spine, a grand affair lined with designer shops and ritzy cafés and punctuated by the city's most elegant piazzas, most notably **Piazza San Carlo**. Around the corner, the **Museo Egizio** (Tues–Sun 8.30am–7.30pm; €6.50; ⓦwww.museoegizio.org) holds a superb collection of Egyptian antiquities, including gorgeously decorated mummy cases, erotic papyri, and the Tomb of Kha, the burial chamber of a 1400-BC architect, and his wife, Merit. Above the museum, the **Galleria Sabauda** (Tues–Sun 8.30am–7.30pm; €4) was built around the Savoy dukes' private collection and is still firmly stamped with their taste – a miscellany of Italian paintings, supplemented by a fine Dutch and Flemish collection, including works by Memling, Brueghel, David Teniers Jnr and Van Dyck. A ten-minute walk northwest brings you to the fifteenth-century **Duomo** housing the **Turin Shroud**, which is usually kept under wraps and only shown to the public during holy years, though a copy is on display by the altar. This piece of cloth, imprinted with the image of a man's body, had long been claimed as the shroud in which Christ was wrapped after his crucifixion. However, in 1989 carbon-dating tests showed it to be a medieval fake, made between 1260 and 1390.

Turin has a good selection of modern art museums, the best of which is the **GAM** on Via Magenta 31 (Tues–Sun 9am–7pm; €6; ⓦwww.gamtorino.it), with works from the eighteenth century to the present day, by artists such as Giorgio de Chirico and Lucio Fontana. For more contemporary art, the **Castello di Rivoli**, 20km outside Turin (Tues–Sun 10am–5pm; €6.50; ⓦwww .castellodirivoli.org), is home of the most important collection of postwar art in Italy, with works by Jeff Koons, Carl Andre and Mario Merz. On weekdays, take bus #36 from Piazza Statuto and then a 20-minute walk; at weekends, there's an (infrequent) direct shuttle bus from Piazza Castello. Less impressive is the **Pinacoteca Agnelli** (Tues–Sun 9am–7pm, ⓦwww .pinacoteca-agnelli.it; €7.50), on top of the Lingotto factory building, on Via Nizza. Designed by Renzo Piano and opened in 2002, the gallery has a fairly thin permanent collection but is worth checking out for the building itself and its visiting exhibitions: take buses #1 or #35 from the train station along Via Nizza.

### Practicalities

Turin's main **train station**, Porta Nuova, is on Corso Vittorio Emanuele, at the foot of Via Roma, convenient for the city centre and hotels. There are two **tourist offices** – the main one in the Atrium built for the 2006 Winter Olympics at Piazza Solferino (Mon–Sun 9.30am–7pm; ☎ 011.535.181, ⓦwww .turismotorino.org), and a smaller one at the train station (Mon–Sat 9.30am–7pm, Sun 9.30am–3pm). The **Torino Card** (€15/two days, €17/three days) gives free transport on buses, entrance to all museums and discounts on theatre and concert tickets. There's **Internet access** at Internet Train, Via Carlo Alberto 18.

▲ Docks Dora

**ACCOMMODATION**
| Mobledor | A |
| Ostello Torino | C |
| Paradiso | D |
| San Carlo | B |

**EATING & DRINKING**
| Baratti e Milano | 3 |
| Caffè San Carlo | 4 |
| Fiorio | 1 |
| Porto di Savona | 2 |
| Vecchio Piemonte | 5 |

**TURIN**

▼ Pinacoteca Agnelli

### Accommodation

Many of Turin's budget hotels are in the sleazy quarter off Via Nizza, convenient enough but not an advisable choice. Somewhat safer, but more expensive, are the streets opposite Porta Nuova, close to Piazza Carlo Felice. There are also a number of fairly reasonably priced hotels west of Piazza Castello.
**Mobledor** Via Accademia Albertina 1 ☎011.888.445. A small friendly one-star hotel in an excellent location. ❹

**Ostello Torino** Via Alby 1 ☎011.660.2939. Friendly HI hostel with small rooms and Internet access; 30min walk from Porta Nuova or take bus #52. €14.
**Paradiso** Via Berthollet 3 ☎011.669.8678. Extremely clean one-star hotel close to the train station with friendly proprietors. ❸
**San Carlo** Piazza San Carlo 167 ☎011.562.7846, ⓦwww.albergosancarlo.it. Clean, neat hotel; some rooms have a view over the piazza. ❻

### Cafes and restaurants

**Baratti e Milano** Piazza Castello 29. *Fin-de-siècle* café, where genteel Torinese sip tea in a rarefied ambience of mirrors, chandeliers and carved wood.
**Caffè San Carlo** Piazza San Carlo 156. A favoured

haunt of politicians and industrialists, this glitzy café is particularly good for an aperitif with nibbles.
**Fiorio** Via Po 8. A *fin-de-siècle* café, worth a visit particularly for its ice cream.

**Porto di Savona** Piazza Vittorio Veneto 2.
Popular and reasonably priced restaurant serving
excellent regional cooking.

**Vecchio Piemonte** Corso Vinzaglio 21. Known for
its classic Piemontese dishes such as *fritto misto
alla piemontese*. Closed Sunday.

## Bars, clubs and live music

In summer, the liveliest areas are Via Carlo Alberto,
Via San Quintino, Docks Dora on Lungo Dora and
the Murazzi bordering Parco San Valentino, where
people congregate at bars with outside tables.
Student night is Thursday. For what's on, look out
for the events pamphlet *Zero*, free from bars.
**AEIOU** Via Spanzotti 3. Big warehouse-style club
for dancing all night; rock, Cuban, jam sessions,
art and theatre projects. Entrance usually free.
**The Beach** Arcate Murazzi del Po. One of the
coolest clubs in Italy; Tuesday is "Socrates night"
featuring music and drinks from a different
country each week.
**The Frog** Via Mercanti 19. Central disco bar with
restaurant and live DJs.
**Hiroshima Mon Amour** Via Bossoli 83. Avant-
garde music and alternative theatre and art.
Entrance around €12.
**Officine Belfort** Corso Venezia 30, in Docks Dora,
beyond Stazione Dora, ⓦ www.barrumba.com.
Industrial-style club with a good reputation. Open
Thurs–Sat.

# Milan (Milano)

The dynamo behind the country's economic miracle, **MILAN** (Milano) is the
capital of Italy's fashion and design industry, a fast-paced business city in which
consumerism and the work ethic rule. The swanky shops and nightlife are a big
draw, but Milan is also a historic city, and a monument to the prestige-building
of the Viscontis and their successors, the Sforzas, who ruled here in Renaissance
times. The Gothic cathedral has few peers in Italy, while paintings in the Pinacoteca di Brera and Leonardo da Vinci's iconic fresco of *The Last Supper*, on show in
a Milan church, are unmissable treats.

## Arrival, information and accommodation

Most international **trains** pull in at the monumental Stazione Centrale, northeast of the centre on Piazza Duca d'Aosta (metro lines MM2 or MM3). **Buses**
arrive at and depart from Piazza Castello, in front of the Castello Sforzesco. Of
Milan's two **airports**, Linate is the closer, 7km from the city centre and connected by the airport bus to Stazione Centrale (every 30min, 6.05am–9.35pm;
journey time 20min; €2.50). There are also ordinary city buses (#73; €1) until
around midnight from Linate to Piazza San Babila. The other airport, Malpensa,
is 50km away towards Lago Maggiore, connected by train to Cadorna station
(every 30min; €9) and by bus with Stazione Centrale (until 10.30pm; €5.50).
The main **tourist offices** are at the Stazione Centrale (Mon–Sat 9am–6pm,
Sun 9am–1pm & 2–5pm; ☏ 02.7252.4301/2/3, ⓦ www.milanoinfotourist
.com) and Via Marconi 1, off Piazza Duomo (daily 9am–1pm & 2–5pm; same
number). Both have the free **listings** guide, *Milano Mese* in Italian and English
and the *Milan by Night* map. **Public transport** consists of an efficient network
of trams, buses and metro (stations denoted below as MM) that runs from 6am
to midnight, with night buses until 1am. Tickets (normally valid 1hr 15min;
€1) can be used for one journey only on the metro; alternatively buy a *blochetto*
of ten tickets (€9.20), or a 24-hour ticket (€3) from the Centrale or Duomo
metro stations.

## Accommodation

Milan is more a business than a tourist city, with summer being low season, and
its accommodation is geared to the expense-account traveller. However, there are
plenty of one-star hotels, mostly concentrated in the area around Stazione Centrale, and along Viale Vittorio Veneto and Corso Buenos Aires.

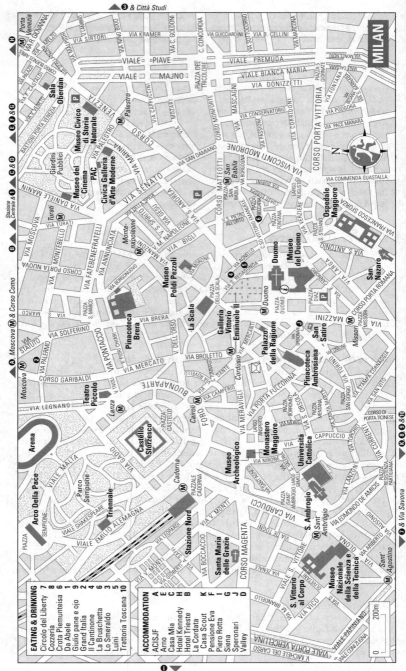

& Città Studi

MILAN

**EATING & DRINKING**

| Circolo del Liberty | 7 |
| Cozzeria | 8 |
| Crota Piemunteisa | 6 |
| Da Abele | 9 |
| Giulio pane e ojo | 1 |
| Grand Italia | 2 |
| Il Cantinone | 4 |
| La Bruschetta | 6 |
| Lo Smeraldo | 3 |
| Luini | 5 |
| Trattoria Toscana | 10 |

**ACCOMMODATION**

| ACISJF | A |
| Arno | E |
| Casa Mia | C |
| Hotel Kennedy | H |
| Hotel Trieste | B |
| La Cordata | K |
| Casa Scout | F |
| Pensione Eva | I |
| Piero Rotta | G |
| Siena | J |
| Speronari | D |
| Valley | |

0   200m

N

ACISJF Corso Garibaldi 121 ☎02.290.00164. Hostel run by nuns and open to women under 25 only. Accommodation in four-bedded rooms. Metro Moscova. €22

Arno Via Lazzaretto 17 ☎02.670.5509. Very friendly one-star hotel near the station, run by the helpful Patrizio. Free Internet access; gets packed from March to July. Metro Repubblica, Porta Venezia or Stazione Centrale. ⑤

Casa Mia Viale V. Veneto 30 ☎02.657.5249, Ⓦwww.casamiahotel.it. Comfortable rooms with satellite TV, and prices to match. Metro Repubblica. ⑨

La Cordata Casa Scout Via Buigozzo 11, ☎02.5831.4675, Ⓔostello@lacordata.it. Well-equipped hostel with kitchen, free Internet and no curfew; ten minutes' walk from Metro Misoni. €18.

Hotel Kennedy Viale Tunisia 6 ☎02.2940.0934, Ⓦwww.kennedyhotel.it. Clean family-run one-star hotel close to the station. Metro Porta Venezia. ⑥

Pensione Eva Via Lazzaretto 17 ☎02.670.6093.
Another basic one-star hotel near the station, next door to Arno. Metro Repubblica, Porta Venezia or Stazione Centrale. ⑥

Piero Rotta HI Hostel ☎02.3926.7095. Though in a red-light district and with a midnight curfew, this huge hostel is comfortable inside. Metro QT8. €18.

Siena Via P. Castaldi 17 (entrance on Via Lazzaretto) ☎02.2951.6108. Small and clean, well-equipped rooms, with young, friendly staff. Metro Repubblica, Porta Venezia or Stazione Centrale. ⑧

Speronari Via Speronari 4 ☎02.8646.1125. Friendly and very central hotel, close to the cathedral. ⑦

Hotel Trieste Via M. Polo 13 ☎02.655.4405, Ⓦwww.htrieste.it. Comfortable two-star hotel in tranquil area of town, near the centre. Metro Repubblica. ⑨

Valley Via Soperga 19 ☎02.669.2777. Clean, family-run one-star hotel very close to the station. Metro Stazione Centrale. ⑥

## The City

A good place to start a tour of Milan is **Piazza del Duomo**, the city's historic centre and home to the world's largest Gothic cathedral, the **Duomo**, begun in 1386 and not finished till almost five centuries later. From the outside it's notable as much for its decoration as its size, with a front that's a strange mixture of Baroque and Gothic – though much of this is currently obscured thanks to ongoing restoration work. The gloomy interior gives access to the cathedral's fourth-century **baptistery** (Tues–Sun 9.45am–12.45pm & 2–5.45pm; €1.50) where St Ambrose baptized St Augustine in AD 387. But the highlight is the cathedral **roof** (9am–4.15/5.45pm; €5 by elevator, €3.50 on foot), where you are surrounded by a forest of lacy Gothic carving, and have superb views of the city. The **Museo del Duomo** (daily 10am–1.15pm & 3–6pm; €6), on the southern side of the piazza, holds casts of a good many of the three thousand or so statues and gargoyles that spike the cathedral. On the opposite side of the piazza is the opulent **Galleria Vittorio Emanuele**, a cruciform glass-domed gallery designed in 1865 by Giuseppe Mengoni, who was killed when he fell from the roof a few days before the inaugural ceremony. The circular mosaic beneath the cupola is composed of the symbols of the cities of the then newly unified Italy – it's considered good luck to spin round on the testicles of the bull (which represents Turin). The Galleria leads through to the world-famous eighteenth-century **La Scala** opera house.

The shopping quarter to the northeast of La Scala – the so-called **Quadrilatero d'Oro** – is home to all the big fashion names, along with design studios and contemporary art galleries. You'll also find here the **Museo Poldi Pezzoli**, Via Manzoni 12 (Tues–Sun 10am–6pm, €7), an intriguing private collection containing, amongst other things, lace, jewellery and clocks, with its highlight, Pollaiuolo's idealised *Portrait of a Young Woman*. A couple of blocks west, **Via Brera** sets the tone for the city's arty quarter with its fancy galleries and art shops, and, at its far end, Milan's most prestigious gallery, the **Pinacoteca di Brera** (Tues–Sun 8.30am–7.30pm; €5), filled with works looted from the churches and aristocratic collections of French-occupied Italy. Venetian painters are well represented, with works by Paolo Veronese, Tintoretto and Giovanni Bellini whose *Pietà* is deemed one of the most moving paintings in the history of art. However, it's Piero della Francesca's *Pala Montefeltro* that is perhaps the most famous painting here.

To the west, the **Castello Sforzesco** rises imperiously from the mayhem of Foro Buonaparte, laid out by Napoleon as part of a grand plan for the city. An arena and triumphal arch remain from the scheme, behind the castle in the **Parco Sempione** (a notorious hangout for junkies and prostitutes), but otherwise the red-brick castle is the main focus of interest, with its crenellated towers and fortified walls. Begun by the Viscontis and rebuilt by their successors, the Sforzas, whose court was one of the most powerful and cultured of the Renaissance, the castle houses the **Museo d'Arte Antica** and **Pinacoteca** (both Tues–Sun 9am–5.30pm; €3) – the former including Michelangelo's *Rondanini Pietà*, the latter a cycle of monochrome frescoes illustrating the Griselda story from Boccaccio's *Decameron* and paintings by Vincenzo Foppa, the leading Milanese artist before Leonardo da Vinci. South of the castle, the church of **Santa Maria delle Grazie** is the main attraction. A Gothic pile, partially rebuilt by Bramante (who added the massive dome), it is famous for its fresco of the **Last Supper** by Leonardo da Vinci, which covers one wall of the refectory. Advance booking is essential (call ☎02.8942.1146; viewing Tues–Sun 8am–7pm; €8).

### Eating, drinking and nightlife

**Food** in workaholic Milan, at lunchtime at least, is more of a necessity than a pleasure, with the city centre dominated by *paninoteche* and fast-food outlets. **Nightlife** is some of the best in Italy, and centres on the streets around the Brera gallery, the club-filled Corso Como, and the Navigli and Ticinese quarters, clustered around Milan's thirteenth-century canals. Listed below are some of the mainstream places where you'll need to dress up, but you won't have to be on the guest-list to get in. Foreign students can often get free admission to clubs, especially on Tuesdays, while there's a day-by-day schedule of concerts and events in *Milan Mese* and the *Zero* pamphlet available free in bars.

The season at **La Scala** (☎02.860.775, ✉www.teatroallascala.org), one of the world's most prestigious opera houses, runs from December to July. Although seats are expensive and can sell out months in advance, there is often a reasonable chance of picking up a seat in the gods an hour or so before a performance.

### Snacks, sandwiches and pizzas

**Crota Piemunteisa** Piazza Beccaria 10. A vast array of chunky sandwiches for around €4.40, and a few tables. Metro Duomo.
**Grand Italia** Via Palermo 5. Cheaper for pizza than *La Bruschetta* and just as good. Metro Moscova.
**La Bruschetta** Piazza Beccaria 12. One of the best-known city-centre pizzerias, though you'll have to wait for a table. Metro Duomo.
**Lo Smeraldo** Via Boccherini 9, Città Studi. Serves thirty types of pizza. Closed Sat and Sun. Metro Loreto/Pasteur.
**Luini** Via S. Radegonda 16. Justifiably popular for its delicious *panzerotti*. Metro Duomo.

### Restaurants

**Circolo del Liberty** Via Savona 20. Eccentric, intimate restaurant run by a talkative Neapolitan. Metro S. Agostino/ Porta Genova.
**Cozzeria** Via Muratori Lodovico 7. Mussels by the kilo; also does a delicious lemon and *peperoncino* sorbet. Metro Porta Genova.
**Da Abele** Via della Temperenza 5. A long-established, cosy and very popular haunt that specializes in risotto. Closed Mon. Metro Pasteur.
**Giulio pane e ojo** Via Muratori Lodovico 10. Trendy but inexpensive trattoria. Closed Sat lunch and Sun. Metro Porta Genova.
**Il Cantinone** Via Agnello 19. Famous old trattoria and bar, with homemade pasta and some choice wines. Metro Duomo.
**Trattoria Toscana** Corso di Porta Ticinese 58. Very trendy club-style restaurant, with a live DJ: gets packed at aperitif time, but also does excellent food. Closed Sun and lunch. Metro Missori/ Porta Genova.

## Bars and clubs

**La Banque** Via Porrone 6. Formerly a bank, this fashionable bar and nightspot is close to the cathedral. Metro Duomo.

**Loolapaloosa** Corso Como 15. Popular pub-style student hangout offering aperitifs from 5–10pm and solid tables to dance on to a mixture of pop, revival and latin. Metro Garibaldi.

**Bar Magenta** Via Carducci 13. Liberty-style bar, timelessly posey and usually packed. Metro Cadorna FN.

**Magazzini Generali** Via Pietrasanta 14 ⓦ www.magazzinigenerali.it. Huge gay-friendly warehouse, playing dance, club and alternative sounds.

**Old Fashion** Viale Alemagna 6 ⓦwww .oldfashion.it. Elegant club/restaurant popular among celebrities, with an outdoor disco in summer. Metro Cadorna.

**Plastic** Viale Umbria 120. A gay-friendly venue with house, electronic, pop and avant-garde music: Friday night is Britpop night. Metro Porta Vittoria.

**Rolling Stone** Corso XXII Marzo. An enormous place that plays a wide range of music, and sometimes hosts big-name rock bands. Metro Dateo/ Porta Vittoria.

**Rocket** Via G Pezzotti 52 ⓦ www.therocket.it. Small and trendy disco bar in the Ticinese area, a favourite among Milan clubbers. Metro Romolo/ Famagosta.

**Scimmie** Via Ascanio Sforza 49. A popular stage, small and buzzy and mainly hosting jazz. Metro Romolo/ Porta Genova.

## Listings

**Consulates** Australia, Via Borgogna 2 ☏02.7770.4217; Canada, Via V. Pisani 19 ☏02.67.581; UK, Via San Paolo 7 ☏02.723.001; US, Via Principe Amedeo 2/10 ☏02.290.351.

**Exchange** The office in Stazione Centrale is a good bet.

**Hospitals** Fatebenefratelli, Corso Porta Nuova 23 ☏02.63.631; Ospedale Maggiore Policlinico, Via Francesco Sforza 35 ☏02.55.031.

**Internet** *Terzomilennio*, Via Lazaretto 2, near the station (Mon–Sat 9am–6pm; €7/hour).

**Laundry** Lavanderia, Via Vigevano 20, near Porta Genova.

**Pharmacy** 24-hour at Stazione Centrale.

**Police** Via Montebello ☏02.62.261.

**Post office** Piazza Cordusio 2.

# Mantua (Mantova)

**MANTUA** (Mantova) is undeniably evocative – the birthplace of Vergil, scene of Verdi's Rigoletto and with a history of equally operatic plots, most of them perpetrated by the Gonzagas, who ruled the town for three centuries and left two splendid palaces. The town centres on four interlinking squares. **Piazza Mantegna** is dominated by the church of **Sant'Andrea**, inside which are wall-paintings designed by Mantegna and executed by his students, one of whom was Correggio. Opposite Sant'Andrea, sunk below the present level of the busy **Piazza dell'Erbe**, is Mantua's oldest church, the beautiful eleventh-century **Rotonda**, still containing traces of its early medieval frescoes. The dark underpassage beneath the red-brick **Broletto**, the medieval town hall, leads into Piazza Broletto, beyond which the sombre Piazza Sordello is flanked by the Baroque Duomo and the **Palazzo Ducale** (Tues–Sun 8.45am–7.15pm; €6.50, bookings essential on ☏041.241.1897), an enormous complex that was once the largest palace in Europe. When it was sacked by the Habsburgs in 1630 eighty carriages were needed to carry the two thousand works of art contained in its five hundred rooms. In the Salone del Fiume there's a *trompe l'oeil* garden complete with painted creepers and two fountains, while the Sala degli Specchi has a notice outside signed by Monteverdi, who worked as court musician to Vincenzo I. Vincenzo also employed Rubens, whose *Adoration of the Magi* in the Salone degli Arcieri shows the Gonzaga family of 1604. However, the palace's real treasure is in the **Castello di San Giorgio** beyond, where you can see Mantegna's frescoes of the Gonzaga family, splendidly restored in the Camera degli Sposi. Mantua's other main sight, the **Palazzo Tè**, on the opposite side of town (Mon 1–6.30pm, Tues–Sun 9am–6.30pm; €10), was designed for Federico

Gonzaga and his mistress, Isabella Boschetta, by Giulio Romano. In the Sala dei Cavalli, horses stand before an illusionistic background in which simulated marble, fake pilasters and mock reliefs reveal distant landscapes. The function of the Salotta di Psiche, further on, is undocumented, but the sultry frescoes, and its proximity to Federico's bedroom, might give a few clues. Beyond, the extraordinary Sala dei Giganti shows the destruction of the giants by the gods, with cracking pillars, toppling brickwork and screaming giants appearing to crash down into the room.

The city centre is a ten-minute walk from the **train station** down Via Solferino. The **tourist office** (Mon–Sat 8.30am–12.30pm & 3–6pm, Sun 9.30am–12.30pm; ☎0376.328.253, ☻www.aptmantova.it) is around the corner from Sant'Andrea, and can provide a list of B&Bs (around ❺), your best bet for budget **accommodation** in Mantua. Alternatively, there are some reasonable three-star hotels, the best of which are the pleasant *Bianchi Stazione*, a former convent opposite the station on Piazza Don Leoni (☎0376.326.465, ☻www.hotelbianchi.mantova.com; ❻); the clean, neat *ABC*, next door at no.25 (☎0376.323.347, ☻www.hotelabcmantova.it; ❾); and the well-kept, comfortable *Broletto,* at Via Accademia 1 (☎0376.223.678; ❻). Otherwise, you'll have to stay out of town – the *Marago*, 3km away in Virgiliana, has cheap doubles (☎0376.370.313, ☻www.ristorantemarago.com; ❸; bus #25).

For inexpensive **food**, try *Il Punto* self-service (closed Sun) at Via Solferino 36, near the train station, or *I Due Cavallini*, Vicolo Salnitro 5 (booking recommended ☎0376.322.084; closed Tues), serving really good local fare at reasonable prices. Alternatively, there's *Quattrotette da Angelo* (literally, four tits) on Vicolo Nazione 4, a basic, crowded place that draws a loyal local clientele (open lunchtime daily Mon–Sat, plus evenings Wed–Fri 7–9.30pm). For **Internet** access, there's the News Slot Internet Cafe at the Galleria Ferry on Corso della Libertá (daily noon–8/10pm). For **nightlife,** the central *Borsacaffe*, Corso della Libertá 6 (☻www.borsartcaffe.it), is a cool place with a DJ from Wed–Sat: otherwise evenings are best spent over a few glasses at the *enoteca Buca della Gabbia*, Via Cavour 91.

# Genoa (Genova)

**GENOA** (Genova) is a marvellously eclectic city of Renaissance palaces and narrow, winding streets. It was one of the five Italian maritime republics, and reached the height of its power in the fifteenth and sixteenth centuries; later, during the Unification era, the city was a base for radical thought. After a long period of economic decline, Genoa has been gradually cleaned up – with the city's architect son, Renzo Piano, playing a leading role. But the planners have neither sanitized the slightly menacing air of the narrow alleys around the seafront, nor eradicated the characteristic port smells – brine and fish – that permeate the lower town.

### The City

Genoa spreads outwards from its **old town** around the port in a confusion of tiny alleyways and old palaces; its people speak an impenetrable dialect – a mixture of Neapolitan, Calabrese and Portuguese. From 1384 to 1515, except for brief periods of foreign domination, the doges ruled the city from the ornate stuccoed **Palazzo Ducale** in Piazza Matteotti (Tues–Sun 9am–9pm; price varies; ☻www.palazzoducale.genova.it), across from which the dour **Gesù** church, designed by Pellegrino Tibaldi at the end of the sixteenth century, contains Guido Reni's *Assumption* and two paintings by Rubens. Close by, the Gothic **Cattedrale di San Lorenzo** is home to the Renaissance chapel of St John the Baptist, whose remains once rested in the thirteenth-century sarcophagus. After a particularly bad storm, priests carried his casket through the city to placate the sea, and a commemorative procession takes place each June 24 to honour him. His reliquary is in the **treasury** (tours Mon–Sat 9am–noon & 3–6pm; €5.50), along with a polished quartz plate on which, legend says, Salome received his severed head.

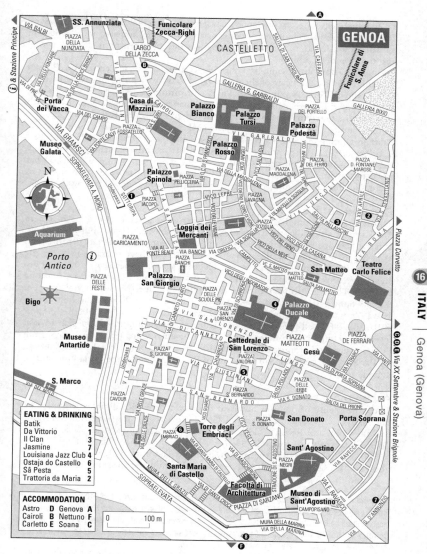

CASTELLETTO

SS. Annunziata

Funicolare
Zecca-Righi

Funicolare di
S. Anna

PIAZZA
DELLA
NUNZIATA

LARGO
DELLA ZECCA

GALLERIA G. GARIBALDI

PIAZZA
DEL PORTELLO

GALLERIA BIXIO

Porta
dei Vacca

Casa di
Mazzini

Palazzo
Bianco

Palazzo
Tursi

Palazzo
Podestà

Museo
Galata

Palazzo
Rosso

VIA GARIBALDI

PIAZZA
D. FONTANE
MAROSE

Palazzo
Spinola

PIAZZA
PELLICCERIA

PIAZZA
MADDALENA

Porto
Antico

Loggia dei
Mercanti

PIAZZA
CARICAMENTO

San Matteo

Teatro
Carlo Felice

Aquarium

Bigo

PIAZZA
DELLE
FESTE

Palazzo
San Giorgio

PIAZZA
BANCHI

Palazzo
Ducale

PIAZZA
DE FERRARI

Museo
Antartide

Cattedrale di
San Lorenzo

Gesù

PIAZZA
MATTEOTTI

S. Marco

PIAZZA
CAVOUR

San Donato

Porta Soprana

EATING & DRINKING
Batik                     8
Da Vittorio               1
Il Clan                   3
Jasmine                   7
Louisiana Jazz Club       4
Ostaja do Castello        6
Sâ Pesta                  5
Trattoria da Maria        2

Torre degli
Embriaci

Sant' Agostino

ACCOMMODATION
Astro     D   Genova   A
Cairoli   B   Nettuno  F
Carletto  E   Soana    C

Santa Maria
di Castello

Facoltà di
Architettura

Museo di
Sant'Agostino

0        100 m

Down on the waterfront, ruined by a hideous concrete overpass, the sea once came up to the vaulted arcades of **Piazza Caricamento**, a hive of activity, fringed by African and Middle Eastern cafés and market stalls. Customs inspectors, and subsequently the city's elected governors, set up in the **Palazzo San Giorgio** on the edge of the square, some rooms of which are open to the public (Sat only 10am–6pm; free). Beyond, the waterfront has been the subject of a massive restoration project, manifest most obviously in the huge **Aquarium** (Mon–Fri 9.30am–7.30pm, Sat & Sun 9.30am–8pm; €13; @www.acquariodigenova.it), and the recently opened **Museo Galata,** Calata de Mari 1 (Tues–Sun 10am–6/7.30pm;

€12), which tells the story of Genoa's naval triumphs, achieved largely using slaves. The museum displays a full-size reconstruction of a galley and also has a section on transatlantic emigration, for which Genoa was the main centre in Italy until well into the twentieth century.

Behind Piazza Caricamento is a thriving commercial zone centred on **Piazza Banchi**, formerly the heart of the medieval city, off which the long Via San Luca leads to the **Galleria Nazionale di Palazzo Spinola** (Tues–Sat 8.30am–7.30pm, Sun 1-8pm; €4), with work by the Sicilian master Antonello da Messina. North of here, **Via Garibaldi** is lined with frescoed and stuccoed Renaissance palaces, whose courtyards and buildings you can peek into. Two are now museums: the **Palazzo Bianco** (Tues–Fri 9am–7pm, Sat & Sun 10am–7pm; joint ticket with Palazzo Rosso €7) holds paintings by Genoese artists and others, including Van Dyck and Rubens, while **Palazzo Rosso** across the road (same hours and ticket) has works by Titian, Caravaggio and Dürer, but it's the decor here that really impresses – fantastic chandeliers, mirrors, an excess of gilding and frescoed ceilings.

## Practicalities

**Trains** from Ventimiglia and points west arrive at Stazione Principe in Piazza Acquaverde, just above the port; trains from La Spezia, Rome and points south arrive at Stazione Brignole in Piazza Verdi, on the east side of the city centre; trains from Milan and Turin usually stop at both, but if you have to travel between the two, take bus #28 or #33 (tickets available from *tabacchi* or newspaper stands). **Ferries** arrive at the Stazione Marittima, ten minutes' walk downhill from Stazione Principe. There are **tourist offices** at Stazione Principe (Mon–Sun 9.30am–1pm & 2.30–6pm; ☎010.246.2633, ⊛www.apt.genova.it), at Piazza delle Feste (daily 10am–7pm; ☎010.248.5710), and at Piazza Mateotti (daily 9.30am–7.45pm; ☎010.868.7452): all give out the free **listings** guide *Passport*. If you plan to visit several museums or tourist attractions, get a **Museum Card** (€29/three days) from the train station or tourist office, that also covers the buses. For **Internet** access, try Bar Superba, on Salita San Giovanni di Pre 25r, opposite the Porta Nuova train station.

## Accommodation

There are plenty of one-star hotels in the city centre with doubles around €40, but many are grim and depressing. Good areas to try are the roads bordering the old town, and Piazza Colombo and Via XX Settembre, near Stazione Brignole. For **camping**, the *Villa Doria*, Via Al Campeggio Villa Doria 15, Pegli (☎010.696.9600, ⊛www.camping.it/liguria/villadoria), 8km from Genoa, is a good bet. It's set in parkland, with its own café, shop and solarium: take a train to Pegli and then bus #93.

**Astro** Via XX Settembre 3/21 ☎010.481.533. Friendly family-run one-star hotel, clean and very close to Stazione Brignole. ❸

**Cairoli** Via Cairoli 14/4 ☎010.246.1454, ⊛www .hotelcairoligenova.com. A very pleasant two-star hotel, handy for the old town and Stazione Principe. ❻

**Carletto** Via Colombo 16/4 ☎010.588.412, ⊛hotelcarletto@libero.it. Simple, clean hotel, a good fallback option if the *Soana* is full. ❺

**Genova** Via Costanzi 120 ☎010.242.2457. Friendly, clean and well-run HI hostel with great views over the port, and Internet access; take bus #40 or (evening) #640 from Stazione Brignole. €15.

**Nettuno** Via Mercantini 16 ☎010.362.8106. Hotel on the seaview walkway on Corso Italia. ❻

**Soana** Via XX Settembre 23/8/a ☎010.562.814, ⊛www.hotelsoana.it. Friendly two-star hotel ten minutes' walk from Stazione Brignole. ❻

## Restaurants

For cheap lunches, **snacks and picnic** ingredients, try the Via de Pre near the station and the covered Mercato Orientale, halfway down Via XX Settembre in the old cloisters of an Augustinian monastery.

**Ostaja do Castello** Salita Santa Maria di Castello 32. Family-run trattoria.

**Sâ Pesta** Via Giustiniani 16. Well-known for its good local cooking, including *farinata*, a thin chick-pea-based pancake, but it closes early. Closed Sun and Mon.

**Trattoria da Maria** Via Testadoro 14/b, just off Via XXV Aprile. No-nonsense, endearingly chaotic place which serves up simple Ligurian cooking at rock-bottom prices.

**Da Vittorio** on Sottoripa, opposite Piazza Carica-mento. A hectic fish restaurant: it's very popular, so can be difficult to get a table.

## Bars and clubs

For late-night drinking, head to the bars around Piazza delle Erbe or down Via di Ravecca.

**Batik** Piazza Sarzano. Eastern-styled disco with classic tunes, free entry, and a pretty upstairs chillout room.

**Il Clan** Salita Pallavicini 16. Trendy bar packed to the rafters with the young and hip. Arrive early to bag one of the loft bed-seats.

**Jasmine** Via Gabriele D'Annunzio 19. The most popular club of the moment. Standard music, hefty entrance fee, students free on Thursday.

**Louisiana Jazz Club** Via S. Sebastiano 36R. Established jazz venue with live music.

# The Riviera di Levante

The stretch of coast east from Genoa, the **Riviera di Levante**, is not the place to come for a relaxing beach holiday. The ports that once survived on navigation, fishing and coral diving have now experienced thirty years of upmarket tourism: the coastline is still wild and beautiful in parts, but the sense of remoteness has gone. All the resorts can be reached by train except for Portofino, for which take bus #82 from Santa Margherita Ligure.

**PORTOFINO**, at the extremity of the Monte Portofino headland, manages to be both attractive and off-putting at the same time, a wealthy resort but a beautiful one. It's well worth making the two-and-a-half-hour walk to the beach and thirteenth-century **San Fruttuoso abbey** (Tues–Sun 10am–4/6pm; €4); boats run there too, for €8.50. The #82 bus route also passes the sparkling cove at **PARAGGI**, a good place for a swim, with a couple of bars set back from the beach. Or take the bus to Ruta, then walk to the summit of **Monte Portofino** (about 20min), from where the views are fantastic on a clear day.

**SANTA MARGHERITA LIGURE** is a small, thoroughly attractive resort, with palm trees along its front and a minuscule pebble beach and concrete jet-ties to swim from. **Accommodation** options include the comfortable *Albergo Annabella*, Via Costasecca 10, just off Piazza Mazzini (☎0185.286.531; ⑤); the welcoming hotel *Nuova Riviera*, Via Belvedere 10/2, in Art Nouveau style with an annexe of cheaper rooms (☎0185.287.403, ⓦwww.nuovariviera.com; ⑦); and the luxurious, but friendly, *Albergo Fasce*, further up the road at Via L. Bozzo 3 (☎0185.286.435, ⓦwww.hotelfasce.it; ⑦), which lends out bikes free. For good local **food**, try *Il Faro*, Via Merigliano (closed Tues), or the long-established *Da Pezzi*, at Via Cavour 21 (closed Sat), a canteen-like locals' hangout serving pasta and grills, and takeaway snacks for lunch. The **tourist office** is on Via XXV Aprile (daily 9.30am–12.30pm & 2/3–5/7.30pm; ☎0185.287.485, ⓦwww .apttigullio.liguria.it).

**RAPALLO** is a highly developed, though still attractive, resort popular with writers: Max Beerbohm lived here, attracting a vast coterie, and Ezra Pound wrote the first thirty of his Cantos here between 1925 and 1930. There's decent **accommodation** in the town centre, most notably *Pensione Bandoni*, Via Marsala 24/3 (☎0185.50.423; ④), where some of the clean, comfortable rooms have views; alternatively, try the *Fernanda*, along the front at Via Milite Ignoto 9 (☎0185.50.244; ⑥), cosy enough, but more expensive for less pleasant rooms.

There are a couple of **campsites**, *Rapallo* at Via San Lazzaro 4 (☎0185.262.018, ⓦwww.campingrapallo.it), and the *Miraflores* at Via Savagna 10 (☎0185.263.000, ⓦwww.campingmiraflores.it). Perhaps the least expensive and most authentic place to **eat** is *Bansin* at Via Venezia 49, in the heart of the old town, while *Da Mario*, Piazza Garibaldi 23, is a good, moderately priced fish restaurant.

Further east is the **CINQUE TERRE** (ⓦwww.aptcinqueterre.sp.it), a series of five small villages perched on tiny cliff-bound inlets. You can get round the lot in a day, if you're a fast walker, though while the views are justifiably famous, you won't be alone, with hundreds of walkers treading the same trail in both directions. Good shoes are recommended for most of the way, though there is a paved stretch between Manarola and Riomaggiore. The Cinque Terre Card allows access to the path for €3 a day, or €5.60 including the train and buses. Each of the five villages has a **tourist office** with Internet access at its train station. **Manarola** is the best of the villages for budget **accommodation**, with the very friendly, neat hostel *Ostello Cinque Terre* in Via Riccobaldi 21 (☎0187.920.215; ⓦwww.hostel5terre.com; €22): head to the top of the town and turn left at the church.

# Northeast Italy

The appeal of **Venice** hardly needs stating: it's one of Europe's truly unique urban landscapes, and is an unmissable part of any European tour. The region around Venice – the **Veneto** – is a prosperous one, where virtually every acre still bears the imprint of Venetian rule. **Padua** and **Verona** are the main attractions, with their masterpieces by Giotto, Donatello and Mantegna, and a profusion of great buildings from Roman times to the Renaissance. Much of the countryside is dull and flat, only perking up to the north with the high peaks of the Dolomite range. South, between Lombardy and Tuscany, stretching from the Adriatic coast almost to the shores of the Mediterranean, **Emilia-Romagna** is the heartland of northern Italy, a patchwork of ducal territories formerly ruled by a handful of families, whose castles and fortresses remain in well-preserved medieval towns. Carving a straight route through the heart of the region, from Milan to Rimini on the coast, the Via Emilia is a Roman military road, constructed in 187 BC, that was part of the medieval pilgrim's route to Rome and the way east for crusaders to Ravenna and Venice. **Bologna**, the region's capital, is one of Italy's largest cities, but despite having one of the most beautifully preserved centres in the country, it's relatively neglected by tourists. Nearby is **Parma**, a wealthy provincial town that is worth visiting for its paintings by Parmigianino and Correggio. The coast is less interesting, and the water polluted, but just south of the Po delta, **Ravenna** boasts probably the finest set of Byzantine mosaics in the world.

## Verona

The easygoing city of **VERONA**, with its Roman sites and streets of pink-hued medieval buildings, stands midway between Milan and Venice at a rail junction for the long trans-Alpine line from Innsbruck (Austria). It reached its zenith as an independent city-state in the thirteenth century under the Scaligeri family. Ruthless in the exercise of power, the Scaligeri were at the same time energetic patrons of the arts, and many of Verona's finest buildings date from the century of their rule.

The city centre clusters in a deep bend in the River Adige, the main sight of its southern reaches the central hub of **Piazza Brà** and its mighty Roman **Arena** (Mon 1.30–7.15pm, Tues–Sun 8.30am–7.15pm; July & Aug closes 3.30pm; €4).

Dating from the first century AD, and originally with seating for some twenty thousand, this is the third-largest surviving Roman amphitheatre, and offers a tremendous panorama from the topmost of the 44 marble tiers. Nowadays it is used as an opera venue (ticket information ☎045.800.5151, ⊛www.arena.it) for big summer productions. To the north, **Via Mazzini**, a narrow traffic-free street lined with expensive shops, leads to a group of squares, most noteworthy of which is the Piazza dei Signori, flanked by the medieval **Palazzo degli Scaligeri** – the residence of the Scaligeri. At right angles to this is the fifteenth-century **Loggia del Consiglio**, the former assembly hall of the city council and Verona's outstanding early Renaissance building, while, close by, the twelfth-century **Torre dei Lamberti** (same hours as Arena; €3 by elevator, €2 on foot) gives dizzying views of the city. Beyond the square, in front of the Romanesque church of Santa Maria Antica, the **Arche Scaligere** are the elaborate Gothic funerary monuments of Verona's first family, in a wrought-iron palisade decorated with ladder motifs, the emblem of the Scaligeri. Mastino I ("Mastiff"), founder of the dynasty, is buried in the simple tomb against the wall of the church; Mastino II is to the left of the entrance, opposite the most florid of the tombs, that of **Cansignorio** ("Top Dog"); while over the side entrance of the church is an equestrian statue of **Cangrande I** ("Big Dog"). Towards the river from here is the church of **Sant'Anastasia** (Tues–Sat 9am–6pm, Sun 3–6pm; €2.50, €5 combined ticket for all Verona churches), a mainly Gothic church, completed in the late fifteenth century, with Pisanello's delicately coloured fresco of St George and the Princess to the right of the altar. Verona's **Duomo** (Tues–Sat 10am–5.30pm, Sun 1.30–5.30pm; €5) lies just around the river's bend, a mixture of Romanesque and Gothic styles that houses an *Assumption* by Titian. In the opposite direction, off Piazza delle Erbe at Via Cappello 23, is the **Casa di Giulietta** (Tues–Sun 8.30am–7.30pm; €4), a well-preserved fourteenth-century structure, though there's no connection between this house and the historical character to whom Shakespeare's Juliet is distantly related. West of here, at the junction of Via Diaz and Corso Porta Borsari, the **Porta dei Borsari** is a fine Roman monument, with an inscription that dates it to 265 AD, though it's almost certainly older than that. Some way down Corso Cavour from here, the **Arco dei Gavi** is a first-century Roman triumphal arch, beyond which the **Castelvecchio** (same hours as Arena; €4) houses a collection of paintings, jewellery and weapons. A kilometre or so to the northwest, the **Basilica di San Zeno Maggiore** (Mon–Sat 8.30am–6pm, Sun 1–6pm; €2.50) is one of the most significant Romanesque churches in northern Italy. Its rose window, representing the Wheel of Fortune, dates from the twelfth century, as does the magnificent portal, while the door has bronze panels depicting scenes from the Bible and the miracles of San Zeno. The simple interior is covered with frescoes, but the most compulsive image is the altar's luminous Madonna and saints by Mantegna.

## Practicalities

The **train station** is twenty minutes outside the city centre, connected with Piazza Brà by bus #11, #12, #13 or #14. There's a **tourist office** at the train station (Mon–Sat 9am–6pm, Sun 9am–3pm; ☎045.800.0861, ⊛www.tourism.verona.it), and at Via degli Alpini 9 (Mon–Sat 9am–7pm, Sun 9am–3pm): both sell the Verona Card (€8), that covers all Verona's museums and churches.

## Accommodation

**Al Castello** Corso Cavour 43 ☎045.800.4403. A central one-star hotel; most rooms have private bathrooms and TV. ❻

**Casa della Giovane** Via Pigna 7 ☎045.596.880; wwww.casadellagiovane.com. For women under 26 only, this simple, clean hostel is right in the old centre. €14.

**Catullo** Via Catullo 1 ☎045.800.2786. One-star hotel in a central position just off Via Mazzini; some rooms have shared bath. ❹

**HI Hostel** Via Fontana del Ferro 15 ☎045.590.360. Hostel in a frescoed palazzo on the north side of the river; curfew 11.30pm; bus #72, #73 or #90 from the station. €13.50 including breakfast.

### Eating, drinking and nightlife

**Al Carro Armato** Vicolo Gatto 2a. An old-fashioned *osteria* , serving good food and drink.
**Alter Ego** Via Torricelle 9, ⌨www.alteregoclub .it. Verona's most cutting-edge disco is a cab ride from the centre; check the website to see what's on each night.
**Bottega del Vino** Vicolo Scudo di Francia, off north end of Via Mazzini. Friendly but pricey bar where you can sample wines from all over Italy.
**Cappa Cafe** Piazzetta Bra' Molinari 1. Fusion pub, with eastern trappings, floor cushions and occasional live music.

**Osteria al Duomo** Via Duomo 7a. Old-fashioned *osteria*, where the food and drink are recommended.
**Pero d'Oro** Via Ponte Pignolo 25. Restaurant serving inexpensive but genuine Veronese dishes.
**Pizzeria Arena** Vicolo Tre Marchetti. The best place in town for pizzas.
**Square** Via Sottoriva 15. A very modern bar oozing urban chic, and strong on cocktails. There's a DJ on several evenings, magazines galore and free Internet. Open from 6pm.

# Padua (Padova)

Extensively rebuilt after World War II bomb damage, and hemmed in by industrial sprawl, **PADUA** (Padova) is not the most alluring city in northern Italy. However, it is one of the most ancient, and makes a good base for seeing Venice (35min away by frequent trains). A former Roman settlement, the city was a place of pilgrimage following the death of St Anthony here, and it later became an artistic and intellectual centre: Donatello and Mantegna both worked here, and in the seventeenth century Galileo researched at the university. Just outside the city centre, through a gap in the Renaissance walls off Corso Garibaldi, the Giotto frescoes in the **Cappella degli Scrovegni** (daily 9am–6/7pm; appointment only, book at least 72hr in advance; €8, or €12 for joint ticket with Musei Civici; ☎049.201.0020, ⌨www .cappelladegliscrovegni.it) are the main reason for coming to Padua, although you get just ten minutes to see them. Commissioned in 1303 by Enrico Scrovegni in atonement for his father's usury, the chapel's walls are covered with illustrations of the life of Mary, Jesus and the story of the Passion – one of the high points in the development of European art in its innovative attention to the inner nature of its subjects. The adjacent **Musei Civici** (Tues–Sun 9am–7pm; €10) contains an assembly of fourteenth- to nineteenth-century art from the Veneto and further afield, the high point being a *Crucifixion* by Giotto that was once in the Scrovegni chapel. South of here, on the other side of the centre, the main sight of the Piazza del Santo is Donatello's **Monument to Gattamelata** of 1453, the earliest large bronze sculpture of the Renaissance. On one side of the square, the basilica of San Antonio or **Il Santo** was built to house the body of St Anthony. The Cappella del Santo has a sequence of panels showing scenes from his life, while the Cappella del Tesoro (daily 9am–12.30pm & 2.30–5pm) houses the saint's tongue and chin in a head-shaped reliquary. From the basilica, Via Umberto leads back towards the **University**, established in 1221, and older than any other in Italy except Bologna. The main block is the **Palazzo del Bò**, where Galileo taught physics from 1592 to 1610, declaiming from a lectern that is still on show, though the major sight is the sixteenth-century **anatomy theatre** (March–Oct, tours Mon, Wed & Fri at 3pm, 4pm & 5pm; Tues, Thurs & Sat at 9am, 10am & 11am; €3). While the **Duomo** is an unlovely church whose design was cribbed from drawings by Michelangelo, the adjacent Romanesque **Baptistery** is one of the unproclaimed delights of the city, lined with fourteenth-century frescoes by Giusto de'Menabuoi – a cycle which makes a fascinating comparison with Giotto's in the Cappella degli Scrovegni.

## Practicalities

Padua **train station** is at the far end of Corso del Popolo, a few minutes' walk north of the city walls. There's a **tourist office** at the station (Mon–Sat 9am–7pm, Sun 9am–noon), but the main office is in Galleria Pedrocchi, just off Via 8 Febbraio (Mon–Sat 9am–12.30pm & 3–7pm; ☏049.876.7927, ✆www.turismopadova.it). It sells the 48-hour **Padova Card** (€14), which buys museum access, free bus travel and a parking space.

Padua's HI **hostel**, Via A. Aleardi 30 (☏049.875.2219; curfew 11pm; bus #3, #8, or #18 from the station; €14), is an unremarkable place with a curfew, and is sometimes used as homeless hostel overspill. You're better off trying one of the **hotels**, such as the one-star *Hotel Dante*, Via San Polo 5 (☏049.876.0408, ✆hotel.dante@virgilio .it; ➌), with clean, old-fashioned rooms, a stone's throw from the sights. Slightly pricier is the two-star *Casa del Pellegrino*, Via Cesarotti 21 (☏049.823.9711, ✆www .casadelpellegrino.com; ➍), which is clean, central and very pleasant, and the friendly *Hotel Eden*, Via C Battisti 255 (☏049.650.484, ✆www.hoteledenpadova.it; ➎), near the Il Santo basilica. The nearest **campsite** is 15km away, at Via Roma 123 in Montegrotto Terme, served by frequent trains (15min).

For **food**, the *Casa del Pellegrino* has an excellent-value restaurant, while the inexpensive *Osteria l'Anfora*, Via dei Soncin 13, has a superb wine list which attracts locals even at lunchtime; the service is leisurely, but the meal is well worth the wait. On summer evenings, the **bars** around Prato della Valle or near the university are lively, including *Miniera*, Via S. Francesco 144, a fashionable late-night spot, while the bars on Piazza delle Erbe are the place to head for an early evening *spritz*. The most popular **club** for students, currently on Wednesday and Saturday, is the *Pachuca* club, Via Bernina 18, a twenty-minute walk behind the train station.

# Venice (Venezia)

The first-time visitor to **VENICE** (Venezia) arrives with a heavy burden of expectations, most of them well founded. It is an extraordinarily beautiful city, and the major sights are all they are cracked up to be. The downside is that Venice is expensive and deluged with tourists. At the height of its prosperity in the fifteenth century the city had a huge mainland empire. It later found new popularity as a destination on the Grand Tour and in the nineteenth century John Ruskin's book "The Stones of Venice" made her architecture famous around the world. Today, nearly twenty million visitors come here each year, most seduced by the famous motifs – carnival time, glass ornaments, singing gondoliers and the fabulously pricey cafés – though others come in search of the quieter quarters of a city that always has the capacity to surprise.

## Arrival, information and accommodation

The city's **Marco Polo** airport is on the edge of the lagoon, linked to the city centre by ACTV bus #5 (€2), ATVO bus (€3), and the more expensive waterbus (from €10). All road traffic comes into the city at **Piazzale Roma**, at the head of the Canal Grande, from where waterbus services run to the San Marco area, stopping off at Santa Lucia **train station**, the next stop along the Canal Grande. The main **tourist office** is at San Marco 71/f, a couple of minutes' walk east of the square (daily 9am–3.30pm; ☏041.529.8711, ✆www.turismovenezia.it & ✆www.comune.venezia. it), and there are also desks at the train station and airport (daily 8am-6.30pm). All three hand out the free English-language **listings** magazine *Leo* or, for nightlife, *Venezia da Vivere*, and sell the **Museum Pass** (€15.50), which gives entry to some of the main museums (but not the Accademia or Guggenheim), the **Chorus Pass** (€9), which gives entry to fourteen churches, and the **Venezia Card** (✆www.venicecard .it; €47/68 for 3/7 days), which covers the waterbuses and most museums.

Walking is the fastest way of getting around and you can cross the whole city in an hour. Tickets for the **waterbus** (*vaporetto*) are available from most landing stages. Flat-rate fares are €5 for any one continuous journey including the Canal

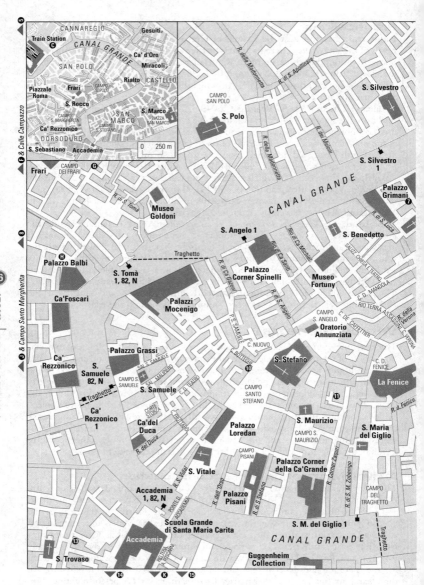

Grande, or €3.50 excluding it. There are also one-day (€10.50) and three-day (€22) tickets available. The **traghetti** that cross the Canal Grande (€0.50 a trip) are a cheap way of getting a ride on a gondola. Otherwise, **gondolas** are ludicrously expensive, though split between six people they become more affordable: the official tariff is €73 for 50 minutes but you may be quoted up to €100 for 45 minutes and an extra €100 for a singer.

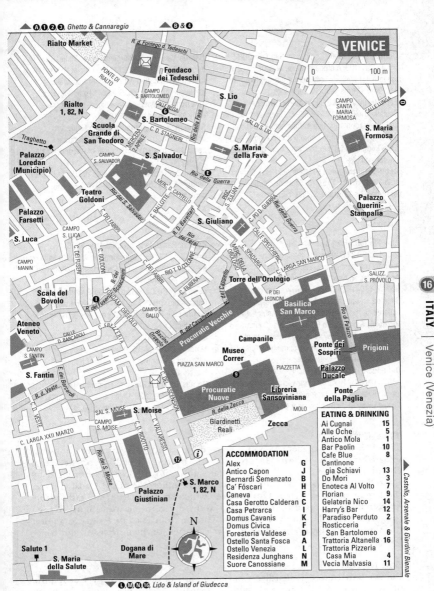

**VENICE**

Rialto Market

R. d. Fontego d. Tedeschi

PONTE DI RIALTO

0 ——— 100 m

Fondaco dei Tedeschi

CAMPO S. BARTOLOMEO

S. Lio

CALLE FIUBIA

Rialto 1, 82, N

CAMPO SANTA MARIA FORMOSA

CALLE LUNGA

Ⓓ

Traghetto

S. Bartolomeo

Scuola Grande di San Teodoro

C. D. STAGNERI

Rio della Fava

SAL DI S. LIO

S. Maria Formosa

Palazzo Loredan (Municipio)

MERCERIA 2 APRILE

CAMPO S. SALVADOR

S. Salvador

S. Maria della Fava

Teatro Goldoni

C. DE FABBRI

Rio della Guerra

Ⓔ

Rio della Guerra

Palazzo Querini-Stampalia

Palazzo Farsetti

CAMPO S. LUCA

MERC. D. CAPITELLO

C. BALLOTTE

S. Giuliano

C. PO D. GUERRA

RISS S. ZULIAN

S. Luca

CAMPO MANIN

C. DEI FUSERI

C. GOLDONI

C. DEI FABBRI

Rio dei Ferali

CALLE SPECCHIERI

C. SPADARIA

C. LARGA SAN MARCO

SALIZZ. S. PROVOLO

Scala del Bovolo

Ⓛ

R. del Fuseri

FONDAM. ORSEOLO

CAMPO S. GALLO

MERC. DELL' OROLOGIO

Torre dell'Orologio

P. DEI LEONCINI

16

Ateneo Veneto

CALLE D. BARCAROLI

FREZZERIA

Bacino Orseolo

Rio del Cavalletto

Procuratie Vecchie

Basilica San Marco

Rio di Palazzo

**ITALY** | Venice (Venezia)

S. Fantin

CAMPO S. FANTIN

Campanile

Ponte dei Sospiri

Prigioni

F. dei Barcaroli

R. d. VESTE

C. D. VESTE

SAL S. MOISE

C. D. ASCENSION

Museo Correr

PIAZZA SAN MARCO

Ⓙ

Procuratie Nuove

PIAZZETTA

Libreria Sansoviniana

Palazzo Ducale

Ponte della Paglia

Castello, Arsenale & Giardini Bienale

C. LARGA XXII MARZO

S. Moise

CAMPO S. MOISE

C. VALLARESSO

R. della Zecca

MOLO

Zecca

**EATING & DRINKING**

| | |
|---|---|
| Ai Cugnai | 15 |
| Alle Oche | 5 |
| Antico Mola | 1 |
| Bar Paolin | 10 |
| Cafe Blue | 8 |
| Cantinone gia Schiavi | 13 |
| Do Mori | 3 |
| Enoteca Al Volto | 9 |
| Florian | 7 |
| Gelateria Nico | 14 |
| Harry's Bar | 12 |
| Paradiso Perduto | 2 |
| Rosticceria San Bartolomeo | 6 |
| Trattoria Altanella | 16 |
| Trattoria Pizzeria Casa Mia | 4 |
| Vecia Malvasia | 11 |

Giardinetti Reali

Palazzo Giustinian

Ⓜ

Ⓘ

S. Marco 1, 82, N

N

Salute 1

S. Maria della Salute

Dogana di Mare

**ACCOMMODATION**

| | |
|---|---|
| Alex | G |
| Antico Capon | J |
| Bernardi Semenzato | B |
| Ca' Fóscari | H |
| Caneva | E |
| Casa Gerotto Calderan | C |
| Casa Petrarca | I |
| Domus Cavanis | K |
| Domus Civica | F |
| Foresteria Valdese | D |
| Ostello Santa Fosca | A |
| Ostello Venezia | L |
| Residenza Junghans | N |
| Suore Canossiane | M |

**Accommodation** is the major expense in Venice and you should always book ahead. The cheapest option is a **hostel**, most owned by religious foundations, or you may want to stay in nearby Padua or Trieste. There are **booking offices** (all open daily 9am–8pm) at the station, the Tronchetto, Piazzale Roma, airport and at the autostrada's Venice exit.

## Hostels

**Domus Civica** Calle Campazzo, San Polo 3082
☏041.721.103. A student house in winter, open
to women travellers only from June-Sept. Curfew
11.30pm. Dorms €28.50, rooms ④
**Foresteria Valdese** Santa Maria Formosa,
Castello 5170 ☏041.528.6797. Three large dorms,
and a few rooms for two to four people. Difficult to
find – go from Campo Santa Maria Formosa along
Calle Lunga, and it's at the foot of the bridge at
the far end. ③
**Ostello Santa Fosca** S. Maria dei Servi, Cannaregio 2372, ☏041.715.775. Student-run hostel in
an atmospheric former Servite convent. €22.

**Ostello Venezia** Fondamenta delle Zitelle, Giudecca 86 ☏041.523.8211. The official HI hostel,
in a superb location with views of San Marco from
the island of Giudecca. Curfew 11pm. Waterbus
#82 from the station. Large place, but get there
early morning or book. €18.50
**Residenza Junghans** Isola della Giudecca
☏041.521.0801, ⓦwww.residenzajunghans.
com. Neat, modern student hall of residence with
singles for €35 and doubles ④
**Suore Canossiane** Fondamenta del Ponte Piccolo,
Giudecca 428 ☏041.522.2157. Women only, no
booking. €15.

## Hotels

**Alex** Rio Terra Frari San Polo 2606,
☏041.523.1341, wwww.hotelalexinvenice.com. A
recently refurbished one-star hotel. ⑤
**Antico Capon** Campo S. Margherita, Dorsoduro
3004/B ☏041.528.5292, ⓦwww.anticocapon.com.
Situated on one of the city's most atmospheric
squares, in the heart of the student district. ⑥
**Bernardi Semenzato** Calle dell'Oca, Cannaregio
4366 ☏041.522.7257; ⓦwww.hotelbernardi
.com. Two-star place with welcoming and helpful
English-speaking owners. ⑤
**Ca' Fóscari** Calle della Frescada, Dorsoduro
3887B ☏041.710.401. ⓦwww.locandacaforscari
.com; Quiet, well-decorated and relaxed place,
tucked away in a tiny alley near San Tomà. ⑥

**Caneva** Ramo della Fava, Castello 5515
☏041.522.8118. Overlooking the Rio della Fava on
the approach to the busy Campo San Bartolomeo,
yet very peaceful. ⑥
**Casa Gerotto Calderan** Campo S. Geremia 283,
Cannaregio ☏041.715.361. Welcoming place not
far from the train station. Dorm beds sometimes
available. ⑥
**Casa Petrarca** Calle delle Colonne, San
Marco 4394 ☏041.520.0430. Friendly place
with just six rooms. The cheapest near the
Piazza. ⑦
**Domus Cavanis** Rio Terrà Foscarini, Dorsoduro
896 ☏041.522.2826. Clean and central; buffet
breakfast in *Hotel Belle Arti* opposite. ⑦

## The City

The 118 islands of central Venice are divided into six districts known as
*sestieri*, with that of **San Marco** (enclosed by the lower loop of the Canal
Grande) home to most of the essential sights. On the east it's bordered by
**Castello**, to the north by **Cannaregio**. On the other side of the Canal Grande,
the largest of the *sestieri* is **Dorsoduro**, which stretches from the fashionable
quarter at the southern tip of the canal to the docks in the west. **Santa Croce**
roughly follows the curve of the Canal Grande from Piazzale Roma to a point
just short of the Rialto, where it joins the smartest of the districts on this bank,
**San Polo**.

### San Marco

**Piazza San Marco** is signalled from most parts of the city by the **Campanile**
(daily 9.30am–4.15/7pm; €6), which began life as a lighthouse in the ninth
century, but is in fact a reconstruction: the original tower collapsed on July 14,
1902. It is the tallest structure in the city, and from the top you can make out virtually every building, but not a single canal. Across the piazza, the **Basilica di San
Marco** (Mon–Sat 9.45am–4.30/5.30pm, Sun 2–4pm; €1.50) is the most exotic
of Europe's cathedrals, modelled on Constantinople's Church of the Twelve
Apostles, finished in 1094 and embellished over the succeeding centuries with trophies brought back from abroad – proof of Venice's secular might and thus of the

spiritual power of St Mark. The Romanesque carvings of the central door were begun around 1225 and finished in the early fourteenth century, while the mosaic above the doorway on the far left – *The Arrival of the Body of St Mark* – was made around 1260 and includes the oldest-known image of the basilica. Inside, the narthex holds more mosaics, together with *The Madonna with Apostles and Evangelists* in the niches of the bay in front of the main door – dating from the 1060s, the oldest mosaics in San Marco. A steep staircase goes from the church's main door up to the **Museo Marciano** and the **Loggia dei Cavalli** (daily 9.45am–5pm; €3), where you can enjoy fine views of the city and the Gothic carvings along the apex of the facade. However, it's the **Sanctuary**, off the south transept (Mon–Sat 10am–5.30pm, Sun 2–4pm; €1.50), that holds the most precious of San Marco's treasures, the **Pala d'Oro** or golden altar panel, commissioned in 976 in Constantinople. The **Treasury** (same times; €2) is a similarly dazzling warehouse of chalices, reliquaries and candelabra, while the tenth-century Icon of the Madonna of Nicopeia (in the chapel on the east side of the north transept) is the most revered religious image in Venice.

The adjacent **Palazzo Ducale** (daily 9am–5/7pm; €11 combined ticket with Piazza San Marco museums) was principally the residence of the doge. Like San Marco, it has been rebuilt many times since its foundation in the first years of the ninth century, but the earliest parts of the current structure date from 1340. Parts of it can be marched through fairly briskly, although you should linger in the **Anticollegio**, one of the palace's finest rooms and home to four pictures by Tintoretto and Veronese's characteristically benign *Rape of Europa*. Veronese features strongly again in the most stupendous room in the building – the Sala del Maggior Consiglio - where his ceiling panel of the *Apotheosis of Venice* is suspended over the dais from which the doge oversaw the sessions of the city assembly. The backdrop is the immense *Paradiso* painted at the end of his life by Tintoretto, with the aid of his son, Domenico. From here you descend quickly to the underbelly of the Venetian state, crossing the **Ponte dei Sospiri** (Bridge of Sighs) to the prisons, and then back over the water to the Pozzi, the cells for the most hardened malefactors.

## West of San Marco: Dorsoduro

Some of the finest architecture in Venice is to be found in **Dorsoduro**, but few visitors wander off the strip that runs between the main sights of the area, the first of which is the **Galleria dell'Accademia** (Mon 8.15am–2pm, Tues–Sun 8.15am–7.15pm; €6.50). This has one of the finest collections of European art, following the history of Venetian painting from the fourteenth to the eighteenth centuries. Five minutes' walk from the Accademia is the unfinished Palazzo Venier dei Leoni, home of the **Guggenheim Collection** (10am–6pm, closed Tues; €10), and of Peggy Guggenheim for thirty years until her death in 1979. Her private collection is an eclectic mix of pieces from her favourite modernist movements and artists, including works by Brancusi, De Chirico, Max Ernst and Malevich. Continuing along the line of the Canal Grande, you'll come to the church of **Santa Maria della Salute**, which houses a hoard of Titian paintings in the sacristy (€2.50), along with the *Marriage at Cana* by Tintoretto, featuring portraits of some of the artist's friends.

## Northwest of San Marco: San Polo and Cannaregio

On the northeastern edge of **San Polo** is the former trading district of **Rialto**. It still hosts the Rialto market on the far side of the Rialto Bridge, a lively affair and one of the few places in the city where it's possible to hear nothing but Italian spoken. The main reason people visit San Polo, however, is to see the mountainous brick church, **Santa Maria Gloriosa dei Frari**, west of here (Mon–Sat 9am–6pm, Sun 1–6pm; €2.50), whose collection of artworks includes a rare couple of paintings by Titian – most notably his *Assumption*, painted in 1518, a swirling piece of compositional bravura for which there was no precedent in Venetian art. Titian is also buried in the church. At the rear of the Frari is the **Scuola Grande di San Rocco** (daily 9–7pm; €5.50), home to a cycle of more than fifty major paintings by Tintoretto – including, in the main hall, three large ceiling panels featuring Old Testament references to the alleviation of physical suffering (coded declarations of the Scuola's charitable activities), while around the walls are New Testament themes.

In the northernmost section of Venice, **Cannaregio**, you can go from the bustle of the train station to some of the quietest and prettiest parts of the city in a matter of minutes. The district boasts one of the most beautiful *palazzi* in Venice, the **Ca D'Oro** or Golden House (Mon 8.15am–2pm, Tues–Sun 8.15am–6pm; €5), whose facade once glowed with gold leaf; and what is arguably the finest Gothic church in Venice, the **Madonna dell'Orto** (€2.50), which contains Tintoretto's tomb and two of his paintings. Cannaregio also has the dubious distinction of containing the world's first **ghetto**: in 1516, all the city's Jews were ordered to move to the island of the Ghetto Nuovo, an enclave which was sealed at night by Christian curfew guards. Even now it looks quite different from the rest of Venice, many of its buildings relatively high-rise due to the restrictions on the growth of the area. The **Jewish Museum** in Campo Ghetto Nuovo organizes interesting tours of the area that leave on the half-hour (museum Mon–Fri & Sun 10am–6/7pm; tours till 4.30pm; museum €3, tours €8), and the Campo's cafés are worth visiting too. East of here, the **Miracoli** church (€2.50) was built in the 1480s to house a painting of the Madonna that was believed to have performed a number of miracles, such as reviving a man who had spent half an hour lying at the bottom of the Giudecca canal.

### Northeast of San Marco: Castello
**Campo Santi Giovanni e Paolo** is the most impressive open space in Venice after Piazza San Marco, dominated by the huge brick church of **Santi Giovanni e Paolo** (San Zanipolo), founded by the Dominicans in 1246 and best known for its funeral monuments to 25 doges. The other essential sight in this area is to the east of San Marco – the **Scuola di San Giorgio degli Schiavoni** (Tues–Sat 9.30am–12.30pm & 3.30–6.30pm, Sun 9.30am–12.30pm; €3), set up by Venice's Slav population in 1451. The building has a superb cycle by Vittore Carpaccio on the ground floor.

### Venice's other islands
Immediately south of the Palazzo Ducale, Palladio's church of **San Giorgio Maggiore** stands on the island of the same name and has two pictures by Tintoretto in the chancel – *The Fall of Manna* and *The Last Supper*, perhaps the most famous of all his images, painted as a pair in the last years of the artist's life. On the left of the choir a corridor leads to the **Campanile** (€3), rebuilt in 1791 after the collapse of its predecessor and one of the best vantage points in the city. The long island of **La Giudecca**, to the west, was where the wealthiest aristocrats of early Renaissance Venice built their villas. The main reason to come is the Franciscan church of the **Redentore** (€2.50), designed by Palladio in 1577 in thanks for Venice's deliverance from a plague that killed a third of the population. You can see its best paintings in the sacristy, as well as a curious gallery of eighteenth-century wax heads of illustrious Franciscans.

### Eating, drinking and entertainment
Venice is awash with places to eat seafood, and there are also plenty of cheapish pizzerias and **bars and pubs** for the student population. The city's **opera house**, La Fenice, has been completely rebuilt after a calamitous fire (☎041.786.511, ⊚www.teatrolafenice.it), though the most famous annual event is **Carnevale**, which occupies the ten days leading up to Lent, finishing on

Shrove Tuesday with a masked ball, dancing in the Piazza, street parties, plus pageants and performances.

## Cafés and pasticcerie

**Gelateria Nico** Záttere ai Gesuati, Dorsoduro. Celebrated for its artery-clogging *gianduiotto* – a block of praline ice cream in whipped cream. Closed Thurs.

**Florian** Piazza San Marco. Museum-piece café with astonishing prices and a live music surcharge. Think twice before sitting down.

**Bar Paolin** Campo Santo Stefano, San Marco. Reputed to make the best ice cream in Venice, with outside tables in one of the finest settings in the city. Closed Fri.

## Restaurants

**Ai Cugnai** Piscina del Forner, Dorsoduro. Good-value trattoria close to the Accademia. Get there by 8pm or be prepared to queue. Closed Mon.

**Alle Oche** Calle del Tintor (south side of Campo S. Giacomo dell'Orio), Cannaregio. Eighty-odd varieties of inexpensive pizza.

**Antico Mola** Fondamenta degli Ormesini, Cannaregio. Originally a family-run, local place, but becoming trendier by the year. Still good food and good value. Closed Wed.

**Paradiso Perduto** Fondamenta della Misericordia, Cannaregio. Fronted by a popular bar, with a lively relaxed atmosphere and occasional live music. Closed Wed.

**Rosticceria San Bartolomeo** Calle della Bissa, San Marco. Glorified snack bar serving superb seafood.

**Trattoria Altanella** Calle dell'Erbe, Giudecca. Succulent fish dishes, and a terrace overlooking the island's central canal. Good for a treat. Closed Mon & Tues.

**Trattoria Pizzeria Casa Mia** Calle dell'Oca, Cannaregio. Very popular trattoria-pizzeria close to St Apostoli Chuch. Closed Tues.

## Bars and nightlife

Apart from the cheesy **disco** Casanova on Lista di Spagna near the station, Venice is short on dance action. However, it does have a lively artistic scene and bars a-plenty, particularly around the buzzing Campo Santa Margherita and Campo San Giacomo.

**Cafe Blue** Calle dei Preti 3778, Dorsoduro, between S.Pantalon and S.Rocco. Popular music-pub, good for beer, tea and Internet access. Closed Sun.

**Cantinone gia Schiavi** Fondamenta Maravegie, Dorsoduro. Great wine shop and bar opposite San Trovaso church. Closed Sun.

**Do Mori** Calle do Mori, San Polo. Narrow, standing-only bar, catering for the Rialto traders and serving delicious snacks. Closed Wed afternoon & all day Sun.

**Enoteca Al Volto** Calle Cavalli, San Marco, near Campo S. Luca. Stocks 800 wines from Italy and elsewhere; good snacks, too. Closed Sun.

**Harry's Bar** Calle Vallaresso 1323, San Marco. Historic watering hole for the rich. Stay at the bar and after three cocktails (about €36) they'll bring you free finger food.

**Vecia Malvasia** San Marco 2586, behind the Fenice opera house. Dance till dawn at this trendy spot for alternative music and art.

## Listings

**Exchange** American Express, Salizzada San Moisè, San Marco.

**Hospital** Ospedale Civili Riuniti di Venezia, Campo Santi Giovanni e Paolo ☎041.523.0000.

**Internet** San Pantalon, Crosera San Pantalon (Mon–Sat 10.30am–8.30pm, €9/hour).

**Laundry** Ai Tre Ponti, Santa Croce 274; Salizzada del Pistor, Cannaregio 4553, near Santi Apostoli.

**Left luggage** At the train station.

**Pharmacies** Farmacia Baldiserotto, Via Garibaldi 1778; or consult *Un Ospite di Venezia* for full list.

**Police** Via Nicoldi 24, Marghera ☎041.271.5511.

**Post office** Fondaco dei Tedeschi, by the Rialto Bridge.

# Bologna

**BOLOGNA** is the oldest university town in Europe and teems with students and bookshops. Up until the last elections, when it fell to the right, "Red Bologna" had been the Italian Communist Party's stronghold and spiritual home since World War II. It also boasts some of the richest food in Italy, a busy cultural life and a café and bar scene that is one of the most convivial in northern Italy.

The compact, colonnaded city centre is still startlingly medieval in plan. Buzzing **Piazza Maggiore** is the obvious place to make for first, dominated by the church of **San Petronio**, intended originally to have been larger than St Peter's in Rome. You can see the beginnings of the planned side aisle on the left of the building and there are models of what the church was supposed to look like in the **museum** (Mon–Sat 9.30am–12.30pm & 2.30–5.30pm; Sun 2.30–5.30pm); otherwise the most intriguing feature is the astronomical clock – a long brass meridian line set at an angle across the floor, with a hole left in the roof for the sun to shine through on the right spot. Bologna's university – the **Archiginnasio** – was founded at more or less the same time as the Piazza Maggiore was laid out, predating the rest of Europe's universities, though it didn't get a special building until 1565. The most interesting part is the **Teatro Anatomico** (Mon–Fri 9am–7pm Sat 9am–1pm; free), the original medical faculty dissection theatre, whose tiers of seats surround a professor's chair, covered with a canopy supported by figures known as *gli spellati* – the skinned ones. South, down Via Garibaldi, Piazza San Domenico is the site of the church of **San Domenico**, built in 1251 to house the relics of St Dominic. The saint's bones rest in the Arca di San Domenico, a fifteenth-century work that was principally the creation of Nicola Pisano, though the angel and figures of saints Proculus and Petronius were the work of a very young Michelangelo. North of here, the eastern section of Bologna's *centro storico* preserves many of the older university departments, housed in large seventeenth- and eighteenth-century palaces. At Piazza di Porta Ravegnana, the **Torre degli Asinelli** (daily 9am–6pm; €3) and perilously leaning **Torre Garisenda** are together known as the Due Torri, the only survivors of literally hundreds of towers that were scattered across the city during the Middle Ages. From here, Via San Stefano leads down past a complex of four churches, collectively known as **Santo Stefano**. The striking polygonal church of San Sepolcro, reached through the church of Crocifisso, is the most interesting: the basin in its courtyard was reputedly used by Pilate to wash his hands after he condemned Christ to death. A doorway leads through to San Vitale e Agricola, Bologna's oldest church, built from discarded Roman fragments in the fifth century; while the fourth church, the Trinitá, lies across the courtyard. Further east, on Via delle Belle Arti, is the city's most important art collection in the **Pinacoteca Nazionale** (Tues–Sun 9–7pm; €4), a body of paintings from 1300–1700, particularly strong on the Riminese and Romagnolo schools, and featuring some lovely works by Vitale de Bologna.

## Practicalities

Bologna's **airport** is northwest of the centre, linked by Airbus (€4.50) to the **train station** on Piazza delle Medaglie d'Oro, at the end of Via dell'Indipendenza. There are **tourist information** booths at the airport (Mon–Sat 9am–8pm) and at the train station (Mon–Sat 8.30am–7.30pm, Sun 9am–1pm), and a main office at Piazza Maggiore 6 (daily 9am–8pm; ☎051.246.541, ⊛www.comune.bologna.it/bolognaturismo for hotel bookings): all provide the free English-language **listings** magazines *Talkabout* and *Zero*, as well as *2night* for nightlife and *L'Ospite di Bologna* (A Guest of Bologna). The biggest and liveliest of the city's **markets** is Mercato delle Erbe, Via Ugo Bassi 2; there's a smaller market on Via Draperie.

## Accommodation

Book ahead as regular trade fairs rapidly fill hotels. The best local **campsite**

is the *Camping Hotel and Residence*, Via Romita 12/4a (☎051.325.016, ⊛www
.hotelcamping.com), near the exhibition centre, and with a swimming pool.

**Accademia** Via delle Belli Arti 6 ☎051.232.318
⊛www.hotelaccademia.it. Grand two-star in a
good location, with modern rooms and car parking.
Includes breakfast. **7**
**Garisenda** Via Rizzoli 9, Galleria del Leone 1
☎051.224.369. A tiny hotel in the heart of Bologna, with just seven rooms; also has a TV/reading
room. **5**
**HI Hostels Due Torri and San Sisto** 6km outside
the centre, at Via Viadagola 5 and 14 ☎051.501

.810; take bus #93 from Via Irnerio till 8pm and 21B
after. Popular hostels with 11.30pm curfew. €15.
**Minerva** Via de Monari 3 ☎051.239.652. Next to
Piazza Maggiore, the basic rooms have basins but
shared bathrooms. No breakfast. **4**
**Panorama** Via Livraghi 1 ☎051.221.802,
⊛www.hotelpanoramabologna.it. A pretty hotel
near Piazza Maggiore: ask for a room with "*vista
delle colline*" rooftop views to the hills around
Bologna. **5**

## Restaurants and bars

There are plenty of good bars on Via Pratello and in the student quarter, and the
late-opening *osterie* all over town that have been the mainstay of Bolognese life for
a few hundred years are still the places to eat and drink.

**Bar Wolf** Via Massarenti 118. Music bar 1km out
of the city, with live jazz on Sundays.
**Broccaindosso**, Via Broccaindosso 7a. A
legendary restaurant serving as much as you
can eat for about €25 – leave room for dessert;
8.30pm–3am; closed Sun.
**Golem Cafe D'Arte** Piazza S. Martino 3/B
⊛www.golemcafe.com. Live music, art and book
exchanges are brought together in this cool
café/bar; open daily to 2 am.
**Marieina** Via San Felice 137. An old, dark *osteria*
close to the city gate, with good wine and snacks.

**Matusel** Via Bertoloni 2. Formerly a brothel, this
lively and noisy *osteria* is close to the university.
Also has Internet access.
**Mario** Via Musolesi 9. Traditional *osteria* popular
with intellectuals and singer-song writers.
**Osteria Senzanome** Via Senzanome 42. Rustic
*osteria* serving good meals and with a wide choice
of beers and wines.
**La Scuderia** Piazza Verdi 2 ⊛www.lascuderia
.bo.it. Student-friendly live music club/restaurant
in former stables; go for Sunday brunch, from
11.30am. or daily aperitifs from 6.30pm.

# Parma

**PARMA**, about 80km northwest of Bologna, is about as comfortable a town as
you could wish for. The measured pace of its streets, the abundance and quality of its restaurants, and the general air of provincial affluence are undeniably
pleasant. There is also plenty to see, not least the works of two key late-Renais-
sance artists – Correggio and Parmigianino. **Piazza Garibaldi** is the fulcrum
of Parma; its cafés and surrounding alleyways are home to much of the town's
nightlife. The mustard-coloured **Palazzo del Governatore** flanks the square,
behind which stands the Renaissance church of **Madonna della Steccata**.
Inside there are frescoes by a number of sixteenth-century painters, notably
Parmigianino, who spent the last ten years of his life on this work, and was
eventually sacked for breach of contract by the disgruntled church authorities.
Nearby in the Romanesque **Duomo**, one of Correggio's most famous works, a
1534 fresco of *The Assumption*, can be seen in the central cupola. You should also
visit the Duomo's octagonal **Baptistery** (Mon-Sun 9am-12.30pm & 3-6.30pm
€4), considered to be Benedetto Antelami's finest work, built in 1196. Antelami
sculpted the frieze that surrounds the building, and was also responsible for the
reliefs inside, including a series of fourteen statues representing the months and
seasons. More Correggio frescoes can be seen in the **Camera di San Paolo**
(Tues-Sun 8.30am-1.45pm; €2) of the former Benedictine convent off Via
Melloni, a few minutes' walk north. East of the cathedral square, it's hard to miss
Parma's biggest monument, the **Palazzo della Pilotta**, begun for Alessandro
Farnese in the sixteenth century and rebuilt after World War II bombing. It

now houses the city's main art gallery, the **Galleria Nazionale** (Tues–Sun 8.30am–1.45pm; €6), whose massive collection, rich in fifteenth- and sixteenth-century works, includes more paintings by Correggio and Parmigianino.

## Practicalities

Parma's **train station** is fifteen minutes' walk from Piazza Garibaldi, with the main **tourist office** on Strada Melloni (Mon–Sat 9am–1pm, 2.30–6pm, Sun 9am–1pm; ☎0521.218.889, ☒turismo.comune.parma.it/turismo. For **Internet** access, there's Libreria Fiaccadori, Via Duomo 8. Parma's best **hostel** is *Foresteria Edison*, Largo Otto Marzo 9a (☎0521.967.088; ☒solares@solaresonline .it), an arts foundation where comfortable dorms are €18-25; to get there take bus #2 from the Teatro Regio to the *capolinea* (end of line) and head right – it's round the back of the building opposite the arts cinema. There's also a spartan HI hostel with **campsite** at Parco Cittadella 5 (☎0521.961.434; €10; closed Oct–March; curfew 11pm); take bus #19 from the station. Of the **hotels**, try the basic *Leon d'Oro* at Viale A. Fratti 4 (☎0521.773.182; ❹), left out of the station, or the neat, old-fashioned *Moderno*, Via A Cecchi 4 (☎0521.772.647; ❺), second right out of the station.

The best bet for food is the superb, inexpensive **restaurant**, *Il Gallo D'Oro*, Borgo Salina 3. At night, head for the *enoteca Bottiglia Azzura*, Borgo Felino 63, or *Ombre Rosse*, Vicolo Giandemaria 4, both of which also do food. It is also worth trying the **bars** along Via Farini, such as the cool *Gavasasa* at no.22, where people gather for a nightly aperitif from 7.30–9pm, or the swish basement bar *Tribeca*, Strada G Mazzini 1, for a dressy night out. Free summer concerts are held in the Parco Vero Pellegrini (the tourist office has details), and there's an annual Verdi **festival** in May/June, while the Teatro Regio on Via Garibaldi (☎0521.039.300) is renowned for its **opera**.

# Ravenna

**RAVENNA's** colourful sixth-century mosaics are acknowledged to be one of the crowning achievements of Byzantine art – they are the sole reason for visiting the town, these days a pretty but provincial backwater. The mosaics are the legacy of a quirk of fate 1500 years ago, when Ravenna briefly became capital of the Roman Empire, and the best of them can be seen in a day. Aim for the basilica of **San Vitale**, ten minutes northwest of the centre, completed in 548 AD. The mosaics are in the apse, arranged in a rigid hierarchy, with Old Testament scenes across the semicircular lunettes of the choir, Christ, the Apostles and sons of San Vitale on the arch, and, on the semidome of the apse, a beardless Christ presenting a model of the church to San Vitale and Bishop Ecclesius. On the side walls of the apse are portraits of the Emperor Justinian and his wife Theodora, Justinian's foot resting on that of his general, Belisarius, who reclaimed the city from the Goths, while Theodora looks on, her expression giving some hint of the cruelty for which she was apparently notorious. Across from the basilica is the tiny **Mausoleo di Galla Placidia**, whose mosaics glow with a deep blue lustre, most in an earlier style than San Vitale's, full of Roman and naturalistic motifs. Adjacent to San Vitale, the **National Museum of Antiquities** (Tues–Sun 8.30am–7pm; €4) displays a sixth-century statue of Hercules capturing a stag, and the so-called "Veil of Classis", decorated with portraits of Veronese bishops of the eighth and ninth centuries. East of here, on the busy Via di Roma, in the sixth-century basilica of **Sant'Apollinare Nuovo**, mosaics run the length of the nave, depicting processions of martyrs bearing gifts for an enthroned Christ and Virgin through an avenue of date palms. Five minutes' walk up Via di Roma, the **Arian Baptistery**, also known as the Basilica dello Spirito Santo, has a fine mosaic ceiling showing the twelve Apostles and the baptism of Christ.

A **combined ticket** (€9.50) covers most of Ravenna's sights, including San Vitale, the Mausoleo di Galla Placidia, Sant'Apollinare Nuovo and the Arian Baptistery. It's available from any of the participating museums, and is valid for a week. Opening times for all the sights are daily 9am–5pm.

It's only a short walk from the **train station** on Piazza Farini, along Viale Farini and Via A. Diaz, to the central Piazza del Popolo. The **tourist office**, Via Salara 8/12 (Mon–Sat 8.30am–6pm, Sun 10am–4pm; ☎0544.35.404, ⓦwww.turismo .ravenna.it), stocks maps, guides and the *Mega Coolissimo* (ⓦwww.coolissimo .it) booklet which has details of club nights. The best place to stay is the pretty **B&B** *Locanda del Melarancio*, on Via Mentana 33 near Piazza del Popolo (☎0544. 215.258, ⓦwww.locandadelmelarancio.it; ❹): it's also popular for **food** and an evening **drink**. If it's full try the **HI hostel**, the *Ostello Dante*, at Via Aurelio Nicolodi 12 (☎0544.421.164; €14), ten minutes' walk out of town or bus #1 from outside the station.

# Central Italy

The Italian heartland of Tuscany represents the archetypal image of the country – its walled towns and rolling, vineyard-covered hills the classic backdrops of Renaissance art. **Florence** is the first port of call, from the Uffizi gallery's master-pieces to the great fresco cycles in the churches. **Siena** is one of the great medieval cities of Europe and also the scene of Tuscany's one unmissable festival – the Palio – which sees bareback horse riders careering around the cobbled central square. Another major city, **Pisa** has its medieval splendours too – the Leaning Tower and cathedral – and there are, of course, the smaller hill towns, of which **San Gimig-nano**, the "city of the towers", is the best known. To the east lies Umbria (ⓦwww .umbria2000.it), a beautiful region of rolling hills, woods and valleys; most visitors head for the capital, **Perugia**, for **Assisi** – with its extraordinary frescoes by Giotto in the Basilica di San Francesco – or **Orvieto**, where the Duomo is one of the greatest Gothic buildings in the country, though lesser-known places like **Spoleto** are worth taking in too. Further east still, in the Marche region, is **Urbino**, with its superb Renaissance ducal palace.

## Florence (Firenze)

Ever since the nineteenth-century revival of interest in Renaissance art, **FLOR-ENCE** (Firenze) has been a shrine to the cult of the beautiful. It is a city of incomparable indoor pleasures, its chapels, galleries and museums embodying the complex, exhilarating and often elusive spirit of the Renaissance more fully than any other town in the country. The city became the centre of artistic patronage in Italy under the Medici family, who ruled Florence as an independent state for three centuries, most auspiciously during the years of Lorenzo de' Medici, dubbed "Lorenzo Il Magnifico". On display here are some of the most famous pieces in Western art, including Michelangelo's *David* in the **Accademia** and Botticelli's *Birth of Venus* in the Uffizi – but note that these and other big attractions can get very overcrowded; in high summer, you could easily wait in line for two or three hours to enter the Uffizi or the **Duomo**. You may find visiting some lesser-known (but just as high-quality) museums more enjoyable: the **Bargello** and

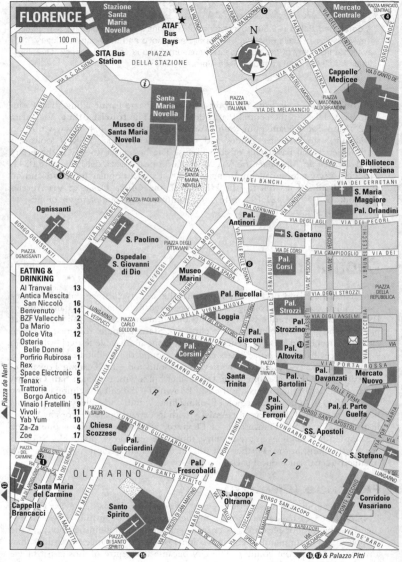

**Museo dell'Opera del Duomo** have a miscellany (the former with a memorably camp *David* by Donatello), the **Cappelle Medicee** house superb Michelangelo sculptures, and the **Cappella Brancacci** is lined with breathtakingly vivid frescoes by Masaccio. For a taste of Florentine life, head for the Mercato Centrale food hall and adjacent street markets, or window-shop on classy Via de' Tornabuoni. Yet exploring Florence can be a stressful business: the sheer number of tourists is

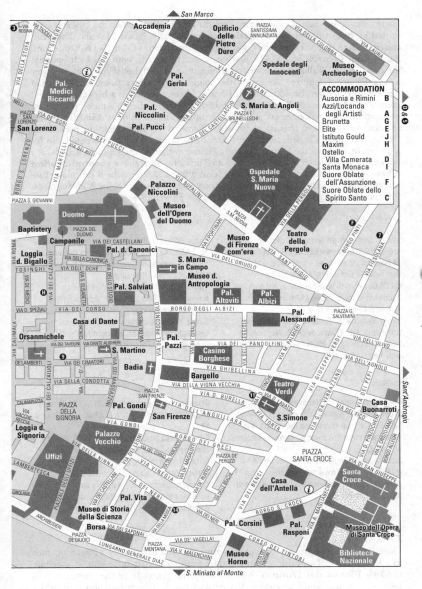

overwhelming for much of the year and many of the pavements are too narrow to cope with the flow of people.

### Arrival, information and accommodation

Pisa's international **airport** is connected by a regular train service (1hr) with Florence's central Santa Maria Novella **train station** (given on timetables as "Firenze SMN").

Flights also come into Florence's tiny Perètola airport, 5km out of the city and connected by bus to the main **bus station**, alongside Santa Maria Novella. The main **tourist office** is at Via Cavour 7r, just north of the Duomo (Mon–Sat 8.30am–7pm, Sun 8.30am–2pm; ☎055.290.832, ✆www.firenzeturismo.it), with a branch opposite the train station. **Walking** is the best way of getting around, but if you want to cover a long distance in a hurry, take one of the orange ATAF **buses**; tickets (€1) are valid for one hour and can be bought from *tabacchi*. Alternatively, rent a **bicycle** using the council's "*Mille e una bici*" scheme (€1.50/hr, €8/day) – there's a pick-up/drop-off point at the train station, or ask at the tourist office. Florence's most affordable **hotels** are close to the station, in particular along and around Via Faenza and the parallel Via Fiume, and along Via della Scala and Piazza Santa Maria Novella; you could also try Via Cavour, north of the Duomo, or the Oltrarno district on the south bank. Advance booking is advisable, or try the Informazioni Turistiche Alberghiere **accommodation office** at the train station (daily 8.45am–8pm; ☎055.282.893), which can make last-minute reservations for a fee. There's a centrally located **campsite**, the *Michelangelo* on Piazzale Michelangelo, Viale Michelangelo 80 (☎055.681.197).

## Hostels

**Istituto Gould** Via dei Serragli 49, Oltrarno ☎055.212.576. ✆www.istitutogould.it. A hostel with all the comforts of a hotel – book early. €21–41.
**Ostello Villa Camerata** Viale Righi 2 ☎055.601.451. HI hostel in a beautiful park, 30min out of town on bus #17 from the train station, midnight curfew. €17.
**Santa Monaca** Via Santa Monaca 6, Oltrarno ☎055.268.338, ✆www.ostello.it. Very popular hostel in a converted fifteenth-century convent, with 1am curfew. €17.

**Suore Oblate dell'Assunzione** Via Borgo Pinti 15 ☎055.248.0582. Not far from the Duomo, and run by missionaries. Singles and doubles only. Midnight curfew. €38 single.
**Suore Oblate dello Spirito Santo** Via Nazionale 8 ☎055.239.8202. Very clean and pleasant women-only place, close to the station. Single, double and triple rooms; 11pm curfew; two-night minimum stay. Closed Nov to mid-June. ❺

## Hotels

**Ausonia e Rimini** Via Nazionale 24 ☎055.496.547, ✆www.kursonia.com. Halfway between the train station and the market, this welcoming place has some en suites and Internet access. ❼
**Azzi/Locanda degli Artisti** Via Faenza 56 ☎055.213.806, ✆www.hotelazzi.com. Beautiful *pensione* that supplies musical instruments and paints on request. ❽

**Brunetta** Borgo Pinti 5 ☎055.247.8134. Friendly place in the historic centre, just east of the Duomo. ❻
**Elite** Via della Scala 12 ☎055.215.395. Friendly two-star hotel near Santa Maria Novella, with some en-suite rooms. ❺
**Maxim** Via Dei Calzaiuoli 11 ☎055.217.474, ✆www.hotelmaximfirenze.it. Very smart two-star hotel near the Duomo, in 1600s building; all en-suite. ❼

## The City

Florence's major sights are contained within an area that can be crossed on foot in a little over half an hour. From the train station, all first-time visitors gravitate towards **Piazza del Duomo**, beckoned by the pinnacle of the dome, which lords it over the whole cityscape. Via dei Calzaiuoli, which runs south from the Duomo, is the main catwalk of the Florentine *passeggiata*, a broad pedestrianized avenue lined with shops and activity. It ends at Florence's other main square, **Piazza della Signoria**, fringed on one side by the graceful late-fourteenth-century Loggia della Signoria and dotted with statuary, most famously a copy of Michelangelo's *David*. The streets west of the square retain their medieval character.

## The Duomo

The **Duomo** (Mon–Sat 10am–5pm) was built between the late thirteenth and mid-fifteenth centuries to an ambitious design, originally the brainchild of Arnolfo di Cambio and realized finally by Filippo Brunelleschi, who completed the majestic dome. The fourth largest church in the world, its ambience is more that of a great assembly hall than of a devotional building, its most conspicuous pieces of decoration being the two memorials to *condottieri* – Uccello's monument to Sir John Hawkwood, painted in 1436, and Castagno's monument to Niccolò da Tolentino, created twenty years later – and seven stained-glass roundels designed by Uccello, Ghiberti, Castagno and Donatello. These are best inspected from a gallery that forms part of the route to the top of the dome (€6), from where the views are stupendous. Next door to the Duomo, the **Campanile** (daily 8.30am–7pm; €6) was begun in 1334 by Giotto and continued after his death by Andrea Pisano and Francesco Talenti. The only part of the tower built exactly as Giotto designed it is the lower storey, studded with two rows of remarkable bas-reliefs, the lower one illustrating the *Creation of Man and the Arts and Industries* carved by Pisano. Opposite, the **Baptistery** (Mon–Sat noon–7pm, Sun 8.30am–2pm; €3), generally thought to date from the sixth or seventh century, is the oldest building in the city. Its most famous embellishments, the gilded bronze doors, were cast in the early fifteenth century by Lorenzo Ghiberti, and were described by Michelangelo as "so beautiful they are worthy to be the gates of Paradise". They're a primer of early Renaissance art, innovatively using perspective, gesture and sophisticated grouping of subjects to convey the human drama of each scene. Ghiberti included a self-portrait in the frame of the left-hand door – his is the fourth head from the top of the right-hand band. Inside, the Baptistery is equally stunning, with a thirteenth-century mosaic floor and ceiling and the tomb of Pope John XXIII, draped by a superb marble canopy, the work of Donatello and his pupil Michelozzo.

## The Palazzo Vecchio, Uffizi and Bargello

The tourist-thronged Piazza della Signoria is dominated by the colossal **Palazzo Vecchio**, Florence's fortress-like town hall (Mon–Sun 9am–7pm, Thurs closes 2pm; €6), begun in the last year of the thirteenth century as the home of the *Signoria*, the highest tier of the city's republican government. The huge Salone dei Cinquecento, built at the end of the fifteenth century, is full of heroic murals by Vasari, though it is redeemed by the presence of Michelangelo's *Victory*, facing the entrance door, originally sculpted for Pope Julius II's tomb but donated to the Medici by the artist's nephew.

Immediately south of the piazza, the **Galleria degli Uffizi** (Tues–Sun 8.15am–6.50pm; summer Sat till 10pm; booking advisable on ☎055.294.883; €6.50) is the greatest picture gallery in Italy, with a collection of masterpieces that is impossible to take in on a single visit. Works from the early Renaissance include three altarpieces of the *Madonna Enthroned* by Cimabue, Duccio and Giotto, though it's Filippo Lippi's *Madonna and Child with Two Angels* that's one of the best-known Renaissance images of the Madonna. Some of Botticelli's most famous works are here too, notably *Primavera* and the *Birth of Venus*, and while the Uffizi doesn't own a finished painting that's entirely by Leonardo da Vinci, there's a celebrated *Annunciation* that's mainly by him, as well as the angel in profile that he painted in Verrocchio's *Baptism*. Room 18 houses the most important of the Medici sculptures, first among which is the *Medici Venus*, while Michelangelo's *Doni Tondo* is his only completed easel painting, its contorted gestures and vivid colours later imitated by the Mannerist painters of the sixteenth century. The Uffizi also has a number of compositions by Raphael and Titian, while later rooms include some large works by Rubens, Van Dyck, Caravaggio and Rembrandt.

The **Bargello** museum (Tues–Sat 8.15am–1.50pm; €4) lies just north of the Uffizi in Via del Proconsolo. The first part of its collection focuses on Michelangelo. Beyond, the more flamboyant art of Cellini and Giambologna is exhibited, including Giambologna's best-known creation, the nimble figure of *Mercury*. Upstairs is Donatello's sexually ambiguous bronze *David*, the first freestanding nude figure since classical times, cast in the early 1430s. Upstairs, the Sala dei Bronzetti houses Italy's best collection of small Renaissance bronzes, with plentiful evidence of Giambologna's virtuosity.

## North: San Lorenzo and around

The church of **San Lorenzo** (daily 10am–5pm, €2.50), north of Piazza del Duomo, has good claim to be the oldest church in Florence, and for the best part of three hundred years was the city's cathedral. At the top of the left aisle and through the cloisters, the **Biblioteca Medicea-Laurenziana** (Mon–Sat 9am–1.30pm; free) was designed by Michelangelo in 1524; its most startling feature is the vestibule, a room almost filled by a flight of steps resembling a solidified lava flow. Michelangelo's most celebrated contribution to the San Lorenzo buildings, however, is the Sagrestia Nuova, part of the **Cappelle Medicee** (Tues–Sun 8.15am–5pm; €5; separate entrance behind church), which contains the fabulous Medici tombs, carved between 1524 and 1533. To the left is the tomb of Lorenzo, duke of Urbino, the grandson of Lorenzo il Magnifico, bearing figures of *Dawn* and *Dusk* to sum up his contemplative nature. Opposite is the tomb of Lorenzo il Magnifico's youngest son, Giuliano, his supposedly more active character symbolized by *Day and Night*. Just east of here, the **Accademia** (Tues–Sun 8.15am–6.50pm; €6.50), Europe's first school of drawing, is swamped by people come to view **Michelangelo's David**. Finished in 1504, when the artist was just 29, and carved from a gigantic block of marble, it's an incomparable show of technical bravura. The gallery also houses his remarkable unfinished *Slaves*.

## East: Santa Croce

Down by the river, the church of **Santa Croce** (Mon–Sat 9.30am–5.30pm, Sun 1–5pm; €4, including museum), begun in 1294, is full of tombstones and commemorative monuments, including Vasari's monument to Michelangelo and, on the opposite side of the church, the tomb of Galileo, built in 1737 when it was finally agreed to give the great scientist a Christian burial. Most visitors, however, come to see the frescoes by Giotto in the Cappella Peruzzi and the Cappella Bardi (on the right of the chancel), which show scenes from the lives of St John the Baptist and St John the Evangelist. The **Museo dell'Opera di Santa Croce**, off the first cloister (9.30am–5.30pm, Sun 1–5pm, closed Wed), houses a miscellany of works of art, the best of which are Cimabue's flood-damaged *Crucifixion* and Donatello's enormous gilded *St Louis of Toulouse*. Brunelleschi's harmonious Cappella dei Pazzi, at the end of the first cloister, was designed in the 1430s and completed in the 1470s, several years after the architect's death; it features decorations by Luca della Robbia.

## South: Oltrarno and beyond

The photogenic thirteenth-century **Ponte Vecchio**, loaded with jewellers' shops overhanging the water, leads from the city centre across the river to the district of Oltrarno. Head west, past the relaxed, café-lined square of Santo Spirito, to the church of Santa Maria del Carmine – an essential visit for the superbly restored frescoes by Masaccio in its **Cappella Brancacci** (Mon & Wed–Sat 10am–5pm, Sun 1–5pm; €4), including an iconic *Expulsion of Adam & Eve* on the left of the entrance arch: Adam presses his hands to his face in despair, Eve raises her head and screams. St Peter is the focus of all the other scenes; the most famous, the *Tribute Money*, on the upper left wall, shows three separate events within a single frame – in the centre is Christ at Capernaum, being asked to pay a tribute to the city; on the left, St Peter fetches coins from the mouth of a fish on the left, and on the right, he pays the tax official.

South of Santo Spirito is the massive bulk of the **Palazzo Pitti**. Nowadays the fifteenth-century palace contains six separate museums, of which the best is the

**Galleria Palatina** (Tues–Sun 8.15am–6.50pm; summer Sat till 10pm; €6.50), which features superb displays of the art of Raphael and Titian, including a number of Titian's most trenchant portraits. Much of the rest of the first floor comprises the state rooms of the Appartamenti Monumentali (included in the Galleria Palatina ticket). The Pitti's enormous formal garden, the delightful **Giardino di Bóboli** (Tues–Sun 8.15am–4.30/7.30pm; €4), is full of Mannerist embellishments, including the Grotta del Buontalenti – among its fake stalactites are shepherds and sheep and replicas of Michelangelo's *Slaves*. Beyond here, the multicoloured facade of **San Miniato al Monte** (daily 8am–12.30pm & 2.30–7pm) lures troupes of visitors up the hill. The interior is like no other in the city, and its general form has changed little since the mid-eleventh century. In the lower part of the church, don't overlook the intricately patterned panels of the pavement, from 1207, and the tabernacle between the choir stairs, designed in 1448 by Michelozzo.

## Eating, drinking and nightlife

The best place to find picnic food and snacks is the **Mercato Centrale**, just east of the train station, which also has bars charging prices lower than elsewhere in the city. Otherwise, try a **vinaio**, a wine cellar/snack bar that serves *crostini* and other snacks. A Florentine speciality, though not for the faint-hearted, is the **trippai**, that sells tripe-filled rolls – there's one at Mercato Centrale and a stall at Piazza de' Nerli. For **listings** information, call in at Box Office, Via Alamanni 39 (℡055.210.804), or consult *Firenze Spettacolo* and *Informa Città*. As for **festivals**, in May there's the *Maggio Musicale* (⊛www.maggiofiorentino.com), while the *Festa di San Giovanni* on 24 June, Florence's saint's day, sees a massive fireworks display. Throughout the summer free concerts and events take place around the city.

### Restaurants and cafés

**Al Tranvai** Piazza T. Tasso 14/r. Good, inexpensive Florentine specialities.
**Antica Mescita San Niccolò** Via San Niccolò 60/r. Unrivalled cheese and wine selection, plus superb Tuscan soups. Closed Sun.
**Benvenuto** Via della Mosca 16/r, off Via de' Neri. Looks more like a delicatessen than a trattoria from the street; the *gnocchi* and *arista* are delicious. Closed Sun.
**Da Mario** Via Rosina 2r. Popular with students and market workers – be prepared to queue and share a table. Closed evenings.
**Osteria Belle Donne** Via delle Belle Donne 16/r.

Flowers and fruit drip from the walls of this lovely *osteria*; blackboard menu featuring local dishes.
**Trattoria Borgo Antico** Piazza Santo Spirito 6r. Busy trattoria on a quiet Oltrarno square, with excellent seafood, homemade pasta and tables outside in summer.
**Vinaio I Fratellini** Via dei Cimatori 38. A typical Florentine *vinaio*.
**Vivoli** Via Isola delle Stinche 7r, near Santa Croce. Best in town for ice cream; closed Mon.
**Za-Za** Piazza del Mercato Centrale 26r. A few tables on ground level, and a bigger canteen below.

### Bars and clubs

**BZF Vallecchi** Via Panicale 61/R Beautiful bookshop/bar/cafe with live music and DJs, aperitifs and film shows, free Internet; daily 4pm–2am.
**Dolce Vita** Piazza del Carmine. Trendy late-night hangout that also stages small-scale art exhibitions. Daily except Sun 5.30pm–1.30am.
**Porfirio Rubirosa** Viale Strozzi 38r. Where the *bella gente* drop in before heading for a late dinner or club; Tues–Sun 8pm–1am.
**Rex** Via Fiesolana 25r, Santa Croce. Good music, a varied clientele, and serves snacks and cocktails; Wed–Mon 5pm–2.30am.

**Space Electronic** Via Palazzuolo 37, ⊛www.spaceelectronic.com. The favourite club for young foreigners, open nightly from 10pm. Bus #6 from Duomo past the Palazzetto dello Sport.
**Tenax** Via Pratese 47. The city's biggest club and one of its leading venues for new and established bands; open Fri & Sat from 10pm. Bus #29 or #30.
**Yab Yum** Via de' Sassetti 5r. City-centre club near the Duomo playing the best of new dance music; Mon–Sat from 8pm.
**Zoe** Via dei Renail 13/r, Oltrarno. Atmospheric red-painted cocktail bar for poseurs, with outside area.

## Listings

Consulates UK, Lungarno Corsini 2
☏055.284.133; US, Lungarno Vespucci 38
☏055.239.8276.
Hospitals Santa Maria Nuova, Piazza Santa Maria
Nuova 1 ☏055.27.581. English-speaking doctors
on 24-hour call at the Tourist Medical Service, Via
Lorenzo il Magnifico 59 ☏055.475.411.
Internet access Internet Train, Via Guelfa

54/56, Via dell'Oriuolo 40r, and Borgo San
Jacopo 30r.
Laundry Onda Blu, Via degli Alfani 24/r; Wash &
Dry, Via della Scala 52–54r.
Pharmacies All-night pharmacy at the train sta-
tion; Molteni, Via dei Calzaiuoli 7r; All' Insegna del
Moro, Piazza San Giovanni 20r.
Police Via Zara 2 ☏055.49.771.
Post office Via Pellicceria 3.

# Pisa

There's no escaping the Leaning Tower in **PISA**. The medieval bell tower is one
of the world's most familiar images and yet its beauty still comes as a surprise. It is
set in chessboard formation alongside the Duomo and Baptistery on the manicured
grass of the **Campo dei Miracoli**, where most buildings belong to the city's
"Golden Age" – the twelfth and thirteenth centuries, when Pisa was one of the
great Mediterranean powers. Perhaps the strangest thing about the **Leaning Tower**
(daily 8.30am–8.30pm; €15), begun in 1173, is that it has always tilted; subsidence
disrupted the foundations when it had reached just three of its eight storeys. For the
next 180 years a succession of architects were brought in to try to correct the tilt,
until 1350 when the angle was accepted and the tower completed. Eight centuries
on, it was thought to be nearing its limit: the overhang is more than 5m, and the
tower, supported by steel wires, was closed to the public in the 1990s – though
it's open for visits once again now that the tilt has been successfully halted. The
**Duomo** (Mon–Sat 10am–7.30pm, Sun 1–7.30pm; €2) was begun a century earlier, its facade – with its delicate balance of black and white marble, and tiers of
arcades – setting the model for Pisa's highly distinctive brand of Romanesque. The
interior continues the use of black and white marble, and with its long arcades of
columns has an almost oriental aspect. Its acknowledged highlight is the astonishingly detailed Gothic pulpit by Giovanni Pisano. The third building of the Miracoli
ensemble, the circular **Baptistery** (daily 8/9am–4.30/7.30pm; €5), is a slightly
bizarre mix of Romanesque and Gothic, embellished with statuary (now displayed
in the museum) by Giovanni Pisano and his father Nicola. Along the north side
of the Campo is the **Camposanto** (same hours; €5), a cloistered cemetery built
towards the end of the thirteenth century. Most of the cloister's frescoes were
destroyed by Allied bombing in World War II, but two masterpieces survived
relatively unscathed – a fourteenth-century *Triumph of Death* and *Last Judgement* in
the Cappella Ammanati, a ruthless catalogue of horrors painted around the time of
the Black Death. At the southeast corner of the Campo, a vast array of pieces from
the Duomo and Baptistery are displayed in the **Museo dell'Opera del Duomo**
(daily 8/9am–5.20/7.20pm; €5), a huge collection that includes statuary by each of
the Pisano family.

Away from the Campo dei Miracoli, Pisa takes on a very different character, as
tourists give way to students at the still-thriving university. It's nonetheless a quiet
place, eerily so at night, set around a series of erratic squares and arcaded streets,
and with clusters of Romanesque churches and, along the banks of the Arno, a
number of fine *palazzi*. The **Piazza dei Cavalieri** is an obvious first stop, a large
square that was the centre of medieval Pisa, before being remodelled by Vasari as
the headquarters of the Knights of St Stephen, whose palace, the curving **Palazzo
dei Cavalieri**, topped with busts of the Medici, faces the order's church of **San
Stefano**. A short walk east along the river, the **Museo Nazionale di San Matteo**
(Tues–Sat 8.30am–7pm, Sun 8.30am–1.30pm; €4) has a superb collection of
religious art housed in a twelfth-century convent.

## Practicalities

Pisa's **train station** is south of the centre on Piazza della Stazione, a ten-minute walk (or bus #3) to Campo dei Miracoli. From the **airport**, take the hourly Florence train for the five-minute journey. There are two **tourist offices**: one to the left of the station (Mon–Fri 9am–7pm, Sat 9am–1.30pm; ☎050.42.291, ⊛www .opapisa.it), and another in the northeast corner of Campo dei Miracoli (Mon–Sat 9am–6pm, Sun 10.30am–4.30pm; ☎050.560.464). Both sell a tourist **ticket** (€10.50) giving admission to most of Pisa's museums, bar the Leaning Tower.

There are plenty of budget **hotels** within a few minutes' walk of Campo dei Miracoli. Alternatively, try the gracious family-run one-star *Locanda Galileo*, on Via Santa Maria (☎050.40.621; ❹) near the Leaning Tower, or the *Pensione Helvetia*, Via G. Boschi 31, off Piazza Arcivescovado (☎050.553.084; ❸), whose charming rooms are furnished in typical Tuscan style. The two-star *La Torre*, Via C. Battisti 17 (☎050.25.220; ❹), is a well-equipped pastel place near the station – the rooms without bath or breakfast are the best deal. The nearest **hostel** is at Via Pietrasantina 15 (☎050.890.622; €21); take bus #3 from the station or Campo dei Miracoli. The city **campsite**, *Campeggio Torre Pendente*, is 1km west of Campo dei Miracoli at Viale delle Cascine 86 (☎050.561.704; closed Nov–March) – a large, well-maintained site, with a restaurant and shop.

There are some good-value **places to eat** a few blocks south of the tower, around the market on Piazza delle Vettovaglie. One of the best is *Vineria di Piazza*, Piazza delle Vettovaglie 13, which does good soups, or try the slightly dearer trattoria *La Mescita*, Via Cavalca 2, on the corner of the piazza. Over to the west, *Pizzeria da Cassio*, Piazza Cavallotti 14, serves decent canteen-style hot food. Pisa is known for its **Gioco del Ponte**, held on the last Sunday in June, when teams from the north and south banks of the city stage a series of "battles", including pushing a seven-tonne carriage over the Ponte di Mezzo. But the town's most magical event is the **Luminara** on June 16, when buildings along the river are festooned with candles to celebrate San Ranieri, the city's patron saint.

# Siena

**SIENA**, 78km south of Florence, is the perfect antidote to its better-known neighbour. Self-contained and still rural in parts behind medieval walls, its great attraction is the cityscape – a majestic Gothic whole that you can roam around and enjoy without venturing into a single museum. It is also a lively university town, so there is no shortage of places to go in the evening. To get the most from it you'll need to stay, especially if you want to see its spectacular horse race, the **Palio** – though you'll definitely need to book during this time (see box on p.624). During the Middle Ages Siena was one of the major cities of Europe. The size of Paris, it controlled most of southern Tuscany and its flourishing wool industry dominated the trade routes from France to Rome. The city developed a highly sophisticated civic life, with its own written constitution and a quasi-democratic government.

## Arrival, information and accommodation

**Buses** stop along Viale Curtatone, by the Basilica of San Domenico, and are much faster and more frequent from Florence than the trains (change at Empoli). The **train station** is down in the valley 2km northeast; to get into town, either walk or cross the road from the station and take just about any city bus heading left, which all drop off about 100m north of Piazza Matteotti near the city centre. The **tourist office** is at Piazza del Campo 56 (daily 9am–7pm; ☎0577.280.551, ⊛www.terresiena.it), and has a hotel list. If you plan on doing a lot of sight-seeing, the *Biglietto Cumulativo* includes entrance to most of Siena's museums (€10/16 valid for 3/7 days), and can be bought at any of the participating museums. There's **Internet access** at Internet Train, Via di Città 121 and Via S. Martino 102.

It's worth phoning ahead for **accommodation**, or booking rooms at the Siena Hotels Promotion booth opposite San Domenico (Mon–Sat 9am–8pm; ℡0577.288.084, ⓦwww.hotelsiena.com). There's a well-maintained **campsite**, *Campeggio Siena Colleverde*, Strada di Scacciapensieri 47, 2km north of the city (℡0577.280.044; closed mid-Nov to mid-March; bus #3 from Piazza Gramsci).

## Hostels and hotels

**Bernini** Via della Sapienza 15 ℡0577.289.047, ⓦwww.albergobernini.com. Charming old fashioned one-star hotel; a few rooms have stunning views of the Duomo. ⑤
**HI Hostel** Via Fiorentina 89 ℡0577.52.212. A comfortable hostel, 2km northwest of the centre; take bus #10 from the train station or Piazza Gramsci, or if you're coming from Florence, ask the bus driver to let you off at "Lo Stellino". €16.
**La Perla** Via delle Terme 25 ℡0577.47.144,

ⓦwww.albergolaperla.191.it. Basic *pensione* in a very central location, two blocks north of the Campo. ⑤
**Piccolo Hotel Etruria** Via Donzelle 3 ℡0577.288.088, wwww.hoteletruria.com. Well-equipped two-star hotel next to *Tre Donzelle* in the centre. ⑥
**Tre Donzelle** Via Donzelle 5 ℡0577.280.358. Historic hotel with simple, clean rooms right in the heart of town. ④

## The City

The **Campo** is the centre of Siena in every sense: the main streets lead into it, the Palio takes place around its café-lined perimeter, and it's the natural place to gravitate towards. It's been called the most beautiful square in the world – an assessment that seems pretty fair; taking a picnic onto the stones to watch the shadows move around the square while topping up your tan is as authentic a Sienese experience as any. The **Palazzo Pubblico** (daily 10am–5.30/7pm) – with its 107m bell-tower, the **Torre del Mangia** (€6) – occupies virtually the entire south side, and although it's still in use as Siena's town hall, its principal rooms have been converted into a **museum** (€7), frescoed with themes integral to the secular life of the medieval city. Best of these are the Sala del Mappamondo, on the wall of which is the fabulous *Maestà* of Simone Martini (1315), an acknowledged masterpiece of Sienese art, and the Sala della Pace, decorated with Lorenzetti's *Allegories of Good and Bad Government* (1377), commissioned to remind the councillors of their duties. Between buildings at the top end of the Campo, the fifteenth-century **Loggia di Mercanzia**, built as a dealing room for merchants, marks the intersection of the city centre's principal streets. From here Via Banchi di Sotto leads east to the Palazzo Piccolomini and on into the workaday quarter of San Martino.

## The Siena Palio

The Siena **Palio** is the most spectacular festival event in Italy, a bareback horse-race around the Campo contested twice a year (July 2 at 7.45pm; and Aug 16 at 7pm) between the ancient wards – or *contrade* – of the city. Each of the seventeen *contrade* has its own church, social centre and museum, and a heraldic animal motif. There's a big build-up, with trials and processions for days before the big event, even though the race itself lasts little more than ninety seconds. It's a hectic and violent spectacle with few rules: each *contrada* has a traditional rival, and ensuring it loses is as important as winning yourself (and it's the horse that wins the prize, whether or not a jockey is on board). For the best view, you need to have found a position on the inner rail by 2pm and to keep it for the next seven hours. Beware that toilets, shade and refreshments are minimal, the swell of the crowd can be overwhelming, and you won't be able to leave the Campo for at least two hours after the race. If you come to town for the Palio but haven't booked a hotel room, reckon on staying up all night.

▲ *Porta Camollia & Via Garibaldi (leading to train station)*

# SIENA

DRAGO

PIAZZA GRAMSCI

VIALE FEDERICO TOZZI

VIALE DELLO STADIO

VIA MALAVOLTI

V.D. STUFASECCA

VIA DI VALLEROZZI

VIA DEL MONTANINI

VIA DEGLI ORBACHI

VIA D. ORTI

N

San Donato

PIAZZA ABBADIA

V. DELL'ABBADIA

VIA DEI ROSSI

San Pietro a Ovile

V. PROVENZANO

VIA DELL'ABBADIA

VIA DEI MONTUCCI

VIA DEI BARONCELLI

PIAZZA G. MATTEOTTI

Palazzo Tantucci

Santa Maria delle Nevi

VIA PIANIGIANI

PIAZZA SALIMBENI

Palazzo Salimbeni

BANCHI DI SOPRA

VIA DI REFENERO

MORO

Palazzo Spannocchi

Santa Maria di Provenzano

PROVENZANO SALVANI   VIA DEL FOSSO

GIRAFFA

Bus stops ★★★

VIALE CURTATONE

VIA DEL PARADISO

Oratorio delle Suore

V.D. PALLA A CORDA

San Pellegrino

VIA DELLA SAPIENZA

VIA DEI PITTORI

VIA DI CAMOLLIA

Biblioteca Comunale

COSTE FONTANI

V.D. ROSA

San Cristoforo

VIA LUCHERINI

VIA DEI TERMINI

TORRE

San Vigilio

VIA SALLUSTIO BANDINI

Palazzo Piccolomini

CIVETTA

VIA CECCO ANGIOLIERI

PIAZZA MADRE TERESA DI CALCUTTA

VIA CAMPOREGIO

Santa Caterina

VIA S. ANTONIO

VID. TIRATOIO

Palazzo Tolomei

VIC. P. PETTINAIO

VISCIONE

VIA DI CALZOLERIA

BANCHI DI SOTTO

San Domenico

Fonte Branda

VIC. D. MACINA

VIA DELLA GALLUZZA

PIAZZA INDIPENDENZA

Loggia della Mercanzia

VIA DELLE TERME

VIC. D. FORCONE

VIA S. CATERINA

VIA DI BECCHERIA

Palazzo Arcivescovile

V.D. COSTONE

VIA ESTERNA DI FONTEBRANDA

VIA DI FONTEBRANDA

Palazzo Tolomei

OCA

SELVA

V. D. VALLEPIATTA

PIAZZA S. GIOVANNI

Baptistery

VIA FRANCIOSA

VIA DI DIACCETO

VIA DI PORTA SALARIA

PIAZZA DEL CAMPO — IL CAMPO

Fonte Gaia

PIANO DEI MANTELLINI

BANCHI DI SOTTO

VIA RINALDINI

VIA DI SALICOTTO

VIA DEL PORRIONE

VIC. D. SCOTTE

VIE LE LOMBARDI

VIA DI SAN GIROLAMO

Duomo

Prefettura

Museo dell'Opera del Duomo

Police

Palazzo Chigi-Saracini

Palazzo Pubblico

PIAZZA DEL MERCATO

VIA DEI MALCONTENTI

AQUILA

San Sebastiano

SS Annunziata

PIAZZA D. SELVA

Santa Maria della Scala

PIAZZA DEL DUOMO

Palazzo delle Papesse

VIA DEL CASATO DI SOTTO

VIA DI CITTÀ

PIAZZA DI POSTIERLA

COSTA LARGA

Pinacoteca Nazionale

16

ITALY | Siena

**ACCOMMODATION**

| Bernini | A | Piccolo Hotel Etruria | C |
| La Perla | D | Tre Donzelle | B |

**EATING & DRINKING**

| Barone Rosso | 3 |
| Carla e Franca | 6 |
| Cubano | 7 |
| Gallo Nero | 5 |
| La Costarella | 9 |
| Nannini Gelateria | 2 |
| Osteria Chiacchieria | 1 |
| Osteria Le Logge | 8 |
| Pizzicheria Morbidi | 4 |

0 ___ 50 m

From the Campo, **Via di Città** cuts west across the oldest quarter of the city, fronted by some of Siena's finest private *palazzi*. At the end of the street, Via San Pietro leads to the **Pinacoteca Nazionale** (Sun & Mon 8.30am–1.30pm, Tues–Sat 8.30am–7.30pm; €4), a fourteenth-century palace housing a rollcall of Sienese Gothic painting. Alleys lead north up to the **Duomo**, completed to virtually its present size around 1215; plans to enlarge it withered with Siena's medieval prosperity, and the vast skeleton of an unfinished extension still stands at the east end of the cathedral square. The Duomo is in any case a delight, its style an amazing conglomeration of Romanesque and Gothic, delineated by bands of black and white marble on its facade. This theme is continued in the sgraffito marble pavement, which begins with geometric patterns outside the church and

625

takes off into a startling sequence of 56 panels within, completed between 1349 and 1547; virtually every artist who worked in the city tried his hand at a design. Midway along the nave, the **Libreria Piccolomini** (daily 9.30am–5/7.30pm; €3), signalled by Pinturicchio's brilliantly coloured fresco of the *Coronation of Pius II*, has further superbly vivid frescoes. Opposite the Duomo is the complex of **Santa Maria della Scala** (daily 10.30am–4.30/6.30pm; €6), the city's hospital for over 800 years, and now a vast museum that includes the frescoed Sala del Pellegrinaio (once used as a hospital ward) and, way down in the basement, the dark and strangely spooky Oratorio di Santa Caterina della Notte chapel. Make time for the **Museo dell'Opera del Duomo** (daily 9am–1.30/7.30pm; €6), tucked into a corner of the abandoned Duomo extension; on display are Pisano's original statues from the facade; the cathedral's original altarpiece, a haunting Byzantine icon known as the *Madonna dagli Occhi Grossi* (Madonna of the Big Eyes); and Duccio's glittering gold *Maestà*, completed in 1311 and acclaimed as the climax of the Sienese style – but the best reason to visit is to follow "Panorama dal Facciatone" signs to steep spiral stairs that climb up to the top of the building; the views are sensational but the topmost walkway is narrow and scarily exposed.

### Restaurants cafés and bars

For **snacks and picnics,** pizza can be bought by weight at Via delle Terme 10, and there's an extravagantly stocked deli, the *Pizzicheria Morbidi*, at Via Banchi di Sotto 27. For a cheap sit-down meal try the unpretentious café *Carla e Franca*, Via di Pantaneto 138, which serves pizza and pasta. **Restaurants** cost a bit over the odds in Siena, especially if you want to eat in the Campo. *Gallo Nero*, Via del Porrione 65–67, serves meals that follow medieval recipes; or for more conventional local fare try *Osteria Le Logge*, in an old pharmacy along the street at no. 33. Out towards San Lorenzo at Corso San Antonio 4, *Osteria Chiacchieria* is a rustic and welcoming spot. For delicious **ice cream**, there's *Nannini Gelateria*, at the Piazza Matteotti end of Banchi di Sopra, or *La Costarella*, just off the Campo near the corner of Via di Città and Via dei Pellegrini. At night, students congregate in **bars** such as the *Barone Rosso*, Via delle Terme 9, with a dance floor, or the Cuban-themed *Cubano* pub on Via San Martino 31.

## San Gimignano

**SAN GIMIGNANO** is one of the best-known villages in Tuscany. Its skyline of towers, framed against classic Tuscan countryside, has caught the tourist imagination. From May to October, it is very busy and to really get a feel for the place you should come out of season. If you can't, aim to spend the night here – in the evenings the town takes on a very different pace and atmosphere. A **combined ticket** (€7.50) covers all the town's civic museums, available at any of the participating sites. The village was a force to be reckoned with in the Middle Ages, with a population of fifteen thousand (twice the present number). Nowadays you could walk across it in fifteen minutes, and around the walls in an hour. The main entrance gate, facing the bus terminal on the south side of town, is **Porta San Giovanni**, from where Via San Giovanni leads to the town's interlocking main squares, **Piazza della Cisterna** and Piazza del Duomo. You enter the Piazza della Cisterna through another majestic gateway, the **Arco dei Becci**, part of the original fortifications before the town expanded in the twelfth century. The more austere **Piazza Duomo**, off to the left, is flanked by the **Collegiata** cathedral (Mon–Sat 9.30am–5/7.30pm, Sun 1–5pm; €3.50), frescoed with Old and New Testament scenes – best, though, is the superb fresco cycle by Ghirlandaio in the Cappella di Santa Fina, depicting the trials of a local saint. There's more work by Ghirlandaio to the left of the cathedral – a fresco of *The Annunciation* on the courtyard loggia – while the **Palazzo del Popolo**, next door (daily 9.30/10am–5.30/7pm; €5), gives you the chance to climb the **Torre Grossa** (€4.10), the town's highest surviving tower and the only one you can ascend. The same building is home to a number of rooms given over to the **Museo Civico**, the first of which, frescoed with hunting scenes, is known as the *Sala di Dante* and houses Lippo Memmi's *Maestà*, modelled on that of Simone Martini in Siena. North from Piazza Duomo, **Via San Matteo** is one of the grandest and best preserved of the city streets, with quiet alleyways running down to the walls.

The nearest **train station** is Poggibonsi, on the Siena–Empoli line, from where **buses** run to San Gimignano every hour (€1.60). Accommodation lists are available from the **tourist office** on Piazza del Duomo (daily 9am–1pm & 2/3–6pm; ℡0577.940.008, ⊛www.sangimignano.com), but from March to October you'll save a lot of frustration by using the Associazione Extralberghiere at Piazza della Cisterna 6 (daily 10am-1pm & 2-7pm; ℡0577.943.111), or the Siena Hotels Promotion on Via San Giovanni 125 just inside Porta San Giovanni (Mon-Sat 9.30am–7pm; ℡0577.940.809), both of which arrange **private rooms** (❻) without commission. One of the cheapest **hotels** is the three-star *Da Graziano*, Via Matteotti 39/a (℡0577.940.101, ⊛www.hoteldagraziano.it; ❺) – ask for a room without breakfast. The nearest **campsite** is *Il Boschetto*, 3km downhill at Santa Lucia (℡0577.940.352; ⊛www.boschettodipiemma.it). Probably the most authentic Tuscan **restaurant** in town is the *Mandragola*, Via Berignano 58.

# Perugia and around

**PERUGIA**, the Umbrian capital, is an attractive medieval university town that buzzes with young people of every nationality, many of them students at the Università per Stranieri (Foreigners' University). Buitoni, the pasta people, are based here, and it's also where Italy's best known chocolate, Perugini, is made – though since its takeover by Nestlé, locals favour Vannucci, made by a former Perugini employee. Perugia hinges on a single street, **Corso Vannucci**, a broad pedestrian thoroughfare, at the far end of which the austere Piazza Quattro Novembre is backed by the plain-faced **Duomo San Lorenzo** (daily 8am–noon & 4pm–sunset). The interior – home to the so-called Virgin's "wedding ring", an unwieldy piece of agate that changes colour according to the character of the person wearing it – isn't especially interesting, and the ring is kept locked up in fifteen boxes fitted into one another like Russian dolls, each opened with a key held by a different person; it's brought out for public viewing every July 30. The centrepiece of the piazza is the **Fontana Maggiore**, sculpted by the father-and-son team Nicola and Giovanni Pisano and describing episodes from the Old Testament, classical myth, Aesop's fables and the twelve months of the year. Opposite rises the gaunt mass of the **Palazzo dei Priori**, worth a glance inside for its frescoed **Sala dei Notari** (Tues–Sun 9am–1pm & 3–7pm; free). A few doors down at Corso Vannucci 25 is the **Collegio di Cambio** (daily 9am–12.30pm & 2.30–5.30pm; €2.60), the town's medieval money-exchange, frescoed by Perugino and said to be the most beautiful bank in the world. The palace also houses the **Galleria Nazionale di Umbria** (daily 8.30am–7.30pm; closed first Mon of each month; €6.50), one of central Italy's best galleries – a twelve-room romp through the history of Umbrian painting, with works by Perugino and Pinturicchio along with one or two stunning Tuscan masterpieces. The best streets to wander around to get a feel of the old city are either side of the Duomo. **Via dei Priori** is the most characteristic, leading down to Agostino di Duccio's colourful **Oratorio di San Bernardino**, whose richly embellished facade is by far the best piece of sculpture in the city. From here you can wander through the northern part of the centre, along Via A. Pascoli, to the **Arco di Augusto**, whose lowest section is now one of the few remaining monuments of Etruscan Perugia. On the other side of town, along **Corso Cavour**, is the large church of **San Domenico**, one of whose chapels holds a superb carved arch by Agostino di Duccio, and, to the right of the altar, the tomb of Pope Benedict XI. In the church's cloisters, the **Museo Archeo-logico Nazionale dell'Umbria** (Mon 2.30–7.30pm, Tues–Sun 8.30am–7.30pm; €4) has one of the most extensive Etruscan collections around.

## Practicalities

**Trains** arrive well away from the centre of Perugia on Piazza V. Veneto; buses #6, #7, #9, #11, #15 make the fifteen-minute journey to Piazza Italia or Piazza Matteotti. The **tourist office** is on Piazza IV Novembre 3 (Mon–Sat 8.30am–1.30pm & 3.30–6.30pm, Sun 9am–1pm; ☏075.573.6458, ⊛www.umbria2000.it), and provides the free *Little Blue What To Do* book for inside information on Perugia. There are two **HI hostels**: *Spagnoli*, 1km from the station on Via Cortonese 4 (☏075.501.1366; €16), and *Ponte Felcino*, in a historic building in a park, at Via Manicomi 97 (☏075.591.3991; €16); it's a 20 minute bus ride (#8) from the train station. A pleasant and more central alternative is the *Centro Internazionale di Accoglienza per la Gioventú* on Via Bontempi 13 (☏075.572.2880, €12), two minutes from the Duomo. As for **hotels**, try the old fashioned, clean two-star *Rosalba*, at Via del Circo 7 in the historic centre (☏075.572.0626, ⊛www.hotelrosalba.com; ⑤), with air-conditioning and free parking; the *Etruria*, an elegant one-star just off the Corso at Via della Luna 21 (☏075.572.3730; ④); or the central, pretty one-star *Anna*, at Via dei Priori 48 (☏075.573.6304; ④), in a former 1600s convent.

On the **food** front, *Osteria del Gambero*, Via Baldeschi 17 (closed Mon), serves Umbrian specialities, while *La Botte*, Via Volte della Pace 33 (closed Sun), is a decent pizzeria. *Dal mì Cocco*, Corso Garibaldi 12 (closed Mon), offers traditional cuisine at rock bottom prices and is popular with students. Two of the liveliest **bars** are the funky, arty *Kandinsky*, Via Enrico del Pozzo 22, with good drinks deals and occasional live music, and *Shamrock* on Piazza Dante 18, an Irish pub with a solid rock soundtrack (daily from 6pm). *Bratislava*, Via Fiorenzuola 12, near Corso Cavour, has **live music** on selected nights, and *Caffè Morlacchi*, Piazza Morlacchi 6–8, features live jazz. There's **Internet** access at Internet Point, Via Ulisse Rocchi 4.

## Assisi

Thanks to St Francis, Italy's premier saint and founder of the Franciscan order, **ASSISI** is Umbria's best-known town, crammed with people for ten months of the year. But it has a medieval hill-town charm and quietens down in the evening. An earthquake in 1997 caused extensive damage to parts of the town, most notably to the **Basilica di San Francesco**, at the end of Via San Francesco (daily 8.30am–6pm; ⊛www.sanfrancescoassisi.org), but restoration is now complete and the basilica is almost back to its original splendour. Justly famed as Umbria's single greatest glory, the basilica houses one of the most overwhelming collections of art outside a gallery anywhere in the world. Begun in 1228, two years after the saint's death, it was financed by donations that flooded in from all over the world. The sombre **Lower Church** is the earlier of the two churches that make up the basilica, its complicated floor plan and claustrophobic vaults intended to create a mood of meditative introspection. Francis lies under the floor in a crypt only brought to light in 1818. Frescoes cover almost every available space, and span a century of continuous artistic development, from the anonymous early works above the altar, through Cimabue's *Madonna, Child and Angels with St Francis* in the right transept to work by the Sienese School painters, Simone Martini and Pietro Lorenzetti. The **Upper Church**, built to a light and airy Gothic plan, is richly decorated, too, with dazzling frescoes on the life of St Francis, some of which at least are considered to be the work of Giotto. There's not a great deal else to see in Assisi's small centre, though a short trek up the steep Via di San Rufino leads to the thirteenth-century **Duomo**, which has the font used to baptize St Francis and St Clare. Close by is the **Basilica di Santa Chiara**, a virtual facsimile of the basilica up the road and home to the macabre blackened body of Clare herself.

Assisi's **train station** is 5km south of town, connected to it by half-hourly buses. The **tourist office**, at Piazza del Comune 12 (summer Mon–Sat 8am–6.30pm, Sun 10am–1pm & 2–5pm; winter Mon–Fri 8am–2pm, 3–6pm, Sat 9am–1pm & 3-6pm, Sun 9am–1pm; ☏075.812.450, www.umbria2000.it), can help with **private rooms**, though do book especially around Easter; or try the pilgrim **hostels** (*Case Religiose di Ospitalità*) dotted around town (❸) – the *Suore del Giglio*, Via San Francesco 13 (☏075.816.258), has the best location. Alternatively, the HI hostel, *Ostello della Pace*, Via di Valecchie (☏075.816.767, ☏www.assisihostel.com; €15), is clean and beautifully located, just below the town. Of the **hotels**, try *Anfiteatro Romano*, Via Anfiteatro Romano 4 (☏075.813.025; ❸), a one-star with parking, or *La Rocca*, Via Porta Perlici 27 (☏075.812.284, ☏www.hotelarocca.it; ❸), 300 metres from the centre, with en-suite rooms and parking. There's also a big **campsite** and hostel at Fontemaggio (☏075.813.636; €20; bus #20 or #34l), 3km out on the road to the monastery of Eremo delle Carceri.

For **food**, try the reasonably priced pizzeria, *Il Pozzo Romano*, on Via Sant'Agnese near Santa Chiara (closed Thurs); *Pallotta*, Via San Rufino 4 (closed Tues), or *I Monaci*, Piazzetta Verdi 10, off Via Fontebella on the Scaletti del Metastasio (closed Wed). Otherwise, the *La Rocca* hotel has a good no-frills restaurant. For **Internet** access, try Internet World at Via Gabriele dell'Addolorata 25 (☏075.812.327), towards Porta Nuova from Piazza del Comune).

# Spoleto

**SPOLETO** is Umbria's most compelling town, remarkable for its extremely pretty position and several of Italy's most ancient Romanesque churches. The lower town, where you arrive, was badly damaged by World War II bombing, and doesn't hold much of interest, so it's best to take a bus straight to the upper town. There's no single, central piazza, but the place to head for is **Piazza della Libertà**, site of a much-restored first-century **Roman Theatre**, visible at all times, but also visitable more closely in conjunction with the **Museo Archeologico** (Mon–Sun 8.30am–7.30pm; €2). The adjoining **Piazza della Fontana** has more Roman remains, best of which is the **Arco di Druso**, built to honour the minor campaign victories of Drusus, son of Tiberius. The homely **Piazza del Mercato**, beyond, is a fine opportunity to take in some streetlife, and from here it's a short walk to the **Duomo**, whose facade of restrained elegance is one of the most memorable in the region. Inside, various Baroque embellishments are eclipsed by the superlative apse frescoes of the fifteenth-century Florentine artist Fra Lippo Lippi, dominated by his final masterpiece, a *Coronation of the Virgin*. He died shortly after their completion (amid rumours that he was poisoned for seducing the daughter of a local noble family) and was interred here in a tomb designed by his son, Filippino. You should also take the short walk out to the **Ponte delle Torri**, a picture-postcard favourite, and an astonishing piece of medieval engineering, best seen as part of a circular walk around the base of the **Rocca** – everyone's idea of a cartoon castle, with towers, crenellations and sheer walls.

Spoleto's **train station** is 1km north of the town centre, with the **tourist office** on central Piazza della Libertà (Mon-Sat 9am–1pm & 4–7pm, Sun 10am-1pm; ☏0743.238.920). For **accommodation**, the best budget choice is the central and reasonably priced *Il Panciolle*, Via del Duomo 3 (☏0743.456.77; ❹), a well equipped two-star hotel. If that's full, the only other vaguely affordable place in the upper town is the two-star *Pensione Aurora*, off Piazza della Libertà at Via dell'Apollinare 3 (☏0743.220.315, ☏www.hotelauroraspoleto.it; ❻). The lower town is very much a second choice, although its hotel-like **hostel**, *Villa Redenta*, Via di Villa Redenta 1, in the converted stables of a seventeenth-century villa (☏0743.224.936, ☏www.villaredenta.com; dorms €20, rooms ❹), is excellent value. The closest **campsite** is the tiny but very pleasant *Camping Monteluco*, behind San Pietro (☏0743.220.358; closed Oct–March). The best basic **trattoria** is *Trattoria del Festival*, Via Brignone 8 (closed Fri); *Il Panciolle*, Via del Duomo 3–4 (closed Wed), is also a popular choice. If you are staying in the lower town, head for *Dei Pini*, Via 3 Settembre (closed Mon), near the hostel, for authentic home cooking at bargain prices.

## Urbino

For the second half of the fifteenth century, **URBINO** was one of the most prestigious courts in Europe, ruled by the remarkable Federico da Montefeltro, who employed a number of the greatest artists and architects of the time to build and decorate his palace in the town. These days, however, it is notable mainly for its excellent museums; the best time to go is mid-week when the university students are around. In the centre of town, the **Palazzo Ducale** is a fitting monument to Federico, home now to the **Galleria Nazionale delle Marche** (Mon 8.30am–2pm, Tues–Sun 8.30am–7.15pm; €4), although it's building itself that makes the biggest impression. Among the paintings in the Appartamento del Duca are Piero della Francesca's strange *Flagellation*, and the *Ideal City*, a famous perspective painting of a symmetrical and deserted cityscape long attributed to Piero but now thought to be by one of his followers. The most interesting and best preserved of the *palazzo's* rooms is Federico's **Studiolo**, a triumph of illusory perspective created by intarsia (wood inlaid as mosaic) – shelves appear to protrude from the walls, cupboard doors seem to swing open to reveal lines of books, a letter lies in an apparently half-open drawer. Even more remarkable are the delicately hued landscapes of Urbino as it might appear from one of the surrounding hills, and the life-like squirrel perching next to a bowl of fruit. Urbino's pleasant jumble of Renaissance and medieval houses is a welcome antidote to the rarefied atmosphere of the Palazzo Ducale. You can wind down in one of the many bars and trattorias, or take a picnic up to the gardens within the **Fortezza Albornoz**, from where you'll get great views of the town and countryside, out to **San Bernardino**, a fine Renaissance church 2km away that is the resting place of the Montefeltros.

Urbino is notoriously difficult to reach – the best approach is by **bus** from Pésaro, about 30km away on the coast (last around 8pm; €2.05). Buses stop in Borgo Mercatale, at the foot of the Palazzo Ducale, which is reached either by lift or by Francesco di Giorgio Martini's spiral staircase. For accommodation, the cheapest options are **private rooms** – lists are available from the **tourist office** on Piazza Rinascimento (Mon–Sat 9am–1pm & 3–6pm; ☎0722.2613, ✆www.comune.urbino.ps.it). The most convenient **hotels** are the three-star *Italia*, Corso Garibaldi 32 (☎0722.2701, ✆www.albergo-italia-urbino.it; ❽), and the slightly dingy *San Giovanni*, Via Barocci 13 (☎0722.2827; ❹; closed July).

For **food**, the university *mensa* on Piazza San Filippo is the best value, while the *Bar Caffe degli Angeli*, Borgo Mercenate 21/22, serves great panini and nibbles. For **restaurants** try the friendly *Il Cantuccio*, Via Budassi 64, where the *strozzapreti* pasta is delicious, or, if your budget's not too tight, *La Taverna degli Artisti*, Via Bramante 52, which serves tasty local dishes. At aperitif time the most popular haunts are the **cafés** around Piazza della Repubblica: *Cocktail & Drink* has a buzzing upstairs lounge and lively music. For a quieter **drink**, try the friendly bar *L'Isola*, Via dei Veterani 18, then, later on, head with Urbino's beautiful people to the disco-pub *Bus Bar*, Via Nazionale Bocca Trabaria 6, a half-hour walk out of the centre.

# Rome (Roma)

Of all Italy's historic cities, **ROME** (Roma) exerts the most compelling fascination. For the traveller, it is the sheer weight of history in the city that is most evident, its various eras crowding in on each other to an almost breathtaking degree. There are the classical features – the Colosseum, the Forum and spectacular Palatine Hill – and relics from the early Christian period in ancient basilicas; while the fountains and churches of the Baroque period go a long way to determining the look of the city centre. But there are also swathes of Fascist-era concrete palaces, and even the occasional modern masterpiece such as Renzo Piano's acclaimed new Auditorium. Rome has a vibrant, chaotic life of its own, the crowded streets thronged with traffic, locals, tourists and students.

## Arrival, information and accommodation

The main **train station** is Termini, meeting-point of the metro lines and city bus routes. Rome has two **airports**: Leonardo da Vinci, better known as Fiumicino, handles all scheduled flights; Ciampino is mainly for charter services. Two train services link Fiumicino to Rome: one to Termini (every 30min; €8.80), the other to Trastevere, Ostiense and Tiburtina stations (every 20min; €4.70). A taxi costs at least €40. From Ciampino, take a Cotral bus to Anagnina on metro line A, from where it's a twenty-minute metro ride to Termini. Information is available from the **Tourist Call Centre** (daily 9am–7pm; ☎06.3600.4399), which has up-to-the-minute information in five languages; the **tourist information** booth at Fiumicino airport (Mon–Sat 8am–7pm; ☎06.6595.4471); and the **main tourist office** at Via Parigi 5 (Mon–Sat 9am–7pm; ☎06.4889.9200). There are also information kiosks dotted around the city (daily 9am–6pm.) Various **museum cards** give reduced or free entry, but you need to know what you want to see to get the best out of them – the Roma Archeologia card is the best for ancient sites including the Colosseum and Palatine (€20/7 days).

The best way to get around Rome is to **walk**. That said, **public transport** is both reliable and cheap. A day-pass (BIG; €4) or single ticket (BIT; €1) can be bought from any newspaper stall or *tabaccaio*, or from the ATAC booth on Piazza dei Cinquecento, which also sells decent transport maps. The buses and the metro stop around 11.30pm (Sat night 12.30am), though metro line A currently ends at 9pm while maintenance work is done, after which a network of **night buses** takes over, serving most parts of the city until about 5.30am. **Taxis** are costly, with the meter starting at €2.33. You can hail one in the street, or try the ranks at Termini, Piazza Venezia, Piazza San Silvestro; alternatively call ☎06.3570, 06.5551 or 06.6645 to book one.

In summer Rome is very crowded, so book **accommodation** as far in advance as possible. If you can't, make straight for the tourist office. Many of the city's cheaper hotels are located close to Termini station.

### Hostels & religious houses
**Alessandro Palace** Via Vicenza 42 ☎06.446.1958, ⓦwww.hostelalessandro.com. Buzzing, friendly, international staff, full use of kitchen and bar. Near station, free Internet. No curfew. €19–24.

**Colors** Via Boezio 31 ☎06.687.4030, ⓦwww.colorshotel.com. In Prati, near St Peter's. Pretty, clean, friendly, good value, use of kitchen and terrace. €23.

**Fawlty Towers** Via Magenta 39 ☎06.445.4802, ⓦwww.fawltytowers.org. Near the station, efficient, clean, with all amenities, including free Internet, kitchen use, satellite TV. €22.

**M&J Place Hostel** Via Solferino 9 ☎06.446.2802, ⓦwww.mejplacehostel.com. Just out of the station and to the right; basic but facilities include kitchen and free Internet access, and conveniently on top of Living Room nightclub. €22.

**Nostra Signora di Lourdes** Via Sistina 113 ☎06.474.5324. Plain convent near the Spanish Steps, singles and rooms for married couples; 10.30pm curfew. €33.

**Ostello del Foro Italico** Viale delle Olimpiadi 61 ☎06.324.2571, ⓦwww.hostelbooking.com. Rome's vast HI hostel. Breakfast included. 12.30am curfew. Metro Ottaviano, then bus #32. €17.

**Hotel Ottaviano** Via Ottaviano 6 ☎06.3973.7253, ⓦwww.pensioneottaviano.com. Basic but friendly private hotel/hostel, excellently situated just outside the Vatican walls. Metro line Ottaviano. €19–24.

**Hotel Sandy** Via Cavour 136 ☎06.488.4585, ⓦwww.sandyhostel.com. Good-value, central young people's hotel/hostel. Metro Cavour. €20.

**Suore Pie Operaie** Via di Torre Argentina 76
⌖06.686.1254. Superbly located and friendly
women-only convent, though with 10.30/11pm
curfew. Closed Aug. €16–24.

**YWCA** Via C. Balbo 4 ⌖06.488.3917. Smart, plain
hostel, for all travellers, and more conveniently
situated than the HI hostel; 10min walk from
Termini. Breakfast included (not Sun). Midnight
curfew. €26–47.

### Hotels

**Davos** Via degli Scipioni 239, ⌖06.321.7012.
Simple, clean *pensione* in Prati area. Metro
Lepanto. ⑤

**Della Lunetta** Piazza del Paradiso 68
⌖06.686.1080, ⌖www.albergodellalunetta
.it. In a great location, this hotel has some superb
refurbished rooms. ⑥

**Katty** Via Palestro 35 ⌖06.490.079. One of the
cheaper, more pleasant options east of the station:
it's worth bargaining for reductions, or ask for the
more basic rooms downstairs. ⑤

**Monaco** Via Flavia 84 ⌖06.474.4335. Very
welcoming and clean; between the station and Via
Veneto. ⑤

**Perugia** Via del Colosseo 7 ⌖06.679.7200,
⌖www.hperugia.it. Smart place on a peaceful but
central street. Metro Colosseo. ⑨

**Rosetta** Via Cavour 295 ⌖06.4782.3069. Good
location close to the Colosseum. Metro Colosseo.
⑥

**Trastevere** Via Luciano Manara 24a
⌖06.581.4713. Simple, pretty place handily
located for the nightlife of Trastevere. ⑧

# The City

Rome's city centre is divided neatly into distinct blocks. The warren of streets
that makes up the **centro storico** (historic centre) occupies the hook of land on
the east bank of the River Tiber, bordered to the east by Via del Corso and to the
north and south by water. From here, Rome's central core spreads east: across Via
del Corso to the major shopping streets and alleys around the **Spanish Steps** and
on down to the main artery of Via Nazionale; and south to the major sites of the
**Roman Forum** and **Palatine Hill**. The west bank of the river is oddly distanced
from the main hum of the city, home to the **Vatican** and **St Peter's** and, to the
south of these, **Trastevere** – even in ancient times a distinct entity from the city
proper, as well as nowadays a focus of nightlife.

## The Capitoline Hill and around

The best place to start a tour of Rome is the **Capitoline Hill**, formerly the
spiritual and political centre of the Roman Empire, which hides behind the Neoclassical Vittorio Emanuele Monument on the traffic-choked Piazza Venezia. The
Capitoline is home to one of Rome's most elegant squares, **Piazza del Campi-
doglio**, designed by Michelangelo in the 1550s for Pope Paul III, and flanked by
the two branches of one of the city's most important museums of antique art – the
**Capitoline Museums** (Tues–Sun 9am–8pm; €7.80). On the left, the **Palazzo
Nuovo** concentrates on some of the best of the city's Roman and Greek sculpture,
and on Renaissance painting, including Caravaggio's *St John the Baptist*. Behind the
square, a road skirts the Forum down to the small church of **San Giuseppe dei
Falegnami**, built above the prison where St Peter is said to have been held – you
can see the bars to which he was chained, along with the spring the saint is said to
have created in which to baptize other prisoners. At the top of the staircase is an
imprint claimed to be of St Peter's head as he was tumbled down the stairs.

Via del Plebiscito forges west from Piazza Venezia past the church of **Gesù**, a high,
wide Baroque church of the Jesuit order, notable for the richness of its interior.
Crossing over, streets wind down to **Piazza di Campo dei Fiori**, home to a
morning market and surrounded by bars. South of the Campo, at the end of Via dei
Balestrari, the **Galleria Spada** (Tues–Sun 8.30am–7.30pm; €5.50) is decorated in
the manner of a Roman noble family and displays a small collection of paintings,
best of which are a couple of portraits by Reni. To the left off the courtyard is a
crafty trompe-l'oeil tunnel by Borromini, whose trick perspective makes it appear
four times its actual length. Across Via Arenula, through and beyond the Jewish

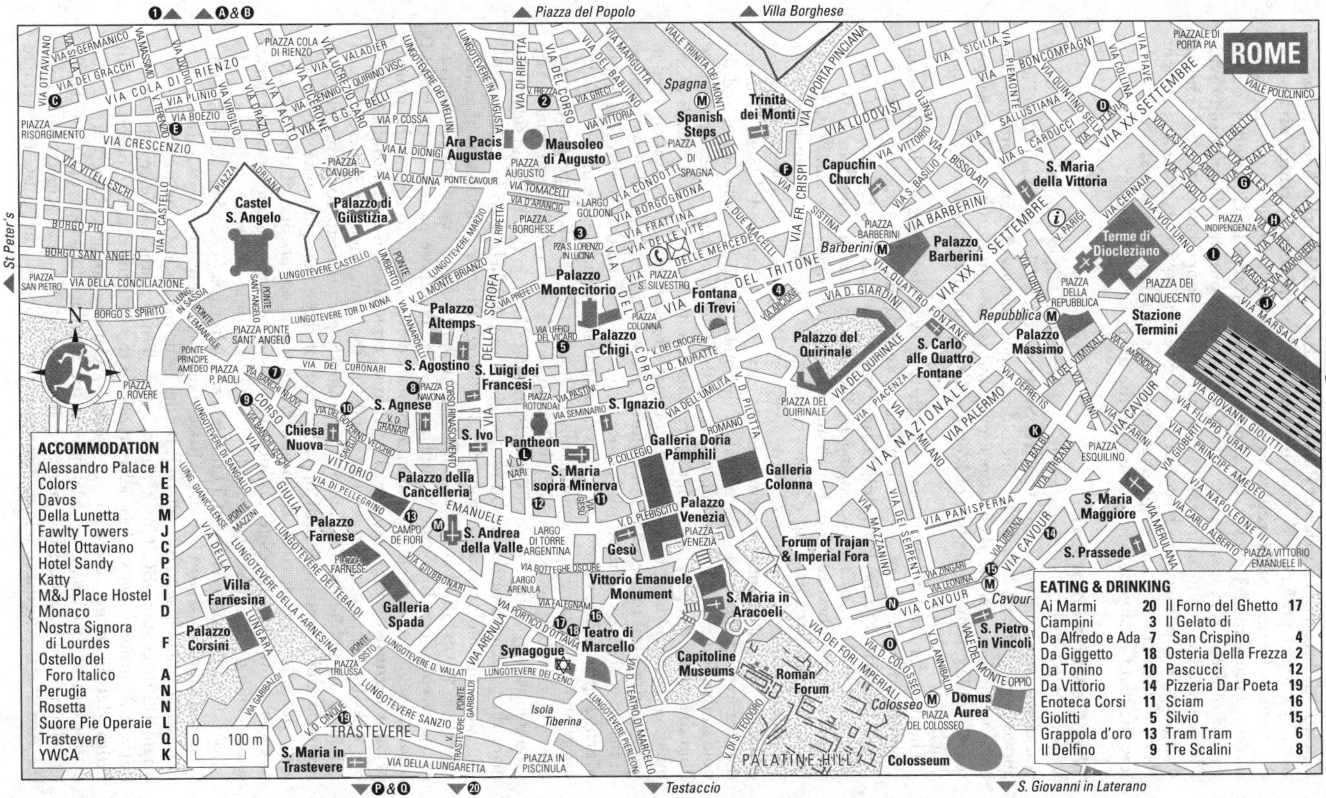

**ACCOMMODATION**

| | |
|---|---|
| Alessandro Palace | H |
| Colors | E |
| Davos | B |
| Della Lunetta | M |
| Fawlty Towers | J |
| Hotel Ottaviano | C |
| Hotel Sandy | P |
| Katty | G |
| M&J Place Hostel | I |
| Monaco | D |
| Nostra Signora di Lourdes | F |
| Ostello del Foro Italico | A |
| Perugia | N |
| Rosetta | O |
| Suore Pie Operaie | L |
| Trastevere | Q |
| YWCA | K |

**EATING & DRINKING**

| | |
|---|---|
| Ai Marmi | 20 |
| Ciampini | 3 |
| Da Alfredo e Ada | 7 |
| Da Giggetto | 18 |
| Da Tonino | 10 |
| Da Vittorio | 14 |
| Enoteca Corsi | 11 |
| Giolitti | 5 |
| Grappola d'oro | 13 |
| Il Delfini | 9 |
| Il Forno del Ghetto | 17 |
| Il Gelato di San Crispino | 4 |
| Osteria Della Frezza | 2 |
| Pascucci | 12 |
| Pizzeria Dar Poeta | 19 |
| Sciam | 16 |
| Silvio | 15 |
| Tram Tram | 6 |
| Tre Scalini | 8 |

**ITALY** | Rome (Roma)

16

633

Ghetto, the broad open space of **Piazza della Bocca di Verità** is home to two of the city's better-preserved Roman temples, the **Temple of Fortuna Virilis** and the circular **Temple of Hercules Victor**, both of which date from the end of the second century BC. However, the church of **Santa Maria in Cosmedin**, on the far side of the square, is more interesting, a typically Roman medieval basilica with a huge marble altar and an ingenious Cosmati mosaic floor – one of the city's finest. Outside in the portico, the Bocca di Verità gives the square its name, an ancient Roman drain cover in the shape of an enormous face that tradition says will swallow the hand of anyone who doesn't tell the truth.

## The Centro Storico

You need to walk a little way northwest from the Capitoline Hill to find the real city centre of Rome, the **Centro Storico**, circled by a bend in the Tiber, above Corso Vittorio Emanuele. The old Campus Martius of Roman times, it later became the heart of the Renaissance city, and is now an unruly knot of narrow streets holding some of the best of Rome's classical and Baroque heritage, as well as much of its nightlife.

The boundary of the historic centre to the east, **Via del Corso**, is Rome's main shopping street. Walking north from Piazza Venezia, the first building on the left is the **Galleria Doria Pamphilj** (10am–5pm; closed Thurs, €8), one of many galleries housed in palaces belonging to Roman patrician families. Its collection includes Rome's best cache of Dutch and Flemish paintings, canvases by Caravaggio and Velázquez's painting of Pope Innocent X. Five minutes from here is the **Pantheon** (daily 8.30/9am–7.30pm; free) on Piazza della Rotonda, the most complete ancient Roman structure in the city, finished around 125 AD. Inside, the diameter of the dome and height of the building are precisely equal, and the hole in the dome's centre is a full 9m across; there are no visible arches or vaults to hold the whole thing up; instead, they're sunk into the concrete of the walls of the building. It would have been richly decorated – the coffered ceiling was covered in solid bronze until the seventeenth century, and the niches were filled with statues of the gods. There's more artistic splendour on view behind the Pantheon in **Santa Maria sopra Minerva**, one of the city's art-treasure churches, crammed with the tombs and gifts of wealthy Roman families. Of these, the Carafa chapel, in the south transept, is the best known, holding Filippino Lippi's fresco of *The Assumption*. You should look, too, at the figure of *Christ Bearing the Cross*, on the left-hand side of the main altar, a serene work painted for the church by Michelangelo in 1521.

In the opposite direction from the Pantheon, **Piazza Navona** is the most appealing square in Rome, and follows the lines of the Emperor Domitian's chariot arena. Pope Innocent X built most of the grandiose palaces that surround it in the seventeenth century and commissioned Borromini to design the church of **Sant'Agnese** on the west side. The church, typically squeezed into the tightest of spaces by Borromini, supposedly stands on the spot where St Agnes, exposed naked to the public in the stadium, miraculously grew hair to cover herself. The **Fontana dei Quattro Fiumi** opposite, one of three that punctuate the square, is by Borromini's arch-rival, Bernini; each figure represents one of the four great rivers of the world – the Nile, Danube, Ganges and Plate – though only the horse, symbolizing the Danube, was actually carved by Bernini himself.

Just out of the north end, you'll find **Palazzo Altemps** (Tues–Sun 9am–7.45pm; €7), functioning as part of the Museo Nazionale Romano and featuring the unmissable ancient statuary collected by the Ludovisi family. The highlight is the original fifth-century-BC Greek throne, embellished with a delicate relief of the birth of Aphrodite. Down Via della Scrofa, in the French national church of **San Luigi dei Francesi**, there's early work by Caravaggio describing the life and martyrdom of St Matthew – Matthew is the dissolute-looking youth on the far left, illuminated by a shaft of sunlight. A little way up Via della Ripetta from here, the **Ara Pacis Augustae** (closed for restoration) was built in 13 BC to celebrate

Augustus' victory over Spain and Gaul. It supports a fragmented frieze showing Augustus himself, his wife Livia, Tiberius, Agrippa, and various children clutching the togas of the elders, the last of whom is said to be the young Claudius.

At the far end of Via di Ripetta the **Piazza del Popolo** provides an impressive entrance to the city, all symmetry and grand vistas, although its real attraction is the church of **Santa Maria del Popolo**, which holds some of the best Renaissance art of any Roman church. Two pictures by Caravaggio get most attention – the *Conversion of St Paul* and the *Crucifixion of St Peter*.

## The Spanish Steps, Palazzo Barberini and Trevi fountain

The area immediately southeast of Piazza del Popolo is travellers' Rome, historically the artistic quarter of the city, with a distinctly cosmopolitan air. At the centre of the district, **Piazza di Spagna** is a long, thin square centring on the distinctive boat-shaped Barcaccia fountain, the last work of Bernini's father. The **Spanish Steps** – a venue for international posing – sweep up from the piazza to the **Trinità dei Monti**, a sixteenth-century church that holds a couple of works by Daniel da Volterra, notably a soft flowing fresco of *The Assumption* in the third chapel on the right, which includes a portrait of his teacher Michelangelo.

From the church, follow Via Sistina to **Piazza Barberini**, a busy traffic junction, in the centre of which is Bernini's Fontana del Tritone. Via Veneto bends north from here, its pricey bars and restaurants once the haunt of Rome's "beautiful people" but now the home of high-class tack. A little way up, the Capuchin **Church of the Immaculate Conception** is worth visiting for its cemetery (9am–noon & 3–6pm, closed Thurs; donation requested); the bones of four thousand monks line the walls of a series of chapels in rococo patterns or as fully clothed skeletons, their faces peering out of their cowls in expressions of agony.

Back across Piazza Barberini, the **Palazzo Barberini** contains the **Galleria d'Arte Antica** (Tues–Sat 8.30am–1.30pm, Sun 8.30am–7pm; €5; book on ☏06.328.101), which displays a rich patchwork of mainly Italian art from the early Renaissance to late Baroque period. In addition to canvases by Tintoretto, Titian and El Greco, highlights include Filippo Lippi's warmly maternal *Madonna and Child*, painted in 1437, and Raphael's beguiling *Fornarina*. But perhaps the most impressive feature of the gallery is the building itself, the epitome of Baroque grandeur worked on at different times by the most favoured architects of the day: Bernini, Borromini and Maderno. West down Via del Tritone from Piazza Barberini, hidden among a tight web of narrow, apparently aimless streets, is one of Rome's more surprising sights – the **Fontana di Trevi**, a huge Baroque gush of water over statues and rocks built onto the back of a Renaissance palace, that can barely be seen for the crowds.

## Piazza della Repubblica and Museo Nazionale Romano

Via Nazionale, one of Rome's main shopping streets, lined with boutiques, leads up to **Piazza della Repubblica**, a stern but rather tawdry semicircle of buildings that occupies part of the site of Diocletian's Baths, the scanty remains of which lie across the square in the church of **Santa Maria degli Angeli**. Michelangelo is also said to have had a hand in modifying another part of the baths, the courtyard that makes up part of the **Museo Nazionale Romano** behind the church (Tues–Sun 9am–7.45pm; €7). The museum's collection of Greek and Roman antiquities is second only to the Vatican's and is now partly housed in the Palazzo Altemps, Palazzo Braschi and the Palazzo Massimo across the square at Piazza dei Cinquecento 68, a recently restored building featuring a series of Roman busts, mosaics and fresco fragments. The top floor gallery contains stunning, sylvan frescoes from a country villa that belonged to the emperor Augustus's wife Livia, and some of the best examples of mosaics from Roman villas around the world.

## The Forum, Palatine Hill, Colosseum and around

In ancient times, the **Roman Forum, Palatine Hill and Colosseum** (Tues–Sun 9am–6pm/1hr before sunset; forum free, rest €10) formed the centre of what was a very large city. Following the downfall of the city to various barbarian invaders, the area was left in ruin, its relics quarried for construction in other parts of Rome during medieval and Renaissance times.

Running through the core of the Forum, the **Via Sacra** was the best-known street of ancient Rome. At the bottom of the Capitoline Hill, the **Arch of Septimius Severus** was built in the early third century AD to commemorate the emperor's tenth anniversary in power, and the grassy, wide-open scatter of paving and beached columns in front of it was the place where most of the life of the city took place. At the nearby **Curia** – begun in 80 BC, restored by Julius Caesar, and rebuilt by Diocletian in the third century AD – the Senate met during the Republican period, and augurs would come to announce the wishes of the gods. On the opposite side is the **House of the Vestal Virgins**, where lived the six women charged with the responsibility of keeping the sacred flame of Vesta alight. On the far side of the site, the **Basilica of Constantine and Maxentius** is probably the Forum's most impressive remains. From the basilica, the Via Sacra climbs to the **Arch of Titus** on a low arm of the Palatine Hill – its reliefs showing the spoils of the sacking of Jerusalem being carried off by eager Romans.

Turning right at the Arch of Titus takes you up to the **Palatine Hill**, now a stunningly beautiful archeological garden. In the days of the Republic, the Palatine was the most desirable address in Rome (from it is derived our word "palace"). The gargantuan **Domus Augustana** spreads to the far brink of the hill and you can look down from here onto its vast central courtyard and maze-like fountain, and wander through a handful of its bare rooms. From close by, steps lead down to the **Cryptoporticus**, a passage built by Nero to link the Palatine with his palace on the far side of the Colosseum, and decorated along part of its length with well-preserved Roman stuccowork. A left turn leads to the **House of Livia**, originally believed to have been the residence of the wife of Augustus, whose courtyard and rooms are decorated with scanty frescoes. Turn right down the passage and up some steps and you're in the **Farnese Gardens**, laid out by Alessandro Farnese in the mid-sixteenth century and now a tidily planted refuge from the exposed heat of the ruins. The terrace here looks back over the Forum, while the terrace at the opposite end looks down on the real centre of Rome's ancient beginning – an Iron Age hut, known as the **House of Romulus**, the best preserved part of a ninth-century village, and the so-called **Lupercal**, beyond, which tradition says was the cave where Romulus and Remus were suckled by the she-wolf.

Immediately outside the Forum, the fourth-century **Arch of Constantine** marks the end of the Via Sacra. Across from here, the **Colosseum** is Rome's most awe-inspiring ancient monument, begun by the Emperor Vespasian around 72 AD and finished by his son Titus about eight years later – an event celebrated by 100 days of games. The Romans flocked here for gladiatorial contests and cruel spectacles – they even had mock sea battles, as the arena could be flooded in minutes. After the games were outlawed in the fifth century, the Colosseum was pillaged for building material, and is now little more than a shell. The structure of the place is still easy to see, however, and has served as a model for stadia around the world ever since.

Close by is Nero's **Domus Aurea** (Weds–Mon 9am–7.45pm; €5, booking fee €1.50; ☎06.3996.7700), whose entrance is opposite the Colosseum, off Via Labicana, a short walk up some steps on the Oppian Hill. Built by Nero as his private house, the palace covered a full square mile and its extravagant halls were decorated in the most lavish style, though little remains today. Stripped of its marble decor and filled with rubble after Nero's death, when the site was first rediscovered hundreds of years later it was thought to be some sort of mystical cave or grotto. It's a short walk from here down to the church of **San Clemente**, a light, twelfth-century basilica that encapsulates the continuity of history in the city.

The ground-floor church is a superb example of a medieval basilica, with some fine mosaics; downstairs (€3), there's the nave of an earlier church, dating back to 392 AD; and at the eastern end and down another level are the remains of a Roman apartment building – a labyrinthine set of rooms including a Mithraic temple of the late second century. The same street leads to the basilica of **San Giovanni in Laterano**, Rome's cathedral and the seat of the pope until the Unification of Italy. There has been a church on this site since the fourth century, and the present building, reworked by Borromini in the mid-seventeenth century, evokes Rome's staggering wealth of history. The doors were taken from the Curia of the Roman Forum. Inside, the first pillar on the left of the right-hand aisle shows a fragment of Giotto's fresco of Boniface VIII, proclaiming the first Holy Year in 1300, while further on, a monument commemorating Sylvester I (bishop of Rome during much of Constantine's reign) incorporates part of his original tomb, said to sweat and rattle its bones when a pope is about to die. Behind the papal altar are the reliquaries for the heads of saints Peter and Paul, though the relics themselves were stolen in the early 1800s. The **Baptistery** is the oldest surviving in the Christian world, an octagonal structure built by Constantine, rebuilt during the fifth century, and now carefully restored after a 1993 car bomb damaged the stonework and some of the frescoes. On the other side of the church the **Scala Santa** is claimed to be the staircase from Pontius Pilate's house down which Christ walked after his trial. The 28 steps are protected by boards, and the only way you're allowed to climb them is on your knees.

## Trastevere

Across the Tiber from the centre of town, **Trastevere** is a small, tightly knit neighbourhood that was once the artisan quarter of the city and has since become gentrified. It is now home to much of the city's most vibrant and youthful night-life – and some of Rome's best restaurants. The best time to come is on Sunday morning, when the **Porta Portese** flea market stretches down Via Portuense to Trastevere station in a congested medley of junk, antiques and clothing. Afterwards, stroll north up Via Anicia to the church of **Santa Cecilia in Trastevere**, built over the site of the second-century home of the patron saint of music. Locked in the hot chamber of her own baths for several days, she sang her way through the ordeal until her head was hacked half off with an axe. If you get the chance, have a peek at the Singing Gallery's beautifully coloured and tender late-thirteenth-century **frescoes** by Piero Cavallini (Tues–Thurs 10am–noon, Sun 11.30am–12.15pm; donation expected). Santa Cecilia is situated in the quieter part of Trastevere, on the southern side of Viale Trastevere, the wide boulevard that cuts through the centre of the district. There's more life on the other side centred on Piazza Santa Maria in Trastevere, named after the church of **Santa Maria in Trastevere** – held to be the first official church in Rome, built on a site where a fountain of oil is said to have sprung on the day of Christ's birth. North towards the Tiber, the **Villa Farnesina** is known for its Renaissance murals, including a Raphael-designed painting of *Cupid and Psyche*, completed in 1517 by the artist's assistants. Raphael did, however, manage to finish the *Galatea* next door. The other paintings in the room are by Sebastiano del Piombo and the architect of the building, Peruzzi, who also decorated the upstairs Salone delle Prospettive, which shows trompe-l'oeil galleries with views of contemporary Rome – one of the earliest examples of the technique.

## St Peter's and the Vatican

Across the Tiber is the **Vatican City**, a tiny territory surrounded by high walls on its far side and on the near side opening its doors to the rest of the city and its pilgrims in the form of Bernini's **Piazza San Pietro**. The basilica of **St Peter's** (daily 7am–6/7pm; free) is the replacement of a basilica built during the time of Constantine, to a plan initially conceived at the end of the fifteenth century by Bramante and finished off over a century later by Carlo Maderno, bridging the

Renaissance and Baroque eras. The inside is full of features from the Baroque period, although the first thing you see, on the right, is Michelangelo's *Pietà*, completed when he was just 24 and, following an attack in 1972, displayed behind glass. On the right-hand side of the nave, the bronze statue of St Peter was cast in the thirteenth century by Arnolfo di Cambio. Bronze was also the material used in Bernini's massive 28m high baldacchino, the centrepiece of the sculptor's embellishment of the interior. Bernini's feverish sculpting decorates the apse, too, his *cattedra* enclosing the supposed chair of St Peter in a curvy marble and stucco throne. An entrance off the aisle leads to the **treasury** (daily 9am–5/6pm; €4.20), while back at the central crossing, steps lead down to the **Vatican Grottoes** (daily 7/8am–5/6pm), where a number of popes are buried in grandiose tombs – in the main, those not distinguished enough to be buried up above. Under the portico, to the right of the main doors, you can ascend by lift to the **roof and dome** (€4.20), from where the views over the city are glorious.

A five-minute walk out of the northern side of Piazza San Pietro takes you up to the only part of the Vatican City you can visit independently, the **Vatican Museums** (Mon–Sat 8.45am–1.45pm, €12; last Sun of the month 8.45am–1.45pm, free) – quite simply the largest, richest museum complex in the world, stuffed with booty from every period of the city's history. If you have little time, start off at the **Raphael Stanze**, at the opposite end of the building to the entrance, a set of rooms decorated for Pope Julius II by Raphael among others. Of these, the **Stanza Eliodoro** is home to the *Expulsion of Heliodorus from the Temple*, an allusion to the military success of Julius II, depicted on the left in portrait. Not to be outdone, Leo X, Julius's successor, in the *Meeting of Attila and St Leo* opposite, ordered Raphael to substitute his head for that of Julius II, turning the painting into an allegory of the Battle of Ravenna at which he was present; thus he appears twice, as pope and as the equally portly Medici cardinal just behind. From here it is impossible to miss the **Sistine Chapel**, built for Pope Sixtus IV in 1481, which serves as the pope's private chapel and hosts the conclaves of cardinals for the election of each new pontiff. The paintings down each side wall are contemporary with the building, depictions of scenes from the lives of Moses and Christ by Perugino, Botticelli and Ghirlandaio among others. But it's the ceiling frescoes of Ghirlandaio's pupil, Michelangelo, depicting the *Creation*, that everyone comes to see, executed almost single-handed over a period of about four years, again for Pope Julius II. Whether the ceiling has been improved by the controversial recent restoration is a moot point. The *Last Judgement*, on the west wall of the chapel, was painted by Michelangelo over twenty years later. The nudity caused controversy from the start, and the pope's zealous successor, Pius IV, would have had the painting removed had not Michelangelo's pupil, Daniele da Volterra, carefully added coverings – some of which have been left by the restorers – to the more obvious nudes, earning himself the nickname of the "breeches-maker".

## Eating, drinking and nightlife

There are some excellent **restaurants** in Rome around Campo dei Fiori and Piazza Navona, but Trastevere is Rome's traditional restaurant ghetto and home to some fine, reasonably priced eateries. In the places listed below, expect to pay around €15 in pizzerias and €25 in trattorias.

The two main areas to go for **bars and clubs** are Monte Testaccio and Trastevere, although there is a good sprinkling of places in the river loop to the west of Piazza Navona. Clubs run the gamut from vast glittering palaces with stunning lights and sound systems, to the down-to-earth student-run **social centres** in the suburbs, many of which first opened in abandoned public buildings in the 1990s; they offer a cheap, alternative programme of concerts, films and parties – some have evolved to be as slick and professional as the commercial alternatives, although others are little more than dope-filled dives.

Tuesday – after 11pm – is one of the trendiest nights in central Rome clubs such as *Bloom, Supperclub* and *La Maison*, but many operate a list-only policy: be prepared to smooth talk your way in.

Rome's **rock scene** is a fairly limp affair, and the city is much more in its element with **jazz**. Most clubs close during July and August, or move to the coast, but the council organizes a series of inexpensive summer entertainments known as **Estate Romana** – outdoor concerts, discos, bars and cinemas throughout Rome - a more appealing option than the clubs on a hot summer's night. The city's best **listings** source is *Roma C'è* (issued on Friday with a section in English). There's also the *TrovaRoma* supplement published with the Thursday edition of *La Repubblica*.

## Snacks, cakes and ice cream

**Ciampini** Piazza San Lorenzo in Lucina. Expensive, but very good: the ice cream here is so popular that they don't even need to put it out on display.

**Giolitti** Via degli Uffici del Vicario 40. A wonderful Italian institution, with a choice of seventy ice-cream flavours. Closed Mon.

**Il Delfino** Corso V. Emanuele 67. Central and very busy cafeteria with a huge choice of snacks and full meals.

**Il Forno del Ghetto** Via del Portico d'Ottavia 1. Unmarked Jewish bakery with marvellous ricotta, and dried fruit-filled cakes. Closed Sat.

**Il Gelato di San Crispino** Via della Panetteria 42. Close to the Trevi fountain and selling some of Rome's best ice cream. Closed Tues.

**Pascucci** Via di Torre Argentina 20. Just the thing after hours of sightseeing – a Roman *frullato*, the local version of a milkshake.

**Sciam** Via del Pellegrino 56. A Middle Eastern-style tea room, done up in truly lavish style, offering exotic teas and treats.

**Tre Scalini** Piazza Navona. Renowned for its absolutely remarkable *tartufo*. Closed Wed.

## Restaurants

**Ai Marmi** Viale di Trastevere 53–59. Rome's most traditional pizzeria, with regional extras such as deep-fried stuffed olives and batter-fried cod. Closed Wed.

**Da Alfredo e Ada** Via dei Banchi Nuovi 14. Genuine home cooking at great prices. Closed Sat and Sun.

**Da Giggetto** Via del Portico d'Ottavia 21a. Much pricier than most, but worth it for great Romano–Jewish cooking. Closed Mon.

**Da Tonino** Via del Governo Vecchio 18/19 Excellent Roman cooking at low prices; packed at lunch and supper.

**Da Vittorio** Via San Cosimato 14a. Neapolitan pizza in the heart of Trastevere. Closed Mon.

**Enoteca Corsi** Via del Gesù. Lunch only, but great home cooking and good wines, with a well-stocked wine shop next door.

**Grappola d'oro** Piazza della Cancelleria 80. Curiously untouched place with genuine Roman cuisine and a timeless trattoria feel. Closed Sun.

**Osteria Della Frezza** Via della Frezza 16. New *osteria* in traditional style, with huge selection of cheeses and casked wine.

**Pizzeria Dar Poeta** Vicolo del Bologna 45, Trastevere. One of the best pizzerias in Rome, so expect to queue. Closed Mon.

**Silvio** Via Urbana 67–69. Classic Italian cooking at this unpretentious restaurant, near Metro Cavour. Closed Mon.

**Tram Tram** Via dei Reti 44–46. San Lorenzo district's top student favourite, featuring regional Pugliese cooking. Closed Mon.

## Bars and birrerias

**Bar della Pace** Via della Pace 5. Just off Piazza Navona, this is the summer bar to be seen in, with outside tables full of Rome's self-consciously beautiful people.

**Enoteca Cavour** Via Cavour 313. At the Forum end of Via Cavour, a handy retreat with an easy-going studenty feel, lots of wine and bottled beers.

**Il Fico** Piazza del Fico. Late at night the piazza thrums with young Romans; escape inside for a cocktail-bar atmosphere.

**Jonathan's Angels** Via della Fossa 18, next door to *Il Fico*. This colourful bar presents an explosion of kitsch decor.

**La Scala** Piazza della Scala. The most popular Trastevere *birreria* – big, bustling and crowded.

**Le Coppelle** Piazza delle Coppelle. Urban design, expensive drinks and leather sofas in a tiny square that's become a summer living room for rich Romans. Good for people-watching.

**Ombre Rosse** Piazza Sant'Egidio 12. Trastevere's liveliest venue, offering a huge menu of drinks and good light snacks, plus newspapers in several languages.

**Vineria** Campo dei Fiori 15. Fashionable *vineria* that spills out into the square during the summer;

drink indoors at a third of the price. If this is packed, try the elegant wine bar *Nolano*, a couple of doors to the left.

## Social Centres

**Brancaleone** Via Levanna 11 ⓦwww .brancaleone.it. In a mansion on Montesacro, the Brancaleone stages concerts, films and political events: it's one of the most successful *centri sociali*, though increasingly like a conventional club.

**Forte Prenestino** Via F. del Pino. Situated in an abandoned nineteenth-century fortress, with two big arenas for concerts and a beehive of smaller spaces used for exhibitions, cinema, a disco and a bar.

**Villaggio Globale** Ex-Mattatoio, Testaccio ⓦwww.ecn.org/villaggioglobale/pages/campo_ boario.htm. Concerts, parties and exhibitions take place in an old slaughterhouse, partly run by the Senegalese community in Rome, and with an interesting café and bookshop. Try to spend at least part of any night out here, but check the website first.

## Discos and clubs

**Art Cafe** Via del Galoppatoio, 33 ☎06.3600.6578. Currently among the trendiest clubs in Rome, with great music, and held in an underground car park at Villa Borghese. Book, or expect to queue.

**Black Out Club** Via Saturnia 18. Popular disco playing a mix of house, punk and grunge.

**Bloom** Via del Teatro Pace 30. Swish disco-bar near Piazza Navona that's hot on design, with a well-heeled clientele. €10 a drink, €15 to sit down; go late.

**Goa** Via Libetta 13. An ethnic feel to accentuate the house, techno and trance high-energy dance atmosphere.

**Groove** Vicolo Savelli 10. Cool candlelit bar with live music that draws an older crowd from all over the world. Good vibe, informal dancing, and expensive drinks. Open Thurs–Sat.

**Il Locale** Vicolo del Fico 3. Local bands, packed with students, dancing usually starts after midnight.

**L'Alibi** Via Monte Testaccio 44. Predominantly but not exclusively male venue that's one of Rome's best gay clubs. Downstairs cellar disco and upstairs open-air bar.

**La Maison** Vicolo da Granari 4, near Piazza Navona ☎06.683.3312. Very glossy disco, home to Rome's gilded youth and minor celebs. Book or queue.

**Supperclub** Via de' Nari 14 ⓦwww.supperclub .com. Overpriced restaurant that turns into a club after 11pm, attracting Rome's beautiful people. No entry fee, cocktails €10.

**Qube** Via di Portonaccio 212. Popular place with solid rock, soul and ethnic music.

## Live music: rock, jazz and Latin

**Alexanderplatz** Via Ostia 9 ☎06.3974.2171. Rome's foremost jazz club-restaurant. Reservations recommended.

**Alpheus** Via del Commercio 36–38. A four-roomed venue with concerts, a disco, theatrical performances and a bar.

**Berimbau** Via dei Fienaroli 30/b. Live Latin-American music and Brazilian drinks.

**Big Mama** Vicolo San Francesco a Ripa 18. Trastevere-based jazz/blues club of long standing. Closed July–Sept.

**Blue Knight** Via delle Fornaci 8–10. Bar and *gelateria* on the ground floor; downstairs there's live music Thurs–Sat.

**Caffè Latino** Via di Monte Testaccio 96. Multi-event club in the hip area near the Protestant cemetery. Best at weekends when it's crowded and more atmospheric.

**Circolo degli Artisti** Via Casilina Vecchia 42. Huge bar and disco with more alternative live music. Cheap and fun.

**Fonclea** Via Crescenzio 82a. Long-running jazz/salsa outfit, with live music most nights. Metro Ottaviano.

## Culture, arts and festivals

For **classical music**, the city's churches host a wide range of choral, chamber and organ recitals, many of them free. International names appear at Rome's snail-shell shaped **Auditorium** (☎800.90.70.80), while the opera scene concentrates on the **Teatro dell'Opera**, Via Firenze, Piazza B. Gigli in winter (box office Mon–Sat 9am–5pm; ☎06.481.601) and at various outdoor venues in summer. Purists should be prepared for a carnival atmosphere and plenty of unscheduled intervals. Rome's two **English-language cinemas** are the Pasquino, Piazza Sant'Egidio 10, Vicolo del Piede in Trastevere, and the Quirinetta at Via Minghetti 4. Other cinemas occasionally showing English-language films are the Nuovo Sacher, Largo Ascianghi 1, and Alcazar, Via Cardinal Merry di Val 14.

## Festivals

**La Festa di Noantri** Viale Trastevere and around. Medieval Trastevere's traditional summer festival in honour of the Virgin, with street stalls selling snacks and trinkets, and a grand finale of fireworks. Main event is the Virgin's effigy being hauled joyously from the church of Sant' Agata to that of San Crisogono, and back again. Last two weeks of July.

**La Festa dell'Unità** Venues change annually; check *Roma C'è* for details. Throughout the summer, this cheery hotchpotch of music, film, eateries, games and other attractions – much of it free – is the refounded Communist Party's way of reminding people of what fun the Left can be.

**Fiesta Capannelle** Via Appia Nuova 1245. Based at Rome's racecourse in the southeast of the city, with a Latin American flavour. Metro A to Subagosto, then bus #354 to Ippodromo Capannelle. Mid-June to Aug.

**Testaccio Village** Viale del Campo Boario. Just behind the old Testaccio slaughterhouse, this nightly festival draws a young crowd for the bars and stalls, live bands and DJs. Metro B to Piramide, night bus #40N back. June–Sept.

**Tevere Expo** Tiber Embankment, main entrance by Castel Sant'Angelo. Atmospheric annual handicrafts fair along the river; nighttime stalls, bars and live entertainment. Mid-June to July.

## Listings

**Embassies** Australia, Via Alessandria 215 ☏06.852.721; Canada, Via G.B. de Rossi 27 ☏06.445.981; New Zealand, Via Zara 28 ☏06.441.7171; UK, Via XX Settembre 80 ☏06.4220.0001; US, Via V. Veneto 121 ☏06.46.741.

**Exchange** Two offices at Termini station operate out of banking hours; also Cambio Rosati, Via Nazionale 186 ☏06.488.5498.

**Hospitals** ☏06.884.0113 for 24-hour assistance. Most central hospital: Santo Spirito, Lungotevere in Sassia 1 ☏06.68.351; International Medical Centre ☏06.488.2371.

**Left luggage** At Termini station.

**Pharmacies** PIRAM, Via Nazionale 228; at Stazione Termini. Rota posted on pharmacy doors.

**Police** Questura, Via S. Vitale ☏06.4686.

**Post office** Piazza San Silvestro 18–20.

# Southern Italy

The Italian **south** or *mezzogiorno* is quite a different experience from the north; indeed, few countries are more tangibly divided into two distinct, often antagonistic, regions. While the north is rich, the south is among the poorest areas in Europe, with a rate of unemployment around twice that of the north. The dialect down here is different, too, sounding almost Arabic sometimes. For most people, **Naples** is the obvious focus, an utterly compelling city just a couple of hours south of Rome. In the **Bay of Naples**, apart from the resort of **Sorrento**, the highlight is the island of **Cápri**, swarmed over by tourists these days but still so beautiful to be worth your time; while the ancient sites of **Pompeii** and **Herculaneum** are Italy's best-preserved and most revealing Roman remains. South of Naples, the **Amalfi Coast** is probably Europe's most dramatic stretch of coastline, harbouring some enticing – if crowded – beach resorts. In the far south, **Matera** is the jewel of the Basilicata region, with its ancient cave dwellings dug into a steep ravine. Puglia – the long strip of land that makes up the "heel" of Italy – was for centuries a strategic province, invaded and colonized by just about every major power of the day. However, apart from the Baroque wonders of **Lecce**, Puglia is really a province you pass through on the way elsewhere – not least by sea to Greece or Croatia.

## Naples (Napoli)

Wherever else you travel south of Rome, the chances are that you'll wind up in **NAPLES** (Napoli). It's the kind of city people visit with preconceptions, and it rarely disappoints: it is filthy, large and overbearing; it is crime-infested; and it

Ferries from Greece and Croatia to **BARI** dock at the Stazione Maríttima, next to the old city. From here, it is a short bus ride or 45-minute walk to the **tourist office** on Piazza Aldo Moro (Mon–Fri 8am–2pm, Tues & Thurs also 3-6pm; ☎080.524.2361, ⊕www.pugliaturismo.com/aptbari) and the nearby **train station.** **BRÍNDISI**, 100km southeast of Bari, has ferries to Greece from the Stazione Maríttima on Via del Mare; from here it's a few minutes' walk to the bottom of Corso Garibaldi, and another twenty minutes on foot (or a short bus ride) to Bríndisi's **train station** in Piazza Crispi. The **tourist office** is at Viale Regina Margherita 43 (daily Mon–Fri 8am–8pm; Sat 8am–1pm; ☎0831.523.072, ⊕www .pugliaturismo.com/aptbrindisi).

is most definitely like nowhere else in Italy – something the inhabitants will be keener than anyone to tell you. One thing, though, is certain: a couple of days here and you're likely to be as staunch a defender of the place as its most devoted inhabitants. Few cities on earth excite such fierce loyalties.

### Arrival, information and accommodation

Naples' **Capodochino Airport** is northwest of the centre at Viale Umberto Maddalena, connected with Piazza Garibaldi by buses #14 and #15 (every 15min; journey time 30min). There's also a blue official airport bus (6am–midnight, every 30min), which takes you straight to the port, Piazza Municipio and Piazza Garibaldi. **Trains** arrive at Napoli Centrale on Piazza Garibaldi, the main hub of all transport services. There's tourist information at the train station (Mon–Sat 9am–7pm, Sun 9am–1pm) and the airport (daily 9am–7pm), but the **main tourist office** is at Piazza Gesù Nuovo dei Martiri 58 (Mon–Sat 9am-1.30pm & 2.30-7pm; ☎081.551.2701, ⊕www.inaples.it). Pick up the free **listings** booklet *Qui Napoli*, handy for ferry and bus times.

Naples is a large sprawling city and while walking is the best option in the centre, you'll also need to get acquainted with the sparkling new **metropolitana** underground network and the city **buses** (tickets €1 from *tabacchi*). **Funiculars** scale the hill of the Vómero from stations at piazzas Montesanto, Amedeo and Augusto. For **trips around the bay** there are three rail systems, the most useful of which is the **Circumvesuviana**, which runs from its station on Corso Garibaldi around the Bay of Naples as far as Sorrento in about an hour. A more entertaining way to travel is the **Metro di Mare** ferry network from Molo Beverello (summer only) which goes to Cápri and south as far as Amalfi and is probably the cheapest way to get a sea trip. If you are around for more than a day, invest in the **Artecard** (from €13), which is valid on various combinations of transport, including a return trip on the Metro di Mare ferries, along with museum entrance.

Many of the city's cheaper **hotels** are situated around Piazza Garibaldi, within spitting distance of the train station and not badly placed for the rest of town. A word of warning: don't go with any of the touts in the station, and try to book accommodation in advance. The best **campsite** is the well-equipped *Vulcano Solfatara*, Via Solfatara 161, Pozzuoli (☎081.526.7413; closed Nov–March ), with a swimming pool, restaurant and Internet access: take the metro to Pozzuoli then it's a ten-minute walk uphill.

### Hostels

**Hostel Pensione Mancini** Via Mancini 33 ☎081.553.6731, ⊕www.hostelpensionemancini .com. Small, basic place right across the piazza from the station. Breakfast included. No curfew. Has singles, dorm beds (€18), and ten percent discount on doubles with this book. ➍

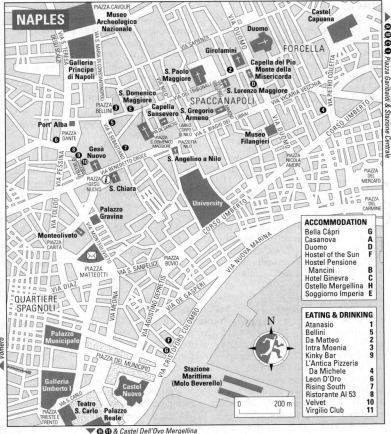

▲ Galleria Nazionale di Capodimonte

**NAPLES**

PIAZZA CAVOUR
Museo
Archeologico
Nazionale

Castel
Capuana

Duomo

Galleria
Principe
di Napoli

Girolamini

FORCELLA

S. Paolo
Maggiore

Capella del Pio
Monte della
Misericorda

S. Domenico
Maggiore

S. Lorenzo Maggiore

Capella
Sansevero

SPACCANAPOLI

Port' Alba

PIAZZA
BELLINI

S. Gregorio
Armeno

PIAZZA
DANTE

Gesù
Nuovo

Museo
Filangieri

S. Angelino a Nilo

PIAZZA
GESU
NUOVO

S. Chiara

Palazzo
Gravina

University

Monteoliveto

PIAZZA
CARITÀ

PIAZZA
MATTEOTTI

PIAZZA
BOVIO

**QUARTIERE
SPAGNOLI**

Palazzo
Municipale

PIAZZA DEL MUNICIPIO

N

Galleria
Umberto I

Stazione
Marittima
(Molo Beverello)

Teatro
S. Carlo

Castel
Nuovo

Palazzo
Reale

PIAZZA
TRIESTE E
TRENTO

0    200 m

▼ & Castel Dell'Ovo Mergellina

Piazza Garibaldi & Stazione Centrale

**ITALY** | Naples (Napoli)

16

### ACCOMMODATION
| | |
|---|---|
| Bella Cápri | G |
| Casanova | A |
| Duomo | D |
| Hostel of the Sun | F |
| Hostel Pensione Mancini | B |
| Hotel Ginevra | C |
| Ostello Mergellina | H |
| Soggiorno Imperia | E |

### EATING & DRINKING
| | |
|---|---|
| Atanasio | 1 |
| Bellini | 5 |
| Da Matteo | 2 |
| Intra Moenia | 3 |
| Kinky Bar | 9 |
| L'Antica Pizzeria Da Michele | 4 |
| Leon D'Oro | 6 |
| Rising South | 7 |
| Ristorante Al 53 | 8 |
| Velvet | 10 |
| Virgilio Club | 11 |

**Ostello Mergellina** Salita della Grotta 23
☏081.761.2346. Popular HI hostel with a view of the bay; curfew is usually 12.30am, but can be flexible. Breakfast included. Metro or train to Mergellina. €14–16.

**Hostel of the Sun** Via Melisurgo 15
☏081.420.6393, ⊛www.hostelnapoli.com. Colourful, clean hostel with kitchen, next to the main ferry dock. Well placed for bars and clubs: ask for Luca and Alfredo's nightlife map. No curfew; breakfast included. Dorms €18, and ten percent discount on doubles with this book. ❹

### Hotels

**Bella Cápri** Via Melisurgo 4 ☏081.552.9494, ⊛www.bellacapri.it. Naples' cheapest rooms

with views over the bay, and right by the port; ten percent discount with this book. ❼

**Casanova** Corso Garibaldi 333 ☏081.268.287, ⊛www.hotelcasanova.com. Close to Piazza Garibaldi, with its own roof garden. ❹

**Duomo** Via Duomo 228 ☏081.265.988, ⊛www.hotelduomonapoli.it. Neat, clean rooms near the Cathedral. ❼

**Hotel Ginevra** Via Genova 116 ☏081.554.1757, ⊛www.hotelginevra.it. Basic, clean one-star close to the station. Internet access at €5/hour. ❺

**Soggiorno Imperia** Piazza Luigi Miraglia 386
☏081.459.347. Homely, clean hotel, with young, friendly staff right in the *centro storico*. On fifth floor, no lift. ❹

## The City

The area between the vast and busy Piazza Garibaldi, where you will arrive, and Via Toledo, the main street a mile or so west, makes up the old part of the city – the **centro storico**. Buildings rise high on either side of the narrow, crowded streets; there's little light, not even much sense of the rest of the city outside – certainly not of the proximity of the sea. The two main drags here are Via dei Tribunali and Via San Biagio dei Librai, both a maelstrom of hurrying pedestrians, revving cars and buzzing scooters. Via dei Tribunali cuts through to Via Duomo, where you'll find the tucked-away **Duomo**, a Gothic building from the early thirteenth century dedicated to San Gennaro, the patron saint of the city. San Gennaro was martyred in 305 AD. Two phials of his blood miraculously liquefy three times a year – on the first Saturday in May (when a procession leads from the church of Santa Chiara to the cathedral) and on September 19 and December 16. If the blood refuses to liquefy – which luckily is rare – disaster is supposed to befall the city. The first chapel on the right as you walk into the cathedral holds the precious phials and Gennaro's skull in a silver bust-reliquary from 1305. Downstairs, the **Crypt of San Gennaro** is one of the finest examples of Renaissance art in Naples, founded by Cardinal Carafa and holding the tombs of both San Gennaro and Pope Innocent IV.

Across Via Duomo, Via dei Tribunali continues on into the heart of the old city: the **Spaccanapoli**, the city's busiest and architecturally richest quarter. Cut down to its other main axis, Via San Biagio dei Librai, which leads west to Piazza San Domenico Maggiore, marked by the **Guglia di San Domenico** – built in 1737, it is one of many whimsical Baroque obelisks that pop up all over the city. The **church** of the same name flanks the north side of the square, an originally Gothic building from 1289, one of whose chapels holds a miraculous painting of *The Crucifixion* which is said to have spoken to St Thomas Aquinas during his time at the adjacent monastery. North, Via de Sanctis leads off right to one of the city's odder monuments, the **Cappella Sansevero** (Mon & Wed–Sat 10am–5.40pm, Sun 10am–1.10pm; €5), the tomb-chapel of the di Sangro family, decorated by the sculptor Giuseppe Sammartino in the mid-eighteenth century with some remarkable carving including a starkly realistic dead *Christ*. The chapel downstairs, commissioned by alchemist Prince Raimondo, contains the gruesome results of some of his experiments: two bodies under glass, their capillaries and organs preserved by a mysterious liquid developed by the prince. Continuing west, the **Gesù Nuovo** church is most notable for its lava-stone facade, prickled with pyramids that give it an impregnable, prison-like air. Facing the Gesù church, the church of **Santa Chiara** is quite different, a Provençal-Gothic structure built in 1328 (and rebuilt after World War II). The attached **cloister** (Mon–Sat 9.30am–5.30pm, Sun 9.30–1.30pm; €4), covered with colourful majolica tiles depicting bucolic scenes of life outside, is one of the gems of the city.

**Piazza del Municipio** is a busy traffic junction that stretches down to the waterfront, dominated by the brooding hulk of the **Castel Nuovo**. Built in 1282 by the Angevins and later the royal residence of the Aragon monarchs, it now contains the **Museo Civico** (Mon–Sat 9am–7pm; €5), which holds periodic exhibitions in a series of elaborate Gothic rooms. The entrance of the Castel incorporates a triumphal arch built in 1454 to commemorate the taking of the city by Alfonso I, the first Aragon ruler. Just beyond the castle, on the left, **Teatro San Carlo** (☎081.797.2331, ⊛www.teatrosancarlo.it) is still the largest opera house in Italy, and one of the most distinguished in the world. Beyond, at the bottom of the main shopping street of Via Toledo, the dignified **Palazzo Reale** (9am–8pm, closed Wed; €4) was built in 1602 to accommodate a visit by Philip III of Spain. Upstairs, the palace's first-floor rooms are decorated with gilded furniture, trompe-l'oeil ceilings, overbearing tapestries and lots of undistinguished seventeenth- and eighteenth-century paintings.

West of Via Toledo, the **Quartiere Spagnoli** is one of the most characteristic parts of the city, its narrow streets home to the infamous slum dwellings known as *bassi*. It is an edgy area, but if you are used to big cities, there's no reason not to take a discreet walk around here: don't go at night, however, and take care not to flash valuables.

Via Toledo leads north from Piazza Trieste e Trento to the **Museo Archeologico Nazionale** (9am–7.30pm, closed Tues; €6.50) – Naples' most essential sight, home to the best of the finds from the nearby Roman sites of Pompeii and Herculaneum. The ground floor concentrates on sculpture, including the *Farnese Bull* and *Farnese Hercules* from the Baths of Caracalla in Rome. The mezzanine floor at the back houses the museum's collection of mosaics, remarkably preserved works giving a superb insight into ordinary Roman customs, beliefs and humour. Upstairs, the wall paintings from the villas of Pompeii and Herculaneum are the museum's other major draw, rich in colour and invention; and don't miss the "secret" room of erotic Roman pictures and sculptures, once thought to be a hazard to public morality and only recently opened. The other side of the first floor has sculptures in bronze from the Villa dei Papiri in Herculaneum, including a superb *Hermes at Rest*, a languid *Resting Satyr* and a convincingly woozy *Drunken Silenus*. At the top of the hill is the city's other major museum, the **Museo Nazionale di Capodimonte** (Thurs–Tues 8.30am–7.30pm; €7.50; buses #160, #161, #157, #178 from Piazza Cavour), the former residence of the Bourbon King Charles III, built in 1738. This has a huge and superb collection of Renaissance paintings, including a couple of Brueghels, *The Misanthrope* and *The Blind*, canvases by Perugino and Pinturicchio, an elegant *Madonna and Child with Angels* by Botticelli and Lippi's soft, sensitive *Annunciation*.

**Vómero**, the district topping the hill immediately above the old city, can be reached on the Montesanto funicular. Go up to the star-shaped fortress of **Castel Sant'Elmo** (Thurs–Tues 8.30am–7.30pm; €3), occupying Naples' highest point. Built in the fourteenth century, it now hosts exhibitions and concerts, and boasts the very best views of Naples.

## Eating, drinking and nightlife

When in Naples, you can't miss its speciality, **pizza**, which should cost around €3 to take away: the best are *marinara*, with tomato, garlic and oil, or *margherita*, with tomato and mozzarella cheese. For a quiet **drink**, head to Chaia, a sedate area near Mergellina with good wine bars, such as *Enoteca Belledonne*, Vico Belledonne a Chaia 18. For a more lively time, in the centre, check out the cheerful studenty **discopubs** on Via Paladino. In July and August most discos close and move to the beach, while the Neapolitans who remain congregate for a beer in Piazza del Gesù and Piazza San Domenico, or the **gay-friendly cafés** on Piazza Bellini, where tables spill out onto the square. For details of particular evenings check *Zero*, a pamphlet available in bars, or for big club events see ⓦwww.angelsoflove .it, Italy's answer to the Ministry of Sound.

### Cafés, pizzerias and restaurants

**Antica Pizzeria Da Michele** Via Cesare Sersale 1–3, corner of Via Colletta. The cheapest pizza in town and possibly the most authentic. Closed Sun.

**Atanasio** Vico della Ferrovia, off Via Milano near the station. *Pasticceria* near the station selling delicious fresh *sfogliatelle*, ricotta and orange-filled pastries.

**Bellini** Via Santa Maria di Constantinopoli 80. One of the city's longest-established restaurants, good for a splurge. Closed Sun eve.

**Da Matteo** Via Tribunali 94. Superb for pizza and also offers a deep-fried ricotta-filled alternative. Closed Sun.

**Intra Moenia** Piazza Bellini 70. A left-wing literary café and publishing house, that also offers Internet access.

**Leon D'Oro** Piazza Dante 48. Great pizza, superb antipasti and moderate prices.

**Ristorante Al 53** Piazza Dante 53. One of the oldest restaurants in town, great antipasti and good local specialities such as *minestra maritata*. Ask Mario for advice.

### Bars and clubs

**Kinky Bar** Via Cisterna dell'Olio 16. Popular reggae bar in the centre of Naples; does not offer what its name promises.

**Rising South** 19 Via S Sebastiano. The coolest
club in Naples, with a velvet Baroque interior
and fruit-based cocktails. You'll need to be on
the list Thursday, Friday and Saturday – call
℡335.811.7107. Tuesday buffet and drink €5
from 9pm; after lunch on Sunday 'Dessert' brings
together music and puddings.

**Velvet** Via Cisterna dell'Olio 11 ⊛www
.velvetnapoli.it. Small and buzzing place with arty
ambience; house and electronic music.
**Virgilio Club** Via Lucrezio Caro 6, near Parco della
Rimembranza. A leafy outdoor disco open from
June to September.

## Listings

**Consulates** UK, Via dei Mille 40 ℡081.423.8911;
US, Piazza della Repubblica ℡081.583.8111.
**Exchange** At Stazione Centrale (daily 7am–9pm).
**Hospital** Ospedale Nuovo Pellegrini, Via FM
Briganti 255 ℡081.254.5291.

**Laundry** Largo Donnaregina 5.
**Pharmacy** At Stazione Centrale (24hr).
**Police** Via Medina 75 ℡081.794.1111.
**Post office** Piazza Matteotti, off Via Toledo.
**Radiotaxi** ℡081.570.7070 or ℡081.556.4444.

# The Bay of Naples

For the Romans, the **Bay of Naples** was the land of plenty, a blessed region with
a mild climate, gorgeous scenery and hence a favourite vacation and retirement
area for the city's nobility. Later, when Naples became the final stop on the Grand
Tour, the relics of its heady Roman period only added to the charm. However,
these days it's hard to tell where Naples ends and the countryside begins, the city
sprawling around the Bay in an industrial and residential mess that is quite at odds
with the region's popular image. It's only when you reach **Sorrento** in the east, or
the islands that dot the bay, that you really feel free of it all. Of the islands, **Cápri**
is the best place to visit if you're here for a short time. There's also, of course,
the ever-brooding presence of **Vesuvius**, and the incomparable Roman sites of
**Herculaneum** and **Pompeii**.

## Herculaneum and Vesuvius

The town of **ERCOLANO** is the modern offshoot of the ancient site of **Herculaneum**, which was destroyed by the eruption of Vesuvius on August 2, 79 AD.
It's worth stopping here for two reasons: to see the excavations and to climb to
the summit of **Vesuvius** – to which buses run from outside the train station. If
you're planning to visit both in one day, be sure to see Vesuvius first, and set off
reasonably early – buses stop running up the mountain at lunchtime, leaving you
the afternoon free to wander around the site.

Situated at the seaward end of Ercolano's main street, **HERCULANEUM** (daily
8.30am–5pm; €10, €18 including Pompeii) was a residential town in Roman
times, much smaller than Pompeii, and as such it's a more manageable site – less
architecturally impressive, but with better preserved buildings and more easily
taken in on a single visit. Because it wasn't a commercial town, there is no central
open space or forum, just streets of villas and shops, cut as usual by two very straight
main streets. The **House of the Mosaic Atrium** retains its mosaic-laid courtyard,
corrugated by the force of the tufa, behind which the **House of the Deer** contains
corridors decorated with richly coloured still lifes and a bawdy statue of a drunken
Hercules. There's also a large **thermae** or bath complex with a domed *frigidarium*
decorated with frescoes of fish and a *caldarium* containing a plunge bath at one end
and a scallop-shell apse complete with washbasin and water pipes. Opposite, the
**House of Neptune and Amphitrite**, holding a sparklingly preserved wall mosaic
of the god and goddess, and frescoes of flowers and vegetables, served in lieu of
a garden. Under the house is a wine shop, stocked with amphorae in wooden
racks, left as they lay when disaster struck. Close by in the **Casa del Bel Cortile**
are some skeletons poignantly lying in the same attitude as they were in 79 AD.

Further down on the opposite side of the road in the **House of the Wooden Partition**, there's a room with the marital bed still intact, and in the house nearby a perfectly preserved coiled rope. However, the rest of the contents are in Naples' archeological museum.

Since its first eruption in 79 AD, when it buried the towns and inhabitants of Pompeii and Herculaneum, **VESUVIUS** has dominated the lives of those who live on the Bay of Naples. It's still an active volcano, the only one on mainland Europe, and there have been hundreds of eruptions over the years, but only two of real significance: one in December 1631 that engulfed many nearby towns and killed three thousand people; and the last, in March 1944, which caused wide-spread devastation, though no one was actually killed. The people who live here still fear the reawakening of Vesuvius, and with good reason – scientists calculate it should erupt every thirty years or so, and it hasn't since 1944. Trasporti Vesuviani run bus services from Ercolano train station to a car park and huddle of souvenir shops and cafés close to **the crater**. The walk up to the crater from the car park where the bus stops takes about half an hour, across barren gravel on marked-out paths. At the top (admission €6), the crater is a deep, wide, jagged ashtray of red rock emitting the odd plume of smoke, though since the last eruption effectively sealed up the main crevice, this is much less evident than it once was. You can walk most of the way around, but take it easy – the fences are old and rickety.

## Pompeii

The other Roman town destroyed by Vesuvius, **POMPEII** (daily 8.30am– 5/7.30pm; €10; ☎081.857.5347, ⊛www.pompeiisites.org) was one of Campania's most important commercial centres. Out of a total population of twemty thousand, it's thought that two thousand perished, asphyxiated by the toxic fumes of the volcanic debris, their homes buried in several metres of volcanic ash and pumice. In effect, the eruption froze Pompeii in time, and the excavations here have probably yielded more information about the life of Roman citizens during the imperial era than any other site. The full horror of their way of death is apparent in plaster casts made from the shapes their bodies left in the volcanic ash. Again, though, most of the best mosaics and murals have found their way to the archeological museum in Naples.

The site covers a wide area, and seeing it properly takes half a day at least. Entering the site from the Pompeii-Villa dei Misteri side, the **Forum** is the first real feature of significance, a slim open space surrounded by the ruins of what would have been some of the town's most important official buildings. North from here, the **House of the Tragic Poet** is named after its mosaics of a theatrical production and a poet inside, though the "Cave Canem" (Beware of the Dog) mosaic by the main entrance is more eye-catching. Close by, the residents of the **House of the Faun** must have been a friendlier lot, its "Ave" (Welcome) mosaic outside beckoning you in to view the atrium and the copy of a tiny bronze dancing faun that gives the villa its name. On the street behind, the **House of the Vettii** (currently closed for restoration) is one of the most delightful houses in Pompeii, a merchant's villa ranged around a lovely central peristyle that gives the best possible impression of the domestic environment of the city's upper middle classes. The first room on the right off the peristyle holds the best of Pompeii's murals viewable in situ: the one on the left shows the young Hercules struggling with serpents, while, through the villa's kitchen, a small room that's normally kept locked has erotic works showing various techniques of lovemaking, together with a potent-looking statue of Priapus from which women were supposed to drink to ensure fertility.

On the other side of the site, the **Grand Theatre** is very well preserved and still used for performances, as is the **Little Theatre** on its far left side. Walk up to the **Amphitheatre**, one of Italy's most intact and also its oldest, dating from 80 BC. Next door, the **Palestra** (currently closed for restoration) is a vast parade ground that was used by Pompeii's youth for sport and exercise. A short walk from the Porta Ercolano is the **Villa dei Misteri**, probably the best preserved of all Pompeii's palatial houses. It derives its name from a series of excellently preserved paintings in one of its larger chambers: depictions of the initiation rites of a young woman into the Dionysiac Mysteries, an orgiastic cult transplanted to Italy from Greece in the Republican era and at times partially outlawed for its excesses.

To **reach Pompeii from Naples**, take the Circumvesuviana to Pompeii-Villa dei Misteri (direction Sorrento; journey time roughly 30min); this leaves you right outside the western entrance to the site. The Circumvesuviana also runs to Pompeii-Santuario, outside the site's eastern entrance (direction Sarno), or you can take the main-line train (direction Salerno) to the main Pompeii FS station, on the south side of the modern town. It makes most sense to see the site from Naples, but there is an **HI hostel**, *Casa del Pellegrino*, at Via Duca d'Aosta 4 (℡081.850.8644; €14), 200m from Pompeii-Santuario station on the Circumvesuviana line, and a large and well-equipped **campsite**, *Zeus*, right outside the Pompeii-Villa dei Misteri station.

## Sorrento

Topping the rocky cliffs close to the end of its peninsula, **SORRENTO** is una-shamedly a resort, its inspired location and mild climate having drawn foreigners from all over Europe for two hundred years. Nowadays it caters mostly to the package-tour industry, but is none the worse for it – a bright, lively place that retains its southern Italian roots. Accommodation and food, though not exactly cheap, are much better value than most of the other resorts along the Amalfi coast, making it a good base from which to explore the area. Sorrento's centre is **Piazza Tasso**, five minutes from the train station along the busy Corso Italia, the streets around which are pedestrianized for the lively evening *passeggiata*. Sorrento isn't particularly well provided with beaches: most people make do with the rocks and a tiny, crowded strip of sand at **Marina Grande** – fifteen minutes' walk or a short bus ride from Piazza Tasso – or simply use the wooden jetties. If you don't fancy this, try the beaches further along, such as the tiny **Regina Giovanna** at Punta del Capo, again connected by bus from Piazza Tasso, where a natural pool by the ruins of the Roman Villa Pollio Felix makes a unique place to bathe.

The **tourist office** in the large yellow Circolo dei Foresteri building at Via de Maio 35, just off Piazza Sant'Antonino (Mon–Sat 8.30am–6.30pm; ℡081.807.4033, Ⓦwww.sorrentotourism.com), can help with accommodation. There's an independent **hostel**, *Le Sirene* (℡081.807.2925; €18), close to the station at Via degli Aranci 158; it's a little cramped, but there's Internet access at €5/hour, and no curfew. Alternatively, try *City*, Corso Italia 221 (℡081.877.2210; ⑤), a good-value but basic central **hotel**, or *Mami Camilla*, Via Cocomella 4 (℡081.878.2067, Ⓦwww.mamicamilla.com; ④), a B&B run by the cookery school above it, with a family atmosphere and great food. There are a couple of options further out beyond Marina Grande along Via del Capo, *Desiree* at 31 (℡081.878.1563; ⑥), with sea views, private beach and extremely friendly owners, or the family-run *Elios*, next door at 33 (℡081.878.1812; ⑤), with sea or garden views. For **camping** try the *Nube d'Argento*, Via del Capo 12 (closed Nov–March), ten minutes' walk from Piazza Tasso in the direction of Marina Grande, which has sea views.

For **eating**, the *Ristorante Sant'Antonino*, off Piazza Antonino, is good value; or call Peppe at *Mami Camilla* (see above) before noon to book a three-course dinner with wine at his cookery school for just €15. For late-night **drinking** and **nightlife**, there's the cheerful disco-bar *Matilda* on Piazza Sant'Antonino, which has Internet access, or the live-music joint *Artis Domus*, Via S. Nicola 56; for local wines and superb grappa try *Le Bollicine* on Via Accademia, a stylish wood-panelled *enoteca*. Otherwise Sorrento is rife with pubs such as the *English Inn*, Corso Italia 55.

## The island of Cápri

Rising from the sea off the far end of the Sorrentine peninsula, the island of **CÁPRI** has long been the most sought-after part of the Bay of Naples. During

Roman times the emperor Tiberius retreated here to indulge in legendary debauchery until his death in 37 AD. Later, the discovery of the Blue Grotto and the island's remarkable natural landscape coincided with the rise of tourism; the island has attracted a steady flow of artists, writers and tourists ever since. Inevitably, Cápri is a crowded and expensive place, and in July and August it's sensible to give it a miss. But it would be hard to find a place with more inspiring views, and it's easy enough to visit on a day-trip. There are regular **ferries** to Cápri from Naples' Molo Beverello, at the bottom of Piazza Municipio, and regular **hydrofoils** from the Mergellina jetty a couple of miles north of here and also from Sorrento. Prices range from €5.80 to €13 one-way, with the cheapest deals tending to be from the state-run ferry Caremar and the Metro di Mare.

Ferries and hydrofoils dock at Marina Grande, the waterside extension of **CÁPRI TOWN**, which perches on the hill above, connected by funicular. Cápri town is a very pretty place, with winding, hilly alleyways converging on the titchy main square of Piazza Umberto. The **Certosa di San Giacomo** (Tues–Sat 9am–2pm, Sun 9am–1pm; free) on the far side of the town is a run-down old monastery with a handful of paintings, and the Giardini Augustos next door give tremendous views of the coast below and the towering jagged cliffs above. From here you can wind down to **MARINA PICCOLA**, a huddle of houses and restaurants around a few patches of pebble beach – pleasantly uncrowded out of season, though in season it's heaving. You can also reach the ruins of Tiberius' villa, the **Villa Jovis**, from Cápri town (daily 9am–1hr before sunset; €2), a steep thirty-minute trek east. The site is among Cápri's most exhilarating, with incredible vistas of the bay, although there's not much left of the villa. The island's other main settlement, **ANACÁPRI**, is less picturesque than Cápri town, its tacky main square flanked by souvenir shops, boutiques and touristy restaurants. But during the season, a chair-lift operates up **Monte Solaro** (596m), the island's highest point, and you can also get to the island's most famous attraction, the **Blue Grotto**, from here – a good 45-minute trek down Via Lo Pozzo or reachable by bus from the main square. At €10, with tip expected, it's a bit of a rip-off, with boatmen whisking visitors through the grotto in five minutes flat, but in the evening, after the tourists have gone, you may be able to swim into the cave for nothing – change at the bar next to the entrance. A better option is Axel Munthe's **Villa San Michele** (daily 9.30am–3.30/6pm; €5), a light, airy house with enviable views that was home to the Swedish writer for a number of years, and is filled with his furniture and knick-knacks, as well as Roman artefacts pillaged from a villa on the site.

The main **tourist office** is on Piazza Umberto in Cápri town (Mon–Sat 9am–8.30pm, Sun 9am–1pm & 3.30–6.45pm; ☎081.837.0686), with another useful branch on Via G. Orlandi in Anacápri (same times; ☎081.837.1524). The best-value place to stay is the pretty **hotel** Bussola di Hermes, Via Traversa La Vigna 14 in Anacápri (☎081.838.2010; ④). Run by the very helpful Rita, it has some dorms for €30 a head, laundry facilities and Internet: call ahead to get picked up from Anacápri. A trek below Anacápri, Villa Eva, Via La Fabbrica 8 (☎081.837.1549; ⑦), consists of a series of fantastical villas designed and built by Eva's artist husband, complete with pool and overgrown garden: they may also pick up from Anacápri if you call. The best central option is Stella Maris, Via Roma 27 (☎081.837.0452; ⑦), a clean, neat hotel in the heart of Cápri, opposite the bus station. Bring a picnic to avoid inflated **restaurant** prices, though if you want to splash out try the excellent Buca di Bacco in Cápri town, Via Longano 35, where a two-course meal with wine will come to around €30.

## The Amalfi Coast

Occupying the southern side of Sorrento's peninsula, the **Amalfi Coast** lays claim to being Europe's most beautiful stretch of coast, its corniche road winding around the towering cliffs. There are no trains; the bus from Sorrento joins the coast road a little west of Positano for the incredible ride east through a handful of villages to Amalfi. If the road is closed due to forest fires or landslides, it takes an alternative route, zigzagging up over a crest and down again in a series of crazy hairpins to Amalfi.

**AMALFI** has been an established seaside resort since Edwardian times, when the British upper classes spent their winters here. An independent republic in Byzantine times, Amalfi was one of the great naval powers with a population of some seventy thousand. Vanquished by the Normans in 1131, it was devastated by an earthquake in 1343. A few remnants of Amalfi's past glories survive, and the town has a crumbly attractiveness that makes it fun to wander through. The **Duomo**, at the top of a steep flight of steps, dominates the main piazza, its decorated, almost gaudy facade topped by a glazed tiled cupola that's typical of the region. The body of St Andrew is buried in its crypt, though the most appealing part of the building is the cloister (daily 9am–9pm; €2.50) – oddly Arabic in feel, with its whitewashed arches and palms. Close by, the **Museo Civico** (Mon–Fri 9am–2pm; free) displays the original *Tavoliere Amalfitane* – the book of maritime laws which governed the republic, and the rest of the Mediterranean, until 1570. Beyond these, the focus is along the busy seafront, where there's a crowded **beach**. The **tourist office** is at Corso delle Repubbliche Marinare 27–29 (Mon–Fri 8am–1.30pm & 3–5pm, Sat 8am–1pm; ☏089.871.107, ⓦwww.amalfitouristoffice.it), next door to the post office. Almost all the **hotels** here are expensive: one pleasant, central option is the *Sant'Andrea*, on the main square (☏089.871.145, ⑥), with views of the *duomo* from some rooms. The only budget option is the popular **hostel–cum–hotel** *A' Scalinatella*, five minutes' walk out of town at Piazza Umberto I 5–6, Atrani (☏089.871.492, ⓦwww .hostelscalinatella.com; dorms €21), with a beach close by. For **eating**, you'll find picnic ingredients at grocery stores along Via delle Cartiere, or try the family-run *Trattoria Il Mulino* on the same street.

The best views of the coast can be had inland from Amalfi, in **RAVELLO**. This was also an independent republic for a while, and for a time an outpost of the Amalfi city-state; now it's not much more than a large village, but its unrivalled location, spread across the top of one of the coast's mountains, makes it more than worth the thirty-minute bus ride (€1) up from Amalfi. Buses drop off on the main Piazza Vescovado, outside the **Duomo**. It's an eleventh-century church dedicated to St Pantaleone, a fourth-century saint whose blood – kept in a chapel on the left-hand side – is supposed to liquefy like that of Naples' San Gennaro, twice a year on May 19 and August 27. Ten minutes away, the gardens of the **Villa Cimbrone** (daily 9am–5pm; €5) spread across the furthest tip of Ravello's ridge. Most of the villa itself is not open to visitors, though it's worth peeking into the crumbly, flower-hung cloister as you go in, and the open crypt down the steps from here. Best bit of the gardens is the belvedere at the far end of the main path, giving marvellous views over the sea below. **Tourist information** is at Via Roma 19 (daily 8am–7pm; ☏089.857.096, ⓦwww.ravellotime.it), which also has a programme for Ravello's famous arts festival (ⓦwww.ravellofestival.com).

## Matera

Tucked into the instep of Italy in the Basilicata region, **Matera** is one of the south's most fascinating cities, principally for its *sassi*, rock dwellings dug out of a ravine. Carlo Levi's book *Christ Stopped at Eboli* compared the *sassi* to Dante's Inferno describing their disease-ridden, poverty-stricken inhabitants as having "the wrinkled faces of old men, emaciated by hunger, with hair crawling with lice and encrusted with scabs". During the 1950s and 60s the residents were forcibly evicted, but in 1993 the area was declared a World Heritage Site and has since been slowly repopulated with hotels, restaurants and workshops.

The warren of rock streets that makes up the *sassi* district is divided into two sections – the Sasso Caveoso and Sassi Barisano – with the main focus of both being the **chiese rupestri** or rock-hewn churches (all churches open daily 10am–1.30pm & 2.30–6.30pm; €3 each, or €5 for four). The most spectacular of the churches is **Madonna de Idris**, perched on the conical Monte Errone that rises in the midst of the *sassi*, with frescoes dating from the fourteenth century. But possibly the most interesting interior is within the **Convincinio S. Antonio**, a complex of four interlinking churches dating from 1200. In 1700, the four churches were converted into cellars – look out for the spouts for red and white wine emerging from what appears to be an altar – then later into houses. Of particular interest are tombs in the floor that were converted into water tanks, demonstrating considerable ingenuity – the porous stone had to be waterproofed, and rainwater channelled into the tanks.

For an insight into what life was like for the *sassi*-dwellers, look into the **Casa Grotta**, just below Madonna de Idris (daily: April–Oct 9am–8pm; Nov–March 9am–5pm; €1.50).

### Practicalities

Matera's **train station** is on Piazza Matteotti and is served by the FAL line to Altamura (for connections to Bari and Gravina) and to Ferrandina (for connections to Metaponto or Potenza); **buses** also stop here. Trailing down from Piazza Matteotti is Via Roma, with the **tourist office** just off it at Via de Viti de Marco 9 (Mon & Thurs 9am–1pm & 4–6.30pm, Tues, Wed, Fri & Sat 9am–1pm; ☎0835.331.983, ⓦwww.aptbasilicata.it). At the bottom of Via Roma is the main Piazza Veneto, off which leads Via del Corso, where you'll find the **telephone** office and the **main post office**.

If you want to stay in Matera, it's worth spending a bit more on one of the atmospheric new cave **hotels**: the best is *Antica Locanda San Martino*, Via San Martino 22 (☎0835.256.600, ⓦwww.locandadisanmartino.it; ❽), a cool, fragrant *sassi* conversion. Slightly cheaper is the original cave hotel, *Sassi*, San Giovanni Vecchio 89 (☎0835.331.009, ⓦwww.hotelsassi.it; ❻), in the heart of the Sasso Barisano and with great views: it also doubles as an unofficial hostel, with dorm beds at €16 a night, or €20 with breakfast. Alternatively, there's the **B&B** *Casa D'Imperio*, Via d'Addozio 39 (☎0835.330.503, ⓦwww.casadimperio.it; ❺), a beautifully refurbished sixteenth-century house. There are cheap **restaurants** all over town, with the rowdy pizzeria *La Panca* (closed Mon) at Piazza Sedile, one of the most popular: it's a ten-minute walk from Piazza Vittorio Veneto up Via XX Settembre and Via Annunziatella. For an evening **drink**, *Caffè del Cavaliere* (closed Sunday and Mon) at Piazza San Pietro Barisano, is the place to gather.

# Lecce

**LECCE**, 40km south of Bríndisi port, has been called the "Baroque Florence" of the south; walking its alleys, there's still a sense of jaw-dropping excitement at discovering its buildings, with forests of vines, flowers and statues enveloping the stonework. Carved from a soft sandstone, the buildings are one of the high-points in Italian architecture, and very different from the heavy Baroque of Rome. Built for wealthy families, churchmen and merchants during the fifteenth to seventeenth centuries, when Lecce was at the height of its power, these buildings are some of the most beautiful examples of the style – some of the most impressive were designed by Giuseppe Zimbale, known as Lo Zingarello. A short walk from the central Piazza Sant'Oronzo is **Santa Croce** (daily 8am–noon & 5–7pm), most famous of the Lecce churches, where delicate engravings and a riot of putti and grotesques soften the Baroque outline of the building. Inside, the excess continues with a riot of stars, flowers and foliage covering everything from the top of columns to chapel altarpieces. Next door, the yellow stone **Palazzo del Governo**, a former Celestine monastery, is another Zingarello building. On **Piazza del Duomo**, a harmonious square surrounded by Baroque *palazzi*, is the **Duomo** itself (daily 8am–noon & 5–7pm), an explosion of Baroque detail – although its main entrance, on the Piazza Vescovile, is much more restrained.

The **train station** is 1km south of the centre on Via Oronze Quarta, while the **tourist office** is at Corso Vittorio Emanuele 24, near the Duomo (Mon–Fri daily 9am–1pm, Tues & Thurs also 4–7pm; ☎0832.248.092, ⓦwww.pugliaturismo .com/aptlecce), and has a list of **B&Bs**. The cheapest **hotel** is the two-star *Cappello*, in Via Montegrappa near the station (☎0832.308.881; ❸), or try the *Centro Storico B&B*, Via Vignes 2b (☎0832.242.828; ⓦwww.bedandbreakfast.lecce.it, ❹). Lecce's nearest **campsite** is *Torre Rinalda* at Litoranea Salentina 152 (☎0832.382.161; closed Oct–May; bus from Piazza Sant'Oronzo). For **food** try the cheap student haunt *Osteria da Angiulino*, hidden along Via Principe di Savoia 24, or the popular old-fashioned *Trattoria Casareccia*, Via Costadura 9. In the evening follow the crowd to one of the many bars around Via Vittorio Emanuele, where the *passeggiata* takes place. There's **Internet access** at Chatwin Netcafé, Via Isabella Catriota 8.

# Sicily (Sicilia)

Perhaps the most captivating of Italy's islands, **SICILY** (Sicilia) feels socially and culturally separate from Europe. Occupying a strategically vital position, the largest island in the Mediterranean has a history and outlook that has less in common with its modern parent than with its erstwhile rulers – from the Greeks who first settled the east coast in the eighth century BC, through a dazzling array of Romans, Arabs, Normans, French and Spanish, to the Bourbons, seen off by Garibaldi in 1860. Substantial relics of these ages remain – temples, theatres and churches are scattered across the island. And there are other, more immediate hints of Sicily's unique past – a hybrid Sicilian language is still widely spoken in the countryside, the food is noticeably spicier, and its sweets (candied fruits and marzipan), have a Middle-Eastern flavour. The capital, **Palermo**, is a bustling city with an unrivalled display of Norman art and architecture and Baroque churches. The most obvious other target is the chic eastern resort of **Taormina**, although if you are looking for fewer people and cleaner water you'd be advised to go to the west or south coasts. Near Taormina you can skirt around the foothills and even up to the craters of **Mount Etna**, or travel south to the ancient Greek centre of **Siracusa**, with its wonderful architecture and ancient remains. To the west, the greatest draw is the grouping of temples at **Agrigento**, the biggest concentration of the island's Greek remnants.

## Palermo and around

In its own wide bay beneath the limestone bulk of Monte Pellegrino, **PALERMO** is stupendously sited. Originally a Phoenician, then a Carthaginian colony, this remarkable city was long considered a prize worth capturing, and under Saracen and Norman rule in the ninth to twelfth centuries it became the greatest city in Europe, famed for the wealth of its court and peerless as a centre of learning. Nowadays it's a brash, exciting city, whose lively markets, unique series of Baroque and Arab-Norman churches, mosaic work and museums are the equal of anything on the mainland. The heart of the old city is the Baroque **Quattro Canti** crossroads,

---

**Getting to Sicily**

To get to Sicily, you simply take a train from the mainland – they travel across the Straits of Messina on the ferries from Villa San Giovanni and continue on the other side. First stop is Messina, after which services either run west to Palermo (change for Agrigento) or south to Taormina and Siracusa. There are also comfortable couchette trains if you are coming down overnight from Rome, Naples or further north.

with **Piazza Pretoria** and its racy fountain just around the corner. In nearby Piazza Bellini, the church of **La Martorana** (Mon–Sat 8am–1pm & 3.30–5.30pm, Sun 8.30am–1pm) is one of the finest survivors of the medieval city. Its slim twelfth-century campanile and series of spectacular mosaics make a marked contrast to the adjacent squat chapel of **San Cataldo** (same hours; €1) with its little Saracenic red golfball domes. In the district of Albergheria, a warren of tiny streets to the southwest, you'll find the deconsecrated church of **San Giovanni degli Eremiti** (Mon–Sat 9am–7pm, Sun 9am–1pm; €4.50), built in 1148 and the most obviously Arabic of the city's Norman relics, with five ochre domes topping a small church that was built upon the remains of an earlier mosque. A path leads up through citrus trees to the church, behind which are its celebrated late-thirteenth-century cloisters. From here it's a few paces north to the **Palazzo dei Normanni**, seat of the Sicilian regional parliament; entrance on Piazza Indipendenza. It was originally built by the Saracens and was enlarged considerably by the Normans, under whom it housed the most magnificent of medieval European courts. The beautiful **Cappella Palatina** (Mon–Sat 8.30am–noon & 3–4.15pm, Sun 8.30am–noon; €5), the private royal chapel of Roger II, built between 1132 and 1143, is almost entirely covered in glorious twelfth-century mosaics. North of here, the **Castello di Zisa**, in Piazza Guglielmo il Buono (Mon–Fri 9am–7pm, Sun 9am–1pm, €2.50), is an amazing piece of twelfth-century Arab architecture with clever heating and cooling systems as well as some lovely mosaics.

Down Corso Vittorio Emanuele from the palace, the **Cattedrale** (Mon–Sat 8.30am–noon and 2–4.30pm, Sun 8.30am–1.30pm) is a more substantial Norman relic, though much restored in the eighteenth century. Still, the triple-apsed eastern end and the lovely matching towers are all original; the interior is cold and Neo-classical, the only items of interest the fine portal and wooden doors and the royal tombs, containing the remains of some of Sicily's most famous monarchs (€1). Away to the northeast, off Via Roma, the **Museo Archeologico Regionale** (Tues–Sat 8.30am–6.45pm, Sun 8.30am–1.45pm; €4.50) is a magnificent collection of artefacts, mainly from the island's Greek and Roman sites. Two cloisters hold anchors and other retrieved hardware from the sea off the Sicilian coast, and there are rich stone carvings from the temple site of Selinunte.

Be sure to walk south through the sprawling **Vucciria market** area (daily from 8am) for a glimpse of old Palermo, before making your way to Sicily's **Galleria Regionale** (Mon–Sun 9am–1pm & 2.30–7pm; €4.50), on Via Alloro in the rough-and-ready La Kalsa district. It's a stunning medieval art collection that includes a magnificent fifteenth-century fresco of the *Triumph of Death*, work by the fifteenth-century sculptor Francesco Laurana and paintings by Antonello da Messina. Near here, at Via Butera 1, is the engaging **Museo delle Marionette** (Mon–Fri 9am–1pm & 3–5pm, Sat 9am–1pm; €4), the definitive collection of traditional Sicilian puppets – in summer, there are free shows (currently Fri 5.30pm), centring on the swashbuckling exploits of Orlando in his battles against the Saracens.

**Trains** arrive at Stazione Centrale, at the southern end of Via Roma, from where buses #101 and #102 run to the centre. **Ferry and hydrofoil** services dock just off Via Francesco Crispi, from where it's a ten-minute walk up Via E. Amari to Piazza Castelnuovo. There are **tourist offices** inside the train station (Mon–Fri 8.30am–2pm & 3–6pm; ⑩www.palermotourism.com) and at Piazza Castelnuovo 34 (same hours; ℡091.583.847). For **Internet access** try Al Falah, Corso Vittorio Emanuele 304 (Mon–Sun 9am–11pm).

Most of Palermo's budget **hotels** are on and around the southern ends of Via Maqueda and Via Roma, near the train station, though it's a rather sleazy area at night. Two of the better options here are the welcoming *Olimpia*, on Corso Vittorio Emanuele (℡091.616.1276; ❸), with clean rooms overlooking Piazza Cassa di Risparmio and a great breakfast, and the simple, family-run *Vittoria*, Via Maqueda 8 (℡091.616.2437; ❹), near the station. You may prefer, however, one of the modern **B&Bs** in the centre of town: north of the main square is welcoming

*A Casa di Amici* on Via Volturno 6 (☎091.584.884, ✆www.acasadiamici.com; ❺), with attractive rooms, use of kitchen and Sky TV as well as young and vivacious hosts. Alternatively, there's the excellent-value *La Dimora Del Guiscardo*, on Via della Vetriera 85 off Piazza Magione in the Kalsa district (☎328.662.6074, ✆www .ladimoradelguiscardo.it; ❸), a lovely, clean place in a restored *palazzo*, with free bicycle loan. In addition, two student halls of residence offer **hostel** accommodation: in August only, *Ostello San Saverio* on Via G di Cristina 39 (☎091.654.7099) has singles for €19 including breakfast, while *Casa Marconi*, Via Monfenera 140 (☎091.657.0611; ❹) has year-round, basic hotel-quality doubles and triples with bath, and a student canteen. A seaside alternative is the well-equipped HI hostel *Baia del Corallo*, out at Sferacavallo, Via Plauto 27 (☎091.6797.807; €18); to reach it, take bus #101 from the station of Piazza Alcide de Gasperi then bus #628.

For authentic Sicilian **street food**, look out for *frittorie* – stalls with large metal pans – selling *pane ca' meusa* (spleen in rolls), and *pane e panelle* (rolls filled with chickpea fritters), or try *Antica Focacceria*, Via A. Paternostro 58, off Corso Vittorio Emanuele. For **pizzas**, head to *Pizzeria Italia*, Via Orologio 54, off Via Maqueda (eves only). The city's cheapest sit-down **restaurant** is *Trattoria-Pizzeria Enzo*, Via Maurolico 17/19, close to the station, while the *Trattoria Primavera* on Piazza Bologni, near the cathedral (closed Mon), serves excellent homestyle cooking. There are a couple of good **pubs** and **clubs** on Via dei Candelai, and late-opening **bars** for drinks and panini on Piazza Bara all'Olivella. *I Candelai*, Via dei Candelai 65, has some of the hottest live music and DJs in Palermo, while *Kursaal Kalhesa*, Foro Umberto I 21 (✆www.kursaalkalhesa.it), is a pricey but cool restaurant/winebar, with live music, bookshop and a garden bar by the sea. There's also a major theatrical and **puppetry** tradition in Sicily, and Palermo has five puppet theatres with regular performances at Cuticchio, Via Bara all'Olivella 95. For details of what's on, check out *Zero* and the fortnightly listings guide *Lapis Palermo*.

## Taormina and around

On Sicily's eastern coast, and dominating two grand sweeping bays, **TAORMINA** is the island's best-known resort. The outstanding remains of its classical theatre, with Mount Etna as an unparalleled backdrop, arrested passing travellers when Taormina was no more than a medieval hill village, and these days it's virtually impossible to find anywhere to stay between June and August. It is rather chi-chi, packed with designer shops and pricey cafes, but still has some charm, with its main traffic-free street, Corso V. Emanuele, lined with fifteenth- to nineteenth-century *palazzi* interspersed with small, intimate piazzas. The **Teatro Greco** (daily 9am–1hr before sunset; €4.50), however – signposted from just about everywhere – is the only real sight, founded by Greeks in the third century BC, though most of what's left is a Roman rebuilding from the first century AD, when the stage and lower seats were cut back to provide room and a deep trench dug in the orchestra to accommodate the animals and fighters used in gladiatorial contests. These days it has a summer season of Greek plays (in Italian). The **train station** is way below town, from where it's a steep thirty-minute walk up or a short bus ride to the centre (€1.30). There's a **tourist office** at the station (Mon–Sat 8am–noon & 4–7pm), with the main office in Palazzo Corvaja, Piazza Santa Caterina (same hours; ☎0942.23.243, ✆www.taormina-ol.it). For **Internet** access try Las Vegas Internet Cafe, Salita Alex Humboldt 7, off Corso Umberto.

The best budget **accommodation** is the pretty hostel *Taormina's Odyssey*, Travessa A, Via G.Martino, off Via Capuccini (☎0942.24.533; €15), with sea-views, a terrace and kitchen, ten minutes' walk from Porta Messina. There are also good possibilities along Via Bagnoli Croce: *Il Leone*, at no. 124–126 (☎0942.23.878; ❹), run by a family of sculptors and artists, has clean, neat rooms, some with a sea view, and the cafe downstairs serves cheap food and drink. Taormina's **HI Hostel**, the small *Ulisse*, Vico San Francesco de Paola 9 at the Porta Catania end of town (℡0942.23.193; €16), is central but basic.

Eating in Taormina is relatively pricey compared to the rest of Sicily – if money is tight, try the good **rosticceria** just up from Porta Messina, on the corner of Via Timeo and Via Patrizio. Among the less expensive **trattorias** are *La Botte*, Piazza Santa Domenica 4, and *Il Baccanale* in Piazza Filea, which has outdoor tables and similar prices – both close to Via Bagnoli Croce. There are several **bars** and discos in the centre, of which the coolest is probably *Q Lounge Bar*, off the main Corso on Piazzetta F Paladini 6. Alternatively, it's a thirty-minute walk along an overgrown path from Porta Catania up to the cheeky *Turrisi* bar (daily 4pm–2/3am) in the sleepy hill-top village of Castelmola. Popular with Taormina's many gay tourists, it's a penis-themed affair on four floors, with superb sea views from the top terrace.

The closest beach to Taormina is at **MAZZARÓ**, with its much-photographed islet, **Isola Bella**: it's a scenic thirty-minute descent on foot, or use the cable car (every 15min; €1.80 single) from Via Pirandello. The beach-bars and restaurants at **SPISONE**, 1km or so further north, are also reachable by path from Taormina, this time from below the cemetery in town.

## Mount Etna

**Mount Etna's** massive bulk looms over much of the coastal route south of Taormina. If you don't have the time to reach the summit, the **Circumetnea rail service** (around €10 return; InterRail passes not valid) provides alternative volcanic thrills in a ride around the base of the volcano from **GIARRE-RIPOSTO**, thirty minutes by train or bus from Taormina; if you make the entire trip to Catania, allow four hours. However, the **ascent** is a spectacular trip, worth every effort to make. At 3323m, Etna is a fairly substantial mountain; the fact that it's also one of the world's biggest volcanoes (and still active) only adds to the draw. On **public transport**, you'll need to come via Catania by bus: there's only one a day (8am from Catania train station) that continues up to the huddle of souvenir shops and restaurants at the *Rifugio Sapienza*, giving you enough time to make it to the top and back for the return bus to Catania (4.30pm). If it is considered safe, a **guide** can take you further up the mountain by jeep or minibus (approximately March–Oct; €42.50 return); if you are given the go-ahead to walk, take warm clothes, good shoes and glasses to keep the flying grit out of your eyes. In any case you will not be allowed beyond 2,900m, marked off by a rope slung across the track. A **tourist office** in Catania train station can help with accommodation, though if you are travelling alone the cheapest option is the easy-going **hostel**, *Agora*, Piazza Curro 6, near the cathedral (℡095.723.3010; ⓦwww.agorahostel.com; dorms €17–20, rooms ❸).

## Siracusa

Further down Sicily's eastern seaboard, **SIRACUSA** (ancient Syracuse) was first colonized by Greeks in 733 BC and grew to become their main power base in Sicily. Today the city boasts some of the best Greek archeological remains anywhere, and also has a strong Baroque character in its old town, squeezed onto the island of **Ortygia**, by the harbour. At the centre of the island, the most obvious attraction is the **Duomo**, set in a conch-shaped piazza studded with Baroque architecture, and itself incorporating twelve fluted columns belonging to the temple that originally stood here. Round the corner, the severe thirteenth-century Palazzo Bellomo houses the **Museo di Palazzo Bellomo** (currently closed for restoration), an outstanding collection of medieval art and paintings by Caravaggio. North of the train station, the city is mainly new and commercial, though there are also the best of Siracusa's archeological sights here. It's a twenty-minute walk, or a short bus ride from Piazza delle Posta (#1, #3, #6, #8, #12, or #25) to Viale Teocrito, from where you walk east for the **Museo Archeologico** (Tues–Sat 9am–1pm & 3–6pm, Sun 9am–1pm; €4.50), housing a wealth of material from the early Greek colonies. Round the corner, the ruined church of **San Giovanni Evangelista** has interesting catacombs (Tues–Sun 9am–12.30pm & 2.30–5.30pm; €3.50), though the church itself was destroyed by an earthquake in 1693 and never rebuilt.

Siracusa's extensive **Parco Archeologico** (daily 9am–2hr before sunset; €4.50) is a twenty-minute walk west of the Museo Archeologico (bus #10 from Piazza Archimede). Here, the **Ara di Ierone II**, an enormous third-century-BC altar, is the first thing you see, though the main highlight of the park is the **Teatro Greco**, cut out of the rock and looking down towards the sea. It's much bigger (though less impressive scenically) than the one at Taormina, capable of holding around fifteen thousand people, and also has a summer season of Greek plays. Nearby, the **Latomia del Paradiso**, a leafy quarry, is best known for the **Orecchio di Dionigi**, an S-shaped cave, 65m long, that Dionysius is supposed to have used as a prison: Caravaggio, a visitor in 1586, coined the name after the shape of the entrance, but the acoustic properties are such that it's not impossible to imagine Dionysius eavesdropping on his prisoners from a vantage point above. The last section of the park contains the neglected-looking **Roman amphitheatre**.

A good **day-trip** out of Siracusa is the half-hour train ride to the tumbledown town of **NOTO**, whose deserted station and crumbling suburbs give way to a lovely Baroque town centre that was recently named a UNESCO World Heritage Site.

### Practicalities

Siracusa's **train station** is on the mainland, a twenty-minute walk from Ortygia. AST **buses** arrive either in Piazza delle Poste, just over the bridge on Ortygia, or else in Piazzale Marconi, in the modern town; SAIS buses stop in Via Trieste, close by Piazza delle Poste. The **main tourist office** is in Ortygia at Via Maestranza 33 (Mon–Sat 9am–1.30pm & 2.30–5.30/7pm; ☎0931.481.200, ☻www.apt-siracusa .it), and there's **Internet access** at the bookshop Libreria Aleph, Corso Umberto 106. In high season you'll need to book **accommodation** in advance. There are no cheap options in Ortygia, but if you're prepared to splash out the *Hotel Alla Giudecca*, Via Alagona 52 (☎0931.222.55, ☻www.allagiudecca.it; ❽), has beautiful apartments with Roman-era Jewish ritual baths in the cellar. On the mainland, the *Aretusa*, Via Francesco Crispi 75 (☎0931.24.211; ❹), is a clean, old-fashioned hotel by the station, with the *Centrale*, Corso Umberto 141 (☎0931.60.528; ❹), a similar, basic hotel just around the corner. The nearest **campsite**, *Agriturist Rinaura* (☎0931.721.224), is 5km away – bus #21, #22 or #23 from Corso Umberto or Piazza delle Poste. As for **restaurants**, *La Siciliana*, Via Savoia 17, does superb value pizzas, while the *Trattoria Archimede*, Via Gemmellaro 8, frequented by locals, is inexpensive and good for fish. *Spaghetteria do Scogghiu*, Via Scina 11, has a huge selection of cheap pasta and is popular at night, with the *Trattoria Da Antonio*, Via Gimillaro 34, serving good home cooking. Piazza S Rocco, Via delle Vergini and Via Roma are the areas to head for a **drink**, with bars such as the old-fashioned *enoteca Solaria* and the pricey cocktail bar *747*. *Lungolanotte*, Lungomare Alfeo, is a popular bar/**club** overlooking the sea, while *Punta del Pero* is a legendary summer bar in Siracusa, served by boats from the harbour in Ortygia (last back around 11pm; €1). *Ultimo Atto*, Via Elorina 120 (☻www.ultimoatto.com), is a reasonable disco near the station playing classic tunes.

## Agrigento

Halfway along Sicily's southern littoral, **AGRIGENTO** is primarily of interest for the substantial remains of Pindar's "most beautiful city of mortals", strung out along a ridge facing the sea a few kilometres below town. The series of Doric temples here, mostly dating from the fifth century BC, are the most evocative of Sicilian remains. They are also the focus of a constant procession of tour buses, so budget accommodation should be booked in advance (though Agrigento could be a day-trip from Palermo). A road winds down from the modern city to the **Valle dei Templi**, buses #1, #2 or #3 dropping you at a car park between the two separate zones of **archeological remains** (daily 8.30am–7.30pm €4.50, or €6 with the museum). The eastern zone is home to the scattered remains of the oldest of the temples, the **Tempio di Ercole**, probably begun in the last decades of the sixth century BC, and the better-preserved **Tempio della Concordia**, dated to around 430 BC, with fine views of the city and sea. There's also the **Tempio di Giunone**, an engaging half-ruin standing at the very edge of the ridge. The western zone, back along the path and beyond the car park, is less impressive but still worth wandering around. Most notable here is the mammoth construction that was the **Tempio di Giove**, or Temple of Olympian Zeus, the largest Doric temple ever known, though never completed, left in ruins by the Carthaginians and further damaged by earthquakes. The small piece that is standing is a nineteenth-century reconstruction. Around the site there are also some early Christian and Byzantine tombs. Via dei Templi leads back to the town from the car park via the excellent **Museo Nazionale Archeo-logico** (Tues–Sat 9am–7pm, Sun–Mon 9am–1pm; €4.50) – an extraordinarily rich collection devoted to finds from the city and the surrounding area.

**Trains** arrive at the edge of the old town, outside which – on Piazza Marconi – buses leave for the temples. The **tourist office** is in the station (Mon–Fri 8am–2pm & 3–7pm; Sat 8am–2pm; ☎0922.22.780 ⊛www.agrigentoweb.it), and there's also an information box at the Valle dei Templi site. The best budget **accommodation** is the friendly and very pleasant B&B *Camere A Sud*, Via Ficani 6, off the main street Via Atenea (☎349.384.424; ❺), with a tiny breakfast terrace where aperitifs are served in summer. Of the hotels, try the new, clean one-star *Hotel Amici*, Via Acrone 5, immediately right out of the station (☎0922.402.831, ⊛www.hotelamici.com; ❹), or the less attractive but central *Concordia*, at Piazza San Francesco 11 (☎0922.596.266; ❹). You can **camp** 5km away at the coastal resort of San Leone; take bus #2 or #2/ from outside the train station. The **trattoria** *Black Horse,* off Via Atenea, serves good-value set meals, while *Chez Jean 2*, Via Cicerone, does the best **pizza** in town.

# Sardinia (Sardegna)

A little under 200km from the Italian mainland, **SARDINIA** (Sardegna) is way off most tourist itineraries, although it boasts some of the country's loveliest beaches and holds fascinating vestiges of the various civilizations that have passed through. In addition to Roman and Carthaginian ruins, Genoese fortresses and a string of lovely Pisan churches, there are striking remnants of Sardinia's only significant native culture, known as the nuraghic civilization after the 7000 *nuraghi*, tower-like stone constructions, that litter the landscape. The capital, **Cágliari**, is worth exploring for its excellent museums and some of the island's best nightlife. The other main ferry port and airport is **Olbia** in the north, little more than a transit town for the **Costa Smeralda** or Emerald Coast, the Aga Khan's exclusive resort stretching from Porto Cervo to Porto Rotondo in the south. There's a third major airport at the bustling package resort of **Alghero** in the northwest. In the interior, **Nuoro** makes a useful stopover for visiting some of the more remote mountain areas, where you can find what remains of the island's traditional culture, best embodied in the numerous village **festivals**.

## Cágliari

Rising up from its port and crowned by an old citadel squeezed within a protective ring of fortifications, **CÁGLIARI** has been Sardinia's capital at least since

To **get to Sardinia**, there are frequent daily **flights** from the Italian mainland to Cágliari, Olbia and Fertília/Alghero. Cheaper but slower are the overnight **ferries** to Cágliari, Arbatax (halfway up the island's eastern coast), Olbia, Golfo degli Aranci (near Olbia) and Porto Torres (on Sardinia's northwestern corner) from mainland Italy (Civitavécchia, Genoa, Livorno, Naples) – as well as from Sicily, Corsica and France. In summer, **fast ferries** connect Genoa, Piombino, Civitavécchia and Fiumicino to the island, though fares are higher than on the regular ferries, and seats quickly get booked up. Getting around Sardinia without a car is best done using a mixture of buses and trains, though connections to some of the more remote areas can be few and far between. Note that Interail/Eurail passes are not valid for the smaller, private rail lines run by Ferrovie della Sardegna (FdS). For up-to-date transport timetables check the back pages of the *Unione Sarda* newspaper.

Roman times and is still the island's biggest town. Nonetheless, its centre is easily explored on foot, with almost all the wandering you will want to do encompassed within the citadel. The most evocative entry to this is from the monumental **Bastione San Remy** on Piazza Costituzione (currently closed for restoration). From here, you can wander off in any direction to enter the intricate maze of Cágliari's citadel, traditionally the seat of the administration, aristocracy and highest ecclesiastical offices. It has been little altered since the Middle Ages, though the tidy Romanesque facade on the mainly thirteenth-century **Cattedrale** (Mon–Sat 8am–12.30pm & 4–7pm, Sun 8am–1pm & 4–8pm) in Piazza Palazzo is in fact a fake, added in the twentieth century in the old Pisan style. At the opposite end of Piazza Palazzo a road leads into the smaller Piazza dell'Arsenale, site of several museums including the **Museo Archeologico Nazionale** (Tues–Sun 9am–8pm; €4), a must for anyone interested in Sardinia's past. The island's most important Phoenician, Carthaginian and Roman finds are gathered here, but everything pales beside the museum's greatest pieces, from Sardinia's **nuraghic** culture. Of these, the most eye-catching is a series of bronze statuettes. In the same complex, the **Pinacoteca Nazionale** (same hours; €2) features some glowing fifteenth-century altarpieces, and a sparkling *Madonna della Cintola* in vivid pinks, greens and oranges by the fifteenth-century Sienese painter Carlo di Giovanni, while the **Museo delle Cere** (daily 9am–1pm, Tues–Sat also 4–7pm; €1.55) displays a series of beautifully executed anatomical waxworks by Clemente Susini for nineteenth-century medical students. Off the piazza stands the **Torre San Pancrazio** (Tues–Sun 9am–4.30pm; €2), from where it's only a short walk to Via dell'Università and the **Torre dell'Elefante** (as San Pancrazio), named after the small carving of an elephant on one side; climb to the top for stupendous views over the city and coast. Nearby, Viale Buon Cammino leads to the **Anfiteatro Romano** (Tues–Sun: April–Oct 9am–1pm & 3–7pm; Nov–March 9am–4pm; free). Cut out of solid rock in the second century AD, the amphitheatre could hold the city's entire population of twenty thousand. Below the Bastione San Remy and to the east is Cágliari's yellow-stone Basilica of **San Saturno**, on Piazza San Cosimo (Mon–Sat 9am–1pm). This ancient cross-shaped church has sixth-century foundations, though the basilica here now was mostly built in the tenth century.

Cágliari's **port** lies in the heart of the town, opposite Via Roma. The **airport** sits beside the Stagno di Cágliari, the city's largest lagoon, fifteen minutes' bus ride west of town. There are **tourist offices** at the port, and opposite the **train and bus stations** on Piazza Matteotti (April–Sept Mon–Sat 8.30am–7.30pm; Oct–March Mon–Fri 9am–1.30pm & 3–6pm, Sat 9am–2pm; ☎070.669.255, ⓦwww.aast.ca.it). Cágliari has a good selection of budget **hotels**, with an HI hostel due to open during 2006: check the latest details with the tourist office. Via

Sardegna has several basic hotels including the neat family-run *La Perla* at no. 18 (℡070.669.446; ❸), with doubles and triples, and the clean one-star *Palmas* at no. 14 (℡070.651.679; ❸). If you can afford to splash out, *AeR Bundes Jack*, Via Roma 75 (℡070.667.970; ❺), is a gem of a hotel right on the seafront, with original 1930s furnishings.

Most of Cágliari's **restaurants** are clustered around Via Sardegna: *Da Serafino*, at no. 109, pulls in the locals for Sardinian specialities such as *spaghetti al bottariga*, while *Da Fabio*, at no. 90, offers good tourist menus and has an English-speaking boss. Seafood-lovers will enjoy the *Ristorante Italia*, no. 30, though prices are relatively high. Away from the port area, try *La Damigiana*, a simple trattoria with low prices, at Corso Vittorio Emanuele 115. Piazza Yenne has numerous outdoor cafés for a **snack** and a beer, and there's a great gelateria, *L'Isola del Gelato*. Via Mameli is a good place for **bars** – the funky *Linea Notturna* at no. 154 (✆www .lineanotturna.it) hosts live music on Thurs-Sat, and also has a restaurant so get there after 10.30pm if you just want to drink. Alternatively, *De Candia*, on Bastione San Remy, has open-air music on summer nights. Cágliari's best bar within the citadel is the cool, underground *Karel*, Via della Università 37, which serves great-value lunches and is popular with students at night. Nearer the port, *Amparias* on Via Savoia 4, has cheap pizzas and buzzing music. There are a couple of **clubs** a cab ride from the centre (both only open at weekends) – *Charlie*, Via de' Carroz (✆www.gclass.it), plays pop and revival on Friday, and revival and lounge on Saturday, while the popular discobar *Spazio Newton*, Via Newton 11, plays revival and alternative music. For events **listings**, check the newspaper *L'Unione Sarda*. For **Internet** access, try the bookshop Le Librerie della Costa, Via Roma 63.

## Su Nuraxi

If you have no time to see any other of Sardinia's ancient stone *nuraghi*, make a point of visiting **Su Nuraxi**, the biggest and most famous of them and a good taste of the primitive grandeur of the island's only indigenous civilization. The snag is access: the site lies 1km outside the village of **BARÚMINI**, 50km north of Cágliari, to which there is only one daily Arst bus (2pm). At Barúmini, turn left at the main crossroads and it's a ten-minute walk to Su Nuraxi (daily 9am–4/7pm; obligatory guided tour €4.20). Its dialect name means simply "the nuragh" and not only is it the biggest nuraghic complex on the island, but it's also thought to be the oldest, dating probably from around 1500 BC. Comprising a bulky fortress surrounded by the remains of a village, Su Nuraxi was a palace complex at the very least – possibly a capital city. The central tower once reached 21m (now reduced to less than 15m), and its outer defences and inner chambers are connected by passageways and stairs. The whole complex is thought to have been covered with earth by Sards and Carthaginians at the time of the Roman conquest, which may account for its excellent state of preservation. To return to Cágliari, get the FdS bus at 6pm from outside Barúmini's bar (buy tickets in Cágliari) to San Luro train station, for a connection at 7.15pm.

## Nuoro

Superbly sited beneath the soaring peak of Monte Ortobene, opposite the stark heights of Sopramonte, **NUORO** is the only one of Sardinia's provincial centres that expresses the island's mountain culture. Much of the town has been disfigured by modern construction, however, and there is little tourist infrastructure, though it can boast some first-class museums. Nuoro's old quarter is the most compelling part of town, spread around the pedestrianized hub of **Corso Garibaldi**. The town's chief attraction is the **Museo della Vita e Tradizioni Popolari** (daily: mid-June to Sept 9am–8pm; Oct to mid-June 9am–1pm & 3–7pm; €5) on Via Mereu, a ten-minute walk from the Corso south of Piazza Vittorio Emanuele, which contains Sardinia's most comprehensive collection of local handicrafts. The museum is currently under restoration, so only six rooms are open, but you can still see the highlight, an astonishing array of carnival costumes and masks made from animal skins and bells, traditionally put on by shepherds to exorcise the fear of turning into beasts themselves. For a more contemporary perspective, the **Museo d'Arte Nuorese** (MAN), just off the Corso (Tues–Sun 10am–1pm & 4.30–8.30pm; €2.60), displays modern art from the whole island. At the bottom of the Corso, on Via Mannu, the new **Museo Archeologico** (Tues–Sat 9am–1pm & 3–5.30pm; free) contains a reconstruction of one of the nuraghic culture's sacred fountains thought to be used for purificatory rites, and a skeleton from around 1100BC which demonstrates some early medical expertise – there's a hole in its skull which has healed, showing the patient survived the operation.

Nuoro's biggest annual festival, the **Festa del Redentore**, takes place on the penultimate Sunday of August, featuring elaborately costumed participants from all over the island. The religious festivities are held on August 29, when a procession from town weaves up to the 955m summit of **Monte Ortobene**, 8km away, where a bronze statue of the Redeemer stands poised above the gorge separating Nuoro from the Sopramonte.

Nuoro's **train station** is a twenty-minute walk from the centre of town along Via Lamármora, and the **bus station** lies a further ten minutes south of here on Via Sardegna. Nuoro's **tourist office** is on Piazza Italia (Mon & Tues 9am–1.30pm & 2.30–7pm; Wed–Sun 8.30am–2pm & 2.30–8pm; ☎0784.30.083, ⊛www.nuoro .com), and is useful for a street-map and list of B&Bs. The few **hotels** in town are mostly aimed at business travellers, such as the characterless *Sandalia*, near the train station on Via Einaudi (☎0784.38.353; ❺). A better bet are the two **B&Bs** on Monte Ortobene, enjoying lofty hilltop views: *Casa Solotti* (☎328.602.8975; ❹) and *Su Redentore* (☎328.022.5518; ❹) – for both, ring ahead to be met. A hostel is due to open in Nuoro soon: ask the tourist office for details. Nuoro's **restaurants** offer good-quality, meaty fare at reasonable prices, such as *Tascusi*, near the top end of the Corso at Via Aspromonte 13, where local dishes are served in simple white rooms decorated with Sard art, and the livelier *Il Rifugio*, Via Mereu 28, a good trattoria-pizzeria. **Nightlife** options are limited – try one of the bars along Corso Garibaldi, or the *New Age* disco, on Via Roma.

## Alghero

In the northwest of Sardinia, **ALGHERO** owes its predominantly Catalan flavour to a wholesale Hispanicization that followed the overthrow of the Genoese Doria family by Pedro IV of Aragón in 1354. The traces are still strong in the old town today, with its flamboyant churches, wrought-iron balconies and narrow cobbled streets named in both Italian and Catalan. A walk around the old town should include the seven defensive **towers** that dominate Alghero's centre and surrounding walls. From the **Giardino Púbblico**, the **Porta Terra** is the first of these massive bulwarks, erected at the expense of the prosperous Jewish community before their expulsion in 1492. Via Roma runs down from here through the old town's puzzle of lanes to the pedestrianized Via Carlo Alberto, holding most of the bars and shops. Turn right to reach **Piazza Cívica**, the old town's main square, at one end of which rises the grand Neoclassical facade of Alghero's mainly sixteenth-century **Cattedrale**. Inside, the lofty nave's alternating pillars and columns are topped by an impressive octagonal dome. The best excursions you can make are west along the coast past the long bay of Porto Conte as far as the point of **Capo Caccia**, where the spectacular sheer cliffs are riddled by deep marine caves. The most impressive of these is the **Grotta di Nettuno**, or Neptune's Grotto (daily 9/10am–2/7pm; €10), a long snaking passage delving far into the rock, into which hourly tours are led, single-file, past dramatically-lit and fantastical stalagmites and stalactites. The return boat trip from the port costs €11, or take the bus from the Giardino Púbblico to Capo Caccia (June–Sept; three daily from 9am; Oct–May one daily), from where it's a 654-step descent.

   **Trains** arrive 3km north of the centre and are connected to the port by regular local buses. Long-distance **buses** arrive in Via Catalogna, on the Giardino Púbblico. Alghero's **tourist office** is on the corner of the Giardino Púbblico (April–Sept Mon–Sat 8am–8pm, Sun 9am–1pm; Nov–March Mon–Sat 8am–2pm; ☎079.979.054, ⊛www.infoalghero.it). There are two good **accommodation** options in the heart of the old town: the decent B&B *Mamjuana*, Vicolo Adami 12 (☎339.136.9791, ⊛www.mamajuana.it; ❺), and the *San Francesco Hotel*, Via Machin 2 (☎079.980.330, ⊛www.sanfrancescohotel.com; ❻), a graceful former monastery with comfortable rooms ranged around a cloister. Five minutes' walk from the old town, at Via Sassari 53, is a lovely B&B (☎079.978.218; ❹), run by Lucia Van Alphen, an inviting family place with a breakfast terrace. The HI **hostel** *Alguer* (☎079.930.478; €16) is in a tranquil spot 6km along the coast at Fertilia, reachable by hourly local bus from Alghero, while *La Mariposa* **campsite** (☎079.950.480; ⊛www.lamariposa.it; April to mid-Oct), is 2km north of town, with direct access to the beach. Alghero's **restaurants** are renowned for seafood, at its best in spring and winter. *La Lépanto* on Via Carlo Alberto, off Piazza Sulis, is one of the finest fish restaurants, though expensive. *Trattoria Maristella* at Via Kennedy 9 is a cheaper alternative, popular with locals, who also flock to *Casablanca*, a more casual pizzeria at Via Umberto 76. *Caffe Teatro* on Piazza del Teatro, is popular for an evening **drink**, and there's **live music** at pizzeria *Poco Loco*, Via Gramsci 9. There are a few **disco/clubs** on Lungomare Dante, or follow the road south to the swanky *Colonial Cafe* on Via Carbia 13, off Viale Resistenza. The bookshop il Labirinto on Via Carlo Alberto has **Internet** access (daily 9am–1pm & 4–9pm).

# Travel details

## Trains

**Alghero** to: Olbia (6 daily; 3hr, via Sassari); Nuoro (3 daily; 3hr 30min–7 hr via Sassari and Macomer).

**Bari** to: Bríndisi (hourly; 1hr 30min).

**Bologna** to: Ferrara (every 30min; 30min); Florence (every 30 min; 1hr); Milan (every 30 min; 2hr); Ravenna (hourly; 1hr 20min).

**Cágliari** to: Alghero (4 daily via Sassari; 5hr); Olbia (4 daily; 4hr–4hr 40min); Nuoro (2 daily; 3hr 30min, via Oristano and Macomer).

**Florence** to: Bologna (every 30min; 1hr); Genoa (hourly; 3–4hr); Milan (every 30min; 3hr); Naples (every 30min; 4hr); Perugia (hourly; 2hr); Pisa (every 15min; 1hr); Rome (every 30 min; 1hr 40min–2hr 30min); Venice (hourly; 2hr 50); Verona (hourly; 3hr).

**Genoa** to: Bologna (hourly; 3hr 30min); Milan (every 30min; 1hr 30min); Naples (10 daily; 8hr); Pisa (hourly; 2–3hr); Rome (hourly; 5hr 20min).

**Milan** to: Bologna (every 20min; 2hr); Rome (hourly; 4hr 30min); Venice (every 30min; 3hr).

**Naples** to: Bríndisi (9 daily; 5hr); Palermo (5 daily; 9hr); Siracusa (5 daily; 9hr).

**Padua** to: Bologna (every 30min; 1hr 20min); Milan (every 30min; 2hr 30min); Verona (every 20min; 1hr).

**Palermo** to: Agrigento (13 daily; 2hr); Catania (6 daily; 3–5hr).

**Perugia** to: Assisi (hourly; 20min); Florence (hourly; 2hr); Rome (hourly; 2hr).

**Pisa** to: Florence (every 15min; 1hr); Lucca (every 15min; 20min).

**Rome** to: Bologna (every 15min; 2hr 40min); Florence (every 15min; 1hr 30min); Milan (every 30min; 4–5hr); Naples (every 15min; 2–3hr).

**Turin** to: Genoa (every 30min; 1hr 50min); Milan (every 30min; 1hr 50min).

**Venice** to: Bologna (every 30min; 2hr); Florence (hourly; 3hr); Milan (every 30min; 3hr); Padua (every 10min; 30min); Verona (every 30min; 1hr 30min).

**Verona** to: Milan (every 30min; 1hr 30min); Padua (every 30min; 55min); Rome (hourly; 5hr); Venice (every 30min; 1hr 30min).

## Buses

**Cágliari** to: Nuoro (4 daily; 3hr 30min); Barumini

for Su Nuraxi (1 daily; 1hr 30min). For more information on buses in Sardinia, see ® www .arst.sardegna.it.

## Ferries

**Cágliari** to: Civitavécchia (1 daily; 14hr 30min–16hr 30min); Genoa (mid-July to Aug 2 weekly; 20hr); Livorno (1 weekly; 7hr); Naples (1–2 weekly; 16hr); Palermo (1 weekly; 13hr 30min); Trápani (1 weekly; 11hr).
**Genoa** to: Bastia (1 weekly; 9hr); Cágliari (2 weekly in summer; 20hr); Olbia (at least 7 weekly in summer; 13 hr); Palermo (6 weekly; 20hr); Porto Torres (7 weekly; 12hr).
**Naples** to: Cápri (6 daily; 1hr 15min); Palermo (daily; 9hr); Sorrento (daily; 1hr 15min); Aeolian Islands (2–3 per week; 9hr overnight to Strómboli).
**Olbia** to: Civitavécchia (1–3 daily; 8hr); Genoa (3–22 weekly; 8–13hr); Livorno (1–4 daily; 10–13hr).

**Porto Torres** to: Genoa (6–14 weekly; 11hr); Marseille, France (2–4 weekly; 12–16hr).
**Reggio di Calabria** to: Messina (12 daily; 20min).
**Santa Teresa di Gallura** to: Bonifacio, Corsica (2–14 daily; 55min).
**Sorrento** to: Cápri (4 daily; 50min).
**Villa San Giovanni** to: Messina (every 15min; 45min).

## Hydrofoils and fast ferries

**Naples** to: Cápri (17 daily; 40min); Sorrento (7 daily; 40min); Aeolian Islands (2–4 per day; 4hr to Strómboli).
**Olbia** to: Civitavécchia (June to early Sept 1–4 daily; 4–6 hr).
**Palermo** to: Naples (daily; 4hr).
**Reggio di Calabria** to: Messina (12 daily; 20min); Naples (summer 1 daily; 6hr).
**Sorrento** to: Cápri (12 daily; 20min).

# 17

# Latvia

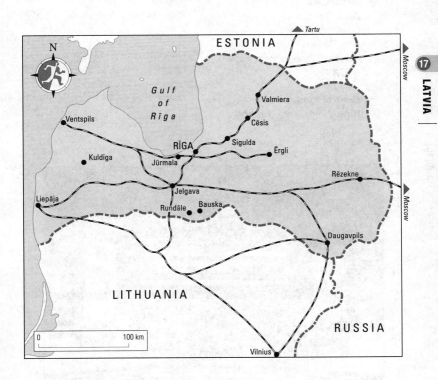

# Latvia highlights

✳ **Milda, the freedom monument, Rīga** A stylized female figure holds aloft three stars; Latvia's symbol of independence. See p.672

✳ **Jugendstil architecture, Rīga** The Latvian capital contains one of Europe's finest arrays of Art Nouveau architecture. See p.672

✳ **Central food market, Rīga** Sights, sounds and pungent smells in gigantic former Zeppelin hangars. See p.673

✳ **Jūrmala coastline** Fresh air, sand dunes, pine forests and faded elegance, all just forty minutes from Rīga. See p.674

✳ **Rundāle Palace** Spectacular Baroque palace, highlight of southern Latvia. See p.675

△ Jugendstil architecture, Rīga

# Introduction and basics

The history of **Latvia**, like that of its neighbour Estonia, is largely one of foreign occupation. The indigenous Balts were overwhelmed at the start of the thirteenth century by German crusading knights, who continued to dominate both land and trade even after political control passed to the Polish-Lithuanian Commonwealth, then Sweden and finally Russia. Latvian independence after a 1918–20 war against the Soviets and the Germans ended with Soviet annexation in 1940, though the country endured a brief but brutal occupation by the Nazis during World War II. On August 21, 1991, as the attempted coup against Gorbachev disintegrated in Moscow, Latvia declared its independence for the second time.

A new member of the European Union, Latvia is these days enjoying impressive economic growth, although the legacy of Soviet occupation, which left the country with a Russian minority population of thirty percent, means it is entering the new era as a culturally divided country.

The most obvious destination is the capital, **Rīga**, a city of architectural treasures. Places within easy reach of the capital include the palace of **Rundāle**, the resort area of **Jūrmala**, and the gently scenic **Gauja Valley** with the attractive small towns of Sigulda and Cēsis. Latvia also has hundreds of miles of unspoilt coast as well as numerous forests inland.

## Information & maps

**Tourist information centres** run by the Latvian tourist board (ⓦ www.latviatourism .lv) are in major centres. The Kümmerly & Frey 1:1,000,000 **map** of the Baltic States includes Latvia, and has a basic street plan of Rīga. Jāṇa Sēta, Elizabetes 83–85, Rīga, is well-stocked with guides, and publishes its own maps. The Falkplan of Rīga includes enlarged sections and public transport routes. **Rīga in your Pocket** is an excellent English-language **listings** guide and **The Baltic Times** weekly (ⓦ www.baltictimes .com) provides you with up-to-date info on news and events.

## Money and banks

Latvia's currency is the **lats** (plural lati) – normally abbreviated to Ls – which is divided into 100 santīmi. Coins come in 0.01, 0.02, 0.05, 0.10, 0.20, 0.50, 1 and 2Ls and notes in 5, 10, 20, 50, 100 and 500Ls. **Bank** (*banka*) hours vary, but in Rīga there should be some open Mon–Fri 9am–5pm, Sat 10am–3pm. Outside the capital, many close at 1pm and all are closed on Saturday and Sunday. Most major banks such as the Hansa Banka, Rīgas Komercbanka and Unibanka will cash **travellers' cheques** (Thomas Cook and American Express preferred) and some give advances on **credit cards**. In Rīga the bigger hotels will also cash travellers' cheques and accept credit cards, which you can use in an increasing number of establishments.

**Exchanging cash** is straightforward, even outside banking hours, as Rīga is full of cur-

---

### Latvia on the net

ⓦ**www.lv** General portal offering links to all manner of Latvia-related subjects.
ⓦ**www.virtualriga.com** Information on travel, entertainment and accommodation.
ⓦ**www.latviansonline.com** News and features in English.
ⓦ**www.tvnet.lv/en** Welcome to Latvia site with useful links.
ⓦ**www.rigathisweek.lv** Site for the free *Riga This Week* listings magazine.
ⓦ**www.latinst.lv** The Latvian Institute's homepage.

rency exchange offices (*valūtas apmaiņa*), but shop around to get the best rate. ATMs are nationwide accepting most international cash cards. At the time of writing, €1 was equal to 0.6Ls, $1 to 0.7Ls and £1 to 1Ls.

## Communications

**Post offices** (*pasts*) are generally open Mon–Fri 8am–8pm, Sat 8am–6pm. There are modern digital public **phones** on the streets operated with either credit cards or magnetic cards (*telekarte*) which come in 2, 3, 5 and 10Ls denominations and can be bought at post offices and most newsagents. There are plenty of **Internet** cafés in Rīga and they are starting to appear in other parts of Latvia as well. Prices are around 1Ls/hr in the capital and 0.60Ls elsewhere.

## Getting around

Buy **train** tickets in advance: stations have separate windows for long-distance (*starppilsētu*) and suburban (*piepilsētu*) trains. Long-distance services are divided into "passenger" (*pasažieru vilciens*) and "fast" (*ātrs*) – both are painfully slow but the latter, usually requiring a reservation, stops at fewer places. On timetable boards, look for *atiet* (departure) or *pienāk* (arrival).

**Buses** are slightly quicker and cheaper than trains but the local services are harder to fathom. Buy long-distance tickets in advance from the ticket counter and opt for an express (*ekspresis*) bus if possible. Both Eurolines and Ecolines offer frequent services linking Rīga with Tallinn (Estonia), Vilnius (Lithuania) and St Petersburg (Russia).

## Accommodation

Outside Rīga and Jūrmala, **accommodation** is limited: even in tourist areas, towns will often only have a couple of hotels and perhaps a campsite. Budget travellers still have a limited choice but **hostel** beds in the centre of Rīga are easily obtained (check ⓦ www.hostellinglatvia.com). It's also possible to find rooms in **student** halls of residence during college vacations – although staff are unlikely to understand English. A number of small-sized, good-value hotels and guest houses are emerging, but rooms are often in short supply and advance reservations are required in summer. In Rīga and Jūrmala there are agencies offering **private rooms**, which are well-priced and should be of a reasonable standard. There's a handful of decently equipped campsites in Rīga, Jūrmala and Sigulda, although they're few and far between elsewhere.

## Food and drink

Whilst meat or fish and potatoes remain the bedrock of Latvian cuisine and there's still enough cream around to clog up your arteries, new restaurants offering dishes from far-flung regions are arriving with greater frequency. Popular national **starters** include the filling cabbage soup (*kāpostu zupa*), sprats with onions (*šprotes ar sīpoliem*) and *pelēkie zirņi* (mushy peas in pork fat). Slabs of pork garnished with potatoes and sauerkraut constitute the typical **main course**, although freshwater fish (*zivs*) is common too. *Rasols* (cubes of potato, ham and gherkin drenched in cream) is the staple salad. There is a Russian presence on many a menu – *pelmeņi* (Russian ravioli) is fairly ubiquitous.

Eating out, particularly in Rīga's classier joints, is often **expensive**, but there are numerous self-service fast-food places around, offering filling meals for around 2Ls. In Rīga you'll also find a few ethnic restaurants offering vegetarian options. Plenteous supermarkets and markets allow for a comfortable self-catering existence.

Rīga has excellent **bars**, though some are expensive. Imported **beer** (*alus*) is widely available, but the local brews are fine and also cheaper – the most common brands are Aldaris and Cēsu. Worth trying once (and probably only once) is Rīga Melnais Balzāms, or Rīga black balsam, a kind of bitter liqueur (45 percent) made from various roots and herbs. Outside the capital, most towns will have at least one bar, café or restaurant. Coffee (*kafija*) and tea (*tēja*) are usually served black – if you want milk (*piens*) and/or sugar (*cukurs*) you'll have to ask.

# Opening hours and holidays

**Shops** are usually open Mon–Fri 8/10am–6/8pm, Sat 10am-–7pm. Some food shops are open until 10pm and are also open on Sunday. In Rīga there are a few 24hr shops, which sell food and alcohol. Most shops and all banks close on the following **public holidays**: Jan 1, Good Fri, Easter Sun, Easter Mon, May 1, second Sun in May, June 23 & 24, Nov 18, Dec 25, 26 & 31.

# Emergencies

**Theft** is the biggest hazard. If you're

## Latvian

In **Latvian**, the stress always falls on the first syllable of the word. The exception is the word for thank you (*paldies*) which has the stress on the second.

|  | Latvian | Pronunciation |
|---|---|---|
| Yes | *Jā* | Jah |
| No | *Nē* | Neh |
| Please | *Lūdzu* | Loodzoo |
| Thank you | *Paldies* | Paldeeass |
| Hello/Good day | *Labdien* | Labdeean |
| Goodbye | *Uz redzēšanos* | Ooz redzehshanwas |
| Excuse me | *Atvainojiet* | Atvainoyet |
| Where? | *Kur?* | Kur? |
| Good | *Labs* | Labs |
| Bad | *Slikts* | Slikts |
| Near | *Tuvs* | Tuvs |
| Far | *Tāls* | Taals |
| Cheap | *Lēts* | Laets |
| Expensive | *Dārgs* | Dahrgs |
| Open | *Atvērts* | Atvaerts |
| Closed | *Slēgts* | Slaegts |
| Today | *Šodien* | Shwadien |
| Yesterday | *Vakar* | Vakar |
| Tomorrow | *Rīt* | Reet |
| How much is....? | *Cik tas maksā...?* | Tsik tas maksah? |
| What time is it? | *Cik ir pulkstenis?* | Tsik ir pulkstenis? |
| I don't understand | *Es nesaprotu* | Es nesaprwatoo |
| Do you speak English? | *Vai Jūs runājat angliski?* | Vai yoos roonahyat angliski? |
| One | *Viens* | Viens |
| Two | *Divi* | Divi |
| Three | *Trīs* | Trees |
| Four | *Četri* | Chetri |
| Five | *Pieci* | Pietsi |
| Six | *Seši* | Seshi |
| Seven | *Septiņi* | Septinyi |
| Eight | *Astoņi* | Astonyi |
| Nine | *Deviņi* | Devinyi |
| Ten | *Desmit* | Desmit |

## Emergency numbers

Police ☏02; Ambulance ☏03; Fire ☏01.

staying in a cheap hotel, don't leave valuables in your room. Muggings and casual violence are not unknown in Rīga; avoid parks and backstreets after dark and don't stagger home alone drunk. **Police** (*policija*) are unlikely to speak much, if any, English. Emergency **medical** care is free, though if you fall ill you'd do best to head for home: Latvian medical facilities tend to be run-down.

# Rīga

**RĪGA**, a major port and industrial centre with nearly a million inhabitants, is the undisputed Baltic metropolis. The city was founded by Albert von Buxhoeveden, a German canon who arrived in 1201 to convert the Latvian tribes to Christianity. Rīga was the main Hanseatic outpost in the region and urban life was from the outset controlled by German nobles and merchants even when wider political control passed to other powers, starting with the Polish-Lithuanian Commonwealth in the late sixteenth century. After a subsequent period of Swedish rule, Rīga became part of the Russian Empire in 1710, and during the second half of the nineteenth century developed into a major manufacturing centre. Badly damaged during World War I, the city made a swift economic recovery during the first period of Latvian independence and remained a major manufacturing centre after the country was swallowed up by the Soviet Union in 1940. Some Latvians hoped a German regime might return their independence and saw the Nazi invasion in June 1941 as a lesser evil to the Soviets. However, Rīga once again suffered under its oppressors: the local population was subdued, and its Jewish community was almost totally annihilated. Back under the Soviets, the influx of Russian immigrants reduced the Latvians to a minority in their own capital – even now thirty percent of the city's population is Russian. Denied citizenship unless they pass a Latvian language test, many Russians remain reluctant to assimilate and risk being left behind by a forward-looking, western-oriented Latvian state.

## Arrival, information and accommodation

Rīga's main **train station** (Centrālā Stacija) and **bus station** (Autoosta) are just south of Old Rīga and within easy walking distance of the centre. The ferry terminal (Jūras pasažieru stacija) is to the north of the centre. Trams #5, #7 or #9 run from the stop in front of the terminal on Ausekļa iela into the centre of town (two stops). There are **tourist offices** at the bus station (daily 9am–6pm, Sat–Sun 10am–5pm; ☎720 0555) and on Rātslaukums square in the centre of the Old Town (daily 10am–7pm; ☎704 4377, ⊕www.rigatourism.com). They have hotel lists and also sell the **Rīga Card** (8/12/16Ls for 24/48/72hr) which gives unlimited use of public transport and museum discounts, but it's worth doing a few sums to see whether it will save you any money on your planned itinerary. The excellent English-language guide *Rīga in Your Pocket* (1.20Ls; ⊕www.inyourpocket.com) is available from kiosks and bookshops. Both Old Rīga and the New Town are easily walkable. Outlying attractions are reached by bus, tram or trolleybus: flat-fare single-journey **tickets** cost 0.20Ls, bought from the conductor. **Taxis** should cost 0.30Ls per kilometre during the day and 0.40Ls between 10pm and 6am, but watch out for rip-offs or non-functioning meters. Rīga Taxi (☎800 1010) is usually reliable.

Rīga has no shortage of expensive **hotels** and its budget accommodation is increasing, but very slowly. Reserve in advance in summer. The Riga City **campsite**, behind the Ķīpsala exhibition centre at Ķīpsalas 8 (May–Sept only; ☎706 5000, ⊕www.bt1.lv), offers tent space for 8Ls per pitch, 5Ls per person. It's 2km northwest of the Old Town – catch bus #5, #7 or #21 from Valdemāra iela and get off once you've crossed the river.

### Hostels

**Argonaut** Kalēju 50 ☎614 7214, ⊕www.argonaut hostel.com. Frequently cramped and a bit rough round the edges, but friendly and decent. Dorms from 10Ls and a handful of 3- and 4-person rooms. **Elizabeth's Hostel** Elizabetes 101 ☎721 7891, ⊕www.youthhostel.lv. Immediately north of the stations, another basic but welcoming place with bunk-bed dorms (10Ls per person) and a handful of doubles (**2**).
**Posh Backpackers** Pupolu 5 ☎721 0917. Frumpily-decorated but otherwise clean place, situated in an old warehouse behind the Central Market. Dorms 8Ls, some doubles **2**

❶ & Art Nouveau buildings

**EATING & DRINKING**

| | | | |
|---|---|---|---|
| Alus Sēta | 6 | Paddy Whelan's | 18 |
| Dickens | 16 | Pelmeņi XL | 8 |
| Double Coffee | 10 | Pizza Lulū | 12 |
| Emihla Gustava Shokolahde | 11 | Rāma | 13 |
| Lido-Staburags | 21 | Rīgas balzams | 5 |
| Lido-Vērmanitis | 3 | Šalt 'n' Pepper | 22 |
| Lidojošā Varde | 1 | Šefpavārs Vilhelms | 7 |
| Mazie Balti Krekli | 20 | Sievasmates pirādziņi | 9 |
| Melnie Mūki | 14 | Skyline Bar | 4 |
| Olé | 19 | Spalvas pa gaisu | 17 |
| Orange Bar | 15 | Zelta Krogs | 2 |

**ACCOMMODATION**

| | |
|---|---|
| Argonaut | G |
| Elizabeth's Hostel | J |
| Homestay | A |
| Laine | D |
| Posh Backpackers | L |
| Radi un Draugi | F |
| Riga City Camping | E |
| Riga Old Town Hostel | H |
| Saulīte | I |
| Tia | B |
| Valdemārs | C |
| Viktorija | K |

0    100 m

17

LATVIA | Rīga

670

**Riga Old Town Hostel** Valņu 43 ☎722 3406, ⓦwww.rigaoldtownhostel.lv. Newest of the backpacker places, with clean bright dorms, central location and a lively bar. 10Ls.

## Hotels

**Homestay** Stokholmas 1 ☎755 3016, ⓦwww.homestay.lv. Welcoming family-run B&B offering 4 rooms in the leafy garden suburb of Mežaparks, some 8km northeast of the Old Town. Internet access available. Take tram 11 from Radio iela to Vizbijas prospekts. ❸

**Laine** Skolas 11 ☎728 8816, ⓦwww.laine.lv. A friendly and comfortable mid-range hotel, ten minutes' walk northeast of the old town, with en suites and shared facilities. ❸

**Radi un Draugi** Mārstaļu 1/3 ☎728 0200, ⓦwww.draugi.lv. One of the few affordable places in the old town, offering cosy en suites with TV. Very popular, so ring well in advance. ❺

**Saulīte** Merķeļa 12 ☎722 8219, ⓦwww.hotel-saulite.lv. Basic but friendly place opposite the train station, with some rooms prone to street noise. More expensive rooms come with modern shower/WC, cheaper ones are unrenovated. ❷–❹

**Tia** Valdemāra 63 ☎733 1407, ⓦwww.tia.lv. Recently renovated with satellite TV amongst other mod-cons but still essentially "no frills". ❻

**Valdemārs** Valdemāra 23 ☎733 4462, ⓦwww.valdemars.lv. A flaky facade but the rooms are spacious and clean, if a little uninspiring. A 10-min walk northeast of the centre. ❹

**Viktorija** Čaka 55 ☎701 4111, ⓦwww.hotel-viktorija.lv. Dowdy but comfortable en-suites a short bus ride or brisk walk from the train station. ❹

# The City

Vecrīga or **Old Rīga**, centred around Cathedral Square and neatly cut in two from east to west by Kaļķu iela, forms the city's nucleus and is home to most of its historic buildings. To the east Old Rīga is bordered by Bastejkalns Park, beyond which lies the **New Town**, the nineteenth- and early twentieth-century extension of the city which contains some remarkable Jugendstil architecture.

## Old Rīga

Cathedral Square (Doma laukums) is edged by government offices and a sprinkling of cafés, and is dominated by the red-brick **Rīga Cathedral** (Tues–Fri 1–5pm, Sat 10am–2pm; Sun services only; 0.50Ls), established in 1211, a towering agglomeration of Romanesque, Gothic and Baroque architecture. The interior is relatively unadorned, the most eye-catching features being a florid pulpit from 1641 and a magnificent nineteenth-century organ with 6768 pipes. The east wing of the cathedral houses the **Rīga Museum of History and Navigation** (Rīgas vēstures un kuģniecības muzejs; Palasta 4; May–Sept Wed–Sun 10am–5pm, Oct–April Wed–Sun 11am–5pm; 1Ls), an absorbing collection of nautical and archeological finds.

From Cathedral Square, Pils iela runs down to leafy **Castle Square** (Pils laukums) and the nondescript **Rīga Castle** (Rīgas pils), built in 1515 and now home to both the Latvian president and the **Latvian History Museum** (Latvijas vēstures muzejs; Wed–Sun 11am–5pm; 1Ls), where you'll find an attractive display of iron-age artefacts and nineteenth-century folk costume. Stroll down Mazā Pils iela from Pils laukums, and you'll see the **Three Brothers** (Trīs brāli), three charming medieval houses, one of which is thought to be the oldest house in Latvia, dating from the fifteenth century. Further north up Jēkaba, at no. 11 is Latvia's **Parliament** (Saeima), housed in an unspectacular late nineteenth-century Renaissance-style building. Nearby on Torņa iela you'll find the seventeenth-century **Swedish Gate** (Zviedru vārti), built – not surprisingly – when Rīga was ruled by the Swedes, and which is the sole surviving city gate. At the end of Torņa iela is the **Powder Tower** (Pulvertornis), a vast, fourteenth-century bastion which is today home to the **Museum Of War** (Wed–Sun 10am–5pm; 0.50Ls), a well-presented account of the country's turbulent history. This tidy, serene little street is also perfect for a quick alfresco drink in one of its inviting cafés.

**Bastion Hill** (Bastejkalns) – the park that slopes down to the city canal on the eastern edge of Old Rīga – is a reminder of Rīga's more recent history: on

January 20, 1991, four people were killed here by sniper fire as Soviet OMON troops stormed the Latvian Ministry of the Interior on nearby Raiņa bulvaris during an attempted crackdown on Latvia's independence drive. Stones bearing the names of the victims mark where they fell near the Bastejas bulvaris entrance. From the Swedish Gate Meistaru iela runs down to the **Great Guild Hall** (Lielā Ģilde) at Amatu 6, once the centre of commercial life in Hanseatic Rīga. Though from the fourteenth century, the building owes its present neo-Gothic appearance to a nineteenth-century facelift and now houses the Latvia State Philharmonic (details of concerts can be found at ⓦwww.music.lv/en). Follow the urban throng west along Kaļķu iela and turn left into Skārņu iela to find **St Peter's Church** (Pēterbaznīca; Tues–Sun 10am–5.15pm), a large red-brick structure with a graceful three-tiered spire and dedicated to the city's patron saint. Climb the tower (same times; 1.60Ls) for panoramic views of the city.

West of St Peter's Church, the Town Hall Square (Ratslaukums) is dominated by the **House of the Blackheads** (Melngalvju nams; Tues–Sun 10am–5pm; 1Ls), a masterpiece of red-brick Gothic architecture which once served as the boozy headquarters of Rīga's bachelor merchants. Almost totally destroyed in 1941, it was lovingly reconstructed in time for the 800th anniversary of Rīga's foundation in 2001. In the southwestern corner of the square, an ugly concrete structure built to house a communist history museum now accommodates the **Occupation Museum of Latvia** (Latvijas okupācijas muzejs; May–Sept daily 11am–5pm, Oct–April Tues–Sun 11am–5pm; donations; ⓦwww.occupationmuseum.lv), a hugely rewarding collection devoted to Latvia's occupation by the Nazis and Soviets. Well presented and with some English-language texts, the display is an excellent introduction to Latvian contemporary history. Nearby at Grēcinieku 18 is **Menzendorff's House** (Mencendorfa nams; Wed–Sun 10am–5pm; 1.20Ls), an impeccably restored late-seventeenth-century merchant's house.

### The New Town and the Central Market

The boulevards of the **New Town** bear witness to a period of rapid urban expansion that began in 1857 and lasted right up until World War I. As Rīga grew into a major industrial centre, four- and five-storey apartment buildings – many of them decorated with extravagant Jugendstil motifs – were erected to house the expanding middle class. As you head east out along Kaļķu, which widens out and becomes Brīvības bulvāris, the modernist **Freedom Monument** (Brīvības piem-ineklis) dominates the view. This stylized female figure, placed here in 1935 and known as "Milda", holds aloft three stars symbolizing the three regions of Latvia. Incredibly, the monument survived the Soviet era, and nowadays two soldiers stand guard here in symbolic protection of Latvia's independence.

Running north from Brīvības bulvāris to the east of the Freedom Monument is the formal **Esplanade Park** with the **Cathedral of Christ's Nativity** (Kristus dzimsanas katedrāle) just inside its grounds. This late nineteenth-century mock-Byzantine creation was returned to the city's Orthodox community after serving as a planetarium during the Soviet period. At the far end of the park is the **State Museum of Latvian Art** (Valsts mākslas muzejs), Valdemāra iela 10 (Mon & Fri–Sun 11am–5pm, Thurs 11am–7pm; 1.20Ls), housed in a grandiose Neoclassical building. Among the numerous nineteenth- and twentieth-century Latvian works inside, look out for the post-impressionist landscapes of Vilhems Purvītis and the agitprop photo-montages of Bolshevik sympathiser Gustavs Klucis.

Jugendstil architecture – florid stucco swirls surrounding doorways, stylized human faces branded into facades, and towers fancifully placed on top of build-ings – can be seen on virtually every street of the New Town. One of the most famous examples is at **Elizabetes 10a and 10b**, an apartment building designed by Mikhail Eisenstein, the father of film director Sergei. Adorned with plaster flourishes and gargoyles, it is topped by two vast impassive faces. An even more impressive group of his buildings can be seen a block north of here on **Alberta iela** on the even numbered side of the street. To get an idea of what these fin-de-siècle homes were like on the inside, visit the **Janis Rosentāls Museum** at Alberta 12 (Wed–Sun 11am–6pm; 0.60Ls), occupying the flat where Latvia's most famous artist lived in the years prior to World War I.

On the southeastern side of Old Rīga, just beyond the bus and train stations, lies the clamour of the **Central Market** (Centrālais tirgus) in a row of 1930s former Zeppelin hangars, where you can find everything from farm produce to fake designer watches. Beware of pickpockets here.

Heading southeast of the market along Gogoļa iela or Prāgas iela you'll some come face to face with the glowering **Academy of Sciences** (Zinātņu Akadēmija), a ruddy-brown slab of 1950s Soviet Baroque, further examples of which can be found in Moscow and Warsaw.

# Eating, drinking and nightlife

Many bars and cafés do cheap and filling **food** and there are also plenty of inexpensive fast-food places, some of which are part of local chains providing Latvian fare. For **drinking**, the Old Town offers innumerable opportunities for bar hopping, with a multiplicity of supping venues (many of which serve decent food) filling up with fun-seeking locals seven nights a week.

## Cafés and snack bars

**Double Coffee** Raiņa 25. Best of the home-grown coffee chains. Sushi (for less than 2Ls) and cocktails alongside cappuccino on the menu. Mon–Thurs 8am–midnight, Fri–Sat 8am–2am, Sun 11am–midnight.

**Emihla Gustava Shokolahde** Marijas 13/VI (Inside the Berga bazārs arcade). The smell of home-made chocolate will make you swoon. Come to with a stiff espresso. Mon–Sat 10am–10pm, Sun 10am–8pm.

**Lido–Staburags** Čaka 55. Big portions for 3Ls. Traditional Latvian food served amid old-fashioned oak rooms. Daily noon–midnight.

**Lido–Vērmanītis** Elizabetes 65. All manner of tasty Baltic meat-and-potato dishes, plus salads and fruit bars on the ground floor, pizza and fast food in the cellar. Daily 8am–11pm.

**Olé** Audēju 1. Offers generous servings at breakfast and dinner, for 3Ls or less, from an eclectic menu despite its Spanish name. 7.30am–5pm, closed Sat & Sun.

**Pelmeņi XL** Kaļķu 7. Popular fast-food joint on the old town's main street offering Slavic ravioli: blobs of dough (*pelmeņi*) filled with meat or cheese. Daily 9am–4am.

**Pizza Lulū** Ģertrūdes 27. Fashionable little pizzeria with reasonable prices. 24hr.

**Šefpavārs Vilhelms** Skūņu 6. Self-service, create-your-own-pancake place near Cathedral Square. Mon–Thurs 9am–10pm, Fri 9am–11pm, Sat 10am–11pm, Sun 10am–10pm.

**Sievasmātes Pīrādziņi** Kaļķu 10. Cheap and cheerful canteen specializing in traditional Latvian pasties stuffed with various fillings. Closes 9pm.

## Restaurants

**Lidojošā Varde** Elizabetes 31a. The name means "The Flying Frog" but you can choose chicken wings and burgers from the menu. Courses from around 3Ls. Daily 10am–midnight.

**Mazie Balti Krekli** Kalēju 54. Relaxing bar-restaurant stuffed with Latvian pop-rock memorabilia. Value-for-money pork-and-potatoes fare. 11am–11pm.

**Melnie Mūki** Jāņa sūta 1. High class international cuisine at affordable prices, with the medieval exposed-brick interior providing plenty of atmosphere. Daily noon–2am.

**Rāma** Barona 56. Hare-Krishna-run veggie place in the New Town with a tasty range of dirt-cheap Asian dishes. One of the few places in the city catering for vegans. Daily 9am–9pm.

**Salt 'n' Pepper** 13. Janvāra 33. Laid-back bar-restaurant with a bit of everything: hearty breakfasts, lunchtime soups and an international array of main meals. Mon–Fri 8am–midnight, Sat–Sun 9am–midnight.

**Zelta Krogs** Citadeles 12. Mixed European-Latvian cuisine in a bright, relaxing spot just north of the Old Town. Plenty of salads, pasta and vegetarian pancakes, all at reasonable prices. Closes 10pm.

## Bars

**Alus Sēta** Tirgoņu iela 6. Sample good, cheap Latvian ales accompanied by the national beer-snack – peas (*zirņi*) sprinkled with bacon bits. Outdoor seating when warm. Daily 11am–1am.

**Dickens** Grēcinieku 11. Brit-pub with a wide range of beers. The cosiest place to watch a match

– from gridiron to the Premier League. Sun–Thurs
11am–1am, Fri & Sat 11am–3am.
**Orange Bar** Jāṇa sēta 5. Post-industrial decor,
alternative sounds, a mildly arty crowd and cheap
bar food. Sun–Thurs noon–1am, Fri 11am–5am,
Sat noon–5am.
**Paddy Whelan's** Grēcinieku 4. Big, lively Irish
pub, popular with young locals and expats alike.
Sun–Thurs noon–midnight, Fri–Sat noon–2am.
**Rīgas Balzams** Torņa 4. Convivial cellar bar
serving up Rīga's favourite firewater – the
black, syrupy *balzams* – either on its own or in
a mind-boggling number of mixer combinations.
Sun–Thurs 9am–midnight, Fri–Sat 9am–1am.
**Skyline Bar** Elizabetes 55. Behold Rīga's splendour from a window-side seat in the bar on the
26th floor of the *Reval Hotel Latvija*. A must. Open
daily 3pm-2am.
**Spalvas pa gaisu** Grēcinieku 8. Snazzy and spacious café-bar with loungey corners, loud music
and good cocktails. Sun–Tues 11am–midnight,
Wed–Thurs 11am–2am, Fri–Sat 11am–5am.

### Live music and clubs
**Pulkvedim Neviens Neraksta** Peldu 26/28. The
hippest club in Rīga: edgy music and an easygoing, fun-seeking clientele. Mon–Thurs noon–3am,
Fri & Sat noon–5am, Sun 4pm–1am.

**Bites Blūzs Klubs** Dzirnavu 34a. Laid-back, unpretentious blues pub with regular gigs and a decent
food menu. Mon–Thurs till 1am, Fri & Sat till 2am.
**Četri Balti Krekli** Vecpilsētas 12. Large upmarket
cellar bar known for its Latvian-only music policy.
Regular gigs by domestic rock-pop acts. No train-
ers. Daily noon–5am.
**Club Essential** Skolas 2. Relatively new in town.
Plays adventurous music and provides chill-out
zone. Thurs–Sun 10pm–6am.
**Depo** Vaļņu 32. Post-industrial cellar space with
alternative DJ nights and live bands. Functions
as a laid-back café during the day. Mon–Thurs
9pm–3am, Fri & Sat 9pm–5am.
**PuPu Lounge** Mārstaļu 14. Cheeky club where
waitresses show off their cleavages. On two
levels. Sun–Wed noon–2am, Thurs–Sat noon–6am.
**Purvs** Matīsa 60. Stylish gay club whose name
means "Swamp". Erotic performances, sometimes
with audience participation. Wed–Sun 8pm till
late; 1–3Ls.
**Roxy** Kaļķu 24. Popular with Russian speakers,
expats and beautiful young things. Bar, billiards
and dancing. Daily 9pm–6am; 5Ls.
**XXL** Kalniņa 4. Gay club and restaurant attracting a mixed, dance-oriented crowd. Good food
and wild decor. Daily 6pm–7am; cover charge
Tues–Sat 1–5Ls.

## Listings

**Bike rental** Gandrs, Kalnciema 28 ☏761 4775.
**Embassies** Canada, Baznīcas 20/22 ☏781 3945;
UK, Alunāna 5 ☏777 4700; US, Raiņa bulvaris 7
☏703 6200.
**Exchange** Marika: Basteja 14, Brīvības 30, Marijas
5, Merķeļa 10 (all 24hr).
**Hospital** Ars, Skolas 5 ☏720 1001. Some
English-speaking doctors.
**Internet access** Interneta Planeta Kafe, Vaļņu iela
41 (24hr); Internet Klubs, Kalku 10 (24hr).

**Left luggage** At the bus station (daily 6.30am–
11pm). Lockers at the left-luggage office (Rokas
Bagāias) in the train station basement (0.50–1Ls
per day, 4.30am–midnight).
**Pharmacy** Rudens aptieka, Ģertrūdes 105 ☏724
4322 (24hr).
**Post office** Brīvības bulvāris 19 (Mon–Fri
7am–10pm, Sat & Sun 8am–8pm).

## Day-trips from Rīga

**JŪRMALA** or "Seashore" is the collective name for a string of small seaside
resorts that line the Baltic coast for about 20km west of Rīga. Originally favoured
by the tsarist nobility, it became the haunt of Latvian intellectuals between the
wars. Today, its sandy beaches backed by dunes and pine woods seethe with
people at weekends and on public holidays. Trains for Jūrmala leave the suburban
terminus of Rīga's central station from platforms 3 and 4; **Majori**, about 10km
beyond Rīga city limits, is the main stop, but you might have to ask someone
where to get off because the stations are badly signposted. Here you'll find a
number of restaurants and cafés along Jomas iela, the pedestrianized main street
running east from the station square, including the Internet café Datorclubs at no.
62. Head north from here to Jūras iela, from where a few paths lead to the beach.

The **tourist office**, Lienes 5 (June–Aug daily 11am–9pm; Sept–May Mon–Fri 9am–5pm; ☏714 7900, ⊛www.jurmala.lv), will fix you up with a **private room** or B&B (❷–❸). The *Nemo* **campsite**, five stops further up the line from Majori at Vaivari (☏773 2350, ⊛www.nemo.lv), enjoys a pleasant middle-of-the-forest location just behind the beach.

The concentration camp at **SALASPILS**, 22km southeast of Rīga, is where most of Rīga's Jewish population perished during World War II. Around one hundred thousand people died here, including Jews from other countries, who had been herded into the Rīga Ghetto after most of the indigenous Jewish population had been wiped out. Today the site is marked by monumental sculptures and a memorial, with the former locations of the barrack buildings outlined by white stones. To get here take a suburban train from Rīga central station in the direction of Ogre and alight at Dārziņi station (little more than a halt in the middle of a forest, it's easy to miss) from where a clearly signposted path leads to the memorial, a walk of about fifteen minutes.

**RUNDĀLE PALACE** or Rundāles Pils (daily 10am–5/6pm; 1.50Ls), 77km south of Rīga, is one of the architectural wonders of Latvia. This 138-room Baroque palace, built in two phases during the 1730s and 1760s, was designed by Bartolomeo Rastrelli, the architect who created the Winter Palace in St Petersburg. It was privately owned until 1920 when it fell into disrepair, but meticulous restoration, begun in 1973, has largely returned it to its former glory. To get here take the bus to **Bauska** (⊛www.bauska.lv) and then a local service to Pilsrundāle, where the palace stands on the other side of the hedge from the bus stop. Should you want to stay overnight, try the plain but comfortable *Viesnīca Bauska*, Slimnīcas 7, Bauska (☏392 4705; ❸), by the bus station.

## Sigulda and Cēsis

**SIGULDA**, dotted with parks and clustered above the southern bank of the River Gauja around 50km northeast of Raga, is **the Gauja National Park**'s main centre and a good jumping-off point for exploring the rest of the Gauja Valley. From the train station Raiņa iela runs north into town, passing the bus station on the way. After about 800m a right turn into Baznaca iela brings you to **Sigulda Church** (Siguldas Baznaca), built over seven hundred years ago, though much altered since. A left turn after the church leads, by way of **Sigulda New Castle** (Siguldas Jaunā Pils), a nineteenth-century manor house masquerading as a medieval castle, to the ruins of **Sigulda Castle** (Siguldas Pilsdrupas), a former stronghold of the German crusading order known as Knights of the Sword. From here you can admire **Turaida Castle** (Turaidas Pils), perched on a bluff 3km away. Although more romantic from a distance you can reach the castle by bus (for Turaida or Krimulda) from Sigulda bus station. The 45-minute walk from Sigulda to Turaida begins by taking J. Poruka iela northwest from Sigulda church; descend the wooden staircase at the end to the bridge across the Gauja river and on the far side of the bridge an asphalt path slopes down to the left, and runs past several sandstone caves before rejoining the main road just short of Turaida itself. Built on the site of an earlier stronghold by the bishop of Raga in 1214, Turaida Castle was destroyed when lightning hit its gunpowder magazine in the eighteenth century. These days it houses a local history **museum** (Tues–Sun 10am–5/6pm; 0.80Ls) and there's a pleasant café where you can rest your legs. Just before the castle is the eighteenth-century **Turaidas Church** (Turaidas Baznacas), an appealing little wooden church with a Baroque tower that's one of the best-preserved examples of Latvian native architecture in the country. Sigulda is also the centre for a range of activities from bobsledding and bungy jumping to bike rental – pick up information from the Sigulda **tourist office**, just west of the train and bus stations at Valdemāra 1a (Mon–Fri 8am–7pm, Sat 9am–2pm; ☏797 1335, ⊛www.sigulda.lv) who can also book you into **private rooms** for 7Ls per person. The Siguldas Pludmale **campsite** (May–Sept only; ☏924 4948, ⊛www.makars.lv; 1Ls per person, 1Ls per pitch) occupies a shady riverside spot downhill from the town centre to the north.

The well-preserved little town of **CĒSIS**, 35km northeast of Sigulda, is considered by many Latvians to have an atmosphere as close to that of prewar small-town Latvia as it's possible to get. From the **train** and **bus** stations walk down Raunas iela to Vienības Laukums, the town's main square. The attractive but run-down old town – a few narrow streets lined with flaking wooden buildings – lies to the south of here. On Rīgas iela just south of the square the remains of the old town gates have been excavated. Nearby, on Skolas iela, is the thirteenth-century **St John's Church** (Svēta Jāņa Baznīca), which contains the tombs of several masters of the Livonian order. East of the square are the remains of **Cēsis Castle** (Cēsu Pils) founded by the Knights of the Sword in 1209. If you decide to stay, the Cēsis **Tourist Information Centre** at Pils laukums 1 (Sept 16–May 14 Mon–Fri 9am–6pm; May 15–Sept 15 Mon–Fri 9am–6pm; Sat 10am–5pm; ☏412 1815, ⓦwww.tourism.cesis.lv) will sort you out with **accommodation**.

# Travel details

## Trains

**Rīga** to: Majori-Jūrmala (every 30min; 40min); Moscow, Russia (1 daily; 16hr); Sigulda (6 daily; 1hr); St Petersburg, Russia (1 daily; 12hr).

## Buses

**Rīga** to: Bauska (every 30min; 1hr 10min–1hr 30min); Cēsis (20 daily; 2hr); Kaunas, Lithuania (3 daily; 4hr 30min); Klaipēda, Lithuania (2 daily; 5hr); Pärnu, Estonia (8 daily; 3hr 30min); Sigulda (hourly; 1hr); Tallinn, Estonia (8 daily; 5hr 30min); Tartu, Estonia (1 daily; 5hr); Vilnius, Lithuania (5 daily; 6hr).
**Sigulda** to: Turaida (12 daily; 10min).

# Lithuania

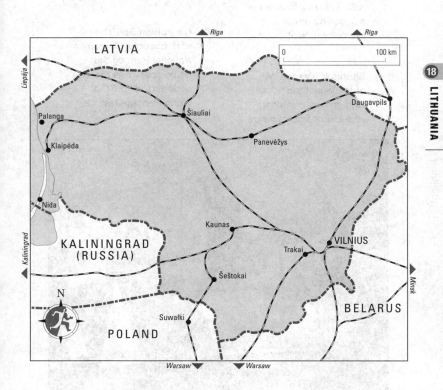

# Lithuania highlights

* **St Anne's church, Vilnius** Napoleon wanted to take this little late-Gothic masterpiece home to Paris. See p.684

* **Genocide museum, Vilnius** In the former KGB HQ, this museum is a shocking reminder of man's inhumanity. See p.686

* **Skonis ir Kvapas, Vilnius** Elegant tea house with gorgeous interiors and an impressive range of teas and coffees. See p.687

* **Trakai** A fairy-tale medieval castle sitting on its own little island amongst lush green countryside a little west of Vilnius. See p.688

* **Couronian Spit** The wild, beautiful Couronian National Park on the Baltic coast was recently added to UNESCO's World Heritage List. See p.690

△ Trakai Castle

# Introduction and basics

Unlike its Baltic neighbours, Lithuania was once a major European power, carving out an extensive east-European empire in the fourteenth century. In 1569, it united with Poland, but the Great Northern War of 1700–21, in which Poland-Lithuania, Russia and Sweden battled for control of the Baltics, left the country devastated. By the end of the eighteenth century most of Lithuania had fallen into Russian hands, but Russia's collapse in World War I enabled the Lithuanians to re-establish their independence – until effective annexation by the USSR in 1940. The country declared its independence on March 11, 1990, way ahead of the other Baltic States.

Travel in Lithuania presents no real hardships, and even in well-trodden destinations the volume of visitors is low, leaving you with the feeling that there's still much to discover here. **Vilnius**, with its Baroque old town, is the most architecturally beautiful of the Baltic capitals, while the second city, **Kaunas**, also has an attractive centre and a couple of unique museums, along with a handful of surprisingly good restaurants and bars. The port city of **Klaipėda** is a convenient stopping-off point en route to the resorts of **Neringa**, a unique spit of sand dunes and forest that shields Lithuania from the Baltic.

## Information & maps

Most major towns have **tourist offices** (ⓦ www.tourism.lt), often offering accommodation listings and events calendars in English. The **In Your Pocket** guides to Vilnius, Kaunas and Klaipėda (available from bookshops, newsstands, tourist offices and some hotels; ⓦ www.inyourpocket.com; 5–8Lt) are indispensable sources of practical information. Regional **maps** and detailed street plans of Vilnius are available in bookshops and kiosks.

## Money and banks

Lithuania's currency is the **litas** (usually abbreviated to Lt), which is divided into 100 centai. Coins come as 0.01, 0.02, 0.05, 0.10, 0.20, 0.50, 1, 2 and 5Lt, with notes of 10, 20, 50, 100 and 200Lt. The litas is pegged to the euro (€1 = 3.45Lt). **Bank** (*bankas*) opening hours vary, though branches of the Vilniaus Bankas usually open Mon–Fri 8am–3/4pm. They generally give advances on Visa/MasterCard/AmEx cards and cash travellers' cheques (commission 2–3 percent). Outside banking hours, find an exchange office (*valiutos keitykla*). There are ATMs in all major towns and credit cards are widely accepted.

## Communications

In major towns, **post offices** (*paštas*) are open Mon–Fri 8am–6pm, Sat 8am–3pm; in smaller places hours are more restricted. Stamps are also available at some kiosks and tourist offices. Public phones operate with cards (*telefono kortelė*; 9Lt, 13Lt, 16Lt and 30Lt) from post offices and kiosks. To make a long-distance call, dial ☏8 before the area code. When calling Lithuania from

## Lithuania on the net

ⓦ **www.tourism.lt** National tourist board site with useful information.
ⓦ **www.tourism.vilnius.lt** Vilnius tourist information.
ⓦ **www.search.lt** Lithuanian search engine.
ⓦ **www.muziejai.lt** Portal of Lithuanian museums.
ⓦ **www.lietuva.lt** General information about the country.

abroad, omit the initial 8. For international calls, dial ⊕8, wait for the tone, then dial 10, then the country code as usual. There's a good choice of **Internet** cafés in Vilnius and a few in Kaunas.

# Getting around

Buses are slightly quicker and slightly more expensive than trains. You should buy **train** tickets in advance – stations have separate windows for long-distance and suburban (*priemiestinis* or *vietinis*) trains. Long-distance services are divided into "passenger" (*keleivinis traukinys*) and "fast" (*greitas*); the latter usually require a reservation. On time-table boards, look for *išvyksta* (departure) or *atvyksta* (arrival).

It's best to buy long-distance **bus** tickets in advance, and opt for an express (*ekspresas*), to avoid frequent stops. You can also pay for your ticket on board, although this doesn't guarantee you a seat. Normally

## Lithuanian

|  | Lithuanian | Pronunciation |
|---|---|---|
| **Yes** | *Taip* | Tape |
| **No** | *Ne* | Ne |
| **Please** | *Prašau* | Prash**au** |
| **Thank you** | *Ačiu* | **Ach**oo |
| **Hello/Good day** | *Labas* | **Lab**ass |
| **Goodbye** | *Viso gero* | Viso gero |
| **Excuse me** | *Atsiprašau* | Atsiprash**au** |
| **Where?** | *Kur?* | Kur? |
| **Good** | *Geras* | Gerass |
| **Bad** | *Blogas* | Blogass |
| **Near** | *Artimas* | Artimass |
| **Far** | *Tolimas* | Tolimass |
| **Cheap** | *Pigus* | Piguss |
| **Expensive** | *Brangus* | Branguss |
| **Open** | *Atidarytas* | Atidaritass |
| **Closed** | *Uždarytas* | Uzhdaritass |
| **Today** | *Šiandien* | Shyandyen |
| **Yesterday** | *Vakar* | Vakar |
| **Tomorrow** | *Rytdiena* | Ritdyena |
| **How much is....?** | *Kiek kainuoja ...?* | Kyek kainwoya? |
| **What time is it?** | *Kiek valandū?* | Kyek valandoo? |
| **I don't understand** | *Nesuprantu* | Nessuprantu |
| **Do you speak English?** | *Ar jūs kalbate angliškai?* | Ar yoos kalbate anglishkay? |
| **One** | *Vienas* | Vyenass |
| **Two** | *Du/dvi* | Du/Dvee |
| **Three** | *Trys* | Triss |
| **Four** | *Keturi* | Keturee |
| **Five** | *Penki* | Penkee |
| **Six** | *Šeši* | Sheshee |
| **Seven** | *Septyni* | Septinee |
| **Eight** | *Aštuoni* | Ashtuonee |
| **Nine** | *Devyni* | Devinee |
| **Ten** | *Dešimt* | Deshimt |

luggage is taken on board, though large bags may have to go in the luggage compartment for a small charge. Buses are also useful for travelling to Lithuania's Baltic neighbours.

# Accommodation

The best way to keep **accommodation** costs down is by staying in **private rooms**, as budget hotels tend to be pretty grim. The most reliable agency is Litinterp, with offices in Vilnius, Klaipėda and Kaunas. Spartan double rooms in Soviet-era budget hotels cost as little as 70Lt. Smaller, mid-range places charge upwards of 200Lt a double. In Vilnius and Kaunas you'll find many international business hotels charging 400Lt and upwards.

There are a few **hostels**, charging 30–35Lt per night. Space is limited and it's best to ring individual establishments in advance. There's a lot of **campsites** in rural areas but few near major cities; those that do exist charge around 10Lt per person, 10–15Lt per tent.

# Food and drink

Lithuanian **cuisine** is based on traditional peasant dishes, with pork, potatoes and sour cream featuring heavily in most main meals. Typical **starters** include marinated mushrooms (*marinuoti grybai*), herring (*silkė*) and smoked sausage (*rukyta dešra*) along with cold beetroot soup (*šaltibarščiai*). Most common of the potato-based dishes is *cepelinai*, or zeppelins – cylindrical potato dumplings stuffed with meat, mushrooms or cheese. Also popular are potato pancakes (*bulviniai blynai*), and cabbage leaves stuffed with minced meat (*balandėliai* or "pigeons"). **Desserts** include stewed fruit (*kompotas*), sweet fruit sauce (*kisielius*), and innumerable varieties of pancakes (*blynai*, *blyneliai*

or *lietiniai* are synonyms for more or less the same thing). Western fast food is making inroads, and Vilnius has a sprinkling of Chinese places. It's possible to find meat-free options on menus. Most cafés and bars do reasonably priced food.

**Beer** (*alus*) is popular, while the leading local firewaters are Starka, Trejos devynerios and Medžiotojū – invigorating spirits flavoured with herbs. Lively **bars** sprout up daily in Vilnius and Kaunas. Many ape American or Irish models, although there are also plenty of folksy Lithuanian places, while cafés (*kavinė*) come in all shapes and sizes. **Coffee** (*kava*) and tea (*arbata*) are usually served black.

# Opening hours and public holidays

**Opening hours** for shops are 9/10am–6/7pm. Outside Vilnius, some places take an hour off for lunch; most usually close on Sun (though some food shops stay open). Most shops and all banks will be closed on the following **public holidays**: Jan 1, Feb 16, March 11, Easter Sun, Easter Mon, May 1, July 6, Aug 15, Nov 1, Dec 25 & 26.

# Emergencies

You're unlikely to meet trouble; car theft and late-night mugging are the most common crimes. The cash-starved **police** expect to be taken seriously – be polite if you have dealings with them. A few of the younger ones may speak a little English. Emergency **health care** is free but if you get seriously ill, head home.

# Vilnius

"Narrow cobblestone streets and an orgy of Baroque: almost like a Jesuit city somewhere in the middle of Latin America," wrote the author Czesław Miłosz of prewar **VILNIUS**. Soviet-era satellite suburbs aside, it's a description which still rings true today. Despite being the capital of the medieval Lithuanian state, Vilnius was occupied by Poland between the wars, and was inhabited mainly by Poles and Jews, who played such a prominent role in the city's life that it was known as the "Northern Jerusalem". Vilnius is still a cosmopolitan place – around twenty percent of its population is Polish and another twenty percent is Russian – though with just 543,000 inhabitants it has an almost village-like atmosphere, making it an easy place to get to know.

## Arrival, information and accommodation

The main **train station** is at Geležinkelio 16, just south of the Old Town, and the main **bus station** is just across the road. There are exchange facilities at both. Trolleybus #2 takes you from the train station to the main Cathedral Square, or it's a fifteen-minute walk into the Old Town. The **tourist offices** at Vilniaus 22 (Mon–Fri 9am–6pm; ☎5/262 9660, ✉tic@vilnius.lt), the railway station and the town hall (both Mon–Fri 9am–6pm, Sat & Sun 10am–4pm) offer advice on hotels and can also book you into private rooms. The best source of listings and yellow pages-style information is the excellent *Vilnius in Your Pocket* city guide (🌐www.inyourpocket.com), costing 5Lt from newspaper kiosks. Vilnius is well served by **public transport** with buses and trolleybuses covering most of the city. Tickets cost 0.80Lt from newspaper kiosks or 1Lt from the driver; validate your ticket by punching it in the machine on board. Alternatively, hail a minibus at any bus stop in the direction you're going, pay the driver 2Lt and you'll be dropped off at the stop you require. **Taxi** prices are usually reasonable and fares should cost no more than around 2–3Lt per kilometre. Phoning for a taxi is one way of ensuring a fair rate; try Vilnius Taxi (☎5/212 8888).

Best-value accommodation is in **private rooms**. Litinterp, Bernardinū 7/2 (Mon–Fri 8.30am–5.30pm, Sat 9.30am–3pm; ☎5/212 3850, 🌐www.litinterp.lt), is the longest-established agency, offering rooms in the Old Town – either with a host family or in *Litinterp*, the agency's own self-contained guest house – with singles from 80Lt and doubles from 140Lt. Similar deals are offered by the Vilnius tourist offices.

## Hostels

**Filaretai** Filaretū 17 ☎5/215 4627. HI-affiliated hostel, with kitchen, common room and washing machine. Fifteen minutes' walk east of the Old Town, or bus #34 from the train station. 24–40Lt.

**JNN Hostel** Konstitucijos 25 ☎5/272 2270, 🌐www.jnn.lt. Neat, en-suite triples and quads in a concrete building north of the river. Take bus #2 from the airport or trolleybus #5 from the train station to žaliasis Tiltas followed by bus #2 or #46. 80–190Lt.

**Old Town Hostel** Aušros Vartū 20–10 ☎5/262 5357, ✉oldtownhostel@lithuanianhostels.com. Cramped, rowdy, but comfortable HI-affiliated hostel near the train and bus stations; reservations essential. 32Lt.

## Hotels

**Apia** Šv Ignoto 12 ☎5/212 3426, 🌐www.apia.lt.

Friendly, twelve-room guest house in superb Old Town location. **❻**

**Domus Maria** Aušros Vartū 12 ☎5/264 4880, 🌐http://domusmaria.vilnensis.lt. Central guest house in a former monastery. Some of the bright, comfortable rooms look out on the Gate of Dawn. **❺**

**Ecotel** Slucko 8 ☎5/210 2700, 🌐www.ecotel.lt. Minimally furnished but soothing en-suites in a new hotel just north of the river. **❹**

**Mikotel** Pylimo 63 ☎5/260 9626, 🌐www.mikotel.lt. Small hotel a few steps away from the train and bus stations, with pristine, modern en-suites and quirky decor. **❹**

**Žemaitēs** Žemaitēs 15 ☎5/213 5453, 🌐www.hotelzemaites.lt. Modern block 2km southwest of the centre offering sparsely furnished but cosy rooms with TV. Trolleybus #15 or #16 from the train and bus stations. **❺**

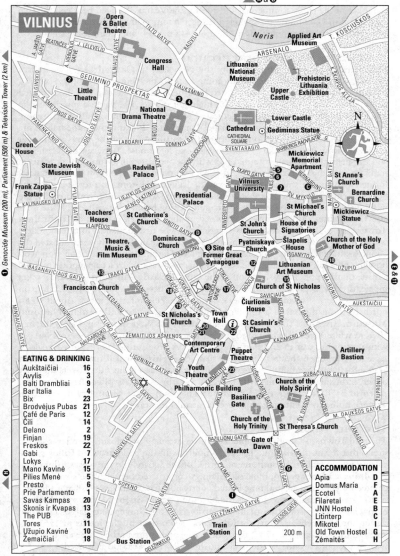

VILNIUS

Opera & Ballet Theatre

Neris    Applied Art Museum

Congress Hall

ARSENALO

Lithuanian National Museum

Upper Castle    Prehistoric Lithuania Exhibition

Little Theatre

GEDIMINO PROSPEKTAS

National Drama Theatre

Cathedral    Lower Castle
CATHEDRAL SQUARE    Gediminas Statue

Green House

State Jewish Museum

Radvila Palace

Vilnius University

Mickiewicz Memorial Apartment

St Anne's Church

Bernardine Church

Frank Zappa Statue

Presidential Palace

Mickiewicz Statue

Teachers' House

St Catherine's Church

St Michael's Church

St John's Church

House of the Signatories

Church of the Holy Mother of God

Theatre, Music & Film Museum

Dominican Church

Site of Former Great Synagogue

Pyatniskaya Church

Šlapelis House

UŽUPIO

Franciscan Church

Lithuanian Art Museum

Church of St Nicholas

Čiurlionis House

St Nicholas's Church

Town Hall

St Casimir's Church

Artillery Bastion

Contemporary Art Centre

Puppet Theatre

Youth Theatre

Philharmonic Building

Basilian Gate

Church of the Holy Spirit

Church of the Holy Trinity    St Theresa's Church

Gate of Dawn

Market

Train Station

Bus Station

**EATING & DRINKING**

| Aukštaičiai | 16 |
| Avylis | 3 |
| Balti Drambliai | 9 |
| Bar Italia | 4 |
| Bix | 23 |
| Brodvėjus Pubas | 21 |
| Café de Paris | 12 |
| Čili | 14 |
| Delano | 2 |
| Finjan | 19 |
| Freskos | 22 |
| Gabi | 7 |
| Lokys | 17 |
| Mano Kavinė | 15 |
| Pilies Menė | 5 |
| Presto | 6 |
| Prie Parlamento | 1 |
| Savas Kampas | 20 |
| Skonis ir Kvapas | 13 |
| The PUB | 8 |
| Tores | 11 |
| Užupio Kavinė | 10 |
| Žemaičiai | 18 |

**ACCOMMODATION**

| Apia | D |
| Domus Maria | F |
| Ecotel | A |
| Filaretai | E |
| JNN Hostel | B |
| Litinterp | C |
| Mikotel | I |
| Old Town Hostel | G |
| Žėmaitės | H |

0        200 m

*Left margin:* Genocide Museum (200 m), Parliament (500 m) & Television Tower (2 km)

18

LITHUANIA | Vilnius

## The City

At the centre of Vilnius, poised between the medieval and nineteenth-century parts of the city, is **Cathedral Square** (Katedros aikštė). To the south of here along Pilies gatvė and Didžioji gatvė is the Old Town, containing perhaps the most impressive concentration of Baroque architecture in northern Europe. West of the square in the New Town is **Gedimino prospektas**, a nineteenth-century boulevard and the focus of the city's commercial and administrative life. Wedged between the Old Town and the Gedimino prospektas areas, the traditionally **Jewish areas** of Vilnius were shorn of their populations in the 1941–45 period, but retain some sights.

## Cathedral Square and around

**Cathedral Square** is dominated by the Neoclassical **Cathedral** (Arkikatedros bazilika; daily 7am–8pm), its origins going back to the thirteenth century, when a wooden church is thought to have been built here on the site of a temple dedicated to Perkūnas, the god of thunder. The highlight of the airy, vaulted interior is the opulent **Chapel of St Casimir**, dedicated to the patron saint of Lithuania, whose remains lie in a silver casket in the chapel's main altar. Next to the cathedral on the square is the white **belfry**, once part of the fortifications of the vanished Lower Castle but now looking like a stranded Baroque lighthouse. Between the Cathedral and the belfry lies a small coloured tile with the word *stebuklas* (miracle) written on it. This marks the spot from where, in 1989, two million people from the Baltic states formed a chain that stretched all the way to Tallinn in Estonia to protest against the Soviet occupation of the Baltic States. Locals can be seen spinning around on the tile in the belief that their wishes will be granted. Rising behind the cathedral is the tree-clad **Gediminas Hill**, its summit crowned by the red-brick octagon of **Gediminas Tower**, one of the city's best-known landmarks. The first substantial fortification here was founded by Grand Duke Gediminas, the Lithuanian ruler who consolidated the country's independence. According to legend, Gediminas dreamt of an iron wolf howling on a hill overlooking the River Vilnia and was told by a pagan priest to build a castle on the spot. The tower houses the **Upper Castle Museum** (Aukštinės pilies muziejus; May–Sept daily 10am–7pm; Oct–April Tues–Sun 11am–5pm; 4Lt, free on Wed in winter), showing the former extent of the Vilnius fortifications. About 100m north of the cathedral in a former arsenal building is the **Lithuanian National Museum**, Arsenalo 1 (Lietuvos nacionalinis muziejus; Wed–Sun 10am–6pm; 4Lt; free Wed in winter), covering the history of Lithuania from prehistoric times to 1940 but with mostly Lithuanian and Russian labelling. A little further north on Arsenalo, a separate department houses the much snazzier **Prehistoric Lithuania exhibition** (Tues–Sat 10am–5pm, Sun 10am–3pm; 4Lt) which, despite its title, covers the story of the Lithuanians up to the Middle Ages. Nearby is the **Applied Art Museum**, Arsenalo 3 (Taikomosios dailės muziejus; Tues–Sun 11am–6pm; 4Lt, free Wed in winter), home to a glittering array of ecclesiastical treasures.

## The Old Town

The **Old Town**, just south of Cathedral Square, is a network of narrow, often cobbled streets that forms the Baroque heart of Vilnius, with the pedestrianized **Pilies gatvė** cutting into it from the southeastern corner of the square. To the west of this street is **Vilnius University**, a jumble of buildings constructed between the sixteenth and eighteenth centuries around nine linked courtyards that extend west as far as Universiteto gatvė. Within its precincts is the beautiful, ornate **St John's Church** (Šv Jono bažnyčia) – access from the main university gate on Universiteto gatvė. Founded during the fourteenth century, St John's was taken over by the Jesuits in 1561 and given to the university in 1737. Reconstruction after a fire in the same year has left it with its present Baroque facade, and a no-holds-barred Baroque altar inside.

The **Presidential Palace**, just west of the university on **Daukanto aikštė**, was originally built during the sixteenth century as a merchant's residence and remodelled into its present Neoclassical form at the end of the eighteenth century, going on to serve as the residence of the Russian governor-general during the Tsarist period. Napoleon Bonaparte stayed here briefly during his ill-fated campaign against Russia in 1812. The emperor is said to have been so impressed by **St Anne's Church** (Šv Onos bažnyčia; May–Sept daily 10am–1pm & 2–7pm) on Maironio gatvė, to the east of Pilies gatvė, that he wanted to take it back to Paris on the palm of his hand. Studded with skeletal, finger-like towers, its facade overlaid with intricate brick traceries and fluting, this late-sixteenth-century structure is the finest Gothic building in Vilnius. Rising behind St Anne's is the Gothic facade of the much larger **Bernardine Church** (Bernardinū bažnyčia) from 1520. Its once fine Baroque interior suffered during its Soviet-era incarnation as home to the Vilnius Art Academy, and the building is now undergoing a much-needed renovation.

Just south of St Anne's and the Bernardine church is a statue commemorating the Polish Romantic poet Adam Mickiewicz (1798–1855), author of *Pan Tadeusz*, the Polish national epic. Here a bridge over the river Vilnia forms the border of the self-declared independent republic of Užupis, home to a flourishing population of artists, bohemians and yuppies. Heading south, Pilies becomes Main Street (Didžioji gatvė), with the restored Baroque palace at no. 4 housing the **Lithuanian Art Museum** (Tues–Sat noon–6pm, Sun noon–5pm; 5Lt; free on Wed in winter), a marvellous collection of sixteenth- to nineteenth-century paintings and sculptures from around the country. The colonnaded Neoclassical building standing at the end of **Town Hall Square** (Rotušės aikštė) has recently been restored to its original function as the town hall. The modern building behind it houses the **Contemporary Art Centre** (Šuolaikinio meno centras or ŠMC; Tues–Sun 11am–6.30pm; 4Lt; free on Wed in winter), which hosts changing exhibitions.

East of the square, **St Casimir's Church** (Šv Kazimiero bažnyčia; Mon–Fri 10am–6.30pm, Sun 8.15am–1.30pm), dating from 1604 and the oldest Baroque church in the city, remains a striking building – its central cupola topped by an elaborate crown and cross symbolizing the royal ancestry of St Casimir, the son of King Casimir IV of Poland. South of here, Didžioji becomes **Aušros Vartū gatvė**, a short distance along which a gateway on the left-hand side leads to the seventeenth-century **Church of the Holy Spirit**, Lithuania's main Orthodox church, a Baroque structure built on a low hill in the grounds of a monastery. In front of the large iconostasis, the bodies of three fourteenth-century martyred saints are displayed in a glass case, their faces swathed in cloth. A little further along Aušros Vartū gatvė the seventeenth-century **St Theresa's Church** (Šv Teresės bažnyčia) rises to the left of the street, another soaring testimony to the city's dominating architectural style. The end of the street is marked by the **Gate of Dawn** (Aušros vartū), the sole survivor of nine city gates that once studded the walls of Vilnius. A chapel above the gate houses the city's most celebrated religious monument, the *Madonna of the Gates of Dawn*, an image of the Virgin Mary said to have miraculous powers and revered by Polish Catholics. East of Aušros Vartū gatvė on Boksto 20/18 is the **Artillery Bastion** (Artilerijos bastėja), a seventeenth-century bastion that was once part of the city's outer fortification ring and which now houses a **museum** (Wed–Sat 10am–5pm, Sun 10am–3pm; 2Lt, free on Wed in winter) of weapons and armour, though the setting is more interesting than the contents.

### Jewish Vilnius

Before World War II Vilnius was one of the most important centres of Jewish life in eastern Europe. The Jews – first invited to settle in 1410 by Grand Duke Vytautas – made up around a third of the city's population, mainly concentrated in the eastern fringes of the Old Town around present-day Vokiečiū gatvė, Žydū gatvė and Antokolskio gatvė. The **Great Synagogue** was located just off Žydū gatvė, on a site now occupied by a kindergarten. Massacres of the Jewish population began soon after the Germans occupied Vilnius on June 24, 1941, and those who survived the initial killings found themselves herded into two **ghettos**. The smaller of these ghettos centred around Žydū, Antokolskio, Stikliū and Gaono streets and was liquidated in October 1941, while the larger occupied an area between Pylimo, Vokiečiū, Lydos, Mikalojaus, Karmelitū and Arkliū streets and was liquidated in September 1943. Most of the Jews of Vilnius perished in Paneriai forest on the southwestern edge of the city (see p.688).

Today, the Jewish population of Vilnius numbers only a few thousand and, out of the 96 that once existed, the city has just one surviving **synagogue**, at Pylimo 39 (Sun–Fri 10am–2pm). To find out about the history of Jewish Vilnius head for the

**Lithuanian State Jewish Museum** (Lietuvos valstybinis Žydų muziejus), housed in various parts of the labyrinthine Jewish community offices at Pylimo 4 (Mon–Thurs 9am–5pm, Fri 9am–4pm; 4Lt, free on Wed in winter). The display includes items salvaged from the Great Synagogue and some of the exhibits are captioned in English. A second branch of the museum occupies the so-called **Green House** (Žalias namas) nearby at Pamenkalnio 12 (Mon–Thurs 9am–5pm, Fri 9am–4pm; donations), and contains a harrowing display about the fate of Vilnius Jews during the war. The museum can also arrange "history of Jewish Vilnius" tours (☎5/262 0730).

Nearby, the otherwise nondescript Kalinausko street is worth a visit to see the bronze head of rocker **Frank Zappa** perched on a column. Civil servant Saulis Paukstys founded the local Zappa fan club and commissioned the socialist realist sculptor Konstantinas Bogdanas, more accustomed to forging likenesses of Lenin, to create this unique tribute to Zappa.

## Gedimino prospektas

**Gedimino prospektas**, named after the founder of the city, runs west from Cathedral Square, and was, in the past, named after St George, Mickiewicz, Stalin and Lenin, reflecting the succession of foreign powers that controlled the city. It was the main thoroughfare of nineteenth-century Vilnius, and remains the most important commercial street. **Lukiškiū aikštė**, around 900m west of Cathedral Square, is the former location of the city's Lenin statue, removed after the failed 1991 coup which precipitated the final break-up of the Soviet Union. The square has long played an infamous role in city history. After the 1863–64 uprising against the Russians, a number of rebels were publicly hanged here, while Gedimino 40, on the southern side of the square, was Lithuania's **KGB headquarters**. The building also served as Gestapo headquarters during the German occupation and more recently the Soviets incarcerated political prisoners in the basement. It's now the **Genocide Museum** (Genocido aukū muziejus; entrance at Aukū 2a; Tues–Sun 10am–4/6pm; 2Lt), with dank green cells and the courtyard where prisoners were tortured and executed preserved in their pre-1991 state. The English-language cassette-tape commentary (10Lt) provides detailed background on the prison and its inmates.

At the far end of Gedimino prospektas stands Lithuania's graceless modern **Parliament Building** (Seimas). Thousands gathered here on January 13, 1991, when Soviet troops threatened to occupy it following the killing of a dozen people at the TV Tower, in the bloodiest event of the struggle for Baltic independence. Facing the river some of the barricades built to defend the building have been preserved, complete with anti-Soviet graffiti; there's also a moving memorial commemorating those who died at the TV Tower and the seven border guards killed by Soviet special forces in July 1991. The 326-metre **TV Tower** (Televizijos bokštas; 10am–9pm; 15Lt) itself is around 3km west of the centre in the Karoliniškės district – trolleybus #16 from the train station or #11 from Lukiškiū aikštė; alight at the Televizijos bokštas stop on Sausio 13-osios gatvė. At the tower's base, wooden crosses commemorate those killed here.

# Eating, drinking and nightlife

There's a fast-growing range of **eateries** in Vilnius offering everything from Lithuanian to Lebanese cuisine – although the majority of places serve the standard meat-and-potatoes. There's little difference between eating and drinking venues: **bars** and **cafés** invariably serve both snacks and meals and often represent better value for money than restaurants. Vilnius has a few **clubs** and discos, though you may have a better (and cheaper) time in some of the bars mentioned below.

### Cafés and snack bars

Bar Italia Gedimino 3a. Strong coffee and an excellent selection of both sandwiches and cakes.
Delano Gedimino 24. Huge subterranean self-service cafeteria; pile your plate high with calorific meat-and-potatoes dishes or head for the healthy salads.
Gabi Šv Mykolo 6. Inexpensive drinks and solid home cooking in a relaxed, no-smoking atmosphere.

18

LITHUANIA | Vilnius

**Mano Kavinė** Bokšto 7. Stylish place in the Old Town with chic, modernist decor, trendy young clientele, a wide range of snacks and speciality teas.

**Pilies Menė** Pilies 8. Flash modern café/bar famous for its extensive pancake menu. Good place for a daytime coffee or night-time drink.

**Presto** Pilies 10. Bright modern coffee bar with an impressive assortment of brews, as well as salads and sumptuous cakes.

**Skonis ir Kvapas** Trakų 8. The most beautiful vaulted interior in town. Big pots of tea, excellent coffee, and an affordable range of hot meals.

**Užupio Kavinė** Užupio 2. Relaxed, mildly Bohemian place on the eastern fringes of the Old Town, with a lime-tree-shaded outdoor terrace overlooking the Vilnia River.

## Restaurants

**Aukštaičiai** Antokolskio 13. Traditional, hearty pork-and-potatoes fare in fun, faux-rustic surroundings.

**Balti Drambliai** Vilniaus 41. Vegetarian restaurant with friendly service, unusual non-smoking policy in the cellar and lively beer garden.

**Čili** Didžioji 5. Popular place for an inexpensive bite, with thin-crust and deep-pan pizzas. Six more branches, one at Gedimino 23.

**Finjan** Vokiečiu 18. Middle-Eastern place that looks like a fast-food café but offers restaurant-quality kebabs, shawarma and falafel.

**Freskos** Didžioji 31. Imaginative, well-presented modern European cuisine behind the Town Hall. Good-value lunchtime salad buffet.

**Lokys** Stiklių 8/10. Reasonably priced Lithuanian cellar restaurant serving boar, elk and beaver meat alongside more traditional meat-and-potato favourites.

**Tores** Užupio 40. Splendid Spanish food in the funky Užupis district. Marvellous views of the old town from the terrace.

**Žemaičiai** Vokiečiu 24. One of the top places for traditional Lithuanian cuisine, serving up *cepelinai* (potato dumplings stuffed with meat), *žemaičiu blynai* (potato pancakes with mincemeat filling), and a range of strong beers. Warren of cellar rooms in winter, outdoor courtyard seating in summer.

## Bars

**Avylis** Gedimino 5. Smartish but atmospheric brick-clad basement with beer brewed on site and a range of Lithuanian food.

**Bix** Etmonū 6. Great bar with industrial decor, karaoke nights and an enjoyable disco in the cellar – run by members of legendary post-punk band Bix. Food available.

**Brodvėjus Pubas** Mėsiniū 4. Popular drinking/dancing venue with live bands (Thurs–Sun) and DJs, and a full menu of snacks and hot meals including lunchtime specials.

**Cafe de Paris** Didžioji 1. Snug, arty and entertaining, you're likely to hear poetry proclaimed from the tabletops here – good pancakes too.

**Prie Parlamento** Gedimino 46. Big, popular café/bar with restaurant-standard food (excellent veggie options) and pub-style bar.

**Savas Kampas** Vokiečiū 4. A cosy wood-furnished interior and extensive list of alcohol, plus good pizzas.

**The PUB** Dominikonū 9. British bar with dark interior and covered courtyard. Frequent live music, big-screen sport and extensive food menu.

## Clubs and live music

**Džiazo Klubas (Jazz Club)** Vilniaus 22. Brick-lined cellar bar with decent jazz and blues bands at weekends. Also does decent food.

**Intro** Maironio 3. Minimally decorated warehouse-style club with a wide-ranging schedule of cutting-edge DJ nights.

**Gravity** Jasinskio 16. Ultra-cool joint offering a mixture of commercial dance and lesser-known music. Attracts the best big-star DJs. Thurs–Sat.

**Neo Men's Factory** Ševčenkos 16. Flamboyantly decorated gay bar and disco, twenty minutes' walk west of the Old Town. Bar Wed & Thurs, disco Fri & Sat.

**Ministerija** Gedimino 46. In the cellar below *Prie Parlamento*, playing newish dance stuff as well as popular classics. Popular with expats and beautiful young things.

**Metelica** Goštauto 12. Trendy place catering for a younger, often Russian crowd. Pop during the week and techno on Sat. Thurs–Sat.

# Listings

**Embassies and consulates** Australia, Vilniaus 23 ☎5/212 3369; Canada, Jogailos 4 ☎5/249 0950; US, Akmenū 6 ☎5/266 5500; UK, Antakalnio 2 ☎5/246 2900.

**Exchange** Parex, outside the station at Geležinkelio 6 (24hr).

**Hospital** Vilnius University Emergency Hospital, Šiltnamiū 29 ☎5/216 9140.

**Internet access** Bazė, Gedimino 50 (entrance round the corner on Rotundo); Collegium, Pilies 22; Netcafe, Antakalnio 36.

**Pharmacy** Gedimino Vaistinė, Gedimino 27 (24hr).

**Police** Jogailos 3 ☎5/261 6208.

**Post office** Gedimino prospektas 7 (Mon–Fri 7am–9pm, Sat 9am–4pm).

Beyond Vilnius, several places merit a day-trip. **PANERIAI**, the site where the Nazis and their Lithuanian accomplices murdered one hundred thousand people during World War II, lies within Vilnius city limits in a forest at the edge of a suburb, 10km southwest of the centre. Seventy thousand of those killed at Paneriai were Jews from Vilnius, who were systematically exterminated from the time the Germans arrived in June 1941 until they were driven out by the Soviet army in 1944. To get to Paneriai, take a southwest-bound suburban train from Vilnius station and alight at Paneriai. From the station platform descend onto Agrastū gatvė, turn right and follow the road through the woods for about a kilometre. The entrance to the site is marked by the **Paneriai Memorial** – two stone slabs with Russian and Lithuanian inscriptions commemorating the murdered "Soviet citizens", flanking a central slab with an inscription in Hebrew commemorating "seventy thousand Jewish men, women and children". From the memorial a path leads to the **Paneriai Museum**, Agrastū 15 (Mon & Wed–Sun 9am–5pm; call to check ☎5/260 2001; donations), with a small display detailing what happened here. Paths lead to the pits in the woods where the Nazis burnt the bodies of their victims and to another eight-metre pit where the bones of the dead were crushed.

The sleepy little town of **TRAKAI**, 25km west of Vilnius, is the former capital of the Grand Duchy of Lithuania. Founded during the fourteenth century and standing on a peninsula jutting out between two lakes, it's the site of two medieval castles. From the **train** and **bus** stations follow Vytauto gatvė to reach the main sights. After about 500m turn right down Kęstučio gatvė to the remains of the **Peninsula Castle**, thought to have been built by Duke Kęstutis, son of Gediminas and father of Vytautas. Trakai is home to the Karaim, members of a Judaic sect whose ancestors were brought here from the Crimea by Grand Duke Vytautas to serve him as bodyguards, and whose distinctive wooden cottages line Karaimū gatvė, the northern continuation of Vytauto gatvė. Around two hundred inhabitants of Trakai are Karaim; Lithuania's smallest ethnic minority, they recognize the Old Testament but not the Talmud. The **Karaim Ethnographic Exhibition**, down the street at no. 22 (Karaimū etnografinė paroda; Wed–Sun 10am–6pm; 2Lt), holds a small but fascinating display of costumes and furnishings. Nearby stands the Karaim prayer house or Kenessa, and beyond that two wooden footbridges lead to the **Island Castle** (Šalos pilis). This cluster of red-brick towers built around 1400 on a small offshore island is one of Lithuania's most famous monuments. Built by Grand Duke Vytautas, under whom Lithuania reached the pinnacle of its power during the fifteenth century, it fell into ruin from the seventeenth century until a 1960s restoration returned it to its former glory. It now contains a worthwhile **museum** (daily: May–Sept 10am–7pm; Oct–April 10am–6pm; 8Lt). The main tower, built around a galleried courtyard, houses exhibits covering the history of the castle, plus examples of medieval weaponry and wooden carvings. Trakai's culinary claim to fame is the *kibinas*, a mincemeat pasty served up at speciality **cafés** such as *Kibininė*, Karaimū 65, and *Kybynlar*, Karaimū 29.

# The rest of Lithuania

Lithuania is predominantly rural – a gently undulating, densely forested landscape scattered with lakes. However, it does boast at least one more major city, **Kaunas**, a genuine rival to Vilnius in terms of its historical importance. Further west, the main highlight of the coast is the holiday village of **Nida**, whose dramatic dunescapes and traditional timber architecture are reachable by ferry and bus from **Klaipėda**, the country's major port.

# Kaunas

**KAUNAS**, 80km west of Vilnius and easily reached by bus or rail, is Lithuania's second city and seen by many Lithuanians as the true heart of their country. It served as provisional capital during the interwar period when Vilnius was occupied by Poland, and remains a major commercial and industrial centre. Nevertheless it's an attractive, easygoing city, with enough sights to merit a full day's visit.

## Arrival, information and accommodation

Kaunas' **train** and **bus** stations are at the southeastern end of the centre, a fifteen-minute walk from Laisvės alėja; a thirty-five minute walk (or short ride on trolleybus #1, #3, #5 or #7) to the Old Town. There's a helpful **tourist office** at Laisvės 36 (Sept–May Mon–Thurs 9am–6pm, Fri 9am–5pm; June–Aug same times plus Sat–Sun 9am–6pm; ☎37/323 436, ✉turizmas@takas.lt) doling out English-language leaflets and a free map. You can also pick up a copy of *Kaunas and Klaipeda in Your Pocket* here (✆www.inyourpocket.com; 8Lt). For **accommodation** the ever-reliable Litinterp, Gedimino 28–7 (☎37/228 718, ✆www.litinterp.lt), can sort you out with a room in the centre from 80Lt single, 140Lt double. Best of the **hotels** is the brand-new *Apple*, Valančiaus 19 (☎37/321 404, ✆www.applehotel.lt), offering simple but comfy en-suites in the Old Town. Options in the New Town include the charmingly olde-worlde *Metropolis*, just off Laisvės alėja at Daukanto 21 (☎37/205 992, ✆www.takiojineris.com; ❷); and the hulking concrete *Takioji Neris*, with comfortable, recently renovated rooms, off Laisvės to the north at Donelaičio 27 (☎37/306 100, ✆www.takiojineris.com; ❼).

## The Town

The most picturesque part of Kaunas is the **Old Town** (Senamiestis), centred around **Town Hall Square** (Rotušės aikštė), on a spur of land between the Neris and Nemunas rivers. The square is lined with fifteenth- and sixteenth-century merchants' houses in pastel stucco shades, but the overpowering feature is the magnificent **Town Hall**, its tiered Baroque facade rising to a graceful 53-metre tower. The other most eye-catching structure on the square is the seventeenth-century **Jesuit Church** on the southern side. Originally part of a larger college and monastery complex, the church was built in 1666. In 1825 the Russians handed it over to the Orthodox church, and later the Soviets turned it into a trade school, but the Baroque interior remains intact.

Occupying the northeastern shoulder of the square, the red-brick tower of Kaunas' austere **Cathedral** stands at the western of Vilniaus gatvė. Dating back to the reign of Vytautas the Great, the cathedral was much added to in subsequent centuries. After the plain exterior, the lavish gilt and marble interior comes as a surprise. There are nine altars, though the large, statue-adorned Baroque high altar (1775) steals the limelight. Predating the cathedral by several centuries is **Kaunas Castle**, whose scant remains survive just northwest of the square. Little more than a restored tower and a couple of sections of wall are left, the rest washed away by the Neris, but in its day the fortification was a major obstacle to the Teutonic Knights. South of the town square, the **Perkūnas House** at Aleksoto 6 is an elaborately gabled Gothic red-brick structure thought to have been built as an office of the Hanseatic League, standing on the reputed site of a temple to Perkūnas, the pagan god of thunder. From here Aleksoto descends to the banks of the Nemunas and the glowering Vytautas Church, built by Vytautas the Great in around 1399.

The main thoroughfare of Kaunas' **New Town** is Laisvės alėja (Freedom Avenue), a broad pedestrianized shopping street running east from the Old Town. At the junction with L. Sapiegos the street is enlivened by a bronze statue of Vytautas the Great, which faces the **City Garden** where, on May 14, 1972, the 19-year-old student Romas Kalanta immolated himself in protest against Soviet rule. Kalanta's death sparked anti-Soviet rioting, and he is commemorated by a contemporary memorial composed of horizontal metal shards. Towards the eastern end of Laisvės alėja, the silver-domed **Church of St Michael the Archangel** looms over Independence Square (Nepriklausomybės aikštė), while the striking modern building in the northeast corner is one of the best art galleries in the country, the **Mykolas Žilinskas Art Museum** (Tues–Sun 11am–5pm; closed last Tues of every month; 5Lt), housing a fine collection of Egyptian artefacts, Chinese porcelain and Lithuania's only Rubens, a sombrely effective *Crucifixion*.

Kaunas celebrates its role in sustaining Lithuanian national identity on **Unity Square** (Vienybės aikštė), at the junction of S. Daukanto and K. Donelaičio, a block north of Laisvės. Here a **monument** depicting liberty as a female figure faces an eternal flame flanked by traditional wooden crosses and busts of prominent nineteenth-century Lithuanians. Just north of the square, Kaunas has two unique art collections. The **A. Žmuidzinavičius Art Museum**, Putvinskio 64 (Tues–Sun 11am–5pm; closed last Tues of every month; 5Lt), better known as the **Devil's Museum**, houses a vast collection of devil figures put together by the artist Antanas Žmuidzinavičius. Though most of the images are comic, there's a sinister representation of Hitler and Stalin as devils dancing on a Lithuania composed of skulls. Diagonally opposite, at Putvinskio 55, the dreamy, symbolist paintings of Mikalojus Čiurlionis, Lithuania's cultural hero, are on display in the **M. K. Čiurlionis State Art Museum** (same times; 5Lt). Heading east down Putvinskio and turning uphill to the left brings you to the Žaliakalnis district to the north of the city centre, where the **Church of Christ's Resurrection**, a 1930s modernist edifice with a very tall white tower, stands near the top of the hill.

Before World War II Kaunas, like Vilnius, had a large Jewish population, but nearly all were killed during the war and little remains to remind of their presence, except the city's sole surviving **synagogue** at Ožeskienės 17 in the New Town, which sports a wonderful sky-blue interior (daily 9am–5pm). To find out about the fate of the Jews of Kaunas, head out of town to the **Ninth Fort Museum**, Žemaičiū plentas 73 (Mon, Wed–Sun 10am–4pm; 4Lt), housed in the tsarist-era fortress where the Jews were kept while awaiting execution. Take any westbound inter-city bus from Kaunas bus station and get off at the IX Fortas stop.

### Eating and drinking

For quick, cheap **eating** head for *Viva Blynai*, *Viva Koldūnai*, Laisvės 53, a snazzy self-service buffet specializing in pancakes and *koldūnai* (Lithuanian ravioli). For something more substantial try the *Bernelių Uzeiga*, Valančiaus 9, where you can dine on meaty Lithuanian staples in an attractive rustic interior. *Pizza Jazz*, Laisvės alėja 68, does delicious thin-crust pizzas while *Žalias Ratas*, in a courtyard behind the tourist office at Laisvės 36, is the place to pig out on traditional country cooking. Cafés and **bars** are often a good bet for eating too: *Avilys*, Vilniaus 34, is a chic establishment with a full range of meals and its own beer; *Miesto Sodas*, Laisvės 93, offers drinking and dining in an elegant park-side pavilion. The *Skliautas*, Rotušės aikštė 26, and the nearby *B.O.*, Muitinės 9, are the best places to hook up with a young, arty crowd. *Los Patrankos*, Savanoriū 124, is the biggest and most enjoyable of the techno-oriented clubs. You can access the **Internet** at Kavinė Internetas, Vilniaus 24 (6Lt/hr).

## Klaipėda

**KLAIPĖDA**, Lithuania's third largest city and most important port, lies on the Baltic coast, a long and tedious 275km by road or rail northwest of Vilnius. Though it has a handful of sights, the city is of more interest as a staging post en route to **Neringa**, the Lithuanian name for the Couronian Spit which shields much of Lithuania's coast from the open Baltic. Founded in the Middle Ages by crusading German knights, Klaipėda (or Memel as it was known in German) only became part of Lithuania in 1923 when paramilitaries moved in to occupy the city. The main sights are in the **Old Town** on the southern bank of the River Danē, an area of half-timbered buildings and cobbled streets, at the heart of which is **Theatre Square** named after the ornate Neoclassical Theatre building on its northern side. In front of the theatre is **Anna's Fountain**, a replica of a famous prewar monument to the German poet Simon Dach (1605–1659), which depicts the heroine of his folksong *Ännchen von Tharau*. Southeast of the square, the **History Museum of Lithuania Minor**, Didžioji vandens 6 (Tues–Sat 10am–6pm; also Sun in summer; 3Lt), has local archeological finds, national costumes and ancient domestic implements. In the **New Town**, on the northern side of the Danē, at Liepū 16, is Klaipēda's splendid red-brick Gothic-revival post office. Built between 1883 and 1893, it is a vivid reminder of imperial German civic pride.

Klaipēda's ultra-helpful **tourist office** is in the middle of the Old Town at Turgaus 7 (July–Aug Mon–Fri 9am–7pm, Sat 10am–4pm; Sept–June Mon–Fri 9am–6pm; ☎46/412 186, ✉tic@one.lt). *Kaunas and Klaipeda in Your Pocket* (8Lt, from the tourist office or bookstores) is a good source of listings information. Litinterp (see above) has a guest house at Puodžiū 17 (Mon–Fri 8.30am–5.30pm; Sat 9.30am–3pm; ☎46/410 644, ⊛www.litinterp.lt) with singles from 70Lt, doubles from 140Lt; it can also provide central private rooms (❷) as well as rooms in Nida. *Klaipeda Travellers' Guesthouse*, Butkū Juzēs 7–4 (☎46/211 879, ✉guestplace@yahoo.com; 35Lt), is a basic but friendly hostel right next to the bus station. Reasonable mid-range **hotels** include the *Aribē*, just east of the Old Town at Bangū 17a (☎46/490 940, ❹), a mid-sized hotel with neat en-suites; and the *Prūsija*, Šimkaus 6 (☎46/412 081; ❹), a welcoming family-run pension between the Old Town and the stations. Good **places to eat** include *Čili Kaimas*, Manto 17, where you can feast on *cepelinai*, potato pancakes and more in a rustic-themed interior; and *Būrū Užeiga*, Kepējū 17, which serves up excellent, meat-heavy Lithuanian and German dishes in homely surroundings. For **drinking**, *Memelis*, Žvejū 4, is a superbly converted warehouse and boutique brewery with roomy bar downstairs and a late-night club on the top floor; while *Kurpiai*, Kurpiū 1, is a traditional woody pub that also functions as the best jazz bar in the Baltics.

## Neringa

**NERINGA**, or the Kuršiū Nerija, is the Lithuanian section of the Couronian Spit, a 97-kilometre spit of land characterized by vast sand dunes and pine forests. Much of the area can be seen as a day-trip from Klaipēda, though you need to stay a day or two to soak up the unique atmosphere. Ferries from the quayside towards the end of Žvejū gatvē in Klaipēda (every 30min, 5am–3am; 1.50Lt return) sail to **Smiltynē** on the northern tip of the spit. From the landing stage, frequent minibuses (7.50Lt) run south towards the scenic, dune-dominated parts of the spit, terminating at Nida, 35km south.

**NIDA** is the most famous village on the spit – a small fishing community boasting several streets of attractive wooden houses, although there's some lumpen Soviet resort architecture at its heart. To get a feel for the old fishing settlement head for **Nagliū gatvē** and **Lotmiškio gatvē** (5min south of the village centre bus stop). The roads are lined with single-storey blue- and brown-painted wooden houses, many with traditional thatched roofs. The **Fisherman's House**, Nagliū 4 (May–Sept Tues–Sun 10am–5pm; 2Lt), is a recreated nineteenth-century cottage with simple wooden furnishings. From the end of Nagliū, a shore path runs to a flight of wooden steps leading up to the top of the **dunes** south of the village. From the summit you can gaze out across a Saharan sandscape to the Kaliningrad province, part of German East Prussia until 1945 but now belonging to the Russian Federation. Nida's long, luxuriant beach stretches along the opposite, western side of the spit, a 30min walk through the forest from the village. The **tourist office**, in the centre of the village at Taikos 4 (June–Aug daily 9am–8pm; Sept–May Mon–Fri 9am–1pm & 2–6pm, Sat 10am–3pm; ☎469/52345, ⊛www.neringainfo.lt), will find you a **private room** (**①**). Litinterp in Klaipēda can book rooms in advance, but for a slightly higher fee. **Camping** *Nida*, 2km southwest of town at Taikos 45a (follow Taikos gatvē out of town and follow the signs; ☎469/52045, ◉www .kempingas.lt) has clean facilities and tent space under the trees for 10Lt per pitch, 10Lt per person – or you can opt for a swanky self-catering apartment (**④**) in the administration building if you fancy splashing out. Among the cheaper **hotels**, *Nidos Smiltē*, Skruzdynēs 2 (☎469/52221, ◉www.is.lt/smilte; **③**), offers simple doubles with shared facilities and spartan cabins in the Nidos Pušynas holiday settlement nearby. For **food**, head for *Seklyčia*, Lotmiškio 1, which does traditional dishes such as *cepelinai* as well as more sophisticated meat and fish dishes. *Senasis uostas*, just behind the bus station at Nagliū 18, is a good place to try the delicious, locally smoked fish *rukyta zuvis*.

# Travel details

| Trains | Buses |
|---|---|
| **Kaunas** to: Klaipēda (2 daily; 3hr 30min); Vilnius (12 daily; 1hr 15min–2hr). | **Kaunas** to: Klaipēda (6 daily; 3hr); Rīga (2 daily; 4hr 30min); Vilnius (every 20–30min; 1hr 30min–2hr). |
| **Klaipēda** to: Kaunas (2 daily; 3hr 30min); Vilnius (3 daily; 5hr). | **Klaipēda** to: Kaunas (16 daily; 3hr); Nida (departures from Smiltynē; 8 daily; 50min); Rīga (2 daily; 5hr); Vilnius (10–12 daily; 5hr). |
| **Vilnius** to: Kaunas (12 daily; 1hr 15min–2hr); Klaipēda (3 daily; 5hr); Šeštokai (1 daily; 3hr 30min); Warsaw (3 weekly; 10hr). | **Vilnius** to: Kaunas (every 20–30min; 1hr 30min–2hr); Klaipēda (8 daily; 4hr); Rīga (4 daily; 5hr–5hr 30min); Tallinn (2 daily; 11hr 40min); Warsaw (3 daily; 12hr). |

# 19

# Morocco

**Note:** This chapter covers only the most easily accessible towns in northern Morocco. The map therefore shows only the northern regions, not the whole of the country

# Morocco highlights

✳ **Chefchaouen** Beautiful and very friendly little town in the Rif mountains, where the houses look like they're made of blue meringue. See p.702

✳ **Medina, Fes** An incredible labyrinth of alleys, sights and smells in the world's best-preserved medieval city. See p.706

✳ **Djemaa el Fna, Marrakesh** A spontaneous live circus in a large square in the middle of town, featuring everything from snake charmers to tooth pullers. See p.715

✳ **Essaouira** Arty, laidback seaside and surfing resort where Jimi Hendrix once played impromptu concerts on the beach. See p.717

△ Town walls, Essaouira

# Introduction and basics

Just an hour's ferry ride from Spain, Morocco seems very far from Europe, with a deeply traditional Islamic culture. Throughout the country, despite its 44 years of French and Spanish colonial rule, a more distant past constantly makes its presence felt. Travel here is, if not always easy, an intense and rewarding experience.

**Berbers**, the indigenous population, make up over half of Morocco's population. Only around ten percent of Moroccans claim to be "pure" **Arabs**, though with a population shift to the industrialized cities, such distinctions are becoming less significant. More telling is the legacy of the **colonial** period: until independence in 1956, the country was divided into Spanish and French zones, the latter building **Villes Nouvelles** (new towns) alongside the long-standing **Medinas** (old towns) in all the country's main cities.

Most visitors' introduction to Morocco is **Tangier** in the north, still shaped by its heyday of "international" port status in the 1950s. To its south, in the Rif mountains, the town of **Chefchaouen** is a small-scale and enjoyably laid-back place, while inland lies the enthralling city of **Fes**, the greatest of the four imperial capitals (the others are Meknes, Rabat and Marrakesh). The sprawl of **Meknes**, with its ancient walls, makes an easy day-trip from Fes.

The power axis of the nation lies on the coast in **Rabat** and **Casablanca**, respectively the seats of government and of industry and commerce. "Casa" looks more like Marseille than anything Moroccan, while the elegant, orderly capital, Rabat, houses some gems of Moroccan architecture. Further south, **Marrakesh** is an enduring fantasy that won't disappoint. The country's loveliest resort,

**Essaouira**, a charming walled seaside town, lies within easy reach of Marrakesh and Casablanca.

## Information, guides and maps

There's a **tourist office** (Délégation du Tourisme) run by the Office National Marocain du Tourisme (**ONMT**) in every major city, and sometimes also a locally funded Syndicat d'Initiative. They stock leaflets and maps, and can put you in touch with official guides. There are scores of "**unofficial guides**", some are genuine students, while others are out-and-out hustlers (though these have been clamped down on). If they do find you, be polite but firm. Note that it's illegal to harass tourists. Good **maps** of Moroccan cities are hard to obtain locally or abroad. The most functional are those in the *Rough Guide to Morocco*.

## Money and banks

The unit of currency is the **dirham** (dh), divided into 100 centimes; in markets, prices may well be in centimes rather than dirhams. There are coins of 10c, 20c, 50c, 1dh, 5dh and 10dh, and notes of 10dh,

---

### Morocco on the net

ⓦ**www.tourisme-marocain.com** Moroccan tourist board's website.

ⓦ**www.geocities.com/thetropics/4896/morocco.html** A selection of information for visitors.

ⓦ**www.arab.net/morocco** Arab.net's Morocco section has pages on history, culture and anything from people to pottery.

ⓦ**www.morocco.com** Huge collection of links to sites about every aspect of Morocco.

20dh, 50dh, 100dh and 200dh. You can get dirhams in Algeciras (Spain) and Gibraltar, and can usually change foreign notes on arrival at major sea- and airports. It can be difficult to change travellers' cheques anywhere but a bank. For **exchange** purposes, the most useful and efficient chain of banks is the **BMCE** (Banque Marocaine du Commerce Extérieur). Post offices will also change cash. **Travellers' cheques** incur a 10.70dh commission except at the state-run Bank al-Maghrib. Many banks give cash advances on credit cards, which can also be used in tourist hotels (but not cheap unclassified ones) and the **ATMs** of major banks. Banking hours are: summer Mon–Fri 8am–2pm; winter Mon–Thurs 8.15–11.30am & 2.15–4.30pm, Fri 8.15–11.15am & 2.45–4.45pm. During the holy month of Ramadan, banks open Mon–Fri 9am–2pm. Morocco is inexpensive but poor, and **tips** can make a lot of difference; it's customary to tip café waiters a dirham or two. At the time of writing, €1 was equal to around 11dh, $1 to 9dh, and £1 to 16dh.

## Communications

**Post offices** (PTT) open Mon–Thurs 8.30am–12.15pm & 2.30–6.30pm, Fri 8.30–11.30am & 3–6.30pm. Central post offices in large cities will be open longer hours, except in summer and Ramadan. You can also buy **stamps** at postcard shops and sometimes at tobacconists. Always post items at a PTT. International **phone calls** are best made with a phonecard (from post offices and some tobacconists). Alternatively, there are privately run *téléboutiques*, open late. You must dial all nine digits of Moroccan phone numbers. **Internet** access is available pretty much everywhere, and at low rates: 10dh/hr is typical.

## Getting around

The **train** network is limited, but for travel between the major cities, trains are the best option. Major stations have free timetables, printed by ONCF (Ⓦwww.oncf.org.ma), the national train company. Couchettes (90dh extra) are available on trains from Tangier to Marrakesh (9hr 30min), and are worth the money for extra comfort and security.

Collective **grands taxis** are usually big Peugeots or Mercedes, plying set routes for a set fare and are much quicker than buses, though the drivers can be reckless. Make clear you only want *une place* (one seat), otherwise drivers may assume you want to charter the whole car. Within towns **petits taxis** do short trips, carrying up to three people. They queue in central locations and at stations and can be hailed on streets when they're empty. Payment – usually no more than 15dh – relates to distance travelled.

**Buses** are marginally cheaper than *grands taxis*, and cover longer distances, but are much slower. CTM (the national company) are most reliable. An additional express service is run by Supratours.

## Accommodation

**Accommodation** is inexpensive, generally good value and usually pretty easy to find, although it's more difficult in main cities and resorts in the peak seasons (August, Christmas and Aïd el Kebir in January). Cheap, unclassified hotels and *pensions* (charging about 80–150dh for a double) are mainly to be found in each town's Medina (old town), while hotels with stars tend to concentrate in the Ville Nouvelle (new town). At their best, **unclassified** Medina hotels are beautiful, traditional houses with whitewashed rooms grouped around a central patio. The worst can be extremely dirty, and many have problems with water. Few have en-suite bathrooms, though a *hammam* (public Turkish bath) is usually close at hand. **Classified** hotels' star-ratings are fairly self-explanatory and prices are reasonable. Except in Marrakesh, most hotels do not include breakfast in their room price. HI **hostels** (*auberges de jeunesse*), often bright, breezy and friendly, generally require you to be in by 10pm or 11pm and out by 10am daily. **Campsites** are usually well out of town. They tend to charge around 15dh per person plus the same again for your tent.

# Food and drink

If your funds are limited, you'll probably be **eating** mainly in cheap local diners. Fancier restaurants, definitely worth an occasional splurge, are mostly to be found in the Ville Nouvelle, which is where you'll also find any bars. Moroccan cooking is good and filling. The main dish is usually a **tajine**, essentially a stew. Classic *tajines* include chicken with lemon and olives, and lamb with prunes and almonds. The most famous Moroccan dish – Berber rather than Arab in origin – is **couscous**, a huge bowl of steamed semolina piled with vegetables, mutton, chicken or fish. Restaurant **starters** include *salade marocaine*, a finely chopped salad of tomato and cucumber, or soup, most often the spicy, bean-based *harira*, followed by couscous, *tajine*, kebab (*brochette*), or something like a Western meat-and-two-veg main course. **Dessert** will probably be fruit, yoghurt or a pastry. Restaurants at all levels may offer a set menu, often a bargain at 60–100dh in even quite fancy places. **Vegetarianism** is not widely understood and meat stock may be added even to vegetable dishes. If **invited to a home**, you're unlikely to use a knife and fork; copy your hosts and eat only with your **right hand**.

The national drink is **thé à la menthe** – green tea with a large bunch of mint and a massive amount of sugar. Coffee (*café* in French; *qahwa* in Arabic) is best in French-style cafés. Many cafés and street stalls sell fresh-squeezed orange juice and **mineral water** is readily available. As an Islamic nation, Morocco gives alcohol a low profile, and it's generally impossible to buy any in the Medinas. Moroccan **wines**, usually red, can be very drinkable, while the best **beer** is Flag Speciale. Most **bars** are totally male domains. Exceptions are a few modern bars in Marrakesh, and those in tourist hotels.

## Language in Morocco

**Moroccan Arabic** is the country's official language, with three Berber dialects, but much of the country is bilingual in **French**. For some useful French words and phrases see p.356.

|  | Moroccan Arabic |  | Moroccan Arabic |
|---|---|---|---|
| **Yes** | *Eyeh* | **Tomorrow** | *Ghedda* |
| **No** | *La* | **How much is....?** | *Shahal...?* |
| **Please** | *Minfadlak* | **What time is it?** | *Shahal fisa'a?* |
| **(to a man)** | | **I (m) don't** | *Ana mish fahim* |
| **Please** | *Minfadlik* | **understand** | |
| **(to a woman)** | | **I (f) don't** | *Ana mish* |
| **Thank you** | *Shukran* | **understand** | *fahma* |
| **Hello** | *Assalam aleikum* | **Do you (m) speak** | *Takellem ilngleezi?* |
| **Goodbye** | *Bissalama* | **English?** | |
| **Excuse me** | *Issmahli* | **Do you (f) speak** | *Takelma ingleezi?* |
| **Where?** | *Fayn?* | **English?** | |
| **Good** | *Mezziyen* | **One** | *Wahad* |
| **Bad** | *Mish Mezziyen* | **Two** | *Jooj* |
| **Near (here)** | *Krayb (min hina)* | **Three** | *Tlata* |
| **Far** | *Baeed* | **Four** | *Arba'a* |
| **Cheap** | *Rkhis* | **Five** | *Khamsa* |
| **Expensive** | *Ghalee* | **Six** | *Sitta* |
| **Open** | *Mahlul* | **Seven** | *Seba'a* |
| **Closed** | *Masdud* | **Eight** | *Temeniya* |
| **Today** | *El Yoom* | **Nine** | *Tisaoud* |
| **Yesterday** | *Imbarih* | **Ten** | *Ashra* |

# Opening hours and holidays

**Shops** and stalls in the *souk* (bazaar) areas open roughly 9am–1pm & 3–6pm. Ville Nouvelle shops are also likely to close for lunch, and also once a week, usually Sunday. Islamic **religious holidays** are calculated on the lunar calendar and change each year. In 2006 they fall (provisionally) as follows: Jan 11 and Dec 31 are **Aïd el Kebir** (when Abraham offered to sacrifice his son for God); Jan 31 is the Muslim New Year; April 11 is **Mouloud** (the birthday of Muhammad); **Ramadan** (when all Muslims fast from sunrise to sunset) falls roughly Sept 24–Oct 24. Non-Muslims are not expected to observe Ramadan, but should be sensitive about not breaking the fast in public. The end of Ramadan is celebrated with **Aïd es Seghir** (aka Aïd el Fitr), a two-day holiday. **Secular holidays** are considered less important, with most public services (except banks and offices) operating normally even during the two biggest ones – the Feast of the Throne (July 30), and Independence Day (Nov 18).

# Cultural hints

Morocco is a Muslim country, and in rural areas particularly, people can be quite **conservative** about dress and displays of affection. It's not the done thing to kiss and cuddle in public, nor even for couples to hold hands. Shorts or skirts above the knee are frowned upon, and women are best advised to wear baggy clothes, long sleeves and long skirts.

Be sensitive when **taking photographs**, and always ask permission. In certain places, particularly the Djemaa el Fna in Marrakesh, people may demand money from you just for happening to be in a shot you have taken. Also note that it is illegal to photograph anything considered strategic, such as an airport or a police station.

When invited into people's homes, remove footwear before entering the reception rooms. If invited for a meal, take a gift: a box of sweets from a posh patisserie usually goes down well.

# Emergencies

Street **robbery** is rare but not unknown, especially in Tangier and Casablanca. Hotels are generally secure for depositing money; campsites less so. There are two main types of **police** – grey-clad gendarmes, with authority outside city limits; and the navy-clad sûreté in towns. There's sometimes a brigade of "tourist police" too. Moroccan **pharmacists** are well trained and dispense a wide range of drugs. In most cities there is a night pharmacy, often at the town hall, and a rota of *pharmacies de garde* which stay open till late and at weekends. You can get a list of English-speaking **doctors** in major cities from consulates. Steer clear of **marijuana** (*kif*) and hashish – it's illegal, and buying it leaves you vulnerable to scams, as well as potentially large fines and prison sentences.

## Emergency numbers

Police – Sûreté ☏19, Gendarmes ☏177, Fire and ambulance ☏15.

# Northern Morocco

The northern tip of Morocco contains enough on its own to justify the short ferry ride over from Spain: in three days or so you could check out the delightfully seedy city of **Tangier** and the picturesque, extremely laid-back little mountain town of **Chefchaouen** in the Rif mountains. There are two crossings from Algeciras: direct to Tangier, which is the easiest way, and takes you straight to a place that is an interesting city in its own right with direct transport connections nationwide; or to the Spanish enclave of **Ceuta**, from which you still have to reach and cross the border.

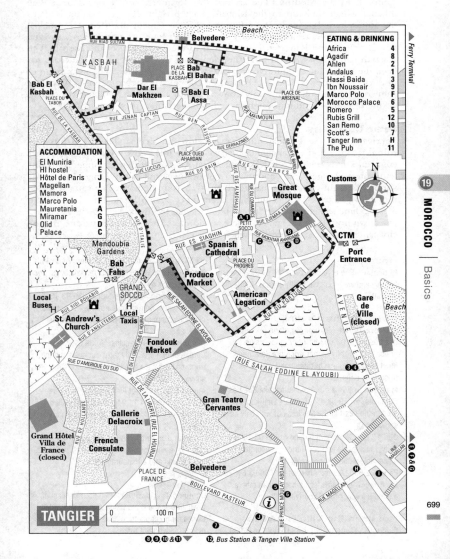

EATING & DRINKING
| | |
|---|---|
| Africa | 4 |
| Agadir | 8 |
| Ahlen | 2 |
| Andalus | 1 |
| Hassi Baida | 3 |
| Ibn Noussair | 9 |
| Marco Polo | F |
| Morocco Palace | 6 |
| Romero | 5 |
| Rubis Grill | 12 |
| San Remo | 10 |
| Scott's | 7 |
| Tanger Inn | H |
| The Pub | 11 |

ACCOMMODATION
| | |
|---|---|
| El Muniria | H |
| HI hostel | E |
| Hôtel de Paris | J |
| Magellan | I |
| Mamora | B |
| Marco Polo | F |
| Mauretania | A |
| Miramar | G |
| Olid | D |
| Palace | C |

TANGIER

0    100 m

# Tangier

For the first half of the twentieth century **TANGIER** (Tanja in Arabic; Tanger in French) was an "International City" with its own laws and administration, plus an eclectic community of expats and refugees. With independence in 1956, this special status was removed and the expat colony dwindled. Today Tangier is a major port, halfway to becoming a mainstream tourist resort, but with hints of its decadent past.

The **Grand Socco**, or Zoco Grande – once the main market square (and, since Independence, officially Place du 9 avril 1947) – offers the most straightforward approach to the **Medina**. The arch at the northwest corner opens onto Rue d'Italie, which leads up to the Kasbah. To the right, Rue es Siaghin leads to the atmospheric but seedy **Petit Socco**, or Zoco Chico, the Medina's principal landmark. From here, though not easy to follow, Rue des Almohades (aka Rue des Chrétiens) and Rue Ben Raisouli lead to the lower gate of the Kasbah. The **Kasbah** (citadel), walled off from the Medina on the highest rise of the coast, has been the palace and administrative quarter since Roman times. The main point of interest is the former Sultanate Palace, or **Dar el Makhzen** (Mon & Wed–Sun 9am–1pm & 3–6pm; 10dh), now converted into a museum, which gives you an excuse to look around it, though the exhibits are rather sparse.

## Practicalities

**Ferries** dock at the terminal immediately below the Medina. The **CTM bus terminal** is at the port entrance, but the *gare routière* **bus station** used by private bus companies and *grands taxis* is 1.5km inland on Av Youssef Ben Tachfine. All **trains** terminate at Tanger Ville station (2km east of town) and call at Tanger Moghogha station (4km out on the Tetouan road; bus #13 from the port). The **tourist office** is at 29 Bd Pasteur (Mon–Thurs 8.30am–noon & 2.30–6.30pm, Fri 8.30–11.30am & 3–6.30pm; sometimes open lunch and weekends in July & Aug; ☎039 94 80 50), just down from Place de France. There are dozens of **hotels** and **pensions**, but the city can get crowded in summer, when some places double their prices.

### Hostel

**HI hostel** 8 Rue El Antaki ☎039 94 61 27. Clean, friendly and well-run. 35dh with HI card, 40dh without.

### Hotels in the Medina

**Mamora** 19 Rue Mokhtar Ahardane (aka Rue des Postes) ☎039 93 41 05. A good-value option in a slightly higher price bracket than most Medina hotels, but has hot water (mornings only). ❶

**Mauretania** 2 Rue des Almohades (aka Rue des Chrétiens) ☎039 93 46 77. Clean, well-kept and right in the heart of the Medina, but with only cold showers. ❶

**Olid** 12 Rue Mokhtar Ahardane ☎039 93 13 10. Tatty, ramshackle and eccentrically decorated, but reasonable value for money. ❶

**Palace** 2 Rue Mokhtar Ahardane ☎039 93 61 28. A variety of rooms, some better than others, around a lovely central courtyard. ❶

### Hotels in the Ville Nouvelle

**El Muniria (Tanger Inn)** 1 Rue Magellan ☎039 93 53 37. A quiet, family-run pension, where William Burroughs wrote his most famous book, *The Naked Lunch*. ❶

**Hôtel de Paris** 42 Bd Pasteur ☎039 93 18 77. A good-value, comfortable hotel with spotless, spacious rooms, good breakfasts and helpful staff. ❷

**Magellan** 16 Rue Magellan ☎039 37 23 19. Carpeted rooms, slightly tatty, but quiet and the front rooms have a fine view of the port area. Hot showers 10dh. ❶

**Marco Polo** corner of Av d'Espagne and Rue El Antaki ☎039 94 11 24. A well-established, German-run hotel, with a good restaurant and lively bar. ❷

**Miramar** 168 Av des FAR ☎039 94 17 15. Old and a little shabby, but on the seafront, with quite large rooms and a restaurant. ❷

### Campsite

**Camping Tingis** ☎039 32 30 65. 6km east of town, beside the Oued Moghogha lagoon. Often closed for no apparent reason, so call ahead before trekking out there.

## Eating, drinking and nightlife

As with most Moroccan cities, the cheapest places to **eat** are in the **Medina**, and an authentic Tangier experience is people-watching over a mint tea at one of the Petit Socco **cafés**. Of the Medina's **restaurants**, the small and simple *Andalus*, 7 Rue du Commerce, off the Petit Socco, has excellent, low-priced swordfish steak or fried shrimps. *Ahlen*, 8 Rue Mokhtar Ahardane (aka Rue des Postes), serves traditional Moroccan dishes. The cheap diners in the Grand Socco are worth a look too; most stay open until midnight or later. Alcoholic drinks are not served in the Medina or Grand Socco.

### Ville Nouvelle Restaurants

**Africa** 83 Rue Salah Eddine el Ayoubi (aka Rue de la Plage). Best of the restaurants on this street, with a 50dh set menu and a drinks licence.

**Agadir** 21 Rue Prince Héritier Sidi Mohammed, uphill from Place de France. Small and friendly, serving French and Moroccan dishes, with a good 58dh set menu.

**Hassi Baida** 83 Rue Salah Eddine el Ayoubi (aka Rue de la Plage). Bright, tiled restaurant serving fish, couscous and *tajine*, with a 45dh set menu.

**Ibn Noussair** 37 Rue Moussa Ben Noussair. Immaculate and inexpensive diner with freshly grilled fish, paella, couscous and tasty *tajines*.

**Marco Polo** corner of Av d'Espagne and Rue el Antaki. Generous servings at a fair price, with snappy service and good views of the bay.

**Romero** 12 Rue Prince Moulay Abdallah. Licensed restaurant specializing in seafood, including vast portions of paella.

**Rubis Grill** 3 Rue Ibn Rochd, off Rue Prince Moulay Abdallah. Fine European dishes amid candlelit hacienda decor with exemplary service.

**San Remo** 15 Rue Ahmed Chaouki. Good-value Spanish, French and Italian cooking, with a take-away pizzeria opposite.

### Bars and nightlife

**Morocco Palace** Av du Prince Moulay Abdallah. A strange, sometimes slightly manic place with traditional Moroccan music and a belly-dancing floorshow.

**Scott's** Rue el Moutanabi (aka Rue Sanlucar). Used to be largely a gay disco, but nowadays very mixed, and worth a look if only for its unusual paintings of Berber boys in Highland military uniform. Usually quiet until after midnight; take care leaving late at night – the best idea is to tip the doorman 5dh to order you a taxi.

**Tanger Inn** 1 Rue Magellan. An institution since the days of the International Zone, decorated with photos of the Beat Generation authors (Burroughs, Ginsberg and Kerouac) who stayed at the hotel, but quiet midweek off-season.

**The Pub** 4 Rue Sorolla. British-run pub with hunting scenes on the walls, a cosy atmosphere and decent bar food.

## Listings

**American Express** Voyages Schwartz, 54 Bd Pasteur ☏ 039 37 48 37.

**Consulates** UK, Trafalgar House, Rue d'Amérique du Sud ☏ 039 93 69 39 or 40.

**Exchange** BMCE, 19 Bd Pasteur is the most efficient with a bureau de change and ATM.

**Internet** Cybercafé Adam, 4 Rue Ibn Rochd (off Bd Pasteur); River-Net, 20 Bd Pasteur (on the corner of Rue Prince Moulay Abdallah).

**Pharmacies** There are several English-speaking pharmacies on Place de France and Bd Pasteur.

**Post office** Main PTT, 33 Bd Mohammed V.

**Police** The Brigade Touristique are based at the former train station by the port ☏ 039 93 11 29.

# Ceuta and Tetouan

A Spanish enclave which dates back to the sixteenth century, the port of **CEUTA** (Sebta in Arabic) is politically and culturally part of Spain. As the crossing here from Algeciras is quicker than to Tangier, this drab outpost has become a popular point of entry. Try to arrive early in the day so that you have plenty of time to move on. The Moroccan border is 3km south of town, reached by local bus from the seafront. Once across, there are shared taxis for the 2km to **FNIDEQ**, where there are buses and shared *grands taxis* to Tetouan and Tangier. There are cash-only exchange places at the frontier.

Coming from Ceuta, you usually need to pick up onward transport at **TET-OUAN**, a town with a walled Medina and a reputation for having the worst hustlers in Morocco – but a *grand taxi* from Fnideq will leave you close enough to Tetouan's bus station to head straight out again. There are regular **buses** to Meknes, Fes and destinations nationwide. For Tangier, Chefchaouen or Ceuta it's easiest to travel by **grand taxi**; those for Fnideq (Ceuta) leave from Boulevard de Mouquaouama, a stone's throw from the bus station, but those for Tangier and Chefchaouen leave from a stand some 2km west, up Boulevard de Mouquaouama to Place Moulay el Mehdi, then west along Av Mohammed V to the end and ask someone. The ONCF office on Av 10 Mai, alongside Place Al Adala, sells **train** tickets that include a shuttle bus to the station at Tnine Sidi Lyamani. If you're stuck in Tetouan, cheap hotels include the friendly *Principe*, 20 Av Youssef Ibn Tachfine (☎066 55 38 20; ❶), on the corner of Boulevard de Mouquaouama midway between the bus station and Place Moulay el Mehdi.

## Chefchaouen

Shut in by a fold of the Rif mountains, **CHEFCHAOUEN** (sometimes abbreviated to Chaouen or Xaouen) had, until the arrival of Spanish troops in 1920, been visited by just three Europeans. It's a town of extraordinary light and colour, its whitewash tinted with blue and edged by golden stone walls. *Pensions* are friendly and cheap and a few days here is one of the best introductions to Morocco. Buses and *grands taxis* drop you outside the town walls; the main entrance to the Medina is a tiny arched entrance, **Bab el Ain**. Through the gate a dominant but narrow lane winds up to the main square, the elongated **Place Outa el Hammam**. This is where most of the town's evening life takes place, while by day the town's focus is the **Kasbah** (Mon & Wed–Sun 9am–1pm & 3–6pm, Fri 9am–noon; 10dh), a quiet ruin with shady gardens and a small museum, which occupies one side of the square. Beyond, the smaller **Place El Makhzen** is an elegant clearing with an old fountain and tourist pottery stalls.

Along and just off the main route through the Medina is a series of small **hotels**, the quietest of which is *Abie Khancha*, 75 Rue Lala el Hora (☎039 98 68 79; ❶), a converted house with a courtyard and terrace. Outside the Medina, nearer to transport, is the immaculate *Madrid*, Av Hassan II (☎039 98 74 96, ⊛www.moroccanhousehotels .com; ❷), and nearby is the cosy *Sevilla*, Av Allal Ben Abdallah (☎039 98 72 85; ❷). The **campsite** (☎039 98 69 79), up on the hill above town, by the modern *Hôtel Asma*, is inexpensive and can be crowded in summer. A very inexpensive but basic and inconveniently located **HI hostel** adjoins the campsite (same number as campsite; dorms 20dh). **Café-restaurants** in the Place Outa el Hammam serve good-value Moroccan meals; one of the best is the *Ali Baba*. Slightly pricier is *Tissemlal* (aka *Casa Hassan*), 22 Rue Targui, just up from Place Outa el Hammam, which serves delicious food in elegant surroundings. Outside the Medina, on Rue Moulay Ali Ben Rachid, *Moulay Ali Ben Rachid* and *Al Jazira* are popular with local residents. **Buses** to Fes and Meknes are sometimes full, so it's worth buying tickets a day in advance. Buses to Tetouan are very frequent, or you can share a *grand taxi*.

# Central Morocco

Between the mountain ranges of the Rif to the north and the Atlas to the south lie the great cities that form Morocco's heart: the great imperial cities of **Meknes** and **Fes**, the modern capital, **Rabat**, and the country's largest city and commercial capital, **Casablanca**.

# Meknes

More than any other Moroccan town, **MEKNES** is associated with a single figure, the Sultan Moulay Ismail, in whose reign (1672–1727) the city went from provincial centre to spectacular capital with over fifty palaces and fifteen miles of exterior walls. A prosperous city today, its monuments reward a day's exploration, with the main sights concentrated in the Medina.

**Place El Hedim** originally formed the western corner of the Medina, but Moulay Ismail had the houses here demolished to provide a grand approach to his palace quarter. The **Dar Jamai** (Mon, Wed, Thurs, Sat & Sun 9am–noon & 3–6.30pm, Fri 9–11.30am & 3–6.30pm; 10dh), at the back of the square, is one of the best examples of a nineteenth-century Moroccan palace, and the museum inside is one of the best in Morocco, with a fantastic display of Middle Atlas carpets. The lane immediately to the left of the Dar Jamai takes you to the Medina's major market street: on your left is **Souk en Nejjarin**, the carpet souk; on your right, leading to the Great Mosque and Bou Inania Medersa, are the fancier goods offered in the **Souk es Sebbat**. The **Bou Inania Medersa** (daily 9am–noon & 3–6.30pm; 10dh), constructed around 1340–50, has an unusual ribbed dome over the entrance hall and from the roof you can look out to the tiled pyramids of the Great Mosque. Behind the magnificent **Bab Mansour** (open for occasional exhibitions) is Place Lalla Aouda. Straight ahead bearing left, you come into another open square, on the right of which is the green-tiled dome of the **Koubba el Khayatine**, once a reception hall for ambassadors to the imperial court (daily 9am–noon & 3–6pm; 10dh). Below it, a stairway descends into a vast series of subterranean vaults, known as the **Prison of Christian Slaves**, though it was probably a storehouse or granary. Ahead of the Koubba, within the wall and at right angles to it, are two modest

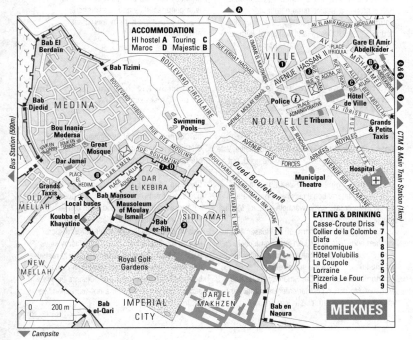

gates. The one on the left opens onto a corridor of walls and, a few metres down, the entrance to **Moulay Ismail's Mausoleum** (daily 9am–12.30pm & 3–6.30pm, closed Fri am; 10dh donation expected), where you can approach the sanctuary. Past the mausoleum, a long-walled corridor leads to the **Heri as-Souani**, a series of storerooms and granaries once filled with provisions for siege or drought. From the roof garden café, you can gaze out across much of the Dar el Makhzen (Royal Palace) and the wonderfully still **Agdal Basin**, built as an irrigation reservoir and pleasure lake.

## Practicalities

Meknes has two **train stations**, both in the Ville Nouvelle. All trains stop at both stations, but **Gare Amir Abdelkader** is more central than **Gare de Ville**. Private **buses** and most **grands taxis** arrive west of the Medina by Bab el Khemis; **CTM buses** arrive at their terminal on Av de Fès, near the Gare de Ville, and some *grands taxis* from Fes also drop you here. The **tourist office** is at 27 Place Administrative (Mon–Thurs 8.30am–noon & 2.30–6.30pm, Fri 8.30–11.30am & 3–6.30pm; ☎055 52 44 26).

### Hostel

**HI hostel** Av Okba Ben Nafi ☎055 52 46 98. An easy 1.5km walk northwest of the city centre, well-maintained and friendly with small dorms and some double rooms around a pleasant courtyard (dorms 45dh with HI card, 50dh without). ❶

### Hotels

**Maroc** 7 Rue Rouamzine, Medina ☎055 53 00 75. Pick of the Medina hotels, with plain but decent rooms around a shaded patio garden. ❶

**Touring** 34 Av Allal Ben Abdallah, Ville Nouvelle ☎055 52 23 51. Central and congenial, with some en-suite rooms. ❶

**Majestic** 19 Av Mohammed V, Ville Nouvelle ☎055 52 20 35. A good one-star: old, but good-value, comfortable, friendly and handy for El Amir Abdelkader train station. ❷

### Campsite

**Camping Aguedal** opposite the Heri as-Souani (no phone). South of the Imperial City, a twenty-minute walk from Place El Hedim, arguably the best campsite in Morocco, with good facilities and hot showers, though prices are high by Moroccan standards.

## Eating and drinking

There are good places to **eat** in all price categories in Meknes, and plenty of **bars**, several in Ville Nouvelle hotels, including the 1930s-style bar of the Art Deco *Hôtel Volubilis* at 45 Av des FAR.

### Restaurants

**Casse-Croute Driss** 34 Rue Emir Abdelkader, Ville Nouvelle. Fresh fried fish – cheap and good, but a little bit cramped.

**Collier de la Colombe** 67 Rue Driba, Medina. Outstanding international cuisine at moderate prices in an ornate early twentieth-century Medina mansion.

**Diafa** 12 Rue Badr el Kobra (off Av Hassan II at its western end), Ville Nouvelle. Great home cooking, though not a massive choice, in what looks like a private house in a residential street.

**Economique** 123 Rue Dar Smen, opposite Bab Mansour, Medina. A popular café/restaurant serving straight Moroccan food at low prices.

**La Coupole** corner of Av Hassan II and Rue Ghana, Ville Nouvelle. Reasonably-priced Moroccan and European food with a bar and nightclub.

**Lorraine** 34 Rue Emir Abdelkader, Ville Nouvelle, two doors from *Casse-Croute Driss*. Good-value set menus, with chicken and meat dishes.

**Pizzeria Le Four** 1 Rue Atlas, Ville Nouvelle. Decent pizzas, pasta and other Italian dishes, though the interior is a bit on the gloomy side.

**Riad** 79 Ksar Chaacha, Medina. A lovely restaurant serving well-prepared Moroccan dishes in beautifully restored rooms or outdoors beside a sunken garden – good for a not-too-expensive splurge.

# Fes (Fez)

The most ancient of the imperial capitals, **FES** (Fez in English) stimulates the senses and seems to exist somewhere between the Middle Ages and the modern world. Some 200,000 of the city's half-million inhabitants live in the oldest part of the Medina, **Fes el Bali**, which has a culture and atmosphere quite different from anywhere in mainland Europe.

## Arrival, information and accommodation

The **train station** is in the Ville Nouvelle, fifteen minutes' walk north of the hotels around Place Mohammed V. If you prefer to stay in the Medina, take a *petit taxi*, or walk down to Place de la Résistance (aka La Fiat) and pick up bus #9 to Dar Batha/Place de l'Istiqlal, near the western gate to Fes el Bali, Bab Boujeloud. The *gare routière* **bus station** is just outside the walls near Bab Boujeloud. The terminal for CTM buses is off Rue de l'Atlas, which links the far end of Av Mohammed V with Place de l'Atlas. **Grands taxis** mostly operate from the *gare routière*; exceptions include those serving Meknes (from the train station). The **tourist office** is on Place de la Résistance (Mon–Thurs 8.30am–noon & 2.30–6.30pm, Fri

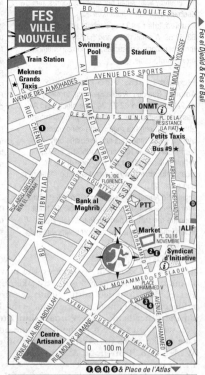

| ACCOMMODATION | | | EATING & DRINKING | | | |
|---|---|---|---|---|---|---|
| Amor | C | Mounia G | Chamonix | 2 | La Cheminée | 1 |
| De la Paix | B | Nouzha H | Chez Vittorio | | Le Nautilus | B |
| Grand | E | Rex F | Pizzeria | 3 | Marrakech | 6 |
| HI hostel | D | Royal A | Eden Chope Bar | 4 | Zagora | 5 |

8.30–11.30am & 3–6.30pm; ☎055 62 34 60), with a Syndicat d'Initiative on Place Mohammed V (same hours plus Sat 8.30am–noon). Both can tell you about June's seven-day **Festival of World Sacred Music**; more details from the secretariat (☎055 74 05 35, ⓦwww.fesfestival.com). There's a shortage of **hotel** space in all categories, so be prepared for higher-than-usual prices; booking ahead is advisable. For atmosphere and character, the Medina is the place to be, though you'll need an easy-going attitude towards size and cleanliness. The less engaging Ville Nouvelle has a wider choice of hotels.

### Hostel

**HI hostel** 18 Rue Abdeslam Seghrini ☎055 62 40 85. One of Morocco's best hostels – well-kept, friendly and spotlessly clean (dorms 45dh with HI card, 50dh without). ❶

### Hotels in the Medina

**Cascade** Just inside Bab Boujeloud, Fes el-Bali ☎055 63 84 42. An old building, with a useful

public *hammam* (bath house) behind. Small rooms, but clean and friendly. ❶

**Du Commerce** Place des Alaouites, Fes el-Djedid, facing the doors of the royal palace ☎055 62 22 31. Still owned by a Jewish family in what was the Jewish quarter; old, but comfortable and friendly, with a lively café at street level. ❶

**Lamrani** Talâa Seghira, Fes el-Bali ☎055 63 44

11. Friendly with small but spotless rooms, mostly doubles, opposite a *hammam*. **①**

**Pension Talaa** 14 Talâa Seghira, Fes el Bali ☎055 63 33 59. A small place and slightly pricier than the other Medina cheapies, but correspondingly more comfortable. **①**

### Hotels in the Ville Nouvelle

**Amor** 31 Rue de l' Arabie Saoudite, formerly Rue du Pakistan ☎055 62 27 24. One block from Av Hassan II, behind the Bank al-Maghrib. Comfortable though sombre rooms with good bathroom but hot water mornings and evenings only. **②**

**De la Paix** 44 Av Hassan II ☎055 62 50 72, ℮hoteldelapaix@iam.net.ma. Tour-group hotel, nicely refurbished, with a good seafood restaurant and a bar. **③**

**Grand** Bd Abdallah Chefchaounei ☎055 93 20 26, ℮grandhotel@fesnet.net.ma. Old colonial hotel opposite the sunken park on Place Mohammed V. Refurbished, en-suite rooms, some very large. **③**

**Mounia** 60 Bd Zerktouni ☎055 65 07 71 or 72, ℮www.hotelmouniafes.com. Modern hotel with friendly management, plus restaurant and a popular bar (which can be noisy). **⑤**

**Nouzha** 7 Av Hassan Dkhissi ☎055 64 00 02 or 12, ℮ametisnouzha@menara.ma. Splendidly decorated public areas and comfortable rooms, slightly out-of-centre but convenient for the CTM terminal. **③**

**Rex** 32 Place de l'Atlas ☎055 64 21 33. Small, congenial hotel built in 1910, but clean, pleasant and near the CTM terminal. **①**

**Royal** 36 Rue es Soudan ☎055 62 46 56. Handy for the train station. All rooms have a shower (some have toilets too), but hot water 7–9am only, and rooms vary in quality; look before you accept. **①**

### Campsite

**Camping International** Route de Sefrou ☎055 61 80 61. Some 4km south of town, this site is pricey but has good facilities, including a pool in summer. Take bus #38 from Place de l'Atlas.

## The City

The Medina is actually two cities: the newer section, **Fes el Djedid**, established in the thirteenth century, is mostly taken up by the Royal Palace. The older part, **Fes el Bali**, founded in the eighth century on the River Fes, was populated by refugees from Tunisia on one bank – the **Kairouine quarter** – and from Spain on the other bank – the **Andalusian quarter**. In practice, almost everything you will want to see is in the Kairouine quarter. For a view over the whole city, take a hike up to the **Arms Museum** in the fort above the bus station (Mon & Wed–Sun 8.30am–noon & 2.30–6pm; 10dh), from which the whole of Fes el Bali is laid out at your feet.

**Getting lost** is one of the great joys of the Fes Medina, and a **guide** is not really necessary; if you get in difficulties, you can always ask people for directions to Bab Boujeloud, Place Nejjarine or the Medersa el Attarin. Should you want to engage one, official guides wear a medallion to identify themselves, unofficial guides do not; both can be found at Bab Boujeloud. Never go shopping with either kind of guide however, as prices are liable to double.

**Talaa Kebira**, the Medina's main artery, can be accessed by entering Bab Boujeloud, taking the first left and then turning right. About 100m down is the most brilliant of Fes's monuments, the **Medersa Bou Inania** (daily 8.30am–1pm & 2.30–5.30pm; 10dh), which comes close to perfection in every aspect of its construction, with beautiful carved wood, stucco and *zellij* tilework – well worth a visit. Continuing down Talâa Kebira you reach the entrance to the **Souk el Attarin** (Souk of the Spice Vendors), the formal heart of the city. To the right, a street leads past the charming **Souk el Henna** – a tree-shaded square where traditional cosmetics are sold – to Place Nejjarin (Carpenters' Square). Here, next to the geometric tilework of the **Nejjarin Fountain**, is the imposing eighteenth-century **Nejjarin Fondouk**, now a woodwork museum (daily 10am–5pm, during Ramadan closes 4pm; 20dh), though the building is rather more interesting than its exhibits. Immediately to the right of the fountain, Talâa Seghira is an alternative route back to Bab Boujeloud, while the alley to the right of that is the aromatic **carpenters' souk**, ripe with the scent of sawn cedar, and top on the list of great Medina smells.

The street opposite the Nejjarin Fountain leads to the **Zaouia Moulay Idriss II**, one of the holiest buildings in the city. Buried here is the son and successor of

FES EL BALI

▲ *Ouezzane & Chaouen*       *Taza & Oujda* ▲

**ACCOMMODATION**
| | |
|---|---|
| Cascade | C |
| Du Commerce | D |
| Lamrani | A |
| Pension Talaa | B |

**EATING & DRINKING**
| | |
|---|---|
| Des Jeunes | 2 |
| La Kasbah | 1 |

N

300 m

Oued Fes

ROUTE DU TOUR DE FES

Bab Sidi Bujida

Bab Ftouh

Andalusian Mosque

Medersa Es Sahrija

Medersa El Oued

Tanneries

Seffarine Medersa

Kairaouine Mosque

Medersa Mishahiya

Attarin Medersa

Medersa Ech Cherratin

Mosque Er Rsif

Local Buses & Petits Taxis

PLACE ER RSIF

Kissaria

Zaouia Moulay Idriss II

Bab Jamaï

Bab El Guissa

Mosque Bab Guissa

Fondouk Guissa

Nejjarin Fondouk

Cherabliyin Mosque

Hammam

Fountain

Fondouk

Merenid Tombs

FES EL BALI

Borj Nord (Arms Museum)

Medersa Bou Inania

Bab Boujeloud

Dar Batha

PLACE DE L'ISTIQLAL

AVE DE LA LIBERTÉ

Lycée

PLACE BAGHDADI

Bab Mahrouk

KASBAH EN NOUAR

Bus Station & Grands Taxis

Bab Ahmed

Jardins de Boujeloud

ROUTE DU TOUR DE FES

AVENUE DES MERINIDS

RUE FAID KHAMMAR

RUE SIDI AL BOUGHALEB

RUE SEFFAH

RUE SIDI BOUJIDA

RUE SIDI YOUSSEF

SOUK EL ATTARIN

RUE HORMIS

RUE CHERABLIYIN

RUE BEN SAFI

RUE SEGHIRA

RUE SIDI EL KHIYAT

RUE FED DOUH

RUE DES FRANÇAIS

ROUTE DU TOUR DE FES

▼ *Ville Nouvelle*

⊙ *Fes el Djedid & Ville Nouvelle*

19

MOROCCO | Central Morocco

707

Fes's founder, who continued his father's work. Only Muslims may enter to check out the *zellij* tilework, original wooden *minbar* (pulpit) and the tomb itself. Just to its east is the **Kissaria**, where fine fabrics are traded. Meanwhile, over to your left (on the other side of the Kissaria), Souk el Attarin comes to an end opposite the fourteenth-century **Attarin Medersa** (daily 9am–6pm; during Ramadan closes 4pm; 10dh), the finest of the city's medieval colleges after the Bou Inania. To the right of the Medersa, a narrow street runs along the north side of the **Kairaouine Mosque**. Founded in 857 AD by a refugee from Kairouan in Tunisia, the Kaiaouine is one of the oldest universities in the world, and the fountainhead of Moroccan religious life. Its present dimensions, with sixteen aisles and room for twenty thousand worshippers, are essentially the product of tenth- and twelfth-century reconstructions. Non-Muslims can look into the courtyard through the main door.

The street emerges in **Place Seffarine**, almost wilfully picturesque with its faience fountain, gnarled fig trees and metalworkers hammering away. On the west side of the square, the thirteenth-century **Seffarine Medersa** is still in use as a hostel for students at the Kairaouine (visitors may enter for a look at any reasonable hour without paying). If you're beginning to find the medieval prettiness of the central *souks* and *medersas* slightly unreal, then the area beyond the square should provide the antidote. The dyers' market – **Souk Sabbighin** – is directly south of the Seffarine Medersa, and is draped with fantastically coloured yarn and cloth drying in the heat. Below, workers in grey toil over cauldrons of multicoloured dyes. Place er Rsif, nearby, has buses and taxis to the Ville Nouvelle. The street to the left (north) of the Seffarine Medersa leads to the **tanneries**, constantly visited by tour groups with whom you could discreetly tag along if you get lost. Inside the tanneries (pay a tip to the *gardien*, usually 10dh, to enter), water deluges through holes that were once windows of houses, and hundreds of skins lie spread out on the rooftops, above vats of dye and the pigeon dung used to treat the leather, reminiscent of the pits of hell from Dante's *Inferno*. Straight on, the road eventually leads back round to the Attarin Medersa.

## Eating and drinking

**Cafés** are plentiful in the Ville Nouvelle, with some of the most popular along Av Mohammed es Slaoui and Av Mohammed V. Fes el Bali has two main areas for **budget eating**: around Bab Boujeloud and along Rue Hormis (running from Souk el Attarin towards Bab Guissa), and in the Ville Nouvelle, try the café/restaurants near the municipal market, on the left-hand side of Av Mohammed V as you walk from the post office. For **bars**, you have to look a little harder. *Eden Chope Bar*, 55 Av Mohammed V, south of Place Mohammed V, with its 1930s mock-classical interior, does good bar snacks, or try the hotel bars.

### Fes el Bali

**Des Jeunes** (aka *Chez Hamid*), inside Bab Boujeloud. Cheap and basic – soups, kebabs, couscous and *pastilla* (poultry-filled pie – a Fes speciality).

**La Kasbah** inside Bab Boujeloud. Two terraces with views over Bab Boujeloud, great *pastilla* and delicious *tajines*.

### Ville Nouvelle

**Chamonix** 5 Rue Moukhtar Soussi, off Av Mohammed V. A reliable restaurant serving Moroccan and European dishes. Attracts a young crowd, and stays open late in summer.

**Chez Vittorio Pizzeria** 21 Rue du Nador, nearly opposite *Hôtel Central*. Pizza and pasta; reliable and good value, but not very exciting.

**La Cheminée** 6 Rue Chenguit (aka Av Lalla Asma). Small and friendly licensed restaurant, moderate prices.

**Le Nautilus** basement of *Hôtel de la Paix*. Classy restaurant renowned for fish and seafood; expensive but worth it.

**Marrakech** 11 Rue Abes Tazi (between *Hôtel Mounia* and the old CTM terminal). Small, but good and inexpensive, with a limited menu of tasty food.

**Zagora** 5 Av Mohammed V in a small arcade, behind the Derby shoe shop. Upmarket and a little pretentious, but the food and service are well above average.

## Listings

**Exchange** BMCE, Place Mohammed V, Place de l'Atlas and Place Florence (all with ATMs).
**Internet** Cyber Club, 70 Rue Bou Khessissat, Fes el Djedid; Cyber la Colombe, Av Mohammed V opposite *Hôtel Central*; London Cyber, Place Batha, nearly opposite the #9 bus stop.

**Pharmacies** Night pharmacy in the *baladiya* (town hall) on Av Moulay Yousef (daily 9.30pm–8.30am).
**Police** Commissariat Central is on Av Mohammed V behind the post office.
**Post office** Corner of avenues Mohammed V and Hassan II.

# Rabat

Capital of Morocco since 1912, **RABAT** is elegant, slightly self-conscious in its modern ways, and a little bit dull. However, its monuments punctuate the span of Moroccan history, and are among the country's most picturesque.

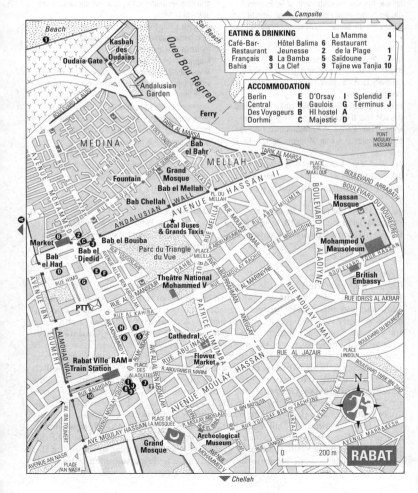

**EATING & DRINKING**

| | |
|---|---|
| Café-Bar- | Hôtel Balima **6** |
| Restaurant | Jeunesse **2** |
| Français **8** | La Bamba **5** |
| Bahia **3** | La Clef **9** |
| La Mamma **4** | |
| Restaurant | |
| de la Plage **1** | |
| Saïdoune **7** | |
| Tajine wa Tanjia **10** | |

**ACCOMMODATION**

| | | | |
|---|---|---|---|
| Berlin **E** | D'Orsay **I** | Splendid **F** |
| Central **H** | Gaulois **G** | Terminus **J** |
| Des Voyageurs **B** | HI hostel **A** | |
| Dorhmi **C** | Majestic **D** | |

## Arrival and accommodation

Rabat Ville **train station** is at the heart of the Ville Nouvelle, with most classified hotels situated only a few minutes' walk away (don't get off at the smaller Rabat Agdal train station, 2km from the centre). The main **bus terminal** is 5km west of the centre, served by local buses #17, #30 and #41, and by *petits taxis*. It's easier, if you're arriving by bus from the north, to get off in Salé across the river, and take a *grand taxi* from there into Rabat. *Grands taxis* for non-local destinations operate from outside the main bus station; those to Casa cost only a couple of dirhams more than the bus and leave more or less continuously. **Local bus** services radiate from the corner of Rue Nador and Bd Hassan II, where *petits taxis* and local *grands taxis* can be found. **Accommodation** can fill up in midsummer and during festivals; it's best to phone ahead.

### Hostel

**HI hostel** 43 Rue Marrassa ☏037 72 57 69. Just outside the Medina walls north of Bd Hassan II. Closed 10am–noon (30dh per person with HI card, 35dh without). Some double rooms available. ➊

### Hotels

**Berlin** 261 Av Mohammed V ☏037 70 34 35. Small hotel with hot showers. Centrally located above the Chinese restaurant *Hong Kong*. ➊

**Central** 2 Rue Al Basra ☏037 70 73 56. Central position near train station and alongside better-known *Hôtel Balima* on Av Mohammed V. A good budget choice and, with 34 rooms, likely to have space. ➊

**Des Voyageurs** 8 Souk Semarine, Medina, near Bab Djedid ☏037 72 37 20. Inexpensive, popular and often full. Clean, airy rooms but no showers. ➊

**Dorhmi** 313 Av Mohammed V, Medina, just inside Bab Djedid ☏037 72 38 98. Above *Café Essalem* and Banque Populaire. Well furnished and maintained. ➊

**D'Orsay** 11 Av Moulay Youssef, on Place de la Gare ☏037 70 13 19. Convenient for train station and café/restaurants, this is a friendly, helpful and efficient hotel. ➋

**Gaulois** 1 Rue Hims ☏037 72 30 22. Two-star with grand entrance and decent, value-for-money rooms, some en suite. ➊

**Majestic** 121 Av Hassan II ☏037 72 29 97, ⊛www.hotel.majestic.ma. Popular and good value, with bright, spotless rooms, some overlooking the Medina. ➋

**Splendid** 8 Rue Ghazza ☏037 72 32 83. Nice place whose best rooms overlook a courtyard, but hot water 10pm–10am only. *Café-Restaurant Ghazza* opposite is good for breakfast. ➋

**Terminus** 384 Av Mohammed V ☏037 70 06 16. A good alternative to the *D'Orsay* round the corner. A large, featureless block, but the interior has been updated. ➌

### Campsites

**Camping de la Plage** ☏063 59 36 63. Across the river at Salé. Basic but well-managed, with a shop opposite for supplies.

## The City

Rabat's compact **Medina** – the whole city until the French arrived in 1912 – is wedged on two sides by the sea and the river, on the others by the twelfth-century Almohad and fifteenth-century Andalusian walls. Laid out in a simple grid, its streets are very easy to navigate. North lies the **Kasbah des Oudaïas**, a charming and evocative quarter whose principal gateway – Bab el Kasbah or **Oudaïa Gate**, built around 1195 – is one of the most ornate in the Moorish world. Its interior is now used for art exhibitions. Down the steps outside the gate, a lower, horseshoe arch leads directly to **Moulay Ismail's Palace** (daily except Tue 9am–noon & 3–5.30pm; 10dh), which hosts exhibitions on Moroccan art and culture. The adjoining **Andalusian Garden** – one of the most delightful spots in the city – was actually constructed by the French in the last century, though true to Arab Andalusian tradition, with deep, sunken beds of shrubs and flowering annuals.

The most ambitious of all Almohad buildings, the **Hassan Mosque** (daily 8.30am–6.30pm; free), with its vast minaret, dominates almost every view of the city. Designed by the Almohad ruler Yacoub el Mansour as the centrepiece of the new capital, the mosque seems to have been more or less abandoned at his death in 1199. The minaret, despite its apparent simplicity, is among the most complex of all Almohad structures: each facade is different, with a distinct combination of patterning, yet the whole intricacy of blind arcades and interlacing curves is based on just two formal designs. Facing the tower are the **Mosque and Mausoleum of Mohammed V**, begun on the sultan's death in 1961 and dedicated six years later. On the opposite side of the Ville Nouvelle from the mausoleum is the **Archeological Museum**, Rue Brihi (daily except Tue 8.30am–noon & 2.30–6pm; 10dh), the most important in Morocco. Although small, it has an exceptional and beautiful collection of Roman-era bronzes, found mainly at Volubilis. The most beautiful of Moroccan ruins, the royal burial ground, called the **Chellah** (daily 8.30am–6pm; 10dh), is a startling sight as you emerge from the long avenues of the Ville Nouvelle, with its circuit of fourteenth-century walls, legacy of **Abou el Hassan** (1331–51), the greatest of the Merenid rulers. Off to the left of the main gate are the partly excavated ruins of the Roman city that preceded the necropolis. A set of Islamic ruins are further down to the right, situated within a second inner sanctuary, approached along a broad path through half-wild gardens.

### Eating and drinking

Rabat has a wide range of good **restaurants** serving both Moroccan and international dishes. As ever, the cheapest ones are to be found in the **Medina**. Avenues Mohammed V and Allal Ben Abdallah have some good **cafés**, but **bars** are few and far between outside the main hotels. The one at the *Hôtel Balima* is as good a place as any. Late-night options include a string of disco-bars around Place de Melilla and on Rue Patrice Lumumba.

**Café-Bar-Restaurant Français** 3 Ave Moulay Youssef, just off Place de la Gare. A downstairs bar and upstairs restaurant that is one of the best places to eat around the train station.

**Café Taghazoute** 7 Rue Sebbahi, Medina. Simple fare, including tasty fried fish, and also omelettes, which makes it a good option for breakfast.

**El Bahia** Bd Hassan II, built into the Andalusian wall, near the junction with Ave Mohammed V. Reasonably priced *tajines*, kebabs and salads, in a pleasant courtyard, upstairs or on the pavement outside, though service can be slow.

**Jeunesse** 305 Ave Mohammed V, Medina. One of the city's best budget eateries, with generous portions of couscous, and decent *tajines*.

**La Bamba** 3 Rue Tanta, behind the *Hôtel Balima*. European and Moroccan dishes, with good-value set menus (80dh European, 100dh Moroccan). Licensed.

**La Clef** Rue Hatim, alongside *Hôtel d'Orsay*. Quiet upstairs restaurant serving good French and Moroccan dishes including excellent *pastilla*.

**La Mamma** 6 Rue Tanta, behind the *Hôtel Balima*. Good pizzas and pasta dishes. *La Dolce Vita*, next door, is owned by the same patron and provides luscious Italian-style ice cream for afters.

**Restaurant de la Plage** on the beach below the Kasbah des Oudaïas ☎037 20 29 28. A fine fish restaurant overlooking the beach, offering the latest catch cooked to perfection.

**Saïdoune** in the mall at 467 Ave Mohammed V, opposite the *Hôtel Terminus*. A good Lebanese restaurant run by an Iraqi; licensed, but closed Friday lunchtime.

**Tajine wa Tanjia** 9 Rue Baghdad. A lovely little place with a wide range of excellent *tajines* and *tanjia* (jugged beef or lamb).

### Listings

**Embassies** Australia represented by Canada; Canada, 13bis Rue Jaâfar as Sadiq, Agdal ☎037 67 74 00; New Zealand represented by the UK; UK, 17 Bd Tour Hassan ☎037 72 96 96; USA, 2 Av Mohammed el Fassi ☎037 76 22 65. Irish citizens covered by their embassy in Lisbon (see p.808), but may get emergency help from the UK embassy.

**Exchange** Along Av Allal Ben Abdallah and Av Mohammed V. BMCE also has a *bureau de change* in Ville train station.

**Internet** Student Cyber, 83 Av Hassan II; ETSI Net, 12 Av Prince Moulay Abdallah; Phobos, 113 Bd Hassan II, by *Hôtel Majestic*.

**Police** Av Tripoli, near the Cathedral. Police post at Bab Djedid.

**Post office** Halfway down Av Mohammed V.

# Casablanca

Morocco's main city and economic capital, **CASABLANCA** (or "Casa") is also North Africa's largest port. Its Westernized image – with fancy beach clubs and almost no women wearing the veil – masks what is still substantially a "first-generation" city with some of Morocco's most intense social problems. Film buffs will be disappointed to learn that Bogart's *Casablanca* wasn't shot here (it was filmed entirely in Hollywood) – the *Bar Casablanca* commemorates it as a gimmick in the luxury *Hyatt Regency* hotel on Place des Nations-Unies, with T-shirts and baseball caps available. The city's main monument, the **Grande Mosquée Hassan II** (tours daily except Fri 9am, 10am, 11am & 2pm; 120dh, students 60dh), opened in 1993, is the world's second largest mosque after the one in Mecca, with space for one hundred thousand worshippers, and a minaret that soars to a record 200m. Commissioned by the last king, who named it after himself, it cost an estimated £320m/US$500m, raised by not wholly voluntary public subscription. It's a twenty-minute walk northwest from the centre. The French colonial buildings grouped around **Place Mohammed V** are built in a style called Mauresque, a French idealization of Moorish design, heavily influenced by Art Deco. The **Medina**, above the port and recently gentrified, is largely the product of the late nineteenth century, when Casa began its modest growth as a commercial centre.

## Practicalities

Some trains stop only at the **Gare des Voyageurs** (2km southeast of the centre) rather than continuing to the better-situated **Gare du Port**, between the town centre and the port. Bus #2 runs into town from the Voyageurs; otherwise, it's a twenty-minute walk or a *petit taxi* ride. Coming by **bus**, take the CTM if possible as it drops you downtown on Rue Léon l'Africain, behind *Hôtel Safir* on Av des FAR; other buses arrive at the *gare routière*, southeast of town on Route des Ouled Ziane. **Grands taxis** from Rabat arrive a block east of the CTM terminal, while those from points south come into a station south of town on the Route de Jadida in Beauséjour. The **tourist office** is inconveniently located south of the centre at 55 Rue Omar Slaoui (Mon–Thurs 8.30am–noon & 2.30–6.30pm, Fri 8.30–11.30am & 3–6.30pm; ☎022 27 11 77); more convenient is the **Syndicat d'Initiative**, 98 Bd Mohammed V (Mon–Fri 8.30am–noon & 3–6.30pm, Sat 8.30am–noon & 3–5pm, Sun 9am–noon; ☎022 22 15 24). **Hotels** are plentiful, though often near capacity, and cheaper rooms in the centre can be hard to find by late afternoon.

### Hostel

**HI hostel** 6 Place Ahmed Bidaoui ☎022 22 05 57. A friendly, well-maintained place just inside the Medina and signposted from the nearby Gare du Port (45dh per person). ❶

### Hotels

**Du Centre** 1 Rue Sidi Belyout, corner of Av des FAR ☎022 44 61 80 or 81. A golden oldie, cheered up with a splash of paint and new en-suite bathrooms. ❷

**Foucauld** 52 Rue Araibi Jilali ☎022 22 26 66. Great value, with en-suite rooms, near several good café/restaurants. ❶

**Mon Rêve** 7 Rue Chaouia ☎022 31 14 39. Long-standing budget travellers' favourite, though many rooms are at the top of a steep spiral staircase. ❶

**Plaza** 18 Blvd Felix Houphouët Boigny ☎022 29 78 22, ⓔhotel_plaza2000@yahoo.fr. Very central with big rooms, some en suite. ❷

**Terminus** 184 Blvd Ba Hamad ☎022 24 00 25. Handy for the Gare des Voyageurs: clean, decent rooms with hot showers on the corridor. ❶

**Touring** 87 Rue Allal Ben Abdallah ☎022 31 02 16. Refurbished old French hotel, friendly and excellent value; the best option in an area of cheap hotels. ❶

### Campsite

**Camping Oasis** Ave Jean Mermoz, Beauséjour ☎022 23 42 57. 4km south of the centre in the suburb of Beauséjour (bus #31 from Place Oued el Makhzine), and a little run-down.

## Eating and drinking

Casa has the reputation of being the best place to **eat** in Morocco, and if you can afford the fancier restaurant prices, this is certainly true. For those on a budget, some of the best possibilities lie in the smaller streets off Bd Mohammed V.

**Chhiouati Port** Rue Bab Rkha, where it meets Rue Sidi Bou Smara and Bd Houphouët Boigny at the edge of the Medina. A cheap hole-in-the-wall eatery with basic but filling meals at low prices.

**Le Buffet** 99 Blvd Mohammed V. Quick, bright and popular, with a reasonable 75dh *menu du jour*.

**Le Dauphin** 115 Blvd Felix Houphouët Boigny ☎022 22 12 00. Long-established and very popular fish restaurant, worth queuing for.

**Ostrea** Port de Pêche (in the fishing port). Superb freshly caught fish, plus oysters from just down the coast, expensive by local standards but much less than you'd pay for the same back home.

**Petit Poucet** 86 Blvd Mohammed V. Old and very reasonably priced French restaurant with a cheaper snack bar next door – one of the best places for some serious drinking.

**Retro 1900** Centre 2000, by Casa Port station. The most upmarket choice in this gone-to-seed 1980s open-air shopping centre, serving French cuisine with flair; pricey but good.

**Rôtisserie Centrale** 36 Rue Chaouia. best of a bunch of cheap chicken-on-a-spit joints on this little stretch of road opposite the Marché Central.

**Snack Amine** 32 Rue Chaouia. Inexpensive fish dishes including sole, whiting, squid, prawns and paella.

# Marrakesh

**MARRAKESH** (Marrakech in French) is a city of immense beauty, low, pink and tent-like before a great shaft of mountains. It's an immediately exciting place, especially around the vast space of its central square, the **Djemaa el Fna**, the stage for a long-established ritual in which shifting circles of onlookers gather around groups of acrobats, drummers, pipe musicians, dancers, storytellers and comedians. Unlike Fes, for so long its rival as the nation's capital but these days stagnating, Marrakesh's population is growing and it has a thriving industrial area; the city remains the most important market and administrative centre of southern Morocco.

The Djemaa el Fna (referred to simply as "el Djemaa", or even "la Place") lies right at the heart of the Medina, and almost everything of interest is concentrated in the web of alleyways around it. Just to the west of the Djemaa, an unmistakable landmark is the minaret of the great **Koutoubia Mosque** (enchanting under floodlights at night), in the shadow of which begins Avenue Mohammed V, leading out of the Medina and up the length of the new city, **Gueliz**. It's a fairly long walk between Gueliz and the Medina, but there are plenty of taxis and the regular buses #1 and #16 between the two.

## Arrival, information and accommodation

From the **train station**, by Gueliz, cross the street and take bus #3/#4/#8/#10/#16/#66 or a *petit taxi* (10–15dh) for Place Foucauld by the Djemaa. The **bus terminal** is just outside the northwestern walls of the Medina by Bab Doukkala; from here it's a 20-minute walk to the Djemaa, or take bus #3/#4/#5/#8/#10/#14/#16/#17/#26/#66 (opposite Bab Doukkala), or a *petit taxi* (8–10dh). CTM buses take you to their office in Gueliz. The **airport**, 4km southwest, is served by the erratic bus #11 (supposedly every half-hour to the Djemaa) – *petits* or *grands taxis* (30–60dh by day, 60dh by night) are a better option. The **tourist office** on Place Abdelmoumen Ben Ali (Mon–Thur 8.30am–noon & 2.30–6.30pm, Fri 8.30–11.30am & 3–6.30pm, also usually Sat 9am–noon & 3–6pm; ☎044 43 62 39) keeps current details of services you might need. There's a branch office at Place Vénus by the Koutoubia (same hours but closed Sat). The Medina, as ever, has the main concentration of cheap **accommodation** – most

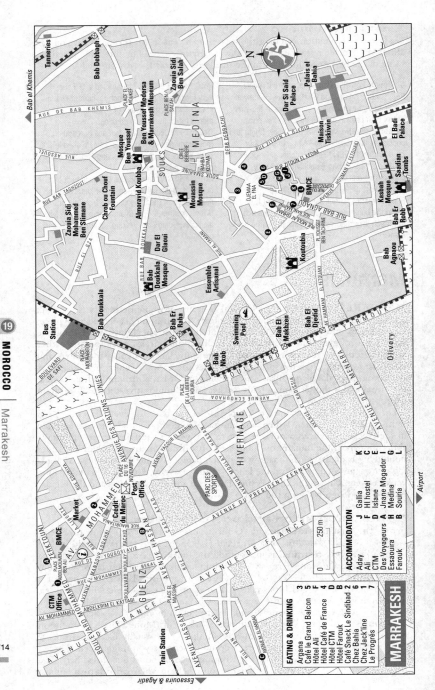

**19**

**MOROCCO** | Marrakesh

**MARRAKESH**

Tanneries

Bab el Khemis ▲

Bab Debbagh

RUE DE BAB EL KHEMIS

RUE ASSOUEL

PLACE EL MOUKEF

Zaouia Sidi Ben Salah

Zaouia Sidi Ben Salah

Ben Youssef Medersa & Marrakesh Museum

PLACE BEN SALAH

Mosque Ben Youssef

Dar Si Said Palace

Palais el Bahia

N

RUE BAB TAGHZOUT

Zaouia Sidi Mohammed Ben Slimane

Chrob ou Chouf Fountain

Almoravid Koubba

SOUKS

CHEE BERBERE

RAHBA KEDIMA

MEDINA

DERB DEBBACHI

RUE ZITOUN EL DJEDID

Maison Tiskiwin

El Badi Palace

RUE EL GZA

SOUK SMARINE

Mouassin Mosque

DJEMAA EL FNA

RUE ZITOUN EL KEDIM

4

5

6

BMCE

Saadian Tombs

RUE DE DUKKALA

Dar El Glaoui

3

Kasbah Mosque

RUE BAB DOUKKALA

RUE AL YAMANI

RUE MOULAY ISMAIL

F

RUE BAB AGNAOU

RUE DE BERIMA

Bab Er Robb

Bab Doukkala

Bab Doukkala Mosque

Ensemble Artisanal

Koutoubia

E

Bab Agnaou

Bus Station

PLACE MOBHABATION

Bab Er Raha

Swimming Pool

Bab El Makhzen

Bab El Djedid

Olivery

BOULEVARD DE SAFI

Bab Nkob

BOULEVARD

EL YARMOUK

Airport ▲

PLACE DE LA LIBERTE EL HOUBA

AVENUE ECHOUHADA

AVENUE EL KADISSIA

AVENUE DE LA MENARA

HIVERNAGE

BOULEVARD

AVENUE DES NATIONS - UNIES

PLACE DU 16 NOVEMBRE

Post Office

Crédit du Maroc

B

AVENUE YACOUB EL MARINI

AVENUE MOHAMED V

AVENUE DU PRESIDENT KENNEDY

PARC DES SPORTS

CTM Office

BMCE

Market

A

i

MOHAMMED

RUE DE MAURITANIA

AVENUE HASSAN II

AVENUE DE FRANCE

Train Station

Essaouira & Agadir ▲

AV. MOHAMMED ABDELKRIM EL KATTABI

AVENUE MOHAMMED VI

PLACE EL MASSIRA

BOULEVARD DE FRANCE - GUELIZ

0   250 m

**ACCOMMODATION**
| | | |
|---|---|---|
| Aday | J | |
| Ali | F | |
| CTM | D | |
| Des Voyageurs | H | |
| Essaouira | A | |
| Farouk | B | |
| Gallia | K | |
| HI hostel | C | |
| Islane | E | |
| Jnane Mogador | I | |
| Medina | G | |
| Souria | L | |

**EATING & DRINKING**
| | |
|---|---|
| Argana | 3 |
| Café le Grand Balcon | 5 |
| Hôtel Ali | F |
| Hôtel Café de France | 4 |
| Hôtel CTM | B |
| Hôtel Farouk | 2 |
| Café Snack Le Sindibad | 6 |
| Chez Bahia | 1 |
| Chez Jack'line | |
| Le Progrès | 7 |

places quite pleasant – and, unusually, has a fair number of classified hotels too. Given the attractions of the Djemaa el Fna and the *souks*, this is the first choice. Booking in advance is advisable. All our recommendations are in the Medina unless stated otherwise.

### Hostel

**HI hostel** Rue El Jahid, Gueliz ☏044 44 77 13. Immaculate, refurbished and close to the train station. Closed 9am–2pm. 40dh. ❶

### Hotels

**Aday** 111 Derb Sidi Bouloukat ☏044 44 19 20. A small hotel near the Djemaa, clean, friendly and well-kept. ❶

**Ali** Rue Moulay Ismail ☏044 44 49 79, ⓦwww .hotelali.com. Popular with overlanders and High Atlas trekkers (guides can be found here). Rooms have showers, and there's cheap dorm accommodation (50dh). ❷

**CTM** Djemaa el Fna ☏044 44 23 25. Above the old bus station, with decent-sized rooms, some with shower (hot water mornings and evenings, in en-suite showers only); rooms 28–32 overlook the square, as does the roof terrace. ❶

**Des Voyageurs** 40 Bd. Mohammed Zerktouni ☏044 44 72 18. Pleasant, old-fashioned hotel, with big, clean rooms and a nice little garden, but hot water mornings only. ❶

**Essaouira** 3 Derb Sidi Bouloukat ☏044 44 38 05, Ⓔhotelessaouira@hotmail.com. Well-run, popular cheapie, with laundry service, baggage deposit and rooftop café. ❶

**Farouk** 66 Av Hassan II, on the corner with Rue Mauretania, Gueliz ☏044 43 19 89, Ⓔhotelfarouk@hotmail.com. Excellent hotel with en-suite rooms and a popular restaurant, within walking distance of the train station. ❶

**Gallia** 30 Rue de la Recette ☏044 44 59 13, ⓦwww.ilove-marrakesh.com/hotelgallia. Pleasant building in a quiet road; airy and spotless rooms (all en suite and with air-con) off two tiled court-yards. Highly recommended – reserve by fax well ahead if possible Ⓕ044 44 48 53. ❸

**Islane** 279 Av Mohammed V, facing the Koutoubia minaret ☏044 44 00 81 or 83, ⓦwww.hotelislane .com. Views of the Koutoubia and comfortable modern rooms (en suite, a/c and satellite TV) compensate for the traffic noise. ❸

**Jnane Mogador** Derb Sidi Bouloukat, by 116 Riad Zitoun Kadem ☏044 42 63 23, ⓦwww .jnanemogador.com. Beautifully restored old house with charming but fully-equipped rooms around a lovely patio. ❷

**Medina** 1 Derb Sidi Bouloukat ☏044 44 29 97. Clean, friendly and good value, with an English-speaking proprietor and breakfast on the roof terrace. ❶

**Souria** 17 Rue de la Recette ☏072 77 18 47, Ⓔlkwika@hotmail.com. Deservedly popular family-run *pension*, spotless and very homely. ❶

## The City

There's nowhere in the world like the **Djemaa el Fna**: by day it's basically a market, with a few snake charmers and an occasional troupe of acrobats; in the late afternoon it becomes a whole carnival of musicians, storytellers and other entertainers; and in the evening dozens of stalls set up to dispense hot food to crowds of locals, while the musicians and performers continue. If you get tired of the spectacle, or if things slow down, you can move over to the rooftop terraces of the *Café de France* or the *Restaurant Argana* to gaze at it all from above. The absence of any architectural feature in the Djemaa serves to emphasize the drama of the **Koutoubia Minaret**. Nearly 70m high and visible for miles, it was begun shortly after the Almohad conquest of the city, around 1150, and displays many features that were to become widespread in Moroccan architecture – the wide band of ceramic inlay, the pyramid-shaped merlons, and the alternation of patterning on the facades.

### The northern Medina

A lane opposite the *Café de France* on the Djemaa el Fna leads to a stuccowork arch that marks the beginning of the crowded **Souk Smarine**, an important thorough-fare traditionally dominated by textiles. Just before the red ochre arch at its end, Souk Smarine narrows and you get a glimpse through the passageways to its right of the **Rahba Kedima**, a small and fairly ramshackle square whose most interesting features are its apothecary stalls. At the end of Rahba Kedima, a passageway to the left gives access to another, smaller square – a bustling, carpet-draped area known as la **Criée Berbère**, which is where slave auctions used to be held.

Cutting back to **Souk el Kebir**, which by now has taken over from the Smarine, you emerge at the **kissarias**, the covered markets at the heart of the *souks*. Kissarias traditionally sell more expensive products, which today means a predominance of Western designs and imports. Off to their right is **Souk des Bijoutiers**, a modest jewellers' lane, while at the north end is a convoluted web of alleys comprising the **Souk Cherratin**, essentially a leatherworkers' market.

If you bear left through this area and then turn right, you should arrive at the open space in front of the Ben Youssef Mosque. The originally fourteenth-century **Ben Youssef Medersa** (daily 9am–6.30pm; 30dh; combined ticket for this, the Marrakesh Museum and Almoravid Koubba 50dh) – the annexe for students taking courses in the mosque – stands off a side street just to the east. It was almost completely rebuilt in the sixteenth century under the Saadians, with a strong Andalusian influence. Parts have exact parallels in the Alhambra Palace in Granada, and it seems likely that Muslim Spanish architects were employed in its construction. Next door, the **Marrakesh Museum** (daily 9am–6.30pm; 30dh; combined ticket 50dh) exhibits jewellery, art and sculpture, both old and new, in a beautifully restored nineteenth-century palace. Almost facing it, just south of the Ben Youssef Mosque, the small **Almoravid Koubba** (daily 9am–6pm; 10dh; combined ticket 50dh) is easy to pass by, but it is the only building in the whole of Morocco from the eleventh-century Almoravid dynasty still intact, and at the root of all Moroccan architecture. The motifs you've just seen in the *medersa* – the pine cones, palms and acanthus leaves – were all carved here first.

If you're keen to buy the best in the *souks*, you should study the more-or-less fixed prices of the range of crafts in the excellent **Ensemble Artisanal** (Mon–Sat 8.30am–1pm & 2.30–7pm, Sun 8.30am–noon), just inside the ramparts on Av Mohammed V.

## The southern Medina

South of Djemaa el Fna there are two places not to be missed: the Saadian Tombs and El Badi Palace, the ruined palace of Ahmed el Mansour. For the tombs, the simplest route from the Djemaa is to follow Rue Bab Agnaou outside the ramparts, then aim for the conspicuous minaret of the **Kasbah Mosque** – the minaret looks gaudy and modern but is in fact contemporary with the Koutoubia, and was restored to its original state in the 1960s. The narrow passageway to the tombs is well signposted from the right-hand corner of the mosque.

Sealed up by Moulay Ismail after he had destroyed the adjoining El Badi Palace, the sixteenth-century **Saadian Tombs** (daily 8.30–11.45am & 2.30–5.45pm; 10dh) lay half-ruined and half-forgotten for centuries but are now restored to their full glory. There are two main mausoleums in the enclosure. The finer is on the left as you come in, a beautiful group of three rooms built to house El Mansour's own tomb and completed within his lifetime. The tombs of over a hundred more Saadian princes and royal household members are scattered around the garden and courtyard, their gravestones likewise brilliantly tiled and often elaborately inscribed.

Though substantially in ruins, enough remains of Ahmed el Mansour's **El Badi Palace** (daily 8.30–11.45am & 2.30–5.45pm; 10dh) to suggest that its name – "The Incomparable" – was not entirely immodest. It took a later ruler, Moulay Ismail, over ten years of systematic work to strip the palace of everything movable or of value, and, even so, there's a lingering sense of luxury. What you see today is essentially the ceremonial part of the palace complex, planned for the reception of ambassadors. To the rear extends the central court, over 130m long and nearly as wide, and built on a substructure of vaults in order to allow the circulation of water through the pools and gardens. In the southwest corner of the complex is an ancient *minbar* (pulpit) from the Dwiria, or Koutoubia mosque; both mosque and *minbar* have been lovingly restored (admission is an extra 10dh).

Heading north from El Badi Palace, **Rue Zitoun el Djedid** leads back to the Djemaa, flanked by various nineteenth-century mansions. Many of these have been converted into carpet shops or tourist restaurants, but one of them has been kept as a museum, the **Palais El Bahia** (Sat–Thurs 8.45–11.45am & 2.45–5.45pm, Fri 8.45–11.30am & 3–5.45pm; 10dh), former residence of a grand vizier. The name of the building means "The Brilliance", an exaggeration perhaps, but it's a beautiful old palace with two lovely patio gardens and some classic painted wooden ceilings. Also on this route is the **Dar Si Said** palace, which houses the **Museum of Moroccan Arts** (daily except Tue 9am–12.15pm & 3–6.15pm; 20dh). A further superb collection of Moroccan and Saharan artefacts is housed in the **Maison Tiskiwin** (daily 9.30am–12.30pm & 3.30–5.30pm; 15dh), which lies between the El Bahia and Dar Si Said palaces at 8 Rue de la Bahia.

## Eating and drinking

The most atmospheric place to **eat** is the Djemaa el Fna, where foodstalls set up around sunset and serve up everything from *harira* soup and couscous or *tajine* to stewed snails and sheep's heads, all eaten at trestle tables. For tea with a view, the terrace cafés of the *Hôtel CTM* and neighbouring *Café le Grand Balcon* overlook the Djemaa el Fna, as do two relatively reasonable rooftop restaurants: *Argana* and *Hôtel Café de France*. As usual in Morocco, cheap restaurants tend to gather in the Medina, with posher places uptown in Gueliz, along with French-style cafés and virtually all the city's bars.

**Café Snack Le Sindibad** 216 Av Mohammed V, near the post office, Gueliz. Couscous, *tajine* or brochettes at 30–50dh a plate. Open 24hr.

**Chez Bahia** Riad Zitoun el Kadim, 50m from Djemaa el Fna. Café/diner offering *pastilla*, *tajine*, breakfast and snacks at low prices.

**Chez Jack'line** 63 Av Mohammed V, Gueliz. Italian, French and Moroccan dishes at moderate prices, with an 80dh set menu.

**Hotel Ali** Rue Moulay Ismail. The eat-all-you-like buffet here, served 7–11pm, is justifiably popular and great value at 60dh. There are also lunchtime menus.

**Hotel Farouk** 66 Av Hassan II, Gueliz. Pizzas or an excellent-value set menu with soup or salad, then couscous, *tajine* or brochettes, followed by fruit or home-made yoghurt, for 50dh.

**Le Progrès** 20 Rue Bani Marine. The best of several decent choices in a street of cheap eateries.

## Listings

**Doctor** Dr Abdelmajid Ben Tbib, 171 Av Mohammed V ☎ 044 43 10 30.

**Exchange** BMCE has branches with adjoining *bureaux de change* and ATMs in the Medina (Rue Moulay Ismail, facing Place de Foucauld) and Gueliz (114 Av Mohammed V).

**Internet** Plenty around Djemaa el Fna, including Super Cyber de la Place in an arcade off Rue Bani

Marine by the *Hôtel Ichbilia*; Cyber Mohammed Yassine, 36 Rue Bab Aganou.

**Mountain trekking guides** Ask at the *Hôtel Ali*.

**Pharmacies** Pharmacie du Progrès, Place Djemaa el Fna at the top of Rue Bab Agnaou; Pharmacie de la Liberté, just off Place de la Liberté (or Houria).

**Post offices** Place du 16 Novembre, midway along Av Mohammed V, and on the Djemaa el Fna.

# Essaouira

**ESSAOUIRA**, the nearest beach resort to Marrakesh, is a lovely eighteenth-century walled seaside town. A favourite with the likes of Frank Zappa and Jimi Hendrix back in the 1960s, its tradition of hippie tourism has created a much more laid-back relationship between local residents and foreign visitors than you'll find in the rest of Morocco, and made Essaouira a centre for arts and crafts in addition to being the country's top surfing and windsurfing spot. Still largely contained within its ramparts, Essaouira is a simple place to get to grips with. At the northeast end of town is the **Bab Doukkala**; at the southwest is the town's pedestrianized main square, **Place Prince Moulay el Hassan**, and the fishing **harbour**. Between them run two main parallel streets: Av de l'Istiqlal/Av Mohammed Zerktouni and Rue Sidi Mohammed Ben Abdallah.

Essaouira is a great place just to walk around and the **ramparts** are the obvious place to start. Heading north along the lane at the end of Place Prince Moulay el Hassan, you can access the **Skala de la Ville**, the great sea bastion topped by a row of cannons, which runs along the northern cliffs. At the end is the circular **North Bastion**, with panoramic views (closes at sunset). Along the Rue de la Skala, built into the ramparts, are the **wood-carving workshops**, where artisans use thuja, a distinctive local hardwood. Marquetry and other woodwork, past and present, is displayed at the **Musée Sidi Mohammed Ben Abdallah** (closed at time of writing), on Rue Derb Laâlouj, the road running down from the ramparts to Av de l'Istiqlal. The town's other **souks** spread around and to the south of two arcades, on either side of Rue Mohammed Zerktouni, and up towards the Mellah (former Jewish ghetto), in the northwest corner of the ramparts. Worth particular attention are the **Marché d'Épices** (spice market) and **Souk des Bijoutiers** (jewellers' market). Art studios and hippie-style clothing shops centre around Place Chefchaouni by the clocktower. By the harbour is another impressive sea bastion, the **Skala du Port** (daily 8.30am–noon & 2.30–6pm; 10dh). The southern **beach** (the northern one is less attractive) extends for miles, past the Oued Ksob riverbed and the ruins of an old fort known as the **Bordj el Berod**, which seems almost to dissolve into the sand.

### Practicalities

The helpful **tourist office** is on Av du Caire (Mon–Fri 9am–noon & 3–6.30pm, June to mid-Sept open Sat same hours; ☏044 78 35 32). **Buses** arrive at a new bus station, about 500m (ten minutes' walk) northeast of Bab Doukkala. Especially at night, it's worth taking a *petit taxi* (about 5dh) or horse-drawn *calèche* (about 10dh). **Grands taxis** also operate from the bus station, though they will drop arrivals at Bab Doukkala or Place Prince Moulay el Hassan. **Accommodation** can be tight over Easter and in summer, when advance booking is recommended. Local residents may approach you with offers of rooms, and Jack's Kiosk, a newspaper shop on Place Prince Moulay el Hassan, displays ads for apartments. For an informal **meal**, you can do no better than eat at the line of grills down at the port, an Essaouira institution. A couple of snack bars on Av de l'Istiqlal offer the cheapest eats in town. Among the regular restaurants, try the budget *Essalam*, on Place Prince Moulay el Hassan, or the moderately-priced *Café-Restaurant Laayoune*, 4bis Rue Hajjali, with well-prepared dishes in a traditional setting. For a seafood splurge, you can't beat the two fish restaurants by the port, the long-established *Chez Sam's* and upmarket newcomer *Le Coquillage*, which is the first you come to.

### Hotels

**Beau Rivage** 4 Place Prince Moulay el Hassan ☏044 47 59 25, ⊕www.essaouiranet .com/beaurivage. Former backpackers' favourite, newly refurbished with spotless en-suite rooms right on the main square. ❸
**Majestic** 40 Rue Laâlouj, opposite the museum ☏044 47 49 09. The former French colonial courthouse, with good, clean rooms, though a little cheerless. ❶
**Sahara** Av Okba Ibn Nafia ☏044 47 52 92, ☏044 47 61 98. Big rooms around a central well, some en suite. ❶

**Shahrazed** 1 Rue Youssef el Fassi, entrance on Rue du Caire ☏044 47 29 77, ⊕hotelshahrazed@yaho.fr. Comfortable and well-equipped, with spacious rooms, most en suite. ❷
**Souiri** 37 Rue Attarine ☏044 47 53 39, ⊕souiri@menara.ma. Popular, colourful Medina hotel with a range of rooms, the cheaper ones with shared bathroom facilities. ❶
**Tafraout** 7 Rue Marrakech ☏044 47 62 76. Clean and friendly with some en-suite rooms. Hot water mornings and evenings only, but public showers for both sexes right next door. ❶

**Campsite**

**Camping Sidi Magdoul** 1km south of town behind the lighthouse ☎044 47 21 96. Clean, friendly and well-managed, with hot showers and bungalows, though the ground is rather hard and shade is sparse.

# Travel details

## Trains

Only direct trains are listed here; for connections, consult ⊛www.oncf.org.ma. Any station ticket office will issue a table of direct and connecting services to any other station.

**Casablanca Port** to: Rabat (half-hourly 6.30am–8.30pm; 1hr).

**Casablanca Voyageurs** to: Fes (9 daily; 4hr 20min); Marrakesh (9 daily; 3hr 15min); Meknes (9 daily; 3hr 30min); Mohammed V airport (hourly 6am–10pm; 35min); Rabat (14 daily; 1hr); Tangier (3 daily; 5hr 40min).

**Fes** to: Casablanca Voyageurs (9 daily; 4hr 15min); Marrakesh (5 daily; 7hr 40min); Meknes (10 daily; 50min); Rabat (9 daily; 3hr 20min); Tangier (1 daily; 5hr 10min).

**Marrakesh** to: Casablanca Voyageurs (9 daily; 3hr 10min); Fes (6 daily; 7hr 35min); Meknes (6 daily; 6hr 45min); Rabat (9 daily; 4hr 15min); Tangier (1 daily; 10hr).

**Meknes** to: Casablanca Voyageurs (9 daily; 3hr 30min); Marrakesh (6 daily; 6hr 50min); Fes (10 daily; 50min); Rabat (9 daily; 2hr 30min); Tangier (1 daily; 4hr 15min).

**Rabat** to: Casablanca Voyageurs (14 daily; 1hr); Casablanca Port (half-hourly 6.30am–9pm; 1hr); Fes (9 daily; 3hr 20min); Marrakesh (8 daily; 4hr 25min); Meknes (9 daily; 2hr 30min); Tangier (3 daily; 4hr 40min).

**Tangier** to: Casablanca Voyageurs (3 daily; 5hr 15min–6hr 05min); Fes (1 daily; 5hr 10min); Meknes (1 daily; 4hr 10min); Marrakesh (1 daily; 9hr 40min); Rabat (3 daily; 4hr 45min).

## Buses

**Casablanca** to: Essaouira (37 daily; 6hr); Fes (25 daily; 5hr 30min); Marrakesh (half-hourly; 4hr); Meknes (20 daily; 4hr 30min); Mohammed V airport (12 daily; 1hr); Rabat (frequent; 1hr 20min); Tetouan (26 daily; 6hr); Tangier (30 daily; 6hr 30min).

**Chefchaouen** to: Casablanca (5 daily, 9hr); Fes (6 daily; 5hr); Meknes (3 daily; 5hr 30min); Rabat (7 daily; 8hr); Tangier (8 daily; 3hr 30min); Tetouan (26 daily; 2hr).

**Essaouira** to: Casablanca (37 daily; 6hr); Rabat (10 daily; 8hr 30min); Marrakesh (14 daily; 3hr 30min).

**Fes** to: Casablanca (25 daily; 5hr 30min); Chefchaouen (6 daily; 5hr); Marrakesh (10 daily; 10hr); Meknes (approximately half-hourly; 1hr); Rabat (approximately half-hourly; 4hr); Tangier (17 daily; 5hr 45min); Tetouan (14 daily; 5hr 20min).

**Marrakesh** to: Casablanca (half-hourly 4am–9pm; 4hr); Essaouira (14 daily; 3hr 30min); Fes (10 daily; 10hr); Meknes (6 daily; 9hr); Rabat (hourly; 5hr 30min); Tangier (6 daily; 10hr).

**Meknes** to: Casablanca (20 daily; 4hr 30min); Chefchaouen (3 daily; 5hr 30min); Fes (approximately half-hourly; 1hr); Marrakesh (6 daily; 9hr); Rabat (approximately half-hourly; 3hr); Tangier (12 daily; 7hr); Tetouan (7 daily; 6hr).

**Rabat** to: Casablanca (frequent; 1hr 20min); Essaouira (10 daily; 7hr 30min); Fes (approximately half-hourly; 4hr); Marrakesh (hourly; 5hr 30min); Meknes (approximately half-hourly; 3hr); Salé (frequent; 15min); Tangier (30 daily; 5hr).

**Tangier** to: Casablanca (30 daily; 6hr); Chefchaouen (8 daily; 3hr 30min); Fes (17 daily; 5hr 45min); Fnideq (for Ceuta) (16 daily; 1hr); Marrakesh (6 daily; 10hr); Meknes (12 daily; 7hr); Rabat (30 daily; 5hr); Tetouan (50 daily; 1hr 30min).

**Tetouan** to: Casablanca (26 daily; 6hr); Chefchaouen (26 daily; 2hr); Fnideq (for Ceuta) (17 daily; 1hr); Fes (14 daily; 5hr 20min); Marrakesh (8 daily; 10hr); Meknes (7 daily; 6hr); Rabat (25 daily; 5hr); Tangier (50 daily; 1hr 30min).

## Ferries and hydrofoils

**Ceuta** to: Algeciras, mainland Spain (16–20 daily; 35min).

**Tangier** to: Algeciras, Spain (18–25 daily; 1hr–2hr 30min); Tarifa, Spain (5 daily; 35min); Gibraltar (2 weekly; 1hr 20min).

# The Netherlands

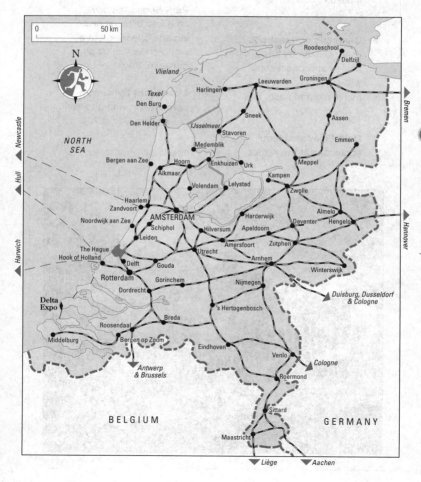

# Netherlands highlights

* **Amsterdam's canals and art** Cruise your way to famous art venues such as the Rijksmuseum and Van Gogh Museum. See p.731 & p.732

* **Cannabis coffeeshops** Every Dutch city has a choice of "coffeeshops", where you can buy marijuana and hash. See p.734

* **Delft** Enjoy wonderful applecake at the Kobus Koch Café, beside the old market square in this picturesque town. See p.740

* **Hoge Veluwe National Park** Spend the day on a free bike, picnicking and checking out a world-class Van Gogh museum. See p.744

* **Maastricht** Dynamic border town with a lovely old quarter. See p.745

△ Amsterdam canal

# Introduction and basics

**The Netherlands** is a country partly reclaimed from the waters of the North Sea, and around half of it lies at or below sea level. Land reclamation has been the dominant motif of its history, resulting in a country of unique images – flat, fertile landscapes punctuated by windmills and church spires; ornately gabled terraces flanking peaceful canals; and mile upon mile of grassy dunes, backing onto stretches of pristine sandy beach.

Most people travel only to uniquely atmospheric **Amsterdam**. Nearby is a group of towns known collectively as the **Randstad** (literally "rim town"), including **Haarlem** and **Delft** with their old canal-girded centres, and **Den Haag** (The Hague), a stately city with fine museums and easy beach access. Outside the Randstad, life moves more slowly. To the south, the landscape undulates into heathy moorland, best experienced in the **Hoge Veluwe National Park**. Further south still lies the compelling city of **Maastricht**, squeezed between the German and Belgian borders.

## Information & maps

"VVV" **tourist offices** are usually in town centres or by train stations, and have information in English, including maps and accommodation lists (a fee is payable); they will also book rooms, again for a small charge. The best general **map** is Kümmerley and Frey's.

## Money and banks

Dutch currency is the **euro** (€). **Banking hours** are Mon 1–4/5pm, Tues–Fri 9am–4/5pm; in larger cities some banks also open Thurs 7–9pm and occasionally on Sat mornings. GWK **exchange offices** at train stations open late daily; they change money and travellers' cheques, and give cash advances. You can also change money at most VVV tourist offices, post offices and *bureaux de change*, though rates are worse. **ATMs** are widespread. Smaller places (including B&Bs) may not accept cards.

## Communications

**Post offices** open Mon–Fri 9am–5pm, Sat 9am–noon. Post international items in the "Overige" slot. Most public **phones** take phonecards (available from post offices and VVVs) or credit cards. The operator is on ☎0800/0410 (free). Many cafés and public libraries offer **Internet** access.

## Getting around

**Trains** (ⓦ www.ns.nl) are fast, fares relatively low, and the network comprehensive. Various **passes** cut costs – ask at a station (passport needed for ID). With any ticket, you're free to stop off en route and continue later that day.

Urban **buses** and **trams** are very efficient. You only need one kind of ticket: a **strippenkaart**. You can buy 2- and 3-strip *strippenkaarts* from bus drivers, or better-value 15-strip (€6.60) or 45-strip (€19.50) *strippenkaarts* in advance from train stations, tobacconists and public transport offices. One *strippenkaart* can be used by any number of people, cancelling the requisite number of strips each.

### The Netherlands on the net

ⓦ **www.holland.com** National tourist board.
ⓦ **www.holland.com/rembrandt400** All about Rembrandt year 2006.
ⓦ **www.ns.nl** Train information.
ⓦ **www.bookings.nl** Online hotel bookings.

There's a nationwide system of **cycle** paths. You can rent bikes cheaply from main train stations and also from outlets in almost any town and village. Theft is rife: never leave your bike unlocked, and don't leave it on the street overnight – most stations have a storage area.

# Accommodation

**Accommodation** can be pricey, especially in places like Amsterdam and Haarlem. Book ahead during the summer and over holiday periods, especially Easter. The cheapest one- or two-star **hotel** double room starts at around €50. Three-star hotel rooms average out at around €80. Prices usually include a reasonable breakfast. You can reserve for free through the Netherlands Reservation Centre (www .hotelres.nl), or at VVV offices (for a small charge). There are 30 excellent HI **hostels** nationwide ( www.stayokay.com), charging €20–25 per person including breakfast. Larger cities often have independent hostels with similar prices, though standards are sometimes not as reliable. There are plenty of well-equipped **campsites**: expect to pay around €4 per person, plus €3–5 for a tent. Some sites also have **cabins** for up to four people, for around €35 a night.

## Dutch Language

| | Dutch | Pronunciation |
|---|---|---|
| **Yes** | *Ja* | Yah |
| **No** | *Nee* | Nay |
| **Please** | *Alstublieft* | Alstooblee-eft |
| **Thank you** | *Dank u/Bedankt* | Dank yoo/Bedankt |
| **Hello/Good day** | *Hallo* | Halloh |
| **Goodbye** | *Dag/Tot ziens* | Dahg/Tot Zeens |
| **Excuse me** | *Pardon* | Pardon |
| **Where?** | *Waar?* | Waah? |
| **Good** | *Goed* | Gud |
| **Bad** | *Slecht* | Slecht |
| **Near** | *Dichtbij* | Dichtbye |
| **Far** | *Ver* | Vare |
| **Cheap** | *Goedkoop* | Gudkoop |
| **Expensive** | *Duur* | Dooer |
| **Open** | *Open* | Open |
| **Closed** | *Dicht* | Dicht |
| **Today** | *Vandaag* | Vandahg |
| **Yesterday** | *Gisteren* | Histehren |
| **Tomorrow** | *Morgen* | Morgen |
| **How much is....?** | *Wat kost...?* | Wat kost…? |
| **What time is it?** | *Hoe laat is het?* | Hoo laht iss het? |
| **I don't understand** | *Ik begrijp het niet* | Ick bechripe het neet |
| **Do you speak English?** | *Spreekt u Engels?* | Spraicht oo Engells? |
| **One** | *Een* | Ayn |
| **Two** | *Twee* | Tway |
| **Three** | *Drie* | Dree |
| **Four** | *Vier* | Veer |
| **Five** | *Vijf* | Vife |
| **Six** | *Zes* | Zess |
| **Seven** | *Zeven* | Zayven |
| **Eight** | *Acht* | Acht |
| **Nine** | *Negen* | Nehen |
| **Ten** | *Tien* | Teen |

# Food, drink and drugs

Dutch **food** tends to be plain but thanks to its colonial history, the Netherlands boasts the best **Indonesian** cuisine outside Indonesia. *Nasi goreng* and *bami goreng* (rice or noodles with meat) are good basic dishes; chicken or beef in peanut sauce (*sateh*) is always available. A *rijsttafel* is rice or noodles served with a huge range of tasty side-dishes.

**Breakfast** (*ontbijt*) is filling, made up of rolls, cheese, ham, eggs, jam and honey, chocolate spread or peanut butter. **Snacks** include chips – *frites* or *patat* – smothered with mayonnaise, curry, satay or tomato sauce, *kroketten* (bite-size chunks of meat goulash coated in breadcrumbs and deep fried) and *fricandel* (a frankfurter-like sausage). **Fish** specialities sold from street kiosks include salted raw herrings, smoked eel (*gerookte paling*), mackerel in a roll (*broodje makreel*) and mussels. Other common snacks are kebab (*shoarma*) and falafel. Most bars serve sandwiches and rolls (*boterham* and *broodjes – stokbrood* if made with baguette) and, in winter, *erwtensoep*, a thick pea soup with smoked sausage, and *uitsmijter* fried eggs on buttered bread, topped with ham or roast beef. In **restaurants**, stick to the dish of the day (*dagschotel*). Train station restaurants serve good meals for €7, student places for under €9. Many places have at least one meat-free item, and you'll find veggie restaurants in most towns.

Sampling the Dutch and Belgian **beers** in every region is a real pleasure, often done in a cosy brown café (*bruine kroeg*, named because of the colour of the tobacco-stained walls); the big brands Heineken, Amstel, Oranjeboom and Grolsch are the tip of the iceberg. A standard, small glass (*een pils*) costs about €1.60; a bigger glass is *een vaasje*. You may also come across *proeflokalen* or tasting houses, small, old-fashioned bars that close around 8pm, and specialize in **jenever**, Dutch gin, drunk straight; *oud* (old) is smooth, *jong* (young) packs more of a punch. **Coffee** is normally good and strong, while **tea** generally comes with lemon. **Chocolate** is also popular, served hot or cold.

## Drugs

Purchases of up to 5g of cannabis, and possession of up to 30g (the legal limit) are tolerated; in practice, many "**coffeeshops**" offer discounted bulk purchases of 50g with impunity. Coffeeshops in city centres – plasticky, neon-lit dives, pumping out mainstream rock, reggae or techno – are worth avoiding. Less touristy districts house more congenial, high-quality outlets. When you walk in, ask to see the **menu** which lists the different hashes and grasses on offer. Take care with spacecakes (cakes or biscuits baked with hash), mainly because you can never be sure what's in them, and don't ever buy from street dealers. All other narcotics are illegal, and don't even entertain the notion of taking a "souvenir" home with you.

# Opening hours and holidays

Many **shops** stay closed on Mon morning, although markets open early. Otherwise, opening hours tend to be 9am–5.30/6pm. In major cities, night shops (*avondwinkels*) open 4pm–1/2am. **Museum** times are generally Tues–Sat 10am–5pm, Sun 1–5pm. Shops and banks are closed, and museums adopt Sunday hours, on **public holidays**: Jan 1, Good Fri, Easter Sun & Mon, April 30, May 5, May 13, Whitsun & Mon, Dec 25 & Dec 26.

# Emergencies

If you are wary of pickpockets and badly lit streets at night, you're unlikely to come into contact with the police. **Pharmacies** (*apotheek*) open Mon–Fri 8.30am–5.30pm; there'll be a note of the nearest open pharmacy on the door. Duty **doctors** at the Centrale Doktorsdienst (☏0900/503 2042) offer advice; otherwise head for any hospital (*ziekenhuis*).

## Emergency numbers

Police, fire and ambulance ☏112.

# Amsterdam

**AMSTERDAM** is a beguiling capital, with a compact mix of the provincial and the cosmopolitan, a welcoming attitude towards visitors and a uniquely youthful orientation. For many, its array of world-class museums and galleries – notably the **Rijksmuseum**, with its collection of seventeenth-century Dutch paintings, and the **Van Gogh Museum** – are reason enough to visit.

Amsterdam started out as a fishing village at the mouth of the River Amstel, and then, when the river was dammed in the thirteenth century, it grew as a trading centre. During the Reformation it rose even further in stature, taking trade away from Antwerp and becoming a haven for its religious refugees. The city went from strength to strength in the seventeenth century, becoming the centre of a vast trading empire with colonies in Southeast Asia. Amsterdam accommodated its expansion with the cobweb of **canals** that gives the city its distinctive and elegant shape today. By the eighteenth century, Amsterdam was in gentle decline, re-emerging as a fashionable focus for the alternative movements of the 1960s. Despite a backlash in the 1980s, the city still takes a progressive approach to social issues and culture, with a buzz of open-air summer events, intimate clubs and bars, and relaxed attitude to soft drugs.

## Arrival, information and accommodation

Schiphol **airport** is connected by train with the main **Centraal Station** (every 15min; hourly at night), which is at the hub of all **bus** and **tram** routes and just five minutes' walk from central Dam Square. International buses arrive at Amstel Station, ten minutes south of Centraal Station by metro. For **information**, the main VVV is outside Centraal Station, Stationsplein 10 (daily 9am–5pm; ☎0900/400 4040, ⓦwww.visitamsterdam.nl); there's another inside the station (Mon–Sat 8am–8pm, Sun 9am–5pm); a smaller kiosk on the Leidseplein corner of Leidsestraat (daily 9am–5pm); and an office in the airport (daily 7am–10pm). Any of these can sell you an **Amsterdam Pass** (€33/43/53 for 1/2/3 days), which gives free or reduced entry to major attractions as well as free public transport and selected restaurant discounts. The VVV has a monthly **listings** guide, *Day by Day – Amsterdam* (€1.75).

The excellent network of **trams**, **buses** and the **metro** (all daily 6/7am–midnight) isn't expensive. The GVB public transport office in front of Centraal Station (Mon–Fri 7am–7/9pm, Sat & Sun 8am–7/9pm; ☎0900/8011) has free route maps and an English guide to the *strippenkaart* ticketing system (see "Getting around"). After midnight, **night buses** take over, running roughly hourly from Centraal Station to most parts of the city. **Bikes** can be rented from Centraal Station or from a number of firms around town (see "Listings", p.736).

### Hostels

**Bob's Youth Hostel** Nieuwezijds Voorburgwal 92 ☎020/623 0063. Lively and smoky, with small dorms, cheap meals and Internet access, this is an old backpackers' favourite, 10min walk southwest from Centraal Station. Dorms €19, rooms ⓺

**Bulldog Low-Budget Hotel** Oudezijds Voorburgwal 220 ☎020/620 3822, ⓦwww.bulldog.nl. Part of the Bulldog coffeeshop chain, this super-smart hostel has a bar and DVD lounge, dorms with TV and showers, doubles and apartments. Tram #4, #9, #16 or #24 to Dam, then a 3min walk east. Dorms €26, rooms ⓺

**Durty Nelly's** Warmoesstraat 115–117 ☎020/638 0125, ⓦwww.xs4all.nl/~nellys/. Good-quality dorms above a packed Irish pub. Eight minutes' walk along Damrak, then turn right at Beursplein from Centraal Station. €25.

**Flying Pig Downtown** Nieuwendijk 100 ☎020/420 6822, ⓦwww.flyingpig.nl. Clean, large establishment well run by ex-backpackers, with free kitchen facilities, Internet access, an

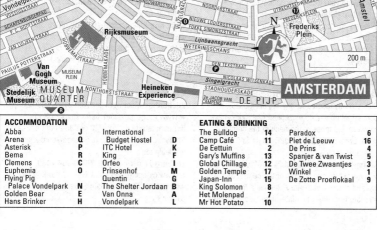

**ACCOMMODATION**

| | | | |
|---|---|---|---|
| Abba | **J** | International | |
| Arena | **Q** | Budget Hostel | **D** |
| Asterisk | **P** | ITC Hotel | **K** |
| Bema | **R** | King | **F** |
| Clemens | **C** | Orfeo | **I** |
| Euphemia | **O** | Prinsenhof | **M** |
| Flying Pig | | Quentin | **G** |
| Palace Vondelpark | **N** | The Shelter Jordaan | **B** |
| Golden Bear | **E** | Van Onna | **A** |
| Hans Brinker | **H** | Vondelpark | **L** |

**EATING & DRINKING**

| | | | |
|---|---|---|---|
| The Bulldog | **14** | Paradox | **6** |
| Camp Café | **11** | Piet de Leeuw | **16** |
| De Eettuin | **2** | De Prins | **4** |
| Gary's Muffins | **13** | Spanjer & van Twist | **5** |
| Global Chillage | **12** | De Twee Zwaantjes | **3** |
| Golden Temple | **17** | Winkel | **1** |
| Japan-Inn | **15** | De Zotte Proeflokaal | **9** |
| King Solomon | **8** | | |
| Het Molenpad | **7** | | |
| Mr Hot Potato | **10** | | |

all-night bar and no curfew; not for faint-hearted non-smokers. Five-minute walk from Centraal Station. €23.40.

**Flying Pig Palace Vondelpark** Vossiusstraat 46 ☎020/400 4187, ⓦwww.flyingpig.nl. On the edge of the city's big park, a clean and well-maintained place with free kitchen facilities and Internet access, no curfew and good tourist information. Tram #1/#2/#5 to Leidseplein. Dorms €22.90, rooms ❺

**Hans Brinker** Kerkstraat 136 ☎020/622 0687, ⓦwww.hans-brinker.com. Well-established and raucously popular cheapie, though a little more upmarket than some. Café with cheap dishes available. Tram #1/#2/#5 to Prinsengracht. €21.

**International Budget Hostel** Leidsegracht 76 ☎020/624 2784, ⓦwww.internationalbudget hostel.com. Excellent, homely budget option on a peaceful little canal in the heart of the city. Tram #1/#2/#5 to Prinsengracht. Dorms €30, rooms ❹

**The Shelter City** Barndesteeg 21 ☎020/625 3230, ⓦwww.shelter.nl. Non-evangelical Christian hostel smack in the middle of the Red-Light District, with single-sex dorms, lockers and a midnight curfew (1am weekends). Metro Nieuw-markt. €19.

**The Shelter Jordaan** Bloemstraat 179 ☎020/624 4717, ⓦwww.shelter.nl. Another easy-going Christian hostel tucked away in the Jordaan district. No smoking. Tram #13/#17 to Marnixstraat. €19.

**Stadsdoelen** Kloveniersburgwal 97 ☎020/624 6832, ⓦwww.stayokay.com. The more accessible of the two HI hostels, with clean semi-private dorms. HI members have priority in high season. Tram #4/#9/#16/#24/#25 to Muntplein. €23.50.

**Vondelpark** Zandpad 5 ☎020/589 8996, ⓦwww.stayokay.com. For facilities, the better of the two HI hostels, with bar, restaurant, TV lounge and kitchen; well located on the edge of the park. Secure lockers and a lift. Tram #1/#2/#5 to Leidseplein, then walk. Dorms €24, rooms ❻

### Hotels

**Abba** Overtoom 120 ☎020/618 3058. Conveniently located for the big art museums, Concertgebouw and Leidseplein. All rooms have showers and those at the back of the hotel are quiet. Breakfast is included. Tram #1 to Constantijn Huygenstraat.

**Arena** 's-Gravesandestraat 51 ☎020/850 2410, ⓦwww.hotelarena.nl. East of the centre, this hip and minimalist 3-star hotel has a lively bar, intimate restaurant and late-night club. All rooms

are en suite. Metro Weesperplein, then walk or tram #9. ❾

**Asterisk** Den Texstraat 16 ☎020/624 1768, ⓦwww.asteriskhotel.nl. Good-value budget hotel, just across the canal from the Heineken Brewery. Tram #16/#24/#25 to Weteringcircuit. ❺

**Bema** Concertgebouwplein 19b ☎020/679 1396, ⓦwww.hotel-bema.demon.nl. Small, clean place with characterful, if not modern, rooms. Handier for concerts and museums than nightlife. Tram /#5/#16 to Museumplein. ❻

**Clemens** Raadhuisstraat 39 ☎020/624 6089, ⓦwww.clemenshotel.nl. One of many options on this hotel strip. Clean, neat and value for money. Ask for a quieter room at the back. Tram #13/#17 to Westermarkt. ❻

**Euphemia** Fokke Simonszstraat 1 ☎020/622 9045, ⓦwww.euphemiahotel.com. A likeable, laid-back atmosphere, and big, basic rooms at reasonable prices, which means it's usually full. Tram #16/#24/#25 to Weteringcircuit. ❺

**King** Leidsekade 85–86 ☎020/624 9603. Clean but tiny rooms in a small hotel. Breakfast included. Minimum three nights during summer. Tram #1/#2/#5 to Leidseplein. ❻

**Prinsenhof** Prinsengracht 810 ☎020/623 1772, ⓦwww.hotelprinsenhof.com. Only two rooms are en-suite, but a hearty breakfast is included and service couldn't be friendlier. ❺

**Quentin** Leidsekade 89 ☎020/626 2187, ⓦwww.quentinhotels.com. Stylish small hotel, often a stopover for bands performing at the Melkweg, and well regarded among gay and lesbian visitors. Tram #1/#2/#5 to Leidseplein. ❼

**St Nicolaas** Spuistraat 1a ☎020/626 1384, ⓦwww.hotelnicolaas.nl. Very pleasant, well-run little hotel housed in a former mattress factory (with a king-size lift to prove it). Breakfast included. ❽

**Van Onna** Bloemgracht 104 ☎020/626 5801, ⓦwww.hotelvononna.com. A quiet, comfort-able, family-run place on a tranquil canal in the Jordaan. Tram #13/#17 to Westermarkt. Breakfast included. ❻

### Campsites

**Vliegenbos** Meeuwenlaan 138 ☎020/636 8855, ⓦwww.vliegenbos.com. In Amsterdam North, a ten-minute ride on bus #32 or #36 from Centraal Station. Closed Oct–March. Four-person cabins available too.

**Zeeburg** Zuider IJdijk 20 ☎020/694 4430, ⓦwww.campingzeeburg.nl. Bus #22 to Kramat-weg or tram #14 from Dam Square. Two-person cabins ❸

# The City

Amsterdam's compact centre contains most of the city's leading attractions but it takes only about forty minutes to stroll from one end to the other. **Centraal Station**, where you're most likely to arrive, lies on the centre's northern edge, its back to the River IJ, and from here the city fans south in a web of concentric canals, surrounded by expanding suburbs. Just wandering around to get the flavour of the place is often the most enjoyable way to proceed.

At the heart of the city is the vivacious **Old Centre**, an oval-shaped area featuring a jumble of antique streets and beautiful, narrow little canals. This is the unlikely setting for the sleazy, infamous **Red-Light District**. Forming a ring around it is the first of the major canals, the Singel, followed closely by the Herengracht, Keizersgracht and Prinsengracht. This is the Amsterdam you see in the brochures: still, dreamy canals, crisp reflections of seventeenth-century town houses, cobbled streets, railings with chained bicycles. To the south is the city's main square, **Leidseplein**, with the world-class trio of the **Rijksmuseum** (closed until 2008), the **Van Gogh Museum** and the **Stedelijk Museum** (closed until 2008) just beyond, forming a prelude to the lovely **Vondelpark** nearby. The **Jordaan** to the west features mazy streets and narrow canals. To the east is the **Old Jewish Quarter**, housing the first-rate Jewish Historical Museum.

## The Old Centre

Amsterdam is a small city, and, although the concentric canal system can be initially confusing, finding your bearings is straightforward. The medieval core boasts the best of the city's bustling streetlife and is home to shops, many bars and restaurants, fanning south from the nineteenth-century **Centraal Station**, one of Amsterdam's most resonant landmarks. From here, the busy thoroughfare **Damrak** marches into the heart of the city, lined with overpriced restaurants and bobbing canal boats, and flanked on the left first by the Modernist stock exchange or **Beurs** (now a concert hall), and then by the enormous De Bijenkorf department store.

East of Damrak, the infamous **Red-Light District**, stretching across two canals – Oudezijds (abbreviated to O.Z.) Voorburgwal and O.Z. Achterburgwal – is one of the real sights of the city, thronged in high season with visitors keen to discover just how shocking it all is. The two canals, with their narrow connecting passages, are crammed with neon-lit "window brothels", where scantily clad women often stand or sit behind glass for up to twelve hours a day.

Behind the Beurs, off Warmoesstraat, the precincts of the **Oude Kerk** (Mon–Sat 11am–6pm, Sun 1–5pm; €4.50; ⑩www.oudekerk.nl) offer a reverential peace after the excesses of the Red-Light district; it's a bare, mostly fourteenth-century church with the memorial tablet of Rembrandt's first wife, Saskia van Uylenburg. Just beyond, Zeedijk leads to the **Nieuwmarkt** square, centred on the turreted **Waag** building, an original part of the city's fortifications. **Kloveniersburgwal**, heading south, was the outer of the three eastern canals of sixteenth-century Amsterdam and boasts, at no. 29, one of the city's most impressive canal houses, built for the Trip family in 1662. Further along on the west side, the Oudemanhuispoort passage is filled with secondhand bookstalls.

At the southern end of Damrak, the **Dam** (or Dam square) is the centre of the city, its War Memorial serving as a meeting place for tourists. On the western side, the **Koninklijk Paleis** (Royal Palace; open for guided tours and exhibitions; ⑩www.klijkhuis.nl) was originally built as the city hall in the mid-seventeenth century. Vying for importance is the adjacent **Nieuwe Kerk** (open for exhibitions only, usually daily 10am–6pm; €10; ⑩www.nieuwekerk.nl), a fifteenth-century church rebuilt several times, and now exhibiting works from the Rijksmuseum and Stedelijk Museum, both of which are currently under renovation.

South of Dam square, **Rokin** follows the old course of the Amstel River, lined with grandiose nineteenth-century mansions. Running parallel, Kalverstraat is a

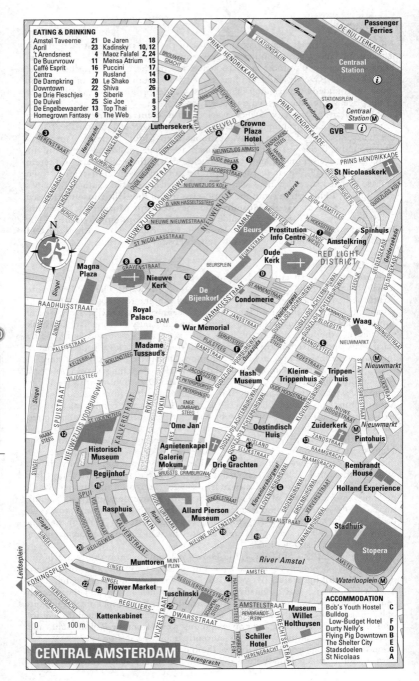

**EATING & DRINKING**

| | | | |
|---|---|---|---|
| Amstel Taveerne | 21 | De Jaren | 18 |
| April | 23 | Kadinsky | 10, 12 |
| 't Arendsnest | 4 | Maoz Falafel | 2, 24 |
| De Buurvrouw | 11 | Mensa Atrium | 15 |
| Caffé Esprit | 16 | Puccini | 17 |
| Centra | 7 | Rusland | 14 |
| De Dampkring | 20 | Le Shako | 19 |
| Downtown | 22 | Shiva | 26 |
| De Drie Fleschjes | 9 | Siberië | 1 |
| De Duivel | 25 | Sie Joe | 8 |
| De Engelbewaarder | 13 | Top Thai | 3 |
| Homegrown Fantasy | 6 | The Web | 5 |

**ACCOMMODATION**

| | |
|---|---|
| Bob's Youth Hostel | C |
| Bulldog | F |
| Low-Budget Hotel | D |
| Durty Nelly's | B |
| Flying Pig Downtown | E |
| The Shelter City | G |
| Stadsdoelen | A |
| St Nicolaas | A |

0    100 m

**CENTRAL AMSTERDAM**

monotonous strip of clothes shops, halfway down which, at no. 92, a gateway forms the entrance to the former orphanage that's now the **Amsterdams Historisch Museum** (Mon–Fri 10am–5pm, Sat & Sun 11am–5pm; €6; ⓦwww.ahm.nl), where artefacts, paintings and documents survey the city's development from the thirteenth century. Just around the corner, off Sint Luciensteeg, the **Begijnhof** is a small court of seventeenth-century buildings where the poor and elderly celebrated Mass in a concealed Catholic church. The plain English Reformed Church, taking up one side of the Begijnhof, has pulpit panels designed by the famous twentieth-century artist Piet Mondriaan. Close by, the **Spui** (pronounced "spow") is a lively corner of town whose mixture of bookshops and packed bars centres around a statue of a young boy known as *'t Lieverdje* (Little Darling). In the opposite direction, Kalverstraat comes to an end at **Muntplein** and the Munttoren – originally a mint and part of the city walls, topped with a seventeenth-century spire. Across the Singel canal is the fragrant daily **Bloemenmarkt** (Flower Market), while in the other direction Reguliersbreestraat turns towards the loud restaurants of **Rembrandtplein**. To the south is Reguliersgracht, an appealing canal with seven distinctive steep bridges stretching in line from Thorbeckeplein.

## Around Leidseplein

Amsterdam's expansion in the seventeenth century was designed around three new canals, **Herengracht**, **Keizersgracht** and **Prinsengracht**, which formed a distinctive cobweb shape around the centre. Development was strictly controlled, resulting in the tall, very narrow residences with decorative gables you see today. The appeal lies in wandering along, taking in the calm tree-lined waterways, while looking into people's windows – Amsterdammers tend not to bother with curtains, a habit which lends the city an open and cosy atmosphere. For shops, bars and restaurants, you're better off exploring the crossing-streets that connect the canals.

From the Spui, trams and pedestrians cross Koningsplein onto Amsterdam's main drag, **Leidsestraat** – a long, slender shopping street that cuts across the main canals. On the corner with Keizersgracht, the designer department store Metz & Co has a top-floor café with one of the best views of the city. Leidsestraat broadens at its southern end into **Leidseplein**, the bustling hub of Amsterdam's nightlife, a cluttered and disorderly open space criss-crossed by tram lines. The square has a frenetic feel, and is flanked by dozens of bars, restaurants and clubs, creating a bright jumble of jutting signs and neon lights. On the far corner, the **Stadsschouwburg** is the city's prime performance space after the Muziektheater, while behind, the fairy-castle *American Hotel* has a bar whose carefully co-ordinated furnishings are a fine example of Art Nouveau.

If you head straight to Leidseplein, however, you'll miss out on the grand canal frontages of Herengracht, especially between Leidsestraat and Vijzelstraat, a stretch known as the Golden Curve. To see the interior of one of the canal houses, head for the **Museum Willet-Holthuysen**, Herengracht 605 (Mon–Fri 10am–5pm, Sat & Sun 11am–5pm; €4; ⓦwww.willetholthuysen.nl), splendidly decorated in Rococo style and containing a collection of glass and ceramics and a seventeenth-century kitchen.

One of the city's loveliest neighbourhoods lies on and around Prinsengracht, focused on the gracious 1631 tower of the **Westerkerk** – north of Leidseplein, and a short stroll west of Dam square. Directly outside, a statue of Anne Frank by the sculptor Marie Andriessen signals the fact that the **Anne Frank House** (daily: April–Aug 9am–9pm; Sept–March 9am–7pm; closed Yom Kippur; €8; ⓦwww.annefrank.nl), where the young diarist lived, is just a few steps away at Prinsengracht 267. It's deservedly one of the most popular tourist attractions in town, so arrive before 9am (or at the end of the day) and be prepared to queue. Anne, her family and friends went into hiding from the Nazis in 1942, staying in the house for two years until they were betrayed and taken away to labour camps, an experience which only Anne's father survived. Anne Frank's diary was among the few things left behind, and was published in 1947, since when it has sold over thirteen million copies worldwide. The rooms the Franks lived in are left much as they were, even down to the movie-star pin-ups in Anne's bedroom and the marks on the wall recording the children's heights.

Across Prinsengracht to the west, the **Jordaan** is a beguiling area of narrow canals, narrower streets and architecturally varied houses. With some of the city's best bars and restaurants, alternative clothes shops and good outdoor markets, especially those on the square outside the Noorderkerk (which hosts an antique and household goods market on Mondays and a popular farmers' market on Saturdays), it's a wonderful area to wander through. The hottest contemporary artists show work at the **Stedelijk Museum Bureau Amsterdam** gallery, Rozenstraat 59 (Tues–Sun 11am–5pm; ⊛www.smba.nl).

## The Museum Quarter and south

Immediately south of Leidseplein begins the **Vondelpark**, the city's most enticing open space, a regular forum for drama and other performance arts on summer weekends, when young Amsterdam flocks here to meet friends, laze by the lake and listen to music; in June, July and August there are free concerts every Sunday at 2pm. Southeast of the park is a residential district, with designer shops and delis along chic **P.C. Hooftstraat** and **Van Baerlestraat** and some of the city's major museums grouped around the grassy wedge of **Museumplein**.

The **Rijksmuseum**, Stadhouderskade 42 (daily 9am–6pm but undergoing major renovation until 2008, so check first with the VVV; €9; ⊛www.rijksmuseum.nl), has fine collections of medieval and Renaissance applied art, displays on Dutch history, a fine Asian collection and an array of seventeenth-century Dutch paintings that is among the best in the world. Most people head straight for one of the museum's great treasures, Rembrandt's *The Night Watch*, but there are many other examples of his work, along with portraits by Frans Hals, landscapes by Jan van Goyen and Jacob van Ruisdael, the riotous scenes of Jan Steen and the peaceful interiors of Vermeer and Pieter de Hooch. Just south is the **Vincent Van Gogh Museum**, Paulus Potterstraat 7 (daily 10am–6pm, Fri 10am–10pm; €10; ⊛www .vangoghmuseum.nl). Long queues can be a problem in high season so arrive early. The collection includes the early years in Holland, continuing to the brighter works he painted after moving to Paris and then Arles, where he produced vivid canvases like *The Yellow House* and the *Sunflowers* series. Along the street, at Paulus Potterstraat 13, the modern-art **Stedelijk Museum** (⊛www.stedelijk.nl) is currently closed for refurbishment until 2008, though its permanent collection, including pieces by Picasso, Matisse, Van Gogh, Chagall, Kandinsky and Braque, can be seen in the former post office on Oosterdokskade (daily 10am–6pm, Thurs till 9pm; €9), just east of Centraal station.

Further along Stadhouderskade from the Rijksmuseum, the **Heineken Experience** at no. 78 (Tues–Sun 10am–6pm, last entry 5pm; €10; ⊛www .heinekenexperience.nl) provides an overview of Heineken's history and the brewing process; afterwards you're given snacks, free **beer** and free Internet access. South of here is the neighbourhood known as **De Pijp** (The Pipe) after its long, sombre canyons of brick tenements. This has always been one of the city's closest-knit communities, and one of its liveliest, with numerous inexpensive Surinamese and Turkish restaurants and a cheerful hub in the long slim thoroughfare of **Albert Cuypstraat**, whose food and clothes **market** (Mon–Sat 9.30am–5pm) is the largest in the city.

## East of the centre

East of Rembrandtplein across the Amstel, the large, squat **Muziektheater** and **Stadhuis** flank **Waterlooplein**, home to the city's excellent **flea market** (Mon–Sat). Behind, Jodenbreestraat was once the main street of the Jewish quarter (emptied by the Nazis in the 1940s); no. 6 is **Het Rembrandthuis** (Rembrandt House; Mon–Sat 10am–5pm, Sun 1–5pm; €7.50; ⊛www.rembrandthuis.nl), which the painter bought at the height of his fame, living here for over twenty years. The interior displays a large number of the artist's engravings. In 2006, look out for events celebrating the four-hundredth anniversary of Rembrandt's birth – for more info see ❽www.holland.com/rembrandt400/press/gb/ or ❽www.rembrandt400 .com. Across the way, the excellent, award-winning **Joods Historisch Museum** (Jewish Historical Museum; daily 11am–5pm; closed Yom Kippur; €6.50; ❽www .jhm.nl) is cleverly housed in a complex of Ashkenazi synagogues dating from the late seventeenth century and gives an imaginative introduction to Jewish life and beliefs.

Down Muiderstraat from here, the prim **Hortus Botanicus**, Plantage Middenlaan 2 (Mon–Fri 9am–4/5pm, Sat & Sun 11am–4/5pm; €6), is a pocket-sized botanical garden with eight thousand plant species; stop off for a relaxed coffee and cakes in the orangery. The eye-catching Plancius Building at Plantage Kerklaan 61 houses the excellent **Verzetsmuseum** (Dutch Resistance Museum; Tues–Fri 9am–5pm, Sat–Mon 10am–5pm; €5.50), where a variety of exhibits depict the ways in which the Dutch people opposed Nazi oppression. A short walk north brings you to Kattenburgerplein and the **Nederlands Scheepvaartmuseum** (Maritime Museum; Tues–Sun 10am–5pm; mid-June to mid-Sept also Mon 10am–5pm; €7.50; ❽www .scheepvaartmuseum.nl), housed in a seventeenth-century arsenal, crammed with maps, weapons and large models of sailing ships.

## Eating and drinking

Amsterdam has an extensive supply of ethnic **restaurants**, especially Indonesian and Chinese, as well as *eetcafés* and bars that serve decent, well-priced food in an unpretentious setting. We've also listed a handful of places to get a snack, as well as the best of the so-called **coffeeshops**, where smoking dope is the primary pastime (ask to see "the menu"). You must be 18 or over to enter these, and don't expect alcohol to be served. Most open at 9am and close at 1am (2/3am at weekends). Check out the widely available *Smokers Guide* (€6.50; ❽www.smokersguide.com) for advice on the varieties available, strengths, prices and new places to smoke.

### Cafés and snacks

**Caffé Esprit** Spui 10a. Swish modern café, with wonderful sandwiches and superb salads.

**Gary's Muffins** Prinsengracht 454, near Leidseplein; also Reguliersdwarsstraat 53. The best muffins and bagels in town, with big cups of coffee (half-price refills).

**Maoz Falafel** Leidsestraat 85, near Leidseplein; also Reguliersbreestraat 45 and Muntplein 1. The best street-food in the city – falafel and as much salad as you can eat for €3.50.

**Mr Hot Potato** Leidsestraat 44. Baked potatoes for €2.50 in a 1950s-style diner.

**Puccini** Staalstraat 17–21, near Waterlooplein. Dreamy cakes, pastries and chocolates, all handmade.

**Winkel** Noordermarkt 43, opposite the Noorderkerk. Popular local hangout on Saturday mornings during the farmers' market. Famously delicious apple cake.

### Restaurants

**Centra** Lange Niezel 29. Wonderful Spanish food and genial atmosphere in this *cantina* near the Oude Kerk. One of Amsterdam's best.

**De Eettuin** 2e Tuindwarsstraat 10, Jordaan. Hefty portions of Dutch food with DIY salad.

**Golden Temple** Utrechtsestraat 126 ☏020/626 8560. Laid-back lacto-vegetarian joint south of Rembrandtplein. No smoking and no alcohol.

**Japan-Inn** Leidsekruisstraat 4. Cheap and cheerful Japanese restaurant near the busy Leidseplein. Open until 11.45pm daily.

**King Solomon** Waterlooplein 239. Grilled meats, falafel and veggie options in this canteen-style kosher place near the Jewish Historical Museum.

**Mensa Atrium** Oudezijds Achterburgwal 237. Amsterdam University's self-service cafeteria with meals under €5. Open to all; extra discounts for students.

**Piet de Leeuw** Noorderstraat 11. Superb steakhouse off Vijzelgracht, dating from the 1940s. Good desserts too.

**Shiva** Reguliersdwarsstraat 72. Outstanding Indian restaurant, with well-priced, expertly prepared food, and veggie options.

Sie Joe Gravenstraat 24. Small Indonesian café-restaurant with a limited menu but well-made *gado gado*, *sateh* and *rending*. Great value for money.

**Top Thai** Herenstraat 22. Some of the best-value authentic Thai food in Amsterdam. Popular, with a friendly atmosphere.

### Bars

**'t Arendsnest** Herengracht 90. Eight Dutch beers on tap, all enthusiastically selected and poured by the owner; from 4pm onwards.

**De Buurvrouw** St Pieterspoortsteeg 29. Dark, noisy bar, just south of Dam Square with a wildly eclectic crowd.

**De Drie Fleschjes** Gravenstraat 16, near Dam Square. Tasting house for spirits and liqueurs. No beer, and no seats either. Closes 8.30pm.

**De Duivel** Reguliersdwarsstraat 87. Amsterdam's only hip-hop café, near the Rembrandtplein. Opposite the hip-hop coffeeshop.

**De Engelbewaarder** Kloveniersburgwal 59. Relaxed and informal haunt of Amsterdam's bookish types, with live jazz on Sunday afternoons.

**De Jaren** Nieuwe Doelenstraat 20–22, near Muntplein. Grand café overlooking the river – one of the best places to peruse the Sunday paper.

**De Prins** Prinsengracht 124. Roomy and welcoming *bruine kroeg*, also popular for its great-value food.

**Het Molenpad** Prinsengracht 653. One of the city's most atmospheric brown cafés, with remarkably good food. Fills with young professionals after 6pm.

**Spanjer & van Twist** Leliegracht 60. Perfect for laid-back summer afternoons, with chairs overlooking the quietest canal in Jordaan.

**De Twee Zwaantjes** Prinsengracht 114. Tiny oddball Jordaan bar where locals sing along raucously to accordion music – you'll either love it or hate it.

**De Zotte Proeflokaal** Raamstraat 29. Belgian hangout just north of Leidseplein with food, liqueurs and hundreds of different kinds of beers.

### Smoking coffeeshops

**The Bulldog** Leidseplein 15-17 and other central outlets. One of the oldest, biggest and brashest coffeeshops – not the place for a thoughtful smoke, though the dope is reliably good.

**De Dampkring** Handboogstraat 29. With colourful decor and a refined menu, this coffeeshop is known for its good-quality hash – a favourite with both tourists and locals, it can get busy.

**Global Chillage** Kerkstraat 51. Celebrated slice of tie-dyed dope culture, with friendly staff.

**Homegrown Fantasy** Nieuwezijds Voorburgwal 87a. Part of the Dutch Passion seed company, selling the widest range of (mostly Dutch) marijuana in Amsterdam.

**Kadinsky** Zoutsteeg 9 & Rosmarijnsteeg 9, both in the old centre. Sensational chocolate chip cookies, scrupulously accurate deals and a background of jazz dance.

**Paradox** 1e Bloemdwarsstraat 2, Jordaan. Satisfies the munchies with outstanding natural food, including spectacular fresh-fruit concoctions. Closes 8pm.

**Rusland** Rusland 16. A cramped but vibrant place just north of Muntplein, serving up 43 different kinds of tea. A cut above the rest.

**Siberië** Brouwersgracht 11. Slightly off the beaten tourist track, very relaxed and very friendly – worth a visit whether you want to smoke or not.

# Nightlife

Amsterdam is a gathering spot for fringe performances, and buzzes with places offering a wide and inventive range of **entertainment**. Drinks cost around fifty percent more than in a bar, but entry prices are low and there's rarely any kind of door policy. Most places open around 10pm and close around 4am. **Cinemas** screen English-language movies, subtitled in Dutch, and rarely show foreign-language films without English subtitles. Check out the lavish Art-Deco interior of the Tuschinski, Reguliersbreestraat 26, or cult and classic flicks at The Movies, Haarlemmerdijk 161, and Kriterion, Roeterstraat 170. Boom Chicago (@www.boomchicago.nl) is a hugely popular rapid-fire **comedy** troupe, performing nightly in English at the Leidseplein Theatre. The best source of listings information is the **Uitburo**, or **AUB**, in the Stadsschouwburg theatre on the corner of Marnixstraat and Leidseplein (daily 10am–6pm, Thurs until 9pm; ☎0900/0191). Wednesday's *Het Parool* newspaper has a good entertainment supplement, *Uit en Thuis*.

## Rock, jazz and world music venues

**Akhnaton** Nieuwezijds Kolk 25 ☎ 020/624 3396, ⓦ www.akhnaton.nl. A Centre for World Culture, specializing in African and Latin American music and dance parties.

**Café Alto** Korte Leidsedwarsstraat 115, near Leidseplein ☎ 020/626 3249, ⓦ www.jazz-cafe-alto.nl. Legendary jazz café-bar, with free live music every night from 10pm until 3am. Big on atmosphere, not space.

**Arena** s'-Gravesandestraat 51, near Oosterpark ☎ 020/694 7444, ⓦ www.hotelarena .nl. Multimedia centre featuring live music every weekend, cultural events, a bar, coffeeshop and restaurant.

**Bimhuis** Piet Heinkade 3 ☎ 020/788 2150, ⓦ www.bimhuis.nl. Premier jazz venue. Free impro sessions 8pm Tues. First stop on IJ-tram from Centraal Station.

**Hof van Holland** Rembrandtplein 7. Traditional brown café with live performances of Dutch music throughout the week, when locals sing Dutch songs.

**Melkweg** Lijnbaansgracht 234a, near Leidseplein ☎ 020/624 1777, ⓦ www.melkweg.nl. Amsterdam's most famous entertainment venue, with a young, hip clientele. Live music from reggae to rock, as well as excellent DJs at the weekend, a monthly film programme, theatre, gallery, bar and restaurant.

**Paradiso** Weteringschans 6–8 ☎ 020/626 4521, ⓦ www.paradiso.nl. Set in a lovely old church, this atmospheric haunt of musos features both biggish names and up-and-coming bands. Near Leidseplein.

**Winston** Warmoesstraat 129 ☎ 020/623 1380, ⓦ www.winston.nl. Small venue with rock, jazz-poetry, R'n'B and punk/noise nights.

## Clubs

**Escape** Rembrandtplein 11. Huge place packed at weekends, with several floors and top DJs. Closed Sun.

**iT** Amstelstraat 24, near Rembrandtplein. Large disco with popular and glamorous gay nights, attracting a dressed-up, uninhibited crowd. Friday is mixed gay/straight night.

**Mazzo** Rozengracht 114, Jordaan. Perhaps the city's hippest and most laid-back club, with a choice of music to appeal to all tastes.

**Melkweg** Lijnbaansgracht 234a, near Leidseplein. After the bands, this multimedia centre hosts theme nights from African dance parties to experimental jazz-trance.

**Ministry** Reguliersdwarsstraat 12. A well-established club near Rembrandtplein which features quality DJs playing speed garage, house and R'n'B to party people. Monday night jam session with the local jazz talent.

**Paradiso** Weteringschans 6–8. One of the principal venues in the city, which on Fridays hosts an unmissable club night, from midnight onwards. Check listings for one-off events. Near Leidseplein.

## Classical music and opera

**Beurs van Berlage** Damrak 277, city centre. The splendid interior of the former stock exchange hosts a wide selection of music from the Dutch Philharmonic and Dutch Chamber orchestras.

**Concertgebouw** Concertgebouwplein 2–6 ☎ 020/ 671 8345, ⓦ www.concertgebouw.nl. Home to the Borodin Quartet. Catch world-renowned orchestras playing amid wonderful acoustics for as little as €15. Summer concerts and free lunchtime performances Wed Sept to May.

**Engelse Kerk** Begijnhof 48. Three to four performances a week, lunchtime, afternoon and evening, with the emphasis on period instruments.

**Muziektheater** Waterlooplein ☎ 020/625 5455, ⓦ www.hetmuziektheater.nl. Full and reasonably priced opera programme. Tickets sell quickly.

**Stadsschouwburg** Leidseplein 26. Somewhat overshadowed by the Muziektheater, but still a significant stage for opera and dance.

# Gay Amsterdam

Amsterdam has one of the biggest and best-established **gay** scenes in Europe: attitudes are tolerant and facilities unequalled. The nationwide organization COC, Rozenstraat 14 (☎ 020/626 3087, ⓦ www.cocamsterdam.nl), can provide on-the-spot **information**, and has a café and popular discos (Sat: women under 24 only). For further advice contact the English-speaking Gay & Lesbian Switchboard (daily 2–10pm; ☎ 020/623 6565, ⓦ www.switchboard.nl) or check ⓦ www .gayamsterdam.com. The gay and lesbian bookshop **Vrolijk** is just behind Dam square at Paleisstraat 135.

### Gay hotels

**Golden Bear** Kerkstraat 37 ☎020/624 4785
ⓦwww.goldenbear.nl. Clean and spacious rooms, not far from the busy Leidseplein. Trams #1, #2 & #5 to Kerkstraat. ⑥
**ITC Hotel** Prinsengracht 1051 ☎020/623 0230, ⓦwww.itc-hotel.com. Friendly hotel in lovely old house, not far from Rembrandtsplein and main gay areas. Tram #4 to Prinsengracht. ⑥
**Orfeo** Leidsekruisstraat 12-14 ☎020/623 1347, ⓦwww.hotelorfeo.com. Very pleasant gay and lesbian hotel behind Leidseplein. Decent breakfasts served until midday. Tram #1, #2 or #5 to Prinsengracht. ⑥

### Gay cafés and bars

**Amstel Taveerne** Amstel 54. Perhaps the best-established bar, at its most vivacious in summer when the guys spill out onto the street.
**April** Reguliersdwarsstraat 37. Large and trendy, with newspapers, coffee and cakes as well as booze.
**Camp Café** Kerkstraat 45. Agreeable mix of tourists and locals, with tasty dishes on offer.
**Downtown** Reguliersdwarsstraat 31, off Rembrandtplein. A favourite with visitors. Relaxed and friendly, with inexpensive meals.
**Le Shako** 's-Gravelandseveer 2. Friendly bar in a quiet street on the Amstel,
**The Web** St Jacobsstraat 6. Strict rubber, leather and denim bar with a dance floor, darkrooms and a pool table. From 2pm.

## Listings

**Bike rental** Cheapest from main train stations. Also try: Bike City, Bloemgracht 70 ☎020/626 3721; Damstraat Rent-a-Bike at Damstraat 20 ☎020/625 5029; or MacBike, Mr Visserplein 2 ☎020/620 0985, Weteringschans 2 ☎020/528 76 88 and Stationsplein east ☎020/624 8391. All charge around €8 a day plus €50 deposit with ID.
**Bike tours** Yellow Bike, Nieuwezijds Kolk 29 ☎020 620 6940, ⓦwww.yellowbike.nl (€18.50/person).
**Embassies and consulates** Note that most of the following are in Den Haag, not Amsterdam. Australia, Carnegielaan 4, Den Haag ☎070/310 8200; Canada, Sophialaan 7, Den Haag ☎070/311 1600; Ireland, Dr Kuyperstraat 9, Den Haag ☎070/363 0993; New Zealand, Carnegielaan 10, Den Haag ☎070/365 8037; UK, Lange Voorhout 10, Den Haag, ☎070/427 0427; US, Museumplein 19, Amsterdam ☎020/575 5309.
**Exchange** GWK in Centraal Station and Leidseplein; Thomas Cook at Dam 23, Damrak 1–5 and Leidseplein 31a; American Express at Damrak 66.
**Hospital** De Boelelaan 1117 ☎020/444 444.
**Laundry** The Clean Brothers, Kerkstraat 56 and Jacob van Lennepkade 179.
**Left luggage** Centraal Station.
**Police** Elandsgracht 117 ☎020/559 9111.
**Post office** Singel 250 (Mon–Fri 9am–6pm, Thurs until 8pm, Sat 10am–1.30pm).

# The Randstad

The string of towns known as the **Randstad**, or "rim town", situated amid a typically Dutch landscape of flat fields cut by canals, forms the country's most populated region and still recalls the landscapes painted in the seventeenth-century heyday of the provinces. Much of the area can be visited as day-trips from Amsterdam, but it's easy and more rewarding to make a proper tour. **Haarlem** is worth a look, while to the south, the university centre of **Leiden** makes a pleasant detour before you reach the refined tranquillity of **Den Haag** (The Hague) and the busy urban centre of **Rotterdam**. Nearby **Delft** and **Gouda** repay visits too, the former with one of the best-preserved centres in the region.

## Haarlem

Just over fifteen minutes from Amsterdam by train, **HAARLEM** is a handsome, mid-sized city that sees itself as a cut above its neighbours. It makes a good alternative base for exploring North Holland, or even Amsterdam itself. The core of the city is **Grote Markt** and the adjoining Riviervischmarkt, flanked by the gabled, originally fourteenth-century **Stadhuis** and the impressive bulk of the **Grote Kerk** or **Sint Bavokerk** (Mon–Sat 10am–4pm; €1.50). Inside, the mighty Christian Müller organ of 1738 is said to have been played by Handel and Mozart. The town's main attraction is the outstanding **Frans Hals Museum**, Groot Heiligland 62 (Tues–Sat 11am–5pm, Sun noon–5pm; €7; ⓦwww.franshalsmuseum.nl), a five-minute stroll from Grote Markt in the Oudemannhuis almshouse. It houses a number of his lifelike seventeenth-century portraits, including the *Civic Guard* series which established his reputation.

### Practicalities

Haarlem **train station**, connected to Amsterdam and to Leiden by four trains an hour, is on the north side of the city, about ten minutes' walk from the Grote Markt; **buses** stop right outside. The **VVV** is attached to the station (April–Sept Mon–Fri 9am–5.30pm, Sat 10am–4pm, Oct–March Mon–Fri 9.30am–5pm, Sat 10am–2pm; ☎0900/616 1600, ⓦwww.vvvzk.nl). Haarlem has a few reasonably priced and central **hotels**, including *Amadeus*, Grote Markt 10 (☎023/532 4530; ❻), and *Carillon*, Grote Markt 27 (☎023/531 0591, ⓦwww.hotelcarillon.com; ❻), both in the central square. Further out there's an HI **hostel** at Jan Gijzenpad 3 (☎023/537 3793, ⓦwww.stayokay.com; €25; 10min on bus #2 from the station), and **campsites** among the dunes west of town (bus #81 from the station), including *Bloemendaal*, Zeeweg 72, in Bloemendaal-aan-Zee (☎023/573 2178; closed Oct–March), and the sprawling *De Lakens*, Zeeweg 60 (☎0900/384 6226, ⓦwww .kennemerduincampings.nl; closed Nov–March).

The best **restaurant** in town is the slightly pricy *Lambermon's*, Spaarne 96 (☎023/542 7804), a *Kooktheater* ("cook-theatre") providing a unique experience and excellent French food. For more traditional Dutch dishes and pastas, try the popular and affordable *Restaurant La Plume*, Lange Veerstraat 1 (☎023/531 3202), or the slightly more upmarket *Applause*, at Grote Markt 23a (☎023/531 1425), a chic Italian bistro with main courses around €20. The long-standing, popular *Café 1900*, Barteljorisstraat 10, serves drinks and light meals in an attractive setting while the *Grand Café Fortuyn*, Grote Markt 23, is quieter, with charming 1930s decor. *Ze Crack*, at the junction of Lange Veerstraat and Kleine Houtstraat, is a dim, smoky **bar** with good music and beer by the pint. For a little traditional character, try the **proeflokaal** *In den Uiver*, Riviervischmarkt 13, or the intimate and typically Dutch *Het Proeflokaal* at Lange Veerstraat 7.

## Leiden and around

The charm of **LEIDEN** lies in the peace and prettiness of its gabled streets and canals, though the town's museums are varied and comprehensive enough to merit a visit in themselves. Its most appealing quarter is Rapenburg, a peaceful area of narrow pedestrian streets and canals that is home to the city's best-known attraction at no. 28 Rapenburg, the **Rijksmuseum Van Oudheden** (National Museum of Antiquities; Tues–Fri 10am–5pm, Sat & Sun noon–5pm; €7.50), the country's principal archeological museum. Outside sits the first-century AD Temple of Teffeh while inside are more Egyptian artefacts, along with classical Greek and Roman sculpture and exhibits from prehistoric, Roman and medieval times. Across Rapenburg, a network of narrow streets converges on the Gothic **Pieterskerk**. East of here, **Breestraat** marks the site of a vigorous **market** (Wed & Sat), which sprawls right over the sequence of bridges into Haarlemmerstraat, the town's major shopping street. Close by, the **Burcht** (daily 10am–10pm; free) is a shell of a fort, whose battlements you can clamber up for views **of the town centre**. Leiden's municipal museum, **Lakenhal**, Oude Singel 28–32 (Tues–Fri 10am–5pm, Sat & Sun noon–5pm; €4), has rooms of furniture, tiles, glass and ceramics and a collection of paintings by Rembrandt and others. Around the corner on Molenwerf, the **Molenmuseum de Valk**, 2e Binnenvestgracht 1 (Tues–Sat 10am–5pm, Sun 1–5pm; €2.50), displays the history of windmills.

Leiden's **train** and **bus stations** are no more than ten minutes' walk from the centre. The **VVV** is a short walk from the stations at Stationsweg 2d (Mon 11am–5.30pm, Tue–Fri 9am–5.30pm, Sat 10am–4.30pm; ☎0900/222 2333, ⓦwww.leiden.nl). Check here for Rembrandt 400 events (see also p.723). Central **accommodation** includes *The Rose*, Beestenmarkt 14 (☎071/514 6630; ❻), and the more appealing *Nieuw Minerva*, a cosy and central canalside hotel at Boommarkt 23 (☎071/512 6358, ⓦwww.nieuwminerva.nl; ❼). The closest **campsite** is *Koningshof* (☎071/402 6051), 6km north of Leiden (bus #40). For **eating**, *M'n Broer*, by the Pieterskerk at Kloksteeg 7, has a reasonable Dutch menu, while *Barrera*, at Rapenburg 56, has good sandwiches. In the evening, the studenty *La Bota*, Herensteeg 9–11, by the Pieterskerk, serves great-value food and beers, while *Jazzcafé The Duke*, at Oude Singel 2, has a busy bar and live jazz most nights.

### The bulbfields

Along with Haarlem to the north, Leiden and Delft are the best bases for seeing the Dutch **bulbfields** which flourish here in spring. The view from the train as you travel from Haarlem to Leiden can be sufficient in itself as the line cuts directly through the main growing areas, the fields divided into stark geometric blocks of pure colour. Should you want to get closer, make a bee-line for **LISSE**, home to the **Keukenhof** (March 23–May 19 daily 8am–7.30pm; €12.50; ⓦwww.keukenhof.nl), the largest flower gardens in the world. Some six million blooms are on show for their full flowering period, complemented by 5000 square metres of greenhouses. Special buses (#54) run daily to the Keukenhof from Leiden bus station twice an hour.

## Den Haag (The Hague)

With its urbane atmosphere, **DEN HAAG** (**THE HAGUE**) is different from any other Dutch city. Since the sixteenth century it has been the Netherlands' political capital though its older buildings are a rather subdued collection with little of Amsterdam's flamboyance. Diplomats and multinational businesses ensure that many of the city's hotels and restaurants are in the expense-account category, and the nightlife is similarly packaged. But amongst all this, Den Haag does have cheaper and livelier bars and restaurants, as well as some excellent museums. Right in the centre, the **Binnenhof** is the home of the Dutch parliament with roots in the thirteenth-century castle. The present complex is a rather mundane affair, the small **Hof Vijver** lake mirroring the symmetry of the facade; inside there's little to see except the **Ridderzaal**, a slender-turreted structure that can be viewed on regular guided tours from the information office at Binnenhof 8a (Mon–Sat 10am–3.45pm; €5/6). Immediately east of the Binnenhof, the **Mauritshuis** picture gallery, Korte Vijverberg 8 (Tues–Sat 10am–5pm, Sun 11am–5pm, plus April–Sept Mon 10am–5pm; €7.50; ⓦwww.mauritshuis.nl), located in a magnificent seventeenth-century mansion, is of more interest, famous for its extensive range of Flemish and Dutch paintings including work by Vermeer, Rubens, Bruegel the Elder and Van Dyck. Down the street at Buitenhof 35, the **Galerij Prins Willem V** (closed for renovation until Jan 2007) has paintings by Rembrandt, Jordaens and Paulus Potter. About fifteen minutes' walk from the Mauritshuis, **Panorama Mesdag** at Zeestraat 65 (Mon–Sat 10am–5pm, Sun noon–5pm; ⓦwww.panorama-mesdag.com; €5) is an astonishing 360-degree painting of seaside scenes of Scheveningen from the 1880s. North, the **Gemeente-museum**, Stadhouderslaan 41 (Tues–Sun 11am–5pm; €8; bus #4/#14 from Centraal Station), contains superb collections of musical instruments and Islamic ceramics, and an array of modern art tracing the development of Dutch painting, with the world's largest collection of Mondriaan paintings. Halfway between Den

Haag and its adjacent beach resort of **SCHEVENINGEN** is one of the city's most hyped attractions, the **Madurodam Miniature City** (daily 9am–6/8/10pm; €12; ⓦ www.madurodam.nl; tram #1/#9), a mildly interesting scale model of a Dutch town.

## Practicalities

The city has two **train stations** – Den Haag HS (short for Hollands Spoor) and, about 1km to the north, Den Haag CS (Centraal Station). Trains from the UK, France and Belgium stop at the former which is convenient for cheaper accommodation as staying in Den Haag can be expensive. The **VVV** is at Hofweg 1, next to the Binnenhof (Mon–Fri 10am–6pm, Sat 10am–5pm, Sun noon–5pm; ☎0900/340 3505; ⓦwww .denhaag.com) and has a small stock of private rooms. There's a cluster of seedy but reasonably priced **hotels** just outside Den Haag HS station including *Aristo*, Stationsweg 164–166 (☎070/389 0847; ❹), and *Astoria*, Stationsweg 139 (☎070/384 0401; ❹). About 500m to the east is the smart HI **hostel** at Scheepmakersstraat 27 (☎070/315 7878, ⓦwww.stayokay.com; €25). You might get a better deal on accommodation 4km north of Den Haag at Scheveningen; ask at the VVV on the seafront at Gevers Deynootweg 1134 (Mon–Sat 9/10am–5/5.30pm; April–Sept also Sun 1–5pm; ☎0900/340 3505). Most **embassies** and consulates are in Den Haag (see p.736).

There are plenty of classy places to **eat** around Denneweg and Frederikstraat, just north of Lange Voorhout: amongst them *Limon*, Denneweg 39a, is always full of people hungry for the superb tapas, while *Malienkolder*, Maliestraat 9, is an inexpensive French/Dutch bistro. South of the Paleis Noordeinde, *HNM*, at Molenstraat 21a, has tasty Dutch, Indonesian, French and Italian specials for just €7. For **drinking**,

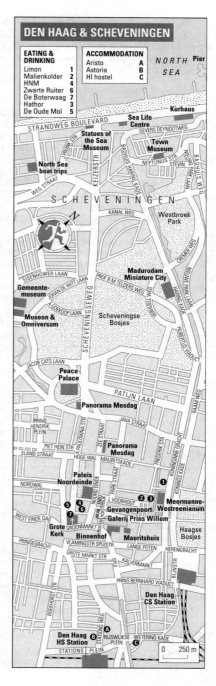

DEN HAAG & SCHEVENINGEN

EATING & DRINKING
Limon 1
Malienkolder 2
HNM 4
Zwarte Ruiter 6
De Boterwaag 7
Hathor 3
De Oude Mol 5

ACCOMMODATION
Aristo A
Astoria B
HI hostel C

try the studenty bar *Zwarte Ruiter* (also with good food) at Grote Markt 27, or nearby *De Boterwaag*, Grote Markt 8a, an appealing brick-vaulted café-bar. Near Denneweg, the canalside *Hathor*, Maliestraat 22, has a convivial atmosphere, as does *De Oude Mol*, a traditional bar tucked down a narrow sidestreet at Oude Molstraat 61.

## Delft

**DELFT**, 2km inland from Den Haag, is perhaps best known for Delftware, the delicate blue and white ceramics to which the town gave its name in the seventeenth century. With its gabled red-roofed houses standing beside tree-lined canals, the pastel colours of the pavements, its brickwork and bridges, the town has a faded tranquillity – though one that can suffer beneath the tourist onslaught during summer. A good starting point is to follow the Historic Walk around the old town with a map from the VVV. A fifteen-minute walk south of the centre at Rotterdamsweg 196 is the **Koninklijke Porceleyne Fles**, a factory producing Delftware (daily 9am–5pm; Nov to mid-March closed Sun; €4; ⊛www. royaldelft.com), while the **Huis Lambert van Meerten Museum**, Oude Delft 199 (Tues–Sat 10am–5pm, Sun 1–5pm; €3.50), has a large collection of Delft and other tiles. The **Markt** is also worth exploring for its collection of small speciality art shops and galleries, with the **Nieuwe Kerk** (Mon–Sat 9/11am–4/6pm; €2.50) at one end and the Renaissance **Stadhuis** opposite. William the Silent – leader of the struggle for Dutch independence in the seventeenth century – is buried in this fine old church and you can climb the 370 steps of the tower for spectacular views. West of here, **Wynhaven**, an old canal, leads to Hippolytusbuurt and the Gothic **Oude Kerk** (same hours and ticket as Nieuwe Kerk), perhaps the town's finest building, with an unhealthily leaning tower. The nearby **Prinsenhof**, William the Silent's base for his revolt against the Spanish and also where he was assassinated, has a decent collection of early Dutch art.

### Practicalites

From Delft's train station, aim for the big steeple you see on exit and it's a ten-minute walk north to the Markt. Delft's **VVV**, here called TIP, is just north of the Markt at Hippolytusbuurt 4 (Tues–Sat 9/10am–4/6pm, Sun & Mon 10am–4pm; ☎015/215 4051; ⊛www.delft.com). The town has some delightful family **B&Bs**: highly recommended is the friendly and welcoming *Oosteinde*, at Oosteinde 156 (☎015/213 4238; ❺), with lovely rooms, while the *Soul Inn,* at Williamstraat 55 (☎015/215 7246; ⊛www.soul-inn.nl; ❹), is sharply decorated and a great place to stay. The **campsite**, *Delftse Hout*, is at Kortftlaan 5 (☎015/213 0040; bus #64 from station).

The least expensive **eating** is at a number of student canteens (term-time only) such as *De Koornbeurs* near the main square and *Jansbrug*, Kornmarkt 50–52. *Het Stadspannekoeckhuys*, 113–115 Oude Delft, also provides a budget stomach-filler of pancakes for around €7. *Kobus Kuch* is a gem of a café/restaurant on the Beestenmarkt – don't miss the tasty *appeltart met slagroom* (apple cake with cream) – while *Uit de Kunst*, at Oude Delft 140, near Oude Kerk, is a charming little café decorated with 1940s memorabilia and offering home-made cakes and biscuits. *Locus Publicus*, Brabantse Turfmarkt 67, is a popular local **bar**, serving a staggering array of beers and a good selection of sandwiches. Further **nightlife** is provided by the nearby club *Speakers*, Burghwal 45–49, which often features live music; and a jazz bar, *Bebop Jazz Café*, Kromstraat 33.

## Rotterdam

Just south of Delft lies **ROTTERDAM**, at the heart of a maze of rivers and artificial waterways that together form the outlet of the rivers Rijn (Rhine) and Maas

(Meuse). After devastating damage during World War II, Rotterdam has grown into a vibrant, forceful city dotted with first-division cultural attractions. Redevelopment also hasn't obliterated the city's earthy character: its tough grittiness is part of its appeal, as are its boisterous bars and clubs.

## Arrival, information and accommodation

Rotterdam's large centre is bordered by its main rail terminal, **Centraal Station**, also the hub of a useful **tram** and **metro** system, though best avoided late at night. The main **VVV** office is a ten-minute walk away at Coolsingel 67 (Mon–Thur 9.30am–6pm, Fri 9.30am–9pm, Sat 9.30am–5pm; ☎010/414 0000, ⓦwww.vvvrotterdam.nl), where you can pick up free maps and brochures. There are plenty of central, reasonably priced **hotels**. Southwest of the station is *Wilgenhof*, Heemraadssingel 92–94 (☎010/425 4892; ❺; tram #1/#7 from Centraal Station), while the lively and agreeable *Bazar*, near the Museumpark at Witte de Withstraat 16 (☎010/206 5151 ⓦwww.bazarhotel.nl; ❻), also has a great café-restaurant. A five-minute walk from Wilhelminaplein metro, on the south bank of the Nieuwe Maas, is the *New York*, Koninginnenhoofd 1 (☎010/439 0500; ⓦwww.hotelnewyork.nl; ❼), with a great atmosphere and excellent restaurant. The HI **hostel** is a 25-minute walk from the station, at Rochussenstraat 107 (☎010/436 5763, ⓦwww.stayokay.com; €23; tram #4 or metro stop Dijkzigt), while the nearest **campsite**, *Stadscamping* (☎010/415 3440), is north of the station at Kanaalweg 84 (bus #33).

## The city

A good feel for the city can be had by walking from the station (or taking #5 tram from just outside) down to the Museumpark. Here, the enormous **Boijmans Van Beuningen Museum**, Mathenesserlaan 18–20 (Tues–Sat 10am–5pm, Sun 11am–5pm; €7 or €12 during exhibitions; ⓦwww.boijmans.nl), has a superb collection of works by Monet, Van Gogh, Picasso, Gauguin and Cézanne, while its earlier canvases include several by Bosch, Bruegel the Elder and Rembrandt. A stroll through the Museumpark brings you to the **Nattuurmuseum Kunsthal** (Tues–Sat 10am–5pm, Sun 11am–5pm; €8.50; ⓦwww.kunsthal.nl), which showcases first-rate exhibitions of contemporary art, photography and design.

Water taxis (€2.50) leave the Veerhaven and the Leuvehaven

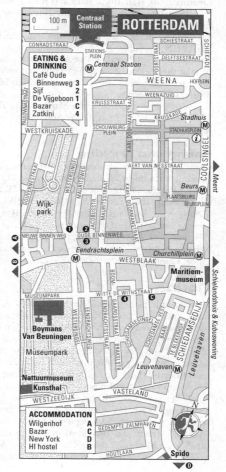

for the splendid *Hotel New York*, occupying the building where transatlantic cruise liners once docked. From here you can walk back to the centre over the futuristic bridge, the Erasmusbrug, an ideal spot for photos. There are also numerous **boat trips** from the Leuvehaven through the harbour (year-round; 1hr 15min; €8.50). In July and August, day-trips also run to Dordrecht, Schoonhoven, the array of 19 windmills at Kinderdijk, and the Delta Project from €39–49 per person; contact the VVV or Spido for details (☎010/275 9988, ⊛www.spido.nl). Ten minutes' walk **north** from Spido is the entertaining **Maritiem Museum** (Maritime Museum; Tues–Fri 10am–5pm, Sat & Sun 11am–5pm; €5) at the Leuvehaven. Close by at Korte Hoogstraat 31 is a seventeenth-century mansion housing the **Museum Het Schielandshuis** (Tues–Sat 10am–5pm, Sun 11am–5pm; €2.70), with displays on the city's history. Another short walk away is Blaak, a pocket-sized area that was levelled in World War II, but has since been rebuilt. The architectural highlight is a remarkable series of topsy-turvy, cube-shaped houses, the *kubuswoningen*, completed in 1984. One of them, at No.70, the **Kijk–Kubus** (Show Cube; daily 11am–5pm; Jan & Feb Fri–Sun only; €1.80; ⊛www.kubuswoning.nl), at Overblaak 70, near Blaak train and metro station, offers somewhat disorientating but compelling tours. Nearby, the Binnenrote **market** (every Tues and Sat) sells fresh cheese, fish and flowers.

If little in Rotterdam city centre can exactly be called picturesque, **DELF-SHAVEN**, a couple of kilometres southwest of Centraal Station, makes up for it – to get here, catch tram #4 or #6 (direction Schiedam, tram stop Spanjaardstraat), or take the metro. Once the harbour that served Delft, it was from here that the Pilgrim Fathers set sail for the New World in 1620. Most of the buildings lining the district's two narrow canals are eighteenth- and nineteenth-century warehouses. Formerly a *jenever* distillery, the **Museum de Dubbelde Palmboom**, Voorhaven 12 (Tues–Fri 10am–5pm, Sat & Sun 11am–5pm; €2.70), is now a wide-ranging historical museum.

### Eating and drinking

Oude and Nieuwe Binnenweg host a number of affordable and tasty **eating** options, including *Café Oude Binnenweg* at Oude Binnenweg 110; *Sijf* at no. 115; and *De Vijgeboon* further along at no. 146a. Witte de Withstraat is also worth wandering along: the *Bazar* at no. 16 does excellent kebabs and vegetarian food, while *Zatkini* at no. 88 is a Barcelona-esque bar. Rotterdam has a lively **club** scene; two current hotspots are *Off Corso*, near Centraal Station at Kruiskade 22, with top DJs, and *Now & Wow* (with popular gay nights) in a huge converted grain silo at Maashaven Metro. Tickets for rock gigs and concerts are on sale at the main post office, Coolsingel 42 (☎0900/300 1250, ⊛www.ticketservice.nl).

## Gouda

A pretty little place some 25km northeast of Rotterdam, **GOUDA** is almost everything you'd expect of a Dutch country town: a ring of quiet canals encircling ancient buildings and old quays. Its **Markt** is the largest in Holland, a reminder of the town's prominence as a centre of the medieval cloth trade, and later of the manufacture of cheeses and clay pipes. A touristy **cheese market** is held here every Thursday morning from June to August. Slap bang in the middle, the elegant Gothic **Stadhuis** dates from 1450; on the north side is the **Waag**, a tidy seventeenth-century building whose top two floors house a cheese museum (April–Oct Tues–Sun 1–5pm, Thurs 10am–5pm; €2). South, off the Markt, the sixteenth-century **St Janskerk** (Mon 1–5.30pm, Tues–Fri 9.30am–5.30pm, Sat 10am–4pm; €2) is famous for its magnificent stained-glass windows depicting both Biblical and secular scenes.

Gouda's **train** and **bus stations** are north of the centre, ten minutes from the **VVV**, Markt 27 (Mon–Fri 9am–5pm, Sat 10am–4pm; June–Aug also Sun noon–3pm; ☎0900/468 32888, ⊛www.vvvgouda.nl), which has a limited supply of private rooms. The nicest **hotel** is *De Utrechtsche Dom*, fifteen minutes' walk from the train station at Geuzenstraat 6 (T0182/528 833, Wwww.hotelgouda.nl; ❻); otherwise, try the hotel *De Keizerskroon*, Keizerstraat 11–13 (T0182/528 096; ❺). For **food**, there are plenty of cafés catering to the swarms of summer day-trippers. You can eat cheaply at *'t Groot Stedelijk*, Markt 44, or *Hof Van Sint Jan*, Achter de Kerk 9a, which does great vegetarian fare, and the attractive *Eetcafé De Beursklok*, Hoge Gouwe 19, offers good-quality Dutch food. For a **drink**, check out the excellent *Eetcafé Vidocq*, Koster Gijzensteeg 5, or *Café Central*, Markt 23.

## Utrecht

"I groaned with the idea of living all winter in so shocking a place," wrote Boswell in 1763, and **UTRECHT**, surrounded by shopping centres and industrial developments, still promises little as you approach. But the centre, with its distinctive sunken canals – whose brick cellar warehouses have been converted into chic cafés and restaurants – is one of the country's most pleasant. The focal point is the **Dom Tower**, built between 1321 and 1382, which at over 110m is the highest church tower in the country, soaring to a delicate octagonal lantern. A guided tour (May–Sept Mon–Sat 10am–5pm, Sun noon–5pm; €7.50) takes you unnervingly close to the top, from where you can see Rotterdam and Amsterdam on a clear day. Below is the Gothic **Dom Kerk**; only the eastern part of the cathedral remains today after the nave collapsed in 1674, but it's worth peering inside (Mon–Fri 10/11am–4/5pm, Sat 10am–3.30pm, Sun 2–4pm; free) and wandering through the Kloostergang, the fourteenth-century cloisters that link the cathedral to the chapterhouse. South of the church at Nieuwegracht 63, the national collection of ecclesiastical art, the **Catharijne Convent Museum** (Tues–Fri 10am–5pm, Sat & Sun 11am–5pm; €7; Wwww.catharijneconvent.nl), has wonderful paintings, manuscripts and church ornaments from the ninth century on.

Utrecht's **train** and **bus stations** both lead into the Hoog Catharijne shopping centre. The main **VVV** office is a short walk away at Vinkenburgstraat 19 (Mon–Fri 9.30am–6.30pm, Sat 9.30am–5pm, June–Sept Sun 10am–2pm; T0900/128 8732, Wwww.utrecht-city.com/gb). For **accommodation**, the pleasant HI **hostel** (T030/656 1277, Wwww.stayokay.com; €24.50) lies 5km southeast, in an old country manor house at Rhijnauwenselaan 14, Bunnik – take bus #40/#41 from the train station. More central is the pleasant guesthouse, *Strowis*, Boothstraat 8 (T030/238 0280, Wwww.strowis.nl; €13; ❹), a fifteen-minute walk northeast towards Janskerk from Centraal Station or a short ride on bus #3/#4/#8/#11 to the Janskerkhof stop, plus a two-minute walk. The well-equipped **campsite**, *De Berekuil*, Arienslaan 5 (T030/271 3870), is served by bus #57. **Restaurants** are mainly situated along Oudegracht; the best is the moderately priced *Stadskasteel Oudaen* at no. 99, the oldest house in town, which serves beer from its own brewery downstairs. *De Oude Muntkelder* at no. 112 serves inexpensive pancakes, while vegetarians should seek out *De Werfkring* at no. 123, or *Milky*, a laid-back restaurant off the canal at Zakkerdragssteeg 22. The city's best **bars** cluster around the junction of Oude Gracht and the Lijnmarkt; one to visit on a weekend is *De Winkel van Sinkel* at Oudegracht 158, with regular dance nights and a chill-out room downstairs.

# Beyond the Randstad

Outside the Randstad towns, the Netherlands is relatively unknown territory to visitors. To the north, there's superb cycling and hiking to be had through scenic **dune reserves** and delightful villages, with easy access to pristine beaches, while the island of **Texel** offers the country's most complete beach experience, and has plenty of birdlife. The **Hoge Veluwe National Park**, near Arnhem, boasts one of the country's best modern art museums and has cycle paths through a delightful landscape. Further south, in the provinces of North Brabant and Limburg, the landscape slowly fills out, moving into a rougher countryside of farmland and forests and eventually into the hills around **Maastricht**, a city with a vibrant, pan-European air.

## Texel

The largest of the islands off the north coast – and the easiest to get to (2hr from Amsterdam) – **TEXEL** (pronounced tessel) offers diverse and pretty landscapes, and is one of Europe's most important bird breeding-grounds. **Ferries** from the town of Den Helder on the mainland depart every hour (€3; coming from Amsterdam, ask for an all-in discounted *Waddenbiljet*). Once there, Texel's main settlement, **DEN BURG**, makes a convenient base and has bike rental outlets. On the coast 3km southeast of Den Burg is **OUDESCHILD**, home to the **Maritiem en Juttersmuseum** (Beachcombers' Museum; Tues–Sat 10am–5pm, July & Aug also Mon 10am–5pm; €4.50), a fascinating collection of marine junk from wrecks. In the opposite direction is **DE KOOG**, with a good sandy beach and the **EcoMare** nature centre, at Ruijslaan 92 (daily 9am–5pm; €7.50), a bird and seal sanctuary as well as natural history museum: from here you can visit the Wad, the banks of sand and mud to the east of the island, where seals and birds gather.

Den Burg's **VVV** is at Emmalaan 66 (Mon–Fri 9am–6pm, Sat 9am–5pm; ☎0222/314 741, ⓦwww.texel.net); nearby is the island's cheapest **hotel**, *'t Koogerend*, Kogerstraat 94 (☎0222/313 301; ⑤). There's also an HI **hostel** on the road to Oudeschild, at Schanseweg 7 (☎0222/315 441, ⓦwww.stayokay.com; €25). **Campers** are spoilt for choice: close to Den Burg is the small, well-run *De Koorn Aar*, Grensweg 388 (☎0222/312 931; closed Nov–March); among the beachside dunes in De Koog is *Kogerstrand*, Badweg 33 (☎0222/317 208; closed Nov–March); and there's *De Krim*, at Roggeslootweg 6 in De Cocksdorp, a hamlet at the island's north tip (☎0222/390 111). The best **food** in Den Burg is *De Worsteltent*, Smitsweg 6, while in De Koog plump for *Vogelhuis Oranjerie*, Dorpsstraat 204 (☎0222/317 279), with main courses for around €17.

## Hoge Veluwe National Park

Some 70km southeast of Amsterdam, and just north of the town of Arnhem, is the huge and scenic **Hoge Veluwe National Park** (daily: April–Aug 8am–8/10pm; Sept–March 9am–5.30/8pm; ⓦwww.hogeveluwe.nl; €6 park only, or €12 with Kröller-Müller museum). Formerly the estate of wealthy local couple Anton and Helene Kröller-Müller, it has three entrances – one near the village of **Otterlo** on the northwest perimeter, another near **Hoenderloo** on the northeast edge, and a third to the south at **Rijzenburg**, near the village of Schaarsbergen. The easiest way to get here is by bus #107 from Arnhem's train station, then change at Otterlo to bus #110 which runs direct to the **Bezoekerscentrum** (Visitors' Centre; daily 10am–5pm): here, you can pick up free **white bicycles**, by far the best way to explore the park, and visit the terraced café/restaurant, *De Koperen Kop*. Within the park is the **Museonder** (daily 10am–5pm), an underground natural history museum, and the **St Hubertus Hunting Lodge** (daily 10am–5pm; guided tours only; €2), the former Art Deco home of the Kröller-Müllers. The park's unmissable highlight is the **Kröller-Müller Museum** (Tues–Sun 10am–5pm; ⓦwww .krollermuseum.nl; free with park admission), a superb collection of fine art including nearly three hundred paintings by Van Gogh, plus works by Picasso, Seurat, Léger and Mondriaan. Behind the museum is a lovely and imaginative **sculpture garden** (Tues–Sun 10am–4.30pm; same ticket).

**Trains** run from Amsterdam to nearby **ARNHEM**, from where you can catch the bus to the park. Arnhem's **VVV** office is near the station, at Willemsplein 8 (Mon 11am–5.30pm, Tues–Fri 9am–5.30pm, Sat 10am–5pm; ☎0900/202 4075; ☻www.vvvarnhem.nl). There's an HI **hostel** at Diepenbrocklaan 27 (☎026/442 0114, ☻www.stayokay.com; €25.50), just north of town towards the park (bus #3). You can **camp** by the park's northeastern Hoenderloo entrance (☎055/378 2232; closed Nov–March).

## Maastricht

Squashed between the Belgian and German borders, **MAASTRICHT** is one of the most delightful cities in the Netherlands. A cosmopolitan place, where three languages happily coexist, it's also one of the oldest towns in the country. The busiest of Maastricht's many squares is **Markt**, at its most crowded during the Wednesday and Friday morning **market**, with the mid-seventeenth-century **Stadhuis** (Mon–Fri 8.30am–12.30pm & 2–5.30pm; free) at its centre. Just west, **Vrijthof** is a grander open space flanked by a line of café terraces on one side and on the other by **St Servaaskerk** (daily 10am–5/6pm; €3.50), a tenth-century church. Next door is **St Janskerk** (Easter–Oct Mon–Sat 11am–4pm; free), with its tall fifteenth-century Gothic tower (€1.50). Maastricht's other main church, the **Onze Lieve Vrouwe Basiliek** (€1.60 for treasury) is a short walk south of Vrijthof, down Bredestraat, in a small, shady square crammed with café tables. On the other side of the square lies the appealing district of **Stokstraat Kwartier**, with narrow streets winding out to the fast-flowing River Jeker and the **Helpoort** fortress gateway of 1229. Continuing south, the casemates in the **Waldeck Park** (guided tours: July–Sept daily 2pm; Oct–June Sat & Sun 2pm; €3.75) are further evidence of Maastricht's once-impressive fortifications. Fifteen minutes' walk further south is the 110m hill of **St Pietersberg**. Of the two ancient defensive tunnel systems under the hill, the **Zonneberg** is probably the better, situated on the far side of the hill at Casino Slavante (hourly guided tours: July–Sept Mon–Sat 11am–4pm, Sun at 2pm & 3pm; €3.75). Just outside the city lies the busy tourist town of **VALKENBURG**, which provides a base for walking the nearby hills and forests.

### Practicalities

The centre of Maastricht is on the west bank of the river. You're likely to arrive, however, on the east bank, in the district known as Wijk, home to the **train** and **bus stations** and many of the city's hotels. The central **VVV**, Kleine Straat 1, at the end of the main shopping street (Mon–Sat 9am–6pm, Sun 11am–3pm; Nov–March closed Sun; ☎043/325 2121, ☻www.vvvmaastricht.nl), has copies of a tourist guide with map and a list of private rooms. There are several good central **hotels**, including *La Cloche*, Bredestraat 41, although check-in is at *Café Cloche*, round the corner at Vrijthof 12 (☎043/321 2407, ☻www.lacloche.com; ⑥). The *Botel Maastricht* (☎043/321 9023; ④) is moored on the river at Maasboulevard 95, not far from the Helpoort, and does an excellent breakfast. The HI **hostel** is at Dousbergweg 4 (☎043/346 6777, ☻www.stayokay.com; €24.55), with access to open-air and indoor swimming pools; it's a ten-minute ride from the station on bus #11 (after 6.25pm, take bus #28 towards Pottenburg and ask the driver). A new hostel is due to open in the centre of town (Maasboulevard 101; ☻www.stayokay.com) in September 2005; ring the VVV to check. For **camping**, *De Bosrand* (☎043/409 1544; closed Nov–March) is at Moerslag 4, twenty-five minutes south of town on bus #57.

For cheap **food**, head for any of the good-value cafés along Koestraat. Alternatively, *Pizzeria Napoli*, at Markt 71, gives a twenty-percent student discount, while *Il Giardino*, Onze Lieve Vrouweplein 15, offers pizzas and pasta from €10 and has a view of the church. Late-night snack attacks can be assuaged at *'t Witte*

*Bruudsje*, Platielstraat 12, which serves baguettes and hot meals until 2am (3am on Fri & Sat). The **bars** on the east side of Vrijthof are packed in summer; *In den Ouden Vogelstruys*, at no. 15, is one of the nicest. Away from Vrijthof, *De Bóbbel*, at Wolfstraat 32, is a bare-boards bar that gets lively in the early evening; in the student area around Tongesestraat both *Van Sloun*, at no. 3, and *Tribunal*, opposite, are excellent. For **live music**, try *D'n Auwestiene*, Kesselskade 43 (Wed–Sun 10pm–5am).

# Travel details

## Trains

**Amsterdam to:** Arnhem (for Hoge Veluwe National Park; every 30min; 1hr 10min); Haarlem (every 10min; 15min); Den Haag (every 15min; 50min); Leiden (every 15min; 45min); Maastricht (hourly; 2hr 35min); Rotterdam (every 10min; 1hr); Schiphol Airport (every 15min; 20min); Texel (via Den Helder; every 30min; 1hr 10min); Utrecht (every 15min; 30min).

**Arnhem** (for Hoge Veluwe National Park) to: Amsterdam (every 30min; 1hr 10min); Utrecht (every 15min; 35min).

**Den Haag to:** Delft (every 15min; 15min); Gouda (every 20min; 20min); Rotterdam (every 15min; 25min); Utrecht (every 20min; 40min).

**Leiden** to: Amsterdam (every 15min; 45min); Den Haag (every 10min; 15min).

**Maastricht** to: Amsterdam (hourly; 2hr 35min).

**Rotterdam** to: Gouda (every 20min; 20min); Utrecht (every 20min; 45min).

**Utrecht** to: Arnhem (every 15min; 35min).

# Norway

# Norway highlights

* **Vigeland Sculpture Park, Oslo** Scandinavia's finest – and most extraordinary – open-air sculpture park. See p.756

* **Vikingskipshuset** This Oslo museum displays a trio of superbly preserved ninth-century Viking boats. See p.756

* **The fjords** Take the ferry across the Sognefjord to Balestrand for the quintessential fjordland experience. See p.758

* **The Jostedalsbreen glacier** Hike to this magnificent glacier or view it near Fjærland. See p.763

* **The Lofoten Islands** Quite simply, some of the finest mountain scenery in the world. See p.767

△ Vikingskipshuset

# Introduction and basics

With its extraordinary ice-sculpted landscape, **Norway** remains a wilderness outpost, whose mountainous tracts stand apart from the tamed and heavily populated continent of Europe. Comparatively quiet for a thousand years since the Vikings stamped their mark on Europe, the country can often seem more than just geographically distant even today. Beyond Oslo and the famous fjords the rest of the country might as well be blank for all many visitors know – and, in a manner of speaking, large parts of it are. Vast stretches in the north are sparsely populated, and here it's possible to travel for hours without seeing a soul.

Beyond **Oslo**, one of the world's most prettily sited capitals, the major cities of interest are historic **Trondheim**, **Bergen**, on the edge of the fjords, and hilly, northern **Tromsø**. All are likeable, easily walkable cities, worth time for themselves as well as being good bases for exploring the startlingly handsome countryside that surrounds them. The perennial draw is, however, the **western fjords** – every bit as scenically stunning as they're cracked up to be. Dip into the region from Bergen or **Åndalsnes**, both accessible by train from Oslo, or take more time and appreciate the subtleties of the region's innumerable waterside towns and villages. Further north – deep in the Arctic Circle – the awe-inspiring **Lofoten Islands** are well worth the effort for their calm atmosphere and sheer beauty. To the north of here, Norway grows increasingly barren, and the tourist trail focuses on the long journey to the North Cape or **Nordkapp** – the northernmost accessible point of mainland Europe. The route leads through the province of **Finnmark**, a vast, eerily bleak wilderness where the Arctic tundra rolls as far as the eye can see, one of the last strongholds of the Sami and their herds of reindeer.

## Information & maps

Every town has a **tourist office**, usually with a stock of free maps and timetables. Many book private rooms and hotel beds, some rent out bikes and change money. During the high season – late June to August – they normally open daily for long hours, while in the shoulder season they mostly adopt shop hours; many close down altogether in winter. The *Hallwag* **map** (1:1,000,000) comes with an index, although the *Statens Kartverk* maps, available in Norway at several scales, are best.

## Money and banks

Norway's currency is the **krone** (kr), divided into 100 øre. Coins are 50 øre, 1kr, 5kr, 10kr and 20kr; notes are 50kr, 100kr, 200kr, 500kr and 1000kr. At the time of writing, €1 is worth 7.87kr; £1 is 11.75kr; and US$1 is 6.5kr.

**Banking** hours are Mon–Fri 9am–3.30pm, Thurs till 5pm, though many banks close thirty minutes earlier in summer. Most airports and some train stations have exchange offices, open evenings and weekends, and some tourist offices also change money, though at worse rates than banks and post offices. **ATMs** are commonplace even in the smaller towns.

## Communications

**Post office** opening hours are usually

---

### Norway on the net

ⓦ**www.visitnorway.com** Official Norwegian Tourist Board site.
ⓦ**www.odin.dep.no** Government site with good information links.

Mon–Fri 8/8.30am–4/5pm, Sat 8/9am–1pm. Stamps are available from post offices, snack and newspaper kiosks and some bookstores. Some public phones take coins, but increasingly only accept **phonecards**, available in a variety of denominations from kiosks. There are no area codes. Directory enquiries is ☏ 1881 within Scandinavia, ☏1882 international. The international operator is on ☏115. Many hotels have **Internet** access, and most libraries offer free access for around 15 mins.

# Getting around

**Public transport** is extraordinarily reliable. In the winter (especially in the north), services can be cut back severely, but no part of the country is isolated for long. A synopsis of all the main air, train, bus and ferry services is given in the free NRI Guide to Transport and Accommodation brochure, available in advance from the Norwegian Tourist Board; and all local tourist offices have detailed regional public transport timetables. There

## The Norwegian Language

|  | Norwegian | Pronunciation |
|---|---|---|
| **Yes** | Ja | Ya |
| **No** | Nei | Nay |
| **Please** | Vaersågod | Varsaagod |
| **Thank you** | Takk | Takk |
| **Hello/Good day** | Godmorgen/Goddag | Godmorgan/Goddag |
| **Goodbye** | Adjø | Ad-yur |
| **Excuse me** | Unnskyld | un-shy-ld |
| **Where?** | Hvor? | Vor? |
| **Good** | God | God |
| **Bad** | Dårlig | Door-lig |
| **Near** | Inaerheten | Eyenar-he-ten |
| **Far** | LangtBorte | LangtBorte |
| **Cheap** | Billig | Billig |
| **Expensive** | Dyrt | dy-rt |
| **Open** | Åpen | A-pen |
| **Closed** | Stengt | Sten-gt |
| **Today** | Idag | Eye-Dag |
| **Yesterday** | Igår | Eye-gar |
| **Tomorrow** | Imorgen | EyeMor-gen |
| **How much is....?** | Hvormyeer...? | Vorm-yeer? |
| **What time is it?** | Hvormangeerklokken? | VorMadg-eerKlock-en? |
| **I don't understand** | Jegforstårikke | Yegforst-aarik-ke |
| **Do you speak English?** | SnakkerduEngelsk? | Snakk-erduEng-elle-sk? |
| **One** | En | En |
| **Two** | To | To |
| **Three** | Tre | Tree |
| **Four** | Fire | Fire |
| **Five** | Fem | Fem |
| **Six** | Seks | Seks |
| **Seven** | Sju | S-jew |
| **Eight** | Åtte | Or-te |
| **Nine** | Ni | N-eye |
| **Ten** | Ti | Tee |

are four main **train** routes. These link Oslo to Stockholm in the east, to Kristiansand and Stavanger in the southwest, to Bergen in the west and to Trondheim and on to Fauske and Bodø in the north. The nature of the country makes most of the routes worth a trip in their own right. The tiny Flåm branch line and sweeping Rauma run to Åndalsnes are exciting examples, as is the journey from Oslo to Bergen, an impressive six-and-a-half-hour trans–mountain ride.

InterRail, Eurail and ScanRail (◉ www .scanrail.com) **rail passes** are valid in Norway, and also give substantial discounts on some major ferry crossings and certain long-distance bus routes. You'll need to use **buses** principally in the western fjords and the far north. Bus tickets aren't expensive and are usually bought on board; in addition the country's principal bus company, Nor-Way Bussekspress (◉ www.nor-way .no), sells several go-as-you-please passes (10 days 1300kr; 21 days 2400kr). Travelling by **ferry** is one of the real pleasures of a trip to Norway. Rates are fixed nationally on a sliding scale, with a ten- to fifteen-minute ride costing 18–24kr for foot passengers. Bus fares include the cost of any ferry journey made en route. Some of the busier ferry routes have a control kiosk, where you pay on arrival, but for the most part a crew member comes round to collect fares either on the quayside or on board. The **Hurtigrute** – "rapid route" (◉ www.norwegiancoastal voyage.com) boat shuttles up and down the coast, linking Bergen with Kirkenes and stopping off at over thirty ports on the way. Short hops are more expensive than buses – a six-hour jaunt, for instance, costs around 500kr per passenger, 800kr for car and driver. Sleeping in the lounges or on deck is allowed – and you can use a shower on the lower corridors. Each ship has a 24-hour cafeteria and restaurants.

# Accommodation

For budget travellers as well as hikers, climbers and skiers, **hostels** provide the accommodation mainstay; there are about a hundred in total, spread right across the country and run by Norske Vandrerhjem (◉ www.vandrerhjem.no). Prices vary greatly (100–200kr), although the more expensive ones nearly always include a first-rate breakfast. Most places also have a supply of doubles for 250–450kr. Non-members pay an extra 25kr a night. Many HI hostels close 11am–4pm, and there's often an 11pm/midnight curfew; Norway also has a number of excellent independent hostels which are less regimented and with comparable prices. Much of Norway's accommodation is seasonal – the further north and into the Fjords you go, the later they'll open and the earlier they'll close. Between June and mid-September you should always call ahead to check on space.

There are around four hundred official **campsites** listed in the tourist board's free camping brochure (◉ www.camping.no), plenty of them easily reached by public transport. On average expect to pay 80–160kr per night for two people using a tent. Sites also often have **cabins** (*hytter*), usually four-bedded affairs with kitchen facilities and sometimes a bathroom, with prices ranging between 250 and 750kr. You can camp rough in open areas as long as you are at least 150m away from houses or cabins or otherwise have permission from the landowner, and leave no trace. **Hotels** are generally too pricey for travellers on a budget (around 700kr for a double), but there are bargains to be found with many city hotels offering substantial discounts during the summer. **Guest houses** (*pensjonater*) in the more touristy towns are about 500kr a double, with breakfast sometimes extra. Tourist offices in larger towns can often fix you up with a **private room** in someone's house for around 300–350kr a double, though there's a booking fee (15–25kr) on top and rooms are frequently out of the centre. In coastal districts, especially the Lofoten Islands, **sjøhus** (literally "sea houses") and **rorbus** (converted fishermen's cabins) can be rented from about 400kr per cabin.

# Food and drink

Norwegian **food** can be excellent: fish is plentiful, as are reindeer steak and elk. However, eating well on a tight budget can be difficult. Breakfast (*frokost*) – a self-service affair of bread, cheese, eggs, preserves, cold meat and fish, washed down with unlimited tea and coffee – is usually excellent at hostels, and memorable in hotels. If it isn't included in the room rate, reckon on an extra 50–70kr.

**Picnic** food is the best stand-by during the day, although there are **fast-food** alternatives. The indigenous Norwegian variety, served up at street stalls (*gatekjøkken*), consists mainly of rather unappetizing hot dogs (*varm pølse*), pizza slices and chicken and chips. A much better choice, and often no more expensive, is simply to get a *smørbrød*, a huge open sandwich heaped with a variety of garnishes. You'll see them in most cafés and bakeries. Good **coffee** is available everywhere and in cafeterias is often half-price after the first cup. **Tea** is usually served with lemon – if you want milk, ask for it. The best deals for sit-down food are at **lunchtime** (*lunsj*), when self-service *kafeterias* offer a limited range of daily specials (*dagens rett*) costing 80–100kr. These include a fish or meat dish with vegetables or salad, often a drink, sometimes bread, and occasionally coffee, too. In the larger towns, you'll also find more original cafés called *kaffistovas*, which serve high-quality Norwegian food at quite reasonable prices. **Restaurants**, serving dinner (*middag*), are out of the range of most budgets – main courses average 180–220kr – but the seafood can be superb. Again, the best deals are at lunchtime, when some restaurants put out a *koldtbord* (the Norwegian *smörgåsbord*), where, for a fixed price (100–200kr), you can eat as much as you like for the three to four hours it's served.

Alcohol prices are among the highest in Europe. Buying from the supermarkets and **Vinmonopolet** (the state–run off-licences) is often the only way you'll afford a tipple: in a bar, **beer** costs around 40kr/500ml. It comes in three strengths: class I is light, class II is what you get in supermarkets and is the most widely served in pubs, while class III is the strongest and only available at Vinmonopolet. In the cities bars stay open until at least 1am; in the smaller towns, they tend to close at around 11pm.

**Emergency numbers**

Police ☎112; Ambulance ☎113; Fire ☎110.

Everywhere, look out for *aquavit*, served ice-cold in little glasses; at forty percent proof, it's real headache stuff. Outside bars and restaurants, **wines** and **spirits** can only be purchased from Vinmonopolet. There's generally one in each town, more in the cities; opening hours are usually Mon–Wed 10am–4/5pm, Thurs 10am–5/6pm, Fri 9am–4/6pm, Sat 9am–1/3pm, and you have to be 18 to buy wine and beer, 20 to buy spirits.

# Opening hours and holidays

**Opening hours** are usually Mon–Wed & Fri 9am–5pm, Thurs 9am–6/8pm, Sat 9am–1/3pm. Almost everything – including the supermarkets – is closed on Sunday, the main exceptions being newspaper and snack-food kiosks (*Narvesen*) and takeaway food stalls. Most businesses are closed on **public holidays**: Jan 1, Maundy Thurs, Good Fri, Easter Sun & Mon, May 1, Ascension Day (mid-May), May 17 (Norway's National Day), Whit Sun & Mon, Dec 25 & 26.

# Emergencies

Norway is well–known for its lack of crime, and the Norwegian people are characteristically friendly and helpful. The **police** are amiable and can normally speak English. Most good hotels as well as pharmacies and tourist offices have lists of local **doctors** and dentists. Norway is not in the EU but reciprocal health agreements mean EU citizens get free hospital treatment with an E111 form. If **Pharmacies** (*apotek*) are closed they usually have a rota in the window advising of the nearest pharmacy that is open.

# Oslo

For a city that offers all the trappings of metropolitan life and is within easy reach of both dense forest and sandy beaches, **OSLO** retains a surprisingly low profile among European capitals. It's also blessed with a clutch of first–rate museums, a lively bar scene and a tempting array of outdoor pursuits, from swimming to skiing.

Oslo is the oldest of the Scandinavian capital cities, founded around 1048 by Harald Hardrada. Several devastating fires and six hundred years later, Oslo upped sticks and shifted west to its present site, abandoning its old name in favour of

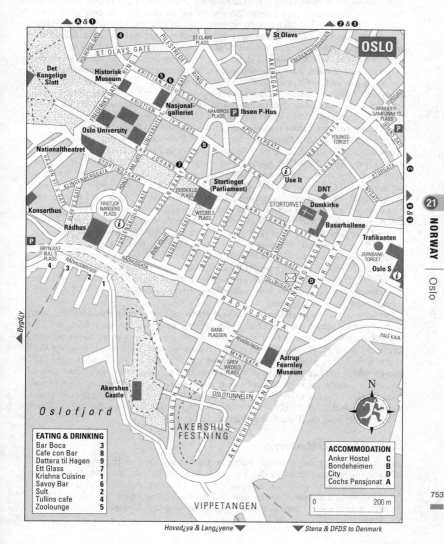

Hoved¿ya & Lang¿yene ▼    ▼ Stena & DFDS to Denmark

**Christiania** – after the seventeenth-century Danish king Christian IV responsible for the move. The new city prospered and by the time of the break with Denmark (and then union with Sweden) in 1814, Christiania – indeed Norway as a whole – was clamouring for independence, something it finally achieved in 1905. Today's city centre is largely the work of the late nineteenth and early twentieth centuries, an era reflected in the wide streets, dignified parks and gardens, solid buildings and long, consciously classical vistas. Its half a million inhabitants have room to spare in a city whose vast boundaries encompass forests, sand and sea.

## Arrival, information and city transport

**Oslo airport** – Gardermoen – is located about 50km north of the city centre: the Airport Express train (every 20min; 20min; 160kr) and the SAS Airport bus (every 20min; 40min; 110kr, 170kr return) run into the city, but the ordinary NSB (Norwegian rail) train is much less expensive (every 30min–1hr; 30min; 77kr). All **trains** arrive at Oslo Sentralstasjon, known as **Oslo S**, at the eastern end of the city centre, with the central **bus terminal** a short walk northeast beneath the Galleriet shopping centre: it handles most long–distance buses, though some services terminate on the south side of Oslo S at the bus stands beside Havnegata. **Car ferries** from Germany and Denmark arrive at either the Vippetangen quays, a fifteen-minute walk south of Oslo S (take bus #60 to the centre), or at Hjortneskaia, some 3km west of the city centre; bus #31 to the centre usually connects with the ferry's arrival.

The main **tourist office** is in the centre, behind the Rådhus at Fridtjof Nansens plass 5 (June–Aug daily 9am–7pm; Sept–May Mon–Sat 9am–4/5pm; ☎24 14 77 00; ⓦwww.visitoslo.com), with a second branch inside Oslo S (May–Aug daily 8am–11pm; Sept Mon–Sat 8am–11pm; Oct–April Mon–Sat 8am–5pm): both issue free city maps, make reservations on guided tours, run a hotel booking service, and sell the useful **Oslo Pass** (195/285/375kr for one/two/three days), which gives free museum admission, limited discounts in shops and restaurants and free city transport. There is also a youth information office, **Use It** (Ungdoms Informasjonen), at Møllergata 3 (Sept–June Mon–Wed & Fri 11am–5pm, Thurs 11am–6pm; July & Aug Mon–Fri 9am–6pm; ☎24 14 98 20; ⓦwww.unginfo.oslo .no). All three provide *Streetwise* – a free budget guide to Oslo – as well as the excellent *Oslo Official Guide* and *What's On in Oslo*. The Norwegian hikers' association, Den Norske Turistforening (**DNT**), has an office in the centre at Storgata 7 (Mon–Fri 10am–4pm, Thurs 10am–6pm, Sat 10am–2pm; ☎22 82 28 00, ⓦwww .turistforeningen.no), where they sell **hiking maps** and give general advice and information on route planning.

The city transport **Trafikanten information office** is on Jernbanetorvet, the pedestrianized square outside Oslo S (Mon–Fri 7am–8pm, Sat 8am–6pm; ☎177, ⓦwww.trafikanten.no), and supplies a useful free transit map and comprehensive timetable booklet, *Rutebok for Oslo*. The **trams** run on eight lines, crossing the centre from east to west, there are also **buses** and an underground Tunnelbanen (**T-bane**), which has eight lines, all of which converge on a common slice of track that crosses the city centre from Majorstuen in the west to Tøyen in the east. Numerous local **ferries** cross the Oslofjord to the south of the centre, connecting the city with its outlying districts and archipelagos. Local transport **tickets** cost a flat-fare of 20kr; a 24hr-travel pass, available from Trafikanten, costs 60kr.

## Accommodation

You're best off **staying** centrally either around Oslo S or near the western reaches of Karl Johans gate, between the Stortinget and the Nationaltheatret. It is always worth calling ahead to check on space. A good budget alternative to the hostels listed below is a **private room**, booked by the tourist office at Oslo S (225kr single, 350kr double), though there's often a minimum two-night stay.

## Hostels

**Anker Hostel** Storgata 55, ☏ 22 99 72 00, ⓦ www.ankerhostel.no. Excellent hostel, in a good location between Oslo S and the hip Grünerløkka district. Lively, clean and friendly, with its own bar, laundry and 24-hour reception. Fifteen minutes' walk from Oslo S or catch tram #11,#12,#13,#15 or #17. Dorms 150–175kr, rooms ❹

**Oslo Haraldsheim Vandrerhjem** Haraldsheimveien 4, Grefsen ☏ 22 22 29 65, ⓦ www.vandrerhjem.no. The best of the HI hostels, 4km northeast of the centre, with 70 rooms, mostly in four-bed dorms, the majority en suite. Take tram #15 or #17 from the bottom of Storgata to the Sinsenkrysset stop, from where it's a signposted five- to ten-minute walk along a footpath. Advance booking necessary in summer. Dorms 175–195kr, rooms ❹

**Oslo Vandrerhjem Holtekilen** Micheletsvei 55, 1368 Stabekk ☏ 67 51 80 40, ⓦ www .vandrerhjem.no. Located 10km west of the city centre, this place has both dorms and one- to four-bedded rooms. Also has kitchen, laundry facilities and restaurant. From Bussterminalen, take bus #151 to the Kveldsroveien bus stop; the hostel is 100m away on the right. Dorms 180kr, rooms ❹

## Hotels and guest houses

**Bondeheimen** Rosenkrantz gate 8 ☏ 23 21 41 00, ⓦ www.bondeheimen.com. One of Oslo's most delightful hotels, tastefully decorated with polished pine everywhere. It's a short walk north of Karl Johans gate – and the buffet breakfast, included in the price, is excellent. ❾

**City** Skippergaten 19 ☏ 22 41 36 10, ⓦ www .cityhotel.no. This modest but pleasant hotel, a long-time favourite with budget travellers, is located above shops and offices in a typical Oslo apartment block near Oslo S. The surroundings are a little seedy, but the hotel is cheerful enough, with small but perfectly adequate rooms. ❻

**Cochs Pensjonat** Parkveien 25 ☏ 23 33 24 00, ⓦ www.cochspensjonat.no. Reasonable guest house with good deals on triples and quads. Mostly shared bathrooms. Pleasant location to the west of the royal palace. ❺

# The city centre and around

Oslo's main street, **Karl Johans gate**, leads west up the slope from Oslo S train station. It begins unpromisingly with a clutter of tacky shops and hang-around junkies, but steps away at the corner of Dronningens gate is the curious **Basarhallene**, a circular building of two tiers, whose brick cloisters once housed the city's food market. With parts dating from the late seventeenth century, the adjacent **Domkirke** (daily 10am–5pm; free) looks plain and dour from the outside: inside, however, the cathedral boasts an elegantly restored interior, its nave and transepts awash with maroon, green and gold paintwork. It's a brief stroll further up Karl Johans gate to the **Stortinget**, the parliament building, an imposing chunk of neo-Romanesque architecture that was completed in 1866. In front of the parliament, a narrow park-piazza flanks Karl Johans gate; in summer it teems with promenading city folk, while in winter people flock to its floodlit open-air skating rinks. Beyond, up the hill, **Det Kongelige Slott** (Royal Palace) is a monument to Norwegian openness; built between 1825 and 1848, when other monarchies were nervously counting their friends, it still stands without railings and walls, and the grounds – **Slottsparken** – are open to the public. The daily changing of the guard (1.30pm) is a snappy affair, well worth a look.

Back on Karl Johans Gate, the nineteenth-century buildings of the **University** fit well into this monumental end of the city centre. Among them, at Universitetsgata 13, you'll find the **Nasjonalgalleriet** (Tues, Wed & Fri 10am–6pm, Thurs 10am–8pm, Sat & Sun 10am–5pm; free; Norwegian–only website ⓦ www .nasjonalgalleriet.no), home to Norway's largest and best collection of fine art. Highlights include some wonderfully romantic, nineteenth-century landscapes by the likes of Johan Christian Dahl and Thomas Fearnley, and a room devoted to Edvard Munch, featuring the original version of the famous *Scream*. Heading south from the University buildings, you can't miss the monolithic brickwork of the massive City Hall, the **Rådhus** (daily 9am–4/5pm; free), opened in 1950 to celebrate the city's 900th anniversary.

## The Bygdøy peninsula

The most enjoyable way to reach the leafy **Bygdøy peninsula**, southwest of the city centre, is by **ferry**. These leave from the Rådhusbrygge (pier 3) behind the Rådhus (late April & Sept every 30min 9am–6.30pm; May–Aug every 15min 8/9am–9.05pm; 20kr). They stop first at the Dronningen (15min from Rådhus-brygge) and then the Bygdøynes piers (20min). The two most popular attractions – the Viking Ships and Folk museums – are within easy walking distance of the Dronningen pier, the others – the Kon-Tiki, the Maritime and the Fram museums – are beside Bygdøynes. It's a (dull) fifteen-minute signposted walk between the two groups of museums. The alternative to the ferry is **bus** #30 (every 15min), which runs all year from Jernbanetorget; the square outside Oslo S. This takes you to the Folk Museum and Viking Ships, and, when the ferry isn't running, to the other three museums as well.

The entertaining **Norsk Folkemuseum**, at Museumsveien 10 (daily: mid-May to mid-Sept 10am–6pm, mid-Sept to mid-May 11am–3/4pm, 90kr; ⊛www .norskfolkemuseum.no), combines indoor collections of furniture, china and silver-ware with an intriguing open-air display of reassembled period farms, houses and other buildings. From here, it's a few minutes walk to the **Vikingskipshuset** (Viking Ships Museum; daily: May–Sept 9am–6pm; Oct–April 11am–4pm; 40kr; ⊛www .ukm.uio.no/vikingskipshuset), housing a trio of ninth-century Viking ships, with viewing platforms to let you see inside the hulls. The three oak vessels were retrieved from ritual burial mounds in southern Norway towards the end of the nineteenth century, each embalmed in a subsoil of clay – hence their excellent state of preservation. The star exhibit is the **Oseberg ship**, thought to be the burial ship of a Viking chieftain's wife. Its ornately carved prow and stern rise high above the hull, where thirty oar-holes indicate the size of the crew. Down by Bygdøynes pier, the **Kon-Tiki museet** (daily: April, May & Sept 10am–5pm; June–Aug 9am–5.30pm; Oct–March 10.30am–4pm; 45kr; ⊛www.kon-tiki.no) displays the balsawood raft on which Thor Heyerdahl made his now legendary 1947 journey across the Pacific to prove that the first Polynesian settlers could have sailed from pre-Inca Peru. Over the road, in front of the **Frammuseet** (daily: May to mid-June & Sept 10am–5.45pm; mid-June to Aug 9am–6.45pm; Oct–April 10am–3.45pm; 40kr), is the *Gjøa*, the one-time sealing ship in which Roald Amundsen made the first successful sailing of the Northwest Passage in 1906. Inside, you can clamber aboard another of Amundsen's ships, the polar vessel *Fram*; this was the ship which carried him to within striking distance of the South Pole in 1911. Complete with most of its original fittings, the interior gives a superb insight into the life and times of these early Polar explorers.

## The Munch Museum and Vigeland Sculpture Park

Also out of the centre but without question a major attraction, the **Munch-museet**, Tøyengata 53 (June to Aug daily 10am–6pm; Sept–May Mon–Fri 10am–4pm, Sat & Sun 11am–5pm; 65kr; ⊛www.munch.museum.no), is reachable by T-bane: get off at Tøyen/Munch-museet and it's a signposted five-minute walk. Born in 1863, **Edvard Munch** is Norway's most famous painter. His lithographs and woodcuts – dark catalogues of swirls and fog – are on display here, as well as his early paintings and the great, signature works of the 1890s. The museum also owns no fewer than fifty versions of *The Scream*.

On the other side of the city and reachable on tram #12 and #15 from the centre (get off at Vigelandsparken), Frogner Park holds one of Oslo's most striking cultural targets in the open-air **Vigeland Sculpture Park** (free access), which com-memorates another modern Norwegian artist, Gustav Vigeland. Vigeland started on the sculptures in 1924 and was still working on them when he died in 1943. A long series of life-size figures frowning, fighting and posing lead up to the central fountain, an enormous bowl representing the burden of life, supported by straining, sinewy bronze Goliaths, while underneath water tumbles out around clusters of playing and standing figures.

## The islands of the inner Oslofjord

The archipelago of low-lying, lightly forested **islands** in the **inner Oslofjord** is the city's summer playground. Although most of the islets are cluttered with summer homes, the least populated are favourite party venues for the city's youth. Ferries to the islands leave from the Vippetangen quay, at the foot of Akershus-stranda – a twenty-minute walk south from Oslo S. The nearest island, **Hovedøya** (reachable by ferries #92, #93 or #94; mid-March to Sept 7.30am–7pm, every 30min–hour; Oct to mid-March three daily; 10min), is also the most interesting, with the overgrown ruins of a twelfth-century Cistercian monastery, and rolling hills covered in farmland and deciduous woods. There are plenty of footpaths to wander, you can swim from the shingle beaches on the south shore, and there's a seasonal café opposite the monastery ruins. Camping is not permitted as Hovedøya is a protected area. The pick of the other islands is wooded **Langøyene** (ferry #94; June–Aug hourly 9.30am–6.45pm; 30min), the most southerly of the archipelago and the one with the best beaches; it has a **campsite**, *Langøyene Camping* (⏿22 36 37 98; June to mid–Aug), and at night the ferries are full of people armed with sleeping bags and bottles, on their way to join swimming parties.

# Eating, drinking and nightlife

Oslo boasts scores of **places to eat**. Those carefully counting the kroner will find it easy to buy bread, fruit and snacks from stalls and shops across the city centre, while fast-food joints offering hamburgers and hot dogs (*pølser*) are legion. For a picnic, buy a bag of freshly cooked, shell-on prawns from one of the fishing boats at the Rådhusbrygge pier, or head to the principal open-air **market** at Youngstorget (Mon–Sat 7am–2pm), a brief stroll north of the Domkirke along Torggata.

Oslo's hippest **cafés** and **bars** can be found in the former working-class area of Grünerløkka along Thorvald Meyersgate and Markveien in particular. To the south, the Grønland district is heading the same way as its trendy neighbour, with a healthy mix of ethnic shops and **restaurants**. Downtown Oslo also has a vibrant bar scene, at its most frenetic on summer weekends. The busiest mainstream bars are concentrated in the side streets near the Rådhus and along the Aker Brygge, while other popular but less assertively heterosexual bars are clustered around Universitetsgata and on Rosenkrantz gate. The busiest **clubs** are on and around Karl Johans gate, with Grønland and Grünerløkka also boasting some good places. Entry can set you back 50–100kr – though drinks prices are the same as anywhere else. Nothing gets going much before 11pm; closing times are generally 3–4am. For entertainment **listings** check *Natt & Dag*, a monthly Norwegian-language broadsheet available free from cafés, bars and shops.

## Cafés and restaurants

**Ett Glass** Karl Johans gate 33, entrance round the corner on Rosenkrantz gate. Trendy, candlelit café/bar. Imaginative inexpensive menu focuses on Mediterranean-influenced light meals and lunches and provides some curious, often mouthwatering delights.
**Kaffistova** Rosenkrantz gate 8. Part of the *Bondeheimen* hotel, this spick-and-span self-service café serves tasty, traditional Norwegian dishes at very fair prices. There's usually a vegetarian option, too.

**Krishna Cuisine** Kirkeveien 59B. In the middle of busy Majorstukrysset, this is the city's best vegetarian option. Closed Sat & Sun.
**Sult** Thorvald Meyersgate 26. Serves innovative dishes using seasonal ingredients, at surprisingly low prices. The attached bar *Tørst* is one of Oslo's most popular spots.
**Tullins cafe** Tullins gate 2. Close to the National Gallery, this fashionable café serves light meals, snacks and coffee in the daytime

and turns into a bar at night. Reasonably priced.

**Zoolounge** Kristian August gate 7B. Stylish modern café/bar with nice snack/meal options, tasty coffee and posh drinks in the evening. Hip young crowd and DJ sessions at night.

## Bars and pubs

**Bar Boca** Thorvald Meyers gate 30. Tiny Fifties-retro bar in Grünerløkka, with the best dry Martinis in Norway. Get there early.

**Cafe con Bar** Brugata 11. As hip as you like, with retro interior and a long bar that can make buying a drink hard work. Good atmosphere, loungy decor.

**Dattera til Hagen** Grønland 10. This trendy Grønland spot is a café by day and a lively bar at night, sometimes with a DJ on its small upstairs dance-floor.

**Savoy Bar** Universitetsgata 11. With its stained-glass windows and wood-panelled walls, this small, intimate bar is an agreeably low-key, if a little more expensive, spot to nurse a beer. Part of the *Savoy* hotel.

## Clubs and music venues

**Blå** Brenneriveien 9c ⊛ www.blx.no. Creative, cultural Grünerløkka nightspot, featuring everything from live jazz and cabaret to public debates and poetry readings. Also boasts some of the best DJs in town, keeping the crowd moving until 3.30am at the weekend. In summer, there's a pleasant riverside terrace and the food is pretty good too.

**Herr Nilsen** C.J. Hambros plass 5, ⊛ www.herrnilsen.no. Great spot for live jazz and blues.

**Original Neilsen** Rosenkrantz gate, at Karl Johans gate. Another excellent jazz venue: cosy and crowded.

**Rockerfeller Music Hall** Torggata 16. This former bathhouse is now one of Oslo's major concert venues, hosting well-known and up-and-coming bands – mostly rock or alternative.

## Listings

**Embassies and consulates** Canada, Wergelandveien 7 ☏ 22 99 53 00; Ireland, Haakon VII's gate 1, 5th Floor ☏ 22 01 72 00; UK, Thomas Heftyes gate 8 ☏ 23 13 27 00; USA, Drammensveien 18 ☏ 22 44 85 50.

**Internet and email** Internet access is available free at the main city library, Henrik Ibsen gate 1 (Mon–Fri 10am–7pm, Sat 9am–3pm).

**Laundry** A Snarvask, Thorvald Meyers gate 18 ☏ 22 37 57 70 (Mon–Fri 10am–8pm, Sat 10am–3pm).

**Left Luggage** Oslo S (daily 4.30am–1.10am); 20/25/30kr for 24hrs.

**Pharmacy** Jernbanetorgets Apotek, Jernbanetorget 4b, is a 24hr pharmacy near Oslo S.

# Bergen and the fjords

The **fjords** are the most familiar and alluring image of Norway – huge clefts in the landscape which occur along the west coast right up to the Russian border, though the most beguiling portion lies between Bergen and Ålesund. **Bergen**, Norway's second largest city, is a handy springboard for the fjords, notably the **Flåm valley** and its inspiring mountain railway, which trundles down to the Aurlandsfjord, a tiny arm of the mighty **Sognefjord**, Norway's longest and deepest. North of the Sognefjord, there is the smaller and less stimulating **Nordfjord**, though there's superb compensation in the **Jostedalsbreen** glacier, which nudges the fjord from the east. The tiny S-shaped **Geirangerfjord**, further north again, is magnificent too – narrow, sheer and rugged – while the northernmost **Romsdalsfjord** and its many branches and inlets reach pinnacles of isolation in the **Trollstigen** mountain highway.

By rail, you can only reach Bergen and Flåm in the south and Åndalsnes in the north. For everything in between – including most of the Sognefjord, Nordfjord and the Jostedalsbreen glacier – **buses** and **ferries** together comprise a complicated but fully integrated system. It's a good idea to pick up full bus and ferry timetables from any local tourist office whenever you can.

# Bergen

Although it's one of the rainiest places in rainy Norway, **BERGEN** does benefit from a spectacular setting among seven hills and is altogether one of the country's most enjoyable cities. There's plenty to see, from fine old buildings to a series of good museums, and Bergen is also within easy reach of some of Norway's most spectacular scenic attractions, both around the city and further north. Founded in 1070, the city was the largest and most important town in medieval Norway, a regular residence of the country's kings and queens, and later a Hanseatic port and religious centre, though precious little of that era survives today. Nowadays, the city centre divides into two main parts: the wharf area, **Bryggen**, adjacent to the Bergenhus fortress, once the working centre of the Hanseatic merchants and now the oldest part of Bergen; and the **modern centre**, which stretches inland from the head of the harbour and takes in the best of Bergen's museums, cafés and bars.

The obvious place to start a visit is the **Torget**, an appealing harbourside plaza that's home to a colourful fish- and fresh-produce market. From here, it's a short stroll round to the **Bryggen**, where a string of distinctive wooden buildings line up along the waterfront. These once housed the city's merchants and now hold shops, restaurants and bars. Although none of these structures was actually built by the Hanseatic Germans – most of the originals were destroyed by fire in 1702 – they carefully follow the original building line. Among them, the **Hanseatic Museum** (May & late Sept daily 11am–2pm; June–Aug daily 9am–5pm; early Sept daily 10am–3pm; Oct–April Tues–Sat 11am–2pm, Sun noon–5pm; 45kr) is the most diverting, an early eighteenth-century merchant's dwelling kitted out in late-Hansa style. Also worth visiting is the **Bryggens Museum** (May–Aug daily 10am–5pm; Sept–April Mon–Fri 11am–3pm, Sat noon–3pm, Sun noon–4pm; 40kr), just along the harbourfront, where a series of imaginative exhibitions attempts a complete reassembly of local medieval life – from domestic implements, handicrafts and maritime objects through to trading items. Nearby you'll also find the **Fløibanen**, a dinky funicular railway (Mon–Fri 7.30am–11pm/midnight, Sat 8am–11pm/midnight, Sun 9am–11pm/midnight; departures every 15 min; return fare 60kr), which runs to the top of **Mount Fløyen** (320m), from where there are panoramic views over the city, and a network of forest walks. Back at the bottom, in the modern centre, Bergen's four main **art museums** are on the south side of a pleasant, artificial lake. The pick of these is the **Rasmus Meyer Samlinger**, Rasmus Meyers Allé 7 (daily 11am–5pm; mid-Sept to mid-May closed Mon; 50kr), which holds an extensive collection of Norwegian painting, including several works by Edvard Munch.

## Practicalities

Bergen is a busy international port and may well be your first stop in Norway. International **ferries** and cruise ships arrive at Skoltegrunnskaien, the quay just beyond Bergenhus fortress, on the east side of the harbour; domestic ferries and catamarans line up on the opposite side of the harbour at the Strandkaiterminalen. The **train** and **bus stations** face Strømgaten, a five-minute walk southeast of the head of the harbour. The **airport**, 20km south of the city, is connected to the bus station by regular *flybussen* (Mon–Fri & Sun 5am–9pm, Sat 5am–4pm, every 15–20min; 45min; 60kr). The city is also the southern terminus of the **Hurtigrute coastal boat**, which leaves from the Frieleneskaien quay behind the university, about 1.5km southwest of the train station – a shuttle bus links the two between April and September (45kr).

The **tourist office** is a few metres from the head of the harbour at Vågsallmenning 1 (May & Sept daily 9am–8pm; June–Aug daily 8.30am–10pm; Oct–April

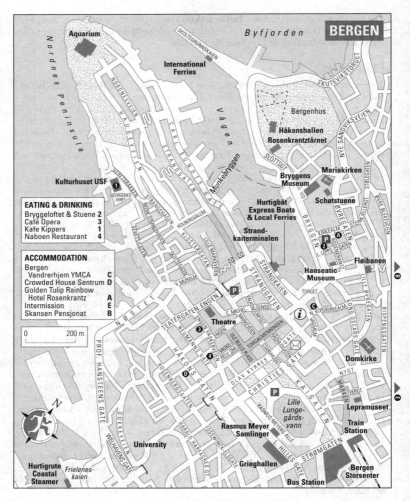

BERGEN

**EATING & DRINKING**
Bryggeloftet & Stuene 2
Café Opera 3
Kafe Kippers 1
Naboen Restaurant 4

**ACCOMMODATION**
Bergen
  Vandrerhjem YMCA   C
Crowded House Sentrum  D
Golden Tulip Rainbow
  Hotel Rosenkrantz   A
Intermission   E
Skansen Pensjonat   B

0        200 m

Mon–Sat 9am–4pm; ☎55 55 20 00; ⊛www.visitbergen.com). It issues maps and sells the Bergen Card (170kr one day/250kr for two days), which allows travel on all the city's buses and free entrance to, or discounts on, most of the city's sights, including sightseeing trips. **Accommodation** is no great problem. As well as the places listed below, there are plenty of **private rooms** (➌) that can be booked through the tourist office. Bergen has a good supply of first-rate **restaurants** concentrated in the Bryggen, with local seafood the speciality. Less expensive – and more fashionable – are the city's **café/restaurants**, which often double up as lively **bars**. Several of the best are located to the southwest of Ole Bulls plass, the main pedestrianized square. In May, the annual **Bergen International Festival** (⊛www.festspillene.no) consists of twelve days of music, ballet, folklore and drama, supplemented by **Nattjazz** (⊛www.nattjazz.no), a prestigious international jazz festival.

## Hostels

**Bergen Vandrerhjem Montana** Johan Blyttsveien 30, Landås ☎ 55 20 80 70, ⊛ www.montana.no. This large and comfortable hostel occupies lodge-like premises in the hills 4km east of the centre, with good views over the city. Singles, doubles and dorms available. Dorms 150kr, rooms ❻
**Bergen Vandrerhjem YMCA** Nedre Korskirkealmenning 4 ☎ 55 60 60 55, ⊛ www.vandrerhjem.no. Close to Torget, a five- to ten-minute walk from the train station. HI hostel with 175 beds – but fills quickly. Facilities include showers, kitchen and laundry. May to mid–Sept only. Dorms 125–170kr, rooms ❺
**Intermission** Kalfarveien 8 ☎ 55 30 04 00. Trim Christian-run hostel close to the train station. Mid-June-mid-August only. 120kr.

## Guest houses and hotels

**Crowded House Sentrum** Håkonsgaten 27 ☎ 55 90 72 00, ⊛ www.crowded-house.com. Lively, appealing place with bright and airy, if spartan, bedrooms. Self-catering facilities too. Halfway along Håkonsgaten, five minutes' walk from the city centre. ❺
**Golden Tulip Rainbow Hotel Rosenkrantz** Rosenkrantzgaten 7 ☎ 55 30 14 00, ⊛ www.rainbow-hotels.no. Efficient hotel in an old building just behind the Bryggen with comfortable rooms and discounts in the summer. ❽
**Skansen Pensjonat** vestrelidsalmenringen 29 ☎ 55 31 90 80, ⊛ www.skansen-pensjonat.no. Simple but cosy little place in a nineteenth-century stone house just above the Fløibanen terminus, near Torget. Has seven rooms and four apartments. ❺

## Cafés, restaurants and bars

**Bryggeloftet & Stuene** Bryggen 11. Slightly staid and expensive restaurant, serving the best and widest range of seafood in town. Main courses around 200kr.
**Café Opera** Engen 24. White wooden building near Ole Bulls plass, bustling with a fashionable crew drinking beer and good coffee. Tasty, filling dishes (from 100kr) including some good veggie options. Crowded club-like venue in the evening.
**Kafe Kippers** Kulturhuset USF, Georgernes verft. Ultra-groovy café/bar in an imaginatively renovated old herring factory, with delicious, inexpensive food and a prime seashore location; the terrace is the place to be on sunny summer days.
**Naboen Restaurant** Neumannsgate 20. Excellent, moderately priced meals at this easy-going restaurant, which features Swedish specialities. A student favourite. Mains from 150kr.

## Listings

**Exchange** The main post office offers competitive exchange rates for foreign currency and travellers' cheques.
**Hiking** The DNT-affiliated Bergen Turlag, Tverrgaten 4–6 (Mon–Wed & Fri 10am–4pm, Thurs 10am–6pm, Sat 10am–2pm; ☎ 55 33 58 10), can advise on hiking trails in the region and sells hiking maps.
**Internet and email** The Cyberhouse Internet Café, just below the funicular at vestrelidsalmenringen 13 (⊛ www.cyberhouse.no), charges 30kr for 30min (daily 9am–10pm).
**Laundry** Jarlens Vaskoteque, Lille Øvregate 17, near the funicular (Mon, Tues & Fri 10am–6pm, Wed & Thurs 10am–8pm; Sat 10am–3pm).
**Pharmacy** Apoteket Nordstjernen, at the bus station (Mon–Sat 8am–11pm, Sun 10am–11pm).
**Post office** On Christies gate, towards the Torget end (Mon–Fri 8am–6pm, Sat 9am–3pm).

# Around Bergen

If you're not journeying through the fjord region – the better option – you can get a taste by taking the train from Bergen to Myrdal, at the head of the remarkable branch line down the valley to **Flåm** and the **Aurlandsfjord** – one of the most popular of all fjord trips. Pick up transport timetables from the tourist office or at the train station before you set out.

## Flåm

If you're short of time, but want to sample a goodly slice of fjord scenery, make the train journey east from Bergen, through Voss, to **Myrdal**, a lonely railway junction, from where specially built trains squeak down a branch line that plummets 900m into the **Flåm valley**. The track took four years to lay and is one of the steepest anywhere in the world, making a wondrously dramatic journey. With a little more time, you might also consider the "Norway in a Nutshell" trip, which, as well as the magnificent train ride, includes a cruise on two of the narrowest "arms" of the Sognefjord between Flåm and Gudvangen plus the spectacular bus ride from Gudvangen back to Voss and Bergen. The round-trip takes seven hours from Bergen and costs 760kr (480kr from Voss); tickets can be bought at any train station. **FLÅM VILLAGE**, the train's destination, lies alongside meadows and orchards on the Aurlandsfjord, a matchstick-thin branch of the Sognefjord. Hikers can get off the train at **Berekvam** station, the halfway point, and stroll down the winding country road from there. Flåm is a tiny village that gets packed with tourists on summer days, but out of season – or on summer evening, when the day-trippers have gone – it can be a pleasantly restful place. There are two good places **to stay**: the homely *Heimly Pensjonat* (☎57 63 23 00, ⊛www.heimly.no; ❻), which provides simple but adequate lodgings in a modern block about 450m along the shore from the train station; and the excellent *Flåm Camping* (☎57 63 21 21, ⊛www.vandrerhjem.no; May–Sept only), a combined **campsite** and **hostel** (dorms 120kr, rooms ❸), 200m from the train station. The **tourist office** is at the ferry dock (daily: May & Sept 8.30am–4.30pm; June, July & Aug 8.30am–8pm; ☎57 63 21 06), by the train station, and has information on local hikes.

## The Sognefjord and the Jostedalsbreen glacier

With the exception of Flåm, the southern shore of the **Sognefjord** remains sparsely populated and relatively inaccessible, whereas the north shore boasts a couple of very appealing resorts. Top-of-the-list **BALESTRAND** is the prettiest base, a tourist destination since the mid-nineteenth century when it was discovered by European travellers in search of cool, clear air and mountain scenery. Buses (and express boats from Bergen and Flåm) arrive at Balestrand's minuscule harbourfront, near which you'll find the **tourist office** (phone for opening hours ☎57 69 12 55). As for somewhere to stay, the comfortable and very appealing *Kringsjå Hotel*, 100m from the tourist office, incorporates the local HI **hostel** (☎57 69 13 03; ⊛www.vandrerhjem.no; hotel doubles ❻; hostel dorms 190kr, hostel doubles ❺; late June to mid-Aug only). Another good choice is the relaxing *Midtnes Pensjonat* (☎57 69 11 33, ⊛www.midtnes.no; ❻), about 300m from the dock behind the little wooden church.

The beauty of the fjord aside, there are few sights as such to see in Balestrand itself, but several lovely places are within easy striking distance, particularly the delightful village of **FJÆRLAND** (also known as Mundal), on the Fjærlandsfjord. The village can be reached direct by ferry from Balestrand from May to early September (two daily; 1hr 30min; passengers 152kr; car & driver 265kr), and by bus throughout the rest of the year (change at Sogndal). Formerly one of the most isolated spots on the Sognefjord, Fjærland is now connected to the road system, but retains its old-fashioned atmosphere and appearance, with a string of handsome clapboard buildings in a wildly beautiful location. Fjærland is also Norway's self-styled book town, and there are various **literature events** held here in the summer (⊛www.bokbyen.no or ⊛www.booktown.net). Fjærland's **tourist office** is in the centre of the village, metres from the ferry dock (late May to early Sept daily 9.30am–5.30pm; ☎57 69 32 33). **Accommodation** is limited: choose from the splendid *Hotel Mundal* (☎57 69 31 01, ⊛www.fjordinfo .no/mundal; ❾; May–Sept only), a quirky, old-fashioned sort of place, and the *Fjærland Fjordstue Hotell* (☎57 69 32 00, ⊛www.fjaerland.no; ❺), a well-tended family hotel with smart modern furnishings. A third option is *Bøyum Camping* (☎57 69 32 52) on the edge of the village near the Bremuseum (glacier museum); they have four-berth huts (from 350kr per night) as well as spaces for tents. Both hotels offer good, wholesome food.

Fjærland's other advantage is its proximity to the southern edge of the **Jostedals-breen glacier**, a vast ice plateau that dominates the whole of the inner Nordfjord region. The glacier's 24 arms – or nodules – melt down into the nearby valleys, giving the local rivers and glacial lakes their distinctive blue-green colouring. The glacier is protected within the **Jostedalsbreen Nasjonalpark**, whose guides take organized **glacier walks** (May–Sept; from around 300kr) on its various arms, ranging from two-hour excursions to all-day, fully-equipped hikes. Equipment is provided, though you'll need good boots, warm clothes, gloves and hat, sunglasses and (usually) your own food and drink. One of the many places that takes bookings is the Fjærland tourist office. You can also reach an arm of the glacier under your own steam – and without too much sweat – by strolling north from Fjærland on Highway 5; about 10km north of the village, just before the tunnel, a signed side road leads the 200m to the Bøyabreen glacier arm, though you're not allowed to walk on it – viewing only.

## The Geirangerfjord

On the north side of the Jostedalsbreen glacier is the **Nordfjord**, but this fjord system doesn't have the scenic lustre of its more famous neighbours and you're much better off pressing on to the S-shaped **Geirangerfjord**, one of the region's smallest and most breathtaking fjords. A convoluted branch of the Storfjord, it cuts deep inland, marked by impressive waterfalls and with a village at either end of its snake-like profile. You can reach the Geirangerfjord in dramatic style by bus from the north or south, but you'd do best to approach from the north if you can. From this direction, the journey begins in Åndalsnes (see below), from where Highway 63 wriggles over the mountains via the wonderful **Trollstigen Highway**, which climbs through some of the country's highest peaks before sweeping down to the tiny Norddalsfjord. From here, it's a quick ferry ride and dramatic journey along the Ørnevegen, the Eagle's Highway, for a first view of the Geirangerfjord and the village that bears its name glinting in the distance. There is little as stunning anywhere in western Norway, and from mid-June to August it can all be seen on a twice-daily bus following this so-called "Golden Route".

**GEIRANGER** village enjoys a commanding position at one end of the fjord. However, it's hopelessly overdeveloped and your best bet, especially in high season, is to pass straight through, taking the ferry on to the hamlet of **HELLESYLT**, an hour's boat ride away through the double bend of the fjord. There's nothing much to the place, but by nightfall Hellesylt makes for a quiet and peaceful **overnight stay**. The ferry terminal is a few steps from the *Grand Hotel* (☎70 26 51 00; ⓦwww .grandhotel-hellesylt.no; ❽), a local landmark since its construction in 1871, though patchily renovated and enlarged – guests are put up in the modern annexe next door. The HI **hostel** (☎70 26 51 28; dorms 125kr, rooms ❸; June–Aug only) is set on the hillside just above the village – just follow the signs. Alternatively, *Hellesylt Camping* (☎70 26 51 88) occupies a shadeless field beside the fjord about 400m from the quay. Usefully, Hellesylt is also on the main Bergen to Loen, Stryn and Ålesund bus route; buses stop near the jetty.

## Åndalsnes

Travelling north from Oslo by train, the line forks at Dombås – the Dovre line continuing northwards over the fells to Trondheim (see opposite), the Rauma line beginning a thrilling, roller-coaster rattle west down through the mountains to the **Isfjord** at Åndalsnes (1hr 30min). Apart from the Aurlandsfjord, an arm of the Sognefjord, reached from Bergen, the Isfjord is the only Norwegian fjord accessible by train, which explains the number of backpackers wandering its principal town of **ÅNDALSNES**, many people's first – sometimes only – contact with fjord country. Despite a wonderful setting between lofty peaks and looking-glass water, the town is unexciting, but it does make a convenient base for further explorations. Åndalsnes has an outstanding HI **hostel** (☎71 22 13 82; ⓦwww.vandrerhjem .no; dorms 200kr, rooms ❺; mid-May to mid–Sept only), which occupies a group of charming wooden buildings in a rural setting 2.5km along the E136 towards Ålesund. Another very good option is the riverside *Åndalsnes Camping og Motell* (☎71 22 16 29; ⊛www.andalsnescamp.no) with cabins (700–750kr per night), rowboats and bikes for rent, a 25-minute walk from the train station – take the first left after the river on the road out to the hostel. The **tourist office**, at the train station (mid–June to mid–Aug Mon–Fri 9am–6pm, Sat & Sun 11am–6pm; mid–Aug to mid–June Mon–Fri 8am–3.30pm; ☎71 22 16 22; ⊛www.visitandalsnes.com), has a free and comprehensive guide to local hikes as well as bus, boat and train timetables.

### Ålesund

At the end of the E136, some 120km west of Åndalsnes, the fishing and ferry port of **ÅLESUND** is immediately – and obviously – different from any other Norwegian town. In 1904, a disastrous fire left ten thousand people homeless and the town centre destroyed. A hectic reconstruction programme saw almost the entire area speedily rebuilt in a style that borrowed heavily from the German Jugendstil movement. Kaiser Wilhelm II, who used to holiday hereabouts, gave assistance, and the architects ended up creating a strange but fetching hybrid of up-to-date foreign influences and folksy local elements, with dragons, faces, flowers and even a decorative pharaoh or two. The finest buildings are concentrated on the main street, **Kongensgate**, and around the slender, central harbour, the **Brosundet**.

The town's **bus station** is by the waterfront, a few metres south of the Brosundet, near the **tourist office** (June–Aug Mon–Fri 8.30am–7pm, Sat 9am–5pm, Sun 11am–5pm; Sept–May Mon–Fri 8.30am–4pm; ☎70 15 76 00, ⊛www.visitalesund.com). The pick of the town's **hotels** is the excellent *Brosundet Gjestehus* at Apotekergata 5 (☎70 12 10 00, ⊛www.brosundet.no; ❼), an old wharfside warehouse that has been beautifully converted into a friendly, family-run place with some nice touches: it has a sauna, kitchen, and laundry facilities as well as free tea, coffee and waffles. There's also a small and central HI **hostel** at Parkgata 14, at the top of Rådstuggata, in an old building that's creaky but clean (☎70 11 58 30, ⊛www.vandrerhjem.no; dorms 170kr, rooms ❺). For **eating**, the *Sjøbua Fiskerestaurant*, Brunholmgata 1, is an expensive but first-rate seafood restaurant, with its own lobster tank. Cheaper if more mundane options include *Smak* at Kipervik gata 5, and *Metz*, a café/restaurant overlooking the Brosundet, with a popular terrace in fine weather.

# Northern Norway

The long, thin counties of **Trøndelag** and **Nordland** mark the transition from rural southern to blustery northern Norway. The main town of Trøndelag, appealing **Trondheim**, is easily accessible from Oslo by train, but north of here travelling becomes more of a slog as the distances between places grow ever greater. In **Nordland** things get wilder still, though save the scenery there's little of interest until you reach the steel town of **Mo-i-Rana**. Just north of here lies the **Arctic Circle**, beyond which the land becomes ever more spectacular, not least on the exquisite, mountainous **Lofoten Islands**, whose idyllic fishing villages (and inexpensive accommodation) richly merit a stop. Back on the mainland, **Narvik** is a modern port handling vast quantities of iron-ore amid some startling rocky surroundings. Further north still, the provinces of **Troms** and **Finnmark** are subtle in their appeal, and the travelling can be hard, with **Tromsø**, a lively urban centre and university town, making the obvious stopping point. As for **Finnmark**, most visitors head straight for **Nordkapp**, from where the Midnight Sun is visible between early May and the end of July.

# Trondheim

**TRONDHEIM**, an atmospheric city with much of its eighteenth-century centre still intact, has been an important Norwegian power base for centuries, its success guaranteed by the excellence of its harbour and its position at the head of a wide and fertile valley. The early Norse parliament, or **Ting**, met here, and the city was once a major pilgrimage centre. The city centre sits on a small triangle of land, a pocket-sized area where the main sights – bar the marvellous cathedral – have an amiable low-key quality. Trondheim also possesses a clutch of good restaurants and a string of busy bars.

The colossal **Nidaros Domkirke** – Scandinavia's largest medieval building, gloriously restored following the ravages of the Reformation and several fires – remains the focal point of the city centre (May to mid-Sept Mon–Fri 9am–3/6pm, Sat 9am–2pm, Sun 1–4pm; mid-Sept to April Mon–Fri noon–2.30pm, Sat 11.30am–2pm, Sun 1–3pm; 40kr). Taking Trondheim's former name (Nidaros means "mouth of the River Nid"), the cathedral is dedicated to King Olav, Norway's first Christian ruler, who was killed at the nearby battle of Stiklestad in 1030, and ultimately buried here. Thereafter, it became the traditional burial place of Norwegian royalty and, since 1814, it has also been the place where Norwegian monarchs are crowned. Highlights of the interior are the Gothic choir and the gargoyles on the pointed arches, as well as the striking choir screen and font, both the work of Norwegian sculptor Gustav Vigeland (1869–1943). Behind the Domkirke lies the heavily restored Archbishop's palace, now housing the **Army and Resistance Museum** (same hours as cathedral; free); its most interesting section recalls the German occupation during World War II, dealing honestly with the sensitive issue of collaboration. Near at hand is **Torvet**, the main city square, a spacious open area anchored by a statue of Olav Tryggvason, perched on a stone pillar like some medieval Nelson. The broad and pleasant avenues of Trondheim's centre radiate out from here; they date from the late seventeenth century, when they doubled as fire breaks. They were originally flanked by long rows of wooden buildings, now mostly replaced by uninspiring modern structures, but one conspicuous survivor is the **Stiftsgården** (guided tours hourly, on the hour till 1hr before closing: early June to late Aug Mon–Sat 10am–3/5pm, Sun noon–5pm; 50kr), the yellow creation just north of Torvet on Munkegata. Built in 1774–78 as the home of a provincial governor, it's now an official royal residence.

## Practicalities

Trondheim is the first major northbound stop of the Bergen-Kirkenes **Hurtigrute coastal boat**, which docks about 600m behind and to the north of Sentralstasjon, the combined **bus and train terminal**. Sentralstasjon is just over the bridge from the town centre, which occupies a small island at the mouth of the River Nid. The **tourist office** is bang in the middle of town on the main square, the Torvet (mid-May to late Aug Mon–Fri 8.30am–6/8pm, Sat & Sun 10am–4/6pm; Sept to early May Mon–Fri 9am–4pm, Sat & Sun 10am–2pm; ☎73 80 76 60, ⊛www .trondheim.com): it runs a room reservation service and has a small supply of **private rooms** (around ❹). Alternatively, there's the large and well-equipped HI **hostel** at Weidemannsvei 41 (☎73 87 44 50, ⊛www.trondheim-vandrerhjem.no; dorms 210kr, rooms ❹), a steep twenty minutes' hike east from the centre over the Bakkebru bridge. A handier option is the *Rainbow Hotel Trondheim*, a well-maintained and modern chain hotel in the centre of town at Kongensgate 15 (☎73 88 47 88, ⊛www.rainbow-hotels.no/trondheim; ❾).

For **eating**, the cafés and restaurants amid the old timber warehouses and homes of the atmospheric Bakklandet area are a good choice. Try the *Dromedar*, Nedre Bakklandet 3, a fashionable café/bar offering tasty snacks and meals with a wholefood slant, or the more central *Credo*, Ørjaveita 4, which has a good restaurant serving innovative seasonal food, with a bar above: it's tucked away on a back street behind the waterside Fjordgata near the junction with Norde gata. Bakklandet is also a good area for **nightlife**, as are the lively bars and clubs along Beddingen, over the Bakkebru bridge. Alternatively, back in the centre, you could try *Brukbar*, Munkegata 26, a lively bar catering for everyone from business folk dropping in after work, to hardcore student boozers.

## The Arctic Circle, Mo-i-Rana and Bodø

North of Trondheim, it's a long haul up the coast to the next major places of interest: Bodø, which is the main ferry port for the Lofoten Islands, and the gritty but likeable town of Narvik, respectively 730km and 908km away. You can cover most of the ground by train, a rattling good journey with the scenery becoming wilder and bleaker the further north you go. From Trondheim, it takes nine hours to reach Fauske, where the railway reaches its northern limit and turns west for the final 65km dash across to Bodø. On the way you cross the **Arctic Circle**, which, considering the amount of effort it takes to get here, is something of an anticlimax. The bare, bleak landscape – uninhabited for the most part – is undeniably impressive, though rather disfigured by the gleaming **Polarsirkelsenteret** (Arctic Circle Centre; daily: May to early June & Aug 9am–8pm; late June & July 8am–10pm; early Sept 10am–6pm; ⑩www.polarsirkelsenteret.no), a giant lampshade of a building plonked by the E6 highway and stuffed with every sort of tourist bauble imaginable, from "Polarsirkelen" certificates to specially stamped postcards.

If you don't fancy making the long journey between Trondheim and Bodø in one hop, you could stop at **MO-I-RANA**, or simply "Mo", just south of the Arctic Circle – although there's little to specifically draw you here. Formerly a grimy steel town, Mo has recently cleaned itself up and its leafy centre holds a pretty eighteenth-century church with a dinky onion dome. If you need **to stay**, head down Ole Tobias Olsens gate, about 300m from the bus and train stations, to the cheerful *Fammy Hotell*, at no. 4 (☎75 15 19 99; ⑩www.fammy.no; ⑥), opposite the **tourist office** (mid-June to mid-Aug Mon–Fri 9am–8pm, Sat 9am–4pm & Sun 1–7pm; mid-Aug to mid-June Mon–Fri 9am–4pm; ☎75 13 92 00, ⑩www.arctic-circle .no). For the adventurous, there are two great options for **cave-walking** here – one fairly straightforward tour to Grønligrotta (mid–June to mid–Aug daily 10am–7pm; 85kr); and a more advanced trip into Setergrotta (early June to mid–Aug; two–hour tours; 165kr): the tourist office has details of both.

Further north, **FAUSKE** is, along with Bodø, an important transport hub and one of the departure points of the **Nord–Norgeekspressen bus** service that continues north as far as Alta. The first step of the route, to Narvik, is a gorgeous four-hour run past fjords and snowy peaks. The buses leave once or twice a day from beside Fauske train station, and tickets are purchased from the driver. In Fauske, Storgata – also the E6 – accommodates the handful of shops that pass for a town centre. It's actually much better to stay in Bodø (see below), but Fauske does have a couple of useful **accommodation** options, including the plush *Fauske Hotell*, Storgata 82 (☎75 60 20 00, ⑩www.fauskehotell.no; ⑨), and the *Lundhøgda* **campsite** (☎75 64 39 66, ⑧lundhogda@c2i.net; May–Sept; cabins 400kr), in a splendid location about 3km west of the town centre along the E80, overlooking the mountains and the fjord. In both cases, advance booking is advised.

An hour or so west of Fauske, **BODØ** is where all trains and many long–distance buses terminate. It's also a stop on the **Hurtigrute** coastal-boat route and the main port of departure for the Lofoten Islands, with car ferries to Moskenes, Værøy and Røst and Hurtigbåt catamarans to Svolvær. All the town's various transport terminals line up along the waterfront within a fifteen–minute walk of each other, with the **bus station** (*Sentrumsterminalen*), at Sjøgata 3, also home to the **tourist office** (mid-May to Aug Mon–Fri 9am–8pm, Sat 10am–8pm, Sun noon–8pm; Sept to mid-May Mon–Wed & Fri 9am–4pm, Thurs 9am–6pm, Sat 10am–3pm; ☎75 54 80 00, ⑩www.visitbodo.com), which has a small supply of **private rooms** (around ❸). Alternatively, the newly-equipped and comfortable HI **hostel** is near the train station at Storgata 90 (☎75 52 11 22, ⊛www.vandrerhjem.no; dorms 150kr, rooms ❸). A good option for **food** is the traditional and inexpensive *Løvolds Kafé* (Mon–Fri 9am–6pm, Sat 9am–3pm), down by the quay at Tollbugata 9: its Norwegian menu features local ingredients, with a daily special from 85kr. You'll find a younger crowd at *Kafé Kafka*, Sandgata 5b, where the menu includes pasta, burgers and salads.

## The Lofoten Islands

Stretched out in a skeletal curve across the Norwegian Sea, the **Lofoten Islands** are perfect for a simple, uncluttered few days. For somewhere so far north the weather is exceptionally mild, and there's plentiful **accommodation** (⊛www .lofoten.info) in *rorbuer*, originally fishermen's shacks, but now more often well-equipped huts sleeping two to six people for around 400kr to 600kr per night, though some of the more deluxe versions can cost 1000kr. In addition, the Lofoten islands have four hostels and plenty of campsites. The **Hurtigrute coastal boat** calls at two ports, Stamsund and Svolvær, while the southern Lofoten ferry leaves Bodø for Moskenes, Værøy and Røst. There are also **passenger express catamarans**, which work out slightly cheaper than the Hurtigrute, linking both Bodø and Narvik with Svolvær. By **bus** the main long-distance services from the mainland to the Lofoten are from Bodø to Svolvær via Fauske and from Narvik to Svolvær.

The main town on **Austvågøy**, the largest and northernmost island of the group, is **SVOLVÆR**, a rather disappointingly modest and modern place, although it is a hub of island bus routes. **Ferries** from Bodø dock about 1km west of the town centre, whereas the Hurtigrute docks in the centre, a brief walk from the **bus station** and the busy **tourist office**, where you can pick up island-wide information and bus schedules (late May to mid-June Mon–Fri 9am–4pm & Sat 10am–2pm; mid-June to mid-Aug Mon–Fri 9am–4pm & 5–7.30/9.30pm, Sat 9/10am–2/4pm, Sun 4–7pm; mid-Aug to late Aug Mon–Fri 9am–7pm, Sat 10am–2pm; Sept to mid-May Mon–Fri 9am–4pm; ☎76 06 98 00). One of the most pleasant places **to stay** in Svolvær is the long-established *Svolvær Sjøhus*, by the seashore at the foot of Parkgata (☎76 07 03 36, ⊛www.svolver-sjohuscamp.no; ❹), five minutes' walk from the square. The accommodation here is in old boathouses with use of a well-equipped kitchen. Alternatively, at the east end of the harbour, a causeway leads out to the slender islet of Svinøya, where accommodation at *Svinøya Rorbuer* (☎76 06 99 30, ⊛www.svinoya.no) ranges from plain and simple *rorbuer* to deluxe en-suite cabins from 500kr per night.

Reachable by bus from Svolvær, **HENNINGSVÆR**, 23km to the southwest, is the most beguiling village, its cramped and twisting lanes of brightly painted wooden houses framing a picture-postcard harbour. It's well worth an overnight **stay** – try *Den siste Viking*, Misværveien 10 (☎76 07 49 11, ✉postmaster@nordnor skklatreskole.no; dorms 175kr, rooms ❹), for charming, cheap, laid-back lodgings, with a lounge and some rooms overlooking the harbour, right in the centre next to the café *Klatrekafeen*.

It is, however, the next large island to the southwest, **Vestvågøy**, which captivates many travellers, due in no small part to the atmospheric village of **STAMSUND**, whose older buildings are strung along a rocky, fretted seashore. It's the first port of call for the **Hurtigrute coastal boat** as it heads north from Bodø and getting here from Austvågøy is reasonably easy, too, with several **buses** making the trip daily (except Sunday), though you do have to change at Leknes, 16km away to the west. In Stamsund, the first place to head for is the smashing HI **hostel** (☎76 08 93 34, ⊛www.vandrerhjem.no; dorms 90kr, rooms ❸; closed mid–Oct to Dec); friendly and very informal, it's made up of several cosy *rorbuer* perched over a pint-sized bay, about 1km up the road from the port and 200m from the nearest bus stop – ask the driver to tell you where to get off. **Fishing** around here is first-class: the hostel rents out rowing boats and lines or you can go on an organized trip (200kr); afterwards, you can cook your catch on the hostel's wood-burning stoves.

By any standard the next two Lofoten islands, **Flakstadøya** and **Moskenesøya**, are extraordinarily beautiful. As the Lofoten archipelago tapers towards its southerly conclusion, rearing peaks crimp a sea-shredded coastline studded with a string of fishing villages. Remarkably, the E10 travels along almost all of this dramatic shoreline, by way of tunnels and bridges, to **MOSKENES**, the **ferry port** midway between Bodø and the remote, southernmost bird islands of Værøy and Røst. Some 6km further on, the E10 ends at the tersely named **Å**, one of the Lofoten's most delightful villages, its huddle of old buildings rambling over a foreshore that's wedged in tight between the grey-green mountains and the surging sea. The same family owns the assortment of smart *rorbuer* (❼–❾) that surround the dock, the adjacent **hostel** (dorms 130kr, rooms ❹), the bar and the only **restaurant**, where the seafood is very good. All accommodation can be reserved on ☏76 09 11 21, ⊛www.lofoten-rorbu.com). Local **buses** run along the length of the E10 from Leknes to Å once or twice daily from late June to late August, less frequently the rest of the year. Buses don't, however, always coincide with sailings to and from Moskenes, so if you're heading from the Moskenes ferry port to Å, you may have to walk – it's 6km – or take a taxi.

## Narvik and beyond

**NARVIK** was established less than a century ago as an ice-free port to handle the iron ore brought by train from northern Sweden, and the rust-coloured machinery of the **iron ore docks** still overwhelms the waterfront. The importance of the industry to the region is well documented in the **Krigsminne Museum** (March to early June & late Aug to Sept daily 10am–4pm; early June to late Aug daily 10am–10pm; 40kr), in the main square. Run by the Red Cross, it documents the wartime German saturation bombing and bitter sea and air battles for control of the iron ore supplies, in which hundreds of foreign servicemen and many locals died.

Narvik's **train station** is at the north end of the town and from here it's a five- to ten-minute walk along the main drag, Kongens gate, to the **bus station**, in the basement of the Amfi shopping centre on the west side of the street. The **tourist office**, at Kongens gate 26 (early to mid-June & mid- to late Aug Mon–Fri 9am–5pm, Sat & Sun 10am–3pm; mid-June to mid-Aug Mon–Fri 9am–7pm, Sat 10am–6pm, Sun 11am–6pm; Sept–May Mon–Fri 8.30am–3.30pm; ☏76 96 56 00; ⊛www.narvikinfo.no), has the full range of bus and ferry timetables and lots of information on outdoor pursuits. In terms of **accommodation**, the best backpacker option is the excellent *Spor 1 Gjestegard* at Brugata 2a (☏76 94 60 20; ⊛www.spor1.no; dorms 160kr, rooms ❸), a welcoming independent hostel with a great atmosphere in a converted railway building; it's central and has kitchen facilities, a sauna and a pub too. Alternatively, the friendly but more traditional *Briedablikk Gjestehus*, Tore Hundsgate 41 (☏76 94 14 18; ⊛www.breidablikk.no, ❺), is a short, steep walk from the tourist office at the top of Kinobakken.

There's a choice of several routes on from Narvik. The **rail link**, cut through the mountains a century ago, runs east and then south into Sweden, reaching Kiruna in three and Stockholm in eighteen hours. It's a beautiful journey, but **bus** travellers, heading north on the Nord-Norgeekspressen to Tromsø and Alta, do no worse with a succession of switchback roads, lakeside forests, high peaks, gentle valleys and plunging, black-blue fjords. In summer, cut grass dries everywhere, stretched over wooden poles forming long lines on the hillsides like so much washing. Narvik is also connected to Svolvær, on the Lofotens, by bus and **catamaran**.

## Tromsø

Rather preposterously, **TROMSØ** was once known as the "Paris of the North", and the city still likes to think of itself as the capital of northern Norway, with two cathedrals, a clutch of interesting museums and an above-average (and affordable) nightlife, patronized by its high-profile student population. Certainly, as a base for this part of the country, it's hard to beat, set in magnificent landscape – dramatic mountains and craggy shoreline. In the centre of town, the **Domkirke** (Tues–Sat noon–4pm, Sun 10am–2/4pm; free) reflects the town's nineteenth-century prosperity, its striking woodwork the result of its barter trade with Russia. From the church, it's a short walk north along the harbourfront to the most diverting of the city's museums, the **Polar Museum** (daily: March to mid-June & mid-Aug to Sept 11am–5pm; mid-June to mid-Aug 10am–7pm; Oct–Feb 11am–3pm; ⊛www .polarmuseum.no; 50kr), whose varied displays include skeletons retrieved from the permafrost of Svalbard and a detailed section on the polar explorer Roald Amundsen. On the other side of the water, over the spindly Tromsø Bridge, the white and ultramodern **Arctic Cathedral** (June to mid-Aug Mon–Sat 10am–8pm, Sun 1–8pm; mid-Aug to May daily 4–6pm; all year Sunday service 11am–noon) is spectacular, made up of eleven immense triangular concrete sections representing the eleven Apostles left after the betrayal. Back in the centre, a ten-minute stroll south along the waterfront from the harbour brings you to the **Polaria** museum, Hjalmar Johansengt 12 (daily: mid-May to mid-Aug 10am–7pm; mid-Aug to mid-May noon–5pm; 80kr), which combines Polar exhibits and an aquarium – complete with walk-through seal tank – with some thought-provoking displays about the region's fragile eco-system.

The **Hurtigrute coastal boat** docks in the centre of town at the foot of Kirkegata; long-distance **buses** arrive and leave from the adjacent car park. The **tourist office** is at Storgata 61, near the Domkirke (mid to late-May & mid-Aug to mid-Sept Mon–Fri 8.30am–3.45pm, Sat & Sun 10.30am–2pm; June to mid-Aug Mon–Fri 8.30am–6pm, Sat 10am–5pm, Sun 10.30am–5pm; mid-Sept to mid-May Mon–Fri 8.30am–4pm; ☏77 61 00 00; ⊛www.destinasjontromso.no), and has a small supply of **private rooms** (❸). The frugal HI **hostel**, *Tromsø Vandrerhjem*, Åsgårdsveien 9, Elverhøy (☏77 65 76 28, ⊛www.vandrerhjem.no; dorms 150kr, rooms ❸; late June to mid-Aug only), is some 2km west of the quay; several city buses go near there (ask at the bus station), or else it's a steep thirty-minute walk. Alternatively, try the *Viking Hotell* at Grønnegt 18 (☏77 64 77 30; ⊛www .viking-hotell.no; ❺), offering central, pleasant, en-suite B&B accommodation. The nearest **campsite**, the year-round *Tromsdalen Camping* (☏77 63 80 37), lies over the bridge on the mainland, about 1800m beyond the Arctic Cathedral.

Tromsø has a great selection of **restaurants**, **cafés** and **pubs**. For excellent coffee, pastries and light snacks, try *Bønna & Rosa*, Strandtorvet 1, while *Aunegården*, at Sjøgata 29, has everything from coffee and mouth-watering cheesecake to traditional Norwegian dishes. The *Sjømatrestauranten Arctandria*, Strandtorvet 13, serves magnificent seafood with main courses averaging around 220kr, while *Il Tabernacolo*, Storgata 36, does excellent, filling – and for Norway – very reasonably priced pasta (three-course set meal from 185kr). **Nightlife** centres on Storgata and the surrounding streets; *Blå Rock Café*, Strandgata 14, is a lively spot with a jukebox and a rock'n'roll crowd, while the terrace of *Skarven*, Strandtorvet 13, is the place to go for summer drinks late into the polar evening.

# Honningsvåg and Nordkapp

Beyond Tromsø, the northern tip of Norway enjoys no less than two and a half months of permanent daylight on either side of the summer solstice. Here, the bleak and treeless island of **Magerøya** is connected to the northern edge of the mainland by an ambitious combination of tunnels and bridges. The island's only significant settlement is the crusty fishing village of **HONNINGSVÅG**, which makes a steady income from accommodating the hundreds of summertime tourists bent on visiting Nordkapp – the North Cape – just 34km away. Of its several **hotels**, one of the more appealing is the *Rica Bryggen*, at the head of the harbour

(☎78 47 28 88; ✆www.rica.no; ⑥). Alternatively, there's *NAF Nordkapp Camping* (☎78 47 33 77; ✆www.nordkappcamping.no; late May to mid-Sept; four–bed cabins 460kr), 8km from Honningsvåg on the road to Nordkapp. Long-distance **buses** arrive in the centre of Honningsvåg and there's a limited bus service on to Nordkapp (late June to mid-Aug one–two daily; 50min). When the buses aren't running, the only option is a taxi (about 1000kr return), though the road is closed throughout the winter and often in spring too. For travellers northbound on the **Hurtigrute coastal boat**, a special coach is laid on to get from Honningsvåg to Nordkapp and back within the two-and-a-half-hour stop. For **food** in Honningsvåg, there are a couple of takeaway kiosks along Storgata and a very good seafood restaurant at the *Honningsvåg Brygge Hotel*.

Whilst **NORDKAPP** is only a 307m-high cliff, with an arguable claim to being the northernmost point of Europe, there *is* something exhilarating about this bleak, wind-battered promontory. Originally a Sami sacrificial site, it was actually named by the English explorer Richard Chancellor in 1553. These days the headland is occupied by **Nordkapphallen** (North Cape Hall; daily: early to mid-May & Sept to mid-Oct noon–4pm; mid-May to mid-June noon–1am; mid-June to July 9am–2am; Aug 9am–midnight; mid-Oct to April 12.30–2pm; 190kr for 48hr, including parking), an extremely flashy complex that contains souvenir shops, cafés, restaurants and huge windows from where you can survey the surging ocean below.

# Travel details

## Trains

**Åndalsnes** to: Dombås (2–3 daily; 1hr 30min); Oslo (2–3 daily; 5hr 30min–6hr 30min).
**Dombås** to: Trondheim (1–4 daily; 2hr 30min).
**Myrdal** to: Flåm (June–Sept 8–10 daily; Oct–May 4 daily; 50min).
**Oslo** to: Åndalsnes (2–3 daily; 5hr 30min–6hr 30min); Bergen (4–5 daily; 6hr 30min); Stockholm (3 daily; 4hr 30min); Trondheim (2–4 daily; 7–10hr); Voss (3–5 daily; 5hr 40min).
**Trondheim** to: Bodø (2 daily; 10hr); Dombås (1–4 daily; 2hr 30min); Fauske (2 daily; 9hr 20min); Mo-i-Rana (2–3 daily; 7hr); Oslo (2–4 daily; 7–10hr).

## Buses

**Ålesund** to: Bergen (daily; 10hr); Hellesylt (1–3 daily; 3hr); Stryn (1–3 daily; 4hr); Trondheim (1–3 daily; 8hr).
**Alta** to: Hammerfest (1–2 daily except Sat; 3hr); Honningsvåg (late June to mid-Aug 1–2 daily; 5hr); Tromsø (April to late Oct 1–2 daily; 7hr).
**Åndalsnes** to: Geiranger (mid-June to late Aug 2 daily; 3–4hr); Ålesund (3–4 daily; 2hr 20min).
**Balestrand** to: Sogndal (2 daily; 1hr).

**Bergen** to: Ålesund (1–2 daily; 10hr); Trondheim (2 daily; 14hr); Voss (4 daily; 1hr 45min).
**Fauske** to: Bodø (1–3 daily; 1hr); Narvik (1–2 daily; 5hr).
**Hammerfest** to: Alta (1–2 daily except Sat; 3hr); Skaidi (1–2 daily except Sat; 1hr 15min).
**Honningsvåg** to: Nordkapp (late June to mid-Aug 1–2 daily; 50min).
**Narvik** to: Tromsø (1–3 daily; 4hr–4hr 40min).
**Oslo** to: Bergen (4–5 daily; 10hr).
**Stryn** to: Bergen (2–4 daily; 7hr); Oslo (1–3 daily; 8hr 30min).
**Tromsø** to: Alta (April to late Oct; 1–2 daily; 7hr); Narvik (1–3 daily; 4hr–4hr 40min); Nordkapp (late June to mid-Aug daily except Sat; 14hr).
**Trondheim** to: Ålesund (1–3 daily; 8hr); Bergen (2 daily; 14hr); Stryn (2 daily; 7hr 20min).
**Voss** to: Bergen (4 daily; 1hr 45min); Sogndal (2 daily; 3hr).

## Catamaran ferries

**Bergen** to: Balestrand (1–2 daily; 4hr); Flåm (May–Sept only; 1–2 daily; 5hr 30min).
**Bodø** to: Svolvær (daily except Sat; 5hr 30min).
**Narvik** to: Svolvær (daily except Sat; 4hr).

# Poland

# Poland highlights

* **Warsaw nightlife** Poland's fast-paced capital boasts a bar and club scene to rival any in Central Europe. See p.782

* **Old Town, Toruń** A lively university town on the Wisła river with a fascinating historic centre. See p.784

* **The beach, Sopot** A vast stretch of white sand near Poland's lively summertime capital, Sopot. See p.784

* **Cloth Hall, Kraków** At the heart of one of Europe's most beautiful main squares. See p.788

* **Auschwitz-Birkenau camps** Sixty years on, the Nazis' most infamous death camps still make a haunting impression. See p.790

* **Tatra Mountains** Hike among the towering peaks and crystal-clear lakes, and eat fresh trout in the bustling mountain resort of Zakopane. See p.791

△ Main square, Kraków

# Introduction and basics

Images of **Poland** flooded the world media throughout the 1980s: strikes at the shipyards of Gdańsk were the harbingers of the disintegration of communism in Eastern Europe. After almost two centuries of foreign domination, Poland's return to democracy at the end of the 1980s brought new freedoms and economic change. Adjustments have proved difficult for some, however, and contrasts abound: on highways, you'll find new cars vying for space with tiny, communist-era models and horse-drawn carts, while unemployment remains high in rural areas. The role of the Catholic Church, however, is as important as ever, with its presence visible in Baroque buildings, roadside shrines and images of both the national icon, the Black Madonna, and the late favourite son Pope John Paul II.

Much of Warsaw, the capital, plumb in the centre of the country, conforms to stereotypes of Eastern European greyness, but its historic centre, beautiful parks and vibrant nightlife are diverting enough. Kraków in the south, the ancient royal capital, is the real crowd-puller, rivalling the elegance of Prague and Vienna, while Gdańsk on the Baltic Sea offers a dynamic brew of politics, commerce and golden beaches in the nearby resort of Sopot. German influences abound in the north and southwest of the country, in Gdańsk itself, in the austere castles and fortified settlements along the River Wisła (Vistula) and in the divided province of Silesia. Yet, to the north of Silesia, quintessentially Polish Poznań is revered as the cradle of the nation. Of the many regions of unspoilt natural beauty, the alpine Tatras on the Slovak border offer exhilarating walking, a unique mountain culture and skiing in the winter.

## Information & maps

Most cities have a tourist office (known as IT or *informacja turystyczna*); sometimes these are run by the local municipality and are good; elsewhere, they're private agencies selling tours and tickets. Bookstores, such as EMPiK, with a branch on most main squares, are well stocked with maps.

## Money and banks

Currency is the złoty (zł or PLN), divided into 100 groszy. Coins come as 1, 2, 5, 10, 20 and 50 groszy, and 1, 2 and 5 złoty; notes as 10, 20, 50, 100 and 200 złoty. Banks (usually open Mon–Fri 7.30am–5pm, Sat 7.30am–2pm) and exchange offices (*kantors*) offer similar exchange rates. Major credit cards are widely accepted, and ATMs are common in cities. At the time of writing, €1 was equal to around 4zł, US$1 to 3.30zł and £1 to 6zł.

## Communications

Post offices are identified by the name *Poczta*, and in larger cities offer poste restante services: anyone addressing mail to you should add "No. 1" after the city's name. Main offices usually open Mon–Sat 8am–8pm; branches close earlier. For public phones you'll need a card (*karta telefoniczna*), available at post offices and some

---

### Poland on the net

ⓦ**www.poland.pl** The official website with many links.
ⓦ**www.inyourpocket.com** Thoroughly researched city guides to Warsaw, Kraków, Gdańsk, Poznań and Wrocław.
ⓦ**www.nwe.com.pl** Weekly national and local Warsaw news, events.

newsagent kiosks. Internet cafés (3–6zł/hr) are widespread.

# Getting around

Polish State Railways (PKP; ⓦ www.pkp.pl) runs three main types of trains. Express services (*ekspresowy*), particularly IC (intercity) or EC (Eurocity), stop at main cities only, and seat reservations (*miejscówka*, 10–18zł/€2.50–4.50) are compulsory. "Fast" trains (*pospieszny*) are cheaper, but not necessarily slower. Normal services (*osobowy*) are less predictable – some are quick, while others stop at every haystack. It's sometimes worth paying fifty percent extra to travel first class, as sardine-like conditions are fairly common. On overnight journeys, second-class sleepers cost around 50zł/€12.50 per person extra. For journeys of over 100km and for international trips you can buy tickets in

## Polish Language

| | Polish | Pronunciation |
|---|---|---|
| **Yes** | *Tak* | Tahk |
| **No** | *Nie* | Nyeh |
| **Please** | *Proszę* | Prosh-eh |
| **Thank you** | *Dziękuję* | Djen-ku-yeh |
| **Hello/Good day** | *Dzień dobry* | Djen doh-brih |
| **Goodbye** | *Do widzenia* | Doh veed-zen-yah |
| **Excuse me** | *Przepraszam* | Prsheh-prash-ahm |
| **Where?** | *Gdzie ?* | G-djeh? |
| **Good** | *Dobry* | Dob-rih |
| **Bad** | *Zły* | Z-wih |
| **Near** | *Blisko* | Blis-koh |
| **Far** | *Daleko* | Dah-leh-koh |
| **Cheap** | *Tani* | Tah-nee |
| **Expensive** | *Drogi* | Droh-gee |
| **Open** | *Otwarty* | Ot-var-tih |
| **Closed** | *Zamknięty* | Zahmk-nee-yen-tih |
| **Today** | *Dzisiaj* | Djyish-eye |
| **Yesterday** | *Wczoraj* | Vchor-eye |
| **Tomorrow** | *Jutro* | Yoo-troh |
| **How much is....?** | *Ile kosztuje...?* | Ill-eh kosh-too-yeh |
| **What time is it?** | *Która godzina?* | Ktoo-rah go-djee-nah |
| **I don't understand** | *Nie rozumiem* | Nyeh roh-zoom-ee-yem |
| **Do you speak English?** | *Pan/i/ mówi po angielsku?* | Pahn/ee/ movee poh ahn-gyel-skoo |
| **One** | *Jeden* | Yed-en |
| **Two** | *Dwa* | Dvah |
| **Three** | *Trzy* | Trshih |
| **Four** | *Cztery* | Chter-ih |
| **Five** | *Pięć* | Pyench |
| **Six** | *Sześć* | Sheshch |
| **Seven** | *Siedem* | Shedem |
| **Eight** | *Osiem* | Oshem |
| **Nine** | *Dziewięć* | Djyev-yench |
| **Ten** | *Dziesięć* | Djyesh-ench |

advance at Orbis travel agencies (branches in all towns and cities). InterRail passes are valid, though you'll still have to pay for seat reservations. Departures (*odjazdy*) are printed on yellow posters; arrivals (*przyjazdy*) on white; "*peron*" means platform.

Intercity buses operated by PKS, the national bus company, are cheap but slow and often overcrowded – only in mountain regions are buses generally faster. Bus stations are usually found next to train stations. The private Polski Express (✆ www.polski express.pl) offers pricier journeys in more comfortable and faster buses – particularly out of Warsaw – but these are still slower than trains. From Gdańsk, PolFerries (✆www .polferries.com.pl) and Stena Line (✆www .stenaline.pl) run regular ferries to Sweden.

# Accommodation

Most Polish towns have at least one budget hotel offering spartan but habitable rooms with communal toilet and shower, usually costing around 90zł/€22 per person, or twice as much for en-suite shower, TV and breakfast. Standards at cheaper places, though, can be unpredictable: some rooms have fittings that haven't changed for decades.

A bed at one of Poland's 200-odd public youth hostels (*schroniska młodzieżowe*) costs around 30zł/€7.50 a head; for a complete list check ✆ www.ptsm.pl. In large cities they're centrally located and open year-round, though usually with lockouts and curfews. Elsewhere they open only in high summer. In addition, Kraków, Warsaw and Gdańsk have excellent year-round private hostels that charge around 50zł/€12.50 per bed and offer amenities like Internet access and laundry service; these should be booked in advance. The Dizzy Daisy chain (✆www .hostel.pl) operates similarly-priced summer hostels in the major cities. Alternatively, ask at tourist offices about summer accommodation in university hostels, which are as cheap as public hostels without the restrictions, though they tend to be located in the suburbs.

You can get a room in a private house (*kwatera prywatna*) almost anywhere in the country. In cities these are often shabby, but in mountain resorts they can be very comfortable. Some of the major cities have a room-finding service (*Biuro Zakwater-owania*), and some tourist offices will also help. Charges start at around 70zł/€18 per person. Houses in holiday areas like Zako-pane post signs reading *noclegi* (lodging) or *pokoje* (rooms); 35zł/€9 a head is the least you can expect to pay. Individuals with rooms to let may approach you at train stations – this can be a bargain, but carries the usual risks of an unofficial deal.

There are hundreds of campsites; for a complete list see the *Campingi w Polsce* map, available from EMPiK and other bookshops. Most open May–Sept only. Charges usually work out at less than 20zł/€5 a head. Many sites have spartan chalets to rent for under 25zł/€6 per person.

# Food and drink

Poles take their food seriously, providing meals of feast-like proportions for the most casual visitors. The cuisine is a complex mix of influences: Russian, German, Ukrainian, Lithuanian and Jewish traditions have all left their mark. Polish meals always start with soups, the best known of which are *barszcz*, beetroot broth, and *żurek*, a sour soup of fermented rye. The basis of most main courses is fried or grilled meat, such as *kotlet schabowy* (pork cutlet). Three inexpensive specialities you'll find everywhere are *gołąbki* (stuffed cabbage), *bigos* (cabbage stewed with meat) and *pierogi*, dumplings stuffed with cottage cheese and onion (*ruskie*), meat (*z mięsem*), or cabbage and mushrooms (*z kapustą i grzybami*). Pancakes (*naleśniki*) often come as a main course, stuffed with cottage cheese (*ze serem*). Fried potato pancakes (*placki ziemniaczane*) are particularly good with sour cream and spicy goulash (*po węgiersku*).

Restaurants are open until at least 9 or 10pm, later in city centres, and prices are low: in most places outside of Warsaw you can have a two-course meal with beer or a soft drink for 30zł/€7.50. In addition to traditional Polish restaurants, the main cities offer a decent selection of places serving various European and world cuisines, many with good vegetarian choices. Anywhere in the country, the cheapest option is to head for a milk bar (*bar mleczny*; usually open morning until 5/6pm), the traditional place for fast and filling daytime meals – though quality and service at such establishments can be poor. The cakes, pastries and other sweets found in cake shops (*cukiernia*) are as good as any in Central Europe. Sernik (*cheesecake*) is a national favourite, as are *makowiec* (poppyseed cake), *szarlotka* (apple pie), and *pączki* (doughnuts filled with rose jam).

Drinking is a national pursuit. Poles can't compete with their Czech neighbours when it comes to beer (*piwo*), but local brands are fairly drinkable and even in Warsaw you won't pay more than 12zł/€3 for a half litre. It's with vodka (*wódka*) that Poles really get into their stride. Ideally served neat and cold, the best clear vodkas are *Żytnia* and *Wyborowa*. Of the flavoured varieties, try *Żubrówka*, infused with bison grass.

# Opening hours and holidays

Most shops open on weekdays from 10am–6pm, and all but the largest close on

Saturday at 2 or 3pm and all day Sunday. RUCH kiosks, selling public transport tickets (*bilety*), open at 6 or 7am. Most museums and historic monuments are closed Monday. Entrance tends to be inexpensive, and is often free one day of the week. Public holidays are: Jan 1, Easter Mon, May 1, May 3, Corpus Christi (May/June), Aug 15, Nov 1, Nov 11, Dec 25 & 26.

# Emergencies

The biggest potential hassles are hotel room thefts and pickpocketing. Safely store your valuables when travelling by night train, and always lock your compartment when sleeping. Polish police (*policja*) are courteous but unlikely to speak English. In medical emergencies most foreigners rely on the pricey private medical centres run by Medicover (℡022/570 1111, ⊛www.medicover.com/pl).

# Warsaw (Warszawa)

First impressions of **WARSAW** (Warszawa) are all too often negative with gleaming new office buildings and hotels sitting uncomfortably amongst the grey, Communist-era apartment blocks. With a little bit of exploring, however, you'll find much more: north of the modern centre are stunning Baroque palaces and the meticulously reconstructed **Old Town**, to the south are two of Central Europe's finest urban **parks**, and east of the centre lie reminders of the rich Jewish heritage extinguished by the Nazis. As compelling as the city's past, however, is Warsaw's vibrant bar, club and restaurant scene.

Warsaw became the capital of Poland in 1596. The city flourished, becoming one of the most prosperous in Central Europe until the eighteenth-century **Partitions** saw Poland systematically devoured by neighbouring Austria, Prussia and Russia. Napoleon's arrival in 1806 brought brief hopes of liberation, but in 1815 the city was integrated into the Russian Empire. The nineteenth century saw a series of rebellions, but all of these were crushed brutally, and it wasn't until the outbreak of World War I that Russian control began to crumble. Polish independence was restored in 1918, and Warsaw once again became the capital. Again independence was short-lived and during World War II the city was virtually wiped out. Hitler, infuriated by the 1943 Ghetto Uprising and the 1944 **Warsaw Uprising**, ordered the total elimination of Warsaw, and by the end of the war 850,000 Varsovians – two-thirds of the city's population – were dead or missing. The task of rebuilding took ten years.

## Arrival, information and accommodation

Okęcie **airport** is 8km southwest of the Old Town: avoid the rip-off taxi drivers and take bus #175 (#611 at night) into town, which passes the main **train station**, Warszawa Centralna, in the modern centre, before arriving in the Old Town. The main **bus station**, Międzynarodowa Dworzec PKS, is located right next to the Warszawa Zachodnia train station, 3km west of Centralna station. To get into town from here catch any eastbound bus. Polski Express **intercity buses** use the bus stop on al. Jana Pawła II, just outside the western entrance of Centralna train station. The best source of **information** is the helpful IT office in the main hall of Centralna station (daily 8am–6/8pm; ☎022/9431, ⊛www.warsawtour.pl), which has excellent free city maps and brochures. There are also IT offices at the airport and main bus station.

**Buses** and **trams** run until around 11pm; after that, night buses leave every thirty minutes from beside the main train station. There is also one **metro** line running north to south through the centre of town. **Tickets** for trams, buses and the metro (2.4zł single trip; 3.6zł 1hr) are bought from green RUCH kiosks or from automatic ticket machines. If you have an ISIC card you can buy 48 percent reduced (*ulgowy*) tickets (1.25zł single trip; 1.9zł 1hr). You'll need two tickets for night buses. Always punch your tickets in the machines on board – Warsaw's zealous inspectors are merciless. Good-value day, three-day and week **passes** are also available and should be punched the first time you use them. **Taxis** cost as little as 1.20zł per kilometre, with a minimum fare of 6zł, but only take taxis that have the company name, telephone number and price per kilometre clearly marked. Don't get a taxi from outside the Centralna Station – go to the nearby ul. Emilii Plater, or better still, book one by phone; English is spoken at Bayer (☎022/9667) and Wawa (☎022/9644).

Warsaw has a few good private **hostels**, several less appealing public ones with curfews, and, in July and August, curfew-free student hostels – ask at the IT offices (see above), who can also give help with **hotel** bookings. Advance booking is essential in summer. Private **rooms** (❷–❸) can be arranged through the Syrena Travel Agency, ul. Krucza 17 (Mon–Fri 9am–6pm; ☎022/629 0537, ⊛www.kwatery-prywatne.pl).

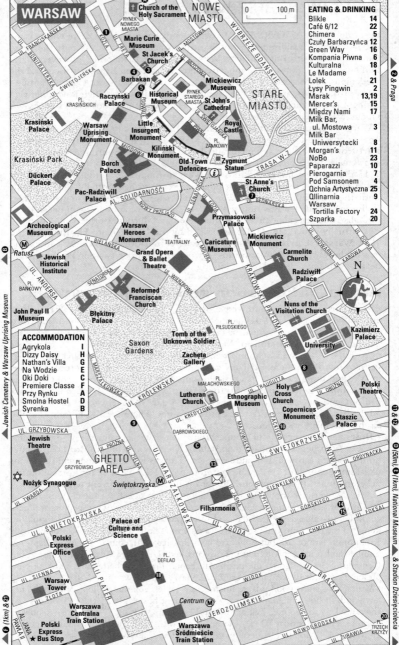

# WARSAW

**EATING & DRINKING**

| | |
|---|---|
| Blikle | 14 |
| Café 6/12 | 22 |
| Chimera | 5 |
| Czuły Barbarzyńca | 12 |
| Green Way | 16 |
| Kompania Piwna | 6 |
| Kulturalna | 18 |
| Le Madame | 1 |
| Lolek | 21 |
| Łysy Pingwin | 2 |
| Marak | 13,19 |
| Mercer's | 15 |
| Między Nami | 17 |
| Milk Bar, | |
| ul. Mostowa | 3 |
| Milk Bar | |
| Uniwersytecki | 8 |
| Morgan's | 11 |
| NoBo | 23 |
| Paparazzi | 10 |
| Pierogarnia | 7 |
| Pod Samsonem | 4 |
| Qchnia Artystyczna | 25 |
| Qllinarnia | 9 |
| Warsaw | |
| Tortilla Factory | 24 |
| Szparka | 20 |

**ACCOMMODATION**

| | |
|---|---|
| Agrykola | I |
| Dizzy Daisy | H |
| Nathan's Villa | G |
| Na Wodzie | E |
| Oki Doki | C |
| Premiere Classe | F |
| Przy Rynku | A |
| Smolna Hostel | D |
| Syrenka | B |

## Hostels

**Agrykola** ul. Myśliwiecka 9 ☎022/622 9110, ⓦ www.hotelagrykola.pl. Bright, modern rooms in a hostel designed for youth athletic groups but open to all. Just east of Łazienki park; bus #151 from the station to the Rozbrat stop before the bridge. Dorms 47zł, rooms ❷

**Dizzy Daisy** ul. Górnośląska ☎022/660 6712, ⓦ www.hostel.pl. Clean and friendly summer hostel near the Łazienki park. Open July 1–Aug 25. Dorms 45zł, rooms ❷

**Nathan's Villa** ul. Piękna 24/26 ☎022/622 2946, ⓦ www.nathansvilla.com. Warsaw branch of the Kraków hostel; clean, well-run and popular. Off Marszałkowska, two tram stops south of Centralna station. 45–50zł.

**Oki Doki** Pl. Dąbrowskiego 3 ☎022/826 5112, ⓦ www.okidoki.pl. The most original hostel in Poland, with eccentric rooms in the Communist-era Agricultural Ministry building. A 10min walk northeast from Centralna station. Dorms 50–60zł, rooms ❸–❹

**Przy Rynku** ul. Rynek Nowego Miasta 4 ☎022/831 5033, ⓦ www.cityhostel.net. The best of the summer hostels, with friendly and helpful staff; July & Aug only. 45zł.

**Smolna Hostel** ul. Smolna 30 ☎022/827 8952. Barrack-like conditions but central location; HI member reductions. Take any tram three stops east of Centralna station. June–Sept curfew 2am; Oct–May 11pm. Dorms 40zł, rooms ❷

**Syrenka** ul. Karolkowa 53a ☎022/632 8829, ⓦ www.ptsm.com.pl/ssmnr6. Old-fashioned, with basic dorms, nicer doubles and a midnight curfew. Tram #12 or #24 west of Centralna station for six stops. Dorms 40zł, rooms ❸

## Hotels

**Na Wodzie** Wybrzeże Kościuszkowskie ☎022/628 5883, ⓦ www.hostel-warsaw.pl. A central "boatel" with small clean rooms, moored next to Poniatowskiego bridge. Take any tram east from Centralna station and get off at the fourth stop, on the bridge. Closed Nov–April. ❷

**Premiere Classe** ul. Towarowa 2 ☎022/624 0800, ⓦ www.premiereclasse.com.pl. The best budget hotel in the city, with bright and clean en-suite doubles with TV. Breakfast 18zł extra. Take any tram 3 stops west from Centralna station. ❸

# The City

Most of what you'll want to see lies on the western bank of the **Wisła** (Vistula) river where you'll find the central business and shopping district, **Śródmieście**, grouped around Centralna station and the nearby Palace of Culture. The more picturesque and tourist-friendly **Old Town** (Stare Miasto) is just to the north.

## The Old Town, New Town and Ghetto

The title Old Town (Stare Miasto) is in some respects a misnomer for the historic nucleus of Warsaw. After World War II this compact network of streets lay in rubble, only to be painstakingly reconstructed in the years afterwards. **Plac Zamkowy** (Castle Square), on the south side of the Old Town, is the obvious place to start a tour. On the east side of the square is the former **Royal Castle**, once home of the royal family and seat of the Polish parliament, now the **Castle Museum** (Tues–Sun 10/11am–4pm; royal apartments 18zł, court rooms 10zł, Sun free). Though a replica, many of the structure's furnishings are originals, having been scooted into hiding during the first bombing raids. After passing the most lavish section of the castle, the Royal Apartments of King Stanisław August, you come to the magnificent Canaletto Room, with its views of Warsaw by Bernardo Bellotto, nephew of the famous Canaletto – whose name he appropriated to make his pictures sell better. Marvellously detailed, these cityscapes were invaluable to the architects rebuilding the city after the war. On Świętojańska, north of the castle, stands **St John's Cathedral**, the oldest church in Warsaw. A few yards away, the **Rynek Starego Miasta** (Old Town Square) is one of the most remarkable bits of postwar reconstruction anywhere in Europe. Flattened during the uprising, its three-storey merchants' houses have been rebuilt in near-flawless imitation of the Baroque originals. It's also home to the **Warsaw Historical Museum** (Tues & Thurs 11am–5.30pm, Wed & Fri 10am–3.30pm, Sat & Sun 10.30am–4.30pm; 5zł, free Sun), which has an important section about the resistance to the Nazis and an impressive English-language film (shown Tues–Sat at noon) with footage of the city in ruins. The nearby sixteenth-century **Barbakan** used to guard the northern entrance to the city. Cross the ramparts from the Barbakan and you're into the **New Town** (Nowe Miasto), which despite its name dates from the early fifteenth century. The heart of the district is the Rynek Nowego Miasta, once a commercial hub, now a soothing change from the bustle of the Old Town. West of here is the former **Ghetto** area. In 1939 there were an estimated 380,000 Jews living in and around Warsaw – one-third of the total population. By May 1945, the ghetto had been razed to the ground and around three hundred Jews were left. The **Nożyk Synagogue** on ul. Twarda is the only one left in Warsaw. You can get an idea of what Jewish Warsaw looked like by walking one block east to the miraculously untouched **ul. Próżna**.

Starting one block north of the synagogue, walk ten minutes west along ul. Grzybowska and then, turning north onto ul. Towarowa, ten minutes more (or take tram #22 from Centralna Station) to ul. Okopowa 49/51 to reach the vast and overgrown **Jewish Cemetery** (Cmentarz Żydowski; Mon–Thurs 9am–4pm, Fri 9am–1pm, Sun 9am–4pm, closed Sat; 4zl), one of the largest in Europe and eerily unchanged since World War II. On the way, just west of the intersection of ul. Grzybowska and ul. Towarowa, the new **Warsaw Uprising Museum** at ul. Przyokopowa 28 (Tues–Sun 10am–6pm; 8zl; tram #22 from Centralna Station to Grzybowska), opened in August 2004 for the Uprising's sixtieth anniversary. Set in a century-old brick power station, the museum traces, in Polish and English and with stunning multimedia displays, the grim story of how Varsovians fought and were eventually crushed by the Nazis in 1944 – a struggle that saw the deaths of nearly two hundred thousand Poles and the destruction of three-quarters of the buildings in the city. Special attention is given to the equivocal role played by Soviet troops in the Uprising – they watched passively from the other side of the river as the Nazis defeated the Polish insurgents, and only after the city was a charred ruin did they move across to "liberate" it from the Germans.

## Śródmieście

The area stretching from the Old Town down towards Łazienki Park – **Śródmieście** – is the fast-paced heart of Warsaw, bisected by the Royal Way thoroughfare, which runs from Plac Zamkowy to the palace of Wilanów. **Krakowskie Przedmieście**, the first part of the Royal Way, is lined with historic buildings. Even in a city not lacking in Baroque churches, the **Church of the Nuns of the Visitation** stands out, with its columned, statue-topped facade; it's also one of the few buildings in central Warsaw to have come through World War II unscathed. Most of the rest of Krakowskie Przedmieście is taken up by **Warsaw University** buildings, including several fine Baroque palaces and the **Holy Cross Church**, wrecked during the Uprising; photos of the figure of Christ standing among the rubble became poignant emblems of Warsaw's suffering. Sealed inside a column to the left side of the nave there's an urn containing Chopin's heart.

South of the university, the main street becomes **Nowy Świat** (New World), with upmarket shopping and a good selection of cafés. East along al. Jerozolimskie is the **National Museum** (Tues–Wed & Fri–Sun 10am–4pm, Thurs 10am–6pm; 11zl, free Sat), housing an impressive collection of Impressionist-era paintings from the Młoda Polska (Young Poland) school, as well as Christian frescoes from eighth-to thirteenth-century Sudan. West of here lies the commercial heart of the city and **Marszałkowska**, the main north-south road cutting across Jerozolimskie. Towering over everything is the **Palace of Culture and Science**, a post-World War II gift from Stalin that the poles including could hardly refuse. The interior contains several thousand rooms, a vast conference hall, theatres, swimming pools and a casino. Outside are basketball courts which turn into a free-to-all ice rink in the winter. The platform on the thirtieth floor (daily 9am–6pm; 18zl) offers an impressive bird's-eye view of the city.

## Out of the centre

South of the commercial district, on the eastern side of al. Ujazdowskie, is the much-loved **Łazienki Park**. Once a hunting ground, the area was bought in the 1760s by King Stanisław August, who turned it into a park and built the Neoclassical **Łazienki Palace** (Tues–Sun 9am–4pm; 12zł) across the park lake. Oak-lined paths lead from the entrance and the ponderous **Chopin Monument** to the palace. Most of the furnishings survived the war intact, but the park itself is the real attraction, pleasantly cool in summer and alive with peacocks and squirrels.

The one must-see on the eastern side of the river is the **Stadion Dziesięciolecia**, the largest outdoor market in Europe, based in Poland's former national football stadium. A sharp contrast to the rapidly westernizing Warsaw on the other side of the river, the market sells everything from life-rafts to hand grenades, and plenty of Russian goods like caviar, icons and smuggled cigarettes. To see the market at its best, arrive by 11am: take any tram heading east from Centralna station, and get off at the first stop over the river. North of the market is the run-down **Praga** district, where much of the Oscar-winning 2002 film *The Pianist* was filmed.

The grandest of Warsaw's palaces, **Wilanów** (Wed–Mon 9.30am–3pm, May–Sept Wed & Sun to 5pm; 20zł), makes an easy excursion from the centre: take bus #116 or #180 south from Krakowskie Przedmieście or Nowy Świat to its terminus. King Jan Sobieski purchased the existing manor house and estate in 1677 and spent nearly twenty years turning it into the "Polish Versailles" – the sixty-odd rooms provide a vast range of decorative styles. The gate on the left side beyond the main entrance opens onto the stately **palace gardens** (daily 9am–sunset; 4.5zł, free Thurs), while to the right before you enter is the **Poster Museum** (Tues–Sun 10am–3.30pm; 8zł, free Wed afternoon), a mishmash of the inspired and the bizarre.

# Eating, drinking and entertainment

For basic meals Warsaw's **milk bars** are cheapest; those at ul. Mostowa 29, overlooking the Barbakan, and the *Bar Uniwersytecki* at Krakowskie Przedmieście 20, by the university, are better than average and have English menus. The **restaurant** and **bar** scene in Warsaw has really taken off in the last few years, and the city now genuinely provides a great night out. Warsaw **festivals** include the Warsaw Summer Jazz Festival, a series of outdoor concerts throughout the summer and the excellent Jazz Jamboree (Oct). Detailed events **listings** can be found in the *Warsaw Insider* (@www.warsawinsider.pl; 6zł) and the bi-monthly *Warsaw In Your Pocket* (@www.inyour pocket.com; 5zł), both available from information centres and at EMPiK stores.

### Cafés and snack bars

**Blikle** Nowy Świat 33. Century-old legend, famous for its doughnuts and pastries.

**Café 6/12** ul. Żurawia 6/12. Café/bar/restaurant that's a favourite among expats for its cool design, attentive service and high-quality drinks, meals and breakfast sets.

**Czuły Barbarzyńca** ul. Dobra 31. Smoky bookstore/café that's always full of students.

**Marak** ul. Świętokrzyska 18. Excellent and affordable soup kitchen, with both Polish classics and exotic soups. There's a second branch at Al. Jerozolimskie 42.

**Mercer's** Nowy Świat 25. The best of the Nowy Świat coffee houses, with aquarium-style windows and great fruit shakes.

**Między Nami** ul. Bracka 20. Relaxed gay-friendly café-bar with good light meals and an excellent atmosphere.

### Restaurants

**Green Way** ul. Szpitalna 6. Deservedly popular vegetarian place, with low prices and generous portions of Polish and Asian dishes.

**Kompania Piwna** ul. Podwale 25. Rowdy grill restaurant, with live traditional music, huge portions of country-style food and Czech beer.

**Pierogarnia** ul. Bednarska 6. Friendly, informal place run by monks and serving a dozen varieties of *pierogi* (till 7pm).

**Pod Samsonem** ul. Freta 3/5. The best of the tourist restaurants around the Old Town, with meat-and-potatoes fare from around 20zł, as well as some Jewish dishes.

Qchnia Artystyczna al. Ujazdowskie 6. In Ujazdowski Castle, with a wonderful view of Łazienki Park from the terrace. Good vegetarian selection.

Qllinarnia ul. Zielna 5, Pavilion 59. Nouveau milk bar that's the best cheap lunch spot in Warsaw. Try *pierogi* with chicken and walnuts (1.50zł each). Mon–Fri till 7pm.

Warsaw Tortilla Factory ul. Wilcza 46. A lively expat watering hole with Tex-Mex food, homemade lemonade and specials on tequila shots.

### Bars

Chimera ul. Podwale 29. Wackily decorated cellar bar that attracts a fun-minded crowd.

Kulturalna plac Defilad 1. Artsy student bar in the southeast wing of the Palace of Culture. DJs at weekends.

Le Madame ul. Koźla 12. Hedonistic gay-friendly bar/club hidden on a quiet street in the New Town. Weekend after-parties run till noon.

Lolek ul. Rokitnicka 20. Garden-restaurant in the middle of a park, with grilled food, beer and live music. Metro: Pole Mokotowskie.

Łysy Pingwin ul. Ząbkowska 12. Tapas and Staropramen in the Praga district. Well worth the trip across the river.

Morgan's ul. Okólnik 1. Warsaw's best Irish pub, with curry night on Tuesdays.

NoBo ul. Wilcza 58a. Unmarked, brothel-like, ultra-trendy spot.

Paparazzi ul. Mazowiecki 12. Where the new middle class come for cocktails.

Szparka plac Trzech Krzyży 16a. One of a row of three comfy late-night openers. Decent food.

### Clubs, discos and live music

Barbie Bar ul. Żurawia 6/12, entrance from ul. Nowogrodzka. Trendy gay club where even the disco balls are pink.

Diuna ul. Dobra 33/35. Eclectic space with a mix of DJs, student jazz bands and Polish hip-hop.

Labo ul. Mazowiecka 11a. Chic city-centre club. Young crowd, nice sofas and they don't just play house. Dress to get in.

Organza ul. Sienkiewicza 4. Large club/restaurant with good pastas and beautiful people.

Piekarnia ul. Młocińska 11. One of Warsaw's best clubs, at the forefront of musical fashion and with frequent big-name DJs. Fri & Sat only.

Tygmont ul. Mazowiecka 6/8. Warsaw's top jazz club, with regular gigs, good food and a smoke-free environment.

## Listings

Embassies Australia, ul. Nowogrodzka 11 ☎022/521 3444; Canada, al. Matejki 1/5 ☎022/584 3100; Ireland, ul. Humańska 10 ☎022/849 6655; New Zealand – matters handled by the UK embassy; UK, al. Róż 1 ☎022/628 1001; US, al. Ujazdowskie 29 ☎022/628 3041.

Internet access Simple Internet, ul. Marszałkowska 99/101 (24hr); Verso, ul. Freta 17 (9am–4/5pm); e-Loco, ul. Krucza 17 (10am–midnight); Top Computer, Nowy Świat 18/20 (9/10am–10/11pm).

Left luggage There's a 24hr left-luggage office at Centralna station, as well as lockers with storage for up to ten days.

Medical services Public Hospital, ul. Marszałkowska 24 ☎022/522 7333; CM Medical Centre, 3rd floor of Marriott Hotel, opposite Centralna Station ☎022/458 7000.

Pharmacies Top floor of Centralna Station in main hall (24hr); ul. Freta 13 (Mon–Fri 8am–8pm, Sat 8am–7pm, Sun 11am–7m).

Post office ul. Świętokrzyska 31/33 (24hr).

# Northern Poland

Even in a country accustomed to shifting borders, northern Poland presents an unusually tortuous historical puzzle. Successively the domain of a Germanic crusading order, of the Hansa merchants and the Prussians, it's only in the last fifty years that the region has really become Polish. **Gdańsk**, **Sopot** and **Gdynia** – the Tri-City, as their conurbation is known – dominate the area from their coastal vantage point. The most enjoyable excursions from Gdańsk are to the medieval centres of **Malbork** and **Toruń**.

# Gdańsk and around

Both the starting point of World War II and the birthplace of the Solidarity movement, **GDAŃSK** has played more than a fleeting role on the world stage. Traces of its past can be seen in the steel skeletons of derelict shipyard cranes and the Hanseatic and Prussian-influenced architecture of the beautifully restored old town. After all the social and political upheavals of the last century the city is now busy reinventing itself as a student and tourist hub.

The **Główne Miasto** (Main Town) is within easy walking distance of the train station. Entering it is like walking straight into a Hansa merchants' settlement, but its ancient appearance is deceptive: by May 1945, the core of Gdańsk was in ruins, leaving the city facing a daunting rebuilding programme. Huge stone gateways guard both entrances to **ul. Długa**, the main thoroughfare. Start from the sixteenth-century gate at the top, **Brama Wyżynna**, and you'll soon come across the huge tower of the Town Hall, which houses a **Historical Museum** (Tues–Sun 10/11am–4pm; 6zł) strong on photos of the city's wartime destruction. Past the Town Hall, the street opens onto the wide expanse of **Długi Targ**, where the sumptuous **Arthur's Court** (Dwór Artusa; Mon–Sun 10/11am–4pm; 6zł) stands out in a square filled with fine mansions. At the end of the street the archways of the **Brama Zielona** open directly onto the waterfront. From the bridge over the Motława Canal you get a good view of the granaries on Spichlerze Island and along the old quay. Halfway down is the largely original fifteenth-century **Gdańsk Crane**, the biggest in medieval Europe, and part of the vast **Central Maritime Museum** (Tues–Sun 10am–4/6pm; 14zł), which spreads out on both banks of the river. Highlights include an exhibition of primitive boats, and photographs illustrating the life of Polish writer Józef Korzeniowski, better known as Joseph Conrad. The streets back into the town from the waterfront are worth exploring, especially **Mariacka**, brimming with amber traders, and ul. Chlebnicka, adjacent to the gigantic **St Mary's Church**, a haven in the 1980s for over twenty thousand members of Solidarity. A few blocks north is the seven-storey **Great Mill**, the biggest in medieval Europe. Further north still loom the cranes of the famous **Gdańsk shipyards**, crucible of the political strife of the 1980s. Outside the gates is the famous anchor-topped **monument** to the workers killed during the 1970s riots, while the nearby **Roads to Freedom** exhibition on ul. Doki 1 (Tues–Sun 10am–4/5pm; 5zł) details the bloody struggle to topple communism. Back on the other side of the old town, in a former Franciscan monastery, the National Museum (Tues–Sun 9/10am–4pm; 9zł) has a fine collection of Gothic art, the highlight of which is a *Last Judgment* by the Dutch painter Hans Memling.

## Practicalities

Gdańsk's main **tourist office** is opposite the Town Hall at ul. Długa 45 (daily 10am–6pm; Oct–April closed Sat & Sun; ☎058/301 9151, ⓦwww.gdansk.pl). The city's best **hostels** are the *Targ Rybny*, near the canal at ul. Grodzka 21 (☎058/301 5627, ⓦwww.gdanskhostel.com; 40zł, rooms ❷) and the *Baltic Hostel*, just north of the train station at ul. 3 Maja 25 (☎058/328 1657, ⓦwww.baltichostel.com; 40zł, rooms ❷). Both offer clean rooms, free Internet access and laundry service as well as complimentary bicycles and kayaks. Less appealing due to its barracks atmosphere and midnight curfew, but still tolerable, is the large red-brick hostel, ten minutes' walk north from the main station at ul. Wałowa 21 (☎058/301 2313, ⓦwww.mokf.com.pl; 29zł, rooms ❶). Central **private rooms** (❷) can be booked at the *Grand Tourist* agency, in the pedestrian mall by the train station (☎058/301 2634, ⓦwww.gt.com.pl).

For cheap **meals**, check out the classic milk bar *Neptun,* at ul. Długa 33/34 (Mon–Fri till 6pm, Sat till 5pm), or the nearby *Bar Pod Rybą*, Długi Targ 35/38, a student institution dishing up baked potatoes daily till 7pm. The more atmospheric

*Mestwin*, at ul. Straganiarska 21/22, offers hearty local meals for 16zł, while *Napoli*, Długa 62/63, is best for pizza and pasta. The popular *Cocktail Bar Capri*, Długa 74, serves excellent cakes. For **drinks**, try *Kamiennica*, ul. Mariacka 37/39, a wonderfully intimate bar, or the wildly decorated *Punkt*, ul. Chlebnicka 2. Best of the **clubs** are the sprawling, mainstream *Parlament*, ul. Św. Ducha 2, and the more cutting-edge *Ggog*, ul. Wajdeloty 12/13. *Gdańsk in Your Pocket* can be bought from the EMPiK store in the pedestrian mall by the train station and includes good **listings**. There's **Internet** access at *Rudy Kot*, ul. Garncarska 18/22.

## Sopot

Some 15km north of Gdańsk is **SOPOT**, Poland's trendiest coastal resort, with a famous pier and a long stretch of white sand. Once regarded as the "Monte Carlo of the Baltics", Sopot is now a magnet for young Polish party animals. Commuter **trains** make the twenty-five minute trip from Gdańsk to Sopot every ten minutes until about 11.30pm. The breezy main artery, ul. Bohaterów Monte Cassino, packed with bars and restaurants, runs east from the train station towards the sea. The **tourist office**, opposite the train station at ul. Dworcowa 4 (daily 8am–6pm; ☎058/550 3783, ◍www.sopot.pl/cit), can help with **accommodation**, which can be hard to come by in summer. *Dom Nauczyciela* (☎058/551 2887; ❸) is an attractive pension near the train station at ul. Kościuszki 64, while *Chemik*, 1km south at ul. Bitwy pod Plowcami 61 (☎058/551 1209; ❷ ❸), is a concrete box with good-value rooms. North of the centre, at ul. Sępia 22, *Maryla* (☎058/551 0034◍www.hotel.sopot.pl; ❸), is a comfortable hotel in a villa that once belonged to Kaiser Wilhelm II; it also has a **campsite** with cabins (❷). *Bar Przystań*, south along the beach at Wojska Polskiego 11, is a cheap, well-known fish **restaurant**, while meat-eaters will delight in the platters at *Harnaś*, ul. Moniuszki 9. Alternatively, *Green Way*, ul. Bohaterów Monte Cassino 67, has decent vegetarian food, while the stylish *Mandarynka*, ul. Bema 6, serves pastas, salads and drinks until late. Film buffs should check out *Galeria Kińsky*, ul. Kościuszki 10, a **bar** situated in the childhood home of actor Klaus Kinski, while expats congregate at the *Language Pub*, ul. Pułaskiego 8. *Sfinks*, generally accepted as Poland's top **nightclub**, is in the middle of the park off Powstańców Warszawy, while *Enzym*, ul. Mamuszki 21 (open Fri–Sun), attracts well-known DJs. There's **Internet** access at the *Cooler Net Cave*, ul Pułaskiego 7a.

## Malbork

Dating from the fourteenth century, the castle of **MALBORK** is one of Poland's most spectacular fortresses. Built to serve as headquarters for the Teutonic Knights, it casts a threatening shadow over what is otherwise a sleepy town. The **train** and **bus stations** are sited next to each other about ten minutes' walk south of the castle; Malbork is on the main Warsaw line, so there are plenty of trains from Gdańsk (30–40min). You approach the **fortress** (Tues–Sun: April 15 – Sept 15 9am–7pm; rest of year 9am–3pm; 19/30zł for mandatory guided tour) through the ruins of the old outer castle. Passing over the moat and through the daunting main gate, you come to the **Middle Castle**. Spread out around an open courtyard, this part of the complex contains the Grand Master's palace, of which the **Main Refectory** is the highlight. From the Middle Castle a passage rises to the **High Castle**, the oldest section of the fortress, harbouring the focus of the Knights' austere monasticism – the vast **Castle Church**.

## Toruń

The biggest and most important of the Hanseatic trading centres along the Wisła, **TORUŃ** miraculously survived recurrent wars, and its historic centre is a rich assembly of architectural styles. Now it's a friendly university city, with bars and cafés sprinkled throughout the tight streets. Highlight of the westerly Old Town is the mansion-lined **Rynek** and its medieval Town Hall, now the **Town Museum** (Tues–Sun 10am–4/6pm; 10zł), with a gorgeous collection of fourteenth-century stained glass. In the western corner of the Rynek stands the impressive **Church of the Blessed Virgin Mary**. South of the Rynek, at ul. Kopernika 15/17, is the **Copernicus Museum** (Tues–Sun 10am–4pm; 10zł), in the brick house where the great man was born and containing a collection of Copernicus artefacts and a sound-and-light show of fifteenth-century Toruń (8zł extra). The font in which Copernicus was baptized in the massive St John's Cathedral (Mon–Sat 9am–5.30pm, Sun 2–5.30pm; 2zł), at the eastern end of ul. Kopernika. To the northeast lies the New Town district, with its illustrious commercial residences grouped around the Rynek Nowomiejski. Ul. Prosta leads north of the square to a park in which stands the former arsenal, now a diverting **Ethnographic Museum** (daily 9/10am–4/6pm; Oct–April closed Mon; 8.5zł), behind which an outdoor display of wooden buildings includes a massive **windmill**.

Toruń Główny, the main **train station**, is 2km away south of the river; buses #22 and #27 (every 10min; 1.8zł) both run to pl. Rapackiego on the edge of the Old Town, the first stop after crossing the river. Exit the station beyond platform 4 and buy tickets from the kiosk beside the bus stop. From the **bus station** on ul. Dąbrowskiego it is a short walk south to the centre. The very friendly **tourist office** at Rynek Staromiejski 25 (Mon & Sat 9am–4pm, Tues–Fri 9am–6pm; May–Sept also Sun 9am–1pm; ☎056/621 0931, ⊛www.it.torun.pl) hands out free maps and can find accommodation and **private rooms** (❷). The best budget **hotel** is the *Hotelik w Centrum*, just east of the centre at ul. Szumana 2 (☎056/652 2246, ⊛www.cku.torun.pl; ❷), where all rooms have TV and there's a kitchen and Internet access. Alternatively, try the simple but clean *Dom Turysty PTTK*, ul. Legionów 24 (☎056/622 3855, ⊛www.pttk.torun.pl; dorm bed 35zł, rooms ❷); take bus #27 four stops north from the main train station. Toruń's best **hostel** is a basic but comfortable setup with no curfew, 3km northeast of the centre in an old fortress at ul. Chrobrego 86 (☎056/655 8236, ⊛www.fort.torun.pl; 15zł; bus #28 or #14). The *Tramp* **campsite** at ul. Kujawska 14 (☎056/654 7187; closed Oct-April), a short walk west of the train station, also has bungalows (❷).

Best for budget **food** is the *Bar Mleczny*, on the corner of Różana and Św. Ducha, offering filling soups, stodgy meals and waffles to take away. Popular with students, *Manekin*, north of Rynek Nowomiejski at ul. Wysoka 5, serves fifty-odd varieties of excellent pancakes. For cheap pasta and pizza, head for the vaulted rooms of *Staromiejska*, at ul. Szczytna 2–4, or to *U Sołtysa*, ul. Mostowa 17, for pricier Polish fare in folksy surroundings. Summer riverbank **cafés** provide pleasant outdoor drinking, while the cellar-**bar** *Pod Aniołem,* under the town hall, sometimes hosts DJs and dancing. Other good choices include *Metropolis*, a lively restaurant, bar and club at ul. Podmurna 28, and *Galeria Krzywa*, a tremendous bar in the Old Town battlements on ul. Bankowa. Be sure to stop in one of the many sweet shops to try *pierniki*, local gingerbread cookies. The *Jeremi* **Internet** café is at Rynek Staromiejski 33.

# Southern Poland

Southern Poland garners more visitors than any other region in the country, and its attractions are clear from a glance at the map. The **Tatra Mountains**, which form the border with Slovakia, are Poland's grandest, snowcapped for much of the year and markedly alpine in feel. **Kraków**, rich in historical associations, is an architectural gem and the country's intellectual heart. Pope John Paul II was Archbishop here until his election in 1978 but equally important are the city's Jewish roots: until World War II, this was one of the great European Jewish centres. This past remains clear in the old Jewish area of Kazimierz, and its culmination is starkly enshrined at the death camps of **Auschwitz–Birkenau**, west of the city.

# Kraków and around

**KRAKÓW** was the only major city in Poland to come through World War II essentially undamaged, and its assembly of monuments has been listed by UNESCO as one of the world's most significant historic sites. Although swarming with visitors in summer, the city's Old Town retains an atmosphere of fin-de-siècle stateliness, its streets a cavalcade of churches and palaces. A university centre, Kraków has a tangible buzz of arty youthfulness and boasts a wealth of nightlife opportunities.

## Arrival, information and accommodation

Kraków Główny, the central **train station**, and the main **bus station** just opposite, are five minutes' walk northeast of the city's historic centre. Everything there is to see is within walking distance; a bus or tram ticket (*bilet normalny*) costs 2.40zł. The city **tourist offices**, one occupying a circular pavilion between the stations and the Old Town (May–Sept Mon–Fri 8am–8pm, Sat & Sun 9am–5pm; Oct–April Mon–Fri 8am–4pm; ☏012/432 0060, ✆www.krakow.pl) and the other in the ground floor of the town hall tower on the main square (same details), have free maps and can find you a place to stay. Just off the main square at ul. Św. Jana 2, the **Cultural Information Centre** (Mon–Fri 10am–6pm, Sat 10am–4pm; ☏012/421 7787, ✆www.karnet.krakow2000.pl) publishes events **listings** in a monthly booklet (*Karnet*; 4zł). The EMPiK store, on the main square, sells the reliable English-language *Kraków in Your Pocket* (✆www.inyourpocket .com). The number of private **hostels** and **pensions** in the centre keeps growing, but if you can't find accommodation, try a **private room**, booked via Jordan (Mon–Fri 8am–6pm, Sat 9am–2pm; ☏012/422 6091, ✆www.jordan.pl), or the adjacent Waweltur (Mon–Fri 8am–8pm, Sat 8am–2pm; ☏012/422 1921, ✆www .waweltur.com.pl), both opposite the train station at ul. Pawia 8. Rooms start at 80zł for a double and can be quite central.

### Hostels

**Bling Bling** ul. Pędzichów 7 ☏012/634 0532, ✆www.blingbling.pl. Well-established and laid-back hostel two blocks north of the Stare Miasto. 55zł.

**Dizzy Daisy** ul. Pędzichów 9 ☏012/292 0171, ✆www.hostel.pl. Adjacent to *Bling Bling*, but also with doubles. Dorms are comfortable but the lounge can get smoky. Two other Dizzy Daisy hostels, *Atlantis* at ul. Dietla 58 and *Dizzy Daily Krakowska* at ul. Krakowska 7, are slightly less appealing. 55zł, rooms ❷

**Greg & Tom Hostel** ul. Pawia 12/15 ☏012/422 4100, ✆www.gregtomhostel.com. Small but amenable fourth-floor hostel by the train station, with free use of bicycles. Coffee and tea but no breakfast. 45zł, rooms ❷

**Mama's** ul. Bracka 4 ☏012/429 5940, ✆www.mamashostel.com.pl. Third-floor hostel with an impressive Stare Miasto location; amenities are first-rate but in summer the courtyard café below is noisy till 2am. 55zł

**Nathan's Villa** ul. Św. Agnieszki ☏012/422 3545, ✆www.nathansvilla.com. Popular private hostel that's well situated between the Stare Miasto and Kazimierz. 45–60zł.

**The Stranger** ul. Kochanowskiego 1/3U ☏012/634 2516, ✆www.thestrangerhostel.com. Famous for its 3m video screen, this well-run hostel attracts a sociable, fun-loving crowd. A few minutes east of the Stare Miasto. 60zł.

**The Traveller's Inn Hostel** ul. J. Sarego 24/2 ☏012/429 4723, ✆www.travellersinn.pl. The most pleasant of Kraków's hostels, on a quiet street, with clean dorms and one double, free use of bicycles and a bright, airy lounge. 50zł, room ❷

### Hotels

**Bed & Breakfast** ul. Wiślna 10 ☏012/421 9871, ✆www.noclegi.tk. Simple, pleasant rooms off the main square, with good breakfast. ❸–❹

**Cybulskiego Guestrooms** ul. Cybulskiego 6/5 ☏012/423 0532, ✆www.freerooms.pl. Spotless en-suite doubles (❷) with bath and kitchen. An easy walk west from the centre. The friendly staff also run the small *Cord Hostel* (dorms 40zł) between Kazimierz and the river at ul. Kordeckiego 3/1.

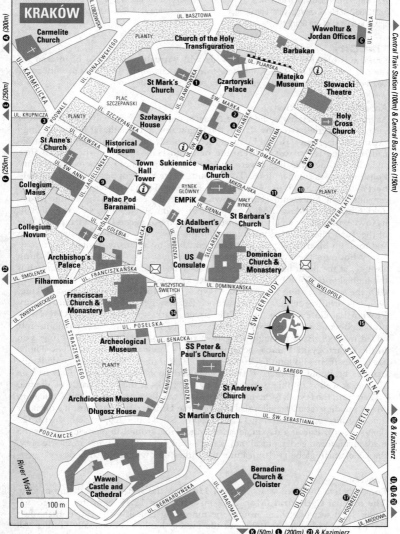

KRAKÓW

**POLAND** | Southern Poland

22

| ACCOMMODATION | | | EATING & DRINKING | | | |
|---|---|---|---|---|---|---|
| Bed & Breakfast | H | | Alchemia | **18** | Dym | **5** |
| Bling Bling | A | | Arka Noego | **16** | Fabryka Pizzy | **19** |
| Cybulskiego | | | Babcia Malina | **1** | Gruzińskie | |
| Guestrooms | F | | Bagelmama | **17** | Czaczapuri | **2** |
| Dizzy Daisy | B | | Balaton | **14** | Łubu Dubu | **15** |
| Dizzy Daisy Atlantis | J | | Black Gallery | **10** | Massolit | **12** |
| Dizzy Daisy Krakowska | L | | Camelot | **6** | Nic Nowego | **8** |
| Greg & Tom Hostel | C | | Chimera | **9** | Pauza | **4** |
| Mama's | G | | Chłopskie Jadło | **7, 13, 21** | Singer | **20** |
| Nathan's Villa | K | | C.K. Browar | **3** | U Stasi | **11** |
| The Stranger | D | | | | | |
| The Traveller's | | | | | | |
| Inn Hostel | I | | | | | |
| Trzy Kafki Plus | E | | | | | |

**Trzy Kafki Plus** ul. Dolnych Młynów 9
℡012/632 4856, ⓦwww.trzykafki.pl. Budget
option just west of the Stare Miasto, with 12
clean en-suite rooms (③). A larger branch, north
of the centre at al. Słowackiego 29, is gloomy
and cheap (②).

## The City

Kraków is bisected by the River Wisla with virtually everything of interest on the north bank. The Rynek Główny forms a focus in the Old Town, with royal Wawel to the south and the Jewish area of Kazimierz beyond.

### Aroung Rynek Główny

At the heart of Kraków is the **Stare Miasto**, the Old Town, with its great central square, the **Rynek Główny**. It was the largest square in medieval Europe: a huge expanse of flagstones, ringed by magnificent houses and towering spires. Its dominant building is the vast **Sukiennice** or Cloth Hall, rebuilt in the Renaissance and still housing a bustling covered market, with a museum of nineteenth-century Polish art on the upper floor. To its south is the tiny copper-domed **St Adalbert's**, the first church to be founded in Kraków. The tall tower nearby is all that remains of the fourteenth-century town hall. On the east side is the Gothic **Mariacki Church** (St Mary's; Mon–Sat 11.30am–6pm, Sun 2–6pm; 4zł), the taller of its towers topped by an amazing ensemble of spires. Legend has it that during one of the Tatar raids, a guard watching from the tower saw the invaders approaching and took up his trumpet; his alarm was cut short by an arrow through the throat. Every hour on the hour a trumpeter plays the sombre *hejnał* melody, halting abruptly at the point he was supposed to have been hit. Highlight of the church is the high altar (1477–89), one of the finest examples of late-Gothic art.

Of the streets leading north off the Rynek, **ul. Floriańska** is the most striking, with colourful medieval and Renaissance façades. The robust fourteenth-century **Floriańska Gate**, at the end of the street, marks the edge of the Old Town proper. Beyond is the **Barbakan** (May–Sept daily 9am–6pm; 4zł), a bulbous fort added in 1498. Back through the gate, a right turn down ul. Pijarska brings you to the **Czartoryski Palace**, housing Kraków's finest art collection (Tues–Thurs, Sat & Sun 10am–3.30pm, Fri 10am–6pm; 7zł, Sun free). Highlights include Rembrandt's brooding *Landscape Before a Storm* and Leonardo da Vinci's *Lady with an Ermine*, as well as trophies surrendered by the Turks at the 1683 Battle of Vienna.

West from the Rynek is the **university area**, whose heart is the Gothic Collegium Maius building, at ul. Jagiellońska 15. Now the **University Museum**, it's open for guided tours only (Mon–Fri 11am–2.20pm, Sat 11am–1.20pm; 7zł; ℡012/422 0549) – book at least a day in advance. Inside, the ground-floor rooms retains the mathematical and geographical murals once used for teaching, while in the treasury, the Jagiellonian globe (1510) features the earliest-known map of America.

### Wawel

For over five hundred years, **Wawel Hill** was the seat of Poland's monarchy. The original **Cathedral** (Mon–Sat 9am–3pm, Sun 12.15–3pm; tombs and bell tower 10zł) was built here around the time King Bolesław the Brave established the Kraków bishopric in 1020, but the present basilica is essentially Gothic. All bar four of Poland's forty-five monarchs are buried, and their tombs and side chapels are like a directory of Central European art, not least the Gothic **Holy Cross Chapel** and the Renaissance **Zygmuntowska chapel**. Arrive early or book ahead to visit the various sections of **Wawel Castle** (ticket office Mon–Sat 9am–3pm, Sun 10am–3pm; ℡012/422 1697), including the **State Rooms** (Tues–Sat 9.30am–3pm, Sun 10am–3pm; 12zł, Sun free), furnished with Renaissance paintings and tapestries, and the king's **Royal Private Apartments** (same times; 15zł). Although much of the contents had been sold by the time of the Partitions to pay off dowries and debts of state, the **Royal Treasury and Armoury** (same times; 12zł) still features some fine items. The **Lost Wawel** exhibition

(Wed–Mon 9.30am–3pm, Sun 10am–3pm; 6zł), beneath the old kitchens south of the cathedral, takes you past the excavated remains of the hill's most ancient buildings, including the foundations of the tenth-century **Rotunda of SS Felix and Adauctus**, the oldest church in Poland. Return to ground level via the **Dragon's Den** (May–Oct daily 10am–5pm; 3zł), a spiral staircase leading to a cavern. Legend has it that Smok the dragon lived here, feeding children, cattle and unsuccessful knights. A clever peasant boy, fed him a sheep stuffed with sulphur; to quench the burning Smok drank half the Wisła, causing him to explode.

## Kazimierz

South from Wawel Hill lies the **Kazimierz** district, which in 1495 became Kraków's Jewish quarter. Kazimierz grew to become one of the main centres of Polish Jewry, but in March 1941 the entire Jewish population of the city was crammed into a tiny ghetto over the river. Waves of deportations to the camps followed and the ghetto was finally liquidated in March 1943, ending seven centuries of Jewish life in Kraków. Today Kazimierz is a fashionable and bohemian residential district, with much to see and plenty of interesting shops, cafés and bars. The tiny **Remu'h Synagogue** at ul. Szeroka 40 (Mon–Fri 9am–4pm; 5zł) is one of two still functioning in the quarter. The tombstones of its cemetery were buried and therefore largely saved from Nazi ransacking. Fragments are collaged together to form an impressive wall just inside the entrance. The **Old Synagogue**, at ul. Szeroka 24, is the oldest surviving Jewish religious building in Poland. Since the war it's been carefully restored and turned into a **Museum of Kraków Jewry** (Wed, Thurs, Sat & Sun 9am–3.30pm, Fri 11am–6pm; 6zł, Wed free), including a permanent exhibition of traditional art by Polish Jews. One block to the southeast, at ul. Dajwór 18, the **Galicia Jewish Museum** (daily 10am–8pm; 6zł) displays a memorable series of photographs evoking the way rural Poland's Jewish heritage has been neglected; there's also a good bookstore, and concerts and lectures are frequently held here. Another interesting visit is the **Synagoga Izaaka** (Isaac Synagogue), at ul. Kupa 18, which has photographs and short silent films illustrating the life of Kazimierz Jews before and during the war (Sun–Fri 9am–7pm; 7zł).

## Eating, drinking and nightlife

Kraków is renowned for its **bars**, **restaurants** and **cafés**, with every street in the old town boasting several places to sit over beer or coffee and cake. For late-night drinking, Kazimierz has a selection of dimly-lit nightspots, while the techno and jazz **clubs** rival those in Warsaw. Important **events** include the Film Festival (May), the Jewish Culture Festival (June) and the Summer Jazz Festival (July/August).

### Cafés, milk bars and snacks

**Babcia Malina** ul. Sławkowska 17. Famous and cheap student milk bar in a mountain-hut-style basement.

**Camelot** ul. Św. Tomasza 17. Upmarket café with the best *szarlotka* (apple pie) in town and folk art decor.

**Chimera** ul. Św. Anny 3. Atmospheric rooms and a terrace in summer. Cheap salads, quiches and the like. Good for vegetarians.

**Dym** ul. Św. Tomasza 17. Dark café favoured by the local intelligentsia.

**Gruziński Czaczapuri** ul. Św. Marka 19. For a late-night snack, this Georgian takeaway serves tasty pittas and pies.

**Massolit** ul. Filicjanek 4. American-owned bookshop/café with superb carrot cake and 25,000 new and used English books.

**U Stasi** ul. Mikołajska 16. Popular and cheap milk bar specializing in *pierogi* and simple meat dishes. With an English menu. Mon–Fri 12.30–5pm.

### Restaurants

**Arka Noego** ul. Szeroka 2. The best-value Jewish restaurant in Kazimierz, with occasional *klezmer* music.

**Balaton** ul. Grodzka 37. Unpromising atmosphere, but fine Hungarian food and wine.

**Bagelmama** ul. Podbrzezie 2. Tiny Kazimierz eatery serving tasty bagels and *burritos*. Closed Mon.

**Chłopskie Jadło** ul. Św. Jana 3, ul. Grodzka 9, ul. Św. Agnieszki 1. Local chain known for hearty, mid-priced peasant cuisine. Book ahead in summer.

Fabryka Pizzy ul. Józefa 34. Stylish, smoke-free pizzeria in Kazimierz; often full.

**Bars**

Alchemia ul. Estery 5. Atmospheric Kazimierz bar catering for curious tourists and permanently sozzled regulars. Open late.

Black Gallery ul. Mikołajska 24. Cellar bar with industrial decor, garden courtyard and lively crowd.

C.K. Browar ul. Podwale 6–7. Excellent beer hall that brews on the premises. Also has a good restaurant and disco.

Łubu Dubu Wielopole 15/1, first floor. Battered old apartment filled with 80s memorabilia, fluorescent lights and drunken Artsy types.

Nic Nowego ul. Św. Krzyźa 15. The most interesting Irish pub in Poland. Sleek, modern, and with sandwiches and salads as well as Guinness.

Pauza ul. Floriańska 18. Unmarked first floor bar-gallery that attracts a discriminating crowd.

Singer ul. Estery 22. One of the oldest and best of Kazimierz's many bars, with a retro ambience and a Singer sewing machine on every table.

**Clubs and live music venues**

Kitsch Wielopole 15/1, second floor. Hedonistic gay club with regular drag shows. Open late.

Pod Jaszczurami Rynek Główny 8. Buzzing university club; student ID sometimes necessary.

Prozac pl. Dominikański 6, in the basement. For breakbeat, house and drum'n'bass; dress up to get in.

Stalowe Magnolie ul. Św. Jana 15. Live rock or jazz in a red velvet lounge, with drinks at Warsaw prices.

U Muniaka ul. Floriańska 3. Jazz sessions, Thurs–Sat at 9.30pm; 20zł cover.

**Listings**

Bike Rental Wypożyczalnia Rowerów, ul. Św. Anny 4 (Mon–Sat 9am–dusk; 4zł/hr, 30zł/day).

Consulates UK, ul. Św. Anny 9 ☎012/421 7030; US, ul. Stolarska 9 ☎012/424 5100.

Internet access Pl@net, Rynek Główny 24 (9am–10pm); Studencki, Rynek Główny 23 (24hr).

Pharmacies Grodzka 26. Rota posted on window.

Post office Ul. Westerplatte 20.

## Wieliczka

Fifteen kilometres southeast of Kraków, the town of **WIELICZKA** is home to a vast, UNESCO-listed **salt mine** (*kopalnia soli*), with 300km of subterranean tunnels reaching a depth of 327m (April–Oct 7.30am–7.30pm; Nov–March 8am–5pm; 50zł; ⊛www.kopalnia.pl; at least six English guided tours daily). Salt was discovered here at least a millenium ago. In the Middle Ages tours were given to visitors of the royal court, and the mine has since drawn such luminaries as Goethe, Balzac and the elder George Bush, as well as thousands of asthmatics who come for the purifying saline air. The tour takes two hours and covers two miles of tunnels and chambers; sights include a salt lake as well as two chapels carved entirely in salt. The larger of these, a 50m chamber with unusual acoustic properties, is sometimes used for concerts and banquets. There's also a display on mining techniques through the ages. Wieliczka is easily reached by **minibus** or **train** from Kraków (20–30min) once there, follow the "Kopalnia" signs.

## Oświęcim (Auschwitz-Birkenau)

In 1940, **OŚWIĘCIM**, a small town 70km west of Kraków, became the site of the Oświęcim-Brzezinka concentration camp, better known by its German name of **Auschwitz-Birkenau**. Of the many camps built by the Nazis, this was the largest and most horrific: something approaching two million people, 85–90 percent of them Jews, died here. You can pick up a detailed guidebook or join a guided group. Get to Auschwitz-Birkenau from Kraków using one of the regular buses to **Oświęcim station** (1hr 30min). From there it's a short bus ride to the gates of Auschwitz, though the last stop for some buses from Kraków is the camp itself. There's an hourly **shuttle-bus** service to the Birkenau section from the car park at Auschwitz; taxis are also available, otherwise it's a 3km walk.

Most of the Auschwitz buildings have been preserved as the **Museum of Martyrdom** (daily: June–Aug 8am–7pm; May & Sept 8am–6pm; Oct & April 8am–5pm; March & Nov to mid-Dec 8am–4pm; mid-Dec to Feb 8am–3pm;

free; ⓦwww.auschwitz-muzeum.oswiecim.pl). The cinema is a sobering starting point, showing film taken by the Soviet troops who liberated the camp in May 1945. The bulk of the camp consists of the prison cell blocks, with the first section dedicated to "exhibits" found in the camp after liberation – rooms full of clothes and suitcases, toothbrushes, glasses, shoes and a huge mound of women's hair. Other barracks are given over to national memorials, and the blocks terminate with the gas chambers and the ovens where the bodies were incinerated. The huge **Birkenau camp** (same hours) is less visited, though it was here that the majority of executions took place. Birkenau was designed purely as a death camp, and the huge gas chambers at the back of the camp were damaged but not destroyed by the fleeing Nazis in 1945. Victims arrived in closed trains to be driven directly into the gas chambers; the railway line is still there, just as the Nazis abandoned it.

## Zakopane and the Tatras

Some 80km long, with peaks of up to 2500m, the **Tatra Mountains** – Tatry in Polish – are the most spectacular part of the chain of ridges extending along Poland's border with Slovakia. The main base for skiing and hiking on the Polish side is the popular mountain resort of **ZAKOPANE**. Skiing here is cheap, with the premier slopes of **Kasprowy Wierch** just a few minutes out of town, and plenty of places in the centre to rent equipment. Hikers may want to avoid the 9km path to the lovely **Morskie Oko** lake in high season, as it gets packed, but there's no shortage of other trails to get you away from the crowds. Zakopane's **market** at the bottom of ul. Krupówki 63 sells local *oscypek* (smoked cheese) as well as handmade souvenirs and Saint Bernard puppies (500zł). Nearby, the wooden **Stary Kościoł** (Old Church) on ul. Kościeliska is a good example of Zakopane architecture, as are the whimsical tombs in the attached **Stary Cmentarz** (Old Cemetery).

Zakopane is easily reached by bus (2hr) or train (3–4hr) from Kraków, with onward buses across the border to Poprad in Slovakia. Both **stations** are a ten-minute walk east of the pedestrianized main street, ul. Krupówki. Uphill, ul. Krupówki merges into ul. Zamoyskiego, which runs out of town towards the Tatra National Park entrance. There's **tourist information** west of the stations at ul. Kościuszki 17 (daily 8am–8pm; ⓦwww.zakopane.pl), with lists of pensions, maps, guidebooks, and details on mountain huts and the weather, while the **Tatra National Park Information Centre**, near the park entrance at ul. Chałubińsk-iego 44 (daily 9am–3pm; ☎018/206 3799), provides more details on hiking.

Accommodation is never a problem in Zakopane, as every third house in town offers **private rooms** (❷). Of the dozens of **pensions**, the modest *Halny*, behind the tourist office at ul. Kamieniec 13a (☎018/201 2041; ❷), is a good choice, as is the more impressive *Api 2*, north of the station at ul. Kamieniec 13a (☎018/206 2931, ⓦwww.api2.pl; ❷), which has bright rooms and a sauna. The *Pod Krokwia* **campsite** (☎018/201 2256) is at the end of ul. Zeromskiego, near the park entrance. **Restaurants** and **cafés** are concentrated on ul. Krupówki, with *Pstrag Górski*, at no. 6a, serving inexpensive fresh trout, while *Sabala*, across the street at no. 11, offers more expensive traditional fare, outside tables and indoor folk music. The best places to drink are the chic *Paparazzi*, just off the main street at ul. Galicy 8, and the affordable and Bohemian *Piano Café*, at ul. Krupówki 63. There's reliable **Internet** access above *Paparazzi*.

# Silesia and Wielkopolska

In Polish it's Śląsk, in Czech Sleszko and in German Schlesien: all three countries hold part of the disputed province of **Silesia**, but since 1945 it has been almost all Polish, a dominance gained as compensation for lands lost to the USSR in 1939. Silesia's main city, **Wrocław**, is one of Central Europe's most enticing centres. To the north, the region known as **Wielkopolska** formed the core of the original Polish nation, and its chief interest is supplied by the vibrant and prosperous city of **Poznań**.

# Wrocław

**WROCŁAW** (pronounced "vrots-wav") is a city used to rebuilding. Through centuries of regularly changing ownership it was largely dominated by Germans and known as Breslau. This all altered after the war, however, when thousands of displaced Poles from **Lwów** (now L'viv in Ukraine), which had been annexed by the Soviets in 1939, were encouraged to take over the severely depopulated Breslau, which in turn had been confiscated from Germany. The influences that shaped the city are reflected in much of its architecture: huge Germanic churches, Flemish-style mansions and Baroque palaces. The latest rebuilding came after a catastrophic flood in the early 1990s, which left most of the centre underwater. Luckily the energy involved in the reconstruction that followed has left the airy Old Town rejuvenated – and without the tourist mobs of Kraków.

### Arrival, information and accommodation

The main **train station**, Wrocław Główny, faces the broad boulevard of ul. Piłsudskiego, about fifteen minutes' walk south of the Rynek; the main **bus station** is behind the train station. The **tourist office** at Rynek 14 (daily: May–Aug 10am–9pm, Sept–April 10am–6pm; ☎071/344 3111, ☜www.wroclaw.pl) can book accommodation. There's a cluster of basic **hotels** near the train station – nearest is the careworn and student-oriented *Piast* at ul. Piłsudskiego 98 (☎071/343 0034, ☜www.odratourist.pl; ❷), with reductions for ISIC holders. Standards improve a bit at the *Savoy*, between the stations and the Old Town at pl. Kościuszki 19 (☎071/340 3219; ❸), but the best deal in the centre is the *Bursa Nauczycielska*, at ul. Kotlarska 42 (☎071/344 3781; ❷), with simple doubles and triples. You're more likely, however, to get a room at the lifeless but clean *Dom Turystyczny Trio*, 1km west of the Rynek at ul. Trzemeska 4 (☎071/355 9446; ☜www.puhot.pl; ❷): take tram #22 from two blocks west of the train station to the stop Młodych Techników. Both of the year-round **hostels** have 10pm curfews; the better of the two, *Tumski* (☎071/322 6099, ☜www.hotel-tumski.com.pl; 30zł), is attached to an expensive hotel of the same name. From July to September you can stay in one of the excellent Orange Hostels (☜www.orangehostels.pl; dorms 30zł, rooms ❶); the central *Nad Fosą* is along the moat at ul. Podwale 27 (☎071/343 9260), while the *Straszny Dwór* is across the river at pl. Grunwaldzki 61 (☎071/328 2287).

### The City

Wrocław's centre is delineated by the River Odra to the north and the bow-shaped ul. Podwale – the latter following the former city walls, whose moat, now bordered by a shady park, largely survives. In the town centre is the vast **Rynek** with its magnificent fifteenth-century Town Hall. The west face and south facade are real show stoppers, while the building itself now serves as the **Historical Museum** (Wed–Sun 10/11am–5/6pm; 7zł). In the northwest corner of the Rynek are two curious Baroque houses known as **Jaś i Małgosia** (Hansel and Gretel), linked by a gateway giving access to St Elizabeth's, the finest of Wrocław's churches. Its ninety-metre tower (Mon–Sat 9am–4pm, Sun 1–4pm; 5zł) is the city's most prominent landmark. Southwest of the Rynek lies the former **Jewish quarter**, whose inhabitants fled or were driven from their tenements during the Third Reich. One of the largest synagogues in Poland, the **Synagoga pod Białym Bocianem** (Mon–Fri 10am–4pm; 4zł), lies hidden in a courtyard at ul. Włodkowica 9.

A specially designed rotunda houses Wrocław's best-known sight, the **Panorama of the Battle of Racławice** (Tues–Sun: April–Nov 8am–7.30pm, Dec–March 9am–5pm; shows every 30min; 20zł, including entrance to the National Museum). This painting, 120m long and 15m high, was commissioned in 1894 for the centenary of the Russian army's defeat by Tadeusz Kościuszko's militia near the village of Racławice, between Kraków and Kielce. At the other end of the park is the **National Museum** (Wed–Sun 9/10am–4/6pm; 15zł, Thurs free), in whose medieval sculpture section is the poignant *Tomb of Henryk the Righteous*, with its group of weeping mourners.

North of the Rynek, the university quarter, packed with historic buildings, is bounded by ul. Uniwersytecka and ul. Grodzka. At the centre of things is the huge **Collegium Maximum**, whose **Aula Leopoldina** assembly hall, upstairs at pl. Uniwersytecki 1 (Mon, Tues & Thurs 10.30am–3.30pm, Fri–Sun 11am–5pm; 4zł), is one of the greatest secular interiors of the Baroque age, fusing architecture, painting, sculpture and ornament into one bravura whole. From the Market Hall, the Piaskowy Bridge leads to the island of **Wyspa Piasek** and the fourteenth-century hall church of St Mary of the Sands, majestically vaulted and featuring a wonderfully kitsch animated children's altar. Two elegant little bridges connect Wyspa Piasek with **Ostrów Tumski**, the city's ecclesiastical heart. Ul. Katedralny leads past several Baroque palaces to the vast and gloomy **Cathedral of St John the Baptist**, which was rebuilt after the war: take the lift up the tower (Mon–Sat 10am–6pm; 4zł) for good views of the city.

### Eating and drinking

For budget **meals**, try *Miś*, ul. Kuźnicza 48 (Mon–Sat till 5/6pm), a student-packed canteen, or *Kurna Chata*, ul. Odrzańska 7, for good, cheap Polish fare in a mountain-style atmosphere. *Vega*, Rynek-Ratusz 27a, serves vegetarian options daily till 5/7pm, while *Le Bistrot Parisien*, ul. Nożownicza 1, offers great quiche, salads and wine well into the evening. Decent **drinking** spots near the university include *Pod Kalamburem*, at ul. Kuźnicza 29a, a Viennese-style café with live bands, and *Kalogródek*, next door at no. 29b, with an airy terrace. *Gumowa Róża*, entered from the Św. Wita alley, is a relaxed basement bar with a bohemian edge, while *PracOFFnia Klub*, Więzienna 6, is a bit more stylish. *Spiż* on the Rynek brews its own beer for an older crowd. Of the **clubs**, the choice venue for house music is *Vulevu*, ul. Świdnicka 53 (open Wed–Sat); a more alternative crowd gathers at the seedy *Wagon Klub*, in the basement of a disused train station at pl. Orlat Lwowskich 20a. There's a 24hr **Internet café** just off the Rynek at ul. Kuźnicza 11/13.

## Poznań

Thanks to its position on the Berlin–Warsaw–Moscow rail line, **POZNAŃ** is many visitors' first taste of Poland. Long identified with Polish nationhood, today it's a city of great diversity and one of Poland's economic successes. For seven centuries the grandiose **Stary Rynek**, lined with attractive bars and restaurants, has been the hub of town life. The turreted Town Hall boasts a vivacious eastern facade, its lime-green pilasters framing a frieze of Polish monarchs. Inside is the **Poznań Historical Museum** (Mon, Tues & Fri 10am–4pm, Wed noon–6pm, Sun 10am–3pm; 5.5zł), worth visiting for the stunning Renaissance Great Hall on the first floor, its vault bearing bas-reliefs with scenes of Samson, King David and Hercules. Many a medieval and Renaissance interior lurks behind the Baroque facades of the houses lining the Stary Rynek – the diverting **Museum of Musical Instruments** at no. 45 (Tues–Sat 11am–5pm, Sun 10am–3pm; 5.5zł, free Sat) is a fine example. West of here, at al. Marcinkowskiego 9, the excellent **National Museum** (Tues–Sat 9/10am–4/6pm; 10zł, free Sat) houses one of Poland's premier collections of old master paintings. East of the Stary Rynek, a bridge crosses to the quiet holy island of **Ostrów Tumski**, dominated by the **Cathedral of SS Peter and Paul**. Most of this cathedral, the country's oldest, was restored to its Gothic shape after wartime devastation. Poland's first two monarchs are buried in the crypt.

## Practicalities

The main **train station**, Poznań Główny, is 2km southwest of the historic quarter; tram #5 runs from the western exit beyond platform 7 to the city centre. The **bus station** is five minutes' walk east of the train station, across the bridge. The city **tourist office**, next to the EMPiK store on the corner of Ratajczaka and 27 Grudnia (Mon–Fri 10am–7pm, Sat 10am–5pm; ☎061/851 9645, ⊛www.cim.poznan.pl), hands out free maps and cultural information. There's also a **regional tourist office** at Stary Rynek 59 (Mon–Fri 9am–5pm, May–Sept also Sat 10am–2pm; ☎061/852 6156). Note that **hotel** prices double during trade fairs, which take place throughout the year, July and August excepted. A cheap and decent option is *Mini-Hotelik*, al. Niepodległości 8 (☎061/863 1416; ❷), or the more central *PTTK Dom Turysty* at Rynek 91 (☎061/852 8893) with basic dorms (60zł) and rooms (❸). Poznań's two **hostels** are reasonable but have 10pm curfews; the better located is just west of the train station at ul. Berwińskiego 2/3 (☎061/866 4040; beds 25zł, rooms ❶). In July and August there's also the *Dizzy Daisy* hostel (☎061/386 1853, ⊛www.hostel.pl; reception open 6–10am and 5–10pm; beds in doubles and triples 40–50zł). Central private **rooms** (❷) can be booked at the Biuro Zakwaterowania Przemysław, opposite the train station's west exit at ul. Głogowska 16 (☎061/866 3560, ⊛www.przemyslaw.com.pl; Mon–Fri 8am–6pm, Sat 10am–2pm), and in the Globtour office in the train station (daily until 10pm).

Cheap Polish **food** can be found at the *Apetyt* milk bar, just off the Rynek on Szkolna, or at the slightly pricier but better quality *Tylko u Nas*, ul. Wrocławska 2. *Dramat*, Stary Rynek 41, is a more atmospheric, good-value, restaurant with tasty pancakes. *Cymes*, off the Rynek at ul. Woźna 2/3, is an affordable and excellent Jewish restaurant that shouldn't be missed, while the wildly popular *Pod Pretekstem*, behind the theatre at ul. Św. Marcin 80/82, is recommended for pasta and drinks. The best **café** is *Za Kulisami*, at ul. Wodna 24, a student hangout with book-lined walls. At night you'll find plenty more students at the **bars** on ul. Nowowiejskiego, especially *Pod Minogą* (no. 8), which hosts bands at weekends, and *W Starym Kinie*, next door. Back on the square, *Tapas*, Stary Rynek 60, is a trendy **club**, complete with VIP section, while *Puzon*, Stary Rynek 9, is great for jazz. **Internet** access is available at *Klik*, south of the Rynek on Jaskółca.

# Travel details

## Trains

**Gdańsk** to: Kraków (5 daily; 7–10hr overnight); Poznań (6 daily; 4hr); Toruń (5 daily; 3hr); Warsaw (12 daily; 4hr); Wrocław (3 daily; 6–7hr).

**Kraków** to: Gdańsk (5 daily; 7hr–10hr overnight); Poznań (4 daily; 6–7hr); Toruń (1 daily; 7hr); Warsaw (11 daily; 2hr 30min–5hr); Wieliczka (9 daily; 20min); Wrocław (12 daily; 4hr–4hr 30min); Zakopane (8 daily; 3–4hr).

**Poznań** to: Gdańsk (6 daily; 4hr); Kraków (6 daily; 6–7hr); Toruń (4 daily; 2–3hr); Warsaw (19 daily; 3hr); Wrocław (23 daily; 2hr).

**Toruń** to: Gdańsk (5 daily; 3hr); Kraków (1 daily; 7hr); Poznań (4 daily; 2–3hr); Warsaw (5 daily; 3hr); Wrocław (2 daily; 4hr 30min).

**Warsaw** to: Gdańsk (12 daily; 4hr); Kraków (15 daily; 2hr 30min–5hr); Poznań (19 daily; 3hr); Toruń (5 daily; 3hr); Wrocław (9 daily; 5–6hr); Zakopane (1 daily; overnight).

**Wrocław** to: Gdańsk (3 daily; 6–7hr); Kraków (12 daily; 4hr–4hr 30min); Poznań (23 daily; 2hr); Toruń (2 daily; 4hr 30min); Warsaw (9 daily; 5–6hr).

**Zakopane** to: Kraków (8 daily; 3–4hr).

## Buses

**Kraków** to: Oświęcim/Auschwitz (22 daily; 1hr 30min); Wieliczka (every 5–10 min; 30min); Zakopane (40 daily; 2hr 30min).

# Portugal

# Portugal highlights

* **A night out in Lisbon**
  Great city for clubbing;
  have a night in the Bairro
  Alto or the club *Lux* to
  find out why. See p.806

* **Óbidos** Picturesque
  village with dazzling
  white-washed houses
  enclosed by medieval
  walls. See p.810

* **Queima das Fitas,
  Coimbra** University town
  that celebrates the end
  of the academic year
  big time every May. See
  p.812

* **Port wine lodges, Porto**
  Various lodges offer free
  tastings. See p.816

* **The Douro rail route**
  One of the most beauti-
  ful lines in Europe, along
  the foot of the steep
  Douro river valley. See
  p.818

* **The Algarve beaches**
  The southern region's
  beaches are second to
  none; the Ilha de Tavira
  has some of the best.
  See p.819

△ Óbidos

# Introduction and basics

**Portugal** has always been influenced by the sea and the Portuguese are very conscious of themselves as a seafaring race; mariners like Vasco da Gama led the way in the exploration of Africa and the Americas, and until thirty years ago Portugal remained a colonial power.

Scenically, the most interesting parts of the country are in the north: the **Minho**, green, damp, and often startling in its rural customs; and the sensational gorge and valley of the **Douro**, followed along its course by the railway, off which antiquated branch lines edge into remote **Trás-os-Montes**. For contemporary interest, spend some time in both **Lisbon** and **Porto**, the two major cities. And if it's monuments you're after, the centre of the country – above all, **Coimbra** and **Évora** – retains a faded grandeur. The coast is virtually continuous beach, and apart from the **Algarve** and a few pockets around Lisbon and Porto, resorts remain low-key. Perhaps the loveliest are along the northern **Costa Verde** or, for isolation, the wild beaches of southern **Alentejo**.

## Information & maps

You'll find a **tourist office** (*turismo*) in almost every town. Staff can help you find a room, and often have local maps and leaflets. For **maps** try those published by the Automóvel Clube de Portugal, GeoCenter or the Michelin #437.

## Money and banks

Currency is the **euro** (€). **Banks** open Mon–Fri 8.30am–3pm; in Lisbon and in some of the Algarve resorts banks and exchange offices may open in the evening to change money. **ATMs** are widespread and **credit cards** are widely accepted; commission on travellers' cheques can be high.

## Communications

**Post offices** (*correios*) are normally open Mon–Fri 9am–6pm, Sat 9am–noon. For **poste restante**, look for a counter marked *encomendas*. International **phone calls** can be made direct from any phone booth or post office. Phonecards cost €3, €6 or €9, from post offices, larger newsagents and tobacconists. The operator is on ☎118 (domestic), ☎098 (international). **Internet** cafés are common (€1.50–3/hr).

## Getting around

CP operates the **trains**. Those designated *Regionais* stop at most stations. *Intercidades* are twice as fast and twice as expensive, and must be reserved. The fastest and most luxurious are the *Rápidos* (known as "Alfa"), which speed between Lisbon, Coimbra and Porto. CP sells its own **rail passes** (valid on any train and in first class), but you'd have to do a lot of travelling to make them worthwhile. Inter-Rail and Eurail are valid, though supplements must be paid on *Intercidades* and *Rápidos*. You can check timetables online (☻www .cp.pt) or call the information line on ☎808 20 82 08. The **bus** network is more comprehensive and services are often faster. On a number of major routes (particularly Lisbon–Algarve) express coaches can knock hours

**PORTUGAL** | Basics

---

## Portugal on the net

- ☻**www.min-cultura.pt** Ministry of Culture, with an agenda of major events.
- ☻**www.portugal.org** Tourist office site, with information and advice.
- ☻**www.portugalvirtual.pt** Comprehensive directory listings.
- ☻**www.algarvenet.com** Detailed site dedicated to the Algarve region.

off the standard multiple-stop bus journeys; ⓦwww.rede-expressos.pt has timetables. For 24hr national bus information call ☎707 22 33 44. **Cycling** is popular, though there are few facilities and little respect from motorists. Bikes can be transported on any *Regional* or *Interregional* train as long as there is space for €1.50–2.50 (free if the bike is dismantled).

# Accommodation

In almost any town you should be able to find **accommodation** in a single room for under €25 and a double for under €50. The main budget stand-bys are **pensions**, or *pensões*. A three-star *pensão* is usually about the same price as a one-star **hotel**. Seaside resorts invariably offer cheaper **rooms** (*quartos* or *dormidas*) in private houses. Tourist offices have lists. At the higher end of the scale are **pousadas** (ⓦwww.pousadas.pt). These charge at least four-star hotel prices, and are often converted from old monasteries or castles.

There are over 40 **hostels** (*Pousadas de Juventude*; ⓦwww.pousadasjuventude.pt); most stay open all year and impose a curfew (usually midnight) and all demand a valid HI card. A dormitory bed costs €5–15, depending on season and location; doubles cost €12–45. Portugal has around 200 **campsites**, most small, low-key and attractively located, and all remarkably inexpensive – you'll rarely pay more than €5 a person. You can get a fairly complete map list from any tourist office. Camping rough is banned; beach areas are especially strict about this.

# Food and drink

Portuguese **food** is excellent, cheap and served in quantity. Virtually all cafés will serve you a basic meal for under €8, and for a little more you have the run of most of the country's restaurants. **Snacks** include *tosta mistas* (cheese and ham toasties); *prego/ bifana* (steak/pork sandwich); *bitoque* (steak, chips, fried egg); *rissóis de carne* (deep-fried meat patties); *pastéis de bacalhau* (codfish cakes); and *sandes* (sandwiches). In **restaurant** you can usually have a substantial meal by ordering a *meia dose* (half portion), or *uma dose* between two. Most serve an *ementa turística* (set meal) which can be good value, particularly in *pensões* that serve meals, or in the cheaper workers' cafés. It's always worth going for the **prato do dia** (dish of the day) and, if you're on the coast, plumping for fish and seafood. Typical **dishes** include *sopa de marisco* (shellfish soup); *caldo verde* (finely shredded green kale leaves in broth); and *bacalhau* (dried cod, cooked in a myriad of different ways). *Caldeirada* is a fish stew cooked with onions and tomatoes, *arroz marisco* a similar stew cooked with rice. Also typical is *carne de porco á Alentejana*, in which fried pork is covered with a clam, tomato and onion sauce or stewed with tomato and onions. Regional **cheeses** are well worth sampling, while **puddings** include *arroz doce* (rice pudding), *salada da fruta* (fresh fruit salad) and *nuvens* (egg custard). Cakes – *bolos* or *pastéis* – are often at their best in *pastelarias* (patisseries), though you'll also find them in cafés and some *casas de chá* (tearooms). Among the best are custard tarts (*pastéis de nata*).

Portuguese **wines** (*tinto* for red, *branco* for white) are very inexpensive and of high quality. The fortified **port** (*vinho do Porto*) and **madeira** (*vinho da Madeira*) wines are the best known. The light **vinhos verdes** are produced in the Minho, and are excellent served chilled. **Brandy** is available in two varieties, Macieiera and Constantino, and like local gin is ridiculously cheap; if you're asking at a bar, always specify "gin nacional", "vodka nacional", etc – it'll save you a fortune. The two most common local **beers** (*cervejas*) are Sagres and Super Bock.

# Opening hours and holidays

Shop **opening hours** are generally Mon–Fri 9am–12.30/1pm & 2/2.30–6/6.30pm, Sat 9am–12.30/1pm. Larger supermarkets tend to stay open until 8pm. Museums, churches and monuments open from around 10am to 6pm; almost all, however, close on Mondays and at Easter and smaller ones often for lunch. The main **public holidays** are: Jan 1, Feb carnival, Good Fri, April 25, May 1, Corpus Christi, June 10, June 13 (Lisbon only), Aug 15, Oct 5, Nov 1, Dec 1, Dec 8, Dec 25.

# Emergencies

Lisbon and the larger tourist areas have seen increases in petty crime. **Police**, though relatively easy-going, carry guns and are not to be argued with. For minor health complaints go to a **pharmacy** (*farmácia*),

normally open Mon–Fri 9am–1pm & 3–7pm, Sat 9am–1pm. A sign at each one will show the nearest 24hr pharmacy. Pharmacists are highly trained and can dispense many drugs without a prescription. You can get the address of an English-speaking doctor from a consular office or, with luck, the local police or tourist office.

## Portuguese

| | Portuguese | Pronunciation |
|---|---|---|
| **Yes** | *Sim* | Sing |
| **No** | *Não* | Now |
| **Please** | *Por favor* | Por favor |
| **Thank you** | *Obrigado [said by men]/ Obrigada [said by women]* | Obrigadoo/obrigada |
| **Hello/Good day** | *Olá* | Orla |
| **Goodbye** | *Adeus* | Adayoosh |
| **Excuse me** | *Desculpe* | Deskulp |
| **Where?** | *Onde?* | Ond? |
| **Good** | *Bom* | Bom |
| **Bad** | *Mau* | Maw |
| **Near** | *Perto* | Pertoo |
| **Far** | *Longe* | Lonje |
| **Cheap** | *Barato* | Baratoo |
| **Expensive** | *Caro* | Karoo |
| **Open** | *Aberto* | Abertoo |
| **Closed** | *Fechado* | Feshardoo |
| **Today** | *Hoje* | Oje |
| **Yesterday** | *Ontem* | Ontaygn |
| **Tomorrow** | *Amanhã* | Amanya |
| **How much is....?** | *Quanto é... ?* | Kwantoo eh? |
| **What time is it?** | *Que horas são?* | Kay orash sow? |
| **I don't understand** | *Não compreendo* | Now compre-ndoo |
| **Do you speak English?** | *Fala Inglés?* | Farla inglayz? |
| **One** | *Um/Uma* | Oom/ooma |
| **Two** | *Dois/Duas* | Doysh/dooash |
| **Three** | *Três* | Treysh |
| **Four** | *Quatro* | Kwatroo |
| **Five** | *Cinco* | Sinkoo |
| **Six** | *Seis* | Saysh |
| **Seven** | *Sete* | Set |
| **Eight** | *Oito* | Oytoo |
| **Nine** | *Nove* | Nove |
| **Ten** | *Dez* | Desh |

# Lisbon (Lisboa)

There are few more immediately likeable capitals than **LISBON** (Lisboa). A lively place, it remains in some ways curiously provincial, rooted as much in the 1920s as the 2000s. Wooden trams clank up outrageous gradients, past mosaic pavements, Art Nouveau cafés and the medieval quarter of Alfama, which hangs below the city's São Jorge castle. The city invested heavily for Expo 98 and the 2004 European Football Championships, reclaiming rundown docks and improving communication links, and today it combines an easy-going, human pace and scale, with a vibrant, cosmopolitan identity.

The city has a huge amount of historic interest. The **Great Earthquake** of 1755 (followed by a tidal wave and fire) destroyed most of the grandest buildings, but frantic reconstruction led to many impressive new palaces and churches, as well as the street grid pattern spanning the seven hills of Lisbon. Several buildings from Portugal's golden age survived the quake – notably the Castelo de São Jorge and the Monastery of Jerónimos at **Belém**. Contemporary sights include the **Fundação Calouste Gulbenkian**, with its superb collections of ancient and modern art.

## Arrival and information

From Portela **airport** the #91 Aerobus (7.45am–8pm, every 20min; takes 20min; €3) runs from outside the arrivals hall to Praça dos Restauradores, Rossio, Praça do Comércio and Cais do Sodré; the ticket is then valid for transport on buses and trams for that day. Local buses #44 and #45 (€1.20) run from the road outside the airport to Rossio and the riverside Cais do Sodré. Long-distance **trains** use **Santa Apolónia station**, on the Azul (marked blue on metro maps) line, or fifteen minutes' walk from the waterfront Praça do Comércio, or a short ride on buses #9, #39, #46 or #90 to Rossio. Local trains from Sintra arrive at **Sete Rios station** right by Jardim Zoológico metro stop, while Rossio station undergoes structural work (expected to be completed in 2006), while trains from the Algarve terminate at **Oriente** station (at the end of the red, Vermelha line) to the northeast of the city, near the airport.

Best place for up-to-date information is the **Lisboa Welcome Centre**, on the corner of Praça do Comércio and Rua do Arsenal (daily 9am–8pm; ☎210 312 700, ⍟www.visitlisboa.com). For information on the rest of the country, visit the main **tourist office** on the western side of Praça dos Restauradores in the Palácio da Foz (daily 9am–8pm; ☎213 463 314, ⍟www.portugalinsite.pt); there's also a small tourist office at the airport (daily 6am–midnight; ☎218 450 660). The **Lisboa Card** (€13.50/23/28 for 1/2/3 days), available from any tourist office, gives unlimited travel, entry to 26 museums plus discounts. Good Lisbon **maps** include the Michelin *Lisboa Planta Roteiro*, which has A–Z street listings.

Most places of interest are within walking distance, but for the outlying areas you'll need to use the fast **metro** (⍟www.metrolisboa.pt); tickets cost €0.70/1

---

### Tram #28

The picture-book **tram #28** is one of Lisbon's greatest and most popular rides. With a travel pass, you can hop on and off where you like. The central section of its route runs from Rua da Conceição in the Baixa, past the Sé and up Rua Augusto Rosa, before rattling through some of Lisbon's steepest and narrowest streets – so close to the shopfronts you could almost take a can of sardines off the shelves. The route is of less interest after you reach Rua de Voz do Operário, from where it's a short walk down to the Feira da Ladra market; or get off at the next stop, in Largo da Graça, for the superb city views.

each (for central/all zones) or €6.15/9.25 for ten. The **trams and buses** (⊛www
.cp.pt) are the most enjoyable way of getting around – tickets (€1.20/1.40, valid
on both) can be used for two journeys when purchased in advance from kiosks, or
cost €1.10 for one journey when bought on board. Much better value though, are
the one-day **travel passes**, available from the tourist office. You need a *Sete Colinas
Card* (Seven Hills card; €0.50) which you then load with a day-pass (*Bilhete um dia;*
€3) that allows unlimited travel on buses, trams, metro and *elevadores* until midnight.
A short hop in a **taxi** shouldn't cost more than €10, but they can be hard to find
at night – if you're leaving a bar or club book one by phone from Rádio Táxis
de Lisboa (☎218 119 000) or Teletáxis (☎218 111 100). **Ferries** cross the River
Tagus (Rio Tejo); most are operated by Transtejo and depart from Belém, Cais do
Sodré and Praça do Comércio. The price – €0.65–1.80 each way – depends on
the route.

## Accommodation

Lisbon has scores of small, cheap **pensions**, most of which are around Rua das
Portas de Santo Antão and Rua da Glória. Most of those listed below are one- or
two-star; addresses, written as 53-3°, for example, show the street number followed by the floor. The Bairro Alto is the most atmospheric neighbourhood,
though rooms can be hard to find and noisy. At Easter and in midsummer, availability is stretched: many single rooms are "converted" to doubles and prices may
start as high as €25. However, during the rest of the year you should have little
difficulty finding a place, and for maybe a third less than the midsummer prices.
For more expensive **hotels**, use the commission-free 24-hour reservation service
(☎213 141 562) at the Praça dos Restauradores tourist office or the airport.

### Hostels
All the following are open 24-hour (reception
8am–midnight).
**Casa de Juventude Lisboa Parque das Nações**
Rua da Moscavide 47–101, Parque das Nações
☎218 920 890. Stuck out in no man's land a good
40min from the centre, but still bustling. Metro to
Oriente. Dorms €13, rooms ❸
**Pousada de Juventude da Catalazete** Estrada
Marginal, Oeiras ☎214 430 638, ⊛www.pousa-
dasjuventude.pt. Overlooking the beach, 15km
outside the city. Take any train from Cais do Sodré
and follow signs from Oeiras station. It's small, so
phone before setting out. Reception open 6–11pm.
Dorms €11, rooms ❷
**Pousada de Juventude de Lisboa** Rua
Andrade Corvo 46 ☎213 532 696, ⊛www
.pousadasjuventude.pt. Lisbon's newly renovated
main hostel, with good facilities. Book in
advance. One block south of Picoas metro stop,
or take buses #1, #21 or #36 from Restauradores or Rossio. Dorms €16, rooms ❸

### Pensions and hotels
**Residencial Camões** Trav. do Poço da Cidade
38-1°, Bairro Alto ☎213 467 510. Brilliant location, though invest in some earplugs for streetside
rooms at weekends. Breakfast included in high
season, English spoken. ❹

**Pensão Coimbra e Madrid** Praça da Figueira
3-3°, Baixa ☎213 424 808. Right on the main
square with superb views, though the rooms are
noisy. Decent proprietors, shabby though clean
furnishings. ❷
**Pensão Ninho das Águias** Costa do Castelo 74,
Alfama ☎218 854 070. Bright, light rooms, some
with private bathrooms, with a lovely garden terrace overlooking the city. ❹
**Pensão Portuense** Rua das Portas de Santo
Antão 151, Baixa ☎213 464 197. One of the city's
best-value establishments, with lots of spotless
rooms and a tasty breakfast. ❹
**Pensão Prata** Rua da Prata 71-3°, Baixa ☎213
468 908. Small rooms, some with showers, up
three extremely steep flights of stairs in a welcoming, family-run apartment. ❷
**Pensão São João de Praça** Rua de São
João de Praça 97-2°, Alfama ☎218 862 591
€218862591@sapo.pt. Clean, quiet and friendly
place in a lovely old town house just below
the cathedral. Front rooms have wrought-iron
balconies. ❹

### Campsites
**Camping Obitur-Guincho** Lugar da Areia,
Guincho ☎214 870 450, ⊛www.orbitur.pt. A well-
located site some way out of the city in surfer's
paradise Guincho, with supermarket, sports facili-

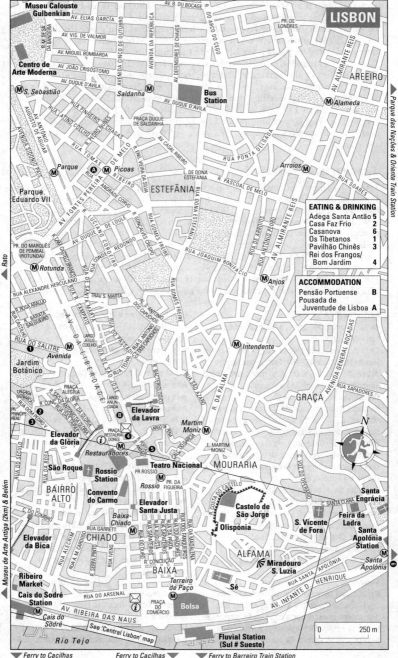

LISBON

**EATING & DRINKING**

| | |
|---|---|
| Adega Santa Antão | 5 |
| Casa Faz Frio | 2 |
| Casanova | 6 |
| Os Tibetanos | 1 |
| Pavilhão Chinês | 3 |
| Rei dos Frangos/ Bom Jardim | 4 |

**ACCOMMODATION**

| | |
|---|---|
| Pensão Portuense | B |
| Pousada de Juventude de Lisboa | A |

ties and cabins to rent. Train from Cais do Sodré to Cascais, then bus to Guincho.

**Parque Municipal de Campismo** Parque Florestal Monsanto ☏217 623 100. Well-equipped main city campsite, complete with pool and shops, in a large park 6km west of the centre. The entrance is on Estrada da Circunvalação on the park's west side. Bus #43 from Praça da Figueira.

# The City

The heart of the capital is the lower town – the **Baixa** – Europe's first great example of Neoclassical design and urban planning. It's an imposing quarter of rod-straight streets, some streaming with traffic but most pedestrianized with mosaic cobbles where buskers and pavement artists ply their trade. Between the Baixa and the Bairro Alto, halfway up the hill, lies an area known as the **Chiado**, which suffered much damage in a fire in 1988 but has been elegantly rebuilt by Portugal's premier architect Álvaro Siza Viera. It remains the city's most affluent quarter, centred on **Rua Garrett** and its fashionable shops and elegant cafés. **Rossio** square is very much a focus for the city, with a couple of great cafés, though its main concession to grandeur is the **Teatro Nacional**, built along the north side in the 1840s. At the waterfront end of the Baixa lies the city's other main square, the beautiful arcaded **Praça do Comércio**.

A couple of blocks east stands the **Sé** or Cathedral (daily 10am–5/6.30pm; free). Founded in 1147 to commemorate the city's reconquest from the Moors, it occupies the site of the principal mosque of Moorish Lishbuna. Like so many of the country's cathedrals, it is Romanesque and extraordinarily restrained in both size and decoration. You'll need to pay to visit the thirteenth-century cloisters (closed Sun; €1) and the treasury museum (closed Sun; €2.50), including the relics of St Vincent. From the Sé, Rua Augusto Rosa and its continuation wind up towards the castle, past the **Miradouro de Santa Luzia**, which offers spectacular views over the Tejo. The **Castelo de São Jorge** (daily 9am–dusk; €3) contains the shell of the Moorish palace that once stood here; part of it hosts **Olispónia**, a multimedia show that makes an excellent introduction to the city's history. The castle itself is an enjoyable place to spend a couple of hours, wandering amid the ramparts and towers.

The **Alfama** quarter, tumbling from the walls of the Castelo to the banks of the River Tejo, is the oldest part of Lisbon. In Arab times it was the city's grandest district, but with subsequent earthquakes the new Christian nobility moved out, leaving it to the fishing community. Despite some commercialization, the quarter still retains a largely traditional life. The **Feira da Ladra**, Lisbon's rambling flea market, fills the Campo de Santa Clara, at the edge of Alfama, every Tuesday and Saturday. Also take a look inside **Santa Engrácia** (Tues–Sun 10am–5/6pm; €2.50), the loftiest and most tortuously built church in the city – begun in 1682, its vast dome was finally completed in 1966. Through the tiled cloisters of nearby **São Vicente de Fora** you can visit the old monastic refectory, since 1855 the pantheon of the Bragança dynasty (Tues–Sun 10am–5.30pm; €3). Here, in more or less complete sequence, are the bodies of all Portuguese kings from João IV, who restored the monarchy in 1640, to Manuel II, who lost it and died in exile in England in 1932.

High above and to the west of the Baixa is **Bairro Alto**, the focus of the city's nightlife. The district can be reached by one of two funicular-like trams – the **Elevador da Glória** from the Praça dos Restauradores or the **Elevador da Bica** from Rua de São Paulo (both €1.20 one-way). The other means of access, the great **Elevador Santa Justa**, built by Eiffel disciple Raul Mésnier de Ponsard, is being renovated, but you can still enjoy the superb views from the café at the top. Hanging almost directly above the exit of Mésnier's funicular are the ruined Gothic arches of the **Convento do Carmo** (Mon–Sat 10am–5/6pm; €2.50). Once the largest church in the city, it was half-destroyed by the 1755 earthquake and is perhaps even more beautiful as a result; its archeological museum contains eclectic treasures from monasteries that were dissolved after the 1834 Liberal revolution.

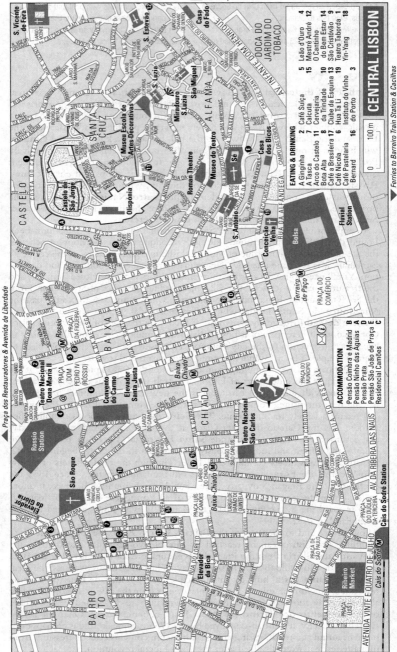

▲ *Santa Apolónia Station*

**CENTRAL LISBON**

0   100 m

▼ *Ferries to Barreiro Train Station & Cacilhas*

**EATING & DRINKING**

| | | | |
|---|---|---|---|
| A Ginginha | 2 | Café Suíça | 4 |
| A Tasca | 7 | Calcuta | 12 |
| Arco do Castelo | 11 | Cervejaria | |
| Bota Alta | 8 | da Trindade | 10 |
| Café a Brasileira | 17 | Clube da Esquina | 13 |
| Café Nicola | 6 | Hua Ta Li | 9 |
| Café Pastelaria | | Instituto do Vinho | |
| Bernard | 16 | do Porto | 3 |

| | |
|---|---|
| Leão d'Ouro | 5 |
| Mestré André | 15 |
| O Cantinho | |
| do Bem Estar | 14 |
| São Cristóvão | 1 |
| Teatro Taborda | 19 |
| Yin-Yang | 18 |

**ACCOMMODATION**

| | |
|---|---|
| Pensão Coimbra e Madrid | B |
| Pensão Ninho das Águias | A |
| Pensão Prata | D |
| Pensão São João de Praça | E |
| Residencial Camões | C |

Praça dos Restauradores & Avenida da Liberdade

S. Vicente de Fora

S. Estevão

Casa do Fado

S. Miguel

S. Luzia

Miradouro S. Luzia

ALFAMA

Museu Escola de Artes-Decorativas

Castelo de São Jorge

Olisponia

SANTA CRUZ

CASTELO

Casa dos Bicos

Museo do Teatro

Roman Theatre

Sé

S. António

Conceição Velha

Bolsa

Fluvial Station

DOCA DO JARDIM DO TOBACO

AV. INFANTE DOM HENRIQUE

Terreiro de Paço

PRAÇA DO COMÉRCIO

RUA DA MADALENA

RUA DOS FANQUEIROS

RUA DA PRATA

RUA DOS CORREEIROS

RUA AUGUSTA

RUA DOS DOURADORES

RUA DOS SAPATEIROS

RUA AUREA

RUA NOVA DO ALMADA

RUA DO CRUCIFIXO

PRAÇA DO MUNICÍPIO

RUA DO ARSENAL

RUA DO COMÉRCIO

RUA DA ALFÂNDEGA

CAMPO DAS CEBOLAS

BAIXA

Praça Dom Pedro IV (Rossio)

Rossio

Teatro Nacional Dona Maria II

PRAÇA DA FIGUEIRA

Rossio Station

Convento do Carmo

Elevador Santa Justa

Baixa-Chiado

CHIADO

Teatro Nacional São Carlos

Baixa-Chiado

São Roque

Elevador da Glória

BAIRRO ALTO

PRAÇA LUÍS DE CAMÕES

Cais do Sodré Station

Ribeiro Market

Elevador da Bica

Cais do Sodré

AVENIDA VINTE E QUATRO DE JULHO

AV. DA RIBEIRA DAS NAUS

RUA DA MISERICÓRDIA

RUA DO SÉCULO

N

## Parque Eduardo VII and the Gulbenkian

North of Praça dos Restauradores are the city's principal gardens, the **Parque Eduardo VII** (metro Marquês de Pombal or Parque). Though there are some pleasant cafés here, the big attraction is the **Estufa Fria** (daily 9am–4.30/5.30pm; €2), a huge and wonderful glasshouse filled with tropical plants, flamingo pools, and endless varieties of palms and cacti. The **Fundação Calouste Gulbenkian** is ten minutes' walk north of the Parque Eduardo VII – or take bus #31 or #46 from Restauradores or the metro to São Sebastião or Praça de Espanha. The Fundação helps finance various aspects of Portugal's cultural life – including an orchestra, three concert halls and two galleries for temporary exhibitions on the site. Established by the Armenian oil magnate Calouste Gulbenkian, the centre's **Museu Calouste Gulbenkian** (Tues–Sun 10am–6pm; €3, joint ticket with Centro de Arte Moderna €5, free Sun am) is the great museum of Portugal, divided into two distinct parts – the first devoted to Egyptian, Greco-Roman, Islamic and Oriental arts, the second to European, including paintings from all the major schools. There's also a stunning room full of Art Nouveau jewellery by René Lalique. Across the gardens, the separate **Centro de Arte Moderna** (same hours; €3, joint ticket with Museu Calouste Gulbenkian €5) has all the big names from the twentieth-century Portuguese scene and some top British artists such as Anthony Gormley.

## Museu Nacional de Arte Antiga and Belém

Lisbon's other top museum is the national art collection, the **Museu Nacional de Arte Antiga** (Tues 2–6pm, Wed–Sun 10am–6pm; €3), situated near the riverfront to the west of the city at Rua das Janelas Verdes 95 (bus #40 or #60 from Praça do Comércio). Its core is formed by fifteenth- and sixteenth-century Portuguese works, the acknowledged masterpiece being Nuno Gonçalves' *St Vincent Altarpiece*, a brilliantly marshalled canvas depicting Lisbon's patron receiving homage from all ranks of its citizens.

Further west lies the suburb of **Belém** from where, in 1497, Vasco da Gama set sail for India. Partly funded by a levy on the fruits of da Gama's discovery – a five-percent tax on all spices other than pepper, cinnamon and cloves, whose import had become the sole preserve of the Crown – the **Monastery of Jerónimos** here (daily 10am–5/6.30pm, free; cloisters same hours €4.50; tram #15 from Praça do Comércio or bus #14 from Praça da Figuera) was begun in 1502 and is the most ambitious achievement of Manueline architecture. The main entrance to the church is a shrine-like hierarchy of figures centred around Henry the Navigator. Vaulted throughout and fantastically embellished, the cloister is one of the most original and beautiful pieces of architecture in the country, holding Gothic forms and Renaissance ornamentation in an exuberant balance. The turreted **Torre de Belém** (Tues–Sun 10am–5/6.30pm; €3), on the edge of the river around 500m from the monastery, has become the tourist board's symbol for Lisbon, built over the last five years of Dom Manuel's reign (up to 1520) to guard the entrance to Lisbon's port. Back towards the monastery are a number of museums, of which the best is the **Museu do Design** (daily 11am–7pm; €3.50) in the pink marble Centro Cultural de Belém, featuring design classics from the twentieth century. Opposite is the vast concrete **Monument to the Discoveries** (Tues–Sun 9am–5/6.30pm; €2; closed for renovation at time of writing) erected in 1960 to commemorate the 500th anniversary of the death of Henry the Navigator; inside, a small exhibition space has changing displays on the city's history. The lift takes you to the top for spectacular views.

## Parque das Nações and the Oceanarium

Built on reclaimed docklands for Expo '98, the **Parque das Nações** (Park of Nations), 5km east of the centre, has become a popular entertainment park, complete with concert venues, theatres and Lisbon's main exhibition centre. All of this is laid out in a traffic-free riverside zone punctuated by water features, cafés and some dazzling modern architecture. The site's main attraction is the **Oceanário de Lisboa** (daily 10am–7pm; €10), Europe's second largest oceanarium, an awe-inspiring collection of fish and sea mammals based around a central tank the size of four Olympic swimming pools. To reach the park, take the metro to Oriente station. You can walk around the park, or use the toy train that circles every twenty minutes or so (€2.50).

## Eating, drinking and nightlife

Lisbon has some great **cafés and restaurants** serving large portions of food at sensible prices. Seafood is widely available – there's an entire central street, Rua das Portas de Santo Antão, which specializes in it. Lisbon also has a rich vein of inexpensive foreign restaurants featuring food from the former colonies (including Angola, Goa and Macau). Many restaurants are **closed on Sundays**, while on Saturday nights you may need to book for the more popular places. The best **food market** is Mercado da Ribeira, Avda 24 de Julho, Cais do Sodré (Mon–Sat 5am–2pm).

The densest concentration of designer bars and clubs is in **Bairro Alto** – Lisbon's traditional nightlife centre. Late-night (though pricier) action can also be found out in the **Docas** (Docklands) district, just east of the 25 de Abril bridge (train to Alcântara Mar from Cais do Sodré or tram #15 or #18). Here, converted warehouses at the **Doca de Santo Amaro** host waterfront bars and cafés, while a little closer to the city centre the **Doca de Alcântara** has emerged as the hangout for Lisbon's chic. Clubs don't really get going until around 2am and tend to stay open till 6am. Admission fees are usually about €10 (usually including one or two drinks), although some clubs leave the cover charge to the doorman's discretion – anything from €5–10. To sample local **fado**, a mournful, romantic singing style somewhere between the blues and flamenco, try clubs in the Bairro Alto or Alfama and expect to pay over €15. If you check out the posters around Restauradores there's a good chance of catching **African music**. What's-on **listings** are in the free *Agenda Cultural*, issued monthly, or in the Friday supplements of the *Independente* or *Diario de Noticias* newspapers.

### Cafés

**Antiga Confeitaria de Belém** Rua de Belém 90, Belém. Historic tiled café famous for its delicious custard tarts or *pastéis de nata*.

**Café a Brasileira** Rua Garrett 120, Chiado. The most famous of Rua Garrett's old-style coffee houses. Open until 2am.

**Café Nicola** Praça Dom Pedro IV 26, Baixa. On the west side of Rossio, this grand old place is a good stop for breakfast. Closed Sat pm & all Sun.

**Café Pastelaria Bernard** Rua Garrett 104, Chiado. Superb cakes and an outdoor terrace.

**Café Suíça** Praça Dom Pedro IV 96. Famous for cakes and pastries, with outdoor seats facing Lisbon's two main squares.

### Restaurants

**Adega Santo Antão** Rua das Portas de Santo Antão 42, Baixa. Good value *adega* with local character, offering great grilled meat and fish. Closed Mon.

**Arco do Castelo** Rua do Chão da Feira 25. Cheerful place by the castle entrance with tempting Goan cooking. Closed Sun.

**Bota Alta** Trav. da Queimada 37, Bairro Alto. Old tavern restaurant that pulls in the punters for its large portions of traditional Portuguese food. Closed Sat lunch & Sun.

**Calcuta** Rua do Norte 17, Bairro Alto. Indian restaurant with chicken, seafood and lamb curries, tandooris, and good vegetarian options. Closed Sun.

**Casa Faz Frio** Rua Dom Pedro V 96, Bairro Alto. Beautiful, very traditional restaurant, with tiny cubicles. Around €12 for a full meal and wine.

**Casanova** Armazém B, Cais da Pedra à Bica do Sapato, Santa Apolónia. Fashionable riverside restaurant serving pizza and pasta with great views from its terrace. You can't book, so turn up early. Closed all Mon & Tues lunch.

**Cervejaria da Trindade** Rua Nova da Trindade 20, Bairro Alto. Wonderful, vaulted beer-hall restaurant, the oldest in the city, with a tiny patio garden. Expensive seafood, but other more moderate dishes.

**Floresta Belém** Praça Afonso de Albuquerque 1, Belém. One of the least expensive of the restaurants near the monastery, with outdoor tables. Closed Sat.

**Hua Ta Li** Rua dos Bacalhoeiros 119, Baixa. Very good, affordable Chinese/Macau restaurant near the Sé – seafood scores highly. Popular for Sunday lunch.

**Leão d'Ouro** Rua 1° de Dezembro 65 ☏213 469 195. Lushly tiled restaurant that offers plentiful servings of grilled meat and fish. Popular, so booking advised.

**Mestré André** Calçadinha de Santo Estêvão 4–6, Alfama. A fine neighbourhood tavern, with good grills (*churrasco*). Outdoor seating in summer. Closed Sun.

**O Cantinho do Bem Estar** Rua do Norte 46, Bairro Alto. Inexpensive Alentejan restaurant that's friendly, bustling and inexpensive.

**Os Tibetanos** Rua da Salitre 117, Rato. Fine vegetarian restaurant run by Buddhists serving organic food. Closed Sat & Sun.

**Rei dos Frangos/Bom Jardim** Trav. de Santo Antão 11–18, Baixa. Excellent for spit-roast chicken at around €10.

**São Cristóvão** Rua de São Cristóvão 28, Alfama ☏218 885 578. Tiny all-day Cape Verdean restaurant which crams in tables, a TV, and live music Fri–Sun eve. Booking advised.

**Teatro Taborda** Costa do Castelo 75, Alfama. Fashionable theatre café/restaurant with fine views from the terrace, serving fresh vegetarian dishes and Greek salads. Closed Mon.

**Yin-Yang** Rua dos Correeiros 14, Baixa. When all the animal protein gets too much, find tofu and fresh juice here. Closes 5pm Mon & Tues.

### Bars

**A Ginginha** Largo de São Domingos, Baixa. Small stand-up bar specializing in *ginginha*, a lethal cherry brandy worth sampling at least once.

**A Tasca** Trav. da Queimada 13–15, Bairro Alto. Cheerful and welcoming tequila bar.

**Clube da Esquina** Rua da Barroca 30, Bairro Alto. Fashionable little corner bar decorated with old transistors – great for people watching.

**Instituto do Vinho do Porto** Rua de São Pedro de Alcântara 45, Bairro Alto. Over 200 types and vintages of port, from €1 a glass. Closed Sun.

**Pavilhão Chinês** Rua Dom Pedro V 89, Bairro Alto. Overly decorated bar, completely lined with cabinets of bizarre artefacts. Daily till 2am. Very expensive.

### Clubs

**Doca de Santo** Doca de Santo Amaro, Alcântara. Large palm-fringed bar, restaurant and club, overlooking the 25 de Abril bridge.

**Frágil** Rua da Atalaia 126, Bairro Alto. Full of poseurs but great fun, in a fine old building. Closed Sun.

**Incognito** Rua dos Poiais de Sao Bento 37. Tiny house/electropop bar whose even tinier dance floor gets rammed with bright young things well into the night.

**Kapital** Avda. 24 de Julho 68, opposite Santos station. Sweaty, fashionable dance venue where you can have a laugh until 6am.

**Kremlin** Escadinhas da Praia 5, Santos. One of the city's most snobbish nightspots, packed with flash young Lisboetas. Techno still rules. Closed Sun & Mon.

**Lux** Doca do Jardim do Tobaco 1100, opposite Santa Apolónia station. The city's best and most fashionable club, boasting top DJs and occasional live bands. Closed Mon.

**Salsa Latina** Gare Marítima de Alcântara, Doca de Santo Amaro. A bar/restaurant and club in a fantastic 1940s cruise-ship terminal, offering salsa (Tues–Sat) and live music at weekends. Closed Sun.

**Trumps** Rua da Imprensa Nacional 104b, Rato. The biggest gay disco in Lisbon with a reasonably relaxed door policy. Closed Mon.

### Fado and live music

**Adega do Ribatejo** Rua do Diário de Notícias 23, Bairro Alto. Popular *fado* venue with a lower-than-usual minimum charge. Singers include a couple of professionals, the manager and even the cooks. Closed Sun.

**Atlantic Pavilion** Parque das Nações. Portugal's largest indoor venue hosting big-name stars.

**B.leza** Largo do Conde Barão 50, Santos. Live African music most nights in a sixteenth-century building, with space to dance and Cape Verdean food. Closed Sun.

**Chafarica** Calçada de São Vicente 79, Alfama. Tiny, long-established Brazilian bar with live music every night. Best after midnight, especially after a few *caipirinhas*.

**Hot Clube de Portugal** Praça da Alegria 39, off Avda. da Liberdade. Tiny basement jazz club, which hosts local and visiting artists. Closed Mon.

**Paradise Garage** Rua João de Oliveira Miguens 38, Alcântara. Big on the club scene, also hosts regular gigs. It's on a tiny side road off Rua da Cruz à Alcântara. Closed Sun–Wed.

**O Senhor Vinho** Rua do Meio a Lapa 18, Lapa. Famous club in the diplomatic quarter west of the centre, sporting some of the best *fado* singers in Portugal. Closed Sun.

**A Severa** Rua das Gáveas 51–61, Bairro Alto. A city institution featuring big *fado* names at big prices. Closed Thurs.

# Listings

**Embassies** Australia, Avda. da Liberdade 198–2°
℡213 101 500; Canada, Avda. da Liberdade
196–200 ℡213 164 600; Ireland, Rua da Imp-
rensa à Estrela 1–4° ℡213 929 440; UK, Rua de
São Bernardo 33 ℡213 924 000; US, Avda. das
Forças Armadas ℡217 273 300.
**Exchange** Main bank branches in the Baixa.
Exchange office at the airport (24hr) and at Santa
Apolónia station (daily 8.30am–3pm).

**Hospital** British Hospital, Rua Saraiva de Carvalho
46 ℡213 955 067.
**Internet** PT Comunicaçoes, Praça Dom Pedro iV
68, Baixa; Web C@fe, Rua do Diário de Notícias
126, Bairro Alto.
**Laundry** Lava Neve, Rua de Alegría 37, Bairro Alto
(closed Sat pm & all Sun).
**Post office** Praça dos Restauradores 58. Also has
email point.

# Day-trips from Lisbon

Half an hour south of Lisbon, dunes stretch along the **Costa da Caparica**, which
the quirks of the River Tejo's currents have largely spared from the pollution that
plagues the city. Travelling north instead you'll reach the lush wooded heights and
royal palaces of **Sintra** and the monastery of **Mafra**, one of the most extraordinary
buildings in the country. These places can all be seen on a day-trip from Lisbon,
but to do justice to Sintra you'll need to stay overnight.

## Caparica

A short journey south of the capital, **CAPARICA** is a thoroughly Portuguese
resort, popular with surfers and crammed with restaurants and beach cafés, yet
solitude is easy enough to find, thanks to the mini-railway (*transpraia*) that runs
along the 8km of dunes in summer. The most enjoyable way to get to Caparica
is to take a **ferry** from the Fluvial station by Praça do Comércio, or from Cais
do Sodré, to Cacilhas, and then pick up the connecting bus. In summer, **buses**
stop at a bus park by the beach. At other times, get off at the first stop in town,
just before Praça da Liberdade, the main square, around which there's a **tourist
office** (Mon–Fri 9am–1pm & 2–5.30pm, Sat 9am–1pm; ℡212 900 071), market,
cinema and bank. There are dozens of good, relaxed, cheap **fish and seafood**
places, as well as beach bars, along the main Rua dos Pescadores, which leads from
the square to the beach; the best place for seafood on the front is *O Barbas* (closed
Tues evening).

## Sintra

**SINTRA**'s cool, hilltop woodland once attracted Moorish lords and the kings of
Portugal from Lisbon during the hot summer months, and the place remains one
of Portugal's most spectacular sights. The layout – an amalgamation of three villages
– can be confusing, but the extraordinary **Palácio Nacional** (10am–5.30pm, closed
Wed; €4, free Sun 10am–2pm), about fifteen minutes' walk from the train station,
is an obvious landmark. The palace was probably in existence under the Moors, but
takes its present form from the rebuilding commissioned by Dom João I and his
successor, Dom Manuel, in the fourteenth and fifteenth centuries. Its style is a fusion
of Gothic and the latter king's Manueline additions. The chapel and its adjoining
chamber – its floor worn by the incessant pacing of the half-mad Afonso VI who
was confined here for six years by his brother Pedro I – are well worth seeing.

Two of Sintra's best sights can be reached on bus #434 – the €3.70 ticket allows
you to get on and off as much as you like. Starting at the train station, the bus stops
at the ruined ramparts of the **Moorish Castle** (daily 10am–7pm; €3.50), from
where the views over the town and surrounding countryside are extraordinary.
Further on, the bus stops at the lower entrance to the immense **Pena Park**, at
the top end of which rears the fabulous **Palácio de Pena** (Tues–Sun 10am–6pm;
€6, gardens only €3.50), a wild nineteenth-century fantasy of domes, towers and

a drawbridge that doesn't draw. The interior has been preserved exactly as left by the royal family on their flight from Portugal in 1910.

Back in town, and walkable from the centre, is another must-see site, the **Quinta da Regaleira** (daily 10am–5.30/8pm; €5, or €10 for guided visits), one of Sintra's most elaborate private estates, five minutes' walk west out of the Palácio Nacional on the Seteais–Monserrate road. The palace and its fantastic gardens were built at the beginning of the last century by a theatrical set designer for one of the richest industrialists in Portugal. The highlight is the **Initiation Well**, inspired by the initiation practices of the Knight Templars and Freemasons. Entering via an Indiana Jones-style revolving stone door, you can walk down a moss-covered spiral stairway to the foot of the well and to a tunnel, which eventually resurfaces at the edge of a lake. Beyond Quinta da Regaleira, the road leads past a series of beautiful private estates to **Monserrate** – about an hour's walk – whose vast **gardens** (daily 9am–5/7pm; €3.50), filled with endless varieties of exotic trees and subtropical shrubs and plants, extend as far as the eye can see.

**Trains** run regularly to Sintra from Lisbon's Sete Rios station (45min; €1.40 one-way). There's a **tourist office** at the station or try the extremely helpful one (daily 9am–7/8pm; ☎219 231 157) just off the central Praça da República, which books cheap **private rooms** (❷). Finding **accommodation** in summer can be a problem, though if you arrive early you should be all right. The best-value pension is probably *Adelaide*, Rua Guilherme Gomes Fernandes 11 (☎219 230 873; ❸), midway between the train station and Sintra village. *Pielas* (☎219 241 691; ❸), Rua João de Deus 70–72, near the station, offers superb rooms above a café, but phone ahead first as it's due to move to a new nearby location. A little further out, in São Pedro, *Residencial Sintra*, Travessa dos Alvares (☎219 230 738; ❼), is a fantastic place with a rambling garden, swimming pool and giant rooms which can easily accommodate extra beds. The **hostel** (☎219 241 210; €12; closed noon–5pm) is at Santa Eufemia in the hills above Sintra, 5km from town. It's possible to get within 2km of the hostel on bus #433 (until 8pm) to São Pedro from outside the train station, after that you'll have to take a taxi. **Restaurants** are generally poor value, relying heavily on day-trippers. Try *Casa da Avo*, Rua Visconde de Monserrate 46 (closed Thurs), or the grilled fish at *Adega de Caves*, Rua de Pendora 8, in the main square.

## Mafra

Connected by regular buses from Sintra train station and from outside Campo Grande metro stop in Lisbon, **MAFRA** is dominated by one building: the vast, pink marble **Palace-Convent** (daily except Tues 10am–4.30pm; €3), built in emulation of Madrid's El Escorial in 1717 by João V, the wealthiest and most extravagant of all Portuguese monarchs. The convent was initially intended for just thirteen Franciscan friars, but as more gold poured in from Brazil, João expanded it into the world's largest basilica, with two royal wings and monastic quarters for three hundred monks and 150 novices. The sheer magnitude of the building is what stands out: there are 5200 doorways, 2500 windows, and two bell towers each containing over fifty bells. The highlight is the magnificent Rococo library, rivalling that of Coimbra in both design and grandeur. The basilica is no less imposing, with the multicoloured marble designs of its floor mirrored in the ceiling decoration.

# Central Portugal

The **Estremadura** region has played a crucial role in each phase of the nation's history – and the monuments are here to prove it. A comparatively small area of fertile rolling hills, it boasts an extraordinary concentration of vivid architecture and engaging towns. **Alcobaça**, **Batalha**, **Óbidos** and **Tomar** – home to the most exciting buildings in Portugal – all lie within ninety minutes' bus ride of one another, as does the pilgrimage centre of **Fátima**. The otherwise rather dull town of **LEIRIA** makes a handy centre for excursions in this area, with buses to the main sights. The **tourist office** (daily 10am–1pm & 2/3–6/7pm; ☎244 848 770) and **bus station** are on opposite sides of a park overlooking the river in the modern city centre. The **train station** is about 4km out of town, with a connecting bus service. For accommodation, check the **pensions**, such as the functional but friendly *Pensão Dom Dinis*, Trav. de Tomar 2 (☎244 815 342; ❸ including breakfast),

North of Estremadura, life on the fertile plain of the **Beira Litoral** has been conditioned over the centuries by the twin threats of floodwaters from Portugal's highest mountains and silting by the restless Atlantic. The highlight here is **Coimbra**, an ancient university town stacked high on the right bank of the Mondego.

## Óbidos

Linked to Lisbon by bus and train, **ÓBIDOS** is a small town of whitewashed houses draped in bougainvillea and encircled by lofty medieval walls. "The Wedding Town" was the traditional bridal gift of the kings of Portugal to their queens, a custom begun in 1282 by Dom Dinis. The town – a couple of hours from Lisbon by train – can hardly have changed in appearance since then: its cobbled streets and steep staircases wind up to the ramparts, from where you can gaze across a fable-like countryside of windmills and vineyards. The parish church, **Igreja de Santa Maria**, in the central *praça*, was chosen for the wedding of the ten-year-old child-king Afonso V and his eight-year-old cousin, Isabel, in 1444. The interior, lined with seventeenth-century blue *azulejos*, contains a retable in a side chapel to the right painted by Josefa de Óbidos, one of the finest Portuguese painters and one of the few women artists afforded any reputation by art historians. One corner of the triangular fortifications is occupied by a massively towered **castle** built by Dom Dinis and now converted into an expensive *pousada*. Other **hotels** in Óbidos also tend to be expensive. Your cheapest option is to consult the list of **private rooms** posted in the **tourist office**, in the main bus station, just south of the town walls (daily 9.30am–6/7pm; ☎262 959 231); there are comfortable rooms at Rua Direita 83 (☎262 959 328; ❸). *Hospedaria Louro*, five minutes' walk south of the coach park, has smart rooms, superb breakfasts, a lovely garden and a pool (☎262 955 100; ❺). One of the better budget places to **eat** is the *Café 1º de Dezembro*, next to the church of São Pedro.

## Alcobaça

From the twelfth century until the middle of the nineteenth, the Cistercian **Abbey of Alcobaça** (daily 9am–5/7pm; €4.50) was one of the greatest in the Christian world. Owning vast tracts of farmland, orchards and vineyards, it held jurisdiction over a dozen towns and three seaports until its ultimate dissolution in 1834. The monastery was originally founded by Dom Afonso Henriques in 1147 in celebration of the liberation of Santarém from the Moors, and is a truly vast complex – its main **church** (free) is one of the largest in Portugal. The exterior is disappointing, as the Gothic facade has been superseded by unexceptional Baroque additions. Inside, however, all later adornments have been swept away, restoring the narrow soaring aisles to their original vertical simplicity. The only exception to this Gothic purity is the frothy Manueline doorway to the sacristy, hidden behind the high altar. The abbey's most precious treasures are the fourteenth-century **tombs** of Dom Pedro and Dona Inês de Castro, sculpted with phenomenal wealth of detail to show the story of Pedro's love for Inês de Castro, the daughter of a Galician nobleman. Fearing Spanish influence over the Portuguese throne, Pedro's father, Afonso V, forbade their marriage. The ceremony nevertheless took place in secret, whereupon Afonso sanctioned his daughter-in-law's murder. When Pedro succeeded to the throne in 1357 he exhumed the corpse of his lover, forcing the entire royal circle to acknowledge her as queen by kissing her decomposing hand. The tombs – inscribed with the motto "*Até o Fim do Mundo*" (Until the End of the World) – have been placed foot to foot so that on the Day of Judgement the lovers may rise and immediately feast their eyes on one another. The most amazing room in the building is the **kitchen**, with its cellars and gargantuan conical chimney, supported by eight trunk-like iron columns. A stream tapped from the River Alcôa still runs straight through the room: it was used not merely for cooking and washing but also to provide a constant supply of fresh fish. The **Sala dos Reis** (Kings' Room), off the beautiful **Cloisters of Silence**, displays statues of virtually every king of Portugal down to Dom José, who died in 1777.

Alcobaça's **bus station** is five minutes' walk from the abbey in the centre of town across the bridge. Alcobaça's **tourist office** (daily 10am–1pm & 2/3–6/7pm; ☎262 582 377) is opposite the abbey on Praça 25 de Abril. The best budget **pension** is *Pensão Corações Unidos* (☎262 582 142; ❸), around the corner at Rua Frei António Brandão 39, and there's a **campsite** (☎262 582 265; closed Jan), ten minutes north of the bus station along Avenida Professor Vieira Natividade. Good-value **restaurants** include the touristy *Frei Bernado*, Rua D Pedro V 17–19, a huge place serving copious meals, and *Taverna o Capadar* at Praça 25 de Abril 41 where locals and tourists enjoy the tables that spill out onto the square in front of the abbey.

## Batalha

The Mosteiro de Santa Maria da Vitória, better known as the **Mosteiro de Batalha** (daily 9am–5/6pm; €4.50), is the finest building in Portugal, an enduring symbol of national pride. It was originally founded to commemorate the Battle of Aljubarrota (1385), which sealed Portugal's independence after decades of Spanish intrigue. It's easily reached on a day-trip from Leiria (4–5 buses daily). The honey-coloured abbey was transformed by Manueline additions in the late fifteenth and early sixteenth centuries, but the bulk was completed between 1388 and 1434 in a profusely ornate version of French Gothic. Within this flamboyant framework there are also strong elements of the English Perpendicular style, an influence explained by the **Capela do Fundador** (Founder's Chapel), directly to the right upon entering the church: beneath the octagonal lantern rests the tomb of Dom João I and Philippa of Lancaster, their hands clasped in the ultimate expression of harmonious relations between Portugal and England. Their four younger sons are buried along the south wall of the Capela do Fundador in a row of recessed arches. Second from the right is the **Tomb of Prince Henry the Navigator**, who guided the exploration of Madeira, the Azores and the African coast. The **Claustro Real** (Royal Cloister) dates from this period of burgeoning self-confidence under Manuel I (1495–1521), its intricate stone grilles being added by Diogo de Boitaca, architect of the cloisters at Belém and the prime genius of Manueline art. Off the east side, the early-fifteenth-century **Sala do Capítulo** (Chapter House) is remarkable for the unsupported span of its ceiling. The Church authorities were convinced that the whole chamber would come crashing down and only employed as labourers criminals already condemned to death. The **Capelas Imperfeitas** (Unfinished Chapels) form a separate structure tacked on to the east end of the church and accessible only from outside the main complex. Dom Duarte, eldest son of João and Philippa, commissioned them in 1437 as a royal mausoleum but the original design was transformed beyond all recognition by Dom Manuel's architects. It is unique among examples of Christian architecture in its evocation of the great shrines of Islam and Hinduism: perhaps inspired by the tales of Indian monuments that filtered back along the eastern trade routes.

## Fátima

**FÁTIMA** is one of the most important centres of pilgrimage in the Catholic world, a status deriving from six **Apparitions of the Virgin Mary**. On May 13,

1917, three children from the village were tending their parents' flock when, in a flash of lightning, they were confronted with "a lady brighter than the sun" sitting in the branches of a tree. The vision returned on the thirteenth day of the next five months, culminating in the so-called Miracle of the Sun on October 13, when a swirling ball of fire cured lifelong illnesses. To commemorate these extraordinary events a vast white **Basilica** and gigantic esplanade have been built, more than capable of holding the crowds of 100,000 who congregate here for the main **pilgrimages** (May 12 & 13; Oct 12 & 13). In the church the tombs of two of the children, who died in the European flu epidemic of 1919–20, are the subject of constant attention. Hospices and convents have sprung up in the shadow of the basilica, and inevitably the fame of Fátima has resulted in its commercialization. Pensions and restaurants abound, but there's little reason to stay except during the big pilgrimages to witness the midnight processions. Regular **bus services** to Fátima from Tomar make a day-trip easy.

## Tomar

**TOMAR**, 34km east of Fátima, is famous for the Convento de Cristo, an artistic tour de force which entwines the main military, religious and imperial strands in the history of Portugal. However, it's an attractive town in its own right – especially during the **Festas dos Tabuleiros**, in the first week of July, when the place goes wild – and is worth a day or two.

Built on a simple grid plan, Tomar's old quarters preserve all their traditional charm, with whitewashed cottages lining narrow cobbled streets. On the central Praça da República stands an elegant seventeenth-century town hall, a ring of houses of the same period and the Manueline church of **São João Baptista**, remarkable for its octagonal belfry and elaborate doorway. Nearby, at Rua Joaquim Jacinto 73, you'll find an excellently preserved fourteenth-century synagogue, now the **Museu Luso–Hebraicoa Abraham Zacuto** (daily 10am–5pm; free); in 1496, Dom Manuel ordered the expulsion or conversion of all Portuguese Jews, and the synagogue at Tomar was one of the few to survive. The **Convento de Cristo** (daily 9am–5.30pm; €3) is set among pleasant gardens with splendid views, about a fifteen-minute walk uphill from the centre of town. Founded in 1162 by Gualdim Pais, first Master of the Knights Templar, it was the headquarters of the Order. The heart of the complex remains the **Charola**, the temple from which the knights drew their moral conviction, a strange place that's more suggestive of the occult than of Christianity. The highlight of the convent is the ornamentation of the windows on the main facade of its **Chapter House**, where maritime motifs form a memorial to the sailors who established the Portuguese empire. The adjoining two-tiered **Great Cloisters** comprise one of the purest examples of the Renaissance style in Portugal. Tomar's **tourist office** (Mon–Fri: winter 10am–1pm & 2–6pm; summer 10am–8pm; ☎249 322 427) is at the top of Avenida Dr Cândido Madureira. There's a number of reasonable **pensions**: nicest of all is the very popular *Residencial União*, Rua Serpa Pinto 94 (☎249 323 161; **③**). *Luz*, a few doors down at Rua Serpa Pinto 144 (☎249 312 317; **③**), has the added bonus of the excellent *Restaurant Tabuleiro*. Close by is the smart *Residencial Sinagoga,* Rua Gil Avô 31 (☎249 323 083, ⓔresidencialsinagoga@clix.pt; **③**).

## Coimbra

**COIMBRA** was Portugal's capital from 1143 to 1255 and it ranks behind only the cities of Lisbon and Porto in historic importance. Its university, founded in 1290, was the only one existing in Portugal until the beginning of the last century. For a provincial town it has remarkable riches, and it's an enjoyable place to stay – especially in May, when the students celebrate the end of the academic year in the **Queima das Fitas**, tearing or burning their gowns and faculty ribbons. This is when you're most likely to hear the Coimbra *fado*, distinguished from the Lisbon version by its mournful pace and complex lyrics.

Old Coimbra sits on a hill on the right bank of the River Mondego, with the university crowding its summit. The main buildings of the **Old University** (daily: summer 8.30am–7pm; winter 9.30am–5pm; €4), dating from the sixteenth century, are set around a courtyard dominated by a Baroque clocktower and a statue of João III. The **chapel** is covered with *azulejos* and intricate decoration, but takes second place to the **Library**, a Baroque fantasy presented to the faculty by João V in the early eighteenth century. Below the university is the **Museu Machado de Castro** (currently closed for restoration), housed in the former archbishop's palace above a Roman crypto-portico, just down from the unprepossessing **Sé Nova** (New Cathedral). Of more interest is the **Sé Velha** (Old Cathedral; Mon–Thurs, Sat & Sun 10am–1pm & 2–6pm; cloister €1), halfway down the hill, one of Portugal's most important Romanesque buildings. Solid and square on the outside, it's also stolid and simple within, the decoration confined to a few giant conch shells and some unobtrusive *azulejos*. Restraint and simplicity certainly aren't the chief qualities of the **Igreja de Santa Cruz** (daily 8.30am–6.30pm; free), at the bottom of the hill past the city gates. Although it was founded before the Old Cathedral, nothing remains that has not been substantially remodelled. In the early sixteenth century, Coimbra was the site of a major sculptural school; the new tombs for Portugal's first kings, Afonso Henriques and Sancho I, and the elaborately carved pulpit, are among its finest works.

### Practicalities

Most mainline **trains** stop at Coimbra B, 3km north of the city, from where there are frequent connecting services to Coimbra A, right at the heart of things. The main **bus station** is on Avenida Fernão de Magalhães, fifteen minutes' walk from the centre – turn right out of the bus station and head down the main road. The **tourist office** (Mon–Fri 9am–5/7pm, Sat & Sun 9/10am–1pm & 2–5/5.30pm; ☎239 488 120, ⓦwww.turismo-centro.pt) is opposite the bridge in the Largo da Portagem. Near the station, the sleazy Rua da Sota and its side streets have a few **pensões** that aren't as bad as they look – try the comfortable *Pensão Vitória* at Rua da Sota 9 & 19 (☎239 824 049; ❹), or the *Residencial Domus* at Rua Adelino Veiga 62 (☎239 828 584; ❹). Alternatively, there are several options east of the university; beneath the aqueduct, *Antunes*, Rua Castro Matoso 8 (☎239 854 720, ⓦwww.residencialantunes.pt; ❹), offers cool, high-ceilinged rooms and parking. The **hostel**, above the park at Rua Henrique Seco 14 (☎239 822 955, ⓦwww .pousadasjuventude.pt; €11), is friendly and immaculately run – it's a twenty-minute walk from Coimbra A, or take bus #7, #29 or #46. For really basic **food**, served up with loads of atmosphere, try the little dives tucked into the alleys between Largo da Portagem, Rua da Sota and Praça do Comércio. *Adega Paço do Conde* at Rua Paço do Conde 1 is a cavernous, locally renowned **churrasqueira** (grill house), while *Café Santa Cruz*, housed in a former monastery on Praça 8 de Maio, is one of the town's best traditional **cafés** – others can be found round Largo da Portagem.

# Northern Portugal

**Porto**, the country's second largest city, is an attractive and convenient centre from which to begin an exploration of the region. Magnificently set on a rocky cliff astride the River Douro, it is perhaps most famous for the port-producing suburb of **Vila Nova de Gaia**, supplied by vineyards further inland along the river. The

**Douro Valley** is traced by a spectacular rail route, with branch lines following valleys north along the River Tâmega to Amarante and along the Corgo to **Vila Real** – the main centre for transport connections into the ancient, isolated region of **Trás-os-Montes** and its old capital of **Bragança**. In the northwest, the **Minho**, considered by many to be the most beautiful part of the country, is a lush wilderness of rolling mountain forests and rugged coastlines (the Costa Verde), with some of the most unspoilt beaches in Europe. A quietly conservative region, its towns have a special charm and beauty, amongst them the religious centre of **Braga**, and the self-proclaimed birthplace of the nation, **Guimarães**.

# Porto (Oporto)

Capital of the north, **PORTO** (sometimes called Oporto in English) is very different from Lisbon – unpretentious, inward-looking, unashamedly commercial. As the local saying goes: "Coimbra sings; Braga prays; Lisbon shows off; and Porto works." The attraction of the city lies largely in the contrast between the prosperous business core and the earthy charm of its Ribeira area, where the cobbled warren of steep alleys and passages appears to have changed little in centuries.

## Arrival, information and accommodation

From the Francisco Sá Carneiro **airport**, 10km north of the city, an Aerobus (7.30am–7pm; every 30min; €4, free for TAP passengers) runs to Avenida dos Aliados, a few yards north of São Bento train station. Most trains from the south stop at the distant **Estação de Campanhã**; you may need to change here for a connection to the central **Estação de São Bento** (5min), or the Vermelha metro line (marked red on maps) will take you into the centre. The main **bus terminal** is on Rua Alexandre Herculano, a short walk east of Estação de São Bento. The most helpful of three central **tourist offices** is just north of Avenida dos Aliados on Rua Clube dos Fenianos 25 (summer daily 9am–7pm; winter Mon–Fri 9am–5.30pm, Sat & Sun 9am–4.30pm; ☏222 393 472, ⊛www.portoturismo .pt). **Internet** access is available at *Onweb*, Avenida dos Aliados 291. The cheapest **rooms** are on Rua do Loureiro and Rua Cimo do Vila, around the corner from São Bento, though this is something of a red-light district. For more salubrious places, head west or east of Avenida dos Aliados; most of the hotels listed below are to the west. There are also some bargain rooms around lively Praça da Batalha.

### Hostel
**Pousada de Juventude** Rua Paulo Gama 552 ☏226 177 257. Large and clean, with a great view of the mouth of the Douro. Bus #35 from Largo dos Loios. €15.

### Pensions and hotels
**Grande Hotel de Paris** Rua da Fábrica 27–29 ☏222 073 140. Not quite so grand anymore, but the rooms are huge and it has a nice central location. Breakfast included. ❸
**Pensão Residencial Duas Nações** Praça Guilherme Gomes Fernandes 59 ☏222 081 616, ⊜duasnacoes@mail.telepac.pt. A deservedly popular option, with cheap and bright en-suite accommodation and Internet access. Book in advance. ❷
**Pensão Estoril** Rua de Cedofeita 193 ☏222 002 751, ⊛www.pensaoestoril.com. Wonderful value en-suite rooms. ❸

**Pensão Monte Sinai** Rua Alexandre Herculano 146 ☏222 008 218. East of Praça da Batalha, inexpensive, but a little dingy and noisy. ❸
**Pensão Oporto Chique** Rua Conde de Vizela 26 ☏222 080 069. One of the cheapest in town, great if you don't mind a lack of natural light. ❷
**Residencial Porto Novo** Rua Alexandre Herculano 185 ☏222 055 739. Clean, modern rooms with TV and bath, back rooms with balconies and great views of the river. Highly recommended. ❸

### Campsites
**Marisol** Rua Alto das Chaquedas 82 ☏227 135 942. Peaceful location south of the river; Espirito Santo bus from Rua Infante D. Henrique.
**Prelada** Rua Monte dos Burgos ☏228 312 616. The closest of the campsites; bus #87 from Cordoaria or the airport (both run until midnight) or #6 from Avda. dos Aliados.

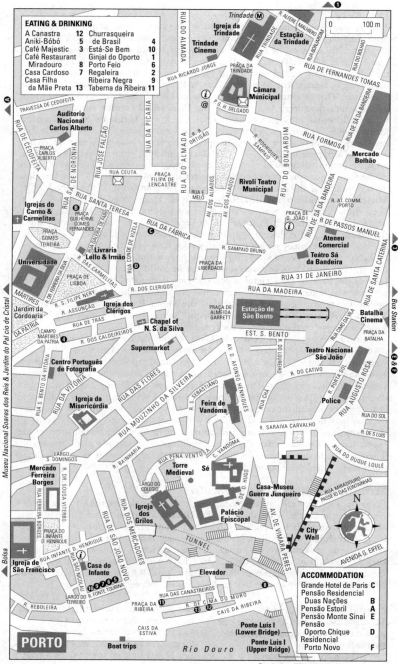

**EATING & DRINKING**

| | | | |
|---|---|---|---|
| A Canastra | 12 | Churrasqueira | |
| Aniki-Bóbó | 5 | de Brasil | 4 |
| Café Majestic | 3 | Está-Se Bem | 10 |
| Café Restaurant | | Ginjal do Oporto | 1 |
| Miradouro | 8 | Porto Feio | 6 |
| Casa Cardoso | 7 | Regaleira | 2 |
| Casa Filha | | Ribeira Negra | 9 |
| da Mãe Preta | 13 | Taberna da Ribeira | 11 |

**ACCOMMODATION**

Grande Hotel de Paris **C**
Pensão Residencial
Duas Nações **B**
Pensão Estoril **A**
Pensão Monte Sinai **E**
Pensão
Oporto Chique **D**
Residencial
Porto Novo **F**

**PORTO**

Boat trips

*Rio Douro*

Port Lodges ▼  ▼ Vila Nova de Gaia

## The City

A great way to get your bearings in Porto is to take a **boat trip** up the Douro from Cais da Estiva, by Cais da Ribeira (around €8). Another good way is to climb the 250 steps of the tower in the Baroque **Igreja dos Clérigos** (Mon–Sat 9am–noon & 3.30–7.30pm, Sun 10am–1pm & 8.30/9am–10/10.30pm; €1), once the tallest building in Portugal. From the tower, it's a ten–minute walk south to the attractive square that bears the name of Porto's most famous son, Henry the Navigator. There's a statue of Henry in the middle of the square and on its north side is a sprawling fresh-food market, the **Mercado Ferreira Borges**. On the west side lurks the most extraordinary church in Porto, **Igreja de São Francisco** (daily 9am–5/6pm; €3 including museum). It's rather plain from the outside, but the interior underwent a fabulously opulent eighteenth-century refurbishment, with gold dripping from every corner. Don't miss the church's small **museum**, set in an eerie underground crypt, and containing an *ossário*, a collection of bones dating from before the time of public cemeteries. Tram #1 departs for the **beaches** by the mouth of the Douro every half hour from in front of the church. The **Museu Nacional Soares dos Reis** at Rua de Dom Manuel II (Tues 2–6pm, Wed–Sun 10am–6pm; €3), over to the west behind the city hospital, was the first national museum in Portugal. Its collection includes glass, ceramics and a formidable array of eighteenth- and nineteenth-century paintings, as well as the late-nineteenth-century sculptures of Soares dos Reis – his *O Desterro* (*The Exile*) is probably the best-known work in Portugal. Follow the road past the museum, or take any bus from the Cordoaria stop except #6 and #18, and you'll come to the **Jardim do Palácio de Cristal**, a peaceful park dominated by a space-age domed pavilion which now serves as a sports centre. In summer the park is home to a vast funfair. On the far side of the park, below the Museu Romântico, is the **Solar do Vinho do Porto** (Mon–Sat 2pm–midnight), where you can sample hundreds of varieties of port on the relaxing river terrace.

South of the river, **Vila Nova de Gaia**, essentially a city in its own right, is dominated by the port trade. From the north bank the names of the various companies (Croft's, Taylor's, Sandeman, Graham's), spelled out in neon letters across the terracotta roofs of the lodges, leave you in no doubt as to what awaits you when you cross. You can walk to Gaia across the **Ponte Luís I**: the most direct route to the wine lodges is across the lower level from the Cais da Ribeira, but if you've a head for heights it's an amazing sensation to walk over the upper deck; otherwise, take bus #32, #57 or #91 from São Bento station. Almost all the companies offer free **tasting and tours** of their lodges, although some of the bigger names like Sandeman charge €3, redeemable against the price of a bottle. There's little pressure to buy anything – but do try the dry white ports, which are often unobtainable elsewhere.

## Eating, drinking and nightlife

Porto has a strong **café culture**, which includes some elegant rivals to the fin-de-siècle places in Lisbon, while the **Cais da Ribeira** waterfront offers a vibrant scene at night with its lively bars and clubs. Most of the city's big nightclubs are in the outlying **Matosinhos** district. Porto's culinary speciality is *tripas* (tripe), though there are always plenty of alternatives on the menu. There are lots of places where you can eat cheaply, particularly **workers' cafés**, which have wine on tap and often offer a set menu for the day. Prime areas are Rua do Almada and Rua de São Bento da Vitória. All are busy at midday and invariably close around 7.30pm and all Sunday.

### Cafés and restaurants

**A Canastra** Cais da Ribeira 37. One of the least pricey of the riverside restaurants, serving solid Portuguese nosh.

**Café Majestic** Rua de Santa Catarina 112. Porto's best café-restaurant with ornate surroundings and delicious breakfasts and teas. Closed Sun.

**Café Restaurant Miradouro** Cais da Ribeira, on the arches by the entrance to the bridge. A popular local hangout with great salads and cheap meals.

**Casa Cardoso** Rua da Fonte Tourina 60. A great place for inexpensive fish, just off the waterfront. Closed Sun.

**Casa Filha da Mãe Preta** Arcos do Douro 2–3, Cais da Ribeira. Bustling restaurant with excellent views over the river. Closed Mon.

**Churrasqueira de Brasil** Campo dos Mártires da Pátria 136, near Torre dos Clérigos. Cheap workers' diner serving ample portions. Closed Tues.

**Ginjal do Oporto** Rua do Bonjardim 724. Bargain local specialities in a no-frills setting. Closed Sun.

**Regaleira** Rua do Bonjardim 87. An unassuming restaurant but one of the best places for fish and seafood, with a decent bar and TV for company.

### Bars

**Aniki-Bóbó** Rua da Fonte Tourina 36. Upbeat late-night acid jazz/house bar. Occasional alternative happenings (eg theatre). Until 4am. Closed Sun.

**Está-Se Bem** Rua da Fonte Tourina 70–72. Attracts an arty crowd until 2am. Closed Sun.

**Ribeira Negra** Rua da Fonte Tourina 66. Lively bar popular with students.

**Porto Feio** Rua da Fonte Tourina 52–54. Laid-back bar-cum-gallery, open earlier than most on this stretch. Thurs–Sat.

**Taberna da Ribeira** Praça da Ribeira. Prime riverside spot with outdoor tables. Until 2am.

### Clubs

All the clubs below are out of the centre, though there are night buses to most if you can't afford a taxi.

**Act** Rua Manuel Pinto de Azevedo 15, Matosinhos. Current hot spot with a warehouse atmosphere and visiting DJs playing drum'n'bass and trance. Open Weds, Fri & Sat midnight til 6am.

**Dadans** Cançada João do Carmo 31, Massarelos. Pricey entrance fee and strict dress code but worth it for the chilled, jazzy atmosphere. Wed–Sat.

**Hard Club** Cais de Gaia, Vila Nova de Gaia. Porto's main venue for DJs and live music, including a good number of British and Stateside acts. Night bus #91.

# Braga

**BRAGA** is Portugal's religious capital – the scene of spectacular **Easter celebrations** with torchlight processions. You can't miss the **Archbishop's Palace**, a great fortress-like building, right at the centre of the old town. Nearby is the **Sé**, which, like the palace, encompasses Gothic, Renaissance and Baroque styles. Founded in 1070, its south doorway is a survivor from this earliest building; its most striking element, however, is the intricate ornamentation of the roofline. A guided tour of the interior (daily 9am–1pm & 2–6.30pm; cathedral free, museum and Capela dos Reis €2) takes you through three Gothic chapels, of which the outstanding specimen is the **Capela dos Reis** (Kings' Chapel), built to house the tombs of Henry of Burgundy and his wife Teresa, the cathedral's founders. The **tourist office** (Mon–Fri 9am–6.30pm, Sat & Sun 9am–12.30pm & 2–5.30pm; ☎253 262 550, ⊛www.cm-braga.pt) is at the corner of Praça da República. Large, comfortable rooms are to be found just round the corner at the *Grande Residencial Avenida*, Av. Da Liberdade 738–2° (☎253 616 363, ✉r.avenida@netcabo.pt; ❸). Braga's well-equipped **hostel** is at Rua Santa Margarida 6 (☎253 616 163; €5), off Avenida Central; the **campsite** (☎253 273 355) is a two-kilometre walk along the Guimarães road, but is very cheap and right next to the municipal swimming pool. *Casa Pimenta*, Praça Conde de Agrolongo 46 (closed Thurs), serves reasonably priced, quality **food** in generous quantities, as does the *Restaurante Moçambicana* at Rua Andrade Corvo 8, one of several excellent cheap restaurants grouped around the Arco da Porta Nova. By far the best of the old **coffee houses** is the mahogany-panelled *Café Astória*, Praça da Republica.

The glorious ornamental stairway of **Bom Jesus**, 3km outside Braga, is one of Portugal's best-known images. Set on a wooded hillside, high above the city, it's a monumental place of pilgrimage created by Braga's archbishop in the early eighteenth century. The #2 **bus** runs from in front of the Cristal Farmácia on Avda da Liberdade in Braga to the foot of the stairway about every thirty minutes at weekends, when half the city piles up there to picnic. If you resist the temptation of the **funicular** (€1) and climb up the **stairway**, Bom Jesus's simple allegory unfolds. Each landing has a fountain: the first symbolizes the wounds of Christ, the next five the Senses, and the final three represent the Virtues. At each corner are chapels with mouldering wooden tableaux of the life of Christ, leading to the Crucifixion at the altar of the church. Beyond are wooded gardens, grottoes and miniature boating pools, and several cheap, lively **restaurants**.

## Guimarães

The first capital of Portugal, **GUIMARÃES** remains a lively and atmospheric university town. The town's chief attraction is the **castelo** (daily 9.30am–12.30pm & 2–5pm; free), whose square keep and seven towers are an enduring symbol of the emergent Portuguese nation. Built by the Countess of Mumadona and extended by Henry of Burgundy, it became the stronghold of his son, Afonso Henriques. From here the Reconquest began along with the creation of a kingdom that, within a century of Afonso's death, was to stretch to its present borders. Afonso is said to have been born in the keep, and may have been baptized in the font of the Romanesque chapel of **São Miguel** on the grassy slope below. Guimarães's **bus station** is fifteen minutes' walk west of town in a vast shopping centre. From the **train station** south of town you'll pass one **tourist office** (Mon–Fri 9.30am–6.30pm, Sat 10am–6pm, Sun 10am–1pm; ☏253 412 450, ✆www.cm-guimaraes.pt) as you walk up Avenida D. Alfonso Henriques to the centre; the other office is in the centre of the old town in Praça de Santiago (Mon–Fri 9.30am–6.30pm, Sat 10am–6pm, Sun 10am–1pm; ☏253 518 790). There's excellent-value **accommodation** at the *Residencial das Trinas,* Rua das Trinas 29, ☏253 517 358; ❸). For **food**, *Oriental* on Largo do Toural has very good regional specialities. Guimarães has a lively **nightlife**, with a number of bars around Praça de Santiago. *Secos Bar* at no. 14 is recommended.

## The Douro rail route

The valleys of the **River Douro** and its tributaries are among the most spectacular landscapes in Portugal, and the Douro Valley itself, a narrow, winding gorge for the majority of its long route, is the most beautiful of all. The **Douro rail route**, which joins the river about 60km inland and then sticks to it across the country, is one of those journeys that needs no justification other than the trip itself. There are regular connections along the line as far as Peso da Régua, first capital of the demarcated port-producing region; beyond Régua, there are less frequent connections to Tua and Pocinho, which marks the end of the line.

At **Livração**, about an hour from Porto, the Tâmega line cuts off for the lovely mountain town of **AMARANTE**. The journey is spectacular, the rickety, single-carriage train struggling through pine woods and vineyards on the climb, with the river visible like a piece of lapis lazuli far below. Amarante is a fine place to stop, with much of its history revolving around the thirteenth-century hermit **Gonçalo**, who is credited with a hand in the founding of just about everything in the town. Although it has a nice church and unusual modernist museum, the main attraction is the setting, the peaceful family atmosphere and relaxing old streets. A good cheap **hotel** is *Residencial A Raposeira*, Largo António Cândido 53 (☏255 432 221; ❷), above the restaurant of the same name, which serves huge, if basic, meals. Shortly after Livração, the main line finally reaches the Douro and heads upstream until, at Mesão Frio, the valley broadens into the little plain commanded by **PESO DA RÉGUA**, the depot through which port wine must pass on its way from Pinhão – the centre of production – to Porto. Beyond Peso da Régua begin the terraced slopes where the **port vines** are grown: they look their best in August, with the grapes ripening, and in September when the harvest has begun. The scenery continues in this vein, craggy and beautiful, with the softer hills of the interior fading dark green into the distance, to Tua (junction for the Corgo line with services to the transport centre of **Vila Real**, the gateway to Trás-os-Montes) and Pocinho, where buses take over for routes east towards Miranda do Douro.

## Trás-os-Montes and Bragança

Perhaps more than anywhere else in Portugal, the province of **Trás-os-Montes** – literally "behind the mountains" – still upholds its traditional customs and farming methods.

On a hillock above **BRAGANÇA**, the small and remote provincial capital, stands a pristine circle of walls, the extraordinary **Cidadela**, enclosing a medieval village and castle. The **Domus Municipalis** here, a fifteenth-century pentagonal Romanesque civic building, is the only one of its kind in Europe. Next to it is the church of **Santa Maria**, with its eighteenth-century barrel-vaulted, painted ceiling – a feature common to several churches in Bragança. Towering above these two is the **castle** itself (Mon–Wed & Fri–Sun 9am–noon & 2–5pm; €1.50, free Sun morning), which the Portuguese royal family rejected as a residence in favour of their vast estate in the Alentejo. At its side a curious pillory rises from the back of a prehistoric granite pig, or *porca*, thought to have been a fertility idol of a prehistoric cult. Celtic-inspired medieval tombstones rub shoulders with a menagerie of *porcas* in the gardens of **Museu do Abade de Baçal**, between the citadel and cathedral in Rua Abílio Beça (Tues–Fri 10am–5pm, Sat & Sun 10am–6pm; €2.50, free Sun). The **tourist office** (Mon–Sat 10am–12.30pm & 2–5/6.30pm; ☎273 381 273) is on an extension of Avenida Cidade de Zamora, a couple of hundred metres north of the cathedral. Comfortable **accommodation** can be found at *Residencial Poças*, Rua Combatentes da G. Guerra 200 (☎273 331 428; ❷) and *Residencial Sra da Ribeira*, Travessa da Misericórdia (☎273 300 550; ❸). The nearest **campsite** (☎273 351 535; May–Sept) is 6km out of town on the França road; another option is the plush, private site *Cepo Verde* (☎273 999 371; May–Sept), 8km down the Vinhais road, with good facilities and a pool. As for **restaurants**, two favourites are *Restaurante Poças*, next to the *residencial*, serving big, wholesome meals, and the beautifully located *Restaurante D. Fernando*, Cidadela 197, inside the walled old town. South of Bragança, hugging the border with Spain in the east, is the vast and beautiful wilderness of the **Parque Natural do Douro Internacional**, home to Europe's largest concentration of Egyptian vultures and a huge number of other birds of prey. The best place to base yourself for a visit is the town of **MOGADOURO**, site of the park's headquarters and connected by daily weekday bus from Bragança (1hr 40min). **Accommodation** is plentiful: try the *Pensão Russo* (☎279 342 134; ❷), on Rua das Eiras.

# Southern Portugal

The huge, sparsely populated plains of the **Alentejo**, southeast of Lisbon, are overwhelmingly agricultural, dominated by vast cork plantations well suited to the low rainfall, sweltering heat and arid soil. This impoverished province is divided into vast estates that provide nearly half of the world's cork but only a sparse living for its rural inhabitants. Visitors to the Alentejo often head for **Évora**, the province's dominant and most historic city. But the **Alentejo coast**, the Costa Azul, is a breath of fresh air after the stifling plains of the inland landscape.

With its long, sandy beaches and picturesque rocky coves, the southern coast of the **Algarve** is the most visited region in the country. West of **Faro**, the lively capital of the Algarve, you'll find the classic postcard images of the province – a series of tiny bays and coves, broken up by weird rocky outcrops and fantastic grottoes, at their most exotic around the resort of **Lagos**. To the east of Faro lie the less developed sandy offshore islets, **the Ilhas** – which front the coastline for some 25 miles – and the lower-key resorts of **Olhão** and **Tavira**. Or head inland where you'll find a more Portuguese way of life at **Silves**, the impressive former capital of the Moors. Throughout the Algarve, accommodation can be a major problem in summer, with hotels block-booked by package companies and pensions filling up early in the day.

## Évora

**ÉVORA**, a UNESCO World Heritage site, is one of the most impressive cities in Portugal. The Romans were in occupation for four centuries and the Moors, who settled for just as long, left their stamp in the tangle of narrow alleys that rise steeply among the whitewashed houses. Most of the monuments, however, date from the fourteenth to the sixteenth centuries, when, with royal encouragement, the city was one of the leading centres of Portuguese art and architecture. The **Templo Romano** in the central square is the best-preserved Roman temple in Portugal, its stark remains consisting of a small platform supporting more than a dozen granite columns with a marble entablature. Next to the temple lies the church of the **Convento dos Lóios**. The convent is now a luxury *pousada*, but the church (Tues–Sun 9.30am–12.30pm & 2–5pm; €3), dedicated to **São João Evangelista**, contains beautiful *azulejos* and an ossuary under the floor. The adjacent palace is the private property of the ducal Cadaval family, though parts of it are sometimes open to visitors for exhibits (usually €2 extra). Nearby, the Romanesque cathedral, or **Sé** (daily 9am–12.30pm & 2–4.30/5pm, cloisters and museum €3), was begun in 1186, about twenty years after the reconquest of Évora from the Moors. The most memorable sight in town, however, is the **Capela dos Ossos** (daily 9am–1pm & 2.30–5.30pm; €1) in the church of **São Francisco**, just south of Praça do Giraldo. A gruesome reminder of mortality, the walls and pillars of this chilling chamber are entirely covered with the bones of more than five thousand monks; an inscription over the door reads, *Nós ossos que aqui estamos, Pelos vossos esperamos* – "We bones here are waiting for your bones". Just below the church lies a beautiful park with a drinks kiosk and picnic tables under the trees.

Évora's **bus** and **train stations** are 1km west of the old town, a twenty-minute walk from the central Praça do Giraldo, centre of Évora's lively student scene. The **tourist office** (daily 9am–6/7pm in winter; ☎266 730 030) is sited here, along with a couple of outdoor cafés. Évora's tourist appeal pushes **accommodation** prices way over the norm. Best options are *Pensão Invicta*, Rua Romão Ramalho 37a, with some rooms overlooking São Francisco (☎266 702 047; ❶); *Pensão Giraldo* has rooms of varying size and comfort at Rua dos Mercadores 15 & 27 (☎266 705 833; ❷); or the lovely, rambling *Residencial Policarpo*, Rua Freiria de Baixo 16 (☎266 702 424, ❺www.pensaopolicarpo.com; ❸), which also has rooms sleeping three or four. The **hostel** here has been closed for some time, but there are plans for a new one, check with the Turismo. If you're stuck for a room, the tourist office will sometimes arrange accommodation in **private homes**. The **campsite** (☎266 705 190) is 2km out of town on the Alcáçovas road; take the hourly buses #5 and #8 from Praça 1 de Maio. For inexpensive **restaurants** try *Restaurante Repas*, 23 Praça 1 de Maio, a lovely outdoor spot for bargain regional dishes, or the homely *O Portão*, on Rua do Cano 27 alongside the aqueduct. Always popular is the reliable Italian food at *Pane & Vino*, Patio do Salema (entrance on Rua Diogo Focardo). *Bar Oficina*, Rue da Moeda 27, offers some laid-back late-night action.

## The Alentejo coast

The coast south of Lisbon features towns and beaches as inviting as those of the Algarve. Admittedly, it's exposed to the winds and waves of the Atlantic, and the waters are colder, but it's fine for summer swimming and far quieter. Local bus services and roughly three express buses daily from Lisbon take you within easy range of the whole coastline, stopping at the beaches of Vila Nova de Milfontes, Porto Côvo and Zambujeira do Mar. Six to eight buses daily run from Lisbon to **SANTIAGO DO CACÉM**, a pleasant little town overlooked by a castle. In turn, there are five buses daily (in summer) from Santiago to **Lagoa de Santo**

André and the adjoining **Lagoa de Melides**, with two of the best beaches in the country. The **campsites** at both places are of a high standard and there are masses of signs offering **rooms**, chalets and houses to let. Beyond the beach-cafés and ice-cream stalls, miles and miles of sand stretch all the way to Comporta in the north and Sines in the south. There are high waves and good surf, but take local advice as the undertow can be fierce. If you'd rather base yourself at Santiago than at the beaches, there's no shortage of good **food and accommodation**. The *Restaurante Covas*, by the bus station at Rua Cidade de Setúbal 10 (℡269 822 675; ❸), is recommended both for its rooms and for its outstanding meals. Some 40km southwest of Santiago do Cacém lies the popular resort of **PORTO CÔVO**, which, although overdeveloped, has plentiful accommodation, a campsite and beautiful beaches to the south. The larger resort of **VILA NOVA DE MILFON-TES** lies a little to the south on the estuary of the River Mira, whose sandy banks gradually expand and merge into the coastline. This is the most popular resort in the Alentejo, with lines of villas and hotels radiating from the centre of the old village. It's still a pretty place, though, with a handsome little castle and an ancient port, reputed to have harboured Hannibal and his Carthaginians during a storm. Finding reasonable **rooms** shouldn't be a problem, and there are a couple of large **campsites** to the north of the village: *Parque de Fontemira Milfontes* (℡283 996 140) and the more modest *Campiférias* (℡283 996 409).

The main inland base is **ODEMIRA**, a quiet, unspoilt country town, connected by eight daily buses to Vila Nova de Milfontes. **Pensions** include *Residencial Rita*, on Estrada da Circunvalação (℡283 322 531; ❹), and *Residencial Idálio*, Rua Eng. Arantes Oliveira 28 (℡283 322 156; ❸), just to the left when you come out of the bus station. Of the **restaurants**, try *O Tarro*, facing the river south of the bus station. South of Odemira at **ZAMBUJEIRA DO MAR**, a large cliff provides a dramatic backdrop to the beach, more than compensating for the winds. There are only a few small **pensions**, such as the *Mar-e-Sol* (℡283 961 171; ❸), a few *dormidas* and a couple of bars, as well as a reasonable **campsite** (℡283 961 172), about 1km from the cliffs.

## Lagos

**LAGOS** is a thriving fishing port and one of the most popular tourist destinations in the Algarve, with some superb beaches and, nearby, extraordinary rock formations around **Ponta da Piedade**, a headland that can be viewed by boat (around €10) from the harbour. The port was a favoured residence of Henry the Navigator, who used it as a base for African trade. Europe's first slave market was here in 1441 in the arches of the **Customs House**, which still stands in the Praça da República near the waterfront. On the waterfront and to the rear of the town are the remains of Lagos's once impregnable fortifications, devastated by the Great Earthquake. One rare and beautiful church which did survive was the **Igreja de Santo António**; decorated around 1715, its gilt and carved interior is wildly obsessive, every inch filled with a private fantasy of cherubic youths struggling with animals and fish. The church forms part of a visit to the adjacent **Museu Municipal** (Tues–Sun 9.30am–12.30pm & 2–5pm; €2), housing an extraordinarily eclectic collection of artefacts including Roman busts and deformed animal foetuses. The promontory south of town is fringed by extravagantly eroded cliff faces that shelter a series of tiny cove beaches. **Praia de Dona Ana** is considered the most picturesque, though its crowds make the smaller coves of **Praia do Pinhão**, down a track just opposite the fire station, and **Praia Camilo**, a little further along, more appealing. Over the river east of Lagos is a splendid sweep of sand – **Meia Praia** – where there's space even at the height of summer.

The **train station** is across the river, fifteen minutes' walk from the centre via a swing bridge in the marina; the **bus station** is a bit closer in, a block back from the main Avenida dos Descobrimentos. The **tourist office** (Mon–Fri

9.30am–5.30/7pm, also Apr–Sept Sat & Sun 9.30am–7pm; ☎282 763 031) is an inconvenient twenty-minute walk east of the bus station – follow the harbour front until you reach the second roundabout. They can help find a room for you, but most economical are the **private rooms** (❷) touted at the bus station. Two of the more convenient and pleasant **pensions** are *Pensão Caravela*, Rua 25 de Abril 16 (☎282 763 361; ❸), and *Pensão Rubimar*, at Rua da Barroca 70 (☎282 763 165, ✉rubimar01@hotmail.com; ❹), which has rooms for up to five people. There's a modern **hostel** at Rua de Lançarote de Freites 50 (☎282 761 970; €15), which also has **Internet** access. Lagos's **campsite**, *Campismo da Trindade* (☎282 763 893), is on the way to Praia de Dona Ana but gets very crowded. In season a regular bus service marked "D. Ana/Oporto de Mós" connects it to town; on foot, follow the main road beyond the fort. For **food**, the popular *Casa do Zé* has outdoor seating near the market. For authentic *piri-piri* chicken try the inexpensive *O Franguinho* at Rua Luís de Azevedo 25 (closed Mon). *Casa Rosa*, Rua do Ferrador 22, is a back-packers' favourite serving inexpensive international food, while *Mullens* **bar**, Rua Cândido dos Reis 86, opposite the cinema, is an atmospheric bar-restaurant with lively music, and *Eddie's Bar*, Rua 25 de Abril 99, is friendly, with a pumping sound system; both open till 2am. For contemporary **club** sounds, there's *Bon Vivant*, Rua 25 de Abril 105, with its "tropical" roof terrace (till 4am).

## Silves

**SILVES** is an inland Algarve town that merits a detour. Capital of the Moorish kings of the al-Gharb (now Algarve), it's still an imposing place and has a lively summer beer festival. The **train station**, on the Lagos–Faro rail line, lies 2km outside the town; there's a connecting bus. Under the Moors, Silves was a place of grandeur and industry, described in contemporary accounts as being "of shining brightness". In 1189 an army led by Sancho I put an end to this splendour, killing some six thousand Moors in the process. The impressively complete sandstone walls of the Moorish **fortress** (daily 10am–6/8pm; €1.80) retain their towers and elaborate communication system, but the inside will remain something of a building site until substantial renovation is complete. Just below the fortress is Silves' **cathedral** (daily 8.30am–6.30pm, Sun between masses only), built on the site of the mosque in the thirteenth century. The nearby **Museu Arqueologia** (Mon–Sat 9am–6pm; €1.50) is an engaging museum that romps through the history of Silves from the year dot to the sixteenth century. The **tourist office**, in the heart of the town at Rua 25 de Abril 26 (Mon–Fri 9.30/10am–1.30pm & 2.30–6/7pm; ☎282 442 255), will help you find a **private room**. Recommended are those at Rua Cândido dos Reis 36 (☎282 442 667; ❸), where you share the use of a kitchen, or try *Residencial Ponte Romana*, over the Roman bridge (☎282 443 275; ❸). Inexpensive **restaurants** cluster round the riverside market building, and on Friday evenings, visit the Fábrica Inglês, where shows are laid on in a former factory packed with cafés and bars.

## Faro

**FARO** is the capital of the Algarve, close to the international airport, 6km west of town. Excellent beaches are within easy reach, and thanks to its university there's a lively nightlife scene too. Despite its modern suburbs, it retains a historic centre to the south and west of an attractive marina. The **Cidade Velha**, or old town, is a semi-walled quarter entered through the eighteenth-century town gate, the **Arco da Vila**. Here you'll find the majestic **Sé** (Mon–Sat 9am–5pm; €1.50), which offers superb views from its belltower. The nearby **Museu Arqueológico** (Tues–Fri 9.30/10am–5.30/6pm, Sat & Sun 11.30am/2–5.30/6pm; €2) is installed in a fine sixteenth-century convent; the most striking exhibit is a third-century Roman mosaic of Neptune and the four winds, unearthed near Faro train station. Faro's most curious sight is the Baroque **Igreja do Carmo** (Mon–Fri 10am–1pm

& 3–5/6pm, Sat 10am–1pm) near the central post office on Largo do Carmo. A door to the right of the altar leads to a macabre **Capela dos Ossos** (€1), its walls decorated with bones disinterred from the adjacent cemetery.

## Practicalities

Taxis from the **airport** to the centre cost around €10, or take bus #16 or #14 (daily 7am–8/11pm, every 45min; €1.20), a twenty-minute journey to town. The **bus station** is right in the centre, behind the *Hotel Eva*, north of the marina; you'll find the **train station** a few minutes beyond, up Avenida da República. There's a **tourist office** at the airport (daily 8am–11.30pm; ☏289 818 582), though the main office is near the harbour at Rua da Misericórdia 8 (Mon–Fri 9.30am–5.30/7pm, Sat & Sun 9.30am–12.30pm & 2–5.30/7pm; ☏289 803 604, ⌨www.rtalgarve.pt). Among the better **places to stay** are the spruce *Residencial Adelaide* (☏289 802 383; ❹), near the Igreja de São Pedro at Rua Cruz de Mestras 7–9, which opens its roof in summer as a dorm with beds for €10; *Pensão Madalena* (☏289 805 806; ❹), Rua C. Bivar 109; and *Residencial Pinto*, Rua 1° de Maio 27 (☏289 807 417; ❷). Faro's **hostel** is east of the centre at Rua da Polícia de Segurança Pública, off Avenida 5 de Outubro (☏289 826 521; €5). The **campsite** (☏289 817 876) is at Praia de Faro (bus #16 from town) but was closed for renovation at the time of writing. There are **restaurants** to meet most budgets: inexpensive options include *Fim do Mundo*, Rua Vasco da Gama 53 (closed Mon), and *Adega Nova*, Rua Francisco Barreto 24, which is close to the train station and always crammed with locals. The town's **nightlife** centres around cobbled Rua do Prior; *Millennium III* is the best club.

## Olhão and the islands

**OLHÃO**, 8km east of Faro, is the largest fishing port on the Algarve and an excellent base for visiting the local sandbank islands. **Train** and **bus** stations are near each other off Avenida da República northeast of town, an easy walk from the **tourist office**, just off Rua do Comércio (Oct–May Mon–Fri 10am–1.30pm & 2.30–6pm; June–Sept daily 9.30am–7pm; ☏289 713 936). For **accommodation**, try the highly rated *Pensão Bela Vista* (☏289 702 538; ❸), right out of the tourist office then first right; or the *Pensão Boémia*, slightly further out of the centre at Rua da Cerca 20, off Rua 18 de Junho (☏289 714 513; ❸). The nearest **campsite** (☏289 700 300) is at Marim, 3km east – buses hourly till 7pm from the main station. There are clusters of **restaurants** around the superb seafront market buildings; *A Bote*, nearby on Avda 5 de Outubro, is also good (closed Sun), or go for the excellent local dishes at the *Bela Vista* restaurant, underneath the Pensão of the same name. **Ferries** leave for the *ilhas* (islands) of Armona and Culatra from the jetty at the far end of Olhão's municipal gardens, five minutes from the market. The service to **Armona** (15min; €2 return) drops you off at a long strip of holiday chalets and huts that stretches right across the island on either side of the main path. The only type of **accommodation** available here is in chalets (April–Oct only; ☏289 714 173), and you'll be lucky to get one in summer. On the ocean side, the beach disappears into the distance and a short walk will take you to totally deserted stretches of sand and dune. Boats to the more distant **Culatra** (35–45min; €2–2.60 return) call first at unattractive Culatra town, then at **FAROL**, a pretty village of holiday homes edged by beautiful beaches on the ocean side.

## Tavira

**TAVIRA** is a good-looking little town with superb island beaches within easy reach, and despite ever-increasing numbers of visitors it continues to make its living as a fishing port. **Buses** pull up at the terminal by the river, a two-minute walk from the central square, Praça da República; the **train station** is 1km from the centre of town, straight up the Rua da Liberdade. From July to mid-September, boats to the beach on **Ilha de Tavira** depart from the quayside at the town side of the flyover (daily 8am–9pm; €2 return). In addition, year-round boats cross from Quatro Águas (every 15min–1hr; €1 return), 2km east of town. The beach is backed by dunes and stretches west almost as far as Fuzeta, 14km away. Despite increasing development – a small chalet settlement, a **campsite** (☎281 324 455; April–Sept) a minute from the sands, watersports, beach umbrellas and half a dozen bar/restaurants facing the sea – it's an enjoyable spot in which to hang out. The best **accommodation** in Tavira is the *Residencial Lagoas Bica*, north of the river at Rua Almirante Cândido dos Reis 24 (☎281 322 252; ❸), with the bonus of the budget eatery, *Bica*, below. Alternatives include the roomy *Pensão do Castelo* (☎281 320 790; ❸) at Rua da Liberdade 22, faded *Residencial Mirante* at Rua da Liberdade 83 (☎281 322 255; ❹ with breakfast) just up the main road (though it can be a bit noisy), and the *Residencial Princesa do Gilão*, across the river on the quayside (☎281 325 171; ❹, with breakfast), whose front rooms have balconies overlooking the river. The **tourist office** just off the main Praça da República (daily 9.30am–1pm & 2–5.30/7pm; ☎281 322 511) might also be able to find you a **private room**. **Bars** and **restaurants** line the gardens along the bank of the River Gilão, which flows through the centre of town. Best choice is *Restaurante João Belhi* at Rua José Padinha 96, which serves seafood at fairly reasonable prices, or the more expensive *Imperial* at no. 22. Over the river, *Beira Rio*, at Rua Borda da Àgua de Assêca 44–46, has tree-shaded tables serving pizza, pasta and salads. The *Arco* (closed Mon), at Rua Almirante Cândido dos Reis 67, is a laid-back, gay-friendly **bar**. Tavira's only **club**, *UBI* (closed Mon in summer, open weekends only in winter), is on Rua Vale Caranguejo, reached by following Rua Almirante Cândido dos Reis to the outskirts of town; it's the huge metallic warehouse on the right.

# Travel details

## Trains

**Coimbra** to: Lisbon (hourly; 2–3hr); Porto (hourly; 1hr 20min–2hr).
**Faro** to: Lagos (7 daily; 1hr 40min); Lisbon (4 daily; 5hr 30min–6hr); Olhão (16 daily; 10min); Silves (7 daily; 1hr–1hr 15min); Tavira (12–17 daily; 35–45min).
**Lagos** to: Faro (7 daily; 1hr 40min); Lisbon (4 daily; 5hr 15min); Silves (13 daily; 30–50min).
**Lisbon** to: Braga (2 daily; 4hr 40min); Coimbra (hourly; 2–3hr); Évora (2 daily; 3hr); Faro (4 daily; 5hr 30min–6hr); Leiria (5 daily; 2–3hr); Porto (hourly; 3hr 30min–4hr); Sintra (every 15min; 45min); Tavira (4 daily; 6–7hr); Tomar (7 daily; 2hr).
**Porto** to: Braga (13–16 daily; 1hr–1hr 45min); Coimbra (hourly; 1hr 20min–2hr); Guimarães (hourly; 1hr 40min); Lisbon (hourly; 3hr 30min–4hr); Madrid, Spain (2 daily; 12hr); Vigo, Spain (3 daily; 4hr 30min).

## Buses

**Braga** to: Bragança (2 daily; 5hr); Guimarães (every 30min; 30min–1hr); Porto (hourly; 1hr 20min).

**Coimbra** to: Fátima (5 daily; 1hr–1hr 30min); Lisbon (hourly; 2hr 20min); Leiria (10 daily; 1hr); Porto (8–10 daily; 1hr 30min); Tomar (2 daily; 2hr).
**Faro** to: Évora (3–4 daily; 4hr–4hr 30min); Huelva (for connections to Sevilla, Spain; 2–4 daily; 3hr 30min); Lagos (8 daily; 1hr 45 min); Lisbon (7–9 daily; 4hr–4hr 30min); Olhão (every 15min–1hr; 20min); Tavira (7–11 daily; 1hr).
**Leiria** to: Alcobaça (4 daily; 50min); Batalha (5 daily; 15min); Coimbra (10 daily; 1hr); Fátima (9 daily; 25min); Tomar (2 daily; 1hr 10min–2hr).
**Lisbon** to: Alcobaça (3–4 daily; 2hr); Coimbra (hourly; 2hr 20min); Évora (hourly; 2hr–2hr 30min); Faro (7–9 daily; 4hr–4hr 30min); Fátima (hourly; 1hr 30min); Lagos (6–9 daily; 4hr–4hr 30min); Leiria (hourly; 2hr); Mafra (hourly; 1hr 30min); Óbidos (hourly; 1hr); Odemira (3 daily; 4hr); Porto (hourly; 3hr); Porto Côvo (2–3 daily; 3hr 30min); Santiago do Cacém (6–8 daily; 2hr 30min); Tomar (2–4 daily; 1hr 45min–2hr); Vila Nova de Milfontes (3–4 daily; 3hr 30min–4hr); Zambujeira do Mar (1 daily; 4hr 45min).
**Porto** to: Braga (hourly; 1hr 20min); Bragança (3 daily; 1hr 50min–3hr); Coimbra (8–10 daily; 1hr 30min); Guimarães (12 daily; 2hr).

# 24

# Romania

# Romania highlights

✻ **Bucharest** Hectic traffic, Stalinist architecture, pretty residential streets and good dining and nightlife: love it or hate it, Bucharest is unmissable. See p.830

✻ **The Carpathians** Stunning mountain scenery, under two hours from the capital. See p.835

✻ **Sighişoara** Beautiful medieval citadel in the heart of Transylvania, with authentic Dracula connections. See p.837

✻ **Muzeul Astra, Sibiu** A fascinating open-air museum of Romanian village architecture, set in a scenic landscape. See p.838

△ Carpathian mountains

# Introduction and basics

Nowhere in Eastern Europe defies preconceptions quite like **Romania**. The country suffers from a poor image, but don't be put off – outstanding landscapes, a surprisingly efficient train system, a huge diversity of wildlife and a bizarre mix of cultures and people await you if you seek them out.

Romanians trace their ancestry back to the Romans, and a mix of Latin and Balkan traits prevails. In addition to ethnic Romanians, there are communities from half a dozen other races and cultures: Saxons (Transylvanian Germans) live around the fortified towns and churches built to guard the mountain passes during the Middle Ages; so do some one and a half million Magyars (Hungarians), many of whom pursue a traditional lifestyle long since vanished in Hungary.

The capital, **Bucharest**, is perhaps daunting for the first-time visitor – its savage history is only too evident – but parts of this once-beautiful city retain a voyeuristic appeal. More attractive by far, and easily accessible on public transport, is **Transylvania**, a region steeped in history, offering some of the most beautiful mountain scenery in Europe.

## Information & maps

Local authorities are now obliged to have **tourist information centres**, but you're best off going to privately run **tourist agencies**, many of which have English-speaking staff. Most bookshops and street vendors have up-to-date maps (*harta*), though it's best to buy them at home.

## Money and banks

The currency, the **leu** (plural lei), comes in notes of 10,000, 50,000, 100,000, 500,000 and 1,000,000 lei, with coins of 500, 1000 and 5000 lei. In July 2005 new notes, for the so-called 'heavy leu', with four zeroes knocked off (so that one leu is equal to 10,000 old lei) were introduced, as well as bani (hundredths of a leu) coins; the two denominations will work in parallel for a couple of years. At time of writing, €1 was equal to 36 lei, US$1 to 28 lei, and £1 to 53 lei. Hotels, rental agencies and other services quote prices in euros. There are plenty of **ATMs** in towns. **Changing money** is best done at private exchange offices (*casa de schimb*). Travellers' cheques are seldom accepted, a hassle to change, and have high commission rates. Never change money on the streets. **Credit cards** are generally accepted at hotels and upmarket shops.

## Communications

**Post offices** (*pošta*) are open Mon–Fri 7am–8pm, Sat 8am–noon. You can phone from the orange cardphones or post offices. Phonecards (100,000, 150,000 or 200,000 lei – get the last for international calls) are available from post offices and news kiosks. Rates are lower from 11pm to 7am. Internet access is available in every town; it's cheap, though not fast.

## Getting around

*InterCity* **trains** are the most comfortable;

---

## Romania on the net

ⓦ **www.turism.ro** Official tourism site.

ⓦ **www.ici.ro/romania** General information and news.

ⓦ **www.inyourpocket.com** Online guide to Bucharest.

ⓦ **http://leosuteu.rdsor.ro** Hiking information and links.

ⓦ **www.eco-romania.ro** Association of ecotourism operators.

they're followed by *Rapid* and *Accelerat* services, which stop more often. *Personal* trains stop everywhere and are generally grubby and crowded. Some overnight trains have **sleeping carriages** (*vagon de dormit*) and **couchettes** (*cuşet*) for a modest surcharge. Seat reservations are required for all fast trains, and are automatically included with locally purchased tickets. You'll also need one for **international trains** that do not require a reservation before entering Romania, so make sure to buy one before departure or face fines. The best place to **buy tickets** and book seats is at the local Agenţia SNCFR (generally open Mon–Fri 8am–7pm); at the station tickets are slightly cheaper but available only one hour in advance. Wasteels – in some major stations – offer discounts for under-26s. **InterRail** is valid, **Eurail** is not.

Only resort to rural **bus** (*autobuz*) services if a train doesn't serve your destination. A number of new **minibus** (*maxitaxi*) services compete on intercity routes – they usually depart from near the train station. Expect to pay the same as the *Accelerat* train fare. **Taxis** are very cheap and an attractive alternative to crowded public transport. Most are honest, but be sure to choose a taxi with a clearly marked company name, and make sure the meter is working.

# Accommodation

**Accommodation** is affordable. Apart from a

## Romanian

|  | Romanian | Pronunciation |
| --- | --- | --- |
| **Yes** | *Da* | Da |
| **No** | *Nu* | Noo |
| **Please** | *Vă rog* | Ve rog |
| **Thank you** | *Mulţumesc* | Mult-sumesk |
| **Hello/Good day** | *Salut/bună ziua* | Saloot/boona zhewa |
| **Goodbye** | *La revedere* | La re-ve-dairy |
| **Excuse me** | *Permiteţi-mi* | Per-mi-tets-may |
| **Where?** | *Unde?* | Oun-day? |
| **Good** | *Bun/bine* | Boon/Bee-ne |
| **Bad** | *Rău* | Rau |
| **Near** | *Apropriat* | A-prope-reeat |
| **Far** | *Departe* | D'par-tay |
| **Cheap** | *Ieftin* | Yeftin |
| **Expensive** | *Scump* | Scoomp |
| **Open** | *Închis* | Un-keez |
| **Closed** | *Deschis* | Des-keez |
| **Today** | *Azi* | Az |
| **Yesterday** | *Ieri* | Ee-airy |
| **Tomorrow** | *Mâine* | Mwee-ne |
| **How much is....?** | *Cât costa...?* | Cuut costa? |
| **What time is it?** | *Ce ora este?* | Che ora est? |
| **I don't understand** | *Nu înţeleg* | Noo unts-eledge |
| **Do you speak English?** | *Vorbiţi Englezeste?* | Vor-beetz eng-lay-zeste? |
| **One** | *Un, una* | Oon, oona |
| **Two** | *Doi, doua* | Doy, doo-a |
| **Three** | *Trei* | Tray |
| **Four** | *Patru* | Pat-ru |
| **Five** | *Cinci* | Chinch |
| **Six** | *Şase* | Shass-er |
| **Seven** | *Şapte* | Shap-tay |
| **Eight** | *Opt* | Opt |
| **Nine** | *Nouă* | No-ar |
| **Ten** | *Zece* | Zay-chay |

growing number of four- and five-star hotels offering Western comforts (and prices), standards tend to be fairly low. Cheaper **hotels** cost 250–425 lei/€7–13 per person per night, for a reasonably clean room and shared shower; breakfast is normally an extra 80 lei/€2.50. An alternative is to take a **private room** (*cazare la persoane particulare*), which will probably be the only option in smaller towns and villages. You'll usually come across people offering accommodation at the train or bus station. Expect to pay around 350 lei/€9. **Hostels** (✆www.dntcj.ro /yhr) are becoming less rare. University towns have **student accommodation** (*caminul de studenţi*) from late June to August, for around 80 lei/€2.50 per night. **Campsites** are usually very basic. Expect to pay around 120 lei/€3.50 per night for tent space, with little more than a tap and dirty loo. Outside national parks, most officials will turn a blind eye if you are discreet about camping wild.

# Food and drink

**Breakfast** (*micul dejun*) is typically a light meal, featuring rolls and butter (*chifle cu unt*) and an *omleta* washed down with a coffee (*cafea*) or tea (*ceai*). The most common **snacks** are flaky pastries (*pateuri*) filled with cheese (*cu brânză*) or meat (*cu carne*), and a variety of spicy grilled sausages and meatballs such as *mici* and *chiftele*. Menus in most **restaurants** concentrate on grilled meats, or *friptura*. *Cotlet de porc* is the common pork chop, while *muşchi de vacă* is fillet of beef. Traditional **Romanian dishes**, can be delicious. The best-known of these is *sarmale* – pickled cabbage stuffed with rice, meat and herbs, usually served with sour cream. Stews (*tocană*) and other dishes often feature a combination of meat and dairy products. **Vegetarians** could try asking for *caşcaval pane* (hard cheese fried in breadcrumbs); *ghiveci* (mixed fried veg); *ardei umpluţii* (stuffed peppers); or vegetables and salads. Establishments called **cofetărie** serve coffee and cakes, and sometimes beer and ice cream. Coffee, whether *cafea naturală* (finely ground and cooked Turkish fashion), *filtru* (filtered) or *nes* (instant), is usually drunk black and sweet; ask for it *cu lapte* or *fără zahăr* if you prefer it with milk or without sugar. **Cakes** and **desserts** are sweet and sticky, as throughout the Balkans. Romanians enjoy pancakes (*clătite*) and pies (*plăcintă*) with various fillings.

Evening **drinking** takes place in outdoor beer gardens, *cramas* (beer cellars), restaurants (where boozers often outnumber the diners), and in a growing number of Western-style cafés and bars. Try **tuica**, a powerful plum brandy taken neat; in rural areas, it is home-made and often twice distilled to yield fearsomely strong *palincă*. Most **beer** (*bere*) is German-style lager. Romania's best **wines** are Grasa and Feteasca Neagră, and the sweet dessert wines of Murfatlar. Expect to pay 50–120 lei/€1–3 for a good quality bottle.

# Opening hours and holidays

Shop **opening hours** are Mon–Fri 9am–6pm, Sat 9am–1pm, with many food shops open until 10pm (or even 24hr) including weekends. Museums and castles also open roughly 9am–6pm (though most are closed on Mon or Tues); **admission charges** are minimal hence we've not quoted them in the Guide unless they are above the norm. **National holidays** are: Jan 1 & 2, Easter Monday, May 1, Dec 1, Dec 25 & 26.

# Emergencies

Watch for pickpockets in crowded buses and trams. Do not believe anyone claiming to be a policeman and asking to see your passport and/or the contents of your wallet. Make sure you have health insurance. Bucharest's central emergency **hospital** is up to Western standards, while Medicover, Calea Plevnei 96 (✆021/310 4410), also offers Western-standard care, with English-speaking doctors. **Pharmacies** (*farmacie*) are usually well-stocked and open Mon–Sat 9am–6pm

| Emergency number |
| --- |
| In all emergencies call ✆112. |

# Bucharest (Bucuresti)

Arriving in **BUCHAREST** (Bucuresti), most tourists want to leave as soon as possible, but to do so would mean missing the heart of Romania. Bucharest does have its charm and elegance – it's just that it does things in its own way. What's more, it's a dynamic city, changing faster than any other in Romania. Old, dusty residential areas with beautiful but crumbling eclectic architecture surround the centre and show what the city was like in a bygone era. Head south and you'll come across unfinished projects from Ceauşescu's reign, frozen in time but still littering the landscape. Seeing the true scale of what a dictatorship can do is something you won't forget. Love it or hate it, Bucharest is unmissable.

## Arrival, information and accommodation

**Henri Coandâ Airport** is at Otopeni, 16km north of the centre; the only reliable taxis are marked FlyTaxi (outside International Arrivals or ☎9440/1), charging a fixed L20,000/km (€0.50); alternatively, head for the #783 bus stop just outside – buy your two-ride ticket from the RATB kiosk. Virtually all **trains** terminate at the much-improved Gara de Nord, from where it's a thirty-minute walk into the centre, or a short ride on the **metro** (change lines at Piaţa Victoriei to reach Piaţa Universităţii). Taxis (see below) can be found outside the main entrance beyond the Wasteels ticket office.

Bucharest has no **tourist office**, so you should pick up a copy of the excellent, English-language **city guide** *Bucharest In Your Pocket* (ⓦwww.inyourpocket.com; €2), with essential reviews of accommodation, restaurants, nightlife and sights; buy it at Gara de Nord's Wasteels office, the airport kiosk or from hotels and bookstores. **Public transport**, although crowded, is efficient and very cheap. The most useful lines of the metro system are the M2 (north–south) and M3 (a near-circle). There's also an array of trams, buses and trolleybuses. **Tickets** must be bought from kiosks located near the bus stops, and validated in the machine on board. After 11.30pm, you'll have to depend on **taxis**, which remain incredibly cheap, at about €0.20/km; the most reputable companies are Cristaxi (☎9461), Cobalcescu (☎9451) or Meridian (☎9444) – make sure the meter is running.

Bucharest now has a good choice of **hostels**, but if you don't fancy those, there are a handful of budget **hotels** to choose from, as well as a growing number of **private apartments**; these cost from around €35 per night and are often better and more spacious than hotel rooms – try *Adrian Accommodation* (☎0723/347192, ⓦwww.bucharest-accommodation.ro), *GrandAccommodation* (☎0722/367 568, ⓦwww.for-rent.ro) or *UNID* (☎021/320 8080, ⓦwww.accommodation.ro).

### Hostels

**Elvis' Villa** Str Avram Iancu 5 ☎021/312 1653, ⓦwww.elvisvilla.ro. Elvis is alive, and runs this bright and lively HI hostel with air-conditioned rooms sleeping 2–8 people. Laundry, breakfast, drinks and Internet are all included, and there's a kitchen and TV room. Their information kiosk at the station will help you get here, otherwise take trolleybus #85 from Piaţa Universităţii east to the Calea Mosilor stop, and continue on foot past the roundabout, turning right at the Greek church. €12.

**Funky Chicken Guesthouse** Str Gen. Berthelot 63 ☎021/312 1425, ✉funkychickenhostel @hotmail.com. The *Villa Helga*'s little sister, conveniently located just north of Cişmigiu Park, between Gara de Nord and the centre. Clean communal bathrooms, TV room, kitchen, laundry service (€2.25), but no longer a chicken. No reservations, but guaranteed accommodation for everyone who turns up. From Gara de Nord, follow B-dul Golescu, cross Str Berzei and enter the street next to the pharmacy. €8

**Villa Helga** Str Salcâmilor 2 ☎021/610 2214, ⓦwww.rotravel.com/hotels/helga. For years the only hostel in town, *Helga* remains a popular and friendly HI hostel, and a good place to meet up with other travellers. Beds in doubles as well as in mixed and female-only dorms, a kitchen, TV room,

# BUCHAREST

CALEA GRIVIŢEI

STR. GEN. BERTHELOT

CALEA VICTORIEI

STRADA P. AMZEI

Amzei Market

STR. MENDELEEV

STRADA TACHE IONESCU

STRADA ENESCU

B-DUL GENERAL MAGHERU

STR. JULLES MICHELET

British Embassy

STRADA PICTOR ARTUR VERONA

STR. ICOANEI

STR. LUTERANA

Athénée Palace

Romanian Atheneum ❹

Royal Palace

PIAŢA REVOLUŢIEI

STRADA C. A. ROSETTI

STR. MARIA ROSETTI

STRADA ŞTIRBEI VODĂ

University Library

PIAŢA REVOLUŢIEI

Cişmigiu Park

STR. ION CÂMPINEANU

PIAŢA WALTER MĂRĂCINEANU

Creţulescu Church

Senate

US Embassy

STR. BATIŞTEI

STRADA TUDOR ARGHEZI

B-DUL N. BĂLCESCU

National Theatre of Bucharest

Enei Church

STR. CÎMPINEANU

STRADA ACADEMIEI

STR. M. MILLO ❼

STR. BREZOIANU

STR. C. MILLE

Cercul Militar

STRADA EDGAR QUINET

University

PIAŢA UNIVERSITĂŢII

B-DUL CAROL I

PIAŢA ROSETTI

B-DUL REGINA ELISABETA

CFR

STRADA EFORIE

STRADA LIPSCANI

Police Headquarters

Doamnei Church

STRADA ACADEMIEI

Bucharest History Museum

Students' Church

Colţea Church

STRADA MIHAI VODĂ

Sf Nicolae-Mihai Vodă Church

River Dâmboviţa

PASAGIUL VILACROSSE

CALEA VICTORIEI

STRADA DOAMNEI

SMÂRDAN

ŞELARI

STR. BLĂNARI

PIAŢA SF. GHEORGHE

St Gheorghe Nou Church

STR. SF. VINERI

CALEA MOŞILOR

Stavropoleos Church

STR. STAVROPOLEOS

STRADA LIPSCANI

STRADA GABROVENI ❽

STRADA COVACI

National History Museum

B-DUL LIBERTĂŢII

Palatul Parlamentului

Arcade

St Apostoli Church

Domniţa Bălaşa Church

B-DUL NAŢIUNILE UNITE

SPLAIUL INDEPENDENŢEI

STRADA FRANCEZĂ

Curtea Veche

Hanul Lui Manuc

Choral Temple

Unirea Market

Unirea Department Store

Piaţa Unirii

BULEVARDUL UNIRII

| ACCOMMODATION | |
|---|---|
| Andy | B |
| Carpaţi | G |
| Cerna | C |
| Elvis Villa | I |
| Funky Chicken | F |
| Marna | D |
| Hostel Miorița | J |
| Muntenia | H |
| Villa 11 | A |
| Villa Helga | E |

| EATING & DRINKING | |
|---|---|
| Barka Saffron | 1 |
| Bistro Atheneu | 4 |
| Burebista | 5 |
| Hanul Hangitei | 8 |
| La 'mpinge Tava | 6 |
| Nicoreşti | 2 |
| Smarts | 3 |
| Vatra | 7 |

N

0        100 m

24

ROMANIA | Bucharest (Bucureşti)

Despite Bucharest's reputation for scams, it's safer than it was. Still, never pay anything to anyone in advance, never change money without knowing the exchange rate, and never hand your passport or wallet to anyone claiming to be a policeman.

courtyard with barbecue and free laundry. Take bus #79, #86 or #133 from Gara de Nord to Piaţa Gemeni, two stops after Piaţa Romana; then take the first right off B-dul Dacia into Str Viitorului. Dorms €10, rooms ②

**Villa 11** Str Institutul Medico Militar 11 ☎0722/495 900, ✉vila11bb@hotmail.com. This friendly and quiet family-run twelve-bed hostel, just five minutes' walk from Gara de Nord, offers standard facilities including free laundry. Phone ahead for airport and station pick-ups. €12.50.

### Hotels

**Andy** Str Witing 2 ☎021/212 7154. Cheap hotel (still better known as the *Bucegi*) near the station, with cramped doubles with shared facilities and larger en-suites. ②

**Carpaţi** Str Matei Millo 16 ☎021/315 0140, ⒲www.carpatihotel.compace.ro. Near Cişmigiu park, quiet and with helpful staff. Rooms with

shared showers or toilet and some en-suites. ③
**Cerna** B-dul Golescu 29 ☎021/311 0535. Opposite the *Andy*; rooms are clean and light; more expensive en-suite doubles also include breakfast. ②
**Hostel Miorița** Lipscani 12 ☎021/312 0361. A new place right in the centre with spacious rooms (and beds), with cable TV and breakfast included. ③
**Marna** Str Buzeşti 3 ☎021/212 7582. Best of the budget hotels near Gara de Nord, with en-suites and shared showers. ②
**Muntenia** Str Academiei 19–21 ☎021/314 6010, ⒲www.muntenia.kappa.ro. Old-fashioned hotel in a good central location 100m northwest of Piaţa Universităţii. En-suites and shared showers. ②

### Campsite

**Băneasa** ☎021/230 4525. Out towards the airport – take bus #301 from Piaţa Romana and get off at the Casa Alba tourist complex.

## The City

"A savage hotchpotch" was Ferdinand Lasalle's verdict on inter-war Bucharest, with its boulevards and nightlife, its slums and beggars, its aristocratic mansions and crumbling Orthodox churches. The extremes of wealth and poverty, once mitigated, have now returned thanks to burgeoning capitalism and corruption. But among the ruptured roads and disintegrating buildings, you'll find leafy squares, shaded parks and dressed-up Romanian girls adding a touch of glamour to the surroundings. Freezing in winter and hot and dusty in the summer, the northern outskirts, beyond the familiar-looking Arc de Triumf, are cooled by woodlands and a girdle of lakes.

Most inner-city sights are within walking distance of **Calea Victoriei**, an avenue of vivid contrasts, scattered with vestiges of *ancien régime* elegance interspersed with apartment blocks, glass and steel facades and cake shops. Fulcrum of the avenue is **Piaţa Revoluţiei**, created during the 1930s on Carol II's orders to ensure a field of fire around the Royal Palace. The palace now contains the excellent **National Art Museum** (Wed–Sun 10/11am–6/7pm; ⒲www.art.museum.ro; €3, free on 1st Wed of month) with fantastic works by El Greco, Rembrandt, Brueghel and Brâncuşi, plus a huge and marvellous collection of medieval and modern Romanian art. North of the palace, the **Athénée Palace Hotel** (now a *Hilton*) has always been a hive of intrigue, but was a veritable "intelligence factory" in the 1950s, with bugged rooms, tapped phones and informer prostitutes. Opposite the palace stands the grand **Romanian Atheneum**, the main concert hall, which can be visited by asking the concierge, and the **University Library**, torched, allegedly by the Securitate, in the confusion of the 1989 revolution, but now rebuilt and reopened. Just south of here is the former Communist Party HQ, now the **Senate**, which dominated TV screens worldwide in 1989. The low balcony is where Nicolae Ceauşescu made his last speech on December 21. Minutes into his speech the booing took over and the dictator's disbelief was broadcast to the nation just before the screens went blank. The next day Ceauşescu and his wife Elena escaped by helicopter from the roof, fleeing only to their eventual execution on Christmas Day. Opposite, the restored eighteenth-century **Creţulescu Church** fronts a tangle of streets wending west towards **Cişmigiu Park**, Bucharest's oldest, containing a boating lake, playgrounds, summer terrace cafés and animated chess players.

Beyond the grand **Cercul Militar** building on the junction with B-dul Regina Elisabeta, the main east–west boulevard, Calea Victoriei continues southwards past the police headquarters. Directly opposite is the **Pasagiul Vilacrosse** arcade, one of the remnants of the Bucharest that used to be known as the "Paris of the East". A little further down, at no. 1, the **Muzeul National de Istorie** (National History Museum; Tues–Sun 10am–6pm) is worth visiting for the vault of superb gold-and silverware left by Romania's ancient inhabitants, the Dacians. The remainder of the museum is likely to be closed for renovation for at least another year. Nearby is Bucharest's **historic centre**: a maze of dusty cobblestone streets with decrepit houses and tiny shops, centred on the pedestrianized Strada Lipscani. The whole area is slated for a major EU-funded renovation project, urgently necessary to save what's left, even if it causes the area to lose some of its authenticity. Just south of Strada Lipscani stands the small **Stavropoleos Church**, built in the 1720s, it has gorgeous, almost arabesque, patterns decorating its facade, and an elegant columned portico. Further south are the modest remains of the **Curtea Veche** (Old Court; daily 10am–4pm), Vlad the Impaler's fifteenth-century citadel. Dating from 1559, the adjacent Old Court church is Bucharest's oldest church. Inside the large white building opposite the church you'll find the lush courtyard of the **Hanul lui Manuc** inn, now home to a hotel and an over-priced restaurant. The inn's southern wall forms one side of **Piaţa Unirii**, which is where the old Bucharest makes way for the new.

## The Centru Civic, Piaţa Universităţii and north

The infamous **Centru Civic** was Ceauşescu's pet urban project. After an earthquake in 1977 damaged much of the city, Ceauşescu took the opportunity to remodel the entire southern portion of central Bucharest as a monument to Communism. By the early 1980s bulldozers had moved in to clear the way for the Victory of Socialism Boulevard (now **Bulevardul Unirii**), taking with them thousands of architecturally significant houses, churches and monuments. The eastern end of the boulevard is now a banking district, while the other end is dominated by the **Palatul Parlementului** (Parliament Palace), supposedly the second-largest administration building in the world. Started in 1984 – but still not complete despite the toil of 100,000 workers – the building contains 1100 rooms and a nuclear shelter, and now houses the Romanian Parliament and a conference centre. **Guided tours** in English (daily 10am–4pm; €3) start at the entrance in the centre of its north side (to the right as you face the building).

Returning northwards from Piaţa Unirii along B-dul Brătianu, you'll see the *Hotel Intercontinental* towering above busy **Piaţa Universităţii**. This is where students pitched their post-revolution City of Peace encampment, which was violently overrun, together with the illusion of true democracy, by the miners that President Iliescu had called in to "restore order" in June 1990. The miners returned to Bucharest in 1991, this time in protest against the government rather than as its storm troopers. When they advanced again in 1999, the government had riot police prevent them from approaching the capital. Just to the east rises Elena Ceauşescu's **Teatrul National** (National Theatre), resembling an Islamicized reworking of the Colosseum. Across the boulevard, **Bucharest University** is surrounded by students, snack stands and book vendors. The bulbous domes of the **Students' Church**, originally a Russian church, appear through a gap in the grand buildings to its south.

Stretching north from Piaţa Victoriei, Şoseaua Kiseleff leads into the more pleasant, leafy suburbs. At no. 3, the **Muzeul Ţăranului Român** (Museum of the

Romanian Peasant; Tues–Sun 10am–6pm, last entry 5pm; ⓦ www.itcnet.ro/mtr) is a must-see, giving an insight into the country's varied rural traditions, with exhibits on everything from costume and textiles to wood and glass painted icons; to the rear there's a beautiful wooden church of the type found in Maramureş, as well as an excellent souvenir shop. At the northern end of the Şoseaua is the **Arc de Triumf**, commemorating Romania's participation on the side of the Allied victors in World War I, while just to the north of here is **Herăstrău Park**, the city's largest. Inside the park, by the northern end of Şoseaua Kiseleff, is the **Muzeul Satului** (Village Museum; daily 9am–6pm), a fabulous ensemble of wooden houses, churches, windmills and other structures from various regions of the country.

## Eating, drinking and nightlife

Traditional fresh **snacks**, such as *gogoşi* (Romanian doughnuts), *pateuri* (pastries, usually with cheese) and *covrigi* (pretzels), are sold all over the city. Bucharest's restaurant scene has improved dramatically in recent years, and there's now a wide selection of ethnic cuisines to choose from aside from the traditional Romanian fare. Beware, though, that some restaurants still have the nasty habit of charging food by weight – if the menu shows the cost per 100 grams, check the real price with the waiter. **Nightlife** is becoming increasingly varied, too, offering something for pretty much all tastes. In the historic centre the area around Strada Gabroveni attracts many new bars and crowds, while, in summer, the clubs and restaurants around Herăstrău lake are popular. *Bucharest in Your Pocket* (see p.830) has complete **listings**. The weekly Romanian-language *şapte Seri* magazine, found free at bars, has events and cinema listings.

### Restaurants

**Barka Saffron** Str Av Sănătescu 1, just west of the Arc de Triumf ☎021/224 1004. Trendy establishment with first-class international, Indian and vegetarian food, and charming staff. Worth the trip north of the centre, and the higher prices.

**Bistro Atheneu** Str Epsicopiei 3 ☎021/313 4900. Across from the Atheneum concert hall, this homely little place has been feeding its Franco-Romanian food to concert-goers and others for a decade.

**Burebista** Str Batistei 14 ☎021/211 8929. One of the best Romanian places in town; huge menu featuring hearty portions of game, rustic surrounds and a live folk band – good central location near the *Intercontinental* hotel, also at Calea Mosilor 195 and B-dul Titulescu 39.

**Hanul Hangitei** Str Gabroveni 16 ☎021/314 7046. A neighbourhood restaurant serving good Romanian cuisine to local residents and workers – busy at lunchtime.

**La 'mpinge Tava** Piaţa Rosetti 4 (on B-dul Carol I). Cheap and popular self-service restaurant serving Romanian food and a few vegetarian options until 6pm. Closed Sat & Sun.

**Nicoreşti** Str Maria Rosetti 40 ☎021/211 2480. All the traditional Romanian dishes at rock-bottom prices with accompanying live music. Near *Villa Helga*.

**Smarts** Str Al. Donici 14 ☎021/211 9035. In a beautiful tree-lined street, this quiet and friendly restaurant serves fine French food alongside the more usual local dishes. Nice bar downstairs.

**Vatra** Str Brezoianu 23. Very central, very affordable, with great Romanian dishes such as *ciorba*.

### Cafés and bars

**Amsterdam Grand Café** Str Covaci 22. Chilled-out, Dutch-run café in the historic centre, with good service, a reading table, inexpensive food, and Dutch and Belgian beer.

**Caffe and Latte** B-dul Schitu Magureanu 35. Small, colourful café opposite Cişmigiu Gardens serving a fabulous range of coffees, shakes, sandwiches and cakes (to 10pm).

**Jukebox** Str Şepcari 22. Opposite Hanul lui Manuc, this raucous cellar bar has nightly live music and karaoke sessions.

**Lăptăria lui Enache** 4th floor of the National Theatre, Piaţa Universităţii. One of Bucharest's most popular bars; live music in winter, and free films on the rooftop terrace in summer. Entrance near the *Intercontinental* hotel near the *Café Deko* sign.

**Planter's Club** Str Mendeleev 10, south of Piaţa Romana. Immensely popular bar-cum-club with a small dance floor.

**Yellow Bar** Str E. Quinet 10, near Piaţa Universităţii. Trendy cellar-lounge bar with comfortable sofas and lots of beautiful people.

### Clubs

**Club A** Str Blănari 14. Catering to a studenty crowd, this good-time party place is the city's most established club.
**Exit** Str Covaci 22. Smooth, chill-out sounds below the *Amsterdam Grand Café.* Fri & Sat only.
**Studio Martin** B-dul Iancu de Hunedoara 41, near Piaţa Victoriei. Brings in the ravers with its international guest DJs (playing techno and house) and gay-friendly atmosphere.
**The Office** Str Tache Ionescu 2. Fashionable club, with a hip crowd and great music, but pricey and posy.
**Twice** Str Sf. Vineri 4. Banging techno tunes at Bucharest's biggest club; heaving and very popular.

## Listings

**Embassies and consulates** Australia, B-dul Unirii 74, 5th floor ☎021/320 9802; Canada, Str N. Iorga 36 ☎021/307 5000; UK, Str J. Michelet 24 ☎021/312 0303; US, Str T. Arghezi 7–9 ☎021/210 4042.
**Gay and lesbian** For information, contact Accept, Str Lirei 10 ☎021/252 1637, ⊛www .accept-romania.ro.

**Hospital** Spitalul Clinic de Urgenţa, Calea Floreasca 8 ☎021/230 0106. Medicover, Calea Plevnei 96 ☎021/310 4410.
**Internet** Brit Café, Calea Dorobantilor 14; PC-Net Café, Calea Victoriei 136 and B-dul Regina Elisabeta 25.
**Post office** Str M. Millo 10.

# Transylvania

Thanks to Bram Stoker's novel, **Transylvania** is famed abroad as the homeland of Count Dracula, but you'll find there's a lot more to explore here than the story of a bloodthirsty nobleman. From Bucharest, trains carve their way through the spectacular **Carpathian** mountain range, which offers Europe's cheapest skiing in winter and wonderful hiking during the summer; from Braşov two routes lead west into Hungary via either Arad or Cluj. It's well worth setting aside some time to explore the rest of Transylvania's caves, alpine meadows, dense forests sheltering bears, and lowland valleys with quaint villages and buffalo cooling off in the rivers. The population is a mix of Romanians, Magyars, Germans, Gypsies and others, thanks to centuries of migration and colonization. The Trianon Treaty of 1920 placed Transylvania within the Romanian state, but the character of many towns still reflects past patterns of settlement. Most striking are the former seats of Saxon power with their medieval streets, defensive towers and fortified churches. **Sighişoara** is the most picturesque but could be the Saxons' cenotaph: their culture has evaporated here, as it threatens to do in **Braşov**, **Sibiu** and in the old German settlements around.

## Braşov

With an eye for trade and invasion routes, the medieval Saxons sited their largest settlements near Transylvania's mountain passes. **BRAŞOV**, which they called Kronstadt, grew prosperous as a result, and for centuries the Saxons constituted an elite whose economic power long outlasted its feudal privileges. The Communist government brought thousands of Moldavian villagers to Braşov to work in the new factories. As a result, there are two parts to Braşov: the quasi-Gothic bit coiled beneath Mount Tâmpa, which looks great, and the surrounding sprawl of flats, which doesn't. The park beside B-dul Eroilor meets the eastern end of the pedestrianized Str Republicii, the hub of Braşov's social life. At the top of Str Republicii, sturdy buildings line Piaţa Sfatului, the main square. The fifteenth-century council house in the centre now houses the **Tourist Office** and **History Museum** (Tues–Sun 10am–5pm). The museum's exhibits illustrate the power of the Saxon guilds, whose main hangout was the red **Merchants' Hall** opposite.

The Gothic pinnacles of the city's most famous landmark, the **Black Church** (Mon–Sat 10am–5pm), stab upwards like a series of daggers: an endearingly monstrous hall-church that took almost a century to complete (1383–1477), it is so called for its soot-blackened walls, the result of being torched by the Austrian army in 1689. Inside, by contrast, the church is startlingly white, with Oriental carpets creating splashes of colour along the walls of the nave. In summer (June–Sept Tues, Thurs & Sat at 6pm), the church's 4000-pipe **organ** is used for concerts. A length of fortress wall runs along the foot of Mount Tâmpa, behind which a **cable car** whisks tourists up to the summit. Of the original seven bastions the best preserved is that of the weavers, on Str Coşbuc. This complex of wooden galleries and bolt-holes now contains the **Museum of the Bârsa Land Fortifications** (Tues–Sun 10am–4pm). Inside are models and weaponry recalling the bad old days when the region was repeatedly attacked by Tatars, Turks and by Vlad the Impaler, who left hundreds of captives on sharp stakes to terrorize the townsfolk. The Saxons' widely publicized stories of Vlad's cruelty unwittingly contributed to Transylvania's dark image and eventually caught Bram Stoker's attention as he conceived *Dracula*.

### Practicalities

Braşov's **train station** is northeast of the old town, 2km from the centre – take bus #4 into town or spend €1 on a taxi. You'll probably be approached by a ball of fire called Maria Bolea or her husband Grig (⌕0744/816 970) offering private rooms or apartments (❶) in the centre or near the station. Don't be fazed, the rooms are fine and she's a mine of information on the local area. They also own the new *Rolling Stone Hostel*, Strada Piatra Mare 2A (⌕/⌕0268/513 965, ⓔoffice@rollingstone.ro; €8); this is near the Piaţa Unirii terminal of bus #4 in the historic Schei district. A similar place is the *Villa Kismet Dao* at Str Democraţiei 2B (⌕0268/514 295,ⓦwww.kismetdao.com; €10), just off Piaţa Unirii, which has a barbecue in the garden and free perks such as Internet access and laundry. Also beyond Piaţa Unirii is the *Casa Speranţei* at Str Piatra Mare 101 (⌕0268/472 415, ⓔcshospice@hospice.bv.astral.ro; €10), where your payment helps cancer victims. Further into town, the *Beke Guesthouse*, Str Cerbului 32 (⌕0723/461 888; ❶), is cosy and quiet. Cheapest of the **hotels** is the basic *Aro Sport*, between Str Republicii and Str Mureşenilor at Str Sfântu Ioan 3 (⌕0268/478 800; ❷). The *Dârste* **campsite** to the southeast of town at Calea Bucureşti 285 (⌕0268/315 863) has cabins as well as tent-space; it's best reached by taxi. The old town is dotted with affordable **restaurants** and **cafés**. Good Romanian food is served at *Sergiana*, in the cellars of Str Mureşenilor 22 (⌕0268/419 775). At Piaţa Enescu 11, through the archway next to the Orthodox church on Piaţa Sfatului, the *Bistro De L'Arte* (⌕0268/473 994) has bistro dishes and breakfasts. A great **place to drink** is *Festival 39*, Str Mureşenilor 23, which is full of the strangest things – from badly stuffed animals and fake plastic trophies to a barman from Cuba; a few doors up the street, *Harley Club Saloon* at no. 13 has more seating and bar food. The Romanian-language magazine *Zile şi Nopţi*, free at bars, lists **events**. There's **Internet** access at Str Republicii 41.

## Bran, Râşnov and Zărneşti

Cosy little **BRAN**, 28km southwest of Braşov, is situated at the foot of the stunning Bucegi mountains. Despite what you may hear, its **castle** (Tues–Sun 9am–5pm) has only tenuous associations with Dracula – aka Vlad the Impaler, who may have attacked it in 1460. Hyperbole is forgivable, though, as Bran really does look like a vampire-count's residence. The castle was built in 1377 by the Saxons of Braşov to safeguard what used to be the main route into Wallachia, and it rises in tiers of towers and ramparts from amongst the woods, against a glorious mountain background. A warren of stairs, nooks and chambers around a small courtyard, the interior is filled with elaborately carved four-poster beds, throne-like chairs and portraits of grim-faced boyars. For a more authentic experience than Bran, jump off the Braşov bus in nearby **RÂŞNOV**, where the hilltop fortress and the views are stunning. North of Bran is **ZĂRNEŞTI**, where **Carpathian Nature Tours** (℡0745/512 096, ✆www.cntours.de) can organize **guided walks** tracking brown bears, wolves, lynx and wild boar (advance booking required) and provide information on hiking, as well as accommodation. You can also stay at Pensiunea Mosorel, Str Dr Senchea 162 (℡/✆0268/222 774, ✉george@ecoland-ro.com; ❷).

**Buses** to Bran and Zărneşti leave at least hourly (less often at weekends) from bus station #2, 3km north of central Braşov at the end of Str Lungă; take bus #12 from the centre or bus #10 from the train station, and get off opposite the stadium. There's no shortage of **private rooms** in Bran; Ovi-Tours, Str Bologa 16 (℡0268/236 666; ❷), have some clean and rustic-style rooms or can help book one elsewhere. For a near-medieval mountain escape, spend a night at *Cabana Montana* (℡0744/801 094; ❷), in the picturesque hamlet of **MAGURĂ**, on the flanks of the Piatra Craiului mountains just south of Zărneşti. Be sure to phone ahead and they'll pick you up from Zărneşti's bus station.

## Sighişoara

A forbidding silhouette of battlements and needle spires looms over the citadel of **SIGHIŞOARA**, perched on a hill overlooking the Tărnave Mare valley; it seems fitting that this was the birthplace of Vlad Ţepeş, the man known to posterity as **Dracula**. Ill-conceived plans to build a "Dracula-land" theme park here were abandoned after widespread protest – yet another illustration of Romania's inability to decide what kind of tourism it wishes to promote. Look out for the Medieval Arts and the Inter-ethnic Cultural **festivals** held annually in July and August, when Sighişoara may be overrun by thousands of beer-guzzlers.

The route from the train station to the centre passes the **Romanian Orthodox Cathedral**, its gleaming white, multifaceted facade a striking contrast to the dark interior. Across the Tărnave Mare river, the **Citadel** dominates the town from a hill whose slopes support a jumble of ancient houses. Steps lead up from the lower town's main square, Piaţa Hermann Oberth, to the main gateway, above which rises the mighty **Clock Tower**. This was built in the fourteenth century when Sighişoara became a free town controlled by craft guilds – each of which had to finance the construction of a bastion and defend it in wartime. Sighişoara grew rich on the proceeds of trade with Moldavia and Wallachia, as attested by the regalia and strongboxes in the tower's **museum** (daily 9am–3.30/6.30pm). The ticket also gives access to the seventeenth-century **torture chamber** and the **Museum of Armaments** next door with its small and poorly presented Dracula Exhibition. In 1431 or thereabouts, the child later known as **Dracula** was born in a two-storey house near the clock tower at Str Muzeului 6. At the time his father – Vlad Dracul – was commander of the mountain passes into Wallachia, but the younger Vlad's privileged childhood ended eight years later, when he and his brother Radu were sent to Anatolia as hostages to the Turks. There Vlad observed the Turks' use of terror, which he would later turn against them, earning the nickname of "The Impaler". Nowadays, Vlad's birthplace is a mediocre tourist restaurant.

Sighişoara's **train station** is on the northern edge of town, on Str Libertaţii. Backpackers are met at the station by runners for the town's many excellent private rooms; perhaps the best are with the Faur family in the citadel at Str Cojocarilor 1 (℡0744/119 211; ❷). Also good value is the *Berg Hostel* in the citadel's oldest house at Str Bastionului 4–6 (℡0265/772 234, ✆www.ibz.org.ro; €9), with dorm rooms, doubles, and a dingy bar in the cellar. The *Steaua* **hotel**, Str 1 Decembrie 12 (℡0265/771 000; ❷), is slightly tatty but affordable. Romantics will appreciate the *Casa cu Cerb* at Str Şcolii 1 (℡0265/774 625, ✆www.casacucerb.ro; ❸), as the bathtubs fit two and the contents of the minibar are included in the price (but breakfast isn't). The nicely restored *Casa Wagner*, Piaţa Cetăţii 7 (☎0265/506 014, ⓦwww.casa-wagner.com; ❹), has comfortable rooms with antique furniture. The **restaurants** in the *Casa cu Cerb* and *Sighişoara* hotels, both on Piaţa Cetăţii, are the best dining options in the citadel, while in the lower town *Joe*, overlooking the field at Str Goga 12, and *La Strada*, Str Morii 7, have good pizzas and outdoor seating. The home-made sandwiches and cakes in the *International Café*, Piaţa Cetăţii 8 (where there's also **tourist information**), are yummy and filling, and you'll find just about the only quiche in Transylvania here. *Rustic*, Str 1 Decembrie 1918 5, offers fairly good Romanian food and becomes a popular **bar** at night. The *Music Pub* in the basement of the *Berg Hostel* has some live music, while *No Limits*, below the Clock Tower, is the most central club. The fastest **Internet** access is in the basement below the *International Café*.

# Sibiu

The narrow streets and old gabled houses of **SIBIU**'s older quarters look like they've come straight off the page of a fairytale. Sibiu was the Saxons' main town, and nowadays has stronger and more lucrative links with Germany than any Transylvanian town, with many people speaking German. Like Braşov, Sibiu was founded by Germans invited by the Hungarian King Géza II to colonize strategic regions of Transylvania in 1143. Its inhabitants came to dominate trade in Transylvania and Wallachia, forming exclusive guilds under royal charter. Alas for the Saxons, their citadels were no protection against the tide of history, which eroded their influence after the eighteenth century. Within the last decades almost the entire Saxon community has left Romania. Set aside most of a day to explore Sibiu's wonderful open-air **Muzeul Astra** museum of traditional cultures.

To reach the centre from the main train station, cross the square and follow Str Gen. Magheru until you hit **Piaţa Mare**. Traditionally the hub of public life, it's surrounded by the houses of sixteenth- and seventeenth-century merchants. On its western side stands the **Muzeul Brukenthal** (Tues–Sun 9am–5pm), one of the finest in Romania with an evocative collection of works by Transylvanian painters. The city's **Muzeul de Istorie** (History Museum; Tues–Sun 9am–5pm) is housed in the impressive Old City Hall, just to the north. On the north side of Piaţa Mare, the huge Catholic church stands next to the **Council Tower** (daily 10am–6pm), which offers fine views over Sibiu's rooftops to the Carpathians. To the north, Piaţa Mică is surrounded by arcaded medieval houses. Just beyond, on Piaţa Huet, the **Evangelical Cathedral** (9am–6pm, Sun from 10am) – a massive hall-church raised during the fourteenth and fifteenth centuries – dominates its neighbours. You can climb the tower (Mon–Sat noon–4pm). The crypt, entered from outside, contains impressive tombstones of local mayors, priests and other notables as well as the tomb of Mihnea the Bad, the Impaler's son, who was stabbed to death outside here in 1510. Head down into the rambling **lower town** using one of two staircases behind the cathedral – one overshadowed by arches and the medieval citadel wall. Alternatively use the road from Piaţa Mică, which is spanned by the elegant **Liars' Bridge** – so called because of the legend that no one can stand on it and tell a lie without the structure collapsing – or from the corner of the square via another ancient stairway, pock-marked with medieval windows, doorways and turrets. Sibiu's open-air museum, the **Muzeul Astra** (Tues–Sun 9am–5pm) on Calea Răşinari, south of the centre, is even better than that of Bucharest; take trolleybus #1 to the end of the line. Scenically set to a backdrop of mountains, the museum offers a fantastic insight into Romanian rural life, with authentic wooden houses, churches and mills, all of which are lovingly tended to and proudly shown off by an array of old gentlemen. The houses' simple interiors, brightly furnished with traditional rugs, often contain the workshop of a trade such as candlemaking. The grounds hold a pleasant lake for boating, and a traditional inn serving local food and drink.

## Practicalities

Sibiu's **train and bus stations** are next to each other on Piața 1 Decembrie 1918, 400m northeast of the main square. Sibiu's **tourist office**, inside the Schiller bookstore on Piața Mare (☎0269/211 110, ⓦwww.sibiu.ro/en), also sells maps and hands out the *Sibiu Live* and *Șapte Seri* **listings magazines**. The new *Black Cat* **hostel** is above a historic pharmacy at Piața Mică 26 (☎0269/431 246, ⓔhostelsibiu@rdslink.ro; €8). Otherwise the best-value **accommodation** is in the lower town at *Hotel Ela*, Str Nouă 43 (☎0269/215 197; ❷), which is friendly and family-run, with a pleasant garden, nine spotless en-suite rooms and guest kitchen. From the train station take Strada 9 Mai, turn right onto Str Rebreanu, then first left onto Str Nouă. More central, although still in the lower town, is the tiny, family-run *Podul Minciunilor* at Str Azilului 1, by the Liars' Bridge (☎0269/217 259; ❷), with adequate but small doubles. The *Evangelisches Pfarrhaus* next to the cathedral at Piața Huet 1 (8am–3pm, or call in advance so a key can be left for you; ☎0269/211 203; €8) has a **hostel** with simple rooms sleeping two to four. *Gasthof Clara*, Str Râului 24 (☎0269/222 914; ❸), is a pleasant new **hotel**, with large beds and en-suite bathrooms and breakfasts; it also dishes out decent pizzas and spaghetti as well as Romanian and German dishes. Excellent local **food** is served up at *Mara*, Str Bălcescu 21, and at *La Turn*, at Piața Mare 1, next to the Council Tower. *Ciao Italia*, Piața Mică 23, offers excellent Italian (of course) food. For something typically Romanian, complete with live folk music, head for the cosy *Crama Sibiu Vechi*, Str Ilarian 3, off Str Bălcescu. Sibiu is quiet after 9pm; however, the smoky *Art Café*, Str Filarmonicii 2 (till 2am), has occasional **jazz** gigs and is full of arty types, while the *Chill Out Club* at Piața Mică 23 holds out till 6am, playing mostly house music.

# Timişoara

The engaging city of **TIMIŞOARA**, 250km west of Sibiu near the Serbian border, and 50km south of the rail junction at Arad, evolved around a Magyar fortress, and from the fourteenth century onwards functioned as the capital of the **Banat** region in the far west of Romania. The Turks conquered the town in 1552, and ruled the surrounding area from here until 1716. The Habsburgs who ejected them proved relatively benign masters, and during the late nineteenth century the municipality rode a wave of progress, becoming one of the first towns in the world to have horse-drawn trams and the first in Europe to install electric street-lighting. Nowadays, Timişoara is one of the most westward-oriented cities of Romania, its good location and multilingual inhabitants attracting many foreign investments. The city's fame abroad rests on its crucial role in the **overthrow** of the Ceauşescu regime. A local Hungarian minister, Lászlo Tökes, took a stand on the rights of his community, and when the police came to turf him out of his house on December 16, 1989, his parishioners barred their way. The five-day battle that ensued provided crucial inspiration for the people of Bucharest, so that Timişoara now regards itself as the guardian of the revolution.

Approaching from the train station, you'll enter the centre at Piața Victoriei, an attractive pedestrianized area, with fountains and flowerbeds strewn along its length. Its obvious focal point is the huge **Romanian Orthodox Cathedral**, completed in 1946 and comprising a blend of neo-Byzantine and Moldavian architectural elements. At the opposite end, the unattractive **Opera House** stands near the **castle** which now houses the stuffy and very missable Museum of the Banat. Antiquated trams trundle past the Baroque **Town Hall** on the central Piața Libertății, while two blocks north the vast Piața Unirii is dominated by the monumental **Roman Catholic and Serbian Orthodox cathedrals**. Built between 1736 and 1773, the former (to the east) is a fine example of Viennese Baroque, the latter is roughly contemporaneous and almost as impressive. In 1868, the municipality demolished most of the redundant citadel, leaving two **bastions** to the east and west of Piaţa Unirii. The part to the east is occupied by an **Ethnographic Museum** (Tues–Sun 10am–5pm; entrance at Str Popa Şapcă 4). Varied folk costumes, painted glass icons and furnished rooms illustrate the region's ethnic diversity effectively, but in an anodyne fashion – for example, there's no mention of the thousands of Serbs deported in 1951 when the Party turned hostile towards Tito's neighbouring Yugoslavia.

## Practicalities

Timişoara Nord **train station** is a fifteen-minute walk west of the centre, along B-dul Republicii. The small **tourist office** (Mon–Sat 10am–8pm, Sun 10am–2pm; ☏0256/437 973), hidden away in the Bazaar courtyard (opposite the Bega shopping centre) on B-dul Revoluţiei, has basic maps and copies of the free English-language **listings magazine** *Timişoara What Where When*. The **hostel** *Timişoara* is on the third floor of the largely derelict *Casa Tineretului* youth centre at Str Arieş 19 (☏0256/191 170, ✉fitt@xnet.ro; €7); take trolleybus #15 south from near the castle – it's not a particularly appealing option for solo women. Otherwise, the cheapest **hotel** is the bright and clean *Hotel Nord* (☏0256/497 504, ✉receptie@hotelnord.ro; ❷), conveniently located opposite the train station at B-dul Gen. Dragalina 47. The well-kept **campsite**, 4km west of town on Aleea Pădurea Verde (☏0256/208 925), also has huts (❷–❸) sleeping two to four people (trolleybus #11 from the train station or centre). For good Romanian **food** try *Club XXI*, Piaţa Victoriei 2, which offers large, hearty meals, or *Grizzly*, Str Ungureanu 7, which has a great selection of dishes, including some for vegetarians. There's also a very useful 24hr **supermarket** on Str Maraşeşti (at Str Lazăr), a short walk northwest of Piaţa Libertăţii. A concentration of **cafés and bars** can be found south of Piaţa Unirii; *Café Corso* at Str Savoya 24 (at Str Maraşeşti) is a popular drinking den (open around the clock) but also pleasant for morning coffee. The *Java Coffee House* and *Baroque*, both at the southeastern corner of Piaţa Unirii are also good places for a relaxing break. There's good jazz, often live, at *Club 30*, at the southern end of Piaţa Victoriei in the Cinema Timiş. Party animals should head for the canalside bars behind the cathedral such as the *Bar Vaporul*, *Bănăteana*, or the *Terasa Boss*. Find out what's going on in the weekly *şapte Seri* **listings magazine**, found free at most bars. There's cheap **Internet** access at Savoya 22, south of Piaţa Unirii.

# Travel details

### Trains

**Braşov** to: Bucharest (22 daily; 2hr 20min–4hr); Sibiu (8 daily; 2hr 15min–3hr 55min); Sighişoara (15 daily; 1hr 40min–3hr); Timişoara (1 daily; 8hr 45min).
**Bucharest** to: Braşov (22 daily; 2hr 25min–4hr); Sibiu (2 daily; 5hr 30min–5hr 50min); Sighişoara (9 daily; 4hr 10min–5hr); Timişoara (6 daily; 7hr 30min–8hr 50min).
**Sibiu** to: Braşov (8 daily; 2hr 10min–3hr 50min); Bucharest (2 daily; 5hr 25min); Sighişoara (change at Copşa Mică or Mediaş; 5 daily; 2hr 15min–3hr); Timişoara (3 daily; 5hr 10min–6hr).
**Sighişoara** to: Braşov (15 daily; 1hr 45min–2hr

45min); Bucharest (9 daily; 4hr 15min–5hr); Sibiu (change at Copşa Mică or Mediaş; 6 daily; 2hr 5min–2hr 45min).
**Timişoara** to: Braşov (1 daily; 9hr); Bucharest (6 daily; 7hr 30min–8hr 45min); Sibiu (3 daily; 5hr 5min–6hr 30min).

### Buses

**Braşov** to: Bran (every 30min 7am–6pm Mon–Fri, hourly Sat/Sun; 45min); Zărneşti (hourly Mon–Fri, 8 Sat, 2 Sun; 1hr).
**Bran** to: Braşov (every 30min 7am–6pm Mon–Fri, hourly Sat/Sun; 45min); Zărneşti (9 daily; 30min).

# Russia

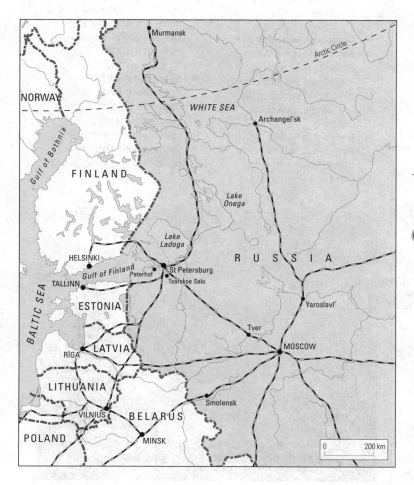

# Russia highlights

* **The Kremlin, Moscow** A whole complex of political, architectural and artistic associations. See p.849

* **Open-air swimming in winter, Moscow** When the air temperature is -15° C and the air above the heated pool is thick with steam. See p.855

* **Banya** If in Russia, do as the Russians do, and beat yourself with birch twigs in a truly local bath-house. See p.854 and p.861

* **Hermitage, St Petersburg** Defines the heart of the city architecturally, intellectually and historically. See p.858

* **Kunstkammer, St Petersburg** Don't miss Peter the Great's eighteenth-century collection of monstrosities and curiosities. See p.859

△ The Kremlin, Moscow

# Introduction and basics

European Russia stretches from the borders of Belarus and Ukraine to the Ural mountains, over 1000km east of Moscow; even without the rest of the vast Russian Federation, it constitutes by far the **largest country** in Europe. Although **visas** are obligatory and accommodation often has to be booked in advance, independent travel grows hugely every year. Moscow and St Petersburg are connected to the rest of Europe by fast trains and buses, and remain the easiest places to visit.

**Moscow**, the capital, is chaotic – not a beautiful city as such. The central core, however, reflects Russia's fascinating history, whether in the Kremlin with its palaces and churches of the tsars, the wooden buildings still tucked away in back streets, in the relics of the Communist years, or in the massive building projects which have radically changed the face of the city since the 1990s. By contrast, **St Petersburg**, Russia's second city, is Europe at its most gracious, an attempt by the eighteenth-century tsar Peter the Great to re-create the best of Western European elegance in what was then a far-flung outpost. Its position in the delta of the River Neva is unparalleled, full of watery vistas of huge and faded palaces. The city has not been revamped anywhere near as much as Moscow, and it preserves a unity of style and mood and a stability lacking in the capital.

## Information & maps

Russia has few **tourist offices**, none of them particularly useful. Most travellers use the **information desks** at hotels and hostels, and there are English-language **newspapers** such as the *Moscow Times* (daily) and the *St Petersburg Times* (twice weekly), and free quarterly magazines available at leading hotels. High-quality **maps** in English are widely available at low prices so there's no need to waste money on expensive foreign ones.

## Money and banks

Currency is the **ruble**, divided into 100 kopeks. There are coins of 1, 5, 10 and 50 kopeks and 1, 2 and 5 rubles, and notes of 5, 10, 50, 100, 500 and 1000 rubles. Everything is charged and paid for in rubles – it's illegal to pay in foreign currency – but to give a stable idea of costs we've quoted prices in **euros** (at time of writing, €1 was equal to 36 rubles). Never **change money** anywhere except in an official bank or currency exchange – the only profit made is by the non-official dealers who – literally – rob you. Most **exchange offices** are open Mon–Sat 10am–6/8pm or later, and **ATMs** are plentiful (the most reliable are those inside metro stations and branches of Sberbank). Both cities are expensive if you choose familiar Western shops and brands – or really quite cheap (particularly St Petersburg) if you look out for the excellent local shops, eateries and clubs.

25

---

### Russia on the net

ⓦ **www.infoservices.com**, ⓦ **www.ru/eng/index.html**, ⓦ **www.geocities.com /Colosseum/Track/7635/russians.html** Directories to Russia on the Net.

ⓦ **www.themoscowtimes.com**, ⓦ **www.sptimesrussia.com** English-language newspapers on the Net, with useful tourist information and current listings.

ⓦ **www.metro.ru** All in Russian, but a stunning introduction to the famous metro.

ⓦ **www.moscow-city.ru**, ⓦ **www.city-guide.spb.ru** The official city guides.

ⓦ **www.museum.ru** Museums all over Russia. The entries are of varying quality, but a fuller list is not to be found.

# Communications

Most **post offices** are open Mon–Sat 8am–7pm. All district post offices have poste restante (do vostrébovaniya) services. Local postal services are reliable and quaint but take ages, so for urgent letters or documents use express-letter companies, such as Westpost, which despatches mail via Finland for moderate sums. Street **phones** take phonecards, but for international calls get a Zebra card, usable from any phone and considerably cheaper. All cards are available from kiosks or branches of the savings bank Sberbank. The numerous **Internet** cafés are cheap. Non-Russian **mobiles** work on roaming via local providers, but you will pay an arm and a leg for the pleasure. If in Russia for any length of time, get a local SIM card, or stick to SMS.

# Getting around

The network of **trains** and buses is extensive and relatively efficient. More than twenty trains a day in each direction connect the two main cities; the journey takes around eight hours (6hr for the popular day train Aurora; 4hr for the evening train). All trains are safe, reliable and cheap (from approx. €20 one way in a four-person compartment; be aware that compartments are mixed male/female), with tickets available in advance from the station. Moscow's and St Petersburg's outlying sights are easily reached by **metro**, suburban **buses** and efficient **minibuses** from the end of a metro line. Fares are also low. Although the practice is declining with the arrival of commercial minibuses, many Russians **hitch** – especially after the public transport system closes down, you'll see people flagging down anything that moves. If the driver finds the destination acceptable, he'll state a price, which may or may not be negotiable. However, you should never accept lifts from anyone who approaches you outside restaurants and nightclubs. Official taxis can be extremely expensive; they are also not particularly reliable, unless you use a dial-a-cab service, for instance when you are in some distant part of town.

# Accommodation and visas

Anyone travelling on a **tourist visa** to Russia must (technically) have accommodation arranged before arrival, but this is increasingly easy to get round. Hostels can usually provide **invitations** for a stay of up to a month as long as you spend (or pay for) just one night there. All hostels, hotels and agencies listed can arrange the necessary visa support for you. Note that it's important to **register** your visa within three working days of your arrival, otherwise you face a fine and considerable inconvenience. On arrival you fill out an **immigration card**: you will be given back the bottom half which you MUST keep and present on departure.

**Hostels** are definitely the best-value accommodation at around €10–25 per person, as well as being safer and cleaner than many more expensive hotels. You should reserve three to four weeks in advance and there is usually no age restriction. Plenty of agencies offer **B&B** in Russian households, from €25 per person per night. Groups of people will find it cheaper to book an apartment with several beds: these are often centrally located. Inexpensive **hotels**

---

## Accommodation and visas: agencies and sites

Ⓦ **www.hostelworld.com** Excellent choice of hostels and mini-hotels at all prices.

Ⓦ **www.cityrealtyrussia.com** Small hotels and B&Bs in St Petersburg and Moscow; visa support.

Ⓦ **www.ostwest.com** Mainly St Petersburg accommodation, including B&B; visa support.

Ⓦ **www.visatorussia.com** Outstanding visa service to Russia and CIS countries.

Ⓦ **www.russianembassy.net** Russian embassies and consulates near you.

Ⓦ **www.infinity.ru** Reliable travel company offering visa service.

and hostels are mainly in characterless modern blocks. Recent years have seen the appearance of central **mini-hotels**, with a tiny number of clean, attractive rooms at €40–70 per night.

# Food and drink

Moscow and St Petersburg abound in cafés and restaurants offering everything from pizza to Indian. Cheap establishments are plentiful, if not always easy to find, and more likely to serve food with a local flavour, but do not accept credit cards. Menus are usually in Russian only. You can always ask what they recommend ("shto-by vy porekomendovali?").

First come the all-important **zakuski** – "tasters" or small dishes consumed before a meal with vodka, as a snack or as a light meal. Herring is a firm favourite (try *selyodka*

| Russian | | |
|---|---|---|
| | **Russian** | **Pronunciation** |
| **Yes** | *Da* | Da |
| **No** | *Net* | Nyet |
| **Please** | *Pozhaluysta* | Pazháaloosta |
| **Thank you** | *Spasibo* | Spaséeba |
| **Hello/Good day** | *Zdravstvuyte* | Zdrávstweetye |
| **Goodbye** | *Do svidaniya* | Da svidáaneya |
| **Excuse me** | *Izvinite* | Izvinéetye |
| **Where?** | *Gde...?* | Gdye...? |
| **Good** | *Khoroshiy* | Khoróshee |
| **Bad** | *Plokhoy* | Plokhóy |
| **Near** | *Blizkiy* | Bléezki |
| **Far** | *Daleko* | Dalyekó |
| **Cheap** | *Deshóvyy* | Deshóvee |
| **Expensive** | *Dorogoy* | Daragóy |
| **Open** | *Otkryt* | Otkryt |
| **Closed** | *Zakryt* | Zakryt |
| **Today** | *Segodnya* | Sevódnya |
| **Yesterday** | *Vchera* | Vcherá |
| **Tomorrow** | *Zavtra* | Závtra |
| **How much is....?** | *Skolko stoit?* | Skóllka stówit? |
| **What time is it?** | *Kotoryy chas?* | Katóree chass? |
| **I don't understand** | *Ya ne ponimayu* | Ya ne ponimáyou |
| **Do you speak English?** | *Vy govorite po-angliyski?* | Vwee gavoréetye po- angléeskee? |
| **One** | *Odin* | Adéen |
| **Two** | *Dva* | Dva |
| **Three** | *Tri* | Tree |
| **Four** | *Chetyre* | Chetéeri |
| **Five** | *Pyat* | Pyat |
| **Six** | *Shest* | Shest |
| **Seven** | *Sem* | Syeem |
| **Eight** | *Vosem* | Vósyem |
| **Nine** | *Devyat* | Dáyvyat |
| **Ten** | *Desyat* | Dáysyat |

*pod shuboy*, herring "in a fur coat" of beetroot, carrot, egg and mayonnaise), as are **pancakes** (*bliny*) with all kinds of savoury or sweet fillings, or indeed with **caviar** (*ikra*); red caviar is relatively cheap. Great emphasis is placed on soup, a daily dose of which is thought to be vital for a healthy body.

Cabbage **soup** (*shchi*), served with a generous dollop of sour cream (*smetana*), is much tastier than it sounds; try the gourmet version, green (or sorrel) soup (*zelyonye shchi*). In summer try cold *borshch* (beetroot soup). **Vegetarians** often have to get by on *zakuski*, since main courses are overwhelmingly based on **meat** (*myaso*), which makes its way into *pelmeny*, a Russian version of ravioli. **Georgian** restaurants always have interesting veggie dishes, such as bean stew or stuffed aubergines. Savoury pies (*pirozhki*) with cabbage or rice are very popular (but never buy from street vendors and don't touch fried pies with meat unless you have a cast-iron stomach). Russian **ice cream** is outstanding, eaten outdoors even when the temperature drops to -20°C.

**Vodka** (*vódka*) is still the national drink, though sales have been overtaken by beer. It's normally served chilled and drunk neat in one gulp, followed by a mouthful of *zakuska*. Connoisseurs stick to the straight stuff, making an exception only for **Pertsovka** (hot pepper vodka – try the Ukrainian version, Nemiroff), whose kick cures all known diseases in seconds. Russians drink **beer** (*pívo*) in the morning to alleviate a hangover, or merely as a thirst quencher. The numerous local brands (in bottles and on tap) have an excellent fresh taste, with few preservatives. Russian wine (*vinó*) is an acquired taste, so most foreigners avoid it. "Soviet Champagne" (*sovetskoe shampanskoe*), however, is a must at any party, and it's well worth trying Georgian dry and semi-sweet wines (such as Stalin's favourite, Khvanchkara) and the fortified wines of the Crimea (*kheres* or sherry and Madeira). Tea (*chay*) is traditionally brewed and stewed for hours, and topped up with boiling water from a samovar (though cafés use teabags); Russians drink it black. Sadly, traditional cafés offering excellent Turkish coffee have mainly been

replaced by the ubiquitous chains of coffee shops.

## Emergency numbers

Police ☎02; ambulance ☎03; fire ☎01.

# Opening hours and holidays

Most **shops** open Mon–Sat 10am–7pm or later; few close for lunch. Department stores, bars and restaurants stay open on Sundays. **Museum** hours are 10am–5/6pm. They are invariably closed one day a week, with one day in the month set aside as a "cleaning day". Ticket offices close one hour earlier. **Churches** are accessible from 8am until the end of evening service. Official **public holidays** are: Jan 1, Jan 6 & 7, Feb 23, March 8, May 1 & 2, May 9, June 12, Nov 7, Dec 12. Russians also informally celebrate the unofficial Julian New Year's Eve, which falls on 13 Jan.

# Emergencies

You really won't be bothered by the so-called Russian "mafia", but beware of **petty crime**, particularly pickpockets. Don't leave valuables in your hotel room, and lock the door before going to sleep. The **police** (*militsia*) wear blue-grey uniforms and are sometimes armed; report a robbery to them ("Menya obokrali" means "I've been robbed"). High-street **pharmacies** (*aptéka*) offer many familiar medicines over the counter. Foreigners tend to rely for treatment on private **clinics**, which charge excessively high rates, so travel insurance is essential. Clinics listed here (see p.855 & p.861) are all recognised by international insurance companies. St Petersburg water contains the giardia parasite, which can cause severe diarrhoea – metranidazol is the cure, but it's better to avoid drinking tap water (whilst not being paranoid about it).

# Moscow (Moskva)

**MOSCOW** (Moskva) is all things to all people. For Westerners, the city may look European, but its unruly spirit seems closer to Central Asia. To Muscovites, however, Moscow is both a "Mother City" and a "big village", a tumultuous community which possesses an underlying collective instinct that shows itself in times of trouble. Moscow has been imbued with a sense of its own destiny since the fourteenth century, when the principality of Muscovy took the lead in the struggle against the Mongol-Tatars who had reduced the Kievan state to ruins. In the fifteenth and sixteenth centuries under Ivan the Great and Ivan the Terrible its realm came to encompass everything from the White Sea to the Caspian, while after the fall of Constantinople to the Turks in 1453, Moscow assumed Byzantium's suzerainty over the Orthodox world. Despite the changes wrought by Peter the Great – not least the transfer of the capital to St Petersburg – Moscow kept its mystique and bided its time until the Bolsheviks made it the fountainhead of a new creed. Since the fall of Communism, Muscovites have given themselves over largely to "Wild Capitalism" and major building programmes have changed the face of the city radically.

## Arrival, information and accommodation

**Planes** from Western Europe arrive either at Sheremetevo, Terminal 2, or the more user-friendly Domodedovo. In both cases, avoid taxi drivers, and take a minibus or official bus to the end of the metro line (Rechnoy Vokzal for Sheremetevo, Domodedovskaya for Domodedovo, which also has an hourly Aeroexpress to the more central Paveletskaya). Trains from Warsaw arrive at **Belarus Station**, 1km northwest of the Garden Ring. Services from Budapest terminate at **Kiev Station**, south of the Moskva River. From St Petersburg, Finland or Estonia, you'll arrive at **Leningrad Station**. To get into the centre take the metro: taxi drivers are notorious for overcharging. Ecolines **buses** from Germany and the Baltic States terminate at **Aerovokzal** on Leningradskoe shosse. General **information** is available from all hostels and hotels, as well as bookshops.

Although the city centre is best explored on foot, Moscow is so big you won't get by without its famous **metro**. Buy a card for a set number of rides. You can travel any distance and change lines as many times as you like for the cost of one ride (€0.40). Stations are marked with a large "M", all signs are in Russian, including "entrance" (vkhód), "exit" (vykhod) and "passage to another line" (perekhód), but maps increasingly have transliterated names as well. **Bus** stops are marked with yellow signs and **trolleybus** stops have blue-and-white signs. Single tickets (*talony* – around €0.35) or batches of ten are available from kiosks by the metro or from the driver of the vehicle. Overground transport in Moscow is inefficient and you're best off sticking with the metro. Official **taxis** come in all shapes and sizes and are often viciously expensive.

Budget travellers will not have an easy time: **hotels** are overpriced. **Mini-hotels**, **hostels** and **bed and breakfast** are all a much better bet (see box, p.844); check out *Uncle Pasha*'s site ®www.cheap-moscow.com for useful information.

### Hostels

**G&R Hostel Asia** Zelenodolskaya ul. 3/2 ☎095/378 0001, ®www.hostels.ru; Ryazanskiy Prospekt metro. Excellent value, with good facilities. Despite its apparent distance from the centre, it's only a short metro ride away. Dorms €18, rooms ❸

**Hostel Snail** Selskokhozyaistvennaya ul. 15/1, office 339 ☎095/795 2335, ®www.hostel-snail

.ru; Botanicheskiy sad metro. A cheap and clean new arrival on the hostel scene. Dorms €16, rooms ❹

**Hostel Sherstone** Gostinichnyy proezd 8/1, 3rd floor ☎095/711 2613, ®www.sherstone.ru; Petrovsko-Razumovskaya metro. A little way from the metro, but very friendly and very cheap. Dorms €17, rooms ❸

Travellers Guest House Bolshaya Pere-
yaslavskaya ul. 50 ☎095/631 40 59, ⌚www
.tgh.ru; Prospekt Mira metro and 10min walk.
American-run hostel on the 10th floor, clean and
fairly central. Dorms €21, rooms ❹

**Hotels**
**Izmailovo Complex** Izmailovskoe shosse
71; Izmailovskiy Park metro: **Gamma-Delta**
☎095/166 4345, ⌚www.gamma-delta.narod

.ru; **Alfa** ☎095/166 0163, ⌚www.alfa-hotel.ru;
**Vega** 71 ☎095/956 0665, ⌚www.hotel-vega.ru.
Complex of high-rise hotels set in a green park,
all with good facilities ❺
**Cosmos** Prospekt Mira 150 ☎095/234 1000,
⌚www.hotelcosmos.ru; VDNKh metro. Right by
stunning Stalinist architectural complex known as
VDNKh, and offering excellent facilities including
a large swimming pool, this hotel is well worth
splashing out on. ❼

# The City

Moscow's general layout is easily grasped – a series of concentric circles and radial
lines emanating from the Kremlin – and the centre is compact enough to explore
on foot. **Red Square** and the **Kremlin** are the historic nucleus of the city, and are
where you'll find Lenin's Mausoleum and St Basil's Cathedral, the famous GUM
department store, and the Kremlin itself, whose splendid cathedrals and Armoury
Museum head the list of attractions. The Kremlin is ringed by two quarters defined
by boulevards built over the original ramparts of medieval times, when Moscow's
residential areas were divided into the inner **Beliy Gorod** and the humbler outer
**Zemlyanoy Gorod**. The cosy **Zamoskvoreche** area to the south is home to the
Tretyakov Gallery of Russian art and Gorky Park. Beyond this core lie some key
sites best reached by metro. To the southwest, **Novodevichiy Convent** nestles
in the loop of the River Moskva and Moscow State University rises high up on
the Sparrow Hills; south is the romantic ex-royal estate of **Kolomenskoe**. In the
north sprawls **VDNKh**, a huge Stalinist exhibition park with amazing statues and
pavilions, while in the east lies the **Andrey Rublev Museum of Old Russian
Art and Culture**.

## Red Square

Every visitor to Moscow is irresistibly drawn to **Red Square**, the historic and
spiritual heart of the city. The name Red Square (Krasnaya ploshchad) has nothing to do with Communism, but derives from *krasnyy*, the old Russian word for
beautiful. On the west side, the Lenin Mausoleum squats beneath the ramparts of
the Kremlin and on the other sprawls **GUM** – what was during Soviet times the
State Department Store – built in 1890–93, and now a hymn to expensive fashion
outlets. In post–Communist Russia, the **Lenin Mausoleum** (Tues, Wed, Thurs,
Sat & Sun 10am–1pm, but occasionally closed for several months at a time;
free) can be seen as either an awkward reminder or a cherished relic of the old
days. Although leaving Lenin's embalmed corpse in situ seems inappropriate, the
Mausoleum itself is a stylish piece of architecture. Behind it, the **Kremlin wall**
– 19m it high and 6.5m thick – contains a mass grave of Bolsheviks who perished
during the battle for Moscow in 1917 and the ashes of an array of luminaries,
including writer Maxim Gorky, first man in space Yuriy Gagarin, and John
Reed, the American Communist who witnessed the Revolution. Beyond lie the
graves of a select group of Soviet leaders, each with his own bust: a pompous
Brezhnev and a benign-looking Stalin. No description can do justice to **St Basil's
Cathedral** (11am–7pm, closed Tues and first Mon of month; €3), silhouetted
against the skyline where Red Square slopes down towards the Moskva River.
Commissioned by Ivan the Terrible to celebrate his capture of the Tatar stronghold of Kazan in 1552, its popular title commemorates a "holy fool", St Basil
the Blessed, who foretold the fire that swept Moscow in 1547. Stalin hated the
building, resenting the fact that it prevented his troops from marching out of Red
Square en masse. At the other end of the square is the **State History Museum**
(10am–6pm, closed Tues and first Mon of month; €5), with a varied collection of

㉕

everything from archeological finds to Soviet badges and textiles on display. Beyond, to the north, is the supreme symbol of Moscow's exchange of Communism for capitalism: in place of the empty space formerly used for parades and displays of military hardware is a vast underground shopping centre buried beneath a mass of tasteless landscaping.

## The Kremlin

Brooding and glittering in the heart of Moscow, the **Kremlin** (10am–5pm, closed Thurs; €10, free entry for under-18s third Mon of month; ® www.kreml.ru) thrills and tantalizes whenever you see its towers against the skyline, or its cathedrals and palaces arrayed above the Moskva River. The founding of the Kremlin is attributed to Prince Yuriy Dolgorukiy, who erected a wooden fort above the confluence of the Moskva and Neglinnaya rivers in about 1147. Under Grand Duke Ivan III (1462–1505) this "kremlin" grew to confirm Moscow's stature as the centre of Russia. A couple of visits are needed to do it all justice: one to see the cathedrals, and another for touring the **Armoury Palace**, which can only be entered at set times.

Roughly two-thirds of the Kremlin is off-limits to tourists, the accessible part beginning around the corner from the Great Kremlin Palace. The **Patriarch's Palace** has changing exhibitions devoted to the seventeenth century. Next, the **Tsar Cannon**, cast in 1586, is one of the largest cannons ever made and was intended to defend the Saviour Gate, but has never been fired. Close by looms the earthbound **Tsar Bell**, the largest bell in the world, cast in 1655. Beyond lies **Cathedral Square**, the historic heart of the Kremlin, dominated by the magnificent, white **Ivan the Great Bell Tower**, the tallest structure within the Kremlin's walls (with excellent small exhibitions on the ground floor; €3), and with four key churches. The most important is the **Cathedral of the Assumption**, used throughout tsarist times for coronations and solemn acts of state. Its exterior is remarkably plain, while the interior is spacious, light and echoing, its walls, roof and pillars entirely covered with icons and frescoes. Next door is the white **Church of the Deposition of the Robe** while the **Cathedral of the Archangel** houses the tombs of Russia's rulers from Grand Duke Ivan I to Tsar Ivan V (later rulers were buried in St Petersburg). Last comes the golden-domed **Cathedral of the Annunciation**, the private royal church, with some of Russia's finest icons, including works by Theophanes the Greek and Andrey Rublev. Situated between the Great Kremlin Palace and the Borovitskiy Gate, the **Armoury Palace** (by ticket purchased in advance; €10) conceals a staggering array of treasures – among them the tsars' coronation robes, carriages, jewellery, dinner services and armour – well worth the trouble.

## The Belyy Gorod

The **Belyy Gorod** (White Town) is the historic name of the residential district that encircled the Kremlin. Multi-domed churches cluster along ulitsa Varvarka, and around Kitay-gorod east of the Kremlin: this was the very heart of the city during the sixteenth century, and even today it has a medieval feel. Its main seventeenth-century thoroughfare, Tverskaya ulitsa, owes its present form to a massive reconstruction programme during the mid-1930s, and yet, despite the scale of some of its gargantuan buildings, the variety of older, often charming side streets gives the avenue a distinctive character. Those interested in Russia's Communist past and turbulent politics should pay a visit to the **Museum of Modern History** (Tues–Sun 10am–6pm; €5), at Tverskaya 21, formerly the Museum of the Revolution. Its bold displays of propaganda posters, photographs and state gifts to Lenin and Stalin are fascinating even if you cannot read Russian. South of Tverskaya, Moscow's **Pushkin Museum of Fine Arts**, Volkhonka ul. 12 (Tues–Sun 10am–7pm; €9; ® www.museum.ru/gmii), has a rich collection of European painting, from Italian High Renaissance works to Rembrandt and Poussin, and

25

▲ Belarus Station & Airport

**EATING & DRINKING**

| | |
|---|---|
| Avocado | 12 |
| Coffee Bean | 5 |
| Gogol | 6 |
| Kish-Mish | 15 |
| Kofe-Inn | 7 |
| Manege Shopping Centre | 14 |
| Moo-Moo | 16 |
| Ogonyok | 10 |
| PiR O.G.I. | 9, 18 |
| Sherbet | 4 |
| Shokoladnitsa | 11 |
| Sindibad | 13 |
| Taras Bulba | 1, 2, 17 |
| Yolki-Palki | 3, 8, 19 |

Tsvetnoy Bulvar

Central Market

Yury Nikulin Circus

Hermitage Gardens

Mayakovskaya

Church of the Nativity of Our Lady in Putinki

Upper Monastery of St Peter

Minsk Hotel

Tchaikovsky Concert Hall

Pushkinskaya

Chekhovskaya

Museum of Modern History

Tverskaya

Tsentralnaya Hotel

Patriarch's Ponds

Zoo Park
Planetarium

Barrikadnaya

Church of the Resurrection of Christ in Jerusalem

Moscow Art Theatre

Bolshoy Theatre

TsUM

Stalin Skyscraper

Chekhov House-Museum

Gorky House-Museum

Museum of Folk Art

Central Telegraph Office

Teatralnaya

House of Unions

Metropol Hotel

Stanislavsky House-Museum

State Duma

Chaliapin House-Museum

US Embassy

House of Writers

Oriental Arts Museum

Moscow Conservatory

National Hotel

Okhotniy Ryad

History Museum

Kazan Cathedral

Tsvetaeva Museum

Lermontov House-Museum

Church of St Simeon the Stylite

Gogol Memorial Room

Moscow University

Biblioteka Imeni Lenina

Manège

Lenin

Scriabin House-Museum

Church of St Saviour in Peski

Arbatskaya Ploshchad

Arbatskaya

Alexandrovskiy Sad

Borovitskaya

Kremlin

Smolenskaya

Melnikov House

Smolenskaya

Pushkin on the Arbat Museum

Pushkin Museum of Fine Arts

River

Ministry of Foreign Affairs

Gagarinskiy Pereulok

Museum of Private Collections

Kropotkinskaya

Pushkin Museum

Cathedral of Christ the Redeemer

Church of St Nicholas

Tolstoy Literary Museum

Tretyakov Gallery

N

0    500 m

MOSCOW

KHAMOVNIKI

Peter the Great (monument)

▼ Novodevichiy Convent & University     ▼ Gorky Park

◄ Kiev Station
◄ White House & Borodino Panorama

---

an outstanding display of Impressionists. It also has the magnificent gold of the lost city of Troy, removed from Germany at the end of World War II and still the subject of conflict between the two countries.

In 1994, Moscow's Mayor Luzhkov took the populist step of announcing the rebuilding of the **Cathedral of Christ the Redeemer** opposite the museum. The vast original structure had been blown up by the Soviet government in 1934 and a swimming pool built on the site. Financed largely by donations and perceived as

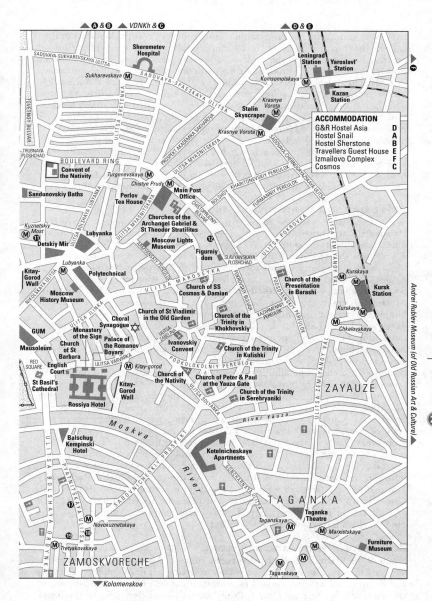

Andrei Rublev Museum (of Old Russian Art & Culture)

a symbol of Moscow's (and Russia's) revival, the cathedral is today a monument to one man's overweening pride and ambition.

### The Zemlyanoy Gorod

In medieval times, the white-walled Belyy Gorod was encircled by a humbler **Zemlyanoy Gorod** (Earth Town). Separated from the Belyy Gorod by the tree-lined "boulevard ring", this is one of the most gentrified parts of Moscow, with Neoclassical and Art Nouveau mansions on every corner. Admirers of Bulgakov, Chekhov, Lermontov, Gorky and Pushkin will find their former homes preserved as museums in the pretty, leafy backstreets around the **Patriarch's Ponds**, southwest of Tverskaya. At Bolshaya Sadovaya ul. 10, a plaque attests that Mikhail Bulgakov lived here from 1921 to 1924; his satirical fantasy *The Master and Margarita* is indelibly associated with this area in particular. Anton Chekhov lived at Sadovaya-Kudrinskaya ul. 6, in what is now the **Chekhov House-Museum** (Thurs, Sat & Sun 11am–5pm, Wed & Fri 2–7pm; €3), while Maxim **Gorky's House-Museum** on the corner of Povarskaya ulitsa and ulitsa Spiridonovka (Wed–Sun 11am–8pm; closed last Thurs of month; free), is worth seeing purely for its amazing Art Nouveau decor, raspberry ice-cream pink both inside and out. West of here, the **Arbat** once stood for bohemian Moscow in the way that Carnaby Street represented swinging London, but today it is aimed more at tourists, with its pricey cafés and antique shops.

## West beyond the Garden Ring

West of the river, patriotic ardour finds an outlet at the immense **Borodino Panorama** at Kutuzovskiy pr. 38 (10am–6pm; closed Fri & last Thurs of month; booked tours only on Wed, independent visits Sat & Sun afternoon; €1.50; ⑩www.1812panorama.ru), housing a painting 115m long and 15m high, with 3000 figures. This monument to the Battle of Borodino, fought against Napoleon in 1812, was completed in 1912, dismantled soon after the Revolution, then re-established thirty years later. South of here, **Moscow State University** occupies the largest of the city's seven 1950s Stalinist-Gothic skyscrapers, dominating the plateau of the Sparrow Hills (Vorobyovye gory), overlooking the Moskva River. Besides the university, the attraction is quite simply the panoramic view of Moscow, with Luzhniki stadium and the Novodevichiy Convent in the foreground, the Kremlin in the middle distance, and six more Stalinist skyscrapers ranged across the city. Visible across the loop of the river, a cluster of shining domes above a fortified rampart proclaims the presence of the lovely **Novodevichiy Convent** (daily 8am–7pm for worship; museum 10am–5pm; closed Tues & first Mon of month; €5). At its heart stands the white Cathedral of the Virgin of Smolensk, with a superb interior. Metro Sportivnaya (ulitsa 10-tiletiya Oktyabrya exit) brings you to within a ten-minute walk of the convent. Beyond its south wall lies the venerable **Novodevichiy Cemetery** (daily 10am–6pm; €2), burial place of numerous famous writers, musicians and artists, including Gogol, Chekhov, Stanislavsky, Bulgakov and Shostakovich. Krushchev is also here – he died out of office, and was denied burial in the Kremlin wall. A little nearer to the centre, **Gorky Park** (daily 10am–10pm; €2, free on weekdays in winter) is famous abroad from Martin Cruz Smith's classic thriller. Inaugurated in 1928, the Soviet Union's first "Park of Culture and Rest" covers three hundred acres and includes funfairs, a large outdoor skating rink and lots of woodland.

## Zamoskvoreche and the south

South of the Kremlin lies **Zamoskvoreche** (simply "Across the Moskva River"), an area dating back to medieval times and preserving a host of colourful churches and the mansions of civic-minded merchants. It can be easily traversed on one of the trams which start from Chistye Prudy metro. Founded in 1892 by the financier Pavel Tretyakov, the **Tretyakov Gallery** (Tues–Sun 10am–7.30pm; €7), five minutes' walk from Tretyakovskaya metro, displays an outstanding collection of Russian art before the Revolution. Russian icons are magnificently displayed. The exhibition continues through to the late nineteenth century, with one vast room filled with the nightmare-like, fantastical works of Mikhail Vrubel. Twentieth-century and contemporary art (dominated by Tatlin, Chagall and Malevich) is at a branch of the gallery opposite the entrance to Gorky Park, at Krymskiy val 10

(Tues–Sun 10am–7.30pm; €7). **Kolomenskoe estate** (grounds daily 8am–9pm, free; museum Tues–Sun 10am–6pm, separate tickets for each building, approx. €6 each, €20 covers all), 10km southeast of the Kremlin, was once a royal summer retreat. Though its legendary wooden palace no longer exists, Kolomenskoe still has one of the finest churches in the whole of Russia, the early sixteenth-century **Church of the Ascension** (services Sun 8am), and vintage wooden structures such as Peter the Great's cabin, set amid hoary oaks above a great bend in the river. Take the metro to Kolomenskaya, fifteen minutes' walk from the site itself.

### East and north of the centre

In the northeast of the city is the fourteenth-century **Andronikov Monastery**, on the steep east bank of the Yauza. At its heart stands Moscow's oldest architectural monument, the **Church of the Saviour** (1420s), which now houses the **Andrey Rublev Museum of Old Russian Art and Culture** at Andronevskaya pl. 10 (11am–6pm, closed Wed and last Fri of month; €3; Ploshchad Ilicha metro). The most famous icons may be in the Tretyakov, but the atmosphere here is something else – you retire from the noise and bustle of the city and enter a peaceful, serene land that feels more truly Russian than the rest of the capital. Even the fact that until the 1950s the church housed the archive of the Ministry of State Security could do nothing to destroy its romance. A few stops north is the Exhibition of Economic Achievements – or **VDNKh** (daily 10am–6pm) – a permanent trade-fair-cum-shopping-centre housed in the magnificent park and grandiose Stalinist architecture of the All-Union Agricultural Exhibition of 1939, a display of the fruits of socialism. Today, cheap imported goods make the whole thing rather tawdry, but when the sun glints off the gilded fountains it still looks magnificent. Near the main entrance stands one of the best-ever Soviet monuments, the **Space Obelisk**, a rocket blasting nearly 100m into the sky on a stylized plume of energy clad in shining titanium. It was unveiled in 1964, three years after Gagarin orbited the earth, an unabashed expression of pride in this unique feat. On the other side of the entrance is the famous monument of the **Worker and Collective Farm Girl**, colossal twin figures intended to embody Soviet industrial progress, though in fact they were handmade.

# Eating, drinking and entertainment

**Cafés** serve plentiful and excellent food, but for true economy in Moscow you have to either go for the many small restaurants offering business lunches for around €5 or stick with **fast food** – full-blown restaurants are all too expensive to be included here. Most places have at least one member of staff with a rudimentary grasp of English. Despite the vast number of clubs, the city's **nightlife** is dominated by the ubiquitous face control, making it difficult to get in to some of the best clubs with the best music. There's a busy schedule of **classical music**, **opera** and **ballet** throughout the year, sometimes held in palaces, churches or – in summer – parks and gardens. **Puppet** and **circus** shows transcend language barriers.

### Cafés, bars and fast food

**Avocado** Chistoprudnyy bulvar 12/2; Chistye Prudy metro. Upmarket, vegetarian, non-smoking restaurant with business lunch for just €4.

**Coffee Bean** Tverskaya ul. 10; Pushkinskaya metro. Bustling, inexpensive place that's cosy despite the chandeliers.

**Gogol** Stoleshnikov pereulok 11; Kuznetskiy Most metro. Cheapest place in the centre and it's stylish, with a free ice-rink in the yard in winter.

**Kish-Mish** Noviy Arbat 28; Smolenskaya metro.

Uzbek food and cheap – a rarity in the centre of Moscow.

**Kofe-Inn** Bolshaya Dmitrovka ul. 16; Teatralnaya metro. A few main meals, but largely great coffee and desserts.

**Manege Shopping Centre** Manezhnaya pl; Teatralnaya metro. Inside this ghastly shopping mall is a surprising variety of cheap fast-food outlets.

**Moo-Moo** ul. Arbat 45/24; Smolenskaya metro. One of those places where you just point at what you want: it's all laid out for you to see. Outdoor terrace in summer.

**Ogonyok** Krasnaya Presnaya ul. 36; 1905-goda metro. Russian food that doesn't limit itself to *pelmeni* and beetroot.

**PiR O.G.I.** Pyatnitskaya ul. 29, Novokuznetskaya metro; also Bolshaya Dmitrovka 12/2, Teatralnaya metro. Great Russian food and beer.

**Sherbet** Petrovka ul. 15/13; Kuznetskiy most metro. Uzbek and Arabic food; cheap and filling business lunches.

**Shokoladnitsa** Pushechnaya ul 7/5; Kuznetskiy most. Chocolate heaven for those with a very sweet tooth.

**Sindibad** Nikitskiy bulvar 14; Arbatskaya metro. Small Lebanese café.

**Taras Bulba** ul. Petrovka 30/7; Pyatnitskaya ul. 14; Sadovaya-Samotechnaya ul. 13/14; and other branches. Chain of Ukrainian cafés where the *borshch* is not to be missed.

**Yolki-Palki** Neglinnaya 8/10; Bolshaya Dmitrovka ul. 23/8; Klimentovskiy per. 14/1; and branches. Eat Russian/Ukrainian/Mongolian food at rock-bottom prices, even if the interior design is a little tacky.

### Clubs and live music

**Art Garbage** Starosadskiy per. 5/6; Kitay-gorod metro. Mixture of disco, contemporary art gallery and live concert venue.

**B2** Bolshaya Sadovaya ul. 8; Mayakovskaya metro. Club with live music and DJs, pop and jazz. Caters to most tastes and popular with locals and expats. Noon–6am.

**Bunker** Tverskaya ul. 12; Pushkinskaya metro. Live rock music most evenings with excellent food too.

**Dom** Bolshoy Ovchinnikovskiy per. 24/4; Novokuznetskaya metro. Just about everything – jazz, blues and experimental - for the "intellectual" crowd. Thurs–Sun. Concerts start 7.30pm.

**Gogol** ul. Arbat 36/2; Arbat metro. Café/club with live music and DJs, and no door policy. Open 24hr.

**Keks** ul. Timura Frunze 11; Park Kultury metro. Everything from electro-jazz to 1960s covers.

**Kitayskiy Letchik Dzhao Dao** Lubyanskiy proezd 25; Kitay-gorod metro. Avoid the Chinese restaurant upstairs and descend to the basement, the coolest club in which to be seen and to hear the best bands. Attached to it is the phenomenally popular *Dom Kukera*, a disco dance club. Open 24hr.

**Project O.G.I.** Potapovskiy per. 8/12; Chistye Prudy metro. Hip club, bar and restaurant with what are often avant-garde and off-the-wall performances as well as sessions for kids in the mornings. Open 24hr.

**Propaganda** Bolshoy Zlatoustinskiy per. 7; Kitay-gorod metro. Shocking face control, but the music's good if you can get in.

**R&B Café** Starovagankovskiy per. 19/2l; Biblioteka im. Lenina metro. Live jazz and blues right at the heart of the city.

**Vermel** Rauschskaya nab. 4/5; Tretyakovskaya metro. A largely student crowd come to listen to live pop and rock.

**Woodstock** Pokrovskiy Bulvar 3; Chistye Prudy metro. Mainly rock, for twenty- and thirtysome-things. Mon–Fri 10am–6am; Sat & Sun 2pm–6am.

### Theatre

**Bolshoy Theatre** Teatralnaya pl. 1 ℡095/250 7317, ⊛www.bolshoi.ru; Teatralnaya metro. The historic main stage is closed until 2008, but the smaller new stage next door is still functioning.

**Helikon Opera** Bolshaya Nikitskaya ul. ℡095/290 6592, ⊛www.helikon.ru; Arbatskaya metro. Prize-winning theatre offering unusual repertoire of small-scale productions.

### Film in English

**America Cinema** *Radisson-Slavyanskaya Hotel* ℡095/941 87 47; Kievskaya metro.

**Dome Cinema** 18/1 Olimpiyskiy pr. ℡095/931 9873; Prospekt mira Kievskaya metro.

### Circus

**Circus on Tsvetnoy** Tsvetnoy bul. 13 ℡095/200 06 68; Tsvetnoy Bulvar metro. Clowns are the forte here.

**Circus on Vernadskiy** pr. Vernadskovo 7 ℡095/930 28 15; Universitet metro. Lots of animal acts.

# Listings

**Bathhouses** Sandunovskiy Banya, Neglinnaya ul. 14, kor. 3–7; Teatralnaya metro.

**Embassies** Australia, Podkolokolniy per. 10A/2 ℡095/956 6070; Canada, Starokonyushenniy per. 23 ℡095/105 6000; Ireland, Grokholskiy per. 5 ℡095/937 5911; New Zealand, Povarskaya ul. 44 ℡095/956 3579; UK, Smolenskaya nab. 10 ℡095/956 7301; US, Bolshoy Deviatinskiy per 8 ℡095/728 5000.

**Internet** Cafemax, ul. Pyatnitskaya 25/1, Novokuznetskaya metro; Nirvana, Rozhdestvenka 29, Kuznetskiy Most metro; Netcity, Kamergersky per. 5/6, Teatralnaya metro.

**Laundry** California Cleaners, Maliyy Gnezdnikovskiy per. 12.

**Left luggage** Most train stations have lockers and/or a 24hr left-luggage office.

**Medical** European Medical Center, Spiridonovskiy per. 1 ☎095/933 6655, ⊛www.emcmos.ru; International SOS Clinic, 31 Grokholskiy per. 10th floor ☎095/937 5760, ⊛www.internationalsos .com. Both recognized by international insurance companies.

**Open-air pools** Chayka, Turchaninov per. 1/3, Park Kultury metro; Luzhniki Luzhnetskaya nab.

24, Vorobyevy Gory metro; Olympic Centre, Ibragimova 30, Semenovskaya metro.

**Pharmacy** StaryArbat, Arbatskaya ul. 25; Multifarma, Turistkaya ul. 27; 24hr pharmacy at pr. Mira 71.

**Post office** Central Telegraph Office, Tverskaya ul. 7; Main Post Office, Myasnitskaya ul. 26/2. Express postal services via Westpost ☎095/ 234 9038, ⊛www.westpost.ru; Courier Service, Bolshaya Sadovaya 10; Mayakovskaya metro ☎095/209 1735.

# St Petersburg (Sankt Peterburg)

**ST PETERSBURG**, Petrograd, Leningrad and St Petersburg again – the city's succession of names mirrors Russia's turbulent history. Founded in 1703 as a "window on the West" by Peter the Great, it was for two centuries the capital of the tsarist empire, synonymous with excess and magnificence, later becoming was the cradle of the revolutions that overthrew the monarchy and brought the Bolsheviks to power in 1917. As Leningrad it epitomized the Soviet Union's heroic sacrifices in World War II, withstanding nine hundred days of Nazi siege. Then, in 1991 – the year the USSR collapsed – the change of name back to St Petersburg proved deeply symbolic of the country's mood. St Petersburg's sense of its own identity owes much to its origins and to the interweaving of myth and reality throughout its history. Intensely proud of itself, of its intellectual – and its workers' revolutionary – past, St Petersburg is an easy and relaxing city. It's also one of contrasts: beautiful yet drab, with beggars and nouveaux riches rubbing shoulders on the main street, **Nevskiy prospekt**. The most celebrated time to visit is during the famous **White Nights** of midsummer (mid-June to mid-July), when darkness never falls, but autumn and winter bathe the city in wonderful lighting effects and the city is much less crowded: apart from anything else, the locals are all out mushroom-hunting or skiing. From May to October all bridges across the Neva are raised from 2–5am – a beautiful sight but inconvenient if you're on the wrong side of the water.

## Arrival, information and accommodation

International **flights** arrive at Pulkovo Airport, Terminal 2. Avoid the waiting taxis and take a bus (#13 or a commercial minibus) to the end of the metro line (Moskovskaya). **Trains** from Helsinki bring you to the new **Ladoga Station** (Ladozhskiy vokzal) while those from Europe and the Baltic States terminate at **Vitebsk Station** (Vitebskiy vokzal). Trains from Moscow draw into **Moscow Station**. All stations are on the metro. Ecolines **buses** from Germany and the Baltic States arrive at Pushkinskaya metro, while Russian intercity buses stop at the "central" bus station at Obvodniy kanal 36 – fifteen minutes' walk from metro Ligovskiy Prospekt. Coaches from Finland all arrive via the centre. In the summer months there are **ferries** from Tallinn, Helsinki and Rostock in Germany, which arrive at the Morskoy vokzal at the western end of Vasilevskiy Island (bus or minibus to the centre). Contact details on ⊛www.silja.fi or ⊛www.tallink.ee. For **information**, pick up the quarterly freebie *Where St Petersburg*, the Friday *St Petersburg Times* and the monthly *Pulse*, available from hotels and shops. The tourist information centre at Sadovaya ul. 14/52 can be helpful but its branch on Palace Square is almost always closed out of high season. Major hostels can provide everything from visa support to theatre tickets.

Petersburgers **walk** everywhere, summer or winter. Yet it is a big city, and you'll need to use its cheap public transport system. Overground transport is more useful in the centre than the fast **metro**. Choose from **trams**, **buses** and **trolleybuses** (tickets from conductor), or efficient commercial **minibuses** (tickets from driver). One of the best ways to see the city is by **boat** (May–Oct) – either a private motorboat from any bridge on Nevskiy prospekt (from €50/hr per boat), or a large tour boat by the Anichkov Bridge (€7 per person). Or take a **walking tour** with Peter's Tours, bookable through the *International Youth Hostel* on ☎812/329 8018.

**Hostels** are reasonably central, with decent facilities and no age restriction. Those listed offer visa support and take credit cards unless otherwise stated. St Petersburg is the home of the relatively inexpensive and cosy **mini–hotel**, abundant short-let **apartments** (perfect for small groups of people) and **B&B** opportunities (see agencies on p.844).

### Hostels

**Hostel All Seasons** Yakovlevskiy per. 11, ☎812/327 1070, ⓦwww.hostel.ru; Park Pobedy metro. About the cheapest place in town, if not in the city centre, but clean and welcoming. Dorms €10.
**Na Muchnom** Sadovaya ul. 25/4 ☎812/310 0412, ⓦwww.namuchnom.ru; Gostinyy dvor metro. At the heart of Dostoyevskian St Petersburg. Dorms €24, rooms ❹
**Nord Hostel** Bolshaya Morskaya ul. 10 ☎812/571 0342, ⓦwww.nordhostel.com; Gostinyy dvor metro. Nothing could be more central. Dorms €24.
**St Petersburg International Hostel** 3-ya Sovetskaya ul. 28 ☎812/329 8018, ⓦwww.ryh. ru; Ploshchad Vosstaniya metro. Popular, so book well ahead for this place which has an excellent student travel agency. Dorms €20, rooms ❸
**Sleep Cheap** Mokhovaya ul. 18–32 ☎812/115 1304, ⓦwww.sleepcheap.spb.ru; Chernyshevskaya metro. Five minutes from the Summer Garden, with just 16 beds. Dorms €19. No credit cards.

### Hotels

**Hotels on Nevsky** ☎812/103 3860, ⓦwww.hon.ru. Not so much a hotel as a series of quite fancy mini-hotels, all of them right on Nevskiy prospekt. ❻
**Neva** Chaykovskovo ul. 17 ☎812/278 0504; Chernyshevskaya metro. Old-fashioned, even quaint, and just a hop away from the Summer Garden. No visa support. ❻

## The City

St Petersburg's centre lies on the south bank of the **River Neva**, with the curving **River Fontanka** marking its southern boundary. The area within the **Fontanka** is riven by a series of wide avenues, which fan out from the most visible landmark on the south bank of the Neva, the **Admiralty**. Many of the city's greatest sights and monuments are located on and around **Nevskiy prospekt**, the main avenue. Across the Neva is **Vasilevskiy Island**, largest of the city's islands, and on the **Strelka**, the island's eastern tip, are found some of St Petersburg's oldest institutions as well as several fascinating museums. On the north side of the River Neva, the Petrograd Side is home to the **Peter and Paul Fortress**, whose construction is seen as marking the foundation of the city itself. Beyond the River Fontanka, the two most popular destinations are the **Smolnyy**, from where the Bolsheviks orchestrated the October Revolution, and the **Alexander Nevskiy Monastery**.

### Nevskiy prospekt to the Winter Palace

Stretching from the Alexander Nevskiy Monastery to Palace Square and the Hermitage, **Nevskiy prospekt** has been the backbone and heart of the city for the last three centuries. Built on an epic scale during the reign of Peter the Great, it manifests every style of architecture from eighteenth-century Baroque to 1950s Stalinist Classicism. Near the striking Dom Knigi bookshop, former emporium of the Singer sewing-machine company, is **Kazan Cathedral**, built between 1801 and 1811 (services daily 9am & 6pm), one of the city's grandest churches, modelled on St Peter's in the Vatican. The cathedral was built to house the venerated icon, *Our Lady of Kazan*, reputed to have appeared miraculously overnight in Kazan in

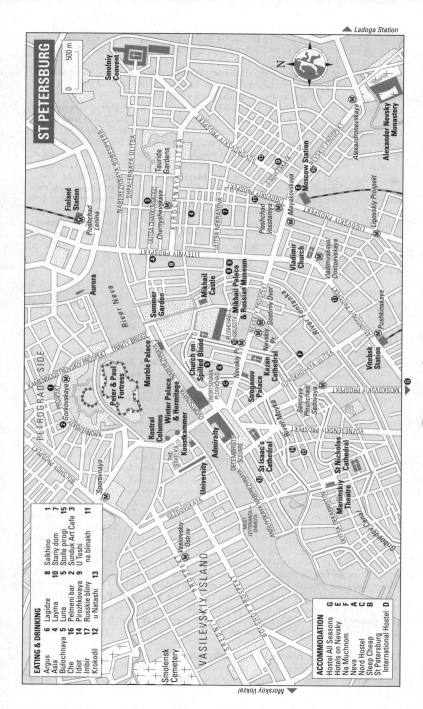

# ST PETERSBURG

▲ Ladoga Station

0 — 500 m

**EATING & DRINKING**

| | |
|---|---|
| Argus | 6 |
| Asia | 4 |
| Bulochnaya | 5 |
| Che | 16 |
| Idiot | 14 |
| Imbir | 17 |
| Krokodil | 12 |

| | |
|---|---|
| Lagidze | 1 |
| Layma | 7 |
| Luna | 10 |
| Pelmeni bar | 15 |
| Pirozhkovaya | 2 |
| Russkie bliny | 3 |
| u Natashi | 13 |

| | |
|---|---|
| Salkhino | 8 |
| Stariy dom | 10 |
| Stolle pirogi | 5 |
| Sunduk Art Cafe | 3 |
| U Teshi | 9 |
| na blinakh | 11 |

**ACCOMMODATION**

| | |
|---|---|
| Hostel All Seasons | G |
| Hotels on Nevsky | E |
| Na Muchnom | F |
| Neva | A |
| Nord Hostel | C |
| Sleep Cheap | B |
| St Petersburg | |
| International Hostel | D |

Smolensk Cemetery

VASILEVSKIY ISLAND

Vasilevskiy Ostrov

University

Kunstkammer

Rostral Columns

THE STRELKA

Peter & Paul Fortress

PETROGRAD SIDE

Aurora

Marble Palace

Summer Garden

Winter Palace & Hermitage

Admiralty

DECEMBRISTS' SQUARE

St Isaac's Cathedral

Marrinsky Theatre

St Nicholas Cathedral

Church on Spilled Blood

Stroganov Palace

Kazan Cathedral

Mikhail Castle

Mikhail Palace & Russian Museum

Nevsky Pr.

Gostiny Dvor

Smolniy Convent

Finland Station

Tauride Gardens

Vladimir Church

Moscow Station

Vitebsk Station

Alexander Nevsky Monastery

River Neva

TRINITY BRIDGE

Ligovskiy Prospekt

857

1579, and transferred by Peter the Great to St Petersburg, where it resided until its disappearance in 1904. In Soviet times the cathedral housed the Museum of Religion and Atheism.

The two-hundred-metre long Baroque **Winter Palace** at the westernmost end of Nevskiy prospekt is the city's largest, most opulent palace. As loaded with history as it is with gilt and stucco, the palace was the official residence of the tsars, not to mention the court and 1500 servants. The main building was finished in 1762 and later new buildings were added to the east: the Small and Large Hermitages were added by Catherine the Great to enable her to be alone with her friends and her paintings, while the New Hermitage was launched as Russia's first public art museum in 1852. Beyond stands the Hermitage Theatre, Catherine the Great's private theatre, now used for concerts. Together these buildings form one of the world's greatest museums, the **Hermitage** (Tues–Sat 10.30am–6pm, Sun 10.30am–5pm; ⓦwww.hermitagemuseum.org; €10). Of awesome size and diversity, it embraces some three million objects, everything from ancient Scythian gold to Cubism. After the state rooms and the Gold Collection (you need to state you want to see the gold when you buy your ticket), the most universally popular section is that covering modern European art from the nineteenth and twentieth centuries, due to move to the majestic General Staff Building on the other side of Palace Square. It includes a fine spread of works by Matisse and Picasso, Gauguin, Van Gogh, Monet and Renoir.

### North of Nevskiy prospekt

Visible from Nevskiy prospekt is the multicoloured, onion-domed **Church on Spilled Blood** (11am–7pm, closed Wed; €8), begun in 1882 to commemorate Tsar Alexander II, assassinated on the site the previous year. In pseudo-traditional Russian style, stuffed full of thousands of metres of mosaics, it is one of St Petersburg's most striking landmarks, quite unlike the dominant Neoclassical architecture. East of the church stands the vast **Mikhail Palace**, main building for the **Russian Museum** (ⓦwww.rusmuseum.ru), containing the finest collection of Russian art in the world. It encompasses fourteenth-century icons, Russian art's coming of age in the late nineteenth century (see the vast historical canvases of Vasiliy Surikov and the socially conscious realism of Ilya Repin), and the movements of the early twentieth century. A little further east is a branch of the Russian Museum, the idiosyncratic and heavily fortified **Mikhail Castle**, built by Paul I in 1801 shortly after he came to the throne, to protect him from the assassination attempt he feared. Indeed, he was murdered in his bedroom there just three weeks after moving in. The **Mikhail Garden** next door (behind the Russian Museum) is much loved by Petersburgers of all ages, who also adore **Marsovo pole** (Field of Mars) on the other side of the River Moyka, heavy with the scent of lilac in spring. At its northwestern corner stands the **Marble Palace**, again part of the Russian Museum, designed by Antonio Rinaldi for Catherine the Great's lover, Count Orlov, and now displaying works by foreign artists living in Russia in the eighteenth and nineteenth centuries, and contemporary art. (All branches of the Russian Museum open Wed–Sun 10am–6pm, Mon 10am–5pm; €9 each branch.) Most popular of all, however, is the **Summer Garden** to the east, commissioned by Peter the Great in 1704 and rebuilt by Catherine the Great in the informal English style that survives today (daily 8/11am–6/10pm). In the northeastern corner, Domenico Trezzini erected a **Summer Palace** (May–Oct Wed–Sun 11am–6pm, Mon 10am–5pm; €5) for Peter the Great in 1710, a modest two-storey building of brick and stucco – one of the first such structures in the city – with fascinating "Dutch" interiors.

### Southwest of Nevskiy prospekt

The **Admiralty** standing at the western end of Nevskiy prospekt is one of the world's most magnificent expressions of naval triumphalism, extending 407m along the waterfront, from Palace Square to Decembrists' Square. Originally founded in 1704 as a fortified shipyard, the Admiralty gradually became purely administrative in function and a suitable building was erected in the early 1820s. Today, the key feature of the building is still its central tower (72.5m high), culminating in a slender spire. The wooded Admiralty Garden leads towards **Decembrists' Square**, named after a group of reformist officers who, in December 1825, marched three thousand soldiers into the square in a doomed attempt to proclaim a constitutional monarchy. Today, the square is dominated by the **Bronze Horseman**, Falconet's renowned 1778 statue of Peter the Great and the city's unofficial symbol, against which newlyweds are traditionally photographed. Looming majestically above the square, **St Isaac's Cathedral** (11am–7pm, colonnade till 5pm, closed Wed; ⊛www.cathedral.ru; €8, colonnade €4) is one of the glories of St Petersburg's skyline, its gilded dome the third largest in Europe. The opulent interior is equally impressive, decorated with fourteen kinds of marble. The cathedral's height (101.5m) and rooftop statues are best appreciated by climbing the 262 steps to the outside colonnade. More intimate in mood is the **St Nicholas Cathedral**, to the south near Theatre Square and the Mariinskiy Theatre. Traditionally the church of naval officers, it is a lovely example of eighteenth-century Russian Baroque – painted ice blue with white Corinthian pilasters, crowned with five gilded onion domes. Its vaulted lower church is festooned with icons, and during services (6pm) the cathedral resounds with the sonorous Orthodox liturgy, chanted and sung amid clouds of incense. The upper church opens only for religious festivals.

## Vasilevskiy Island

Pear-shaped **Vasilevskiy Island** cleaves the River Neva into its Bolshaya and Malaya branches, forming a strategic wedge whose eastern "spit", or **Strelka**, is as much a part of St Petersburg's waterfront as the Winter Palace or Admiralty. Originally, Peter envisaged making the island the centre of his capital, compelling rich landowners and merchants to settle here, but the lack of bridges and hazardous crossing by boat led people to prefer settling on the mainland. Although you can reach the Strelka by numerous buses from Nevskiy prospekt, it's best to walk across **Palace Bridge**, which offers fabulous views of both banks of the Neva (richly illuminated at night). On the Strelka are the **Rostral Columns** and Neoclassical **Stock Exchange** building (now housing the Naval Museum, well worth a visit; Wed–Sun 11am–6pm, closed last Thurs of month; ⊛www .museum.navy.ru; €9), an ensemble created at the beginning of the nineteenth century by Thomas de Thomon, who also designed the granite embankments and cobbled ramps leading down to the Neva – reminders that the city's port and commercial centre were once located here. Not to be missed is the **Kunstkammer** (11am–6pm, closed Mon and last Tues of month, ⊛www.kunstkamera.ru, €7), Russia's oldest public museum, founded by Peter the Great in 1714. Its name (meaning "art chamber" in German) dignified Peter's fascination for curiosities and freaks: he offered rewards for "human monsters" and unknown birds and animals, which were preserved in vinegar or vodka.

## The Peter and Paul Fortress

Across the Neva from the Winter Palace, on a small island, stands the **Peter and Paul Fortress**, built to secure Russia's hold on the Neva delta. Forced labourers toiled from dawn to dusk to construct the fortress in just seven months. The day of its foundation, 27 May 1703, is considered to mark the founding of the city (much celebrated each year). The Fortress (8am–10pm; free) includes a **cathedral** and varied **museums** covering the city's history and Russian life (10am–7pm, closed Wed; ⊛www.spbmuseum.ru; €4 for all the museums). The midday gun, fired daily, resounds across the city centre, making windows shake and setting off car alarms. The Dutch-style **Peter and Paul Cathedral**, completed in 1733, remained the tallest structure in the city until the 1960s. Sited around the nave are the tombs of Romanov monarchs from Peter the Great onwards, excluding Peter II, Ivan VI and Nicholas II. Nicholas and his family, whose bones were discovered in a mineshaft in the Urals in 1989, were finally buried in a chapel here in 1998.

### Beyond the Fontanka

Nestling in a bend of the River Neva, northeast of Nevskiy prospekt, lies the quiet **Smolnyy district**, with an ice-blue cathedral towering on the eastern horizon. This is the focal point of the former **Smolnyy Convent**, founded in the eighteenth century by the Empress Elizabeth. Rastrelli's grandiose Baroque structure hides an austere white interior, used to host temporary exhibitions and concerts. The **Smolnyy Institute**, now the Governor's Headquarters, was built in 1806–08 to house the Institute for Young Noblewomen. Lenin ran the Revolution from here, and for the 74 years of Communist rule, the word "Smolnyy" was synonymous with the Revolution and the Party. At the eastern end of Nevskiy prospekt lies the **Alexander Nevskiy Monastery**, founded in 1713 by Peter the Great and one of only four monasteries in the Russian Empire with the rank of *lavra*, the highest in Orthodox monasticism. Two famous cemeteries lie in the monastery grounds: the **Tikhvin Cemetery**, also known as the Necropolis for Masters of the Arts, with the graves of Dostoyevsky, Rimsky-Korsakov, Tchaikovsky, Rubinstein and Glinka, and, directly opposite, the smaller **Lazarus Cemetery**, the oldest in the city. Tickets are required for entry to both (summer 9.30am–6pm; winter 10am–4pm, closed Thurs; ☎812/274 2635; €2); foreigners are sometimes asked to make a "contribution" before entering the monastery proper. At the gates of the **monastery** (daily dawn to dusk) is Trezzini's **Church of the Annunciation** (11am–5pm, closed Mon & Thurs; €1.50), original burial place of Peter III, Catherine the Great's deposed husband.

## Eating, drinking and entertainment

Avoid big-name cafés imitating Western stereotypes and prices and go for the more intimate **cafés** that serve good food and offer a good feel for local life. They may be harder to find, but are well worth it. Then move on to one of the city's famous clubs: Petersburg is associated with several legendary homegrown bands and the face control is less of an obstacle than in Moscow. If your taste is more classical, beware and stick to the Mariinskiy (formerly Kirov) for **ballet**; other theatres offer poor-quality stagings aimed at the profoundly undiscriminating. **Opera** can also be quite fun at the Zazerkale Children's Theatre or the St Petersburg Opera. For details of what's happening, check the listings papers (see "Arrival").

### Cafés and bars

**Argus** Bolshaya Konyushennaya ul. 15; Nevskiy prospekt metro. Noisy and central, with its own small brewery.

**Asia** Ryleeva ul. 23; Ploshchad Vosstaniya metro. Serving inexpensive and extremely filling Uzbek food, this café gets very full at lunchtimes. Try the delicious *chebureki* (meat patties).

**Bulochnaya** Bolshaya Konyushennaya 15; Nevskiy prospekt metro. Second-best *pirozhki* in town (see *Stolle pirogi*), and the most central.

**Che** Poltavskaya ul. 3; Moskovkiy Vokzal metro. This bar/café fancies itself something rotten, but it's still the place to be seen.

**Idiot** nab. reki Moyki 82; bus or minibus from Nevskiy prospekt. Vegetarian place full of foreigners and social-climbing Russians.

**Krokodil** Galernaya ul. 18; 5min walk from St Isaac's Cathedral. Café with an original menu and fresh food, popular with the in-crowd, and handy for lunch if you're near St Isaac's.

**Lagidze** Belinskovo ul. 3; Chernyshevskaya metro. Just off the Fontanka, this place offers Russian and Caucasian food in quiet surroundings. If it's full, try *Metekhi* next door.

**Layma** nab. kanala Griboedova 16; Gostinyy Dvor/Nevskiy Prospekt metro. Fast food, including steaks and salads, plus beer. Open 24hr.

**Luna** Bolshaya Konyushennaya 7; Nevskiy prospekt metro. Very cheap and relatively cheerful.

**Pelmeni bar** Kronverkskiy pr. 53a; Gorkovskaya metro. Entrance off Vvedenskaya ul. A wide variety of traditional *pelmeni* and some original recipes, freshly made on the premises, at low prices.

**Pirozhkovaya** Liteyniy pr. 47; Mayakovskaya metro. A little bit of the Soviet Union, with chest-high tables (no chairs – you stand), lots of *pirozhki* or pies, and a corner for those in need of a quick shot (or two) of vodka, for tiny sums of money. 8am–7pm.

**Russkie bliny u Natashi** 5-ya Sovetskaya ul. 24. Pig out on the city's most outstanding pancakes at the cheapest known prices.

**Stariy dom** Nekrasova ul. 25; Ploshchad Vosstaniya metro. An original take on Russian and Caucasian cooking.

**Stolle pirogi** ul. Dekabristov 19. Even if you've spent all your money on a ticket to the Mariinskiy you can still afford to stuff yourself with the city's best *pirozhki* (savoury pies) just round the corner.

**Sunduk Art Cafe** Furshtatskaya ul. 42; Cherny-shevskaya metro. Great food and cocktails, live jazz most evenings (small cover charge), welcoming decor.

**U Teshi na blinakh** Ligovskiy pr. 31; Ploshchad Vosstaniya metro. Fast, filling food right by the Moscow station – perfect for late departures and early arrivals.

### Restaurants
**Imbir** Zagorodnyy pr. 15. Mixture of traditional Russian and Japanese dishes at very moderate prices, for the young and modish.

**Salkhino** Kronverkskiy pr. 25; Gorkovskaya metro. Probably the most fashionable Georgian restaurant in town, with all-embracing (sometimes stifling) service.

### Clubs and live music
**Fish Fabrique** Ligovskiy pr. 53; Mayakovskovo metro. Café-club at the heart of the city's famous artists' colony.

**Griboedov** Voronezhskaya ul. 2a; Ligovskiy Prospekt metro. Still the coolest of cool dance clubs, in a former bomb shelter. 5pm–6am.

**JFC Jazz Club** Shpalernaya ul. 33; Cherny-shevskaya metro. The city's most exciting jazz programme, tucked away in a courtyard. 11am–last guest.

**Jimi Hendrix Blues Club** Liteyniy pr. 33; Cherny-shevskaya metro. Mixed-quality bands and good food. 11am–1am.

**Metro** Ligovskiy pr. 174; Ligovskiy Prospekt metro. It's big, it's loud, it's tacky, but it's not that expensive, and everyone keeps coming back. 10pm–6am.

**Moloko** Perekupnoy per. 12; Ploshchad Aleksan-dra Nevskovo metro. Underground rock club with a reputation for discovering great acts. 7pm–midnight, closed Mon.

**PAR.spb** Alexandrovskiy park 5v; Gorkovskaya metro. Electronic music in a very cool and popular venue. Fri–Sun 11pm–8am.

**Zoom Café Club** Gorokhovaya ul. 22; Sadovaya metro. Everything from jazz to medieval plainsong. 11am–midnight.

### Classical, opera and ballet
**Mariinskiy (formerly Kirov) Theatre** Teatralnaya pl. 1 ☎812/114 5264, ⊛www.mariinsky.ru. Prices €8–120. Performances at 7pm, matinees at noon. Due to close for reconstruction mid-2006 (but don't count on it).

**St Petersburg Opera** Galernaya ul. 33 ☎812/315 6769; Nevskiy Prospekt metro. Once an aristo-cratic private theatre; perfect for small chamber operas. Performances at 7pm.

**Zazerkale** Rubinshteyna ul. 13 ☎812/112 5135; Nevskiy Prospekt metro. Supposedly just for children, they also do rather good Italian opera in this 400-seat theatre. Performances at 7pm.

**Philharmonia** Mikhaylovskaya ul. 2 ☎812/110 4290; Nevskiy Prospekt metro. Draws international classical musicians as well as Russia's best. Performances at 7pm.

# Listings

**Bathhouse** Yamskie, Dostoevskovo ul. 9; Vladimir-skaya metro. Closed Mon & Tues.

**Consulates** Canada, Malodetskoselskiy pr. 32 ☎812/325 8448; UK, pl. Proletarskoy diktatury 5 ☎812/320 3200; US, Furshtadtskaya ul. 15 ☎812/331 2600.

**Internet access** Quo Vadis, Nevskiy pr. 24 (24hr); expensive but central. Cafemax, Nevskiy pr. 90/92 (24hr) or inside the Hermitage; very fast link.

**Left luggage** Main stations have lockers and/or a 24hr left-luggage office.

**Medical** International Clinic, Dostoevskovo ul.

19/21 ☎812/336 3333, ⊛www.icspb.com; Euromed, Suvorovskiy pr. 60 ☎812/327 0301, ⊛www.euromed.ru; British-American Family Prac-tice, Grafsky per. 7 ☎812/327 6030, ⊛www .british-americanclinic.com.

**Pharmacy** Petropharm, at Nevskiy pr. 22 (24hr). Other branches at nos. 50, 66 & 83.

**Post office** Main post office at Pochtamskaya ul. closed indefinitely for restoration. Express letter post: Westpost, Nevskiy pr. 86. Letters can be sent cheaply via Finnish post from the *Grand Hotel Europe*.

## Day-trips from St Petersburg

You should aim to make at least one day-trip out of St Petersburg – the locals get out of town whenever they can, to swim in the Gulf in summer, or ski or gather mushrooms in winter. Even if you don't go into the (increasingly expensive) palaces, the parks are full of things to see and do.

In summer, most visitors opt for **Peterhof**, 29km west, famed for its marvellous fountains and cascades at the **Great Palace** (10.30am–6pm, closed Mon; ⊛www .peterhof.ru; palace €12, Lower Park €8). Almost unknown is the charming neo-Gothic **Cottage Palace** (May–Oct daily except Fri 10am–6pm; Oct–April Sat & Sun 10am–5pm, closed last Tues of month; €5) in the nearby Alexandria Park. Travel by hydrofoil in summer (€5 each way) from outside the Winter Palace or take one of the frequent minibuses from Avtovo metro station (€0.70). In winter, try **Tsarskoe Selo** (also known as Pushkin), 17km southeast of St Petersburg. The palace (10am–5pm, closed Tues; €17, park €3) is a vulgar blue-and-white Baroque structure, set in a richly landscaped park, with Scottish architect Charles Cameron's supremely elegant Neoclassical Gallery stretching high above the park. The famous Amber Room, stolen by the Germans during World War II and subsequently "mis-laid", was re-created in time for St Petersburg's 300th anniversary in 2003. To get to Tsarskoe Selo, frequent minibuses (€0.80) run from behind the vast statue of Lenin at Moskovskaya metro station. The same minibuses will take you on to the more intimate **Pavlovsk**, its **Great Palace** (10am–5pm, closed Fri; ⊛www.pavlovsk.org; €12, park €3) a monument to the taste and habits of Paul I's wife Maria Fedorovna. Pavlovsk park is much loved by St Petersburg's inhabitants, who walk here and feed the squirrels in summer, and ski through the grounds in winter.

# Travel details

## Trains

**Moscow** to: Berlin (1 daily; 25hr 30min); Budapest (1 daily; 37hr); Cologne (1 daily; 34hr); Helsinki (1 daily; 12hr 30min); Prague (1 daily; 33hr); Riga (2 daily; 15hr 30min); St Petersburg (frequent; 4hr 30min–8hr); Sofia (1 daily; 56hr); Tallinn (1 daily; 15hr); Warsaw (2 daily; 18hr).

**St Petersburg** to: Helsinki (3 daily; 6hr); Riga (1 daily; 8 hr); Tallinn (1 daily; 5hr 30min); Vilnius (1 every 2 days; 12 hr).

## Buses

**Moscow** to: Riga (2 daily; 20hr); St Petersburg (1 daily; 13hr); Tallinn (1 daily; 18hr 30min).
**St Petersburg** to: Tallinn (7 daily; 8hr 30min); Tartu, Estonia (1 daily; 8hr 30min).

## International ferries

*May–Sept only*
**St Petersburg** to: Helsinki (14hr); Tallinn (13hr); Rostock, Germany (37hr).

# Serbia

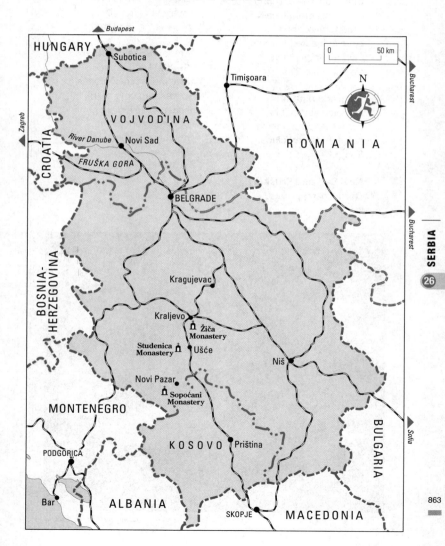

# Serbia highlights

* **Kalemegdan Fortress, Belgrade** The city landmark, this dramatically sited fortification has been subjected to more than a hundred invasions. See p.871

* **Belgrade nightlife** Immerse yourself in the welter of congenial cafés, bars and clubs. See p.873

* **Novi Sad and Fruška Gora** Cosmopolitan, laid-back city on the Danube close to some lovely wooded hills, ideal for walking. See p.875

* **Monasteries, Southern Serbia** Serbia's medieval monastic churches represent some of the finest achievements of the Byzantine era, notably some marvellous frescoes. See p.877

△ Kalemegdan Fortress, Belgrade

# Introduction and basics

For centuries under the thrall of Turkish rule, Serbia only attained independence in 1878, before becoming the hub of the short-lived Kingdom of Serbs, Croats and Slovenes, and then, after World War II, the modern Yugoslav state. Sanctions imposed following the onset of war in Bosnia in 1992 crippled the economy, while a decade of ruinous Milošević rule culminated in NATO air strikes in 1999, and a popular uprising against the Serbian president a year later. While the country continues to struggle with enormous economic and political problems, tourists are, at last, beginning to discover the unexpected delights of this embattled country. Serbia is, in fact, one part of a currently fragile union with the smaller republic of Montenegro, though the latter republic has not been covered in this chapter on this occasion.

Serbia's capital, **Belgrade**, is the quintessential Balkan city, a noisy, vigorous place, whose nightlife is fast gaining a reputation as being amongst the most exciting in Eastern Europe. North of here, on the iron-flat Vojvodina plain, is the charming city of Novi Sad, close to the Fruška Gora hills, which offer fine walking and the chance to visit several historic monasteries. Serbia's most revered monastic churches, however, are located deep in the mountainous tract of land south of Belgrade – namely Žiča, Studenica and Sopoćani. Southeast of here the industrial city of Niš holds a handful of curious sights worth visiting en route to Bulgaria.

## Information & maps

Most towns and resorts have a **tourist information office** (*turističke informacije*), whose staff invariably speak excellent English. Although they do not book rooms they can advise on local accommodation. A good standard of English is spoken pretty much everywhere. Freytag & Berndt publishes a good 1:300,000 country **map**.

## Money and banks

Currency is the **dinar** (usually abbreviated to Din), comprising coins of 1, 2, 5, 10 and 20 dinar (and also 50 para coins – 100 para equals 1 dinar), and notes of 10, 20, 50, 100, 200, 1000 and 5000 dinar. Note that you cannot use the dinar in either Montenegro or Kosovo, where the official currency is the euro – this is also the easiest foreign currency to change in Serbia itself. The best place to change money is at one of the many **exchange offices** (*menjačnica*), or a bank (*banka*), which are generally open Mon–Fri 8am–7pm and Sat 8am–3pm. **ATMs** are increasingly widespread and credit cards are accepted in a growing number of hotels and restaurants. Exchange **rates** are currently around 80Din to the euro, 120Din to the pound, and 70Din to the US dollar.

## Communications

Most **post offices** (*pošta*) are open Mon–Fri 8am–7pm, Sat 8am–3pm. **Stamps** (*markice*) can also be bought at newsstands. Public **phones** use cards (*Halokartice*),

### Serbia on the net

ⓦ **www.serbia-tourism.org** Official tourist board site.

ⓦ **www.beograd.org.yu** Detailed information on sights and events in the capital.

ⓦ **www.novisadtourism.org.yu** Useful site on Serbia's second city.

currently valued at 200 and 300Din and available from post offices, kiosks and tobacconists. It's usually easier to make long-distance and international calls at a post office, where you're assigned a cabin and given the bill afterwards. **Internet** access is fairly widespread; expect to pay around 60Din/hr.

# Getting around

Years of little or no investment has left the public transport system in a rather dilapidated state although, for the most part, it just about does the job. Travelling by **train** in Serbia can be a somewhat purgatorial experience, with slow, dirty and often delayed services the norm, though fares are incredibly cheap and some of the routes extremely scenic. **Serbian Railways** (*Srbije železnice*) run four types of train; *expresni* (express), *poslovni* (rapid), *brzi* (fast) – though there's little distinction between these three – and *putnički* (slow), which are to be avoided wherever possible. Reservations are not necessary, except during summer for the daily (overnight) train from Belgrade to Bar on the Montenegrin coast. Inter Rail and Eurail tickets are valid. Though slightly more expensive, **buses** offer a far quicker and more practical way of getting around, with regular services fanning out from Belgrade to all parts of the country.

# Accommodation

Serbia lags some way behind most other countries in the region in terms of both the range and quality of **accommodation** on offer. This includes **hotels**, many of which are relics of the old state system and in desperate need of privatization. There's no organized **hostel** system as such in Serbia, though some places are now affiliated to Hostelling International (HI) – however, this tends to be basic accommodation in student halls, and is usually only available during the summer. Similarly, **campsites** are few and far between, and of those that do exist most are fairly rudimentary.

# Food and drink

In common with other Balkan countries, Serbian **cuisine** is overwhelmingly dominated by meat, and many dishes manifest Turkish or Hungarian influences. **Breakfast** (*doručak*) typically comprises a coffee, roll and cheese or salami, while also popular is *burek*, a greasy, flaky pastry filled with cheese (*sa sirom*) or meat (*sa mesom*), and which is usually accompanied by a glass of yoghurt (*jogurt*). *Burek* is also served as a **street snack**, as are the ubiquitous *čevapčići* (rissoles of spiced minced meat served with onion), *pljeskavica* (oversized hamburger) and *ražnjići* (shish kebab). You will also find these on just about every **restaurant** (*restoran*) menu, alongside other characteristic Serbian dishes such as the typical starter, *čorba* (a thick meat or fish soup), and **main dishes** such as *pasulj* (a thick bean soup spotted with pieces of bacon or sausage), *sarma* (cabbage leaves stuffed with minced meat and rice), *podvarak* (roast meat in sauerkraut), *kolenica* (leg of suckling pig), and the gut-busting *karađorđe vasnicla*, a breaded veal cutlet, rolled and stuffed with cheese. A popular accompaniment to all these dishes is *pogača*, a large bread cake.

Pizzerias aside, vegetarians will have a fairly tough time of it, though dishes worth trying are *srpska salata* (salad with tomato, onion and hot peppers), *šopska salata* (similar but topped with grated soft cheese), *gibanica* (layered cheese pie) and *zeljanica* (cheese pie with spinach). Typical **desserts** include *strudla* (strudel), *krofna* (plain, jam or chocolate doughnut), and *baklava*, a sweet Turkish pastry smothered with syrup.

Basic **self-catering** and picnic ingredients such as cheese (*sir*), vegetables (*povrče*) and fruit (*voće*) can be obtained from a supermarket (*samoposluga*) or market (*piaca*), while bread (*hleb*) and pastries can be bought from a bakery (*pekara*).

### Drink

Few Serbs get by without a strong cup of **coffee** (*kafa*) to kick-start the day, traditionally served Turkish-style (black, thick and with the grinds at the bottom), though you'll find decent instant coffee (*nes*), espressos and cappuccinos in most cafés (*kafič*) – often accompanied by a glass of mineral water (*mineralna voda*). **Fruit juice** (*voćni sok*) comes in various guises, such as *gusti* (thick), a natural, dense pulp.

The best domestic **beers** (*pivo*) are actually those brewed in Montenegro, such as Nikšićko, which comes in both light and dark varieties, while the best **wines**, such as the red Vranac, also hail from Montenegro. *Spricer* (white wine with soda or sparkling mineral water) is a refreshing alternative on hot summer days. Above all, though, Serbia is renowned for its *rakija*, a ferociously powerful brandy served neat, the most common of which is the plum variety, *šljivovica*. Another popular drink is *pelinkovac*, a bittersweet aperitif-type liqueur.

## Serbian

| | Serbian | Pronunciation |
|---|---|---|
| **Yes** | *Da* | Da |
| **No** | *Ne* | Ne |
| **Thank you** | *Hvala* | Hvala |
| **Hello/Good day** | *Zdravo/Dobar Dan* | Zdravo/Dobar Dan |
| **Goodbye** | *Doviđenja* | Doveejenya |
| **Excuse me** | *Izvinite* | Eezveeneete |
| **Where?** | *Gde?* | Gede |
| **Good** | *Dobro* | Dobro |
| **Bad** | *Loše* | Loshe |
| **Near** | *Blizu* | Bleezoo |
| **Far** | *Daleko* | Daaleko |
| **Cheap** | *Jeftino* | Yefteeno |
| **Expensive** | *Skupo* | Skoopo |
| **Open** | *Otvoreno* | Otvoreno |
| **Closed** | *Zatvoreno* | Zatvoreno |
| **Today** | *Danas* | Danas |
| **Yesterday** | *Juće* | Yooche |
| **Tomorrow** | *Sutra* | Sootra |
| **How much is....?** | *Koliko Košta...?* | Koleeko Koshta...? |
| **What time is it?** | *Koliko je sati?* | Koleeko ye satee? |
| **I don't understand** | *Ne razumem* | Ne razoomem |
| **Do you speak English?** | *Da li pričate engleski?* | Da lee Preechate engleskee? |
| **One** | *Jedan* | Yedan |
| **Two** | *Dva* | Dva |
| **Three** | *Tri* | Tree |
| **Four** | *Četiri* | Cheteeree |
| **Five** | *Pet* | Pet |
| **Six** | *Šest* | Shest |
| **Seven** | *Sedam* | Sedam |
| **Eight** | *Osam* | Osam |
| **Nine** | *Devet* | Devet |
| **Ten** | *Deset* | Deset |

SERBIA | Basics

26

# Opening hours and holidays

Most **shops** open Mon–Fri 8am–8pm (sometimes with a break for lunch), and Sat 8am–2pm. Museum times vary, but most are usually closed on Monday. All shops and banks are closed on **public holidays**: Jan 1 & 7, April 27, and May 1 & 2. The Orthodox Church celebrates Easter between one and five weeks later than the other churches.

# Emergencies

The crime rate, even in Belgrade, is low by European standards, though the usual precautions apply. The **police** (*policija*) are generally easygoing and may speak some basic English. Routine checks on identity cards and documents are not uncommon, so always carry your passport or a photocopy. **Pharmacies** (*apoteka*) tend to follow shop hours, and a rota system covers night-time and weekend opening; details are posted in the window of each pharmacy. Opening hours are generally Mon–Fri 8am–8pm, Sat 8am–3pm. If the pharmacy can't help, they will direct you to a hospital (*bolnica*).

**Emergency numbers**

Police ☎92; Ambulance ☎94; Fire ☎93.

# Belgrade

By no stretch of the imagination can **BELGRADE** (White City) be described as one of Europe's most attractive cities. Nor can it boast world-class museums, galleries or architecture. Yet the raw vigour of its streets, the warmth and humour of its citizens, and a bar and club scene unmatched anywhere else in the Balkans, will ensure that a day or two spent here will be one of the unexpected high points on any European itinerary.

Occupying a strategic point on the junction of the **Danube** and **Sava rivers**, Belgrade was the property of a warlike succession of Celts, Romans, Huns and Avars until the Turks wrenched it from the Hungarians in 1521. The city has since been repeatedly burned, sacked and bombed, including heavy shelling during World War II which razed much of it, and in 1999, when it withstood more than two months of NATO air strikes.

## Arrival, information and city transport

Belgrade's **airport** is 18km northwest of the city in Surćin, and connected to the city by regular Yugoslav airlines (JAT) buses (hourly 5am–9pm; 160Din) which drop off at the train station and Trg Slavija, and bus #72 (5.15am–midnight; 30Din), which terminates at the Zeleni Venac market. A taxi should cost no more than 600Din. The main **train** (železnička stanica) and **bus** (autobuska stanica) stations are located adjacent to each other on Savski trg and Železnička respectively, just fifteen minutes' walk southeast of the centre.

The city's main **tourist information centre** is located in the subway under Terazije – the entrance is on the corner of Kneza Mihailova near the Albanija building (Mon–Fri 9am–8pm, Sat 9am–5pm, Sun 10am–4pm; ☎11/635-622, ⊛www .belgradetourism.org.yu), with further offices at Kneza Mihailova 18 (Mon–Fri 9am–9pm, Sat 9am–5pm, Sun 10am–4pm; ☎11/2629-992) and the railway station (Mon–Fri 9am–8pm, Sat 9am–5pm, Sun 10am–4pm). All these can furnish you with a copy of the free listings magazine *This Month in Belgrade*.

An efficient, if chaotic and overcrowded, system of **buses**, **trolleybuses** and **trams** operates throughout the city. Tickets can be bought from a kiosk or newsstand (20Din) or on the vehicle itself (30Din) – either way, tickets must be validated in the machine on board. Night buses operate between midnight and 4am. **Taxis** provide a far more comfortable means of getting around town, with a starting rate of around 35Din plus 50Din per kilometre – the most reliable companies are Eurotaxi (☎334-4747) and Žuti taxi (☎9802), which can also be flagged down in the street.

## Accommodation

Years of negligible investment and no tourists has left many of Belgrade's **hotels** in a depressed state. Those at the lower end of the spectrum, of which there are many, are almost indistinguishable from one another, though most offer value for money.

At present Belgrade doesn't have any official **hostels**, though the centrally located *Jelica Milovanović* summer hostel at Krunska 8 (☎11/323-1268, ☎322-0762; mid-June to Aug) has three- to six-bed rooms, with and without private shower – you need to be a HI hostel member to stay here. The city's only **campsite** is the *Dunav* (☎11/199-072), though it's actually located some 12km from the centre at Batajnički put bb, in Zemun (bus #704 or #706 from Zeleni Venac market).

### Hotels

**Beograd** Balkanska 52 ☎11/645-199, ☎687-959. A short walk uphill from the train station, this dull place has bog-standard, but clean, rooms. ❸

**Bristol** Karađorđeva 50 ☎11/668-400, ☎631-895. Grimy brown hulk right next to the bus station, but with surprisingly decent rooms. ❸

**Centar** Savski trg 7 ☎11/264-4055, ☎657-838.

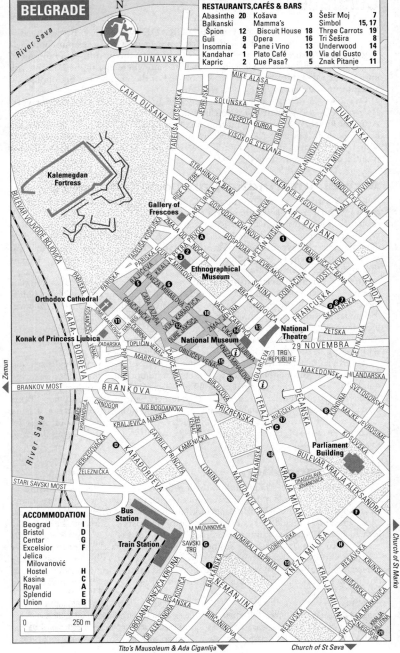

# BELGRADE

**N**

River Sava

## RESTAURANTS, CAFÉS & BARS

| | | | |
|---|---|---|---|
| Abasinthe | 20 | Košava | 3 |
| Balkanski | | Mamma's | |
| Špion | 12 | Biscuit House | 18 |
| Guli | 9 | Opera | 16 |
| Insomnia | 4 | Pane i Vino | 13 |
| Kandahar | 1 | Plato Café | 10 |
| Kapric | 2 | Que Pasa? | 5 |
| Šešir Moj | 7 |
| Simbol | 15, 17 |
| Three Carrots | 19 |
| Tri Šešira | 8 |
| Underwood | 14 |
| Via del Gusto | 6 |
| Znak Pitanje | 11 |

DUNAVSKA

CARA DUŠANA

MIKE ALASA

JEVREJSKA · SOLUNSKA

DESPOTA ĐURĐA

VISOKOG STEVANA

DUNAVSKA

**Kalemegdan Fortress**

BULEVAR VOJVODE BOJOVIĆA

STRAHINJIĆA BANA

RIGE OD FERE

KNIĆANINOVA

KAPETAN MIŠINA

GUNDULIĆEV VENAC

ZMAJ JOVINA

SKENDER-BEGOVA

**Gallery of Frescoes**

TADEUŠA KOŠĆUŠKA

ZMAJA OD NOĆAJA

GOSPODAR JOVANOVA

GOSPODAR JEVREMOVA

CARA DUŠANA

STRAHINJIĆA BANA

DOSITEJEVA

PARISKA

UZUN MIRKOVA

KRALJA PETRA

VIŠNJIĆEVA

**Ethnographical Museum**

ⓐ

③

②

①

④

ⓓ

ⓒ

FRANCUSKA

ŠKADARSKA

DŽORDŽA

RAJIĆEVA

KNEZA MIHAILOVA

SIMINA

BRAĆE JUGOVIĆA

DOBRAČINA

ZETSKA

**Orthodox Cathedral** ✝

CARA LAZARA

GRAČANIČKA

VUKA KARADŽIĆA

⑫

VASE ČARAPIĆA

ZMAJ JOVINA

ČIKA LJUBINA

⑭

⑬

**National Theatre**

29 NOVEMBRA

**Konak of Princess Ljubica**

SIME MARKOVIĆA

IVAN-BEG

DUBROVA

ĐURE JAKŠIĆA

**National Museum**

⑩

ZADARSKA

TOPLIČIN VENAC

OBILIĆEV VENAC

KNEZA MIHAILA

KOLARČEVA

ⓘ

TRG REPUBLIKE

MAKEDONSKA

HILANDARSKA

SVETOGORSKA

POP LUKINA

MARŠALA

CARICE MILICE

BIRJUZOVA

⑯

ⓘ

DEČANSKA

**BRANKOV MOST**

**BRANKOVA**

CRNOGOR

JUG BOGDANOVA

KRALJEVIĆA MARKA

ZELENI VENAC

BALKANSKA

PRIZRENSKA

TERAZIJE

NUŠIĆEVA

⑰

KONDINA

MAJKE JEVROSIME

KOSOVSKA

Zemun ▲

River Sava

BRAĆE KRSMANOVIĆA

HERCEGOVAČKA

GAVRILA PRINCIPA

KAMENIČKA

LOMINA

NARODNOG FRONTA

**Parliament Building**

BULEVAR KRALJA ALEKSANDRA

ⓔ

DRAGOSLAVA JOVANOVIĆA

ⓕ

Church of St Marko ▲

ŽELEZNIČKA

**STARI SAVSKI MOST**

ⓓ

KARAĐORĐEVA

⑱

KRALJA MILANA

RESAVSKA

KRUNSKA

## ACCOMMODATION

| | |
|---|---|
| Beograd | I |
| Bristol | D |
| Centar | G |
| Excelsior | F |
| Jelica | |
| Milovanović | |
| Hostel | H |
| Kasina | C |
| Royal | A |
| Splendid | E |
| Union | B |

**Bus Station**

**Train Station**

M. MILOVANOVIĆA

SAVSKI TRG

ⓖ

ⓗ

ADMIRALA GEPRATA

DOBRINJSKA

KNEZA MILOŠA

⑲

ⓘ

BALKANSKA

NEMANJINA

DRINSKA

SLOBODANA PENEZIĆA KRCUNA

RISANSKA

BIRČANINOVA

RESAVSKA

MIŠARSKA

SVETOZARA MARKOVIĆA

KRALJA MILANA

⑳

SVETOGA NJEGOŠA

0 — 250 m

Tito's Mausoleum & Ada Ciganlija ▼          Church of St Sava ▼

Directly opposite the train station, this is as grubby as it gets, but it is the cheapest place going. ❷

**Excelsior** Kneza Miloša 5 ☎11/323-1381, ℻323-1951. A stone's throw from the Parliament building, this place is not pretty, but no worse than anything else around. ❸

**Kasina** Terazije 25 ☎11/323-5574, ℻323-8257. Very central, but located on one of the city's noisiest streets – ask for a room at the rear. Rooms are dreary but have a/c. ❺

**Royal** Kralja Petra 56 ☎11/634-222, ☺www .hotelroyal.co.yu. Well-located hotel with slightly

careworn rooms, though they do at least retain a modicum of character. One of the better budget options. ❸

**Splendid** Dragoslava Jovanovića 5 ☎11/323-5444, ☺www.splendid.co.yu. Secreted away down a quiet street near the city council building, the rooms here are unspectacular but generally fine. ❸

**Union** Kosovska 1 ☎11/324-8022, ℻322-4480. The best of the city's lower-end hotels, with spacious, tidy and decently furnished rooms. ❹

## The City

The city's chief attraction is the **Kalemegdan Fortress**, which sweeps around a wooden bluff overlooking the wayward swerve of the Danube. Just outside the park boundary is the **Old City**, whose dense lattice of streets conceals Belgrade's most interesting sights. South of here is Belgrade's central square, **Trg Republike**, and the old Bohemian quarter of **Skadarlija**, beyond which lie several more worthwhile sites, including one of the world's largest Orthodox churches. For something a bit more relaxing head east across the Sava to the village-like suburb of **Zemun**, or further south still towards the island of **Ada Ciganija**, the city's prime recreational spot.

## Kalemegdan Fortress and the Old Centre

Splendidly sited on an exposed nub of land overlooking the confluence of the mighty Sava and Danube rivers is **Kalemegdan Park**, dominated by the substantial remains of the **Kalemegdan Fortress**. Originally built by the Celts, expanded upon by the Romans, and rebuilt in the Middle Ages, most of what remains is the result of a short-lived Austrian occupation in the early part of the eighteenth century, before the Ottomans handed it over to Serbia. Some of the subterranean passageways are occasionally used for art exhibitions, while, appropriately enough, the fortress also houses a **Military Museum** (Tues–Sun 10am–5pm; 50Din), containing an array of ferocious-looking weaponry. Otherwise, the park, frequented by walkers, joggers and elderly gentlemen participating in impromptu games of chess, is a lovely place to stroll around. Exiting the park and crossing Pariska, you'll find yourself in the oldest part of the city. At Kralja Petra 7 is the **Orthodox Cathedral**, which, until the completion of the Church of St Sava (see p.872), was the city's most important place of worship. A rather stark Neoclassical edifice built in 1840 on the orders of the Serbian prince Miloš Obrenović, it features a fine Baroque tower and, inside, a beautiful iconostasis. Built around the same time is the oddly titled **?** Café just across the road. It received its name on account of a row amongst a group of church leaders who objected to its then name, the *Café at the Cathedral* – hence, and as a temporary solution, the owner hung out a question mark, which remains to this day.

Just around the corner, at Sime Markovića 8, is the **Konak of Princess Ljubica** (Mon–Fri 10am–5pm, Sat & Sun 9am–4pm; 150Din), the one-time residence of Princess Ljubica Obrenović, wife of Miloš. Restored in the 1970s, the interior of this early eighteenth-century house reflects the style and opulence of the upper classes at that time, each room sporting an intriguing blend of Turkish and Oriental flourishes in the form of carpets, period furniture, objets d'art and paintings.

Two more interesting museums lie a short walk southeast of the park. At Cara Uroša 20, the **Gallery of Frescoes** (Tues–Sat 10am–5pm, Sun 10am–2pm; 50Din) keeps an impressive display of copies of medieval frescoes from the most important Serbian and Macedonian monasteries. Beyond here, at Studentski trg 13, the **Ethnographical Museum** (Tues–Sat 10am–5pm, Sun 9am–2pm; 60Din) is the city's most worthwhile museum, with superb displays of folk art, costumes and textiles.

## Trg Republike and around

The main street leading south from Kalemegdan is Kneza Mihailova, a slicked-up, pedestrianized *korzo* accommodating the city's most stylish shops. Its southern end opens up onto **Trg Republike** (Republic Square), the city's main square, an irregularly shaped space flanked by glassy modern blocks and remnants from more monumental architectural times. On the north side stands the imposing **National Museum**, currently closed pending a huge renovation project.

East of Trg Republike is **Skadarlija**, once a favoured hangout for artists, actors and writers. Although this small enclave still retains vestiges of a bygone Bohemian era – centred around sloping, cobbled Skadarska – it is today the location for the city's most established restaurants, as well as a handful more cafés and bars. South of Trg Republike is the wide swathe of Terazije, which slices through the commercial and business hub of the city.

## South of Trg Republike

A left turn part way down Terazije brings you to the **Parliament Building** (Skupština), an inelegant Classical-style structure dating from the early part of the twentieth century. The building has seen its fair share of drama over the years, most recently in October 2000 when hundreds of people crashed their way in to retrieve thousands of fraudulent ballot papers following the presidential election (in which Milošević was defeated), in the process setting fire to parts of the building and making off with various mementoes – most of which were returned upon request. Beyond the Parliament Building is the **Church of St Marko**, a solid neo-Byzantine structure built between the wars and modelled on the church of Gračanica in Kosovo. Its hollow shrine, supported by four enormous pillars, is distinguished only by some eighteenth- and nineteenth-century icons and the tomb of the Serbian Emperor, Czar Dušan. If you want some idea of what precision bombing can do, take a look immediately behind the church, where the wrecked building of the state television studios still stands – NATO missiles struck here on April 23 1999, killing sixteen people. A small memorial and a couple of headstones are located nearby.

Dominating the skyline south of Terazije is the huge gilded dome of the **Church of St Sava**, which stakes fair claim to being one of the largest Orthodox churches in the world. Named after the founder of the Serbian Orthodox Church, and sited on the spot where his bones were supposed to have been burnt by the Turks in 1594, this immense structure has been under construction since 1894, albeit with some rather lengthy pauses along the way. Even now it still remains incomplete, though you can pop your head inside for a quick peek. One other site worth making the effort to get to is **Tito's Mausoleum** (Tues–Sun; free), located around 1.5km south of the centre on Bulevar Mira (trolleybus #42 from Studentski trg). Also known as Kuca cvece (House of Flowers), the great man's tombstone stands in a large, cool hall bordered by flowers and watched over by a stern-faced guard.

## Beyond the centre

For a peaceful escape from the city centre, head across the Sava river to the suburb of **Zemun**, an attractive jumble of low-slung houses, narrow winding streets and market squares. Zemun's main sights are centred around the hilly waterside district of Gardoš, which holds the remnants of a Gothic-style fortress, and the Baroque **Nikolajevska Church**, the city's oldest Orthodox church, featuring a beautiful iconostasis. Another good reason to come here is to visit one of the many superb fish restaurants along the banks of the Danube. To get here take bus #15 or #84 from Zeleni Venac, or bus #83 from outside the train station. Either way, alight on Glavna, the main street. During the summer, Belgraders flock to **Ada Ciganlija** (Gypsy Island), a long wooded strip stretching along the bank of the Sava just south of the centre. Aside from its sandy beaches (including a naturist area at the southern end), cafés and restaurants, there are opportunities aplenty to partake in various sporting activities such as sailing and windsurfing. To get here, take bus #53 or #56 from Zeleni Venac.

## Eating and drinking

Belgrade's **restaurant** scene is evolving fast, and there are an increasing number of ethnic restaurants hitting town. For those seeking the most authentic Serbian eating experience, head to Skadarska. Belgraders like to party hard, and the city's **nightlife** is currently amongst the most varied and exciting in Eastern Europe, much to the surprise of many a visitor. There are a staggering number of places to drink and dance, with particularly heavy concentrations along Strahinjića bana, Obilićev venac and Njegoševa. Hugely popular amongst Belgraders during the summer months are the many **river rafts** (*splavovi*), variously housing restaurants, bars and discos, most of which are concentrated on the bank of the Danube behind the *Hotel Jugoslavija* towards Zemun, and along the Sava around the Brankov Bridge.

### Fast food, self-service and snack bars

**Amica** Mišarska 7. Up near Slavija, this place offers a terrific range of sweet and sour pancakes.

**Fast Food Aquarium** Nušićeva. Large kiosk doling out seafood bites and salads.

**Pekara Centar Pizza** Kolarčeva 10. Huge range of pastries and pizzas at this busy bakery just off Trg Republike.

**Ruski Car** Obilićev venac 28. Takeaway counter in the venerable "Russian Csar" café offering freshly made *burek* and *gibanica*.

### Restaurants

**Kapric** Kralja Petra 44. The best Italian food in town – including gnocchi and risotto – at this florally-decorated spaghetteria. Good veggie options.

**Košava** Kralja Petra 36. Homely little trattoria on two levels with simple decor and great pizzas.

**Opera** Obilićev venac 30. Neat outfit offering a mix of Serbian and Italian food in classy surroundings – pleasant outdoor seating, too.

**Pane i Vino** Dobraćina 5. This stylishly simple restaurant is the place to try pasta, *bruschette* and *panini*.

**Que Pasa?** Kralja Petra 13–15. Swanky cellar restaurant for high-class Serbian grills, and a loungey upstairs place offering *tortillas* and pancakes.

**Šešir Moj** Skadarska 27. "My Hat" is typical of the many national restaurants along this street – big, juicy portions of *ćevapi*, *pljeskavica* and grilled peppers served by waiters in costume with gypsy bands to boot.

**Tri Šešira** Skadarska 29. Steps from *Šešir Moj*, the "Three Hats" offers a barely distinguishable menu, but its tree-shaded courtyard is better for outdoor seating.

**Via del Gusto** Knez Mihailova 48. Three-in-one patisserie, café and restaurant – delicious Mediterranean food at reasonable prices.

**Znak Pitanje "?"** Kralja Petra 6. Built in 1832, the city's oldest restaurant is a characterful peasant-style inn (with low wooden tables and stools) providing solid Serbian fare.

### Cafés and bars

**Abasinthe** Kralja Milutina 33. Candle-topped tables, good drinks and attractive waiting staff keep the youthful, beautiful crowd happy.

**Balkanski Špion** Vuka Karadića 7. Just off Knez Mihailova, the film-themed "Balkan Spy" café is ideal for a quieter daytime or evening drink.

**Guli** Skadarska 13. The liveliest bar on this street, with a hip crowd and a raucous atmosphere.

**Insomnia** Strahinjića Bana 66. Cool brown-leather sofas and big windows make this trendy hangout an ideal spot for people watching.

**Kandahar** Strahinjića Bana 48. Beautifully designed, orientally-themed café whose teas are the best in town. It also has the most atmospheric terrace on the street.

**Mamma's Biscuit House** Terazije 40. Some of the best coffees, cakes and hot sandwiches in the city.

**Plato Café** Akademski Plato 1. This long-standing favourite doubles up nicely as a daytime terrace

café and chill-out evening venue with live jazz music most nights.
**Simbol** Nušićeva 4 and Obilićev venac 27. Busy, Roman-themed café that more than suffices for a coffee, beer or glass of wine.
**Three Carrots** Kneza Miloša 16. The city's token Irish pub isn't a bad place at all, with tasty beers on tap and simple pub food available.
**Underwood** Vasina 5. Busy and popular wood-furnished café also offering a good choice of wines.

### Clubs and live music

**Acapulco** Bulevar Nikole Tesla bb. If you want to experience a night of Serbia's infamous Turbo-folk (an excruciating hybrid of electronic pop and Balkan folk music), then this rocking raft behind the *Hotel Jugoslavija* is the place to come.
**Beggars Banquet** Resavska 24. So named after the Stones' album, this barn-like venue has regular live rock music.
**Bus** Aberdareva 1. As the name implies, this red double-decker bus, across from the bombed-out TV studios, has regular DJ nights, with discounted prices on Tuesday.
**Oh, Cinema!** Kalemegdan Terasa (during summer) and Gračanička 18 (during winter). Both these venues – one an atmospheric indoor hall, the other an outdoor terrace – are popular party places with frequent live music, and remain open later than most.
**Tramvaj** Ruzveltova 2. Energetic pub/club place that puts on live jazz/blues once or twice a week. A 10min walk south of St Marko's church.
**Underground** Pariski 1. Well established on the local club scene, *Underground* is a warren of vast rooms under the fortress accommodating thumping house and techno tunes alongside chill-out areas.

## Entertainment

Belgrade offers a rich cultural programme, most of which takes place at the **National Theatre** on Trg Republike – tickets for theatre (100–600Din) and opera/ballet (100–800Din) can be purchased from the box office inside the theatre (10am–2pm & 5pm till performance). The **Belgrade Philharmonia** play at the Kolarčev Concert Hall, Studentski trg 5 (box office 10am–2pm & 2.30–7.30pm; tickets 200–500Din). What few big-name groups that do come to Belgrade usually play at the Sava Centar, across the river in Novi Beograd, though the Dom Omladine Youth Cultural Centre at Makedonska 22 (@www.domomladine.org) often has a good cross-section of Serbian and international music as well as film and other multimedia events. Tickets for events at all the above venues can be obtained from the Bilet Servis ticket agency at Trg Republike 5 – inside the IPS shop (Mon–Fri 9am–8pm, Sat 9am–3pm).

## Listings

**Embassies and consulates** Australia, Čika Ljubina 13 ☎11/624-655; Canada, Kneza Miloša 13 ☎11/306-3000; Ireland ☎11/302-9600; New Zealand ☎11/428-2208; UK, Resavska 46 ☎11/2645-055; US, Kneza Miloša 50 ☎11/3619-344.
**Hospital** Pasterova 2 ☎11/361-8444.

**Internet** Dom Omladine (Youth Centre), Makedonska 22; Plato Plus, Vasina 19.
**Pharmacy** Kralja Milana 9 and Nemanjina 2 – both 24hr.
**Police** Savski trg 2 ☎11/645-764.
**Post office** Zmaj Jovina 17. Mon–Sat 8am–7pm.

# Northern Serbia

North of Belgrade to the Hungarian border is the Vojvodina, a flat, fertile, and largely featureless plain that contains the country's most disparate mix of peoples, including a large Hungarian minority. The region's main draw is **Novi Sad**, a friendly, graceful city that makes for an easy and enjoyable day-trip from the capital. It's also an excellent base for forays into **Fruška Gora**, a series of gently undulating hills to the south, peppered with ancient Orthodox monasteries.

# Novi Sad

The cosmopolitan city of **NOVI SAD**, some 75km north of Belgrade on the main road and rail routes towards Budapest, is Serbia's most appealing urban centre, with much to show for its centuries of Austro-Hungarian rule. The city developed in tandem with the huge **Petrovaradin Fortress** on the Danube's south bank. There had been fortifications here since Roman times, but the fortress took its present shape in the eighteenth century when the Austrians turned it into a barrier against Turkish expansionism. In the event, no assault was ever made on the fortress and it eventually became a jail, its most celebrated inmate being a young Tito, briefly imprisoned for propagating socialist ideas. A vast enterprise, it took a hundred years to build, and contains four subterranean levels with a total of sixteen kilometres of tunnels, around one kilometre of which is open to visitors (daily 9am–6pm; 100Din). Otherwise you can stroll along the fortress walls and take in the splendid views of the town and surrounding countryside, and visit the artists' studios secreted away inside the citadel stables.

Across the river, the hub of the city is Trg Slobode (Freedom Square), a spacious square with an ostentatious town hall on one side and the neo-Gothic, brick-clad Catholic **Church of the Virgin Mary** on the other. Head straight on past the cathedral towards pedestrianized Zmaj Jovina, a popular *korso* teeming with busy pavement cafés. At the head of the street stands the nineteenth-century Archbishop's Palace, a curiously fanciful red-tiled building with Moorish arched windows and a pinnacled roof. Here the street forks – to the left, in Svetozara Markovica, is the **Orthodox Church**, originally designed in 1740 by the Hungarian architect Mihailj Harminic but rebuilt between 1840–60 and harbouring some thirty beautifully decorated icons. Turn right and you enter Dunavska, a quaint, cobbled street and setting for more boutique shops, cafés and restaurants.

At the bottom end of Dunavska, at no. 35, is the excellent **Museum of Vojvodina** (Tues–Fri 9am–7pm, Sat & Sun 9am–2pm; 50Din), which details life in the region from the Paleolithic period, and features a prolific archeological section and a fine ethnographical section incorporating a colourful assemblage of Serbian folk costumes and some lovely icons on glass.

Sun lovers should head for the **Štrand** (May–Sept), a tidy expanse of sandy beach and extensive lawns on the Danube's north bank, opposite the fortress. The beachy atmosphere is enhanced by the plethora of cafés, bars and kiosks dotted along the front.

## Practicalities

Arriving at the adjacent **bus** and **train** stations, 1km north of the centre on Bulevar Jaše Tomića, it's an easy fifteen-minute walk into town – head straight down Bulevar Oslobođenja and then left down Jevrejska (by the market). Alternatively you can take one of the regular buses #4 or #11 from the train station forecourt to Uspenska opposite the National Theatre. The helpful **tourist information** centre is a five-minute walk away at Mihaila Pupina 9 (Mon–Fri 8.30am–8pm, Sat 8.30am–1pm; ☎21/421-811, ⊛www.novisadtourism.org.yu), the town's main thoroughfare.

The city's one **hostel** is the *Brankovo Kolo*, Episkopa Visariona 3 (☎21/528-263, ⊛www.hostelns.com; 1100Din; July–Aug only). Best of the **hotels** is the smart, colourful and friendly *Hotel Zenit* at Zmaj Jovina 8 (☎21/621-444, ⊛www .hotelzenit.co.yu; ❺) – it's actually just off this street through a narrow passage. Otherwise there's the venerable but fading *Hotel Vojvodina* on Trg Svobode (☎21/622-122, ⓔvojvodinahtl@neobee.net; ❸), or the down-at-heel, though perfectly acceptable, *Pansion Fontana*, Nikole Pašićeva 27 (☎21/621-760; ❸).

Two of the best **restaurants** in town are *Arhiv*, a bright outfit next to the *Hotel Zenit* offering a classy international menu, and *Alla Lanterna* at the bottom of

Dunavska, whose pasta dishes are the best in town. Another good place with Italian food is *Pomodoro Rosso*, Nikole Pašićeva 14. The most obvious **drinking** spots are the pavement cafés ranged along Zmaj Jovina. For more discreet consumption, head to Laze Telečkog, just off Zmaj Jovina, where you'll find *Divan Dućan*, a lovely tea house at no. 6, and *Kuća Mala* next door (which also serves snacks), while there's more lively fare at *Marsha's Pub* opposite, and at *Cuba Libre*, no.13. Alternatively, during the summer, there are dozens of open-air bars along the Štrand (see p.875). For four days at the beginning of July each year the grounds of Petrovaradin Fortress play host to the **Exit Noise Festival** (⊛www.exitfest.org), now established as the premier music event in southeastern Europe, attracting some of the biggest names in rock, hip-hop and techno.

## Around Novi Sad

Shadowing the city to the south are the low rolling hills of the **Fruška Gora** (Holy Mountain), a densely wooded region of farms, orchards and vineyards carved up by a well-worn nexus of simple hiking trails. Moreover, the Fruška Gora shelter some seventeen monasteries, the most interesting of which lie in fairly close proximity to each other on the southeastern rim of the hills – none of them has specific opening hours, but you should be able to look around freely at any time of the day. Just off the main road before the village of Irig, about 15km south of Novi Sad, is **Hopovo**, the largest and most Byzantine in style, frescoed with seventeenth-century works of an unknown monk-artist from Mount Athos, and decorated outside with a graceful twelve-sided dome supported by columns. Some 8km southeast, the church at **Krušedol** dates from the sixteenth century, though, with the exception of some excellent frescoes from the Russian school, most paintings are from the mid-eighteenth century, as the Turks burned the original building. During World War II the church was used as a prison by the Ustaše – the wartime Croatian terrorist organization – who summarily murdered many partisans here. Dating from the sixteenth century, the monastery of **Vrdnik**, west of Hopovo, once held the relics of the heroic Serbian leader Tsar Lazar, brought here from Ravanica monastery in the migration of 1683 – his remains have since been returned to Ravanica, except for part of his collar bone which is now concealed within a glass box. Without wheels, visiting the monasteries is a tricky business – the closest you can get to Fruška Gora by public transport from Novi Sad is bus #61 or #62 (from the local bus station on Gimnazijska, just north of Zmaj Jovina) to the small town of Sremski Karlovci, or any bus to Irig. All in all you're better off going on an organized visit arranged through one of the agencies in town, such as Magelan, Zmaj Jovina 23 (☎21/420-680, ⊛www.magelancorp.co.yu).

# Southern Serbia

South of Belgrade, the landscape becomes increasingly more appealing, the green rolling heartland of its central hills and mountains the setting for a sprinkling of fine sights. Chief amongst these are Serbia's revered medieval monasteries, the best possible illustration of an age that Serbs, even today, look back on with pride. Three of the most important are **Žiča**, **Studenica** and **Sopoćani**, all of which belong to the so-called Raška School, a style dating from the foundation of the Serbian state in the late twelfth century and which are distinguished by some fine Romanesque architecture and monumental frescoes. Elsewhere, the region's main city, **Niš**, conveniently straddles major road and rail routes to Bulgaria and Macedonia further south, and has a few worthy sights in its own right.

# The monasteries of Žiča, Studenica and Sopoćani

Four kilometres southeast of the grimy industrial town of Kraljevo (itself about 170km south of Belgrade) lies the monastery of **Žiča**. Founded in the early thirteenth century by St Sava – Serbia's patron saint – Žiča was the fulcrum of his master plan to establish the great and holy kingdom of Serbia. The church itself has been heavily restored over the years, though the frescoes remain in a rather parlous state, with patches around the cupola and the *Crucifixion* in the south transept all that remain from Sava's time. To get here take a local bus headed towards the village of Mataruška Banja, or a taxi or, if you're in the mood, you can walk from Kraljevo in about forty-five minutes – it's signposted from town.

From Kraljevo the road weaves its way south around the sleek wooded spurs of the Ibar Valley down to Ušće, where a smaller road branches off to the monastery of **Studenica**, the first and greatest of the Serbian monasteries. Established at the end of the twelfth century by Stefan Nemanja, the complex comprises three churches (there were nine at one time) enclosed within an oval paddock. The largest, and most important, of these is the church of Sv Bogdorica (Church of Our Lady), whose paintings represent the first flowering of Serbian fresco painting, manifest in such pieces as the remarkably well-preserved *Crucifixion* on the west wall of the nave. The inner sanctum holds the marble tomb of Stefan Nemanja, below a fresco that shows him being presented to Christ and the Virgin. Either side of Sv Bogdorica is the much smaller, fourteenth-century Kraljeva Crkva (King's Church), also containing some impressive frescoes, and the Church of Sv Nikola (Church of St Nicholas), which also keeps a couple of well-preserved frescoes, such as *Three Marys at Christ's Grave*. If you wish to **stay**, there's an adjoining hotel, which has accommodation in multi-bed dorms (**②**). Studenica is reachable on one of the irregular buses from Ušće or by a forty-five-minute walk.

From Ušće buses rumble southwards to **Novi Pazar**, a humdrum town whose many Turkish monuments recall the town's one-time status as the capital of the Sandžak, a remote Muslim region that remained a solitary island of Turkish rule until the late nineteenth century. The main attraction, though, lies 16km southwest of town; built in the thirteenth century by King Uroš, the monastery of **Sopoćani** was largely destroyed by rampaging Turks in the seventeenth century, and mostly remained that way until its restoration in the 1920s. Sopoćani holds what are considered to be the finest Serbian fresco paintings, the best known of which is the *Dormition of the Virgin* covering the west wall. Uroš is buried in the nave. Unfortunately there are no buses to Sopoćani, so you'll have to rely on getting a taxi from Novi Pazar. If you're looking to stick around, then Novi Pazar has a handful of reasonable **hotels** including the *Kan*, Rifata Burdževića 10 (☏20/25-250; **②**), and the more comfortable *Tadž* at no. 79 (☏20/311-904; **④**).

# Niš

The largest town in southern Serbia, and the third largest in the country, **NIŠ** is a hard-nosed, gritty industrial centre that retains a rather depressed air – a situation not helped by the pounding the city took during the 1999 NATO air strikes. It does, though, hold several curious sights, while its location on the main road and rail routes into Macedonia and Bulgaria make it a convenient place to stop off.

The heart of the city is the main square, Trg oslobođenja, from where it's a short walk north across the Nišava River to **Niš Fortress**. Originally built on the site of a Roman fortress, the current fortifications date from the beginning of the eighteenth century. The most interesting parts are the well-preserved Istanbul Gate (now the entrance), and the Mosque of Bali Beg, an arsenal converted to a modern art gallery. Most people, though, come here for the bars and cafés crammed inside the courtyard. Niš's most appealing sights, however, are located out on the fringes of town, the most curious of which is the **Ćele Kula** (Tower of Skulls; Mon–Sat 9am–4pm, Sun 10am–2pm; 100Din), east of the centre on Braće Taskovića (bus #24). Surrounded by the Turkish army on nearby Čegar Hill in 1809, Stevan Sinđelić and his men chose death before dishonour and ignited their gunpowder supplies, blowing to pieces most of the Turks, and all of the Serbians. As a grisly statement of Turkish sovereignty, the Pasha ordered around a thousand Serbian heads to be stuffed and mounted on the tower, around sixty of which now remain. No less morbid is the World War II **Crveni Krst (Red Cross) Concentration Camp** (daily 9am–6pm; 100Din) sited 2km northwest of town, out beyond the bus station on Bulevar 12 Februar. Built as an army depot, it's a sombre grey memorial to the bravery of its inmates – partisans, Communists, gypsies and Jews – rounded up here prior to their torture and execution or deportation to the death camps. On February 12, 1942, a suicidal escape attempt left fifty prisoners machine-gunned on the walls – the bullet holes are still visible – but also saw a hundred or so managing to scale the barriers in one of the biggest breakouts of the war. The perimeter walls, barbed-wire fences and watchtowers all remain, though there's little to see in the building itself, save for some dusty old photographs of prisoners on the cell walls. Many of those who passed through Crveni Krst met their deaths at **Bubanj**, a wooded hill located to the southwest of town. Although the exact total is unknown, it's estimated that some 12,000 people were shot here – the site is now commemorated by an inelegant concrete memorial, comprised of three giant clenched fists.

## Practicalities

The **bus station** is located just outside the citadel on Februar 12 Bulevar, while the **train station** is west of town on Dimitrija Tucovica. You can get information from the **tourist office** at Voždova 7 (Mon–Fri 8.30am–7pm, Sat 8.30am–1pm; ☎18/523-118). The only really central, and cheap, **place to stay** is the *Hotel Ambasador* on Trg oslobođenja (☎18/25-650; ❸). More distant alternatives consist of the *Hotel Centroturist*, next to the football stadium east of the centre at IX Brigade 10 (☎18/22-468; ❸), and the *Hotel Lion*, also east of the city (but on the north side of the river) at Knaževačka 28a (☎18/570-010; ❸).

The town possesses some very good **restaurants** including *Hamam*, just inside the fort entrance, and the *Sinđelić* at Nikole Pašica 25, which offers perhaps the best Serbian food in town. For evening **drinking**, make a beeline for the cluster of cafés and bars inside the fortress. Beyond here try *Porto Bello*, a café-boat on the Nišava by the bridge leading to the fortress, and *Broz*, Pobode 20, a funky bar with good background music and photos of Tito adorning the walls.

# Travel details

| Trains |
|---|
| **Belgrade** to: Kraljevo (2 daily; 4hr 15min); Niš (8 daily; 4–5hr); Novi Sad (10 daily; 1hr 30min); Ušče (2 daily; 5hr). |
| **Kraljevo** to: Belgrade (3 daily; 4hr 15min); Niš (2 daily; 3hr 45min). |
| **Niš** to: Belgrade (7 daily; 4–5hr); Kraljevo (2 daily; 3hr 45min). |
| **Novi Sad** to: Belgrade (10 daily; 1hr 30min). |

| Buses |
|---|
| **Belgrade** to: Kraljevo (every 60–90min; 2hr); Niš (hourly; 3hr); Novi Pazar (every 60–90min; 3hr); Novi Sad (every 30–50min; 1hr 20min–1hr 45min). |
| **Kraljevo** to: Belgrade (every 60–90min; 2hr); Novi Pazar (hourly; 1hr 30min). |
| **Niš** to: Belgrade (hourly; 3hr); Novi Pazar (4 daily; 3hr). |
| **Novi Pazar** to: Belgrade (every 60–90min; 3hr); Kraljevo (hourly; 1hr 30min); Niš (4 daily; 3hr). |
| **Novi Sad** to: Belgrade (hourly; 1hr 15min). |

# Slovakia

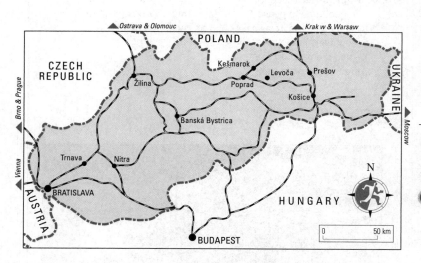

# Slovakia highlights

**Bratislava** The Slovak capital has a small but beautifully restored old town full of Baroque palaces, leafy squares and lively pavement cafés. See p.885

**High Tatras** These jagged, granite peaks – the most spectacular mountains in Slovakia – rise dramatically from the Poprad plain. See p.890

**Levoča** An attractive walled medieval town, originally settled by Saxons. See p.892

**Spišský hrad** This sprawling medieval castle in the east of the country is Slovakia's most stunning hilltop ruin. See p.892

△ Tatras Mountains

# Introduction and basics

**Slovakia** consists of the long, narrow strip of land that stretches from the fertile plains of the Danube basin up to the peaks of the High Tatras, Europe's most exhilarating mountain range outside the Alps. The country's mountain chains have long formed barriers to industrialization and modernization, and parts of Slovakia remain surprisingly rural and unspoilt.

Before 1918, present-day Slovakia was known as Upper Hungary and lay under Magyar rule for roughly a millennium; Bratislava even became the Hungarian capital when the Turks occupied the rest of Hungary. In 1918, however, the Slovaks threw in their lot with their Slav neighbours, the Czechs, forming **Czechoslovakia**, a union that, with the exception of the war years, lasted 75 years until the countries' "velvet divorce" in 1993 (the Czech Republic is covered in Chapter 7). Slovakia's independence is now assured and it joined the EU in May 2004.

The republic has a diverse population, with over half a million ethnic **Hungarians** in the south, as well as thousands of **Romanies** (Gypsies), who live a fairly miserable existence throughout the country, and several thousand **Ruthenians** (Rusyns) in the east.

**Bratislava**, the capital, has been much maligned but its compact old town has been beautifully restored in the last decade and it's now a rewarding, lively place. Poprad provides the transport hub for the **High Tatras**, and is also the starting point for exploring the intriguing medieval towns of the **Spiš** region. Further east still, **Prešov** is the cultural centre of the Ruthenian minority; while **Košice**, Slovakia's vibrant second city, boasts a fine Gothic cathedral, ethnic diversity and a lively independence from much of the rest of the country.

## Information & maps

Just about every town has some kind of tourist office (*informačné centrum*), most with English speakers. In summer they're generally open Mon–Fri 9am–6pm, Sat & Sun 9am–2pm; in winter they tend to close an hour earlier and all day Sunday (sometimes also Sat). **Maps** are available, often very cheaply, from bookshops and some hotels (a town plan is *plán mesta* or *orientačná mapa*). The VKÚ's excellent 1:50,000 series details hiking paths.

## Money and banks

Currency is the **Slovak crown** or *Slovenská koruna* (Sk), which is divided into 100 heller or *halér* (h). Coins are 10h, 20h, 50h, 1Sk, 2Sk, 5Sk and 10Sk; notes are 20, 50, 100, 200, 500 and 1000Sk. The crown is not fully convertible, which theoretically means you can't buy any currency until you arrive. **Credit and debit cards** are accepted in most upmarket hotels and restaurants and some shops, and there are plenty of **ATMs** in all the larger towns. **Exchange offices** (*zmenáreň*) can be found in all major hotels, travel agencies and department stores. At time of writing, €1 was equal to 40Sk, 1$ to 31Sk and £1 to 59Sk.

## Communications

Most **post offices** (*pošta*) open Mon–Fri 8am–5pm – you can also buy stamps (*známky*) from some tobacconists (*tabák*) and street kiosks. Poste restante is available in major towns; write Pošta 1 (the main

### Slovakia on the net

ⓦ **www.slovakspectator.sk** English-language weekly, with news and listings.

ⓦ **www.tatry.sk** Excellent guide to the High Tatras, with plenty of travel and accommodation info.

ⓦ **www.sacr.sk** Tourist board site, with basic but useful information.

office), followed by the name of the town. Cheap local calls can be made from any **phone**, but for international calls it's best to use a card phone; buy a card (*telefonná karta*) from a tobacconist or post office. Internet cafés have appeared in the larger towns; expect to pay 50–100Sk/hr.

# Getting around

Train services are slow, but some of the journeys are worth it for the scenery alone. Slovak Railways (*Železnice Slovenskej republiky* or *ŽSR*) runs fast *rýchlik* trains that stop at major towns; the *osobný vlak*, or local train, stops everywhere. You can buy tickets (*lístok*) for domestic journeys at the station (*stanica*) before or on the day of departure. Supplements are payable on all EuroCity (EC) trains, and occasionally for InterCity (IC) and Expres (Ex) trains. ŽSR runs reasonably priced sleepers (*lužkový vozeň*) and couchettes (*ležadlový vozeň*) – book in advance, no later than six hours before departure. **InterRail** is valid; **Eurail** requires supplements. You can search train timetables online at ⓦ www.zsr.sk.

Travelling by **bus** (*autobus*) is quicker and covers a more extensive network. In most cities the bus and train stations are adjacent. The state bus company is *Slovenská automobilová doprava* or *SAD*. The usual practice is to buy your ticket from the driver. Book in advance if you're travelling at the weekend or early in the morning on one of the main routes.

# Accommodation

Arrange **accommodation** as far in advance as possible. Some hotels have double pricing, with higher rates for foreigners, but a basic room for €9 per head is not hard to find anywhere outside Bratislava. While the old state hotels and spa complexes are slowly being refurbished, their rooms are usually box-like and overpriced; the new hotels and pensions that have opened up are often better value for money. **Private rooms** are a good option in many towns – keep your eyes peeled for *Zimmer frei* or *Priváty* signs or book through the local tourist information office. Prices start at around €7.50 per person per night.

There is no real network of **hostels**, though a few are affiliated to HI and others come under CKM, the student travel agency (ⓦ www.ckm.sk). Bratislava has a few private hostels offering varying degrees of discomfort. Elsewhere, CKM or local tourist offices can give information on cheap **student accommodation** in the university towns during July and August. In the High Tatras, you can find a fair number of chalet-style **refuges** (*chata*) scattered about the hillsides. Some are practically hotels and cost around €15 a bed, while simpler, more isolated wooden shelters cost much less. **Campsites** are plentiful, and many feature simple **bungalows** (*chata* again), often available for upwards of €7.50 a bed.

# Food and drink

Slovak **food** is no-nonsense, filling fare; traces of Hungarian, Polish and Ukrainian influences can be found in different regions. The usual mid-morning snack at the **bufet** (stand-up canteen) is *párek*, a hot frankfurter dipped in mustard or horseradish and served inside a white roll. The national dish is *bryndzové halušky* – dumplings with a thick sheep's-cheese sauce and crumbled grilled bacon – but Hungarian influences are strong here, too: goulash is very popular, as are *langoše* – deep-fried dough smothered in a variety of toppings. Most menus start with **soup** (*polievka*). **Main courses** are based on pork, beef or chicken, but trout and carp are usually featured somewhere on the menu. Most main courses are served with delicious potatoes (*zemiaky*) – but fresh salads or green vegetables are still a rarity in local restaurants. In addition to *palačinky* (cold pancakes) filled with chocolate, fruit and cream, Slovak **desserts** invariably feature apple or cottage-cheese strudel and ice cream. In outlying regions closing time will still be 9 or 10pm, the bigger cities have restaurants open till 11pm or later. **Coffee** (*káva*) is drunk black – espresso-style in the big cities, but sometimes simply hot water poured over grounds (described rather hopefully as "Turkish" or *turecká*). The cake shop (*cukráreň*) is an important part of social life, particularly on Sunday mornings when it's often the only place that's open in town. Whatever the season, Slovaks love their daily fix of ice cream (*zmrzlina*), available at *cukráreň* or dispensed from little window kiosks in the sides of buildings.

Vineyards in the south of Slovakia produce some pretty good white **wines**. The most famous local firewaters are *slivovice*, a plum **brandy** available just about everywhere, and *borovička*, made with juniper berries. Slovaks love draught **beer**, but the *pivnica*, where most heavy drinking goes on, is still less common in Slovakia than in the Czech Republic. Slovaks tend to head instead for restaurants or wine bars (*vináreň*), which usually have slightly later opening hours and often double as nightclubs.

# Opening hours and holidays

**Opening hours** for shops are Mon–Fri 9am–6pm, Sat 8am–noon, with some shops and most supermarkets staying open later. In large towns, supermarkets and out-of-town hypermarkets also open on Sunday. Smaller shops take an hour or so for lunch between noon and 2pm. The basic opening hours for **castles** and **monasteries** are Tues–Sun 9am–5pm. Out of the season

## Slovak

| | Slovak | Pronunciation |
|---|---|---|
| **Yes** | *Áno* | Uh-no |
| **No** | *Nie* | Nyeh |
| **Please** | *Prosím* | Pro-seem |
| **Thank you** | *D'akujem vam* | Dya-koo-yem vam |
| **Hello/Good day** | *Dobrý deň/Ahoj* | Dob-rie den[y]/a-hoy |
| **Goodbye** | *Dovidenia* | Do-vid-en-ya |
| **Excuse me** | *Prepáčte* | Pre-patch-teh |
| **Where** | *Kde* | Gde |
| **Good** | *Dobrý* | Dob-rie |
| **Bad** | *Zle* | Zleh |
| **Near** | *Blízko* | Bli-sko |
| **Far** | *D'aleko* | D[y]a-lek-o |
| **Cheap** | *Lacný* | Lats-nie |
| **Expensive** | *Drahý* | Dra-hie |
| **Open** | *Otvorený* | Ot-vor-eh-nie |
| **Closed** | *Zatvorený* | Zat-vor-eh-nie |
| **Today** | *Dnes* | Dnes |
| **Yesterday** | *Včera* | Ftch-er-a |
| **Tomorrow** | *Zajtra* | Zuyt-ra |
| **How much is....?** | *Kol'ko stát'...?* | Kol-ko stat[y] |
| **What time is it?** | *Kol'ko je hodín?* | Kol-ko ye hod-in |
| **I don't understand** | *Nerozumiem* | Ne-ro-zoom-yem |
| **Do you speak English?** | *Hovoríte po Anglicky?* | Hov-or-i-te po ang-lits-ky |
| **One** | *Jeden* | Yed-en |
| **Two** | *Dva* | Dva |
| **Three** | *Tri* | Tri |
| **Four** | *Štyri* | Shtir-i |
| **Five** | *Pät'* | Pyat[y] |
| **Six** | *Šest'* | Shest[y] |
| **Seven** | *Sedem* | Sed-em |
| **Eight** | *Osem* | Oss-em |
| **Nine** | *Devät'* | Dev-yat[y] |
| **Ten** | *Desat'* | Dess-at[y] |

SLOVAKIA | Basics

27

opening hours are often restricted to weekends and holidays. Most castles are closed in winter. When visiting a sight, always ask for an *anglický text*, an often unintentionally hilarious English resumé. **Museums** are usually open Tues–Sun year-round, though most close early in winter. **Admission** rarely costs more than 100Sk – hence we've only quoted prices greater than this. **Public holidays** include Jan 1, Jan 6, Good Fri, Easter Mon, May 1, May 8, July 5, Aug 29, Sept 1, Sept 15, Nov 1, Dec 24, 25 and 26.

# Emergencies

The state **police** (*polícia*) wear khaki-green uniforms, and the local municipal or *mestská polícia* wear a variety of outfits. Theft from cars and hotel rooms is your biggest worry, though pickpocketing is also common in the larger towns. You should carry your **passport** with you at all times, though you're most unlikely to get stopped. Minor ailments can be easily dealt with by the **pharmacist** (*lekáreň*), but language is likely to be a problem. If the pharmacy can't help, they'll direct you to a **hospital** (*nemocnica*).

## Emergency numbers

Police ☏158; Ambulance ☏155; Fire ☏150.

# Bratislava

**BRATISLAVA** – just 60km east of Vienna – has two distinct sides: the old quarter is an attractive slice of Habsburg Baroque, while the rest of the city has the drab, concrete looks of the average East European metropolis. Indeed, more buildings have been destroyed here since World War II than were bombed out during it. Much has been done recently, however, to spruce the city up, and the paved streets and squares of the old town are now abuzz with cafés and bars. Thanks to its large student population, the city has a lively, cosmopolitan atmosphere – and with sparser sightseeing crowds than Prague, it makes for a pleasant place to spend a couple of days.

## Arrival, information and accommodation

The scruffy main **train station**, Bratislava–Hlavná stanica, is about a kilometre north of the centre. From the tram terminus below you can hop on tram #1 into town (tickets from the platform machines). Some trains, particularly those heading for west Slovakia, pass through Bratislava Nové Mesto station, 4km northeast of the centre, which is linked by tram #6. **Buses** usually arrive at the main bus station, Bratislava autobusová stanica, on Mlynské nivy, fifteen minutes' walk east of the centre; trolleybus #210 will take you across town to the main train station, while #206 and #208 will drop you on Hodžovo námestie. The **tourist office**, BKIS, at Klobucnícka 2 (June–Sept Mon–Fri 8.30am–7pm, Sat 9am–5pm, Sun 9.30am–4pm; Oct–May Mon–Fri 8.30am–6pm, Sat 9am–2pm; ☎02/5443 3715, ⓦwww.bkis.sk, ⓦwww.bratislava.sk), is good for general queries and getting hold of a map and the monthly listings magazine, *Kam do mesta* (free) or the English-language *What's on Bratislava & Slovakia* (40Sk); it also books accommodation (50Sk fee). There's another smaller office in the main train station. The weekly *Slovak Spectator*, available from kiosks and hotels, has news and some listings. *MEGAiNET*, Klariská 5, has **Internet** access.

**Walking** is the only way to see the mainly pedestrianized Staré Mesto (Old Town). If you need to use the **public transport system** a 14Sk ticket from a yellow machine or kiosk near the stop lasts long enough for most journeys; validate the ticket as soon as you get on and use a fresh ticket each time you change. You'll also need a half-fare ticket for any bulky luggage. The booth to the left of the train station's main exit sells one/two-day passes (90/170Sk).

**Hotels** are more expensive than anywhere else in the country, making **hostels** and **private rooms** the most popular options for budget travellers. You can book centrally located rooms (❸) through the tourist office. The tourist office can also help with finding rooms in Bratislava's various **student hostels**, though these are open only in summer.

### Hostels

**Downtown Backpacker's** Panenská 31 ☎02/5464 1191, ⓦwww.backpackers.sk. Friendly HI-affiliated place near Hodžovo námestie, with a few doubles and lockers in rooms. Open all year. Dorms 600Sk, rooms ❹

**J.Hronca** Bernolákova 1 ☎02/5249 7723. The liveliest student hostel in the city – with a bar on site – is only a short tram ride northeast of the centre. Breakfast included. June–Aug only. Tram #11 from Kamenné námestie. Dorms 283Sk, rooms ❷

**Patio** Špitálska 35 ☎02/5292 5797, ⓦwww .patiohostel.com. Five minutes' walk from Kamenné námestie, this refurbished hostel has dorms and rooms, a laundry and Internet access. Open all year. Dorms 530Sk, rooms ❸

**Svoradov** Svoradova 13 ☎02/5441 1908. Another bustling student hostel, centrally located just two blocks north of the castle. Open all year. Dorms 350Sk, rooms ❷

### Hotels and pensions

**Arcus** Moskovská 5 ☎02/5557 2522. Small quiet pension within walking distance of the old town, just east of Americké námestie. Take any tram heading up Špitálska from Kamenné námestie. ❺

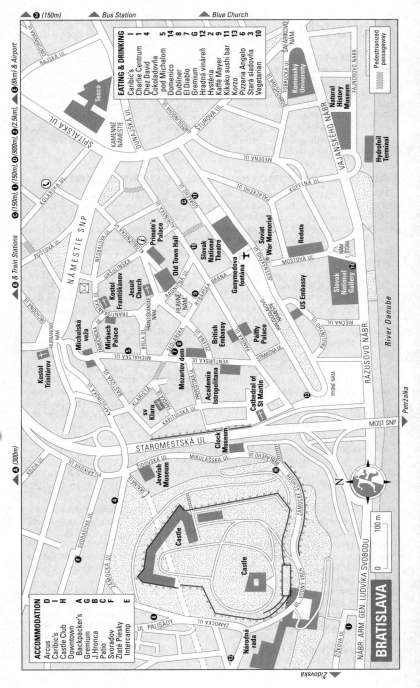

**BRATISLAVA**

ACCOMMODATION
Arcus — D
Caribic's — I
Castle Club — H
Downtown — A
Gremium — G
J.Hronca — B
Patio — C
Svoradov — F
Zlaté Piesky Intercamp — E

EATING & DRINKING
Caribic's — 1
Charlie Centrum — 4
Chez David — 14
Čokoladovňa pod Michalom — 5
Domenico — 8
Dubliner — 7
El Diablo — G
Gremium — 12
Hradná vináreň — 9
Hystéria — 11
Kaffé Mayer — 13
Kikaku sushi bar — 6
Korzo — 3
Pizzeria Angelo — 10
Stará sladovňa
Vegetarian

**Caribic's** Žižkova 1a ☎ 02/5441 8334, ⊛ www
.caribics.sk. Pleasant rooms in an old fisherman's
lodge and pretty good value given its proximity
to the old town, though rather noisy thanks to
passing trams. ❹
**Castle Club** Zámocké schody 4 ☎ & 🅵 02/5464
1472, ✉ castleclub@stonline.sk. One atmospheric
apartment and two simple rooms with shared
facilities, on a quiet site just below the castle, with
views over the Danube. ❺
**Gremium** Gorkého 11 ☎ 02/5413 1026, ⊛ www
.gremium.sk. The only halfway decent, relatively

inexpensive option in the old town. Clean, with
extremely basic en-suite bathrooms, plus a café
and sports bar on the bottom two floors. ❸

### Campsites
**Zlaté Piesky Intercamp** ☎ 02/4425 7373,
⊛ www.intercamp.sk. Two fairly grim campsites,
8km northeast of the city centre, near the swimming lake of the same name. Tent camping May
to mid-Oct. Also offers year-round bungalows
❶–❷. Tram #2 from the main train station or #4
from town.

## The City

Trams from the main train station offload behind the *Hotel Fórum* on Obchodná
– literally Shop Street – which descends into Hurbanovo námestie, a busy junction
on the northern edge of the old town. Here you'll find the hefty mass of the **Kostol
trinitárov**, one of the city's finest churches, its exuberant trompe-l'oeil frescoes
creating a magnificent false cupola. Opposite the church, a footbridge crosses a
small section of what used to be a moat towards the city's last remaining double
gateway. The tower above the gateway's second arch, the **Michalská veža** (Tues–Fri
9.30/10am–4.30/5pm, Sat & Sun 11am–6pm), provides an evocative and impressive
entrance to the old town and is now a weapons museum – worth visiting if only
for the view from the top. Michalská and Ventúrska, which run into each other, have
both been beautifully restored and are lined with some of Bratislava's finest Baroque
palaces. There are usually plenty of students milling about amongst the shoppers,
as the main university library is on this thoroughfare. The palaces of the Austro-
Hungarian aristocracy continue into Panská, starting with the **Pálffy Palace**, at
Panská 19, today an art gallery (Tues–Sun 11am–6pm), housing a patchy collection
of Slovak paintings from the nineteenth and twentieth centuries.

A little northeast of here are the adjoining main squares of the old town – **Hlavné
námestie** and **Františkánske námestie** – on the east side of which is the Old
Town Hall, a lively hotchpotch of Gothic, Renaissance and nineteenth-century
styles containing the main **City Museum** (Tues–Fri 10am–5pm, Sat & Sun 11am–
6pm), which features a medieval torture exhibition in the basement dungeons. Up
Františkánska from Františkánska námestie, you'll find the Counter-Reformation
**Jesuit Church** and the **Mirbach Palace** (Tues–Sun 11am–6pm), one of the best
preserved of Bratislava's Rococo buildings. The permanent collection of Baroque
and Rococo art isn't up to much but there are good temporary exhibitions. Round
the back of the Old Town Hall is **Primaciálne námestie**, dominated by the
Neoclassical **Primate's Palace** (Tues–Sun 10am–5pm), whose pediment frieze is
topped by a cast-iron cardinal's hat. The palace's main claim to fame is its Hall of
Mirrors, where Napoleon and the Austrian emperor signed the Peace of Pressburg
(as Bratislava was then called) in 1805.

The most insensitive of Bratislava's postwar developments took place on the west
side of the old town. After the annihilation of the city's Jewish population by the
Nazis, the Communist authorities tore down almost all of the Jewish quarter in order
to build the brutal showpiece SNP Bridge, now known as the **Nový most** or New
Bridge. Its one support column leans at an alarming angle, topped by a saucer-like,
pricey penthouse café reminiscent of the Starship Enterprise (under reconstruction
at the time of writing). The traffic which now tears along Staromestská has seriously
undermined the foundations of the **Cathedral of St Martin**, the Gothic coronation
church of the kings and queens of Hungary for over 250 years, whose ill-propor-
tioned steeple is topped by a tiny gilded Hungarian crown. Having passed under the
approach road for the Nový most, you'll come to the **Clock Museum** at Židovská

1 (Tues–Fri 9.30/10am–4.30/5pm, Sat & Sun 9.30/11am–4.30/6pm), with a display of brilliantly kitsch Baroque and Empire clocks. The large prewar Slovak Jewish population is commemorated at the **Jewish Museum** at Židovská 17 (Mon–Fri & Sun 11am–5pm), with a display of Judaica and a brief history of Slovak Jewry. The **castle** (daily 9am–6/8pm) is an unwelcoming giant box built in the fifteenth century by Emperor Sigismund, burnt down by its own drunken soldiers in 1811 and restored in the 1950s and 1960s. It houses two museums (Tues–Sun 9am–5pm): the **Slovak Historical Museum**, which displays a hotchpotch of eighteenth- and nineteenth-century furniture, portraits, (more) clocks, weaponry and some modern Slovak art, and the **Music Museum**, with local folk instruments, scores and recordings. You can also climb to the top of one of the castle's four corner towers, for an incredible view south across the Danube plain and over the river to the Petržalka housing estate, where a third of the city's population lives.

Despite the fast road on the embankment, it is just about possible to enjoy a stroll along the **River Danube** – *Dunaj* in Slovak. It gets quieter and more pleasant as you walk away from the Nový most back towards the old town and the moorings for ferries to Budapest and Vienna. About halfway down is the **Slovak National Gallery** (Tues–Sun 10am–5.30pm). There are two entrances: the one on the embankment lets you into the main building, a converted naval barracks, while the one on Stúrovo námestie gives access to the Esterházy Palace wing, used for temporary exhibitions, mostly focusing on modern art (currently closed for renovation). The permanent collection in the main building features a rundown of Slovak Gothic and Baroque art. Right by the ferries is the **Natural History Museum** (Tues–Sun 9am–5pm). Carry on to Safárikovo námestie, and up Bezručova to Ödön Lechner's concrete, sky-coloured Art Nouveau **Blue Church**, a lost monument to this once-Hungarian city, abandoned in the Slovak capital and dedicated to St Elizabeth, the city's one and only famous saint, born here in 1207.

# Eating, drinking and nightlife

There's an excellent choice of **places to eat** and prices are generally low. The most memorable aspect of the whole experience, however, is often the ambience, and exploring the atmospheric streets of the old town by night is all part of the fun. Bratislava's nightlife is heavily biased towards high culture, with opera and ballet at the Slovak National Theatre (ⓦwww.snd.sk) and classical music at the Reduta concert hall, both on Hviezdoslavovo námestie, as well as the varied programme put on at the modern Istropolis complex on Trnavské myto (tram #2 from the station; tram #4 or #6 from the centre). The most prestigious festival is the Bratislava Music Festival (ⓦwww.hc.sk), held in October. There are few out-and-out dance clubs, but you'll find plenty of late-opening pubs and bars helping to fill the gap.

### Cafés and restaurants

**Caribic's** Žižkova 1 ☏02/5441 8334. Known also as *Rybársky cech*. Reliably good but pricey fish restaurant on the ground floor of a former fisherman's house by the waterfront below the castle (there's a posher, more expensive version upstairs). Reservations recommended.

**Chez David** Zamocká 13 ☏02/5441 3824. Classy kosher restaurant serving fresh, beautifully prepared Jewish cuisine.

**Čokoladovňa pod Michalom** Michalská 6. Small, dark café near the Michalská veža, with 60 kinds of hot and ice chocolate on offer.

**Domenico** Námestie L.Štura 4. Quality café near the river with quirky decor, air-conditioning and a good-value lunch menu.

**Hradná vináreň** Dubčekovo námestie 1. Smart restaurant and bar in the castle grounds, with breathtaking views, serving excellent Slovak specialities and wine.

**Kaffé Mayer** Hlavné námestie 4. A resurrected century-old café that emulates its Viennese-style ancestor – very popular with the city's older cake-and-coffee fans.

**Kikaku sushi bar** Gorkého 6. Slightly clinical Japanese bar serving the usual raw fish and rice.

**Korzo** Hviezdoslavovo námestie 11. Passable shot at a Viennese-style café and a good place for breakfast, with tables outside overlooking Rybné námestie and the Nový most.

**Pizzeria Angelo** Zámocká 3. Offering over 20 sorts of pizza in a pleasantly decorated interior, near the castle.

**Vegetarian** Laurinská 8. Plain and simple vegetarian lunch spot, with a short list of salads and soya-based main dishes. Closed Sat & Sun.

### Bars and clubs

**Charlie Centrum** Špitálska 4. Bratislava's longest-serving nightspot, with a multiscreen art-house cinema and a late-night bar/club in the basement.

**Dubliner** Sedlárska 6. Very popular, stereotypical Irish bar – complete with cobbled floor – which sometimes stages live music.

**El Diablo** Sedlárska 4. Mexican-themed bar with lively late nights at weekends.

**Gremium** Gorkého 11. Busy sports bar, with a big screen, betting shop and a gallery area, along with a café upstairs.

**Hystéria** Odbojárov 9. Located behind the ice-hockey stadium (tram #4 or #6 from Kamenné námestie), this place is worth the trek for its Tex-Mex food, pool and regular live music.

**Stará sladovňa** Cintorínska 32. The city's malthouse until 1976, *Mamut*, as it's known, is Bratislava's most famous (and largest) pub. Czech Budvar on tap, big band and country & western music Thurs–Sat, and a bingo hall and slot-machine room on site.

# Slovakia's mountain regions

The great virtue of Slovakia is its mountains, particularly the **High Tatras**, which, in their short span, reach alpine heights and have a bleak, stunning beauty. By far the country's most popular destination, they are, in fact, the least typical of Slovakia's mountains, which are predominantly densely forested, round-topped limestone ranges. In the heart of the mountains is **Banská Bystrica**, one of the many towns in the region originally settled by German miners in the thirteenth century, and still redolent of those times. Rail lines, where they exist, make for some of the most scenic **train** journeys in the country.

## Banská Bystrica

Lying at the very heart of Slovakia's mountain ranges, the old German mining town of **BANSKÁ BYSTRICA** is a useful introduction to the area and is also a handsome historic town in its own right – once you've made it through the tangled suburbs of the burgeoning cement and logging industries. **Námestie SNP**, the former medieval marketplace, is still the centre of life here and a great place for just hanging out and people watching. Down the centre of the square are a column dedicated to the Virgin Mary, the black obelisk of the Soviet war memorial and a fountain that enthusiastically chucks water over a pile of mossy rocks. Take a close look at the ornate burgher houses around the square, in particular the **Venetian House** at no. 16. Opposite, at no. 4, the honey-coloured Thurzo Palace is decorated like a piece of embroidery and now houses the **town museum** (Mon–Fri 8am–noon & 1–4pm, Sun 10am–5pm). The best exhibits are the folk furniture and costumes on the top floor – villagers in the area were still wearing these clothes in the 1960s. At the top end of the square there's a strange mishmash of buildings including the remains of the town castle, a **barbican** curving snugly round a Baroque tower. Next door the former **town hall** (Tues–Fri 10am–5pm, Sat & Sun 10am–4pm) is the town's main art gallery and puts on interesting temporary exhibitions of contemporary and twentieth-century Slovak art. Behind the town hall is the rouge-red church of **Panna Mária**, which dates back to the thirteenth century; the north side-chapel contains the town's greatest art treasure, a carved late-Gothic altarpiece by Master Pavol of Levoča. About 200m southeast of námestie SNP is the **SNP Museum** at Kapitulská 23 (Tues–Sun: May–Sept 9am–6pm; Oct–April 9am–4pm), dating from 1969 and looking like an intergalactic mushroom chopped in half. The museum deals as best it can with the complex issues raised by the Slovak National Uprising (SNP) against the Nazis (and the Slovak puppet regime), which began on August 29, 1944, in Banská Bystrica, and was eventually crushed by the Germans two months later, just a month or so before the town's liberation. Outside, amid the bushes, you'll notice an exhibition of tanks and guns from the uprising and the town's last two surviving medieval bastions.

Banská Bystrica's main **bus** and **train stations** are in the new part of town, ten minutes' walk east of the centre; if you arrive on a slow train, you can alight at Banská Bystrica mesto train station, just five minutes' walk south of the main square. There's a **tourist office** inside the barbican (Mon–Fri 8/9am–5/7pm; mid-May to mid-Sept also Sat 9am–1pm; ☎048/16 186, ⊛www.kisbb.sk), which can help arrange **accommodation**. The best of the **hotels** is the luxurious *Arcade* (☎048/430 21 11, ⊛www.arcade.sk; ❺), conveniently located in a Renaissance building near the town museum. Also centrally located, the late nineteenth-century *Národný dom* (☎048/412 37 37; ❷), at Národná 11, has its own café and restaurant. The cheapest rooms in town are at the basic hostel *Milvar* at Školská 9 (☎048/413 87 73; 440Sk for a double), 2km west of the main square. There are plenty of cafés, bars and **restaurants** around the námestie SNP: try the *Pilzner restaurant*, on the northern side of the square, which serves local food washed down with Pilsner Urquell. Alternatively, the *Červený rak* (closed Sun), at the southwestern end of the square, offers pizzas and Slovak dishes in a pleasant interior or, in summer, on a shady patio. For a **coffee**, there's no better place than the atmospheric, two-storey *Iné Kafe*, at Lazovná 16, some 200m north of the main square.

## The High Tatras

Rising like a giant granite reef above the patchwork Poprad plain, the **High Tatras** are the main reason for venturing this far into Slovakia. Even after all the tourist-board hype, they are still an inspirational sight. A wilderness, however, they are not; all summer, visitors are shoulder to shoulder in the necklace of resorts which sit at the foot of the mountains, and in winter skiers take over. But once you're above the tree line, surrounded by bare primeval scree slopes and icy blue tarns, nothing can take away the exhilaration or the breathtaking views.

The mainline train station for the Tatras is Poprad-Tatry in **POPRAD**. Though there is a small Old Town, Poprad's not worth a major halt. If you do need to stay, the **tourist office** (Mon–Fri 9am–5pm, Sat 9am–noon; July & Aug Mon–Fri 8am–6pm, Sat 9am–1pm, Sun 1–4pm; ☎052/16 186, ⊛www.poprad.sk) at the western end of námestie sv Egidia can organise **private rooms**. The *Hotel Satel* (☎052/716 11 11, ⊛www.satel-slovakia.sk; ❸), on Mnoheľova, halfway between the stations and the centre, has plain, decent rooms, a restaurant and a sauna.

From the high-level platform at Poprad-Tatry, cute red tram-like trains (the TEZ) trundle across the fields, linking Poprad with the string of resorts and spas halfway up the Tatras within the **Tatra National Park** or **TANAP**. There's a whole range of **accommodation** from private rooms (❶) and top-notch hotels (❾) set among the pine woods, to the mountain huts (300–400Sk per person) up above the tree line. The best base is the scattered settlement of **STARÝ SMOKOVEC** (30min from Poprad-Tatry), whose nucleus is the stretch of lawn between the half-timbered supermarket and the sandy-yellow *Grand Hotel*. You can get help with accommodation at the **tourist office** (Mon–Fri 8/9am–4/5pm; in summer also Sat & Sun 8am–2pm; ☎052/442 34 40, ⊛www.tatry.sk) in the modern white building about 100m to your left as you face the *Grand*. For camping your best bet is *Eurocamp FICC*, just south of **Tatranská Lomnica** with bungalows, a restaurant and café, hot showers and many other facilities. The campsite has its own train station: either take the ordinary train from Poprad-Tatry via Studený Potok or the TEZ, changing at Starý Smokovec and Tatranská Lomnica.

The ski season runs from December to March and there are plenty of places in Starý Smokovec to rent equipment. Walking's best from July to September when the air's clearest and views are at their most spectacular. Many paths are open year round, though high-level paths, above the mountain huts, are open mid-June to October only. The walking trails are fantastic and clearly marked. If you're planning a hike don't go without the green 1:25 000 Vysoké Tatry hiking map (available from the tourist office), walking boots, water, food and waterproofs. For daily weather reports and more information on walking go to the **Horská služba** (mountain rescue), just uphill from Starý Smokovec station (℡052/442 28 20, ✪www.hzs.sk).

The most straightforward and rewarding climb from Starý Smokovec is to follow the blue-marked path that leads from behind the *Grand* to the summit of **Slavkovský štít** (2452m), a return journey of nine hours. Alternatively, a narrow-gauge funicular, again starting from behind the *Grand* (daily 7.30am–7pm, closed May & Nov), climbs 250m to **HREBIENOK**. The charming wooden mountain hut *Bilíkova chata* (℡052/442 24 39; ❸) is a five-minute walk from the top of the funicular – even if you don't stay there you should stop for a drink on the balcony for the views. Beyond the *chata*, the path continues through the woods before passing the gushing waterfalls of the **Studenovodské vodopády**. Just past the waterfall, a whole variety of trekking possibilities opens up. The right-hand fork takes you up the **Malá Studená dolina** and then zigzags above the tree line to the *Téryho chata* (℡052/442 52 45; ❷), set in a lunar landscape by the shores of the **Päť Spišských plies**. Following the spectacular trail over the Priečne sedlo (not recommended for those with acrophobia) to *Zbojnicka chata* (℡0903/619 000; ❷), you can return via the **Vejká studená dolina** – an eight-hour round trip from Hrebienok. If you don't have the time or inclination to hike, you can still enjoy some fabulous views by taking a series of cable cars (daily 8.30am–3.50/5.50pm; book at least two or three days in advance; closed May & Nov) from Tatranská Lomnica to the summit of **Lomnický štít** (2632m), the Tatras' second-highest peak.

# East Slovakia

Stretching from the High Tatras east to the Ukrainian border, the landscape of **East Slovakia** is decidedly different from the rest of the country. Ethnically, this is probably the most diverse region in the country, with different groups coexisting even within a single valley. The majority of the country's Romanies live here, mostly on the edge of Slovak villages, in shantytowns of almost medieval squalor. In the ribbon-villages of the north and east, the Rusyn minority struggle to preserve their culture and religion, while along the southern border there are large numbers of Hungarians. After spending time in the rural backwaters, **Košice**, Slovakia's second city, can be a welcome though somewhat startling return to city life. Gradually realizing its potential as a diverse and vibrant cosmopolitan centre, it certainly contains enough of interest for at least a day's stopover.

## The Spiš region

The land that stretches northeast up the Poprad Valley to the Polish border and east along the River Hornád towards Prešov is known as the **Spiš region**, for centuries a semi-autonomous province within the Hungarian kingdom. After the devastation of the mid-thirteenth-century Tatar invasions, the Hungarian Crown encouraged Saxon families to repopulate the area. The wealthy settlers built some wonderful Gothic churches, and later enriched almost every town and village with the distinctive touch of the Renaissance. Today, with only a few of its ethnic Germans and Hungarians remaining, the Spiš shares the low-living standards of the rest of East Slovakia. But the region's architectural richness offers a glimmer of hope in the growth of tourism – indeed during high season, in towns such as **Levoča**, you can often hardly move for tour buses.

27

## Levoča and around

Some 25km east of Poprad, across a broad sweep of undulating Spiš countryside, the ravishingly beautiful walled town of **LEVOČA**, set on a slight incline, has a wonderfully medieval look. The main square is **námestie Majstra Pavla**. To the north is the square's least distinguished but most important building, the municipal weigh-house; a law of 1321 obliged every merchant passing through the region to hole up at Levoča for fourteen days, pay various taxes and allow the locals first refusal on their goods. Towering over the weigh-house is the Catholic church of **sv Jakub** (Mon 11/11.30am–4/5pm, Tues–Sat 8.30/9am–4/5pm, Sun 1–4/5pm; Nov–Easter closed Sun & Mon), which is crammed with religious art, the star attraction being the magnificent sixteenth-century wooden altarpiece by Master Pavol of Levoča – at 18.6m, reputedly the tallest of its kind in the world. The church can be visited only with a guide, and tours (every 30min, hourly in winter) leave from the ticket office opposite the main entrance. A small **museum** (daily 9am–5pm) dedicated to Master Pavol stands opposite the church on the eastern side of the square. South of the church is the **town hall** (daily 8/9am–4/5pm), built in a sturdy Renaissance style. On the first floor, there's a museum on the Spiš region, and some fine examples of Spiš handicrafts on the top floor. The last building in the centre of the square is the oddly squat Lutheran church, built in an uncompromisingly Neoclassical style. Take some time to wander round the **back streets** where it's the unrestored buildings that evoke Levoča's past most vividly.

Train services to Levoča were suspended at the time of writing, but there are several buses a day from Poprad, Prešov and Košice. The **bus station** (and train station) is a ten-minute walk southeast of the old town. If you're coming from the east get off one stop earlier at the Košice gate. The **tourist office** (May–Sept Mon–Fri 10am–4.30pm, Sat & Sun 9.30am–1.30pm; Oct–April Mon–Fri 9am–4.30pm, Sat 9am–noon; ☏053/451 37 63, ✆www.levoca.sk) is located in the northwest corner of the main square. Outside the annual Catholic pilgrimage in early July to the church on Marianska Hora, the sacred hill to the north of town, **accommodation** shouldn't be hard to find. A reasonable option is the *Hotel Barbakan* at Košická 15 (☏053/451 43 10, ✆www.barbakan.sk; ❹), which includes a buffet breakfast in the price; alternatively, there are several cheaper pensions in town, including the *Penzión pri Košickej bráne* (☏053/451 28 79; ❸), next door to the *Barbakan*. There's also a good campsite, *Kováčova vila*, 3km north of Levoča. Authentic Slovak pub **food** can be had from the cheap *Biela pani*, which occupies two cellars at the southern end of the main square, and from the atmospheric *U troch apoštolov* on the east side of the main square. There's a self-service lunchtime-only vegetarian restaurant, *Vegeterián*, at Uholná 3 (closed Sat & Sun), northwest of the main square, and the self-explanatory *Pizzeria* nearby at Vetrová 4.

The road east from Levoča takes you to the edge of Spiš territory, clearly defined by the Branisko ridge, which blocks the way to Prešov. Even if you're not going any further east, you should at least take the bus as far as **SPIŠSKÉ PODHRADIE**, for perhaps the most spectacular sight in the whole country – the **Spišský hrad** (May–Oct daily 9am–6pm). This pile of chalk-white ruins, strung out on a bleak hill, is irresistibly photogenic and finds its way into almost every tourist brochure. The ruins themselves don't quite live up to expectations, though the view from the top is pretty spectacular. The *Penzión Podzámok* at Podzámková 28 (☏053/454 17 55; ❷) is a good **place to stay**, with superb views up to the castle.

## Prešov

Capital of the Slovak Šariš region and a cultural centre for the Rusyn (Ruthenian) minority, **PREŠOV** has been treated to a wonderful face-lift over the last few years. There's not much of interest beyond its main square, but it's a refreshingly youthful and vibrant town, partly due to its university. The lozenge-shaped main square, **Hlavná ulica**, is flanked by creamy, pastel-coloured eighteenth-century facades. At the square's southern tip is the **Greek-Catholic Cathedral**, a wonderful Rococo affair with a huge iconostasis. Further along, on the same side of the square, is Prešov's **town hall**, from whose unsuitably small balcony Béla Kun's Hungarian Red Army declared the short-lived Slovak Socialist Republic in 1919. Further north along the square, the **town museum**, situated in the dogtooth-gabled Rákócziho dom at no. 86 (Tues 9am–6pm, Wed–Fri 9am–5pm, Sun 1–6pm), offers a thorough account of the history of the town and the Šariš region. Prešov's Catholic and Protestant churches vie with each other at the widest point of the square. The fourteenth-century Catholic church of **sv Mikuláš** has the edge, not least for its modern Moravian stained-glass windows and its sumptuous Baroque altarpiece. Behind sv Mikulás, the much plainer **Lutheran church**, built in the mid-seventeenth century, bears witness to the strength of religious reformism in the outer reaches of Hungary at a time when the rest of the Habsburgs' lands were suffering the full force of the Counter-Reformation. Lastly, the town's ornate fin-de-siècle **synagogue** in the northwest corner of the old town – access from Okružná – has been turned into a small **Museum of Judaica** (Tues & Wed 11am–4pm, Thurs & Fri 10am–1pm, Sun 1–5pm), with an exhibition on Judaism and the region's Jewish community, 6000 of whom perished in the Holocaust. The **bus** and **train stations** are opposite each other about 1km south of the main square; the best buses and trolleybuses into town are those which stop at Na Hlavnej. There's a **tourist office** (Mon–Fri 9am–6pm, Sat 9am–1pm; ☏051/773 11 13, ✉www.presov.sk) near the town hall. The *Pension Antonio* at Jarková 22, a block west of the main square (☏051/772 32 25, ✉www .antoniopension.sk; ❸), has seven en-suite doubles with satellite TV and a restaurant; otherwise there's the *Senator*, at Hlavná 67 (☏051/773 11 86; ❹), above the tourist office, with some rooms overlooking the main square. There are **restaurants** and cafés all along Hlavná, including the inexpensive but decent *Baltic*, upstairs at no. 26, or the pleasant and unpretentious *Slovenská reštaurácia* (closed Sat eve & Sun), at no. 11. If you fancy a complete change try the *Vegetarian Club* Indian restaurant at Hlavná 70. For **Internet access** go to the *Film Café* at no. 121.

# Košice

Slovak towns rarely amount to much more than their one long main square, and even **KOŠICE**, the country's second-largest city, is no exception. Rather like Bratislava, Košice was, until relatively recently, a modest little town on the edge of the Hungarian plain. Then, in the 1950s, the Communists established a giant steelworks on the outskirts of the city. Fifty years on, Košice has a population of around 250,000, a number of worthwhile museums and what is arguably Slovakia's finest cathedral. Just 21km north of the Hungarian border, Košice also acts as a magnet for the Hungarian community – to whom the city is known as Kassa – and the underemployed Romanies of the surrounding region, lending it a diversity and vibrancy absent from small-town Slovakia.

Almost everything of interest is situated on or around Košice's long pedestrianized main square, which is called **Hlavná ulica**. Lined with handsome Baroque and Neoclassical palaces, it's dominated by the city's unorthodox Gothic **Cathedral of St Elizabeth**, its charcoal-coloured stone recently sandblasted back to its original honeyed hue. Begun in 1378, it's an unusual building from the outside, with striped roof tiles and two contorted towers – one of them serves as a vantage point (Mon–Fri 9.30am–4.30pm, Sat 9am–1.30pm). Inside, imposing Gothic furnishings add an impressive touch to an otherwise plain nave, and the main gilded altar depicts scenes from the life of the cathedral's patron saint. On the busy north side of the cathedral is the fourteenth-century **Urbanova veža**, the town tower, standing on its own set of mini-arcades. The public park and fountains beyond are a favourite spot for hanging out and make an appropriately graceful approach to the city's grand Austro-Hungarian **theatre**. The peculiar **Vojtech Löffler Museum** at Alžbetina 20 (Tues–Sat 10am–6pm, Sun 1–5pm), west off the main square, features the work and private collections of Košice's most prominent Communist-sanctioned sculptor. Another unusual attraction is the **Mikluš Prison** (Tues–Sat 9am–5pm, Sun 9am–1pm), east off the square down Univerzitna, whose original dimly lit dungeons and claustrophobic cells graphically transport you into its history as the city prison and torture chamber. At the northern tip of the main square, námestie Maratónu mieru is flanked to the east and west by the bulky nineteenth-century **East Slovak Museum** (Tues–Sat 9am–5pm, Sun 9am–1pm). The western building is worth visiting for its basement collection of fifteenth- to seventeenth-century gold coins – 2920 in all – minted at Kremnica, but stashed away by city burghers and discovered by accident in 1935. Hidden round the back of the museum is a wooden **Greek-Catholic church**, brought here from the Ukrainian borderlands.

The **train** and **bus stations** are opposite each other, ten minutes' walk east of the old town. There's a small but helpful **tourist office** (Mon–Fri 8am–7pm, Sat 8am–1pm; ☎055/16 186, ⊛www.mickosice.sk) in the Dargov department store on the corner of Hlavná and Štúrova, and another branch (Mon–Fri 8am–7pm, Sat & Sun 8am–4.30pm) inside Tesco at the far end of Hlavná. Both can help with finding **rooms** and sorting out accommodation in **student hostels** in the summer holidays. The best-located place is *Ubytovňa*, Jesenského 20 (☎055/633 59 12; 214Sk), to the east of the main square. There's another bigger student hostel, *Domov mládeže*, at Medická 2 (☎055/643 56 88; 215Sk). This is best reached by going up Vojenská then taking the steep flight of steps: it's the rather gloomy block to your left but much nicer inside. The nearest **campsite** (open all year) is 5km south of the city centre and also rents out bungalows; take tram #1, #3 or #4 from the *Slovan* hotel to the flyover, then get off and walk 500m west along Alejová, the road to Rožňava. For **hotel** accommodation *Centrum*, Južná trieda 2 (☎055/678 31 01; ❹), a five-minute walk south of the main square, occupies an ugly high-rise, but inside it's pretty comfortable. Handy for the train and bus stations, though rather soulless, is *Pension Krmanová*, Krmanová 14 (☎055/623 05 65; ❸). The best **places to eat** are located in the streets to the east of the main square: *Ajvega*, Orlia 10, is a popular vegetarian place with a summer terrace, and serves soya versions of standard Slovak dishes, washed down with fresh juices. *Sedliacky dvor*, at Biela 3, is a hymn to Slovak folk culture and cuisine, while the dark-red *Bakchus*, roughly opposite the Kostol františkánov, dishes out Slovak and Hungarian specialities. *Kleopatra Pizza Bar*, at Hlavná 24, is great in summer with outdoor tables overlooking the gardens to the south of the cathedral. Košice's nightlife revolves around the main square, where there are plenty of options for **drinking**, like the *Music Pub Diesel* at Hlavná 92, which serves Guinness, and the pub *Nebo-Peklo* at Vrátna 4, which has live music on Friday. You can also catch **live jazz** most nights at the city's smoky *Jazz Club*, Kováčska 39. Mainstream culture predominates in Košice, though the city also boasts a **Hungarian theatre**, Thália, on Mojmírova, and Slovakia's one and only **Romany theatre**, Romathan, Štefánikova 4, which puts on a range of events from concerts to plays. The tourist office stocks the free **listings** booklet *Kultúrny informátor*. You can access the **Internet** at Net Club, Hlavná 9.

# Travel details

| Trains |
| --- |
| **Bratislava** to: Banská Bystrica (2 daily; 3hr 10min–3hr 45min); Poprad-Tatry (every 2hr; 3hr 40min–7hr 40min); Košice (13 daily; 5hr 15min–9hr 50min). |
| **Košice** to: Prešov (11 daily; 40min). |
| **Poprad-Tatry** to: Starý Smokovec (hourly; 35min); Košice (hourly; 1hr 5min–2hr 10min). |

| Buses |
| --- |
| **Levoča** to: Spišské Podhradie (every 30min; 25min). |
| **Košice** to: Poprad (every 1–2hr; 2hr 15min–2hr 45min); Prešov (every 10–20min; 35–55min). |
| **Poprad** to: Levoča (hourly; 25–55min); Spišské Podhradie (hourly; 35min–1hr 10min); Prešov (hourly; 1hr 20min–2hr). |

# 28

# Slovenia

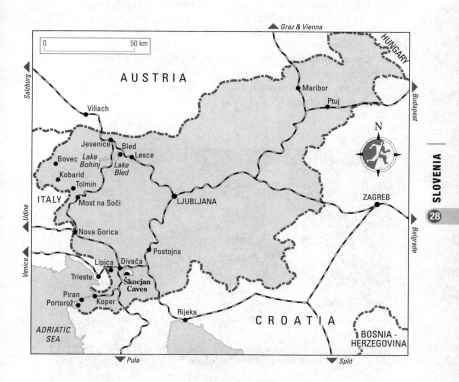

# Slovenia highlights

* **Old Town, Ljubljana** Stunning architecture, a hilltop castle and leafy riverside cafés adorn the alluring Slovenian capital. See p.902

* **Škocjan Caves** Magnificent underground canyon, highlight of the Karst region. See p.905

* **Lake Bohinj** Pearl of Slovenian lakes, less visited and more serene than Bled. See p.906

* **Piran** Historic coastal town strewn with gorgeous Venetian Gothic architecture, pretty squares and churches. See p.906

* **Kobarid Museum, Soča Valley** Immensely beautiful valley, compelling museum. See p.908

* **Ptuj** Slovenia's oldest and prettiest town. See p.909

△ Mestni Trg fountain, Ljubljana

# Introduction and basics

**Slovenia** is the most stable, prosperous and welcoming of all Europe's erstwhile Communist countries. It was always the richest and most Westernized of the Yugoslav federation, and managed to avoid much of the strife which plagued the republics to the south. Administered by German-speaking overlords until 1918. Slovenes absorbed the culture of their rulers while managing to retain a strong sense of ethnic identity through their Slavic language.

Slovenia's sophisticated capital, **Ljubljana**, is easily the best of the cities, manageably small and cluttered with Baroque and Habsburg buildings. Elsewhere, the Julian Alps provide stunning mountain scenery, most accessible at **Lake Bled** and **Lake Bohinj**, and most memorable along the **Soča Valley**. Further south are spectacular caves like those at **Postojna** and **Škocjan**, while the short stretch of Slovenian coast is punctuated by a couple of attractive towns, **Piran** and **Portorož**. On the main route east towards Budapest is **Ptuj**, Slovenia's oldest and most well-preserved town.

## Information & maps

Most towns and resorts have a **tourist information office**, some of which rent private rooms. A high standard of English is spoken pretty much everywhere. Freytag & Berndt publishes a good 1:300,000 country map, while the Slovene Alpine Association's excellent **hiking maps** (ⓦwww.pzs.si) are widely available in bookshops.

## Money and banks

Currency is the **tolar** (SIT), divided into 100 stotini. There are coins of 1, 2, 5 and 10SIT; and notes of 10, 20, 50, 100, 200, 500, 1000, 5000 and 10,000SIT. The exchange rate at the time of writing was 230SIT to €1, 190SIT to $1, and 350SIT to £1. **Banks** (*banka*) generally open Mon–Fri 8.30am–12.30pm & 2–5pm, Sat 8.30am–11am/noon. You can also change money in tourist offices, post offices, travel agencies and exchange bureaux (*menjalnica*). **Credit cards** are accepted in a large number of hotels and restaurants, and **ATMs** are widespread.

## Communications

Most **post offices** (*pošta*) are open Mon–Fri 8am–6/7pm and Sat 8am–noon/1pm. Stamps (*znamke*) can also be bought at newsstands. Public **phones** use cards (*telekartice*; 700, 1000, 1700 and 3500SIT), available from post offices, kiosks and tobacconists. Make long-distance and international calls at a post office, where you're assigned to a cabin and given the bill afterwards. **Internet** access is now fairly widespread – expect to pay around 350SIT/hr.

## Getting around

Slovene Railways (Slovenske železnice; ⓦ www.slo-zeleznice.si) is smooth and efficient. **Trains** (*vlaki*) are divided into slow (*potniški*), and Intercity (IC) express trains, as well as the fast Inter City Slovenia trains (ICS) between Ljubljana and Maribor. Reservations (*rezervacije*) are obligatory on all ICS trains, for all services marked on a timetable

## Slovenia on the net

ⓦ**www.bled.si** Useful site to Slovenia's most popular destinations.

ⓦ**www.slovenia-tourism.si** Official tourist board site.

ⓦ**www.ljubljana.si** Detailed information on sights and events in the capital.

ⓦ**www.burger.si** Superb interactive maps and panoramic photos.

with a boxed R, and optional for those trains designated by just an R. Most timetables have English notes, and "Departures" is *odhodi*, "arrivals" is *prihodi*. Eurail and Inter-Rail passes are valid.

The **bus** network consists of an array of local companies. Towns such as Ljubljana, Maribor and Koper have big bus stations with computerized booking facilities, where you can buy your tickets several hours in advance – recommended if you're travelling between Ljubljana and the coast in high season. Elsewhere, simply pay the driver or conductor. You'll be charged extra for cumbersome items of baggage.

# Accommodation

**Accommodation** is universally clean and good quality. Expect to pay from €40/9600SIT for a double at two-star **hotels**, from €56/13500SIT for a three-star. Family-run **pensions** in rural areas, especially the mountains, offer the same facilities as hotels but usually at a lower price. **Private rooms**

## Slovene

|  | Slovene | Pronunciation |
|---|---|---|
| **Yes** | *Ja* | Ya |
| **No** | *Ne* | Ne |
| **Please** | *Prosim* | Proseem |
| **Thank you** | *Hvala* | Huala |
| **Hello/Good day** | *Živijo/dober dan* | Jeeveeyo/dober dan |
| **Goodbye** | *Nasvidenje* | Nasveedenye |
| **Excuse me** | *Oprostite* | Oprosteete |
| **Where?** | *Kje?* | Kye |
| **Good** | *Dobro* | Dobro |
| **Bad** | *Slabo* | Slabo |
| **Near** | *Blizu* | Bleezoo |
| **Far** | *Daleč* | Daalech |
| **Cheap** | *Poceni* | Potzenee |
| **Expensive** | *Drago* | Drago |
| **Open** | *Odprto* | Odpurto |
| **Closed** | *Zaprto* | Zapurto |
| **Today** | *Danes* | Danes |
| **Yesterday** | *Včeraj* | Ucheray |
| **Tomorrow** | *Jutri* | Yutree |
| **How much is....?** | *Koliko stane...?* | Koleeko stane...? |
| **What time is it?** | *Koliko je ura?* | Koleeko ye oora? |
| **I don't understand** | *Ne razumem* | Ne razoomem |
| **Do you speak English?** | *Ali govorite angleško?* | Alee govoreete angleshko? |
| **One** | *Ena* | Ena |
| **Two** | *Dve* | Dve |
| **Three** | *Tri* | Tree |
| **Four** | *Štiri* | Shteeree |
| **Five** | *Pet* | Pet |
| **Six** | *Šest* | Shest |
| **Seven** | *Sedem* | Sedem |
| **Eight** | *Osem* | Osem |
| **Nine** | *Devet* | Devet |
| **Ten** | *Deset* | Deset |

(*zasebne sobe*) are available throughout Slovenia, with bookings usually made by travel agents like Globtour or Kompas (usually open daily 9am–7/8pm in summer). Rooms are pretty good value at about €20–28/4800–6750SIT a double, although stays of three nights or less are invariably subject to a thirty-percent surcharge. Self-catering **apartments** (*apartmaji*) are also plentiful in the mountains and on the coast.

Hostels are thin on the ground, although there's a scattering of student dorms (*dijaški dom*) open over the summer. Advance booking is advised. Expect to pay about €11–16/2880–4800SIT per person per night. **Campsites** are plentiful in the mountains and on the coast and have good facilities, restaurants and shops. Two people travelling with a tent can expect to pay €11–14/2880–3600SIT. The majority of campsites are open from May to September. Camping rough without permission is punishable by a fine.

# Food and drink

Slovene **cuisine** draws on Austrian, Italian and Balkan influences. There's a native tradition, too, based on age-old peasant recipes. For **breakfast** and **snacks**, *okrepčevalnice* (snack bars) and street kiosks dole out *burek*, a flaky pastry filled with cheese (*sirov burek*) or meat (*burek z mesom*). Sausages come in various forms, most commonly hot dogs, *hrenovke* (Slovene frankfurters), or *kranjska klobasa* (big spicy sausages). **Menus** in a *restavracija* (restaurant) or *gostilna* (inn) are dominated by roast meats (*pečenka*) and schnitzels (*zrezek*). Goulash (*golaž*) is found almost everywhere. Two traditional dishes are *žlikrofi*, ravioli filled with potato, onion and bacon; and *žganci*, once the staple diet of rural Slovenes, a buckwheat or maize porridge often served with sauerkraut. *Ocvrti sir* (cheese fried in breadcrumbs) is one of the few dishes that will appease vegetarians. On the coast you'll find plenty of fish (*riba*), mussels (*školjke*) and squid (*kalamari*). Italian pasta dishes appear on most menus, and no high street is without at least one pizzeria. Typical **desserts**

include strudel filled with apple or rhubarb; *štruklji*, dumplings with fruit filling; *potica*, a doughy roll filled with nuts and honey; and *prekmurska gibanica*, a delicious local cheesecake.

Daytime **drinking** takes place in small café/bars, or in a *kavarna*, where a range of cakes, pastries and ice cream is usually on offer. **Coffee** (*kava*) is generally served black unless specified otherwise – ask for *mleko* (milk) or *smetana* (cream). **Tea** (*čaj*) is usually served black. Evening haunts include bars or the more traditional *pivnica* (beer hall) or *vinarna* (wine cellar). Slovene **beer** (*pivo*) is usually excellent (*Laško Zlatorog* is considered the best), although most breweries also produce *temno pivo* ("dark beer"), a Guinness-like stout. The local **wine** (*vino*) is either *črno* (red) or *belo* (white) and has an international reputation. Favourite aperitifs include *slivovka* (plum brandy), *vilijemovka* (pear brandy), the fiery *sadjevec*, a brandy made from various fruits, and the gin-like *brinovec*.

# Opening hours and holidays

Most **shops** open Mon–Fri 8am–7pm and Sat 8am–1pm; an increasing number open on Sun. Museum times vary, but most are usually closed on Mon. All shops and banks are closed on the following **public holidays**: Jan 1 & 2, Feb 8, Easter Mon, April 27, May 1 & 2, June 25, Aug 15, Oct 31, Nov 1, Dec 25 & 26.

# Emergencies

The **police** (*policija*) are generally easygoing and likely to speak some English. **Pharmacies** (*lekarna*) follow shop hours, and a rota system covers night-time opening; details are in the window of each pharmacy.

| Emergency numbers |
| --- |
| Police ☏113; Ambulance & Fire ☏112. |

# Ljubljana

The Slovene capital **LJUBLJANA** curls under its castle-topped hill, an old centre marooned in the shapeless modernity that stretches out across the plain, a vital and fast-growing capital. The city's sights are only part of the picture; first and foremost Ljubljana is a place to meet people and to get involved in the nightlife – the buildings just provide the backdrop.

## Arrival, information and accommodation

Your likely point of arrival (and drop-off point for buses from Brnik airport, 23km north of the city) is the main **train and bus station**, located on Trg Osvobodilne fronte, ten minutes' walk north of the centre. The **Slovenian Tourist Information Centre (STIC)** is at Krekov trg 10 (daily 8am–7/9pm; ☎01/306-4575), with the main **Ljubljana Tourist Information Office (TIC)** in the old town on Stritarjeva next to the Triple Bridge (daily 8/10am–6/8pm; ☎01/306-1215, ⊛www.ljubljana.si); there's a further branch at the train station (Mon–Fri 8/10am–5.30/9pm; June–Sept also Sat & Sun; ☎01/433-9475). Ljubljana's **buses** are cheap and frequent; you pay on the bus – put your money in a box next to the driver (280SIT per journey) – or buy tokens (*žetoni*; 190SIT) in advance from post offices and most newspaper kiosks. If you're staying for a few days, the Ljubljana **Tourist Card** (3000SIT), available from all the above tourist offices, entitles you to three days' unlimited travel on the city's public bus network, and discounted entrance fees to selected museums, galleries and restaurants. The TIC has a limited stock of central **private rooms** (❸), which can only be booked on the day.

### Hostels

**Celica Youth Hostel** Metelkova 9 ☎01/430-1890, ⊛www.souhostel.com. Brilliantly original hostel in a refurbished former military prison, with two-bed "cells" and multi-bedded rooms. A 10min walk from the stations. Reservations essential. 3750–5000SIT.

**Dijaški Dom Ivana Cankarja** Poljanska 26 ☎01/474-8600. Largest of the student hostels, open July & Aug only. 3000SIT.

**Dijaški Dom Poljane** Potošnikova 3 ☎01/300-3137. Smallest and cleanest of the student hostels, open mid-June & July only. 3000SIT.

**Dijaški Dom Tabor** Vidovdanska 7 ☎01/234-8840. Most central, and busiest, of the student hostels, open July & Aug only. 3000SIT.

**Fluxus Hostel** Tomšičeva 4 ☎031/852921, ⊛www.fluxus-hostel.com. Clean, bright and spacious hostel with a six- and eight-bed dorm. Reservations essential. 4900SIT.

### Hotels

**BIT Center** Litijska 57 ☎01/548-0055, ⊛www.bit-center.net. Modern, functional rooms in this sports centre 2km east of the centre; 50 percent discount on sporting facilities. Buses #5, #9 and #13. ❸

**City Hotel Turist** Dalmatinova 15 ☎01/234-9130, ⊛www.hotelturist.si. Decent, if a little pricey, downtown hotel, a 5min walk from the stations. ❻

**Emonec** Wolfova 12 ☎01/200-1520, ⊛www.hotel-emonec.com. Great-value place in the heart of town, with simple, modern rooms, and beautifully designed bathrooms. ❹

**M Hotel** Derševa 4 ☎01/513-7000, ⊛www.m-hotel.si. Neat and bright modern hotel, 2.5km northwest of the city centre off Celovška cesta. Buses #1, #3 and #15. ❺

**Park** Tabor 9 ☎01/232-1398, ⊛www.hotelpark.si. High-rise located amidst a jumble of apartment buildings a few blocks east of the station with shabby, bare rooms, some en-suite. ❸–❹

**Pri Mraku** Rimska 4 ☎01/421-9600, ⊛www.daj-dam.si. Perky downtown pension, with colourful, cosy rooms. Ten percent discount for stays of more than three nights. ❻

### Campsite

**Ježica** Dunajska 270 ☎01/568-3913, ⊜ljubljana.resort@gpl.si. Pleasant site 5km north of the centre, which also has a few bungalows (❸). Buses #6 or #8.

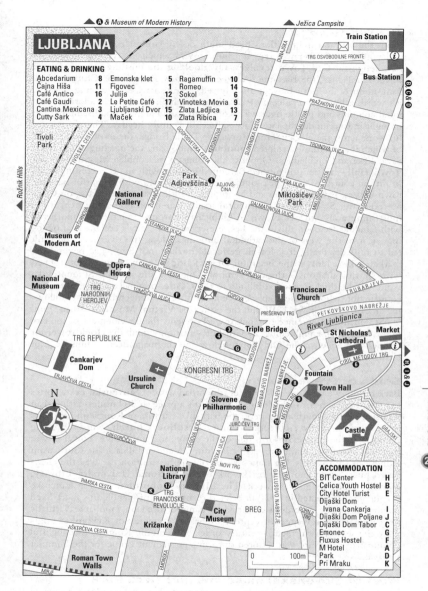

# LJUBLJANA

Train Station

TRG OSVOBODILNE FRONTE

Bus Station

## EATING & DRINKING

| | | | | | |
|---|---|---|---|---|---|
| Abcedarium | 8 | Emonska klet | 5 | Ragamuffin | 10 |
| Čajna Hiša | 11 | Figovec | 1 | Romeo | 14 |
| Café Antico | 16 | Julija | 12 | Sokol | 6 |
| Café Gaudi | 2 | Le Petite Café | 17 | Vinoteka Movia | 9 |
| Cantina Mexicana | 3 | Ljubljanski Dvor | 15 | Zlata Ladjica | 13 |
| Cutty Sark | 4 | Maček | 10 | Zlata Ribica | 7 |

Tivoli Park

Rožnik Hills

Park Adjovščina

National Gallery

Miklošičev Park

Museum of Modern Art

National Museum

Opera House

TRG NARODNIH HEROJEV

Franciscan Church

River Ljubljanica

Triple Bridge

St Nicholas' Cathedral

Market

TRG REPUBLIKE

Cankarjev Dom

KONGRESNI TRG

Fountain

Town Hall

Ursuline Church

Slovene Philharmonic

JURČIČEV TRG

Castle

National Library

NOVI TRG

TRG FRANCOSKE REVOLUCIJE

City Museum

BREG

Križanke

Roman Town Walls

MIRJE

0      100m

## ACCOMMODATION

| | |
|---|---|
| BIT Center | H |
| Celica Youth Hostel | B |
| City Hotel Turist | E |
| Dijaški Dom Ivana Cankarja | I |
| Dijaški Dom Poljane | J |
| Dijaški Dom Tabor | C |
| Emonec | G |
| Fluxus Hostel | F |
| M Hotel | A |
| Park | D |
| Pri Mraku | K |

SLOVENIA | Ljubljana

28

# The City

Ljubljana's main point of reference is **Slovenska cesta**, a busy north–south thoroughfare that slices the city down the middle. Most of the sights are within easy
walking distance of here, with the **Old Town** straddling the River Ljubljanica
to the south and east and the nineteenth-century quarter to the west, where the
principal museums and galleries are to be found.

## The Old Town

From the bus and train stations head south down Miklošičeva for ten minutes and you're on **Prešernov trg**, the hub around which everything in Ljubljana's delightful **Old Town** revolves. Overlooking the bustling square and the River Ljubljanica, the Baroque seventeenth-century **Franciscan Church** (daily 9am–noon & 3–7pm), blushes a sandy red; despite its weary-looking interior, it's worth a look for Francesco Robba's marble high-altar, richly adorned with spiral columns and plastic figurines. Robba, an Italian architect and sculptor, was brought in to remodel the city in its eighteenth-century heyday. There's more of his work across the elegant Tromostovje, or Triple Bridge, the most distinguished of which is a beautifully sculpted **fountain**, symbolizing the meeting of the rivers Sava, Krka and Ljubljanica. Opposite the fountain on cobbled Mestni trg is the **Town Hall** – an undistinguished Baroque building, with some interesting sgraffiti in the courtyard. The area south of here is crammed with colourful Baroque town houses, pavement cafés and boutiques. A little east of Mestni trg, on Ciril-Metodov trg, **St Nicholas' Cathedral** (daily 6am–noon & 3–6pm; free) is the most sumptuous and overblown of Ljubljana's Baroque statements. Smothered with fabulous frescoes, this is the best preserved of the city's ecclesiastical buildings. Just to the west of the cathedral buildings, along the riverside, you can't fail to miss the brash, free-for-all **general market** (not Sun). Just beyond the market, take a look at the beautiful Dragon Bridge, each corner pylon topped with spitting dragons – the city symbol. Opposite the market, Studentovska winds up the thickly wooded hillside to the **Castle**, originally a twelfth-century construction whose present appearance dates from the sixteenth century, following an earthquake in 1511. Within the castle, the **Virtual Museum** (10am–7pm; 900SIT including entrance to clock tower) presents the development of the city in the form of an enlightening 3D visual presentation. Climb the **clock tower** for a superlative view of the Old Town below and the magnificent Kamniške Alps to the north.

## South of Prešernov trg

Back on the western side of the river, the broad slash of **Slovenska cesta** forms the commercial heart of Ljubljana, though it's a place to do business rather than sightsee. Further south along here, the park-like expanse of Kongresni trg slopes away from the early eighteenth-century **Ursuline Church**, whose looming Baroque coffee-cake exterior is one of the city's most impressive. Lower down, by the side of the main university building, Vegova Ulica leads south from Kongresni trg towards Trg francoske revolucije, passing on the way the chequered pink, green and grey brickwork of the **National University Library**, arguably Plečnik's greatest work. The **Illyrian Monument** on Trg francoske revolucije was erected in 1930 in belated recognition of Napoleon's short-lived attempt to create a fiefdom of the same name centred on Ljubljana. Virtually next door is the seventeenth-century monastery complex of **Križanke**: originally the seat of a thirteenth-century order of Teutonic Knights, its delightful colonnaded courtyard was restored to form a permanent venue for the Summer Festival.

## West of Slovenska: museums and Tivoli Park

West of Slovenska, Cankarjeva heads down towards a neatly ordered corner of town that contains the city's most important museums. The **National Museum** (Tues–Sun 10am–6pm, Thurs till 8pm; 800SIT; ✆www.narmuz-lj.si), at Muzejska 1, has its permanent collection under wraps until at least 2006, but it does host some excellent temporary exhibitions. The building also houses the **Natural History Museum** (same hours and ticket), notable for having the only complete mammoth skeleton found in Europe. The **National Gallery** at Prešernova 24 (Tues–Sun 10am–6pm; 800SIT, free Sat pm; ✆www.ng-slo.si) is housed in the former Narodni Dom, built in the 1890s to accommodate Slovene cultural institutions in defiance of the Habsburgs. The gallery is rich in local medieval Gothic work, although most visitors gravitate towards the halls devoted to the Slovene Impressionists, and in particular the outstanding works by Ivan Grohar and Rihard Jakopič. Diagonally across from here the **Museum of Modern Art** at Cankarjeva 15 (Tues–Sun 10am–6pm; 1000SIT; ⓦ www.mg-lj.si) carries on where the National Gallery left off, showing how the Slovene Impressionists developed more experimental styles in the early years of the twentieth century. Beyond the galleries lies **Tivoli Park**, an expanse of lawns and tree-lined walkways backed by dense woodland, perfect for a short ramble. A villa above the centre contains the most enjoyable of Ljubljana's museums, the **Museum of Modern History** (Tues–Sun 10am–6pm; 800SIT; ⓦ www.muzej-nz.si) with dioramas, video screens and period music combining to produce an evocative journey through twentieth-century Slovene history, including the Ten-Day War of Independence in 1991.

## Eating, drinking and nightlife

Ljubljana boasts a tight concentration of **restaurants**, most of which offer excellent value for money. The best choice for **snacks** are the many kiosks and stands near the stations and scattered elsewhere throughout town, selling *burek*, hot dogs and the local *gorenjska* sausages. The **market** is on Vodnikov trg. On summer evenings the **cafés and bars** of Ljubljana's Old Town spill out onto the streets, and a wander along the riverbanks will yield one enticing place after another. The free English-language magazine *Ljubljana Life* (ⓦ www.ljubljanalife.com), available from the tourist offices, contains bar and club **listings**. Cankarjev Dom, Prešernova 10, is the scene of major orchestral and theatrical events, as well as occasional folk and jazz concerts (ticket office Mon–Fri 10am–2pm & 4.30–8pm, Sat 10am–1pm; also 1hr before performance). The **Slovenska Filharmonija orchestra** performs at Kongresni trg 9, while the **National Opera and Ballet Theatre** is at Župančičeva 1 (ticket office Mon–Fri 2–5pm, Sat 6–7pm; also 1hr before performance). The **International Summer Festival** (July to mid-Sept; ☎01/241-6026, ⓦ www.festival-lj.si) features orchestral concerts at major venues. The free monthly *Where To?* pamphlet, from the tourist offices, has complete listings.

### Restaurants

**Abcedarium** Ribji trg 2. Located within Ljubljana's oldest house, this modern outfit offers a good range of food including Slovene staples, salads, soups and the best breakfasts in town.

**Cantina Mexicana** Knafljev prehod. Colourful and lively place serving Mexican standards, in addition to a fancy cocktail bar.

**Emonska klet** Plešnikov trg 1. Once the halls of the Ursuline convent, this capacious cellar restaurant serves up pizzas, salads and Slovenian dishes. Nightly live music and a cracking bar turns this into a bit of a party place in the evenings.

**Figovec** Gosposvetska 1. Charmingly old-fashioned downtown restaurant specializing in pony steaks, horsemeat goulash and traditional Slovene standards.

**Julija** Stari trg 9. A simple eatery in a lovely Old Town location, with decent salads, pasta and seafood dishes.

**Ljubljanski Dvor** Dvorni trg 1. Best thin-crust pizzas in town at this fast and furious place, which also has a great terrace overlooking the Ljubljanica.

**Romeo** Stari trg 6. Opposite *Julija*, appropriately enough, knocking up cheap and filling Mexican dishes; one of the best places to go for post-pub munchies. Open late.

**Sokol** Ciril Metodov trg 18. Busy and atmospheric inn-style place, serving hearty, inexpensive portions of traditional Slovene food.

**Zlata Ribica** Cankarjevo Nabrežje 5. With a great outdoor dining area, this modest and inexpensive fish restaurant by the River Ljubljanica is delightful.

### Cafés and bars

**Café Antico** Stari trg 27. Lovely Old Town hangout with a pleasantly dated ambience, offering a decent range of coffee, wine and draught beer.

**Čajna Hiša** Stari trg 3. Bijou café serving the best

teas in town, excellent sandwiches and cakes, and decent breakfasts. Closed Sun.

**Café Gaudí** Nazorjeva 10. Delightful interior and a seductive range of coffees.

**Cutty Sark** Knafljev prehod 1. Straightforward drinking venue, with draught beers and a raucous atmosphere.

**Le Petite Café** Trg francoske revolucije 4. Wonderful place, ideal for a coffee and croissant during the day or a glass of wine in the evening.

**Maček** Krojaška 5. Hip café with large outdoor terrace; the place to be seen on Ljubljana's riverfront, and consequently crammed.

**Ragamuffin** Krojaška 4. Small, reggae-oriented café/bar, good for a daytime chill-out or more boisterous evening drink.

**Vinoteka Movia** Mestni trg 2. Cosy little bar that's the best place to sample some of Slovenia's exceptional wines.

**Zlata Ladjica** Juršišev trg 1. Youthful, pub-type place in a lovely spot on the left bank of the Ljubljanica.

### Clubs and discos

**Bacchus** Kongresni trg 3. Stylish, three-in-one restaurant, lounge bar and club.

**Gajo Jazz Club** Beethovnova 8 ⓦ www .jazzclubgajo.com. Refined late-night jazz club with quality offerings by both domestic and foreign acts.

**Global** Slovenska (top of the Nama department store). Standard disco with lots of spangly silver and gold decor. Access is via a glass elevator on the street.

**K4** Kersnikova 4. Stalwart of Ljubljana's alternative scene, offering different styles of music on different nights – including at least one gay night a week.

**KUD Prešeren** Karunova 14. Superb gig venue that also hosts regular literary events, workshops and art exhibitions.

**Metelkova mesto** Metelkova cesta. Ljubljana's alternative cultural Mecca, consisting of a cosmopolitan cluster of clubs and bars (collectively entitled Metelkova), is located in the former army barracks next to the *Celica* youth hostel.

**Orto Bar** Grabloviševa 1. Loud and groovy bar-cum-club east of the train station with pumping disco tunes and frequent live-rock evenings.

## Listings

**Embassies and consulates** Australia, Trg republike 3 ⓣ01/425-4252; Canada, Miklošiševa 19 ⓣ01/430-3570; UK, Trg republike 3 ⓣ01/200-3910; US, Prešernova 31 ⓣ01/200-5500.
**Exchange** At the train station and *Menjalnica* on Pogaršarjev trg.
**Hospital** Bohoriševa 4 ⓣ01/232-3060.
**Internet access** Cybercafe Xplorer, Petkovškovo Nabrežje 23 (Mon–Fri 10am–10pm, Sat & Sun 2–10pm); Cyber City, Trg Osvobodilne 5 (Mon–Sat

8am–11pm, Sun noon–11pm); Kiber Pipa, Kersnikova 6 (Mon–Fri 10am–10pm); Slovenian Tourist Information Centre, Krekov trg 10 (daily 8am–7/9pm).
**Laundry** Chemo-express, Wolfova 12 (closed Sat & Sun; ⓣ01/251-4404).
**Left luggage** At the train station.
**Pharmacy** Lekarna Miklošiš, Miklošiševa 24 ⓣ01/231-4558 (24hr).
**Post office** Slovenska 32 and Trg Osvobodilne fronte 5.

# The rest of Slovenia

Emphatically not to be missed while you're in Ljubljana is a visit to either the **Postojna** or **Škocjan caves** – both of which are easily managed either as a day-trip from the capital or en route south to Slovene Istria, to Croatia or to Italy. A more low-key alternative to the caves is **Lipica**, where the celebrated white Lipizzaner horses are bred, or **Predjama Castle**, near Postojna, an atmospherically sombre castle high above a cave entrance in the midst of a dramatic landscape. Close to the Italian and Croatian borders, the towns of **Slovene Istria** have long been popular resorts, yet have still managed to retain some charm and identity. Much of this stems from their Italian character, a legacy of four hundred years of Venetian rule. The main draw is **Piran**, which, with its cobbled piazzas, shuttered houses and back alleys laden with laundry, is almost overwhelmingly pretty, while **Portorož** is Slovenia's brashest beach resort. Within easy reach northwest of Ljubljana are the stunning mountain lakes of **Bled** and **Bohinj**. The magnificent **Soča valley**, on the western side of the Slovene Alps, is much less touristy, although small towns like **Kobarid** and **Bovec** make excellent bases for hiking and adventure sports. East of Ljubljana on the main route to Hungary, **Ptuj** is Slovenia's oldest town.

## Postojna and Predjama Castle

**POSTOJNA** is on the main rail route south, 65km from Ljubljana, but as the walk to the caves from Postojna train station is further than from the bus stop, most people go by one of the regular buses. Once in the town, signs direct you to the **caves** (daily 9/10am–4/6pm; tours every 1–2hr, last tour 1hr before closing; 3700SIT; ⓦwww.postojna-cave.com). Inside, a railway whizzes you through 2km of preliminary systems before the guided tour starts. The vast and fantastic jungles of rock formations are quite breathtaking. Your best bet for **accommodation** in Postojna are private rooms (❷), arranged by Kompas, Titov trg 2a (Mon–Fri 8am–7pm, Sat 9am–1pm; ☎05/721-1480, ✆info@kompas-postojna.si), who are also the best source of information on the town and the caves. The *Kras* **hotel** at Tržaška 1 (☎05/726-4071; ❹) is extremely drab, but the *Pivka* **campsite** (☎05/726-5382), 4km beyond the cave entrance en route to Predjama Castle, also has four-person bungalows (❹). *Pizzeria Minutka*, northwest of the main square at Ljubljankska 14, is a pleasant alternative to the tourist eateries by the caves.

Well signposted 7km northwest of the caves, but not served by public transport, is **Predjama Castle** (daily 9/10am–4/7pm; 1100SIT). Pushed up high against a cave entrance in the midst of karst landscape, this sixteenth-century castle is an impressive sight and affords excellent views of the surrounding countryside. Its damp and rather melancholy interior is less rewarding, though there are a few interesting exhibits from this and an earlier castle that stood nearby. There are **guided tours** of the cave below the castle (May–Sept daily 11am, 1pm, 3pm & 5pm; 1100SIT).

## Lipica and Škocjan Caves

Located 7km west of the drab railway-junction town of Divača near the Italian border, **LIPICA** gave its name to the **Lipizzaner** horses associated with Vienna's Spanish Riding School. There are three hundred horses here, the results of fastidious breeding that can be dated back to 1580, when the Austrian Archduke Charles established the farm in order to add Spanish and Arab blood to the Lipizzaner strain that was first used by the Romans for chariot races. Tours are given round the **stud farm** (daily 9/11am–3/6pm; 1400SIT; ⓦwww.lipica.org), and the horses give the elegant displays for which they're famous (April Fri & Sun 3pm; May–Oct Tues, Fri & Sun 3pm; 2800SIT). Public **transport** is poor: a few buses run from Sežana, 5km north of Lipica, on weekday mornings, but you have little time to look around before catching the last bus back. The alternatives include spending a (pricey) night here in one of the hotels – the *Klub* or *Maestoso* (both ☎05/739-1580; ❺), walking or hitching.

Getting to the **ŠKOCJAN CAVES**, 5km south of Divača, is no less problematic, but absolutely worth the effort. Much less visited (but more rewarding) than Postojna, the Škocjan Caves are a stunning system of vast chambers, secret passages and collapsed valleys carved out by the Reka River, which begins its journey some 50km south near the Croatian border. Daily **tours** (10am, 11.30am, then hourly between 1–5pm; 2500SIT; ⓦwww.park-skocjanske-jame.si) take you through several stalactite-infested chambers and halls, before you reach the breathtaking **Murmuring Cave**, a three-hundred-metre-long, one-hundred-metre-high gorge – reputedly the world's largest subterranean canyon. From Divača train station, it's a forty-five minute walk (signposted); if you're coming from Ljubljana by bus, get the driver to set you down by the access road, from where it's a reasonable 1.5km walk to the caves. If you need to stay, there's the *Pension Risnik* (☎05/763-0008; ❸), 200m up from the train station in Divača.

## The coast: Portorož and Piran

Easily reached by bus from the train terminus in Koper, **PORTOROŽ** ("Port of Roses") sprawls at the end of a long, tapering peninsula that projects like a lizard's tail north into the Adriatic. Known since the end of the nineteenth century for its mild climate and the health-inducing properties of its salty mud baths, the resort is now a vibrant strip of hotels and beaches. Combining Portorož's modernity with the charm of Piran (a short bus ride or forty-minute walk away; see below) is the key to enjoying this brash, consumption-oriented place. The **tourist office** (daily: July & Aug 9am–1.30pm & 3–9pm; Sept–June 10am–5pm; ☎05/674-0231, ⓦwww.portoroz.si) is on the main coastal strip, Obala Maršala Tita, just down from the bus terminal; the best **private rooms** (❷) are available from Tourist Service Portorož (☎05/674-0360, ⓦwww.tourist-portoroz-sp.si), next to the bus terminal.

  **PIRAN**, at the tip of the peninsula, 4km from Portorož's bus station, couldn't be more different. Its web of arched alleys, tightly packed ranks of houses and little Italianate squares is simply delightful. The centre, 200m around the harbour from the bus station, is **Tartinijev trg**, named after the eighteenth-century Italian violinist and composer Giuseppe Tartini, who was born in a house on the square and is commemorated by a bronze statue in the centre. With its striking oval-shaped interior, it's one of the loveliest squares on this coast, fringed by a mix of Venetian palaces and a grand-looking Austrian town hall. Across the harbour, in the Gabrielli Palace, the **Maritime Museum** (Tues–Sun 9am–noon & 3/6–6/9pm; 700SIT) houses a collection of fine model ships, along with an interesting display on Piran's salt industry. From the square's southeastern corner, follow Ulica IX Korpusa up to the barnlike Baroque **Church of Sv Jurij**, crowning a commanding spot on the far side of Piran's peninsula – the adjacent **belfry** (100SIT) offers wonderful views of the town and Adriatic, as do the towers punctuating the formidable sixteenth-century **walls** five minutes' walk beyond.

  Piran's **tourist office** is on Tartinijev trg (July & Aug daily 9am–1.30pm & 3–9pm; Sept–June Mon–Fri 9am–5pm, Sat 10am–2pm; ☎05/673-0220). **Rooms** can be booked through Maona, at Cankarjevo nabrežje 7, between the bus station and the square (☎05/673-4520, ⓦwww.maona.si), whilst the **hostel** *Val*, in the old town at Gregorčičeva 38a (☎05/673-2555, ⓦwww.hostel-val.com; ❸), has excellent facilities and a delightful restaurant. The *Fiesa* **campsite** (☎05/674-6230) is 1km away – follow the path from the church. For **eating**, the main square offers a couple of good possibilities: *Batana*, on Kidričevo Nabrežje, is a stylish pizzeria with pleasant terrace, and *Mario*, up a flight of steps from Tartinijev trg, has good-value fish and meat dishes. Numerous more expensive seafood restaurants line the seafront. The best **drinking** spots are the waterfront *Café Teater*; the *Da Noi* bar, a cellar-like space next to the *Pavel* restaurant on the seafront; and *Kavana Galerija Tartini*, on Tartinijev trg.

## Bled and Bohinj

Some 50km northwest of Ljubljana, towards Austria and at the eastern end of the Julian Alps, are the stunning **mountain lakes** of **Bled** and **Bohinj**, Slovenia's premier tourist attractions. If you're interested in serious **hiking**, good maps are essential: your best bets are the 1:50,000 *Triglav National Park*, the 1:25,000 *Mount Triglav* and the 1:25,000 *Bled and environs* – all published by the Slovene Alpine Association. Pick them up in Ljubljana bookshops or from the tourist offices in Bled and Ribčev Laz. **Buses** are the easiest way to get here (hourly from Ljubljana; 1hr 15min to Bled, 2hr to Bohinj). **Rail** access to the region is either via the main northbound line from Ljubljana, which calls at Bled-Lesce 3km southeast of Bled (and linked to Bled by a regular bus), or a branch line which leaves the main

Ljubljana–Villach route at Jesenice and crosses the mountains towards Italy and the coast, calling at Bled-Jezero and Bohinjska Bistrica. The trip from Jesenice, chugging steadily through the mountains and karst, is wonderful.

## Bled

There's no denying that the lake resort of **BLED** has all the right ingredients for a memorable visit – a placid mirror lake with a romantic island, a fairy-tale castle high on a bluff, leafy lanes and a backdrop of snow-tipped mountains. In summer, the lake, fed by warm-water springs that take the water temperature up to 26°C, forms the setting for a whole host of water sports – major rowing contests are held here throughout summer – and in winter the surface becomes a giant skating rink. During the day a constant relay of stretched gondolas leaves from below the *Park Hotel*, the *Pension Mlino*, and the bathing resort below the castle, ferrying tourists back and forth to Bled's picturesque **island** (2400SIT return). With an early start (and by renting your own rowing boat from *Mlino*) you can beat them to it. Crowning the island, the Baroque-decorated **Church of Sv Marika Božja** is the last in a line of churches on a spot that's long held religious significance: under the present building are remains of early graves and, below the north chapel, a pre-Roman temple. From the bathing resort on the north shore a couple of paths run uphill to **Bled Castle** (daily 8am–5/7pm; 1200SIT), originally an eleventh-century fortification but whose present appearance dates from the seventeenth; the museum, containing local artefacts, is pretty dull, but the lovely chapel decorated with frescoes is worth a look, and the views across the lake and towards the Alps are terrific. The main attraction in the outlying hills is the **Vintgar Gorge** (mid-April to Oct daily 8am–8pm; 600SIT), 5km north of town, an impressive defile accessed via a series of wooden walkways and bridges suspended from the rock face. To get there, head northwest out of Bled on the Vintgar road (just up from the bus station), turning right on the outskirts of town towards the villages of Gmajna and Zasip. Head uphill through Zasip to the hilltop chapel of Sv Katarina before picking up a path through the forest to the gorge entrance. Alternatively you can get there by bus (mid-June to Sept daily at 10am) from the bus station.

**Trains** from Ljubljana stop at Bled-Lesce, some 4km southeast of Bled itself and connected to the town by regular buses. The **bus station** is a five-minute walk northeast of the lake on Grajska cesta. Bled's **tourist office** is at Cesta svobode 10 (July & Aug daily 8am–9pm; Sept–June Mon–Sat 8am–5/8pm, Sun 10am/noon–5/6pm; ☎04/574-1122, ⊛www.bled.si), in the casino building opposite the *Park Hotel*. **Private rooms** are available through Kompas, in the shopping centre at Ljubljanska 4 (☎04/572-7501, ⊛www.kompas-bled.si). The outstanding *Bledec* **hostel** (☎04/574-5250, ⊛www.mlino.si; 4000SIT) is just above the bus station at Grajska 17, and there's another, the *Kuralt* (☎04/572-5833, ⊛www.ats.si; 4000SIT), in Spodnje Gorje 4km north of Bled (hourly bus from Bled). There are also some good **pensions** scattered around the lake, such as the *Pletna* at Cesta svobode 37 (☎04/574-3702; ❸), and the *Mlino*, 200m further along at no. 45 (☎04/574-1404; ❹). Bled **campsite** (☎04/575-2000) is beautifully located at the western end of the lake amid the pines; catch a bus towards Bohinj and ask to be set down by the *Vila Bled*, from where it's a ten-minute walk. The best places for **eating** are in the hillside area between Bled's bus station and castle: *Gostilna Pri Planincu*, Grajska 8, offers solid Slovene home cooking, whilst *Okarina*, just up from here at Rikljeva 9, has a varied menu including some exceptional vegetarian dishes; the hostel restaurant is pretty decent too.

## Lake Bohinj

From Bled hourly buses make the 30km trip through the verdant, mist-laden Sava Bohinjka Valley to **Lake Bohinj**. In appearance and character Lake Bohinj is utterly different from Bled: the lake crooks a narrow finger under the wild mountains, woods slope gently down to the water, and a lazy stillness hangs over all.

**RIBČEV LAZ** (often referred to as Jezero on bus timetables), at the eastern end of the lake, is where most facilities are based, including the **tourist office** (July & Aug daily 8am–8pm; Sept–June Mon–Sat 8am–6pm, Sun 9am–3pm; ℡04/574-6010, Ⓦwww.bohinj.si), which offers a plentiful choice of **rooms** (❷) and apartments (❸–❹) around Ribčev Laz and in the idyllic villages of **STARA FUŽINA** and **STUDOR**, 1km and 2.5km north respectively. The star attraction in Ribčev Laz is the **Church of Sv Janez** (July & Aug daily 9am–noon & 5–8pm; other times contact the tourist office; 100SIT), a chunky-looking structure whose nave and extraordinary frescoes date back to the fourteenth century. **Walking trails** lead round both sides of the lake, or north onto the eastern shoulders of the Triglav range. One route leads north from Stara Fužina into the Voje valley, passing through the dramatic **Mostnica Gorge**, a popular local beauty spot.

About 5km from Ribčev Laz at the western end of the lake is the hamlet of **UKANC** (sometimes referred to as Zlatorog), where there's a lakeside **campsite** (℡04/572-3483) and a **cable car** (daily 8am–6pm every 30min; closed Nov; 2000SIT return), which whizzes you up to the summit of **Mount Vogel** (1540m) in just five minutes – if the Alps look dramatic from the lakeside, from Vogel's summit they're breathtaking. Ukanc is also the starting point for a 45-minute walk north to the photogenic **Savica Waterfalls** (April to Oct 8am–6pm; 400SIT). The falls themselves mark the start of one of the most popular hiking routes up Mount Triglav, which zigzags up the mountain wall to the north before bearing northwest into the **Valley of the Seven Lakes** – an area strewn with eerie boulders and hardy firs – before continuing to the summit of Triglav itself. It's not a hike of great technical difficulty, though it's steep in parts and good maps, careful planning and a watchful eye on the weather are required. The Seven Lakes can be treated as a day-long hiking expedition from Bohinj, but the assault on Triglav itself necessitates at least one night in a mountain hut. The tourist office in Ribčev Laz will supply details and book you a place, although huts on Triglav are only open from late June to late September – the upper stretches of the mountain shouldn't be tackled outside these times.

## The Soča valley

On the other, less-touristy side of the mountains from Bohinj, the River Soča cuts through the western spur of the Julian Alps, running parallel with the Italian border. During World War I, the Soča marked the front line between the Italian and Austro-Hungarian armies; memorial chapels and abandoned fortifications abound, located incongruously amidst awesome alpine scenery. The valley is also a major centre for activity-based tourism, with the foaming river itself providing the ideal venue for **rafting** and **kayaking** throughout the spring and summer. The main tourist centres are **Kobarid** and **Bovec**, both small towns boasting a range of walking possibilities. The 1:50,000 *Posočje* **map** covers trails in the region: it's best to pick it up in Ljubljana if you can, as not all local shops have it. Approaching the Soča valley from the Bled-Bohinj area involves catching one of six daily trains from Bled-Jezero or Bohinjska Bistrica to **Most na Soči**, where five buses daily run onwards up the valley. Getting here from the coast entails catching buses plying the Koper-Sežana-Nova Gorica-Tolmin-Kobarid route (min. 4hr, depending on connections), although you might have to change at each stage of the journey.

It was at the little alpine town of **KOBARID** that German and Austrian troops finally broke through Italian lines in 1917, almost knocking Italy out of World War I in the process. Ernest Hemingway, then a volunteer ambulance driver on the Italian side, took part in the chaotic retreat that followed, an experience that resurfaced in his novel *A Farewell to Arms*. A processional way leads up from Kobarid's main square to a monumental, three-tiered **Italian War Memorial** officially opened by Benito Mussolini in 1938, and a fitting place from which to enjoy views of the surrounding alps and ponder Kobarid's violent past. Back in town, the **Kobarid**

**museum**, at Gregorčičeva 10 (Mon–Fri 9/10am–5/6pm, Sat & Sun 9am–6/7pm; 800SIT; ✆www.kobariski-muzej.si), doubles as the **tourist office** (✆05/389-0000, ✆www.kobarid.si), and presents a thoughtful and balanced record of the war with a gripping collection of photographs, maps and mementos. Continue past the museum, head downhill and take the Drežnica road across the River Soča to pick up trails to the **Kozjak waterfall** (50min), less impressive for its height than for the cavern-like space which it has carved out of the surrounding rock. Numerous paths branch off from here into the wooded hills, passing trench systems dug by the Italians during the war. The tourist office can help out with private **rooms** (❷) in Kobarid and surrounding villages, and there are two **campsites** – the *Koren* (✆05/389-1311) and the *Lazar* (✆05/388-5333) – located on opposite banks of the River Soča, 500m east of town on the way towards the Kozjak waterfall. Kobarid's only budget **eating** is at *Pizzeria pri Vitku*, hidden away in a residential district at Pri Malnik 41 (take the road south out of town and follow the signs), though if you fancy a splurge, there's one of Slovenia's best seafood restaurants, *Kotlar*, at Trg svobode 11. The main **rafting** company is X-Point (✆05/388-5308, ✆x.point@siol.net), just north of Trg svobode at Stresova 1; they also organize a range of other outdoor activities. Expect to pay around €30 for a rafting trip.

Some 25km up the valley from Kobarid, the village of **BOVEC** straggles between imperious mountain ridges. A useful base for the Soia valley, it has more accommodation than Kobarid because of its status as a winter ski resort. It's also the location of most of the rafting and adventure-sport companies, and departure point for alpine walks. The quickest route into the mountains is provided by the **gondola** 1km south of the village (July & Aug Sat & Sun; 2800SIT return), which ascends to the pasture-cloaked Mount Kanin over to the west. The **tourist office** is just around the corner from the bus stop at Trg golobarskih žrtev 8 (July & Aug daily 9am–8pm; Sept–June Mon–Fri 9am–5pm, Sat & Sun 9am–noon; ✆05/384-1919, ✆www.bovec.si). Private **rooms** (❷) and apartments are available from either Go tours, at Trg golobarskih žrtev 50 (✆05/389-6366, ✆www.gotourbovec.com), or Avrigo, at no. 47 (✆05/384-1150). The nearest **campsite** is *Polovnik*, Ledina 8 (✆05/388-6069); follow the road north out of the village and it's signed to the right after 500m. The best place to **eat** around the main square is *Stari Kovai*, at Rupa 3, with a long list of inexpensive pizzas alongside the usual schnitzels, while good coffees and ices can be had at the hotel *Alp*, also on the square. Bovec Rafting Team (✆05/388-6128, ✆www.brt-ha.si), located in a small hut on the main square, is one of the many companies in town offering **rafting** trips (with prices much the same as in Kobarid). It also organizes kayaking (€25) and canyoning (€40) and rents out mountain bikes.

# Ptuj

Located 120km northeast of Ljubljana, **PTUJ** is the oldest town in Slovenia and about the most attractive as well, rising up from the Drava valley in a flutter of red roofs and topped by a friendly looking castle. But the best thing is its streets, with scaled-down mansions standing shoulder to shoulder on scaled-down boulevards, medieval fantasies crumbling next to Baroque extravagances. Ptuj is on the main rail line from Ljubljana to Budapest (the Venice–Ljubljana–Budapest express passes through here once a day in both directions), and can also be reached by bus from Slovenia's second-largest city, **Maribor**, which is on the Ljubljana–Vienna line. On arriving at Maribor, turn left outside the train station and head downhill – the bus station is on the other side of the crossroads.

Ptuj's main street is Prešernova cesta, an attractive thoroughfare which snakes along the base of the castle-topped hill. At its eastern end is a fine-looking sixteenth-century bell tower and the **Church of St George**, a building of twelfth-century origin that holds a statue of its patron nonchalantly killing a rather friendly-looking dragon, and numerous exceptional frescoes. From here Prešernova cesta leads to

28

the **Archeological Museum** (mid-April–Dec daily 10am–5pm; 800SIT), housed in what was once a Dominican monastery, gutted in the eighteenth century and now hung with spidery decoration, and worth a look for the carvings and statuary around its likeably dishevelled cloisters. A path opposite the monastery winds up to the **castle**. There's been a fortification of sorts here for as long as there's been a town, since Ptuj was the only bridging point across the Drava for miles around, holding the defences against the tribes of the north. An agglomeration of styles from the fourteenth to the eighteenth centuries, the castle was home to a succession of noble families, the most prominent of which were the Herbersteins, Austro–Slovene aristocrats who made their fortune in the Habsburg Empire's wars against the Turks. The castle **museum** (daily 9am–5/6pm; July & Aug Sat & Sun till 8pm; 800SIT) contains dull collections of period furniture, tapestries and paintings, though the exhibition on the *Kurenti*, an extravagant and unusual Shrovetide (late Feb/early March) carnival that celebrates the rite of spring, is entertaining.

Ptuj's **train station** is 500m northeast of the centre on Osojnikova cesta, the **bus station** 200m nearer town on the same road. From both points, walk down Osojnikova to its junction with ul Heroja Lacka: a right turn here lands you straight in the centre. The **tourist office** is at Slovenski trg 14 (July & Aug Mon–Fri 8am–6pm, Sat 8am–4pm, Sun 10am–3pm; Sept–June closed Sun; ☏02/779-6011, ⊛www.ptuj-tourism.si), though you'll get more assistance from the friendly **Centre for Free Time Activities (CID)**, across from the bus station at Osojnikova 9 (Mon–Thurs 8am–8pm, Sat 10am–1pm; ☏02/771-0814, ⊛www.cid.si); they also run the superb **hostel** (same tel; 4000SIT) in the same building, and have **Internet access**. There are two reasonably priced **hotels**: the *Mitra*, Prešernova 6 (☏02/787-7455, ⊛www.hotel-mitra-fm.si; **⑤**), and the *Poetovio*, near the bus station at Trstenjakova 13 (☏02/779-8201; **③**). The **campsite** is 2km across the river at Pot v Toplice 9 (☏02/782-7821, ⊛www.terme-ptuj.si). The best **restaurants** are *Amadeus*, near the Archeological Museum at Prešernova 36, which serves great Slovene dishes, and *Ribič*, a delightful fish place down by the riverside at Dravska ulica 9; a cheap and cheerful alternative is the *Perutnina Ptuj* on Novi trg. By far the liveliest venue for a **drink**, by day or night, is *Café Evropa*, on Mestni trg, though *Čajni Kotiček* on Murkova ulica, and *Café Orfei* on Prešernova, are equally enjoyable places.

# Travel details

## Trains

**Bohinjska Bistrica** to: Most na Soči (6 daily; 45min).
**Ljubljana** to: Divača (hourly; 1hr 30min); Koper (5 daily; 2hr 30min); Maribor (hourly; 2hr 20min–3hr 20min); Postojna (hourly; 1hr); Ptuj (7 daily; 2hr 30min).

## Buses

**Kobarid** to: Bovec (5 daily; 40min); Ljubljana (3–4 daily; 4hr); Nova Gorica (3 daily; 1hr 15min).

**Koper** to: Piran (every 20min; 30min); Portorož (every 20min; 20min).
**Ljubljana** to: Bled (hourly; 1hr 15min); Bohinj (hourly; 2hr); Bovec (4 daily; 4hr 45min); Divača (10 daily; 1hr 30min); Kobarid (3–4 daily; 4hr); Koper (8 daily; 2hr); Maribor (7 daily; 3hr 45min); Piran (6 daily; 2hr 40min); Portorož (6 daily; 2hr 30 min); Postojna (hourly; 1hr).
**Maribor** to: Ptuj (every 30min; 40min).
**Piran** to: Ljubljana (6 daily; 2hr 40min); Portorož (every 20min; 10min); Trieste (Mon–Sat hourly; 1hr).

# Spain

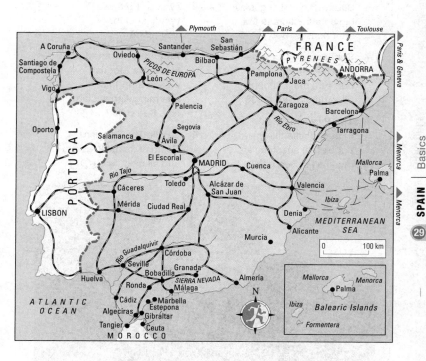

# Spain highlights

* **Madrid** World-class museums and legendary nightlife. See p.917

* **Plaza Mayor, Salamanca** The finest square in a beautiful town. See p.931

* **Guggenheim Museum, Bilbao** The building is as big an attraction as the art it houses. See p.937

* **Santiago de Compostela** The end-point of Europe's most famous pilgrim trail. See p.938

* **The Pyrenees** Trek through these thinly populated, spectacular mountains. See p.940

* **Dalí museums, Costa Brava** Get into the mind of the master. See p.946

* **Barcelona** Perhaps Europe's most alluring city. See p.948

* **Ibiza** Dance the night away in Europe's trendiest clubs. See p.958

* **Alhambra, Granada** Evocative Moorish palace atop this charming Andalucian city. See p.968

* **Seville** The Spanish South at its most vibrant and alluring. See p.971

△ Guggenheim Museum, Bilbao

# Introduction and basics

**Spain** might appear from the brochures to be no more than a clichéd whirl of bullfights and crowded beaches, castles and Moorish palaces. Travel for any length of time, however, and the sheer variety of this huge country cannot fail to impress. The separate kingdoms that made up the original Spanish nation remain very much in evidence, in a diversity of language, culture and traditions.

Of the regions, **Catalonia** (Catalunya) in the northeast is vibrant and go-ahead; **Galicia** in the northwest a verdant rural idyll; the **Basque country** around Bilbao a remarkable contrast between post-industrial depression and unbridled optimism; **Castile** and the south still, somehow, quintessentially "Spanish". There are definite highlights: the three great cities of **Barcelona**, **Madrid** and **Seville**; the Moorish monuments of **Andalucía** in the south and the Christian ones of **Old Castile** in the west; beach-life on the island of **Ibiza** or on the more deserted sands around **Cádiz**; and, for some of the best trekking in Europe, the **Pyrenees**.

Cartogràfic de Catalunya (ⓦ www.icc.es), which covers the Pyrenees in five sheets.

## Money and banks

**Currency** is the euro (€). **Banks** and *cajas de ahorro* have branches in all but the smallest towns, open Mon–Fri 8.30am–2pm, also Sat in low season. You can usually change cash at larger hotels (bad rates, but low commission), at travel agents, and at most El Corte Inglés department stores. In tourist areas you'll also find **casas de cambio**, with more convenient hours, but worse exchange rates. **ATMs** are widespread.

## Information & maps

The **Spanish National Tourist Office** (*Información* or *Oficina de turismo*) has a branch in virtually every major town, giving away maps and accommodation lists. There are also provincial or municipal Turismos. Both types are usually open Mon–Fri 9/10am–1pm & 4–7/8pm, Sat 9am–1/2pm. Good touring and city **maps** are published by Editorial Telstar (ⓦ www.distrimapas-telstar.es) and Editorial Almax (ⓦ www.almax-editores.com). Serious **trekkers** should look for topographical maps issued by Editorial Alpina (ⓦ www.editorialalpina.com), or the Mapas Excursionistas produced by the Institut

## Communications

**Post offices** (*correos*) open Mon–Fri 8.30am–2pm, Sat 9am–noon; big branches in cities open later. **Stamps** are also sold at tobacconists (*estancos*). Poste restante should be addressed to "Lista de Correos", followed by the name of the town and province. You can make international calls from almost any public **phone**. The various discount cards for domestic and overseas calls are the cheapest way to pay (available from tobacconists, *locutorios* and many Internet cafés). Most phone boxes accept coins as well as cards. The operator is on ☎1003 domestic, ☎025 international. Within Spain, dial all nine digits. **Internet** access is widely available.

---

### Spain on the net

ⓦ **www.tourspain.co.uk** Comprehensive website of the Spanish tourist board.
ⓦ **www.spain.info** Information on almost every aspect of Spain.
ⓦ **www.guiadelocio.com** Nationwide restaurant and entertainment listings, updated weekly (in Spanish only).
ⓦ **www.gospain.org** Useful links directory.

# Getting around

RENFE (🌐 www.renfe.es) operates **trains**, with three types of service: *Cercanías* (red) are local commuter trains in the major cities; *Regionales* (orange) run between cities, and are equivalent to buses in speed and cost – *regional exprés* and *delta* trains can cover longer distances; and *Largo recorrido* express trains (grey) come as – in ascending order of luxury – *Diurno, Intercity (IC), Estrella (*), Talgo, Talgo Pendular, Talgo 200 (T200),* and *Trenhotel*. Anything above Intercity can cost twice as much as standard second class. There are also private high-speed trains such as the sleek and efficient *AVE* to Seville, *Alaris* to Valencia, and *Euromed* and *Altaria* to Alicante. A good way to avoid queuing at stations is to buy tickets at travel agents that display the RENFE sign – they can also make seat reservations (€3, the same as at the station), which are obligatory on *largo recorrido* trains. **InterRail** and **Eurail** passes are valid on all RENFE trains and also on *EuroMed*; supplements are charged on the fastest trains, as well as a reservation fee. Book well in advance, especially at weekends and holidays.

Many smaller villages are accessible only by **bus**, almost always leaving from the capital of their province. Service varies in quality, but buses are often faster than trains and prices pretty standard at around €6 per 100km. Services are drastically reduced on Sundays and holidays.

## Spanish

| | Spanish | Pronunciation |
|---|---|---|
| **Yes** | *Si* | See |
| **No** | *No* | Noh |
| **Please** | *Por favor* | Por fabor |
| **Thank you** | *Gracias* | Grath-yass |
| **Hello/Good day** | *Hola* | Ola |
| **Goodbye** | *Adiós* | Ad-yoss |
| **Excuse me** | *Con permiso* | Con pairmeeso |
| **Where?** | *Donde?* | Donday? |
| **Good** | *Bueno* | Bwayn |
| **Bad** | *Malo* | Mal |
| **Near** | *Próximo* | Prox-eemo |
| **Far** | *Lejos* | Layhoss |
| **Cheap** | *Barato* | Bar-ato |
| **Expensive** | *Caro* | Caro |
| **Open** | *Abierto* | Ab-yairto |
| **Closed** | *Cerrado* | Thairrado |
| **Today** | *Hoy* | Oy |
| **Yesterday** | *Ayer* | A-yair |
| **Tomorrow** | *Mañana* | Man-yana |
| **How much is....?** | *Cuánto cuesta?* | Kwanto kwesta |
| **What time is it?** | *Tiene la hora?* | Tee-eynay-la ora |
| **I don't understand** | *No entiendo* | Ent-yendo |
| **Do you speak English?** | *Habla ingles?* | Ablay een-glayss |
| **One** | *Un/Uno* | Oon/Oona |
| **Two** | *Dos* | Doss |
| **Three** | *Tres* | Tress |
| **Four** | *Cuatro* | Kwatro |
| **Five** | *Cinco* | Theenko |
| **Six** | *Seis* | Say-eess |
| **Seven** | *Siete* | See-eytay |
| **Eight** | *Ocho* | O-cho |
| **Nine** | *Nueve* | Nwaybay |
| **Ten** | *Diez* | D-yeth |

# Accommodation

Simple, reasonably priced **rooms** (*habitaciones*) or *camas* (beds) are widely available in rural Spain, advertised in private houses or above bars, often with the phrase "*camas y comidas*" (beds and meals). In most towns you'll be able to get a double for around €30, €20 a single. Prices in popular areas drop in low season. Tourist offices always have lists of places to stay, but often miss the cheaper deals. **Hotels** go by various names. Cheapest of all are *fondas* (identifiable by a square blue sign with a white F on it), closely followed by *casas de huéspedes* (CH) and *pensiones* (P), though these days all are officially designated as *pensiones*, and anything calling itself a *fonda* may only offer meals. Slightly more expensive, but far more common, are *hostales* (marked Hs) and *hostal-residencias* (HsR), categorized from one- to three-stars. Finally, *hoteles* (H) are again star-graded, with one-stars costing no more than three-star *hostales* – sometimes they're actually cheaper. Near the top end of this scale there are also state-run **paradores** (⊛ www.parador.es): beautiful places, often converted from castles, monasteries and other minor Spanish monuments.

HI **hostels** (*albergues juveniles*; ⊛ www.reaj.com) are rarely very practical. In most of the country, few stay open all year, and in towns and cities they can be inconveniently located, suffer from curfews and are often block-reserved by school groups. At around €12–25 per person, usually including breakfast, they are rarely cheaper than sharing a double room in a *fonda* or *casa de huéspedes*. On the other hand some cities, including Barcelona, have a growing network of centrally located **backpacker** hostels with good facilities, no curfew, and the prospect of meeting like-minded travellers. Beds are €17–23, membership not required: check ⊛ www.hostelspain.com for lists of budget hotels and hostels. Nationwide, **agroturismo** and **casa rural** programmes offer excellent cheap accommodation in rural areas. Tourist offices have full lists. There are hundreds of **campsites**, mostly on the coast, charging about €3 per person plus the same for a tent. The National Tourist Board has the free *Mapa de Campings* and the complete *Guía de Campings* (€6); or see ⊛ www.vayacamping.net. **Camping rough** is not a good idea; you can be fined for camping near a tourist beach or campsite.

# Food and drink

Bars and cafés are best for **breakfast**, which can consist of a brioche/croissant, *churros con chocolate* – long tubular doughnuts with thick drinking chocolate – *tostadas* (toasted bread) with oil (*con aceite*) or butter and jam (*con mantequilla y mermelada*), or *tortilla* (omelette). **Coffee** and **pastries** are available at the many excellent *pastelerías* and *confiterías*, while sandwiches (*bocadillos*), filled with sliced meats, cheese or *tortilla*, are available everywhere. *Tabernas*, *tascas*, *bodegas*, *cervecerias* and bars all serve **tapas** or *pinchos*: mini portions of meat, fish, tortilla or salad for €1.30–3.00 a plate. Their big brothers, **raciones** (€4–10), make a sufficient meal in themselves. Good value two- or three-course main meals (*cubierto*, *menú del día* or *menú de la casa*) with wine are served at **comedores** or **cafeterías** (€7–10). *Cafeterías* serve rather bland *platos combinados* such as egg and fries or *calamares* and salad, with bread and a drink included (€5–8). At a **restaurant**, the cheapest full meal plus wine costs €7–10. **Fish and seafood** are fresh and excellent, particularly regional specialities such as Galician fish stews (*zarzuelas*) and Valencian paellas (which also contain meat). Restaurants serving exclusively fish and seafood are called **marisquerías**. The big cities, notably Madrid, Barcelona and Valencia, are fab for **vegetarians**, with scores of veggie restaurants plus fusion cuisine and Asian specialities widely available.

**Wine**, either *tinto* (red), *blanco* (white) or *rosado/clarete* (rosé), is usually very good. The best red is Rioja, though you should also look out for Ribera del Duero from Castilla or Somontano from Aragón. Catalonia produces the best whites, especially Penèdes or Peralada; alternatively, try the refreshing Galician Albariño or the more economical Ribeiro. *Vino de Jerez*, Andalucian **sherry**, is served chilled and either *fino/jerez seco* (dry), *amontillado* (medium), or *oloroso/jerez dulce* (sweet). *Cerveza*, lager-type **beer**, is more expensive than wine but also good. **Sangría**, a wine-and-fruit punch, and **sidra**, a dry farmhouse cider most typical in the Basque Country and Asturias, are worth sampling. Spaniards often take a *copa* of liqueur with their coffee; the best are *anís* (like Pernod) or *coñac*, local vanilla-flavoured brandy. There are cheaper Spanish equivalents (*nacional*) of most spirits. **Coffee** is invariably espresso, unless you specify *cortado* (with a drop of milk), *con leche* (a more generous dollop) or *americano* (weaker black coffee). **Tea** is drunk black. If you want milk, ask afterwards: ordering *té con leche* might get you a glass of milk with a teabag floating on top. Herbal teas, such as *tila* (lime blossom), *menta* (mint) and *manzanilla* (camomile), are very good.

# Opening hours and holidays

Certain **shops** stay open all day, especially department stores, but basic summer hours are Mon–Sat 9.30am–1.30pm & 4.30–8pm. **Museums**, with few exceptions, take a break between 1 and 4pm, and are closed Sun afternoon and all day Mon. The important **churches** operate similarly; others open only for worship in the early morning and/or evening. As well as scores of local **holidays**, national ones are: Jan 1, Jan 6, Maundy Thurs or Easter Mon, Good Fri, Easter Sun, May 1, Aug 15, Oct 12, Nov 1, Dec 6, Dec 8, Dec 25.

# Emergencies

The paramilitary **Guardia Civil** (green uniforms and kepis) still police some rural areas, borders and most highways. In cities, you'll find the **Policía Nacional** (talk to them if you get robbed) and the **Policía Municipal** (traffic police), and there's a **Patrulla Rural** in some outlying areas. Petty theft can be particularly bad in some cities and during fiestas; use common sense and keep an eye (and an arm) on your things at all times. For minor **health** complaints go to a pharmacy (*farmacia*), which you'll find in almost any town. In more serious cases head to *Urgencias* at the nearest **hospital**, or get the address of an English-speaking doctor from the nearest consulate, *farmacia*, local police or tourist office.

## Emergency numbers

All emergencies ☏112; ambulance ☏061.

# Madrid

**MADRID** became Spain's capital thanks to its geography; when Philip II moved the seat of government here in 1561, his aim was to create a symbol of Spanish unification and centralization. However, the city has few natural advantages – it is 300km from the sea on a 650-metre-high plateau, freezing in winter, baking in summer – and it was only the determination of successive rulers to promote a strong central capital that ensured its success. Today, Madrid's streets are a beguiling mix of old and new, with narrow, atmospheric alleys and wide, open boulevards. It is also home to some of Spain's best artworks, from the outstanding pictures acquired by the monarchs, which went on to form the basis of the Prado's world-renowned collection, to the impressive modern works at the Reina Sofía museum. Galleries and sights aside, much of Madrid's charm comes from immersing yourself in the daily life of the city: hanging out in the traditional cafés and *chocolaterías* or the summer *terrazas*, packing the lanes of the Sunday Rastro flea market, or playing hard and very late in a thousand bars, clubs, discos and *tascas*.

## Arrival, information and city transport

Barajas **airport** is 16km out of town and connected with the central Nuevos Ministerios **metro** station (12 min) by line #8. Alternatively, **bus** #200 leaves terminals 1 and 2 (6/7am–11.30pm; weekdays every 10min; weekends & holidays every 20min; €1) for the Avenida de America interchange, where you can get the metro into the centre. A **taxi** from the airport to central Madrid should cost no more than €25 – check the driver's meter is switched on.

**Trains** from the north and Portugal arrive at the **Estación de Chamartín**, in the north of the city but connected to the centre – and all major city locations – via metro line #10. **Estación de Atocha** serves the south, east and west of Spain. Local trains use the Estación de Príncipe Pío, more widely known as **Estación del Norte**, below the central Plaza de España. **Bus terminals** are scattered throughout the city, but the largest – used by all international services – is the **Estación del Sur** (Metro Mendez Alvaró) on c/Mendez Alvaró, south of Atocha station.

The main municipal **tourist office** is at Plaza Mayor 3 (Mon–Sat 10am–8pm, Sun 10am–3pm; ☎915 881 636), with branches at Duque de Medinaceli 2, near Plaza de las Cortes (Mon–Fri 8am–8pm, Sat 9am–1pm; ☎914 294 951), and at the airport (daily 8am–8pm; ☎913 058 656).

For details of **what's on**, check the weekly *Guía del Ocio* (available from newsstands), the Friday and Saturday editions of *El País* and *El Mundo* (which has a listings magazine on Friday), and the free monthly *En Madrid*, available at tourist offices and bars. The websites ⓦwww.gomadrid.com and ⓦwww.munimadrid.es are also useful.

The centre is comfortably walkable, but Madrid also has an efficient **metro system** that runs from 6am until 1.30am (flat fare €1.15; €5.80 for the metrobus ten-ride ticket, valid on buses too). The urban **bus network** is more comprehensive but more complicated – the **transport information** stand in Plaza de Cibeles is more reliable than the quickly outdated handouts. Buses run from 6am to 11.30pm, but there are also several nightbus lines in the centre, from Plaza de Cibeles and Puerta del Sol (midnight–5am every 15min). Hop-on hop-off **tour bus** companies have stops at all the major sights (€10/12 for one/two days).

## Accommodation

The cheapest **accommodation** is around the Estación de Atocha, though places closest to the station are rather grim, and the area can feel threatening at night. A better option is to head up c/Atocha towards Sol, to the streets surrounding the buzzing, pedestrianized Plaza Santa Ana. Prices rise as you reach the Plaza Mayor and Puerta del Sol, but even here there are affordable options. Other promising

**SPAIN**

**29**

▲ A   ▲ B   ▲ 1

**ACCOMMODATION**

| | | | |
|---|---|---|---|
| High Tec | G | Hostal Los Amigos | F |
| Hostal Aguilar | H | Hostal Miau | L |
| Hostal Alcazar Regis | C | Hostal Mondragon | H |
| Hostal Armesto | N | Hostal Plaza D'Ort | M |
| Hostal Barbieri | D | Hostel Richard Schirman | A |
| Hostal Cantabrico | J | Hostal Santa Cruz | |
| Hostal Horizonte | I | de Marcenado | B |
| Hotel Lisboa | I | Hostal Villar | K |
| | | Rafael Hotel Ventas | E |

Conv. de las Comendadoras

Montserrat

Las Maravillas

S. Marcos

Torre de Madrid

Museo Cerralbo

Edificio España

PLAZA DE ESPAÑA

Parque del Oeste

Templo de Debod

Parque de la Montaña

Jardines de Ferraz

Casa de Campo

CUESTA DE

Jardines de Sabatini

Convento de la Encarnación

Jardines del Cabo Noval

Palacio Real

Armería Real

Campo del Moro

Catedral Ntra. Sra. de la Almudena

PLAZA DE ORIENTE

Teatro Real

Iglesia de Santiago

San Nicolás

Casa de Cisneros

Los Lujanes

Muralla árabe

Capitania General

Ayuntamiento

San Miguel

PLAZA MAYOR

Minist. de Asuntos Exteriores

Parque Emir Mohamed

Las Vistillas

Capilla del Obispo

San Pedro

San Andrés

San Isidro

San Francisco el Grande

Gran Vía

Noviciado

S. Antonio de los Alemanes

San Plácido

S. Martín

Palacio de la Prensa

Sto. Domingo

Cine Callao

Descalzas Reales

El Carmen

San Ginés

PUERTA DEL SOL

Sol

Hemeroteca Nacional

Tirso de Molina

La Latina

PLAZA DE CASCORRO

La Corrala

**RESTAURANTS, CAFÉS & TAPAS BARS**

| | | | | | |
|---|---|---|---|---|---|
| Arroceria Gala | 27 | Casa Lucio | 25 | La Bio-Tika | 26 |
| Arti | 3 | Cerveceria Alemana | 16 | La Dolores | 19 |
| Bodega Angel Sierra | 4 | Cervecería Santa Ana | 17 | La Gloria de Montera | 7 |
| Botin | 20 | Ducados Café | 11 | La Truncha | |
| Café Comercial | 1 | El Abuelo | 13 | La Musa de Latina | 24 |
| Café Gijon | 5 | El Brilliante | 31 | La Valencia | 12 |
| Casa Alberto | 21 | El Estragon | 23 | Los Gabrieles | 14 |
| Casa Ciriaco | 10 | Fresc Co | 2 | Melo's | 29 |

| | | |
|---|---|---|
| Museo de Jamon | 8 |
| Star Café | 6 |
| Taberna de Antonio Sanchez | 30 |
| Taberna de Cienvinos | 18 |
| Taverna Maceira | 22 |
| Vina P | 15 |
| Viuda de Vacas | 28 |

0    100 m

▼ Estadio Vicente Calderon

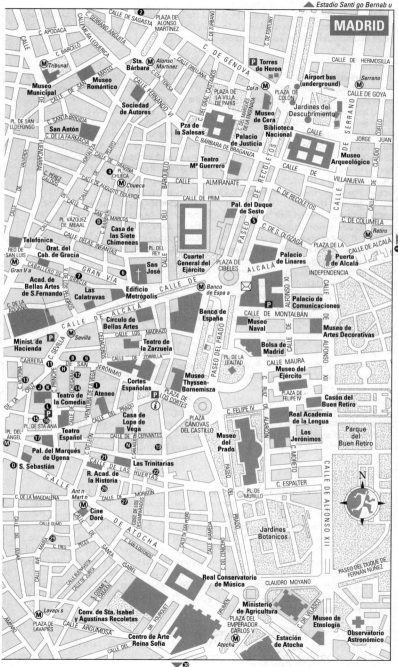

▲ Estadio Santigo Bernabu

# MADRID

- Sta. Bárbara
- Alonso Martínez
- Torres de Heron
- Airport bus (underground)
- Serrano
- Museo Municipal
- Museo Romántico
- Sociedad de Autores
- San Antón
- Plaza de la Salesas
- Museo de Cera
- Biblioteca Nacional
- Jardines del Descubrimiento
- Palacio de Justicia
- Palacio de Braganza
- Teatro Mª Guerrero
- Chueca
- Museo Arqueológico
- Casa de las Siete Chimeneas
- Pal. del Duque de Sesto
- Telefónica
- Orat. del Cab. de Gracia
- San José
- Cuartel General del Ejército
- Palacio de Linares
- Puerta de Alcalá
- Retiro
- Acad. de Bellas Artes de S.Fernando
- Las Calatravas
- Edificio Metrópolis
- Banco de España
- Palacio de Comunicaciones
- Mínist. de Hacienda
- Círculo de Bellas Artes
- Sevilla
- Teatro de la Zarzuela
- Museo Naval
- Museo de Artes Decorativas
- Bolsa de Madrid
- Museo Thyssen-Bornemisza
- Museo del Ejército
- Cortes Españolas
- Ateneo
- Teatro de la Comedia
- Casón del Buen Retiro
- Casa de Lope de Vega
- Museo del Prado
- Real Academia de la Lengua
- Los Jerónimos
- Parque del Buen Retiro
- Teatro Español
- Las Trinitarias
- Pal. del Marqués de Ugena
- S. Sebastián
- R. Acad. de la Historia
- Cine Doré
- Real Conservatorio de Música
- Conv. de Sta. Isabel y Agustinas Recoletas
- Centro de Arte Reina Sofía
- Ministerio de Agricultura
- Estación de Atocha
- Museo de Etnología
- Jardines Botánicos
- Observatorio Astronómico

**SPAIN**

29

919

areas include Gran Vía, where the huge old buildings hide a vast array of hotels and *hostales*, and north of here up noisy c/Fuencarral towards Chueca and Malsaña. The price at all hostels listed below includes breakfast.

## Hostels

**Hostal Barbieri** c/Barbieri 15 ☎915 310 258, ⓦwww.barbierihostel.com. Basic dorm accommodation plus kitchen in youthful, hip Chueca. €16.

**Hostal Los Amigos** Campomanes 6 ☎915 471 707, ⓦwww.losamigoshostel.com. Friendly hostel with full kitchen on a quiet street between Sol and the Palacio Real. Metro Opera. Dorm-beds €16, doubles ❸.

**Hostal Mondragón** c/San Jerónimo 32 ☎914 296 816. Low-cost accommodation in a good location. Rooms have en-suite cold showers and a sink. No curfew. €11.

**Hostel Richard Schirmann** Casa del Campo ☎914 635 699, ⓦwww.reaj.com. Friendly, comfortable and clean HI place, but way out of the city in a seedy area – taxis advisable at night. Roughly 1km from Metro El Lago. €12.

**Hostel Santa Cruz de Marcenado** c/Santa Cruz de Marcenado 28 ☎915 474 532, ⓦwww .reaj.com. North of the Plaza de España near the Palacio Liria; modern, quiet HI place. Some reports about unfriendly staff. Curfew 1.30am. Metro Argüelles. €12.

## Hotels

**High Tec** c/Arenal 4 ☎915 210 542, ⓦwww .hthoteles.com. Part of a well-regarded chain, with stylish rooms in a beautiful building in the heart of the old town. ❽

**Hostal Aguilar** c/San Jerónimo 32 ☎914 295 926, ⓦwww.hostalaguilar.com. One of several sound choices in an old building packed with possibilities. Good central location. ❹

**Hostal Alcázar Regis** Gran Vía 61 ☎915 479 317. Near the Plaza de España, characterful hostal in a beautiful old building. Deservedly popular and often full. ❹

**Hostal Armesto** c/San Agustin 6 ☎914 299 031. Small, very pleasant *hostal*, well positioned for the Santa Ana area and the art galleries. ❹

**Hostal Cantabrico** c/Cruz, 5 ☎915 310 130, ⓦwww.hostalcantabricomadrid.com. Well-located, family-run place with restaurant serving traditional home-cooked food. ❹

**Hostal Horizonte** c/Atocha 28 ☎913 690 996, ⓦwww.hostalhorizonte.com. Well-maintained and characterful rooms near the Plaza Santa Ana, though can be noisy.❸

**Hostal Lisboa** c/Ventura de la Vega 17 ☎914 299 894, ✉hostallisboa@inves.es Good three-star *hostal* in modernized town house, central but not too hectic. ❹

**Hostal Miau** c/Principe, 26 ☎913 697 120, ⓦwww.hotelmiau.com. Soundproofed and air-conditioned rooms in a lovely eighteenth-century building overlooking Plaza Santa Ana. ❻

**Hostal Plaza D'ort** Plaza del Angel 13 ☎914 299 041, ⓦwww.plazadort.com. Spacious rooms, just off Plaza de Jacinto Benavente. ❹

**Rafael Hotel Ventas** c/Alcala, 269 ☎913 261 620, ⓦwww.rafaelhoteles.com. Spacious en-suite rooms in friendly business hotel near the bullring. Café and restaurant on-site. Bargain weekend rates. ❽

**Hostal Villar** c/del Principe 18 ☎915 316 600, ⓦwww.villar.arrakis.es. A comfortable, elegant old building, in a great location off Plaza Santa Ana. ❸

# The City

Central **Puerta del Sol**, with its bustling crowds and traffic, is as good a place as any to start. This is officially the centre of the nation: a stone slab in the pavement outside the main building on the south side marks **Kilometre Zero**, from where six of Spain's National Routes begin. A statue of a bear pawing a *madroño* bush lies on the north side; this is both the emblem of the c ity and a favourite meeting place. Immediately north of Sol, c/de Preciados and c/del Carmen head towards the Gran Vía; both are pedestrianized and constitute the most popular **shopping area** in Madrid. West, c/del Arenal heads directly towards the Opera and Royal Palace, but there's more of interest along **c/Mayor**, one of Madrid's oldest thoroughfares, which runs southwest through the heart of the medieval city, also to end close to the Royal Palace.

### Plaza de la Villa and Plaza Mayor

About two-thirds of the way along c/Mayor is the **Plaza de la Villa**, almost a casebook of Spanish architectural development. The oldest survivor here is the

**Torre de los Lujanes**, a fifteenth-century building in Mudéjar style; next in age is the **Casa de Cisneros**, built by a nephew of Cardinal Cisneros in sixteenth-century Plateresque style; and to complete the picture is the **Ayuntamiento** (free tours in Spanish only, Mon at 5pm), begun in the seventeenth century, but later remodelled in Baroque mode. Baroque is taken a stage further around the corner in c/San Justo, where the church of **San Miguel** shows the unbridled imagination of its eighteenth-century Italian architects. Walking straight from the Puerta del Sol to the Plaza de la Villa, it's easy to miss altogether the **Plaza Mayor**, the most important architectural and historical landmark in Madrid. This almost perfectly preserved, extremely beautiful, seventeenth-century arcaded square, set back from the street, was planned by Philip II and Juan Herrera as the public meeting place of the new capital: *autos-da-fé* (trials of faith) were held by the Inquisition here, kings were crowned, festivals and demonstrations staged, bulls fought and gossip spread. The more important of these events would be watched by royalty from the frescoed **Casa Panadería**, named after the bakery that it replaced. Along with its popular but pricey cafés, the plaza still performs several public functions today: in summer, it's an outdoor theatre and music stage; in autumn, a book fair; and just before Christmas it becomes a bazaar for festive decorations and religious regalia.

## Palacio Real

Calle del Arenal ends at the Plaza Isabel II opposite the **Teatro Real** (ⓦwww .teatro-real.com) or Opera House, which is separated from the Palacio Real by the newly renovated **Plaza de Oriente**. The chief attraction of the area is the grandiose **Palacio Real**, or Royal Palace (Mon–Sat 9.30am–5.30pm, Sun 9am–2pm; €8, free Wed to EU citizens). Built after the earlier Muslim Alcázar burned down on Christmas Day 1734, this was the principal royal residence until Alfonso XIII went into exile in 1931. The present royal family inhabits a more modest residence on the western outskirts of the city, using the Palacio Real only on state occasions. The building scores high on statistics: it claims more rooms than any other European palace; a **library** with one of the biggest collections of books, manuscripts, maps and musical scores in the world; an **armoury** with an unrivalled and often bizarre collection of weapons dating back to the fifteenth century; and an original **pharmacy**, a curious mixture of alchemist's den and early laboratory. Take your time to contemplate the extraordinary opulence of the place: acres of Flemish and Spanish tapestries, endless Rococo decoration, bejewelled clocks and pompous portraits of the monarchs. In the **Sala del Trono** (Throne Room) there's a magnificent frescoed ceiling by Tiepolo representing the glory of Spain – an extraordinary achievement for an artist by then in his seventies.

## The Gran Vía

North from the palace, c/Bailén runs into the Plaza de España, longtime home of the tallest skyscrapers in the city. From here join **Gran Vía**; it was once the capital's major thoroughfare and effectively divides the old city to the south from the newer parts. Permanently crowded with shoppers and sightseers, the street is appropriately named, with splendidly quirky Art Nouveau and Art Deco facades fronting its banks, offices and apartments, and huge posters on the cinemas. At its far end, by the magnificent cylindrical **Edificio Metropolis**, it joins with c/Alcalá on the approach to Plaza de la Cibeles. Just across the junction is the majestic old **Círculo de las Bellas Artes**, a contemporary art space with a trendy café/bar (€1). On an entirely different plane, the **Monasterio de las Descalzas Reales** (Tues–Thurs & Sat 10.30am–12.45pm & 4–5.45pm, Fri 10.30am–12.45pm, Sun 11am–1.45pm; €5), one of the hidden treasures of the city, lies just south of the Gran Vía on the Plaza de las Descalzas. It's an amazingly rich and beautiful locale, the tranquillity within its thick walls making an extraordinary contrast to the frenzied commercialism all around. A whistle-stop guided tour (in Spanish) takes you through the cloisters and up an overly ornate stairway to a series of chambers packed with art and treasures of every kind.

## The Prado

Just across the Paseo del Prado from the Círculo de la Bellas Artes lies Madrid's **Museo del Prado** (Tues–Sat 9am–7pm, Sun 9am–2pm; €6, free Sun; ☎913 79 5 299; ⊛wwwmuseoprado.es), which has been one of Europe's key art galleries ever since it opened in 1819. It houses over three thousand paintings in all, including the world's finest collections of Goya, Velázquez and Bosch. Pick up a leaflet at the entrance to find your way round. The early **Flemish masters** are displayed on the ground floor. The great triptychs of Hieronymus Bosch are familiar from countless reproductions, while the museum's collection of over 160 works of later Flemish and Dutch art has been imaginatively re-housed in a suite of twelve rooms off the main gallery on the first floor. Rubens is extensively represented – by the beautifully restored *Three Graces* among others – as are van Dyck and Jan Brueghel. The central downstairs gallery houses the **early Spanish collection**, and a dazzling array of portraits and religious paintings by El Greco, among them his mystic and hallucinatory *Crucifixion* and *Adoration of the Shepherds*. Beyond this are the Prado's **Italian** treasures: superb Titian portraits of Charles V and Philip II, as well as works by Tintoretto, Bassano, Caravaggio and Veronese. Upstairs are Goya's unmissable Black Paintings, best seen after visiting the rest of his work on the top floor. Outstanding presence among Spanish painters is **Velázquez** – among the collection are intimate portraits of the family of Felipe IV, most famously his masterpiece *Las Meninas*. The top floor of the building is devoted almost entirely to **Francisco de Goya**, whose many portraits of his patron, Charles IV, are remarkable for their lack of any attempt at flattery, while those of Queen María Luisa, whom he despised, are downright ugly. He was an enormously versatile artist: contrast the voluptuous Majas with the horrors depicted in *The Second of May* and *The Third of May*, on-the-spot portrayals of the rebellion against Napoleon and the subsequent reprisals.

## Thyssen-Bornemisza collection

The **Colección Thyssen–Bornemisza** (Tues–Sun 10am–7pm; temporary collection €5, whole collection €9; ⊛www.museothyssen.org) occupies the old Palacio de Villahermosa, diagonally opposite the Prado. In 1993, this prestigious site played a large part in Spain's acquisition of what was perhaps the world's greatest private art collection, with important works from every major period and movement - from Duccio and Holbein, through El Greco and Caravaggio, to Schiele and Rothko; from a strong showing of nineteenth-century Americans to some very early and very late Van Goghs; and side-by-side hangings of parallel Cubist studies by Picasso, Braque and Mondrian. There's a **bar and café** in the basement and re-entry is allowed, so long as you get your hand stamped at the exit desk.

## Centro de Arte Reina Sofía

The **Centro de Arte Reina Sofía** (Mon & Wed–Sat 10am–9pm, Sun 10am–2.30pm; €3, free Sat after 2.30pm, ☎914 675 062 ⊛www.museoreinasofia.mcu .es), facing Atocha station at the end of Paseo del Prado, keeps different opening hours and days from its neighbours, which is fortunate because this leading exhibition space, and permanent collection of modern Spanish art, is another essential stop on the Madrid art scene. The museum, a massive former convent and hospital, is a kind of Madrid response to the Pompidou centre in Paris. Transparent lifts shuttle visitors up the outside of the building, whose levels feature a cinema, excellent art and design bookshops, a print, music and photographic library, restaurant, bar and café, as well as the exhibition halls (top floor) and the collection of twentieth-century art (second floor). It is for **Picasso's Guernica** that most visitors come to the Reina Sofía, and rightly so. Superbly displayed along with its preliminary studies, this icon of twentieth-century Spanish art and politics – a response to the fascist bombing of the Basque town of Guernica in the Spanish Civil War – carries a shock that defies all familiarity. Other halls are devoted to **Dalí** and Surrealism, early-twentieth-century Spanish artists including **Miró** and post-World War II figurative art, mapping the beginning of abstraction through to Pop and avant-garde.

## The Rastro

The area south of the Plaza Mayor and c/Atocha has traditionally been a tough, working-class district and in many places the old houses survive, huddled together in narrow streets. However, an influx of youthful, fashionable residents has changed the character of **La Latina** and **Lavapiés** over the last decade, making it pleasantly hip. Partly responsible for this change is the **Rastro** (Metro La Latina), which is as much part of Madrid's weekend ritual as a Mass or a *paseo*. This gargantuan, thriving, thieving shambles of a **street market** sprawls south from Metro La Latina to the Ronda de Toledo, and is particularly busy along c/Ribera de Curtidores; crowds flood through between 10am and 3pm on Sundays and holidays. Don't expect to find fabulous bargains; the serious antiques trade has mostly moved off the streets and into the shops. Keep a tight grip on your bags, pockets, cameras and jewellery. Afterwards head over to the bars and *terrazas* around Puerta de Moros for an *aperitivo* and to while away the afternoon.

## Retiro and other parks

Madrid's many parks provide great places to escape the sightseeing for a few hours. The most central and most popular is the **Parque del Buen Retiro** behind the Prado, a stunning mix of formal gardens and wilder spaces. You can jog, row a boat, picnic, have your fortune told and, above all, promenade – on Sunday afternoon half of Madrid turns out for the paseo. You can also visit the newly-built 'Hill of the Absents' – a mound constructed in memory of those who died in the Atocha bombing of 2004. Travelling art exhibitions are frequently housed in the beautiful **Palacio de Velázquez** and the nearby **Palacio de Cristal** (times and prices vary according to exhibition). The nearby **Jardines Botánicos** (daily 10am–sunset; €2.50; Metro Atocha), whose entrance faces the southern end of the Prado, are also delightful.

# Eating and drinking

There can be few places in the world that can rival the area around Puerta del Sol in either quantity or variety of outlets for **eating and drinking**. And the feasts continue in all directions, especially towards Plaza Santa Ana and along c/de las Huertas to Atocha, but also south in the neighbourhood haunts of La Latina and Lavapiés, and north in the gay *barrio* Chueca and the alternative Malsaña. The streets between Lope de Vega, Plaza Santa Ana and c/Echegary are especially pleasant for bar-hopping. In summer, all areas of the city have pavement café/bars, where coffees are taken by day and drinks pretty much all night. The prime area is Paseo Castellana, where many of the top discos can be found. Smaller scenes are in Plaza de Chueca, Paseo Rosales del Pintor along the Parque del Oeste, the more relaxed and pleasant c/Argumosa in Lavapiés/Atocha, Puerta de Moros in La Latina and Las Vistillas, on the south side of the viaduct on c/Bailén, due south of the royal palace. Check out, too, the numerous tantalizing chocolate shops, such as *Chocolateria San Gines*, at Pasadizo de San Ginés, 5.

### Cafés and tapas bars

**Arti** Maestro Guerrero 4, just off the Plaza España. Decent place for a light breakfast. Cheap food and good music make it a popular spot for students and backpackers.

**Bodega Ángel Sierra** Plaza Chueca. Great old bar right on the square, just the place for an apéritif.

**Café Comercial** Glorieta de Bilbao. Traditional café and meeting place; linger over coffee, *coñac* or cakes.

**Café Gijon** c/Paseo de Recoletos 21. Long famous as a centre for literary gatherings, this beautiful glass-fronted café is a must for a leisurely drink or meal.

**Casa Alberto** c/de las Huertas 18. One of the most traditional Huertas bars: very friendly and huge portions, with a restaurant out back.

**Cervecería Alemána** Plaza Santa Ana. One of Hemingway's favourite haunts and consequently full of Americans; good traditional atmosphere none the less.

**Cervecería Santa Ana** Plaza de Santa Ana 10. Excellent spot for alfresco or indoor tapas and beers.

**Ducados Cafe** Plaza de Canalejas, 3. Young, funky bar/café, serving good salads and pizza, as well as decent cocktails. A popular spot for the first drink of the night.

**El Abuelo** c/Victoria 12. This legendary family-owned tapas bar serves only two tapas: grilled prawns and prawns cooked with garlic.

**El Brilliante** c/Santa Maria de la Cabeza, just in front of Atocha station. Renowned for its squid and calamari *bocadillos*.

**La Dolores** Plaza de Jesús 4. A typical Madrid drinking bar, popular during the day among locals.

**La Musa de Latina** Costanilla de San Andrés 12. Brings Spanish cooking to the next level with a new way of making tapas.

**Los Gabrieles** c/Echegaray 17. One of the most spectacular tiled bars in Madrid, with fabulous nineteenth-century drinking scenes on the ceramic tiles, including a great version of Velázquez's *Los Borrachos* (The Drunkards).

**Melo's** c/Ave María 44. Excellent-value Galician place serving huge portions. A Lavapiés institution.

**Museo del Jamón** c/San Jerónimo 6, Puerta del Sol end. Extraordinary place where hundreds of hams hang from the ceiling, and you can sample the different (expensive) varieties over a glass or two; also serves full meals and the best breakfast deals in town. Numerous other branches.

**Star Café** c/Marqués de Valdeiglesias 5. Hip, happening gay/mixed bar. Funky grooves in the basement at weekends. Closed Sun.

**Taberna de Antonio Sànchez** c/Mesón de Parades 13. Quality tapas served up at this 100-year-old bar.

**Taberna de Cienvinos** c/Nuncio, 17 Wonderfully atmospheric old taverna serving a huge variety of wines plus tapas and *raciones*.

**Taberna Maceira** c/Huertas 66. Tasty tapas and seafood; *pulpo a la Gallega* (octopus with red paprika) is one of its specialties.

**La Venencia** c/Echegaray 7. Marvellous old wooden bar, serving sherry only and the most basic of tapas – cheese and pressed tuna. A must.

## Restaurants

**Arroceria Gala** c/Moratin 22. Excellent value paella restaurant with a lovely conservatory at the back.

**Botin Restaurant** c/Cuchilleros 17. Claims to be the world's oldest restaurant, dating from 1725, and frequented by Hemingway. Popular with tourists and Spaniards alike for its excellent food, including *cochinillo asado* (roast suckling pig): three-course menu is €30.

**Casa Ciriaco** c/Mayor 84. Good, traditional restaurant, not too expensive for the area.

**Casa Lucio** Cava Baja 35. One of Madrid's most prestigious restaurants, popular with celebrities and politicians. Worth a visit if your pockets are deep enough.

**El Estragón** Plaza de la Paja 10. Good vegetarian tapas and an economical *menú del día* in an attractive plaza.

**Fresc Co** Sagasta 30. Eat-as-much-as-you-like buffet for €9 at this popular chain restaurant.

**La Bio-Tika** Amor de Dios 3. Specializes in macrobiotic vegetarian food. Reasonable menu and a health food shop on the premises.

**La Gloria de Montera** Caballero de Gracia 10. Very popular restaurant serving quality Mediterranean food. No advance booking.

**La Trucha** c/Manuel Fernandez y Gonzalez, 3. Fun, buzzy bistro serving up such treats as trucha à la truchana (trout stuffed with garlic and ham) and chopitos (baby squid). The two-course menus cost €12 or €17.50.

**L'Hardy** c/de San Jerónimo, 10. The best restaurant in Madrid for *Cocido Madrileño*, a traditional dish made of chickpeas, vegetables and meat.

**Vina P** Plaza Santa Ana, 4. Good moderately priced restaurant offering a good selection of tapas and mains.

**Viuda de Vacas** c/Cava Alta 23. Good-value no-frills Castilian restaurant in an area packed with great bars.

# Nightlife

Madrid parties late, with **clubs** starting around 1am and staying open until well beyond dawn. For diving in and out of clubs, as Madrileños like to do, the student area of Malsaña, focused on Plaza del Dos de Mayo, holds most promise, with the music in the clubs here leaning more towards grunge: the key street to start off in is c/San Vicente Ferrer. Chueca, the mainly gay area, is always on the go, with new bars and clubs opening up all the time. It is one of the best places for partying in Madrid, with c/Fuencarral seeing the main action. The multi-cultural Lavapiés/Anton Martín area, south of Sol, is also the centre of a buzzing nightlife. Big **rock concerts** are usually held at Palacio Vistalegre, Utebo 1 (Metro Oporto), and La Peineta stadium, Avenida Arcentales (Metro Las Musas). **Flamenco** can also be heard at its best in the summer, especially at the *noches de flamenco* in the beautiful courtyard of the old barracks on c/del Conde Duque. What's-on **listings** are detailed in the English-language magazine *En Madrid*, *Guia del Ocio*, *El País*, and *Metropoli*, which comes free with *El Mundo* on a Friday, while gigs are advertised on posters around Sol. In July and August the city council sponsors a **Veranos de la Villa** programme of concerts and free cinema in some attractive outside venues.

**Film** is a passion in Madrid, reflected in the queues outside the huge-capacity cinemas on Gran Vía. The Spanish routinely dub foreign movies, but a few cinemas specialize in original-language screenings. These include the Alphaville and Renoir theatres at c/Martín de los Heros 14 and 12, near Plaza de España; Ideal Yelmo Cineplex at c/del Doctor Cortezo 6; and the Círculo de Bellas Artes, on c/del Marqués de Casa Riera. A bargain (€1.35) programme of classic films is shown at the lovely Art Deco Filmoteca at c/Santa Isabel 3, which has a pleasant bar and, in summer, an outdoor *cine-terraza*. Cultural events in English are held from time to time at the British Institute, c/Miguel Angel 1 (☎913 337 3501, ⌨www.britishcouncil.es; Metro Alonso Martínez), which can also be a useful point for contacts.

## Music bars and clubs

**Buddha del Mar** Ctra.de la Coruña, ⌨www .buddhadelmar.com. Very trendy club with Asian decor on the outskirts of Madrid. Cheap to get to by taxi.

**Cool** c/Isabel La Católica 6. Disco and house dominate the dance floor. Metro Santo Domingo.

**Macumba** Above Chamartín station. Weekend favourite where the likes of Ministry of Sound hit the decks until 9am. Metro Chamartín.

**Maxim** Puerta de Toledo 1. Another biggie, hosting both underground and celebrity techno and house DJs. Metro Puerta de Toledo.

**Moma Bar** c/José Abascal 56. Up-market club where well-heeled Madrileños go to party. Metro Gregorio Marañón.

**Ohm** Pl del Callao 4. Perennially popular mixed/ gay night. Metro Callao.

**Palacio de Gaviria** c/de Arenal 9, ⌨www .palaciogaviria.com. Classic eighteenth-century palace converted into a club. Popular with foreign-exchange students. Metro Sol.

**Pasapoga** Gran Vía 37. This elegant theatre was a popular dance hall venue in the 1950s. It now hosts everything from mixed/gay to oriental nights. Metro Callao.

**Stella** c/de Arlabán 7. Light house and handbag rule at the Room session on Friday and Saturday nights. Metro Sevilla.

## Live music

**Arena** c/Princesa 1. Top DJs and big-name bands play at this club. Metro Plaza de España.

**Café Central** Plaza del Angel, 10. One of the best places in Madrid to hear live jazz. Open from noon for drinks, with music nightly from 10.30pm. Metro Sol.

**Gruta 77** c/Nicolas Morales, s/n & c/Cucillo 6. Cool foreign indie bands often play here. Metro Oporto.

**La Boca del Loba** c/Echegaray 11. Good gig venue with a reputation for showcasing new acts. Metro Sevilla.

**Moby Dick** c/Avda. de Brasil 5. Popular nautically-themed venue attracting foreign bands. Excellent dance floor. Metro Santiago Bernabéu.

**Siroca** c/San Dimas 3. Late-night music venue with bands playing everything from pop and rock to hip-hop, jazz and funk. Metro San Bernardo.

## Flamenco

**Café de Chinitas** c/ Torija 7. Authentic music and spectacular shows at this long-established club. The €25 entrance price includes the first drink. Metro Santo Domingo.

**Candela** c/ del Olmo 2. Legendary bar frequented by musicians, with occasional performances. Metro Tirso de Molino.

**Casa Patas** c/de Cañizares 10. Classic Flamenco club with bar and restaurant. Best nights Thurs & Fri. Entrance €12, or €25–30 with dinner. Metro Antón Martín.

**Las Carboneras** Plaza del Conde de Miranda 1 ☎ 915 428 677. Authentic, untouristy Flamenco bar and restaurant. Reserve a table ahead. Metro Sol.

## Listings

**Bullfights** Madrid's Plaza de Toros – *Las Ventas* – hosts some of the year's most prestigious events, especially during the May/June San Isidro festivities. Tickets for all but the biggest events are available at the box office ☎913 562 200, ⊕www .las-ventas.com.

**Embassies** Australia, Plaza Descubridor Diego de Ordás 3 ☎914 416 025; Canada, Nuñez de Balboa 35 ☎914 233 250; Ireland, Paseo de la Castellana 46 ☎914 364 093; New Zealand, Plaza de la Lealtad 2 ☎915 230 226; UK, c/de Fernando el Santo 16 ☎913 190 200; US, c/Serrano 75 ☎915 872 200.

**Exchange** Large branches of most major banks on c/Alcalá and Gran Vía. Round-the-clock currency exchange at the airport; Banco Central is best for AmEx cheques.

**Hospitals** La Paz del Insalud, Paseo de la Castellana 261 ☎917 277 000 (Metro Begoña); Hospital de Madrid, Plaza Conde del Valle de Suchil 16 ☎914 476 600 (Metro Quevedo or San Bernardo).

**Laundry** Onda Blue c/ Léon 3 (Metro Anton Martín) also has Internet; c/Cervantes 1 (Metro Anton Martín); c/Pelayo 44 (Metro Chueca).

**Pharmacies** Farmacía Atocha, c/Atocha 114 ☎915 273 415; Farmacía Lopez Vicente, Gran Vía, 26 ☎915 213 148; Farmacia c/ Mayor 11 ☎913 664 616 (24hr). All have a list of night pharmacies posted outside.

**Post office** Palacio de Comunicaciones, Plaza de Cibeles.

# Around Madrid

Surrounding the capital are some of Spain's most fascinating cities, all an easy day-trip from Madrid or a convenient stop-off on the main routes out. From **Toledo** you can turn south to Andalucía or strike west towards Extremadura. To the northwest the roads lead past **El Escorial**, from where a bus runs to Franco's tomb at **El Valle de los Caídos**, and through the dramatic scenery of the Sierra de Guadarrama to **Segovia**.

## Toledo

Capital of medieval Spain until 1560, **TOLEDO** remains the seat of the Catholic primate and a city redolent of past glories. Set in a desolate landscape, it rests on a rocky mound isolated on three sides by a looping gorge of the Río Tajo (Tagus). Every available inch of this outcrop has been built on: houses, synagogues, churches and mosques are heaped upon one another in a haphazard spiral, which the dark, somewhat claustrophobic cobbled lanes infiltrate as best they can. To see the city at its best, lose yourself in the back streets or stay the night; by 6pm the tour buses have all gone home. Right at the heart of the city sits the **cathedral** (daily 10.30am–noon & 4–7pm, free; museum Mon–Sat 10.30am–6pm, Sun 2–6pm, €8), a robust Gothic construction that took over 250 years to complete (1227–1493). Inside, at the heart of the church is the Choir (closed Sun am), with two tiers of magnificently carved wooden stalls. Directly opposite stands the gargantuan altarpiece of the Capilla Mayor, one of the triumphs of Gothic art, while directly behind the main altar is an extraordinary piece of fantasy, the Baroque *Transparente*, with marble cherubs sitting on fluffy marble clouds - it's especially magnificent when the sun reaches through the hole punched in the roof (designed specifically for that purpose). In the Capilla Mozárabe, Mass is still celebrated daily (9.30am) according to the ancient Visigothic rites. You should also see the Capilla de San Juan, housing the riches of the cathedral treasury; the Sacristía, with the cathedral's finest paintings, including works by El Greco, Velázquez and Goya; and the New Museums, with more work from El Greco, who was born in Crete but settled in Toledo in about 1577.

Toledo is dominated by the imposing **Alcázar** (which is closed for restoration until at least 2007), east of the cathedral. In 1936, during the Civil War, six hundred barricaded Nationalists held out against relentless Republican attack for over two months until finally relieved by one of Franco's armies. Franco's regime completely rebuilt the fortress as a monument to the endurance and glory of its defenders. An excellent collection of El Grecos can be seen to the north of here in the **Museo de Santa Cruz** (Mon–Sat 10am–6.30pm, Sun 10am–2pm; free), while the **Museo de los Concilios y de la Cultura Visigótica** (Tues–Sat 10am–2pm & 4–6.30pm, Sun 10am–2pm; free), in the Mudéjar church of **San Román**, a short way northwest of the cathedral, is also well worth a visit. The building, a delightful combination of Moorish and Christian elements, perhaps even outshines the Visigothic artefacts within. However, El Greco's masterpiece, *The Burial of the Count of Orgaz*, is housed in an annexe to the nearby fourteenth-century church of **Santo Tomé** (daily 10am–5.45pm; €1.90), whose tower is one of the finest examples of Mudejar architecture in Toledo.

From Santo Tomé, c/de San Juan de Dios leads down to the old Jewish quarter and, on c/Reyes Católicos, the synagogue of **El Tránsito**, built along Moorish lines by Samuel Levi in 1366. The only other surviving synagogue, **Santa María la Blanca** (daily 10am–5.45/6.45pm; €1.90), is a short way down the same street, though it looks more like a mosque. If you leave the city by the **Puerta de Cambrón** you can follow the Paseo de Recaredo, which runs alongside a stretch of Moorish walls towards the **Hospital de Tavera** (10.30am–1.30pm & 3.30–6pm; €3), a Renaissance palace with beautiful twin patios. Heading back to town, pass through the main city gate, the **Nueva Puerta de Bisagra**, marooned by a constant swirl of traffic. The main road bears to the left, but on foot you can climb towards the centre of town by a series of stepped alleyways, past the intriguing Mudéjar church of **Santiago del Arrabal** and the tiny mosque of **Santo Cristo de la Luz**, one of the oldest Moorish monuments surviving in Spain.

### Practicalities

From Toledo's **train station** it's a beautiful (but uphill) twenty-minute walk to the central Plaza Zocódover (bus #5 or #6). The **bus station** is on Avenida de Castilla la Mancha in the modern, lower part of the city, a ten-minute walk from the Plaza. Cercanía trains run from both Atocha and Chamartín stations in Madrid (last train back to Madrid at 8.58pm); buses depart from Estación del Sur, with the last bus back to Madrid leaving Toledo at 10pm (Sun 11.30pm). The main **tourist office** is in Plaza Ayuntamiento (daily 10.30am–2.30pm & 4.30–7pm, closed Mon pm; ☎925 254 030), with a branch at the Zococentre, Silleria (daily 10.30am–6/7pm; ☎925 220 300).

In summer, **accommodation** can be very hard to find, so it's worth arriving early. There are a couple of sound budget options on C/Recoletos: *Pension Segovia* at no.2 (☎925 211 124; ❷) and *Pension Castilla* at no.6 (☎925 256 318; ❷) with basic, clean rooms. Alternatively, try the friendly, central *Hostal Santa Tome* c/Santo Tome, 13 (☎925 221 712, ◍www.hostalsantotome.com; ❸), with spacious, spotless rooms, or *Posada de Zocadover* c/Cordonerias 6 (☎925 255 814; 3), with smaller rooms. The slightly pricer *Hospederia de Los Reyes,* Perela 37 ☎925 28 3667; ❹), has comfortable rooms, on the way up from station. Toledo's **campsite** *El Greco Camping,* C/Cordonerias 6 (☎925 220 090), is on the road to Puebla de Montalban, with good views of the city.

Toledo's **restaurants** are plentiful but relatively expensive and not always very good quality. Just uphill from Puerta Bisagra, *La Bisagra*, c/Arrabal 14, and *Arrabal*, opposite, are touristy but reasonably priced. For cheap set menus, particularly at lunchtime, try *Casa Ludeña*, Plaza Magdalena 13, southwest of Zocódover, or *Restaurante Palacios*, c/Alfonso X El Sabio 3. Good quality tapas can be found at *El Trébol*, Santa Fe 15, and *Enebro* 2, Plaza San Justo 9. For something a little different, *Dar Al-chal Teteria* is a Moorish bar next to the Santa La Maria synagogue, serving a selection of teas. Northeast of Zocodover, c/Santa Fe has several **outdoor cafes** popular with a young crowd in the evenings, or head out of town to Plaza Cuba

29

(bus #1), which is full of lively **bars** and **clubs**. Other clubs worth trying are *TBEO*, Corralillo de San Miguel; *Camelot*, Cristo de la Luz; and *Venta de Alma*, housed in an old farmhouse across the Puente de San Martín on Carretera de Piedrabuena.

## El Escorial

Northwest of Madrid is the line of mountains formed by the Sierra de Guadarrama and the Sierra de Gredos, snow-capped and forbidding even in summer. Beyond them lies Segovia, but on the near side, in the foothills of the Guadarrama, are **SAN LORENZO DEL ESCORIAL** and the monastery of **El Escorial** (Tues–Sun 10am–5pm; €9, free on Wed for EU citizens; ☎918 905 313). Enormous and overbearing, its severe grandeur can be impressive, but all too often it's just depressing. Planned by Philip II as a monastery and mausoleum, it was the centre of his web of letters, a place from which he boasted he could "rule the world with two inches of paper". To avoid the worst of the crowds, come just before lunch, or at least head for the royal apartments – focus of all the bus tours – then, and try not to visit on a Wednesday. The west gateway leads into the **Patio de los Reyes**, where to the left is a school, to the right the monastery, both of them still in use, and straight ahead the **church**. Back outside and around to the left are the **Sacristía** and the **Salas Capitulares** (Chapterhouses), which contain many of the monastery's religious treasures, including paintings by Titian, Velázquez and Ribera. Beside the sacristy a staircase leads down to the **Panteón de los Reyes**, the final resting place of virtually all Spanish monarchs since Charles V. Just above the entrance is the *Pudrería*, where their bodies are laid to rot for twenty years or so before the cleaned skeletons are moved. The younger Royal corpses are laid in the **Panteón de los Infantes**. Nearby are the **Library**, with probably the most valuable collection of books in Spain, and the so-called **New Museums**, where much of the Escorial's art collection – works by Bosch, Gerard David, Dürer, Titian, Zurbarán and many others – is kept in an elegant suite of rooms. Finally, there's the **Palace** itself, including the spartan quarters inhabited by Philip II. Later, less ascetic monarchs enlarged and richly decorated the palace apartments, but Philip's simple rooms, with the chair that supported his gouty leg and the deathbed from which he could look down into the church where Mass was constantly celebrated, remain the most fascinating.

**Trains** run every hour from Madrid Atocha to El Escorial (1hr), though **buses** leaving from Madrid's Moncloa area (every 15 min; 50min) are slightly cheaper and take you right to the monastery. If you arrive by train, take the connecting local bus up to the town centre; it leaves promptly and it's a long uphill walk if you miss it. The **tourist office** is near the monastery at c/Grimaldi 2 (Mon–Fri 10am–6pm, Sat & Sun 10am–7pm; ☎918 905 313; ⓦwww.sanlorenzoturismo .org). If you want **to stay** overnight in El Escorial, there are a couple of decent budget options, the *Hostal Cristina*, Calvirio 45 (☎918 901 961; ❸) and Hostal Vasco, Plaza Santiago 11 (☎918 901 619; ❸), as well as an HI **hostel**, c/Residencia 14 (☎918 905 924; dorm-beds €12). There's also a **campsite** (☎918 902 412, ⓦwww.campingelescorial.com), 5km out on the road to Segovia, with bungalows sleeping five (minimum five night stay). **Eating** is pricey, although there are several inexpensive places along c/Juan de Toledo, off Plaza Virgen de Gracia, and up the hill on c/Pozas. *Bar Monasterio*, opposite the tourist office, is a good spot for snacks and drinks.

## Segovia

For such a small city, **SEGOVIA**, 100km northwest of Madrid, has a remarkable number of outstanding architectural monuments. Most celebrated are the Roman aqueduct, the cathedral and the fairy-tale Alcázar, but the less obvious attractions

29

– the cluster of ancient churches and the many mansions found in the lanes of the old town, all in a warm, honey-coloured stone – are what really make it worth visiting. In winter, at over 1000m, it can be very cold here.

The imposing **cathedral** (daily 9.30am–2pm & 4–8pm; €2) was the last major Gothic building in Spain and it takes that style to its logical extreme, with pinnacles and flying buttresses tacked on at every conceivable point. The treasures are almost all confined to the **museum,** which opens off the cloisters. Beside the cathedral, c/de Daoiz leads past a line of souvenir shops to the church of San Andrés and on to a small park in front of the **Alcázar** (daily 10am–6/7pm; Ⓦwww.alcazardesegovia.com, €3.50). It's an extraordinary fantasy of a castle, which, with its narrow towers and turrets, looks like something out of Disneyland. And indeed it is a sham – originally built in the fourteenth and fifteenth centuries but almost completely destroyed by fire in 1862 and rebuilt as a hyperbolic parody of the original. The **Aqueduct,** over 800m long and at its highest point towering 30m above the Plaza de Azoguejo, stands up without a drop of mortar or cement. No one knows exactly when it was built, but it was probably around the end of the first century AD under the emperor Trajan. Segovia is an excellent city for walking, with some fine views and beautiful churches to be enjoyed just outside the boundaries. Perhaps the most interesting church is **Vera Cruz** (Tues–Sun 10.30am–1.30pm & 3.30–6/7pm; €1.50), a remarkable twelve-sided building in the valley facing the Alcázar, erected by the Knights Templar in the early thirteenth century. Inside, the nave is circular, its heart occupied by a strange two-storeyed chamber – again twelve-sided – in which the knights, as part of their initiation, stood vigil. Climb the tower for a highly photogenic vista of the city. While you're over here you could also visit the prodigiously walled **Convento de los Carmelitas** (daily 10am–1.30pm & 4–8.30pm, closed Mon am; ℡921 431 349; free) and the ramshackle fifteenth-century **Monasterio del Parral**, literally 'Monastery of the Grape' (Mon–Sat 10am–12.30pm & 4.15–6.30pm, Sun 10–11.30am and 4–6.30pm; ℡921 431 298; free).

Cercanía **trains** run to Segovia from Atocha or Chamartín stations every two hours, or there's a **bus** from Madrid's main bus station. The train station is a fifteen minute walk out of town – turn right out of the station and follow the left hand fork, or take any bus (every 30min) marked "Puente Hierro/Estación Renfe" to the central Plaza Mayor. The main **tourist office** is at Plaza del Azoguejo 1 (daily 9am–8pm; ℡921 466 070; Ⓦwww.turismocastillayleon.com), with the local branch at Plaza Mayor 10 (Sun–Thurs 9am–8pm, Fri & Sat 9am–9pm; ℡921 460 334). The best budget **accommodation** is the central *Hostal Aragón,* Plaza Mayor 4 (℡921 460 914; ❷), or try *Hostal Plaza,* Cronista Lecea 11 (℡921 460 303, Ⓦwww .hostal-plaza.com; ❸), or *Hostal Fornos,* Infanta Isabel 13 (℡921 460 198; ❸), with classic, airy rooms. For larger budgets, there's the *Hotel Infanta Isabel* in a great location at Plaza Mayor 12 (℡921 461 300, Ⓦwww.hotelinfantaisabel.com; ❻). The **campsite**, *Camping Acueducto* (℡921 425 000; April–Sept), is 2km out on the road to La Granja. Calle de la Infanta Isabella, which opens off the Plaza Mayor is packed with noisy **bars** and cheap **restaurants**. Mesón de Cándido, on Plaza del Azonguejo next to the aqueduct, is one of the best – pricey, but well worth it. Cheaper alternatives include *La Cueva de San Esteban,* Plaza San Estaban, and *La Almuzara,* c/Marqués del Arco 3, for decent vegetarian dishes. *Bar Santana,* Infant Isabel 18, is a good venue for live music.

# Extremadura

The harsh environment of **Extremadura**, west of Madrid, was the cradle of the *conquistadores*, men who opened up a new world for the Spanish Empire. Remote before and forgotten since, Extremadura enjoyed a brief golden age when the heroes returned with their gold to live in a flourish of splendour. **Cáceres** preserves an entire town built with *conquistador* wealth, the streets crowded with the ornate mansions of returning empire builders. An even more ancient past becomes tangible in the wonders of **Mérida**, the most completely preserved Roman city in Spain.

## Cáceres

Old **CÁCERES**, 350km southwest of Madrid, was largely built on the proceeds of American exploration. Today the town has been immaculately restored, yet it remains a rapidly growing provincial capital, and home to the University of Extremadura. Any visit should begin with **the Plaza Mayor**, opposite the tourist office, in the old town. Almost every building here is magnificent. It features ancient walls pierced by the low **Arco de la Estrella**, the **Torre del Bujaco** – whose foundations date back to Roman times – and the **Torre del Horno**, one of the best-preserved Moorish mud-brick structures in Spain. Another highlight, through the Estrella gate, is the **Casa de Toledo-Montezuma** to which a follower of Cortés brought back one of the New World's more exotic prizes – a daughter of the Aztec emperor as his bride. In the Casa de las Valetas, on Plaza San Mateo, is the **Museo Provincial** (Tues–Sat 9am–2.30pm & 5–8.15pm, Sun 10.15am–2.30pm; free to EU citizens with passport, €1.20 for non-EU), whose highlight is the cistern of the original Moorish Alcázar, with rooms of wonderful horseshoe arches. Cáceres' **train and bus stations** face each other across the Carretera Sevilla, some way out of town; bus #1 runs (every 15min) to Plaza de San Juan, a square near the centre, with signs leading on towards the Plaza Mayor and the **tourist office** (Mon–Fri 9.30am–2pm & 4–7pm, Sat & Sun 9.30am–2pm; ☎927 322 677, ⊛www.turismoextremadura .com). The best **places to stay** are all on or near Plaza Mayor – try *Pensión Carretero* at no. 22 (☎927 247 482; ❷), or the stylish *Hostal Alameda Palacete* at c/General Margallo 45 (☎927 211 674, ⊛www.alamedapalacete.com; ❹). Good **restaurant** options include *El Tablón*, c/Donoso Cortés 13-15; *El Figón*, Plaza San Juan 14; and *Torre de Sande*, c/Conde, 3. For **bar-hopping**, head to the Plaza Mayor or c/de Pizarro, just outside the walls on the west side of the old town.

## Mérida

**MÉRIDA**, 70km south of Cáceres, contains one of Europe's most remarkable concentrations of Roman monuments: scattered in the midst of the modern city are remains of everything from engineering works to domestic villas. With the aid of a map and a little imagination, it's not hard to reconstruct the Roman city within the not especially attractive modern town.

A **combined ticket** (€8) gives access to all the sites (all open daily 9.30am–1.45pm & 4/5–6.15/7.15pm). The **Teatro Romano and Anfiteatro** was a present to the city from Agrippa in around 15 BC. The stage is in a particularly good state of repair and in July it plays host to a season of classical plays. In its day the adjacent amphitheatre could accommodate up to fifteen thousand people – almost half Mérida's population today. Also worth seeing is the magnificent **Puente Romano**, the Roman bridge across the islet-strewn Guadiana – sixty arches long, and defended by an enormous, plain, Moorish **Alcazaba**. Nearby is the sixteenth-century **Plaza de España**, the heart of the modern town. Just across from it, the vast, red-brick bulk of the **Museo Nacional de Arte Romano** (Tues–Sat 10am–2pm & 4–6/9pm, Sun 10am–2pm; €2.40, free on Sat pm & Sun for EU citizens, ⊛www.mnar.es) does full justice to its high-class collection, including portrait statues of Augustus, Tiberius and Drusus, and some glorious mosaics. Of the two Roman villas in Mérida, the **Casa Romana Anfiteatro**, which lies immediately below the museum, has perhaps the best mosaics.

Mérida's **tourist office** is at the entrance to the Roman theatre site on Paseo José Saenz de Burnaga (Mon–Fri 9am–1.45pm & 4/5–6.30/7.15pm, Sat & Sun 9.30am–2pm; ☎924 315 353, ⊛www.turismoextremadura.com). Budget **accommodation** is limited – try *Hostal Nueva España*, Avda. Extremadura 6 (☎924 313 356; ❸), or *Hostal Salud*, c/Vespasiano 41 (☎924 31 22 59, ⊜hsalud@blunet.com; ❸). There's a **campsite**, *Camping Mérida* (☎924 303 453, ⓟ924 300 398), not far east of town on the Madrid-Lisbon highway, and a more attractive site at *Proserpina* (☎924 123 055; closed Oct–May), 5km north, where you can swim in the reservoir. Mérida is a lively place, and the whole area between the train station and the Plaza de España is full of **bars and restaurants**. Good food can be found at *Restaurante Briz*, c/Félix Valverde Lillo 5, just off the main plaza, and *Via Flavia*, Plaza del Rastro 9.

# Old Castile

The foundations of modern Spain were laid in the kingdom of **Castile**, west and north of Madrid. A land of frontier fortresses – the *castillos* from which it takes its name – it became the most powerful and centralizing force of the Reconquest, extending its domination through military gains and marriage alliances. The monarchs of this triumphant and expansionist age were enthusiastic patrons of the arts, endowing their cities with superlative monuments above which, quite literally, tower the great Gothic cathedrals of **Salamanca** and **León**.

## Salamanca

**SALAMANCA** is probably the most graceful city in Spain, home to what was once one of the most prestigious universities in the world and still boasting an unmistakable atmosphere of erudition. It's a small place, given a gorgeous harmony by the golden sandstone from which almost the entire city seems to be constructed. Two cathedrals, one Gothic, the other Romanesque, vie for attention with Renaissance palaces; the Plaza Mayor is the finest in Spain; and the surviving university buildings are tremendous. And as if that weren't enough, Salamanca's student population ensure their town is always lively at night. Two great architectural styles were developed, and see their finest expression, in Salamanca. **Churrigueresque**, a particularly florid form of Baroque, takes its name from José Churriguera (1665–1723), the dominant member of a prodigiously creative family. **Plateresque** came earlier, a decorative technique of shallow relief and intricate detail named for its alleged resemblance to the art of the silversmith (*platero*).

A postcard-worthy overview of Salamanca is easy to attain: go to the extreme south of the city and cross its oldest surviving monument, the much-restored, 400-metre-long **Puente Romano** (Roman Bridge). To explore Salamanca from the inside, though, make for the grand **Plaza Mayor**, its bare central expanse enclosed by a four-storey building decorated with iron balconies and medallion portraits. Nowhere is the Churrigueresque variation of Baroque so refined as here, the restrained elegance of the designs heightened by the changing strength and angle of the sun. From the south side, Rua Mayor leads to the vast Baroque church of **La Clerecía**, seat of the Pontifical University (open for visits Sun 12.30pm), and the celebrated fifteenth-century **Casa de las Conchas**, or House of Shells (Mon–Fri 9am–9pm, Sat & Sun 10am–2pm & 4–7pm; free), so called because its facades are decorated with rows of carved scallop shells, symbol of the pilgrimage to Santiago. From the Casa de las Conchas, c/de los libreros leads to the **Patio de las Escuelas** and the Renaissance entrance to the **University** (Mon–Sat 9.30am–1pm & 4–7pm, Sun 10am–1pm; €4, free Mon morning). The ultimate achievement of Plateresque art, this reflects the tremendous reputation of Salamanca in the early sixteenth century, when it was one of Europe's greatest universities.

As a further declaration of Salamanca's standing, the Gothic **Catedral Nueva** (daily 9am–8pm; free) was begun in 1512, and acted as a buttress for the Old Cathedral, which was in danger of collapsing. Joaquín Churriguera and his brother Alberto both worked here – the former on the choir stalls, the latter on the dome. Entry to the **Catedral Vieja** (daily 10am–7.30pm; €3) is through the first chapel on the right. Tiny by comparison and a stylistic hotch-potch of Romanesque and Gothic, its most striking feature is the huge fifteenth-century retable. Another faultless example of Plateresque art, the **Convento de San Esteban** (daily 9.30am–1pm and 4–8pm; €1.50), is a short walk down c/del Tostado from the Plaza de Anaya at the side of the Catedral Nueva. The monastery's cloisters, through which you enter, are magnificent, but the most beautiful cloisters in the city stand across the road in the **Convento de las Dueñas** (Mon–Sat 10.30am–12.45pm & 4.30–7pm, Sun 11am–12.45pm; €1.50). Built on an irregular pentagonal plan, its upper-storey capitals are wildly carved with writhing demons and human skulls. The latest jewel in Salamanca's crown is no less spectacular. The **Museo Casa Lis** (Tues–Fri 11am–2pm & 4/5–7/9pm, Sat & Sun 11am–8/9pm; €2.50; ⓦwww .museocasalis.org) near the Roman Bridge, at c/Gibraltar 14, houses a spectacular collection of Art Nouveau and Art Deco furniture, ornaments and glass; the building itself – with its extravagant use of stained glass and light – is an extra treat.

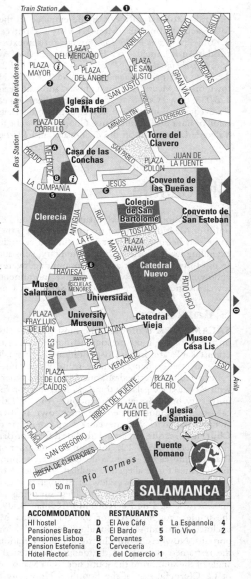

### Practicalities

The **bus and train stations** are on opposite sides of the city, each about fifteen minutes' walk from the centre. The municipal **tourist office** is at Plaza Mayor

14 (Mon–Fri 9am–2pm & 4.30–8pm, Sat 10am–8pm, Sun 10am–2pm; ☎923 218 342), with the regional office in the Casa de las Conchas (daily 9am–2pm & 5–8pm; ☎923 268 571). **Accommodation** is reasonably priced, but can be hard to find in high season – especially at fiesta time in September, and touts tend to be out in force at the train station in summer. The area around Plaza Mayor is the best place to look, with small, cobbled streets housing scores of small *fondas* and *hostales*, most of a high standard: good-value options are *Pensión Estefania*, c/de Jesús 3 (☎923 217 372; ❷), *Pensiones Lisboa*, c/Melendez 1 (☎923 214 333; ❷), and *Pensiones Barez*, c/Melendez 19 (☎923 217 495; ❷). For a splurge, there's the elegant *Hotel Rector*, Paseo Rector Esperabe 10 (☎923 218 48; ❽), in an aristocratic house. Salamanca's HI **hostel** is at c/Escoto 13–15 (☎923 269 141, ⊛www.alberguesalamanca.com; €11.90), with six-bed dorms and excellent facilities. There are several **campsites** nearby: the *Don Quijote* in Cabrerizos (☎923 209 052) is by a river 4km out – reached by bus #2 from Gran Vía – and serves good food in its on-site restaurant; while *Camping La Capea*, at Aldeaseca de la Armuña (☎923 251 066), is just off the road to Zamora, 4km out of the city and surrounded by woodlands.

The **cafés** in Plaza Mayor are pricey, but worth it for the splendour and atmosphere of the square – *Cervantes* at no.15 has great tapas and window tables overlooking the Plaza. The university area has loads of good-value bars and **restaurants** catering to student budgets: cheap and cheerful places include *El Ave Café*, c/delos Libreros 24; *Cervecería del Comercio*, c/Pozo Amarillo 23; and *El Bardo*, c/Compañía 8, for decent vegetarian food. Salamanca is lively at night, particularly along Bordadores, where *Gatsby* at no. 16, *La Hacienda* at no. 4, and *Camelot* at no. 3, are all good choices. *Tio Vivo*, Clavel 3–5, is worth a visit for its interior alone, while *La Espannola*, Gran Via 51, is a must for cocktails. For **clubbing**, try *Morgano*, c/de Iscar Peyra 30; *Bar Plutos*, c/Varillas 12; or the *Barco de Salamanca*, Paseo Fluvial, a late-night music venue set on a boat.

# León

The stained glass in the cathedral of **LEÓN** and the Romanesque wall paintings in its Royal Pantheon are reason enough for many people to visit the city, but León also has an attractive and enjoyable modern quarter. The city has a rich history: in 914, as the Reconquest edged its way south from Asturias, this became the Christian capital, and along with its territories it grew so rapidly that by 1035 the county of Castile had matured into a fully fledged kingdom. For the next two centuries León and Castile jointly spearheaded the war against the Moors, but by the thirteenth century Castile's power had eclipsed that of even her mother territory.

León's **cathedral** (daily 8.30am–1.30pm & 4–7/8pm) dates from the city's final years of greatness. It is said to be a miracle that it's still standing: it has the largest proportion of glass to stone of any Gothic cathedral. The kaleidoscopic stained-glass windows present one of the most magical and harmonious spectacles in Spain, and the colours used – reds, golds and yellows – could only be Spanish; the bewildering sensation of refracting light was further enhanced by the addition last century of a glass screen, allowing a clear view up to the altar. The west facade, dominated by a massive rose window, is also magnificent. The city's other great attraction is the **Real Colegiata de San Isidoro**, which houses the bodies of the early kings of León and Castile. Ferdinand I, who united the two kingdoms in 1037, commissioned the complex as a shrine for the bones of St Isidore, which lie in a reliquary on the high altar, and a mausoleum for himself and his successors. The **pantheon** (Mon–Sat 10am–1.30pm & 4–6.30pm, Sun 10am–1.30pm; €3, free Thurs pm), a pair of small crypt-like chambers, is in front of the west facade. One of the earliest Romanesque buildings in Spain (1054–63), it was decorated towards the end of the twelfth century with some of the most imaginative and impressive paintings of Romanesque art. They are extraordinarily well preserved and their biblical and everyday themes are perfectly adapted to the architecture of the vaults. Also worth seeing is the opulent **Monasterio de San Marcos**, at Plaza de San Marcos, 7, built in 1168 for the Knights of Santiago, one of several chivalric orders founded in the twelfth century both to protect pilgrims on their way to Santiago de Compostela and to lead the Reconquest. Fittingly, it has been converted into a parador (T987 237 300, ⓦwww.parador.es; ❾), where guests enjoy the luxury of a magnificent church of their own, the **Iglesia San Marcos**. The church can be visited by non-patrons too; its sacristy houses a small **museum** (Tues–Sat 10am–2pm & 4/5–7/8pm, Sun 10am–2pm; €1.20) of priceless exhibits, housed in a room separated from the hotel lobby by a thick pane of glass.

### Practicalities

The train and bus stations are both just south of the river: the **train station** at the end of Avenida de Palencia, the bridge across into town, and the **bus station** on Paseo Ingeniero Saenz de Miera – from here, turn left onto the Paseo to reach the bridge. From the roundabout, just across the river at Glorieta Guzmán El Bueno, you can see straight down Avenida de Ordoño II and across the Plaza de Santo Domingo to the cathedral. Directly opposite the cathedral's west facade stands the **tourist office** (Mon–Fri 9am–2pm & 5–7pm, Sat & Sun 10am–2pm & 5–8pm; T987 237 082, ⓦwww.jcyl.es/turismo). There are plenty of **places to stay**, particularly on the main roads leading off the Glorieta, Avda. de Roma and Avda. Ordoño II. Good budget options include *Hostal Oviedo* at Avda. de Roma 26 T987 222 236; ❷); *Hostal Bayon* at Alcázar de Toledo 6 (T987 231 446; ❷); *Hostal Guzmán el Bueno*, Lopez Castrillón 6 (T987 236 412; ❸); and *Pensión Puerta del Sol*, overlooking the Plaza Mayor (T987 211 966; ❷). There are also a couple of **hostels**: a summer-only HI hostel with a pool at c/de la Corredera 4 (T987 203 414; ❶) – follow Avda. de Independencia from Plaza de Santo Domingo – and an independent one at c/Campos Góticos 3, by the bullring (T987 261 174; ✉alberguedeleon@hotmail .com; ❶), about twenty minutes' walk from the cathedral.

The liveliest time of year to be in León is for the **fiesta** of St Peter in the last week of June, though at any time the **bars and restaurants** in the small square of San Martín, behind Plaza Mayor, and the area around it, known locally as Barrio Húmedo, are pretty lively. Try *Zuloaga*, Sierra Pambley 3, and *Boccalino*, Plaza de San Isidora 9, for the best food.

# Spain's north coast

Spain's **north coast** veers wildly from the typical conception of the country, with a rocky, indented coastline full of cove beaches and fjord-like *rías*. It's an immensely beautiful region – mountainous, green and thickly forested, with frequent rains often shrouding the countryside in a fine mist. The summers are temperately warm and, if you don't mind the occasional shower, provide a glorious escape from the unrelenting heat of the south. In the east, butting against France, is **Euskadi** – the **Basque Country** – which, despite some of the heaviest industrialization on the peninsula, remains remarkably unspoiled: neat and quiet inland, rugged and enclosed along the coast, with easy, efficient transport connections. **San Sebastián** is the big seaside attraction, a major resort with superb but crowded beaches, but there are any number of lesser-known, equally attractive coastal villages all the way to **Bilbao** and beyond. Note that the Basque language, Euskera, bears almost no relation to Spanish (we've given the alternative Basque names where popularly used) – it's perhaps the most obvious sign of Spain's strongest separatist movement. To the west lies **Cantabria**, centred on the port of **Santander**, with more good beaches and superb trekking in the mountains of the **Picos de Europa**. The mountains extend into **Asturias**, the one part of Spain never conquered by the Moors. Its high, remote valleys are mining country, providing the raw materials for the heavy industry of the three cities: Gijón, Avilés and Oviedo. In the far west, **Galicia** looks like Ireland, and there are further parallels in its climate, culture and – despite its fertile appearance – its history of famine and poverty. While right-wing Galicia may not share the radical traditions of the Basque country or Asturias it does treasure its independence, and Gallego is still spoken by around 85 percent of the population – again, we've given Gallego place names in parentheses. For travellers, the obvious highlight is **Santiago de Compostela**, the greatest goal for pilgrims in medieval Europe.

If you're not in a great hurry, you may want to make use of the independent **FEVE rail line** (☎902 100 818, ✆www.feve.es; rail passes not valid). The 650km rail line begins at Bilbao and follows the coast, with inland branches to Oviedo and León, all the way to El Ferrol in Galicia. Despite recent major repairs and upgrading, it's still slow but it's cheap and a terrific journey, skirting beaches, crossing rivers and snaking through a succession of limestone gorges.

## San Sebastián

The undisputed queen of Basque resorts, **SAN SEBASTIÁN** (Donostia), just an hour by road from Bilbao, is a picturesque – though expensive – town with excellent beaches, restaurants and bars, and is acknowledged by Spaniards as an unrivalled gastronomic centre. Along with Santander, San Sebastian has always been a fashionable place to escape the heat of the southern summers, and in July and August it's packed with well-to-do-families. Its summer **festivals** include annual rowing races between the villages along the coast, and an International Jazz Festival (late July; ✆www.jazzaldia .com), that attracts top performers to play in different locations around town.

Set around the deep, still bay of La Concha and enclosed by rolling low hills, San Sebastián is beautifully situated; the old town sits on the eastern promontory, its back to the wooded slopes of Monte Urgull, while newer development has spread inland along the banks of the River Urumea and around the edge of the bay to the foot of Monte Igüeldo. The **old quarter**'s cramped and noisy streets are where crowds congregate in the evenings to wander among the small bars and shops and sample the shellfish from the traders down by the fishing harbour. Here too are the town's chief sights: the gaudy Baroque facade of the church of **Santa María**, and the more elegantly restrained sixteenth-century **San Vicente**. The centre of the old part is the Plaza de la Constitución, known locally as "La Consti"; the numbers on the balconies of the buildings around the square refer to the days when it was used as a bullring. Just behind San Vicente, the excellent **Museo de San Telmo** (July & Aug Tues–Sat 10.30am–8.30pm, Sun 10.30am–2pm; Sept–June Tues–Sat 10.30am–1.30pm & 4–7.30pm, Sun 10.30am–2pm; free) is a fascinating jumble of Basque folklore, funerary relics and assorted artworks. Behind this, **Monte Urgull** is criss-crossed by winding footpaths to the top. From the mammoth figure of Christ on its summit there are great views out to sea and back across the bay to the town. Still better views across the bay can be had from the top of **Monte Igüeldo**; take bus #16 or walk around the bay to its base, from where a **funicular** (daily: July & Aug 10am–10pm; Sept–June 11am–6/8pm; closed Wed in winter; €1.60 return) will carry you to the summit, the home of a **funfair** (€1.30). **La Concha** beach is the most central and the most celebrated, a wide crescent of yellow sand stretching round the bay from the town. Out in La Concha bay is a small island, **Isla de Santa Clara**, which makes a good spot for picnics; a boat leaves from the Paseo Mollaberria (July & Aug 10am–8.30pm, every 30min; Sept–June 10am–8pm, hourly; €2.60). **Ondaretta**, considered the best beach for swimming and never quite as packed as La Concha, is a continuation of the same strand beyond the rocky outcrop that supports the **Palacio Miramar** (gardens open 9/10am–sunset; free), once a summer home of Spain's royal family. The atmosphere here is rather more staid – it's known as *La Diplomática* for the number of Madrid's "best" families who holiday here. Far less crowded, and popular with surfers, **Playa de Zurriola** and the adjacent **Playa de Gros** have breakwaters to shield them from dangerous currents. Should you tire of sun and antiquity, head for the sparkling conference and cultural centre, the **Palacio Kursaal** (guided tours Mon–Fri at 1.30pm, Sat & Sun 11.30am, 12.30pm & 1.30pm; €3) on Avenida de Zurriola. Designed by Rafael Moneo, and set on the banks of the River Urumea by Playa de Zurriola, the building consists of two translucent glass cubes not dissimilar to Japanese lanterns – an elegant sight at night.

## Practicalities

National **buses** use the terminal at Plaza Pío XII, twenty minutes' walk inland along the river (tickets can be bought from the terminal or the respective bus company offices around the city centre), while regional ones go from either Plaza de Guipúzcoa or Estación Amara. The main-line **train station** is across the River Urumea on Paseo de Francia, although local lines to Hendaye and Bilbao (rail passes not valid) have their terminus on c/Easo. The **tourist office**, at c/Reina Regente 3 in the old town (June–Sept daily 8am–8pm; Sept–June Mon–Sat 9am–1.30pm & 3.30–7pm, Sun 10am–2pm; ☎943 481 166, ❽www.sansebastianturismo .com), is very helpful in finding a place to stay, or use the **online reservations service** at ❽www.paisvasco.com/centralreservas.

   **Accommodation**, though plentiful, is not cheap and can be very hard to come by in season and at weekends. In the old town, look around La Consti and c/San Jerónimo; in the central district there's better value around the cathedral, especially calles Easo, San Martín and San Bartolomé; or on the other side of the river try behind the Plaza de Cataluña, where you'll also find excellent tapas bars. *Pension Amaiur*, c/de Agosto 31 (☎943 429 654, ❽www.pensionamaiur.com; ❸), is a good-value budget choice with a kitchen and Internet access: alternatively, try *Pensión Anne*, c/Esterlines 15  (☎943 421 438, ❽www.pensionanne.com; ❹) in a pedestrianized area; *Pensión La Perla*, c/Loyola 10 (☎943 428 123; ❹); or *Pensión San Martín*, c/San Martín 10 (☎943 428 714; ❹). *La Sirena* **hostel** (☎943 310 268, ❽www.paisvasco.com/albergues; €10.44 for under 26s, or €12 for over 26s) is out of the centre on Paseo de Igüeldo, just a few minutes' walk back from the end of Ondarreta beach.

   San Sebastián has some of the best **restaurants** in the country, with top-quality seafood a speciality. Prices reflect the popularity of the area, especially in the waterside restaurants, but it's no hardship to survive on the delicious **tapas**, which are laid out in all but the fanciest bars – check the prices first, but around €1.20 per *pintxo* is the norm. *Gaztelu*, c/31 de Agosto 22, is worth a try for well-priced *raciones*, as is *Beti-Jai*, on c/Narrika, in the old town. Alternatively, there are good fixed-price menus at *Ardandegi*, c/Reyes Católicos 7, *La Barranquesa*, c/Larramendi 21, or *Morgan* on c/Narrika Kalea.

   The fanciest **bars and clubs** are along the promenade by the beach, Paseo de la Concha, and charge €12–18 to get in; the cheaper places are mostly in the old town where people normally start the evening off – later everyone heads to the area along c/Reyes Católicos behind the cathedral or c/San Bartolomé. For late nights, head for *Etxekalte* at c/Mari Kalea 11, overlooking the port and beach, where a young clientele grooves to jazz, urban soul and hip-hop (free entry). A recent addition to San Sebastián's night scene are "growshops", a blend of Amsterdam café, art gallery and bar – *Soma 107*, on c/Larramendi 4, is one of the best.

# Bilbao

Although traditionally an industrial city, **BILBAO** (Bilbo) has given itself a makeover and is now a priority destination on any Spanish tour. And no surprise: a state-of-the-art metro (designed by Britain's Lord Foster) links the city's widespread attractions; the breathtaking Guggenheim Museum by Frank Gehry – along with Jeff Koons' puppy sculpture in flowers – is a major draw; the airport and one of the many dramatic river bridges are Calatrava-designed; and there are various bids to further develop the riverfront with university buildings and public parks. The city's vibrant, friendly atmosphere, elegant green spaces and some of the best cafés, restaurants and bars in Euskadi, combine to make Bilbao an appealing destination.

The **Casco Viejo**, the old quarter on the east bank of the river, is focused on the beautiful **Teatro Arriag**, the elegantly arcaded **Plaza Nueva**, the fourteenth-century Gothic **Catedral de Santiago** (Tues–Sat 10am–1.30pm & 4pm–7pm, Sun 10.30am–1.30pm; free), and the interesting **Basque Museum** on Plaza Miguel de Unamuno 4 (Tues–Sat 11am–5pm, Sun 11am–2pm; €3). However, it is along the Río Nervión that a whole number of exciting new buildings have appeared. A good route leads from the Casco Viejo down the river past the Campo Volantín footbridge and the more imposing Zubizuri bridge to the sensual, billowing titanium curves of the **Guggenheim Museum** (daily 10am–8pm; Sept–June closed Mon; ⓦwww.guggenheim-bilbao.es; €10), described as "the greatest building of our time" by architect Philip Johnson. The building and exterior sculptures are arguably more of an attraction than most of the art inside: the permanent collection, which includes works by Kandinsky, Klee, Mondrian, Picasso, Chagall and Warhol, to name a few, is housed in traditional galleries; temporary exhibitions and individual artists' collections are displayed in the huge sculpted spaces nearer the river. Further along from the Guggenheim, on the edge of the Parque de Doña Casilda de Hurriza, is the **Museo de Bellas Artes** (Tues–Sat 10am–8pm, Sun 10am–2pm; ☎944 396 060; €4.50, combined ticket with the Guggenheim €11; free on Wed), which houses works by Goya and El Greco and some fine temporary exhibitions.

## Practicalities

The FEVE and RENFE **train stations** are located just over the river from the Casco Viejo, while most **buses** arrive some way out of the centre at Estación Termibús in San Mamés – from here catch the metro to the centre or walk (twenty minutes). From the **airport**, (☎944 869 664) a bus (daily 6am–10pm, every 30min; €1) runs to Plaza Moyua in the centre. The main **tourist office** is at c/Rodriguez Arias 3 (Mon–Fri 9am–2pm & 4–7.30pm; ☎944 795 760, ⓦwww.bilbao.net), with branches in the basement of the Teatro Arriag, at Plaza Arriaga 1 (Mon–Fri 9am–2pm & 4–7.30pm, Sun 9.30am–2pm), and outside the Guggenheim (July & Aug 10am–3pm & 4–7pm, Sun 10am–3pm; Sept–June Tues–Sat 11am–2.30pm & 3.30pm–6pm, Sun 11am–2pm.). There's **Internet** access at Laser, c/Sendaja 31.

The best place for **accommodation** is the Casco Viejo – especially along and around the streets leading off c/Bidebarrieta, which leads from Plaza Arriaga to the cathedral. In summer and at weekends, booking ahead is advisable. Good possibilities include the friendly and helpful *Hostal Gurea*, c/Bidebarrieta 14 (☎944 163 299; ❸), *pensiones Ladero*, c/Lotería 1 (☎944 150 932; ❸), and *Mendez*, c/Santa Maria 13; ☎944 160 364; ❸), where some rooms have balconies; *Pensión Serantes*, c/Somera 14 (☎944 151 557; ❷); and *Iturrianea Ostatua*, c/Santa Maria (☎944 161 500. ❹).

**Eating and drinking** are also good in Casco Viejo, where the most enjoyable way to eat is to move from bar to bar, snacking on *pintxos*: Plaza Nueva and the area known as the *siete calles* have numerous options, including *Café Boulevard*, Paseo del Arenal, for great breakfasts, and the Moorish-style *Café Iruña*, c/Jardines de Albia 5, for mid-afternoon coffee. For a sit-down meal, there's the highly recommended Basque restaurant *Bar Rio-Oja*, c/Perro 4, just west of the cathedral. Bilbao can be very lively indeed at night, with the streets around c/Licenciado Poza and c/Ledesma harbouring a clutch of buzzy **bars**. The whole city goes totally wild during the August **fiesta and** bullfighting extravaganza, *La Semana Grande* (from first Sat after Aug 15), with scores of open-air bars, live music and impromptu dancing.

29

# Picos de Europa National Park

The **Picos de Europa** offer some of the finest hiking, canoeing and other mountain activities in Spain. The densely forested national park boasts two glacial lakes, a series of peaks over 2400m high, and wildlife including otters and bears. From Santander, about 80km to the east, the park is reached by passing through San Vicente de la Barquera, Unquera and Cares; alternative access is from Oviedo in the south, a spectacular drive of 80km along winding, narrow roads. **CANGAS DE ONÍS**, a major gateway to the park, has a helpful **tourist office** (June–Sept daily 10am–10pm; Oct–May Mon–Sat 10am–2pm & 4–7pm; ☎985 848 005, ⊛www .picosdeeuropa.com) and **accommodation**, at *Hospedaje Torreón* (☎985 848 211, ⊛www.iespana.es/pensiontorreon; ❸). There's also a **campsite** at Soto de Cangas, 3.5km west (☎985 940 097), and a private **hostel**, *Albergue La Posada del Monasterio* (☎985 848 553, ⊛www.posadadelmonasterio.com), offering dorms (€14) and private rooms (❷), in an atmospheric old monastery in La Vega-Villanueva, 2km northwest of Cangas de Onís; the management organizes canoeing, hiking and other activities in the park. Alternatively, you can stay at **COVADONGA** in the park at the *Hospedería del Peregrino* (☎985 846 047, ⊛www.picosdeeuropa.com /incatur/elperegrino; ❸).

# Santiago de Compostela

**SANTIAGO DE COMPOSTELA**, built in a warm golden granite, is one of the most beautiful of all Spanish cities. The whole of this medieval place has been declared a national monument and it remains remarkably uniform in its charm, the more so for being almost wholly pedestrianized. The **pilgrimage to Santiago** (see box opposite) captured the imagination of medieval Christian Europe on an unprecedented scale; during the eleventh and twelfth centuries, when the city was at the height of its popularity, it received half a million pilgrims each year. People of all social backgrounds came to visit the supposed shrine of St James the Apostle (Santiago to the Spanish), making this the third-holiest site in Christendom, after Jerusalem and Rome. These days, tourists are as likely to be attracted by art and history as by religion, but the all-round atmosphere of the place must not be dissimilar to that of the pilgrim days. Once host to kings and all manner of society, Santiago is by no means a dead city now – it's the seat of Galicia's regional government, and houses a great contemporary art gallery and a large student population. It's also a manageable size – fifteen minutes' walk from the centre, you're in open countryside.

All roads lead to the **cathedral** (daily 7.30am–9pm, visits allowed outside Mass), whose sheer grandeur you first appreciate upon venturing into the vast expanse of the Praza do Obradoiro. Directly ahead stands a fantastic Baroque pyramid of granite, flanked by immense bell towers and everywhere adorned with statues of St James in his familiar pilgrim guise with staff, broad hat and scallop-shell badge. This Obradoiro facade was built in the mid-eighteenth century by an obscure Santiago-born architect, Fernando Casas y Novoa, and no other work of Spanish Baroque can compare with it. The building's highlight is the **Pórtico de Gloria**, the original west front, which now stands inside the cathedral behind the Obradoiro. So many millions have pressed their fingers into the roots of the *Tree of Jesse* below the saint that five deep and shiny holes have been worn into the solid marble. The spiritual climax of the pilgrimage was the approach to the **High Altar**. This remains a peculiar experience: you climb steps behind the altar, embrace the Most Sacred Image of Santiago, kiss his bejewelled cape, and are handed, by way of certification, a document in Latin called a *Compostela*. The statue has stood there for seven centuries and the procedure is quite unchanged. The elaborate pulley system in front of the altar is for moving the immense incense-burner – *El Botafumeiro* – which, operated by eight priests, is swung in a vast ceiling-to-ceiling arc across

## The Camino de Santiago

The most famous Christian pilgrimage in the world, the **Camino de Santiago** – or Way of St James – traces routes through France and Spain to Santiago de Compostela. If you're travelling in this part of the world, you will doubtless see many pilgrims, identified – mainly to each other – by the coquille St Jacques, a large effigy of a scallop shell, that they wear attached to their backpack. "Santiago de Compostela" comes from the Latin meaning "St James of the Field of Stars"; it's named after a peasant who had a vision in a field of stars near where the town now lies; soon after, the Catholic Church miraculously discovered that the disciple James had been buried in that very spot. There are those that scoff at the notion that James was ever in Spain, never mind buried here; some see it as an early church PR exercise to garner some enthusiasm against the Moors. Whether you believe or not, the reality is that millions *do* – if not in the legend, at least in the physical and mental challenge of a pilgrimage on foot. Should you be interested in walking, cycling or taking the train, check ⊛www.xacobeo.es.

the transept. It is stunning to watch, but takes place only during certain festival services – check with the tourist office. You can also visit the treasury, archeological museum, cloisters and crypt (daily 10.30am–1.30pm & 4–6.30/8pm, closed Aug; €5).

The enormous Benedictine **San Martín Pinario monastery** stands close to the cathedral, the vast altarpiece in its church depicting its patron riding alongside St James. Nearby is **San Francisco**, reputedly founded by the saint himself during his pilgrimage to Santiago. In the north of the city are Baroque **Santa Clara**, with a unique curving facade, and a little beyond it, **Santo Domingo**. This last is perhaps the most interesting of the buildings, featuring a magnificent seventeenth-century triple stairway, each spiral leading to a different storey of a single tower, and a fascinating museum of Gallego crafts and traditions, the **Museo do Pobo Gallego** (Tues–Sat 10am–2pm & 4–8pm, Sun 11am–2pm; free). A symbol of Santiago's enduring creativity and charm lies just next door, in the **Centro Galego de Arte Contemporánea** (Tues–Sun 11am–8pm; free), a beautiful gallery designed by Portuguese architect Álvaro Siza and host to a revolving triumvirate of challenging visiting exhibitions.

### Practicalities

Arriving at Santiago **bus station** you're 1km or so north of the town centre; bus #10 runs to Praza Galicia at the southern edge of the old city. The **train station** is a walkable distance south of the plaza along Rúa do Horreo. The **airport**, 12 km northeast of town (☎981 547 501, ⊛www.aena.es), is linked to the centre by hourly buses (€1.55). The **tourist office** is at Rúa do Vilar 63 (daily: summer 9am–9pm; winter 10am–3pm & 4–7pm; ☎981 555 129, ⊛www.santiagoturismo .com), and there's **Internet access** at Cibernova, Rúa Nova 50.

You should have no difficulty finding inexpensive **accommodation**, but note that *pensiones* here are often called *hospedajes*. The biggest concentration of places is on the three parallel streets leading down from the cathedral, Rúa Nova Rúa do, Rúa do Vilar and Rúa do Franco, with *Hostal Barbantes II*, Rúa do Franco 3 (☎981 576 520; ❹) having a lively bar and restaurant. *Residencia La Estela*, Rúa de. Raxoi 1 (☎981 582 796; ❸), is in a great position on the corner of Praza do Obradoiro, or try *Hospedaje Viño*, Praza de Mazarelos 7 (☎981 585 185; ❷), whose owner also has dozens of other rooms across town. *Hostal Costavella*, Rúa Porta da Pena 17 (☎981 569 530, ⊛www.costavella.com; ❺) is more upmarket with fourteen attractive rooms and a tranquil garden. There's a **pilgrim refuge** at Avda. Quiroga Palacios 2a (☎981 589 200; €5), though you can only stay for one night, or a **hostel** with good facilities, 3km out of town at Monte de Gozo (☎981 558 942; €7 if under 30, otherwise €11) – take bus #C1, #6 or #7 from Praza Galicia. The excellent

**campsite** *As Cancelas* (℡981 580 266) is 2.5km north of the cathedral; take city bus #4 or #6.

Thanks, perhaps, to the students, there are plenty of cheap **restaurants** and excellent bars; it's also the best place in Galicia to hear local Breton-style music, played on *gaitas* (bagpipes). Seafood and fish are good at *Bodegón de Xulio*, Rúa do Franco 24, and there are good **tapas bars** nearby, such as *Tacita de Juan* at Rúa do Horreo 31, and the gorgeous green-tiled and mirrored *Cafetería Paradíso*, Rúa do Vilar 29, where you'll even get a few tapas for free. Good **bars** include the inebriated *El Retablo* at Rúa Nova 13, the alternative *Bar Tolo* on Fonte de San Miguel, or the popular *A Reixa* at Tras de Salomé 3.

# The Pyrenees

With the singular exception of **Pamplona** at the time of its bull-running fiesta, the area around the Spanish Pyrenees is little visited – most people who come here at all travel straight through. In doing so they miss out on some of the most wonderful scenery in Spain, and some of the country's most attractive trekking. You'll also be struck by the slower pace of life, especially in **Navarra** (in the west, a partly Basque region) and **Aragón** (in the centre); the Catalan Pyrenees (for which, see p.945) are more developed. There are few cities here – Pamplona itself and **Zaragoza**, with its fine Moorish architecture, are the only large centres – but there are plenty of attractive small towns and, of course, the mountains themselves, with several beautiful **national parks** as a focus for exploration.

## Pamplona

**PAMPLONA** (Iruña) has been the capital of Navarra since the ninth century, and long before that was a powerful fortress town defending the northern approaches to Spain. Even now it has something of the appearance of a garrison city, with its hefty walls and elaborate pentagonal citadel. The compact and lively streets of the old town offer plenty to look at – the elaborately restored **cathedral** with its magnificent cloister and interesting **Museo Diocesano** (Mon–Sat 10am–1.30pm & 4–7pm; June–Sept 10am-7pm; €3), the colossal **city walls** and **citadel**, the display of regional archeology, history and art in the **Museo de Navarra** (Tues–Sat 9.30am–2pm & 5–7pm, Sun 11am–2pm; €2, free Sat pm & all Sun; ⓦwww.cfnavarra.es/cultura/museo), and much more – but most visitors come here for just one thing: the thrilling week of the Fiestas de San Fermín (see box opposite).

The **train station** (℡948 130 202) is 2.5km from the old part of town, but bus #9 runs every fifteen minutes to the end of Paseo de Sarasate, a few minutes' walk from the central Plaza del Castillo – there is a RENFE ticket office at c/Estella 8. The **bus station** is on c/Conde Oliveto in front of the citadel, while the **tourist office** (Mon–Sat 10am–2pm & 4–7pm, Sun 10am–2pm; ℡848 420 420, ⓦwww .navarra.es) is at c/Eslava 1, on Plaza San Francisco.

**Rooms** are in short supply during summer, and at fiesta time you've virtually no chance of a place without booking. As most hotels at least double their prices during San Fermín, you may be better off staying in San Sebastián or other nearby towns and travelling to Pamplona in the evening to enjoy the night-long festivities and early morning running of the bulls. Outside fiesta time, good options are the *Hostal Otano*, c/San Nicolás 5 (℡948 227 036; ❹), or *Hostal Arriazu*, c/Comedias 14 (℡948 210 202; ⓦwww.hostalarriazu.com; ❹), next to Plaza del Castillo. The *Ezcaba* **campsite**, ℡948 330 315; bus #4), is 7km out of town on the road to France, but fills several days before the fiesta. If you end up **sleeping rough**, remember that there is safety in numbers – head for one of the many parks such as Vuelta del Castillo or Media Luna and bring a sleeping bag, as the nights are cool. For a hot shower or bath, there are **public baths** at c/Eslava (Tues–Sat 8.30am–8pm, Sun 8.30am–1pm).

Pamplona's nightlife scene is one of the most boisterously cheerful in Spain; best **bars** are on and around c/San Nicolás, and during San Fermín on c/Jarauta and c/San Lorenzo too, as well as a number of grungy late-night dives on Calderia S. Augustín on the other side of the square. Food is expensive in Pamplona and you'll be hard pressed to find a set menu for less than €8. C/San Nicolás has several reasonable **restaurants** including *Dom Lluis* at no.1 and the excellent vegetarian *Sarasate* at no.19. Alternatively, there's *Erburu*, c/San Lorenzo 19, something of a local institution, or *El Mesón del Navarrería*, c/Navarrería 15, serving massive baguettes. For tapas, head to *Café Roch*, c/Comedias, or *Bar Mesón Caballo Blanco*, c/Redin, up above the ramparts behind the cathedral. The elegant *Café Iruña*, on Plaza del Castillo, is the place to sit over a leisurely coffee.

# Zaragoza

**ZARAGOZA** is the capital of Aragón, and easily its largest and liveliest city, with over half the province's one million people and the majority of its industry. There are some excellent bars and restaurants tucked in among its remarkable monuments, and it's also a handy transport centre, with good connections into the Pyrenees and east towards Barcelona. Try and be here for **Semana Santa** – the week before Easter – for the spectacular street processions. Zaragoza's highlight, which you should see even if you plan to do no more than change trains or buses, is the city's only surviving legacy from Moorish times. From the tenth to the eleventh century this was the centre of an independent dynasty, the Beni Kasim. Their palace, the **Aljafería** (Mon–Wed & Sat 10am–2pm & 4.30–6.30/8pm, Fri 4.30–6.30/8pm, Sun 10am–2pm; €4), surrounded by moat and gardens, was built in the heyday of their rule in the mid-eleventh century, and thus predates the Alhambra in Granada as well as Seville's Alcázar. From the original design the foremost relic is a tiny and beautiful mosque adjacent to the ticket office.

Further on is an intricately decorated court, the Patio de Santa Isabella. Crossing from here, the Grand Staircase (added in 1492) leads to a succession of rooms remarkable chiefly for their carved ceilings. The most imposing of the city's churches, majestically fronting the Río Ebro, is the **Basilica de Nuestra Señora del Pilar** (daily 5.45am–8.30/9.30pm), one of Zaragoza's two cathedrals. It takes its name from the column that the Virgin is said to have brought from Jerusalem during her lifetime to found the first Marian chapel in Christendom. Topped by a diminutive image of the Virgin, the pillar forms the centrepiece of the Holy Chapel and is the focal point for pilgrims, who line up to kiss an exposed section encased in a silver sheath. However, in terms of beauty the basilica can't compare with the nearby Gothic-Mudéjar old cathedral, **San Salvador**, or La Seo (Tues–Fri 10am–2pm & 4–7pm, Sat & Sun 10am–noon/1pm & 4–6/7pm; Oct–June closed Sun; €2), at the far end of the pigeon-thronged Plaza del Pilar. Just south of the cathedral, at c/Espoz y Mina 23, lies the wonderful **Museo Camón Aznar** (Tues–Fri 9am–2.15pm & 6–9pm, Sat 10am–2pm & 6–9pm, Sun 11am–2pm; €1), housed in a sixteenth-century building and an absolute must for Goya fans. The city has recently been bringing to light its Roman past in several underground excavations: the **Forum** and **river port** (just off the Plaza del Pilar) and the **Roman Baths** (all Tues–Sat 10am–2pm & 5–8pm, Sun 10am–2pm; €2) and the **amphitheatre** in c/Verónica (Tues–Sat 10am–9pm, Sun 10am–2pm; €3.25). You can visit all of them with a combined ticket (€7). Following the semicircle of c/Coso and c/Cesar Augusto, the **Roman walls** are steadily being excavated; best place to view them is at c/Echegaray at the junction with c/Coso, where remains of towers and ramparts can be seen.

### Practicalities

Zaragoza's stunning modern **train station**, Intermodal Delicias, serving all destinations, including the new high-speed AVE line to Madrid, is on Avda Navarra, about a 30-minute walk to the centre, or take bus #51 (every 10min). Most local and national **bus** services use the Agreda terminal at Paseo María Agustín 7 (a ten-minute walk along Avda. Cesar Augusto to the centre). The main **tourist office** is in Plaza del Pilar (daily 10am–8pm; ☏976 393 537, ⓦwww.turismozaragoza.com), with another at the Torreón de la Zuda (daily 10am–2pm & 4.30pm-8pm; ☏976 201 200) – part of the city fortifications overlooking the river.

There are **rooms** – and some cheap restaurants – in the streets off c/Madre Sacramento, parallel to Paseo María Agustín, with *Pensión Miramar*, c/Capitán Casado 17 (☏976 281 094; ❻) better than most. However, there's more atmosphere in the area known as El Tubo, between c/de Alfonso I and c/de Don Jaime I, close to Plaza del Pilar, with good bets here including *Pensión Peñafiel*, c/Méndez Núñez 38 (☏976 299 712; ❸) and *El Borjano* at c/Estébanes 4 (☏976 394 875; ❷). The HI **hostel** is out of the centre on c/Franco y Lopez 4 (☏976 306 692; under 25s €10, over 25s €13; hostel cards required; bus #22). For **food** in El Tubo, try the atmospheric *Casa Lac* on c/Mártires, supposedly the oldest restaurant in Spain and not too costly, or *La Tasquilla de Pedro*, c/Cinegio 3, for tapas. Alternatively, *Casa Dominó*, on Plaza Santa Marta, serves over 200 types of tapas, while *El Fuelle* on c/Mayor near Plaza del Pilar, is a good bet.

## Jaca

Heading towards the Pyrenees from Zaragoza, **JACA** is Aragon's northernmost significant town and a principal base for exploring the Aragonese Pyrenees. It's also a place of considerable interest – an early capital of the kingdom of Aragón that lay astride one of the main medieval pilgrim routes to Santiago. Accordingly, a magnificent **cathedral** (daily 11am–1pm & 4–8pm), the first in Spain to be built in the Romanesque style, dominates the town centre from its position at the north edge of the old quarter. It remains impressive despite much internal remodelling over the centuries, and there's a powerful added attraction in its **Museo Diocesano** (Easter–Sept daily 10am–1.30/2pm & 4–7/8pm; Oct–Easter Tues–Sun 11am–1.30pm & 4–7pm; €2). The shady cloisters are home to a collection of beautiful Romanesque and Gothic religious sculpture and frescoes, gathered from village churches in the area and from higher up in the Pyrenees. As well as being a popular Pyrenean ski resort (800m), Jaca is primarily an army town, with recruits attending the local mountain warfare academy. The military connection is nothing new: the **Ciudadela**, a sixteenth-century fort built to the stellar ground plan in vogue at the time, still offers good views of surrounding peaks. You can visit parts of the interior (daily: April–June & Sept–Oct 11am–12.30pm & 5–6.30pm; July–Aug 11am–noon & 6–8pm; Nov–March 11am–noon & 4–5pm; €4) on a guided tour only – though, frankly, the exterior is far more compelling.

Arriving in Jaca by **train**, you'll find yourself 1km or so north of centre; an urban shuttle bus takes you to the **bus station** on Avda. Jacetania, 200m northwest of the cathedral. The **tourist office** (summer Mon–Fri 9am–2pm & 4.30–8pm, Sat 9am–1.30pm & 5–8pm, Sun 10am–1.30pm; winter Mon–Fri 9am–1.30pm & 4.30–7pm, Sat 10am–1pm & 5–7pm; ☎974 360 098, ⓦwww.aytojaca.es) is on Avda. Regimiento de Galicia, just downhill from the Ciudadela, and stocks a range of leaflets on outdoor activities and cultural events.

Jaca's **accommodation** prices are pushed up by the ski- and cross-border trade, and reservations are advisable in August and during winter. All the budget options are in the northern half of the old town: two good clean, quiet options are *Hostal Paris*, Plaza de San Pedro 5 (☎974 361 010, ⓦwww.jaca.com/hostalparis; ❷) and *Hostal Somport*, Echegaray 11 (☎ & ☎974 363 410; ❸). There's also a **hostel** on Avda.Perimetral (☎973 369 536; dorm-beds €14; doubles ❶), next to the ice rink. There are two **campsites**, the basic *Victoria Camping* (☎974 360 323), 1.5km west of town on the Pamplona road, and *Pena Oroel Camping* (☎974 360 215; Easter and summer only), 3km down the Sabiñanigo road. As for **restaurants**, *Mesón Corbacho*, c/Ramiro Primero 2, has decent set menus, while *El Arco*, c/San Nicolas 4 (closed Sun off-season) is a good option for vegetarians. If you want to splash out, *Mesón Cobarcho*, c/Ramiro 1, is full of character for a special occasion.

# The Aragonese Pyrenees

If you're not a keen trekker or skier, then the foothill villages of **ANSÓ** and **ECHO** (formerly "Hecho") set in their beautiful namesake valleys are your best target in the **Aragonese Pyrenees**: they're noted for their distinctive, imposing architecture, and are accessible by bus from Jaca (Mon–Sat 6.30pm), returning early in the morning (Ansó 6am; Echo 6.45am). There are summer-only **tourist offices** in both villages: on c/Santa Bárbara in Ansó (☎974 370 210, ⓦwww.pyreneesguide.com), and Plaza del Conde Xiquena 1, Echo (☎974 375 329). Echo, to the east, is more visited, with a wider range of **accommodation** and **food**: try *Casa Chuanet* (☎974 375 033; ❸) above *Bar Danubio* on the west side of town; *Bar Subordán* on Plaza Palacio de la Fuente is the place for excellent, affordable snacks. There's also a delightful **campsite**, *Valle de Echo* (☎974 375 361), and an *albergue* in the village of **SIRESA**, 4km north (☎974 375 385, ⓔalbsiresa@arrakis.es; €10). In the westerly valley, less-frequented Ansó offers several reasonable places to stay and eat, including *Hostal Restaurante Aisa*, on Plaza Domingo Miral (☎974 370 009; ❷), and another riverside, summer-only **campsite** (☎974 370 003), next to the swimming pool. For meat-oriented **meals**, try *Kimboa*, at the north edge of the village.

Worthwhile targets for a winter visit to alpine Aragón are the adjacent ski resorts of **ASTÚN** and **CANDANCHU**, north of Jaca, which are easily reached by bus. If your budget is limited and/or you're primarily interested in skiing, then either of two *albergues* should suit – the highly rated *El Aguila* (☎974 373 291; closed

May, June & Sept–Nov; €11–16), or *Valle de Aragón* (☎974 373 222; €12–17), with half-board offered at both.

For summertime walking, there's no better destination than the **Parque Nacional de Ordesa**, focused on a vast, trough-like valley flanked by imposingly striated limestone palisades. The bus (Mon–Sat 10.15am) from Jaca reaches **Sabiñánigo** in time to connect with a year-round 11am onward service (also July & Aug Mon–Sat at 6.30pm; Sept–June Fri & Sun at 5.30pm) to Torla, the best base for the park (see below). Approaching Sabiñánigo by bus or train from Zaragoza, you'll need departures before 8.30am and 7.15am respectively to make the 11am connection. From Torla, a regular shuttle bus services covers the 5km further **into the park**, but trekkers should opt instead for the lovely trail (1hr 30min) on the far side of the river, well marked as the GR15.2. Further **treks** can be as gentle or as strenuous as you like, the most popular outing being an all-day trip to the **Circo de Soaso** waterfalls. For detailed information on the park, contact either Torla's tourist office (summer only Mon–Fri 10am–1pm & 6–8pm, Sat & Sun 9.30am–1.30pm & 5–8.30pm; ☎974 229 804) or the park's **Centro de Visitantes**, 3km north above the Puente de los Navarros (☎974 486 472, @pnomp.torla@terra.es).

**TORLA** itself, a formerly sleepy, stone-built village, has been overwhelmed in its contemporary role as gateway to the park, though older corners are still visually attractive. Don't hope for a **room** or refuge bed from mid-July to late August, without reserving well in advance – even the three **campsites**, *San Antón* (☎974 486 063), *Río Ara* (☎974 486 248), and *Ordesa* (☎974 486 146), strung out between 1km and 3km north, often fill up. At other times of the year you can usually find space at the central *Hostal Alto Aragón* (☎974 486 172; ❸); otherwise try the *Refugio Lucien Briet* (☎974 486 221, @www.ordesa.net/refugio-lucienbriet; dorm-beds €8.50, doubles ❸) or the 21-place *Refugio L'Atalaya* (☎974 486 022; €10), both in the village centre. Both the hostal and the *Bar Brecha*, at *Lucien Briet*, serve good-value **meals**.

**BENASQUE** – several valleys east of Torla, and cradled between the two highest summits in the Pyrenees – serves as another favourite jump-off point for mountain rambles. There is a regular bus service from Barbastro (daily at 11am, Mon–Sat at 5.20pm), which tends to wait for arriving services from Jaca and Zaragoza, and there's a marginally better chance of finding a bed here during high season, although hotels usually demand a minimum five-night stay. The **tourist office** is at c/San Sebastián 5 (daily 9/10am–2pm & 4/5–9pm; ☎974 551 289, @www.turismobenasque.com), dispensing pamphlets on local walks as well as information about local activities. For **accommodation**, try *La Fonda de Vescelia*, c/Mayor 5 (☎974 551 654, @vescelia@terra.es; dorm-beds €23, doubles ❺), which also serves cheap meals, or *Hostal Valero* (☎974 551 061, @www.hoteles-valero.com; ❸), on Ctra. Anciles. Decent hearty **food** can be found at *Bar Bardanca*, c/Las Plazas 6, or the slightly livelier, pricer *Bar Sayó* on c/Mayor 13.

# Catalonia (Catalunya)

With its own language, culture and, to a degree, government, **Catalonia** (Cataluña in Castilian Spanish, Catalunya in Catalan) has a unique identity. **Barcelona**, the capital, is very much the main event, one of the most vibrant and exciting cities in Europe. Inland, the monastery of **Montserrat**, Catalonia's premier "sight", is perched on one of the most unusual rock formations in Spain, while the **Catalan Pyrenees**, though more developed than their western neighbours, are easier to access and breathtaking nonetheless. The coast immediately either side of Barcelona is rather plain, with the exception of the Modernist buildings and gay nightlife of **Sitges**, a thirty-minute train ride southwest. Further north, the rugged **Costa**

**Brava** is slowly shedding its erstwhile unfortunate image and boasts the best beaches in the region. Since the use of the Catalan language is so widespread, we've used Catalan spellings, with Castilian equivalents in parentheses. **Hostels** can be booked online or by a central reservations phone service (Ⓣ934 838 363, Ⓦwww.tujuca.com).

## The Catalan Pyrenees

The **Catalan Pyrenees**, every bit as spectacular as their Aragonese neighbours, have been exploited for far longer. While this has resulted in numerous less-than-aesthetic ski resorts and hydroelectric projects, it also means good public transport and a well-developed tourism infrastructure. In the less frequented corners, such as the westerly **Parc Nacional**, the scenery is the equal of any in Europe, while even the touristy train ride up to **Núria** to the east rarely fails to impress.

### The Parc Nacional

After Ordesa, the most popular target of trekkers in the Pyrenees is the **Parc Nacional d'Aigüestortes i Estany de Sant Maurici**, covering nearly 200 square kilometres of forest, lakes and cirques, presided over by 3000-metre snow-capped peaks. For the less adventurous, there are lower-altitude tracks through fine scenery and visits to several villages around the park. For more information about outdoor activities, contact the **Park Information Offices** at the edge of Boí (April–Oct daily 9am–1pm & 3.30–6.45pm, Nov–March Mon–Sat 9am–2pm & 3.30–6pm, Sun 9am–2pm; Ⓣ973 696 189), or in central Espot (same hours; Ⓣ973 624 036). The main access towns are **La Pobla de Segur**, reached by train from Barcelona, and **El Pont de Suert**, a two-hour bus ride northwest from La Pobla. The best bases, however, are Boí, Taüll and Espot, 60km north of La Pobla and, west and east of the park boundaries respectively, with Capdella to the south a less busy alternative; all are set in their own gorgeous valleys. **BOÍ** is just off the main road up to the Viella tunnel, served by daily bus from La Pobla via El Pont de Suert. In the town itself, the tiny old quarter is dwarfed by modern construction, and tourism facilities are expensive. Exceptions include *Pensión Pascual* (Ⓣ973 696 014; ❸) down by the bridge, with *Casa Higinio*, 200m up the road to Taüll, being the best place to **eat**. You may have more luck, however, in the handsome neighbouring village of **TAÜLL**, 3km uphill to the east. It has a friendly **pension** – *Sant Climent*, c/Les Feixes 8 (Ⓣ973 696 052; ❸), and an attractive **campsite** (Ⓣ973 696 174). The village of **CAPDELLA** is served by just three buses a week from La Pobla, but if you stay at the well-run *Refugio Tacita*, just above the village (Ⓣ973 663 121; Ⓦwww.tacitahostel.com; €15; Jan–May Sat & Sun only), the owners will pick you up from La Pobla. Within the park itself, camping is forbidden and accommodation is limited to five **mountain refuges** (€13–14), with seven more just outside the boundaries – you can reserve space at nine of them on the website Ⓦwww.carrosdefoc.com, which also gives details on the trails between them – you rarely have to walk for more than four hours between huts.

### Núria and beyond

For a beautiful but easy way to see the Pyrenees, look no further than the rack-and-pinion rail line up to the cirque and shrine at **NÚRIA**. After a leisurely start from Ribes de Freser (see p.946), the tiny two-carriage train lurches up into the mountains, following a river between great crags. Once through a final tunnel, the train emerges alongside a small lake, at the other side of which is a giant building combining church, café, ski centre and the *Hotel Vall de Núria* (Ⓣ972 732 000; ❼ half-board; two nights minimum). There's also a basic **campsite** behind the hotel (pay in advance at the tourist office; Ⓣ972 732 020), plus a **hostel**, *Pic de l'Àliga* (Ⓣ972 732 048; €15.50), at the end of the cable car. You'll need good equipment, even in summer, since it gets cold at night. For **food**, *Bar Finestrelles* serves hot snacks and breakfast, or there's self-service place for lunch only, and the pricier dining room at the *Vall de Núria*.

The privately owned **Núria train** (☎972 732 020, ⊛www.valldenuria.com) runs year-round except Nov, from Ribes-Enllaç, via Ribes de Freser and Queralbs village, where there are also places **to stay**, such as the *Porta de Núria* (☎972 727 137; ❸) in Ribes de Freser. Trains from Barcelona connect with the Núria train at Ribes-Enllaç. Mainline trains continue to Puigcerdà, on the French frontier – the only surviving rail link over the Pyrenees to France. Four trains a day currently leave for La Tour de Carol, 3km over the border, but if you miss them it's easy enough to walk a slightly shorter distance east to Bourg-Madame, the actual border town. **PUIGCERDÀ** is cheaper than anywhere in France, should schedules compel an **overnight stay**: try the friendly, newly refurbished *Pensió Maria Belvedere*, c/Carmelites 6–8 (972 880 356; ❸), or *Pensió Maria Victoria*, c/Querol 7 (☎972 880 300; ❸). For a splurge, there's the family-run *Hotel Del Prado*, with a pool (☎972 880 400; ❺). **Restaurant** prices are slightly inflated by the cross-border trade, but good bets include *Pizzeria del Reg* on Plaça del Reg, and *Sant Remo* on c/Ramón Cosp 9.

# The Costa Brava

Stretching for 145km from the French border to the town of Blanes, the **Costa Brava** (Rugged Coast) boasts wooded coves, high cliffs, pretty beaches and deep blue water. Struggling under its image as the first developed package-tour coast in Spain, it is very determinedly reinventing itself by revitalizing its local essence and shifting away from mass tourism. Broadly, the coast is split into three areas: the southern tip, clustered around brash **Lloret de Mar**, which most closely resembles the area's once-popular image; the stylish central area between **Palamós** and **Pals**, popular with the chic Barcelona crowd; and the more rugged northern part, dominated by the spectacular **Cap de Creus** headland and park, and the bohemian **Cadaqués**, which attracts an arty crowd paying tribute to Salvador Dalí. Inland are the twin hubs of **Girona**, the beautiful medieval capital of the region, and **Figueres**, Dalí's birthplace and home to his outrageous museum. **Buses** in the region are almost all operated by SARFA (☎972 364 295) with an office in every town. To visit the smaller, and more beautiful coves, a car or bike is useful, or you could walk the fabulous **camí de ronda** necklace of footpaths running along the coastline.

## Figueres and Cadaqués

The northernmost parts of the Costa Brava are reached via **FIGUERES**, a provincial Catalan town with a lively Rambla and plenty of cheap food and accommodation. The place would pass almost unnoticed, however, were it not for the most visited museum in Spain after the Prado, the surreal **Museu Dalí** (July–Sept daily 9am–7.15pm; Oct–Jun Tues–Sun 10.30am–5.15pm; ⊛www.salvador-dali. org; €10). Born in Figueres, Dalí also died here and is now buried in a stone sarcophagus inside the museum, which contains a range of his work and will appeal to everyone's innate love of fantasy, absurdity and participation.

To make your way into the middle of town, simply follow the "Museu Dalí" signs from the **train station**. The **tourist office** (March–June & Oct Mon–Fri 8.30am–3pm & 4.30–8pm, Sat 9.30am–1.30pm & 3.30–6.30pm; July & Aug, Mon–Sat 8.30am–9pm, Sun 9am–3pm; Nov–Feb Mon–Fri 8.30am–3pm; Sept Mon–Fri 8.30am–8pm, Sat 9am–8pm; ☎972 503 155, ⊛www.figueresciutat.com) is in front of the post office building by the Plaça del Sol, and runs English-language guided walks of the town in summer. For a comfortable **room**, try *Pensió Isabel II*, c/Isabel II 16 (☎972 504 735; ❷), or *Hostal Androl* (☎972 675 496, ⊛www.androl .internet-park.net; ❸), with year-round camping as well as double and triple rooms and a restaurant/bar. There's a gaggle of cheap tourist **restaurants** in the narrow streets around the Dalí museum and some nice, but pricier, pavement cafés lining the Rambla.

The beautiful fishing village of **CADAQUÉS**, an hour by regular SARFA bus from Figueres, was the artist's home from 1930 until his death, and has attracted an arty crowd ever since. The stunning **Casa-Museu Dalí** (mid-June to Sept daily 10.30am–9pm; Oct–Dec & March to mid-June Tues–Sun 10.30am–6pm; booking required ☎972 251 015; €8), the museum set up in his jumble of a home, lies 1km northeast in the tiny Portlligat cove and offers an enthralling glimpse into his private life.

Cadaqués itself is a whitewashed village with tiny beaches and narrow cobbled streets straddling a hill topped by an imposing church. **Accommodation** can be found at the comfortable *Hostal Cristina*, c/Riera 1 (☎972 258 138; ❺), near the seafront, and at *Hotel Llane Petit*, Platja Llane Petit (☎972 251 020, ⓦwww .llanepetit.com; ❺), where the rooms have a terrace with sea or mountain views. For a **drink** or a **meal**, the areas around c/Miguel Rosset and below the church are the liveliest.

## Girona and around

**GIRONA**, 37km south of Figueres, is one of Spain's loveliest unsung cities, with alleyways winding around its compact old town, the **Barri Vell**, through the atmospheric streets of **El Call**, the beautifully preserved medieval Jewish quarter. Fought over every century since the Romans first set foot here, and dominated by its towering cathedral, Girona's eclectic past is tangible in its enchanting **Banys Arabs** (Arab Baths) and the medieval walls, which provide a great afternoon's walk. On the Rambla, the **tourist office** (Mon–Fri 8am–8pm, Sat 8am–2pm & 4–8pm, Sun 9am–2pm; ☎972 226 575, ⓦwww.ajuntament .gi/turisme) dispenses maps and there's also an information stand at the train station. Good, central **accommodation** can be found at the *Pensió Viladomat*, c/Ciutadans 5 (☎972 203 176; ❸), with light, well-furnished rooms, or at *Hotel Historic* c/Bellmirall 4 (☎972 223 583, ⓦwww.hotelhistoric.com; ❼), beneath the cathedral. The Rambla is fine for a relaxing **drink**, but it's best to go into the Barri Vell or the area around Plaça Independència for more interesting places to **eat** at night.

Regular buses serve the central coast, where your best bet is to head for **BEGUR**, a hill-town nestling around a seventeenth-century church in the lee of its ruined medieval castle. Its five small beaches are all served by bus from Pl. Forgas. Favoured by an affluent Barcelona crowd, it's pricey, but serves as a good base for trips up and down the coast. Best-value **accommodation** is the friendly *Hotel Rosa*, c/Pi i Ralló 11 (☎972 623 015, ⓦwww.hotel-rosa.com; ❻), in a lovely old building, and you're never far from good **restaurants** or a sophisticated **bar** scene, centred on the streets around the church. From Begur you're within striking distance of **EMPÚRIES** (daily 10am–6/8pm; €2.40), one of the most interesting archeological sites in Spain. It started life in 550 BC as Greek *Emporion* (literally "Trading Station") and for three centuries conducted a vigorous trade throughout the Mediterranean. Later a splendid Roman city with an amphitheatre, fine villas and a broad marketplace grew up above the old Greek town. The remains of the original Greek colony occupy the lower ground, where the ruins of temples, the town gate, agora and several streets can easily be made out, along with a mass of house foundations (some with mosaics). The site lies behind a sandy bay about 2km north of **L'ESCALA**. A very good **hostel**, *Empúries*, c/Les Coves 41 (☎972 771 200; €20 including breakfast), offers a tranquil base, but you'll either need your own transport or be willing to walk the two kilometres into neighbouring L'Escala to catch a SARFA bus to get around with any ease.

# Barcelona

**BARCELONA**, the self-confident and progressive capital of Catalonia, is a tremendous place to be. Though it boasts outstanding Gothic and Art Nouveau buildings, and some great museums − most notably those dedicated to Picasso, Miró and Catalan art − its main appeal lies in getting lost in the narrow side streets of the **Barri Gòtic** (Gothic Quarter), rising, eating and drinking late, hitting the beach or lazing in the parks, and generally soaking up the atmosphere. A thriving port and the most prosperous commercial centre in Spain, it has a sophistication and cultural dynamism way ahead of the rest of the country. But Barcelona has also evolved an individual and eclectic cultural identity, most perfectly and eccentrically expressed in the architecture of **Antoni Gaudí**. As in any large city, be aware that there are problems with pickpockets − some areas around the Ramblas are pretty seedy. Keep your camera hidden, leave passports and tickets locked up in your hotel, and zip bags up.

## Arrival, information and city transport

The **airport**, 12km southwest, is linked by train (daily 5.30am−10.45pm, every 30min; €2.25) to the main train station, Barcelona Sants, from where you can take the metro to the city centre (line #3 to Liceu for the Ramblas). Many trains from the airport also run on to Plaça de Catalunya, a more direct way of reaching the Barri Gòtic. Alternatively, the Airbus (5.30/6am−11/11.30pm, every 12min; €3.60) runs to Plaça d'Espanya, Gran Vía de les Corts Catalanes and Plaça de Catalunya. A taxi to the centre will cost around €22. **Barcelona Sants** is the city's main **train station**, for national and some international arrivals − many national buses also stop here. **Estació de França**, near Parc de la Ciutadella, is the terminal for long-distance Spanish and European express and intercity trains. Leaving França either take the metro (line #4) from nearby Barceloneta, or simply walk (5min) into the Barri Gòtic, up Vía Laietana and into c/Jaume. The main **bus** terminal is the **Estació del Nord** (three blocks north of Parc de la Ciutadella; Metro Arc de Triomf). Balearics ferries dock at the **Estació Marítima** (Metro Drassanes) at the bottom of the Ramblas.

The best **tourist office** is beneath Plaça de Catalunya (daily 9am−9pm; ☎932 853 834, ⑩www.barcelonaturisme.com; Metro Catalunya). Other branches can be found at Plaça de Sant Jaume in the Barri Gòtic (Mon−Fri 9am−8pm, Sat 10am−8pm, Sun 10am−2pm; Metro Jaume I); at Barcelona Sants (Mon−Fri 8am−8pm, Sat & Sun 8am−2pm); and at the airport (daily 9am−9pm). The quickest way of getting around is by **metro** (5/6am−midnight, 2am at weekends) as **bus** routes (5am−10.30pm, plus night bus network) are far more complicated − though every bus stop does display a comprehensive route map. There's more information on ⑩www.tmb.net, or pick up a free **transport map** at TMB customer service centres at Barcelona Sants or Universitat and Diagonal metro stations. There's a flat **fare** on both metro and buses (€1.15), but it's cheaper to buy a ten-ride **targeta** (T-10; €6), available at any metro station, which covers the metro, buses, and some regional train lines. Similarly, there are **daily passes** which offer unlimited travel (T-Dia; €4.60/one day to €18.20/five days), or the **Barcelona Card**, available from any tourist office (€18/one day to €30/five days), covering transport to/from the airport, all city transport, plus discounts at museums, shops and restaurants. The **Bus Turístic** links 27 of Barcelona's major sights, at which you can hop off and on at your leisure (€17/day; €21/two days); tickets are available at tourist offices or on the bus itself. Black and yellow **taxis** are plentiful and very useful late at night. There's a minimum charge of €1.15, €1.30 after 10pm and at weekends, with an average cross-town journey costing €6−7.

## Accommodation

**Accommodation** in Barcelona is among the most expensive in Spain and in summer you'll be hard pushed to find a hostel bed for under €20, or a double

29

room for under €50. You're also strongly advised to book ahead, at least for the first couple of nights. Most of the cheapest accommodation is to be found in the side streets off and around the Ramblas, particularly in the **Barri Gòtic** between the Ramblas and Plaça de Sant Jaume, in the area bordered by c/Escudellers and c/de la Boqueria. **El Raval**, on the other side of the Ramblas, also has some cheap choices, especially around c/Junta del Comerç, though this neighbourhood has a slightly edgier feel at night. The tourist office at Plaça de Catalunya can help find rooms (though not hostel space), or you can use **Barcelona Online** (☎933 437 993, ⓦwww.barcelona-on-line.es) or the online hostel and budget hotel **reservation service** ⓦwww.hostelbarcelona.com. For longer stays, the English-run Barcelona Home Search (mobile ☎605 609 707, ⓦwww. barcelonahomesearch. com) rents out well-maintained **apartments** in various city-centre locations. There are hundreds of **campsites** on the coast in either direction, but none less than 11km from the city.

### Hostels

**Albergue Verge de Montserrat** Pg. Mare de Déu del Coll 41–51, Horta ☎932 105 151, ⓦwww .tujuca.com. A lovely HI mansion hostel with gardens and views, around 30min from the centre. Five-night maximum stay. Metro Vallcarça. Dorms €23, breakfast included.

**Barcelona Mar** c/Sant Pau 80, El Raval ☎933 248 530, ⓦwww.youthostel-barcelona.com. Large, secure hostel with mixed dorms and Internet, close to MACBA and the Raval nightlife, but in a bit of a feisty neighbourhood. Metro Paral.lel /Drassanes. Dorms €23, breakfast included.

**Center Ramblas** c/Hospital 63, El Raval ☎934 124 069, ⓦwww.center-ramblas.com. Very popular HI hostel, just off the Ramblas, with bar, laundry and no curfew. Metro Liceu. Dorms €16 (over 26s €20), includes breakfast.

**Gothic Point** c/Vigatans 5–9, La Ribera ☎932 687 808, ⓦwww.gothicpoint.com. Stunning conversion of an old building, with en-suite dorm rooms, bike rental and organized social events. Recommended. Metro Jaume I. Dorms €21, includes breakfast and free Internet.

**Itaca** c/Ripoll 21, Barri Gòtic ☎933 019 751, ⓦwww.itacahostel.com. Funky little hostel near the cathedral, with spacious mixed dorms (though women-only dorm available), plus Internet, kitchen and breakfast (€2). Metro Jaume I. Dorms €18.

**Sea Point** Pl. del Mar 1–4, Barceloneta ☎932 247 075, ⓦwww.seapointhostel.com. Beachfront accommodation with en-suite dorms, and café looking right out onto the boardwalk. Metro Barceloneta. Dorms €21, includes breakfast and free Internet.

### Hotels

**Hostal Centric** c/Casanova 13, Eixample ☎934 267 573, ⓦwww.hostalcentric.com. Good-value rooms (cheapest on the upper floors with shared bathroom) in a quiet street that's close to the action nonetheless. Metro Universitat. ❺

**Hostal Fernando** c/de Ferran 31, Barri Gòtic ☎933 017 993, ⓦwww.barcelona-on-line.es/ fernando. Well-kept rooms in the *hostal*, plus top-floor dorm accommodation (€19). Metro Liceu. ❸

**Hostal Gat Raval** c/Joaquím Costa 44, El Raval ☎934 816 670, ⓦwww.gataccommodation.com. Sleek minimalist design and helpful, friendly staff in this refreshingly clean, bright and youthful hotel. Metro Universitat. ❹

**Hostería Grau** c/Ramelleres 27, El Raval ☎933 018 135, ⓦwww.hostalgrau.com. Charming place with a friendly, welcoming café/bar (breakfast €3–7), laundry service and Internet. Metro Catalunya. ❹

**Hotel La Terrassa** c/Junta del Comerç 11, El Raval ☎933 025 174. Basic budget favourite, with plain singles, doubles and triples, some en suite, and a pleasant terrace. Metro Liceu. ❸

## The City

Scattered as Barcelona's main sights may be, the greatest area of interest is the **old town**, whose cramped streets above the harbour can be easily explored on foot. The twisting alleys of the **Barri Gòtic** contain the superb cathedral and several excellent museums, while bisecting the old town, at the western edge of the Barri Gòtic, are the famous **Ramblas**, the city's main thoroughfare. At the Ramblas' northern end is **Plaça de Catalunya**; at the southern end, the harbour and the revitalised **Port Vell** (old port). West of the Ramblas lies the warren-like **El Raval**, once a notorious red-light district, now an up-and-coming arty, nightlife

▲ *Parc Güell*

SAGRADA FAMILIA

FONTANA

PL. MOLINA
Casa Vicens

GRACIA

GRÀCIA

Casa Macaya

Casa de les Punxes

VERDAGUER

Casa Thomas

Palau Quadras

Palau Robert
Casa Serra

Casa Milà (La Pedrera)

Palau Montaner

DIAGONAL

GIRONA

Jardins Torres de les Aigües

PASSEIG DE GRACIA

EIXAMPLE

PROVENÇA

Casa Batlló

Casa Amatller

Casa Lleó Morera

Casa Calvet

Fundació Antoni Tàpies

HOSPITAL CLINIC

El Corte Inglés

Escola Industrial

Universitat de Barcelona

CATALUNYA

PLAÇA DE CATALUNYA

El Triangle

PLAÇA DE L'UNIVERSITAT

ENTENÇA

UNIVERSITAT

MACBA

LICEU

Preso Model

Hospital de la S. Creu

SANTS-ESTACIÓ

Mercat de la Boqueria

TARRAGONA

ROCAFORT

SANT ANTONI

Liceu

Barcelona Sants

Parc de Joan Miró

ESPANYA

PLAÇA D'ESPANYA

PARAL·LEL

AVINGUDA DEL PARAL·LEL

POBLE SEC

Caixa Forum

Funicular de Montjuïc

Museu d'Arqueologia

Fundació Joan Miró

Poble Espanyol

MIRAMAR

Museu Etnològic

MONTJUÏC

MNAC

Teleféric

Anella Olímpica

Estadi Olímpic

950

Palau Sant Jordi

Castell de Montjuïc

▲ Tibidabo

▲ Madrid

▲ Airport

SPAIN

29

# BARCELONA

SPAIN

29

Sagrada Família

PLAÇA DE LES GLÒRIES CATALANES

GLÒRIES

POBLE NOU

PLAÇA DE LA HISPANITAT

Teatre Nacional de Catalunya

LLACUNA

Cementiri de Poble Nou

MARINA

Estació del Nord

BOGATELL

TETUAN

PLAÇA DE TETUAN

VILA OLÍMPICA

Nova Icària

ARC DE TRIOMF

Palau de Justícia

PASSEIG MARINA

Arc de Triomf

Parc de la Ciutadella

URQUINAONA

Museu de Zoologia

Hivernacle

Parlament de Catalunya

Torre Mapfre

Museu Geologia

CIUTADELLA

Mercat del Born

Parc Zoològic

Hotel Arts

Port Olímpic

Museu Picasso

Estació de França

La Seu

JAUME I

Santa Maria del Mar

PASSEIG CIRCUMVAL·LACIÓ

Barceloneta

BARCELONETA

CIUTAT VELLA

RONDA LITORAL

PLAÇA D'ANTONI LÓPEZ

Palau del Mar

PL. BARCELONETA

MAQUINISTA

Sant Sebastià

DRASSANES

IMAX

BARCELONETA

ADMIRALL AIXADA

PORT VELL

L'Aquàrium

PLAÇA PORTAL DE LA PAU

JOAN DE BORBÓ

Drassanes (Museu Marítim)

Estació Marítima

Maremàgnum

Torre Sant Sebastià

MOLL D'ESPANYA

Torre Jaume I

Telefèric

MOLL DE BARCELONA

Torre Miramar

World Trade Centre

MAR MEDITERRÁNEO

MOLL DE PONIENTE

N

0      500 m

neighbourhood but still with a few rough edges. Medieval streets continue either side of the Ramblas, reaching northeast through **La Ribera** (site of the Picasso Museum) and southwest to the fortress-topped hill of **Montjuïc**. A cable car connects Montjuïc with **Barceloneta**, the waterfront restaurant district east of the harbour. Beyond Plaça de Catalunya stretches the modern commercial area, known as the **Eixample**, within which lies some extraordinary architecture, including Gaudí's **Sagrada Familia**.

### The Ramblas and El Raval

Only in Barcelona could a street – or, strictly, streets – be a highlight. But the **Ramblas** are not just any street – here you will find everything from flower markets to fire eaters, performers to pet shops, and in the evening, all of Barcelona out taking a stroll. Don't miss the glorious **La Boqueria**, the city's main food market (Mon–Sat 6am–8pm), a splendid gallery of sights and smells with several excellent snack and tapas bars on its fringes and a good restaurant at the back. A little further down is the **Liceu**, Barcelona's celebrated opera house, with daily tours of the interior (10am, 11am, noon & 1pm; €5.50; ☏934 859 900, ☖www.liceubarcelona .com). Further down still, hidden behind an archway just off the Ramblas, lies the elegant but seedy nineteenth-century **Plaça Reial**. Decorated with tall palm trees and iron lamps (designed by the young Gaudí), it's the haunt of crusties, Catalan eccentrics, the odd drunk and hundreds of alfresco diners and drinkers. Right at the harbour end of the Ramblas, Columbus stands pointing out to sea from the top of a tall, grandiose column, the **Mirador de Colón** (Mon–Fri 9/10am–1.30pm & 3.30–6.30/8.30pm, Sat & Sun 10am–6.30/8.30pm; €2). Take the lift to his head for a fine view of the city. Opposite here are the **Drassanes**, medieval shipyards dating from the thirteenth century, whose stone-vaulted buildings house the fine **Museu Marítim** (daily 10am–7pm; €5.40), with its impressive sixteenth-century Royal Galley.

North of the Drassanes, on the west side of the Ramblas, **El Raval** has a few sights of note, starting with Gaudí's **Palau Guell** (Mon–Sat 10am–1pm & 4–7.30pm; €3) at c/Nou de la Rambla 3. Here, the wrought-iron supports blend magnificently with granite, marble, ceramics, woodwork and stained and etched glass, and the roof is particularly impressive. Carrer de Sant Pau cuts west to Barcelona's oldest church, **Sant Pau del Camp**, which once stood in open fields beyond the city walls. For a taste of the regenerated side of El Raval, you can then walk up along the **Rambla de Raval** – a new boulevard with pavement cafés and bars – on your way to the stunning **Museu d'Art Contemporani de Barcelona** or MACBA (Mon & Wed–Fri 11am–7.30pm, Sat 10am–8pm, Sun 10am–3pm; €7, Wed €3; ☖www .macba.es), with exciting displays by international and national artists.

### The Barri Gòtic, La Ribera and Ciutadella

The **Barri Gòtic** dates principally from the fourteenth and fifteenth centuries, when Catalunya reached the height of its commercial prosperity. The quarter is centred on **Plaça de Sant Jaume**, on one side of which stands the restored town hall, the **Ajuntament**, and on the other, the **Palau de la Generalitat**, home of the Catalan government. Just behind the square **La Seu**, Barcelona's cathedral (daily 8am–1pm & 4/5–7.30pm; €4), is one of Spain's great Gothic buildings, its magnificent **cloisters** (9am–1pm & 4–7pm) looking over a lush tropical garden with soaring palm trees and white geese. Barcelona's finest Roman remains were uncovered nearby, beneath the beautiful **Plaça del Rei**, and now form part of the **Museu d'Història de la Ciutat** (Tues–Sat 10am–8pm, Sun 10am–3pm; Oct–May closed Mon–Fri 2–4pm; €4, free first Sat of month), entered from c/del Veguer. You'll also be able to see the interiors of the Plaça del Rei's finest buildings – including the famous **Saló del Tinell**, on whose steps Ferdinand and Isabella stood to receive Columbus on his triumphant return from his famous voyage of 1492. Behind the *plaça*, the **Museu Frederic Marés** (Tues–Sat 10am–7pm, Sun

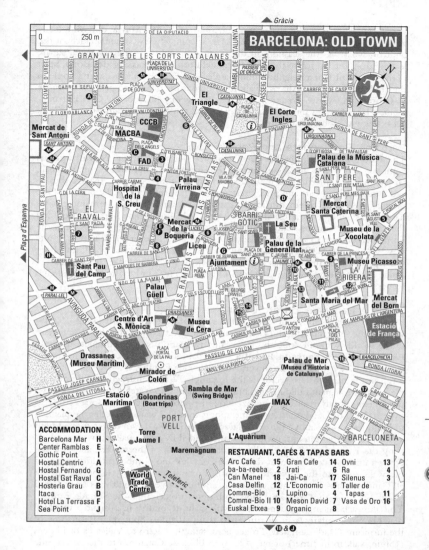

▲ Gràcia

**BARCELONA: OLD TOWN**

0   250 m

**ACCOMMODATION**

| | |
|---|---|
| Barcelona Mar | H |
| Center Ramblas | E |
| Gothic Point | I |
| Hostal Centric | A |
| Hostal Fernando | G |
| Hostal Gat Raval | C |
| Hosteria Grau | B |
| Itaca | D |
| Hotel La Terrassa | F |
| Sea Point | J |

**RESTAURANT, CAFÉS & TAPAS BARS**

| | | | | | |
|---|---|---|---|---|---|
| Arc Cafe | 15 | Gran Cafe | 14 | Ovni | 13 |
| ba-ba-reeba | 2 | Irati | 6 | Ra | 4 |
| Can Manel | 18 | Jai-Ca | 17 | Silenus | 3 |
| Casa Delfin | 12 | L'Economic | 5 | Taller de | |
| Comme-Bio | 1 | Lupino | 4 | Tapas | 11 |
| Comme-Bio II | 10 | Meson David | 7 | Vasa de Oro | 16 |
| Euskal Etxea | 9 | Organic | 8 | | |

▼ ❶❽ & ❿

10am–3pm; €3, free Wed afternoon & first Sun of month; ⓦwww.museumares
.ben.es) consists of a fascinating personal collection of social and historical oddities
gathered over fifty years of travel, and has a lovely shaded courtyard café in the
grounds.

Heading east from Plaça de Sant Jaume, you cross Vía Laietana into **La Ribera**
and reach the **Carrer de Montcada**, crowded with beautifully restored old
buildings. One of these houses the **Museu Picasso** (Tues–Sat 10am–8pm, Sun
10am–3pm; €6, free first Sun of month, ⓦwww.museupicasso.bcn.es), one of
the world's most important collections of Picasso's work, providing a unique
opportunity to trace the artist's development from his early paintings as a young
boy in Barcelona to the major works of later years. Continue down the street and

you'll come out opposite the stunning basilica of **Santa María del Mar** (daily 9am–1.30pm & 4.30–8pm; Sun choral Mass at 1pm; ⓦwww.santamariadelmar.tk), built on what was the seashore in the fourteenth century. The elongated square leading from the church to the old Mercat del Born is the **Passeig del Born**, heart of the trendy **El Born** neighbourhood, a pleasant area for wandering, and home to the city's best nightlife. An easy walk from here is the green and peaceful **Parc de la Ciutadella,** whose attractions include the meeting place of the Catalan parliament, a lake, Gaudí's monumental fountain and the city **zoo** (daily 10am–5/7pm; €14; ⓦwww.zoobarcelona.com).

## Port Vell, Barceloneta and Port Olímpic

The whole **Port Vell** area has been revitalized, notably by the **Maremàgnum** complex, and is now a pleasant, attractive place with an upmarket shopping mall, an overpriced aquarium (ⓦwww.acquariumbcn.com), cinema, IMAX theatre and a multitude of bars and pricey restaurants. The other side of the port, past the marina, the **Barceloneta** district, in contrast, is one of the few remaining *barris* harbouring genuine local Catalan life: here, you'll find cleaned-up **beaches**, and the city's most famous seafood restaurants. A **cable car** (*telefèric*) runs from the tip of Barceloneta to Montjuïc (daily 10.45am–7/8pm, every 15min; €7.50 one way, €9 return). Walk 1km east along the beach promenade and you'll find **Port Olímpic** with its myriad bars and restaurants. At night the tables are stacked up, dance floors emerge and the area hosts one of the city's most vibrant bar and club scenes.

## Sagrada Família and Parc Güell

Barcelona offers – above all through the work of **Antoni Gaudí** (1852–1926) – some of the most fantastic and exciting modern architecture to be found anywhere in the world. Without doubt his most famous creation is the incomplete **Temple Expiatori de la Sagrada Família** (daily 9am–6/8pm; €8, €10.50 including guided tour, €2 to go up the tower; Metro Sagrada Família; ⓦwww.sagradafamilia .org), in the northeastern sector of the Eixample. With construction still ongoing, the interior is a giant building site, but it's fascinating to watch Gaudí's last-known plans being slowly realized. The size alone is startling, with eight spires rising to over 100m. For Gaudí these were metaphors for the Twelve Apostles; he planned to build four more above the main facade and to add a 180m tower topped with a gallery over the transept, itself to be surrounded by four smaller towers symbolizing the Evangelists. Take the lift, or climb up one of the towers, and you can enjoy a dizzy view down over the whole complex and clamber still further round the walls and into the towers. The tourist office issues a handy leaflet describing all Gaudí's works, with a map of their locations. Above all, don't miss **Parc Güell** (daily 10am–6/9pm; free), his most ambitious project after the Sagrada Família. This almost hallucinatory experience, with giant decorative lizards and a vast Hall of Columns, contains a small **museum** (daily 10am–6/8pm; €3) with some of the furniture Gaudí designed. To get here, take the metro to Vallcarça or Lesseps (15min walk from either) or bus #24 from Plaça de Catalunya to the eastern side gate.

## Montjuïc

The hill of **Montjuïc** has yet more varied attractions – half a dozen museums, the "Spanish Village", Olympic arena, a superbly sited castle, and spectacular views of the sprawling city below. The most obvious approach is to take the metro to **Plaça d'Espanya** and walk from there up the imposing Avda. de la Reina María Cristina, past the 1929 International Fair buildings and the rows of fountains. If you'd rather start with the castle, take the **Funicular de Montjuïc** (daily 9am–10pm every 10min; €2.20 return), which runs from Paral.lel metro station to the start of the **Telefèric de Montjuïc** (April–Oct daily 11am–7/9pm, Nov–March Sat &

Sun only; €3.60, €5 return), which in turn leads to the **castle** (June–Aug daily 10am–8pm, April & May daily 10am–2pm, Sept–March Sat & Sun 10am–2pm; ☎932 892 830). Alternatively, take bus #50 from Plaça Universitat along Gran Vía to Montjuïc.

If you start at Plaça d'Espanya, you'll pass **Caixa Forum** (Tues–Sun 10am–8pm; free) – a superb arts and cultural centre set within an old textile factory – before climbing the steps and escalators to the **Palau Nacional**, centrepiece of Barcelona's 1929 International Fair and now home to one of Spain's great museums, the **Museu Nacional d'Art de Catalunya** (Tues–Sat 10am–7pm, Sun 10am–2.30pm; €4.80, free first Thurs of month; ⓦwww.mnac.es). Its enormous collection includes a Romanesque collection that is the best of its kind in the world: 35 rooms of eleventh- and twelfth-century frescoes, meticulously removed from a series of small Pyrenean churches and beautifully displayed. There is also a substantial collection of Gothic, Baroque and Renaissance works. Nearby, to the east, is the **Fundació Joan Miró** (Tues–Sat 10am–7/8pm, Thurs till 9.30pm, Sun closes 2.30pm; €7.20; ⓦwww.bcn.fjmiro.es), the most adventurous of Barcelona's art museums, devoted to one of the greatest Catalan artists. The beautiful white building houses a permanent collection of paintings, graphics, tapestries and sculptures donated by Miró himself and covering the period from 1914 to 1978.

A short walk over to the other side of the Palau Nacional brings you to the **Poble Espanyol** or "Spanish Village" (Mon 9am–8pm, Tues–Thurs 9am–2am, Fri & Sat 9am–4am, Sun 9am–noon; ⓦwww.poble-espanyol.com; €7), consisting of replicas of famous or characteristic buildings from all over Spain, and with a lively club scene at night. From the Poble Espanyol, the main road climbs around the hill to what was the principal **Olympic arena** in 1992. The Olympic Stadium itself, the **Estadi Olímpic** (daily 10am–6/8pm; free), built originally for the 1929 Exhibition, was completely refitted to accommodate the 1992 opening and closing ceremonies. The **Galeria Olímpica** at the stadium (Mon–Fri 10am–1/2pm & 4–6/7pm; €2.70) is a hands-on affair covering the staging of the Games in the city. Finally, atop **Montjuïc** and offering magnificent views across the city, stands the eighteenth-century **Castell de Montjuïc**, with an outdoor café within the ramparts, a mediocre military museum (€2.50) and a walk along a panoramic pathway into the surrounding woods.

## Eating, drinking and nightlife

With more than ten thousand places to eat, Barcelona boasts a huge variety of **restaurants**, and even low-budget travellers can eat well. Be aware that a lot of places close on Sundays and throughout August, and that the great-value *menú del día* is only available at lunchtime. For picnics, head for the Boqueria **covered market**, off the Ramblas. There are hundreds of excellent **bars and cafés**, including the lively **tapas** places in the Barri Gòtic (look on and around c/de la Mercè) and the fashionable bars in the Passeig del Born. **Gràcia** (Metro Fontana), north of the Eixample, is the most studenty area in Barcelona, great for a drink around the main Plaça del Sol, while **Barceloneta** is the place for seafood restaurants. Barcelona's **nightlife** is some of Europe's most exciting, though it's not cheap – in the most exclusive places even a beer costs roughly ten times as much as in the neighbourhood bar next door. The hi-tech theme palaces are concentrated mainly in the Eixample, especially in the rich kids' stamping ground bordered by c/Ganduxer, Avda. Diagonal and Vía Augusta, west of Gràcia. Laid-back and/or alternative places can be found in the streets of El Raval, around MACBA and south, while the waterfront Port Olímpic area is a more mainstream summer-night playground. Music bars close at 3am, the clubs at 4/5am, though some open between 5am and 9am at weekends. For **listings**, buy the weekly *Guía del Ocio* from any newsstand (ⓦwww.guiadelociobcn.com) or pick up a copy of the quarterly entertainment guide *See Barcelona* (ⓦwww.seebarcelona.com), from hotels or tourist offices. There's a thriving **gay scene** in Barcelona (ⓦwww.gaybarcelona.net), particularly

29

in the so-called Gaixample, a few square blocks northwest of the main university: *SexTienda*, at c/Rauric 11 (near Plaça Reial), supplies free maps of gay Barcelona with a list of bars, clubs and contacts.

## Tapas bars

**ba-ba-reeba** Pg. de Gràcia 28, Eixample. Typical uptown tapas barn with a huge range of food, open until 1.30am. Metro Pg. de Gràcia.

**Euskal Etxea** Pl. Montcada 1–3, La Ribera. Specializing in mouthwatering *pintxos* (Basque tapas). Metro Jaume I. Closed Mon.

**Irati** c/Cardenal de Casanyes 17. Excellent tapas bar and restaurant, serving new-wave Basque cuisine. Metro Liceu.

**Jai-Ca** c/Ginebra 13, Barceloneta. Small cornerside bar with some of the best tapas in town. Metro Barceloneta.

**Taller de Tapas** c/de l'Argentería. One of several city-centre branches of this popular chain of tapas bars/restaurants offering simple, quality food in elegant, relaxed surroundings. Highly recommended. Metro Jaume I.

**Vaso de Oro** Carrer de Balboa 6. Some of the city's best tapas, in a tiny but lively bar, oozing noise and character. Metro Barceloneta.

## Restaurants

**Arc Café** c/Carabassa 19, Barri Gòtic. Students, travellers and artists all hang out in this old-town brasserie-bar, serving breakfasts until 1pm. Metro Drassanes.

**Can Manel** Pg. Joan de Borbó 60, Barceloneta. Probably the best value by the harbour, though the weekday €8.25 *menú del día* features disappointingly little seafood. Metro Barceloneta.

**Casa Delfin** Pg. del Born 36, La Ribera. Paper-tablecloth bar-restaurant that packs in the locals for a cheap and cheerful *menú del día*. Closed Sun. Metro Barceloneta.

**Comme-Bio & Comme-Bio II** Via Laietana, La Ribera, Metro Jaume I; and Gran Vía 603, corner Rambla de Catalunya, Eixample, Metro Catalunya. Sibling vegetarian restaurants that double as health-food stores. Buffet lunch is €8.50.

**Gran Cafe** c/Avinyo, 9, Barri Gotic. Elegant Barcelona institution offering exceptional service and good Catalan/French food. Metro Liceu.

**L'Economic** Pl. Sant Agustí Vell 13, La Ribera. The beautiful tiled dining room is the backdrop for one of the city's bargains – an excellent three-course lunch for under €8, wine included. Metro Jaume I. Closed weekends.

**Lupino** c/Carme 33, El Raval. Elegant, airy and sophisticated restaurant on Placa Gardunya, serving an exceptional €8.50 lunch menu. Highly recommended. Metro Liceu.

**Meson David** c/Carrates 65. Lively, bustling, family-run Galician restaurant. Open for lunch and dinner, closed Weds. Metro Paral-lel.

**Organic** c/Junta de Comerc 11. Trendy organic vegetarian restaurant serving tasty meals, including salads, soups, pizzas, vegan dishes and home-made bread. Metro Liceu.

**Ovni** c/Via Laietana 32. Stylish, fantastic value vegetarian restaurant serving all-you-can eat buffet for €6.60 or €7.95 at weekends. Free internet access for 30min. Metro Jaume I.

**Ra** c/Carme 34. Trendy bar/restaurant serving excellent €10 lunch menu. Metro Liceu.

**Silenus** c/Angels 8, El Raval. Just round the corner from the MACBA and with a decidedly hip clientele, this billowing white space serves delicious food. Come for lunch and you can eat for just over €10. Closed Sun. Metro Liceu.

## Cafés and bars

**Canigó** Pl. de la Revolució, Gràcia. Family-run neighbourhood bar, packed out with a hip local crowd. Closed Mon. Metro Fontana.

**Cereria** Bxda. de Sant Miquel 3, Barri Gòtic. So laid-back it's horizontal – a literary café with good cakes and daily specials. Metro Jaume I.

**Fira** c/Provença 171, Eixample. Only in Barcelona – fairground rides and circus paraphernalia adorn this longstanding theme bar. Opens 11pm, closed Sun & Mon. Metro Provença.

**Kasparo** Pl. Vincenç Martorell, El Raval. Bar with terrace in a lovely arcaded square, very popular for good-value food. Metro Catalunya.

**Muebles Navarro** c/Riera Alta 4–6, El Raval. Converted furniture store with big, comfy sofas and big, strong drinks. Popular with a gay crowd. Opens 6pm, closed Mon. Metro Sant Antoni.

**Parnasse** c/Gignàs 21, Barri Gòtic. Listen to jazz, and drink modestly priced single-malt whiskies or the legendary absinthe. Opens 8pm, closed Sun & Mon. Metro Jaume I.

**Téxtil Café** c/Montcada 12, La Ribera. In the atmospheric medieval courtyard of the textile museum, with braziers in winter. Closed Mon. Metro Jaume I.

**Travel Bar** c/Boqueria 27, Barri Gòtic. A popular dive for backpackers: one-stop shop for cheap food, Internet access, fun city tours and general chilling out. Metro Liceu.

**Virreina** Pl. de la Virreina 1, Gràcia. Gracia's favourite bar on the neighbourhood's nicest square – Belgian beers and sandwiches a speciality.

### Clubs and live music venues

**KGB** c/Alegre de Dalt 55, Gràcia. Warehouse bar-club with good alternative rock and pop acts and after-hours techno club. Metro Joanic.

**Loft** c/Pamplona 88, Poble Nou. The place to go for hard, fast house. Fri & Sat only. Metro Bogatell.

**Metro** c/Sepúlveda 185, Eixample. The original Barcelona gay club has seen everyone from Marc Almond to Jean Paul Gaultier through its doors, and it's still pulling in the crowds. Metro Universitat.

**Moog** c/Arc del Teatre 3, El Raval. Techno temple with regular appearances from top UK and Euro DJs. Best on Wed & Sun; €8 entry. Metro Drassanes.

**Razz Club** c/Almogàvers 122, Poble Nou. Underground rock, punk, Indie and electro, Fri & Sat only. Metro Bogatell.

**Sala Apolo/Club Nitsa** c/Nou de la Rambla 113, Poble Sec. Regular live gigs by biggish names and burgeoning stars from the worlds of alternative rock, electronica and techno – *Nitsa* club night rules the roost at weekends. Metro Paral.lel.

### Listings

**Consulates** Australia, Gran Vía Carles III 98, Les Corts ☎933 309 496; Canada, c/Elisenda de Pinós 10, Sàrria ☎932 042 700; Ireland, Gran Vía Carles III 94, Les Corts ☎934 915 021; New Zealand, Trav. de Gràcia 64, Gràcia ☎932 090 399; UK, Avda. Diagonal 477, Eixample ☎934 199 044; US, Passeig de la Reina Elisenda 23, Sàrria ☎932 802 227.

**Exchange** Most banks located in Pl. de Catalunya and Pg. de Gràcia. ATMs and money exchange at the airport, Barcelona Sants, the tourist office at Pl. Catalunya, and at *casas de cambio* throughout the centre.

**Hospitals** 24hr accident and emergency centres at: Centre Perecamps, Avda. Drassanes 13, El Raval ☎934 410 600; Hospital Clinic, c/Villaroel 170, Eixample ☎932 275 400; Hospital del Mar, Pg. Marítim 25, Vila Olímpica ☎932 489 011.

**Internet access** Ciberopcion, Gran Via de les Corts Catalanes 602, Eixample; easyEverything, Ronda de l'Universitat, Eixample, and Ramblas 31; Internet Gallery Café, Barra de Ferro 3.

**Laundry** Lavomatic, Pl. Joaquim Xirau, Barri Gòtic, and c/Consolat del Mar 43, La Ribera.

**Left luggage** Lockers at all the stations, €3–4.50 per day.

**Lost property** ☎934 023 161.

**Pharmacies** At least one *farmacía* (marked with a green cross) in each neighbourhood is open 24hr – look in the window of any pharmacy for addresses.

**Police** Guardia Urbana (city police), Ramblas 43 ☎933 441 300; open 24hr.

**Post office** Correus, Pl. Antoni Lòpez, at the bottom of Vía Laietana (Mon–Sat 8.30am–9.30pm, Sun 8.30am–2.30pm).

# The Balearic islands

The four chief **Balearic islands** – Ibiza, Formentera, Mallorca and Menorca – maintain a character distinct from the mainland and from each other. **Ibiza**, firmly established among Europe's hippest resorts, has an intense, outrageous street life and a floating summer population that includes clubbers, fashion victims and gay visitors from every corner of Europe, and beyond. Tiny neighbouring **Formentera** is relatively undeveloped and tranquil by comparison, with miles of breathtaking sandy beaches bathed by waters turquoise enough to rival the Caribbean. **Mallorca**, the largest of the Balearics, still battles with its image as a mass market tourism destination, though in reality you'll find all the clichés crammed into the sprawling resorts of the Bay of Palma. Away from here, there are soaring pine-forested mountains, traditional villages, lively fishing ports, some beautiful coves and the Balearics' one real city, **Palma**.

**Ferries** from mainland Spain (and Marseille) and inter-island connections are overpriced considering the distances involved: the cheapest mainland **ferry and catamaran** connections are from Denia (south of Valencia), with daily services to Ibiza and Mallorca (from €30 one way to either island). For the latest schedules and lowest prices, see ⓦwww.iscomarferrys.com or ⓦwww.balearia.com, though

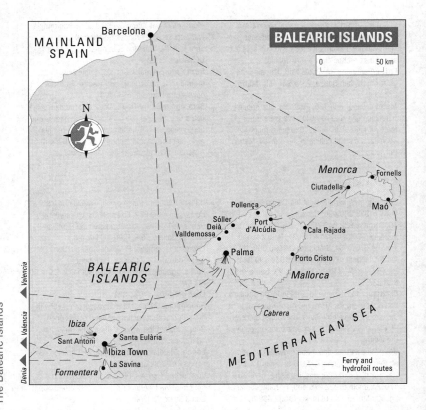

BALEARIC ISLANDS

MAINLAND SPAIN

Barcelona

0      50 km

N

Menorca    Fornells

Ciutadella

Maó

Pollença

Sóller    Port
Deià    d'Alcúdia
Valldemossa     Cala Rajada

BALEARIC
ISLANDS

Palma

Porto Cristo

Mallorca

Cabrera

Ibiza

Santa Eulària

Sant Antoni

Ibiza Town

La Savina

Formentera

MEDITERRANEAN SEA

Ferry and
hydrofoil routes

Valencia

Valencia

Denia

special **flight** deals mean it can be cheaper to fly. **Prices** on all the Balearic islands are considerably above the mainland, and from mid-June to mid-September budget **rooms** are in extremely short supply, so book in advance.

## Ibiza

**IBIZA** (Eivissa in Catalan) is an island of excess. Beautiful and indented with scores of barely accessible coves, it's nevertheless the islanders and their visitors who make it special. However outrageous you may want to be (and outrageousness is the norm), the locals have seen it all before. For years it was the European hippy escape, but nowadays it is as synonymous with the European club scene as with its 1960s denizens, who keep coming back.

In physical as well as atmospheric terms, **IBIZA TOWN** is the most attractive place on the island. Set around a dazzling natural harbour, it's one of the Mediterranean's most cosmopolitan small capitals. Approach by sea and you'll get the full effect of the old town's walls rising like a natural extension of the rocky cliffs that protect the port. Within the walls is the ancient quarter of **Dalt Vila**, first settled by the Phoenicians, and today topped by a sturdy Gothic cathedral and castle. From the **ferry terminal**, the old streets of the Sa Penya and La Marina quarters (known as 'the port') extend out before you – a maze of tottering houses and whitewashed lanes where the bars and boutiques buzz with life in the summer.

The **airport** is 6km out; there's a regular bus from here (7.30am–10.30pm; €1.20), or you can take a taxi (€16). There's a **tourist desk** at the airport (May–Oct Mon–Sat 9am–2pm & 4–9pm, Sun 9am–2pm), but the main office is directly opposite the ferry building, at c/Antoni Riquer 2 (June–Sept Mon–Fri 8.30am–2.30pm & 5–7.30pm, Sat 9.30am–1.30pm; Oct–May Mon–Fri 8.30am–2.30pm; ☎971 301 900). Alternatively, check out ⓦwww.ibiza-spotlight.com for excellent up-to-date information about the island. **Internet** cafés in Ibiza Town include Surf@net, c/Riambau 4.

Most of the cheaper **hotels** are around Passeig Vara del Rey: *Casa de Huespédes*, Vara de Rey 7 (☎971 301 376; ❸) has pleasant, artistically-furnished rooms., while the *Hostal Sol y Brisa*, Avgda. Bartomeu Vicent Ramon 15 (☎971 310 818; ❸) is clean, cheap and friendly. Close by, *Hostal Ripoll*, c/Vicente Cuervo 14 (☎971 314 275; ❸) is also a good-value place, with *Hostal Parque*, Plaça des Parque 4 (☎971 301 358; ⓦwww.hostalparque.com; ❹), a notch up in quality with bright air-con rooms.

Down in the port area, *Hostal La Marina*, c/Barcelona 7 (☎971 310 172, ⓦwww.ibiza-spotlight.com/hostal-lamarina; ❺) has attractive, individually styled rooms. The best of the island's **campsites** are *Camping Cala Bassa*, 15km out of town near Sant Josep (☎971 344 599), and *Camping Cala Nova*, 20km to the north (☎971 331 774), both adjoin excellent beaches.

For cheap **food** in the port area try *C'an Costa* at c/Creu 19, or *La Victoria*, just along the road at c/Riambau 1. The *Croissant Show*, Mercat Vell, only closes between five and seven in the morning in summer, and there are several other good cafés on Plaça des Parc. Most **bars** in the port area are overpriced by Spanish standards, though the harbourfront *Can Bar Pou*, c/Lluis Tur i Palau 19, is affordable and popular with locals, while the *Base Bar* and *Rock Bar* (both May–September only), 250m further east along the portside road, attract a raucous crowd. Alternatively, kick off first on the cheaper Plaça del Parc, at *Sunset Café* or *Madagascar*.

Ibiza's globally renowned **club** scene needs little introduction. The season is short however (mid-June to September), with August being particularly busy. The main night venues – where the beats go on till well past dawn – are the swanky *Pacha*; cavernous *Privilege* (home to the *Manumission* night); and the innovative *Amnesia*. After that you can party on at the day venue *Space*, with its legendary terrace, and the inimitable *DC 10*. The **Discobus** links them with the centre and runs through the night (€2 single fare). Be prepared to spend a lot of money, though, with entrance fees upwards of €35 and astronomical bar prices. Look out for the free invites distributed in the hip port bars each night or head to the legendary free party scene at *Bora Bora*, a clubby beach bar in nearby Platja d'en Bossa. Ibiza has one of the best **gay scenes** in Europe (ⓦwww.gayibiza.net), with the action centred on one wild street: the c/de la Verge "village" in the port. Here you'll find around twenty bars, including the intimate *Capricho* at no.42. There's another cluster just off here on c/d'Alfons XII, where *Dôme*, at no. 5, is an uber-trendy favourite. The only dedicated gay club (men only) is *Anfora*, c/San Carlos 7, in Dalt Vila, but many clubs hold a gay night once a week; the most popular is *La Troya Asesina* at *Amnesia* (Wed), Europe's largest gay night.

## Formentera

For a complete contrast with Ibiza's hedonism, **FORMENTERA** makes for a relaxing day-trip. Just three nautical miles south of its neighbour and smallest of the inhabited islands, its uncrowded beaches are a haven for anyone seeking escape, with little in the way of sophistication. **Boats** from Ibiza (€16 return, €25 by catamaran) dock at the tiny harbour of **LA SAVINA**, where you can rent mopeds or bicycles, while the island's only **tourist office** is by the quay (Mon–Fri 10am–2pm & 5–7pm; ☎971 322 057). The whitewashed capital, **SANT FRANCESC**, is 2km from La Savina, along a narrow road that continues on to the easternmost point at La

Mola. Along it, or just off it, are almost all of the island's settlements, including the village of **SANT FERRAN**, and the small resort of **Es Pujols**. The best beaches are the stunning white sands of **Platja Illetes** on the slim spur of land which stretches out to the north of La Savina, and **Platja de Migjorn**, a five-kilometre stretch of sand occupying most of southern Formentera and broken only by the occasional bar or hotel – it's popular with nude sunbathers. For **accommodation** in La Savina, the stylish *Hostal La Sabina*, near the port at Avda. Mediterranea 22–40 (☎971 322 279; ➎), has a small terrace restaurant and backs onto a tranquil lagoon speckled with yachts. In Sant Ferran try *Hosta-Residencia Illes Pitiüses* (☎971 328 189; ➍), or the basic, clean *Pensión Bon Sol*, c/Major 84–76 (☎971 328 882; ➋). **Camping** is illegal. For a **meal** or **drink**, hippy favourite *Fonda Pepe* in Sant Ferran is something of a local institution, or try the fantastic *Blue Bar*, at the end of a dirt track on Platja de Migjorn, signposted off the main Sant Ferran to La Mola road.

# Mallorca

**MALLORCA** has a split identity. As one of Europe's most popular tourist resorts it pulls in around three million tourists a year, and there are sections of its coast where the concrete curtain of high-rise hotels and shopping centres is continuous. But the spread of development is limited to the **Bay of Palma**, a forty-kilometre strip flanking the island's capital; to the north and east, things are very different. Not only are there good cove beaches and wonderful rural hotels, but there's a startling variety and physical beauty to the land itself, which makes the island many people's favourite in the Balearics.

## Palma

**PALMA** is an attractive, modern and ambitious city. Its centre, where the evening *paseo* is ingrained, is a vibrant and urbane place of stylish boutiques and pavement cafés – a world away from the heaving holiday sprawl of the surrounding bay. Arriving by sea, it's beautiful and impressive, with the grand limestone bulk of the cathedral towering above the old town and the remnants of medieval walls.

The large **ferry** port is 3.5km west of the city centre, connected to Palma by bus #1; Palma **airport**, 8km east of the city, is also served by bus #1 (every 15min; €2) to the Passeig Mallorca. Around the cathedral, containing Gaudí features, is the **Portela quarter**, "Old" Palma, a cluster of alleyways and lanes that become more spacious and ordered as you move towards the zigzag of avenues built beside or in place of the city walls. Cutting up from the sea, beside the cathedral, is **Passeig d'es Born**, garden promenade as well as boulevard, and way up the hill to the northeast lies the **Plaça Mayor**, target for most of the day-tripping tourists. The **tourist office** is at Plaça de la Reina 2 (Mon–Fri 9am–8pm, Sat 9am–2pm; ☎971 712 216, ⊛www.visitbalears.com). For **Internet** access, head to La Red cybercafé, c/Concepció 5, just off Avgda Jaume III.

The best areas to look for **accommodation** are around the Passeig Mallorca, on c/Apuntadores or c/Sant Feliu running west from Passeig d'es Born (cheaper), and on c/Sant Jaume (mid-range). Some decent options include *Hostal Apuntadores*, c/Apuntadores 8 (☎971 713 491; ✉apuntadores@jet.es; ➋), with a roof terrace overlooking the harbour; *Hostal Pons*, c/Vi 8 (☎971 722 658; ➋), in a traditional house; and the sixteenth-century *Hotel Born*, on c/Sant Jaume 3 in the heart of the old town (☎971 712 942, ⊛www.hotelborn.com; ➍). There are no official **campsites** on the island, but there is a **hostel** at c/Costa Brava 13 in El Arenal (☎971 260 892; €18), though it's often booked by school groups; take bus #15 from Plaça d' Espanya or Plaça de la Reina.

There are plenty of touristy **restaurants** along Passeig d'es Born, but for bags of local atmosphere and great tapas try the fantastic *El Pilon*, c/Cifre 4, in a tiny alley just off here. Good fare is also available nearby in the La Llotja area between c/Apuntados and the seafront. Here you'll find several inexpensive places, including *Vecchio Giovani*, c/Sant Joan 3. For **nightlife**, start the evening in the La Llotja area, then move on to the waterfront venue *Pacha*, Avda. Gabriel Roca 42, which has guest DJs from Ibiza and the UK. *Tito's*, Placa Gomila 3, is another hardy perennial of the Palma scene.

### Around Mallorca

When you feel you've exhausted the city's possibilities head north to **SÓLLER**, **DEIÁ**, **POLLENÇA**, **PORT D'ALCÚDIA** or to one of the small towns around **PORT CRISTO** on the southeast coast. Accommodation is reasonably priced in each of these towns, though in July or August it'll be almost impossible to find. Mallorca's **bus service** is good, but for a real treat you need to take the delightful hour-and-a-quarter **train** ride from Palma to Sóller (5 daily; €6 one-way). Built in 1911 to carry fruit to Palma, the line rattles and rolls in wooden carriages through the dusty outskirts of the capital before a cross-country climb into mountain passes and tunnels, passing almond groves, unruffled lakes and craggy peaks topping a thousand metres. For a different route back to Palma, catch one of the five daily buses from Plaça America in Sóller, which wind their way along the coast to delightful **Deià**, where writer Robert Graves is buried in the tiny churchyard. Three kilometres away is the clifftop mansion of **Son Marroig** (Mon–Sat 9.30am–2pm & 3–5pm; €4), that once belonged to Archduke Ludwig Salvator and is remarkable for its gardens and the headland below. Cutting inland, the route takes in **Valldemossa**, where George Sand and Chopin stayed for four months in the 1830s at the Real Cartuja de Jesús de Nazaret monastery (Mon–Sat 9.30am–4.30/6pm, Sun 10am–1pm; €8), before heading across the plain to Palma. Without stops the bus ride from Sóller to Palma takes fifty minutes.

# Valencia and the east coast

Much of Valencia's coast has been insensitively overdeveloped, a strip of concrete apartment blocks and vacation homes linked by the southbound highway. But the area still has its attractions: the stretch of coast between Jávea and Altea has escaped the worst excesses, and the cities – vibrant **Valencia** and relaxed **Alicante** – are well worth a visit.

## Valencia

**Valencia** is emerging as one of the nation's most progressive cities. Spain's third largest, it has yet to approach the vitality of Barcelona or the cultural variety of Madrid, but the city is fast shaking off a slightly provincial reputation and reinventing itself at a heady pace. In the last few years a vast, iconic new arts and science complex has emerged, a state-of-the-art metro has opened, the city beaches have been revitalized, while dozens of hip new bars, restaurants and boutiques have injected new life into the historic centre. It is particularly lively during the *Fallas* **festival** (in early March), when the city's population swells by two million, as visitors flock to see dozens of giant wooden caricatures ceremoniously burned amidst a riot of fireworks. The most interesting area for wandering is undoubtedly the maze-like **Barrio del Carmen**, with its arty, underground atmosphere. Stretching north of the Mercado Central up to the Río Turia, it's full of historic buildings being renovated and stylish cafés opening up next to crumbling town houses.

Traditional Valencian architecture is characterized by its elaborate Baroque facades – you'll see them all over town, but none so extraordinary or rich as the **Palacio del Marqués de Dos Aguas**, a short walk north of the train station. Hipólito Rovira, who designed its amazing alabaster doorway, died insane in 1740, which should come

VALENCIA

**I.V.A.M.**

**Museo Etnológico**

**Torres de Serrano**

**Museo de Bellas Artes**

Jardines del Turia

PLAZA DE LOS FUEROS

Bus Station

**Torres de Quart**

**San Nicolás**

**Catedral y Miguelete**

**Basilica de los Desamparados**

**San Esteban**

**Palacio Monaterio del Temple**

**Lonja de los Mercaderes**

**Santa Catalina**

**San Martín**

**Mercado Central**

**Palacio de Dos Aguas**

**Corpus Christi**

**Santo Domingo**

Balearic Ferry Terminal

**San Juan de la Cruz**

**Universidad**

**Palacio de Justicia**

ALBEREDA

**Ayuntamiento**

**San Agustín**

**RENFE Station**

**Plaza de Toros**

PL. ESPANYA

N

0    100 m

**ACCOMMODATION**
High Tech                    C
Petit Palace Bristol         A
Home                         B
Hostal El Rincón             E
Hostal Universal             D
Pensión Paris

**RESTAURANTS, CAFÉS & BARS**
Café Sant Jaume              2
Cocina de Marcado            5
Gásmar                       3
Moma                         7
Radio City Bar               4
Seu-Xerea                    1
The Lounge                   6

*La Ciudad de las Artes y Ciencias* ▼

as no surprise to anyone who's seen it. Inside is the **Museo Nacional de Cerámica** (Tues–Sat 10am–2pm & 4–8pm, Sun 10am–2pm; €2.40, free Sat am & Sun), with a vast collection of ceramics from all over Spain. Nearby, in the **Plaza Patriarca**, is the Neoclassical former university, with beautiful cloisters and a series of classical concerts in July, plus a small art **museum** (daily 11am–1.30pm; €1.20), displaying excellent works by El Greco, Morales and Ribalta. From here, up c/de la Paz, is the **Plaza de la Reina**, home to the impressive thirteenth-century **Cathedral**, whose bell-tower, the **Miguelete** (Mon–Sat 10am–1pm & 4.30–8pm, Sun 10am–1pm & 5–7pm; €1.20), gives stunning city views. Just west of the cathedral is the enormous **Mercado Central**, a huge iron and glass structure housing over one thousand stalls selling local fruit, vegetables and seafood until 2pm (closed Sundays).

Other museums worth visiting include **IVAM**, the modern art museum at c/ Guillém de Castro 118 (Tues–Sun 10am–8pm; ⓦwww.ivam.es; €2, free Sun), and the **Museo de Bellas Artes**, on c/San Pío V (Tues–Sun 10am–8pm; ⓦwww.cult .gva.es/mbav/mbav; €5), whose collection includes pieces by Bosch and Goya. The real highlight, however, is the **Ciudad de las Artes y las Ciencias** (City of Arts and Sciences; ⓦwww.cac.es; daily 10am–8pm, closes midnight in summer; €28.80 for two-day pass), sitting in a huge landscaped park that was built in the old riverbed of the Río Turia. This breathtaking collection of concrete, steel and glass futuristic architecture comprises five main buildings, four of which were designed by local architect Santiago Calatrava. The complex includes an eyeball-shaped IMAX **cinema**, a vast **science museum**, a huge **oceographic park** (with beluga whales, sharks and turtles) and a dramatic pistachio nut-shaped **arts centre**.

## Practicalities

Valencia's **train station** is centrally located: cross the busy c/Xátiva ring road and up Avda. Marqués de Sotelo for the Plaza del Ayuntamiento, and continue north to the old quarters of the city. The **bus station** is further out on the far bank of the Río Turia riverbed; take local bus #8, the metro to Turia, or allow thirty minutes if you walk. Bus #19 connects the Balearic **ferry terminal** with the central Plaza del Ayuntamiento. There are **tourist offices** (Ⓦwww.turisvalencia .es) at c/Paz 48 (Mon–Sat 9am–6.30pm; ☎963 986 422), and at Plaza de la Reina 19 (Mon–Sat 9am–7pm, Sun 10am–2pm; ☎963 153 931): both hand out the free English-language **listings** guide *24-7 Valencia* and *Hello Valencia*.

Most budget **accommodation** is spread around the historic centre: first choice are the three superb *Hôme* hostels, all near the Mercado Central – head to the main branch at c/La Lonja 4 (☎963 916 229; Ⓦwww .likeathome.net; dorms €14, doubles ❷), and the helpful staff will direct you from there. Nearby is *Hostal El Rincón*, c/Carda 11 (☎963 916 083; ❷), or head into the streets around Plaza del Ayuntamiento to the good-value *Pensión Paris*, c/Salva 12 (☎963 526 766; ❷), or *Hostal Universal*, c/Barcas 5 (☎963 515 384; ❷). For those on a bigger budget, the *High Tech Petit Palace Bristol*, c/Abadia de San Martín 3 (☎963 945 100, Ⓦwww.hthoteles.com; ❼) has designer rooms in a fantastic old-town location.

The quality of Valencia's **restaurants** has improved in recent years, with a new wave of trendy places opening across the city. There are plenty of decent options near the Mercado Central and in the Barrio del Carmen, including *Cocina del Mercado* at c/Carda, 6, offering hearty stews and traditional mountain food; stylish *Moma* at c/Correjeria 12, for modern Spanish cooking; and *Gásmar*, c/Palafox 9, right by the Mercado Central, for a good cheap *menú del día*. For a treat, *Seu-Xerea*, Conde de Almodova 4, offers imaginative Mediterranean/Oriental cuisine and a great €14 three-course lunch. To sample great **paella** in its home town, head to *La Pepica*, at Paseo Neptuno 6 on Malvarossa beach.

Valencia can seem dead at night, but only because the action is widely dispersed. The best of the city-centre **nightlife** is in the Barrio del Carmen (c/Caballeros, c/Quart and c/Alta). *Café Sant Jaume*, c/Caballeros 52, is an excellent place to start, then move on to *Radio City Bar*, c/Santa Teresa 19, with a mainly young clientele, or the trendy *The Lounge* café-bar, c/Estamineria Vieja 2, with free Internet access. The university area, around Avda. Blasco Ibáñez, is also popular: *Warhol* at no. 111 plays alt rock, while nearby *Woodstock,* Poly y Peyrolón 37, is a student hangout playing indy tunes. For salsa head to *Café Bachata*, c/Jesús 36, or the bars on c/Juan Llorens. One good central **club** is the unpretentious *Latex Community,* located 200m south of the train station on Gran Vía Germanias 31, with electronica and house DJs. The best **gay bars and clubs** are in and around c/Quart; for dancing try *Venial* at no. 26, or *La Goulue*, a few doors down.

## Listings

**Consulates** UK, c/Colon 22, Valencia ☎963 520 710, or Plaza Calvo Sotelo 1–2, Alicante ☎965 216 022; US, c/Romagosa 1, Valencia ☎963 516 973.
**Exchange** Main branches of banks are around Pl. del Ayuntamiento or along c/Játiva 24. Outside banking hours, try: Caja de Ahorros, c/Játiva 14, to the left as you come out of the train station.
**Hospital** Avda. Cid, at the Tres Cruces junction ☎963 862 900.

**Internet** ONO, c/San Vicente Mártir 22; Work center, C/Xativa, 19, opposite the station (24hr).
**Laundry** Pl. del Mercado 12, by the Mercado Central.
**Left luggage** At the train station (24hr).
**Pharmacies** Pl. del Mercado 37; at corner of Pl. del Ayuntamiento and c/Periodista Azzati.
**Police** Gran Vía Ramón y Cajal 40 ☎963 539 539.
**Post office** c/San Vicente Mártir 23.

# The Costa Blanca

South of Valencia stretches the **Costa Blanca**, with – between Gandía and Benidorm – some of the best beaches on this coast. Much of it, though, suffers from the worst excesses of package tourism and in the summer it's hard to get a room anywhere – in August virtually impossible – though there are hundreds of campsites. A rattling narrow-gauge **rail line** (FGV) runs hourly down the coast from Alicante past Benidorm and Denia. Continuing south, beneath the wooded capes, bypassed by the main road, stretch probably the most beautiful beaches on this coastline, centred on Javea – though you'll need a car to get to any of them, and even if you have a vehicle there's barely a cheap room to be found.

### Alicante

**ALICANTE** is a living, thoroughly Spanish city, despite its proximity to a strip of package holiday resorts. With good beaches nearby, lively nightlife and plenty of cheap hotels and restaurants it makes a pleasant stop. Wide esplanades give the town an elegant air, and around the Plaza de Luceros and along the seafront *paseo* you can relax beneath palm trees at terrace cafés. If you can, time your visit to coincide with the *Hogueres* **fiesta** of processions, fire and fireworks which culminates in an orgy of burning on the night of 23/24 June. The towering fortress **Castillo de Santa Bárbara** (Mon–Sat 10am–2pm & 4/5pm–8pm, Sun 10am–3pm; €2.50 for the lift), on the bare rock behind the town beach, is Alicante's only real "sight", with pleasant park areas and a tremendous view from the top. Access it from Playa Postiguet via a tunnel, then a lift shaft cut straight up through the rock. For the best local **beaches** head for **Playa Arenales**, 12km south of town reached by hourly Baile buses from the main bus terminal.

The main **train station** is on Avda. Salamanca, but trains on the private **FGV** line to Benidorm and Denia leave from the small station at the far end of the Playa del Postiguet. Buses from the **airport**, 12km south (6.30am–11.30pm; every 30min), stop opposite the **bus station** on c/Portugal. The huge helpful main **tourist office** (Mon–Sat 10am–7/8pm; ☎965 200 000; ⊛www.alicanteturismo .com) is at Avda. Rambla Méndez Nuñez 23; there are also offices inside the train and bus stations, and airport.

Outside July and August, you shouldn't have too much trouble finding **accommodation**, with the bulk of the options concentrated at the lower end of the old town, above the Esplanada de España – especially on c/San Fernando, c/Jorge Juan and c/Castaño. *Hostal Ventura*, c/San Fernando 10 (☎965 208 337; ❷), and *Hostal San Fernando*, c/San Fernando 34 (☎965 213 656; ❷), are both close to the promenade, but be prepared for the noisy nightclubs nearby. Slightly pricier is the lovely, comfortable *Les Monges*, c/San Agustín 4 (☎965 215 046; ❹). There are several **campsites**, including *El Molino* at Playa de San Juan to the north (connected by FGV train and bus #21) and *La Marina*, 29km south of town in woods on a good beach and connected by Costa Azul buses.

Cheap **restaurants** are clustered around the Ayuntamiento and on c/Mayor, with a couple of places serving couscous on c/Miguel Soler. For great **tapas and** *raciones*, try the atmospheric *Mesón de Labradores*, near the cathedral at c/Labradores 19. For **bars** and the best **nightlife**, head into the Barrio Santa Cruz, whose narrow streets lie roughly between the cathedral, Plaza Carmen and Plaza San Cristóbal.

# Andalucía

The southern region of Andalucía is likely to both meet and defy your preconceptions of Spain. Everywhere there is evidence of this passionate, parched country

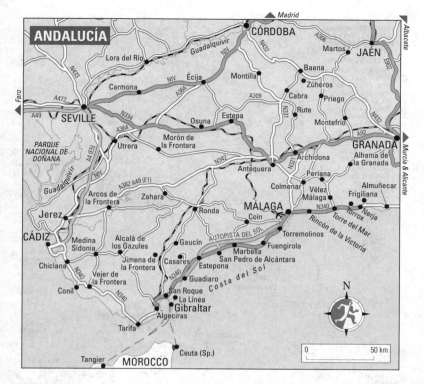

at its most exuberant: it is the home of flamenco and the bullfight, tradition and fierce pride. But it's also much more than the cliché. Evidence of the Moors' sophistication remains visible to this day in **Córdoba**, in **Seville** and, particularly, in **Granada**'s Alhambra. On the coast you could despair. Extending to either side of **Málaga** is the **Costa del Sol**, Europe's most developed resort area, with its beaches hidden behind a remorseless curtain of concrete. But there is life beyond the Costa del Sol, especially the beaches of the Costa de la Luz. Here, **Tarifa** sits on the most southerly tip of Europe, its exposed position drawing swarms of windsurfers. Andalucía is also where Europe stops and Africa begins; in places the mountains of that great continent appear almost close enough to touch, in reality they are just half an hour away by ferry.

## Granada

If you see only one town in Spain it should be **GRANADA**, with its wonderful backdrop of the Sierra Nevada. For here stands Spain's most visited monument, the Alhambra – the spectacular and serene climax of Moorish art in Spain. Granada was established as an independent kingdom in 1238 by **Ibn Ahmar**, a prince of the Arab Nasrid tribe, who had been driven south from Zaragoza. The Moors of Granada maintained their autonomy for two and a half centuries, but by 1490 only the city itself remained in Muslim hands. **Boabdil**, the last Moorish king, appealed in vain for help from his fellow Muslims in Morocco, Egypt and Turkey, and in the following year Ferdinand and Isabella marched on Granada with an army said to total 150,000 troops. For seven months, through the winter of 1491, they lai

# GRANADA

**ACCOMMODATION**
Albergue Juvenil Granada **F**
Hotel Casa Capitel **A**
Hostal Fonda Sanchez **G**
Hostal Londres **C**
Hostal Olympia **D**
Hostal Zacatin **E**
Hostal Zurita **I**
Pension Los Montes **B**
Pension Romero **H**

**RESTAURANTS,
CAFÉS & BARS**
Bodegas Castaneda **2**
Café Bar Soria **4**
La Chicota **3**
Nueva Bodega **1**
Bar Reca **5**

N

SACROMONTE

Casa del Chapiz

ALBAICÍN

Iglesia del Salvador

Mirador de San Nicolás

S. Juan de los Reyes

San Bartolomé

Arco de las Pesas

PL. DE S. NICOLÁS

Cvto. de la Concepción

San Cristóbal

MIRADOR DE ROLANDITO

CENICEROS

PILAR SECO

Palacio de Dar-al-Horra

Casa de Porras

Murallas de Albaycín

Cvto. de Sta. Isabel la Real

San José

Mirador del Carril de la Lona

San Gregorio Bético

Hospital Real

Iglesia de San Ildefonso

PL. DE LA MERCED

CRUZ DE QUIROS

ZENETE

AVENIDA

AV. CAP. MORENO

Arco o Puerta de Elvira

PLAZA DEL TRIUNFO

PL. DE LOS NARANJOS

ELVIRA

B

CAPUCHINOS

HOSPICIO

Fuente Del Triunfo

GRAN VÍA DE COLÓN

GRAN VÍA DE COLÓN

D

C

SAN AGUSTÍN

PL. DE S. AGUSTÍN

AVDA. DE LA CONSTITUCIÓN

P

P

ACERA DEL TRIUNFO

SAN JUAN DE DIOS

MENDOZA

MANO DE HIERRO

ARRIOLA

Igl. de los Santos Justo y Pastor

JERÓNIMO

SAN

Colegio de Niñas Nobles

S. Felipe Neri

Hospital e Iglesia de San Juan de Dios

ARGUETA

G

DR. SEVERO OCHOA

SANTA BARBARA

RECTOR

LOPEZ

Monasterio e Iglesia de San Jerónimo

Colegio de San Bartolomé y Santiago

Universidad

DUQUESA DE LA TRINIDAD

CONDE INFANTES

4

5

I

MÁLAGA

FÁBRICA VIEJA

BUENSUCESO

PLAZA LOBOS

Guadix & Murcia

Jaén, Madrid & Bus Station

Train Station, Airport & Seville

Antequera & Málaga

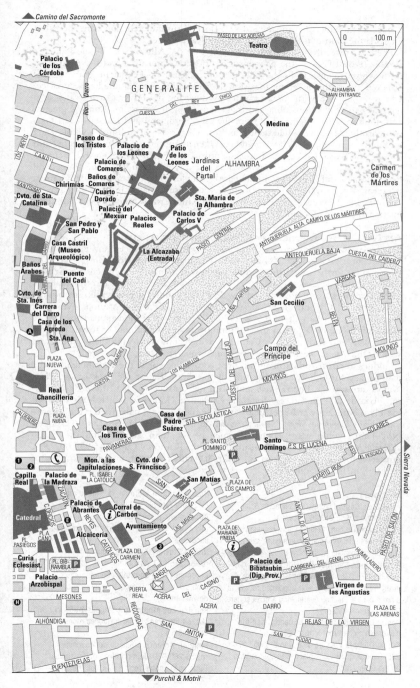

PASEO DE LAS ADELFAS

Teatro

0    100 m

Palacio
de los
Córdoba

GENERALIFE

Río Darro

CUESTA DEL REY CHICO

ALHAMBRA
MAIN ENTRANCE

Medina

Paseo de
los Tristes

Palacio de
los Leones

Patio
de los
Leones

Jardines
del
Partal

ALHAMBRA

Carmen
de los
Mártires

Palacio de
Comares

Baños de
Comares

Chirimías

Cuarto
Dorado

Cvto. de Sta.
Catalina

Palacio del
Mexuar

Palacios
Reales

Sta. María de
la Alhambra

San Pedro y
San Pablo

Palacio de
Carlos V

Casa Castril
(Museo
Arqueológico)

Baños
Árabes

La Alcazaba
(Entrada)

PASEO CENTRAL

ANTEQUERUELA ALTA CAMPO DE LOS MÁRTIRES

Puente
del Cadí

ANTEQUERUELA BAJA    CUESTA DEL CAIDERO

Cvto. de
Sta. Inés

PEÑA PARTIDA

VARGAS

Carrera
del Darro

Casa de los
Ágreda

San Cecilio

Sta. Ana

BELÉN

MOLINOS

PLAZA
NUEVA

Campo del
Príncipe

LOS ALAMILLOS

CUESTA DEL REALEJO

MOLINOS

Real
Chancillería

CUESTA DE GOMÉREZ

PLAZA
NUEVA

SANTIAGO

SOLARES

CALDERERÍA

Casa del
Padre
Suárez

STA. ESCOLÁSTICA

Casa de
los Tiros

P.S. DE LUCENA

CUESTA DEL PESCADO

PAVANERAS

Santo
Domingo

SPAIN

❶

☎

Mon. a las
Capitulaciones

Cvto. de
S. Francisco

PL. SANTO
DOMINGO

29

❷

Capilla
Real

Palacio de
la Madraza

PL. ISABEL
LA CATÓLICA

San Matías

PLAZA DE
LOS CAMPOS

CUARTO REAL

Sierra Nevada

ZACATÍN

Palacio de
Abrantes

Corral de
Carbón

SAN MATÍAS

LAS NAVAS

Catedral

CÓRDOBAS

REYES

ⓘ

Ayuntamiento

PLAZA DE
MARIANA
PINEDA

ANCHA DE LA VIRGEN

PASEO DEL SALÓN

Ⓔ

Alcaicería

CATÓLICOS

❸

GANIVET

ⓘ

HUMILLADERO

PL. A.
CANO

PLAZA DEL
CARMEN

Curia
Eclesiást.

PL. BIB-
RAMBLA

P

Palacio de
Bibataubín
(Dip. Prov.)

P

PL.
PASIEGOS

ÁNGEL

CARRERA   DEL   GENIL

Palacio
Arzobispal

ACERA

DEL

CASINO

P

Virgen de
las Angustias

Ⓗ

MESONES

PUERTA
REAL

ACERA    DEL    DARRO

PLAZA DE
LAS ARENAS

ALHÓNDIGA

RECOGIDAS

SAN
ANTÓN

P

REJAS   DE   LA   VIRGEN

SAN    ISIDRO

PUENTEZUELAS

d siege to the city. On January 2, 1492, Boabdil surrendered, and with the fall of Granada the Christian Reconquest of Spain was complete.

There are three distinct groups of buildings on the **Alhambra** hill: the **Palacios Reales** (Royal Palace), the palace gardens of the **Generalife**, and the **Alcazaba**, from whose reddish walls the hilltop took its name: al-Hamra in Arabic means "the red". Ibn Ahmar rebuilt the Alcazaba and within the walls he began a palace, which he supplied with running water by diverting the River Darro; water is an integral part of the Alhambra and this engineering feat was Ibn Ahmar's greatest contribution. After their conquest of the city, Ferdinand and Isabella lived for a while in the Alcazaba, while their grandson, Charles V, demolished a whole wing to build an incongruous and grandiose Renaissance palace. By the eighteenth century the Royal Palace was in use as a prison. In 1812 it was taken and occupied by Napoleon's forces, who looted and damaged whole sections of the palace, and tried, unsuccessfully, to blow up the entire complex. The Alhambra aside, Granada is a great place to wander, with evidence of its Moorish past still very much alive in the souk-like labyrinth of narrow streets and whitewashed houses of the **Albaicín** quarter, off Via de Colon.

### Arrival, information and accommodation

The **train station** is 1km out of town on Avda. de Andaluces, and is connected to the centre by buses #8, #4 and #11. The main **bus station**, on Carretera de Jaén, is a bit further out; bus #3 runs into town. A bus also connects the **airport** with Gran Vía de Colón (8am–6pm, up to 7 daily; €3). Details and timetables of all buses and trains are posted on the walls of the **tourist office** within the beautiful Corral del Carbon on c/Mariana Pineda, off c/Reyes Católicos (Mon–Sat 9am–7pm, Sun 10am–2pm; ☎958 247 146; ⊛www.turismodegranada.org). The **Gran Vía** is Granada's main street, cutting through the middle of town. It forms a "T" at its end with c/Reyes Católicos, which runs east to the Plaza Nueva and west to the Puerta Real, the city's two main squares.

Finding **accommodation** in this area is easy, except at the very height of the season. Try the streets to either side of the Gran Vía, at the back of the Plaza Nueva, around the Puerta Real and Plaza del Carmen (particularly c/de Navas), the Plaza de la Trinidad, or along the Cuesta de Gomérez, which leads up from the Plaza Nueva towards the Alhambra. The most central **campsite** is the surprisingly leafy *Camping Sierra Nevada*, Avda. de Madrid 107 (☎958 150 062; closed Nov–Feb), within easy walking distance of the train station, with the handy *Albergue Juvenil Granada* **hostel** nearby on Avda. Ramón y Cajal 2 (☎958 002 900, ⊜reservas.iti@iuntadeandalucia.es; €12): it's rather institutional, but has lots of facilities, including a pool.

### Hotels

**Hotel Casa Capitel** c/Cuesta Aceituneros 6, off Plaza Nueva ☎958 215 260, ⊛www .hotelcasacapitel.com. Beautiful newly-opened hotel in a sixteenth-century mansion in a quiet, safe and atmospheric location on the edge of the Albaicín. **❼**

**Hostal Fonda Sanchez** Plaza de la Universidad 1 ☎958 278 235, ⊛www.fondasanchez.com. A lovely mansion with airy, well-appointed rooms, in a great central location overlooking a quiet square. Highly recommended. **❸**

**Hostal Londres** Gran Vía 29. Friendly, well-run place with a great roof terrace. **❸**

**Hostal Olimpia** c/Alvaro de Bazán 6 ☎958 278 238. Central, good-value place with shared bath off the Gran Vía. **❷**

**Hostal Zacatin** c/Ermita 11, signed off Plaza Bib-Rambla ☎958 221 155. Atmospheric place with tiny rooms, in the midst of the Alcaicería labyrinth of medina-style shops. **❷**

**Hostal Zurita** Plaza de la Trinidad 7 ☎958 275 020. Airy, family-run accommodation on pretty square; some rooms with bath. There's a lively café-bar downstairs. **❸**

**Pensión Los Montes** c/Arteaga 3 ☎958 277 930. Just off the Gran Vía, old-fashioned rooms, some with baths. **❸**

**Pensión Romero** c/Silleria de Mesones 1 ☎958 266 079. Just off Plaza de la Trinidad. Quite basic, some rooms overlook the square. **❸**

## The City

The standard approach to the **Alhambra** (daily: March–Oct 8.30am–8pm; Nov–Feb 8.30am–6pm; €11) is on foot along the Cuesta de Gomérez, the road that climbs uphill from Plaza Nueva, or take the Alhambrabus from Plaza Nueva (every 10min; €0.88). Tickets are limited, so buy in advance from any Banco BBVA in Spain (including the one in town at Plaza Isabel la Católica); by phone (☎902 224 460; credit cards only; €0.88 booking fee); or online (✆www.alhambratickets .com). A hot tip is to buy a *bono turístico Granada* (tourist voucher; €20) from the tourist office, which lets you jump the lengthy queues and gets you into a range of museums and sights throughout the city, as well as allowing ten bus trips. Tickets are timed for the Palacios Nazaries; if you get the choice, opt for later in the day, after most tour groups have left. Ideally you should start your visit with the earliest, most ruined, part of the fortress – the **Alcazaba**. At the summit is the **Torre de la Vela**, named after a huge bell on its turret, from where there's a fine overview of the whole area. The buildings in the **Palacios Nazaries** show a brilliant use of light and space with ornamental stucco decoration, in rhythmic repetitions of supreme beauty. Arabic inscriptions feature prominently: some are poetic eulogies of the buildings and rulers, but most are taken from the Koran. The sultans used the **Mexuar**, the first series of rooms, for business and judicial purposes. In the **Serallo**, beyond, they received distinguished guests: here is the royal throne room, known as the **Hall of the Ambassadors**, the largest room of the palace. The last section, the **Harem**, formed their private living quarters. These are the most beautiful rooms of the palace, and include the **Court of the Lions**, which has become the archetypal image of Granada. You can exit the Palacios Nazaries through the courtyard of the **Charles V's Palace**, once the scene of bullfights, which now houses a museum and, although wilfully out of place here, is a distinguished piece of Renaissance design. A short walk takes you to the **Generalife,** the gardens and summer palace of the sultans. Paradise is described in the Koran as a shaded, leafy garden refreshed by running water where the "fortunate ones" may take their rest under tall canopies. It is an image that perfectly describes the Generalife, whose name means "garden of the architect".

From just below the entrance to the Generalife the **Cuesta del Rey Chico** winds down towards the River Darro and the old Arab quarter of the Albaicín, where you'll find the marvellous eleventh-century **Baños Árabes**, at Carrera del Darro 31 (Tues–Sat 10am–2pm; free). From here, you can wind your way up to the **Mirador de San Nicolás** for the quintessential Alhambra view with the Sierra Nevada backdrop, particularly stunning at sunset. Back down in the city centre, the **Capilla Real** (Mon–Sat 10.30am–1pm & 3.30–6.30pm, Sun 10am–noon & 4–8pm; €3) was built in the first decades of Christian rule as a mausoleum for Ferdinand and Isabella. Although their tombs are simple, above is the fabulously elaborate monument erected by their grandson, Charles V. For all its stark Renaissance bulk, Granada's **cathedral**, adjoining the Capilla Real and entered from the door beside it (Mon–Sat 10.30am–1.30pm & 4–8pm, Sun 4–8pm; €3), has a simple but imposing grandeur.

## Eating, drinking and nightlife

You don't come to Granada for the cuisine, though the centre has plenty of animated bars serving good, cheap food and staying open late. The open-air **cafés** on Plaza Nueva are great to while away some time, but pricey if you eat. Better-value **restaurants**, and numerous late-night bars, can be found in "Little Morocco", the warren of streets between here and the Gran Vía: good-value choices here include the *Nueva Bodega*, at c/Cetti Merién 3, and, just around the corner, *Bodegas Castañeda*, on c/Almireceros. There's a further nucleus of reasonable eateries around Plaza del Carmen (near the Ayuntamiento) and along c/Navas, where *La Chicota*, at no.20, serves great tapas. For people-watching and local atmosphere, head to the bars around Plaza Bib-Rambla, or the tiny *Café Bar Soria* and *Bar Reca*, on the nearby Plaza de la Trinidad. Moroccan-style teashops, known as **teterías**, are increasingly popular, particularly with students, and serve a wide choice of herb teas (*infusiones*), accompanied by sticky Arab pastries. Try the delightful *Kasbah*, at Calderia Nueva 4, an intriguing alleyway of craft shops, and the cheap falafel, hummous and kebabs at *Al-Andalus*, on the corner of nearby Calle Elvira. There are several **Internet** cafés around c/Santa Escolástica, including Net Internet, Plaza de los Girones 3.

**Nightlife** is focused on c/Elvira, with its large number of bars; one of the most atmospheric is *Taberna Salinas* at c/Elvira 13. Another good area for drinking is around the university, on c/Gran Capitán and c/Pedro Antonio de Alarcón. In term-time, students also gather in **pubs** near the bus station around the Campo del Príncipe, a square on the southern slopes of the Alhambra, where you'll also find good tapas. At the weekend, the best **disco** in town is *El Camborio* inside the caves at the end of Camino del Sacramento. Granada is also one of the best places in Spain to hear **flamenco**, though finding the real thing can be difficult. Avoid the touristy *espectaculares* around Sacromonto, and head to the city's oldest bar, the atmospheric *Eshavira*, c/Postigo de la Cinca 2, off c/Elvira in the Albaicín, which also hosts live jazz.

## Córdoba

Now a minor provincial capital, **CÓRDOBA** was once the largest city of Roman Spain, and for three centuries the heart of the great medieval caliphate of the Moors. It's an engaging, atmospheric city, easily explored and with some excellent budget accommodation. For visitors, its main attraction comes down to a single building: La Mezquita – the grandest and most beautiful mosque ever constructed by the Moors. This stands right in the centre of the city, surrounded by the labyrinthine Jewish and Moorish quarters, and is a building of extraordinary mystical and aesthetic power.

Córdoba's domination of Moorish Spain began thirty years after the conquest, in 756 AD, when the city was placed under **Abd ar-Rahman I**, who established control over all but the north of Spain. It was he who began the building of the Great Mosque – in Spanish, **La Mezquita** (Mon–Sat 10am–7.30pm, Sun am for worship & 2–7.30pm; €6.50) – which is approached through the Patio de los Naranjos, a classic Islamic court preserving both its orange trees and fountains for ritual purification before prayer. Inside, a thicket of nearly a thousand twin-layered red and white pillars combine to mesmeric effect, the harmony culminating only at the foot of the beautiful Mihrab (prayer niche). North of La Mezquita lies the **Judería**, Córdoba's old Jewish quarter, a fascinating network of lanes that are more atmospheric and less commercialized than Seville's. Near the heart of the quarter, at c/Maimonides 18, is a tiny **synagogue** (Tues–Sat 10am–1.30pm & 3.30–5.30pm, Sun 10am–1.30pm; €0.50, free for EU citizens), one of only three in Spain that survived the Jewish expulsion of 1492. East of the Judería, the **Museo Arqueológico** (Tues 3–8pm, Wed–Sat 9am–8pm, Sun 9am–3pm; €1.50, free for EU citizens) occupies a small Renaissance mansion in which Roman foundations have been incorporated into an imaginative display. Northeast of here, you can watch craftsmen at work in the **Museo Regina**, on Plaza Luís Venegas (Mon–Sat 10am–3pm & 5–8pm; €3), which is devoted to the history of jewellery.

Close to the **train and bus stations**, the broad Avda. del Gran Capitán leads down to the old quarters and La Mezquita – a 25-minute walk, or short ride on bus #3. The **tourist office** is at the Palacio de Congresos y Exposiciones, c/Torrijos 10, alongside La Mezquita (Mon–Fri 9.30am–6pm, Sat 10am–6pm, Sun 10am–2pm; ☎957 471 235, ⊛www.ayuncordoba.es), and there's **Internet** access at Ch@t-is, Claudio Marcelo 15, near Plaza Tendillas.

The best **places to stay** are concentrated in the maze of streets northeast of La Mezquita, many with beautifully tiled courtyards – try *Heredia*, c/Ray

Heredia 26 (☎957 474 182; ❸), with quiet, spacious rooms. Close to La Mezquita itself are. *Hotel-Restaurante Los Patios*, Cardenal Herrero 14 (☎957 478 340; ❸), and *Hostal Deanes*, c/Deanes 6, ☎957 293 744; ❸), with simple rooms and a central patio. Slightly further out is the *Hotel Maestre*, c/ Romero Barros 16 (☎957 475 395; ⓦ www.hotelmaestre .com; ❷), with traditional Cordoban architecture and pretty patios. The HI **hostel** is in the Judería, a few minutes' walk from La Mezquita, at Plaza Juda Levi (☎957 290 166; under 26 €13.50, over 26 €18.25), while the main **campsite**, *Campamento Municipal El Brillante* (☎957 282 165; bus #10 or #11), is 2km north on the road to Villaviciosa.

Avoid the touristy places around La Mezquita, and you'll find **bars** and **restaurants** reasonably priced. Loads of alternatives can be found in the Judería and in the old quarters off to the east, above Paseo de la Ribera: try *El Extremeño*, at Plaza Agrupación de Cofradías, just north of La Mezquita. *Taberna Plateros*, opposite *Hostel Maestre*, does main courses from €6. The local barrelled **wine** is mainly Montilla or Moriles – both are magnificent, resembling mellow, dry sherries. To sample them, head for *Taberna San Miguel*, Plaza San Miguel 1, a Córdoba institution with a room devoted to bullfighting history. **Flamenco** performances take place at *Tablao Cardenal*, c/Torrijos 10 (from 10pm; €18, bookings on ☎957 483 320; closed Sun), but it's poor fare compared to displays in Seville or Granada.

## Seville (Sevilla)

**SEVILLE** (Sevilla) is the great city of the Spanish south, intensely hot in summer and with an abiding reputation for exuberance and intensity. It has three important monuments – the Giralda tower, the cathedral and the Alcázar – and an illustrious history, but it's the living self of this city of Carmen, Don Juan and Figaro that remains the great attraction. It is expressed on a phenomenally grand scale at the city's two great festivals – **Semana Santa**, during the week before Easter, and the **April Feria**, which lasts a week at the end of the month. Seville is also Spain's second most important centre for **bullfighting** after Madrid. It remains a poor city and petty crime is a big problem. While it has an upbeat modern dimension to its buildings and infrastructure, the soul of the city still lies in its historic latticework of narrow streets, patios and plazas, where minarets jostle for space among cupolas and palms.

**CÓRDOBA**

| ACCOMMODATION | | RESTAURANTS | |
|---|---|---|---|
| Hostal Deanes | D | El Extremeño | 2 |
| Heredia | A | Taberna Plateros | 3 |
| HI Hostel | B | Taberna San Miguel | 1 |
| Hotel Maestre | E | | |
| Hotel-Restaurante Los Patios | C | | |

La Cartuja

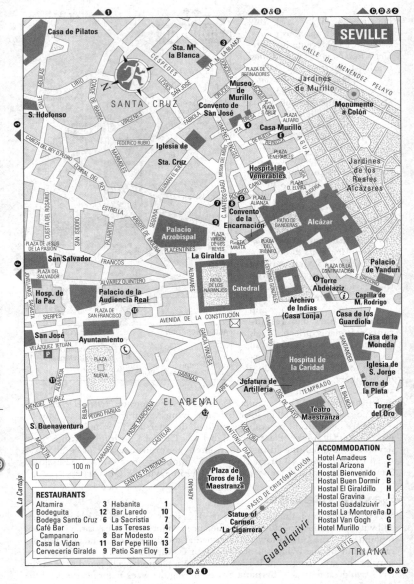

**SEVILLE**

**RESTAURANTS**

| | | | |
|---|---|---|---|
| Altamira | 3 | Habanita | 1 |
| Bodeguita | 12 | Bar Laredo | 10 |
| Bodega Santa Cruz | 6 | La Sacristía | 7 |
| Café Bar | | Las Teresas | 4 |
| Campanario | 8 | Bar Modesto | 2 |
| Casa la Vidan | 11 | Bar Pepe Hillo | 13 |
| Cervecería Giralda | 9 | Patio San Eloy | 5 |

**ACCOMMODATION**

| | |
|---|---|
| Hotel Amadeus | C |
| Hostal Arizona | F |
| Hostal Bienvenido | A |
| Hostal Buen Dormir | B |
| Hostal El Giraldillo | I |
| Hostal Gravina | H |
| Hostal Guadalzuivir | J |
| Hostal La Montoreña | D |
| Hostal Van Gogh | G |
| Hotel Murillo | E |

## Arrival, information and accommodation

The San Justa **train station** is out of the centre on Avda. Kansas City, which is also the airport road; bus #C1 connects it to the centre and to the San Sebastián bus station. There is an hourly bus service (6.15am–9.30pm; €2.30) connecting the **airport** to the town. The main **bus station** is at Plaza de Armas, beside the river by the Puente del Cachorro, but buses for destinations within Andalucía (plus

Barcelona, Alicante and Valencia) leave from the more central terminal at Plaza de San Sebastián. Bus #C4 connects the two terminals. The **tourist offices** are at Plaza San Francisco, 19 (Mon–Fri 8am–8pm; ☏954 595 288, ⓦwww.turismo .sevilla.org) and Avda. de la Constitución 21 (Mon–Fri 9am–7pm, Sat 10am–2pm & 3–7pm, Sun 10am–2pm; ☏954 221 404, ⓦwww.andalucia.org).

The most attractive but pricey area to **stay** is the maze-like Barrio Santa Cruz, near the cathedral. Cheaper options can be found in c/Farnesio, on the periphery of the Barrio, or slightly further out beyond Plaza Nueva, towards the river and the Plaza de Armas bus station. During Easter week and the April fair, prices double, and you'll need to book six months in advance. There's an HI **hostel** *Albergue Juvenil Sevilla*, c/Isaac Peral 2 (☏955 056 500; under 26 €13.50, over 26 €18.25), some way out in the university district (take bus #34 from Puerta de Jerez or Plaza Nueva), and a **campsite** *Camping Sevilla* by the airport (☏954 514 379), with its own pool, and a minibus link to central Seville three times a day.

### Hotels

**Hotel Amadeus** c/Farnesio 6 ☏954 501 443, ⓦwww.hotelamadeussevilla.com. Beautifully furnished hotel in an eighteenth-century building in the heart of the Barrio Santa Cruz. ❻

**Hostal Arizona** c/Pedro del Torro 14 ☏954 216 042. Near the Plaza de Armas bus station, basic rooms, with and without bath; gets busy so arrive early or phone ahead. ❷

**Hostal Bienvenido** c/Archeros 14, Barrio Santa Cruz ☏954 413 655. Small rooms, with a pleasant roof terrace. ❸

**Hostal Buen Dormir** c/Farnesio 8, Barrio Santa Cruz ☏954 217 492. Good value, friendly place, with a roof terrace, in a street with several possibilities. ❸

**Hostal El Giraldillo** c/Gravina 23 ☏954 224 275. Has some airy rooms with tiny balconies. ❸

**Hostal Gravina** c/Gravina 46 ☏954 216 414. Basic but cheap and clean. ❸

**Hostal Guadalquivir** c/Pages del Corro 53 ☏954 332 100. Friendly place, with excellent value rooms across the river in Triana. ❸

**Hostal La Montoreña** c/San Clemente 12 ☏954 412 407. No-frills rooms with shared bath, in a good location. ❷

**Hostal Van Gogh** c/Miguel de Manara 1 ☏954 563 727, ⓦwww.grupo-piramide.com. A great location beside the cathedral, though variable rooms. ❺

**Hotel Murillo** c/Reinoso 6 ☏954 210 959, ⓦwww.hotelmurillo.com. Attractive rooms and newly refurbished one and two bedroom apartments, in a quiet, central location. ❻

## The City

Seville was one of the earliest Moorish conquests (in 712 AD) and, as part of the Caliphate of Córdoba, became the second city of al-Andalus. When the caliphate broke up in the early eleventh century it was the most powerful of the independent states to emerge and, under the Almohad dynasty, became the capital of the last real Moorish empire in Spain from 1170 until 1212. The Almohads rebuilt the Alcázar, enlarged the principal mosque and erected a new and brilliant minaret – the **Giralda** (Mon–Sat 11am–5pm, Sun 2.30–6pm; €7, including entrance to cathedral, free Sun) – topped with four copper spheres. It still dominates the skyline today and you can ascend the minaret for a remarkable view of the city. The Giralda was so venerated by the Moors that they wanted to destroy it before the Christian conquest of the city. Instead in 1402 it became the bell tower of the **cathedral** (same hours as Giralda, ⓦwww.catedralsevilla.org), the world's largest Gothic church, and third largest cathedral. Its centre is dominated by a vast retable composed of 45 carved biblical scenes, making up the largest altarpiece in the world. Across Plaza del Triunfo from the cathedral lies the **Alcázar** (Tues–Sat 9.30am–6/7pm, Sun 9.30am–1.30/5pm; €5), a site that rulers of Seville have occupied from the time of the Romans. Under the Almohads, the complex was turned into an enormous citadel, forming the heart of the town's fortifications. Parts of the walls survive, but the palace was rebuilt in the Christian period by Pedro the Cruel (1350–1369). His works, some of the best surviving examples of Mudéjar architecture, form the nucleus of the Alcázar today. Later additions include a wing in which early expeditions to the Americas were planned. Don't miss the beautiful and rambling Alcázar **gardens**.

Ten minutes' walk south of the cathedral, **Plaza de España** and adjoining **María Luisa Park** are an ideal place to spend the middle part of the day. En route you pass the **Fábrica de Tabacos**, the old tobacco factory that was the setting for Bizet's Carmen, and today is part of the university. Towards the end of the María Luisa Park, some grand pavilions house museums. The furthest contains the city's **archeology** collections (Tues 3–8pm, Wed–Sat 9am–8pm, Sun 9am–2pm; €1.50, free for EU citizens), while opposite is the **Popular Arts Museum** same details with interesting displays relating to the April *feria*.

A further twenty minutes' walk northwest along the river, the Río Guadalquivir, takes you to the twelve-sided **Torre del Oro** (Tues–Fri 10am–2pm, Sat–Sun 11am–2pm; €1), built in 1220 as part of the Alcázar fortifications. The tower later stored the gold brought back to Seville from the Americas – hence its name. Across from here is the **Hospital de la Caridad** (Mon–Sat 9am–1.30pm & 3.30–6.30pm, Sun 9am–1pm; €4) founded in 1676 by Don Miguel de Manara, the inspiration for Byron's Don Juan, who repented his youthful excesses and set up this hospital for the relief of the dying and destitute. There are some magnificent paintings by Murillo and Valdés Leal inside. There's more superb art at the **Museo de Bellas Artes** on Plaza del Museo (Tues 3–8pm, Wed–Sat 9am–8pm, Sun 9am–2pm; €1.50, free for EU citizens), housed in a beautiful former convent. Highlights include paintings by Murillo, as well as Zurbarán's *Carthusian Monks at Supper* and El Greco's portrait of his son.

Across the river lies the **Triana** barrio that was once home to the city's gypsy community and is still a lively and atmospheric place. At Triana's northern edge lies **La Cartuja** (Tues–Fri 10am–8pm, Sat 11am–8pm, Sun 10am–3pm; €1.80), a fourteenth-century former Carthusian monastery, and home to the **Museo del Arte Contemporáneo** (Tues–Sat 9am–8.30pm, Sun 9am–2.30pm; €1.50, free on Tues), which displays work by local artists and hosts international exhibitions.

### Eating, drinking and nightlife

Seville is packed with lively bars and restaurants, but it can be expensive, particularly in the Barrio Santa Cruz. Calle Mateus Gago has some good options, notably *Cervecería Giralda*, at no. 1, for its stuffed baked potatoes; the chic *La Sacristía*, at no. 18, for delicious croquettes with mushrooms and bacon; and the *Café Bar Campanario*, opposite, where two large bulls' heads will watch you eat. Other central areas to try are the streets around Plaza Nueva: the atmospheric *Casa la Vidan,* on c/Albareda, serves a tasty breakfast for a few euros and cheap eats later on, while just east of the square on Plaza de San Francisco, *Bar Laredo* makes filling *bocadillos* for around €3. North of the Alcàzar, the *Altamira,* Plaza Santa María La Blanca 4, is also a good bet, while **vegetarians** should head for the Cuban vegan restaurant *Habanita*, on c/Golfo, just off c/Pérez Galdos, in the Alfalfa area.

For straight drinking and occasional tapas there are **bars** all over town – a high concentration of them with barrelled sherries from nearby Jerez and Sanlúcar (the locals drink the cold, dry fino). In the centre of Santa Cruz one of the liveliest places is *Las Teresas* at c/Santa Teresa 2, while *Bodega Santa Cruz* on c/Rodrigo Caro has loads of atmosphere and tasty tapas. Another good choice, especially for fish tapas, is *Bar Modesto* at c/Cano y Cuento 5, in the northern corner of Santa Cruz by Avda. Menéndez Pelayo. The less expensive *Bodeguita* at c/Arfe 5, south of Plaza Nueva, is also worth searching out, while the *Patio San Eloy* at c/San Eloy 9 is a classic tiled warren serving fabulous small filled rolls. In Triana, the buzzy *Bar Pepe Hillo*, c/Adriano 24, has its own terrace.

The Alfalfa area, north of the cathedral, is lively at night with numerous **music** bars: *Bar Nao* and *Sopa de Ganso* in c/Pérez Galdos both attract a student crowd. The other main area for nightlife, popular with tourists, is just across the river in Triana on c/Betis. **Flamenco** – or more accurately *Sevillanas* – music and dance can be seen at dozens of places in the city, though many are tacky and expensive: head instead to the excellent, rambling bar *La Carbonería* at c/Levías 18, just northeast of the Iglesia de San Juan, which often has spontaneous flamenco, or *Bar Casa Anselma*, c/Pages del Corro 49 in Triana, for authentic dancing (after 11.30pm). Alternatively, try the regular performances at the **Casa de la Memoria de Al-Andalus**, c/Ximenez de Enciso 28 (℡954 560 670; nightly at 9pm; €11), or head to Triana's c/Rodrigo de Triana, home to a handful of Flamenco academies, such as Academia de Baile Manolo, at no. 30, where you can watch the students in action.

## Listings

**Bullfighting** The season starts with the April *feria* and continues until Sept, with most *corridas* held on Sun evenings. Tickets from the Maestranza bullring, Paseo de Colón 12 (℡954 501 382), which also houses a museum; from as little as €10.

**Consulates** Australia, Federico Rubio 14 ℡954 220 971; Ireland, Plaza de Santa Cruz 6 ℡954 216 361; US, Paseo de las Delicias 7 ℡954 231 885.

**Exchange** Banks and *cambios* can be found around the tourist office on Avda. de la Constitución.

**Hospital** Hospital Universitario, Avda. Dr. Fedriani 3 ℡954 557 400. Also, emergency clinic just behind the Alcázar, at corner of Menendez Pelayo and Avda. de Cádiz.

**Internet** Sevilla Internet Center, c/Almirantazgo 2, just off Avda. de la Constitución.

**Laundry** c/Castelar 2.

**Left luggage** At the train station (24hr).

**Pharmacies** Opposite the cathedral on Avda. de la Constitución; in the Barrio de Santa Cruz, on the corner of c/Mateos Gago and c/Rodrigo Caro.

**Police** Plaza de la Gavidia ℡954 228 840.

**Post office** Avda. de la Constitución 32.

# Cádiz

**CÁDIZ** is among the oldest settlements in Spain and has long been one of the country's principal ports. Its heyday was the eighteenth century, when it enjoyed a virtual monopoly on the Spanish-American trade in gold and silver. Central Cádiz, built on a peninsula-island, remains much as it must have looked in those days, with its grand open squares, narrow alleyways and high, turreted houses. It's also the spiritual home of flamenco, and you get a sense of that to this day; the city, crumbling from the effect of sea air on soft limestone, has a tremendous atmosphere – slightly seedy, definitely in decline, but still full of mystique. Cádiz's big party time is its annual **carnival**, normally held in February and early March; expect frenzied celebrations, masked processions and satirical digs at the local big shots.

With its blind alleys, back streets and cafés, Cádiz is fascinating to wander around. To understand the city's layout, climb the **Torre Tavira**, Marqués del Real Tesoro 10 (daily 10am–6/8pm; ⊛www.torretavira.com; €4), tallest of the 160 lookout towers in the city, with an excellent camera obscura. Some specific sites to check out are the huge **Catedral Nueva** (Tues–Fri 10am–1.30pm & 4.30–7pm, Sat 10am–12.30pm, Sun 11am-1pm; €4) – an unusually successful blend of High Baroque and Neoclassical styles, decorated entirely in stone. The oval, eighteenth-century chapel of **Santa Cueva,** c/Rosario (Tues–Fri 10am–1pm & 4.30–7.30pm, Sat & Sun 10am–1pm; €1.50), has eight magnificent arches decorated with frescoes by Goya.

By **train** you'll arrive on the periphery of the old town, close to the Plaza de San Juan de Dios, the busiest of the squares, and home to the **tourist office** (Mon–Fri 9am–2pm & 4–7pm; ℡956 241 001, ⊛www.cadizayto.es). By **bus** you'll be dropped a few blocks further north, along the waterfront. There's plenty of budget **accommodation** in the dense network of alleys around Plaza de San Juan de Dios, protruding across the neck of the peninsula from the port. The best options are the lovely tiled *Pensión Colon*, c/Marqués de Cádiz 6 (℡956 285 351; ❸), with a roof terrace; *Hostal España*, a few doors down at no.9 (℡956 285 500; ❷);

and *Pensión Fantoni*, c/Flamenco 5, (☎956 282 704; ❸), also with a roof terrace. There's a **hostel**, *Quo Vádis*, c/Diego Arias 1 (☎956 221 939; ❷), ten minutes' walk from the train station. Plaza de San Juan de Dios has several **cafés** and cheap **restaurants**, notably *La Caleta*, whose interior is built like the bow of a ship.

## Tarifa

If there is one thing that defines **TARIFA**, it is the wind. This is the most southerly point in mainland Europe and in the summer the prevailing, massively powerful, levant has made it one of the world's most popular **wind-and-kite-surfing** destinations. The elements aside, there's a good feel to the place – with its funky, laid-back atmosphere and maze of narrow streets. Africa feels very close, too, with the Rif Mountains clearly visible. The ten-kilometre white, sandy beaches, **Playa de los Lances** and **Playa Valdevaqueros**, are the places to head for wind- and kite-surfing. In summer they're connected to the town by a shuttle bus. Just to the east of town are the dramatic rocky coves of **La Caleta**. If you're not an experienced surfer, remember these winds can reach storm force ten: be sure to join a course such as the one run by Tarifa Spinout (☎956 236 352; from €50/2hr). You can also **whale- and dolphin-watch** from Tarifa: book in advance through one of the two, non-profit-making organizations: Whale Watch España, Avda. de la Constitución 6 (☎639 476 544; €27), or Tarifa, Pedro Cortez 4 (☎956 627 008; €27).

**Buses** drop off at the stop on the main Cádiz-Algeciras road, Batalla del Salado: head downhill for the ancient archway into the old town. EU citizens can take the **ferry to Tangier** in Morocco (€24.50 one way). The **tourist office** is on the fringes of the old town at Paseo de la Alameda (Mon–Sat 10am–2pm & 6–8pm, Sun 10am–2pm; ☎956 680 993; ⊛www.tarifaweb.com). In the summer finding **accommodation** can be tricky, making it advisable to book in advance. A good bet is *Hostal Africa*, c/María Antonia Toledo 12 (☎956 680 220; ❸), in the old town with a fantastic view of Africa from its large roof terrace. Also in the old town, near San Mateo church, is the lovely *Pensión Correo*, c/Coronel Moscardó 8 (☎956 680 206; ❹). There are several **campsites** near the main windsurfing beaches, such as *Tarifa* (☎956 684 778), *Paloma* (☎956 684 203) and *Torre de la Pena* (☎956 684 903). The central Plaza de Oviedo is home to the cosmopolitan *Café Central*, as well as a kiosk by the church selling *bocadillos*, falafal and kebabs; nearby *La Trattoría*, Paseo de la Alameda, serves decent pizza and pasta. There are plenty of **bars** – in the old town one of the best is *La Ruina*, c/Trinidad, which has an open rooftop terrace in the summer. Away from the centre, **clubs** include the funky *Far Out*, and the seasonal *Jungle Playa* and *La Jaima*; to get there take the free night buses.

## Málaga and the Costa del Sol

Perhaps the outstanding feature of the **Costa del Sol,** the richest and fastest-growing resort area in the Mediterranean, is its ease of access. Hundreds of charter flights arrive here every week, which means that it's often possible to get an absurdly cheap ticket from London. Málaga airport is positioned midway between **Málaga**, the main city on the coast, and **Torremolinos**, its much maligned resort. A train (every 30min) runs along the coast between Málaga and Fuengirola, while Granada, Córdoba and Sevilla are all within easy reach, as are Ronda and the white villages (*pueblos blancos*). In some ways then, this coast's enormous popularity isn't surprising: what is surprising is that the **beaches** are generally grit-grey rather than golden and the sea is none too clean.

    **MÁLAGA** is the second city of the south after Seville, and also one of the poorest. Yet though the clusters of high-rises look pretty grim as you approach, the historic centre has plenty of charm. Around the old fishing villages of El Palo and Pedregalejo, to the east of the centre, are a series of small beaches and a promenade lined with some of the best fish and seafood restaurants in the province. Overlooking the town and port are the Moorish citadels of the **Alcazaba** (Tues–Sun 9.30am–7/8pm; €1.80), where the lengthy excavation of a **Roman amphitheatre** continues, and the **Gibralfaro castle** (daily 9am–7/8pm; €1.80, €3 including Alcazaba), just fifteen minutes' walk from the train or bus stations, and visible from most central points. Málaga's most famous native son, born here in 1881, is honoured in the new **Museo Picasso**, on c/San Agustín (Tues–Thurs 10am–8pm, Fri–Sat 10am–9pm, Sun 10am–8pm; €6), which displays works spanning Picasso's entire career, from his earliest sketches to some of his last paintings created shortly before his death in 1973.

Buses #5 and #18 connect the main **train and bus stations** to the centre. Arriving at the **airport**, catch the electric train (every 30min) to the main train station, or continue another stop to Málaga Centro: Alameda for the city centre. The **tourist office** is at Pasaje Chinitas 4 (Mon–Fri 8am–1.30pm & 4.30–7pm, Sat & Sun 9.30am–1.30pm; ☎952 213 445, ⊛www.malagaturismo.com), with a second branch at Avenida de Cervantes 1 (Mon–Fri 8am–2.30pm & 4–7pm, Sat & Sun 9.30am–1.30pm; ☎952 604 410).

Málaga has a number of reasonably priced **rooms**, especially in the streets north and south of the Alameda. Alternatively, try *Hostal La Palma*, c/Martínez 7 (☎952 226 772; ❷), or the more upmarket *Hotel Lis*, c/Córdoba 7 (☎952 227 300; ⊛www .costadelsol.spa.es/hotel/hotelis; ❺). There's also a **hostel**, *Albergue Juvenil Málaga*, at Plaza Pío XII 6 (☎952 308 500; under 26 €13.50, over 26 €18.25). The closest **campsite** (☎952 382 602) is at Torremolinos on Ctra. Nacional; take the Málaga-Torremolinos bus from the train station. Malaga's cuisine - fried fish and sweet Málaga wine – can be enjoyed at a vast choice of **tapas bars and restaurants**. One of the most atmospheric spit 'n' sawdust-style bodegas is *Antigua Casa de Guardia*, Alameda Principal 16, the oldest bar in town, with wine served straight from the barrel. *Bar Logueno*, on c/Marín Garcia, is a local favourite with over 75 tapas to choose from. You'll find plenty of other bars in the area between Plaza de la Merced and Plaza de los Mártires, which is buzzing till late at the weekend.

Approached in the right kind of spirit, it's possible to have fun in **TORREMO-LINOS**, whose reputation as a haven for beer-swilling youths and coach tours of grannies is somewhat overplayed. There is still a relatively unspoilt old part of town, plus La Carihuela, the former fishermen's district, now better known for its excellent seafood restaurants and traditional low-rise buildings. For **accommodation**, try *Hostal Flor Blanco*, Paseo Marítimo La Carihuela 4 (☎952 382 071; ❸). A good time costs more in chic **MARBELLA**, where there are bars and nightclubs galore alongside a surprisingly well-preserved old village and some wonderfully conspicuous consumption. At **ESTEPONA** there's a **campsite** and a number of **hostales**, including the *Vista al Mar*, c/Real 154 (☎952 803 247; ❷). Just south of here, **SAN PEDRO DE ALCANTARA** provides something of a haven amid the sea of development, with its pleasant Plaza de la Iglesia. For **accommodation**, try *Dona Catalina*, Avda. Oriental 14 (☎952 853 120; ⊛www.hotasa.es; ❸), offering en-suite rooms with little balconies, or *Hostal La Colonia*, Avda. Oriental 18 (☎952 783 765; ❸). There's inexpensive food at *Maccherone* Italian **restaurant** on Avda. Oriental or the *Café Bar Picasso* on Avda. Pablo Ruiz Picasso, near the church on the plaza, which also offers **Internet** access.

# Ronda

Andalucía is dotted with small, brilliantly whitewashed villages known as the **pueblos blancos**, most often straggling up hillsides towards a castle or towered church. The most spectacular lie in a roughly triangular area between Málaga, Algeciras and Seville, at whose centre is the startling town of **RONDA**, connected by a scenic road and rail line from Algeciras, the latter a wonderful ride.

Built on an isolated ridge of the sierra, and ringed by dark, angular mountains, Ronda is split in half by a gaping river gorge with a sheer drop, spanned by an eighteenth-century arched bridge. The town itself is fascinating to wander around and has sacrificed surprisingly little of its character to the flow of day-trippers from the coast. Crossing the Puente Nuevo from Plaza de España takes you from the modern **Mercadillo** quarter to the old Moorish town, the **Ciudad**, centred on the church of **Santa María la Mayor**, originally the mosque. Turning off the main street to the left takes you steeply down to the old bridges – the **Puente Viejo** of 1616 and the Roman single-span **Puente Arabe**. Nearby, on the southeast bank of the river, are the distinctive **Baños Árabes** (daily 10am–7pm, Sat & Sun 10am-3pm; €2). Crossing the old bridge takes you back to the modern town via the **Jardín de la Mina**, which ascends the gorge in a series of stepped terraces with superb views of the river, new bridge and remarkable stairway of the **Casa del Rey Moro** (daily 10am–8pm; €4), an early eighteenth-century mansion built on Moorish foundations. Don't miss the delightful, tiled garden of the **Casa Don Bosco** (daily 9am–5.30pm; €1) at Calle San Juan de Lefran 20. Behind the church is the **Palacio de Mondragón** (Mon–Fri 10am–7pm, Sat & Sun 10am-3pm; €2), probably the palace of the Moorish kings and now home to the Museo Municipal – a steep path descends to the river from here. The principal gate of the town, through which the Christian conquerors passed, stands beside the **Alcázar**, destroyed by the French in 1809. Back in the Mercadillo quarter is the **bullring** (daily 10am–8pm; €4, including museum) – one of the most prestigious in Spain – and the beautiful clifftop *paseo*, facing the open valley and the dramatic mountains of the Serrenía de Ronda.

Ronda's **tourist office** is opposite the entrance to the bullring at Plaza de Toros (Mon-Fri 9.30am–7.30pm, Sat & Sun 10am–2pm & 5.30–6.30pm; ☎952 187 119, ⓦwww.turismoderonda.es), with the regional office nearby at Paseo de Blas Infante 29 (Mon–Fri 9.30am-7.30pm; Sat & Sun 10am-2pm and 3.30-6.30pm; ☎952 187 119; www.andalucia.org).

All the **accommodation** is in the Mercadillo quarter. Calle Almendra (a continuation of c/Lorenzo Borrego) has several options including the basic but cheap *Hostal Ronda Sol*, c/Almendra 11 (☎952 874 497; ❷), and *Pensión Hostal Biarritz*, c/Almendra 7 (☎952 872 910; ❷), a few doors down at no. 7. Nearby, the basic *La Purisima*, c/Sevilla 10 (☎952 871 050; ❸), is recommended, as is the pleasant *Hotel Macias*, c/Pedro Romero 3 (☎952 874 238; ❹), and the *Hotel Virgen de los Reyes*, c/Lorenzo Borrego 13 (☎952 871 140; ❸), both with comfortable en-suite rooms. The best of the **campsites** is *El Sur* (☎952 875 939, ⓦwww.camping-elsur .es), 1.5km down the Algeciras road.

Budget **restaurants** are mainly found around Plaza del Socorro, on c/Almendra. *El Brillante* on c/Sevilla is friendly and cheap, as is *Pizzeria Michel Angelo* at c/Lorenzo Borrego 5. Alternatively, try *Taberna de Santo Domingo*, on the road of the same name, just across the Puente Nuevo into the old town, or *Hotel-Restaurante Don Miguel*, on Plaza de España, with great views of the gorge. For pastries, coffee and the **Internet**, there's Planet Adventure, just off the Plaza del Socorro at c/Molino 6. At the weekend, Ronda's **nightlife** kicks off along c/Niño and c/Jerez, and around Plaza de C. Abela. For the energetic, Pangea Active Nature, c/Dolores Ibarruri 4 (☎952 873 496, ⓦwww.pangea-ronda.com), arranges **hiking**, **mountain-biking** and **kayaking** through the spectacular local scenery; a half-day bike-trip costs €30, half-day kayaking €35.

## Algeciras

The main reason to visit **ALGECIRAS**, a bus ride along the coast from Cádiz, is for the **ferry to Morocco**, though the old town has some pleasant plazas and parks. The crossings are to Tangier (10 daily; 2hr 30min; €25 one way; ⓦwww .trasmediterranea.es) and tickets are available at scores of travel agents along the waterside on Avda. Virgen del Carmen and on most approach roads. Wait till Tangier before buying any Moroccan currency. The number of people passing through Algeciras guarantees plenty of inexpensive **rooms**. Try the family-run *Pensión Tetuan* at Duque de Almodóvar 9 (☎956 652 854; ❷), or the modern *Hotel Jusa Alarde* (☎956 660 408; ❺), in the business district. If you have trouble finding space, check the list in the **tourist office** near the port on Avda. Villa Nueva (Mon–Fri 9am–2pm; ☎956 572 636; ⊛www.andalucia.org). A good bet for cheap **restaurants** is c/Emilio Castelar in the centre.

# Travel details

## Trains

**Algeciras** to: Madrid (2 daily; 6hr); Granada (3 daily; 4hr); Ronda (5 daily; 1hr 40min).
**Barcelona** to: Bilbao (2 daily; 9hr–10hr 20min); Girona (hourly; 1hr 15min–1hr 30min); Puigcerdà (6 daily; 3hr); Tarragona (every 30min; 1hr); Valencia (14 daily; 3–5hr); Zaragoza (15 daily; 3hr 40min–4hr 30min).
**Bilbao** to: León (1 daily; 4hr 40min); Madrid (1–2 daily; 5hr 10min–8hr 30min); San Sebastián (6–7 daily; 2hr 30min).
**Córdoba** to: Madrid (8 daily; 1hr 40min–4hr 30min); Málaga (8–10 daily; 2hr 10min–3hr 30min); Seville (20 daily; 1hr–1hr 30min).
**Granada** to: Madrid (2 daily; 6hr); Ronda (1 daily; 4hr 20min); Valencia (1–2 daily; 8hr 20min).
**León** to: Barcelona (3–4 daily; 9hr 30min–11hr 40min); Madrid (5–7 daily; 4hr–6hr 20min); Oviedo (5 daily; 2hr); Salamanca (6 daily; 3–5hr); San Sebastián (1 daily; 5hr); Santiago (1 daily; 6hr).
**Madrid** to: Algeciras (2 daily; 6hr); Alicante (6–7 daily; 3hr 45min–4hr); Barcelona (6–7 daily; 4hr 45min–9hr); Bilbao (1–2 daily; 5hr 10min–8hr 30min); Cáceres (5–6 daily; 3hr 25min–5hr); Cádiz (2 daily; 5hr); Córdoba (8 daily; 1hr 40min–4hr 30min); Granada (2 daily; 6hr); Jaca (1 daily; 7hr); León (5–7 daily; 4hr–6hr 20min); Málaga (5–6 daily; 4–7hr); Mérida (4–5 daily; 4hr 20min–7hr 30min); Oviedo (2–3 daily; 5hr 45min–8hr 10min); Pamplona (2–3 daily; 3hr 30min); Salamanca (5 daily; 2hr 30min); San Sebastián (3 daily; 6hr 30min–9hr); Santiago (2 daily; 8–9hr); Segovia (7–9 daily; 2hr); Seville (18 daily; 2hr 30min); Toledo (7–10 daily; 1hr); Valencia (11 daily; 3hr 30min); Zaragoza (13 daily; 1hr 45min–4hr 30min).
**Málaga** to: Córdoba (8–10 daily; 2hr 10min–3hr 30min); Madrid (5–6 daily; 4–7hr); Ronda (1 daily; 2hr); Seville (6 daily; 3hr).
**San Sebastián** to: Bilbao (6–7 daily; 2hr 30min);

Madrid (3 daily; 6hr 30min–9hr); Pamplona (2–3 daily; 1hr 45min); Salamanca (2 daily; 6–7hr); Valencia (1 weekly; 11hr); Zaragoza (2–3 daily; 4–5hr).
**Santiago** to: León (1 daily; 6hr); Madrid (2 daily; 8–9hr ).
**Valencia** to: Barcelona (17 daily; 3hr); Granada (2 daily; 9hr); Madrid (10 daily; 3-6hr).
**Zaragoza** to: Barcelona (14–16 daily; 3–6hr); Canfranc (2 daily; 3hr 30min); Jaca (3 daily; 3hr 10min); Madrid (13 daily; 1hr 45min–4hr 30min); Pamplona (4–5 daily; 2hr).

## Buses

**Alicante** to: Barcelona (7 daily; 8hr); Granada (3–5 daily; 5hr); Madrid (5 daily; 6hr); Málaga (5 daily; 8hr); Valencia (hourly; 4hr).
**Barcelona** to: Alicante (7 daily; 8hr); Madrid (7–15 daily; 7hr 30min); Valencia (14–17 daily; 4–5hr); the Vall d'Aran (1 daily; 6hr 30min); Zaragoza (15–25 daily; 3hr 30min–5hr).
**Bilbao** to: San Sebastián (1–2 hourly; 1hr 10min); Santiago de Compostela (3 daily; 11–12hr).
**Córdoba** to: Granada (7 daily; 3hr); Madrid (6 daily; 4hr 30min); Málaga (5 daily; 3hr–3hr 30min); Seville (10 daily; 2hr 30min).
**Figueres** to: Barcelona (3–6 daily; 2hr 15min); Cadaqués (3 daily; 1hr); L'Escala (5 daily; 45min); Palafrugell (4 daily; 1hr 30min).
**Girona** to: Barcelona (3–7 daily; 2hr 15min); Begur (4 daily; 1hr 30min); Cadaqués (3 daily; 1hr 50min).
**Granada** to: Alicante (3–5 daily; 5hr); Cádiz (2 daily; 6hr); Córdoba (7 daily; 3hr); Madrid (6–9 daily; 6hr); Seville (7–9 daily; 3hr 30min–4hr 30min); Valencia (3 daily; 7hr).
**Madrid** to: Algeciras (4 daily; 8hr 30min); Alicante (8 daily; 5hr); Barcelona (7–15 daily; 7hr 30min); Bilbao (11 daily; 4hr 45min); Cáceres (7–10 daily; 4hr); Cádiz (6 daily; 7hr); Córdoba (6 daily; 4hr 30min); El Escorial (hourly; 1hr); Granada (6–9

daily; 6hr); León (11 daily; 4hr); Málaga (7 daily; 7hr); Oviedo (12 daily; 5hr 30min); Pamplona (4 daily; 6hr); Salamanca (16 daily; 2hr 30min); San Sebastián (8–9 daily; 6hr 30min); Santander (8 daily; 6hr); Santiago (6 daily; 8–9hr); Segovia (every 30min; 1hr 30min); Seville (11 daily; 6–8hr); Toledo (every 30min; 1hr); Valencia (14 daily; 4hr).

**Málaga** to: Algeciras (10 daily; 3hr); Córdoba (5 daily; 3hr–3hr 30min); Granada (14 daily; 2hr); Ronda (6 daily; 3hr); Seville (11 daily; 3hr); Torremolinos (every 30min; 30min).

**Salamanca** to: Mérida (5 daily; 4hr 30min); Seville (5 daily; 8hr).

**San Sebastián** to: Bilbao (1–2 hourly; 1hr 10min); Madrid (8–9 daily; 6hr 30min); Pamplona (13 daily; 2hr).

**Santiago** to: Porto (4 weekly; 2hr 30min); Madrid (6 daily; 8hr).

**Seville** to: Cádiz (11 daily; 2hr); Córdoba (10 daily; 2hr 30min); Granada (7–9 daily; 3hr 30min–4hr 30min); Madrid (11 daily; 6–8hr).

**Valencia** to: Alicante (hourly; 4hr); Barcelona (14–17 daily; 4–5hr); Denia (8 daily; 1hr 45min); Madrid (13 daily; 4hr); Seville (3 daily; 11hr).

**Zaragoza** to: Barcelona (15–25 daily; 3hr 30min–5hr); Madrid (19 daily; 3hr 30min); Pamplona (7–8 daily; 2hr–2hr 45min).

## Ferries

**Barcelona** to: Ibiza (4–6 weekly; 9hr 30min); Palma (2–4 daily; 8hr 30min).

**Denia** to: Ibiza (1–2 daily; 2hr 15min–4hr 30min); Palma (2 daily; 5hr–10hr 30min).

**Ibiza** to: Formentera (6–9 daily; 30min–1hr); Palma (1–3 weekly; 6hr 30min); Valencia (1–6 weekly; 9hr).

**Tarifa** to: Tangier, Morocco (summer 4 daily; winter 5 weekly; 30–45min).

**Palma** to: Ibiza (1–3 weekly; 6hr 30min).

**Valencia** to: Ibiza (1–6 weekly; 7hr); Palma (6–13 weekly; 9h).

# Sweden

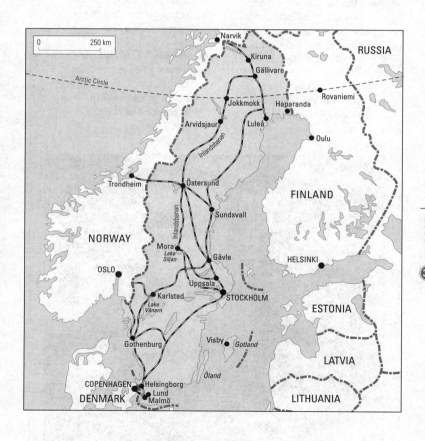

# Sweden highlights

* **Gamla Stan, Stockholm**
One of Europe's most
elegant and best pre-
served medieval centres.
See p.988

* **Lilla Torg, Malmö** This
beautiful cobbled square
in the city centre is a fine
place to down a beer or
two and chill. See p.996

* **Inlandsbanan** Single
track rail line that winds
its way through virgin
forest and past crystal-
clear streams en route to
Lapland. See p.999

* **Orsa Grönklitt bear
park, Dalarna** A rare
chance to come face to
face with the King of the
Forest. See p.999

* **Jokkmokk, Arctic
Circle** An excellent base
from which to explore
the wilds of Swedish
Lapland. See p.1000

△ Gamla Stan, Stockholm

# Introduction and basics

**Sweden** is one of Europe's best kept secrets. This vast land of coniferous forests and crystal clear mountain lakes boasts not only sophisticated cities but also some of the continent's best beaches. And forget about legendary high prices, devaluation has now made Sweden one of the best bargains in Europe.

The west coast harbours a host of historic ports – **Gothenburg**, **Helsingborg** and **Malmö**, linked by bridge to Copenhagen – but it is **Stockholm**, the capital, that is the country's supreme attraction, a bundle of islands housing monumental architecture, fine museums and the country's most active culture and nightlife. The two university towns, **Lund** and **Uppsala**, demand a visit too, while, moving northwards, **Östersund** both makes justified demands on your time. This area, central and northern Sweden, is the country of tourist brochures: great swathes of forest, inexhaustible lakes (some 96,000 of them) and some of the best wilderness hiking in Europe.

## Information & maps

Almost all towns have a **tourist office**, giving out maps and timetables, and usually able to book private rooms, rent bikes and change money. The best **map** is the Motormännens *Sveriges Atlas*.

## Money and banks

Currency is the **krona** (plural kronor), made up of 100 öre. There are coins of 50öre, 1kr, 5kr and 10kr; and notes of 20kr, 50kr, 100kr,

500kr, 1000kr and 10,000kr. At the time of writing €1 was worth 9kr, US$1 was 7.5kr, and £1 was 14kr. **Banks** are open Mon–Fri 9.30am–3pm, Thurs also 4–5.30pm. Outside hours you can **change money** at airports and ferry terminals, as well as at Forex offices, which usually offer the best rates (minimum 30kr commission). **ATMs** are plentiful and **credit cards** are accepted just about everywhere.

## Communications

**Post office** services can now be found in supermarkets, newsagents, tobacconists and hotels. **Public phones** take cards (*telefonkort*), available from newsagents and kiosks. You can also use credit cards in payphones marked "CCC". Directory enquiries is on ☎118 118 (domestic), ☎118 119 (international). **Internet** cafés are surprisingly rare, though you should find at least one in the larger towns (40–60kr/hr). Access is free in local libraries.

## Getting around

Swedish State Railways (SJ; ⊛ www.sj.se) has an extensive **train** network, running as far north as Sundsvall and Östersund.

SWEDEN | Basics

---

### Sweden on the net

⊛**www.cityguide.se** Up-to-date guide to events and entertainment in the main Swedish cities.

⊛**www.visit-sweden.com** The largest single source of information in English on Sweden, its provinces, nature, culture and society.

⊛**www.stockholmtown.com** Everything you ever wanted to know about the Swedish capital.

⊛**www.svenskaturistforeningen.se** Tips and ideas on where to visit in Sweden, courtesy of the Swedish Youth Hostel Association.

InterRail and Eurail are valid, as is the ScanRail pass (see p.51). The famous Inlandsbanan line (@ www.inlandsbanan.se), which runs through central and northern Sweden, operates from mid-June to mid-September. The *SJ Tågtider* timetable, from any station, lists many useful train services (not the Inlandsbanan or Pågatågen line, on both of which InterRail is valid). It's a good idea to reserve your seat. If you're travelling on a pass, you must reserve seats separately before your journey (65kr). For all train travel north of the line between Sundsvall and Östersund, above the Arctic Circle and on into Norway, service is provided by Connex (@ www.connex.se). SJ will not book tickets on Connex lines or give out information.

# Accommodation

Sweden has 315 **hostels** operated by STF (@ www.svenskaturistforeningen.se). There are usually doubles as well as dorms, and virtually all have self-catering kitchens and serve a buffet breakfast. Prices are low (120–200kr); non-HI members pay about an extra 50kr a night. There are also many non-STF hostels, mostly run by SVIF (@ www.svif.se).

**Hotels** come cheaper than you'd think, especially in Stockholm and the bigger towns during the summer, when hotels slash their prices. Reduced summer prices are identical to price – an average for an en-suite double room is 650kr. All hotels include breakfast in the price. Package

## Swedish

|  | Swedish | Pronunciation |
|---|---|---|
| Yes | Ja | Ya |
| No | Nej | Nay |
| Please | Var så god | Vaa-show-go |
| Thank you | Tack | Tak |
| Hello/Good day | Hej | Hay |
| Goodbye | Hejdå | Hay-doe |
| Excuse me | Ursäkta | Urh-shekta |
| Where? | Var? | Vaar? |
| Good | Bra | Braa |
| Bad | Dålig | Doe-lee |
| Near | Nära | Nera |
| Far | Avlägsen | Arv-lessen |
| Cheap | Billig | Billi |
| Expensive | Dyr | Deer |
| Open | Öppen | Upp-en |
| Closed | Stängd | Stengd |
| Today | I dag | Ee daa |
| Yesterday | I går | Ee gor |
| Tomorrow | I morgon | Ee morron |
| How much is....? | Vad kostar det...? | Vaa kostar day? |
| What time is it? | Hur mycket är klockan? | Hoor mucker er clockan? |
| I don't understand | Jag förstår inte | Yaa fur-stor inte |
| Do you speak English? | Talar du engelska? | Taalar doo eng-ul-ska? |
| One | Ett | Ett |
| Two | Två | Tvo |
| Three | Tre | Tray |
| Four | Fyra | Feera |
| Five | Fem | Fem |
| Six | Sex | Sex |
| Seven | Sju | Shoo |
| Eight | Åtta | Otta |
| Nine | Nio | Nee-o |
| Ten | Tio | Tee-o |

deals in Malmö, Stockholm and Gothenburg, bookable through the tourist office, get you a hotel bed for one night, breakfast and a city discount card from 450–550kr per person (mid-June to mid-Aug & weekends year-round). In larger towns you can book a **private room** through the tourist office for about the same as a hostel bed.

Practically every village has at least one **campsite**, generally of a high standard. Pitching a tent costs 100–200kr in July & Aug (plus a 10–20kr fee per person), a little less at other times. Most sites are open June to Sept, some year-round; all are listed in the book *Camping Sverige*, available at larger sites and bookshops. Many sites have **cabins**, usually with bunk beds and kitchen equipment but not sheets, for 350–500kr for a four-bedded affair.

# Food and drink

Swedish **food** is largely meat-, fish- and potato-based – varied and generally tasty; eating and drinking is not as expensive as it used to be. **Breakfast** (*frukost*) is invariably a help-yourself buffet of juice, cereals, bread, boiled eggs, jams, salami, tea and coffee (hostels 55kr, hotels free). **Coffee** is usually filter and can be bitter; it's often free after the first cup. **Tea** is weak but costs the same (15–20kr). For **snacks**, a *gatukök* (street kitchen) or *korvstånd* (hot-dog stall) will serve hot dogs, burgers, chips and the like for around 40kr. A hefty burger-and-fries meal costs 55–60kr. Coffee shops always display a range of freshly baked pastries (coffee and cake for 40–60kr), and also serve *smörgåsar*, **open sandwiches** piled high with toppings for 30–60kr. Eating in a **restaurant** is great value at lunchtime (11am–2pm), when most places offer a set meal (*dagens rätt*) of a main dish with bread and salad at 65–75kr. Specialities include northern Swedish delicacies – reindeer and elk meat, and wild berries – and herring in many different guises. More expensive are restaurants and hotels that put out the **smörgåsbord** at lunchtime for 150–200kr, where you help yourself to unlimited portions of herring, smoked and fresh salmon, hot and cold meats, potatoes, salad, cheese and fruit. Otherwise meals in restaurants, especially at **dinner** (*middag*), can be expensive: 200–250kr for two courses, plus 35–55kr for a beer. Better value are pizzerias and Chinese restaurants.

**Drinking** costs the same as in most European capitals. You'll pay 40–55kr for half a litre of lager-type **beer** – a *storstark*. Unless you specify, it will be *starköl*, the strongest beer, or the slightly weaker *mellanöl*; *folköl* is the cheaper and weaker brew; cheapest (around half the price) is *lättöl*, a concoction that is virtually non-alcoholic. A glass of **wine** in a bar or restaurant costs around 50–60kr, while you can buy a whole bottle for a little more in a state bottle shop. The local firewater is **akvavit**, served ice-cold in tiny shots and washed down with beer. Bars and pubs close around midnight, a little later in Malmö, Gothenburg and Stockholm.

# Opening hours and holidays

**Shops** open Mon–Fri 9am–6pm, Sat 9am–1/4pm. Some larger stores stay open until 8/10pm, and open Sun noon–4pm. Banks, offices and shops close on **public holidays** (and may close early on the preceding day): Jan 1, Jan 6, Good Fri, Easter Sun & Mon, May 1, Ascension, Whit Sun & Mon, June 20 & 21, Nov 1, Dec 24–26 & 31.

# Emergencies

The **police** are courteous and fluent in English. In case of **health problems** go to a hospital with your passport, where for a maximum of around 500kr you'll receive treatment; if you have to stay it costs an extra 85kr per day. Urgent treatment is free for anyone with a European Health Insurance Card. A **pharmacist** (*apotek*) opens shop hours (Stockholm has a 24-hour pharmacy; see p.991); larger towns operate a rota system, with the address of the nearest late-opener posted on each pharmacy's door.

**Emergency numbers**

All emergencies ☏112.

# Stockholm

Built on fourteen islands, **Stockholm** was a natural site for the fortifications, erected in 1255, that grew into the current city. In the sixteenth century, the city fell to King Gustav Vasa, a century later becoming the centre of the Swedish trading empire that covered present-day Scandinavia and beyond. Following the waning of Swedish power it only rose to prominence again in the nineteenth century when industrialization took off.

## Arrival and information

Stockholm has three **airports**, all linked to the city by bus or train. Ryanair flies into Stockholm Skavsta and Västerås, both 100km from the capital and connected by bus (both 130kr single; 199kr return; 80min) to the Cityterminalen. From the main airport, Arlanda, buses (89kr single; 170kr return) and trains (190kr single) run frequently into the city arriving at the Cityterminalen and Central Station respectively. By **train**, you arrive at **Central Station**, a cavernous structure on Vasagatan in Norrmalm. All branches of the Tunnelbana, Stockholm's metro, meet at T-Centralen, the station directly below Central Station. **Cityterminalen**, adjacent, handles all **bus** services, both domestic and international. Viking Line **ferries** arrive at **Tegelvikshamnen** in Södermalm, in the south of the city, a thirty-minute walk from the centre, or connected by bus to Slussen and then by Tunnelbana to T-Centralen. The Silja Line terminal is in the northeastern reaches of the city, a short walk from Gärdet or Ropsten underground stations. The useful **tourist office** (Mon–Fri 9am–6pm, Sat & Sun 10am–3pm; ☎08/508 28 508, ⓦwww.stockholm town.com) is at Hamngatan 27 near Sergels Torg square, and sells the **Stockholm Card** (260/390/540kr for 24/48/72 hours), which gives unlimited city transport (except on direct airport buses) and free museum entry and boat tours.

The best way to explore is to **walk** – it takes about 25 minutes to cross central Stockholm on foot. Alternatively, Storstockholms Lokaltrafik (SL; ⓦwww.sl.se) operates buses and trains (underground and local) – quickest is the **Tunnelbana** (T-bana) metro, based on three main lines. **Buses** can be less direct. **Ferries** also link some of the central islands: Djurgården is connected with Nybroplan in Norrmalm (summer only) and Skeppsbron in Gamla Stan (all year). Individual tickets are relatively expensive so buy a **pass**. Don't confuse the Stockholm Card (see above) with the more limited **24-hour** and **72-hour cards** (95/180kr), which give unlimited travel on public transport within Stockholm county. A strip of twenty transferable SL **ticket coupons** (*Rabattkuponger*; 145kr) is also an option; you'll need two coupons for any single journey in the centre. You can hail **taxis** in the street, or book on ☎08/15 00 00. A daytime trip across the city centre costs 170–200kr; women get a 5–10 percent discount at weekends.

## Accommodation

There's plenty of **accommodation**, but booking in advance is always a good idea. The cheapest choices lie north of Cityterminalen, in the streets west of Adolf Fredriks Kyrka. **Hotellcentralen**, a booking service on the lower level of Central Station (daily 8/9am–4/6/8pm; ☎08/508 28 508, ⓔhotels@svb.stockholm.se), charges a fee of 60kr per room, 25kr for a hostel if you go in person, but is free over the phone. Hotelltjänst, Nybrogatan 44 (☎08/10 44 37, ⓦwww.hotelltjanst .com), can fix you up with a double **private room** for around 600kr.

### Hostels

**Af Chapman** Skeppsholmen ☎08/463 22 66, ⓦwww.stfchapman.com. Official hostel on an atmospheric sailing ship moored at Skeppsholmen. Without a reservation, the chances of a bed in summer are negligible. Dorms 155kr, rooms ⑤

**City Backpackers** Upplandsgatan 2A, Norra

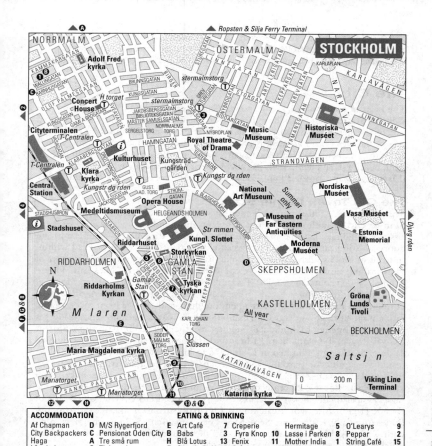

**STOCKHOLM**

| ACCOMMODATION | | EATING & DRINKING | | | | | |
|---|---|---|---|---|---|---|---|
| Af Chapman | **D** | Art Café | **7** | Creperie | Hermitage | **5** | O'Learys | **9** |
| City Backpackers | **C** | Babs | **3** | Fyra Knop | **10** | Lasse i Parken | **8** | Peppar | **2** |
| Haga | **A** | Blå Lotus | **13** | Fenix | **11** | Mother India | **1** | String Café | **15** |
| Långholmen | **G** | Cosmic Café | **12** | Gråmunken | **6** | Muffin Bakery | **4** | Söders Hjärta | **14** |
| M/S Rygerfjord | **E** | | | | | | | |
| Pensionat Oden City | **B** | | | | | | | |
| Tre små rum | **H** | | | | | | | |
| Zinkensdamm | **F** | | | | | | | |

Bantorget ☎08/20 69 20, ⊛www
.citybackpackers.se. Curfewless non-STF hostel
with four-bed rooms and cheaper eight-bed dorms.
Free internet. Dorms 190kr, rooms ⑧

**Långholmen** Kronohäktet, Långholmen ☎08/720
85 00, ⊛www.langholmen.com. Stockholm's
grandest official hostel, in an old prison on Långholmen island, with ordinary doubles in summer
as well as hostel beds. T-bana to Hornstull. Turn
left and follow the signs. Dorms 205kr, rooms ⑤

**M/S Rygerfjord** Söder Mälarstrand-Kaj 12
☎08/84 08 30, ⊛www.rygerfjord.se. Comfortable
hostel-ship moored on Södermalm close to Slussen T-bana station. 185kr.

**Zinkensdamm** Zinkens väg 20, Södermalm
☎08/616 81 00, ⊛www.zinkensdamm.com. Huge
official hostel, nicely situated by the water, with
kitchen facilities. Zinkensdamm T-bana. Dorms
185kr, rooms ⑤

### Hotels and pensions

**Haga** Hagagatan 29 ☎08/545 473 00, ⊛www
.hagahotel.se. Modern, good-value rooms within
easy walking distance of the northern edge of the
city centre. Odenplan T-bana. ⑦

**Pensionat Oden City** Kammakargatan 62
☎08/796 96 00, ⊛www.pensionat.nu. Superb location right in the city centre and at a good price. ⑥

**Tre små rum** Högbergsgatan 81 ☎08/641 23
71, ⊛www.tresmarum.se. Seven bright modern
non-smoking rooms in the heart of Södermalm. No
en-suites. Mariatorget T-bana. ⑥

### Campsites

**Ängby** ☎08/37 04 20. West of the city on Lake
Mälaren and near the beach. T-bana to Ängbyplan,
then a 300m walk. Open all year.

**Bredäng** ☎08/97 70 71. Pricey place with a hostel
and restaurant on site. 10km southwest of the

centre by Lake Mälaren. Take T-bana to Bredäng from where it's a 700m walk. April–Oct only. **Östermalms Citycamping** Fiskartorpsvägen 2

⊕ 08/10 29 03. Stockholm's most centrally located campsite at the Östermalm sports ground surrounded by woodland. Late June to late Aug only.

# The City

The heart of Stockholm is the old town, Gamla Stan, a 200m walk south from the **Central Station** across Vasabron Bridge. The main commercial districts are located east of the station along Klarabergsgatan, Sveavägen and Hamngatan. However, one of the city's main attractions lies next door to the station right at the water's edge: the **Stadshuset**, Hantverkargatan 1 (guided tours 10am & noon; June–Sept 2pm; 60kr; T-Centralen). With its gently-tapering 106-metre high red-brick **tower** (May–Sept daily 10am–4.30pm; 15kr), it has the best fix on the city's layout.

## The Old Town: Gamla Stan,

Three islands – Riddarholmen, Staden and Helgeandsholmen – make up **Gamla Stan** or **Old Stockholm**, a clutter of seventeenth- and eighteenth-century Renaissance buildings, hairline medieval alleys and tall, dark houses whose intricate doorways still bear the arms of the wealthy merchants who once dwelled within. In front of the Swedish parliament building, Riksdagshuset, accessible by a set of steps leading down from Norrbro, the **Medeltidsmuseum** (Tues–Sun 11am–4/6pm; guided tours 2pm; 60kr; T-Gamla Stan) is the best city-related historical collection in Stockholm. Ruins of medieval tunnels and walls were discovered during excavations under the parliament building, and they've been incorporated into a walk-through underground exhibition here. Over a second set of bridges is the most distinctive monumental building in Stockholm, the **Kungliga Slottet** (Royal Palace; T-Gamla Stan), a beautiful Renaissance successor to the original castle of Stockholm. Finished in 1760, it's a striking achievement, outside sombre, inside a magnificent Baroque and Rococo swirl. The **apartments** (mid-May to Aug daily 10am–4pm; Sept to mid-May Tues–Sun noon–3pm; 80kr) form a relentlessly linear collection of furniture and tapestries; the **Treasury** (same times as apartments; 80kr) has ranks of jewel-studded crowns, the oldest that of Karl X (1650). Also worth catching is **Livrustkammaren**, the Royal Armoury (June–Aug daily 10am–5pm; Sept–May Tues–Sun 11am–5/8pm; free), less to do with weapons than with ceremony – suits of armour, costumes and horse-drawn coaches from the sixteenth century onwards.

Beyond the palace lies Gamla Stan proper, where the streets suddenly narrow and darken. The first major building is the **Storkyrkan** (daily 9am–4/6pm; 10kr, free in winter), consecrated in 1306 and technically Stockholm's cathedral – the monarchs of Sweden are married and crowned here. The Baroque interior is marvellous, with an animated fifteenth-century sculpture of *St George and the Dragon*, the royal pews, more like golden billowing thrones, and a monumental black and silver altarpiece. **Stortorget**, Gamla Stan's main square, is handsomely proportioned and crowded with eighteenth-century buildings. The surrounding narrow streets house a succession of arts and craft shops, restaurants and discreet fast-food outlets, clogged by summer buskers and evening strollers. Keep right on as far as the handsome Baroque **Riddarhuset** (Mon–Fri 11.30am–12.30pm; 40kr), in whose Great Hall the Swedish aristocracy met during the seventeenth-century Parliament of the Four Estates. Their coats of arms – around 2500 of them – are splattered across the walls. From here it's a matter of seconds across the bridge onto **Riddarholmen**, and to **Riddarholms Kyrkan** (mid-May–Sept daily 10am–4pm; 20kr), originally a Franciscan monastery and long the burial place of Swedish royalty. You'll find the unfortunate Gustav II Adolf in the green marble sarcophagus.

## Skeppsholmen, Norrmalm and Östermalm

Off Gamla Stan's eastern reaches on the way to the island of **Skeppsholmen**, you'll find the **National Art Museum** on Strömkajen (Tues–Sun 11am–5/8pm; free; some exhibitions 30–60kr; T-Kungsträdgården), an impressive collection of applied art – beds slept in by kings, cabinets used by queens, alongside Art Nouveau coffee pots and vases and examples of Swedish furniture design. Upstairs there is a plethora of European sculpture, mesmerizing sixteenth- and seventeenth-century Russian Orthodox icons, and a quality selection of paintings. Skeppsholmen's **Moderna Muséet** (Tues–Sun 10am–6/8pm; free), one of the better modern art collections in Europe, has a comprehensive selection of works by some of the twentieth century's leading artists including Dalí, Warhol and Matisse.

Modern Stockholm lies immediately north of Gamla Stan. It's split into two distinct sections: the central **Norrmalm** and the classier, residential streets of **Östermalm** to the east – though there's not much apart from a couple of specialist museums to draw you here. On the waterfront, at the foot of Norrbro, is **Gustav Adolfs Torg**, more a traffic island than a square, with the eighteenth-century **Opera House** its proudest and most notable building. It was at a masked ball here in 1792 that King Gustav III was shot; you'll find Gustav's ball costume, as well as the assassin's pistols and mask, displayed in the royal armoury in Gamla Stan. Norrmalm's eastern boundary is marked by **Kungsträdgården**, the most fashionable and central of the city's numerous parks; once royal gardens, they are now Stockholm's main meeting place and there's almost always something going on, especially in summer. On the opposite side of Norrmalm in Östermalm is the **Historiska Muséet** (Tues–Sun 11am–5/8pm, also Mon mid-May to Sept; 60kr; T-Karlaplan). Ground-floor highlights include a Stone Age household and a mass of Viking weapons, coins and boats, while upstairs there's a worthy collection of medieval church art and architecture, evocatively housed in massive vaulted rooms.

### Djurgården

A former royal hunting ground, **Djurgården** is Stockholm's nearest large expanse of park. You could walk to the park from Central Station, but it's quite a hike: you can take the bus instead – #44 from Karlaplan or #47 and #69 from Nybroplan – or in summer, the ferry from Nybroplan, or year round from Slussen. In the northeast of the park you can get excellent views from 155-metre-high **Kaknäs TV tower** (daily 10am–9pm; 30kr), one of Scandinavia's tallest structures. South over Djurgårdsbron are numerous museums. Palatial **Nordiska Muséet** (daily 10am–4/5pm; free) is a good attempt to represent Swedish cultural history in an accessible fashion, with a particularly interesting Sámi section. Close by, the **Vasa Muséet** (daily 10am–5/7/8pm; 80kr) is an essential stop, displaying the *Vasa* warship which sank in Stockholm harbour after just twenty minutes of its maiden voyage in 1628. Preserved in mud, the ship was raised along with 12,000 objects in 1961. Walkways bring you nose to nose with the cannon hatches and restored decorative relief, exhibition halls display the retrieved bits and pieces, while films and videos explain the social and political life of the period – all with excellent English notes and regular English-language **guided tours**.

## Eating, drinking and nightlife

The three main areas for decent **eating**, day or night, are Norrmalm, Gamla Stan and Södermalm – the island south of Slussen. The Hötorgshallen in Hötorget is a cheap and varied indoor **market**, awash with small cafés and ethnic snacks. Outside is an excellent daily fruit and veg market too. Many cafés, restaurants and bars offer food during the day and entertainment in the evening. As well as the weekend, Wednesday night is an active time, as there's usually plenty going on and queues at the more popular **nightlife** haunts. Live music venues charge 60–100kr admission. The city's main **gay** centre, RFSL, Sveavägen 57 (℡08/457 13 22; T-bana Rådmansgatan), has information about the ever-changing bar and club scene in Stockholm and throughout the rest of the country.

## Cafés and restaurants

**Art Café** Västerlånggatan 60, Gamla Stan. A fifteenth-century arty cellar-café with sandwiches, good coffee and cakes.

**Babs** Birger Jarlsgatan 37, near Nybroplan. Lively, young and laid-back atmosphere at this quirky restaurant/bar. Interesting – mostly meat – dishes include duck terrine with pear and raisin.

**Blå Lotus** Katrina Bangata 21, Södermalm. The hangout of the alternative crowd – always has an intellectual buzz.

**Cosmic Café** Wollmar Yxkullsgatan 5B, Södermalm, opposite Mariatorget T-bana. A tiny, fun, wholefood vegetarian café with very good-value salads, pastas and great fresh fruit milkshakes.

**Creperie Fyra Knop** Svartensgatan 4, Södermalm. Excellent-value crêpes served in this dark, evocative restaurant which is fashionably tatty and plays the likes of Leonard Cohen.

**Hermitage** Stora Nygatan 11, Gamla Stan. Excellent vegetarian place with delicious fresh salads and breads.

**Lasse i Parken** Högalidsgatan 56, Södermalm. Beautiful daytime café in an eighteenth-century house with a pleasant garden. Summer daily 11am–5pm. Hornstull T-bana.

**Mother India** Wallingatan 40, Norrmalm. Really good Indian food at sensible prices with masses of vegetarian options. T-bana T-Centralen.

**Muffin Bakery** Fridhemsgatan 3, Kungsholmen. Muffins, cakes and tasty Mediterranean-style sandwiches at this popular neighbourhood café with outdoor seating in summer. Fridhemsplan T-bana.

**Peppar** Torsgatan 34, Norrmalm. Cajun and creole food are served up at this good-value restaurant near Central Station, which also doubles as a popular bar.

**String Café** Nytorgsgatan 38, Södermalm. Ultra laid-back retro café full of posey young studenty types. Lots of big, cheapish coffees with muffins, brownies and the like.

## Bars, brasseries and pubs

**Fenix** Götgatan 40, Södermalm. Trendy and lively American-style bar. Good selection of beers and cheapish food.

**Gråmunken** Västerlånggatan 18, Gamla Stan. Cosy café with live jazz several nights a week.

**O'Learys** Götgatan 11, Södermalm. A good bar/restaurant for watching sport on the widescreen TV.

**Söders Hjärta** Bellmansgatan 22, Södermalm. Swanky restaurant with a less intimidating and friendly bar on the mezzanine floor.

## Live music

**Engelen** Kornhamnstorg 59, Gamla Stan. Jazz, rock and blues nightly.

**Fasching** Kungsgatan 63, Norrmalm. Stockholm's premier jazz venue, with local acts and big names.

**Kaos** Stora Nygatan 21, Gamla Stan. Good live music from 9pm nightly; rock bands on Fri and Sat in the cellar and reasonable late-night food.

**Nalen Stacken** Regeringsgatan 74, Norrmalm. The place to go for boogie, R&B, swing and rock'n'roll bands playing regularly.

**Stampen** Stora Nygatan 5, Gamla Stan. Long-established and rowdy jazz club.

## Discos and clubs

**Berns** Berzelii Park, Kungsträdgården. One of the hottest places for locals to hang out. The stunning decor here is a mix of nineteenth century Baroque and the very latest Nordic designs. T-Bana Kungsträdgården.

**Kharma** Sturegatan 10, Norrmalm. All the latest tunes in an elegant club noted for its black and white chequered floor and sensual blood red drapes and sofas. T-bana Östermalmstorg.

**StureCompagniet** Sturegatan 4, Norrmalm. Terrific light show with house and techno sounds blaring on three floors of bars. T-bana Östermalmstorg.

## Gay venues

**Bysis** Hornsgatan 82, Södermalm. A friendly neighbourhood bar always packed out. Summer terrace with decent food. Open Wed (mostly women) & Fri. Zinkensdamm T-bana.

**Chokladkoppen** Stortorget 18, Gamla Stan. Popular mixed gay café right in the heart of the old town renowned for its pretty waiters and great hot chocolate. Gamla Stan T-bana.

**Lino** Södra Riddarholmshamnen 19, Riddarholmen. Currently the hippest spot playing house and Eighties/Nineties hits. Sat till 3am.

**Patricia** Stadsgårdskajen, Slussen. Drag shows, dancing and comedy on what was the Queen Mother's royal yacht. Also an excellent restaurant on the upper deck. Gay on Sun only. Slussen T-bana.

**Side Track** Wollmar Yxkullsgatan 7, Södermalm. A dark and smoky bar on Söder popular with leather and denim boys, though everyone is welcome.

**Torget** Mälartorget 13, Gamla Stan. A superbly elegant and fun place to drink at any time of the evening – and always packed with beauties.

# Listings

## Uppsala

Forty minutes' train ride north of Stockholm, **UPPSALA** is regarded as the historical and religious centre of Sweden. It's a tranquil alternative to the capital, with a delightful river-cut centre, not to mention an active student-geared nightlife. At the centre of the medieval town, a ten-minute walk from the train station, is the great **Domkyrkan** (daily 8am–6pm; free), Scandinavia's largest cathedral. The echoing interior remains impressive, particularly the French Gothic ambulatory, with its tiny chapels, one of which contains a lively set of restored fourteenth-century wall paintings that tell the legend of St Erik, Sweden's patron saint, while another contains his relics. Poke around and you'll also find the tombs of Reformation rebel monarch Gustav Vasa and his son Johan III, and that of the great botanist Carl Von Linné (self-styled as Carolus Linnaeus), who lived in Uppsala. Opposite the cathedral is the **Gustavianum** (daily 10/11am–4/5pm; closed Mon Sept–May; 40kr), built in 1625 as part of the university, and much touted for its tidily preserved anatomical theatre. The same building houses small collections of Egyptian, Classical and Nordic antiquities and the **Uppsala University Museum**, which contains the glorious Augsburg Art Cabinet, an ebony treasure chest presented to Gustav II Adolf. The **castle** (June–Aug English guided tours at 1pm & 3pm; 60kr) is worth a visit, although a 1702 fire that destroyed three-quarters of the city did away with all but one side and two towers of this opulent palace. You can wander around the excavations and peruse the waxworks in authentic costumes.

Uppsala's **train** and **bus stations** are beside each other, not far from the **tourist office**, Fyris Torg 8 (Mon–Fri 10am–6pm, Sat 10am–3pm; mid-June to mid-Aug also Sun noon–4pm; ☎018/727 48 00, ⊛www.res.till.uppland.nu), which has an English map and handout. Uppsala now has a new central STF **youth hostel** at Kungsgatan 27 (☎018/480 50 55; ❹). For a **hotel** try *Hotel Uppsala*, Kungsgatan 27 (☎018/480 50 00, ⊛www.basichotel.com; ❻), with bright, clean rooms and weekend reductions. The best **cafés** are *Ofvandahls*, Sysslomansgatan 5, a student classic, but only fun for smokers; *Güntherska*, Östra Ågatan 31, another favourite and strictly non-smoking; and *Wayne's Coffee*, Smedsgränd 4, with vast windows looking out onto the street. However, for something more substantial head for *Svenssons krog/bakficka*, Sysslomansgatan 15, the best **restaurant** for traditional fare. During the summer, the outdoor café/bar *Lilla Helgonet*, right by the river at Eriks Torg, is a popular spot.

### Gamla Uppsala

About 5km north of town, three huge **barrows**, atmospheric royal burial mounds dating back to the sixth century, mark the original site of Uppsala, **GAMLA UPPSALA**, reached on frequent buses #2, #24 or #54 from Uppsala's main square, Stora Torget. This was a pagan settlement and a place of ancient sacrificial rites: every ninth year a festival demanded the death of nine men, hanged from a nearby tree until their corpses rotted. The pagan temple where this took place is marked by the Christian **Gamla Uppsala Kyrka** (daily 9am–4/6pm), built when the Swedish

**SWEDEN | Stockholm**

③⓪

kings first took baptism in the new faith. Look for the faded wall paintings and the tomb of Celsius of thermometer fame. The worthwhile **Gamla Uppsala Museum** (May–Aug daily 11am–5pm; Sept–April Wed, Sat & Sun noon–3pm; 50kr) explains the origin of local myths from Roman times and Uppsala's era of greatness.

# Southern Sweden

**Southern Sweden** is a nest of coastal provinces, extensive lake and forest regions, gracefully ageing cities and superb beaches. Much of the area, especially the south-west coast, is the target of Swedish holidaymakers, with a wealth of campsites and cycle tracks, yet retaining a sense of space and tranquillity as well as plenty of historical and cultural high points. The grandest coastal city is charming **Gothenburg**, well deserving exploration. South of here, **Helsingborg**, a stone's throw from Denmark, and **Malmö**, still sixteenth-century at its core, are both worth a day or two. **Lund**, a medieval cathedral and university town, lies conveniently between the two.

## Gothenburg (Göteborg)

Although **GOTHENBURG** is Scandinavia's largest port, shipbuilding has long since taken a back seat to ferry arrivals – those from Newcastle (England) alongside the dock-strewn river, and those from Denmark right in the centre of the port and shipyards. Beyond the shipyards, Gothenburg is the prettiest of Sweden's cities, with broad avenues split and ringed by an elegant seventeenth-century, Dutch-designed canal system.

### Arrival, information and transport

DFDS **ferries** from England dock at Frihamnen, opposite the Opera House. From here it's a fifteen-minute walk across the Göta river into the city centre. Stena Line ferries from Frederikshavn in Denmark dock within twenty minutes' walk of the centre. Trams #3 and #9 run past to the centre. **Trains** arrive at Central Station on Drottningtorget. **Buses** from all destinations use the adjoining Nils Ericson-splatsen bus terminal. Gothenburg has two **tourist offices**: a kiosk (Mon–Fri 10am–6pm, Sat 10am–5pm, Sun noon–4pm) in Nordstan, the shopping centre next to Central Station, and a main office on the canal front at Kungsportsplatsen 2 (June–Aug daily 9.30am–6/8pm; rest of year Mon–Sat 9.30am–2/5pm; ☎031/61 25 00, ⓦwww.goteborg.com). They sell the **Gothenburg Pass** (210/295kr for 24/48hr), giving unlimited bus and tram travel, free or half-price museum entry and concessions including a free boat trip to Elfsborg Fortress and fifty-percent discount on a day trip to Frederikshavn in Denmark. Gothenburg is the most attractive Swedish city around which to **walk**, though you may well use the **public transport** system of trams and buses. Each city journey costs 20kr for adults, though it's a third cheaper to buy a ten-trip "Maxirabatt 100" for 100kr. Tickets can be bought from the driver or from Tidpunkten and Pressbyrån kiosks around the city. Just get on and punch "2" for city rides and "BYTE" if you are continuing on another bus or tram. **Night** bus/tram tickets are double the daytime rates. **Taxi** rides (☎031/65 00 00) within the city centre cost around 75kr, and there are twenty-percent discounts for women travelling after 9pm at night, but check with the driver first. The best **Internet** cafés are Gameonline, Magasin-sgatan 26, and Game Net, at Viktoriagatan 22.

### Accommodation

Of the **hostels**, the most central and best appointed is the excellent *Slottssko-gen*, Vegagatan 21 (☎031/42 65 20, ⓦwww.sov.nu; 110kr), two minutes' walk

from Linnégatan; take tram #1 or #6 to Olivedalsgatan. Another fine option, and well placed for ferries to Denmark, is *Stigbergsliden*, Stigbergsliden 10 (☏031/24 16 20, ⊛www.hostel-gothenburg.com; 120kr). If you want something a little more peaceful try *Kvibergs*, Kvibergsvägen 5 (☏031/43 50 55, ⊛www .vandrarhem.com; 155kr), housed in an old barracks building and close to Gothenburg's largest weekend fleamarket – take tram #6, #7 or #11 to Kviberg. The tourist office's **Gothenburg package** (from 485kr/person) gets you a room in a central hotel, with breakfast and a free Gothenburg Pass. The tourist office can also book **private rooms** for around 175kr a head. Alternatively, try the friendly *Lilton*, Föreningsgatan 9 (☏031/82 88 08, ⊛www.hotellilton.com; ⑥), in a charming old house tucked away close to the Haga area and offering a cosy atmosphere. For character and great location, opt for the very comfortable 1907 sailing ship *Barken Viking* (☏031/63 58 00, ⊛www.liseberg.se; ⑦), moored on Gullbergskajen outside the Opera House. The all-year *Kärralund* **campsite** (⊛www.liseberg.se; 180kr/pitch) is 4km out on Olbergsgatan (tram #5 to Welandergatan).

## The City

King Gustav II Adolf, looking for western trade, founded Gothenburg in the early seventeenth century as a response to the high tolls charged by the Danes for using the narrow sound between the two countries. As a Calvinist and businessman, Gustav much admired Dutch merchants, inviting them to trade and live in Gothenburg, and it's their influence that shaped the city, parts of which have an oddly Dutch feel. The area defined by the central canal represents what's left of old Gothenburg, centring on **Gustav Adolfs Torg**, a windswept square flanked by the nineteenth-century **Börshuset** (Exchange Building), and the fine **Rådhus** (town hall), originally built in 1672. Around the corner, the **Kronhuset**, off Kronhusgatan, was built in 1643 and is a typical seventeenth-century Dutch construction,. The cobbled courtyard outside is flanked by the mid-eighteenth-century **Kronhusbodarna** (Mon–Fri 11am–4pm, Sat 11am–2pm), now done up as period craft shops selling sweets and souvenirs. The **Stadsmuseum**, Norra Hamngatan 12 (daily 10am–5/8pm; closed Mon Sept–April; 40kr), is worth a visit for its rich collection of archeological, cultural and industrial exhibits. Close by, the **Maritima Centrum** (March–Oct daily 10am–4/6pm; Nov Fri–Sun only; 75kr) allows you to clamber aboard a destroyer and submarine moored at the quayside. It's worth coming down here just to look at the shipyards beyond, like a rusting Meccano set put into sharp perspective by the striking **Opera House** (daily noon–6pm; ☎031/10 80 00; tickets from 50kr), a graceful and imaginative ship-like structure. Back south from the Opera House, through Kungsportsplatsen and across the canal, Kungsportsavenyn is Gothenburg's showiest thoroughfare. Known simply as **Avenyn**, this wide strip was once flanked by private houses fronted by gardens and is now lined with overpriced, posey yet popular pavement restaurants and brasseries. About halfway down, the excellent **Röhsska Museum of Arts and Crafts** at Vasagatan 37–39 (Tues–Sun 11am/noon–5pm, Tues till 8pm; 40kr) celebrates Swedish design through the ages, among other things. At the top end, **Götaplatsen** is the modern cultural centre of Gothenburg, home to a concert hall, theatre and **Art Museum** (daily 11am–5/6pm, Wed till 9pm; 40kr) whose enormous collections include a good selection of Impressionist paintings, pop art and – most impressively – superb Swedish work in the Furstenburg galleries on the sixth floor. Just a few minutes' walk west of Avenyn, the old working-class district of **Haga** is now a picturesque area of gentrified chic with plenty of daytime cafés and boutiques, while **Linnégatan**, a few steps further, is a more charismatic and cosmopolitan version of Avenyn with the most diverse places to eat, drink and stroll. Five minutes' walk southeast of Götaplatsen, on the edge of the centre, is **Liseberg**, a surprisingly aesthetic amusement park (mid-April to late Aug daily noon/3–11pm, also Sat & Sun in Sept noon/1pm–8pm/11pm; *Åkpass*: 265kr for free rides all day) with some high-profile rides and acres of gardens, restaurants and fast food. In the opposite direction, great views of the harbour and surrounding area can be had from the excursion boats that run from Lilla Bommen to the **Nya Elfsborg Fortress** (mid-May to Aug daily 9.30am–4.20pm; 110kr, including guided tour of fortress), a seventeenth-century island defence guarding the harbour entrance, whose surviving buildings have been turned into a museum and café.

### Eating and drinking

There's no shortage of places to **eat**; the city's range of ethnic restaurants is particularly good, reflecting its trading past. For **picnic food** try Saluhallen, the indoor market in Kungstorget, which also houses the two cheapest snack bars in town. In Linné, Saluhall Briggen, Tredje Långgatan, is smaller but brimming with mouthwatering fish, cheeses and cheap cafés. Many of the glitziest places to eat flank Avenyn, though with the exception of *Jungans Café* at no. 37 – a Gothenburg institution – they are generally busy and overpriced; less obvious, and usually cheaper, places can be found in the streets clustered around Haga Nygatan: the cheapest, offering filling lunches, is *Café Konditori Kringlan*, Haga Nygatan 13. For friendly, laid-back atmosphere in the centre head for *Tintin Café*, Engelbrektsgatan 22, off Avenyn – open round the clock. Another good choice is *Cyrano*, Prinsgatan 7 (☎031/14 31 10), an authentic Provençal bistro. For **vegetarian** and vegan meals, the classic place is *Solrosen* (☎031/711 66 97), Kaponjärgatan 4, in Haga district, which turns into a lively drinking venue at night. For superb Indian food look no further than *Mother India*, Köpmansgatan 27, off Nils Ericsonsplatsen, which also has lunch for 65kr. The area around Avenyn is the focal point for **night-time** Gothenburg. At Vasagatan 23, *Java Kaffebar* is a studenty coffee house with a Parisian feel. *Napoleon* at Vasagatan 11 has a lovely, mellow interior and is set in a fabulous old house with exterior wall paintings. *Greta's*, Drottninggatan 35, is a stylish yet casual bar/restaurant, very popular as a **gay** venue and also serving good food. There's live music at *The Dubliner* at Östra Hamngatan 50b, which claims to have been established in 1870 and serves Guinness and whisky. *Nefertiti*, Hvitfeldtsplatsen 6, is one of the best places to see live jazz and world **music**. The city's large student community means lots of local **live bands**. The best place to hear them is at *Kompaniet Underground*, Kungsgatan 19, which has a bar on the top floor and dancing downstairs.

## Helsingborg

At **HELSINGBORG** only a narrow sound separates Sweden from Denmark; indeed, Helsingborg was Danish for most of the Middle Ages, with a castle controlling the southern regions of what is now Sweden. The town's enormously important strategic position meant that it bore the brunt of repeated attacks and rebellions, the Swedes conquering the town on six separate occasions, only to lose it back to the Danes each time. Finally, in 1710, a terrible battle saw off the Danes for the last time, and the battered town lay abandoned for almost two hundred years. Only in the nineteenth century, when the harbour was expanded and the railway constructed, did Helsingborg find new prosperity. Today, the dramatically redeveloped harbour area has breathed new life into this likeable, relaxed town. Directly south of the North Harbour café-bars, the strikingly designed **Henry Dunker Cultural House** (Tues–Sun 10am–5pm; free), Kungsgatan 11, named after the city's foremost industrialist benefactor, aims to provide a full vision of Helsingborg's history. East from Hamntorget and the harbours, the massive, neo-Gothic **Rådhus** marks the bottom of **Stortorget**, the long thin square sloping up to the lower battlements of what's left of Helsingborg's castle, the **kärnan** or keep (daily: June–Aug 11am–7pm; Sept–May Tues–Sun 9am/11am–3/4pm; 20kr), a fourteenth-century brick tower, the only survivor from the original fortress. The views from the top are worth the entrance fee although you don't miss much from the lower (free) battlements. Off Stortorget, **Norra Storgatan** contains Helsingborg's oldest buildings, attractive seventeenth- and eighteenth-century merchants' houses with quiet courtyards.

Apart from the HH Ferries passenger ferry from Helsingør (Denmark), which pull up across an arm of the docks, all **ferries**, **trains** and **buses** arrive at Knutpunkten, the harbourside **central terminal**. It's just a couple of minutes' walk from here to the **tourist office** inside the town hall at the corner of Stortorget and Järnvägsgatan (Mon–Fri 9/10am–6/8pm, Sat 9/10am–2/5pm; mid-June to Aug also Sun 10am–3pm; ☎042/10 43 50, ✆www.helsingborgsguiden.com), which has free city maps and masses of brochures. The cheapest of the central **hotels** is *Linnéa*, Prästgatan 4 (☎042/37 24 00; ●), which drops prices in summer and at weekends. The official **hostel** (☎042/13 11 30, ✆www.stfvandrarhem.helsingborg .nu; 190kr) is at Planteringsvägen 69-71 (bus #1). Alternatively, the *Villa Thalassa* hostel (☎042/38 06 60, ✆www.villathalassa.com; 180kr; bus #219) is 4km north along Drottninggatan. For **camping**, try the waterfront site on Kustgatan in Råå Vallar, 5km southeast; take bus #1 from outside the Rådhus. Daytime **cafés** include the classic *Fahlmans* at Stortorget 11 and the charismatic *Ebbas Fik*, Bruksgatan 20, decked out with authentic 1950s memorabilia. There are plenty of harbour-front bars. A good cheap **restaurant** is *Papadam* at Bruksgatan 10 in the centre with a good selection of balti and biriani dishes, though *Olsons Skafferi* at Mariagatan 6, serving top quality Italian fare, is better. The best **club** is the justifiably popular, and noisy, *The Tivoli*, Hamntorget 11, where you'll get the very best in Swedish and European dance music for a 75kr entrance.

## Lund

Forty minutes south of Helsingborg and fifteen minutes from Malmö, **LUND** is a beautiful university town with a picturesque medieval centre and a unique buzz

when the students are around. Its weather-beaten **Domkyrkan** (Mon–Fri 8am–
6/7.15pm, Sat & Sun 9.30am–5/7.30pm; free), consecrated in 1145, is considered
by many to be Scandinavia's finest medieval building. Its plain interior culminates
in a delicate, semicircular apse with a gleaming fifteenth-century altarpiece and a
mosaic of Christ surrounded by angels – although what draws most attention is a
fourteenth-century astronomical clock, revealing an ecclesiastical Punch and Judy
show (daily noon & 3pm). Outside the cathedral, **Kyrkogatan**, lined with staunch,
solid, nineteenth-century civic buildings, leads into the main square, **Stortorget**,
off which **Kattesund** is home to a glassed-in set of excavated medieval walls.
Adjacent at Kattesund 6 is the **Drottens museum** (Mon–Fri 9am–4pm, Sat 10am–
2pm, Sun noon–4pm; 30kr), the remains of a medieval church in the basement of
another modern building, but the real interest is in the powerful atmosphere of the
old streets behind the Domkyrkan. In this web of streets, **Kulturen** (daily 11am/
noon–4/5pm; Oct to mid-April closed Mon; 50kr) is a village in itself of indoor
and open-air collections of southern Swedish art, silverware, ceramics and musical
instruments. Finish off your meanderings with a visit to the **Botaniska Trädgård**
(daily 6am–8pm; free) just beyond, an extensive botanical garden.

    **Trains** arrive on the western edge of town, an easy walk from the centre. The
**tourist office** is opposite the Domkyrkan at Kyrkogatan 11, and is well signposted
from the train station (June–Aug Mon–Fri 10am–6pm, Sat & Sun 10am–2pm;
Sept–May Mon–Fri 10am–5pm, May & Sept also Sat 10am–2pm; ☎046/35 50 40,
🌐www.lund.se). **Internet access** is available at the city library, St Petri Kyrkogata
6, as well as at Noll Ett, Lilla Gråbrödersgatan 2. Lund makes an appealing alternative stopover to Malmö or Helsingborg by virtue of **private rooms** which the
tourist office can book for 225kr (50kr booking fee). The town's unusual **hostel**,
*Tåget*, Vävaregatan 22 (☎046/14 28 20; 130kr), packs you into three-tiered sleeping
compartments of six 1940s carriages parked on a branch line behind the train station;
turn right and follow the signs. For a good-value central **hotel**, check into *Ahlström*,
Skomakaregatan 3 (☎046/211 01 74; ❻), or *Hotel Överliggaren*, Bytaregatan 14
(☎046/15 72 30; ❻). There are plenty of cheap places to **eat**. *Café Ariman*, attached
to the Nordic Law Department at Kungsgatan 2, has been updated, but maintains its
shabby, left-wing coffee-house appeal with good, cheap, light food; while *Conditori
Lundagård*, Kyrkogatan 17, is the classic student café. *Fellini*, opposite the train station
at Bangatan 6, is a popular Italian eatery. *Tegnérs*, next to the student union at Sand-
gatan 2, serves really fine food at student prices. Lund's most popular meeting place is
the *Stortorget* on Stortorget with a bar, restaurant and club. The best **club**, however,
is *Basilika*, Stora Södergatan 13, just south of Stortorget – minimum age 22.

## Malmö

**MALMÖ**, won back for Sweden from Denmark by Karl X in the seventeenth
century, is a handsome city, with a cobbled medieval core that has a lived-in,
workaday feel, worlds apart from the museum-piece quality of most other Swedish
town centres. With the **Øresund Link**, a sensational seventeen kilometre long
road and rail bridge, Malmö really is the Swedish gateway from continental Europe,
and after years in the doldrums, is enjoying an economic revival. The city's canals,
parks and largely pedestrianized streets and squares make it a great place to stroll
around. Most of the medieval centre was taken apart in the early sixteenth century
to make way for **Stortorget**, a vast market square. It's as impressive today as it must
have been when it first appeared, flanked on one side by the **Rådhus**, built in 1546
and covered with statuary and spiky accoutrements; there are tours of the well-preserved interior (check with the tourist office for times). **Södergatan**, Malmö's main
pedestrianized shopping street, runs south from here towards the canal. Behind the
Rådhus stands the **St Petri Kyrka** (daily 8/10am–6pm; free), a fine Gothic church
with an impressively decorative pulpit and a four-tiered altarpiece. **Lilla Torg** is
everyone's favourite part of the city – indeed, it's been voted the most popular

square in Sweden. A late-sixteenth-century spin-off from an overcrowded Stortorget, it's usually full, with a roaring trade from jewellery stalls and summer buskers.
The southern side of the square is formed by a row of mid-nineteenth-century
brick and timber warehouses; the shops around here sell books, antiques and gifts,
though the best place to drop into is the nearby **Saluhallen**, an excellent indoor
market. Further west still lie the **Kungsparken** and the **Malmöhus** (daily 10am/
noon–4pm; 40kr), a low fortified castle defended by a wide moat, two circular
keeps and grassy ramparts, raised by Danish king Christian III in 1536. For a time
a prison (Bothwell, third husband of Mary, Queen of Scots, was the most notable
inmate), the castle and its outbuildings now constitute a series of exhibitions including Malmö's main **museum**, though unfortunately with no information in English.
The pleasant grounds are peppered with small lakes and an old windmill.

## Practicalities

**Trains** arrive at Central Station, including the local Pågatåg services (to and from
Helsingborg and Lund; rail passes valid). The train station also has showers (20kr) and
beds (5.30am–11pm; 25kr/hour). The main **bus terminal** is outside Central Station,
in Centralplan. The **tourist office** is inside the station (Mon–Fri 9am–5/6/7pm, Sat
9/10am–2/3/5pm; May–Sept also Sun 10am–3/5pm; ☎040/34 12 00, ◍www
.malmo.se/turist). It stocks the handy *Malmö This Month* and sells the **Malmö Card**
(130kr/160kr/190kr for one/two/three days), which gives free museum entry, free
travel on city buses, free car parking in public places and a free sightseeing tour by
bus. For **Internet** use, head for Surfer's Paradise, Amiralsgatan 14, or Cyber Space,
Engelbrektsgatan 13a. Malmö is one of the easier places in the south to find cheap
accommodation. A good choice of **hotel** is *Comfort Hotel Malmö* (☎040/33 04 50,
◍www.choicehotels.se; ❺) at Carlsgatan 10c. There is just one HI **hostel**, the
inconveniently placed *STF Vandrarhem*, Backavägen 18 (☎040/822 20; 130kr; closed
Christmas and New Year), 5km out – take bus #21 from Central Station. A better
bet is *Bosses Gästvåningar*, Södra Förstadsgatan 110b (☎040/32 62 50, ◍www.bosses
.se; ❹), a comfortable **B&B**, twenty minutes' walk south from the station or bus
#15 or #20 to Södervärn. The nearest **campsite** is *Sibbarps Camping* (☎040/15 51
65) on Strandgatan; bus #12B from Central Station.

The Saluhall on Landbygatan by Lilla Torget stocks a marvellous array of **picnic**
supplies. For **lunch**, a delightful option is the quirky *Café Siesta*, Hjorttackegatan 1
– turn right at the western end of Landbygatan off Lilla Torg – a fun café serving
filling sandwiches and home-made apple cake. *Bageri Café* at Saluhallen is excellent
for filled baguettes and bagels. *Spot*, Stora Nygatan 33 (Mon–Fri 9am–6pm, Sat
10am–5pm), is a chic Italian and very good for cheese, fish and meat. Another
fabulous **restaurant** is the unlicensed *Krua Thai*, Möllevångstorget, which serves
tasty Thai mains from an unbelievable 60kr, while, across the square at no. 8,
*Nyhavan* is an excellent Danish restaurant with a good range of open sandwiches
from 65kr. For **drinking**, Lilla Torg is first choice and swarms with bustling
venues through the evening. The liveliest bars here, with outside tables in summer,
are *Mello Yello* and *Moosehead*. The best place for occasional **live music** is *Mattssons
Musikpub*, Göran Olsgatan 1, behind the Rådhus. The unforgettably named *Wonk*
is the **gay club** of choice at Amiralsgatan 20 (Sat only), however, it's also worth
searching out the bar/club *Indigo* at Monbijougatan 15.

# Central and northern Sweden

The long wedge of land that comprises **central and northern Sweden** – from
the northern shores of Lake Vänern to the Finnish border – is Sweden as seen in

the brochures: lakes, holiday cottages, forests and reindeer. On the eastern side, Sweden's coast forms one edge of the **Gulf of Bothnia**. With its jumble of erstwhile fishing towns and squeaky-clean contemporary urban planning, this corridor of land together with its regional town, **Sundsvall**, is worth stopping off in if you're travelling north or have just arrived from Finland by ferry. Though the weather isn't as reliable as further south, you are guaranteed clean beaches, crystal-clear waters and fine hiking. To the west, folklorish **Dalarna** province is the most picturesque region, with sweeping green countryside and inhabitants who maintain a cultural heritage (echoed in contemporary handicrafts and traditions) that goes back to the Middle Ages. This is the place to spend midsummer, particularly Midsummer's Night (June 21) when the whole region erupts in celebration. The **Inlandsbanan**, the great Inland Railway, cuts right through this area from Lake Siljan through the modern lakeside town of **Östersund** to **Gällivare** above the Arctic Circle. An enthralling 1300-kilometre, two-day ride, it ranks with the best European train journeys.

## Sundsvall

Known as the "Stone City", **SUNDSVALL** is immediately and obviously different to other northern Swedish towns. Once home to a rapidly expanding nineteenth-century sawmill industry, the whole city burned down in 1888 and a new centre built completely of stone emerged within ten years. The result is a living document of early-twentieth-century urban architecture, designed by architects who were engaged in rebuilding Stockholm's residential areas at the same time. The materials are limestone and brick, the style simple and the size often overwhelming. The **Esplanaden**, a wide central avenue, cuts the grid in two, itself crossed by **Storgatan**, the widest street. The area around **Stortorget** is still the roomy commercial centre that was envisaged. Behind the mock-Baroque exterior of the **Kulturmagasinet**, on Hamngatan (Mon–Thur 10am–7pm, Fri 10am–6pm, Sat 10am–4pm; free), four late nineteenth-century warehouses have been developed into a cultural complex devoted to art exhibits and city history. The **Gustav Adolfs Kyrkan** (daily 11am/noon–3/4pm; free) – a soaring red-brick structure whose interior looks like a large Lego set – marks one end of the new town. To get the best perspective on the city's layout, climb to the heights of the **Norra Bergets Hantverksmuseum** (daily 11am–5pm; free), an open-air crafts museum down Storgatan and over the main bridge. From the **train station** the centre is five minutes' walk away, with the **tourist office** in the main Stortorget (Mon–Fri 10am–6pm, Sat 10am–2pm; ☎060/61 04 50, ⓦwww.sundsvallturism.com). The HI **hostel** (☎060/61 21 19; 185kr) at Norra Berget takes about half an hour to walk to from the centre. Of the **hotels**, *Svea Hotel*, Rådhusgatan 11 (☎060/61 16 05; ❺), and *Lilla Hotellet* (☎061/61 35 87; ❺) at no.15 have the cheapest doubles in town. For **eating**, Storgatan is lined with restaurants, most offering daily lunch menus, while *La Spezia*, Sjögatan 6, has bargain pizzas from 40kr and *Dragon House*, at Rådhusgatan 34, serves authentic Asian meals including a good value Mongolian barbecue.

## Dalarna

The **Dalarna** region holds a special, misty-eyed place in the Swedish heart and should certainly be seen, though not to the exclusion of points further north. **Lake Siljan**, at the heart of the province, is the major draw, its gentle surroundings, traditions and local handicrafts weaving a subtle spell. If you've only got time to see part of the lake, **MORA** is as good a place as any, and a starting point for the Inlandsbanan rail route (see below). At the northwestern corner of Lake Siljan, the little town is a showcase for the work of Anders Zorn, the Swedish painter who lived in Mora and whose work is exhibited in the **Zorn Museum**, Vasagatan 36 (Mon–Sat 9am/noon–5pm, Sun 11am/1–5pm; 40kr), along with his small but well-chosen personal collection. Zorn's oils reflect a passion for Dalarna's pastoral lifestyle, but it's his earlier watercolours of southern Europe and North Africa that really stand out. The **tourist office** (Mon–Sat 10am–5pm; ☎0250/59 20 20, ⊛www.siljan.se) is at Mora station, and the HI **hostel** at Fredsgatan 6 (☎0250/381 96, ⊜info@maalkullann.se; 145kr). **LEKSAND** is perhaps the most popular and traditional of the Dalarna villages and certainly worth making the effort to reach at midsummer, when the festivals recall age-old maypole dances, the celebrations culminating in the **church boat races**, an aquatic procession of decorated longboats which the locals once rowed to church every Sunday. The **tourist office** in the train station building (Mon–Fri 10am–5pm; mid-June to mid-Aug Mon–Fri until 7pm, Sat & Sun 10am–5pm; ☎0247/79 61 30, ⊛www.siljan.se) has lots of information on the area, as does the **hostel** (☎0247/152 50; 125kr), 2km south of the centre at Parkgården.

# The Inlandsbanan

The **Inlandsbanan** (Inland Railway; ☎0771/53 53 53, ⊛www.inlandsbanan.se), linking central Sweden with Gällivare, 1300km further north, is the most charismatic of Scandinavian rail routes. InterRail pass holders under the age of 26 travel for free (those older pay full fare). With a ScanRail Pass there is a 25-percent discount off an Inland Railway Card which otherwise costs 1195kr and which offers unlimited travel on the line for fourteen days. The full fare, travelling second class from Östersund to Gällivare, costs 697kr, plus an optional 50kr seat reservation.

## Mora to the Arctic Circle

The Inlandsbanan begins in Mora, making its first stop at **ORSA**, fifteen minutes up the line, where the nearby **Grönklitt bear park** (mid-May to mid-Sept daily 10am–3/6pm; 95kr) provides the best chance to see the bears that roam the countryside. The **hostel** at the park (☎0250/462 00; 310kr) has fine facilities. Several hours north of here, the line's halfway point is marked by **ÖSTERSUND**. It's a welcoming place, and its **Storsjön** – or Great Lake – gives it a holiday atmosphere unusual this far north. The lake is also alleged to be the home of a Loch Ness-style monster. In summer, you can make a tour of the lake on a **steamboat cruise**, stopping off on the small island of Verkön (check with tourist office for times; 100kr). Otherwise, the main thing to do in town is to visit **Jamtli** (June–Aug daily 11am–5pm; Sept–May 10/11am–4/5pm; closed Mon; 60kr), an impressive open-air **museum** fifteen minutes' walk north from the centre along Rådhusgatan, full of volunteers milling around in traditional country costume encouraging visitors to join in baking, tree-felling and grass-cutting. On the way in, the museum proudly shows off the ninth-century **Överhogdal tapestries**, whose simple handwoven patterns of horses, dogs and other beasts is quite breathtaking. It's also home to a small collection of monster-catching gear from the nineteenth century. Back in the centre, the town slopes steeply down to the water, and it's tiring work strolling the pedestrianized streets that run around Stortorget. From the **harbour** you can take the bridge over the lake to **Frösön** island, site of the original Viking settlement here. The **tourist office** is at Rådhusgatan 44 (Mon–Fri 9am–5pm; June–Aug until 7/9pm and also open Sat & Sun 10am–3/7pm; ☎063/14 40 01, ⊛www.turist.ostersund.se) and sells the **Östersundskortet**, valid nine days (June–Aug; 140kr), giving free access to the town's sights, half-price sightseeing tours and half-price on the steamboat cruise. For a central **hotel**, try either *Hotell Jämteborg*, Storgatan 54 (☎063/51 01 01; ❻), or the *Hotell Jemtlandia*, along the same road at Storgatan 64 (☎063/51 73 35; ❺). The STF **hostel** in Östersund (☎063/13 91 00; 165kr) is a ten-minute walk from the train station at Södra Gröngatan 36 in the town centre. More atmospheric is the **hostel** at Jamtli (☎063/12 20 60; 140kr; take bus #2 to the end of the line). **Campers** can stay at either *Östersunds Camping*, 2km down Rådhusgatan (☎063/14 46 15), at Krondikesvägen 95, or on Frösön island at *Frösö Camping* (☎063/432 54; June to early Aug only; bus #3 or #4 from the centre). For **food**, try the young and trendy *Brunkullans* restaurant with its outdoor garden at Postgränd 5, or the daily specials at the *Australian Captain Cook*, Hamngatan 9

– cheaper than *Brunkullans*, with live entertainment on Wed & Sat, and very popular for **drinking** too. Another good bar to check out is *News* at Samuel Permansgatan 9.

Further north, **ARVIDSJAUR** contains Sweden's oldest surviving Sámi village, **Lappstaden** (daily tours in July at 5pm; 30kr, otherwise just walk in), dating from the late eighteenth century, a huddle of houses that was once the centre of a great winter market. They were not meant to be permanent homes, but rather a meeting place during festivals, and the last weekend in August is still taken up by a great celebratory shindig. There's a cosy private **hostel** at Västra Skolgatan 9 (☎0960/124 13; 130kr), and *Camp Gielas*, beside one of the lakes 1km south of the station, has cabins from 400kr. The **tourist office** (Mon–Fri 8.30am–noon & 1–4.30pm; June to mid-Aug daily 9.30am–6pm; ☎0960/175 00; ◎www.arvidsjaurlappland.com) is at Östra Skolgatan 18c. Three and a half hours north of Arvidsjaur, the Inlandsbanan finally crosses the **Arctic Circle**, signalled by a bout of whistle-blowing as the train pulls up. Painted white rocks curve away over the hilly ground, a crude but popular representation of the Circle.

### Jokkmokk

In the midst of remote, densely forested, marshy country, **JOKKMOKK** is a welcome oasis. Once wintertime Sámi quarters, the town is today a renowned handicraft centre, with a Sámi educational college keeping the language and culture alive. The **Ájtte Museum** (Mon–Fri 9/10–4/6pm, Sat & Sun 9am/noon–4/6pm; Oct–April closed Sat; 50kr) on Kyrkgatan is the place to see some of the intricate work. Have a glance, too, at the so-called **Lapp Kyrka**, enclosed by a wide wooden fence, in which corpses were interred during winter, waiting for the thaw when the Sámi could go out and dig graves. The great **winter market** still survives, now nearly 400 years old, held on the first Thursday, Friday and Saturday of each February, when 30,000 people gather in town. It's the best time to be in Jokkmokk, and staying means booking accommodation a good six months in advance. A smaller, less traditional autumn fair at the end of August is an easier though poorer option. The **tourist office** is at Stortorget 4 (mid-June to mid-Aug daily 9am–6pm; mid-Aug to mid-June Mon–Fri 8.30am–4pm; ☎0971/222 50, ◎www.turism.jokkmokk.se). In summer there should be no problem getting a place at the HI **hostel** at Åsgatan 20 (☎0971/559 77; 120kr); just follow the signs from the station. The **campsite** is 3km east on route 97.

# Travel details

## Trains

**Gällivare** to: Narvik, Norway (2 daily; 3hr 50min).
**Gothenburg** to: Copenhagen (10 daily; 4hr); Helsingborg (10 daily; 2hr 40min); Lund (10 daily; 3hr 15min); Malmö (10 daily; 3hr 30min); Oslo (2 daily; 4hr).
**Malmö** to: Helsingborg (at least hourly; 50min); Lund (at least hourly; 15min).
**Stockholm** to: Gothenburg (hourly; 3hr); Helsingborg (hourly, change at Lund; 5hr); Lund (hourly; 4hr 40min); Malmö (hourly; 4hr 30min); Mora (2 daily; 4hr); Narvik (2 daily; 20hr); Östersund (5 daily; 6hr); Sundsvall (8 daily; 3hr 20min); Uppsala (half hourly; 40min).

**Sundsvall** to: Östersund (4 daily; 2hr 20min).
**Uppsala** to: Mora (2 daily; 2hr 15min), Stockholm (half-hourly; 40min).

## International ferries

**Gothenburg** to: Frederikshavn, Denmark (4–8 daily; 3hr 15min); Newcastle, Britain (4 weekly; 24hr); Kiel, Germany (1 daily; 14hr).
**Helsingborg** to: Helsingør, Denmark (3 hourly; 25min).
**Stockholm** to: Helsinki (Helsingfors), Finland (2 daily; 15hr); Tallinn, Estonia (3-4 weekly; 15hr); Turku (Åbo), Finland (4 daily; 13hr).
**Trelleborg** to: Rostock, Germany (3 daily; 6hr); Travemünde, Germany (2 daily; 7–9hr).

# 31

# Switzerland and Liechtenstein

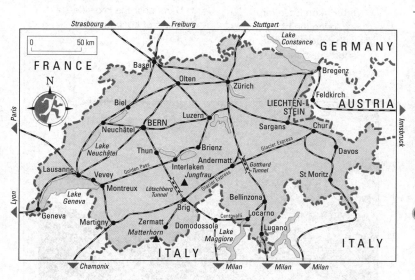

31

# Switzerland highlights

* **Lausanne** Geneva's unsung neighbour, with bags of style, sass and lakeside charm. See p.1013

* **Lake Luzern** Take a cruise on Switzerland's most scenic lake, nestling between high peaks. See p.1019

* **Interlaken** Base for exploring the high Alps, with access to adventure sports plus the superb Schilthorn cable-car ride. See p.1022

* **The Matterhorn** World-famous mountain peak, with guaranteed skiing and snowboarding year-round. See p.1024

* **World's highest bungee jump** A death-defying 220m off the Verzasca Dam, near the lakeside resort of Locarno. See p.1026

△ Gornergrat, above Zermatt

# Introduction and basics

**Switzerland** is one of Europe's most visited countries, but one of its least understood. Pass through for a day or two and you'll get all the quaint stereotypes – cheese, chocolate and clocks – but not much else. Stay a bit longer and another much more rewarding Switzerland will emerge. Sights are breathtaking, transport links are excellent and almost everyone speaks some English along with at least one of the official languages (German, French, Italian, and, in the southeast, Romansh).

The most visited Alpine area is the picturesque **Bernese Oberland**, but the loftiest Alps are further south, where the Toblerone-peaked **Matterhorn** looms above **Zermatt**. In the southeast, forested mountain slopes surround chic **St Moritz**. Of the northern German-speaking cities, **Zürich** has tons of sightseeing and nightlife and provides easy access to the tiny principality of **Liechtenstein** on the Rhine. **Basel** and the capital **Bern** are quieter, each with an attractive historic core, while **Luzern** lies in an appealing setting of lakes and mountains. In the French-speaking west, the cities of **Lake Geneva** – notably **Geneva** and **Lausanne** – make up the heart of Suisse-Romande. South of the Alps, sunny, Italian-speaking Ticino can seem a world apart, particularly the palm-fringed lakeside resorts of **Lugano** and **Locarno**.

## Information & maps

All towns have a **tourist office** (*Verkehrsverein* or *Tourismus*; *Office du Tourisme*; *Ente Turistico*), invariably located near the train station and always extremely useful. Most staff speak English, but **opening hours** in smaller towns allow for a long lunch and can be limited at weekends and in the off-season. All have accommodation and transport lists, and **maps**. *Swiss Backpacker News* (ⓦ www.backpacker.ch)

is an excellent free paper widely available. ⓦ www.swisstopo.ch has 1:50,000 and 1:25,000 walkers' maps.

## Money and banks

Both countries use the **Swiss franc** (CHF or Fr.), divided into 100 Rappen (Rp), centimes or centisimi (c). There are coins of 5c, 10c, 20c, 50c, Fr.1, Fr.2 and Fr.5, and notes of Fr.10, Fr.20, Fr.50, Fr.100, Fr.200 and Fr.1000. Train stations are the best places for **changing money**. **Banks** usually open Mon–Fri 8.30am–4.30pm; some in cities and resorts also open Sat 9am–4pm. Post offices give a similar exchange rate to banks, and **ATMs** are everywhere. Many shops and services, especially in tourist hubs, accept **euros**. At the time of writing, €1 was roughly equal to Fr.1.50, US$1 to Fr.1.20 and £1 to Fr.2.20.

## Communications

Main **post offices** tend to open Mon–Fri 7.30am–noon & 1.30–6.30pm, Sat 8–11am. Most **public phones** take phonecards (*taxcards*), available from post offices and news kiosks (Fr.5, Fr.10 or Fr.20), as well as credit cards; some take Swiss and euro coins. Kiosks also sell good-value discount

---

### Switzerland and Liechtenstein on the net

ⓦ **www.MySwitzerland.com** Tourist office site – vast, detailed and authoritative.
ⓦ **www.postbus.ch** Details of the postbus network, including Alpine routes.
ⓦ **www.museums.ch** Information on museums nationwide.
ⓦ **www.swissinfo.org** News database in English, with good links.
ⓦ **www.tourismus.li** The Liechtenstein tourist board.

cards for calling internationally. The expensive **operator** is on ☏ 111 (domestic) or ☏ 1141 (international). **Internet access** is widespread, at cafés (Fr.4–12/hr) or free at many hotels and hostels.

# Getting around

**Public transport** is comprehensive. Main stations keep a public copy of the national timetable, which covers all rail, bus, boat and cable-car services. Travelling by **train** is comfortable, hassle-free and extremely scenic, with many mountain routes an attraction in their own right. The main network, run by SBB-CFF-FFS, covers much of the country, but many routes, especially Alpine lines, are operated by smaller companies. **Buses** take over where train track runs out – generally yellow **postbuses**, which depart from train-station forecourts. InterRail and Eurail are valid on SBB and most smaller lines, but the discounts they bring are patchy on boats, cable cars and mountain railways (specified in the text as "**IR**" for InterRail and "**ER**" for Eurail). Postbuses are free with all Swiss passes (specified as "**SP**") – although Alpine routes command a Fr.8–15 supplement, along with seat reservation – but not to Eurail and InterRail pass-holders. Most lake **ferries** run only in summer (June–Sept), and duplicate routes which can be covered more cheaply and quickly by rail.

# Accommodation

**Accommodation** isn't as expensive as you might think, and is nearly always excellent.

Tourist offices can often book rooms for free in their area; they often have a display-board (with a courtesy phone) on the street or at the train station, giving details of every hotel. When you check in, ask for a **guest card**, which can give substantial discounts on local attractions and transport. A **hostel** (*Jugendherberge; Auberge de Jeunesse; Albergo/Ostello per la Gioventù*) represents great value for money (always book ahead June–Sept). **HI hostels** (☻www.youthhostel .ch) are of a universally high standard, with doubles as well as small dorms. Non-HI members pay Fr.6 extra. A rival group known as **Swiss Backpackers** (☻www .backpacker.ch) has lively hostels that are less institutional, often in prime town-centre locations and priced to compete; they're specified in the text as **SB hostels**. **Campsites** are clean and well equipped. Prices are about Fr.8 per person plus Fr.8–12 per pitch and per vehicle. Many sites require an international camping carnet. Camping outside official sites is illegal. **Hotels** are everywhere, invariably excellent, and not expensive. Shared-bath doubles start around Fr.85 (average Fr.110), en suites around Fr.135.

# Food and drink

**Eating out** can punch a hole in your budget. Burgers, pizza slices, kebabs and falafel are universal **snack** standbys, as are pork *Bratwürste* sausages. **Dairy products** find their way into most Swiss dishes. Cheese **fondue** – a pot of wine-laced molten cheese into which you dip cubes of bread or potato – is the national dish. It's usually priced as a two-person (or more) meal, or as an

## Adventure sports in Switzerland

With its landscape of mountains, glaciers, deep gorges and fast-flowing rivers, Switzerland is ideal territory for **adventure sports**. Dozens of companies, based in all the main resorts, offer activities through the summer, such as **canyoning** (Fr.100/half-day), **river-rafting** (Fr.100/half-day), **bungee-jumping** (Fr.85 from 100m; Fr.230 from 180m), **zorbing** (where you're strapped inside a giant plastic sphere and rolled down a mountainside; Fr.50), **house-running** (where you hook a rope round yourself and run full-tilt down the side of a tall building; Fr.75), and **flying fox** (where you glide down a vertical cliff on a rope; Fr.80). Hang-gliding (Fr.130), **paragliding** (Fr.170) and **skydiving** from 4000m (Fr.400) can all be done alone or in tandem with an instructor. Tourist offices and ☻www.MySwitzerland.com have full details.

Almost everyone you meet will be able to converse in English, though a word or two of the local lingo never goes amiss. **French** (see p.356) is used in the western third of the country. From roughly Bern eastwards, **German** (see p.430) will be understood, although people actually speak **Swiss German**, an entirely different language where the standard greeting is *Grüezi* (sometimes *Grüss Gott*) and every town has its own unique dialect. The southern Ticino region is **Italian**-speaking (see p.589), while **Romansh**, a direct descendant of Latin, survives in the Alpine valleys around St Moritz.

all-you-can-eat deal (*fondue à discrétion* or *à gogo*). Another speciality is **raclette** – piquant molten cheese spread on a plate and scooped up with bread or potato. A Swiss-German staple is **Rösti**, grated potatoes topped with cheese, chopped ham or a fried egg. Almost everywhere offers **vegetarian** set menus. Alternative diners, many in squats in the major towns, offer budget veggie and vegan meals as standard. **Cafés** and **restaurants** usually serve meals at set times (noon–2pm & 6–10pm), with only snacks available in between. To get the best value, make lunch your main meal, and always opt for the dish of the day (*Tagesmenu*, *Tagesteller*, *Tageshit*; *plat/assiette du jour*; *piatto del giorno*) – substantial nosh for Fr.15 or less. The same meal in the evening, or choosing *à la carte* anytime, can cost double. **Department stores** have excellent **self-service** restaurants, where pick-and-choose meals are great value: you pay about Fr.6/10 for a small/large plate, with no limit on the quantity of fresh salad or hot daily special you can pile onto it. Some offer a twenty-percent discount to students. Cafés are open from breakfast till midnight/1am and often sell alcohol; **bars** and **pubs** tend to open their doors for late-afternoon and evening business only. **Beers** are invariably excellent, at Fr.3–4 for a glass (*e'Schtange*, *une pression*, *una birra*). Even the simplest places have **wine**, most affordably as *Offene Wein*, *vin ouvert*, *vino aperto* – a handful of house reds and whites chalked up on a board (small glass Fr.3–5).

# Opening hours and holidays

**Shop hours** are Mon–Fri 9am–6.30pm, Sat 8.30am–4pm, sometimes with a lunch-break and earlier closing in smaller towns. **Museums** and attractions generally close on Mon. Almost everything is closed on **public holidays**: Jan 1, Good Fri & Easter Mon, Ascension Day, Whit Mon, Dec 25 & 26. In Switzerland, shops and banks close for all or part of the national holiday (Aug 1) and on a range of local holidays. Liechtenstein keeps May 1 as a public holiday, and Aug 15 as the national holiday.

# Emergencies

Swiss **police** – who may not speak English – are courteous enough to white people, sometimes less so to everyone else. Form You'll have to pay **hospital** (*Spital*, *hôpital*, *ospedale*) bills upfront and claim expenses back later. Every district has one local **pharmacy** (*Apotheke*, *pharmacie*, *farmacia*) open outside normal hours; each pharmacy has a sign telling you where the nearest open one is.

## Emergency numbers

Police ☏117; fire ☏118; ambulance ☏144.

**SWITZERLAND AND LIECHTENSTEIN** | Basics

**31**

# Zürich

Not so long ago, **ZÜRICH** was famed for being the cleanest, most icily efficient city in Europe: apocryphal stories abound of tourists embarking on efforts to find a cigarette butt or food wrapper discarded on the streets – and drawing a blank every time. But there's a lot more to Zürich these days than its obsessive cleanliness: this most beautiful of cities, astride a river and turned towards a crystal-clear lake and distant snowy peaks, has plenty to recommend it, not least bars and clubs as hip and varied as those in more celebrated European cities. The steep, cobbled alleys of the Old Town are great to wander around, with an engaging café culture and a wealth of nightlife. You could easily spend days here.

## Arrival, information and accommodation

Zürich's main station, the giant **Hauptbahnhof** (HB), is served by trains from all over Europe, and from the **airport** (Flughafen), 11km northeast. The building extends three storeys below ground, taking in a shopping mall, supermarket and some good eateries; the main concourse is the haunt of pickpockets and bag-snatchers, so keep your valuables safe. The international **bus station** is 50m north on Sihlquai. The **tourist office** on the station concourse (Mon–Sat 8/8.30am–7/8.30pm, Sun 8.30/9am–6.30pm; ☎044 215 40 00, ⊛www.zuerich.com) will book rooms for free, and sells the **Zürich Card** (Fr.15/30 one/three days), which entitles you to free rides on public transport and free entry to museums. You can cover most sights by walking, but the **tram and bus** system is easy to use (⊛www.vbz.ch), with all tickets valid on trams, buses, some boats and local "S-Bahn" city trains. The most important hubs are the city squares of Bahnhofplatz and, on the east side of the river, Central and Bellevue. Buy tickets from machines at every stop: choose between the green button (24hr; Fr.7.20); blue button (1hr; Fr.3.60); or yellow button (short one-way hop; Fr.2.10). You'll need a multizone ticket to get to or from the airport.

### Hostels

**City Backpacker (SB)** Niederdorfstr. 5 ☎044 251 90 15, ⊛www.city-backpacker.ch. Good atmosphere and central location, plus free kitchen use, laundry and Internet (though a Fr.20 key deposit). No check-in after 10pm. Dorms Fr.31 (exc. breakfast), rooms ❹

**Jugendherberge (HI)** Mutschellenstr. 114 ☎043 399 78 00, ⊛www.youthhostel.ch. Rather institutional hostel, out in a southwestern suburb. Tram #7 (direction Wollishofen) to Morgental, then walk 5min. Dorms Fr.37.50 (inc. breakfast), rooms ❺

### Hotels

**Etap** Technoparkstr. 2 ☎044 276 20 00, ⊛www.etaphotel.com. Generic, functional hotel out west in the old industrial quarter, behind the trendy Schiffbau arts centre. ❹

**Limmathof** Limmatquai 142 ☎044 267 60 40, ⊛www.limmathof.com. Central riverside two-star with decent, compact rooms. ❼

**Martahaus** Zähringerstr. 36 ☎044 251 45 50, ⊛www.martahaus.ch. Clean, safe Old Town budget hotel with dorms (Fr.38) and rooms, plus a women-only annexe. ❺

**Otter** Oberdorfstr. 7 ☎044 251 22 07, ⊛www.wueste.ch. Relaxed, friendly Old Town joint with a clientele of students and artists. Rooms are decked in murals, drapes and plants. Also has a dreamy top-floor apartment. ❺

**Villette** Kruggasse 4 ☎044 251 23 35, ⊛hotelvillette@bluewin.ch. Simple rooms above a good city-centre fondue restaurant. Efficient, friendly service too. ❺

**X-tra** Limmatstr. 118 ☎044 448 15 00, ⊛www.x-tra.ch. Postmodern-styled rooms above the lively *X-tra* bar and nightclub, a little northwest of the centre. ❻

### Campsite

**Seebucht** Seestr. 559 ☎044 482 16 12, ⊛www.camping-zurich.ch. Well-serviced site on the lakeside, 2km south of the centre. Bus #161 or #165 from Bürkliplatz to Stadtgrenze. Closed Oct–April.

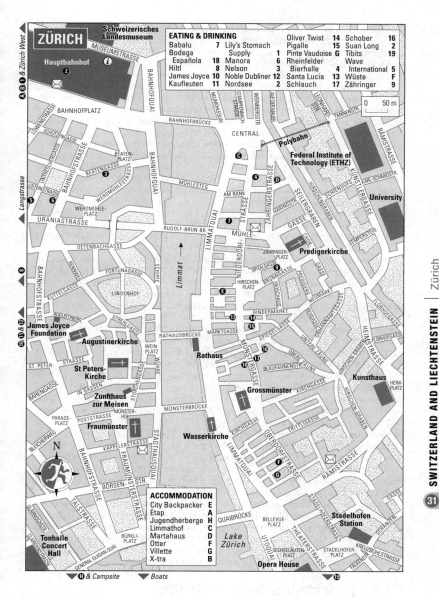

**ZÜRICH**

Schweizerisches Landesmuseum
MUSEUMSTRASSE
Hauptbahnhof ℹ️

**EATING & DRINKING**

| | | | | | |
|---|---|---|---|---|---|
| Babalu | 7 | Lily's Stomach | | Oliver Twist | 14 | Schober | 16 |
| Bodega | | Supply | 1 | Pigalle | 15 | Suan Long | 2 |
| Española | 18 | Manora | 6 | Pinte Vaudoise | G | Tibits | 19 |
| Hiltl | 8 | Nelson | 3 | Rheinfelder | | Wave | |
| James Joyce | 10 | Noble Dubliner | 12 | Bierhalle | 4 | International | 5 |
| Kaufleuten | 11 | Nordsee | 2 | Santa Lucia | 13 | Wüste | F |
| | | Schlauch | 17 | Zähringer | 9 |

0    50 m

**ACCOMMODATION**

| | |
|---|---|
| City Backpacker | E |
| Etap | A |
| Jugendherberge | H |
| Limmathof | C |
| Martahaus | D |
| Otter | F |
| Villette | G |
| X-tra | B |

▼ H & Campsite     ▼ Boats     ▼ 19

## The City

Across the River Limmat from the station, the narrow lanes of the medieval **Nied-erdorf** district stretch south, quiet during the day and bustling after dark. The waterfront is lined with fine Baroque *Zunfthäuser* (guildhalls), arcaded lower storeys fronting the quayside, their extravagantly decorated dining-rooms now mostly upmarket restaurants. One block in is **Niederdorfstrasse**, initially tacky, but offering plenty of opportunities to explore atmospheric cobbled side-alleys and secluded courtyards: Lenin lived at Spiegelgasse 14 in 1917 (pre-Revolution), while a café at Spiegelgasse 1 once housed the Cabaret Voltaire, birthplace of the Dada art movement. Just south is Zürich's trademark **Grossmünster** (Great Minster; Mon–Sat 9/10am–5/6pm), where Huldrych Zwingli, father of Swiss Protestantism, began preaching the Reformation in 1519. Its exterior is largely fifteenth-century, while its twin towers were topped with distinctive octagonal domes in the seventeenth century. The interior is austere but for the intensely coloured choir windows (1933) by Augusto Giacometti and the Roman-esque crypt which contains an oversized fifteenth-century statue of Charlemagne, popularly associated with the foundation of the church in the ninth century. A door, to the right on exiting, gives into the atmospheric **cloister**. Alleys behind the church lead up the hill to Switzerland's best gallery, the **Kunsthaus** (Tues–Thurs 10am–9pm, Fri–Sun 10am–5pm; Fr.6, free on Wed; more for temporary exhibits; ⓦwww .kunsthaus.ch). Some fascinating late-Gothic paintings are fleshed out by a roomful of Venetian masters and fine Flemish pieces. The collection of twentieth-century art is stunning: works by Miró, Dalí and De Chirico head a wonderful Surrealist overview; Picasso, Chagall, Klee and Kandinsky all have rooms to themselves; there are two of Monet's most beautiful waterlily canvases, plenty of Warhols, an array of Giacometti's sculpture, and the largest Munch collection outside Norway.

The **west bank** is the main commercial district, while further west of the centre are the coolest hangouts and the best streetlife. Tram #2 or #3 to Bezirksgebäude will deliver you to relaxed **Helvetiaplatz**, from where funky **Langstrasse** heads north – lowlife bars rubbing shoulders with avant-garde galleries, the smells of kebabs and pizza mixing with the pungent aroma of marijuana. This whole fascinating street is a mingle of styles and cultures – Swiss-German blending with French-African, Turkish, Balkan, East Asian and Latin American. Leading south from the station, **Bahnhofstrasse** is one of the most prestigious shopping streets in Europe. This is the gateway into the modern city, and is where all of Zürich strolls, to browse at the inexpensive department stores that crowd the first third of the street, or to sign away Fr.25,000 on a Rolex watch or a Vuitton bag at the understated super-chic boutiques further south. Two-thirds of the way down is **Paradeplatz**, a tram-packed little square offering some of the best people-watching in the city. The narrow lanes between Bahnhofstrasse and the river lead up to the **Lindenhof**, site of a Roman fortress and customs post. James Joyce wrote *Ulysses* in Zürich (1915–19), and the **Joyce Foundation**, nearby at Augustinergasse 9 (Tues–Fri 10am–5pm; free), can point you to his various hangouts, and his grave. Steps away is **St Peters-Kirche** (Mon–Fri 8am–6pm, Sat 9am–4pm), renowned for its enormous sixteenth-century clock face – the largest in Europe. Immediately south rises the slender-spired Gothic **Fraumünster** (Mon–Sat 9/10am–4/6pm), which began life as a convent in the ninth century; its spectacular stained glass by Marc Chagall is unmissable.

A tasty diversion heads south to the Lindt & Sprüngli **chocolate factory**, Seestrasse 204, Kilchberg (Wed–Fri 10am–noon & 1–4pm; free). Frustratingly, the company refuses to let anyone near the production line; instead, you're diverted to a small museum, shown a video and then let loose to sample the company's wares for free. Kilchberg is 6km south along the lake's western shore from Bürkliplatz by bus #165 or boat, also reachable by S-Bahn suburban train from Zürich.

## Eating, drinking and nightlife

A wander through the Niederdorf district will turn up dozens of **eating** options – falafel, sausage, noodle and french-fry stands, plus beerhalls serving daily specials for about Fr.13. Supplementing its lively **music** venues, Zürich's **club** scene has skyrocketed recently, and you'll find dance floors heaving. The hip quarter around Langstrasse, west of the centre, is full of DJ bars, and the industrial quarter to the northwest is where the best clubs hide themselves. August sees the **Street Parade**

(ⓦwww.street-parade.ch), a hedonistic weekend of techno street-dancing. **Listings** are in *ZüriTipp* (ⓦwww.zueritipp.ch), available at the tourist office.

### Snack meals

**Nordsee** Train station concourse. Good-value fish dishes and snacks, eat in or take away.

**Suan Long** Train station lower level. Cheap, filling stir-fries – meat and veggie.

**Wave International** At Jelmoli dept store on Uraniastr. Swiss, Asian, Turkish and Arabic nosh.

### Cafés and restaurants

**Bodega Española** Münstergasse 15. Atmospheric tapas bar and paella restaurant.

**Hiltl** Sihlstr. 28. Top-quality vegetarian buffet, with budget prices for takeaway.

**Lily's Stomach Supply** Langstr. 197. Clean, modern place in a multicultural district, churning out fresh-cooked Asian specialities (from Fr.10). The German menu marks dishes that are extra-spicy *!!!* and those that are an acquired taste *\*\*\**.

**Manora** 5th floor of Manor store, Bahnhofstr. 75. Good, varied self-service fare for under Fr.13.

**Pinte Vaudoise** In *Hotel Villette*, Kruggasse 4. Traditional place serving what some say is the best fondue in Zürich. Closed Sat in summer, & Sun.

**Santa Lucia** Marktgasse 21. Wide selection of good-value pasta and pizza. Serves until 2am.

**Schlauch** Upstairs at Münstergasse 20. Health food (Fr.12–17) served in a quiet atmosphere.

**Schober** Napfgasse 4. Don't leave Zürich without sampling a mug of hot chocolate here.

**Tibits** Seefeldstr. 2, beside the Opera House. Chic, healthy veggie fast food. Daily till midnight.

**Zähringer** Zähringerplatz 11. Co-operative-run café-bar with an alternative-minded clientele and cheap food.

### Bars

**Babalu** Schmidgasse 6. Tiny, chic DJ-bar.

**James Joyce** Pelikanstr. 8. Original nineteenth-century interior, transported piece by piece from Dublin. Closed Sat from 7pm & all Sun.

**Kaufleuten** Pelikanstr. 18. Modish venue for mixing with designers, musicians and the idle rich.

**Nelson** Beatengasse 11. Massive, noisy pub near the station; cheap beer & late opening.

**Noble Dubliner** Talacker 43/Talstr. 82. Good beer, good service and a talkative atmosphere.

**Oliver Twist** Rindermarkt 6. Small English pub on an Old Town lane.

**Pigalle** Marktgasse 14. Legendary little bar filled with the elegantly wasted.

**Rheinfelder Bierhalle** Niederdorfstr. 76. Best of the hearty beerhalls. Closed Sun.

**Wüste** In *Hotel Otter*, Oberdorfstr. 7. Mellow, comfortable den near the Grossmünster.

### Clubs and music venues

**Abart** Manessestr. 170. Regular choice of local and foreign bands.

**Casa Bar** Münstergasse 20. Live jazz nightly in the Old Town.

**Dynamo** Wasserwerkstr. 21. Alternative, punkish bands and dance nights.

**Labyrinth** Pfingstweidstr. 70. Hard house at this mixed gay/straight venue.

**Oxa** Andreasstr. 70. Techno and house; famed after-hours parties (Sun 5am–noon).

**Rote Fabrik** Seestr. 395. Alternative bands, big-name DJs, cheap food and a great riverside bar.

**Toni Molkerei** Förrlibuckstr. 109. Eclectic dance club in a vast industrial space.

**X-tra** Limmatstr. 118. Very popular club and live music venue.

# Listings

**Bike rental** Free (with photo-ID & Fr.20 deposit) from "Velogate", next to platform 18 of the station (daily 7.30am–9.15pm).

**Consulates** Ireland, Claridenstr. 25 ☏044 289 25 15; UK, Hegibachstr. 47 ☏044 383 65 60; USA, Dufourstr. 101 ☏044 422 25 66. Embassies are in Bern.

**Hospital** Permanence Medical Centre, Bahnhof-platz 15 ☏044 215 44 44.

**Laundry** Mühlegasse 11, Niederdorf.

**Pharmacy** Bellevue: Theaterstrasse 14 (24hr).

**Post office** Kasernenstrasse, beside the station.

# The Rhine falls

A great fine-weather excursion from Zürich is the half-day trip north to the **Rhine falls** (ⓦwww.rhinefalls.com), Europe's largest waterfalls, which tumble

3km west of **SCHAFFHAUSEN**. They are truly magnificent, not so much for their height (a mere 23m) as for their impressive breadth (150m) and the sheer drama of the place, with spray rising in a cloud of rainbows above the forested banks. The turreted castle **Schloss Laufen** on the south bank completes the spectacle. Be here on August 1, Switzerland's national day, for a famous fireworks display. Damp steps lead down from the castle souvenir shop to platforms at the water's edge (Fr.1), where the falls roar inches from your nose. In summer, the best views are from daredevil boats, which scurry about in the spray (Fr.7–9). Take a **train** from Zürich either to Winterthur, from where hourly trains serve Schloss Laufen's own little station (April–Oct only), or to Schaffhausen, from where you can walk (20min) or take bus #1 or #6 to Neuhausen Zentrum, 5min from the falls.

# Lake Geneva (Lac Léman)

French-speaking Switzerland, or Suisse Romande, occupies the western third of the country, comprising the shores of **Lake Geneva** (⊛www.lake-geneva -region.ch) and the hills and lakes leading north almost to Basel. The ambience here is thoroughly Gallic: historical animosity between Geneva and France has nowadays given way to a yearning on the part of most francophone Swiss to abandon their bumpkin compatriots in the east and embrace the EU. **Geneva**, at the southwestern tip of the lake, was once a haven for free-thinkers from all over Europe; now it's a city of diplomats and big business. Halfway around the lake, **Lausanne** is full of young people, a cultured, energetic town acclaimed as the skateboarding capital of Europe. Further east, the shore features vineyards and opulent villas – **Montreux** is particularly chic – and the stunning medieval **Château de Chillon**, which drew Byron and the Romantic poets. Mont Blanc, western Europe's highest mountain (4807m), is visible from Geneva city centre, while Montreux and neighbouring **Vevey** have breathtaking views across the water to the French Alps. On a sunny day, the train ride around the beautiful northern shore is memorably scenic, but the lake's excellent **boat** service (IR no discount; ER & SP free; ⊛www.cgn.ch) helps bring home the full grandeur of the setting.

## Geneva (Genève)

The Puritanism of **GENEVA** (Genève) is inextricably linked with the city's struggle for independence. Long ruled by the dukes of Savoy, sixteenth-century Genevans saw the Reformation as a useful aid in their struggle to rid themselves of Savoyard influence. By the time the city's independence was won in 1602, its religious zeal had painted it as the "Protestant Rome". Geneva remained outside the Swiss Confederation until 1815 (the Catholic cantons opposed its entry), and acquired a reputation for joylessness which it still struggles to shake off. Today, it's a working city, sharply focused on its prominent role in international diplomacy and big business. It's all very pretty, but – unlike its neighbour Lausanne – you need time to penetrate the facade of money and power.

### Arrival, information and accommodation

The main **train station**, Gare de Cornavin, lies at the head of Rue du Mont-Blanc in the city centre. Expresses from Paris, Lyon and Grenoble arrive in a separate French section (passport control), while local French trains from Annecy/ Chamonix terminate at Gare des Eaux-Vives on the east side of town (tram #12 or #16 into the centre). From the **airport**, 5km northwest, trains and bus #10

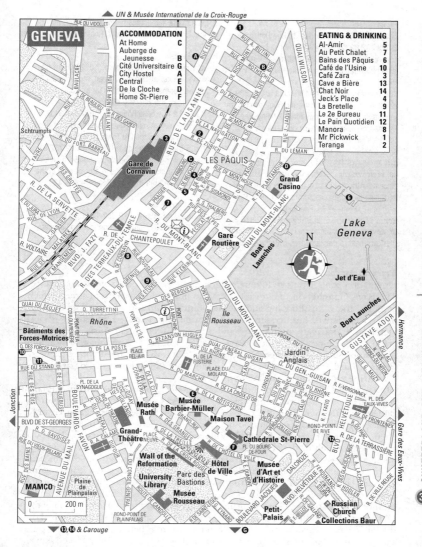

**GENEVA**

**ACCOMMODATION**

| | |
|---|---|
| At Home | C |
| Auberge de Jeunesse | B |
| Cité Universitaire | G |
| City Hostel | A |
| Central | E |
| De la Cloche | D |
| Home St-Pierre | F |

**EATING & DRINKING**

| | |
|---|---|
| Al-Amir | 5 |
| Au Petit Chalet | 7 |
| Bains des Pâquis | 6 |
| Café de l'Usine | 10 |
| Café Zara | 3 |
| Cave a Bière | 13 |
| Chat Noir | 14 |
| Jeck's Place | 4 |
| La Bretelle | 9 |
| Le 2e Bureau | 11 |
| Le Pain Quotidien | 12 |
| Manora | 8 |
| Mr Pickwick | 1 |
| Teranga | 2 |

Lake Geneva (Lac Léman)

SWITZERLAND AND LIECHTENSTEIN

**31**

run into the city. The international **bus station** (Gare Routière) is on Place Dorcière in the centre. **Boats** dock at several central quays. The **tourist office** is in the main post office at 18 Rue du Mont-Blanc (daily 9/10am–6pm; Sept to mid-June closed Sun; ☎022 909 70 00, ⊛www.genevatourism.ch), and there's also a desk within the municipality's information office, on the Pont de la Machine (Mon noon–6pm, Tues–Fri 9am–6pm, Sat 10am–5pm; ☎022 311 99 70, ⊛www .ville-ge.ch). Both have stacks of material in English, including the useful *Young People* brochure listing budget hotels and ideas. During the summer, a bus parked at the station end of Rue du Mont-Blanc houses the "CAR" info-centre (mid-June to early Sept daily 9am–11pm; ☎022 731 46 47).

### Hostels

**Auberge de Jeunesse (HI)** 30 Rue Rothschild
☎022 732 62 60, ⊛www.youthhostel.ch &
⊛www.yh-geneva.ch. Big, bustling, well-maintained 330-bed hostel in a central location, with
cheap meals. Bus #1 to Wilson. Fr.26.
**Cité Universitaire** 46 Av Miremont ☎022 839
22 22, ⊛www.unige.ch/cite-uni. Huge place 3km
south (bus #3), with dorms for Fr.22 July–Sept
(dorms Oct–June are groups only). Plenty of
cut-price singles, doubles and studios year-round.
Breakfast extra. Rooms ❹
**City Hostel (SB)** 2 Rue Ferrier ☎022 901 15
00, ⊛www.cityhostel.ch. Excellent backpacker
place near the HI hostel, with plenty of services
(including laundry), plus dorms and rooms. Bus #4
to Prieuré. Dorms Fr.28. Rooms ❹
**Home St-Pierre** 4 Cour St-Pierre ☎022 310 37
07, ⊛www.homestpierre.ch. In the heart of the
Old Town next to the cathedral, with two dorms
plus single and double rooms (all women-only);
breakfast extra. Dorms Fr.27. Rooms ❸

### Hotels

**At Home** 16 Rue de Fribourg ☎022 906 19 00,
⊛www.hotel-at-home.ch. Clean, modern Pâquis-
district rooms, with discounts for students, though
a bit small and soulless. ❻
**Central** 2 Rue de la Rôtisserie ☎022 818 81 00,
⊛www.hotelcentral.ch. Quiet, good-value top-floor
rooms just below the Old Town, all with balcony. ❹
**De la Cloche** 6 Rue de la Cloche ☎022 732 94
81, ⊛www.geneva-hotel.ch/cloche. Eight characterful, high-ceilinged rooms in a quiet area of the
Pâquis 50m from the lake. Regularly full. ❺

### Campsite

**Pointe-à-la-Bise** ☎022 752 12 96, ⊛www.tcs
.ch. Good-quality site 7km northeast in Vésanaz;
bus #E. April–Sept.

## The City

Orientation centres on the Rhône, which flows from the lake west into France.
The **Rive Gauche**, on the south bank, takes in a grid of waterfront streets which
comprise the main shopping and business districts and the adjacent high ground
of the Old Town. Further south lies **Carouge**, characterized by artisans' shops,
picturesque Italianate architecture and a lively, independent spirit. Behind the
grand hotels lining the northern **Rive Droite** waterfront is the main station and
the cosmopolitan (and sometimes sleazy) Les Pâquis district, filled with cheap restaurants. Further north are the offices of the dozens of international organizations
headquartered in Geneva, including the UN.

On the Rive Gauche, beyond the ornamental flowerbeds of the **Jardin Anglais**,
erupts the roaring 140-metre-high plume of Geneva's trademark **Jet d'Eau**. Nearby
is the main thoroughfare of the Old Town, the cobbled, steeply ascending **Grande
Rue**. Here, among the secondhand bookshops and galleries, you'll find the atmospheric seventeenth-century **Hôtel de Ville** and the arcaded **armoury**, backed by a
lovely terrace with the longest wooden bench in the world (126m). A block away is
the huge late-Romanesque **Cathédrale St-Pierre** (Mon–Sat 9/10am–5/7pm, Sun
11am–5/7pm), with an incongruous eighteenth-century portal and a plain, soaring
interior. The frescoes of the internal Chapelle des Macchabées, with their intricate
floral patterns and lute-strumming angels, are modern versions of the faded fifteenth-
century originals now in Geneva's main museum. Round the corner is the hub of the
Old Town, **Place du Bourg-de-Four**, a picturesque split-level square perched on
the hillside and ringed by cafés. Alleys wind down from here to the university park
and its austere **Wall of the Reformation** (1909–17) alongside busy Place Neuve.
A stroll east of the Old Town is the gigantic **Musée d'Art et d'Histoire**, 2 Rue
Charles Galland (Tues–Sun 10am–5pm; free; ⊛mah.ville-ge.ch). Upstairs are three
stunning sculptures – a graceful *Venus and Adonis* by Canova and two powerful pieces
by Rodin. The fine-art collection is crowned by Konrad Witz's famous altarpiece,
made for the cathedral in 1444, showing Christ and the fishermen transposed onto
Lake Geneva. Other highlights are by local artist Félix Vallotton; Cézanne, Renoir
and Modigliani; and some striking Swiss landscapes by Bern-born Ferdinand Hodler.
The basement holds the massive archeological collection, including Egyptian mummies and Greek and Roman statuary. Nearby is the **Collections Baur**, 8 Rue
Munier-Romilly (Tues–Sun 2–6pm; Fr.5), the country's premier collection of

East Asian art, featuring luminescent yellow Yongzhang ceramics and spectacular porcelain and jade. Make time also for **MAMCO**, a top-quality museum of modern and contemporary art housed in an old factory west of the Old Town at 10 Rue des Vieux-Grenadiers (Tues–Fri noon–6pm, Sat & Sun 11am–6pm; Fr.8).

About 1km north of the station, opposite the UN complex on Avenue de la Paix, is the thought-provoking **Musée International de la Croix-Rouge** (Mon & Wed–Sun 10am–5pm; Fr.10; @www.micr.ch; bus #8 or #F to Appia), which documents the origins, growth and achievements of the Red Cross without resorting to self-congratulation. Carefully chosen audiovisual material combines with quietly dramatic exhibits – such as the 34 footprints in a tiny cell-space where a delegate found seventeen people crammed together – to leave a powerful impression.

Twenty minutes south of the centre by tram #12 or #13 lies the late-Baroque suburb of **Carouge**, built by the king of Sardinia in the eighteenth century as a separate town. Its low Italianate houses and leafy streets are now largely occupied by fashion designers and small galleries, and the area's reputation as an outpost of tolerance and hedonism beyond Geneva's jurisdiction lives on in its numerous cafés and music bars. Carouge hosts a colourful **market** (Wed & Sat); the flea market at Plainpalais, near Geneva's Old Town, is also worth a browse (same days).

## Eating and drinking

### Cafés and bars
**Bains des Pâquis** 30 Quai du Mont-Blanc. Popular café-bar attached to the lakefront swimming area. Summer only.

**La Bretelle** 15 Rue des Etuves. Camp, kitsch tavern, with live accordion and/or drag cabaret Thurs–Sat.

**Café de l'Usine** In L'Usine squat, Place des Volontaires. Graffitied, upstairs café-bar, serving meals for around Fr.10. Closed Sun & Mon.

**Cave a Bière** 19 Rue Ancienne, Carouge. Bar with almost 400 beers from around the world. Closed Sun & Mon.

**Chat Noir** 13 Rue Vautier, Carouge @www.chatnoir.ch. Bar and cellar venue with live music (anything from folk to metal) and DJs. Wed–Sat until 4am.

**Le 2e (Deuxième) Bureau** 9 Rue du Stand. Sleek bar thumping with deep beats.

**Mr Pickwick** 80 Rue de Lausanne. Homely English pub with TV football.

### Restaurants
**Al-Amir** 12 Rue des Alpes. Excellent Lebanese kebabs and falafel from Fr.8.

**Au Petit Chalet** 6 Rue Chaponnière. Unpretentious place for Swiss fondues and rösti. Closed Mon.

**Café Zara** 25 Rue de Lausanne. Simple little Eritrean/Ethiopian café-restaurant near the station.

**Jeck's Place** 14 Rue de Neuchâtel. Affordable Thai food, with lunches from Fr.15. Closed Sat lunch.

**Manora** 4 Rue de Cornavin. Excellent self-service nosh, with plentiful veggie selections and meals from Fr.12.

**Le Pain Quotidien** 21 Boulevard Helvétique. No-nonsense café with superb breakfasts (Fr.7 or Fr.12) and lavish weekend brunches (Fr.28). Closed Tues eve.

**Teranga** 38bis Rue de Zurich. Tiny backstreet Senegalese place, with good service and great food. Closed Sat lunch & Sun.

## Listings

**Consulates** Australia, 2 Chemin des Fins ☎022 799 91 00; Canada, 5 Ave de l'Ariana ☎022 919 92 00; New Zealand, 2 Chemin des Fins ☎022 929 03 50; UK, 37 Rue de Vermont ☎022 918 24 00; USA, 7 Rue Versonnex ☎022 840 51 60. Embassies are in Bern.

**Hospital** Hôpital Cantonal, 24 Rue Micheli-du-Crest ☎022 372 33 11.

**Laundry** Lavseul, 29 Rue de Monthoux.

**Post office** 18 Rue du Mont-Blanc.

# Lausanne

Geneva's neighbour **LAUSANNE** is interesting, attractive, worldly and well aware of how to have a good time – in short, Switzerland's sexiest city. It's tiered above the lake on a succession of south-facing terraces, with the Old Town at the top, the train station and commercial districts in the middle, and the one-time fishing village of **Ouchy**, now prime territory for waterfront café-lounging and strolling, at the bottom. The hills are incredibly steep; copy the locals and catch a bus into the Joret forests above the city, and then blade or **skateboard** your way down to Ouchy: aficionados have been clocked doing 90kph through the streets. Switzerland's biggest university aids the youthful spirit, and a wealth of international student programmes feeds an unusually diverse, multi-ethnic makeup. For lively streetlife and uniquely chilled-out bars, head for the converted warehouses of the city-centre **Flon** district.

To get to the central **Place St-François** from the train station, either walk up the steep Rue du Petit-Chêne, or take the metro to Flon; from the metro platforms, lifts shuttle you up to the level of the giant **Grand Pont**, between Place Bel-Air on the left and St François on the right. Glitzy **Rue de Bourg** entices shoppers uphill from St François; beside it, Rue St-François drops down into the valley and up the other side to the cobbled **Place de la Palud**, an ancient, fountained square flanked by the arcades of the Renaissance town hall. From here the medieval **Escaliers du Marché** lead up to the **Cathedral** (daily 8am–7pm), a fine Romanesque-Gothic jumble, its clean lines only peripherally adorned with memorials and fifteenth-century frescoes. Opposite, in the former bishop's palace, is the **Musée Historique** (Tues–Thurs 11am–6pm, Fri–Sun 11am–5pm; Fr.8), which houses a model of old Lausanne – invaluable for grasping the city's confusing topography. Lausanne suffered from many medieval fires, and is the last city in Europe to keep alive the tradition of the nightwatch: every night, on the hour (10pm–2am), a sonorous-voiced civil servant calls out from the cathedral tower *"C'est le guet; il a sonné l'heure"* ("This is the night-watch; the hour has struck"), assuring the lovers and assorted drunks below that all is well. West of the cathedral hill is **Place de la Riponne**, an arid expanse of concrete dominated by the splendidly ostentatious Palais de Rumine, housing the university library and various museums. Save your francs for the outstanding **Collection de l'Art Brut**, 11 Ave des Bergières (Tues–Sun 11am–6pm; July & Aug also Mon 11am–6pm; Fr.8; ⊛www.artbrut.ch), ten minutes' walk northwest of Riponne on Ave Vinet, or bus #2 or #3 to Jomini. This unique gallery is devoted to "outsider art", the creative output of ordinary people with no artistic training at all – often loners, psychotics or the criminally insane – who for some reason suddenly began making their own art. It's utterly absorbing. In a park on the Ouchy waterfront sits Lausanne's flagship **Olympic Museum** (daily 9am–6pm; Oct–April closed Mon; Fr.14), a vacuous and expensive place that trumpets the Olympic ideal by means of snippets of archive footage, stirring music and Cathy Freeman's old running shoes. Bypass it for the **Musée de l'Elysée**, an excellent museum of photography in the same park (daily 11am–6pm; Fr.8; free on first Sat of month).

## Practicalities

Lausanne has two **tourist offices** (☎021 613 73 73, ⊛www.lausanne-tourisme .ch): one in the train station (daily 9am–7pm), the other beside Ouchy metro station (daily 9am–8pm; Oct–March closes 6pm). Both have stacks of information on the whole lake region. Ouchy's waterfront hosts regular free **music** events all summer, and people come down here to do a spot of café sunbathing or blade-cruising (rent blades or skates from beside Ouchy metro). Lausanne's big party is the **Festival de la Cité** in early July (⊛www.festivaldelacite.ch), featuring music, dance, drama and mime on several open-air stages in the old town. Also check out July's big-name **Paleo Rock Festival** in nearby Nyon (⊛www.paleo.ch).

### Accommodation

**Pension Bienvenue** 2 Rue du Simplon ☎021 616 29 86, ⊛www.pension-bienvenue.ch. Respectable women-only guesthouse behind the station. **⑤**

**Jeunotel (HI)** 36 Chemin du Bois-de-Vaux ☎021

626 02 22, ⊛www.youthhostel.ch. Huge place beside *Vidy* campsite with four-bed dorms and rooms. Dorms Fr.33. Rooms **⑤**

**Lausanne Guest House (SB)** 4 Epinettes ☎021 601 80 00, ⊛www.lausanne-guesthouse.ch.

**31**

Quality no-smoking hostel with lake views, four-bedded dorms and rooms. Dorms Fr.35. Rooms ❹

**Old Inn** 11 Av de la Gare ☎ 021 323 62 21, ✉ old _inn@bluewin.ch. Quiet, spartan little pension. ❹

**Du Raisin** 19 Place de la Palud ☎ 021 312 27 56. Seven plain rooms above an old café in the heart of the Old Town. ❹

**Vidy** ☎ 021 622 50 00, ⓦ www.campinglausan-nevidy.ch. Bus #1 to Maladière and walk 5min ahead to this decent lakeside campsite.

### Restaurants and cafés

**Au Couscous** 2 Rue Enning. Couscous and *tajine* (from Fr.23), mezze (Fr.26), plus daily specials (Fr.16) and veggie and macrobiotic dishes. Closed Sat & Sun lunchtimes.

**Bleu Lézard** 10 Rue Enning. Fashionable, lively café-bar on a busy corner.

**La Bossette** 4 Pl du Nord. Friendly local café on a patch of green beneath the château, serving speciality beers plus excellent food.

**Café de l'Évêché** 4 Rue Curtat. Haunt of talkative students and local old-timers, just below the cathedral.

**Laxmi** 5 Escaliers du Marché. Indian/veggie. All-you-can-eat lunches are Fr.17, less for vegetarian dishes, or Fr.12 for cold dishes; evening *menus*

cost no more. Student discount. Closed Mon lunch & Sun.

**Ma Jong** 3 Escaliers du Grand-Pont. Just down from *Manora*, with freshly wok-fried meals for Fr.14. Sushi too. Closed Sun.

**Manora** 17 Pl St-François. Self-service place with a wide range of cheap food.

**Café Romand** Pl St-François (under *Pizza Hut*). Bustling, heartwarming place with cosy alcoves for beer, coffee or heavy Swiss fare. Closed Sun.

### Bars and nightlife

**Au Château** 1 Pl du Tunnel. Bar with funky music and flavourful home-brewed beers.

**D!** Pl Centrale. Happening basement club playing house and drum 'n' bass. Closed Mon–Wed.

**Lecaféthéâtre** 10 Rue de Genève. Café-bar with live cabaret or music most nights. Closed Sun & Mon.

**Le Loft** 1 Escaliers Bel-Air. Techno club with international DJs.

**MAD (Moulin à Danse)** 23 Rue de Genève, ⓦ www.mad.ch. Cutting-edge dance club with adjoining theatre, art galleries and alternative-style café.

**VO Le Jazz Café** 11 Pl du Tunnel. Café-bar and live venue with regular DJ nights.

## Vevey, Montreux and Chillon

East of Lausanne, trains meander through steep vineyards to **VEVEY**, a small market town looking over to the French Alps. It holds a **Street Artists' Festival** in late August, jugglers, acrobats and mime artists performing on the lakeside (ⓦ www .artistesderue.ch). Vevey's charm centres on the huge lakeside **Grande Place**, a few minutes' walk southeast of the station – known also as Place du Marché and packed with market stalls (Tues & Sat) – and the narrow streets which lead off into the old town to the east. The excellent fine-art museum, **Musée Jenisch** on Rue de la Gare (Tues–Sun 11am–5.30pm; Fr.12), has Europe's largest collection of Rembrandt lithographs, as well as graphic works by Dürer, Corot, Le Corbusier and others. East of Place du Marché is a statue of Charlie Chaplin, "The Tramp", who moved to Vevey from the US in the 1950s to escape McCarthyism. To head on to Montreux and Chillon, ditch the train in favour of **bus #1**, which plies the coast road every 10min. If you have time, walk the floral lakeside path. **MONTREUX**, 6km east of Vevey, is a snooty place, full of money and not particularly exciting, but it enjoys spectacular views of the Dents-du-Midi peaks opposite and hosts a colourful Friday market. The town is protected from chill northerly winds by a wall of mountains and so basks in its own microclimate, boasting lakeside palm trees and exotic flowers. The zigzagging streets of the old quarter above the train station provide more interest than the Grand-Rue below (head 100m left out of the station and cut down the stairs between buildings), although you should make time for the statue of one-time resident **Freddie Mercury** silently serenading the swans on the lakefront. The star-studded **Montreux Jazz Festival** (ⓦ www .montreuxjazz.com) packs the town out in early July; check online for tickets (Fr.50–150) or just join the street parties and free entertainment on the lake.

The climax of a journey around Lake Geneva is the stunning thirteenth-century **Château de Chillon** (daily 9/10am–5/6pm; Fr.10; ⓦ www.chillon.ch), one of the best-preserved medieval castles in Europe. Whether you opt for the 45-minute shoreline walk east from Montreux, or bus #1 from Vevey or Montreux, or a local train, a bike, or, best of all, a lake steamer, your first glimpse of the castle is unforgettable – an elegant, turreted pile jutting out into the water, framed by trees and craggy mountains. At the gate you'll get a follow-the-numbers pamphlet, which starts you off in the dungeons where the dukes of Savoy imprisoned François Bonivard, a Genevan priest, from 1530 to 1536 (he was manacled to the fifth pillar along); Lord Byron, after a sailing trip here with Shelley in 1816, was so affected by the story that he spent the next day in his Ouchy hotel room writing his poem *The Prisoner of Chillon*. Byron's signature, scratched on the dungeon's third pillar, probably isn't genuine. As you look out onto the lake from the castle, it's sobering to realize how sheer the rock is: just below the castle walls yawns 300m of cold water, enough to swallow the Eiffel Tower without a trace. Upstairs you'll find more wonders: gloriously grand knights' halls, secret twisting passages between lavish bedchambers, Gothic windows with dreamy views and a frescoed chapel.

The **tourist offices** of Vevey and Montreux (☏0848 868 484, ⓦwww.montreux -vevey.com) have the same information: Vevey's is in the pillared Grenette building on Grande-Place (June–Sept Mon–Fri 9am–6pm, Sat 9am–4pm; Oct–May Mon–Fri 8.30am–12.30pm & 1.30–6pm, Sat 8.30am–noon); Montreux's is beside the ferry landing-stage (June–Sept daily 9.30am–6pm; Oct–May Mon–Fri 9am–12.30pm & 1.30–6pm). Their brochure *On The Trail of Hemingway* pinpoints local sites with famous-name associations. The pristine *Riviera Lodge* SB **hostel**, 5 Grande-Place in Vevey (☏021 923 80 40, ⓦwww.rivieralodge.ch; dorms Fr.31; ➍), is better-value than the HI hostel at 8 Passage de l'Auberge, beside Territet station 1500m east of Montreux (☏021 963 49 34, ⓦwww.youthhostel.ch; dorms Fr.31; ➍). Of the **hotels**, go for cosy *Les Négociants*, 27 Rue du Conseil in Vevey (☏021 922 70 11, ⓦwww.hotelnegociants.ch; ➏), or basic *Elite*, 25 Ave du Casino in Montreux (☏021 966 03 03; ➑). Lakeside *La Pichette* **campsite** (☏021 921 09 97; April–Sept) is 2km west of Vevey. Vevey has a self-service *Manora* **restaurant** in the St Antoine mall outside the station, and plenty of pavement cafés in the centre. The food at *Hôtel des Négociants* is good. Montreux has plenty of eateries outside the station on Ave des Alpes, including some with lakeview terraces.

# The Swiss heartland

The Mittelland – the populated countryside between Lake Geneva and Zürich, flanked by the Jura range to the north and the high Alps to the south – is a region of gentle hills, lakes and some high peaks. There's a wealth of cultural and historical interest in the German-speaking cities of **Basel**, **Luzern** and the federal capital, **Bern**. Wherever you base yourself, the mountains are never more than a couple of hours away by train.

## Basel (Bâle)

You might expect **BASEL** (Bâle in French), situated on the Rhine exactly where Switzerland, Germany and France touch noses, to hum with pan-European energy, but the close proximity of foreign languages and cultures seems to have introverted the city rather than energized it: it's a curiously measured place, where equilibrium is everything. With both a gigantic port and the HQs of several pharmaceutical multinationals, Basel cherishes its reputation as Switzerland's wealthiest city. Its long-standing patronage of the arts has resulted in some first-rate museums and galleries and superb contemporary architecture. However, unless you're here for the massive three-day February **carnival** (⊛www.fasnacht.ch) – which begins at 4am on the Monday after Mardi Gras – you may find Basel a tough nut to crack.

The River **Rhine** describes a right-angled curve through the centre of Basel, flowing from east to north. On the south/west bank (1km north of the main station) is the historic Old Town, which is centred on the hectic main square **Barfüsserplatz**, ringed by higgledy-piggledy medieval buildings. The city's cultural pre-eminence in the fifteenth and sixteenth centuries is amply demonstrated in the splendid Barfüsserkirche, now home to the **Historisches Museum** (Mon & Wed–Sun 10am–5pm; Fr.7); don't miss the sumptuous medieval tapestries, hidden behind protective blinds. Sixteenth-century lanes lead up behind the Historisches Museum to Basel's cathedral, the **Münster** (Mon–Sat 10/11am–4/5pm, Sun 1/2–4/5pm). Medieval stone carving above the main portal shows the cathedral's founder, Emperor Heinrich II, holding a model of the church; beside him is a Foolish Virgin. Inside, in the north aisle, is the tomb of the Renaissance humanist Erasmus, and behind the church is the Pfalz terrace, a fine spot for a picnic with a view. From Barfüsserplatz, shop-lined Gerbergasse and Freiestrasse run north to **Marktplatz**, dominated by the elaborate scarlet façade of the sixteenth-century **Rathaus**. Just beyond Marktplatz is the **Mittlere Brücke**, which for many centuries was the only bridge across the Rhine between its source and the sea. **Boats** still depart regularly from here for pleasure trips. The working-class quarter across the river, known as **Kleinbasel**, was traditionally the object of scorn for the merchants of the city centre: their Lällekönig bust still faces down the bridge, sticking out its tongue at the Kleinbaslers. Don't be put off: humdrum Kleinbasel is worth a wander (especially the Rhineside lanes), and its riverbank steps are a great spot to catch the sunset.

Back at Barfüsserplatz, Steinenberg climbs east past a sputtering Jean Tinguely fountain – another sunny hangout spot – to a traffic junction, from where St Alban-Graben heads northeast to the river. The venerable **Antikenmuseum** is at no. 5 (Tues–Sun 10am–5pm; Fr.7), with superb Greek and Etruscan pottery and Egyptian antiquities. Opposite at no. 16 is the absorbing **Kunstmuseum** (Tues–Sun 10am–5pm; Fr.7, or joint ticket Fr.15 includes entry to Museum für Gegenwartskunst; free on 1st Sun of month), its dazzling array of twentieth-century art surpassed by an outstanding medieval collection. Down to the river, then right, is the **Museum für Gegenwartskunst** (Tues–Sun 11am–5pm, Wed until 7pm; joint admission with Kunstmuseum), with installations by Frank Stella and Joseph Beuys sharing space with video art. A stroll away, at St Alban-Tal 37, is the restored **Basler Papiermühle** (Papermill), housing the wonderful Museum of Paper, Writing and Printing (Tues–Sun 2–5pm; Fr.12), where you can make your own paper, from pulp to final product. A walk away on the north bank, in Solitude Park, is the beautifully designed **Museum Jean Tinguely** (Wed–Sun 11am–7pm; Fr.7; ⊛www.tinguely .ch), dedicated to one of Switzerland's best-loved artists. Tinguely used scrap metal, plastic and bits of everyday junk to create room-sized Monty-Pythonesque machines that – with the touch of a foot-button – judder into life, squeaking, clanking and scraping in a parody of the slickness of our performance-driven world.

Out in the suburbs is Basel's finest gallery – **Fondation Beyeler** (daily 10am–6pm, Wed until 8pm; Fr.18; tram #6; ⊛www.beyeler.com), sympathetically designed by Renzo Piano, architect of Paris's Pompidou Centre. A small but exceptionally high-quality collection features some of the best works by Picasso, Giacometti, Rothko, Rodin, Bacon, Miró and others. Sink into a huge white sofa opposite a giant Monet, to indulge in dreamy contemplation of the waterlilies in front of you and also the watery gardens outside.

## Practicalities

Basel has two **train stations** straddling three countries. **Basel SBB** is the main one, most of it in Switzerland; at one end, past passport control, is a section in French territory entitled **Bâle SNCF** which handles trains from Paris and Strasbourg. Trams #8 and #11 shuttle to Barfüsserplatz. Some trains from Germany terminate at Basel Badischer Bahnhof (**Basel Bad.** for short), in a German enclave on the north side of the river (passport control), from where tram #6 runs to Barfüsserplatz. The **tourist office** is in a side entrance of the Stadt Casino on Barfüsserplatz (Mon–Fri 8.30am–6.30pm, Sat 10am–5pm, Sun 10am–4pm; ☏061 268 68 68, ✆www.baseltourismus.ch), with a branch office inside the main SBB train station (Mon–Fri 8.30am–6.30pm, Sat & Sun 9am–2pm). If you stay overnight you're entitled to a **Mobility Card**, giving free city transport; pick it up from your hotel at check-in. The **Basel Card** (Fr.20/27/35 for 24/48/72 hours) covers free museum entry, free city tours, discounts at restaurants, bars and clubs, and more. Basel thrives on conference business, so accommodation prices drop at weekends.

### Accommodation
**Au Violon** Im Lohnhof 4 ☏061 269 87 11, ✆www.au-violon.com. Comfortable, stylish little hotel above a quiet Old Town courtyard. ❼
**Basel Backpack (SB)** Dornacherstr. 192 ☏061 333 00 37, ✆www.baselbackpack.ch. Friendly hostel just behind the station. Dorms Fr.31. Rooms ❺
**Hecht am Rhein** Rheingasse 8 ☏061 691 22 20. Friendly, unfussy small hotel. Pay a bit more for a riverside room. ❺
**Jugendherberge City (HI)** Pfeffingerstr. 8 ☏061 365 99 60, ✆www.youthhostel.ch. Comfortable hostel on a quiet street behind the station, opening in January 2006. No dorms. Rooms ❹
**Jugendherberge St Alban (HI)** St Alban-Kirchrain 10 ☏061 272 05 72, ✆www.youthhostel.ch. Quiet hostel on the river, closed for renovation in the first part of 2006, expected to re-open in the autumn. Dorms Fr.31. Rooms ❹

### Cafés and restaurants
**Manora** Greifengasse. Excellent-value self-service hot meals, salads and snacks.

**Mr Wong** Steinenvorstadt 3. Popular Asian fast-food joint just off Barfüsserplatz.
**Pfalz** Münsterberg 11. Small café with fresh juices and a salad buffet. Closed Sat & Sun.
**Parterre** Klybeckstr. 1. Friendly Kleinbasel café hangout serving excellent food. Closed Sun.
**Zum Isaak** Münsterplatz 16. Tranquil café on this old-town square for snacks and full meals. Closed Mon.
**Zum Roten Engel** Andreasplatz. Pleasant vegetarian café with snacks, full meals and fresh juices.

### Bars, clubs and music venues
**Atlantis** Klosterberg 10. Club-bar with regular music and dance.
**Bird's Eye** Kohlenberg 20. Lively jazz venue.
**Fischerstube** Rheingasse 45. Atmospheric backstreet beerhall with a hearty clientele.
**Hirscheneck** Lindenberg 23. Co-op owned budget café/bar/restaurant. Loud music and generous portions of simple food.
**Kaserne** Klybeckstr. 1. Alternative hangout offering veggie food. Mutates on Tues into Basel's premier gay/lesbian meeting-point.

## Luzern (Lucerne)

An hour south of Basel and Zürich is beautiful **LUZERN** (Lucerne), offering captivating mountain views, lake cruises and a picturesque medieval quarter. The giant Mount Pilatus rears up behind the town, which is split by the River Reuss, flowing rapidly out of the northwestern end of the oddly shaped **Vierwaldstättersee** ("Lake of the Four Forest Cantons" or plain Lake Luzern). Altdorf, just around the lake, was where **William Tell** shot the apple from his son's head; the Tell legend lies at the core of Swiss national identity, and the semi-mystical Vierwaldstättersee is the spiritual as well as the geographical centre of the country. But Luzern is no museum piece; the large population of young people love their café culture, and on a weekend night, the main Pilatusstrasse boulevard has the buzz of any European capital.

The **train station** is perfectly located on the waterfront. You'll want to stop and gawp at the views of snowy mountains across the lake, and at the **KKL** just alongside, a stunning concert hall with a giant roof that seems to float unsupported. From the station, busy Pilatusstrasse storms southwest away from the river. About 100m along is the absorbing **Sammlung Rosengart** gallery (daily 10/11am–5/6pm; Fr.15) with a superb collection of twentieth-century art. The ground floor is devoted to Picasso, the basement to Paul Klee, and the upper floor to Chagall, Monet, Renoir and others. Behind it, on both riverbanks, spread the Old Town alleys. A stroll through the alleys leads to the fourteenth-century **Kapellbrücke**, a covered wooden bridge angled around the squat mid-river **Wasserturm**. After a disastrous fire in 1993, it was reconstructed with the medieval paintings fixed to its roof-beams replaced by facsimiles (although a few charred originals remain) – check out no. 31's William Tell. The north bank is home to a medieval ensemble of cobbled, fountained squares ringed by colourful facades and packed with shops and cafés. Northeast of the Old Town is Löwenplatz, dominated by a glass building housing the diverting **Bourbaki Panorama** (daily 9am–6pm; Fr.8), a 110m-by-10m circular mural depicting a scene in the 1870–71 Franco-Prussian War. Just off the square is the moving **Löwendenkmal**, a dying lion hewn out of a cliff-face to commemorate 700 Swiss mercenaries killed by French revolutionaries in 1792. The **Verkehrshaus** is 2km east of town at Lidostrasse 5 (daily 10am–5/6pm; Fr.24; ⓦwww.verkehrshaus.org); if you're not taking the boat, hop on bus #6 or #8, or else it's a pleasant lakeside stroll. The complex, inadequately translated as "Transport Museum", is a vast area that could keep you amused all day, complete with original space capsules, railway locomotives, aeroplanes, cable cars and more. An incongruous highlight is an excellent section housing the whimsical and attractive works of the Swiss contemporary artist **Hans Erni**.

## Practicalities

Luzern's **train station** is on the south bank, with the **tourist office** on platform 3 (Mon–Fri 8.30am–6/8.30pm, Sat & Sun 9am–6/8.30pm; ☎041 227 17 17, ⓦwww .luzern.org). The decent HI **hostel** is 1km northwest of town by Lake Rotsee, Sedelstr. 12 (☎041 420 88 00, ⓦwww.youthhostel.ch; bus #18 to Jugendherberge; dorms Fr.32.50, rooms ❹); there's also the friendly SB *Backpackers*, Alpenquai 42 (☎041 360 04 20, ⓦwww.backpackerslucerne.ch; bus #6/7/8 to Weinbergli, then cut left; dorms Fr.28, rooms ❹). Of the **hotels**, the central *Tourist Hotel*, St Karliquai 12 (☎041 410 24 74, ⓦwww.touristhotel.ch; ❺), also has dorms for around Fr.35. The characterful *Schlüssel*, Franziskanerplatz 12 (☎041 210 10 61; ❺), is the city's oldest hotel, with some rooms overlooking formal gardens alongside. The *Lido* **campsite** is near the Verkehrshaus, at Lidostr. 19 (☎041 370 21 46, ⓦwww.camping-international.ch). A **visitors' card**, available from your hotel, grants plenty of discounts around town. **Eating** and **drinking** venues crowd the waterfront and the Old Town squares. *Manora* has a rooftop terrace at Weggisgasse 11; *Hug*, on Mühlenplatz, is a great café for breakfast or lunch; *Hofgarten*, Stadthofstr. 14, has excellent veggie food; relaxed *Parterre*, Mythenstr. 7, is another good option. Top **bars** include the buzzing *Jazz Kantine*, Grabenstr. 8, with DJs and live bands downstairs; *Wärchhof*, Werkhofstr. 11, with women-only nights (Mon); and frenetic *Schüür*, Tribschenstr. 1, with excellent music and cheap weekday lunches. Luzern's raucous **Carnival**, ending on Ash Wednesday, is the biggest and best in Switzerland, a six-day round of drinking, dancing and partying.

## Engelberg and Lake Luzern

Luzern is a major centre for **adventure sports**; the main operator is Outventure (☎041 611 14 41, ⓦwww.outventure.ch), which offers canyoning, bungee-jumping and more, bookable direct or through any of the hostels. Most activities take place at the Alpine resort of **ENGELBERG**, a picturesque hour-long train ride from Luzern, and worth a visit in its own right. Signposted from its train station is a four-stage cable car serving the snowbound summit of **Mount Titlis** (3239m), the highest point in Central Switzerland (ⓦwww.titlis.ch), which hosts snowsports all summer long. ER, IR and SP bring discounts on the eyepopping trip up and down, and there are countless offers and all-in rental deals for mountain-bikes, scooters, DevilBikes and snowboarders to take advantage of.

You shouldn't leave Luzern without taking a trip on the **lake** (ferry routings at ⓦwww.lakelucerne.ch; ER & SP free, IR half-price; tourist info at ⓦwww .lakeluzern.ch), Switzerland's most beautiful and dramatic by far, the thickly wooded slopes rising sheer from the water. Of the lakeside towns, **VITZNAU** (1hr from Luzern) is the base-station of the oldest rack-railway in the world, serving the majestic **Mount Rigi** (SP, IR & ER 25-percent discount; ⊛www.rigi.ch); and **KEHRSITEN** (35min) has a funicular up to **Bürgenstock**, from where a twenty-minute clifftop walk brings you to Europe's fastest outdoor elevator, swishing you in seconds to the Hammetschwand summit. From **ALPNACHSTAD** (1hr 40min), the steepest rack-railway in the world climbs to the top of **Mount Pilatus** (ER 35-percent discount; SP 25-percent discount; IR no discount; ⊛www.pilatus .com). Taking a leisurely boat ride to the far point of the lake at **FLÜELEN** (2hr 50min) connects with mainline trains running west to Luzern and Basel, north to Zürich and south to Lugano and Milan.

# Bern

Of all Swiss cities, **BERN** is the most immediately charming. Crammed onto a steep-sided peninsula in a crook of the fast-flowing River Aare, the city's quiet, cobbled lanes, lined with sandstone arcaded buildings, have changed little in five hundred years. It's sometimes hard to remember that this quiet, attractive town of just 130,000 people is the nation's capital.

Bern's old centre is best explored from the focal east–west **Spitalgasse**. As it leads away from the train station, Spitalgasse becomes Marktgasse, Kramgasse and then Gerechtigkeitsgasse, but all the way down is lined with seventeenth- and eighteenth-century houses, fountains and arcaded shops. Some 200m east of the station, the street crosses **Bärenplatz**, scene of much outdoor daytime drinking and a lively Saturday-morning market; to the right of it is the domed **Bundeshaus** or Federal Parliament Building. Beyond Bärenplatz, Marktgasse continues under the **Käfigturm** (prisoners' tower), a thirteenth-century town gate. Further along is an eleventh-century gate that was converted in the sixteenth century into the **Zytglogge** – a distinctively top-heavy clocktower. (To the left, in Kornhausplatz, is the most famous of Bern's many ornate fountains, the horrific **Kindlifresserbrunnen**, depicting an ogre devouring a struggling baby.) Münstergasse, one block south, leads to the fifteenth-century Gothic **Münster** (Tues–Sat 10am–4/5pm, Sun 11.30am–2/5pm), noted for the magnificently gilded high-relief *Last Judgement* above the main entrance and the elegant buttressed terrace on its south side. Its 254-stepped **tower** (closes 30min earlier; Fr.4), the tallest in Switzerland, offers terrific views. The terraced **Münsterplattform** garden behind, perched above the river, is a prime hangout spot for Bern's wasted youth. At the eastern end of the centre, the Nydeggbrücke crosses the river to the **Bärengraben** (open access), Bern's famed bear-pits, which have housed generations of morose shaggies since the early sixteenth century. Legend has it that the town's founder Berchtold V of Zähringen named Bern after killing one of the beasts during a hunt; the bear has remained a symbol of the town ever since. The current layout is due to be overhauled in the next few years, becoming the centrepiece of a much larger park-like enclosure. The walk back over the bridge and up to the city centre is eased by bus #12, which usefully runs through the old town to the station.

Bern's **Kunstmuseum**, near the station at Hodlerstrasse 8–12 (Tues 10am–9pm, Wed–Sun 10am–5pm; Fr.7), is especially strong on twentieth-century art, with works by Matisse, Kandinsky, Braque and Picasso. More museums are grouped around **Helvetiaplatz**, south of the river: the **Alpines Museum** (Mon 2–5pm, Tues–Sun 10am–5pm; Fr.9) houses interesting displays exploring mountain culture, and you could spend hours in the fascinating **Historisches Museum** (Tues–Sun 10am–5pm, Wed until 8pm; Fr.13); check out the "Dance of Death" sequence in the basement. East of the centre at Ostring, the superb **Paul Klee Centre** (Tues–Sun 10am–5pm, Thurs until 9pm; Fr.16) has the world's largest collection of works by the whimsical twentieth-century artist, who spent much of his life in Bern. The building is a stunning, triple-arched design by the star Italian architect Renzo Piano.

## Practicalities

Within Bern's **train station** is the **tourist office** (Mon–Sat 9am–6.30/8.30pm, Sun 9/10am–5/8.30pm; ☏031 328 12 12, ⊛www.berninfo.com), with a branch at the Bärengraben (June–Sept daily 9am–6pm; shorter hours in winter). Both sell the BernCard (Fr.10/13.50/17 for 1/2/3 days), giving free transport and many discounts. The riverside HI **hostel** is at Weihergasse 4 (☏031 311 63 16, ⊛www .jugibern.ch; dorms Fr.30, rooms ❹); the pleasant SB *Landhaus*, Altenbergstr. 4 (☏031 331 41 66, ⊛www.landhausbern.ch; dorms Fr.35, rooms ❺), is near the Bärengraben; while the SB *Bern Backpackers/Hotel Glocke* is very central at Rathausgasse 75 (☏031 311 37 71, ⊛www.bernbackpackers.com; dorms Fr.29, rooms ❻). Good-value *Eichholz* **campsite** is at Strandweg 49 (☏031 961 26 02, ⊛www.campingeichholz.ch; April–Sept). For **eating**, *Manora*, just off Bahnhofplatz, has filling cheap food; the popular *Reitschule*, a dilapidated squat arts centre beside the train tracks on Bollwerk, offers a Fr.5 meal in its restaurant *Sous Le Pont*, along with cheap beer and a liberal attitude to dope-smoking. There's no shortage of good **café/bars**, including *Café des Pyrénées*, a jovial hangout on Kornhausplatz, and *Altes Tramdepot*, a microbrewery beside the Bärengraben. The *Reitschule* (see above) and *Dampfzentrale*, Marzilistr. 47, are the premier venues for **live music** and clubbing. Bern hosts a huge open-air rock event in July (⊛www .gurtenfestival.ch).

## Listings

**Bike rental** Free (with photo-ID & Fr.20 deposit) from "Bern rollt", in front of the station (daily 7.30am–9.15pm).

**Embassies** Australia, embassy in Berlin ☏004930/880 0880, consulate in Geneva ☏022 799 91 00; Canada, Kirchenfeldstr. 88, Bern ☏031 357 32 00; Ireland, Kirchenfeldstr. 68, Bern ☏031 352 14 42; New Zealand, embassy in Berlin ☏004930/20 6210, consulate in Geneva ☏022 929 03 50; UK, Thunstr. 50, Bern ☏031 359 77 00; USA, Jubiläumstr. 93, Bern ☏031 357 70 11.

**Hospital** Inselspital, Freiburgstr. ☏031 632 24 64.

**Laundry** Jet Wash, Dammweg 43.

**Pharmacy** Hörning, in the station.

**Post office** Schanzenstr., behind the station.

# The Swiss Alps

South of Bern and Luzern, and east of Montreux, lies the grand Alpine heart of Switzerland, a massively impressive region of classic Swiss scenery – high peaks, sheer valleys and cool lakes – that makes for great summer hiking and world-class winter sports. The Bernese Oberland, centred on the **Jungfrau Region**, is the most accessible and touristed area, but beyond this first great wall of peaks is another even more daunting range in which the **Matterhorn**, marking the Italian border, is star attraction. The wild summits and remote valleys in the southeastern corner of Switzerland shelter the world-famous mountain resort of **St Moritz**.

Note that very little happens in the mountains in the **off-seasons** (April, May, Oct & Nov); shops and hotels may be shut at these times, cable cars closed for renovations, and smaller resorts virtually deserted.

## The Jungfrau Region

The spectacular **Jungfrau Region** is named after a grand triple-peaked ridge – the Eiger, Mönch and Jungfrau – which crests 4000m. Endlessly touted hereabouts is the rack-railway excursion up to the **Jungfraujoch**, the highest train station in Europe at 3454m ("Top of Europe"). The cable-car ride up the **Schilthorn** (2970m) gets second billing, but is in fact quicker, cheaper, offers a more scenic ride up, and has better views from the top: don't be misled. A round-trip from Interlaken takes six hours to the Jungfraujoch, four hours to the Schilthorn (both including an hour at the summit). Setting off on the first train of the day (6.30am) brings discounts on both routes. Most beautiful part of the region's countryside is the **Lauterbrunnen valley**, overlooked by the resort of **Mürren**, which provides an excellent base for winter skiing and summer hiking, as does **Grindelwald**, in its own valley slightly east. **Interlaken** is the main transport hub for the region, but the sheer volume of tourist traffic passing through the town can make it a less-than-restful place to stay.

## Interlaken

**INTERLAKEN** is centred on its long main street, Höheweg, which is lined with cafés and hotels and has a train station at each end, though the best way to arrive is by boat. The town lies on a neck of land between two of Switzerland's most attractive lakes, and it exists chiefly to amuse the trippers passing through on their way to the mountains. **Interlaken Ost** station is the mainline terminus and the departure point for trains into the mountains (see below); coming from Luzern, you could get out at Brienz and do the last stretch to Interlaken Ost by boat. Trains from the Bern/Zürich direction pass first through **Interlaken West** (docking point for boats from Thun), and this station is nearer to the **tourist office**, which sits beneath the town's tallest building at Höheweg 37 (Mon–Fri 8am–6/6.30pm, Sat 8/9am–4/5pm; July & Aug also Sun 10am–noon & 5–7pm; shorter hours in winter; ☎033 826 53 00, ✆www.interlakentourism.ch). Interlaken is a hub for **adventure sports**: Alpin Raft (☎033 823 41 00, ✆www.alpinraft.ch) is the local leader, with loads of daily activities from skydiving to horse trekking, bookable direct and at hostels. **Accommodation** fills up quickly in the high seasons; there are hotel lists and courtesy phones at both stations. The worthy HI **hostel** is 2km east (bus #1), at Aareweg 21 in Bönigen (☎033 822 43 53, ✆www.youthhostel.ch; dorms Fr.30, rooms ❹); you'd do better joining the backpacker crowd at the excellent SB *Balmer's Herberge*, fifteen minutes south of town at Hauptstr. 23, Matten (☎033 822 19 61, ✆www.balmers.com; dorms Fr.27, rooms ❸). Pick of the quieter places in town is the excellent SB *Backpackers Villa Sonnenhof*, Alpenstr. 16 (☎033 826 71 71, ✆www.villa.ch; dorms Fr.33, rooms ❺). SB *Happy Inn*, Rosenstr. 17 (☎033 822 32 25, ✆www.happy-inn.com; dorms Fr.30, rooms ❺), is a backup option. The nearest **campsite** is well-equipped *Sackgut* behind Ost station (☎033 822 44 34, ✆www.campinginterlaken.ch; May–Oct). For budget **food**, *Migros* opposite West station has self-service staples (closed Sun); *PizPaz* on Centralstr. does pizza and pasta (closed Mon); *El Azteca*, Jungfraustr. 30, has Mexican set-meals from Fr.14. *Positiv Einfach*, Centralstr. 11, is a hip music **bar**; and *Balmer's* hostel has cheap beer.

## Lauterbrunnen

It's hard to overstate just how stunning the **Lauterbrunnen valley** is. An immense U-shaped cleft with bluffs on either side rising 1000m sheer, doused by some 72 waterfalls, it is utterly spectacular. The **Staubbach falls**, the highest in Switzerland at nearly 300m, tumble just beyond the village of **LAUTERBRUNNEN** at the valley entrance, whose train station (served by trains from Interlaken Ost) is opposite both the funicular station for Mürren and the **tourist office** (Mon–Fri 8am–5/7pm; June–Sept also Sat & Sun 9am–12.30pm & 1.30–4/5pm; ☎033 856 85 68, ✆www.lauterbrunnen.ch). **Accommodation** is down by the tracks at the cosy SB *Valley Hostel* (☎033 855 20 08, ✆www.valleyhostel.ch; dorms Fr.25) or up at the excellent *Mountain Hostel* in Gimmelwald (see below).

From Lauterbrunnen, it's a scenic half-hour walk, or an hourly postbus, 3km up the valley to the spectacular **Trümmelbach falls** (April–Nov daily 8/9am–5/6pm; Fr.10), a series of thunderous waterfalls – the runoff from the mountain glaciers – which have carved corkscrew channels into the valley walls. The postbus continues 1.5km to **STECHELBERG** at the end of the road, starting point for the **cable-car ride** up to Gimmelwald, Mürren and the Schilthorn; the huge base station complex is 1km before the hamlet.

## Mürren and up to the Schilthorn

The cable car from Stechelberg leaps the valley's west wall to reach the quiet hamlet of **GIMMELWALD**, a little-visited spot with the superb self-catering *Mountain Hostel* (☎033 855 17 04, ⊚www.mountainhostel.com; Fr.20). Further up is the car-free village of **MÜRREN**. It's worth the journey for the views: from here, the valley floor is 800m straight down, and the panorama of snowy peaks filling the sky is dazzling. Mürren is also accessible from Lauterbrunnen on the BLM Bergbahn, comprising a steep funicular to Grütschalp and a spectacular little cliff-edge **train** from there (IR no discount; ER 25-percent discount; SP free). It's easy to do a round-trip by cable-car and train. The cable car continues from Mürren on a breathtaking ride (20min) up to the 2970m summit of the **Schilthorn** (⊚www.schilthorn.ch), where you can enjoy exceptional panoramic views and sip cocktails in the revolving *Piz Gloria* summit restaurant. Schilthornbahn **prices**, compared to the Jungfraujoch ride, are a bargain. From Stechelberg to the top is Fr.96 round-trip, from Mürren Fr.66 (IR no discount; ER Fr.72/49; SP free to Mürren, then Fr.49). Going up before 9am or after 3pm knocks a further 25 percent off.

## Grindelwald

Valley-floor trains from Interlaken Ost also run to the more popular holiday centre of **GRINDELWALD**, nestling under the craggy trio of the Wetterhorn, Mettenberg and Eiger. Numerous trails around **Pfingstegg** and especially **First** – both at the end of gondola lines from Grindelwald – provide excellent hiking. The **tourist office** (daily 8/9am–noon & 1.30–5/6pm; shorter hours in April & Nov; ☎033 854 12 12, ⊚www.grindelwald.com) is 200m east of the station, alongside the **Bergsteigerzentrum** (Mountaineering Centre; ☎033 854 12 80, ⊚www.gomountain .ch), which offers bungee jumps, canyon leaps and guided ascents. Tandem Flights (⊚www.paragliding-grindelwald.ch) arranges accompanied **paragliding** jumps from Fr.160. A steep fifteen-minute walk will get you to Terrassenweg, a quiet lane running above the village, where there's an excellent HI **hostel** (☎033 853 10 09, ⊚www.youthhostel.ch; dorms Fr.30, rooms ❺) and a less studenty *Naturfreundehaus* (☎033 853 13 33; dorms Fr.34, rooms ❹). The well-run SB *Mountain Hostel* (☎033 853 39 00, ⊚www.mountainhostel.ch; dorms Fr.35, rooms ❹) is on the valley floor beside Grindelwald-Grund station. (Trains from Grindelwald pass through Grund on their way up to Kleine Scheidegg.) You can **camp** at *Aspen* (☎033 854 40 00, ⊚www.hotel-aspen.ch; March–Oct).

## To the Jungfraujoch

Switzerland's most popular (and expensive) mountain railway trundles through lush countryside south from Interlaken before coiling up across mountain pastures, breaking the treeline and tunnelling clean through the Eiger to emerge at the **JUNGFRAUJOCH** (3454m), an icy, windswept col just beneath the Jungfrau summit. The journey up – touted endlessly under the shoutline "Top of Europe" – is scenic in parts, but very long (2hr 20min from Interlaken, with the last 40min climbing in a pitch-dark tunnel), and the top station is a tourist circus of ice sculptures, husky sleigh rides, canteen restaurants and a post office, all overflowing with tour-groups. Nonetheless, on a clear day and with time to spare, it's worth the expense. Panoramic views from the Sphinx Terrace (3571m) to Germany's Black Forest in one direction and across a gleaming wasteland to the Italian Alps in the other are heart-thumping – as is the thin air up here. Don't forget your sunglasses.

There are two **routes** to the top. Trains head southwest from Interlaken Ost along the valley floor to Lauterbrunnen, from where you pick up the mountain line which climbs through Wengen; trains also head southeast from Interlaken Ost to Grindelwald, where you change for the climb, arriving from the other direction. All trains terminate at the spectacularly located hamlet of Kleine Scheidegg, where you must change for the final pull to Jungfraujoch; the popular practice is to go up one way and down the other. The adult round-trip **fare** from Interlaken is a budget-crunching Fr.173 (IR no discount; ER 25-percent discount; SP free to Wengen or Grindelwald then 25-percent discount) – but the discounted **Good Morning ticket**, valid if you travel up on the first or second trains of the day (which start from Interlaken Ost at 6.30am/6.35am & 7.20am), is Fr.149. **Walking** some sections, up or down, is perfectly feasible in summer, and can also save plenty. The Good Morning ticket from Lauterbrunnen or Grindelwald is Fr.130, from Grindelwald-Grund Fr.125, from Wengen Fr.118 and from Kleine Scheidegg Fr.80. Excellent transport networks and vista-rich footpaths linking all stations mean that with a hiking map and timetable you can see and do a great deal in a day and still get back to Interlaken, or even Bern or Zürich, by bedtime.

## Zermatt and the Matterhorn

The shark's-tooth **Matterhorn** (4478m) is the most famous of Switzerland's mountains, and no other natural or human structure in the whole country is so immediately recognizable: in most people's minds, the Matterhorn stands for Switzerland like the Eiffel Tower stands for France. One reason it's so famous is that it stands alone, its impossibly pointy shape sticking up from an otherwise uncrowded horizon above **ZERMATT** village; another is that the quintessential Swiss chocolate, Toblerone, was modelled on it. The only way to reach Zermatt is on the spectacular narrow-gauge MGB train line (ER no discount, IR half-price, SP free; www.mgbahn.ch). Coming from Bern, Zürich or Milan change at **Brig** (Briga in Italian); coming from Geneva, Lausanne or Paris change at **Visp**. The most celebrated way to arrive is on the long east–west St Moritz-to-Zermatt **Glacier Express**, a day-long journey by panoramic train (reserve at any train station; ER & SP free; IR half-price; www.glacierexpress.ch).

Zermatt's main street throngs year-round with an odd mixture of professional climbers, tour-groups, backpackers and fur-clad socialites. Electric minibuses ferry people between the train station at the northern end of the village and the cable-car terminus 1km south. Opposite the station, GGB Gornergrat-Bahn trains (ER no discount, IR half-price, SP free) climb above the village, giving spectacular Matterhorn views (sit on the right) all the way up to the **Gornergrat**, a vantage point with a magnificent Alpine panorama including Switzerland's highest peak, the Dufourspitze (4634m). In summer, GGB trains leave Zermatt once-weekly at dawn to arrive in time for a breathtaking Alpine sunrise. At the south end of Zermatt village a cable car heads up via Furi to the **Schwarzsee** (2583m), the most popular point from which to view the peak and, in summer, the trailhead for a zigzag walk (2hr) to the *Berghaus Matterhorn* inn (3260m), right below the mountain. All of Zermatt's cable cars and trains bring you to trailheads and spectacular views, while lifts to **Trockener Steg** give access to 21km of ski runs and a snowboard half-pipe that are open all **summer** long (day-pass Fr.62).

There's a hotel list and courtesy phone in Zermatt station; otherwise consult the helpful **tourist office** nearby (Mon–Sat 8.30am–6pm; June–Sept & Dec–April also Sun 9.30am–noon & 4–6pm; ☎027 966 81 00, www.zermatt.ch). **Alpin Center** (☎027 966 24 60, www.zermatt.ch/alpincenter), on the main street, runs canyoning, snowshoeing and guided climbs. The excellent HI **hostel** is on the east side of the village (☎027 967 23 20, www.youthhostel.ch; dorms Fr.47 inc. half-board, rooms ❻); nearby is the SB *Matterhorn Hostel* (☎027 968 19 19, www.matterhornhostel.com; dorms Fr.36, rooms ❺). The good *Matterhorn* **campsite** is north of the station (☎027 967 39 21; June–Sept). **Hotel** *Mischabel*, down by the river, is quiet and characterful (☎027 967 11 31, www.zermatt.ch/mischabel; ❺). There are plenty of places to **eat** all along Zermatt's main drag: *Hotel Post* has budget pizza/pasta, as does the lively *North Wall* bar, on the other side of the river. Pleasant *Café du Pont*, just past the church, serves affordable fondues.

## St Moritz

**ST MORITZ** is all you expect and more – a brassy, in-your-face reminder of the hotshot world beyond the mountain walls. The town sits in the wild and beautiful Engadine Valley that runs for 100km along the south side of the Alps. For a century or more, it's been the prime winter retreat of social high-flyers, minor European royalty and the international jetset, who've sparked the arrival of Vuitton, Cartier and Armani amidst this stunningly romantic setting of forest, lake and mountains; when the tourist office trumpets St Moritz's "champagne climate", they don't necessarily mean the sparkling sunshine (although there's an amazing 322 days of that a year, on average). The town spans two villages, St Moritz-Bad on the lake and St Moritz-Dorf on the hillside 2km above, linked by the main Via dal Bagn. Dorf is the upmarket one, while Bad – site of a Roman spa – is more down-to-earth. The area boasts legendary bob and toboggan courses, including the death-defying 1.2km **Cresta Run** (end-Dec to Feb; Fr.450 for 5 rides; men only, no women allowed; ⓦwww.cresta-run.com). You can rent wooden sleds for the famous winter **Preda–Bergün toboggan run** (daily 10am–5pm; one ride Fr.12; day ticket Fr.32; ⓦwww.berguen.ch), starting from Preda train station and taking a zigzag 5km course down through the scenic Albula valley to Bergün, where trains cart you back to the beginning. The course is floodlit at night (Tues–Sun 7–11.30pm).

Via Serlas winds up from the **train station** below Dorf to a central square, from where the **tourist office** is 100m east at Via Maistra 12 (Mon–Sat 9am–6pm, Sun 4–6pm; April–June, Oct & Nov Sat closes noon, closed Sun; ☎081 837 33 33, ⓦwww.stmoritz.ch). The genial HI **hostel** *Stille*, Via Surpunt 60 (☎081 833 39 69, ⓦwww.youthhostel.ch; dorms Fr.46 inc. half board, rooms ⑥), is a twenty-minute walk around the lake next to the *Stille* sports **hotel** (☎081 833 69 48, ⓦwww.hotelstille.ch; ⑦) and near the *Olympiaschanze* **campsite** (☎081 833 40 90; June–Sept). Spartan *Hotel Bellaval* (☎081 833 32 45; ⑦) is beside the station. Most **restaurants** are ridiculously expensive; affordable ones include *Boccalino* pizzeria, Via dal Bagn 6, but with this kind of scenery all around, you'd do better to picnic. Best bet for a **drink** is *Bobby's Pub* at Via dal Bagn 52.

# Ticino

The Italian-speaking region of **Ticino** (*Tessin* in German and French) occupies the balmy, lake-laced southern foothills of the Alps. It's radically different from the rest of Switzerland in almost every way: culture, food, architecture, attitude and driving style owe more to Milan than Zürich, and the glamour of the place – its lushly wooded hills, azure lakes and palm trees – often blinds visitors with romance. Switzerland has controlled the area since the early 1500s, when it defeated the Duke of Milan's army. Nowadays it's a cruel irony that the patriotic Ticinesi suffer Switzerland's highest unemployment rates even though service industries thrive, staffed by Italian guest-workers and paid for by thousands of Swiss-German tourists and second-home-owners. The main attractions are the lakeside resorts of **Locarno** and **Lugano**, where mountain scenery merges with the subtropical flora encouraged by the warm climate.

Unless you approach from Italy, there's only one train line in – through the 16km **Gotthard Tunnel**, on the main line from Zürich or Luzern. The track's spiralling contortions on the approach climb are famous: trains pass the onion-domed church at Wassen three times, first far above you, then on a level, and finally far below, before entering the subalpine tunnel.

# Locarno

Mainline trains speed south to Lugano and Milan, while a branch line heads west from Bellinzona to **LOCARNO**, a characterful old town on a broad sweeping bay in Lake Maggiore, its piazzas overlooked by subtropical gardens of palm trees, camellias and bougainvillea. It can get overrun with the rich and wannabe-famous on summer weekends yet manages to retain its sun-drenched cool. The focus of town is **Piazza Grande**, just off the lakefront, where on warm summer nights exquisitely groomed locals parade to and fro. The Renaissance **Old Town** is ranged on gently rising ground behind the piazza: wandering through the alleys with an ice cream is the best way to blend in with Locarno life. The church of **Madonna del Sasso** (daily 6.30am–7pm) is an impressive ochre vision floating above the town on a wooded crag, consecrated in 1487. The walk up (or down) through a wooded ravine and past decaying shrines is glorious; or take the funicular from just west of the station to Ticino's greatest photo-op, looking down on the church and lake. From the top station, an ear-poppingly steep cable car climbs to **Cardada**, set amidst fragrant pine woods, with walking routes and a spectacular, silent chairlift whisking you up to **Cimetta**, where the restaurant terrace offers a view you won't forget in a hurry. A short bus-ride east of Locarno is **Valle Verzasca**, where deathwish freaks can re-enact the opening scene of the James Bond film *Goldeneye*, by **bungee-jumping** a world-record 220m off the Verzasca Dam (April–Oct daily; Fr.255; book on ☎0848 808 007, ⊛www.trekking.ch) – in June, July & August, you can jump by moonlight; see the website.

Locarno's **train station** is 150m northeast of Piazza Grande. Between the two is the landing-stage; summer boats run to nearby Swiss lakeside resorts such as Ascona, and south to Italian ones such as Stresa (on the main line to Milan). The **tourist office** is in the Casino complex opposite the landing-stage (Mon–Fri 9am–6pm; April–Oct also Sat 9am–5pm, Sun 10am–noon & 1–3pm; ☎091 791 00 91, ⊛www .maggiore.ch). Stay at the friendly HI **hostel**, *Ostello Palagiovani*, Via Varenna 18 (☎091 756 15 00, ⊛www.youthhostel.ch; ❹; dorms Fr.39.50; bus #31/36 to Cinque Vie); central *Città Vecchia*, Via Torretta 13 (☎091 751 45 54, ⊛www.cittavecchia .ch; dorms Fr.33, rooms ❺; March–Oct); or serviceable *Delta* **campsite** (☎091 751 60 81, ⊛www.campingdelta.com; March–Oct), a 15min walk south along the lakeshore. *Manora* has good self-service **food** across from the train station, open late and Sundays, and Piazza Grande is full of cafés and pizzerias buzzing from morning until after midnight. In the alleys, *Cittadella*, Via Cittadella 18, serves affordable pizzas and fish dishes; *Cantina Canetti* off Piazza Grande has plain local cooking and live accordion on weekend nights. Early August's **Locarno International Film Festival** (⊛www.pardo.ch) is stealing a march on Cannes for star-appeal; catch nightly offerings on Europe's largest movie screen, set up in Piazza Grande.

# Lugano

With its cluster of piazzas and tree-lined promenades, **LUGANO** is the most alluring of Ticino's lake resorts, less touristic than Locarno but with, if anything, double the chic. Centre of town is **Piazza della Riforma**, a huge café-lined square just by the exceptionally beautiful Lago di Lugano. Through the maze of steep lanes northwest of Riforma, Via Cattedrale dog-legs up to **Cattedrale San Lorenzo**, characterized by a fine Renaissance portal, fragments of interior frescoes, and spectacular views from its terrace. Also from Riforma, narrow Via Nassa – home of big-name designer boutiques – heads southwest to the medieval church of **Santa Maria degli Angioli**, containing a stunning wall-sized fresco of the Crucifixion. A little further south is the **Museo d'Arte Moderna**, Riva Caccia 5 (Tues–Sun 9am–7pm; entry varies), with world-class exhibitions; and a little further still is the modestly named district of **Paradiso**, from where a funicular rises to **San Salvatore**, a rugged rock pinnacle offering fine views of the lake and surrounding countryside. The best of the lake is behind (south of) San Salvatore on the Ceresio peninsula, accessed by boats or postbuses. Here you'll find tiny **Montagnola**, where the writer Hermann Hesse lived for 43 years; his first house, Casa Camuzzi, is now a small museum (Tues–Sun 10am–12.30pm & 2–6.30pm; Nov–Feb Sat & Sun only; Fr.6), with an excellent 45-minute English film on Hesse's life in Ticino. Jewel of the lake is **Morcote** on the southern tip of the peninsula; tranquil stepped lanes lead up to its photogenic church of Santa Maria del Sasso, and several walks explore the woods, including a trail back to San Salvatore (2hr 30min).

Lugano's **train station** overlooks the town from the west, linked to the centre by a short funicular or by steps down to Via Cattedrale. The **tourist office** is in Palazzo Civico, off Riforma (Mon–Fri 9am–5/7pm; April–Oct also Sat 9am–5pm, Sun 10am–3pm; ☎091 913 32 32, ⓦwww.lugano-tourism.ch); **boats** around the lake (IR & ER no discount, SP free) depart from directly opposite. An excellent HI **hostel** (with swimming pool) is at Via Cantonale 13, Savosa (☎091 966 27 28, ⓦwww.youthhostel.ch; dorms Fr.31, rooms ❸; March–Oct; bus #5 to Crocifisso from the stop 200m left out of the train station). The SB *Montarina* is behind the station, Via Montarina 1 (☎091 966 72 72, ⓦwww.montarina.com; dorms Fr.29, rooms ❺). *La Piodella* (☎091 994 77 88) is one of several lakeside **campsites** in Agno, a short train-ride west. For **eating**, central Piazza Cioccaro is home to a big *Manora* and *Sayonara* serving inexpensive staples; *La Tinèra*, off Via dei Gorini, behind Riforma, has tasty Ticinese chicken stews. The many cafés around Riforma are packed with evening **drinkers**, while in the warren of the Quartiere Maghetti nearby is *Etnic*, with Mediterranean-style food, beer, cocktails and a cosy studentish atmosphere. From Lugano, the **Palm Express** bus (ⓦwww.postbus.ch) follows a lovely route up to St Moritz.

# Liechtenstein

Only slightly larger than Manhattan island, **Liechtenstein** is the world's fourth-smallest country. It's an unassuming place squashed between Switzerland and Austria, ruled over by His Serene Highness Prince Hans Adam II, and has made a mint from nursing some Fr.90 billion in its numbered bank accounts. The main reason to visit is the novelty value – at less than two hours from Zürich, you can see the whole country in a day. Swiss francs are legal tender, but the phone system is separate (country code ☎423).

From **Sargans** train station on the Zürich–Chur line, bus #1 shuttles over the Rhine (no border controls) in half-an-hour to the capital **VADUZ**, a tiny town bulging with glass-plated banks and squadrons of aimless visitors. Central hub is the post office, where all buses stop, midway between the two parallel main streets, Äulestrasse and pedestrianized Städtle. Facing it is the sleek **Kunstmuseum** (Tues–Sun 10am–5pm, Thurs till 8pm; Fr.8), displaying modern pieces as well as the private art collection inherited – and added to – by the prince, which includes works by Rubens and Rembrandt. Perched on the forested hillside above is the prince's restored sixteenth-century **castle** (no public access). The **tourist office**, Städtle 37 (daily 9am–noon & 1.30–5pm; Nov–April closed Sat & Sun; ☎239 63 00, ⓦwww.tourismus.li), will bang a stamp into your passport as a memento (Fr.2). There's an **HI hostel** at Untere Rüttigasse 6, beside Mühleholz bus stop in Schaan, 2km north (☎232 50 22; dorms Fr.31, rooms ❹; March–Oct); tranquil *Mittagsspitze* **campsite** (☎392 36 77) is 5km south in the countryside near Triesen. *Cesare*, Städtle 15 (closed Sat & Sun), has good Italian **food**; and stand-up deli *Eredi Florini*, Herrengasse 9 (closed Sun), has delicious point-and-choose meals.

Postbuses from Vaduz serve all points in Liechtenstein – if you have time to spare, catch bus #10 to the mountain resort of **MALBUN**, at 1602m. Buses also serve

**Feldkirch** just across the border in **Austria** (passport needed), from where trains run on to Bregenz, Innsbruck and Vienna.

# Travel details

## Trains

**Basel** to: Bern (every 30min; 55min); Geneva (hourly; 2hr 45min); Interlaken Ost (every 30min; 2hr 10min); Lausanne (every 30min; 2hr 10min); Lugano (hourly; 3hr 50min); Luzern (hourly; 1hr 5min); Zürich (every 15min; 1hr).

**Bern** to: Basel (every 30min; 55min); Geneva (every 30min; 1hr 45min); Interlaken Ost (every 30min; 55min); Lausanne (every 30min; 1hr 10min); Luzern (every 30min; 1hr 20min); Zürich (every 30min; 1hr).

**Geneva** to: Basel (hourly; 2hr 45min); Bern (every 30min; 1hr 45min); Lausanne (every 15min; 35min); Montreux (every 30min; 1hr 5min); Vevey (every 30min; 1hr); Zürich (every 30min; 2hr 45min).

**Interlaken Ost** to: Bern (every 30min; 55min); Grindelwald (hourly; 35min); Jungfraujoch (hourly; 2hr 20min – change at Grindelwald or Lauterbrunnen, then Kleine Scheidegg); Lauterbrunnen (hourly; 20min); Luzern (hourly; 1hr 55min); Zürich (every 30min; 2hr 5min).

**Lausanne** to: Basel (every 30min; 2hr 10min); Bern (every 30min; 1hr 10min); Geneva (every 15min; 35min); Montreux (every 15min; 20min); Vevey (every 15min; 15min); Zürich (every 30min; 2hr 10min).

**Lugano** to: Luzern (hourly; 2hr 45min); Zürich (hourly; 2hr 55min).

**Luzern** to: Basel (hourly; 1hr 5min); Bern (every 30min; 1hr 20min); Interlaken Ost (hourly; 1hr 55min); Lugano (hourly; 2hr 45min); Zürich (every 30min; 45min).

**Montreux** to: Geneva (every 30min; 1hr 5min); Interlaken (every 30min; 2hr 45min – change at Zweisimmen & Spiez); Lausanne (every 15min; 20min); Vevey (3 hourly; 5min).

**Vevey** to: Geneva (every 30min; 1hr); Lausanne (every 15min; 15min); Montreux (3 hourly; 5min).

**Zürich** to: Basel (every 15min; 1hr); Bern (every 30min; 1hr); Geneva (every 30min; 2hr 45min); Interlaken Ost (every 30min; 2hr 5min); Lausanne (every 30min; 2hr 10min); Lugano (hourly; 2hr 55min); Luzern (every 30min; 45min); Sargans (every 30min; 1hr); St Moritz (hourly; 3hr 20min – change at Chur).

## Buses

**Lugano** to: St Moritz (mid-June to mid-Oct daily, other times 3 weekly; 3hr 45min).

**Sargans** to: Vaduz (every 20min; 30min).

**Vaduz** to: Malbun (hourly; 30min).

## Boats

*The following times are for May–Sept only; very few boats run outside these months.*

**Geneva** to: Lausanne (3 daily; 3hr 30min); Montreux (3 daily; 5hr); Vevey (3 daily; 4hr 30min).

**Lausanne** to: Geneva (3 daily; 3hr 30min); Montreux (5 daily; 1hr 30min); Vevey (5 daily; 1hr).

**Luzern** to: Alpnachstad (6 daily; 1hr 40min); Flüelen (8 daily; 2hr 50min); Kehrsiten (hourly; 35min); Vitznau (hourly; 1hr).

# 32

# Turkey

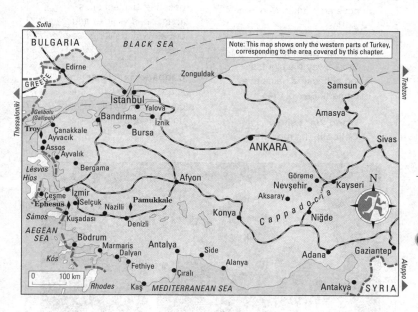

# Turkey highlights

* **Aya Sofya, Istanbul**
Stunning sixth-century cathedral. A fascinating glimpse into the city's Byzantine past. See p.1038

* **Covered Bazaar, Istanbul**
With over 3000 shops, stalls and workshops, this is the world's largest covered market. See See p.1040

* **Turkish bath, Istanbul**
Soak away the sightseeing aches and pains in a hamam. See p.1043

* **World War I sites, Gelibolu** The moving cemeteries and monuments of Gallipoli attract thousands every ANZAC Day (April 25). See p.1045

* **Ephesus** The largest and best-preserved archeological site in Turkey. See p.1052

* **Fethiye** A great base for beaches, ancient sites, abandoned villages and Lycian Way trekking. See p.1056

* **Cappadocia** A lunar landscape, replete with eerie caves, rock dwellings and underground cities. See p.1063

△ Ephesus

# Introduction and basics

**Turkey** has multiple identities, poised uneasily between East and West: mosques coexist with churches, and Roman remnants crumble alongside ancient Hittite sites. The country is an explicitly secular republic, though the majority of its people are Muslim, and is an immensely rewarding place to travel, not least because of the people, whose reputation for friendliness and hospitality is richly deserved.

The old imperial capital **Istanbul**, straddling the Bosphorus straits and the Marmara coast, is a heady mix of the European and Oriental. Flanking Istanbul on opposite sides of the Sea of Marmara are the two earlier Ottoman capitals, **Bursa** and **Edirne**, and the former Byzantine capital of **Iznik**, with, just beyond, the World War I battlefields of the **Gelibolu** peninsula (**Gallipoli**). Moving south, small country towns are swathed in olive groves, while the area is littered with ancient sites, including **Assos**, **Pergamon** and **Ephesus**. Beyond the functional city of **Izmir**, the Aegean coast is Turkey at its most developed, with large numbers drawn to resorts such as **Bodrum** and **Marmaris**. Beyond here, the aptly named **Turquoise Coast** is home to more resorts, such as **Fethiye**, **Kaş**, **Olympos** and **Xanthos**, with its remnants of the Lycians, and **Antalya**, one of Turkey's fastest-growing cities. Inland from here is the spectacular **Cappadocia**, with its famous rock churches, subterranean cities and landscape studded with cave dwellings. Further north, **Ankara**, Turkey's capital, is a planned city whose contrived Western feel gives some indication of the priorities of the modern Turkish Republic.

## Information & maps

Most towns of any size have a **tourist office** (*Turizm Danışma Bürosu*) generally open Mon–Fri 8.30am–12.30pm & 1.30–5.30pm. Staff may not speak English, but they often have good brochures and maps, and should be able to help you with accommodation. The best **maps** are by Geo Centre/RV ("Turkey West" and "Turkey East"). City tourist offices normally stock reasonable street plans.

## Money and banks

Currency is the **new Turkish lira** (ytl), divided into 100 kuruş. There are coins of 1, 5, 10, 25, 50 kuruş, and 1 ytl, and notes of 1, 5, 10, 20, 50, 100 ytl. Exchange rates for foreign currency are always better inside Turkey. Many pensions and hotels, particularly in the popular destinations, also quote prices in euros, and you can usually pay in either euros or Turkish lira. The current **exchange rate** is 2.50ytl to £1; 1.40ytl to US$1; and 1.70ytl to €1.

**Banks** open Mon–Fri 8.30am–noon & 1.30–5pm; some, notably Garanti Bankasi, are open at lunchtimes and on Sat. Most charge a commission of about €3.50 for travellers' cheques. Some of the **exchange booths** run by banks in coastal resorts, airports and ferry docks charge a small commission. Private exchange offices have competitive rates and no commission. Almost all banks have **ATMs**. Post offices in sizeable towns also sometimes change cash and cheques, for a one-percent commission.

**TURKEY** | Basics

**32**

# Communications

Most **post offices** (PTT) open Mon–Sat 8.30am–5.30pm, with main branches opening till 7/8pm and on Sun. Use the **yurtdışı** (overseas) slot on postboxes. **Phone calls** can be made from Turk Telecom booths and the PTT. Post offices and kiosks sell phonecards (30, 60 and 100 units) and also have metered phones. Some payphones accept credit cards. Numerous private **phone shops** (*Köntürlü telefon*) offer metered calls at dubious, unofficial rates. The international operator is on ☎ 115. There are **Internet** cafés in most towns, charging €0.50–2/hr.

# Getting around

The **train** system, run by TCDD, is limited. The most useful services are the expresses between Istanbul and Ankara, and other long-distance links to main provincial cities such as Edirne, Konya, Denizli and Izmir. Cheap sleeper cabins are available on overnight services. Reservations are only necessary at weekends or on national holidays. An ISIC card gets a 20 percent discount. InterRail passes are valid, Eurail aren't.

Long-distance **bus** is a more reliable way of getting around. Most routes are covered by several competing firms, which all have ticket booths at the bus station (*otogar* or *terminal*) from which they operate, as well as an office in the town centre. Fares vary only slightly between companies: expect to pay €5/100km. An ISIC card gets a small discount with some firms. Top companies (such as Kamil Koç, Pamukkale, Uludag and Varan) are worth paying the bit extra for comfort, punctuality, service and safety. For short hops you're most likely to use a **dolmuş**, a car or minibus that follows a set route, picking up and dropping off along the way. Sometimes the destination will be posted on a sign at the kerbside, and sometimes within the *dolmuş* itself, though you'll generally have to ask. Fares are very low.

Nearly all **ferries** are run by Türkiye Denizcilik İşletmesi (TDI), who operate everything from inner-city shuttles and inter-island lines to international routes. Overnight services are popular, and you should buy tickets in advance through authorized TDI agents. A third-class double cabin from Istanbul to Izmir costs about €50 per person. Students get a 30 percent discount with an ISIC card.

# Accommodation

Finding **accommodation** is generally no problem, except in high season at the busier coastal resorts and in the larger towns. A double room in a one-star **hotel** costs €15–40 in season depending on the location, with breakfast sometimes included. Basic ungraded hotels or **pansiyons** (pensions) may offer spartan rooms, with or without bathroom, for as low as €10. A new type of "bijou" hotel/pension, often in historic buildings, offers high levels of comfort, sometimes at surprisingly reasonable prices. There's also a well-established network of **backpacker hotels**. Most rooms tend to be sparse but clean, at €4–10 for a dorm bed, €10–20 for an en-suite double. Most resort-based places close in winter, so it's wise to call ahead or check with the local tourist office. Similar in price and facilities is the small chain of **hostels** under the banner "Turkish YHA", though of these only one is actually HI-affiliated (the Interyouth hostel in Istanbul). **Campsites** are common only on the coast and in national parks; tourist offices stock a map of them all. Per-person charges run from €2 to €10, plus €3–4 per tent. Campsites often rent out tents or provide **chalet accommodation** for €10–20.

# Food and drink

At its finest, Turkish **food** is one of the world's great cuisines, yet prices are on the whole affordable. **Breakfast** (*kahvaltı*) served at hotels and *pansiyons* is usually a buffet, offering bread with butter, cheese, jam, honey, olives and tea or coffee. Many workers start the morning with a **börek** or a **poça**, pastries filled with meat, cheese or potato that are sold at a tiny **büfe** (stall/café) or at street carts. Others make do with a simple **simit** (sesame-seed bread ring). **Snack** vendors hawk **lahmacun**, small "pizzas" with meat-based toppings, and, in coastal cities, **midye tava** (deep-fried mussels). Another option is **pide**, or Turkish pizza – flat bread with various toppings.

**Restaurants** (*lokanta*) serve more substantial hot dishes. Meat dishes include several variations on the kebab (**kebap**). Fish and seafood are good, if usually pricey, and sold normally by weight. **Mezes** – an extensive array of cold appetizers – come in all shapes and sizes, the most common being **dolma** (peppers or vine leaves stuffed with rice), **patlícan salata** (aubergine in tomato sauce), and **acılı** (a mixture of tomato paste, onion, chilli and parsley), which along with **sebze turlu** (vegetable stew), and **nohut** (chickpeas) are the few dishes available for vegetarians. Most budget restaurants are alcohol-free; some places marked **içk ili** (licensed) may be more expensive.

## Turkish

|  | **Turkish** | **Pronunciation** |
|---|---|---|
| **Yes** | *Evet* | Evet |
| **No** | *Hayır/yok* | Hi-uhr/yok |
| **Please** | *Lütfen* | Lewtfen |
| **Thank you** | *Teskküler/mersi/sağol* | Teshekkewrler/sa-ol |
| **Hello/Good day** | *Merhaba* | Merhabuh |
| **Goodbye** | *Hoşça kalın* | Hosh-cha kaluhn |
| **Excuse me** | *Pardon* | Pardon |
| **Where?** | *...nerede?* | ...Neredeh? |
| **Good** | *Iyi* | Eeyee |
| **Bad** | *Kötü* | Kurtew |
| **Near** | *Yakın* | Yakuhn |
| **Far** | *Uzak* | Oozak |
| **Cheap** | *Ucuz* | Oojooz |
| **Expensive** | *Pahalı* | Pahaluh |
| **Open** | *Açık* | Achuhk |
| **Closed** | *Kapalı* | Kapaluh |
| **Today** | *Bugün* | Boogewn |
| **Yesterday** | *Dün* | Dewn |
| **Tomorrow** | *Yarın* | Yaruhn |
| **How much is....?** | *Ne kadar...?* | Ne kadar |
| **What time is it?** | *Saatiniz var mı?* | Saatiniz var muh |
| **I don't understand** | *Anlamıyorum* | Anlamuh-yoroom |
| **Do you speak English?** | *Ingilizce biliyor musunuz?* | Eengeeleezjeh beeleeyor moosoonooz |
| **One** | *Bir* | Bir |
| **Two** | *Iki* | Iki |
| **Three** | *Uç* | Ewch |
| **Four** | *Dört* | Durt |
| **Five** | *Beş* | Besh |
| **Six** | *Altı* | Altuh |
| **Seven** | *Yedi* | Yedi |
| **Eight** | *Sekiz* | Sekiz |
| **Nine** | *Dokuz* | Dokuz |
| **Ten** | *On* | On |

For **dessert**, there's every imaginable concoction at a **pastane** (sweet-shop): best are the honey-soaked **baklava**, and a variety of milk puddings, most commonly **sütlaç**. Other sweets include **aşure** (Noah's pudding), a sort of rosewater jelly laced with pulses, raisins and nuts: and **lokum** or **Turkish delight**.

**Tea** (*çay*) is the national drink, with sugar on the side but no milk. **Turkish coffee** (*kahve*) is served in tiny cups. Instant coffee is losing ground to fresh filter coffee in trendier cafés. **Fruit juices** (*meyva suyu*) can be excellent but are usually sweetened. **Mineral water**, either still (*su*) or fizzy (*maden suyu*), is found on the table in most restaurants. You'll also come across **ayran**, watered-down yoghurt, which makes a refreshing drink. The main locally brewed brands of **beer** (*bira*) are Efes Pilsen and Tuborg; imported beers are available, but at a horrendous mark-up. The national aperitif is anis-flavoured **rakí** – stronger than Greek ouzo, it's usually drunk with ice and topped up with water.

# Opening hours and holidays

**Shops** are generally open Mon–Sat 9am–7/8pm, and possibly Sun, depending on the owner. The two **religious holidays** are Kurban Bayram (the Feast of the Sacrifice), which falls on Jan 10–14 in 2006: and the Şeker Bayram (Sugar Holiday), which marks the end of the Muslim fasting month of Ramadan (Nov 3–6 in 2006). If either falls midweek, the government may choose to extend the holiday period to as much as nine days, announcing this only a couple of weeks beforehand. In big resorts, museums generally stay open but in smaller towns they may close. Many shops and restaurants also close as their owners return to their home towns for the holiday. Banks and public offices are also closed on the **secular holidays**: Jan 1, April 23, May 19, Aug 30, Oct 29.

# Emergencies

Street **crime** is uncommon and theft is rare, apart from passport theft (see box below) and the odd phone-snatching in Istanbul. The authorities usually treat tourists with courtesy, and all **police** wear dark blue uniforms with baseball caps, with their division – *trafik*, *narkotik*, etc – clearly marked. In rural areas, you'll find the camouflage-clad **Jandarma**, a division of the regular army. For minor health complaints head for the nearest **pharmacy** (*eczane*). Night-duty pharmacists are known as **nöbet(ci)**; the current rota is posted in every pharmacy's front window. For more serious ailments, go to a **hospital** (*klinik*) – either public (*Devlet Hastane* or *SSK Hastanesi*), or the much higher-quality and cleaner private (*Özel Hastane*).

## Emergency numbers

Police ☎155; Ambulance ☎112; Fire ☎110.

# Istanbul

Arriving in **ISTANBUL** can come as a shock. Most visitors head for the old city in and around Sultanahmet, where back streets teem with traders pushing handcarts, stevedores carrying burdens twice their size, and omnipresent shoeshine boys. Yet this is merely one aspect of modern Istanbul; only a couple of kilometres to the north you'll find the former European quarter of Beyoğlu, with its trendy bars and cutting-edge dance clubs. Further north again are the pavement cafés and restaurants of Ortaköy and a series of swish Bosphorus suburbs.

Istanbul is the only city in the world to have played capital to consecutive Christian and Islamic empires, and retains features of both. **Byzantium**, as the city was formerly known, was an important trading centre, but only gained power in the fourth century AD, when Constantine chose it as the new capital of the **Roman Empire**. Later, as **Constantinople**, the city became increasingly dissociated from Rome, adopting the Greek language and Christianity and becoming the capital of an independent empire. In 1203 the city was sacked by the Crusaders. As the Byzantines declined, the **Ottoman Empire** prospered, and in 1453 the city was captured by Mehmet the Conqueror. In the following century, the victory was reinforced by the great military achievements of Selim the Grim and by the reign of Süleyman the Magnificent. By the nineteenth century, however, the glory days of Ottoman domination were firmly over. Defeat in World War I was followed by the **War of Independence**, after which Atatürk created a new capital in Ankara – although Istanbul retained its importance as a centre of trade and commerce. In recent years, the population of the city has reached fifteen million, almost a fifth of the country's total, and is still on the rise, adding further to the cacophony and congestion.

The city is divided in two by the **Bosphorus**, which runs between the Black Sea and the Sea of Marmara, dividing Europe from Asia. At right angles to it, the inlet of the **Golden Horn** cuts the European side in two. The old centre of **Sultanahmet**, occupying the tip of the peninsula south of the Golden Horn, is home to the city's main sightseeing attractions: the cathedral of Aya Sofya, Topkapı Palace and the Blue Mosque. Annoying hustlers mean first impressions can be negative, though problems rarely occur: if they do, tourist police are usually quick to respond. Further west, near the **city walls**, lies the **Kariye Camii**, which contains the city's finest surviving Byzantine mosaics and frescoes. Across the Golden Horn to the north, the **Galata Tower** offers superb panoramic views over the city.

## Arrival, information and accommodation

Istanbul's **airport** is 24km west of the city. Buses run to Taksim Square northeast of Beyoğlu (€4). Taxis taking the direct route along the seafront road (Sahil Yolu) cost €15; make sure they use the meter. The airport metro runs to the city centre at Aksaray, but for Sultanahmet it's best to change onto the tramway at Zeytinburnu;

TURKEY | Istanbul

this entire journey costs around €1. Trains from Europe terminate at **Sirkeci station**, linked to Sultanahmet by a short tram ride; trains from Asia terminate at **Haydarpaşa station** on the east bank of the Bosphorus, from where you can get a ferry to Eminönü and a tram from there to Sultanahmet. From Istanbul's **bus station** at Esenler, 15km northwest, the better bus companies run courtesy minibuses to various points in the city, although if you're heading for Sultanahmet it's often quicker to take the **metro** (actually an express tramway; €0.60) to Aksaray and change to the Kabataş-bound tram line which passes through Sultanahmet and Sirkeci. Some buses also stop at the Harem bus station on the Asian side, from where there are regular *dolmuşes* to Haydarpaşa station. The most central **tourist office** is in Sultanahmet, near the Hippodrome on Divanyolu Cad (daily 9am–5pm; ☎0212/518 8754), with smaller, less informative branches at the airport (24hr) and the two train stations.

Two **bus services** operate on the same city routes, either the private Halk Otobus service (pay conductor on entry; €0.60) or the more common municipality buses (marked IETT), for which you have to buy tickets (€0.60) in advance from bus stations, newspaper kiosks or fast-food booths; some longer routes, usually served by double-deckers, require two advance tickets (look for the sign *iki bilet geçerlidir*). There are route maps at main bus stops. The European side has two **tram** lines, one running from Kabataş through Sultanahmet to Topkapı and outlying suburbs, the other running along Istiklâl Caddesi from Beyoğlu to Taksim using an antique tram; buy tokens (*jetons*; €0.60) from a booth before you enter the platform. There's also a **municipal train** network running along the Marmara shore – west from Sirkeci station on the European side, and east from Haydarpaşa on the Asian (allow at least an hour to get to the Asian station from the centre). On the European side you buy a token (€0.60) to let you through the turnstile onto the platform, while on the Asian side you buy a ticket (same price). There are also **dolmuşes**, which have their point of departure and destination displayed somewhere about the windscreen. **Ferries** run between Eminönü and Karaköy on the European side, and Üsküdar, Kadıköy and Haydarpaşa in Asia; buy your ticket (€0.60) from the dockside kiosks. There are special **sightseeing boats** along the Bosphorus throughout the year from Eminönü (€10; 1hr 30min) but you'll see many of the same sights on the regular ferry to Anadolu Kavağı for less than half the price (€4 return). Last return boat from Anadolu Kavağı in summer is at 5pm, after which you must resort to a bus or *dolmuş*.

## Accommodation

Finding **accommodation** is rarely a problem, but in high season anything up to a week's advance booking is advisable. Some of the city's best small hotels and *pansiyons* are situated in **Sultanahmet**, particularly around Yerebatan Caddesi and the back streets between the Blue Mosque and the sea. It's worth shopping around for a good deal: most hotels include breakfast in the price and some offer air-con and cable TV, while some hostels offer inclusive deals and free Internet access. **Taksim** is also a convenient base, and comes into its own at night as a centre of cultural and culinary activity; take bus #T4 from Sultanahmet, which runs via Karaköy. From Eminönü and Aksaray, many buses pass through either Karaköy or Taksim, or both.

### Sultanahmet

**And** Yerebatan Cad, Cami Cikmazi 36–40 ☎0212/512 0207. Central hotel near Aya Sofya. Faded rooms, but stunning rooftop views. ❹

**Antique** Kutlugün Sok 51 ☎0212/638 1637, ⓦwww.antiquehostel.com. Quiet, comfortable hotel with large, traditionally furnished rooms; with TV, en suite and air-con. ❸

**Buhara** Küçük Ayasoyfa Cad, Yeğen Sok 11 ☎0212/517 3427. Pleasant but basic hotel with outstanding views from its rooftop terrace. ❸

**Fehmi Bey** Üçler Sok 15 ☎0212/638 9083. Large, friendly hotel with period furniture. Rooms are en suite with cable TV, air-con and some with balconies. Ten percent discount for cash. ❺

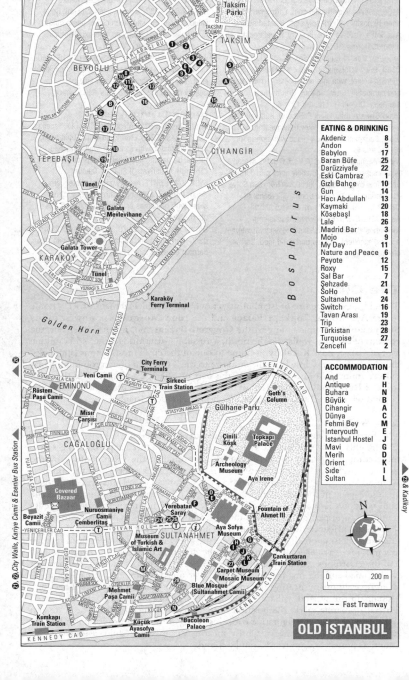

**EATING & DRINKING**

| | |
|---|---|
| Akdeniz | 8 |
| Andon | 5 |
| Babylon | 17 |
| Baran Büfe | 25 |
| Darüzziyafe | 22 |
| Eski Cambraz | 1 |
| Gızlı Bahçe | 10 |
| Gun | 14 |
| Hacı Abdullah | 13 |
| Kaymaki | 20 |
| Kösebaşı | 18 |
| Lale | 26 |
| Madrid Bar | 3 |
| Mojo | 9 |
| My Day | 11 |
| Nature and Peace | 6 |
| Peyote | 12 |
| Roxy | 15 |
| Sal Bar | 7 |
| Şehzade | 21 |
| SoHo | 4 |
| Sultanahmet | 24 |
| Switch | 16 |
| Tavan Arası | 19 |
| Trip | 23 |
| Türkistan | 28 |
| Turquoise | 27 |
| Zencefil | 2 |

**ACCOMMODATION**

| | |
|---|---|
| And | F |
| Antique | H |
| Buhara | N |
| Büyük | B |
| Cihangir | A |
| Dünya | C |
| Fehmi Bey | M |
| Interyouth | E |
| İstanbul Hostel | J |
| Mavi | G |
| Merih | D |
| Orient | K |
| Sıde | I |
| Sultan | L |

**TURKEY** | Istanbul

**32**

**OLD İSTANBUL**

0 ——— 200 m

------ Fast Tramway

N

**Interyouth Hostel** Caferiye Sok 6/1 ☎0212/513 6150, ⊛www.yucelthostel.com. Large, well-managed HI hostel with friendly staff, located next to Aya Sofya. Café, terrace, laundry, travel agent and Internet. Dorms €6, rooms ②

**Istanbul Hostel** Kutlugün Sok 35 ☎0212/516 9380, ⊛www.istanbul-hostel.com. Friendly long-running hostel, with Internet access, terrace, bar and competent travel agency. Ground-floor rooms are noisy. Dorms €7, rooms ①

**Mavi Guesthouse** Ishak PaŞa Cad, Kutlugün Sok 3 ☎0212/516 5878, ⊛www.maviguesthouse .com. Backpacker-friendly place with dorms for €7, rooms ②

**Merih** Alemdar Cad 20 ☎0212/526 9708, €meri hotel@superonline.com. Friendly hotel with dorms and a few dingy doubles, just down from Aya Sofya; front rooms can be noisy. Dorms €7, rooms ②

**Orient International Youth Hostel** Akbıyık Cad 13 ☎0212/518 0789, ⊛www.hostels.com /orienthostel. Long-established hostel with Internet access, excellent roof bar and good food. Dorms €9, rooms ②

**Sıde Hotel and Pansiyon** Utangaç Sok 20 ☎0212/517 2282, ⊛www.sidehotel.com. Good value, welcoming staff, with clean rooms ranging from basic to well equipped, and excellent sea views from the terrace. ②–④

**Sultan Hostel** Akbıyık Cad 21 ☎0212/516 9260. Large, well run, recently refurbished backpackers' joint with roof terrace and street-side bar – the nearby rooms are noisy. Dorms €8, rooms ②

### Beyog*lu and Taksim

**Büyük Londra Oteli** Meşrutiyet Cad 117, Tepebaşi ☎0212/249 1025. Century-old Italian-built hotel, full of character, with spacious, well-furnished rooms. Bargaining could halve the price. ⑥

**Cihangir** Arslanyatağı Sok 33, Taksim ☎0212/251 5317, ⊛www.cihangirhotel.com. Smart hotel on quiet back street with a/c rooms, some with balconies enjoying outstanding Bosphorus views. ⑤

**Dünya** Meşrutiyet Cad 79, Tepebaşi ☎0212/244 0940. Run-down and slightly seedy, but with clean, bargain en-suite rooms with TV. ②

# The City

The old imperial centre of Istanbul stretches from the Sultanahmet district – home to the **Aya Sofya**, **Topkapı Palace** and the **Blue Mosque** – northwest to the **Süleymaniye** mosque complex, the **Covered Bazaar** and, much further out, the remains of the **city walls**. To the north, across the Galata Bridge, the old Levantine area of Galata, now **Karaköy**, is home to one of the city's most famous landmarks, the Galata Tower. Close by is the entrance to the **Tünel**, an underground funicular railway running from Karaköy up to the start of Istiklâl Caddesi. This is the main street of **Beyoğlu**, home to many of the city's restaurants and much of the nightlife, beyond which lies **Taksim Square**, the heart of modern Istanbul.

## Aya Sofya

The former Byzantine cathedral of **Aya Sofya** (Tues–Sun 9.15am–4.30/6pm; €9), readily visible thanks to its massive domed structure, is perhaps the single most compelling sight in the city. Commissioned in the sixth century by the Emperor Justinian, it was converted to a mosque in 1453, after which the minarets were added; it's been a museum since 1934. For centuries this was the largest enclosed space in the world, and the interior – filled with shafts of light from the high windows around the dome – is still profoundly impressive. Scaffolding currently obscures part of the dome's interior, but nevertheless helps bring home the scale of the place. Between the four great piers that hold up the dome, columns of green marble support the galleries. There are a few features left over from its time as a mosque – a *mihrab* (niche indicating the direction of Mecca), a *mimber* (pulpit) and the enormous wooden plaques which bear sacred names of God, the prophet Muhammad and the first four caliphs. The balconies, pediments and capitals are of white marble, many bearing the monograms of Justinian and his wife Theodora. Upstairs in the western gallery (closes 1hr before museum) a large circle of green Thessalian marble marks the position of the throne of the empress. There are also remains of abstract and figurative **mosaics**. Two of the most beautiful can be seen upstairs, where the figures of Christ and the Virgin with Child, as depicted on countless posters and postcards, can be found.

## Topkapı Palace and around

Immediately north of Aya Sofya, **Topkapı Palace** (daily except Tues 9am–5pm; €7) is Istanbul's other unmissable sight. Built between 1459 and 1465, the palace was the centre of the Ottoman Empire for nearly four centuries. Ongoing restoration work means parts of the museum and some less important palace rooms are often closed, but this is unlikely to spoil your visit – there's still plenty to see. The **ticket office** is in the first courtyard, with the second courtyard the site of the beautifully restored **Divan**, containing the Imperial Council Hall and the couch that gave the institution its name. The **Divan tower** is a useful landmark, visible from many vantage points across the city. In the **Inner Treasury** there's an exhibition of arms and armour, while across the courtyard are the **palace kitchens**, with their magnificent rows of chimneys. Around the corner is the **Harem**, well worth the obligatory guided tour (9am–noon & 1–4pm, every 30min; €6; buy your ticket at least 15min in advance). The only men once allowed in here were eunuchs and the imperial guardsmen, who were only employed at certain hours and even then blinkered. Many rooms have never been opened to the public and are awaiting restoration, but the tour takes in a good part of the 400-room complex, including the **Hünkar Sofası** (Imperial Hall) where the sultan entertained his visitors, and the bedchamber of Murat III, covered in sixteenth-century Iznık tiles and kitted out with a marble fountain and bronze fireplace. Back in the main body of the palace, in the third courtyard, the **throne room** was where the sultan awaited the outcome of sessions of the Divan in order to give his assent or otherwise to their proposals. Nearby, the **Pavilion of the Conqueror** (9am–5pm; €6) houses the Topkapı treasury, where you can see such famous items as the Topkapı Dagger, decorated with three enormous emeralds, and the Spoonmaker's Diamond, the fifth largest in the world. In the **Pavilion of the Holy Mantle** are the holy relics brought home by Selim the Grim after his conquest of Egypt in 1517. The fourth courtyard consists of gardens graced with various pavilions, including the **circumcision room** and the sumptuously decorated **Mecidiye Köşkü**, which commands the best view of any of the Topkapı pavilions.

Just west of Topkapı, **Gülhane Parkı**, once the palace gardens, now houses three museums all covered by one €6 ticket. In the **Archeological Museum** (Tues–Sun 9am–5pm) is a superb collection of sarcophagi, sculptures and other remains of past civilizations. The adjacent **Çinili Köşk** is the oldest secular building in Istanbul, now a **Museum of Ceramics** (Tues–Sun 9.30am–5pm), housing a select collection of Iznık ware and Selçuk tiles. Nearby, the **Museum of the Ancient Orient** (Wed–Sun 9.30am–5pm) contains a small but dazzling collection of Anatolian, Egyptian and Mesopotamian artefacts.

## The Blue Mosque and around

With its six minarets, the Sultanahmet Camii, or **Blue Mosque** (daily 9am–7pm; closed prayer times), is instantly recognizable; inside, its four "elephant foot" pillars obscure parts of the building and dwarf the dome they support. It's the 20,000-odd blue tiles inside that lend the mosque its name - fine examples of late sixteenth-century Iznık ware, they include flower and tree panels as well as more abstract designs. Outside the precinct wall is the **Tomb of Sultan Ahmet** (daily 8.30am–5pm), where the sultan is buried along with his wife and three of his sons. Behind the mosque is the **Vakıf Carpet Museum** (Tues–Sat 9am–4pm; free), which houses antique carpets and kilims from all over Turkey.

West of the Blue Mosque the **Hippodrome** arena was constructed by Septimus Severus in 200 AD. The **Egyptian Obelisk** at its southern end was originally 60m tall, but only the upper third survived shipment from Egypt in the fourth century. The scenes carved on the base record its erection in Constantinople under the direction of Theodosius I. Nearby, the **Serpentine Column** comes from the Temple of Apollo at Delphi and was brought here by Constantine.

On the west side of the Hippodrome, the former palace of Ibrahim Paşa, completed in 1524 for the grand vizier of Süleyman the Magnificent, is a fitting home for the **Museum of Turkish and Islamic Art** (Tues–Sun 9am–5pm; €2.50), containing one of the best-exhibited collections of Islamic artefacts in the world. Ibrahim Paşa's magnificent audience hall is devoted to a collection of Turkish carpets, while on the ground floor, in rooms off the central courtyard, is an exhibition of the folk art of the Yörük tribes of Anatolia.

To the north, on the corner of Yerebatan Caddesi, the **Yerebatan Saray** or "Sunken Palace" (daily 9am–4.30/5.30pm; €6) is one of several underground cisterns that riddle the foundations of the city. Probably built by Constantine and enlarged by Justinian, the cistern is thought to have supplied water to the Great Palace of the Byzantine emperors. Raised pathways allow you to walk through the cistern's forest of columns, and gaze upon the monumental Medusa heads that support two of them. On the east side of the Blue Mosque, the **Mosaic Museum** (Tues–Sun 9.15am–4.30pm; €2.50), on Torun Sokak, displays some of the magnificent mosaics that once decorated the floors of the Great Palace, a vast complex which once stretched from the Hippodrome down to the sea walls.

## Covered Bazaar, Süleymaniye Camii and Spice Bazaar

West of Sultanahmet, head along busy Divan Yolu to **Cemberlitaş**, or the Column of Constantine, erected in 330 AD to mark the city's dedication as capital of the Roman Empire. Off the main street to the right lies the district of Beyazıt, centred on the **Kapalı Çarşı**, or Covered Bazaar (Mon–Sat 8.30am–6.30/7.30pm; ⊛www.kapali-carsi.com), a huge web of passageways housing over 4000 shops. It has long since spilled out of the covered area, sprawling into the streets that lead down to the Golden Horn. There are carpet shops everywhere catering for all budgets, shops selling leather goods around Kurkçular Kapı and Perdahçılar Caddesi, and gold jewellery on Kuyumcular Caddesi. Don't forget to haggle. When you need a break, the *Fes Café* on Halıcılar Caddesi is a comfortable spot to gloat over your booty.

West of the bazaar, peek into the **Beyazit Camii**, the oldest surviving imperial mosque in the city (1506), with a beautiful courtyard full of richly coloured marble. Beyond the Covered Bazaar, in a pleasant area of shady courtyards behind the university, stands one of the finest of all the Ottoman mosque complexes, the **Süleymaniye Camii**. The cemetery here (Wed–Sun 9.30am–6.30pm) holds the tomb of Süleyman the Magnificent and of Roxelana, his wife. Süleyman's tomb is particularly impressive, with doors inlaid with ebony and ivory, silver and jade. The rest of the complex is made up of the famous **Süleymaniye Library**, and the **Tomb of Mimar Sinan**, built for the master imperial architect, its magnificent carved turban a measure of his rank.

The area sloping down to the river behind the Covered Bazaar is known as **Eminönü**, where, on the waterfront, stands the last of Istanbul's imperial mosques, **Yeni Camii**. Next door, the **Mısır Çarşısı** (Egyptian Bazaar), also known as the **Spice Bazaar**, sells everything from saffron to aphrodisiacs. A short walk west, the **Rüştem Paşa Camii** is one of the most attractive of Istanbul's smaller mosques, with tiles from the finest period of Iznik tile production. On the waterfront, the most prominent landmark is the **Galata Bridge**, a modern two-tier structure that provides access to the opposite bank of the Golden Horn.

## Kariye Camii and the city walls

West of Beyazit, Istanbul becomes tattier and more intimate, almost like a collection of villages intersected by major roads. **Kariye Camii** (9.30am–4.30pm, closed Wed; €6), the former church of St Saviour in Chora, was built in the early twelfth century and has some superbly preserved fourteenth-century frescoes and mosaics. It can be reached by taking the metro to Topkapı (a western district, not the city-centre palace) and walking north beside the city walls as far as the Edirnekapa gate, from where it's signposted.

Over 6km long, Istanbul's western **city walls** are among the most fascinating Byzantine remains in Turkey; they barred the peninsula to attackers for 800 years. First raised by the Emperor Theodosius II, they are the result of a hasty rebuilding to repel Attila the Hun's forces in 447 AD; an ancient edict was brought into effect whereby all citizens, regardless of rank, were required to help, and 16,000 men finished the project in just two months. Most of the outer wall and its 96 towers are still standing, and although long sections have been rebuilt and closed off, untouched sections can still be examined in detail if you're willing to clamber in the dirt and brick dust. Do pay attention to your personal security here, especially in the evening.

Plenty of **buses** run this way from Eminönü and Sultanahmet, including bus #80 to Yedikule, #84 to Topkapı and #86 to Edirnekapı, while the **tram** line runs west from Aksaray to the Topkapı gate. However, the best way to get here is to take the scenic **train** ride along the coast from Eminönü to **Yediküle**, a district lying at the southern end of the walls in the attractive former Greek quarter of Samatya. This also has a few reasonable restaurants and cafés where you can stop before setting off on your exploration of the walls. The Ottoman fortress of Yediküle is closed for restoration until late 2006.

## Across the Golden Horn: Karaköy and Beyoğlu

Across the Galata Bridge from Eminönü is **Karaköy** (formerly Galata). In 1261 Galata became a Genoese trading colony, and during the early centuries of Ottoman rule it functioned as the capital's "European" quarter, home to Jewish, Greek and Armenian minorities. Overcrowding during the subsequent centuries saw the Europeans gradually spread from Galata into neighbouring **Beyoğlu**, but after the exodus of much of the Greek population from Beyoğlu in the 1960s the area began to lose its cosmopolitan flavour, becoming home to brothels, pick-up joints and sex cinemas. It has since cleaned up its appearance and now plays host to trendy café-bars, restaurants and clubs, coexisting alongside a seedy red-light district.

The **Galata Tower** (daily 9am–7pm; €3.50), built in 1348, is the area's most obvious landmark; its viewing galleries, café and ridiculously expensive restaurant offer the best panoramas of the city. Up towards **Istiklâl Caddesi**, Beyoulu's main boulevard, an unassuming doorway leads to the courtyard of the **Galata Mevlevi-hane** (9am–4.30pm, closed Wed; €1.50), a former monastery and ceremonial hall of the **Whirling Dervishes**, a sect founded in the thirteenth century. Exhibits include instruments and dervish costumes, and the building itself has been beautifully restored to late eighteenth-century splendour. Staged dervish ceremonies take place most Sundays throughout the year (information on ☎0212/245 4141), and also at the Sirkeci Central Train Station Exhibition Hall (every Sun, Wed & Fri; ☎0212/485 8834; €12). The best way to continue along Istiklâl Caddesi is to hop on the **antique tram** which trundles for 1km or so to **Taksim Square**, taking in the sumptuous fin-de-siècle architecture along the way.

# Eating, drinking and nightlife

Sultanahmet has some decent **restaurants**, although the principal concentrations are in Beyoğlu and Taksim. The **Balık Pazar**, particularly, behind the Çiçek Pasajı (off Istiklâl Cad), is a great area for *mezes*, kebabs and fish, while **Çiçek Pasajı** itself offers similar fare but is overpriced and touristy. **Snacks** include the dubious fish sandwiches served off boats in Kadıköy, Karaköy and Eminönü; *kokoreç* (skeins of sheep's innards) sold from street stalls; and delicious corn on the cob sold by vendors everywhere. Western-style **bars and clubs** – invariably trendy and expensive – have all but taken over the city, with **house** being the current music of choice. **Traditional music**, however, is still popular, particularly in the laid-back bar-restaurants around Taksim and in nearby suburbs, and along the Bosphorus (particularly the district of Ortaköy, just beyond Beşiktaş), where you can eat accompanied by an ever-changing crowd of musicians. Backpackers, especially Antipodeans, tend to gather in the bars on Akbıyık Caddesi in Sultanahmet.

## Restaurants

### Sultanahmet and around

**Baran Büfe** Divan Yolu Cad 7. Good spot to watch the world go by whilst enjoying some cheap tasty eats or a *nargile*. Open 24hr.

**Darüzziyafe** Şifahane Cad 33. Reasonably priced Ottoman cuisine next to Süleymaniye mosque. Live traditional music most evenings.

**Kaymaki Kahvaltı** Celebioğin Cad 6, Beşiktaş. Small, plain local restaurant serving the best *menemen* in town. Popular at weekends.

**Lale** Divan Yolu Cad 6. Bustling lunchtime-buffet restaurant, popular with tourists and locals alike.

**Şehzade Mehmet Efendi** Şehzade Camii, Şehzadebaşı Cad. Wonderfully atmospheric restaurant located in the *medrese* of the Şehzade mosque. Excellent-value *pide*, kebabs and stews.

**Sultanahmet Köftecisi** Divan Yolu Cad 12/a. Busy, basic restaurant; good for tasty traditional Turkish dishes.

**Türkistan Aşevi** Tavukhane Sok 36, behind the Blue Mosque. Central Asian cuisine with a good set menu. You'll be asked to take off your shoes.

**Turquoise** Akbıyık Cad 40. Small, cosy Mediterranean restaurant serving quality, reasonably priced fare.

### Beyoğlu

**Andon** Siraselviler Cad 89, Beyoğlu. Plush French restaurant and café on four floors serving a variety of coffees; also free Wi-Fi connection.

**Gun** Tarichi Beyoğlu Balık Pazarı 60. Well placed in the midst of the covered market, good for fish dishes or just a beer.

**Hacı Abdullah** Sakızağcı Cad 17. A local legend - stunning home cooking at reasonable prices. No alcohol.

**KöŞebaŞi** Istiklâl Cad 405. Trendy, tasty, ultra-modern take on traditional Turkish dishes.

**Nature and Peace** Büyükparmakkapı Sok 21, Istiklâl Cad. Vegetarian place three blocks from Taksim, offering lentil *köfte* and other veggie dishes.

**Tavan Arası** Asmalımescit Sok 5, Tünel. Large portions of good-quality home-made Turkish food. Popular with students due to the small prices.

**Zenceful** Kurabiye Sok 3. Two branches opposite each other, serving cheap Turkish and vegetarian dishes. Popular with expats.

## Bars

**Akdeniz** Nevizade Sok 25, Beyoğlu. Rambling, multi-storey student bar, playing rock music and serving cheap drinks.

**Eski Cambraz** Mıs Sok 32, Beyoğlu. Small, cosy bar on two floors, frequented by art students. Mixed pop music played at levels conducive to conversation.

**Gızlı Bahçe** Nevizade Sok 27, Istiklâl Cad, Beyoğlu. Cutting-edge dance music in a dilapidated Ottoman town-house bar. Mixed trendy crowd, and a deliciously illicit atmosphere.

**Madrid Bar** Ipek Sok 20, Beyoğlu. Cheap bar popular with students and impecunious expats alike.

**My Day** Balo Sok 18, Beyoğlu. Small, modern, trendy bar with DJs playing a wide selection of sounds.

**Sal Bar** Büyükparmakkapı Sok 18, Istiklâl Cad, Beyoğlu. Traditional Turkish music and beer. For more of the same try *Ekin* and *Barabar* on the same street.

**Trip** Kadife Sok 10, Kadıkoy. Shabby-chic converted Ottoman house with a sliding roof on the terrace and a good selection of alternative pop.

## Clubs

**Babylon** Şeyhbender Sok 3, Asmalımescit, Tünel. Regular stints by foreign bands and DJs. Expensive, but occasionally has special offers.

**Mojo** Büyükparmakkapı Sok, Istiklâl Cad, Beyoğlu. Trendy basement dive with live bands most nights. Closes 4am.

**Peyote** Sahne Sok 24, Beyoğlu. Small, modern club playing deep/hard house to a trendy crowd.

**Roxy** Arslanyatağı Sok 113, Siraselviler Cad,

Taksim. DJs and regular live bands in a pricey, professional-oriented bar/disco.

**SoHo** MeŞelik Sok 14, Beyoğlu. The current hard-house dance club to be seen in, with inflated bar prices to match. Good DJs. Very popular at weekends.

**Switch** Muammer Karaca Çıkmazı, Istiklal Cad, Taksim. Underground dance club with local and foreign DJs.

## Listings

**Consulates** Australia, Tepecik Yolu 58, Etiler ☎0212/257 7050; Ireland, Cumhuriyet Cad 26a, Elmadağ ☎0212/246 6025; New Zealand, Yeşil Çimen Cad 75, Ihlamur ☎0212/258 8722; UK, Meşrutiyet Cad 34, Tepebaşı, Beyoğlu ☎0212/334 6400; US, Kaplicalar Mevkii Sok 2, Istinye ☎0212/335 9000.

**Hospitals** American Hospital, Güzelbahçe Sok 20, Nişantaşı ☎0212/231 4050; International Hospital, Istanbul Cad 82, Yeşilköy ☎0212/663 3000.

**Internet** Internet Café, 2nd floor, Incili Çavuş Sok 31, Divan Yolu; Blue Internet Café, Yerbatan Cad 54; Seycom, Divan Yolu Cad 54/4, Sultanahmet.

**Laundry** Amfora, Binbirdirek Mah. Peykhane Cad 53/1.

**Left luggage** Sirkeci and Haydarpaşa train stations.

**Police** Tourist Police, Yerebatan Cad, Sultanahmet ☎0212/527 4503.

**Post office** Yeni Posthane Cad, Sirkeci.

**Turkish baths** The most central, and most frequented by tourists, are the 400-year-old Çemberlitaş Hamam on Divan Yolu (daily 6am–midnight; €15), and Cağaoğlu Hamam, Hilali Ahmed Cad 34 (daily: men 8am–10pm; women 8am–8pm; €10–30). Outside the main tourist areas *hamams* are much cheaper: the 500-year-old Tophane Hamam on the Bosphorus at Tophane costs only €4 (daily 7am–10pm).

# Around the Sea of Marmara

Despite their proximity to Istanbul, the shores and hinterland of the **Sea of Marmara** are relatively neglected by foreign travellers – but there are good reasons to come: not least the border town of **Edirne** which was once the Ottoman capital. To the southeast the quaint country town of **Iznik** was briefly the Byzantine capital and boasts extensive ruins, while nearby **Bursa**, the first Ottoman capital, has some of the finest monuments in the Balkans. Many visitors also stop off at the extensive World War I battlefields and cemeteries of the **Gelibolu peninsula** (Gallipoli), using either the port of **Eceabat** as a base, or, more commonly, **Çanakkale** – from where it's also easy to visit the ruins of ancient Troy.

## Edirne

**EDIRNE** boasts an impressive number of elegant monuments and makes for an easily digestible introduction to Turkey. Bordering both Greece and Bulgaria, it's a lively place, albeit somewhat seedy thanks to vast numbers of truck drivers and traders who pass through. The city springs to life for the week-long **oil wrestling festival** of Kırkpınar (end of June).

You can see the sights on foot in a day. The best starting point is the **Eski Camii** bang in the centre, the oldest mosque in town, begun in 1403. Just across the way, the **Bedesten** was Edirne's first covered market, though the plastic goods it now touts are no match for the building itself. Nearby, the **Semiz Ali Paşa Çarşısı** is the other main bazaar, while a short way north of here is the beautiful **Üç Şerefeli Camii**, dating from 1447; its name means "three-balconied", derived from the presence of three galleries for the muezzin on the tallest of the four idiosyncratic minarets. A little way east, the masterly **Selimiye Camii** was designed by Minar Sinan. Its four slender minarets, among the tallest in the world, also have three balconies; the interior is most impressive, its dome planned to surpass that of Aya Sofya in Istanbul. Next door, the **Museum of Turkish and Islamic Arts** (Tues–Sun 8.30am–noon & 1–5.30pm; €0.50) houses assorted wooden, ceramic and martial knick-knacks from the province. The main **Archeological Museum** (Tues–Sun 8.30am–noon & 1–5.30pm; €0.50), just northeast of the mosque, contains an assortment of Greco-Roman fragments, some Neolithic finds and an ethnographic section that focuses on local crafts.

The **bus station** is 9km southeast of the centre, from where there are frequent *dolmuşes* and city buses into town. The **train station** is 1km further in the same direction. There are two **tourist offices** (both daily 8.30am–5.30pm; ☎0284/213 9208), both on Talat Paşa Caddesi, the main one about 500m west towards the Gazi Mihal bridge at no. 76a, and a helpful annexe up near Hürriyet Meydanı by the traffic signals. Edirne's few budget **hotels** are either grim dosshouses or booked solid by truck drivers. Best of the cheapies is *Saray* (☎0284/212 1457; ❷), with a TV in each room; more comfortable are *Şaban Açikgöz*, Çilingirler Cad 9 (☎0284/213 0313; ❸), and *Efe Hotel*, Maarif Cad 13 (☎0284/213 6080, ⊛www.efehotel.com; ❹), which also has air-conditioning. The *Rüştem Paşa Kervanseray*, on Iki Kapılı Han Cad (☎0284/225 2195, ⊛k.saray@netone.com; ❹), has reasonable rooms in a restored Ottoman *karavanserai* though bargaining is recommended. For **snacks**, look out for the tiny *ciğerci* shops serving the city's speciality, deep-fried liver. The lower end of Saraçlar Caddesi offers some decent **cafés and restaurants**, with *Ak Piliç* at no. 14 serving good chicken dishes, and the nearby *Urfa Gaziantep* offering excellent *lahmucan* and *şiş kebab*; all along the street you'll also find stalls selling Turkish desserts. The *English Pub*, near the *Efe Hotel*, makes a passable attempt at its namesake. **Internet** access is at Eska Internet Café, Ilk Kapalıhan Cad 5.

## Çanakkale

Although celebrated for its setting on the Dardanelles, **ÇANAKKALE** has little to detain you. However, it is a popular base for visiting the Gelibolu (Gallipoli) sites and the sparse ruins of Troy. Almost everything of interest in town – park, naval museum (daily 8am–noon & 1–5pm; €1) and archeological museum (daily 8am–noon & 1–5.30pm; €2) – is within walking distance of the **ferry docks**, close to the start of the main Demircioğlu Caddesi. The **bus station** is out on the coastal highway, Atatürk Caddesi, a fifteen-minute walk from the waterfront; if you're arriving on the bus from Istanbul, get off at the ferry rather than going out to the bus station. At the **tourist office** beside the ferry docks (daily 8am–noon & 1–5/8pm; ☎0286/217 1187) you can pick up a free map of the Gallipoli battlefields.

Except for a crowded couple of weeks during the **Çanakkale/Troy Festival** (mid-Aug), or on **ANZAC Day** (April 25), when the town is inundated with Antipodeans, you'll have little trouble finding budget **accommodation**: try the clean and airy *Yellow Rose*, Yeni Sok 5 (☎0286/217 3343, ⊛www.yellowrose.4mg .com; dorms €6, rooms ❷), or the similar *Anzac House*, Cumhuriyet Meydanı 61 (☎0286/213 5969, ⊛www.anzachouse.com; dorms €5, rooms ❶), with small but neat rooms, Internet access and good Gallipoli tours. The friendly and homely *Efes Hotel*, Fetvahane Sok 15 (☎0286/217 3256; ❷), is excellent value, more so than the upmarket *Anafartalar*, overlooking the ferry landing (☎0286/217 4454; ❹ including breakfast). There are several local **campsites** – at Güzelyalı, Dardanos and Kepez – all accessible by minibus.

On the quayside south of the ferry jetty, both the *Rıhtim* and *Liman Yalova* **restaurants** offer excellent, but pricey, fish and scenic views. *Gaziantepe*, Fetvahane Sok 8, serves up cheap and tasty Turkish specialities, whilst further along the street the female-run *Köy Ev* provides a taste of real Turkish home cooking. There's a burgeoning **café** and **bar** scene on Yalı Caddesi and Fetvahane Sokak, with the latter boasting the current top spot, *Depo*. The *TNT* bar on Saat Kule Meydanı is popular with the Anzac crowd, while *Lodos*, Nara Cad 1 near the ferry terminal, is good for dance music and has regular live sets.

## The Gelibolu (Gallipoli) peninsula

Though endowed with splendid scenery and beaches, the slender **Gelibolu (Gallipoli) peninsula**, which forms the northwest side of the Dardanelles, is known chiefly for its grim military history. In April 1915 it was the site of a plan, devised by Winston Churchill, to land Allied troops, many of them Australian and New Zealand units, with a view to putting Turkey out of the war. It failed miserably, with massive casualties. Nevertheless, this was the first time Australians and New Zealanders had seen action under their own commanders; the date of the first landings, April 25, is celebrated as **ANZAC Day**. The battlefields and cemeteries have no admission fees or restricted hours, but since there's little public transport you'll have to take a tour unless you have your own vehicle. Various local companies offer **battlefield tours** (around €33 per person, including lunch), the best operated by *TJ's* hostel based in Eceabat (☎0286/814 3121, ⓦwww.anzacgallipolitours .com). For a group of four or five, renting a car and doing it yourself would work out cheaper.

The World War I battlefields and Allied cemeteries are by turns moving and numbing in the sheer multiplicity of graves, memorials and obelisks. However, it's difficult now to imagine the bare desolation of 1915 given the lush landscape of much of the area. The first stop on most tours is the **Kabatepe Orientation Centre and Museum** (daily 8am–6pm; €1), beyond which are the **Beach**, **Shrapnel Valley** and **Shell Green** cemeteries, followed by **Anzac Cove** and **Arıburnu**, site of the ANZAC landing. Beyond Arıburnu, a left fork leads towards the beaches and salt lake at **Cape Suvla**, today renamed Kemikli Burnu; most tourists bear right for Büyük Anafartalar village and **Çonkbayırı Hill**, where there's a massive New Zealand memorial and a Turkish memorial detailing Atatürk's words and deeds. Working your way back down towards the orientation centre, you pass **The Nek**, **Walker's Ridge** and **Quinn's Post**, where the trenches of the opposing forces lay within a few metres of each other: the modern road corresponds to no-man's-land. From here the perilous supply line ran down-valley to the present location of **Beach Cemetery**.

# Troy

Although not the most spectacular archeological site in Turkey, **TROY** (Truva) is probably the most celebrated, thanks to its key role in Homer's *Iliad*. The ruins of the ancient city, just west of the main road around 20km south of Çanakkale, are on a much smaller scale than other sites, consisting mainly of defensive walls, a small theatre and the remains of a temple. Some come away disappointed, but it's worth remembering that the settlement dates back to the late Bronze Age, making Troy far older than most other Classical cities. The oldest layer of remains, Troy I, dates back to about 3600 BC, while the final development, Troy IX, was built between 300 BC and 300 AD, during the heyday of the Roman Empire. Çanakkale is the most sensible base: take one of the frequent *dolmuşes* (€1), which run from its minibus station direct to the site, rather than forking out €21 to join an organized tour. And, in any case, the information panels go some way to bringing the scant ruins to life. At the site (daily 8am–5/7pm; €7) entrance, a road leads to a giant wooden horse. Just beyond is the ruined city itself, a craggy outcrop overlooking the plain, which stretches about 8km to the sea. It's a fantastic view, and despite the sparseness of the remains, as you stand on what's left of the ramparts and look out across the plain, it's not too difficult to imagine a besieging army camped out below.

# Iznik

Tucked away at the eastern end of the lake that bears its name, the sleepy little town of **IZNIK** boasts extensive, well-preserved ruins. Originally the ancient Greek city of Nicaea, it became the Byzantine capital when Istanbul fell to the Crusaders in 1204. Under the Ottomans, the city became a centre for ceramic production, an art that has recently been revived. You're free to wander the length of the Byzantine city walls that enclose almost everything of interest. In the centre sits the **Aya Sofya Museum** (daily 8am–noon & 1–5pm; €1.50), the remains of a Byzantine church originally founded by Justinian. To the northeast lies the fourteenth-century **Nilüfer Hatun Imareti**, a religious hostel that nowadays houses Iznik's **Archeological Museum** (daily 8am–noon & 1–5pm; €1.50), displaying some fabulous examples of Ottoman Iznik ceramics. The **Iznik Foundation** (Mon–Fri 9am–7pm; ⊛www.iznik.com) has restarted local ceramic production using original materials and techniques, to great success. Given that each tile takes seventy days to make, it's no wonder that they cost around €150 each; you can see the painstaking process on the free tour. The factory, located amidst olive groves near the lake, southwest of the old city walls, is signposted as *Iznik Vakfi* from Sahil Yolu.

    **Buses** arrive at Iznik's bus station, southeast of the centre, from where everything is within walking distance. The **tourist office** is east of the Aya Sofya, at Kılıçaslan Cad 130 (Mon–Fri 8.30am–noon & 1–5.30pm; ☎0224/757 1933). In summer, what **accommodation** there is tends to fill up fast, so reserve in advance where possible. Unfortunately, you can't at the backpacker-friendly *Kaynarca Pansiyon*, Gündem Sok 1 (☎0224/757 1753, ⊛www.kaynarca.s5.com; dorms €7, rooms ❷), with TV in every room and an attached Internet café, but it's worth turning up early. For views over the lake, try the refurbished *Çamlık Motel*, Sahili Cad 11 (☎0224/757 1631; ❸), which has a decent restaurant, or the better-value *Cem Pansiyon*, Sahili Cad 20 (☎0224/757 1687; ❸). The fish **restaurants** on the coast road, Sahil Yolu, are so-so, but *Balıkçı* at no. 22 serves excellent grilled local fish. There's a row of cheap restaurants clustered around Aya Sofya, including *KarPi*, which is renowned for its *pide*.

# Bursa

Draped along the leafy lower slopes of Uludağ, which towers more than 2000m above, **BURSA** – first capital of the Ottoman Empire and the burial place of several sultans – does more justice to its setting than any other Turkish city besides Istanbul. Gathered here are some of the finest early Ottoman monuments in Turkey, in a tidy and appealing city centre, though traffic congestion can make getting around a daunting experience.

    Flanked by the busy Atatürk Caddesi, the compact **Koza Parkı**, with its fountains, benches and cafés, is the real heart of Bursa. On the far side looms the fourteenth-century **Ulu Camii**, whose interior is dominated by a huge *şadırvan* pool for ritual ablutions. Close by is Bursa's covered market, the **Bedesten**, given over to the sale of jewellery and precious metals, and the **Koza Hanı**, flanking the park, still entirely occupied by silk and brocade merchants. Across the river to the east, the **Yeşil Camii** (daily 8am–8.30pm) is easily the most spectacular of Bursa's imperial mosques. The hundreds of green tiles inside line every available vertical surface up to 5m in height. The nearby hexagonal **Yeşil Türbe** (daily 8am–noon & 1–7pm) contains the sarcophagus of Çelebi Mehmet I and assorted offspring. The immediate environs of the mosque are a busy tangle of cafés and souvenir shops. The *medrese*, the largest surviving dependency of the mosque, now houses Bursa's recently renovated **Museum of Turkish and Islamic Art** (Tues–Sun 8.30am–noon & 1–5.30pm; €1), with Iznik ware, Çanakkale ceramics, glass items and a mock-up of an Ottoman circumcision chamber. West of the centre, the **Hisar** ("citadel") district was Bursa's original nucleus. Narrow lanes wind up past dilapidated Ottoman houses, while walkways clinging to the rock face offer fabulous views. The best-preserved dwellings are a little way west in medieval **Muradiye**, where the **Muradiye Külliyesi** mosque and *medrese* complex was begun in 1424. This is the last imperial foundation in Bursa, although it's most famous for its tombs, set in lovingly tended gardens. Out beyond the Kültür Parkı, the **Yeni Kaplıca** (daily 9am–11pm; €6) are the nearest of Bursa's baths, a faded reminder of the days when the town was patronized as a spa.

    Bursa's **bus terminal** is 5km north on the main road to Istanbul, from where bus #38 (every 15min) runs to Koza Parkı, at one corner of which is Bursa's **tourist**

**office** (Mon–Fri 8.30am–5.30pm; ☏0224/220 1848). Avoid the few grim **hotels** around the old bus station, now the main *dolmuş* garage: better options lie in the centre and the leafy spa suburb of Çekirge, a *dolmuş* ride to the northwest. In the centre a cheap, clean and friendly option is *Guneş*, Inebey Cad 75 (☏0224/224 1404; ❶), while *Hotel Dikmen*, Maksem Cad 78 (☏0224/224 1840; ❹), is also clean and friendly and has cable TV in all rooms. The female-run *Çeşmeli* at Heykel Gümüşçeken Cad 6 (☏0224/224 1512; ❸) has great views from the upper rooms, or there's the comfortable *Hotel Efehan*, Heykel Gümüşçeken Cad 34 (☏0224/225 2260, ⓦwww.efehan.com.tr; ❸). In Çekirge, try the unpretentious *Demirci Otel*, Hammamlar Cad 33 (☏0224/236 5104; ❷), with its own *hamam*.

For **food**, in the central Heykel district, *Iskender*, Unlu Cad 7, offers Bursa's speciality, *Iskender kebap*, while on the same street, *Palmiye* at no. 34 is a cheap and lively alternative. The *Fasil* at Yaşıl Cad 2 has comfortable Ottoman decor and low seating. Close to the tourist office at Belediye Cad 15, the more elegant *Çiçek Izgara* offers a decent take on many Ottoman dishes, while for a good view overlooking the river there's *Yener Ocakbasi*, set in terraced gardens. The old fish market on Sakarya Caddesi, at the foot of the citadel, is dominated by lively **fish restaurants**, of which *Arap Şükrü*, at no. 6, is reasonably priced. This street also has a number of reasonable **bars**, including *Piccolo*. A more central option, housed within the Setbaşi, is the dark, pub-like *La Bella*, complete with dartboard.

# Turkey's Aegean coast

The **Aegean coast** is, in many ways, Turkey's most enticing destination, home to some of the best of its Classical antiquities and the most appealing resorts. Tiny **Assos** with its ancient ruins is one of the gems of the coast. **Bergama**, 70km to the southeast, makes a charming place to stop for a few days. Further south, the city of **Izmir** serves as a base for day-trips to adjacent sights and beaches. The territory to the south is home to the best concentration of Classical, Hellenistic and Roman ruins, notably **Ephesus** and the remains inland at **Hierapolis** – sitting atop the famous pools and mineral formations of **Pamukkale**. The coast itself is better down south, too, and although the larger resorts, including **Kuşadası** and **Marmaris**, have been marred by the developers, **Bodrum** still has a certain charm.

## Assos

**ASSOS**, 70km south of Çanakkale, is a tiny stone village built on a hill around the ruins of the ancient town of the same name, founded in the sixth century BC and once home to Aristotle. The old-town ruins (daily 8.30am–5/7pm; €3) are for the most part blissfully quiet; the **Temple of Athena** has had its Doric columns re-erected, and there are breathtaking views from here to the Greek island of Lésvos. The only transport is a **minibus** from Ayvacik, 25km to the north, which passes through both the upper village of Assos and its twin settlement downhill around the fishing harbour; it runs according to demand, so out of season and at off-peak times you may have a long wait. Before Assos, beside an antique bridge is the popular and immaculate *Old Bridge House* (☏0286/721 7426; dorms €11, rooms ❹), with cabins set in landscaped gardens. **Pansiyons** in the upper village are all in restored stone houses and include the delightful *Timur Pansiyon*, just below the entrance to the ruins (☏0286/721 7449, ⓦwww.hitit.co.uk/timur; ❷), with excellent views, and *Dolunay* (☏0286/721 7172; ❷), next to the *dolmuş* stop. Down on the harbour are several beautiful but expensive stone-built **hotels**, which can generally be bargained down in midweek; alternatively, there's the cheaper *Antik*

*Pansiyon* (☎0286/721 7101; **❷**), just behind. Further along the shore to the east, are several small **campsites** including *Çakır* (☎0286/721 7048). At Kadırga, to the east of the harbour, there's a good, relatively undeveloped shingle **beach**.

## Bergama

**BERGAMA** is the site of the Hellenistic – and later Roman – city of Pergamon, ruled for several centuries by a powerful local dynasty. Excavations were completed here in 1886, but unfortunately much of what was found has since been carted off to Germany. However, the acropolis of Eumenes II remains a major attraction, and there are a host of lesser sights and an old quarter of ramshackle charm that deserve a day or two. The old town lies at the foot of the acropolis, about ten minutes' walk from the bus station. Its foremost attraction is the **Kızıl Avlu** (daily 8.30am–5.30pm; €3), a huge edifice on the river not far from the acropolis, originally built as a temple to the Egyptian god Osiris and converted to a basilica by the early Christians, when it was one of the Seven Churches of Asia Minor addressed by St John in the Book of Revelation. South along the main street is the **Archeological Museum** (Tues–Sun 8.30am–6pm; €2.50), which has a large collection of locally unearthed booty, including busts of Zeus and Socrates and a model of the Zeus altar. Bergama has a particularly good **hamam**, the *Hacı Hekim*, Bankalar Cad 32 (from €5). **Pergamon**, the ancient city of kings, is set on top of a rocky bluff towering over modern Bergama. Taking a short cut through the old town still means an uphill walk of around half an hour. By taxi, the ride costs €6 or more; a taxi-tour around all Bergama's sights costs about €15 but is only recommended if you are pushed for time. The first attraction on the **acropolis** (daily 9am–5/7pm; €6) is the huge horseshoe-shaped **Altar of Zeus**, built during the reign of Eumenes II to commemorate his father's victory over the Gauls. North of the Zeus altar lie the sparse remains of a **Temple of Athena**, above which loom the restored columns of the **Temple of Trajan**, where the deified Roman emperor and his successor Hadrian were revered in the imperial era. From the Temple of Athena a narrow staircase leads down to the theatre, the most spectacular part of the ruined acropolis, capable of seating 10,000 spectators, and a **Temple of Dionysos**, just off-stage to the northwest.

Bergama's **bus station** is on the main road, 500m from the town centre, and within fifteen minutes' walk of most accommodation. The **tourist office** (daily 8.30am–noon & 1–5.30pm; ☎0232/633 1862) is further along the same road. Budget **hotels** are thin on the ground but most are clustered behind the bus station. *Böblingen*, Askeplion Cad 2 (☎0232/633 2153; **❷**), has cheap doubles with shower, while *Manolya*, at Tanpinar Sok 11 (☎0232/633 1763; **❷**), features modern rooms with TV and a/c. Slightly more upmarket is the large *Efsane*, Ataturk Bul 82 (☎0232/633 6350, ⊛www.efsanehotel.com; **❸**). Restaurant options abound, such as the excellent-value *Arzu Pide*, Istiklal Meydanı 10; *Sağlam 3*, Hükümet Meydanı 89, with a good range of traditional Turkish food; and *Pala* at Mescit Karacac 4, renowned for its *köfte*. The hottest **bar** in town is the *Pergamon*, Bankalar Cad 5, housed in an old mansion, with live music at weekends.

## Izmir

**IZMIR** – ancient Smyrna – is home to nearly three million people. Mostly burned down in the Turkish–Greek war of 1922, Izmir has been built pretty much from scratch and is nowadays booming, cosmopolitan and relentlessly modern. Its hot climate is offset by its location, straddling a fifty-kilometre-long gulf fed by several streams and flanked by mountains on all sides. Orientation can be confusing – many streets are unmarked – but most points of interest lie near each other and walking is the most enjoyable way of exploring. Izmir cannot be said to have a single centre, although **Konak**, the busy park, bus terminal and shopping centre on the waterfront, is where visitors spend most time. It's marked by the ornate **Saat Kulesi** (clock tower), the city's official symbol, and the **Konak Camii**, distinguished by its facade of enamelled tiles. Southwest of here, the **Archeological Museum** (Tues–Sun 8.30am–5.30pm; €2.50) features an excellent collection of finds from all over Izmir province, including some stunning marble statues and sarcophagi. Immediately east of Konak is Izmir's **bazaar**. The main drag, Anafartalar Caddesi, is lined with clothing, jewellery and shoe shops; Fevzipaşa Bulvarı and the alleys just south are strong on leather garments. Worth seeking out is the handsome **Kızılara Gazi Kervanseray** on 871 Sok, which has antique and carpet shops, and houses a popular café. East, across Gaziosmanpaşa Bulvarı, the **Agora**

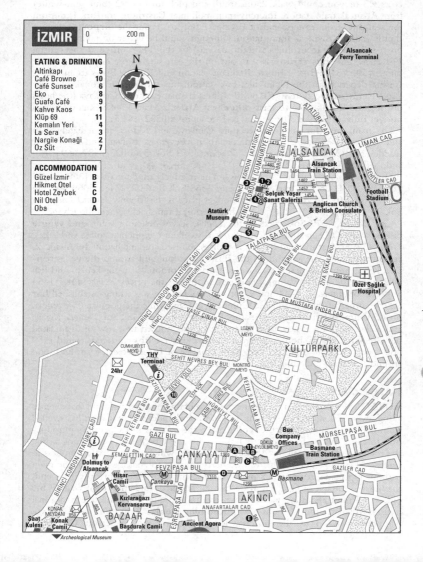

(daily 8.30am–5.30pm; €2), commercial centre of the Classical city, dates back to the early second century BC. Above this is the **Kadifekale**, an irregularly shaped fortress dating from Byzantine and Ottoman times that gives great views over the city from its pine-shaded tea garden (daily 9am–9pm). The less energetic can take a red-and-white city bus #33 from Konak, but it's worth walking up from the agora, threading through once-elegant narrow streets.

### Practicalities

Ferries anchor at the **Alsancak terminal**, 2km north of the centre, where there's also a Turkish Maritime Lines office selling onward boat tickets; a taxi into town costs €5 or you could walk 250m south and pick up bus #2 (blue-and-white) from Alsancak train station. Intercity trains pull in at **Basmane station**, 1km from the seafront at the eastern end of Fevzipaşa Bulvarı. From the **airport**, there's a shuttle train to Alsancak train station, although you'd be better off taking a Havaş bus (which runs according to flight arrivals) to the THY office at the central *Efes Hotel*. The **bus station** is way out on the east side of the city, from where buses #50, #51 and #54 run to Basmane station and Konak. Buses to and from Çeşme depart from the Uçkuyular bus station: bus #169 from Konak. There's also a handy **metro** system (€0.60) that links Basmane station, Çankaya (the hotel district) and Konak. The **tourist office** is at Akdeniz Mah, 1344 Sok 2, off Cumhuriyet Bulvari (daily 8.30am–noon & 1–5.30pm; ☎0232/483 5117).

The main areas for budget **hotels** are Çankaya and Akinci, immediately west and southwest of Basmane station, or around Fevzipaşa Bulvarı and Anafartalar Caddesi. In Çankaya, there's *Hotel Zeybek*, 1368 Sok 5 (☎0232/489 6694; ❷), and *Nil Otel*, Fevzipaşa Bul 155 (☎0232/483 5228; ❷), with TV and air-con, though rooms at the front can be noisy. The relatively modern *Oba*, 1369 Sok 27 (☎0232/441 9605; ❷), and *Güzel Izmir*, 1368 Sok 8 (☎0232/483 5069; ❷), are also worth a try. In Akinci, the best budget place is the friendly *Hikmet Otel*, 945 Sok 25 (☎0232/484 2672; ❶), in a characterful, if ramshackle, neighbourhood.

*Café Browne*, 1379 Sok, next to the *Hilton*, serves delicious soups and **veggie** dishes, while *Oz Süt*, Atatürk Cad 180, has excellent continental coffee and cakes. *Guafe Café* at Atatürk Cad 216, is a well-established student haunt. In Alsancak, **restaurants** and bars abound on the Birinci Kordon, and around the pedestrianized Kıbrıs Şehit Caddesi – try *La Sera*, Birinci Kordon 190a, for kebabs and fish plus live music in the evenings. For seafood, there's the pricey *Kemal' ın Yeri*, 1453 Sok 20a; or *Altınkapı*, 1444 Sok 9, for its *inegöl kofte*. *Eko* is a long-established **bar** on the corner of Pilevne Bul and Cumhuriyet Cad, while the popular *Café Sunset*, on Ali Çetinkaya, lives up to its name. Further along on 1482 Sok, *Nargile Konağı* and *Kahve Kaos* are inexpensive student hangouts housed in a row of dilapidated old Greek merchants' houses. There are several dance **clubs** clustered around 1459 Sok, or try *Klüp 69* on 1367 Sok 5. A number of **Internet** cafés can be found around Alsancak, including Internet House, 1378 Sok 26b.

## Kuşadası

**KUŞADASI** is Turkey's most bloated resort, a brash coastal playground that extends along several kilometres of seafront. In just three decades its population has swelled from 6000 to around 50,000. Unfortunately, the town is many people's introduction to the country: ferry services link it with the Greek island of Sámos, while the resort is a port of call for Aegean cruise ships, which disgorge vast numbers in summer. Liman Caddesi runs from the ferry port up to Atatürk Bulvarı, the main harbour esplanade, from which pedestrianized Barbaros Hayrettin Bulvarı ascends the hill. To the left of here, the **Kale** district, huddled inside the town walls, is the oldest and most appealing part of town, with a mosque and some fine traditional houses. Kuşadası's most famous beach, **Kadınlar Denizi**, 3km southwest of town, is a popular strand, usually too crowded for its own good in season. **Güvercin**

**island**, closer to the centre, is mostly landscaped terraces dotted with tea gardens and snack bars. For the closest sandy beach, head 500m further south, just before **Yılancı Burnu**, or alternatively try **Tusan** beach, 7km north of town, served by all Kuşadası–Selçuk *dolmuşes*, as well as more frequent ones labelled *Şehir İçi*. Much the best beach in the area is **Pamucak**, at the mouth of the Küçük Menderes River, 15km north, an exposed 4km stretch of sand that is as yet little developed; in season it's served by regular *dolmuşes* from both Kuşadası and Selçuk.

The **tourist office** (Mon–Fri 8am–6pm; summer also Sat & Sun; ☎0256/614 1103) is right by the ferry port. The combined **dolmuş** and long-distance **bus station** is about 2km out, past the end of Kahramanlar Caddesi on the ring road to Söke, while the *dolmuş* stop is closer to the centre on Adnan Menderes Bulvarı. **Ferries to Samos** (€25 single, €30 day return, €50 open return) are subject to demand, with no scheduled services in winter: Diana on Kıbrıs Cad (☎0256/614 3859) runs up to two boats daily in summer, with an extra Turkish boat, *Sultan*, in the mornings, operated by Azim, on Liman Cad, Yayla Pasajı (☎0256/614 1553).

There's plenty of **accommodation**, though some hotels and *pansiyons*, especially in areas favoured by backpackers, are used by prostitutes and their pimps. Most of the good *pansiyons*, as well as some to be avoided, are just south of the town centre, uphill from Barbaros Hayrettin Bulvarı. *Golden Bed* on Aslanlar Cad, Uğurlu Çıkmazı 4 (☎0256/614 8708, Ⓦwww.kusadasihotels.com/goldenbed; ❷), is the best value with characterful en-suite rooms. *Sezgin Hotel* at Aslanlar Cad 68 (☎0256/614 4225, Ⓦwww.sezginhotel.com; ❶) has comfortable en-suite rooms and a swimming pool, while lively *Sammy's Palace*, Kıbriş Cad 14 (☎0256/612 2588, Ⓦwww.sammystravel.com; ❷), is firmly on the ANZAC circuit. Up on the hill *Stella Hostel* on Bezirgan Sok 44, (☎0256/614 1632, wwww.stellahostel.com; dorms €9, rooms ❷), has presentable en-suite rooms with private balconies and a roof bar.

For **food**, there are a couple of long-established places on Cephane Sok in the Kale district: *Öz Urfa* has excellent-value *lahmacun* and *pide*, while *Avlu* serves a wide range of kebab and steam-tray food in an outdoor courtyard. If you want to eat by the water without emptying your wallet, the *Holiday Inn*, along Kahramanlar Caddesi, serves great-value dishes from eastern Turkey. The numerous **bars** on Barlar Sok are frankly not worth the effort – *Alize*, on Karagöz Sok 7, is better, and popular with young locals after live music. **Internet** access is at m@ilhouse, opposite the Kale Camii on Barbarosh Bul.

# Selçuk

**SELÇUK** has been catapulted into the limelight of premier-league tourism by its proximity to the ruins of Ephesus. The flavour of tourism here, though, is different from that at nearby Kuşadası, its location and ecclesiastical connections making it a haven for a disparate mix of backpackers and pilgrims from every corner of the globe, with Pamucak beach easily accessible by a short *dolmuş* ride. **Ayasoluk hill** (daily 8.30am–5.30pm; €2.50), the traditional burial place of St John the Evangelist, who died here around 100 AD, boasts the remains of a basilica built by Justinian that was one of the largest Byzantine churches in existence; various colonnades and walls have been re-erected, giving a hint of the building's magnificence. The tomb of the evangelist is marked by a slab at the former site of the altar; beside the nave is the baptistry, where religious tourists pose in the act of dunking their heads for the camera. Just behind the tourist office, the Efes **Archeological Museum** (Tues–Sun 8.30am–5.30pm; €2.50) has galleries of finds from Ephesus, while beyond the museum, 600m along the road toward Ephesus, are the scanty remains of the **Artemision** or sanctuary of Artemis. This massive Hellenistic structure was considered one of the Seven Wonders of the Ancient World, though this is hard to believe today. Some 9km southwest of Selçuk lies **Meryemana** (daily dawn–dusk; €6), a tiny Greek chapel (Mass, summer daily 7.15am, Sun also 10.30am) where some Orthodox theologians believe the Virgin Mary passed her last years, having travelled to the region with St John the Evangelist. Evidence of Mary's residence is somewhat circumstantial but that doesn't stop coach tours to Ephesus making the detour.

At the base of the castle hill in town, a pedestrian precinct leads east to the **train station**. Following the main highway a bit further south brings you to the **bus** and **dolmuş** terminal, opposite which is the friendly **tourist office** (daily 8.30am–noon & 1–5.30pm; winter closed Sat & Sun; ☎0232/892 6945). Most **pansiyons and hotels** will pick you up from the bus station if you call on arrival, and many arrange free lifts to Ephesus and other local sights. *Homeros Pansiyon*, Asmalı Sok 17 (☎0232/892 3995; ❷), has wonderful rooms crammed with local fleamarket finds, while *Barım Pansiyon*, Turgut Reis Sok 34 (☎0232/892 6923; ❷), is also highly recommended, with good doubles in a rambling, quirky old house. The large *Jimmy's Place,* Atatürk Mah, 1016 Sok 19 (☎0232/892 7558, ✆www.jimmysplaceephesus .com; dorms €5, rooms ❶), has Internet access, a cosy restaurant and the only swimming pool in town. The antique-strewn *Nazhan*, St Jean Cad 2 (☎0232/892 8731; ❸), is more upmarket but still good value. Classier still is the beautifully furnished *Nilya*, Atatürk Mah, 1051 Sok 7 (☎0232/892 9081, ✉nilya_ephesus@hotmail.com; ❹), which has splendid views over the Artemision. Selçuk's **campsite**, *Garden* (☎0232/892 2489), lies 300m beyond the Isa Bey mosque.

Along the vine-covered 1006 Sokak are a number of good-value **restaurants** including *Okulmuş* and *Okumuzlar Pide*. Alternatively, there's the cheap and unpretentious *Sirin*, Sieburg Cad 17/C. *Natural Pastanesi*, 1005 Sok 13/b, serves a wide selection of cakes and pastries, while the bar-bistro *Aloa Vera*, Cengiz Topel 18, is good for lunch or an evening drink. For further nocturnal activities, 1005 Sokak has a number of small **bars** with outdoor seating, including the long-established *Bar Ba* and *Casa Café*. Cheap **Internet** facilities are at NetHouse, Sieburg Cad 4b. The **hamam** (Sat–Thurs 7am–11pm; Friday women only; full treatment €9, plus small tip for masseur), next to the main police station, offers a cheap introduction to a good Turkish scrub and massage.

To stay outside Selçuk in the countryside, take one of the hourly minibuses to **ŞIRINCE**, a 600-year-old Greek stone village whose wine-making tradition has been continued by Muslim Turks who settled here in the 1920s. You can sleep overnight in one of the beautifully restored village houses. The friendly and accommodating *Şirince Pansiyon* (☎0232/898 3163; ❹) is wonderfully atmospheric, and run by a friendly retired engineer.

# Ephesus

With the exception of Pompeii, **EPHESUS** (Efes in Turkish) is the largest and best-preserved ancient city around the Mediterranean. Not surprisingly, the ruins are busy in summer, although with a little planning it's possible to tour the site in relative peace. Certainly, it's a place you should not miss. You'll need at least three partly shady hours, and a water bottle. Originally situated close to a temple devoted to the goddess Artemis, Ephesus' location by a fine harbour was the secret of its success in ancient times, eventually making it the wealthy capital of Roman Asia, ornamented with magnificent public buildings. During the Byzantine era the city went into decline, owing to the abandoning of Artemis worship, Arab raids, and (worst of all) the final silting up of the harbour, leading the population to move to the nearby hill crowned by the tomb and church of St John, future nucleus of the town of Selçuk.

Approaching from Kuşadası, get the *dolmuş* to drop you at the *Tusan Motel* junction, 1km from the gate. From Selçuk, it's a 3km walk. In the centre of the **site** (daily 8am–6pm; €9) is the **Arcadian Way**, which was once lined with hundreds of shops and illuminated at night. The nearby **theatre** has been partly restored to allow its use for open-air concerts and occasional summer festivals; it's worth the climb to the top for the views over the surrounding countryside. **Marble Street** passes the main **agora**, and a **Temple of Serapis** where the city's Egyptian merchants would have worshipped. About halfway along is a footprint, a female head and a heart etched into the rock – an alleged signpost for a brothel. On the side of the terraced hill, the **Terrace Houses** were once the preserve of the rich: currently under excavation, they are due to open to the public in early 2006. Across the intersection looms the **Library of Celsus**, erected by the consul Gaius Julius Aquila between 110 and 135 AD as a memorial to his father, Celsus Polemaeanus. The elegant, two-storey facade was fitted with niches for statues of the four personified intellectual virtues; today they are filled with copies (the originals are in Vienna). Just uphill, a Byzantine fountain looks across the Street of the Curetes to the **public latrines**, a favourite with visitors. Continuing along, you'll come to the **Temple of Hadrian**, behind which sprawl the **Baths of Scholastica**, named after a fifth-century Byzantine woman whose headless statue adorns the entrance. On the far side of the street from the Hadrian shrine lies a huge pattern **mosaic**, which once fronted a series of shops. Further up Street of the Curetes you pass the **Temple of Domitian** – the lower floor of which houses a mildly interesting **Museum of Inscriptions** – on the way to the large, overgrown **upper agora**, fringed by a colonnade to the north, and a restored *odeion* and *prytaneum* or civic office.

# Bodrum

In the eyes of its devotees, **BODRUM** – ancient Halicarnassos – with its white-washed houses and subtropical gardens, is the most attractive Turkish resort, a quality outfit in comparison to its upstart Aegean rivals. And it is a pleasant town in most senses, despite having no real beach, although development has proceeded apace over the last couple of decades. The centrepiece is the **Castle of St Peter** (Tues–Sun 8.30am–noon & 1–5.30pm; €6), built by the Knights of St John over a Selçuk fortress between 1437 and 1522. Inside, the various towers house a **Museum of Underwater Archeology**, which includes coin and jewellery rooms, Classical and Hellenistic statuary, and Byzantine relics retrieved from two wrecks, alongside a diorama explaining the salvage techniques. The **Carian princess hall** (Tues–Fri 10am–noon & 2–4pm; €2.50 extra) displays the skeleton and sarcophagus of a fourth-century BC noblewoman unearthed in 1989. There is also the **Glass Wreck Hall** (Tues–Fri 10am–noon & 2–4pm; €2.50 extra) containing the wreck and cargo of an ancient Byzantine ship, which sank near Marmaris. Immediately north of the castle lies the **bazaar**, from where you can stroll up Türkkuyusu Caddesi and turn left to the town's other main sight, the **Mausoleum** (daily 8am–5pm; €2.50). This is the burial place of Mausolus, who ruled Halicarnassos in the fourth century BC, greatly increasing its power and wealth, although the bulk of his tomb (from which we derive the word "mausoleum") is now in London's British Museum. The town's ancient **amphitheatre** (Tues–Sun 8.30am–noon & 1–5.30pm; €2.50), just above the main highway to the north, was begun by Mausolus and was modified in the Roman era; it's used during the annual September festival.

**Ferries** dock at the jetty west of the castle, close to the **tourist office** on Iskele Meydanı (Mon–Fri 8.30am–5.30pm; summer also Sat & Sun). The **bus station** is 500m up Cevat Şakir Caddesi, which divides the town roughly in two. Bodrum Ferryboat Association (☎0252/316 0882) run **ferries to Kos** (€23 one way, €23 day return, €45 open return), as well as domestic services to Datça, while Bodrum Express Lines (☎0252/316 1087) handle **hydrofoils to Kos** (€23 one way, €23 day return), **Rhodes** (€45 one way, €50 day return, €100 open return) and domestic services to Marmaris. There's a port tax (€10), payable on arrival in Greece if you're not returning the same day. Some of the cheapest **accommodation** is southeast of the bus station in Kumbahçe and either side of Türkkuyusu Cad: *Dönen*, Türkkuyusu Cad 21 (☎0252/316 4017; ❷), is very clean and all rooms have a homely touch, while *Sevin*, Türkkuyusu Cad 5 (☎0252/316 7682; ❷), is well run with a pleasant shady garden and restaurant. Alternatively, there's the new *Bodrum Backpackers*, Ataturk Cad 31b (☎0252/316 1564; dorms €9, rooms ❷), aimed at the English party crowd. West of the centre opposite the marina, *Bahçeli Ağar Aile*, Neyzen Tevfik Cad 1402, Sok 4 (☎0252/316 1648; **❷**), is a family-run place in a quiet neighbourhood. *Dolmuşes* from the bus station head to nearby Akyarlar, where you'll find the best sandy beach around, some quiet *pansiyons* and restaurants, and a **campsite**.

**Eating out** in Bodrum is pricey: the best of the budget places is *Nazik Ana*, on Eski Hukumet Sok 7, which serves traditional Turkish cuisine in a vine-covered restaurant, while *Gemibaşi*, opposite the yacht harbour, on the corner of Firkayten Sok and Neyzen Tevfik, is good for simple meat or fish dishes. The walled *Secret Garden*, on Sanat Okullu Cad 1019 Sok, makes for a good romantic splurge. Dr Alim Bey Caddesi is lined with seafront restaurants and cafés: both *Seagul* and *Moonlight* have tables on the sand. At night head to Cumhuriyet Caddesi, where *Roka* at no. 100 has an upmarket rooftop **bar** with great views; *Café del Mar* at no. 170 has a small **club** upstairs playing hard house; and *Halikarnas*, at the eastern end, is the Aegean's best-known club. **Internet** access is at Hakim's Internet on Atatürk Caddesi.

## Marmaris

**MARMARIS** rivals Kuşadası as the largest and most developed Aegean resort – there is little left of the sleepy fishing village that it was a mere two decades ago. Its huge marina and proximity to Dalaman airport mean that tourists pour in more or less nonstop during the warmer months. According to legend, the place was named when Süleyman the Magnificent, not finding the castle here to his liking, was heard to mutter *Miman as* ("Hang the architect") – a command which should perhaps still apply to the designers of the seemingly endless high-rises. Ulusal Egemenlik Bulvarı cuts Marmaris in half, and the maze of narrow streets east of it is home to most things of interest. The **Kaleiçi** district, the warren of streets at the base of the tiny castle, offers a pleasant wander, and the **castle museum** (Tues–Sun 8am–noon & 1–5.30pm; €1) has a worthwhile archeology and ethnography collection.

From the **bus station**, 2km east of the centre on the Muğla road, pick up a *dolmuş* to take you into town. Many of the bus companies also offer a free transfer minibus to the centre. The **ferry** dock abuts Iskele Meydanı, on one side of which stands the helpful **tourist office** (Mon–Fri 8.30am–noon & 1–5/7pm; summer also Sat & Sun). **Ferries to Rhodes** (€40 one way, €40 day return, €70 open return) run daily in high season, weekly in winter. Agents include Yeşil Marmaris, Barbaros Cad 13 (☎0252/412 2290), and Engin Turizm, 3rd floor, G. Mustafa Cad 16 (☎0252/412 6944).

Package tourism ensures that **hotels** here are expensive, and welcoming *pansiyons* few and far between, but the tourist office is tuned in to the needs of backpackers and can help out. The cheapest option is the *Interyouth Hostel* at Tepe Mahallesi 42, Sok 45, in the bazaar close to the Atatürk statue (☎0252/412 3687, ✉interyouth@turk.net; dorms €6, rooms **❷**), with a lively rooftop café, Internet access and a competitively priced travel service. Behind the huge Tansaş shopping centre is the *Nadir* (☎0252/412 1167; **❷**), which has en-suite rooms with air-conditioning. Another good budget *pansiyon* is the *Yeşim*, west of the centre towards Uzunyalı beach at Atatürk Cad 60, Sok 3 (☎0252/412 3001; **❶**). More upmarket, but still great value, is the *Marina* motel (☎0252/412 6598, ⊛www.marmaris marinahotel.com; **❸**), which has clean en-suite rooms and a breakfast terrace. The fabulous *Kırçiçeği* on Kübilay Alpagün Caddesi, behind the bazaar, offers excellent traditional Turkish **food** at reasonable prices; while Barbaros Caddesi is lined with quality restaurants, such as *Caria*, which serves a good range of *meze*. For **drinking**, try one of the many bars along the nearby Hacı Mustafa Sokağl, such as *Scorpios Bar*, or head up the castle hill to *Panorama*, with great views.

## Pamukkale and Hierapolis

The rock formations of **PAMUKKALE** (literally "Cotton Castle"), 140km northeast of Marmaris, are the most-visited attraction in this part of Turkey, a series of white terraces saturated with dissolved calcium bicarbonate, bubbling up from the feet of the Çal Dağı mountains beyond. As the water surges over the edge of the plateau and cools, carbon dioxide is given off and calcium carbonate precipitated as hard chalk or travertine. The spring emerges in what was once the ancient city of Hierapolis, the ruins of which would merit a stop even if they weren't coupled with the natural phenomenon. The **travertine terraces** (daily 24hr; €3) are deservedly the first item on most visitors' agendas, but you should bear in mind the fragility of this natural phenomenon. Nowadays most of the pools are very shallow and closed off, with tourists confined to walking on specially marked routes, though this is, thankfully, having a positive effect, as the travertines slowly return to their former pristine whiteness, enhanced by night-time **illumination** (8–11pm). Up on the plateau is what is spuriously billed as the **sacred pool** (daily 8am–8pm; €11) of the ancients, open for bathing in the 35°C mineral water. In reality, though, it's little more than a few big lumps of carved marble submerged in a concrete swimming pool.

The archeological zone of **HIERAPOLIS** lies west of the village of Pamukkale Köyü, via a narrow road winding up past the *Turism Motel*. Its main features include a **Temple of Apollo** and the adjacent **Plutonium** – the latter a cavern emitting a toxic mixture of sulphur dioxide and carbon dioxide, capable of killing man and beast alike. There's also a restored **Roman theatre** dating from the second century AD, with most of the stage buildings and their elaborate reliefs intact. Arguably the most interesting part of the city, though, is the **colonnaded street** which once extended for almost 1km, terminating in monumental portals a few paces outside the walls – of which only the most northerly, a triple arch, still stands. Just south of the arch is the elaborate tomb of Flavius Zeuxis – the first of more than a thousand tombs constituting the **necropolis**, and the largest in Asia Minor. At the summit of the terraces, near the car park is the **tourist office** (April–Oct Mon–Sat 8am–noon & 1–5.30pm; ☎0258/272 2077). Opposite is the **museum** (Tues–Sun 9am–12.30pm & 1.30–5.30pm; €1.50), housed in the restored, second-century baths, but the collection of statuary, sarcophagi and masonry fragments is disappointing.

There are more than forty **pansiyons** in the village of **PAMUKKALE KÖYÜ**, though touts at the bus stand can be particularly aggressive. One of the best and friendliest is the air-conditioned *Koray* (☎0258/272 2222; ❷), which has a pleasant garden, buffet meals and TV in every room. Alternatively, try *Meltem Guest House*, Kuzey Sok 9 (☎0258/272 3134; dorms €7, doubles ❷), or the family-owned *Kervanseray*, up the hill (☎0258/272 2209, ✉kervanseray2@superonline.com.tr; ❷), both with en-suite doubles and Internet access. A little out of town is the rock-bottom cheapie *Allgau* (☎0258/272 2250; ❶), with basic doubles, good **food**, tent space and smarter doubles (❷) in an attached new hotel. Other than here, you are probably best off eating at your *pansiyon*.

# Turkey's Mediterranean coast

The first stretch of Turkey's **Mediterranean coast**, dominated by the Akdağ and Bey mountain ranges of the Taurus chain and known as the "**Turquoise Coast**", is its most popular, famed for its pine-studded shore, minor ruins and beautiful scenery. Most of this is connected by Highway 400, which winds precipitously above the sea from Marmaris to Antalya. In the west, **Fethiye**, along with the nearby lagoon of **Ölüdeniz**, give good access to the pick of the region's Lycian ruins, such as **Xanthos**. The scenery becomes increasingly spectacular as you head towards the site of **Olympos**, and **Kaş**, which offers great scuba-diving, before reaching the port and major city of **Antalya**.

# Fethiye and around

**FETHIYE** is well sited for access to some of the region's ancient sites, many of which date from the time when this area was the independent kingdom of Lycia. The best beaches, around the Ölüdeniz lagoon, are now much too crowded for comfort, but Fethiye is still a market town and has been able to spread to accommodate increased tourist traffic. Fethiye itself occupies the site of the Lycian city of **Telmessos**, little of which remains other than the impressive ancient theatre, which was only unearthed in 1992, and a number of Lycian rock tombs on the hillside above the bus station. You can also visit the remains of the medieval fortress, on the hillside behind the harbour area of town. In the centre of town, off Atatürk Caddesi, the small **museum** (Tues–Sun 8.30am–5.30pm; €2.50) has some fascinating exhibits from local sites and a good ethnographic section.

One of the most dramatic sights in the area is the ghost village of **KAYA KÖYÜ** (Levissi), 7km out of town, served by *dolmuşes* from the old bus station. The village was abandoned in 1923, when its Anatolian-Greek population was relocated, and all you see now is a hillside covered with more than two thousand ruined cottages and an attractive basilica. **Ölüdeniz** is about two hours on foot from Kaya Köyü – through the village, over the hill and down to the lagoon – or a *dolmuş* ride from Fethiye. The warm waters of this lagoon make for pleasant swimming, if you don't mind paying the small entrance fee, although the crowds can reach saturation level in high season – in which case the nearby beaches of Belceğiz and Kidrak are better bets. Ölüdeniz is also the starting point for the **Lycian Way** trekking route, which starts from near the *Montana Holiday Village* on the Fethiye–Ölüdeniz road and winds along the coast almost as far as Antalya.

East of Fethiye lies the heartland of **ancient Lycia**, home to a number of important archeological sites. The closest is the **LETOÖN**, accessible by *dolmuş* from Fethiye to Kumluova, the site lying 4km off the main highway. The Letoön (daily 7am–7.30pm; €2.50) was the official sanctuary of the Lycian Federation, and the extensive remains bear witness to its importance. The low ruins of three **temples** occupy the centre of the site, and there is also a large, well-preserved **theatre**, entered through a vaulted passage. On the other side of the valley, the remains of the hilltop city of **XANTHOS** are perhaps the most fascinating of the Lycian sites, though the most important relic discovered at the site, the fourth-century Nereid Monument, is now in the British Museum. Buses between Fethiye and Patara drop you off in Kanak, from where it's a ten-minute walk up to the **ruins** (daily 7am–7.30pm; €2.50). West of the car park are the acropolis, agora and a Roman theatre, beside which are two Lycian tombs – the so-called **Harpy Tomb**, decorated with pairs of bird-woman figures carrying children in their arms, and a **sarcophagus** standing on a pillar tomb. Northeast of the agora looms a structure known popularly as the **Xanthian obelisk** – in fact the remains of a pillar tomb covered on all four sides by the longest-known Lycian inscription.

## Practicalities

Fethiye's **bus station** is 2km east of the centre; *dolmuşes* to and from Ölüdeniz, Çalış beach and Kaya Köyü use the old station, east of the central market. The **tourist office** is close to the theatre, near the harbour at Iskele Meydanı 1 (daily 8.30am–5.30/7.30pm; ☎0252/612 1527). BigBackpackers Yachting, Zafer Cad 1 (☎0242/612 7834, ⊛www.guletcruiseturkey.com), can organize four-day **boat trips** in a traditional Turkish *gulet* from Fethiye to Olympos (Demre) for around €140 per person.

Most of Fethiye's budget **hotels** are concentrated around the quieter suburb of Karagözler, overlooking the marina to the west: there are direct *dolmuşes* here from the bus station (€0.50), though some hotels run a complimentary shuttle service. The highly organized, family-run *Ferah Pension*, Orta Yol 21 (☎0252/614 2816, ⊛www.ferahpension.com; dorms €6, rooms ❷), has good facilities and stunning views, while a little futher west, *Irem*, Fevzi Çakmak Cad 45 (℡0252/614 3985; ❷), has clean doubles with sea views. The *Ideal Pension*, Zafer Cad 1 (℡0252/614 1981, ⓦwww.idealpension.net; dorms €7, rooms ❷), is popular with backpackers, and has a great terrace and Internet access; or try the good-value, friendly *Alish* above the yacht harbour on Birinci Karagözler (℡0252/612 3518; dorms €9, rooms ❶). One of the best **campsites** is the *Ölüdeniz*, with its own beach and restaurant; it's just past the entrance to Ölüdeniz lagoon on the left.

For **meals**, try *Çoban*, Sok 37, with outdoor tables, good *çorba* and other traditional Turkish dishes, or the more touristy *Meğri*, Likya Sok, for excellent *pide*. Paspartu Sokak is lined with **bars**, the best of which is the *Ottoman Dance Bar* in an Ottoman house, or try the trendy, yachting-themed *4 Corners* where Eski Camii meets Atatürk Caddesi. The cheapest **Internet** access is at Trend, Kayaiş Hani 6.

## Kaş

**KAŞ** sprang to prominence after about 1850, when it established itself as a Greek fishing and timber port. It is beautifully located, nestled in a small curving bay below rocky cliffs – the name itself means "eyebrow" or "something curved". But what was once a sleepy fishing village is fast becoming an adventure-sports centre for backpackers, with nightlife to match, and provides a handy base for paragliding, mountain biking and some of the cheapest and best **scuba-diving** in Turkey. Many of the *pansiyons* listed below can organize such activities, or try one of the numerous operators in town, such as the professionally run Bougainville (℡0242/836 3737, ⓦwww.bougainville-turkey.com) or Sun Diving (℡0242/836 2637).

Scattered around the streets and to the west are the remains of ancient **Antiphellos**, one of the few Lycian cities to bear a Greek name, small in number but nevertheless impressive. Five hundred metres west of town lies an almost complete Hellenistic theatre, behind which is a unique Doric tomb named *Kesme Mezar*, again almost completely intact. Kaş is also well situated for the nearby ruins of **Kekova** and **Patara**.

All **buses** and *dolmuşes* arrive at the small bus station just north of the town at the top of Elmalı Caddesi. The **tourist office** is in the town square at Cumhuriyet Maydanı 5 (April–Oct Mon–Fri 8.30am–7pm, Sat & Sun 10am–7pm; ℡0242/836 1238). Most of the budget **accommodation** is situated a five-minute walk from the bus station near the mosque. *Ateş*, Yeni Cami Sok 3 (℡0242/836 1393; dorms €7, doubles ❷), is a backpacker favourite, with a popular rooftop bar, good breakfasts and an attached quality hotel (❸). Alternatively, there's the nearby *Meltem*, along a sidestreet off Elmalı Caddesi (℡0242/836 1055; ❷), with large rooms and great views, or the good-value *Ani* at Resep Bilgin Cad 12 (℡0242/836 1791; ❷).

For **restaurants**, *Sofra* on Gürsoy Sok serves good-quality, excellent-value Turkish dishes, while *Seçkin*, opposite the Marina Mosque, is a popular local cheapie. Most of the **bars** are clustered to the east of town, including the popular *Mavi*, on the waterfront, with a small dance club, *Deep Bar*, above. Another favourite, packed most weekends, is *Red Point*, tucked away on Süleyman Topçu Sok. Reliable **Internet** access can be found at NetHouse and Magicom on Çukurbaulı Caddesi.

## Olympos and Çıralı

There's another Lycian site, **OLYMPOS**, 50km before Antalya, located on a beautiful sandy bay and the banks of a largely dry river. It's an idyllic location with a small village that is now firmly on the backpacker circuit. The site itself (€1.50 when someone is manning the ticket office) features some recently excavated tombs, the walls of a Byzantine church, and a theatre, most of whose seats have gone. On the north side of the river are more striking ruins, including a well-preserved marble temple entrance. Beyond is a Byzantine bath house with mosaic floors, and a Byzantine canal which would have carried water to the heart of the city. A pleasant 1.5km walk away is the holiday village of **Çıralı.** About an hour's

32

well-marked stroll above the village's citrus groves flickers the dramatic **Chimaera** (open 24hr; €1.50), a series of eternal flames issuing from cracks in the bare rock. The fire has been burning since antiquity, and inspired the Lycians to worship the god Hephaestos (or Vulcan to the Romans). The mountain was also associated with a fire-breathing monster, also known as the Chimaera, with a lion's head, a goat's rear and a snake for a tail.

There are one or two **minibuses** a day from Antalya to Çıralı in season; otherwise you'll have to take a taxi (€10) from the main road. To get directly to Olympos, catch any Kaş–Antalya bus to the minibus stop on the main highway, 8km up from the shore; in season there are hourly minibuses from there to Olympos. Çıralı boasts around forty **pansiyons** catering largely for families, all hidden in the citrus groves behind the beach – but the area is a national park and nesting turtles mean that camping on the beach, and night access in general, is forbidden. Best of the budget options is *Bariş Pansiyon* (☎0212/825 7080; ❷), set around a pretty garden. *Yavuz* (☎0242/825 7021; ❷) is a moderately priced two-storey place tucked inside a grove of poplars. Back along the beach and ranged along the road behind the ruins are a group of backpacker **"tree-house" camps**, pick of the crop being the family-run *Şaban* (☎0242/892 1265, ⓦwww.sabanpansion.com; dorms €8.50, doubles ❶), with excellent homemade food and a friendly, relaxed atmosphere. Towards the main highway the large and well-run *Kadir's* (☎0242/892 1250, ⓦwww.olympostreehouse.com; dorms €9, doubles ❷) has good facilities including an alfresco nightclub. Closer to the beach *Bayram's* (☎0242/892 1243, ⓦwww .bayrams.com; ❷) has tightly packed well-made bungalows, while the small *Sheriff* (☎0242/892 1301, ⓦwww.sheriffolympos.com; ❸) has good-quality bungalows. All of these places are half-board with a variety of huts and Internet access. There are a handful of pleasant beach **restaurants** including *Yavuz* and *Olympos*, or for excellent lunchtime *gözleme* try *Pehlivan*, close to the ticket office. *Orange*, nestled amongst the rocks in a small side valley, is the best of the three bars in the area. Note, too, that there are no **banks** or ATMs in Olympos or Çıralı, so make sure you have enough cash before arriving. Many of the *pansiyons* can accept card payment for accommodation.

## Antalya

**ANTALYA** is blessed with an ideal climate and a stunning setting, and, despite the grim appearance of its concrete sprawl, it's an agreeable place – although the main area of interest for visitors is confined to the relatively small old quarter; its beaches don't rate much consideration. The intersection of Cumhuriyet Caddesi and Sarampol is dominated by the **Yivli Minare** or "Fluted Minaret", erected in the thirteenth century. Downhill from here is the **old harbour**, recently restored and site of the evening promenade. North is the disappointing bazaar, while south, beyond the Saat Kalesi (clock tower), lies **Kaleiçi** or the old town, with every house now a carpet shop, café or *pansiyon*. On the far side, on Atatürk Caddesi, the triple-arched **Hadrian's Gate** recalls a visit by the emperor in 130 AD; while Hesapçı Sokak leads south past the **Kesik Minare** to a number of tea gardens and the **Hıdırlık Kulesi**, indisputably Roman but of ambiguous function – it could have been a lighthouse, bastion or tomb. The one thing you shouldn't miss is the **Archeological Museum** (Tues–Sun 9am–6.30pm; €9), one of the top five archeological collections in the country; it's on the western edge of town at the far end of Kenan Evren Bulvarı, easily reachable by a tram that departs from the clock tower in Kaleiçi. Highlights include an array of Bronze Age urn burials, second-century statuary, an adjoining sarcophagus wing, and a number of mosaics, not to mention an ethnography section with ceramics, household implements, weapons and embroidery.

Antalya's main **bus station** is 8km north of town, although regular *dolmuşes* and city buses run from here to a terminal at the top of Kazım Özalp Caddesi (still known by its old name of Sarampol), which runs for just under 1km down to the clock tower on the fringe of the old town. About 5km west of the centre is the **ferry dock**, connected to the centre by *dolmuş*. The **airport** is 12km northeast; Havaş buses into town depart from the domestic terminal, five minutes' walk from the international terminal, while city-centre-bound *dolmuşes* pass nearby. The main **tourist office** is a fifteen-minute walk west from the clock tower on Cumhuriyet Cad (daily 8am–6/7pm; ☎0242/241 1747). Most travellers stay in the atmospheric old town, where almost every other building is a **pansiyon**. The backpacker favourite *Sabah Pansiyon*, Hesapçı Sok 60a (☎0242/247 5345, ⓦwww .sabahpansiyon.8m.com; dorms €8, doubles ②), is clean and well-run, and the owner speaks good English; book ahead in high season. Another popular option is *White Garden Pansiyon*, Hasapçı Geçidi (☎0242/241 9115; ②), with efficient and pleasant staff. *Antique Pansiyon* at Tuzcular Mah, Paşa Camii Sok 28 (☎0242/242 4615, ⓔantique@ixir.com; ③), is housed in a characterful old Ottoman house, albeit with erratic plumbing, and has an English-speaking owner. There are unparalleled rooftop sea views from both *Keskin 1*, Hadarlak Sok 35 (☎0242/244 0135; ②), with air-conditioning, and the friendly family-run *Senem*, Zeytingeçidi Sok 9 (☎0242/247 1752; ②).

Many Kaleiçi *pansiyons* have their own **restaurants**, with the *Antique Pansiyon* the best for elegant evening dining. The covered pedestrian precinct, Eski Sebzeciler Içi Sokak, is packed with restaurants serving the local speciality *tandır kebap* (mutton roasted in a clay pot). *Gaziantep*, at the edge of the bazaar through the *pasaj* at Ismet Paşa Cad 3, is excellent, or try *Can Can* opposite the plaza cinema for huge, cheap and tasty *durum* kebabs. *The Castle* near Hıdılık Kulesi is popular in the evenings for food and drinks with great views. **Nightlife** is mostly based around the harbour, with the long-running *Rock Bar* on Uzun ÇarşışI a favourite student hangout hosting bands at the weekend. In the warren of streets behind the harbour, the laidback *Gizli Bahçe* bar on Karadaysi Sok 5 is another student favourite, while the nearby *Türkü* is a smart place to hear live Turkish music. Back up the hill near the clock tower, the chic lounge-bar/**club** *Roof*, Tuzcular Uzuncarsi Sok 14, has hard-house dj's most weekends. *Moonlight Café*, on 1291 Sok opposite Hadrian's Gate, has cheap, fast **Internet** access.

# Central Turkey

When the first Turkish nomads arrived in **Anatolia** during the tenth and eleventh centuries, the landscape must have been strongly reminiscent of their Central Asian homeland. The terrain that so pleased the tent-dwelling herdsmen of a thousand years ago, however, has few attractions for modern visitors: monotonous, rolling vistas of stone-strewn grassland, dotted with rocky outcrops, hospitable only to sheep. In winter it can be numbingly cold, while in summer, temperatures can rise to unbear-able levels. It seems appropriate that the heart of original Turkish settlement should be home to the political and social centre of modern Turkey – **Ankara**, a modern European-style capital, symbol of Atatürk's dream of a secular Turkish republic. The south-central part of the country draws more visitors, not least for **Cappadocia** in the far east of the region, where water and wind have created a land of fantastic forms from the soft tufa rock, including forests of cones, table mountains and canyon-like valleys. Further south still, **Konya** is best known as the birthplace of the mystical **Sufi** sect and is a good place to stop over between Cappadocia and the coast.

## Ankara

Modern **ANKARA** is really two cities, a double identity that is due to the break-neck pace at which it has developed since being declared capital of the Turkish

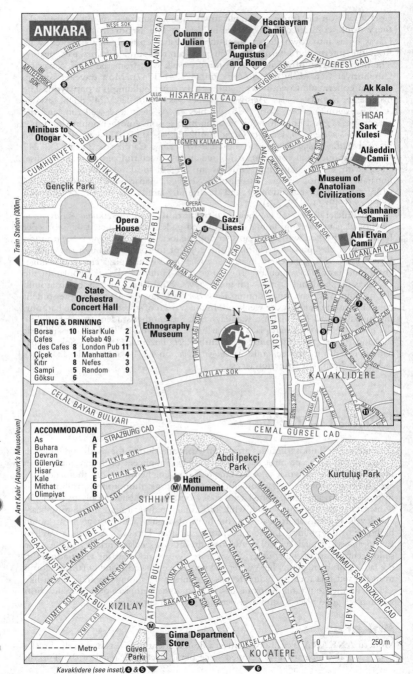

# ANKARA

Hacıbayram Camii

Column of Julian

Temple of Augustus and Rome

NEŞE SOK

SINASI

SOK

ÇANKIRI CAD

RUZGARLI CAD

İBİ MÜTEFERRIKA SOK

BENTDERESİ CAD

HİSARPARKI CAD

ULUS MEYDANI

KEVGİRLİ SOK

Ak Kale

HİSAR

Şark Kulesi

Aläeddin Camii

**Minibus to Otogar**

CUMHURİYET BUL

İSTİKLÂL CAD

ULUS

TEĞMEN KALMAZ CAD

SUSAM SOK

KONYA SOK

IŞIKLAR CAD

ALATEN SOK

KADİFE SOK

Gençlik Parkı

SANAYİ CAD

ÇERKES SOK

ANAFARTALAR CAD

SARAÇLAR SOK

ÇIKRIKÇILAR YOK.

**Museum of Anatolian Civilizations**

**Aslanhane Camii**

**Opera House**

OPERA MEYDANI

**Gazi Lisesi**

ATATÜRK BUL

KOSOVA SOK

DERMAN SOK

DENİZCİLER CAD

AÇIÇEŞME SOK

**Ahi Elvan Camii**

ULUCANLAR CAD

TALATPAŞA BULVARI

**State Orchestra Concert Hall**

TÖRK OCAĞI SOK

**Ethnography Museum**

HASIR CILAR SOK

N

HESTEPE SOK

TUNUS CAD

KENNEDY CAD

ESAT CAD

BOKLUM CAD

BÜLTEN SOK

BÜYÜK ELÇİ SOK

KONYA SOK

BİLLUR SOK

ATATÜRK BUL

## EATING & DRINKING

| | | | |
|---|---|---|---|
| Borsa | **10** | Hisar Kule | **2** |
| Cafes | | Kebab 49 | **7** |
| des Cafes | **8** | London Pub | **11** |
| Çiçek | **1** | Manhattan | **4** |
| Kıtır | **8** | Nefes | **3** |
| Sampi | **5** | Random | **9** |
| Göksu | **6** | | |

KAVAKLIDERE

KIZILAY SOK

CELÂL BAYAR BULVARI

CEMAL GÜRSEL CAD

STRAZBURG CAD

ILKIZ SOK

CİHAN SOK

Abdi İpekçi Park

TUNA CAD

**Kurtuluş Park**

## ACCOMMODATION

| | |
|---|---|
| As | **A** |
| Buhara | **F** |
| Devran | **H** |
| Güleryüz | **D** |
| Hisar | **C** |
| Kale | **E** |
| Mithat | **G** |
| Olimpiyat | **B** |

HANIMELİ SOK

SIHHIYE

**Hatti Monument**

GAZİ-MUSTAFA-KEMAL-BUL.

NECATİBEY CAD

ÇAKMAK SOK

İZMİR CAD

FEVZİ ÇAKMAK SOK

MENEKŞE SOK

SÜMER SOK

İZMİR CAD

KIZILAY

MARMARA SOK

HALK SOK

TUNA CAD

SAĞLIK SOK

MİTHAT PAŞA CAD

ADAKALE SOK

BAYINDIR SOK

SAKARYA CAD

İNKILAP SOK

ATAÇ SOK

ZİYA-GÖKALP-CAD.

LİBYA CAD

UMUT SOK

SELVİ SOK

MAHMUT ESAT BOZKURT CAD

ÇALDIRAN SOK

LİBYA CAD

**Gima Department Store**

Güven Parkı

KOCATEPE

YÜKSEL CAD

--- Metro

0        250 m

◄ Train Station (300m)

◄ Anıt Kabir (Atatürk's Mausoleum)

Kavaklıdere (see inset), ❹ & ❺ ▼        ▼❻

**32**

Republic in 1923. Until then Ankara – known as Angora – had been a small provincial city, famous chiefly for the production of soft goat's wool. This city still exists, in and around the old citadel that was the site of the original settlement. The other Ankara is the modern metropolis that has grown up around a carefully planned attempt to create a seat of government worthy of a modern, Western-looking state. It's worth visiting just to see how successful this has been, although there's not much else to the place, and the nightlife, museums and other sights need only detain you for a day or two at most.

## Arrival, information and accommodation

Ankara's Esenboğa **airport** is 33km north of town. Havaş buses (€4) meet incoming Turkish Airlines flights; a taxi will set you back €30. The **bus station** lies 5km to the southwest; some minibuses run service minibuses to the centre, otherwise take a *dolmuş* or the **Ankaray** rapid transit system (€0.50) to Kızılay and change onto the **metro** (same ticket) for Ulus, where most of the budget hotels are located. The **train station** is at the corner of Talat Paşa Caddesi and Cumhuriyet Bulvarı, from where frequent buses run to Kızılay and Ulus. As well as the Ankaray and metro there are plenty of **buses** running the length of the main Atatürk Bulvarı. Buy bus tickets in advance from kiosks next to the main bus stops (it's a good idea to stock up on tickets, as some areas have no kiosks). There's a **tourist office** across from the train station at Gazi Mustafa Kemal Bulvarı 121, just outside Maletepe station on the Ankaray (Mon–Fri 9am–5pm, Sat & Sun 10am–5pm; winter closed Sun; ☎0312/231 5572). Most of the cheaper **hotels** are in the streets east of Atatürk Bulvarı between Ulus and Opera Meydanı; there are a few more upmarket places north of Ulus, and on and around Çankırı Caddesi, and further options banded along Gazi Mustafa Kemal Bulvarı in Maltepe and on Atatürk Bulvarı south of Kızılay, with prices increasing as you move south.

### Hotels

**As** Rüzgarlı Sok 4, Ulus ☎0312/310 3998. Well-priced, clean and pleasant en-suite rooms with TV. ❸

**Buhara** Sanayi Cad 13, Ulus ☎0312/310 7999. One of the better choices in Ulus, with en-suites and TV. ❸

**Devran** Sanayi Cad, Tavus Sok 8, Ulus ☎0312/311 0485. Best value of the cheaper choices with bright, clean en-suite rooms with TV. ❷

**Güleryüz** Sanayı Cad 37, Ulus. Comfortable, if a little overpriced, en-suite rooms with TV. ❷

**Kale** Anafartalar Cad, Alataş Sok 13, Ulus ☎0312/311 3393. Basic but reasonably clean double rooms with bathrooms and TV; breakfast extra. ❷

**Mithat** Itfaiye Meydanı, Tavus Sok 2, Ulus ☎0312/311 5410, ⊛www.Otelmithat.com.tr. Professionally run, offering singles and doubles with bathrooms,TV, breakfast and plenty of hot water. ❷

**Olimpiyat** Rüzgarlı Eşdost Sok 14, Ulus ☎0312/324 3331. Reasonably priced with good en-suite rooms. ❷

## The City

The city is bisected north–south by **Atatürk Bulvarı**, and everything you need is in easy reach of this broad and busy street. At the northern end, **Ulus Meydanı**, a large square and an important traffic intersection marked by a huge equestrian Atatürk statue, is the best jumping-off point for the old part of the city - a village of narrow cobbled streets and ramshackle wooden houses centring on the **Hisar**, Ankara's old fortress and citadel. Most of what can be seen today dates from Byzantine times, with substantial Selçuk and Ottoman additions. There are tremendous views of the rest of the city from inside, as well as a twelfth-century mosque, the **Alâeddin Camii**. The **Aslanhane Camii** and **Ali Elvan Camii** bazaar areas to the south are more impressive, built by the Selçuks during the thirteenth century. Follow Kadife Sokak from here towards the modern city and you come to the **Museum of Anatolian Civilizations** (Tues–Sun 9am–5.30pm; €6), which boasts an incomparable collection of archeological objects housed in a restored

Ottoman *bedesten*, or covered market. Hittite carving and relief work form the most compelling section of the museum, mostly taken from Carchemish, near the present Syrian border. There are also Neolithic finds from Çatal Höyük, the site of one of Anatolia's oldest settlements and widely regarded as the world's first "city".

North of Ulus Meydanı is what's left of Roman Ankara, namely the **Column of Julian** on Hükümet Meydanı. Close by, the **Hacıbayram Camii**, built in 1400, was erected on the ruins of the **Temple of Augustus and Rome**, built by the Phrygians during the second century BC in honour of Cybele. South down Atatürk Bulvarı, **Gençlik Parkı** was built on the orders of Atatürk to provide a recreational spot for the hard-working citizens of his model metropolis; it features an artificial lake, funfair, cafés and an **Opera House** near the entrance. Further down Atatürk Bulvarı, the **Ethnography Museum** (Tues–Sun 9am–5pm; €1.50) boasts archives of the great man's funeral, as well as a good collection of folk costumes, Ottoman art and Selçuk woodcarving.

Across the main west–east rail line lies **Sıhhıye Meydanı** and the real heart of modern Ankara, which focuses on the large square of Kızılay, the main transport hub of the city. A few streets east rise the four minarets of the **Kocatepe Camii**, a modern mosque built in Ottoman style that ranks as one of the biggest in the world. Beyond lies Turkey's parliament building, a strip of embassies, and the **Presidential Palace** (Çankaya Köşku; guided tours Sun 1.30–5pm; free), Atatürk's Ankara residence, whose grounds are home to the Çankaya Atatürk Museum (same times and ticket). Northeast of here, **Anıt Kabir** is the site of **Atatürk's mausoleum** (daily 9am–4/5pm; free; bus #265 from Ulus and near Tandoğan Ankaray station), at the end of a long colonnaded avenue lined by Hittite lions. It's almost bare inside except for the forty-tonne sarcophagus and the guards. At the southeastern end of the courtyard is a **museum** (Sun 1.30–4.30pm) containing various pieces of Atatürk memorabilia, including a number of Lincoln limousines, which served as his official transport.

### Eating and drinking

Standard *pide* and kebab places can be found on just about every street in Ankara and there's an abundance of good sweet and **cake shops**. Ulus, particularly along Çankırı Caddesi, is the place to look for cheap lunchtime venues, although most night-time eating and drinking takes place in the modern centre around Kızılay, where Sakarya, Selanik and Bayindir sokaks harbour a range of possibilities. Or try south in the well-heeled district of Kavaklıdere, particularly Tunali Hilmi and Bestekar sokaks. Further south still is upmarket Çankaye. Ankara's citizens are proud of the **Opera House** at Opera Meydanı, which is great value: admission is usually €10 or under for lively and well-attended performances of works such as *Madame Butterfly* and *La Bohème*. **Clubs** can be found at *Kashmere* and *Complex*, both on Farabi Sok, Çankaya.

### Cafés and restaurants

**Cafes des Cafes** Tunali Hilmi Cad 83/a, Kavaklıdere. Small trendy café serving decent coffee and pastries but no alcohol. Good weekend breakfasts.

**Çiçek Lokantası** Çankırı Cad 12a, Ulus. One of Ankara's mainstays, serving traditional dishes in regal splendour, albeit at a price.

**Göksu** Bayindir Sok 22, Kavaklıdere. Reasonably priced fish restaurant that's also good for drinks .

**Hisar Kule** On the left inside the entrance to the Kule. One of several old-citadel restaurants in restored houses. Wonderful views from the terrace.

**Kebab 49** Bulten Sok 5, Kavaklıdere. Large, popular kebab restaurant, with a range of traditional dishes at reasonable prices.

**Sampi** Simon Bolivar Cad 40, Çankaya. One of four branches specializing in dishes from the Black Sea coast.

### Bars

**Borsa** Tunali Hilmi Cad 49, Kavaklıdere. Sophisticated older students' bar. Prices change according to the ticker-tape display above the bar.

**Kıtır** Opposite the cinema on Tunali Hilmi Cad, Kavaklıdere. Alternative rock bar with a wide-ranging playlist, packed at the weekends.

**London Pub** Arjantin Cad 40, Kavaklıdere.

Frequented by more affluent students, artists and professionals; busy most weekends.
**Manhattan** Cinnah Cad, Cevre Sok 2, Kavaklıdere. Popular rock venue with live bands and large crowds at the weekends.

**Nefes Bar** Sakarya Cad 25/a, Kızılay. Busy music venue hosting a wide range of artists from reggae to Latin Jazz.
**Random** below *Kıtır* on Tunali Hilmi Cad, Kavaklıdere. Slightly smarter, older and more pricey version of *Kıtır*.

## Listings

**Embassies** Australia, Nenehatun Cad 83, Gaziosmanpaşa ☎ 0312/459 9500; Canada, Cinnah Cad 58, Çankaya ☎ 0312/409 2700; New Zealand, Iran Cad 13/4, Kavaklıdere ☎ 0312/467 9054; UK, Şehit Ersan Cad 46a, Çankaya ☎ 0312/468 6230; US, Atatürk Bul 110, Kavaklıdere ☎ 0312/455 5555.
**Hamams** Karacabey Hamami, Talat Paşa Bul 101 (men 6am–11pm; women 7am–7pm; from €10).

**Hospital** Hacettepe University Medical Faculty, west of Hasırcılar Sok, Sıhhıye ☎ 0312/305 5000.
**Internet** Intek Internet Café, Karanfil Sok 47a, Kızılay; Internet Café, next to PTT, Maltepe.
**Left luggage** At the bus and train stations.
**Post office** Merkez Postahane, on Atatürk Bulvarı, Ulus.

# Cappadocia

A land created by the complex interaction of natural and human forces over vast spans of time, **CAPPADOCIA**, around 150km southeast of Ankara, is initially a disturbing place, the great expanses of bizarrely eroded volcanic rock giving an impression of barrenness. It is in fact an exceedingly fertile region, and one whose weird formations of soft, dusty rock have been adapted over millennia by many cultures, from Hittites to later Christians hiding away from Arab marauders. There are more than a thousand rock-churches in Cappadocia, dating from the earliest days of Christianity to the thirteenth century, and some caves are still inhabited. It's a popular area with tourists, and getting more so, but the crowds are largely confined to a few areas. For a breathtaking perspective on this complex geological wonderland you could splash out on a **hot air balloon** ride: Goreme Balloons (☎0384/341 5662, ⊛www.goremeballoons .com) have offices in Göreme and Ürgüp and fly every morning between April and November.

The best-known sites are located within the triangle delineated by the roads connecting Nevşehir, Avanos and Ürgüp. Within this region are the valleys of fairy **chimneys**, formed when patches of hard lava settled on top of the soft greyish bedrock (composed of compacted volcanic ash); the areas topped by lava chunks resisted erosion, eventually forming fifty-metre-high cones which dot the landscape. Also here are the rock-cut churches of the **Göreme Open-Air Museum**, with their amazing selection of frescoes, and the **Zelve** monastery, a complex of troglodyte dwellings and churches hewn out of the

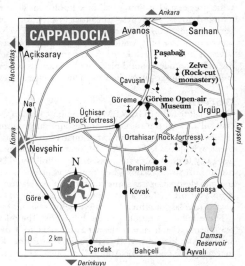

rock. **Göreme** itself and nearby **Ürgüp** both make attractive bases to tour the area, though most public transport comes via the regional centre of **Nevşehir**. Outside the triangle to the south are the underground cities of **Derinkuyu** and **Kaymaklı**, fascinating warrens attesting to the ingenuity of the ancient inhabitants.

## Nevşehir

Though said to be Turkey's richest community, thanks to its abundant grain farming, **NEVŞEHIR**, at the very heart of the region, can hardly be accused of ostentatious wealth. As many of Cappadocia's frequent bus services use the town as a hub, you'll probably find yourself detouring through when travelling between other neighbouring towns. The **Ottoman castle** at the heart of the old city, southwest of the modern centre, is a good landmark. The new city below is divided by two main streets, Atatürk Bulvarı, on which are situated most of the hotels and restaurants, and Lale Caddesi, turning into Gülzehir Caddesi to the north, where you'll find the main **dolmuş station**. The **tourist office** is on Atatürk Bulvarı, on the right as you head downhill towards Ürgüp (daily 8am–6pm; winter closed Sat & Sun; ☏0384/213 3659). **Pansiyons** in Nevşehir are neither as cheap nor as good as elsewhere in Cappadocia: try the good-value *Hotel Viva* (☏0384/213 1326; ❷), or the more upmarket, friendly and clean *Hotel Seven Brothers* (☏0384/213 4979; ❸), just round the corner. The nicest of the **campsites** in the region, the *Koru Mocamp*, is signposted off to the right as you turn from Nevşehir into Üçhisar.

## Derinkuyu and Kaymaklı

Among the most extraordinary phenomena of the Cappadocia region are the remains of a number of **underground settlements**, some of them large enough to have accommodated up to 30,000 people. The cities are thought to date back to Hittite times, though the complexes were later enlarged by Christian communities, who added missionary schools, churches and wine cellars. A total of forty such settlements have been discovered, and the most thoroughly excavated is **DERINKUYU** (daily 8am–5.30pm; €6), 29km from Nevşehir and accessible by *dolmuş*. The city is well lit and the original ventilation system still functions remarkably well, though some of the passages are small and cramped. The excavated area (only a quarter of the total) consists of eight floors and includes stables, wine presses and a dining hall or schoolroom with two long, rock-cut tables, plus living quarters, churches, armouries, a cruciform church, meeting hall and dungeon. Some 10km north of Derinkuyu is **KAYMAKLI** (daily 8am–5.30pm; €6), where only five of its underground levels have been excavated to date. The layout is very similar to Derinkuyu, with networks of streets and small living spaces leading off into underground plazas with various functions, the more obvious of which are stables, smoke-blackened kitchens, storage spaces and wine presses.

## Göreme

The small town of **GÖREME** is the best known of the few remaining Cappadocian villages whose rock-cut houses and fairy chimneys are still inhabited. In the last few years these ancient living quarters have slowly been destroyed by development, which has led to a "Save Göreme" campaign. However, it is still possible to get away from what is now essentially a holiday village, and the tufa landscapes are just a short stroll away. When buying your bus ticket to Göreme be sure to check the end destination, as some bus firms may sell you a ticket there but will actually drop you off in Nevşehir, from where you'll have to continue by local bus or *dolmuş* (the last of which leaves Nevşehir at about 6pm).

There are two churches in the hills above the village, the **Durmuş kadir kilisesi**, clearly visible across the vineyard next to a cave-house with rock-cut steps, and the double-domed **Karşıbucak yusuf koç kilisesi**, which houses frescoes in very good condition. About 2km outside the village, the **Göreme Open-Air**

**Museum** (daily 8am–5/6pm; €7) is the site of over thirty other churches, mainly dating from the ninth to the end of the eleventh century and containing some of the best of all the frescoes in Cappadocia. Most are barely discernible from the outside, apart from a few small holes serving as windows or air shafts. But inside, the churches re-create many of the features of Byzantine buildings, with domes, barrel-vaulted ceilings and cruciform plans supported by mock pillars, capitals and pendentives. The best-preserved church is the **Tokalı kilise** (€2.50 extra), located away from the others on the opposite side of the road, about 50m back towards the village. It's in fact two churches, both frescoed: an old church, dating from 920 AD, and a new church, whose frescoes represent some of the finest examples of tenth-century Byzantine art. The most famous of the churches in the main complex are the **Elmalı kilise**, the **Karanlık kilise** whose frescoes have recently been restored, and the **Carıklı kilise** – all eleventh-century churches heavily influenced by Byzantine forms and painted with superb skill. Look, too, at the church of **St Barbara**, named after the depiction of the saint on the north wall.

Göreme's **tourist office** (daily 5am–9pm) in the **bus station** has a useful **accommodation** list and maps of the local area. One of the best budget *pansiyons* is *Shoestring* (☎0384/271 2450; dorms €5.50, doubles ❶), which has good-sized cave rooms and a characterful dorm, while up the hill, *Panoramic* (☎0384/271 2040, ⊛www.panoramiccave.com; dorms €6, doubles ❷) has large rooms and commanding views. Upmarket *Kelebeck* (☎0384/271 2531, ⊛www.kelebeckhotel .com; ❷) has well furnished, immaculate cave rooms and good food, though the best of the non-cave options is the English-owned *Köse Pension* (☎0384/271 2294, ⊛dawn@kosepension.com; dorms €7, doubles ❷), with its own swimming pool. For more luxury try *Göreme House* (☎0384/271 2668; ❸), up a cobbled road behind the mosque, which has excellent en-suite rooms, central heating and some rooms with Jacuzzis (❹). There are several **campsites** on the fringes of Göreme, the best being *Panorama*, 1km out on the Üçhisar road, with a pool. The plush *Alaturca* on Muze Caddesi has a decent **café** serving quality traditional food, while *Local* and *Cappi* at the crossroads to the museum are popular lunchtime options. *Silk Road* in the centre dishes up cheap and tasty kebabs, while the large *Pacha*, behind the bus station, and the *Flintstones Bar*, at the start of the museum road, provide low-key nocturnal entertainment. Oz Cappadocia Tour, next to the bus station, rent **bikes** for €6. There's expensive but reliable **Internet** access at the *Flintstones Café* behind the bus station.

## Ürgüp

There is also plenty of accommodation in **ÜRGÜP**, a pretty old town with its own cave dwellings 5km east of Göreme. In some ways, it's a more sophisticated base than Göreme as it has managed to combine tourism successfully with the more traditional aspects of Turkish life. Ürgüp's **tourist office** (May–Sept daily 8.30am–8pm; winter closed Sat & Sun; ☎0384/341 4059) on the main shopping street, Kayseri Caddesi, maintains an up-to-date price list of **hotels and pansiyons**. One of Ürgüp's most attractive buildings houses *Asia Minor* (☎0384/341 4645, ⊛www.cappadociahouse.com; ❸), with a courtyard, while *Hotel Hitit* (☎0384 341 4481, ⊛www.hitithotel.com; ❷) has decent rooms, and a lovely rose garden and cave bar. Out of the centre on the Nevşehir road, the *Otel Melis* (☎0384/341 2495, ⊛www.melishotel.com; ❹) has a variety of upmarket rooms and an impressive swimming pool, while *Sun Pansiyon*, behind the *hamam* on İstiklâl Cad (☎0384/341 4493; ❷), has a few cave rooms reputed to be a thousand years old, and the *Yıldız Hotel*, just past the police station on the Kayseri road (☎0384/341 4610; ❸), has basic, spacious en-suites. There are numerous **tour operators** in Ürgüp; try Magic Valley, next to the bus station at Güllüce Cad 7 (☎0384/341 2163).

**Eating** options include *Cirağan Restaurant* and *Şömine*, serving well-prepared specialities, both in the central square. *Cumhuriyet Meydani*, beside the *hamam*, serves traditional Turkish dishes, while the excellent, affordable *Ahra* courtyard restaurant dishes up quality home-cooking. The nearby *Tanhani* specializes in good-value steam-tray food. The *Prokopi* bar, Istikal Cad 46, is an atmospheric place for a **drink**, or try *Murat* bar opposite the bus station. *Eftelya*, near the bus station, offers **Internet** access.

## Konya

Roughly midway between Antalya and Nevşehir, **KONYA** is a place of pilgrimage for the Muslim world – the home of Celalledin Rumi or the **Mevlâna** ("Our Master"), the mystic who founded the Mevlevî or **Whirling Dervish** sect, and the centre of **Sufic** mystical practice and teaching. It was also a capital during the Selçuk era, many of the buildings from which are still standing, along with examples of their highly distinctive crafts and applied arts, now on display in Konya's museums. The **Mevlâna Müzesi** (daily 10am–5pm; €2.50) is housed in the first lodge (*tekke*) of the Mevlevî dervish sect, at the eastern end of Mevlâna Bulvarı, easily recognizable by its distinctive fluted turquoise dome. The main building of the museum holds the mausoleum containing the tombs of the Mevlâna, his father and other notables – as with mosques, shoes must be left at the door, women must cover their heads, and whether you're male or female, if you're wearing shorts you'll be given a skirt-like garment to cover your legs. You can take photographs of the mausoleum, but remember to be respectful; it is an extremely holy site. The original *semahane* (ceremonial hall) exhibits some of the musical instruments of the first dervishes, the original illuminated poetical work of the Mevlâna, and a 500-year-old silk carpet from Selçuk Persia that is supposedly the finest ever woven. In the adjoining room, a casket containing hairs from the beard of the Prophet Muhammad is displayed alongside illuminated medieval Korans. A separate building houses an exhibition of dervish memorabilia and some bizarre waxwork figures. West of the Alâeddin Parkı lies the other monument of interest: the **Ince Minare Medresesi** (Tues–Sun 9am–5pm; €1.50), with a distinctive minaret and an ornate Selçuk stone portal featuring Koranic script.

Konya's **bus station** is 10km out of town, from where the Konak *dolmuş* and tramway connects with the town centre; the **train station** is 2km out of the centre at the far end of Istasyon Caddesi, connected to the centre by regular *dolmuşes*. The **tourist office** is at Mevlâna Cad 21 (Mon–Fri 8am–5.30pm; ☎0332/351 1074). Konya's better **hotels** are on or just north of Mevlâna Caddesi; outside the annual Mevlâna festival (Dec) rates can usually be bargained down. Behind the post

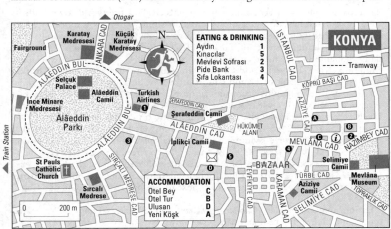

**KONYA**

▲ Otogar

**EATING & DRINKING**
| | |
|---|---|
| Aydın | 1 |
| Kınacılar | 5 |
| Mevlevi Sofrası | 2 |
| Pide Bank | 3 |
| Şifa Lokantası | 4 |

----- Tramway

Karatay Medresesi
Küçük Karatay Medresesi
Fairground
Selçuk Palace
Ince Minare Medresesi
Alâeddin Camii
Turkish Airlines
Alâeddin Parkı
Şerafeddin Camii
İplikçi Camii
HÜKÜMET ALANI
St Pauls Catholic Church
Sırcalı Medrese
BAZAAR
Selimiye Camii
Aziziye Camii
Mevlâna Museum

▲ Train Station

**ACCOMMODATION**
| | |
|---|---|
| Otel Bey | C |
| Otel Tur | B |
| Ulusan | D |
| Yeni Köşk | A |

0    200 m

office, *Ulusan*, Kurşuncular Sok 4 (☎0332/351 5004; ❷), is spotlessly clean, has free Internet and is excellent value. Closer to the Mevlâna, *Otel Bey*, Ayanbey Sok 25 (☎0332/352 0173; ❸), is another clean, affordable option, while the friendly *Otel Tur*, Esarizade Sok 13 (☎0332/351 9825; ❷), has quiet, comfortable rooms. Another good-value option is the *Yeni Köşk*, Kadılar Sok 28 (☎0332/352 0671; ❸).

As for **eating**, the *Şifa Lokantası*, Mevlâna Cad 29, is reasonably priced; *Aydın*, near the Turkish Airlines office on Mevlâna Caddesi, serves great-value *pide* in a dark interior; and *Pide Bank*, Araboğlu Makası 8, is good for coffee and breakfast *börek*. For excellent views over the Mevlâna museum and decent Turkish dishes, try *Mevlevi Sofrası*, on Nazimbey Caddesi, or *Kınacılar Tatlıcısı*, on Çıkrıkçılar içi Merkez at the start of the bazaar, for *baklava*. Express Internet, Alâeddin Bulvarı 21, is one of a number of **Internet** places southwest of Alâeddin Tepesi.

# Travel details

## Trains

Ankara to: İzmir (2 daily; 10hr).
Istanbul to: Ankara (6 daily; 8–9hr 30min); Edirne (1 daily; 6hr 30min); Denizli (1 daily; 14hr 30min); İzmir (1 daily; 11hr); Konya (1 daily; 14hr).
İzmir to: Selçuk (7 daily; 1hr).

## Buses and dolmuşes

Ankara to: Antalya (12 daily; 10hr); Bodrum (10 daily; 10hr); Bursa (hourly; 7hr); Fethiye (2 daily; 12hr); Istanbul (every 30min; 7hr); İzmir (hourly; 8hr); Konya (14 daily; 3hr 30min); Marmaris (14 daily; 13hr); Nevşehir (12 daily; 4hr 30min).
Antalya to: Antakya (3 daily; 12hr); Denizli (6 daily; 5hr 30min); Fethiye, by inland route (6 daily; 4hr); Istanbul (4 daily; 12hr); İzmir (6 daily; 9hr 30min); Kaş (6 daily; 5hr); Konya (6 daily; 5hr 30min); Side (3 hourly; 1hr 15min); Nevşehir (1 daily; 11hr); Olympos (every 30min; 2hr 30min).
Bodrum to: Fethiye (6 daily; 4hr 30min); İzmir (hourly; 4hr); Kaş (3 daily; 6hr); Kuşadası (3 daily; 3hr); Marmaris (14 daily; 3hr 15min); Selçuk (hourly; 3hr).
Bursa to: Çanakkale (hourly; 5hr).
Denizli to: Bodrum (2–3 daily; 4hr 30min); Fethiye (5 daily; 4hr); Konya (several daily; 7hr 15min); Marmaris (6 daily; 4hr).
Edirne to: Çanakkale (4 daily; 4hr 30min);

Fethiye to: Kaş (hourly; 4hr); Marmaris (every 30min; 3hr); Patara (10 daily; 1hr 30min).
Istanbul to: Alanya (hourly; 14hr); Antalya (4 daily; 12hr); Bodrum (5 daily; 12hr); Bursa (hourly; 5hr); Çanakkale (hourly; 5hr 30min); Datça (1 daily; 17hr); Denizli (hourly; 15hr); Edirne (hourly; 3hr); Fethiye (hourly; 15hr); İzmir (hourly; 10hr); Iznik (Orhangazi; hourly; 5hr); Göreme (5 daily; 12hr 30min); Kuşadası (3 daily; 11hr); Marmaris (4 daily; 13hr); Nevşehir (3 daily; 12hr); Ürgüp (5 daily; 12hr 30min); Kaş (2 daily; 12hr); Konya (7 daily; 11hr).
İzmir to: Ankara (every 30min; 8hr); Bergama (hourly; 2hr); Bodrum (hourly; 4hr); Bursa (6 daily; 7hr); Çanakkale (4 daily; 5hr); Datça (hourly; 7hr); Denizli (hourly; 4hr); Fethiye (12–18 daily; 7hr); Konya (1 daily; 8hr); Kuşadası (every 30min; 1hr 40min); Marmaris (hourly; 5hr); Nevşehir (1 daily; 12hr); Selçuk (every 40min; 1hr).
Kuşadası to: Pamukkale (12 daily; 3hr 30min).
Marmaris to: Kaş (4 daily; 5hr); Nevşehir (1 daily; 14hr).
Nevşehir to: Konya (4 daily; 3hr).

## Domestic ferries

Bodrum to: Datça (April–Oct 3 daily; 1hr 30min).
Gelibolu to: Lapseki (15 daily; 20min).
Istanbul to: Yalova (for Bursa or Iznik, 8daily; 1hr 30min).
Kilitbahir to: Çanakkale (hourly; 10min).

TURKEY | Travel details

32

# Travel
# store

# Rough Guides travel...

TRAVEL STORE

# ...music & reference

Mexico
Peru
St Lucia
South America
Trinidad & Tobago
Yúcatan

## Africa & Middle East

Cape Town & the
Garden Route
Egypt
The Gambia
Jordan
Kenya
Marrakesh
DIRECTIONS
Morocco
South Africa, Lesotho
& Swaziland
Syria
Tanzania
Tunisia
West Africa
Zanzibar

## Travel Theme guides

First-Time Around the
World
First-Time Asia
First-Time Europe
First-Time Latin
America
Travel Online
Travel Health
Travel Survival
Walks in London & SE
England
Women Travel

## Maps

Algarve
Amsterdam
Andalucia & Costa
del Sol
Argentina
Athens
Australia
Baja California
Barcelona
Berlin
Boston

Brittany
Brussels
California
Chicago
Corsica
Costa Rica & Panama
Crete
Croatia
Cuba
Cyprus
Czech Republic
Dominican Republic
Dubai & UAE
Dublin
Egypt
Florence & Siena
Florida
France
Frankfurt
Germany
Greece
Guatemala & Belize
Hong Kong
Iceland
Ireland
Kenya
Lisbon
London
Los Angeles
Madrid
Mallorca
Marrakesh
Mexico
Miami & Key West
Morocco
New England
New York City
New Zealand
Northern Spain
Paris
Peru
Portugal
Prague
Rome
San Francisco
Sicily
South Africa
South India
Sri Lanka
Tenerife
Thailand

Toronto
Trinidad & Tobago
Tuscany
Venice
Washington DC
Yucatán Peninsula

## Dictionary Phrasebooks

Croatian
Czech
Dutch
Egyptian Arabic
European Languages
(Czech, French,
German, Greek,
Italian, Portuguese,
Spanish)
French
German
Greek
Hindi & Urdu
Hungarian
Indonesian
Italian
Japanese
Latin American
Spanish
Mandarin Chinese
Mexican Spanish
Polish
Portuguese
Russian
Spanish
Swahili
Thai
Turkish
Vietnamese

## Music Guides

The Beatles
Bob Dylan
Cult Pop
Classical Music
Elvis
Frank Sinatra
Heavy Metal
Hip-Hop
Jazz
Opera
Reggae

Rock
World Music (2 vols)

## Reference Guides

Babies
Books for Teenagers
Children's Books, 0–5
Children's Books, 5–11
Comedy Movies
Conspiracy Theories
Cult Fiction
Cult Football
Cult Movies
Cult TV
The Da Vinci Code
Ethical Shopping
Gangster Movies
Horror Movies
iPods, iTunes & Music
Online
The Internet
James Bond
Kids' Movies
Lord of the Rings
Macs & OS X
Muhammad Ali
Music Playlists
PCs and Windows
Poker
Pregnancy & Birth
Sci–Fi Movies
Shakespeare
Superheroes

Unexplained
Phenomena
The Universe
Weather
Website Directory

## Football

Arsenal 11s
Celtic 11s
Chelsea 11s
Liverpool 11s
Newcastle 11s
Rangers 11s
Tottenham 11s
Man United 11s

TRAVEL STORE

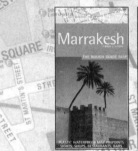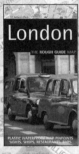

# small print and
# Index

# A Rough Guide to Rough Guides

In the summer of 1981, Mark Ellingham, a recent graduate from Bristol University, was travelling round Greece and couldn't find a guidebook that really met his needs. On the one hand there were the student guides, insistent on saving every last cent, and on the other the heavyweight cultural tomes whose authors seemed to have spent more time in a research library than lounging away the afternoon at a taverna or on the beach.

In a bid to avoid getting a job, Mark and a small group of writers set about creating their own guidebook. It was a guide to Greece that aimed to combine a journalistic approach to description with a thoroughly practical approach to travellers' needs – a guide that would incorporate culture, history, and contemporary insights with a critical edge, together with up-to-date, value-for-money listings. Back in London, Mark and the team finished their Rough Guide, as they called it, and talked Routledge into publishing the book.

That first *Rough Guide to Greece*, published in 1982, was a student scheme that became a publishing phenomenon. The immediate success of the book – with numerous reprints and a Thomas Cook Prize shortlisting – spawned a series that rapidly covered dozens of destinations. Rough Guides had a ready market among low-budget backpackers, but soon also acquired a much broader and older readership that relished Rough Guides' wit and inquisitiveness as much as their enthusiastic, critical approach. Everyone wants value for money, but not at any price.

Rough Guides soon began supplementing the "rougher" information about hostels and low-budget listings with the kind of detail on restaurants and quality hotels that independent-minded visitors on any budget might expect, whether on business in New York or trekking in Thailand.

These days the guides – distributed worldwide by the Penguin Group – offer recommendations from shoestring to luxury and cover more than 200 destinations around the globe, including almost every country in the Americas and Europe, more than half of Africa, and most of Asia and Australasia. Our ever-growing team of authors and photographers is spread all over the world, particularly in Europe, the USA, and Australia.

In 1994, we published the *Rough Guide to World Music* and *Rough Guide to Classical Music*, and a year later the *Rough Guide to the Internet*. All three books have become benchmark titles in their fields – which encouraged us to expand into other areas of publishing, mainly around popular culture. Rough Guides now publish:

- Travel guides to more than 200 worldwide destinations
- Dictionary phrasebooks for 22 major languages
- History guides ranging from Ireland to Islam
- Maps printed on rip-proof and waterproof Polyart™ paper
- Music guides running the gamut from Opera to Elvis
- Restaurant guides to London, New York, and San Francisco
- Reference books on topics as diverse as the Weather and Shakespeare
- Sports guides from Formula 1 to Man Utd
- Pop culture books from *Lord of the Rings* to Cult TV
- World Music CDs in association with World Music Network

Visit **www.roughguides.com** to see our latest publications.

# Rough Guide credits

**Text editors**: Clifton Wilkinson, Amanda Tomlin, Chloe Thomson
**Layout**: Umesh Aggarwal, Dan May, Amit Verma
**Cartography**: Ed Wright
**Picture editor**: Mark Thomas
**Production**: Julia Bovis
**Proofreader**: Stewart Wild
**Editorial: London** Kate Berens, Claire Saunders, Geoff Howard, Ruth Blackmore, Polly Thomas, Richard Lim, Alison Murchie, Sally Schafer, Karoline Densley, Andy Turner, Ella O'Donnell, Keith Drew, Edward Aves, Nikki Birrell, Helen Marsden, Joe Staines, Duncan Clark, Peter Buckley, Matthew Milton; **New York** Andrew Rosenberg, Richard Koss, Steven Horak, AnneLise Sorensen, Amy Hegarty, Hunter Slaton
**Design & Pictures: London** Simon Bracken, Diana Jarvis, Harriet Mills, Jj Luck, Chloë Roberts; **Delhi** Madhulita Mohapatra, Ajay Verma, Jessica Subramanian, Ankur Guha
**Production**: Sophie Hewat, Katherine Owers

**Cartography: London** Maxine Repath, Katie Lloyd-Jones; **Delhi** Manish Chandra, Rajesh Chhibber, Jai Prakash Mishra, Ashutosh Bharti, Rajesh Mishra, Jasbir Sandhu, Karobi Gogoi, Animesh Pathak
**Online: New York** Jennifer Gold, Suzanne Welles, Kristin Mingrone; **Delhi** Manik Chauhan, Narender Kumar, Shekhar Jha, Rakesh Kumar, Lalit Sharma, Chhandita Chakravarty
**Marketing & Publicity: London** Richard Trillo, Niki Hanmer, David Wearn, Demelza Dallow, Louise Maher; **New York** Geoff Colquitt, Megan Kennedy, Milena Perez; **Delhi** Reem Khokhar
**Custom publishing and foreign rights**: Philippa Hopkins
**Manager India**: Punita Singh
**Series editor**: Mark Ellingham
**Reference Director**: Andrew Lockett
**PA to Managing and Publishing Directors**: Megan McIntyre
**Publishing Director**: Martin Dunford
**Managing Director**: Kevin Fitzgerald

# Publishing information

This twelfth edition published October 2005 by
**Rough Guides Ltd,**
80 Strand, London WC2R 0RL
345 Hudson St, 4th Floor,
New York, NY 10014, USA
14 Local Shopping Centre, Panchsheel Park, New Delhi 110017, India.
**Distributed by the Penguin Group**
Penguin Books Ltd,
80 Strand, London WC2R 0RL
Penguin Putnam, Inc.,
375 Hudson St, NY 10014, USA
Penguin Group (Australia)
250 Camberwell Road, Camberwell,
Victoria 3124, Australia
Penguin Books Canada Ltd,
10 Alcorn Avenue, Toronto, ON,
M4V 1E4 Canada
Penguin Group (New Zealand),
Cnr Rosedale and Airborne Roads,
Albany, Auckland, New Zealand

Typeset in Bembo and Helvetica to an original design by Henry Iles.

Printed in Italy by LegoPrint S.p.A

© Rough Guides

No part of this book may be reproduced in any form without permission from the publisher except for the quotation of brief passages in reviews.

1096pp includes index
A catalogue record for this book is available from the British Library.

ISBN-13: 978-1-84353-511-9
ISBN-10: 1-84353-511-4

# Help us update

We've gone to a lot of effort to ensure that the twelfth edition of **The Rough Guide to Europe** is accurate and up to date. However, things change – places get "discovered," opening hours are notoriously fickle, restaurants and rooms raise prices or lower standards. If you feel we've got it wrong or left something out, we'd like to know, and if you can remember the address, the price, the time, the phone number, so much the better.

We'll credit all contributions, and send a copy of the next edition (or any other Rough Guide if you prefer) for the best letters. Everyone who writes to us and isn't already a subscriber will receive a copy of our full-colour thrice-yearly newsletter. Please mark letters: "**Rough Guide Europe update**" and send to: Rough Guides, 80 Strand, London WC2R 0RL, or Rough Guides, 4th Floor, 345 Hudson St, New York, NY 10014. Or send an email to **mail@roughguides.com**.

Have your questions answered and tell others about your trip at **www.roughguides.atinfopop.com**.

## Acknowledgements

The editor would like to thank everyone who updated this edition: Slawomir Adamczak (Czech Republic and Slovakia); Thomas Brown (Estonia and Poland); Jon Bousfield (Latvia and Lithuania); Tim Burford (Romania); Lucia Cockcroft (Spain); Sarah Gear (Bulgaria, Croatia and Greece); Lucia Graves (Italy); Michael Harcourt (Britain); Rob Humphreys (Austria); Daniel Jacobs (Basics and Morocco); Phil Lee (Belgium, Luxembourg and Norway); Norm Longley (Hungary, Serbia and Slovenia); Lucy Mallows (the Netherlands); Claire Morsman (Germany); Lone Mouritsen (Denmark); Roger Norum (Andorra and France); Catherine Phillips (Russia); James Proctor (Finland and Sweden); Emma Rees (Portugal); Paul Sentobe (Turkey); Matthew Teller (Switzerland and Liechtenstein) and Geoff Wallis (Ireland).

**SMALL PRINT**

# Photo credits

All photos © Rough Guides except the following:

## Cover

Main front: Piazza San Marco, Venice © Getty
Small front top picture: Metro sign, Madrid © Alamy
Small front lower picture: Portuguese Cafe © Corbis
Back top picture: Jungfrau railway, Switzerland © Corbis
Back lower picture: Eiffel Tower, Paris © Alamy

## Introduction

Jungfrau train, Switzerland © Ray Juno/Corbis
Gellért Baths, Budapest © Oliver Benn/Getty Images
Mini clogs © Peter Adams/Getty Images
The Court of the Lions, the Alhambra, Granada © Nedra Westwater/Getty Images
Trevi Fountain, Rome © Glen Alison/Getty Images
Woman on pebbled beach © Antonio Mo/Getty Images
FIFA World Cup 2006 © David Crausby/Alamy
Hot air balloon in Cappadocia, Turkey © TNT Magazine/Alamy
Pint of Guinness, photography by Mark Thomas © Rough Guides
Sultanahmet Camii Mosque © Shaun Egan/Getty Images
Moules Frites, photography by Mark Thomas © Rough Guides
Dancing on Sa Trinchas Beach, Ibiza © Jamie Baker/Everynight images
Aerial view of Old Town Prague, Czech Republic © Andrea Pistolesi/Getty Images

## Itineraries

Close up of Big Ben, London, photography by Mark Thomas © Rough Guides
Couple on bridge, Paris © Will & Deni McIntyre/Getty Images
Bundestag, Berlin © Mark Thomas
Koutoubia Mosque, Marrakesh © Preston/Schlebusch/Getty Images
Santoríni, Greece © Sylvain Grandadam/Getty Images
Parliament, Budapest © Pulfer/Getty Images
Midnight Sun, Sweden © Hans Strand/Getty Images
Saint Basil's Cathedral, Moscow © Harald Sund/Getty Images
Coffee and Croissants © Carlos Spaventa/Getty Images

## Black and whites

**p.76** Sant Joan Caselles, Andorra © Roger Norum
**p.90** Schönbrunn Palace, Vienna © Gavin Hellier/Robert Harding Picture Library
**p.118** Kayaking, River Lesse © Tourism Brussels-Ardennes
**p.144** The Sherlock Holmes pub, London © Superstock
**p.224** Aleksandâr Nevsky Cathedral, Sofia © Kyle Clapham
**p.246** Dubrovnik, Croatia © Ken Gillham/Robert Harding Picture Library/Getty Images
**p.270** Prague Castle, Czech Republic, photography by Helena Smith © Rough Guides
**p.294** Skagen, Denmark © Bob Kirst/Crobis
**p.320** Alexander Nevsky Cathedral, Tallinn © Robert Harding Picture Library
**p.336** Reindeer, Finland © James Proctor
**p.354** Chenonceaux, Loire Valley © Chris Coe/Axiom
**p.428** Oktoberfest, Munich © David Sanger Photography/Alamy
**p.484** The Acropolis, photography by Paul Hellander © Rough Guides
**p.532** People playing chess at the Széchenyi Baths, Budapest © Sergio Pitamitz/Alamy
**p.554** Barrels at the Guinness Factory, Dublin, photography by Mark Thomas © Rough Guides
**p.586** The Palio, Siena © Loriat Ly/Robert Harding Picture Library
**p.664** Art Nouveau detail on a building in Rīga, Latvia © Travelog Picture Library/Alamy
**p.678** Trakai Castle, Lithuania © G.R. Richardson/Robert Harding Picture Library
**p.694** Town Walls, Essaouira © Hamish Brown
**p.722** Herengracht, Amsterdam © Anthony Cassidy
**p.748** Vikingskipshuset, Oslo © AM Corporation/Alamy
**p.772** Main Square, Old Town, Kraków © K. Gillham/Robert Harding Picture Library
**p.796** Óbidos © Jeremy Philips/Travel Ink
**p.826** Carpathian Mountains, Romania © W. Jacobs/Trip
**p.842** Red Square and St Basil's Cathedral © Focus Russia/Alamy
**p.864** Despot Gate and Dizar Tower, Belgrade © DIOMEDIA/Alamy
**p.880** Tatras Mountains, Slovakia © N. McDiarmid/Trip
**p.896** Mestni Fountain, Ljubljana © Phil Robinson/Robert Harding Picture Library
**p.912** Guggenheim Museum, Bilbao © Neil Setchfield
**p.982** Gamla Stan, Stockholm © Paul van Riel, Robert Harding Picture Library
**p.1002** View toward the Matterhorn © Andre Jenny/Alamy
**p.1030** Ancient Ephesus, Library Ephesus © Izzet Keribar

# Index

Map entries are in colour

**INDEX**

# Map symbols

Maps are listed in the full index using coloured text

| | | | | |
|---|---|---|---|---|
| ┅┅┅ | International boundary | ✡ | Synagogue |
| ┅ ┅ ┅ | Province boundary | ☪ | Mosque |
| ──▭── | Railway | ⊞ | Hospital |
| ┉┉┉ | Funicular | ⊠ | Post office |
| ●┄┄● | Cable car | ⓘ | Information office |
| ▬▬▬ | Motorway | ⓒ | Telephone office |
| ═══ | Tolled motorway | @ | Internet access |
| ══ | Road | ★ | Bus stop |
| ═══ | Pedestrianized street | Ⓜ | Metro station |
| ▥▥▥ | Steps | Ⓡ | RER station |
| ┄┄┄ | Path | Ⓢ | S-Bahn |
| ── ── | Ferry route | Ⓣ | Tram stop |
| ──── | Waterway | Ⓤ | U-Bahn |
| ▪▪▪▪▪ | Wall | ⊖ | London Underground Station |
| ⌃⌃ | Mountains | ⊜ | FGC station |
| ▲ | Peak | ℗ | Parking |
| ☀ | Hill | ⊠ | Gate |
| ⌢⌢⌢⌢ | Rocks | ⏖ | Swimming pool |
| ∴ | Ruins | ⊙ | Statue |
| ◠ | Cave | ▬ | Building |
| ⚒ | Waterfall | ⊞ | Church (town) |
| ⵣ | Fountain | ◯ | Stadium |
| ⚶ | Viewpoint | ▦ | Park |
| ⵟ | Lighthouse | ⊞ | Christian cemetery |
| ♦ | Point of interest | ⵟ | Muslim cemetery |
| ⚑ | Museum | ⊔ | Jewish cemetery |
| 血 | Stately house | ▦ | Beach |
| ⌂ | Monastery | ▨ | Glacier |
| ⵜ | Church (region) | ▨ | Forest |

MAP SYMBOLS

Ⓘ